1998 Standard Catalog of

FIREARMS

THE COLLECTOR'S PRICE & REFERENCE GUIDE

8TH EDITION

From the publishers of
GUN LIST

NED SCHWING

Published by

**krause
publications**

700 E. State Street • Iola, WI 54990-0001
Telephone: 715/445-2214

Please call or write for our free catalog of publications.
Our toll-free number to place an order or obtain a free catalog is 800-258-0929
or please use our regular business telephone 715-445-2214
for editorial comment and further information.

Library of Congress Catalog Number: 90-62405
ISBN: 0-87341-553-1
Printed in the United States of America

CONTENTS

—— FIREARMS DIRECTORY ——

FIREARMS DIRECTORY

──── FIREARMS DIRECTORY ────

FIREARMS DIRECTORY

FIREARMS DIRECTORY

━━━ FIREARMS DIRECTORY ━━━

——— FIREARMS DIRECTORY ———

FIREARMS DIRECTORY

FIREARMS DIRECTORY

FIREARMS DIRECTORY

ACKNOWLEDGMENTS

Orvel Reichert is a collector World War II-era semi-automatic pistols, especially the P38, and has been an invaluable help in sorting out a sometimes confusing array of pistol variations. He can be reached at P.O. Box 67, Vader, WA 98593, 360-245-3492

John Dougan, Ruger expert, who supplied us with information on the Great Western Arms Co.

Dave Kidd, experienced Winchester collector, helped with Model 1890 prices.

Ottis Spigelmyer shared with us his in-depth knowledge of Remington arms.

Burt O'Neil is an experienced collector of Browning "P" Grades and helped with that pricing. He can be reached at 610-793-3256

Thanks to Smith & Wesson experts Roy Jinks, of Smith & Wesson, who wrote the introduction to that section in this book.

C.W. Slagle, of Scottsdale, Arizona, for his expertise in antique firearms.

Thanks to John Kronschnabl, former advertising manager of *Gun List* magazine (Krause Publications), for his invaluable assistance throughout the year.

Thanks to Eric M. Larson for his knowledgeable information on Federal gun laws.

A special thanks to Simeon Stoddard, assistant curator of the Cody Firearms Museum, for his research and contribution on the M1 Garand rifle.

A special thanks to all the manufacturers and importers who supplied us with information and photographs on their products.

Thanks to the Lew Horton Distributing Company for their invaluable information on Colt Custom Shop products and Smith & Wesson Performance Center products.

Thanks to Jerry Cummings of Manawa, Wisconsin, and William "Pete" Harvey of Falmouth, Massachusetts, who contributed photos and research information.

Many thanks to Harold Hamilton of Hershey, Pennsylvania, for his invaluable assistance with Hamilton rifles.

Tony Galazan and Dick Perrett of Galazan's assisted with the early Ithaca and Lefever shotgun prices. They can be reached at 203-225-6581.

Michael McIntosh gave generously of his expert knowledge of A.H. Fox Company and its guns.

Ed Buehlman, a long time firearms dealer, shared his knowledge of Colt New Frontier Models. He can be reached at 847-381-2276.

Thanks to Rick Kennerknecht, Randall Historian, and Steve Comus for writing the Randal Story.

Special appreciation to Joe McBride of McBride's Guns in Austin, Texas, for his invaluable assistance.

Walter C. Snyder is the "Chronicler of the Ithaca Gun Company" and has devoted a great deal of time and effort to making the Ithaca section the most comprehensive of any price guide on the market.

Tom Turpin is a big help with his invaluable knowledge of F.W. Heym Company and its product line.

Horst Held of Midlothian, Texas, provided us with information on interesting and seldom seen antique semi-automatic pistols.

Thanks to all the readers who have taken the time to contact the editor with corrections, omissions and additional information.

PHOTO CREDITS

John Gallo, president of Butterfield and Butterfield auction house in San Francisco, made available a wealth of fine photographs and other auction information that has improved the quality of this publication. Through the efforts of Butterfield's, firearms collecting has reached a level of interest on par with the fine art world.

Thanks to the Milwaukee Public Museum, 800 W. Wells St., Milwaukee, WI 53233; and the Buffalo Bill Historical Center, Cody Firearms Museum, P.O. Box 1000, Cody, WY 82414, for supplying us with photographs. We also wish to thank the Remington Arms Company for their kind assistance in providing us with photos of out of production Remington firearms.

Many thanks to the following who lent us their firearms to photograph for this book:

Thomas W. Radcliffe

Brook Davis

Thomas F. Swearengen

Chip Johnson of Direct Firearms, St. Joseph, Missouri

C. Roy Jones of C. Roy's Gunsmithing, Kaiser, Missouri

Mike and Wanda Moutray of Mike's Gun Sales, Grant City, Missouri

Will Parsons of Parsons Gun Shop

Joe Lech of Ironwork Armco, Raytown, Missouri

Guns of the World, Kansas City, Missouri

J.M. Stanley of Stan's Gun Shop, Joplin, Missouri

H.L. Hoeflicker of HLH Enterprises, Shawnee Mission, Kansas

S.T. Sinclair

Pat Morgan

Steve Comus

William H. Lehman of B & B Guns, Brighton, Colorado

James D. McKenzie and Samuel Baum of Kentucky Rifle, Union City, Pennsylvania

Dean Parr of Dean's Gun Shop, St. Joseph, Missouri

E.K. Tryon of Philadelphia, Pennsylvania

Bob's Gun Rack of Lee's Summit, Missouri

Pat McWilliams

J.M. Stanley

Ken Waughtal of Merriam, Kansas

Armond Beetch of Quapaw, Oklahoma

Jim Rankin

Eric M. Larson

Jim Taylor of Mt. Vernon, Missouri

C. Hadley Smith

Walter C. Snyder

Ithaca Gun Company

Tom Turpin

Horst Held

INTRODUCTION

This last few editions of the *Standard Catalog of Firearms* represents a somewhat new direction for the editor and the publisher. The *Catalog* is now more than just a valuable price guide. It is a comprehensive compilation of values, technical data, historical information, useful articles, accurate photographs, and the latest in selected auction results of unique firearms that will inform and educate the reader. Now it is possible for the reader of this volume to have a wealth of information, not just prices, at his fingertips. This information is further enhanced by quality photos, many of them of rare and seldom encountered examples.

The editor's and publisher's goal is to furnish the reader with an encyclopedia of information that will enable the collector to gain additional insight into all aspects of firearms collecting. Collectors have sought to acquire firearms for a multitude of reasons. From firearms that are historically important, to firearms that were the innovators in design and function, to firearms that were admired for their grace and beauty; all of these factors are considered in this book.

In many cases it is impossible to price certain firearms due to their uniqueness, historical importance, or embellishments. The inclusion of selected auction results will give the reader an insight into the rarified atmosphere of rare and valuable collectable firearms. Most of us will not have the opportunity to own many of these beautiful specimens, but we can vicariously, through this book, appreciate these fine guns.

This publication not only attempts to provide high quality photographs that illustrate the firearms in question, but to furnish the reader with detailed descriptions of each firearm and to break down these explanations into useful categories. A simplified grading system that is easily understandable is an additional aid to the collector. This 8th Edition, with the addition of more than 1,400 photos, is a significant improvement over the 7th Edition. The editor and publishers have made a commitment to refine each subsequent publication in a substantial fashion. Time and space constraints have not allowed us to make each category definitive, but that is our goal in ensuing editions. This is a work in progress.

I would also like to comment about letters and calls I have received from readers of this publication. Almost without exception the vast majority are extremely knowledgeable about a firearm or group of firearms and willingly and constructively lend their expertise to this book. I want to thank each one of them for their time and interest in helping make this price and reference guide the best on the market today.

In the last analysis we believe that the reader will benefit from the information presented in this book, not only from a pricing standpoint but as a reference source as well.

Good luck with your collecting and be safe in your shooting,

Ned Schwing
Editor

GRADING SYSTEM

In the opinion of the editor all grading systems are subjective. It is our task to offer the collector and dealer a measurement that most closely reflects a general consensus on condition. The system we present seems to come closest to describing a firearm in universal terms. We strongly recommend that the reader acquaint himself with this grading system before attempting to determine the correct price for a particular firearm's condition. Remember, in most cases condition determines price.

NIB-New in Box
This category can sometimes be misleading. It means that the firearm is in its original factory carton with all of the appropriate papers. It also means the firearm is new; that it has not been fired and has no wear. This classification brings a substantial premium for both the collector and shooter.

Excellent
Collector quality firearms in this condition are highly desirable. The firearm must be in at least 98 percent condition with respect to blue wear, stock or grip finish, and bore. The firearm must also be in 100 percent original factory condition without refinishing, repair, alterations or additions of any kind. Sights must be factory original as well. This grading classification includes both modern and antique (manufactured prior to 1898) firearms.

Very Good
Firearms in this category are also sought after both by the collector and shooter. Firearms must be in working order and retain approximately 92 percent metal and wood finish. It must be 100 percent factory original, but may have some small repairs, alterations, or non-factory additions. No refinishing is permitted in this category. Both modern and antique firearms are included in this classification.

Good
Modern firearms in this category may not be considered to be as collectable as the previous grades, but antique firearms are considered desirable. Modern firearms must retain at least 80 percent metal and wood finish, but may display evidence of old refinishing. Small repairs, alterations, or non-factory additions are sometimes encountered in this class. Factory replacement parts are permitted. The overall working condition of the firearm must be good as well as safe. The bore may exhibit wear or some corrosion, especially in antique arms. Antique firearms may be included in this category if their metal and wood finish is at least 50 percent original factory finish.

Fair
Firearms in this category should be in satisfactory working order and safe to shoot. The overall metal and wood finish on the modern firearm must be at least 30 percent and antique firearms must have at least some original finish or old re-finish remaining. Repairs, alterations, nonfactory additions, and recent refinishing would all place a firearm in this classification. However, the modern firearm must be in working condition, while the antique firearm may not function. In either case the firearm must be considered safe to fire if in a working state.

Poor
Neither collectors nor shooters are likely to exhibit much interest in firearms in this condition. Modern firearms are likely to retain little metal or wood finish. Pitting and rust will be seen in firearms in this category. Modern firearms may not be in working order and may not be safe to shoot. Repairs and refinishing would be necessary to restore the firearm to safe working order. Antique firearms will have no finish and will not function. In the case of modern firearms their principal value lies in spare parts. On the other hand, antique firearms in this condition may be used as "wall hangers" or as an example of an extremely rare variation or have some kind of historical significance.

Pricing Sample Format

NIB	Exc.	V.G.	Good	Fair	Poor
550	450	400	350	300	200

PRICING

The prices given in this book are <u>RETAIL</u> prices.

Unfortunately for shooters and collectors, there is no central clearinghouse for firearms prices. The prices given in this book are designed as a guide, not as a quote. This is an important distinction because prices for firearms vary with the time of the year and geographical location. For example, interest in firearms is at its lowest point in the summer. People are not as interested in shooting and collecting at this time of the year as they are in playing golf or taking a vacation. Therefore, prices are depressed slightly and guns that may sell quickly during the hunting season or the winter months may not sell well at all during this time of year. Geographical location also plays an important part in pricing. For instance, a Winchester Model 70 in a .264 caliber will bring a higher price in the Western states than along the Eastern seaboard. Smaller gauges and calibers seem to be more popular along both coasts and mid-sections of the United States than in the more open western sections of the country.

It is not practical to list prices in this book with regard to time of year or location. What is given is a reasonable price based on sales at gun shows, auction houses, *Gun List* prices, and information obtained from knowledgeable collectors and dealers. The firearms prices listed in this book are **RETAIL PRICES** and may bring more or less depending on the variables discussed above. If you choose to sell your gun to a dealer you will not receive the retail price but a wholesale price based on the markup that particular dealer needs to operate. Also, in certain cases there will be no price indicated under a particular condition but rather the notation "**N/A**" or the symbol "—". This indicates that there is no known price available for that gun in that condition or the sales for that particular model are so few that a reliable price cannot be given. This will usually be encounter only with very rare guns, with newly introduced firearms, or more likely with antique firearms in those conditions most likely to be encountered. Most antique firearms will be seen in the good, fair and poor categories.

One final note. The prices listed here come from a variety of sources: retail stores, gun shows, individual collectors, and auction houses. Due to the nature of business one will usually pay higher prices at a retail store than at a gun show. In some cases auctions will produce excellent buys or extravagant prices, depending on any given situation. Collectors will sometimes pay higher prices for a firearm that they need to fill out their collection when in other circumstances they will not be willing to pay market price if they don't have to have the gun. The point here is that prices paid for firearms is an ever changing affair based or a large number of variables. The prices in this book are a **GENERAL GUIDE** as to what a willing buyer and willing seller might agree on. You may find the item for less, and then you may have to pay more depending on the variables of your particular situation.

Sometimes we loose sight of our collecting or shooting goals and focus only on price. Two thoughts come to mind. First, one long time collector told me once that, "you can never pay to much for a good gun." Second, Benjamin Franklin once said, "the bitterness of poor quality lingers long after the sweetness of a low price."

In the final analysis, the prices listed here are given to assist the shooter and collector in pursuing their hobby with a better understanding of what is going on in the marketplace. If this book can expand one's knowledge, then it will have fulfilled its purpose.

ADDITIONAL CONSIDERATIONS

As stated in the pricing section, this publication offers a general guide to prices. There are many factors that may affect the value of a firearm. We have attempted to be as comprehensive as possible but we cannot cover all possible factors that may influence the worth of any given firearm. Some of these circumstances will be discussed so that the shooter and collector will have a better idea of how certain factors may affect prices.

Firearms have been admired and coveted, not only for their usefulness, but also for their grace and beauty. Since the beginning of the 19th century, firearms' makers have adorned their guns with engraving, fine woods, or special order features that set their products apart from the rest. There is no feasible way to give the collector every possible variation of the firearms presented in this book. However, in a general way certain special factors will significantly influence the price of a firearm.

Perhaps the most recognizable special feature collectors agree affects the price of a firearm is engraving. The artistry, beauty, and intricate nature of engraving draw all collectors toward it. But, firearms engraving is a field unto itself requiring years of experience to determine proper chronological methods and the ability to identify the engraver in question. Factory engraving generally brings more of a premium than aftermarket engraving. To be able to determine factory work is a difficult task full of pitfalls. In some cases, factories like Colt and Winchester may have records to verify original factory engraving work. Whereas, other manufacturers such as Parker, Remington, or Savage do not have these records. Whenever a firearm purchase is to be made with respect to an engraved gun, it is in the collector's best interest to secure an expert opinion and/or a factory letter prior to the purchase. Engraved firearms are expensive. A mistake could cost the collector thousands of dollars; proceed with caution.

The 18th century was also a time when pistols and rifles were purchased by or given to historically important individuals. Firearms have also been an important part of significant historical events such as the Battle of the Little Bighorn or the Battle of Bull Run or some other meaningful event in our nation's history. Many of these firearms are in museums where the public can enjoy, see and appreciate them. Others are in private collections that seldom, if ever, are offered for sale. If the collector should ever encounter one of these historically important firearms, it cannot be stressed strongly enough to secure an expert determination as to authenticity. Museum curators are perhaps the best source of information for these types of firearms. As with engraved guns, historical firearms are usually expensive, and without documentation their value is questionable.

Special features and variations are also a desirable part of firearms collecting. As with engraving, special order guns can bring a considerable premium. The Colt factory has excellent records regarding their firearms and will provide the collector with a letter of authenticity. Winchester records are not as comprehensive, but rifles made prior to 1908 may have documentation. Other firearm manufacturers either do not have records or do not provide the collector with documentation. This leaves the collector in a difficult position. Special order sights, stocks, barrel lengths, calibers, and so forth must be judged on their own merits. As with other factors an expert should be consulted prior to purchase. Sometimes this can be difficult. Experienced collectors, researchers, and museums will generally provide the kind of information a collector needs before purchasing a special order or unique firearm.

Perhaps the best advice is for the collector to take his time. Do not be in a hurry and do not allow yourself to be rushed into making a decision. Learn as much as possible about the firearms you are interested in collecting or shooting. Try to keep current with prices through the *Gun List* and this publication. Go to gun shows, not just to buy or sell but to observe and learn. It is also helpful to join a firearms club or association. These groups have older, experienced collectors who are glad to help the beginner or veteran. Firearms collecting is a rewarding hobby. Firearms are part of our nation's history and represent an opportunity to learn more about their role in that American experience. If done skillfully, firearms collecting can be a profitable hobby as well.

AUCTION HOUSE CREDITS

The following auction houses were kind enough to allow the Catalog to report unusual firearms from their sales. The directors of these auction concerns are acknowledged for their assistance and support.

Butterfield & Butterfield
220 San Bruno Avenue
San Francisco, CA 94103
Attention: James Ferrell
415-861-7500 ext. 327
415-861-8951 FAX

J.C. Devine, Inc.
P.O. Box 413
Milford, NH 03055
Attention: Joe Devine
603-673-4967
603-672-0328

Faintich Auction Service
10902 St. Charles Rock Rd.
St. Louis, MO 63074
Attention: Jeff Faintich
314-739-7796
314-739-3086

Old Town Station Ltd.
P.O. Box 15351
Lenexa, KS 66285
Attention: Jim Supica
913-492-3000
913-492-8951 FAX

Rock Island Auction Company
1050 36th Avenue
Moline, IL 61265
Attention: Patrick Hogan
800-238-8022
309-797-1655 FAX

CONTRIBUTING EDITORS

Bob Ball
Springfield Armory & Mauser rifles
P.O. Box 255
Unionville, CT 06085

Thomas Barker
Laurona, Ugartechea
P.O. Box 3361
Victoria, TX 77903
512-573-GUNS

J.B. Barnes
Stevens single shot rifles and pistols
29 Ridgeview Dr.
Dry Ridge, KY 41035
606-824-5086

David Bichrest
Winchester lever action rifles
P.O. Box 6039
Falmouth, ME 04105
207-781-3360
207-781-4437 FAX

Douglas Carlson
Colt precussion & Colt conversions revolvers
Antique Remington handguns
P.O. Box 71035
Des Moines, IA 50325
515-224-6552

Jim Cate
J.P. Sauer pistols
406 Pine Bluff Dr.
Chattanooga, TN 37412
423-892-6320

Kevin Cherry
Winchester And Colt Commemoratives
3402 West Wendover Avenue
Greensboro, NC 27407
919-854-4182

Don Criswell
Winchester Model 21 shotguns
Parker shotguns
P.O. Box 277
Yorba Linda, CA 92686
714-970-5934

John Diemer
Belgium Browning shotguns and rifles
3304 Mayfield Court
Winston-Salem, NC 27104
910-760-0257

John Dougan
Ruger & Great Western
2000 Saul Kleinfeld Dr. #110
El Paso, TX 79936
915-857-1992

Jeff Faintich
Colt pre-war semi-automatic pistols
Colt antique long arms
10902 St. Charles Rock Rd.
St. Ann, Mo 63074
314-739-0399

Richard Freer
Belgium Browning shotguns
Winchester pre-64 shotguns
8928 Spring Branch Drive
Houston, TX 77080
713-467-3016

Chad Hiddleson
Ruger
1945 Clover Street
Perry, IA 50220

David Hunter
Marlin lever action rifles
6618 Parker Road
Wadesville, IN 47638
812-985-7448

Rick Kennerknecht
Randall 1911 A1 Pistols
228 Columbine Dr.
Casper, WY 82609
307-234-2400
e mail: rekenn@trib.com

Eric Larson
H&R Handy Guns
Smoothbore Pistols
P.O. Box 5497
Takoma Park, MD 20913
301-270-3450

Roger Lenzmeier
Ithaca Shotguns
2322 Vicking Cr. N.W.
Rochester, MN 55901

Karl Lippard
Perazzi, Fabbri, Famars
P.O. Box 60719
Colorado Springs, CO 80960
719-444-0786

Duke McCaa
Kimber, Current Brownings, Colt SAA,
& Winchester
5243 Gulf Breeze Parkway
Gulf Breeze, FL 32561
904-932-4867

Gale Morgan
Luger and Mauser pistols
Pre-World War I pistols
P.O. Box 72
Lincoln, CA 95648
916-645-1720

Doug Murray
Savage Model 99 and early Savage rifles
20 Polo Lane
Westbury, NY 11590
516-333-6874

Nick Niles
Stevens, Savage Fox B, and Davis doubles
P.O. Box 46
Southport, CT 06490
203-259-2396

Larry Orr
Remington & Winchester rifles & shotguns
105 N. 8th.
Beresford, SD 57004
605-763-5090

Jim Rankin
Walther pistols
3615 Anderson Road
Coral Gables, FL 33134
305-446-1792

Orvel Reichert
World War II-era semi-automatic pistols
P.O. Box 67
Vader, WA 98593
360-245-3492

Richard M. Kumor Sr.
c/o Rickey's Gun Room
WWII era military firearms
P.O. Box 286
Chicopee, MA 01021
413-592-5000

Dan Sheil
Merkel shotguns and rifles
9240 Southwest 140 Street
Miami, FL 33176
305-253-5984

Don Stika
CZ pistols
BRNO and Mauser sporting rifles
Mannlicher rifles
P.O. Box 882
Bensenville, IL 60106
630-766-4617

Jim Supica
Smith & Wesson
P.O. Box 15351
Lenexa, KS 66285
913-492-3000

Walt Snyder
Ithaca shotguns
225 South Valley Rd.
Southern Pines, NC 28387
910-692-7324

Allan Wilson
Winchester Model 70
109l Backhill
Plainfield, NH 03781
603-298-8085

WHAT TO DO BEFORE YOU BUY A GUN; ADVICE FOR ALL

So you want to buy a gun. For the veteran shooter or collector, the series of events leading up to a purchase is almost taken for granted. You know what you want and all you have to do is find the type and style at the price you want to pay. But what about the beginner or the experienced hand who is branching off into new territory? We all need to be reminded, from time to time, of certain steps we need to take to make a successful purchase; one that we will be happy with for a long time.

If you are about to purchase a handgun, rifle, or shotgun for practical reasons, the one recommendation that should *always* be kept in mind is to read about the types of firearms you might be interested in and the conditions that they are intended for. You wouldn't want to buy a trap gun if you are going to hunt ducks; or a .22 auto pistol to hunt brown bear in Alaska. There are almost as many opinions on what to use for any given hunting or shooting situation as there are hunters and shooters, but reading about the guns is a good place to start. Next, ask your friends what they use and why. Are they happy with the quality, performance, and reliability of the gun they use? If so, why? Ask a lot of "whys." If you are able, try to test fire the gun. That is a good start, or, better yet, use the gun under actual shooting conditions.

Remember, much of what you read and hear boils down to personal preference on the part of the user and nothing more. Occasionally, a rifle or shotgun or pistol may not fit you, may be too heavy or too light. These are all factors you should strive to find out before you buy; not after.

Where you buy is also important. Most towns and cities have at least one gun store with a competent, knowledgeable staff that is able to offer sound advice and help if you are in the market for what they carry in stock. Of course, they want to sell you a gun, so you have to keep that fact in mind. Buying a gun at a gun show is another approach that works for many people. This technique works best when you have already made up your mind what you want. Before you buy a gun at a gun show, make sure that it is what you want and it is in safe operating condition. Buy from a reputable dealer. If you get home and the gun doesn't work as it should, make sure you can return it in the same condition as when you purchased it. You can also buy a gun through the mail from publications such as *Gun List.* This avenue has its bumps in the road as well. You must purchase the gun through a licensed FFL holder. Buy from a reliable person. Ask for references and inquire about the seller. Bad reputations usually precede disreputable people. Make sure you have at least a three-day inspection period after you receive the gun to make up your mind.

For the collector, the options are similar but the circumstances are a bit more complicated. The collecting of arms, whether they be military or sporting, American or foreign, modern or antique, can be an extremely rewarding experience. It does, however, like any other collecting field, have its pitfalls. Many of these can be avoided by simply following a tried and true set of guidelines; *read, look, touch, compare, question, and read some more.* Before you buy, learn as much as you can. Read about your interest, and look and handle as many examples as possible. Ask questions about finish, markings, grips, stocks, barrel lengths, and so on. Take what you see and review what you have already read; it will clarify many of your questions. For example, you can read about Winchester's stock finish used before 1915 and think you understand the difference between shellac and a finish with chemical compounds; but you really don't know the difference until you see it and feel it.

When at last you are ready to make a purchase, investigate the seller's reputation and always demand a detailed receipt noting the make, model, serial number, special features, and so forth. Disreputable sellers are less likely to provide you with such a receipt than honest dealers. When you inquire about a particular dealer, ask collectors, not other dealers. Don't get in a hurry. You should also determine whether the seller will allow you to return the item should it not be genuine in any respect. If you follow the above steps and ask for help from an expert or knowledgeable collector, even if a fee is involved, your risk will be minimized. The expenditure of a few dollars to ensure an item's authenticity is money well spent should the item not be as advertised. In certain cases, antique firearms can be authenticated by factory letters. Some Winchesters and Colts can be "lettered" in this manner. Inquire if this can be done and have it so before you buy. If in doubt about the firearm or the seller, don't buy.

Another opportunity where collectors can purchase firearms is at auction. Though many fine pieces can be acquired in this way, extreme caution must be exercised. Since auctioneers only act as an agent for the seller, items are sold "as is," and purchases are final. Consequently it is absolutely necessary to examine material offered for sale before purchasing to ensure its authenticity. If you cannot attend an auction personally, secure the services of a trusted representative to perform the examination. To avoid becoming caught in the excitement of an auction, set the amount you are willing to pay beforehand and stick to it. As with any purchase, caution and prudence must be exercised.

Whether you are a shooter or collector and whatever approach you take, there are two keys that you should always keep in mind; *let knowledge and patience be your guide.*

VIOLENT CRIME CONTROL AND LAW ENFORCEMENT ACT OF 1994

The following portions of the assault weapon law are excerpted from the final bill as signed by President Clinton. It is an attempt by the editor to keep the gun buying public informed of current federal guns laws. The Crime Bill passed the Congress in August of 1994 and was signed into law on September 13, 1994. It is an important piece of legislation that all gun owners should be aware of. The provisions of this law are significant and should be understood in order to be in compliance with the law. The penalties are severe: up to ten years in a federal prison and up to a $10,000 fine.

TITLE XI

Subtitle A-Assault Weapons

It shall be unlawful for a person to manufacture, transfer, or possess a semiautomatic assault weapon unless otherwise lawfully possessed under Federal law on the date of the enactment of this subsection *[September 13, 1994]. This law does not apply to firearms specified in Appendix A to this section, as such firearms were manufactured on October 1, 1993. Also exempt are any firearms that are operated by bolt, pump, lever, or slide action; or firearms that have been rendered permanently inoperable; or any firearm that is classified as an antique. Also exempt are firearms that cannot accept a detachable magazine that holds more than 5 rounds of ammunition; or any semiautomatic shotgun that cannot hold more than 5 rounds of ammunition in a fixed or detachable magazine.*

The term "semiautomatic assault weapon" means:
Any firearm, or copies or duplicates of the firearms in any caliber known as:
1. *Norinco, Mitchell, and Poly Technologies Automat Kalashnikovs (all models)*
2. *Action Arms Israeli Military Industries UZI and Galil.*
3. *Beretta Ar70(SC-70).*
4. *Colt AR-15.*
5. *Fabrique National FN/FAL, FN/LAR, and FNC.*
6. *SWD M-10, M-11, M-11/9, and M-12.*
7. *Steyr AUG.*
8. *INTRATEC TEC-9, TEC-DC9, and TEC-22.*
9. *Any revolving cylinder shotguns, such as (or similar to) the Street Sweeper and Striker 12.*

What follows is an important set of rules that govern firearms not named above. These rules account for the potential ban on an additional 184 firearms if they meet the following conditions.
A. *A semiautomatic rifle that has an ability to accept a detachable magazine and has at least two of the following:*
   1. *A folding or telescoping stock.*
   2. *A pistol grip that protrudes conspicuously beneath the action of the weapon.*
   3. *A bayonet mount.*
   4. *A flash suppressor or threaded barrel designed to accommodate a flash suppressor.*
   5. *A grenade launcher.*

B. A semiautomatic pistol that has an ability to accept a detachable magazine and has at least two of the following:

1. *An ammunition magazine that attaches to the pistol outside of the pistol grip.*
2. *A threaded barrel capable of accepting a barrel extender, flash suppressor, forward handgrip, or silencer.*
3. *A shroud that is attached to, or partially or completely encircles, the barrel and that permits the shooter to hold the firearm with the nontrigger hand without being burned.*
4. *A manufactured weight of 50 ounces or more when the pistol is unloaded.*
5. *A semiautomatic version of an automatic firearm.*

C. A semiautomatic shotgun that has at least two of the following:

1. *A folding or telescoping stock.*
2. *A pistol grip that protrudes conspicuously beneath the action of the weapon.*
3. *A fixed magazine capacity in excess of 5 rounds.*
4. *An ability to accept a detachable magazine.*

A.A. Arms AR9
AP-9 Assault Pistol
American Arms AKY39 Rifle
American Arms AKF39 Rifle
American 180
AMT Lightning 25/22
Anschutz Deluxe Model 520/61
AR-10 Semi-Auto Rifle
Argentine FALs
Armalite AR-180 Sporter Carbine
Armscor Model 1600
Armscor AK-22
Armscorp M-14 Semi-Auto Rifle
Australian Automatic Arms SAR
Australian Automatic Arms SAC
Australian Automatic Arms SAP
Australian Automatic Arms SP Hunting Rifle
Australian Automatic Arms SP-20 Hunting Rifle
Australian L1A1 FAL
Auto-Ordnance Mod 1927A-3
Auto-Ordnance 1927-A5 Pistol
Barrett Light-Fifty
Benelli MI Super 90 Defense Shotgun
Beretta AR-70 Sporter
Beretta SC-70 Carbine
Bushmaster Auto Rifle
Bushmaster Rifle
Bushmaster Auto Pistol
Calico Model 100 Carbine
Calico Model 100 Pistol
Calico Model 900 Carbine
Calico Model 951 Tactical Carbine
CETME Rifle
Clayco AKS Rifle
Cobray M-11
Cobray M-11/9
Cobray 9mm Carbine
Cobray M-12
Colt AR-15
Colt AR-15 9mm Carbine
Colt AR-15A2 Sporter 11
Colt AR-15A2 Carbine
Colt AR-15A2 H-BAR
Colt AR-I5A2-Delta H-BAR
Colt Match Delta H-BAR
Colt Sporter Lightweight
Colt Sporter Target
Commando Arms Carbine

Daewoo AR110C
Daewoo AR100
Demro TAC-1 Carbine
Demro XF-7 Carbine
Eagle Arms EA-15 Action Master Auto Rifle
Eagle Arms EA-15 Auto Rifle
Eagle Arms EA-15 El Carbine
Eagle Arms EA-15 E2 Carbine
Eagle Arms EA-15 E2 H-BAR
Eagle Arms EA-15 Golden Eagle Auto Rifle
Egyptian Maadi AKM
Egyptian Maadi "Thumbhole AKM"
EMF AP-74
Encom Mk IV
FAMAS Semi-Auto Rifle
Feather AT-9 Carbine
Feather AT-22
Feather Mini-AT
Feather SAR-180 Carbine Feather Saturn 30 Rifle
Federal Model XC-220
Federal XC900 Pistol
Federal XC450 Pistol
Fed Ord M-14 Rifle
F.I.E./Franchl Para Carbine FN-FNC
FN "G series" FAL
FN-LAR Competition Auto FN-LAR Heavy Barrel .308 Match
FN-LAR Paratrooper Model 50-64 FN-LAR
  Model 50-63
Franchi SPAS-12 Shotgun
Galil AR
Galil ARM
Galil Sniper Rifle
Galil Sporter
Goncz High-Tech Carbine
Goncz High-Tech Long Pistol
Grendel P-31 Auto Pistol
Grendel R-31 Auto Carbine
Heckler & Koch PSG-1 Marksman Rifle
Heckler & Koch SP89
Heckler.& Koch VP 70Z Pistol
Heckler & Koch 91
Heckler & Koch 93
Heckler & Koch 94
Holmes MP-22
Holmes MP-38
Holmes MP-83
Intratec Scorpion
Intratec TEC-9

Intratec TEC-DC9
Intratec TEC-22
Israeli FALs
Iver Johnson Enforcer Model 3000 Auto
Iver Johnson PM30HB Carbine
Kassnar SA 85M AKM
Kassnar SA 85M "Thumbhole AKM"
MAC-10 Semi Auto
MAC-11 Semi-Auto
Micro Uzi Pistol
Mini Uzi Pistol
Mitchell AKM
Mitchell AK-22
Mitchell Galil/22
Mitchell Heavy Barrel AKM
Mitchell MAS-22
Mitchell M-16/22
Mitchell M-76 Counter Sniper Rifle
any MI Carbine with folding stock
Norinco MAK-90 Rifle
Norinco MAK-91 Legend Rifle
Norinco Officer's Nine Carbine
Norinco RPK Rifle
Norinco Type 81S Rifle
Norinco Type 81MGS Rifle
Norinco Type 84S AK
Norinco Type 86S "Bullpup" AK Rifle
Norinco Type 86S-7 Rifle
Norinco Type 88SB Rifle
Olympic Arms CAR-9
Olympic Arms CAR-15
Olympic Arms CAR-40
Olympic Arms CAR-45
Olympic Arms CAR-310
Olympic Arms K-4 AR-15 Rifle
Partisan Avenger
Poly Technologies AK-47/S
Poly Technologies AKS-762
Poly Technologies AKS-762 Down Folder
Poly Technologies AKS-762 Side Folder
Poly Technologies M-14/S
Poly Technologies RPKS-74 Assault Rifle
Ruger Mini-14/5

Ruger Mini-14 with folding stock
Scarab Skorpion Pistol
SIG AMT
SIG PE-57
SIG SG 550-2 SP Rifle
SIG SG 550-2 SP Carbine
Smith Enterprises M-14 Semi-Auto Rifle
Spectre Carbine
Spectre DA pistol
Springfield Armory SAR-3
Springfield Armory SAR-48 Standard
Springfield Armory SAR-48 Bush Rifle
Springfield Armory SAR-48 Heavy Barrel
Springfield Armory SAR-48 Para
Springfield Armory SAR-4800
Springfield Armory MIA
Springfield Armory MIA Super Match
Springfield Armory M1A-A1 Bush Rifle
Springfield Armory BM-59 Italian Model
Springfield Armory.BM-59 Alpine Model
Springfield Armory BM-59 Alpine Paratrooper Model
Springfield Armory BM-59 Nigerian Mk IV Model
Springfield Armory M-21 Sniper Rifle
Sterling Carbine
Steyr AUG-SA
Street Sweeper Shotgun
Striker 12 SE-12 Shotgun
SVD "Tiger" Sniper Rifle
Universal 100 Carbine
USAS-12 Auto
Uzi Pistol
Uzi Carbine
Valmet M-62/S Rifle
Valmet M-71/S Rifle
Valmet M-76 Standard Rifle
Valmet M-78 Rifle
Valmet M-82 Bullpup Rifle
Valmet Hunter Rifle
Weaver Arms Nighthawk
Wilkinson "Linda" Pistol
Wilkinson "Terry" Carbine
XM 231S Semi-Auto Pistol

The law further stipulates that "any semiautomatic assault weapon manufactured after the date of enactment [9/13/94] shall clearly show the date on which the weapon was manufactured."

BAN OF LARGE CAPACITY AMMUNITION FEEDING DEVICES.

The term large capacity ammunition feeding device means:

A magazine, belt, drum, feed strip, or similar device manufactured after the date of enactment of the Violent Crime Control and Law Enforcement Act of 1994 [9/13/94] that has the capacity of, or that can be readily restored or converted to accept more than 10 rounds of ammunition. It does not include an attached tubular device designed to accept, and capable of operating only with .22 caliber rimfire ammunition.

A large capacity feeding device manufactured after the date of enactment [9/13/94] shall be identified by a serial number that clearly shows that the device was manufactured or imported after the effective date of the subsection, and such other identification as the Secretary may by regulation prescribe.

The ban on magazines capable of holding more than 10 rounds does not apply to magazines produced or imported prior to September 13, 1994. These pre-ban magazines are still legal to own and sell. Again the regulations supporting this portion of the law have yet to be written and may contain provisions with unknown effects.

1997 . . . THE YEAR IN REVIEW

by Dave Tinker

"After two years of drought, there has to be some kind of increase in demand. If the consumer is interested, the dealer starts buying. Then the wholesaler starts his buying. And it should all trickle back to the manufacturer in a few months." **(A firearms manufacturer on his 1997 prospects.)**

As far as we can tell, that manufacturer may still be waiting for his market observation to be fulfilled, because none of the parties—consumers, dealers or distributors—showed enough buying interest to make 1997 much more than a third consecutive year of drought. But unlike the dry spells of 1995 and 1996, the industry in 1997 was unable to convince itself that better times were just a hot new gun or a sales incentive or two around the corner. Firearms executives were instead forced to acknowledge that this industry has problems that go far beyond one year's consumer, dealer and distributor demand.

One of the largest problems the industry had to deal with in 1997—and one it will face for the next several years unless drastic changes are made soon—is a shrinking and aging base of customers for its wares.

"The average age of our ultimate customer keeps going up," a marketing manager observed. "We're all fighting to sell rifles to these people right up until five minutes before they die. The result is that distributors are basically selling guns for the payment terms—3 percent, 5 percent or whatever. That's not going to change until we find some new customers."

Several manufacturers, especially long gun producers, had that point driven home early in the year when they were forced to sell at ridiculously low margins just to keep the lines moving. Others, like U.S. Repeating Arms Company, shut down their factories and furloughed workers for a month during the middle of the year.

Although the low margin sales were generally restricted to the major brand names, lower volume long gun producers also felt the effect on their business.

"Smaller companies like us end up getting whiplash," a marketing vice president observed. "Our customers are getting good sell-through on our products, and they're making money on them. But they owe the big companies so much that they can't re-order. One year you have legislative pressure, the next year you have a reduction in the number of FFL dealers and then you have the overall market go like this," he said. "Not that the industry is very good at it anyway, but this makes it hard to plan."

It was no better in the handgun business. If the truth were to be told, it was probably much worse but the market was better prepared for weak sales than it was in the previous two years. Manufacturers and distributors carved out niche markets for themselves, concentrating on exclusive deals and guns they could fit into the crowded but still profitable concealed carry field.

Various manufacturers' sales incentives helped the flow, although there was concern (and still is) that the market was being built on false promises and by artificial means.

"Some people call it distress marketing, but I call it good marketing," said a multi-store retailer, who estimated that his sales for the year were down about a percentage point from 1996. "If there is a trend in marketing right now, it is that high priced items are selling well and low priced products are doing nicely. It is the product lines in the middle, which covers the bulk of the market, that has people worried because they just aren't moving. Most of the new products coming out are at one end of the scale or the other. Few companies are even trying the middle ground."

The "middle ground" was the most crowded part of the handgun market, and an area in which most of the bargains were found. Most of the excess inventory apparently was at the distributor level, which backed things up to the manufacturers.

"We just bought about $12 million worth of inventory from other distributors and have another $8 or $9 million committed," said a major wholesaler, who called himself a scavenger. "We've had some manufacturers complain that we're down as much as $1 million in order dollars with them this year, but we're actually selling more of their products than we were last year. We're just buying from their other distributors."

Handgun manufacturers took steps to make sure that there won't be as many inventory-driven bargains on the market by the end of the year. Sigarms has cut back on production to shrink its inventory levels while Glock recently made large sales to New Zealand and Israel that tightened its supply to the point of being sold out here for the rest of 1997.

The ongoing problems with the handgun markets took their toll on accessories as well, especially lasers and electronic dot sights. Certain brands, according to distributors, moved along at the rate of about 20 a month for much of the year, compared to about 200 a year ago.

"We never anticipated this much of a drop. Nobody did," an optics manufacturer lamented. "It involves anything that has to do with handguns. The trend is that it isn't getting any better and that will lead to some problems as we go along."

Nowhere was the trend more clearly defined than in mid-summer announcements from Sturm, Ruger & Company and Smith & Wesson.

Ruger bought Callaway Golf's interest in the recently completed Antelope Hills foundry in Prescott, Arizona for $7 million. Callaway also agreed to purchase an additional one million cast titanium golf club heads from Ruger over and above present orders with the company. Shipments will be made on a monthly basis beginning in early 1998, Ruger said.

"This new arrangement makes Ruger the sole owner of the most complete and efficient foundry of its kind specializing in large production of titanium components," said chairman William B. Ruger. "Ruger becomes an active and strongly committed member of the golf industry and we will have the capacity to be of service to many other industries."

Smith & Wesson signed an agreement to produce a new set of forged irons for Snake Eyes Golf Clubs, which said the gun manufacturer is "an ideal match." The new clubs hit the market at the end of 1997.

When major news from the two largest companies in the handgun business involves golf clubs, you know there is a problem.

Ownership and Management Changes Abound

While many companies were concentrating on finding new ways of salvaging an otherwise bad year, others worked on building market share the old-fashioned way: They bought it.

Colt's Manufacturing Company, Inc., which has made the list of top industry news stories in past years for its bankruptcy troubles and a controversial new pistol, signed letters of intent to purchase FN Herstal from Giat Industries, the French-government owned defense conglomerate. The deal would make Colt's the owner of such notable American companies as U.S. Repeating Arms Company, Browning Arms Company and FN Manufacturing, the lead supplier of the military's M16 rifle and related hardware.

"The acquisition of Herstal would represent an important step in creating the premier small arms manufacturer to the armed forces of the world and unite four important worldwide brands: Colt, FN Herstal, Winchester and Browning," Colt's chairman Donald Zilkha said.

"Purchasing FN Herstal does several things for Colt's in addition to making it the sole supplier of the M16," said a source familiar with the company. "It would allow the company to get out of Hartford and move into the USRAC facility. Colt's could consolidate all of its overhead into one state-of-the-art property."

Another scenario being discussed has Colt's moving all of its operations to FN's Columbia factory. While it is obviously cheaper to do business in South Carolina, a move out of Connecticut would require Colt's to pay back more than $10 million to the Connecticut Development Authority. CDA invested that amount in the company in 1994 in return for a pledge that Colt's stay in the state for 10 years.

Blount, Inc. continued its run of picking up new companies for its Sporting Equipment division when it inked a deal to purchase ammunition manufacturer Federal Cartridge Company from Pentair, Inc. The deal could bump the Blount division's sales to as much as $300 million by the end of 1998.

Federal, which employs approximately 900 people at plants in Anoka, Minnesota and Richmond, Indiana, had net sales of about $130 million in 1996. Those sales figures rank Federal third among the "Big Three" in ammunition manufacturing behind Olin Winchester and Remington Arms. The acquisition could easily move Blount's division into second place ahead of Remington in the ammunition sales game. By adding Federal's sales to those generated by Blount's existing CCI, Blazer, Lawman and Gold Dot lines, Blount ammunition revenues should surpass Remington's 1996 sales of $160.2 million.

"Federal Cartridge is one of the premier brands in the shooting sports industry," said Blount president and chief executive officer John M. Panettiere. "We believe that their strong name recognition will greatly enhance and expand our existing product offerings. Federal's excellent product lines, sound management team, and talented workforce will provide us with tremendous opportunities for growth and further enhance our competitive position in the shooting sports industry."

"This acquisition is another demonstration of Blount's commitment to its corporate strategy of expanding our core businesses through acquisitions, investments in people and technology, and strategic partnerships," Panettiere said.

That corporate strategy has been particularly evident in Blount's Sporting Equipment group over the last few years. In that time, the company has acquired Ram-Line, Inc., Simmons Outdoor Corp., Jon-E and Bar-Buoy. Rumors persist that Blount is also looking for a firearms manufacturing company although no deal has been done. (Browning has been prominently mentioned on many occasions.)

Hoppe's, one of the most recognized brands of cleaning supplies and accessories in the business, also has a new corporate home. The company was sold to Brunswick, where it will be part of the corporation's outdoor recreation group.

Several leading companies may not be under new ownership in 1998, but they will be under new management or operating under different partnership arrangements.

Heckler & Koch and Italian shotgun manufacturer Benelli Armi did not extend their exclusive U.S. commercial distribution agreement when it expired at the end of the year, saying each company has "grown to the point where they must concentrate all their sales efforts in their specialized areas of expertise from both a product and market standpoint." The Benelli line accounted for about 60-65 percent of HK's American sales.

Beginning this January, Benelli will handle its own importing, marketing and distribution through a newly-formed operation called Benelli, Inc., which is jointly owned by Benelli Armi and Beretta Holding. The new company will be headquartered in a separate facility at Beretta's Accokeek, Maryland location. Piero Gussalli Beretta, managing director of Beretta Holding, will be president of the new venture. Stephen Otway was appointed vice president and general manager.

Beretta said he has been pleased with the consumer acceptance and steady growth of Benelli products achieved through the H&K distribution arrangement, but added that "it was simply time for Benelli to have its own independent operation and direct control of its future in the important U.S. market.

Sigarms, Inc. replaced its top management early in 1997, hiring George Schneider, former general manager of the Beretta U.S.A. operation in Maryland, as president and chief executive officer of Sigarms, Inc. Herman Kloetzer is the new general manager and executive vice president of the Exeter, New Hampshire-based facility.

Interarms named industry veteran Ron Stillwell, who had been president of Colt and Houston-based High Standard Manufacturing, as its chief operating officer in a late summer management shake-up. Sales and marketing executive Gene Lumsden and vice president/treasurer David McGilvey left the company in that purge.

Alson C. Cornell was named executive vice president of sales and marketing for O.F. Mossberg & Sons, Inc. Cornell, who previously worked for Beretta U.S.A., will direct all of Mossberg's domestic, export and mass merchant sales functions as well as external communications and product service. He will also manage law enforcement and government sales for Mossberg's Uzi America subsidiary operation.

Taurus International vice president Bruce Savane announced his retirement in late September after 20 years with the Brazilian manufacturer. He was replaced by Bob Morrison, an industry veteran who most recently was the firm's western region representative.

The management shuffle was not restricted to firearms-related companies. The ammunition world had its share of movement as well, with Olin Winchester and Fiocchi of America naming new top executives as they tried to turn around extremely sluggish sales.

Olin appointed Thomas M. Gura, Jr. to the Winchester presidency. Gura, who was vice president of sales and marketing for Olin's brass division, has been with Olin since 1968 in a variety of sales and marketing jobs. Gura succeeds Douglas J. Cahill, who resigned as Winchester president. Marketing vice president Harlan Kent resigned earlier while Tom Conroy was transferred to another job within Olin.

Focchi named Michael Shea vice president of sales. He succeeds Craig Alderman as the top executive of the Italian manufacturer's U.S. subsidiary. Market sources said Alderman's contract was not renewed.

Those new executives will be asked to correct a downward trend in ammunition sales that has been ongoing for the better part of three years. Excise tax collection data showed that ammo companies paid $52.4 million through the end of 1996. That is down from $54.2 million in 1995 and $69.2 million in 1994.

Winchester's sales, like just about every other company's, were less than stellar through the same period, although the company entered several "strategic alliances" with other manufacturers in 1997, designed to perk up business. Sources said those ties with Nosler, Delta Frangible Ammunition and Bismuth Cartridge are strong and performing positively enough to keep them intact despite the management change.

Next Case, Please...

The industry did a little better in court during 1997 than it did in the market, winning a pair of troublesome liability cases in California and New York while disposing of at least one major internal patent fight that had been ongoing for nearly three years.

Glock Inc. and Smith & Wesson reached an out-of-court settlement of Glock's patent infringement and trade dress lawsuit over S&W's Sigma pistol series. The settlement came just hours before trial was to begin in the federal action, which Glock brought in July 1994 shortly after Smith & Wesson introduced the polymer-framed Sigma. Trade dress allegations were resolved at the same time when Glock granted Smith & Wesson a worldwide trade dress license for the Sigma pistols. S&W will pay an undisclosed amount for the license.

The companies said they agreed to "amicably resolve the lawsuit rather than continuing with the arduous and expensive course of litigation and inevitable appeals process. The settlement resolves all issues between the parties respecting the Sigma Series pistols on a worldwide basis."

Glock's claims of infringement hinged on Smith & Wesson's alleged use of a "positive guide means" in the Sigma pistols, something Glock says is protected under its patent. S&W has "maintained from the outset, and continues to maintain today, that the Sigma Series do not contain a positive guide means" in the sense of the Glock patent. Those contentions aside, Smith & Wesson agreed to remove the subject of Glock's assertions, a surface located just below the sear on the Sigma pistols. Glock agreed that the modification would resolve the patent claims.

On the liability front, California Superior Court Judge James Warren dismissed a lawsuit that claimed Intratec TEC 9 and TEC DC-9 pistol manufacturer Navegar, Inc. was to blame for a murderer's use of its guns in a 1993 mass killing at a San Francisco law firm.

Relatives of the victims, aided by lawyers from the Center to Prevent Handgun Violence, sued Navegar, U.S.A. Magazines, Inc., Hellfire Systems, and a Las Vegas pawn shop. The pawn shop settled its portion out of court, Hellfire went into bankruptcy and U.S.A. was dismissed from the action in 1995.

The plaintiffs claimed that Navegar was liable because its guns were prohibited under California's Roberti-Roos assault weapons ban. Navegar lawyers pointed out that the guns were "legally manufactured in Florida, legally put into commerce, and legally purchased in Nevada by the homicidal maniac who perpetrated the rampage."

Warren rejected the plaintiffs' assertion that advertisements for the Intratec pistols led to Ferri's deadly rampage, saying the attempts to link the murders to the ads "amount to little more than guesswork." He concluded that there is no evidence that the advertisements were a "substantial factor" in the killings.

"Even if Navegar violated California's assault weapons ban by advertising outlawed weapons (in the state), plaintiffs have adduced no direct evidence that establishes a causal link between Navegar's conduct and the plaintiffs' damages," Warren said. He also denied the plaintiffs' position that Navegar should not have sold the firearm because it could be used criminally, saying he found no legal precedent to support the claim.

"In case after case and jurisdiction after jurisdiction, courts have refused to impose a duty upon firearms manufacturers not to sell their products merely because of the potential misuse of the product by a third party," the judge said.

Industry attorneys were pleased if not a little surprised by Warren's decision, especially after he had ruled two years earlier that the plaintiffs could pursue their lawsuit against Navegar.

"It's a big win for the firearms industry," said Robert Ricker of the American Shooting Sports Council. "It's going to slam the door on these defectless product liability claims."

The 2nd U.S. Court of Appeals slammed the door on another case when it affirmed the dismissal of a $1.49 billion lawsuit brought against Olin Corporation by a freshman Congressman whose husband was among nine killed in a 1993 Long Island Railroad shooting spree.

The three judge panel voted 2-1 to uphold a lower court's ruling in the suit brought by Rep. Carolyn McCarthy, who rode an anti-gun campaign to Congress. The decision on the suit, which claimed Olin Winchester's marketing strategy for the Black Talon cartridge influenced the shooter, means state courts cannot hear McCarthy's case.

Another federal appeals court ruled in favor of gun shows in a California case, finding that Santa Clara County's attempt to ban gun sales on its fairgrounds violates the constitutional right of free speech.

The county's restriction on transactions during gun shows at the fairgrounds, approved in January 1996, was an attempt to suppress truthful speech about a legal product, said the 9th U.S. Circuit

Court of Appeals. The court upheld a federal judge's decision last July to strike down the ban and let gun sales continue.

"A proposal to engage in (a gun sale) is protected as commercial speech under the First Amendment," said Judge Joseph Sneed, who wrote the panel's opinion in the 3-0 decision.

The judge said that while commercial speech can be restricted to protect a substantial, legitimate concern of the government, the county did not show the necessity for the ban on gun sales. Prohibiting sales only at the fairgrounds, while allowing them elsewhere in the county, does not reduce the supply of guns and is not a legitimate way for the county to send a message to the public that it opposes gun use, he added.

"The county has not presented a shred of evidence that any county resident, or anyone else, has somehow gotten the mistaken impression that the county promotes gun use," or that any such impression was caused by gun sales at the fairgrounds, Sneed opined. "The record suggests that (the policy) is at best an inept response to residents who strongly support the cause of gun control."

Looking to Next Year...

It is never easy to predict what the firearms industry will do from one year to the next, but it is safe to assume that 1998 will bring even more change to an already shaken business. Barring major legislative or regulatory actions, none of the changes should hinder your ability to buy guns when you want to. But several hundred companies are hoping you'll do it soon!

1997: THE YEAR THE FOG LIFTED

by Jim Schneider

In many ways, 1997 truly was the year the fog lifted on a variety of firearms issues.

The U.S. Supreme Court issued its long-awaited decision on the Brady Law, striking down part of it as unconstitutional and hinting there may eventually be a ruling on the true meaning of the Second Amendment.

America's richest man threw his weight behind gun control, and it became apparent that the great smoke screen for virtually any anti-gun proposal these days involves the words "safety" or "public health."

Also in '97, a pro-gun source in the Justice Department leaked a paper outlining all the goodies the Clinton / Gore Administration has in mind for America's gun owners and collectors. Meanwhile, it became clear that what is occurring actually represents a global push for gun control.

The year also saw a gun dealer / collector learn that even when you win in court you sometimes lose the gun, and Ray Carn was among hundreds of Australian gun collectors who learned that it really could happen to them.

The Brady Decision

The "gun story" that grabbed the most headlines in '97 came when the Supreme Court ruled that the federal government cannot compel local police to determine whether buyers are fit to purchase a handgun.

Although the 5-4 decision was a victory for pro-gun groups, it was less than total since the court did nor rule the waiting period itself unconstitutional.

Writing for the court, Justice Antonin Scalia stated, "The federal government may neither issue directives requiring the states to address particular problems, nor command the states' officers, or those of their political subdivisions, to administer or enforce a federal regulatory program.

"Such commands are fundamentally incompatible with our constitutional system of dual sovereignty."

Associated Press said at the time that, "The ruling is further evidence of the conservative court's determination to shift the balance of power from the federal government toward the states."

Ironically, late in '98 the Brady Law becomes a federal instant check, something pro-gun groups like the National Rifle Association have supported for years. If the computer finds the would-be purchaser is clean, he buys the gun on the spot. On the other hand, if it finds he is a felon, he may be arrested within minutes.

In those states that have an instant check in place, dozens of felons have been arrested attempting to buy a handgun — compared to the handful actually arrested under the Brady Law. In the congressional battle over passage of the Brady Bill, the NRA was actually pushing for a tougher and more effective law than Handgun Control Inc. But you didn't see that reported in many newspapers.

Nor were you likely to see Justice Clarence Thomas' concurring opinion in the Printz v. U.S. (Brady) case suggesting that sometime in the future the Supreme Court may be ruling on the true meaning of the Second Amendment.

In that opinion, Thomas stated, "The Second Amendment similarly appears to contain an express limitation on the government's authority. The Second Amendment provides '(a) well regulated Militia, being necessary to the security of a free state, the right of the people to keep and bear arms, shall not be infringed.'

"This court has not had recent occasion to consider the nature of the substantive right safeguarded by the Second Amendment.

"If, however, the Second Amendment is read to confer a personal right to 'keep and bear arms,' a colorable argument exists that the federal government's regulatory scheme, at least as it pertains to the purely intra-state sale or possession of firearms, runs afoul of that amendment's protections.

"As the parties did not raise this argument, we need not consider it here.

"Perhaps, at some future date, this Court will have the opportunity to determine whether Justice Story was correct when he wrote that the right to bear arms 'has justly been considered as the palladium of the liberties of the republic....'"

If that opportunity arises, Justices Scalia and Thomas seem to be leaning toward interpreting the Second Amendment as an individual right. Whether we could garner three more votes on the court remains to be seen.

Following the Brady decision, I talked with Second Amendment scholar and attorney Dr. Stephen Halbrook, who argued the case before the Supreme Court. He understandably was quite pleased with the decision.

"It's a great victory not just for gun owners but for the American people generally because it helps stem the tide of increasing federal encroachment on the powers of the states and localities and hence the sovereignty of this country," Halbrook said.

"I don't like the fact that the waiting period remains; but it is a small price to pay to prevent Brady II from being enacted, which would have conscripted the states and localities to set up registration of all firearms, to have arsenal licenses for two bricks of .22 ammo and all the other things that were in Brady II. It puts the skids on that."

Dr. Stephen Halbrook

Halbrook noted that immediately following the Supreme Court's decision, President Clinton ordered Attorney General Janet Reno and Treasury Secretary Robert Rubin to contact local law enforcement officials and tell them that local officials could still conduct background checks of their own.

Halbrook fired off a letter to Clinton and Reno pointing out that what they were advising is illegal in many states.

Currently, Halbrook is collecting information on what he claims are illegal background fees still being charged in some states. He is considering class action lawsuits to recover the illegally collected fees still being charged some handgun purchasers.

America's Richest Man

While the Brady decision generated some positive news for our side, here's one 1997 headline that could scare you: "America's Richest Man Pushing Gun Control."

And it should! Because according to newspapers in the state of Washington, that's exactly what's happening.

The Seattle Post-Intelligencer and other Washington newspapers have reported that Microsoft mogul Bill Gates — reportedly worth more than $16 billion — helped bankroll Initiative 676 that appeared on the ballot in that state on Nov. 4. Earlier this year Gates and his family spent over $36,000 to help get the initiative on the ballot — not counting money spent sponsoring fund-raising events to solicit contributions from other wealthy anti-gunners.

Indeed, writing in the Bellevue East Side Journal, Adele Ferguson noted how Gates and a handful of other rich residents are driving the social agenda in Washington State.

Not only was Gates successful in getting $10,000 donations for Initiative 676 from his wealthy friends, but the major media outlets were more than happy to help portray this as a "gun safety" initiative.

In fact, the initiative was just another example of how the anti-gunners are attempting to disguise every gun control measure imaginable as a "safety" measure.

Among other things, Initiative 676 was set to register everyone in the state who "possesses or controls" a handgun, as well as their spouses, require triggerlocks accompany all handgun transfers and prohibit teaching of firearms safety to a spouse or children except in officially designated shooting areas.

Federal Level

On the federal level, triggerlock and "safe" storage legislation held center stage for much of '97. And the other side has attempted to paint us into a corner on this issue.

On one hand, every responsible gun owner and collector believes in the safe storage of firearms where a child is not going to accidentally find them. However, some of the more extreme proposals that say you must keep firearms locked securely in one room and ammunition locked securely in another room also say: "No gun will be used for self-defense in this house."

While reasonable laws may sound okay, there's also the broader question of how much do we compromise? Unfortunately, if we review what has happened in the United Kingdom and Australia we see that the anti-gunners there often played the "safety card" until they were strong enough to simply ban large groups of firearms outright.

I chatted with Joe Phillips, director of the Federal Affairs Division of the NRA's Institute for Legislative Action (NRA-ILA), shortly after the House passed its Juvenile Justice Bill without a triggerlock provision, much to the chagrin of the Clinton Administration.

Phillips said, "Speaking professionally — knowing where the other side wants to go with this, which is mandatory safety, education and training, and mandatory requirements for safe storage at home, ultimately leading to what Great Britain has, which is you can't even have a firearm in your home — I have no problem whatsoever with drawing the line in the sand and trying to defend the line.

"Personally, I think this is outrageous what they are trying to do. A government mandate."

Why all the interest in triggerlocks?

Phillips pointed out, "The Democrats have polled in this. When you ask the average person on the street, 'Do you think you should be able to put devices on firearms that keep children from accidentally discharging the firearms?,' the question polls out real high.

"What we found is that you can very quickly move people in the other direction when you say, 'Do you believe government should be mandating how you store your firearms?' and 'Do you believe that safe firearms education and training is a good thing and would you support increased funding for education, safety and training?' That number moves right back over.

"So they like education and training. They hate government mandates. They hate the idea of the government substituting its judgment for theirs. And they particularly like the idea that responsible people act responsibly, but they're not punished by government for not doing so."

In the face of this "safety" hysteria, it should be remembered that the annual number of fatal firearms accidents has decreased 56% since 1930 — even though the number of Americans has more than doubled during that period.

As usual with its legislative initiatives, the Clinton Administration had a carefully designed study ready to support its push for triggerlocks and safe storage provisions.

As the debate raged in Congress, a study conducted back in 1994 was released reportedly showing that an "unlocked gun" can be found in about one in every six American households.

"A locked gun can avoid a family tragedy," Attorney General Janet Reno said in a statement accompanying the report on the Justice Department study.

Now It's 'Junk Guns'

Of course, there were other anti- and pro-gun federal legislative proposals in 1997.

Among them were "junk gun" bills. "Junk gun" is simply the 1990's term used to revive the much discredited "Saturday Night Special" proposals of the '70s and '80s.

And some of the same old players were at it again in Congress. Sen. Barbara Boxer (D-CA) filed her much publicized bill, SB-70, to ban "junk guns."

At the same time Rep. Charles Schumer (D-NY) filed HB-492, a similar bill, which would impose the 1968 "sporting use" standard that banned the importation of small or inexpensive handguns to domestically-manufactured handguns. Boxer claimed that the 1968 Gun Control Act imposed a double standard by imposing criteria for prohibiting guns with similar characteristics to be made and sold in the US.

Interestingly, S-70 would allow police and government agencies to have these "unsafe" guns, often carried as a back-up or off-duty gun.

Unfortunately, the "junk gun" push has spread to state legislatures.

With anti-gunners attempting to portray all police officers as anti-gun, it was good to see one national police group blast S-70.

"U.S. Sen. Barbara Boxer's proposal to ban inexpensive, so-called 'junk' handguns is discriminatory, opposed by law enforcement and a proven crime reduction failure," declared James Fotis, executive director of the 50,000-member Law Enforcement Alliance of America (LEAA) with headquarters in Falls Church, VA.

"Sen. Boxer's plan to ban smaller, less expensive handguns is backdoor discrimination against the poor who often live in tough, high-crime neighborhoods infested with drug dealers and gangs. Sen. Boxer's proposed handgun ban will eliminate an affordable, self-defense tool for America's honest poor....

"I challenge the media and all members of Congress to ask America's honest poor if they believe Sen. Boxer's income-based gun ban will reduce crime, protect them from criminal attack, take more criminals off the street or clean up drug-gang crime in their neighborhoods."

Fotis pointed out, "It will also ban some high quality, expensive firearms used everyday by America's law enforcement professionals, security officers, shop owners and citizens."

BATF on Bullets

President Clinton's push for a new armor-piercing bullet law took a shot from an unexpected source in '97 when BATF issued a draft of a study on ammunition and protective vests.

BATF said that since passage of the nation's current laws regarding armor-piercing ammunition, "...no police officer in the United States has died as a result of a round of armor-piercing ammunition, as defined, having been fired from a handgun, subsequently penetrating an officer's protective body armor causing lethal injuries."

BATF concluded, "Combined with the availability of sensible defensive strategies, the existence of laws restricting the common availability of armor-piercing ammunition are clearly working to protect law enforcement officers and no attempt to discard the existing laws should be undertaken.

"At the same time, because the existing laws are working, no additional legislation regarding such laws is necessary. In this matter, to err on the conservative side of the existing status quo laws is to avoid any experimentation with police officer lives that could conceivably lead to numerous additional police fatalities."

However, not all the news regarding bullet legislation was good in '97. There were bills to ban and place prohibitively high taxes on ammunition.

And while the federal government is studying placing taggants in explosive materials for tracing purposes, some state legislators have been playing with taggant legislation. Some of these proposals — none of which passed — would ban even possession of ammunition not containing taggants.

If your collection includes ammunition — and there's no exemption in the bill for collectors — guess what happens.

On another front, the domestic violence misdemeanor law rushed through Congress in 1996 came back to haunt civilians and police officers in '97. The law prohibits possession of a firearm by anyone ever convicted of a domestic violence misdemeanor — even though in some states that is defined as yelling at one's spouse.

Two Pro-Gun Bills

On our side of the coin, two gun bills of special interest to everyone concerned with personal and home defense were filed in the House in '97.

HR-27 would provide civil penalties for anyone who denies people the right to have firearms in their home for defensive purposes.

The bill was filed Rep. Roscoe Bartlett (R-MD) and affirms the right to obtain firearms for security and to use firearms in defense of self, family or home.

The bill gives a person whose rights have been violated in any manner the authority to bring a civil action in any U.S. district court against the United States, any state or any person for damages, injunctive relief and other relief deemed appropriate by the court, including attorney's fees.

The other bill was HR-339, a measure which would permit people who have been issued concealed carry licenses in their state to have licenses honored in every other state, including those which do not issue carry licenses to their own residents.

Introduced by Rep. Cliff Stearns (R-FL), HR-339 would provide that anyone who is not prohibited by federal law from possessing, transporting, shipping or receiving a firearm may carry in another state notwithstanding any law of the state being visited or traveled through. While in such other state, the state laws governing concealed carry will apply to the nonresident.

For those states which do not have clear statutes regarding licensing, or who may carry concealed, the Stearns bill would establish minimum federal standards.

Justice Department Paper

It was not a specific anti- or pro-gun bill but a January, 1997, Department of Justice paper that was leaked to the gun press that should have received headlines across the country.

Despite President Clinton's early claims about loving duck hunters, the true intentions of the Clinton/ Gore Administration regarding gun owners were revealed in the paper.

A high Justice Department source, who for obvious reasons wished to remain unnamed, said these provisions would not be presented as one massive bill but introduced in Congress one or two at a time. In fact, a number already have been.

The Justice Department paper was a complete laundry list of anti-gun proposals

Well known Second Amendment scholar and lawyer Dave Hardy noted, "It looks to me like this list basically took every anti-gun proposal of the last five years and tried to roll them into one long list.

"Basically, this is a proposal to outlaw gun ownership through the means of making it so burdensome that no one can afford to own firearms."

Perhaps the greatest threat comes from two proposals that appear under the "Gang Violence" section of the Justice Department paper:

— Amend the RICO statute to add certain federal offenses involving the illegal transfer of firearms to the list of RICO predicates.

— Increase the penalty for certain RICO violations and facilitate the prosecution of certain RICO cases by providing the prosecutors need not prove that a defendant personally agreed to commit any acts of racketeering.

Hardy pointed out RICO "is the government's neutron bomb" designed to take out Mafia bosses.

"Then you're going to turn that loose on the average FFL (holder)?" he asked. "It's designed that way. You can confiscate all of his assets, tie up everything, massive penalties, civil liability.

"As I said, RICO is designed as the neutron bomb for the most serious of offenders. And they want to turn that loose on Joe Blow's Gun Shop."

International Front

Perhaps nowhere did the fog lift more in '97 than on the international front. The major media had been ridiculing the National Rifle Association for its concerns over what the United Nations might be doing.

Then on July 18 members of the United Nations Panel of Governmental Experts on Small Arms agreed on their recommendations. According to the anti-gun British American Security Information Council, these recommendations included urging nations:

— to ensure "effective" control over possession and transfer of small arms and "light weapons" by imposing requirements on all civilian possession of small arms and "light weapons" in their territory;

— to develop laws regarding which arms are permitted for civilian possession and under which conditions they can be used;

— to initiate laws, regulations and administrative procedures to exercise effective control over the legal possession of small arms and "light weapons" and over their transfer;

— to evaluate the feasibility of marking arms at the time of manufacture;

— to restrict the manufacture and sales of small arms and "light weapons" to government-authorized manufacturers and dealers;

— to destroy surplus firearms;

— to improve border controls and training for customs officials; and

— to continue and expand regional gun buy-up programs.

In other words, total control of all firearms worldwide. The question is: Will global gun registration be followed by global gun confiscation?

We do know that British handgun owners kissed their firearms good-bye in '97, as did Australians who owned semiautomatic long guns and pump action shotguns.

The news form overseas wasn't all bad. The Polish government is preparing to liberalize its gun laws — apparently with the support of police officials. And up in Canada, tribal chiefs are going to court to challenge that nation's new gun control laws unless native hunters are exempted.

Waiting 30 Years

Then there were a couple of gun collectors who had their own traumas in 1997. One was Loring Hill of Elkins Park, PA, who has been trying to get back his prized Al Capone-era Thompson submachinegun since authorities confiscated a portion of his gun collection back in 1968.

But the former Philadelphia police officer has been told the gun has mysteriously disappeared from the arsenal of Chester County, PA, detectives.

Naturally, Hill, now 57, wants an explanation.

Hill was a gun dealer who sold firearms to police departments when the Pennsylvania State Police arrested him for trafficking in automatic weapons.

At his trial, Hill argued that his federal dealer's license allowed him to sell automatic firearms. A county judge ruled that the Pennsylvania law banning the practice superseded Hill's license — even if he was selling to police departments. Hill was convicted of unlawful trafficking, put on two years' probation and fined $200.

The 18 guns he had confiscated included four Thompsons. He put the value of the collection at $50,000.

Hill applied for and was granted a pardon by Gov. Shapp in 1975. He successfully petitioned the Treasury Department to reinstate his firearms license. And two decades later he's still trying to reclaim his collection.

Hill estimated the now missing Thompson was worth $5,000.

Ray Carn's Story

Of course, thousands of Australian gun collectors can sympathize with Hill. One such collector I had the opportunity to interview in '97 was Ray Carn, 56, an architect from Adelaide who has been collecting firearms for 35 years.

"I had a very large collection of self-loading, military-style firearms," Carn told me. "In South Australia, there probably only would have been maybe one or two other people who had anything near the volume that I had of them — the number and type.

"I started collecting a long time ago. It increased in intensity as I became more affluent. I've been really seriously building up a collection of this stuff since about the mid-70s. I had a full range of the self-loading style firearms."

Carn's collection included 35 such firearms that had to be turned in — including American rifles (among them M-1 Garands), Australian, European, Russian, Chinese, etc.

"Those guns sat in a strong room, not even in the capital city but in the country," Carn said. "They only ever saw the light of day for an authorized club shoot — if I was prepared to fire them. Some of them were new, and I wasn't prepared to fire them. Or for a display because the association to which I belong, which is the Antique and Historical Arms Association of South Australia, is a collecting body which has just had its 25th anniversary.

"We hold annual arms fairs and gun shows where our displays are put on. In fact, three years ago was rather prophetic.

"I had a display which was, 'Moms and dads, show your children these because we may not be allowed to hold them much longer.' I didn't realize it would come that quickly.

"This is history, which some people are trying to ban, and you may never see them again. All I've got now are photographs of them."

So when the fog lifted for Ray Carn in 1997, a major part of his firearms collection was gone.

But now that the view is clear and the story of the Ray Carns of Australia is out, perhaps collectors around the world will have a view of the fate that could be theirs if they are not politically diligent — and active.

So in that sense, perhaps we should be thankful that 1997 was the year the fog lifted.

(Jim Schneider is legislative editor of *Gun Week*. He has monthly legislative columns in *Muzzle Blasts*, *The Message* and *Trap & Field*. He also contributes to *Gun News Digest*, *Guns & Ammo*, *Shooting Industry* and *Women & Guns*.)

TRENDS IN GUN COLLECTING

By Jeff Faintich

As a second generation arms dealer who has been actively engaged in this business for the better part of the last thirty five years, I am often asked "What trends do you see for the future of this business?"

To that I respond "The most consistent thing I see for the future is change." I have seen the general climate of the industry and the manner in which this business is conducted change dramatically in the last decade.

To begin, let's talk about supply and demand. Demand today seems to be waning from where it has been for the last several years. I believe this is attributable to the older collector beginning to lose some interest in the hobby he has pursued over the last several decades. He may have either filled out his collection or begun to lose interest because it is becoming increasingly more difficult and expensive to locate items for his collection. Let's face it, we are all aware that the nature of gun shows has changed the later part of this decade. As a matter of fact, I had noticed that the trend was beginning to move away from shows during the later part of the '80s. When the business was at its peak, Columbus Ohio was probably the mecca for most collectors and dealers. You could almost always count on going to an Ohio Gun Collectors Show and either buying or selling a ton of merchandise.

The greatest change of all in the last several decades has been the political climate around the world towards firearms in general. This attitude has contributed to the greatest amount of decay in the business probably since before the hobby really took off in the late 1950s and early '60s. The current administrations' policy towards the firearms business in general has hung like a cloud around almost every aspect of the trade. Until we all unite to make the necessary changes that can stabilize the marketplace we will all suffer from the current trend. Just look at what has transpired in England, Australia and Canada for the reality of what could ultimately happen to us. In these countries anything that resembles a gun is either coming under so many restrictions that is impossible to possess anything to keep in your home or literally coming under new confiscation laws. That's not to indicate that this sort of legislation is pending here but be certain that it is being looked at in several legislative arenas. Until the public accepts more responsibility we can potentially all come under greater scrutiny.

It also seems to me that there just aren't as many dollars in the market place as there were formerly. You can look at the widespread development of the gaming industry around the country and assume that a certain percentage of disposable dollars has shifted from the gun market to the gaming industry. Obviously, most individuals with average incomes only have so many disposable dollars to go around. I believe this shift is definitely contributing to a certain percentage of this loss. This may apply more towards the contemporary merchandise than to the collectible market place but the collectible market place has gone unscathed. Additionally, the unbelievable rise in the stock market has appeared to have been consistent for the last four years. Hard assets, such as collectibles have not been nearly as attractive as they were previously.

In the last several years retailing in contemporary merchandise has slowed down close to 25 or 30 percent. Dealers in almost every part of the country have told me similar stories. And although we have seen a slight resurgence in the last six months, business in general merchandise is still off and I don't anticipate the type of recovery we need to revitalize the market place as yet. I believe individuals' saturation with merchandise has ultimately caught up with the market place. Everyone can afford or needs just so many items before there becomes a limit to it. Even with the introduction of new products, I don's see consumers running out to add to their collections.

If you look at the market place you can see what has happened to the major manufacturers. As more of them became involved in mass merchandising they became more vulnerable. Ultimately, this top heavy structure they created literally fell apart. Today, we see companies such as Colt's buying up Browning and Winchester USRAC and attempting to establish themselves under a new umbrella in what they hope will become a more profitable business climate. This could happen but it will require a new strategy, one which has not existed previously. If they can establish this climate and the market place does turn around they may very well find that they are entrenched in a very profitable arena. If they can maintain this strategy without losing perspective they may stay healthy and profitable for years to come.

On the other side of the coin, the merchandise that does become available for those who are still in pursuit of quality collectibles is doing extremely well. In fact, I would have to say that some of this merchandise is doing considerably better than almost anyone could expect. The big problem for general dealers today though is that the shows are not the medium which is contributing the most to the collectible market. Instead it is the auction circuit. This means that these dealers will need to participate in the auctions as well and purchase either for their inventories or for their clientele. I have seen many dealers at every auction I attend buy a good amount of merchandise, just as they might have at any of the shows they would have previously attended. Gun shows in general have continued to deteriorate with more and more tables filled with peripheral and general merchandise. Good collectible merchandise is just not showing up at gun shows as a rule. Several of the major shows still seem to be doing well but on the whole that climate is just not healthy either and has not been for a number of years. It has been profitable for the promoters and perhaps some of the dealers who set up at these shows but on the whole that climate for continued growth in the area of collectibles is just not healthy and could potentially come under greatest scrutiny. Shows such as the Las Vegas Antique Arms Shows, the Colorado Gun Collectors' Show, the Tulsa Gun Show, and Collectors Arms Dealers Association shows held in Denver, Chicago, and Orlando, the colt Collectors Association show and the Winchester Arms Collectors show are among just some of the major collector shows that are still prolific. This does not mean that a great many other shows are no longer good but for those dealers and collectors that travel around the country these seem to be consistently the better shows to attend.

Again, the auction houses seem to be the beneficiaries of more and more collectible merchandise. Their ability to attract a specific arena of clientele who are able to preview the merchandise through their catalogues has given them a decided advantage over shows in general. In this manner, you will be able to "see the entire show" before you consider attending. In today's climate, where it might cost you several hundred dollars to as much as a thousand dollars to attend a show it has become potentially a new and perhaps more efficient avenue to find the merchandise you are looking for. If the auction houses continue to get more and more collectible merchandise then they may indeed become more of an avenue for this type of item. Gun shows as we knew them may continue to take on an entirely different look and we could see a larger segregation of the types of merchandise available in both arenas.

This has given you a general overview of the marketplace as I see it but now let's talk about things in more specific terms. Such as what is still doing well and what isn't and what trends do I see on the horizon.

Of course, Winchesters and Colts still reign as the major items everyone is pursuing everywhere. But the other major manufacturers are not trailing as far behind as they once were. As a matter of fact, we are seeing other manufacturers really come into their own depending upon the quality of the items they produced. Even items, which were once considered "lower end" are now first starting to come into their own.

In the area of Colts, the .38 caliber martial double actions have really started to come into their own. A record price was set this year for an unaltered 1889 Navy (one of 5000 produced and all but 364 were altered) at $18,000.00. Several others of this vintage such as the Models 1892, 1894, 1895, 1901, 1903 etc. are following suite, although not necessarily to this extreme. This is happening without hardly any written text to help spur on the marketplace. They usually go hand in hand but they have been a most pleasant surprise.

Later this fall, Don Wilkerson will be publishing a new book on the Model 1878 and I look for a follow through with this area as new interest is created. Additionally, Doug Sheldon will have a new book out on the .38 Supers and I would anticipate a certain amount of stimulation again coming into this arena.

Most other Colt double actions and automatics have been doing a nice job of holding their own in this arena. Some of the models such as the Officers Models have become somewhat soft but on the whole most of the other models are doing quite well. The early Colt long slides are encountering a resurgence after being soft for the last several years. Of course, they experienced a meteoric rise after Sheldon's first book in 1989. The classic 1911s and 1911 A1s have really continued to be highly sought after with more and more pressure on the earlier, original examples.

Percussion Colts have continued to climb into the stratosphere and sales on the whole are softening but the more moderately priced examples with lesser finish are doing very well. But those examples that are rarely encountered such as Pattersons, Dragoons, Walkers and models with exception condition are exceptions to this rule. Similar sales results are being experienced with Colt long arms as the Lightning Rifle market went off the charts several years ago for outstanding condition or rare examples.

This past summer The Buffalo Bill Historic Society in Cody, Wyoming presented a display of wonderful antique Remington firearms in conjunction with the Remington Collectors Association. A book on Remingtons will be forthcoming and I certainly anticipate this market to really take off for the fine condition and rare examples.

Merwin, Hulbert & Co. products are another examples of a group of firearms that went nearly unnoticed for many years and today they are truly showing the results of gathering more strength.

Smith & Wessons have been showing continued strength in the antique section of their market but the more contemporary merchandise has been more stable.

European automatics for the most part have been showing a relatively stable rise for the last few years with many of the more popular collectible models naturally showing considerable strength. However, some of the antique European arms have shown some softness but again condition should be considered when this evaluation is being made, in addition to overall rarity.

Classic American shotguns are still doing well considering that this is really a lost art form. The more well known and higher grade models still seem to be attracting the most interest with the most desirable classic English and European makers also on the top of the heap. More contemporary and field grade models have seen some softening in the market place as their desirability may be somewhat waning.

Overall, all of these items are still most desirable, given the nature of the market place. Nothing is going without interest when it comes to the antique aspect of this business. And don't just take my word for it. Even those analysts who are not interested in firearms but do relate to the various other market places in the world have made notice that firearms and other collectible objects are ready to be looked at with much more interest than in the immediate past. Especially with the rise of the various investment market places, ultimately an alternative avenue to place these assets will make this market place all that much more attractive to many other individuals. If you felt that perhaps the market was showing some softness then perhaps this might be the appropriate time for you to act. If investing in these items is what you are after then why wait until the markets are moving before you buy that item you like. If on the other hand you collect because you have an appreciation for the merchandise then I would recommend you use the philosophy I have used for so many years: Buy what you like when it becomes available and always buy the best condition you can afford. So much of this merchandise only comes around once in awhile and when the opportunity arises you need to step up to it and take advantage of it. Remember, as Will Rogers once said about land: "They ain't making the stuff any more."

Good collecting.

Jeff Faintich

A Colt factory engraved pre-war/post-war single action revolver sold for $22,400. Faintich Auction Service, October 1996.

A second generation Colt single action with a signed card and photograph from Elvis Presley to Chief Edward Davis. Auction price was $14,000. Faintich Auction Service, October 1996.

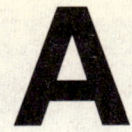

A

A.A.
Azanza & Arrizabalaga
Eibar, Spain

Pistols by this manufacturer are readily identifiable by the presence of the trademark "AA" on their frames.

A.A.

A 7.65mm caliber semiautomatic pistol with a 9-shot magazine. The slide marked "Modelo 1916 Eibar (Espana)."

Exc.	V.G.	Good	Fair	Poor
150	100	75	50	35

Reims

A 6.35mm or 7.65mm caliber semiautomatic pistol. The slide marked "1914 Model Automatic Pistol Reims Patent".

Exc.	V.G.	Good	Fair	Poor
140	90	65	45	25

A.A.A.
Aldazabal
Eibar, Spain

Modelo 1919

A 7.65mm semiautomatic pistol.

Exc.	V.G.	Good	Fair	Poor
150	100	75	50	35

A & R SALES SOUTH
El Monte, California

45 Auto

An alloy-frame version of the Colt Model 1911 semiautomatic pistol.

NIB	Exc.	V.G.	Good	Fair	Poor
300	200	175	150	125	100

Mark IV Sporter

A semiautomatic copy of the M-14 military rifle. Manufactured in .308 cal. (7.65mm Nato) only.

NIB	Exc.	V.G.	Good	Fair	Poor
500	300	200	175	150	100

AFC
Auguste Francotte
Liege, Belgium

This was one of the most prolific makers of revolvers in Liege during the last half of the 19th century. It is estimated that over 150 different revolvers were made and marketed by them before they were forced out of business by the German occupation of 1914. Francotte produced many variations from Tranter copies to pinfires, early Smith & Wesson designs to the 11mm M1871 Swedish troopers revolver. They made break-open revolvers and produced only one semi-auto, a 6.35mm blowback design. A good portion of their pistols were produced for the wholesale market and were sold under other names. These particular revolvers will bear the letters "AF" stamped somewhere on the frame. Because of the vast number and variety of pistols produced by this company, cataloging and pricing is beyond the scope of this or any general reference book. It is suggested that any examples encountered be researched on an individual basis. The lone semi-auto, produced in 1912, can be priced rather easily since it is the only one the company ever manufactured.

Semi-Auto

A 6.35mm, 6-shot detachable magazine pocket pistol with blue finish. This model was marked "Francotte Liege."

Exc.	V.G.	Good	Fair	Poor
300	225	175	125	85

A. J. ORDNANCE

This is a delayed blowback action that is unique in that every shot was double action. This pistol was chambered for the .45 ACP cartridge and had a 3.5" stainless steel barrel with fixed sights and plastic grips. The detachable magazine held 6 shots, and the standard finish was matte blue. Chrome plating was available and would add approximately 15 percent to the values given.

NIB	Exc.	V.G.	Good	Fair	Poor
500	450	400	350	275	150

AMAC
American Military Arms Corporation
formerly
Iver Johnson
Jacksonville, Arkansas

The Iver Johnson Arms Co. was founded in 1871 in Fitchsburg, Massachusetts. It was one of the oldest and most successful of the old-line arms companies on which our modern era has taken its toll. In 1984 the company moved to Jacksonville, Arkansas; in 1987 it was purchased by the American Military Arms Corporation. This company has released some of the older designs as well as some new models. In 1993 the company went out of business. The original Iver Johnson line will be listed under its own heading later in this text.

U.S. Carbine .22

This is a semiautomatic, military-style carbine that is patterned after the M1 of WWII fame. It is chambered for the .22 l.r. cartridge, has an 18.5" barrel and features military-style peep sights and a 15-shot detachable magazine.

NIB	Exc.	V.G.	Good	Fair	Poor
200	150	125	100	75	50

Wagonmaster Lever Action Rifle

This model is chambered for the .22 rimfire cartridge, has an 18.5" barrel and is styled after the Win. 94. The stock has a straight grip; and the forend, a barrel band. There are adjustable sights and a tube magazine that holds 15 l.r. cartridges.

NIB	Exc.	V.G.	Good	Fair	Poor
175	150	120	100	75	50

Wagonmaster .22 Magnum

This model is the same as the Wagonmaster except that it is chambered for the .22 rimfire magnum.

NIB	Exc.	V.G.	Good	Fair	Poor
175	150	120	100	75	50

Targetmaster Pump Action Rifle

This model is a slide- or pump-action that is chambered for the .22 rimfire cartridges. It has an 18.5" barrel with adjustable sights and a straight-grip stock. It holds 12 l.r. cartridges.

NIB	Exc.	V.G.	Good	Fair	Poor
175	150	120	100	75	50

Li'L Champ Bolt Action Rifle

This model is a scaled-down single shot that is chambered for the .22 rimfire cartridges. It has a 16.25" barrel, adjustable sights, a molded stock, and nickel-plated bolt. This model is 33" overall and is designed to be the ideal first rifle for a young shooter.

NIB	Exc.	V.G.	Good	Fair	Poor
100	75	60	45	35	20

M .30 Cal. Carbine

A military-style carbine styled after the M1 of WWII fame. It is chambered for the .30 Carbine cartridge and has an 18" barrel with military-style sights and hardwood stock. There are detachable 5-, 15-, and 30-round magazines available.

NIB	Exc.	V.G.	Good	Fair	Poor
275	225	200	175	125	90

Paratrooper .30 Carbine

This model is similar to the M1 model with a folding stock.

NIB	Exc.	V.G.	Good	Fair	Poor
325	250	225	200	150	100

Enforcer .30 Carbine

This is a 9.5" pistol version of the M1 Carbine. It has no buttstock.

NIB	Exc.	V.G.	Good	Fair	Poor
350	300	250	200	150	100

Long Range Rifle System

This is a specialized long-range, bolt-action rifle chambered for the .50 Cal. Browning Machine gun cartridge. It has a 33" barrel and a special muzzle brake system. A custom order version in the .338 or .416 caliber is also available.

NIB	Exc.	V.G.	Good	Fair	Poor
8500	7000	5000	3500	2000	1000

TP-22 and TP-25

This model is a compact, double-action, pocket automatic that was styled after the the Walther TP series. Chambered for either the .22 rimfire or the .25 centerfire cartridges, it has a 2.75" barrel, fixed sights and black plastic grips. The detachable magazine holds 7 shots and the finish is either blue or nickel-plated. The nickel-plated version is worth 10 percent more than the blue .

NIB	Exc.	V.G.	Good	Fair	Poor
225	175	150	100	75	50

AMAC -22 Compact or 25 Compact

This is a compact, single-action, semiautomatic pocket pistol that is chambered for the .22 rimfire or the .25 ACP cartridge. It has a 2" barrel, 5-shot magazine, plastic grips and blue or nickel finish. The nickel finish is 10 percent higher in cost than the blue .

NIB	Exc.	V.G.	Good	Fair	Poor
175	125	100	80	55	35

AMT
Arcadia Machine and Tool
Irwindale, California

Lightning

A single-action, semiautomatic, .22 caliber pistol. Available with barrel lengths of 5" (Bull only), 6.5", 8.5", 10.5" and 12.5" (either Bull or tapered), and adjustable sights, as well as the trigger. The grips are checkered black rubber. Manufactured between 1984 and 1987 this model resembled the Ruger.

Exc.	V.G.	Good	Fair	Poor
250	200	175	125	85

Bull's Eye Regulation Target

As above, with a 6.5" vent-rib bull barrel, wooden target grips, and an extended rear sight. Manufactured in 1986 only.

Exc.	V.G.	Good	Fair	Poor
350	300	250	200	100

Baby Automag

Similar to the above with an 8.5" ventilated rib barrel, and Millett adjustable sights. Approximately 1,000 were manufactured.

Exc.	V.G.	Good	Fair	Poor
450	350	275	225	150

Automag II

A stainless steel, semiautomatic .22 Magnum Pistol. Available with 3-3/8", 4.5", and 6" barrel lengths and Millett adjustable sights, grips of black, grooved, plastic. Was first manufactured in 1987. Still in production.

NIB	Exc.	V.G.	Good	Fair	Poor
375	300	225	150	100	80

Automag III

This semiautomatic pistol is chambered for the .30 Carbine cartridge and the 9mm Winchester Magnum cartridge. Barrel length is 6.37" and overall length is 10.5". The magazine capacity is 8 rounds. Fitted with Millett adjustable rear sight and carbon fiber grips. Stainless steel finish. Pistol weighs 43 oz.

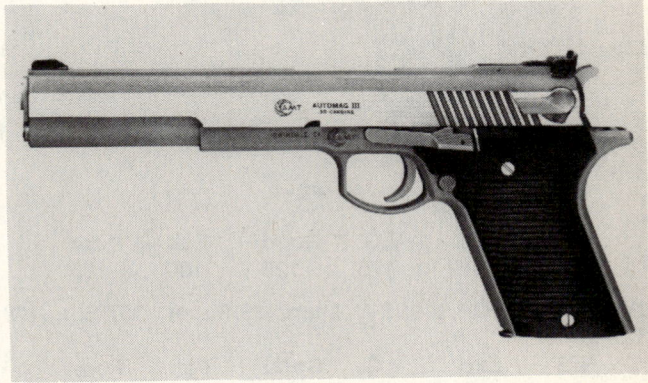

NIB	Exc.	V.G.	Good	Fair	Poor
425	350	250	225	100	80

Automag IV

Similar in appearance to the Automag III this pistol is chambered for the .45 Winchester Magnum. Magazine capacity is 7 rounds and weight is 46 oz.

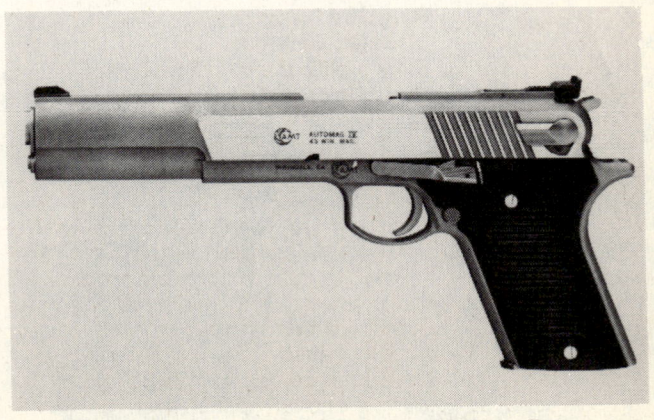

NIB	Exc.	V.G.	Good	Fair	Poor
650	525	400	300	200	100

Automag V

Introduced in 1993 this model is similar in appearance to the Automag models but is chambered for the .50 caliber cartridge. A limited production run of 3000 pistols with special serial number from "1 of 3000 to 3000 of 3000". Barrel length is 6.5" and magazine capacity is 5 rounds. Weighs 46 oz. Production stopped in 1995.

NIB	Exc.	V.G.	Good	Fair	Poor
750	600	500	400	300	150

Back Up Pistol

This is a small semiautomatic pocket pistol chambered for the .22 l.r. and the .380 ACP cartridges. This is fitted with a 2.5" barrel and is offered with either black plastic or walnut grips. The pistol weighs 18 oz. Magazine capacity is 5 rounds. Originally manufactured by TDE, then Irwindale Arms Inc., it is now currently produced by AMT.

NIB	Exc.	V.G.	Good	Fair	Poor
275	225	175	125	100	85

Back Up-.45ACP, .40S&W, 9mm, .38 Super, .357 Sig, .400 Cor Bon

NIB	Exc.	V.G.	Good	Fair	Poor
425	350	300	250	150	100

.380 Back Up II

Introduced in 1993 this pistol is similar to the Back Up model but with the addition of a double safety, extended finger grip on the magazine, and single action only.

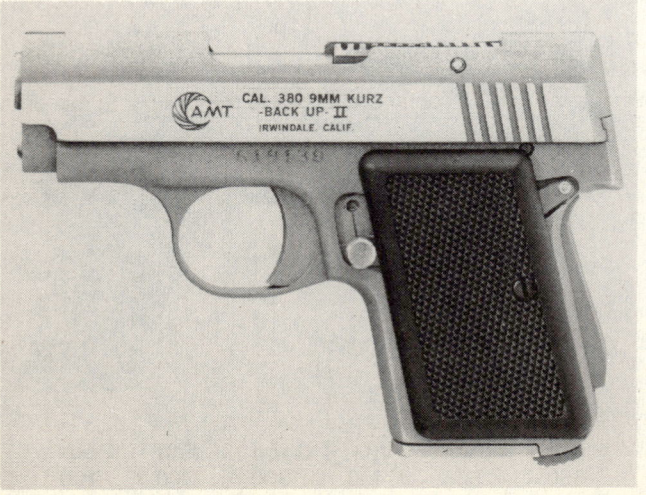

NIB	Exc.	V.G.	Good	Fair	Poor
250	200	150	125	100	85

Hardballer/Government Model

This model is similar to the Colt Gold Cup .45 ACP. It is offered in two versions. The first has fixed sights and rounded slide top while the second has adjustable Millett sights and Matte rib. Magazine capacity is 7 rounds. Wraparound rubber grips are standard. Long grip safety, beveled magazine well, and adjustable trigger are common to both variations. Weight is 38 oz.

Hardballer-Adjustable sights

NIB	Exc.	V.G.	Good	Fair	Poor
450	400	350	275	200	125

Government Model-Fixed sights

NIB	Exc.	V.G.	Good	Fair	Poor
425	375	300	250	150	100

Hardballer Longslide

Similar to the Hardballer Model but fitted with a 7" barrel. Magazine capacity is 7 rounds. Pistol weighs 46 oz.

NIB	Exc.	V.G.	Good	Fair	Poor
475	425	325	275	200	125

On Duty

This semiautomatic pistol features a double-action-only trigger action or double action with decocker and is chambered for the 9mm, .40S&W, or .45 ACP calibers. Barrel length is 4.5" and overall length is 7.75". The finish is a black anodized matte finish. Carbon fiber grips are standard. Furnished with 3-dot sights. Weighs 32 oz. No longer in production.

NIB	Exc.	V.G.	Good	Fair	Poor
450	350	250	200	150	100

Skipper

Identical to the Hard Baller with a 1" shorter barrel and slide, discontinued in 1984.

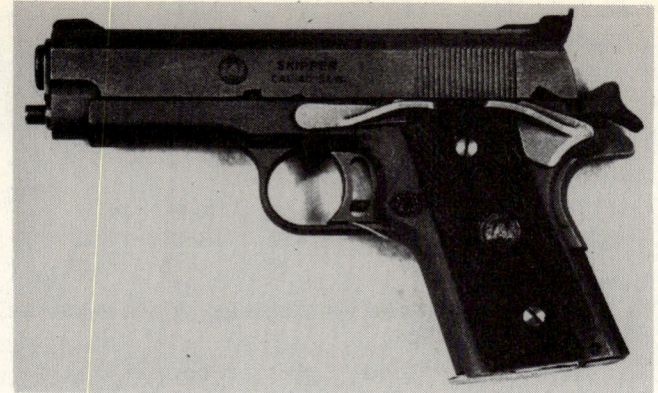

Exc.	V.G.	Good	Fair	Poor
400	325	275	200	125

Combat Skipper
Similar to the Colt Commander. Discontinued in 1984.

Exc.	V.G.	Good	Fair	Poor
350	300	250	200	125

Lightning Rifle
Patterned after the Ruger 10/22, this rifle has a 22" barrel and a 25-round, detachable magazine with a folding stock. Introduced in 1986.

NIB	Exc.	V.G.	Good	Fair	Poor
300	225	175	150	125	100

Small Game Hunter
As above with a full stock and 10-round magazine. Introduced in 1986.

NIB	Exc.	V.G.	Good	Fair	Poor
300	225	175	150	125	100

Small Game Hunter II
This semiautomatic rifle is chambered for the .22 Long Rifle cartridge. Stock is a checkered black matte nylon and is fitted with a removable recoil pad for ammo, cleaning rod, and knife. Rotary magazine holds 10 rounds. Stainless steel action and barrel. Barrel is a heavy weight target type 22" long. Weight is 6 lbs. No longer in production.

NIB	Exc.	V.G.	Good	Fair	Poor
300	225	175	150	125	100

Hunter Rifle
This semiautomatic rifle is chambered for the .22 Rimfire Magnum cartridge. Stock is checkered black matte nylon. Other features are similar to the Small Game Hunter 11 including weight.

NIB	Exc.	V.G.	Good	Fair	Poor
350	250	200	150	125	100

Magnum Hunter

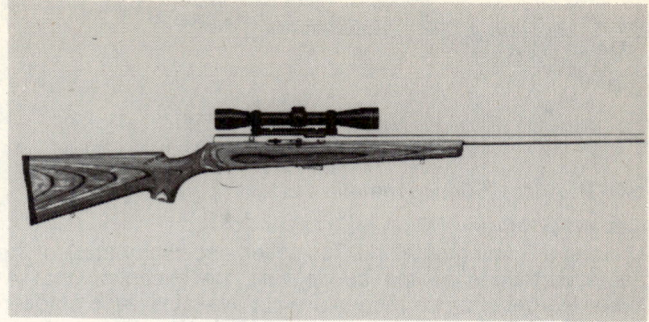

Introduced in early 1993 this new addition to the AMT line is chambered for the .22 Magnum cartridge and is fitted with a 22" accurized barrel. Barrel and action are stainless steel. It comes standard with a 5-round magazine and composite stock but a laminated stock is available at an extra as is a 10-round magazine.

NIB	Exc.	V.G.	Good	Fair	Poor
500	400	350	250	200	150

Challenge Edition
This is a custom ordered .22 caliber semi-automatic rifle built on a Ruger 10/22 like receiver. Offered in eitherr 18" or 22" barrel lengths with all stainless steel construction, McMillan fiberglass stock, and Weaver style scope mounts.

NIB	Exc.	V.G.	Good	Fair	Poor
990	800	—	—	—	—

Single Shot Standard Rifle
Custom-built rifle with choice of barrel length, composite stock adjustable trigger, post '64 Winchester action all in stainless and chromemoly steel. Chambered for all standard calibers. First offered in 1996.

NIB	Exc.	V.G.	Good	Fair	Poor
840	675	—	—	—	—

Single Shot Deluxe Rifle
Custom built rifle on a Mauser type action with choice of match grade barrel lengths and custom Kevlar stock. Built from stainless and chromemoly steel. Chambered for all standard calibers. First offered in 1996.

NIB	Exc.	V.G.	Good	Fair	Poor
1800	1400	—	—	—	—

Bolt Action Repeating Rifle-Standard
Similar in construction and features to the Standard Single shot rifle.

NIB	Exc.	V.G.	Good	Fair	Poor
840	675	—	—	—	—

Bolt Action Repeating Rifle-Deluxe
Similar in construction and features to the Deluxe Single shot rifle.

NIB	Exc.	V.G.	Good	Fair	Poor
1800	1400	—	—	—	—

A-SQUARE
Bedford, Kentucky

Hannibal Grade
Utilizing the P-17 Enfield action, with a 22" to 26" barrel, this rifle is chambered for 32 calibers from 7mm Rem. Mag. up to and including the 500 A-Square Mag. and .577 Tyrannosaur. Blued with a checkered walnut pistol grip stock. Introduced in 1986. Weights range from 9 lbs. to 13.25 lbs. depending on caliber.

NIB	Exc.	V.G.	Good	Fair	Poor
2900	2400	1500	950	500	300

NOTE: Add $350 for synthetic stock.

Caesar Grade

Utilizing a Remington Model 700 action and chambered for the same cartridges as the above with the exception that A-Square proprietary cartridges are not available. Also made in the left-hand version. Introduced in 1986. Weights are in the 8.5 to 11 lbs. range.

NIB	Exc.	V.G.	Good	Fair	Poor
2900	2400	1500	950	500	300

NOTE: Add $350 for synthetic stock.

Hamilcar Grade

This model is a smaller and lighter version of the Hannibal Grade. It was introduced in 1994. It is designed to be chambered in cartridges in the 30-.06 size. Weights are around 8 to 8.5 lbs. Introduced in 1994.

NIB	Exc.	V.G.	Good	Fair	Poor
2900	2400	1500	950	500	300

Genghis Khan Model

This model is designed for varmint shooting and is fitted with a heavy weight barrel. Offered in .22-250, .243 Win., 6mm Rem., .25-06, 257 Wby., and .264 Win. Barrel length is to customers specifications as is length of pull. No iron sights are fitted to this model. Weight is approximately 11 lbs.

NIB	Exc.	V.G.	Good	Fair	Poor
2900	2400	1500	950	500	300

NOTE: These rifles are offered with a number of options that can effect price.

ATCSA
Armas De Tiro Y Casa
Eibar, Spain

Colt Police Positive Copy

A .38 caliber 6-shot revolver resembling a Colt Police Positive.

Exc.	V.G.	Good	Fair	Poor
175	125	100	60	40

Target Pistol

A .22 caliber single shot target pistol utilizing a revolver frame.

Exc.	V.G.	Good	Fair	Poor
225	175	125	100	55

AGUIRREY ARANZABAL (AYA)
Eibar, Spain
Side x Side Shotguns
Current Importer-Armes de Chasse

SIDE BY SIDE

Matador Side x Side

A 12, 16, 20, 28 or .410 bore boxlock double barrel shotgun with 26", 28" or 30" barrels, single selective trigger and automatic ejectors. Blued with a walnut stock. Manufactured from 1955 to 1963.

28 gauge and .410-Add 20 %.

Exc.	V.G.	Good	Fair	Poor
475	400	350	300	200

Matador II Side x Side

As above, in 12 or 20 gauge with a ventilated rib.

Exc.	V.G.	Good	Fair	Poor
500	425	375	300	200

Matador III Side x Side

As above, with 3" chambers.

NIB	Exc.	V.G.	Good	Fair	Poor
950	750	600	450	350	250

Bolero Side x Side

As above, with a non-selective single trigger and extractors. Manufactured until 1984.

Exc.	V.G.	Good	Fair	Poor
450	380	300	250	200

Iberia Side x Side

A 12 or 20 gauge Magnum boxlock double barrel shotgun with 26", 28" or 30" barrels, double triggers and extractors. Blued with a walnut stock. Manufactured until 1984.

NIB	Exc.	V.G.	Good	Fair	Poor
575	500	425	325	250	200

Iberia II Side x Side

Similar to the above, in 12 or 16 gauge with 28" barrels and 2-3/4" chambers. Manufactured in 1984 and 1985.

NIB	Exc.	V.G.	Good	Fair	Poor
575	500	425	325	250	200

Model 106 Side x Side

A 12, 16, or 20 gauge boxlock double barrel shotgun with 28" barrels, double triggers and extractors. Blued with a walnut stock. Manufactured until 1985.

NIB	Exc.	V.G.	Good	Fair	Poor
550	500	400	300	250	200

Model 107-LI Side x Side

As above, with the receiver lightly engraved and an English-style stock. In 12 or 16 gauge only.

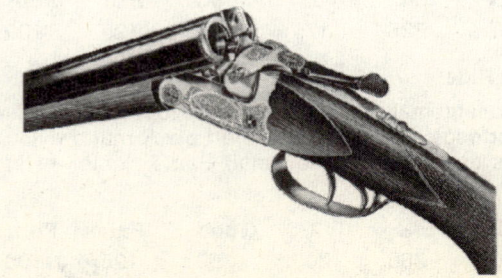

NIB	Exc.	V.G.	Good	Fair	Poor
650	600	525	450	300	250

Model 116 Side x Side

A 12, 16 or 20 gauge sidelock double barrel shotgun with 27" to 30" barrels, double triggers and ejectors. Engraved, blued with a walnut stock. Manufactured until 1985.

NIB	Exc.	V.G.	Good	Fair	Poor
950	800	600	475	350	275

Model 117 Side x Side

As above, with 3" chambers.

NIB	Exc.	V.G.	Good	Fair	Poor
850	700	500	425	300	250

Model 117 "Quail Unlimited" Side x Side

As above in 12 gauge only with 26" barrels and the receiver engraved "Quail Unlimited of North America". Forty-two were manufactured.

NIB	Exc.	V.G.	Good	Fair	Poor
1500	1200	875	650	425	300

Model 210 Side x Side

An exposed hammer, 12 or 16 gauge, boxlock shotgun with 26" to 28" barrels and double triggers. Blued with a walnut stock. Manufactured until 1985.

NIB	Exc.	V.G.	Good	Fair	Poor
800	675	550	400	325	225

Model 711 Boxlock Side x Side

A 12 gauge boxlock double barrel shotgun with 28" or 30" barrels having ventilated ribs, single selective trigger and automatic ejectors. Manufactured until 1984.

NIB	Exc.	V.G.	Good	Fair	Poor
900	800	700	500	350	250

Model 711 Sidelock Side x Side

As above, with sidelocks. Manufactured in 1985 only.

NIB	Exc.	V.G.	Good	Fair	Poor
1000	900	750	500	400	300

Senior Side x Side

A custom order 12 gauge double barrel sidelock shotgun, gold inlaid and engraved. Made strictly to individual customer's specifications.

NIB	Exc.	V.G.	Good	Fair	Poor
15000	12500	9000	7000	4500	2250

OVER/UNDERS

Model 79 "A" Over/Under

A 12 gauge boxlock Over/Under double barrel shotgun with 26", 28" or 30" barrels, single selective trigger and automatic ejectors. Blued with a walnut stock. Manufactured until 1985.

NIB	Exc.	V.G.	Good	Fair	Poor
1250	1050	925	750	500	300

Model 79 "B" Over/Under

As above, with a moderate amount of engraving.

NIB	Exc.	V.G.	Good	Fair	Poor
1350	1150	950	800	575	350

Model 79 "C" Over/Under

As above, with extensive engraving.

NIB	Exc.	V.G.	Good	Fair	Poor
2000	1800	1500	1150	675	400

Model 77 Over/Under

As above, patterned after the Merkel shotgun.

NIB	Exc.	V.G.	Good	Fair	Poor
3000	2700	2000	1500	1000	500

Coral "A Over/Under

A 12 or 16 gauge Over/Under boxlock double barrel shotgun with 26" or 28" barrels having ventilated ribs, double triggers and automatic ejectors. Fitted with a Kersten cross bolt. Manufactured until 1985.

NIB	Exc.	V.G.	Good	Fair	Poor
1250	900	700	500	300	200

Coral "B" Over/Under

As above, with an engraved French case hardened receiver.

NIB	Exc.	V.G.	Good	Fair	Poor
1400	1100	750	600	350	250

CURRENTLY IMPORTED SHOTGUNS
**Importer-Armes De Chasse
Chadds Ford, PA**

SIDELOCK/SIDE BY SIDE

AYA sidelock shotguns use the Holland and Holland system. They feature double triggers, articulated front trigger, cocking indicators, bushed firing pins, replaceable firing pins, replaceable hinge pins, and chopper lump barrels. Frame and sidelocks are case-colored. These shotguns weigh between 5 and 7 pounds depending on gauge and barrel length. Barrel lengths are offered in 26", 27", 28", and 29" depending on gauge. All stocks are figured walnut with hand checkering and oil finish. These guns are available with several extra cost options that may effect price. Also influencing price of new guns is the fluctuating dollar in relation to Spanish currency.

Model No. 1

This model is offered in 12 gauge and 20 gauge with special English scroll engraving. Fitted with automatic ejectors and straight grip stock with exhibition quality wood.

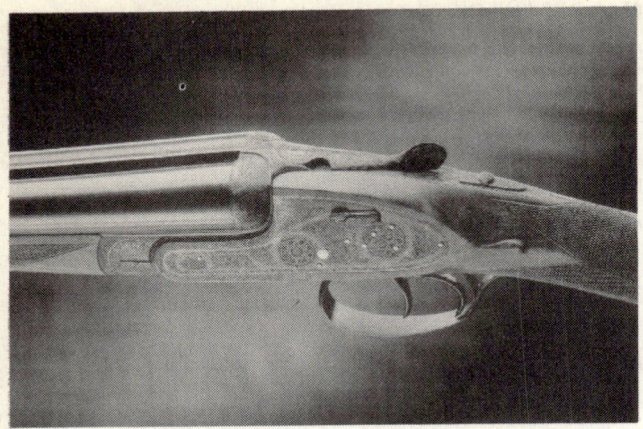

NIB	Exc.	V.G.	Good	Fair	Poor
5500	3000	1500	1000	750	500

Model No. 2

The Model 2 is offered in 12, 16, 20, and 28 gauge as well as .410 bore. It has automatic ejectors and straight grip select walnut stock.

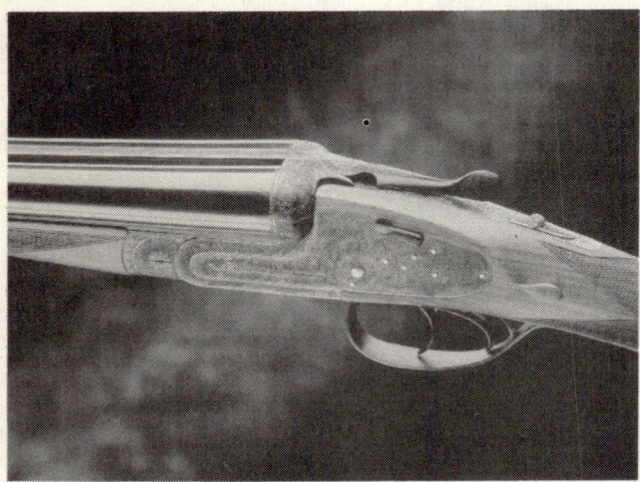

NIB	Exc.	V.G.	Good	Fair	Poor
2500	1500	1000	750	600	450

Model No. 53

Chambered for 12, 16, and 20 gauge, this model features three locking lugs and side clips. It also has automatic ejectors and straight grip stock.

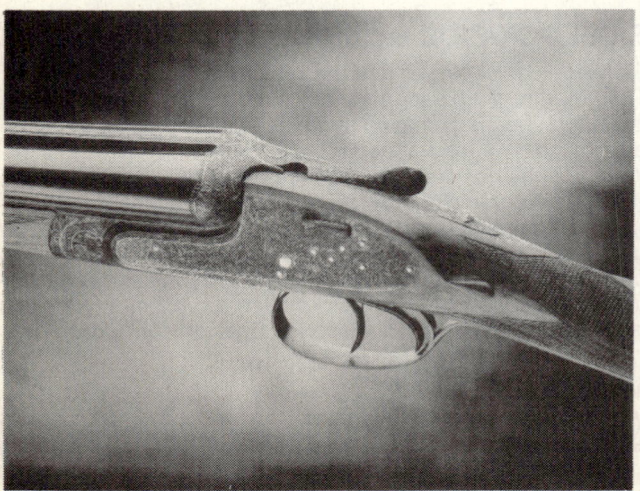

NIB	Exc.	V.G.	Good	Fair	Poor
3750	2250	1500	950	650	400

Model No. 56

This model is available in 12 gauge only and features three locking lugs, side clips, special wide action body, and raised matted rib. Select walnut straight grip stock.

NIB	Exc.	V.G.	Good	Fair	Poor
6500	4000	2500	1200	800	400

Model XXV-sidelock

Offered in 12 gauge and 20 gauge only this model is fitted with a Churchill-type rib. Automatic ejectors and select straight grip walnut stock are standard.

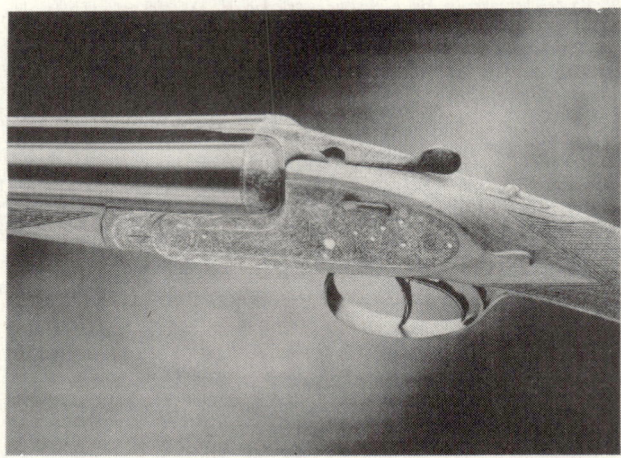

NIB	Exc.	V.G.	Good	Fair	Poor
3250	1750	1200	750	500	300

BOXLOCK SIDE BY SIDE

These AYA guns utilize an Anson and Deeley system with double locking lugs with detachable cross pin and separate trigger plate that gives access to the firing mechanism. Frame is case-colored. The barrels are chopper lump, firing pins are bushed, automatic safety and automatic ejectors are standard. Barrel lengths are offered in 26", 27", and 28" depending on gauge. Weights are between 5 and 7 pounds depending on gauge.

Model XXV-Boxlock

This model is available in 12 and 20 gauge only. The select walnut stock is hand checkered with straight grip stock.

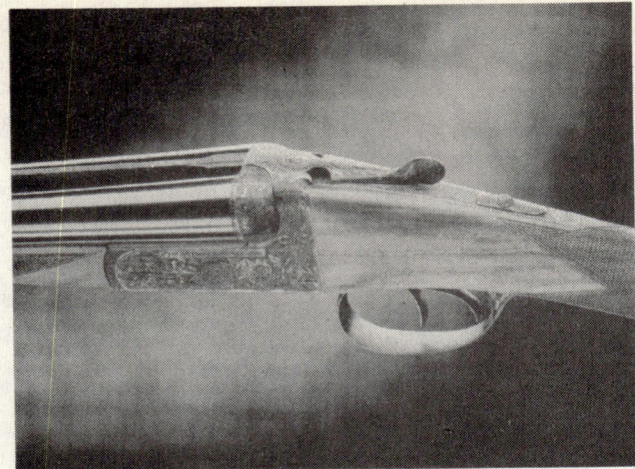

NIB	Exc.	V.G.	Good	Fair	Poor
2500	1250	800	600	350	250

Model No. 4

This model is available in 12, 16, 20, and 28 gauge as well as .410 bore. It is fitted with select hand checkered walnut stock with straight grip. Light scroll engraving on this model.

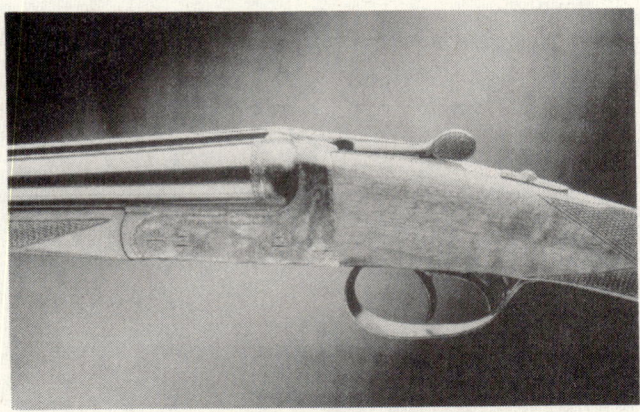

NIB	Exc.	V.G.	Good	Fair	Poor
1500	800	650	450	350	200

Model No. 4 Deluxe

Same as above but with select walnut stock and slightly more engraving coverage.

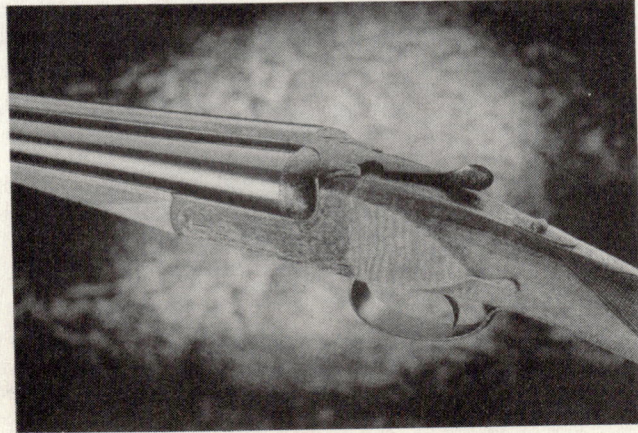

NIB	Exc.	V.G.	Good	Fair	Poor
2500	2000	1500	1000	550	350

OVER/UNDER

These AYA shotguns are similar in design and appearance to the Gebruder Merkel over and under sidelocks with three part forend, Kersten cross bolt, and double under locking lugs.

Model No. 37 Super

This model is available in 12 gauge only with ventilated rib, automatic ejectors, internally gold plated sidelocks. Offered with three different types of engraving patterns: ducks, scroll, or deep cut engraving.

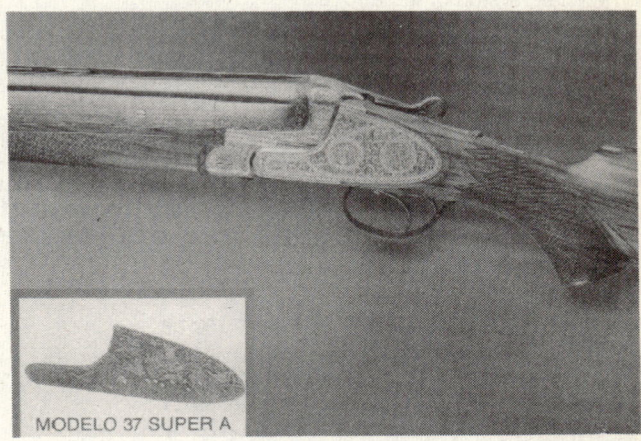

MODELO 37 SUPER A

NIB	Exc	V.G.	Good	Fair	Poor
11000	8500	5000	3500	2000	1000

Model Augusta

This is the top-of-the-line AYA model offered in 12 gauge only. It features presentation wood and deep cut scroll engraving.

NIB	Exc.	V.G.	Good	Fair	Poor
20000	15000	8000	4500	3500	1500

NOTE: For extra cost options add approximately:
- Pistol grip-$90
- Rubber recoil pad-$190
- Left-hand gun-$775
- Length of pull longer than 15"-$125
- Select wood-$235
- Deluxe Wood-$550
- Single non-selective trigger-$400
- Single selective trigger-$600
- Chrome lined barrels-$140
- Churchill rib-$375
- Raised rib-$180
- Extra set of barrels-$ 1500

ABADIE
Liege, Belgium

System Abadie Model 1878

A 9mm double-action revolver with a 6-shot cylinder, octagonal barrel and integral ejector rod.

Exc.	V.G.	Good	Fair	Poor
300	225	175	125	90

System Abadie Model 1886

A heavier version of the above.

Exc.	V.G.	Good	Fair	Poor
275	200	150	110	75

ABBEY, F.J. & CO.
Chicago, Illinois

The Abbey Brothers produced a variety of percussion rifles and shotguns which are all of individual design. The prices listed below represent what a plain F.J. Abbey & Company firearm might realize.

Rifle

Exc.	V.G.	Good	Fair	Poor
800	600	400	200	125

Shotgun

Exc.	V.G.	Good	Fair	Poor
1000	800	500	300	150

ABBEY, GEORGE T.
Utica, New York, and Chicago, Illinois

George T. Abbey originally worked in Utica, New York, from 1845 to 1852. He moved to Chicago in 1852 and was in business until 1874. He manufactured a wide variety of percussion and cartridge firearms. The values listed below represent those of his most common products.

Single Barrel .44 Cal.

Exc.	V.G.	Good	Fair	Poor
1000	750	450	335	200

Side x Side Double Barrel-.44 Cal.

Exc.	V.G.	Good	Fair	Poor
1750	1350	800	525	275

Over/Under Double Barrel-.44 Cal.

Exc.	V.G.	Good	Fair	Poor
2000	1500	900	700	350

ACCU-MATCH
Mesa, Arizona

Accu-Match Custom Pistol

This is a competition pistol built on the Colt 1911 design. Chambered for the .45 ACP it is fitted with a 5-1/2" match grade stainless steel barrel, stainless steel slide and frame with extended slide release and safety. Fitted with a beavertail grip safety and wraparound finger groove rubber grips this pistol has a threaded three port compensator and dual action recoil spring system with three dot sight system.

NIB	Exc.	V.G.	Good	Fair	Poor
840	700	—	—	—	—

ACHA
Domingo Acha
Vizcaya, Spain

Acha Model 1916

A 7.65mm caliber semiautomatic pistol with internal hammer. Normally marked "F de Acha Hrs C 7.65."

Exc.	V.G.	Good	Fair	Poor
200	150	125	90	65

Atlas

A 6.35mm caliber semiautomatic pistol marked either "Domingo Acha y Cia" or "Pistolet automatique 6.35 Atlas."

Exc.	V.G.	Good	Fair	Poor
150	100	80	60	40

Looking Glass

A 6.35mm caliber semiautomatic pistol marked "Looking Glass."

Exc.	V.G.	Good	Fair	Poor
200	150	125	90	65

ACME
**SEE—Davenport Arms Co., Maltby Henley & Co.,
and Merwin & Hulbert & Co.**

ACME ARMS
New York, New York

A trade name found on .22, .32 caliber revolvers and 12 gauge shotguns marketed by the Cornwall Hardware Company.

.22 Revolver

A 7-shot single-action revolver.

Exc.	V.G.	Good	Fair	Poor
350	275	175	125	75

.32 Revolver

A 5-shot single-action revolver.

Exc.	V.G.	Good	Fair	Poor
375	300	200	150	100

Shotgun

A 12 gauge double barrel shotgun with external hammers.

Exc.	V.G.	Good	Fair	Poor
350	275	175	125	75

ACME HAMMERLESS
**Made by Hopkins & Allen
Norwich, Connecticut**

Acme Hammerless

A .32 or .38 caliber 5-shot revolver with either exposed hammer or enclosed hammer. Sometimes known as the "Forehand 1891."

Exc.	V.G.	Good	Fair	Poor
200	125	90	60	45

ACTION
**Eibar, Spain
Maker—Modesto Santos**

Action

A 6.35mm or 7.65mm semiautomatic pistol marked on the slide "Pistolet Automatique Modele 1920." Often found bearing the trade name "Corrientes" as well as the maker's trademark "MS".

Exc.	V.G.	Good	Fair	Poor
200	150	100	80	60

ACTION ARMS LTD.
Philadelphia, Pennsylvania

AT-84, AT-88
A 9mm or .41 Action Express caliber semiautomatic pistol with a 4.75" barrel and either 15-shot (9mm) or 10-shot (.41) magazine. Blued or chrome plated with walnut grips.

NIB	Exc.	V.G.	Good	Fair	Poor
600	500	425	350	300	150

AT-84P, AT-88P
As above, with a 3.7" barrel and smaller frame.

NIB	Exc.	V.G.	Good	Fair	Poor
700	600	525	450	400	200

AT-88H
As above with a 3.4" barrel and smaller frame.

NIB	Exc.	V.G.	Good	Fair	Poor
600	500	425	350	300	150

Timber Wolf Carbine
Introduced in 1989, this slide-action carbine features an 18.5" barrel with adjustable rear sight and blade front sight. Chambered for the .357 Magnum or .38 Special cartridges it is offered in either blue or hard chrome finish. Weight is approximately 5.5 lb. Built in Israel by Israel Military Industries.

NIB	Exc.	V.G.	Good	Fair	Poor
450	400	300	200	150	100

ADAMS
Deane, Adams & Deane
London, England
London Armoury Co. (After 1856)

Revolvers based upon Robert Adams' patents were manufactured by the firm of Deane, Adams & Deane. Although more technically advanced than the pistols produced by Samuel Colt, Adams' revolvers were popular primarily in England and the British Empire.

Adams Model 1851 Self-Cocking Revolver
A .44 caliber double-action percussion revolver with a 7.5" octagonal barrel and 5-shot cylinder. The barrel and frame are blued, the cylinder case hardened and the grips are walnut. The top strap is marked "Deane, Adams and Deane 30 King William St. London Bridge." This revolver does not have a hammer spur and functions only as a double action.

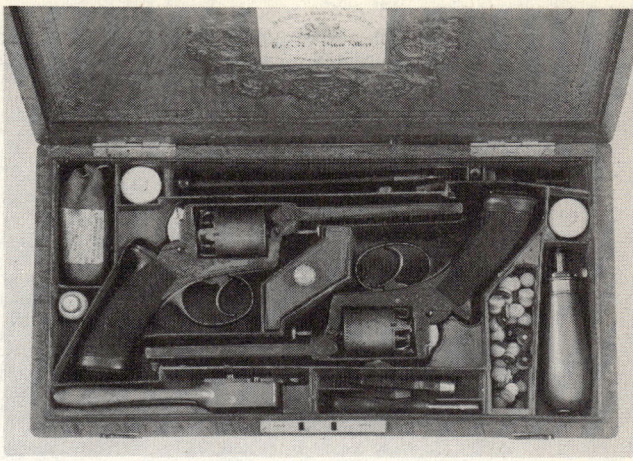

Exc.	V.G.	Good	Fair	Poor
—	1500	1000	700	400

Adams Pocket Revolver
As above, in .31 caliber with a 4.5" barrel.

Exc.	V.G.	Good	Fair	Poor
—	1750	1200	850	400

Beaumont-Adams Revolver
As above, fitted with a Tranter Patent loading lever and the hammer made with a spur.

Exc.	V.G.	Good	Fair	Poor
—	1450	850	625	300

ADAMY GEBRUDER
Suhl, Germany

Over/Under Shotgun
A 12 or 16 gauge double barrel Over/Under shotgun with 26" to 30" barrels, double triggers and a walnut stock.

Exc.	V.G.	Good	Fair	Poor
1850	1500	1100	750	400

ADIRONDACK ARMS CO. or A.S. BABBITT CO.
Plattsburgh, New York

Orvil M. Robinson Patent Rifle
The Robinson tube-fed repeating rifle was made in New York between 1870 and 1874. The early models, 1870-1872, are marked "A.S. Babbitt"; the later models, 1872-1874, "Adirondack Arms Co." The Company was sold to Winchester in 1874, but they never produced the Robinson after that date. The rifle has been found in two styles: The first with small fingers on the hammer to cock and operate the mechanism; the second with buttons on the receiver to retract the bolt and cock the hammer. The rifle was made in .44 cal. with an octagonal

barrel usually found in 26" or 28" length. The frames were predominantly brass; but some iron frames have been noted, and they will bring a premium of approximately 25 percent. The barrel and magazine tube have a blued finish.

First Model

Exc.	V.G.	Good	Fair	Poor
—	—	6000	3500	950

Courtesy Buffalo Bill Historical Center, Cody, Wyoming

Second Model

Exc.	V.G.	Good	Fair	Poor
—	—	6000	3500	950

ADLER
Engelbrecht & Wolff
Blasii, Germany

An extremely rare and unusually designed semiautomatic pistol adapted for the 7.25mm Adler cartridge. Produced in very limited numbers. Prospective purchasers are advised to secure a qualified appraisal prior to acquisition.

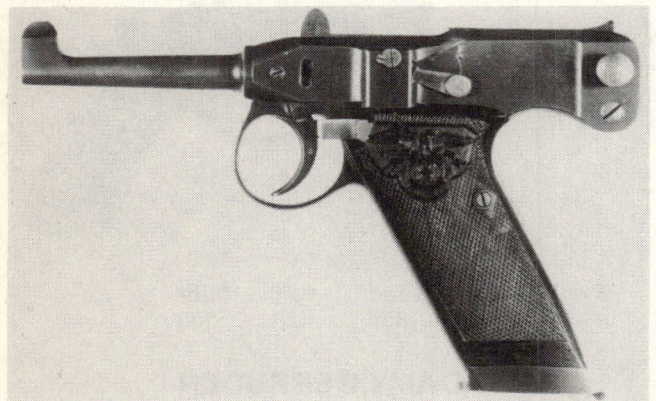

Courtesy James Rankin

Courtesy James Rankin

Exc.	V.G.	Good	Fair	Poor
—	5000	2500	1000	500

ADVANCED SMALL ARMS INDUSTRIES
Solothurn, Switzerland
Imported by Magnum Research
Minneapolis, Minnesota

one Pro .45

Introduced in 1997 and built in Switzerland by ASAI this pistol features a 3" barrel chambered for the .45 ACP cartridge. It is based on a short recoil operation and is available in double action or double action only. Also available is a kit (purchased seperatly) to convert the pistol to .400 Cor-Bon caliber. The pistol weighs about 24 oz. empty. The conversion kit has a retail price of $209.00.

NIB	Exc.	V.G.	Good	Fair	Poor
650	—	—	—	—	—

ADVANTAGE ARMS U.S.A., INC.
Distributed by Wildfire Sports
St. Paul, Minnesota

Model 422

A .22 or .22 Magnum caliber 4 barrel derringer with 2.5" barrels. Entirely made of an aluminum alloy. Finished in either blue or nickel-plate. Manufactured in 1986 and 1987.

NIB	Exc.	V.G.	Good	Fair	Poor
175	125	100	85	65	45

AETNA ARMS CO.
New York

A .22 caliber spur trigger revolver with an octagonal barrel and 7-shot cylinder. The barrel marked "Aetna Arms Co. New York". Manufactured from approximately 1870 to 1880.

Exc.	V.G.	Good	Fair	Poor
—	—	1500	950	450

AFFERBACH, W. A.
Philadelphia, Pennsylvania

This maker is known to have produced copies of Henry Derringer's percussion pocket pistols. Though uncommon, their values would be approximately as listed below.

Exc.	V.G.	Good	Fair	Poor
—	—	1800	1450	650

AGNER (SAXHOJ PRODUCTS INC.)
Copenhagen, Denmark
Importer: Beeman Arms
Santa Rosa, California

Model M 80

A .22 caliber single shot stainless steel target pistol with a 5.9" barrel, adjustable sights and walnut grips. This pistol is fitted with a dry fire mechanism. Also available in a left-hand version. Imported from 1981 to 1986.

Exc.	V.G.	Good	Fair	Poor
1000	700	500	300	150

AGUIRRE
Eibar, Spain

Basculant

A 6.35mm semiautomatic pistol marked on the slide "Cal. 6.35 Automatic Pistol Basculant".

Exc.	V.G.	Good	Fair	Poor
200	125	100	75	50

LeDragon

As above, with the slide marked "Cal. 6.35 Automatic Pistol LeDragon" and a stylized dragon molded into the grips.

Exc.	V.G.	Good	Fair	Poor
200	125	100	75	50

AIR MATCH
Importer: Kendall International
Paris, Kentucky
Air Match 500

A .22 caliber single shot target pistol with a 10.5" barrel, adjustable sights and adjustable front-mounted counterweights. Blued with walnut grips. Imported from 1984 to 1986.

NIB	Exc.	V.G.	Good	Fair	Poor
700	550	400	300	250	125

AJAX ARMY

Single Action Unknown

A spur-trigger, single-action, solid-frame revolver that was chambered for the .44 rimfire cartridge. It had a 7" barrel and was blued with walnut grips. It was manufactured in the 1880s.

Exc.	V.G.	Good	Fair	Poor
1000	750	425	300	150

ALAMO RANGER
Alamo Ranger Spain

A typical low-quality, early Spanish copy of the Colt Police Positive, chambered for the .38 caliber centerfire, and the cylinder held 6 shots. The finish was blued; grips were checkered hard rubber. The maker of this pistol is unknown.

Exc.	V.G.	Good	Fair	Poor
150	125	100	75	45

ALASKA
SEE—Hood Firearms Co.
Norwich, Connecticut

ALDZABAL
Eibar, Spain
Aldazabal, Leturiondo & CIA.

Aldazabal

Another typical low-quality, "Eibar"-type semiautomatic. It was a Browning blowback copy, chambered for the 7.65mm cartridge. It had a 7-shot detachable magazine and blued finish with checkered wood grips. This company ceased production before the Spanish Civil War.

Exc.	V.G.	Good	Fair	Poor
175	125	95	65	40

ALERT
SEE—Hood Firearms Co.
Norwich, Connecticut

ALEXIA
SEE—Hopkins & Allen
Norwich, Connecticut

ALFA
SEE—Armero Especialistas Reunides
Eibar, Spain

ALKARTASUNA FABRICA DE ARMAS
Guernica, Spain

This company began production during World War I to help Gabilondo y Urresti supply sidearms to the French. After the hostilities ceased, they continued to produce firearms under their own name. They manufactured the typical poor quality, unimaginative weapons usually associated with Spain during this era. They produced a number of variations in both 6.35mm and 7.65mm marked "Alkar." Collector interest is very thin. The factory burned down in 1920, and by 1922 business had totally ceased.

Exc.	V.G.	Good	Fair	Poor
200	175	125	95	50

ALLEN, ETHAN
Grafton, Massachusetts

The company was founded by Ethan Allen in the early 1800s. It became a prolific gunmaking firm that evolved from Ethan Allen to Allen & Thurber, as well as the Allen & Wheelock Company. It was located in Norwich, Connecticut, and Worcester, Massachusetts, as well as Grafton. It eventually became the Forehand & Wadsworth Company in 1871 after the death of Ethan Allen. There were many and varied firearms produced under all of the headings described above. If one desires to collect Ethan Allen firearms, it would be advisable to educate oneself, as there are a number of fine publications available on the subject. The basic models and their values are as follows:

First Model Pocket Rifle

Manufactured by Ethan Allen in Grafton, Massachusetts. It was a bootleg-type, under-hammer, single shot pistol chambered for .31 percussion. Larger-caliber versions have also been noted. It had barrel lengths from 5" to 9" that were part-octagon in configuration. It had iron mountings and was blued with walnut grips. The barrel was marked, "E. Allen/Grafton/Mass." as well as "Pocket Rifle/Cast Steel/ Warranted." There were approximately 2,000 manufactured from 1831 to 1842.

Exc.	V.G.	Good	Fair	Poor
—	2000	1000	400	200

Second Model Pocket Rifle

A rounded-frame, round-grip version of the First Model.

Exc.	V.G.	Good	Fair	Poor
—	2000	1000	400	200

Bar Hammer Pistol

A double-action pistol with a top-mounted bar hammer. It was chambered for .28 to .36 caliber percussion. The half-octagon barrels were from 2" to 10" in length. They screwed out of the frame so it was possible to breech load them. The finish was blued with rounded walnut grips. They were marked, "Allen & Thurber/Grafton Mass." There were approximately 2,000 manufactured between the early 1830s and 1860.

Exc.	V.G.	Good	Fair	Poor
—	2000	1000	400	200

Tube Hammer Pistol

This version was similar to the Bar Hammer with a curved hammer without a spur. There were only a few hundred manufactured between the early 1830s and the early 1840s.

Exc.	V.G.	Good	Fair	Poor
—	3000	1500	750	300

Side Hammer Pistol

A single-shot, target-type pistol that was chambered for .34, .41, and .45 caliber percussion. It had a part-octagon barrel that was from 6" to 10" in length. There was a wooden ramrod mounted under the barrel. This model had a good quality rear sight that was adjustable. The ornate triggerguard had a graceful spur at its rear. The finish was blued with a rounded walnut grip. The barrel was marked, "Allen & Thurber, Worchester." There were approximately 300 manufactured in the late 1840s and early 1850s.

Exc.	V.G.	Good	Fair	Poor
—	1250	600	225	125

Center Hammer Pistol

A single-action chambered for .34, .36, or .44 percussion. It had a half-octagon barrel from 4" to 12" in length. It had a centrally mounted hammer that was offset to the right side to allow for sighting the pistol. The finish was blued with walnut grips. It was marked, "Allen & Thurber, Allen Thurber & Company." Some specimens are marked, "Allen & Wheelock." There were several thousand manufactured between the late 1840s and 1860.

Exc.	V.G.	Good	Fair	Poor
1500	800	400	200	100

Double Barrel Pistol

A SxS, double-barrel pistol with a single trigger. It was chambered for .36 caliber percussion with 3" to 6" round barrels. The finish was blued with walnut grips. Examples with a ramrod mounted under the barrel have been noted. The flute between the barrels was marked, "Allen & Thurber," "Allen Thurber & Company," or "Allen & Wheelock." There were approximately 1,000 manufactured in the 1850s.

Exc.	V.G.	Good	Fair	Poor
—	1000	500	250	100

Allen & Wheelock Center Hammer Pistol

A single-action pocket pistol chambered for .31 to .38 caliber percussion. It had octagon barrels from 3" to 6" in length. The finish was blued with square-butt walnut grips. The barrel was marked, "Allen & Wheelock." There were approximately 500 manufactured between 1858 and 1865.

Exc.	V.G.	Good	Fair	Poor
—	800	400	150	100

Allen Thurber & Company Target Pistol

A deluxe, single-action target pistol that was chambered for .31 or .36 caliber percussion. It had a heavy, octagon barrel that was from 11" to 16" in length. There was a wooden ramrod mounted underneath the barrel. The mountings were of German silver, and there was a detachable walnut stock with a deluxe, engraved patchbox. This weapon was engraved, and the barrel was marked, "Allen Thurber & Co./Worchester/Cast Steel." This firearm was furnished in a fitted case with the stock, false muzzle, and various accessories. It was considered to be a very high grade target pistol in its era. The values shown are for a complete-cased outfit. There were very few manufactured in the 1850s.

Exc.	V.G.	Good	Fair	Poor
—	15000	6500	2000	750

NOTE: For pistols without attachable stock deduct 80%.

Ethan Allen Pepperboxes

During the period from the early 1830s to the 1860s, this company manufactured over 50 different variations of the revolving, pepperbox-type pistol. They were commercially quite successful and actually competed successfully with the Colt revolving handguns for more than a decade. They were widely used throughout the United States, as well as in Mexico, and during our Civil War. They are widely collectible because of the number of variations that exist. The potential collector should avail himself of the information available on the subject. These pepperboxes can be divided into three categories.

No. 1—Manufactured from the 1830s until 1842, at Grafton, Massachusetts.

No. 2—Manufactured from 1842 to 1847, at Norwich, Connecticut.

No. 3—Manufactured from 1847 to 1865, at Worchester, Massachusetts.

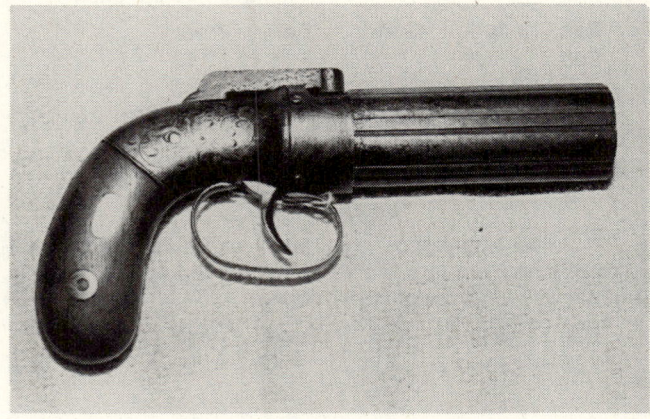

There are a number of subdivisions among these three basic groups that would pertain to trigger type, size, barrel length etc. It would be impossible to cover all 50 of these variations in a text of this type. We strongly suggest that qualified, individual appraisal be secured if contemplating a transaction. The values of these pepperbox pistols in excellent condition would be between $1,500 and $5,000. Most examples will be seen in the fair to good condition and will bring $1,000 to 2,000 depending on variation.

Large Frame Pocket Revolver

A double-action pocket revolver that was chambered for .34 caliber percussion. It had an octagon barrel from 3" to 5" in length. There were no sights. The 5-shot, unfluted cylinder was game scene-engraved. The finish was blued with rounded walnut grips. It had a bar-type hammer. This was the first conventional revolver manufactured by this company, and it was directly influenced by the pepperbox pistol for which Ethan Allen had become famous. It was marked, "Allen &

Wheelock" as well as "Patented April 16, 1845." There were approximately 1,500 manufactured between 1857 and 1860.

Courtesy Milwaukee Public Museum, Milwaukee, Wisconsin.

Exc.	V.G.	Good	Fair	Poor
—	1000	500	200	125

Small Frame Pocket Revolver

This version was similar to the Large Frame Pocket Revolver except chambered for .31 caliber percussion, with a 2" to 3.5" octagon barrel. It was slightly smaller in size, finished and marked the same. There were approximately 1,000 made between 1858 and 1860.

Exc.	V.G.	Good	Fair	Poor
—	1000	500	150	100

Side Hammer Belt Revolver

A single-action revolver chambered for .34 caliber percussion. It had an octagon barrel from 3" to 7.5" in length. It featured a hammer that was mounted on the right side of the frame and a 5-shot, engraved, unfluted cylinder. The cylinder access pin is inserted from the rear of the weapon. The finish is blued with a case-colored hammer and triggerguard and flared-butt walnut grips. It is marked, "Allen & Wheelock." There were two basic types. Values for the early model, of which 100 were manufactured between 1858 and 1861, are as follows:

Exc.	V.G.	Good	Fair	Poor
—	—	800	400	200

Standard Model

The second type was the Standard Model, with a spring-loaded catch on the triggerguard as opposed to a friction catch on the early model. There were approximately 1,000 manufactured between 1858 and 1861.

Courtesy Milwaukee Public Museum, Milwaukee, Wisconsin.

Exc.	V.G.	Good	Fair	Poor
—	1500	600	325	150

Side Hammer Pocket Revolver

This version was chambered for .28 caliber percussion and had a 2" to 5" octagon barrel. The frame was slightly smaller than the belt model.

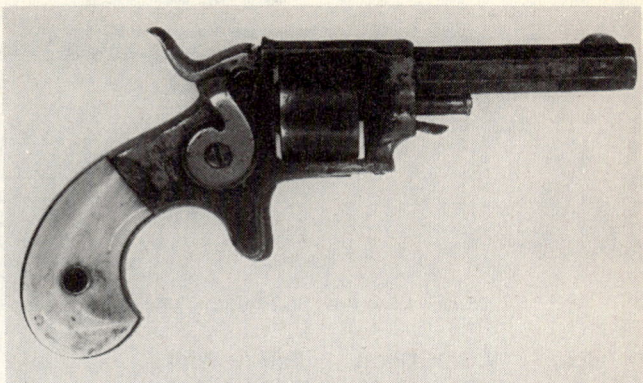

Courtesy Milwaukee Public Museum, Milwaukee, Wisconsin.

Early Production, 100 Manufactured

Exc.	V.G.	Good	Fair	Poor
—	—	800	325	150

Standard Production, 1,000 Manufactured

Exc.	V.G.	Good	Fair	Poor
—	1500	600	200	100

Side Hammer Navy Revolver

This was a large-frame, military-type revolver that was similar to the Side Hammer Belt Model, chambered for .36 caliber percussion. It features an octagon, 5.5" to 8" barrel with a 6-shot, engraved cylinder. There was an early-production type with a friction catch on the triggerguard. There were approximately 100 manufactured between 1858 and 1861.

Exc.	V.G.	Good	Fair	Poor
—	—	2500	1500	500

Standard Model, 1,000 Manufactured

Exc.	V.G.	Good	Fair	Poor
—	4000	2000	1000	500

Center Hammer Army Revolver

A large, military-type, single-action revolver that was chambered for .44 caliber percussion. It had a 7.5", half-octagon barrel and a 6-shot, unfluted cylinder. The hammer was mounted in the center of the frame. The finish was blued with a case-colored hammer and triggerguard and walnut grips. The barrel was marked, "Allen & Wheelock. Worchester, Mass. U.S./Allen's Pt's. Jan. 13, 1857. Dec. 15, 1857, Sept. 7, 1858." There were approximately 700 manufactured between 1861 and 1862.

Courtesy Milwaukee Public Museum, Milwaukee, Wisconsin.

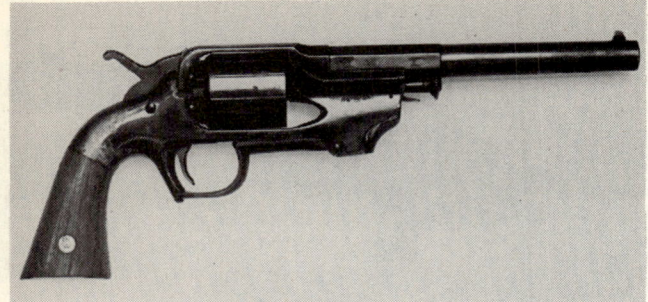

Courtesy Milwaukee Public Museum, Milwaukee, Wisconsin.

Exc.	V.G.	Good	Fair	Poor
—	5000	2500	1000	500

Center Hammer Navy Revolver

Similar to the Army Revolver except chambered for .36 caliber percussion with a 7.5", full-octagon barrel. Examples have been noted with 5", 6", or 8" barrels. Otherwise, it was similar to the Army model.

Exc.	V.G.	Good	Fair	Poor
—	3000	1500	750	400

Center Hammer Percussion Revolver

A single-action revolver chambered for .36 caliber percussion. It had an octagonal, 3" or 4" barrel with a 6-shot, unfluted cylinder. The finish was blued with walnut grips. This model supposedly was made for the Providence, Rhode Island, Police Department and has become commonly referred to as the "Providence Police Model." There were approximately 700 manufactured between 1858 and 1862.

Exc.	V.G.	Good	Fair	Poor
—	1500	800	300	125

Lipfire Army Revolver

A large, military-type, single-action revolver that was chambered for the .44 lipfire cartridge. It had a 7.5", half-octagon barrel with a 6-shot, unfluted cylinder that had notches at its rear for the cartridge lips. The finish was blued with a casecolored hammer and triggerguard and square-butt walnut grips. The barrel was marked, "Allen & Wheelock, Worchester, Mass." It resembled the Center Hammer Percussion Army Revolver. There were two basic variations, with a total of 250 Lipfire Army Revolver manufactured in the early 1860s.

Early Model Top Hinged Loading Gate

Exc.	V.G.	Good	Fair	Poor
—	4000	2000	1000	500

Late Model Bottom Hinged Loading Gate

Exc.	V.G.	Good	Fair	Poor
—	3000	1500	750	400

Lipfire Navy Revolver

Similar to the Army model, except chambered for the .36 lipfire cartridge, with an octagonal, 4", 5", 6", 7.5", or 8" barrel. There were approximately 500 manufactured in the 1860s.

Exc.	V.G.	Good	Fair	Poor
—	3000	1500	750	500

Lipfire Pocket Revolver

A smaller version chambered for the .32 lipfire cartridge, with an octagonal, 4", 5", or 6" barrel. There were approximately 200 manufactured in the early 1860s.

Exc.	V.G.	Good	Fair	Poor
—	2000	750	400	200

.32 Side Hammer Rimfire Revolver

A single-action, spur-trigger, pocket revolver chambered for the .32 caliber rimfire cartridge. It had octagonal barrels from 3" to 5" in length. The finish was blued with flared-butt, walnut grips. It was marked, "Allen & Wheelock Worchester, Mass." There were three variations with a total of approximately 1,000 manufactured between 1859 and 1862.

First Model—Rounded Top Strap

Exc.	V.G.	Good	Fair	Poor
—	1250	500	250	125

Second Model—July 3, 1860 Marked on Frame

Exc.	V.G.	Good	Fair	Poor
—	1000	400	200	100

Third Model—1858 and 1861 Patent Dates

Exc.	V.G.	Good	Fair	Poor
—	1000	400	200	100

.22 Side Hammer Rimfire Revolver

A smaller version of the .32 revolver, chambered for the .22 rimfire cartridge. It has octagonal barrels from 2.25" to 4" in length. It has a 7-shot, unfluted cylinder. There were approximately 1,500 manufactured between 1858 and 1862. There were many variations.

Early Model First Issue—Access Pin Enters from Rear

Exc.	V.G.	Good	Fair	Poor
—	900	450	200	100

Second Issue—Access Pin Enters from Front

Exc.	V.G.	Good	Fair	Poor
—	850	400	200	100

Third Issue—Separate Rear Sight

Exc.	V.G.	Good	Fair	Poor
—	1500	700	300	150

Fourth to Eighth Issue—Very Similar, Values the Same

Exc.	V.G.	Good	Fair	Poor
1000	500	250	150	100

Single Shot Center Hammer

A single-shot derringer-type pistol that was chambered for the .22 caliber rimfire cartridge. It had part-octagon barrels from 2" to 5.5" in length that swung to the right side for loading. Some had automatic ejectors; others did not. The frame was either brass or iron with birdshead or squared-butt walnut grips. It was marked, "Allen & Wheelock" or "E. Allen & Co." There were very few manufactured in the early 1860s.

Early Issue

Full-length, octagon barrel and a round, iron frame. It is rarely encountered.

Exc.	V.G.	Good	Fair	Poor
—	1000	500	225	100

Standard Issue—Squared Butt or Birdshead

Exc.	V.G.	Good	Fair	Poor
1250	500	250	200	100

.32 Single Shot Center Hammer

A larger-frame pocket pistol chambered for the .32 rimfire cartridge. It has a part-octagon or full-octagon barrel of 4" or 5" in length. It swung to the right side for loading. Otherwise, this model was similar to the .22-caliber version.

Exc.	V.G.	Good	Fair	Poor
—	1000	400	200	100

Vest Pocket Derringer

A small pocket pistol chambered for the .22 rimfire cartridge. It had a 2", part-octagon barrel that swung to the right-hand side for loading. The cartridges were manually extracted. It featured a brass frame with a blued or plated barrel and walnut, birdshead grips. The barrel was marked, "Allen & Co. Makers." This was an extremely small firearm, and there were approximately 200 manufactured between 1869 and 1871.

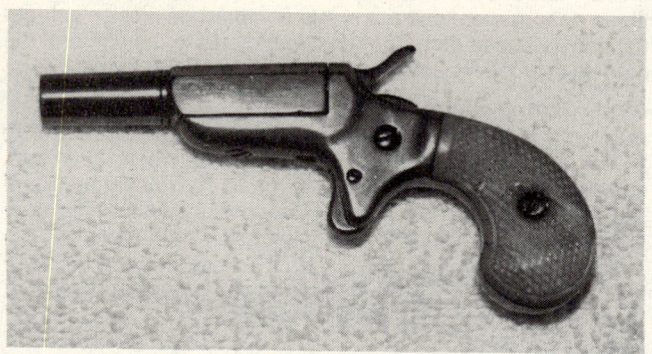

Exc.	V.G.	Good	Fair	Poor
—	1000	400	200	100

.32 Derringer

Similar to the Vest Pocket Version, larger in size, and chambered for the .32 rimfire cartridge. It had a part-octagon barrel from 2" to 4" in length that swung to the right for loading. This version featured an automatic extractor. The barrel was marked, "E. Allen & Co. Worchester, Mass." This was a very rare firearm, made between 1865 and 1871.

Exc.	V.G.	Good	Fair	Poor
—	1500	600	450	250

.41 Derringer

The same size and configuration as the .32 caliber model except it was chambered for the .41 rimfire cartridge with barrel lengths of 2.5" to 2.75" in length. The markings were the same. There were approximately 100 manufactured between 1865 and 1871.

Exc.	V.G.	Good	Fair	Poor
—	—	1000	500	250

Center Hammer Muzzle-loading Rifle

A single-shot rifle chambered for .44 caliber percussion. It had a 36" round barrel with an octagonal breech. It had a center-mounted hammer that was offset to the right for sighting. It had iron mountings. The finish was browned with a case-colored lock. There was a ramrod mounted under the barrel. It had a walnut buttstock with a crescent buttplate and no forearm. There were approximately 100 manufactured in the 1850s.

Exc.	V.G.	Good	Fair	Poor
—	—	1000	500	250

Side Hammer Muzzle-loading Rifle

Similar to the Center Hammer model, with the hammer mounted on the right side of the lock. It was chambered for .38 caliber percussion, with an octagon barrel from 28" to 32" in length. It is occasionally found with a patchbox. The barrel is browned with a case-colored lock and a walnut stock with crescent buttplate. There were several hundred manufactured from the early 1840s to the 1860s.

Exc.	V.G.	Good	Fair	Poor
—	3500	1500	700	350

Combination Gun

Either an Over/Under or SxS rifle chambered for 12 gauge and .38 caliber percussion. The barrels were from 28" to 34" in length. It had two hammers and double triggers with a ramrod mounted either beneath or on the right side of the barrels. The finish was browned with a walnut stock. Examples with a patchbox have been noted. Production was very limited, with

the Over/Under versions worth approximately 10 percent more than the SxS values given. They were manufactured between the 1840s and the 1860s.

Exc.	V.G.	Good	Fair	Poor
—	4000	2500	1000	450

Side Hammer Breech-loading Rifle

A unique rifle chambered for .36 to .50 caliber percussion. It was offered with various-length, part-octagon barrels. It had an unusual breech mechanism that was activated by a rotating lever which resembled a water faucet. The barrel was browned with a case-colored lock and a walnut stock. It was marked, "Allen & Wheelock/ Allen's Patent July 3, 1855." There were approximately 500 manufactured between 1855 and 1860.

Courtesy Buffalo Bill Historical Center, Cody, Wyoming.

Exc.	V.G.	Good	Fair	Poor
—	3000	1500	650	250

Drop Breech Rifle

This single-shot rifle was chambered for the .22 through the .44 rimfire cartridges. It had a part-octagon barrel from 23" to 28" in length. The breech was activated by the combination triggerguard action lever. Opening the breech automatically ejected the empty cartridge. The external hammer was manually cocked, and it featured an adjustable sight. The barrel was blued with a case-colored frame and a walnut stock. It was marked, "Allen & Wheelock/ Allen's Pat. Sept. 18, 1860." There were approximately 2,000 manufactured between 1860 and 1871.

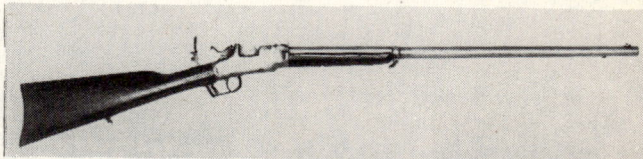

Courtesy Milwaukee Public Museum, Milwaukee, Wisconsin.

Exc.	V.G.	Good	Fair	Poor
3500	1500	750	475	300

Lipfire Revolving Rifle

A six-shot, cylinder-type rifle chambered for the .44 caliber lipfire cartridge. It had an unfluted cylinder with slots at its rear to allow for the cartridge lips. The round barrels were 26" to 28" in length with an octagon breech. The finish was blued with a case-colored frame and a walnut buttstock. This model was not marked with the maker's name. There were approximately 100 manufactured between 1861 and 1863.

Courtesy Buffalo Bill Historical Center, Cody, Wyoming.

Exc.	V.G.	Good	Fair	Poor
—	—	10000	5000	2000

Double Barrel Shotgun

A SxS gun chambered for 10 or 12 gauge. The barrel length was 28". It was loaded by means of a trapdoor-type breech that had a lever handle. The finish was blued with checkered walnut stock. There were a few hundred manufactured between 1865 and 1871.

Exc.	V.G.	Good	Fair	Poor
—	1000	800	400	200

ALLEN & THURBER
SEE—Ethan Allen

ALLEN & WHEELOCK
SEE—Ethan Allen

ALLEN FIREARMS
Santa Fe, New Mexico
SEE—Aldo Uberti

ALL RIGHT F. A. CO.
Lawrence, Massachusetts

Little All Right Palm Pistol

Squeezer-type pocket pistol invented by E. Boardman and A. Peavy in 1876, was made in .22 cal. and had a 5-shot cylinder with a 1-5/8" or 2-3/8" barrel. The barrel is octagonal with a tube on top of it which houses the sliding trigger. The finish is nickel. The black hard rubber grips have "Little All Right" & "All Right Firearms Co., Manufacturers Lawrence, Mass. U.S.A." molded into them. There were several hundred produced in the late 1870s.

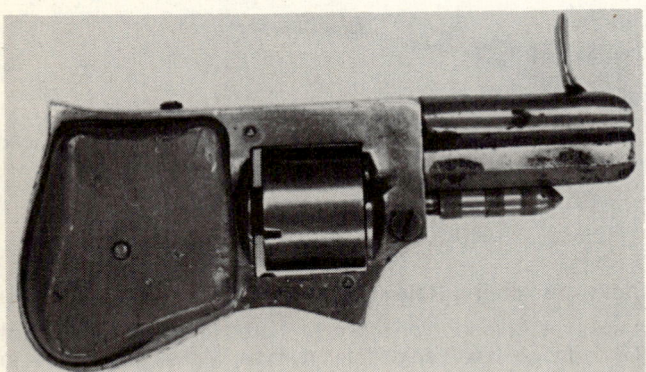

Courtesy Milwaukee Public Museum, Milwaukee, Wisconsin.

Exc.	V.G.	Good	Fair	Poor
—	2000	1000	500	250

ALPHA ARMS CO.
Flower Mound, Texas

Alpha Arms Co. produced high-grade bolt-action rifles on a semi-custom basis. It manufactured a number of standard models but offered many options at additional cost. Some of these options were custom sights and finishes and an octagonal barrel. These extra features would add to the value of the models listed. This company operated from 1983 until 1987.

Alpha Jaguar Grade I

Built on a Mauser-type action with barrel lengths from 20" to 24". It was chambered for most calibers between .222 Rem. and .338 Win. Mag. The stock was made from a synthetic laminated material that the company called Alphawood. This model was introduced in 1987 and only produced that year.

NIB	Exc.	V.G.	Good	Fair	Poor
900	750	500	400	300	200

Jaguar Grade II

Similar to the Grade I with a Douglas Premium barrel.

NIB	Exc.	V.G.	Good	Fair	Poor
1000	850	650	500	400	250

Jaguar Grade III

Has the Douglas barrel plus a hand-honed trigger and action and a three-position safety like the Winchester Model 70.

NIB	Exc.	V.G.	Good	Fair	Poor
1200	1000	850	700	400	200

Jaguar Grade IV

Has all the features of the Grade III with a specially lightened action and sling-swivel studs.

NIB	Exc.	V.G.	Good	Fair	Poor
1300	1100	950	800	500	250

Alpha Grand Slam

Features the same high quality as the Jaguar models and is available in a left-hand model. It has a fluted bolt, laminated stock, and a matte blue finish.

NIB	Exc.	V.G.	Good	Fair	Poor
1200	1000	850	700	450	250

Alpha Custom

Similar to the Grand Slam with a select grade stock.

NIB	Exc.	V.G.	Good	Fair	Poor
1500	1275	1000	750	500	250

Alpha Alaskan

Similar to the Grand Slam but chambered for the .308 Win., .350 Rem. Mag., .358 Win. and the .458 Win. Mag. It features all stainless steel construction.

NIB	Exc.	V.G.	Good	Fair	Poor
1500	1275	1000	750	500	250

Alpha Big - Five

Similar to the Jaguar Grade IV chambered for the .300 Win. Mag., .375 H&H Mag. and the .458 Win. Mag. It had a reinforced through-bolt stock to accommodate the recoil of the larger caliber cartridges for which it was chambered. It also had a decelerator recoil pad. This model was manufactured in 1987 only.

NIB	Exc.	V.G.	Good	Fair	Poor
1600	1375	1100	850	600	300

ALSOP, C.R.
Middletown, Connecticut

This firearms manufacturer made revolvers during 1862 and 1863. They made two basic models, the Navy and the Pocket model. Some collectors consider the Alsop to be a secondary U.S. martial handgun, but no verifying government contracts are known to exist.

First Model Navy Revolver

A .36 cal. revolver with a 3.5", 4.5", 5.5", or 6.5" barrel length and a 5-shot cylinder. It has a blued finish, wood grips, and a peculiar hump in its backstrap. The first model has a safety device which blocks the spur trigger. This device is found on serial numbers 1-100. Markings are as follows: "C.R. Alsop Middletown, Conn. 1860 & 1861" on the barrel. The cylinder is marked "C.R. Alsop" & "Nov. 26th, 1861"; the sideplate, "Patented Jan. 21st, 1862."

Exc.	V.G.	Good	Fair	Poor
—	5000	2500	1000	500

Standard Model Navy Revolver

Exactly the same as the First Model without the safety device. They are serial numbered 101 to 300.

Exc.	V.G.	Good	Fair	Poor
—	4500	2000	700	300

Pocket Model Revolver

A .31 cal. 5-shot revolver with spur trigger, 4" round barrel, blued finish, and wood grips. It is very similar in appearance to the Navy model but smaller in size. It is marked "C.R. Alsop Middletown, Conn. 1860 & 1861" on the barrel. The cylinder is marked "C.R. Alsop Nov. 26th, 1861." They are serial numbered 1-300.

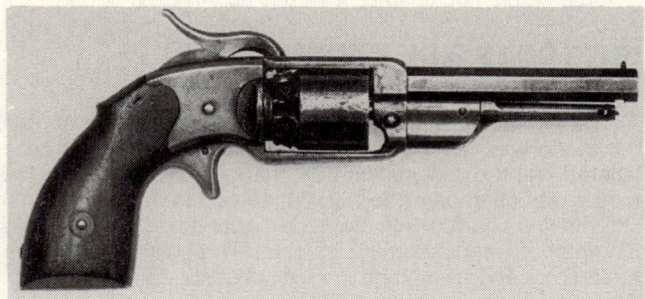

Courtesy Milwaukee Public Museum, Milwaukee, Wisconsin.

Exc.	V.G.	Good	Fair	Poor
—	2500	1000	500	200

AMERICAN ARMS
Garden Grove, California

Eagle .380

This pistol was a stainless steel copy of the Walther PPKS. It was a semi-auto blowback that was chambered for the .380 ACP. It was double-action and had a 3.25" barrel and a 6-shot detachable magazine. An optional feature was a black teflon finish that would increase the value by 10 percent. This company ceased production in 1985.

Exc.	V.G.	Good	Fair	Poor
300	225	175	150	100

AMERICAN ARMS CO.
Boston, Massachusetts

The history of American Arms is rather sketchy, but it appears the company was formed in 1853 as the G. H. Fox Co. and then became the American Tool & Machine Co. in 1865. In 1870 they formed a new corporation called American Arms Company with George Fox as the principle stockholder. This corporation was dissolved in 1873; a second American Arms Co. was incorporated in 1877 and a third in 1890. It is unclear if these corporations had essentially the same owners, but George H. Fox appears as a principal owner in two of the three. One could assume that financial problems forced them to bankrupt one corporation and reorganize under another. American Arms manufactured firearms in Boston, Massachusetts, from 1866 until 1893. In 1893 they moved to Bluffton, Alabama and manufactured guns until 1901.

Fox Model "Swing Out" Hammer Double

Manufactured from 1870 to 1884, designed by George H. Fox, not to be confused with A.H. Fox. This model is unusual in that the barrel swings to the right for loading and the barrel release is located on the tang. It comes in 10 and 12 gauge, 26", 28", 30" and 32", with twist, Damascus or laminated barrels. Early production models have conventional soldered together barrels. Later variations after 1878 feature a unique design in that the barrels are dovetailed together. These guns could be ordered with several options and choices of finish; this would add premium value to a particular gun.

Exc.	V.G.	Good	Fair	Poor
1000	900	600	300	150

Semi-Hammerless Double

Manufactured from 1892 to 1901. This model features a cocking lever that cocks an internal firing pin. It comes in 12 gauge with 30" twist barrels.

Exc.	V.G.	Good	Fair	Poor
750	600	400	250	150

Whitmore Model Hammerless Double

Manufactured from 1890 to 1901. It comes in 10, 12, and 16 gauge with 28", 30" or 32" twist, laminated or Damascus barrels. It is marked Whitmore's patent.

Exc.	V.G.	Good	Fair	Poor
850	700	650	250	150

Semi-Hammerless Single Barrel

Manufactured from 1882 to 1901. It comes in 10, 12, and 16 gauge with 28", 30" or 32" twist or Damascus barrel.

Exc.	V.G.	Good	Fair	Poor
800	600	400	200	100

Top Break Revolvers

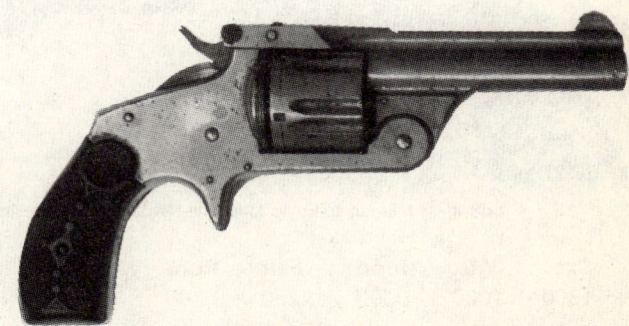

Courtesy Milwaukee Public Museum, Milwaukee, Wisconsin.

Spur Trigger - Single Action Five Shot Revolver

These revolvers were made between 1883 and 1887 in .38 S&W only. They feature an unusual manual ring extractor and double-fluted cylinder. They are nickel plated with hard rubber grips and are marked "American Arms Company Boston Mass."

Exc.	V.G.	Good	Fair	Poor
850	500	250	150	100

Standard Trigger Double Action Model 1886 Revolver

This model has a standard trigger and triggerguard, comes in .32 short and .38 S&W with a 3.5-inch barrel, in blue or nickel finish. The early models are equipped with the ring extractor and double fluted cylinder. Later variations have a standard star extractor and single fluted cylinder.

Exc.	V.G.	Good	Fair	Poor
850	500	250	150	100

Hammerless Model 1890 Double Action

These guns were manufactured from 1890 to 1901. It has an adjustable single or double-stage trigger pull and several unusual safety devices. It comes in .32 and .38 S&W with a 3.25" ribbed barrel, fluted cylinder, nickel finish, hard rubber grips with logo and ivory or mother of pearl grips. It is marked "American Arms Co. Boston/Pat. May 25, 1886." The top strap is marked "Pat. Pending" on early models and "Pat's May 25'86/Mar 1 1'89/June 17'90:" on later models.

Exc	V.G.	Good	Fair	Poor
1500	800	400	200	100

American Arms Co. manufactured a two-barrel derringer-style pocket pistol. The barrels were manually rotated to load and fire the weapon. The pistol had a nickel-plated brass frame, blued barrels, and walnut grips. The markings were as follows: "American Arms Co. Boston, Mass." on one barrel and "Pat. Oct. 31, 1865" on the other barrel. There were approximately 2,000-3,000 produced between 1866 and 1878.

Combination .22 caliber R.F. and .32 caliber R.F.

A two-caliber combination with 3" barrel, square butt only. The most common variation.

Exc.	V.G.	Good	Fair	Poor
1500	1000	500	250	100

.32 cal. R.F., Both Barrels

3" barrel with square butt.

Courtesy Milwaukee Public Museum, Milwaukee, Wisconsin.

Exc.	V.G.	Good	Fair	Poor
1500	1000	500	250	100

.32 caliber R.F. Both Barrels

2-5/8" barrel with birdshead grips.

Exc.	V.G.	Good	Fair	Poor
1750	1250	600	300	150

.38 caliber R.F. Both Barrels

2-5/8" barrel with birdshead grips. A rare variation.

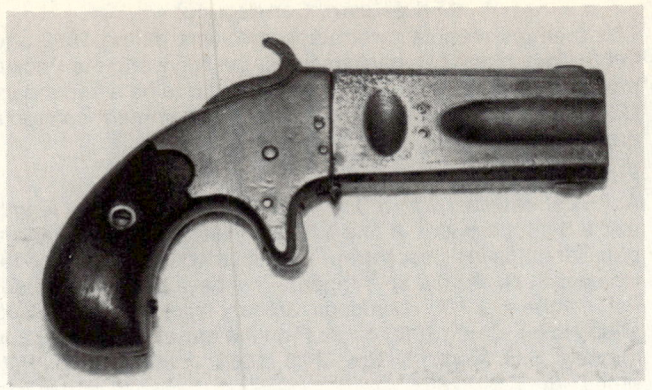

Exc.	V.G.	Good	Fair	Poor
—	—	1500	800	500

.41 caliber R.F. Both Barrels

2-5/8" barrel with square butt only.

Exc.	V.G.	Good	Fair	Poor
2000	1500	800	400	200

AMERICAN ARMS, INC.
North Kansas City, Missouri

Basically an importer of firearms: shotguns from Spain, rifles from Yugoslavia, and handguns from Germany and Yugoslavia. They also manufacture in the U.S.A. There are certain rifles that they are no longer allowed to import because of the Bush administration's ban on foreign semiautomatic rifles. These weapons are listed for reference but are not priced due to the extreme fluctuations in values as this is written.

SHOTGUNS SIDE X SIDE

Gentry - York

These two designations cover the same model. Prior to 1988 this model was called the York. In 1988 the receiver was case-colored and the designation was changed to the Gentry. This model was chambered for 12, 20, 28 gauge and .410. It had chrome-lined barrels from 26" to 30" in length, double triggers, 3" chambers, and automatic ejectors. The boxlock action featured scroll engraving, and the walnut stock was hand-checkered. It was introduced in 1986.

NIB	Exc.	V.G.	Good	Fair	Poor
700	625	450	300	200	150

10 Gauge Magnum Shotgun

A 10 gauge with 3.5" chambers and 32" barrels. It featured a scroll-engraved, chromed boxlock action and double triggers. It was imported from Spain in 1986 only.

NIB	Exc.	V.G.	Good	Fair	Poor
900	800	550	350	250	150

12 Gauge magnum Shotgun

As above but chambered for 12 gauge 3-1/2" magnum shell.

NIB	Exc.	V.G.	Good	Fair	Poor
700	625	450	300	200	150

Brittany

Chambered for 12 and 20 gauge with 27" or 25" barrels with screw-in choke tubes. It had a solid matted rib and a casecolored, engraved boxlock action. Automatic ejectors and a single selective trigger were standard on this model as was a hand-checkered, walnut, straight-grip stock with semi-beavertail forend. This model was introduced in 1989.

NIB	Exc.	V.G.	Good	Fair	Poor
850	750	600	450	375	200

Turkey Special

A utilitarian model designed to be an effective turkey hunting tool. It is chambered for the Magnum 10 and 12 gauges and has 26" barrels. The finish is parkerized, and the stock is also finished in a non-glare matte. Sling-swivel studs and a recoil pad are standard. This model was introduced in 1987.

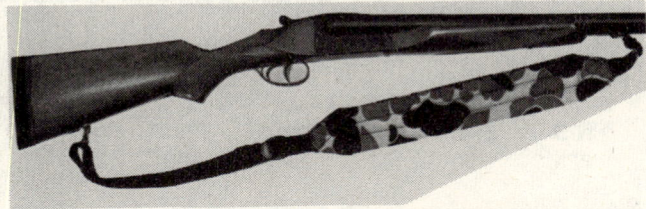

NIB	Exc.	V.G.	Good	Fair	Poor
525	475	425	350	250	150

Waterfowl Special

This model is similar to the Turkey Special but chambered for the 10 gauge only. It is furnished with a camouflaged sling. It was introduced in 1987.

NIB	Exc.	V.G.	Good	Fair	Poor
525	475	425	350	250	150

Specialty Model

Similar to the Turkey Special and offered in 12 gauge 3-1/2" magnum.

NIB	Exc.	V.G.	Good	Fair	Poor
700	625	450	300	200	150

Derby

Chambered for the 12 and 20 gauge. It has 26" or 28" barrels with 3" chambers and automatic ejectors. Either double or single selective triggers are offered, and the sidelock action is scroll engraved and chromed. The checkered straight-grip stock and forearm are oil-finished. This model was introduced in 1986.

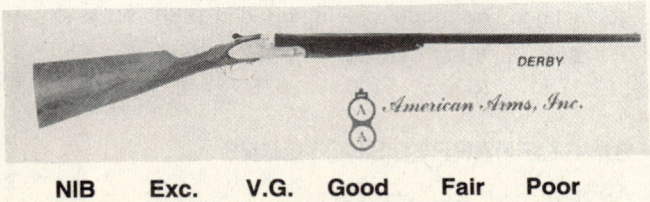

NIB	Exc.	V.G.	Good	Fair	Poor
825	700	600	500	350	200

Grulla #2

Top-of-the-line model chambered for 12, 20 and 28 gauge and .410. The barrels are 26" or 28" with a concave rib. The hand-fitted full sidelock action is extensively engraved and casecolored. There are various chokes, double triggers, and automatic ejectors. The select walnut, straight-grip stock and splinter forend is hand-checkered and has a hand-rubbed oil finish. This model was introduced in 1989.

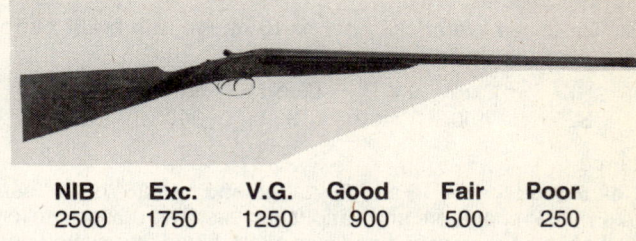

NIB	Exc.	V.G.	Good	Fair	Poor
2500	1750	1250	900	500	250

SHOTGUNS O/U

F.S. 200

A trap or skeet model that was chambered for 12 gauge only. It had 26" Skeet & Skeet barrels or 32" full choke barrels on the trap model. The barrels were separated and had a vent rib. The boxlock action had a Greener crossbolt and was either black or matte chrome-plated. It featured a single selective trigger, automatic ejectors, and a checkered walnut pistol-grip stock. The F.S. 200 was imported in 1986 and 1987 only.

Exc.	V.G.	Good	Fair	Poor
675	575	465	350	150

F.S. 300

Similar to the F. S. 200 with lightly engraved side plates and a 30" barrel offered in the trap grade. It was imported in 1986 only.

Exc.	V.G.	Good	Fair	Poor
800	675	565	450	250

F.S. 400

Similar to the F.S. 300 with an engraved, matte chrome-plated receiver. It was imported in 1986 only.

Exc.	V.G.	Good	Fair	Poor
1100	950	800	650	350

F.S. 500

Similar to the F.S. 400 with the same general specifications. It was not imported after 1985.

Exc.	V.G.	Good	Fair	Poor
1150	1000	850	700	350

Waterfowl Special

Chambered for the 12 gauge Magnum with 3.5" chambers. It has 28" barrels with screw-in choke tubes. There are automatic ejectors and a single selective trigger. The finish is parkerized with a matte finished stock, sling swivels, and camouflaged sling and a recoil pad. It was introduced in 1987.

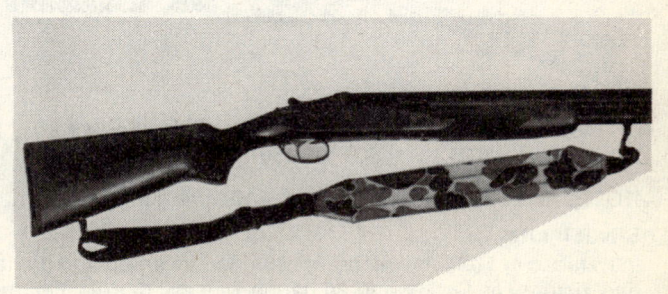

NIB	Exc.	V.G.	Good	Fair	Poor
575	475	400	350	300	150

Waterfowl 10 Gauge

The same as the Waterfowl Special but is chambered for the 10 gauge Magnum with double triggers.

NIB	Exc.	V.G.	Good	Fair	Poor
750	600	500	350	300	200

Turkey Special

Similar to the Waterfowl Special 10 gauge with a 26" barrel with screw-in choke tubes.

NIB	Exc.	V.G.	Good	Fair	Poor
525	450	400	350	300	200

Lince

Chambered for the 12 and 20 gauge and had 26" or 28" barrels with 3" chambers and various chokes. The boxlock action had a Greener crossbolt and was either blued or polished and chrome-plated. The barrels were blued with a ventilated rib. It had a single selective trigger and automatic ejectors. The Lince was imported in 1986 only.

Exc.	V.G.	Good	Fair	Poor
500	425	350	300	200

Silver Model

Similar to the Lince with a plain, unengraved, brushed-chrome-finished receiver. It was imported in 1986 and 1987.

Exc.	V.G.	Good	Fair	Poor
500	425	350	300	200

Silver I

Similar to the Silver but is available in 28 gauge and .410, as well as 12 and 20 gauge. It also has a single selective trigger, fixed chokes, extractors, and a recoil pad. It was introduced in 1987.

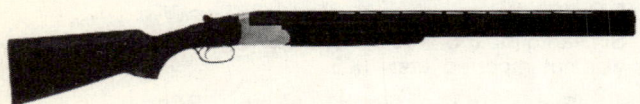

NIB	Exc.	V.G.	Good	Fair	Poor
550	475	325	275	200	175

NOTE: Add $25 for 28 gauge and .410 bore guns.

Silver II

Similar to the Silver I with screw-in choke tubes, automatic ejectors, and select walnut. It was introduced in 1987.

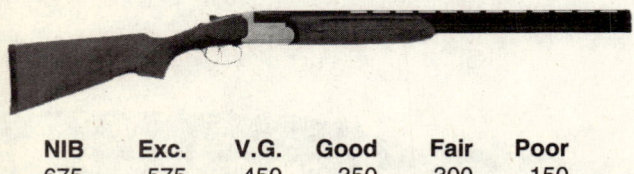

NIB	Exc.	V.G.	Good	Fair	Poor
675	575	450	350	300	150

NOTE: Add $25 for 28 gauge and .410 bore guns.

Silver II Lite

Introduced in 1994 this model is designed as an upland game gun. Offered in 12, 20, and 28 gauge with 26" barrels. Chambered for both 2-3/4" and 3" shells. Frame is made from a lightweight steel alloy.

NIB	Exc.	V.G.	Good	Fair	Poor
875	775	550	400	300	150

Silver Competition/Sporting

Offered in 12 gauge with a choice of 28" or 30" barrels which are made from chrome moly. Barrels have elongated forcing cones, chromed bores and are ported to help reduce recoil. Comes with interchangeable choke tubes. The single selective trigger is mechanical. Weighs about 7-1/2 pounds. In 1996 a 20 gauge model was added with 28" barrel and 3" chambers.

NIB	Exc.	V.G.	Good	Fair	Poor
875	775	550	400	300	150

Bristol

Chambered for 12 and 20 gauge. It has various barrel lengths with a vent rib and screw-in choke tubes. The chambers are 3", and the chrome-finished action is a boxlock with Greener crossbolt and gamescene-engraved side plates. There are automatic ejectors and a single selective trigger. It was introduced in 1986, and in 1989 the designation was changed to the Sterling.

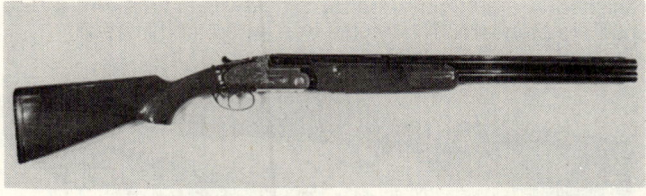

NIB	Exc.	V.G.	Good	Fair	Poor
825	750	675	500	400	200

Sir

Chambered for the 12 and 20 gauge with 3" chambers, various barrel lengths and chokings and a ventilated rib. The chrome-finished sidelock action has a Greener crossbolt and is engraved with a gamescene. There are automatic ejectors and a single selective trigger. This model was imported in 1986.

Exc.	V.G.	Good	Fair	Poor
875	750	625	500	250

Royal

Chambered for the 12 and 20 gauge. It is manufactured in various barrel lengths and chokes with a vent rib and 3" chambers. The chrome-finished sidelock action has a Greener crossbolt and is profusely scroll-engraved. It has automatic ejectors and a single selective trigger. The select pistolgrip walnut stock is hand-checkered and oil-finished. This model was imported in 1986 and 1987.

Exc.	V.G.	Good	Fair	Poor
1500	1275	1000	800	400

Excelsior

Similar to the Royal with extensive deep relief engraving and gold inlays. This model was imported in 1986 and 1987.

Exc.	V.G.	Good	Fair	Poor
1750	1500	1200	875	450

SINGLE BARREL SHOTGUNS

AASB

The standard single-barrel, break-open, hammerless shotgun. It is chambered for 12 and 20 gauge and .410. It has a 26" barrel with various chokes and 3" chambers. It has a pistol-grip stock and a matte finish. It was introduced in 1988.

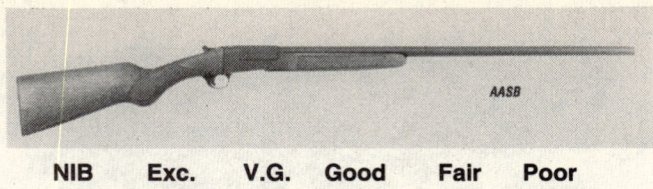

AASB

NIB	Exc.	V.G.	Good	Fair	Poor
100	85	75	60	45	25

Campers Special

Similar to the standard model with a 21" barrel and a folding stock. It was introduced in 1988.

NIB	Exc.	V.G.	Good	Fair	Poor
107	95	85	70	50	35

Single Barrel Shotguns Youth Model

Chambered for the 20 gauge and .410 and has a 12.5" stock with a recoil pad. It was introduced in 1989.

NIB	Exc.	V.G.	Good	Fair	Poor
115	100	80	65	50	35

Slugger

This version has a 24" barrel with rifle sights. It is chambered for the 12 and 20 gauge and has a recoil pad.

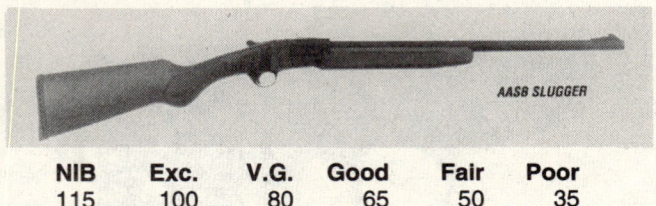

AASB SLUGGER

NIB	Exc.	V.G.	Good	Fair	Poor
115	100	80	65	50	35

10 Gauge Model

Chambered for the 10 gauge 3.5" Magnum. It has a 32" full choke barrel and a recoil pad. This model was introduced in 1988.

NIB	Exc.	V.G.	Good	Fair	Poor
150	135	100	85	60	45

Combo Model

Similar in appearance to the other single-barrel models but is offered in an interchangeable-barreled rifle/shotgun combination—the 28" barreled .22 Hornet and the 12 gauge, or the 26" barreled .22 l.r. and 20 gauge. This model was furnished with a fitted hard case to hold the interchangeable barrels. It was introduced in 1989.

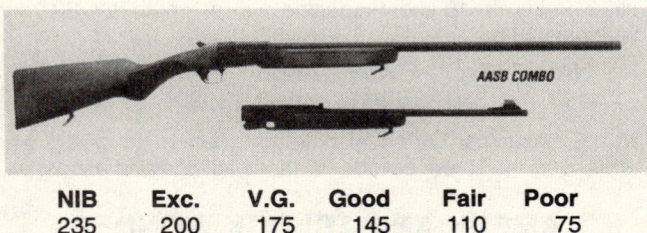

AASB COMBO

NIB	Exc.	V.G.	Good	Fair	Poor
235	200	175	145	110	75

RIFLES

Model ZCY.223

A gas-operated, semiautomatic rifle that is chambered for the .223. It is the civilian version of the Yugoslavian Military rifle and was never actually imported — only advertised. This is another model that would have wildly fluctuating values; and if one were to be located for sale, it would be a market-will-bear situation.

NOTE: These rifles are listed for reference purposes only. An independent appraisal should be secured if a transaction is contemplated.

Model ZCY.308

Essentially the same rifle as the ZCY.223 — only it is chambered for the .308 cartridge. This model was imported in 1988 only.

AKY39

The semiautomatic version of the Soviet AK-47 as it is manufactured by Yugoslavia. It is offered with folding tritium night sights and a wooden fixed stock. It was imported in 1988 and is now banned from further importation.

AKF39

The same rifle as the AKY39 with a metal folding stock.

AKC47

Basically the same rifle as the AKY39 without the tritium night sights. Importation is no longer allowed.

AKF47

The same rifle as the AKC47 with a metal folding stock.

EXP-64 Survival Rifle

A .22 caliber, semiautomatic takedown rifle. It is self-storing in a floating, oversized plastic stock. The rifle has a 21" barrel with open sights and a crossbolt safety. There is a 10-shot detachable magazine. Importation by American Arms began in 1989.

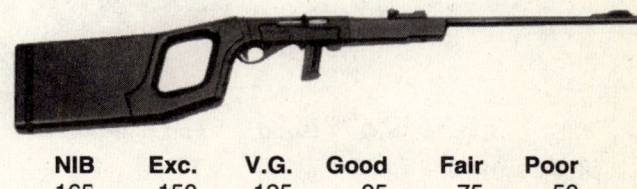

NIB	Exc.	V.G.	Good	Fair	Poor
165	150	125	95	75	50

SM-64 TD Sporter

A .22 l.r. semiautomatic with a takedown 21" barrel. It has adjustable sights and a checkered hardwood stock and forend. Importation commenced in 1989.

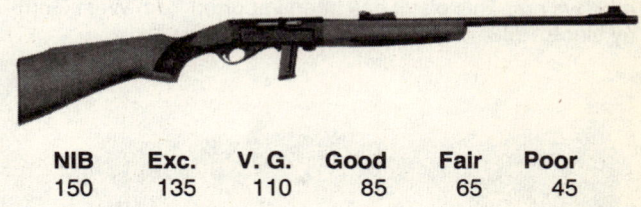

NIB	Exc.	V.G.	Good	Fair	Poor
150	135	110	85	65	45

HANDGUNS

Model TT Tokarev

The Yugoslavian version of the Soviet Tokarev chambered for 9mm Parabellum and with a safety added to make importation legal. It has a 4.5" barrel, 9-shot magazine and a blued finish with checkered plastic grips. Importation began in 1988.

TT9MM

NIB	Exc.	V.G.	Good	Fair	Poor
290	265	225	175	140	100

Model ZC-.380

A scaled-down version of the Tokarev that is chambered for the .380 ACP. It has a 3.5" barrel and holds 8 shots. The finish and grips are the same as on the full-sized version. Importation from Yugoslavia began in 1988.

NIB	Exc.	V.G.	Good	Fair	Poor
275	250	225	175	125	100

Model EP-.380

A high-quality, stainless steel pocket pistol that is chambered for the .380 ACP cartridge. It is a double-action semiautomatic that holds 7 shots and has a 3.5" barrel. The grips are checkered walnut. This pistol has been imported from West Germany since 1988.

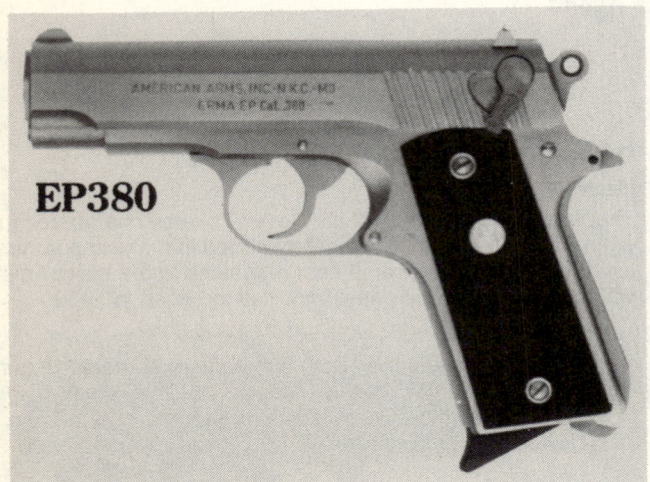

NIB	Exc.	V.G.	Good	Fair	Poor
450	400	350	275	225	100

Model PK-22

A domestic semiautomatic that is chambered for the .22 l.r. It is a double action with a 3.5" barrel and an 8-shot finger extension magazine. It is made of stainless steel and has black plastic grips. This model is manufactured in the U.S.A. by American Arms.

NIB	Exc.	V.G.	Good	Fair	Poor
200	175	150	125	100	75

Model CX-22

A compact version of the PK-22 with a 2.75" barrel and a 7-shot magazine. Manufacture began in 1989.

NIB	Exc.	V.G.	Good	Fair	Poor
200	175	150	125	100	75

Aussie Model

Introduced in 1996 this is an Austrialian designed semi-automatic pistol made in Spain. Chambered for the 9mm or 40S&W cartridge it has a polymer frame with nickeled steel slide. Sold with 10 shot magazine. Barrel length is 4-3/4" and weight is 23 oz.

NIB	Exc.	V.G.	Good	Fair	Poor
400	350	300	250	200	100

NOTE: American Arms also imports Uberti revolvers and rifles. See the Uberti section for those listings and prices.

AMERICAN BARLOCK WONDER
SEE-Crescent Arms Co.

AMERICAN DERRINGER CORP.
Waco, Texas

Model 1 Derringer

Fashioned after the Remington O/U derringer this is a high quality, rugged pistol. It is built from high tensile strength stainless steel. There are over 60 different rifle and pistol calibers to choose from on special order. The upper barrel can be chambered different from the lower barrel on request. Available in a high polish finish or a satin finish. Offered with rosewood, bacote, walnut, or blackwood grips. Ivory, bonded ivory, stag, or pearl are available at extra cost. Overall length is 4.8", barrel length is 3", width across the frame is .9", width across the grip is 1.2". Typical weight is 15 oz. in .45 caliber. All guns are furnished with French fitted leatherette case. Prices are determined by caliber.

Caliber: .22 Long Rifle through .357 Mag. and .45 ACP

NIB	Exc.	V.G.	Good	Fair	Poor
210	180	150	125	100	75

Calibers: .41 Mag., .44-40, .44 Special, .44 Mag., .45 Long Colt, .410 Bore, .22 Hornet, .223 Re., 30-30, and .47-70 Gov't.

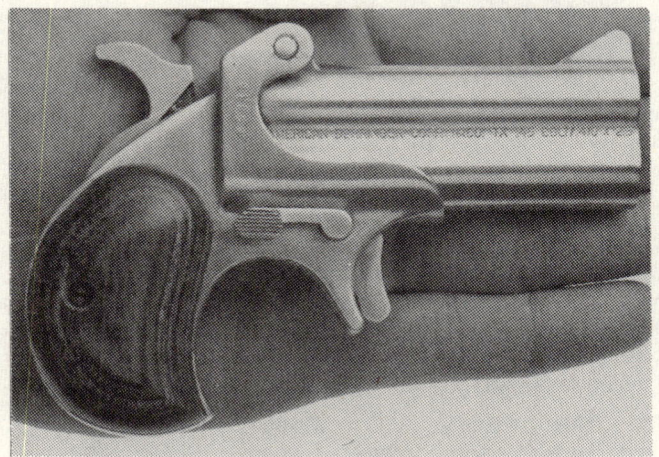

NIB	Exc.	V.G.	Good	Fair	Poor
300	275	250	200	150	100

Model 1 Texas Commemorative

Built with a solid brass frame and stainless steel barrel. Dimensions are same as Model 1. Grips are stag or rosewood and offered in .45 Colt, .44-40, or .38 Special. Barrels marked, "Made in the 150th Year of Texas Freedom". Limited to 500 pistols in each caliber.

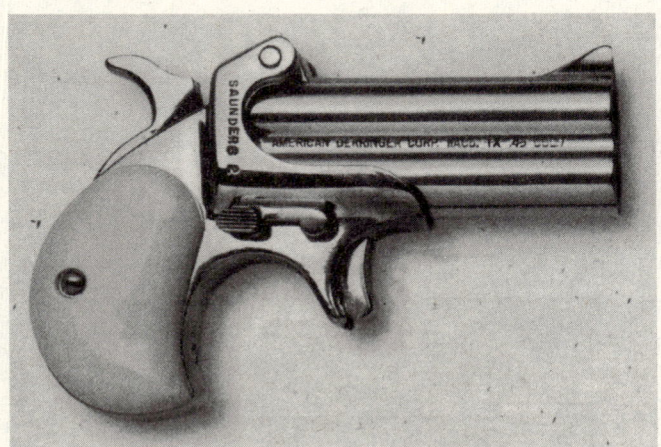

Caliber: .38 Special

NIB	Exc.	V.G.	Good	Fair	Poor
185	150	125	100	80	70

Calibers: .45 Colt and .44-40

NIB	Exc.	V.G.	Good	Fair	Poor
275	250	200	150	125	100

Deluxe Engraved

Special serial number engraved on back strap.

NIB	Exc.	V.G.	Good	Fair	Poor
900	750	550	350	250	150

Model 1 Lady Derringer

Similar to the Model 1 but chambered for the .38 Special, .32 Magnum, .45 Colt, or .357 Magnum. Offered in two grades.

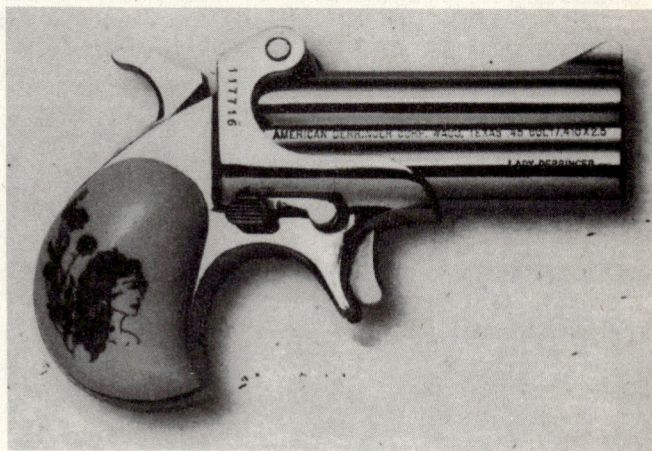

Deluxe Grade

High polished stainless steel with scrimshawed ivory grips with cameo or rose design.

NIB	Exc.	V.G.	Good	Fair	Poor
200	175	150	125	100	75

Deluxe Engraved Grade

Same as above but hand engraved in 1880s style.

NIB	Exc.	V.G.	Good	Fair	Poor
650	550	500	450	250	150

Model 1 125th Anniversary Commemorative

Built to commemorate the 125th anniversary of the derringer, 1866 to 1991. Similar to the Model 1 but marked with the patent date December 12, 1865. Brass frame and stainless steel barrel. Chambered for .440-40, .45 Colt, or .38 Special.

NIB	Exc.	V.G.	Good	Fair	Poor
275	250	225	175	125	100

Deluxe Engraved

NIB	Exc.	V.G.	Good	Fair	Poor
650	550	500	450	250	150

Model 1 NRA 500 Series

Limited edition of 500. Also available in gold and blue finishes over stainless steel.

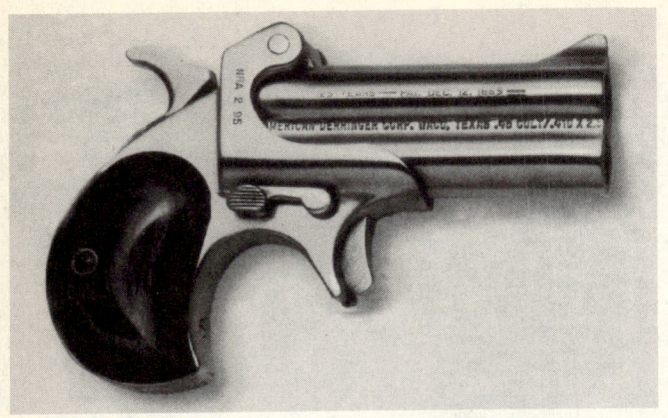

NIB	Exc.	V.G.	Good	Fair	Poor
350	300	250	200	150	100

Model 2-Pen Pistol

Introduced in 1993 this is a legal pistol that cannot be fired from its pen position but requires that it be pulled apart and bent 80 degrees to fire. Made from stainless steel it is offered in .22 LR, .25 ACP, and .32 ACP. The length in pen form is 5.6" and in pistol form is 4.2". Barrel length is 2". Diameter varies from 1/2" to 5/8". Weight is 5 oz.

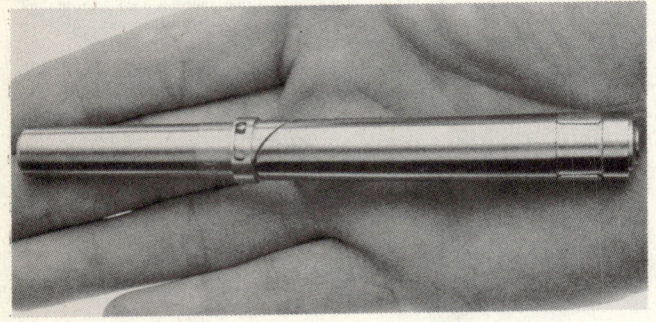

NIB	Exc.	V.G.	Good	Fair	Poor
225	175	135	115	100	85

Model 3

This model is a single barrel derringer. Barrel length is 2.5" and swing down to load. Frame and barrel are stainless steel. Offered in .38 Special or .32 Magnum. Weighs about 8 oz. Production of this model has been temporary halted.

NIB	Exc.	V.G.	Good	Fair	Poor
120	100	85	75	65	50

Model 4

Similar in appearance to the Model 3 but fitted with a 41" barrel. Overall length is 6" and weight is about 16.5 oz. Chambered for 3" .410 bore, .45 Long Colt, .44 Magnum, or .357 Magnum.

NIB	Exc.	V.G.	Good	Fair	Poor
325	300	275	250	200	125

Model 4-Engraved

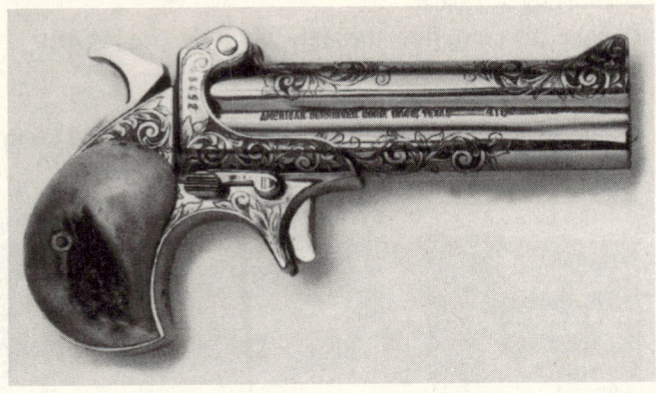

NIB	Exc.	V.G.	Good	Fair	Poor
1500	1200	—	—	—	—

Model 4-Alaskan Survival Model

Similar to the Model 4 but with upper barrel chambered for .45-70 and lower barrel for .45 LC or .410. Both barrels can also be chambered for .44 Magnum or .45-70. Comes with oversized rosewood grips.

NIB	Exc.	V.G.	Good	Fair	Poor
350	300	250	200	150	100

NOTE: For extra high polish add $25.00.

Model 6

This double barrel derringer is fitted with a 6" barrel chambered for the .45LC or .410 bore. Weighs about 21 oz. Rosewood grips are standard. Optional calibers are .357 Magnum or .45 ACP. Oversize grips are optional and add about $35 to value.

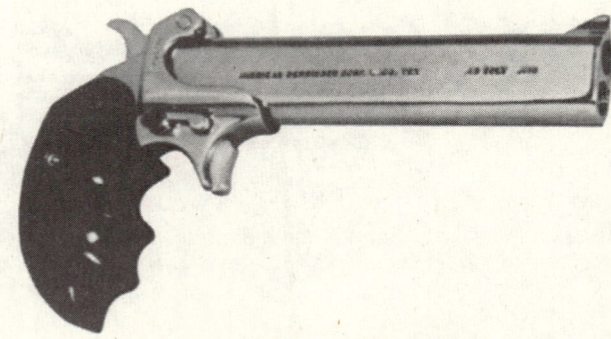

NIB	Exc.	V.G.	Good	Fair	Poor
350	300	250	200	150	100

Model 6-Engraved

NIB	Exc.	V.G.	Good	Fair	Poor
1700	1400	—	—	—	—

High Standard Double Action Derringer

This double barrel derringer is chambered for the .22 Long Rifle or .22 Magnum cartridge. Its barrel length is 3.5" and overall length is 5.125". Weighs approximately 11 oz. The finish is blue with black grips. Production temporarily halted.

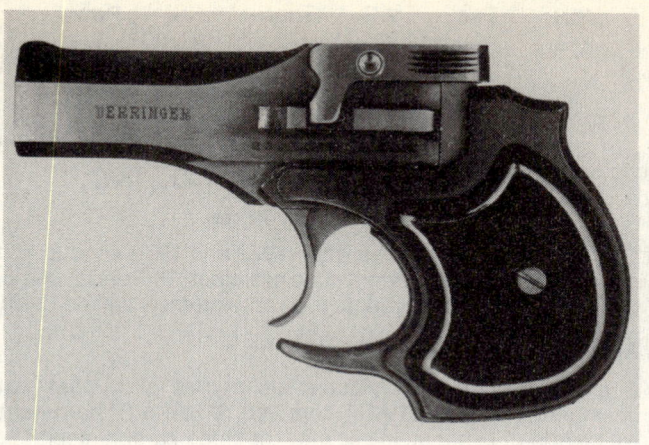

NIB	Exc.	V.G.	Good	Fair	Poor
170	150	125	100	85	75

DA 38 Double Action Derringer

This is a two-barrel model featuring a double action trigger. Overall length is 4.9" and barrel length is 3". Weight is about 15 oz. Chambered for .38 Special, .357 magnum, 9mm Luger, and .40 S&W. Finish is satin stainless. Grip is made from aluminum. Grips are rosewood or walnut.

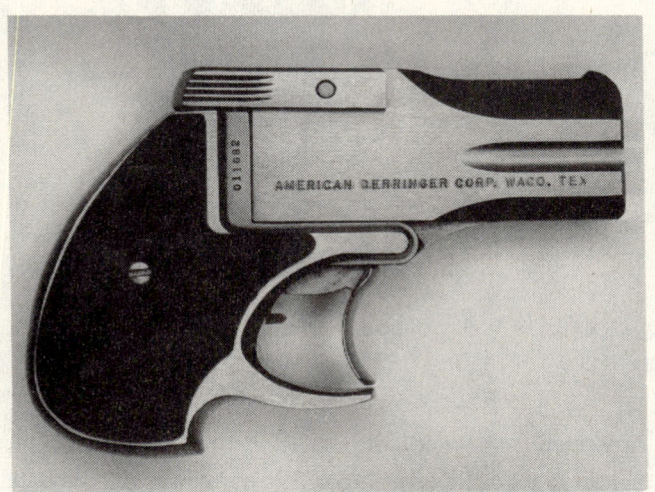

NIB	Exc.	V.G.	Good	Fair	Poor
225	200	175	150	125	100

MINI COP-4 SHOT

This is a four-barrel derringer chambered for the .22 Magnum Rimfire cartridge. Production is temporarily halted.

NIB	Exc.	V.G.	Good	Fair	Poor
310	285	250	225	175	125

COP-4 SHOT

Same as above but chambered for the .357 Magnum cartridge. Production is temporarily halted.

NIB	Exc.	V.G.	Good	Fair	Poor
375	350	325	300	225	150

Model 7 Derringer-Lightweight

Manufactured as a backup gun for police officers. The frame and barrels are made of aircraft aluminum alloy; the other parts are stainless steel. This gun weighs 7.5 oz. Its appearance and function are similar to the Model 1. The finish is a gray matte with thin, matte-finished grips of rosewood or bacote. This model is chambered for and priced as follows:

.32 S&W Long/.32 Magnum

NIB	Exc.	V.G.	Good	Fair	Poor
170	140	120	100	80	50

.38 S&W and .380 ACP

NIB	Exc.	V.G.	Good	Fair	Poor
170	140	120	100	80	50

.22 L.R. and .38 Special

NIB	Exc.	V.G.	Good	Fair	Poor
170	140	120	100	80	50

.44 Special

NIB	Exc.	V.G.	Good	Fair	Poor
425	400	375	325	265	200

Model 8

This is a single action two shot target pistol with a manually operated hammer block safety. Safety automatically disengages when the hammer is cocked. Barrel length is 8". Chambered for the .45 Colt and .410 shotshell. Weight is 24 oz.

NIB	Exc.	V.G.	Good	Fair	Poor
375	300	250	200	—	—

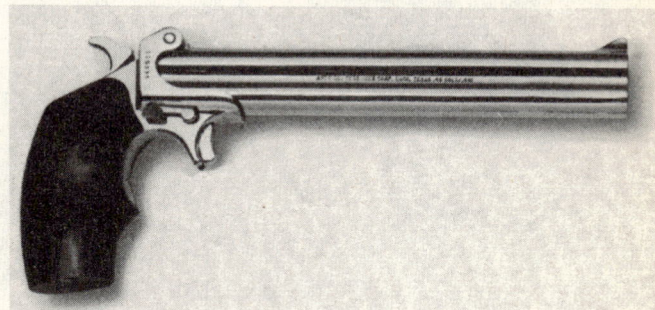

Model 8-Engraved

NIB	Exc.	V.G.	Good	Fair	Poor
1850	1500	—	—	—	—

Model 10 Derringer

Similar to the Model 1 with a frame of aluminum alloy and all other parts, including the barrels, stainless steel. It has a grey matte finish and thin grips of rosewood or bacote. It weighs 10 oz. and is chambered for the .38 Special, .45 ACP or the .45 Colt. For .45 Colt-Add 10%.

NIB	Exc.	V.G.	Good	Fair	Poor
240	200	175	140	110	80

Model 11 Derringer

A stainless steel barrel and all other parts aluminum. It weighs 11 oz. and is chambered for the .38 Special, .380 Auto, .32 Mag., .22 LR, and .22 Magnum. The grips and finish are the same as on the Model 10.

NIB	Exc.	V.G.	Good	Fair	Poor
225	175	150	125	100	75

Semmerling LM-4

This gun has been in production for approximately 10 years, built by various companies. This latest offering by American Derringer may, with the right marketing and manufacturing approach, be the one that makes a commercial success of this fine firearm concept. The LM-4 was designed as the ultimate police backup/defense weapon. It is a manually operated, 5-shot repeater only 5.2" long, 3.7" high, and 1" wide. It is chambered for the .45 ACP and is undoubtedly the smallest 5-shot .45 ever produced. The LM-4 is made of a special tool steel and is either blued or, at extra cost, hard chrome-plated. A stainless steel version is also available. The LM-4 is not a semi-automatic, although it physically resembles one. The slide is flicked forward and back after each double-action squeeze of the trigger. This weapon is virtually hand-built and features high visibility sights and a smooth trigger. It is an extremely limited production item, and the company produces only two per week. The price and availability may fluctuate, so the company should be contacted for accurate figures. The values for the guns produced before American Derringer's involvement will be found in the section dealing with the Semmerling. These values are for the latest production by American Derringer. Prices listed below may change due to supply and demand.

Hard Chrome-Add $200.00.

Stainless steel-Add 35%.

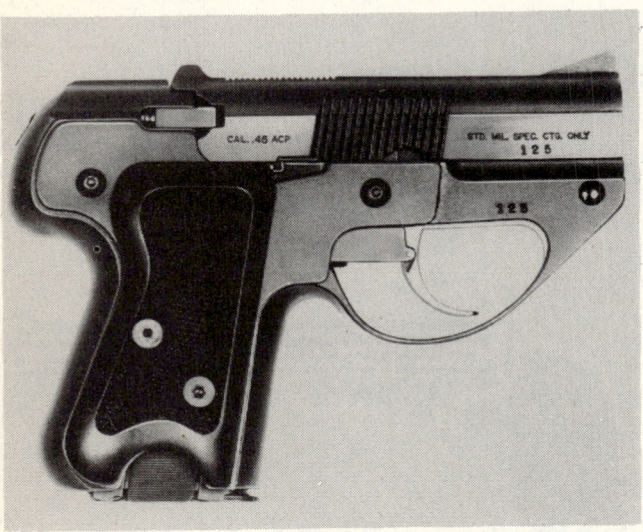

NIB	Exc.	V.G.	Good	Fair	Poor
2100	1750	1250	750	500	300

LM-5

Built of stainless steel this semiauto is chambered for the .32 Mag or .25 Auto. The barrel length is 2.25" and the overall length is 4", height is 3". Wooden grips are standard. Offered in limited quanities Weight is approximately 15 oz.

NIB	Exc.	V.G.	Good	Fair	Poor
325	250	200	150	100	75

AMERICAN F.A. MFG. CO., INC.

San Antonio, Texas

This company operated between 1972 and 1974, producing a .25 ACP pocket pistol and a stainless steel .38 Special derringer. A .380 auto was produced on an extremely limited basis.

American .25 Automatic

A small, blowback, semiautomatic pocket pistol that was chambered for the .25 ACP cartridge. It had a 2" barrel and was made of either stainless steel or blued carbon steel. The grips were of plain uncheckered walnut, and the detachable magazine held 7 shots. It was manufactured until 1974.

Stainless Steel-Add 20%.

Exc.	V.G.	Good	Fair	Poor
200	150	125	100	75

American .380 Automatic

Similar to the .25 except larger. The barrel was 3.5", and the gun was made in stainless steel only. The grips were of smooth walnut, and it held 8 shots. There were only 10 of these .380's manufactured between 1972 and 1974. They are extremely rare, but there is little collector base for this company's products, and the value is difficult to estimate.

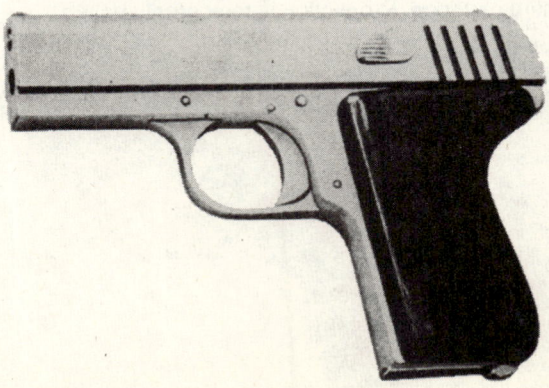

Exc.	V.G.	Good	Fair	Poor
600	550	475	375	200

American .38 Special Derringer

A well-made, stainless steel O/U derringer that was similar in appearance and function to the old Remington O/U. It had 3" barrels, that pivoted upward for loading. This gun was a single-action that had an automatic selector and a spur trigger. The smooth grips were of walnut. There were approximately 3,500 manufactured between 1972 and 1974.

Exc.	V.G.	Good	Fair	Poor
200	180	150	125	90

AMERICAN FRONTIER FIREARMS
Aguanga, California

This firm began importing Italian-made parts for its single action revolver line in 1996. These parts are then fitted and finished in its California facility. The first of these metallic cartridge revolvers was ready for delivery in late 1996. In addition to its standard guns the company also offers special finishes and is ready to fill special orders. For this reason only standard prices are given. For this edition only manufacturer's suggested retail prices are quoted as no secondary market has yet been established.

1871-72 Open Top Standard Model

Offered in .38 or .44 caliber with non-rebated cylinder. Barrel lengths are 7.5" or 8" in round. Blued finish except silver backstrap and trigger guard. Walnut grips.

NIB	Exc.	V.G.	Good	Fair	Poor
795	—	—	—	—	—

1871-72 Open Top Tiffany Model

Same as above but with additional round barrel lengths of 4.75" and 5.5". Tiffany grips with gold and silver finish with engraving.

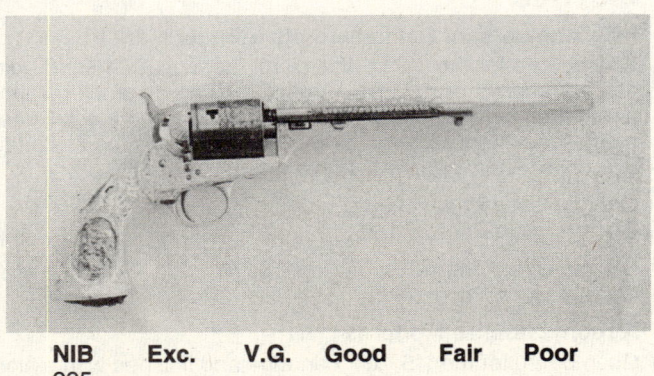

NIB	Exc.	V.G.	Good	Fair	Poor
995	—	—	—	—	—

Richards 1860 Army Conversion Standard Model

Offered in .38 or .44 calibers with rebated cylinder and with or without ejector assembly. Available in 4.75", 5.5", or 7.5" round barrel lengths. Blued finish with silver plated brass trigger guard and backstrap. Walnut grips.

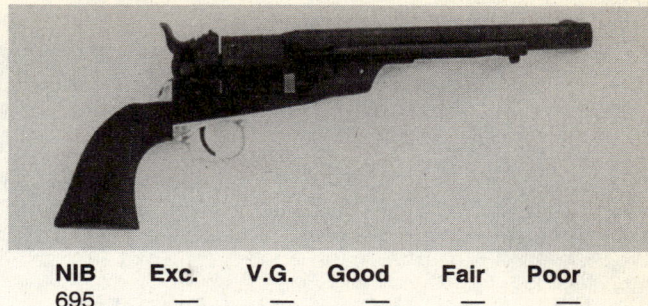

NIB	Exc.	V.G.	Good	Fair	Poor
695	—	—	—	—	—

Richards 1851 Conversion Standard Model

Available in .38 or .44 calibers with non-rebated cylinder in octagon barrel lengths 4.75", 5.5", or 7.5". Blued steel backstrap and trigger with walnut grips. There is no ejector rod assembly on this model.

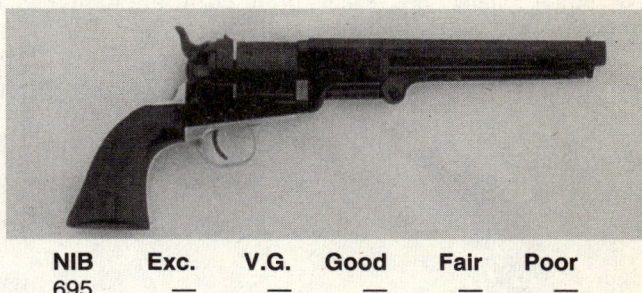

NIB	Exc.	V.G.	Good	Fair	Poor
695	—	—	—	—	—

Richards & Mason Conversion 1851 Navy Standard Model

Offered in .38 and .44 calibers with Mason ejector assembly and non-rebated cylinder with a choice of octagon barrels in 4.75", 5.5", or 7.5". Blued finish with blued backstrap and trigger guard. Walnut grips.

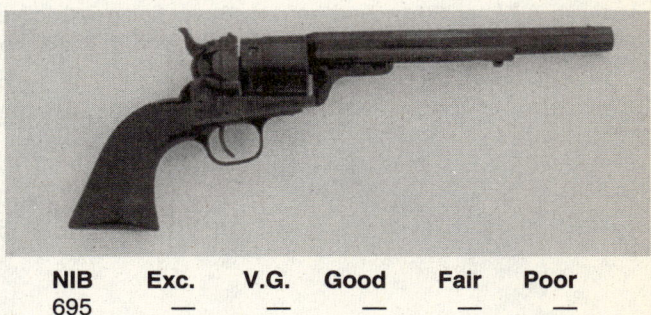

NIB	Exc.	V.G.	Good	Fair	Poor
695	—	—	—	—	—

Remington New Model Army Standard

Offered in .38, .44, and .45 calibers with 5.5", 7.5", or 8" barrels. The finish is blue and this model comes with an ejector assembly, loading gate, and government cartouche on the left grip.

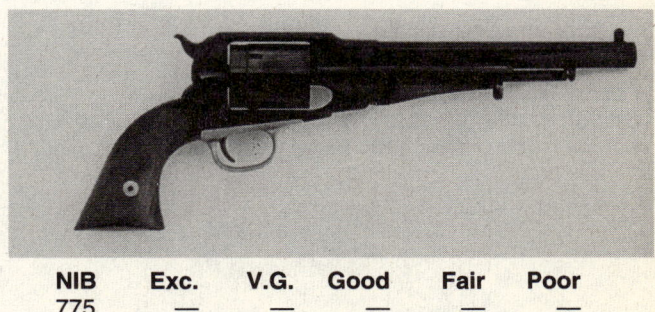

NIB	Exc.	V.G.	Good	Fair	Poor
775	—	—	—	—	—

Remington New Model Standard

Offered in .38, .44, or .45 calibers with 5.5" or 7.5" octagon barrel. Furnished with or without ejector rod. Walnut grips.

NIB	Exc.	V.G.	Good	Fair	Poor
695	—	—	—	—	—

1871-72 Pocket Model

This is a five-shot .32 caliber revolver based on the Colt 1862 Police Model. Offered with 4.75" or 5.5" round barrels. Blued finish with silver plated brass backstrap and trigger guard. Walnut or Tiffany grips. Prices given below are for the base model.

NIB	Exc.	V.G.	Good	Fair	Poor
495	—	—	—	—	—

Pocket Richards & Mason Navy Conversion

Offered in .32 caliber with a five shot non-rebated cylinder. Fitted with 4.75" or 5.5" round barrels. Blued finish with silver plated backstrap and trigger-guard with ejector assembly. Walnut grips.

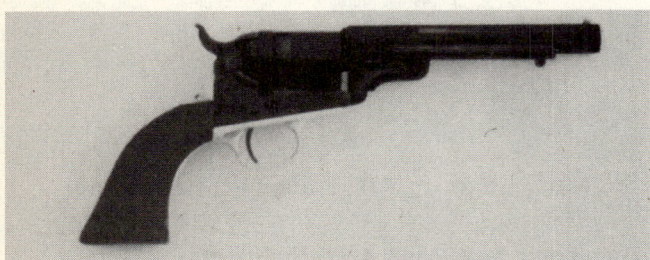

NIB	Exc.	V.G.	Good	Fair	Poor
495	—	—	—	—	—

Pocket Richards Conversion Model

Same as above but fitted with rebated cylinder.

NIB	Exc.	V.G.	Good	Fair	Poor
495	—	—	—	—	—

Pocket Remington

Offered in .22, .32, and .38 calibers with 3.5" barrel with or without ejector rod or gate. Blued finish with Walnut grips.

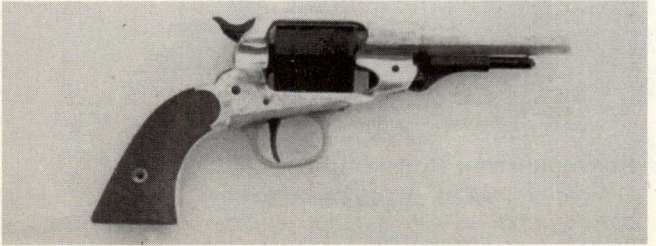

NIB	Exc.	V.G.	Good	Fair	Poor
495	—	—	—	—	—

NOTE: Guns shipped without ejector assembly will be supplied with a ramrod and plunger typical of the period.

AMERICAN GUN CO.
Norwich, Connecticut
Crescent Firearms Co.—Maker
H. & D. Folsom Co.—Distributor

Side x Side Shotgun

A typical trade gun made around the turn of the century by the Crescent Firearms Co. to be distributed by H. & D. Folsom. These are sometimes known as "Hardware Store Guns," as that is where many were sold. This particular gun was chambered for 12, 16, and 20 gauges and was produced with or without external hammers. The length of the barrels varied, as did the chokes. Some were produced with Damascus barrels; some, with fluid steel. The latter are worth approximately 25% more.

Knickerbocker Pistol
(See Knickerbocker)

NOTE: For a full listing of most of the variations of the Crescent Arms Co., and shotguns marked with American Gun Co. see "Crescent F.A. Co.".

AMERICAN HISTORICAL FOUNDATION
Richmond, Virginia

The American Historical Foundation is a private organization that commissions historical commemoratives in conjunction with leading manufacturers and craftsmen around the world. The values listed below show the Foundation's original issue prices and the last known retail price. Secondary market sales are infrequent and are difficult to confirm. The American Historical Foundation sells only direct and not through dealers or distributors. Nevertheless, the last retail price can be useful to both the buyer and seller when neither is compelled to buy or sell. When applicable, a separate price will be given for a display case. Issues that have been sold out will be so stipulated.

The collector should be aware that these firearms are valuable for their beauty and historical significance. AHF commemoratives are collectible only if they remain in the exact same condition in which they were issued: new, unfired, and with all of the original packing material and papers.

PISTOLS

40th Anniversary Commemorative Ruger Mark II

Chambered for the .22 l.r. this pistol features a 24-karat gold etched receiver and barrel with gold plating on small component parts, polymer ivory grips with both red and black Ruger medallions. Manufactured by Sturm, Ruger Co. and limited to 950 units. Serial numbers 40th 1 through 40th 950.

Original Issue Price: $995
Current Issue Price: $1095

Display Case Original Issue Price: $119
Current Issue Price: $149

Airborne Jubilee Model 1911A1

Chambered for the .45 ACP cartridge and finished with a high polish blue with etched commemorative inscriptions. Selected parts are gold plated. Manufactured by Auto-Ordnance Corp. and limited to 500 units.

Original Issue Price: $995
Current Issue Price: $1095

Display Case Original Price: $119
Current Issue Price: $149

Allied Victory Browning Hi-Power

This Browning-manufactured 9mm pistol features 24-karat gold plating, checked walnut grips with cloisonne medallion. The slide has deeply etched inscriptions and scenes. An extra magazine and cleaning rod are also gold plated. Issue limited to 500 units.

Current Issue Price: $1795
Display Case Current Issue Price: $179

Armed Forces Model 1911A1

This is a set of four Model 1911A1s representing each of the U.S. armed forces branches. Each pistol is chambered for the .45 ACP and features custom designed etchings and grips of different woods and medallions. Manufactured by Auto Ordnance Corp. and and limited to 1911 sets.

Original Issue Price: $995
Current Issue Price: $1095

Display Case Original Issue Price: $85
Current Issue price: $149

Armed Forces Ruger

Chambered for the .22 l.r. cartridge and fitted with a bull barrel, it is available in the four military branches: Army, Navy, Marine, and Air Force. Each features a high-polish blue finish with 24-karat gold foliate motif covering the full length of the barrel and receiver. There are twelve gold plated parts. A cloisonne medallion is featured in the wooden grips. Manufactured by Sturm, Ruger & Co. this issue is limited to 250 pistols per service branch.

Current Issue Price: $1095
Display Case Current Issue Price: $139

D-Day Commemorative Model 1911A1

This .45 ACP caliber pistol has gold plated parts, polymer ivory grips with medallions, and is serially numbered DDAY0001 through DDAY1000. Built by Auto-Ordinance Corp. and limited to 1000 units.

Original Issue Price: $995
Current Issue Price: $1095

Display Case Original Issue Price: $85
Current Issue Price: $149

ETO Luger

This European Theater of Operations commemorative issue used original P.08 Lugers manufactured by Eurfort, Simpson & Co.. The collector's edition has a contrasting mirror and matte blue finish. Etched tributes and gold gilt are applied. Six component parts are gold plated and the grips are of select walnut with high gloss finish. This edition is limited to 750 units.

Current Issue Price: $1795
Display Case Current Issue Price: $179

Deluxe Edition has 24-karat gold plating with oak leaf scroll engraving with 75 percent coverage. This Deluxe Edition is limited to 10 units.

Original Issue Price: $3995
Display Case Original Price: $179

Five Star General Series

This M15 is chambered for the .45 ACP cartridge. This is an ongoing series commemorating the five star generals of World War 11. Editions are limited to 500. The blue finish has a contrasting high mirror and matte finish with seven gold plated component parts. Millett sights are fitted. Etched commemorative markings with 24-karat gold infill. First in series honors General Eisenhower and the second in the series is for General MacArthur. Manufactured by Auto Ordnance Corp.

Current Issue Price: $1295
Display Case Current Issue Price: $149

Smith & Wesson Tactical Competition

Chambered for the .40 S&W cartridge this pistol was built by the Performance Center at Smith & Wesson. It has a match grade barrel with custom tuned action and hand fitted. The slide and frame are hand engraved with a high polish blue while the frame top is a blue matte. Compensated.

Deluxe Edition limited to 10 units.
Last Issue Price: $3795
Sold Out

Collector Edition limited to 40 units
Current Issue Price: $2795

UZI Pistol

Chambered for the 9mm Parabellum cartridge the receiver and barrel are 24-karat gold plated with hand engraving. Produced by the AHF custom shop and limited to 100 units. Includes display case.

Last Issue Price: $2495
Sold Out

Vietnam War Limited Edition 1911A1

Chambered for the .45 ACP cartridge this Auto Ordnance pistol features an etched frame with high polish blue finish. Slide has 24-karat gold etchings and small parts are gold plated.

Original Issue Price: $1095
Display Case Original Issue Price: $85
Current Issue Price: $149

World War II Colt .45 Series

There are twelve .45s in this series, each commemorating a major campaign of WWII. They are etched and have a high blue polish. Each of the 12 pistols is limited to 250 units. Includes display case.

Current Issue Price: $995

Second Amendment Browning Hi-Power

Introduced in 1994, this Browning Hi-Power is chambered for the .40 S&W cartridge. The frame is plated in silver while the hammer, trigger, magazine release, safety, slide release, and grip screws are gold plated. The frame and slide are etched in vine scroll patterns. The grips are rosewood with the left grip inset with a cloisonne medallion. This series is limited to 500 pistols with special serial numbers from SA001 through SA500 engraved on the right side of the frame.

Current Issue Price: $1995
Display Case Current Issue Price: $179

American Eagle Hi-Power

Manufactured by Browning this 9mm pistol is etched and selectively plated with gold. Ivory polymer grips are scrimshawed with oak leaves and scroll. Serially numbered from AE001 through AE750, this issue is limited to 750 units.

Current Issue Price: $2195
Display Case Current Issue Price: $179

Showcase Edition Inglis High Power

Based on the Inglis-built WWII pistol this 1996 edition is limited to 250 pistols. Both the slide and frame are nickel plated and lightly engraved. Grips are rosewood. Serial numbered between 001 and 250.

Current Issue Price: $1295
Display Case Current Issue Price: $149

Golden Centurion Beretta

This 1996 limited edition pistol is restricted to 250 units. This Model 96D is chambered for the .40S&W. The slide and frame are hand engraved and both are plated in gold. Grips are a high polished Ebony. Serial numbers are between 001 and 250 with a prefix of "GC".

Current Issue Price: $2,195
Display Case Current Issue Price: $149

Colt Gold Cup

Introduced in 1996 this limited edition .45 ACP pistol is completely gold plated. The slide is etched and the grips are American walnut. This edition is limited to 1,000 pistols. Serial numbers from GCE0001 to GCE1000.

Current Issue Price: $2,195
Display Case Current Issue Price: $149

REVOLVERS

200th Constitution Commemorative Revolver

Chambered for the .44 Magnum cartridge this handgun features extensive 24-karat gold inlays and etchings. Fitted with a 10" barrel and Ivory polymer grips. Collector's Edition serial numbered from CC001 through CC950. Manufactured by Wesson Firearms and limited to 950 units.

Collector's Edition Original Price: $995
Collector's Edition Last Issue Price: $1295
Sold Out

Deluxe Museum Edition serial numbered CD001 through CD500. Limited to 500 units.
Deluxe Museum Edition Original Issue Price: $1295
Deluxe Museum Edition Last Issue Price: $1595
Sold Out

1847 Model Walker

This revolver is the second issue in the "Samuel Colt Golden Tribute Collection." Limited to 950 units.

Original Issue Price: $1895
Current Issue Price: $2195
Display Case Original Issue Price: $229
Current Issue Price: $249

American Deer Hunter Commemorative

Chambered for .44 Magnum and fitted with a 10" barrel. The Deluxe Trophy Edition features a deeply blued finish with 24-karat gold plated hammer, trigger, front sight, cylinder release, and grip screws. Grips are Herrett finger groove. Serial numbered DEER001T through DEER250T. Manufactured by Wesson Firearms and limited to 250 units.

Original Issue Price: $1995
Display Case Original Issue Price: $149
Current Issue Price: $179

Sportsman's Edition is a field grade version with high polish blue finish and gold gilt etching on barrel. Serial number DEER001S through DEER750S. Limited to 750 units.

Original Issue Price: $995
Current Issue Price: $1095
Display Case Original Issue Price: $149
Current Issue Price: $179

Civil War Colt Dragoons

Chambered for .44 caliber cartridge this revolver is available in either Union Model with hand engraved and 24-karat gold plating or Confederate Model with hand engraved and silver plating. Limited to 125 units of each.

Last Issue Price: $2495 Sold Out

Jefferson Davis Model 1851 Navy

Patterned after the Colt 1851 Navy pistol presented to Jefferson Davis in 1858, this handgun is chambered for the .36 caliber cartridge and features hand engraving with sterling silver plated selected parts. Comes complete with detachable shoulder stock. Manufactured by A. Uberti and limited to 250 units.

Current Issue Price: $2995

Col. J.S. Mosby Model 1860 Army

This is a stainless steel revolver chambered for the .44 caliber cartridge. It is hand engraved with selected 24-karat gold plated parts. Manufactured by Colt and limited to 150 units.

Last Issue Price: $2495
Sold Out

Old West Sheriffs Model Colt

This Colt single action army is chambered for the .45 Long Colt cartridge. The ivory cylinder pin is custom made and there are three areas of 24-karat gold inlay on a blue finish which is extensively hand engraved. The Ivory grips are scrimshawed. An AHF custom shop edition limited to only 10 units. Includes display case.

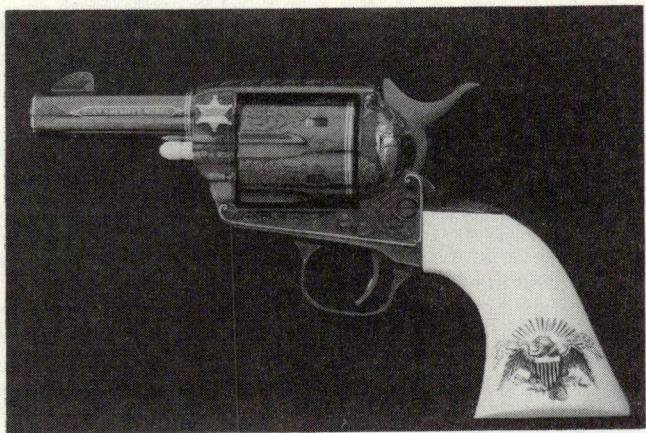

Current Issue Price: $10995

General Patton Single Action Army

Fitted with a 5.5" barrel and chambered for the .45 Long Colt, this handgun features a silver plated finish with extensive scroll hand engraving. Polymer grips combined with ivory and lanyard ring. Serial numbered P001 through P2500. Manufactured by A. Uberti and limited to 2500 units.

Original Issue Price: $1495
Last Issue Price: $1895
Display Case Last Issue Price: $169

Teddy Roosevelt Single Action Army

Hand engraved with 24-karat gold inlay of Roosevelt's initials on left recoil shield this SAA is chambered for the .44-40 caliber cartridge. Entire gun is 24-karat and sterling silver plated. Manufactured by A. Uberti and limited to 750 units.

Original Issue Price: $1995
Display Case Original Issue Price: $149
Current Issue Price: $179

Texas Patterson

This is a hand engraved 24-karat gold plated 5 shot pistol chambered for the .36 caliber cartridge. It is the first issue of the "Samuel Colt Golden Tribute Collection." Manufactured by D. Pedersoli of Italy and limited to 950 units.

Original Issue Price: $1495
Current Issue Price: $2195
Display Case Original Issue Price: $225
Current Issue Price: $259

> A Texas Patterson revolver was sold at auction for $1,210. It was NIB with glass top case. Two digit #.
> J.C. Devine, Inc., September 1996

Second Amendment Commemorative Revolver

Manufactured by Wesson Firearms this pistol is chambered for the .44 Magnum and fitted with a 10" barrel. Grips are walnut with medallions. Collector's Edition limited to 1500 units and is fully etched with blued frame and barrel. Small parts are gold plated. Serial numbered 2A0001 through 2AC1500

Collector's Edition Original Issue Price: $1295
Collector's Edition Current Issue Price: $1695
Display Case Original Issue Price: $149
Current Issue Price: $179

Deluxe Museum Edition features a fully etched frame and barrel with all parts gold plated. Serial numbered 2AD001 through 2AD750. Limited to 750 units.
Deluxe Museum Edition Original Issue Price: $1595
Deluxe Museum Edition Current Issue Price: $1895
Display Case Original Issue Price: $149
Current Issue Price: $179

J.E.B. Stuart LeMat

Chambered for .44 caliber cartridge this nine-shot revolver also includes a single shot .65 caliber shotgun barrel. Finish is blued with selective etching and 24-karat gold plating. Manufactured by Navy Arms and limited to 500 units.

Original Issue Price: $2195
Current Issue Price: $2695
Display Case Original Issue Price: $179
Current Issue Price: $225

Wild Bill Hickok Model 1851 Navy

Reproduction of 1851 Navy revolver chambered for .36 caliber cartridge. Hand engraved with sterling silver plating. Manufactured by A. Uberti and limited to 500 units.

Current Issue Price: $1995
Display Case Original Issue Price: $119
Current Issue Price: $179

World War II Commando Enfield

This is a No.2 Mark I Enfield revolver. The flats are polished to high mirror blue finish while the recessed areas are matte finished. Etched commemorative markings and 24-karat gold filling. A walnut display and Commando knife are included. Limited to 250 units.

Current Issue Price: $995

American Flag Tribute

Two hand built editions honoring the American flag; a Wesson Arms .44 Magnum and a Sturm, Ruger & Co. .22. Each edition features a 10" target length barrel with the entire Pledge of Allegiance etched and selectively plated in gold. Each has Ivory polymer grips and is serially numbered AF0001 through AFIOOO.

.44 Magnum

Current Issue Price: $1495
Display Case Current Issue Price: $179

Ruger .22

Current Issue Price: $1095
Display Case Current Issue Price: $179

Smith & Wesson 629 Tactical

Chambered for the .44 magnum this pistol was built by the S&W Performance Center. It features a compensation port across the top of the barrel and a machined expansion chamber inside the muzzle. The frame is hand engraved. This is the first 3" barrel Model 629 ever made. The edition is limited to 25 units. Shooters case included.

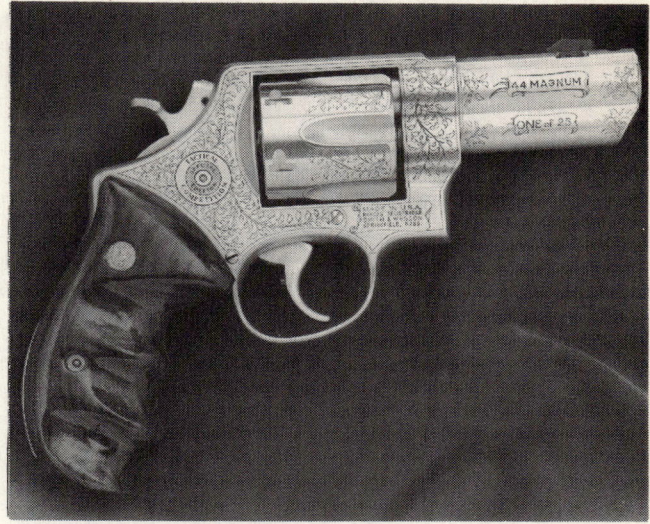

Current Issue Price: $2795
Sold Out

Smith and Wesson 629 Hunter

Built by the S&W Performance Center this 6" magnaported barrel revolver has hand engraved frame and Nikon scope. Edition is limited to 50 units.

Current Issue Price: $3795

Patton .357

This hand engraved Smith & Wesson .357 Magnum Model 27 is available in two editions: the Deluxe Edition and Collector's Edition. The Deluxe Edition is plated in sterling silver and has full hand engraving. It is limited to 100 units and is serial numbered from P001D through P100D.

Deluxe Edition
Current Issue Price: $2495
Display Case Current Issue Price: $195

Collector Edition has a high blue polish with the cylinder silver plated and etched with Patton's military units, insignia, and rank. This edition is limited to 950 units and is serially numbered from POO 1C through P950C.

Current Issue Price: $995
Display Case Current Issue Price: $195

North/South 3rd Model Dragoons

This .44 caliber revolver is offered in either the blued North Model or French grayed South Model. Two editions are available: the Deluxe and the Collector. The Deluxe Edition is manufactured by Colt and features hand engraving and gold inlays.

Limited to 50 models of North and South each. Serial numbered from USA01D through USA50D or CSA01D through CSA50D.

Current Issue Price: $2495
Display Case Current Issue Price: $179

Collector Edition is hand engraved and built by the Italian firm Uberti. Limited to 250 units of both the North and South models. Serial numbered from USA001C through USA250C or CSA001C through CSA250C.

Current Issue Price: $1595
Display Case Current Issue Price: $179

The Old West Gambler

This .45LC 3" barrel revolver is silver plated and hand engraved. Ivory polymers are scrimshawed. A compartmentalized display case with playing cards, dice, chips, and flask is included.

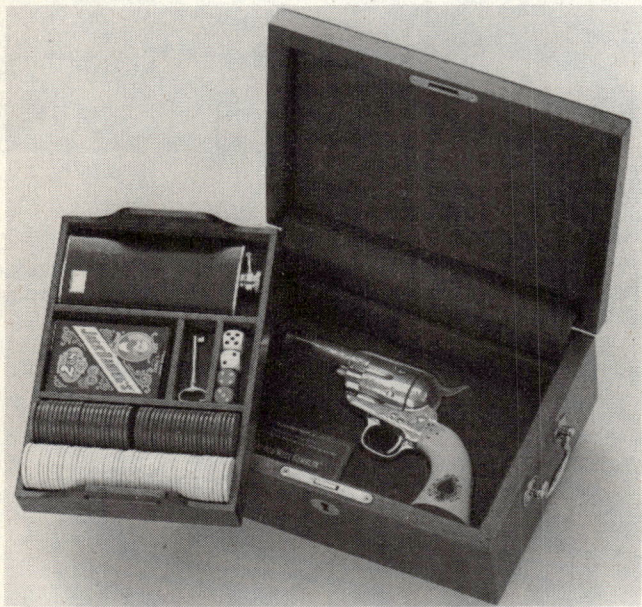

Current Issue Price: $2195

Wyatt Earp Single Action Army

The Uberti built 7.5" barrel revolver is chambered for the .45 LC and features nickel plating and etching and gold infilled banner. Fitted with walnut grips. Limited to 750 units and serially numbered from WE001 through WE750.

Current Issue Price: $1595
Display Case Current Issue Price: $179

Colt Anaconda

This Colt revolver is chambered for the .357 Magnum cartridge and plated in gold and black titanium. This limited edition of 1,000 revolvers has an 8" barrel. Serial numbered from LE0001 to LE1000.

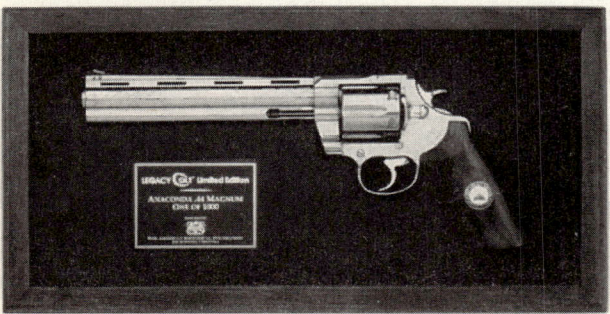

Current Issue Price: $1595
Display Case Current Issue Price: $179

Colt Python .357 Magnum

This model has a gold finish with engraveing on an 8" barrel with silver cylinder, hammer, and sights. Fitted with rosewood grips. Edition limited to 1,000 revolvers with serial numbers from 0001 to 1000.

Current Issue Price: $2,795
Display Case Current Issue Price: $179.

Smith & Wesson Model 625

This edition is limited to 100 revolvers. The barrel length is 3" and the cylinder and frame are engraved in the bank note style. The grips are Hogue Bill Jordan style. Edition includes custom polymer carrying case. Serial numbered from 001 to 100.

Current Issue Price: $2195

Cowboy Ruger

This is a Ruger-built single action revolver chambered for the .45 Long Colt or .44 Magnum cartridge. All steel surfaces are engraved and gold plated. Rosewood grips with "old style" red medallions for the .45 and black for the .44. Barrel leength is 7.5". Limited to 500 units with serial number 001 to 500. Prefix .45LC or .44M.

Current Issue Price: $1,895
Display Case Current Issue Price: $179

Smith & Wesson .44 magnum-Fifty States Edition

This model is fitted with a 8.25" barrel and features 100 revolvers per state. Each state name is etched in gold on the barrel and frame. Total edition is 5,000 guns.

Current Issue Price: $1,895
Display Case Current Issue Price: $179

RIFLES AND CARBINES

50 States Henry

A faithful copy of the famous repeating rifle chambered for the .44-40. This is the rare iron frame version with blued finish inlaid with 24-karat gold. The receiver, upper and lower tangs, buttplate, loading lever, barrel and hammer are hand engraved in addition to the 7"s of gold inlaid borders. The magazine follower, trigger, and breech block are gold plated. The stock is select walnut. Manufactured by A. Uberti and limited to 2 rifles per state with a limit of 100 units. Each rifle is marked with the state's outline and motto.

Current Issue Price: $11995
Display Case Current Issue Price: $499

1885 Deer Hunter

This Browning copy of the Winchester Model 1885 is chambered for the .45-70 cartridge. The receiver is French grayed with custom designed hand engraving. Collector Issue limited to 100 units.

Collector Original Issue Price: $2975

Civil War Commemorative Henrys:

Similar to the Constitution Henry with choice of either Abraham Lincoln with hand engraved brass frame with gold plating and blued barrel or Jefferson Davis with hand engraved brass frame with silver plating and brown barrel. Manufactured by A. Uberti and limited to 250 of each model.

Original Issue Price: $3495
Current Issue Price: $3995
Display Case Current Issue Price: $249

Constitution Commemorative Henry

Patterned after the Henry rifle with brass frame and hand engraved 24-karat plating. Manufactured by A. Uberti and limited to 200 units.

Last Issue Price: $2395
Sold Out
Display Case Original Issue Price: $249

ETO/PTO Thompson

A semiautomatic reproduction of the Model 192A1 Thompson chambered for the .45 ACP. Special roll markings with gold in-fill. Stocks are made from select walnut and have a high polish with two cloisonne medallions. There are five gold-plated component parts including the Cutts Compensator. Manufactured by Auto-Ordnance and limited to 500 for each theater of operation.

Current Issue Price: $1595
Display Case Current Issue Price: $249

Korean War Semi-Auto Thompson

Chambered for the .45 ACP this model is also available in full auto for Class III license holders. Special finish select walnut stock and forearm. Multiple gold plated parts. Serial numbered from KW0001 through KW1500. There were 2000 manufactured in 1984. Manufactured by Auto-Ordnance and limited to 1,500 units.

Last Issue Price: $1195
Display Case Last Issue Price: $225

Law Enforcement Thompson

This set contains a policeman and sheriff model with gold etchings and gilting. Deluxe walnut stocks are fitted with custom medallions. Manufactured by Auto-Ordnance and limited to 1,500 of each model.

Current Issue Price: $1595
Display Case Original Issue Price: $225

Current Issue Price: $249

M16 Airborne

This rifle is chambered for the .223 caliber cartridge and features hand engraving and gold plated selected parts. The specially finished stock has a heavy textured black finish. Issue limited to 950 units.

Original Issue Price: $2495
Last Issue Price: $2795
Display Case Original Issue Price: $225
Last Issue Price: $249

M16 Vietnam War Commemorative

This issue commemorates the Vietnam War veteran. It is chambered for the .223 cartridge, is hand engraved, and has gold plated small parts. A bipod is included. Serial numbered from VN000L through VN1000. Issue limited to 1,000.

Last Issue Price: $1995
Sold Out
Display Case Last Issue Price: $225

> **A cased Vietnam War commemorative M16 sold at auction for $1380. The condition was NIB.**
> **Rock Island Auction Company, September 1997.**

Model 1861 Springfield Musket

Issued to commemorate the 125th anniversary of the Civil War this rifle is a .58 caliber. Selected parts are hand engraved and gold plated. Select grade walnut stock. Manufactured by Ezechiele and Rino Chiappa and limited to 125 units.

Original Issue Price: $3495
Display Case Original Issue Price: $295
Current Issue Price: $399

Special Forces MAC-10

Chambered for the .45 ACP this semiautomatic commemorates the 25th anniversary of the MAC-10.

Original Issue Price: $1195
Current Issue Price: $1595
Display Case Original Issue Price: $169

Vietnam M14 Rifle

Chambered for the .308 Win. cartridge this rifle is manufactured by Federal Ordnance. It features gold etching and gilted metal parts. Issue is limited to 500 units for each of two editions.

Collector's Edition Original Issue Price: $2195 Collector's Edition Last Issue Price: $2495

Deluxe Museum Edition Original Issue Price: $2495
Deluxe Museum Edition Last Issue Price: $2895
Display Case: $249 either edition.

> **A cased Vietnam War commemorative M14 sold at auction for $1495. Condition was NIB.**
> **Rock Island Auction Company, September 1997.**

Winchester Model 94

This issue commemorates the centennial of the closing of the American West. Chambered for the .30-30 cartridge the Collector Edition features eight gold plated parts with walnut stocks fitted with custom medallions. One side of the receiver is hand engraved. Limited to 750 units.

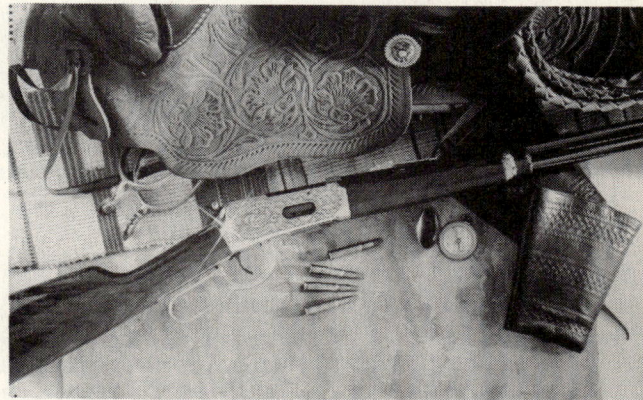

Original Issue Price: $1795
Last Issue Price: $1895
Display Case Original Issue Price: $249
Last Issue Price: $299

Deluxe Museum Edition features extensive hand engraving. Stocks are custom walnut by Fajen with rounded style butt plate that is also engraved and gold plated. Issue is limited to 250 units.

Deluxe Original Issue Price: $2495
Current Issue Price: $2895

Display Case Original Issue Price: $225
Current Issue Price: $249

World War II Springfield

Original WWII bolt action Model 1903 Springfield chambered for the .30-06 cartridge features a deeply blued finish on receiver and bolt with contrasting mirror and satin finishes on small parts. Stock is custom made. Issue limited to 500 units.

Original Issue Price: $1495
Current Issue Price: $1695
Display Case Original Issue Price: $249

World War II Garand Rifle

These original WWII Garand rifles are chambered for the .30-06 cartridge and feature gold plated parts with a high-polish blue. Released in 1984 and serial numbered from WW0001 through WW2500. Limited to 2500 units.

Original Issue Price: $1695
Current Issue Price: $1895
Display Case Original Issue Price: $225
Current Issue Price: $249

Airborne Golden Jubilee Thompson

This issue commemorates the 50th anniversary of the Airborne. It features special etchings and medallions. Manufactured by Auto Ordnance Corp. and limited to 500 units.

Last Issue Price: $1995
Display Case Last Issue Price: $249

American Armed Forces

This is a semiautomatic carbine version that has gold plated small parts and several gold inlays. Serial numbered from UZI001 through UZI1500. Includes detachable shoulder stock. Limited to 1500 units.

Last Issue Price: $2195
Sold Out

Armed Forces M16s

This issue is similar to the Vietnam War M16 except that it has four models to commemorate the four branches of service. Limited to 100 units for each branch.

Last Issue Price: $2995
Many branches sold out.
Display Case Last Issue Price: $249

Armed Forces Semi-Auto Thompson

Semi-Auto reproduction of the military Thompson submachine gun. Special finish high grade walnut, gold plated parts. Four models to commemorate the four service branches. Manufactured by Auto-Ordnance and limited to 750 for each service branch.

Current Original Issue Price: $1895
Current Issue Price: $1995

Airborne Golden Jubilee M1A1 Carbine

This issue uses an original WWII carbine chambered for the .30 caliber carbine cartridge. It features a folding stock, special commemorative etchings and gold plated selective parts. Limited to 500 carbines.

Current Issue Price: $1295
Display Case Current Issue Price: $249

SHOTGUNS

Annual Federal Duck Stamp Browning Shotguns

For the year 1991/1992 three grades were available in the Browning over and under shotgun. Hand engraved with gold inlays each is commissioned on an individual basis to customer specifications.

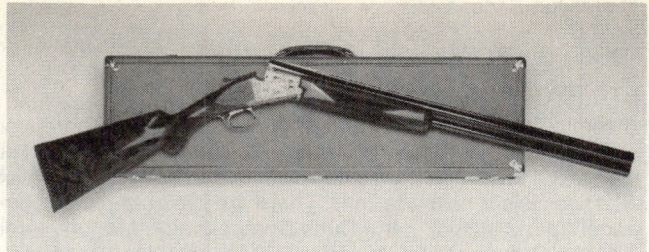

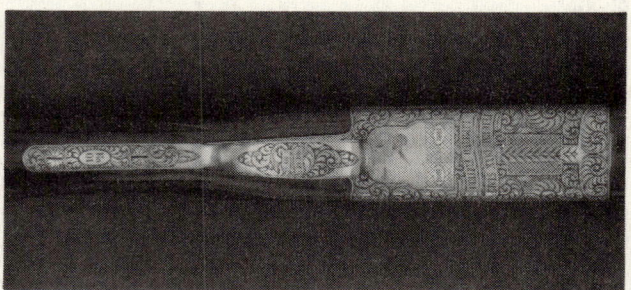

B-25 Edition limited to 50 guns.
Original Issue Price: $14500
Current Issue Price: $14995

B-125 Edition limited to 100 guns.
Original Issue Price: $9995
Current Issue Price: $10495

Citori Edition limited to 200 guns.
Original Issue Price: $4995
Current Issue Price: $5495

For the year 1992/1993 the same three grades are available.

B-25 Edition limited to 50 guns.
Original Issue Price: $14500
Current Issue Price: $14995

B-125 Edition limited to 100 guns.
Original Issue Price: $9995
Current Issue Price: $10495

Auto-5 Magnum Edition limited to 250 guns.
Current Issue Price: $2495

French Revolution Shotgun

This is a custom made shotgun built by Renata Gamba. They are hand engraved and signed by Cesare Giovnelli. The left side of the receiver shows the storming of the Bastille and the right side shows the march on Versailles. Limited to 200 guns. Display case included in price.

Last Issue Price: $10995

Vietnam War Combat Shotgun

Manufactured by Savage this 12 gauge shotgun has a hand engraved receiver with gold plated small parts. Produced in 1988 and serial numbered from VN001 through VN750. Limited to 750 guns.

Last Issue Price: $1595
Sold Out
Display Case Last Issue Price: $249

Generals Ulysses S. Grant Henry and Robert E. Lee Henry

This quality Uberti copy of the rare iron frame repeating rifle is chambered for the .44-40. It is hand engraved and selectively gold plated. Limited to 250 units per General.

Current Issue Price: $2495
Display Case Current Issue Price: $299

Vietnam Tribute Colt M16

This model is the Match HBAR version and is chambered for the .223 cartridge. It is etched and gold gilt infilled. This issue commemorates the Vietnam veteran and has eleven component parts gold plated. Serially number from VT0001 through VT1500 this issue is limited to 1,500 units.

Current Issue Price: $1995
Display Case Current Issue Price: $249

AMERICAN INDUSTRIES
Cleveland, Ohio
Renamed CALICO
Bakersfield, California

Calico M-100

A semiautomatic carbine that has a 16.1" barrel with a flash suppressor. It is chambered for the .22 l.r. and features a folding stock, full shrouding hand-guards, a 100-round capacity, helical feed, and detachable magazine. It features an ambidextrous safety, pistol grip storage compartment, and a black finished alloy frame and adjustable sights. This model was introduced in 1986.

NIB	Exc.	V.G.	Good	Fair	Poor
400	300	250	175	125	100

Calico M-100P/M-110

Similar to the M-100 .22 rimfire with a 6" barrel with muzzle brake and no shoulder stock.

NIB	Exc.	V.G.	Good	Fair	Poor
325	275	225	175	100	75

Calico M-100S Sporter/M-105

Similar to the Model 100 with a futuristically styled walnut buttstock and forearm.

NIB	Exc.	V.G.	Good	Fair	Poor
350	275	250	200	100	75

Calico M-101 Solid Stock Carbine

Introduced in 1994 this rifle features a 100-round magazine and a composite buttstock that is removable.

NIB	Exc.	V.G.	Good	Fair	Poor
375	300	275	200	100	75

Calico M-900

A black polymer-stocked rifle that is similar to the M-100S, chambered for the 9mm Parabellum. It has a delayed blowback action and features a stainless steel bolt and alloy receiver. The cocking handle is non-reciprocating, and the rear sight is fixed with an adjustable front. There is a 50-round magazine standard and a 100-round capacity model optional. This model was introduced in 1989.

NIB	Exc.	V.G.	Good	Fair	Poor
500	425	375	300	225	100

Calico M-950 Pistol

Similar to the Model 900 rifle with a 6" barrel and no shoulder stock.

NIB	Exc.	V.G.	Good	Fair	Poor
475	400	350	275	200	100

Calico M-951

The M-951 is a tactical carbine with a sliding buttstock. The barrel is 16" in length. It weighs about 7 pounds.

NIB	Exc.	V.G.	Good	Fair	Poor
500	425	375	300	225	100

Calico M-951S

Same as above but furnished with more conventional buttstock. Referred to as a light tactical carbine. Weighs about 7-1/4 pounds.

NIB	Exc.	V.G.	Good	Fair	Poor
500	425	375	300	225	100

AMERICAN INTERNATIONAL
Salt Lake City, Utah
A/K/A American Research & Development

American 180 Carbine

This firearm, imported from Austria, is a semiautomatic, 16.5" barreled carbine chambered for the .22 l.r. The sights are adjustable, and the stock is made of high-impact plastic. The unique drum magazine holds 177 rounds and is affixed to the top of the receiver. There is a select-fire version available for law enforcement agencies only and an optional laser lock sight system. This firearm was discontinued and recently has become available again from Feather Industries in Boulder, Colorado. It is now known as the SAR-180.

NIB	Exc.	V.G.	Good	Fair	Poor
650	500	400	300	200	100

N.P. AMES PISTOLS
Springfield, Massachusetts

Overall length-11-5/8"; barrel length-6"; caliber-.54. Markings: on lockplate, forward of hammer "N.P. AMES/SPRING-FIELD/MASS", on tail, either & "USN" or "USR" over date; on barrel, standard U.S. Navy inspection marks. N. P. Ames of Springfield, Massachusetts received a contract from the U.S. Navy in September 1842 for the delivery of 2,000 single shot muzzleloading percussion pistols. All are distinguished by having a lock mechanism that lies flush with the right side of the stock. On the first 300 Ames pistols, this lock terminates in a point; the balance produced were made with locks with a rounded tail. This "box lock" had been devised by Henry Nock in England, and was adapted to the U.S. Navy for the percussion pistols they ordered from Ames and Derringer. In addition to the 2,000 pistols for the Navy, the U.S. Revenue Cutter Service purchased 144 (distinguished by the "U S R" marks) for the forerunner of the U.S. Coast Guard. The latter commands triple the price over the "U S N" marked pistols, while the Navy pistols with pointed tails quadruple the value.

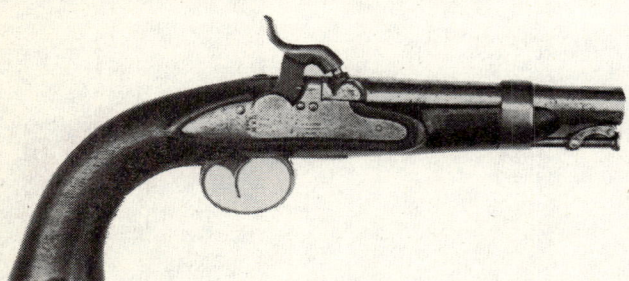

Courtesy Milwaukee Public Museum, Milwaukee, Wisconsin.

Courtesy Milwaukee Public Museum, Milwaukee, Wisconsin.

Exc.	V.G.	Good	Fair	Poor
—	3000	1500	750	400

AMES SWORD CO.
Chicopee Falls, Massachusetts

Turbiaux Le Protector

Ames Sword Co. became one of three U.S. companies that produced this unique, French palm-squeezer pistol. The design consists of a round disk with a protruding barrel on one side and a lever on the other. The disk contains the cylinder that holds either seven 8mm rimfire or ten 6mm rimfire cartridges. The barrel protrudes between the fingers, and the le-

ver trigger is squeezed to fire the weapon. The design was patented in 1883 and sold successfully in France into the 1890s. In 1892 Peter Finnegan bought the patents and brought them to Ames Sword. He contracted with them to produce 25,000 pistols for the Minneapolis Firearms Company. After approximately 1,500 were delivered, Finnegan declared insolvency, and after litigation, Ames secured the full patent rights. The Ames company produced Protector Revolvers until at least 1917.

(See Chicago Firearms Co. and Minneapolis Firearms Co.)

Exc.	V.G.	Good	Fair	Poor
2500	1500	900	500	250

ANCION & CIE
(of Liege, Belgium
See French Military Firearms)

ANCION MARX
Liege, Belgium

This company began production in the 1860s with a variety of cheaply made pinfire revolvers. They later switched to solid-frame, centerfire, "Velo-Dog" type revolvers chambered for 5.5mm or 6.35mm. They were marketed in various countries under many different trade names. Some of the names that they will be found under are Cobalt, Extracteur, LeNovo, Lincoln, and Milady. The quality of these revolvers is quite poor; and collector interest, almost non-existent. Values do not usually vary because of trade names.

Exc.	V.G.	Good	Fair	Poor
175	125	100	65	45

ANDERSON
Anderson, Texas

Anderson Under Hammer Pistol

An unmarked, under hammer percussion pistol that was chambered for .45 caliber. It had a 5" half-round/half-octagonal barrel with an all steel, sawhandle-shaped frame. There was a flared butt with walnut grips. The finish was blued. There is little information on this pistol, and its origin is strongly suspected but not confirmed.

Exc.	V.G.	Good	Fair	Poor
—	—	500	250	100

ANDRUS & OSBORN
Canton, Connecticut

Andrus & Osborn Under Hammer Pistol

This pistol is of the percussion type and chambered for .25 caliber. The part-round/part-octagonal barrel is 6" long and features small silver star inlays along its length. The barrel is marked "Andrus & Osborn/Canton Conn." with an eagle stamped beside it. It is marked "Cast Steel" near the breech. The grips are of walnut, and the finish is browned. Active 1863 to 1867.

Exc.	V.G.	Good	Fair	Poor
—	900	600	300	100

ANSCHUTZ
Ulm, Germany
Importer—Precision Sales International
Westfield, Massachusetts

Mark 10 Target Rifle

A single-shot, bolt-action rifle that is chambered for the .22 l.r. cartridge. It has a 26" heavy barrel with adjustable target-type sights. The finish was blued, and the walnut target stock had an adjustable palm rest. It was manufactured between 1963 and 1981.

NIB	Exc.	V.G.	Good	Fair	Poor
350	300	250	210	150	100

Model 1407

Similar to the Mark 10 but is furnished without sights. It was known as the "I.S.U." model. It was discontinued in 1981.

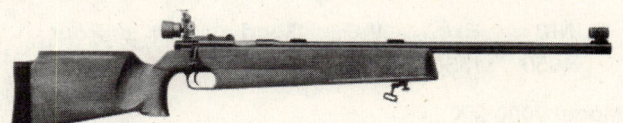

NIB	Exc.	V.G.	Good	Fair	Poor
375	325	275	235	175	100

Model 1408

A heavier-barrelled version of the Model 1407.

NIB	Exc.	V.G	Good	Fair	Poor
375	325	275	235	175	100

Model 1411

Designed specifically to be fired from the prone position.

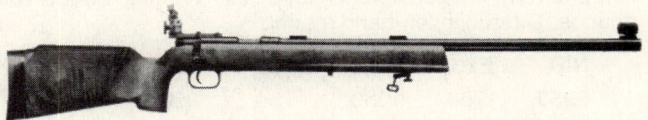

NIB	Exc.	V.G.	Good	Fair	Poor
350	300	250	210	150	100

Model 1413 Match

A high-grade, competition version with a heavy target barrel that is furnished without sights. The walnut stock has an adjustable cheekpiece.

NIB	Exc.	V.G.	Good	Fair	Poor
550	500	450	400	275	150

Model 1416D Classic

This sporting rifle is chambered for the .22 Long Rifle cartridge and is fitted with an American-style stock of European walnut or hardwood. Built on Anschutz Match 64 action. Left handed model also offered.

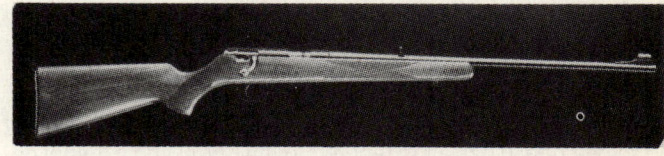

NIB	Exc.	V.G.	Good	Fair	Poor
550	450	350	300	200	100

Model 1516D Classic

Same as above but chambered for .22 Magnum cartridge.

NIB	Exc.	V.G.	Good	Fair	Poor
560	460	350	300	200	100

Model 1416D Custom

Chambered for the .22 Long Rifle cartridge, this model features a European style stock with Monte Carlo cheekpiece, and Schnabel forend.

NIB	Exc.	V.G	Good	Fair	Poor
585	425	375	300	200	100

Model 1516D Custom

Same as above but chambered for .22 Magnum cartridge.

NIB	Exc.	V.G.	Good	Fair	Poor
600	450	400	300	200	100

Model 1733D Mannlicher

Introduced in 1993 this model features a Mannlicher stock built on a Match 54 action. The stock has a rosewood Schnabel tip and checkering is done in a skip-line pattern. Chambered for .22 Hornet. Weighs about 6-1/4 pounds.

NIB	Exc.	V.G.	Good	Fair	Poor
1250	950	700	500	300	200

Model 1418D Mannlicher

A hunting rifle with a full-length, Mannlicher-type stock made with hand-checkered walnut. Chambered for .22 Long Rifle.

NIB	Exc.	V.G.	Good	Fair	Poor
850	625	500	300	200	150

Model 1518D Mannlicher

Same as above but chambered for the .22 Magnum.

NIB	Exc.	V.G.	Good	Fair	Poor
850	625	500	300	200	150

Model 1418/19

A lower-priced sporter model that was formerly imported by Savage Arms.

NIB	Exc.	V.G.	Good	Fair	Poor
300	250	200	150	125	85

Model 184

A high-grade, bolt-action sporting rifle chambered for the .22 l.r. cartridge. It has a 21.5" barrel with a folding-leaf sight. The finish is blued with a checkered walnut, Monte Carlo stock with a Schnabel forend. It was manufactured between 1963 and 1981.

NIB	Exc.	V.G.	Good	Fair	Poor
375	335	280	220	150	100

Model 54 Sporter

A high-grade, bolt-action sporting rifle chambered for the .22 l.r. cartridge. It has a 24" tapered round barrel and a 5-shot detachable magazine. It features a folding leaf-type rear sight. The finish is blued with a checkered walnut, Monte Carlo stock. It was manufactured between 1963 and 1981.

NIB	Exc.	V.G.	Good	Fair	Poor
650	575	500	350	250	125

Model 54M

This version is chambered for the .22 rimfire Magnum cartridge.

NIB	Exc.	V.G.	Good	Fair	Poor
700	600	525	375	275	125

Model 141

A bolt-action sporter chambered for the .22 l.r. cartridge. It has a 23" round barrel with a blued finish and walnut Monte Carlo stock. It was manufactured between 1963 and 1981.

NIB	Exc.	V.G.	Good	Fair	Poor
350	300	250	200	150	100

Model 141M

Chambered for the .22 rimfire Magnum cartridge.

NIB	Exc.	V.G.	Good	Fair	Poor
375	325	275	225	175	100

Model 153

A bolt-action sporting rifle chambered for the .222 Remington cartridge. It has a 24" barrel with folding-leaf rear sight. The finish is blued with a checkered French walnut stock featuring a rosewood forend tip and pistol grip cap. It was manufactured between 1963 and 1981.

NIB	Exc.	V.G.	Good	Fair	Poor
575	500	385	300	225	150

Model 153-S

This version was offered with double-set triggers.

NIB	Exc.	V.G.	Good	Fair	Poor
625	550	435	350	275	150

Model 64

A single shot, bolt-action rifle that is chambered for the .22 l.r. cartridge. It has a 26" round barrel and is furnished without sights. The finish is blued, and the walnut target-type stock featured a beaver-tail forearm and adjustable buttplate. It was manufactured between 1963 and 1981.

NIB	Exc.	V.G.	Good	Fair	Poor
375	300	250	200	150	100

Model 64MS

This version was designed for silhouette shooting and has a 21.25" barrel, blued finish, and a target-type walnut stock with a stippled pistol grip.

NIB	Exc.	V.G.	Good	Fair	Poor
750	600	525	400	300	200

Model 54.18MS

A high-grade silhouette rifle chambered for the .22 l.r. cartridge. It has a 22" barrel and a match-grade action with fully adjustable trigger. It is furnished without sights. The finish is blued with a target-type walnut stock.

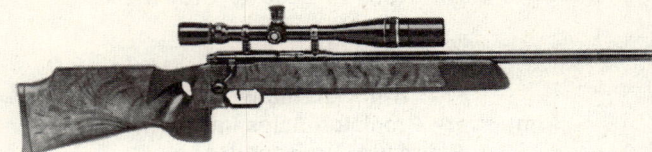

NIB	Exc.	V.G.	Good	Fair	Poor
1250	950	750	500	300	200

Model 54.MS REP

A repeating rifle with a 5-shot, detachable magazine with a thumbhole stock with vented forearm.

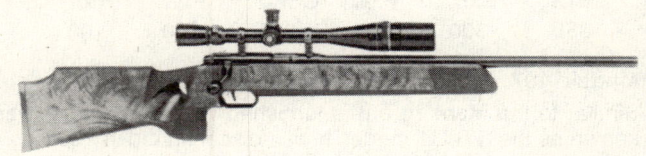

NIB	Exc.	V.G.	Good	Fair	Poor
1650	1350	900	500	300	200

Model 2000 MK

This single shot rifle was chambered for the .22 l.r. cartridge. It has a 26" round barrel with target-type sights. The finish was blued and has a checkered walnut stock. It was not imported after 1988.

NIB	Exc.	V.G.	Good	Fair	Poor
350	300	250	200	150	100

Model 2007 Supermatch

Introduced in 1993 this target rifle is chambered for the .22 Long Rifle cartridge. It has a 19-3/4" barrel fitted to a Match 54 action. Trigger is a two-stage. The stock is standard ISU configuration with adjustable cheekpiece. Weighs about 10.8 pounds. Offered in left-hand model.

NIB	Exc.	V.G.	Good	Fair	Poor
2250	1750	1250	750	350	200

Model 2013 Supermatch

Similar to the above model but fitted with an International stock with palm rest and buttstock hook. Weighs about 12.5 pounds.

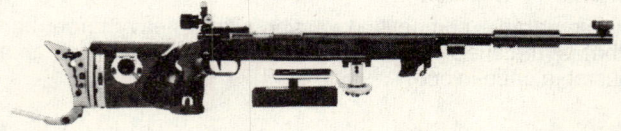

NIB	Exc.	V.G.	Good	Fair	Poor
3100	2500	1750	1250	600	300

Model 1403D

A single-shot target rifle chambered for the .22 l.r. cartridge. It has a 26" barrel and is furnished without sights. It has a fully adjustable trigger and a blued finish with a walnut target-type stock.

NIB	Exc.	V.G.	Good	Fair	Poor
700	650	575	500	375	250

Model 1803D

A high-grade target rifle chambered for the .22 l.r. cartridge. It has a 25.5" heavy barrel with adjustable target sights. It features an adjustable trigger. The finish is blued with a light-colored wood stock with dark stippling on the pistol grip and forearm. The stock features an adjustable cheekpiece and buttplate. It was introduced in 1987.

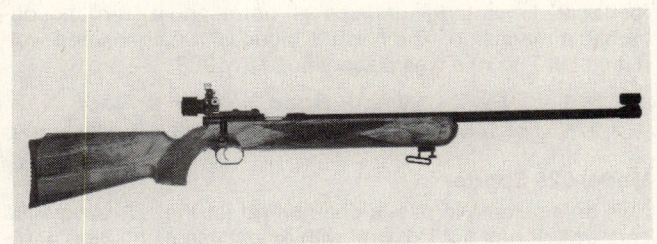

NIB	Exc.	V.G.	Good	Fair	Poor
810	750	675	600	450	200

Model 1808DRT Super

A single shot, running-boar type rifle that is chambered for the .22 Long Rifle cartridge. It has a 32.5" barrel furnished without sights. The finish is blued with a heavy target-type walnut stock with thumb hole. It is furnished with barrel weights. Rifle weighs about 9.4 pounds. Also available in a left-hand version.

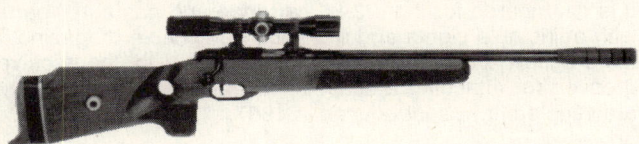

NIB	Exc.	V.G.	Good	Fair	Poor
1400	1200	1050	750	450	250

Model 1903D

Designed for the advanced junior shooter this target rifle has a 25-1/2" barrel on a Match 64 action with a single stage trigger. The walnut stock is fully adjustable. Weighs about 9.5 pounds and is offered in a left-hand model.

NIB	Exc.	V.G.	Good	Fair	Poor
850	700	600	400	300	200

Model 1907ISU Standard Match

Chambered for the .22 Long Rifle cartridge this rifle is designed for both prone and position shooting with a weight of 11.2 pounds. Built on a Match 54 action and fitted with a 26" barrel this rifle has a two-stage trigger with a removable cheekpiece and adjustable buttstock.

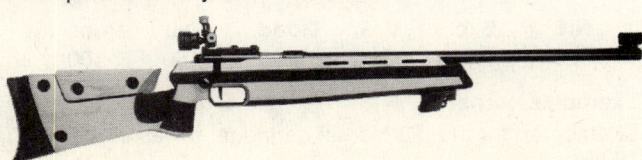

NIB	Exc.	V.G.	Good	Fair	Poor
1500	1250	900	450	300	200

Model 1910 Super Match II

A high-grade, single shot target rifle chambered for the .22 Long Rifle cartridge. It has a 27.25" barrel and is furnished with diopter-type target sights. The finish is blued with a walnut thumbhole stock with adjustable cheekpiece and buttplate. Hand rest and palm rest are not included.

NIB	Exc.	V.G.	Good	Fair	Poor
2200	1750	1300	900	500	250

Model 1911 Prone Match

This version has a stock designed specifically for firing from the prone position.

NIB	Exc.	V.G.	Good	Fair	Poor
1750	1450	950	650	400	250

Model 1913 Super Match

A virtually hand-built, match target rifle. It is chambered for the .22 l.r. cartridge and features a single shot action. It has adjustable, diopter-type sights on a 27.25" heavy barrel. This is a custom-made gun that features every target option conceivable. The finish is blued with a fully adjustable walnut stock.

NIB	Exc.	V.G.	Good	Fair	Poor
2600	2000	1500	1000	500	250

Model 1827B Biathlon

A repeating, bolt-action target rifle chambered for the .22 l.r. cartridge. It is specially designed for the biathlon competition. Production is quite limited and on a custom basis.

NIB	Exc.	V.G.	Good	Fair	Poor
1750	1400	1050	800	400	250

Model 1827BT Biathlon

Similar to the above model but features a straight pull Fortner bolt system. Available in left-hand model.

NIB	Exc.	V.G.	Good	Fair	Poor
2800	2250	1650	1000	500	250

Model 1433D

This is a centerfire version of the Model 54 target rifle chambered for the .22 Hornet. It is a special-order item and features a set trigger and a 4-round, detachable magazine. The finish was blued with a full-length, Mannlicher stock. It was discontinued in 1986.

NIB	Exc.	V.G.	Good	Fair	Poor
1000	850	600	400	200	100

Achiever

Introduced in 1993 this target rifle is chambered for the .22 Long Rifle cartridge. Designed for the beginning shooter it is furnished with a 5-shot clip but can be converted to a single shot with an adaptor. Barrel length is 19-1/2". Action is Mark 2000 with two-stage trigger. Stock pull is adjustable from 12" to 13". Weighs about 5 pounds.

NIB	Exc.	V.G.	Good	Fair	Poor
325	250	200	150	125	100

Achiever Super Target

Designed for the advanced junior shooter this model has a 22" barrel. Weighs about 6-1/2 pounds.

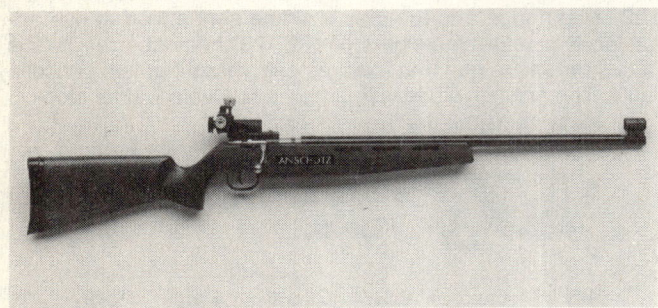

NIB	Exc.	V.G.	Good	Fair	Poor
400	325	250	175	125	100

Bavarian 1700

A classic-style sporting rifle chambered for the .22 l.r., .22 rimfire Magnum, .22 Hornet, and the .222 Remington cartridges. It features a 24" barrel with adjustable sights. It has a detachable magazine and a blued finish with a checkered walnut, European-style Monte Carlo stock with cheekpiece. It was introduced in 1988.

NIB	Exc.	V.G.	Good	Fair	Poor
800	650	500	400	300	200

Classic 1700

Similar in appearance to the Bavarian but furnished with an American style stock with fluted comb. Furnished in same calibers as Bavarian but weighs 6-3/4 pounds.

NIB	Exc.	V.G.	Good	Fair	Poor
800	650	500	400	300	200

Custom 1700

Similar to the Bavarian and Classic in caliber offerings but offered with a fancy European walnut stock with roll-over cheekpiece with Monte Carlo. The pistol grip has a palm swell and is fitted with a white lined rosewood grip cap with a white diamond insert. Forend is Schabel type and stock is checkered in ship line pattern.

NIB	Exc.	V.G.	Good	Fair	Poor
800	650	500	400	300	200

Model 1700 FWT

This model has same specifications as the 1700 Custom but is fitted with a McMillan laminated fiberglass stock. Weighs about 6-1/4 pounds.

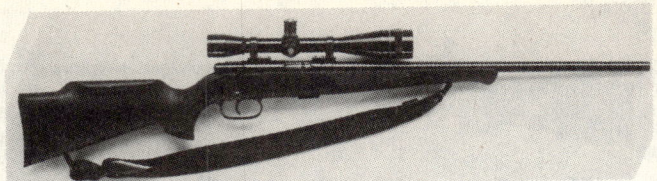

NIB	Exc.	V.G.	Good	Fair	Poor
950	800	700	500	300	200

Model 1700 FWT Deluxe

Same as above but fitted with a laminated wood grain stock.

NIB	Exc.	V.G.	Good	Fair	Poor
1125	900	800	550	300	200

Model 520/61

A blowback-operated, semiautomatic rifle that is chambered for the .22 l.r. cartridge. It has a 24" barrel and a 10-round, detachable magazine. The finish is blued with a checkered walnut stock. This rifle was discontinued in 1983.

NIB	Exc.	V.G.	Good	Fair	Poor
275	200	150	125	100	85

Model 525 Sporter

This semiautomatic rifle is chambered for the .22 Long Rifle cartridge. It has a 24" barrel with adjustable sights and a 10-round, detachable magazine. The finish is blued with a checkered Monte Carlo-type stock. It was introduced in 1984. A carbine version with a 20" barrel was originally offered but was discontinued in 1986.

NIB	Exc.	V.G.	Good	Fair	Poor
435	375	300	225	175	100

Exemplar

A bolt-action pistol that is built on the Model 64 Match Action. It is chambered for the .22 l.r. cartridge and has a 10" barrel with adjustable sights and a 5-shot, detachable magazine. It features an adjustable two-stage trigger with the receiver grooved for attaching a scope. The walnut stock and forend are stippled. It was introduced in 1987.

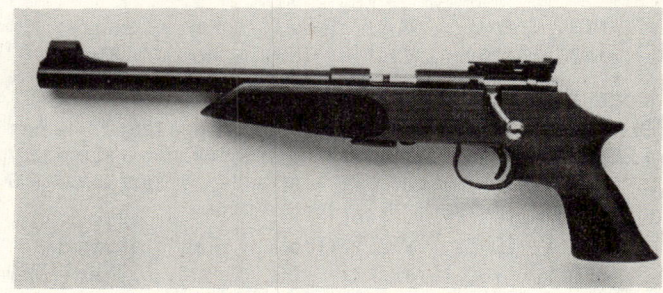

NIB	Exc.	V.G.	Good	Fair	Poor
400	325	275	210	150	100

Exemplar XIV

Similar to the standard Exemplar with a 14" barrel. It was introduced in 1988.

NIB	Exc.	V.G.	Good	Fair	Poor
420	370	275	200	150	100

Exemplar Hornet

Chambered for the .22 Hornet cartridge. It was introduced in 1988.

NIB	Exc.	V.G.	Good	Fair	Poor
750	600	400	300	200	100

ANTI GARROTTER
English

Percussion belt pistol, marked Balls Pat. Steel oval is 7 inches long and the barrel protrudes 1-1/2 inches, approximately 45 caliber. A cord runs from the lock up and through the sleeve and is fired by pulling the cord.

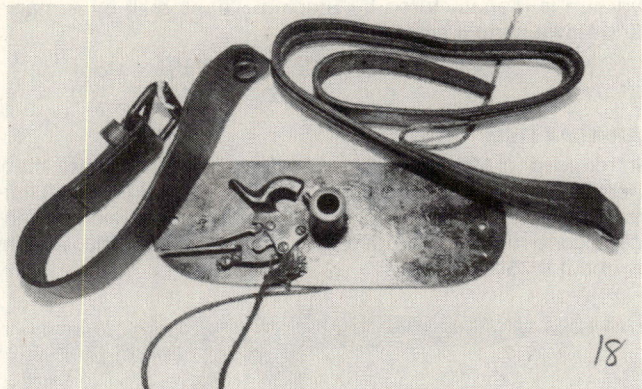

Exc.	V.G.	Good	Fair	Poor
5500	4000	1500	800	400

APACHE
Eibar, Spain
SEE—Ojanguren Y Vidosa

APALOZO HERMANOS
Zumorraga, Spain

Spanish manufacturer from approximately 1920 to 1935. Their trademark, a dove-like bird, is normally found impressed into the grips.

Apaloza
Copy of a Colt Police Positive Revolver.

Exc.	V.G.	Good	Fair	Poor
175	125	100	65	45

Paramount
Copy of the Model 1906 Browning chambered for the 6.35mm. Standard marking, "Paramount Cal. .25" normally found on the slide.

Exc.	V.G.	Good	Fair	Poor
175	125	100	65	45

Triomphe
The slide is inscribed "Pistolet Automatique Triomphe Acier Comprime."

Exc.	V.G.	Good	Fair	Poor
175	125	100	65	45

ARIZAGA, G.
Eibar, Spain

Spanish manufacturer during the first half of the twentieth century.

Arizaga
7.65mm semiautomatic pistol.

Exc.	V.G.	Good	Fair	Poor
175	125	100	65	45

Mondial
Resembling a Savage semiautomatic pistol externally, this model is based on John M. Browning's design. Examples are known with and without a grip safety. The grips are stamped with an owl in a circle trademark and "Mondial".

Exc.	V.G.	Good	Fair	Poor
175	125	100	75	50

Pinkerton
Arizaga's standard model known to exist with a cartridge counter. Slide is marked "Pinkerton Automatic 6.35".

Exc.	V.G.	Good	Fair	Poor
150	100	75	50	35

Warwinck
As above but chambered for 7.65mm cartridges, the slide is marked "Automatic Pistol 7.65 Warwinck".

Exc.	V.G.	Good	Fair	Poor
175	125	100	75	50

ARIZMENDI
Eibar, Spain

Originally founded in the 1890s, the company was reformed in 1914 and manufactured semiautomatic pistols.

Singer
Chambered for both the 6.35mm and 7.65mm. Manufactured from 1913 onward. Standard markings include the trademark "AG" with a crown and crescent on the slide and frame.

Exc.	V.G.	Good	Fair	Poor
200	150	100	65	45

Teuf - Teuf
A 7.65mm semiautomatic pistol marked "Automatic Teuf Teuf. Pistol 7.65mm."

Exc.	V.G.	Good	Fair	Poor
200	150	100	65	45

Walman
Chambered for 6.35, 7.65, and 9mm short. This pistol is normally marked "American Automatic Pistol Walman Patent".

Exc.	V.G.	Good	Fair	Poor
200	150	100	65	45

Arizmendi
Solid-frame, folding-trigger revolver chambered for 7.65mm or .32 caliber revolver. Normal markings are the trademark "FA" and a circled five-pointed star.

Exc.	V.G.	Good	Fair	Poor
175	125	80	50	25

Boltun
The 6.35mm version is marked "Automatic Pistol Boltun Patent", while the 7.65mm model is marked "Automatic Pistol Boltun Patent Marca Registrada 7375 Cal. 7.65."

Exc.	V.G.	Good	Fair	Poor
175	125	80	50	25

Puppy
A variation of the "Velo-Dog" revolver with the barrel stamped "Puppy" and the frame bearing the "FA" trademark.

Exc.	V.G.	Good	Fair	Poor
175	125	80	50	25

Pistolet Automatique
Normal markings include the "FA" trademark.

Exc.	V.G.	Good	Fair	Poor
175	125	80	50	25

Kaba Spezial
This pistol is normally marked "Pistol Automatique Kaba Spezial," with the "Kaba" cast into the grips.

Exc.	V.G.	Good	Fair	Poor
175	125	80	50	25

Roland

Chambered for 6.35 and 7.65mm cartridges, this model was manufactured during the 1920s.

Exc.	V.G.	Good	Fair	Poor
200	150	100	75	50

Ydeal

Patterned after the Model 1906 Browning pistol. It is chambered for the 6.35mm or 7.65mm cartridges. Standard markings are "Pistolet Automatique Ydeal" and "Ydeal" cast in the grips.

Exc.	V.G.	Good	Fair	Poor
200	150	100	75	50

ARIZMENDI ZULAICA
Eibar, Spain

Cebra

A semiautomatic 7.65mm pistol, the slide marked "Pistolet Automatique Cebra Zulaica Eibar," together with the letters "AZ" in an oval.

Exc.	V.G.	Good	Fair	Poor
200	150	100	65	35

Cebra Revolver

Copy of a Colt Police Positive revolver marked "Made in Spain" with the word "Cebra" cast in the grips.

Exc.	V.G.	Good	Fair	Poor
175	125	125	75	50

ARMALITE, INC.
Costa Mesa, California
Geneseo, Illionis (current production)

In 1995 Eagle Arms purchased the Armalite trademark and certain other assets. The new companies are organized under the Armalite name. The original company, formed in the mid 1950s, developed the AR-10, which in turn led to the development of the M-16 series of service rifles still in use today. All current models are produced at the Geneseo, Ilinois, facility.

AR-17 Shotgun

A gas-operated semiautomatic 12 gauge shotgun, with a 24" barrel and interchangeable choke tubes. The receiver and the barrel are made of an aluminum alloy, with an anodized black or gold finish. The stock and forearm are of plastic. Approximately 2,000 were manufactured during 1964 and 1965.

NIB	Exc.	V.G.	Good	Fair	Poor
550	450	400	300	225	100

AR-7 Explorer Rifle

A .22 l.r. semi-auto carbine with a 16-inch barrel. The receiver and barrel are partially made of an alloy. The most noteworthy feature of this model is that it can be disassembled and the component parts stored in the plastic stock. Manufactured between 1959 and 1973.

NIB	Exc.	V.G.	Good	Fair	Poor
100	85	70	60	50	25

AR-7 Custom

As above with a walnut cheekpiece stock, manufactured between 1964 and 1970.

NIB	Exc.	V.G.	Good	Fair	Poor
150	125	100	80	60	35

AR-180

A gas-operated semiautomatic rifle chambered for the .223 or 5.56mm cartridge. The AR-180 is the civilian version of the AR18 that is fully automatic. It is a simple and efficient rifle that was tested by various governments and found to have potential. This rifle was also manufactured by Howa Machinery Ltd. and Sterling Armament Co. of England. The most common version is manufactured by Sterling. Those built by Armalite and Howa bring a small premium.

NIB	Exc.	V.G.	Good	Fair	Poor
750	700	650	550	450	200

AR-10A4 Rifle

Introduced in 1995 this model features a 20" stainless steel heavy barrel chambered for the .308 Win. cartridge. Has a flat-top receiver, optional two-stage trigger, detachable carry handle, scope mount. Equipped with 10-round magazine. Weight is about 9.75 lbs.

NIB	Exc.	V.G.	Good	Fair	Poor
1300	1050	750	—	—	—

AR-10A2 Rifle

This model has a 20" heavy barrel chambered for the .308 cartridge but without the removable carry handle.

NIB	Exc.	V.G.	Good	Fair	Poor
1300	1050	750	—	—	—

AR-10T Rifle

This model features a 24" heavy barrel with a two stage trigger. The front sight and carry handle are removable. The handguard is fiberglass. Weight is approximately 10.4 lbs.

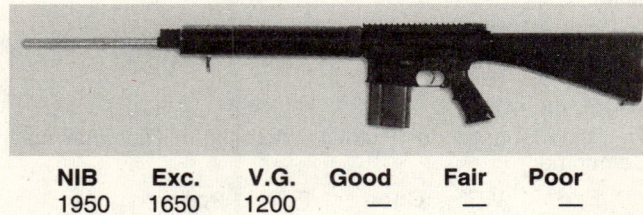

NIB	Exc.	V.G.	Good	Fair	Poor
1950	1650	1200	—	—	—

AR-10T Carbine

Similar to the AR-10T but fitted with a 16.25" target weight barrel. Weight is approximately 8.5 lbs.

NIB	Exc.	V.G.	Good	Fair	Poor
1850	1550	1100	—	—	—

M15A2 HBAR

This model was introduced in 1995 and features a 20" heavy barrel chambered for .223 cartridge. A2 style forward assist, recoil check brake. Sold with a 10-round magazine. Weight is approximately 8.2 lbs.

NIB	Exc.	V.G.	Good	Fair	Poor
850	700	500	—	—	—

M15A2 National Match

Chambered for the .223 cartridge this variation features a 20" stainless steel match barrel with two stage trigger, A2 style forward assist and hard coated anodized receiver. Equipped with a 10-round magazine. Weight is about 9 lbs.

NIB	Exc.	V.G.	Good	Fair	Poor
1200	950	700	—	—	—

M15A2- M4A1C Carbine

Similar to the M15A2 heavy barrel but with a 16" heavy barrel. Flattop receiver with detachable carry handle. Introduced in 1995.

NIB	Exc.	V.G.	Good	Fair	Poor
900	750	550	—	—	—

M15A2-M4C Carbine

Similar to the M4A1C Carbine but with the flattop receiver and detachable carry handle.

NIB	Exc.	V.G.	Good	Fair	Poor
850	700	500	—	—	—

M15A4(T)-Eagle Eye

Chambered for the .223 cartridge and fitted with a 24" stainless steel heavy weight barrel this rifle has a National Match two stage trigger, Picatinny rail, NM fiberglass handguard tube. Sold with a 7-round magazine and 4-section cleaning rod with brass tip, sling, owner's manual, and lifetime warranty.

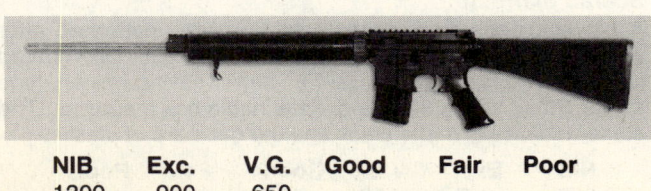

NIB	Exc.	V.G.	Good	Fair	Poor
1300	900	650	—	—	—

M15A4 Special Purpose

This model is fitted with a 20" heavy barrel with detachable front sight, detachable carry handle with NM sights, Picatinny rail. Weight is about 7.8 lbs.

NIB	Exc.	V.G.	Good	Fair	Poor
975	750	600	—	—	—

M15A4-Action Master

This variation features a 20" stainless steel heavy barrel with two stage trigger, Pictinny rail, and fiberglass handguard tube. Weight is approximately 9 lbs.

NIB	Exc.	V.G.	Good	Fair	Poor
1175	850	700	—	—	—

M15A4-Eagle Spirit

This version is similar to the Action Master above but fitted with a 16" stainless steel barrel. Weight is about 7.6 lbs.

NIB	Exc.	V.G.	Good	Fair	Poor
1175	850	700	—	—	—

PRE-BAN MODELS

Golden Eagle

Fitted with a 20" stainless extra heavy barrel with NM two stage trigger and NM sights. Sold with a 30-round magazine. Weight is about 9.4 lbs.

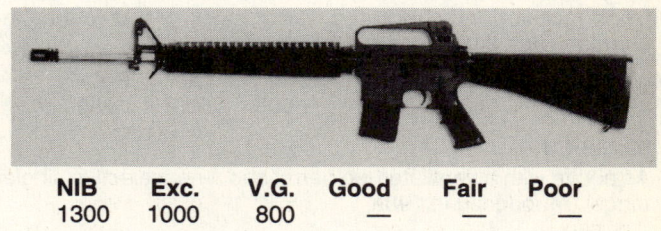

NIB	Exc.	V.G.	Good	Fair	Poor
1300	1000	800	—	—	—

HBAR

This pre-ban rifle has a 20" heavy barrel, a 30-round magazine, and sling. Weight is approximately 8 lbs.

NIB	Exc.	V.G.	Good	Fair	Poor
1100	850	700	—	—	—

M4C Carbine

This pre-ban variation is fitted with a 16" heavy barrel, collapsible stock, and fixed flash suppressor. Weight is about 6.2 lbs.

NIB	Exc.	V.G.	Good	Fair	Poor
1100	850	700	—	—	—

ARMAS DE FUEGO
Guernica, Spain
Believed to have been in business from 1920 to 1924.

Alkar
A 6.35mm copy of the Model 1906 Browning pistol distinguishable by eight slots cut into the left side of the grip.

Exc.	V.G.	Good	Fair	Poor
200	150	100	75	50

ARMERO ESPECIALISTAS
Eibar, Spain

Alfa
"Alfa" was a trademark given a number of revolvers based upon both Colt and Smith & Wesson designs in calibers ranging from .22 to.44.

Exc.	V.G.	Good	Fair	Poor
200	150	100	75	50

Omega
A semiautomatic 6.35 or 7.65mm pistol marked "Omega" on the slide and grips.

Exc.	V.G.	Good	Fair	Poor
200	150	100	75	50

ARMES DE CHASSE
Chadds Ford, Pennsylvania
Importer of firearms manufactured by P. Beretta, and other arms manufactured in Germany.

Model EJ
An O/U Anson & Deeley action 12 gauge shotgun with double triggers as well as automatic ejectors. Blued barrels, silver finished receiver and checkered walnut stock. Manufactured in Germany and introduced in 1989.

NIB	Exc.	V.G.	Good	Fair	Poor
1000	950	800	650	500	250

Model EU
As above with a ventilated-rib barrel and a nonselective single trigger. Introduced in 1989.

NIB	Exc.	V.G.	Good	Fair	Poor
1200	1000	850	650	500	250

Highlander
A side-by-side double-barrel 20 gauge shotgun with a boxlock action. Available in various barrel lengths and choke combinations, with double triggers and manual extractors. Blued with a checkered walnut stock. Manufactured in Italy and introduced in 1989.

NIB	Exc.	V.G.	Good	Fair	Poor
700	600	500	350	250	125

Chesapeake
As above but chambered for the 3.5", 12 gauge shell. The bores are chrome-lined and suitable for steel shot. Fitted with automatic ejectors and double triggers. Manufactured in Italy, it was introduced in 1989.

NIB	Exc.	V.G.	Good	Fair	Poor
800	700	600	475	400	200

Balmoral
English style straight grip 12, 16, or 20 gauge boxlock shotgun, fitted with false sideplates. Receiver and sideplates case-hardened, the barrels blued. Fitted with a single trigger and automatic ejectors. Manufactured in Italy and introduced in 1989.

NIB	Exc.	V.G.	Good	Fair	Poor
800	725	625	500	400	200

Model 70E
A 12, 16, or 20 gauge side-by-side shotgun fitted with 27" or 28" barrels. The action based upon the Anson & Deeley design with a Greener crossbolt. The receiver is case-hardened, barrels are blued and the walnut stock checkered. Manufactured in Germany and introduced in 1989.

NIB	Exc.	V.G.	Good	Fair	Poor
800	725	625	500	400	200

Model 74E
As above with gamescene engraving and more fully figured walnut stock. Introduced in 1989.

NIB	Exc.	V.G.	Good	Fair	Poor
1000	925	775	625	500	250

Model 76E
As above with engraved false sideplates and fully figured walnut stock. Introduced in 1989.

NIB	Exc.	V.G.	Good	Fair	Poor
1500	1150	900	750	600	300

ARMINEX LTD.
Scottsdale, Arizona

Tri-Fire
A semiautomatic pistol chambered for 9mm, .38 Super or .45 ACP cartridges. Available with conversion units that add approximately $130 if in excellent condition. Fitted with 5", 6", or 7" stainless steel barrels. Presentation cases were available at an extra cost of $48. Approximately 250 were manufactured from 1981 to 1985.

NIB	Exc.	V.G.	Good	Fair	Poor
400	325	225	175	125	90

Target Model
As above with a 6" or 7" barrel.

NIB	Exc.	V.G.	Good	Fair	Poor
450	400	325	275	200	100

ARMINIUS
SEE-Freidrich Pickert
Zelia-Mehlis, Germany
Hermann Weirauch
Melrichstadt, Germany
F. 1. E.
Hialeah, Florida

ARMITAGE INTERNATIONAL, LTD.
Seneca, South Carolina

Scarab Skorpion
A blowback-operated, semiautomatic pistol, patterned after the Czechoslovakian Scorpion submachine gun. Chambered for the 9mm cartridge with a 4.6" barrel having military-type sights. Fitted with a 32-round, detachable box magazine. The standard finish is matte black and the grips are of plastic.

NIB	Exc.	V.G.	Good	Fair	Poor
350	250	200	150	125	90

ARMS CORPORATION OF THE PHILIPPINES
Armscor Precision
Foster City, California

Armscor Precision is an importer of a variety of firearms made in the Philippines.

SHOTGUNS

Model 30D

A slide-action 12 gauge shotgun fitted with either 28" or 30" barrels with various chokes. The magazine holds 6 cartridges. Weight is about 7.6 lbs.

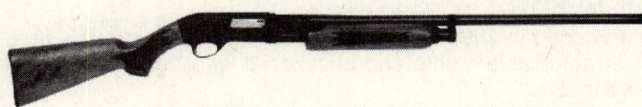

NIB	Exc.	V.G.	Good	Fair	Poor
200	175	150	125	100	75

Model 30DG

As above with a 20" barrel, fitted with rifle sights and a 7-shot magazine. Weight is about 7.2 lbs.

NIB	Exc.	V.G.	Good	Fair	Poor
175	150	125	100	80	70

Model 30R

As above with shotgun bead sights, 20" or 18.5" barrel. Weight is between 7 and 7.2 lbs depending on barrel length.

NIB	Exc.	V.G.	Good	Fair	Poor
175	150	125	100	80	70

Model 30RP

As above with an auxiliary black composition pistol-grip and an 18.5" barrel.

NIB	Exc.	V.G.	Good	Fair	Poor
175	150	125	100	80	70

RIFLES

Model M14P

A .22 caliber bolt-action rifle fitted with a 23" barrel, open sights, and a 5-shot detachable magazine. Stock of mahogany.

NIB	Exc.	V.G.	Good	Fair	Poor
100	90	75	50	35	25

Model M14D

As above with an adjustable rear sight and checkered stock. Manufactured in 1987 only.

NIB	Exc.	V.G.	Good	Fair	Poor
125	100	85	60	40	25

Model 14Y

This bolt action rifle is chambered for .22 long rifle cartridge. It is fitted with an 18" barrel and 10-round magazine. Weight is approximately 5.2 lbs.

NIB	Exc.	V.G.	Good	Fair	Poor
150	125	100	—	—	—

Model 12Y

This bolt action rifle is a single shot and chambered for the .22 long rifle. It is fitted with an 18" barrel. Weight is about 5 lbs.

NIB	Exc.	V.G.	Good	Fair	Poor
125	100	75	—	—	—

Model 1400

This is a bolt action rifle chambered for the .22 long rifle cartridge. Fitted with a 22.5" barrel and a 10-round magazine. Weight is about 6.5 lbs.

NIB	Exc.	V.G.	Good	Fair	Poor
200	175	150	125	100	75

Model M1500

A .22 Magnum bolt-action rifle fitted with a 22.5" barrel, open sights, 5-shot magazine and checkered mahogany stock. Weight is approximately 6.5 lbs.

NIB	Exc.	V.G.	Good	Fair	Poor
200	175	150	125	100	75

Model M1600

A .22 caliber copy of the U.S. M16 rifle having an 18" barrel and detachable 15-round magazine. Weight is about 6.2 lbs.

NIB	Exc.	V.G.	Good	Fair	Poor
110	100	85	60	40	25

Model M1600R

As above with a stainless steel collapsible stock and shrouded barrel. No longer in production.

NIB	Exc.	V.G.	Good	Fair	Poor
125	105	90	70	50	35

Model M1600C

As above with a 20" barrel and fiberglass stock. No longer in production.

NIB	Exc.	V.G.	Good	Fair	Poor
135	110	90	70	50	35

Model M1600W

As above with a mahogany stock. No longer in production.

NIB	Exc.	V.G.	Good	Fair	Poor
135	110	90	70	50	35

Model M1800

A .22 Hornet bolt-action rifle fitted with a 22.5" barrel, 5-shot magazine and a mahogany Monte Carlo style stock. Weight is approximately 6.6 lbs.

Exc.	V.G.	Good	Fair	Poor
150	125	100	75	50

Model 20C

Chambered for .22 long rifle with a 15-round magazine and fitted with an 18.25" barrel. Weight is about 6.2 lbs.

NIB	Exc.	V.G.	Good	Fair	Poor
95	80	65	50	35	25

Model M20P

A .22 caliber 15-shot semiautomatic rifle fitted with a 20.75" barrel, open sights and plain mahogany stock. Weight is about 6.3 lbs.

NIB	Exc.	V.G.	Good	Fair	Poor
95	80	65	50	35	25

Model M2000

As above with adjustable sights and a checkered stock. Weight is approximately 6.4 lbs.

Exc.	V.G.	Good	Fair	Poor
80	60	50	35	25

Model AK22S

A .22 caliber semiautomatic rifle resembling the Russian AKA47. Barrel length of 18.5", 15-round magazine and mahogany stock. Weight is about 7.5 lbs.

NIB	Exc.	V.G.	Good	Fair	Poor
160	140	125	100	75	50

Model AK22F

As above with a folding stock. No longer in production.

NIB	Exc.	V.G.	Good	Fair	Poor
200	175	150	100	75	50

HANDGUNS

Model M100

A double-action, swing-out cylinder revolver chambered for .22, .22 Magnum, and the .38 Special cartridges. Having a 4" ventilated-rib barrel. Six-shot cylinder and adjustable sights. Blued with checkered mahogany grips. No longer in production.

NIB	Exc.	V.G.	Good	Fair	Poor
200	175	150	110	80	50

Model 200P

Introduced in 1990 this 6-shot revolver is chambered for the .38 Special cartridge. It is fitted with a 4" barrel, fixed sights and wood or rubber grips. Weighs about 26 ozs.

NIB	Exc.	V.G.	Good	Fair	Poor
180	150	125	100	85	60

Model 200TC

Introduced in 1990 this model is similar to above but is fitted with adjustable sights and checkered wood grips. Weight is about 28 oz.

NIB	Exc.	V.G.	Good	Fair	Poor
200	175	150	125	100	75

Model 200DC

Similar to the Model 200 P but fitted with a 2.5" barrel. Weight is about 22 oz.

NIB	Exc.	V.G.	Good	Fair	Poor
175	150	125	100	85	60

Model 201S

Similar to the Model 200 P but in stainless steel.

NIB	Exc.	V.G.	Good	Fair	Poor
200	175	150	125	100	75

Model 1911-A1

A semiautomatic pistol similar in design to the Colt Model 1911 pistol. Chambered for the .45 ACP cartridge and fitted with a 5" barrel. Blued finish. Magazine capacity is 8 rounds. Weight is about 39 oz.

NIB	Exc.	V.G.	Good	Fair	Poor
500	400	—	—	—	—

Model 1911-A2

Same as above but fitted with a double column magazine with a 13-round capacity. Weight is approximately 43 oz.

NIB	Exc.	V.G.	Good	Fair	Poor
600	500	—	—	—	—

ARMSCORP OF AMERICA
Baltimore, Maryland

RIFLES

M-14R

A civilian version of the U.S. M14 rifle manufactured from new and surplus parts. Introduced in 1986.

NIB	Exc.	V.G.	Good	Fair	Poor
600	500	400	300	200	100

M-14 National Match

As above but built to A.M.T.U. MIL specifications. Introduced in 1987.

NIB	Exc.	V.G.	Good	Fair	Poor
1500	1150	800	500	400	200

FAL

A civilian version of the FN FAL rifle assembled from new and Argentine surplus parts. Introduced in 1987.

NIB	Exc.	V.G.	Good	Fair	Poor
800	650	500	400	300	150

M36 Israeli Sniper Rifle

A specialized weapon built upon the Armscor M-14 receiver in the Bullpup style. Barrel length 22" and of free floating design for accuracy, chambered for the .308 cartridge. There is an integral flash suppressor and a bipod. It is furnished with a 20-shot detachable magazine. This civilian version was first offered for sale in 1989.

NIB	Exc.	V.G.	Good	Fair	Poor
3000	2500	2000	1500	850	400

Expert Model

A .22 caliber semiautomatic rifle with a 21" barrel, open sights, and 10-shot magazine. Introduced in 1989.

NIB	Exc.	V.G.	Good	Fair	Poor
225	200	175	145	100	80

HANDGUNS

Hi-Power

An Argentine-made version of the Browning semiautomatic pistol chambered for 9mm with a 4.75" barrel. Matte finished with checkered synthetic grips. Introduced in 1989.

NIB	Exc.	V.G.	Good	Fair	Poor
400	350	300	250	200	100

Detective HP - Compact

As above with a 3.5" barrel.

NIB	Exc.	V.G.	Good	Fair	Poor
450	400	350	275	200	100

SD9

An Israeli-made 9mm double-action semiautomatic pistol with a 3" barrel. Assembled extensively from sheet-metal stampings. Loaded chamber indicator and 6-round magazine. This model is also known as the Sirkus, SD9 manufactured by Sirkus Industries in Israel. Introduced in 1989.

NIB	Exc.	V.G	Good	Fair	Poor
300	250	200	150	100	75

P22

A copy of the Colt Woodsman .22 caliber semiautomatic pistol available with either 4" or 6" barrels and a 10-shot magazine. Finish blued, grips of checkered hardwood. Introduced in 1989.

NIB	Exc.	V.G.	Good	Fair	Poor
200	150	125	100	75	50

ARNOLD ARMS
Arlington, Washington

Alaskan Bush Rifle

This is a bolt action rifle chambered for calibers from .223 to .338 Win. Mag. Barrel lengths are from 22" to 26" depending on caliber. Stocks are synthetic in black woodland or arctic camo. Sights are optional. Rifle is drilled and tapped for scope mounts. Trigger is fully adjustable. Choice of Chrome-moly steel or stainless steel. Introduced in 1996.

NIB	Exc.	V.G.	Good	Fair	Poor
3000	2500	—	—	—	—

Alaskan Trophy Rifle

Similar to the Bush Rifle except chambered for .300 Magnums to .458 Win. Mag. Barrel lengths are 24" to 26" depending on caliber. Choice of walnut, synthetic, or fibergrain stock. Fitted with iron sights. Choice of stainless or Chrome-moly steel. Introduced in 1996.

Fibergrain or Synthetic stock

NIB	Exc.	V.G.	Good	Fair	Poor
3750	3000	—	—	—	—

Walnut Stock

NIB	Exc.	V.G.	Good	Fair	Poor
5200	4000	—	—	—	—

Grand Alaskan Rifle

This version is fitted with AAA fancy select or exhibition wood. Built in calibers from 300 Mag to .458 Win. Mag.

NIB	Exc.	V.G.	Good	Fair	Poor
6500	5000	—	—	—	—

High Country Mountain Rifle

Similar to the Alaskan Bush Rifle except chambered for the .257 to .337 Magnum calibers. Choice of AA select walnut or synthetic stock. Introduced in 1996.

Synthetic Stock

NIB	Exc.	V.G.	Good	Fair	Poor
3000	2500	—	—	—	—

Walnut Stock

NIB	Exc.	V.G.	Good	Fair	Poor
4650	3750	—	—	—	—

Safari Rifle

Introduced in 1996 this model features calibers from .223 to .458 Win. Mag. Barrel lengths are from 22" to 26" depending on caliber. The Appolo is a controlled or push feed type with one piece cone head bolt. Fully adjustable trigger with Chrome-moly or stainless steel construction. Sights are optional but the rifle is drilled and tapped for scope mounts. Choice of A fancy English or AA fancy English walnut.

A Fancy English Walnut

NIB	Exc.	V.G.	Good	Fair	Poor
4600	3700	—	—	—	—

AA Fancy English Walnut

NIB	Exc.	V.G.	Good	Fair	Poor
4800	3900	—	—	—	—

African Trophy Rifle

Similar to the Safari Rifle except stocked in AAA fancy walnut with wrap around checkering.

NIB	Exc.	V.G.	Good	Fair	Poor
6200	5000	—	—	—	—

Grand African Rifle

Similar to the Safari rifle with the addition of Exhibition Grade wood. Calibers are from .338 to .458.

NIB	Exc.	V.G.	Good	Fair	Poor
7700	6200	—	—	—	—

Serengeti Synthetic Rifle

Similar to the Safari rifle with a fibergrain stock in classic or Monte Carlo style. Checkering or stipple finish. Calibers are .243 to 300 Magnum. Introduced in 1996.

NIB	Exc.	V.G.	Good	Fair	Poor
3100	2500	—	—	—	—

Arfican Synthetic Rifle

Similar to the Safari rifle with fibergrain stock, checkering or stipple finish. Calibers are .338 Mag. to .458 Mag.

NIB	Exc.	V.G.	Good	Fair	Poor
3100	2500	—	—	—	—

AROSTEGUI
Eibar, Spain

Azul, Royal

This semiautomatic pistol is a first-rate copy of the Mauser Model C96, and is very collectible.

Exc.	V.G.	Good	Fair	Poor
1375	1000	800	600	300

E.A.

A 6.35mm semiautomatic pistol copied after the Model 1906 Browning. The frame is marked with the letters "EA" in a circle and a retriever is molded in the grips.

Exc.	V.G.	Good	Fair	Poor
175	150	100	75	50

Velo-Dog

A folding trigger 5.5mm or 6.35mm revolver bearing the trademark "EA" on the grips.

Exc.	V.G.	Good	Fair	Poor
125	100	75	50	30

ARRIETA S.L. ELQOLBAR
Spain
Importer-Morton's Ltd.
Lexington, Kentucky

This company produces a wide variety of double-barrel shotguns in a price range from $450 to above $14,000. It is recommended that highly engraved examples as well as small bore arms be individually appraised.

490 Eder

A double barrel boxlock shotgun with double triggers and extractors. Discontinued in 1986.

Exc.	V.G.	Good	Fair	Poor
475	425	325	250	100

500 Titan

A Holland & Holland-style sidelock double-barrel shotgun with French case-hardened and engraved locks. Double triggers on extractors. No longer imported after 1986.

Exc.	V.G.	Good	Fair	Poor
575	500	400	300	150

501 Palomara

As above, but more finely finished. Discontinued in 1986.

Exc.	V.G.	Good	Fair	Poor
700	600	500	400	200

505 Alaska

As above, but more intricately engraved. Discontinued in 1986.

Exc.	V.G.	Good	Fair	Poor
800	700	600	500	250

510 Montana

A Holland & Holland-style sidelock double barrel shotgun with the internal parts gold plated.

NIB	Exc.	V.G.	Good	Fair	Poor
2200	1750	1250	850	500	250

550 Field

As above, without the internal parts being gold plated.

NIB	Exc.	V.G.	Good	Fair	Poor
2200	1750	1250	850	500	250

557 Standard

As above, but more finely finished.

NIB	Exc.	V.G.	Good	Fair	Poor
2600	2000	1750	1250	800	400

558 Patria

As above, but more finely finished.

NIB	Exc.	V.G.	Good	Fair	Poor
2650	2150	1750	1250	800	400

560 Cumbre

As above, but featuring intricate engraving.

NIB	Exc.	V.G.	Good	Fair	Poor
2800	2200	1800	1200	800	400

570 Lieja

NIB	Exc.	V.G.	Good	Fair	Poor
3000	2500	2000	1500	750	500

575 Sport

NIB	Exc.	V.G.	Good	Fair	Poor
3250	2750	2250	1700	1200	750

578 Victoria

This model is engraved in the English manner with floral bouquets.

NIB	Exc.	V.G.	Good	Fair	Poor
3500	2750	2000	1250	750	350

585 Liria

As above, but more finely finished.

NIB	Exc.	V.G.	Good	Fair	Poor
3800	3000	2250	1500	900	400

588 Cima

NIB	Exc.	V.G.	Good	Fair	Poor
3800	3000	2250	1500	900	400

590 Regina

NIB	Exc.	V.G.	Good	Fair	Poor
4250	3500	2700	1750	1000	500

595 Principe

As above, but engraved with relief-cut hunting scenes.

NIB	Exc.	V.G.	Good	Fair	Poor
6500	5000	4000	3000	2000	1000

600 Imperial

This double-barrel shotgun has a self-opening action.

NIB	Exc.	V.G.	Good	Fair	Poor
5750	4250	3250	2000	1000	500

601 Tiro

As above, but nickel-plated.

NIB	Exc.	V.G.	Good	Fair	Poor
6500	5000	4000	3000	2000	1000

801

A detachable sidelock, self-opening action, double-barrel shotgun engraved in the manner of Churchill.

NIB	Exc.	V.G.	Good	Fair	Poor
9500	8000	6500	4000	3000	1500

802

As above, with Holland & Holland-style engraving.

NIB	Exc.	V.G.	Good	Fair	Poor
9500	8000	6500	4000	3000	1500

803

As above, with Purdey-style engraving.

NIB	Exc.	V.G.	Good	Fair	Poor
6500	5000	4000	3000	2000	1000

875

A custom manufactured sidelock, double-barrel shotgun built solely to the customer's specifications.

NIB	Exc.	V.G.	Good	Fair	Poor
14000	12000	8500	6750	5000	2000

ARRIZABALAGA
Eibar, Spain

Arrizabalaga
A 7.65mm semiautomatic pistol with a 9-shot magazine and a lanyard ring fitted to the butt.

Exc.	V.G.	Good	Fair	Poor
200	125	100	65	40

Campeon
A 6.35mm or 7.65mm semiautomatic pistol with the slide marked "Campeon Patent 1919" and the plastic grips "Campeon".

Exc.	V.G.	Good	Fair	Poor
200	125	100	65	40

Sharpshooter
A 6.35mm, 7.65mm or 9mm Corto (short) semiautomatic pistol fitted with a cocking lever. The barrel tips up for cleaning or when using the pistol as a single shot.

Exc.	V.G.	Good	Fair	Poor
300	250	200	125	85

JoLoAr
As above, but chambered for either the 9mm Bergman Bayard or .45ACP cartridges.

Exc.	V.G.	Good	Fair	Poor
300	250	200	150	90

NOTE: The .45 caliber version is worth approximately 40% more than the values listed above.

ASCASO
Cataluna, Spain
A copy of the Astra Model 400. The barrel marked "F. Ascaso Tarrassa" in an oval.

Exc.	V.G.	Good	Fair	Poor
375	275	200	150	90

ASHEVILLE ARMORY
Asheville, North Carolina

Enfield Type Rifle
A .58 caliber percussion rifle with a 32.5" barrel and full stock secured by two iron barrel bands. Finished in the white brass triggerguard and buttplate with a walnut stock. The lockplate is marked "Asheville, N.C." Approximately 300 were made in 1862 and 1863. Prospective purchasers are advised to secure a qualified appraisal prior to acquisition.

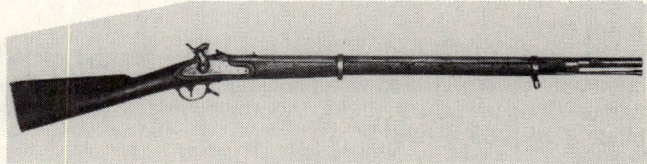

Courtesy Milwaukee Public Museum, Milwaukee, Wisconsin.

Exc.	V.G.	Good	Fair	Poor
—	—	15000	6000	2000

PETER & WILLIAM ASHTON
Middletown, Connecticut

Ashton Under Hammer Pistol
A .28 to .38 caliber single shot percussion revolver with 4" or 5" half-octagonal barrels marked "P.H. Ashton" or "W. Ashton." Blued or browned with walnut grips. Active 1850s.

Exc.	V.G.	Good	Fair	Poor
—	1500	500	250	100

H. ASTON/H. ASTON & CO. PISTOLS
Middleton, Connecticut
Overall length 14"; barrel length 8-1/2"; caliber .54. Markings: on lockplate, forward of hammer "U S/H. ASTON" or "U S/H. ASTON & CO.," on tail "MIDDTN/CONN/(date)"; on barrel, standard government inspection marks. Henry Aston of Middleton, Connecticut received a contract from the U.S. War Department in February 1845 for 30,000 single shot percussion pistols. These were delivered between 1846 and 1852, after which Ira N. Johnston continued production under a separate contract. Three thousand of these pistols were purchased for Navy usage and many of these were subsequently marked with a small anchor on the barrel near the breech. These Navy purchases will command a slight premium.

Courtesy Milwaukee Public Museum, Milwaukee, Wisconsin.

Exc.	V.G.	Good	Fair	Poor
4000	2000	1500	600	300

ASTRA-UNCETA SA
Guernica, Spain
Astra is a brand name placed on guns built by Esperanza y Unceta and then Unceta y Cia. This Spanish company has now incorporated its trade name into its corporate name and is now know as Astra-Unceta SA. The firm under the direction of Don Pedron Unceta and Don Juan Esperanza began business in Eibar on July 17, 1908 and moved to Guernica in 1913. The Astra trademark was adopted on November 25, 1914. Esperanza began production of the Spanish army's Campo Giro pistol in 1913. The Model 1921 was marketed commercially as the Astra 400. After the Spanish Civil War Uncerta was one of only four handgun companies permitted to resume manufacturing operations. An interesting and informative side note is that pistols with 1000 to 5000 model numbers were made after 1945.

Victoria
A 6.36mm semiautomatic pistol with a 2.5" barrel. Blued with black plastic grips. Manufactured prior to 1913.

Exc.	V.G.	Good	Fair	Poor
350	250	200	150	100

Astra 1911
As above, renamed in November of 1914 and chambered additionally for the 7.65mm cartridge.

Exc.	V.G.	Good	Fair	Poor
350	250	175	100	75

Astra 1924

A 6.35mm semiautomatic pistol with a 2.5" barrel. The slide marked "Esperanza y Unceta Guernica Spain Astra Cal 6.35 .25." Blued with black plastic grips.

Exc.	V.G.	Good	Fair	Poor
300	200	125	100	75

Astra 100

A different tradename for the Model 1911 in 7.65mm caliber.

Exc.	V.G.	Good	Fair	Poor
350	225	200	150	100

Astra 200

A 6.35mm semiautomatic pistol with a 2.5" barrel and 6-shot magazine fitted with a grip safety. Also known as the "Firecat" in the United States. Manufactured from 1920 to 1966.

Exc.	V.G.	Good	Fair	Poor
300	200	125	100	75

Astra 400 or Model 1921

A 9x23 Bergman caliber semiautomatic pistol with a 6" barrel. Blued with black plastic grips. This model was adopted for use by the Spanish Army. Approximately 106,000 were made prior to 1946. Recent importation has depressed the price of these guns. Any with Nazi proofs marks are worth a 100% premium, but caution is advised.

Exc.	V.G.	Good	Fair	Poor
325	275	150	75	40

Astra 300

As above, in 7.65mm or 9mm short. Those used during World War II by German forces bear Waffenamt marks. Approximately 171,000 were manufactured prior to 1947.

Nazi-Proofed-Add 25%.

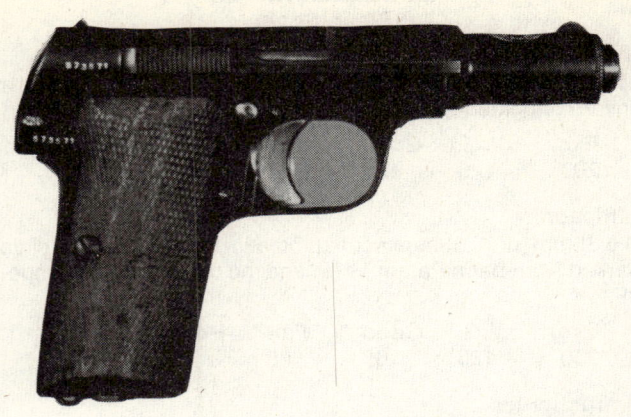

Courtesy Orvel Reichert.

Exc.	V.G.	Good	Fair	Poor
350	300	200	150	100

Astra 600

Similar to the Model 400, but in 9mm Parabellum. In 1943 and 1944 approximately 10,500 were manufactured. Some of these World War II guns will have Nazi proof stamp and bring a premium. A further 49,000 were made in 1946 and commercially sold.

Exc.	V.G.	Good	Fair	Poor
350	250	200	150	100

Astra 700

The Model 400 in 7.65mm caliber. Approximately 4,000 were made in 1926.

Exc.	V.G.	Good	Fair	Poor
600	450	400	300	150

Astra 800

Similar to the Model 600 with an external hammer and loaded chamber indicator. Blued with plastic grips having the tradename "Condor" cast in them. Approximately 11,400 were made from 1958 to 1969.

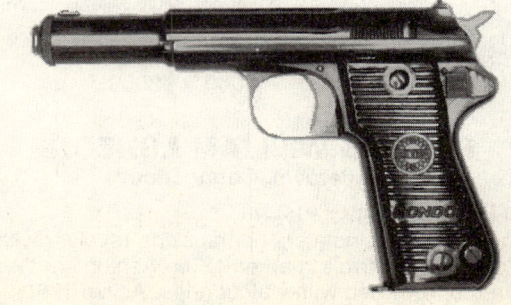

Exc.	V.G.	Good	Fair	Poor
1250	850	750	500	250

Astra 900

A copy of the Mauser Model C96 semiautomatic pistol. Blued with walnut grips.

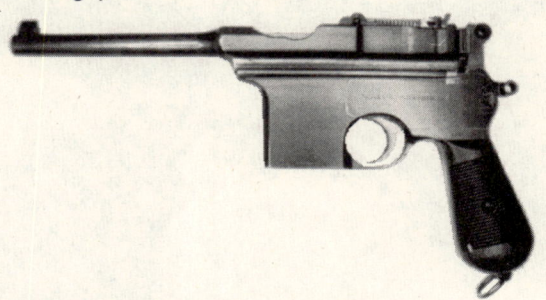

Exc.	V.G.	Good	Fair	Poor
2250	1750	1250	750	500

Astra 1000

A postwar version of the Model 200 with a 4" barrel and 12-shot magazine.

Exc.	V.G.	Good	Fair	Poor
550	450	400	300	150

Astra 2000

As above, in .22 or 6.35mm caliber without a grip safety and with an external hammer. Blued with plastic grips.

Exc.	V.G.	Good	Fair	Poor
350	250	200	150	90

Astra 3000

The Model 300 in 7.65mm or 9mm short with a 6- or 7-shot magazine and loaded chamber indicator. Manufactured from 1948 to 1956.

Exc.	V.G.	Good	Fair	Poor
400	300	250	200	100

Astra 4000

As above, with an external hammer and also chambered in .22 caliber. Blued with plastic grips.

Exc.	V.G.	Good	Fair	Poor
300	225	200	150	75

Astra 5000

A .22, 7.65mm or 9mm short semiautomatic pistol (resembling a Walther PP Pistol) with a 3.5" barrel. Blued, chrome-plated or stainless steel with plastic grips. Also available with a 6" barrel as a sport model. Introduced in 1965.

Exc.	V.G.	Good	Fair	Poor
350	250	200	150	75

Astra 7000

An enlarged version of the Model 2000 in .22 caliber.

Exc.	V.G.	Good	Fair	Poor
300	250	200	150	75

Constable A-60

A .380 caliber double-action semiautomatic pistol with a 3.5" barrel, adjustable sights and 13-shot magazine. Blued with plastic grips. Introduced in 1986.

NIB	Exc.	V.G.	Good	Fair	Poor
400	300	200	150	100	75

Astra A-80

A .38 Super, 9mm or .45 caliber double-action semiautomatic pistol with a 3.75" barrel and either a 9- or 15-shot magazine depending upon the caliber. Blued or chrome-plated with plastic grips. Introduced in 1982.

NIB	Exc.	V.G.	Good	Fair	Poor
450	350	300	250	200	100

Astra A-90

As above, in 9mm or .45 caliber only. Introduced in 1986.

NIB	Exc.	V.G.	Good	Fair	Poor
400	350	300	250	200	100

Astra Cadix

A .22 or .38 Special double-action swing-out cylinder revolver with a 4" or 6" barrel and either 9- shot or 5-shot cylinder. Blued with plastic grips. Manufactured from 1960 to 1968.

Exc.	V.G.	Good	Fair	Poor
200	150	125	90	70

.357 Double Action Revolver

As above, in .357 Magnum caliber with a 3", 4", 6", or 8.5" barrel, adjustable sights and 6-shot cylinder. Blued or stainless steel with walnut grips. Manufactured from 1972 to 1988.

Stainless steel-Add 10%.

NIB	Exc.	V.G.	Good	Fair	Poor
250	200	150	125	100	75

.44/.45 Double Action Revolver

As above, in .41 Magnum, .44 Magnum or .45 ACP caliber with 6" or 8.5" barrels and a 6-shot cylinder. Blued or stainless steel with walnut grips. Manufactured from 1980 to 1987.

Stainless steel-Add 25%.

Exc.	V.G.	Good	Fair	Poor
350	300	250	200	100

Terminator

As above, in .44 Special or .44 Magnum with a 2.75" barrel, adjustable sights and 6-shot cylinder. Blued or stainless steel with rubber grips.

Stainless steel version-Add 10%.

Exc.	V.G.	Good	Fair	Poor
350	300	250	200	100

Convertible Revolver

Similar to the .357 D/A revolver but accompanied by a cylinder chambered for 9mm cartridges. Barrel length 3". Blued with walnut grips. Introduced in 1986.

Exc.	V.G.	Good	Fair	Poor
300	250	200	150	100

CURRENTLY IMPORTED PISTOLS
IMPORTER-EUROPEAN AMERICAN ARMORY
Hialeah, FL

Model A-100

This semiautomatic service pistol is chambered for the 9mm Parabellum, .40 S&W, or .45 ACP cartridges. The trigger action is double action for the first shot, single action for follow-up shots. Equipped with a decocking lever. The barrel is 3.8" long and the overall length is 7.5". Magazine capacity for the 9mm is 17 rounds, .40 S&W is 13 rounds, while the .45 holds 9 rounds. A blue or nickel finish is standard. Weight is approximately 34 oz. Also available in a featherweight model 9mm only at 26.5 oz.

NIB	Exc.	V.G.	Good	Fair	Poor
400	350	300	250	200	100

NOTE: Add $35 for nickel finish.

Model A-100 Carry Comp

Similar to the Model A-100 but fitted with a 4.25" barrel and 1" compensator. Blue finish only. Weight is approximately 38 oz. Magazine capacity for 9mm is 17 rounds and for the .40 S&W and .45 ACP 10 rounds.

NIB	Exc.	V.G.	Good	Fair	Poor
475	375	—	—	—	—

Model A-70

This is a lightweight semiautomatic pistol chambered for the 9mm cartridge or .40 S&W cartridge. It is fitted with 3-dot combat sights. The barrel is 3.5" long and the magazine capacity is 8 rounds for 9mm and 7 rounds for the .40 S&W. Black plastic grips and blue finish are standard. Weight is 29 oz.

NIB	Exc.	V.G.	Good	Fair	Poor
325	275	225	175	150	100

NOTE: Add $35 for nickel finish.

Model A-75

Introduced in 1993 this model features all of the standard features of the Model 70 plus selective double or single trigger action and decocking lever. Chambered for 9mm, .40 S&W, or .45 ACP. Offered in blue or nickel finish and steel or alloy frame in 9mm only. Weight for steel frame in 9mm and .40 S&W is 31 oz., for .45 ACP weight is 34.4 oz. Featherweight 9mm weight is 23.5 oz.

NIB	Exc.	V.G.	Good	Fair	Poor
375	325	250	200	150	100

NOTE: Add $35 for nickel finish.

AUER, B.
Louisville, Kentucky

Auer Pocket Pistol

A .60 caliber percussion pocket pistol with a 4" octagonal barrel and a long tang extending well back along the grip. Browned, silver furniture and a checkered walnut stock. The lock is marked "B. Auer". Produced during the 1850s.

Exc.	V.G.	Good	Fair	Poor
—	2500	1000	500	250

AUGUSTA MACHINE WORKS
Augusta, Georgia

1851 Colt Navy Copy

A .36 caliber percussion revolver with an 8" barrel and 6-shot cylinder. Unmarked except for serial numbers with either 6 or 12 stop cylinder slots. Blued with walnut grips. This is a very rare revolver. Prospective purchasers are advised to secure a qualified appraisal prior to acquisition.

Exc.	V.G.	Good	Fair	Poor
—	—	25000	7500	2500

AUSTRALIAN AUTOMATIC ARMS LTD.
Tasmania, Australia
Importer-North American Sales International, Inc.
Midland, Texas

SAR

A 5.56mm semiautomatic rifle with a 16.25" or 20" barrel, 5-shot or 20-shot magazine, black plastic stock and forend. Imported from 1986 to 1989.

NIB	Exc.	V.G.	Good	Fair	Poor
700	600	450	350	250	125

SAP

A 10.5" barrelled pistol version of the above. Imported from 1986 to 1989.

NIB	Exc.	V.G.	Good	Fair	Poor
700	600	450	350	250	125

SP

A sporting rifle version of the SAR, fitted with a wood stock and 5-shot magazine. Introduced in 1989.

NIB	Exc.	V.G.	Good	Fair	Poor
775	650	500	400	300	150

AUSTRIAN MILITARY FIREARMS

The end of the Napoleonic Wars found the army of the Austria Hungarian Empire armed with a variety of flintlock firearms. The foot troops carried either the MI798 or the M1807 musket or the M1807 yager rifle. The mounted forces were armed with either the MI 798 dragoon carbine, the MI798 Hussarcarbine, the M1798 rifled cavalry carbine, the M1781 Cuirassier musketoon, and the M1798 pistol. In 1828 a new flintlock musket superseded the M1798 pattern, only to be modified again in 1835. In the latter years, however, the Austrian military also began experimenting with a variation of the percussion system invented by Giuseppe Console, utilizing a small elongated copper cylinder filled with fulminate. In 1840, the flintlock muskets adopted in 1835 were adapted to a variation of this percussion system as modified by Baron von Augustin. This system was made army-wide in 1842 with the adoption of a new musket and yager rifle with locks specifically manufactured for the Augustin tubelocks. In 1849, a new rifle replaced the M1842 pattern; both of these rifles were based on the Devilgne chambered breech. In 1850, a cavalry carbine and a horse pistol were added to the tubelock series. All of these arms were either .69 or .71 caliber. The tubelock, however, was shortlived; in 1854, Austria abandoned the tubelock system in favor of standard percussion cap then widely used by the armies of Europe. At the same time it adopted a new smaller caliber (.54) which it applied to the new M1854 rifle-musket and the M1855 yager rifle. A horse pistol based on the same system (Lorenz's compressed, elongated ball) was adopted in 1859.

Large numbers of the Austrian longarms were imported to the United States in the first two years of the American Civil War. Beginning in 1863, the Confederate States also imported large numbers of the M1854 series rifle-muskets. Most of the tubelocks first being modified to standard percussion in Belgium before importation, arms of prime interest to American collectors, accordingly demand higher prices.

In 1867, the Austria-Hungarian Empire adopted two different breechloading mechanisms and the self-contained metallic cartridge. Those muzzleloading arms deemed acceptable for alteration (the M1854 series of rifle-muskets and rifles) were adapted to the Wanzel system. Newly made arms (the M1867 rifle) were made in conformity with Werndl's breechloading design.

During the period within the scope of this catalog, Austrian arms were generally made on contract with the major gunmakers in and near Vienna ("Wien" in Austrian). These makers usually marked their products with their name upon the barrel of the arm, near the breech. The major makers included BENTZ, FERD. FRUWIRTH (who also simply marked his arms "F. F."), CARL HEISER, JOSEF JESCHER, ANNA OSTERLIEN, PIRKO, TH. ROTTME, G. SCHLAGER, TH. SEDERE, F. UMFAURER, WANZEL, and ZEILINGER (with the "Z" usually backwards). Lockplates were marked with the government ownership mark (a small double-headed eagle) and the date of manufacture (deleting the number "1" from the year, such as "847" for "1847".) Since the arms were not interchangeable, mating numbers are usually found on all the metal parts.

Austrian Musket, M1828

Overall length 57-3/4"; barrel length 42-1/2"; caliber .69. Basically following the pattern of the French M1822 musket, this arm still accepted the quadrangular M1799 bayonet, distinguished by having a solid socket with a hook ring at its rear, like the Prussian bayonet for the M1808 musket.

Exc.	V.G.	Good	Fair	Poor
800	700	650	550	400

Austrian Musket, M1835

Overall length 57-3/4"; barrel length 42-1/2"; caliber .69. The M1835 musket follows the pattern of the Austrian M1807 musket, but is adapted for the Consule tubelock percussion system, which essentially replaced the frizzen and pan with a hinged tube retainer. This arm still uses the M1799 quadrangular bayonet.

Exc.	V.G.	Good	Fair	Poor
1200	750	700	600	350

Austrian Musket, M1840

Overall length 57-3/4"; barrel length 42-1/2"; caliber .69. The M1840 musket was manufactured in flint. Its primary differences from the M1828 musket lie in its furniture (mainly the front band) and the bayonet attachment, which consists of a lug beneath the barrel and an elongated hook projecting from the forend of the stock to accept the new M1840 quadrangular bayonet. The bayonet is distinguished by having a straight slot in its socket, closed by a bridge.

Exc.	V.G.	Good	Fair	Poor
1050	850	750	600	350

Austrian Musket, M1842

Overall length 57-3/4"; barrel length 42-1/2"; caliber .69 (.71) The M1842 musket was manufactured in Augustin tubelock. Its main distinction from the M1840 flintlock musket is the lock, which in addition to having the integral hinged tubelock mechanism in lieu of the frizzen, has a distinctly rounded rear tail. Although 25,000 of these muskets were imported into the United States for use by Fremont's forces in Missouri in 1861, many were subsequently altered to percussion. The Cincinnati contractors, Hall, Carroll & Co. or Greenwood & Co. accounted for 10,000 of these arms, all of which were altered to percussion by means of the cone-in-barrel system. These were also rifled and a portion of them sighted with a long range rear sight similar to the Enfield P1853 rifle-musket. Many of the balance were subsequently sent to the Frankfort Arsenal in Philadelphia, where they were subcontracted to Henry Leman of Lancaster for alteration to standard percussion. Those altered by Leman are distinguished by having a new breechpiece with integral bolster, the latter with a cleanout screw through its face. In addition to the 25,000 imported for Fremont, the firm of M, Boker & Co. of New York imported approximately 8,000 Austrian M1842 muskets which it had altered to percussion in Belgium. The French method of adding a reinforced bolster to the top right-hand side of the barrel was used. Many of those were also rifled and sighted in the manner of the French adaptations fashionable in Europe. George Heydecker of New York City imported another 4,000 in 1863 that were seized in transit to Canada, reputedly for delivery to Mexican republican forces.

Courtesy Milwaukee Public Museum, Milwaukee, Wisconsin.

In original tubelock!

Exc.	V.G.	Good	Fair	Poor
1450	950	900	850	500

Altered to percussion (Cincinnati contractors)

Exc.	V.G.	Good	Fair	Poor
700	550	500	450	250

Altered to percussion (Leman)

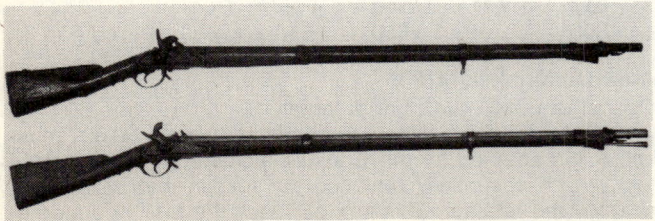

Courtesy Milwaukee Public Museum, Milwaukee, Wisconsin.

Exc.	V.G.	Good	Fair	Poor
600	450	400	350	200

Altered to percussion and rifled (Boker)

Exc.	V.G.	Good	Fair	Poor
600	450	375	325	200

Austrian M1844 "Extra Corps" Musketoon

Overall length 48-3/8"; barrel length 33-1/2"; caliber .69 (.71) Is essentially a shortened version of the Austrian M1842 musket. In original Augustin tubelock, it is virtually unknown. Most of the production is thought to have been purchased by arms speculators at the beginning of the American Civil War and altered to standard percussion in Liege, Belgium. The Belgian alteration followed the second pattern adopted by that government to alter arms to percussion and consisted of brazing a "lump" of metal to the upper right hand side of the barrel, into which a cone was threaded. The arms so altered were also rifled and sighted. The sights either copied the Austrian M1854 riflemusket folding sight or the French "ladder" rear sight using the pattern utilized on the M1829 rifled cavalry musketoon. Over 10,000 of these arms were imported into the United States in 1861-1862 by Herman Boker & Co. of New York City.

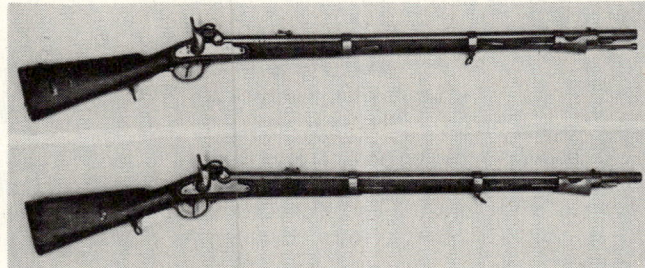

Courtesy Milwaukee Public Museum, Milwaukee, Wisconsin.

Altered to percussion and rifled (Boker)

Exc.	V.G.	Good	Fair	Poor
500	400	325	275	200

Austrian M1842 yager rifle

Overall length 48-1/4"; barrel length 33-1/4"; caliber .69/.71. The Austrian M1842 yager rifle ("Kammer Busche") was originally manufactured in tubelock for the rifle battalions of the Austrian Army. Its bore terminated in a Delvigne breech, i.e. a chamber of lesser diameter than the caliber whose lip served as a base for disfiguring the projectile to fill the rifling. Made obsolete by the Thouvenin and Minie systems, many M1842 yager rifles were altered in 1860 in Belgium to standard percussion and sold to the Italian revolutionaries led by Giuseppe Garibaldi, giving the gun that nickname. Two methods of alteration were applied. One, the "Belgian" system, brazed a "lump" of iron to the upper right surface of the breech, which was tapped for a standard percussion cone. The other, the "Prussian," involved fitting the breech with a new barrel section incorporating a new bolster. At least 500 of these altered arms were imported into the United States during the American Civil War, where they (and the M1849 yager rifles similarly altered) were called "Garibaldi Rifles."

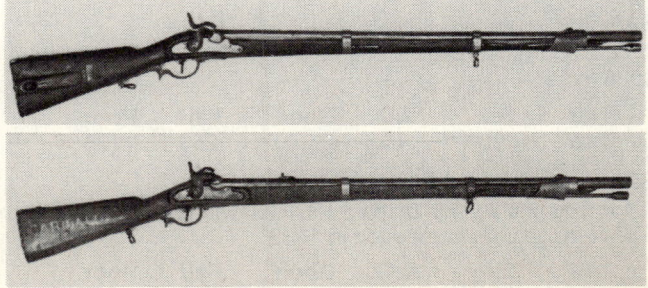

Courtesy Milwaukee Public Museum, Milwaukee, Wisconsin.

Exc.	V.G.	Good	Fair	Poor
500	400	350	250	150

Austrian M1849 yager rifle

Overall length 48"; barrel length 33-1/4"; caliber .71. The successor to the M1842 Austrian "Kammer Busche," the M1849 model is distinguished by having its barrel wedge fastened rather than retained by bands. Both the M1842 and the M1849 yager rifles were adapted to socket bayonets having long straight knife blades; both socket types were slotted. That of the M1842 was secured to the barrel by the same method as the M1842 Austrian musket; that of the M1849, however, locked onto a lug on the right side of the barrel and was secured by a rotating ring on the back of the socket. Adapted to standard percussion in the same manner as the M1842 yager rifles, more than 25,000 were sold to the U.S. War Department in 1862 and 1863.

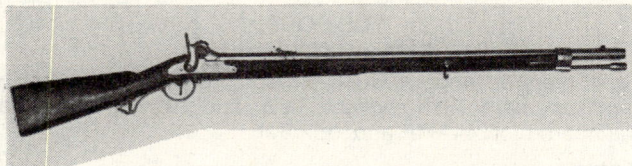

Courtesy Milwaukee Public Museum, Milwaukee, Wisconsin.

Austrian M1850 horse pistol

Overall length 16"; barrel length 8-7/8"; caliber .69. A bulky brass mounted pistol with lanyard ring, this arm was made originally in tubelock. However, a small quantity appear to have been altered to standard percussion locks in Liege, Belgium. In the process the double-strapped front bands of the original were removed and the forestock cut away to adapt the stock to an iron ramrod. (In Austrian service the ramrod was hung from the crossbelt of the mounted trooper.) Quantities imported into the United States are uncertain but may have been included among the 346 foreign horse pistols purchased by the U.S. War Department from P.S. Justice in 1861.

Exc.	V.G.	Good	Fair	Poor
450	350	300	225	150

Austrian M1850 carbine

Overall length 30"; barrel length 14-1/2"; caliber .71. Originally manufactured in tubelock for Austrian cavalry service, this large caliber, short-barrelled rifled carbine (12-groove rifling) saw service in the United States when 10,000 were purchased by U.S. purchasing agent George Schuyler in 1861. Those purchased for U.S. service, however, had been altered in Liege, Belgium for standard percussion locks in the same manner that the Austrian M1842 and M1849 yager rifles had been altered.

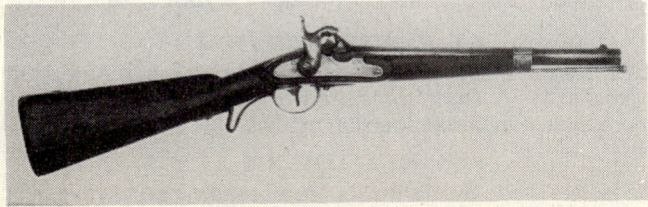

Courtesy Milwaukee Public Museum, Milwaukee, Wisconsin.

M1854 rifle-musket (The "Lorenz")

Overall length 52"; barrel length 37-1/4"; caliber .54 (and .58). Adopted in 1854 as a replacement for its smoothbore muskets, the Austrian M1854 rifle-musket was made in three variants. The standard infantry arm had a simple block sight for mass volley fire. The rifles for the "rear rank" men were similar but with a folding leaf sight with windows graduated to 900 paces. A similar sight was also applied to the rifles for sharpshooter battalions, which also had a cheekpiece built into the buttstock. The quadrangular socket bayonet locked onto the front sight, whose sides were angled to accept the diagonal slot in the bayonet's socket. The Austrian M1854 rifle-musket was the second most prolifically imported arm during the American Civil War, with some 89,000 being imported into the Confederacy and more than 175,000 into the Union. Thousands of the latter were bored up to .58 caliber before being imported.

Courtesy Milwaukee Public Museum, Milwaukee, Wisconsin.

Exc.	V.G.	Good	Fair	Poor
650	550	450	300	200

M1854 yager rifle

Overall length 43"; barrel length 28"; caliber .54. Designed for the rifle battalions of the Austrian army to replace the M1842 and M1849 rifles, the M1854 yager rifles are distinguished by having an octagonal, wedge-fastened barrel turned round near the muzzle to accept a socket bayonet with a long straight knife blade. An angled lug on the turned section engaged the diagonal slot in the bayonet's socket. The rear sight for these rifles is unusual, consisting of a curved slide that traverses two upright walls and can be locked with a turn key on its right side for various ranges up to 900 paces. These rifles were made for Austrian service without provision for a ramrod (that device being affixed to a crossbelt of the individual soldier). But the approximately 2,500 that were imported for U.S. service during the American Civil War were adapted for a ramrod by inletting a channel under the forestock.

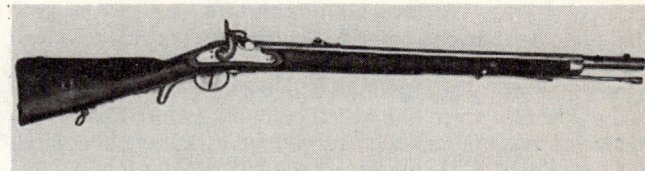

Courtesy Milwaukee Public Museum, Milwaukee, Wisconsin.

Exc.	V.G.	Good	Fair	Poor
800	600	500	275	200

Austrian M1859 horse pistol

Overall length 16" (less stock); barrel length 10-3/8"; caliber .54. The M1850 tubelock pistol was replaced in the Austrian service in 1859 with a new standard percussion rifled horse pistol firing the Lorenz "compression" elongated ball. Like the U.S. M1855 horse pistol, this new pistol had a detachable shoulder stock so that it could be used as a carbine. Like its predecessors, no provision was made for a ramrod, which continued to be attached to a belt crossing the trooper's torso.

Exc.	V.G.	Good	Fair	Poor
550	450	350	250	200

Austrian M 1854/67 "Wanzel" alteration to breechloader

Overall length 52-1/4"; barrel (bore) length; 34-1/2"; caliber .54. The "Wanzel" breechloading mechanism applied to the Austrian M1854 rifle-muskets is much like the Allin "trapdoor" applied in the U.S. to long arms during the period 1865-1873. A breech block that hinges forward upon the barrel is released by a lever on the right side of the block, permitting insertion of a brass cartridge. In the process of altering these arms to breechloaders the sling swivels were moved from the middle band and triggerguard bow to the middle of the forestock and the buttstock.

Courtesy Milwaukee Public Museum, Milwaukee, Wisconsin.

Exc.	V.G.	Good	Fair	Poor
450	350	300	275	200

Austrian M 1867 "Werndl" breechloading rifle

Overall length 48-1/4"; barrel (bore) length 31-1/4"; caliber 11mm. In 1867 the Austrian military adopted the breechloading system that had been invented by Joseph Werndl, director of the Austrian armory at Steyr. The breech of Werndl's design is rotated by means of a lever on its left side to expose the chamber for loading and extraction of cartridges. WERNDL appears on the top of the barrel in recognition of the designer's invention. In 1888 the Werndl rifles were superseded by the Mannlicher smokeless powder arms.

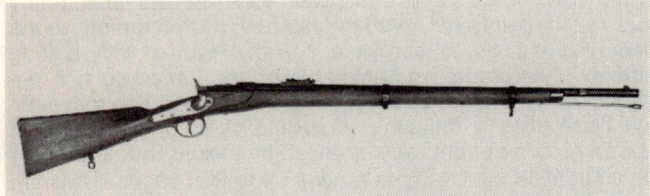

Courtesy Milwaukee Public Museum, Milwaukee, Wisconsin.

Exc.	V.G.	Good	Fair	Poor
500	400	350	250	200

AUTO MAG
Various Manufacturers

This popular stainless steel semiautomatic pistol was developed by the Sanford Arms Company of Pasadena, California, in the 1960s and was chambered for a special cartridge known as the .44AMP which had a 240 grain .44 caliber bullet. Production of this arm has been carried out by a number companies over the past 30 years. It is believed that less than 10,000 have been produced by the eight manufacturers involved.

AUTO MAG CORP.
Pasadena, California

Serial number range A0000 through A3300, made with a 6.5" vent-rib barrel, chambered in .44AMP only.

NIB	Exc.	V.G.	Good	Fair	Poor
2250	1700	1200	850	600	300

TDE CORP.
North Hollywood, California

Serial number range A3400 through A05015, made with a 6.5" vent-rib barrel, chambered in .44AMP and .357AMP.

.44AMP

NIB	Exc.	V.G.	Good	Fair	Poor
1950	1500	1100	850	600	300

.357AMP

NIB	Exc.	V.G.	Good	Fair	Poor
2150	1650	1200	900	600	300

TDE CORP.
El Monte, California

Serial number range A05016 through A08300, 6.5" vent-rib barrel standard. Also available in 8" and 10" barrel lengths chambered for .44AMP and .357AMP.

.44AMP

NIB	Exc.	V.G.	Good	Fair	Poor
1800	1450	1000	800	600	300

.357AMP

NIB	Exc.	V.G.	Good	Fair	Poor
1600	1200	900	700	500	300

> An Auto Mag Custom Model 100 Series with 8.5" barrel was sold at auction for $4,400. Only one of ten built in this configuration. Caliber is .44AMP. Condition excellent. Rock Island Auction, December 11, 1995.

HIGH STANDARD
New Haven, Connecticut

High Standard made 113 guns, all with "H" prefix serial numbers.

NIB	Exc.	V.G.	Good	Fair	Poor
2000	1750	1250	900	600	300

TDE-OMC

This is known as the solid-bolt or "B" series. The serial number range is B00001 through B00370. Either 6.5" vent-rib or 10" tapered barrels are available.

NIB	Exc.	V.G.	Good	Fair	Poor
2400	2000	1500	1000	600	300

AMT "C" SERIES

There were 100 guns produced in this series. The first 50 were serial numbered with a "C" prefix. The second 50 were serial numbered "LAST 1" through "LAST 50." They were available with a 6.5" vent-rib or 10" tapered barrel.

NIB	Exc.	V.G.	Good	Fair	Poor
2400	2000	1500	1250	700	350

L. E. JURRAS CUSTOM

This custom maker produced a limited number of Auto Mag pistols in 1977. These arms are worth approximately 35-50% more than standard production models.

KENT LOMONT

As pistols made by this maker are essentially prototypes, it is advised that potential purchasers secure a qualified appraisal.

AUTO ORDNANCE CORP.
West Hurley, New York

Thompson 1911 A1-Standard

A 9mm, .38 Super or.45 caliber, copy of the Colt Model 1911 A1. Pistol weighs 39 oz.

NIB	Exc.	V.G.	Good	Fair	Poor
375	300	250	200	150	100

NOTE: For 9mm and .38 Super add $20 to above prices.

Thompson 1911 A1-Deluxe

Same as above but Hi-profile 3 white dot sight system. Grips are black textured, rubber wraparound grips.

NIB	Exc.	V.G.	Good	Fair	Poor
400	325	275	225	150	100

Thompson 1911 A1-10mm

Same as above but chambered for the 10mm cartridge. Magazine capacity is 8 rounds.

NIB	Exc.	V.G.	Good	Fair	Poor
425	350	300	250	175	100

Thompson 1911 A1-Duo Tone

Chambered for the .45 ACP, the slide is blued and the frame is satin nickel.

NIB	Exc.	V.G.	Good	Fair	Poor
400	325	275	225	150	100

Thompson 1911 A1-Satin Nickel

Chambered for .45 ACP or .38 Super the finish is a satin nickel on both frame and slide. Blade front sight and black checkered plastic grips.

NIB	Exc.	V.G.	Good	Fair	Poor
400	325	275	225	150	100

Thompson 1911 A1-Competition

Chambered for .45 ACP or .38 Super the pistol is fitted with a 5" barrel with compensator and other competition features such as custom Commander hammer, flat mainspring hous-ing, beavertail grip safety, full length recoil guide rod, and ex-tended ejector, slide stop and thumb safety. Pistol weight 42 oz. and is 10" overall.

NIB	Exc.	V.G.	Good	Fair	Poor
600	525	400	350	300	150

NOTE: For .38 Super add $10 to above prices.

Thompson 1911 A1-Parkerized

NIB	Exc.	V.G.	Good	Fair	Poor
375	295	250	225	200	150

Thompson 1911 A1-Pit Bull

Chambered for .45 ACP and fitted with a 3-1/2" barrel this model has high profile sights and black textured rubber wrap-around grips. Magazine capacity is 7 rounds and weight is 36 oz.

NIB	Exc.	V.G.	Good	Fair	Poor
400	350	300	250	200	150

Thompson 1911 A1-General

This is a Commander size pistol with 4-1/2" barrel, high profile sights. Chambered for .45ACP or .38 Super. Weighs 37 oz.

NIB	Exc.	V.G.	Good	Fair	Poor
400	325	275	225	150	100

ZG-51 "Pit Bull"

Same as above, with a 3.5" barrel in .45 caliber. Introduced in 1988 and renamed "PIT BULL" in 1994.

NIB	Exc.	V.G.	Good	Fair	Poor
375	325	275	225	200	150

Thompson 1927 A1 Standard

A semiautomatic version of the Thompson submachine gun, chambered for the .45 ACP cartridge with a 16-1/2" barrel that is 18" with compensator. Blued with walnut stock. Weight is 13 lbs. Manufactured until 1986.

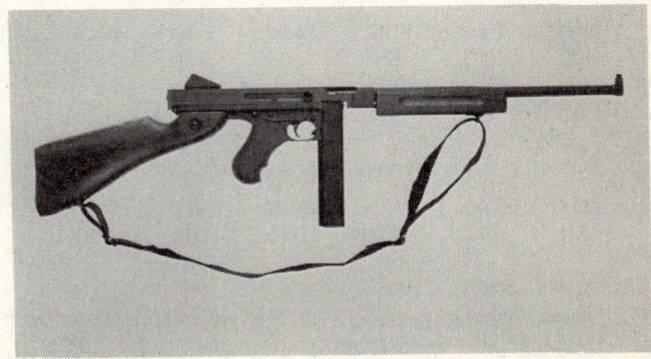

NIB	Exc.	V.G.	Good	Fair	Poor
550	450	300	250	200	150

1927 A1 Deluxe

As above, with a finned barrel, adjustable sights, pistol-grip forearm, and a 50-round drum magazine costing an additional $140. The violin-shaped carrying case adds approximately $115 to the values listed below.

NFA 1934 requires their registration and a $200 tax payment for each transfer of ownership.

The original wholesale price of each model was $525 ($750 retail). Their manufacture was discontinued in 1986, when the law was amended to prohibit the transfer or possession of any machine gun which was not registered on May 19, 1986. West Hurley Thompsons are considered "shooters" rather than collector's items, but their limited supply suggests there may be some collector potential, particularly for the M1 variation. Some early production Model 1928 guns may not be as well machined or hand fitted as the late-production ones. Current prices are approximate and will vary by local demand.

Model 1928 serial numbered from 100A (?) to 2700A (?)

Exc.	V.G.	Good	Fair	Poor
2,300	2,000	1,700	1,600	1,500

M1 serial numbered from M100A to M174A (609 manufactured)

Exc.	V.G.	Good	Fair	Poor
2,500	2,200	1,900	1,800	1,600

The Violent Crime Control and Law Enforcement Act of 1994 (Public Law 103-322) has affected the price and availability of magazines for Thompson submachine guns, to the extent they have a capacity of more than 10 rounds of ammunition, because the 1994 Act prohibits their manufacture in the United States. Standard 20-round magazines that once sold for $6 may command $20 or more. Pre-1994 Act prices for modern reproduction 50-round "L" and 100-round "C" drums, which were expensive to begin with, have experienced similar increases and cannot be reliably priced at this time.

NIB	Exc.	V.G.	Good	Fair	Poor
750	650	575	500	350	150

1927 A1C

As above, with an aluminum alloy receiver. Introduced in 1984.

NIB	Exc.	V.G.	Good	Fair	Poor
725	625	550	500	350	150

1927 A5

A reduced-size version of the Model 1927 A1 with a 13" finned barrel, aluminum alloy receiver and no shoulder stock.

NIB	Exc.	V. G.	Good	Fair	Poor
725	625	550	500	350	150

1927 A3

A .22 caliber variation of the Model 1927 A1 with a 16" barrel and aluminum alloy receiver. No longer in production.

NIB	Exc.	V.G.	Good	Fair	Poor
450	400	350	275	200	100

Thompson Submachine Gun NFA

Fully automatic reproductions of the .45 caliber Thompson Submachine Gun were manufactured during the 1980s by Auto Ordnance Corporation of West Hurley, New York, in Model 1928 and M1 variations. The M1 designation "is actually incorrect, as the guns are in the M1A1 Thompson configuration" (see "The West Hurley M1 Thompson SMG," by Frank Iannamico, *Machine Gun News*, June 1995, pages 40-42). All "West Hurley" Thompsons have the letter "A" suffix on the serial number and the West Hurley, New York address on the receivers' right side. The Model 1928 has a 10.5" finned barrel and Cutts compensator (which adds about an additional 2"); the M1 has a 10.5" unfinned barrel and no compensator. The

AUTO POINTER

Yamamoto Co.

Tokyo, Japan

Auto - Pointer Shotgun

A 12 or 20 gauge semiautomatic shotgun with 26", 28" or 30" barrels and an aluminum alloy frame. Blued with a checkered walnut stock. Originally imported by Sloan's but no longer available.

Exc.	V.G.	Good	Fair	Poor
350	250	200	150	100

AZPIRI

Eibar, Spain

Avion

A 6.35mm semiautomatic pistol copied after the model 1906 Browning. Marked "Pistolet Automatique Avion Brevete." Manufactured from 1914 to 1918.

Exc.	V.G.	Good	Fair	Poor
250	150	125	95	65

Colon

As above, in 6.35mm caliber and marked "Automatic Pistol Colon".

Exc.	V.G.	Good	Fair	Poor
200	125	100	75	50

B

B.R.F.
South Africa

B.R.F.
This is a .25 caliber semiautomatic pistol similar to the P.A.F. with a 2" barrel and 6 shot magazine. Little is known about the manufacturer of this pistol, its origins, or dates of manufacture.

Exc.	V.G.	Good	Fair	Poor
200	175	125	100	70

BSA GUNS LTD.
Birmingham, England
Birmingham Small Arms

Established in 1861, this firm has produced a wide variety of firearms over the years. The more common of these arms that are currently available in the United States are as follows:

SINGLE SHOT

No. 12 Cadet Martini
A .310 caliber single shot Martini action rifle with a 29" barrel, adjustable sights and straight-gripped walnut stock. Approximately 80,000 were manufactured from 1911 to 1913. Many of those imported into the United States were altered to .22 caliber.

Exc.	V.G.	Good	Fair	Poor
375	300	200	150	100

Centurian Match Rifle
As above, in .22 caliber with a 24" barrel, adjustable sights and a pistol-grip walnut stock.

Exc.	V.G.	Good	Fair	Poor
475	350	300	200	100

Model 13 Sporter
As above, in .22 Hornet with hunting sights.

Exc.	V.G.	Good	Fair	Poor
450	325	300	225	100

Martini International Match
As above, with a heavy match barrel, ISU style sights and a match stock. Manufactured from 1950 to 1953.

Exc.	V.G.	Good	Fair	Poor
450	375	325	250	125

Martini International Light
As above, with a 26" barrel of lighter weight.

Exc.	V.G.	Good	Fair	Poor
450	375	325	250	125

Martini International ISU
As above, meeting ISU specifications with a 28" barrel. Manufactured from 1968 to 1976.

Exc.	V.G.	Good	Fair	Poor
525	450	400	325	200

BOLT ACTIONS

Royal
A bolt-action sporting rifle manufactured in a variety of calibers and a 24" barrel, with a checkered French walnut stock.

Exc.	V.G.	Good	Fair	Poor
375	300	250	200	100

Majestic Deluxe
A .22 Hornet, .222, .243, 7x57mm, .308 or .30-06 bolt action sporting rifle with a 22" barrel, having a folding rear sight and a checkered walnut stock with a Schnabel forend tip. Imported from 1959 to 1965.

Exc.	V.G.	Good	Fair	Poor
375	300	250	200	100

Majestic Deluxe Featherweight
As above, in .270 or .458 Magnum with a thinner barrel.

Exc.	V.G.	Good	Fair	Poor
375	300	250	200	100

Monarch Deluxe
As above, drilled and tapped for telescopic sight and also available in a heavy barrelled varmint version in .222 or .243 caliber. Imported from 1966 to 1974.

Exc.	V.G.	Good	Fair	Poor
400	325	275	225	100

Herters U9
The firm of Herters, Inc. of Waseca, Minnesota, imported BSA rifle actions beginning in 1965 which were used for custom made rifles. Commencing in 1986, BSA began production of a new line of bolt action sporting rifles on the Model CF-2 action. The standard production models are as follows:

Sporter/Classic
A hunting rifle available in a variety of calibers with a checkered walnut stock. Introduced in 1986.

Exc.	V.G.	Good	Fair	Poor
375	325	275	200	100

Varminter
As above, with a matte-finished heavy barrel in .222, .22-250 or .243 caliber. Introduced in 1986.

Exc.	V.G.	Good	Fair	Poor
350	275	225	175	100

Stutzen Rifle
As above, with a 20.5" barrel and a Mannlicher style stock.

Exc.	V.G.	Good	Fair	Poor
400	350	275	225	100

Regal Custom

As above, with an engraved receiver, checkered walnut stock and an ebony forend. Imported only in 1986.

Exc.	V.G.	Good	Fair	Poor
850	750	600	500	250

CFT Target Rifle

A .308 caliber single shot version of the above with a 26.5" barrel and adjustable sights. Imported only in 1987.

Exc.	V.G.	Good	Fair	Poor
700	600	550	400	200

BABCOCK, MOSES
Charlestown, Massachusetts
Babcock Under Hammer Cane Gun

A .52 caliber percussion cane gun having a 27" barrel and overall length of approximately 33". Folding trigger, under hammer with a wood handle. The hammer is marked "Moses Babcock/Charlestown." Active 1850s and 1860s.

Exc.	V.G.	Good	Fair	Poor
550	400	300	250	125

BABBIT, A. S.
Plattsburgh, New York
SEE-Adirondack Arms

BACON ARMS CO.
Norwich, Connecticut

Bacon Arms operated from 1862 until 1891. They have become known primarily for the production of cheaply made, solid-frame, rim-fire revolvers known as "Suicide Specials." Bacon manufactured and sold under a number of different trademarks. They were: Bacon, Bonanza, Conqueror, Express, Gem, Governor, Guardian, and Little Giant. Collector interest is low, and values for all trademarks are quite similar.

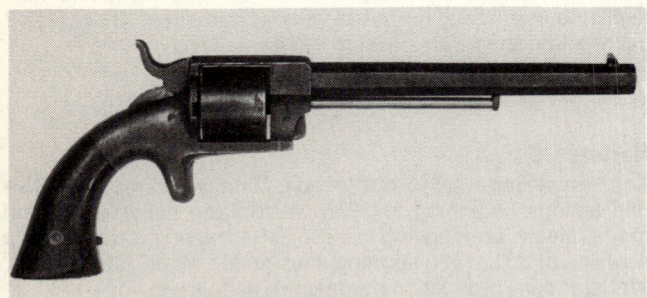

Courtesy Milwaukee Public Museum, Milwaukee, Wisconsin

Exc.	V.G.	Good	Fair	Poor
125	100	80	65	35

BAER CUSTOM, LES
Hillsdale, Ilinois

This long standing 1911 pistolsmith is now producing custom quality 1911 pistols on a semi-production basis. Each pistol features a large number of custom characteristics such as forged steel frame and full slide recoil rod, double serrated slide, beveled magazine well, checkered front strap, beavertail safety, extended magazine release button, Bo-Mar sights, and many others depending on the specififc model.

COMPETITION PISTOLS

Baer 1911 Ultimate Master Combat Pistol-Compensated

Chambered for the .45 ACP and fitted with a triple port, tapered cone compensator.

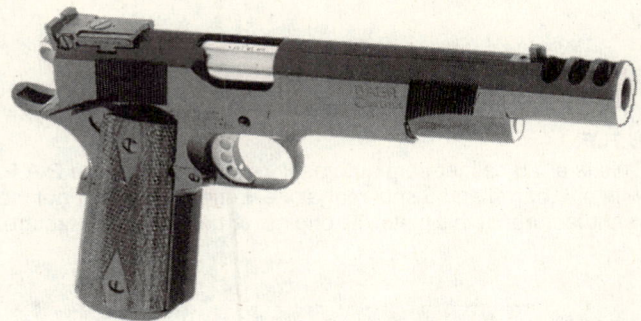

NIB	Exc.	V.G.	Good	Fair	Poor
2300	1750	1000	750	600	300

Baer 1911 Ultimate Master Steel Special

Designed for steel targets and Bianchi style competition this model is similar to above but designed for light loads. Chambered for .38 Super. Hard Chrome finish.

NIB	Exc.	V.G.	Good	Fair	Poor
2900	2250	1500	950	750	350

Baer 1911 Ultimate Master Combat Pistol

Similar to the other Baer Master series pistols this model is offered in .45 ACP, .400 COR-BON, and .38 Super. It is fitted with a large number of special features. Offered in a 5" or 6" version. The 5" version is also offered in 9x23 caliber.

6" Model

NIB	Exc.	V.G.	Good	Fair	Poor
2400	1900	1300	850	650	350

5" Model

NIB	Exc.	V.G.	Good	Fair	Poor
2500	1800	1200	800	600	350

Baer 1911 Ultimate Master Para

Designed for IPSC competition and offered either in Unlimited version with compensator and scope or Limited version with iron sights and no compensator.

Unlimited Model-.45ACP, .38 Super, 9x23

NIB	Exc.	V.G.	Good	Fair	Poor
3200	2500	1750	1200	850	400

Limited Model-.45ACP, .38 Super, 9x23

NIB	Exc.	V.G.	Good	Fair	Poor
2700	2000	1500	900	650	300

Baer 1911 IPSC Action Pistol

Chambered for .45ACP with blued slide and frame.

NIB	Exc.	V.G.	Good	Fair	Poor
1500	1150	850	600	450	300

Baer 1911 Nationale Match Hardball Pistol

Designed for DCM matches. Chambered for .45 ACP

NIB	Exc.	V.G.	Good	Fair	Poor
1225	900	700	500	400	200

Baer 1911 Bullseye Wadcutter Pistol

Designed for use with wadcutter loads only. Chambered for .45 ACP.

NIB	Exc.	V.G.	Good	Fair	Poor
1500	1100	800	600	500	250

NOTE: This version is also offered with a Baer Optical mount. Add $125 for this option. For a 6" slide with LoMount BoMars sight add $200.

Baer 1911 Target Master

Designed for NRA centerfire matches. Chambered for .45ACP

NIB	Exc.	V.G.	Good	Fair	Poor
1250	1000	750	550	450	250

DUTY & DEFENSE PISTOLS

Baer 1911 Premier II

Designed as a duty or defense pistol this model is chambered for the .45 ACP, .400 COR-BON, and 9x23 cartridges. Fitted with a 5" slide.

NIB	Exc.	V.G.	Good	Fair	Poor
1425	1150	900	600	450	250

NOTE: For stainless steel version add $150 to above prices. Add $100 for .400 COR-BON and $250 for 9x23.

Baer 1911 Premier II-6" barrel

Same as above but fitted with a 6" match grade barrel.

NIB	Exc.	V.G.	Good	Fair	Poor
1700	1450	1100	900	700	350

NOTE: Add $100 for .400 COR-BON and $300 for .38 Super. 9x23 not offered with 6" slide.

Baer 1911 Custom Carry-Commanche Length

Chambered for .45ACP this model has several options including 4-1/2" barrel, stainless steel slide and frame, lightweight aluminum frame with blued steel slide.

NIB	Exc.	V.G.	Good	Fair	Poor
1640	1200	950	600	450	250

NOTE: For stainless steel add $40. For lightweight frame add $130.

Baer Custom Carry-5"

Same as above but offered with 5" slide. Not offered in aluminum frame.

NIB	Exc.	V.G.	Good	Fair	Poor
1620	1200	950	600	450	250

NOTE: Add $40 for stainless steel.

Baer 1911 Prowler III

Similar to the Premier II but with a tapered cone stub weight, a full length guide rod, and a reverse plug.

NIB	Exc.	V.G.	Good	Fair	Poor
1800	1500	1200	950	700	350

Baer 1911 Prowler IV

Chambered for .45ACP or .38 Super this model is built on a Para-Ordnance oversize frame . Fitted with a 5" slide.

NIB	Exc.	V.G.	Good	Fair	Poor
2300	1750	1250	900	650	300

NOTE: For optional 6" barrel and slide add $300.

Baer S.R.P.(Swift Response Pistol)

Chambered for .45ACP and built on a Para-Ordnance frame this unit is similar to the one supplied to the FBI. Supplied with wooden presentation box.

NIB	Exc.	V.G.	Good	Fair	Poor
2800	2350	1750	1200	850	400

NOTE: For S.R.P. models built on a Baer frame or shorter 4-1/2" frame subtract $300 from NIB through Fair prices.

NEW CONCEPTS PISTOLS

This line of 1911 pistols offers custom features at a slightly lower cost. Each succeeding grade offers a few more features.

Baer 1911 Concept I

Chambered for .45ACP and fitted with Bo-Mar sights.

NIB	Exc.	V.G.	Good	Fair	Poor
1400	1150	900	750	550	300

Baer 1911 Concept II

Same as above but fitted with Baer adjustable sights.

NIB	Exc.	V.G.	Good	Fair	Poor
1400	1150	900	750	550	300

Baer 1911 Concept III

Same as above but with stainless steel frame with blued steel slide with Bo-Mar sights.

NIB	Exc.	V.G.	Good	Fair	Poor
1520	1250	950	800	550	300

Baer 1911 Concept IV

Same as above but with Baer adjustable sights.

NIB	Exc.	V.G.	Good	Fair	Poor
1500	1250	950	800	550	300

Baer 1911 Concept V

This model has both stainless steel slide and frame with Bo-Mar sights.

NIB	Exc.	V.G.	Good	Fair	Poor
1550	1350	1000	850	600	300

Baer 1911 Concept VI

Same as above but fitted with Baer adjustable sights.

NIB	Exc.	V.G.	Good	Fair	Poor
1550	1350	1000	850	600	300

Baer 1911 Concept VII

Features all blued 4-1/2" steel frame and slide with Baer adjustable sights.

NIB	Exc.	V.G.	Good	Fair	Poor
1500	1250	950	800	550	300

Baer 1911 Concept VIII

Same as above but with stainless steel slide and frame.

NIB	Exc.	V.G.	Good	Fair	Poor
1550	1350	1000	850	600	300

Baer 1911 Concept IX

This version has a lightweight aluminum frame with 4-1/2" steel slide.

NIB	Exc.	V.G.	Good	Fair	Poor
1600	1350	1000	850	600	300

Baer 1911 Concept X

This model featurs a 4-1/2" stainless steel slide with a lightweight aluminum frame.

NIB	Exc.	V.G.	Good	Fair	Poor
1600	1350	1000	850	600	300

Baer Lightweight .22 caliber 1911 Models

4-1/2" Model with fixed sights

NIB	Exc.	V.G.	Good	Fair	Poor
1425	1200	950	800	550	300

5" Model with fixed sights

NIB	Exc.	V.G.	Good	Fair	Poor
1425	1200	950	800	550	300

5" Model with Bo-Mar sights

NIB	Exc.	V.G.	Good	Fair	Poor
1500	1275	1000	850	600	300

BAFORD, ARMS, INC.
Bristol, Tennessee
C.L. Reedy & Assoc.-Distributors
Melbourne, Florida

Thunder Derringer

A .410 bore or .44 Special single shot pistol with 3" interchangeable barrels and a spur trigger. Additional interchangeable barrels are chambered in calibers from .22 to 9mm. Also available with a scope. Blued with a walnut grip. Introduced in 1988.

NIB	Exc.	V.G.	Good	Fair	Poor
130	100	85	70	55	35

NOTE: Add $100 for interchangeable barrel.

Fire Power Model 35

A 9mm semiautomatic pistol with a 4.75" barrel, Millett adjustable sights and 14-shot magazine. Fitted with a combat safety and hammer, and Pachmayr grips. Stainless steel. Introduced in 1988.

NIB	Exc.	V.G.	Good	Fair	Poor
475	425	350	300	250	125

BAIKAL
U.S.S.R.
Commercial Trading Imports
Bloomington, Minnesota

Baikal IJ-27E1C

A 12 or 20 gauge Magnum O/U shotgun with 26" skeet-skeet or 28" modified-full ventilated rib barrels, single selective trigger and extractors. Blued with a walnut stock.

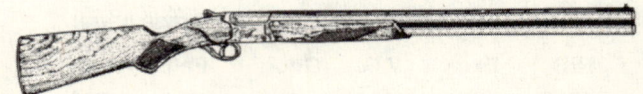

Mfg. List Price
$449.95

NIB	Exc.	V.G.	Good	Fair	Poor
350	275	200	150	100	75

Baikal TOZ - 34

A 12 or 28 gauge double-barrel shotgun with 26" or 28" barrels, double triggers, cocking indicators and extractors. Blued with a checkered walnut stock. This model was also available with a silver-plated receiver.

Mfg. List Price
$465.95

NIB	Exc.	V.G.	Good	Fair	Poor
375	300	250	200	100	75

Model MC-8-0

A 12 gauge double barrel shotgun with 26" skeet-skeet or 28" full-modified barrels, hand fitted action and engraved receiver.

Mfg. List Price
$2,295.00

NIB	Exc.	V.G.	Good	Fair	Poor
1800	1250	950	700	500	250

Model MC-5-105

The Model TOZ-34 with an engraved receiver.

Mfg. List Price
$1,325.00

NIB	Exc.	V.G.	Good	Fair	Poor
1050	850	700	500	300	150

Model MC-7

As above, with a relief engraved receiver.

Mfg. List Price
$2,695.00

NIB	Exc.	V.G.	Good	Fair	Poor
2100	1750	1200	800	550	250

Model MC-109

A custom made O/U shotgun with detachable sidelocks. Produced in limited quantities and most often to the purchaser's specifications.

Mfg. List Price
$3,695.00

NIB	Exc.	V.G.	Good	Fair	Poor
2850	2000	1500	950	600	300

BAILONS GUNMAKERS, LTD.
Birmingham, England

Most of the products of this company are produced strictly on custom order.

Hunting Rifle

A bolt-action sporting rifle produced in a variety of calibers with a 24" barrel having open sights, double-set triggers and a 3- or 4-shot magazine. Blued with a well figured walnut stock. The values listed below are for a standard grade rifle.

NIB	Exc.	V.G.	Good	Fair	Poor
1850	1500	1150	900	600	300

BAKER GAS SEAL
London, England

A .577 caliber percussion revolver with a 6.5" octagonal barrel and 6-shot cylinder. When the hammer is cocked, the cylinder is forced forward tightly against the barrel breech, thus creating a gas seal. Blued, case-hardened with walnut grips.

Exc.	V.G.	Good	Fair	Poor
900	700	600	475	250

BAKER GUN & FORGING CO.
Batavia, New York

The Baker Gun & Forging Company was founded in early 1890, by Elias Baker, brothr of William Baker (see below). Made from drop forged parts, Baker single and double barrel shotguns quickly gained a reputation for strength and reliabil-

ity among shooters of the period. Offered in a wide variety of grades, from plain utilitarian to heavily embellished models, Baker shotguns have in recent years become highly collectable. The company was sold on December 24, 1919, to H. & D. Folsom Arms Company of Norwich, Connecticut. The Folsom company had for almost 20 years been the Baker company's sole New york City agent and had marketed at least one Baker model that was only made for them. From 1919 to approximately 1923, Folsom continued to assemble and make Baker shotguns.

The Baker Gun & Forging Company was the first American arms manufacturer to:

1. Make a single barrel trap shotgun.

2. Make a single barrel trap shotgun with a ventilated rib.

3. Make arms with an intercepting firing pin block safety.

4. Make a double barrel shotgun with hammers directly behind the firing pins.

5. Use a long swinging sear that once adjusted gave consistent trigger pull throughout the working life of an arm.

Those Baker shotguns manufactured between 1913 and 1923 that were engraved by Rudolph J. Kornbrath command substantial price premiums over the values listed below. prospective purchasers of Kornbrath decorated Bakers are advised to secure a qualified appraisal prior to acquisition.

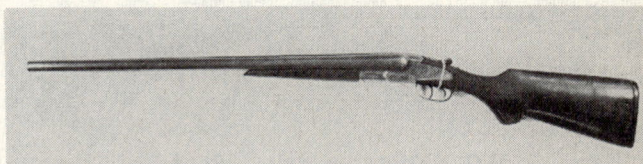

Baker Trap Gun

A 12, gauge single barrel boxlock shotgun with either a 30" or 32" barrel. Blued, case-hardened with a walnut stock.

Exc.	V.G.	Good	Fair	Poor
1500	1250	900	500	250

Elite Grade (standard scrollwork and simple game scenes engraved on receiver)

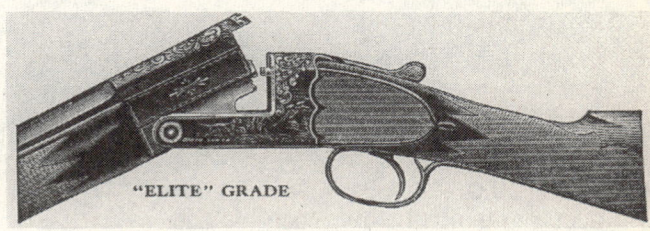

Exc.	V.G.	Good	Fair	Poor
2000	1500	1000	500	250

Superba (heavily engraved on receiver and sides of barrel breech)

Exc.	V.G.	Good	Fair	Poor
4000	3000	1500	750	500

Black Beauty Double Shotgun

Made solely for H. & D. Folsom Arms Company. A 12 or 16 gauge double barrel shotgun with sidelocks and 26", 28", 30", or 32" barrels in 12 gauge and 26", 28", or 30" barrels in 16 gauge. the barrels blued, the receiver casehardened, the sideplates finished with black oxide and the stock of walnut. Automatic ejectors and single trigger extra cost options.

Exc.	V.G.	Good	Fair	Poor
850	750	650	500	250

Grade S Double Shotgun

As above, with simple engraving.

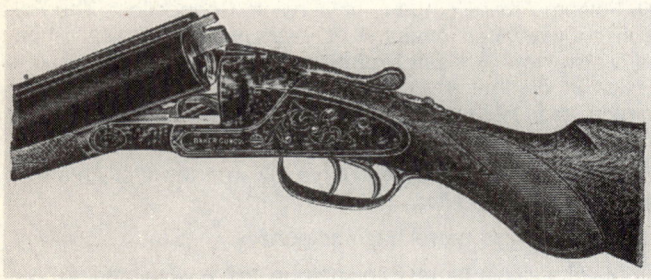

Exc.	V.G.	Good	Fair	Poor
1200	1000	750	400	250

Grade R Double Shotgun

As above, with casehardened sideplates and engraved with simple scrollwork as well as game scenes.

Exc.	V.G.	Good	Fair	Poor
1500	1250	900	500	300

Paragon Grade Shotgun

As above, with finely cut scrollwork and detailed game scenes engraved on the sideplates. The stock of inely figured walnut.

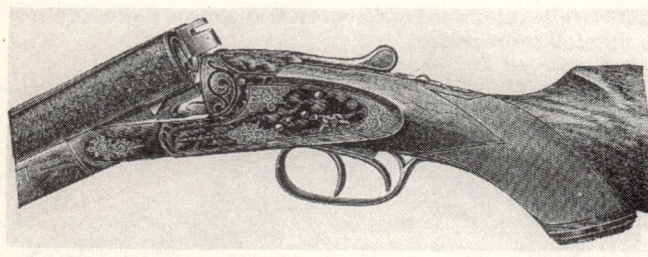

Exc.	V.G.	Good	Fair	Poor
2000	1750	1200	900	500

Paragon Grade - Model NN

As above, but more finely engraved. Built on special order only. Automatic ejectors.

Exc.	V.G.	Good	Fair	Poor
3000	2250	1400	900	500

Expert Grade Double Shotgun

The highest grade shotgun manufactured by the Baker Gun & Forging Company. General specifications as above. The stock of imported English or French walnut. The engraving of full coverage type and partially chiselled. Automatic ejectors and single trigger if requested. Built on special order only.

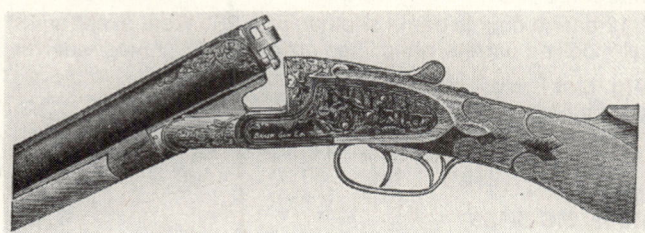

Exc.	V.G.	Good	Fair	Poor
5000	4000	2000	1500	750

Deluxe Grade Double Shotgun

The designation given those Expert Grade shotguns produced by H. & D. Folsom from 1919 to 1923. Characteristics and values identical to those listed for the Baker Expert grade Double Shotgun.

Batavia Special

A 12 or 16 gauge double barrel shotgun with sidelocks and 28", 30", or 32" barrels in 12 gauge and 28" or 30" barrels in 16 gauge. Blue, casehardened with a walnut stock and double triggers.

Exc.	V.G.	Good	Fair	Poor
500	325	275	225	175

Batavia Brush Gun

A 12 or 16 gauge double barrel shotgun with sidelocks and 26" barrels. Blue, casehardened with walnut stock. Sling rings and swivels optional.

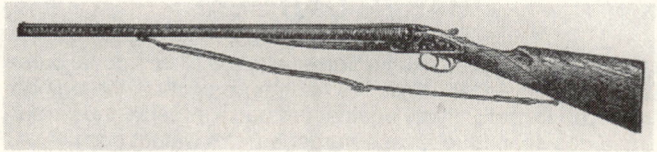

Exc.	V.G.	Good	Fair	Poor
400	325	275	225	175

Batavia Leader

A 12 or 16 gauge double barrel shotgun with sidelocks and 26", 28", 30", or 32" barrels in 12 gauge and 26", 28", or 30" barrels in 16 gauge. Blue, casehardened with a walnut stock and double triggers.

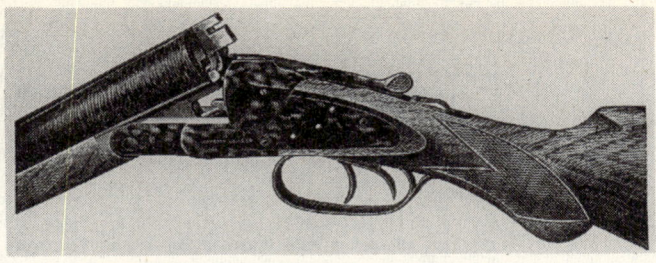

Exc.	V.G.	Good	Fair	Poor
500	425	375	325	275

Batavia Damascus

As above with Damascus barrels.

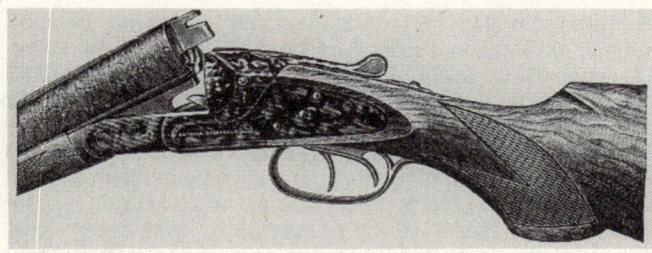

Exc.	V.G.	Good	Fair	Poor
400	325	275	225	175

Baker Hammer Gun

A 10, 12, or 16 gauge double barrel shotgun with sidehammers and 30" and 32" barrels in 10 gauge, 26" to 32" barrels in 12 gauge and 26" to 30" barrels in 16 gauge. Browned, casehardened with walnut stock and double triggers.

Baker Hammer Gun—Twist Barrels

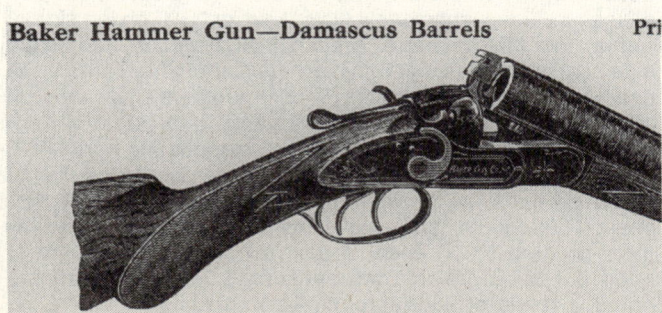

Baker Hammer Gun—Damascus Barrels

Exc.	V.G.	Good	Fair	Poor
300	250	175	125	100

Batavia Automatic Rifle

A .22 caliber semiautomatic rifle with a 24" round barrel and a detachable 7-shot magazine. Blue with a walnut stock.

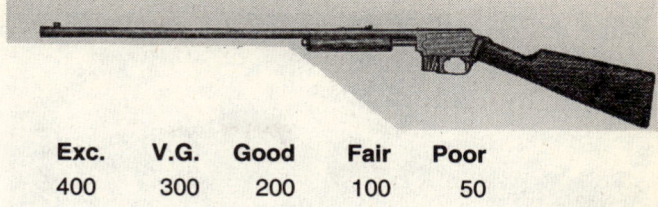

Exc.	V.G.	Good	Fair	Poor
400	300	200	100	50

BAKER, WILLIAM
Marathon, Syracuse and Ithaca, New York

William Baker designed and built double barrel shotguns from approximately 1869 until his death in 1889. His hammerless designs were used by the Baker Gun & Forging Company of Batavia, New York, which was established by his brother Elias in early 1890.

BAKER, M.A.
Fayetteville, North Carolina

In business from 1857 through 1862, Baker produced sporting arms prior to the Civil War. During the Civil War Baker altered muskets and "common rifles." In addition, it is thought that Baker made rifles for the State of North Carolina with lockplates stamped M.A. BAKER/FAYETTEVILLE/N.C. These rifles resembled the U.S. Model 1841 Rifle and had the following characteristics: Overall length 51-1/2"; Barrel length 35-1/8"; Caliber .50. Number made in excess of 65. Prospective purchasers are strongly advised to secure a qualified appraisal prior to acquisition.

Exc.	V.G.	Good	Fair	Poor
—	7000	3500	2000	1000

BAKER, THOMAS

Baker shotguns and rifles were extensively imported into the United States during the nineteenth and early twentieth centuries. As these arms are often marked with his address, the following list of the London premises he occupied should prove useful.

1 Stonecutter Street	1838-1844
Bury Street, St. Jame's	1844-1850
34 St. James's Street	1850
88 Fleet Street	1851-1881
88 Fleet Street & 21 Cockspur Street	1882-1898
88 Fleet Street & 29 Glasshouse Street	1899-1905
29 Glasshouse Street	1905-1915
64 Haymarket	1915

BALL REPEATING CARBINE
Lamson & Co.
Windsor, Vermont

Ball Repeating Carbine

A .50 caliber lever-action repeating carbine with a 20.5" round barrel and 7-shot magazine. The receiver is marked "E.G. Lamson & Co./Windsor, Vt./U.S./Ball's Patent/June 23, 1863/Mar. 15, 1864." Blued, case-hardened with a walnut stock. Late production examples of this carbine have been noted with browned or bright barrels. In excess of 1,500 were made between 1864 and 1867.

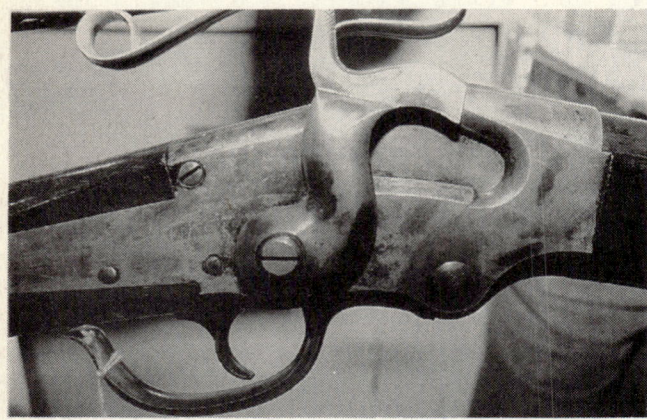

Courtesy Milwaukee Public Museum, Milwaukee, Wisconsin

Exc.	V.G.	Good	Fair	Poor
—	5000	2500	750	400

BALLARD PATENT ARMS
(until 1873; after 1875, see MARLIN)

On Nov. 5, 1861, C.H. Ballard of Worcester, Massachusetts, received a patent for a breechloading mechanism that would remain in production for nearly thirty years. Ballard patented a breechblock that tilted down at its front to expose the breech by activating the lever/triggerguard. During the twelve years that followed, Ballard rifles, carbines, and shotguns were produced by five interrelated companies. Four of these were successive: Ball & Williams, R. Ball & Co. (both of Worcester, Massachusetts), Merrimack Arms & Manufacturing Co. and Brown Manufacturing Company (both of Newburyport, Massachusetts). These four companies produced Ballard arms in a successive serial range (1 through approximately 22,000), all marked upon the top of the frame and the top of the barrel where it joins the frame. In 1863, another company, Dwight, Chapin & Company of Bridgeport, Connecticut also produced Ballard rifles and carbines in a larger frame size, but in a different serial range (1 through about 1,900), usually marked on the left side of the frame below the agents' mark. The large frame carbines and rifles were produced to fulfill a U.S. War Department contract initially for 10,000 of each, subsequently reduced to 1,000 of each, issued to Merwin & Bray, the sole agents for the Ballard patent arms between 1862 and 1866. Most of the production during this period concentrated on military contracts, either for the U.S. War Department or the state of Kentucky, although the state of New York also purchased 500 for its state militia.

Ballard (Ball & Williams) sporting rifles, first type. (Serial numbers 1-100)

Barrel length 24"; caliber .38 rimfire. Markings: BALL & WILLIAMS/Worcester, Mass., and BALLARD'S PATENT/Nov. 5, 1861 on octagonal barrel. The distinctive feature of the earliest production of the Ballard rifles is the presence of an internal extractor conforming to the patent specifications. After approximately 100 rifles, this feature was dropped in favor of a manual extractor located under the barrel.

Courtesy Milwaukee Public Museum, Milwaukee, Wisconsin

Exc.	V.G.	Good	Fair	Poor
1500	1200	1000	800	450

Ballard (Ball & Williams) sporting rifles, second type. (Serial numbers 200-1600, and 1600 through 14,000, interspersed with martial production)

Barrel length 24", 28", or 30", usually octagonal, but part round/part-octagonal as well; calibers .32, .38, and .44 rimfire. Markings: BALL & WILLIAMS/Worcester, Mass., BALLARD'S PATENT/Nov. 5, 1861, and MERWIN & BRAY, AGT'S/ NEW YORK, on facets of barrel until about serial no. 9000, thereafter the patent name and date on the right side of the frame and the manufacturer and agents on the left side of the frame. On early production (200 to 1500), the extractor knob is smaller and crescent shaped. Early production (prior to about serial no. 10,000) have solid breechblocks; after that number breechblocks are made in two halves. A few of these arms were made with bronze frames to facilitate engraving and plating. These should command a higher premium.

Exc.	V.G.	Good	Fair	Poor
800	700	500	350	200

Ballard (Ball & Williams) sporting rifles, third type. (Serial numbers 14,000 to 15,000)

These arms are essentially the same as the second type in characteristics but have Merwin & Bray's alternate percussion mechanism built into the breechblock. The hammer is accordingly marked on the left side "PATENTED JAN. 5, 1864."

Exc.	V.G.	Good	Fair	Poor
800	700	500	350	200

Ballard (Ball & Williams) military carbines. (Serial numbers 1500 through 7500, and 8500 through 10,500)

Overall length 37-1/4"; barrel (bore) length 22"; caliber .44 rimfire. Markings: same as Ballard/Ball & Williams sporting rifles, second type. Additional marks on U.S. War Department purchases include inspector's initials "MM" or "GH" on left side of frame, and "MM" on barrel, breechblock, buttplate, and on left side of buttstock in script within an oval cartouche. Three thousand of the earlier production (serial numbers 1700 through about 5000) of these carbines were sold to the state of Kentucky under an August 1862 contract, extended in April 1863. In November 1863, Kentucky contracted for an additional 1,000 carbines. In the interim, the state of New York purchased 500 for distribution to its militia. The U.S. War Department ordered 5,000 under a contract signed in January of 1864, but Ball & Williams delivered only 1,500 (serial numbers noted in range of 9800 through 10,600) while concentrating production on their more lucrative Kentucky contract. Another 600 of the federal contract were partially inspected (serial numbers about 6500 to 7100-MM in cartouche in stock only) but were rejected because the barrels had been rifled prior to proofing; these were sold to Kentucky in September 1864 on an open market purchase. The carbines marked with federal inspection marks usually bring a premium.

Courtesy Milwaukee Public Museum, Milwaukee, Wisconsin

Exc.	V.G.	Good	Fair	Poor
650	500	400	350	250

Ballard (Ball & Williams) "Kentucky" half-stock rifles

Overall length 45 3/8"; barrel (bore) length 30"; caliber .44 rimfire. These half-stock rifles bear the standard Ball & Williams markings upon their barrels and in addition have the state ownership mark ("KENTUCKY") on the barrel forward of the rear sights. A total of 1,000 (serial numbers about 7100 through 8550) were contracted for by Kentucky in November 1863 and delivered between January and April 1864.

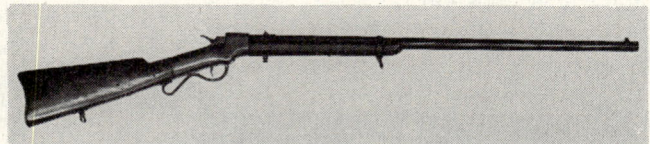

Courtesy Milwaukee Public Museum, Milwaukee, Wisconsin

Exc.	V.G.	Good	Fair	Poor
700	600	450	375	275

Ballard (Ball & Williams) "Kentucky" full stock rifles

Overall length 45-1/4"; barrel (bore) length 30"; caliber .46 rimfire. Marked on the frame with standard Ball & Williams manufacturer (left), agent (left), and patent (right) markings, these rifles are additionally distinguished by the state ownership mark "KENTUCKY" stamped into the top of the frame near the breech. Kentucky contracted for 3,000 of these arms in November 1863, initially in .56 caliber. However, by mutual consent of the state and the contractors, in February 1864 the caliber of the arms was changed to .46. All deliveries were made in this caliber, beginning in July 1864 and continuing until March 1865 (serial numbers 10,400 to 14,500).

Courtesy Milwaukee Public Museum, Milwaukee, Wisconsin

Exc.	V.G.	Good	Fair	Poor
700	600	475	350	250

Ballard (Dwight, Chapin & Co.) carbines

Overall length 37-3/4"; barrel (bore) length 22"; caliber .56 rimfire. Markings: On left side of round-topped frame "BALLARD'S PATENT/NOV. 5 1861"; on right side of frame "DWIGHT, CHAPIN & CO./BRIDGEPORT CONN." (through serial no. about 125, deleted after that number) over "MERWIN & BRAY/AGT'S N.Y." over serial no. Inspection letters "D" frequently appear on carbines with the Dwight, Chapin, & Co. markings, indicative of preliminary inspection by E. M. Dustin, of the U.S. Ordnance Department.

Often mistaken as early Ballard production from a fictitious Fall River, Massachusetts factory, these carbines and their complementing rifles were in fact not placed into production until 1863, as evident by the split, two-piece breechblocks. Both carbines and rifles originated from a contract entered into between the U.S. War Department and Merwin & Bray in October 1862 for 10,000 of each arm, subsequently reduced to 1,000 of each by the Commission on Ordnance and Ordnance Stores. Because Ball & Williams facilities were tied up with Kentucky contracts, Merwin & Bray turned to the small parts maker of Dwight, Chapin & Co. in Bridgeport, Connecticut. Although they tooled for production, they fell short of scheduled delivery dates, and although about 100 carbines had been inspected, no deliveries were accepted (due to caliber problems) by the U.S. government, effectively bankrupting Dwight, Chapin & Co. The completed carbines and unfinished parts were sent to Worcester and assembled by Ball & Williams, and Merwin & Bray sold all 1,000 carbines in Kentucky in April 1864 on an open market purchase.

Courtesy Milwaukee Public Museum, Milwaukee, Wisconsin

Exc.	V.G.	Good	Fair	Poor
700	600	450	350	275

Ballard (Dwight, Chapin & Co.) full-stock rifle

Overall length 53"; barrel (bore) length 30"; caliber .56 rimfire. Markings: same as Dwight, Chapin & Co. carbines, but none found with "DWIGHT, CHAPIN & CO./BRIDGEPORT, CONN." stamping above agents marks. The history of these rifles is the same as the .56 caliber carbines, with serial numbers interspersed in the production of the carbines (1 through 1850). Evidently only about 650 of the rifles were completed of the 1,000 set up. Of these, 35 were sold to a U.S. agent in Florida in February 1864 and 600 to Kentucky in April 1864 with the 1,000 carbines.

Exc.	V.G.	Good	Fair	Poor
800	700	500	400	300

Ballard (R. Ball) & Co. sporting rifles

Overall length varies according to barrel length; barrel (bore) length usually 24", 28", and 30"; calibers .32, .38, .44, and .46 rimfire. Markings: The frame markings of R. Ball & Co. rifles are similar to Ball & Williams production, only eliminating the Ball & Williams marking on the left side. Cartridge size, e.g. "No. 44", usually also stamped upon the top of the barrel or frame. Merwin & Bray's patented alternate ignition device usually present with left side of hammer usually marked "PATENTED JAN. 5, 1864." Serial numbers (which follow in sequence with Ball & Williams production. i.e. after no. about 15,800) appear on top of barrel and top of frame. After William Williams withdrew from the Ball & Williams partnership in mid-1865, the business continued under the name of R. Ball & Co., with Richard Ball's son-in-law, E.J. Halstead, in charge after the former's paralytic stroke in the fall of 1865.

Ballard (R. Ball) & Co. carbines

Overall length 37-1/4"; barrel (bore) length 22" caliber .44 rimfire. Markings: same as R. Ball & Co. sporting rifles; "No. 44" on top of frame near breech. Although firm evidence is elusive, approximately 1,000 of these carbines were manufactured in anticipation of a Canadian contract, which never came to fruition. Serial numbers are interspersed with sporting rifles, in the

16,400 through 17,700 range. All are equipped with the Merwin & Bray dual ignition block.

Exc.	V.G.	Good	Fair	Poor
600	500	400	300	250

Ballard (Merrimack Arms & Manufacturing Co.) sporting rifles

Overall length varies with barrel length; usual barrel lengths 24", 28", 30"; calibers .22, .32, .44, .46, .50 rimfire. Markings: left side of frame marked with both manufacturing and patent marks, "MERRIMACK ARMS & MFG. CO./NEWBURYPORT, MASS." over "BALLARD'S PATENT/ NOV. 5, 1861". Caliber usually marked on top of barrel or frame, e.g. "No. 38" together with serial no. Left side of hammer marked "PATENTED JAN. 5, 1864" if breech fitted with Merwin & Bray's alternate ignition device. In the spring of 1866, Edward Bray of Brooklyn, New York, and former partner of Joseph Merwin purchased the Ballard machinery from R. Ball & Co. and set up a new plant in Newburyport, Massachusetts, primarily for the production of sporting rifles. The glut of surplus arms on the market following the American Civil War, however, forced him into bankruptcy in early 1869, after producing only about 2,000 Ballard rifles, carbines and a limited number of 20 gauge shotguns. Serial numbers continue in the sequence of the Ball & Williams/R. Ball & Co. production (serial numbers about 18,000 through 20,300). Prices of these rifles will vary considerably depending on the degree of finish or engraving.

Exc.	V.G.	Good	Fair	Poor
1500	1200	900	400	275

Ballard (Merrimack Arms & Manufacturing Co.) carbines

Overall length 37-1/4"; barrel (bore) length 22"; caliber .44 rimfire. Markings: same as Merrimack Arms & Mfg. Co. sporting rifles. In March 1866, the state of New York purchased 100 Ballard carbines (serial numbers about 18,500 to 18,600) for use by its prison guards. In January 1870, an additional 70 (serial numbers 19,400 to 19,500) were purchased from New York City arms merchants Merwin, Hulbert & Co. to arm guards at Sing Sing Prison. Between these two purchases Merrimack Arms & Mfg. Co. had shortened its new "tangless" frames by 1/8", the prime distinction between the two purchases. Despite the rarity of both types of carbines, they do not command high prices.

Exc.	V.G.	Good	Fair	Poor
500	400	350	275	200

Ballard (Brown Manufacturing Co.) sporting rifles

Dimensions: same as Merrimack Arms & Mfg. Co. sporting rifles. Markings: left side of frame marked with manufacturer, "BROWN MFG. CO. NEWBURYPORT, MASS." over patent, "BALLARD'S PATENT/ NOV. 5, 1861." Serial no. on top of barrel and frame. Upon the failure of Merrimack Arms & Manufacturing Company in early 1869, the plant was purchased by John Hamilton Brown, who continued producing Ballard patent rifles until 1873 in a serial range consecutive with that of its three predecessors (Ball & Williams, R. Ball & Co., and Merrimack Arms & Mfg. Co.) Approximately 2,000 Ballard arms were produced during the period of Brown's manufacture of the Ballard (serial numbers about 20,325 through 22,100). Brown made Ballards tend to exhibit finer finishing than earlier produced rifles, accounting for their average higher value. Special features, such as breakdown facility and side extractors (on .22 cal. rifles) will also positively affect the prices.

Exc.	V.G.	Good	Fair	Poor
1500	1250	850	450	275

Ballard (Brown Mfg. Co.) full-stock military rifles

Overall length 52-1/2" barrel (bore) length 30"; caliber .46 rimfire. Markings: The same as Brown Mfg. Co. sporting rifles, with the addition of the caliber marking, "No. 46", on the top of the barrel forward of the rear sight. The cause for the production of the Ballard/Brown military rifle has yet to be determined, but it has been speculated that they were possibly manufactured in anticipation of a sale to France during the Franco-Prussian War. In any event, the sale was not culminated, and many, if not most, of the estimated 1,000 produced were "sporterized" by shortening the forestock and sold by commercial dealers in the United States. Serial numbers concentrate in the 20,500 through 21,600 range, with sporting rifles interspersed in the sequence. Rifles that have not been sporterized command a premium.

Exc.	V.G.	Good	Fair	Poor
600	475	375	300	200

BALLARD, C. H.
Worcester, Massachusetts

Single Shot Derringer

A .41 caliber rimfire spur trigger single shot pistol with a 2.75" barrel marked "Ballard's". Blued with silver-plated frame and walnut grips. Manufactured during the 1870s.

Iron Frame Model-Add 25%.

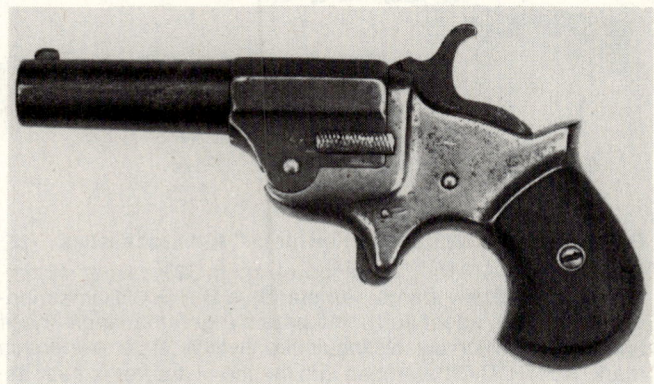

Exc.	V.G.	Good	Fair	Poor
1750	950	450	200	100

BALLESTER—MOLINA
SEE-Hafdasa

BARNETT
SEE-English Military Firearms

BARRET F.A. MFG. CO.
Murfreesboro, Tennessee

Model 82 Rifle

A .50 caliber Browning semiautomatic rifle with a 37" barrel and 11-shot magazine. The barrel fitted with a muzzle brake, and the receiver with a telescope. Approximate weight 35 lbs. Parkerized. Manufactured from 1985 to 1987.

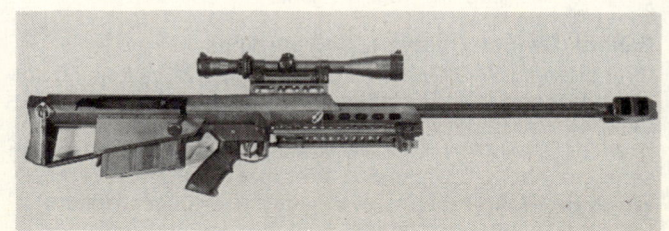

NIB	Exc.	V.G.	Good	Fair	Poor
4200	3500	2750	2250	1750	1000

Model 82Al

As above, with a 29" barrel without sights, and a 10 round magazine. A 10X telescope and iron sights are optional. Comes with hard carrying case. Weight is 28.5 lbs.

NIB	Exc.	V.G.	Good	Fair	Poor
6500	5200	4000	2750	2000	1000

Model 95

Introduced in 1995 this .50 caliber BMG bolt action model features a 29" barrel and 5 round magazine. Scope optional. Weight is 22 lbs.

NIB	Exc.	V.G.	Good	Fair	Poor
4500	4000	3000	2000	1000	500

BARRETT, J. B. and A.B. & CO.
Wytheville, Virginia

Barrett Muskets and Rifled Muskets

Overall length 57-3/4"; barrel length 41-1/2" - 42"; caliber .69. Markings: Although the Barretts placed no marks of their own on their alterations, most were effected on Virginia Manufactory muskets, whose lockplates are marked "VIRGINIA/Manufactory" forward of the hammer and "RICHMOND/(date)" on the tail.

For many years collectors considered the adaptations of Hall rifles and carbines from breechloaders to muzzleloaders to be the product of J.B. Barrett & Co. of Wytheville. Recent evidence, however, confirms that those adaptations were actually effected in Danville, Virginia, by another firm (see READ & WATSON). Nevertheless, the Barretts of Wytheville did adapt arms during the early years of the American Civil War. The adaptation, effected almost exclusively upon Virginia Manufactory flintlock muskets consisted of percussioning by means of the cone-in-barrel and rifling of the barrels with seven narrow grooves. In 1861 and 1862, the Barretts percussioned a total of 1250 muskets, of which 744 were rifled.

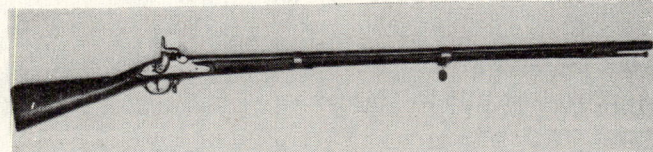

Courtesy Milwaukee Public Museum, Milwaukee, Wisconsin

Exc.	V.G.	Good	Fair	Poor
—	—	8000	3500	1000

BAR-STO PRECISION MACHINE
Burbank, California

Bar-Sto 25

A .25 caliber semiautomatic pistol with a brushed stainless steel receiver and slide. Walnut grips. Produced in 1974.

Exc.	V.G.	Good	Fair	Poor
200	175	150	125	100

BASCARAN
Eibar, Spain

Martian

A 6.35mm or 7.65mm caliber semiautomatic pistol. The slide is marked "Automatic Pistol Martian". Blued with black plastic grips having the monogram "MAB" cast in them.

Exc.	V.G.	Good	Fair	Poor
225	175	135	100	75

Thunder

As above, in 6.35mm caliber. The slide is not marked, but the tradename "Thunder" is cast in the grips.

Exc.	V.G.	Good	Fair	Poor
250	200	165	125	90

BAUER F. A. CORP.
Fraser, Michigan

Bauer 25 Automatic

A .25 caliber semiautomatic pistol made of stainless steel with a 2.5" barrel and 6-shot magazine. Walnut or imitation pearl grips. Manufactured from 1972 to 1984.

Exc.	V.G.	Good	Fair	Poor
200	175	150	110	80

The Rabbit

A .22 caliber by .410 bore combination rifle/shotgun, with a tubular metal stock. Manufactured between 1982 and 1984.

Exc.	V.G.	Good	Fair	Poor
150	110	90	75	50

BAYARD
SEE—Pieper, H. & N.
Herstal, Belgium

BAYONNE, MANUFACTURE D'ARMES
Bayonne, France
A/K/A MAB

MAB Modele A

A 6.35mm semiautomatic pistol with a 2" barrel. Blued with black plastic grips having the monogram "MAB" cast in them. Manufactured from 1921 to date.

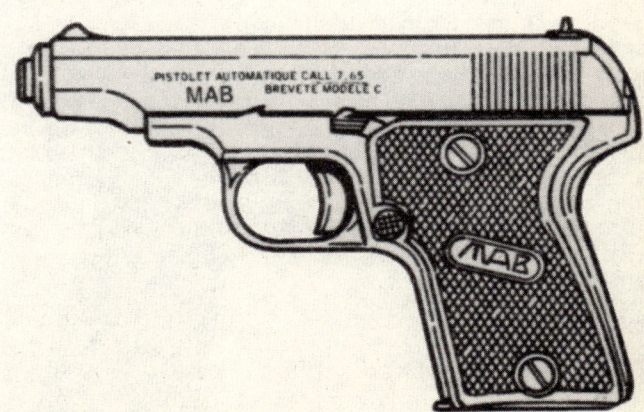

Exc.	V.G.	Good	Fair	Poor
200	150	125	100	75

MAB Modele B

Similar to the above, with the slide marked "Pistolet Automatique MAB Brevete." Manufactured from 1932 to 1949.

Exc.	V.G.	Good	Fair	Poor
250	225	200	125	90

MAB Modele C

Patterned after the Model 1910 Browning, in 7.65mm or .380 ACP. Manufactured after 1933.

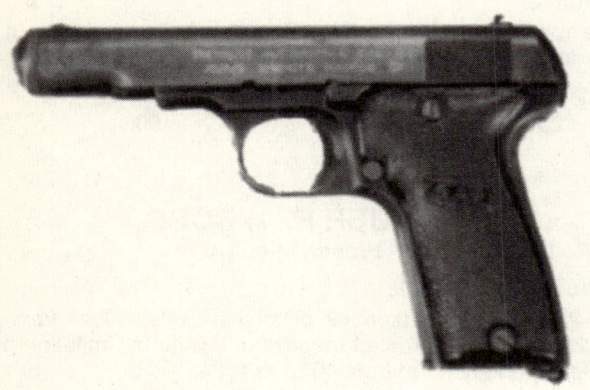

Exc.	V.G.	Good	Fair	Poor
250	225	200	125	90

MAB Modele D currently imported by Century International

As above, with a 4" barrel. Manufactured from 1933 to date.

NOTE: Add 100% for Nazi marked pistols.

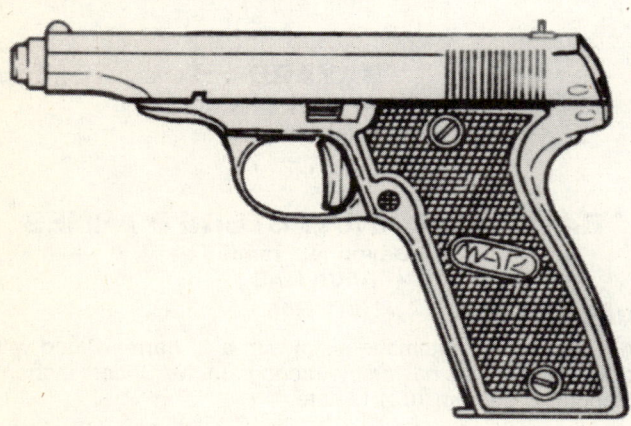

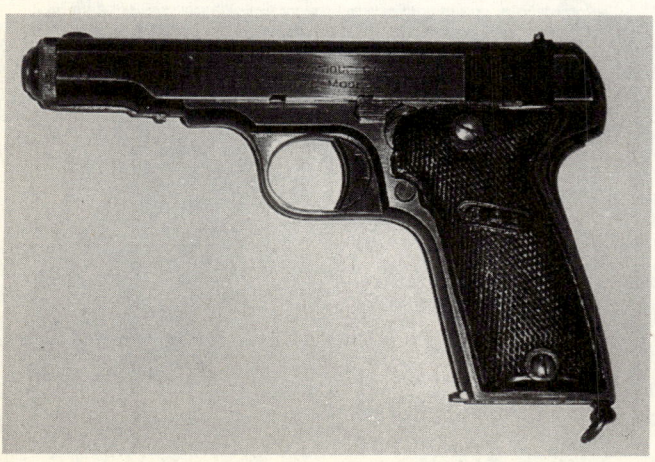

Courtesy Richard M. Kumor, Sr.

Exc.	V.G.	Good	Fair	Poor
175	150	125	100	75

MAB Modele E

Similar to the above, in 6.35mm caliber. Introduced in 1949.

Exc.	V.G.	Good	Fair	Poor
250	200	175	125	90

MAB Modele F

Similar to the Model B, but with interchangeable barrels from 2.65" to 7.25" in length and in .22 caliber.

Exc.	V.G.	Good	Fair	Poor
225	175	150	100	75

MAB Modele GZ

Manufactured by Arizmendi of Eibar, Spain, and in 7.65mm caliber. The slide marked "Echasa Eibar (Espana) Cal. .32 Modelo GZ-MAB Espanola."

Exc.	V.G.	Good	Fair	Poor
225	175	150	100	75

MAB Modele R

Similar to the Model D, with an external hammer and in 7.65mm or 7.65mm long caliber.

Exc.	V.G.	Good	Fair	Poor
300	250	200	150	100

MAB Modele R Para

As above, in 9mm caliber.

Exc.	V.G.	Good	Fair	Poor
400	350	300	225	125

MAB Modele PA-15

As above, with a 15-shot magazine.

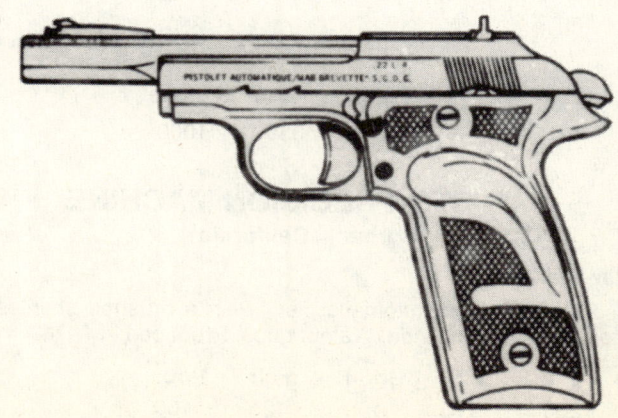

Exc.	V.G.	Good	Fair	Poor
425	375	300	225	125

Modele "Le Chasseur"

The Model F with an external hammer and in .22 caliber. Offered in a variety of barrel lengths and sight styles. Introduced in 1953.

Exc.	V.G.	Good	Fair	Poor
250	200	175	150	100

NOTE: MAB pistols that were sold in the U.S.A. were retailed by the Winfield Arms Company of Los Angeles, California, and are marked "Made in France for WAC." This does not affect values to any appreciable degree.

BEATTIE, J.
London, England

Beattie produced a variety of revolvers during the percussion period, some of which were imported into the United States. During the period this firm was in business, it was located at the following London addresses:

43 Upper Marylebone Street	1835-1838
52 Upper Marylebone Street	1838-1842
52 Upper Marylebone Street & 223 Regent Street	1842-1846
205 Regent Street	1851-1882
104 Queen Victoria Street	1882-1894

Beattie Gas Seal Revolver

A .42 caliber single-action percussion revolver with a 6.25" octagonal barrel. When the hammer is cocked, the cylinder is forced forward against the barrel breech, thus effecting a gas seal. Blued, casehardened with walnut grips.

Exc.	V.G.	Good	Fair	Poor
4500	4000	3250	2500	1000

BEAUMONT
Maastrict, Netherlands

1873 Dutch Service Revolver, Old Model

A 9.4mm double-action 6-shot revolver weighing 2 lbs.-12 oz.

Exc.	V.G.	Good	Fair	Poor
250	225	185	145	100

1873 Dutch Service Revolver, New Model

As above, with a 6-shot cylinder.

Exc.	V.G.	Good	Fair	Poor
250	225	185	145	100

1873 KIM, Small Model

As above, with an octagonal barrel and 5-shot cylinder.

Exc.	V.G.	Good	Fair	Poor
275	250	200	150	100

BEAUMONT, ADAMS
SEE—Adams

BEAUMONT-VITALI
Holland

Beaumont-Vitali

An 11mm caliber bolt-action rifle with a 30" barrel and full stock secured by two barrel bands. Essentially this rifle is a modification of the Dutch Model 1871 single shot rifle fitted with a Vitali box magazine.

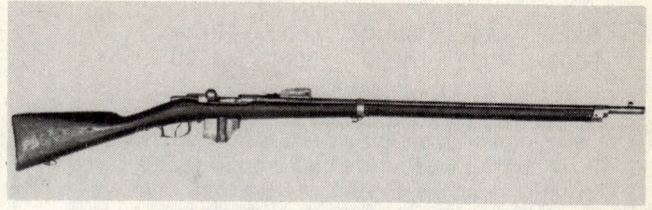

Courtesy Milwaukee Public Museum, Milwaukee, Wisconsin

Exc.	V.G.	Good	Fair	Poor
200	175	125	90	65

BECKER AND HOLLANDER
Suhl, Germany

Beholla

A 7.65mm caliber semiautomatic pistol produced under contract for the German War Department. The right side of the slide is marked "Becker U Hollander Waffenbau Suhl" and the left side "Selbstlade Pistol Beholla Cal. 7.65."

Exc.	V.G.	Good	Fair	Poor
400	275	225	175	100

BEEMAN PRECISION ARMS, INC.
Santa Rosa, California

Although primarily known as an importer and retailer of airguns, Beeman Precision Arms, Inc. has marketed several firearms.

MP-08

A .380 caliber semiautomatic pistol with a 3.5" barrel and 6-shot magazine, resembling the German Luger. Blued. Introduced in 1968.

NIB	Exc.	V.G	Good	Fair	Poor
400	350	250	200	175	100

P-08

As above, in .22 caliber with an 8-shot magazine and walnut grips. Introduced in 1969.

NIB	Exc.	V.G	Good	Fair	Poor
400	350	250	200	175	100

SP Standard

A .22 caliber single shot target pistol with 8" to 15" barrels. Fitted with adjustable sights and walnut grips. Imported in 1985 and 1986.

NIB	Exc.	V.G.	Good	Fair	Poor
225	200	175	150	125	75

SP Deluxe

As above, with a walnut forend.

NIB	Exc.	V.G.	Good	Fair	Poor
250	225	200	175	125	75

BEERSTECHER, FREDERICK
Philadelphia, Pennsylvania (1846-1856)
Lewisburg, Pennsylvania (1857-1868)

Superposed Load Pocket Pistol

A .41 caliber superposed load percussion pistol with an average barrel length of 3", German silver mounts and walnut stock. The hammer is fitted with a moveable twin striker head so that the first charge in the barrel can be fired and then the second fired. The lock is normally marked "F. Beerstecher's/Patent 1855". Prospective purchasers are advised to secure a qualified appraisal prior to acquisition.

Exc.	V.G.	Good	Fair	Poor
5000	4500	4000	3000	1500

> A .90 caliber Plains type percussion rifle with 41-1/2" barrel was sold at auction for $550. Condition was good. Back action lock marked "Beerstecher/Centreville". Stock has iron trigger guard with pewter forend tip.
> J.C. Devine, Inc. August 1996.

BEHOLLA
SEE-Becher and Hollander

BEISTEGUI, HERMANOS
Eibar, Spain

Beistegui "RUBY"

A 7.65mm caliber semiautomatic pistol copied after the Ruby. The slide marked "1914 Model Automatic Pistol Beistegui Hermanos Eiber (Espana)."

Exc.	V.G.	Good	Fair	Poor
200	150	125	80	50

Bulwark #1

The Bulwark is a fixed-barrel, external-hammer, blowback semiautomatic chambered for the 7.65mm cartridge. It bears no external markings except the monogram "B&H" molded into the grips.

Exc.	V.G.	Good	Fair	Poor
150	125	100	75	50

Bulwark #2

A copy of the Browning .25 caliber semiautomatic pistol. The slide marked "Fabrique de Armes de Guerre de Grand Precision Bulwark patent Depose No. 67259."

Exc.	V.G.	Good	Fair	Poor
150	125	100	75	50

Libia

As above, with the mark "Libia".

Exc.	V.G.	Good	Fair	Poor
150	125	100	75	50

BENELLI
Italy
Importer-Heckler & Koch
Sterling, Virginia

SHOTGUNS

Model SL-121 V

This is a semiautomatic 12 gauge with 3" chambers and various barrel lengths and chokes. It has a black anodized alloy receiver and was discontinued in 1985.

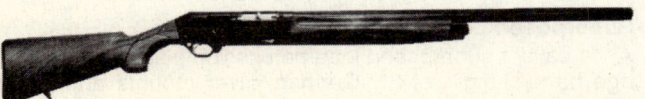

NIB	Exc.	V.G.	Good	Fair	Poor
475	450	400	350	300	150

Model SL 121 Slug

This model is similar to the SL-121 V with a 21" cylinder-bore barrel and rifle sights. It, too, was discontinued in 1985.

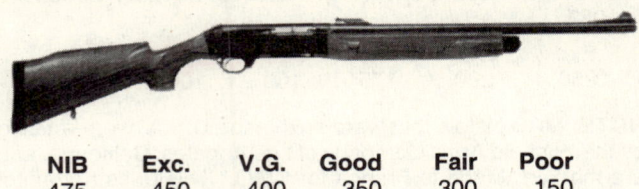

NIB	Exc.	V.G.	Good	Fair	Poor
475	450	400	350	300	150

Model SL-123 V

This model has the improved, fast, third-generation action. Otherwise it resembles the earlier SL-121.

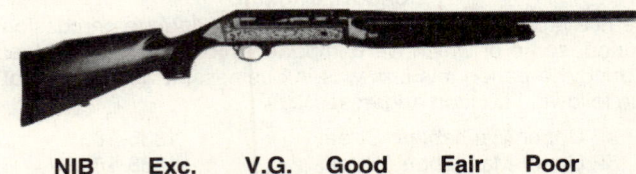

NIB	Exc.	V.G.	Good	Fair	Poor
500	475	425	350	300	150

Model SL 201

This is a 20 gauge with a 26", improved cylinder barrel. It is similar in appearance to the SL-123.

NIB	Exc.	V.G.	Good	Fair	Poor
500	475	425	350	300	150

M3 Super 90

This is an improved version of the Benelli pump action and semiautomatic inertia recoil system. The shotgun can be converted from pump to semiautomatic by turning a spring loaded ring located at the end of the forearm. It has a rotating bolt system and is chambered for 12 gauge, with a 3" chamber. This model has a 19.75" barrel with cylinder bore and rifle sights with a 7-round tubular magazine. It has a matte black finish and a black fiberglass pistol grip stock and forearm. This model was introduced in 1986.

NIB	Exc.	V.G.	Good	Fair	Poor
1000	750	700	600	450	300

M3 Super 90 Folding Stock

Same as above but furnished with a folding tubular steel stock.

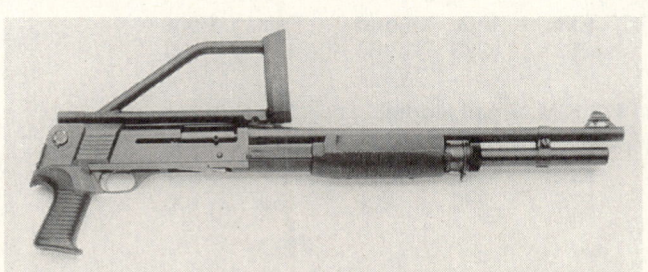

NIB	Exc.	V.G.	Good	Fair	Poor
2000	1500	1150	850	600	300

M1 Super 90 Tactical

This is a semiautomatic 12 gauge shotgun with an inertia recoil system. It features a 18.5" plain barrel with 3 screw in choke tubes. Available in either standard polymer stock or pistol grip stock. Ghost ring sights are standard. Gun weighs 6.5 lbs. First introduced in 1993.

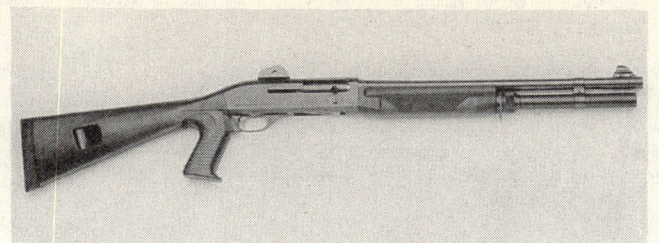

NIB	Exc.	V.G.	Good	Fair	Poor
800	650	550	450	350	250

M1 Super 90 Defense Gun

Comes standard with polymer pistol grip stock, 19.75" barrel, plain sights, or ghost ring sights. Offered in 12 gauge only. Weighs 7.1 lbs.

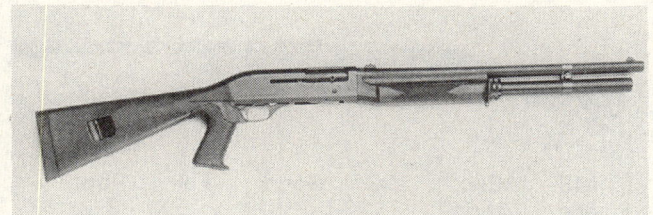

NIB	Exc.	V.G.	Good	Fair	Poor
800	650	550	450	350	250

M1 Super 90 Slug Gun

Equipped with a standard black polymer stock with 19.75" plain barrel. Fitted with a 7-shot magazine. Ghost ring sights are an option. Weighs 6.7 lbs.

NIB	Exc.	V.G.	Good	Fair	Poor
800	650	550	450	350	250

M1 Super 90 Entry Gun

This model is fitted with a black polymer pistol grip stock with 14" plain barrel. Magazine holds 5 shells. Plain or ghost ring sights available. **CAUTION: Restricted sale, Class III Transfer** required. Manufacturer's retail price is $900.

M1 Super 90 Field

This model is similar to other Super 90 series guns with a 21", 24", 26", or 28" vent rib barrel with screw-in choke tubes.

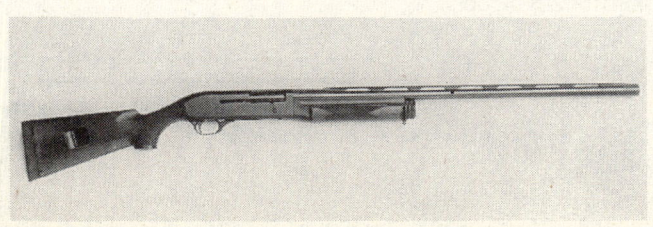

NIB	Exc.	V.G.	Good	Fair	Poor
825	600	500	400	350	200

M1 Super 90 Camo Field

Same as above but with camouflage receiver, barrel, butt stock and forearm. Offered in 24", 26", and 28" vent rib barrels. Introduced in 1997.

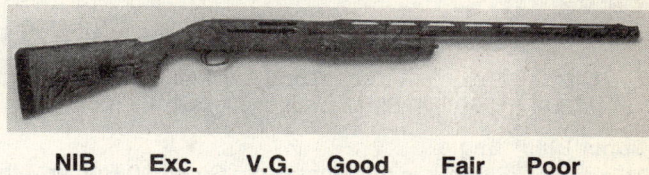

NIB	Exc.	V.G.	Good	Fair	Poor
900	700	—	—	—	—

M1 Super 90 Sporting Special

Introduced in 1993 this 12 gauge shotgun is similar to the Super 90 with the addition of non-reflective surfaces, 18.5" plain barrel with 3 choke tubes (IC, Mod, Full). The gun is fitted with ghost ring sights.

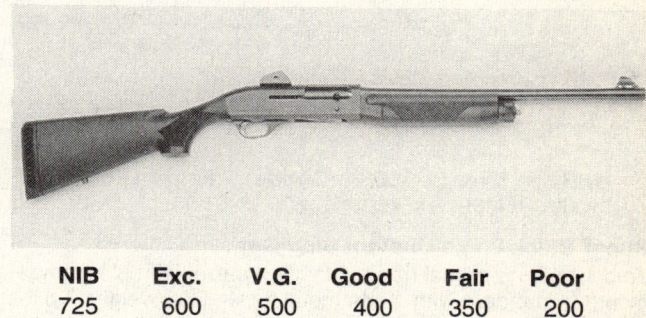

NIB	Exc.	V.G.	Good	Fair	Poor
725	600	500	400	350	200

Montefeltro Super 90

Introduced in 1987, this model is similar to the Super 90 Field with a checkered walnut stock and forearm with gloss finish. Offered with 21", 24", 26", or 28" vent rib barrel. Available in 12 gauge only with 3" chambers. This shotgun offered in left-hand model also.

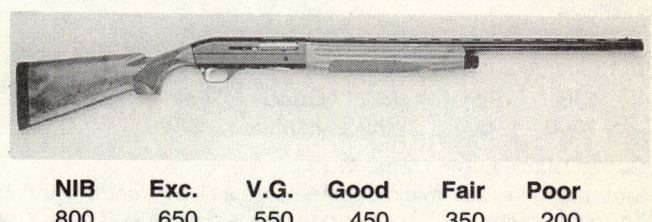

NIB	Exc.	V.G.	Good	Fair	Poor
800	650	550	450	350	200

Montefelto 20 Gauge

Introduced in 1993, this model features a walnut checkered stock with 26" vent rib barrel. In 1995 a 24" vent rib barrel was offered as well. Gun weighs 5.75 lbs.

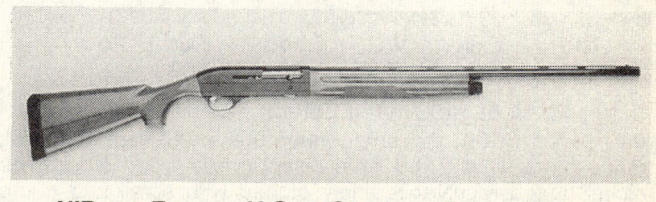

NIB	Exc.	V.G.	Good	Fair	Poor
800	650	550	450	350	200

Montefelto 20 Gauge Limited

Introduced in 1995 this version features a finely etched nickel plate receiver with scroll and game scenes highlighted in gold. The stock is a select grade walnut and is fitted with a 26" vent rib barrel.

NIB	Exc.	V.G.	Good	Fair	Poor
1750	1250	800	500	350	250

Super Black Eagle

This model is similar to the Montefeltro Super 90 Hunter with a polymer or walnut stock and forearm. It is offered with a 24", 26", or 28" vent rib-barrel with 5 screw-in choke tubes. Chambered for 12 gauge from 2-3/4" to 3-1/2". It was introduced in 1989. The 24" barrel was introduced in 1993.

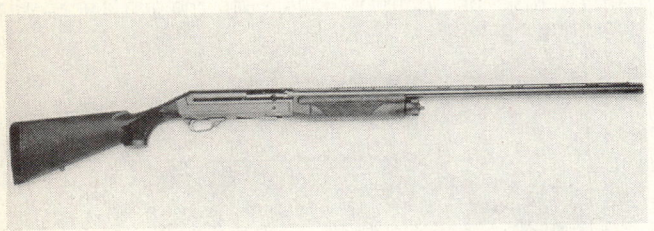

NIB	Exc.	V.G.	Good	Fair	Poor
1000	800	750	600	500	250

Super Black Eagle Custom Slug Gun

This 12 gauge model has a 24" rifled barrel with 3" chamber. It comes standard with matte metal finish. Gun weighs 7.6 lbs.

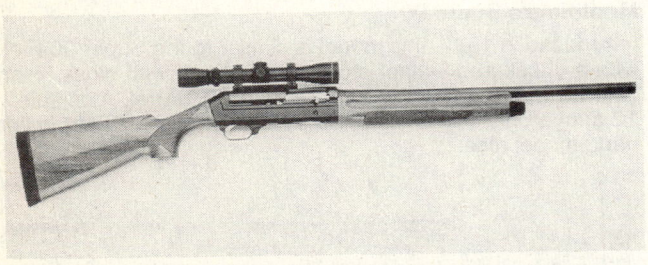

NIB	Exc.	V.G.	Good	Fair	Poor
1000	800	750	600	500	350

Super Black Eagle Camo Gun

Introduced in 1997 this model features 24", 26", or 28' vent rib barrels chambered for 12 gauge shells. Has a Realtree Xtra Brown camo finish. Stock is camo polymer as is forearm.

NIB	Exc.	V.G.	Good	Fair	Poor
1200	900	700	600	500	250

Super Black Eagle Limited Edition

Introduced in 1997 this shotgun features a 26" vent rib barrel, matte metal finish, and satin select grade wood stock. The nickel plated receiver is finely etched with scroll and game scenes. Limited to 1,000 guns.

NIB	Exc.	V.G.	Good	Fair	Poor
2000	1500	—	—	—	—

Black Eagle Competition Gun

Offered in 12 gauge only this model is fitted with an etched receiver, mid rib bead, competition stock, and 5 screw-in choke tubes. Available in either 26" or 28" vent rib barrel. The upper receiver is steel while the lower receiver is lightweight alloy. Weighs 7.3 lbs.

NIB	Exc.	V.G.	Good	Fair	Poor
1200	800	750	600	500	250

Black Eagle

Similar to the Black Eagle Competition Model but with standard grade wood and matte black finish on the receiver. Introduced in 1997.

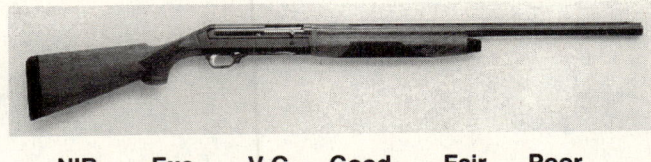

NIB	Exc.	V.G.	Good	Fair	Poor
900	600	—	—	—	—

Black Eagle Executive Series

Offered in 12 gauge only this is a special order only shotgun. It is offered with a choice of 21", 24", 26", 28" vent rib barrels. Each grade or level of gun is engraved with increasing levels of coverage. The stock is fancy walnut.

Type I

NIB	Exc.	V.G.	Good	Fair	Poor
3750	2750	1250	750	500	300

Type II

NIB	Exc.	V.G.	Good	Fair	Poor
4250	3250	1500	750	500	300

Type III

NIB	Exc.	V.G.	Good	Fair	Poor
4750	3500	1700	800	600	400

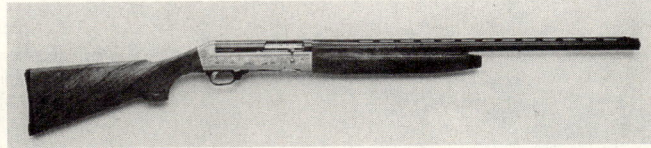

Sport Model

This model was introduced in 1997 and is the first shotgun with removable, interchangeable carbon fiber vent ribs. This model is offered in 12 gauge only with choice of 26" or 28" barrels. Butt pad is adjustable. Weight is 7 lbs. for 26" models and 7.3 lbs. for 28" models.

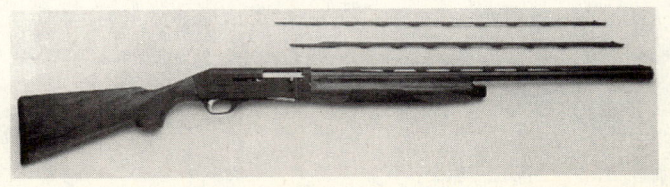

NIB	Exc.	V.G.	Good	Fair	Poor
1100	850	—	—	—	—

HANDGUNS

Model B-76

This is an all-steel, double-action semiautomatic chambered for the 9mm Parabellum. It has a 4.25" barrel, fixed sights, and an 8-round detachable magazine.

NIB	Exc.	V.G.	Good	Fair	Poor
450	400	350	300	200	100

Model B-76S

This is the target version of the B-76. It has a 5.5" barrel, adjustable sights, and target grips.

NIB	Exc.	V.G.	Good	Fair	Poor
550	500	400	300	200	100

Model B-77

This model is similar to the B-76 except that it is chambered for the .32 ACP.

NIB	Exc.	V.G.	Good	Fair	Poor
350	300	250	200	150	100

Model B-80

This is another model similar to the B-76 except that it is chambered for the .30 Luger cartridge.

NIB	Exc.	V.G.	Good	Fair	Poor
400	350	300	200	150	100

Model B-80S

This is the target version of the B-80 with a 5.5" barrel and adjustable sights. It also features target grips.

NIB	Exc.	V.G.	Good	Fair	Poor
500	450	400	300	200	100

Model MP90S Match

This is a semi-automatic single action pistol chambered for the .22 Short, .22 Long Rifle, or .32 S&W wadcutter. It is fitted with a 4 3/8" barrel with walnut match style fully adjustable grips, blade front sight and fully adjustable rear sight. Barrel has adjustable weights below . Magazine capacity is 5 rounds. Weight is about 39 oz. Imported by European American Armory.

NIB	Exc.	V.G.	Good	Fair	Poor
1250	950	—	—	—	—

Model MP95E Match

Similar to the above model but with anatomically shaped grips. Imported by European American Armory.

NIB	Exc.	V.G.	Good	Fair	Poor
550	450	—	—	—	—

BENSON FIREARMS
Seattle, Washington
SEE—Aldo Uberti

Formerly the importer of the fine Italian Uberti firearms. Their arrangement ended in 1989, and these guns are now imported by Uberti U.S.A., Inc.

BENTLEY, DAVID
Birmingham

Bentley was a prolific maker of both percussion and cartridge arms between 1845 and 1883. Those arms in cases can be dated by the addresses listed.

New Church Street	1845-1849
55 Hockley Street	1849-1854
5 Lower Loveday Street	1855-1860
61 & 62 Lower Loveday Street	1860-1863
44 Shadwell Street	1863-1871
Tower Works, Aston	1871-1883

BENTLEY, JOSEPH
Birmingham and Liverpool

Best known for his transitional and later patented percussion revolvers, Bentley worked at the following addresses:

Birmingham	11 Steelhouse Lane	1829-1837
	14 St. Mary's Row	1840-1864
Liverpool	143 Dale Street	1840-1842
	12 South Castle Street	1842-1851
	40 Lime Street & 65 Castle	1852-1857
	65 Castle & 37 Russell Street	1857-1862

Bentley Revolver

A .44 caliber double-action percussion revolver with a 7" barrel and 5-shot cylinder. Blued, casehardened with walnut grips.

Exc.	V.G.	Good	Fair	Poor
3500	3000	2500	1750	900

BENTZ
SEE-Austrian Military Firearms

BERETTA, DR. FRANCO.
Brescia, Italy

Black Diamond Field Grade

A boxlock O/U shotgun produced in a variety of gauges and barrel lengths with single triggers and automatic ejectors. Blued, French casehardened with a walnut stock.

NIB	Exc.	V.G.	Good	Fair	Poor
975	850	700	575	450	200

The above model is produced in four embellished grades as follows:

Grade One

NIB	Exc.	V.G.	Good	Fair	Poor
1150	900	700	550	400	200

Grade Two

NIB	Exc.	V.G.	Good	Fair	Poor
1700	1250	900	700	500	300

Grade Three

NIB	Exc.	V.G.	Good	Fair	Poor
2500	1750	1200	850	600	300

Grade Four

NIB	Exc.	V.G.	Good	Fair	Poor
3250	2750	2200	1250	700	350

Gamma Standard

A 12, 16, or 20 gauge boxlock O/U shotgun with 26" or 28" barrels, single trigger and automatic ejectors. Blued, French casehardened with a walnut stock. Imported from 1984 to 1988.

NIB	Exc.	V.G.	Good	Fair	Poor
450	375	300	225	150	100

Gamma Deluxe

As above, but more finely finished.

NIB	Exc.	V.G.	Good	Fair	Poor
650	575	500	400	250	125

Gamma Target

As above, in a trap or skeet version. Imported from 1986 to 1988.

NIB	Exc.	V.G.	Good	Fair	Poor
600	500	450	375	300	150

America Standard

A .410 bore boxlock O/U shotgun with 26" or 28" barrels. Blued, French case hardened with a walnut stock. Imported from 1984 to 1988.

NIB	Exc.	V.G.	Good	Fair	Poor
325	275	225	175	150	100

America Deluxe

As above, but more finely finished.

NIB	Exc.	V.G.	Good	Fair	Poor
400	325	275	220	175	100

Europa

As above, with a 26" barrel and engraved action. Imported from 1984 to 1988.

NIB	Exc.	V.G.	Good	Fair	Poor
400	325	275	225	175	100

Europa Deluxe

As above, but more finely finished.

NIB	Exc.	V.G.	Good	Fair	Poor
475	375	300	250	200	125

Francia Standard

A .410 bore boxlock double-barrel shotgun with varying barrel lengths, double triggers and manual extractors. Blued with a walnut stock. Imported from 1986 to 1988.

NIB	Exc.	V.G.	Good	Fair	Poor
250	200	175	150	125	100

Alpha Three

A 12, 16, or 20 gauge boxlock double-barrel shotgun with 26" or 28" barrels, single triggers and automatic ejectors. Blued, French casehardened with a walnut stock. Imported from 1984 to 1988.

NIB	Exc.	V.G.	Good	Fair	Poor
400	350	300	225	150	100

Beta Three

A single-barrel, break-open, field-grade gun chambered for all gauges and offered with a ventilated rib barrel from 24" to 32" in length. The receiver chrome-plated, and the stock of walnut. Imported from 1985 to 1988.

NIB	Exc.	V.G.	Good	Fair	Poor
150	125	100	75	60	40

Beretta U.S.A.

BERETTA, PIETRO
Brescia, Italy
IMPORTER - Beretta U.S.A. Corp.
Accokeek, Maryland

Fabbrica d'Armi Pierto Beretta, of Gardone Val Trompia, near Milan, Italy is one of the world's oldest industrial concerns. A leading maker of sporting, military, and civilian firearms, this firm has been in existence for almost 500 years. Founded by Bartolomeo Beretta, a master gunbarrel maker, in 1526. His son Giovannino followed his father's footsteps and subsequent generations have developed this firm into a worldwide success. Beretta manufactured its first pistol, the Model 1915, in 1915 as a wartime project.

Spread over 500,000 square feet and employing 2,200 employees this old world firm captured the United States military contract in 1985 for its standard issue sidearm, the Model 92F. These pistols are currently manufactured at Beretta U.S.A.'s plant in Maryland. Besides the affiliate in the United States, Beretta has three others located in France, Greece, and Rome.

The American affiliate was formed in 1977 to handle U.S. demand. A year later it began to manufacture some firearms, namely the Model 92F. At the present time Beretta has delivered over 250,000 Model 92F pistols to the U.S. military. Beretta continues to produce sidearms for the U.S. military and law enforcement agencies throughout the U.S.

NOTE: In 1994 Beretta changed its model designations with a new nomenclature system that brings back some of the old product names and the addition of new names instead of numbered models. Beretta will continue to use the numbered model designation along with the new product names so that both will complement the other.

PISTOLS

Model 1910

A 6.35mm caliber semiautomatic pistol with 2" barrel, fixed sights and 7-shot magazine. Blued with walnut grips. Manufactured between 1910 and 1934.

Exc.	V.G.	Good	Fair	Poor
325	275	200	150	100

Model 1915

A 7.65mm caliber semiautomatic pistol with 3.5" barrel, fixed sights and 8-shot magazine. Blued with walnut grips. The slide is marked "Pietro Beretta Brescia Casa Fondata nel 1680 Cal. 7.65mm Brevetto 1915." Manufactured between 1915 and 1919.

Exc.	V.G.	Good	Fair	Poor
325	275	200	150	100

Model 1915 2nd Variation

As above, in 9mm Glisenti caliber.

Exc.	V.G.	Good	Fair	Poor
400	325	250	200	125

Model 1915/1919

This model is an improved version of the above pistol but chambered for the 7.65mm cartridge. It also incorporates a new barrel-mounting method and a longer cutout in the top of the slide.

Courtesy Orvel Reichert

Courtesy Orvel Reichert

Exc.	V.G.	Good	Fair	Poor
325	275	200	150	100

Model 1919

Similar to Model 1915, in 6.35mm caliber. Manufactured between 1920 and 1939.

Exc.	V.G.	Good	Fair	Poor
325	275	200	150	100

Model 1923

A 9mm caliber semiautomatic pistol with 4" barrel and 8-shot magazine. Blued with steel grips. The slide is marked, "Brev 1915-1919 Mlo 1923." Manufactured from 1923 to 1935.

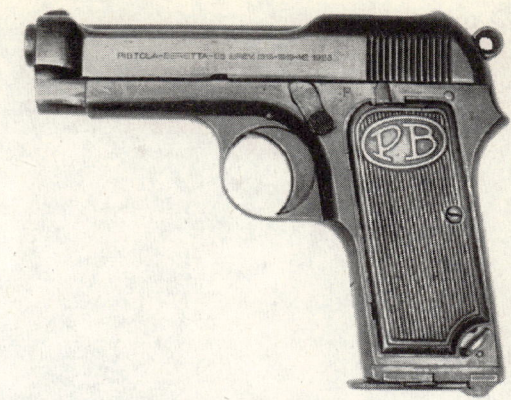

Exc.	V.G.	Good	Fair	Poor
500	400	325	225	150

Model 1931

A 7.65mm caliber semiautomatic pistol with 3.5" barrel and open-top slide. Blued with walnut grips and marked, "RM" separated by an anchor.

Exc.	V.G.	Good	Fair	Poor
425	350	250	200	150

Model 1934

As above, with 9mm short caliber. The slide is marked, "P. Beretta Cal. 9 Corto-Mo 1934 Brevet Gardone VT." This inscription is followed by the date of manufacture that was given numerically, followed by a Roman numeral that denoted the year of manufacture on the Fascist calendar which began in 1922. Examples are marked, "RM" (Navy), "RE" (Army), "RA" (Air Force), and "PS" (Police). Manufactured between 1934 and 1959.

Courtesy Orvel Reichert

Courtesy Orvel Reichert

Exc.	V.G.	Good	Fair	Poor
350	300	200	150	100

Model 1934 Rumanian Contract

This model is identical to the Model 1934 except the slide is marked "9mm Scurt" instead of 9mm Corto.

Exc.	V.G.	Good	Fair	Poor
450	400	300	225	125

Model 1935

As above, in 7.65mm caliber. Postwar versions are known. Manufactured from 1935 to 1959.

Courtesy Orvel Reichert

Exc.	V.G.	Good	Fair	Poor
350	300	200	150	100

Model 318

An improved version of the old Model 1919 with the butt reshaped to afford a better grip. Chambered for the .25 ACP cartridge and has a 2.5" barrel. Variety of finishes with plastic grips. In the United States it is known as the "Panther." Manufactured between 1935 and 1946.

Exc.	V.G.	Good	Fair	Poor
300	250	200	150	100

Model 418

As above, with a rounded grip and a cocking indicator. It is known as the "Bantam" in the U.S. Introduced in 1947.

Exc.	V.G.	Good	Fair	Poor
250	200	150	125	90

Model 420

An engraved and chrome-plated Model 418.

Exc.	V.G.	Good	Fair	Poor
350	300	275	200	150

Model 421

An engraved, gold-plated Model 418 with tortoise-shell grips.

Exc.	V.G.	Good	Fair	Poor
475	425	325	250	150

Model 948

A .22 l.r. version of the Model 1934. It has either a 3.5" or 6" barrel.

Exc.	V.G.	Good	Fair	Poor
350	300	200	125	90

Model 949 Olympic Target

A .22 caliber semiautomatic pistol with 8.75" barrel, adjustable sights and muzzle break. Blued with checkered, walnut grips. Manufactured from 1959 to 1964.

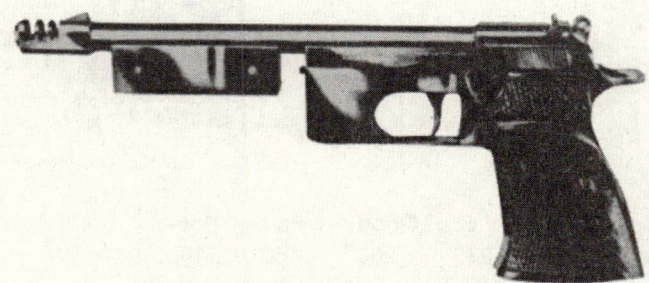

Exc.	V.G.	Good	Fair	Poor
750	600	500	400	200

Model 950/Jetfire

A .22 caliber semiautomatic pistol with 2.25" barrel hinged at the front that could be pivoted forward for cleaning or loading, making this either a semiauto or single-shot pistol. Blued with plastic grips. Introduced in 1955. A 4" barrel version also available. This model was known as the "Minx" in the U.S.

plastic grips. Introduced in 1955. A 4" barrel version also available. This model was known as the "Minx" in the U.S.

NIB	Exc.	V.G.	Good	Fair	Poor
200	150	135	110	85	50

Model 950B/Jetfire

As above, in .25 caliber, known as the "Jetfire" in the United States.

NIB	Exc.	V.G.	Good	Fair	Poor
200	150	135	110	85	50

Model 3032 Tomcat

This is a double action semi-automatic pistol similar in appearance to the Model 950 but chambered for the .32 ACP cartridge. Barrel length is 2.45" and overall length is 5". Fixed blade front sight and drift adjustable rear sight. Plastic grips. Seven round magazine. Blued or matte black finish. Weight is 14.5 oz.

NIB	Exc.	V.G.	Good	Fair	Poor
250	175	150	125	100	75

NOTE: For matte black finish add $50.

Model 951

A 9mm caliber semiautomatic pistol with 4.5" barrel and fixed sights. Blued with plastic grips. It is also known as the "Brigadier." Manufactured from 1952 to present day.

Exc.	V.G.	Good	Fair	Poor
350	300	200	150	100

Model 70

The Model 948 with cross-bolt safety, hold-open device, and a push-button magazine release. There are a number of sub-variations available chambered for the .22 l.r., .32 ACP, and the .380 ACP cartridges. Available with a 3.5" or 6" barrel and has a detachable magazine. Also known as the "Puma" or the "Cougar." It was introduced in 1958 and discontinued in 1985.

NIB	Exc.	V.G.	Good	Fair	Poor
325	275	200	175	125	85

Model 101

Another name for the Model 70T pistol.

NIB	Exc.	V.G.	Good	Fair	Poor
350	275	225	175	150	100

Model 20

A .25 ACP double-action pistol with 2.5" barrel and 9-shot magazine. Blued with either walnut or plastic grips. Discontinued in 1985.

NIB	Exc.	V.G.	Good	Fair	Poor
200	175	150	125	90	75

Model 21/21 Bobcat

This small frame semiautomatic pistol, chambered for the .22 Long Rifle or .25 ACP cartridge, features a 2.4" tip-up barrel with fixed sights and a magazine capacity of 8 rounds (.25 ACP) or 7 rounds (.22 L.R.). Comes with either plastic or walnut grips and a deluxe version with gold line engraving. Pistol weighs about 1 to 1.5 oz. depending on caliber.

Standard model

NIB	Exc.	V.G.	Good	Fair	Poor
200	175	150	125	100	75

Model 21EL-Gold Engraved Model

NIB	Exc.	V.G.	Good	Fair	Poor
275	225	175	150	100	75

Model 71/Jaguar

Similar to above model and chambered for .22 l.r. cartridge. Frame is alloy and is fitted with a 3.5" barrel. Barrels with 6" lengths are encountered but have more value and are known as Model 72.

NIB	Exc.	V.G.	Good	Fair	Poor
300	225	200	175	125	100

Model 72-6" barrel

NIB	Exc.	V.G.	Good	Fair	Poor
350	300	275	225	150	125

Model 90

A double-action, semiautomatic pocket pistol with a 3.5" barrel and 8-round magazine. Manufactured from 1969 to 1983.

Exc.	V.G.	Good	Fair	Poor
275	250	200	150	125

Model 92

A 9mm caliber double-action, semiautomatic pistol with a 5" barrel, fixed sights and a 16-round, double-stack magazine. Blued with plastic grips. Introduced in 1976 and is now discontinued.

NIB	Exc.	V.G.	Good	Fair	Poor
450	400	375	300	250	200

Model 92SB-P

As above, but with a polished finish. Manufactured from 1980 to 1985.

NIB	Exc.	V.G.	Good	Fair	Poor
475	425	375	325	250	200

Model 92SB Compact

As above, with a 4.3" barrel and a shortened grip frame that holds a 14-shot magazine. Either blued or nickel-plated with wood or plastic grips. The nickel version would be worth an additional 15 percent. The wood grips would add $20 to the value. Introduced in 1980 and discontinued in 1985.

NIB	Exc.	V.G.	Good	Fair	Poor
475	425	375	325	250	200

Model 92FS

The current production Model 92 chambered for the 9mm Parabellum cartridge. Barrel length is 4.9" and rear sight is a 3-dot combat drift adjustable. The magazine capacity is 15 rounds. This semiautomatic pistol features a double or single action operation. The safety is manual type. The frame is a light alloy sandblasted and anodized black. The barrel slide is steel. Grips are plastic checkered with black matte finish. Equipped with spare magazine cleaning rod, and hard carrying case. Pistol weighs 34.4 oz. empty.

NIB	Exc.	V.G.	Good	Fair	Poor
450	400	350	300	200	150

Model 96

Identical to Model 92Fs but fitted with a 10-round magazine and chambered for the .40 S&W. Introduced in 1992.

NIB	Exc.	V.G.	Good	Fair	Poor
450	400	350	300	200	150

Model 96 Combat

Introduced in 1997 this model is single action only with a competition tuned trigger. The barrel length is 5.9" and is supplied with a weight as standard. Rear sight is adjustable target type. Weight is 40 oz.

NIB	Exc.	V.G.	Good	Fair	Poor
1550	1150	—	—	—	—

Model 96 Stock

Similar to the Model 96 but in double/single action with a half-cock notch for cocked and locked carry. Fitted with a 4.9" barrel with fixed sights. Three interchangeable front sights are supplied as standard. Weight is 35 oz. Introduced in 1997.

NIB	Exc.	V.G.	Good	Fair	Poor
1350	950	—	—	—	—

Model 92/96FS Inox

Same as above except the barrel, slide, trigger, extractor, and other components are made of stainless steel. The frame is made of lightweight anodized aluminum alloy. The Model 96FS was discontinued in 1993.

NIB	Exc.	V.G.	Good	Fair	Poor
550	500	450	350	300	200

Model 92/96FS Centurion

Chambered for either the 9mm or .40 S&W this model features a 4.3" barrel but yet retains a full grip to accommodate a 15-round magazine (9mm) or 10 rounds (.40 S&W). Pistol weighs approximately 33.2 oz. Introduced in 1993. Black sandblasted finish.

NIB	Exc.	V.G.	Good	Fair	Poor
450	400	350	300	200	150

Model 92F

A 9mm Parabellum caliber double action semiautomatic pistol with a 4.9" barrel, fixed sights and a 15-shot double-stack magazine with an extended base. Matte-blued finish with walnut or plastic grips. Introduced in 1984. No longer in production.

NIB	Exc.	V.G.	Good	Fair	Poor
450	400	350	300	200	150

Model 92F Compact

As above, with a 4.3" barrel and a 13-shot magazine. No longer in production.

NIB	Exc.	V.G.	Good	Fair	Poor
450	400	350	300	200	150

Model 92 FS Compact "Type M"

Essentially the same as the Model 92FS Compact but with the exception of a single column magazine that holds 8 rounds and reduces the grip thickness of the pistol. Pistol weighs 30.9 oz. Discontinued in 1993.

NIB	Exc.	V.G.	Good	Fair	Poor
450	400	350	300	200	150

Model 92FS Deluxe

Identical dimensions to the full size Model 92FS with the addition of gold plated engraved frame with gold plated extra magazine in fitted leather presentation hard case. Grips are walnut briar with gold initial plate. Introduced in 1993.

NIB	Exc.	V.G.	Good	Fair	Poor
3750	3000	2000	1000	750	500

Model 92/96D

Same specifications as the standard Model 92 and Model 96 except that this variation has no visible hammer and is double action only. This model has no manual safety. Pistol weighs 33.8 oz.

NIB	Exc.	V.G.	Good	Fair	Poor
425	375	325	275	200	150

Model 92/96DS

Same as above but with the same manual safety as found on the 92FS pistol. Introduced in 1994.

NIB	Exc.	V.G.	Good	Fair	Poor
425	375	325	275	200	150

Model 92/96G

Designed for the French Gendarmerie, this model has now been adopted for the French Air Force as well as other government agencies. This model features a hammer drop lever that does not function as a safety when the lever is released but lowers the hammer and returns to the ready to fire position automatically. Offered to law enforcement agencies only.

Model 92 Competition Conversion Kit

The kit includes a 7.3" barrel with counterweight and elevated front sight, semiautomatic, walnut grips, and fully adjustable rear sight. Comes in special carrying case with the basic pistol.

Kit Price Only:

NIB	Exc.	V.G.	Good	Fair	Poor
500	350	300	200	150	100

Model M9 Limited Edition

Introduced in 1995 to commemorate the 10th anniversary of the U.S. military's official sidearm this 9mm pistol is limited to 10,000 units. Special engraving on the slide with special serial numbers.

Standard Model

NIB	Exc.	V.G.	Good	Fair	Poor
625	475	400	300	200	100

Deluxe Model-Walnut grips with gold plated hammer and grip screws.

NIB	Exc.	V.G.	Good	Fair	Poor
750	600	450	350	200	100

Model 8000/8040 Cougar

This is a compact size pistol using a short recoil rotating barrel. It features a firing pin lock, chrome lined barrel, anodized aluminum alloy frame with Bruniton finish. Overall length is 7", barrel length is 3.6", overall height 5.5", and unloaded weight is 33.5 oz. Offered in double/single action as well as double action only. Magazine holds 10 rounds. Available in 9mm or 40 S&W.

NIB	Exc.	V.G.	Good	Fair	Poor
600	525	400	350	250	150

Model 8000/8040 Mini Cougar

This pistol was introduced in 1997 and is similar in design to the full size model. Offered in 9mm or 40 S&W the pistol is fitted with a 3.6" barrel. Empty weight is 27 oz. Offered in double/single action or double action only. Magazine capacity is 10 rounds for 9mm and 8 rounds for .40 S&W model.

NIB	Exc.	V.G.	Good	Fair	Poor
650	550	—	—	—	—

Model 84/Cheetah

This is a small semiautomatic pistol chambered for the .380 cartridge. It has a double column magazine that holds 13 rounds. Offered in blue or nickel finish. Grips are checkered black plastic or checkered wood.

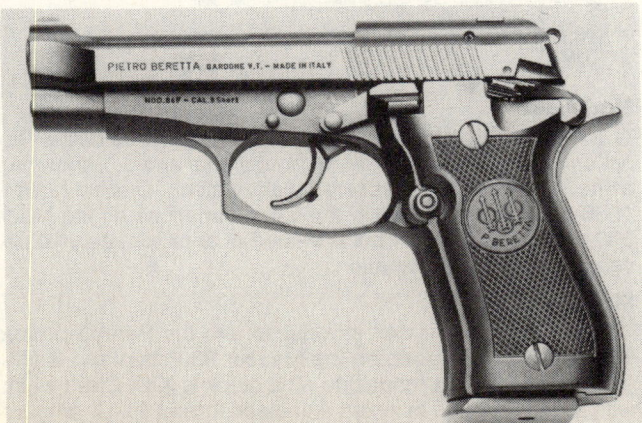

NIB	Exc.	V.G.	Good	Fair	Poor
450	375	325	275	200	150

Model 84BB

Similar to the Model 84 but incorporates different features such as a firing pin blocking device and loaded chamber indicator. Single column magazine holds 8 rounds of .380 shells. Discontinued in 1993.

NIB	Exc.	V.G.	Good	Fair	Poor
425	375	325	275	200	150

Model 85/Cheetah

Similar in appearance to the Model 84 but features a single column magazine with a capacity of 8 rounds. Available in blue or nickel finish. Grips are checkered black plastic. Pistol weighs 22 oz.

NIB	Exc.	V.G.	Good	Fair	Poor
405	375	325	275	200	150

Model 86/Cheetah

This .380 ACP semiautomatic pistol has a 4.4" tip-up barrel. Magazine capacity is 8 rounds. Furnished with checkered wood grips. Pistol weighs 23 oz.

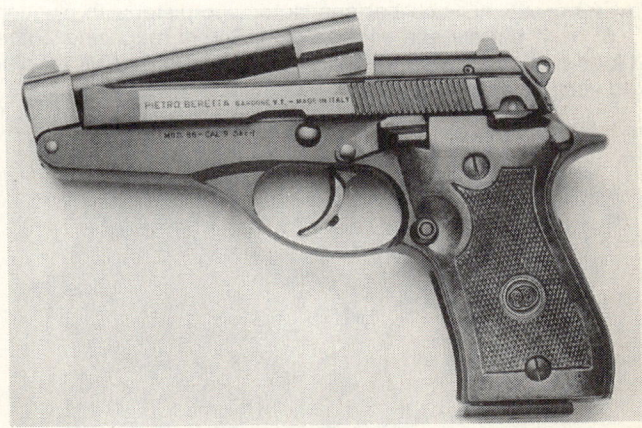

NIB	Exc.	V.G.	Good	Fair	Poor
425	350	300	250	200	150

Model 87/Cheetah

A .22 caliber double-action, semiautomatic target pistol with a 3.8" or 6" barrel, adjustable sights with a 7-shot magazine. Blued with checkered walnut grips. Introduced in 1986.

NIB	Exc.	V.G.	Good	Fair	Poor
425	350	300	250	200	150

Model 89/Gold Standard

A .22 caliber, semiautomatic target pistol with adjustable sights, and 10-shot, detachable magazine. Matte finish with hand-fitting walnut grips. Introduced in 1988.

NIB	Exc.	V.G.	Good	Fair	Poor
650	575	475	400	300	150

Model 950 BS/Jetfire

A .22 or .25 ACP caliber semiautomatic pistol with pivoting, 2.5" or 4" barrels and either a 6- or 8-shot magazine. Either blued or nickel-plated with black plastic grips. The nickel-plated version is worth an extra 15 percent.

NIB	Exc.	V.G.	Good	Fair	Poor
150	125	100	75	60	45

RIFLES

AR-70

A .222 or .223 caliber, semiautomatic rifle with a 17.7" barrel, adjustable diopter sights, and a 5, 8, or 30-shot magazine. Black epoxy finish with a synthetic stock

NIB	Exc.	V.G.	Good	Fair	Poor
1850	1500	1050	750	600	300

Model 500 Custom

A bolt-action sporting rifle chambered for a variety of calibers with a 24" barrel, open sights, three action lengths and a 3- or 4-shot magazine. Blued with a checkered walnut stock.

500 Custom

Exc.	V.G.	Good	Fair	Poor
600	525	400	325	275

This model was offered in five grades:

Model 500S
Exc.	V.G.	Good	Fair	Poor
625	550	425	350	300

Model 500DL
Exc.	V.G.	Good	Fair	Poor
1400	1250	1000	775	650

Model 500DEELL
Exc.	V.G.	Good	Fair	Poor
1600	1450	1200	975	800

Model 500DEELLS
Exc.	V.G.	Good	Fair	Poor
1625	1475	1225	1000	825

Model 501

A .243 or .308 caliber bolt-action rifle with a 23" barrel, furnished without sights and a 6-shot magazine. Blued with a checkered walnut stock. It was discontinued in 1986. It was offered in the same variations as the Model 500 series-501S, 501DL, 501DLS, 501EELL, and 501EELLS. The values for this series are the same as for the 500 series rifles.

501 Deluxe

Model 502

A .270, 7mm Remington Magnum, and the .30-06 caliber bolt action rifle with a 24" barrel, without sights and a 5-shot magazine. Blued with a checkered walnut stock. Discontinued in 1986. It is also available in the same variations as the Model 500 and the Model 501 but is valued at approximately 10 percent higher in each variation.

Mato Deluxe

This bolt action rifle was introduced into the Beretta product line in 1997. It is based on the Mauser 98 action and is fitted with a drop-out box magazine. The stock is XXX Claro walnut with a hand rubbed oil finish and black forend tip. Chambered for .270 Win., .280, .30-06, 7mm magnum, .300 magnum, .338 magnum, and .375 H&H. Weight is about 8 lbs.

NIB	Exc.	V.G.	Good	Fair	Poor
2000	—	—	—	—	—

Mato Standard

Same as above but fitted with a matte gray Kevlar and graphite composite stock. Weight is approximately 7.9 lbs.

NIB	Exc.	V.G.	Good	Fair	Poor
1550	—	—	—	—	—

Model S689

A 9.3x74R or the .30-06 caliber O/U rifle with a boxlock action, 23" ribbed barrels and express-type sights. Blued, casehardened or nickel-plated with checkered walnut stock. Double triggers and automatic ejectors.

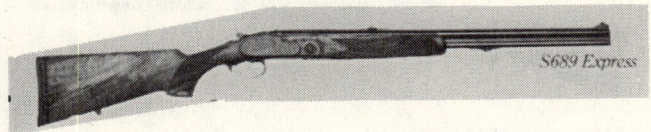

S689 Express

NIB	Exc.	V.G.	Good	Fair	Poor
4950	3750	2750	1800	1250	1000

SSO Express

A .375 Holland & Holland and .458 Winchester Magnum caliber O/U, double-barrel rifle with 23" barrels, folding express sights, double triggers, and automatic ejectors. Furnished with a fitted case. This firearm is available on a custom-order basis and should be individually appraised.

NIB	Exc.	V.G.	Good	Fair	Poor
18000	13000	9500	6500	5000	4000

SS05 Express

A more finely finished version of the above.

NIB	Exc.	V.G.	Good	Fair	Poor
20000	15000	11000	8500	7000	5500

SHOTGUNS

Beretta shotguns are marked with a symbol or 0 stamping to indicate the type of fixed choke in the barrel or barrels. Usually this stamping is on the side of the barrel in the rear near the receiver on semiautomatics and near the ejectors on double barrel shotguns. Beretta shotguns with screw-in Mobilchoke tubes will have notches cut in them to indicate the amount of choke placed in the tube.

Fixed Chokes & Beretta Mobilchoke Designations		Mobilchoke Rim Notches
O(*)	F(Full)	I
OO(**)	IM(Improved Modified)	II
OOO(***)	M(Modified)	III
OOOO(****)	IC(Improved Cyl.)	IIII
COOOO(C****)	CL(Cylinder)	IIIII
SK	SK(Skeet)	No Notches

The BL series of O/U shotguns were manufactured between 1968 and 1973. They are chambered for 12 or 20 gauge and were offered with 26", 28", or 30" vent-ribbed barrels with various choke combinations. They feature boxlock actions and were offered with either single or double triggers, and manual extractors or automatic ejectors. The finishes are blued with checkered walnut stocks. The configurations differ basically in the quality of materials and workmanship and the degree of ornamentation.

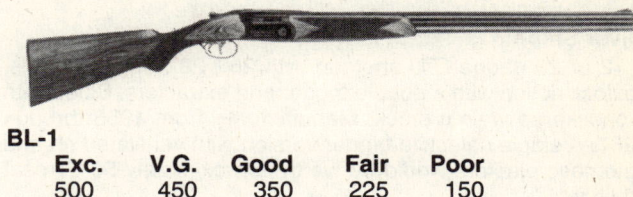

BL-1

Exc.	V.G.	Good	Fair	Poor
500	450	350	225	150

BL-2

Exc.	V.G.	Good	Fair	Poor
425	375	300	250	200

BL-2/S (Speed Trigger)

Exc.	V.G.	Good	Fair	Poor
450	400	325	275	225

BL-2 Stakeout (18" Barrel)

Exc.	V.G.	Good	Fair	Poor
400	350	275	225	175

BL-3

Exc.	V.G.	Good	Fair	Poor
600	550	475	425	350

BL-3 Competition

Exc.	V.G.	Good	Fair	Poor
650	600	525	475	400

BL-4

Exc.	V.G.	Good	Fair	Poor
800	750	650	525	425

BL-4 Competition

Exc.	V.G.	Good	Fair	Poor
850	800	700	575	450

BL-5

Exc.	V.G.	Good	Fair	Poor
900	850	725	575	450

BL-5 Competition

Exc.	V.G.	Good	Fair	Poor
950	900	775	600	475

BL-6 (Sidelock)

Exc.	V.G.	Good	Fair	Poor
1250	1150	1000	850	675

BL-6 Competition

Exc.	V.G.	Good	Fair	Poor
1300	1200	1050	900	725

Model S55B

A 12 or 20 gauge O/U shotgun with 26", 28", or 30" ventilated-rib barrels, various choke combinations and boxlock action with a single selective trigger and extractors. Blued with a checkered walnut stock.

Exc.	V.G.	Good	Fair	Poor
550	500	400	325	275

Model S56 E

As above, but more finely finished.

Exc.	V.G.	Good	Fair	Poor
600	550	450	375	325

Model S58 Competition

As above, with either 26" or 30" barrels, wide vent ribs and competition-type stocks.

Exc.	V.G.	Good	Fair	Poor
700	650	550	475	400

Silver Snipe

A 12 or 20 gauge O/U shotgun with 26", 28", or 30" barrels, boxlock action with a double trigger and extractors. Blued with a checkered walnut stock. Manufactured from 1955 through 1967. A single selective trigger version with ventilated rib and automatic ejectors would be worth approximately 50 percent additional.

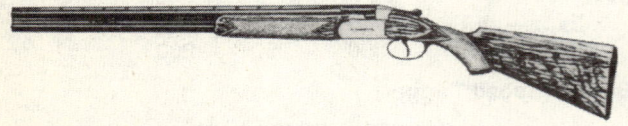

Exc.	V.G.	Good	Fair	Poor
400	375	325	275	200

Golden Snipe

As above with a ventilated rib and automatic ejectors. If it has a single selective trigger, add 10%.

Exc.	V.G.	Good	Fair	Poor
675	600	500	350	200

Model 57 E

As above, but more finely finished. Manufactured between 1955 and 1967.

Exc.	V.G.	Good	Fair	Poor
825	775	600	475	250

ASEL Model

A 12 or 20 gauge O/U shotgun with 26", 28", or 30" ventilated rib barrel with various choke combinations. Single selective trigger and automatic ejectors. Blued with a checkered pistol grip stock. Manufactured between 1947 and 1964.

Exc.	V.G.	Good	Fair	Poor
3500	2150	1200	750	400

NOTE: For 12 gauge guns deduct $1000 from Exc. condition price.

Model 409 PB

A 12, 16, 20, and 28 gauge boxlock, double-barrel shotgun with 27", 28", or 30" barrels with double triggers and extractors and various choke combinations. Blued with a checkered walnut stock. Manufactured between 1934 and 1964.

Exc.	V.G.	Good	Fair	Poor
775	700	625	500	250

Model 410 E

As above, but more finely finished.

Exc.	V.G.	Good	Fair	Poor
900	825	650	500	275

Model 410

As above, with a 32" full-choke barrel. Blued with a checkered walnut stock. Introduced in 1934.

Exc.	V.G.	Good	Fair	Poor
1000	925	750	600	300

Model 411 E

The Model 410 with false sideplates and more heavily engraved. Manufactured between 1934 and 1964.

Exc.	V.G.	Good	Fair	Poor
1200	1125	950	800	425

Model 424

A 12 and 20 gauge boxlock shotgun with 26" or 28" barrels, double triggers, various choke combinations, and extractors. Blued with a checkered walnut stock. In 20 gauge it is designated the Model 426 and would be worth an additional $100.

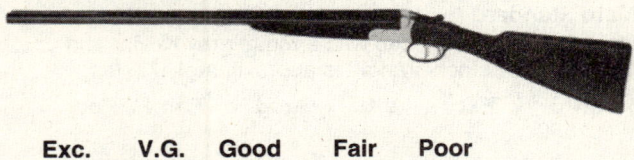

Exc.	V.G.	Good	Fair	Poor
950	875	675	500	225

Model 426 E

As above, with silver inlays and heavier engraving, single selective trigger and automatic ejectors. Not imported after 1983.

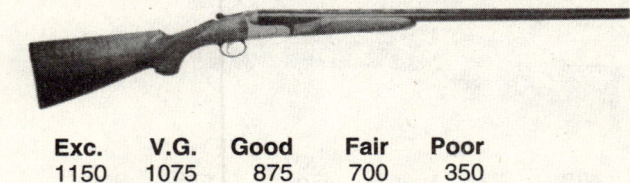

Exc.	V.G.	Good	Fair	Poor
1150	1075	875	700	350

Model 625

A 12 or 20 gauge boxlock, double-barrel shotgun with 26", 28", or 30" barrels, various choke combinations, double triggers and extractors. Moderately engraved and blued with a checkered walnut grip. Imported between 1984 and 1986.

Exc.	V.G.	Good	Fair	Poor
800	750	600	500	250

Silver Hawk

A 10 or 12 gauge boxlock, double-barrel shotgun with 30" barrels, double triggers and extractors. Blued with a silver-finished receiver and a checkered walnut stock. The 10 gauge version would be worth an additional 20 percent. Discontinued in 1967.

Exc.	V.G.	Good	Fair	Poor
500	450	375	250	150

Model 470 Silver Hawk

Introduced in 1997 to commemorate Beretta's 470 years in the gunmaking business, this shotgun is offered in either 12 or 20 gauge configurations. The receiver is silver chrome with engraving. The top lever is checkered with a gold inlaid hawk's head. The gun is fitted with a straight grip stock with splinter forearm of select walnut with oil finish. Choice of 26" or 28" barrels with auto ejection or manual extraction. Weight of 12 gauge about 6.5 lbs. The 20 gauge weighs approximately 6 lbs.

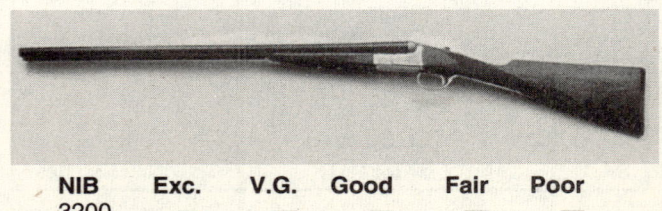

NIB	Exc.	V.G.	Good	Fair	Poor
3200	—	—	—	—	—

Beretta "SO" Series

These over and under shotguns were fitted with side locks, automatic ejectors, single or double triggers. Barrel ranges in length from 26" to 30" with a wide variety of choke combinations. These guns were introduced in 1948 in 12 gauge only and no longer imported as a production gun in 1986. Many of these SO guns were sold through the firm of Garcia, a sporting goods firm and distributor. The various grades are priced according to quality of wood, finish engraving coverage, and the like. Do not confuse these earlier Beretta shotguns with the present line of premium grade Berettas now being imported into the U.S.

Model SO-1

Exc.	V.G.	Good	Fair	Poor
2000	1600	1200	800	400

Model SO-2

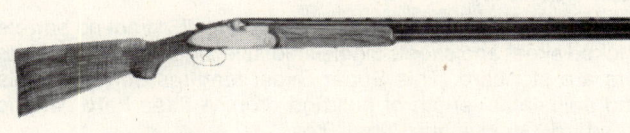

Exc.	V.G.	Good	Fair	Poor
2500	1900	1500	900	500

Model SO-3

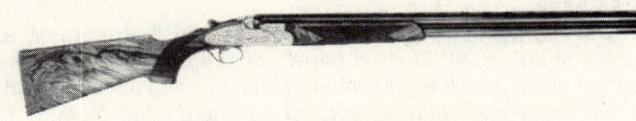

Exc.	V.G.	Good	Fair	Poor
3500	2500	1750	1200	600

Model SO-4

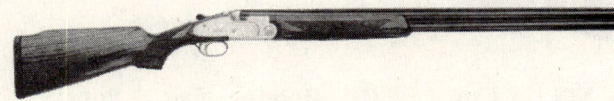

Exc.	V.G.	Good	Fair	Poor
4500	3250	2200	1500	750

Model SO-5 (503EELL)

Exc.	V.G.	Good	Fair	Poor
8000	6000	4000	2000	1000

Model SO-6 (450 or 451EL) SideXSide

This model is fitted with Holland and Holland-style side locks and third fastner.

Exc.	V.G.	Good	Fair	Poor
8000	6000	4000	2000	1000

Model SO-7 (451EELL)

Exc.	V.G.	Good	Fair	Poor
9500	7000	5000	2500	1200

SO-5 Trap

A premium grade Beretta over and under shotgun built for competition trap shooting. Available in 12 gauge with 30" vent rib barrels standard. Barrels in 28" and 32" may be special ordered. Receiver is silver with light scroll engraving. The stock is select highly figured walnut with pistol grip and offered in International or Monte Carlo dimensions. Special trap rubber recoil pad is furnished. Weighs 8 lbs., 2 oz. Furnished with leather case and tools.

NIB	Exc.	V.G.	Good	Fair	Poor
12000	8000	5000	3500	2500	1500

SO-5 Trap 2 BBL Set

NIB	Exc.	V.G.	Good	Fair	Poor
15500	11000	8500	6000	4500	2500

SO-5 Skeet

Same general specifications as above but furnished to skeet dimensions. Offered in 12 gauge only with 26" or 28" vent rib barrels choked sheet. Weighs 7 lbs., 8 oz.

NIB	Exc.	V.G.	Good	Fair	Poor
12000	8000	5000	3500	2500	1500

SO-5 Sporting Clays

Offered in 12 gauge only with choice of 28" or 30" barrels; 26" on special order. Sporting clay dimension walnut stock with pistol grip and rubber recoil pad. Weighs 7 lbs., 8oz.

NIB	Exc.	V.G.	Good	Fair	Poor
12000	8000	5000	3500	2500	1500

SO-6

This is a premium grade Beretta that is available in several different configurations similar to the SO-5. Available in 12 gauge only. It features a true side lock action, single selective or non-selective trigger, fixed or screw-in choke tubes. The receiver is offered either in silver finish or casehardened without engraving. The walnut is highly select walnut with fine line checkering. A choice of pistol grip or straight grip is offered. Supplied with a leather fitted hard case. Weighs about 7 lbs., 4 oz. depending on barrel length.

SO-6 Trap

NIB	Exc.	V.G.	Good	Fair	Poor
16500	12000	8000	5000	3500	2000

SO-6 Skeet

NIB	Exc.	V.G.	Good	Fair	Poor
16500	12000	8000	5000	3500	2000

SO-6 Sporting Clays

NIB	Exc.	V.G.	Good	Fair	Poor
16500	12000	8000	5000	3500	2000

SO-6 EELL

A higher grade in the SO-6 series that features a silver receiver with custom engraving with scroll or game scenes. Gold inlays are available on request. Choice of barrel lengths from 26" to 30". All of the same features of the SO 6, but with higher fit and finish. Offered in 12 gauge only.

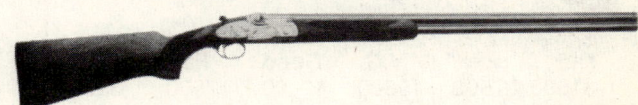

NIB	Exc.	V.G.	Good	Fair	Poor
26000	20000	12500	8000	5000	2500

SO-7

One of Beretta's best-grade, sidelock, double-barrel shotgun. It is elaborately engraved and has the highest grade walnut in the stock.

Exc.	V.G.	Good	Fair	Poor
9500	7850	6750	5500	4500

SO-9

This model O/U is Beretta's highest grade. Offered in 12, 20, and 28 gauge, and .410 bore. The true side lock (removable) receiver is highly engraved with scroll or game scenes by Italy's finest craftsmen. Barrel lengths are offered from 26" to 30" with solid hand filed rib. The walnut stock is the finest available with either pistol grip or straight grip. Stock dimensions to customers request. A custom fitted leather case with accessories is supplied with gun.

NIB	Exc.	V.G.	Good	Fair	Poor
28500	23500	18500	10000	5000	2500

SS06

This is a premium grade sidelock over and under express rifle. Equipped with double triggers. It is offered in 9.3x74R, .375 H&H Magnum, and .458 Win. Magnum. It is fitted with a 24" barrel with express sights. Claw mounts and Ziess are available from the factory. The receiver is case-colored with light scroll engraving. Special select walnut is used in the stock and forearm with fine line checkering. Stock comes with cheekpiece and rubber recoil pad. Furnished with leather case. Rifle weighs about 11 lbs.

NIB	Exc.	V.G.	Good	Fair	Poor
21000	15000	10000	7500	3500	2500

SS06 EELL

Offered in the same calibers as above but furnished with hand engraved game scenes with gold inlays. Walnut stock is special select briar with fine diamond line checkering.

NIB	Exc.	V.G.	Good	Fair	Poor
23000	17500	12500	10000	4500	3000

Model 452

This is a premium grade side by side shotgun fitted with slide locks (removable). Offered in 12 gauge only with 26", 28", or 30" solid rib barrels. The receiver is a highly polished silver finish without engraving. Triggers may be double, single selective, or single non-selective. The stock and forearm are special select walnut with fine line checkering with a choice of pistol or straight grip. Comes with leather hard case. Weighs about 6 lbs., 13 oz.

NIB	Exc.	V.G.	Good	Fair	Poor
22000	17000	12500	8500	4500	2500

Model 452 EELL

Same as above but furnished with fine scroll or game scene engraving. The highest grade of walnut is furnished for the stock and forearm. Leather case with accessories furnished.

NIB	Exc.	V.G.	Good	Fair	Poor
31000	27500	19500	12000	7500	3500

Model 455

This is a premium grade side by side express rifle with slide locks. Available in the following calibers: .375 H&H Magnum, .458 Win. Magnum, .470 Nitro Express, .500 Nitro Express, and .416 Rigby. The receiver is case-colored without engraving and the walnut stock is highly figured with fine line checkering. Comes supplied with express sights. Claw mounts and Zeiss scope offered at customers request only on .375, .458, and .416. Weighs about 11 lbs.

Model 455 EELL

Same as above model but furnished with case-colored game scene engraving with gold inlays. Walnut briar stock with fine diamond line checkering. Supplied with leather case and accessories.

NIB	Exc.	V.G.	Good	Fair	Poor
47000	37500	27500	17500	9500	4500

Model 682/682 Gold

This is a high grade, quality built O/U shotgun. Offered in 12 and 20 gauge, it is also available in some configurations in 28 gauge and .410 bore with barrel lengths from 26" to 34" depending on the type of shooting required. It is fitted with single selective trigger and automatic ejectors. Barrels are fitted with ventilated rib and various fixed or screw-in choke combinations are available. The stock is a high grade walnut with fine checkering in stock dimensions to fit the function of the gun. The frame is silver with light scroll borders on most models. This model covers a wide variety of applications and these are listed below by grade and/or function:

NOTE: The Beretta Competition series shotguns have been renamed as of 1994. These shotguns are also referred to as the 682 Gold Competition Series guns, such as Model 682 Gold Trap or Model 682 Gold X Trap Combo and so forth.

682 Super Skeet

This model is offered in 12 gauge only with 28" vent rib barrels choked skeet and skeet. Single selective trigger and auto ejectors are standard. This Super Skeet features ported barrels and adjustable length of pull and drop. A fitted hard case is standard. Gun weighs 7 lbs., 8 oz.

NIB	Exc.	V.G.	Good	Fair	Poor
2300	1850	1500	1250	950	750

682 Skeet

This is the standard 12 gauge skeet model that features a choice of 26" or 28" vent rib barrels choked skeet and skeet. Walnut stock is of International dimensions with special skeet rubber recoil pad. Gun is supplied with hard case. Weighs 7 lbs., 8 oz.

NIB	Exc.	V.G.	Good	Fair	Poor
2000	1850	1500	1250	950	700

682 4 BBL Set

This skeet gun is fitted with 4 barrels in 12, 20, 28 gauge, and .410 bore. Each barrel is 28", choked skeet and skeet, and fitted with a vent rib.

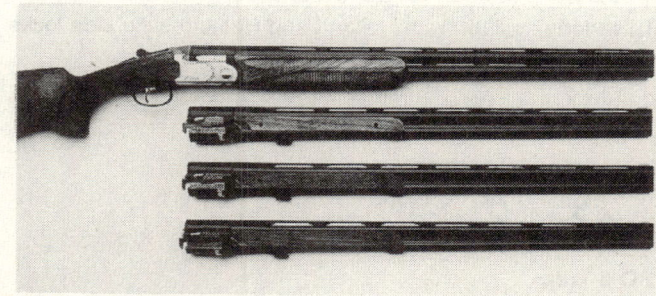

NIB	Exc.	V.G.	Good	Fair	Poor
4500	4000	3500	3000	2000	950

682 Super Sporting/682 Gold Sporting Ported

Built for sporting clays this 12 gauge or 20 gauge model features ported barrel and adjustable length of pull and drop. Fitted with 28" or 30" vent barrel with screw-in chokes; fixed chokes on special order. Checkered walnut stock with pistol grip and recoil pad. Supplied with case. Introduced in 1993. Weight of 12 gauge is 7 lbs-8 oz. and 20 gauge weighs 6 lbs.-3 oz.

NIB	Exc.	V.G.	Good	Fair	Poor
2300	1850	1500	1250	950	350

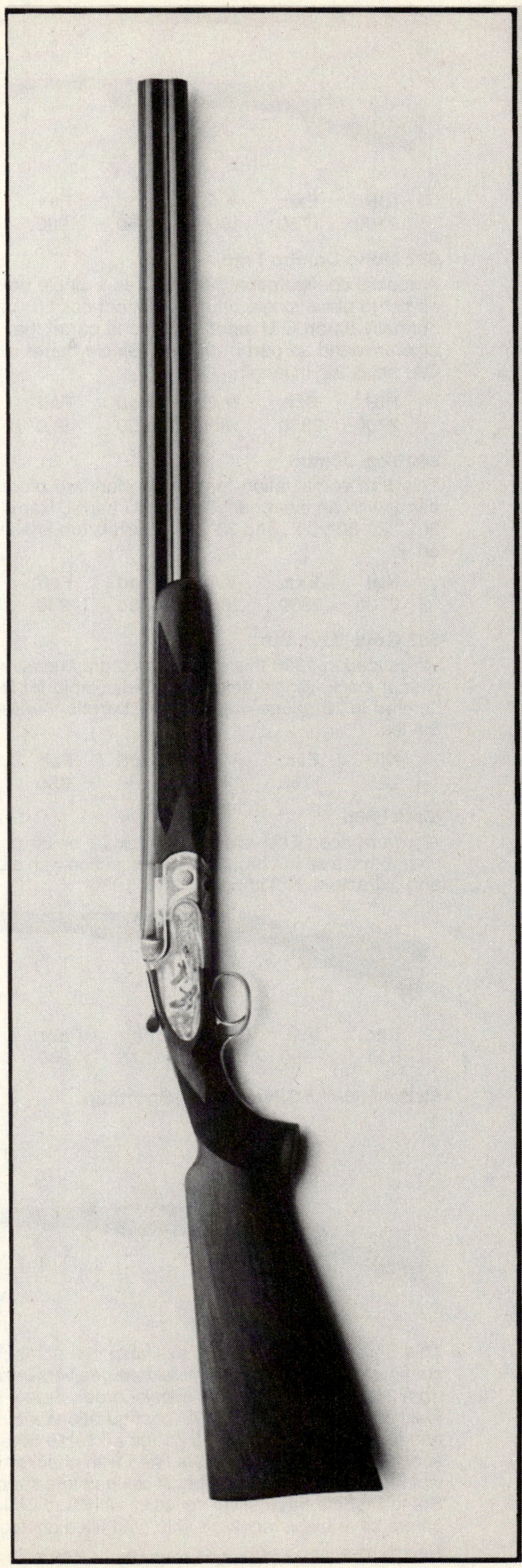

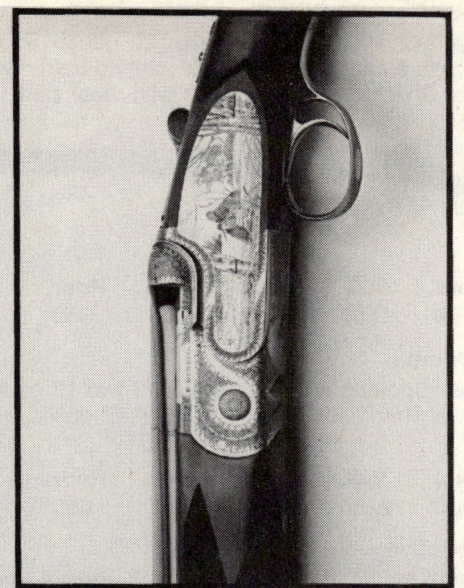

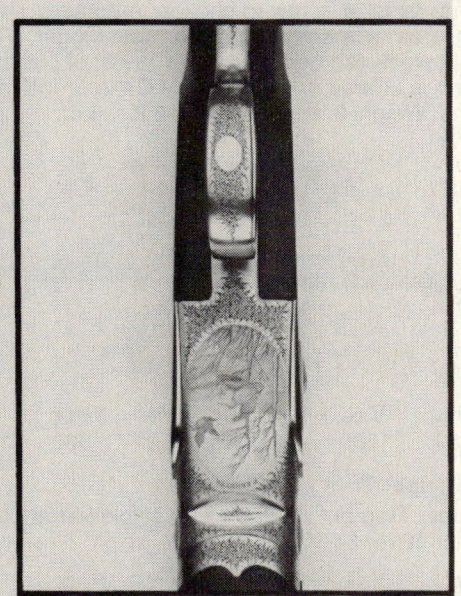

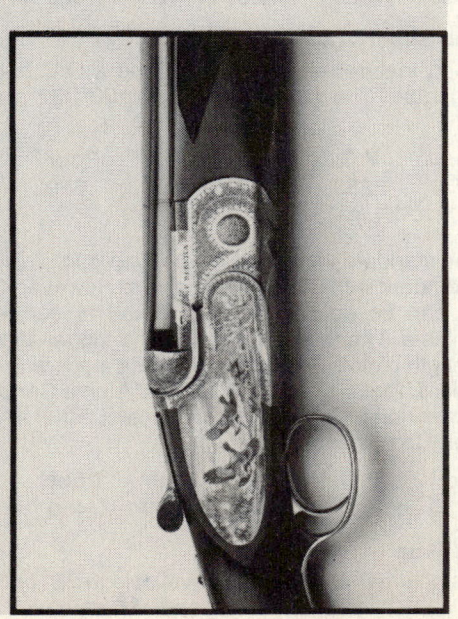

BERETTA PREMIUM GRADES
Shown above: The Beretta S09 20 gauge Over/Under shotgun. Beretta Premium Grades feature hand detachable sideplates. European walnut stocks and fore-ends, Boehler high-nickel antinit steel barrels, true sidelock actions, closed receivers and a variety of engraving patterns.

682 Sporting/682 Gold Sporting

The standard version of the 12 gauge or 20 gauge Super Sporting model with a choice of 28" or 30" vent rib barrel with screw-in chokes. Checkered walnut stock with recoil pad. Introduced in 1993.

NIB	Exc.	V.G.	Good	Fair	Poor
2100	1750	1500	1250	950	350

682 Sporting Combo

Similar to the 682 Sporting with the addition of two 12 gauge 28" and 30" barrel fitted with screw-in chokes. Supplied with hard case.

NIB	Exc.	V.G.	Good	Fair	Poor
2800	2500	2250	1750	1250	650

682 Super Trap

This 12 gauge trap model (a 20 gauge set of barrels is available on special order) features ported 30" or 32" ventilated rib barrels with either fixed or screw-in chokes. Automatic ejectors are standard as is a single non-selective trigger. The checkered walnut stock can be adjusted for length of pull and drop of comb and is offered in either Monte Carlo or International dimensions. Weight is approximately 8 lbs.,6 oz.

NIB	Exc.	V.G.	Good	Fair	Poor
2300	1850	1500	1250	950	500

682 Top Single Super Trap

Same as the Super Trap but available in a single barrel configuration of either 32" or 34".

NIB	Exc.	V.G.	Good	Fair	Poor
2400	1950	1600	1350	950	500

682 Top Combo Super Trap

This configuration features a single barrel and a O/U barrel both interchangeable. The combinations are: 30", 32", and 30", 34".

NIB	Exc.	V.G.	Good	Fair	Poor
3000	2750	2250	1750	1250	650

682 Trap

This model is the standard variation Beretta Trap gun. This 12 gauge comes standard with 30" vent rib barrels. However, 28" and 32" barrel can be special ordered. Fixed or screw-in chokes are available. The three-position sliding trigger allows for adjustable length of pull. A checkered walnut stock with recoil pad is standard. Stock is available in either Monte Carlo or International dimensions. Customer has choice of either silver or black receiver. Comes cased.

NIB	Exc.	V.G.	Good	Fair	Poor
2200	1750	1500	1250	900	450

682 Top Single Trap

This 12 gauge single barrel trap gun is available in 32" or 34" vent rib barrel.

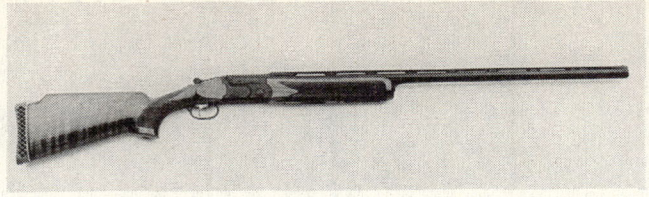

NIB	Exc.	V.G.	Good	Fair	Poor
2100	1750	1500	1250	900	450

682 Mono Combo Trap

A special configuration that features a single barrel with vent rib set to place single barrel in bottom position of what would normally be an O/U setup. A second barrel that is an O/U is also provided as part of the set. Single barrel is 34" and the O/U set is 32" in length.

NIB	Exc.	V.G.	Good	Fair	Poor
2700	2350	1850	1350	950	500

682 Top Combo

This trap combination features a standard placement single barrel with an interchangeable O/U barrel. Barrel available in 30", 32"; 30", 34"; and 32", 34". Barrels are fitted with ventilated rib.

NIB	Exc.	V.G.	Good	Fair	Poor
2700	2350	1850	1350	950	500

682 Gold "Live Bird"

Introduced in 1995 this model has a gray receiver with select walnut stock. Single selective is adjustable for length of pull. Offered in 12 gauge only with 30" barrels. Average weight is 8.8 lbs.

NIB	Exc.	V.G.	Good	Fair	Poor
2250	1750	1450	1150	850	400

Model 685

A lower-priced O/U chambered for 12 or 20 gauge with 3" chambers, a satin-chromed boxlock action with a single trigger and extractors. Not imported after 1986.

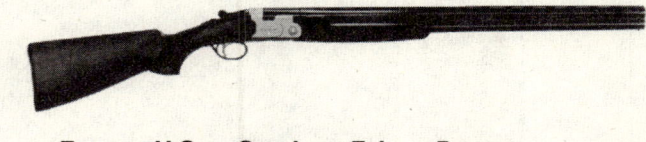

Exc.	V.G.	Good	Fair	Poor
650	600	500	375	200

Model 686/686 Silver Perdiz Sporting

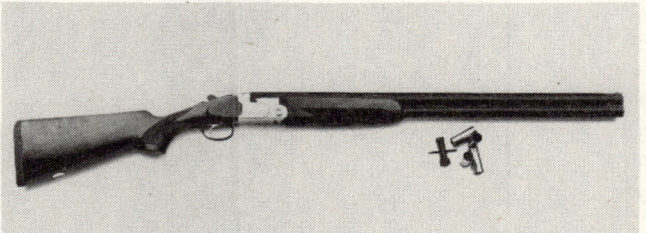

This Beretta O/U shotgun is available in a number of different configurations. This basic model features ventilated rib barrels from 24" to 30"; 30" being a special order. Screw-in chokes or fixed chokes are available. All configurations are offered in 12 gauge and 20 gauge with 28 gauge and .410 bore available in special order only. The gun is fitted with checkered American walnut stock with black rubber recoil pad and special grip cap. Some models have silver receiver with scroll engraving and others have black receivers with gold filled contours.

NOTE: This 686 series also renamed in 1994.

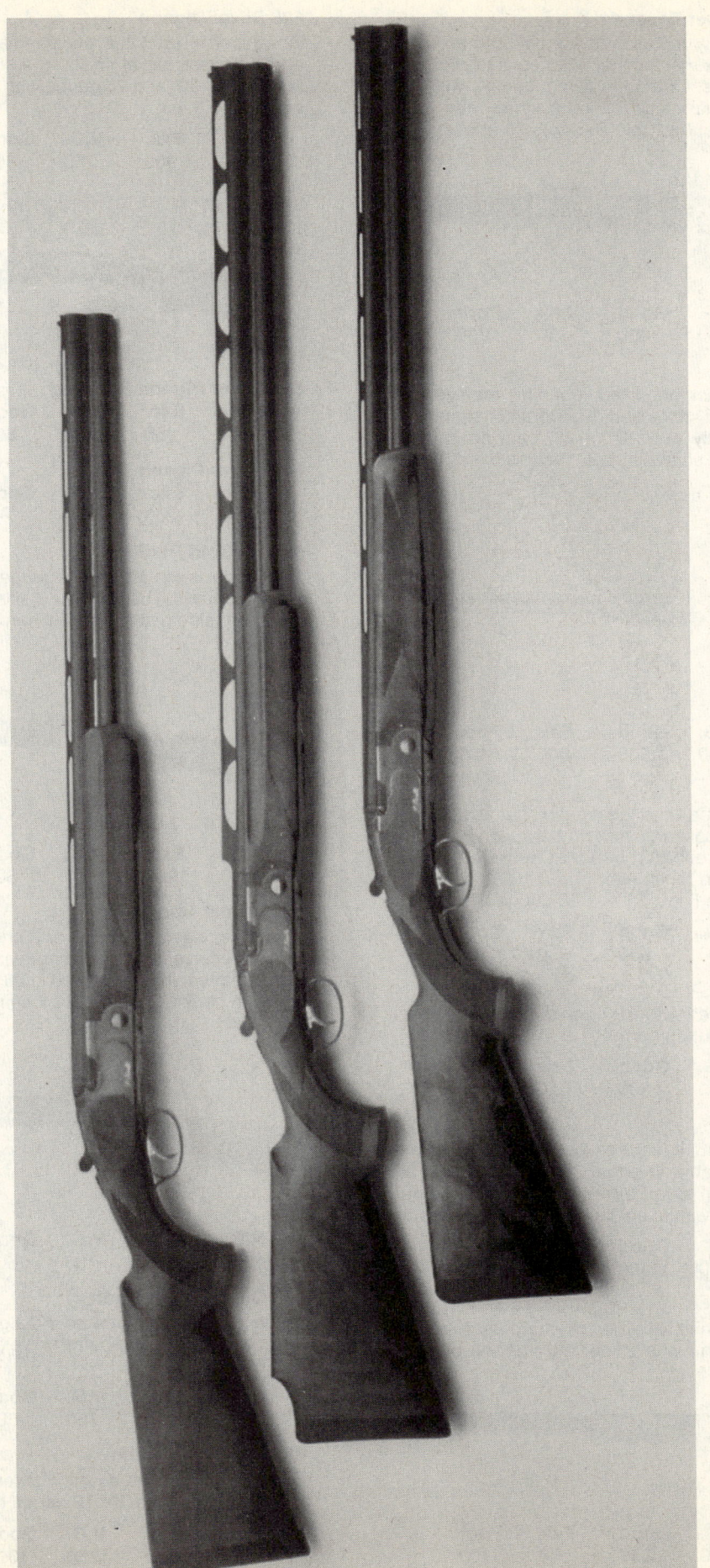

Models 682 Skeet (top), 682 Super Trap (middle) and 682 Trap (bottom)

Model 686 Essential/Silver Essential

Introduced in 1994 this 686 model is designed to be an entry level 686. It offers all of the mechanical features of the 686 series without any of the frills. Offered in 12 gauge only with 26" or 28" barrels. Plain walnut stock with checkering and plain blue receiver. Weighs about 6.7 lbs. Renamed the Silver Essential in 1997.

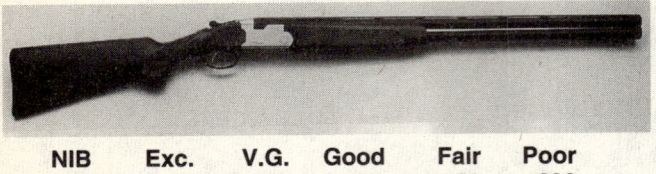

NIB	Exc.	V.G.	Good	Fair	Poor
900	750	600	450	350	200

686 Ultra Light Onyx

This model features a black anodized light alloy receiver accented with an engraved gold-filled "P. Beretta" signature. Available in 12 gauge only with 26" or 28" vent rib barrels. Chokes are either fixed or screw-in type. Weighs 5 lbs., 1 oz.

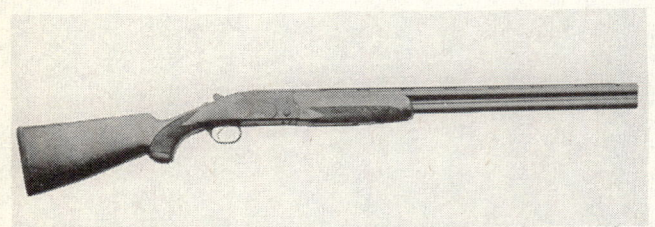

NIB	Exc.	V.G.	Good	Fair	Poor
1050	850	750	600	500	400

686 Onyx

Similar in appearance to the Ultra Light Onyx, but available in either 12 gauge or 20 gauge with vent rib barrel lengths from 26" to 28". Chambers are either 3" or 3.5". Checkered walnut stock offered in pistol grip or straight grip. Choice of choke types. Weight of 12 gauge 6 lbs., 13 oz.; 20 gauge 6 lbs., 3 oz.

NIB	Exc.	V.G.	Good	Fair	Poor
950	850	750	650	500	400

686 Onyx 2 BBL Set

Same as above but supplied with a 20 gauge 28" vent rib barrel and a 28 gauge 26" vent rib barrel.

NIB	Exc.	V.G.	Good	Fair	Poor
1450	1250	1000	800	650	500

686 Silver Receiver

This model is the basic 686. It features a plain semi-matte silver receiver and is available in either 12 or 20 gauge; 28 gauge available on special order. Vent rib barrels are offered in lengths from 24" to 30" with fixed chokes or choke tubes.

NIB	Exc.	V.G.	Good	Fair	Poor
950	850	750	650	500	400

686 L/686 Silver Perdiz

Same as above but furnished with a scroll engraved silver receiver. Offered in 28 gauge with 26" or 28" vent rib barrels. Gun weighs 5 lbs., 5 oz.

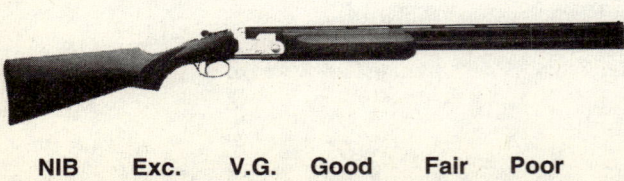

NIB	Exc.	V.G.	Good	Fair	Poor
950	850	750	650	500	400

686 Silver Pigeon

Introduced in 1996 this model replaces the Silver Perdiz. It has an electroless nickel finish on a scroll engraved receiver. Offered in 12, 20, and 28 gauge with 26" or 28" barrels. Average weight is 6.8 lbs.

NIB	Exc.	V.G.	Good	Fair	Poor
1150	900	750	600	500	300

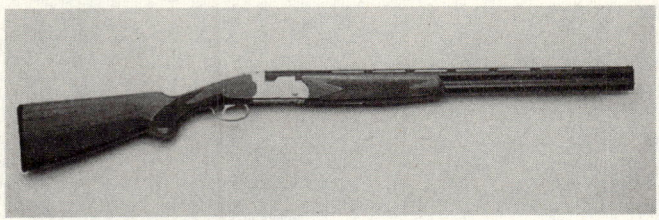

686 Silver Pigeon Sporting

NIB	Exc.	V.G.	Good	Fair	Poor
1250	950	750	600	500	300

686 Silver Pigeon Trap

NIB	Exc.	V.G.	Good	Fair	Poor
1600	1200	—	—	—	—

686 EL/Gold Perdiz

This model is available in 12 gauge or 20 gauge with 26" or 28" vent rib barrels. The receiver is silver with scroll engraving and fitted with side plates. A fitted hard case comes with the gun.

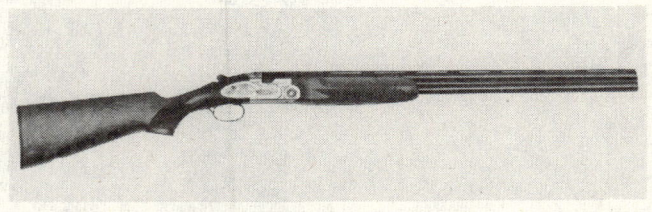

NIB	Exc.	V.G.	Good	Fair	Poor
1550	1250	1000	800	700	350

686 Hunter Sport

A sporting clays 12 gauge or 20 gauge shotgun that features a silver receiver with scroll engraving. Wide 12.5mm target rib. Radiused recoil pad. Offered in 26" or 28" vent rib barrels with screw-in chokes. Offered for the first time in 1993.

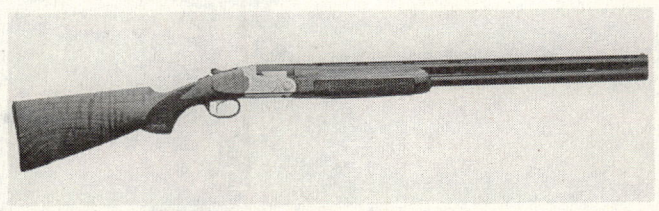

NIB	Exc.	V.G.	Good	Fair	Poor
1000	850	750	600	500	250

686 Onyx Hunter Sport

Same as above but offered in 12 gauge only with matte black finish on receiver and barrels. Weighs 6 lbs., 13 oz. Introduced in 1993.

NIB	Exc.	V.G.	Good	Fair	Poor
1000	850	750	600	500	250

686 Sporting Combo

Same specifications as the Hunter Sport with the addition of an interchangeable 30" 12 gauge barrel.

NIB	Exc.	V.G.	Good	Fair	Poor
1800	1500	1250	1000	800	550

686 Collection Trap

Introduced in 1996 this model features a special multu-colored stock and forend. Offered in 12 gauge only with 30" barrels. Factory recoil pad standard. Average weight is 7.7 lbs.

NIB	Exc.	V.G.	Good	Fair	Poor
1250	900	750	500	400	300

686 Collection Sport

Similar to above but offered with 28" barrels.

NIB	Exc.	V.G.	Good	Fair	Poor
1250	900	750	500	400	300

Model 687/687 Silver Pigeon Sporting

This model is similar to the Model 686 but in a slightly more ornate version.

NOTE: This series renamed in 1994.

687 L/Silver Pigeon

This model is offered in 12 gauge or 20 gauge with 26" or 28" vent rib barrels. The box lock receiver is scroll engraved with game scenes. Auto ejectors and double or single triggers are offered.

NIB	Exc.	V.G.	Good	Fair	Poor
1500	1100	950	800	650	300

687 Silver Pigeon Sporting

A sporting clays version available in 12 or 20 gauge with 28" or 30" barrels.

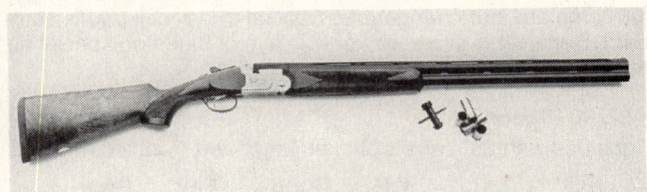

NIB	Exc.	V.G.	Good	Fair	Poor
1900	1400	1000	700	550	350

687 Sporting Combo

Offered in 12 gauge only with two sets of 12 gauge interchangeable vent rib barrels in 28" and 30".

NIB	Exc.	V.G.	Good	Fair	Poor
2400	2100	1850	1500	1150	600

687 EL/687 Gold Pigeon

This model is offered with scroll engraved gold inlaid game animals. Fitted with side plates. The stock is highly figured walnut with fine line checkering. Available in 12, 20, 28 gauge or .410 bore in 26" or 28" vent rib barrels with screw-in chokes. Comes with fitted hard case. Weights for 12 gauge: 6 lbs., 13 oz.; 20 gauge: 6 lbs., 3 oz.; 28/.410: 5 lbs., 5 oz.

NOTE: Series renamed in 1994.

687 EL 12 gauge and 20 gauge

NIB	Exc.	V.G.	Good	Fair	Poor
2750	2450	1800	1200	750	350

687 EL 28/.410

NIB	Exc.	V.G.	Good	Fair	Poor
2800	2500	1850	1250	800	400

687 EL Gold Pigeon Sporting

A sporting clays model chambered for 12 gauge and fitted with 28" or 30" vent rib barrels. Offered new in 1993. Comes with fitted hard case.

NIB	Exc.	V.G.	Good	Fair	Poor
2800	2250	1750	1250	900	450

687 EELL/Diamond Pigeon

Same as above, including gauge and barrel offerings, but furnished with more fully figured walnut and finer checkering. Fitted with slide plates that are scroll engraved with fine cut game scenes. This grade is also available in a straight grip English stock version in 20 gauge as well as a combo set of 20 gauge and 28 gauge interchangeable 26" barrels. All 687 EELL Models are fitted with hard case.

NOTE: Series renamed in 1994.

687 EELL 12 and 20 gauge

NIB	Exc.	V.G.	Good	Fair	Poor
5000	2850	2000	1500	1000	500

687 EELL 28 gauge and .410 bore

NIB	Exc.	V.G.	Good	Fair	Poor
5000	3000	2200	1700	1100	550

687 EELL Combo

NIB	Exc.	V.G.	Good	Fair	Poor
5500	3750	2750	2000	1500	1000

687 Skeet

Same as above with the addition of a skeet configuration. A 12 gauge version is offered with 28" vent rib barrels choked skeet and skeet. Weighs about 7 lbs., 8 oz. A 4 barrel set is also offered with interchangeable 12, 20, 28 gauge, and .410 bore barrels choked skeet and skeet.

687 EELL 12 gauge

NIB	Exc.	V.G.	Good	Fair	Poor
3200	2850	2250	1500	1000	800

687 EELL 4 BBL Set

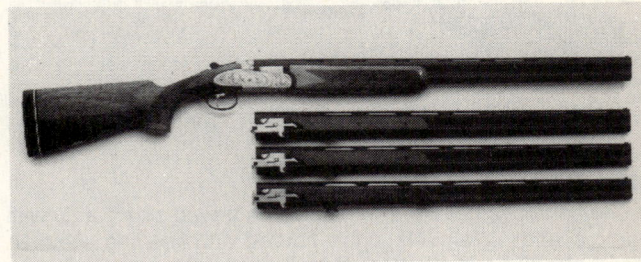

NIB	Exc.	V.G.	Good	Fair	Poor
5750	5000	4500	3750	2500	1500

687 EELL Diamond Pigeon Sporting

A sporting clays version of the 687 EELL in 12 gauge only with 28" vent rib barrels fitted with screw-in chokes.

NIB	Exc.	V.G.	Good	Fair	Poor
4100	3250	2500	1700	1100	600

687 EELL Trap

This model is fitted with either International or Monte Carlo trap stock dimensions. Offered in 12 gauge with 30" vent rib barrels fixed or screw-in choke tubes. Weighs about 8 lbs.,6 oz.

NIB	Exc.	V.G.	Good	Fair	Poor
3500	3000	2500	2000	1500	1000

687 EELL Top Combo

A single barrel trap gun with choice of one single barrel set and one Over/Under steel rod barrel in either 30" and 32" or 32" and 34".

NIB	Exc.	V.G.	Good	Fair	Poor
4000	3500	3000	2250	2000	1000

Model 626 Field Grade

A 12 or 20 gauge boxlock double-barrel shotgun with a 26" or 28" barrel, various choke combinations, single-trigger and automatic ejectors. Engraved, blued with a checkered walnut stock. Imported between 1984 and 1988.

Exc.	V.G.	Good	Fair	Poor
900	825	700	575	475

626 Onyx

This model is a box lock side by side shotgun offered in 12 gauge and 20 gauge. With choice of 26" or 28" solid rib barrels with screw-in chokes. Double triggers are standard but single trigger is available on request. Receiver is anti-glare black matte finish. Stock is walnut with hand checkering and pistol grip. The 12 gauge weighs 6 lbs., 13 oz. and the 20 gauge weighs 6 lbs., 13 oz.

NIB	Exc.	V.G.	Good	Fair	Poor
1250	950	850	750	500	400

627 EL

This model is offered in 12 gauge only with choice of 26" or 28" solid rib barrels. The walnut is highly figured and fine cut checkered. The receiver is silver with slide plates engraved with scroll. Comes with hard case.

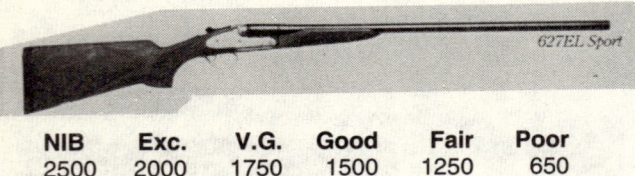

627EL Sport

NIB	Exc.	V.G.	Good	Fair	Poor
2500	2000	1750	1500	1250	650

627 EELL

Same as above but fitted with scroll engraved side plates with game scenes. Walnut is highly figured with fine line checkering. A straight grip stock is also offered in this model. Comes with hard case.

NIB	Exc.	V.G.	Good	Fair	Poor
3750	3500	3000	2500	1500	1000

Model 451 Series

A custom order sidelock shotgun. The lowest-priced version would be worth approximately $6,000 in excellent condition; and the top-of-the-line model, approximately $25,000. Prospective purchasers are advised to secure a qualified appraisal prior to acquisition.

Model FS-1

A single-barrel boxlock shotgun in all gauges and a 26" or 28", full-choke barrel. Blued with a checkered walnut stock. This model was also known as the "Companion."

Exc.	V.G.	Good	Fair	Poor
250	225	175	125	90

TR-1 Trap

A 12 gauge, single-barrel boxlock trap gun, 32" ventilated-rib, full-choke barrel. Blued with a checkered, Monte Carlo stock. Manufactured between 1968 and 1971.

Exc.	V.G.	Good	Fair	Poor
275	250	200	150	100

TR-2 Trap

As above, with a high, competition-type vent rib. It was manufactured between 1969 and 1973.

Exc.	V.G.	Good	Fair	Poor
300	275	225	175	125

Mark II Trap

A 12 gauge, boxlock single-barrel trap shotgun with a 32" or 34", full-choke barrel, competition-type rib and automatic ejector. Blued with a checkered, Monte Carlo type, walnut stock. Manufactured between 1972 and 1976.

Exc.	V.G.	Good	Fair	Poor
700	625	525	450	275

Model ASE 90/Gold Series

This is a competition trap model Over/Under shotgun. It features a trigger lock assembly that is removable in the field so a spare can be used in the event of failure. The single non-selective trigger has a three way adjustment. The ventilated rib is wide and the side ribs are also ventilated. Walnut stock and forearms are interchangeable. Special trap recoil pad is standard. Receiver is silver with gold inlays or blued on special order. The ASE 90 weighs about 8 lbs., 6 oz.

ASE 90 Pigeon

Equipped with 28" barrels choked Improved Modified and Full.

NIB	Exc.	V.G.	Good	Fair	Poor
5750	5250	3750	2750	1500	1000

ASE 90 Trap

Comes standard with 30" vent rib barrels.

NIB	Exc.	V.G	Good	Fair	Poor
5750	5250	3750	2750	1500	1000

ASE 90 Gold X Trap Combo

Introduced in 1993 this set features a single barrel and interchangeable Over/Under barrels in 30", 32" and 30", 34" combinations.

NIB	Exc.	V.G	Good	Fair	Poor
6750	5500	4000	3000	1500	1000

ASE 90 Skeet

This model is a skeet version of the ASE 90 series. Features the same basic specifications as the trap model but configured for competition skeet. Offered in 12 gauge only with 28" skeet and skeet chokes. Weighs about 7 lbs., 11 oz.

NIB	Exc.	V.G.	Good	Fair	Poor
5750	5250	3750	2750	1500	1000

ASE 90 Sporting Clay

Configured for sporting clay competition. Offered in 12 gauge only with 28" or 30" vent rib barrels.

NIB	Exc.	V.G.	Good	Fair	Poor
6750	5500	4000	3000	1500	1000

Model SL-2

A 12 gauge slide action shotgun, 26", 28", or 30", ventilated rib barrels with various chokes. Blued with a checkered walnut stock. Manufactured between 1968 and 1971.

Exc.	V.G.	Good	Fair	Poor
350	300	250	200	150

Pigeon Series

As above, in three grades.

Silver Pigeon

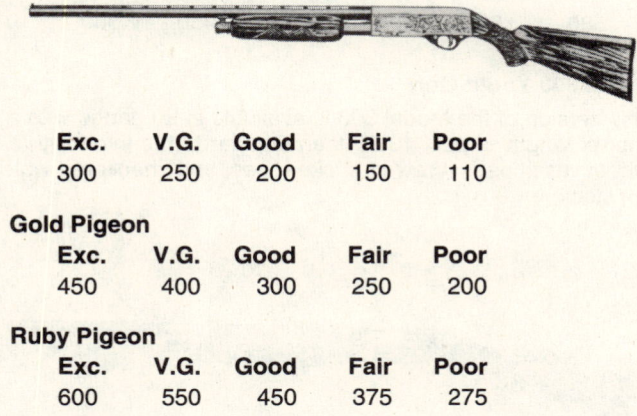

Exc.	V.G.	Good	Fair	Poor
300	250	200	150	110

Gold Pigeon

Exc.	V.G.	Good	Fair	Poor
450	400	300	250	200

Ruby Pigeon

Exc.	V.G.	Good	Fair	Poor
600	550	450	375	275

AL Series

A 12 or 20 gauge semiautomatic shotgun with 26", 28", or 30" barrels and various choke combinations. Blued with a checkered walnut stock. Manufactured between 1969 and 1976.

AL-1

Exc.	V.G.	Good	Fair	Poor
400	375	300	225	150

AL-2

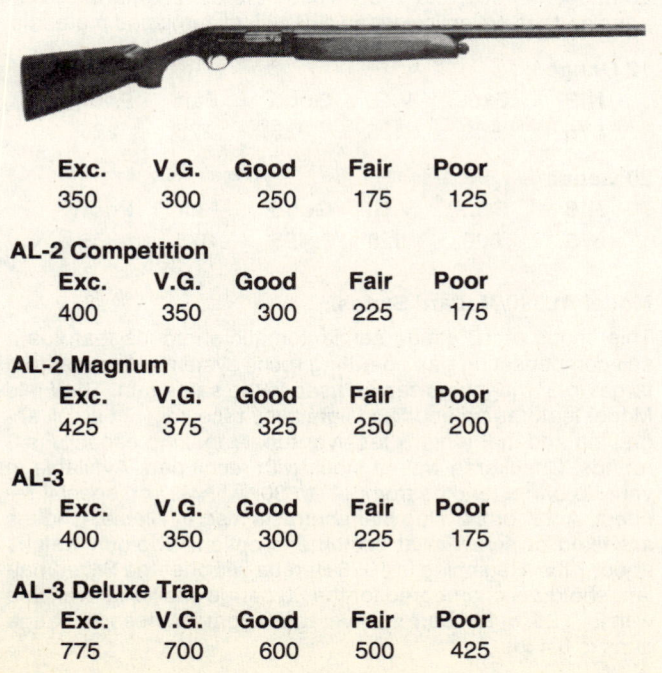

Exc.	V.G.	Good	Fair	Poor
350	300	250	175	125

AL-2 Competition

Exc.	V.G.	Good	Fair	Poor
400	350	300	225	175

AL-2 Magnum

Exc.	V.G.	Good	Fair	Poor
425	375	325	250	200

AL-3

Exc.	V.G.	Good	Fair	Poor
400	350	300	225	175

AL-3 Deluxe Trap

Exc.	V.G.	Good	Fair	Poor
775	700	600	500	425

Model 301

Improved version of the AL Series manufactured between 1977 and 1982. It is also available as a slug gun with a 22" barrel with rifle sights.

Exc.	V.G.	Good	Fair	Poor
400	350	300	225	175

Model 1200 Field Grade

A 12 gauge semiautomatic shotgun, 28" ventilated-rib barrel, screw-in choke tubes and a 4-round, tubular magazine. Matte blued with either a checkered walnut or black synthetic stock. Introduced in 1984.

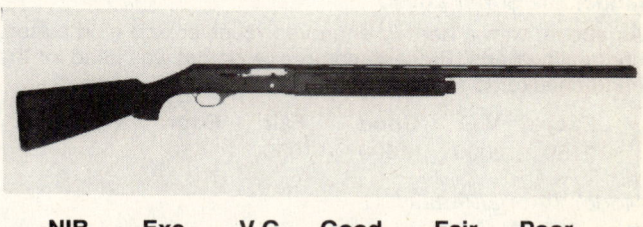

NIB	Exc.	V.G.	Good	Fair	Poor
585	525	425	325	250	200

Model 1200 Magnum (3" Chamber)

NIB	Exc.	V.G.	Good	Fair	Poor
585	525	425	325	250	200

Model 1200 Riot (20" Cyl. Bore Barrel)

NIB	Exc.	V.G.	Good	Fair	Poor
585	525	425	325	250	200

Model 1201

This 12 gauge semiautomatic shotgun has a short recoil system and features a synthetic stock with matte black finish and lightweight alloy receiver. Available in two basic configurations: the Field Grade with choice of 24", 26", and 28" vent rib barrel with screw-in chokes and Riot Models with 18" plain cylinder choked barrel with either full stock or pistol grip only stock (introduced in 1993). Field Grade weighs about 6 lbs.,12 oz. and the Riot Model about 6 lbs., 5 oz.

Field Grade

NIB	Exc.	V.G.	Good	Fair	Poor
450	400	350	300	200	150

Riot Model

NIB	Exc.	V.G.	Good	Fair	Poor
650	500	400	350	250	175

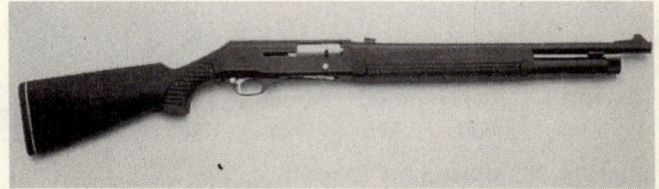

NOTE: For Riot Models with pistol grip add $40. For Riot Models with Tritium sights add $75.

Model 302

A 12 or 20 gauge semiautomatic shotgun using 2.75" or 3" shells interchangeably, various barrel lengths and screw-in choke tubes. Blued with a checkered walnut stock. Manufactured between 1982 and 1987.

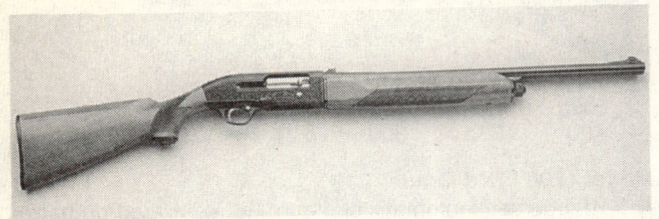

Exc.	V.G.	Good	Fair	Poor
400	350	275	200	150

Model 302 Super Lusso

As above, with a heavily engraved receiver and gold plated, contrasting parts. Presentation-grade walnut was used for the hand-checkered stock. Discontinued in 1986.

Exc.	V.G.	Good	Fair	Poor
2150	2000	1600	1050	850

Model Vittoria/Pintail

This semiautomatic 12 gauge shotgun was introduced to the Beretta product line in 1993. It has a short recoil operation and is offered with a 24" or 26" vent rib barrel with screw-in chokes. A 24" rifled choke tube version for slugs is also available. A nonreflective matte finish is put on all wood and metal surfaces. Equipped with sling swivels and walnut stock. Weighs about 7 lbs.

NOTE: Renamed in 1994.

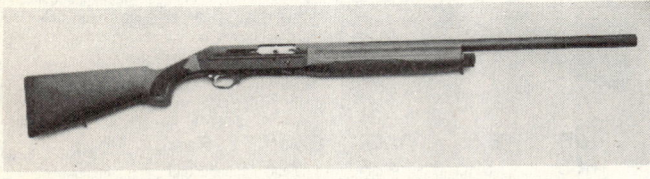

NIB	Exc.	V.G.	Good	Fair	Poor
600	550	500	400	350	250

A-303 Series

A 12 or 20 gauge semiautomatic shotgun, 26", 28", 30", or 32" ventilated rib barrels with screw-in choke tubes. Blued with a checkered walnut stock. Introduced in 1987. The various models offered differ slightly in configuration and/or quality of materials.

Model A-303

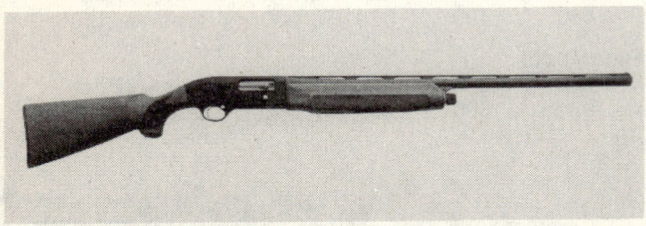

NIB	Exc.	V.G.	Good	Fair	Poor
650	600	475	375	300	250

Model A-303 Upland (24" Barrel)

NIB	Exc.	V.G.	Good	Fair	Poor
680	650	525	425	350	300

Model A-303 Sporting Clays

NIB	Exc.	V.G.	Good	Fair	Poor
735	700	575	475	400	350

Model A-303 Competition (Trap or Skeet)

NIB	Exc.	V.G.	Good	Fair	Poor
675	650	530	425	350	300

Model A-303 Slug Gun (22" Barrel with Sights)

NIB	Exc.	V.G.	Good	Fair	Poor
680	650	525	425	350	300

Model 303 Youth Gun

This version of the Model 303 is available in 20 gauge with a shorter length of pull, 13.5", than standard. It is fitted with a rubber recoil pad, screw-in choke tubes, and checkered walnut stock.

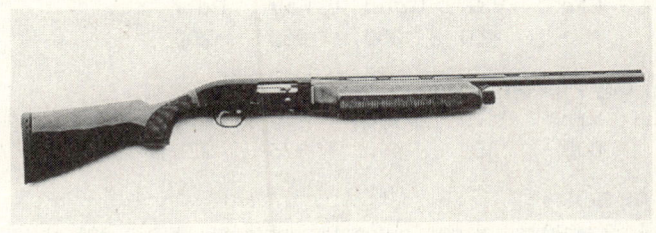

NIB	Exc.	V.G.	Good	Fair	Poor
500	450	400	300	250	200

Model A-303 Ducks Unlimited

A commemorative version of the Model 303. It is chambered for 12 or 20 gauge. There were 5,500 manufactured in 12 gauge in 1986 and 1987. There were 3,500 manufactured in 20 gauge in 1987 and 1988. These are commemorative firearms and are collectible when NIB with all furnished materials.

12 Gauge

NIB	Exc.	V.G.	Good	Fair	Poor
575	500	425	325	275	225

20 Gauge

NIB	Exc.	V.G.	Good	Fair	Poor
675	600	525	425	375	325

Model AL390/Mallard Series

This series of 12 gauge semiautomatic shotguns features a self compensating gas operating recoil system. All loads from target to 3" magnums can be used in the same gun. The Field Model features an anodized light alloy receiver with scroll engraving and matte black receiver top. Magazine capacity is 3 rounds. Checkered walnut stock with recoil pad. Available in vent rib barrel lengths from 24" to 30" with 32" on special request. A 22" or 24" slug plain barrel is also available. Chokes are fixed or screw-in at customer's option. Shotgun weighs about 7 lbs. Beginning in 1996 Beretta will offer the Silver mallard shotguns chambered for the 20 gauge shell and available with 24", 26, or 28" barrels. Average weight for these 20 gauge guns is 6.4 lbs.

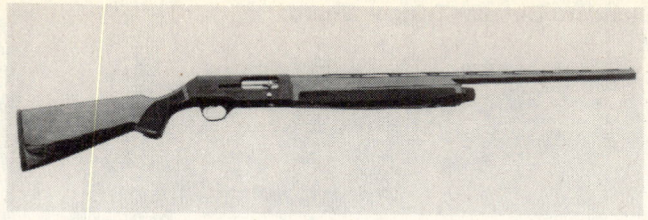

Field Grade/AL390 Silver Mallard

NIB	Exc.	V.G.	Good	Fair	Poor
800	600	450	350	300	200

Slug Gun/AL390 Silver Mallard

NIB	Exc.	V.G.	Good	Fair	Poor
800	600	450	350	300	200

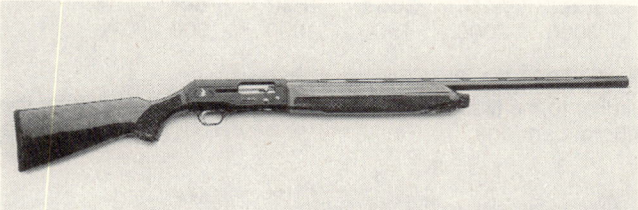

AL390 Silver Mallard-Synthetic Stock

NIB	Exc.	V.G.	Good	Fair	Poor
800	600	450	350	300	200

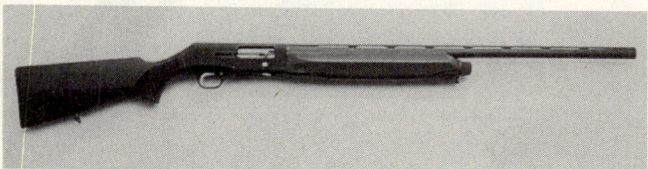

AL390 Silver Mallard-Camouflage

NIB	Exc.	V.G.	Good	Fair	Poor

Deluxe Grade/Gold Mallard

Gold filled game animals and select walnut stock.

NIB	Exc.	V.G.	Good	Fair	Poor
700	650	500	350	300	200

AL390 Trap

NIB	Exc.	V.G.	Good	Fair	Poor
675	600	500	400	300	200

AL390 Super Trap

Features ported barrels in 30" or 32", adjustable length of pull, adjustable comb.

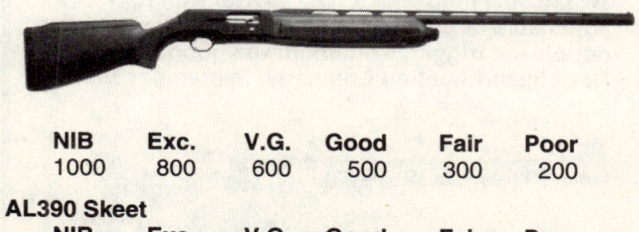

NIB	Exc.	V.G.	Good	Fair	Poor
1000	800	600	500	300	200

AL390 Skeet

NIB	Exc.	V.G.	Good	Fair	Poor
625	550	450	350	250	200

AL390 Super Skeet

Features ported barrel, adjustable cast and length of pull, and adjustable drop. 12 gauge only.

NIB	Exc.	V.G.	Good	Fair	Poor
1000	800	600	500	300	200

AL390 Sporting

NIB	Exc.	V.G.	Good	Fair	Poor
700	550	450	350	250	200

AL390 Sporting-20 gauge

Same as above but in 20 gauge. Introduced in 1997. Weight about 6.8 lbs.

NIB	Exc.	V.G.	Good	Fair	Poor
800	600	—	—	—	—

AL390 Sporting Ported

NIB	Exc.	V.G.	Good	Fair	Poor
725	650	550	400	300	200

AL390 Sport Gold Sporting

Introduced in 1997 this model is similar to above models but with silver sided receiver with gold engraving. Select walnut stock. 12 gauge only with choice of 28" or 30" vent rib barrels. Weight about 7.6 lbs.

NIB	Exc.	V.G.	Good	Fair	Poor
1100	900	—	—	—	—

AL390 Sport Sporting Youth

This semi-automatic shotgun is offered in 20 gauge only with 26" vent rib barrel. Length of pull is 13.5" with adjustable drop and cast on the butt stock. Introduced in 1997. Weight is approximately 6.7 lbs.

NIB	Exc.	V.G.	Good	Fair	Poor
825	675	—	—	—	—

AL390 Sport Sporting Youth Collection

Same as above but with multi-colored stock and forearm. Introduced in 1997.

NIB	Exc.	V.G.	Good	Fair	Poor
N/A	—	—	—	—	—

AL390 Camo

This 12 gauge shotgun is offered with either a 24" or 28" vent rib barrel. Barrel, receiver, stock and forearm have woodland camo finish. Weight is about 7.5 lbs. Offered for first time in 1997.

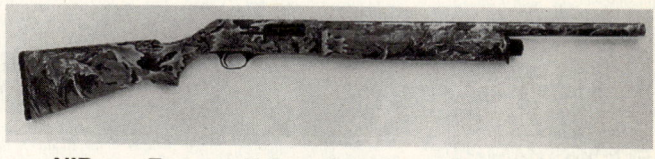

NIB	Exc.	V.G.	Good	Fair	Poor
995	—	—	—	—	—

Waterfowl/Turkey Model-Matte Finish

NIB	Exc.	V.G	Good	Fair	Poor
550	500	450	350	300	250

Super Trap-Ported barrels, adjustable comb and L.O.P.

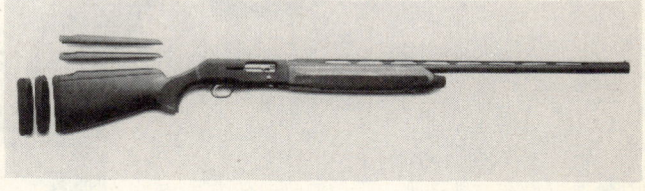

NIB	Exc.	V.G.	Good	Fair	Poor
975	925	850	700	500	400

Super Skeet-Ported barrels, adjustable comb and L.O.P.

NIB	Exc.	V.G.	Good	Fair	Poor
950	900	825	700	500	400

BERGMANN, THEODOR WAFFENFABRIK
Suhl, Germany

Model 1894-Bergmann Schmeisser

This model was produced in 5mm, 6.5mm, 7.5mm, and 8mm mainly as prototypes. The 5mm caliber will demand a premium. This pistol is extremely rare and as such cannot be accurately priced. Prices up to $22,000 have been noted over the last two years. An independent appraisal by an expert is strongly recommended before a sale.

Model 1896

Similar to the Model 1894 with the recoil spring located inside the butt instead of beneath the barrel. The magazine has two slots machined in its cover and holds five rounds. It can be found chambered for the 5mm and 6.5mm cartridges.

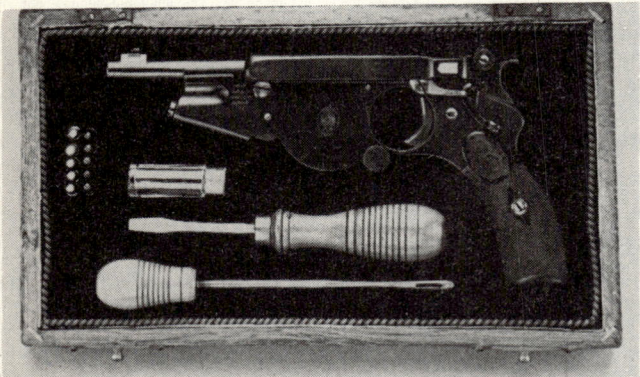

Courtesy Butterfield & Butterfield, San Francisco, California

Exc.	V.G.	Good	Fair	Poor
3000	2000	1800	1000	500

Model 1896, Number 2

There are two version of this small pocket pistol, both chambered for the 5mm cartridge:

Folding Trigger:

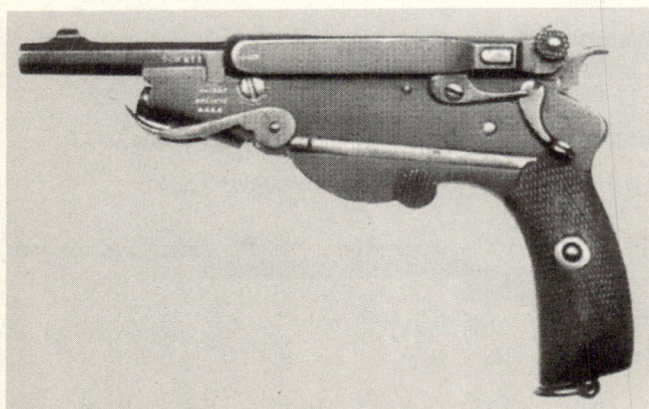

Courtesy Rock Island Auction Company

Exc.	V.G.	Good	Fair	Poor
3500	2500	2000	1000	500

Standard Circular Trigger Guard:

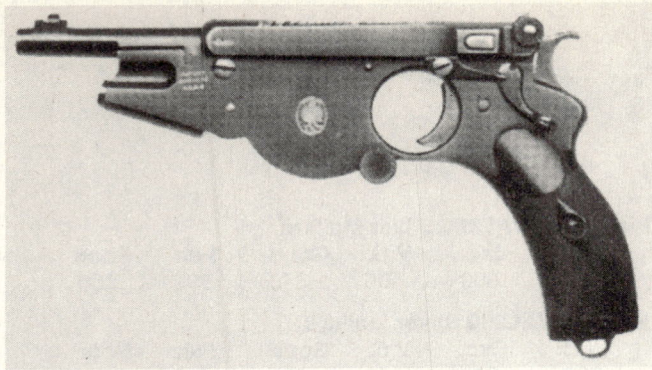

Courtesy Rock Island Auction Company

Exc.	V.G.	Good	Fair	Poor
3000	2000	1500	1000	500

Model 1896 No. 3

Similar to the Number 2 version but larger. Chambered for the 6.5mm cartridge.

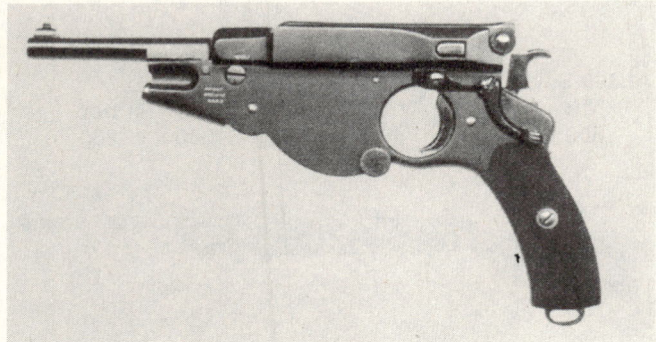

Courtesy Rock Island Auction Company

Exc.	V.G.	Good	Fair	Poor
4000	2000	1500	1000	500

A Bergmann No. 3 1896 pistol chambered for 6.5mm cartridge was sold at auction for $9,775. The pistol was cased with two magazines, screwdriver, cleaning rod and oil bottle. Condition was excellent to mint.
Butterfield & Butterfield, July 1996

A Bergmann No. 3 Target pistol sold at auction for $6,325.00. Fitted with a 7.25" barrel with fully adjustable target sights. Also fitted with adjustable double set trigger. Condition was good.
Rock Island Auction Company, September 1997

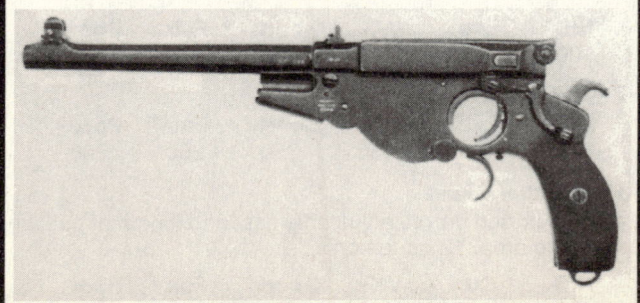

Model 1896 No. 4

As above, but in 8mm Bergmann caliber. Approximately 200 manufactured.

Exc.	V.G.	Good	Fair	Poor
4500	3500	2500	1500	1000

NOTE: There were target models of the Number 3 and Number 4 produced in very small quantities. Prices for this pistol have exceeded $15,000 over the last three years. A very rare variation!

Model 1897 No. 5

A locked-breech, semiautomatic pistol chambered for the 7.8mm Bergmann cartridge. This version has a box magazine that is located in front of the trigger guard similar to that found on a "Broomhandle" Mauser. The magazine is detachable but it can also be loaded with a stripper clip.

Exc.	V.G.	Good	Fair	Poor
7000	6000	4000	1500	1000

Model 1897, Number 5, "Karabiner Bergmann" (Carbine)

Of the nearly 1000 Model 1897, Number 5 pistols produced, fewer than 10% were carbines, making this version highly desirable.

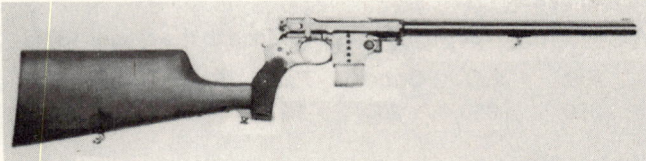

Courtesy Rock Island Auction Company

Exc.	V.G.	Good	Fair	Poor
20000	15000	8000	4500	3000

Model 1899 No. 6

Similar to the No. 5 with the early, side-loaded magazine. It was chambered for the 8mm cartridge and later chambered for the 7.5mm.

Exc.	V.G.	Good	Fair	Poor
2500	2250	1600	1300	850

Simplex

Manufactured between 1898 and 1905, this small pocket pistol is chambered for the 8mm cartridge. It has an 8 round removable magazine located in front of the trigger guard. There are three sub-variations, all with similar values. All versions have black hard rubber grips with the "Simplex" name cast into both sides.

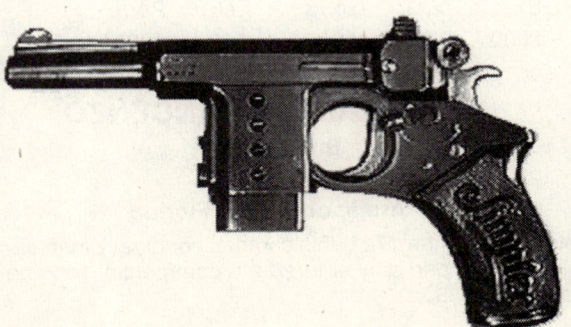

Exc.	V.G.	Good	Fair	Poor
3000	2300	1800	1500	900

Mars

Chambered for the 9mm Bergmann cartridge that was also known as the 9mm Largo in Spain, this pistol was adopted by

the Spanish army as their service pistol in 1905. Bergman had contracted the manufacture of this model to the firm of Schilling & Company. In 1904 Heinrich Krieghoff took over the Schilling Company and cancelled the Bergmann contract. This left Bergmann with the Spanish contract and no manufacturing facility. He attempted to manufacture this model in his own factory but failed, and the Mars was licensed to the firm of Pieper in Liege, Belgium. There were approximately 1000 Mars pistols made by Bergmann. The first 100 of these were chambered for the .30 Mauser cartridge. In 1921 the company firm was sold to a group headed by the firm of Lignose, and they began manufacture of the Lignose one-handed pistol that is covered in its own section of this text.

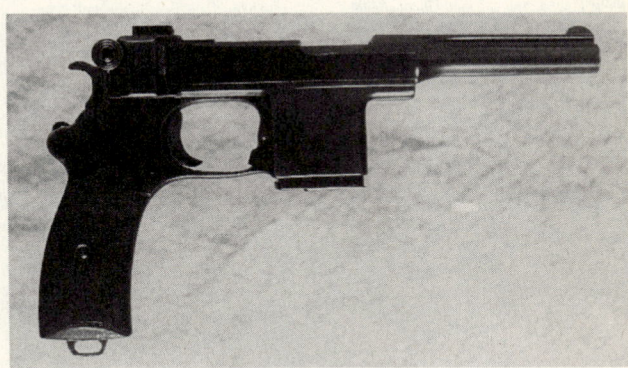

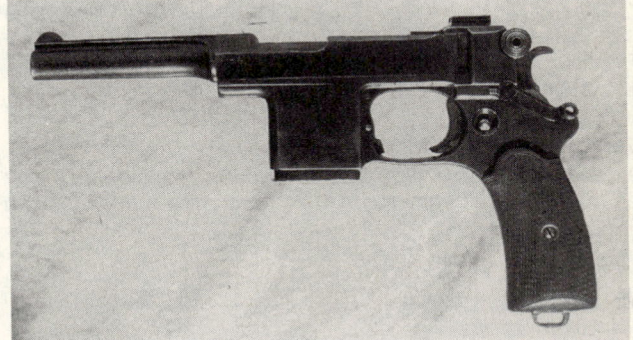

Courtesy Orvel Reichert

Exc.	V.G.	Good	Fair	Poor
4000	3200	2000	1500	1000

NOTE: There were a few prototype/test guns produced in 11mm.

Model 2

Similar to the 1906 Browning. Is a 6.35mm caliber semiautomatic pistol with a 2.5" barrel. Blued with plastic grips.

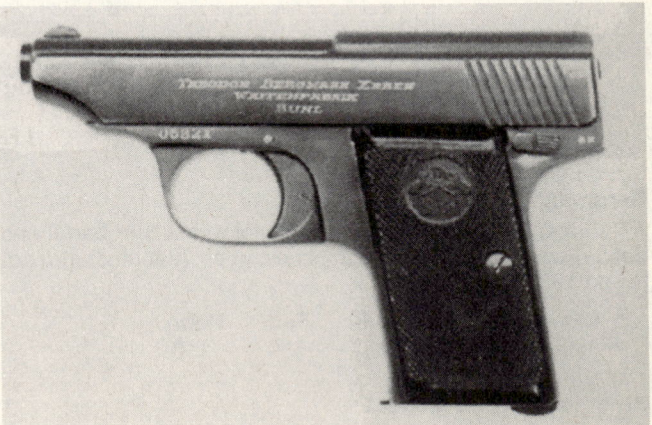

Courtesy Rock Island Auction Company

Exc.	V.G.	Good	Fair	Poor
300	250	175	110	80

No. 3

As above, with a 9-round, detachable magazine.

Exc.	V.G.	Good	Fair	Poor
300	250	175	110	80

Bergmann-Bayard Model 1908

Built by the Belgium firm of Pieper SA from 1908 to about 1914.

Caliber is 9mm with 4" barrel. Many foreign contracts were built in this model.

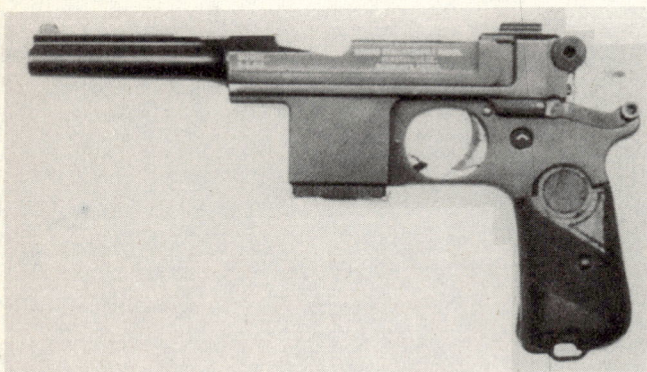

Courtesy Rock Island Auction Company

Exc.	V.G.	Good	Fair	Poor
2500	2000	1500	800	400

Bergmann-Bayard Model 1910-21

Similar to the Model 1908 but this model is coonsidered a Danish manufacture beginning in 1921, hence the model designation 1921.

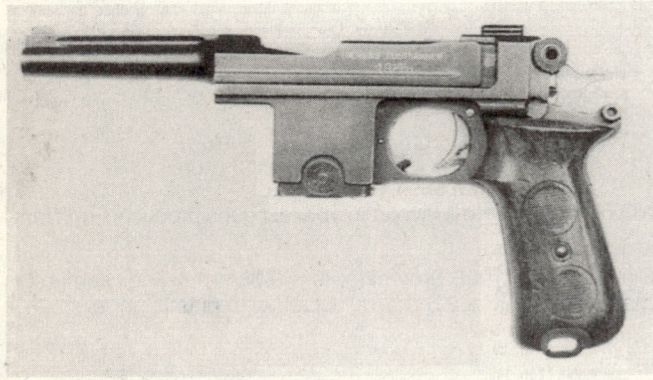

Courtesy Rock Island Auction Company

Exc.	V.G.	Good	Fair	Poor
2500	2000	1500	800	400

Bergmann-Erben

A 7.65mm caliber semiautomatic pistol with a 3.5" barrel and double-action lock. Blued with plastic grips. Manufactured between 1937 and 1939.

Exc.	V.G.	Good	Fair	Poor
350	300	225	150	110

Bergmann-Erben Model 2

As above, in 6.35mm caliber. Manufactured between 1937 and 1939.

Exc.	V.G.	Good	Fair	Poor
350	300	225	150	110

BERN, WAFFENFABRIK
Bern, Switzerland

The Swiss Military Arsenal in Bern produced a variety of military arms for that country's armed forces. A total of 47,732 Parabellum semiautomatic pistols were made there, most of which were in 7.65mm caliber.

Swiss Ordnance Revolver M 1878

A 10.4mm caliber double-action revolver with an octagonal barrel and 6-shot cylinder. The left sideplate of this revolver is hinged so that it may be swung forward to clean the lockwork. The grips are impressed with the Swiss Cross.

Exc.	V.G.	Good	Fair	Poor
800	700	575	450	300

M1872/78

A 10.4mm rimfire or 10.4mm centerfire Chamelot-Delvigne revolver.

Exc.	V.G.	Good	Fair	Poor
550	450	375	300	200

Model 1882

A 7.5mm revolver similar in appearance to the Model 1878.

Exc.	V.G.	Good	Fair	Poor
350	250	200	150	125

Model 1889

As above, with a more acutely angled butt and an improved sideplate release mechanism.

Exc.	V.G.	Good	Fair	Poor
350	250	200	150	125

Pistol 06 W + F (Model 06/24)

A Swiss-made copy of the German Model 1900/06 Luger semiautomatic pistol, marked "Waffenfabrik Bern."

Exc.	V.G.	Good	Fair	Poor
4000	3000	2100	1800	1300

Pistol 1929

Similar to the above, with the exception that the toggle finger pieces are smooth, the grip frame is uncurved, safety lever is a flat configuration and the grip safety is of inordinate size. Fitted with plastic grips.

Exc.	V.G.	Good	Fair	Poor
3000	2700	2000	1500	1000

BERNARDELLI, VINCENZO
Brescia, Italy
Importer
Armsport-Miami, Florida

Established in the 1721, this company originally manufactured military arms and only entered the commercial sporting arms market in 1928.

HANDGUNS

Vest Pocket Model

Similar to the Walther Model 9, in a 6.35mm caliber semiautomatic pistol with a 2.25" barrel, and 5-shot magazine. An extended 8-shot version was also available. Blued with plastic grips. Manufactured between 1945 and 1948.

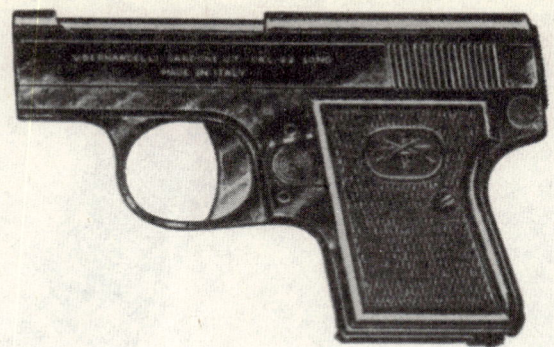

Exc.	V.G.	Good	Fair	Poor
300	225	155	100	75

Pocket Model

As above, in 7.65mm caliber. This model was also offered with extended barrels that protruded beyond the end of the slide. Introduced in 1947.

Exc.	V.G.	Good	Fair	Poor
275	200	150	100	75

Baby Model

As above, in .22 short or long rifle. Manufactured between 1949 and 1968.

Exc.	V.G.	Good	Fair	Poor
275	200	150	100	75

Sporter Model

A .22 caliber semiautomatic pistol with 6", 8", or 10" barrels and adjustable sights. Blued with walnut grips. Manufactured between 1949 and 1968.

Exc.	V.G.	Good	Fair	Poor
300	225	175	125	100

Revolvers

A .22 rimfire and .32 caliber double-action revolver with 1.5", 2", or 5" barrels. A .22 caliber, 7" barrel version with adjustable sights also available. Manufactured between 1950 and 1962.

Exc.	V.G.	Good	Fair	Poor
225	150	125	100	75

Model 60

A .22, .32 ACP or .380 ACP caliber semiautomatic pistol with 3.5" barrel and fixed sights. Blued with plastic grips. Manufactured since 1959.

Exc.	V.G.	Good	Fair	Poor
250	175	150	125	90

Model 68

A .22 rimfire caliber or .25 ACP semiautomatic pistol with a 2" barrel and 5-shot magazine. Blued with plastic grips. No longer imported into the U.S.

Exc.	V.G.	Good	Fair	Poor
175	125	100	75	50

Model 80

A .22 or .380 ACP caliber semiautomatic pistol with a 3.5" barrel and adjustable sights. Blued with plastic grips. Imported between 1968 and 1988.

Exc.	V.G.	Good	Fair	Poor
225	175	125	100	80

Model USA

A .22, .32 ACP or .380 ACP caliber semiautomatic pistol with a 3.5" barrel, adjustable sights, steel frame and a loaded chamber indicator. Blued with plastic grips.

NIB	Exc.	V.G.	Good	Fair	Poor
450	350	200	150	100	90

Model AMR

As above, with a 6" barrel.

NIB	Exc.	V.G.	Good	Fair	Poor
450	350	200	150	100	90

Model 69

A .22 caliber semiautomatic target pistol with a 6" heavy barrel, and a 10-shot magazine. Blued with checkered walnut grips.

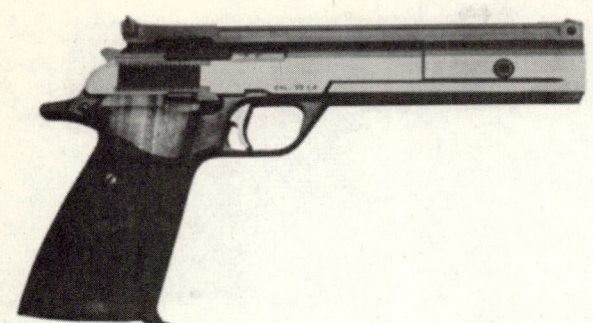

NIB	Exc.	V.G.	Good	Fair	Poor
450	375	300	225	150	100

Model P010

A .22 caliber, single-action, semiautomatic target pistol with a 6" barrel, adjustable target sights, barrel weights, and an adjustable trigger. Matte-black finish with stippled walnut grips. Introduced in 1989. Weight 40 oz. sold with special hard case.

NIB	Exc.	V.G.	Good	Fair	Poor
800	700	500	300	200	100

Model PO 18

A 7.65mm or 9mm Parabellum caliber, double action, semiautomatic pistol with a 4.75" barrel and a 16-shot, double stack, detachable magazine. All-steel construction. Blued with plastic grips. Walnut grips are available for an additional $40. Introduced in 1985.

NIB	Exc.	V.G.	Good	Fair	Poor
650	550	400	275	200	100

Model PO 18 Compact

As above, with a 4" barrel and a shorter grip frame with a 14-shot, double-column magazine. Introduced in 1989.

NIB	Exc.	V.G.	Good	Fair	Poor
650	550	400	275	200	100

Model P One

A full size semi-automatic pistol chambered for the 9mm or 40S&W calibers. Fitted with a 4.8" barrel. Can be fired double action or single. 10 shot magazine. Weight is 2.14 lbs. Available in black or chrome finish. Add $50 for chrome finish.

NIB	Exc.	V.G.	Good	Fair	Poor
625	525	400	275	200	100

Model P One-Compact

Same as above but with 4" barrel and offered in .380 caliber as well as 9mm and 40S&W. Weight is 1.96 lbs.

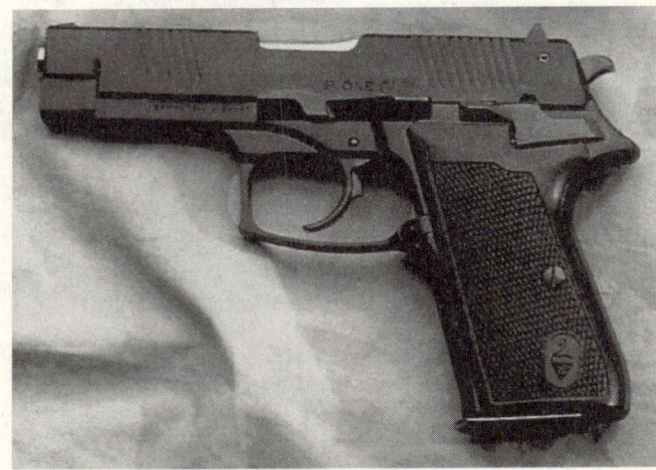

NIB	Exc.	V.G.	Good	Fair	Poor
650	550	400	275	200	100

Practical VB Target

Designed for Practical shooting this 9mm pistol has a 6" barrel with choice of 2 or 4 port compensator. It is fitted with numerous extra features. Weights is 2.2 lbs.

NIB	Exc.	V.G.	Good	Fair	Poor
1500	1200	850	600	400	200

Practical VB Custom

As above but designed for IPSC rules.

NIB	Exc.	V.G.	Good	Fair	Poor
2250	1900	1400	900	600	300

SHOTGUNS

Model 115 Series

A 12 gauge Over/Under, boxlock, double-barrel shotgun with various barrel lengths and choke combinations, single triggers and automatic ejectors.

Model 115

NIB	Exc.	V.G.	Good	Fair	Poor
1525	1250	900	700	550	300

Model 115S

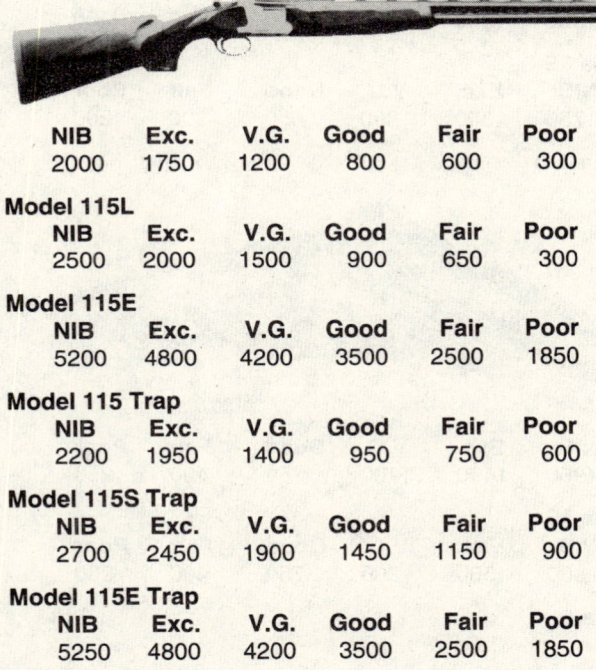

NIB	Exc.	V.G.	Good	Fair	Poor
2000	1750	1200	800	600	300

Model 115L

NIB	Exc.	V.G.	Good	Fair	Poor
2500	2000	1500	900	650	300

Model 115E

NIB	Exc.	V.G.	Good	Fair	Poor
5200	4800	4200	3500	2500	1850

Model 115 Trap

NIB	Exc.	V.G.	Good	Fair	Poor
2200	1950	1400	950	750	600

Model 115S Trap

NIB	Exc.	V.G.	Good	Fair	Poor
2700	2450	1900	1450	1150	900

Model 115E Trap

NIB	Exc.	V.G.	Good	Fair	Poor
5250	4800	4200	3500	2500	1850

Model 190 Series

A 12 gauge, Over/Under shotgun with various barrel lengths and choke combinations, a single selective trigger and automatic ejectors. Engraved and silver-finished with a checkered walnut stock. Introduced in 1986. The various versions differ in the degree of ornamentation and quality of materials utilized in construction.

Model 190

NIB	Exc.	V.G.	Good	Fair	Poor
1050	950	750	600	475	400

Model 190MC

NIB	Exc.	V.G.	Good	Fair	Poor
1150	1050	850	700	575	500

Model 190 Special

NIB	Exc.	V.G.	Good	Fair	Poor
1350	1150	950	800	675	600

Model 190 Combo Gun

A .243, .308 or .30-06 caliber and 12, 16, or 20 gauge combination Over/Under rifle shotgun with a boxlock action, double triggers and automatic ejectors. Blued with a checkered walnut stock. Introduced in 1989.

NIB	Exc.	V.G.	Good	Fair	Poor
1325	1125	925	775	650	575

Orione Series

A 12 gauge boxlock Over/Under shotgun with various barrel lengths and choke combinations. Finishes and triggers were optional, as were extractors or automatic ejectors.

Orione

NIB	Exc.	V.G.	Good	Fair	Poor
1150	900	700	500	400	200

Orione S

NIB	Exc.	V.G.	Good	Fair	Poor
1150	900	700	500	400	200

Orione L

NIB	Exc.	V.G.	Good	Fair	Poor
1250	1000	800	600	500	250

Orione E

NIB	Exc.	V.G.	Good	Fair	Poor
1350	1150	850	600	500	250

S. Uberto I Gamecock

A 12, 16, 20, or 28 gauge boxlock side by side shotgun with either 25.75" or 27.5" barrels, various chokes, double triggers and extractors. Automatic ejectors were available and would be worth a 20 percent premium. Blued with a checkered stock.

Exc.	V.G.	Good	Fair	Poor
950	700	500	350	250

Brescia

A 12, 16, or 20 gauge sidelock double-barrel shotgun with exposed hammers, various barrel lengths, choke combinations, a sidelock action, double triggers, and manual extractors. Blued with an English-style, checkered walnut stock.

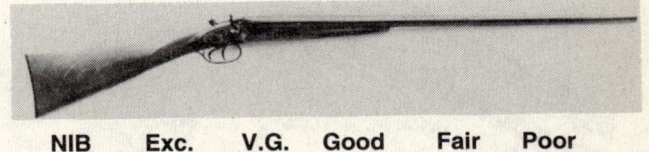

NIB	Exc.	V.G.	Good	Fair	Poor
1850	900	700	450	350	225

Italia

This is a higher-grade version of the Brescia.

NIB	Exc.	V.G.	Good	Fair	Poor
2250	1250	750	600	400	250

Italia Extra

This is the highest grade hammer gun that Bernardelli produces.

NIB	Exc.	V.G.	Good	Fair	Poor
5900	2750	1500	1000	750	300

Uberto Series

A 12, 16, 20 or 28 gauge, Anson & Deeley boxlock double-barrel shotgun with various barrel lengths and choke combinations. The increased value of the various models depends on the degree of engraving, options, and quality of materials and workmanship utilized in their construction.

S. Uberto I

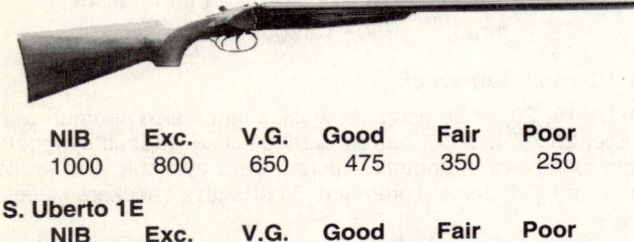

NIB	Exc.	V.G.	Good	Fair	Poor
1000	800	650	475	350	250

S. Uberto 1E

NIB	Exc.	V.G.	Good	Fair	Poor
1100	900	700	500	350	250

S. Uberto 2

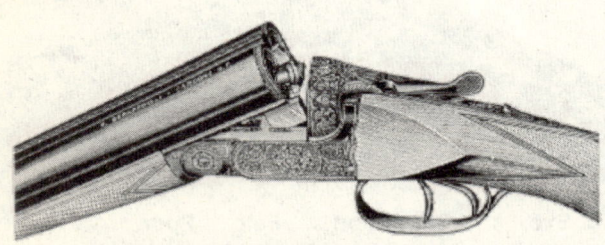

NIB	Exc.	V.G.	Good	Fair	Poor
1500	1100	800	500	350	250

S. Uberto 2E

NIB	Exc.	V.G.	Good	Fair	Poor
1750	1350	950	600	400	250

S.Uberto F.S.

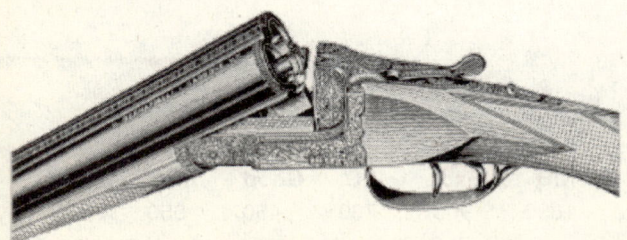

NIB	Exc.	V.G.	Good	Fair	Poor
2000	1500	1100	800	400	250

S. Uberto F.S.E.

NIB	Exc.	V.G.	Good	Fair	Poor
2250	1750	1200	800	400	250

Roma Series

Similar to the S. Uberto Series with false sideplates. The value of the respective variations result from the degree of ornamentation and quality of materials and workmanship utilized in the construction.

Roma 3

NIB	Exc.	V.G.	Good	Fair	Poor
1550	1200	800	600	300	200

Roma 3E

NIB	Exc.	V.G.	Good	Fair	Poor
1750	1300	900	650	300	200

Roma 4

NIB	Exc.	V.G.	Good	Fair	Poor
1950	1400	1100	750	400	250

Roma 4E

NIB	Exc.	V.G.	Good	Fair	Poor
2000	1500	1200	750	400	250

Roma 6

NIB	Exc.	V.G.	Good	Fair	Poor
2100	1750	1400	850	500	250

Roma 6E

NIB	Exc.	V.G.	Good	Fair	Poor
2200	1800	1400	850	500	250

Roma 7

NIB	Exc.	V.G.	Good	Fair	Poor
2900	2500	1800	1200	700	350

Roma 8

NIB	Exc.	V.G.	Good	Fair	Poor
3500	3000	2250	1550	850	400

Roma 9

NIB	Exc.	V.G.	Good	Fair	Poor
4000	3500	2750	1700	950	450

Elio

A 12 gauge, boxlock double-barrel shotgun with various barrel lengths and choke combinations, lightweight frame, double triggers and extractors. Scroll-engraved, silver finished receiver, blued barrels and a select, checkered walnut stock.

NIB	Exc.	V.G.	Good	Fair	Poor
1000	800	600	500	350	250

Elio E

As above, with automatic ejectors.

NIB	Exc.	V.G.	Good	Fair	Poor
1100	900	700	550	350	250

Hemingway

As above, with coin-finished receiver, engraved with hunting scenes, 23.5" barrels, double triggers or single trigger and a select, checkered walnut stock. Available in 12, 20 and 28 gauge.

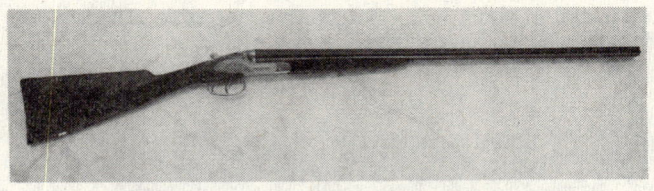

NIB	Exc.	V.G.	Good	Fair	Poor
1750	1350	900	700	400	250

Hemingway Deluxe

Same as above but fitted with full side plates.

NIB	Exc.	V.G.	Good	Fair	Poor
2250	1750	1200	800	400	250

Las Palomas Pigeon Model

A live Pigeon gun in 12 gauge with single trigger.

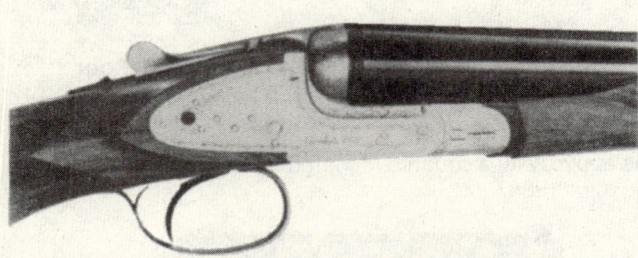

NIB	Exc.	V.G.	Good	Fair	Poor
3800	3250	2500	2000	1500	750

Holland V.B. Series

A 12 or 20 gauge sidelock shotgun with various barrel lengths, detachable Holland & Holland-type locks, single triggers, and automatic ejectors. The various models listed below vary in the amount of engraving and the quality of their wood. Prospective purchasers are advised to secure a qualified appraisal prior to acquisition.

Holland V.B. Liscio

NIB	Exc.	V.G.	Good	Fair	Poor
8000	5500	4000	3000	2000	1000

Holland V.B. Inciso

NIB	Exc.	V.G.	Good	Fair	Poor
10250	7500	5250	4000	2500	1250

Holland V.B. Lusso

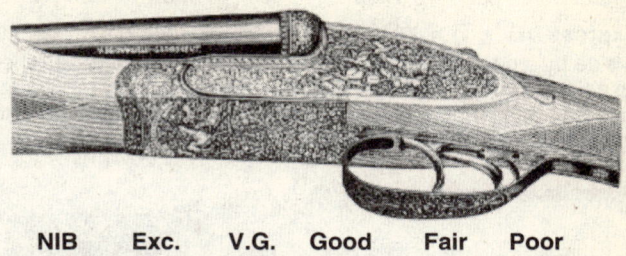

NIB	Exc.	V.G.	Good	Fair	Poor
11000	8000	6000	4500	2500	1250

Holland V.B. Extra

NIB	Exc.	V.G.	Good	Fair	Poor
13000	10000	7500	5500	3000	1500

Holland V.B. Gold

NIB	Exc.	V.G.	Good	Fair	Poor
45000	30000	22500	15000	7500	3000

Luck

An over and under shotgun with single selective trigger or double triggers, automatic ejectors with choice of fixed chokes or choke tubes. Available in 12 gauge. Blued or coin finish receiver.

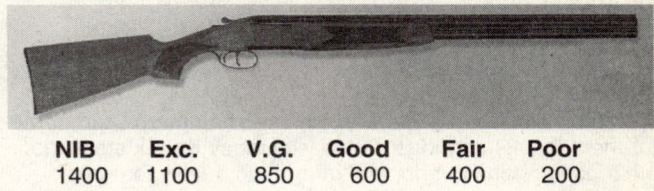

NIB	Exc.	V.G.	Good	Fair	Poor
1400	1100	850	600	400	200

Giardino

This is a semiautomatic shotgun chambered for the 9mm shot cartridge. Fitted with a 4 round magazine. Weight is 5 lbs.

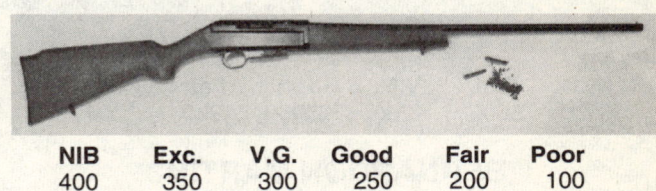

NIB	Exc.	V.G.	Good	Fair	Poor
400	350	300	250	200	100

RIFLES

Carbina VB Target

A semiautomatic carbine chambered for the .22LR cartridge. Barrel is 20.8" and magazine capacity is 10 rounds.

NIB	Exc.	V.G.	Good	Fair	Poor
650	550	400	300	200	100

Comb 2000

A rifle shotgun combination in 12 or 16 gauge with a variety of centerfire calibers to choose from. Barrels are 23.5" long. Set trigger special rib for scope mount and cheekpiece stock with pistol grip. Weight is 6-3/4 lbs.

NIB	Exc.	V.G.	Good	Fair	Poor
2200	1700	1200	800	400	250

Express 2000

An over and under double rifle chambered for a variety of European calibers Express with automatic ejectors, double set triggers or single trigger, muzzle adjustment device. Barrel length is 23.5".

NIB	Exc.	V.G.	Good	Fair	Poor
2750	2350	1700	1200	600	300

Express VB

A side by side double rifle chambered for a variety of European calibers up to .375 H&H. Double or single trigger auto ejectors, and finely engraved receiver with beavertail forearm and cheekpiece stock with pistol grip.

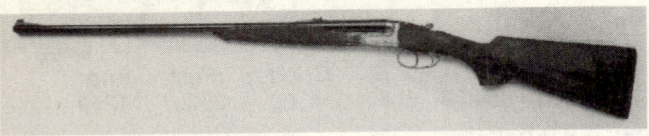

NIB	Exc.	V.G.	Good	Fair	Poor
5500	4700	3750	2000	1000	750

Express VB Deluxe

Same as above but with side plates and select walnut stock finely checkered.

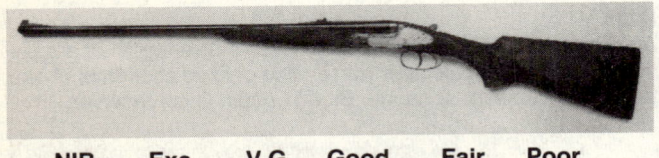

NIB	Exc.	V.G.	Good	Fair	Poor
5600	4800	3750	2000	1000	750

Minerva

A side by side double rifle with exposed hammers chambered for the 9.3x74R cartridge. Fitted with fancy walnut stock, double triggers, hand cut rib, and other high quality features.

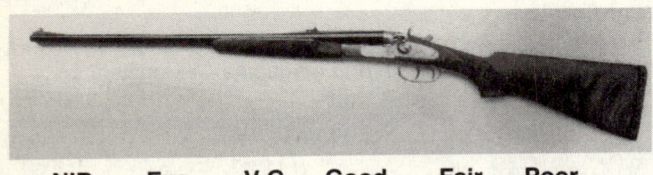

NIB	Exc.	V.G.	Good	Fair	Poor
6000	5600	4250	2500	1200	750

BERNARDON MARTIN
St. Etienne, France

1907/8 Model

A 7.65mm caliber semiautomatic pistol. The left side of the slide is marked "Cal. 7.65mm St. Etienne." The trademark "BM" is molded into the grips.

Exc.	V.G.	Good	Fair	Poor
450	300	225	175	100

1908/9 Model

As above, with a grip safety.

Exc.	V.G.	Good	Fair	Poor
450	300	225	175	100

Occasionally the Bernardon Martin pistol will be noted with the word "Hermetic" stamped on the slide in letters that do not match the other markings on the weapon.

BERNEDO, VINCENZO
Eibar, Spain

BC

A 6.35mm caliber semiautomatic pistol, having a completely exposed barrel. The slide marked "Pistolet Automatique Bernedo Patent No. 69952."

Exc.	V.G.	Good	Fair	Poor
250	200	150	125	75

BERSA
Ramos Mejia, Argentina
Importer-Eagle Imports

The firm Fabrica de Armas Bersa SA has been selling pistols in this country since about the mid-1970s.

Model 644

This model is a blowback pocket pistol chambered for the .22 Long Rifle. The trigger system is single action. Barrel length is 3.5", overall length is 6.57", and empty weight is approximately 28 oz. This is the basic Bersa model from which its other models derive their design and function.

NIB	Exc.	V.G.	Good	Fair	Poor
225	175	150	125	100	75

Model 622

Similar to the Model 644 but with a slightly longer barrel.

NIB	Exc.	V.G.	Good	Fair	Poor
225	175	150	125	100	75

Model 23

A .22 rimfire caliber, double-action, semiautomatic pistol with a 3.5" barrel and 10-shot detachable magazine. Either blued or satin nickel-plated with checkered walnut grips.

NIB	Exc.	V.G.	Good	Fair	Poor
225	200	150	125	100	75

Model 223

As above, with a squared triggerguard and nylon grips. Imported after 1988.

Exc.	V.G.	Good	Fair	Poor
225	175	125	100	75

Model 224

As above, with a 4" barrel. Imported after 1988.

Exc.	V.G.	Good	Fair	Poor
225	175	125	100	75

Model 225

As above, with a 5" barrel. Discontinued in 1986.

Exc.	V.G.	Good	Fair	Poor
225	175	125	100	75

Model 226

As above, with a 6" barrel. Discontinued in 1988.

Exc.	V.G.	Good	Fair	Poor
225	175	125	100	75

Model 323

A .32 ACP caliber single-action semiautomatic pistol, with a 3.5" barrel, fixed sights and a 7-shot detachable magazine. Blued with molded plastic grips. Not imported after 1986.

Exc.	V.G.	Good	Fair	Poor
150	125	100	75	50

Model 383

As above, in .380 caliber. Discontinued in 1988.

Exc.	V.G.	Good	Fair	Poor
175	150	125	90	75

Model 383A

A .380 ACP caliber double-action semiautomatic pistol with a 3.5" barrel with fixed sights and 7-shot magazine. Blued with checkered walnut grips. Overall length is 6.6" and weight is about 24 oz. Available in blue or nickel finish.

NIB	Exc.	V.G.	Good	Fair	Poor
225	200	150	125	100	75

Model 83

Similar to the above model but with double action operating system. Weighs about 26 oz. Introduced in 1988.

NIB	Exc.	V.G.	Good	Fair	Poor
225	200	150	125	100	75

Model 85

As above, with a double-column magazine. Introduced in 1988.

NIB	Exc.	V.G.	Good	Fair	Poor
275	250	200	150	100	75

Model 97

This model is a slightly larger version of the Model 644 chambered for the 9mm Short.

NIB	Exc.	V.G.	Good	Fair	Poor
200	175	150	125	100	75

Model 86

Similar to the Model 85 .380 caliber, but features a matte blue or satin nickel finish, wrap around rubber grips, and three-dot sight. Magazine capacity is 13 rounds.

NIB	Exc.	V.G.	Good	Fair	Poor
295	250	225	200	150	100

Thunder 9

Introduced in 1993 this model is a double action 9mm pistol that features ambidextrous safety, reversible extended magazine release, ambidextrous slide release, adjustable trigger stop, combat style hammer, three-dot sights, and matte blue finish. Magazine capacity is 15 rounds.

NIB	Exc.	V.G.	Good	Fair	Poor
300	275	250	200	150	100

BERTHIER
French State

The Berthier bolt-action rifle was adopted as the French service rifle in 1890 and was made in two styles: a Carbine with a 17.5" barrel, and a rifle with a 31.5" barrel. Both were chambered for the 8mm Lebel cartridge and originally had three-shot magazines. After World War I, many of these arms were modified so that a 5-shot magazine could be used.

Berthier Carbine

Exc.	V.G.	Good	Fair	Poor
300	250	175	125	75

Berthier Rifle

Exc.	V.G.	Good	Fair	Poor
275	225	150	100	50

BERTRAND, JULES
Liege, Belgium
Le Novo

A 6.35mm caliber double-action revolver. Manufactured in the 1890s. The only identifying markings are the "JB" trademark on the grips.

Exc.	V.G.	Good	Fair	Poor
150	100	50	35	20

Lincoln

As above, in 7.65mm caliber.

Exc.	V.G.	Good	Fair	Poor
150	100	50	35	20

Le Rapide

A 6.35mm caliber, semiautomatic pistol marked "Man Gr/d'Armes et Munitions Cal. Browning 6.35 Le Rapide." The grips are marked "Le Rapide" and "JB."

Exc.	V.G.	Good	Fair	Poor
175	125	90	50	25

BERTUZZI
Brescia, Italy
Importer-New England Arms
Kittery Point, Maine

SHOTGUNS OVER/UNDER

Zeus

A 12 gauge sidelock shotgun with automatic ejectors, single selective trigger, and deluxe checkered walnut stock. Custom order in various barrel lengths and chokes. Engraved. Rarely seen on the used gun market.

NIB	Exc.	V.G.	Good	Fair	Poor
10000	8500	6500	4500	3500	2500

Zeus Extra Lusso

As above, but available on special order only.

NIB	Exc.	V.G.	Good	Fair	Poor
15000	12000	8500	6000	4500	3500

SHOTGUNS SIDE-SIDE

Orione

A 12-gauge boxlock shotgun with Anson & Deeley through bolt, in various barrel lengths and chokes, single selective trigger and automatic ejectors. Hand-checkered, walnut stock with a semi-beavertail forearm.

NIB	Exc.	V.G.	Good	Fair	Poor
3500	3000	2500	1850	1500	1000

Best Quality Sidelock

A custom order sidelock shotgun in various gauges with barrel lengths and chokes to suit the customer. Extensively engraved with a walnut stock.

NIB	Exc.	V.G.	Good	Fair	Poor
7500	7000	6000	4500	3500	2500

BIGHORN ARMS CO.
Watertown, South Dakota

Target Pistol

A .22 caliber single shot pistol resembling a semiautomatic. Ventilated-rib barrel 6" in length. Stock of molded plastic.

Exc.	V.G.	Good	Fair	Poor
150	125	100	85	65

Shotgun

A single shot 12 gauge shotgun with a 26" barrel. Blued with a plastic stock.

Exc.	V.G.	Good	Fair	Poor
100	85	65	50	30

BIGHORN RIFLE CO.
Orem, Utah

Bighorn Rifle

Custom order in any caliber, double-barrel, bolt-action rifle with optional barrel lengths and finishes. Double trigger and walnut stock.

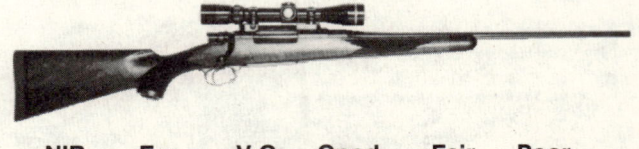

NIB	Exc.	V.G.	Good	Fair	Poor
2000	1750	1500	1000	750	400

BILHARZ, HALL, & CO.
CONFEDERATE CARBINES

During the American Civil War, the Southern Confederacy made valiant but often futile efforts to produce small arms for its forces. The small firm of Bilharz, Hall, & Co. of Pittsylvania Court House (currently Chatham), Virginia, exemplifies one such effort to furnish the Confederate cavalry with arms. Unfortunately, because their arms were never marked with the name of the manufacturer, they have been mistaken for the products of other small arms makers of the Confederacy.

Bilharz, Hall & Co. breechloading ("Rising Breech") carbine

Overall length 40"; barrel length 21"; caliber 54. Markings: either "P" or "P/CS" on upper left side of barrel and top of rising breech. The peculiar feature of this carbine is the manner in which the breechblock exposes the chamber. A box-like chamber at the rear of the barrel rises vertically to expose the chamber for a paper cartridge by activating the lever/trigger-guard mechanism. Only 100 of this type were delivered to the Confederacy in September 1862. Two types of front sight blades are known, but neither affects the value.

Courtesy Milwaukee Public Museum, Milwaukee, Wisconsin

Exc.	V.G.	Good	Fair	Poor
—	12500	8500	5000	3500

Bilharz, Hall & Co. muzzleloading carbine

Overall length 37-1/2"; barrel length 22"; caliber .58. Markings: "P/CS" on upper left of barrel near breech; "CSA" on top near breech. Modeled after the Springfield U.S. M1855 rifle carbine, the Bilharz, Hall & Co. muzzleloading carbine has often been mistakenly identified as a product of D.C. Hodgkins & Sons of Macon, Georgia. Serial numbers (found internally) belie that identification. Instead these arms are part of deliveries made to Richmond from the middle of 1863 until March 1864. Serial numbers, noted in excess of 700, suggest that about 1,000 were produced. Two basic types, the earlier (through serial number 300) were made with brass nosecaps; the later type (about serial number 310 through at least 710) have pewter nosecaps on the short forestock; neither type affects value.

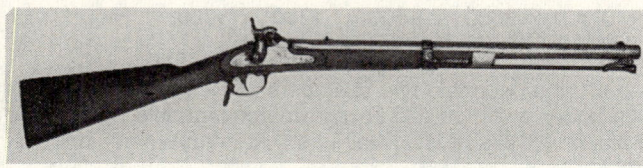

Exc.	V.G.	Good	Fair	Poor
—	12000	8000	4500	3000

BILLINGHURST, WILLIAM
Rochester, New York

Billinghurst originally worked for James and John Miller of Rochester. After James Miller's death in 1837, Billinghurst established his own shop where he produced revolving rifles based upon Miller's 1829 patent. While these arms were originally made with percussion ignition systems (either pill or percussion cap), later examples using self-contained metallic cartridges are sometimes encountered. Billinghurst also established a well-deserved reputation for making extremely accurate percussion target pistols and rifles.

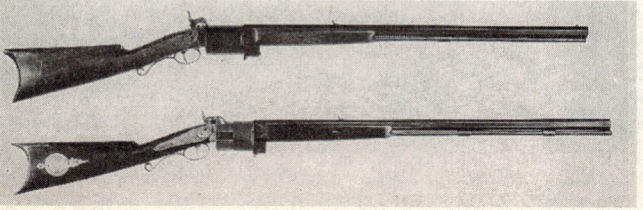

Revolving Rifle

Calibers vary from .40 to .50 with barrels from 24" to 29"; walnut stocks. The barrels marked: "W. Billinghurst, Rochester, N.Y.," or "W. Billinghurst."

Exc.	V.G.	Good	Fair	Poor
—	15000	9500	5000	2000

W. Billinghurst Under Hammer Pistol

This pistol is somewhat different than most of the under hammers encountered. The barrels are 12" to 18" in length and of a heavy octagonal construction. They are chambered from .30 to .38 caliber and utilize the percussion ignition system. Higher grade versions feature a part-round barrel, and it is important to note that no two pistols are alike. These pistols were furnished with detachable shoulder stocks, and a good many were cased with telescopic sights and false muzzles. This is a high quality weapon; and if encountered with the optional accessories, it would definitely warrant an individual appraisal. This firearm was manufactured in the 1850s and 1860s.

Shoulder Stock-Add 30%-50%.

Exc.	V.G.	Good	Fair	Poor
—	5000	3000	1500	800

BILLINGS
Location Unknown

Billings Pocket Pistol

A .32 rimfire caliber single shot spur trigger pistol with a 2.5" round barrel and an unusually large grip. The barrel is stamped "Billings Vest Pocket Pistol Pat. April 24, 1866." Blued with walnut grips. Manufactured between 1865 and 1868.

Exc.	V.G.	Good	Fair	Poor
—	1500	700	500	275

BINGHAM LTD.
Norcross, Georgia

PPS 50

A .22 rimfire caliber semiautomatic rifle patterned after the Soviet PPSH submachine gun with 16" barrel and a 50-round drum magazine. Blued, walnut or beech stock with a vented handguard. Manufactured between 1976 and 1985.

Exc.	V.G.	Good	Fair	Poor
350	250	175	125	100

AK-22

A .22 rimfire caliber semiautomatic rifle patterned after the Soviet AK-47 with either a 15- or 29-shot magazine. Walnut or beech stock. Manufactured between 1976 and 1985.

Exc.	V.G.	Good	Fair	Poor
250	200	150	100	75

Bantam

A .22 rimfire or .22 rimfire Magnum caliber bolt-action rifle with an 18.5" barrel. Manufactured between 1976 and 1985.

Exc.	V.G.	Good	Fair	Poor
100	85	70	50	35

BISMARCK
Location Unknown

Bismarck Pocket Revolver

A .22 caliber spur trigger revolver with a 3" round-ribbed barrel and a 7-shot, unfluted cylinder. Brass frame and the remainder was plated with rosewood grips. The barrel is marked "Bismarck." Manufactured in the 1870s.

Exc.	V.G.	Good	Fair	Poor
350	300	200	150	90

BITTERLICH, FRANK J.
Nashville, Tennessee

A .41 caliber single shot percussion pistol in a variety of octagonal barrel lengths, German silver mounts, walnut stock. The barrel and locks are marked "Fr.J. Bitterlich/Nashville, Tenn." Produced between 1861 and 1867.

Exc.	V.G.	Good	Fair	Poor
—	3000	1000	750	300

BITTNER, GUSTAV
Wieport, Bohemia

Bittner

A 7.7mm Bittner caliber self-loading pistol with a 4.5" barrel. The bolt containing the firing pin is fully mounted within the frame and is operated by the finger lever trigger. Manufactured in 1893. Less than 500 were made.

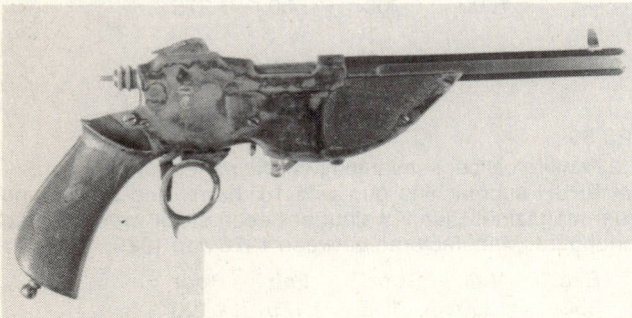

Exc.	V.G.	Good	Fair	Poor
—	5000	2500	1200	500

BLAKE, J. H.
New York, New York

Blake Bolt Action Rifle

A .30-40 Krag caliber bolt-action rifle with a 30" barrel, and a 7-shot magazine. The stock is secured by three barrel bands. Blued with a walnut stock. Manufactured between 1892 and 1910.

Courtesy Milwaukee Public Museum, Milwaukee, Wisconsin

Exc.	V.G.	Good	Fair	Poor
750	675	500	375	200

BLANCH, JOHN
London, England

Blanch Percussion Pistol

A .69 caliber single shot, percussion pistol with a 5" Damascus barrel. Engraved frame and hammer with a walnut grip. Manufactured in the 1830s.

Exc.	V.G.	Good	Fair	Poor
—	5000	2500	1300	800

BLAND, THOMAS & SONS
London, England

Established in 1840, this firm has produced or marketed a wide variety of percussion and cartridge arms. Over the years, the firm has occupied a variety of premises in London, some of them concurrently.

41 Whittall Street	1840-1867
41, 42, 43 Whittall Street	1867-1886
106 Strand	1872-1900
430 Strand	1886-1900
2 William IV Street	1900-1919
4-5 William IV Street	1919-1973
New Row, St. Martin's Lane	1973-

T. Bland & Sons is perhaps best known for their double barrel rifles and shotguns, which were made in a variety of grades.

Exc.	V.G.	Good	Fair	Poor
3500	2500	1750	1250	700

BLASER JAGDWAFFEN
Germany

Model K77

A single shot rifle chambered in a variety of calibers with a 24" barrel and silver plated as well as engraved receiver. Walnut stock. Introduced in 1988.

Extra Barrels-Add $750 Per Barrel.

NIB	Exc.	V.G.	Good	Fair	Poor
2300	1850	1500	1200	900	450

Model R-84

A bolt-action sporting rifle chambered in a variety of calibers with either a 23" or 24" barrel. Interchangeable barrels are available for this model. Walnut stock. Imported beginning in 1988.

NIB	Exc.	V.G.	Good	Fair	Poor
2300	1850	1500	1200	900	450

Ultimate Bolt Action

As above, with a silver-plated and engraved receiver as well as a set trigger.

NIB	Exc.	V.G.	Good	Fair	Poor
1500	1300	1050	825	700	375

Special Order Ultimate

The above model is available in a variety of finishes and degrees of decoration as follows:

Ultimate Deluxe

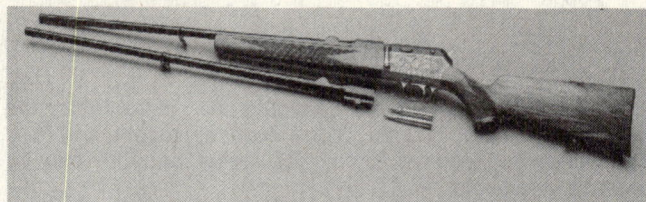

NIB	Exc.	V.G.	Good	Fair	Poor
1600	1400	1150	925	800	400

Ultimate Super Deluxe

NIB	Exc.	V.G.	Good	Fair	Poor
4250	3750	3250	2500	2000	1000

Ultimate Exclusive

NIB	Exc.	V.G.	Good	Fair	Poor
5700	5000	4500	3500	2600	1300

Ultimate Super Exclusive

NIB	Exc.	V.G.	Good	Fair	Poor
8900	7900	6800	5000	4000	2000

Ultimate Royal

NIB	Exc.	V.G.	Good	Fair	Poor
11500	9500	7500	6000	4000	2000

NOTE: Extra interchangeable caliber barrels for the above rifles are available at $700 to $1,200 per barrel depending on the grade.

BLISS, F. D.
New Haven, Connecticut

Bliss Pocket Revolver

A .25 caliber spur trigger revolver with a 3.25" octagon barrel, 6-shot magazine, and a square butt. Blued with either hard rubber or walnut grips. The barrel is stamped "F.D. Bliss New Haven, Ct." There was an all-brass framed version made early in the production, and this model would be worth approximately 50 percent more than the values listed here for the standard model. Approximately 3,000 manufactured circa 1860 to 1863.

Exc.	V.G.	Good	Fair	Poor
—	1000	500	300	100

BLISS & GOODYEAR
New Haven, Connecticut

Pocket Model Revolver

A .28 caliber percussion revolver with a 3" octagonal barrel, 6-shot magazine, unfluted cylinder and a solid frame with a removable sideplate. Blued with a brass frame and walnut grips. Approximately 3,000 manufactured in 1860.

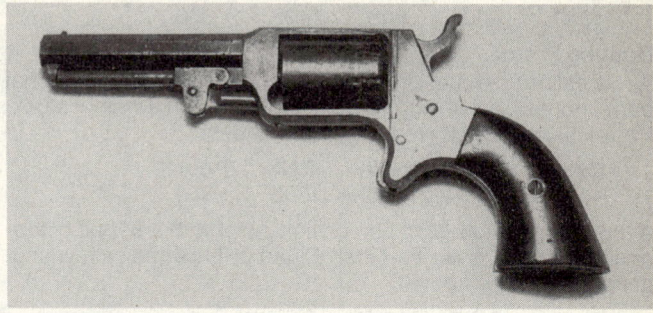

Exc.	V.G.	Good	Fair	Poor
—	2000	750	450	200

BLISSETT
SEE-English Military Firearms

BLUNT & SYMS
New York, New York

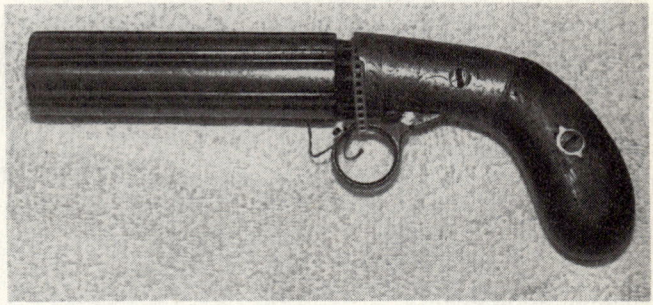

Under Hammer Pepperbox

Pepperboxes produced by Blunt & Syms are noteworthy for the fact that they incorporate a ring trigger cocking/revolving mechanism and a concealed under hammer. They were produced in a variety of calibers and the standard finish was blued. Normally these pistols are found marked simply "A-C" on the face of the barrel group. Some examples though are marked "Blunt & Syms New York".

This firm was in business from approximately 1837 to 1855.

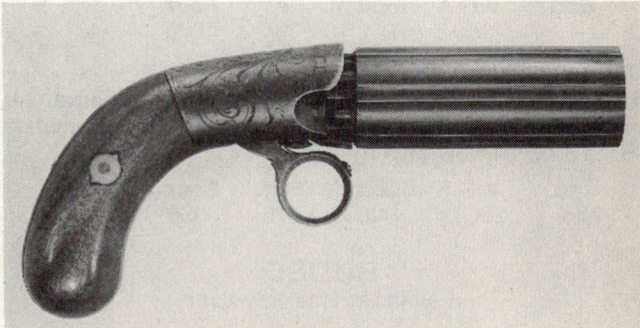

Small Frame Round Handle .25-.28 Caliber

Exc.	V.G.	Good	Fair	Poor
750	400	350	275	175

Medium Frame Round Handle .31 Caliber

Exc.	V.G.	Good	Fair	Poor
700	350	300	225	150

Round Handle Dragoon .36 Caliber

Exc.	V.G.	Good	Fair	Poor
1000	650	550	400	300

Medium Frame Saw Handle .31 Caliber

Exc.	V.G.	Good	Fair	Poor
850	450	400	325	250

Saw Handle Dragoon .36 Caliber

Exc.	V.G.	Good	Fair	Poor
1600	800	600	425	350

Dueling Pistol

A .52 caliber percussion single shot pistol with an octagonal barrel normally of 9" length. Steel furniture with a walnut stock. Barrel marked "B&S New York/Cast Steel".

Exc.	V.G.	Good	Fair	Poor
—	2500	1000	500	350

A .36 caliber single-shot percussion pistol with a 6" half octagonal barrel and a bar hammer. Blued or browned with walnut grips. Marked as above.

Exc.	V.G.	Good	Fair	Poor
—	1750	800	400	200

Side Hammer Pocket Pistol

A .31 or .35 caliber single shot percussion pistol with a 2.5" to 6" octagonal barrel. Blued with walnut grips.

Exc.	V.G.	Good	Fair	Poor
—	1500	500	225	175

Side Hammer Belt Pistol

As above, in calibers ranging from .36 to .44 with barrel lengths of 4" or 6".

Exc.	V.G.	Good	Fair	Poor
—	1750	700	350	250

Ring Trigger Pistol

A .36 caliber percussion single shot pistol with a 3" to 5" half octagonal barrel and a ring trigger. Blued with walnut grips.

Exc.	V.G.	Good	Fair	Poor
—	1000	500	250	200

Double Barrel Pistol

A .36 to .44 caliber percussion double barrel pistol with 7.5" barrels and walnut grips. A ring trigger variation of this model is known.

Exc.	V.G.	Good	Fair	Poor
—	800	500	275	225

Double Barrel Under Hammer Pistol

As above, with two under hammers and in .34 caliber with 4" barrels.

Exc.	V.G.	Good	Fair	Poor
—	1250	600	300	250

Derringer Style Pistol

A .50 caliber single shot percussion pistol with a 3" barrel, German silver mounts and a walnut stock. The lock is marked "Blunt & Syms/New York".

Exc.	V.G.	Good	Fair	Poor
—	2000	1000	475	350

BODEO
Italian Service Revolver

System Bodeo Modello 1889 (Enlisted Model)

A 10.4mm caliber revolver with a 4.5" octagonal barrel, and 6-shot cylnder. This revolver was adopted as the Italian service revolver in 1889 and was replaced by the Glisenti in 1910. Manufactured by various Italian arms companies.

Exc.	V.G.	Good	Fair	Poor
200	175	150	100	75

Modello 1889 (Officers Model)

Essentially the same as the enlisted man's model with a round barrel, non-folding trigger, and conventional triggerguard.

Exc.	V.G.	Good	Fair	Poor
200	175	150	100	75

BOLUMBURO, G.
Eibar, Spain

A 6.35 and 7.65mm caliber semiautomatic pistol under the trade name Bristol, Giraida, Gloria, Marina, Regent, and Rex. The values on these would be quite similar, and they may be regarded the same.

Exc.	V.G.	Good	Fair	Poor
200	125	85	65	45

BOND
SEE-English Military Firearms

BOOM
SEE-Shaftuck, C.S.
Hatfield, Massachusetts

BORCHARDT
Berlin, Germany
Waffenfabrik Lowe

DWM

A 7.65mm semiautomatic pistol with a 6.5" barrel and an 8-shot magazine. Blued with walnut grips and a detachable walnut shoulder stock. This pistol was designed by Hugo Borchardt and was manufactured by Ludwig Lowe of Berlin. It is the immediate predecessor of the Luger. Later models were manufactured by DWM. Prospective purchasers should secure a qualified appraisal prior to acquisition.

NOTE: Lowe Manufacture-Add 15%.

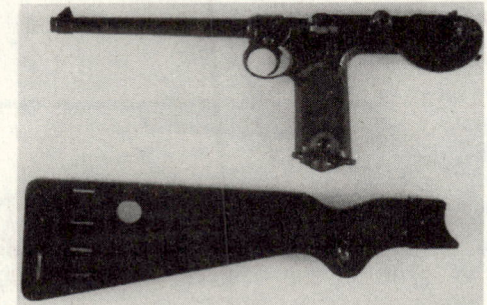

Courtesy J.C. Devine, Inc.

Exc.	V.G.	Good	Fair	Poor
12500	9000	7000	5000	2000

A 7.62 Borchardt with 7-1/2" barrel marked with B, U, and G proofs sold at auction for $25,300. The pistol came with a factory leather case with shoulder stock, removable walnut cheekpiece, and other accessories. Butterfield & Butterfield, July 1996.

BORSIG
East Germany

The Borsig is the East German version of the Soviet Makarov pistol. It is a double-action, chambered for the Soviet 9X18mm cartridge. Its appearance is nearly identical to the Makarov.

Exc.	V.G.	Good	Fair	Poor
200	175	150	100	75

BOSS & CO.
London, England

The firm of Boss & Co. has been in the firearms business since 1832 and enjoys a reputation for producing some of the finest shotguns in the world. The prices of these guns are quite high, and setting a value in a publication of this nature is nearly impossible. There are not enough bought and sold to give an accurate market value. There were less than 10,000 ever manufactured, and anyone contemplating purchase should secure an individual and expert appraisal. For reference purposes we list the basic models and their prices.

Side x Side

This is a custom order shotgun available in any gauge with barrel lengths and chokes to the customer's specifications. It has automatic ejectors and either a single or double trigger. The stock is made of the best-grade walnut and made to order with or without a pistol grip. The small-gauge guns would bring a sizable premium as few were made.

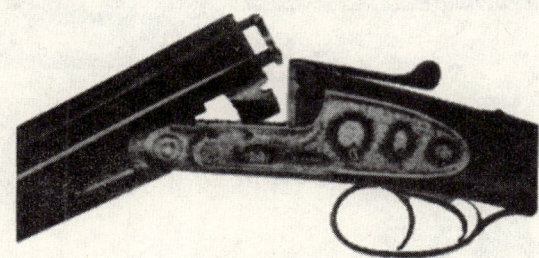

NIB	Exc.	V.G.	Good	Fair	Poor
40000	30000	15000	10000	8000	5500

Over/Under

The Over/Under was built to order and is similar in quality to the side x side.

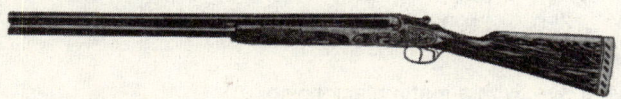

NIB	Exc.	V.G.	Good	Fair	Poor
60000	40000	20000	15000	10000	7500

The following is applicable to both models:

20 Gauge-Add 25%.
28 Gauge-Add 30%.
.410-Add 50%.
Cased with accessories-Add $1500.

BOSWELL, CHARLES
London, England

One of England's more established makers of best-quality rifles and shotguns. In 1988 the company was purchased by an American consortium and the Cape Horn Outfitters of Charlotte, North Carolina, was appointed their sole agent.

Double Rifle, Boxlock

A .300 Holland & Holland, .375 Holland & Holland or .458 Winchester Magnum double-barrel boxlock rifle with double triggers and a walnut stock. Other features were made to the customer's specifications. A .600 Nitro Express version was also available.

.600 Nitro Express-Add 25%.

Exc.	V.G.	Good	Fair	Poor
40000	32500	25000	17500	12500

Double Rifle, Sidelock

As above, with Holland & Holland-style sidelocks.
.600 Nitro Express-Add 25%.

Exc.	V.G.	Good	Fair	Poor
55000	40000	30000	20000	17500

Shotgun, Boxlock

A boxlock double-barrel shotgun produced in a variety of gauges, barrel lengths and degrees of decoration.

.28 Gauge and .410-Add 20%.

Exc.	V.G.	Good	Fair	Poor
8500	7000	5500	4000	3000

Shotgun, Sidelock

As above, with Holland & Holland-style sidelocks.
.28 Gauge and .410-Add 20%.

Exc.	V.G.	Good	Fair	Poor
9500	8000	6500	5000	3750

BOSWORTH, B. M.
Warren, Pennsylvania

Bosworth Under Hammer Pistol

A .38 caliber single-shot percussion pistol with an under hammer and a 6" half octagonal barrel. The frame is marked "BM Bosworth". Browned with brass grips forming part of the frame. Made circa 1850 to 1860.

Exc.	V.G.	Good	Fair	Poor
—	1000	500	275	200

BRAENDLIN ARMOURY
London, England

A .450 caliber 8-barrel pistol with hinged barrels, rotating firing pin and double-action lock. Manufactured during the 1880s.

Exc.	V.G.	Good	Fair	Poor
—	7500	4500	2750	1500

BRAND
E. Robinson, Maker
New York

Brand Breech Loading Carbine

A .50 rimfire caliber carbine with a 22" barrel secured by one barrel band. The frame is marked "Brand's Patent July 29,1862/E. Robinson Manfr/New York." This carbine was produced in limited numbers, primarily for trial purposes.

Exc.	V.G.	Good	Fair	Poor
—	8000	3500	2000	900

BREDA, ERNESTO
Milan, Italy
Importer-Diana Imports Co.
San Francisco, California

Andromeda Special
A 12 gauge boxlock shotgun with various barrel lengths and chokes, single selective triggers and automatic ejectors. Engraved, satin-finished with checkered walnut stock.

Exc.	V.G.	Good	Fair	Poor
700	650	550	425	300

Vega Special
A 12 gauge boxlock Over/Under shotgun with 26" or 28" barrels, various choke combinations, single selective trigger and automatic ejectors. Engraved and blued with a checkered walnut stock.

Exc.	V.G	Good	Fair	Poor
650	600	500	375	275

Vega Special Trap
As above with a competition-styled stock and 30" or 32" barrels with full chokes.

Exc.	V.G.	Good	Fair	Poor
1150	900	750	500	350

Sirio Standard
Similar to the Vega with extensive engraving and a higher degree of finishing. There is a 28" barreled skeet version available in this model.

Exc.	V.G.	Good	Fair	Poor
2250	2000	1750	1250	650

Standard Semiautomatic
A 12 gauge semiautomatic shotgun with 25" or 27" ventilated rib barrels, screw-in choke tubes, an engraved receiver, and checkered walnut stock.

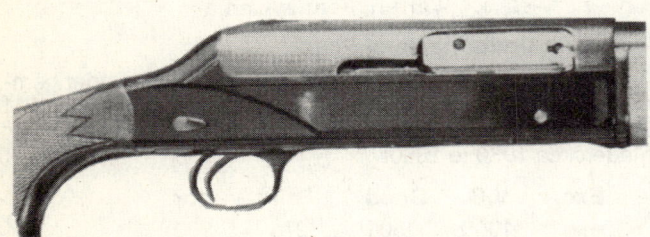

Exc.	V.G.	Good	Fair	Poor
325	275	225	175	125

Grade I
As above, with more engraving and finer wood.

Exc.	V.G.	Good	Fair	Poor
550	475	325	225	175

Grade II
A more elaborately engraved version of the Grade I.

Exc.	V.G.	Good	Fair	Poor
675	600	450	375	250

Grade III
The most deluxe version in this line with select walnut and extensive engraving.

Exc.	V.G.	Good	Fair	Poor
875	800	650	575	250

Magnum Model
Same as the standard, 12 gauge Magnum.

Exc.	V.G.	Good	Fair	Poor
475	400	350	275	200

Gold Series Antares Standard
A 12 gauge semiautomatic shotgun with a 25" or 27" ventilated-rib barrel and screw-in choke tubes. Blued with a checkered walnut stock.

Exc.	V.G.	Good	Fair	Poor
500	400	350	275	225

Gold Series Argus
As above, with alloy frame.

Exc.	V.G.	Good	Fair	Poor
525	425	375	300	250

Gold Series Aries
As above, except in 12 gauge Magnum.

Exc.	V.G.	Good	Fair	Poor
550	450	400	325	275

BREN 10
Dornaus & Dixon Inc.
Huntington Beach, California
Manufactured from 1983 until 1986.

Standard Bren 10
A 10mm caliber double-action semiautomatic pistol with a 5" barrel and 11-shot magazine. Stainless frame and satin-blued slide. Manufactured between 1983 and 1986.

NIB	Exc.	V.G.	Good	Fair	Poor
1350	1100	800	500	300	200

M & P Model
As above, with a matte black finish.

NIB	Exc.	V.G.	Good	Fair	Poor
1350	1000	800	500	300	200

Pocket Model
As above, with a 4" barrel and 9-shot magazine.

NIB	Exc.	V.G.	Good	Fair	Poor
1300	1150	850	500	300	200

Dual-Master Presentation Model
As above, with a .45 caliber, extra barrel and slide and a fitted walnut case.

NIB	Exc.	V.G.	Good	Fair	Poor
1750	1500	1050	700	400	250

Marksman Model

Similar to the Standard Model but in .45 caliber. There were 250 manufactured for the "Marksman Shop" in Chicago, Illinois.

NIB	Exc.	V.G.	Good	Fair	Poor
1100	1000	750	500	300	200

Initial Commemorative

There were supposed to be 2,000 of these manufactured in 1986, but no one knows how many were actually produced. They are chambered for the 10mm and have a high-gloss blue finish with 22 kt. gold-plated details. The grips are laser engraved, and the whole affair is furnished in a walnut display case.

NIB	Exc.	V.G.	Good	Fair	Poor
3000	2500	2000	900	400	250

BRETTON
Ste. Etienne, France
Importers—Quality Arms, Inc.
Houston, Texas
Mandall Shooting Supplies
Scottsdale, Arizona

Baby Standard

A 12 or 20 gauge Over/Under shotgun with various barrel lengths and choke combinations and double triggers. Blued, checkered walnut stock.

NIB	Exc.	V.G.	Good	Fair	Poor
800	725	625	500	400	325

Deluxe Grade

A 12, 16, and 20 gauge Over/Under shotgun. Engraved, coin-finished receiver with walnut stock.

NIB	Exc.	V.G.	Good	Fair	Poor
1000	800	650	500	400	325

BRIGGS, H. A.
Norwich, Connecticut

Briggs Single Shot Pistol

A .22 caliber single shot spur trigger pistol with a 4" part-round/part-octagonal barrel with a downward rotating breech-block. Blued with walnut grips. Frame is marked "H.A. Briggs/Norwich, Ct." Manufactured in the 1850s and 1860s.

Exc.	V.G.	Good	Fair	Poor
750	600	525	400	275

BRILEY
Houston, Texas

El Presidente Model-Unlimited

This 1911 style pistol can be built on a Caspian Arms, STI, or SVI frame. Includes scope mount, compensator, match barrel, cocking sight, lowered and flared ejection port, front and rear serrations, aluminum guide rod, and numerous other custom features. Offered in most calibers. Blued finish.

NIB	Exc.	V.G.	Good	Fair	Poor
2400	2000	—	—	—	—

Versatility Plus Model-Limited

Built on a 1911 frame with BoMar sight, checkered mainspring housing and checkered front strap. Many other custom features. Available in .45 ACP, .40 S&W, and 9mm.

NIB	Exc.	V.G.	Good	Fair	Poor
1750	1500	—	—	—	—

Versatility Model -Limited

Similar to the above model but without several features such as the checkered front strap. Available in .45 ACP, .40 S&W, 9mm.

NIB	Exc.	V.G.	Good	Fair	Poor
1250	1000	—	—	—	—

Lightning Model-Action Pistol

Built on a 1911 frame this pistol features many custom components including a titanium compensator. Weight no more than 40 oz. Available in 9mm and .38 Super only.

NIB	Exc.	V.G.	Good	Fair	Poor
2200	1800	—	—	—	—

Carry Comp Model-Defense

Built on a 1911 frame this model features a dual port cone compensator with many custom features. Barrel length is about 5". Offered in .45 ACP only.

NIB	Exc.	V.G.	Good	Fair	Poor
2150	1800	—	—	—	—

BRIXIA
Brescia, Italy

Model 12

A commercial version of the Model 1910 Glisenti in 9mm caliber. The only markings are the monogram "MBT" cast in the grips.

Exc.	V.G.	Good	Fair	Poor
375	325	275	200	150

BRNO ARMS
Uhersky Brod, Czech Republic
Importer-CZ-USA
Oakhurst, California

Brno rifles and shotguns are built in the same factory as CZ pistols.

ZH-Series

A double barrel Over/Under boxlock series of shotguns with interchangeable barrels in shotgun and rifle configurations, of various lengths, double triggers and automatic ejectors. The models listed below represent the different gauges and/or calibers offered.

ZH-300

NIB	Exc.	V.G.	Good	Fair	Poor
800	675	575	400	325	250

ZH-301

Exc.	V.G.	Good	Fair	Poor
725	600	500	375	300

ZH-302

Exc.	V.G.	Good	Fair	Poor
725	600	500	375	300

ZH-303

Exc.	V.G.	Good	Fair	Poor
725	625	500	375	300

ZH-304

Exc.	V.G.	Good	Fair	Poor
875	725	575	450	375

ZH-305

Exc.	V.G.	Good	Fair	Poor
875	775	625	475	375

ZH-306

Exc.	V.G.	Good	Fair	Poor
875	775	625	500	400

ZH-321

Exc.	V.G.	Good	Fair	Poor
700	600	475	375	300

ZH-324

Exc.	V.G.	Good	Fair	Poor
800	675	525	450	375

Model 300 Combo

The model ZH-300 with 8 interchangeable barrels in a fitted case. Introduced in 1986.

NIB	Exc.	V.G.	Good	Fair	Poor
5800	5000	4000	2750	2000	1500

Model 500

The model ZH-300 with acid etched decoration, automatic ejectors and in 12 gauge.

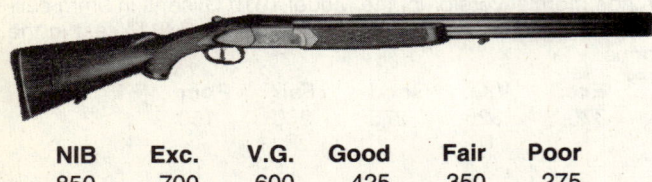

NIB	Exc.	V.G.	Good	Fair	Poor
850	700	600	425	350	275

CZ-581

A 12 gauge O/U double barrel boxlock shotgun with 28" ventilated-rib barrels, single-trigger, and automatic ejectors. Blued with a walnut stock.

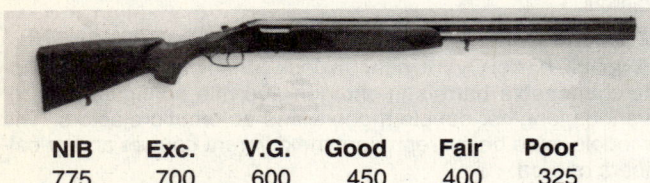

NIB	Exc.	V.G.	Good	Fair	Poor
775	700	600	450	400	325

CZ-584

A combination 12 gauge/7x57Rmm, .222 or .308 caliber Over/Under combination rifle/shotgun with 24.5" ventilated-rib barrels, single-triggers and automatic ejectors. Blued with a walnut stock. Discontinued in 1986.

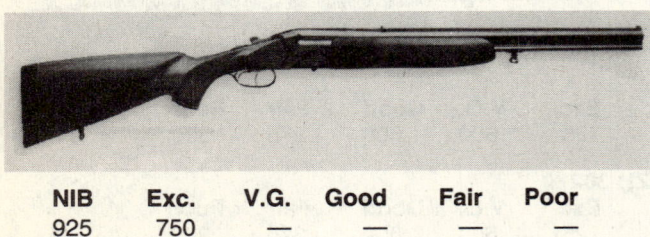

NIB	Exc.	V.G.	Good	Fair	Poor
925	750	—	—	—	—

ZP-49

A 12 gauge sidelock double-barrel shotgun with double triggers and automatic ejectors. Blued with a walnut stock. Imported in 1986 only.

Exc.	V.G.	Good	Fair	Poor
675	575	475	350	300

ZP-149

As above, without engraving.

NIB	Exc.	V.G.	Good	Fair	Poor
650	575	500	350	325	250

ZP-349

As above, with the buttstock having a cheekpiece and a beavertail forearm.

Exc.	V.G.	Good	Fair	Poor
675	600	500	350	250

RIFLES

ZKW-465 (Hornet Sporter)

A .22 Hornet caliber bolt-action rifle with a 23" barrel, express sights and double set triggers. Blued with a walnut stock.

Exc.	V.G.	Good	Fair	Poor
1200	1000	850	700	550

Model 21H

A 6.5x57mm, 7x57mm or 8x57mm caliber bolt-action sporting rifle with a 28.5" barrel, express sights and double set triggers. Blued with a walnut stock.

Exc.	V.G.	Good	Fair	Poor
1000	900	800	600	500

Model 22F

As above, with a Mannlicher-style stock.

Exc.	V.G.	Good	Fair	Poor
1250	1100	900	650	500

Model I

A .22 caliber bolt-action rifle with a 22.75" barrel having folding leaf rear sights. Blued with a walnut stock.

Exc.	V.G.	Good	Fair	Poor
600	500	400	325	250

Model II

As above, with a more finely figured walnut stock.

Exc.	V.G.	Good	Fair	Poor
650	550	450	375	275

ZKM-452

As above, with a 25" barrel and either a 5- or 10-shot magazine. Blued with a beechwood stock.

Exc.	V.G.	Good	Fair	Poor
250	200	150	125	100

ZKM-452-2E Lux

A more finely finished version of the basic ZKM 452 rifle chambered for the .22 Long Rifle or .22 WRM cartridge. Checkered fancy walnut stock. Open sights. Five round magazine standard. Add $35.99 for .22 WRM version.

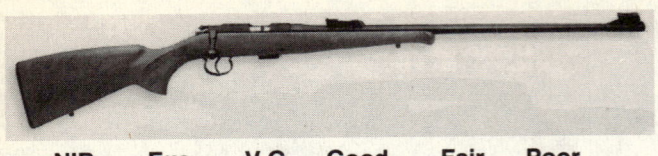

NIB	Exc.	V.G.	Good	Fair	Poor
325	275	—	—	—	—

ZKM-452D

As above, with a walnut, Monte Carlo-style stock.

Exc.	V.G.	Good	Fair	Poor
350	300	250	175	125

ZKM 611

This is a semi-automatic rifle chambered for the .22 WRM cartridge. It is fitted with a 20" barrel and has a magazine capacity of 6 rounds. Weight is approximately 6.2 lbs.

NIB	Exc	V.G.	Good	Fair	Poor
450	400	300	200	175	125

ZKB 680

A .22 Hornet or .222 caliber bolt-action rifle with a 23.5" barrel, double set triggers and 5-shot magazine. Blued with a walnut stock.

NIB	Exc.	V.G.	Good	Fair	Poor
750	650	500	350	300	200

ZKK 600

Offered in 7x57mm, 7x64mm, .270, or .30-06. Features a Mauser-type bolt action with controlled feed, non-rotating extractor, and dovetailed receiver in three action lengths.

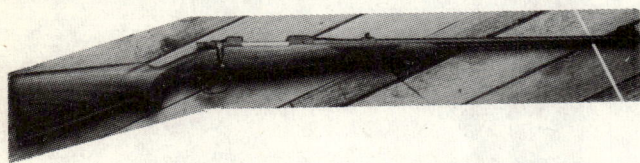

NIB	Exc.	V.G.	Good	Fair	Poor
650	550	450	400	300	225

NOTE: Add $100 to prices for pop-up receiver sight that was discontinued in 1977.

ZKK 601

As above, in .243 or .308 caliber.

NIB	Exc.	V.G.	Good	Fair	Poor
650	550	450	400	300	225

ZKK 602

As above, in .300 Holland & Holland, .375 Holland & Holland or .458 Winchester Magnum.

NIB	Exc.	Good	Good	Fair	Poor
750	675	525	500	425	325

CZ-511

A .22 caliber semiautomatic rifle with adjustable sights. Blued with a walnut stock. Discontinued in 1986. Reintroduced in 1997.

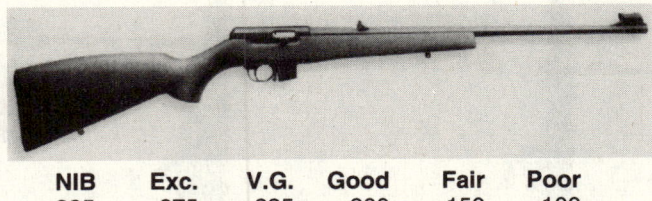

NIB	Exc.	V.G.	Good	Fair	Poor
325	275	225	200	150	100

Model 581

Similar to the above, but more finely finished.

Exc.	V.G.	Good	Fair	Poor
650	550	500	400	325

Model 537

This bolt action rifle is chambered for the .270, .308, and .30-06 cartridges. The rear sight is adjustable and the stock is checkered walnut. Barrel length is 23.6". Magazine capacity is 5 rounds. Weight is approximately 7.9 lbs.

NIB	Exc.	V.G.	Good	Fair	Poor
600	500	400	300	225	175

CZ Model 527

This bolt action model is chambered for the .22 Hornet, .222 Rem., and the .223 Rem. The rear sight is adjustable and the checkered stock is walnut. Barrel length is 23.6" and magazine capacity is 5 rounds. Weight is approximately 6.2 lbs.

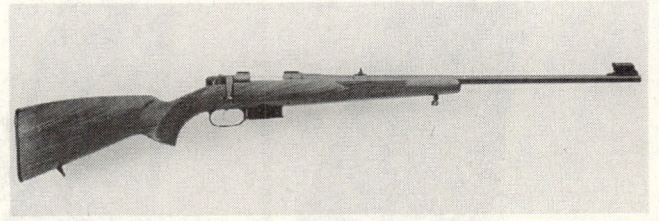

NIB	Exc.	V.G.	Good	Fair	Poor
600	500	400	300	225	175

CZ Model 527 FS

Same as above but fitted with a full one-piece stock.

NIB	Exc.	V.G.	Good	Fair	Poor
650	550	425	300	225	175

CZ Model 550

Chambered for the .243, .270, .308, and .30-06 cartridges this bolt action rifle features a 24" barrel and high comb walnut stock. No open sights. Weight is about 7.25 lbs.

NIB	Exc	V.G.	Good	Fair	Poor
600	500	400	300	225	175

CZ Model 550 Batteu Lux

Chambered for the .30-06 cartridge. Ramp rear sight. Barrel length is 20.25". Weight is approximately 7.25 lbs. Checkered walnut stock.

NIB	Exc.	V.G.	Good	Fair	Poor
675	550	—	—	—	—

CZ Model 550 FS Battue

Same as above but with full length stock.

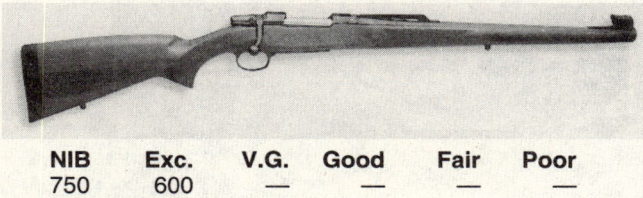

NIB	Exc.	V.G.	Good	Fair	Poor
750	600	—	—	—	—

CZ Model 550 Minnesota

This model is chambered for the .270 Win. and .30-06 calibers. Barrel length is 23.5". Weight is approximately 7.25 lbs. No sights. Supplied with recoil pad.

NIB	Exc.	V.G.	Good	Fair	Poor
650	550	—	—	—	—

CZ Model 550 Minnesota DM

Same as above but with detachable magazine. Calibers are .270 Win. and .308.

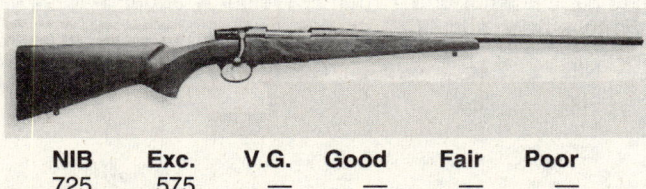

NIB	Exc.	V.G.	Good	Fair	Poor
725	575	—	—	—	—

Super Express Rifle

An Over/Under sidelock double barrel rifle, with 23.5" barrels, double triggers and automatic ejectors. Engraved, blued with a walnut stock. Available in 6 grades as below:

Standard Model

NIB	Exc.	V.G.	Good	Fair	Poor
4500	3750	3000	2500	1750	1250

Grade I

NIB	Exc.	V.G.	Good	Fair	Poor
6500	5500	4750	4500	3600	3250

Grade II

NIB	Exc.	V.G.	Good	Fair	Poor
5500	4750	4000	3500	2750	2250

Grade III

NIB	Exc.	V.G.	Good	Fair	Poor
5250	4500	3950	3250	2750	2250

Grade IV

NIB	Exc.	V.G.	Good	Fair	Poor
5000	4000	3500	3000	2500	2250

Grade V

NIB	Exc.	V.G.	Good	Fair	Poor
4750	3850	3250	2750	2250	1750

Grade VI

NIB	Exc.	V.G.	Good	Fair	Poor
4600	3950	3100	2600	1950	1500

BROLIN ARMS
Le Verne, California

This California company began business in 1995 with the manufacturing of 1911 type pistols. These pistols are manufactured and assembled in the U.S. Because these pistols were first introduced in 1996 only limited prices will be given. Very little price history has been established.

LEGEND SERIES-1911 AUTO PISTOL

Model L45-Standard Auto Pistol

This is the standard model with 5" barrel chambered for the .45 ACP. Fitted with throated match barrel, polished feed ramp, lowered ejection port, beveled magazine well and fixed sights. Other custom features as well. Finish is matte blue with 7-round magazine. Weight is about 36 oz.

NIB	Exc.	V.G.	Good	Fair	Poor
450	350	—	—	—	—

Model L45C-Compact Auto Pistol

Similar to the above standard model with the same features but with a 4.5" barrel. Weight is about 32 oz.

NIB	Exc.	V.G.	Good	Fair	Poor
460	350	—	—	—	—

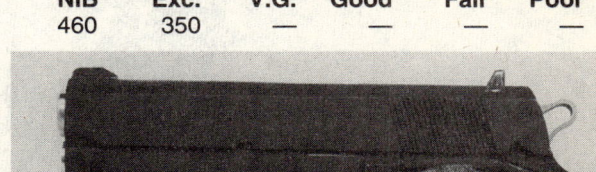

Model L45T

This version of the L45 series was introduced in 1997 and is fitted with a compact slide on a full size frame. Weight is 36 oz.

NIB	Exc.	V.G.	Good	Fair	Poor
460	350	—	—	—	—

NOTE: For Novak sights add $50.

PATRIOT SERIES-DPC CARRY-COMP PISTOLS

Model P45 Comp-Standard Carry Comp

This model features a 4" barrel with integral compensator cut into the slide. Other features are a custom beavertail grip safety, adjustable aluminum trigger, flat top slide, and checkered wood grips. Weight is about 37 oz. For two-tone finish add $20.

NIB	Exc.	V.G.	Good	Fair	Poor
650	500	—	—	—	—

Model P45C Comp-Compact Carry Comp

Similar to the above model but fitted with a 3.25" barrel. Weight is about 33 oz. For two-tone finish add $20.

NIB	Exc.	V.G.	Good	Fair	Poor
680	500	—	—	—	—

Model P45T

This addition to the Patriot Series was introduced in 1997 and has all of the features of the Patriot pistols but is fitted with a compact slide and full size frame. Weight is about 35 oz. Also available in two-tone finish for an additional $20.

NIB	Exc.	V.G.	Good	Fair	Poor
690	500	—	—	—	—

NOTE: For Novak sights add $50.

TAC SERIES-TACTICAL 1911 PISTOLS

Model TAC-11

This series and model were introduced in 1997 and have all of the features of the L45 series with the additions of a special 5" conical match barrel, Novak Low Profile sights, black rubber contour grips, "iron claw" extractor, and optional night sights. Chambered for the .45 ACP the pistol is supplied with an 8-round magazine. Weight is approximately 37 oz.

NIB	Exc.	V.G.	Good	Fair	Poor
650	—	—	—	—	—

NOTE: For Tritium night sights add $90.

PRO SERIES-COMPETITION PISTOL

Model Pro-Stock-Competition Pistol

Chambered for the .45 ACP, this pistol is designed for the competition shooter. Many special features are standard such as full length recoil guide, front strap high relief cut, serrated flat mainspring housing, ambidextrous thumb safety and fully adjustable rear sight. Barrel length is 5" and weight is about 37 oz. For two-tone finish add $20.

NIB	Exc.	V.G.	Good	Fair	Poor
780	600	—	—	—	—

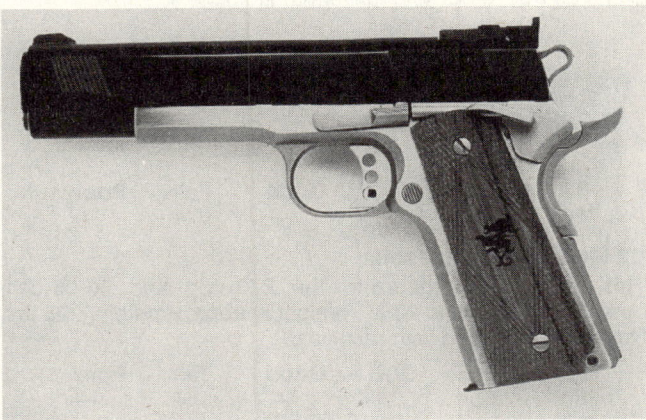

Model Pro-Comp-Competition Pistol

Similar to the competition model above but fitted with an integral compensator and 4" barrel. Weight is about 37 oz. For two-tone finish add $20.

NIB	Exc.	V.G.	Good	Fair	Poor
900	700	—	—	—	—

SHOTGUNS

LAWMAN SERIES--PERSONAL SECURITY SHOTGUN

Model HL18SB
This is a pump action 12 gauge shotgun with an 18.5" barrel with black synthetic stock with bead sights. Weight is about 7 lbs. Introduced in 1997.

NIB	Exc.	V.G.	Good	Fair	Poor
250	—	—	—	—	—

Model HL18SR
Same as above but fitted with rifle sights.

NIB	Exc.	V.G.	Good	Fair	Poor
260	—	—	—	—	—

Model HL18SBN
Same as above but with nickel finish and bead sights.

NIB	Exc.	V.G.	Good	Fair	Poor
270	—	—	—	—	—

Model HL18WB
This version has a wood stock and bead sights.

NIB	Exc.	V.G.	Good	Fair	Poor
250	—	—	—	—	—

Model HL18WR
Same as above but fitted with rifle sights.

NIB	Exc.	V.G.	Good	Fair	Poor
260	—	—	—	—	—

FIELD SERIES-PUMP ACTION FIELD GUN

Model HF24SB
This is a 12 gauge pump action shotgun with a 24" barrel, matte finish, and black synthetic stock with bead sights. Weight is about 7.3 lbs. Introduced in 1997.

NIB	Exc.	V.G.	Good	Fair	Poor
270	—	—	—	—	—

Model HF28SB
Same as above but fitted with a 28" barrel. Weight is 7.4 lbs.

NIB	Exc.	V.G.	Good	Fair	Poor
270	—	—	—	—	—

Model HF24WB
This model features a 24" barrel with wood stock.

NIB	Exc.	V.G.	Good	Fair	Poor
270	—	—	—	—	—

Model HF28WB
Same as above but with 24" barrel.

NIB	Exc.	V.G.	Good	Fair	Poor
270	—	—	—	—	—

FIELD COMBO-TWO BARREL COMBO SET

Model HC28SB
This set consists of an 18.5" barrel and 28" barrel with synthetic stock pistol grip, and bead sights.

NIB	Exc.	V.G.	Good	Fair	Poor
300	—	—	—	—	—

Model HC28SR
Same as above but with rifle and bead sights.

NIB	Exc.	V.G.	Good	Fair	Poor
320	—	—	—	—	—

Model HC28WB
This model features a wood stock, pistol grip, and bead sights.

NIB	Exc.	V.G.	Good	Fair	Poor
300	—	—	—	—	—

Model HC28WR
Same as above but with wood stock with rifle and bead sights.

NIB	Exc.	V.G.	Good	Fair	Poor
320	—	—	—	—	—

BRONCO
SEE—Arizmendi
Eibar, Spain

BROOKLYN F. A. CO.
Brooklyn, New York

Slocum Pocket Revolver
A .32 caliber spur trigger revolver with a 3" round barrel. The frame is silver-plated brass and scroll engraved; the remainder is either blued or plated with walnut grips. The barrel is marked "B.A. Co. Patented April 14, 1863." Approximately 10,000 were manufactured in 1863 and 1864. The cylinder has five individual tubes that slide forward to open for loading and then for ejecting the spent cartridges.

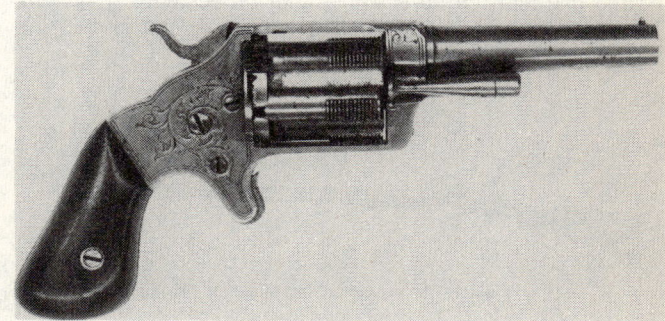

Exc.	V.G.	Good	Fair	Poor
1250	700	400	200	100

Slocum Unfluted Cylinder Pocket Revolver
As above, but in .22 or .32 caliber with 5- or 7-shot cylinder. Approximately 250 were manufactured in .32 rimfire and 100 in .22 rimfire.

.22 Caliber-Add 25%.

Exc.	V.G.	Good	Fair	Poor
—	800	400	250	200

BROWN MANUFACTURING CO.
Newburyport, Massachusefs
SEE-also Ballard

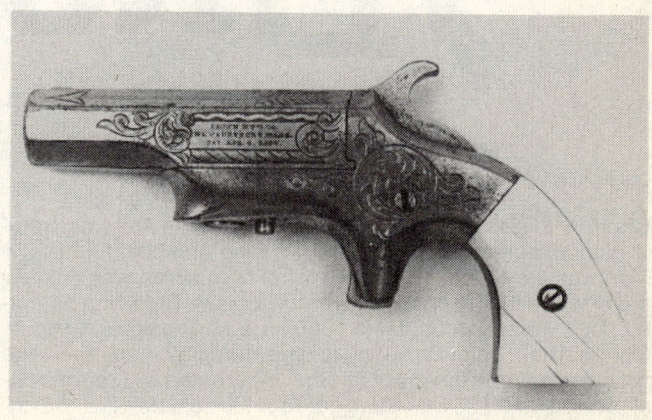

Courtesy W. P. Hallstein III and son Chip

Southerner Derringer

A .41 caliber spur trigger single shot pocket pistol with a pivoted 2.5" or 4" octagonal barrel marked "Southerner". Silver plated or blued with walnut grips. This pistol was manufactured by the Merrimack Arms Co. from 1867 to 1869 and by the Brown Manufacturing Co. from 1869 to 1873.

Brass Framed 2.5" Barrel

Exc.	V.G.	Good	Fair	Poor
—	1200	500	250	125

Iron Frame 2.5" Barrel (Brown Mfg. Only)

Exc.	V.G.	Good	Fair	Poor
—	1700	750	400	200

Brass Frame 4" Barrel

Exc.	V.G.	Good	Fair	Poor
—	1500	750	425	300

Brown Mfg. Co./Merrill Patent breechloading rifles

Overall length 54-3/4"; barrel (bore) length 35"; caliber .577. Markings: On breechblock-bolt mechanism, "BROWN MFG. CO. NEWBURYPORT, MASS./PATANTED OCT. 17, 1871." The patent issued to George Merrill in 1871, permitted the Brown Manufacturing Co. to alter probably up to 1,000 English P1853 rifle-muskets to a single shot breechloading system. The large bolt handle projecting upward at the end of the breech readily distinguishes these arms.

Courtesy Milwaukee Public Museum, Milwaukee, Wisconsin

Exc.	V.G.	Good	Fair	Poor
—	2250	1000	500	275

BROWN PRECISION, INC.
Los Molinos, California

Although known as a manufacturer of stocks, this company also produces custom order rifles.

High Country Standard

A .243 to .30-06 bolt-action rifle with a 22" barrel and Kevlar stock. Gray Camo Stock, Stainless Barrel and Leupold 2.5 x 10 Scope-Add $650.

NIB	Exc.	V.G.	Good	Fair	Poor
985	925	775	575	450	375

Open Country Varmint Rifle

Similar to the above, with a heavy barrel. Introduced in 1989.

NIB	Exc.	V.G.	Good	Fair	Poor
1100	1000	850	650	500	400

Law Enforcement Model

A .308 caliber Remington Varmint action rifle with a 20" barrel, Zeiss telescope and Kevlar stock.

NIB	Exc.	V.G.	Good	Fair	Poor
1050	950	800	600	450	375

Pro-Hunter

A .375 Holland & Holland or .458 Winchester Magnum bolt action rifle. Blued, electroless nickel-plated or Teflon coated.

NIB	Exc.	V.G.	Good	Fair	Poor
1800	1700	1450	1250	1000	750

A .270 or .30-06 bolt-action rifle with a 22" featherweight barrel and Kevlar stock.

NIB	Exc.	V.G.	Good	Fair	Poor
600	525	450	350		250

Blaser Rifle

Built on the Camex-Blaser action with a Brown Precision stock.

NIB	Exc.	V.G.	Good	Fair	Poor
1400	1250	1000	750	650	500

BROWNING ARMS CO.
Morgan, Utah

Contrary to popular belief, the firm of Browning Arms has really manufactured only one gun in its long and colorful history. This was the Model 1878 single shot rifle, which was actually the first gun that the prolific inventor John M. Browning patented. This firm was founded in 1880 as J. M. Browning & Bro. in Ogden, Utah. John Browning is considered by many to be the greatest firearms genius of all time. He created 80 firearms designs and held 128 individual patents. He sold designs to Winchester, Stevens, Remington, and Colt, as well as to the Belgian firm of Fabrique Nationale (FN). He was directly responsible for designing many of the firearms with which we have come to be familiar, including the 1911 Colt Government Model, the 1885 Winchester Single Shot (evolved from the Model 1878 that was actually Browning-manufactured), the Models 1886, 1892, 1894, and 1895 Lever Action Rifles, as well as the Model 1897 Shotgun. He was also directly responsible for producing the Model 1935 Hi-Power that achieved worldwide service pistol acceptance. In the 1890s Browning had difficulty dealing with the American arms corporations, so he went to Europe and established a lasting relationship with the firm of Fabrique Nationale in Herstal, Belgium. This agreement has lasted until 1977 when FN purchased the Browning Company. In the early 1970s, the Browning corporation contracted with the firm of B. C. Miroku in Japan and has since marketed guns produced by them. In 1991 GIAT, a French state-owned firm, purchased FN and Browning. One should be cognizant of the fact that in the opinion of many experts Miroku-produced Browning firearms are as high in quality as any others produced; collector interest dictates greater values on the Belgian-manufactured versions.

CAUTION
Certain Browning long guns and pistols used wood that was salt-cured, causing a rusting problem to the underside of barrels and actions. This problem occured from about 1966 to 1972. This should be carefully checked before purchase.

Early Semiautomatic Pistols
In the period between 1900 and the development of the Model 1935 Hi-Power Pistol, Browning had a number of semiautomatic pistols manufactured by Fabrique Nationale of Herstal, Belgium. They were the Models 1900, 1903, 1905, 1910, 1922, the Baby, and the 1935 Model Hi-Power. These firearms will be listed in more detail with their respective values in the Fabrique Nationale section of this text.

Hi-Power Modern Production
This version of the FN Model 1935 is quite similar in appearance to the original described in the FN section. It is chambered for the 9mm Parabellum cartridge and has a 4.75" barrel. Models built before the passage of the crime bill have a double column, 13-round, detachable box magazine and is blued with checkered walnut grips. It has fixed sights and has been produced in its present configuration since 1954. Add a 10 percent premium for adjustable sights. A matte-nickel version is also available and would be worth approximately 5 percent additional.

Spur Hammer Version
NIB	Exc.	V.G.	Good	Fair	Poor
475	400	350	300	275	200

Round Hammer Version
NIB	Exc.	V.G.	Good	Fair	Poor
600	500	400	350	300	200

Hi-Power-.30 Luger
This version is similar to the standard Hi-Power except that it is chambered for the .30 Luger cartridge. There were approximately 1,500 imported between 1986 and 1989. The slide is marked "FN." The Browning-marked versions are quite rare and worth approximately 10 percent additional.

Exc.	V.G.	Good	Fair	Poor
425	300	250	200	100

Tangent Sight Model
This version is similar to the standard Hi-Power with the addition of an adjustable rear sight calibrated to 500 meters. There were approximately 7,000 imported between 1965 and 1978. If the grip frame is slotted to accept a detachable shoulder stock, add approximately 20 percent to the value; but be wary of fakes. Add an additional 10% for "T" series serial numbers.

Exc.	V.G.	Good	Fair	Poor
750	675	500	400	300

Renaissance Hi-Power
This is a heavily engraved version with a matte-silver finish. It features synthetic-pearl grips and a gold-plated trigger. Import on this model ended in 1980.

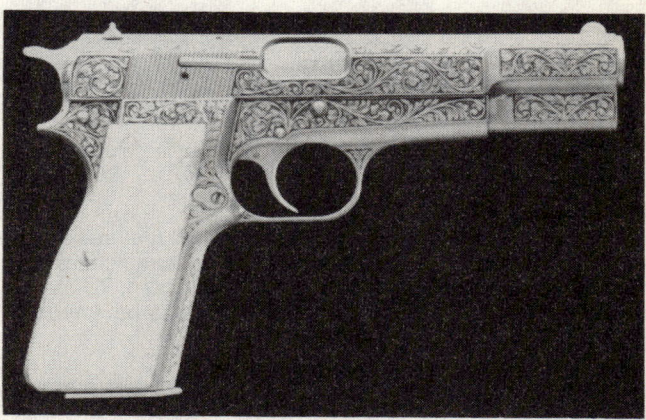

Spur Hammer Model
NIB	Exc.	V.G.	Good	Fair	Poor
1500	1200	1050	800	250	100

Ring Hammer Model
NIB	Exc.	V.G.	Good	Fair	Poor
1600	1400	1000	800	500	250

Adjustable Sight Spur Hammer Model
NIB	Exc.	V.G.	Good	Fair	Poor
1675	1150	850	600	500	250

Renaissance .25 Caliber
NIB	Exc.	V.G.	Good	Fair	Poor
900	750	600	400	300	150

Renaissance .380 Caliber
With pearl grips

NIB	Exc.	V.G.	Good	Fair	Poor
1400	1150	850	600	400	200

Renaissance .380 Caliber (Model 1971)
With wood grips and adjustable sights.

NIB	Exc.	V.G.	Good	Fair	Poor
1000	800	600	400	325	175

Cased Renaissance Set
This features one example of a fully engraved and silver-finished .25 ACP "Baby," one .380 ACP pistol, and one Hi-Power. The set is furnished in a fitted walnut case or black leatherette and was imported between 1955 and 1969.

NIB	Exc.	V.G.	Good	Fair	Poor
3750	3000	2100	1500	1100	900

Louis XVI Model

This is a heavily engraved Hi-Power pistol that features a leaf-and-scroll pattern. It is satin-finished and features checkered walnut grips. It is furnished in a fitted walnut case. To realize its true potential, this pistol must be NIB. It was not imported after 1984.

Diamond Grip Model

NIB	Exc.	V.G.	Good	Fair	Poor
900	775	650	550	300	200

Medallion Grip Model

NIB	Exc.	V.G.	Good	Fair	Poor
800	700	600	350	225	150

Hi-Power Centennial Model

This version is similar to the standard fixed-sight Hi-Power but is chrome-plated with the inscription, "Browning Centennial/1878-1978" engraved on the slide. It is furnished with a fitted case. There were 3,500 manufactured in 1978. As with all commemorative pistols, in order to realize its collector potential, this model should be NIB with all supplied material. Prices are for pistols built in Belgium

NIB	Exc.	V.G.	Good	Fair	Poor
700	500	400	300	200	150

Hi-Power Capitan

This is a new verions of the Hi-Power model fitted with tangent sights. Introduced in 1993. Furnished with walnut grips. Weighs about 32 oz. Assembled in Portugal.

NIB	Exc.	V.G.	Good	Fair	Poor
475	400	350	300	250	200

Hi-Power Practical

First introduced in 1993 this version is furnished with a blued slide and chrome frame. Has Pachmayr wraparound rubber grips, round style serrated hammer, and removable front sight. As available with adjustable sights. Weighs 36 oz. Assembled in Portugal

NIB	Exc.	V.G.	Good	Fair	Poor
475	400	350	300	250	200

Hi-Power Silver Chrome Model

Furnished in hard chrome and fitted with wraparound Pachmayr rubber grips. Weighs 36 oz. Assembled in Portugal. Add 10% for models with all Belgian markings.

NIB	Exc.	V.G.	Good	Fair	Poor
600	375	325	275	225	200

Hi-Power Mark III

The pistol has a matte blued finish with low profile fixed sights, and two-piece molded grips with thumb rest. Weighs 32 oz.

NIB	Exc.	V.G.	Good	Fair	Poor
380	325	275	225	200	175

Hi-Power 40 S&W

Introduced in 1994, this new version of the Hi-Power is furnished with adjustable sights, molded grips, 5" barrel and a 10-round magazine. Weighs about 35 oz.

NIB	Exc.	V.G.	Good	Fair	Poor
475	400	350	300	250	200

BDA-380

This is a double-action, semiautomatic pistol chambered for the .380 ACP cartridge. It features a 3.75" barrel with a 14-round, double-stack, detachable magazine. The finish is either blued or nickel-plated with smooth walnut grips. This pistol was manufactured in Italy by Beretta and introduced in 1982. Add 5% for nickel finish.

NIB	Exc.	V.G.	Good	Fair	Poor
450	375	325	275	200	150

Model BDA

This is a double-action, semiautomatic pistol manufactured for Browning by Sig-Sauer of Germany. It is identical to the Sig-Sauer Model 220. It is chambered for 9mm Parabellum, .38 Super, and the .45 ACP cartridges. The .38 Super would be worth approximately 30 percent additional. This model was only produced for a short time.

Exc.	V.G.	Good	Fair	Poor
500	425	375	300	235

BDM Pistol

This is a double-action, semiautomatic pistol chambered for the 9mm cartridge. The pistol is fitted with a selector switch that allows the shooter to choose between single action model or double action model. It features a 4.75" barrel with adjustable rear sight. The magazine capacity is 15 rounds. Weighs 31 oz.

NIB	Exc.	V.G.	Good	Fair	Poor
560	500	450	400	300	200

Model BDM Silver Chrome

This variation of the BDM was introduced in 1997 and features a silver chrome finish on the slide and frame. The balance of the pistol is in a constrasting matte blue finish.

NIB	Exc.	V.G.	Good	Fair	Poor
560	500	450	400	300	200

Model BDM Practical

This model, also introduced in 1997, is the same as above but with the silver chrome on the frame only.

NIB	Exc.	V.G.	Good	Fair	Poor
560	500	450	400	300	200

Model BPM-D

Introduced in 1997 this new version of the BDM (Browning Pistol Model Decocker) features a double action pistol with the first shot fired double action and subsequent shots fired single action. There is no manual safety. A decock lever also releases the slide.

NIB	Exc.	V.G.	Good	Fair	Poor
525	475	425	375	275	200

Model BRM-DOA

This 9mm pistol is a redesigned version of the Model BDM but the initials stand for "Browning Revolver Model-Double Action Only". This pistol also has a finger support trigger guard for two-handed control. All other features are the same as the BPM-D pistol. Weight is approximately 31 oz.

NIB	Exc.	V.G.	Good	Fair	Poor
525	475	425	375	275	200

Nomad

This is a blowback-operated, semiautomatic pistol chambered for the .22 l.r. cartridge. It was offered with a 4.5" or 6.75" barrel. It has a 10-round, detachable magazine with adjustable sights and all-steel construction. The finish is blued with black plastic grips. It was manufactured between 1962 and 1974 by FN.

NIB	Exc.	V.G.	Good	Fair	Poor
300	250	200	150	75	50

Challenger

This is a more deluxe target pistol chambered for the .22 l.r. cartridge. It was offered with a 4.5" or 6.75" barrel and has a 10-round magazine. It is constructed entirely of steel and has adjustable sights. The finish is blued with a gold-plated trigger and checkered, wraparound, walnut grips. It was manufactured between 1962 and 1975 by FN.

NIB	Exc.	V.G.	Good	Fair	Poor
500	375	300	250	200	140

Renaissance Challenger

This version is fully engraved with a satin-nickel finish and furnished with a fleece lined pouch.

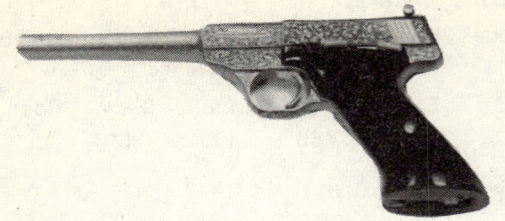

NIB	Exc.	V.G.	Good	Fair	Poor
1400	1100	750	600	400	275

Gold Line Challenger

This version is blued and has a gold-inlaid line around the outer edges of the pistol. It was cased in a fleece lined pouch. Built in Belgium.

NIB	Exc.	V.G.	Good	Fair	Poor
1600	1300	1000	750	500	350

Challenger II

This is a blowback-operated, semiautomatic pistol chambered for the .22 l.r. cartridge. It has a 6.75" barrel with an alloy frame. The finish is blued with phenolic impregnated hardwood grips. This pistol was manufactured between 1975 and 1982 in Salt Lake City, Utah.

Exc.	V.G.	Good	Fair	Poor
250	225	175	140	100

Challenger III

This version features a 5.5" bull barrel with adjustable sights. It was manufactured between 1982 and 1985 in Salt Lake City, Utah. A 6.75", tapered-barrel version was also available and known as the Sporter.

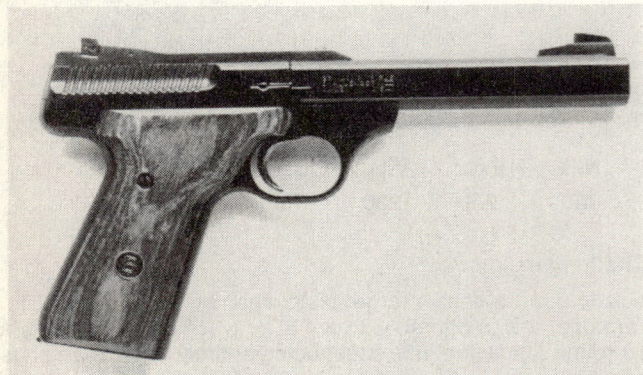

Exc.	V.G.	Good	Fair	Poor
225	200	150	125	90

Medalist

This is a high-grade, semiautomatic target pistol chambered for the .22 l.r. cartridge. It has a 6.75", vent-rib barrel with adjustable target sights. It was supplied with three barrel weights and a dry-fire-practice mechanism. The finish is blued with target type, thumbrest, walnut grips. It was manufactured between 1962 and 1975 by FN. There were four additional high-grade versions of this pistol that differed in the degree of ornamentation.

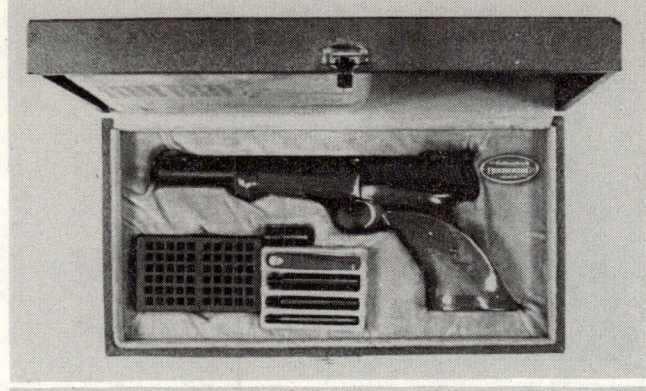

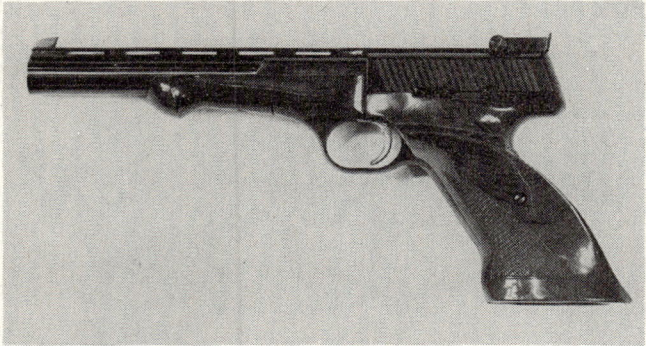

NIB	Exc.	V.G.	Good	Fair	Poor
800	650	575	475	375	250

International Medalist

About 700 were sold in the U.S. from 1970 to 1974. Barrels were 5 7/8" long. Built in Belgium.

NIB	Exc.	V.G.	Good	Fair	Poor
750	525	425	300	200	150

Second Model International Medalist.

Same as above but with flat-sided barrel, dull finish, and adjustable palm rest. Built in Belgium.

NIB	Exc.	V.G.	Good	Fair	Poor
650	450	350	275	200	150

Gold Line Medalist

Introduced in 1962 and discontinued in 1974 with only an estimated 400 guns produced.

NIB	Exc.	V.G.	Good	Fair	Poor
1750	1600	1250	1000	750	500

Renaissance Medalist

This model was built entirely in Belgium from 1970 to 1974.

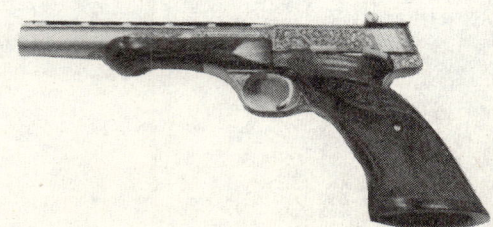

NIB	Exc.	V.G.	Good	Fair	Poor
2250	1900	1500	1200	900	700

Browning Collector's Edition-Non-Engraved, 38 Manufactured

NIB	Exc.	V.G.	Good	Fair	Poor
1500	1250	1000	750	500	400

Browning Collector's Edition-Engraved, 22 Manufactured

NIB	Exc.	V.G.	Good	Fair	Poor
2500	2000	1600	1250	900	700

Buck Mark

This is a blowback-operated, semiautomatic pistol chambered for the .22 l.r. cartridge. It has a 5.5" bull barrel with adjustable sights. It has an 11-round, detachable magazine and is matte blued with skip-line checkered synthetic grips. It was introduced in 1985. Produced in the U.S.

NIB	Exc.	V.G.	Good	Fair	Poor
210	175	150	135	110	85

Buck Mark Plus

This version is similar to the standard with plain wood grips. It was introduced in 1987. Produced in the US.

NIB	Exc.	V.G.	Good	Fair	Poor
250	210	185	150	120	100

Buck Mark Plus Nickel

Introduced in 1996. Add $30 to above price.

Buck Mark Varmint

This version has a 9.75" bull barrel with a full length ramp to allow scope mounting. It has no sights. It was introduced in 1987 and produced in the U.S.

NIB	Exc.	V.G.	Good	Fair	Poor
320	285	250	200	175	125

Buck Mark Silhouette

This version features a 9.75" bull barrel with adjustable sights.

NIB	Exc.	V.G.	Good	Fair	Poor
350	325	285	220	185	140

Buck Mark 22 Micro

This version of the Buck Mark 22 is fitted with a 4" bull barrel. Available in blue, matte blue, or nickel finish. Also available in Micro Plus variation with walnut grips. Weighs 32 oz.

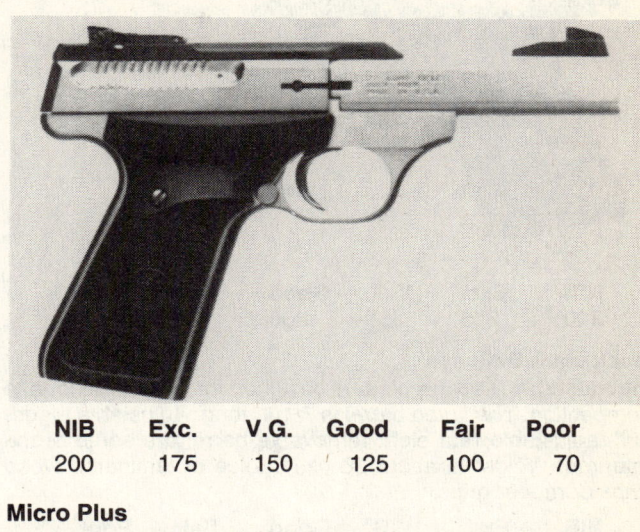

NIB	Exc.	V.G.	Good	Fair	Poor
200	175	150	125	100	70

Micro Plus

NIB	Exc.	V.G.	Good	Fair	Poor
225	200	175	150	125	90

Micro Plus Nickel

Introduced in 1996. Add $30 to above price.

Buck Mark 5.5

This .22 caliber pistol has a 5.5" heavy bull barrel fitted with target sights. It is offered in three separate models.

5.5 Blued Target

This version has a blued finish, contoured walnut grips, target sights. Weighs 35.5 oz.

NIB	Exc.	V.G.	Good	Fair	Poor
300	275	250	200	150	100

5.5 Gold Target

Same as above but has a gold anodized frame and top rib. Slide is blue. Walnut grips.

NIB	Exc.	V.G.	Good	Fair	Poor
325	300	275	225	175	125

5.5 Field

Same action and barrel as the Target Model but with adjustable field sights. Sights are hoodless. Slide and barrel is blued while the rib and frame are anodized blue. Grips are walnut.

NIB	Exc.	V.G.	Good	Fair	Poor
300	275	250	200	150	100

Buck Mark Bullseye

Introduced in 1996 this pistol is designed for metallic silhouette competition. The fluted barrel is 7-1/4" long. Adjustable trigger pull, adjustable rear sight removable barrel are some of the features. Weight is about 36 oz. Choice of laminated wood grips or rubber grips.

NIB	Exc.	V.G.	Good	Fair	Poor
325	275	225	175	125	75

NOTE: For Rosewood target grips add $90.

Buck Mark Unlimited Match

This pistol is fitted with a 14" barrel with top rib. The front sight hood is slightly rearward of the muzzle for a maximum sight radius of 15". All other features are the same as the Silhouette model. Weighs 64 oz.

NIB	Exc.	V.G.	Good	Fair	Poor
375	325	275	225	175	125

> ## CAUTION
> Certain Browning long guns used wood that was salt-cured, causing a rusting problem to the underside of barrels and actions. This should be carefully checked before purchase. This problem is most prevalent during the years 1966 to 1972

SHOTGUNS

SUPERPOSED SHOTGUNS

This series of Over/Under, double-barrel shotguns is chambered for 12, 20, and 28 gauges, as well as the .410 bore and is offered with vent-rib barrels from 26.5" to 32" in length. It features various choke combinations. This shotgun is built on a boxlock action and features either double or single selective triggers and automatic ejectors. There were a number of versions offered that differ in the amount of ornamentation and the quality of the materials and workmanship utilized in manufacture. Values for small-bore models are generally higher. This series was introduced in 1930 and is manufactured by Fabrique Nationale in Belgium. For factory restored guns or very fine non-factory restorations Superposed guns will bring close to factory orginal prices.

For extra factory installed barrels add $1000.

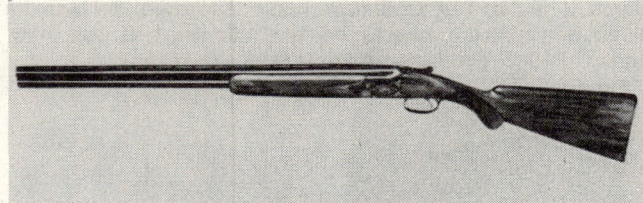

PREWAR SUPERPOSED, 1930-1940

Browning Superposed shotgun prices are divided into three different categories. The first category is for prewar guns built from 1930 to 1940. <u>These prewar Superposed guns were manufactured in 12 gauge only</u> from serial number 1 to around 17,000. These shotguns were offered in four different grades: Grade I, Pigeon, Diana, and Midas.

Grade I

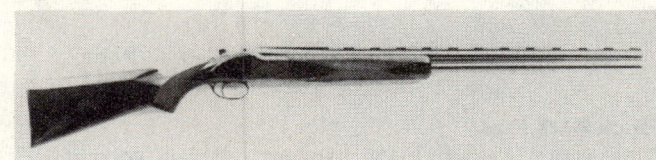

Exc.	V.G.	Good	Fair	Poor
1400	1100	750	400	300

Pigeon

Exc.	V.G.	Good	Fair	Poor
2500	1600	1100	500	400

Diana

Exc.	V.G.	Good	Fair	Poor
3500	2750	1700	750	500

Midas

Exc.	V.G.	Good	Fair	Poor
5500	3950	2950	1000	750

NOTE: For Twin-Single triggers add 15%.
For Vent Rib add 10%.
For recoil pads or shorter than standard stocks deduct 25%.

SUPERPOSED FROM 1947-1959

The second category of Superposed was produced and sold from 1947 to 1959. These were built in 12 and 20 gauge as well as the 28 gauge and .410 bore which were introduced in 1959. These shotguns were graded using a Roman numeral system instead of names. They are: Grade I, Grade II, Grade III, Grade IV, Grade V, and Grade VI. The values listed below are for 12 gauge. Add the premium or deductions as listed below.

20 Gauge-Add 20%.
28 Gauge- Add 60% (1959 only).
.410-Add 25% (1959 only).

Standard Weight 12 or 20 gauge Grade I-Deduct 10%.

Grade I (marked Lightning on frame)

NIB	Exc.	V.G.	Good	Fair	Poor
2000	1500	900	800	300	200

Grade II

NIB	Exc.	V.G.	Good	Fair	Poor
3200	2500	1600	900	550	300

Grade III

NIB	Exc.	V.G.	Good	Fair	Poor
3500	3000	2100	1400	600	300

Grade IV

NIB	Exc.	V.G.	Good	Fair	Poor
4500	3900	3000	1800	1000	500

Grade V

NIB	Exc.	V.G.	Good	Fair	Poor
5000	4250	3250	1800	1200	600

Grade VI (Built in 1957 through 1959 only)

NIB	Exc.	V.G.	Good	Fair	Poor
8000	6500	4500	3000	2000	700

NOTE: The number of Grade VIs sold in North America is unknown, but it was most likely very small. This is a very rare grade. Proceed with caution.

The number of 28 gauge and .410 bore guns sold in late 1959 number less than 100.

SUPERPOSED FROM 1960-1976

Browning Superposed shotguns built from 1960 to 1976 revert back to the older grade names. They are Grade I, Pigeon, Pointer, Diana, and Midas. These shotguns were available in 12, 20, and 28 gauge as well as .410 bore. This last production period is a little more complicated due to manufacturing changes that some collectors consider important such as round knobs, long tangs.

Prices below reflect Superposed field guns produced from 1960 to 1965 in round pistol grip knob with long trigger guard tang in 12 gauge. For all other variations during this period one should consider the following:

For salt wood damage deduct a minimum of 50%.
For round knob short tang (circa 1966-1969) deduct 25%.
For flat knob short tang (circa 1969-1971) deduct 30%.
For flat knob long tang (circa 1971-1976) deduct 15%.
For New Style Skeet and Lightning Trap (recoil pad, flat knob, full beavertail forearm) with long trigger guard tang (1971-1976) deduct 25%; with short trigger guard tang deduct 40%; if Broadway rib deduct an additional 10%.
For skeet chokes on field guns deduct 5%.
For recoil pads on 2-3/4" chambered field guns deduct 10%.
For Master engraver signed guns (Funken, Watrin, Vrancken) add 10%.
For Standard Weight Grade I guns deduct 10%.
For shorter than standard stock length deduct 25%.
For 20 gauge add 25%.
For 28 gauge add 60%.
For .410 bore add 25%.

Grade I (Lightning marked on frame)

NIB	Exc.	V.G.	Good	Fair	Poor
2000	1500	900	500	300	200

Pigeon Grade

NIB	Exc.	V.G.	Good	Fair	Poor
3200	2500	1600	950	600	300

Pointer Grade

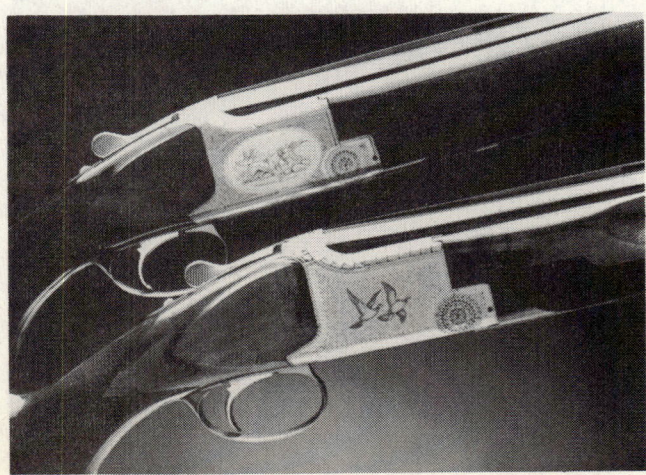

NIB	Exc.	V.G.	Good	Fair	Poor
4800	3400	2500	1400	1000	600

Diana Grade

NIB	Exc.	V.G.	Good	Fair	Poor
5000	3500	2750	1700	1200	600

Midas Grade

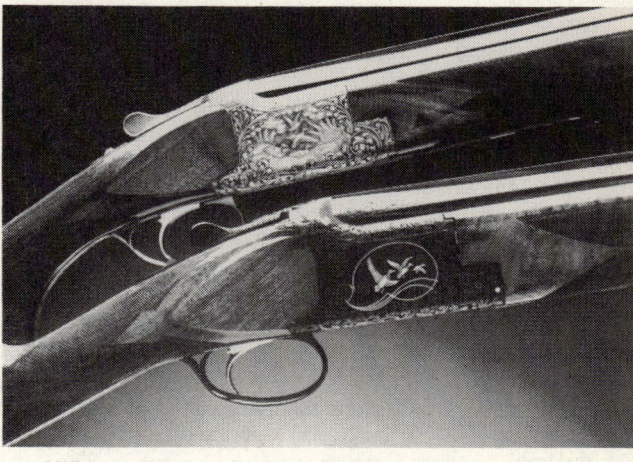

NIB	Exc.	V.G.	Good	Fair	Poor
6500	4000	3500	2250	1500	700

Comment: FN also built Exhibition Grades that were sold in this country under the Browning name. Collectors consider a true Exhibition Grade as one not having a "C" prefix in the serial number. These particular guns are considered quite desirable and should be appraised on an individual basis. Superposed in this catagory exceed $10,000 in price depending on gauge, engraving coverage, and options.

The second type of Exhibition Grade is know as the "C" type that was first sold in the United States in about 1973 and is so called because of the "C" prefix in the serial number. There were about 225 of these guns sold in the United States and are not considered as valuable as the pure Exibition Grade by the collector. These "C" grade guns should also be appraised individually.

SUPERPOSED SUPERLIGHT

This model was first introduced in 1967 in 12 gauge and 1969, in 20 gauge. Special order 28 gauge as well as .410 bore are also seen. It was offered in 26.5" barrel lengths with 27.5" barrls in 12 gauge and 28" barrels in smaller bores available on special order. It features a rounded frame and straight grip stock with tapered solid or vent rib barrels. Regular production on the Superlight ended in 1976 for the grades listed below. Production did continue for the Superlight in the P series begun in 1977.

NOTE: For 20 gauge guns add a 20% premium.
For 28 gauge guns add a 50% premium.
For .410 bore guns add 10% premium for high grades guns 30% for Grade I.

Grade I

NIB	Exc.	V.G.	Good	Fair	Poor
2000	1500	950	500	300	200

Pigeon Grade

NIB	Exc.	V.G.	Good	Fair	Poor
3250	2500	1750	950	550	300

Pointer Grade

NIB	Exc.	V.G.	Good	Fair	Poor
5000	3500	2750	1500	1000	600

Diana Grade

NIB	Exc.	V.G.	Good	Fair	Poor
5500	3500	2750	1500	1000	600

Midas Grade

NIB	Exc.	V.G.	Good	Fair	Poor
6500	5000	3750	2250	1750	700

SUPERPOSED PRESENTATION GRADE SERIES

The following superposed shotguns were manufactured between 1977 and 1984 by FN in Belgium. The following models differ in the amount of ornamentation and the quality of materials and workmanship utilized in construction. This series was also available in a superlight configuration.

NOTE: The following values would be increased approximately 25 percent for Superlight variation with all options including oil finish, checkered butt, three-piece forend, and hand-filed rib. Add the following percentages to the values listed below:

For Presentation Grade guns with extra sets of barrels add approximately $1,250 to $1,500 depending on gauge and combination.

For 20 gauge guns-20%.
For .28 gauge guns-50%.
For .410 bore-20%.

Presentation I (without gold inlays)

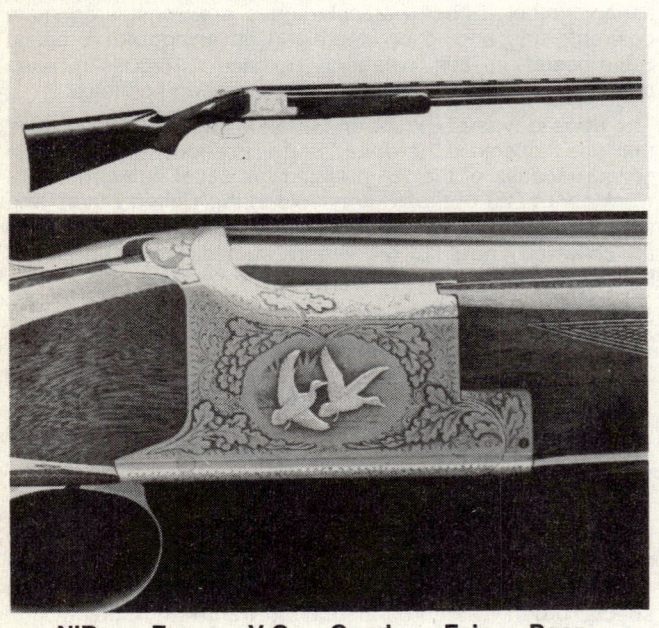

NIB	Exc.	V.G.	Good	Fair	Poor
2500	1900	1400	900	500	400

Presentation 1 Gold-inlaid

NIB	Exc.	V.G.	Good	Fair	Poor
3000	2500	1750	1000	600	400

Presentation 2 (without gold inlays)

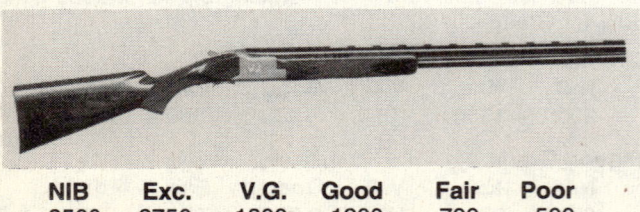

NIB	Exc.	V.G.	Good	Fair	Poor
3500	2750	1800	1200	700	500

Presentation 2 Gold-inlaid

NIB	Exc.	V.G.	Good	Fair	Poor
4500	3500	2500	1500	800	500

NOTE: For early hand-engraved P3 models (approximately 25 produced) add 40%. These early guns are rare, proceed with caution.

Presentation 3 Gold-inlaid

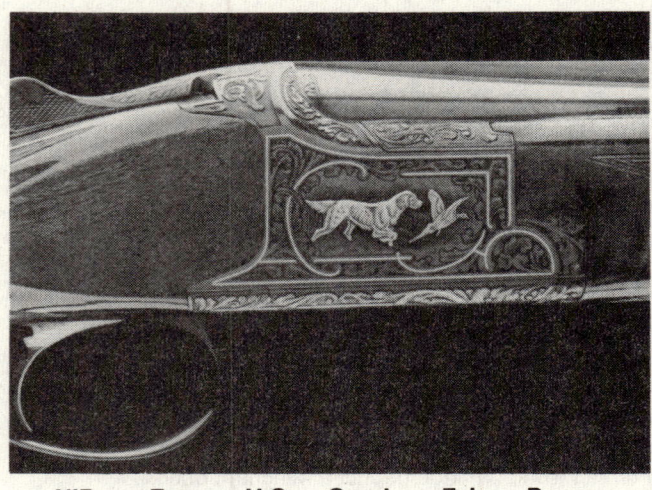

NIB	Exc.	V.G.	Good	Fair	Poor
5500	4000	3000	2250	1000	600

Presentation 4 Gold-inlaid

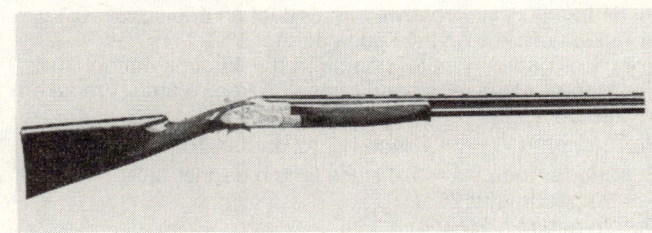

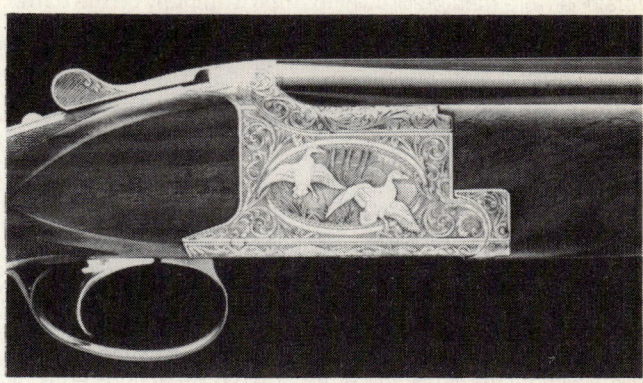

1983 Black Duck Issue

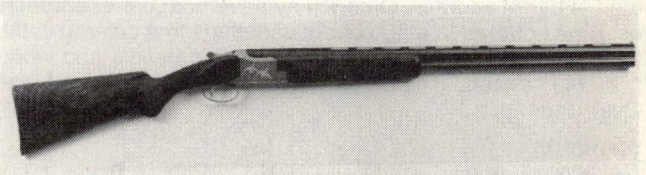

NIB	Exc.	V.G.	Good	Fair	Poor
5250	3250	2500	1800	1300	900

Bicentennial Model

Produced in 1976 to commemorate the 200 year anniversary of America. A total of 53 guns were built in this special edition. All of these Superposed were 12 gauge with 28" barrels and each was numbered for one of the fifty states plus the District of Columbia. Two additional guns were built for the Smithsonian Institution and the Liege Firearms Museum. All were fitted with side plates with gold inlays. To reflect true value guns must be in unfired condition in their original case with all the papers.

NIB	Exc.	V.G.	Good	Fair	Poor
8000	6000	4000	2750	1500	—

NOTE: A number of FN Browning Superposed B-25 shotguns were imported into this country by Browning in various grades. These Superposed were intended orginally for FN's European market. There are a large number of variations and grades. It is strongly suggested that an expert appraisal be sought prior to the sale. As a general rule these prices for NIB guns are: A grade-$1,200-1,600; B grade $1,600-2,500; C grade $2,500-3,500; D grade $3,500-5,000. These guns are marked with both the Browning and FN barrel address.

Classic

Produced in 1986 this model was offered in 20 gauge with 26" barrels. About 2,500 guns were produced. Silver gray receiver with engraving.

NIB	Exc.	V.G.	Good	Fair	Poor
1750	1250	—	—	—	—

Gold Classic

This shotgun was similar to the above model but more finely finished and engraved with gold inlays. About 350 of these guns were built in 1986.

NIB	Exc.	V.G.	Good	Fair	Poor
7500	5500	—	—	—	—

Liege

This is an Over/Under shotgun chambered for 12 gauge. It was offered with 26.5", 28", or 30" vent-rib barrels with various choke combinations. It features a boxlock action with a nonselective single trigger and automatic ejectors. The finish is blued with a checkered walnut stock. There were approxi-

NIB	Exc.	V.G.	Good	Fair	Poor
7500	6000	5000	3500	2000	1200

NOTE: For P4 Grade guns with no gold deduct approximately 20%.

SUPERPOSED WATERFOWL LIMITED EDITION SERIES

This model was issued in three different versions; Mallard, Pintail, and Black Duck. Each edition was limited to 500 guns, all in 12 gauge. It has been observed that some of these guns were stocked with salt cured wood. Salt wood stocks will drastically affect price. Caution should be exercised when a sale is contemplated. Prices reflect the absence of salt wood damage.

1981 Mallard Issue

NIB	Exc.	V.G.	Good	Fair	Poor
5250	3250	2500	1800	1300	900

1982 Pintail Issue

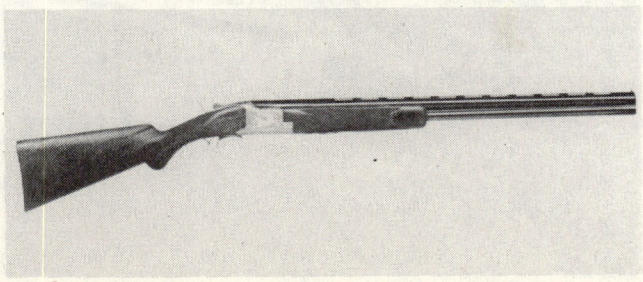

NIB	Exc.	V.G.	Good	Fair	Poor
5250	3250	2500	1800	1300	900

mately 10,000 manufactured between 1973 and 1975. U.S. versions were marked Browning Arms Company on the barrel.

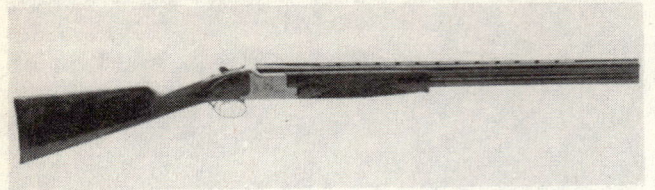

NIB	Exc.	V.G.	Good	Fair	Poor
750	600	500	400	300	200

B27

This improved version of the Liege was imported into the U.S., some without the Browning Arms Company markings and only the FN barrel address. Others may have both barrel addresses. It was offered in a number of variations that differed in the amount of ornamentation and quality of materials and workmanship utilized. It features the same action as the Liege Over/Under gun.

Standard

NIB	Exc.	V.G.	Good	Fair	Poor
650	500	400	300	250	200

Deluxe

NIB	Exc.	V.G.	Good	Fair	Poor
900	850	600	450	350	250

Deluxe Trap

NIB	Exc.	V.G.	Good	Fair	Poor
850	750	500	400	300	250

Deluxe Skeet

NIB	Exc.	V.G.	Good	Fair	Poor
850	750	500	400	300	250

Grand Deluxe

NIB	Exc.	V.G.	Good	Fair	Poor
1200	1000	700	600	500	400

City of Liege Commemorative-250 Manufactured

NIB	Exc.	V.G.	Good	Fair	Poor
1150	950	650	550	450	300

ST-100

This is an Over/Under trap gun that features separated barrels with an adjustable point of impact. It is chambered for 12 gauge and has a 30" or 32" barrel with full choke and a floating ventilated rib. It features a single trigger and automatic ejectors. The finish is blued with a checkered walnut stock. It was manufactured by FN between 1979 and 1983.

NIB	Exc.	V.G.	Good	Fair	Poor
2000	1700	1400	1000	700	400

Citori Series

This is an Over/Under, double-barrel shotgun chambered for all gauges and offered with vent rib barrels of 26" through 30" in length. It has a boxlock action with a single selective trigger and automatic ejectors. The various grades differ in the amount of ornamentation and the quality of materials and workmanship utilized in construction. This series is manufactured in Japan by B.C. Miroku and was introduced in 1973.

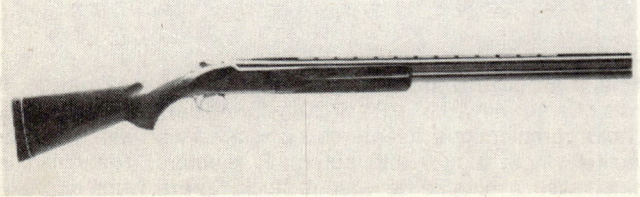

Grade I

NIB	Exc.	V.G.	Good	Fair	Poor
900	800	725	550	425	300

Upland Special-Grade I

Offered with straight grip stock and 24" rib barrels. Available in 12 gauge or 20 gauge. Weighs 6 lbs., 11 oz. in 12 gauge and 6 lbs. in 20 gauge.

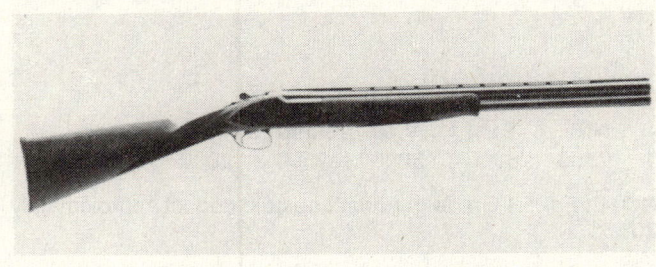

NIB	Exc.	V.G.	Good	Fair	Poor
935	850	700	600	400	300

Grade II-Discontinued 1983

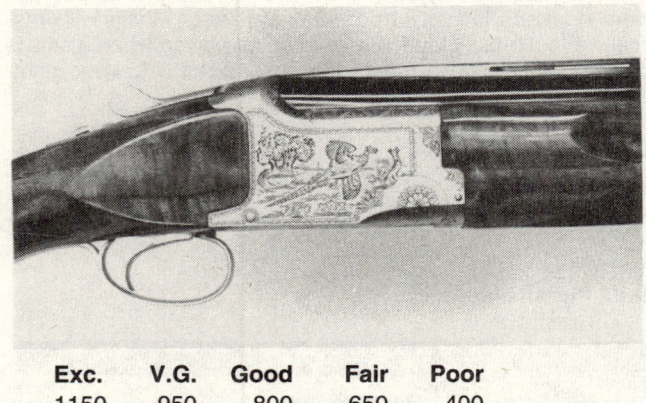

Exc.	V.G.	Good	Fair	Poor
1150	950	800	650	400

Grade II-Choke Tubes

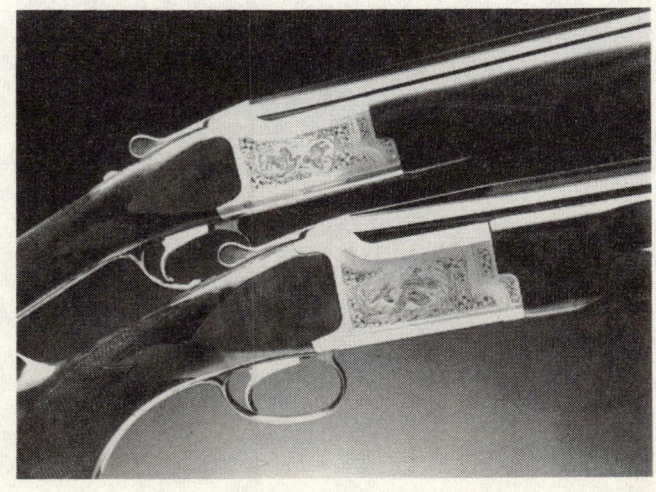

NIB	Exc.	V.G.	Good	Fair	Poor
1400	1250	950	775	650	400

Grade V-Discontinued 1984

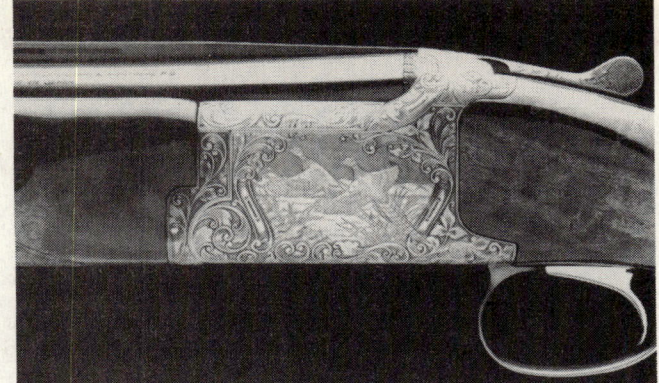

NIB	Exc.	V.G.	Good	Fair	Poor
1750	1600	1250	950	750	400

Grade V-with side plates

NIB	Exc.	V.G.	Good	Fair	Poor
2000	1750	1350	1000	800	400

Grade VI-Choke Tubes

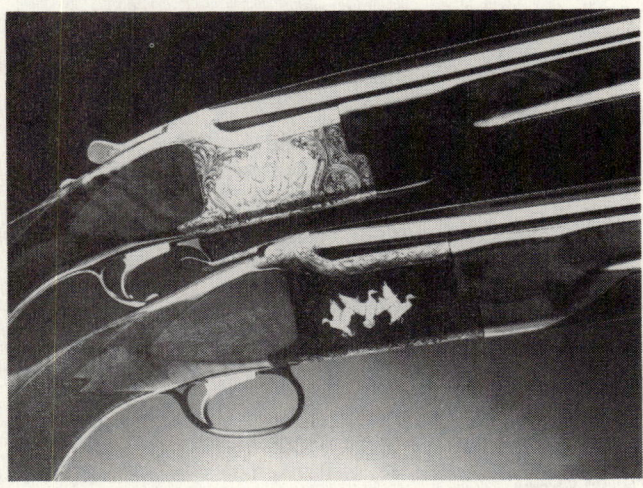

NIB	Exc.	V.G.	Good	Fair	Poor
1750	1500	1200	1000	750	500

Citori Lightning

This is a lightweight version that features a slimmer profile and has a checkered, round-knob, pistol-grip stock. It is offered in all gauges and in the same barrel lengths as the standard Citori. It features screw-in choke tubes known as invectors. It was introduced in 1988. The models differ in the amount of ornamentation and quality of materials and workmanship utilized.

Grade I

NIB	Exc.	V.G.	Good	Fair	Poor
995	850	700	575	450	375

Grade III

NIB	Exc.	V.G.	Good	Fair	Poor
1400	1250	950	775	650	500

Grade VI

NIB	Exc.	V.G.	Good	Fair	Poor
1750	1500	1200	1000	750	500

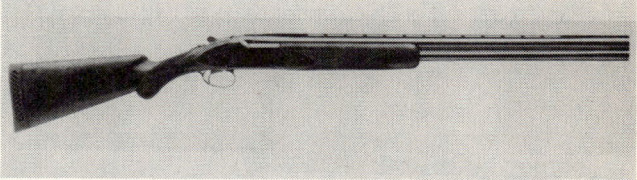

Citori Sporting Clays

Specifically design for sporting clays shooting. Offered in 12 gauge only, each model is back-bored, ported and fitted with Invector-Plus choke tubes. Barrels are chrome-plated. Receiver is blued with gold inscription. Pigeon Grade has gold detailing and high grade gloss walnut stock. Signature Grade features a red and black print on the stock with gold decals. Trigger is adjustable to three length of pull positions. Comes with three interchangeable trigger shoes. Each model is fitted with rubber recoil pad.

Lightning Sporting Model

This model features a rounded pistol grip and Lightning forearm with choice of high or low vent rib. Chambered for 3" shells. Offered in 28" or 30" barrels. Weighs about 8.5 lbs.

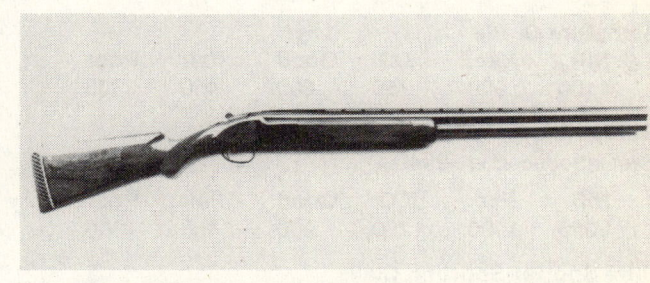

NIB	Exc.	V.G.	Good	Fair	Poor
1100	900	750	600	450	300

Pigeon Grade

NIB	Exc.	V.G.	Good	Fair	Poor
1200	1000	800	650	450	300

Golden Clays

First introduced in 1994.

NIB	Exc.	V.G.	Good	Fair	Poor
2350	1950	1500	900	450	300

Citori Plus

This model features an adjustable point of impact from 3" to 12" above point of aim. Receiver on Grade I is blued with scroll engraving. Walnut stock is adjustable and forearm is a modified beavertail style. Available in 30" or 32" barrels that are backbored and ported. Non-ported barrels are optional. Weighs about 9 lbs., 6 oz.

Grade I

NIB	Exc.	V.G.	Good	Fair	Poor
1100	900	700	500	400	300

Pigeon Grade

NIB	Exc.	V.G.	Good	Fair	Poor
1600	1350	900	700	500	300

Signature Grade

NIB	Exc.	V.G.	Good	Fair	Poor
1500	1300	900	700	500	300

Golden Clays

First introduced in 1994.

NIB	Exc.	V.G.	Good	Fair	Poor
2750	2250	1500	900	450	300

Trap Combination Set

This version is offered in Grade I only and features a 34" single barrel and a 32" set of Over/Under barrels. It is furnished in a fitted case and has been discontinued.

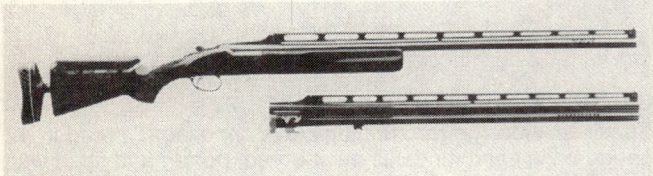

Exc.	V.G.	Good	Fair	Poor
1200	1050	950	800	700

GTI Model

This model features a 13mm wide rib, ventilated side ribs, pistol grip stock, semi-beavertail forearm. Offered in 28" or 30" barrel. Weighs about 8 lbs. This model not offered in Pigeon Grade.

Grade I

NIB	Exc.	V.G.	Good	Fair	Poor
1100	900	750	600	450	300

Signature Grade

NIB	Exc.	V.G.	Good	Fair	Poor
1100	900	750	600	450	300

Golden Clays

First introduced in 1994.

NIB	Exc.	V.G.	Good	Fair	Poor
2350	1900	1250	900	450	300

Ultra Sporter-Sporting Clays

This model was introduced in 1995 and replaces the GTI model. It features a 10mm to 13mm tapered rib and is offfered with either a blued or grey receiver with walnut stock with pistol grip and semi-beavertail forearm. Fitted with adjustable comb. Adjustable length of pull. Offered in 12 gauge only with 28" or 30" barrels. Average weight is 8 lbs.

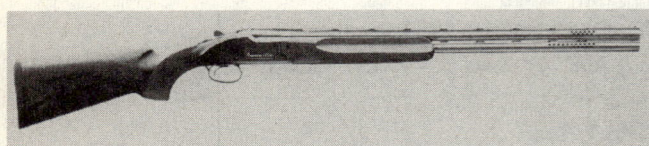

NIB	Exc.	V.G.	Good	Fair	Poor
1450	1100	800	550	400	300

Ultra Sporter Sporting Clays-Golden Clays

NIB	Exc.	V.G.	Good	Fair	Poor
2750	2200	1600	1100	750	400

Citori Superlight

This is a lighter-weight version of the Citori chambered for all gauges and offered with the same features as the Lightning Series. The grades differ in the amount of ornamentation and quality of materials and workmanship utilized. This series was introduced in 1983.

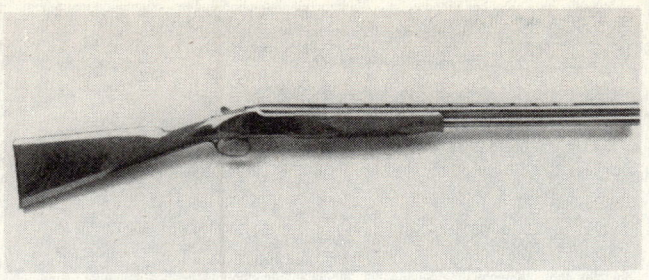

Micro Lightning

Offered in 20 gauge only and has reduced dimensions for smaller shooters. Available with 24" vent rib barrels. Weighs 6 lbs., 3 oz.

NIB	Exc.	V.G.	Good	Fair	Poor
950	850	700	600	400	300

Gran Lightning

This is essentially a Grade I Lightning with a high grade select walnut stock with satin finish. Receiver and barrels are blued. Offered in 12 gauge and 20 gauge with choice of 26" or 28" vent rib barrels. Choke tubes standard. Weighs about 8 lbs. in 12 gauge and 6 lbs., 11 oz. in 20 gauge.

NIB.	Exc.	V.G.	Good	Fair	Poor
1250	1000	800	650	450	300

Grade I

NIB	Exc.	V.G.	Good	Fair	Poor
1000	900	750	500	425	350

Grade III

NIB	Exc.	V.G.	Good	Fair	Poor
1400	1300	1050	750	550	450

Grade V-Discontinued 1984

Exc.	V.G.	Good	Fair	Poor
1450	1350	1100	800	500

Grade VI

NIB	Exc.	V.G.	Good	Fair	Poor
1800	1600	1300	1000	800	500

Citori Skeet

This series of guns was chambered for all gauges and was designed for competition skeet shooting. It is similar to the standard Citori with a high-post target rib and 26" or 28" barrels. The versions differ in the amount of engraving and the quality of materials and workmanship utilized.

Grade I

NIB	Exc.	V.G.	Good	Fair	Poor
1000	925	750	550	425	350

Grade II-Discontinued 1983

Exc.	V.G.	Good	Fair	Poor
1000	900	750	450	300

Grade III

NIB	Exc.	V.G.	Good	Fair	Poor
1500	1200	900	750	450	300

Grade V-Discontinued 1984

NIB	Exc.	V.G.	Good	Fair	Poor
1600	1200	900	750	450	300

Grade VI

NIB	Exc.	V.G.	Good	Fair	Poor
2000	1750	1200	900	450	300

Golden Clays

First introduced in 1994.

NIB	Exc.	V.G.	Good	Fair	Poor
2400	2000	1500	900	450	300

3 Gauge Set
Consists of 20 gauge, 28 gauge, and .410 bore interchangeable 28" vent rib barrels.

Grade I
NIB	Exc.	V.G.	Good	Fair	Poor
2100	1950	1700	1250	900	700

Grade III
NIB	Exc.	V.G.	Good	Fair	Poor
2500	2250	1900	1400	1100	800

Grade VI
NIB	Exc.	V.G.	Good	Fair	Poor
2950	2500	2000	1500	1200	900

4 Gauge Set
This set has a 12 gauge, 20 gauge, 28 gauge, and .410 bore interchangeable vent rib barrels in either 26" or 28" lengths.

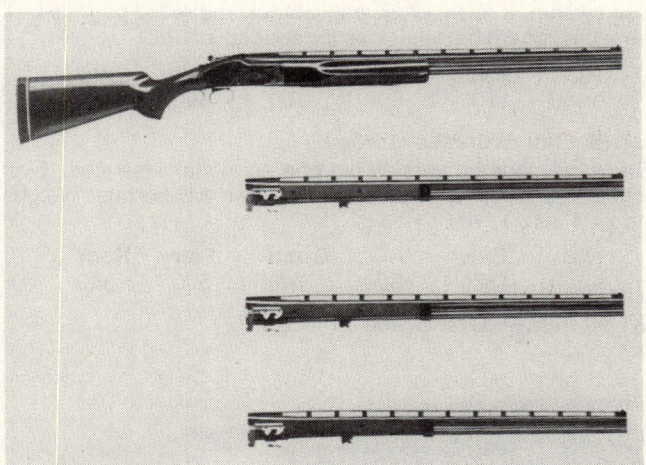

Grade I
NIB	Exc.	V.G.	Good	Fair	Poor
3300	2750	2250	1700	1250	900

Grade III
NIB	Exc.	V.G.	Good	Fair	Poor
3400	2900	2500	1900	1350	900

Grade VI
NIB	Exc.	V.G.	Good	Fair	Poor
3800	3300	2900	2250	1400	950

Citori Trap
This version is similar to the standard Citori, offered in 12 gauge only with 30" or 32" barrels. It features a high rib and a Monte Carlo-type stock with recoil pad. The versions differ as to the amount of ornamentation and the quality of materials and workmanship utilized.

Grade I
NIB	Exc.	V.G.	Good	Fair	Poor
1000	900	750	550	425	350

Plus Trap-Adjustable Rib and Stock
NIB	Exc.	V.G.	Good	Fair	Poor
1500	1350	1000	750	600	500

Grade II-Discontinued 1983

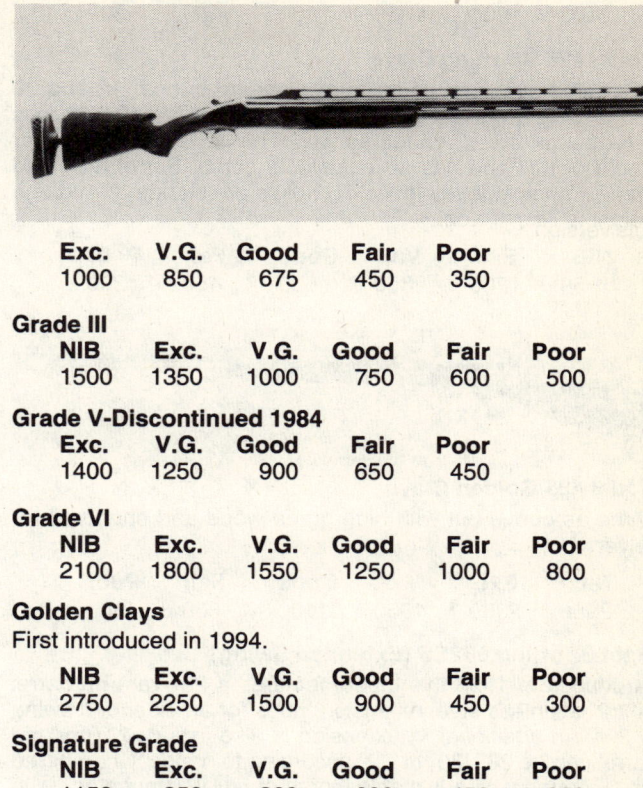

Exc.	V.G.	Good	Fair	Poor
1000	850	675	450	350

Grade III
NIB	Exc.	V.G.	Good	Fair	Poor
1500	1350	1000	750	600	500

Grade V-Discontinued 1984
Exc.	V.G.	Good	Fair	Poor
1400	1250	900	650	450

Grade VI
NIB	Exc.	V.G.	Good	Fair	Poor
2100	1800	1550	1250	1000	800

Golden Clays
First introduced in 1994.
NIB	Exc.	V.G.	Good	Fair	Poor
2750	2250	1500	900	450	300

Signature Grade
NIB	Exc.	V.G.	Good	Fair	Poor
1150	950	800	600	450	300

Model 325 Sporting Clays
Introduced in 1993 this model has a European design that features a grayed receiver scroll engraved, Schnabel forearm, 10mm wide vent rib, three interchangeable and adjustable trigger shoes, back-bore barrels that are ported and fitted with choke tubes. Available in 12 gauge and 20 gauge. The 12 gauge is offered with 28", 30", or 32" barrels while the 20 gauge is offered with 28" or 30" barrel fitted with conventional chokes. The 12 gauge weighs about 7 lbs., 14 oz., while the 20 gauge weighs about 6 lbs., 12 oz.

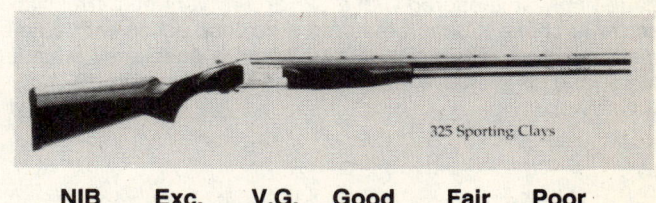

325 Sporting Clays

NIB	Exc.	V.G.	Good	Fair	Poor
1350	1200	900	700	450	300

Special Sporting
Similar to the Sporting model but fitted with a 2-3/4" chamber and choice of 28", 30", or 32" barrels. Barrels are ported. Barrels are also fitted with a high post rib. Stock has a full pistol grip and optional adjustable comb. Depending on barrel length weighs about 8.3 lbs.

Grade I
NIB	Exc.	V.G.	Good	Fair	Poor
1150	900	750	600	450	300

Signature Grade
NIB	Exc.	V.G.	Good	Fair	Poor
1150	900	750	600	450	300

Pigeon Grade
NIB	Exc.	V.G.	Good	Fair	Poor
1300	1100	850	600	450	300

Golden Clays

NIB	Exc.	V.G.	Good	Fair	Poor
2400	1900	1250	900	450	300

Model 425 Sporting Clays

This Citori over and under gun is offered in both 12 and 20 gauge with a choice of 28" and 30" barrel with 32" barrels available on the 12 gauge as well. The 425 is adjustable for length of pull and has an adjustable comb. Barrel are fitted with a 10mm wide rib. Invector chokes are standard. Average weight is 7lbs. 14 oz.

NIB	Exc.	V.G.	Good	Fair	Poor
1550	1200	850	600	450	300

Model 425 Golden Clays

Same as above but with high grade wood and engraved receiver.

NIB	Exc.	V.G.	Good	Fair	Poor
2950	2350	1650	1100	600	300

Light Sporting 802ES (Extended Swing)

Introduced in 1996 this model features a 28" vent rib barrel with 2" stainless steel extension tubes for an extended swing of 30". An additional 4" extension is also included. Thus the barrel can be 28", 30" or 32" according to needs. Chambered for 12 gauge with adjustable length of pull. Walnut stock with pistol grip and schnabel forearm. Weight is about 7.5 lbs.

NIB	Exc.	V.G.	Good	Fair	Poor
1700	1400	900	700	500	250

BT-99

This is a break-open, single-barrel trap gun chambered for 12 gauge only. It is offered with a 32" or 34", vent-rib barrel with screw-in choke tubes. It features a boxlock action with automatic ejectors. The finish is blued with a checkered walnut stock and beavertail forearm. It was introduced in 1971 by B.C. Miroku.

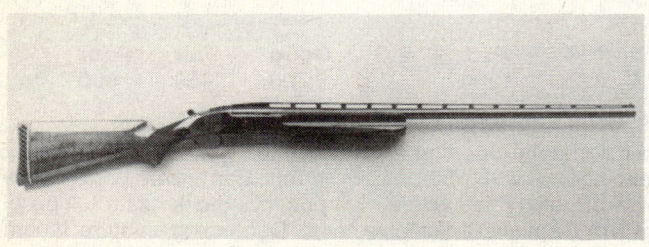

NIB	Exc.	V.G.	Good	Fair	Poor
1000	850	675	500	400	350

Citori Plus Combo

This model features a single barrel trap and an interchangeable Over/Under set of barrels. Other features are similar to Citori Plus Grade 1. Barrel combinations are 32" Over/Under with 34" single barrel or 30" Over/Under barrel with 32" or 34" single barrel.

NIB	Exc.	V.G.	Good	Fair	Poor
2500	2100	1750	1 100	700	450

BT-99 Stainless

First introduced in 1993.

NIB	Exc.	V.G.	Good	Fair	Poor
1275	1150	900	700	550	350

BT-99 Signature Grade I

First introduced in 1993.

NIB	Exc.	V.G.	Good	Fair	Poor
975	850	700	600	500	300

BT-99 Pigeon Grade

First introduced in 1993.

NIB	Exc.	V.G.	Good	Fair	Poor
1200	950	800	650	500	300

BT-99 Golden Clays

First introduced in 1994.

NIB	Exc.	V.G.	Good	Fair	Poor
2250	1750	1250	900	450	300

BT-99 Plus

This version features an adjustable vent rib and a recoil reduction system. It has an adjustable stock and recoil pad, as well as a backboard barrel. It was introduced in 1989.

NIB	Exc.	V.G.	Good	Fair	Poor
1350	1200	900	700	500	300

BT-99 Plus Stainless-Grade I

Same as standard version but offered in stainless steel. First introduced in 1993. Available in 32" and 34" barrels. Weighs about 8 lbs., 11 oz.

NIB	Exc.	V.G.	Good	Fair	Poor
1600	1350	900	700	500	350

BT-99 Plus-Pigeon Grade

NIB	Exc.	V.G.	Good	Fair	Poor
1500	1200	900	800	550	350

BT-99 Plus-Signature Grade

NIB	Exc.	V.G.	Good	Fair	Poor
1400	1100	850	700	500	300

BT-99 Plus-Golden Clays

First introduced in 1994.

NIB	Exc.	V.G.	Good	Fair	Poor
2600	2250	1750	900	450	300

BT-99 Plus Micro

Slightly reduced dimensions and offered in barrel lengths from 28" to 34". Weighs about 8 lbs., 6 oz.

NIB	Exc.	V.G.	Good	Fair	Poor
1350	1100	900	700	500	300

BT-99 Plus-Pigeon Grade

NIB	Exc.	V.G.	Good	Fair	Poor
1500	1200	900	800	550	350

BT-99 Plus-Signature Grade

NIB	Exc.	V.G.	Good	Fair	Poor
1400	1150	900	750	500	300

Model BT-100

First introduced in 1995 this single barrel trap features an adjustable trigger pull and length of pull. The stock has either a Monte Carlo version or an adjustable comb version. Barrel is either 32" or 34". Choice of blue or stainless finish. Weight is about 8.9 lbs.

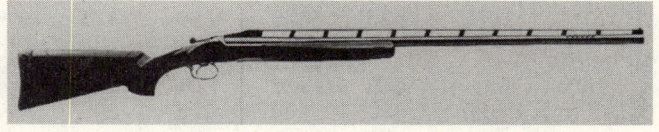

NIB	Exc.	V.G.	Good	Fair	Poor
1850	1200	900	700	500	300

Recoilless Trap

First introduced in 1993 this model features an advanced design that eliminates recoil up to 72 percent. The receiver is a special bolt action single shot. Receiver is black anodized. It is fitted with an adjustable ventilated rib so the point of impact can be moved. Adjustable length of pull. The Standard Model is a 12 gauge with 30" barrel while the Micro Model is fitted with 27" barrels. Choke tubes are supplied. Standard Model weighs 9 lbs., 1 oz., while the Micro Model weighs 8 lbs., 10 oz.

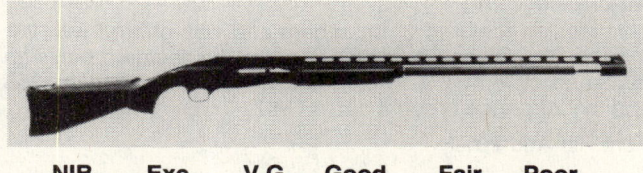

NIB	Exc.	V.G.	Good	Fair	Poor
1500	1300	900	700	500	350

BSS

This is a SxS, double-barrel shotgun chambered for 12 or 20 gauge. It was offered with a 26", 28", or 30" barrel with various choke combinations. It features a boxlock action and automatic ejectors. Early guns had a nonselective single trigger; late production, a selective trigger. The finish is blued with a checkered walnut stock and beavertail forearm. It was manufactured between 1971 and 1988 by B.C. Miroku.

Single-Selective Trigger-Add 20%.
20 Gauge-Add 20%.

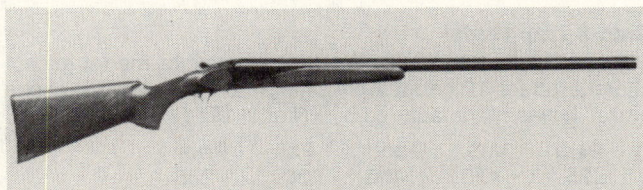

Exc.	V.G.	Good	Fair	Poor
750	650	575	400	200

BSS Sporter

This version features an English-style, straight-grip stock and a splinter forearm. The stock was oil-finished. It was offered with a 26" or 28" barrel.

For 20 gauge-Add 20%.

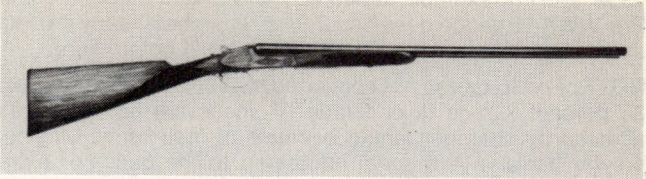

Exc.	V.G.	Good	Fair	Poor
850	750	650	450	250

BSS Grade II

This version features game scene engraving and a satin, coin finished receiver. It was discontinued in 1983.

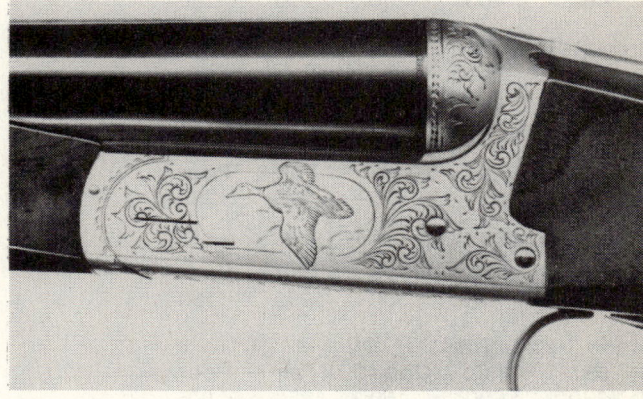

Exc.	V.G.	Good	Fair	Poor
1250	1000	750	600	400

BSS Sidelock

This version features an engraved sidelock action and was offered in 12 or 20 gauge. It was offered with a 26" or 28" barrel and has a straight-grip stock and splintered forearm. It was manufactured in Korea between 1983 and 1988.

NIB	Exc.	V.G.	Good	Fair	Poor
2400	2100	1600	1250	800	500

NOTE: Add 10% to above prices for 20 gauge guns.

AUTO-5 SHOTGUN

Early Production Auto-5

This series of recoil-operated, semiautomatic shotguns was designed by John M. Browning and was offered in 12 or 16 gauge. The barrel lengths were 26", 28", 30", or 32" with various chokes and ribs. It has a unique, square-back action that has become instantly recognizable. The finish is blued with a checkered, walnut, round-knob stock. The various versions differ in the amount of ornamentation, type of rib, and quality of materials and workmanship utilized in construction. This series was manufactured in Belgium by FN between 1903 and

1939. The first example appeared in the United States in 1923. Pre-WWII 16 gauge guns had 2-9/16" chambers; early models should be inspected by a qualified gunsmith before firing.

NOTE: For 16 gauge not converted to 2-3/4" chamber deduct 30 percent. Grade III or Grade IV prices are not nearly as affected by chamber length because of their rarity. Original prewar barrels were serial numbered to the gun. For extra barrels serial numbered to the gun add $100 for plain barrels, $200 for matte rib barrels, $275 for vent rib barrels. For extra barrels on Grade IV guns add an additional 30% to these barrel prices. Prices given below are for guns with original barrels serial numbered to the gun.

Grade I-Plain Barrel

Exc.	V.G.	Good	Fair	Poor
450	400	300	250	150

Grade I-Matte Rib

Exc.	V.G.	Good	Fair	Poor
550	500	375	300	175

Grade I-Vent Rib

Exc.	V.G.	Good	Fair	Poor
650	600	475	375	200

Grade II-Plain Barrel

Exc.	V.G.	Good	Fair	Poor
475	425	300	250	150

Grade II-Matte Rib

Exc.	V.G.	Good	Fair	Poor
650	600	450	350	175

Grade II-Vent Rib

Exc.	V.G.	Good	Fair	Poor
900	800	600	400	200

Grade III-Plain Barrel

Exc.	V.G.	Good	Fair	Poor
1500	1100	850	500	250

Grade III-Matte Rib

Exc.	V.G.	Good	Fair	Poor
2500	2100	1000	500	250

Grade III-Vent Rib

Exc.	V.G.	Good	Fair	Poor
2650	2250	1250	600	300

Grade IV-Plain Barrel

Exc.	V.G.	Good	Fair	Poor
3600	3000	2250	850	350

Grade IV-Matte Rib

Exc.	V.G.	Good	Fair	Poor
4300	3800	3000	1000	400

Grade IV-Vent Rib

Exc.	V.G.	Good	Fair	Poor
4500	4100	3250	1500	500

American Browning Auto-5

This recoil-operated, semiautomatic shotgun was another variation of the early-production Auto-5. It was chambered for 12, 16, or 20 gauge and was manufactured by the Remington Company for Browning. It is quite similar to Remington's Model 11 shotgun but features the Browning logo and a different type of engraving. There were approximately 45,000 manufactured between 1940 and 1942.

Vent Rib-Add 20%.
20 Gauge-Add 10%.

Exc.	V.G.	Good	Fair	Poor
450	350	300	200	170

Mid-Production Auto-5-FN Manufacture
Standard Weight

This version of the recoil-operated, semiautomatic Auto-5 shotgun was manufactured by FN in Belgium between 1952 and 1976. It was offered in 12 or 16 gauge with 26" through 32" barrels with various chokes. The finish is blued with a checkered walnut stock and a black buttplate that was marked "Browning Automatic" with "FN" in center oval. Guns made prior to 1967 will be found with round knob pistol grips. The flat-bottom variation was introduced in 1967.

NOTE: Add 20 percent for guns with round knob pistol grip or straight grip stock.

Plain Barrel

NIB	Exc.	V.G.	Good	Fair	Poor
575	475	425	375	250	175

Matte Rib

NIB	Exc.	V.G.	Good	Fair	Poor
600	550	450	400	275	200

Vent Rib

NIB	Exc.	V.G.	Good	Fair	Poor
675	575	500	400	300	250

Auto-5 Lightweight

This version was chambered for 12 or 20 gauge and featured a lighter-weight, scroll-engraved receiver. It was manufactured between 1952 and 1976 by FN. The 20 gauge was not introduced until 1958.

Vent Rib-Add 20%.
For 20 Gauge-Add 20%.

NIB	Exc.	V.G.	Good	Fair	Poor
750	650	550	450	275	200

Auto-5 Magnum

This version featured 3" chambers and was offered with 26" through 32", full-choke barrels. It was manufactured between 1958 and 1976 by FN. The 12 gauge was introduced in 1958 and the 20 gauge brought out in 1967.

Vent Rib-Add 20%.

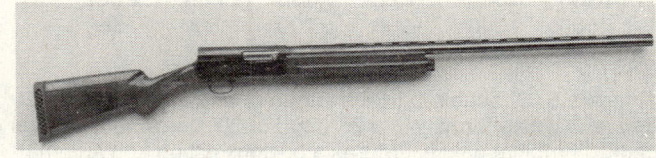

Exc.	V.G.	Good	Fair	Poor
675	575	475	375	250

Auto-5 Skeet

This version is similar to the Lightweight Model, chambered for 12 or 20 gauge with a 26" or 28", vent-rib, skeet-choked barrel.

Exc.	V.G.	Good	Fair	Poor
675	575	525	425	250

Auto-5 Trap Model

This version is similar to the standard-weight model except chambered for 12 gauge only, with a 30", vent-rib, full-choke barrel. It was manufactured by FN until 1971.

Exc.	V.G.	Good	Fair	Poor
525	475	400	300	225

Sweet Sixteen

This version is similar to the standard-weight and is chambered for 16 gauge only. It has a gold plated trigger and was manufactured by FN between 1953 and 1976.

Matte Rib-Add 25%.
Vent Rib-Add 50%.

NIB	Exc.	V.G.	Good	Fair	Poor
850	650	550	400	300	200

Buck Special

This version features a 24", cylinder-bore barrel with adjustable rifle sights. It was produced in 12 and 20 gauge 2-3/4" and 3" magnum, and in 16 gauge with 2-3/4" chambers. It was manufactured by FN between 1963 and 1976. Prices are for 12 gauge guns.

Exc.	V.G.	Good	Fair	Poor
600	550	475	350	250

Two Millionth Commemorative

This version commemorated the two millionth Auto-5 shotgun produced by FN. It was engraved with a special high-polish blue finish and high-grade, checkered walnut in the stock. It was furnished in a black fitted case along with a book on the Browning Company. There were 2,500 manufactured between 1971 and 1974. As with all commemoratives, it must be NIB to realize its top potential.

NIB	Exc.	V.G.	Good	Fair	Poor
1250	1000	850	500	350	250

Late Production Auto-5-B.C. Miroku Manufacture

In 1976 production of the Auto-5 shotgun was begun by B.C. Miroku in Japan. This move was accomplished after approximately 2,750,000 Auto-5 shotguns were manufactured by FN in Belgium between 1903 and 1976. The Japanese manufactured guns in the opinion of many knowledgeable people show no less quality or functionality but are simply not as desirable from a collector's standpoint. The variations and their values are as follows:

Auto-5 Light 12

This version is chambered for 12 gauge 2-3/4" chamber only and is offered with a lightweight receiver. The barrel has a vent rib and choke tubes. It was introduced in 1975.

NIB	Exc.	V.G.	Good	Fair	Poor
525	450	400	300	250	150

Auto-5 Light 20

This version is similar to the Light 12 except chambered for 20 gauge only.

NIB	Exc.	V.G.	Good	Fair	Poor
575	450	400	300	250	150

Auto-5 Magnum

This version features 3" chambers and is offered with 26", 28", 30", or 32" barrels. It was introduced in 1976 by Miroku and discontinued in 1996.

NIB	Exc.	V.G.	Good	Fair	Poor
550	450	400	300	250	150

Auto-5 Buck Special

This version has a 24" barrel cylinder-bored with adjustable sights. It was introduced by Miroku in 1976.

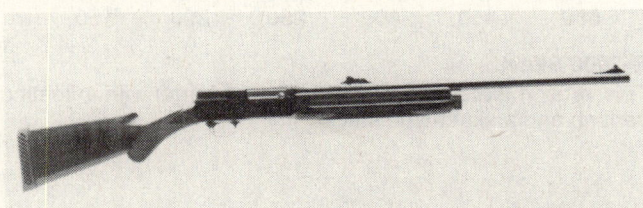

NIB	Exc.	V.G.	Good	Fair	Poor
550	450	400	300	250	150

Auto-5 Skeet

This is a competition model that features 26" or 28", skeet-bored barrels with a vent rib. It was manufactured between 1976 and 1983 by Miroku.

NIB	Exc.	V.G.	Good	Fair	Poor
675	425	375	275	225	150

Sweet Sixteen

This version is similar to the Belgian-produced Sweet Sixteen, but is offered standard with a vent rib and screw-in invector choke tubes. It was introduced in 1987 by Miroku.

NIB	Exc.	V.G.	Good	Fair	Poor
675	500	400	300	250	150

A-5 DU 50th Anniversary

This was a high-grade version of the Auto-5 produced to commemorate the 50th anniversary of Ducks Unlimited. It is highly engraved and features high-gloss bluing and a fancy checkered walnut stock. There were approximately 5,500 manufactured by Miroku in 1987. They were auctioned by the Ducks Unlimited chapters to raise money for the organization, and because of this fact, it is difficult to furnish an accurate value. This is a commemorative firearm and, as such, must be NIB with all furnished materials to command premium collector value. We furnish what we feel is a general value.

NIB	Exc.	V.G.	Good	Fair	Poor
1100	950	750	500	350	250

A-5 DU Sweet Sixteen

This was a special version of the Miroku-manufactured Sweet Sixteen that was auctioned by the Ducks Unlimited chapters in 1988. There were 5,500 produced. All specifications and cautions that were furnished for the 50th Anniversary gun also apply here.

NIB	Exc.	V.G.	Good	Fair	Poor
1100	950	750	500	350	250

Auto-5 Classic

This is a special limited edition series of A-5 shotguns built in 12 gauge only. The Classic is photo-etched with game scenes on a silver gray receiver. 5,000 of these guns were manufactured in 1984. The Gold Classic is similar in appearance but features gold inlays and is limited to 500 guns.

Classic

NIB	Exc.	V.G.	Good	Fair	Poor
1150	950	750	650	500	300

Gold Classic-Produced by FN

NIB	Exc.	V.G.	Good	Fair	Poor
3695	3000	2500	2000	1000	500

Auto-5 Light Buck Special

This model is a lightweight version of the Buck Special. Chambered for the 2-3/4" shell and fitted with a 24" vent rib barrel. Conventional choked for slug or buckshot. Barrel has adjustable rear sight and ramp front sight. Weighs 8 lbs.

NIB	Exc.	V.G.	Good	Fair	Poor
550	475	400	300	225	150

Auto-5 Stalker

New for 1993 this model is available in either a lightweight version or a Magnum version. The Light Stalker is available in 12 gauge with either 26" or 28" barrel with choke tubes. The Magnum Stalker is offered in 12 gauge (3" chamber) with 28" or 30" barrel and choke tubes. The Light Stalker weighs 8 lbs., 4 oz. and the Magnum Stalker weighs 8 lbs., 11 oz.

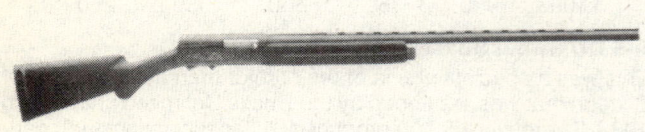

Light Stalker

NIB	Exc.	V.G.	Good	Fair	Poor
575	500	425	325	250	150

Magnum Stalker

NIB	Exc.	V.G.	Good	Fair	Poor
575	500	425	325	250	150

Double Automatic Shotgun

This is a short recoil-operated, semiautomatic shotgun chambered for 12 gauge only. It was offered with a 26", 28", or 30" barrel that was either plain or vent-ribbed. It has various chokes. The receiver is steel, and the finish is blued or silver with a checkered walnut stock. The tubular magazine holds only two shots—hence its name. It was manufactured between 1952 and 1971.

Vent Rib-Add 25%.

Exc.	V.G.	Good	Fair	Poor
450	400	325	250	200

Twelvette Double Auto

This version is similar to the Double Automatic except that it has an aircraft aluminum alloy frame color-anodized in either blue, silver, green, brown, or black. Red-, gold-, or royal blue-colored receivers were the rarest colors and would command approximately a 50 percent premium. It was offered with either a plain or vent rib barrel. There were approximately 65,000 produced between 1952 and 1971.

Vent Rib-Add 25%.

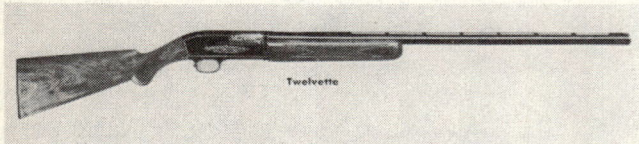

Exc.	V.G.	Good	Fair	Poor
475	425	350	275	225

Twentyweight Double Auto

This version is similar in all respects to the Twelvette except that it is three-quarters of a pound lighter and was offered with a 26.5" barrel. It was manufactured between 1952 and 1971.

Vent Rib-Add 25%.

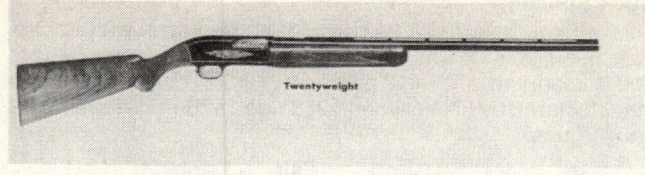

Exc.	V.G.	Good	Fair	Poor
500	435	375	300	250

B-2000

This is a gas-operated, semiautomatic shotgun chambered for 12 or 20 gauge and offered with a 26", 28", or 30", vent rib barrel with various chokes. The finish is blued with a checkered walnut stock. This shotgun was assembled in Portugal from parts that were manufactured by FN in Belgium. There were approximately 115,000 imported between 1974 and 1983.

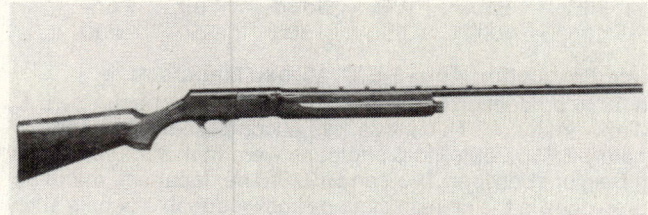

NIB	Exc.	V.G.	Good	Fair	Poor
550	450	400	250	200	150

B-2000 Magnum

This version features a barrel with 3" chambers and was offered standard with a recoil pad.

NIB	Exc.	V.G.	Good	Fair	Poor
550	450	400	250	200	150

B-2000 Buck Special

This version has a 24", cylinder-bored barrel with rifle sights.

NIB	Exc.	V.G.	Good	Fair	Poor
550	450	400	250	200	150

B-2000 Trap

This version has a 30", full-choke barrel with a floating rib and a Monte Carlo-type trap stock.

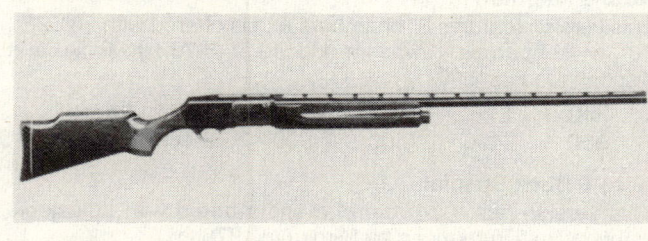

NIB	Exc.	V.G.	Good	Fair	Poor
550	450	400	250	200	150

B-2000 Skeet

This version features a 26", skeet-bored barrel with a floating vent rib and a skeet-type stock.

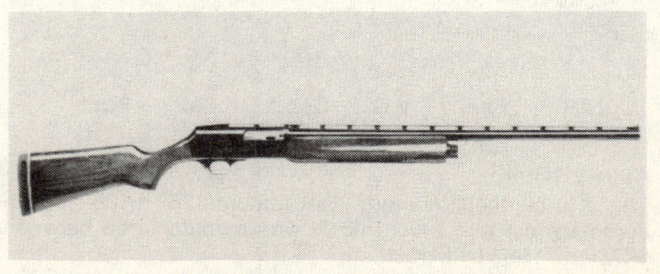

Exc.	V.G.	Good	Fair	Poor
400	340	300	250	175

Model B-80

This is a gas-operated, semiautomatic shotgun chambered for 12 or 20 gauge. It features 3" magnum potential by simply exchanging the barrel. It features various-length barrels and was offered with screw-in invector chokes as of 1985. The receiver is either steel or lightweight aluminum alloy. The finish is blued with a checkered walnut stock. This gun was assembled in Portugal from parts manufactured by Beretta in Italy. It was manufactured between 1981 and 1988.

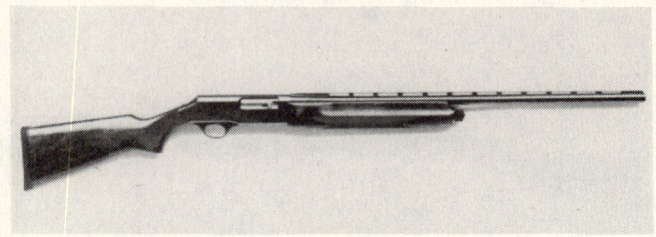

Exc.	V.G.	Good	Fair	Poor
450	400	350	300	200

Model B-80 Buck Special

This version features a 24", cylinder-bored barrel with rifle sights. It was discontinued in 1984.

Exc.	V.G.	Good	Fair	Poor
450	400	350	300	200

Model B-80 DU Commemorative

This version was produced to be auctioned by American Ducks Unlimited chapters. In order to realize the collector potential, it must be NIB with all supplied materials. Values supplied are general.

NIB	Exc.	V.G.	Good	Fair	Poor
900	700	500	375	300	250

Model Gold 10

Introduced for the first time in 1993 this is a gas operated 5-shot semiautomatic shotgun chambered for the 10 gauge shell. Offered with 26", 28", or 30" vent rib barrel. The standard model has a walnut stock, blued receiver and barrel while the Stalker Model is fitted with a graphite composite stock with nonglare finish on receiver and barrel. Both models are fitted with choke tubes. Weighs about 10 lbs., 10 oz.

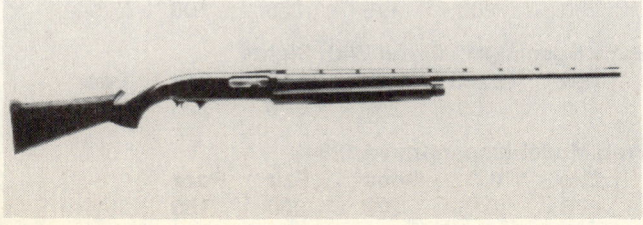

NIB	Exc.	V.G.	Good	Fair	Poor
725	650	550	450	300	150

Stalker Model

NIB	Exc.	V.G.	Good	Fair	Poor
725	650	550	450	300	150

Gold 3-1/2" 12 Gauge

Introduced in 1997 this model features a 3-1/2" chamber. It can operate 2-3/4", or 3" shells as well. The weight is approximately 7 lbs. 10 oz.

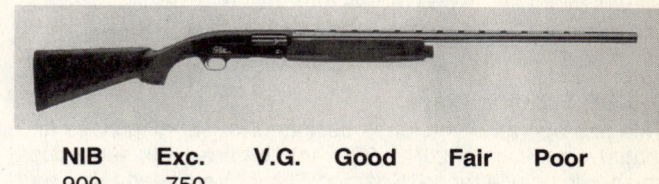

NIB	Exc.	V.G.	Good	Fair	Poor
900	750	—	—	—	—

Gold 12 Gauge Hunter

Introduced in 1994 this semi-automatic shotgun is built on the same gas operating system as the Gold 10. Offered with 26", 28", or 30" barrel it has a magazine capacity of four 3" shells. Walnut stock has full checkered pistol grip with black rubber recoil pad. Invector plus choke tubes supplied. Weighs about 7.5 lbs.

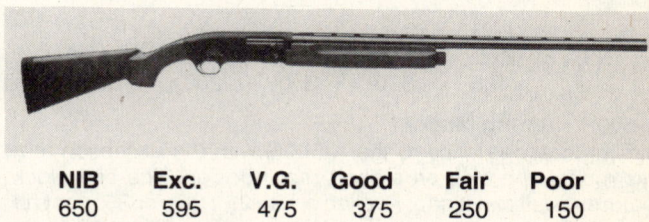

NIB	Exc.	V.G.	Good	Fair	Poor
650	595	475	375	250	150

Gold Deer Hunter

Introduced in 1997 this model features a choice of a fully rifle barrel or a smooth bore barrel with invector choke system. Both versions come with a cantilever scope mount. Stock and forearm are of select walnut. Receiver has non-glare black finish. Barrel is satin finish. Barrel length is 22" on both barrels. Weight is about 7 lbs. 12 oz. Price below is for smooth bore barrel.

NIB	Exc.	V.G.	Good	Fair	Poor
725	650	550	450	300	150

NOTE: For fully rifle version add $40.

Gold 20 Gauge Hunter

Same as above but chambered for 20 gauge and offered in 26" or 28" barrel lengths. Weighs about 6.8 lbs.

NIB	Exc.	V.G.	Good	Fair	Poor
650	575	475	375	250	150

Gold Sporting Clays

Introduced in 1996 this model features a ported barrel in 28" or 30" lengths. Recoil pad is standard. Weight is about 7.5 lbs.

NIB	Exc.	V.G.	Good	Fair	Poor
675	600	500	400	300	150

A-500

This is a self-adjusting, gas-operated, semiautomatic shotgun chambered for 12 gauge only. It is offered with 26", 28", or 30" barrels with a vent rib and screw-in invector choke tubes. It has 3" chambers and can fire any load interchangeably. The finish is blued with a checkered walnut stock and recoil pad. It features light engraving. It was introduced in 1987.

NIB	Exc.	V.G.	Good	Fair	Poor
560	490	425	350	275	225

A-500G Sporting Clays

This gas operated version is designed for sporting clays and features a choice of 28" or 30" vent rib barrel with semi-gloss finish with gold lettering "Sporting Clays". Ventilated recoil pad standard. Weighs about 8 lbs.

NIB	Exc.	V.G.	Good	Fair	Poor
520	425	350	300	200	150

A-500R Hunting Model

Similar in appearance to the A-500G with the exception that this model operates on a short recoil design. The butt stock features a full pistol grip. Available with 26", 28", or 30" vent rib barrels. Choke tubes standard. Weighs about 7 lbs., 13 oz.

NIB	Exc.	V.G.	Good	Fair	Poor
475	385	300	250	200	150

A-500R Buck Special

Same as Hunting Model with the addition of adjustable rear sight and contoured front ramp sight with gold bead. Choke tubes standard as is 24" barrel. Weighs 7 lbs., 11 oz.

NIB	Exc.	V.G.	Good	Fair	Poor
500	425	350	300	225	150

BPS Model

This is a slide action shotgun chambered for 10, 12, or 20 gauge. It is offered with various length vent rib barrels with screw-in invector chokes. It features 3" magnum chambers and a bottom-ejection system that effectively makes it ambidextrous. It has double slide bars and a 5-shot tubular magazine. It is constructed of all steel. It was introduced by B.C. Miroku in 1977.

Field Grade

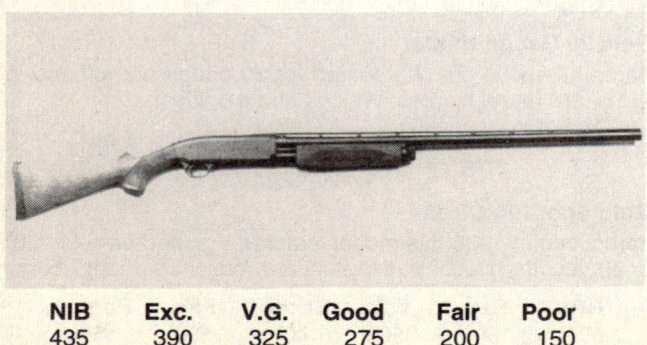

NIB	Exc.	V.G.	Good	Fair	Poor
435	390	325	275	200	150

Field Grade-28 Gauge

Introduced in 1994.

NIB	Exc.	V.G.	Good	Fair	Poor
475	425	350	275	200	150

Magnum Model-10 or 12 Gauge, 3.5" Chambers

NIB	Exc.	V.G.	Good	Fair	Poor
510	450	375	325	250	200

Upland Special-22" Barrel, Straight Stock

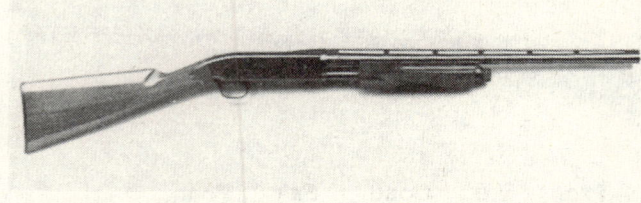

NIB	Exc.	V.G.	Good	Fair	Poor
435	390	325	275	200	150

Stalker Model-Matte Finish, Black Stock

NIB	Exc.	V.G.	Good	Fair	Poor
435	390	325	275	200	150

Pigeon Grade

Furnished in 12 gauge only with high grade walnut stock and gold trimmed receiver.

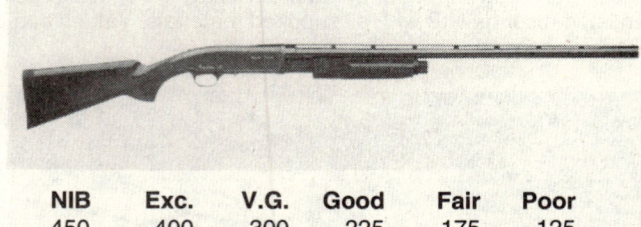

NIB	Exc.	V.G.	Good	Fair	Poor
450	400	300	225	175	125

Game Gun

Offered in 12 gauge only this model is available in either a Turkey Special or a Deer Special. Both have 20.5" plain barrel and drilled and tapped receivers. The stock is walnut. The turkey gun is fitted with an extra full choke. The deer gun has a special rifled choke tube for slugs. Both weigh about 7 lbs., 7 oz.

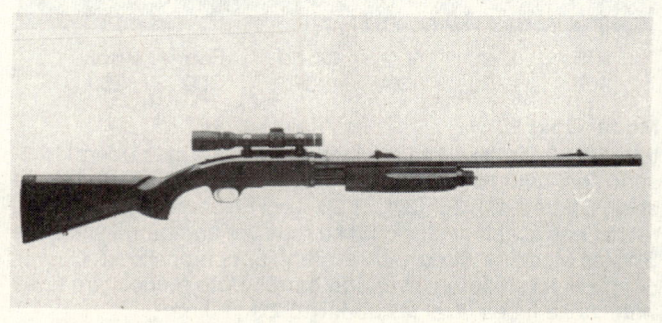

NIB	Exc.	V.G.	Good	Fair	Poor
250	200	175	125	100	50

Buck Special-24" Barrel With Sights

NIB	Exc.	V.G.	Good	Fair	Poor
450	400	350	300	225	175

Trap Model-discontinued 1984

Exc.	V.G.	Good	Fair	Poor
375	325	275	200	150

Youth Model-Short Stock, 22" Barrel

NIB	Exc.	V.G.	Good	Fair	Poor
435	390	325	275	200	150

Waterfowl Deluxe

This version is chambered for 12 gauge with a 3" chamber and features an etched receiver with a gold-plated trigger. Otherwise, it is similar to the standard BPS.

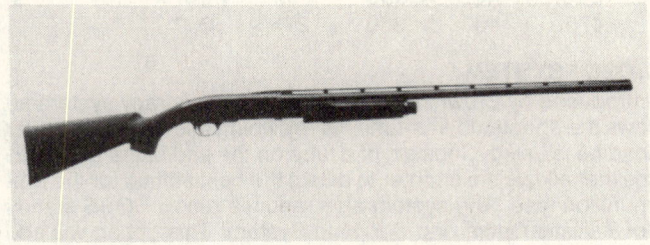

Exc.	V.G.	Good	Fair	Poor
600	525	425	325	250

Ducks Unlimited Versions

These were limited-edition guns produced to be auctioned by Ducks Unlimited. They were furnished with a case and must be NIB with furnished materials to realize their collector potential.

NIB	Exc.	V.G.	Good	Fair	Poor
650	525	425	325	250	175

BROWNING CHOKE TUBE SELECTION

Rim Notches	Pattern w/Lead Shot	Pattern w/Steel Shot
12 Gauge Invector-Plus for Back-Bored Guns		
Knurled	X-Full Turkey	Do not use
I	Full	Do not use
II	Imp. Modified	Full
III	Modified	Full
IIII	Imp. Cylinder	Modified
IIIII	Skeet	Imp. Cylinder
No Notches	Cylinder	Cylinder
10 Gauge Invector		
Knurled	X-Full Turkey	Do not use
I	Full	Do not use
II	Modified	Full
III	Imp. Modified	Modified
16 Gauge Invector		
I	Full	Do not use
II	Modified	Full
III	Imp. Cylinder	Modified
IIII	Skeet	Imp. Cylinder
No Notches	Cylinder	Imp. Cylinder
20 Gauge Invector		
I	Full	Full
II	Modified	Imp. Modified
III	Imp. Cylinder	Modified
IIII	Skeet	Modified
No Notches	Cylinder	Imp. Cylinder

CAUTION: Do not interchange invector choke tubes with Invector-Plus choke tubes. May cause personal injury.

Model 12-Grade I

This is a slide-action shotgun chambered for 20 gauge with a 26", modified choke, vent rib barrel. It is a reproduction of the Winchester Model 12 shotgun. It has a 5-round, tubular magazine with a floating, high-post rib. It has a takedown feature and is blued with a walnut stock. Introduced in 1988, total production will be limited to 8,500 guns.

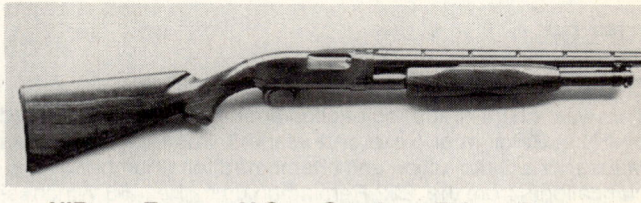

NIB	Exc.	V.G.	Good	Fair	Poor
675	575	400	300	250	200

Model 12-Grade V

This is an extensively engraved version of the Grade I Model 12. It features a select walnut stock with deluxe checkering and a high-gloss finish. There are gold inlays. It was introduced in 1988, and production will be limited to 4,000 guns.

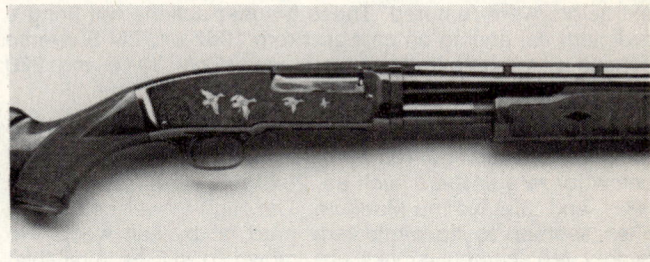

NIB	Exc.	V.G.	Good	Fair	Poor
1150	850	650	450	300	200

Limited Edition Model 42

A new version of the .410 bore pump shotgun that was last produced by Winchester in 1963. Available in two grades both fitted with 26" vent rib barrels. The Grade I features a plain blued receiver with walnut stock. The Grade V features a blued receiver with scroll engraving and gold inlays. Both models are choked full and weigh 6 lbs., 4 oz.

Grade I

NIB	Exc.	V.G.	Good	Fair	Poor
650	600	500	400	300	200

Grade V

NIB	Exc.	V.G.	Good	Fair	Poor
1050	900	700	500	350	200

A-Bolt

Introduced in 1995 this bolt action shotgun is offered in 12 gauge with 3" chamber. Rifled barrel version is 22" long while the invector barrel version is 23" long with a 5" rifle tube installed. Has a 2-shot detachable magazine. Average weight is about 7 lbs.

Hunter Version

NIB	Exc.	V.G.	Good	Fair	Poor
775	700	600	500	400	200

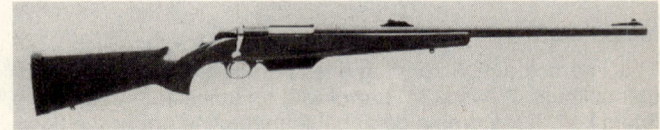

Stalker Version

NIB	Exc.	V.G.	Good	Fair	Poor
650	575	500	400	300	150

NOTE: For invector rifled choke tube model deduct $50.

RIFLES

High-Power Bolt Action Rifle

This was a high-grade, bolt-action sporting rifle manufactured by FN in Belgium or Sako on Finland It was built on either a Mauser or a Sako action and chambered for a number of popular calibers from the .222 Remington up to the .458 Winchester Magnum. There were three basic grades that differed in the amount of ornamentation and the quality of materials and workmanship utilized. Certain calibers are considered to be rare and will bring a premium from collectors of this firearm. We recommend securing a qualified appraisal on these rifles if a transaction is contemplated. We furnish general values only.

NOTE: From 1960 through 1966 FN Mauser actions with long extractors were featured. These Mauser actions will bring a premium depending on caliber. From 1967 on, FN Supreme actions with short extractors were used. *Only .30-06 and .270 calibers continued with long extractor Mauser actions.*

CAUTION: For buyer and seller alike some rare calibers may be worth as much as 100 percent or more over prices listed below for rare calibers such as .284 Win., .257 Roberts, 300 H&H, and .308 Norma Magnum. The High-Power bolt action rifles seemed to be particularly hard hit by salt wood. No factory replacement stocks are known to still be available. Proceed with caution.

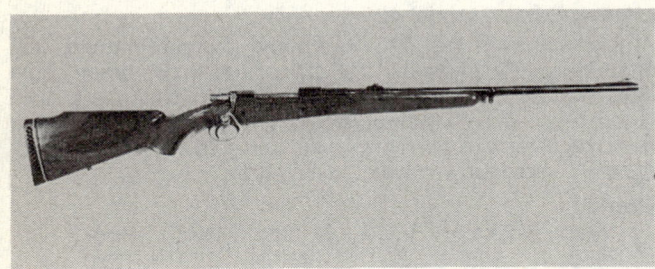

Safari Grade-Standard Model, Standard Calibers

Exc.	V.G.	Good	Fair	Poor
900	750	575	450	300

Medallion Grade-Scroll Engraved

Exc.	V.G.	Good	Fair	Poor
1500	1250	1000	750	500

Olympian Grade-Extensive Engraving

Exc.	V.G.	Good	Fair	Poor
2750	2000	1750	1450	1000

Model BBR

This is a bolt-action sporting rifle chambered for various popular calibers. It has a 24" barrel with an adjustable trigger and fluted bolt. It features a detachable magazine under the floorplate and was furnished without sights. The finish is blued with a checkered, walnut, Monte Carlo stock. It was manufactured between 1978 and 1984 by Miroku.

Exc.	V.G.	Good	Fair	Poor
475	400	350	275	200

BOSS™ SYSTEM

Introduced by Browning in 1994 this new accuracy system allows the shooter to fine-tune his Browning rifle to the particular load he is using. Consists of a tube on the end of the rifle muzzle that allows the shooter to select the best setting for the ammunition type. The system also reduces recoil. BOSS stands for Ballistic Optimizing Shooting System. This option will add approximately $80 to the value of the particular Browning rifle on which it is fitted.

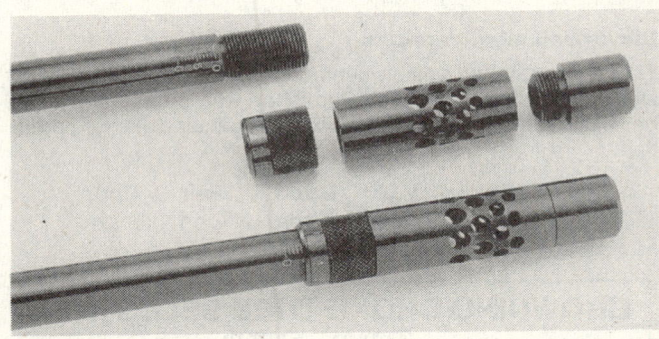

A-Bolt Hunter

This is the current bolt-action rifle manufactured by B.C. Miroku. It is chambered for various popular calibers and offered with a 22", 24", or 26" barrel. It has either a short or long action, an adjustable trigger, and a detachable box magazine that is mounted under the floorplate. It is furnished without sights and is blued with a checkered walnut stock. It was introduced in 1985.

NIB	Exc.	V.G.	Good	Fair	Poor
450	400	350	300	250	200

A-Bolt II Hunter

Introduced in 1994 this new model features a newly designed anti-bind bolt and improved trigger system.

NIB	Exc.	V.G.	Good	Fair	Poor
450	400	350	300	250	200

Composite Stalker

Supplied with composite stock and matte finish bluing. Offered in .338 Win. Mag., .300 Win. Mag., 7mm Rem. Mag., .25-06, .270, .280, .30-06.

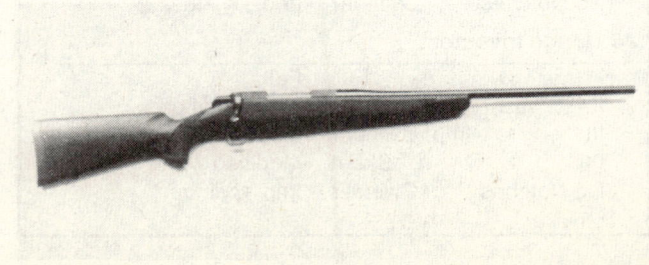

NIB	Exc.	V.G.	Good	Fair	Poor
400	350	300	250	200	150

A-Bolt II Composite Stalker
Same as above but with 1994 improvements.

NIB	Exc.	V.G.	Good	Fair	Poor
450	400	350	300	250	200

Stainless Stalker
This version is chambered for the .270, .30-06, and the 7mm Remington Magnum cartridges. It is constructed of stainless steel and has a black, painted wood stock. It was introduced in 1987.

NIB	Exc.	V.G.	Good	Fair	Poor
580	525	450	350	300	250

A-Bolt II Composite Stainless Stalker
Same as above but with 1994 improvements.

NIB	Exc.	V.G.	Good	Fair	Poor
580	525	450	350	300	250

A-Bolt II Heavy Barrel Varmit
Introduced in 1994 this model features all of the A-Bolt II improvements in a heavy barrel varmint rifle. Offered in .22-250 and .223 Rem. calibers with 22" barrel. Equipped with black laminated wood stock.

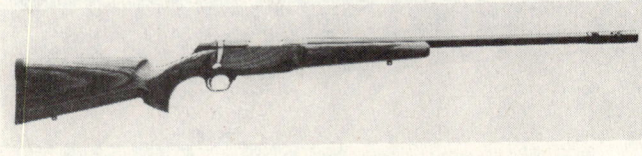

NIB	Exc.	V.G.	Good	Fair	Poor
685	600	525	425	325	250

A-Bolt Eclipse M-1000
This version of the Eclipse was introduced in 1997 and is offered in .300 Win. Mag. The rifle is fitted with a 26" barrel with BOSS system. The stock is a laminated hardwood with gray/black finish. The forearm is a benchrest style. Weight is approximately 9 lbs. 13 oz.

NIB	Exc.	V.G.	Good	Fair	Poor
900	700	600	450	350	250

A-Bolt Eclipse Varmint
Introduced in 1996 this model features a thumbhole stock made from gray/black laminated hardwood. Offered in two version: a short action heavy barrel version and a long and short action with standard weight barrel. Eclipse varmint weighs about 9 lbs. and the standard barrel version weighs about 7.5 lbs. depending on caliber.

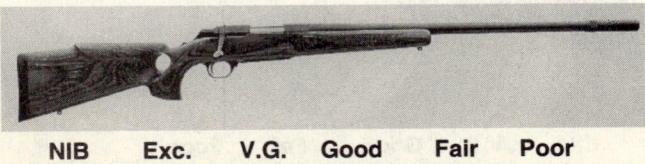

NIB	Exc.	V.G.	Good	Fair	Poor
950	800	600	500	400	250

Euro-Bolt
First introduced in 1993 this A-Bolt variation features a rounded bolt shroud, Mannlicher-style bolt handle, continental style stock with cheekpiece, Schnabel style forearm. The finish is a low luster blue. Offered in .270, .30-06, and 7mm Rem. Mag. calibers. Weighs about 7 lbs.

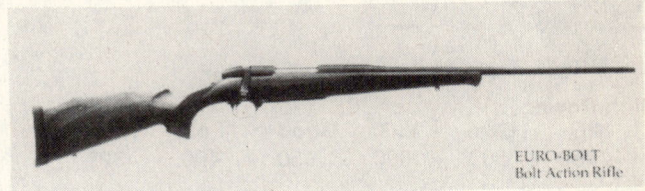

EURO-BOLT
Bolt Action Rifle

NIB	Exc.	V.G.	Good	Fair	Poor
550	500	450	350	250	150

A-Bolt II Euro Bolt
Same as above but with 1994 improvements.

NIB	Exc.	V.G.	Good	Fair	Poor
550	500	450	350	250	150

Medallion Model
This is a deluxe version of the A-Bolt Hunter with a high-polish blue finish and a select walnut stock with rosewood pistol-grip cap and forend tip.

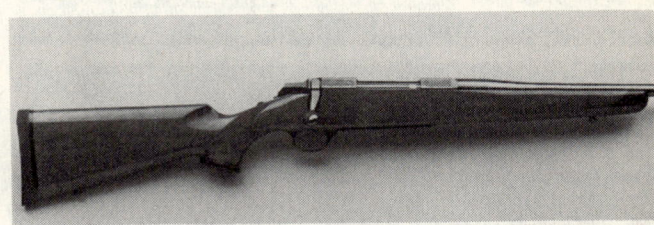

NIB	Exc.	V.G.	Good	Fair	Poor
525	475	400	350	300	250

A-Bolt II Medallion
Same as above but with 1994 improvements.

NIB	Exc.	V.G.	Good	Fair	Poor
525	475	400	350	300	250

Gold Medallion
This version has a fancy-grade walnut stock with a cheekpiece. It is lightly engraved and has gold-inlaid letters. It was introduced in 1988.

NIB	Exc.	V.G.	Good	Fair	Poor
690	625	550	450	400	325

A-Bolt II Gold Medallion
Same as above but with 1994 improvements.

NIB	Exc.	V.G.	Good	Fair	Poor
690	625	550	450	400	325

Big Horn Sheep Issue
This is a high-grade version of the A-Bolt chambered for the .270 cartridge. It features a deluxe skip-line checkered walnut stock with a heavily engraved receiver and floorplate. It has two gold sheep inlays. There were 600 manufactured in 1986 and 1987.

NIB	Exc.	V.G.	Good	Fair	Poor
1050	800	600	450	400	325

Pronghorn Issue

This is a deluxe version of the A-Bolt chambered for the .243 cartridge. It is heavily engraved and gold inlaid and features a presentation-grade walnut stock with skipline checkering and pearl-inlaid borders. There were 500 manufactured in 1987.

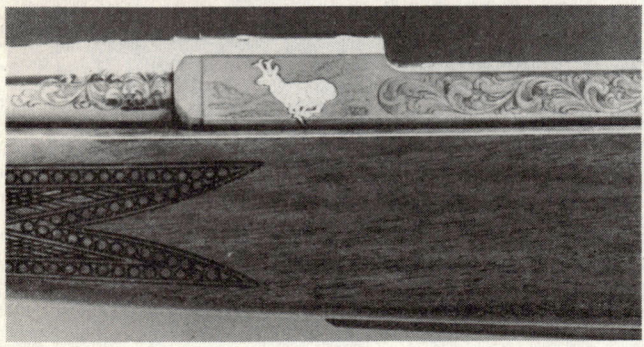

NIB	Exc.	V.G.	Good	Fair	Poor
1300	1000	750	500	400	325

Micro-Medallion Model

This is a smaller version of the A-Bolt Hunter chambered for popular cartridges that fit a short action. It has a 20" barrel without sights and a 3-round magazine. It was introduced in 1988.

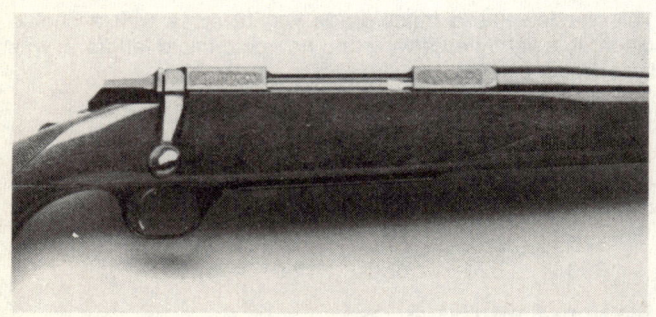

NIB	Exc.	V.G.	Good	Fair	Poor
525	475	400	350	300	250

A-Bolt II Micro-Medallion

Same as above but with 1994 improvements.

NIB	Exc.	V.G.	Good	Fair	Poor
525	475	400	350	300	250

Grade I A-Bolt .22

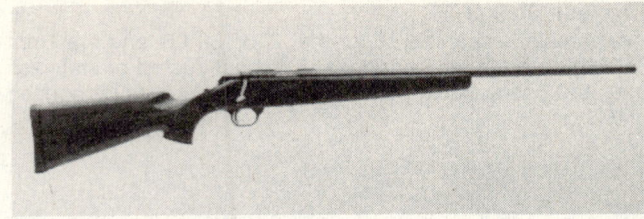

This is a bolt-action sporting rifle chambered for the .22 l.r. or .22 Magnum cartridges. It features a 60-degree bolt and a 22" barrel available either with or without open sights. It has a 5-round, detachable magazine and an adjustable trigger. The finish is blued with a checkered walnut stock. It was introduced in 1986.

.22 Magnum-Add 15%.

NIB	Exc.	V.G.	Good	Fair	Poor
340	275	210	150	125	100

Gold Medallion A-Bolt.22

This deluxe, high-grade version features a select stock with rosewood pistol-grip cap and forend tip. It is lightly engraved and has gold-filled letters. It was introduced in 1988.

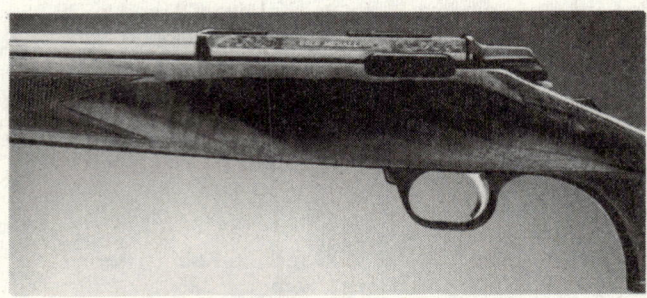

NIB	Exc.	V.G.	Good	Fair	Poor
450	400	350	300	225	175

T-Bolt Model T-1

This is a unique, straight-pull, bolt-action sporting rifle chambered for .22 caliber cartridges. It has a 22" barrel with open sights and a 5-round magazine. The finish is blued with a plain walnut stock. It was manufactured between 1965 and 1974 by FN. Many T-Bolt rifles were affected by salt wood. Proceed with caution.

Exc.	V.G.	Good	Fair	Poor
350	300	250	150	100

T-Bolt Model T-2

This version is similar to the T-1 with a select, checkered walnut stock and a 24" barrel.

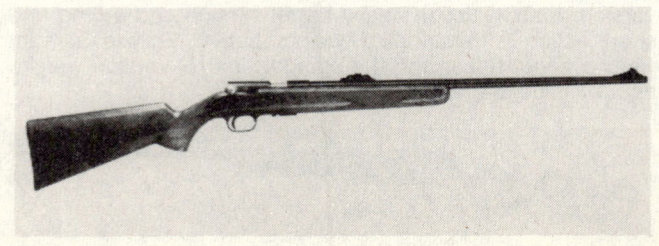

Exc.	V.G.	Good	Fair	Poor
450	380	300	250	200

Trombone Model

This is a slide-action rifle chambered for the .22 l.r. cartridge. It has a 24" barrel with open sights and a takedown design. It has a tubular magazine and a hammerless action. There were approximately 150,000 manufactured by FN between 1922 and 1974. Approximately 3,200 were imported by Browning in the 1960s. They are marked with either the FN barrel address or the Browning Arms address. The Browning marked guns are worth approximately 20 percent additional. The values given are for FN-marked guns.

NIB	Exc.	V.G.	Good	Fair	Poor
750	550	500	450	375	275

BPR-22

This is a short-stroke, slide action rifle chambered for the .22 Magnum cartridge. It has a 20.25" barrel with open sights and an 11-round, tubular magazine. The finish is blued with a checkered walnut stock. It was manufactured between 1977 and 1982.

Exc.	V.G.	Good	Fair	Poor
275	200	150	125	95

NOTE: Add $100 for models chambered for .22 Magnum.

BPR-22 Grade II

This version is engraved and has a select walnut stock.

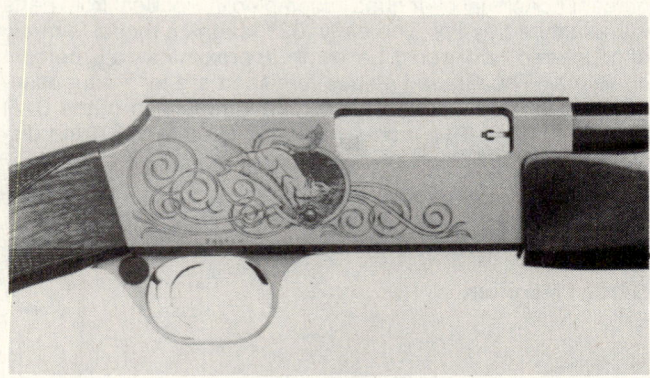

Exc.	V.G.	Good	Fair	Poor
500	375	275	225	150

NOTE: Add 20% for models chambered for .22 Magnum.

.22 CALIBER SEMI-AUTO

This is a blowback-operated, semiautomatic rifle chambered for the .22 Long Rifle or Short cartridge. It features a takedown barrel design with a 19.25" barrel and an 11-round, tubular magazine inside the buttstock. It is loaded through a hole in the middle of the buttstock. The finish is blued with a checkered walnut stock and beavertail forearm. This lightweight, compact firearm was manufactured by FN between 1956 and 1974 for U.S. marked guns. There are a number of versions that differ in the amount of ornamentation and the quality of materials and workmanship utilized.

Early Wheel Sight manufactured 1956-1960-Add 10%.

Grade I

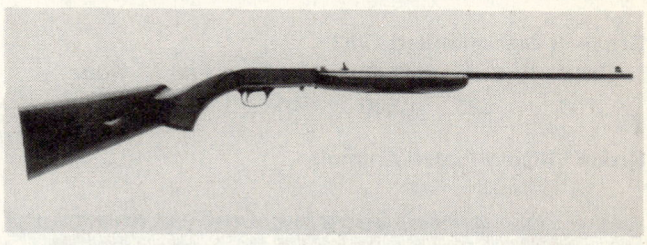

NIB	Exc.	V.G.	Good	Fair	Poor
500	350	300	250	200	125

NOTE: For Grade I short add 20%.

Grade II-French Greyed Receiver

NIB	Exc.	V.G.	Good	Fair	Poor
1000	700	600	400	300	200

NOTE: For Grade II short add 300%.

Grade III-French Greyed Receiver

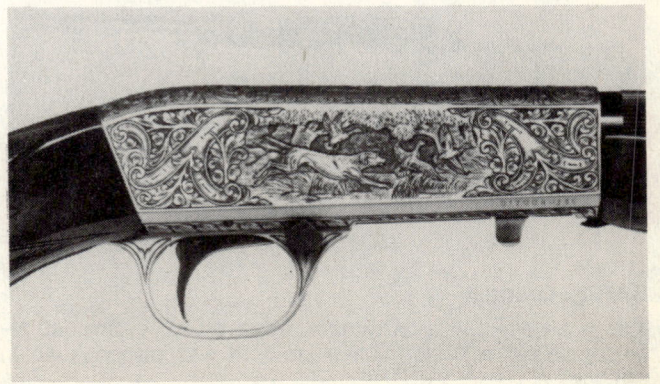

NIB	Exc.	V.G.	Good	Fair	Poor
2000	1400	1050	600	400	300

NOTE: For premium engravers add 40 percent to Grade III. For Grade III short add 500%. For unsigned Grade III, 1956-1960, deduct 20%.

.22 Semi-Auto (Miroku Mfg.)

This model is similar to the Belgian FN except that it was produced as of 1976 by B.C. Miroku in Japan. Collector interest is not as high as in the FN version.

Grade I

NIB	Exc.	V.G.	Good	Fair	Poor
300	250	200	175	125	100

Grade II-Discontinued 1984

NIB	Exc.	V.G.	Good	Fair	Poor
425	375	325	275	225	150

Grade III-Discontinued 1983

NIB	Exc.	V.G.	Good	Fair	Poor
700	625	500	400	300	200

Grade VI-Gold Plated Animals

NIB	Exc.	V.G.	Good	Fair	Poor
675	600	500	425	325	275

BAR-22

This is a blowback-operated, semiautomatic rifle chambered for the .22 l.r. cartridge. It has a 20.25" barrel with open sights and a 15-round, tubular magazine. It features a polished, lightweight alloy receiver. It was finished in blue with a checkered walnut stock. It is manufactured between 1977 and 1985 by Miroku.

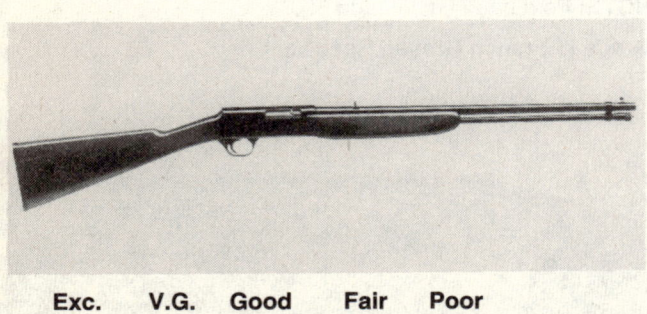

Exc.	V.G.	Good	Fair	Poor
250	210	190	160	125

BAR-22 Grade II

This is a deluxe version with an engraved, silver-finished receiver. It has a select walnut stock. It was discontinued in 1985.

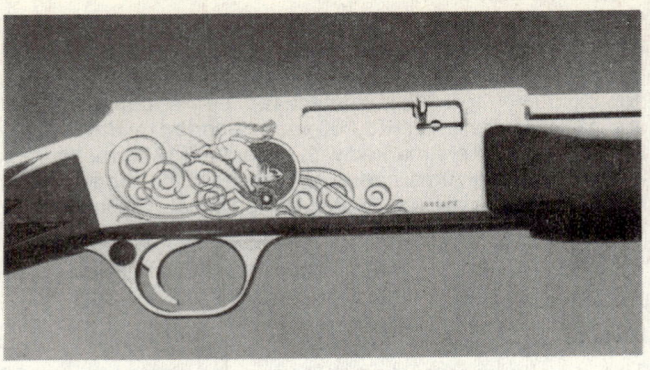

Exc.	V.G.	Good	Fair	Poor
450	250	200	150	120

Patent 1900 High Power

This is a semiautomatic sporting rifle chambered for the .35 Remington cartridge. It is similar in configuration to the Remington Model 8 rifle. It has a 22" barrel with open sights and a 5-round, integral magazine. The finish is blued with a plain walnut stock. There were approximately 5,000 manufactured between 1910 and 1931. A deluxe model with a ribbed barrel and checkered walnut stock was also available and would be worth approximately 15 percent additional.

Exc.	V.G.	Good	Fair	Poor
675	600	500	375	300

BAR HIGH POWER RIFLE

This is a gas-operated, semiautomatic sporting rifle chambered for various popular calibers from the .243 up to the .338 Magnum cartridges. It was offered with either a 22" or 24" barrel with folding leaf sight until 1980. The finish is blued with a checkered walnut stock. The various grades offered differed in the amount of ornamentation and the quality of materials and workmanship utilized. Earlier models were manufactured in Belgium by FN; these guns would be worth approximately 15 percent additional over guns assembled in Portugal from parts manufactured by FN. The early .338 Magnum model is rarely encountered and would be worth approximately 25 percent additional. The Grade I values furnished are for Portuguese-assembled guns from 1977 until the introduction of the BAR Mark II in 1993. This model was introduced in 1967 and discontinued in 1977.

Grade I

NIB	Exc.	V.G.	Good	Fair	Poor
600	425	350	275	225	100

Grade I Magnum

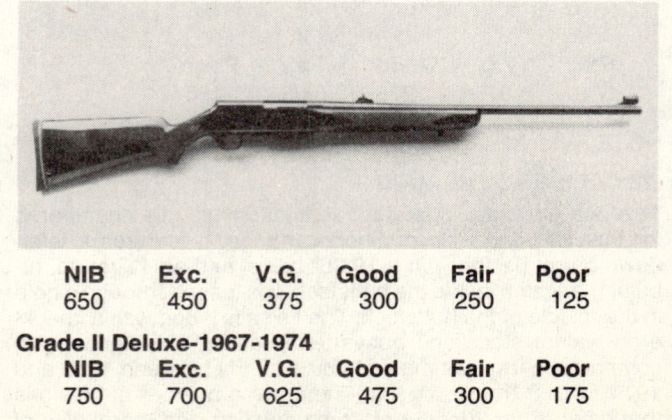

NIB	Exc.	V.G.	Good	Fair	Poor
650	450	375	300	250	125

Grade II Deluxe-1967-1974

NIB	Exc.	V.G.	Good	Fair	Poor
750	700	625	475	300	175

Grade II Deluxe Magnum-1968-1974

NIB	Exc.	V.G.	Good	Fair	Poor
775	700	650	500	325	200

Grade III-Discontinued 1984

NOTE: The Grade III was offered in two variations. The first was hand engraved and produced in Belgium. The second was photo etched and built in Belgium and assembled in Portugal. This second variation will not be as valuable as the first.

NIB	Exc.	V.G.	Good	Fair	Poor
1250	1000	700	550	375	250

Grade III Magnum-Discontinued 1984

NIB	Exc.	V.G.	Good	Fair	Poor
1400	1200	850	600	400	275

NOTE: Prices indicated above are for 1970 through 1974 production. For guns assembled in Portugal deduct 30%. .338 Win. Mag caliber is rare in Grade III. Add 75% premium.

Grade IV-Gamescene Engraved

This grade was hand engraved from 1970 through 1976 then was etched thereafter. Grade IV rifles were discontinued in 1984.

Pre-1977 rifles-Add 40%.
Premium engravers add 10%.

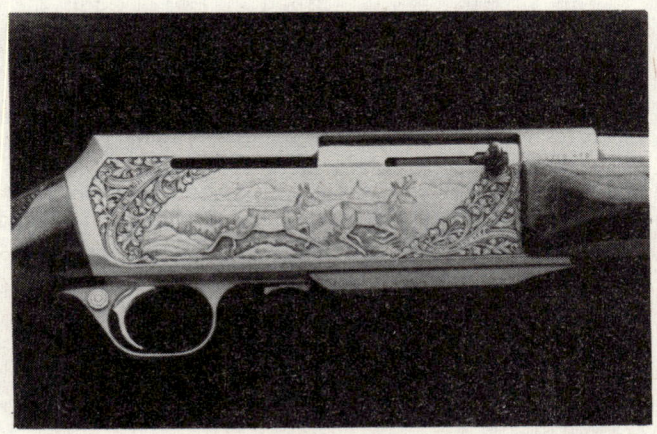

NIB	Exc.	V.G.	Good	Fair	Poor
1700	1300	950	800	650	400

Grade IV Magnum

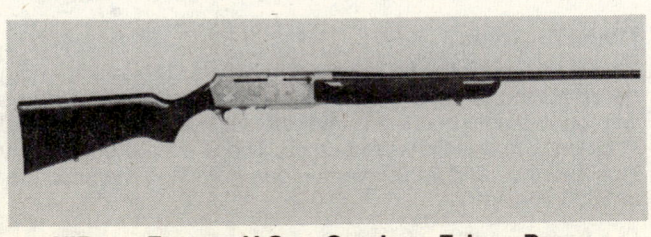

NIB	Exc.	V.G.	Good	Fair	Poor
1800	1300	975	850	650	425

Grade V-Gold Inlaid-1971-1974

NIB	Exc.	V.G.	Good	Fair	Poor
3000	2700	2300	1800	1200	600

Grade V Magnum-1971-1974

NIB	Exc.	V.G.	Good	Fair	Poor
3500	3200	2500	1850	1250	600

NOTE: For special order variations on Grade V rifles add up to 100%

North American Deer Rifle Issue

This is a deluxe version of the BAR chambered for .30-06 only. It features a photo etched, silver-finished receiver and a deluxe, checkered walnut stock. There were 600 produced and furnished with a walnut case and accessories. This model was discontinued in 1983. As with all commemoratives, it must be NIB to command premium values.

NIB	Exc.	V.G.	Good	Fair	Poor
2700	1800	1400	1000	450	250

BAR Mark II Safari Rifle

This is an improved version of the BAR first introduced by Browning in 1967. Announced in 1993 this Mark II design uses a new gas system with a newly designed buffering system to improve reliability. This model also has a new bolt release lever, a new easily removable trigger assembly. Available with or without sights. Walnut stock with full pistol grip and recoil pad on Magnum gun are standard. The receiver is blued with scroll engraving. Rifles with Magnum calibers have a 24" barrel while standard calibers are fitted with a 22" barrel. Available in .243, .308, .270, .30-06, 7mm Rem. Mag., .300 Win. Mag., .338 Win. Mag. Standard calibers weigh about 7 lbs., 9 oz. and Magnum calibers weigh about 8 lbs., 6 oz.

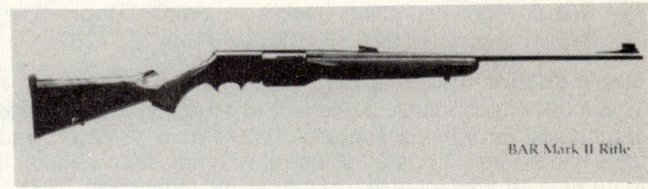

BAR Mark II Rifle

NIB	Exc.	V.G.	Good	Fair	Poor
525	450	400	350	250	150

NOTE: Add 30% for .270 Wby. Mag. which was made for one year only.

BAR Mark II Lightweight

This version of the Mark II was introduced in 1997 and features a lightweight alloy receiver and shortened 20" barrel. It is offered in .30-06, .270 Win., .308 Win., and .243 Win. calibers. It is not offered with the BOSS system. Weight is approximately 7 lbs. 2 oz.

NIB	Exc.	V.G.	Good	Fair	Poor
700	550	—	—	—	—

Model BPR

The initials "BPR" stand for Browning Pump Rifle. It was introduced in 1997 and is similar in appearance to the BAR. Offered in both long action and short action calibers with barrel lengths from 22" to 24". Short action calibers are: .243 Win., and .308 Win. Long Action calibers are: .270 Win., .30-06, 7mm Rem. Mag., and .300 Win. Mag. Weight is about 7 lbs. 3 oz.

NIB	Exc.	V.G.	Good	Fair	Poor
650	475	—	—	—	—

BL-22 Grade I

This is a lever-action rifle chambered for the .22 rimfire cartridge. It has an 18" barrel with a tubular magazine and a folding leaf rear sight. It is a Western-style firearm that features an exposed hammer. The finish is blued with a walnut stock. It was introduced in 1970 by Miroku.

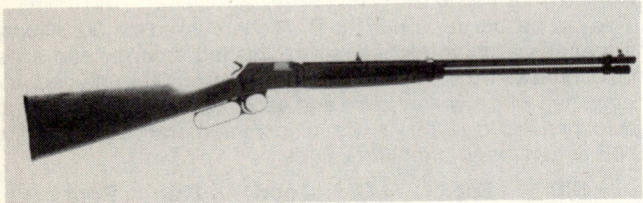

NIB	Exc.	V.G.	Good	Fair	Poor
285	225	020	150	125	100

BL-22 Grade II

This version is similar with a scroll-engraved receiver and a checkered, select walnut stock.

NIB	Exc.	V.G.	Good	Fair	Poor
325	250	225	175	150	125

Model 81 BLR

This is a contemporarily designed, lever-action sporting rifle chambered for various popular calibers from .22-250 up to .358 Winchester. It has a 20" barrel with adjustable sights. It features a 4-round, detachable magazine and a rotary locking bolt. The finish is blued with a checkered walnut stock and recoil pad. It was introduced in 1971 and manufactured that year in Belgium. In 1972 manufacture moved to Miroku in Japan.

Belgian manufactured version-Add 20 %.

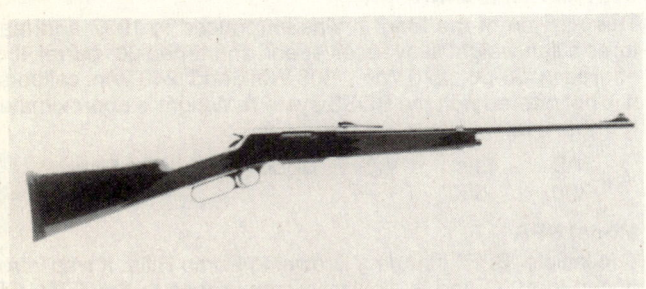

NIB	Exc.	V.G.	Good	Fair	Poor
475	400	325	275	200	150

Model BLR Lightning

Introduced in 1996 this model features a lightweight aluminum receiver with walnut stock with checkered pistol grip. Offered in both long and short action calibers from .223 Rem. to 7mm Rem. Mag. Barrel length is 20" for short action calibers and 22" to 24" for long action calibers. Open sights are standard. Weight is about 7 lbs. depending on caliber.

NIB	Exc.	V.G.	Good	Fair	Poor
550	450	325	275	200	150

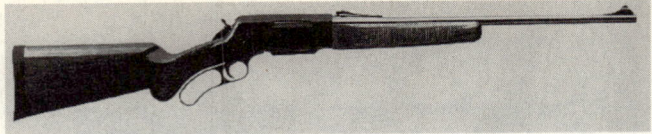

Model 65 Grade I

This was a limited-edition, lever-action rifle chambered for the .218 Bee cartridge. It has a tapered, round, 24" barrel with open sights. It was patterned after the Winchester Model 65 rifle. It has a 7-round, tubular magazine. The finish is blued with a plain walnut stock and metal buttplate. There were 3,500 manufactured in 1989.

NIB	Exc.	V.G.	Good	Fair	Poor
550	475	400	325	250	175

Model 65 High Grade

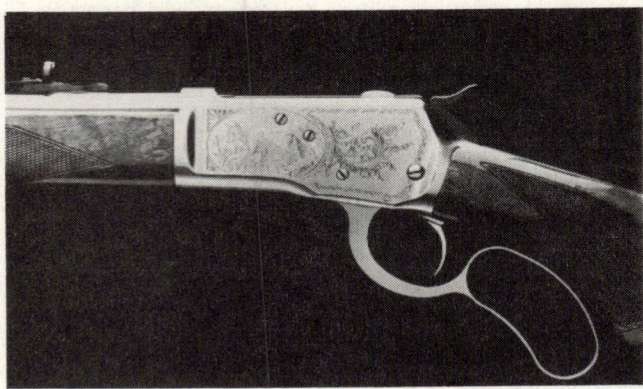

This is a deluxe version that features a silver-finished, scroll engraved receiver with gold animal inlays and a gold-plated trigger. It features a select, checkered walnut stock. There were 1,500 manufactured in 1989.

NIB	Exc.	V.G.	Good	Fair	Poor
850	750	600	500	400	275

Model 53

Offered in 1990 this model is a reproduction of the Winchester Model 53 and like the original is chambered for the .32-20 cartridge. This is a limited edition offering confined to 5,000 rifles. It features hand cut checkering, high grade walnut stock with full pistol grip and semi-beavertail forend. Pistol grip is fitted with a metal grip cap. Barrel length is 22" and the finish is blue.

NIB	Exc.	V.G.	Good	Fair	Poor
675	575	500	400	300	150

Model 71 Grade I

This was a reproduction of the Winchester Model 71, chambered for the .348 cartridge. It has either a 20" or 24" barrel with open sights and a 4-round, tubular magazine. The finish is blued with a plain walnut stock. There were 4,000 twenty-inch carbines and 3,000 twenty-four-inch rifles manufactured in 1986 and 1987.

Exc.	V.G.	Good	Fair	Poor
595	500	400	300	225

Model 71 High Grade

This version was similar to the Grade I except that it had a scroll engraved, grayed receiver with a gold-plated trigger and gold inlays. There were 3,000 rifles and 3,000 carbines manufactured in 1986 and 1987.

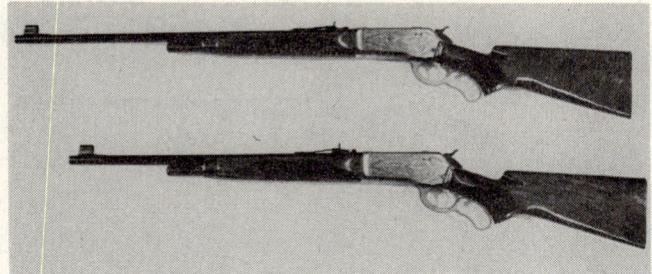

Exc.	V.G.	Good	Fair	Poor
900	750	600	500	400

Model 1878

Based on John M. Browning's first patent this single shot rifle was the only firearm manufactured by the Browning brothers. Offered in several calibers only a few hundred probably exist with the Ogden, Utah, barrel address. This design was later sold to Winchester and sold under that company's name as the Model 1885 High Wall.

Exc.	V.G.	Good	Fair	Poor
4500	3500	2500	1500	500

Model B-78

Introduced in 1973 this single shot, lever action falling block was offered in several calibers from .22-250 to .45-70. Barrel lengths from 24" to 26" in either round or octagonal shape with no sights except .45-70. Checkered walnut stock. Discontinued in 1982.

NOTE: Add 15% for .45-70 caliber.

NIB	Exc.	V.G.	Good	Fair	Poor
800	650	550	300	200	100

Model 1885 High Wall

This is a single shot rifle with falling block action and octagonal free floating barrel similar to the Model 78. Introduced in 1985. The stock is a high grade walnut with straight grip and recoil pad. Furnished with 28" barrel it is offered in the following calibers: .223, .22-250, .270, .30-06, 7mm Rem. Mag., .45-70 Gov't. Weighs about 8 lbs., 12 oz.

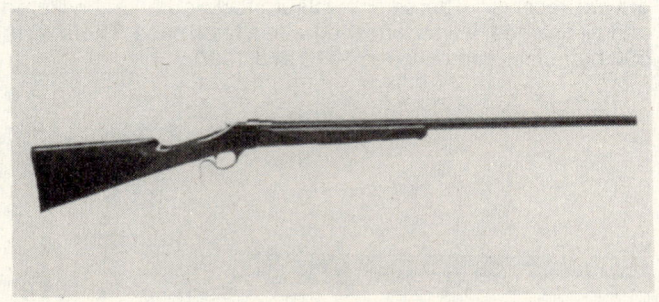

NIB	Exc.	V.G.	Good	Fair	Poor
800	650	550	300	200	100

Model 1885 Low Wall

Introduced in 1995 this rifle is similar to the above but in a more accurate version of the orginal Low Wall. The thin octagon barrel is 24" in length. Trigger pull is adjustable. The walnut stock is fitted with a pistol grip and Schnabel forearm. Offered in .22 Hornet, .223 Rem. and the .243 Win. calibers. Weight is about 6.4 lbs.

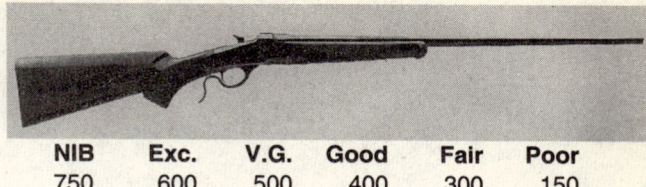

NIB	Exc.	V.G.	Good	Fair	Poor
750	600	500	400	300	150

Model 1885 BPCR (Black Powder Cartridge Rifle)

This model was introduced in 1996 for BPCR metallic silhouette shoots. Chambered for the .45-70 or .40-60 caliber the receiver is case colored and the 28" round barrel is fitted with vernier sight with level. The walnut stock has a checkered pistol grip and is fitted with a tang sight. Weight is approximately 11 lbs.

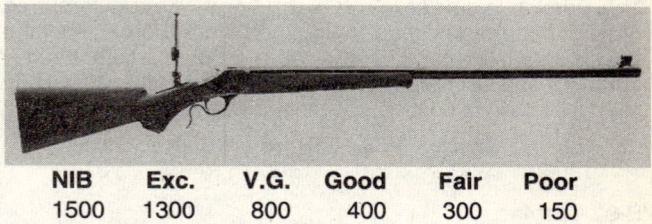

NIB	Exc.	V.G.	Good	Fair	Poor
1500	1300	800	400	300	150

Model 1885 Traditional Hunter

This variation of the Model 1885 series was introduced in 1997. It is fitted with an oil finish walnut stock with crescent buttplate. The barrel is octagonal and 28" in length. The rear sight is buckhorn and the rifle is fitted with a tang mounted peep sight. The front sight is gold bead classic style. The rifle is chambered for the 30-30, .38-55, and .45-70 cartridges. Weight is approximately 9 lbs.

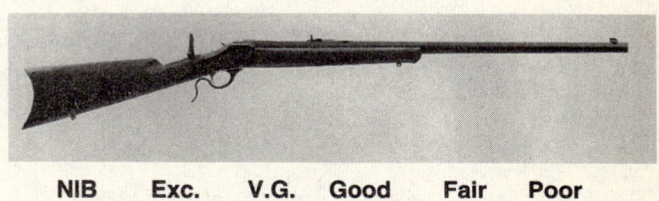

NIB	Exc.	V.G.	Good	Fair	Poor
1100	900	700	—	—	—

Model 1886 Grade I

This was a lever-action sporting rifle patterned after the Model 1886 Winchester rifle. It was chambered for the .45-70 cartridge and has a 26", octagonal barrel with a full-length, tubular magazine. The finish is blued with a walnut stock and crescent buttplate. There were 7,000 manufactured in 1986.

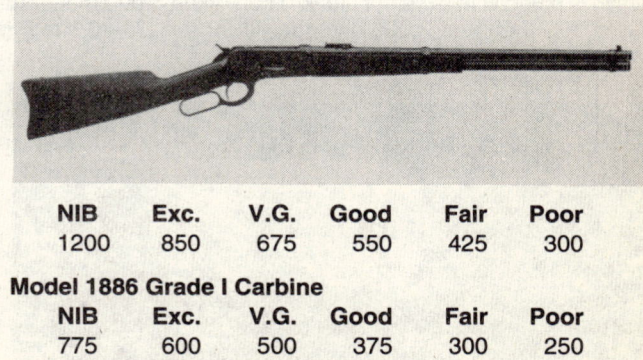

NIB	Exc.	V.G.	Good	Fair	Poor
1200	850	675	550	425	300

Model 1886 Grade I Carbine

NIB	Exc.	V.G.	Good	Fair	Poor
775	600	500	375	300	250

Model 1886 High Grade

This deluxe version of the Model 1886 features game scene engraving with gold accents and a checkered, select walnut stock. "1 of 3,000" is engraved on the top of the barrel. There were 3,000 manufactured in 1986.

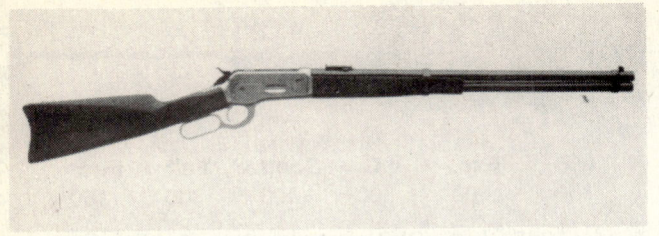

NIB	Exc.	V.G.	Good	Fair	Poor
1600	1150	900	700	550	425

Model 1886 High Grade Carbine

NIB	Exc.	V.G.	Good	Fair	Poor
1200	950	750	600	450	300

Model 1886 Montana Centennial

This version is similar to the High Grade with a different engraving pattern designed to commemorate the centennial of the State of Montana. There were 2,000 manufactured in 1986. As with all commemoratives, it must be NIB with all supplied materials to command collector interest.

NIB	Exc.	V.G.	Good	Fair	Poor
1300	950	750	600	450	375

B-92 Carbine

This is a lever-action sporting rifle patterned after the Winchester Model 92. It was chambered for the .357 Mag. and the .44 Mag. cartridges. It has a 20" barrel with an 11-round, tubular magazine. The finish is blued with a walnut stock. It was discontinued in 1986.

NOTE: Add 10% for Centennial Model

Exc.	V.G.	Good	Fair	Poor
400	325	195	150	120

NOTE: For .357 Magnum add 30 percent.

Model 1895 Grade I

This is a lever-action sporting rifle chambered in .30-.40 Krag and the .30-06 cartridge. It was patterned after the Model 1895 Winchester rifle. It has a 24" barrel and a 4-round, integral box magazine. It has a buckhorn rear sight and a blade front. The finish is blued with a walnut stock. There were 6,000 manufactured in .30-06 and 2,000 chambered for the .30-40 Krag. It was manufactured in 1984.

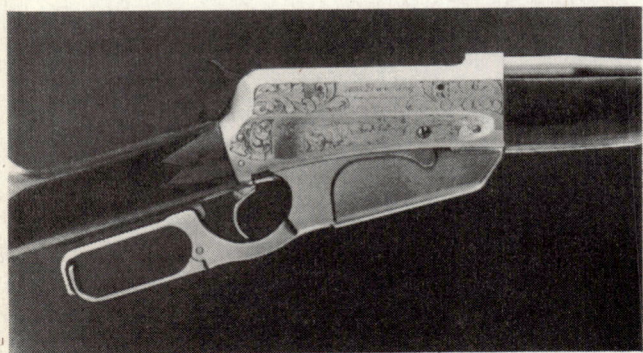

Exc.	V.G.	Good	Fair	Poor
600	525	450	375	275

NOTE: For .30-06 caliber add 15 percent.

Model 1895 High Grade

This is the deluxe engraved version of the Model 1895. It has gold-inlaid game scenes and a gold-plated trigger and features a checkered select walnut stock. There were 2,000 produced in 1984—1,000 in each caliber.

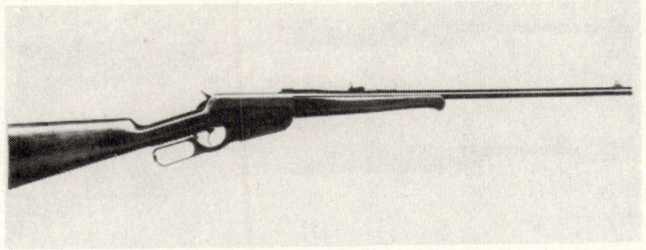

Exc.	V.G.	Good	Fair	Poor
1000	900	700	575	400

NOTE: For .30-40 caliber deduct 20 percent.

Express Rifle

This is an Over/Under, superposed rifle chambered for the .270 Winchester or the .30-06 cartridges. It has 24" barrels with folding express sights and automatic ejectors. It features a single trigger. The receiver is engraved and is finished in blue with a deluxe checkered walnut stock. It was discontinued in 1986.

Exc.	V.G.	Good	Fair	Poor
2200	1800	1500	1100	800

Continental Set

This consists of an Express Rifle chambered for the .30-06 cartridge and furnished with an extra set of 20 gauge, Over/Under barrels. The shotgun barrels are 26.5" in length. There is a single trigger, automatic ejectors, and a heavily engraved receiver. The select walnut stock is hand-checkered and oil-finished. It was furnished with a fitted case. There were 500 manufactured between 1978 and 1986.

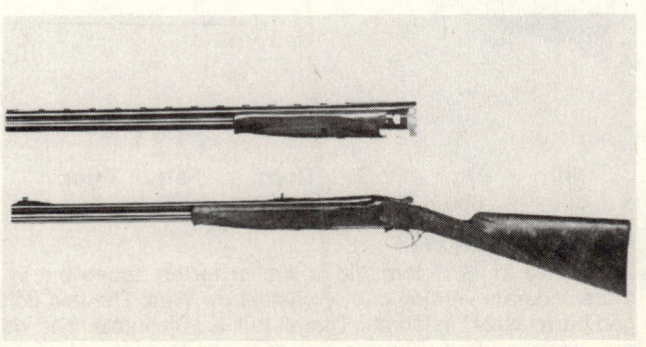

Exc.	V.G.	Good	Fair	Poor
3500	2750	2200	1750	1000

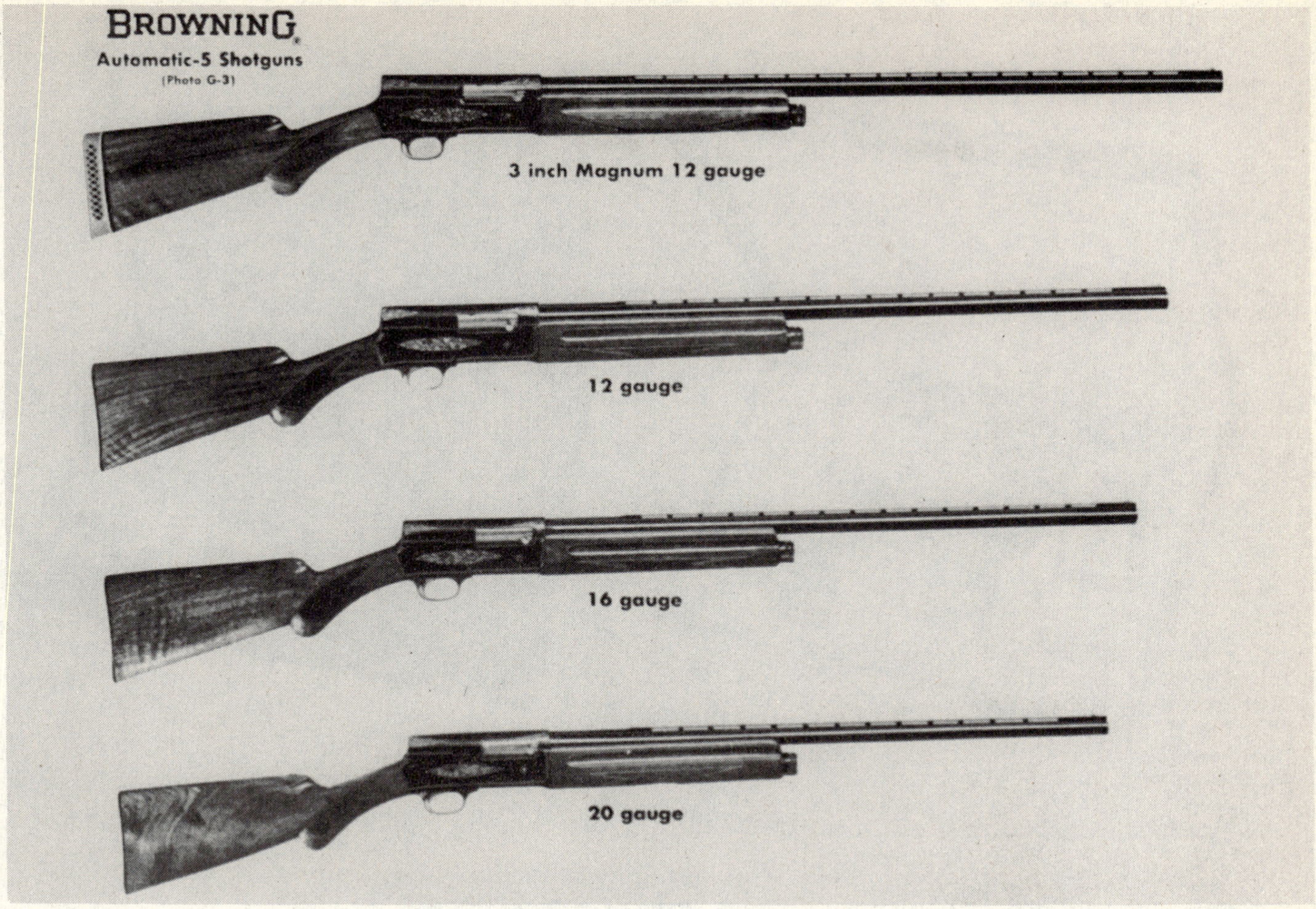

BROWNING.
Automatic-5 Shotguns
(Photo G-3)

3 inch Magnum 12 gauge

12 gauge

16 gauge

20 gauge

Challenger

Medalist

Nomad

BROWNING.
.22 Automatic Pistols
(Photo G-15)

BROWNING
Automatic Pistols
(Photo G-8)

Top 9mm

Center .380 caliber

Bottom .25 caliber

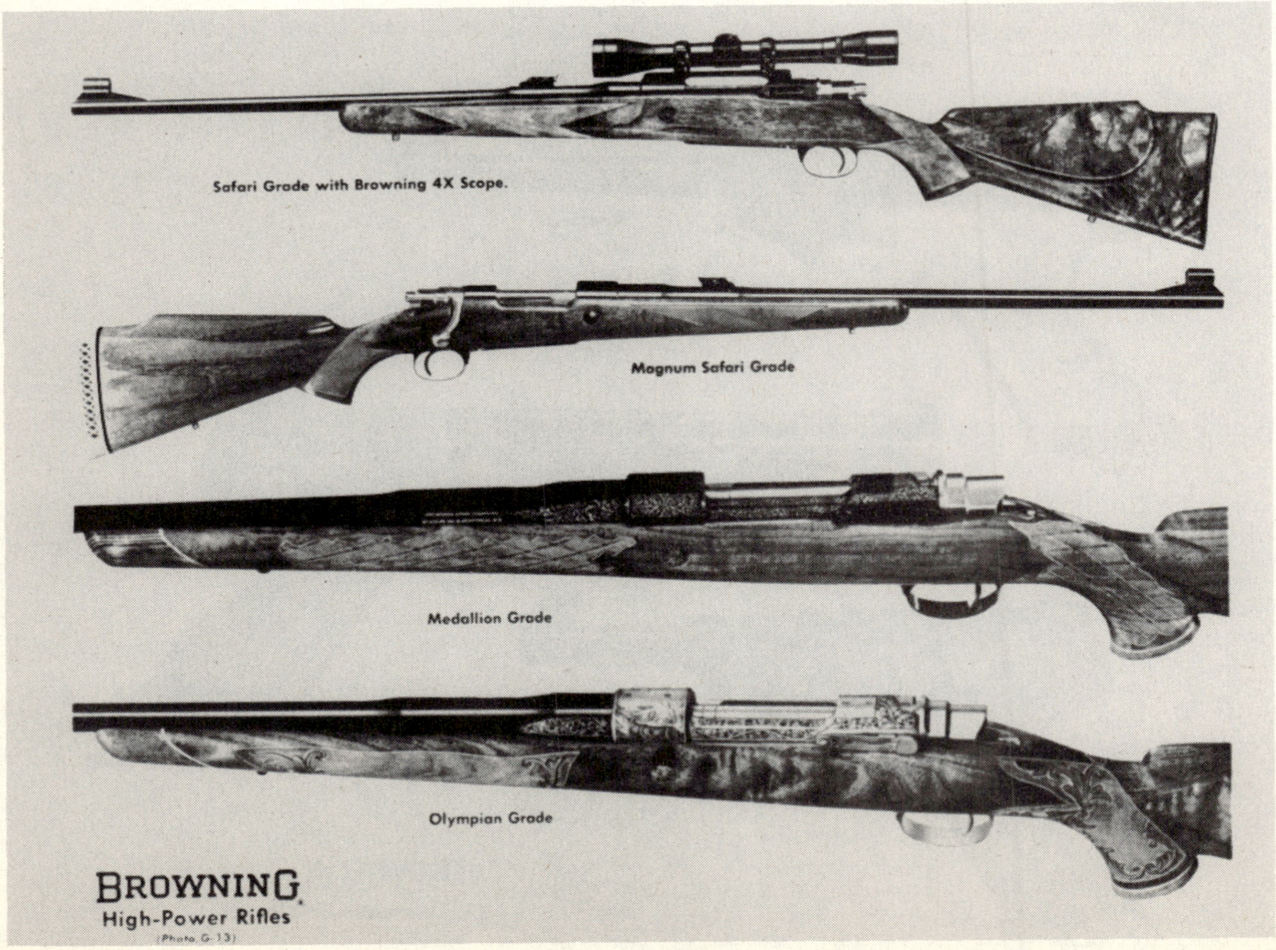

Safari Grade with Browning 4X Scope.

Magnum Safari Grade

Medallion Grade

Olympian Grade

BROWNING
High-Power Rifles
(Photo G-13)

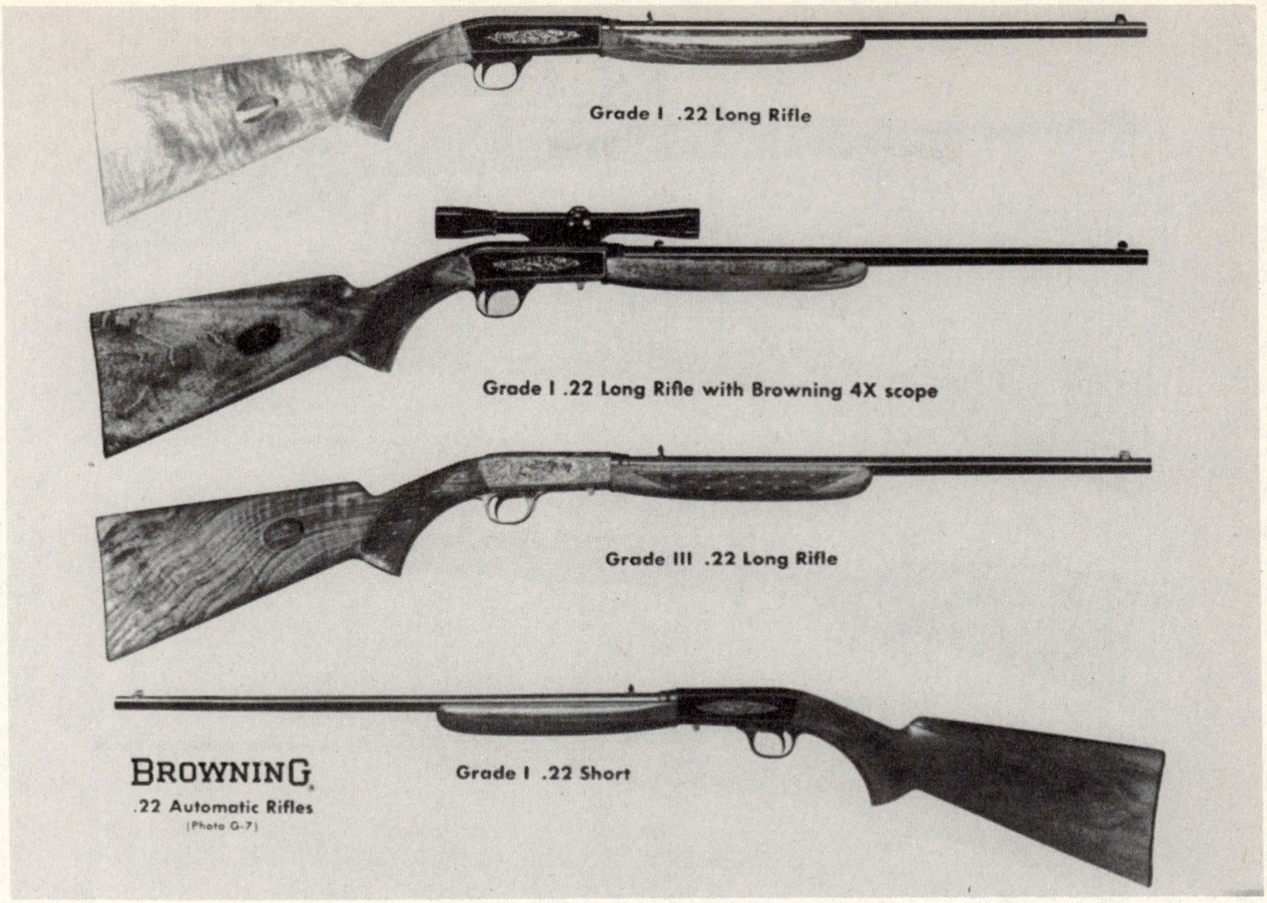

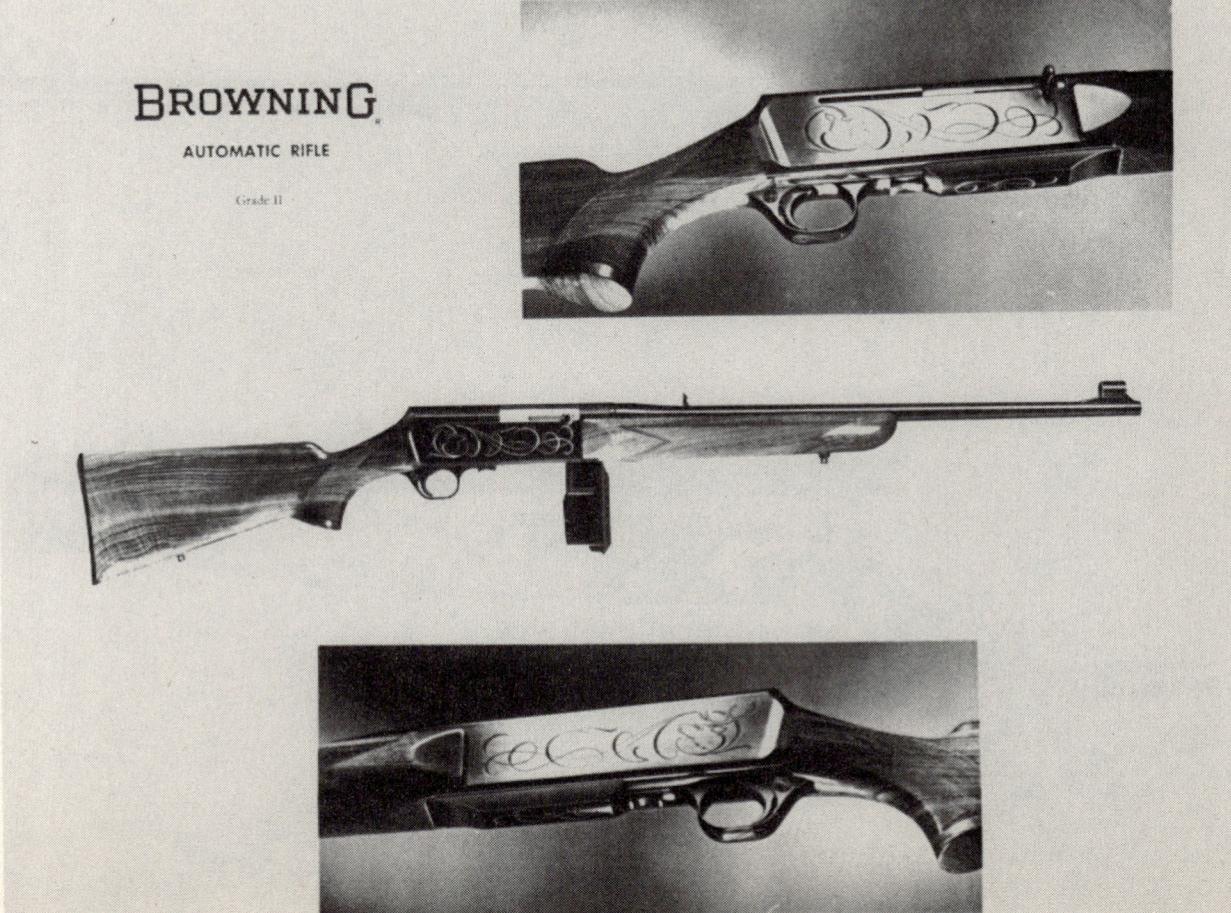

Grade I .22 Long Rifle

Grade I .22 Long Rifle with Browning 4X scope

Grade III .22 Long Rifle

BROWNING.
.22 Automatic Rifles
(Photo G-7)

Grade I .22 Short

BROWNING.

AUTOMATIC RIFLE

Grade II

BROWNING
High-Power Rifles
(Photo G-33)

Safari Grade Rifle and Browning 4X Scope. Calibers available: 270W, 30 06, .308W, .264W.

Safari Grade Rifle and Browning 3X - 9X Variable Scope. Calibers Available: 7mm Rem. Magnum, .300W Magnum, .300H&H Magnum, .308 Norma Magnum, .338W Magnum, .375H&H, .458W Magnum.

Safari Grade Rifle with Lightweight Sporter Barrel and 2X - 7X Variable Scope. Heavy target barrel optional. Calibers Available: .243W or .22 250 (Wildcat)

Safari Grade Rifle with Heavy Target Barrel and Browning 6X Scope. Lightweight Sporter barrel optional. Calibers Available: .222 Remington or .222 Remington Magnum.

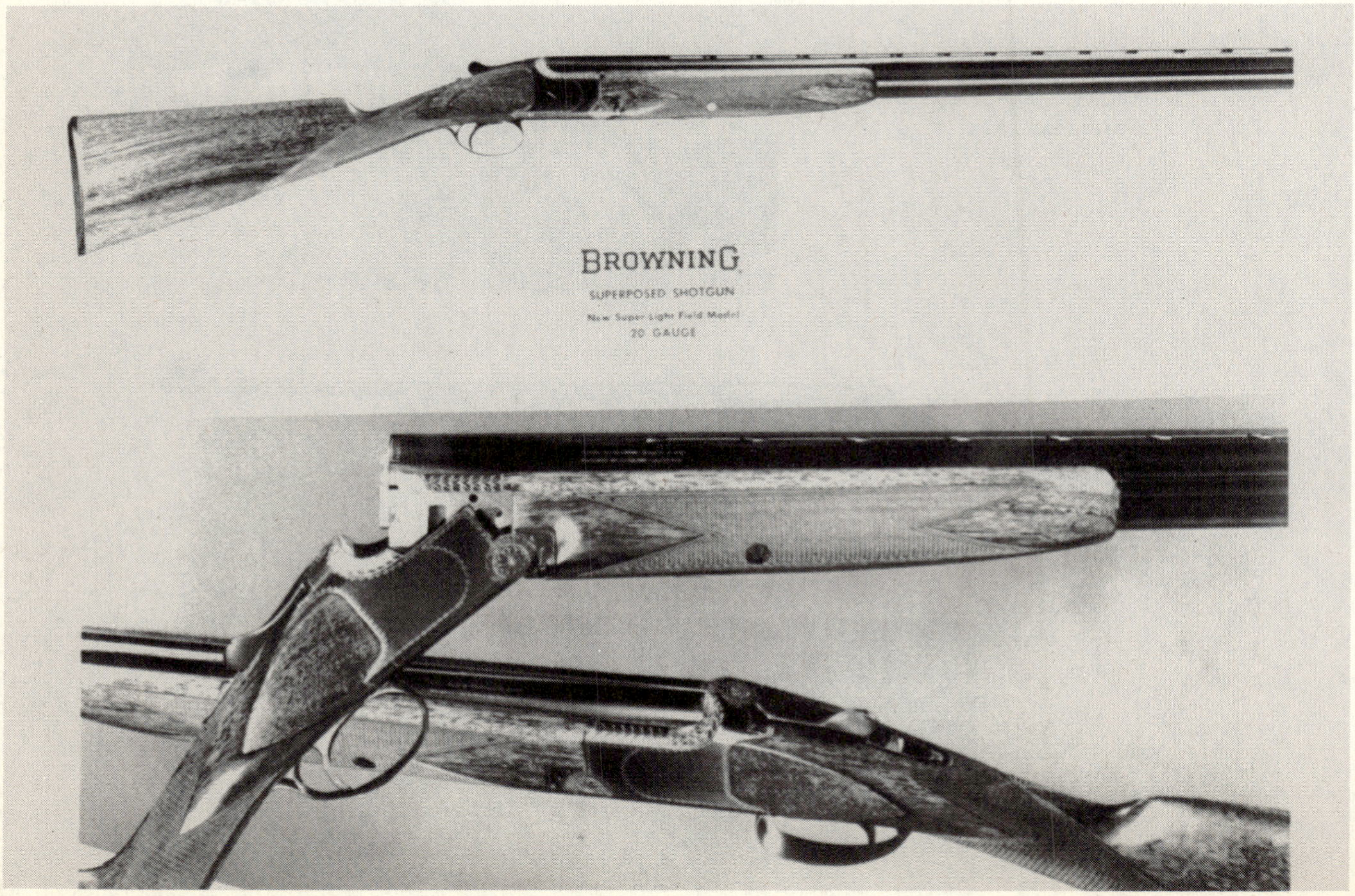

BROWNING
SUPERPOSED SHOTGUN
New Super-Light Field Model
20 GAUGE

BROWNING

T-BOLT .22 CALIBER BOLT ACTION RIFLE

An entirely new concept in bolt action design.

(Photo G-37)

T-1 with Browning 4X .22 Riflescope

T-2

BRUCE & DAVIS
Webster, Massachusetts

Double Barreled Pistol

A .36 caliber double-barrel percussion pistol with 3" to 6" round barrels. The barrel rib marked "Bruce & Davis". Blued with walnut grips. Manufactured during the 1840s.

Exc.	V.G.	Good	Fair	Poor
650	375	300	200	150

BRUCHET
Ste. Etienne, France

Model A Shotgun

A 12 or .410 bore sliding action shotgun with double triggers, and automatic ejectors. The barrel lengths and chokes are to customer specifications. Produced on a limited basis (50 per year) since 1982.

Base Price as Follows; Add 25 Percent Per Grade.

NIB	Exc.	V.G.	Good	Fair	Poor
2000	1750	1500	1250	1000	500

Model B

As above, with a finer finish and a spring assisted action opener. Imported since 1982.

NIB	Exc.	V.G.	Good	Fair	Poor
6250	5250	4000	3000	2250	1250

BRUFF, R.P.
New York, New York

Bruff Pocket Pistol

A .41 caliber single shot percussion pistol with 2.5" to 3" barrels The pistol is marked "R.P. Bruff NY" in an arch and "Cast Steel." German silver with a checkered walnut stock. Manufactured between 1861 and 1870.

Exc.	V.G.	Good	Fair	Poor
1500	1000	500	400	200

BUCO
Germany

Buco Gas Pistol

This odd firearm looks more like a telescope than a pistol. It is chambered for a 10.55mm gas cartridge and is a single shot. Overall it is approximately 5.5" long in its open or cocked position. The barrel is smooth bore and 3.75" in length. This pistol has no sights and no safety—one simply pulls the inner tube back much like extending a telescope, unscrews the end cap, inserts the round, and screws the cap back into place. When it is needed, a thumbnail is used to depress the sear and fire the pistol. They are marked on the end cap "Buco DRGM." No more information is available as to quantity or year of manufacture.

Exc.	V.G.	Good	Fair	Poor
300	250	200	150	100

BUDISCHOWSKY
Mt. Clemens, Michigan

TP-70

A .22 or .25 ACP caliber semi-automatic pistol with a 2.5" barrel, fixed sights and 6-shot magazine. Stainless steel with plastic grips. Manufactured between 1973 and 1977.

.22 Rimfire Caliber

NIB	Exc.	V.G.	Good	Fair	Poor
475	425	350	300	225	150

.25 ACP Caliber

NIB	Exc.	V.G.	Good	Fair	Poor
400	325	250	200	175	125

NOTE: After 1977, Norton Arms produced this pistol; values are approximately 40 percent less than those made by Budischowsky.

BUL TRANSMARK LTD.
Tel-Aviv, Israel
Importer-All American Sales, Memphis, Tennessee

Model M5

Introduced for the first time in the U.S. in 1996 this semi-automatic pistol bears a resemblance to the Model 1911. The frame is polymer and the slide is stainless steel. Available in 9mm, .38 Super, .40 S&W, and .45 ACP. Magazine limited to 10 rounds.

NIB	Exc.	Good	Good	Fair	Poor
750	—	—	—	—	—

BULLARD REPEATING ARMS CO.
Springfield, Massachusetts

Designed by James H. Bullard, the following rifles were manufactured in competition with those produced by the Whitney Arms Company and the Winchester Repeating Arms Company. Approximately 12,000 were made between 1886 and 1890.

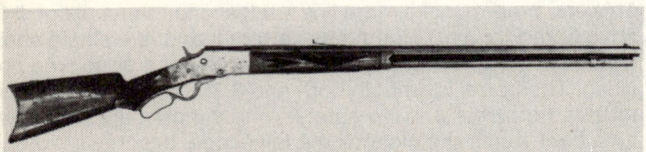

Courtesy Milwaukee Public Museum, Milwaukee, Wisconsin

Small Frame

A .32-40 and .38-45 caliber lever-action rifle with a 26" octagonal barrel and either a half- or full-length magazine tube. Blued or casehardened with a walnut stock. The receiver is stamped "Bullard Repeating Arms Company/Springfield,

Mass., U.S.A. Pat. Aug. 16, 1881." The caliber is marked on top of the frame.

Exc.	V.G.	Good	Fair	Poor
4000	2500	1200	600	375

Large Frame

A .40-75 through .45-85 caliber lever-action rifle with 28" octagonal barrel. Other features and markings as above. Can be custom ordered in .50-95 and .50-115.

Exc.	V.G.	Good	Fair	Poor
6000	3000	1500	800	450

Carbine

A .45-70 caliber lever-action rifle with a 22" round barrel and a sliding dust cover on the receiver. Marking and finish as above.

Exc.	V.G.	Good	Fair	Poor
8500	5000	2750	2000	1000

Musket

A .45-70 caliber lever-action rifle with a 30" round barrel with a full-length stock secured by two barrel bands. There is a rod under the barrel, military sights, and the same sliding cover on the receiver as found on the Carbine. There have been examples noted without the manufacturer's markings.

Exc.	V.G.	Good	Fair	Poor
8000	4500	2750	2000	1000

BULLDOG SINGLE SHOT PISTOL
Connecticut Arms & Manufacturing Co.
Naubuc, Connecticut

Bulldog

A .44 or .50 caliber single shot spur trigger pistol with 4" or 6" barrels, and a pivoting breechblock that moves to the left for loading. Blued, casehardened and stamped "Connecticut Arms & Manf. Co. Naubuc Conn. Patented Oct. 25, 1864." There were only a few hundred manufactured, and the .50 caliber, 6" barrelled versions would be worth an additional 40 percent. Produced between 1866 and 1868.

Exc.	V.G.	Good	Fair	Poor
900	500	400	250	150

BURGESS GUN CO.
Buffalo, New York
ALSO SEE-Colt and Whitney

One of the most prolific 19th century designers was Andrew Burgess who established his own company in 1892. The Burgess Gun Company manufactured slide action shotguns and rifles operated by a unique pistol grip prior to their being purchased by the Winchester Repeating Arms Company in 1899. Arms based on Burgess' patents were manufactured by a variety of American gunmakers. Serial numbers for all Burgess shotguns begin at 1000.

12 Gauge Slide Action Shotgun

A 12 gauge slide action shotgun with a 28" or 30" barrel. Blued with a walnut stock. This model was available with 6 grades of engraving. The values listed below are for the standard, plain model.

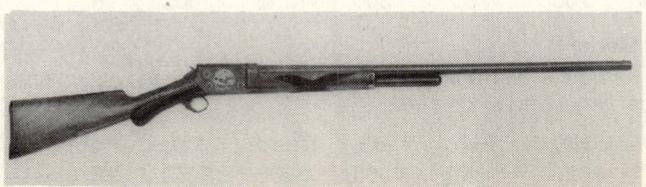

Burgess engraving grades (I -4)

Exc.	V.G.	Good	Fair	Poor
2000	1250	750	250	175

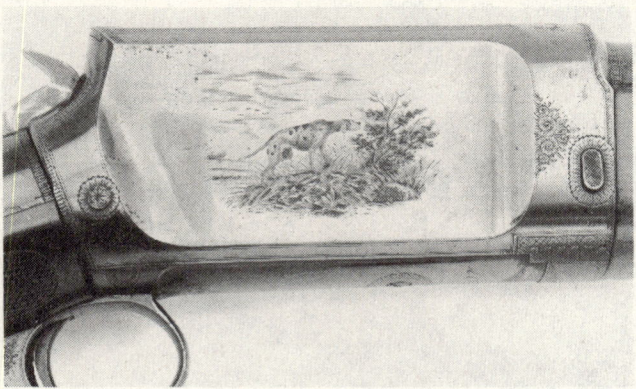

Folding Shotgun

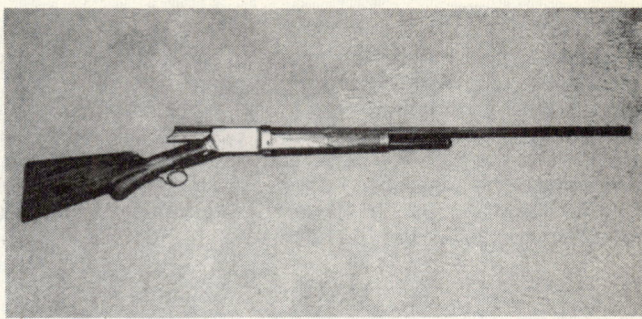

As above, with a 19.5" barrel that is hinged so that it may be folded back against the buttstock.

Exc.	V.G.	Good	Fair	Poor
4000	2500	1250	500	300

Slide Action Rifle

An extremely rare rifle based upon the shotgun design described above. Manufactured in at least three calibers with varying barrel lengths. Blued with a walnut stock.

Exc.	V.G.	Good	Fair	Poor
4000	2500	1250	500	300

BURGSMULLER, K.
Krelensen, Germany

Burgo

The Rohm RGI0 under another name. It is a poor quality, inexpensive, .38 caliber revolver. The examples marketed by Burgsmuller are so marked.

Exc.	V.G.	Good	Fair	Poor
125	100	75	50	25

Regent

The Regent is a .22 caliber revolver that resembles the Colt Police Positive in appearance. It is of a higher quality than the Burgo. The manufacturer is not known.

Exc.	V.G.	Good	Fair	Poor
150	125	100	75	50

BURNSIDE RIFLE CO.
Providence, Rhode Island
Bristol Firearms Co.

Bristol, Rhode Island

This is an historically desirable firearm for Civil War collectors as the designer, Ambrose E. Burnside, was to become a well known Union general. The rifle, of which there were four distinct models, was used quite extensively in the Civil War.

This carbine was manufactured first by the Bristol Firearms Co., which made the entire production of the first model and also some of the second model. In 1862 the Burnside Firearms Co. was formed, and they produced the remainder of the second models and all of the third and fourth models. Production ceased entirely in 1865.

Burnside Carbine 1st Model

This model was produced by Bristol and was chambered for the .54 caliber. It is a breech-loader that uses the percussion ignition system but features a cartridge of sorts made of copper, and a tape priming device that was located inside the frame. It has a 22" round barrel with no forend and a walnut stock with inspector's cartouche. The finish is blued and case-colored, and the frame is stamped "Burnside's /Patent/March 25th/1856." There were approximately 250 1st Models manufactured.

Exc.	V.G.	Good	Fair	Poor
—	—	8000	3500	1200

2nd Model

The 2nd Model features an improved breechblock opening mechanism located inside the triggerguard. The barrel is 21" long, and the other features are similar to the 1st Model. They are marked either "Bristol Firearm Co." or "Burnside Rifle Co./Providence-R.I." The barrel is marked "Cast Steel 1861," and some of the breechblock devices are marked "G.P. Foster Pat./April 10th 1860." There were approximately 1,500 2nd Models manufactured in 1861 and 1862.

Courtesy Milwaukee Public Museum, Milwaukee, Wisconsin

Exc.	V.G.	Good	Fair	Poor
—	—	3500	1500	750

3rd Model

This model differs from the 2nd Model in that it has a forend with a barrel band and a slightly modified hammer. The markings are the same as the Burnside-manufactured 2nd Models. There were approximately 2,000 produced in 1862.

Exc.	V.G.	Good	Fair	Poor
—	—	2500	900	450

4th Model

This model differs from the others in that it features a hinged breech that permits simpler loading of the odd-shaped Burnside percussion cartridge. The frame is marked "Burnside's Patent/Model of 1864." The other features are similar to the 3rd Model. There were approximately 50,000 manufactured between 1862 and 1865.

Courtesy Milwaukee Public Museum, Milwaukee, Wisconsin

Exc.	V.G.	Good	Fair	Poor
—	3500	2000	800	400

BUSHMASTER FIREARMS INC.
Windham, Maine

As of 1996 the company had a limited supply of pre-ban rifles similar to those listed below but fitted with flash suppressor, bayonet lug, and telescoping stocks. These pre-ban guns have a retail price of $1,000. This price may be higher or lower depending on your area and the current mood surrounding "assualt weapons".

Bushmaster XM15-E2S Shorty Carbine

This is a "post-ban" model of the M16 gas operated semiautomatic rifle chambered for the .223 Remington cartridge. It is fitted with a heavy 16" barrel and a 30 round magazine (while supplies last). Overall length is 35" and empty weight is 6.72 lbs.

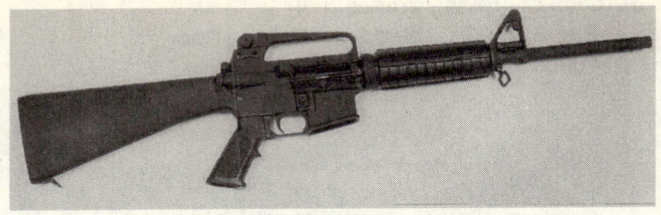

NIB	Exc.	Good	Good	Fair	Poor
730	600	500	400	300	200

NOTE: Add $50 for fluted barrel.

Bushmaster XM15-E2S Dissipator

Similar to the above model with a 16" barrel but fitted with a longer plastic handguard to give a longer sight radius. Weight is 7.2 lbs.

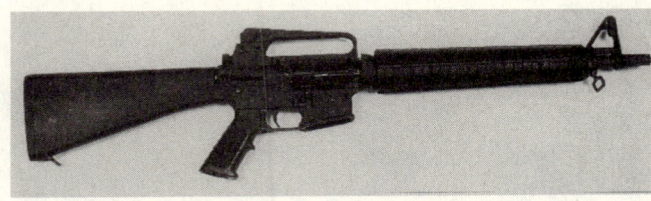

NIB	Exc.	Good	Good	Fair	Poor
740	600	500	400	300	200

Bushmaster XM15-E2S Target Model

Furnished with a 20" heavy barrel and A-2 stock. Weight is 8.35 lbs.

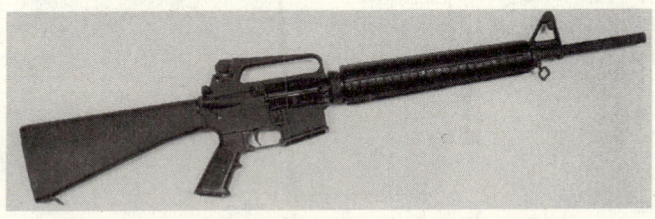

NIB	Exc.	Good	Good	Fair	Poor
740	600	500	400	300	200

NOTE: Add $10 for 24" barrel and $20 for 26" barrel.

Bushmaster XM15-E2S V-Match Competion

This model is a specially designed competiion rifle with 20", 24", or 26" barrel lengths. Fitted with a black anodized aluminum handguard. Weight is about 8.1 lbs.

NIB	Exc.	Good	Good	Fair	Poor
795	675	550	425	325	225

Bushmaster M17S Bullpup

This model is a gas operated semiautomatic rifle in the bull pup design. Chambered for the .223 cartridge and fitted with a 21.5" barrel. Weight is 8.2 lbs.

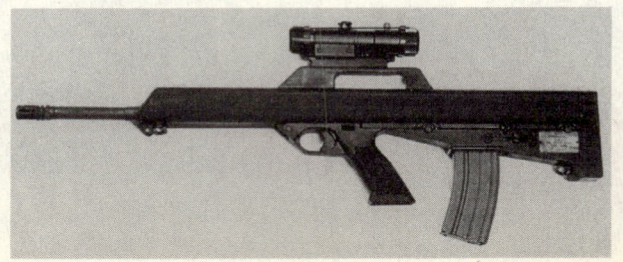

NIB	Exc.	Good	Good	Fair	Poor
575	475	375	275	175	100

BUTLER, WM. S.
Rocky Hill, Connecticut

Butler Single Shot Pistol

A .36 caliber single shot percussion pocket pistol with a 2.5" barrel and the frame and grip made in one piece. The frame marked "Wm. S. Butler's Patent/Patented Feb.3, 1857."

Exc.	V.G.	Good	Fair	Poor
425	350	250	200	150

BUTTERFIELD, JESSE
Philadelphia, Pennsylvania

Butterfield Army Revolver

A .41 caliber revolver with a 7" octagonal barrel, an unfluted 5-shot cylinder and features a special priming device, a disk that was loaded in front of the triggerguard. A brass frame, blued with walnut grips. The frame is stamped "Butterfield's Patent Dec. 11, 1855/Phila." Approximately 650 manufactured in 1861 and 1862.

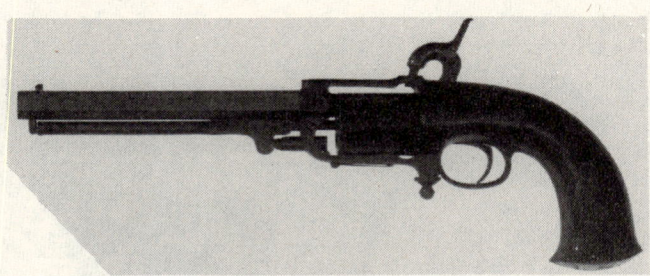

Courtesy Milwaukee Public Museum, Milwaukee, Wisconsin

Exc.	V.G.	Good	Fair	Poor
—	—	4500	1750	750

Butterfield Pocket Pistol

A .41 caliber single-shot percussion pistol with a 2" to 3.5" barrel. German silver with walnut stocks. The lock is marked "Butterfield's/Patent Dec 11, 1855." Extremely rare. Manufactured in the 1850s.

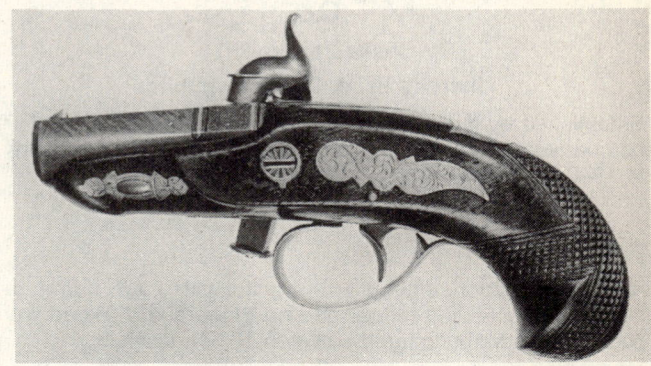

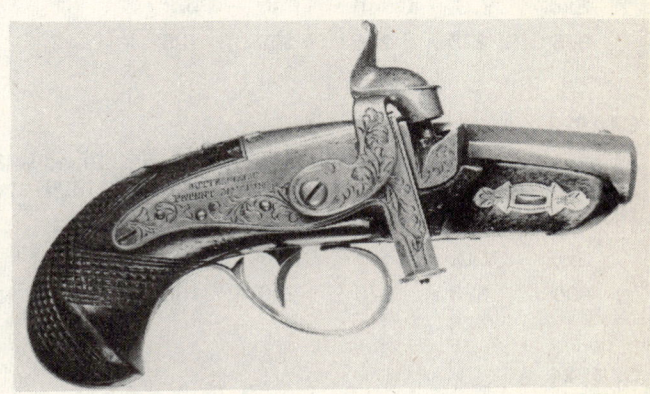

Exc.	V.G.	Good	Fair	Poor
—	—	6000	3500	1500

CZ
(Ceska Zbrojovka)
Uhersky Brod, Czech Republic

Established by Karel Bubla and Alois Tomiska in 1919. This company later merged with Hubertus Engineering Company. In 1949 the company was nationalized.

Fox

A 6.35mm caliber semi-automatic pistol with a 2.5" barrel, tubular slide, a folding trigger and no triggerguard. Blued with plastic grips. Manufactured between 1919 and 1926.

Exc.	V.G.	Good	Fair	Poor
375	275	225	150	125

CZ 1922

As above with a conventional trigger and guard. Blued with checkered plastic grips. Manufactured between 1926 and 1936.

Exc.	V.G.	Good	Fair	Poor
400	325	275	200	150

CZ 1924

The first military pistol produced by CZ. It is a locked-breech pistol with a 3.5" rotating barrel chambered for the 9mm short cartridge, external hammer and a magazine safety. It features a rounded slide and is blued with a wrap-around walnut grip. The slide is marked, "Ceska Zbrojovka A.S. v Praze."

Exc.	V.G.	Good	Fair	Poor
475	375	300	200	100

A limited number of pistols have been noted marked, "CZ 1925" and "CZ 1926." There are various minor design changes on each model, and it is conjectured that they were prototypes that were manufactured on the road to the production of the less complicated, blowback-operated CZ 1927 pistol.

CZ 1927

A semiautomatic pistol chambered for the 7.65mm cartridge, marked the same as the CZ 1924, but the cocking grooves on the slide are cut vertically instead of sloped as on the earlier model. This model was blued with checkered, wrap-around, plastic grips. These early guns were beautifully made and marked, "Ceska Zbrojovka AS v Praze." This version remained in production during the German occupation of Czechoslovakia between 1939 and 1945. Occupation pistols are marked, "Bohmische Waffenfabrik im Prag." The Germans used the code "fnh" on these wartime pistols. The finish declined as the war progressed, with the very late guns rough but functional. After the war, these pistols continued in production until 1951. There were over 500,000 manufactured.

Nazi-Proofed-Add 50%.

Courtesy Orvel Reichert

Courtesy Orvel Reichert-Commercial markings

Exc.	V.G.	Good	Fair	Poor
400	325	250	175	150

NOTE: Some of these pistols were made with an extended barrel for the use of a silencer. This variation brings a large premium. Less than 10 CZ27s were made in .22 caliber. An expert opinion is suggested if a sale is contemplated.

CZ 1936

A 6.35mm caliber semiautomatic pistol with 2.5" barrel, and double-action-only lockwork. Discontinued in 1940 because of wartime production.

Exc.	V.G.	Good	Fair	Poor
350	250	200	125	100

CZ 1938

This odd pistol has been rated as one of the worst military service pistols ever manufactured. It is chambered for the 9mm short cartridge and has a 4.65" barrel. Except for a few examples with a conventional sear and slide safety it is double-action-only with exposed hammer, and difficult to fire accurately. It utilizes an 8-round, detachable box magazine; and the slide is hinged at the muzzle to pivot upward for ease of cleaning and disassembly. It is well made and well finished but is as large in size as most 9mm Parabellum pistols. Production began in 1938, and the Germans adopted it as the "Pistole Mod 39" on paper; but it is doubtful that any were actually used by the German army. It now appears that the P39(t), which is the Nazi designation, were all sent to Finland and a large number with "SA" (Finnish) markings have recently been surplused along with their holsters. A few SA marked guns have been modified by the Finnish Army to function single or double action.

Exc.	V.G.	Good	Fair	Poor
450	400	350	250	175

CZ 45

This model is a small .25 caliber (6.35mm) pocket pistol that is double action only. It was produced and sold after World War II. It is a modified version of the CZ 1936. Approximately 60,000 were built between 1945 and 1949.

Exc.	V.G.	Good	Fair	Poor
350	300	250	175	125

CZ 1950

This is a blowback-operated, semiautomatic, double action pistol chambered for the 7.65mm cartridge. It is patterned after the Walther Model PP with a few differences. The safety catch is located on the frame instead of the slide; and the trigger guard is not hinged, as on the Walther. It is dismantled by means of a catch on the side of the frame. Although intended to be a military pistol designed by the Kratochvil brothers, it proved to be underpowered and was adopted by the police. There were few released on the commercial market.

Exc.	V.G.	Good	Fair	Poor
400	300	250	200	125

Model 1970

This model was an attempt to correct dependability problems with the Model 50. There is little difference to see externally between the two except for markings and the grip pattern. Production began during the 1960s and ended in 1983.

Exc.	V.G.	Good	Fair	Poor
450	350	300	225	175

CZ 1952 currently imported by CIA

Since the Czechoslovakian army was not happy with the underpowered CZ 1950 pistol, they began using Soviet weapons until 1952, when this model was designed. It was designed for a new cartridge known as the 7.62mm M48. It was similar to the Soviet cartridge but loaded to a higher velocity. This is a single-action, semiautomatic pistol with a 4.5" barrel. It has a locked breech that utilizes two roller cams. This was an excellent pistol that has been replaced by the Soviet Makarov, a pistol that is decidedly inferior to it.

Exc.	V.G.	Good	Fair	Poor
150	125	100	75	65

CZ USA

CURRENTLY IMPORTED CZ PISTOLS
CZ-USA
Oakhurst, California

CZ 75

Designed by the Koucky brothers in 1975, this model bears little resemblance to previous CZ pistols. Considered by many to be the best pistol ever to come from the Czech Republic. Chambered for the 9mm Parabellum cartridge it is copied in many countries. This pistol has a breech lock system utilizing a Browning style cam. The slide rides on the inside of the slide rails. Magazine capacity is 15 rounds, barrel length is 4.72", overall length is 8", and the empty pistol weighs 34.5 oz. Offered in black paint, matte or polished blue finish.

NIB	Exc.	V.G.	Good	Fair	Poor
600	500	425	400	325	250

CZ 75 B

Introduced in 1994 this CZ model is an updated version of the original CZ 75. It features a pinned front sight, a commander hammer, non-glare ribbed barrel, and a squared triggerguard. Also offered in 40 S&W chamber.

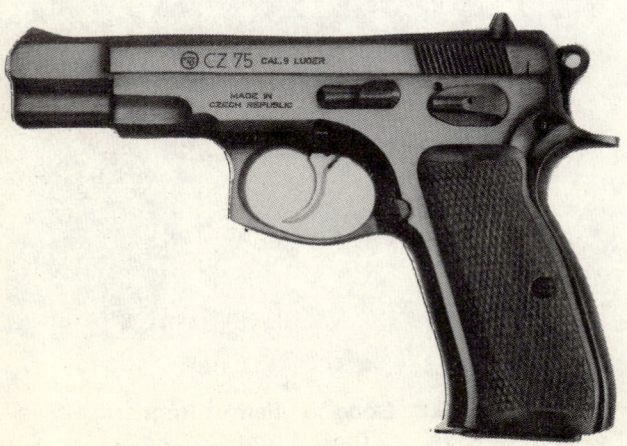

NIB	EXC.	V.G	Good	Fair	Poor
450	350	300	250	175	125

NOTE: For 40 S&W add $30.

CZ 75 Compact

Introduced in 1992 this is a compact version of the CZ 75. The barrel length is 3.9", the overall length is 7.3", and the weight is about 32 oz. Offered in black paint, matte or polished blue finish.

NIB	Exc.	V.G.	Good	Fair	Poor
450	350	300	250	175	125

CZ 75 Semi-Compact

This model was introduced in 1994 and has the same barrel length as the Compact (3.9") but has the same full size grip as the CZ 75. Magazine capacity is 15 rounds of 9mm. Overall length is 7.3".

NIB	Exc.	V.G.	Good	Fair	Poor
450	350	300	250	175	125

CZ 85

This model is similar in appearance to the CZ 75 but offers some new features such as ambidextrous safety and slide stop levers, squared trigger guard, adjustable sight, and ribbed slide. Caliber, magazine capacity, and weight are same as CZ 75.

NIB	Exc.	V.G.	Good	Fair	Poor
450	350	300	250	175	125

CZ 85-Combat

Similar to the CZ 85 but with the addition of adjustable sights, walnut grips, round hammer, and free dropping magazine.

NIB	Exc.	V.G.	Good	Fair	Poor
450	350	300	250	175	125

CZ 75 Kadet

This is a separate conversion kit for the CZ 75/85 series. It converts these pistols to .22 Long Rifle. Adjustable rear sight. supplied with 10-round magazine.

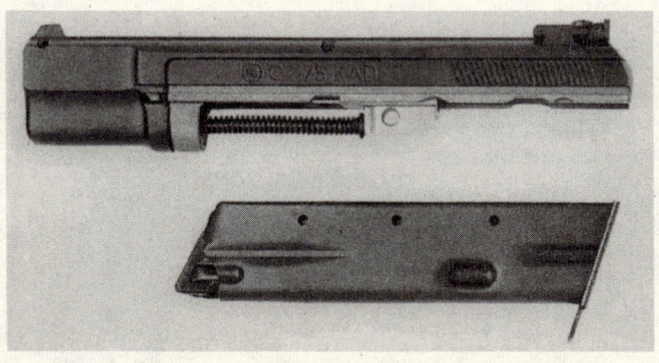

NIB	Exc.	V.G.	Good	Fair	Poor
N/A	—	—	—	—	—

CZ 83

This is a fixed barrel .380 caliber pistol. It features an ambidextrous safety and magazine catch behind the triggerguard. The pistol is stripped by means of a hinged trigger guard. Barrel length is 3.8", overall length is 6.8", and weight is about 23 oz.

NIB	Exc.	V.G.	Good	Fair	Poor
350	300	275	225	150	125

NOTE: In 1993 Special Editions of the above pistols were introduced. These Special Editions consist of special finishes for currently imported CZ pistols. There are high polish blue, nickel, chrome, gold, and a combination of the above finishes. These Special Edition finishes may affect price and the buyer and seller should be aware of the initial extra cost that added between $100 and $250 to the cost of the pistol when new.

CZ 97B

This pistol was planned for production in the summer of 1997. It is chambered for the .45 ACP cartridge. It is fitted with a 4.8" barrel and has a single action double action mode. Magazine capacity is 10 rounds. Wood grips with blue finish. Weight is approximately 40 oz.

NIB	Exc.	V.G.	Good	Fair	Poor
N/A	—	—	—	—	—

CZ 100

This is a semi-automatic pistol, introduced in 1996, chambered for the 9mm or .40 S&W cartridge. It has a plastic frame and steel slide. Barrel length is 3.75". Weight is approximately 24 oz. US magazine capacity is 10 rounds.

NIB	Exc.	V.G.	Good	Fair	Poor
425	375	300	225	175	100

CABANAS, INDUSTRIAS S.A.
Aguilas, Mexico

This company manufactures a variety of bolt-action single shot rifles that utilize .22 caliber blanks to propel a .177 caliber pellet.

Mini-82 Youth

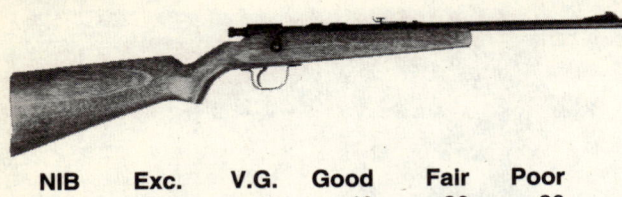

NIB	Exc.	V.G.	Good	Fair	Poor
75	65	50	40	30	20

R-83 Larger Youth

NIB	Exc.	V.G.	Good	Fair	Poor
85	75	60	50	40	30

Safari A

NIB	Exc.	V.G.	Good	Fair	Poor
100	90	75	50	40	30

Varmint

NIB	Exc.	V.G.	Good	Fair	Poor
125	110	90	75	50	35

Espronceda IV

NIB	Exc.	V.G.	Good	Fair	Poor
125	110	90	75	50	35

Leyre

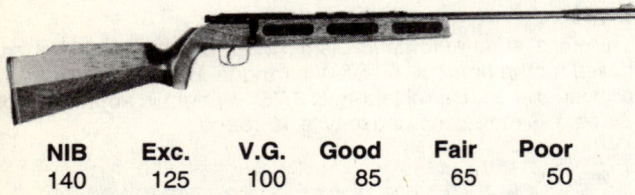

NIB	Exc.	V.G.	Good	Fair	Poor
140	125	100	85	65	50

Master

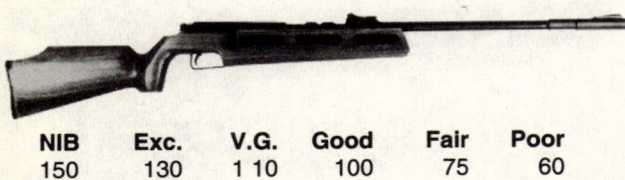

NIB	Exc.	V.G.	Good	Fair	Poor
150	130	1 10	100	75	60

CABELAS, INC.
Sidney, Nebraska

AYA Grade II Custom

A 12, 16, and 20 gauge boxlock shotgun in various barrel lengths and chokes, a single selective trigger, and automatic ejectors. Engraved with a hand-checkered walnut stock. This model is no longer available.

Exc.	V.G.	Good	Fair	Poor
1250	1175	950	700	575

Hemingway Model

A 12 or 20 gauge boxlock shotgun with 28" barrels, various chokes, a single selective trigger and automatic ejectors. Engraved with a hand-checkered walnut stock.

NIB	Exc.	V.G.	Good	Fair	Poor
975	900	750	600	525	450

CALICO
SEE-American Industries, Inc.
Cleveland, Ohio

CAMEX-BLASER USA, INC.
SEE-Blaser Jagwaffen
Ft. Worth, Texas

CAMPO GIRO
Eibar, Spain

Esperanza y Unceta Model 1904

Designed by Lt. Col. Venancio Aguirre. This pistol was produced in limited numbers. Prospective purchasers are advised to secure a qualified appraisal prior to acquisition.

Exc.	V.G.	Good	Fair	Poor
1500	1000	800	600	450

Model 1910

Similar to the above, in 9mm Largo. Tested, but not adopted, by the Spanish army.

Exc.	V.G.	Good	Fair	Poor
1200	800	650	500	450

Model 1913

An improved version of the above.

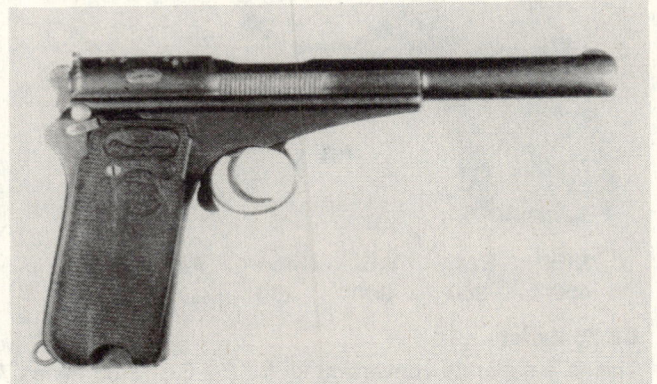

Courtesy James Rankin

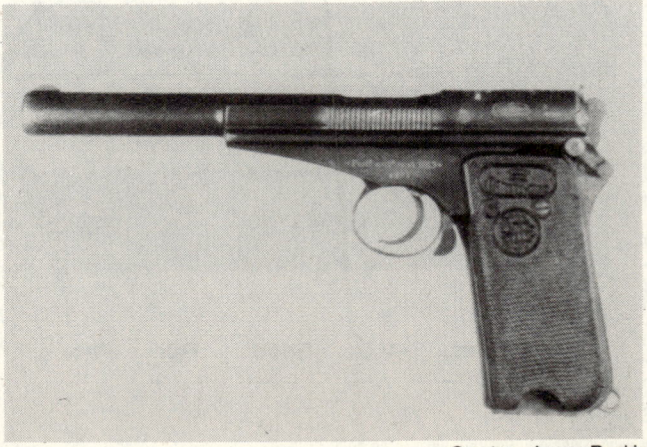

Courtesy James Rankin

Exc.	V.G.	Good	Fair	Poor
950	750	650	500	450

Model 1913/16
An improved version of the above.

Courtesy James Rankin

Courtesy James Rankin

Exc.	V.G.	Good	Fair	Poor
550	450	375	300	200

CARCANO
Turin, Italy
Designed by Salvator Carcano, the Model 1891 was adopted as Italy's standard service rifle in 1892.

Fucile Modello 91
A 6.5mm caliber bolt-action rifle with a 31" barrel, 6-shot magazine, full-length stock, split bridge receiver, and a tangent rear sight with a wooden handguard and barrel bands retaining the stock.

M91 Carbine with Grenade Launcher-courtesy Richard M. Kumor, Sr.

Exc.	V.G.	Good	Fair	Poor
125	100	75	40	20

Cavalry Carbine
As above, with a shorter-barrel, half-stock and a folding bayonet.

Exc.	V.G.	Good	Fair	Poor
100	80	65	40	20

Fucile Modello 38
A 7.35 caliber bolt-action rifle.

Exc.	V.G.	Good	Fair	Poor
100	80	65	40	20

Cavalry Carbine
As above, with a shorter barrel, a folding bayonet and a fixed rear sight.

Exc.	V.G.	Good	Fair	Poor
150	125	90	60	40

Italian Youth Rifle
Smaller version of full size military and chambered for 6.5mm cartridge. Barrel length is 14.4". Add $75 for dedication plaque.

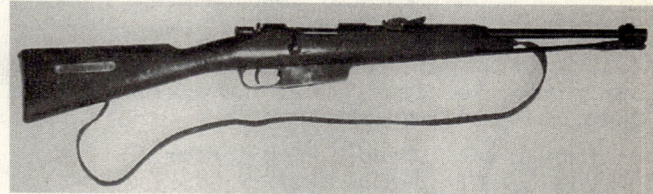

Courtesy Richard M. Kumor, Sr.

Exc.	V.G.	Good	Fair	Poor
450	375	250	150	75

CARD, S. W.
Unknown

Under Hammer Pistol
A .34 caliber single shot percussion pocket pistol with a 7.75" half octagonal barrel marked "S.W. Card" and "Cast Steel". Blued with walnut grips.

Exc.	V.G.	Good	Fair	Poor
700	325	275	200	125

CARLTON, M.
Haverhill, New Hampshire

Under Hammer Pistol
A .34 caliber percussion under hammer single shot pistol with a 3.5" to 7.75" half-octagonal barrel marked "M. Carleton & Co." Browned with walnut grips. Active 1830s and 1840s.

Exc.	V.G.	Good	Fair	Poor
800	425	350	250	175

CASARTELLI, CARLO
Brescia, Italy
Importer-New England Arms Co.
Kittery Point, Maine

Sidelock Shotgun
Custom order sidelock shotgun that is available in any gauge, barrel length, choke, automatic ejectors and single selective trigger and choice of engraving style.

NIB	Exc.	V.G.	Good	Fair	Poor
15000	13500	10000	8250	6000	4000

Kenya Double Rifle
Custom order, full sidelock rifle that is available in all standard and magnum calibers. The customer may literally design this firearm if one desires and if one can afford it.

NIB	Exc.	V.G.	Good	Fair	Poor
30000	27000	22500	18000	13000	9000

Africa Model

A bolt-action rifle built on a square-bridge magnum Mauser action. It is chambered for the heavy magnum calibers and can be taken down for transport. The other features are on a custom order basis.

NIB	Exc.	V.G.	Good	Fair	Poor
8750	8000	7000	5750	4750	3750

Safari Model

Built on a standard Mauser bolt-action and is chambered for the non-magnum calibers.

NIB	Exc.	V.G.	Good	Fair	Poor
7000	6500	5500	4500	3250	2500

CASE WILLARD & CO.
New Hartford, Connecticut

Under Hammer Pistol

A .31 caliber single shot percussion pistol with a 3" half-octagonal barrel marked "Case Willard & Co./New Hartford Conn." Blued, brass frame with walnut grips.

Exc.	V.G.	Good	Fair	Poor
750	375	300	225	150

CASPIAN ARMS, LTD.
Hardwick, Vermont

Government Model

Similar to the Colt 1911, a .45 ACP caliber semiautomatic pistol with interchangeable slides for 9mm and .38 Super available. This model features high profile sights, an adjustable trigger, carbon steel or stainless steel and walnut grips. Manufactured since 1986.

NIB	Exc.	V.G	Good	Fair	Poor
550	475	425	375	300	225

Model 110

A fully customized version of the Colt 1911, .45 ACP or .38 Super caliber semi-automatic pistol with all the custom features one could cram on the Government Model. Manufactured since 1988.

NIB	Exc.	V.G.	Good	Fair	Poor
900	825	700	600	475	300

Viet Nam Commemorative

Government Model engraved by J.J. Adams and nickel-plated. The walnut grips have a branch service medallion inlaid, and gold plating was available for an additional $350. There were 1,000 manufactured in 1986.

NIB	Exc.	V.G.	Good	Fair	Poor
1200	1000	800	600	475	300

CENTURY GUN CO.
Greenfield, Indiana

This was formerly a handmade revolver produced in Evansville, Indiana, and chambered for the .45-70 cartridge. This model was discontinued after only 524 were manufactured. They are now back in production as of 1986. The original guns are valued separately from the new production version.

Model 100 Revolver

A .30-30, .375 Winchester, .444 Marlin, .45-70, and .50-70 caliber revolver with barrel lengths from 6.5" to 15", 6-shot steel cylinder and a manganese bronze alloyed frame, a crossbolt safety, adjustable sights, and walnut grips. A limited-production item, with only 600 produced since 1976. The .45-70 is considered the standard caliber, and all other calibers are custom-order only.

.45-70 Caliber

NIB	Exc.	V.G.	Good	Fair	Poor
750	700	600	500	400	325

All Other Calibers

NIB	Exc.	V.G.	Good	Fair	Poor
1600	1400	1200	1000	800	600

Original Evansville Model 100

NIB	Exc.	V.G.	Good	Fair	Poor
2500	2250	2000	1600	1250	950

CENTURY INTERNATIONAL ARMS CO.
St. Albans, Vermont

Century International Arms is a leading importer of military firearms primarily of foreign manufacture. These low-cost firearms are excellent shooters and many have been restocked to make satisfactory hunting rifles. The listing below offers a representative sample of imports from Century. The company is always providing new surplus firearms that may not appear in this edition.

Centurion Shotgun

This is a new Over/Under shotgun in 12 gauge with 2-3/4" chambers. The walnut stock is checkered. The receiver is blue. Offered in 26" or 28" vent rib barrels in full and modified chokes. Weight is about 7 lbs.

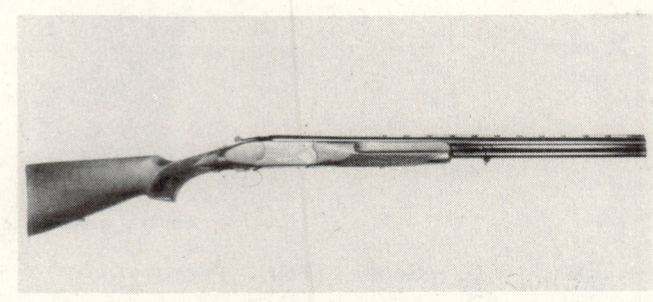

Exc.	V.G.	Good	Fair	Poor
280	225	200	175	125

Centurion 98 Sporter

This is a refinished and rebuilt on a surplus German Mauser 98 action with new commercial 22" barrel. No sights. A synthetic stock with recoil pad is standard. Chambered for .270 or .30-06. Weighs about 7 lbs., 13 oz.

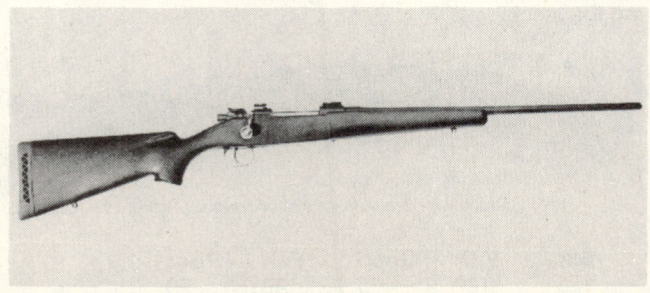

Exc.	V.G.	Good	Fair	Poor
230	200	175	150	100

Enfield Sporter No. I Mark III

This refinished rifle has a cut down Sporter style stock. Action and sights are original. Caliber is .303.

Exc.	V.G.	Good	Fair	Poor
120	80	60	50	40

Enfield Sporter No. 4 Mark I
Similar to above with cut down stock. Caliber .303.

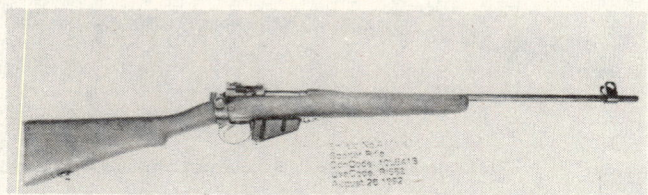

Exc.	V.G.	Good	Fair	Poor
120	80	60	50	40

With new walnut stock.

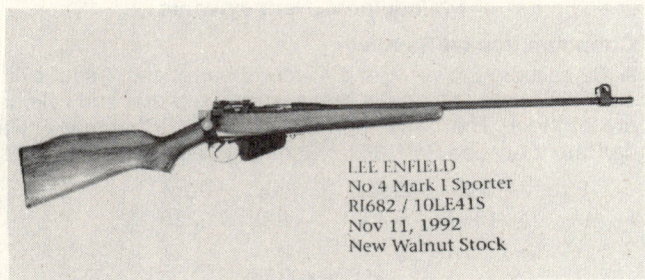

LEE ENFIELD
No 4 Mark I Sporter
RI682 / 10LE41S
Nov 11, 1992
New Walnut Stock

Exc.	V.G.	Good	Fair	Poor
160	125	100	75	50

TOZ-17
An original Russian rifle chambered for the .22 l.r. Has a 21" barrel and 5-round magazine. Checkered stock and iron sights. Weighs about 5.4 lbs.

Exc.	V.G.	Good	Fair	Poor
120	80	60	50	40

TOZ-17-1
Same as above with hooded front sight and tangent rear sight. Receiver is grooved for scope mount.

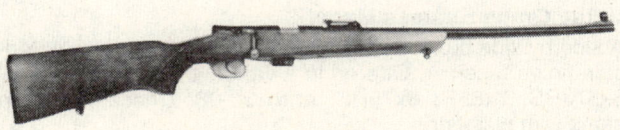

Exc.	V.G.	Good	Fair	Poor
80	65	50	40	35

Mexican Mauser Model 1910 Sporter
This rifle has been converted from a military rifle to a sporter by cutting down the stock. The metal is refinished and the barrel has been rebored and rechambered for the .30-06 cartridge. The box magazine holds 5 rounds. Barrel is 23" and rifle weighs about 8 lbs.

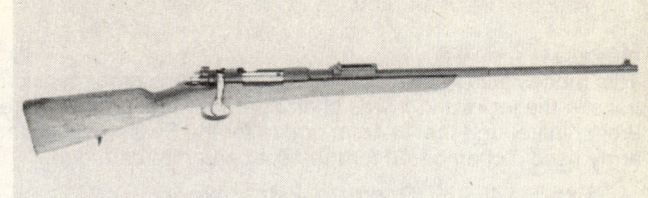

Exc.	V.G.	Good	Fair	Poor
175	140	125	100	75

FAL Sporter
This is a refinished FAL receiver and barrel installed in a synthetic thumbhole stock. The flash suppressor and bayonet lug have been removed. Barrel is 20.75" and weight is approximately 10 lbs.

NIB	Exc.	V.G.	Good	Fair	Poor
625	500	350	300	250	150

M-14 Rifle
Imported from China by Century International this rifle features a 22" barrel chambered for the .308 Win. cartridge. Stock is walnut with rubber pad. Parkerized finish. Weight is approximately 8.25 lbs.

NIB	Exc.	V.G.	Good	Fair	Poor
450	350	250	200	150	100

Tiger Dragunov Rifle
This is a shortened version of the Russian SVD sniper rifle. Fitted with a 20.8" barrel and chambered for the 7.62x54R cartridge the rifle is sold with a 5-round magazine and a 4x range finding scope. Imported from Russia. Weight is about 8.5 lbs.

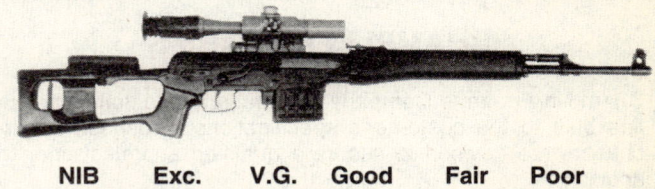

NIB	Exc.	V.G.	Good	Fair	Poor
1350	1100	800	—	—	—

CETME
Madrid, Spain

Cetme Autoloading Rifle
A .308 caliber semiautomatic rifle with a fluted chamber, a 17.74" barrel, an aperture rear sight and a 20-round detachable magazine. Black with a military-style wood stock. It is identical in appearance to the H&K 91 assualt rifle.

NIB	Exc.	V.G.	Good	Fair	Poor
1750	1250	950	750	600	300

CHAMELOT-DELVIGNE
Liege, Belgium

Model 1871 Belgian Troopers Revolver
A large, solid-frame weapon chambered for the 10.4mm centerfire cartridge.

Exc.	V.G.	Good	Fair	Poor
700	400	250	175	125

Model 1872 Swiss

This model, also known as the "Schmidt," had some modifications in the lockwork. It was chambered for the 12mm rimfire, 9mm rimfire, and the 10.4mm rimfire for the Swiss. The Italian army used it chambered for the 10.4 centerfire cartridge.

Exc.	V.G.	Good	Fair	Poor
1200	700	550	400	300

Model 1873

The Netherlands used the Model 1873, chambered for the 9.4mm centerfire, as an officer's revolver. The French had it chambered in 11mm centerfire for the enlisted troopers.

Exc.	V.G.	Good	Fair	Poor
400	250	200	150	100

> A cased gold inlaid presentation Model 1873 revolver was sold at auction for $2,750. No serial number. Condition was excellent. Butterfield & Butterfield, December 1995.

Model 1874

The Model 1874 was used by French officers and was chambered for 11mm centerfire.

Exc.	V.G.	Good	Fair	Poor
600	300	200	150	100

Model 1872/78 Swiss

This model designation signifies a recall of the Swiss Schmidt version. The 10.4mm centerfire caliber was standardized, and all Model 1872 revolvers still in service were converted and re-marked.

Exc.	V.G.	Good	Fair	Poor
750	500	350	275	225

Model 1879 Italian

The Italian army used the Model 1879 chambered for the 10.4mm centerfire as its officers' revolver.

Exc.	V.G.	Good	Fair	Poor
350	200	150	110	80

CHAMPLIN FIREARMS
Enid, Oklahoma

Champlin Firearms Company manufactures custom order rifles built to the customer's specifications. Prospective purchasers are advised to secure a qualified appraisal prior to acquisition.

Bolt Action Rifle

These arms featured round or octagonal barrels, set triggers, a variety of sights and well figured walnut stocks.

NIB	Exc.	V.G.	Good	Fair	Poor
5500	4500	3500	2900	2200	1500

CHAPMAN C.
Unknown

Chapman Rifle

This rare Confederate weapon was patterned after the U.S. Model 1841. It is chambered for .58 caliber and utilizes the percussion ignition system. The round barrel is 33" long, with a full-length stock and two barrel bands. The mountings are brass, and the stock is walnut. "C.Chapman" was stamped on the lock. This weapon was manufactured somewhere in the Confederate States of America during the Civil War, but little else is known.

CHAPMAN CHARLES
Chattanooga, Tennessee

Chapman produced a limited number of percussion carbines and rifles during the Civil War. Carbines had an overall length of 39-1/2" and .54 caliber barrels 24" in length. Their furniture was of brass. Chapman rifles resembled the U.S. Model 1841 Rifle, but did not have patchboxes. Overall length 48-1/2", barrel length 33", caliber .58. Chapman rifles and carbines are marked "C. CHAPMAN" on the lockplates.

Prospective purchasers are strongly advised to secure an expert appraisal prior to acquisition.

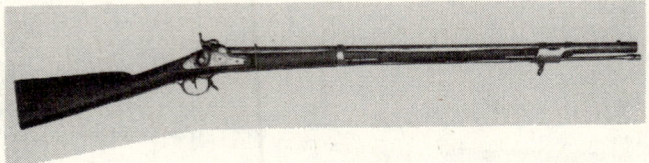

Courtesy Milwaukee Public Museum, Milwaukee, Wisconsin

Exc.	V.G.	Good	Fair	Poor
—	—	15000	7500	2500

CHAPMAN, G. & J.
Philadelphia, Pennsylvania

Chapman Pocket Revolver

A .32 caliber revolver with a 4" round barrel and 7-shot cylinder. The frame is made of brass while the barrel and cylinder are of steel. The barrel is marked "G.& J. Chapman/Philada/Patent Applied For/1861." Manufactured during the1860s.

Exc.	V.G.	Good	Fair	Poor
—	1500	750	400	250

CHAPIUS
France

RG Progress

A 12, 16, or 20 gauge boxlock shotgun. Most options are available on order.

NIB	Exc.	V.G.	Good	Fair	Poor
2500	2250	2000	1800	1250	900

RG Express Model 89

A 7 X 65R, 8 X 57 JRS, 9.3 X 74R, and .375 Holland & Holland caliber sidelock, double-barrelled shotgun. The other features are at the customer's order.

NIB	Exc.	V.G.	Good	Fair	Poor
6500	5750	4800	4000	3000	1500

Utility Grade Express Model

A side by side box lock action double rifle with case colored or coin finish receiver. Offered in a variety of calibers: 9.3x74R, 8x57JRS, 7x65R, 8x75RS, and .30-06. Checkered walnut stock with pistol grip.

NIB	Exc.	V.G.	Good	Fair	Poor
6000	4800	4000	3000	1500	750

St. Bonnet Model

This model is a side by side shotgun with sideplates on a boxlock action. Scroll engraved case colored receiver. Straight grip stock and double triggers. Offered in 12, 16, or 20 gauge.

NIB	Exc.	V.G.	Good	Fair	Poor
4000	3250	2000	1250	800	500

African PH Model Grade I

A box lock action double rifle offered in a wide variety of calibers. Caliber determines retail price. Hand engraved case colored receiver. Pistol grip stock with European style cheek piece.

.470 Nitro & .416 Rigby

NIB	Exc.	V.G.	Good	Fair	Poor
12500	9500	—	—	—	—

375 H&H

NIB	Exc.	V.G.	Good	Fair	Poor
9500	7500	—	—	—	—

.300 Win. Mag.

NIB	Exc.	V.G.	Good	Fair	Poor
8500	6500	—	—	—	—

.30-06, 9.3x74 R

NIB	Exc.	V.G.	Good	Fair	Poor
8000	6000	—	—	—	—

African PH Model Grade II

Same as above but with master engraving with game scenes. Add 20% to 25% to above NIB prices.

CHARLEVILLE
("Manufre Royle de Charleville" SEE-French Military Firearms)

CHARTER ARMS, CORP.
Ansonia, Connecticut

Police Undercovers

This model is chambered for the .38 Special or the .32 Magnum. It is fitted with a 2" barrel in blue or stainless steel finish. Offered with walnut or rubber grips. The overall length is 6.25" and weight is between 16 oz. and 19 oz. depending on grips and finish. This model is currently in production.

NIB	Exc.	V.G.	Good	Fair	Poor
225	200	175	150	100	75

Undercover Stainless Steel

As above, in stainless steel.

NIB	Exc.	V.G.	Good	Fair	Poor
275	250	225	175	125	100

Undercoverette

As above, with a thinner grip and in .32 S&W.

Exc.	V.G.	Good	Fair	Poor
175	150	125	100	75

Pathfinder

Similar to the above, but in .22 or .22 Magnum caliber with a 2", 3", or 6" barrel with adjustable sights.

NIB	Exc.	V.G.	Good	Fair	Poor
225	200	175	150	100	75

Pathfinder Stainless Steel

As above, in stainless steel.

NIB	Exc.	V.G.	Good	Fair	Poor
290	275	200	175	125	100

Bulldog

Similar to the Undercover model, but in .44 Special caliber with a 2.5" or 3" barrel and 5-shot cylinder.

NIB	Exc.	V.G.	Good	Fair	Poor
235	200	175	150	125	100

Stainless Steel Bulldog

As above, in stainless steel.

NIB	Exc.	V.G.	Good	Fair	Poor
285	250	225	175	150	110

Target Bulldog

As above, in .357 Magnum or .44 Special with a 4" barrel fitted with adjustable rear sights. Blued with walnut grips. Manufactured from 1986 to 1988.

NIB	Exc.	V.G.	Good	Fair	Poor
200	185	160	145	110	80

Bulldog Pug

Chambered for the .44 Special cartridge it is fitted with a 2.5" barrel. Available with walnut or neoprene grips in blue or stainless steel finish with choice of spur or pocket hammer. The cylinder holds 5 rounds. Overall length is 7" and weight is between 20 oz. and 25 oz. depending on grip and finish. This model is currently in production.

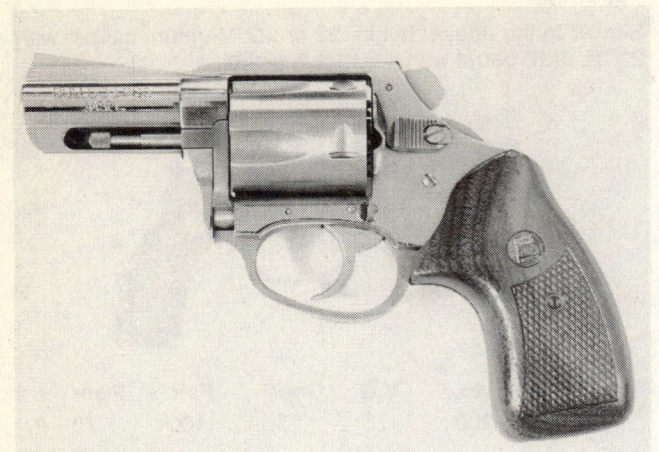

NIB	Exc.	V.G.	Good	Fair	Poor
250	200	175	150	100	75

Stainless Steel Bulldog

As above, in stainless steel.

NIB	Exc.	V.G.	Good	Fair	Poor
300	250	225	175	150	125

Bulldog Tracker

As above, with a 2.5", 4", or 6" barrel in .357 Magnum only.

NIB	Exc.	V.G.	Good	Fair	Poor
250	225	200	165	140	110

Police Bulldog

As above, in .32 H&R Magnum, .38 Special or .44 Special with 3.5" or 4" barrel.

NIB	Exc.	V.G.	Good	Fair	Poor
235	200	175	150	125	100

Stainless Steel Police Bulldog

As above, in stainless steel and available also in .357 Magnum.

NIB	Exc.	V.G.	Good	Fair	Poor
285	250	210	175	145	110

Off Duty

Chambered for the .38 Special or .22 Long Rifle this revolver is fitted with a 2" barrel. Offered with either walnut or rubber grips in blue or stainless steel finish with choice of spur or pocket hammer. Weight of the .38 special version is between 17 oz. and 23 oz., depending on grip and finish. The .22 LR version weighs between 19 oz. and 22 oz. The overall length is 4.75". This model is currently in production. A nickel finish with rubber grips is also offered.

NIB	Exc.	V.G.	Good	Fair	Poor
185	150	125	100	75	60

Pit Bull

A 9mm Federal, .38 Special or .357 Magnum caliber double action revolver with a 2.5", 3.5", or 4" barrel. Blued with rubber grips.

NIB	Exc.	V.G.	Good	Fair	Poor
285	250	200	175	125	90

Explorer 11 Pistol

A .22 caliber semiautomatic pistol with 6", 8", or 10" barrels. Available with a camo, black, silver, or gold finish and plastic grips. Discontinued in 1986.

NIB	Exc.	V.G.	Good	Fair	Poor
110	95	75	65	45	25

Model 40

A .22 caliber double action semiautomatic pistol with a 3.5" barrel and 8-shot magazine. Stainless steel with plastic grips. Manufactured from 1984 to 1986.

Exc.	V.G.	Good	Fair	Poor
250	225	200	150	100

Model 79K

A .32 or .380 caliber double action semiautomatic pistol with a 3.5" barrel and 7-shot magazine. Stainless steel with plastic grips. Manufactured from 1986 to 1988.

Exc.	V.G.	Good	Fair	Poor
325	300	250	180	125

Model 42T

A .22 caliber semiautomatic pistol with a 6" barrel and adjustable sights. Blued with walnut grips. Manufactured in 1984 and 1985.

NIB	Exc.	V.G.	Good	Fair	Poor
500	450	400	325		200

AR - 7 Explorer Rifle

A .22 caliber semiautomatic rifle with a 16" barrel, 8-shot magazine and hollow plastic stock which can house the barrel when detached.

NIB	Exc.	V.G.	Good	Fair	Poor
150	125	100	80	60	40

CHASSEPOT
French Military

MLE 1866

An 11mm caliber bolt-action rifle with a 32" barrel, a full-length walnut stock held on by two barrel bands, a cleaning rod mounted under the barrel and a bayonet lug that allows the attaching of a brass-handled, saber-type bayonet. White with a walnut stock.

Courtesy Milwaukee Public Museum, Milwaukee, Wisconsin

Exc.	V.G.	Good	Fair	Poor
500	300	175	125	100

CHICAGO F. A. CO.
Chicago, Illinois

Protector Palm Pistol

A .32 caliber radial cylinder revolver designed to fit in the palm of the hand and to be operated by a hinged lever mounted to the rear of the circular frame. The sideplates are marked "Chicago Firearms Co., Chicago, Ill." and "The Protector". Blued with hard rubber grip panels or nickel-plated with pearl grip panels. Manufactured by the Ames Manufacturing Company.

Standard Model Nickel-Plated/Black Grips

Exc.	V.G.	Good	Fair	Poor
—	2500	1000	500	250

Blued Finish-Add 50%.
Pearl Grips-Add 20%.

CHIPMUNK, INC.
Medford, Oregon

Chipmunk Single Shot Rifle

A .22 or the .22 rimfire Magnum caliber bolt-action rifle with 16.25" barrel, and open sights.

NIB	Exc.	V.G.	Good	Fair	Poor
130	110	100	80	60	40

Deluxe Chipmunk

As above, with a hand-checkered walnut stock.

NIB	Exc.	V.G.	Good	Fair	Poor
180	160	135	100	80	50

Silhouette Pistol

A .22 caliber bolt-action pistol with a 14.5" barrel, open sights and rear pistol-grip walnut stock.

NIB	Exc.	V.G.	Good	Fair	Poor
150	125	100	80	60	40

CHRISTENSEN ARMS
St. George, Utah

Carbon One

This is a bolt action rifle with Remington 700 action chambered for .17 through .243 caliber. It is fitted with a custom trigger, Match grade stainless steel barrel and black synthitic stock. Weight is about 6 lbs.

NIB	Exc.	V.G.	Good	Fair	Poor
2750	2250	—	—	—	—

Carbon Lite

This model is similar to above but weighs about 5 lbs.

NIB	Exc.	V.G.	Good	Fair	Poor
2750	2250	—	—	—	—

Carbon King

This model utilizes a Remington 700 BDL long action and is chambered for .25 caliber through .30-06. Stainless steel barrel, custom trigger, and black synthetic stock are standard. Weight is approximately 6.5 lbs.

NIB	Exc.	V.G.	Good	Fair	Poor
2750	2250	—	—	—	—

Carbon Cannon

Similar to above model and chambered for belted magnum calibers. Weight is about 7 lbs.

NIB	Exc.	V.G.	Good	Fair	Poor
2750	2250	—	—	—	—

Carbon Challenge I

This rifle is built on a Ruger 10/22 action. It is fitted with a Volquartsen trigger, bull barrel of stainless steel and black synthetic stock. Weight is approximately 3.5 lbs.

NIB	Exc.	V.G.	Good	Fair	Poor
995	800	—	—	—	—

Carbon Challenge II

Similar to above model but fitted with an AMT action and trigger. Weight is about 4.5 lbs.

NIB	Exc.	V.G.	Good	Fair	Poor
1095	900	—	—	—	—

Carbon Tactical

This bolt action model uses a Remington 700 BDL action and is available in most any caliber. It is fitted with a custom trigger, Match grade stainless steel barrel, and black synthetic stock. Weight is about 7 lbs.

NIB	Exc.	V.G.	Good	Fair	Poor
2750	2250	—	—	—	—

CHURCHILL
Importer-Ellet Bros.
Chapin, South Carolina

Windsor I

A 10, 12, 16, 20, 28, and .410 bore Anson & Deeley double barrel boxlock shotgun with barrel lengths from 23" through 32", various choke combinations, double triggers and extractors. Scroll-engraved, silver-finished, with checkered walnut pistol grip and forend.

NIB	Exc.	V.G.	Good	Fair	Poor
650	600	500	400	300	200

Windsor II

As above, in 10, 12, and 20 gauge only with automatic ejectors. Not imported after 1987.

NIB	Exc.	V.G.	Good	Fair	Poor
650	600	550	450	350	250

Windsor VI

As above with sidelocks. Chambered for 12 and 20 gauge only with automatic ejectors. Not imported after 1987.

NIB	Exc.	V.G.	Good	Fair	Poor
900	800	750	650	500	350

Royal

A 12, 20, 28 and .410 bore boxlock double-barrel shotgun with various barrel lengths and chokes, double triggers and extractors. Case hardened with checkered walnut stock. Introduced in 1988.

NIB	Exc.	V.G.	Good	Fair	Poor
550	500	425	350	275	125

OVER/UNDERS

Monarch

A 12, 20, 28, or .410 bore Over/Under shotgun with a boxlock action, 25", 26", or 28" ventilated-rib barrels, either double or a single selective trigger, extractors, and a checkered walnut stock.

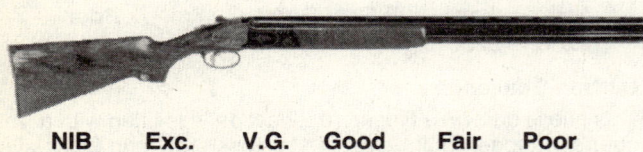

NIB	Exc.	V.G.	Good	Fair	Poor
530	475	425	375	300	150

Windsor III

A 12 and 20 and .410 bore boxlock double-barrel shotgun with 27" or 30" ventilated-rib barrels, extractors, a single selective trigger, scroll-engraved, silver finished and a checkered walnut stock.

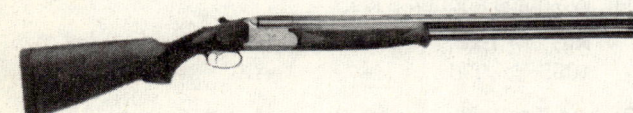

NIB	Exc.	V.G.	Good	Fair	Poor
625	575	525	475	400	200

Windsor IV

As above, with screw-in choke tubes standard. Introduced in 1989.

NIB	Exc.	V.G.	Good	Fair	Poor
850	775	650	500	425	200

Regent

As above, in 12 and 20 gauge with 27" ventilated-rib barrels, screw-in choke tubes, scroll-engraved false sideplates, automatic ejectors, a single selective trigger, and a checkered walnut stock. Not imported after 1986.

NIB	Exc.	V.G.	Good	Fair	Poor
850	750	650	550	450	250

Regent II

As above with finer overall finishing.

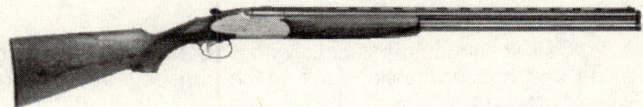

NIB	Exc.	V.G.	Good	Fair	Poor
1100	1000	850	750	500	250

Regent Shotgun Rifle Combination

A .222, .223, .243, .270, .308, or .30-06 caliber/12 gauge Over/Under rifle/shotgun with a 25" ventilated rib, automatic ejectors and single selective trigger. Silver finished, scroll engraved with a checkered walnut stock.

NIB	Exc.	V.G.	Good	Fair	Poor
925	825	725	600	450	250

Windsor Grade Semiautomatic

A 12 gauge semiautomatic shotgun with 26", 28", or 30" ventilated-rib barrels and screw-in choke tubes. An etched and anodized alloy receiver with a checkered walnut stock.

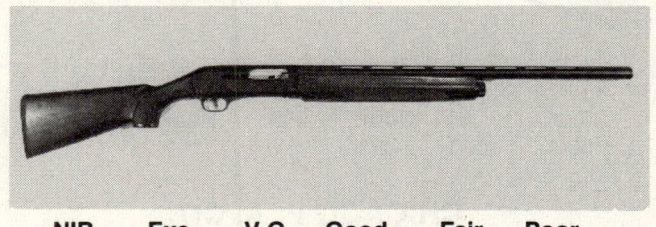

NIB	Exc.	V.G.	Good	Fair	Poor
425	375	325	275	225	175

Regent Grade Semiautomatic

Chambered for 12 gauge with choice of 26", 28", or 30" barrels. Standard chokes or choke tubes. walnut stock with pistol grip. Introduced in 1984 and discontinued in 1986. Weight is about 7-1/2 lbs.

NIB	Exc.	V.G.	Good	Fair	Poor
425	375	325	275	225	175

Windsor Grade Slide Action

A 12 gauge slide action shotgun with a 26" through 30" ventilated-rib barrel, various chokes, double slide rails, and an anodized alloy receiver. Checkered walnut stock. Discontinued in 1986.

Exc.	V.G.	Good	Fair	Poor
400	375	300	250	175

RIFLES

Highlander

A .25-06 through .300 Winchester Magnum caliber bolt-action rifle with a 22" barrel, with or without sights, a 3-shot magazine, and a checkered walnut stock.

NIB	Exc.	V.G.	Good	Fair	Poor
460	420	375	300	250	200

Regent

As above, with a with Monte Carlo-style comb and cheekpiece. Discontinued in 1988.

Exc.	V.G.	Good	Fair	Poor
550	500	425	350	275

CHURCHILL, E. J. LTD.
London, England

One of One Thousand Rifle

A .270 to .458 Magnum caliber bolt-action rifle with 24" barrel and a select French walnut stock with a trap pistol-grip cap and recoil pad. Only 100 produced for the 20th anniversary of Interarms in 1973.

Exc.	V.G.	Good	Fair	Poor
15000	12500	10000	7000	5500

Premier Over/Under Shotgun

A 12, 16, and 20 gauge sidelock Over/Under shotgun with barrel lengths from 25" through 32", any choke combination, automatic ejectors and single selective triggers. Engraved with walnut stock.

Exc.	V.G.	Good	Fair	Poor
17500	15000	12500	8000	5000

Premier Side x Side

As above, in the side x side configuration. Available in all gauges and as a double rifle in most popular calibers at a higher cost.

Double Rifle-Add 40%.

Exc.	V.G.	Good	Fair	Poor
17500	15000	12500	8000	5000

Imperial

The second quality side x side made by this company; and made-to-order available in all gauges, barrel lengths, and chokes. It was also made as a double rifle in most calibers at extra cost.

Double Rifle-Add 40%.

Exc.	V.G.	Good	Fair	Poor
13000	11000	9000	6500	4000

Field Model

The third quality side lock, side x side shotgun available in 12 gauge only, with all other features available on order.

Exc.	V.G.	Good	Fair	Poor
9000	8000	6000	4500	3000

Hercules

The best quality boxlock side x side. Available in any gauge and barrel length. All other options were available on request. There were some produced as small caliber double rifles.

Double Rifle-Add 40%.

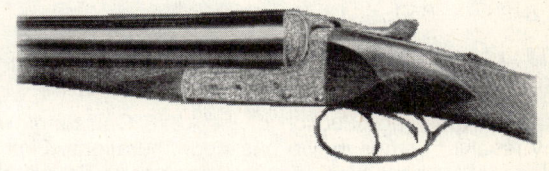

Exc.	V.G.	Good	Fair	Poor
9000	8000	6000	4500	3000

Utility Model

The 2nd quality boxlock—available with custom features similar to the Hercules.

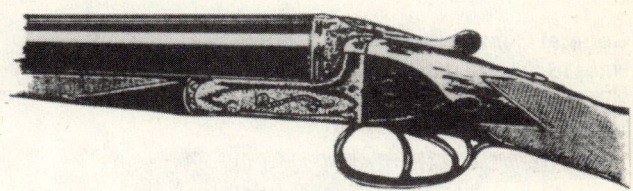

Exc.	V.G.	Good	Fair	Poor
6000	5000	3500	2500	2000

Crown

The third quality boxlock and was available with many custom features.

Exc.	V.G.	Good	Fair	Poor
4000	3000	2500	1750	1200

CHYLEWSKI, WITOLD
Switzerland

A 6.35mm caliber semi-automatic pistol with a 6-round magazine, marked "Brevete Chylewski" and bears the name Neuhausen on the left side of the pistol. Approximately 1,000 were made between 1910 and 1918. This pistol was designed to be cocked with one hand.

Exc.	V.G.	Good	Fair	Poor
850	750	650	500	275

CIMARRON F. A. MFG. CO.
Fredericksburg, Texas

Model No. 3 Schofield

This version of the Schofield is manufactured for Cimarron by Armi San Marco in Italy. Its parts are interchangeable with the orginal. It is offered in several variations and calibers.

Schofield Civilian Model

Fitted with 7" barrel and offered in .38 special, .38 WCF, .44 Russian & Special, .44 WCF, .45 Schofield, .45 ACP, .45 Long Colt.

NIB	Exc.	V.G.	Good	Fair	Poor
849	650	—	—	—	—

Schofield Military Model

Essentially the same as the Civilian Model except for its markings.

NIB	Exc.	V.G.	Good	Fair	Poor
849	650	—	—	—	—

Schofield Wells Fargo

Similar to the Military and Civilian Model but fitted with a 5" barrel. Calibers are the same.

NIB	Exc.	V.G.	Good	Fair	Poor
849	650	—	—	—	—

NOTE: For standard nickel finish add $100.00 and for custom nickel finish add $150.00.

Cimarron Arms reproduction of the 1873 Colt Single Action Army revolver comes in two basic configurations. First is the "Old Model" with the black powder frame screw-in cylinder pin retainer and circular bull's eye ejector head. Second is the "prewar Model" style frame with spring loaded cross-pin cylinder retainer and half moon ejector head. Old Model revolvers are available in authentic old style charcoal blue finish at an extra charge. Unless otherwise stated all of these Colt reproductions are produced by Uberti of Italy. Plain walnut grips are standard unless noted.

General Custer 7th Cavalry Model

Has US military markings and is fitted with 7-1/2" barrel on an old model frame. Offered in .45 Long Colt only.

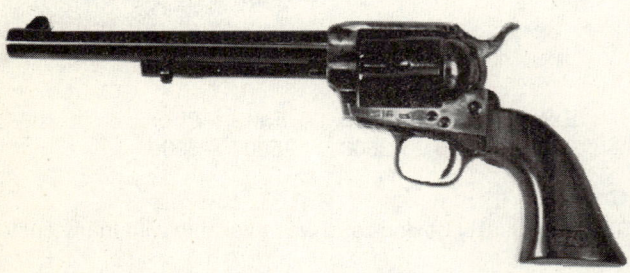

NIB	Exc.	V.G.	Good	Fair	Poor
499	375	—	—	—	—

Rough Rider U.S. Artillery Model

This version of the old model is fitted with a 5-1/2" barrel and chambered for .45 Long Colt.

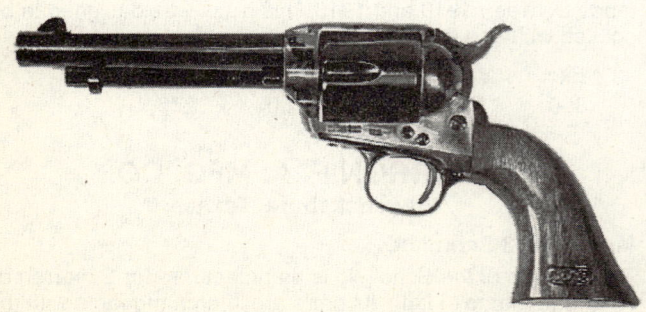

NIB	Exc.	V.G.	Good	Fair	Poor
499	675	—	—	—	—

Frontier Six Shooter

This revolver is offered with a choice of 4-3/4", 5-1/2", or 7-1/2" barrel. It is chambered for .38 WCF, .357 Magnum, .44 WCF, .45 Long colt, or .45LC with extra .45ACP cylinder. For charcoal blue finish add $40.00 to NIB price. For extra .45ACP cylinder add $30.00.

NIB	Exc.	V.G.	Good	Fair	Poor
469	350	—	—	—	—

Sheriff's Model w/No ejector

Fitted with a 3" barrel and chambered in .44 WCF or .45 Long Colt. Built on an Old Model frame.

NIB	Exc.	V.G.	Good	Fair	Poor
469	350	—	—	—	—

New Sheriff's Model w/ejector

This variation is fitted with a 3-1/2" barrel with ejector and is available in .357 Magnum, .44 WCF, .44 Special, and .45 Long Colt. For checkered walnut grips add $35.00.

NIB	Exc.	V.G.	Good	Fair	Poor
469	350	—	—	—	—

New Thunderer

The frame is based on the Old Model fitted with a bird's head grip with a choice of plain or checkered walnut grips. Offered in 3-1/2" or 4-3/4" barrel lengths. First offered for 1997 are barrel lengths in 5-1/2" and 7-1/2". Chambered for .357 Magnum, .44 WCF, .44 special, or .45 Long Colt/.45 ACP. Add $35.00 for checkered grips.

NIB	Exc.	V.G.	Good	Fair	Poor
489	350	—	—	—	—

New Model P

Offered in either Old Model or prewar styles in a choice of 4-3/4", 5-1/2", or 7-1/2" barrel. Chambered for .32 WCF, .38 WCF, .44 WCF, .44 Special, or .45 Long Colt.

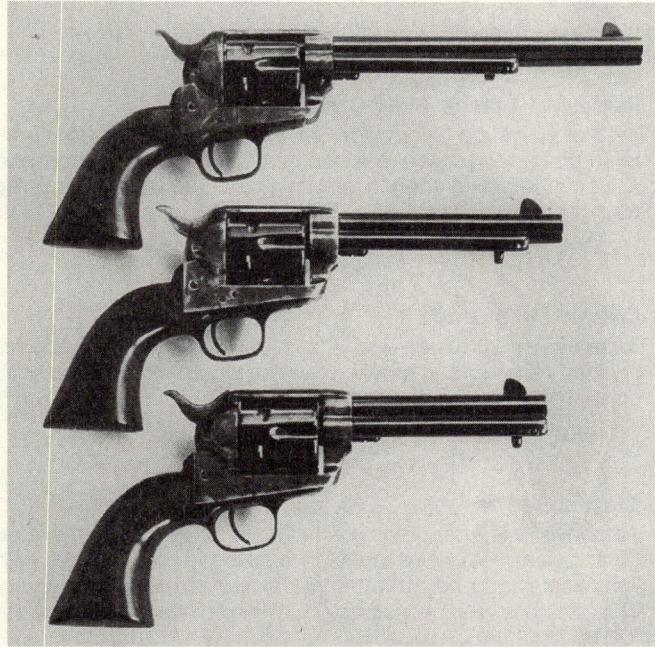

NIB	Exc.	V.G.	Good	Fair	Poor
469	350	—	—	—	—

A.P. Casey Model P U.S. Cavalry

Fitted with a 7-1/2" barrel and chambered for .45 Long Colt this revolver has US markings(APC) on an Old Model frame.

NIB	Exc.	V.G.	Good	Fair	Poor
499	375	—	—	—	—

Rinaldo A. Carr Model P U.S. Artillery

This is a Model P built on an Old Model frame and chambered for .45 Long colt and fitted with a 5-1/2" barrel. US markings (RAC).

NIB	Exc.	V.G.	Good	Fair	Poor
499	375	—	—	—	—

El Pistolero

This budget priced revolver was introduced in 1997 and features a brass backstrap and trigger guard with plain walnut grips. Offered in 4-3/4", 5-1/2", and 7-1/2" barrel lengths. Chambered for .45 Long Colt or .357 Magnum.

NIB	Exc.	V.G.	Good	Fair	Poor
340	250	—	—	—	—

NOTE: Cimarron also sells Uberti manufactured black powder Colt reproductions from the Patterson to the Model 1862 Pocket. For prices and specifications on these models see the Uberti section.

RIFLES

Henry Civil War Model

Offered in .44 WCF or .45 Long Colt with 24-1/4" barrel. For charcoal blue or white finish finish add $80.00.

NIB	Exc.	V.G.	Good	Fair	Poor
1050	850	—	—	—	—

Henry Civilian Model

Same as above but without military markings.

NIB	Exc.	V.G.	Good	Fair	Poor
1025	825	—	—	—	—

Model 1866 Yellowboy Carbine

Reproduction of the Winchester model 1866. Fitted with a 19" barrel and chambered for .38 Special, .44 WCF, or .45 Long Colt. For charcoal blue add $40.00

NIB	Exc.	V.G.	Good	Fair	Poor
825	625	—	—	—	—

Model 1866 Yellowboy Rifle

Same as above but fitted with a 24-1/4" barrel. For charcoal blue add $40.00.

NIB	Exc.	V.G.	Good	Fair	Poor
835	625	—	—	—	—

Model 1873 Winchester Rifle

This lever action rifle is offered in .357 Magnum, .44 WCF, or .45 Long Colt. Fitted with a 24-1/4" barrel. For charcoal blue add $40.00. For pistol grip option add $140.00.

NIB	Exc.	V.G.	Good	Fair	Poor
950	775	—	—	—	—

Model 1873 Long Range Rifle

Similar to the Model 1873 but fitted with a 30" barrel. For pistol grip option add $140.00. For 1 of 1000 engraving option add $1,250.00.

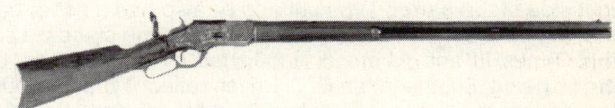

NIB	Exc.	V.G.	Good	Fair	Poor
1000	800	—	—	—	—

Model 1873 Carbine

Same as the standard Model 1873 but fitted with a 19" barrel. Add $40.00 for charcoal blue.

NIB	Exc.	V.G.	Good	Fair	Poor
950	775	—	—	—	—

Model 1873 Short Rifle

This model is fitted with a 20" barrel. Add $40.00 for charcoal blue.

NIB	Exc.	V.G.	Good	Fair	Poor
950	775	—	—	—	—

Model 1874 Sharps

A reproduction of the Model 1874 Sharps rifle chambered for the .45-70 cartridge. Fitted with a 32" tapered octagon barrel. Stock is hand checkered with satin finish walnut. Double set triggers standard. First introduced to the Cimarron product line in 1997.

NIB	Exc.	V.G.	Good	Fair	Poor
1200	1000	—	—	—	—

Remington Rolling Block

This Remington reproduction was introduced to Cimarron in 1997 and represents the Rolling Block Sporting rifle with 30" tapered octagon barrel and chambered for .45-70 cartridge. Hand checkered stock with satin finished walnut stock.

NIB	Exc.	V.G.	Good	Fair	Poor
1100	850	—	—	—	—

CLAPP, HOFFMAN & CO.
CLAPP, GATES & CO. RIFLES.
Alamance, North Carolina

Clapp, Hoffman & Co. and its successor, Clapp, Gates & Co., both of Alamance (Guilford County), North Carolina, entered into several contracts with the state of North Carolina for the delivery of rifles. These contracts included an escalator clause that allowed the contractors to charge costs plus a percentage. Under their contracts, Clapp, Gates & Co. delivered 1,078 rifles in four varieties, before the state bought out the balance of the contract in 1864 due to the exorbitant prices caused by inflation.

Overall length: Types I, II, & III 51-1/4" to 52", Type IV varies between 46-1/2" and 51"; barrel length: Types I, II, & III 35-1/4" to 36", Type IV varies between 31-1/4" and 35-7/8"; caliber: Types I, II, & III .50, Type IV .577; markings: none. Despite the absence of makers marks, the Clapp, Gates & Co. products are readily distinguished by their part-round, part-octagonal (octagonal section on Types I to III, about 4" long, 4-3/4" to 5-1/2" on Type IV rifles) barrels having only a slightly raised bolster projecting from the upper right quarter. This small bolster accommodates the boxlock that distinguished the first 100 rifles produced. This gave way to a standard percussion lock on subsequent production, which required that the hammer bend sharply to the left to strike the cone. Type I and Type II rifles were adapted to a "footprint" saber bayonet lug on the right side of the barrel; Types III and IV also had a saber bayonet lug on the right side of the barrel but of the standard pattern. Types III and IV are distinguished by their caliber, the former being .50, the latter .577. Prices reflect Type II through IV production; Type I (while extant) has never been offered for sale and would presumably bring a significantly higher premium.

Exc.	V.G.	Good	Fair	Poor
12500	10000	8250	5500	3000

CLARK, F. H.
Memphis, Tennessee

Pocket Pistol

A .41 caliber single shot percussion pistol with a 3.5" to 5" barrel, German silver mounts and end cap, and the barrel is stamped "F.H. Clark & Co./Memphis." Manufactured in the 1850s and 1860s.

Exc.	V.G.	Good	Fair	Poor
—	2500	1200	750	500

CLASSIC DOUBLES
Tochigi City, Japan
Importer-Classic Doubles International
St. Louis, Missouri

Importer of the Japanese shotgun formerly imported by Winchester as the Model 101 and Model 23. These models were discontinued by Winchester in 1987.

Model 201 Classic

A 12 or 20 gauge boxlock double-barrel shotgun with 26" ventilated-rib barrels, screw-in choke tubes single selective trigger and automatic ejectors. Blued with checkered walnut stock and beavertail forearm.

NIB	Exc.	V.G.	Good	Fair	Poor
2200	1950	1700	1500	1250	900

Model 201 Small Bore Set

As above, with a smaller receiver and two sets of barrels chambered for 28 gauge and .410. The barrels are 28" in length.

NIB	Exc.	V.G.	Good	Fair	Poor
3650	3200	2750	2250	1750	1250

Model 101 Classic Field Grade I

A 12 or 20 gauge Over/Under shotgun with 25.5" or 28" ventilated-rib barrels, screw-in choke tubes, automatic ejectors and a single-selective trigger. Engraved, blued with checkered walnut stock.

NIB	Exc.	V.G.	Good	Fair	Poor
1900	1750	1500	1250	1000	700

Classic Field Grade II

As above, in 28 gauge and .410, highly engraved with a coin-finished receiver and a deluxe walnut stock with a round knob pistol grip and fleur-de-lis checkering.

NIB	Exc.	V.G.	Good	Fair	Poor
2200	2000	1750	1500	1250	900

Classic Sporter

As above, in 12 gauge only with 28" or 30" barrels, ventilated rib and screw-in choke tubes. The frame is coin-finished with light engraving and a matted upper surface to reduce glare. The stock is select walnut. This model was designed for "Sporting Clays."

NIB	Exc.	V.G.	Good	Fair	Poor
2000	1800	1500	1250	1000	700

Waterfowl Model

As above with 30" barrels having 3" chambers, vent rib, and screw-in choke tubes. The overall finish is a subdued matte with light engraving.

NIB	Exc.	V.G.	Good	Fair	Poor
1500	1350	1000	850	650	500

Classic Trap Over/Under

Designed for competition trap shooting with 30" or 32" barrels having a ventilated center and top rib, automatic ejectors, screw-in choke tubes, and a single trigger. Blued with light engraving and a walnut stock in straight or Monte Carlo style.

NIB	Exc.	V.G.	Good	Fair	Poor
1900	1750	1500	1250	1000	700

Classic Trap Single

As above, with a single 32" or 34" barrel.

NIB	Exc.	V.G.	Good	Fair	Poor
2000	1800	1500	1250	1000	700

Classic Trap Combo
As above, with a single barrel and a set of Over/ Under barrels.

NIB	Exc.	V.G.	Good	Fair	Poor
2800	2500	2000	1750	1250	1000

Classic Skeet
As above, with 27.5" barrels.

NIB	Exc.	V.G.	Good	Fair	Poor
1900	1750	1500	1250	1000	700

Classic Skeet 4 Gauge Set
As above, furnished with four sets of barrels chambered for 12, 20, 28 gauge, and .410.

NIB	Exc.	V.G.	Good	Fair	Poor
3700	3000	2500	2250	1850	1500

CLEMENT, CHAS.
Liege, Belgium

Model 1903
A 5.5mm Clement semiautomatic pistol.

Exc.	V.G.	Good	Fair	Poor
600	500	450	375	250

Model 1907
As above, but in 6.35mm and 7.65mm caliber.

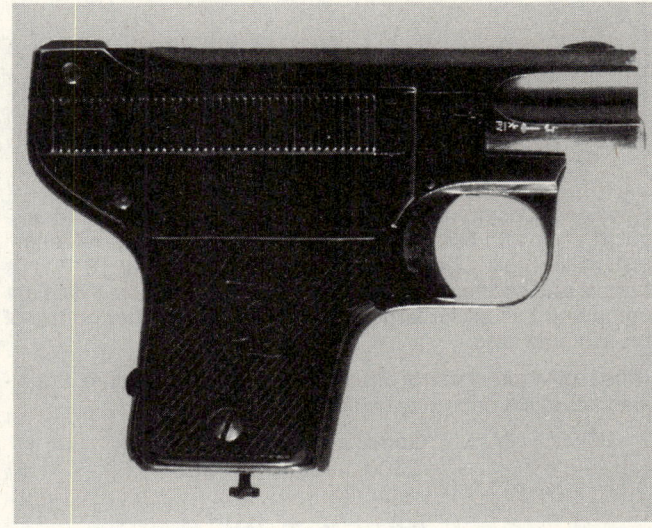

Courtesy Orvel Reichert

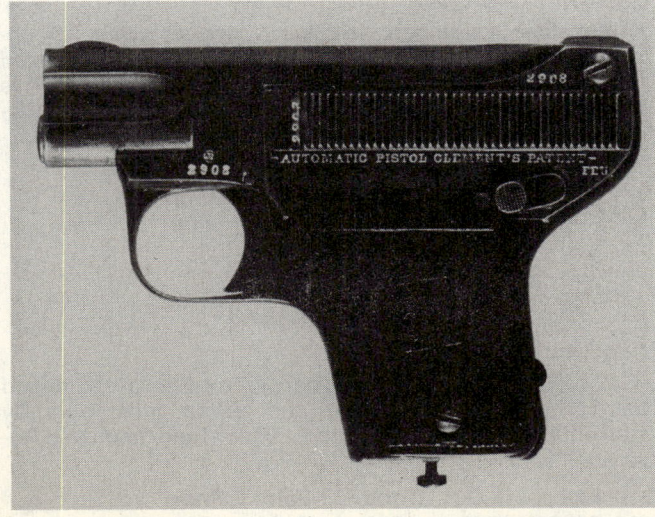

Courtesy Orvel Reichert

Exc.	V.G.	Good	Fair	Poor
350	300	250	200	150

> A Clement pistol with attachable shoulder stock was sold at auction for $11,500. It was chambered for the 9mm cartridge and was fitted with a 8-1/2" barrel. A factory leather holster and walnut shoulder stock with three extra magazines were also included in the sale. The serial number was 13. Condition was excellent to mint. Butterfield & Butterfield, July 1996.

Model 1908
As above with grip frame and a repositioned magazine release.

Exc.	V.G.	Good	Fair	Poor
450	400	350	300	200

Model 1910
Redesigned version of the above with the barrel and housing all one piece. This unit is held in position by the triggerguard.

Courtesy Orvel Reichert

Exc.	V.G.	Good	Fair	Poor
450	400	350	300	250

Model 1912
A 6.35mm caliber semiautomatic rifle marked "Clement's Patent"; others, "Model 1912 Brevet 243839."

Exc.	V.G.	Good	Fair	Poor
750	650	550	400	325

Revolver copy of the Colt Police Positive. It was chambered for .38 caliber.

Exc.	V.G.	Good	Fair	Poor
275	250	200	125	90

CLERKE PRODUCTS
Santa Monica, California

Hi-Wall

A copy of the Winchester Model 1885 High Wall rifle with the action activated by a lever, and the receiver is case colored. This rifle is chambered for almost all of the modern calibers and features a 26" barrel and a walnut stock with a pistol grip and a Schnabel forend. It was manufactured between 1972 and 1974.

NIB	Exc.	V.G.	Good	Fair	Poor
300	250	200	150	100	80

Deluxe Hi-Wall

As above, with a half-round/half-octagonal barrel, select walnut stock, and a recoil pad. It was manufactured between 1972 and 1974.

NIB	Exc.	V.G.	Good	Fair	Poor
350	300	250	200	150	100

CLIFTON ARMS
Grand Prairie, Texas

Although this company primarily is a manufacturer of composite laminated stocks, they will on special order build custom rifles. Due to the unique nature of each rifle, a qualified appraisal is necessary.

COBRAY INDUSTRIES
Atlanta, Georgia
S.W.D., Inc.

MII Pistol

A 9mm caliber semiautomatic pistol. It fires from the closed bolt and is made of steel stampings with a parkerized finish. It is patterned after, though a good deal smaller than, the Ingram Mac 10. It is currently out of production and impossible to accurately price. If purchase or sale is contemplated, please check local values.

MII Carbine

As above, with a 16.25" shrouded barrel and a telescoping metal shoulder stock.

Terminator Shotgun

A single shot 12 or 20 gauge shotgun that fires from an open bolt position. The cocked bolt is released to slam home on the shell when the trigger is pulled. The 18" barrel is cylinder bored. There is a telescoping wire stock and the finish is parkerized.

Exc.	V.G.	Good	Fair	Poor
125	100	80	60	40

COCHRAN TURRET
C. B. Allen
Springfield, Massachusetts

Under Hammer Turret Rifle

A .36 or .40 caliber percussion radial cylinder rifle with 31" or 32" octagonal barrels and walnut stocks. The barrel marked "Cochrans/Many/Chambered/&/Non Recoil/Rifle" and the top strap "C.B. Allen / Springfield." These rifles were produced in the variations listed below. Manufactured during the late 1830s and 1840s.

1st Type

Fitted with a circular top strap secured by two screws. Serial numbered from 1 to approximately 30.

Exc.	V.G.	Good	Fair	Poor
—	—	8000	4000	1250

2nd Type

Fitted with a rectangular hinged top strap, the locking catch of which serves as the rear sight. Serial numbered from approximately 31 to 155.

Exc.	V.G.	Good	Fair	Poor
—	—	7000	3500	1500

3rd Type

As above, with a smaller hammer and a plain triggerguard.

Exc.	V.G.	Good	Fair	Poor
—	—	7000	3500	1500

Pistol

Action similar to above with 4" to 7" barrels.

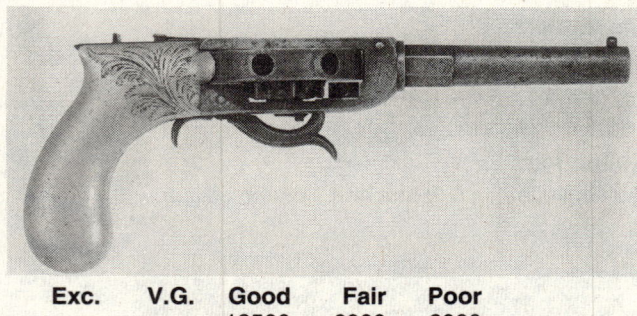

Exc.	V.G.	Good	Fair	Poor
—	—	12500	6000	2000

CODY, MICHAEL & SONS
Nashville, Tennessee

Received a contract with the State of Tennessee for "Mississippi" rifles with brass patchboxes in late 1861. Barrel length 36"; caliber .54. Cody often used reworked Model 1817 Rifle barrels and sporting pattern single screw lockplates. Rifles are unmarked except for large engraved serial number on top of breech plug tang.

Prospective purchasers are strongly advised to secure a qualified appraisal prior to acquisition.

Exc.	V.G.	Good	Fair	Poor
—	—	7500	3000	950

COFER, T. W.
Portsmouth, Virginia

Cofer Navy Revolver

A .36 caliber spur trigger percussion revolver with a 7.5" octagonal barrel and 6-shot cylinder. The top strap is marked "T.W. Cofer's/Patent." and the barrel "Portsmouth, Va." This revolver was manufactured in limited quantities during the Civil War. Prospective purchasers are advised to secure a qualified appraisal prior to acquisition.

Exc.	V.G.	Good	Fair	Poor
—	—	65000	30000	5000

COGSWELL
London, England

Cogswell Pepperbox Pistol

A .47 caliber 6-shot percussion pepperbox with casehardened barrels, German silver frame and walnut grips. Normally marked "B. Cogswell, 224 Strand, London" and "Improved Revolving Pistol."

Exc.	V.G.	Good	Fair	Poor
3000	2200	1750	1250	750

COGSWELL & HARRISON, LTD.
London, England

Markor

A 12, 16, or 20 gauge boxlock double-barrel shotgun with 27" or 30" barrels, various chokes, automatic ejectors and double triggers. The English-style straight stock is select walnut. This model is no longer manufactured.

Auto Ejectors-Add 20%.

NIB	Exc.	V.G.	Good	Fair	Poor
1500	1400	1200	950	700	400

Huntic

As above, with ejectors, a single selective trigger (optional) and a 25" barrel was offered.

NIB	Exc.	V.G.	Good	Fair	Poor
3750	3400	3000	2500	1200	600

Regency Model

A 12, 16, or 20 gauge Anson and Deeley boxlock double-barrel shotgun with 26", 28", or 30" barrels, various chokes, double triggers, automatic ejectors, and an English-style stock. This model has been manufactured since 1970.

NIB	Exc.	V.G.	Good	Fair	Poor
3250	2850	2400	1750	1400	700

Ambassador Model

As above, with false sideplates and a higher degree of engraving.

NIB	Exc.	V.G.	Good	Fair	Poor
4000	3500	3000	2500	2000	1000

Rex

A 12, 16, or 20 gauge boxlock double-barrel shotgun with 25", 27.5", or 30" barrels, automatic ejectors, double triggers, and an English-style stock. It is no longer made.

NIB	Exc.	V.G.	Good	Fair	Poor
1750	1500	1250	1000	750	400

Sandhurst

As above, with false sideplates and more engraving.

NIB	Exc.	V.G.	Good	Fair	Poor
2500	2250	2000	1500	1000	500

Konor

Similar to the Sandhurst with more elaborate engraving and a fancier grade stock. Single selective triggers are available for an additional 15 percent.

NIB	Exc.	V.G.	Good	Fair	Poor
2900	2600	2250	1850	1500	750

Primic

A 12, 16, and 20 gauge sidelock shotgun with various barrel lengths and chokes, hand-detachable full sidelocks, automatic ejectors, and double triggers. A single selective trigger was available for an additional charge. English-style, walnut stock.

NIB	Exc.	V.G.	Good	Fair	Poor
6000	5000	3750	2500	2000	1000

Victor

Similar to the above, but made solely to custom order.

NIB	Exc.	V.G.	Good	Fair	Poor
10000	8750	6250	4500	2750	1250

COLTS PATENTS ARMS MANUFACTURING COMPANY
Hartford, Connecticut

Of all the American firearms manufacturers, perhaps the best known is the Colt Company. Indeed, this recognition is so widespread that some popular writers have used the name Colt to indicate a revolver or semiautomatic pistol.

Originally founded in 1836 as the Patent Arms Manufacturing Company (Paterson, New Jersey) to produce percussion revolvers designed by Samuel Colt, the concern was initially a failure. However, the company formed in 1847 to manufacture revolvers of an improved form was a success. Even after Samuel Colt's death in 1862, his company thrived. With the introduction of the Model 1873 Single Action Army Revolver, the myth of the Colt became part of the American legend for that revolver was to be used by adventurers, cowboys, farmers, soldiers and a host of others for better than 70 years.

In 1897 the Colt's Patent Fire Arms Manufacturing Company entered into an agreement with John M. Browning to produce self-loading pistols of his design. One result of this association was to be the .45 caliber Model 1911 Semi-Automatic Pistol, which was the standard issue sidearm of the U.S. Armed Forces from 1911 to the late 1980s.

Because of their romance, form and variation, Colt revolvers, pistols and longarms are most sought after by collectors. Due to this, however, caution should be exercised and the opinion of experts should be sought when the purchase of rare or pristine examples is contemplated.

COLT PATERSON MODELS
Paterson, New Jersey

Pocket or Baby Paterson Model No. 1

The Paterson was the first production revolver manufactured by Colt. It was first made in 1837. The Model 1 or Pocket Model is the most diminutive of the Paterson line. The revolver is serial numbered in its own range, #1 through #500. The numbers are not visible without dismantling the revolver. The barrel lengths run from 1.75" to 4.75". The standard model has no attached loading lever. The chambering is .28 caliber percussion and it holds five shots. The finish is all blued, and the grips are varnished walnut. It has a roll-engraved cylinder scene, and the barrel is stamped "Patent Arms Mfg. Co. Paterson N.J.Colt's Pt."

Exc.	V.G.	Good	Fair	Poor
35000	25000	20000	10000	—

Belt Model Paterson No. 2

The Belt Model Paterson is a larger revolver with a straight-grip and an octagonal barrel that is 2.5" to 5.5" in length. It is chambered for .31 caliber percussion and holds five shots. The finish is all blued, with varnished walnut grips and no attached loading lever. It has a roll-engraved cylinder scene, and the barrel is stamped "Patent Arms Mfg. Co. Paterson N.J. Colt's Pt." The serial number range is #1-#850 and is shared with the #3 Belt Model. It was made from 1837-1840.

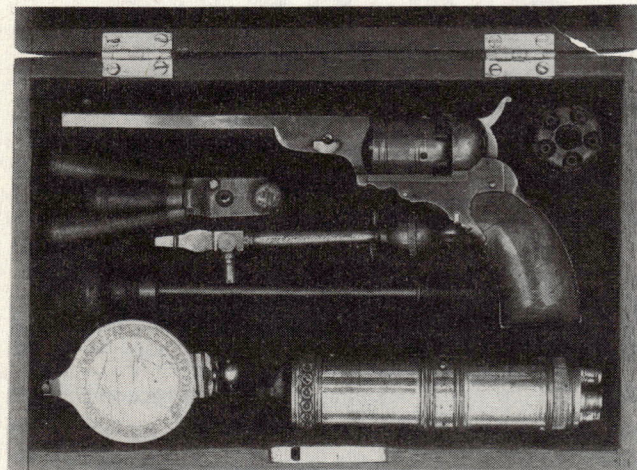

Courtesy Buffalo Bill Historical Center, Cody, Wyoming

Exc.	V.G.	Good	Fair	Poor
35000	25000	12500	5000	—

Belt Model Paterson No. 3

This revolver is quite similar to the Model #2 except that the grips are curved outward at the bottom to form a more hand-filling configuration. They are serial numbered in the same #1-#850 range. Some attached loading levers have been noted on this model, but they are extremely rare and would add approximately 35 percent to the value.

Exc.	V.G.	Good	Fair	Poor
35000	25000	12000	5000	—

A cased Paterson Belt Model, serial number 95, was sold at auction for $99,000. Accessories included extra cylinder numbered to gun, bullet mold, combination tool, and charger flask and rod. Condition excellent.
Butterfield & Butterfield, December 1995.

Ehlers Model Pocket Paterson

John Ehlers was a major stockholder and treasurer of the Patent Arms Mfg. Co. when it went bankrupt. He seized the assets and inventory. These revolvers were Pocket Model Patersons that were not finished at the time. Ehlers had them finished and marketed them. They had an attached loading lever, and the abbreviation "Mfg Co." was deleted from the barrel stamping. There were 500 revolvers involved in the Ehlers variation totally, and they were produced from 1840-1843.

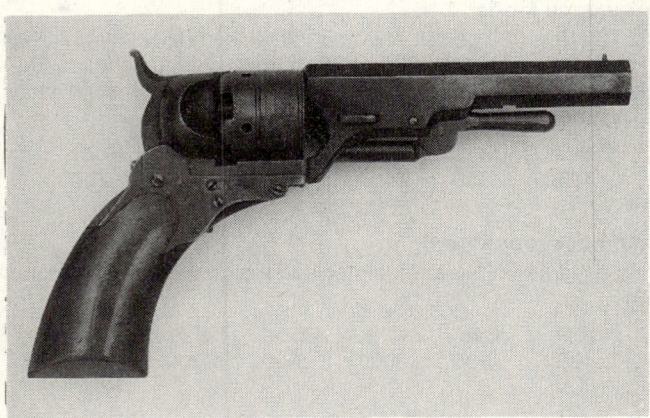

Exc.	V.G.	Good	Fair	Poor
—	—	18000	8000	—

Ehlers Belt Model Paterson

The same specifications apply to this larger revolver as they do to the Ehlers Pocket Model. It falls within the same 500 revolver involvement and is rare.

Exc.	V.G.	Good	Fair	Poor
—	—	20000	10000	—

Texas Paterson Model No. 5

This is the largest and most sought after of the Paterson models. It is also known as the Holster Model. It has been verified as actually seeing use by both the military and civilians on the American frontier. It is chambered for .36 caliber percussion, holds five shots, and has an octagonal barrel that ranges from 4" to 12" in length. It has been observed with and without the attached loading lever, but those with it are rare. The finish is blued, with a case-colored hammer. The grips are varnished walnut. The cylinder is roll-engraved; and the barrel is stamped "Patent Arms Mfg. Co. Paterson, N.J. Colts Pt." Most Texas Patersons are well used and have a worn appearance. One in excellent or V.G. condition would be highly prized. A verified military model would be worth a great deal more than standard, so qualified appraisal would be essential. The serial number range is #1-#1000, and they were manufactured from 1838-1840. The attached loading lever brings approximately a 25 percent premium.

Exc.	V.G	Good	Fair	Poor
50000	35000	25000	8500	—

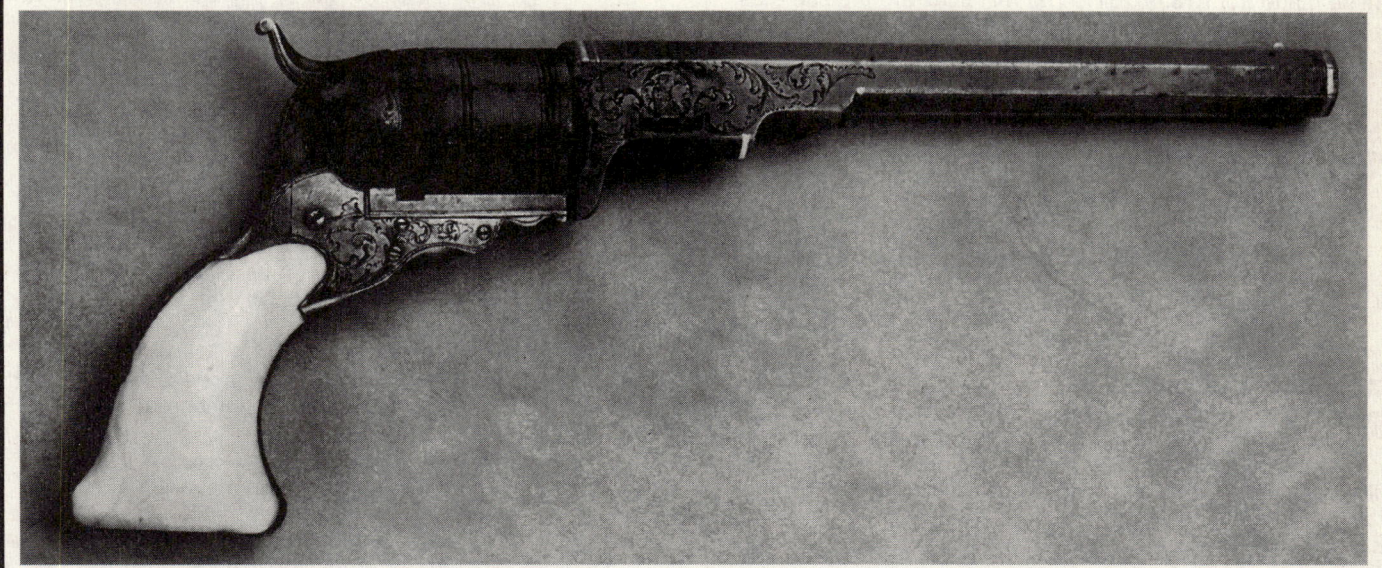

A Texas Paterson No. 5 with six silver bands, scroll engraved frame, recoil shield, hammer, and grip straps. Ivory grips. Barrel length is 7-1/2". Condition is very good. Auction price was $200,500. Butterfield & Butterfield, April 1997.

COLT REVOLVING LONG GUNS 1837-1847

First Model Ring Lever Rifle

This was actually the first firearm manufactured by Colt; the first revolver appeared a short time later. There were 200 of the First Models made in 1837 and 1838. The octagonal barrel of the First Model is 32" long and browned, while the rest of the finish is blued. The stock is varnished walnut with a cheekpiece inlaid with Colt's trademark. The ring lever located in front of the frame is pulled to rotate the 8-shot cylinder and cock the hammer. The rifle is chambered for .34, .36, .38, .40, and .44 caliber percussion. The cylinder is roll-engraved, and the barrel is stamped "Colt's Patent/Patent Arms Mfg. Co., Paterson, N. Jersey." This model has a top strap over the cylinder. They were made both with and without an attached loading lever. The latter is worth approximately 10 percent more.

Courtesy Butterfield & Butterfield, San Francisco, California

Exc.	V.G.	Good	Fair	Poor
20000	12500	8500	5000	—

Second Model Ring Lever Rifle

This model is quite similar in appearance to the First Model. Its function is identical. The major difference is the absence of the top strap over the cylinder. It had no trademark stamped on the cheekpiece. The Second Model is offered with a 28" and a 32" octagonal barrel and is chambered for .44 caliber percussion, holding 8 shots. There were approximately 500 produced from 1838-1841. The presence of an attached cheekpiece would add approximately 10 percent to the value.

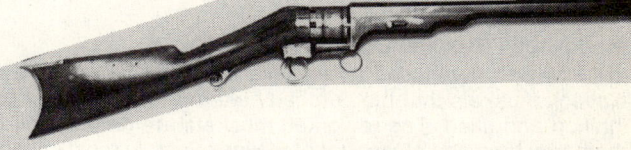

Courtesy Butterfield & Butterfield, San Francisco, California

Exc.	V.G.	Good	Fair	Poor
20000	12500	8500	5000	—

Model 1839 Carbine

This model has no ring but features an exposed hammer for cocking and rotating the 6-shot cylinder. It is chambered for .525 smoothbore and comes standard with a 24" round barrel. Other barrel lengths have been noted. The finish is blued, with a browned barrel and a varnished walnut stock. The cylinder is roll-engraved, and the barrel is stamped "Patent Arms Mfg. Co. Paterson, N.J.-Colt's Pt." There were 950 manufactured from 1838-1841. Later variations of this model are found with the attached loading lever standard, and earlier models without one would bring approximately 25 percent additional. There were 360 purchased by the military and stamped "WAT" on the stock. These would be worth twice what a standard model would bring. Anyone considering the purchase of one would be well advised to proceed with extreme caution.

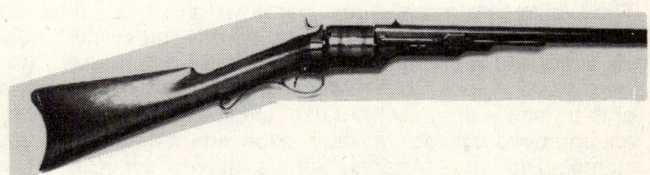

Courtesy Butterfield & Butterfield, San Francisco, California

Exc.	V.G.	Good	Fair	Poor
15000	11000	6500	3000	—

Model 1839 Shotgun

This model is quite similar in appearance to the 1839 Carbine. It is chambered for 16 gauge and holds six shots. It has a Damascus pattern barrel, and the most notable difference is a 3.5" (instead of a 2.5") long cylinder. There were only 225 of these made from 1839-1841. The markings are the same as on the Carbine.

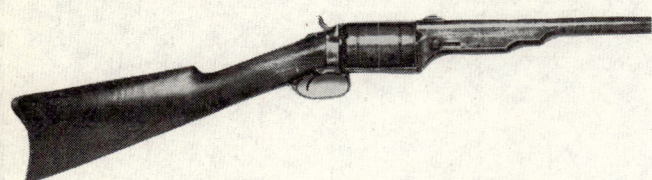

Courtesy Butterfield & Butterfield, San Francisco, California

Exc.	V.G.	Good	Fair	Poor
12500	8500	6500	3500	—

Model 1839/1850 Carbine

In 1848 Colt acquired a number of Model 1839 Carbines (approximately 40) from the state of Rhode Island. In an effort to make them marketable they were refinished and the majority fitted with plain cylinders (brightly polished) having integral ratchets around the arbor hole.

Barrel length 24"; caliber .525; barrel browned; cylinder polished; frame blued; furniture casehardened; walnut stock varnished.

Exc.	V.G.	Good	Fair	Poor
12500	8500	5000	4000	—

Model 1854 Russian Contract Musket

In 1854 Colt purchased a large number of U.S. Model 1822 flintlock muskets that the company altered to percussion cap ignition and rifled. The reworked muskets are dated 1854 on the barrel tang and at the rear of the lockplate. In most instances the original manufactory marks, such as Springfield or Harpers Ferry at the rear of the lockplate, have been removed, while the U.S. and eagle between the hammer and bolster remain. The percussion nipple bolster is marked COLT'S PATENT. Some examples have been noted with the date 1858.

Barrel length 42"; caliber .69; lock and furniture burnished bright; walnut stock oil finished.

Exc.	V.G.	Good	Fair	Poor
4000	3000	2000	1500	750

Breech loading examples made in two styles are also known. Production of this variation is believed to have only taken place on an experimental basis.

Exc.	V.G.	Good	Fair	Poor
6500	6000	5000	2500	1000

COLT WALKER-DRAGOON MODELS
Hartford, Connecticut

Walker Model Revolver

The Walker is a massive revolver. It weighs 4 lbs., 9 oz. and has a 9" part-round/part-octagonal barrel. The cylinder holds six shots and is chambered for .44 caliber percussion. There were 1,000 Walker Colts manufactured in 1847, and nearly all of them saw extremely hard use. Originally this model had a roll-engraved cylinder, military inspection marks, and barrel stamping that read "Address Saml. Colt-New York City." Practically all examples noted have had these markings worn or rusted beyond recognition. Because the Walker is perhaps the most desirable and sought-after Colt from a collector's standpoint and because of the extremely high value of a Walker in any condition, qualified appraisal is definitely recommended.

These revolvers were serial numbered A, B, C, and D Company 1-220, and E Company 1-120.

Courtesy Buffalo Bill Historical Center, Cody, Wyoming

Exc.	V.G.	Good	Fair	Poor
—	—	300000	150000	50000

Civilian Walker Revolver

This model is identical to the military model but has no martial markings. They are found serial numbered 1001 through 1100.

Exc.	V.G.	Good	Fair	Poor
—	—	300000	150000	50000

A Model 1847 Whitneyville Walker Dragoon, serial number B Company No. 8, was sold at auction for $143,000. Condition was good. Which is a rare condition for this revolver. Butterfield & Butterfield, December 1995.

Whitneyville Hartford Dragoon

This is a large, 6-shot, .44 caliber percussion revolver. It has a 7.5" part-round/part-octagonal barrel. The frame, hammer, and loading lever are case colored. The remainder is blued, with a brass triggerguard and varnished walnut grips. There were only 240 made in late 1847. The serial numbers run from 1100-1340. This model is often referred to as a Transitional Walker. Some of the parts used in its manufacture were left over from the Walker production run. This model has a roll-engraved cylinder scene, and the barrel is stamped "Address Saml. Colt New York-City." This is an extremely rare model, and much care should be taken to authenticate any contemplated acquisitions.

Exc.	V.G.	Good	Fair	Poor
—	—	35000	25000	18500

Walker Replacement Dragoon

This extremely rare Colt (300 produced) is sometimes referred to as the "Fluck" in memory of the gentleman who first identified it as a distinct and separate model. They were produced by Colt as replacements to the military for Walkers that were no longer fit for service due to mechanical failures. They were large, 6-shot, .44 caliber percussion revolvers with 7.5" part-round/part-octagonal barrels. Serial numbers ran from 2216 to 2515. The frame, hammer, and loading lever are case-colored; the remainder, blued, The grips, which are longer than other Dragoons and similar to the Walkers, are of varnished walnut and bear the inspectors mark "WAT" inside an oval cartouche on one side and the letters "JH" on the other. The frame is stamped "Colt's/ Patent/U.S." The letter "P" appears on various parts of the gun. This is another model that should definitely be authenticated before any acquisition is made.

Exc.	V.G.	Good	Fair	Poor
—	—	30000	20000	5000

First Model Dragoon

Another large, 6-shot, .44 caliber percussion revolver. It has a 7.5" part-round/part-octagonal barrel. The frame, hammer, and loading lever are case colored; the remainder, blued with a brass grip frame and square backed triggerguard. The triggerguard is silver-plated on the Civilian Model only. Another distinguishing feature on the First Model is the oval cylinder stop notches. The serial number range is 1341-8000. There were approximately 5,000 made. The cylinder is roll-engraved; and the barrel stampings read "Address Saml. Colt, New York City." "Colt's Patent" appears on the frame. On Military Models the letters "U.S." also appear on the frame.

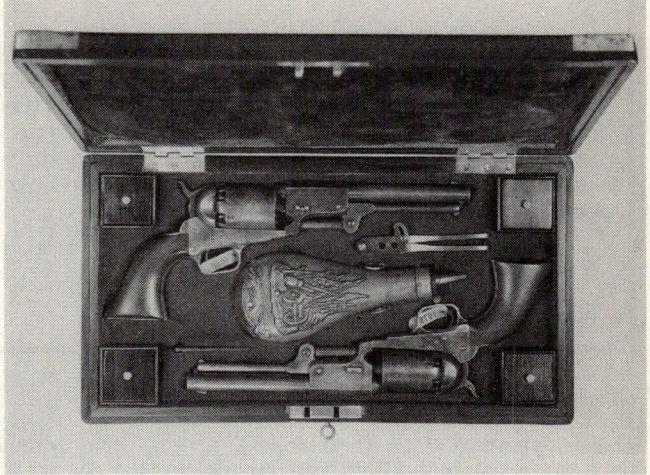

Courtesy Buffalo Bill Historical Center, Cody, Wyoming

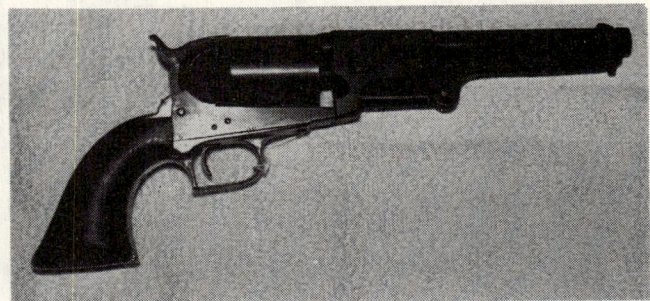

Military Model

Exc.	V.G.	Good	Fair	Poor
—	65000	35000	20000	3000

Civilian Model

Exc.	V.G.	Good	Fair	Poor
—	35000	25000	18000	2500

Second Model Dragoon

Most of the improvements that distinguish this model from the First Model are internal and not readily apparent. The most obvious external change is the rectangular cylinder-stop notches. This model is serial numbered from 8000-10700, for a total production of approximately 2,700 revolvers manufactured in 1850 and 1851. There is a Civilian Model, a Military Model, and an extremely rare variation that was issued to the militias of New Hampshire and Massachussetts (marked "MS."). Once again, caution is advised in acquisition.

Civilian Model

Exc.	V.G.	Good	Fair	Poor
—	55000	35000	25000	3000

Military Model

Exc.	V.G.	Good	Fair	Poor
—	55000	45000	30000	2500

Militia Model

Exc.	V.G.	Good	Fair	Poor
—	55000	45000	30000	2500

Third Model Dragoon

This is the most common of all the large Colt percussion revolvers. Approximately 10,500 were manufactured from 1851 through 1861. It is quite similar in appearance to the Second Model, and the most obvious external difference is the round triggerguard. The Third Model Dragoon was the first Colt revolver available with a detachable shoulder stock. There are three basic types of stocks, and all are quite rare as only 1,250 were produced. There are two other major variations we will note—the "C.L." Dragoon, which was a militia-issued model and is rare, and the late-issue model with an 8" barrel. These are found over serial number 18000, and only 50 were produced. Qualified appraisal should be secured before acquisition as many fakes abound.

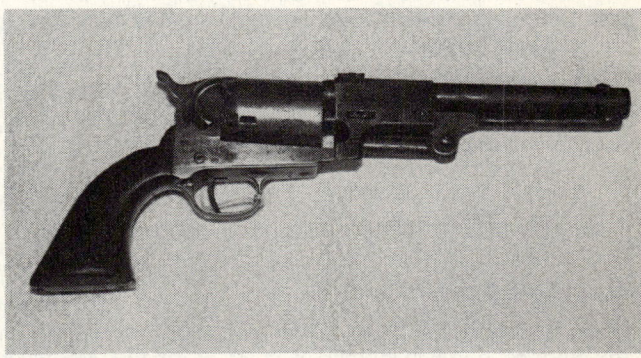

Civilian Model

Exc.	V.G.	Good	Fair	Poor
50000	40000	25000	15000	2000

Military Model

Exc.	V.G.	Good	Fair	Poor
—	45000	27500	17500	2500

> A Martial 3rd Model Dragoon in standard military configuration was sold at auction for $25,300. Condition was very good with traces of the cartouche remaining.
> Butterfield & Butterfield, December 1995.

Shoulder Stock Cut Revolvers

Exc.	V.G.	Good	Fair	Poor
50000	40000	27500	17500	2500

Shoulder Stocks

Exc.	V.G.	Good	Fair	Poor
15000	12000	8000	4000	2000

C.L. Dragoon (Hand Engraved, Not Stamped)

Exc.	V.G.	Good	Fair	Poor
—	55000	35000	15000	2500

8" Barrel Late Issue

Exc.	V.G.	Good	Fair	Poor
55000	45000	35000	25000	4000

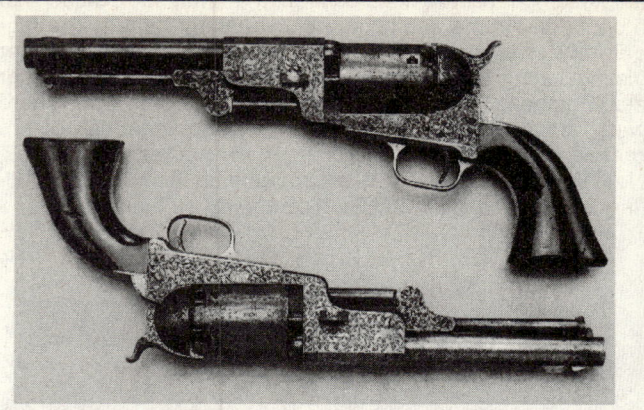

A pair of deluxe engraved presentation Colt Third Model revolvers was sold at auction for $299,500. All metal surfaces of the revolvers were engraved except the barrels by Gustave Young. This pair was consecutively numbered. Donated by Sam Colt as a shooting prize among US mounted troops. Overall condition is excellent. Butterfield & Butterfield, April 1997.

Hartford English Dragoon

This is a variation of the Third Model Dragoon. The only notable differences are the British proofmarks and the distinct #1-#700 serial number range. Other than these two features, the description given for the Third Model would apply. These revolvers were manufactured in Hartford but were finished at Colt's London factory from 1853-1857. Some bear the hand-engraved barrel marking "Col. Colt London." Many of the English Dragoons were elaborately engraved, and individual appraisal would be a must.

Two hundred revolvers came back to America in 1861 to be used in the Civil War. As with all the early Colts, caution is advised in acquisition.

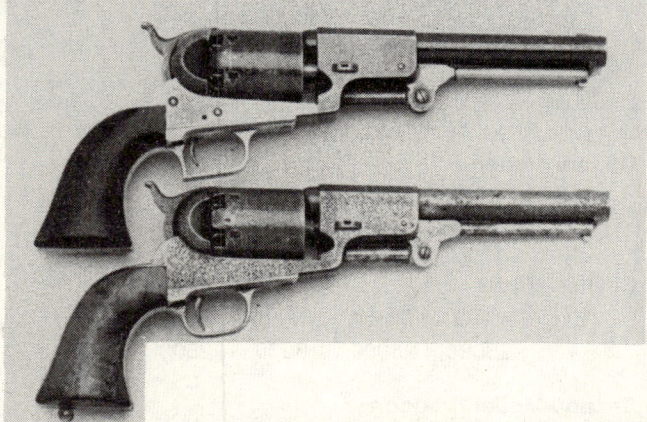

Courtesy Butterfield & Butterfield, San Francisco, California

Exc.	V.G.	Good	Fair	Poor
45000	35000	20000	12000	3000

Model 1848 Baby Dragoon

This is a small, 5-shot, .31 caliber percussion revolver. It has an octagonal barrel in lengths of 3", 4", 5", and 6". Most were made without an attached loading lever, although some with loading levers have been noted. The frame, hammer, and loading lever (when present) are case colored; the barrel and cylinder, blued. The grip frame and triggerguard are silver-plated brass. There were approximately 15,500 manufactured between 1847 and 1850. The serial range is between #1-#5500. The barrels are stamped "Address Saml. Colt/New York City." Some have been noted with the barrel address inside brackets. The frame is marked "Colt's/Patent." The first 10,000 revolvers have the Texas Ranger/Indian roll-engraved cylinder scene; the later guns the stagecoach holdup scene. This is a popular model, and many fakes have been noted.

Attached Loading Lever-Add 15%.

Courtesy Milwaukee Public Museum, Milwaukee, Wisconsin

Texas Ranger/Indian Scene

Exc.	V.G.	Good	Fair	Poor
25000	20000	15000	6000	1500

Stagecoach Holdup Scene

Exc.	V.G.	Good	Fair	Poor
25000	20000	15000	6000	1500

Model 1849 Pocket Revolver

This is a small, either 5- or 6-shot, .31 caliber percussion revolver. It has an octagonal barrel 3", 4", 5", or 6" in length. Most had loading gates, but some did not. The frame, hammer, and loading lever are case colored; the cylinder and barrel are blued. The grip frame and round triggerguard are made of brass and are silver plated. There are both large and small triggerguard variations noted. This is the most plentiful of all the Colt percussion revolvers, with approximately 325,000

manufactured over a 23-year period, 1850-1873. There are over 200 variations of this model, and one should consult an expert for individual appraisals. There are many fine publications specializing in the field of Colt percussion revolvers that would be helpful in the identification of the variations. The values represented here are for the standard model.

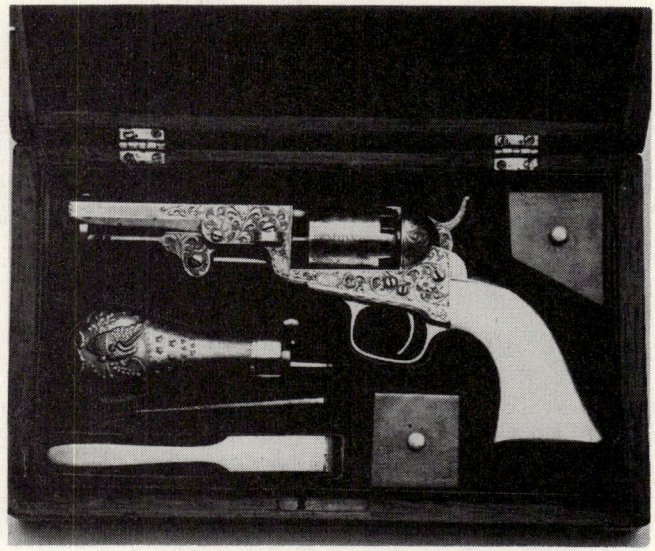

Courtesy Butterfield & Butterfield, San Francisco, California

Exc.	V.G.	Good	Fair	Poor
5000	4500	1800	1000	200

London Model 1849 Pocket Revolver

Identical in configuration to the standard 1849 Pocket Revolver, the London-made models have a higher quality finish and their own serial number range, #1-#11000. They were manufactured from 1853 through 1857. They feature a roll-engraved cylinder scene, and the barrels are stamped "Address Col. Colt/London." The first 265 revolvers, known as early models, have brass grip frames and small round triggerguards. They are quite rare and worth approximately 50 percent more than the standard model that has a steel grip frame and large oval triggerguard.

Exc.	V.G.	Good	Fair	Poor
4250	3500	1500	850	200

> A cased Exhibition Grade factory engraved London Pocket Model 1849 was sold at auction for $44,000. Barrel stamped with London proofs. Condition was excellent to mint. Butterfield & Butterfield, December 1995.

Model 1851 Navy Revolver

This is undoubtedly the most popular revolver Colt produced in the medium size and power range. It is a 6-shot, .36-caliber percussion revolver with a 7.5" octagonal barrel. It has an attached loading lever. The basic model has a case colored frame hammer, and loading lever, with silver-plated brass grip frame and triggerguard. The grips are varnished walnut. Colt manufactured approximately 215,000 of these fine revolvers between 1850 and 1873. The basic Navy features a roll-engraved cylinder scene of a battle between the navies of Texas and Mexico. There are three distinct barrel stampings—serial number 174,000, "Address Saml. Colt New York City"; serial number 74,001-101,000 "Address Saml. Colt. Hartford, Ct."; and serial number 101,001-215,000 "Address Saml. Colt New York U.S. America." The left side of the frame is stamped

"Colt's/Patent" on all variations. This model is also available with a detached shoulder stock, and values for the stocks today are nearly as high as for the revolver itself. Careful appraisal should be secured before purchase. The number of variations within the 1851 Navy model designation makes it necessary to read specialized text available on the subject. We furnish values for the major variations but again caution potential purchasers to acquire appraisals.

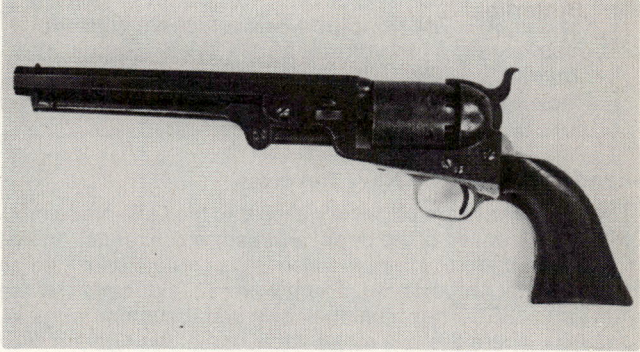

Courtesy Milwaukee Public Museum, Milwaukee, Wisconsin

Square Back Trigger Guard 1st Model Serial # 1-1000

Exc.	V.G.	Good	Fair	Poor
—	—	35000	25000	5000

Square Back Trigger Guard 2nd Model Serial # 1000-4200

Exc.	V.G.	Good	Fair	Poor
—	35000	20000	15000	2500

Small Round Trigger Guard Serial #4201-85000

Exc.	V.G.	Good	Fair	Poor
18000	14000	5000	2000	400

Large Round Trigger Guard Serial #85001-215000

Exc.	V.G.	Good	Fair	Poor
10000	8000	4000	2000	500

> A presentation Deluxe factory engraved Model 1851 Navy was sold at auction for $38,500. It was presented to the Said Pasha of Turkey by Samuel Colt. Condition was excellent. The revolver may be unfired. Butterfield & Butterfield, August 1995.

Martial Model

"U.S." stamped on the left side of frame; inspector's marks and cartouche on the grips.

Exc.	V.G.	Good	Fair	Poor
35000	25000	8000	3000	800

Shoulder Stock Variations

1st and 2nd Model Revolver Cut for Stock Only. An expert appraisial is recommended prior to a sale of these very rare variations.

Stock Only

Exc.	V.G.	Good	Fair	Poor
3500	2500	2000	1750	1250

3rd Model Cut For Stock

Revolver Only

Exc.	V.G.	Good	Fair	Poor
20000	12000	8000	2000	600

Stock

Exc.	V.G.	Good	Fair	Poor
2500	2000	1750	1250	850

> A cased set of Model 1851 Navy revolvers, serial numbers 191694 and 192602, were sold at auction for $38,500. The condition was excellent with the case having all the extras and is in excellent condition.
> Rock Island Auction Co., May 1996.

London Model 1851 Navy Revolver

These revolvers are physically similar to the U.S.-made model with the exception of the barrel address, which reads "Address Col. Colt. London." There are also British proofmarks stamped on the barrel and cylinder. There were 42,000 made between 1853 and 1857. They have their own serial-number range, #1-#42,000. There are two major variations of the London Navy, and again a serious purchaser would be well advised to seek qualified appraisal as fakes have been noted.

1st Model

Serial #1-#2,000 with a small round brass triggerguard and grip frame. Squareback guard worth a 40 percent premium.

Exc.	V.G.	Good	Fair	Poor
8000	7000	3000	2000	500

2nd Model

Serial #2,001-#42,000, steel grip frame, and large round triggerguard.

Exc.	V.G.	Good	Fair	Poor
7000	5500	2500	1500	500

Hartford Manufactured Variation

Serial numbers in the 42,000 range.

Exc.	V.G.	Good	Fair	Poor
20000	16000	4000	2500	500

COLT SIDE HAMMER MODELS

Model 1855 Side Hammer "Root" Pocket Revolver

The "Root", as it is popularly known, was the only solid-frame revolver Colt ever made. It has a spur trigger and walnut grips, and the hammer is mounted on the right side of the frame. The standard finish is a case colored frame, hammer, and loading lever, with the barrel and cylinder blued. It is chambered for both .28 caliber and .31 caliber percussion. Each caliber has its own serial number range-#1-#30000 for the .28 caliber and #1-#14000 for the .31 caliber. The model consists of seven basic variations, and the serious student should avail himself of the fine publications dealing with this model in depth. Colt produced the Side Hammer Root from 1855-1870.

Models 1 and 1A Serial #1-#384

3.5" octagonal barrel, .28 caliber, roll-engraved cylinder, Hartford barrel address without pointing hand.

Exc.	V.G.	Good	Fair	Poor
8000	7000	5000	3000	1000

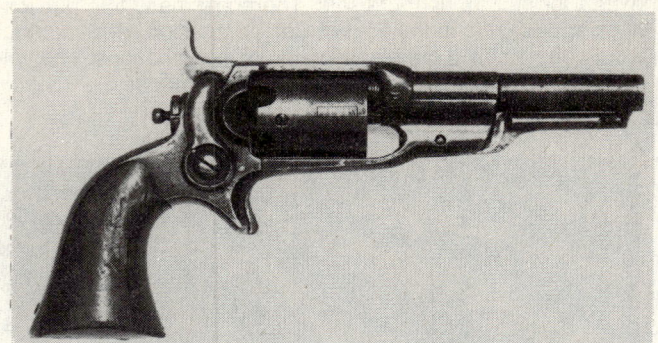

Courtesy Milwaukee Public Museum, Milwaukee, Wisconsin

Model 2 Serial #476-#25000

Same as Model 1 with pointing hand barrel address.

Exc.	V.G.	Good	Fair	Poor
4000	3000	1800	1200	500

Model 3 Serial #25001-#30000

Same as the Model 2 with a full fluted cylinder.

Exc.	V.G.	Good	Fair	Poor
4000	3000	1800	1200	500

Model 3A and 4 Serial #1-#2400

.31 caliber, 3.5" barrel, Hartford address, full fluted cylinder.

Exc.	V.G.	Good	Fair	Poor
6000	5000	3000	1500	600

Model 5 Serial #2401-#8000

.31 caliber, 3.5" round barrel, address "Col. Colt New York."

Exc.	V.G.	Good	Fair	Poor
6000	5000	3000	1500	600

Model 5A Serial #2401-#8000

Same as Model 5 with a 4.5" barrel.

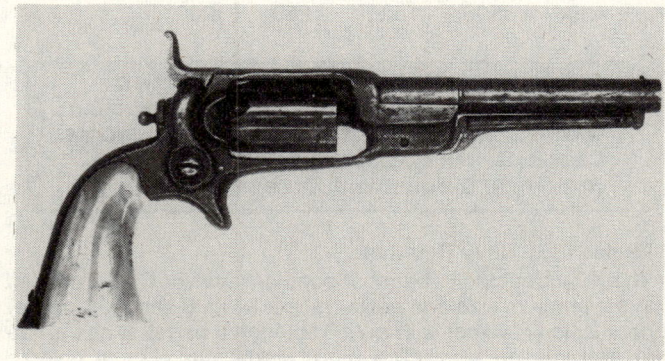

Courtesy Milwaukee Public Museum, Milwaukee, Wisconsin

Exc.	V.G.	Good	Fair	Poor
6000	5000	3000	1500	600

Models 6 and 6A Serial #8001-#11074

Same as Model 5 and 5A with roll-engraved cylinder scene.

Exc.	V.G.	Good	Fair	Poor
6000	5000	3000	1500	600

Models 7 and 7A Serial #11075–#14000
Same as Models 6 and 6A with a screw holding in the cylinder pin.

Exc.	V.G.	Good	Fair	Poor
6500	5500	3500	2000	800

COLT SIDE HAMMER LONG GUNS

1855 Sporting Rifle, 1st Model

This is a 6-shot revolving rifle chambered for .36 caliber percussion. It comes with a 21", 24", 27", or 30" round barrel that is part octagonal where it joins the frame. The stock is walnut with either an oil or a varnish finish. The frame, hammer, and loading lever are case colored; the rest of the metal, blued. The hammer is on the right side of the frame. The lst Model has no forend, and an oiling device is attached to the barrel underlug. The triggerguard has two spur-like projections in front and in back of the bow. The roll-engraved cylinder scene depicts a hunter shooting at five deer and is found only on this model. The standard stampings are "Colt's Pt./1856" and "Address S. Colt Hartford, Ct. U.S.A."

A Colt Model 1855 Sporting Rifle First Model was sold at auction in April of 1997 for $5,750. Fitted with a 30" barrel. Condition was about 40% blue with excellent stock.
Rock Island Auction Company.

Early Model

Low serial numbers with a hand-engraved barrel marking "Address S. Colt Hartford, U.S.A."

Exc.	V.G.	Good	Fair	Poor
15000	8500	3750	2500	1000

Production Model

Exc.	V.G.	Good	Fair	Poor
12500	6500	2750	2000	1000

1855 lst Model Carbine

Identical to the lst Model Rifle but offered with a 15" and 18" barrel.

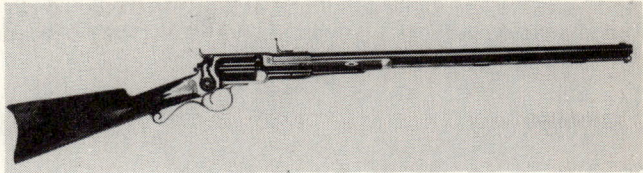

Courtesy Milwaukee Public Museum, Milwaukee, Wisconsin

Exc.	V.G.	Good	Fair	Poor
12500	10000	8000	2750	1000

1855 Half Stock Sporting Rifle

Although this rifle is quite similar in appearance and finish to the lst Model, there are some notable differences. It features a walnut forend that protrudes halfway down the barrel. There are two types of triggerguards—a short projectionless one or a long model with a graceful scroll. There is a 6-shot model chambered for .36 or .44 caliber or a 5-shot model chambered

for .56 caliber. The cylinder is fully fluted. The markings are "Colt's Pt/1856" and "Address Col. Colt/Hartford Ct. U.S.A." There were approximately 1,500 manufactured between 1857 and 1864.

Courtesy Milwaukee Public Museum, Milwaukee, Wisconsin

Exc.	V.G.	Good	Fair	Poor
12000	6500	2000	1500	750

1855 Full Stock Military Rifle

This model holds 6 shots in its .44 caliber chambering and 5 shots when chambered for .56 caliber. It is another side hammer revolving rifle that resembles the Half Stock model. The barrels are round and part-octagonal where they join the frame. They come in lengths of 21", 24", 27", 31", and 37". The hammer and loading lever are case colored; the rest of the metal parts, blued. The walnut butt stock and full length forend are oil finished, and this model has sling swivels. The cylinder is fully fluted. Military models have provisions for affixing a bayonet and military-style sights and bear the "U.S." martial mark on examples that were actually issued to the military. The standard stampings found on this model are "Colt's Pt/1856" and "Address Col. Colt Hartford, Ct. U.S.A." There were an estimated 9,300 manufactured between 1856 and 1864.

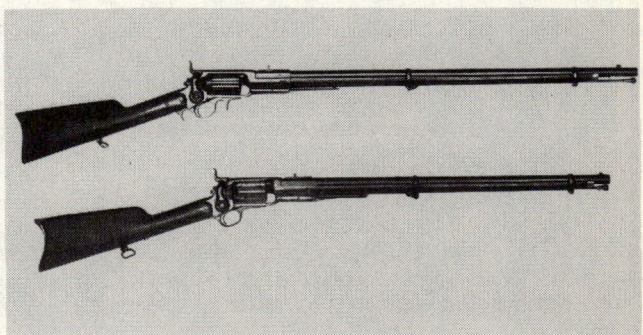

Courtesy Milwaukee Public Museum, Milwaukee, Wisconsin

Martially Marked Models

Exc.	V.G.	Good	Fair	Poor
9500	7500	5500	2500	1000

Without Martial Markings

Exc.	V.G.	Good	Fair	Poor
7500	5500	4000	2000	1000

1855 Full Stock Sporting Rifle

This model is similar in appearance to the Military model, with these notable exceptions. There is no provision for attaching a bayonet, there are no sling swivels, and it has sporting-style sights. The buttplate is crescent shaped. This model has been noted chambered for .56 caliber in a 5-shot version and chambered for .36, .40, .44, and .50 caliber in the 6-shot variation. They are quite scarce in .40 and .50 caliber and will bring a 10 percent premium. The standard markings are "Colt's Pt/1856" and "Address Col. Colt/Hartford Ct. U.S.A." Production on this model was quite limited (several hundred at most) between the years 1856 and 1864.

Exc.	V.G.	Good	Fair	Poor
15000	12000	6000	1750	500

Model 1855 Revolving Carbine

This model is similar in appearance to the 1855 Military Rifle. The barrel lengths of 15", 18", and 21" plus the absence of a forend make the standard Carbine Model readily identifiable. The markings are the same. Approximately 4,400 were manufactured between 1856 and 1864.

Exc.	V.G.	Good	Fair	Poor
12000	10000	6500	2750	1000

Model 1855 Artillery Carbine

Identical to the standard carbine but chambered for .56 caliber only, it has a 24" barrel, full-length walnut forend, and a bayonet lug.

Exc.	V.G.	Good	Fair	Poor
12000	8500	5000	3500	1200

Model 1855 British Carbine

This is a British-proofed version with barrel lengths of up to 30". It has a brass triggerguard and buttplate and is chambered for .56 caliber only. This variation is usually found in the 10000-12000 serial number range.

Exc.	V.G.	Good	Fair	Poor
8500	6500	5500	2250	750

Model 1855 Revolving Shotgun

This model very much resembles the Half Stock Sporting Rifle but was made with a 27", 30", 33", and 36" smoothbore barrel. It has a 5-shot cylinder chambered for .60 or .75 caliber (20 or 10 gauge). This model has a case colored hammer and loading lever; the rest of the metal is blued, with an occasional browned barrel noted. The buttstock and forend are of walnut, either oil or varnish-finished. This model has no rear sight and a small triggerguard with the caliber stamped on it. Some have been noted with the large scroll triggerguard; these would add 10 percent to the value. The rarest shotgun variation would be a full stocked version in either gauge, and qualified appraisal would be highly recommended. This model is serial numbered in its own range, #1-#1100. They were manufactured from 1860-1863.

.60 Caliber (20 gauge)

Exc.	V.G.	Good	Fair	Poor
8500	6500	5000	2000	750

.75 Caliber (10 gauge)

Exc.	V.G.	Good	Fair	Poor
8500	6500	5000	1750	750

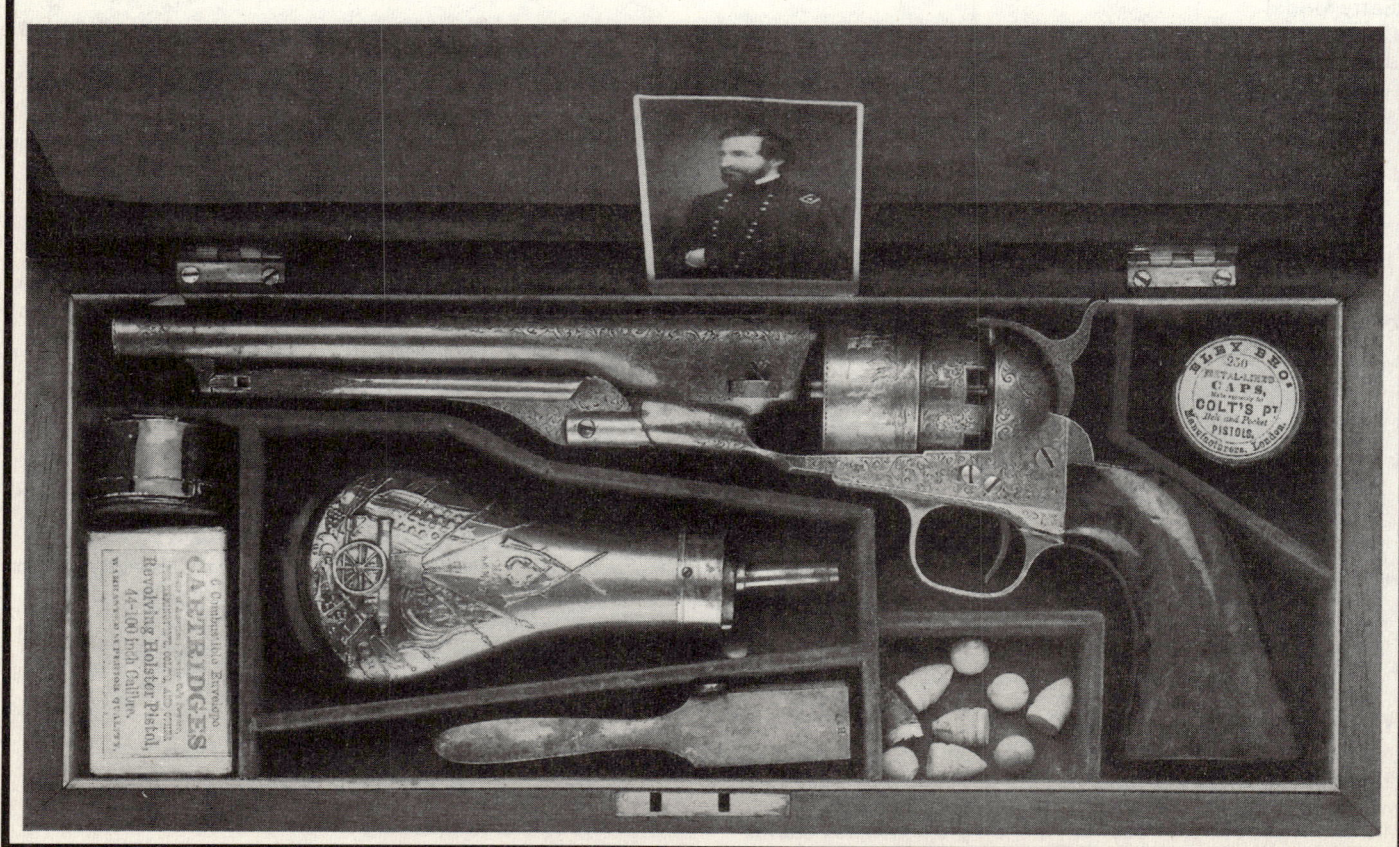

A factory presentation Colt Model 1860 Army revolver with 7-1/2" barrel and three screw frame not cut for a shoulder stock was engraved by Gustave Young. Deluxe burl walnut grips. Presented by Colt to General Rosecrans. Revolver is cased with all accessories. Condition excellent. Auction price was $112,500.
Butterfield & Butterfield, April 1997.

Model 1861 Single Shot Rifled Musket

With the advent of the Civil War, the army of the Union seriously needed military arms. Colt was given a contract to supply 112,500 1861-pattern percussion single shot muskets. Between 1861 and 1865, 75,000 were delivered. They have 40" rifled barrels chambered for .58 caliber. The musket is equipped with military sights, sling swivels, and a bayonet lug. The metal finish is bright steel, and the stock is oil-finished walnut. Military inspector's marks are found on all major parts. "VP" over an eagle is stamped on the breech along with a date. The Colt address and a date are stamped on the lockplate. A large number of these rifles were altered to the Snyder breech loading system for the Bey of Egypt.

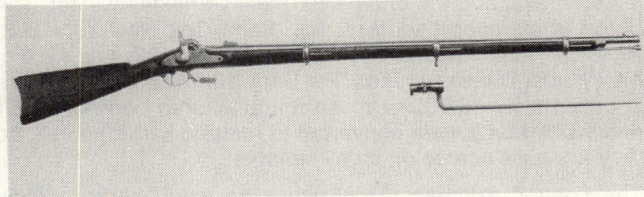

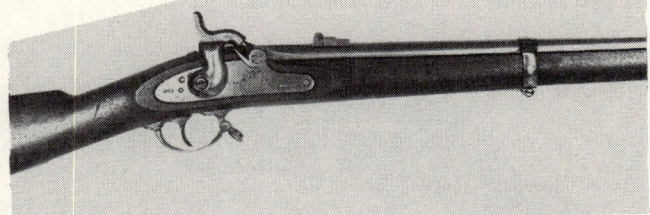

Courtesy Milwaukee Public Museum, Milwaukee, Wisconsin

Production Model

Exc.	V.G.	Good	Fair	Poor
4000	3000	1800	750	450

PERCUSSION REVOLVERS

Model 1860 Army Revolver

This model was the third most produced of the Colt percussion handguns. It was the primary revolver used by the Union Army during the Civil War. Colt delivered 127,156 of these revolvers to be used during those hostilities. This is a 6-shot .44 caliber percussion revolver. It has either a 7.5" or 8" round barrel with an attached loading lever. The frame, hammer, and loading lever are case colored; the barrel and cylinder are blued. The triggerguard and front strap are brass, and the backstrap is blued steel. The grips are one-piece walnut. The early models have the barrels stamped "Address Saml. Colt Hartford Ct." Later models are stamped "Address Col. Saml. Colt New-York U.S. America." "Colt's/Patent" is stamped on the left side of the frame; ".44 Cal.," on the triggerguard. The cylinder is roll engraved with the naval battle scene. There were a total of 200,500 1860 Army Revolvers manufactured between 1860 and 1873.

Martial Marked Model

Exc.	V.G.	Good	Fair	Poor
35000	25000	6000	3000	800

Civilian Model

This model is found in either 3-or-4 screw variations and it may or may not be cut for a shoulder stock. Civilian models are usually better finished.

Courtesy Milwaukee Public Museum, Milwaukee, Wisconsin

Exc.	V.G.	Good	Fair	Poor
15000	10000	5000	3000	800

Full Fluted Cylinder Model

Approximately 4,000 Army's were made with full fluted cylinders. They appear in the first 8,000 serial numbers.

Courtesy Milwaukee Public Museum, Milwaukee, Wisconsin

Exc.	V.G.	Good	Fair	Poor
35000	25000	12000	6000	1800

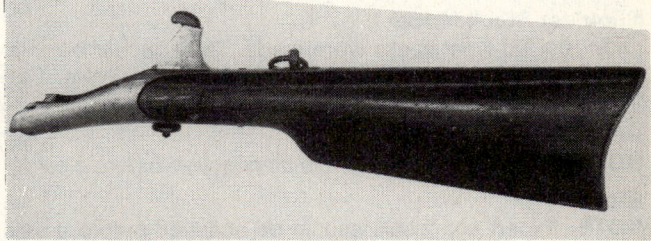

Courtesy Milwaukee Public Museum, Milwaukee, Wisconsin

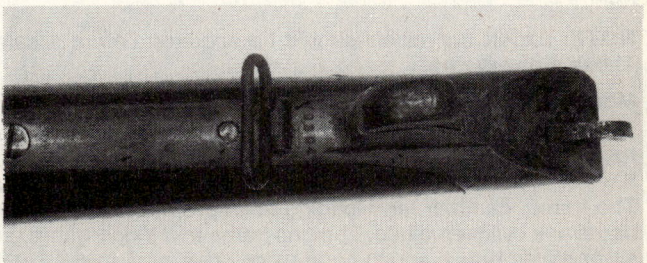

Courtesy Milwaukee Public Museum, Milwaukee, Wisconsin

Shoulder Stock 2nd Type (Fluted Cylinder Model)

NOTE: Expert appraisals should be acquired before a sale. These are rare accouterments.

Shoulder Stock 3rd Type (Standard Model)

NOTE: Expert appraisals should be acquired before a sale. These are rare accoutrements.

Model 1861 Navy Revolver

This model is a 6-shot, 7.5" round-barrelled, .36 caliber percussion revolver. The frame, hammer, and attached loading lever are case colored. The barrel and cylinder are blued. The grip frame and triggerguard are silver-plated brass. The grips are of one-piece walnut. The cylinder has the roll-engraved naval battle scene, and the barrel stamping is "Address Col. Saml. Colt New-York U.S. America." The frame is stamped "Colts/Patent" with "36 Cal." on the triggerguard. There are not many variations within the 1861 Navy model designation, as less than 39,000 were made between 1861 and 1873.

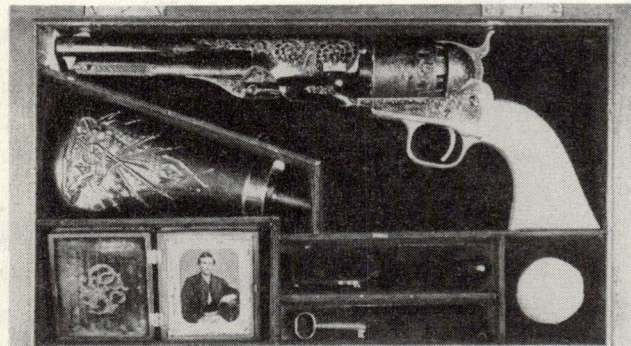

Courtesy Butterfield & Butterfield, San Francisco, California

Civilian Model

Exc.	V.G.	Good	Fair	Poor
35000	25000	5000	3000	800

Military Model

Marked "U.S." on frame, inspector's cartouche on grip. 650 were marked "U.S.N." on the butt.

Exc.	V.G.	Good	Fair	Poor
50000	35000	10000	5000	1500

Shoulder Stock Model

Only 100 3rd-type stocks were made. They appear between serial #11000-#14000. These are very rare revolvers. Cautions should be exercised.

Revolver

NOTE: Expert appraisals should be acquired before a sale.

Stock

NOTE: Expert appraisals should be acquired before a sale. These are rare accouterments.

Fluted Cylinder Model

Approximately the first 100 were made with full fluted cylinders.

NOTE: Expert appraisals should be acquired before a sale. These are very rare.

Model 1862 Pocket Navy Revolver

This is a smaller, 5-shot, .36 caliber percussion revolver that resembles the configuration of the 1851 Navy. It has a 4.5", 5.5", or 6.5" octagonal barrel with an attached loading lever. The frame, hammer, and loading lever are case colored; the barrel and cylinder, blued. The grip frame and triggerguard are silver-plated brass; and the one-piece grips, of varnished walnut. The stagecoach holdup scene is roll-engraved on the cylinder. The frame is stamped "Colt's/Patent"; and the barrel, "Address Col. Saml. Colt New-York U.S. America." There were approximately 19,000 manufactured between 1861 and 1873. They are serial numbered in the same range as the Model 1862 Police. Because a great many were used for metallic cartridge conversions, they are quite scarce today.

The London Address Model with blued steel grip frame would be worth more than the standard model.

Standard Production Model

Exc.	V.G.	Good	Fair	Poor
15000	8000	3000	2000	800

Model 1862 Police Revolver

This is a slim, attractively designed revolver that some consider to be the most aesthetically pleasing of all the Colt percussion designs. It has a 5-shot, half-fluted cylinder chambered for .36 caliber. It is offered with a 3.5", 4.5", 5.5", or 6.5" round barrel. The frame, hammer, and loading lever are case colored; the barrel and cylinder, blued. The grip frame is silver-plated brass; and the one-piece grips, varnished walnut. The barrel is stamped "Address Col. Saml Colt New-York U.S. America"; the frame has "Colt's/Patent" on the left side. One of the cylinder flutes is marked "Pat Sept. 10th 1850." There were approximately 28,000 of these manufactured between 1861 and 1873. Many were converted to metallic cartridge use, so they are quite scarce on today's market.

The London Address Model would be worth approximately twice the value of the standard model.

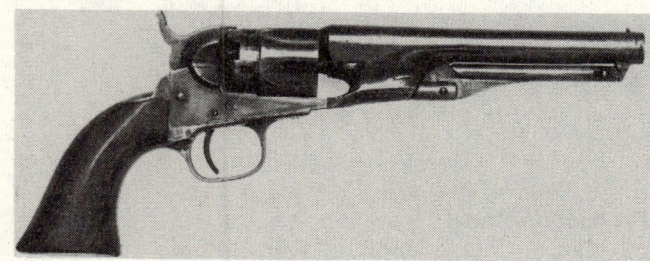

Courtesy Milwaukee Public Museum, Milwaukee, Wisconsin

Standard Production Model

Exc.	V.G.	Good	Fair	Poor
10000	6000	3000	1800	800

> A presentation Colt Model 1862 Police revolver was sold at auction for $8,500. The revolver was fitted with a 6.5" barrel and was silver plated. Inscription dated June 10, 1863. Condition was very good.
> J.C. Devine, Inc., March 1996.

METALLIC CARTRIDGE CONVERSIONS

Thuer Conversion Revolver

Although quite simplistic and not commercially successful, the Thuer Conversion was the first attempt by Colt to convert the percussion revolvers to the new metallic cartridge system. This conversion was designed around the tapered Thuer cartridge and consists of a ring that replaced the back part of the cylinder, which had been milled off. This ring is stamped "Pat. Sep. / 15. 1868." The ejection position is marked with the letter "E." These conversions have rebounding firing pins and are milled to allow loading from the front of the revolver. This conversion was undertaken on the six different models listed below; and all other specifications, finishes, markings, etc., not directly affected by the conversion would be the same as previously described. From a collectible and investment standpoint, the Thuer Conversion is very desirable. Competent appraisal should be secured if acquisition is contemplated.

Model 1849 Pocket Conversion

Exc.	V.G.	Good	Fair	Poor
15000	12000	6000	3000	1500

Model 1851 Navy Conversion

Exc.	V.G.	Good	Fair	Poor
12000	10000	6000	3000	1500

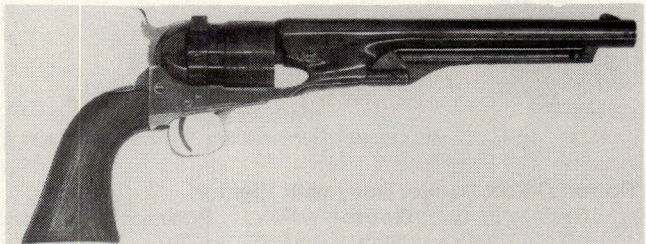

Courtesy Milwaukee Public Museum, Milwaukee, Wisconsin

Model 1860 Army Conversion

Exc.	V.G.	Good	Fair	Poor
12000	8000	6000	3000	1500

Model 1861 Navy Conversion

Exc.	V.G.	Good	Fair	Poor
10000	8000	6000	3000	2000

Models 1862 Police Conversion

Exc.	V.G.	Good	Fair	Poor
10000	8000	6000	3000	2000

Model 1862 Pocket Navy Conversion

Exc.	V.G.	Good	Fair	Poor
10000	8000	6000	3000	2000

NOTE: Blued models will bring higher prices than nickel models in the same condition.

Richards Conversion, 1860 Army Revolver

This was Colt's second attempt at metallic cartridge conversion, and it met with quite a bit more success than the first. The Richards Conversion was designed for the .44 Colt cartridge and has a 6-shot cylinder and an integral ejector rod to replace the loading lever that had been removed. The other specifications pertaining to the 1860 Army Revolver remain as previously described if they are not directly altered by the conversion. The Richards Conversion adds a breechplate with a firing pin and its own rear sight. There were approximately 9,000 of these Conversions manufactured between 1873 and 1878.

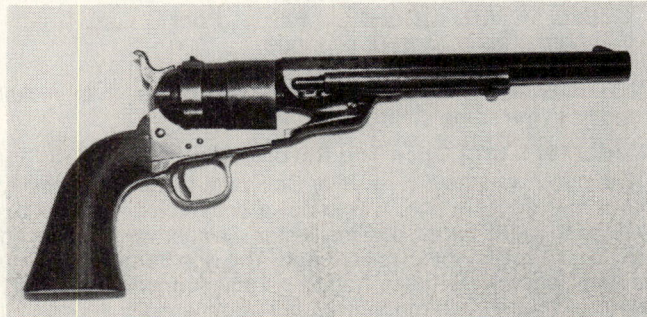

Civilian Model

Exc.	V.G.	Good	Fair	Poor
12000	8000	3000	2000	1000

Martially Marked Variation

This variation is found with mixed serial numbers and a second set of conversion serial numbers. The "U.S." is stamped on the left side of the barrel lug, and inspector's cartouche appears on the grip. This is a very rare Colt revolver.

Exc.	V.G.	Good	Fair	Poor
35000	25000	15000	6000	2500

NOTE: Blued models will bring higher prices than nickel models in the same condition.

Transition Richards Model

This variation is marked by the presence of a firing pin hammer.

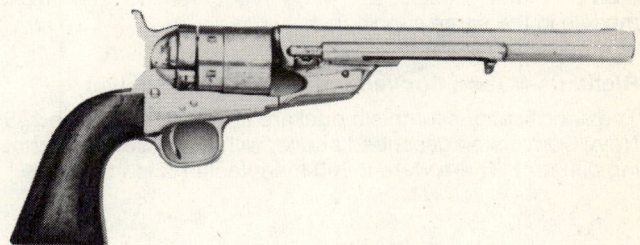

Courtesy Butterfield & Butterfield, San Francisco, California

Exc.	V.G.	Good	Fair	Poor
13500	9000	3500	2500	1000

NOTE: Blued models will bring higher prices than nickel models in the same condition.

Richards-Mason Conversion, 1860 Army Revolver

This conversion is different from the Richards Conversion in a number of readily apparent aspects. The barrel was manufactured with a small lug much different in appearance than seen on the standard 1860 Army. The breechplate does not have its own rear sight, and there is a milled area to allow the hammer to contact the base of the cartridge. These Conversions were also chambered for the .44 Colt cartridge, and the cylinder holds 6 shots. There is an integral ejector rod in place of the loading lever. The barrels on some are stamped either "Address Col. Saml. Colt New-York U.S. America" or "Colt's Pt. F.A. Mfg. Co. Hartford, Ct." The patent dates 1871 and 1872 are stamped on the left side of the frame. The finish of these revolvers, as well as the grips, were for the most part the same as on the unconverted Armies; but for the first time, nickel-plated guns are found. There were approximately 2,100 of these Conversions produced in 1877 and 1878.

Exc.	V.G.	Good	Fair	Poor
15000	9500	4000	3000	1500

NOTE: Blued models will bring higher prices than nickel models in the same condition.

Richards-Mason Conversions 1851 Navy Revolver

These revolvers were converted in the same way as the 1860 Army previously described, the major difference being the caliber .38, either rimfire or centerfire. Finishes are mostly the same as on unconverted revolvers, but nickel-plated guns are not rare.

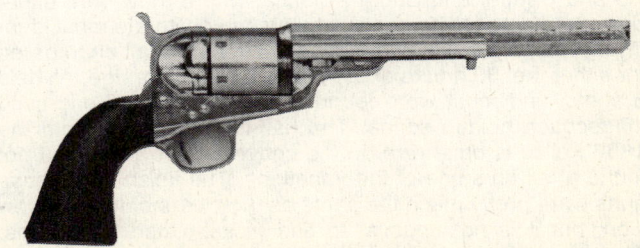

Courtesy Butterfield & Butterfield, San Francisco, California

Production Model Serial #1-3800

Exc.	V.G.	Good	Fair	Poor
10000	8000	3000	2000	1000

U.S. Navy Model Serial #41000-91000 Range

"USN" stamped on butt; steel grip frame.

Exc.	V.G.	Good	Fair	Poor
15000	10000	5000	3000	1500

NOTE: Blued models will bring higher prices than nickel models in the same condition.

Richards-Mason Conversion 1861 Navy Revolver

The specifications for this model are the same as for the 1851 Navy Conversion described above, with the base revolver being different. There were 2,200 manufactured in the 1870s.

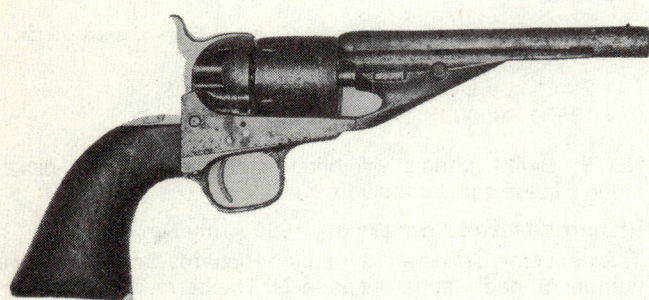

Courtesy Wallis & Wallis, Lewes, Sussex, England

Standard Production Model Serial #100-#3300 Range

Exc.	V.G.	Good	Fair	Poor
8000	6000	3000	2000	1000

U.S. Navy Model #1000-#9999 Serial Range

Exc.	V.G.	Good	Fair	Poor
15000	12000	6000	3000	1500

NOTE: Blued models will bring higher prices than nickel models in the same condition.

Model 1862 Police and Pocket Navy Conversions

The conversion of these two revolver models is the most difficult to catalogue of all the Colt variations. There were approximately 24,000 of these produced between 1873 and 1880. There are five basic variations with a number of sub-variations. The confusion is usually caused by the different ways in which these were marked. Depending upon what parts were utilized, caliber markings could be particularly confusing. One must also consider the fact that many of these conversion revolvers found their way into secondary markets, such as Mexico and Central and South America, where they were either destroyed or received sufficient abuse to obliterate most identifying markings. The five basic variations are all chambered for either the .38 rimfire or the .38 centerfire cartridge. All held 5 shots, and most were found with the round roll-engraved stagecoach holdup scene. The half-fluted cylinder from the 1862 Police is quite rare on the conversion revolver and not found at all on some of the variations. The finishes on these guns were pretty much the same as they were before conversion, but it is not unusual to find nickel-plated specimens. Blued models will bring a premium over nickel in the same condition. The basic variations are as follows.

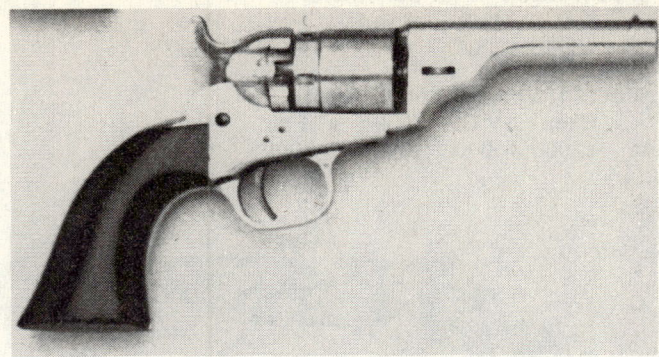

Courtesy Butterfield & Butterfield, San Francisco, California

Round Barrel Pocket Navy with Ejector

Exc.	V.G.	Good	Fair	Poor
4000	3500	2000	1500	750

3.5" Round Barrel Without Ejector

Exc.	V.G.	Good	Fair	Poor
2500	2000	1000	650	300

4.5" Octagonal Barrel

Exc.	V.G.	Good	Fair	Poor
4000	3000	1500	1000	600

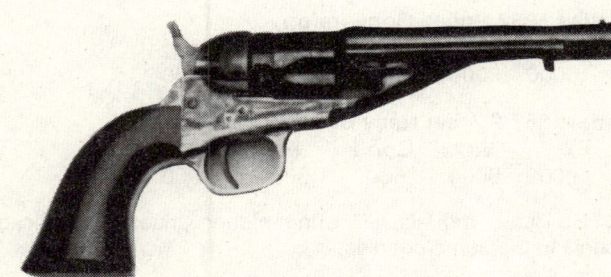

Courtesy Butterfield & Butterfield, San Francisco, California

NOTE: Blued models will bring higher prices than nickel models in the same condition.

Standard Configuration 1862 Police and Pocket Navy

Half-fluted cylinder-Add 20%.

Exc.	V.G.	Good	Fair	Poor
4000	2500	1500	1000	500

Round Barrel Model, with Ejector

Exc.	V.G.	Good	Fair	Poor
4000	2500	1500	1000	500

NOTE: Blued models will bring higher prices than nickel models in the same condition.

Model 1871-1872 Open Top Revolver

This model was the first revolver Colt manufactured especially for a metallic cartridge. It was not a conversion. The frame, 7.5" or 8" round barrel, and the 6-shot cylinder were produced for the .44 rimfire metallic cartridge. The grip frame and some internal parts were taken from the 1860 Army and the 1851 Navy. Although this model was not commercially successful and was not accepted by the U.S. Ordnance Department, it did pave the way for the Single Action Army that came out shortly thereafter and was an immediate success. This model is all blued, with a case colored hammer. There are some with silver-plated brass grip frames, but most are blued steel. The one-piece grips are of varnished walnut. The cylinder is roll-engraved with the naval battle scene. The barrel is stamped "Address Col. Saml. Colt New-York U.S. America." The later production revolvers are barrel stamped "Colt's Pt. F.A. Mfg. Co. Hartford, Ct. U.S.A." The first 1,000 revolvers were stamped "Colt's/Patent." After that, 1871 and 1872 patent dates appeared on the frame. There were 7,000 of these revolvers manufactured in 1872 and 1873.

1860 Army Grip Frame

Exc.	V.G.	Good	Fair	Poor
25000	20000	10000	6000	3000

1851 Navy Grip Frame

Exc.	V.G.	Good	Fair	Poor
11500	9500	7500	4500	2250

NOTE: Blued models will bring higher prices than nickel models in the same condition.

COLT DERRINGERS AND POCKET REVOLVERS

First Model Derringer

This is a small all-metal single shot. It is chambered for the .44 rimfire cartridge. The 2.5" barrel pivots to the left and downward for loading. This model is engraved with a scroll pattern and has been noted blued, silver, or nickel-plated. The barrel is stamped "Colt's Pt. F.A. Mfg. Co./Hartford Ct. U.S.A/ No.1." ".41 Cal." is stamped on the frame under the release catch. There were approximately 6,500 of this model manufactured from 1870-1890. It was the first single shot pistol Colt produced.

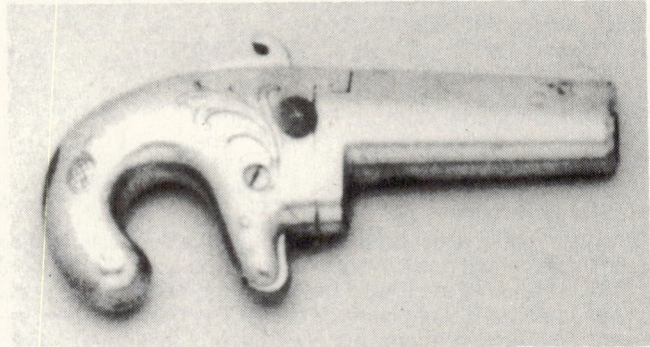

Courtesy Butterfield & Butterfield, San Francisco, California

Exc.	V.G.	Good	Fair	Poor
4000	3000	1800	1200	400

Second Model Derringer

Although this model has the same odd shape as the First Model, it is readily identifiable by the checkered varnished walnut grips and the "No 2" on the barrel after the address. It is also .41 rimfire and has a 2.5" barrel that pivots in the same manner as the First Model. There were approximately 9,000 of these manufactured between 1870 and 1890.

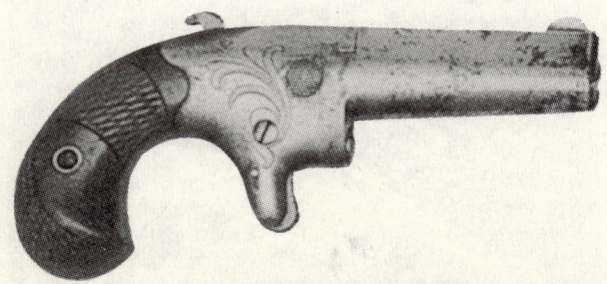

Courtesy Wallis & Wallis, Lewes, Sussex, England

Exc.	V.G.	Good	Fair	Poor
3500	2500	1500	800	400

Third Model Derringer

This model was designed by Alexander Thuer who was also responsible for Colt's first metallic cartridge conversion. It is often referred to as the "Thuer Model" for this reason. It is also chambered for the .41 rimfire cartridge and has a 2.5" barrel that pivots to the right (but not down) for loading. The Third Model has a more balanced appearance than its predecessors, and its commercial success (45,000 produced between 1875 and 1910) reflects this. The barrel on this model is stamped "Colt" in small block letters on the first 2,000 guns. The remainder of the production features the "COLT" in large italicized print. The ".41 Cal." is stamped on the left side of the frame. This model will be found with the barrel blued or plated in either silver or nickel and the bronze frame plated. The grips are varnished walnut.

Courtesy Butterfield & Butterfield, San Francisco, California.

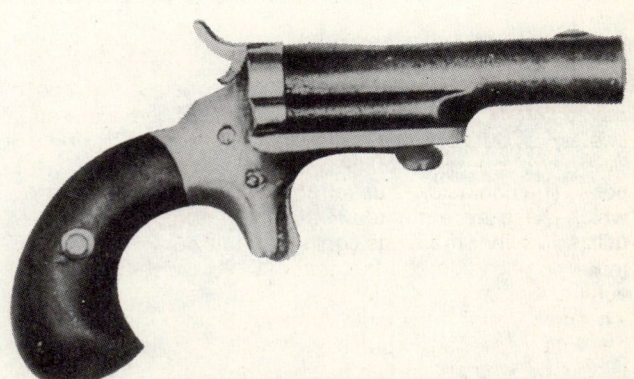

Courtesy Wallis & Wallis, Lewes, Sussex, England

First Variation, Early Production

This has a raised area on the underside of the frame through which the barrel screw passes, and the spur is not angled. Small block "Colt" lettering on barrel.

Exc.	V.G.	Good	Fair	Poor
6000	4000	3000	1500	800

First Variation, Late Production

This is similar to early production but has large italicized "COLT" on barrel.

Exc.	V.G.	Good	Fair	Poor
3000	2500	2000	1500	500

Production Model

Exc.	V.G.	Good	Fair	Poor
1500	1200	600	400	200

House Model Revolver

There are two basic versions of this model. They are both chambered for the .41 rimfire cartridge. The 4-shot version is known as the "Cloverleaf" due to the shape of the cylinder when viewed from the front. Approximately 7,500 of the nearly 10,000 House revolvers were of this 4-shot configuration. They are offered with a 1.5" or 3" barrel. The 1.5" length is quite rare, and some octagonal barrels in this length have been noted. The 5-shot round-cylinder version accounts for the rest of the production. It is found with serial numbers over 6100 and is offered with a 2-7/8" length barrel only. This model is stamped on the top strap "Pat. Sept. 19, 1871." This model has brass frames that were sometimes nickel-plated. The barrels are found either blued or plated. The grips are varnished walnut or rosewood. There were slightly fewer than 10,000 of both variations manufactured from 1871-1876.

Cloverleaf with 1.5" Round Barrel

NOTE: Octagon barrel variation will command a premium

Exc.	V.G.	Good	Fair	Poor
4000	3000	2000	1500	500

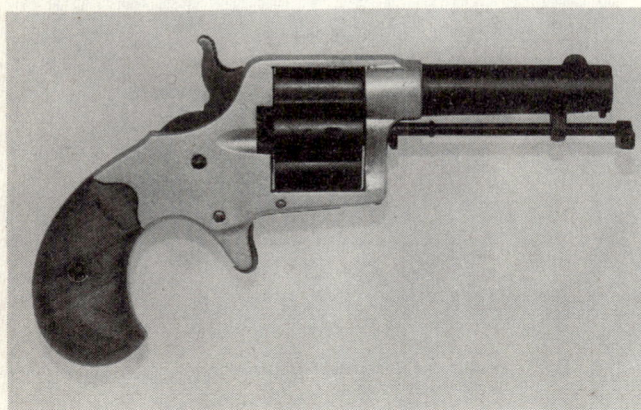

Courtesy Buffalo Bill Historical Center, Cody, Wyoming

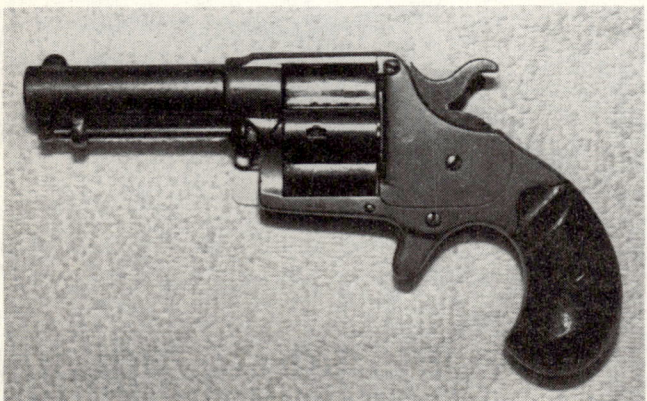

Cloverleaf with 3" Barrel

Exc.	V.G.	Good	Fair	Poor
2500	2000	1200	600	400

House Pistol with 5-Shot Round Cylinder

Exc.	V.G.	Good	Fair	Poor
3000	2500	1500	1000	500

Open Top Pocket Revolver

This is a .22-caliber rimfire, 7-shot revolver that was offered with either a 2-3/8" or a 2-7/8" barrel. The model was a commercial success, with over 114,000 manufactured between 1871 and 1877. There would undoubtedly have been a great deal more sold had not the cheap copies begun to flood the market at that time, forcing Colt to drop this model from the line. This revolver has a silver or nickel-plated brass frame and a nickel-plated or blued barrel and cylinder. The grips are varnished walnut. The cylinder bolt slots are found toward the front on this model. "Colt's Pt. F.A. Mfg. Co./Hartford, Ct. U.S.A." is stamped on the barrel and ".22 Cal." on the left side of the frame.

NOTE: Blued models will bring a premium over nickel in the same condition.

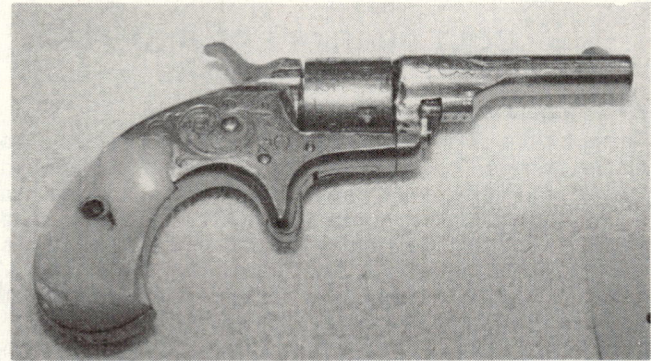

Early Model With Ejector Rod

Exc.	V.G.	Good	Fair	Poor
2500	1800	1200	800	400

Production Model Without Ejector Rod

Exc.	V.G.	Good	Fair	Poor
1200	1000	500	300	150

New Line Revolver .22

This was the smallest framed version of the five distinct New Line Revolvers. It has a 7-shot cylinder and a 2.25" octagonal barrel. The frame is nickel-plated, and the balance of the revolver is either nickel-plated or blued. The grips are of rosewood. There were approximately 55,000 of these made from 1873-1877. Colt also stopped production of the New Lines rather than try to compete with the "Suicide Specials." "Colt New .22" is found on the barrel; and ".22 Cal.," on the frame. The barrel is also stamped "Colt's Pt. F.A. Mfg.Co./Hartford, Ct. U.S.A."

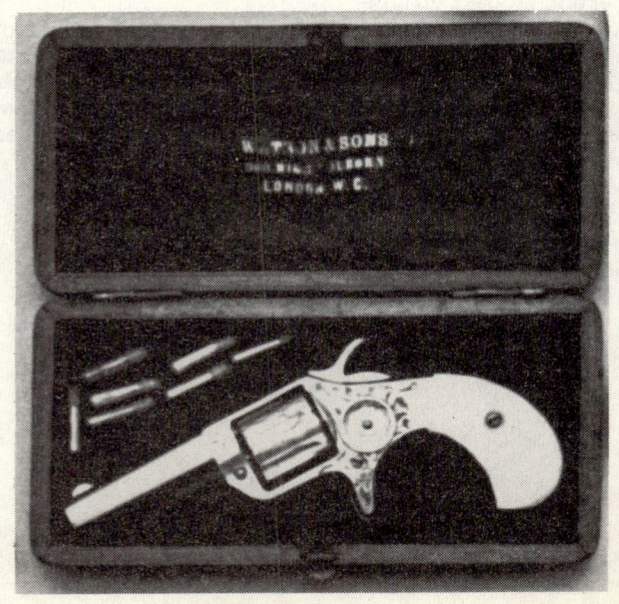

Courtesy Butterfield & Butterfield, San Francisco, California

1st Model
Short cylinder flutes.

Exc.	V.G.	Good	Fair	Poor
1500	1200	600	400	200

2nd Model
Long cylinder flutes.

Exc.	V.G.	Good	Fair	Poor
1500	1200	600	400	200

NOTE: Blued models will bring higher prices than nickel models in the same condition.

New Line Revolver .30
This is a larger version of the .22 New Line. The basic difference is the size, caliber, caliber markings, and the offering of a blued version with case colored frame. There were approximately 11,000 manufactured from 1874-1876.

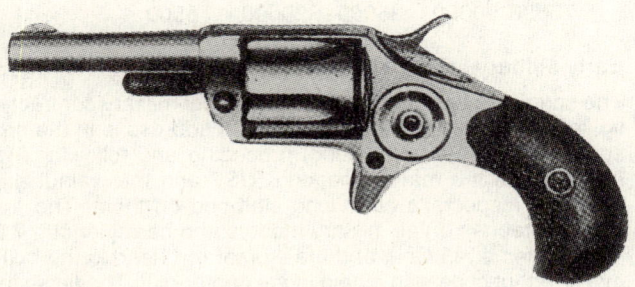

Courtesy Wallis & Wallis, Lewes, Sussex, England

Exc.	V.G.	Good	Fair	Poor
1500	1200	600	400	200

NOTE: Prices above are for nickel finish. Blued models will bring a premium of 100%

New Line Revolver .32
This is the same basic revolver as the .30 caliber except that it is chambered for the .32-caliber rimfire and .32-caliber centerfire and is so marked. There were 22,000 of this model manufactured from 1873-1884. This model was offered with the rare 4" barrel, and this variation would be worth nearly twice the value of a standard model.

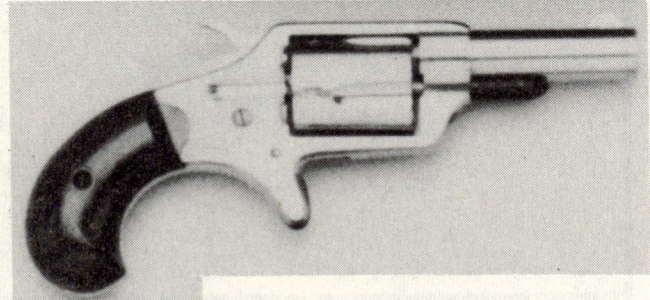

Courtesy Butterfield & Butterfield, San Francisco, California

Exc.	V.G.	Good	Fair	Poor
1200	1000	600	400	200

NOTE: Prices above are for nickel finish. Blued models will bring a premium of 100%

New Line Revolver .38
There were approximately 5,500 of this model manufactured between 1874 and 1880. It is chambered for either the .38 rimfire or .38 centerfire caliber and is so marked. This model in a 4" barrel would also bring twice the value.

Exc.	V.G.	Good	Fair	Poor
1500	1200	800	600	300

New Line Revolver .41
This is the "Big Colt," as it was sometimes known in advertising of its era. It is chambered for the .41 rimfire and the .41 centerfire and is so marked. The large caliber of this variation makes this the most desirable of the New Lines to collectors. There were approximately 7,000 of this model manufactured from 1874-1879. A 4"-barrelled version would again be worth a 100 percent premium.

Exc.	V.G.	Good	Fair	Poor
1800	1400	1000	600	300

NOTE: Prices above are for nickel finish. Blued models will bring a premium of 100%

New House Model Revolver
This revolver is similar to the other New Lines except that it features a square butt instead of the bird's head configuration, a 2.25" round barrel without ejector rod, and a thin loading gate. It is chambered for the .32 (rare), .38, and the .41 centerfire cartridges. The finish was either full nickel-plated or blued, with a case colored frame. The grips are walnut, rosewood or (for the first time on a Colt revolver) checkered hard rubber, with an oval around the word "Colt." The barrel address is the same as on the other New Lines. The frame is marked "New House," with the caliber. There were approximately 4,000 manufactured between 1880-1886. .32 caliber model would bring a 10 percent premium.

Courtesy Milwaukee Public Museum, Milwaukee, Wisconsin

Exc.	V.G.	Good	Fair	Poor
2000	1600	1000	600	300

NOTE: Prices above are for nickel finish. Blued models will bring a premium of 100%

New Police Revolver
This was the final revolver in the New Line series. It is chambered for .32, .38, and .41 centerfire caliber. The .32 and .41 are quite rare. It is offered in barrel lengths of 2.25", 4.5", 5.5", and 6.5". An ejector rod is found on all but the 2.5" barrel. The finish is either nickel or blued and case colored. The grips are hard rubber with a scene of a policeman arresting a criminal embossed on them; thusly the model became known to collectors as the "Cop and Thug" model. The barrel stamping is as the other New Lines, and the frame is stamped "New Police .38." There were approximately 4,000 of these manufactured between 1882-1886.

NOTE: The .32 and .41 caliber versions of this model will bring a 40-50 percent premium. Blued models and models with 5.5" or 6.5" barrels will bring a premium. Short barrel model will bring about 50% of the listed prices.

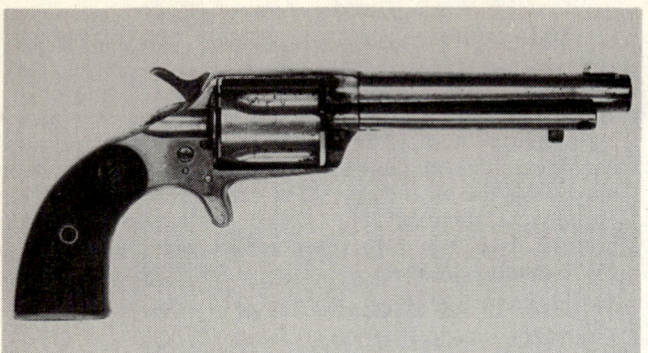

Courtesy Milwaukee Public Museum, Milwaukee, Wisconsin

Long Barrel model with ejector

Exc.	V.G.	Good	Fair	Poor
4000	3000	2000	1200	600

COLT'S SINGLE ACTION ARMY REVOLVER

The Colt Single Action Army, or Peacemaker as it is sometimes referred to, is one of the most widely collected and recognized firearms in the world. With few interruptions or changes in design, it has been manufactured from 1873 until the present. It is still available on a limited production basis from the Colt Custom Shop. The variations in this model are myriad. It has been produced in 30 different calibers and barrel lengths from 2.5" to 16", with 4.75", 5.5", and 7.5" standard. The standard finish is blued, with a case colored frame. Many are nickel-plated. Examples have been found silver- and gold-plated, with combinations thereof. The finest engravers in the world have used the SAA as a canvas to display their artistry. The standard grips from 1873-1883 were walnut, either oil-stained or varnished. From 1883 to approximately 1897, the standard grips were hard rubber with eagle and shield. After this date, at serial number 165000, the hard rubber grips featured the Rampant Colt. Many special-order grips were available, notably pearl and ivory, which were often checkered or carved in ornate fashion. The variables involved in establishing values on this model are extreme. Added to this, one must also consider historical significance, since the SAA played a big part in the formative years of the American West. Fortunately for those among us interested in the SAA, there are a number of fine publications available dealing exclusively with this model. It is my strongest recommendation that they be acquired and studied thoroughly to prevent extremely expensive mistakes. The Colt factory records are nearly complete for this model, and research should be done before acquisition of rare or valuable specimens.

For our purposes we will break down the Single Action Army production as follows:

Antique or Black Powder, 1873-1898, serial #1-#175000

The cylinder axis pin is retained by a screw in the front of the frame.

Prewar, 1899-1940, serial #175001-#357859

The cylinder axis pin is retained by a spring-loaded button through the side of the frame. This method is utilized on the following models, as well.

Postwar 2nd Generation, 1956-1978, serial #0001SA99999SA

3rd Generation, 1978-Present, serial #SA1001. A breakdown of production by caliber will follow the chapter. It is important to note that the rarer calibers and the larger calibers bring higher values in this variation.

COLT *ANTIQUE* SINGLE ACTION ARMY REVOLVER

1st Year Production "Pinched Frame" 1873 Only

It is necessary to categorize this variation on its own. This is one of the rarest and most interesting of all the SAAs-not to mention that it is the first. On this model the top strap is pinched or constricted approximately one-half inch up from the hammer to form the rear sight. The highest surviving serial number having this feature is #156, the lowest #1. From these numbers, it is safe to assume that the first run of SAAs were all pinched-frame models; but there is no way to tell how many there were, since Colt did not serial number the frames in the order that they were manufactured. An educated guess would be that there were between 50 and 150 pinched frame guns in all and that they were all made before mid-July 1873. The reason for the change came about on the recommendation of Capt. J.R. Edie, a government inspector who thought that the full fluted top strap would be a big improvement in the sighting capabilities of the weapon. The barrel length of the first model is 7.5"; the standard caliber, .45 Colt; and the proper grips were of walnut. The front sight blade is German silver. Needless to say, this model will rarely be encountered; and if it is, it should never be purchased without competent appraisal.

Exc.	V.G.	Good	Fair	Poor
75000	50000	35000	20000	6500

Early Military Model 1873-1877

The serial number range on this first run of military contract revolvers extends to #24000. The barrel address is in the early script style with the # symbol preceding and following. The frame bears the martial marking "US," and the walnut grips have the inspector's cartouche stamped on them. The front sight is steel as on all military models; the barrel length, 7.5". The caliber is .45 Colt, and the ejector rod head is the bull's-eye or donut style with a hole in the center of it. The finish features the military polish and case colored frame, with the remainder blued. Authenticate any potential purchase; many spurious examples have been noted.

Exc.	V.G.	Good	Fair	Poor
30000	20000	8500	3750	2000

A Model 1873 with 7-1/2" barrel inspected by Orville W. Ainsworth was sold at auction for $20,700. It was stamped with a 4 digit serial number. This is a very early military model. Condition is good with all markings clear. Rock Island Auction Company, November 18, 19 & 20, 1996.

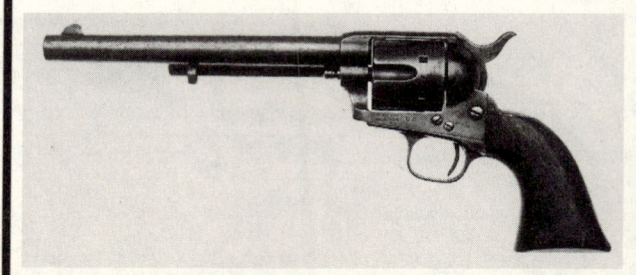

Early Civilian Model 1873-1877

This model is identical to the Early Military Model but has no military acceptance markings or cartouches. Some could have the German silver front sight blade. The early bull's-eye ejector rod head is used on this model. The Civilian Model has a higher degree of polish than is found on the military models, and the finish on these early models could be plated or blued with a case colored frame. The grips are standard one-piece walnut. Ivory-grip models are worth a premium.

Exc.	V.G.	Good	Fair	Poor
20000	12000	8000	2500	1000

.44 Rimfire Model 1875-1880

This model was made to fire the .44 Henry Rimfire cartridge. It was to be used as a compatible companion sidearm to the Henry and Winchester 1866 rifles that were used extensively during this era. However, this was not the case; and the .44 Rimfire was doomed to economic failure as soon as it appeared on the market. By that time, it had already been established that large-caliber centerfire cartridges were a good deal more efficient than their rimfire counterparts. The large-caliber rimfires were deemed obsolete before this Colt ever hit the market. The result of this was that Colt's sales representatives sold most of the production to obscure banana republics in South and Central America, where this model received much abuse. Most had the original 7.5" barrels cut down; and nearly all were denied even the most basic maintenance, making the survival rate of this model quite low. All this adds to its desirability as a collector's item and makes the risk of acquiring a fake that much greater. This model is unique in that it was the only SAA variation to have its own serial number range, starting with #1 and continuing to #1892, the latest known surviving specimen. The block style barrel markings were introduced during this production run. At least 90 of these revolvers were converted by the factory to .22 rimfire, and one was shipped chambered for .32 rimfire.

Exc.	V.G.	Good	Fair	Poor
20000	15000	8500	3750	2000

Late Military Model 1878-1891

The later Military Models are serial numbered to approximately #136000. They bear the block-style barrel address without the # prefix and suffix. The frames are marked "US," and the grips have the inspector's cartouche. The finish is the military-style polish, case colored frame; and the remainder, blued. Grips are oil-stained walnut. On the military marked Colts, it is imperative that potential purchases be authenticated as many fakes have been noted.

Exc.	V.G.	Good	Fair	Poor
25000	15000	8500	2250	1500

> **A military marked Model 1873 revolver, serial number 111933, in .45 caliber was sold at auction for $35,750. Revolver was shipped in 1884. Condition was excellent to mint. Butterfield & Butterfield, December 1995.**

Artillery Model 1895-1903

A number of "US" marked SAAs were returned either to the Colt factory or to the Springfield Armory, where they were altered and refinished. These revolvers have 5.5" barrels and any combination of mixed serial numbers. They were remarked by the inspectors of the era and have a case colored frame and a blued cylinder and barrel. Some have been noted all blued within this variation. This model, as with the other military marked Colts, should definitely be authenticated before purchase. Some of these revolvers fall outside the 1898 antique cutoff date that has been established by the government and, in our experience, are not quite as desirable to investors. They are generally worth approximately 20 percent less.

Exc.	V.G.	Good	Fair	Poor
7500	5000	3000	1750	1000

London Model

These SAAs were manufactured to be sold through Colt's London Agency. The barrel is stamped "Colt's Pt. F.A. Mfg. Co. Hartford, Ct. U.S.A. Depot 14 Pall Mall London." This model is available in various barrel lengths. They are generally chambered for .45 Colt, .450 Boxer, .450 Eley, .455 Eley, and rarely .476 Eley, the largest of the SAA chamberings. A good many of these London Models were cased and embellished, and

they should be individually appraised. This model should be authenticated as many spurious examples have been noted.

Exc.	V.G.	Good	Fair	Poor
8500	6500	4000	1750	1000

Frontier Six-Shooter 1878-1882

Several thousand SAAs were made with the legend "Colt's Frontier Six Shooter" acid-etched into the left side of the barrel instead of being stamped. This etching is not deep, and today collectors will become ecstatic if they discover a specimen with mere vestiges of the etched panel remaining. These acid-etched SAAs are serial numbered #45000-#65000. They have various barrel lengths and finishes, but all are chambered for the .44-40 caliber.

Exc.	V.G.	Good	Fair	Poor
15000	10000	7500	2500	1000

Sheriff's or Storekeeper's Model 1882-1898

This model was manufactured with a short barrel (2.5"-4.75"). Most have 4" barrels. It features no ejector rod or housing, and the frame is made without the hole in the right forward section to accommodate the ejector assembly. The Sheriff's or Storekeeper's Model is numbered above serial #73000. It was manufactured with various finishes and chambered for numerous calibers. This model continued after 1898 into the smokeless or modern era. Examples manufactured in the prewar years are worth approximately 20 percent less. Although faking this model is quite difficult, it has been successfully attempted.

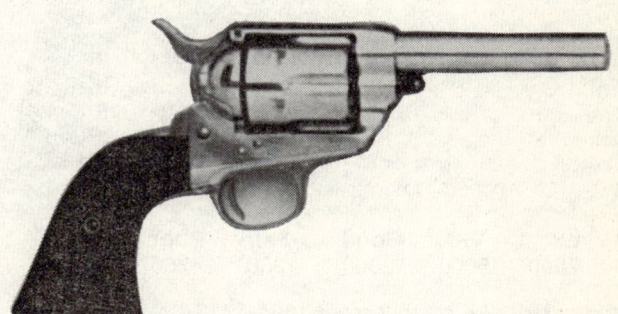

Courtesy Butterfield & Butterfield, San Francisco, California

Exc.	V.G.	Good	Fair	Poor
25000	15000	10000	4500	2000

Flattop Target Model 1888-1896

This model is highly regarded and sought after by collectors. It is not only rare (only 925 manufactured) but is an extremely attractive and well-finished variation. It is chambered for 22 different calibers from .22 rimfire to .476 Eley. The .22 rimfire, .38 Colt, .41, and .45 Colt are the most predominant chamberings. The 7.5" barrel length is the most commonly encountered. The serial number range is between #127000-#162000. Some have been noted in higher ranges. The finish is all blued, with a case colored hammer. The checkered grips are either hard rubber or walnut. The most readily identifying feature of the flattop is the lack of a groove in the top strap and the sight blade dovetailed into the flattop. The front sight has a removable blade insert. The values given are for a standard production model chambered for the calibers previously mentioned as being the most common. It is important to have other calibers individually appraised as variance in values can be quite extreme.

Exc.	V.G.	Good	Fair	Poor
15000	12500	8500	5000	3750

Bisley Model 1894-1915

This model was named for the target range in Great Britain, where their National Target Matches were held since the nine teenth century. The model was designed as a target revolver with an odd humped-back grip that was supposed to better fill the hand while target shooting. It is also easily identified by the wide low profile hammer spur, wide trigger, and the name "Bisley" stamped on the barrel. The Bisley production fell within the serial number range #165000-#331916. There were 44,350 made.

It was offered in 16 different chamberings from .32 Colt to .455 Eley. The most common calibers were .32-20, .38-40, .41, .44-40, and .45 Colt. The barrel lengths are 4.75", 5.5", and 7.5". The frame and hammer are case-colored; the remainder, blued. Smokeless powder models produced after 1899 utilized the push-button cylinder pin retainer. The grips are checkered hard rubber. This model was actually designed with English sales in mind; and though it did sell well over there, American sales accounted for most of the Bisley production. The values we provide here cover the standard calibers and barrel lengths. Rare calibers and/or other notable variations can bring greatly fluctuating values, and qualified appraisals should be secured in such cases. Bisleys manufactured from 1898-1915 are worth approximately 20 percent less.

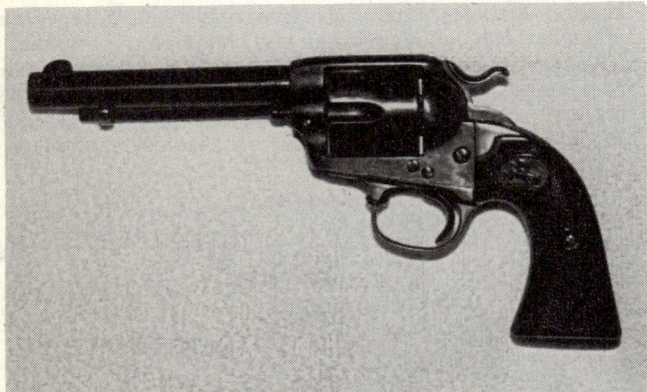

Exc.	V.G.	Good	Fair	Poor
7500	5000	2000	1250	750

Bisley Model Flattop Target 1894-1913

This model is quite similar to the Standard Bisley Model, with the flattop frame and dovetailed rear sight feature. It also has the removable front sight insert. It has an all-blued finish with case-colored hammer only and is available with a 7.5" barrel. Smokeless powder models produced after 1899 utilized the push-button cylinder pin retainer. The calibers are the same as the standard Bisley. Colt manufactured 976 of these revolvers. The advice regarding appraisal would also apply.

Exc.	V.G.	Good	Fair	Poor
12000	10000	6500	2500	1000

Standard Civilian Production Models 1876-1898

This final designated category for the black powder or antique SAAs includes all the revolvers not previously categorized. They have barrel lengths from 4.75", 5.5", and 7.5" and are chambered for any one of 30 different calibers. The finishes could be blued, blued and case colored, or plated in nickel, silver, gold, or combinations thereof. Grips could be walnut, hard rubber, ivory, pearl, stag, or bone. The possibilities are endless. The values given here are for the basic model, and we again strongly advise securing qualified appraisal when not completely sure of any model variation.

Exc.	V.G.	Good	Fair	Poor
20000	15000	8500	2000	1000

NOTE: At this time it is important to note that the Colt's Single Action Army Revolvers we have discussed to this point are in the antique category as established by our federal government. The arbitrary cutoff date of 1898 has been established,

and any weapon made prior to this date is considered an antique and, as such, not subject to the restraints placed on collectors and dealers by the Gun Control Act of 1968. This is important because firearms falling into this category will usually bring higher values due to the demand by pure investors who do not relish paperwork on collectible investments. There will be those who disagree with me on this line of reasoning, but my experience tells me that it is correct.

COLT PREWAR SINGLE ACTION ARMY REVOLVER 1899-1940

Standard Production Prewar Models

The 1899 cutoff has been thoroughly discussed, but it is interesting to note that the actual beginning production date for smokeless models was 1900. The Prewar Colts are, all in all, quite similar to the antiques—the finishes, barrel lengths, grips, etc. Calibers are also similar, with the exception of the obsolete ones being dropped and new discoveries added. The most apparent physical difference between the smokeless powder and black powder models is the previously discussed method of retaining the cylinder axis pin. The prewar Colts utilized the spring-loaded button through the side of the frame. The black powder models utilized a screw in the front of the frame. The values we furnish for this model designation are for these standard models only. The serial number range on the prewar SAAs is 175001-357859. Note that any variation can have marked effects on value fluctuations, and qualified appraisal should be secured.

Exc.	V.G.	Good	Fair	Poor
7500	5500	3000	2000	1000

> In March 1996 a Pre-war Colt single action Army chambered for the .38 WCF cartridge with 4.75" barrel was sold at auction for $14,850. It was the property of Captain John R. Hughes, Texas Ranger and so inscribed. The Gun was shipped in 1902. Condition was overall grey metal with traces of blue in protected areas.
> Faintich Auction Service, LLC.

Long Fluted Cylinder Model 1913-1915

Strange as it may seem, the Colt Company has an apparent credo they followed to never throw anything away. That credo was never more evident than with this model. These Long Flute Cylinders were actually left over from the model 1878 Double Action Army Revolvers. Someone in the hierarchy at Colt had an inspiration that drove the gunsmiths on the payroll slightly mad: to make these cylinders fit the SAA frames. There were 1,478 of these Long Flutes manufactured. They are chambered for the .45 Colt, .38-40, .32-20, .41 Colt, and the .44 Smith & Wesson Special. They were offered in the three standard barrel lengths and were especially well-polished, having what has been described as Colt's "Fire Blue" on the barrel and cylinder. The frame and hammer are case colored. They are fitted with checkered hard rubber grips and are particularly fine examples of Colt's craft.

Exc.	V.G.	Good	Fair	Poor
7500	6000	5000	2500	1000

COLT POSTWAR SINGLE ACTION ARMY REVOLVER

Standard Postwar Model 1956-1975

In 1956 the shooting and gun-collecting fraternity succeeded in convincing Colt that there was a market for a re-introduced SAA. The revolver was brought back in the same external configuration. The only changes were internal. The basic specifications as to barrel length and finish availability were the same. The calibers available were .38 Special, .357 Magnum, .44 Special, and .45 Colt. The serial number range of the re-introduced 2nd Generation, as it is sometimes known, Colt is #000ISA-73000SA. Values for the standard postwar Colts are established by four basic factors: caliber (popularity and scarcity), barrel length, finish, and condition. Shorter barrel lengths are generally more desirable than the 7.5". The .38 Special is the rarest caliber, but the .45 Colt and .44 Special are more sought after than the .357 Magnum. Special feature revolvers, such as the 350 factory-engraved guns produced during this period, must be individually appraised. The ivory situation in the world today has become quite a factor, as ivory grips are found on many SAAs. We will attempt to take these factors into consideration and evaluate this variation as accurately and clearly as possible. Remember as always, when in doubt secure a qualified appraisal.

4.7 5" Barrel-Add 25%.
5.5" Barrel-Add 15%.
Nickel Finish-Add 20%.
Ivory Grips-Add $250.

A Colt factory engraved pre-war/post-war single action revolver chambered for .38 Special and fitted with a 5-1/2" barrel. Pearl grips. Presented to Colt president Graham Anthony. Engraved by Alvin Herbert, Colt master engraver. Price was $22,400. Condition is excellent.
Faintich Auction Service, October 1996.

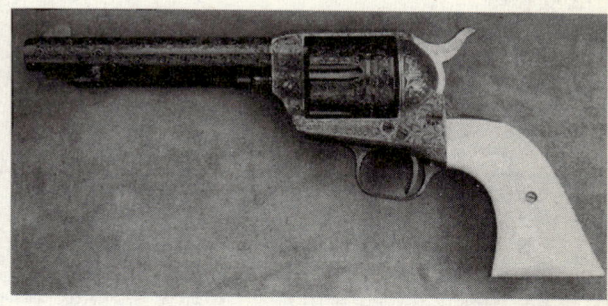

Photo by Paul Goodwin

A second generation Colt single action with a signed card and photograph from Elvis Presley to Chief Edward Davis. The revolver was fitted with a 5-1/2" barrel and engraved with gold and platinum inlays. Carved ivory stocks. Chambered for .45 Colt. Condition was as new. Auction price was $14,000.
Faintich Auction Service, October 1996.

Values for 7.5" Barrel Model

.38+ Special

NIB	Exc.	V.G.	Good	Fair	Poor
1750	1350	900	750	650	550

.357 Magnum

NIB	Exc.	V.G.	Good	Fair	Poor
1500	1100	750	650	600	550

.44 Special

NIB	Exc.	V.G.	Good	Fair	Poor
2000	1400	1050	850	750	650

.45 Colt

NIB	Exc.	V.G.	Good	Fair	Poor
1800	1250	1000	850	750	650

> A consective pair of factory engraved 2nd generation single action army revolvers with 7.5" barrels and chambered for the .45 Colt sold for $8,500. Factory engraving was style C and the stocks were pearlite. Bill Mains was the engraver. Condition is excellent to mint.
> Faintich Auction Service, LLC. March 1996.

Sheriff's Model 1960-1975

Between 1960 and 1975, there were approximately 500 Sheriff's Models manufactured. They have 3" barrels and no ejector rod assemblies. The frames were made without the hole for the ejector rod to pass through. They were blued, with case colored frames; 25 revolvers were nickel-plated and would bring a sizable premium if authenticated. The barrels are marked "Colt Sheriff's Model." The serial number has an "SM" suffix. They are chambered for the .45 Colt cartridge.

Nickel Finish-Add 20%.

NIB	Exc.	V.G.	Good	Fair	Poor
2500	1650	1500	850	600	500

Buntline Special 1957-1975

The "Buntline Special" was named after a dime novelist named Ned Buntline, who supposedly gave this special long barrel revolver to Wyatt Earp. The story is suspected to be purely legend as no Colt records exist to lend it credence. Be that as it may, the Colt factory decided to take advantage of the market and produced the 12" barrelled SAA from 1957-1974. There were approximately 3,900 manufactured. They are chambered for the .45 Colt cartridge and are offered in the blued and case colored finish. Only 65 Buntlines are nickel-plated, making this an extremely rare variation that definitely should be authenticated before purchase. Walnut grips are the most commonly noted, but they are also offered with the checkered hard rubber grips. The barrels are marked on the left side "Colt Buntline Special .45." Nickel Finish-Add 60%.

NIB	Exc.	V.G.	Good	Fair	Poor
1750	1250	950	600	400	350

New Frontier 1961-1975

The New Frontier is readily identified by its flattop frame and adjustable sight. It also has a high front sight. Colt manufactured approximately 4,200 of them. They are chambered for the .357 Magnum, .45 Colt, .44 Special (255 produced), and rarely (only 49 produced) in .38 Special. A few were chambered for the .44-40 cartridge. The 7.5" barrel length is by far the most common, but the 4.75" and 5.5" barrels are also offered. The standard finish is case colored and blued. Nickel-plating and full blue are offered but are rarely encountered. Standard grips are walnut. The barrel is stamped on the left side "Colt New Frontier S.A.A." The serial has the "NF" suffix.

4.75" Barrel-Add 25%.
5.5" Barrel-Add 20%.
Full Blue-Add 50%.

.38 Special-Add 50%.
.44 Special-Add 30%.
44-40-Add 30%

NIB	Exc.	V.G.	Good	Fair	Poor
1500	800	550	450	400	300

New Frontier Buntline Special 1962-1967

This model is rare, as Colt only manufactured 70 during this five-year period. They are similar to the standard Buntline, with a 12" barrel. They are chambered for .45 Colt only.

NIB	Exc.	V.G.	Good	Fair	Poor
3500	2500	1000	750	600	500

COLT THIRD GENERATION SINGLE ACTION ARMY 1976-1981

In 1976 Colt made some internal changes in the SAA. The external configuration was not altered. The serial number range began in 1976 with #80000SA, and in 1978 #99999SA was reached. At this time the suffix became a prefix, and the new serial range began with #SA01001. This model's value is determined in much the same manner as was described in the section on the 2nd Generation SAAs. Caliber, barrel length, finish, and condition are once again the four main determining factors. The prevalence of special-order guns was greater during this period, and many more factory-engraved SAAs were produced. Colt's Custom Shop was quite active during this period. We feel that it is not advisable to undertake evaluation of specially embellished guns and strongly advise that competent appraisal be secured on any firearms that deviate from the standard. There are, quite frankly, too many fraudulent Colt SAAs out there; and the financial risks are great.

4.75" Barrel-Add 25%.
5.5" Barrel-Add 10%.
Nickel Plated-Add 10%.
Ivory Grips-Add $250.

Values with 7.5" Barrel

.357 Magnum

NIB	Exc.	V.G.	Good	Fair	Poor
900	650	600	500	375	300

.44-40

NIB	Exc.	V.G.	Good	Fair	Poor
1100	850	700	600	500	400

.44-40 Black Powder Frame (Screw Retaining Cylinder Pin)

NIB	Exc.	V.G.	Good	Fair	Poor
1400	1100	900	700	600	450

.44 Special

NIB	Exc.	V.G.	Good	Fair	Poor
950	750	650	550	400	350

.45 Colt

NIB	Exc.	V.G.	Good	Fair	Poor
950	750	650	550	400	350

Sheriff's Model 3rd Generation

This model is similar to the 2nd Generation Sheriff's Model. The serial number and the fact that this model is also chambered for the .44-40 are the only external differences. Colt offered this model with interchangeable cylinders—.45 Colt/.45 ACP or .44-40/.44 Special-available in 3" barrel, blued and case colored finish standard.

Interchangeable Cylinders-Add 30%.
Nickel Finish-Add 10%.
Ivory Grips-Add $250.

NIB	Exc.	V.G.	Good	Fair	Poor
950	800	700	600	450	400

Colt Single Action Army Production Breakdown by Caliber Antique and Prewar

CALIBER	SAA	FLATTOP SAA	BISLEY	FLATTOP BISLEY
.22 R.F.	107	93	0	0
.32 R.F.	1	0	0	0
.32 Colt	192	24	160	44
.32 S&W	32	30	18	17
.32-44	2	9	14	17
.32-20	29,812	30	13,291	131
.38 Colt (1914)	1,011	122	412	96
	—	—	—	—
.38 Colt (1922)	1,365	0	0	0
	—	—	—	—
.38 S&W	9	39	10	5
.38 Colt Sp.	82	7	0	0
.38 S&W Sp.	25	0	2	0
.38-44	2	11	6	47
.357 Mag.	525	0	0	0
.380 Eley	1	3	0	0
.38-40	38,240	19	12,163	98
.41	16,402	91	3,159	24
.44 SmBr.	15	0	1	0
.44 R. F.	1,863	0	0	0
.44 Germ.	59	0	0	0
.44 Russ.	154	51	90	62
.44 S&W	24	51	29	64
.44 S&W Sp.	506	1	0	0
.44-40	64,489	21	6,803	78
.45 Colt	150,683	100	8,005	97
.45 SmBr.	4	0	2	0
.45 ACP	44	0	0	0
.450 Boxer	729	89	0	0
.450 Eley	2,697	84	5	0
.455 Eley	1,150	37	180	196
.476 Eley	161	2	0	0
Total	**310,386**	**914**	**44,350**	**976**

The above chart covers the production by caliber of the Single Action Army Revolvers manufactured between 1873 and 1940. These are the antique and the prewar firearms. This chart readily informs us as to which are the rare calibers.

Buntline Special 3rd Generation

This is the same basic configuration as the 2nd Generation with the 12" barrel. Standard finish blued and case-colored, it is chambered for .45 Colt and has checkered hard rubber grips.

Nickel Finish-Add 10%.

NIB	Exc.	V.G.	Good	Fair	Poor
950	800	700	600	450	400

New Frontier 3rd Generation

This model is similar in appearance to the 2nd Generation guns. The 3rd Generation New Frontiers have five-digit serial numbers; the 2nd Generation guns, four-digit numbers. That and the calibers offered are basically the only differences. The 3rd Generations are chambered for the .44 Special and .45 Colt and are rarely found in .44-40. Barrel lengths are 7.5" standard, with the 4.75" and 5.5" rarely encountered.

.44-40-Add 20%.
4.75" Barrel-Add 35%.
5.5" Barrel-Add 25%.

NIB	Exc.	V.G.	Good	Fair	Poor
700	600	500	400	300	250

COLT CURRENT PRODUCTION SINGLE ACTION ARMY 1982-PRESENT

Standard Single Action Army

The SAA, it is sad to note, has all but faded from the firearms picture. They are currently available as a special-order custom shop proposition. The cost is great; and the availability, low. The heyday of one of the most venerable firearms of them all is pretty much at an end. The SAAs have been available in .357 Magnum, .38-40, .44-40, .44 Special, and .45 Colt. Barrels were available in 3" through 10" lengths. The finishes are nickel-plated and blued, with case-colored frames. A number of optional finishes are available on request. Grips are available on a custom order basis. This model is available on special-order only. As of 1997 the Custom Shop is offering this revolver in the following calibers and barrel lengths : .45 Long Colt and .44-40 with 4-3/4" or 5/12" barrels.

Nickel Finish-Add $125.
Royal Blue Finish-Add $200.
Mirror Brite Finish-Add $225.
Gold Plate-Add $365.
Silver Plate-Add $365.
Class A Engraving-Add $875.

Class B Engraving-Add $1,200.
Class C Engraving-Add $1,500.
Class D Engraving-Add $1,750.
Buntline Engraving-Add 15%.

NIB	Exc.	V.G.	Good	Fair	Poor
1150	1000	600	450	400	300

Colt Single Action Army "The Legend"
A limited edition revolver built to commemorate Colt's official PRCA sponsorship. Limited to 1,000. Chambered for .45 Long Colt fitted with a 5-1/2" barrel. Nickel finish Buffalo horn grips with gold medallions. Machine engraved and washed in gold.

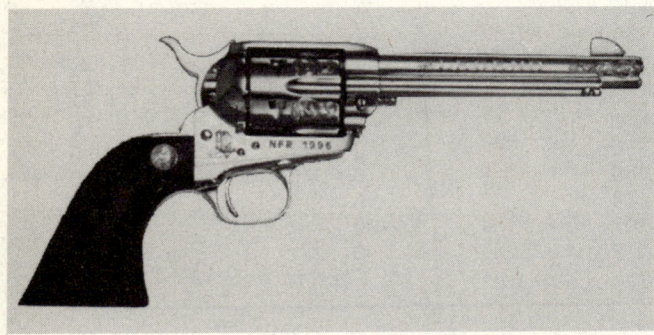

NIB	Exc.	V.G.	Good	Fair	Poor
N/A	—	—	—	—	—

COLT SCOUT MODEL SINGLE ACTION ARMY

New Frontier Scout 1958-1972
This is a scaled-down version of the SAA that is chambered for the .22 l.r. with an interchangeable .22 Magnum cylinder. It is offered with a 4.25", 4.75", or a 9.5" barrel. The frame is alloy; and the finish, either blued or nickel-plated. The grips are hard rubber.

9.5" Buntline-Add 50%.
Extra Cylinder-Add 10%.
Nickel Plated-Add 10%.

NIB	Exc.	V.G.	Good	Fair	Poor
400	300	200	175	125	90

Peacemaker Scout 1970-1977
This model is similar to the New Frontier Scout, with a steel case-colored frame. The barrel lengths offered are 4.75", 6", or 7.5". It also has an interchangeable .22 Magnum cylinder.

NIB	Exc.	V.G.	Good	Fair	Poor
500	450	300	200	150	100

Scout Model SAA
This is basically a scaled-down version of the SAA chambered for the .22 l.r. cartridge. This model is offered with a 4.75", 6", or 7" barrel. The earlier production has case-colored frames with the remainder blued; later production is all blued. Grips are checkered hard rubber. This model was discontinued in 1986.

NIB	Exc.	V.G.	Good	Fair	Poor
350	250	175	150	100	75

NOTE: Anyone wishing to procure a factory letter authenticating a Single Action Army should do so by writing to: COLT HISTORIAN, P.O. BOX 1868, HARTFORD, CT 06101. There is a charge of $35 per serial number for this service. If Colt cannot provide the desired information, $10 will be refunded. Enclose the Colt model name, serial number, and your name and address, along with the check.

COLT ANTIQUE LONG ARMS

Berdan Single Shot Rifle
This is a scarce rifle on today's market. There were approximately 30,200 manufactured, but nearly 30,000 of them were sent to Russia. This rifle was produced from 1866-1870. It is a trapdoor-type action chambered for .42 centerfire. The standard model has a 32.5" barrel; the carbine, 18.25". The finish is blued, with a walnut stock. This rifle was designed and the patent held by Hiram Berdan, Commander of the Civil War "Sharpshooters" Regiment. This was actually Colt's first cartridge arm. The 30,000 rifles and 25 half-stocked carbines that were sent to Russia were in Russian Cyrillic letters. The few examples made for American sales have Colt's name and Hartford address on the barrel.

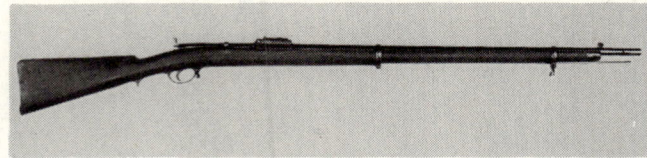

Courtesy Milwaukee Public Museum, Milwaukee, Wisconsin

Rifle Russian Order, 30,000 Manufactured

Exc.	V.G.	Good	Fair	Poor
5000	3500	1500	650	450

Carbine Russian Order, 25 Manufactured

Exc.	V.G.	Good	Fair	Poor
4500	3750	3000	2000	1500

Rifle U.S. Sales, 100 Manufactured

Exc.	V.G.	Good	Fair	Poor
2750	2000	1750	1250	1000

Carbine U.S. Sales, 25 Manufactured

Exc.	V.G.	Good	Fair	Poor
5000	4000	3500	2500	2000

Colt-Franklin Military Rifle
This is a rifle that was not a successful venture for Colt. The patents were held by William B. Franklin, a vice-president of the company. This was a bolt-action rifle with a primitive, gravity-fed box magazine. It is chambered for the .45-70 government cartridge, has a 32.5" barrel, and is blued, with a walnut stock. The rifle has the Colt Hartford barrel address and is stamped with an eagle's head and U.S. inspectors marks. There were only 50 of these rifles produced, and it is believed that they were prototypes intended for government sales. This was not to be, and production ceased after approximately 50 were manufactured in 1887 and 1888.

Exc.	V.G.	Good	Fair	Poor
4500	3750	3000	2000	1500

Colt-Burgess Lever Action Rifle
This represented Colt's only attempt to compete with Winchester for the lever-action rifle market. It is said that when Winchester started to produce revolving handguns for prospective marketing, Colt dropped the Burgess from its line.

This rifle is chambered for .44-40. It has a 25.5" barrel and a 15-shot tubular magazine. The Carbine version has a 20.5" barrel and 12-shot magazine. The finish is blued, with a case-colored hammer and lever. The stock is walnut with an oil finish. The Colt Hartford address is on the barrel, and "Burgess Patents" is stamped on the bottom of the lever. There were 3,775 rifles manufactured—1,219 with round barrels and 2,556 with octagonal barrels. There were also 2,593 Carbines. The Burgess was produced from 1883-1885.

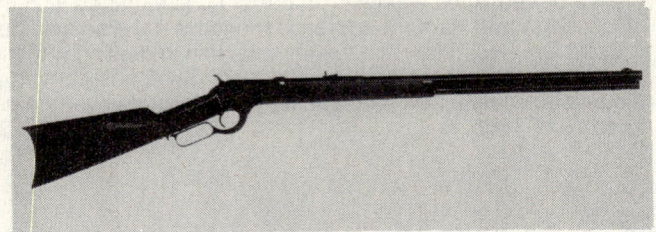

Courtesy Buffalo Bill Historical Center, Cody, Wyoming

Rifle, Octagonal Barrel

Exc.	V.G.	Good	Fair	Poor
9500	6500	2500	1500	550

Rifle, Round Barrel

Exc.	V.G.	Good	Fair	Poor
9500	6500	2000	950	750

Carbine

Exc.	V.G.	Good	Fair	Poor
12500	8500	2500	1250	950

Baby Carbine, Lighter Frame and Barrel (RARE)

Exc.	V.G.	Good	Fair	Poor
12500	8500	2500	1500	1150

In April of 1997 Rock Island Company sold a Colt Burgess rifle at auction for $6,900. Condition is good. Barrel length is 25-1/2". Stock is in excellent condition. Bore is bright.

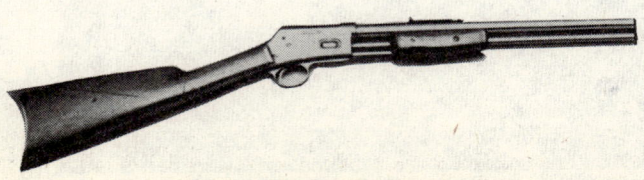

Lightning Slide Action, Medium Frame

This was the first slide action rifle Colt produced. It is chambered for.32-20, .38-40, and .44-40 and was intended to be a companion piece to the SAAs in the same calibers. The rifle has a 26" barrel with 15-shot tube magazine; the carbine, a 20" barrel with 12-shot magazine. The finish is blued, with case-colored hammer; the walnut stock is oil-finished; and the forend, usually checkered. The Colt name and Hartford address are stamped on the barrel along with the patent dates. There were approximately 89,777 manufactured between 1884 and 1902.

Courtesy Butterfield & Butterfield, San Francisco, California

Rifle

Exc.	V.G.	Good	Fair	Poor
5000	2500	1250	750	400

Carbine

Exc.	V.G.	Good	Fair	Poor
5500	3500	1750	800	500

Military Rifle or Carbine

.44-40 caliber, short magazine tube, bayonet lug, and sling swivels.

Exc.	V.G.	Good	Fair	Poor
6500	4000	2750	2000	1500

Baby Carbine, 1 lb., Lighter Version of Standard Carbine

Exc.	V.G.	Good	Fair	Poor
7500	5000	2750	2000	1500

San Francisco Police Rifle

.44-40 caliber, #SFP 1-SFP401 on bottom tang.

Exc.	V.G.	Good	Fair	Poor
4000	3000	1250	800	500

Lightning Slide Action Small Frame

This is a well-made rifle and the first of its type that Colt manufactured. It is chambered for the .22 Short and Long. The standard barrel length is 24"; the finish, blued with a case-colored hammer. The stock is walnut; some were checkered; some, not. The barrel is stamped with the Colt name and Hartford address and the patent dates. There were 89,912 manufactured between 1887 and 1904.

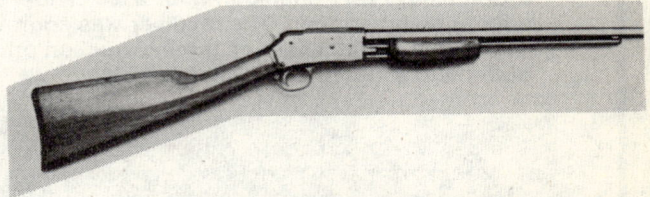

Courtesy Butterfield & Butterfield, San Francisco, California

Exc.	V.G.	Good	Fair	Poor
2000	1250	700	500	300

Lightning Slide Action, Large Frame

This rifle is similar in appearance to the Medium Frame Lightning, though larger in size. It is chambered in larger rifle calibers of the era, from .38-56 up to .50-95 Express. The larger calibers are more desirable from a collector's standpoint. The rifle has a 28" barrel; the carbine, a 22" barrel. The finish is blued, with a case-colored hammer. The stock is oiled walnut; the forend, checkered. The Colt name and Hartford address are stamped on the barrel along with the patent dates. This rifle is quite large and has come to be known as the "Express model." Colt manufactured 6,496 between 1887 and 1894.

Rifle, 28" Octagonal Barrel

Exc.	V.G.	Good	Fair	Poor
6500	4500	2000	750	500

Rifle, 28" Round Barrel

Exc.	V.G.	Good	Fair	Poor
6500	4500	2000	1000	600

Carbine, 22" Barrel

Exc.	V.G.	Good	Fair	Poor
10000	6500	3000	1500	750

Baby Carbine, 22" Barrel 1 lb. Lighter

Exc.	V.G.	Good	Fair	Poor
15000	10000	7500	3000	1750

Model 1878 Double Barrel Shotgun

This model is chambered in 10 or 12 gauge and has 28", 30", or 32" barrels. It is a sidelock double-trigger hammer gun with case-colored locks and breech. The barrels are browned Damacus-patterned. The checkered walnut stock is varnished or oil-finished. The Colt's Hartford address is stamped on the barrel rib; and Colt's name, on the lock. This has been regarded as one of the finest shotguns made in America, although Colt had difficulty competing with the less expensive European imports of the day. They ceased production after only 22,690 were manufactured between 1878 and 1889.

Fully Engraved Model-Add 80%.

Exc.	V.G.	Good	Fair	Poor
3500	3000	2250	1250	650

Model 1883 Double Barrel Shotgun

This model is a hammerless boxlock, chambered for 10 or 12 gauge. The barrels are 28", 30", or 32"; and it features double triggers. The frame and furniture are case-colored; the barrels, browned with Damascus pattern. The checkered walnut stock is varnished or oil-finished. Colt's Hartford address is stamped on the barrel rib. "Colt" is stamped on each side of the frame. Again, as in the Model 1878, this is rated as one of the finest of all American-made shotguns. There were many special orders, and they require individual appraisal. Colt manufactured 7,366 of these guns between 1883 and 1895.

Fully Engraved Model-Add 80%.

Exc.	V.G.	Good	Fair	Poor
3800	3250	2500	1500	750

Double Barrel Rifle

This is one of the rarest of all Colt firearms and is a prize for the Colt collector. There were only 35 of these guns manufactured. They were said to be the special interest of Caldwell Hart Colt, Samuel Colt's son, who was an avid arms collector. It is said that most of the 35 guns produced wound up in his collection or those of his friends. This gun is chambered for .45-70 or one of the larger variations thereof. It is an exposed hammer sidelock with double triggers. The locks, breech, and furniture are case-colored; the barrels, browned or blued. The barrels are 28" in length, and the checkered stock was oil-finished or varnished walnut. The barrel rib is stamped with the Colt name and Hartford address. The locks are also stamped "Colt." One must exercise extreme caution in dealing with this model as there have been model 1878 Shotguns converted into double rifles. Colt manufactured the 35 guns over the period 1879-1885.

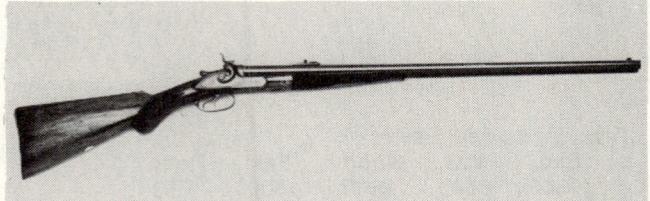

Courtesy Butterfield & Butterfield, San Francisco, California

Exc.	V.G.	Good	Fair	Poor
20000	15000	12500	6500	5000

A Colt Model 1877 chambered for a .38 caliber cartridge and fitted with a 4-1/2" barrel was presented to retiring police captain. The revolver was engraved by Cuno Helfricht. The pistol is cased and is fitted with pearl grips. Condition is near mint. Auction price was $46,000.
Butterfield & Butterfield, October 1996.

COLT DOUBLE ACTION REVOLVERS

Model 1877 "Lightning" and "Thunderer"

The Model 1877 was Colt's first attempt at manufacturing a double-action revolver. It shows a striking resemblance to the Single Action Army. Sales on this model were brisk, with over 166,000 produced between 1877 and 1909. Chambered for two different cartridges, the .38 Colt, known as the "Lightning", and .41 Colt, as the "Thunderer." The standard finishes are blued, with case-colored frame and nickel plate. The bird's-head grips are of checkered rosewood on the early guns and hard rubber on the majority of the production run. The barrel lengths most often encountered are 2.5" and 3.5" without an ejector rod, and 4.5" and 6" with the rod. Other barrel lengths from 1.5" through 10" were offered. The Model 1877 holds 6 shots in either caliber. There were quite a few different variations found within this model designation. Values furnished are for the standard variations. Antiques made before 1898 would be more desirable from an investment standpoint.

.41 Caliber "Thunderer"-Add 10%.
Over 7" Barrel-Add 10%.
London Barrel Address-Add 20%.
.32 Caliber-Add 25%.
Rosewood Grips-Add 10%.

Without Ejector, 2.5" and 3.5" Barrel

Exc.	V.G.	Good	Fair	Poor
3500	1750	1000	500	350

With Ejector, 4.5" and 6" Barrel

Exc.	V.G.	Good	Fair	Poor
3000	1750	1000	750	450

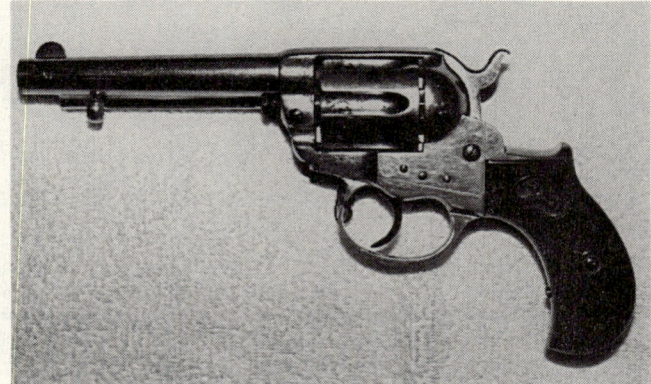

A Colt Model 1877 chambered for .38 caliber and fitted with a 2-1/2" barrel, nickel plated and inscribed "J.B.M. TO J.W.H." (to John Wesley Hardin from his brother-in-law Jim Miller). The condition was very good. Auction price was $189,500.
Butterfield & Butterfield, October 1996.

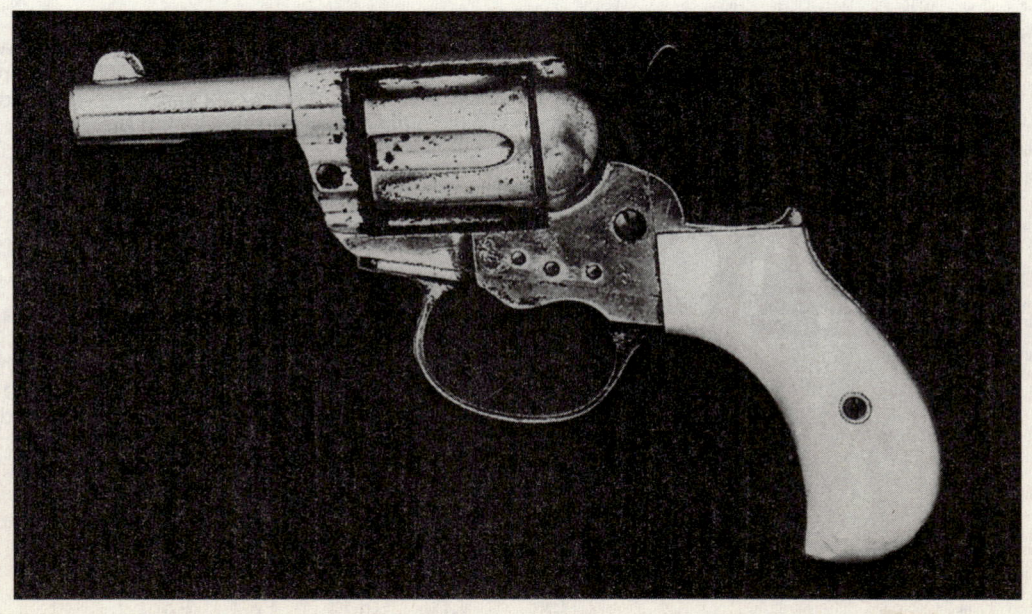

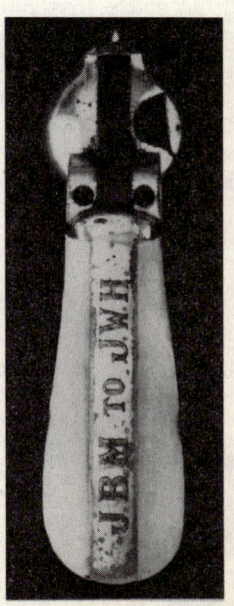

A Colt Model 1877 chambered for .41 caliber and fitted with a 4-1/2" barrel was sold at auction for $167,500. It belonged to Pat Garrett, sheriff of Lincoln County, New Mexico. The revolver was engraved with gold-washed nickel plated finish. Condition was good.
Butterfield & Butterfield, October 1996.

Model 1878 "Frontier"

This model is a large and somewhat ungainly looking revolver. It has a solid frame with a removable triggerguard. The cylinder does not swing out, and there is a thin loading gate. It has bird's-head grips made of checkered hard rubber; walnut would be found on the early models. The finish is either blued and case-colored or nickel-plated. The Model 1878 holds 6 shots, and the standard barrel lengths are 4.75", 5.5", and 7.5" with an ejector assembly and 3", 3.5", and 4" without. The standard chamberings for the Model 1878 are .32-20, 38-40, .41 Colt, .44-40, and .45 Colt. This model was fairly well received because it is chambered for the large calibers that were popular in that era. Colt manufactured 51,210 between 1878 and 1905. Antique models made before 1898 would be more desirable from an investment standpoint.

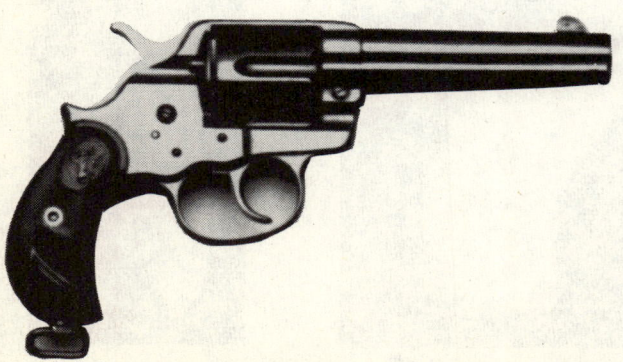

Model 1878 "Frontier" Standard

Exc.	V.G.	Good	Fair	Poor
3500	2500	1000	500	350

Model 1878 "Frontier" Omnipotent

This is a special order version of the model above with the name "Omnipotent" stamped on the barrel.

Exc.	V.G.	Good	Fair	Poor
6500	4000	1650	950	600

Model 1902

This is a U.S. Ordnance contract Model 1878. It has a 6" barrel and is chambered for .45 Colt. The finish is blued, and there is a lanyard swivel on the butt. This model bears the U.S. inspector's marks. It is sometimes referred to as the Philippine or the Alaskan model. The triggerguard is quite a bit larger than standard.

Exc.	V.G.	Good	Fair	Poor
4500	2750	2000	700	500

Model 1889 Navy

The 1889 Navy is an important model from a historical standpoint as it was the first double-action revolver Colt manufactured with a swing-out cylinder. They produced 31,000 of them between 1889 and 1894. The Model 1889 is chambered for the .38 Colt and the .41 Colt cartridges. The cylinder holds 6 shots. It is offered with a 3", 4.5", or 6" barrel; and the finish was either blued or nickel-plated. The grips are checkered hard rubber with the "Rampant Colt" in an oval molded into them. The patent dates 1884 and 1888 appear in the barrel marking, and the serial numbers are stamped on the butt. 3" Barrel-Add 20%.

Exc.	V.G.	Good	Fair	Poor
2000	1200	650	450	200

Colt Model 1889 U.S. Navy revolver marked U.S.N. Caliber is .38 and barrel is 6". Revolver is unaltered and in excellent original condition. Auction price was $20,340. Faintich Auction Service, June 1997.

Photo by Paul Goodwin

U.S. Navy Model

This variation has a 6" barrel, is chambered for .38 Colt, and is offered in blued finish only. "U.S.N." is stamped on the butt. Most of the Navy models were altered at the Colt factory to add the Model 1895 improvements. An original unaltered specimen would be worth as much as 50 percent premium over the altered values shown.

Exc.	V. G.	Good	Fair	Poor
1250	900	500	200	100

U.S. Navy Model

Exc.	V. G.	Good	Fair	Poor
3500	2750	1500	1000	750

Courtesy Butterfield & Butterfield, San Francisco, California

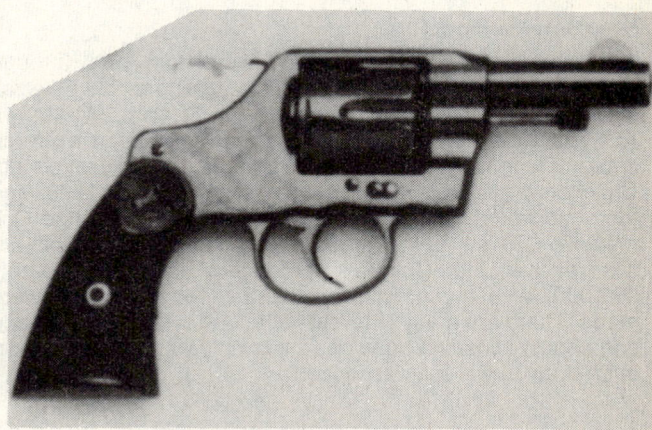

Courtesy Butterfield & Butterfield, San Francisco, California

Exc.	V.G.	Good	Fair	Poor
7500	5000	3000	1000	500

Model 1892 "New Army and Navy"

This model is similar in appearance to the 1889 Navy. The main differences are improvements to the lockwork function. It has double bolt stop notches, a double cylinder locking bolt, and shorter flutes on the cylinder. The .38 Smith & Wesson and the .32-20 were added to the .38 Colt and .41 Colt chamberings. The checkered hard rubber grips are standard, with plain walnut grips found on some contract series guns. Barrel lengths and finishes are the same as described for the Model 1889. The patent dates 1895 and 1901 appear stamped on later models. Colt manufactured 291,000 of these revolvers between 1892 and 1907. Antiques before 1898 are more desirable from an investment standpoint.

NOTE: For 3" Barrel-Add 20%.

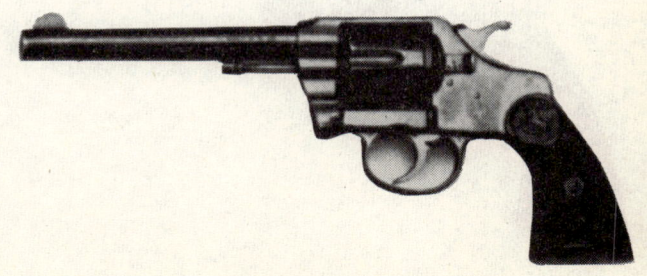

Courtesy Butterfield & Butterfield, San Francisco, California

U.S. Army Model

Exc.	V.G.	Good	Fair	Poor
2000	1200	500	250	150

Model 1905 Marine Corps

This model is a variation of the New Army and Navy Model. It was derived from the late production with its own serial range #10001-10926. With only 926 produced between 1905 and 1909, it is quite rare on today's market and is eagerly sought after by Colt Double Action collectors. This model is chambered for the .38 Colt and the .38 Smith & Wesson Special cartridges. It holds 6 shots, has a 6" barrel, and is offered in a blued finish only. The grips are checkered walnut and are quite different than those found on previous models. "U.S.M.C." is stamped on the butt; patent dates of 1884, 1888, and 1895 are stamped on the barrel. One hundred-twenty-five of these revolvers were earmarked for civilian sales and do not have the Marine Corps markings; these will generally be found in better condition. Values are similar.

Courtesy Butterfield & Butterfield, San Francisco, California

Exc.	V.G.	Good	Fair	Poor
4500	3500	2000	1500	750

New Service Model

This model was in continual production from 1898 through 1944. It is chambered for 11 different calibers: .38 Special, .357 Magnum, .38-40, .44 Russian, .44 Special, .44-40, .45 ACP, .45 Colt, .450 Eley, .455 Eley, and .476 Eley. It is offered in barrel lengths from 2" to 7.5", either blued or nickel-plated. Checkered hard rubber grips were standard until 1928, and then checkered walnut grips were used with an inletted Colt medallion. This was the largest swing-out cylinder double action revolver that Colt ever produced, and approximately 356,000 were manufactured over the 46 years they were made. There are many different variations of this revolver, and one should consult a book dealing strictly with Colt for a thorough breakdown and description.

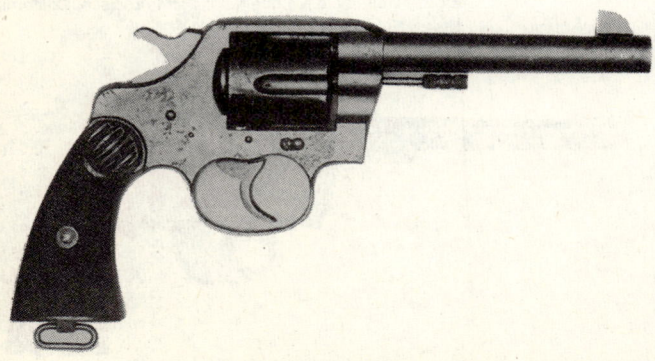

Courtesy Wallis & Wallis, Lewes, Sussex, England

Early Model, #1-#12000

Exc.	V.G.	Good	Fair	Poor
1500	1000	600	350	250

Early Model Target, #6000-#15000

Checkered walnut grips, flattop frame, 7.5" barrel.

Exc.	V.G.	Good	Fair	Poor
3000	1750	850	400	300

Improved Model, #21000-#32500

Has internal locking improvements.

Exc.	V.G.	Good	Fair	Poor
1500	1000	400	300	200

Improved Target model, #21000-#32500

Exc.	V.G.	Good	Fair	Poor
3000	1750	850	350	250

U.S. Army model 1909, #30000-#50000

5.5" barrel, .45 Colt, walnut grips, "U.S. Army model 1909" on butt.

Exc.	V.G.	Good	Fair	Poor
3000	1500	800	300	200

U.S. Navy model 1909, #30000-#50000

Same as above with "U.S.N." on butt.

Exc.	V.G.	Good	Fair	Poor
3500	2000	1000	350	250

U.S. Marine Corps Model 1909, #30000-#50000

Checkered walnut rips,. "U.S.M.C." on butt.

Exc.	V.G.	Good	Fair	Poor
4500	2000	1200	650	450

U.S. Army Model 1917, #150000-#301000

Smooth walnut grips, 5.5" barrel, .45 ACP and .45 Colt, model designation stamped on butt.

Exc.	V.G.	Good	Fair	Poor
750	600	400	300	225

Model 1917 Civilian, #335000-#336000

Approximately 1,000 made in .45 ACP only from Army parts overrun. No military markings.

Exc.	V.G.	Good	Fair	Poor
900	800	650	400	300

Late Model New Service, #325000-#356000

Checkered walnut grips and internal improvements.

Exc.	V.G.	Good	Fair	Poor
1500	1000	600	300	200

Shooting Master, #333000-#350000

Round butt, checkered walnut grips with Colt medallion, 6" barrel, "Colt Shooting Master" on barrel, flattop frame with target sights. Chambered for the .357 Magnum cartridge.

Exc.	V.G.	Good	Fair	Poor
1500	1200	850	400	300

Magnum Model New Service, Over #340000

.357 Magnum, .38 Special.

Exc.	V.G.	Good	Fair	Poor
800	600	350	250	200

New Pocket Model

This was the first swing-out cylinder, double action pocket revolver made by Colt. It is chambered for .32 Colt and .32 Smith & Wesson. It holds 6 shots and is offered with barrel lengths of 2.5", 3.5", 5", and 6". The finish is blued or nickel-plated, and the grips are checkered hard rubber with the oval Colt molded into them. "Colt's New Pocket" is stamped on the frame. 1884 and 1888 patent dates are stamped on the barrel of later-production guns. There were approximately 30,000 of these manufactured between 1893 and 1905. Antiques made before 1898 are more desirable.

Early Production Without Patent Dates-Add 25%.
5" Barrel-Add 10%.

Exc.	V.G.	Good	Fair	Poor
600	450	300	250	150

Pocket Positive

Externally this is the same revolver as the New Pocket, but it has the positive lock feature. It was manufactured between 1905 and 1940.

Exc.	V.G.	Good	Fair	Poor
500	375	275	225	125

New Police Model

This model appears similar to the New Pocket Model. The frame is stamped "New Police." It is chambered for the .32 Colt, .32 Colt New Police, and .32 Smith & Wesson cartridges. The barrel lengths are 2.5", 4", and 6". The finishes are blued or nickel-plated. Colt manufactured 49,500 of this model from 1896-1907. The New York City Police Department purchased 4,500 of these revolvers, and the backstraps are so marked. There was also a target model of this revolver, which features a 6" barrel with a flattop frame and target sights, of which 5,000 were produced.

New York Police Marked-Add 10%.
Target model-Add 20%.

Exc.	V.G.	Good	Fair	Poor
400	250	200	150	100

Police Positive

This is externally the same as the New Police with the addition of the positive lock feature and two new chamberings—the .38 New Police and the .38 Smith & Wesson. They were manufactured from 1905-1947.

Exc.	V.G.	Good	Fair	Poor
350	300	250	200	150

Police Positive Target

This is basically the same as the New Police Target with the positive lock feature. It is chambered in .22 l.r., as well as the other cartridges offered in the earlier model.

Exc.	V.G.	Good	Fair	Poor
650	550	400	300	200

NOTE: A .22 caliber Police Positive chambered for the .22 short and long cartridge may be seen with British proofs. Several such revolvers were sold to London Armory in this configuration during the late 1920s..A NIB example recently sold for $1,200.

Police Positive Special

This model is similar to the Police Positive but has a slightly larger frame to accept the longer cylinder needed to chamber more powerful cartridges such as the .38 Special, in addition to the original chamberings. They were manufactured from 1907-1973.

Exc.	V.G.	Good	Fair	Poor
350	275	225	150	100

Police Positive Special Mark V

Introduced in 1994 this is an updated version of the Police Positive Special. This model features an underlug 4" barrel with rubber grips and fixed sights. The butt is rounded. The revolver is rated to fire .38 caliber +P rounds. Overall length is 9" and weighs approximately 30 oz.

NIB	Exc.	V.G.	Good	Fair	Poor
325	250	200	150	100	85

Army Special Model

This is a heavier-framed improved version of the New Army and Navy revolver. It is chambered for the .32-20, .38 Colt, .38 Smith & Wesson, and .41 Colt. It is offered with a 4", 4.5", 5", and 6" barrel. The finish is blued or nickel-plated, and the grips are checkered hard rubber. The serial number range is #291000-#540000, and they were manufactured between 1908-1927.

Exc.	V.G.	Good	Fair	Poor
550	400	250	200	150

Officer's Model Target 1st Issue

This revolver is chambered for the .38 Special cartridge. It has a 6" barrel and is blued. It has a flattop frame with adjustable target sights. Colt manufactured this model from 1904-1908.

Exc.	V.G.	Good	Fair	Poor
1000	750	350	300	200

Officer's Model Target 2nd Issue

This model is similar to the 1st Issue but is offered in .22 l.r. and .32 Police Positive caliber, as well as in .38 Special. It also is furnished with a 4", 4.5", 5", 6", and 7.5" barrel in .38 Special only. It has checkered walnut grips. Colt manufactured this model between 1908 and 1940.

Exc.	V.G.	Good	Fair	Poor
700	550	300	250	150

Camp Perry Single Shot

This model was created by modifying an Officer's Model frame to accept a special flat single shot "cylinder." This flat chamber pivots to the left side and downward for loading. The pistol is chambered for .22 l.r. and is offered with an 8" (early production) or 10" (late production) barrel. The finish is blued, with checkered walnut grips. The name "Camp Perry Model" is stamped on the left side of the chamber; the caliber is on the barrel. Colt named this model after the site of the U.S. Target Competition held annually at Camp Perry, Ohio. They manufactured 2,525 of these between 1920 and 1941.

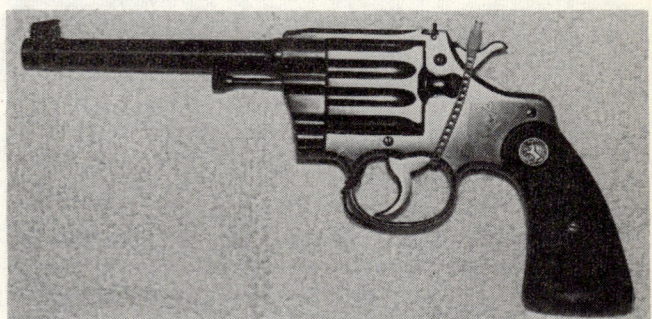

Exc.	V.G.	Good	Fair	Poor
1750	1250	750	500	350

Officers Model Match

Introduced in 1953 this model is similar to the Officers Model Target and chambered for either the .22 caliber cartridge or the .38 Special with 6" barrel. The revolver is fitted with a heavy tapered barrel and wide hammer spur with adjustable rear sight and ramp front sight. It was sold with checkered walnut target grips. Blued finish is standard. Discontinued in 1970. The standard of long action could be fired both double or single action. The .22 caliber version prices are listed below. Officers Model Match in .38 caliber will bring approximately 20% less.

Exc.	V.G.	Good	Fair	Poor
750	600	450	350	250

.22 Caliber in Short Action-Single Action Only

Exc.	V.G.	Good	Fair	Poor
1000	750	600	500	350

Official Police

This was a popular revolver in the Colt line for many years. It was manufactured from 1927 to 1969. It is chambered for .32-20 and .41 Colt. These calibers were discontinued in 1942 and 1930, respectively. The .38 Special was chambered throughout the entire production run, and .22 l.r. was added in 1930. This model holds 6 shots, has a square butt, and is offered with 2", 4", 5", and 6" barrel lengths. The grips are checkered walnut. The finish is either blued or nickel-plated.

Nickel-Plated-Add 10%.
.22 l.r.-Add 20%.

Exc.	V.G.	Good	Fair	Poor
350	300	250	200	150

Commando Model

This model, for all intents and purposes, is an Official Police chambered for .38 Special, with a 2", 4", or 6" barrel. This model is parkerized and stamped "Colt Commando" on the barrel. There were approximately 50,000 manufactured between 1942-1945 for use in World War II.

NOTE: Add 30% for 2" barrel.

Courtesy Richard M. Kumor, Sr.

Exc.	V.G.	Good	Fair	Poor
500	350	225	150	100

Marshall Model

This is an Official Police that is marked "Colt Marshall" on the barrel and has an "M" suffix in the serial number. It has a 2" or 4" barrel and a round butt. The finish is blued. There were approximately 2,500 manufactured between 1954 and 1956.

Exc.	V.G.	Good	Fair	Poor
500	400	300	250	150

Bankers Special

The Bankers Special is a 2" barrelled, easily concealed revolver. It was designed with bank employees in mind. It is chambered for .38 Special and was offered in blued finish. The grips are rounded but full-sized, and Colt utilized this feature in advertising this model. The U.S. Postal Service equipped its railway mail clerks with this model. There were approximately 35,000 manufactured between 1926 and 1943.

Exc.	V.G.	Good	Fair	Poor
1200	800	300	250	150

NOTE: Nickel models will command a premium.

Detective Special 1st Issue

This model is actually a duplication, as it is nothing more than a Police Positive Special with a 2" barrel standard. It was originally chambered for .32 New Police, .38 New Police, (which were discontinued) and .38 Special, which continued until the end of the production run. The finish is blued, and it is offered with wood or plastic grips. There were over 400,000 manufactured between 1926 and 1972.

Exc.	V.G.	Good	Fair	Poor
900	650	250	175	100

Detective Special 2nd Issue

This is basically a modernized, streamlined version of the 1st issue. It is similar except that it has a 2" or 3" barrel with a shrouded ejector rod and wraparound checkered walnut grips and is chambered for .38 Special. It was finished in blue or nickel plate. Reintroduced in 1993.

Left View

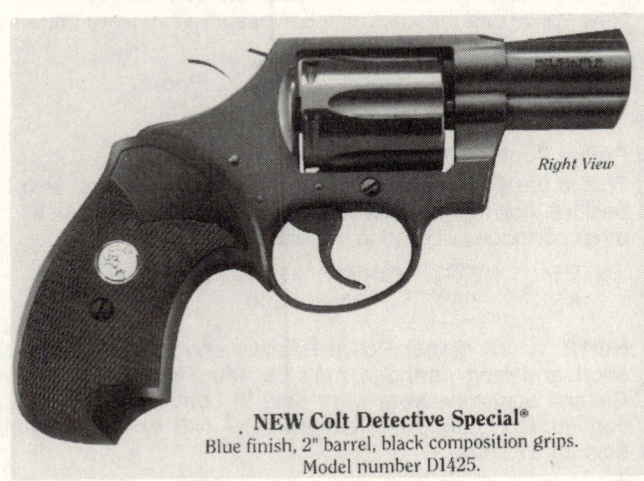

Right View

NEW Colt Detective Special®
Blue finish, 2" barrel, black composition grips.
Model number D1425.

NIB	Exc.	V.G.	Good	Fair	Poor
350	275	225	175	125	75

Add $25 for nickel finish.

Colt .38 SF-VI

Introduced in 1995 this model is essentially a Detective Special in stainless steel with a new internal mechanism. Has a transfer bar safety mechanism. Fitted with a 2" barrel and cylinder holds 6 rounds of .38 Special. A 4" barrel in bright stainless steel is also available. Weight is 21 oz. and overall length is 7".

NIB	Exc.	V.G	Good	Fair	Poor
400	325	275	225	150	100

Colt .38 SF-VI Special Lady

Introduced in 1996 this 2" barrel version is similar to the above model with the addition of a bright finish and bobbed hammer. Weight is 21 oz.

NIB	Exc.	V.G.	Good	Fair	Poor
400	325	275	225	150	100

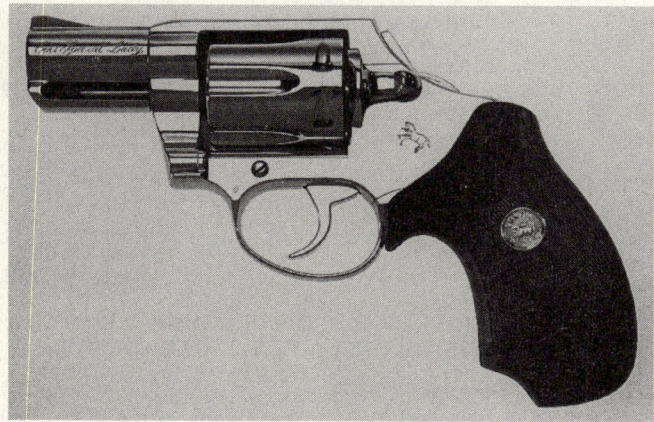

Detective Special II (DS-II)

Introduced in 1997 this version of the Detective special features new internal lock work and a transfer bar safety mechansim. It is fitted with a 2" barrel, has a capacity of six rounds, and is chambered for the .38 Special. Rubber combat style grips are standard. Weight is approximately 21 oz. Stainless steel finish.

NIB	Exc.	V.G.	Good	Fair	Poor
400	300	—	—	—	—

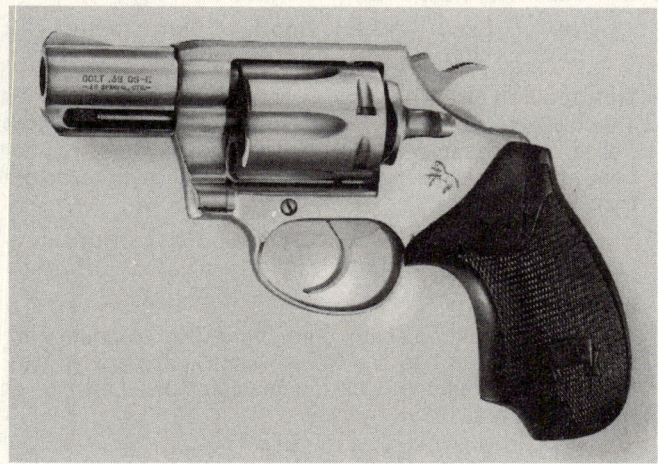

Cobra 1st Issue

The Cobra is simply an alloy-framed lightweight version of the Detective Special. It weighs only 15 oz. The Cobra is chambered for .32, .38 Special, and .22 l.r. This model is available in either a round butt or square butt version with a 4" barrel only. They were manufactured between 1950 and 1973.

Exc.	V.G.	Good	Fair	Poor
500	300	225	150	100

Cobra 2nd Issue

The same as the 1st Issue in .38 Special only, this is streamlined with wraparound walnut grips and shrouded ejector rod.

Exc.	V.G.	Good	Fair	Poor
350	300	225	150	100

NOTE: For nickel add 30%.

Agent 1st Issue

This revolver is basically the same as the 1st Issue Cobra with a shortened grip frame. This was done to make the Agent more concealable. Colt manufactured the Agent 1st Issue from 1955-1973.

Exc.	V.G.	Good	Fair	Poor
400	300	200	125	100

Agent L.W. 2nd Issue

This is a streamlined version with the shrouded ejector rod. In the last four years of its production, it was matte finished. Colt manufactured this model between 1973 and 1986.

Exc.	V.G.	Good	Fair	Poor
250	200	175	125	100

Border Patrol

This model is quite rare, as Colt manufactured only 400 of them in 1952. It is basically a Police Special with a heavy 4" barrel. It is chambered for the .38 Special and was built to be strong. The finish is blued and serial numbered in the 610000 range.

Exc.	V.G.	Good	Fair	Poor
5000	3000	2000	1000	500

Air Crewman Special

This model was especially fabricated for the Air Force to be carried by their pilots for protection. It is extremely lightweight at 11 oz. The frame and the cylinder are made of aluminum alloy. It has a 2" barrel and is chambered for the .38 Special. The finish was blued, with checkered walnut grips. There were approximately 1,200 manufactured in 1951, and they are marked "U.S." or "A.F."

Exc.	V.G.	Good	Fair	Poor
4500	2500	1500	800	250

A Colt Air Crewman with 2" barrel and chambered for .38 Special was sold at auction for $4,802.50. It belonged to General Harrison, U.S.A.F. Condition was very good to excellent. Faintich Auction Service, June 1997.

Photo by Paul Goodwin

Courier

This is another version of the Cobra. It features a shorter grip frame and a 3" barrel. This model is chambered for .32 and .22

rimfire. There were approximately 3,000 manufactured in 1955 and 1956.

.22 Rimfire-Add 20%.

Exc.	V.G.	Good	Fair	Poor
850	750	600	500	350

Trooper

This model was designed specifically by Colt to fill the need for a large, heavy-duty, powerful revolver that was accurate. The Trooper filled that need. It was offered with a 4" or 6" barrel and blued or nickel finishes with checkered walnut grips. The Trooper is chambered for the .38 Special/.357 Magnum, and there is a .22 rimfire version for the target shooters. This model was manufactured between 1953 and 1969.

Exc.	V.G.	Good	Fair	Poor
400	250	200	150	100

Colt .357 Magnum

This is a deluxe version of the Trooper. It is offered with a special target wide hammer and large target-type grips. The sights are the same as Accro target model. It features a 4" or 6" barrel and a blued finish and was manufactured between 1953 and 1961. There were less than 15,000 produced.

Exc.	V.G.	Good	Fair	Poor
500	350	300	200	150

Diamondback

This model is a medium-frame, duty-type weapon suitable for target work. It has the short frame of the Detective Special with the ventilated rib 2.5", 4", or 6" barrel. It is chambered for .38 Special and .22 rimfire for the target shooters. The finish is blued or nickel-plated, with checkered walnut grips. The Diamondback features adjustable target sights, wide target hammer, and a steel frame. It was manufactured between 1966 and 1986.

Nickel Finish-Add 15%.

NIB	Exc.	V.G.	Good	Fair	Poor
500	375	300	250	200	150

NOTE: For .22 caliber 2.5" barrel add $200. If finish is nickel add $500.

Viper

This is an alloy-framed revolver chambered for the .38 Special. It has a 4" barrel and was manufactured between 1977 and 1984. The Viper is essentially a lightweight version of the Police Positive.

NIB	Exc.	V.G.	Good	Fair	Poor
450	375	200	175	125	100

Python

The Python is the Cadillac of the Colt double-action line. It has been manufactured since 1955 and is still the flagship of the Colt line. It is chambered for the .357 Magnum cartridge, holds 6 shots, and has been offered in barrel lengths of 2.5", 3", 4", 6", and 8". This revolver is offered finished in high polished Colt Royal Blue, nickel-plate, matte-finish stainless steel, or what is known as "The Ultimate"—a high polished stainless steel. The 3" barrel, as well as the nickel plating, has been discontinued. The grips are checkered walnut. It is possible that the nickel-plated specimens may bring a 10 percent premium. In my experience this is not always the case as many potential purchasers have a definite preference for the blued finish.

NIB	Exc.	V.G.	Good	Fair	Poor
750	550	450	350	275	225

Matte Stainless Steel

NIB	Exc.	V.G.	Good	Fair	Poor
825	650	550	450	350	275

"The Ultimate" Bright Stainless

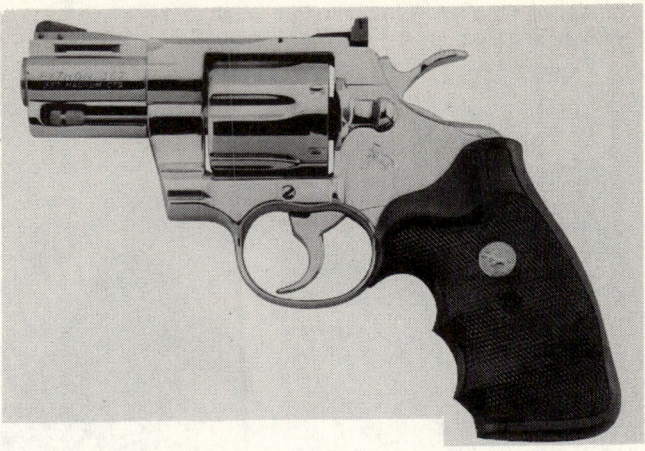

NIB	Exc.	V.G.	Good	Fair	Poor
875	675	575	475	375	300

Python .38 Special

This is an 8" barrelled Python chambered for the .38 Special only. It was a limited-production venture that was not a success. It was offered in blue only.

Exc.	V.G.	Good	Fair	Poor
500	400	325	275	225

Python Hunter

The Hunter was a special 8" .357 Magnum Python with an extended eye relief Leupold 2X scope. The grips are neoprene with gold Colt medallions. The revolver, with mounted scope and accessories, was fitted into a Haliburton extruded aluminum case. The Hunter was manufactured in 1981 only.

NIB	Exc.	V.G.	Good	Fair	Poor
1000	800	650	500	400	300

Metropolitan MK III

This revolver is basically a heavier-duty version of the Official Police. It is chambered for .38 Special and fitted with a 4" heavy barrel. It is finished in blue only and was manufactured from 1969-1972.

NIB	Exc.	V.G.	Good	Fair	Poor
400	300	150	125	100	75

Lawman MK III

This model is offered chambered for the .357 Magnum with a 2" or 4" barrel. It has checkered walnut grips and is either blued or nickel-plated. Colt manufactured the Lawman between 1969 and 1983.

Exc.	V.G.	Good	Fair	Poor
350	300	200	150	100

Lawman MK V

This is an improved version of the MK III. It entailed a redesigned grip, a shorter lock time, and an improved double action. It was manufactured 1982-1985.

NIB	Exc.	V.G.	Good	Fair	Poor
300	250	225	175	125	90

Trooper MK III

This revolver was intended to be the target-grade version of the MK III series. It is offered with a 4", 6", or 8" vent-rib barrel with a shrouded ejector rod similar in appearance to the Python. It is chambered for the .22 l.r. and the .22 Magnum, as well as .357 Magnum. It features adjustable target sights, checkered walnut target grips, and is either blued or nickel-plated. This model was manufactured between 1969 and 1983.

NIB	Exc.	V.G.	Good	Fair	Poor
325	275	250	200	150	100

Trooper MK V

This improved version of the MK III was manufactured between 1982 and 1985.

NIB	Exc.	V.G.	Good	Fair	Poor
325	275	250	200	150	100

Boa

This is basically a deluxe version of the Trooper MK V. It has all the same features plus the high polished blue found on the Python. Colt manufactured 1,200 of these revolvers in 1985, and the entire production was purchased and marketed by Lew Horton Distributing Company in Southboro, Massachusetts.

NIB	Exc.	V.G.	Good	Fair	Poor
450	400	350	300	250	150

Peacekeeper

This model was designed as a duty-type weapon with target capabilities. It is offered with a 4" or 6" barrel chambered for .357 Magnum. It features adjustable sights and neoprene combat-style grips and has a matte blued finish. This model was manufactured between 1985 and 1987.

NIB	Exc.	V.G.	Good	Fair	Poor
300	275	225	200	150	100

King Cobra

This model has become the workhorse of the Colt revolver line. The King Cobra has a forged steel frame and barrel and a full length ejector rod housing. The barrel is fitted with a solid rib. This model is equipped with an adjustable, white outline rear sight and a red insert front sight. Colt black neoprene combat style grips are standard. The blued model is no longer offered.

Blued

NIB	Exc.	V.G.	Good	Fair	Poor
325	300	250	200	150	100

Stainless Steel

Offered in 4" or 6" barrel lengths. In 1997 this model was introduced with optional barrel porting. Also for 1997 all King Cobras are drilled and tapped for scope mounts.

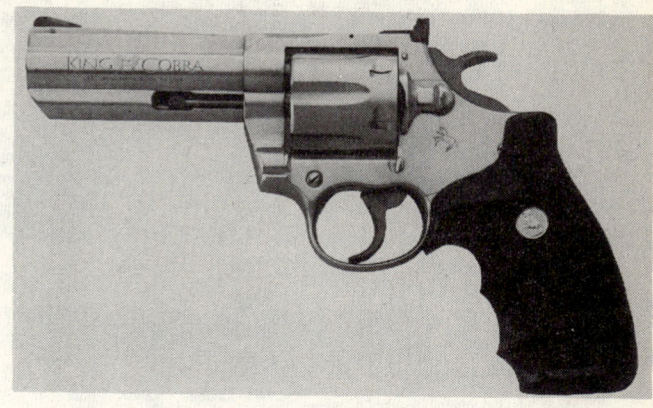

NIB	Exc.	V.G.	Good	Fair	Poor
375	325	300	250	200	125

High Polish Stainless Steel

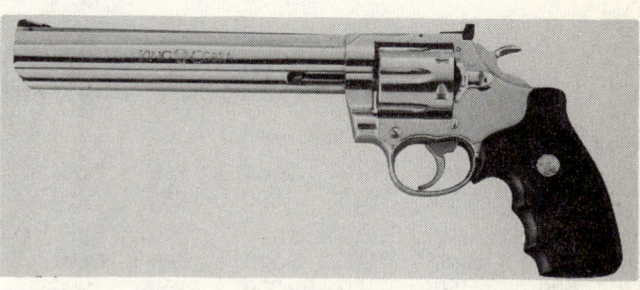

NIB	Exc.	V.G.	Good	Fair	Poor
400	350	300	250	200	125

Anaconda

This double-action .44 Magnum revolver was introduced in 1990. It is offered with 4", 6", or 8" barrel lengths. The 4" model weighs 47 oz., the 6" model weighs 63 oz., and the 8" model weighs 59 oz. The Anaconda holds 6 rounds and is available with a matte stainless steel finish. For 1993 a new chambering in .45 Colt was offered for the Anaconda. This model was offered with a 6" or 8" barrel in a matte stainless steel finish revolver chambered for the .44 Remington Magnum cartridge. It is currently offered with a 6" or 8" barrel and adjustable red-insert front and white-outline rear sights. It is constructed of matte-finished stainless steel and has black neoprene finger-groove grips with gold Colt medallions. In 1996 the Realtree model was offered with 8" barrel. Chambered for the .44 Magnum cartridge. Furnished with either adjustable rear sight and ramp front sights or special scope mount. In 1997 the Anaconda was drilled and tapped for scope mounts and buyers had the option of barrel porting.

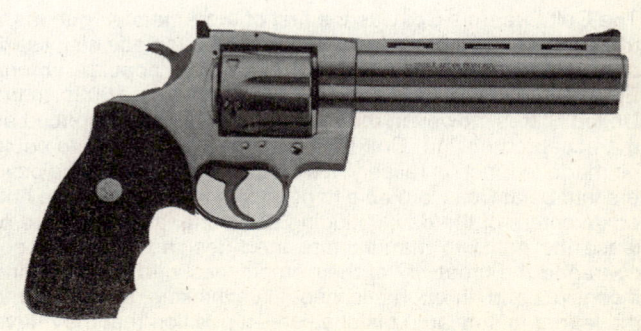

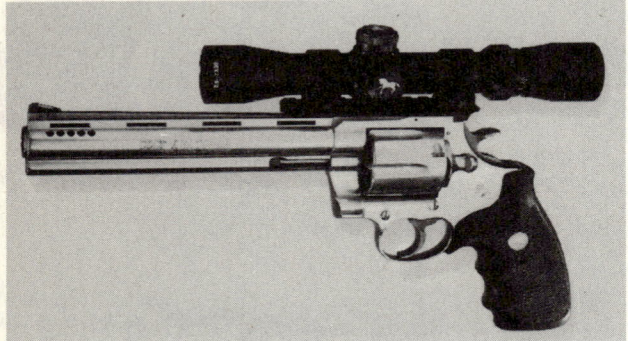

Colt Anaconda with optional ported barrel with oprional Colt optics.

.44 Magnum

NIB	Exc.	V.G.	Good	Fair	Poor
500	450	350	300	250	200

.45 Colt

NIB	Exc.	V.G.	Good	Fair	Poor
500	450	350	300	250	200

Realtree Camo Model-Adjustable sights

NIB	Exc.	V.G.	Good	Fair	Poor
675	625	500	400	300	200

Realtree Camo Model-Scope mounts

NIB	Exc.	V.G.	Good	Fair	Poor
900	800	650	500	400	250

COLT SEMIAUTOMATIC PISTOLS

The Colt Firearms Co. was the first of the American gun manufacturers to take the advent of the semiautomatic pistol seriously. This pistol design was becoming popular among European gunmakers in the late 1880s and early 1900s. In the United States, however, the revolver was firmly ensconced as the accepted design. Colt realized that if the semiauto could be made to function reliably, it would soon catch on.. The powers that be at Colt were able to negotiate with some of the noted inventors of the day, including Browning, and to secure or lease the rights to manufacture their designs. Colt also encouraged the creativity of their employees with bonuses and incentives and, through this innovative thinking, soon became the leader in semiauto pistol sales—a position that they have

never really relinquished to any other American gun maker. The Colt semiautomatic pistols represent an interesting field for the collector of Colt handguns. There were many variations with high enough production to make it worthwhile to seek them out. There are a number of fine books on the Colt semiautomatics, and anyone wishing to do so will be able to learn a great deal about them. Collector interest is high in this field, and values are definitely on the rise.

Model 1900

This was the first of the Colt automatic pistols. It was actually a developmental model with only 3,500 being produced. The Model 1900 was not really a successful design. It was quite clumsy and out of balance in the hand and was not as reliable in function as it should have been. This model is chambered for the .38 Rimless smokeless cartridge. It has a detachable magazine that holds seven cartridges. The barrel is 6" in length. The finish is blued, with a case-colored hammer and safety/sight combination. The grips are either plain walnut, checkered walnut, or hard rubber. This pistol is a Browning design, and the left side of the slide is stamped "Browning's Patent" with the 1897 patent date. Colt sold 200 pistols to the Navy and 200 to the Army for field trials and evaluation. The remaining 3,300 were sold on the civilian market. This model was manufactured from 1900-1903.

Civilian Model with Sight/Safety Combination-Add 40%.

Standard Civilian Production

Exc.	V.G.	Good	Fair	Poor
7500	4000	2250	1250	750

U.S. Navy Military Model

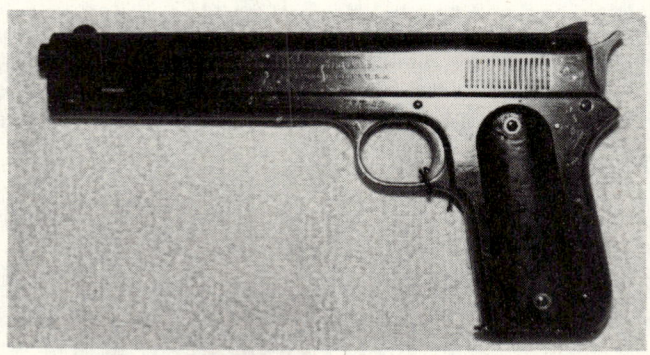

Exc.	V.G.	Good	Fair	Poor
7500	6000	5000	2500	1000

A U.S. Navy Military Model in .38ACP caliber which was factory inscribed and gold inlaid to a Navy inspector. This pistol was the first to leave the factory with rubber stocks. A factory letter was with the pistol. Overall condition of pistol is excellent. Price paid in March 1996 was $20,350. Faintich Auction Service, LLC.

U.S. Army Miliary Model-1st contract

Exc.	V.G.	Good	Fair	Poor
20000	15000	10000	4000	2000

U.S. Army Military Model-2nd contract

Exc.	V.G.	Good	Fair	Poor
10000	7500	5500	2000	1500

Model 1902 Sporting Pistol

This model is chambered for the .38 Rimless smokeless cartridge. It has a 7-round detachable magazine and a 6" barrel and is blued, with checkered hard rubber grips featuring the "Rampant Colt" molded into them. The most notable features of the 1902 Sporting Model are the rounded butt, rounded hammer spur, dovetailed rear sight, and the 1897-1902 patent dates. Colt manufactured approximately 7,500 of these pistols between 1903 and 1908.

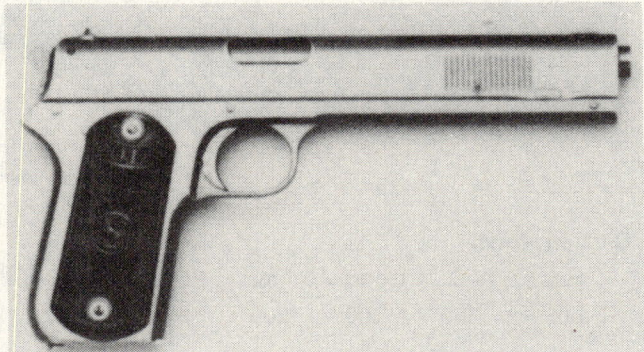

Exc.	V.G.	Good	Fair	Poor
3500	2000	1250	750	450

Model 1902 Military Pistol

This model is a somewhat larger, heavier pistol than the 1902 Sporting Pistol. It has the same .38 ACP chambering and 6" barrel, but the detachable magazine holds 8 rounds. The grip of this model is larger and squared off, and it has a lanyard swivel on the butt. There were approximately 18,000 manufactured between 1902 and 1929.

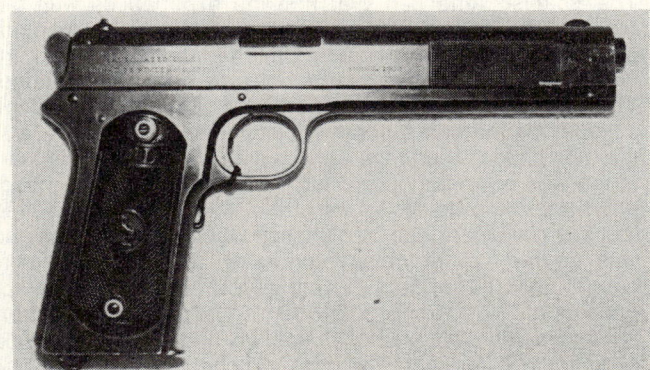

Early Model with Front of Slide Serrated

Exc.	V.G.	Good	Fair	Poor
3500	2000	1250	750	450

Standard Model with Rear of Slide Serrated

Exc.	V.G.	Good	Fair	Poor
2500	1750	1000	500	400

U.S. Army Marked, #15001-#15200 with Front Serrations

Exc.	V.G.	Good	Fair	Poor
6000	5000	2500	1250	600

Model 1903 Pocket Pistol

This was the first automatic pocket pistol Colt produced. It is essentially identical to the 1902 Sporting Model with a shorter slide. The barrel length is 4.5", and it is chambered for the .38 Rimless smokeless cartridge. It is blued, with a case-colored hammer, with checkered hard rubber grips that have the "Rampant Colt" molded into them. The detachable magazine holds 7 rounds. There were approximately 26,000 manufactured between 1903 and 1929.

Exc.	V.G.	Good	Fair	Poor
1100	850	650	350	200

Model 1903 Hammerless, .32 Pocket Pistol

Courtesy Orvel Reichert

This was the second pocket automatic Colt manufactured. It was another of John Browning's designs, and it developed into one of Colt's most successful pistols. This pistol is chambered for the .32 ACP cartridge. Initially the barrel length was 4"; this was shortened to 3.75". The detachable magazine holds 8 rounds. The standard finish is blue, with quite a few nickel plated. The early model grips are checkered hard rubber with the "Rampant Colt" molded into them. Many of the nickel plated pistols had pearl grips. In 1924 the grips were changed to checkered walnut with the Colt medallions. The name of this model can be misleading as it is not a true hammerless but a concealed hammer design. It features a slide stop and a grip safety. Colt manufactured 572,215 civilian versions of this pistol and approximately 200,000 more for military contracts. This model was manufactured between 1903 and 1945.

Early Model 1897 Patent Date-Add 40%.
Nickel Plated With Pearl Grips-Add $100.
4" Barrel to #72,000-Add 20%.

Exc.	V.G.	Good	Fair	Poor
550	500	450	300	200

> **A factory engraved Model 1903 executed by Cuno Helfricht, serial number 00, was sold at auction for $82,500. Presented by the president of Colt Firearms to Kaiser Wilhem II. Shipped in 1906. Condition excellent to mint. Butterfield & Butterfield, December 1995.**

U.S. Military Model

Serial prefix M, marked "U.S. Property" on frame, parkerized finish.

Exc.	V.G.	Good	Fair	Poor
1200	850	400	300	250

Model 1908 Hammerless .380 Pocket Pistol

This model is essentially the same as the .32 Pocket Pistol, chambered for the more potent .380 ACP, also known as the 9mm Browning short. Other specifications are the same. Colt manufactured approximately 138,000 in this caliber for civilian sales. An unknown number were sold to the military.

Standard Civilian Model

Nickel with Pearl Grips-Add $100.

Exc.	V.G.	Good	Fair	Poor
800	650	475	350	250

Military Model

Serial prefix M, marked "U.S. Property" on frame, parkerized finish.

Exc.	V.G.	Good	Fair	Poor
1500	1000	750	500	300

Model 1908 Hammerless .25 Pocket Pistol

This was the smallest automatic Colt made. It is chambered for the .25 ACP cartridge, has a 2" barrel, and is 4.5" long overall. It weighs a mere 13 oz. This is a true pocket pistol. The detachable magazine holds 6 shots. This model was offered in blue or nickel-plate, with grips of checkered hard rubber and checkered walnut on later versions. This model has a grip safety, slide lock, and a magazine disconnector safety. This was another Browning design, and Fabrique Nationale manufactured this pistol in Belgium before Colt picked up the rights to make it in the U.S. This was a commercial success by Colt's standards, with approximately 409,000 manufactured between 1908 and 1941.

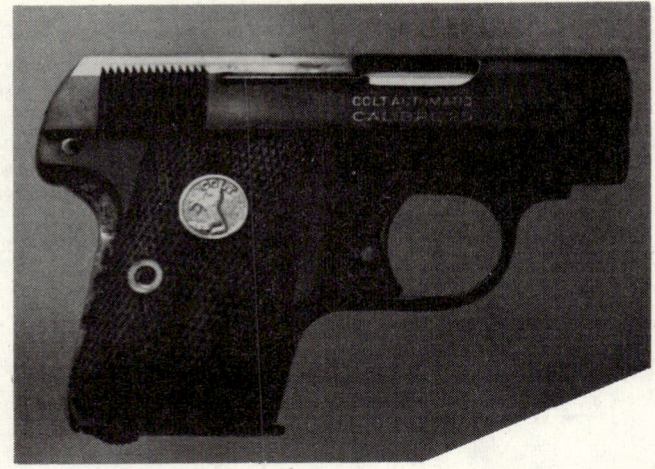

Courtesy Orvel Reichert

Civilian Model

Exc.	V.G.	Good	Fair	Poor
500	350	300	200	100

Military Model

"U.S. Property" marked on right frame. Very rare.

Exc.	V.G.	Good	Fair	Poor
2500	1250	600	450	300

Model 1905 .45 Automatic Pistol

The Spanish American War and the experiences with the Moros in the Philippine campaign taught a lesson about stopping power or the lack of it. The United States Army was convinced that they needed a more powerful handgun cartridge. This led Colt to the development of a .45-caliber cartridge suitable for the semiautomatic pistol. The Model 1905 and the .45 Rimless round were the result. In actuality, this cartridge was not nearly powerful enough to satisfy the need, but it led to the development of the .45 ACP. Colt believed that this pistol/cartridge combination would be a success and was geared up for mass production. The Army actually bought only 200 of them, and the total production was approximately 6,300 from 1905 to 1911. The pistol has a 5" barrel and detachable 7-shot magazine and is blued, with a case-colored hammer. The grips are checkered walnut. The hammer was rounded on the first 3,600 pistols and was changed to a spur hammer on the later models. The right side of the slide is stamped "Automatic Colt / Calibre 45 Rimless Smokeless." This model was not a commercial success for Colt—possibly because it has no safety whatsoever except for the floating inertia firing pin. The 200 military models have grip safeties only. A small number (believed to be less than 500) of these pistols were grooved to accept a shoulder stock. The stocks were made of leather and steel and made to double as a holster. These pistols have been classified "Curios and Relics" under the provisions of the Gun Control Act of 1968.

Civilian Model

Exc.	V.G.	Good	Fair	Poor
4000	3500	1750	950	400

Military Model, Serial #1-201

Known as the 1907 Contract Pistol, it has a lanyard loop, a loaded chamber indicator, and a grip safety and bears the inspector's initials "K.M."

Exc.	V.G.	Good	Fair	Poor
8500	6500	4500	1500	500

COLT 1911

The Colt Government Model is one of the most recognizable handguns in the world. Its popularity is second only to the Single Action Army among firearm collectors in the world today. It was this pistol that established Colt as the leader among handgun manufacturers. Arguably the advent of this fine pistol was timely from a historic point of view. It appeared just in time for the beginning of WWI and was able to prove its worth on the battlefields of Europe and the Pacific in both WWI and WWII. This was undoubtedly John Browning's crowning achievement, as this pistol shall always be the most respected of the Colt Auto line. There were over 200 factory variations and the production run from 1911, and still going strong, is unsurpassed. There were approximately 336,000 civilian and 2,695,212 military versions of the 1911 and 1911A1 manufactured to this point. This model was used in WWI, WWII, the Korean War and Vietnam. Its recent replacement still stirs controversy from some knowledgeable quarters. There are a number of excellent books specializing in this firearm, and one interested in collecting this pistol will have no trouble gaining an education in the field.

Model 1911 Automatic Pistol Commercial Series

The commercial or civilian version of the 1911 is readily recognized by the "C" prefix in the serial number. This variation commenced production in 1911 with serial number C 1 and was replaced in 1925 by its successor, the 1911A1 at serial number C130000. The 1911 is a large-frame semiautomatic with a 5" barrel. The finish is a high polish blue with checkered walnut grips. The grips feature a raised diamond around the screw holes. The 1911 has a thin front sight blade, long trigger, short spur on the hammer, and the grip safety. The mainspring housing is flat, and there is no relief cut on the frame behind the trigger. The pistol is chambered for the .45 ACP and has a 7-round detachable magazine. The words "Government Model" were not stamped on this pistol until the 1911A1 Series after 1946. There are a number of variations of this model. We list the major ones and advise those interested in collecting to procure one of the excellent volumes available on this pistol. Early Models 1897, 1902, 1905, and 1911 Patent Dates Serial numbers through C4500 3 Digit Serial Number-Add 20%.

2 Digit Serial Number-Add 40%.

Exc.	V.G.	Good	Fair	Poor
2500	1500	900	600	400

Standard 1911 Pistol

Exc.	V.G.	Good	Fair	Poor
2500	1500	900	500	300

> A factory inscribed gold banded Model 1911 Government Model, produced 1913, was sold at auction for $8,140. Condition was excellent. Factory letter. Chambered for .45 ACP with 5" barrel, blue finish, diamond checkered walnut stocks, and loop magazine. Faintich Auction Service, LLC.

Argentine Contract

This is part of the commercial serial range and falls between numbers C10000 and C130000. The pistols are marked "Pistola Automatica Sistema Colt, Calibre 11.25mm, modelo 1916." They bear the Argentine Crest and were manufactured between 1917 and 1925.

Exc.	V.G.	Good	Fair	Poor
950	750	550	400	300

1911 Russian Order

This variation is chambered for .45ACP and has the Russian version of "Anglo Zakazivat" stamped on the frame. There were 14,500 of these blued pistols manufactured in 1915-1916. They are found between serial numbers C50000 and C85000.

This variation is rarely encountered today, as they did go to Russia and a lot has happened over there since. One should be extremely cautious and secure qualified appraisal if contemplating a purchase, as fakes have been noted.

Exc.	V.G.	Good	Fair	Poor
2500	1750	1250	650	400

WWI British Contract

This series is chambered for the British .455 cartridge and is so marked on the right side of the slide. The British "Broad Arrow" proofmark will also be found. These pistols were made in 1915-1916 and have their own serial range W10001 through W21000. They are commercial series pistols.

Exc.	V.G.	Good	Fair	Poor
1500	1000	750	550	450

Model 1911 Automatic Pistol, Military Series

The military Model 1911 is basically identical to the commercial series except for the markings that appear on the military version. They both have the blued finish and the diamond checkered walnut grips. The serial number range on 1911 military pistols falls between 1 and 629500 with no prefix. They were manufactured by other subcontractors as well as by Colt and are listed with appropriate values. The standard frame stamping is "United States Property," The right side of the slide is marked "Model of 1911" followed by "U.S.Army," "U.S. Navy," or "U.S.M.C." They were manufactured between 1912 and 1925.

Courtesy Milwaukee Public Museum, Milwaukee, Wisconsin

Colt Manufacture

U.S. Army marked throughout serial range.

Below Serial #10000-Add 10%.

Exc.	V.G.	Good	Fair	Poor
2000	1500	1000	550	450

U.S. Navy Marked

Courtesy Butterfield & Butterfield, San Francisco, California

Exc.	V.G.	Good	Fair	Poor
3500	2000	1250	550	450

Rock Island Auction Company sold a Model 1911 pistol with military and USMC markings. Grips are excellent, bore is excellent, and overall condition is good. Auction price was $3,565. April 1997.

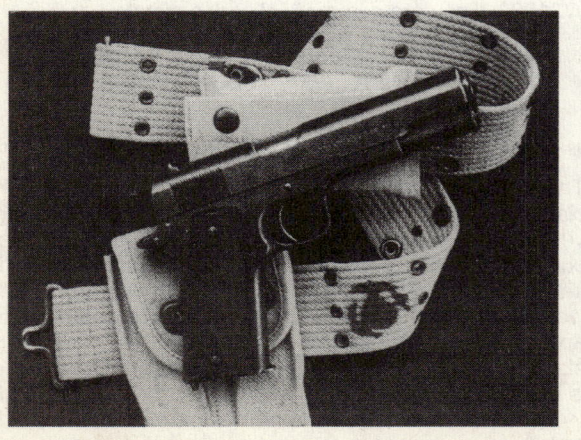

U.S.M.C. Marked

Approximately 13,500 produced in appropriate serial range.

Exc.	V.G.	Good	Fair	Poor
3500	2000	1250	550	450

Springfield Armory Manufacture

There were approximately 25,767 pistols produced by the Springfield Armory. They are within serial number 72751 and #133186. These pistols have the Springfield Eagle and the U.S. Ordnance flaming bomb stamped on the frame and slide.

Exc.	V.G.	Good	Fair	Poor
2500	1500	700	500	400

Springfield Armory D.C.M. Model

There were fewer than 100 of these pistols produced for sale through the Department of Civilian Marksmanship before the beginning of WWI. They are marked "NRA" on the frame. Expert authentication should be secured on this pistol!

Exc.	V.G.	Good	Fair	Poor
2500	1850	1250	800	600

Remington-UMC Manufacture

There were 21,676 of these pistols produced in 1918 and 1919. They have their own serial number range #1-#21676 and are stamped "Remington UMC" on the slide.

Exc.	V.G.	Good	Fair	Poor
3500	2000	1000	500	400

North American Arms Co. Manufacture

This is the rarest variation of the military Colt 1911. Only 100 were produced in Quebec, Ontario, during 1918. These pistols are not serial numbered. A small number, used for record-keeping, can be found on some of the pistols. It appears on the slide just after the serrations end. These pistols are also not marked "U.S Property." One must be wary of fakes when dealing with this model, as it is extremely desirable to collectors.

Exc.	V.G.	Good	Fair	Poor
12000	10000	7500	5000	2750

British RAF Rework

These pistols were made from the British Contract pistols left at the end of WWI. They were simply refinished and stamped by hand "RAF" on the left side of the frame.

Exc.	V.G.	Good	Fair	Poor
1250	900	700	500	400

Arsenal Reworked 1911 Military Models

After WWI the Armed Forces still had a need for handguns. It is estimated that over 50 percent of the 1911s went home in duffel bags as war souvenirs with the returning "Doughboys." The remaining 1911s were sent to Augusta Arsenal, Rock Island Arsenal, or Springfield Armory, where they were refurbished as needed. These guns were parkerized and bear the initials of the arsenal that reworked them, "AA", "RIA," or "SA".

Exc.	V.G.	Good	Fair	Poor
750	650	500	350	250

Norwegian Automatisk Pistol Model 1912

Norway had been seriously considering the adoption of a semiautomatic pistol since 1904, when they established the "Permanent Gun Commission" to test the offerings available at that time. Eventually, after much testing and debate, including the Norwegian Parliament's involvement, the Colt 1911 was settled on. Due to legal ramifications around John Browning's involvement with Fabrique Nationale, the Norwegian government had to negotiate with F.N. instead of Colt. They desired to acquire the rights to manufacture the pistol themselves under license and not merely to purchase it outright. In 1917 the negotiations were complete, and the "Kongsberg Vapenfabrikk" delivered the first pistol. There were 500 pistols in the initial order. They have Norwegian acceptance markings and are designated "M/1912." In all other respects, they are identical to the Colt Model 1911. The last of the "M/1912" pistols was manufactured in 1919.

Exc.	V.G.	Good	Fair	Poor
1200	900	700	550	400

Norwegian Automatisk Pistol Model 1914

In 1919 the Norwegian service pistol was changed slightly. The slide lock lever was enlarged and extended downward, and the hammer spur was made slightly longer. The reasoning behind these modifications was to make the pistol easier to handle. Whether it accomplished this goal or not is debatable. The new model is marked "11.25m/m Aut. Pistol M/1914" on the left side of the slide. Production on the M/1914 continued until the early 1930s. Approximately 20,000 were manufactured.

Exc.	V.G.	Good	Fair	Poor
900	675	600	400	200

Pistole 657(n)-Norw. 14-

After Nazi Germany occupied Norway, the "Kongsberg Vapenfabrikk" was put into operation to produce the M/1914 to be issued to occupation troops. This production ceased in 1943, after approximately 10,000 pistols were produced. The above designation was assigned by the German Heereswaffenamt. These pistols do not exhibit the Norwegian crown cypher; and some, though not all, bear the WAA German Ordnance Office acceptance mark.

Exc.	V.G.	Good	Fair	Poor
900	675	600	400	200

MODEL 1911A1 SEMIAUTOMATIC PISTOL

The Model 1911 A1 was manufactured by Colt until 1971 when it was replaced by the Series 70 Government Model. This modification involved a slightly heavier slide and a modified collet barrel bushing. In 1983 Colt introduced the Series 80 models which had the additional passive firing pin safety lock. The half-cock notch was also redesigned. At the beginning of 1992 another change was made to the Model 1911A1 model in the form of an enhanced pistol. Included were the Government models, the Commander, the Officer's model, the Gold Cup, and the Combat Elite. These modifications are the result of Colt's desire to meet the shooters demand for a more "customized" pistol. The Model 1911A1 may be the most modified handgun in the world. Colt chose some of the most popular modifications to perform on their new enhanced models. They include beavertail safety grip, a slotted Commander style hammer, a relief cut under the triggerguard, a beveled magazine well, a slightly longer trigger, a flat top rib, and angled slide serrations.

Model 1911A1 Automatic Pistol Commercial Series

It is said that the period between the two wars saw the finest of the Colt Automatics produced. The 1911A1 was known as the "Government Model" in its civilian configuration; and with the exception of the fit, finish, and markings, it was identical to the military models. The "C" prefix still designated the commercial series and did so until 1950, when it was changed to a suffix. The "Government Model" is polished and blued. It has checkered walnut grips. There were a number of different commercial models manufactured. We individually list them.

Pre-WWII Commercial

These pistols were manufactured by Colt from 1925-1942. They fall within the #Cl30000-C215000 serial range.

Exc.	V.G.	Good	Fair	Poor
2000	1500	1000	500	350

Post WWII Commercial

Produced 1946-1969. "C" prefix until 1950, when it was changed to a suffix. Approximately 196,000 manufactured.

Exc.	V.G.	Good	Fair	Poor
850	650	450	350	250

Super .38 1929 Model

This pistol is identical in outward physical configuration to the .45 ACP Colt Commercial. It is chambered for the .38 Super cartridge and has a magazine that holds 9 rounds. The right side of the slide is marked "Colt Super .38 Automatic" in two lines, followed by the "Rampant Colt."

Exc.	V.G.	Good	Fair	Poor
3000	2000	1200	1000	600

A pre-war Model 1911 .38 Super was sold at auction for $2,875 in April of 1997. Dual tone magazine. Condition is near mint.
Rock Island Auction Company.

Super Match .38 1935 Model

Only 5,000 of these specially fit and finished target-grade pistols were manufactured. They have Stevens adjustable sights, and the top surfaces are matte-finished to reduce glare. Twelve hundred of these pistols were purchased and sent to Britain in 1939, at the then costly rate of $50 per unit.

Adjustable Sights

Exc.	V.G.	Good	Fair	Poor
6500	4500	1700	1100	800

Fixed Sights

Exc.	V.G.	Good	Fair	Poor
4000	2750	2000	1500	1000

1st Model National Match .45

This pistol was produced so that Colt would have a factory produced target-grade pistol for the 1932 National Matches at Camp Perry. The pistol was made up of specially selected hand-honed and fitted parts. It has a special "Match" grade barrel. The first pistols had fixed sights, but shortly thereafter the "Stevens Adjustable Rear Target Sight" was used. The right side of the slide is marked "National Match." This model possessed exceptional shooting qualities. It was produced until 1941.

Adjustable Sights

Exc.	V.G.	Good	Fair	Poor
4000	2750	1200	750	450

Fixed Sights

Exc.	V.G.	Good	Fair	Poor
2750	2000	1000	600	400

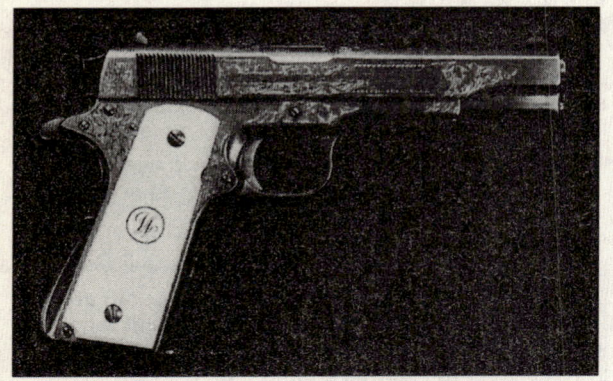

A Colt factory engraved National Match was sold at auction for $13,800. The grips were ivory. Coverage would be about "B." Condition was excellent plus.
Rock Island Auction Company, September 1997.

Ace Model .22 Pistol

In 1930 Colt purchased advertising that, in effect, requested the shooting public to let the company know if they would be interested in a .22 rimfire pistol built similar to the Government Model. The response must have been positive because in 1931 the Colt Ace appeared on the market. The Ace uses the same frame as the Government Model with a modified slide and a heavy barrel. It is chambered for .22 l.r. The size is the same as the larger-caliber version, and the weight is 36 oz. The operation is straight blowback. The Ace has a 10-round detachable magazine and features the "Improved Ace Adjustable Target Sight." The markings on the left side of the slide are the same as on the Government Model; the right side reads "Colt Ace 22 Long Rifle." At first the Army purchased a few pistols (totaling 206) through 1936. It was found, however, that the function of the Ace was less than perfect, as the .22 rimfire lacked the power to consistently and reliably blow back the slide. Approximately 11,000 Ace pistols were manufactured, and in 1941 they were discontinued.

Exc.	V.G.	Good	Fair	Poor
2500	1750	1000	700	500

Service Model Ace .22 R. F. Pistol

In 1937 Colt introduced this improved version of the Ace Pistol. It utilizes a floating chamber invented by David "Carbine" Williams, the firearm's designer who invented the MI carbine while serving time on a Southern chain gang. This loading chamber gave the Service Model Ace the reliability and "feel" that the public wanted. The serial number is prefixed by the letters "SM." The external configuration is the same as the Ace, and the slide is marked "Colt Service Model Ace .22 Long Rifle." Colt sold some to the Army and some on a commercial basis. There was a total of 13,000 manufactured before production ceased in 1944.

Exc.	V.G.	Good	Fair	Poor
3500	2000	1250	800	600

Ace Service Model-Post-War

Introduced in 1978 this model is similar to the pre-war model. Production ceased in 1982.

NIB	Exc.	V.G.	Good	Fair	Poor
800	650	400	300	200	100

Conversion Units .22/.45, .45/.22

In 1938 Colt released a .22-caliber conversion unit. With this kit, one who already owned a Government Model could simply switch the top half and fire inexpensive .22 rimfire ammunition. The unit consists of a slide marked "Service Model Ace", barrel

with floating chamber, ejector, slide lock, recoil spring, and 10-shot magazine. The Conversion Units feature the Stevens adjustable rear sight. Later that same year, a kit to convert the Service Model Ace to .45 ACP was offered. In 1942 production of these units ceased. The .22 kit was reintroduced in 1947; the .45 kit was not brought back.

Prewar Service Model Ace Conversion Unit

Exc.	V.G.	Good	Fair	Poor
3500	2500	1500	450	350

.45/.22 Conversion Unit

Exc.	V.G.	Good	Fair	Poor
450	375	325	250	150

Postwar .22 Conversion Unit

Exc.	V.G.	Good	Fair	Poor
350	300	250	200	150

Drake National Match Pistols

In the 1950s, Springfield Armory used some of these specially machined and hardened slides to construct highly accurate pistols for the Camp Perry Competition. The slides have "NM" and a number on the left side and the Drake name on the right. The "NM" number also appears on the barrel, and the bushing and "NM" is stamped on the triggerguard. "S" (designating Springfield Armory) is stamped on the frame, along with the letter "S" on the barrel link. These high-grade pistols have either adjustable sights or high-profile fixed sights. They are quite scarce and should be authenticated.

Exc.	V.G.	Good	Fair	Poor
950	750	600	450	400

National Match Reworks

These pistols were hand fitted by government armorers for use by the U.S. shooting teams. They have the letters "NM" on all the parts and are either blued or parkerized with target-type sights.

Exc.	V.G.	Good	Fair	Poor
1200	900	600	450	350

Gold Cup National Match

This model is chambered for the .45 ACP, features the flat mainspring housing of the 1911, and has a match-grade barrel and bushing. The parts were hand fitted to target tolerances, and the slide has an enlarged ejection port. The trigger is the long version with an adjustable trigger stop, and the sights are adjustable target type. The finish is blued, with checkered walnut grips and gold medallions. The slide is marked "Gold Cup National Match," and the serial number is prefixed by the letters "NM." This pistol was manufactured from 1957 until 1970.

Exc.	V.G.	Good	Fair	Poor
950	800	550	450	350

Gold Cup MKIII National Match

This pistol is identical to the Gold Cup .45 except that it is chambered for the .38 Mid-Range Wad Cutter round. It was manufactured from 1961 until 1974.

Exc.	V.G.	Good	Fair	Poor
950	800	550	450	350

COLT FOREIGN CONTRACT COMMERCIAL PISTOLS

Mexican Contract Pistols

These pistols were manufactured before 1927. They are marked "Ejercito Mexicano," which translates to "Mexican Army." They have the "C" serial number prefix, and most were well-used.

Exc.	V.G.	Good	Fair	Poor
900	750	600	500	350

Argentine Contract Pistols

These pistols were delivered to Argentina in 1927. The right side of the slide is marked with the two-line inscription "Ejercito Argentino Colt Cal .45 Mod. 1927." There is also the Argentine National Seal and the "Rampant Colt." Colt enjoyed a profitable relationship with Argentina through the late 1920s, delivering approximately 10,000 pistols before failing to meet a delivery date in the early 1930s. This brought about the licensing of the Argentine government to manufacture the Colt pistol on its own.

Exc.	V.G.	Good	Fair	Poor
550	500	400	300	200

Model 1911A1 Automatic Pistol Military Model

As WWII loomed on the horizon and Germany's intentions became ever clearer, it became apparent that we would have an escalated need for weapons once again in this century. We were, however, now better able to fill this need than we had been the time before. Our gun manufacturers had already tooled up and were producing guns for the British "Lend Lease Program." Our government awarded contracts to Colt, Remington-Rand, Ithaca, Union Switch & Signal, and Singer. Their collective efforts resulted in the manufacture of approximately 2,000,000 1911A1s. These pistols were used not only in WWII but in the Korean and Vietnam wars.

It is only recently that the 1911A1 has been replaced, controversially, as our nation's service pistol. Regardless of who manufactured these 1911A1s, they all have 5" barrels and 7-round detachable magazines and are chambered for the .45 ACP cartridge. All but the earliest Colt-produced guns are parkerized and have brown checkered plastic grips. The first 1911A1s produced were a bright polished blue with checkered walnut grips. The authenticity of a WWII 1911A1 can be checked by comparing the manufacturer to the assigned serial number chart that appears at the end of this chapter. There are a number of fine publications that specialize in this model, and the serious student should acquire them and learn.

Colt Manufacture

These pistols were produced from 1924 through 1945. They commenced with serial number 700000, and there were approximately 1,627,000 manufactured.

Early models with Polished and Blued Finish-Add 100%.

Exc.	V.G.	Good	Fair	Poor
1000	700	400	300	250

Remington-Rand Manufacture

Approximate production 948,905; 1943-1945.

Exc.	V.G.	Good	Fair	Poor
950	800	500	350	330

Ithaca Manufacture

Approximate production 441,557; 1943-1945.

Exc.	V.G.	Good	Fair	Poor
850	675	450	350	300

Union Switch & Signal Manufacture

Approximate production 55,100; 1943 only.

Exc.	V.G.	Good	Fair	Poor
1200	1000	800	500	400

Singer Manufacture

Five hundred produced in 1942 only. Exercise caution if contemplating purchase, as the extreme rarity of this model has encouraged fakery.

Exc.	V.G.	Good	Fair	Poor
10000	7500	5500	4500	3500

MKIV Series 70 Government Model

This model is essentially a newer version of the 1911A1. It has the prefix "70G" from 1970-1976, "G70" from 1976-1980, and "70B" from 1980-1983, when production ceased. This model is offered in blue or nickel plate and has checkered walnut grips with the Colt medallion. It is chambered for .45 ACP, .38 Super, 9mm, and 9mm Steyr (foreign export only).

NIB	Exc.	V.G.	Good	Fair	Poor
600	500	400	300	250	200

MKIV Series 70 Gold Cup National Match

This is the newer version of the 1957 National Match. It features a slightly heavier slide and Colt Elliason sights. The chambering is .45 ACP only. The Accurizer barrel and bushing was introduced on this model. It was manufactured from 1970-1983.

NIB	Exc.	V.G.	Good	Fair	Poor
800	700	550	450	300	250

COLT ENHANCED GOVERNMENT MODELS

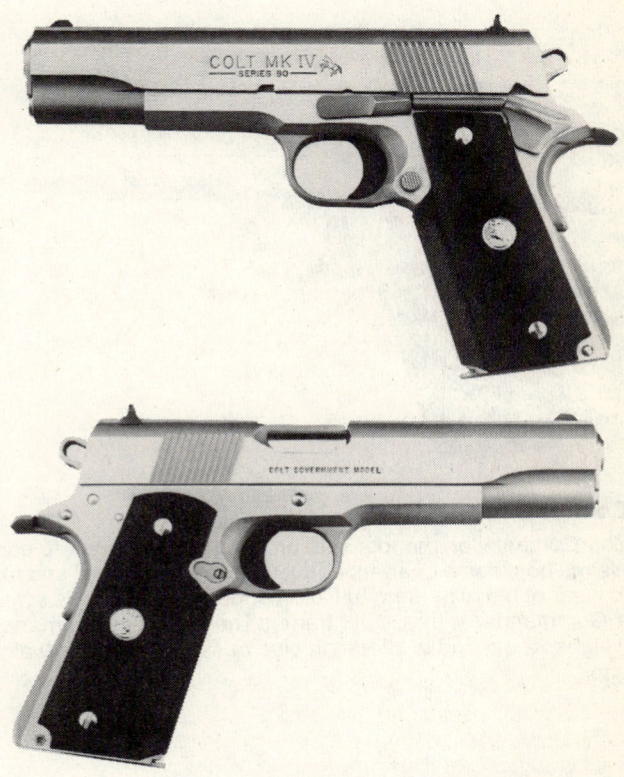

In 1992 Colt introduced a new set of features for its Model 1911A1 series pistols. These new features include: a flattop slide, angled rear slide serrations, scalloped ejection port, combat style hammer, beavertail grip safety, relief cut under triggerguard, and long trigger. The models that are affected by this new upgrade are the: Delta Elite, Combat Elite, Government Model, Combat Commander, Lightweight Commander, Officer's ACP, Officer's ACP Lightweight.

Commander

This is a shortened version of the Government model. It has a 4.25" barrel, a lightweight alloy frame, and a rounded spur hammer. The total weight of the Commander is 27.5 oz. The serial number has the suffix "LW." The Commander is chambered for the .45 ACP, 9mm, and .38 Super. The latter two have been discontinued. Some were chambered for 7.65 Parabellum for export only. The Commander was introduced in 1949 and is still being manufactured.

NIB	Exc.	V.G.	Good	Fair	Poor
550	450	400	350	300	200

Combat Commander

The Combat Commander was produced in response to complaints from some quarters about the excessive recoil and rapid wear of the alloy-framed Commander. This model is simply a Commander with a steel frame. The Combat Commander weighs 32 oz. and is offered in blue or satin nickel with walnut grips.

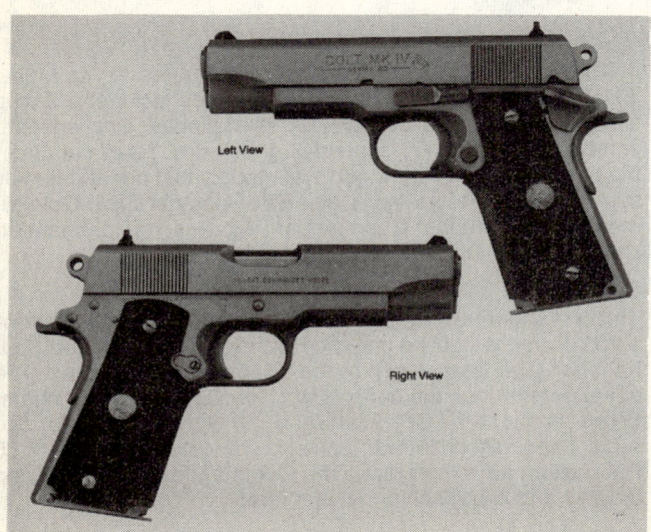

NIB	Exc.	V.G.	Good	Fair	Poor
600	500	450	375	300	200

MK IV Series 80 Government Model

This model was introduced in 1983. It is, for all purposes, the same externally as the Series 70. The basic difference is the addition of the new firing pin safety on this model.

NOTE: In 1997 Colt offered this model with fixed white dot sights.

Blued

NIB	Exc.	V.G.	Good	Fair	Poor
600	500	400	350	300	250

Nickel Plated

Exc.	V.G.	Good	Fair	Poor
550	450	375	300	250

Stainless Steel

NIB	Exc.	V.G.	Good	Fair	Poor
625	575	475	400	325	275

Polished Stainless Steel

NIB	Exc.	V.G.	Good	Fair	Poor
700	600	500	450	350	300

Colt 1991A1

Introduced in 1992 this Colt Government Model is designed to resemble the original GI service issue Government Model. Offered in .45 ACP, a 5" barrel, 7-round magazine, black composition grips, and a special parkerized finish. In 1996 this model was also chambered for the 9x23 cartridge.

Left View

Right View

NIB	Exc.	V.G.	Good	Fair	Poor
475	375	250	200	150	125

NOTE: This pistol was offered in stainless steel in 1996. Add $50 to the above prices.

NIB	Exc.	V.G.	Good	Fair	Poor
500	400	250	200	150	125

M1991A1 Compact

Chambered for the .45 ACP this model has a 3.25" barrel. It is 1.5" shorter than the standard M1991A1 model and .375" shorter in height. Its magazine holds 6 rounds.

NOTE: In 1997 Colt offered this model in stainless steel with fixed white dot sights. Add $50 to NIB price.

Left View

M1991A1 Commander

Chambered for the .45 ACP this model has all of the same features as the standard M1991A1 with a slightly shorter 4.25" barrel.

NOTE: In 1997 Colt offered this model in stainless steel with fixed white dot sights. Add $50 to NIB price.

Right View

NIB	Exc.	V.G.	Good	Fair	Poor
475	375	250	200	150	125

MK IV Series 80 Gold Cup National Match

Externally the same as the Series 70 Gold Cup with the new firing pin safety.

Blued

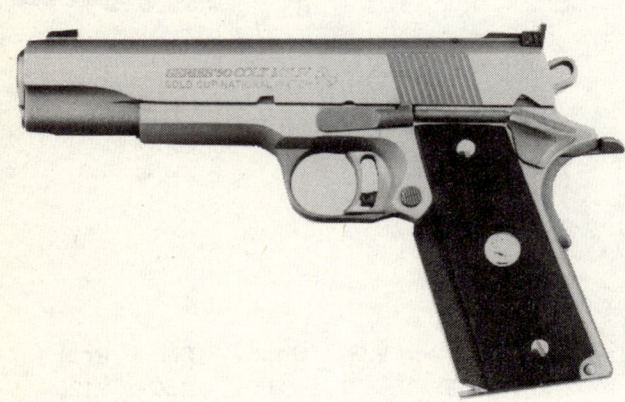

NIB	Exc.	V.G.	Good	Fair	Poor
700	600	500	450	350	250

Stainless Steel

NIB	Exc.	V.G.	Good	Fair	Poor
775	650	550	500	400	300

Polished Stainless Steel

NIB	Exc.	V.G.	Good	Fair	Poor
825	700	600	550	450	350

Officers ACP

This is a shortened version of the Government Model. It has a 3.5" barrel and weighs 37 oz. It is chambered for the .45 ACP only and has checkered walnut grips. The Officers ACP was introduced in 1985.

Blued

NIB	Exc.	V.G.	Good	Fair	Poor
550	450	350	325	250	200

Matte Blued

NIB	Exc.	V.G.	Good	Fair	Poor
525	425	325	300	225	200

Satin Nickel (Discontinued 1985)

Exc.	V.G.	Good	Fair	Poor
400	300	250	200	150

Stainless Steel

NIB	Exc.	V.G.	Good	Fair	Poor
650	550	400	350	300	250

Lightweight Officers ACP

This is an alloy-framed version that weighs 24 oz. It was introduced in 1986.

NIB	Exc.	V.G.	Good	Fair	Poor
600	500	400	375	300	200

Delta Gold Cup

Introduced in 1992 the Delta Gold Cup is chambered for the 10mm, features a 5" barrel, stainless steel finish, adjustable Accro sights, special trigger, and black rubber wraparound stocks. Features all of the new "Enhanced" model features.

NIB	Exc.	V.G.	Good	Fair	Poor
800	750	650	550	400	200

Delta Elite

This model is chambered for the 10mm Norma cartridge. It is offered in blue or stainless steel. The grips are black neoprene with the Delta medallion. It features a high-profile three-dot combat sight system. The Delta Elite was introduced in 1987.

Blued

NIB	Exc.	V.G.	Good	Fair	Poor
550	475	375	325	300	250

Stainless Steel

NIB	Exc.	V.G.	Good	Fair	Poor
600	500	400	350	300	250

Polished Stainless Steel

NIB	Exc.	V.G.	Good	Fair	Poor
675	575	450	400	350	250

Combat Elite

This is a specialized Government model that has a 5" barrel and adjustable Accro sights. It is chambered either in .45 ACP or .38 Super. It weighs 38 oz. and has an 8-round magazine for the .45 ACP and a 9-round magazine for the .38 Super. Finish can be either blue or matte stainless steel.

NIB	Exc.	V.G.	Good	Fair	Poor
650	550	450	350	300	200

Combat Target Model

Introduced in 1996 this 5" barrel 1911 model features a fitted barrel, Gold Cup style trigger, tuned action, flat top slide, relieved ejection port, skeletonized hammer, wide grip safety, high cut trigger guard, beveled magazine well, and adjustable sights. Weight is 39 oz. Offered in both blue and stainless steel. In 1996 this model was also chambered for the new 9x23 cartridge as well as the .45ACP and the .38 Super.

NOTE: In 1997 Colt expanded this Target Model to include a number of different variations. They are listed below.

NIB	Exc.	V.G.	Good	Fair	Poor
700	650	550	500	400	200

NOTE: Add $50 for stainless steel version.

Combat Target Combat Commander

Barrel length is 4-1/4". Chambered for .45 ACP. Stainless steel finish. Weight is 36 oz. Has all other Combat Target features.

NIB	Exc.	V.G.	Good	Fair	Poor
750	675	575	500	400	200

Combat Target Officer's ACP

Fitted with a 3-1/2" barrel and chambered for .45 ACP. Stainless steel finish. Weight is about 34 oz. Has all other Combat Target features.

NIB	Exc.	V.G.	Good	Fair	Poor
750	675	575	500	400	200

Double Eagle

This is a double-action semiautomatic pistol chambered for the 10mm Auto and the .45 ACP cartridges. It has a 5" barrel and an 8-round detachable box magazine. It is constructed of stainless steel and has checkered black synthetic grips. The sights are fixed and utilize the three-dot system.

Left View

Right View

NIB	Exc.	V.G.	Good	Fair	Poor
500	425	350	300	250	200

Double Eagle Officer's Model

This is a compact version of the double-action Double Eagle pistol chambered for .45 ACP only.

NIB	Exc.	V.G.	Good	Fair	Poor
480	425	375	300	250	6200

Double Eagle Combat Commander

Based on the standard Double Eagle design but with a slightly shorter 4.25" barrel, the Double Eagle Combat Commander fits between the standard model and the smaller Officer's Model. Available in .45 ACP and .40 S&W (1993) this model weighs about 36 oz., holds 8 rounds, has white dot sights, and checkered Xenoy grips. The finish is matte stainless steel.

NIB	Exc.	V.G.	Good	Fair	Poor
625	550	500	400	300	200

Double Eagle First Edition

This version of the double-action Double Eagle pistol is chambered for the 10mm Auto and is furnished with a Cordura holster, double-magazine pouch, and three magazines, as well as a zippered black Cordura case.

NIB	Exc.	V.G.	Good	Fair	Poor
700	650	550	475	375	300

.380 Series 80 Government Model

This is a single-action, blowback-operated semiautomatic pistol chambered for the .380 ACP cartridge. It has a 3.25" barrel and a 7-round magazine. The sights are fixed. It is available either blued, nickel plated, or stainless steel. It has synthetic grips and was introduced in 1985.

Nickel Finish-Add 10%.
Stainless Steel-Add 10%.

NIB	Exc.	V.G.	Good	Fair	Poor
350	300	250	200	175	125

Mustang

This is a more compact version of the .380 Government Model. It has a 2.75" barrel and a 5-round detachable magazine.

Nickel Finish-Add 10%.
Stainless Steel-Add 10%.

NIB	Exc.	V.G.	Good	Fair	Poor
350	300	250	200	175	125

Mustang Plus II

This version of the Mustang pistol features the 2.75" barrel with the longer grip frame that accommodates a 7-round magazine. It was introduced in 1988 and is offered in blue, as well as stainless steel.

Stainless Steel-Add 10%.

Left View

Right View

NIB	Exc.	V.G.	Good	Fair	Poor
385	300	250	200	175	125

Mustang Pocket Lite

A lightweight version of the Mustang that features an aluminum alloy receiver. The finish is blued only, and it has synthetic grips. It was introduced in 1987.

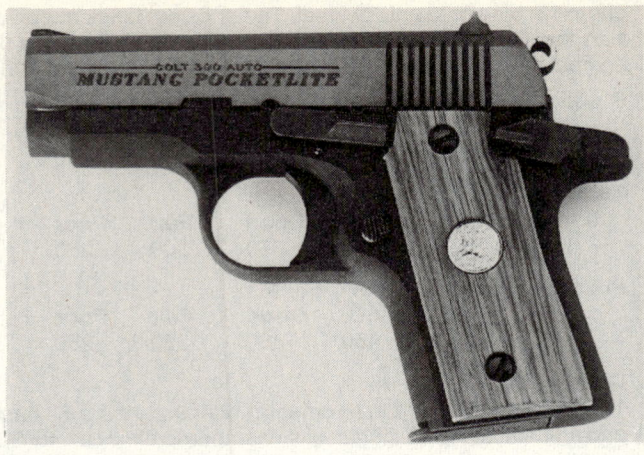

NIB	Exc.	V.G.	Good	Fair	Poor
385	300	250	200	175	125

Colt Pony

Introduced in 1997 this semi-automatic pistol is chambered for the .380 ACP. It is fitted with a 2-3/4" barrel and a bobbed hammer. It is double action only. The grips are black composition. Sights are a ramp front with fixed rear. Finish is Teflon and stainless steel. Magazine capacity is 6 rounds. Overall length is 5-1/2". Weight is 19 oz.

NIB	Exc.	V.G.	Good	Fair	Poor
475	400	—	—	—	—

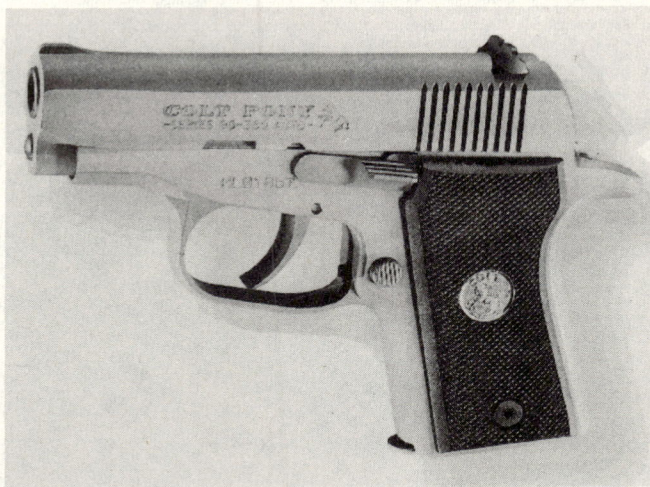

Colt Pony Pocket Lite

Same as above but with aluminum and stainless frame. Weight is 13 oz.

NIB	Exc.	V.G.	Good	Fair	Poor
500	425	—	—	—	—

Colt Model 2000

Introduced in 1992, the Model 2000 is a new departure for Colt from its traditional service style semiautomatic pistols. Chambered for the 9mm, the Model 2000 is a double action only pistol with a 4.5" barrel and a choice between a polymer frame or an aluminum alloy frame. The polymer frame model weighs 29 oz. while the aluminum alloy frame weighs 33 oz. Grips are black composition and sights are white dot. Pistol was dropped from the Colt line in 1994.

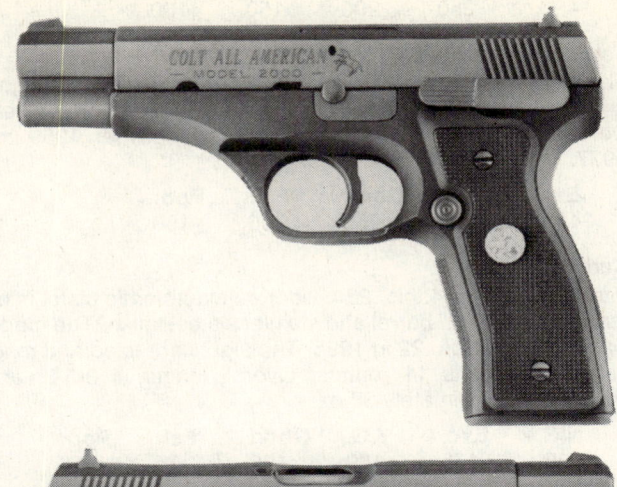

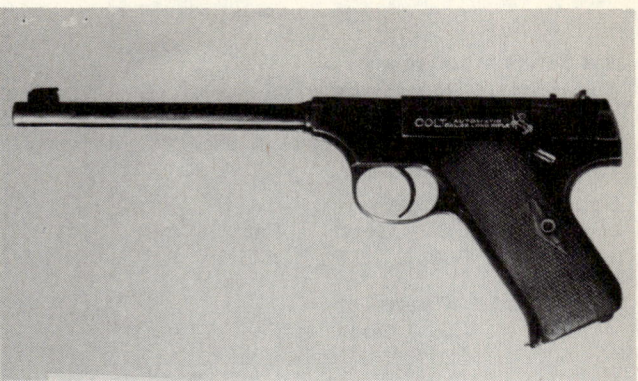

Courtesy Orvel Reichert

Exc.	V.G.	Good	Fair	Poor
1200	750	500	300	200

1st Series Woodsman

This series was manufactured from 1927 until 1947. It was chambered for .22 l.r. standard velocity up to 1932. After that date it was redesigned to fire high-velocity ammunition. The mainspring housing on these high-velocity models is serrated instead of checkered. This change took place at serial number 83790. All Woodsmans after this fired high-velocity ammunition. This model is blued, with checkered wood grips; and the side of the frame is marked "The Woodsman." The 10-shot detachable magazine is released at the bottom. There were approximately 112,000 manufactured.

Sport Model, 4.5" Barrel

Exc.	V.G.	Good	Fair	Poor
850	600	450	300	200

Target Model, 6.5" Barrel

Exc.	V.G.	Good	Fair	Poor
650	475	375	275	200

1st Series Woodsman Match Target

This model has a special 6.5" heavy barrel, target sights, and longer checkered walnut target grips. The side of the receiver has a "Bull's-eye" and the "Match Target" designation stamped on it. There were only 16,000 of these pistols manufactured between 1938 and 1944. They are quite scarce today.

NOTE: A few of these pistols were made for the military. For those that are so marked add 25%.

Exc.	V.G.	Good	Fair	Poor
2000	1500	850	500	400

2nd Series Woodsman

This is a totally redesigned pistol and is different from the preceding models. It has a slide stop, a hold-open device, and a push-button magazine release behind the triggerguard. It is blued, with brown plastic grips. There were approximately 146,000 manufactured between 1948 and 1955.

Sport Model, 4.5" Barrel

Exc.	V.G.	Good	Fair	Poor
550	450	350	250	200

Target Model, 6" Barrel

Exc.	V.G.	Good	Fair	Poor
450	350	300	200	150

Match Target Model, 4.5" Barrel

Exc.	V.G.	Good	Fair	Poor
800	650	575	400	300

NIB	Exc.	V.G.	Good	Fair	Poor
450	400	350	300	250	200

COLT.22 RIMFIRE SEMIAUTOMATIC PISTOLS

Colt Junior Pocket Model

This diminutive unit is only 4.5" long overall and weighs 12 oz. Colt did not manufacture this pistol but rather had it made for them by Astra in Spain. The pistol was introduced in 1958 chambered for .25 ACP. One year later a .22 Short version appeared. Both had external hammers and detachable 6-round magazines. The passage of the 1968 Gun Control Act made import of a weapon of this size illegal, so Colt discontinued its relationship with Astra. The pistol was re-introduced in 1970 as an American-made product and was produced for two more years. Production ceased in 1972. Astra also made this pistol and called it the Cub.

.22 Short-Add 25%.

NIB	Exc.	V.G.	Good	Fair	Poor
300	250	200	175	125	75

Pre-Woodsman Model

This pistol was designed by John Browning. The name Woodsman was not used until 1927, but some collectors use it to describe this pistol as it is of the same pattern. This pistol was designed for general purpose use, hunting, and informal target practice. The pistol has a 6.5" thin barrel and weighs 28 oz. There is a 10-round detachable magazine, and the chambering is .22 Long Rifle standard velocity only. It has a concealed hammer and a sliding thumb safety. The finish is blue, with checkered plastic grips. On early models checkered walnut grips and a brass follower in magazine are seen. It was manufactured between 1915 and 1927, and there were approximately 54,000 produced.

Match Target Model, 6" Barrel

Exc.	V.G.	Good	Fair	Poor
700	600	400	300	250

3rd Series Woodsman

This model is similar to the 2nd Series except that the magazine catch is located at the bottom of the grip. It was manufactured from 1955-1960 with black plastic grips and from 1960-1977 with checkered walnut.

Sport Model, 4.5" Barrel

Exc.	V.G.	Good	Fair	Poor
500	300	250	175	125

Target Model, 6"Barrel

Exc.	V.G.	Good	Fair	Poor
500	325	250	175	125

Match Target Model, 4.5" Barrel

Exc.	V.G.	Good	Fair	Poor
650	500	300	200	150

Match Target, 6" Barrel

Exc.	V.G.	Good	Fair	Poor
600	450	300	200	150

Challenger Model

This pistol is simply a Woodsman with less expensive grips and sights. It has either a 4.5" or a 6" barrel, fixed sights, no hold-open device, and a bottom magazine release. It is chambered for .22 l.r. The production ran to 77,000. It was manufactured between 1950 and 1955.

Exc.	V.G.	Good	Fair	Poor
400	300	250	200	150

Huntsman Model

The only difference between the Huntsman and the Challenger is that the Huntsman utilizes a 3rd Series frame. The Huntsman had black plastic grips until 1960 and checkered walnut after that. There were approximately 100,000 manufactured between 1955 and 1977.

Exc.	V.G.	Good	Fair	Poor
400	250	200	150	100

Targetsman Model

This is essentially the Huntsman with adjustable target sights and a thumbrest grip. It is offered with a 6" barrel only. There were approximately 65,000 manufactured between 1959 and 1977.

Exc.	V.G.	Good	Fair	Poor
400	300	250	200	150

Cadet /Colt .22

Introduced in 1994 this .22 caliber semiautomatic pistol is offered with a 4-1/2" barrel and stainless steel finish. The model was renamed Colt .22 in 1995. The sights are fixed and magazine capacity is 11 rounds. Overall length is 8-5/8" and weight is approximately 33 oz.

NIB	Exc.	V.G.	Good	Fair	Poor
225	175	150	125	75	50

Colt .22 Target

Introduced in 1995 this model features a 6" bull barrel with removable front sight and adjustable rear sight. Black composite monogrip stock. Stainless steel finish. Weight is 40.5 oz.

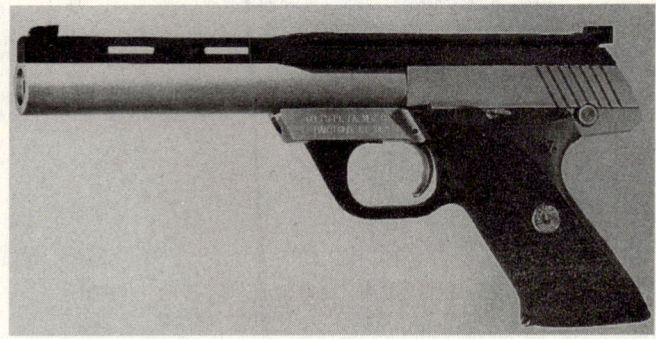

NIB	Exc.	V.G.	Good	Fair	Poor
300	250	200	150	100	75

SERIAL NUMBERS ASSIGNED TO M1911 AND 1911A1 CONTRACTORS

Year	Serial No.	Manufacturer	Year	Serial No.	Manufacturer
1912	1-500	Colt	1914	60401-72570	Colt
	501-1000	Colt USN		72571-83855	Springfield
	1001-1500	Colt		83856-83900	Colt
	1501-2000	Colt USN		83901-84400	Colt USMC
	2001-2500	Colt		84401-96000	Colt
	2501-3500	Colt USN		96001-97537	Colt
	3501-3800	Colt USMC		97538-102596	Colt
	3801-4500	Colt		102597-107596	Springfield
	4501-5500	Colt USN	1915	107597-109500	Colt
	5501-6500	Colt		109501-110000	Colt USN
	6501-7500	Colt USN		110001-113496	Colt
	7501-8500	Colt		113497-120566	Springfield
	8501-9500	Colt USN		120567-125566	Colt
	9501-10500	Colt		125567-133186	Springfield
	10501-11500	Colt USN	1916	133187-137400	Colt
	11501-12500	Colt	1917	137401-151186	Colt
	12501-13500	Colt USN		151187-151986	Colt USMC
	13501-17250	Colt		151987-185800	Colt
1913	17251-36400	Colt		185801-186200	Colt USMC
	36401-37650	Colt USMC			
	37651-38000	Colt			
	38001-44000	Colt USN			
	44001-60400	Colt			

Year	Serial No.	Manufacturer
1917	186201-209586	Colt
	209587-210386	Colt USMC
	210387-215386	Colt Frames
	215387-216186	Colt USMC
	216187-216586	Colt
	216587-216986	Colt USMC
1918	216987-217386	Colt USMC
	217387-232000	Colt
	232001-233600	Colt USN
	233601-594000	Colt
1918	1-13152	Rem-UMC
1919	13153-21676	Rem-UMC
	594001-629500	Colt
	629501-700000	Winchester (Assigned)
1924	700001-710000	Colt
1937	710001-712349	Colt
1938	712350-713645	Colt
1939	713646-717281	Colt USN
1940	717282-721977	Colt

Year	Serial No.	Manufacturer
1941	721978-756733	Colt
1942	756734-800000	Colt
	S800001-S800500	Singer
	800501-801000	H&R (Assigned)
1943	801001-958100	Colt
	958101-1088725	U.S. S.& S.
	1088726-1208673	Colt
	1208674-1279673	Ithaca
	1279674-1279698	Augusta Arsenal (Renumber)
	1279699-1441430	Remington-Rand
	1441431-1471430	Ithaca
	1471431-1609528	Remington-Rand
1944	1609529-1743846	Colt
	1743847-1890503	Ithaca
	1890504-2075103	Remington-Rand
1945	2075104-2134403	Ithaca
	2134404-2244803	Remington-Rand
	2244804-2380013	Colt
	2380014-2619013	Remington-Rand
	2619014-2693613	Ithaca

COLT MODERN LONG ARMS

Colteer I-22

This is a single shot bolt-action rifle chambered for .22 l.r. or .22 Magnum. It has a plain uncheckered walnut stock, 20" barrel, and adjustable sights. There were approximately 50,000 manufactured between 1957 and 1966.

Exc.	V.G.	Good	Fair	Poor
400	300	175	125	90

Stagecoach

This is a semiautomatic, saddle ring carbine. It is chambered for .22 l.r. and has a 16.5" barrel and a 13-shot tubular magazine. The stock is fancy walnut, and the receiver has the stagecoach holdup scene roll-engraved on it. There were approximately 25,000 manufactured between 1965 and 1975.

Exc.	V.G.	Good	Fair	Poor
450	350	200	150	100

Courier

This model is similar to the Stagecoach, with a pistol grip stock and beavertail forearm. It was manufactured between 1970 and 1975.

Exc.	V.G.	Good	Fair	Poor
450	350	200	125	90

Colteer

This is a less expensive version of the Stagecoach. It features a 19.5" barrel, has a 15-shot tubular magazine, and is stocked in a plainer grade walnut. There is no roll engraving. Approximately 25,000 were manufactured between 1965 and 1975.

Exc.	V.G.	Good	Fair	Poor
450	350	200	125	90

Colt "57" Bolt Action Rifle

This rifle was manufactured for Colt by the Jefferson Mfg. Co of New Haven, Connecticut. It utilizes a Fabrique Nationale Mauser action and has a checkered American walnut stock with a Monte Carlo comb. The rifle is offered with adjustable sights. It is chambered for .243 or .30-06. There is also a deluxe version that features higher-grade wood. There were approximately 5,000 manufactured in 1957.

Deluxe Version-Add 20%.

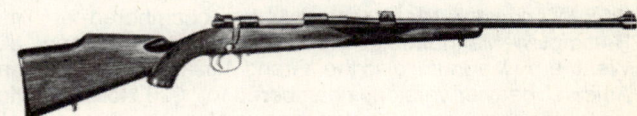

Exc.	V.G.	Good	Fair	Poor
550	450	350	300	225

Coltsman Bolt Action Rifle

The Coltsman was manufactured for Colt by Kodiak Arms. It utilizes either a Mauser or Sako action. The rifle is offered in .243, .308, .30-06, and .300 Winchester Magnum. It has a barrel length of 22", 24" in the Magnum chambering. The stock is checkered American walnut. There were approximately 10,000 manufactured between 1958 and 1966. There is a deluxe version that features a higher-grade, skipline-checkered walnut stock and rosewood forend tip; this is called "The Coltsman Custom."

Coltsman Custom-Add 50%.

Exc.	V.G.	Good	Fair	Poor
650	550	450	350	250

Coltsman Pump Shotgun

This model was manufactured by Jefferson Arms, utilizing an aluminum alloy frame made by Franchi. It is chambered for 12, 16, and 20 gauge and has a 26" or 28" plain barrel. There were approximately 2,000 manufactured between 1961 and 1965.

Exc.	V.G.	Good	Fair	Poor
350	300	275	200	150

Semi-Auto Shotgun

The Semi-Auto Shotgun was manufactured for Colt by the firm of Luigi Franchi in Italy. It features an aluminum alloy receiver and is chambered for 12 or 20 gauge. The barrel length is 26", 28", 30", or 32"—either vent rib or plain. A deluxe version, "The Custom Auto," features a fancy walnut stock and a hand engraved receiver. There were approximately 5,300 manufactured between 1962 and 1966.

Custom Auto-Add 25%.

Exc.	V.G.	Good	Fair	Poor
375	325	300	225	175

Double Barrel Shotgun

During 1961 and 1962, Colt had approximately 50 side-by-side shotguns made for them by a French gun manufacturer. They have the Colt name on the breech area of the barrels and are in the 467000-469000 serial range. There is little information available on this gun, and Colt never went past the test-market stage.

Exc.	V.G.	Good	Fair	Poor
1000	750	650	500	400

Colt Sauer Bolt Action Rifle

This is a high quality and unique rifle manufactured for Colt by the firm of J.P. Sauer & Son of Germany. The rifle features a non-rotating bolt that makes the Colt Sauer action smoother functioning than most. It has a 24" barrel, skipline-checkered walnut stock with rosewood forend tip, pistol grip cap, and recoil pad. There are five basic configurations: the Standard Action, chambered for .25-06, .270 Winchester, and .30-06; the Short Action, chambered for .22-250, .243 Winchester, and .308 Winchester; the Magnum Action, chambered for .7mm Remington Magnum, .300 Winchester Magnum, and .300 Weatherby Magnum; also the "Grand Alaskan" and the "Grand African," heavier versions chambered for .375 Holland & Holland Magnum and .458 Winchester Magnum, respectively. These rifles were all discontinued by Colt in 1985.

Colt Sauer Short Action

Exc.	V.G.	Good	Fair	Poor
900	750	500	400	350

Standard Action-Add $50.
Magnum Action-Add $200.
"Grand Alaskan"-Add $400.
"Grand African"-Add $450.

Colt Sauer Drilling

This is a rather unique firearm and one with which many American enthusiasts are not familiar—a 3-barrelled gun. It features a side-by-side shotgun in 12 gauge over a .30-06 or .243 rifle barrel. The name was based on the German word for three, as this is where the concept was developed. They are quite popular in Europe where the game preserve style of hunting is prevalent but have little use in America where our hunting seasons don't often overlap. This drilling has 25" barrels and pop-up sights for the rifle barrel and is nicely engraved. It was discontinued by Colt in 1985.

Exc.	V.G.	Good	Fair	Poor
3500	2750	2000	1500	1100

Colt-Sharps Rifle

Introduced in 1970 as the last word in sporting rifles, the Colt-Sharps is a falling-block action that was advertised as a modern Sharps-Borchardt. This undertaking was first-class all the way. The finish is high polish blue with a deluxe-grade hand-checkered walnut stock and forend. This rifle is chambered for .17 Remington, .22-250, .243, .25-06, 7mm Remington Magnum, .30-06, and .375 Holland & Holland Magnum; and it was offered cased with accessories. This model was manufactured between 1970 and 1977.

NIB	Exc.	V.G.	Good	Fair	Poor
2500	2000	1200	850	500	300

AR-15 Sporter (Model #6000)

A semiautomatic rifle firing from a closed bolt was introduced into the Colt product line in 1964. Similar in appearance and function to the military version, the M-16. Chambered for the .223 cartridge. It is fitted with a standard 20" barrel with no forward assist, no case deflector, but with a bayonet lug. Weighs about 7.5 lbs. Dropped from production in 1985.

NIB	Exc.	V.G.	Good	Fair	Poor
850	700	600	550	400	300

AR-15 Sporter w/Collapsible Stock (Model #6001)

Same as above but fitted with a 16" barrel and folding stock. Weighs approximately 5.8 lbs. Introduced in 1978 and discontinued in 1985.

NIB	Exc.	V.G.	Good	Fair	Poor
1000	850	700	600	450	400

AR-15 Carbine (Model #6420)

Introduced in 1985 this model has a 16" standard weight barrel. All other features are the same as the previous discontinued AR-15 models. This version was dropped from the Colt product line in 1987.

NIB	Exc.	V.G.	Good	Fair	Poor
1100	900	800	650	450	400

AR-15 9mm Carbine (Model #6450)

Same as above but chambered for 9mm cartridge. Weighs 6.3 lbs.

NIB	Exc.	V.G.	Good	Fair	Poor
1100	900	800	650	450	400

AR-15A2 (Model #6500)

Introduced in 1984 this was an updated version with a heavier barrel and forward assist. The AR sight was still utilized. Weighs approximately 7.8 lbs.

NIB	Exc.	V.G.	Good	Fair	Poor
1100	900	800	650	450	400

AR-15A2 Govt. Model Carbine (Model #6520)

Added to the Colt line in 1988 this 16" standard barrel carbine featured for the first time a case deflector and the improved A2 rear sight. This model is fitted with a 4-position telescoping buttstock. Weighs about 5.8 lbs.

NIB	Exc.	V.G.	Good	Fair	Poor
1250	1000	850	700	500	400

AR-15A2 Gov't. Model (Model #6550)

This model was introduced in 1988 is the rifle equivalent to the Carbine. It features the heavier 20" A2 barrel, forward assist, case deflector, but still retains the bayonet lug. Weighs about 7.5 lbs. Discontinued in 1990.

NIB	Exc.	V.G.	Good	Fair	Poor
1250	1000	850	700	500	400

AR-15A2 H-Bar (Model #6600)

Introduced in 1986 this version features a special 20" heavy barrel. All other features are the same as the A2 series of AR15s. Discontinued in 1991. Weighs about 8 lbs.

NIB	Exc.	V.G.	Good	Fair	Poor
1400	1100	1000	750	500	400

AR- 15A2 Delta H-Bar (Model #6600DH)

Same as above but fitted with a 3x9 scope and detachable cheekpiece. Dropped from the Colt line in 1990. Weighs about 10 lbs.

NIB	Exc.	V.G.	Good	Fair	Poor
1800	1500	1200	900	700	500

Sporter Lightweight Rifle

This lightweight model has a 16" barrel and is finished in a matte black. It is available in either a .223 Rem caliber (Model #6530) that weighs 6.7 lbs., a (Model #6430) 9mm caliber weighing 7.1 lbs., or a (Model #6830) 7.65x39mm that weighs 7.3 lbs. The .223 is furnished with two five-round box magazines as is the 9mm and 7.65x39mm. A cleaning kit and sling are also supplied with each new rifle. The buttstock and pistol grip are made of durable nylon and the handguard is reinforced fiberglass and aluminum lined. The rear sight is adjustable for windage and elevation. These newer models are referred to simply as Sporters and are not fitted with a bayonet lug.

NIB	Exc.	V.G.	Good	Fair	Poor
800	650	550	450	350	300

NOTE: The Model 6830 will bring about $25 less than the above prices.

Sporter Target Model Rifle (Model #6551)

This 1991 model is a full size version of the Lightweight Rifle. The Target Rifle weighs 7.5 lbs. and has a 20" barrel. Offered in .223 Rem caliber only with target sights adjustable to 800 meters. New rifles are furnished with two 5-round box magazines, sling, and cleaning kit.

NIB	Exc.	V.G.	Good	Fair	Poor
900	750	550	450	350	300

Sporter Match H-Bar (Model #6601)

This 1991 variation of the AR-15 is similar to the Target Model but has a 20" heavy barrel chambered for the .223 caliber. This model weighs 8 lbs. and has target type sights adjustable out to 800 meters. Supplied with two 5-round box magazines, sling, and cleaning kit.

NIB	Exc.	V.G.	Good	Fair	Poor
1000	800	650	450	350	300

Colt AR-15 (XM16E1)

This rifle was made upon request for foreign contracts. Very rare. Proceed with caution. this variation will command a premium price over the standard AR-15 rifle. Secure an appraisial before a sale.

Courtesy Richard M. Kumor, Sr.

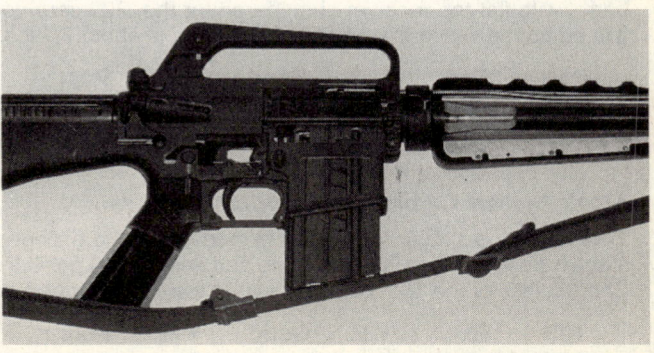

Courtesy Richard M. Kumor, Sr.

Sporter Match Delta H-Bar (Model #6601 DH)

Same as above but supplied with a 3x9 scope. Weighs about 10 lbs. Discontinued in 1992.

NIB	Exc.	V.G.	Good	Fair	Poor
1500	1250	900	700	500	300

Sporter Competition H-Bar (Model #6700)

Introduced in 1992, the Competition H-Bar is available in .223 caliber with a 20" heavy barrel counterbored for accuracy. The carry handle is detachable with target sights. With the carry handle removed the upper receiver is dovetailed and grooved for Weaver style scope rings. This model weighs approximately 8.5 lbs. New rifles are furnished with two 5-round box magazines, sling, and cleaning kit.

NIB	Exc.	V.G.	Good	Fair	Poor
950	750	600	450	350	300

Sporter Competition H-Bar Select w/scope (Model #6700CH)

This variation, also new for 1992, is identical to the Sporter Competition with the addition of a factory mounted scope. The rifle has also been selected for accuracy and comes complete with a 3-9X rubber armored variable scope, scope mount, carry handle with iron sights, and nylon carrying case.

NIB	Exc.	V.G.	Good	Fair	Poor
1350	950	750	500	350	300

AR-15 Carbine Flat-top Heavyweight (Model #6731)

This variation in the Sporter series features a heavyweight 16" barrel with flat-top receiver chambered for the .223 cartridge. It is equipped with a fixed buttstock. Weight is about 7.1 lbs.

NIB	Exc.	V.G.	Good	Fair	Poor
750	650	500	400	300	200

AR-15 Tactical Carbine (Model #6721)

This version is similar to the above model with the exception of the buttstock which is telescoping and adjusts to 4 positions. Chambered for the .223 cartridge with a weight of about 7 lbs.

NIB	Exc.	V.G.	Good	Fair	Poor
1600	1250	1000	—	—	—

Sporter H-Bar Elite (Model #6724)

This variation was introduced in 1996 and features a free floating 24" stainless steel match barrel with an 11 degree target crown and special Teflon coated trigger group. The handguard is all-aluminum with twin swivel studs. Weight is approximately 9.26 lbs.

NIB	Exc.	V.G.	Good	Fair	Poor
1250	950	750	500	350	300

COLT CUSTOM SHOP

The Colt Custom Shop has developed several models over the years that are available to the public. The basis of these offerings are standard Colt Models upgraded to perform special functions.

Special Combat Government Model (Competition)

This is a competition ready model. Chambered for the .45 ACP it comes fitted with a skeletized trigger, upswept grip safety, custom tuned action, polished feed ramp, throated barrel, flared ejection port, cutout commander hammer, two 8-round magazines, hard chromed slide and receiver, extended thumb safety, Bomar rear sight, Clark dovetail front sight, and flared magazine funnel. The pistol has been accurized and is shipped with a certified target.

NIB	Exc.	V.G.	Good	Fair	Poor
1450	1100	800	500	300	200

Special Combat Government Model (Carry)

This model has all of the same features as the competition model except that it has a royal blue finish, special bar-dot night sights, ambidextrous safety. It has also been accurized and shipped with a certified target.

NIB	Exc.	V.G.	Good	Fair	Poor
1250	900	700	400	300	200

Gold Cup Commander

Chambered for the .45 ACP and has the following features: heavy-duty adjustable target sights, beveled magazine well, serrated front strap, checkered mainspring housing, wide grip safety, Palo Alto wood grips, and stainless steel or royal blue finish.

NIB	Exc.	V.G.	Good	Fair	Poor
650	550	450	350	250	150

Gold Cup Trophy

Introduced in 1997 this model features .45 ACP 5" barrel 1911 with a choice of stainless steel or blue finish. Several custom features such as skeletonized hammer and trigger. Adjustable rear sight and wraparound rubber grips are standard. The pistol has been accurized and is shipped with a target. Magazine capacity is 7 or 8 rounds. Weight is approximately 39 oz. Add $60.00 for stainless steel finish.

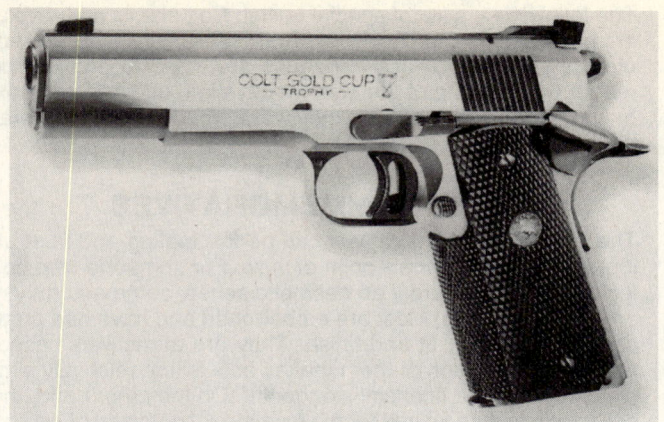

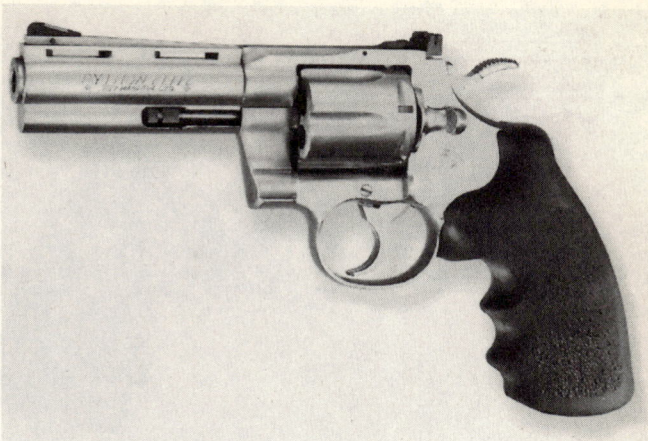

NIB	Exc.	V.G.	Good	Fair	Poor
1000	800	—	—	—	—

McCormick Commander

This is a limited edition pistol made for Lew Horton in 1995 and limited to 100 pistols. It has many special features. The slide is engraved and there is a gold rampant colt on the slide.

Suggested Retail Price: $1125

McCormick Officer

This Lew Horton exclusive pistol has factory installed McCormick parts and a hard chrome finish. A total of 500 guns were built in 1995.

Suggested Retail Price: $950

McCormick Factory Racer

This is a limited edition pistol from Lew Horton. It is a full size government model with hard chrome finish, special barrel, trigger safety, and other custom features. Each gun is rollmarked "McCormick Factory Racer" on the slide. Special serial numbers from MFR001 to MFR500.

Suggested Retail Price: $1100

U.S. Shooting Team Gold Cup

This is a limited edition Gold Cup .45 ACP with special blue, sights, grips. The U.S. Shooting Team logo is rolled on the slide. Limited to 500 pistols and built for Lew Horton.

Suggested Retail Price: $1025

Colt Classic .45 Special Edition

This Lew Horton model is limited to 400 pistols and features a royal blue polish with special "Classic .45" gold etched on the slide. Pearlite grips.

Suggested Retail Price: $960

Ultimate Python

Custom tuned action with both Elliason and Accro sighting systems. Both rubber and walnut grips are included. Bright stainless steel or royal blue finish. Available only with 6" barrel.

NIB	Exc.	V.G.	Good	Fair	Poor
1000	850	750	600	400	250

Python Elite

This model has a hand tuned .357 magnum action with a choice of 4" or 6" barrel with adjustable rear sight and red ramp front sight. On the 4" barrel models grips are rubber service while on the 6" models they are rubber target style. Finish is stainless steel or royal blue. Weight is about 38 oz. with 4" barrel and 43 oz. with 6" barrel.

Suggested Retail Price: $925

Custom Anaconda

Custom tuned action, Magnaported barrel, with Elliason rear sight. The contoured trigger is polished smooth. Comes with Pachmayr grips and brushed stainless steel finish.

NIB	Exc.	V.G.	Good	Fair	Poor
650	575	500	400	300	200

Anaconda Hunter

Comes with a Leupold 2X scope, heavy-duty mounts, cleaning accessories, both walnut and rubber grips, in a hard case. Furnished only with an 8" barrel.

NIB	Exc.	V.G.	Good	Fair	Poor
975	900	800	600	400	250

Bobbed Detective Special

First offered in 1994 this model features a bobbed hammer, a front sight with night sight, and honed action. Available in either chrome or blue finish.

NIB	Exc.	V.G.	Good	Fair	Poor
475	400	300	200	150	100

Limited Class .45 ACP

Designed for tactical competition. Supplied with a parkerized matte finish, lightweight composite trigger, extended ambidextrous safety, upswept grip safety, beveled magazine well, accurized, and shipped with a signed target. Introduced in 1993.

NIB	Exc.	V.G.	Good	Fair	Poor
750	675	600	450	300	200

Compensated Model .45 ACP

This competition pistol has a hard chrome receiver, bumper on magazine, extended ambidextrous safety, blue slide with full profile BAT compensator, Bomar rear sight, and flared funnel magazine well. Introduced in 1993.

NIB	Exc.	V.G.	Good	Fair	Poor
1850	1350	900	650	400	250

Nite Lite .380

Supplied with a bar-dot night sight, special foil mark on barrel slide, Teflon-coated alloy receiver, stainless slide, high capacity grip extension magazine, and a standard magazine. Shipped with a soft carrying case. Introduced in 1993.

NIB	Exc.	V.G.	Good	Fair	Poor
450	400	325	275	225	150

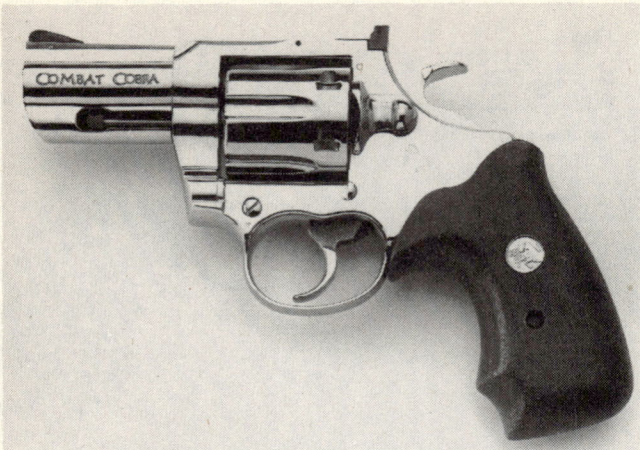

Standard Tactical Model

Built for 20th Anniversary of IPSC competition shooting in 1996. Built on the Colt Government model with round top slide and chamber for .45 ACP. Many special features Special serial numbers. Limited to 1,500 pistols.

Suggested Retail Price: $1400

Superior Tactical Model

Same as above but built on an enhanced frame with many custom features

Special serial numbers limited to 500 pistols.
Suggested Retail Price: $1800

Deluxe Tactical Model

Same as above but with added features. Limited to 250 Pistols.

Suggested Retail Price: $2660

The following is a list of special edition Colt pistols and revolvers produced by the Colt Custom Shop exclusively for distributor Lew Horton. These handguns are listed to provide the reader with an idea of the number of limited edition Colts sold by Lew Horton and the year they were produced with the retail price.

COLT COMMEMORATIVES

The field of commemoratives can be fascinating and frustrating, depending on one's point of view. For someone who collects things from purely an aesthetic sense, commemoratives are quite desirable. Most are embellished and have had great care put into their fit and finish. They are attractively cased, and the proliferation of them makes acquisition relatively simple except from a financial standpoint. On the other hand, the collector who has an eye for the investment potential of his collections has found that the commemorative market has been soft and as investments they historically have not done well. The reason for this is twofold. The limited production appeal is not always what it seems. Many times the amounts produced are greater than one would consider limited. It is also a fact that if one fires a commemorative, its collectibility is gone. Even excessive handling can cause this problem. This means that since the majority of these firearms are kept new in the original boxes, the supply will usually outstrip the demand. Because of the limited numbers built it is difficult to furnish accurate prices for the secondary market.

Few commemoratives are ever lost or worn out. Collectors who seek firearms for their historic significance are usually not interested in the commemoratives, as even though they may have been issued to commemorate a specific historic person or event, they are not a part of the era and are regarded as "instant" collectibles. In some areas one will find that the Colt Commemoratives are not as desirable, saleable, or expensive as the plain out-of-the-box versions. This is especially true in the Single Action Army Models. We list the commemoratives made by Colt in chronological order. Remember that the prices reflect new-in-the-box as it came from the factory—all papers, books, etc., intact and included. We also include the issue price for comparison. If the model with which you are concerned has been fired or is not in its original casing or box, deduct as much as 50 percent from these prices. It is interesting to note that in some areas shooters are taking advantage of the soft commemorative market and are buying SAAs at lower prices than the plain 3rd Generation guns—then shooting them. This can perhaps have a positive effect on appreciation.

Model	Qty. Built	Year Made	Retail Price
Horse Pistol, SAA	100	1983	$1100.00
Ultimate Officer's .45 ACP	500	1989	777.00
Lt. Commander .45 ACP	800	1985	590.00
Combat Cobra 2-1/2"	1000	1987	500.00
Lady Colt (MKIV .380 ACP)	1000	1989	547.00
Night Commander .45 ACP	250	1989	725.00
El Presidente .38 Super	350	1990	800.00
El Comandante .38 Super	500	1991	800.00
El General .38 Super	500	1991	850.00
El Capitan	500	1991	875.00
Colt Boa-4" & 6"	600	1985	525.00
El Dorado	750	1992	1099.00
El Coronel	750	1993	899.00
El Teniente	400	1992	1036.00
Classic Gold Cup	300	1993	1849.95
Night Officer	350	1993	679.95
El Presidente Premier Edition	10	1993	3000.00

COLT COMMEMORATIVES

1961	Issue	NIB	Amount Mfg.
Geneseo, IL. 125th Anniv. Derringer	$ 28	$ 650	104
Sheriff's Model (Blue & Case)	130	1995	478
Sheriff's Model (Nickel)	140	5000	25
Kansas Statehood Scout	75	395	6,197
125th Anniv. Model SAA .45	150	995	7,390
Pony Express Cent. Scout	80	450	1,007
Civil War Cent. Pistol	75	175	24,114

1962			
Rock Island Arsenal Cent. Scout	$ 39	$ 250	550
Columbus, OH. Sesquicent. Scout	100	550	200
Ft. Findlay, OH. Sesquicent. Scout	90	650	110
Ft. Findlay Cased Pair	185	2500	20
New Mex. Golden Anniv. Scout	80	395	1,000
Ft. McPherson, Nebraska Cent. Derringer	29	395	300
West Virginia Statehood Cent. Scout	75	395	3,452

1963			
West Virginia Statehood Cent. SAA .45	$ 150	$1095	600
Ariz. Terr. Cent. Scout	75	395	5,355
Ariz. Terr. Cent. SAA .45	150	1095	1,280
Carolina Charter Tercent Scout	75	395	300
Carolina Charter Tercent .22/.45 Comb.	240	1495	251
H. Cook 1 To 100 .22/.45 Comb.	275	1695	100
Ft. Stephenson, Oh. Sesquicent. Scout	75	550	200
Battle of Gettysburg Cent. Scout	90	395	1,019
Idaho Terr. Cent. Scout	75	395	902
Gen. J.H. Morgan Indiana Raid Scout	75	650	100

1964			
Cherry's 35th Anniv. .22/.45 Comb.	$ 275	$ 1695	100
Nevada Statehood Cent. Scout	75	395	3,984
Nevada Statehood Cent. SAA .45	150	1095	1,688
Nevada Statehood Cent. .22/.45 Comb.	240	1495	189
Nev. Statehood Cent. .22/.45 W/extra Cyls.	350	1595	577
Nevada Battle Born Scout	85	395	981
Nevada Battle Born SAA .45	175	1395	80
Nevada Battle Born .22/.45 Comb.	265	2595	20
Montana Terr. Cent. Scout	75	395	2,300
Montana Terr. Cent. SAA .45	150	1095	851
Wyoming Diamond Jubilee Scout	75	395	2,357
General Hood Cent. Scout	75	395	1,503
New Jersey Terrcent. Scout	75	395	1,001
New Jersey Terrcent SAA .45	150	1095	250
St. Louis Bicent. Scout	75	395	802
St. Louis Bicent. SAA .45	150	1095	200
St. Louis Bicent .22/.45 Comb.	240	1495	250
California Gold Rush Scout	80	395	500
Pony Express Pres. SAA .45	250	1395	1,004
Chamizal Treaty Scout	85	395	450
Chamizal Treaty SAA .45	170	1295	50
Chamizal Treaty .22/.45 Comb	280	1995	50
Col. Sam Colt Sesquicent. SAA .45	225	1095	4,750
Col. Sam Colt Deluxe SAA .45	500	1950	200
Col. Sam Colt Special Deluxe SAA .45	1000	2950	50
Wyatt Earp Buntline SAA .45	250	1995	150

1965			
Oregon Trail Scout	$ 75	$ 395	1,995
Joaquin Murietta .22/.45 Comb.	350	1695	100
Forty-Niner Miner Scout	85	395	500
Old Ft. Des Moines Reconst. Scout	90	395	700
Old Ft. Des Moines Reconst. SAA .45	170	1095	100
Old Ft. Des Moines Reconst. .22/.45 Comb.	290	1695	100
Appomattox Cent. Scout	75	395	1,001
Appomattox Cent. SAA .45	150	1095	250
Appomattox Cent. .22/.45 Comb.	240	1495	250
General Meade Campaign Scout	75	395	1,197
St. Augustine Quadracent. Scout	85	395	500
Kansas Cowtown Series Wichita Scout	85	395	500

1966	Issue	NIB	Amount Mfg.
Kansas Cowtown Series Dodge City Scout	$ 85	$ 395	500
Colorado Gold Rush Scout	85	395	1,350
Oklahoma Territory Scout	85	395	1,343
Dakota Territory Scout	85	395	1,000
General Meade SAA .45	165	1095	200
Abercrombie & Fitch Trailblazer N.Y.	275	1095	200
Abercrombie & Fitch Trailblazer Chic.	275	1095	100
Abercrombie & Fitch Trailblazer S.F.	275	1095	100
Kansas Cowtown Series Abilene Scout	95	395	500
Indiana Sesquicent Scout	85	395	1,500
Pony Express 4-Square Set .45 4 Guns	1,400	5995	N/A
California Gold Rush SAA .45	175	1295	130

1967			
Lawman Series Bat Masterson Scout	$ 90	$ 395	3,000
Lawman Series Bat Masterson SAA .45	180	1295	500
Alamo Scout	85	395	4,250
Alamo SAA .45	165	1095	750
Alamo .22/.45 Comb.	265	1495	250
Kansas Cowtown Series Coffeyville Scout	95	395	500
Kansas Trail Series Chisolm Trail Scout	100	395	500
WWI Series Chateau Thierry .45 Auto	200	695	7,400
WWI Series Chateau Thierry Deluxe	500	1350	75
WWI Series Chateau Thierry Sp. Deluxe	1000	2750	25
WWI Series Chateau Thierry Sp. Deluxe	1000	2750	25

1968			
Nebraska Cent. Scout	$ 100	$ 395	7,001
Kansas Trail Series Chisolm Trail Scout	100	395	500
WWI Series Belleau Wood .45 Auto	200	695	7,400
WWI Series Belleau Wood Deluxe	500	1350	75
WWI Series Belleau Wood Sp. Deluxe	1000	2750	25
Lawman Series Pat Garrett Scout	110	395	3,000
Lawman Series Pat Garrett SAA .45	220	1095	500

1969			
Nathan B. Forrest Scout	$ 110	$ 395	3,000
Kansas Trail Series Santa Fe Trail Sct.	120	395	501
WWI Ser. 2nd Battle of Marne .45 Auto	220	695	7,400
WWI Ser. 2nd Battle of Marne Deluxe	500	1350	75
WWI Ser. 2nd Battle of Marne Sp. Del.	1000	2750	25
Alabama Sesquicent. Scout	110	395	3,001
Alabama Sesquicent. SAA .45	N/A	15000	1
Golden Spike Scout	135	395	11,000
Kansas Trail Ser. Shawnee Tr. Scout	120	395	501
WWI Ser. Meuse-Argonne .45 Auto	220	695	7,400
WWI Ser. Meuse-Argonne Deluxe	500	1350	75
WWI Ser. Meuse-Argonne Sp. Deluxe	1000	2750	25
Arkansas Terr. Sesquicent. Scout	110	395	3,500
Lawman Ser. Wild Bill Hickok Scout	117	395	3,000
Lawman Ser. Wild Bill Hickok SAA .45	220	1095	500
California Bicent. Scout	135	395	5,000

1970			
Kansas Ft. Ser. Ft. Larned Scout	$ 120	$ 395	500
WWII Ser. European Theatre	250	695	11,500
WWII Ser. Pacific Theatre	250	695	11,500
Texas Ranger SAA .45	650	2250	1,000
Kansas Ft. Ser. Ft. Hays Scout	130	395	500
Marine Sesquicent. Scout	120	395	3,000
Missouri Sesquicent. Scout	125	395	3,000
Missouri Sesquicent. SAA .45	220	995	900
Kansas Ft. Ser. Ft. Riley Scout	130	395	500
Lawman Ser. Wyatt Earp Scout	125	450	3,000
Lawman Ser. Wyatt Earp SAA .45	395	2250	500

1971			
NRA Centennial SAA .45	$ 250	$ 1095	5,000
NRA Centennial SAA .357 Mag.	250	850	5,000
NRA Centennial Gold Cup .45 Auto	250	850	2,500
U.S. Grant 1851 Navy	250	595	4,750
Robt. E. Lee 1851 Navy	250	595	4,750
Lee - Grant Set 1851 Navies	500	1350	250
Kansas Ft. Ser. Ft. Scott Scout	130	395	500

1972	Issue	NIB	Amount Mfg.
Centennial Cased Set Florida Terr. Sesquicent. Scout	$ 125	$ 395	2,001
Arizona Ranger Scout	135	395	3,001
1975			
Peacemaker Centennial SAA .45	$ 300	$ 1395	1,500
Peacemaker Centennial SAA .44-40	300	1395	1,500
Peacemaker	625	2895	500
1976			
U.S. Bicentennial Set	$ 1695	$ 1895	1,776
1977			
2nd Amendment .22	$ 195	$ 395	3,020
U.S. Cavalry 200th Anniversary Set	995	1250	3,000
1978			
Statehood 3rd Model Dragoon	$ 12500	$ 6995	52
1979			
Ned Buntline SAA N.F. .45	$ 895	$ 895	3,000
Ohio President's Spec. Edit. .45 Auto	N/A	800	250
Tombstone Cent. .45 SAA	550	1295	300
1980			
Drug Enforcement Agency .45 Auto	$ 550	$ 1100	910
Olympics Ace Spec. Edition .22	1000	1150	200
Heritage Walker .44 Percussion	1495	950	1,847
1981			
John M. Browning .45 Auto	$ 1100	$ 895	3,000
1982			
John Wayne SAA	$ 2995	$ 1995	3,100
John Wayne SAA Deluxe	10000	7500	500
John Wayne SAA Presentation	20000	12000	100
1983			
Buffalo Bill Wild West Show Cent SAA	$ 1350	$ 1350	500
1984			
1st Edition Govt. Model .380 ACP	$ 425	$ 400	1,000
Duke Frontier .22	475	495	1,000
Winchester/Colt SAA .44-40	N/A	2250	4,000
USA Edition SAA .44-40	4995	3500	100
Kit Carson New Frontier .22	550	395	1,000
2nd Edition Govt. Model .380 ACP	525	400	1,000
Officer's ACP Commencement Issue	700	600	1,000
Theodore Roosevelt SAA .44-40	1695	1695	500
No Amer. Oilmen Buntline SAA .45	3900	3500	200
1986			
150th Anniversary SAA .45	$ 1595	$ 1595	1,000
150th Anniv. Engraving Sampler	1613	2500	N/A
150th Anniv. Engraving Sampler .45 Auto	1155	1000	N/A
Texas 150th Sesquicent. Sheriff's .45	836	1095	N/A
Mustang 1st Edition .380 ACP	475	395	1,000
Officer's ACP Heirloom Edition	1575	1550	N/A
Klay-Colt 1851 Navy	1850	1850	150
Klay-Colt 1851 Navy Engraved Edit.	3150	3150	50
Double Diamond Set .357 & .45 Auto	1575	1595	1,000
1987			
Combat Elite Custom Edition .45 Auto	$ 900	$ 750	500
12th Man Spirit of Aggieland .45 Auto	950	750	999
1989			
Snake Eyes Ltd. Edit. 2-2.5" Pythons	$ 2950	$ 1895	500

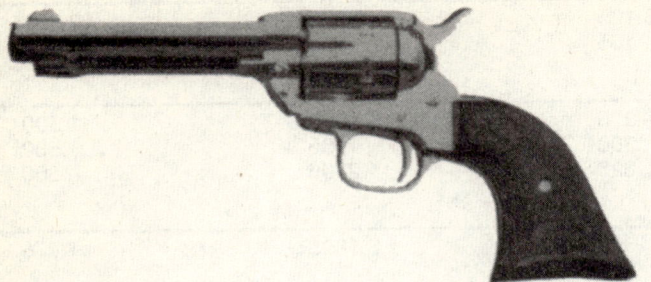

Bat Masterson

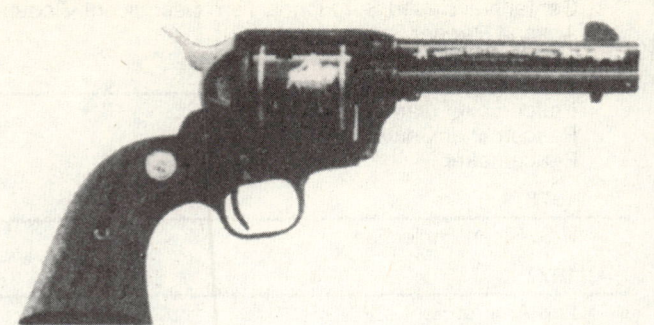

Buffalo Bill Wild West Show

Arizona Territorial Centennial

California Gold Rush

Abilene Commemorative

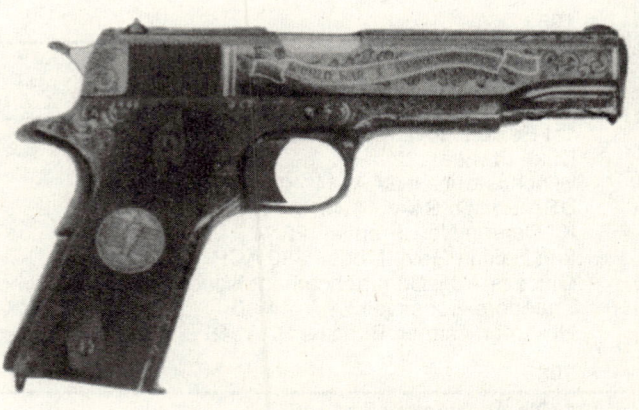

Chateau Thierry Commemorative

Belleau Wood Commemorative

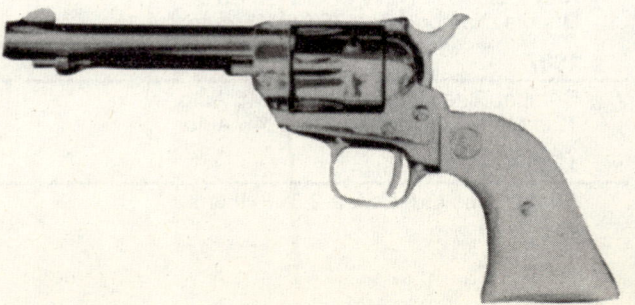

Dodge City Commemorative

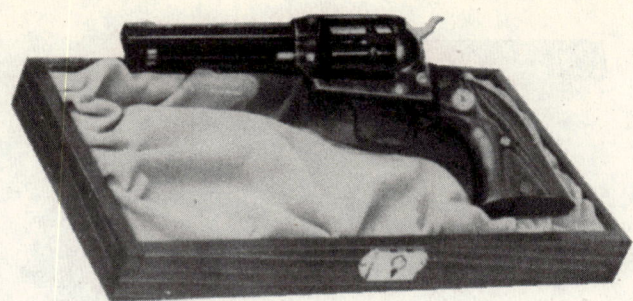

Florida Territorial Sesquicentennial

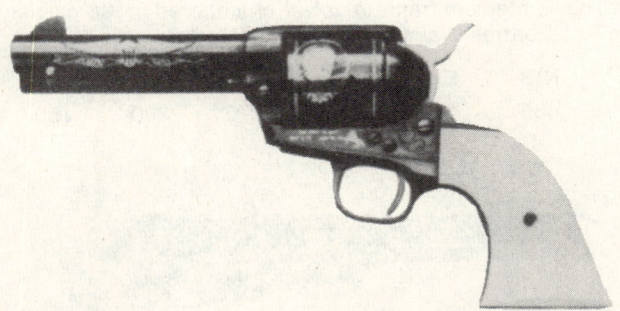

John Wayne Commemorative

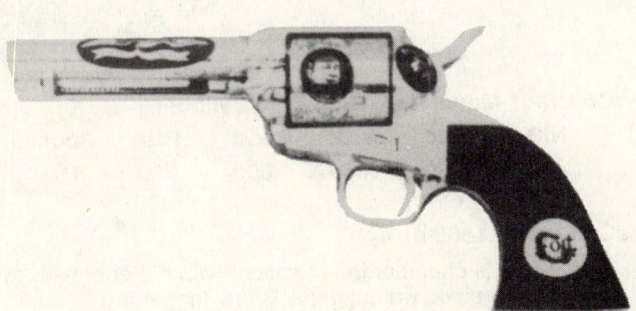

John Wayne Deluxe

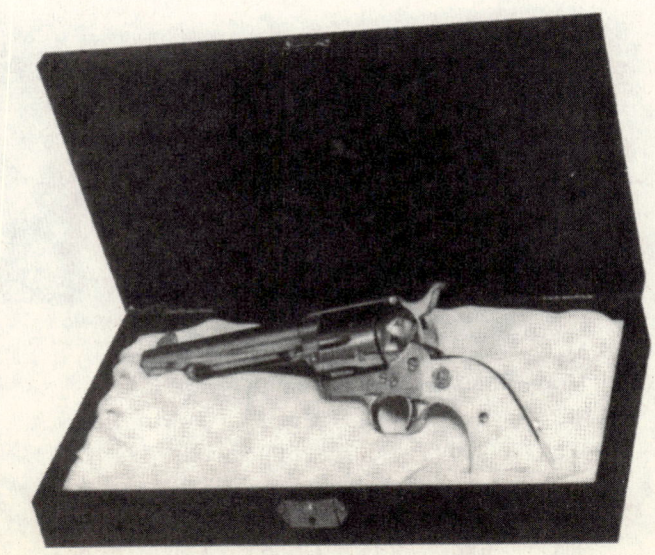

Alabama Sesquicentennial

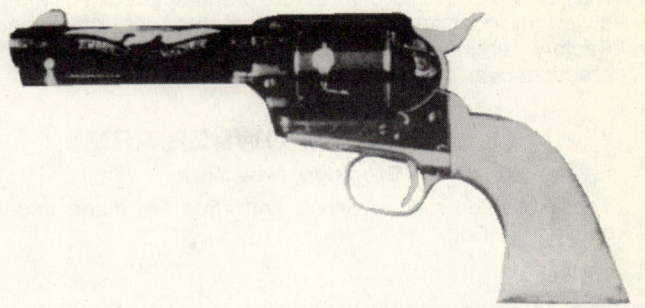

John Wayne Presentation

REPRODUCTION COLT PERCUSSION REVOLVERS

Walker

Made from 1979 to 1981; serial numbers 1200-4120 and 32256 to 32500.

NIB	Exc.	V.G.
895	750	500

Walker Heritage Model

NIB
950

First Model Dragoon

Made from 1980 to 1982; serial numbers 24100-34500.

NIB	Exc.	V.G.
395	300	100

Second Model Dragoon

Made from 1980 to 1982; serial numbers as above.

NIB	Exc.	V.G.
395	300	100

Third Model Dragoon

Made from 1980 to 1982; serial numbers as above.

NIB	Exc.	V.G.
395	300	100

Model 1848 Pocket Pistol

Made in 1981; serial numbers 16000-17851.

NIB	Exc.	V.G.
425	300	100

Model 1851 Navy Revolver

Made from 1971 to 1978; serial numbers 4201-25100 and 24900-29150.

NIB	Exc.	V.G.
395	400	325

Model 1860 Army Revolver

Made from 1978 to 1982; serial numbers 201000-212835.

NIB	Exc.	V.G.
550	500	475

Model 1861 Navy Revolver

Made during 1980 and 1981; serial numbers 40000-43165.

NIB	Exc.	V.G.
500	450	400

Model 1862 Pocket Pistol

Made from 1979 to 1984; serial numbers 8000-58850.

NIB	Exc	V.G.
425	350	300

Model 1862 Police Revolver

Made from 1979 to 1984; serial numbers in above range.

NIB	Exc.	V.G.
425	400	300

NOTE: The above revolvers were manufactured in a variety of styles (cylinder form, stainless steel, etc.) that affect prices. Factory engraved examples command a considerable premium over the prices listed above.

COLT BLACKPOWDER ARMS
Brooklyn, New York

These blackpowder revolvers and rifles are made under license from Colt.

Walker

This .44 caliber large frame revolver is fitted with a 9" barrel.

NIB	Exc	V.G.	Good	Fair	Poor
475	400	350	300	200	150

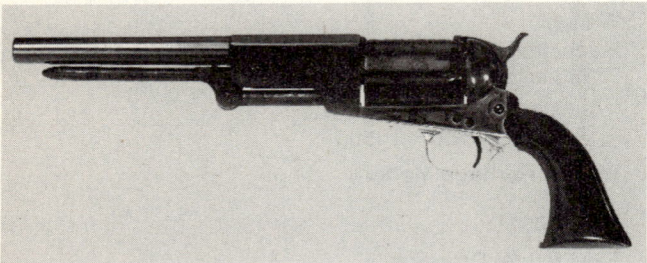

Whitneyville Hartford Dragoon

Similar in appearance to the Walker colt this revolver is fitted with a 7-1/2" barrel and a silver plated iron backstrap and trigger guard. This is a limited edition with a total of 2,400 guns built with serial numbers between 1100 through 1340.

NIB	Exc	V.G.	Good	Fair	Poor
475	400	350	300	200	150

3rd Model Dragoon

Another large frame revolver with 7-1/2" barrel with a brass backstrap, 3-screw frame, and unfluted cylinder.

NIB	Exc	V.G.	Good	Fair	Poor
475	400	350	300	200	150

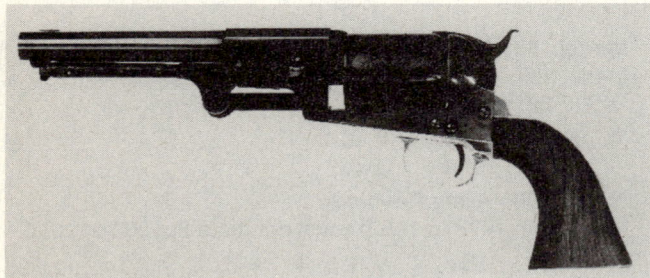

3rd Model Dragoon-Steel Backstrap

NIB	Exc	V.G.	Good	Fair	Poor
500	425	375	325	200	150

3rd Model Dragoon-Fluted Cylinder

NIB	Exc	V.G.	Good	Fair	Poor
510	435	375	325	200	150

Colt 1849 Model Pocket

A small frame revolver chambered in .31 caliber with a 4" barrel. Fitted with one-piece walnut grips.

NIB	Exc	V.G.	Good	Fair	Poor
435	375	325	275	200	150

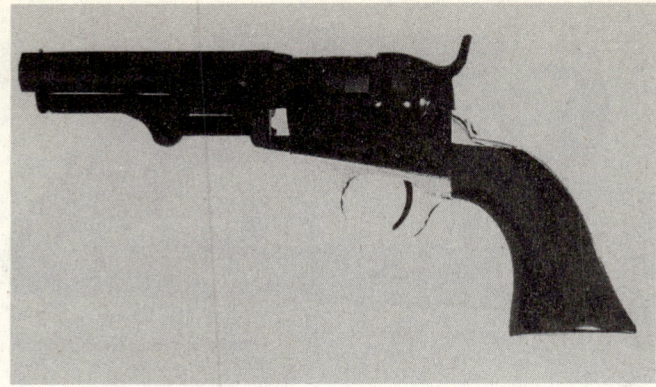

Colt 1851 Model Navy

This is medium frame revolver chambered in .36 caliber with 7-1/2" barrel. Walnut grips and case color frame.

NIB	Exc	V.G.	Good	Fair	Poor
435	375	325	275	200	150

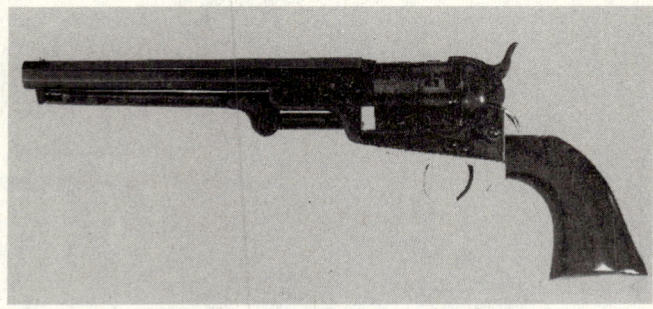

Colt 1851 Model Navy with Dual Cylinder

NIB	Exc	V.G.	Good	Fair	Poor
475	400	350	300	200	150

Colt Model 1860 Army

This model is chamber in .44 caliber with roll engraved cylinder and one piece walnut grips. Barrel length is 8".

NIB	Exc	V.G.	Good	Fair	Poor
435	375	325	275	200	150

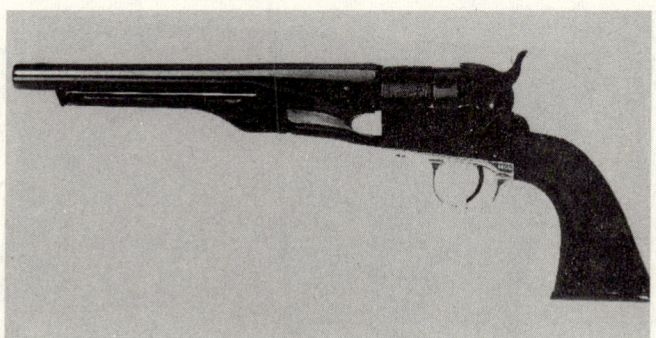

Colt Model 1860 Army with Dual Cylinder

NIB	Exc	V.G.	Good	Fair	Poor
475	400	350	300	200	150

Colt Model 1860 Army-Fluted Cylinder

NIB	Exc	V.G.	Good	Fair	Poor
450	400	350	300	200	150

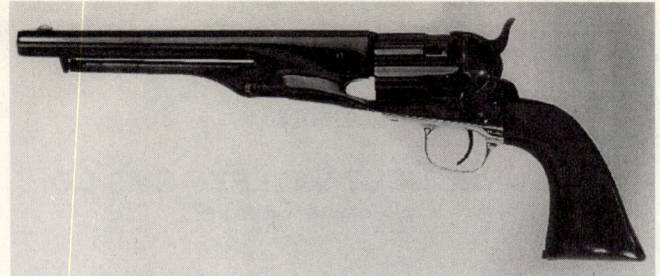

Colt 1860 Officers Model

This is a deluxe version of the standard 1860 with a special blued finish and gold crossed sabres. This is a 4-screw frame with 8" barrel and 6-shot rebated cylinder.

NIB	Exc	V.G.	Good	Fair	Poor
675	575	450	375	250	150

Colt Model 1860 Army Gold U.S. Cavalry

Features a gold engraved cylinder and gold barrel bands.

NIB	Exc	V.G.	Good	Fair	Poor
650	575	450	375	250	150

Colt Model 1860 Army-Stainless Steel

NIB	Exc	V.G.	Good	Fair	Poor
475	400	350	300	200	150

Colt Model 1861 Navy

This .36 caliber revolver features a 7-1/2" barrel with engraved cylinder, case colored frame and one piece walnut grips.

NIB	Exc	V.G.	Good	Fair	Poor
450	400	350	300	200	150

Colt Model 1861 Navy General Custer

Same as above but with engraved frame and cylinder.

NIB	Exc	V.G.	Good	Fair	Poor
975	850	700	500	300	200

Colt Model 1862 Trapper-Pocket Police

This small frame revolver is fitted with a 3-1/2" barrel, silver backstrap, and trigger guard. The cylinder is semi-fluted and chambered in .36 caliber.

NIB	Exc	V.G.	Good	Fair	Poor
435	375	325	275	200	150

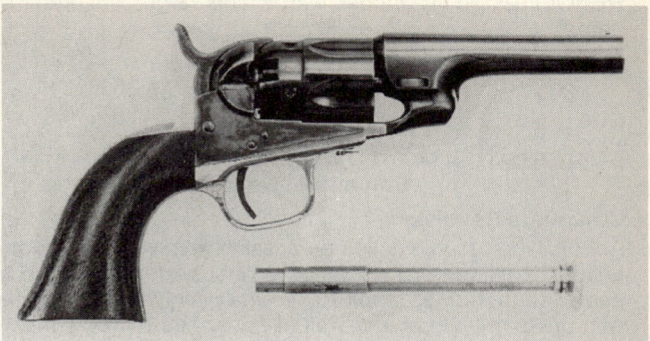

Colt Model 1862 Pocket Navy

This small frame revolver is fitted with a round engraved cylinder with a 5" octagon barrel with hinged loading lever. Chambered for .36 caliber.

NIB	Exc	V.G.	Good	Fair	Poor
435	375	325	275	200	150

Colt 1861 Musket

This Civil War musket is chambered in the .58 caliber. Lockplate, hammer, buttplate, and 3 barrel bands, and 40" barrel are finished bright. The stock is a one-piece oil-finish affair. Bayonet and accessories are extra.

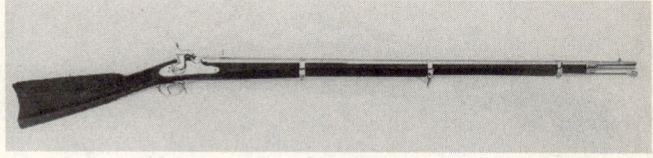

NIB	Exc	V.G.	Good	Fair	Poor
650	550	400	325	275	150

Colt 1861 Musket-Artillery Model

Same as above but fitted with a 31-1/2" barrel.

NIB	Exc	V.G.	Good	Fair	Poor
650	550	400	325	275	150

Colt 1861 Musket Presentation 1 of 1000

Limited to 1,000 guns these are special finished with a high polish and Colt's signature in gold on the trigger guard. Sold with special custom wooden case.

NIB	Exc	V.G.	Good	Fair	Poor
2100	1500	750	600	450	300

Colt 1861 Musket Presentation 1 of 1000-Artillery Model

Same as above but 31-1/2" barrel.

NIB	Exc	V.G.	Good	Fair	Poor
2100	1500	750	600	450	300

Colt Gamemaster .50

Introduced in 1997 this rifle is chambered for the .50 caliber. It is fitted with a 31.5" barrel and weighs about 13 lbs.

NIB	Exc.	V.G.	Good	Fair	Poor
800	650	—	—	—	—

COLUMBIA ARMORY
Columbia, Tennessee

A trade name applied to a variety of solid frame cartridge revolvers made by John T. Smith Company of Rock Falls, Connecticut. They were marked "SAFETY HAMMERLESS

REVOLVER". This model was made under several trade names.

Exc.	V.G.	Good	Fair	Poor
200	125	100	75	50

COLUMBUS F. A. MFG. CO.
Columbus, Georgia

Columbus Revolver
A .36-caliber double action percussion revolver with a 6-shot, unfluted cylinder and a 7.5" octagonal barrel. Similar in appearance to the 1851 Colt Navy. The pistol is browned steel, with brass gripstraps and walnut grips. The barrel is marked "Columbus Fire Arms Manuf. Co/Columbus Ga." 100 revolvers were manufactured in 1863 and 1864.

Exc.	V.G.	Good	Fair	Poor
—	—	50000	25000	5000

COMBLAIN
Belgium and Brazil

Single Shot Rifle
A 11x53Rmm caliber rifle with a falling block action. Manufactured both in a hammerless and hammer version. Full stock secured by two barrel bands.

Courtesy Milwaukee Public Museum, Milwaukee, Wisconsin

Exc.	V.G.	Good	Fair	Poor
750	650	500	350	250

COMMANDO ARMS
Knoxville, Tennessee

Formerly known as Volunteer Enterprises. The name change took place in 1978.

Mark III Carbine
A .45 ACP caliber semiautomatic rifle with a 16.5" barrel, a peep rear sight and a vertical foregrip. Manufactured between 1969 and 1976.

NIB	Exc.	V.G.	Good	Fair	Poor
375	300	250	200	150	100

Mark 9 Carbine
As above, in 9mm caliber.

NIB	Exc.	V.G.	Good	Fair	Poor
400	300	250	200	150	100

Mark.45
The new designation for the Mark III after the company changed its name.

NIB	Exc.	V.G.	Good	Fair	Poor
400	325	250	200	150	100

CONNECTICUT ARMS CO.
Norfolk, Connecticut

Pocket Revolver
A .28 caliber spur trigger revolver with 3" octagonal barrel, 6-shot unfluted cylinder, using a cup-primed cartridge and loads from the front of the cylinder. There is a hinged hook on the side of the frame under the cylinder that acts as the extractor.

Silver-plated brass, blued with walnut grips. The barrel is marked "Conn. Arms Co. Norfolk, Conn." Approximately 2,700 manufactured in the 1860s.

Exc.	V.G.	Good	Fair	Poor
—	—	750	300	100

CONNECTICUT VALLEY ARMS CO.
Norcross, Georgia

RIFLES

Express Rifle
A .50 caliber double barrel percussion rifle with 28" barrels. Blued with a walnut stock.

Deluxe Version-Add 100%.

NIB	Exc.	V.G.	Good	Fair	Poor
525	450	400	350	300	225

Over/Under Rifle
A .50 caliber double-barrel Over/Under rifle with 26" barrels. Blued with a walnut stock.

NIB	Exc.	V.G.	Good	Fair	Poor
575	500	450	400	350	275

Hawken Rifle
A .50 caliber with a 28" octagonal barrel, double set triggers and a walnut stock.

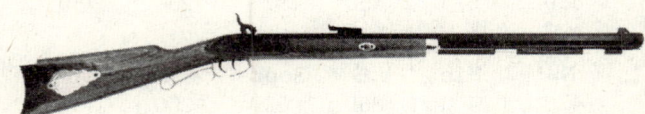

NIB	Exc.	V.G.	Good	Fair	Poor
400	325	275	225	150	100

Presentation Grade Hawken
As above, with an engraved lock, patchbox, and finely figured stock.

NIB	Exc.	V.G.	Good	Fair	Poor
500	425	375	325	275	200

Pennsylvania Long Rifle
A .50 caliber flintlock rifle with a 40" octagonal barrel, double set triggers and a walnut stock.

NIB	Exc.	V.G.	Good	Fair	Poor
475	400	350	300	250	175

Kentucky Rifle
A .45 caliber percussion rifle with a 33.5" octagonal barrel and walnut stock.

NIB	Exc.	V.G.	Good	Fair	Poor
275	225	175	150	100	75

Mountain Rifle
A .50 or .54 caliber percussion half-stock rifle.

NIB	Exc.	V.G.	Good	Fair	Poor
300	225	175	125	100	75

Blazer Rifle
A .50 caliber percussion rifle with a 28" octagonal barrel and walnut stock.

NIB	Exc.	V.G.	Good	Fair	Poor
150	125	100	85	65	45

Apollo Shadow SS

Introduced in 1993 this rifle features an in-line stainless steel bolt spring action, a 24" blued round barrel with octagonal one piece receiver, drilled and tapped. Stock is black hardwood-textured with Dura Grip with pistol grip and recoil pad. Offered in either .50 or .54 caliber. Weighs about 9 lbs.

NIB	Exc.	V.G.	Good	Fair	Poor
175	150	125	100	75	50

Apollo Classic

Similar to the above Apollo Model but with dark brown stained laminated hardwood stock with pistol grip, raised comb, and recoil pad. Weighs about 8-1/2 lbs.

NIB	Exc.	V.G.	Good	Fair	Poor
215	175	150	125	100	75

Apollo Carbelite

Offered in .50 caliber with percussion bolt and 27" blued round taper barrel with octagonal receiver, drilled and tapped. Fitted with Carbelite composite stock with Monte Carlo and cheekpiece with pistol grip. Weighs approximately 7-1/2 lbs.

NIB	Exc.	V.G.	Good	Fair	Poor
280	225	175	150	100	75

Apollo Starfire

Chambered for the .50 caliber bullet this rifle is an in-line type with 24" stainless steel barrel with synthetic stock with checkered pistol grip, raised comb, and cheekpiece. Weight is about 6.5 lbs.

NIB	Exc.	V.G.	Good	Fair	Poor
225	175	150	125	100	75

Apollo Eclipse Rifle

Offered in either .50 or .54 caliber with 24" round barrel with blued steel receiver. Synthetic stock with checkered pistol, raised comb, and cheekpiece. Approximate weight is 6.5 lbs.

NIB	Exc.	V.G.	Good	Fair	Poor
175	150	1250	100	85	65

Apollo Dominator

Fitted with a synthetic thumbhole stock and a 24" round barrel this rifle is chambered for the .50 caliber bullet. Introduced in 1996. Weight is approximately 8.5 lbs.

NIB	Exc.	V.G.	Good	Fair	Poor
300	225	175	150	100	75

Apollo Brown Bear

This .50 caliber rifle is fitted with a hardwood stock with pistol grip with raised comb and cheekpiece. The barrel is round and 24". Introduced in 1996. Weight is about 6.5 lbs.

NIB	Exc.	V.G.	Good	Fair	Poor
200	175	150	125	100	75

Frontier Carbine

Fitted with a 24" blued barrel this rifle is offered in .50 caliber percussion or flintlock. Case-hardened lock with hardwood stock. Weighs about 6-3/4 lbs.

NIB	Exc.	V.G.	Good	Fair	Poor
150	125	100	85	75	50

Plainsman rifle

This .50 caliber percussion rifle has a 26" octagonal barrel with case-hardened lock and hardwood stock. Weight is about 6-1/2 lbs.

NIB	Exc.	V.G.	Good	Fair	Poor
130	115	100	85	75	50

Panther Carbine

This percussion rifle is available in either .50 or .54 caliber. It is fitted with a 24" blued octagonal barrel with Hawken-style case-hardened lock. Stock is textured black Dura Grip over hardwood with Monte Carlo comb, cheekpiece, and pistol grip. Weight approximately 7-1/2 lbs.

NIB	Exc.	V.G.	Good	Fair	Poor
150	125	100	85	75	50

Bushwacker Rifle

This .50 caliber percussion rifle is fitted with a 26" octagonal barrel with case-hardened engraved lock and brown stained hardwood stock with rounded nose. Weight is about 7-1/2 lbs.

NIB	Exc.	V.G.	Good	Fair	Poor
135	115	100	85	75	50

Trophy Carbine

This carbine is fitted with a 24" half-round half-octagon barrel with Hawken style lock. The stock is walnut with Monte Carlo comb, cheekpiece, and pistol grip. Offered in .50 or .54 caliber percussion and weighs about 6-3/4 lbs.

NIB	Exc.	V.G.	Good	Fair	Poor
215	175	150	125	100	75

Varmint Rifle

This is a lightweight percussion rifle in .32 caliber with 24" octagon barrel and case-colored lock. The stock is hardwood. Weighs about 6-3/4 lbs.

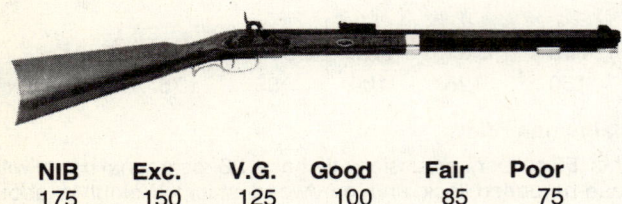

NIB	Exc.	V.G.	Good	Fair	Poor
175	150	125	100	85	75

Woodsman Rifle LS

Introduced in 1994 this rifle features a 26" blued octagon barrel with dark brown stained laminated hardwood stock. Offered in .50 or .54 caliber percussion. Weighs about 6-1/2 lbs.

NIB	Exc.	V.G.	Good	Fair	Poor
135	115	100	85	75	50

Frontier Hunter Carbine

Offered in either .50 or .54 caliber this percussion rifle is fitted with a 24" blued octagon barrel and case-hardened 45° offset hammer. The stock is dark stained laminated hardwood. Weighs about 7-1/2 lbs.

NIB	Exc.	V.G.	Good	Fair	Poor
170	150	125	100	75	50

Grey Wolf Rifle

Offered in either .50 or .54 caliber percussion this rifle is fitted with a 26" matte blue octagon barrel with a case-hardened engraved lock. The stock is matte gray composite with raised comb, checkered pistol grip, and buttplate. Weighs about 6-1/2 lbs.

NIB	Exc.	V.G.	Good	Fair	Poor
160	125	100	85	75	50

Lone Grey Wolf Rifle

Introduced in 1994 this .50 caliber percussion rifle features a 26" matte blued octagon barrel. The triggerguard is oversized. The composite stock is black and has a raised comb, checkered pistol grip, and recoil pad. Weighs about 6-1/2 lbs.

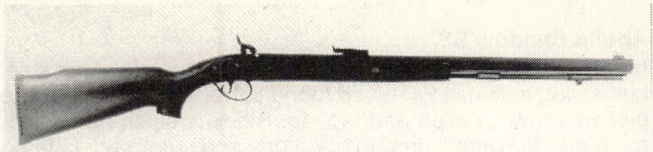

NIB	Exc.	V.G.	Good	Fair	Poor
185	150	125	100	75	50

Timber Wolf Rifle

Introduced in 1994 this model is similar to the above model but is furnished with Realtree composite stock with raised comb, checkered pistol grip, and buttplate. Weighs about 6-1/2 lbs.

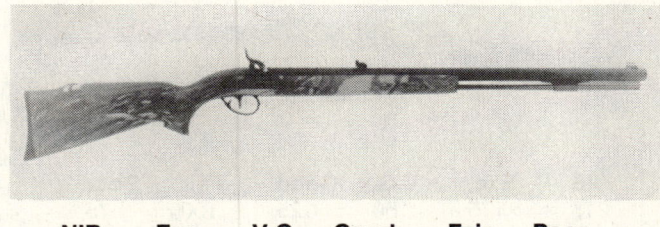

NIB	Exc.	V.G.	Good	Fair	Poor
185	165	140	100	75	50

Tracker Carbine LS

Introduced in 1994 this carbine is fitted with a 21" blued, half-round, half-octagon barrel with a Hawken-style lock. The stock is laminated dark brown with matte finish, and straight grip. Chambered for .50 caliber percussion. Weighs about 6-1/2 lbs.

NIB	Exc.	V.G.	Good	Fair	Poor
185	165	140	100	75	50

Stag Horn

Introduced in 1996 this in-line rifle is chambered for the .50 or .54 caliber bullet. The round barrel is 24" with blued finish. The stock is synthetic with checkered pistol grip, raised comb, and cheekpiece. Weight is about 6.5 lbs.

NIB	Exc.	V.G.	Good	Fair	Poor
175	150	1250	100	85	65

SHOTGUNS

Brittany 11 Shotgun

A .410 bore double-barrel percussion shotgun with 24" barrels, double triggers and a walnut stock.

NIB	Exc.	V.G.	Good	Fair	Poor
170	150	125	100	75	50

Trapper Shotgun

A 12 gauge percussion single barrel shotgun with a 28" barrel threaded for choke tubes and a walnut stock.

NIB	Exc.	V.G.	Good	Fair	Poor
225	200	175	150	100	75

Classic Turkey Double-Barrel Shotgun

This is a 12 gauge percussion breech loading shotgun with 28" barrel. The stock is European walnut with straight grip checkered stock. Weighs about 9 lbs.

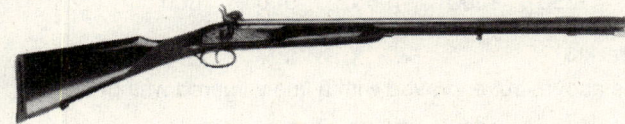

NIB	Exc.	V.G.	Good	Fair	Poor
325	275	225	150	125	100

Trapper Shotgun

This is a single barrel 12 gauge shotgun with a 28" barrel. The stock is a straight grip hardwood with checkering. Supplied with three interchangeable chokes. Weighs about 6 lbs.

NIB	Exc.	V.G.	Good	Fair	Poor
185	165	140	100	75	50

PISTOLS

Siber

A .45 caliber percussion pistol patterned after the Swiss Siber.

NIB	Exc.	V.G.	Good	Fair	Poor
400	325	275	225	150	100

Kentucky

A .45 caliber single shot percussion pistol with a 10" barrel and walnut stock.

NIB	Exc.	V.G.	Good	Fair	Poor
140	125	100	80	60	40

Philadelphia Derringer

A .45 caliber single shot percussion pistol with a 3.25" barrel and walnut stock.

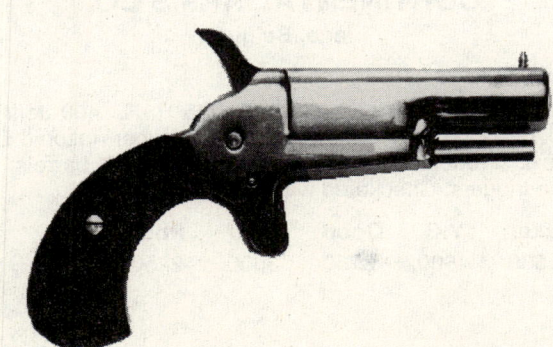

NIB	Exc.	V.G.	Good	Fair	Poor
75	65	50	40	30	20

Sheriff's Model

A .36 caliber percussion revolver, nickel-plated with walnut grips.

NIB	Exc.	V.G.	Good	Fair	Poor
225	200	175	150	125	100

3rd Model Dragoon

NIB	Exc.	V.G.	Good	Fair	Poor
225	200	175	150	125	100

Colt Walker Replica

NIB	Exc.	V.G.	Good	Fair	Poor
275	250	225	200	175	150

Remington Bison

NIB	Exc.	V.G.	Good	Fair	Poor
250	225	200	175	150	125

Pocket Police

NIB	Exc.	V.G.	Good	Fair	Poor
135	110	100	85	65	45

Pocker Revolver

Chambered for .31 caliber. Fitted with 4" octagon barrel. Cylinder holds five bullets. Solid brass frame. Weighs about 15 oz.

NIB	Exc.	V.G.	Good	Fair	Poor
125	100	85	75	60	50

Wells Fargo

NIB	Exc.	V.G.	Good	Fair	Poor
165	145	125	100	75	50

1851 Navy

NIB	Exc.	V.G.	Good	Fair	Poor
135	110	100	85	65	45

1861 Navy

NIB	Exc.	V.G.	Good	Fair	Poor
150	135	110	90	75	50

1860 Army

NIB	Exc.	V.G.	Good	Fair	Poor
220	200	175	150	125	100

1858 Remington

NIB	Exc.	V.G.	Good	Fair	Poor
175	150	125	100	75	50

1858 Remington Target

As above, but fitted with adjustable sights.

NIB	Exc.	V.G.	Good	Fair	Poor
235	200	175	125	100	75

Bison

A 6-shot .44 caliber revolver with 10-1/4" octagonal barrel. Solid brass frame. Weighs about 48 oz.

NIB	Exc.	V.G.	Good	Fair	Poor
160	130	100	85	75	50

Hawken Pistol

This is a .50 caliber percussion pistol with 9-3/4" octagon barrel. The stock is hardwood. Weighs about 50 oz.

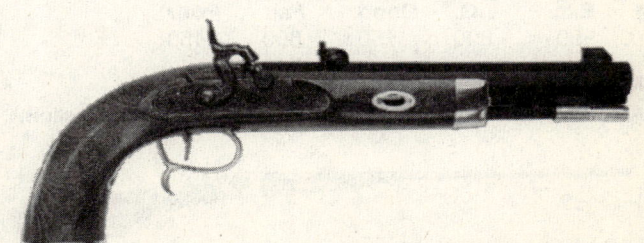

NIB	Exc.	V.G.	Good	Fair	Poor
135	110	85	75	65	50

CONSTABLE, R.
Philadelphia, Pennsylvania

Pocket Pistol

A single shot percussion pistol with a 3" round or octagonal barrel. German-silver mounts and walnut stock. These pistols are marked "R. Constable Philadelphia" and were manufactured during the late 1840s and 1850s.

Exc.	V.G.	Good	Fair	Poor
—	1500	900	500	200

CONTENTO/VENTUR
Importer-Ventura
Seal Beach, California

This high-grade, double-barrel shotgun is no longer imported.

SIDE BY SIDE

Model 51

A 12, 16, 20, 28, and .410 bore boxlock double-barrel shotgun with 26", 28", 30", and 32" barrels, various chokes, extractors and double triggers. Checkered walnut stock. Introduced in 1980 and discontinued in 1985.

Exc.	V.G.	Good	Fair	Poor
500	350	300	225	150

Model 52

As above in 10 gauge.

Exc.	V.G.	Good	Fair	Poor
500	350	300	225	150

Model 53

As above, with scalloped receiver, automatic ejectors and available with a single selective trigger. Discontinued in 1985.

Single-Selective Trigger-Add 25%.

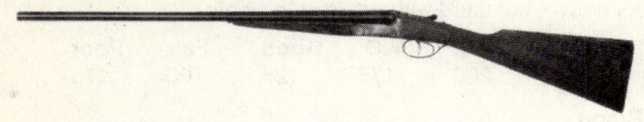

Exc.	V.G.	Good	Fair	Poor
550	400	350	250	200

Model 62

A 12, 20, or 28 gauge Holland & Holland sidelock shotgun with various barrel lengths and chokes, automatic ejectors, cocking indicators, a floral engraved receiver, a checkered, walnut stock. Discontinued in 1982.

Exc.	V.G.	Good	Fair	Poor
950	800	750	600	450

Model 64

As above, but more finely finished. No longer in production.

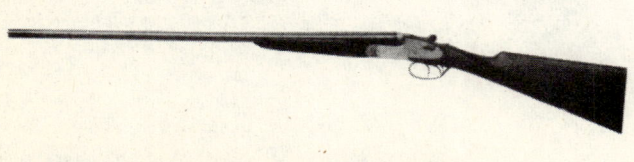

Exc.	V.G.	Good	Fair	Poor
1150	900	850	700	550

OVER/UNDER

A 12 gauge Over/Under shotgun with 32" barrels, screw-in choke tubes, a high ventilated rib, automatic ejectors, and a standard single selective trigger. Checkered, with Monte Carlo walnut stock.

Exc.	V.G.	Good	Fair	Poor
1050	900	750	600	500

Mark 2

As above, with an extra single barrel and fitted in a leather case.

Exc.	V.G.	Good	Fair	Poor
1350	1200	1050	900	800

Mark 3

As above, but engraved with a finely figured walnut stock.

Exc.	V.G.	Good	Fair	Poor
1600	1500	1250	1100	950

Mark 3 Combo

As above, with an extra single barrel and fitted in a leather case.

Exc.	V.G.	Good	Fair	Poor
2800	2600	2250	1750	1300

CONTINENTAL
RWM
Cologne, Germany

Continental Pocket Pistol

A 6.35mm caliber semiautomatic pistol with a 2" barrel, internal hammer, and a 7-shot detachable magazine. Blued with plastic grips, and the slide is marked "Continental Kal. 6.35."

Exc.	V.G.	Good	Fair	Poor
200	150	125	100	75

CONTINENTAL ARMS CO.
Liege, Belgium

Double Rifle

A .270, .303, .30-40, .30-06, .348, 375 H&H, .400 Jeffreys, .465, .475, .500, and .600 Nitro Express caliber Anson & Deeley boxlock double-barreled rifle with 24" or 26" barrels, and double triggers. Checkered walnut stock.

Exc.	V.G.	Good	Fair	Poor
5500	4500	3750	3000	2250

CONTINENTAL ARMS CO.
Norwich, Connecticut

Pepperbox

A .22 caliber 5-barrel pepperbox with a spur trigger and 2.5" barrels marked "Continental Arms Co. Norwich Ct. Patented Aug. 28, 1866." Some examples of this pistol are to be found marked "Ladies Companion."

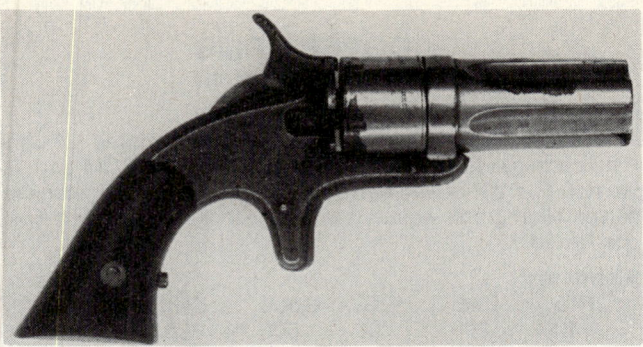

Courtesy Milwaukee Public Museum, Milwaukee, Wisconsin

Exc.	V.G.	Good	Fair	Poor
—	1750	700	350	250

COOK & BROTHER RIFLES AND CARBINES
New Orleans

In early 1861, Ferdinand W.C. Cook and his brother, Francis L. Cook, both English emigres, joined to form Cook & Brother in New Orleans to manufacture rifles and carbines following the English P1853 series for the newly seceded state of Louisiana and its neighbors. Between June 1861 and the federal occupation of New Orleans in April 1862, this firm produced about 200 cavalry and artillery carbines and about 1000 rifles. Having successfully moved the armory's machinery before federal occupation, the firm continued manufacture of rifles in Selma, Alabama, during 1862, probably completing another 1,000 rifles with the New Orleans lock markings from the parts brought with them. Reestablished in Athens, Georgia, in early 1863, the firm continued to build both carbines and rifles, manufacturing more than 5,500 above the New Orleans production through 1864. The firm's products were clearly among the best small arms made within the Confederacy

Cook & Brother Rifles (New Orleans & Selma production)

Overall length 48-3/4"; barrel length 33"; caliber .58. Markings: representation of a Confederate flag ("Stars & Bars") and "COOK & BROTHER/N.O./1861 (or) 1862" on lock; same usually on barrel, together with serial number and "PROVED" near breech. Rifles in the early production have long range rear sights and unusual two piece block and blade front sights as well as an integral bayonet lug with guide on right side of barrel. Later production utilizes a brass clamping ring for the bayonet, a block open rear sight and a simple block and blade front sight. Earlier production will claim a premium if in good condition.

Courtesy Milwaukee Public Museum, Milwaukee, Wisconsin

Exc.	V.G.	Good	Fair	Poor
—	—	15000	7500	3000

Cook & Brother Carbines (New Orleans production)

Overall length 40" (artillery), 37" (cavalry); barrel length 24" (artillery), 21"-21-1/2"; caliber .58. Markings: As on Cook & Brother rifles (New Orleans production) artillery and cavalry carbines were produced in New Orleans in a separate serial range from the rifles. Total production is thought not to have exceeded 225, divided evenly between 1861 and 1862 dates. In addition to the overall and barrel lengths, the main difference between the artillery and cavalry carbines is the manner in which they were carried. The former bears standard sling rings on the upper band and the triggerguard strap, the latter has a bar with a ring on the left side of the stock. Both are exceedingly rare.

Exc.	V.G.	Good	Fair	Poor
—	—	15000	6500	5000

Cook & Brother Rifles (Athens production)

Overall length 49"; barrel length 33"; caliber .58. Markings: representation of a Confederate flag ("Stars & Bars") and "COOK & BROTHER/ATHENS GA./date (1863 or 1864), and serial number on lock; "PROVED" on barrel near breech; serial number on various metal parts. After reestablishing their plant at Athens, Georgia, in the spring of 1863, Cook & Brother continued to manufacture rifles in a consecutive serial range after their New Orleans/Selma production (beginning about serial number 2000) and continued to make arms well into 1864 (through at least serial number 7650) until Sherman's army threatened the plant and necessitated the employment of its workforce in a military capacity as the 23rd Battalion Georgia State Guard.

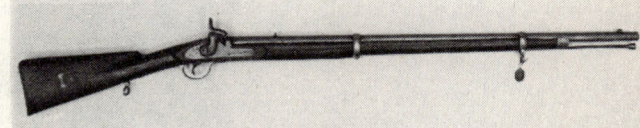

Courtesy Milwaukee Public Museum, Milwaukee, Wisconsin

Exc.	V.G.	Good	Fair	Poor
—	—	15000	7500	3000

Cook & Brother Carbines (Athens production)

Overall length 40" (artillery) or 37" (cavalry); barrel lengths 24" (artillery) or 21"-21-1/2" (cavalry); caliber .58. Markings: same as on Athens production rifles. Artillery and cavalry carbines were manufactured in the same serial range as the Athens production rifles (about 2000 through 7650). As in New Orleans production, the artillery and cavalry carbines are distinguished from one another by their respective lengths. Unlike New Orleans/Selma production, however, some of the cavalry carbines are mounted with sling swivels of the artillery style, while others bear the sling ring on the left side and additionally have a swivel ring to secure the ramrod.

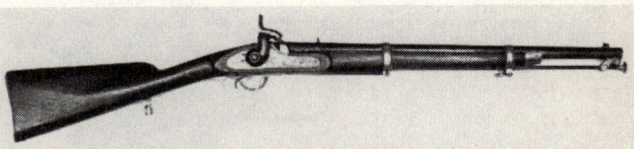

Courtesy Milwaukee Public Museum, Milwaukee, Wisconsin

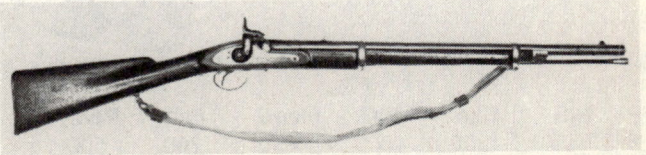

Courtesy Milwaukee Public Museum, Milwaukee, Wisconsin

Exc.	V.G.	Good	Fair	Poor
—	—	15000	6500	5000

COONAN ARMS CO.
St. Paul, Minnesota

Model A

A .357 Magnum semiautomatic pistol with a 5" barrel, a 7-shot, detachable magazine, and fixed sights. Stainless steel with walnut grips. Introduced in 1981 and discontinued in 1984.

NIB	Exc.	V.G.	Good	Fair	Poor
700	600	525	450	400	325

Model B

An improved version of the above with a linkless barrel system, extended grip safety, enclosed trigger bar, and a more contoured grip. A 6" barrel is available, as are adjustable sights, as extra cost options. A .38 Special conversion is also available. Introduced in 1985.

6" Barrel-Add $40.
Bomar Adjustable Sights-Add $130.
.38 Special Conversion-Add $40.

NIB	Exc.	V.G.	Good	Fair	Poor
750	650	600	525	450	375

Comp I

As above, with an attached compensator and a stippled front grip strap. Introduced in 1989.

NIB	Exc.	V.G.	Good	Fair	Poor
1350	1200	1000	850	700	500

Comp I Deluxe

As above, with a blued stainless steel slide, checkered grip straps, and a finer finishing.

NIB	Exc.	V.G.	Good	Fair	Poor
1650	1350	1150	950	800	600

COOPER ARMS
Stevensville, Montana

Model 36 Marksman

This is a premium bolt action rifle chambered for the .22 Long Rifle cartridge and in centerfire calibers of .17 CCM and .22 Hornet. The 23" Shilen barrel is mated to a solid bar stock receiver. High grade walnut is used in stocks that are fine-lined checkered.

Standard

NIB	Exc.	V.G.	Good	Fair	Poor
1400	800	700	500	300	200

Classic

NIB	Exc.	V.G.	Good	Fair	Poor
1600	1100	800	600	400	200

Custom Classic

NIB	Exc.	V.G.	Good	Fair	Poor
1900	1550	1150	850	600	300

BR-50 w/Jewell Trigger

NIB	Exc.	V.G.	Good	Fair	Poor
1800	1450	1100	800	600	300

IR-50-50 w/Jewell Trigger

NIB	Exc.	V.G.	Good	Fair	Poor
1800	1450	1100	800	600	300

Featherweight w/Jewell Trigger

NIB	Exc.	V.G.	Good	Fair	Poor
1800	1450	1100	800	600	300

Model 40

This bolt action rifle is chambered for the .17 AK Hornet, .22 K Hornet, or the .22 Hornet.

Classic

NIB	Exc.	V.G.	Good	Fair	Poor
1800	1500	1100	800	600	300

Custom Classic

NIB	Exc.	V.G.	Good	Fair	Poor
2000	1750	1250	850	600	300

Model 21

This bolt action rifle is chambered for the following cartridges: .221 Fireball, .222, .223, .6x45, 6x47, .17 Mach IV, and the .17 Rem. A 24" stainless steel Shilen match grade barrel is fitted. AAA claro walnut is used with oval forearm, ambidextrous palm swell, 22 line to the inch checkering, oil finish, and Pachmayr butt pad are all standard features. Weighs approximately 8 lbs.

Varmint Extreme

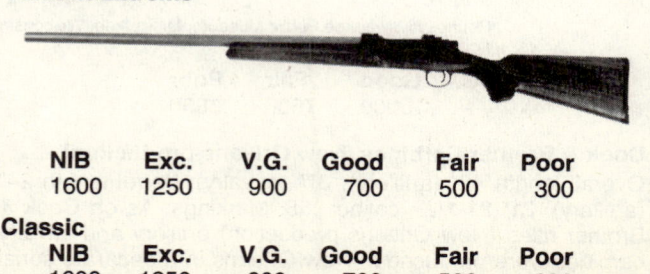

NIB	Exc.	V.G.	Good	Fair	Poor
1600	1250	900	700	500	300

Classic

NIB	Exc.	V.G.	Good	Fair	Poor
1600	1250	900	700	500	300

Custom Classic

NIB	Exc.	V.G.	Good	Fair	Poor
1900	1700	1300	850	600	300

Benchrest w/Jewell Trigger

NIB	Exc.	V.G.	Good	Fair	Poor
2100	1800	1300	900	650	325

Model 22

This is a bolt action single rifle chambered for a variety of calibers: 6.PPC, 22-250, .220 Swift, .243, .25-06, .308, .22 BR, 7.62X39, 6.5X55. A Pachmayr decelerator pad is standard. Weight is approximately 8.5 lbs.

Pro Varmint Extreme

NIB	Exc.	V.G.	Good	Fair	Poor
1750	1500	1200	800	600	300

Benchrest w/Jewell Trigger

NIB	Exc.	V.G.	Good	Fair	Poor
2100	1800	1300	900	650	325

Model 22 Repeater

Same as above but with magazine and chambered for .22-25, .308, 7mm-08, and .243.

Classic

NIB	Exc.	V.G.	Good	Fair	Poor
2400	2000	1750	1250	800	400

Custom Classic

NIB	Exc.	V.G.	Good	Fair	Poor
2650	2200	1850	1400	900	450

NOTE: There are a number of extra cost options that can effect the price of each of these models. Options such as Skelton butt plate, quarter ribs ribbon checkering etc. can add hundreds of dollars to the price of the gun. Check these options carefully before a sale.

COOPER, J. M. & CO.
Philadelphia, Pennsylvania

Pocket Revolver

A .31 caliber percussion double action revolver with 4", 5", or 6" octagonal barrel, and a 6-shot unfluted cylinder. Blued with walnut grips. During the first two years of production they were made in Pittsburgh, Pennsylvania, and were so marked. Approximately 15,000 were manufactured between 1864 and 1869.

Pittsburgh-Marked Models-Add 20%.

Courtesy Milwaukee Public Museum, Milwaukee, Wisconsin

Courtesy Milwaukee Public Museum, Milwaukee, Wisconsin

Exc.	V.G.	Good	Fair	Poor
1500	1000	500	250	150

COOPERATIVA OBRERA
Eibar, Spain

Longines

A 7.65mm caliber semiautomatic pistol. The slide is marked "Cal. 7.65 Automatic Pistol Longines."

Exc.	V.G.	Good	Fair	Poor
225	175	150	110	85

COPELAND, FRANK
Worcester, Massachusetts

Copeland Pocket Revolver .22

A .22 cartridge spur trigger revolver with a 2.5" barrel, 7-shot magazine, an unfluted cylinder and lock notches on the front. Frame is brass, blued walnut, or rosewood grips. The barrel marked "F. Copeland, Worcester, Mass." Manufactured in the 1860s.

Exc.	V.G.	Good	Fair	Poor
—	550	300	125	100

Copeland .32 Revolver

A .32 caliber spur trigger revolver with a 5-shot fluted cylinder and an iron frame. Nickel-plated. The barrel marked "F. Copeland, Sterling, Mass." Manufactured in the 1860s.

Exc.	V.G.	Good	Fair	Poor
—	550	300	150	75

COSMI, A. & F.
Torrette, Italy
Importer-New England Arms
Kittery Pt., Maine

Semiautomatic

A 12 and 20 gauge semiautomatic shotgun with various barrel lengths and chokes, an 8-shot magazine, and a ventilated rib. This is basically a custom-built, made-to-order gun. There is a standard and a deluxe model, with the differences being in the degree of embellishment.

Standard Model

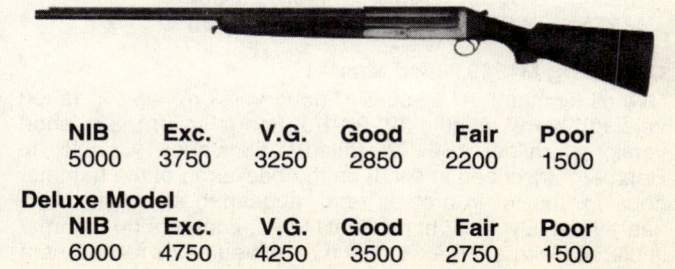

NIB	Exc.	V.G.	Good	Fair	Poor
5000	3750	3250	2850	2200	1500

Deluxe Model

NIB	Exc.	V.G.	Good	Fair	Poor
6000	4750	4250	3500	2750	1500

COSMOPOLITAN ARMS CO.
Hamilton, Ohio

Breech Loading Rifle

A .52 single shot percussion rifle with a 31" round barrel. The frame marked "Cosmopolitan Arms Co. Hamilton 0. U.S./Gross Patent." Blued with a walnut buttstock. Approximately 100 were made between 1859 and 1862.

Exc.	V.G.	Good	Fair	Poor
—		4000	1500	500

COWLES & SON
Chicopee, Massachusetts

Single Shot

A .22 or .30 caliber single shot spur trigger pistol with a 3.25" round barrel. Silver-plated brass frame, blued with walnut grip. Approximately 200 manufactured in 1865.

Exc.	V.G.	Good	Fair	Poor
—	950	400	250	100

CARL PHILLIP CRAUSE MUSKETS AND RIFLES
Herzberg, Germany

Carl Phillip Crause (who signed his products only with his last name) operated a gun manufactory in Herzberg on the Harz in the northwestern German kingdom of Hannover from the close of the Napoleonic Wars until 1857. The main production of his factory was devoted to military arms for Hannover and the surrounding principalities. Weapons of his manufacture included the Brunswick M1835 and M1848 rifles, the Hannovarian M1850 and M1854 rifle-muskets and yager rifles, and the M1840 and M1849 rifle-muskets of the Hanseatic League (a coalition of the north German states of Oldenberg, Hamburg, Bremen, and Lubeck). The latter two arms were subsequently altered to accept the elongated projectiles popular during the 1850s, and a few thousand evidently were imported into the United States and saw service during the American Civil War.

Hanseatic League M1840 Rifled Musket

Overall length 55-1/2"; barrel length 40-1/4"; caliber .70. Markings: on lockplate forward of hammer, "Crause in Herzberg" in script, the "s" in the archaic form, appearing as an "f." Of the 6,000 muskets of this type made, approximately half were sent to the United States in 1861 during the arms crisis that accompanied the outbreak of the American Civil War. A total of 2,680 of these were issued to Ohio and at least one regiment (the 56th Ohio) was armed with these rifled muskets. These arms were misidentified during the period as being Saxon due to the similarity of the large squared off foresection of the lockplate.

Courtesy Milwaukee Public Museum, Milwaukee, Wisconsin

Exc.	V.G.	Good	Fair	Poor
775	650	475	375	250

Oldenberg M1849 Rifled Musket

Overall lengths 55-1/2"-56-5/8" (long version), 49-1/2" (short version); barrel lengths 39"-39-1/8" (long version), 33" (short version); caliber .69-.72 (rifled). Markings: "Crause in Herzberg" inscribed in script on the backstrap of the hammer housing, the "s" in archaic form, appearing as an "f." Nicknamed the "Cyclops" because its large, center-hung hammer is pierced with a large window that served as its rear sight, a

few hundred of these clumsy rifled muskets may have been intermixed with the shipments of "Saxon" muskets imported in 1861 or 1862 into the United States during the American Civil War.

Courtesy Milwaukee Public Museum, Milwaukee, Wisconsin

Exc.	V.G.	Good	Fair	Poor
700	600	500	350	225

CRESCENT F. A. CO.
Norwich, Connecticut

This company manufactured good quality, inexpensive side-by-side and single barrel shotguns and was founded in 1893. They were bought by the H & D Folsom Arms Company of New York, importers and distributors of firearms and sporting goods.

After the purchase of Crescent, the Folsom Company was able to offer a complete range of shotguns, imported English, French, Belgium, and American made Crescents. By the turn of the century Crescent Arms produced huge quantities of "Hardware Guns". It produced guns under direct contract to distributors, mail order houses and hardware distributors with any brand name the customer requested. Crescent also produced guns for its parent company, as Folsom house brands that were sold to customers that did not want their own brand name.

By the late 1890s Crescent was producing basically five grades of double-barrel shotguns offering a model for most tastes. #2641 was a double bolt, top lever action, barlock with armory steel barrels and low circular hammers. This model came in 12 gauge only with either 30- or 32-inch Belgian made Damascus barrels; the rest being American made. #2650 this model is the same as 2641 but it has Damascus Belgian made barrels and was better finished. #2660 was also the same as 2641 however, it was fitted with American made Damascus barrels. #2655 was of the same basic design and was fitted with twist barrels with a Deeley & Edge snap forend. It has engraving on the triggerguard and locks and is somewhat better finished. #2665 has much more and better quality engraving, but was essentially the same as #2655. In 1904 Crescent added hammerless models with fluid steel barrels but they still offered the same line with a choice of hammers or not. Basically Crescent was able to mix and match barrel steels, engraving, checkering, wood and finish to provide a model for most tastes and still use the same basic design by changing the components. Various models could be ordered in 12, 16, 20, and 28 gauge, and .410.

The Crescent/Folsom Arms Company continued this type of business until 1930 when it merged with Davis-Warner Arms Corp. and became the Crescent-Davis Arms Corp. In 1932 its assets and machinery were bought by Stevens Arms Company, a victim of changing tastes and the Depression.

DOUBLES

Triumph-Hammerless Boxlock

Exc.	V.G.	Good	Fair	Poor
700	600	400	300	200

Model 2655-Laminated Barrels Hammer Sidelock

Exc.	V.G.	Good	Fair	Poor
500	400	300	200	150

Model 2665-Damascus Barrels Hammer Sidelock

Exc.	V.G.	Good	Fair	Poor
500	400	300	200	150

Knickerbocker No. 6 Armory-Hammerless Sidelock

Exc.	V.G.	Good	Fair	Poor
400	300	250	200	100

Knickerbocker No. 7 Hammerless Sidelock

Exc.	V.G.	Good	Fair	Poor
400	300	250	200	100

Knickerbocker No. 8-Damascus Barrels Hammerless Sidelock

Exc.	V.G.	Good	Fair	Poor
500	400	300	250	200

American Gun Co. NY No. 1 Armory-Hammerless Sidelock

Exc.	V.G.	Good	Fair	Poor
400	300	250	200	100

American Gun Co. NY No. 2-Hammerless Sidelock

Exc.	V.G.	Good	Fair	Poor
500	400	300	250	200

American Gun Co. No. 3-Damascus Barrels Hammer Sidelock

Exc.	V.G.	Good	Fair	Poor
600	500	400	300	250

American Gun Co. No. 4-Hammer Sidelock

Exc.	V.G.	Good	Fair	Poor
700	600	500	400	300

American Gun Co. No. 5-Damascus Barrels Hammer Sidelock

Exc.	V.G.	Good	Fair	Poor
800	700	600	450	350

American Machine Made 2641-Hammer Sidelock

Exc.	V.G.	Good	Fair	Poor
400	350	300	250	200

American Machine Made 2650-Hammer Sidelock

Exc.	V.G.	Good	Fair	Poor
500	400	350	300	250

American Machine Made 2660-Damascus Barrels Hammer Sidelock

Exc.	V.G.	Good	Fair	Poor
600	500	450	350	300

Folsom Arms Co. No. 0 Armory-Hammer Sidelock

Exc.	V.G.	Good	Fair	Poor
400	300	250	200	100

Folsom Arms Co. No. 2-Hammer Sidelock

Exc.	V.G.	Good	Fair	Poor
500	400	300	200	150

Folsom Arms Co. No. 3 Damascus Barrel

Exc.	V.G.	Good	Fair	Poor
600	450	350	300	200

New Knickerbocker Armory-Hammerless Sidelock

Exc.	V.G.	Good	Fair	Poor
400	300	250	200	100

New Knickerbocker WT-Hammerless Sidelock

Exc.	V.G.	Good	Fair	Poor
450	350	250	200	150

New Knickerbocker Damascus Barrels-Hammerless Sidelock

Exc.	V.G.	Good	Fair	Poor
500	400	300	250	200

American Gun Co. Small Bore No. 28 Straight Stock-Hammer Sidelock

Exc.	V.G.	Good	Fair	Poor
800	700	600	400	300

American Gun Co. Small Bore No. 44 Straight Stock-Hammer Sidelock

Exc.	V.G.	Good	Fair	Poor
900	750	650	450	350

American Gun Co. No. 0 Armory Straight Stock-Hammer Sidelock

Exc.	V.G.	Good	Fair	Poor
350	300	250	200	100

American Gun Co. No. 28 Nitro Straight Stock-Hammer Sidelock

Exc.	V.G.	Good	Fair	Poor
800	650	550	400	300

American Gun Co. No. 44 Nitro Straight Stock-Hammer Sidelock

Exc.	V.G.	Good	Fair	Poor
900	750	600	450	350

American Gun Co. Midget Field No. 28-Hammer Sidelock

Exc.	V.G.	Good	Fair	Poor
800	650	400	400	300

American Gun Co. Midget Field No. 44-Hammer Sidelock

Exc.	V.G.	Good	Fair	Poor
900	750	650	500	350

Crescent 1922 Model No. 66 Quali-Hammerless Sidelock

Exc.	V.G.	Good	Fair	Poor
600	500	450	350	250

Crescent American Hammer Gun No. 0-Hammer Sidelock

Exc.	V.G.	Good	Fair	Poor
350	300	250	200	100

Crescent Firearms Co. No. 0-Hammer Sidelock

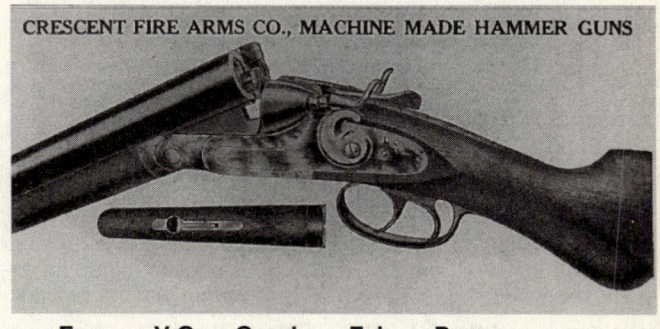

Exc.	V.G.	Good	Fair	Poor
400	350	250	200	150

Crescent Firearms Co. No. 0 Nickel-Hammer Sidelock

Exc.	V.G.	Good	Fair	Poor
500	400	350	250	200

Crescent Firearms Co. No. 6 Peerless-Hammerless Sidelock

Exc.	V.G.	Good	Fair	Poor
400	350	250	200	150

Crescent Firearms Co. No. 6E Peerless Engraved-Hammerless Sidelock

Exc.	V.G.	Good	Fair	Poor
600	450	350	250	200

Crescent Firearms Co. No. 66 Quali-Hammerless Sidelock

Exc.	V.G.	Good	Fair	Poor
650	500	400	300	200

Crescent Firearms Co. No. 60 Empire-Hammerless Sidelock

Exc.	V.G.	Good	Fair	Poor
450	400	350	300	200

Crescent Firearms Co. No. 6 Peerless-Hammerless Sidelock

Exc.	V.G.	Good	Fair	Poor
400	350	300	200	150

Crescent Firearms Co. No. 44 Improved-Hammer Sidelock

Exc.	V.G.	Good	Fair	Poor
700	600	500	400	300

New Crescent Empire Red Butt-Hammerless Sidelock

Exc.	V.G.	Good	Fair	Poor
400	350	250	200	150

Crescent New Empire No. 88-Hammerless Sidelock

Exc.	V.G.	Good	Fair	Poor
400	350	250	200	150

Crescent New Empire No. 9-Hammerless Sidelock

Exc.	V.G.	Good	Fair	Poor
350	300	250	200	100

Crescent Empire No. 60-Hammerless Sidelock

Exc.	V.G.	Good	Fair	Poor
350	300	250	200	100

Crescent Certified Empire No. 60-Hammerless Sidelock

Exc.	V.G.	Good	Fair	Poor
400	300	250	200	150

Crescent Certified Empire No. 9-Hammerless Sidelock

Exc.	V.G.	Good	Fair	Poor
450	350	300	250	200

Crescent Certified Empire No. 88-Hammerless Sidelock

Exc.	V.G.	Good	Fair	Poor
500	450	400	350	300

Crescent Davis No. 600-Hammerless Boxlock

Exc.	V.G.	Good	Fair	Poor
400	350	300	250	200

Crescent Davis No. 900-Hammerless Boxlock

Exc.	V.G.	Good	Fair	Poor
500	450	400	350	300

Single Shot

Made in 12, 16, 20, and 28 gauge and .410. Barrel lengths were 26", 28", 30", and 32", with various chokes. It had an exposed hammer, fluid steel barrel, and walnut pistol grip stock.

Exc.	V.G.	Good	Fair	Poor
150	125	100	75	50

Revolver

A typical S&W copy made by Crescent in Norwich, Connecticut. It was a top-break, double action, that was found either blued or nickel-plated with checkered, black hard rubber grips. The cylinder held 5 shots and was chambered for the .32 S&W cartridge.

Exc.	V.G.	Good	Fair	Poor
175	150	125	85	40

Crescent Certified Shotgun NFA, CURIO OR RELIC

The Crescent Certified Shotgun is a .410 smooth bore shot pistol with a 12.25" barrel manufactured from approximately 1930 to 1932 by the Crescent-Davis Arms Corp., Norwich, Connecticut, and possibly thereafter until 1934 by the J. Stevens Arms Co., which purchased the company. In various distributor catalogs it is termed the "Ever-Ready" Model 200, and advertised with a blued frame. Specimens have been observed with "tiger-stripe" (like an H&R Handy-Gun) or Colt SAA or Winchester-type case hardening. Total production is unknown but serial numbers ranging from 1305 to 3262 have been observed, suggesting it may have been fewer than 4,000. The government ruled the .410 Crescent to be a "firearm" in the "any other weapon" category under the NFA in 1934, when its retail price was about $11.

Exc.	V.G.	Good	Fair	Poor
850	650	500	350	250

NOTE: Add $100 to $300 for original cardboard box.

The barrel is marked **_PROOF TESTED 410 GAUGE_** on top and **2?IN SHELLS** on the middle left side. The receiver's left side is stamped **CRESCENT CERTIFIED SHOTGUN/CRESCENT-DAVIS ARMS CORPORATION/NORWICH, CONN., U.S.A.** The earliest guns also have **.410** stamped at the top of the left side of the receiver near the breech, but this marking does not appear on later guns. It is a rather heavy (57 oz. unloaded) handgun.

These materials are copyright © 1998 by Eric M. Larson, printed in the *Catalog* by permission of the copyright holder, and will appear in a forthcoming book on pre-NFA smooth bore shot pistols (see H&R Handy-Gun entry).

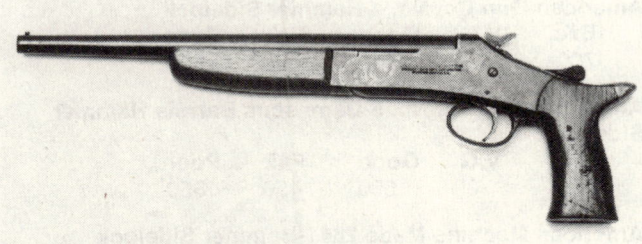

Exc.	V.G.	Good	Fair	Poor
850	650	500	350	250

NOTE: Add $100 to $300 for original cardboard box.

Crescent Auto & Burglar Gun CURIO OR RELIC, NFA

The Crescent Auto & Burglar Gun is a hammerless .410 bore or 20 gauge smooth bore pistol with 12.25" double barrels. The trigger guard and double triggers designs are identical to those of the .410 Crescent Certified Shotgun. An extremely rare firearm whose total production and years of manufacture are unknown at this time, its only known documentation is an advertisement by "Saul Ruben, The Gun Store, 68 E. Long St., Columbus, Ohio," on page 44 of the October 1932 issue of **_Hunter-Trader-Trapper_**, which lists a $14.75 retail price. At this time, four specimens are known, all in .410 bore, bearing serial numbers S-1, S-13, S-18, and S-19. The serial number appears under the forestock on the metal. The left side of its receiver is marked **Crescent Fire Arms Co./Norwich, Conn. U.S.A.**, and the right side is stamped **NEW EMPIRE**. Establishing a reliable value may be difficult, but could be logically expected to approximate those for a nonstandard or special-order Ithaca Auto & Burglar Gun. The Crescent Auto & Burglar Gun may have been distributed by the H.&D. Folsom Arms Co. of New York City through its manufacturing division, the Crescent Firearms Co., Norwich, Connecticut. Crescent's sellers included the Belknap Hardware Co., Louisville, Kentucky, and Hibbard-Spencer-Bartlett Co., Chicago, Illinois. This writer would like to communicate with anyone who may own or have owned a Crescent Auto & Burglar Gun, to better document this firearm.

These materials are copyright © 1998 by Eric M. Larson, printed in the *Catalog* by permission of the copyright holder, and will appear in a forthcoming book on pre-NFA smooth bore shot pistols (see H&R Handy-Gun entry).

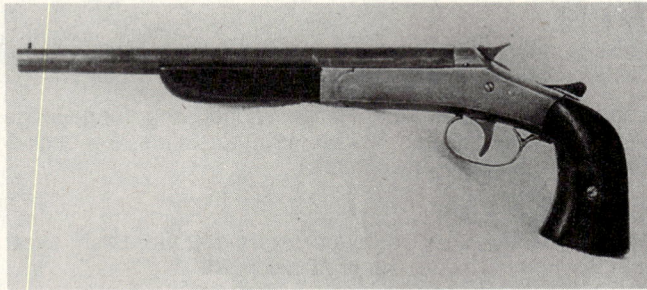

Victor Ejector Pistol NFA

The Victor Ejector Pistol is a .410 smooth bore shot pistol with a 12" barrel manufactured sometime before 1930 by the Crescent Fire Arms Co. of Norwich, Connecticut. This firearm apparently is not listed in any Crescent or other trade catalog, and total production is unknown. It may be a predecessor or factory prototype of the Crescent Certified Shotgun .410 pistol, because both were manufactured by Crescent, and most design features are identical. The single known example of the Victor Ejector Pistol bears serial number 755004. Because of its extreme rarity, a reliable value cannot be determined at this time.

The left side of the receiver is stamped **Victor Ejector/Crescent Fire Arms Co./Norwich, Conn. U.S.A.**; and **.410** is stamped at the top left side of the receiver near the breech, as in the earliest variatons of the Crescent Certified Shotgun. The barrel is stamped GENUINE ARMORY STEEL on the top near the breech, chambered only for 2.5" shells, with serial number 755004 stamped on the left side of the barrel lug. The configuration of the receiver, trigger guard, barrel latch lever, and wooden forend (the number 5004 is stamped on the forend metal) are indistinguishable from that of the Crescent Certified Shotgun.

The major differences between the Victor Ejector and Crescent Certified Shotgun is the latter's (1) pistol grip style, and (2) weight. The Victor pistol grip represents the average that would result from combining the Colt Single Action Army and Colt Bisley grips. The Victor is unusually heavy--exactly 74 oz. (about 4.6 lbs) unloaded, versus 57 oz. (about 3.5 lbs) for the Crescent. Whether the pistol grip part of the receiver was brazed on or cast with the rest of the receiver is unclear, and additional specimens of this firearm may shed some light on this question. The Victor Ejector was probably redesigned to eliminate some of the weight.

These materials are copyright © 1998 by Eric M. Larson, printed in the *Catalog* by permission of the copyright holder, and will appear in a forthcoming book on pre-NFA smooth bore shot pistols (see H&R Handy-Gun entry). This writer would like to communicate with people who own or may have owned other specimens of this firearm so its history can be better documented.

BRAND NAMES USED BY CRESCENT ARMS

American Bar Lock Wonder made for Sears, Roebuck & Co.

American Boy made for Townley Metal & Hardware Co.

American Gun Co. (H & D Folsom house brand)

American Gun Company of New York

American Nitro

Armory Gun Co.

Baker Gun Co. (if no foreign proof marks)

T. Barker New York-if a sidelock hammerless double.

Bellmore Gun Co.

Berkshire No. 3000 made for Shapleigh Hardware Co. of St. Louis, MO

Black Beauty-hammerless doubles

Bluefield Clipper

Bluegrass Arms Co. made for Belknap Hardware Co. of Louisville, KY

Blue Whistler

Bridge Black Prince

Bridge Gun Co.

Bridge Gun Works

Bridgeport Arms Co. (if no foreign proof marks)

Bright Arms Co.

Canadian Belle

Carolina Arms Co. made for Smith Wadsworth Hardware Co. of Charlotte, NC

Caroline Arms

Central Arm Co. made for Shapleigh Hardware Co. of St. Louis, MO

Chatham Arms Co.

Cherokee Arms Co. made for C. M. McClung Co. of Knoxville, TN

Chesapeake Gun Co.

Chicago Long Range Wonder 1908-1918 made for Sears, Roebuck & Co. of Chicago, IL

Colonial

Columbian New York Arms Co.

Compeer made for Van Camp Hardware & Iron Co. of Indianapolis, IN

Connecticut Arms Co.

Cumberland Arms Co.

Crescent Fire Arms Co.

Creve Cour (if no foreign proof marks) made for Isaac Walker Hardware Co. of Peoria, IL

Cruso

Daniel Boone Gun Co. made for Belknap Hardware Co. of Louisville, KY

Delphian Arms Co. (some models without foreign proof marks) made for Supplee-Biddle Hardware Co. of Philadelphia, PA

Delphian Manufacturing Co. (some models)

Diamond Arms Co. (some models) made for Shapleigh Hardware Co. of St. Louis, MO

Dunlap Special made for Dunlap Hardware Co. of Macon, GA

E.C. Mac made for E.C. Meacham Arms Co. of St. Louis, MO

Elgin Arms Co. made for Strauss & Schram and Fred Biffar & Co. both of Chicago, IL

Elmira Arms Co.

Empire Arms Co. made for Sears, Roebuck & Co. of Chicago, IL

Empire State Arms Co.

Enders Oakleaf made for Shapleigh Hardware Co. of St. Louis, MO

Enders Special Service made for Shapleigh Hardware Co.

Enders Royal Service made for Shapleigh Hardware Co.

Essex made for Belknap Hardware Co. of Louisville, KY

Excel made for Montgomery Ward & Co. of Chicago, IL

Farwell Arms Co. made for Farwell, Ozmun & Kirk of St. Paul, MN

Faultless made for John M. Smythe Co. of Chicago, IL

Faultless Goose Gun made for John M. Smyth Co. of Chicago, IL

The Field after 1894

Folsom Arms Co. (also used by H & D Folsom on Belgian imports)

F.F. Forbes (H & D Folsom house brand)

Fort Pitt Arms Co.

Fremont Arms Co. (also used on Belgian imports)

Gold Medal Wonder

Greenfield (some models) made for Hibbard, Spencer, Bartlett & Co. of Chicago, IL

H.B.C. (some models) made for Hudson's Bay Co. of Canada.

H.S.B. & Co. (some models) made for Hibbard, Spencer,

Bartlett & Co. of Chicago, IL

Hanover Arms Co. (if no foreign proof marks)

S.H. Harrington (if no foreign proof marks)

Hartford Arms Co. made for both Simmons Hardware and Shapleigh Hardware Co. of St. Louis, MO

Harvard (H & D Folsom house brand)

Hermitage (some models) made for Grey-Dusley Hardware Co. of Nashville, TN

Hip Spe Bar (some models) made for Hibbard, Spencer, Bartlett & Co. of Chicago, IL

Hibbard (some models) made for Hibbard, Spencer, Bartlett & Co. of Chicago, IL

Howard Arms Co. made for Fred Biffar & Co. of Chicago, IL

Hudson (some models) made for Hibbard, Spencer, Bartlett & Co. of Chicago, IL

Hunter made for Belknap Hardware Co. Louisville, KY

Interstate Arms Co. made for Townley Metal & Hardware Co. of Kansas City, MO

Jackson Arms Co. made for C.M. McClung & Co. of Knoxville, TN

Joseph Arms Co. Norwich, Conn.

K K and Keen Kufter (some models) made for Shapleigh Hardware Co. of St. Louis, MO

Kingsland Special and Kingsland 10 Star made for Geller, Ward & Hasner of St. Louis, MO

Kirk Gun Co. made for Farwell, Ozmun & Kirk of St. Paul, MN

Knickerbocker (up to 1915, H & D Folsom house brand)

Knockabout (before 1925) made for Montgomery Ward & Co. of Chicago, IL

Knoxall (only hammerless doubles)

Laclede Gun Co.

Lakeside made for Montgomery Ward & Co. of Chicago, IL

Leader Gun Co. made for Charles Williams Stores of New York, NY

Lee's Special and Lee's Munner Special made for Lee Hardware Co. of Salina, KS

Long Range Marvel, Long Range Winner, and Long Range Wonder made between 1893 to 1909 for Sears, Roebuck & Co. of Chicago, IL F.A. Loomis

Marshwood

Massachusetts Arms Co. made before 1920 for Blish, Mizet and Silliman Hardware Co. of Atchison, KS

Mears (if no foreign proof marks)

Metropolitan made for Siegal-Cooper Co. of New York, NY

Minnesota Arms Co. made for Farwell, Ozmun, Kirk & Co. of St. Paul, MN

Mississippi Arms Co. St. Louis (some models) made for Shepleigh Hardware Co. of St. Louis, MO

Mississippi Valley Arms Co. (some models) made for Shapleigh Hardware Co. of St. Louis, MO

Mohawk made for Glish, Mizet and Lilliman Hardware Co. of Atchinson, KS

Monitor

R. Murdock, National Firearms Co. (some models)

National Arms Co. hammer doubles (without foreign proof marks) and hammerless doubles made for May Hardware Co. of Washington, D.C. and Moskowitz and Herbach Co. of Philadelphia, PA

New Britain Arms Co.'s Monarch

New Elgin Arms Co.

New Empire

New England (some models after 1914) made for Sears, Roebuck & Co.

New England Arms Co. (some models)

Newport Model CN made for Hibbard, Spencer, Bartlett and Co. of Chicago

Newport Model WN (some models) made for Hibbard, Spencer, Bartlett and Co. of Chicago

New Rival made for Van Camp Hardware and Iron Co. of Indianapolis, IN

New York Arms Co. made for Garnet Carter Co. of Chattanooga, TN

New York Machine Made (some models)

New York Match Gun (some models)

New York Nitro Hammerless

Nitro Bird made for Conover Hardware Co. of Kansas City, MO

Nitro Hunter made for Belknap Hardware Co. of Louisville, KY

Nitro King 1908 to 1917 made for Sears, Roebuck & Co. of Chicago, IL

Norwich Arms Co.

Not-Noc Manufacturing Co. made for Belknap Hardware Co. of Louisville, KY and Canton Hardware Co. of Canton, OH

Osprey made for Lou J. Eppinger, Detroit, MI

Oxford made for Belknap Hardware Co. of Louisville, KY

Peerless (H & D Folsom house brand)

Perfection made for H. G. Lipscomb & Co. of Nashville, TN
Piedmont made for Piedmont Hardware Co. of Danville, PA

Piedmont Arms Co.

Pioneer Arms (if no foreign proof marks) made for Kruse and Baklmann Hardware Co. of Cincinnati, OH

No. 66—410 GAUGE QUAIL MODEL

Quail (H & D Folsom house brand)

Queen City made for Elmira Arms Co. of Elmira, NY

Red Chieftan (model 60) made for Supplee Biddle Hardware Co. of Philadelphia, PA

Rev-O-Noc (some models) made for Hibbard, Spencer, Bartlett & Go. of Chicago, IL

Rich-Con made for Richardson & Conover Hardware Co.

Charles Richter (some models) made for New York Sporting Goods Co. of New York, NY

Rickard Arms Co. made for J. A. Rickard Co. of Schenectady, NY

Rival (some models) made for Van Camp Hardware and Iron Co.of Indianapolis, IN

Rocket Special

Royal Service made for Shapleigh Hardware Co. of St. Louis, MO

Rummel Arms Co. made for A. J. Rummel Arms Co. of Toledo, OH

Ruso (if no foreign proof marks)

St. Louis Arms Co. (sidelock hammerless doubles) made for Shapleigh Hardware Co. of St. Louis, MO

Seminole (hammerless) unknown

Shue's Special made for Ira M. Shue of Hanover, PA

Smithsonian (some models)

John M. Smythe & Co. made for John M. Smythe Hardware Co. of Chicago, IL

Southern Arms Co. (some models)

Special Service made for Shapleigh Hardware Co. of St. Louis, MO

Spencer Gun Co. made for Hibbard, Spencer, Bartlett & Co. of Chicago, IL

Sportsman (some models) made for W. Bingham & Co. of Cleveland, OH

Springfield Arms Co. used until 1930. (H & D Folsom house brand). This brand was also used by Stevens and James Warner guns.

Square Deal made for Stratton, Warren Hardware Co. of Memphis, TN

Star Leader (some models)

State Arms Co. made for J.H. Lau & Co. of New York, NY

sterling Arms Co.

Sullivan Arms Co. made for Sullivan Hardware Co. of Anderson, SC

Superior (some models) made for Paxton & Gallagher Co. of Omaha, NE

Syco (some models) made for Wyeth Hardware Co. of St. Joseph, MO

Ten Star & Ten Star Heavy Duty (if no foreign proof marks) made for Geller, Ward & Hasner Co. of St. Louis, MO

Tiger (if no foreign proof marks) made for J.H. Hall & Co. of Nashville, TN

Townley's Pal and Townley's American Boy made for Townley Metal & Hardware Co. of Kansas City, MO

Trap's Best made for Watkins, Cottrell Co. of Richmond, VA

Triumph (some models) made for Sears, Roebuck & Co. of Chicago, IL

Tryon Special (some models) made for Edward K. Tryon Co. of Philadelphia, PA

U.S. Arms Co. (if no foreign proof marks) made for Supplee-Biddle Hardware Co. of Philadelphia, PA

U.S. Field

Utica Firearms Co. (some models) made for Simmons Hardware Co. of St. Louis, MO

Victor & Victor Special made for Hibbard, Spencer, Bartlett & Co. of Chicago, IL

Virginia Arms Co. made for Virginia-Carolina Co. of Richmond, VA

Volunteer (some models) made for Belknap Hardware Co. of Louisville, KY

Vulcan Arms Co. made for Edward K. Tryon Co. of Philadelphia, PA

Warren Arms Co. (if no foreign proof marks)

Washington Arms Co. (some models)

Wauregan (some models)

Wautauga (some models) made for Wallace Hardware Co. Morristown, TN

Wildwood made for Sears, Roebuck & Co. of Chicago, IL

Wilkinson Arms Co. (if no foreign proof marks) made for

Richmond Hardware Co. of Richmond, VA

Wilshire Arms Co. made for Stauffer, Eshleman & Co. of New Orleans, LA

Winfield Arms Co. (H & D Folsom house brand)

Winoca Arms Co. made for Jacobi Hardware Co. of Philadelphia, PA

Witte Hardware Co. (some models) made for Witte Hardware Co. of St. Louis, MO

Wolverine Arms Co. made for Fletcher Hardware Co. of Wilmington, NC

Worthington Arms Co. made for George Worthington Co. of Cleveland, OH

CRISPIN, SILAS
New York, New York

Crispin Revolver

A .32 Crispin caliber 5- or 6-shot revolver produced in limited quantities. Some are marked "Smith Arms Co., New York City.

Crispin's Pat. Oct. 3, 1865." The most noteworthy feature of these revolvers is that the cylinder is constructed in two pieces so that the belted Crispin cartridge can be used. It is believed that these revolvers were only made on an experimental basis, between 1865 and 1867.

Exc.	V.G.	Good	Fair	Poor
—	—	10000	5000	2500

CRUCELEGUI, HERMANOS
Eibar, Spain

A 5mm, 6.35mm, 7.65mm, and 8mm caliber double-action revolver. The trade names used were; Puppy, Velo-Mith, LeBrong, Bron-Sport, C.H., and Brong-Petit.

Exc.	V.G.	Good	Fair	Poor
125	100	80	60	35

CUMMINGS, O. S.
Lowell, Massachusetts

Cummings Pocket Revolver

A .22 caliber spur trigger revolver with a 3.5" ribbed round barrel, and a 7-shot fluted cylinder. Nickel-plated with rosewood grip. The barrel is stamped "O.S. Cummings Lowell, Mass." Approximately 1,000 manufactured in the 1870s.

Exc.	V.G.	Good	Fair	Poor
—	650	300	150	100

CUMMINGS & WHEELER
Lowell, Massachusetts

Pocket Revolver

Similar to the Cummings Pocket Revolver with subtle differences such as the length of the flutes on the cylinder and the size and shape of the grip. The barrel is slightly longer and is marked "Cummings & Wheeler, Lowell, Mass."

Exc.	V.G.	Good	Fair	Poor
—	700	350	150	100

CUSTOM GUN GUILD
Doraville, Georgia

Wood Model IV

A falling block single shot rifle produced in a number of popular calibers with barrel lengths from 22" to 28". The stock of select checkered walnut. This is a lightweight rifle, at approximately 5.5 lbs. It was manufactured for one year only, 1984, and is not often encountered on today's market.

Exc.	V.G.	Good	Fair	Poor
3250	2750	2500	1750	1000

D

D (anchor) C

(probably either "Dejardine & Cie," "L. Demousse & Cie,"
or
"DeFooze & Cie," all of Liege, Belgium
SEE-English Military Firearms

D. W. M.

Berlin, Germany
ALSO SEE-Luger & Borchardt

Model 22

A 7.65mm caliber semiautomatic pistol with 3.5" barrel. Blued with walnut grips; later changed to plastic grips. Approximately 40,000 manufactured between 1921 and 1931.

Exc.	V.G.	Good	Fair	Poor
750	675	500	400	250

DAEWOO

Pusan, Korea
Importer-Kimber of America
Yonkers, New York

DH-40

This semi-automatic pistol is chambered for the .40 S&W cartridge. It has a 4.13" barrel and a magazine capacity of 11 rounds. Weight is approximately 32 oz.

NIB	Exc.	V.G.	Good	Fair	Poor
425	375	300	250	175	100

DP-51B

This semi-automatic pistol is chambered for the 9mm cartridge and is fitted with a 4.13" barrel. Magazine capacity is 13 rounds. Overall length is 7.5" and weight is approximately 28 oz.

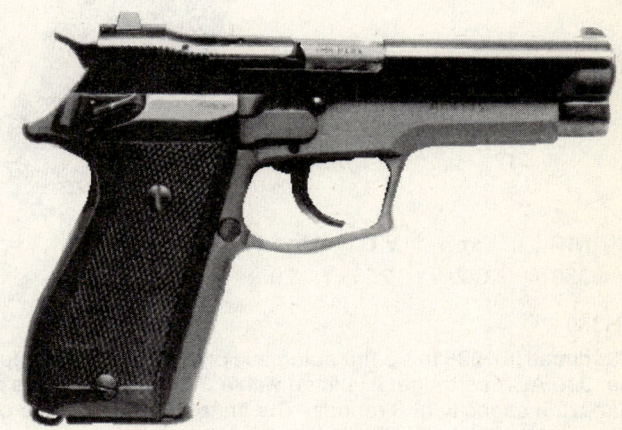

NIB	Exc.	V.G.	Good	Fair	Poor
375	325	275	225	175	100

DP-51SB

This is a more compact design with 3.6" barrel and 10-round magazine. Weight is 27 oz. Stainless steel finish.

NIB	Exc.	V.G.	Good	Fair	Poor
400	350	275	225	175	100

DP-51CB

Same as above but fitted with a 3.6" barrel. Magazine capacity is 10 rounds. Weight is about 26 oz.

NIB	Exc.	V.G.	Good	Fair	Poor
425	375	300	250	175	100

DP-52

This semi-automatic pistol is chambered for the .22 Long Rifle cartridge. It has a 3.82" barrel length and a magazine capacity of 10 rounds. It operates in double action and single action modes. Overall length is 6.7" and weight is approximately 23 oz.

NIB	Exc.	V.G.	Good	Fair	Poor
350	300	250	200	150	100

DH380

Introduced in 1996 this semi-automatic pistol is chambered for the .380 ACP cartridge. It is fitted with a 3.8" barrel and has a magazine capacity of 8 rounds. The firing model is double or single action. Weight is approximately 24 oz.

NIB	Exc.	V.G.	Good	Fair	Poor
375	325	275	225	150	100

DR200

Introduced in 1996 this semi-automatic rifle is chambered for the .223 Rem. cartridge. It features a black matte finish with a synthetic thumbhole stock. Barrel length is 18.3". Uses AR15 magazines not included with the rifle. Weight is about 9 lbs.

NIB	Exc.	V.G.	Good	Fair	Poor
675	625	500	400	300	150

Max I

A 5.56mm caliber semiautomatic rifle with an 18" barrel, gas operated rotary bolt action, magazines interchangeable with those from the M-16. Black. Introduced in 1985, but is no longer imported.

Max II

This rifle is quite similar to the Max I with a folding composite stock.

DAISY
Rogers, Arkansas

WL Rifle

A .22 combustible cartridge single shot rifle with an 18" barrel and plastic stock. Cartridge is ignited by compressed air. Manufactured during 1968 and 1969. It is believed that less than 20,000 were made.

NIB	Exc.	V.G.	Good	Fair	Poor
125	100	85	75	50	25

VL Presentation Model

As above, with a walnut stock. Approximately 4,000 were made in 1968 and 1969.

NIB	Exc.	V.G.	Good	Fair	Poor
175	150	125	100	75	50

WL Cased Presentation Model

As above, with a gold plaque inlaid in the stock and with a fitted case containing 300 VL cartridges.

NIB	Exc.	V.G.	Good	Fair	Poor
250	200	175	125	100	75

Model 2201/2211

A bolt action single shot rifle chambered for .22 long rifle cartridge. Fitted with a 19" barrel with octagon shroud. Ramp blade front sight with adjustable notch rear sight. Synthetic stock on Model 2211 and walnut stock on Model 2201. Trigger is adjustable. Weight is about 6.5 lbs.

NIB	Exc.	V.G.	Good	Fair	Poor
125	100	75	60	50	25

NOTE: Add $10 for synthtic stock.

Model 2202/2212

Similar to the above model in appearance but fitted with a 10-round rotary magazine. The synthetic stock is Model 2212 and the walnut stock is Model 2202. Weight is about 6.5 lbs.

NIB	Exc.	V.G.	Good	Fair	Poor
135	100	75	60	50	25

NOTE: Add $10 for synthetic stock.

Model 2203/2213

This is a semi-automatic rifle chambered for .22 long rifle cartridge. Has a 7-round magazine and a 19" barrel. The synthetic stock is Model 2213 and the walnut stock is Model 2203. Weight is approximately 6.5 lbs.

NIB	Exc.	V.G.	Good	Fair	Poor
135	100	75	60	50	25

NOTE: Add $10 for synthetic stock.

DAKIN GUN CO.
San Francisco, California

Model 100

A 12 and 20 gauge boxlock double-barrel shotgun with 26" or 28" barrels, various chokes, extractors and double triggers. Engraved, blued, with a checkered walnut stock. Manufactured in the 1960s.

Exc.	V.G.	Good	Fair	Poor
400	325	275	200	100

Model 147

As above, with ventilated rib barrels.

Exc.	V.G.	Good	Fair	Poor
450	375	250	200	100

Model 160

As above with a single selective trigger.

Exc.	V.G.	Good	Fair	Poor
475	400	350	250	150

Model 215

As above, but more finely finished.

Exc.	V.G.	Good	Fair	Poor
950	850	700	500	250

Model 170

A 12, 16, and 20 gauge Over/Under shotgun with 26" or 28" ventilated rib barrels, various chokes, and double triggers. Blued and lightly engraved. Discontinued in the 1960s.

Exc.	V.G.	Good	Fair	Poor
500	425	350	275	150

DAKOTA ARMS, INC.
Sturgis, South Dakota

This company was formed by Don Allen, Inc., and H.L. Grisel, Inc. Both were fine craftsmen in the field of custom rifles. They offer four basic models with a number of options to fit the customers' needs or wants. The workmanship and materials are of the highest quality. They have been in business since 1987.

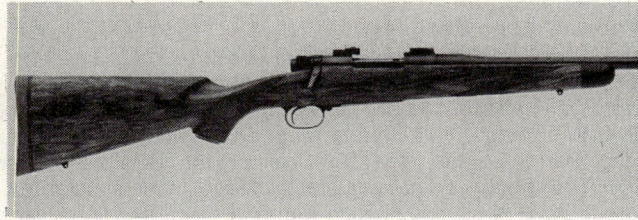

Dakota 76 Classic

A .257 Roberts, .270 Winchester, .280 Remington, .3006, 7mm Remington Magnum, .338, .300 Winchester Magnum, and the .458 Winchester Magnum bolt-action rifle with a 23" barrel, and Mauser-type extractor. Checkered walnut stock. Manufactured in 1987.

NIB	Exc.	V.G.	Good	Fair	Poor
2000	1750	1500	950	800	400

Dakota 76 Varmint

Introduced in 1996 this rifle is chambered for a variety of cartridges from the .22 Hornet to the 6mm PPC. This is a single shot bolt action design available in right or left hand versions. Barrel length is 24". The Varmint style stock is semi-fancy walnut with oil finish and no checkering. Many extra cost options are offered for this model.

NIB	Exc.	V.G.	Good	Fair	Poor
2500	2200	1650	1100	850	400

Varmint Grade

Offered in a wide variety of calibers from the .222 Rem. to the .22-250 Rem. Furnished with X grade English walnut.

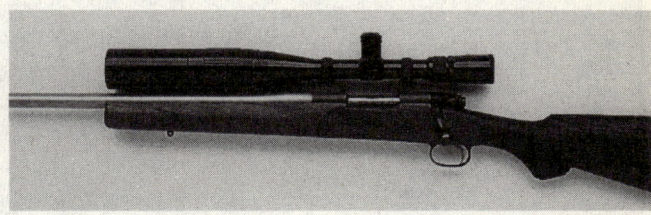

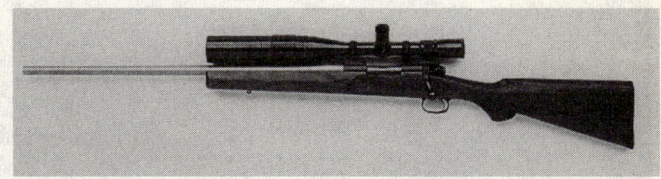

NIB	Exc.	V.G.	Good	Fair	Poor
2000	1850	1500	1200	900	400

Safari Grade

As above, in .375 Holland & Holland, .458 Winchester Magnum, and other short Magnum calibers with an ebony forend tip, one-piece magazine assembly and features open sights. Weighs approximately 8-1/2 lbs.

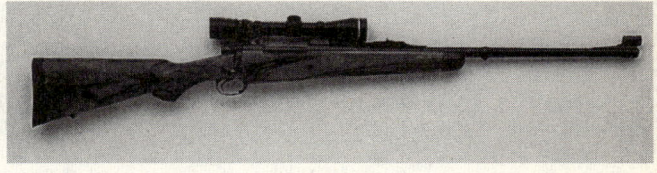

NIB	Exc.	V.G.	Good	Fair	Poor
2750	2200	1700	1200	950	400

Alpine Grade

As above, but lighter in weight and chambered for .22-250, .243, 6mm, 250-3000, 7mm/08, .308, and .358. Introduced in 1989.

NIB	Exc.	V.G.	Good	Fair	Poor
1850	1750	1400	1250	800	400

African Grade

As above in .416 Rigby, .416 Dakota, .404 Jeffery, and .450 Dakota with walnut especially selected for strength, with crossbolts through the stock. Weighs between 9 and 10 lbs.

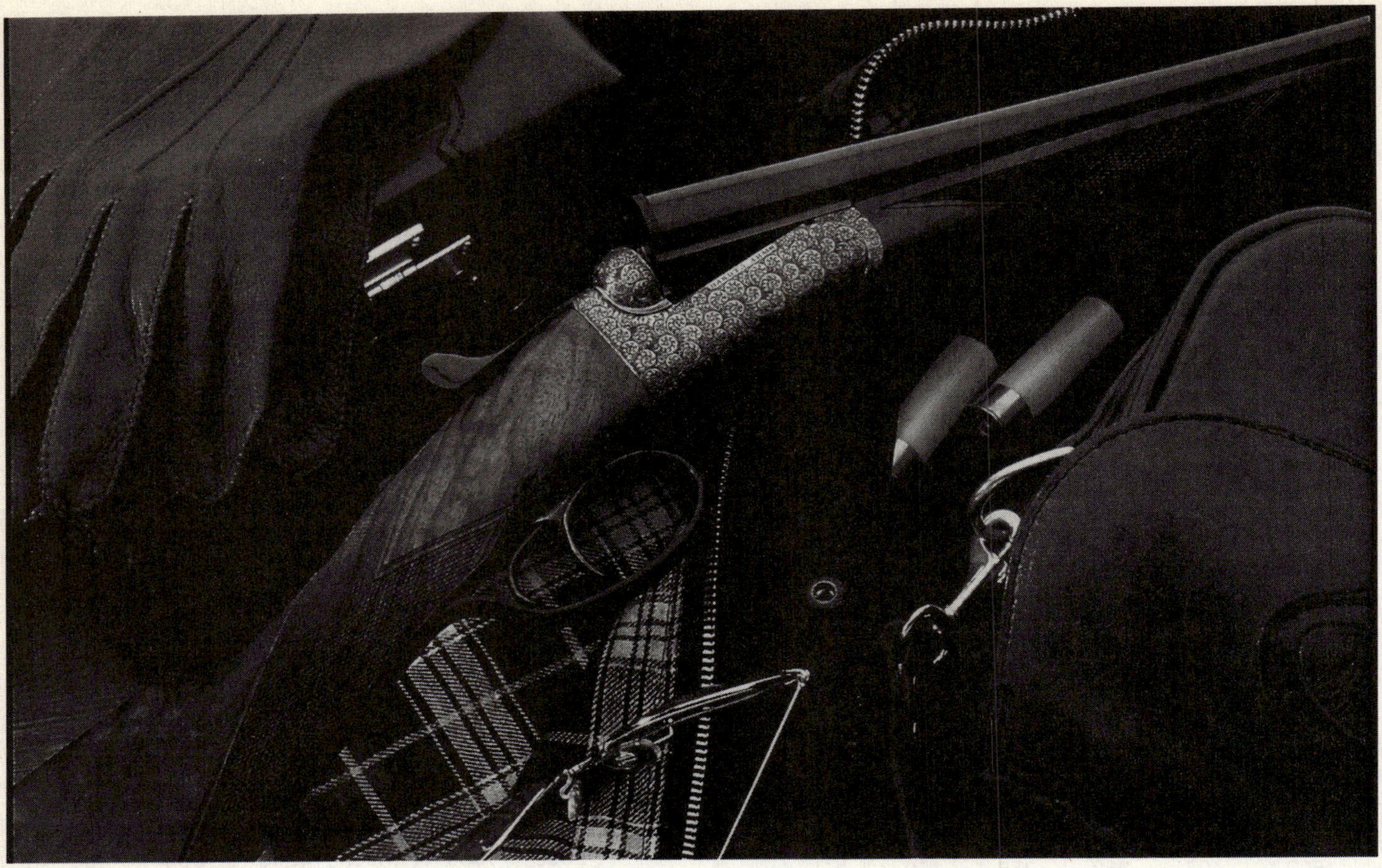

The American Legend

NIB	Exc.	V.G.	Good	Fair	Poor
3500	3250	2750	2500	1200	600

Model 10 Single Shot

Built on a single shot falling action this rifle features a 23" barrel and choice of XX grade wood with oil finish. Fine line checkering, steel gripcap, and 1/2" recoil pad are also standard. Weighs about 6 lbs.

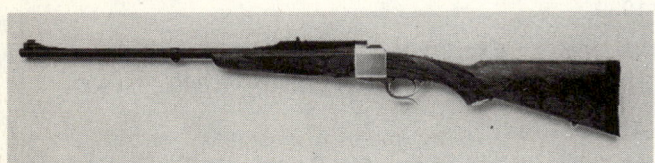

NIB	Exc.	V.G.	Good	Fair	Poor
2250	1950	1500	1200	800	400

Dakota .22 Long Rifle Sporter

Fitted with a 22" barrel and X grade oil finish walnut with fine line checkering and steel gripcap. A 1/2" black recoil pad is standard. Weighs about 6-1/2 lbs.

NIB	Exc.	V.G.	Good	Fair	Poor
1250	1000	800	650	500	300

Model 97 Long Range Hunter

Introduced in 1997 this bolt action rifle is offered in 13 calibers: .250-6, .257 Roberts, .270 Win., .280 Rem., 7mm Rem. Mag., 7mm Dakota Mag., .30-06, .300 Win. Mag., .300 Dakota Mag., .338 Win. mag., .330 Dakota Mag., .375 H&H, .375 Dakota Mag. Barrel lengths depend on caliber but are either 24" or 26". The trigger is fully adjustable. Many other special features. Stock is black synthetic with one-piece bedding. Black recoil pad is standard. Weight is approximately 7.7 lbs.

NIB	Exc.	V.G.	Good	Fair	Poor
1595	1250	—	—	—	—

Model T-76 Longbow Tactical Rifle

This long range tactical bolt action rifle is available in 3 calibers: .338 Lapua, .300 Dakota Mag., and .330 Dakota Mag. The fiberglass stock is an A-2 McMillan in black or olive green. Adjustable length of pull with bipod spike in forearm. The 28" stainless steel is .950 diameter at the muzzle with muzzle brake. The rifle is sold with a number of accessories such as a case with bipod, tool kit and tool box. Weight is about 13.7 lbs.

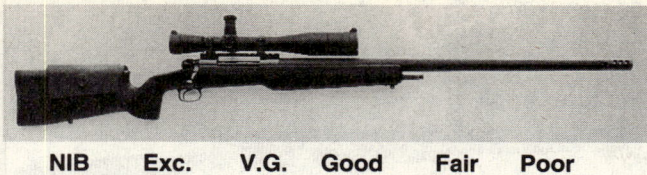

NIB	Exc.	V.G.	Good	Fair	Poor
4250	3000	—	—	—	—

NOTE: Dakota offers a wide variety of options to all of its grades. Some of these options are quite expensive and will add a considerable sum to the value of the gun. It is advisable to secure a knowledgeable appraisal before the sale.

Dakota American Legend

Introduced in 1996, this side by side shotgun is offered in 20 gauge with 27" barrels, concave rib, splinter forearm, double triggers, straight grips stock, and full scroll engraving on the frame. Many additional extra cost options are offered which can greatly affect the price. The base price is listed below.

NIB	Exc.	V.G.	Good	Fair	Poor
18000	—	—	—	—	—

Dakota Shotgun

Similar to the American Legend but offered in two grades of finish. These new grades were first offered in 1997.

Classic Grade

This grade features a case colored round action with straight grip and fancy walnut oil finish stock. Forearm is splinter type. Double trigger standard with choice of chokes.

NIB	Exc.	V.G.	Good	Fair	Poor
7950	6000	—	—	—	—

Premier Grade

This grade features a case colored round action with 50% engraving coverage. Exhibition grade English walnut stock with straight grip and splinter forearm. Oil rubbed finish. Double triggers are standard with choice of chokes.

NIB	Exc.	V.G.	Good	Fair	Poor
9950	7500	—	—	—	—

DALY, CHARLES
Dayton, Ohio

An importer of German, Japanese, and Italian shotguns and combination guns.

CHARLES DALY, EARLY PRUSSIAN GUNS

Commanidor Over/Under Model 100

A boxlock Over/Under Anson & Deeley action shotgun chambered all gauges, choice of barrel length and chokes, double triggers (standard) or single selective trigger. Blued with a checkered walnut stock. Manufactured in Belgium in the late 1930s.

Exc.	V.G.	Good	Fair	Poor
800	600	475	275	200

Commanidor Over/Under Model 200

As above, with a better-grade walnut stock.

Exc.	V.G.	Good	Fair	Poor
900	700	500	300	200

Superior Side-x-Side

As above, with an Anson & Deeley boxlock action and double triggers. Blued with a walnut stock. Not manufactured after 1933.

Exc.	V.G.	Good	Fair	Poor
1200	850	650	450	250

Empire Side-x-Side

As above, but engraved with a better grade of walnut.

Exc.	V.G.	Good	Fair	Poor
2500	2000	1750	1250	600

Diamond Grade Side-x-Side

A deluxe version of the above.

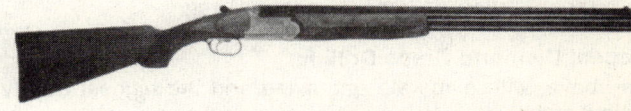

Exc.	V.G.	Good	Fair	Poor
5000	4500	3750	3000	1200

Regent Diamond Grade Side-x-Side

A custom order version of the above.

Exc.	V.G.	Good	Fair	Poor
5500	4750	4000	300	1200

> **A Charles Daly Regent Diamond Grade in 12 gauge with 28" barrels was sold at auction for $5,500. The gun was manufactured in 1908 with steel barrels. Single selective trigger. Condition was excellent.**
> **J.C. Devine, Inc., March 1996.**

Empire Over/Under

A 12, 16, and 20 gauge Anson & Deeley boxlock shotgun with choice of barrel length and choke, double triggers and automatic ejectors. Engraved with fine quality scrollwork and walnut stock. Discontinued in 1933.

Exc.	V.G.	Good	Fair	Poor
2250	2000	1500	1150	500

Diamond Grade Over/Under

As above, but more finely finished.

Exc.	V.G.	Good	Fair	Poor
5000	4500	3750	3000	1250

SEXTUPLE SINGLE BARREL TRAP

Empire Grade

A 12 gauge boxlock single barrel shotgun with 30"-34" full choke barrels, a ventilated rib and automatic ejectors. The action features six locking lugs and is strong. Engraved with a walnut stock. Manufactured after 1933.

Exc.	V.G.	Good	Fair	Poor
2500	2250	1850	1500	750

Regent Diamond Grade

As above, with more engraving and a better grade walnut stock.

Exc.	V.G.	Good	Fair	Poor
3500	3250	2850	2500	1250

DRILLINGS

Superior Grade Drilling

A 12, 16, and 20 gauge Over/Under rifle/shotgun with a rifle barrel in .25-20, .25-35, or .30-30 running beneath them. Engraved with a walnut stock. Not manufactured after 1933.

Exc.	V.G.	Good	Fair	Poor
2500	2250	1800	1450	800

Diamond Grade Drilling

As above, with more engraving and a better grade of walnut in the stock.

Exc.	V.G.	Good	Fair	Poor
4500	4000	3750	3000	1500

Regent Diamond Grade Drilling

As above, with elaborate engraving and the highest quality walnut stock.

Exc.	V.G.	Good	Fair	Poor
5500	5000	4500	4000	2000

CHARLES DALY, B.C. MIROKU GUNS

Empire Grade Side By Side

A 12, 16, and 20 gauge Anson and Deeley boxlock shotgun with 26", 28", and 30" barrels, various chokes, extractors, and a single trigger. Blued with a checkered walnut stock. Manufactured between 1968 and 1971.

Add 10% for ventilated rib barrels and/or 20 gauge.

Exc.	V.G.	Good	Fair	Poor
550	500	450	375	200

Superior Grade Single Barrel Trap

A 12 gauge boxlock shotgun with 32" or 34" ventilated rib barrels, full choke, and automatic ejector. Blued with Monte Carlo walnut stock. Manufactured between 1968 and 1976.

Exc.	V.G.	Good	Fair	Poor
550	500	450	350	200

Over/Unders

A 12, 20, and 28 gauge and .410 bore boxlock shotgun with 26", 28", and 30" barrels with ventilated ribs. Various choke combinations were offered with single selective triggers and automatic ejectors. Blued with checkered walnut stocks. The differences between the grades are the degree and quality of the engraving and the grade of walnut used for the stock. The smaller-bore guns bring a premium as follows. Manufactured between 1963 and 1976 by B.C. Miroku.

20 Gauge-Add 10%.
28 Gauge-Add 20%.
.410-Add 30%.

Venture Grade

Exc.	V.G.	Good	Fair	Poor
550	500	450	375	200

Venture Grade Skeet or Trap

Offered with either 26" Skeet & Skeet or 30" full choke.

Exc.	V.G.	Good	Fair	Poor
575	525	475	375	200

Field Grade

Chambered for 12 and 20 gauge only.

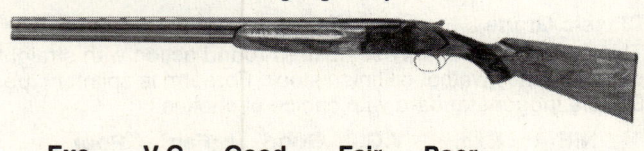

Exc.	V.G.	Good	Fair	Poor
650	575	500	425	200

Superior Grade

Exc.	V.G.	Good	Fair	Poor
750	675	600	525	200

Superior Grade Trap

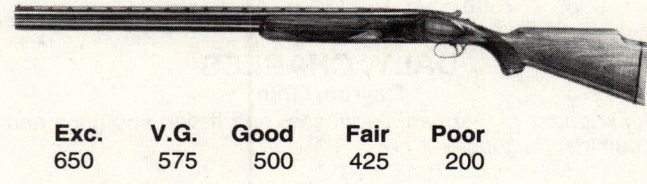

Exc.	V.G.	Good	Fair	Poor
650	575	500	425	200

Diamond Grade

Exc.	V.G.	Good	Fair	Poor
1000	900	750	600	300

Diamond Grade Trap or Skeet

With either 26" Skeet & Skeet or 30" full choke barrels and Monte Carlo stocks.

Wide Rib-Add 5%.

Exc.	V.G.	Good	Fair	Poor
1050	950	800	650	350

CHARLES DALY, ITALIAN MANUFACTURE

Manufactured by the firm of Breda in Milan, Italy. The semiautomatic "Novamatic" was produced in 1968. All other models began Italian production in 1976.

Novamatic Lightweight

A 12 gauge semiautomatic shotgun with a 26" or 28" ventilated-rib barrel and screw-in choke tubes. The receiver is alloy, with checkered walnut stock. Imported under the Daly name in 1968 only.

Exc.	V.G.	Good	Fair	Poor
300	275	225	175	125

Novamatic Trap

As above, with a Monte Carlo stock and a 30" full choke barrel.

Exc.	V.G.	Good	Fair	Poor
350	300	250	200	150

Charles Daly Field Grade Over/Under

A 12 and 20 gauge Over/Under shotgun with 26" or 28" chrome-lined ventilated rib barrels with a crossbolt boxlock action, single selective trigger, and extractors. Blued with a stamped checkered walnut stock. Introduced in 1989.

Exc.	V.G.	Good	Fair	Poor
450	400	350	275	200

Charles Daly Deluxe Over/Under

As above with automatic ejectors, screw-in choke tubes, and a silver-finished receiver. The walnut stock is handcheckered. Introduced in 1989.

Exc.	V.G.	Good	Fair	Poor
650	600	500	400	200

Diamond Grade Over/Under

As above in 12 and 20 gauge Magnum with various barrel lengths and screw-in choke tubes, single trigger, automatic ejectors, and select walnut stock. Discontinued in 1968.

Exc.	V.G.	Good	Fair	Poor
700	625	550	400	200

Diamond Grade Trap or Skeet

As above, with 26" or 30" barrels. Available in 1989 after the Field Model was discontinued.

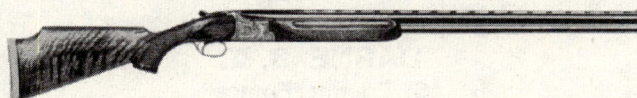

Exc.	V.G.	Good	Fair	Poor
1000	900	750	500	250

Presentation Grade Over/Under

As above, with a Purdy-type boxlock action and engraved false sideplates. The stock is of deluxe French walnut. Discontinued in 1986.

Exc.	V.G.	Good	Fair	Poor
1000	900	750	500	250

Superior II O/U

A 12 and 20 gauge Over/Under shotgun with 26" or 28" ventilated rib barrels, various chokes, single trigger, and automatic ejectors. Engraved, blued with a walnut stock. Discontinued in 1988.

Exc.	V.G.	Good	Fair	Poor
675	600	500	375	200

Superior Grade Side-x-Side

A 12 and 20 gauge boxlock double barrel shotgun with 26" or 28" barrels, various chokes, a boxlock action, and single trigger. Blued, with a walnut stock.

Exc.	V.G.	Good	Fair	Poor
500	425	375	300	200

Charles Daly Automatic

A 12 gauge Magnum semiautomatic shotgun with 26" or 28" ventilated rib barrels, screw-in choke tubes and a 5-shot magazine. There is a slug gun available with rifle sights. Checkered walnut grip in two versions—a pistol grip and an English-style straight grip. The choke-tube model would be worth a 10% premium.

Exc.	V.G.	Good	Fair	Poor
375	325	275	225	150

DAN ARMS OF AMERICA
Allentown, Pennsylvania

These are Italian-made shotguns manufactured by Silmer and imported by Dan Arms of America. They are no longer produced as of 1988.

SIDE-X-SIDES

Field Grade

A boxlock shotgun chambered for all gauges with 26" or 28" barrels, various choke combinations, double triggers and extractors. Blued with a walnut stock.

Exc.	V.G.	Good	Fair	Poor
300	265	225	150	125

Deluxe Field Grade

As above, with a single trigger and automatic ejectors.

Exc.	V.G.	Good	Fair	Poor
450	400	325	250	200

OVER/UNDERS

Lux Grade I

A 12 and 20 gauge Over/Under shotgun with a 26", 28" or 30" ventilated rib barrels, double triggers and extractors. Blued finish with a walnut stock.

Exc.	V.G.	Good	Fair	Poor
275	250	200	150	100

Lux Grade II

As above, in 12 gauge only with a single trigger.

Exc.	V.G.	Good	Fair	Poor
325	300	250	200	150

Lux Grade III

As above, in 20 gauge only with automatic ejectors.

Exc.	V.G.	Good	Fair	Poor
400	325	275	225	175

As above in 12 gauge only with screw-in choke tubes.

Exc.	V.G.	Good	Fair	Poor
450	375	325	275	200

Silver Snipe

A 12 or 20 gauge shotgun manufactured to custom order with engraved false sideplates and a select walnut stock.

Exc.	V.G.	Good	Fair	Poor
1250	1000	800	600	350

DANCE & BROTHERS
CONFEDERATE REVOLVERS
Columbia, Texas

J.H., G.P., and D.E. Dance began production of percussion revolvers for the Confederate States of America in Columbia, Texas, in mid-1862, moving to Anderson, Texas, in early 1864. Based on surviving serial numbers, the combined output at both places did not exceed 350 pistols. Most of these were in the "Army" (.44 caliber) size but a limited number of "Navy" (.36 caliber) were also manufactured. Nearly all are distinguished by the absence of a "recoil shield" on the frame behind the cylinders. As Colt M1851 "Navy" revolvers closely resemble the Dance Navy revolvers, great care must be exercised in examining revolvers purported to be Dance Navies.

.44 Caliber

Exc.	V.G.	Good	Fair	Poor
—	—	25000	8000	2000

.36 Caliber

Courtesy Milwaukee Public Museum, Milwaukee, Wisconsin

Exc.	V.G.	Good	Fair	Poor
—	—	27500	8500	3000

C DANDOY/A LIEGE
SEE French Military Firearms

DANSK REKYLRIFFEL SYNDIKAT
Copenhagen, Denmark

Schouboe 1902/1903

A 7.65mm caliber semiautomatic pistol with a conventional blowback design. Production ended in 1910, with less than 1,000 manufactured.

Exc.	V.G.	Good	Fair	Poor
—	4000	3000	2500	1200

Model 1907

An 11.35mm caliber semiautomatic pistol designed to fire a 55-grain, copper-aluminum-and-wood projectile at a velocity of 1625 ft./sec. Five hundred were manufactured before production stopped in 1917.

Exc.	V.G.	Good	Fair	Poor
—	5000	4000	3000	2000

Combination holster/shoulder stocks were made for this model, but are extremely rare. If present with a pistol, they would add approximately 50% to the value.

DARDICK CORP.
Hamden, Connecticut

Perhaps one of the most unusual firearms to have been designed and marketed in the United States during the 20th century. It utilizes "tround," which is a triangular plastic case enclosing a cartridge. The action of these arms consists of a revolving carrier that brings the trounds from the magazine into line with the barrel. Discontinued in 1962.

Series 1100 (3" barrel)

Chambered in .38 Dardick only.

Exc.	V.G.	Good	Fair	Poor
750	650	550	400	200

Series 1500 (6" barrel)

Chambered for the .22, .30, and the .38 Dardick.

Exc.	V.G.	Good	Fair	Poor
950	850	750	600	300

A carbine conversion kit consisting of a long barrel and shoulder stock was available and would bring a premium of $250 to $400 depending on the condition.

DARLING, B. & B. M.
Belingham, Massachusetts

Darling Pepperbox Pistol

A .30 caliber percussion 6-shot pepperbox with 3.25" length barrels. Blued with walnut grips. This is one of the rarest American pepperboxes and copies are known to have been made. Consequently, prospective purchasers are advised to secure a qualified appraisal prior to acquisition. Manufactured during the late 1830s.

Exc.	V.G.	Good	Fair	Poor
—	—	3500	1000	550

DARNE, S. A.
St. Etienne, France

Darne Side-x-Side Shotguns

A 12, 16, 20, or 28 gauge sliding breech double-barrel shotgun manufactured in a variety of barrel lengths and with numerous optional features. Manufactured from 1881 to 1979.

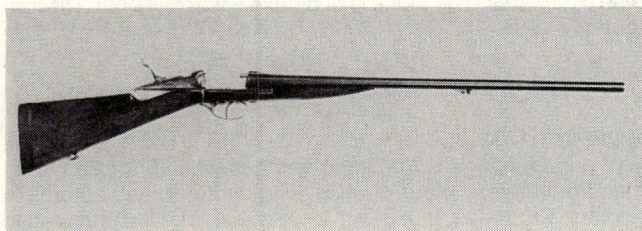

Model R11

Exc.	V.G.	Good	Fair	Poor
1000	900	750	600	350

Model R15

Exc.	V.G.	Good	Fair	Poor
2500	2000	1750	1500	750

Model V19

Exc.	V.G.	Good	Fair	Poor
3250	3000	2750	2250	1250

Model V22

Exc.	V.G.	Good	Fair	Poor
3750	3500	3000	2500	1200

Model V Hors Series No. I

Exc.	V.G.	Good	Fair	Poor
4500	4000	3750	3250	1500

DAUDETEAU
St. Denis, France

Model 1896

A 6.5mm caliber bolt-action rifle with a 26" barrel, full length stock secured by two barrel bands and a fixed magazine. Blued with a walnut stock.

Exc.	V.G.	Good	Fair	Poor
250	175	150	100	75

DAVENPORT FIREARMS CO.
Norwich, Connecticut

Single Barrel Shotgun

A 10, 12, 16, or 20 gauge side hammer single barrel shotgun with 26" to 36" barrels and extractors. Blued, case hardened with a walnut stock. Manufactured from approximately 1880 to 1915.

Exc.	V.G.	Good	Fair	Poor
300	150	125	100	75

8 Gauge Goose Gun

As above, in 8 gauge.

Exc.	V.G.	Good	Fair	Poor
400	250	200	150	100

Falling Block Single Shot Rifle

A .22, .25, or .32 rimfire single shot rifle with a 24" round barrel and exposed hammer. Blued with a walnut stock. The barrel marked "The W.H. Davenport Fire Arms Co. Norwich, Conn. U.S.A. Patented Dec. 15, 1891." Manufactured between 1891 and 1910.

Exc.	V.G.	Good	Fair	Poor
550	500	425	325	200

DAVIDSON F. A.
Eibar, Spain

Arms bearing this name were manufactured in Spain by Fabrica De Armas.

Model 63B

A 12, 16, 20, 28, or .410 bore double barrel boxlock shotgun with 25" to 30" barrels. Engraved, nickel-plated with a walnut stock. Made from 1963 to 1976.

Exc.	V.G.	Good	Fair	Poor
275	225	200	150	100

Model 69 SL

A 12 or 20 gauge sidelock double-barrel shotgun with 26" or 28" barrels and finished as above.

Exc.	V.G.	Good	Fair	Poor
400	350	300	225	125

Stagecoach Model 73

A 12 or 20 gauge Magnum sidelock double-barrel shotgun with 20" barrels and exposed hammers.

Exc.	V.G.	Good	Fair	Poor
275	225	175	150	100

DAVIS, A. JR.
Stafford, Connecticut

Under Hammer Pistol

A .31 caliber single shot under hammer percussion pistol with a 7.5" half octagonal barrel and brass frame. The grips are of maple and formed with a bottom tip. The top strap marked "A. Davis Jr./Stafford Conn."

Exc.	V.G.	Good	Fair	Poor
—	950	600	300	100

DAVIS, N.R. & CO.
DAVIS, N.R. & SONS
Freetown and Assonet, Massachusetts

Manufacturer of percussion, and later, cartridge shotguns from 1853 to 1919. The cartridge shotguns embodied Nathan R. Davis' patented improvements of 1879, 1884, and 1886. Though only made in plain, serviceable grades, Davis shotguns were extremely well made and lived up to the company's motto "As Good as the Best."

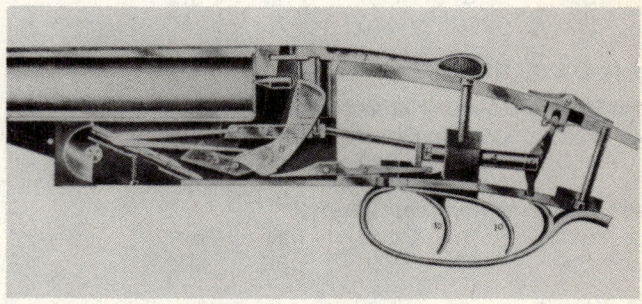

Grade A, B and BS Hammerless Shotguns
Made in 12 or 16 gauge with 28", 30", or 32" barrels.

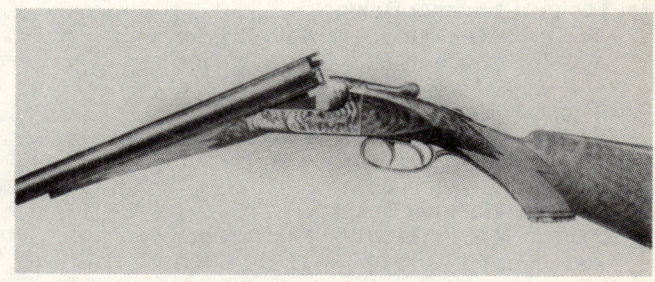

Exc.	V.G.	Good	Fair	Poor
750	600	400	200	100

Grade C Hammerless Shotgun
Made in 10 gauge with 30" or 32" barrels.

Exc.	V.G.	Good	Fair	Poor
750	600	400	200	100

Grade D and DS Hammer Shotguns
Made in 12 or 16 gauge with 28", 30", or 32" barrels.

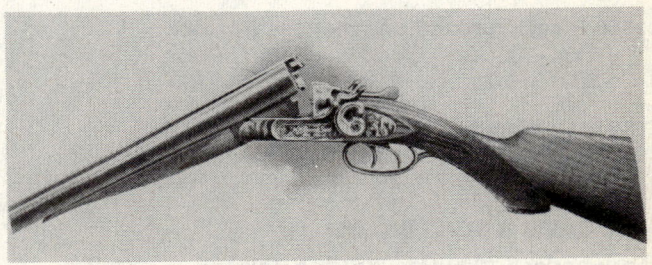

Exc.	V.G.	Good	Fair	Poor
750	600	400	200	100

Grade E and F Single Barrel Shotguns
Made in 12 or 16 gauge with 30" or 32" barrels.

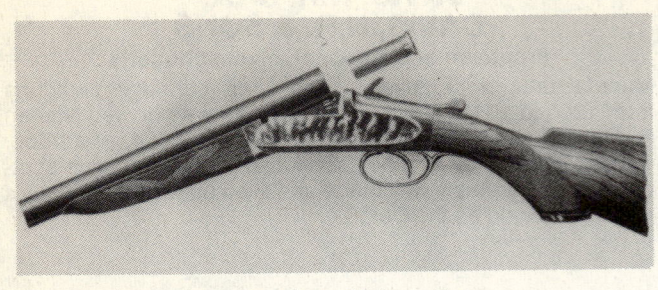

Exc.	V.G.	Good	Fair	Poor
250	200	100	75	50

N.R. DAVIS BRANDS

1st Button Opener-Hammer Boxlock

Exc.	V.G.	Good	Fair	Poor
400	300	250	150	100

1st Sidelever-Hammer Boxlock

Exc.	V.G.	Good	Fair	Poor
400	300	250	150	100

2nd Sidelever-Hammer Boxlock

Exc.	V.G.	Good	Fair	Poor
400	300	250	150	100

1st Toplever-Hammer Boxlock

Exc.	V.G.	Good	Fair	Poor
400	300	250	150	100

2nd Toplever-Hammer Boxlock

Exc.	V.G.	Good	Fair	Poor
400	300	250	150	100

3rd Toplever-Hammer Boxlock

Exc.	V.G.	Good	Fair	Poor
400	300	250	150	100

1879 1st Model-Hammer Boxlock

Exc.	V.G.	Good	Fair	Poor
400	300	250	150	100

1879 2nd Model Damascus Barrels-Hammer Boxlock

Exc.	V.G.	Good	Fair	Poor
400	300	250	150	100

1885 "Hammerless"-Hammerless Boxlock

Exc.	V.G.	Good	Fair	Poor
400	300	250	150	100

1886 Rival-Hammerless Boxlock

Exc.	V.G.	Good	Fair	Poor
300	250	200	150	100

1886 Rival Improved-Hammerless Boxlock

Exc.	V.G.	Good	Fair	Poor
300	250	200	150	100

1897 "G"-Hammer Sidelock

Exc.	V.G.	Good	Fair	Poor
300	250	200	150	100

N.R. DAVIS & SONS BRAND

Hammerless 1900-Hammerless Boxlock

Exc.	V.G.	Good	Fair	Poor
300	250	200	150	100

Hammerless A Damascus Barrels-Hammerless Boxlock

Exc.	V.G.	Good	Fair	Poor
300	250	200	150	100

Hammerless B-Hammerless Boxlock

Exc.	V.G.	Good	Fair	Poor
300	250	200	150	100

Hammerless C Engraved Damascus Barrel-Hammerless Boxlock

Exc.	V.G.	Good	Fair	Poor
350	300	250	150	100

Hammerless D Engraved-Hammerless Boxlock

Exc.	V.G.	Good	Fair	Poor
400	350	300	250	200

New Model-Hammerless Boxlock

Exc.	V.G.	Good	Fair	Poor
300	250	200	150	100

"B.S." Straight Stock-Hammerless Boxlock

Exc.	V.G.	Good	Fair	Poor
300	250	200	150	100

"D.S." Straight Stock-Engraved-Hammerless Boxlock

Exc.	V.G.	Good	Fair	Poor
300	250	200	150	100

Davis Special-Hammerless Boxlock

Exc.	V.G.	Good	Fair	Poor
800	600	500	400	250

Davis "B" Manga Steel-Hammerless Boxlock

Exc.	V.G.	Good	Fair	Poor
800	600	500	400	250

DAVIS-WARNER BRANDS
Expert-Hammerless Boxlock

Exc.	V.G.	Good	Fair	Poor
350	250	200	150	100

"BS"-Hammerless Boxlock

Exc.	V.G.	Good	Fair	Poor
300	250	200	150	100

"Maximin"-Hammerless Boxlock

Exc.	V.G.	Good	Fair	Poor
400	300	250	200	150

"DS"-Hammerless Boxlock

Exc.	V.G.	Good	Fair	Poor
300	250	200	150	100

Deluxe-Hammerless Boxlock

Exc.	V.G.	Good	Fair	Poor
300	250	200	150	100

Premier-Hammerless Boxlock

Exc.	V.G.	Good	Fair	Poor
300	250	200	150	100

Peerless Ejector-Hammerless Boxlock

Exc.	V.G.	Good	Fair	Poor
400	300	250	200	150

Hypower-Hammerless Boxlock

Exc.	V.G.	Good	Fair	Poor
400	300	250	200	150

Ajax-Hammerless Boxlock

Exc.	V.G.	Good	Fair	Poor
300	250	200	150	100

Certified (Savage)

Exc.	V.G.	Good	Fair	Poor
400	300	250	150	100

Deluxe Special (Model 805)-Automatic Ejectors

Exc.	V.G.	Good	Fair	Poor
500	400	300	200	150

Premier Special (Model 802)

Exc.	V.G.	Good	Fair	Poor
500	400	300	200	150

Premier (Model 801)

Exc.	V.G.	Good	Fair	Poor
400	300	250	150	100

Ajax (Model 800)

Exc.	V.G.	Good	Fair	Poor
400	300	250	150	100

CRESCENT-DAVIS BRANDS

Model No. 600-Hammerless Boxlock

Exc.	V.G.	Good	Fair	Poor
600	500	300	200	100

Model No. 900-Hammerless Boxlock

Exc.	V.G.	Good	Fair	Poor
600	500	300	200	100

DAVIS & BOZEMAN
Central, Alabama

Pattern 1841 Rifle

A .58 caliber single shot percussion rifle with a 33" round barrel, full walnut stock, 2 barrel bands, brass furniture and an iron ramrod. The lock marked "D. & B. Ala." as well as the serial number and date of manufacture. Prospective purchasers are advised to secure a qualified appraisal prior to acquisition.

Exc.	V.G.	Good	Fair	Poor
—	—	14000	5000	2000

DAVIS INDUSTRIES
Mira Loma, California

This company was founded in 1982 by Jim Davis in Chino, California. At the present time the company produces all of its handguns in a 50,000 square foot plant in Mira Loma, California. All Davis guns have a lifetime warranty. Any malfunction will be repaired or replaced free of charge.

D-Series Derringer

A .22 Long Rifle, .22 WMR, .25 ACP and .32 ACP caliber double-barrel Over/Under derringer with 2.4" barrels. Black Teflon or chrome plated finish with laminated wood grips. Weighs approximately 9.5 oz.

NIB	Exc.	V.G.	Good	Fair	Poor
60	50	40	30	25	20

Big Bore D-Series

Similar to the above model but chambered for the .38 Special and .32 H&R Magnum. Barrel length is 2.75". Weighs about 11.5 oz.

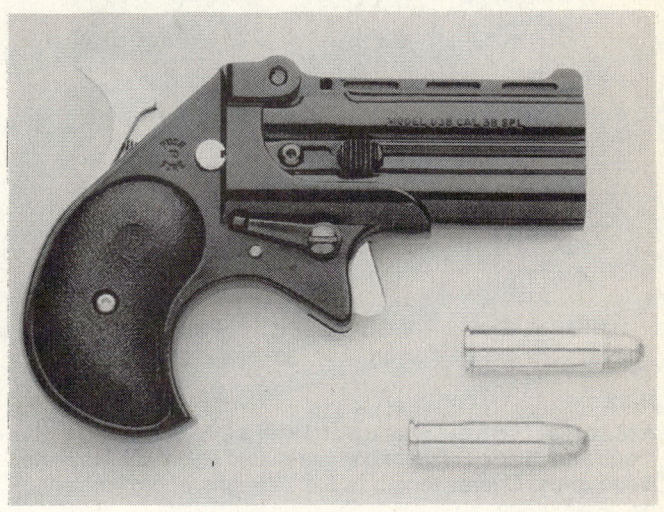

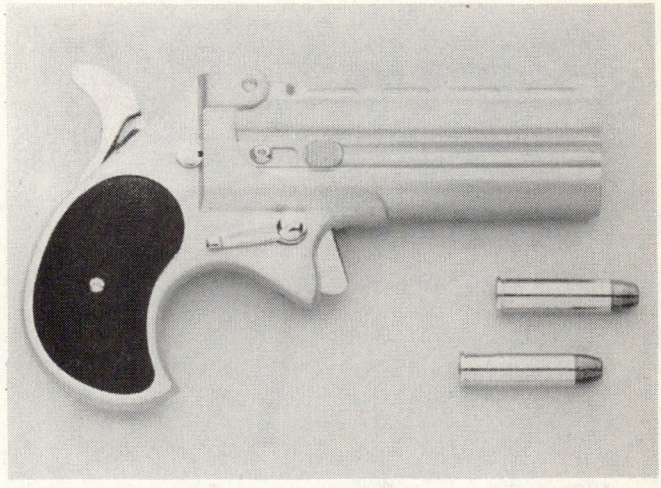

NIB	Exc.	V.G.	Good	Fair	Poor
80	60	45	30	25	20

Long Bore D-Series

Introduced in 1994 this two-shot pistol is chambered for the .22 Long Rifle, .22 WMR, .32 ACP, .32 H&R Mag., .380 ACP, 9mm, and .38 Special cartridges. Barrel length is 3.75", overall length is 5.65" and weight is approximately 13 oz.

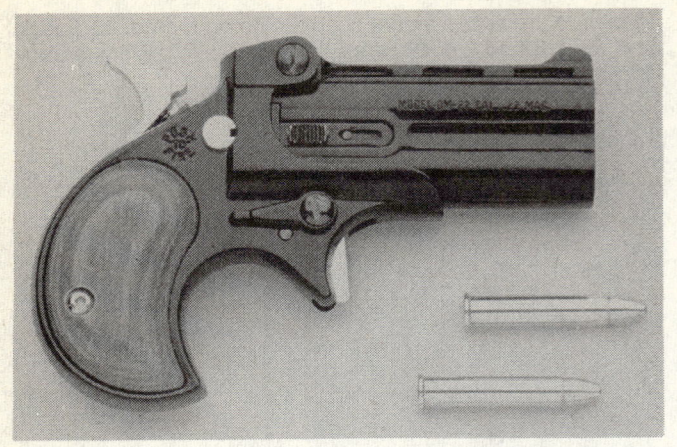

NIB	Exc.	V.G.	Good	Fair	Poor
80	60	45	30	25	20

P-32

A .32 caliber semiautomatic pistol with a 2.8" barrel and 6-shot magazine. Black Teflon or chrome-plated finish with laminated wood grips. Overall length is 5.4". Weighs approximately 22 oz.

NIB	Exc.	V.G.	Good	Fair	Poor
85	75	60	45	35	25

P-380

As above, in .380 caliber.

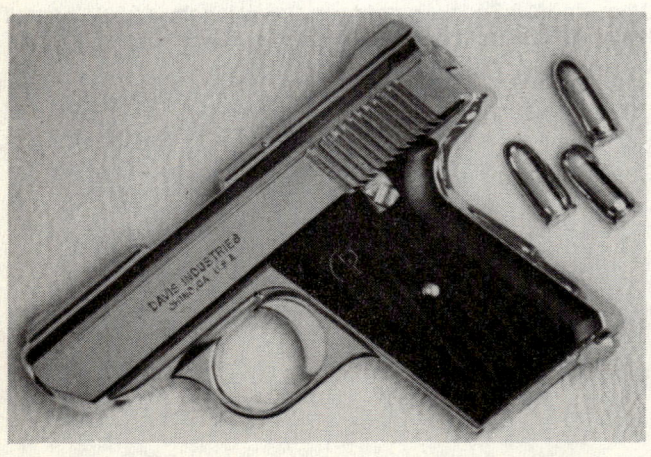

NIB	Exc.	V.G.	Good	Fair	Poor
100	80	65	50	40	30

DAVIS-WARNER ARMS CORPORATION
Norwich, Connecticut

Established in 1917, when N.R. Davis & Sons purchased the Warner Arms Company. Manufactured shotguns, as well as revolvers and semiautomatic pistols. Ceased operations in 1930. The Crescent Arms Company purchased the proprietary rights to the name and briefly assembled shotguns under the name (probably from parts acquired in the purchase) until Crescent was in turn purchased by J.C. Stevens.

Initially, the Davis-Warner shotguns were identical to those made by Davis, (see preceding entry), but they subsequently made a Davis Grade B.S. Hammerless, Davis-Warner Expert and Davis Grade D.S. The pistols made by the company included .32 caliber revolvers and two Browning Patent semiautomatics made in Belgium for the company.

Davis Grade B.S. Hammerless Shotgun

Made in 12, 16, or 20 gauge with 28", 30", or 32" barrels.

Exc.	V.G.	Good	Fair	Poor
750	600	400	200	100

Davis-Warner Expert Hammerless

Made in 12, 16, or 20 gauge with 26", 28", 30", or 32" barrels.

Exc.	V.G.	Good	Fair	Poor
750	600	400	200	100

Davis-Warner Swing Out Revolver

Double action .32 caliber revolver with a 5" or 6" barrel.

Exc.	V.G.	Good	Fair	Poor
150	125	100	75	50

Davis-Warner Semiautomatic Pistols

Browning Patent .25 ACP, .32 ACP or .380 caliber pistols.

Exc.	V.G.	Good	Fair	Poor
300	250	175	125	75

Warner Infallible Semiautomatic Pistol

Freyberg Patent .32 ACP.

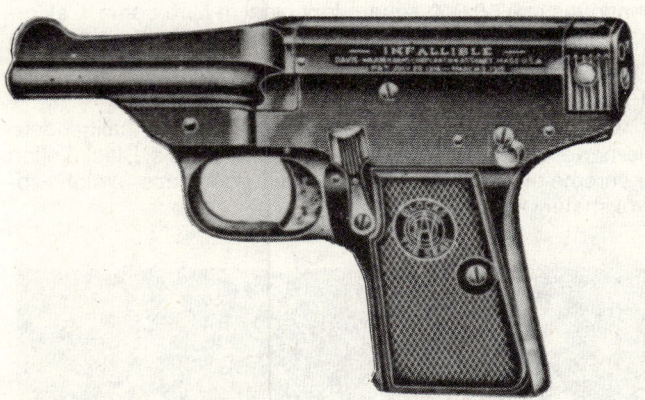

Exc.	V.G.	Good	Fair	Poor
300	250	175	125	75

DAW, G. H.
London, England

Daw Revolver

A .38 caliber double-action percussion revolver with a 5.5" barrel marked "George H. Daw, 57 Threadneedle St. London, Patent No. 112." Blued, with walnut grips. Manufactured in the 1860s.

Exc.	V.G.	Good	Fair	Poor
—	5000	3000	1750	1000

DEANE, ADAMS & DEANE
London, England
SEE Adams

DEANE-HARDING
London, England

Deane-Harding Revolver

A .44 caliber percussion revolver with a 5.25" barrel and 5-shot cylinder. Blued, case hardened with walnut grips. Manufactured during the late 1850s.

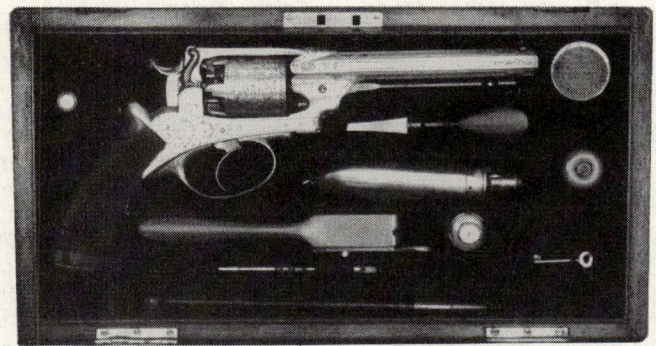

Courtesy Butterfield & Butterfield, San Francisco, California

Exc.	V.G.	Good	Fair	Poor
—	3000	1750	1250	800

DECKER, WILHELM
Zella St. Blasii, Germany

A 6.35mm double-action revolver with a 6-shot cylinder and concealed hammer. Blued with plastic grips. Manufactured prior to 1914.

Exc.	V.G.	Good	Fair	Poor
900	800	700	500	350

DEFIANCE ANTI-BANDIT GUN
California Arms Co.
San Francisco, California

Defiance Anti-Bandit Gun   CURIO OR RELIC, NFA

The Defiance Anti-Bandit Gun is a double-barreled smooth bore shot pistol designed for 20 gauge shotgun or tear gas shells. It was manufactured in 1926-27 by The American Machine Company for the California Arms Co., San Francisco, California, a law enforcement supply manufacturer and distributor, and distributed by them from about 1926-30. Total production is unknown, but apparently was extremely limited; the serial numbers of two known specimens are 49 and 313. Thomas F. Swearengen has identified 3 models in his book, *The World's Fighting Shotguns* (Alexandria, Virginia: Ironside International Publishers, Inc., 1978, pages 88-93), which constitutes the only known published research on this firearm at this time. The Defiance has "twin plunger-type cocking knobs on the rear of an aluminum die-cast frame, a single nonselective trigger, and cylinder-bore barrels mounted in a steel, monobloc, frettage-type chamber housing." Model A has 12.5" barrels and a checkered forearm; Model B has 12.5" barrels and a smooth forearm; Model C has 12.25" barrels and a smooth forearm. Swearengen also terms the Defiance the P-50, a designation used in the California Arms Co. catalog, where "P" numbers were assigned sequentially (but arbitrarily) to the firearms they offered for sale, apparently as stock numbers. Because few specimens of the Defiance Anti-Bandit Gun exist, establishing reliable values may be difficult, but could be logically expected to approximate those for a nonstandard or special-order Ithaca Auto & Burglar Gun. The government ruled the Defiance Anti-Bandit Gun to be a "firearm" in the "any other weapon" category under the NFA.

These materials are copyright © 1998 by Eric M. Larson, printed in the *Catalog* by permission of the copyright holder, and will appear in a forthcoming book on pre-NFA smooth bore shot pistols (see H&R Handy-Gun entry).

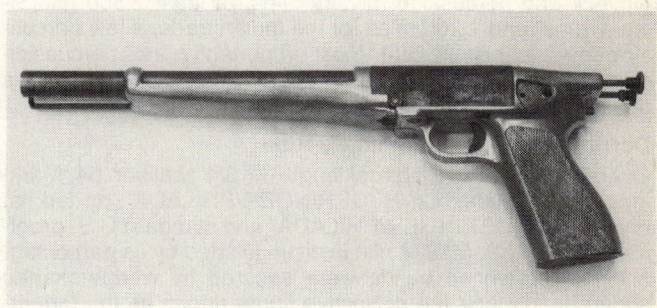

DEMIRETT, J.
Montpelier, Vermont

Under Hammer Pistol

A .27 caliber single shot percussion pistol with 3" to 8" barrels and an under hammer. The barrel marked "J. Demerrit / Montpelier / Vermont." Blued with maple, walnut or stag horn grips. Active from 1866 to the mid-1880s.

Exc.	V.G.	Good	Fair	Poor
—	—	1500	600	300

DEMRO
Manchester, Connecticut

XF-7 Wasp Carbine

A 9mm or .45 caliber semiautomatic carbine with a 16.5" barrel and folding stock.

Exc.	V.G.	Good	Fair	Poor
350	300	250	200	150

T.A.C. Model 1

As above, with a fixed stock.

Exc.	V.G.	Good	Fair	Poor
350	300	250	200	150

DERINGER REVOLVER AND PISTOL CO.
Philadelphia, Pennsylvania

After Henry Deringer's death, his name was used by I.J. Clark who manufactured rimfire revolvers on Charles Foehl's patents between 1870 and 1879.

Derringer Model I

A .22 caliber spur trigger revolver with a hinged octagonal barrel and 7-shot cylinder. Manufactured circa 1873.

Exc.	V.G.	Good	Fair	Poor
600	400	300	200	150

Derringer Model II

As above, with a round barrel and also available in .32 caliber.

Exc.	V.G.	Good	Fair	Poor
500	350	250	175	150

Centennial 1876

A .22, .32, or .38 caliber solid frame revolver.

Exc.	V.G.	Good	Fair	Poor
800	550	350	200	150

HENRY DERINGER RIFLES AND PISTOLS
Philadelphia, Pennsylvania

Henry Deringer Sr. and his son, Henry Jr., were well established in Philadelphia by the close of the War of 1812, having made both sporting and military rifles at that place since the turn of the century. Henry Jr. continued in the gun trade until the outbreak of the American Civil War, primarily producing flintlock and percussion military rifles, at least 2,500 "Northwest guns" and 1,200 rifles for the Indian trade, a few percussion martial pistols, but most importantly the percussion pocket pistols that became so popular that they took on his misspelled name as a generic term, the "derringers."

Derringer U.S. M1814 Military Rifle

Overall length 48-1/2"; barrel length 32-3/4"; caliber .54. Markings: on lockplate, "US/H. DERINGER/PHILADA", on top flat of barrel, "H. DERINGER/PHILADA" and standard U.S. proofmarks. The U.S. M1814 rifle is distinguished by its part octagonal barrel, whose bands were secured by wedge-shaped spring bands, and the distinctive finger ridges on the triggerguard strap. Henry Deringer Sr. received a contract for 2,000 of these rifles in 1814, but delivered only 50 that year, devoting his resources instead to a more lucrative Pennsylvania state contract for rifles.

Exc.	V. G.	Good	Fair	Poor
—	4000	1600	1200	850

Derringer U.S. M1817 Military Rifle (Types I & II)

Overall length 51-1/4"; barrel length 36"; caliber .54. Markings: on lockplate, "US/H. DERINGER/PHILADA" forward of cock, date on tail; standard U.S. proofmarks on barrel. The U.S. M1817 "common" rifle followed much of the same design elements as its predecessor, the U.S. M1814 rifle; however, the barrel is fully round with its bands secured by full band springs, and on the earlier production, the finger ridges on the triggerguard strap were eliminated in favor of a plain strap formed into a handgrip. On the 6,000 rifles manufactured under his 1840 contract, Deringer eliminated the "pistol grip" in favor of a plain strap, distinguishing Type 11 production from Type 1. As one of the four major contractors for the U.S. M1817 rifle, Deringer produced a total of 111,000 rifles for the U.S. War Department. Many of the rifles from first two contracts (2,000 in 1821, 3,000 in 1823) were distributed to Southern states under the 1808 Militia Act. Accordingly, Deringer M1817 rifles altered to percussion by traditional Southern methods may generate a premium.

(in flintlock)

Exc.	V.G.	Good	Fair	Poor
—	4000	1500	1200	800

(altered to percussion)

Exc.	V. G.	Good	Fair	Poor
—	2000	700	550	400

Derringer Original Percussion Martial Rifles (Types I & II).

Overall length 51-1/4"; barrel length 36"; caliber .54. Markings: Type I-on lockplate forward of hammer "DERINGER/PHILA"; also known to exist with standard U.S. M1817 lock markings and barrel marks; Type II-on lockplate forward of hammer "US/DERINGER/PHILADELA" or "DERINGER/PHILADELA" and same on top of barrel.

Although the Type I rifle of this series appears at first glance to be a late contract rifle altered to percussion by means of the cone-in-barrel method, in fact it is an original percussion rifle made by Deringer from modified spare parts that remained after the completion of his 1840 contract. The Type 11 rifle also evidences having been made from modified parts; however, its cone is set in an elongated bolster brazed to the right side of the barrel. Speculation concerning these rifles is rampant; however, the available evidence indicates that Deringer pro-

duced about 600 of these most likely produced at the beginning of the American Civil War.

Courtesy Milwaukee Public Museum, Milwaukee, Wisconsin

Exc.	V.G.	Good	Fair	Poor
—	2500	900	650	450

Derringer Original Percussion Rifle-Muskets

Overall length 57-3/4"; barrel length 42"; caliber .69. Markings: on lock forward of hammer, "US/DERINGER/PHILADELA". Just as the original percussion rifle appears to be an altered arm, the rare Derringer rifle muskets at first appear to have been flintlocks. However, these arms are original percussion, having been made from spare or rejected parts from the U.S. M1816 muskets. The brazed bolsters are identical in style to that of the Type 11 original percussion rifles made by Deringer. Barrels are rifled with seven grooves, and the barrels accordingly bear a rear sight. Deringer probably assembled a hundred of these rifles in 1861 to arm some company of Pennsylvania's early war regiments.

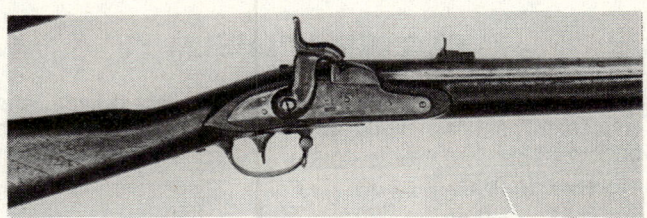

Courtesy Milwaukee Public Museum, Milwaukee, Wisconsin

Exc.	V.G.	Good	Fair	Poor
—	2500	900	650	450

Derringer U.S. Navy Contract "Boxlock" Pistols

Overall length 11-5/8"; barrel length 6"; caliber .54. Markings: on lockplate, "US/DERINGER/ PHILADELIA" or merely "DERINGER/PHILADEL'A" in center, the tail either plain or marked "U.S.N./(date)"; barrels sometimes marked with U.S. Navy inspection marks.

Deringer was granted a contract with the U.S. Navy in 1845 for 1,200 of the new "boxlock" percussion pistols also made by Ames. All of these appear to have been delivered. From the extra parts, Deringer is thought to have assembled several hundred extra pistols, some of which he rifled. The latter bring a premium, even though quantities remain enigmatic.

Exc.	V.G.	Good	Fair	Poor
—	3500	1400	1100	750

Derringer Percussion Pocket Pistols

Overall length varies with barrel length; barrel length 1-1/2" to 6" in regular 1/8" gradients; caliber .41 (usually, other calibers known). Markings: "DERINGER/PHILADELA" on back-action lock and rear section of top barrel flat; "P" impressed in circle with serrated edges on left side of breech; agent marks occasionally on top of barrel.

The most famous of Henry Deringer's products, an estimated 15,000 were produced between the Mexican War through the Civil War, usually in pairs. The popularity of the pistol is attested in the large number of imitations and the nickname "Derringer" applied to them, even when clearly not Deringer's products. Prices can fluctuate widely based on agent marks occasionally found on barrel. Care is advised in purchasing purported "true" derringers.

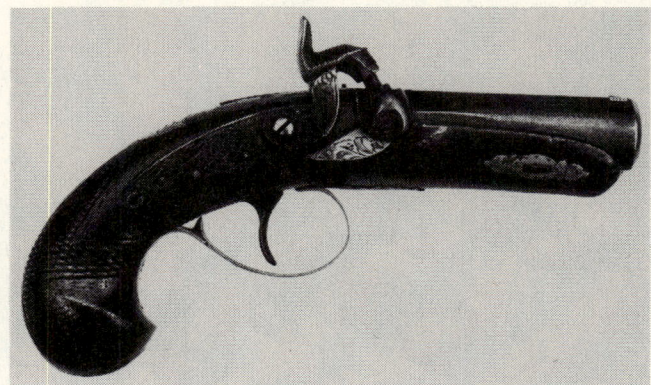
Courtesy Milwaukee Public Museum, Milwaukee, Wisconsin

Exc.	V.G.	Good	Fair	Poor
—	4500	1600	1200	800

Principle Maker of Derringer-Style Pocket Pistols
William AFFLERBACH, Philadelphia, PA
Balthaser AUER, Louisville, KY
Frederick BEERSTECHER, Philadelphia and Lewisburg, PA
Franz J. BITTERLICH, Nashville, TN
BLUNT & SYMS, New York, NY
Richard P. BRUFF, New York, NY
Jesse S. BUTTERFIELD, Philadelphia, PA
Daniel CLARK, Philadelphia, PA
Richard CONSTABLE, Philadelphia, PA
DELONG & SON, Chattanooga, TN
MOSES DICKSON, Louisville, KY
Horace E. DIMICK, St. Louis, MO
Gustau ERICHSON, Houston, TX
B.J. EUSTACE & Company, St. Louis, MO
James E. EVANS, Philadelphia, PA
W.S. EVANS, Philadelphia, PA
FIELD, LANGSTROTH & Company, Philadelphia, PA
Daniel FISH, New York, NY
FOLSOM BROTHERS & Company, New Orleans, LA
August G. GENEZ, New York, NY
George D. H. GILLESPIE, New York, NY
Frederick G. GLASSICK, Memphis, TN
James GOLCHER, Philadelphia, PA
Joseph GRUBB & Company, Philadelphia, PA
John H. HAPPOLDT, Charlestown, SC
John M. HAPPOLDT, Columbus, George, and Charlestown, SC
HAWS & WAGGONER, Columbia, SC
HODGKINS & SONS, Macon, GA
Louis HOFFMAN, Vicksburg, MS
HYDE & GOODRICH, New Orleans, LA
Joseph JACOB, Philadelphia, PA
William W. KAYE, Philadelphia, PA
Benjamin KITTERIDGE, Cincinnati, OH
Peter W. KRAFT, Columbia, SC
John KRIDER, Philadelphia, PA
Jacob KUNTZ, Philadelphia, PA
Martille La FITTE, Natchitoches, LA
A. Frederichk LINS, Philadelphia, PA
C. LOHNER, Philadelphia, PA

John P. LOWER, Denver, CO
A.R. MENDENHALL, Des Arc, AK
John MEUNIER, Milwaukee, WI
William D. MILLER, New York, NY
MURPHY & O'CONNELL, New York, NY
—— NEWCOMB, Natchez, MS
Charles A. OBERTEUFFER, Philadelphia, PA
Stephen O'DELL, Natchez, MS
Henry C. PALMER, St. Louis, MO
R. PATRICK, New York, NY
REID & TRACY, New York, NY
William ROBERTSON, Philadelphia, PA
ROBINSON & KRIDER, Philadelphia, PA
Ernst SCHMIDT & Company, Houston, TX
SCHNEIDER & GLASSICK, Memphis, TN
W.A. SEAVER, New York, NY
Paul J. SIMPSON, New York, NY
SLOTTER & Company, Philadelphia, PA
Patrick SMITH, Buffalo, NY
SPRANG & WALLACE, Philadelphia, PA
Adam W. SPIES, New York, NY
Casper SUTER, Selma, AL
Jacob F. TRUMPLER, Littler Rock, AK
Edward TRYON, Jr., Philadelphia, PA
George K. TRYON, Philadelphia, PA
TUFTS & COLLEY, New York, NY
WOLF, DASH & FISHER, New York, NY
Alfred WOODHAM, New York, NY
Andrew WURFFLEIN, Philadelphia, PA
John WURFFLEIN, Philadelphia, PA
Agent Names Found On Derringer Pocket Pistols
W.C. ALLEN, San Francisco, CA
W.H. CALHOUN, Nashville, TN
CANFIELD & BROTHERS, Baltimore, MD
F. H. CLARK & CO., Memphis, TN
COLEMAN & DUKE, Cahaba, AL
M.W. GALT & BROTHER, Washington, DC
J.B. GILMORE, Shreveport, LA
A.B. GRISWOLD & CO., New Orleans, LA
HYDE & GOODRICH, New Orleans, LA
LULLMAN & VIENNA, Memphis, TN
A.J. MILLSPAUGH, Shreveport, LA
H.G. NEWCOMB, Natchez, MS
A.J. PLATE, San Francisco, CA
J.A. SCHAFER, Vicksburg, MS
S.L. SWETT, Vicksburg, MS
A.J. TAYLOR, San Francisco, CA
WOLF & DURRINGER, Louisville, KY

DESERT EAGLE
Imported by Magnum Research
Minneapolis, Minnesota

The Desert Eagle is a semiautomatic gas operated pistol chambered for the .357 Magnum, .41 Magnum, .44 Magnum, and .50 Action Express. It is produced by Israel Military Industries. The pistols are furnished with a standard 6" barrel but 10" and 14" interchangeable barrels are offered as options. Also available are these interchangeable barrels that are Mag-Na-Ported. The standard material used for frame is steel, but stainless and aluminum are also available. The standard finish for these pistols are black oxide but custom finishes are available on special order. These special finishes are: gold, stainless steel, satin nickel, bright nickel, polished blue, camo, matte chrome, polished chrome, brushed chrome, and matte chrome with gold. All of these special order finishes as well as the optional barrels will affect the prices of the pistols. Prices listed here will reflect standard pistols only.

.357 Magnum
.44 Magnum
.50 A.E.
DESERT EAGLE PISTOL
Mark XIX Component System
MAGNUM RESEARCH, INC.
7110 University Avenue N.E.
Minneapolis, MN 55432
(612) 574-1868

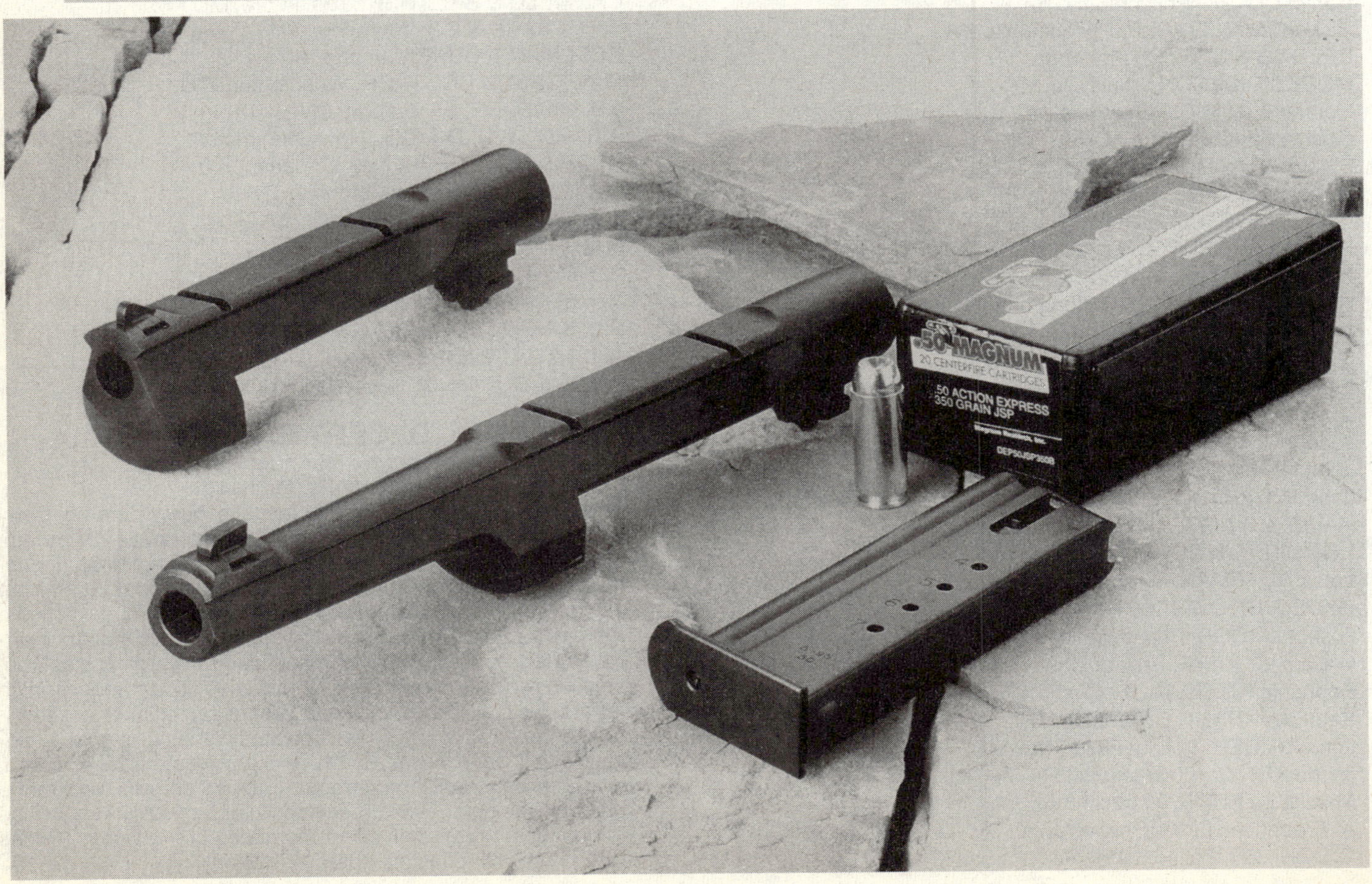
.50 MAGNUM
20 CENTERFIRE CARTRIDGES
.50 ACTION EXPRESS
350 GRAIN JSP

Desert Eagle .357 Magnum

Standard with 6" barrel and black oxide finish. Magazine capacity is 9 rounds. Standard weight is 58 oz.

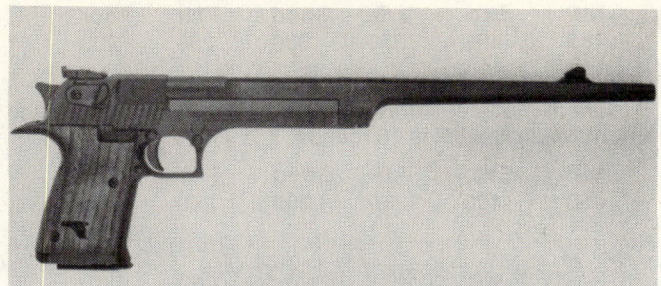

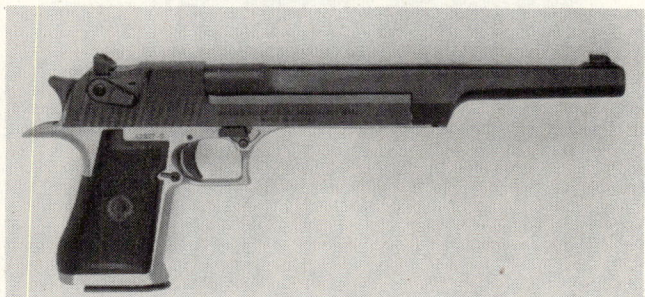

NIB	Exc.	V.G.	Good	Fair	Poor
650	600	550	500	400	250

Desert Eagle .41 Magnum/.44 Magnum

Standard barrel length is 6" with black oxide finish. Magazine capacity is 8 rounds. Weight for standard pistol is 63 oz.

NIB	Exc.	V.G.	Good	Fair	Poor
750	700	600	550	450	275

Desert Eagle .50 Action Express

Standard barrel length is 10" with black oxide finish. Magazine capacity is 7 rounds. Standard weight is 72 oz.

NIB	Exc.	V.G.	Good	Fair	Poor
1200	950	800	700	600	375

Desert Eagle Mark XIX

Introduced in 1996 this new design is manufactured in the U.S. and allows the interchangeability of barrels to switch calibers between the same receiver. A single receiver can be turned into 6 different pistols in 3 Magnum calibers. Available are the .50 A.E., .44 mag., and .357 Mag. in barrel lengths of 6" or 10". Seperate magazines are also required. Eight different finishes are offered as well. A seperate bolt assembly is necessary to convert the .44/.50 calibers to the .357. There are so many different possibilities with this design that only the basic pistol prices are given. Extra barrel assemblies are an additional cost. Prices range from $280 to $160 depending on caliber and length.

.50A.E. w/6" Barrel

NIB	Exc.	V.G.	Good	Fair	Poor
800	650	—	—	—	—

.50A.E. w/10" Barrel

NIB	Exc.	V.G.	Good	Fair	Poor
850	700	—	—	—	—

.44 Mag. w/6" Barrel

NIB	Exc.	V.G.	Good	Fair	Poor
750	600	—	—	—	—

.44 Mag. w/10" Barrel

NIB	Exc.	V.G.	Good	Fair	Poor
800	650	—	—	—	—

.357 Mag. w/6" Barrel

NIB	Exc.	V.G.	Good	Fair	Poor
750	600	—	—	—	—

.357 Mag. w/10" Barrel

NIB	Exc.	V.G.	Good	Fair	Poor
775	600	—	—	—	—

Bolt Assembly-.44/.50 or .357

NIB	Exc.	V.G.	Good	Fair	Poor
125	100	—	—	—	—

Baby Eagle

The Baby Eagle is a smaller version of the Desert Eagle. It is an all steel construction, extra long slide rail, nylon grips, combat style triggerguard, ambidextrous thumb safety, decocking safety. It is a double action design and available in 9mm, .40 S&W, .41 Action Express. Standard finish is black oxide but matte chrome and brushed are offered as optional finishes. Fixed sights are standard. Fixed night sights and adjustable night sights are options.

Baby Eagle 9mm

Fitted with a 4.7" barrel and black oxide finish this model has a magazine capacity of 16 rounds. Empty weight is 35 oz.

NIB	Exc.	V.G.	Good	Fair	Poor
450	400	350	300	250	200

Baby Eagle .40 S&W

Supplied with 4.7" barrel and black oxide finish it has a magazine capacity of 10 rounds. Empty weight is 35 oz.

NIB	Exc.	V.G.	Good	Fair	Poor
450	400	350	300	250	200

Baby Eagle .41 Action Express

This model also has a 4.7" barrel and black oxide finish. Magazine capacity is 11 rounds. Empty weight is 35 oz.

NIB	Exc.	V.G.	Good	Fair	Poor
450	400	350	300	250	200

Baby Eagle Short Barrel

This 9mm model features a 3.6" barrel with frame mounted safety. Magazine holds 10 rounds.

NIB	Exc.	V.G.	Good	Fair	Poor
450	400	350	300	250	200

Baby Eagle Short Barrel/Short Grip

This 9mm version has a 3.6" barrel and shorter grip than standard. Magazine capacity is still 10 rounds. Frame mounted safety.

NIB	Exc.	V.G.	Good	Fair	Poor
450	400	350	300	250	200

Mountain Eagle

This semiautomatic pistol is chambered for the .22 Long Rifle cartridge. It features a 6.5" barrel with adjustable rear sight. The grip is a one-piece molded plastic, checkered with raised side panels. The magazine capacity is 15 rounds with 20-round magazine available as an option. A black oxide finish is standard. The pistol weighs 21 oz.

NIB	Exc.	V.G.	Good	Fair	Poor
200	175	150	125	100	75

Mountain Eagle-Target Edition

Similar to the standard Mountain Eagle but fitted with an 8" accurized barrel, two-stage target trigger, jeweled bolt, adjustable sights with three interchangeable blades, and range case.

NIB	Exc.	V.G.	Good	Fair	Poor
250	200	175	150	125	85

Mountain Eagle Compact Edition

Similar to above but fitted with a 4.5" barrel and short grip.

NIB	Exc	V.G.	Good	Fair	Poor
200	150	125	100	85	70

Lone Eagle

This is a single shot rotating breech pistol designed to fire centerfire cartridges. The standard finish is a black oxide blue luster. The barrel is drilled and tapped for scope mounts. Standard barrel length is 14". Fixed, adjustable, or silhouette sights are offered as options. Stock assembly is made from Lexan. The handgun is offered in the following calibers: .22-250, .223, .22 Hornet, .243, .30-30, .30-06, .308, .357 Mag., .358 Win., .35 Rem., .44 Mag., .444 Marlin, 7mm-08, 7mm Bench Rest. Weighs between 4 lbs., 3 oz. to 4 lbs., 7 oz. depending on caliber.

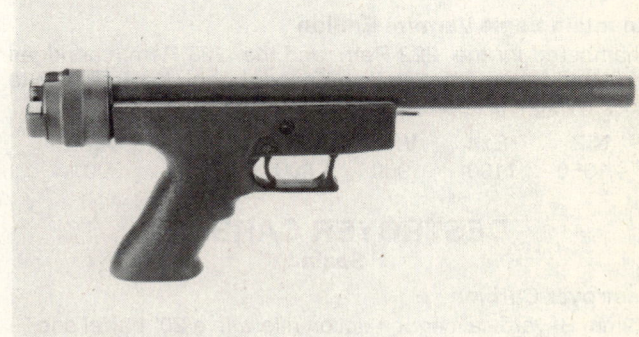

NIB	Exc.	V.G.	Good	Fair	Poor
325	300	275	250	200	125

Lone Eagle (New Model)

Introduced in 1996 this new Lone Eagle model features 15 interchangeable barreled actions from .22 Hornet to .444 Marlin. Available in both black and chrome actions with or without muzzle brake. The 7.62X39 action was introduced in 1996 also. Sights can be fixed, adjustable or silhouette type. Weight is from 4 lbs., 3 oz. to 4 lbs., 7 oz. depending on caliber. Prices below reflect black action and fixed sights.

NIB	Exc.	Good	Good	Fair	Poor
280	225	175	150	125	100

NOTE: Add $80 for muzzle brake; $30 for chrome action; $35 for adjustable sights; $130 for sihouette sights.

Mountain Eagle Rifle

A limited edition rifle (1,000) with a Sako action and composite stock. Chambered for the .270, .280, .30-06, .300 Win., .338 Win, 7mm Mag. Introduced in 1994.

NIB	Exc.	V.G.	Good	Fair	Poor
1250	1000	850	750	500	250

Mountain Eagle Varmint Edition

Chambered for the .222 Rem. and the .223 Rem. cartridges and fitted with a 26" stainless Krieger barrel. Kevlar-graphite stock. Weight is approximately 9 lbs 13 oz.

NIB	Exc	V.G.	Good	Fair	Poor
1350	1100	900	800	500	300

DESTROYER CARBINE
Spain

Destroyer Carbine

A 9mm Bayard caliber bolt-action rifle with a 20" barrel and 7-shot magazine. Full length stock with two barrel bands.

Exc.	V.G.	Good	Fair	Poor
200	125	90	65	35

DETONICS MANUFACTURING CORP.
Bellevue, Washington

This company manufactured semiautomatic pistols based upon the Colt Model 1911.

Mark I

A .45 caliber semiautomatic pistol with a 3.25" barrel and 6-shot magazine. Matte blued with walnut grips. Discontinued in 1981.

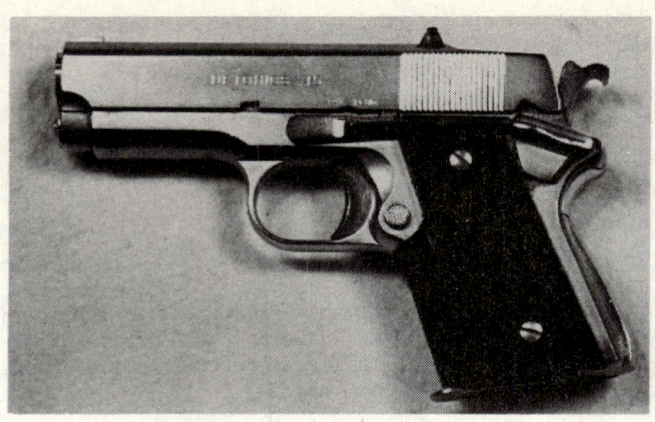

Exc.	V.G.	Good	Fair	Poor
550	450	400	300	200

Mark II

As above, with satin nickel-plated finish. Discontinued in 1979.

Exc.	V.G.	Good	Fair	Poor
550	450	400	300	200

Mark III

As above, with hard chrome plating. Discontinued in 1979.

Exc.	V.G.	Good	Fair	Poor
600	500	450	350	250

Mark IV

As above, with polished blue finish. Discontinued in 1981.

Exc.	V.G.	Good	Fair	Poor
550	450	400	300	200

Combat Master

The Mark I in 9mm, .38 Super, or .45 caliber.

NIB	Exc.	V.G.	Good	Fair	Poor
975	800	600	500	400	250

Combat Master Mark V

As above, in stainless steel with a matte finish. Discontinued in 1985.

NIB	Exc.	V.G.	Good	Fair	Poor
975	800	600	500	400	250

Combat Master Mark VI

As above, with adjustable sights and the sides of the slide polished. 1,000 were made in .451 Detonics Magnum caliber.

.451 Detonics Magnum-Add 40%.

NIB	Exc.	V.G.	Good	Fair	Poor
900	750	600	500	400	250

Combat Master Mark VII

As above, without sights.

.451 Detonics Magnum-Add 40%.

NIB	Exc.	V.G.	Good	Fair	Poor
900	750	600	500	400	250

Military Combat MC2

As above, in 9mm, .38 Super or .45 caliber with fixed sights, dull finish and Pachmayr grips. Discontinued in 1984.

NIB	Exc.	V.G.	Good	Fair	Poor
675	600	500	425	300	200

Scoremaster

As above, in .45 or .451 Detonics Magnum with a 5" or 6" barrel, Millet sights and a grip safety.

NIB	Exc.	V.G.	Good	Fair	Poor
1250	1000	800	600	400	250

Janus Competition Scoremaster

As above, in .45 caliber with a compensated barrel. Introduced in 1988.

NIB	Exc.	V.G.	Good	Fair	Poor
1750	1450	1250	850	650	300

Servicemaster

As above, with a 4.25" barrel, interchangeable sights and matte finish. Discontinued in 1986.

Exc.	V.G.	Good	Fair	Poor
1000	800	600	400	200

Pocket 9

A 9mm double action semiautomatic pistol with a 3" barrel and 6-shot magazine. Matte finish stainless steel. Discontinued in 1986.

Exc.	V.G.	Good	Fair	Poor
400	350	275	225	175

DEUTSCHE WERKE
Erfurt, Germany

Ortgies

A 7.65mm or 9mm short semiautomatic pistol marked on the slide "Deutsche Werke Erfurt". The walnut grips inlaid with a brass medallion cast with an ornate "D".

6.35mm

Exc.	V.G.	Good	Fair	Poor
325	225	175	125	90

DEVISME, F. P.
Paris, France

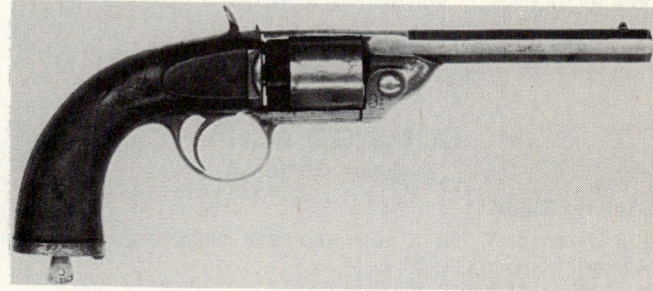

One of the more popular French gunsmiths of the mid-19th century, F.P. Devisme manufactured a wide variety of firearms including single shot percussion pistols, double-barrel percussion rifles and shotguns, percussion revolvers and cane guns. After 1858 this maker manufactured cartridge weapons of the same style as his percussion arms. The quality of all of his products is uniformly high and it is impossible to provide generalized price guide. Prospective purchasers are advised to secure a qualified appraisal prior to acquisition.

DICKINSON
SEE Dickinson, E.L.

DICKINSON, E. L. & J.
Springfield, Massachusetts

Ranger

A .32 caliber spurt rigger revolver with a 6-shot cylinder.

Exc.	V.G.	Good	Fair	Poor
200	175	150	110	80

Single Shot

A .32 caliber single shot pistol with a 3.75" hinged barrel, silver plated brass frame, blued barrel and walnut grips.

Exc.	V.G.	Good	Fair	Poor
400	350	300	225	150

DICKSON, NELSON & CO.
Dawson, Georgia

Dickson, Nelson Rifle

A .58 caliber single shot percussion rifle with a 34" barrel, full stock secured by two barrel bands, brass furniture and iron loading rod. The lock marked "Dickson/Nelson & Co./C.S." as well as "Ala." and the date of manufacture. Prospective purchasers are advised to secure a qualified appraisal prior to acquisition. A carbine version of this arm is known and has a 24" barrel.

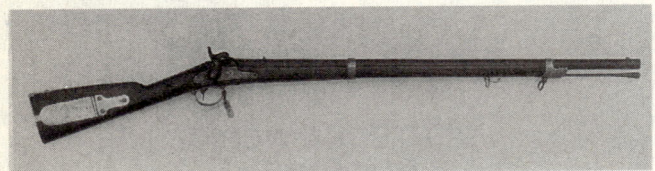

Exc.	V.G.	Good	Fair	Poor
—	—	17500	7500	3000

DIMICK, H.E.
St. Louis, Missouri

While this maker is primarily known for half stock Plains Rifles, he also manufactured a limited number of percussion pistols. These vary in length, caliber, stock form and type of furniture. The values listed below should only be used as a rough guide. Prospective purchasers should secure a qualified appraisal prior to acquisition. Active 1849 to 1873.

Exc.	V.G.	Good	Fair	Poor
—	—	5000	2000	900

DOMINGO ACHA
Eibar, Spain

Looking Glass

A 6.35mm or 7.65mm semiautomatic pistol with the slide marked "Looking Glass".

Exc.	V.G.	Good	Fair	Poor
175	125	100	75	50

DOMINO
Brescia, Italy
Importer - Mandall Shooting Supplies
Scottsdale, Arizona

Model OP 601 Match Pistol

A .22 caliber short semiautomatic pistol with a 5.6" vented barrel, target sights, adjustable and removable trigger. Blued with adjustable walnut grips.

NIB	Exc.	V.G.	Good	Fair	Poor
1300	1150	1000	800	625	450

Model SP 602 Match Pistol

As above, in .22 l.r. caliber.

NIB	Exc.	V.G.	Good	Fair	Poor
1300	1150	1000	800	625	450

DORNHAUS & DIXON
Huntington Beach, California
SEE Bren 10

DORNHEIM, G.C.
Suhl, Germany

Gecado

A 6.35mm or 7.65mm semiautomatic pistol bearing the name "Gecado" on the slide. Marketed by G.C. Dornheim.

Exc.	V.G.	Good	Fair	Poor
200	150	125	75	50

DREYSE
SEE Rheinmetall

DRISCOLL, J.B.
Springfield, Massachusetts

Single Shot Pocket Pistol

A small pistol chambered for .22 rimfire. It has a 3.5" octagonal barrel that pivots downward for loading after a trigger-like hook under the breech is pulled. It has a spur trigger, silver-plated brass frame, and a blued barrel. The square butt is flared at the bottom, and the grips are walnut. There were approximately 200 manufactured in the late 1860s.

Exc.	V.G.	Good	Fair	Poor
—	—	600	200	100

DUBIEL ARMS CO.
Sherman, Texas

Established in 1975 by Joseph Dubiel and Dr. John Tyson. They are engaged in the manufacture of high quality, custom built, bolt-action rifles. The rifles are constructed from patented Dubiel actions that feature a 5-lug bolt locking mechanism and a 36-degree bolt rotation. They are chambered for all calibers from .22-250 through .458 Winchester Magnum. Barrel lengths, weights, and stock styles are made to the customer's order. Douglas Premium barrels and Canjar triggers are used, and there are six basic stock designs available. The rifles are guaranteed to group in 1.5" at 100 yards with factory ammunition. The values listed are basic retail prices, and appraisal should be secured as options will drastically affect prices.

NIB	Exc.	V.G.	Good	Fair	Poor
2500	2250	2000	1750	1500	1200

DUMOULIN
Herstal, Belgium
Importer - Midwest Gunsport
Zebulon, North Carolina

The guns produced by Ernest Dumoulin are essentially handmade to the customer's order. They are of the highest quality, both in materials and workmanship. There are many options available that have a tremendous impact on value fluctuations. The models and values listed here are base prices. If a sale or purchase is contemplated, individual competent appraisal should be secured.

SHOTGUNS

Europa Model

A side-x-side double barrel chambered for 12, 20, and 28 gauge and .410 bore. It is available in any length barrel and choke combination, with an Anson & Deeley boxlock action and automatic ejectors. One has the option of double or single selective triggers and a choice of six different moderate engraving patterns. The select walnut stock is oil-finished. This model was introduced in 1989.

Basic Values:

NIB	Exc.	V.G.	Good	Fair	Poor
3350	3100	2750	2250	1800	1400

Leige Model

A side-x-side double chambered for 12, 16, 20, and 28 gauge. It is similar to the Europa, with a greater degree of finish and more engraving. The walnut is of a higher grade. This model was introduced in 1986.

NIB	Exc.	V.G.	Good	Fair	Poor
5300	5000	4500	4000	3500	3000

Continental Model

A side-x-side chambered for 12, 20, and 28 gauge and .410. Barrel lengths and chokes are on a custom-order basis. This is a true sidelock action with automatic ejectors and choice of triggers. There are six different engraving patterns, and the stock is made of high grade, hand-checkered, oil-finished walnut. This model was introduced in 1989.

NIB	Exc.	V.G.	Good	Fair	Poor
7500	7000	6500	5750	5000	4200

Etendart Model

A side-x-side chambered for 12, 20, and 28 gauge. This best grade side-x-side is built on a purely made-to-order basis. It is profusely engraved and uses exhibition grade walnut in its stock. There are 12 different engraving patterns from which to choose, and the cost is according to embellishments chosen. Values given here are for the basic model.

NIB	Exc.	V.G.	Good	Fair	Poor
14500	12500	10000	8000	6000	4500

Superposed Express International

An Over/Under chambered for 20 gauge and is furnished with a set of rifle barrels in the customer's choice of seven calibers. The walnut is of a deluxe grade, and engraving is available at extra cost. This is a made-to-order gun, and the value here is for the most basic model. This gun was discontinued in 1985.

Exc.	V.G.	Good	Fair	Poor
2500	2250	1750	1250	1000

Boss Royal Model

The best grade Over/Under, chambered for 12, 20, and 28 gauge. It is a full sidelock gun that is made to the customer's specification using the finest materials and workmanship available. This model was introduced in 1987.

NIB	Exc.	V.G.	Good	Fair	Poor
18500	15000	12500	10000	8000	6750

Eagle Model Combination Gun

This model has a rifle barrel or the shotgun barrel that is chambered for 12 or 20 gauge. The rifle calibers available are .22 Hornet, .222 Remington, .222 Remington Magnum, 6mm, .243, .25-06, .30-06, 6.5 x 57R, 7 x 57R, 8 x 57JRS, and 9.3 x 74R. The action is a boxlock with automatic ejectors, and the other specifications are on a custom-order basis. This model was introduced in 1989.

NIB	Exc.	V.G.	Good	Fair	Poor
2750	2500	2000	1750	1250	1000

DOUBLE RIFLES

Europa I

A made-to-order, Over/Under, double-barreled rifle available in the same calibers as the Eagle Combination gun. It has an Anson & Deeley boxlock and all other options to the customer's specifications.

NIB	Exc.	V.G.	Good	Fair	Poor
5000	4750	4000	3500	2900	2250

Continental I Model

A more deluxe Over/Under rifle with a true sidelock action. The calibers are the same as the Europa. The specifications are to the customer's order with 12 engraving patterns to choose from at extra cost. This model was introduced in 1989.

NIB	Exc.	V.G.	Good	Fair	Poor
8500	7800	7000	5500	4500	3750

Pionier Express Rifle

A side-x-side double rifle chambered for the .22 Hornet through the .600 Nitro Express. It has the Anson & Deeley boxlock action and is quite deluxe throughout. The specifications are to the customer's order, and there are basically 12 models available (P-1 through P-XII). The differences among these models are in the degree of ornamentation and quality of the walnut used for the stock. The prices of these models would have to be ascertained through appraisal, as a book of this nature could not possibly consider the variables that one could encounter with a gun of this type. Values range from approximately $8,000 to $12,000 for the basic models.

Aristocrat Model

A low-profile single shot chambered for all calibers up to .375 Holland & Holland. This is a deluxe, made-to-order rifle with exhibition-grade walnut and 12 engraving patterns available.

Exc.	V.G.	Good	Fair	Poor
9000	8000	7000	5500	4800

BOLT ACTION RIFLES

Centurion Model

A custom-order rifle built on a Mauser or Sako action and chambered for all calibers from .270 to .458 Winchester Magnum. The barrel lengths available were 21.5", 24", and 25.5"; and there were many engraving options from which to choose. The stock is of deluxe French walnut, with rosewood forend tip and pistol gripcap. This rifle was discontinued in 1986.

NIB	Exc.	V.G.	Good	Fair	Poor
800	675	600	500	400	300

Centurion Classic

Similar to the Mauser-actioned Centurion chambered for the non-Magnum calibers only. The walnut used for the stock is a better grade.

NIB	Exc.	V.G.	Good	Fair	Poor
950	750	650	550	450	300

Diane

A more deluxe version of the Centurion Classic.

NIB	Exc.	V.G.	Good	Fair	Poor
1550	1400	1150	950	700	600

Amazone

A 20"-barreled, full-length stocked, upgraded version of the Diane.

NIB	Exc.	V.G.	Good	Fair	Poor
1750	1600	1250	1000	750	600

Bavaria Deluxe

Similar to the Centurion, with the same barrel lengths and calibers available. The engraving styles available are more deluxe. This model was discontinued in 1985.

NIB	Exc.	V.G.	Good	Fair	Poor
1900	1750	1500	1250	1000	750

Safari Model

Similar to the Bavaria Deluxe, but it is chambered for the heavy Magnum calibers only.

NIB	Exc.	V.G.	Good	Fair	Poor
2400	2000	1750	1500	1250	1000

Safari Sportsman

Built on a Magnum Mauser action and is chambered for the .375 Holland & Holland, .404 Jeffreys, .416 Rigby, and the .505 Gibbs. This is a true big game rifle that was made available in 1986.

NIB	Exc.	V.G.	Good	Fair	Poor
4000	3750	3250	2750	2500	2000

African Pro

A more deluxe version of the Safari Sportsman, with a folding leaf rear sight, hooded front sight, and an ebony or buffalo horn forend tip.

NIB	Exc.	V.G.	Good	Fair	Poor
4800	4500	4000	3250	2750	2500

NOTE: Again we feel it is important to note that all values furnished in this section are estimates based on the most basic model in each designation. There are many options that will radically affect values, and a competent appraisal should be secured if a sale or purchase is contemplated.

DURLOV
Czech Republic

This company was part of the national co-operative under communist rule when the Czech Republic was part of Czechoslovakia. The company was formed in 1948. The company specialized in low-cost but well made rimfire target pistols.

Durlov Model 70 Standard

This model is a bolt action single shot pistol chambered for the .22 long rifle. A knob at the rear of the frame opened the bolt. When the bolt is closed the firing pin is cocked. The barrel is 9.75" long with an adjustable front sight for windage. The rear sight is adjustable for elevation. Wooden wraparound grips with thumb rest are standard. Weighs about 44 oz.

Exc.	V.G.	Good	Fair	Poor
250	200	175	100	75

Durlov Model 70 Special

Same as above but with the addition of a set trigger.

Exc.	V.G.	Good	Fair	Poor
300	250	200	150	100

Durlov Model 75

This model features a set trigger, better sights, and grip. The rear sight is fully adjustable.

Exc.	V.G.	Good	Fair	Poor
350	300	250	200	150

Pav

This target pistol was introduced between World War I and World War II. It is an inexpensive pistol with a fixed front sight and a notch for the rear sight. Like the other models above it is also a single shot chambered for the .22 long rifle cartridge. The barrel is 10.25" and weighs about 35 oz.

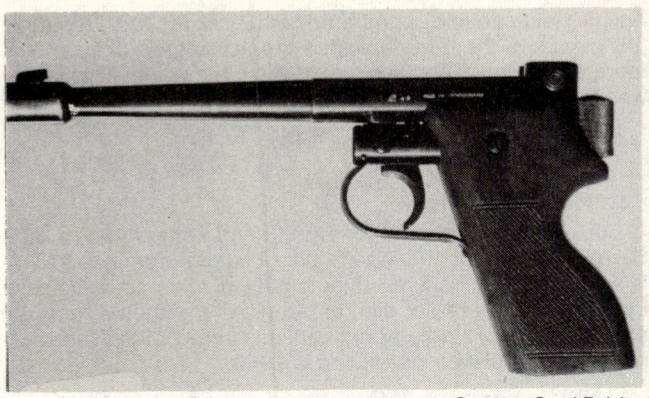

Courtesy Orvel Reichert

Exc.	V.G.	Good	Fair	Poor
175	150	100	75	50

DUSEK, F.
Opocno, Czech Republic

Dusek commenced business in the mid-1920s and continued to make firearms through WWII. They manufactured pistols for Nazi Germany under the contract code "aek." After the war the communists took over, and Dusek's designs were relegated to the CZ factory.

Duo

Introduced in 1926, this 6.35mm pistol is based on the 1906 Browning design. It has a 2.25" barrel and 6-shot detachable magazine. The Duo was successful from a commercial standpoint and was exported throughout the world. During WWII the slide markings were in German; and the name "Eblen", Dusek's German sales agent, may sometimes be found on the slide. The Duo may also be found marked Ideal, Jaga, and Singer.

Nazi-marked examples will bring a 25% premium.

Exc.	V.G.	Good	Fair	Poor
250	200	150	100	80

Perla

This 6.35mm pistol has a fixed barrel and open-topped slide. It resembles a Walther design and is striker-fired. The slide is marked "Automat Pistole Perla 6.35mm"; the grips, "Perla 6.35." Dusek made this model from the early 1930s until WWII.

Exc.	V.G.	Good	Fair	Poor
250	200	150	100	80

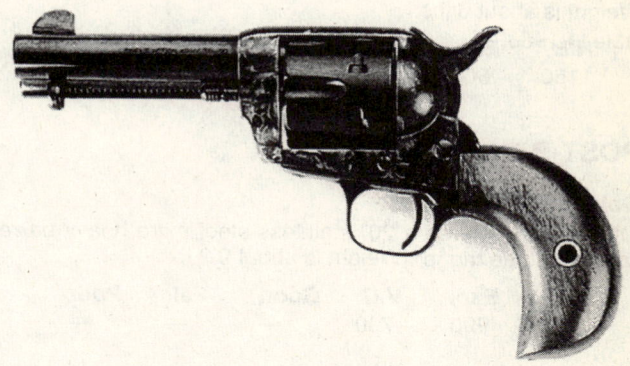

NIB	Exc.	V.G.	Good	Fair	Poor
450	350	—	—	—	—

E.M.F. CO., INC.
Santa Ana, California
SEE Uberti, Aldo

An importer and a distributor of quality Italian-made reproduction firearms. Its offerings are listed in the section dealing with Aldo Uberti firearms. Included below are new products for this company as of 1997.

Hartford Bisley

This single action revolver is fitted with a Colt Bisley grip. Chambered for .45 Long Colt as well as .32-20, .357 Magnum, .38-40, and .44-40 calibers. Barrel lengths are 4-3/4", 5-1/2", and 7-1/2". Plain walnut grips.

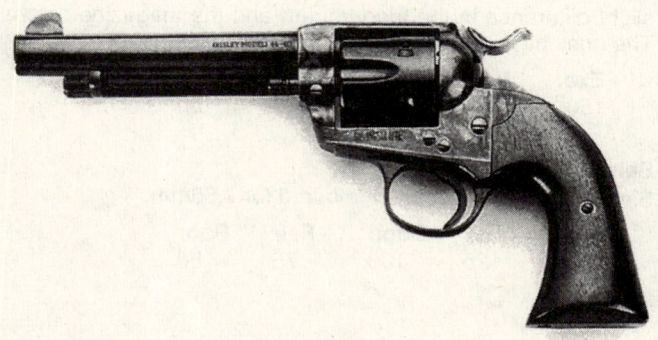

NIB	Exc.	V.G.	Good	Fair	Poor
450	350	—	—	—	—

Hartford Express

A single Colt SAA frame and barrel with a Colt Lightning style grip. Chambered for .45 Long Colt in 4-3/4", 5-1/2", or 7-1/2" barrel lengths.

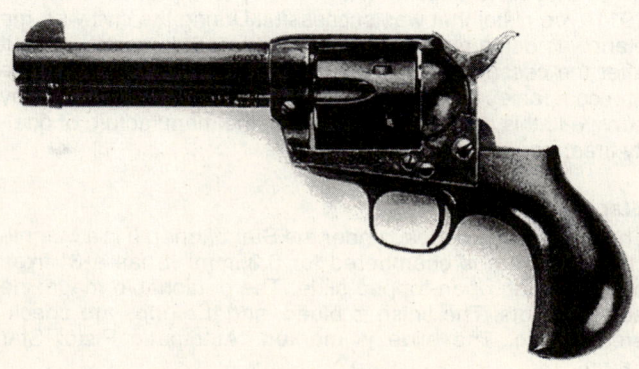

NIB	Exc.	V.G.	Good	Fair	Poor
450	350	—	—	—	—

Hartford Pinkerton

This model features a 4" barrel with ejector and a bird's head grip. Chambered for 45 Long Colt, .32-20, .357 Magnum, .38-40, .44-40, and .44 Special.

EAGLE ARMS CO.
New Haven, Connecticut
SEE Plant Manufacturing Co.

EAGLE ARMS
Division of Armalite
Geneseo, Illinois

PRE-BAN MODELS

Golden Eagle

This model is identical in design to the AR-15. Fitted with a 20" stainless steel extra heavy barrel with National Match sights and two stage trigger. Weight is about 9.4 lbs.

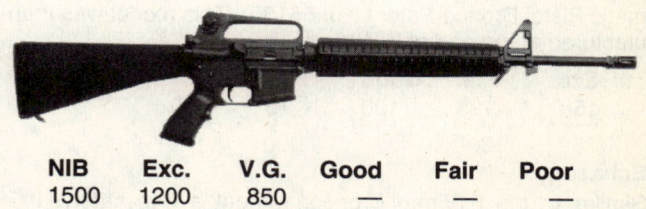

NIB	Exc.	V.G.	Good	Fair	Poor
1500	1200	850	—	—	—

HBAR

Similar to the above model but with a heavy 20" barrel. Weight is approximately 8 lbs.

NIB	Exc.	V.G.	Good	Fair	Poor
1100	800	600	—	—	—

SPR

This is similar to the above model with the exception of a detachable carry handle. Weight is about 7.6 lbs.

M4C Carbine

This model features a 16" barrel with a 4.33" flash suppressor. Retractable stock. Weight is approximately 6.2 lbs.

NIB	Exc.	V.G.	Good	Fair	Poor
1100	800	600	—	—	—

M4A1C Carbine

Similar to the above model but with detachable carry handle. Weight is about 6 lbs.

NIB	Exc.	V.G.	Good	Fair	Poor
1150	800	600	—	—	—

POST-BAN MODEL

Golden Eagle

This model features a 20" stainless steel extra heavy barrel with two stage trigger. Weight is about 9.2 lbs.

NIB	Exc.	V.G.	Good	Fair	Poor
1200	900	700	—	—	—

ECHAVE & ARIZMENDI
Eibar, Spain

Founded in 1911, this company produced the usual poor quality, early Spanish semiautomatic pistols. They did improve their quality later on and were permitted to return to gun manufacturing after the Spanish civil war. They were one of the few pistol makers to survive this period. They imported many models, and their products are not particularly of interest to collectors.

Basque, Echasa or Dickson Special Agent

These two pistols are the same under different names. They are chambered for 7.65mm and are double-action, blowback operated, semiautomatic copies of the Walther PP. The disassembly methods and the quality are the two differences. The finish is blued, and the grips are checkered wood. The slides are marked either "Basque" or "Echasa" and "Made in Spain Cal. .3 2".

Exc.	V.G.	Good	Fair	Poor
200	150	125	100	75

Bronco

A copy of the Browning 1906 chambered for 7.65mm and 6.35mm. It has a grip safety and is marked "1918 Model Automatic Pistol Bronco Patent No. 66130". This model was manufactured at the end of WWI.

Exc.	V.G.	Good	Fair	Poor
150	125	100	75	50

Echasa

Similar to the 6.35mm Bronco, without a grip safety. It is marked "Model 1916".

Exc.	V.G.	Good	Fair	Poor
150	125	100	75	50

Fast

Similar to the Echasa except that it is chambered for the .22 l.r. and the 9mm short, as well as the 7.65mm and the 6.35mm. There is one version that is chrome-plated with white plastic grips.

Exc.	V.G.	Good	Fair	Poor
175	150	125	100	75

Lightning

A renamed version of the Bronco in 6.35mm.

Exc.	V.G.	Good	Fair	Poor
150	125	100	75	50

Lur Panzer

A copy of the Luger toggle-lock action, chambered for .22 rimfire. This is an almost exact copy except for a different trigger assembly and a less robust mainspring. It is marked "Lur Cal.22 LR Made in Spain." The plastic grips have "Panzer" molded into them.

Exc.	V.G.	Good	Fair	Poor
225	200	150	125	100

Pathfinder

The 6.35mm Bronco with another name for export purposes.

Exc.	V.G.	Good	Fair	Poor
150	125	100	75	50

Protector

Similar to the Echasa, chambered for 6.35mm. There is a slight difference in the triggerguard and the magazine catch. The grips have molded flowers and the caliber in a circle.

Exc.	V.G.	Good	Fair	Poor
150	125	100	75	50

Selecta

Similar to the Protector, chambered for 7.65mm.

Exc.	V.G.	Good	Fair	Poor
150	125	100	75	50

ECHEVERRIA, STAR-BONIFACIO SA
Eibar, Spain

An old-line Spanish company that survived the Spanish civil war. It was founded in 1908 by Jean Echeverria, but the early records of the company were lost during the civil war. The early pistols the company produced were patterned after the Mannlicher designs, and the trade name Star was the closest thing to Steyr that could be used. After the close of WWI, the company began production of the open-topped slide Star for which they have become known. They also produced a large 1911-type pistol that was successful. During the civil war, the plant was damaged and the company records destroyed; but after the cessation of hostilities, they were one of only three gun companies that were allowed to remain in business. They survive to this day and are known for the manufacture of quality firearms.

Star Model 1908

The first pistol produced under the Star banner. It is a Mannlicher copy that is chambered for 6.35mm. It has a 3" fixed barrel and an open-topped slide. The detachable magazine holds 8 shots. The finish is blued, and the grips are checkered plastic. The slide is marked "Automatic Pistol Star Patent."

Exc.	V.G.	Good	Fair	Poor
275	250	200	150	100

Star Model 1914

Similar to the Model 1908, with a 5" barrel and larger grips that have the Star name molded into them. This model was the first to have the six-pointed star surrounded by rays of light (that became the Star trademark) stamped on its slide.

Exc.	V.G.	Good	Fair	Poor
275	250	200	150	100

Star Model 1919

Also a copy of a Mannlicher design and differs from its predecessors chiefly in the way the pistol is disassembled. This model has a spring catch at the top of the triggerguard. This model also has a small spur on the hammer, and the magazine release was relocated to a button behind the triggerguard instead of a catch at the bottom of the butt. This model was chambered for 6.35mm, 7.65mm and 9mm short, with various barrel lengths offered. The maker's name, as well as the Star trademark, is stamped into the slide. This model was produced until 1929.

Exc.	V.G.	Good	Fair	Poor
275	250	200	150	100

Modelo Militar

Represents the first pistol Star produced that was not a Mannlicher design copy. This model was copied from the Colt 1911. It was chambered initially for the 9mm Largo in hopes of securing a military contract. When this contract was awarded to Astra, Star chambered the Model 1919 for the .38 Super and the .45 ACP and put it on the commercial market. This model is like the Colt 1911—it has a Browning-type swinging link and the same type of lock up. However there is no grip safety, and the thumb safety functions differently. This model was produced until 1924.

Exc.	V.G.	Good	Fair	Poor
275	250	200	175	125

Star Model A

A modification of the Model 1919, chambered for the 7.63 Mauser, 9mm Largo, and the .45 ACP cartridge. The slide is similar in appearance to the 1911 Colt, and the spur hammer has a small hole in it. Early models had no grip safety, but later production added this feature. Some models are slotted for addition of a shoulder stock.

Exc.	V.G.	Good	Fair	Poor
350	275	175	150	100

Star Model B

Similar to the Model A except that it is almost an exact copy of the Colt 1911. It is chambered for 9mm Parabellum and has a spur hammer with no hole. This model was introduced in 1928.

Courtesy Orvel Reichert

Exc.	V.G.	Good	Fair	Poor
325	250	200	175	125

Star Model C

The Model B chambered for the 9mm Browning long cartridge. It was manufactured in the 1920s.

Exc.	V.G.	Good	Fair	Poor
225	175	150	125	90

Star Model CO

A pocket pistol similar to the early open-topped Star pistols. It is chambered for the 6.35mm cartridge, and the finish is blued with checkered plastic grips that bear the Star name and logo. This model was manufactured between 1930 and 1957.

Exc.	V.G.	Good	Fair	Poor
200	150	125	100	75

Star Model D

A medium-sized pistol that is similar in appearance to a smaller Model A. It is chambered for the 9mm short cartridge and was called the "Police and Pocket Model" after it was adopted by the Spanish police. It was manufactured between 1930 and 1941.

Exc.	V.G.	Good	Fair	Poor
250	175	150	110	80

Star Model E

A pocket pistol chambered for the 6.35mm cartridge. It has a 2.5" barrel and an external hammer. The detachable magazine holds 5 rounds, and the finish is blued with checkered plastic grips. This model was manufactured between 1932 and 1941.

Exc.	V.G.	Good	Fair	Poor
200	175	150	110	80

Star Model F

The first of the .22 caliber Star pistols. It has a 4" barrel, a 10-shot magazine, and fixed sights. The finish is blued, and the plastic grips are checkered. This model was manufactured between 1942 and 1967.

Exc.	V.G.	Good	Fair	Poor
225	175	125	100	75

Star Model F Target

Similar to the Model F, with a 6" barrel.

Exc.	V.G.	Good	Fair	Poor
225	200	150	125	100

Star Model F Sport

Has a 5" barrel and was also manufactured between 1962 and 1967.

Exc.	V.G.	Good	Fair	Poor
225	175	150	125	100

Star Model F Olympic

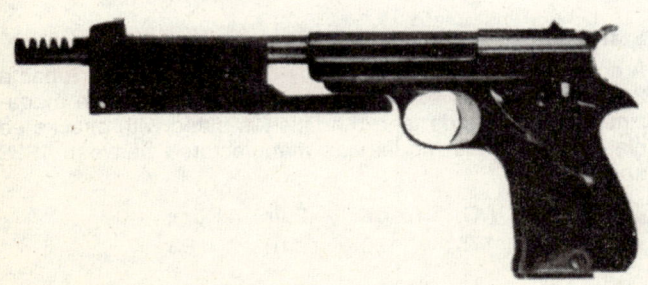

Has a 6" barrel and adjustable sights. It is furnished with a muzzle brake and barrel weights. It was manufactured between 1942 and 1967.

Exc.	V.G.	Good	Fair	Poor
275	225	175	150	125

Star Model F Olympic Rapid Fire

Similar to the Olympic but is chambered for .22 short only.

Exc.	V.G.	Good	Fair	Poor
275	225	175	150	125

Star Model FR

Has an adjustable sight and a slide stop. The 4" barrel is heavier, with flattened sides. It was manufactured between 1967 and 1972.

Exc.	V.G.	Good	Fair	Poor
225	175	145	125	100

Star Model FRS

Similar to the Model FR, with a 6" barrel. It is also available chrome-plated with white checkered plastic grips. It was introduced in 1967 and is still in production.

Exc.	V.G.	Good	Fair	Poor
225	175	145	125	100

Star Model FM

A heavier-framed version of the Model FRS. It has a 4.5" barrel and is available in blue or chrome-plated. It was introduced in 1972 and is still made.

Exc.	V.G.	Good	Fair	Poor
225	175	145	125	100

Star Model H

Similar to the old Model CO—only larger in size. It is chambered for the 7.65mm cartridge and was manufactured between 1932 and 1941.

Exc.	V.G.	Good	Fair	Poor
225	175	150	125	100

Star Model HK

A pocket-sized version of the Model F chambered for .22 short. It has a 2.5" barrel and is quite scarce on today's market.

Exc.	V.G.	Good	Fair	Poor
250	200	150	125	100

Star Model HN

Simply the Model H chambered for the 9mm short cartridge. It was manufactured and discontinued at the same time as the Model H was.

Exc.	V.G.	Good	Fair	Poor
250	200	150	125	100

Star Model I

An improved version of the Model H with a 4" barrel and a re-contoured grip. It was chambered for 7.65mm and was produced until 1941. After the war it was resumed and survived until the mid-1950s, when it was replaced by the modernized Model IR that would be valued approximately the same.

Exc.	V.G.	Good	Fair	Poor
200	150	125	100	75

Star Model M

Similar to the Model B, chambered for the .38 Auto cartridge.

Exc.	V.G.	Good	Fair	Poor
275	225	175	125	100

Star Model P

The postwar version of the Model B, fitted with a 5" barrel and chambered for the .45 ACP cartridge. Checkered walnut grips and blued finish.

Exc.	V.G.	Good	Fair	Poor
350	300	225	175	125

Star Model CU "Starlet"

Similar to the Model CO, with an alloy frame that was anodized in black, blue, gray, green, or gold. It has a steel slide that is blued or chrome-plated. It has checkered, white plastic grips and is chambered for the .25 ACP cartridge. It has a 2.5" barrel, fixed sights, and a 5-shot magazine. This model was introduced in 1975 and was not imported after 1986.

Exc.	V.G.	Good	Fair	Poor
175	150	125	100	75

Star Model BKS "Starlight"

The smallest locked-breech automatic chambered for the 9mm cartridge at the time. It has an alloy frame and a 4.25" barrel. It is similar in appearance to a scaled-down Colt 1911 without a grip safety. It has an 8-shot magazine and is either blued or chrome-plated, with checkered plastic grips. This model was manufactured between 1970 and 1981.

Exc.	V.G.	Good	Fair	Poor
250	225	200	150	125

Star Model PD

Chambered for the .45 ACP cartridge and has a 4" barrel. It has an alloy frame and a 6-shot magazine and adjustable sights and is blued with checkered walnut grips. It was introduced in 1975.

NIB	Exc.	V.G.	Good	Fair	Poor
400	325	275	225	175	125

Star Model BM

A steel-framed 9mm that is styled after the Colt 1911. It has an 8-shot magazine and a 4" barrel. It is available either blued or chrome-plated.

NIB	Exc.	V.G.	Good	Fair	Poor
350	300	250	200	150	125

Star Model BKM

Similar to the BM, with an alloy frame.

NIB	Exc.	V.G.	Good	Fair	Poor
375	325	275	225	175	125

Star Model 28

The first of Star's Super 9s. It is a double-action semiautomatic chambered for the 9mm Parabellum cartridge. It has a 4.25" barrel and a steel frame. The magazine holds 15 shots. The construction of this pistol was totally modular, and it has no screws at all in its design. It is blued with checkered synthetic grips and was manufactured in 1983 and 1984.

NIB	Exc.	V.G.	Good	Fair	Poor
400	300	250	200	150	100

Star Model 30M

An improved version of the Model 28, that is quite similar in appearance. It was introduced in 1985.

NIB	Exc.	V.G.	Good	Fair	Poor
450	350	300	250	200	125

Star Model 30/PK

Similar to the Models 28 and 30M, with a lightweight alloy frame.

NIB	Exc.	V.G.	Good	Fair	Poor
450	350	300	250	200	125

ECHEVERRIA
(Star)
Importer - Interarms
Alexandria, Virginia

Megastar

This is a double-action semiautomatic pistol chambered for the 10mm or .45 ACP cartridge. It features a three position ambidextrous selective decocking lever, rubber grips, combat style triggerguard, slotted hammer, and checkered mainspring housing. Barrel length is 4.6" and the magazine capacity is 12 rounds. Available in either blue or starvel (brushed chrome). The pistol weighs 47.6 oz.

NIB	Exc.	V.G.	Good	Fair	Poor
500	450	350	250	200	100

Firestar-M/43, M/40, and M45

This is a compact large caliber semiautomatic pistol offered in 9mm, the M43, .40 S&W, the M40, and the .45 ACP, the M45. It features an ambidextrous safety, steel frame and slide, checkered rubber grips. The barrel is 3.4" on the M43 and M40 and 3.6" on the M45. Choice of finish is blue or starvel (brushed chrome). A finger rest magazine is optional. Weight for the M43 and M40 is 30 oz. while the M56 weighs 35 oz. Introduced in 1990.

NIB	Exc.	V.G.	Good	Fair	Poor
400	300	250	200	150	100

Firestar Plus

This is a lightweight version of the Firestar Series with the addition of a double column magazine. Offered in the 9mm caliber in either blue or Starvel finish this pistol has a magazine capacity of 10 rounds and weighs 24 oz. Introduced in 1992.

NIB	Exc.	Good	Good	Fair	Poor
450	350	300	250	175	125

Starfire Model 31P

This model evolved from the Models 28 and 30. It is chambered for either the 9mm Parabellum or .40 S&W. The trigger action is double-action/single-action. Barrel length is 3.9". It is fitted with a two position safety/decocking lever. The magazine capacity for the 9mm is 15-rounds while the .40 S&W holds 11 rounds. The pistol weighs 39 oz.

NIB	Exc.	V.G.	Good	Fair	Poor
425	350	300	250	200	100

Starfire Model 31PK

Similar to the Model 31P but built on an alloy frame. Chambered for 9mm only with a 15 round magazine capacity. Weight is 30 oz.

NIB	Exc.	V.G.	Good	Fair	Poor
400	350	300	250	200	100

Ultrastar

Introduced in 1994 this compact 9mm or .40 S&W semiautomatic pistol with a polymer frame features a 3.57" barrel, a 9-round magazine, a blued finish and an overall length of 7". It weighs about 26 oz. It has a double action operating system, a windage adjustable rear sight, and an ambidextrous two-position safety.

NIB	Exc.	V.G.	Good	Fair	Poor
475	375	325	275	200	100

ECLIPSE
Pittsburgh, Pennsylvania
Enterprise Gun Works

Single Shot Derringer

This pocket pistol was made by the firm of James Bown & Son, doing business as the Enterprise Gun Works. It is chambered for .22 or .32-caliber rimfire cartridges. A few in .25 rimfire have been noted and would add approximately 25% to the values listed. The barrel is 2.5" in length and is part-round/part-octagonal. It pivots sideways for loading. It has a spur trigger and a bird's head grip. The barrel is stamped "Eclipse." It is made of nickel-plated iron, with walnut grips. There were approximately 10,000 manufactured between 1870 and 1890.

Exc.	V.G.	Good	Fair	Poor
—	600	250	100	75

84 GUN CO.
Eighty Four, Pennsylvania

In business for a brief time in the early 1970s. They produced three basic bolt-action rifles—each in four grades that differ in amounts of embellishment and grades of wood. There is little known about this company and its products. An accurate appraisal with hands-on would be the only proper way to place a value on these rifles as there are not enough traded in to establish correct values in a book of this nature. The basic models are as follows:

Classic Rifle
Grade 1-Grade 4 available
450—1600

Lobo Rifle
Grade 1-Grade 4 available
425—2500

Pennsylvania Rifle
Grade 1-Grade 4 available
425—2500

ELGIN CUTLASS
Springfield, Massachusetts

Manufactured by two companies—C.B. Allen of Springfield, Massachusetts, and Morill, Mosman and Blair of Amherst, Massachusetts. It is a unique pistol that has an integral knife attachment affixed to the gun barrel. It was designed and patented by George Elgin and simultaneously produced by the two companies. The inspiration for this weapon was supposedly Jim Bowie, who at that time had made a name as a knife fighter with his large "Bowie" knife. The blades for these pistols were supplied by N.P. Ames of the famed Ames Sword Co.

These pistols are much sought after, and one must exercise caution as fraudulent examples have been noted.

C. B. Allen-Made Pistols
U.S. Navy Elgin Cutlass Pistol

Chambered for .54 caliber percussion and has a 5" octagonal smooth-bore barrel. The Bowie-style blade is 11" long by 2" wide and is forged together with the triggerguard and the knuckle guard that protects the grip. The handle is walnut. This pistol was issued to the U.S. Navy's Wilkes-South Sea Exploration Expedition, and the markings are "C.B. Allen / Springfield / Mass." "Elgin's Patent" and the letters "CB", "CBA" along with the date 1837. If the sheath that was issued with this knife pistol is included and in sound condition, it would add approximately $700 to the value. There were 150 manufactured for the U.S. Navy in 1838.

Exc.	V.G.	Good	Fair	Poor
—	10000	8000	6500	4750

Civilian Model

Chambered for .35 or .41 caliber percussion and has a 4" octagonal barrel with a 7.5"-10" knife blade. It has a round triggerguard but does not have the knuckle bow across the grip, as found on the military model. They are marked "C.B. Allen Springfield, Mass." Blades marked "N.P. Ames" have been noted. There were approximately 100 manufactured in 1837.

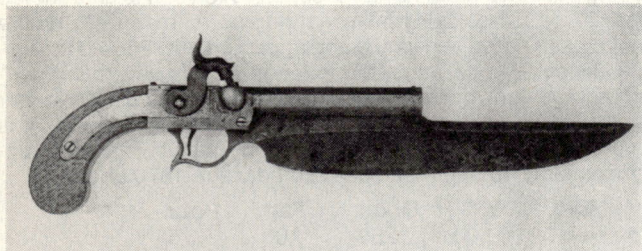

Exc.	V.G.	Good	Fair	Poor
—	9000	6000	3250	2750

Morill, Mosman and Blair-Made Pistols
Small Model

The main difference in the pistols of the two makers is that this model has a round barrel and a square-back triggerguard that comes to a point at the rear. This version is chambered for .32 caliber percussion and has a 2.75" barrel. The knife blade is 7.5" in length and is screwed to the frame. This model is unmarked except for a serial number. The number produced is unknown, and they were manufactured in 1837.

Exc.	V.G.	Good	Fair	Poor
—	9000	6000	3250	2750

Large Model

Chambered for .36 caliber percussion and has a 4" round barrel and a 9" knife blade. The pistol is usually marked "Cast Steel" and serial numbered. The blade is etched with an American eagle, stars, and an urn with flowers. "Elgin Patent" is etched in the center. This model was also manufactured in 1837.

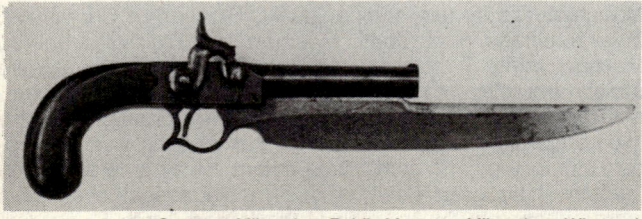

Courtesy Milwaukee Public Museum, Milwaukee, Wisconsin

Exc.	V.G.	Good	Fair	Poor
—	10000	7000	3500	3000

ELLS, JOSIAH
Pittsburgh, Pennsylvania

Pocket Revolver

Three distinct variations of this percussion revolver. They are chambered for .28 and .31 caliber and have 6-shot unfluted cylinders. They have been noted with 2.5", 3", and 3.75" octagonal barrels.

Model 1

The first model has an open-topped frame and is chambered for .28 caliber. The cylinder holds 5 or 6 shots, and the hammer is of the bar type. It was offered with a 2.5" or 3" barrel. The markings are "J. Ells; Patent; 1854." There were approximately 625 manufactured between 1857 and 1859.

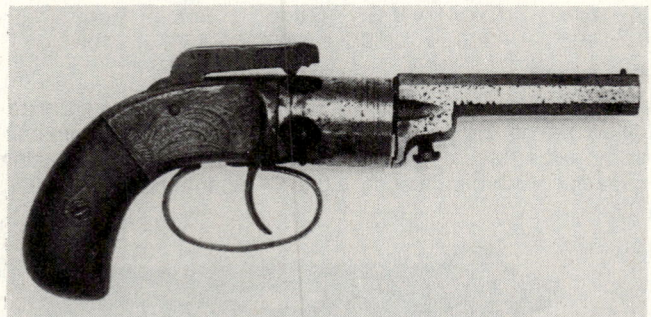

Courtesy Milwaukee Public Museum, Milwaukee, Wisconsin

Exc.	V.G.	Good	Fair	Poor
—	1200	500	275	200

Model 2

The second model is similar to the first, with a solid-topped frame. They have 5-shot cylinders and 3.75" long barrels. There were approximately 550 manufactured.

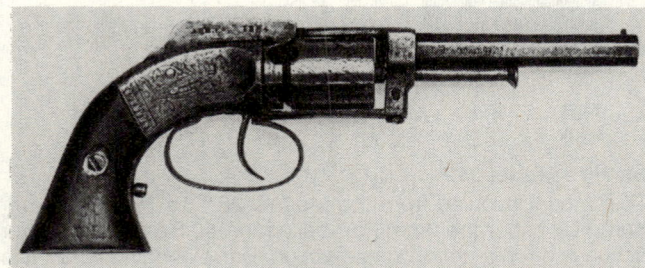

Courtesy Milwaukee Public Museum, Milwaukee, Wisconsin

Exc.	V.G.	Good	Fair	Poor
—	1500	800	350	200

Model 3

The third model is radically different from its forerunners. It has a closed-top frame and a conventional spur-type hammer that strikes from the right side. It functions either as a double- or single-action. It is chambered for .28 caliber and has a 5-shot cylinder and a 3.75" barrel. There were only about 200 manufactured between 1857 and 1859.

Exc.	V.G.	Good	Fair	Poor
—	1500	800	350	200

ENFIELD ROYAL SMALL ARMS FACTORY
Middlesex, England

In 1879 the British Army needed revolvers, and the Royal Small Arms Factory was commissioned to produce them. The result was that on August 11, 1880, the Enfield Mark I was accepted for duty.

Enfield Mark I Revolver

A 6-shot, hinged-frame, break-open revolver. It has an odd ejection system—when the barrel is pulled down, the cylinder moves forward; and the extractor plate remains in place, retaining the spent cartridges. This revolver is chambered for the .476 cartridge and has a 6-shot cylinder. The barrel is 6" long, and the finish is blued with checkered walnut grips.

Exc.	V.G.	Good	Fair	Poor
250	225	175	140	100

Enfield Mark 2

The Mark 2 is similar externally, with some design improvements—such as a rounded front sight, taper-bored cylinders, an integral top strap, and plain grips. The Mark 2 was introduced in 1881 and was replaced by the Webley Mark I in 1887.

Exc.	V.G.	Good	Fair	Poor
250	225	175	140	100

Enfield-Produced Webley Mark 6

This model is identical to the Webley-produced versions. It is of .455 caliber and is stamped "Enfield" on the frame.

Exc.	V.G.	Good	Fair	Poor
300	250	175	140	100

Enfield No. 2 Mark I

Originally chambered for the .38 Webley Special. It is a 6-shot, break-open double action, with a 5" barrel. The finish is blued, with black plastic checkered grips. This model was actually a modified Webley design and was adopted in 1932. In 1938 the bullet was changed from a 200-grain lead "soft-nosed" to a 178-grain jacketed, in response to pressure from the Geneva Conference.

Exc.	V.G.	Good	Fair	Poor
200	175	150	125	100

Enfield No. 2 Mark I

The same as the Mark I with the hammer spur and single-action lockwork omitted in response to the Royal Tank Regiment's fear that the spur would catch on the tank as the crews were entering and exiting their confines.

Exc.	V.G.	Good	Fair	Poor
225	200	175	150	125

During WWII these pistols were manufactured by Albion Motors Ltd. of Glasgow, Scotland. These pistols were produced between 1941 and 1943, and approximately 24,000 were made. They are marked "Albion" on the right side of the frame. These examples would not be valued differently than Enfield-made pistols. Enfield pistols with the marking "SM" or "SSM" will also be noted, and this refers to various parts produced by Singer Sewing Machine Company of England. These pistols were assembled at Enfield. Used until 1957, when the FN-Browning GP35 semiautomatic pistol replaced them.

Enfield Rifles
Lee-Enfield Mark I

Chambered for the .303 cartridge and has a 30" barrel. The attached box magazine holds 10 rounds, and the sights are military-styled. The stock is full-length walnut, and there is a cleaning rod beneath it. There are two barrel bands and a bayonet lug. This model was manufactured between 1895 and 1899.

Exc.	V.G.	Good	Fair	Poor
250	225	200	150	100

Lee-Enfield Mark I

A Mark 3 Martini Henry with a .303-caliber barrel fitted to it. It was introduced in 1899.

Exc.	V.G.	Good	Fair	Poor
250	225	200	150	100

Lee-Enfield Mark I

Simply the Mark I with no attached cleaning rod. It was introduced in 1899.

Exc.	V.G.	Good	Fair	Poor
250	225	200	150	100

Lee-Enfield Mark II SMLE

The Mark I converted by fitting a shorter and lighter barrel, modifying the action to accept a stripper clip, and fitting new sights. The letters SMLE stand for Short Magazine, Lee-Enfield. It was introduced in 1903.

Exc.	V.G.	Good	Fair	Poor
225	200	175	150	100

SMLE Mark III currently imported by CIA

Chambered for .303 British and has a 25" barrel with a 10-round magazine. The magazine has a cut off, and the sights are military-styled. The action is modified to accept a stripper clip and automatically eject it when the bolt is closed. This model was introduced in 1907.

Exc.	V.G.	Good	Fair	Poor
150	100	85	60	30

SMLE No. 5 Mark I

Also known as the Jungle Carbine. It is chambered for the .303 British cartridge and has a 20.5" barrel with an attached flash suppressor and a shorter forend and hand guard. It is furnished with a rubber butt pad and modified rear sight. This was not a popular weapon with the soldiers who carried it as the recoil was excessive due to the lighter weight.

Courtesy Richard M. Kumor, Sr.

Exc.	V.G.	Good	Fair	Poor
400	350	275	175	125

No. 3 Mark I P1914 currently imported by CIA

Built on a modified Mauser-type action and was chambered for the .303 British cartridge. It was a secondary-issue arm during WWI and was simpler to mass-produce than the SMLE. These rifles were also produced in the U.S.A. by Remington and Winchester.

Exc.	V.G.	Good	Fair	Poor
170	120	90	65	35

SMLE No. 4 Mark I currently imported by CIA

An improved version that featured a stronger action with an aperture sight and was easier to mass produce. It was issued in 1939 and was used during WWII. There is a cased and scoped Sniper model of this variation.

Exc.	V.G.	Good	Fair	Poor
150	100	85	60	30

Sniper Model Cased

Exc.	V.G.	Good	Fair	Poor
1200	800	650	425	350

No.3 Mark I

A single-shot, bolt-action training rifle that is chambered for the .22 rimfire cartridge.

Exc.	V.G.	Good	Fair	Poor
350	325	275	200	150

ENFIELD AMERICAN, INC.
Atlanta, Georgia

MP-45

A blowback-operated, semiautomatic assault pistol chambered for the .45 ACP cartridge. It was offered with a barrel length of 4.5" through 18.5". The long barrel features a shroud. The finish is parkerized, and there were four different magazines available in 10, 20, 30, and 50-round capacities. This firearm was manufactured in 1985 only.

Exc.	V.G.	Good	Fair	Poor
300	275	225	175	125

ENGLISH MILITARY FIREARMS
Enfield, England

Until the establishment of the Royal Armory at Enfield in 1816, the government of England relied solely upon the contract system to obtain small arms for its naval and military forces. Even after the Enfield Armory began is first major production in 1823, the contractors continued to dominate the production of arms for the military. These contractors were concentrated in two major cities, Birmingham and London. Although a number of makers from Birmingham were capable of manufacturing arms, "lock, stock, and barrel," and of assembling them, most of the makers of that city specialized in the making of specific parts, which could be assembled into complete arms on the "factory system" then prevalent in Liege. When the English War Department was the purchaser, the parts were usually delivered to the Tower of London for assembly. Most military arms made in Birmingham accordingly are seldom marked with a single maker's name. Rather they bear the English crown and the name "TOWER" on the lock. Those barrels that passed proof at Birmingham after 1813 were marked with the view and proofmarks derived from Ketland's only proofmarks; these consisted of a pair of crowned, crossed scepters, one pair of which had the letter "V" in the lower quarter and the other of which had the letters "B," "C," and "P" respectively in the left, right, and lower quarters. In contrast, the arms manufactured at London were almost always completed by their manufacturers, and bear their names usually upon the lockplates and barrels. The London gunmakers also marked their barrels with a pair of proofmarks, consisting of a crown over a "V" and a crown over an intertwined "G" and "P." Prominent martial arms makers in the London trade through the 1860s included, "BOND," "BARNETT," "BLISSETT," "GREENER," "HOLLIS & SONS," "LONDON ARMORY CO," "KERR," "PARKER, FIELD & SONS," "PRITCHETT," "POTTS & HUNT," "ROBERT WHEELER," "WILSON & CO.," and "YEOMANS." (It should be noted that most of these London makers also manufactured sporting and other trade arms, which will bear similar marks.) During the period of transition from the contract system to the reliance upon the works at Enfield (roughly 1816 through 1867), the arms themselves underwent major transitions, first from flintlock to percussion ignition systems and then from smoothbore to rifled bore, first in large and then in small bore sizes. The major infantry types include:

New Land Pattern Musket

Overall length 58-1/2"; barrel length 42"; caliber .75. The mainstay of the British Army during the Napoleonic Wars, this flintlock arm continued, primarily, in service until 1838, with major quantities (5,000 from each) being ordered from Enfield and from the contractors as late as 1823.

Exc.	V.G.	Good	Fair	Poor
2200	2000	1500	850	600

Pattern of 1839 (P1839) Musket

Overall length 55"; barrel length 39"; caliber .76. In 1838 the British War Department contracted for the parts for 30,000 new flintlock arms. However, before these arms could be assembled, the War Department adopted the percussion system of ignition and ordered that these arms be made as percussion. Obsolete by 1861, large numbers were purchased by the Southern Confederacy and imported for use in the American Civil War. Arms with firm evidence of Confederate military usage increases the value of the arm considerably.

Exc.	V.G.	Good	Fair	Poor
950	850	500	450	350

Pattern of 1842 (P1842) Musket (and Rifled Musket)

Overall length 55"; barrel length 39-1/4"; caliber .75. The first English-made as percussion musket to be issued to the Line Regiments of the British Army, continued in production through the Crimean War. The final production (1851-1855) of 26,400 were made with rifled barrel and a long range rear sight soldered to the barrel, similar in configuration to that of the P1851 rifle-musket. These rifled versions of the P1842 musket will command a premium.

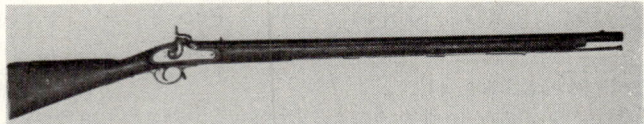

Courtesy Milwaukee Public Museum, Milwaukee, Wisconsin

Exc.	V.G.	Good	Fair	Poor
900	850	650	450	350

"Brunswick" Rifles (first model or P1837) and (second model or P1845)

Overall length 46-1/2" (Pl837), 45-3/4" (Pl845); barrel length 33" (Pl837), 30" (Pl845); caliber .704. The "Brunswick" rifle differed from its predecessors (the "Baker rifle") adopted for the English "Rifle Brigade" in having a large bore cut with only two spiraling grooves. These grooves engaged a specially cast ball having a raised belt circumventing it. The first model of the "Brunswick rifle" adopted in 1837 is primarily distinguished by having a "backaction" percussion lock, which continued in production until 1844 despite having been officially changed to the standard "barlock" in 1841. Those made after 1844 bear the standard percussion lock. The value of these rifles is enhanced by virtue of the importation of at least 2,000 (probably first model variants) into the Southern Confederacy during the American Civil War. (It should be noted that Russia also adopted a variant of the "Brunswick" style rifle, having them made in Liege, Belgium and so marked with Liege proofmarks. These rifles are distinguished by having a distinctive rear sight with an adjustable arcing ladder.)

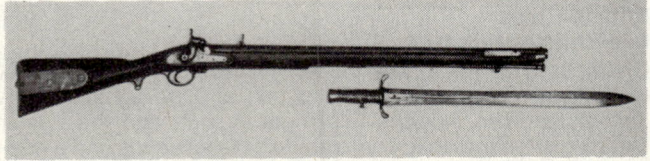

Courtesy Milwaukee Public Museum, Milwaukee, Wisconsin

Exc.	V.G.	Good	Fair	Poor
1250	1100	900	700	450

Pattern of 1851 (P1851) Rifle-Musket

Overall length 55"; barrel length 39"; caliber .702. With the success of the "Minie ball" projectile in France, England in

1851 adopted its first production rifle musket. Externally resembling the P1842 musket, the P1851 is distinguished by the long range rear sight soldered to the barrel and its smaller caliber (.70) rifled bore. Approximately 35,000 were manufactured until 1855, with a substantial number being imported to the United States during the early years of the American Civil War.

Courtesy Milwaukee Public Museum, Milwaukee, Wisconsin

Exc.	V.G.	Good	Fair	Poor
1500	1250	1000	700	450

Pattern of 1853 (PI853) Rifle Musket (first through fourth types)

Overall length 55" (54" on fourth type); barrel length 39"; caliber .577. The P1853 rifle musket underwent several changes during the span of its production. The earliest type (first model) was made with clamping bands. Due to problems with the bands slipping, the bands were modified in late 1855 to solid, spring fastened (second model), the upper wider than the other two. However, in 1858 the government reverted to clamping bands continuing production in this style through 1863. Those made at Enfield after 1859 were one inch shorter in the butt stock, but the contractors continued to deliver them in 55-inch length well into the 1860s. The fourth model is distinguished by the "Baddeley patent" clamping barrel bands, wherein the screwheads are recessed into the bands. The third model saw the greatest production, with more than 600,000 being imported into the north and about 300,000 into the south during the American Civil War. P1853 rifle muskets with early Confederate importation marks on the stock and butt plate will command a premium if authentic.

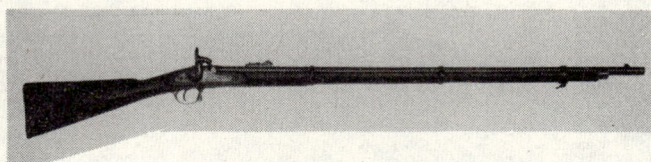

Courtesy Milwaukee Public Museum, Milwaukee, Wisconsin

Exc.	V.G.	Good	Fair	Poor
1300	950	650	450	350

American Made Copies of the English P1853 Rifle Musket

Three firms during the period from 1855 through 1862 produced copies of the P1853 rifle musket, Robbins & Lawrence of Windsor, Vermont; Orison Blunt of New York City; and John Moore of New York City. All three types command a premium over the standard imported muskets and may be distinguished as follows:

Robbins & Lawrence P1853 Rifle Muskets

During the Crimean War, Robbins & Lawrence received a contract for 25,000 P1853 rifle muskets of the second model. Due to production delays, the company had delivered only 10,400 when the war ended. Due to the penalties for non-deliveries, Robbins & Lawrence declared bankruptcy. An additional 5,600 arms were made on the firms machinery while in receivership by the "Vermont Arms Co." before the machinery was sold to Sharps and Eli Whitney, Jr. The Robbins & Lawrence-made P1853 rifle muskets are distinguished by the lock marking "WINDSOR" beneath the date (such as "1856") on the forward part of the lock and by non-English proofmarks on the barrel. Many of these arms saw service in the American Civil

War, with Alabama obtaining several hundred in 1861. Arms with confirmed southern usage will bring substantial premiums.

Exc.	V.G.	Good	Fair	Poor
2000	1800	1300	850	600

Orison Blunt P1853 Rifle Muskets

At the beginning of the Civil War, Orison Blunt of New York City attempted to produce a copy of the P1853 rifle musket but with a 40-inch barrel and in .58 caliber. After making several hundred, his proposed contract with the U.S. War Department was declined. Nevertheless, in mid-1862, it is thought that about 1,000 of his rifle muskets were purchased by the U.S. government and sent to Illinois to arm volunteers. Blunt "Enfields" are distinguished by two distinct markings. While most lockplates are totally unmarked, a few are known with the mark "UNION" on the forward part of the lockplate and an eagle impressed into the rounded tail. More importantly, Blunt barrels bear an oval with the letters "DP/B" near the breech. (Note: Not all P1853 rifle muskets with 40-inch barrels were made by Blunt; Birmingham and Liege contractors supplied the Spanish government with a 40-inch barrel copy of the P1853 English rifle musket as well, and some of these were diverted to the American market during the Civil War. These are usually distinguished by the letter "C" in a diamond near the breech of the barrel surrounded by proofmarks.)

Courtesy Milwaukee Public Museum, Milwaukee, Wisconsin

Exc.	V.G.	Good	Fair	Poor
1200	1100	1000	750	475

John P. Moore P1853 Rifle Muskets

During the American Civil War arms merchant John P. Moore of New York City received a contract for the delivery of 20,000 P1853 rifle muskets, supposedly to be made in the United States. In fact, most of his contract was made in Birmingham, England, with only 1,080 completely made in the United States. These are distinguished by having an unusual script proofmark on the barrel near the breech instead of the standard Birmingham crossed scepters. These script letters have been interpreted as either "V LB" or "EP I" depending on how they are read. All of Moore's P1853 deliveries bear a distinctive lock marking, consisting of the date forward of the hammer ("1861", "1862," or "1863") and an eagle perched on a shield on the tail. The shield bears the letter "M" in its chief. Moore also delivered 999 short rifles (33" barrels) with the same lock markings. Likewise, all of the barrels on the Moore P1853 rifle musket contract are serially numbered, either on the forward side near the muzzle or on the side of the bayonet lug/front sight. Because the Moore rifles have been misidentified as a product of a North Carolina arms merchant, they tend to command higher prices than are warranted by their numbers.

Exc.	V.G.	Good	Fair	Poor
1100	1000	850	600	450

"Brazilian Naval Rifle"

Overall length 48"; barrel length 32"; caliber .58. Markings: on lockplate forward of hammer "D (anchor) C"; the same mark stamped in the wood and metal in various places on the rifle;

on barrel, same mark and Liege proofmarks (an oval encompassing the letters E/LG/(star). Although neither made for the English government nor in England, this rifle copies so many features of the English P1856 series rifles (see next page) as to be easily mistaken for it. The major differences consist of a longer (3-3/8") sight base than the English rifles and a front band/nosecap that also serves as the ramrod funnel. These Liege-made rifles were supposedly made for the Brazilian government, but at the beginning of the American Civil War they were diverted to the United States, about 10,000 being imported. To show their new ownership, a brass shield bearing the U.S. coat of arms was screwed into the wrist of the stock.

Courtesy Milwaukee Public Museum, Milwaukee, Wisconsin

Exc.	V.G.	Good	Fair	Poor
800	725	650	450	275

Patterns of 1856, 1858, 1860, and 1861 (P1856, P1858, P1860, P1861) Sergeant's Rifles

Overall length 49"; barrel length 33"; caliber .577. The four variations of the short rifle adopted for sergeants in the British Army in 1856 are relatively minor. The P1856 is mainly distinguished by having a short (1/2") key forward of the saber bayonet lug on the right side of the barrel. The P1858 rifle moved this lug to the forward band, permitting the extension of the length of the forestock. (A brass furnished rifle also without the key but with the lug on the barrel was also adopted in 1858 for the Navy; it is distinguished by having its rear sling swivel attached to the triggerguard bow instead of the tail of the triggerguard strap.) The P1860 rifle differed from its predecessors by having five groove rifling instead of three groove. The introduction of a new gunpowder in 1861 permitted the resighting of the ladder on the P1861 rifle to 1,250 yards instead of the 1,100 yards that had been previously used. Significant quantities of these rifles were purchased by both belligerents during the American Civil War; those with proven southern history will command a premium.

Courtesy Milwaukee Public Museum, Milwaukee, Wisconsin

Courtesy Milwaukee Public Museum, Milwaukee, Wisconsin

Exc.	V.G.	Good	Fair	Poor
1250	1050	800	650	450

Pattern of 1853 (P1853) Artillery Carbine (First, Second, and Third Models)

Overall length 40"; barrel length 24"; caliber .577. Designed for the gunners of the Royal Artillery, this carbine was meant to be slung over the shoulder and accordingly has a sling swivel on the upper band and upon a lug inset into the buttstock. The first model (adopted in 1853), like the sergeant's rifle has a 112" key forward of the saber bayonet lug on the right side of the barrel; in addition to other minor improvements, this key was eliminated in the second model, adopted in 1858. In 1861, a third model was adopted, having five groove rifling and improved rear sight. Approximately 1,000 of the latter type saw service in the American Civil War. Carbines with Confederate stock and buttplate markings will command a premium.

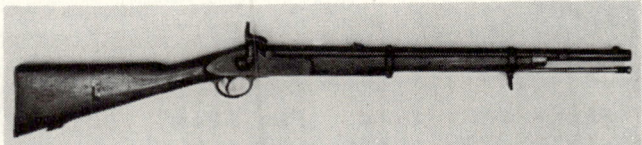

Courtesy Milwaukee Public Museum, Milwaukee, Wisconsin

Exc.	V.G.	Good	Fair	Poor
1100	950	700	550	400

Patterns of 1856 (P1856) and Pattern of 1861 (P1861) Cavalry Carbines

Overall length 37" (Pl856), 36-1/2" (Pl861) barrel length 21"; caliber .577. Due to inadequacies in the various breechloading carbines tried by the British mounted service, in 1856 the War Department adopted a muzzleloading carbine incorporating the features of the P1853 series small arms. The earlier version had three groove rifling and a small rear sight with two leaves. In 1861 this was replaced by a larger ladder sight and five groove rifling adopted. More than 6,000 P1856 carbines were imported by the Southern Confederacy during the Civil War to make up for the inadequate supply of carbines. Carbines with verifiable Southern history will command a premium.

Courtesy Milwaukee Public Museum, Milwaukee, Wisconsin

Exc.	V.G.	Good	Fair	Poor
975	850	725	600	375

ERA
Brazil

Era Double Barrel Shotgun

An inexpensive shotgun chambered for 12 and 20 gauge, as well as .410. It was offered with 26", 28", or 30" barrels with various choke combinations. It has double triggers and extractors, with a checkered hardwood pistol-grip stock. This gun is also available as a Quail model with a 20" barrel and as a Riot model with an 18" barrel. These two models are not offered in .410 bore.

Exc.	V.G.	Good	Fair	Poor
175	150	125	100	75

Era Over/Under Shotgun

Chambered for 12 or 20 gauge, with 28" ventilated rib barrels that were choked full and modified. It is a boxlock with double triggers, extractors, and a hardwood stock. It was also offered in a trap model and a skeet model chambered for 12 gauge only and appropriately choked. These latter two models would be worth a 10% premium over the values shown.

Exc.	V.G.	Good	Fair	Poor
300	275	250	200	150

ERICHSON, G.
Houston, Texas

Erichson Pocket Pistol

A close copy of the Philadelphia-style Henry Deringer. It is chambered for .45-caliber percussion and has a 3.25" barrel. The mountings are German silver and not engraved; the stock is walnut. The hammer is deeply fluted; and the forend, carved. The barrel is marked "G. Erichson / Houston, Texas." The number produced is unknown, but examples are scarce. They were manufactured in the 1850s and 1860s.

Exc.	V.G.	Good	Fair	Poor
—	—	6000	3000	1000

ERMA WERKE WAFFENFABRIK
Erfurt, Germany
Postwar
Dachau, Germany

Known primarily as a manufacturer of submachine guns, but they are also in the handgun and rifle business. In 1933 they answered the German army's need for an inexpensive practice weapon by producing a .22 rimfire conversion unit for the Luger pistol. This was marketed commercially and was available for many years. The success of this unit led the company to produce other inexpensive target and plinking pistols. After the war they were reorganized in the western sector and resumed submachine gun production. In 1964 they returned to the sporting firearms business with the introduction of their .22 rimfire Luger-lookalike pistol. Since then, they have produced many like-quality firearms. They were imported by Excam of Hialeah, Florida. This association is now terminated, and they are currently imported by Beeman Precision in Santa Rosa, California, and Mandell Shooting Supplies in Scottsdale, Arizona.

Erma .22 Luger Conversion Unit

Produced for the German army in 1933 and then became a successful commercial item. It would turn a standard 9mm or 7.65mm Luger into an inexpensive-to-shoot .22 rimfire. The unit consists of a barrel insert, a breech block, and toggle unit with its own lightened recoil spring, and a .22 magazine. This unit was furnished with a wooden box. There were many different sized units to fit various caliber and barrel-length Lugers, but all used the same parts and concept. These units have become desirable to Luger collectors.

Exc.	V.G.	Good	Fair	Poor
500	425	350	275	200

.22 Target Pistol (Old Model)

An inexpensive, blowback-operated, semiautomatic pistol chambered for the .22 rimfire cartridge. This model has a 4" barrel and an open-topped slide. The frame is made from a cast zinc alloy, and there is an external hammer. There are adjustable sights, and balance weights were available. This pistol was manufactured in 1936.

Exc.	V.G.	Good	Fair	Poor
250	225	175	125	100

.22 Target Pistol (New Model)

An improved version of the old model, that features a new grip angle and a magazine and takedown device that is like that of the Luger. There were interchangeable barrels and three basic models—the "Sport," "Hunter," and "Master." The difference was the length of the barrels—4", 5", and 6", respectively. These pistols were manufactured between 1937

and 1940, when they were discontinued due to Erma's involvement in the war effort.

Exc.	V.G.	Good	Fair	Poor
275	250	200	150	125

KGP-Series

Made to resemble the Luger quite closely. They utilized the mechanical features of the .22 conversion unit and developed a pistol around it. There are many different versions of this pistol chambered for .22 rimfire, .32 ACP, and .380 ACP. The original designation was the KGP-68; but the Gun Control Act of 1968 required that a magazine safety be added, and the model was redesignated the KGP-68A. The last designations for the three calibers are KGP-22, KGP-32, and KGP-38. These pistols were manufactured between 1964 and 1986, and their values are as follows:

KGP-68

A 4" barrel and is chambered for the .32 ACP and the .380 ACP cartridges. It has a 6-shot magazine and an anodized alloy receiver. This model is also known as the Beeman MP-08.

Exc.	V.G.	Good	Fair	Poor
500	400	300	200	100

KGP-69

A .22 rimfire version of this series, with an 8-shot magazine capacity. It is also known as the Beeman P-08.

Exc.	V.G.	Good	Fair	Poor
300	200	150	100	75

ET-22 Luger Carbine

A rare firearm. According to some estimates only 375 were produced. It features an 11.75" barrel and is chambered for the .22 rimfire cartridge. It has an artillery Luger-type rear sight and checkered walnut grips, with a smooth walnut forend. The pistol was furnished with a red-felt-lined, black leatherette case.

Exc.	V.G.	Good	Fair	Poor
400	350	300	200	150

KGP-22

The later version of the KGP-69 chambered for .22 rimfire.

Exc.	V.G.	Good	Fair	Poor
350	300	250	200	125

KGP-32 & KGP-38

These two designations are the later versions of the KGP-68 and 68A.

Exc.	V.G.	Good	Fair	Poor
350	300	250	200	125

ESP 85A

A high quality target pistol imported by Mandall Shooting Supply. It features an interchangeable barrel system that converts the chambering from .22 rimfire to .32 S&W long wad cutter. The barrels are both 6" in length, and there are adjustable and interchangeable sights and a 5- or 8-shot detachable magazine. The finish is blued, and the grips are stippled target types. The gun is furnished in a padded hard case with two extra magazines and takedown tools. This unit was introduced in 1989.

NIB	Exc.	V.G.	Good	Fair	Poor
1100	1000	850	700	550	450

RX-22

A .22 rimfire copy of the Walther PPK. It has a 3.25" barrel, an 8-shot detachable magazine, and a blued finish with checkered black plastic grips. It was assembled in the U.S.A. from parts made in West Germany. It was discontinued in 1986.

Exc.	V.G.	Good	Fair	Poor
200	175	150	125	100

REVOLVERS

ER-772 Match

A target revolver chambered for the .22 rimfire and has a 6" shrouded barrel with a solid rib. The swing-out cylinder holds 6 shots, and the sights are adjustable. The finish is blued, with stippled target grips. This model was introduced in 1989.

NIB	Exc.	V.G.	Good	Fair	Poor
500	450	400	350	250	200

ER-773 Match

Similar to the ER-772 except that it is chambered for the .32 S&W long cartridge.

NIB	Exc.	V.G.	Good	Fair	Poor
500	450	400	350	250	200

ER-777

Basically a similar revolver to the ER-773 except that it has a 4.5" or 5" barrel and is chambered for the .357 Magnum car-tridge. The revolver is larger and has standard sport grips. This model was also introduced in 1989.

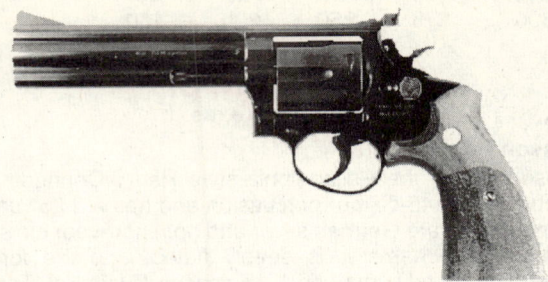

NIB	Exc.	V.G.	Good	Fair	Poor
500	450	400	350	250	200

RIFLES

EMI.22

A semiautomatic .22 rimfire version of the MI Carbine. It has an 18" barrel and a 15-round magazine. It was manufactured between 1966 and 1976.

Exc.	V.G.	Good	Fair	Poor
200	175	150	125	100

EG-72, EG-722

A 15-shot slide action carbine chambered for .22 rimfire, with a 18.5" barrel and open sights. The finish is blued, and it was manufactured between 1970 and 1985.

Exc.	V.G.	Good	Fair	Poor
135	110	100	75	50

EG-712, EG-73

A lever copy of the Winchester 94 Carbine chambered for the .22 rimfire or the .22 rimfire Magnum (EG-73). It has an 18.5" barrel and holds 15 shots in a tubular magazine. It was manufactured between 1973 and 1985.

Exc.	V.G.	Good	Fair	Poor
200	175	150	125	100

SR-100

This is long range precision bolt action rifle chambered for .308 Win., .300 Win. Mag., or .338 Lapua calibers. Barrel length on the .308 Win. caliber is 25.25", other calibers are 29.25". All barrels are fitted with a muzzle brake. Trigger is adjustable. Stock is laminated with thumbhole and adjustable recoil pad and cheekpiece. Weight is approximately 15 lbs.

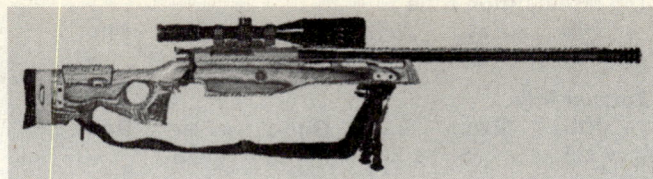

NIB	Exc.	V.G.	Good	Fair	Poor
8800	7000	—	—	—	—

ERQUIAGA
Eibar, Spain

Another Spanish company that commenced business during WWI as a subcontractor on the French "Ruby" contract. They manufactured the usual poor-quality, 7.65mm Eibar-type pistol.

Fiel

The trade name found on the Ruby subcontract pistol described above. It is marked "Erquiaga y Cia Eibar Cal. 7.65 Fiel".

Exc.	V.G.	Good	Fair	Poor
175	150	125	100	75

Fiel 6.35

After the end of WWI, a 1906 Browning copy was made. It is chambered for the 6.35mm cartridge. The markings are "Automatic Pistol 6.35 Fiel No. 1". Later models had "EMC" molded into the grip.

Exc.	V.G.	Good	Fair	Poor
150	125	100	75	50

Marte

Another poor-quality "Eibar"-type pistol that is chambered for the 6.35mm and that was made in the early 1920s.

Exc.	V.G.	Good	Fair	Poor
150	125	100	75	50

ERRASTI, A.
Eibar, Spain

Errasti manufactured a variety of inexpensive yet serviceable pistols from the early 1900s until the Spanish civil war.

Velo-Dog

Usual cheap solid frame folding trigger revolvers one associates with the model designation. They were chambered in 5.5mm and 6.35mm and were made in the early 1900s.

Exc.	V.G.	Good	Fair	Poor
150	125	100	75	50

M1889

In 1915-1916 Errasti produced the 10.4mm Italian army service revolver. The quality was reasonably good. They were marked "Errasti Eiber" on the right side of the frame.

Exc.	V.G.	Good	Fair	Poor
200	175	150	100	75

Errasti

Two "Eibar" type Browning copies were made under this trade name. One was chambered for the 6.35mm, the other the 7.65mm. They were both marked "Automatic Pistol Errasti."

Exc.	V.G.	Good	Fair	Poor
150	125	100	75	50

Errasti Oscillante

Manufactured in the 1920s, these revolvers were copied from the Smith & Wesson Military & Police design. They were chambered for the .32, .38, and .44 calibers with the .38 being the most frequently encountered.

Exc.	V.G.	Good	Fair	Poor
150	125	100	75	50

Dreadnaught, Goliath and Smith Americano

These three trade names were found on a group of poor quality nickel-plated revolvers. They were made from 1905 through 1920 and were obvious copies of the Iver Johnson design. They had break-open actions, ribbed barrel, and were chambered for .32, .38, and .44 calibers. They are scarce today, as most have long since fallen apart.

Exc.	V.G.	Good	Fair	Poor
150	125	100	75	50

ESCODIN, M.
Eibar, Spain

This company made a Smith & Wesson revolver copy from 1924 through 1931. It is chambered for the .32 and the .38 Special. The only marking is a coat of arms stamped on the left side of the frame.

Exc.	V.G.	Good	Fair	Poor
150	125	100	75	50

ESPIRIN, HERMANOS
Eibar, Spain

Euskaro

This poor-quality, often unsafe revolver was manufactured from 1906 until WWI. They are copies of the Iver Johnson design break-open actions, chambered for .32, .38, and .44. This product epitomizes the worst Eibar had to offer during the pre-Civil War era.

Exc.	V.G.	Good	Fair	Poor
125	100	75	50	25

EUROARMS OF AMERICA
Winchester, Virginia

An importer of black powder muzzle-loading firearms, primarily replicas of early American weapons.

REVOLVERS

1851 Navy

A replica of the Colt revolver chambered for .36 or .44 caliber percussion. It has a squareback, silver-plated triggerguard and a 7.5" barrel.

NIB	Exc.	V.G.	Good	Fair	Poor
135	125	110	80	65	45

1851 Navy Police Model

Chambered for .36 caliber with a 5-shot, fluted cylinder and a 5.5" barrel.

NIB	Exc.	V.G.	Good	Fair	Poor
135	125	110	80	65	45

1851 Navy Sheriff's Model

A 5" barrelled version of the Navy Model.

NIB	Exc.	V.G.	Good	Fair	Poor
110	100	80	60	50	35

1851 "Schneider & Glassick" Navy

A replica of the Confederate revolver chambered for .36 or .44 caliber percussion.

NIB	Exc.	V.G.	Good	Fair	Poor
110	100	80	60	50	35

1851 "Griswold & Gunnison" Navy

A replica of this Confederate revolver chambered for .36 or .44 caliber percussion.

NIB	Exc.	V.G.	Good	Fair	Poor
110	90	75	60	40	25

1862 Police

A replica of the Colt Model 1862 chambered for .36 caliber percussion, with a 7.5" barrel and a steel frame.

NIB	Exc.	V.G.	Good	Fair	Poor
150	125	110	90	65	45

1860 Army

A replica of the Colt revolver chambered for .44 caliber percussion. It was offered with a 5" or 8" barrel.

NIB	Exc.	V.G.	Good	Fair	Poor
150	125	100	75	50	30

1861 Navy

A replica of the Colt revolver chambered for .36 caliber percussion.

NIB	Exc.	V.G.	Good	Fair	Poor
160	135	110	80	60	40

1858 Remington Army or Navy

Replicas of the Remington percussion revolvers chambered for .26 or .44 caliber.

NIB	Exc.	V.G.	Good	Fair	Poor
175	150	125	100	75	50

RIFLES

The following rifles are modern replicas of early American and British firearms. They are of good quality and are quite serviceable. There is little collector interest, and we list them along with their values.

Cook & Brother Carbine

NIB	Exc.	V.G.	Good	Fair	Poor
375	325	250	100	150	100

1863 J.P. Murray

NIB	Exc.	V.G.	Good	Fair	Poor
360	310	225	175	125	100

1853 Enfield Rifled Musket

NIB	Exc.	V.G.	Good	Fair	Poor
400	350	300	250	175	125

1858 Enfield Rifled Musket

NIB	Exc.	V.G.	Good	Fair	Poor
375	325	250	200	150	100

1861 Enfield Musketoon

NIB	Exc.	V.G.	Good	Fair	Poor
350	300	225	175	125	90

1803 Harper's Ferry

NIB	Exc.	V.G.	Good	Fair	Poor
500	425	350	300	225	150

1841 Mississippi Rifle

NIB	Exc.	V.G.	Good	Fair	Poor
475	400	325	275	200	125

Pennsylvania Rifle

NIB	Exc.	V.G.	Good	Fair	Poor
300	250	225	200	150	100

Hawken Rifle

NIB	Exc.	V.G.	Good	Fair	Poor
300	250	200	150	100	80

Cape Gun

NIB	Exc.	V.G.	Good	Fair	Poor
400	350	275	225	175	125

Buffalo Carbine

NIB	Exc.	V.G.	Good	Fair	Poor
400	350	300	250	175	100

1862 Remington Rifle

NIB	Exc.	V.G.	Good	Fair	Poor
300	250	225	200	125	60

Zouave Rifle

NIB	Exc.	V.G.	Good	Fair	Poor
325	275	225	175	125	90

Duck Gun

A single-barreled percussion fowling piece chambered for 8, 10, or 12 gauge. It has a 33" smooth-bore barrel and a case-colored hammer and lock. The stock is walnut with brass mountings. This model was introduced in 1989.

NIB	Exc.	V.G.	Good	Fair	Poor
400	350	300	250	175	100

A side-by-side, chambered for 12 gauge percussion. It has 28" barrels with engraved locks and a walnut stock.

NIB	Exc.	V.G.	Good	Fair	Poor
425	375	325	275	200	125

EUROPEAN AMERICAN ARMORY CORP.
Importers
Hialeah, Florida

Witness Pistols

These quality pistols are produced by Tanfoglio, an Italian firm, and imported into the U.S. by European American Armory. These handguns are based on the CZ design and offer many features that are sought after by the shooter such as: competition sights, double-action/single-action trigger system, and internal firing pin lock. The firm was founded by Giuseppe Tanfoglio after WWII. He formed a partnership with Antonio Sabbati and began to manufacture small caliber pistols. During the 1960s the firm also produced derringers and Colt SAA copies. In 1980 the Tanfoglio company decided to enter the service pistol market and copied the respected Czech CZ design. The Tanfoglio company currently produces the P9 series for Springfield Armory and the Desert Eagle line for IMI. In 1993 EAA converted from two frame sizes to one and redesigned the triggerguard and beavertail. This redesigned frame enables all of the different caliber slide assemblies to be interchangeable with one frame. This new configuration began to appear in mid-1993. The buyer should be aware that the EAA Custom Shop offers a wide variety of accessories for its pistols, such as compensators, hammers, ported barrels, grips, etc., that will affect price.

EAA Witness Standard

Available in 9mm, .41 AE, 40 S&W, and .45 ACP with 4.5" barrel. Magazine capacity: 9mm-16 rounds, .41 AE-11 rounds, .40 S&W-12 rounds, .45 ACP-10 rounds. Offered in blue, chrome, two-tone, and stainless steel. Weighs approximately 33 oz.

Old Configuration

NIB	Exc.	V.G.	Good	Fair	Poor
385	325	275	225	175	125

New Configuration

NIB	Exc.	V.G.	Good	Fair	Poor
385	325	275	225	175	125

NOTE: For chrome, two-tone, and stainless steel add 5% to above prices. Pistols chambered for .45 ACP add 10%.

EAA Witness Subcompact

Offered in the same calibers as the standard model but fitted with a 3.66" barrel and shorter grip. Magazine capacity: 9mm-13 rounds, .41 AE-9 rounds, .40 S&W 9-rounds, .45 ACP-8 rounds. Weighs about 30 oz. Offered in blue, chrome, two-tone, and stainless steel.

Old Configuration

NIB	Exc.	V.G.	Good	Fair	Poor
385	325	275	225	175	125

New Configuration

NIB	Exc.	V.G.	Good	Fair	Poor
385	325	275	225	175	125

NOTE: For chrome, two-tone, and stainless steel add 5% to above prices. Pistols chambered for .45 ACP add 10%.

EAA Witness Carry Comp

This model is offered in 9mm, .41 AE, .40 S&W, and .45 ACP. It features a 1" steel compensator. The barrel is 41" long. Overall length is the same as the standard model as is magazine capacity. Offered in blue or blue chrome finish. Weighs 34 oz.

Old Configuration

NIB	Exc.	V.G.	Good	Fair	Poor
500	450	375	325	250	175

New Configuration

NIB	Exc.	V.G.	Good	Fair	Poor
500	450	375	325	250	175

NOTE: For .45 ACP add 15% to above prices.

EAA Witness Combo 9/40

This model offers a 9mm conversion kit, and a .40 S&W conversion kit. These kits consist of a slide, barrel, recoil spring and guide, and magazine. Available in standard or subcompact size in blue, chrome, or two-tone finish.

NIB	Exc.	V.G.	Good	Fair	Poor
550	475	400	350	275	175

NOTE: For chrome or two-tone finish add 5% to above prices.

EAA Witness Sport L/S

This model features a longer slide for its 4.75" barrel. Offered in 9mm, .41 AE, .40 S&W, and .45 ACP. Magazine capacity: 9mm-19 rounds, .41 AE-13 rounds, .40 S&W 14 rounds, and .45 ACP-11 rounds. This model is also fitted with adjustable rear sight and extended safety. Available in two-tone finish. Weighs about 34.5 oz. A ported barrel is offered as an option.

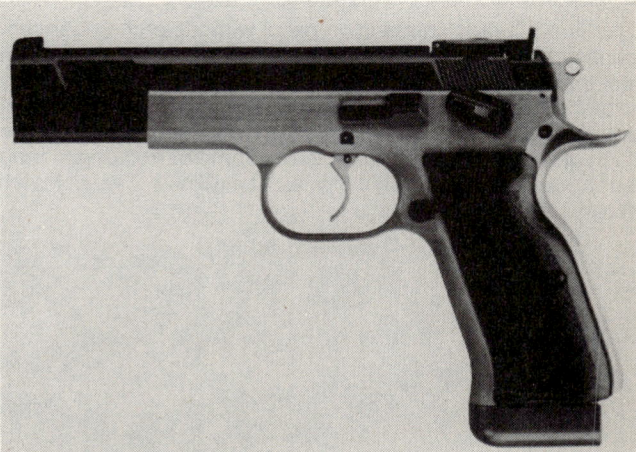

Old Configuration

NIB	Exc.	V.G.	Good	Fair	Poor
625	550	500	400	300	200

New Configuration

NIB	Exc.	V.G.	Good	Fair	Poor
625	550	500	400	300	200

NOTE: For .45 ACP add 10% to prices.

EAA Witness Sport

This model is built on the standard Witness frame with the addition of an adjustable rear sight and extended safety. Offered in 9mm, .41 AE, .40 S&W, .45 ACP in standard model magazine capacity. Weighs 33 oz. Available in two-tone finish.

Old Configuration

NIB	Exc.	V.G.	Good	Fair	Poor
550	475	400	300	200	150

New Configuration

NIB	Exc.	V.G.	Good	Fair	Poor
550	475	400	300	200	150

NOTE: For .45 ACP add 10% to above prices.

EAA Witness Silver Team Match

This is designed as a competition pistol. It is fitted with a 5.25" barrel. It has the following features: dual chamber compensator, single-action trigger, extended safety, competition hammer, paddle magazine release, checkered walnut grips, and adjustable rear sight or drilled and tapped for scope mount. Offered in 9mm-19 rounds, .40 S&W 14 rounds, .41 AE-13 rounds, .45 ACP-11 rounds, and 9 x 21. Finish is blue and weight is approximately 34 oz.

NIB	Exc.	V.G.	Good	Fair	Poor
900	800	700	600	450	300

EAA Witness Gold Team Match

This is a full race competition pistol with triple chamber compensator, beaver tail grip safety, beveled magazine well, adjustable rear sight or drilled and tapped for scope mount, extended safety and magazine release, competition hammer, square triggerguard, checkered front and back strap, competition grips, and hard chrome finish. Same barrel length, magazine capacity, and calibers as the Silver Team Match. Weighs 38 oz.

NIB	Exc.	V.G.	Good	Fair	Poor
1600	1250	900	750	600	400

EAA Witness Limited Class Pistol

This model is built on the Witness Match frame with competition grips, high capacity magazine, extended safety and magazine release, single action trigger, long slide with adjustable rear sight, and match grade barrel. Offered in 9mm, .40 S&W, .38 Super, and .45 ACP with blue finish.

NIB	Exc.	V.G.	Good	Fair	Poor
900	775	650	550	400	300

EAA Witness Multi Class Pistol Package

This package consists of one Witness Limited Class pistol with a complete unlimited class top half. The top half is made up of a standard length slide with super sight, recoil guide and spring, match grade competition barrel (threaded for compensator), and a dual chamber compensator. Available in 9mm, .40 S&W, 9 x 21, .45 ACP, 9 x 23, and .38 Super. Finish is blue.

NIB	Exc.	V.G.	Good	Fair	Poor
1500	1200	850	600	300	200

NOTE: Any of the above EAA Witness pistol can be supplied with double-action only triggers at no additional charge.

OTHER EAA IMPORTED FIREARMS

EAA Big Bore Bounty Hunter

This model is a single action revolver made in Germany. It features three-position hammer, forged barrel, and walnut grips. Offered in .357 Mag., .45 Long Colt, and .44 Mag. in 4.5", 5.5", or 7.5" barrel lengths. Choice of finish includes blue or case-colored frame, chrome, gold, or blue and gold.

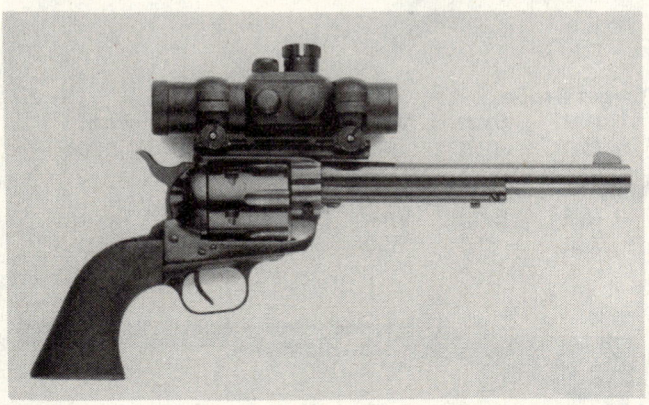

NIB	Exc.	V.G.	Good	Fair	Poor
300	225	175	150	125	100

NOTE: For chrome, gold, or blue and gold finish add 20%.

EAA Small Bore Bounty Hunter

This is a single action .22 caliber revolver. It has wood grips and is available in blue or blue and brass finish. Barrel lengths are 4.75", 6", and 9". It is chambered for .22 Long Rifle or .22 Winchester Rimfire Magnum.

NIB	Exc.	V.G.	Good	Fair	Poor
150	125	100	90	70	60

EAA F.A.B. 92 Pistol

This model is a semiautomatic pistol similar to the Witness, but fitted with a hammer drop safety and slide mounted safety, that is both a double-action or single-action. It is available in either a full size (33 oz.) or compact size (30 oz.). The full size version has a 4.5" barrel while the compact is fitted with a 3.66" barrel. Offered in 9mm or .40 S&W in blue, two-tone, or chrome finish.

NIB	Exc.	V.G.	Good	Fair	Poor
350	275	225	175	125	100

EAA European Standard Pistol

This is a single-action semiautomatic pistol with external hammer, slide grip serrations, wood grips, and single column magazine. The barrels length is 3.2" and overall length is 6.5". Chambered for .22 Long Rifle, 380 ACP, .32 ACP. The magazine capacity is 10 rounds for the .22 LR, 7 rounds for .380, and 7 rounds for .32. Offered in blue, blue/chrome, chrome, blue/gold. Weighs 26 oz.

NIB	Exc.	V.G.	Good	Fair	Poor
165	135	110	95	75	50

EAA European Target Pistol

This model features adjustable rear sight, external hammer, single action trigger, walnut target grips, and adjustable weight system. Chambered for .22 Long Rifle. Offered in blue finish and weighs 40 oz.

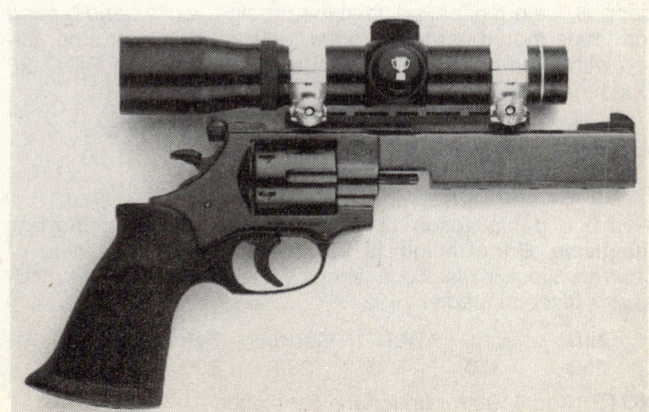

NIB	Exc.	V.G.	Good	Fair	Poor
325	275	225	175	150	100

EAA Windicator Standard Grade

This German built model is a double action revolver chambered for the .22 Long Rifle, .22 Winchester Rimfire Magnum, .32 H&R, and .38 Special. It is offered in 2", 4", and 6" barrel lengths. The cylinder capacity for the .22 LR/.22WRM is 8 rounds, .32 H&R is 7 rounds, and the .38 Special is 6 rounds. The cylinder is unfluted. Finish is blue.

NIB	Exc.	V.G.	Good	Fair	Poor
185	140	120	95	75	60

EAA Windicator Basic Grade

This model is chambered for the .38 Special or the .357 Magnum with 2" barrel. The fluted cylinder holds 6 rounds. Finish is blue.

NIB	Exc.	V.G.	Good	Fair	Poor
175	130	110	85	65	50

EAA Windicator Tactical Grade

This model is similar in appearance to the standard grade but is chambered for the .38 Special with 2" or 4" barrel. The 4" barrel has an integral compensator. Finish is blue.

2" Barrel

NIB	Exc.	V.G.	Good	Fair	Poor
190	150	125	100	80	60

4" Barrel

NIB	Exc.	V.G.	Good	Fair	Poor
250	200	150	125	100	75

EAA Windicator Target Grade

This model has the following special features: adjustable trigger pull, walnut grips, adjustable rear sight, drilled and tapped for scope mount, target hammer, adjustable trigger stop. Fitted with 6" target barrel. Chambered for .22 Long Rifle, .38 Special, .357 Mag. Blue finish.

NIB	Exc.	V.G.	Good	Fair	Poor
350	275	225	200	150	100

EAA PM2 Shotgun

This is a pump action 12 gauge shotgun with 6-round box magazine. Barrel length is 20" and finish is either blue or chrome. Stock is black composite. Weight is 6.8 lbs. This model was discontinued in 1993.

NIB	Exc.	V.G.	Good	Fair	Poor
450	350	300	250	200	150

NOTE: Add $100 for optional night sights.

EAA HW 60 Rifle

This German made target rifle is chambered for the .22 Long Rifle. It features an adjustable trigger and other target and match grade components. The barrel length is 26.8", the stock is stippled walnut, and the finish is blue. Weighs approximately 10.8 lbs.

Target Grade

NIB	Exc.	V.G.	Good	Fair	Poor
670	575	500	400	300	200

Match Grade

NIB	Exc.	V.G.	Good	Fair	Poor
760	650	550	450	350	250

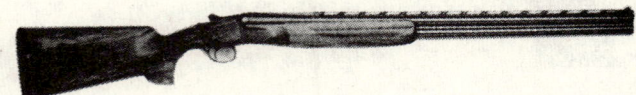

EAA Sabatti

These firearms are made by the Sabatti firm in Gardone, Italy. It is a old line company, having been in the firearms business since 1674. The company also produces and supplies component parts to many of Italy's premier gun makers. These shotguns and rifles are manufactured for the cost-conscious buyer.

EAA Sabatti Falcon

This is a field grade Over/Under shotgun with checkered walnut stock with pistol grip, boxlock action, double triggers, and extractors. Offered in 12 or 20 gauge with 3" chambers. Also available in 28 gauge and .410 bore with 26" or 28" barrels. Barrel lengths are available in 26", 28", or 30". Chokes are fixed.

NIB	Exc.	V.G.	Good	Fair	Poor
575	425	400	350	300	250

28/.410

NIB	Exc.	V.G.	Good	Fair	Poor
625	480	425	375	325	275

EAA Sporting Clay Basic

This model features a single selective trigger, extractors, checkered walnut stock with pistol grip, extra wide rib, and blued receiver with scroll engraving. Offered in 12 gauge only with 28" fixed choke barrel.

NIB	Exc.	V.G.	Good	Fair	Poor
350	275	250	200	150	100

EAA Sporting Clay Pro

This model is similar to the basic sporting clay model with the addition of a select walnut stock, screw in choke tubes, automatic ejectors, recoil pad. Comes with hard shell case.

NIB	Exc.	V.G.	Good	Fair	Poor
950	720	650	550	450	300

EAA Sporting Clay Pro Gold

Same as above but with gold inlay receiver.

NIB	Exc.	V.G.	Good	Fair	Poor
1000	750	650	550	450	300

EAA Saba

This model is a side-x-side shotgun that features an engraved silver boxlock receiver, double or single triggers, selective ejectors, solid raised matted rib, and select European walnut checkered stock. Offered in 12, 20, and 28 gauge as well as .410 bore. Barrel length are 26" or 28" with fixed chokes.

NIB	Exc.	V.G.	Good	Fair	Poor
775	600	500	400	300	250

EAA Rover 870

This is a high quality bolt action rifle. The walnut stock is checkered with rubber recoil pad. Adjustable rear sight and receiver is drilled and tapped for scope mount. Barrel length is 22". Chambered for the following cartridges: .22-250, .243, .25-06, .270, .308, .30-06, 7mm Rem. Mag., .300 and .338 Win. Mag.

NIB	Exc.	V.G.	Good	Fair	Poor
560	425	375	300	200	125

EAA SP 1822

This Sabatti rifle is chambered for the .22 Long Rifle. It is a semiautomatic carbine with a two-piece stock and adjustable stock.

NIB	Exc.	V.G.	Good	Fair	Poor
200	150	125	100	85	60

EAA SP 1822H

This a heavy barrel version of the above model without sights. The receiver is fitted with scope mount base.

NIB	Exc.	V.G.	Good	Fair	Poor
200	150	125	100	85	60

EAA SP 1822TH

This variation also has a heavy barrel without sights but with base mounts. A one-piece Bell and Carlson thumb hole stock is the feature of this model.

NIB	Exc.	V.G.	Good	Fair	Poor
350	260	225	175	125	90

EAA Benelli Silhouette Pistol

This is a specialized competition pistol with a semiautomatic action. The stocks are match type walnut with stippling. The palm shelf is adjustable. The barrel is 4.3" long. Fully adjustable sights. It is chambered for the .22 Long Rifle, .22 Short, and the .32 WC. Supplied with loading tool and cleaning rod. The .22 Caliber version weighs 38.5 oz. Overall length is 11.7".

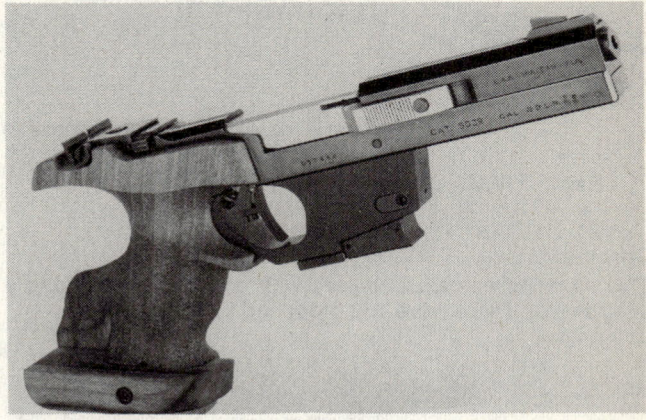

NIB	Exc.	V.G.	Good	Fair	Poor
1850	1250	950	750	600	400

EAA Astra Pistol

see Astra

EVANS REPEATING RIFLE CO.
Mechanic Falls, Maine

Incorporated in 1873, this firm produced repeating rifles based upon patents issued to Warren R. Evans (1868-1871) and later George F. Evans (1877, 1878 and 1879). The most distinctive feature of these arms is that they used a butt magazine operating on the principle of an Archimedean screw. Distributed by Merwin, Hulbert & Company, as well as Schuyler, Hartley & Graham, Evans rifles met with some success. One of their earliest advocates was William F. Cody (Buffalo Bill). The company ceased operations in 1879, after approximately 15,000 arms had been made.

Lever Action Rifle

This rifle is totally unique for a number of reasons. It holds the most rounds of any repeating rifle that did not have a detachable magazine, with capacities up to 38 rounds on some models. This rifle was chambered for its own cartridge—the .44 Evans of which there were two versions: a 1" cartridge in the "Old Model" and the "Transition Model" and a 1.5" cartridge in the "New Model". The finish on these rifles is blued, with nickel-plated levers and buttplates noted on some examples. The stocks are walnut. There were approximately 12,250 of all models manufactured between 1873 and 1879.

Old Model

This variation is chambered for the 1" .44 Evans cartridge and has a butt stock that covers only the top half of the revolving 34-shot magazine located in the butt of the rifle. The buttplate appears as if it is reversed, and the markings on the "Old Model" are "Evans Repeating Rifle/Pat. Dec. 8, 1868 & Sept. 16, 1871." There are three versions of the Old Model as follows. They were manufactured between 1874 and 1876 and serial numbered 1-500.

Military Musket

This version has a 30" barrel, with two barrel bands and provisions for a bayonet. There were only 50 estimated manufactured.

Exc.	V.G.	Good	Fair	Poor
—	—	2500	1500	500

Sporting Rifle

Approximately 300 of this model produced with a 26", 28", or 30" octagonal barrel.

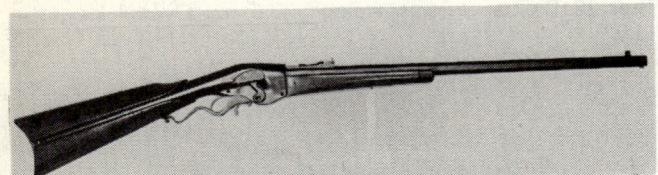

Courtesy Milwaukee Public Museum, Milwaukee, Wisconsin

Exc.	V.G.	Good	Fair	Poor
—	—	1500	800	400

Carbine

This variation has a 22" barrel, with one barrel band and a sling swivel. There were 150 produced.

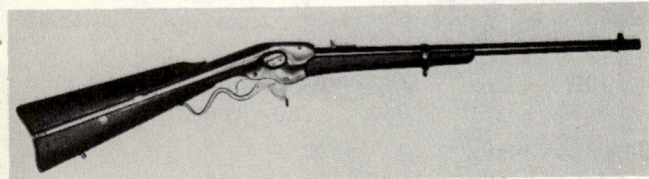

Courtesy Milwaukee Public Museum, Milwaukee, Wisconsin

Exc.	V.G.	Good	Fair	Poor
—	—	1750	900	550

Transitional Model

Has a butt stock that covers both the top and bottom of the rotary magazine, with an exposed portion in the middle of the butt. The buttplate does not have the backward appearance, and the barrel is marked "Evans Repeating Rifle Mechanic Falls Me./Pat Dec. 8, 1868 & Sept. 16, 1871". This version was manufactured in 1876 and 1877 and was serial numbered between 500-2185, for a total of approximately 1,650 manufactured.

Military Musket

Has a 30" barrel and two barrel bands. 150 were produced.

Exc.	V.G.	Good	Fair	Poor
—	—	1800	1200	450

Carbine

Four hundred-fifty of these produced, with a 22" barrel and one barrel band.

Exc.	V.G.	Good	Fair	Poor
—	—	1300	700	375

Sporting Rifle

Has a 26", 28", or 30" barrel. There were 1,050 produced.

Exc.	V.G.	Good	Fair	Poor
—	—	1000	500	300

"Montreal Carbine"

A special issue marked "Montreal," sold by R.H. Kilby, Evans' Canadian sales agent. There were between 50 and 100 produced.

Exc.	V.G.	Good	Fair	Poor
—	—	1800	1000	450

New Model

Approximately 10,000 of the New Model produced, chambered for the 1.5" .44 Evans cartridge with a magazine capacity reduced to 28. The frame was redesigned and rounded at the top, and the forend fit flush to the receiver. The lever and hammer are streamlined, and there is a dust cover over the loading gate. The markings are the same as on the Transitional Model with "U.S.A." added to the last line. This version was not serial numbered, and any numbers found are assembly numbers only.

Military Musket

3,000 produced, with a 30" barrel and two barrel bands.

Courtesy Butterfield & Butterfield, San Francisco, California

Exc.	V.G.	Good	Fair	Poor
—	—	1650	1000	450

Carbine

4,000 produced with a 22" barrel, one barrel band, and a sling swivel.

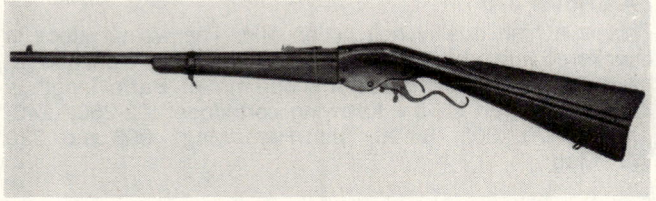

Courtesy Buffalo Bill Historical Center, Cody, Wyoming

Exc.	V.G.	Good	Fair	Poor
—	—	1000	550	400

Sporting Rifle

3,000 produced with 26", 28", or 30" octagonal barrels.

Exc.	V.G.	Good	Fair	Poor
—	1500	750	500	275

EVANS, J. E.
Philadelphia, Pennsylvania

Evans Pocket Pistol

A copy of the Philadelphia-made Henry Deringer pistol and is chambered for .41 caliber. It utilizes the percussion ignition system and has barrels from 2.5" to 3" in length. The stock is of walnut with a checkered grip, and the mountings are scroll-engraved German silver. The barrel is marked "J.E. Evans Philada." These pistols were manufactured in the 1850s.

Exc.	V.G.	Good	Fair	Poor
—	—	1500	550	350

EXCAM
Hialeah, Florida

An importer of firearms is not a manufacturer. The Erma and Uberti products they import are under their own heading in this book. The other products that they import are listed here. They are no longer in business.

TA 76

Patterned after the Colt Single Action Army and is chambered for the .22 rimfire cartridge. It has a 4.75", 6", or 9" barrel and blue finish with wood grips. It is offered with brass triggerguard and backstrap and also offered chrome-plated. A combo model with an extra .22 Magnum cylinder is available and would add 10% to the listed values.

Exc.	V.G.	Good	Fair	Poor
90	75	65	40	25

TA 38 Over/Under Derringer

A two-shot derringer patterned after the Remington derringer. It is chambered for the .38 Special cartridge, has 3" barrels that pivot upward for loading, and is blued with checkered nylon grips. This model was discontinued in 1985.

Exc.	V.G.	Good	Fair	Poor
90	75	65	40	25

TA 90

A double-action, semiautomatic copy of the CZ-75 that some experts rate as the finest combat handgun in the world. It is chambered for the 9mm Parabellum and has a 4.75" barrel. It is constructed of steel and is finished with a matte blue or chrome with checkered wood or rubber grips. The detachable magazine holds 15 rounds.

NIB	Exc.	V.G.	Good	Fair	Poor
415	380	325	275	200	150

BTA-90B

A compact version of the TA 90, that has a 3.5" barrel and a 12-round detachable magazine. It is similar in all other respects to the standard model, with rubber grips only.

NIB	Exc.	V.G.	Good	Fair	Poor
425	400	350	300	225	175

TA 90 SS

A competition version of the TA 90, that is similar to the standard model except that it is compensated and features adjustable sights. It is offered either blued or chrome-plated and was introduced in 1989.

NIB	Exc.	V.G.	Good	Fair	Poor
650	575	500	400	325	225

TA 41, 41C, and 41 SS

This series of pistols is identical to the TA 90 series except that they are chambered for the .41 Action Express cartridge. Their values are about 10 percent higher than the 9mm versions. They were introduced in 1989.

Warrior Model W 722

A double-action revolver chambered for the .22 rimfire and the .22 rimfire magnum with an interchangeable cylinder. It has a 6" barrel, adjustable sights, and an 8-shot cylinder capacity. It is blued, with checkered plastic grips. This model was not imported after 1986.

Exc.	V.G.	Good	Fair	Poor
100	75	50	35	20

Model W384

A double-action revolver chambered for the .38 Special cartridge, with a 4" or 6" vent rib barrel, blued finish, and plastic grips. It was discontinued in 1986.

Exc.	V.G.	Good	Fair	Poor
150	125	100	75	50

Model W357

Similar to the W384 except that it is chambered for the .357 Magnum cartridge. It was discontinued in 1986.

Exc.	V.G.	Good	Fair	Poor
200	150	125	100	75

Targa GT 26

A blowback-operated, semiautomatic pistol chambered for the .25 ACP cartridge. It has a 2.5" barrel and a 6-shot detachable magazine. It is finished in blue or matte chrome, with a choice of alloy or steel frame. The grips are wood.

Steel Frame Version

NIB	Exc.	V.G.	Good	Fair	Poor
110	90	75	50	40	30

Alloy Frame Version

NIB	Exc.	V.G.	Good	Fair	Poor
70	60	50	35	30	25

GT 22

A semiautomatic pistol chambered for the .22 l.r. cartridge. It has a 4" barrel, fixed sights, and a 10-round magazine. It is available either blued or matte chrome-plated and has wooden grips.

NIB	Exc.	V.G.	Good	Fair	Poor
200	175	150	125	90	70

GT 22T

Similar to the GT 22, with a 6" barrel and adjustable target-type sights.

NIB	Exc.	V.G.	Good	Fair	Poor
225	200	175	150	100	75

GT 32

A blowback-operated semiautomatic pistol chambered for the .32 ACP cartridge. It has a 7-round magazine and is either blued or matte chrome-plated with wood grips.

NIB	Exc.	V.G.	Good	Fair	Poor
200	175	150	125	90	75

GT 380

Similar to the GT 32 except that it is chambered for the .380 ACP cartridge.

NIB	Exc.	V.G.	Good	Fair	Poor
215	185	175	135	110	85

GT 380XE

Similar to the the GT 380, with an 11-shot, high-capacity, detachable magazine.

NIB	Exc.	V.G.	Good	Fair	Poor
225	200	185	150	125	100

EXEL ARMS OF AMERICA
Gardner, Massachusetts
SEE Lanber
Laurona & Ugartechia

This firm was engaged in the import of Spanish shotguns. They ceased importing them in 1967, and the specific models will be found listed under the manufacturers' names.

F

F.A.S.
Italy
Importer - Beeman Prec. Arms
Santa Rosa, California
Osbourne's
Cheboygan, Michigan

Model 601

A high-grade, competition target pistol chambered for the .22 short cartridge. It is a semiautomatic, with a 5.5" barrel and adjustable target sights. The detachable magazine holds 5 rounds, and the finish is blued with wraparound target grips. This model was discontinued in 1988.

Exc.	V.G.	Good	Fair	Poor
1150	950	750	550	300

Model 602

Similar to the Model 601 except that it is chambered for the .22 l.r. It was discontinued in 1987.

Exc.	V.G.	Good	Fair	Poor
1100	900	700	525	300

Model 603

Chambered for the .32 S&W wad cutter cartridge and features adjustable grips. It was discontinued in 1987.

Exc.	V.G.	Good	Fair	Poor
1100	950	750	550	300

FEG
(FEGYVERGYAR)
Budapest, Hungary
Importer—Century International Arms Co.
St. Albans, Vermont

Rudolf Frommer was a first-class engineer who became associated with Fegyvergyar in 1896. In 1900 he became the manager and held that position until his retirement in 1935. He died one year later in 1936. His designs were successful and prolific. They were used militarily and sold on the commercial market as well.

Model 1901

An odd pistol that was not successful at all. It was chambered for an 8mm cartridge that was the forerunner of the 8mm Roth Steyr. It has a long, slender barrel, which was actually a collar with the barrel within. It has a rotary bolt and external hammer and is recoil-operated. There is a 10-round integral magazine, and it is loaded from the top via a stripper clip. This pistol was manufactured from 1903 to 1905.

Exc.	V.G.	Good	Fair	Poor
1750	1500	1250	1000	600

Model 1906

An improved version of the 1901, chambered for the 7.65mm Roth cartridge. It is, for all intents and purposes, the same action; but on later models a detachable 10-round magazine was adopted. It was manufactured between 1906 and 1910 in small quantity.

Exc.	V.G.	Good	Fair	Poor
1500	1350	1100	850	500

Model 1910

The final version in this series of pistols and is similar with the addition of a grip safety.

Exc.	V.G.	Good	Fair	Poor
1250	1000	900	700	400

Model Stop

Introduced in 1912 and took a whole new approach compared to any of the pistols this company had produced to that point. It is still unconventional as it uses two recoil springs in a tube above the barrel and resembles an air pistol in this way. It is chambered for 7.65mm or 9mm short and has a 3.75" barrel. The detachable magazine holds 7 rounds, and the sights are fixed. This locked-breech action, semiautomatic pistol was a commercial success. It was used widely by the Austro-Hungarian military during WWI. It was manufactured between 1912 and 1920.

Exc.	V.G.	Good	Fair	Poor
275	225	200	150	100

Baby Model

A smaller version of the Stop that was designed as a pocket pistol with a 2" barrel and chambered for the same calibers. It was manufactured at the same time as the Stop Model.

Exc.	V.G.	Good	Fair	Poor
275	225	175	125	75

Lilliput

This pocket pistol is chambered for 6.35mm and outwardly resembles the Baby. It is actually a simple, blowback-operated, semiautomatic pistol and was a good deal less complex to produce. This model was introduced in 1921.

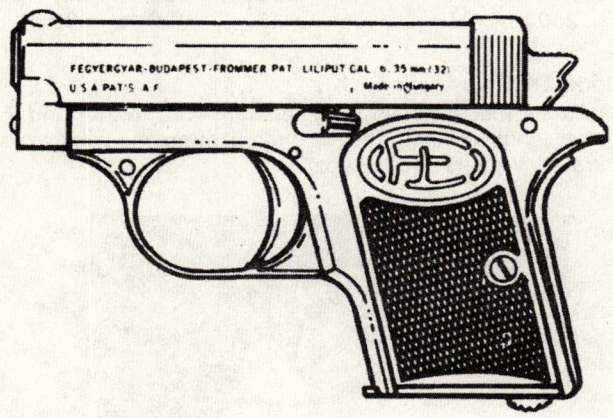

Exc.	V.G.	Good	Fair	Poor
250	200	150	125	75

Model 1929

A blowback-operated semiautomatic chambered for the 9mm short cartridge. It has an external hammer; and the barrel was retained, as the Browning was, by four lugs. This was a simple and reliable pistol, and it was adopted by the military as a replacement for the Stop. This model was manufactured between 1929 and 1937.

Exc.	V.G.	Good	Fair	Poor
225	190	175	125	75

Model 1937

An improved version of the Model 1929 and was the last of Frommer's designs. It appeared a year after his death. This model is similar to the Model 1929, with a grooved slide to make cocking easier. It was adopted as the M1937 by the Hungarian Military, and in 1941 the German government ordered 85,000 pistols chambered for 7.65mm to be used by the Luftwaffe. These pistols were designated the "P Mod 37 Kal 7.65." They were also marked "jhv," which was the German code for the Hungarian company. These German pistols also have a manual safety, which is not found on the Hungarian military version and bears the Waffenamt acceptance marks. This model was manufactured from 1937 until the end of WWII.

Nazi Proofed 7.65mm Version

Exc.	V.G.	Good	Fair	Poor
275	250	200	150	100

9mm Short Hungarian Military Version

Exc.	V.G.	Good	Fair	Poor
250	225	175	125	75

Model R-9

A copy of the Browning Hi-Power semiautomatic pistol. It is chambered for 9mm Parabellum and has a 4.75" barrel. The frame is steel, and the finish is blued with checkered wood grips. The detachable magazine holds 13 shots, and the sights are fixed. This model was imported in 1986 and 1987 only.

Exc.	V.G.	Good	Fair	Poor
275	225	200	150	100

Model PPH

A copy of the Walther PP, chambered for the .380 ACP cartridge. It is a double-action semiautomatic with a 3" barrel, alloy frame, and a blued finish, with thumb rest checkered plastic grips. It was imported in 1986 and 1987 only.

Exc.	V.G.	Good	Fair	Poor
225	175	150	100	75

Model B9R

This semiautomatic pistol is chambered for the .380 ACP cartridge and fitted with a 4" barrel, it features double or single action trigger operation. The frame is alloy and weighs about 25 oz. Magazine capacity is 15 rounds.

NIB	Exc.	V.G.	Good	Fair	Poor
225	200	175	150	125	75

Model AP9

Chambered for the .380 ACP this pistol is a copy of the Walther PP. It has a aluminum alloy frame and a magazine capacity of 7 rounds. The barrel is 3.94" in length and the pistol is 6.89" overall. The trigger is double action.

Exc.	V.G.	Good	Fair	Poor
135	100	85	70	50

Model PA63

Same as above but chambered for the 9mm Makarov (9xl8mm) cartridge.

Exc.	V.G.	Good	Fair	Poor
125	90	75	60	50

Model FP9

This model is a copy of the Browning Hi-Power pistol. Chambered for the 9mm Luger cartridge. It features a walnut checkered grip with blue finish. Barrel is 5" and overall length is 8". The top of the slide features a full length ventilated rib with fixed sights. Weighs 35 oz. Magazine capacity is 14 rounds.

NIB	Exc.	V.G.	Good	Fair	Poor
215	175	150	125	90	70

Model P9R

This is similar to the model above and follows the Browning Hi-Power lines with the exception of the ventilated rib. Barrel length is 4.66" and the pistol is offered in blue or chrome finish. Magazine capacity is 15 rounds.

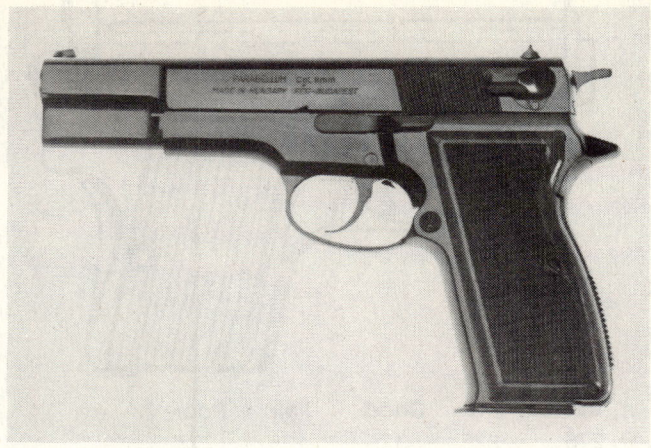

Blue

NIB	Exc.	V.G.	Good	Fair	Poor
225	200	150	125	90	70

Chrome

NIB	Exc.	V.G.	Good	Fair	Poor
250	225	175	150	120	80

Model P9RK

Similar to model above but fitted with 4.12" barrel and 7.5" overall length. Finger grooves on front strap and back strap is serrated. Weighs about 34 oz.

NIB	Exc.	V.G.	Good	Fair	Poor
230	200	150	25	90	70

F.I.E.
Hialeah, Florida

Firearms Import and Export was engaged in the business of importing the Franchi shotgun (which is listed under its own heading) and the Arminius revolver (which is made in Germany). They were also distributors for the Titan semiautomatic pistols, which are manufactured in the U.S.A. They were also importing a series of 9mm pistols from Italy that are produced by Tanfoglio and known as the TZ series. F.I.E. was no longer in business as of 1990.

TZ 75

A copy of the CZ 75 Czechoslovakian combat pistol produced by Tanfoglio in Italy. It is a 9mm, double-action semiautomatic with a 4.75" barrel, all-steel construction, fixed sights, and a 15-shot magazine. It is offered either blued or matte chrome plated, with wood or rubber grips.

NIB	Exc.	V.G.	Good	Fair	Poor
400	350	300	250	200	150

TZ 75 Series 88

An improved version that is also chambered for the .41 Action Express cartridge. It has a firing pin safety and can be carried cocked and locked. There are a few other minor changes. It was introduced in 1988.

NIB	Exc.	V.G.	Good	Fair	Poor
425	375	325	250	200	150

KG-99

A blowback-operated, semiautomatic assault pistol chambered for the 9mm Parabellum cartridge. It has a 36-round magazine. It was discontinued in 1984.

NIB	Exc.	V.G.	Good	Fair	Poor
500	450	350	250	200	150

Spectre Assault Pistol

An assault-type semiautomatic pistol chambered for the 9mm Parabellum. It has a 30- or 50-round magazine available. It was introduced in 1989.

NIB	Exc.	V.G.	Good	Fair	Poor
650	575	475	400	300	200

NOTE: Recent firearms legislation creates an uncertain market for this type of pistol.

Titan II .22

A semiautomatic pistol chambered for the .22 l.r. It has a 10-shot magazine and a blued finish with walnut grips. It is made in the U.S.A.

NIB	Exc.	V.G.	Good	Fair	Poor
200	150	100	75	50	25

Titan E32

A single-action, blowback-operated, semiautomatic pistol that was chambered for the .32 ACP and is now chambered for the .380 ACP cartridge. The finish is blue or chrome-plated, and the grips are walnut.

NIB	Exc.	V.G.	Good	Fair	Poor
200	175	150	125	100	75

Super Titan 11

Similar to the Titan except that it has a 12-round, high-capacity magazine.

NIB	Exc.	V.G.	Good	Fair	Poor
225	200	175	150	100	75

Titan 25

A smaller version of the Titan Series chambered for the .25 ACP cartridge. It is blued or chrome-plated.

NIB	Exc.	V.G.	Good	Fair	Poor
75	65	50	40	30	20

Titan Tigress

Similar to the Titan 25 except that it is gold-plated and cased.

NIB	Exc.	V.G.	Good	Fair	Poor
140	115	90	75	50	30

D38 Derringer

A two-shot, Over/Under, Remington-style derringer chambered for the .38 Special cartridge. It is chrome-plated and was dropped from the line in 1985.

NIB	Exc.	V.G.	Good	Fair	Poor
75	60	45	35	25	20

D86 Derringer

A single-shot derringer with a 3" barrel. It is chambered for the .38 Special cartridge and is chrome-plated. There is an ammunition storage compartment in the butt and a transfer bar safety that makes it safer to carry. This model was introduced in 1986.

NIB	Exc.	V.G.	Good	Fair	Poor
95	80	65	50	35	20

There is a series of single-action, .22 caliber revolvers that were patterned after the Colt Single Action Army. They were manufactured in the U.S.A. or Brescia, Italy. They are inexpensive and of fair quality. The differences between these models are basically barrel lengths, type of sights, and finish. They all are chambered for the .22 l.r. and have interchangeable .22 Magnum cylinders. We list them for reference purposes.

Cowboy

NIB	Exc.	V.G.	Good	Fair	Poor
80	60	50	40	35	20

Gold Rush

NIB	Exc.	V.G.	Good	Fair	Poor
150	125	100	80	75	50

Texas Ranger

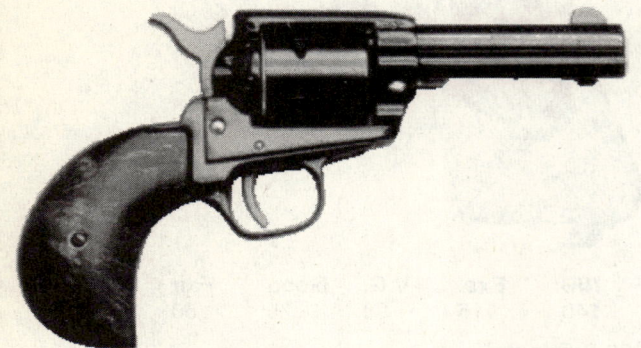

NIB	Exc.	V.G.	Good	Fair	Poor
100	85	75	50	35	20

Buffalo Scout

NIB	Exc.	V.G.	Good	Fair	Poor
95	80	70	50	35	20

Legend S.A.A.

NIB	Exc.	V.G.	Good	Fair	Poor
125	110	85	65	50	30

Hombre

A single-action made in Germany by Arminius. It is patterned after the Colt Single Action Army revolver. The Hombre is chambered for the .357 Magnum, .44 Magnum, and .45 Colt cartridges. It is offered with a 5.5", 6", or 7.5" barrel, case-colored frame, and blued barrel and cylinder, with smooth walnut grips. The backstrap and triggerguard are offered in brass and will bring a 10% premium.

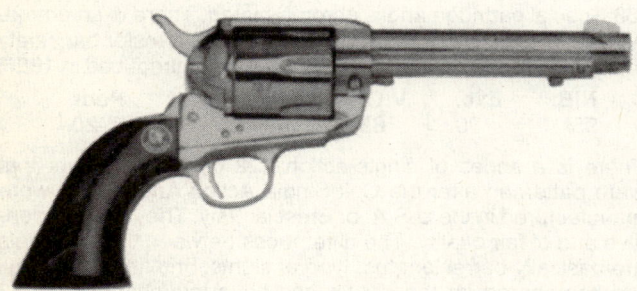

NIB	Exc.	V.G.	Good	Fair	Poor
225	200	175	125	100	75

ARMINIUS REVOLVERS

Model 522TB

A swing-out cylinder, double-action revolver chambered for the .22 rimfire cartridge. It has a 4" barrel and is blued with wood grips.

NIB	Exc.	V.G.	Good	Fair	Poor
150	125	100	75	50	30

722

Similar to the 522, with an 8-shot cylinder and a 6" barrel. It is available with a chrome finish.

NIB	Exc.	V.G.	Good	Fair	Poor
150	125	100	75	50	30

532TB

A 7-shot, double-action revolver chambered for the .32 S&W cartridge. It has a 4" barrel and adjustable sights and is finished in either blue or chrome.

NIB	Exc.	V.G.	Good	Fair	Poor
160	130	110	80	60	40

732B

Similar to the 532TB, with a 6" barrel and fixed sights. It was discontinued in 1988.

NIB	Exc.	V.G.	Good	Fair	Poor
120	100	80	65	50	35

Standard Revolver

A double-action, swing-out cylinder revolver chambered for .32 Magnum or .38 Special. It has a 4" or 6" barrel and fixed sights and is blued with wood grips. This model is made in the U.S.A. and was introduced in 1989.

NIB	Exc.	V.G.	Good	Fair	Poor
125	100	75	50	35	20

Models 384TB and 386TB

These two models are double-action chambered for the .38 Special cartridge. The 384 has a 4" barrel; and the 386, a 6" barrel. They are available in blue or chrome plate and were discontinued in 1985.

NIB	Exc.	V.G.	Good	Fair	Poor
165	125	100	85	65	50

Model 357TB

Similar to the 384TB except that it is chambered for the .357 Magnum cartridge and is offered with a 3", 4", or 6" barrel.

NIB	Exc.	V.G.	Good	Fair	Poor
200	175	150	125	90	75

222, 232, and 382TB

These models are double-action swing-out cylinder revolvers chambered for .22 rimfire, .32 S&W, and .38 Special. They are 2"-barreled snub-nosed revolvers, with either blued or chrome-plated finishes. They were discontinued in 1985.

NIB	Exc.	V.G.	Good	Fair	Poor
125	100	75	50	40	25

Model 3572

A similar revolver to the 382TB except that it is chambered for the .357 Magnum cartridge. It was discontinued in 1984.

NIB	Exc.	V.G.	Good	Fair	Poor
225	200	175	125	100	75

SHOTGUNS AND RIFLES

Model 122

A bolt-action rifle chambered for .22 rimfire, with a 21" barrel and adjustable sights. It has a 10-shot magazine and a walnut Monte Carlo stock. It was introduced in 1986.

NIB	Exc.	V.G.	Good	Fair	Poor
110	95	75	50	35	25

Single Shot

Brazilian made and chambered for 12 or 20 gauge and .410. It is a single-barreled break open, with 25" through 30" barrel and various chokes. It is blued with a wood stock and was introduced in 1985.

NIB	Exc.	V.G.	Good	Fair	Poor
100	80	60	45	35	25

S.O.B.

Similar to the single shot, with an 18.5" barrel and a pistol grip instead of a standard stock. This model was discontinued in 1984.

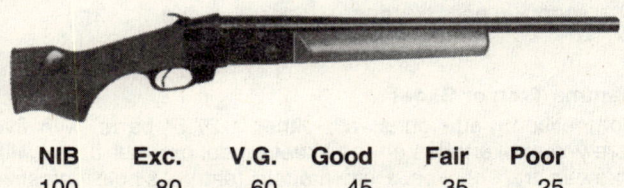

NIB	Exc.	V.G.	Good	Fair	Poor
100	80	60	45	35	25

Sturdy Over/Under

Chambered for 12 and 20 gauge and has 3" chambers and 28" vent rib barrels with various chokes. This is an Over/Under with double triggers and extractors. The frame is engraved and silver finished. It was manufactured in Italy by Maroccini and imported between 1985 and 1988.

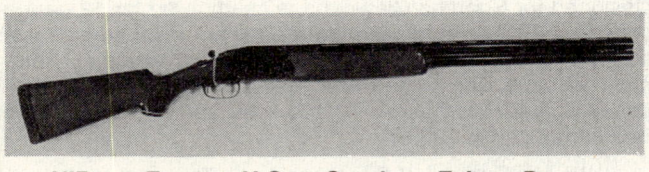

NIB	Exc.	V.G.	Good	Fair	Poor
300	275	225	175	150	100

Brute

A side-x-side chambered for 12 and 20 gauge and .410. It has 19" barrels, double triggers, and extractors. It has a wood stock and was dropped from the line in 1984.

NIB	Exc.	V.G.	Good	Fair	Poor
200	175	125	100	75	50

SPAS-12

A unique shotgun in that it can function as a pump or an automatic with the touch of a button. It is a paramilitary-type shotgun chambered for 12 gauge, with a 21.5" barrel and a 9-shot tube magazine. It has an alloy receiver and a folding stock. The finish is all black. This model is manufactured by Franchi in Italy.

NIB	Exc.	V.G.	Good	Fair	Poor
2000	1500	900	650	400	300

Law-12

A paramilitary-type, 12-gauge, semiautomatic shotgun that is gas-operated and has a 9-shot tube magazine. The barrel is 21.5" in length and choked cylinder bore. It has a military special black finish and a black synthetic stock.

NIB	Exc.	V.G.	Good	Fair	Poor
650	550	400	300	200	100

SAS-12

A paramilitary-type, slide-action shotgun chambered for 12 gauge. It has a 21.5" barrel, choked cylinder bore. The finish is similar to the LAW-12, and it is manufactured by Franchi in Italy.

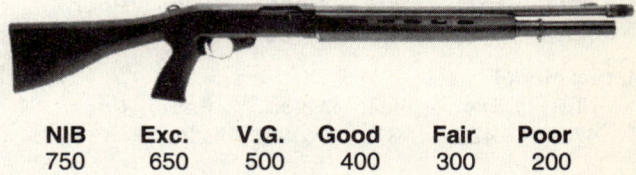

NIB	Exc.	V.G.	Good	Fair	Poor
750	650	500	400	300	200

F&T
(Falise & Trappman of Liege, Belgium)
SEE French Military Firearms

FABARM
Brescia, Italy
Importer - St. Lawrence Sales, Inc.
Lake Orion, Michigan

SEMI-AUTOMATIC SHOTGUNS

Ellegi Standard

A gas-operated, semiautomatic shotgun chambered for 12 gauge. It has a 28" vent rib barrel with choice of choke. The receiver is blue anodized alloy with a photo-etched gamescene, and the stock and forearm are checkered walnut. This model was introduced in 1989.

NIB	Exc.	V.G.	Good	Fair	Poor
700	625	525	450	350	250

The Ellegi Model is available in six other configurations. The differences are in the barrel length and choke, type of choke tubes, and finish. Basically the guns are quite similar to the standard model. These variations are as follows:

Ellegi Multichoke

NIB	Exc.	V.G.	Good	Fair	Poor
700	625	525	450	350	250

Ellegi Innerchoke

NIB	Exc.	V.G.	Good	Fair	Poor
725	650	550	475	375	275

Ellegi Magnum

NIB	Exc.	V.G.	Good	Fair	Poor
725	650	550	475	375	275

Ellegi Super Goose

NIB	Exc.	V.G.	Good	Fair	Poor
800	725	625	550	450	350

Ellegi Slug

NIB	Exc.	V.G.	Good	Fair	Poor
775	700	600	525	425	325

Ellegi Police

NIB	Exc.	V.G.	Good	Fair	Poor
575	500	450	400	300	225

SLIDE ACTION SHOTGUNS

Model S.D.A.S.S.

Chambered for 12 gauge with a 3" chamber. It is offered with a 20" or 24.5" barrel threaded for external choke tubes. This model has an 8-shot tube magazine, twin action bars, an alloy receiver, and a matte black finish. It is a defensive-type shotgun and has been imported since 1989.

NIB	Exc.	V.G.	Good	Fair	Poor
500	450	400	350	250	175

The Special Police and the Martial Model are variations of the basic slide action and differ in barrel length and choke. The Police Model has a shrouded barrel.

Special Police

NIB	Exc.	V.G.	Good	Fair	Poor
525	475	425	350	275	200

Martial Model

NIB	Exc.	V.G.	Good	Fair	Poor
475	425	375	300	225	175

SINGLE SHOT SHOTGUNS

Omega Standard

Has an alloy receiver and is chambered for 12 and 20 gauge, as well as .410. It has 26" or 28" barrels with various chokes. The finish is black with a beech stock. It was introduced in 1989.

NIB	Exc.	V.G.	Good	Fair	Poor
150	125	100	75	50	40

Omega Goose Gun

Chambered for 12 gauge only, with a 35.5" full-choke barrel.

NIB	Exc.	V.G.	Good	Fair	Poor
160	140	125	100	75	50

SIDE-X-SIDE SHOTGUNS

Beta Model

This double-barrel is chambered for 12 gauge only, with choice of barrel length and choke. It has a boxlock action with false side plates. It has a single trigger and automatic ejectors, and the finish is blued with a checkered, select walnut stock. This model was introduced in 1989.

NIB	Exc.	V.G.	Good	Fair	Poor
925	850	750	600	450	300

Beta Europe

A deluxe version that features single selective triggers and a gamescene engraved, coin-finished receiver. The stock is the straight English style with a splinter forend. This model was introduced in 1989.

NIB	Exc.	V.G.	Good	Fair	Poor
1750	1500	1250	1000	750	500

OVER/UNDER SHOTGUNS

Field Model

Chambered for 12 gauge and has 29" vent rib barrels with various chokes. The receiver is coin-finished, and the stock is checkered walnut. This Model was discontinued in 1985.

NIB	Exc.	V.G.	Good	Fair	Poor
900	700	600	500	400	300

Gamma Field

Chambered for 12 or 20 gauge and is offered with 26", 28", or 29" vent rib barrels and various choke combinations. Screw-in choke tubes are available and would be worth a 10% premium. This model has a boxlock, coin-finished receiver that is moderately engraved and a checkered walnut stock.

NIB	Exc.	V.G.	Good	Fair	Poor
925	850	775	650	500	350

Gamma Paradox Gun

Chambered for 12 gauge only, and the top barrel is rifled for accurate placement of slugs. The barrels are 25" long with vent rib, and the bottom barrel has three screw-in choke tubes. This model has a single selective trigger and automatic ejectors. The finish is similar to the Field Model. It was introduced in 1989.

NIB	Exc.	V.G.	Good	Fair	Poor
1000	900	825	750	600	450

Gamma Trap or Skeet

Competition-grade guns with either a 27.5" barrel with five screw-in choke tubes on the skeet model or a 29" barrel with screw-in trap chokes. Both models feature single selective triggers and automatic ejectors; and the trap model has a Monte Carlo stock. They have moderately engraved, coin-finished boxlock actions and were introduced in 1989.

NIB	Exc.	V.G.	Good	Fair	Poor
1000	900	825	750	600	450

Gamma Sporting Competition Model

Designed for Sporting Clays and is chambered for 12 gauge only. The 29" barrel has a wide rib and is furnished with five screw-in choke tubes. It has a single selective trigger, automatic ejectors, and a checkered walnut stock with a competition recoil pad. It is finished like the skeet and trap models and was introduced in 1989.

NIB	Exc.	V.G.	Good	Fair	Poor
1000	900	825	750	600	450

FABBRI, ARMI
Gardone V.T., Italy
Importer-New England Arms
Kiftery Point, Maine

Fabbri Armi currently manufactures one of the best shotguns in the world. They are available as a custom made-to-order item, and they are not often seen in the used gun market. The values for guns of this nature and quality are impossible to accurately establish in a book of this nature as there are so many options and conditions that make the prices fluctuate greatly. We give an estimate figure as a base starting point but strongly urge individual appraisal should a transaction involving one of these fine firearms be contemplated.

A three shotgun set all consecutively serial numbered, all with a 28" barrel in 20 and 28 gauge, and a .410 bore. All three were engraved by the Italian Master Galiazzi. Condition is near mint. Auction price was $34,500. Butterfield & Butterfield, April 1997.

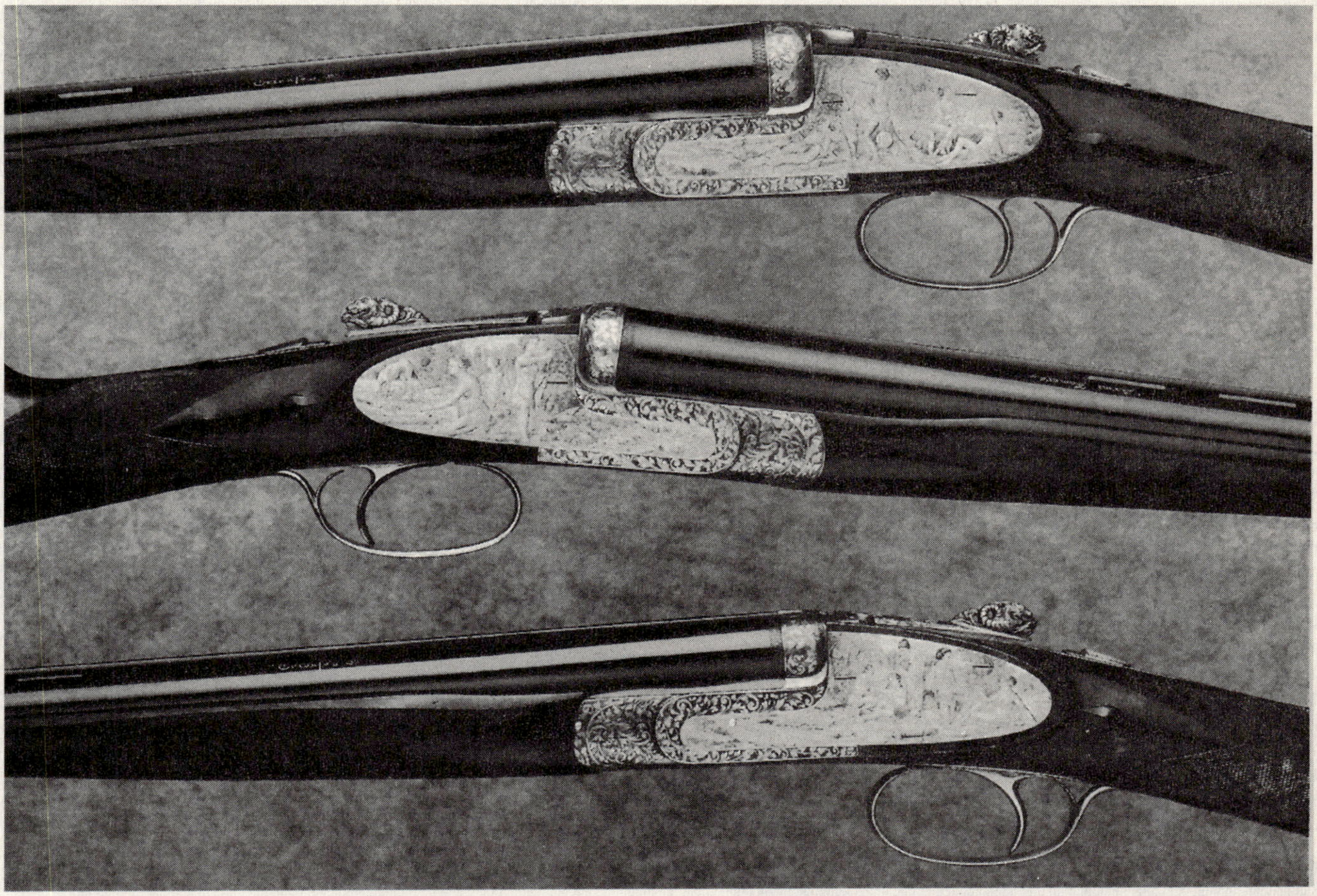

Side-x-Side Shotgun

Chambered for 12 or 20 gauge with all other features on a custom-order basis. This model is no longer in production.

NIB	Exc.	V.G.	Good	Fair	Poor
38000	20000	17500	15000	10000	8000

Over/Under Shotgun

Chambered for 12 or 20 gauge with all other features on a custom-order basis.

NIB	Exc.	V.G.	Good	Fair	Poor
70000	50000	30000	20000	15000	10000

FABRIQUE NATIONALE
Herstal, Belgium

In 1889 Fabrique Nationale (or FN) was founded by a group of Belgian investors for the purpose of manufacturing Mauser rifles for the Belgian army. This was to be accomplished under license from Mauser, with the technical assistance of Kudwig Loewe of Berlin. A few years later, in the late 1890s, John Browning arrived in Europe seeking a manufacturer for his semiautomatic shotgun. He had severed his ties with Winchester after a disagreement. This led to a long association that worked out extremely well for both parties. Later Browning became associated with Colt, and the world market was divided—with the Eastern Hemisphere going to FN and the Western Hemisphere to Colt.

In this section, we list arms that bear the FN banner. The FN-manufactured firearms produced under the Browning banner are listed in the Browning section of this book.

Model 1900

A blowback-operated semiautomatic pistol chambered for the 7.65mm cartridge. It has a 4" barrel and fixed sights and is blued with molded plastic grips. This model is notorious as the pistol that was used to assassinate Archduke Ferdinand, an event that touched off WWI. It was manufactured between 1899 and 1910. This model is referred to as the "Old Model."

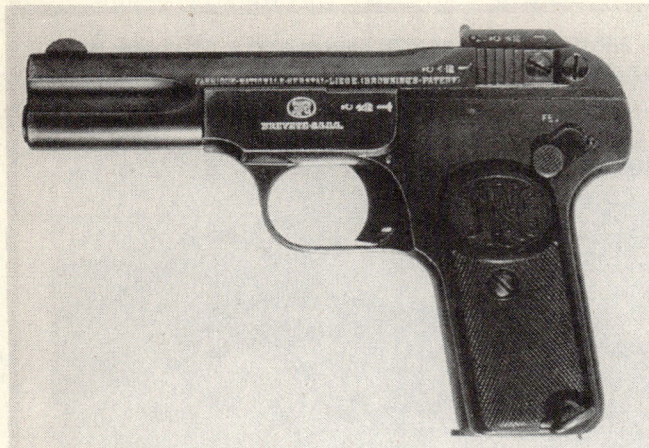

Exc.	V.G.	Good	Fair	Poor
350	325	275	200	150

Model 1903

A considerable improvement over the Model 1900. It is also a blowback-operated semiautomatic; but the recoil spring is located under the barrel, and the firing pin travels through the slide after being struck by a hidden hammer. The barrel is held in place by five locking lugs that fit into five grooves in the frame. This pistol is chambered for the 9mm Browning long cartridge and has a 5" barrel. The finish is blued with molded plastic grips, and the detachable magazine holds 7 rounds. There is a detachable shoulder stock/holster along with a 10-round magazine that was available for this model. These accessories are extremely rare and if present would make the package worth approximately five times that of the pistol alone. There were approximately 58,000 manufactured between 1903 and 1939. This model was one of the Browning patents that the Eibar Spanish gunmakers did so love to copy because of the simplicity of the design.

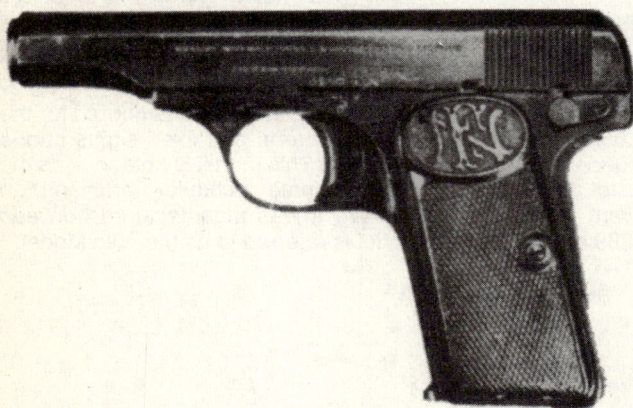

Exc.	V.G.	Good	Fair	Poor
475	425	375	275	175

Model 1906

A smaller version of the Model 1903, designed to be a pocket pistol and chambered for the 6.35mm cartridge. It became known as the "Vest Pocket" model and was also the basis for many Eibar copies. It has a 2.5" barrel and was produced in two distinct variations. The first variation had no safety lever or slide lock and relied on the grip safety. The second variation, that occurred at approximately serial number 100000, added this safety lever and slide lock, which helped simplify dismantling of the pistol. This model was available either blued or nickel-plated. The plated models would bring a 10% premium. There were approximately 1,086,100 manufactured between 1906 and 1959.

1st Variation Under Serial Number 100000
Exc.	V.G.	Good	Fair	Poor
350	300	250	200	125

2nd Variation Over Serial Number 100000
Exc.	V.G.	Good	Fair	Poor
300	275	200	175	100

Model 1910 "New Model"

Chambered for 7.65mm and 9mm short. It has a 3.5" barrel, is blued, and has molded plastic grips. The principal difference between this model and its predecessors is that the recoil spring on the Model 1910 is wrapped around the barrel. This gives the slide a more graceful tubular appearance instead of the old slab-sided look. This model has the triple safety features of the 1906 Model 2nd variation and is blued with molded plastic grips. This model was adopted by police forces around the world. It was manufactured between 1912 and 1954.

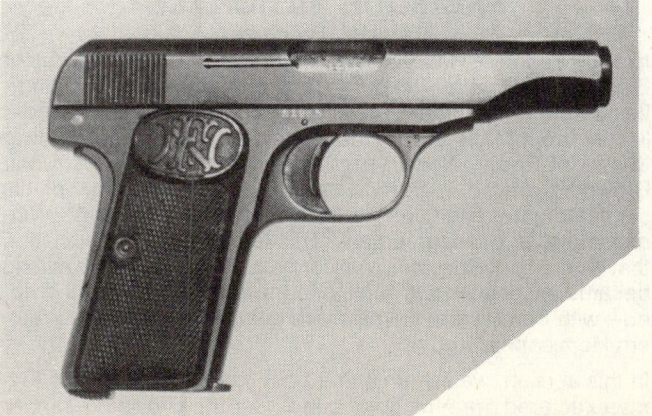

Courtesy Orvel Reichert

Exc.	V.G.	Good	Fair	Poor
350	300	250	175	125

Model 1922

Similar to the Model 1910, with a longer 4.5" barrel and correspondingly longer slide. This model was a military success, and approximately 200,000 were produced during the WWII German occupation of Belgium in 1940-1944. These pistols that bear the Waffenamt acceptance marks are known as the "Pistole Modell 626(b)," and are chambered for 7.65mm only. These pistols would bring a 10% premium. There were also contracts from France, Yugoslavia, and Holland, as well as Belgian military versions. They were manufactured between 1912 and 1959.

Exc.	V.G.	Good	Fair	Poor
275	225	175	125	100

"Baby" Model

A smaller and lighter version of the Model 1906. It is chambered for the 6.35mm cartridge and has a 2" barrel. There is no grip safety or slide lock on this model, and it appears to be more square in shape than the Model 1906. This model was offered in blue, with molded plastic grips. Early models have the word "Baby" molded into the grips; post-1945 versions do not. There is also a nickel-plated version with pearl grips. There were over 500,000 of these manufactured between 1931 and 1983.

Courtesy Orvel Reichert

Courtesy Orville Reichert

Exc.	V.G.	Good	Fair	Poor
400	325	300	225	150

Model 1935

The last design from John Browning and was developed between 1925 and 1935. This pistol is known as the Model 1935, the P-35, High-Power or HP, and also as the GP (which stood for "Grand Puissance") and was referred to by all those names at one time or another. The HP is essentially an improved version of the Colt 1911 design. The swinging link was replaced with a fixed cam, which was less prone to wear. It is chambered for the 9mm Parabellum and has a 13-round detachable magazine. The only drawback to the design is that the trigger pull is not as fine as that of the 1911, as there is a transfer bar instead of a stirrup arrangement. This is necessary due to the increased magazine capacity resulting in a thicker grip. The barrel is 4.75" in length. It has an external hammer with a manual and a magazine safety and was available with various finishes and sight options and was furnished with a shoulder stock. The Model 1935 was used by many countries as their service pistol as such there are many variations. We list these versions and their approximate values. There are books available specializing in this model, and it would be beneficial to gain as much knowledge as possible if one contemplates acquisition of this fine and highly collectible pistol.

Prewar Commercial Model

Found with either a fixed sight or a sliding tangent rear sight and is slotted for a detachable shoulder stock. It was manufactured from 1935 until 1940.

Wood Holster Stock-Add 50%.

Fixed Sight Version

Exc.	V.G.	Good	Fair	Poor
600	525	475	375	275

Tangent Sight Version

Exc.	V.G.	Good	Fair	Poor
1000	850	675	550	400

Prewar Military Contract

The Model 1935 was adopted by many countries as a service pistol, and they are as follows:

Belgium

Exc.	V.G.	Good	Fair	Poor
1200	1050	900	600	375

Canada and China (See John Inglis & Company)

Denmark

Exc.	V.G.	Good	Fair	Poor
1250	1100	950	650	400

Great Britain

Exc.	V.G.	Good	Fair	Poor
1150	1000	850	550	325

Estonia

Exc.	V.G.	Good	Fair	Poor
1200	1050	900	600	375

Holland

Exc.	V.G.	Good	Fair	Poor
1250	1100	950	650	400

Latvia

Exc.	V.G.	Good	Fair	Poor
1500	1350	1050	775	500

Lithuania

Exc.	V.G.	Good	Fair	Poor
1250	1100	950	650	400

Romania

Exc.	V.G.	Good	Fair	Poor
1500	1350	1050	775	500

German Military Pistole Modell 640(b)

In 1940 Germany occupied Belgium and took over the FN plant. The production of the Model 1935 continued, with Germany taking the output. The FN plant was assigned the production code "ch," and many thousands were produced. The finish on these Nazi guns runs from as fine as the Prewar Commercial series to downright crude, and it is possible to see how the war was progressing for Germany by the finish on their weapons. One must be cautious with some of these guns as there have been fakes noted with their backstraps cut for shoulder stocks, producing what would appear to be a more expensive variation. Individual appraisal should be secured if any doubt exists.

Fixed Sight Model

Exc.	V.G.	Good	Fair	Poor
500	450	400	300	250

Tangent Sight Model - 50,000 Manufactured

Courtesy Orvel Reichert

Courtesy Orvel Reichert

Exc.	V.G.	Good	Fair	Poor
800	750	700	550	400

Captured Prewar Commercial Model

These pistols were taken over when the plant was occupied. They are slotted for stocks and have tangent sights. There were few produced between serial number 48,000 and 52,000. All noted have the War 613 Nazi proof mark. Beware of fakes!

Exc.	V.G.	Good	Fair	Poor
1500	1400	1150	750	500

Postwar Military Contract

Manufactured from 1946, and they embody some design changes—such as improved heat treating and barrel locking. Pistols produced after 1950 do not have barrels that can interchange with the earlier model pistols. The earliest models have an "A" prefix on the serial number and do not have the magazine safety. These pistols were produced for many countries, and there were many thousands manufactured.

Fixed Sight

Exc.	V.G.	Good	Fair	Poor
475	425	375	300	250

Tangent Sight

Exc.	V.G.	Good	Fair	Poor
750	675	575	400	300

Slotted and Tangent Sight

Exc.	V.G.	Good	Fair	Poor
1150	1050	750	500	400

Postwar Commercial Model

Introduced in 1950 and in 1954. Those imported into the U.S.A. are marked Browning Arms Co. These pistols have the commercial polished finish.

Fixed Sight

Exc.	V.G.	Good	Fair	Poor
500	425	350	300	250

Tangent Sight

Exc.	V.G.	Good	Fair	Poor
750	650	500	400	350

Slotted and Tangent Sight

Exc.	V.G.	Good	Fair	Poor
1200	1100	800	550	450

WARNING: A large number of counterfeit FN Hi-Powers have been shipped to the United States, possibly from the Balkans. The slides are marked just like the FN originals but the fit and finish is of poor quality. These pistols are missing numerous small proof stamps and markings normally found on FN pistols. These counterfeits have a serial number on the front of the grip strap with a single letter prefix. All are fitted with the late style extractor. Metal finish is either a military matte blue or a commercial high gloss blue.

RIFLES

Model 1889

The Mauser rifle that FN was formed to manufacture. It is chambered for 7.65mm and has a 30.5" barrel. The magazine holds 5 rounds. The unique feature that sets the Belgian rifle apart from the Mausers made by other countries is the thin steel tube that encases the barrel. The sights are of the military type. The finish is blued, with a walnut stock.

Exc.	V.G.	Good	Fair	Poor
275	250	200	125	100

Model 1949 or SAFN 49

A gas-operated semiautomatic rifle chambered for 7x57, 7.92mm, and .30-06. It has a 23" barrel and military-type sights. The integral magazine holds 10 rounds. The finish is blued, and the stock is walnut. This is a well-made gun that was actually designed before WWII. When the Germans were in the process of taking over Belgium, a group of FN engineers fled to England and took the plans for this rifle with them, preventing the German military from acquiring a very fine weapon. This model was introduced in 1949, after hostilities had ceased. This model was sold on contract to Egypt, chambered for 7.92mm; to Venezuela, chambered for 7x57; and to Columbia, Indonesia, Belgium, and Luxembourg chambered for the .30-06. The Egyptian model has recently been imported in large numbers and is worth approximately 20% less.

.30-06 caliber-Add 20%.

Exc.	V.G.	Good	Fair	Poor
400	350	300	225	150

Model 30-11 Sniper Rifle

Chambered for the 7.62 NATO cartridge. It has a 20" heavy barrel and Anschutz sights. There is a flash suppressor mounted on the muzzle. It is built on a highly precision-made Mauser bolt action fed by a 9-round, detachable box magazine. The walnut stock is rather unique in that the butt is made up of two parts, with the rear half being replaceable to suit the needs of different-sized shooters. It is issued with a shooting sling, bipod, and a foam-lined carrying case. This is a rare firearm on the commercial market as it was designed and sold to the military and police markets.

Exc.	V.G.	Good	Fair	Poor
5000	4500	3500	2750	2000

FN-FAL

A gas-operated, semiautomatic version of the famous FN battle rifle. This weapon has been adopted by more free world countries than any other. It is chambered for the 7.62 NATO or .308 and has a 21" barrel with an integral flash suppressor. The sights are adjustable with an aperture rear, and the detachable box magazine holds 20 rounds. The stock and forearm are made of wood or a black synthetic. This model has been discontinued by the company and is no longer manufactured.

50.00-21" Rifle Model

NIB	Exc.	V.G.	Good	Fair	Poor
2800	2400	2000	1800	1200	1000

50.63-18" Paratrooper Model

NIB	Exc.	V.G.	Good	Fair	Poor
2800	2400	2000	1800	1200	1000

50.64-21" Paratrooper Model

NIB	Exc.	V.G.	Good	Fair	Poor
2800	2400	2000	1800	1200	1000

50.41-Synthetic Butt H-Bar

NIB	Exc.	V.G.	Good	Fair	Poor
2800	2400	2000	1800	1200	1000

50.42-Wood Butt H-Bar

NIB	Exc.	V.G.	Good	Fair	Poor
2800	2400	2000	1800	1200	1000

FNC

A lighter-weight assault-type rifle chambered for the 5.56mm cartridge. It is a gas-operated semiautomatic with an 18" or 21" barrel. It has a 30-round box magazine and is black, with either a fixed or folding stock. This model was also discontinued by FN. The same problem with fluctuating values applies to this weapon as to the L.A.R., and we strongly advise that one researches the market in a particular geographic location as prices can fluctuate radically.

Standard-Fixed stock, 16" or 18" barrel

NIB	Exc.	V.G.	Good	Fair	Poor
1500	1300	1100	1000	800	600

Paratrooper Model-Folding stock, 16" or 18" barrel

NIB	Exc.	V.G.	Good	Fair	Poor
1600	1350	1150	1000	800	600

NOTE: The above prices are for Belgian made guns only.

Musketeer Sporting Rifles

A bolt-action rifle built on the Mauser action chambered for various popular cartridges. It has a 24" barrel and is blued, with a checkered walnut stock. It was manufactured between 1947 and 1963.

Exc.	V.G.	Good	Fair	Poor
400	375	325	225	150

Deluxe Sporte

A higher-grade version of the Musketeer with the same general specifications. It was also manufactured between 1947 and 1963.

Exc.	V.G.	Good	Fair	Poor
500	450	400	300	200

FN Supreme

Chambered for the popular standard calibers and has a 24" barrel with an aperture sight and a checkered walnut stock. It was manufactured between 1957 and 1975.

Exc.	V.G.	Good	Fair	Poor
550	500	450	350	225

Supreme Magnum Model

Similar to the standard Supreme except that it is chambered for .264 Win. Mag., 7mm Rem. Mag., and .300 Win. Mag. It is furnished with a recoil pad and was manufactured between the same years as the standard model.

Exc.	V.G.	Good	Fair	Poor
600	550	500	400	250

FAIRBANKS, A. B.
Boston, Massachusetts

Fairbanks All Metal Pistol

This odd pistol was produced of all metal, with a one-piece cast brass frame and handle and an iron barrel and lock system. It is chambered for .33 caliber and utilizes the percussion ignition system. The barrel lengths noted are of 3" to 10". The barrels are marked "Fairbanks Boston. Cast Steel." They were manufactured between 1838 and 1841.

Exc.	V.G.	Good	Fair	Poor
—	—	600	300	150

FALCON FIREARMS
Northridge, California

Portsider

A copy of the Colt 1911 built for a left-handed individual. It is constructed of stainless steel and is similar in all other respects to the Colt. It was introduced in 1986.

NIB	Exc.	V.G.	Good	Fair	Poor
575	500	425	375	300	225

Portsider Set

A matching serial numbered pair consisting of a left-handed and a right-handed version of this model. It was cased, and there were only 100 manufactured in 1986 and 1987.

NIB	Exc.	V.G.	Good	Fair	Poor
1400	1250	1000	750	600	475

Gold Falcon

The frame was machined from solid 17-karat gold. The slide is stainless steel, and the sights have diamond inlays. It was engraved to the customer's order, and there were only 50 manufactured.

NIB	Exc.	V.G.	Good	Fair	Poor
30000	25000	20000	15000	—	—

FAMARS, A. & S.
Brescia, Italy

The Famars shotgun is one of the world's finest and is available on a custom-order basis. This makes it quite difficult to accurately establish values in a book of this nature. Each individual gun must be appraised if a transaction is contemplated as the array of options available makes the values fluctuate greatly. We list them and give an estimated value in their basic form only.

Zeus

An engraved side by side boxlock

In the white

NIB	Exc.	V.G.	Good	Fair	Poor
24200	18750	—	—	—	—

S3 pattern

NIB	Exc.	V.G.	Good	Fair	Poor
28750	20000	—	—	—	—

Tribute

An engraved side by side droplock.

In the white

NIB	Exc.	V.G.	Good	Fair	Poor
26900	20800	—	—	—	—

S3 pattern

NIB	Exc.	V.G.	Good	Fair	Poor
31500	22000	—	—	—	—

Venus

A side by side sidelock shotgun with choice of engraving patterns and coverage.

In the white

NIB	Exc.	V.G.	Good	Fair	Poor
34135	26650	—	—	—	—

S3 pattern

NIB	Exc.	V.G.	Good	Fair	Poor
38785	30000	—	—	—	—

S4 pattern

NIB	Exc.	V.G.	Good	Fair	Poor
44285	34000	—	—	—	—

S5 pattern

NIB	Exc.	V.G.	Good	Fair	Poor
49685	38500	—	—	—	—

S4E pattern

NIB	Exc.	V.G.	Good	Fair	Poor
54885	42500	—	—	—	—

S5E pattern

NIB	Exc.	V.G.	Good	Fair	Poor
60285	46700	—	—	—	—

SXO pattern

NIB	Exc.	V.G.	Good	Fair	Poor
79200	61300	—	—	—	—

Veneri

A side by side sidelock shotgun.

NIB	Exc.	V.G.	Good	Fair	Poor
38000	30000	—	—	—	—

Jorema Royal

An over and under shotgun with sidelocks.

In the white

NIB	Exc.	V.G.	Good	Fair	Poor
26900	20800	—	—	—	—

S3 pattern

NIB	Exc.	V.G.	Good	Fair	Poor
31500	24400	—	—	—	—

S4 pattern

NIB	Exc.	V.G.	Good	Fair	Poor
37000	28600	—	—	—	—

S5 pattern

NIB	Exc.	V.G.	Good	Fair	Poor
42000	32500	—	—	—	—

S4E pattern

NIB	Exc.	V.G.	Good	Fair	Poor
47600	36800	—	—	—	—

S5E pattern

NIB	Exc.	V.G.	Good	Fair	Poor
53000	41000	—	—	—	—

SXO pattern

NIB	Exc.	V.G.	Good	Fair	Poor
79200	61000	—	—	—	—

Excaliber

An over and under shotgun with sidelocks.This is a large frame pigeon or competition model.

NIB	Exc.	V.G.	Good	Fair	Poor
N/A	30000	—	—	—	—

African Express

A side by side boxlock double rifle.

NIB	Exc.	V.G.	Good	Fair	Poor
31900	22500				

Venus Express Professional

A side by side double rifle with sidelocks.

NIB	Exc.	V.G.	Good	Fair	Poor
47900	32500	—	—	—	—

Venus Express Extra

A side by side double rifle with sidelocks.

NIB	Exc.	V.G.	Good	Fair	Poor
N/A	45000	—	—	—	—

FARQUHARSON, JOHN
London, England

Not a gunmaker but the designer of what is perhaps the finest single shot action ever developed. It was patented on May 25, 1872, and has been used as the basis for some of the world's best single shot rifles manufactured by top English gunmakers throughout the years. There will be references to this action under sections dealing with these makers.

FARROW ARMS CO.
Holyoke, Massachusetts
Mason, Tennessee

Farrow Falling Block Rifle

Designed by W.M. Farrow, a target shooter who had worked on the Ballard rifles for the Marlin company. The Farrow rifles are chambered for various calibers and have barrel lengths from 28"-36" of octagonal configuration. They feature tang sights and are either all blued or have a nickel-plated receiver. The stocks are walnut. There were two grades offered that varied according to the grade of wood used. These rifles are quite scarce on today's market, and the number manufactured between 1885 and 1900 is unknown.

No. 1 Model

Fancy walnut with checkering and a Schutzen buttplate.

Exc.	V.G.	Good	Fair	Poor
—	—	6500	3000	1750

No. 2 Model

Plainer wood and no checkering.

Exc.	V.G.	Good	Fair	Poor
—	—	5500	2500	1400

FAYETTEVILLE ARMORY PISTOLS AND RIFLES
Fayetteville, North Carolina

In 1861, the U.S. Arsenal at Fayetteville, North Carolina, was seized by the officials of that state and later turned over to the government of the Confederate States of America. While still controlled by the state of North Carolina, a number of inferior flintlock arms were altered at the arsenal from flint to percussion, including a number of U.S. M1836 pistols and U.S. M1819 Hall rifles (the latter also shortened and remodeled into cavalry carbines). In accordance with an agreement between the governors of Virginia and North Carolina, the rifle machinery seized at the former U.S. Armory at Harpers Ferry, Virginia, was also sent to Fayetteville, where in 1862 the Confederacy began the construction of rifles modeled after the the U.S. M1855 rifle. Production continued until 1865 when the advance of Sherman's Armies necessitated the evacuation of the armory.

Fayetteville Armory Percussion Pistols (U.S. M1836 Pistols, Altered)

Overall length 13-1/4"; barrel length 8-1/2"; caliber .54. Markings: same as U.S. M1836 contact pistols, i.e. the locks either marked with eagle head over "A. WATERS/MILBURY MS./(date)" or "US/R. JOHNSON/MIDDN CONN./(date)" and various barrel proofmarks; also occasionally marked "N. CAROLINA".

The Fayetteville Armory altered approximately 900 U.S. M1836 pistols from flintlock to percussion. These arms were altered by enlarging the flint touchhole and screwing in a cylindrical drum in place of the pan and frizzen. The distinguishing feature of the Fayetteville alteration is the clean-out screw at the face of the cylinder and the "S" shaped hammer, not unlike that used on post-1862 dated rifles.

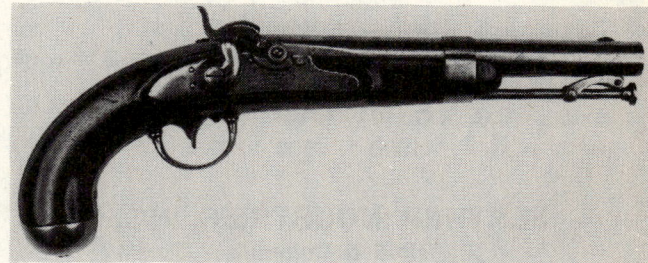

Courtesy Milwaukee Public Museum, Milwaukee, Wisconsin

Exc.	V.G.	Good	Fair	Poor
—	—	2500	1200	900

Fayetteville Armory Rifles (Types I through IV)

Overall length 49-1/8"; barrel length 33"; caliber .58. Markings: on barrel, an eagle over "C.S.A./FAYETTEVILLE" forward of the hammer and the date on the rounded tail. "CSA" also found on buttplates; date on top of barrel; proofmarks (eagle head, "V" and "P") on left quarter of barrel near breech.

From 1862 to early 1865, the Fayetteville Armory produced four variants of the old U.S. M1855 rifle on the machinery that had been lent to North Carolina by Virginia after its capture in April 1861. The earliest 1862 production (Type I) utilized un-milled lockplates captured at Harpers Ferry and are distinguished by having a "hump" (where the Maynard primer would have been milled) that extends to the arc of the hammer. Type II production utilized the newly made locks received from Richmond during the balance of 1862; they had a relatively low "hump" whose upper surface matched the contour of the stock. By the end of 1862, Fayetteville was producing its own lock, the plate of which resembled the U.S. M1861 rifle musket, but with a distinctive "S" shaped hammer. This lock distinguishes both type III and type IV production. All rifles made through 1863 continued to bear a saber bayonet lug on the right side of the barrel. In 1864, however, this was eliminated in favor of a triangular socket bayonet. The absence of the saber bayonet lug and remodeled front sight distinguishes type IV production. Because the barrel machinery went to Richmond, production at Fayetteville was continually hindered, seldom reaching more than 300 per month in the three years that the Fayetteville rifle was manufactured. (Note: The rarity of Type I production will usually generate a premium for that variant.)

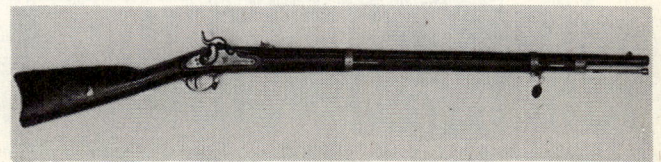

Courtesy Milwaukee Public Museum, Milwaukee, Wisconsin

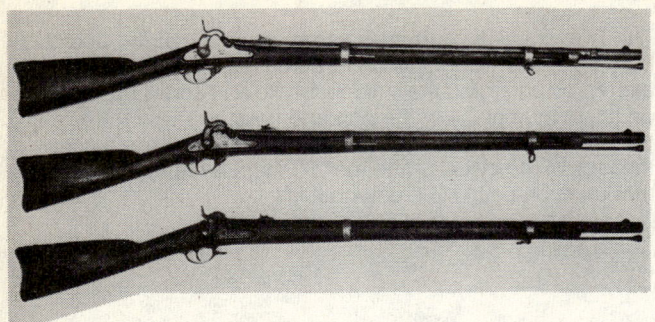

Courtesy Milwaukee Public Museum, Milwaukee, Wisconsin

Exc.	V.G.	Good	Fair	Poor
—	—	11500	4500	3750

FEATHER INDUSTRIES, INC.
Trinidad, Colorado

AT-22

A blowback-operated semiautomatic chambered for the .22 l.r. cartridge. It has a removable, shrouded 17" barrel and a folding metal stock. There are adjustable sights, and the finish is black. There is a detachable 20-round magazine. This model was introduced in 1986.

NIB	Exc.	V.G.	Good	Fair	Poor
250	200	175	150	110	75

AT-9

Similar to the AR-22 except that it is chambered for the 9mm Parabellum cartridge and has a 16" barrel and 32-round magazine. It was introduced in 1988.

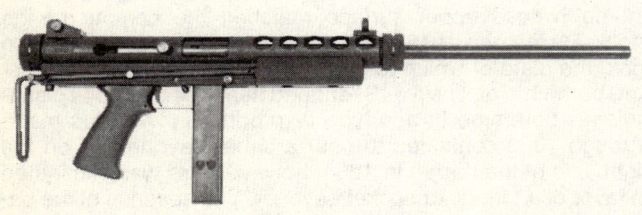

NIB	Exc.	V.G.	Good	Fair	Poor
325	275	250	225	175	125

KG-9

A 9mm, semiautomatic assault rifle that was introduced in 1989.

NIB	Exc.	V.G.	Good	Fair	Poor
575	500	425	375	300	250

KG-22

Similar in appearance to the KG-9 except that it is chambered for .22 l.r. and has a 20-round detachable magazine. It was introduced in 1989.

NIB	Exc.	V.G.	Good	Fair	Poor
300	275	225	175	125	100

SAR-180

The current incarnation of the old American 180, which was manufactured in Austria a number of years ago. It is chambered for .22 l.r. and has a 17.5" barrel. It is a blowback-operated semiautomatic that has a 165-round drum magazine that sits on top of the action on the flat side. The rear sight is adjustable, and the finish is blued with a walnut stock, pistol grip, and forend. This model was revived by Feather Industries in 1989.

NIB	Exc.	V.G.	Good	Fair	Poor
500	450	400	350	275	200

Mini-AT

A blowback-operated semiautomatic pistol chambered for the .22 l.r. cartridge. It is a 5.5"-barreled version of the AT-22 rifle and has a 20-round magazine. This model was manufactured between 1986 and 1989.

NIB	Exc.	V.G.	Good	Fair	Poor
350	200	175	150	125	100

Guardian Angel

A two-shot, Over/Under, derringer-styled pistol. It is chambered for the 9mm Parabellum and can be converted to fire the .38 Super cartridge. It is constructed of stainless steel and has an internal hammer and fully enclosed trigger. It was introduced in 1988.

NIB	Exc.	V.G.	Good	Fair	Poor
150	125	100	75	50	40

FEDERAL ENGINEERING CORP.
Chicago, Illinois

XC-220

A blowback-operated, semiautomatic rifle chambered for the .22 l.r. cartridge. It has a 16.5" barrel and a steel receiver that is blued. The stock is black synthetic. This model was introduced in 1984.

NIB	Exc.	V.G.	Good	Fair	Poor
450	300	275	225	175	125

XC-450

Similar in appearance to the XC-220 except that it is chambered for the .45 ACP cartridge. It has a 30-round detachable magazine.

NIB	Exc.	V.G.	Good	Fair	Poor
650	525	450	400	300	250

XC-900

A 9mm Parabellum version of the same basic firearm. It has a 32-round magazine and was introduced in 1984.

NIB	Exc.	V.G.	Good	Fair	Poor
600	500	425	350	275	200

FEDERAL ORDNANCE, INC.
South El Monte, California

An importer as well as a manufacturer that basically fabricates new and custom firearms out of existing older military parts. The firearms they import are military surplus weapons that will be covered in their own sections of this book. The firearms covered here are of Federal Ordnance manufacture.

M-14 Semiautomatic

A semiautomatic version of the M-14 service rifle. It is constructed of a newly manufactured receiver that has no selector and select surplus G.I. parts. The rifle is refinished to original specifications and furnished with a 20-round magazine and either a wood or fiberglass stock. This model was introduced in 1986. Although this model is a battle rifle and falls into the category affected by the wild price fluctuations we have been experiencing, prices for this gun have stayed fairly stable due to a fairly constant supply. This model has been manufactured since 1986.

Exc.	V.G.	Good	Fair	Poor
650	600	550	450	375

Model 714 Broomhandle Mauser

A remanufactured C96-type pistol chambered for 7.63mm or 9mm Parabellum. It utilizes a new manufactured frame and surplus parts. It features a 10-round detachable magazine, adjustable sights, and walnut grips. A Bolo Model with a smaller grip was produced in 1988 only.

NIB	Exc.	V.G.	Good	Fair	Poor
850	750	650	500	250	100

Model 713 Mauser Carbine

A 16"-barreled version of the Mauser with a fixed walnut stock. It has a standard magazine and is chambered for 7.63mm or 9mm Parabellum. It is refinished and was introduced in 1987.

Exc.	V.G.	Good	Fair	Poor
1250	1000	900	700	575

Model 713 Deluxe

Chambered for 7.63mm and has a 16" barrel with a detachable shoulder stock made of deluxe walnut. It has been modified to accept detachable magazines and is furnished with two 20-shot units. It has a 1000-meter adjustable sight and is furnished in a fitted leather case. There were only 1,500 manufactured in 1986.

NIB	Exc.	V.G.	Good	Fair	Poor
2000	1750	1500	1250	1000	800

Standard Broomhandle

A refurbished surplus C-96 Mauser pistol with a new 7.63mm or 9mm barrel. All springs are replaced, and the entire gun is refinished. It is furnished with a shoulder stock/holster of Chinese manufacture.

NIB	Exc.	V.G.	Good	Fair	Poor
725	650	525	450	350	275

Ranger 1911A1

Federal Ordnance's version of the 1911A1 Colt service pistol. It is made of all steel, is chambered for .45 ACP, and has checkered walnut grips. It was introduced in 1988.

NIB	Exc.	V.G.	Good	Fair	Poor
450	375	325	275	225	150

FEINWERKBAU
Oberndorf, Germany
Importer - Beeman Precision Arms
Santa Rosa, California

Known predominately for the production of high quality, extremely accurate air rifles and pistols. They also produce some of the most accurate target .22 caliber firearms in the world today. These firearms are listed:

Model 2000 Universal

A single-shot, bolt-action target rifle chambered for the .22 rimfire cartridge. It has a 26.5" barrel with adjustable aperture sights and a fully adjustable trigger. There were four different stock configurations offered with stippled pistol grips and forearms. An electronic trigger was available as a $450 option. This model was discontinued in 1988.

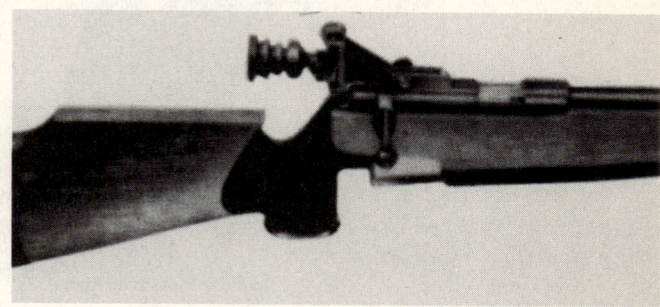

Exc.	V.G.	Good	Fair	Poor
1200	1050	850	650	550

Mini 2000

Has a 22" barrel, and the electronic trigger was available at the additional cost.

Exc.	V.G.	Good	Fair	Poor
1000	850	750	550	450

Running Boar Rifle

Has a thumbhole stock with an adjustable cheekpiece and is furnished without sights. It was specially designed for the offhand Running Boar Competitions.

Exc.	V.G.	Good	Fair	Poor
1200	1050	850	650	550

Match Rifle

Has a 26.75" barrel and an adjustable cheekpiece stock.

Exc.	V.G.	Good	Fair	Poor
1100	950	750	550	450

Model 2600 Ultra Match Free Rifle

Similar to the Model 2000, with a laminated thumbhole stock and a heavy 26" barrel, fully adjustable sights, and trigger. It is offered with an electronic trigger for an additional $400. This model was introduced in 1986.

NIB	Exc	V.G.	Good	Fair	Poor
1400	1200	1000	850	650	550

FEMARU
Budapest, Hungary

Hungary became a communist satellite in the mid-1950s. At this time the Femaru company was designated to replace the firm of Fegyvergyar as the official Hungarian arms manufacturer. The products are of good quality.

Model 37

This semi-automatic pistol was built in both 7.65mm and 9mm Short calibers. It is well designed pistol of quality construction.

It is fitted with a grip safety and exposed hammer. The Hungarian military adopted the pistol in 1937. It was produced until the late 1940s. Early guns were marked "Femaru Fegyver es Gepgyar RT Budapest" but during the war the Nazi code for these guns was "jhv". The 9mm models have a 7-round magazine while the 7.65 models have an 8-round magazine. During World War II the Germans designed this pistol the "Pistol Mod 37 Kal 7.65 (Ung)". Add 75% for Nazi proofed examples.

Courtesy Richard M. Kumor, Sr.

Exc.	V.G.	Good	Fair	Poor
350	275	225	150	100

Hege

A complete copy of the Walther PP. It is chambered for the 7.65mm and manufactured to be sold by Hegewaffen of Germany. The slide is so marked, along with a Pegasus in a circle. The designation "AP 66 Cal.7.65" also appears. The pistol was intended for export sales in the U.S. and other western countries.

Exc.	V.G.	Good	Fair	Poor
250	225	175	125	100

Tokagypt

15,000 of these pistols were built in 1958, under contract for the Egyptian army. It is a modified version of the Soviet TT-33 Tokarev chambered for the 9mm Parabellum with a safety added. This is a well-made, serviceable pistol; and it is difficult to understand why Egypt reneged on the contract. The balance were sold commercially-some under the trademark "Firebird."

Exc.	V.G.	Good	Fair	Poor
400	350	275	200	125

Walam

Another Walther PP copy of excellent quality chambered for the 9mm short or .380 ACP. Egypt was also to be the recipient of this contract, but again they mysteriously cancelled. The pistols were sold on the commercial market—some designated Model 48.

Exc.	V.G.	Good	Fair	Poor
250	225	175	125	100

FERLIB
Gardone V.T., Italy
Importers - Quality Arms
Houston, Texas
New England Arms
Kittery Point, Maine

Model F.VI

A high-grade, side-x-side shotgun chambered for all gauges and is essentially custom-ordered. It is available in various barrel lengths and chokes and has an Anson and Deeley boxlock action, double triggers, and automatic ejectors. The action is case-colored, and the stock is hand-checkered select walnut. Single selective triggers are available for an additional $375.

28 Gauge and .410-Add 10%.

NIB	Exc.	V.G.	Good	Fair	Poor
3800	3500	2800	2250	1700	1450

Model F.VII

Has a scroll-engraved, coin-finished frame but otherwise is similar to the Model F.VI. Single trigger option and small gauge premium are the same.

NIB	Exc.	V.G.	Good	Fair	Poor
5000	4250	3750	3000	2400	1950

Model F.VII/SC

A more deluxe version with gold inlays and a gamescene-engraved receiver. Options and premium are the same.

NIB	Exc.	V.G.	Good	Fair	Poor
6100	5500	4500	3750	2800	2250

Model F. VII Sideplate

Features false sideplates that are completely covered with gamescene engraving. This model is standard with a single-selective trigger, but the small gauge premium is applicable.

NIB	Exc.	V.G.	Good	Fair	Poor
5500	5000	4250	3500	2750	2200

Model F.VII/SC Sideplate

The false sideplate model with gold inlays accenting the full coverage engraving.

28 Gauge and .410-Add 10%.

NIB	Exc.	V.G.	Good	Fair	Poor
7200	6500	5250	4500	3500	2750

Hammer Gun

Features a boxlock action with external hammers. Its other features are custom ordered to the purchaser's specifications.

NIB	Exc.	V.G.	Good	Fair	Poor
2900	2500	1850	1500	1000	750

FERRY, ANDREWS & CO.
Stafford, Connecticut

Under Hammer Pistol

This boot pistol is chambered for .36 caliber percussion and has a 3" part-round, part-octagonal barrel. They are similar to the other under hammer pistols that were produced in Connecticut and Massachusetts. The top strap was marked "Andrews Ferry & Co." The number manufactured is unknown. They were produced in the 1850s.

Exc.	V.G.	Good	Fair	Poor
—	1250	600	350	125

FIALA ARMS COMPANY
New Haven, Connecticut

Fiala Target Pistol

A different type of pistol than what is commonly encountered. Outwardly it resembles a semiautomatic Colt Woodsman; in actuality it is a manually operated firearm that must be cycled by hand after every shot. It was chambered for the .22 rimfire and was offered with interchangeable barrels in lengths of 3", 7.5", and 20". The finish is blued, and the grips are checkered walnut. They are marked "Fiala Arms and Equipment Co. Inc. / New Haven Conn. / Patents Pending". This pistol was furnished with a detachable shoulder stock in a leather trunk case that held the gun, three barrels, stock, and cleaning tools. The government has classified this pistol with its stock as a "Curio and Relic"; and in its complete state it is a very desirable collectible.

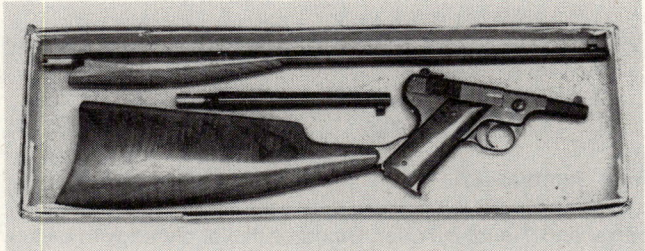

Courtesy Butterfield & Butterfield, San Francisco, California

Complete, Three Barrels, Stock, Tools, and Case

Exc.	V.G.	Good	Fair	Poor
2500	2100	1250	675	550

Gun Only

Exc.	V.G.	Good	Fair	Poor
1500	1250	500	250	150

FINNISH LION
Valmet, Sweden

ISU Target Rifle

A single shot, bolt-action rifle chambered for the .22 rimfire cartridge. It has a 27" heavy barrel and a target stock with accessories. It features target adjustable sights and was manufactured between 1966 and 1977.

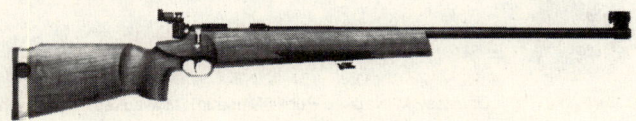

Exc.	V.G.	Good	Fair	Poor
350	300	250	200	125

Champion Free Rifle

Has a 29" heavy barrel and double-set triggers. Otherwise it is similar to the ISU model. It was manufactured between 1965 and 1972.

Exc.	V.G.	Good	Fair	Poor
600	525	450	375	275

Match Rifle

Similar to the Champion rifle, with a thumbhole stock and an adjustable butt plate. It was manufactured between 1937 and 1972.

Exc.	V.G.	Good	Fair	Poor
500	425	350	275	200

FIOCCHI OF AMERICA, INC.
Ozark, Missouri
SEE Pardini and A. Zoli

Imports the above firearms, and they are listed in their own respective sections.

FIREARMS INTERNATIONAL
Washington, D.C.
SEE Star

Was once the importer of the Star Model D as it was sold in the U.S.A. They also imported various other .25 caliber Colt copies that are not considered collectible and would be valued in the $150-and-under range.

FLORENCE ARMORY
Florence, Guilford Counry, North Carolina

Founded in 1862 as a repair facility to alter sporting arms for military use. Majority of work done by H.C. Lamb & Company. In 1862, Captain Z. Coffin ordered stocks, barrels and locks to assemble newly made rifles. Furniture of these arms varied, either being supplied by Glaze & Company or being the remainders from Searcy & Moore's production. Number made estimated to be in excess of 300 rifles in both .50 and .54 calibers. These arms (particularly the barrels) exhibit characteristics of North Carolina contract pieces.

Prospective purchasers are strongly advised to secure an expert appraisal prior to acquisition.

Exc.	V.G.	Good	Fair	Poor
—	—	7500	6000	4000

FOEHL, C.
Philadelphia, Pennsylvania

Foehl Derringer

A .41 caliber percussion single shot pistol with a 2" barrel, German silver mounts and a walnut stock. The lock marked "C. Foehl".

Exc.	V.G.	Good	Fair	Poor
—	—	1750	750	300

FOEHL & WEEKS
Philadelphia, Pennsylvania

Columbian

A .32 or .38 caliber revolver marked with the patent date "20 January 1891".

Exc.	V.G.	Good	Fair	Poor
150	125	100	75	50

Columbian Automatic

A .38 caliber revolver with a hinged barrel and cylinder assembly.

Exc.	V.G.	Good	Fair	Poor
175	150	125	100	75

Perfect

As above, with a concealed hammer and also in .32 caliber.

Exc.	V.G.	Good	Fair	Poor
175	150	125	100	75

FOGARTY
American Repeating Rifle Co.
Boston, Massachusetts

Fogarty Repeating Rifle and Carbine

A limited number of repeating rifles and carbines based upon Valentine Fogarty's patents were produced between 1866 and 1867. The calibers of these arms varies and the normal barrel lengths are 20" and 28". Blued, case-hardened with walnut stocks. The American Repeating Rifle Company was purchased by the Winchester Repeating Arms Company in 1869. Prospective purchasers are advised to secure a qualified appraisal prior to acquisition.

Rifle

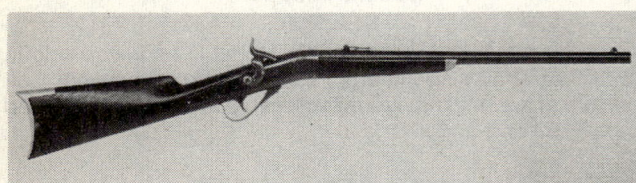

Courtesy Buffalo Bill Historical Center, Cody, Wyoming

Exc.	V.G.	Good	Fair	Poor
—	—	5000	3000	1250

Carbine

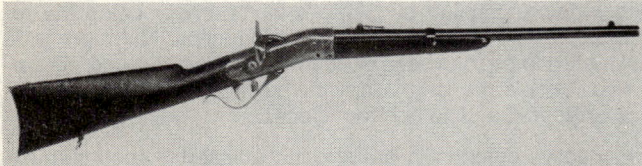

Courtesy Buffalo Bill Historical Center, Cody, Wyoming

Exc.	V.G.	Good	Fair	Poor
—	—	5000	3000	1250

FOLSOM, H.
St. Louis, Missouri
SEE Crescent Arms Co.

Derringer

A .41 caliber single shot percussion pocket pistol with a 2.5" barrel, German silver mounts and a walnut stock. The barrel marked "H. Folsom".

Exc.	V.G.	Good	Fair	Poor
—	—	800	350	275

FOREHAND & WADSWORTH
Worcester, Massachusetts

Established in 1871 and operated under the above name until 1890 when it became the Forehand Arms Company. Hopkins & Allen purchased the company in 1902.

Single Shot Derringer

A .22 caliber single shot pocket pistol with a 2" half-octagonal pivoted barrel, spur trigger and nickel- or silver-plated frame. Walnut grips. The barrel marked "Forehand & Wadsworth Worcester".

Exc.	V.G.	Good	Fair	Poor
—	1250	500	250	100

Single Shot .41 Derringer

As above in .41 caliber with a 2.5" round barrel.

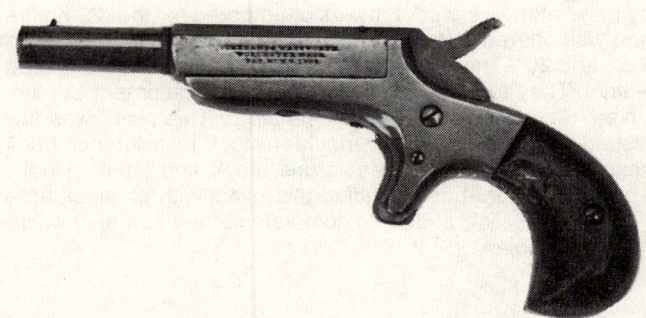

Courtesy Milwaukee Public Museum, Milwaukee, Wisconsin

Exc.	V.G.	Good	Fair	Poor
—	—	750	450	200

Side Hammer .22

A .22 caliber spur trigger revolver with a 2.25" to 4" octagonal barrel and 7-shot cylinder. Blued or nickel-plated with walnut grips.

Exc.	V.G.	Good	Fair	Poor
—	300	200	150	100

Center Hammer

A .32 caliber spur trigger revolver with a 3.5" octagonal barrel and 6-shot cylinder. Blued or nickel-plated with rosewood or walnut grips. The top strap commonly found marked "Terror".

Courtesy Milwaukee Public Museum, Milwaukee, Wisconsin

Exc.	V.G.	Good	Fair	Poor
—	350	150	175	125

Old Model Army Single Action Revolver

A .44 Russian caliber revolver with a 7.5" round barrel and 6-shot cylinder. The barrel marked "Forehand & Wadsworth, Worchester, Mass. U.S. Patd. Oct. 22, '61, June 27, '71 Oct. 28, '73." Blued with walnut grips. Approximately 250 were manufactured between 1872 and 1878.

Exc.	V.G.	Good	Fair	Poor
—	—	1500	850	500

New Model Army Single Action Revolver

Similar to the above, with a 6.5" barrel and half-cock notch on the hammer. Approximately 250 were made between 1878 and 1882.

Exc.	V.G.	Good	Fair	Poor
650	575	475	350	225

Double Action Revolver

A .32 or .38 caliber double-action revolver with a 3.5" barrel and 6-shot cylinder. The .32 caliber version marked "Forehand & Wadsworth Double Action", and the .38 caliber "American Bulldog". Manufactured from 1871 to 1890.

Exc.	V.G.	Good	Fair	Poor
250	225	175	125	75

British Bulldog

A solid frame double-action revolver similar to the above.

Exc.	V.G.	Good	Fair	Poor
250	225	175	125	90

British Bulldog .44

As above in .44 S&W caliber with a 5" barrel and 5-shot cylinder.

Exc.	V.G.	Good	Fair	Poor
275	250	175	125	90

Swamp Angel

A .41 caliber single action revolver with a 3" barrel and 5-shot cylinder. The top strap marked "Swamp Angel".

Exc.	V.G.	Good	Fair	Poor
200	175	150	100	75

Forehand Arms Co. 1898-1902
Perfection Automatic

A .32 or .38 caliber double-action revolver with a hinged barrel and cylinder assembly. Varying barrel lengths. Blued or nickel-plated with hard rubber grips.

Exc.	V.G.	Good	Fair	Poor
200	150	100	75	50

FOWLER, B. JR.
Hartford, Connecticut

Percussion Pistol

A .38 caliber single shot percussion pistol with a 4" half octagonal barrel, iron frame and maple grips. The barrel marked "B. Fowler, Jr." Manufactured between 1835 and 1838.

Exc.	V.G.	Good	Fair	Poor
—	950	500	300	150

FOX, A. H.
Philadelphia, Pennsylvania

Ansley H. Fox established the Fox Gun Company in Baltimore, Maryland, in 1896. Subsequently, he made arms under the name Philadelphia Gun Company. As of 1905, he operated under the name A.H. Fox. In 1930, this company was purchased by the Savage Arms Company who continued manufacturing all grades of Fox shotguns. As of 1942, the Savage Company only made the plainer grades.

NOTE: See Savage Arms for Fox Model B shotguns.

Sterlingworth

A 12, 16, or 20 gauge boxlock double-barrel shotgun with 26", 28", or 30" barrels, double triggers and extractors. Automatic ejectors were also available and would add approximately 30% to the values listed below. Blued, case-hardened with a walnut stock. Manufactured from 1911 to 1946.

20 Gauge-Add 50%.

Exc.	V.G.	Good	Fair	Poor
1250	1000	800	500	275

Sterlingworth Deluxe

As above, with an ivory bead, recoil pad and optional 32" barrel.

20 Gauge-Add 50%.

Exc.	V.G.	Good	Fair	Poor
1450	1250	1000	700	400

SP Grade

A 12, 16, or 20 gauge boxlock double-barrel shotgun with varying length barrels, double triggers and extractors.

20 Gauge-Add 35%.

Automatic Ejectors-Add 15%.

Exc.	V.G.	Good	Fair	Poor
1000	850	750	450	225

HE Grade

Similar to the early A Grade and offered in 12 and 20 gauge. Chambers were 2-1/4" standard with 3" chambers available on request. This model is marked on the barrel "Not Warranted". this referred to pattern density, not barrel quality. Only 60 20 gauge HE Grades appear in factory records. Manufactured from 1923 to 1942.

Single Selective Trigger-Add 20%.

Exc.	V.G.	Good	Fair	Poor
2500	2150	1750	1000	650

High Grade Guns A-FE

The Fox Company as well as the Savage Arms Company produced a variety of shotguns decorated in varying grades. They were available in 12, 16, and 20 gauge. As the value for these arms depends on the particular features of these arms, prospective purchasers are advised to secure a qualified appraisal prior to acquisition.

A Grade-built from 1905 to 1942

Exc.	V.G.	Good	Fair	Poor
1450	1150	850	600	400

AE Grade (Automatic Ejectors)-built from 1905 to 1946

Exc.	V.G.	Good	Fair	Poor
1750	1450	1150	900	700

B Grade-built from 1905 to 1918

Exc.	V.G.	Good	Fair	Poor
2400	2100	1600	1100	500

BE Grade-built from 1905 to 1918

Exc.	V.G.	Good	Fair	Poor
2800	2500	2000	1500	900

C Grade-built from 1905 to 1913

Exc.	V.G.	Good	Fair	Poor
2600	2200	1700	1100	550

CE Grade-built from 1905 to 1946

Exc.	V.G.	Good	Fair	Poor
3000	2600	2100	1550	950

XE Grade-built from 1914 to 1945

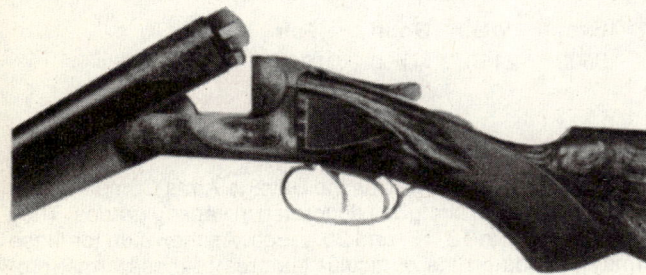

Exc.	V.G.	Good	Fair	Poor
5500	5000	3500	1850	1100

D Grade-built from 1906 to 1913

Exc.	V.G.	Good	Fair	Poor
8000	7000	4500	2500	1000

DE Grade-built from 1906 to 1945

Exc.	V.G.	Good	Fair	Poor
8500	7500	5000	3000	1500

F Grade-built from 1906 to 1913

Exc.	V.G.	Good	Fair	Poor
22500	15000	8000	5000	3000

FE Grade-built from 1906 to 1940

Exc.	V.G.	Good	Fair	Poor
25000	18500	10000	7000	5000

Single Barrel Trap Guns

A 12 gauge single barrel boxlock shotgun with 30" or 32" ventilated rib barrels and automatic ejector. There were approximately 571 single barrel trap guns manufactured. Produced in four grades as listed below:

J Grade-built from 1919 to 1936

Exc.	V.G.	Good	Fair	Poor
1750	1450	950	750	450

K Grade-built from 1919 to 1931
Approximately 75 built

Exc.	V.G.	Good	Fair	Poor
2500	2000	1650	1250	750

L Grade-built from 1919 to 1931
Approximately 25 built

Exc.	V.G.	Good	Fair	Poor
3500	2500	2000	1500	1000

M Grade-built from 1919 to 1932
A total of 9 guns built

Exc.	V.G.	Good	Fair	Poor
8500	6500	4500	3000	2000

Currently manufactured A.H. Fox shotguns

In 1993 the Connecticut Manufacturing Company of New Britain, Connecticut, announced the production of the A.H. Fox shotgun in 20 gauge exclusively. The gun is hand-built and constructed to the same dimensions and standards as the original Fox. The gun is offered in five grades with many standard features and several optional ones as well. Each shotgun is built to order. Because these guns are newly built and have no pricing history, only manufacturer's retail price for the base gun will be given. Extra sets of barrels, single triggers, and other extra costs options will greatly affect price.

CE Grade

Receiver engraved with fine scroll and gamescene engraving with Turkish Circassian walnut stock, fine line hand checkering. Choice of full, half, or straight grip with splinter forend. Double triggers, automatic ejectors, automatic safety, choice of chokes, and barrel lengths in 26, 28, and 30 inches.

Retail price: $5,650

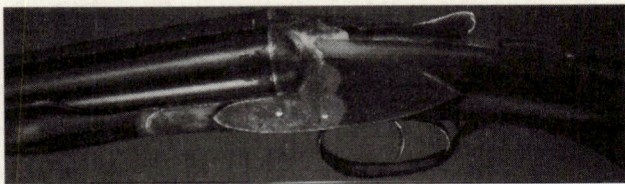

XE Grade

Same features as above with the addition of chiseled scroll work with engraved gamescenes and higher quality Circassian walnut.

Retail price: $8,500

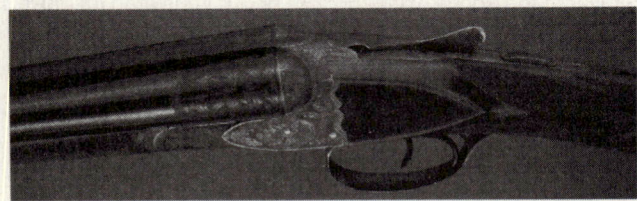

DE Grade

Same features as above with more intricate and extensive engraving. Even higher quality wood with diamond pattern checkering.

Retail price: $12,500

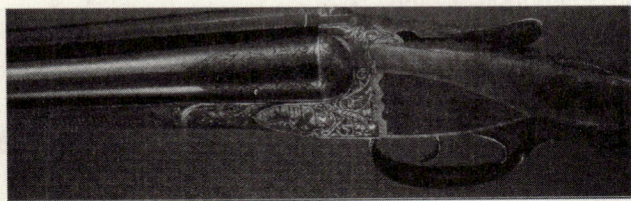

FE Grade

This grade features gold inlays and distinctive scroll work. Best quality wood with very fine line diamond pattern checkering.

Retail price: $17,500

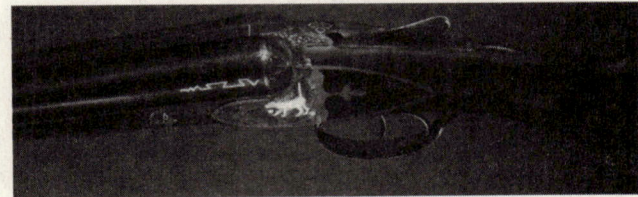

Exhibition Grade

This is the company's highest grade and features any optional detail the customer desires including custom engraving and exhibition quality wood. Each Exhibition Grade Fox will be unique and should be appraised on an individual basis.

Retail price: $25,000

FRANCHI, L.
Brescia, Italy
Importer - American Arms, Inc.
No. Kansas City, Missouri

SIDE-X-SIDE-SHOTGUNS

Astore

A 12 gauge boxlock shotgun manufactured in a variety of barrel lengths with double triggers and automatic ejectors. Blued with a straight walnut stock. Manufactured from 1937 to 1960.

NIB	Exc.	V.G.	Good	Fair	Poor
1000	900	750	500	350	200

Astore II

As above, but more finely finished.

NIB	Exc.	V.G.	Good	Fair	Poor
1250	1100	900	700	450	250

Astore 5

As above, but more finely finished.

NIB	Exc.	V.G.	Good	Fair	Poor
2000	1750	1250	950	600	300

Airone

Similar to the Astore. Manufactured during the 1940s.

NIB	Exc.	V.G.	Good	Fair	Poor
1300	1050	950	750	500	250

Sidelock Double Barrel Shotguns

A 12, 16, or 20 gauge sidelock double-barrel shotgun manufactured in a variety of barrel lengths with a single selective trigger and automatic ejectors. Produced in the following grades they differ as to engraving coverage and quality of wood:

Condor

NIB	Exc.	V.G.	Good	Fair	Poor
7500	6500	4500	3500	2500	1250

Imperial

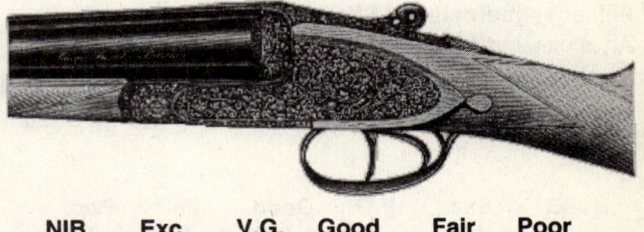

NIB	Exc.	V.G.	Good	Fair	Poor
10000	8500	6000	4500	3250	1500

Imperiales

NIB	Exc.	V.G.	Good	Fair	Poor
10500	9000	6500	5000	3500	1500

No. 5 Imperial Monte Carlo

NIB	Exc.	V.G.	Good	Fair	Poor
15000	12500	9000	7500	5000	2000

No. 11 Imperial Monte Carlo

NIB	Exc	V.G.	Good	Fair	Poor
16000	13500	10000	8000	5500	2000

Imperial Monte Carlo Extra

NIB	Exc.	V.G.	Good	Fair	Poor
20000	17500	12500	9500	7500	3500

OVER/UNDER SHOTGUNS

Priti Deluxe Model

A 12 or 20 gauge Over/Under boxlock double-barrel shotgun with 26" or 28" ventilated rib barrels, single trigger and automatic ejectors. Introduced in 1988.

NIB	Exc.	V.G.	Good	Fair	Poor
400	350	300	250	200	150

Falconet

A 12, 16, 20, and 28 gauge as well as .410 bore boxlock double-barrel shotgun with single selective trigger and automatic ejectors. The receiver was annodized in tan, ebony, or silver finishes. Manufactured from 1968 to 1975.

Silver Receiver-Add 10%.
28 Gauge and .410-Add 25%.

NIB	Exc.	V.G.	Good	Fair	Poor
550	500	425	350	250	200

Falconet Skeet

As above, with a 26" skeet barrel with a wide rib and the receiver case-hardened. Manufactured from 1970 to 1974.

NIB	Exc.	V.G.	Good	Fair	Poor
950	850	700	550	450	250

Falconet International Skeet

As above, but more finely finished.

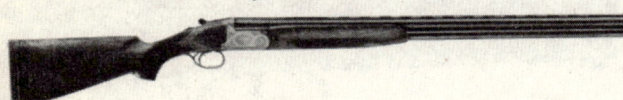

NIB	Exc.	V.G.	Good	Fair	Poor
1000	900	750	600	475	250

Falconet Trap

As above, with a 30" modified and full choke barrel, and trap stock. Manufactured from 1970 to 1974.

NIB	Exc.	V.G.	Good	Fair	Poor
950	850	700	550	450	250

Falconet International Trap

As above, but more finely finished.

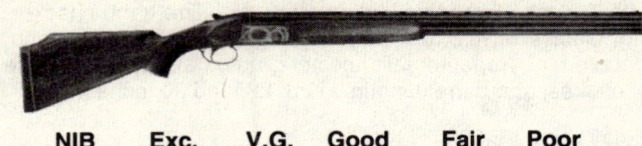

NIB	Exc.	V.G.	Good	Fair	Poor
1000	900	750	600	475	250

Peregrine Model 451

A 12 gauge boxlock double-barrel shotgun with 26" or 28" ventilated rib barrels, alloy receiver, single selective trigger and automatic ejectors. Manufactured in 1975.

NIB	Exc.	V.G.	Good	Fair	Poor
600	525	450	375	275	200

Peregrine Model 400

As above, with a steel frame.

NIB	Exc.	V.G.	Good	Fair	Poor
650	575	500	400	300	200

Aristocrat

Similar to the above, with 26", 28", or 30" ventilated rib barrels. Manufactured from 1960 to 1969.

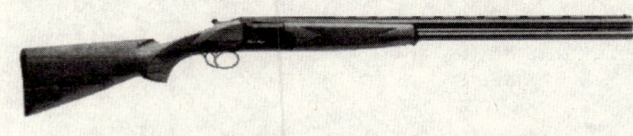

NIB	Exc.	V.G.	Good	Fair	Poor
650	575	500	400	300	200

Aristocrat Magnum

As above, with 3" chambers and 32" full choke barrels.

NIB	Exc.	V.G.	Good	Fair	Poor
650	575	500	400	300	200

Aristocrat Silver King

As above, with a French case-hardened receiver, and available in four grades of decoration.

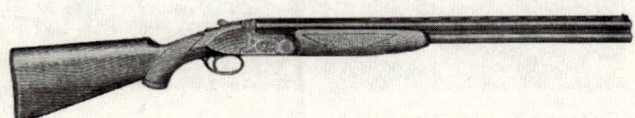

NIB	Exc.	V.G.	Good	Fair	Poor
750	675	575	475	350	200

Aristocrat Deluxe

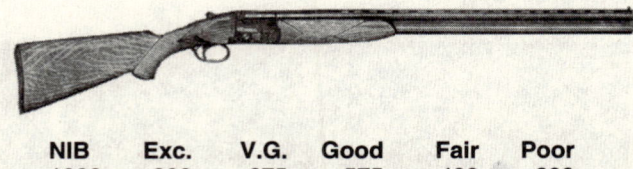

NIB	Exc.	V.G.	Good	Fair	Poor
1000	800	675	575	400	200

Aristocrat Supreme

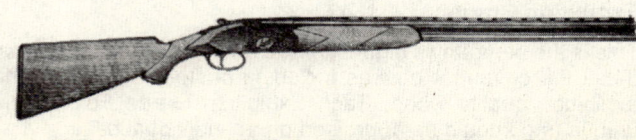

NIB	Exc.	V.G.	Good	Fair	Poor
1450	1200	850	700	575	250

Aristocrat Imperial

NIB	Exc.	V.G.	Good	Fair	Poor
2750	2250	1750	1250	950	450

Aristocrat Monte Carlo

NIB	Exc.	V.G.	Good	Fair	Poor
3500	3000	2750	2000	1500	750

Model 2003 Trap

A 12 gauge boxlock double-barrel shotgun with 30" or 32" ventilated rib barrels, single selective trigger and automatic ejectors. Manufactured in 1976.

NIB	Exc.	V.G.	Good	Fair	Poor
1250	1100	800	650	500	250

Model 2004 Trap

A single-barreled version of the Model 2003.

NIB	Exc.	V.G.	Good	Fair	Poor
1250	1100	800	650	500	250

Model 2005 Combination Trap

The Model 2003 with both a single and set of Over/Under barrels.

NIB	Exc.	V.G.	Good	Fair	Poor
2500	2200	1750	1200	950	450

Model 3000 "Undergun"

As above, with a single barrel fitted with a high ventilated rib so that it fires from the lower barrel position.

NIB	Exc.	V.G.	Good	Fair	Poor
2750	2450	2000	1500	1200	600

Alcione Model

A 12 gauge boxlock double-barrel shotgun with 28" ventilated rib barrels, single selective trigger and automatic ejectors.

NIB	Exc.	V.G.	Good	Fair	Poor
650	550	450	325	250	150

Alcione SL

As above, but more finely finished and with a French case-hardened receiver.

NIB	Exc	V.G.	Good	Fair	Poor
1250	900	700	500	300	150

SEMIAUTOMATIC SHOTGUNS

Standard Model

A 12 or 20 gauge semiautomatic shotgun with 24" to 30" ventilated rib barrels (those made after 1989, threaded for choke tubes) and an alloy receiver. Walnut stock. Manufactured since 1950.

Magnum Model-Add 10%.

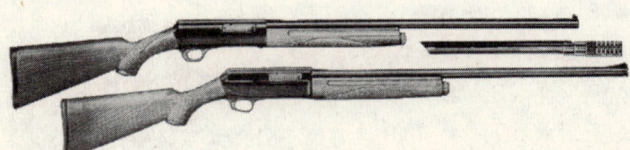

NIB	Exc.	V.G.	Good	Fair	Poor
500	450	350	300	250	150

Hunter Model

As above with an etched receiver and more finely figured wood.

Magnum Model-Add 10%.

NIB	Exc.	V.G.	Good	Fair	Poor
400	350	300	250	200	150

Eldorado

As above, but more finely finished. Manufactured from 1954 to 1975.

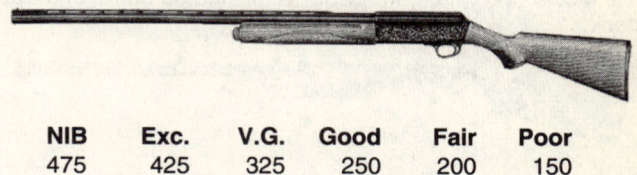

NIB	Exc.	V.G.	Good	Fair	Poor
475	425	325	250	200	150

Crown Grade, Diamond Grade, Imperial Grade

As above, with hand-done engraving and finely figured walnut stocks.

Crown Grade

NIB	Exc.	V.G.	Good	Fair	Poor
1500	1250	1000	700	475	250

Diamond Grade

NIB	Exc.	V.G.	Good	Fair	Poor
2000	1750	1250	900	675	300

Imperial Grade

NIB	Exc.	V.G.	Good	Fair	Poor
2500	2250	1750	1250	950	450

Model 500

A 12 gauge semiautomatic shotgun with a 28" ventilated rib barrel and walnut stock. Introduced in 1976.

Deluxe Version-Add 10%.

NIB	Exc.	V.G.	Good	Fair	Poor
350	325	275	200	150	100

Model 520 "Eldorado Gold"

An engraved and gold inlaid version of the above.

NIB	Exc.	V.G.	Good	Fair	Poor
1000	850	650	450	300	150

Model 530 Trap

The Model 500 with a 30" or 32" ventilated rib barrel and trap stock.

NIB	Exc.	V.G.	Good	Fair	Poor
675	600	500	400	300	150

Prestige Model

A 12 gauge semiautomatic shotgun manufactured in a variety of barrel lengths. After 1989 the barrels threaded for choke tubes. Alloy receiver and walnut stock.

NIB	Exc.	V.G.	Good	Fair	Poor
575	500	425	350	250	150

Elite Model

As above, with an etched receiver and more finely figured stock.

NIB	Exc.	V.G.	Good	Fair	Poor
600	500	425	350	250	150

SPAS12

A 12 gauge slide action or semiautomatic shotgun with a 21.5" barrel and 9-shot magazine. Annodized, black finish with a composition folding or fixed stock.

NIB	Exc.	V.G.	Good	Fair	Poor
950	800	600	500	400	300

Black Magic Game Model

A 12 gauge Magnum semi-iautomatic shotgun with 24" to 28" ventilated rib barrels threaded for choke tubes, gold annodized alloy receiver, blackened barrel and walnut stock. Also available in trap or skeet configuration.

Skeet Model-Add 10%.
Trap Model-Add 15%.

NIB	Exc.	V.G.	Good	Fair	Poor
400	350	275	200	150	100

Black Magic Hunter

A 12 gauge Magnum double-barrel shotgun with 28" ventilated rib barrels threaded for choke tubes, single selective triggers and automatic ejectors. Blued with a walnut stock. Introduced in 1989.

NIB	Exc.	V.G.	Good	Fair	Poor
975	850	650	400	300	150

Black Magic Lightweight Hunter

As above, with 26" barrels and 2.75" chambers.

NIB	Exc.	V.G.	Good	Fair	Poor
975	850	650	400	300	150

RIFLES

Centennial Semiautomatic

A .22 caliber semiautomatic rifle with a 21" barrel, adjustable sights, alloy receiver and walnut stock. Manufactured in 1968 only.

Deluxe Engraved Model-Add 20%.

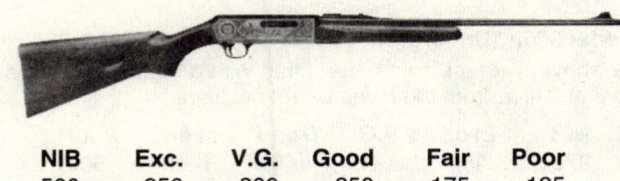

NIB	Exc.	V.G.	Good	Fair	Poor
500	350	300	250	175	125

FRANCOTTE, A.
Liege, Belgium

Jubilee

A 12, 16, 20, and 28 gauge Anson & Deeley boxlock double-barrel shotgun with various barrel lengths and chokes, automatic ejectors, double triggers and walnut stock.

Exc.	V.G.	Good	Fair	Poor
1650	1350	1100	850	450

No. 14

Exc.	V.G.	Good	Fair	Poor
2250	1850	1600	1300	650

No. 18

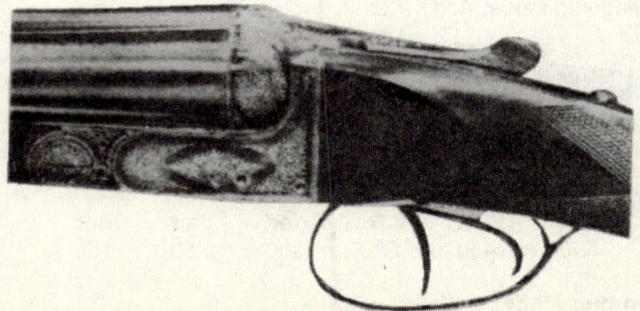

Exc.	V.G.	Good	Fair	Poor
2750	2250	2000	1500	750

No. 20

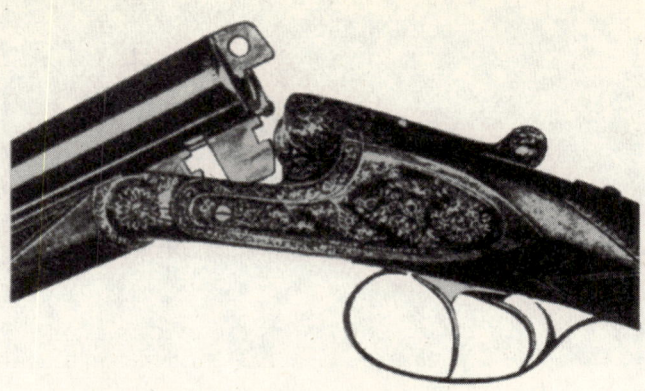

Exc.	V.G.	Good	Fair	Poor
3250	2500	2250	1750	900

No. 25

Exc.	V.G.	Good	Fair	Poor
3750	3000	2750	2000	1000

No. 30

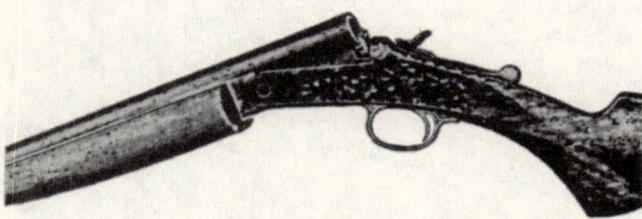

Exc.	V.G.	Good	Fair	Poor
4800	4000	3500	3000	1500

Eagle Grade No. 45

A finer finished Jubilee model.

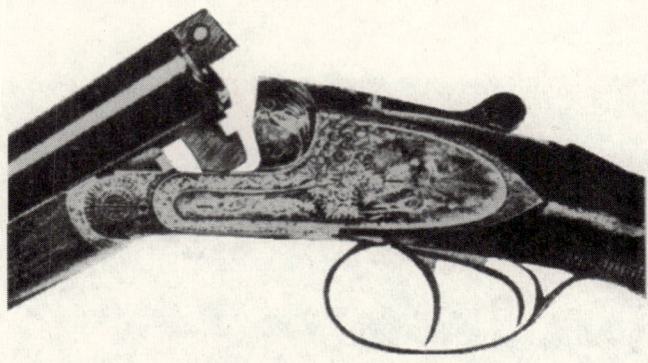

Exc.	V.G.	Good	Fair	Poor
3750	3000	2500	2000	1000

Knockabout

A plain version of the Jubilee Model in 12, 16, 20, 28 and .410 bore.

20 Gauge-Add 20%.
28 Gauge-Add 30%.
.410-Add 40%.

Exc.	V.G.	Good	Fair	Poor
1250	1100	850	650	500

Sidelock Side-x-Side

A 12, 16, 20, and 28 and .410 bore sidelock shotgun ordered per customer's specifications. Extensive scroll engraving, deluxe walnut stock and finely checkered. The .410 will bring a premium of from $1,200-$1,500.

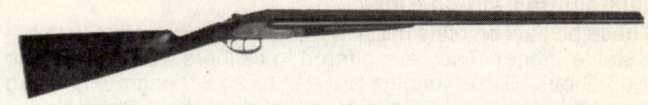

NIB	Exc.	V.G.	Good	Fair	Poor
12650	10000	8000	6500	5000	3500

Deluxe Sidelock Side-x-Side

As above, with gold-inlaid hunting scenes.

NIB	Exc.	V.G.	Good	Fair	Poor
15000	12500	10000	8000	5750	4800

FRANCOTTE, A.
Liege, Belgium
CURRENTLY IMPORTED SHOTGUNS AND RIFLES
Importer - Armes De Chasse
Chadds Ford, Pennsylvania

Francotte currently imports side-by-side boxlock or sidelock shotguns, double rifles, and single shot rifles as well as bolt action rifles into the United States through Armes De Chasse. These shotguns and rifles are all custom built to the customers specifications. Gauge (including 24 and 32 gauge), caliber, barrel length, engraving, wood type and style are all individually produced. No two all alike. These shotguns and rifles should be individually appraised before the sale. Prices listed below reflect a range that the original buyer paid and also reflect the value of the changing dollar.

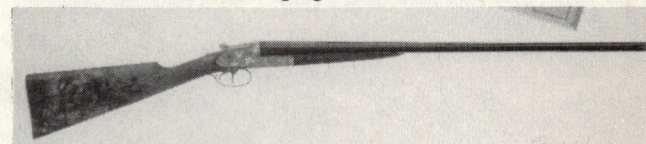

Custom Side-x-Side Shotguns

Available in 12, 16, 20, 28 gauge and .410 bore in either boxlock or sidelock actions. Barrel length, engraving, wood type and style are at the customer's discretion. Retail prices range from:

Basic Boxlock with 27.5" barrels and walnut stock with double triggers in 12, 16, and 20 gauge-$16,000

Basic Boxlock in 28 gauge or .410 bore-$20,000

Basic Boxlock with 26.5" 50 28" barrels and deluxe walnut stock and double triggers in 12, 16, and 20 gauge-$20,000

Basic Boxlock in 28 gauge or .410 bore-$25,000

Prices for 24 and 32 gauge are extra. These prices do not include engraving.

Custom Double Rifles

These custom built double rifles are offered in calibers from 9.3x74R to .470 Nitro Express in boxlock or sidelock actions. Barrel length, engraving, wood type and style are at the customer's discretion. Retail prices range from:

Prices for 24 and 32 gauge are extra. These prices do not include engraving.

Boxlock in 9.3x74R, 8x57JRS and other European calibers-$20,000

Boxlock in .375 H&H and .470 NE-$25,000

Sidelock in 9.3x74R, etc.-$30,000 Sidelock in large calibers-$36,000

Custom Single Shot Mountain Rifles

These single shot rifles are offered in rimmed cartridges but rimless cartridge rifles can be built on special request. Barrel length, engraving, wood type and style are at the customer's discretion. Retail prices range from:

Boxlock in rimmed calibers-Prices start at $15,000

Sidelock in 7x65R and 7mm Rem. Mag.-Prices start at $27,000

Custom Bolt Action Rifles

These bolt action rifles utilize a Mauser 98 type action with adjustable trigger. They are offered in calibers from .17 Bee to .505 Gibbs. Barrel lengths are 21" to 24.5", engraving wood type and style are at the customers' discretion. Retail prices range from:

Standard bolt action calibers: .270, .30-06, 7x64, 8x60S and 9.3x62-Prices start at $9,000

Short action calibers: .222, .223-Prices start at $10,000

Magnum action calibers: 7mm Rem. Mag., .300 Win. Mag., .338 Win. Mag., .375 H&H, and .458 Win. Mag.-Prices start at $15,000

African calibers: .416 Rigby, .460 Wby., .505 Gibbs-Prices start at $15,000

NOTE: Please note that the above prices are for the basic models. They do not reflect the extensive list of options available on these custom firearms.

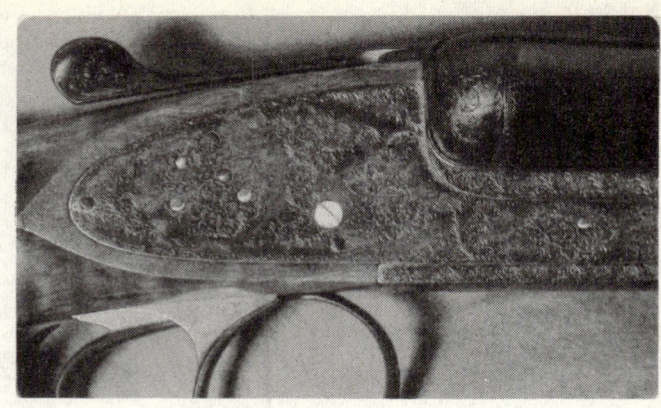

Francotte engraving patterns.

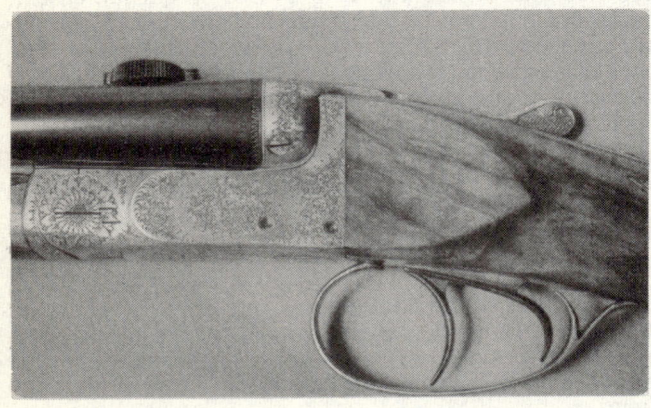

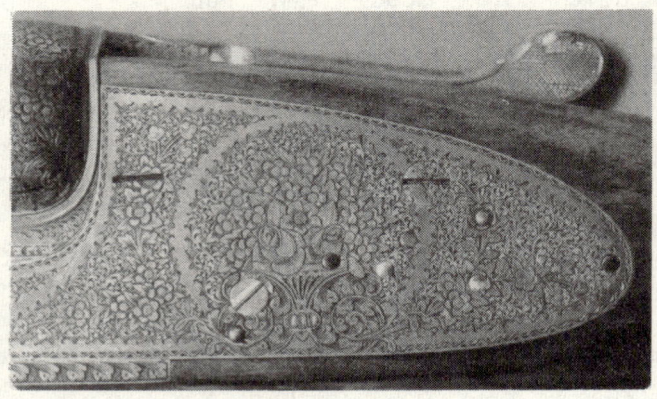

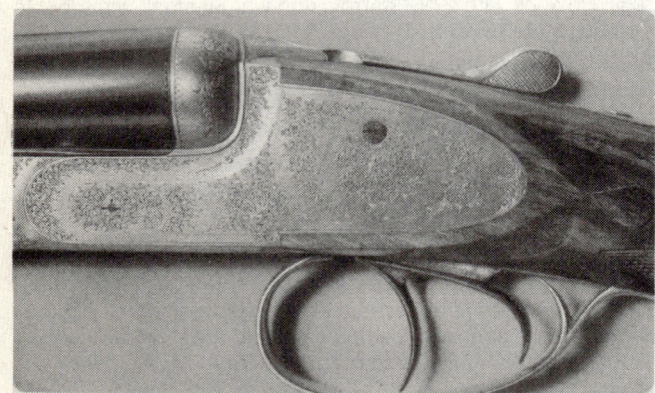

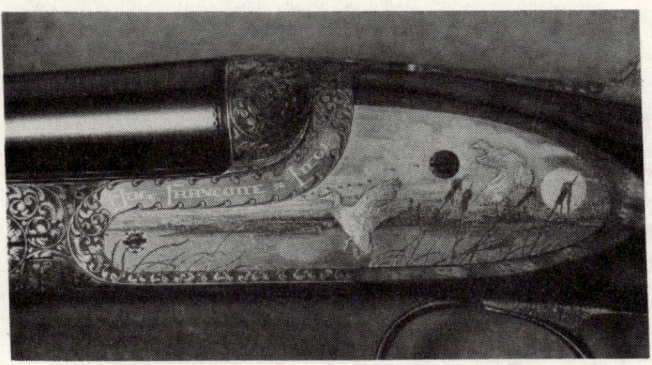

FRANKLIN, C. W.

Liege, Belgium

Manufacturer of utilitarian shotguns with either exposed or enclosed hammers. Circa 1900.

Single Barrel

Exc.	V.G.	Good	Fair	Poor
125	75	50	35	20

Damascus Barrel Double

Exc.	V.G.	Good	Fair	Poor
200	150	125	100	65

Steel Barrel Double

Exc.	V.G.	Good	Fair	Poor
250	175	150	125	90

FRANKONIAJAGD

Favorit Germany

Chambered for various European calibers, this bolt-action rifle has a 24" barrel and set triggers. Blued, with a checkered walnut stock.

Exc.	V.G.	Good	Fair	Poor
300	275	250	175	125

Favorit Deluxe

As above, with a more finely figured stock.

Exc.	V.G.	Good	Fair	Poor
325	300	275	200	150

Safari Model

As above, in Magnum calibers.

Exc.	V.G.	Good	Fair	Poor
475	425	375	275	200

Heeren Rifle

A best quality single shot rifle with a 26" octagonal barrel, double-set triggers, and adjustable sights. Engraved with hand checkered, high-grade walnut. Blued. Produced in a variety of calibers.

Exc.	V.G.	Good	Fair	Poor
3000	2650	2200	1700	1250

FRASER, DANIEL & SON

Edinburgh, Scotland

This renowned rifle maker was an apprentice of Alexander Henry. Fraser had retail stores at the following addresses:

22 Greenside Place	1873-1874
18 Leith Walk	1874-?
4 Leith Street Terrace	?-1916

FRASER F. A. CROP.

Fraser, Michigan

Fraser 25 cal.

A .25 ACP caliber semiautomatic pistol with a 2.25" barrel and 6-round magazine. Stainless steel with black nylon grips. There is a 24 kt. gold-plated model that is worth approximately $100 additional.

NIB	Exc.	V.G.	Good	Fair	Poor
150	125	100	75	50	35

FREEDOM ARMS

Freedom, Wyoming

"Percussion" Mini-Revolver

A .22 caliber spur trigger revolver with 1", 1.75", or 3" barrel lengths, 5-shot cylinder and a bird's-head grip. Stainless steel. A belt buckle is available that houses the pistol for an additional $40.

NIB	Exc.	V.G.	Good	Fair	Poor
200	175	150	125	100	75

Patriot

As above, in .22 l.r. caliber.

NIB	Exc.	V.G.	Good	Fair	Poor
150	125	100	85	65	45

Minuteman

As above, with a 3" barrel. Discontinued in *1988*.

NIB	Exc.	V.G.	Good	Fair	Poor
150	125	100	85	65	45

Ironsides

As above, in .22 Magnum with a 1" or a 1.75" barrel.

NIB	Exc.	V.G.	Good	Fair	Poor
175	150	125	100	80	60

Bostonian

As above, with a 3" barrel.

NIB	Exc.	V.G.	Good	Fair	Poor
175	150	125	100	80	60

Celebrity

As above, with the belt buckle mount for either .22 or .22 Magnum revolvers.

.22 Magnum Model-Add $25.

NIB	Exc.	V.G.	Good	Fair	Poor
325	300	250	200	150	100

Casull Field Grade

A .454 Casull Magnum revolver with a 4.75", 7.5", and a 10" barrel and standard fixed sights. Fires a 225-grain bullet. Also offered in .50 AE and .44 Rem. Mag. Adjustable sights available as a $75 option. Matte stainless steel with black rubber "Pachmayr" grips. Introduced in 1988.

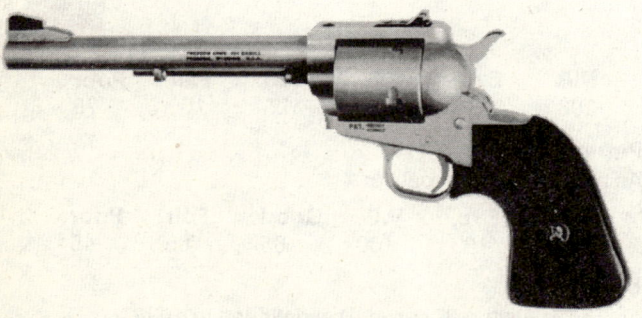

NIB	Exc.	V.G.	Good	Fair	Poor
1100	900	750	550	400	300

Casull Premier Grade

A .454 Mag., .44 Rem. Mag., .45 Win. Mag., .50 AE, and the .45 Colt revolver with replaceable forcing and walnut grips.

The finish is a brush stainless steel. The adjustable sights are an extra cost option on this model as well.

NIB	Exc.	V.G.	Good	Fair	Poor
1500	1250	900	700	500	300

NOTE: Extra cylinders are available for these models in .45 Colt, .45 Win. Mag., and .45 ACP. Add $250 to the price of the gun for each cylinder.

Model 353

Chambered for .357 magnum cartridge with choice of 4.75", 6", 7.5", or 9" barrel length. Adjustable sights.

Field Grade

NIB	Exc.	V.G.	Good	Fair	Poor
1100	900	750	550	400	300

Premier Grade

NIB	Exc.	V.G.	Good	Fair	Poor
1500	1200	900	700	500	300

Signature Edition

As above, with a highly polished finish, rosewood grips, 7.5" barrel only and a fitted case. The serial numbers are DC1-DC2000. (The DC represents Dick Casull, the designer of the firearm.) A total of 2,000 were made.

NIB	Exc.	V.G.	Good	Fair	Poor
2000	1750	1500	1250	900	600

Model 252

This is a stainless steel version of the large frame revolver chambered for the .22 Long Rifle cartridge. Available in 5.12", 7.5", or 10 " barrel lengths. Matte finish. Optional .22 magnum cylinder available for $250.

Silhouette Class-10" barrel

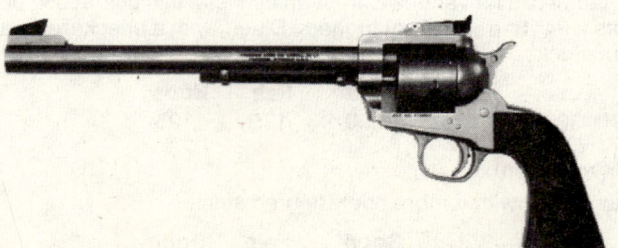

NIB	Exc.	V.G.	Good	Fair	Poor
1400	1150	850	600	450	250

Varmint Class-5.12" or 7.5" barrel

NIB	Exc.	V.G.	Good	Fair	Poor
1350	1100	800	600	450	250

Mid Frame Revolver

Introduced in 1997 this 6-round single action is chambered for the .357 magnum cartridge and is fitted with either a 5.5" or 7.5" barrel. It is offered with adjustable sights or fixed sights. The frame is slightly smaller than the company's large frame revolvers.

NIB	Exc.	V.G.	Good	Fair	Poor
1360	—	—	—	—	—

NOTE: There are a number of extra cost options that will affect the price. Some of these options are extra costs sights, grips, Mag-Na-Port barrels, slings, and trigger overtravel screws.

FREEMAN, AUSTIN T.
Hoard's Armory
Watertown, New York

Freeman Army Model Revolver

A .44 caliber percussion revolver with a 7.5" round barrel and a 6-shot unfluted cylinder with recessed nipples. Blued, case-hardened rammer and hammer, and walnut grips. The frame is marked "Freeman's Pat. Dec. 9, 1862/Hoard's Armory, Watertown, N.Y." Several thousand were manufactured in 1863 and 1864.

Exc.	V.G.	Good	Fair	Poor
—	—	3000	1250	500

FRENCH MILITARY FIREARMS
(including copies made in Liege, Belgium)
Charleville, St. Etienne, Chatellrault,
Mutzig and Tulle Armories

Despite its defeats in the closing battles of the Napoleonic Wars, France maintained a considerable army after the conflict that continued the traditions of Napoleon's leadership and propelled itself into the forefront of 19th century arms development. The diversity of the French Army is reflected in the many variations of the firearms produced during the fifty years following 1815. Most of these firearms were the products of five major armories, the old Charleville Armory and St. Etienne works, and the newer armories at Chatellrault, Mutzig, and Tulle. The armory of manufacture was invariably inscribed in script upon the lock, usually preceded by an abbreviation "Manufactire Roy le de" or "M re R le de" until 1848, "M re N le de" from 1848 until 1852, and "M re Imp ale de" after 1852, respectively representing, "The Royal Manufactory at ..." "The National Manufactory at ...," and, "The Imperial Manufactory at ..." In addition to these lock markings, the specific model year was usually marked upon the barrel tang, preceded by an "M". If the model had been altered, a "T" (for "transformed") was added after the date, and if subsequently remodeled, the script ("bis" was added after that (for "again"). Date of manufacture usually appears upon the barrel, and also within the pressed circle surrounding the "touch mark" on the right side of the buttstock. Numerous inspection marks also appear on the metal parts of the gun.

The arms manufactured for the French military were widely copied in Europe's major firearms center, Liege, Belgium. The Liege gun trade, however, was based on the "factory" system. Each specialist, working out of his own cottage, manufactured one type of part on subcontract and delivered it to an assembler. Many of the final assemblers in Liege did not mark their products or did so only with crowned initials. Those that did usually marked their "products" upon the lockplates. Among the better known Liege assemblers' marks during the middle of the 19th century were ANCION & CIE/A LIEGE, A F (A. Francofte), B F (Beuret Freres), C D (probably for Charles Dandoy), D (anchor) C (probably Dejerdine & Co., Demousse & Co., or DeFooz & Co.), D L (DeLoneux) C. DANDOY/A LIEGE, A. & CH DE LONEUX DRISKET & WAROUX, G M (Gulikers Marquinay), V. GULIKERS/A LIEGE, J L (Joseph LeMille), L (anchor) C or L. LAMBIN & CIE/LIEGE, LE MILLE/A LIEGE, P.J. MALHEREBE & CIE/LIEGE, E. MUNSEUR/LIEGE, J.A. PETRY/A LIEGE, G. SCHOPEN/A LEIGE, TANNER & CIE., T. TILKEN/A/LIEGE, AND V P (Vivario-Plombeur). It should be noted, however, that these makers produced not only copies of French arms, but also accepted contracts for arms from other European powers, notably Russia, Spain, the Piedmont, Saxony, and England. Whether marked on the lock or not, all Liege barrels were required to pass a proof of strength, and having done so were marked near their breech with a small tower and the Liege black powder proof, an oval encompassing the letters "E/LG/"(star). The main French firearms produced or copied during the muzzle-loading era were:

French M 1816 Flintlock Musket
(for Infantry/Light Infantry)

Overall length 58-1/8"/ 56"; barrel length 42-7/8"/ 40-1/2"; caliber .69 This musket is basically the French M1777 musket with minor improvements. Although the French did not subsequently alter this model to percussion, the Kingdom of Wurtemberg obtained several thousand from the Charleville Armory, which were altered to percussion and then rifled and sighted after their own models of 1842 and 1855, the barrel receiving a long range French style rear sight after rifling. As many as 2,000 of these may have been imported into the United States in 1862 by Marcellus Hartley.

(in flintlock)

Exc.	V.G.	Good	Fair	Poor
2200	2000	1700	1350	700

Courtesy Milwaukee Public Museum, Milwaukee, Wisconsin

(altered to percussion, rifled and sighted)

Exc.	V.G.	Good	Fair	Poor
800	650	500	400	275

French M 1822 Flintlock Musket
(for Infantry/Light Infantry)

Overall length 58"/55-7/8"; barrel length 42-5/8"/ 40-5/8" (40-5/8" for both types if "T bis"); caliber .69 (.71 for rifled versions). The French M1822 musket in either full infantry length or the shorter version for light infantry (voltiguers), set the pattern for most of the muskets subsequently adopted by the European powers during the second quarter of the 19th century.

In the 1840s many were "transformed," i.e. altered to percussion by adding a convex bolster to the upper right side of the barrel near the breech for a cone and replacing the flintlock battery with a percussion hammer. With the adoption of the Minie ball projectile, it was determined to further upgrade these arms; however, because a new caliber had been adopted, the old barrels were deemed too thin to both enlarge and rifle. Accordingly new barrels were made in .71 caliber. The percussioned version was copied in Liege (by Ancion, Francotte, and Falise & Trapmann) for the Kingdom of Piedmont as its M1844 musket and M1860 rifle musket. These are distinguished by the enlarged tip of the hammer spur, a peculiar rear sight added to the breech and tang, and Liege markings.

(in flintlock)

Exc.	V. G.	Good	Fair	Poor
2200	2000	1700	1350	700

(altered to percussion, and rifled)

Exc.	V. G.	Good	Fair	Poor
800	650	500	400	275

French M 1822 Cavalry Flintlock Pistol (and "T bis")

Overall length 13-1/4"; barrel length 7-7/8"; caliber .69 (.71 in "T bis"). The M1822 cavalry or horse pistol served as the secondary arm of the French mounted forces, with a pair assigned to each horseman to be kept in saddle holsters astride the pommel of the saddle. Like the M1822 muskets, these were altered ("transformed") to percussion after 1842 in the same manner as the muskets. In 1860, the ordnance department decided to rifle them as well ("transformed again"—hence "Tbis") but this required a new barrel since the adoption of the new caliber (.71) precluded rifling the thin old barrels.

(in flintlock)

Exc.	V. G.	Good	Fair	Poor
900	800	600	450	375

(in percussion and rifled)

Exc.	V. G.	Good	Fair	Poor
575	525	500	375	250

French M1822 Cavalry and Lancer Flintlock Musketoons (and "T")

Overall length 34-5/8"; barrel length 19-5/8"; caliber .69. The main difference between the carbines carried by the cavalry and that of the lancers was the manner of slinging, with the latter having sling rings attached to the upper band and to a projection set into the buttstock. The ramrod was carried separately, consequently there was no inletting of the forestock. After 1842, both types were altered to percussion in the same manner as the M1822 muskets and pistols.

(in flintlock)

Exc.	V. G.	Good	Fair	Poor
950	850	650	450	375

(in percussion and rifled)

Exc.	V. G.	Good	Fair	Poor
600	550	450	350	250

French M1829 Artillery Flintlock Carbine (and "T bis")

Overall length 37-1/4"/38-1/4" (for "T bis"); barrel length 23-5/8"; caliber .69/.71 (for "T bis"). The carbine for artillerists was similar in configuration to that for the cavalry and lancers, differing primarily in having a ramrod in a channel below the barrel. After 1841, these arms were altered to percussion and after 1846 a bayonet lug with long guide was added to the right side of the barrel to accommodate the French M1847 yatagan saber bayonet. At the same time, a number of these arms

were sighted, rifled, and a "tige" (a metal column or pillar) was inserted into the breech of the bore that permitted the arm to fire the Thouvenin projectile. After 1857 new barrels were manufactured that permitted the introduction of the standard Minie projectile of .71 caliber.

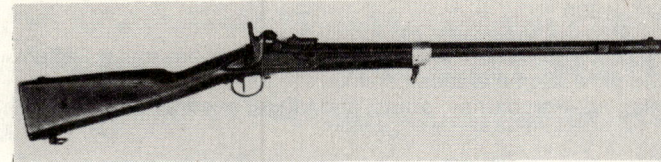

Courtesy Milwaukee Public Museum, Milwaukee, Wisconsin

Exc.	V.G.	Good	Fair	Poor
950	850	650	450	375

(in percussion and rifled)

Exc.	V.G.	Good	Fair	Poor
600	550	450	350	250

French M1837 Rifle 4" Carbine a la Poncharra")

Overall length 51-5/8"; barrel length 34-1/4"; caliber .69. The first of the French percussion arms for the general services, the M1837 rifle was designed on the Poncharra system. In this system, a chamber of lesser diameter than the bore was affixed to the barrel. A projectile of the diameter across the lands and its "sabot" was rammed into the barrel, and upon striking the lip of the chamber theoretically expanded into the rifling.

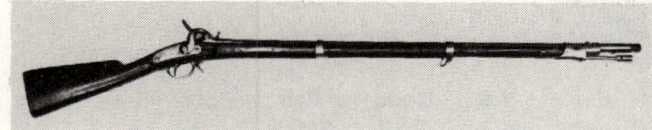

Courtesy Milwaukee Public Museum, Milwaukee, Wisconsin

Exc.	V.G.	Good	Fair	Poor
1600	1500	1250	850	450

French M1840 Rifle ("Carbine de Munition")

Overall length 48-1/8"; barrel 32-5/8"; caliber .71. After the success of the M1837 carbine, the rifle went into production at the armories at Mutzig and Chatellrault as the M1840 "carbine Tierry" or "carbine de munition." It was modified in 1842. The design was modified by adding a projection to the lower end of the buttplate. Herman Boker of New York City imported 25,000 of the M1840 rifles in 1862, but the slow twist of the rifling caused them to be classified as "4th class" weapons and none were issued.

Courtesy Milwaukee Public Museum, Milwaukee, Wisconsin

Exc.	V.G.	Good	Fair	Poor
850	750	600	450	300

French M1840 and M1842 Percussion Muskets (Infantry/Light Infantry)

Overall length 58-1/4" / 55-1/4"; barrel length 42-5/8"/ 40-1/2"; caliber .71. The M1840 and M1842 muskets were the first percussion arms adopted for general infantry service in the French army, both being distinguished by employing back-action percussion locks. The M1840 was distinguished from the M1842 by having a screwed in "patent" breech integrating the bolster, while the bolster of the M1842 musket was forged integral to the barrel, both flush with the right side of the barrel. The M1842 musket was later "transformed" to the M1842T by rifling the barrel with four broad grooves. The Belgian gun trade copied the M1842T both with and without the block rear sight that stood on the breechplug tang.

Courtesy Milwaukee Public Museum, Milwaukee, Wisconsin

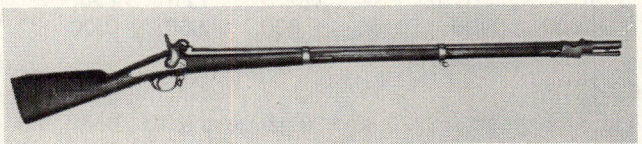

Courtesy Milwaukee Public Museum, Milwaukee, Wisconsin

Exc.	V.G.	Good	Fair	Poor
800	700	475	400	275

French M1853 Musket, M1853 "T" and M1857 Rifle-Muskets

Overall length 58-1/8" (M1853 infantry musket only)/ 55-1/4"; barrels 42-5/8" (MI853 only) /40-1/2"; caliber .71. In 1853, the M1842 series of arms was modified slightly, the most visible difference being the right face of the bolster, which stands away from the right side of the barrel. After the adoption of the "Minie ball" as the main projectile of the French army, the new M1857 rifle musket was introduced. It was essentially the same as the M1853 "T" light infantry musket but its bore was rifled with four broad grooves. Subsequent to the adoption of the M1857 rifle musket the M1853 muskets were "transformed," the light infantry muskets simply by rifling them, and the infantry muskets by shortening them to 55-1/4" with 40-1/2" barrels and rifling them. Both types were widely copied by the Belgian gun trade, who exported thousands to the United States in 1861, many with French style long range sights affixed to the barrels.

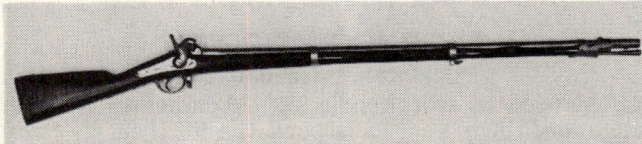

Courtesy Milwaukee Public Museum, Milwaukee, Wisconsin

Exc.	V.G.	Good	Fair	Poor
800	700	475	425	300

French M1846 and M1853 Rifles ("Carbine a tige")

Overall length 49-1/4"; barrel length 34-1/4"; caliber .71. In 1846 the French abandoned the Delvigne chamber rifles in favor of a different method of compressing the projectile into the rifling, that of M. Thouvenin. In Thouvenin's system, the chamber with a lip was replaced with a metal column or pillar "a tige" extending from the breechplug into the bore. After the powder settled around the "tige" the bullet was rammed into the bore and compressed against the tige to expand it into the rifling. The rifle adopted in 1853 differed from the original model adopted in 1846 only in the bolster configuration, the latter extending away from the right side of the barrel. At least a thousand Belgian made "carbines a tige" were imported into the Confederacy in 1861. Accordingly, Belgian "tige" rifles with proven Southern usage should command a premium over those without such history.

Exc.	V.G.	Good	Fair	Poor
900	800	650	475	350

French M1853 "T" and M1859 Rifles ("Carbine de Vincennes")

Overall length 49-1/4"; barrel length 34-1/4"; caliber .71. With the adoption of the self expanding "Minie ball" in 1857, the French ordnance soon adopted a rifle which was suitable for it, the M1859 "carbine de Vincennes." Beginning in 1860, the M1853 "tige" rifles were "transformed" by the removal of the pillars from the breechplugs and fitting them with the rear sight leaves of the M1859 rifle. The M1853 "T" and M1859 French rifle was widely copied in Liege, and thousands were exported to the United States during the American Civil War, while most of the French made M1859 rifles reposed in French arsenals. Like the M1840 and M1846 and M1853 rifles, the M1859 rifle took a long yatagan blade saber bayonet that was affixed to a lug with a guide on the right side of the barrel.

Courtesy Milwaukee Public Museum, Milwaukee, Wisconsin

Exc.	V.G.	Good	Fair	Poor
950	875	700	525	425

FRENCH STATE
Manufactured by MAS
Etienne, France
SACM
Cholet, France
MAC
Chatellerault, France
MAT
Tulle, France

Model 1885

An 11mm caliber percussion revolver with a 5" barrel, solid frame and a 6-shot cylinder with a loading gate. Blued with checkered walnut grips.

Exc.	V.G.	Good	Fair	Poor
300	250	200	150	100

Model 1887

As above, with 8mm caliber.

Exc.	V.G.	Good	Fair	Poor
300	250	200	150	100

Model 1892

An 8mm Lebel caliber solid-frame revolver with a 5" barrel and the 6-shot cylinder. Blued, with checkered walnut grips and a lanyard swivel on the butt.

Courtesy Orvel Reichert

Exc.	V.G.	Good	Fair	Poor
225	200	175	125	75

Model 1892 "A Pompe"

As above, except that the cylinder latch is a sleeve around the ejector rod that can be moved forward to release the cylinder.

Exc.	V.G.	Good	Fair	Poor
225	200	175	125	75

MAS Model 1935A

A 7.65mm long caliber semiautomatic pistol. Eventually became known as the Model 1935A.

German Waffenamt Model

Exc.	V.G.	Good	Fair	Poor
225	175	150	100	75

Standard Model

Exc.	V.G.	Good	Fair	Poor
200	150	125	100	75

Model 1935S

As above, with locking ribs on slide.

Exc.	V.G.	Good	Fair	Poor
200	150	125	100	75

MAS Model 1950

A 9mm Parabellum caliber semiautomatic pistol with a 9-shot magazine. Blued, with ribbed plastic grips.

Exc.	V.G.	Good	Fair	Poor
475	425	350	275	200

FRIGON
Clay Center, Kansas

An importer of guns manufactured by Marocchi of Italy.

FT I

A 12 gauge boxlock single-barrel shotgun with a 32" or 34" ventilated rib barrel, full choke, automatic ejector and interchanged stock. Blued. Introduced in 1986.

NIB	Exc.	V.G.	Good	Fair	Poor
875	750	650	550	450	300

FTC

As above, with two sets of barrels (a single ventilated rib trap barrel and a set of Over/Under ventilated rib barrels). In a fitted case. Introduced in 1986.

NIB	Exc.	V.G.	Good	Fair	Poor
1600	1400	1150	800	650	500

FS-4

A four gauge set (12, 20, and 28 gauge and .410 bore). Introduced in 1986.

NIB	Exc.	V.G.	Good	Fair	Poor
2350	2100	1750	1500	1100	750

FROMMER
SEE Fegyvergyar

FRUHWIRTH
Austria

M1872 Fruhwirth System Rifle

An 11mm bolt-action rifle with a 25" barrel and 6-shot magazine. Blued with a full length walnut stock.

Exc.	V.G.	Good	Fair	Poor
350	300	250	175	100

FURR ARMS
Prescott, Arizona
J. & G. Sale, Inc.
Prescott, Arizona

In addition to producing reproductions of various cannon, this company also manufactured one-tenth to three-quarter scale reproductions of Gatling guns. Prospective purchasers are advised to secure a qualified appraisal prior to acquisition.

FYRBURG, ANDREW
Hopkinton, Massachusetts

A 3"-barreled .32 caliber and a 3.5" .38 caliber revolver with round ribbed barrels and round butts. The grips bear the trademark, "AFCo." This model was most likely made by Iver Johnson for Andrew Fryburg.

Exc.	V.G.	Good	Fair	Poor
200	125	100	75	50

G

G M

(Gulikers Marquinay of Liege, Belgium)
SEE French Military Firearms

GABBET - FAIRFAX, H.
Leamington Spa, England

Mars

Designed by Hugh Gabbet-Fairfax, this semiautomatic pistol was produced on an extremely limited basis by the Webley company, in 1898. The pistol was produced in two calibers; the .380 and the .45 ACP. The pistol was also produced in a propriety 8.5mm cartridge. This was the most powerful handgun cartridge of its time and remained so until well after World War II. It is estimated that only about 80 of these pistols were ever produced the last of which were produced in 1907. This is rare and desirable collectable and prospective purchasers are advised to acquire a qualified appraisal prior to the sale.

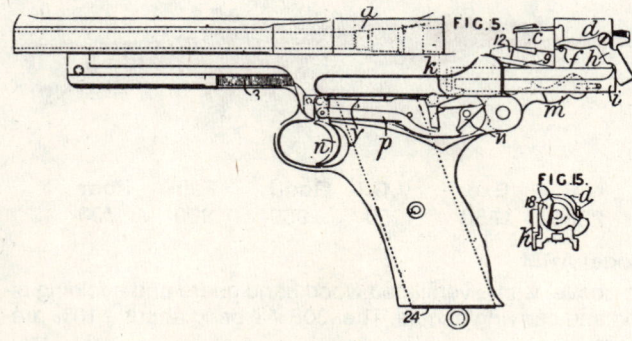

Exc.	V.G.	Good	Fair	Poor
25000	15000	9000	5000	3000

GABILONDO Y CIA
SEE Llama

GABILONDO Y URRESTI
Guernica, Spain
Elgoibar, Spain
SEE Llama

This Spanish firm was founded in 1904 to produce inexpensive revolvers of the Velo-Dog type. Sometime around 1909 the firm began to manufacture the Radium revolver. In 1914 the company produced a semiautomatic pistol distributed as the Ruby. This pistol soon became the mainstay of the company with orders of 30,000 pistols a month for the French army. With the end of WWI Gabilondo Y Urresti moved to Elgoeibar, Spain. The company produced a Browning 1910 replica pistol until the early 1930s. It was at this point that Gabilondo began to manufacture a Colt Model 1911 copy that became known as the Llama. For information of specific Llama models see the Llama section. The pistols listed below reflect the pre-Llama period and are so marked with the trade name of that particular model. The monogram "GC" frequently appears on the grips but not on the slide.

Velo-Dog Revolver

A 6.35mm double-action revolver with a 1.5" barrel, folding trigger and concealed hammer. Blued with walnut grips. Manufactured from 1904 to 1914.

Exc.	V.G.	Good	Fair	Poor
150	125	100	75	50

Radium

A 6.35mm caliber semiautomatic pistol with a 2.5" barrel and 6-shot magazine. The slide is marked "Firearms Manufacturing Automatic Pistol Radium Cal. 6.35." Produced between 1909 and 1914.

Exc.	V.G.	Good	Fair	Poor
175	150	125	100	75

Ruby

A 7.65mm caliber semiautomatic pistol. Discontinued in 1930.

Exc.	V.G.	Good	Fair	Poor
200	175	150	100	75

Bufalo

A 6.35mm, 7.65mm, and 9mm short caliber semiautomatic pistol. Blued with black plastic grips. Marked "Automatica Piastola Espana Bufalo." The caliber is also stamped on the slide. Manufactured between 1919 and 1925 under this name and for a number of years more under different names.

Exc.	V.G.	Good	Fair	Poor
175	150	125	100	75

Danton

As above, without the grip safety. "Danton" stamped on the side. Manufactured between 1925 and 1933.

Exc.	V.G.	Good	Fair	Poor
175	150	125	100	75

Perfect

This semiautomatic pistol was chambered for the 6.35mm and 7.65mm cartridges. It was a cheap, low priced pistol marketed by Mugica. These pistols usually have the word "Perfect" on the grips. The slide may be stamped with the name MUGICA but many are not.

Exc.	V.G.	Good	Fair	Poor
225	175	150	100	75

Plus Ultra

This pistol was chambered for the 7.65mm cartridge and was built from 1925 to 1933. It had a 20-round magazine that gave the pistol an unusual appearance.

Exc.	V.G.	Good	Fair	Poor
250	200	175	125	100

GALAND, C.F.
Liege, Belgium

Galand, Galand & Sommerville, Galand Perrin

A 7mm, 9mm, and 12mm caliber double-action revolver with a 6-shot cylinder, open frame, a unique ejection system that, by means of rotating a lever downward from the triggerguard, causes the barrel and cylinder to slide forward, leaving the ejector and the spent cases behind. Circa 1870.

Exc.	V.G.	Good	Fair	Poor
400	325	275	200	150

Velo-Dog

A 5.5mm Velo-Dog caliber fixed trigger and guard double-action revolver with open-top design. Later models (.22 and 6.35mm caliber) feature folding triggers and no triggerguards.

Exc.	V.G.	Good	Fair	Poor
175	125	100	75	50

Le Novo

As above, with a concealed hammer and in 6.35mm caliber.

Exc.	V.G.	Good	Fair	Poor
225	175	125	100	75

Tue-Tue

A .22 short, 5.5mm Velo-Dog, and 6.35mm caliber double action revolver with a concealed hammer, folding trigger, and a swing-out cylinder with central extractor. Introduced in 1894.

Exc.	V.G.	Good	Fair	Poor
225	175	150	100	75

GALAND & SOMMERVILLE
Liege, Belgium
SEE Galand

GALEF
Zabala Hermanos & Antonio Zoli
Spain

Zabala Double

A 10, 12, 16, and 20 caliber boxlock shotgun with a 22" to 30" barrel and various chokes. Hardwood stock.

Exc.	V.G.	Good	Fair	Poor
300	200	150	100	75

Companion

A folding 12 to .410 bore single shot underlever shotgun with a 28" or 30" barrel.

Exc.	V.G.	Good	Fair	Poor
175	100	75	50	25

Monte Carlo Trap

A 12 gauge underlever single shot shotgun with a 32" ventilated rib barrel.

Exc.	V.G.	Good	Fair	Poor
225	175	150	100	75

Silver Snipe, Golden Snipe, and Silver Hawk
SEE Antonio Zoli

GALESI, INDUSTRIA ARMI
Brescia, Italy

Founded in 1914. The company was recently renamed "Rigarmi."

Galesi

A 6.35mm caliber semiautomatic pistol. A copy of the 1906 Browning, without a grip safety. Introduced in 1914.

Exc.	V.G.	Good	Fair	Poor
275	225	175	125	100

Model 1930

A 6.35mm, 7.65mm or 9mm short caliber semiautomatic pistol. Based on the 1910 Browning design. Blued with plastic grips. The slide marked "Brevetto Mod. 1930." The prewar designation was the Model 6.

Exc.	V.G.	Good	Fair	Poor
275	225	175	125	100

Model 9

A .22 rimfire, 6.35mm, and the 7.65mm caliber semiautomatic pistol. Blue or plated. Marked "Hijo" and imported by Sloan & Co. of New York.

Exc.	V.G.	Good	Fair	Poor
200	150	125	100	75

Rigarmi

A copy of the Walther PP, in .22 l.r., 6.35mm, and the 7.65mm caliber. Finished in a variety of ways and marked "Rigarmi Brescia."

Exc.	V.G.	Good	Fair	Poor
175	125	100	50	25

GALIL
Israel Military Industries
Israel
Importer-Action Arms, Ltd.
Philadelphia, Pennsylvania

Model AR

This rifle is an Israeli variant of the AK-47 based on the Valmet. It is also used by the South African military where it is called the R-4 rifle. It is a .223 or .308 caliber semiautomatic rifle with 16" or 19" barrels. Parkerized with the flip "Tritium" night sights and folding stock. The .308 version would bring about a 10% premium.

NIB	Exc.	V.G.	Good	Fair	Poor
2300	1850	1250	900	800	700

Model ARM

As above, with a ventilated wood hand guard and a folding bipod and carrying handle. The .308 will bring about a 10% premium.

NIB	Exc.	V.G.	Good	Fair	Poor
2500	2000	1500	900	800	700

Sniper Rifle

As above, with a 20" heavy barrel, adjustable wooden stock, and a 6X40 scope is furnished in addition to the Tritium night sights. Supplied with two 25-shot magazines and a fitted case.

NIB	Exc.	V.G.	Good	Fair	Poor
6500	5700	4000	3500	3000	2000

Hadar II

As above, in a walnut, one-piece, thumbhole stock, an 18.5" barrel, 4-shot magazine and adjustable sight. Introduced in 1989.

NIB	Exc.	V.G.	Good	Fair	Poor
1300	1100	800	650	500	400

GALLAGER
Richardson & Overman
Philadelphia, Pennsylvania

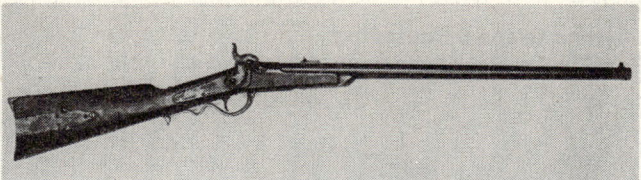

Courtesy Milwaukee Public Museum, Milwaukee, Wisconsin

Gallager Carbine

A .50 caliber single shot percussion carbine with a 22.25" barrel, saddle ring and walnut stock. Blued and case-hardened. Approximately 23,000 were made during the Civil War.

Percussion Model

Exc.	V.G.	Good	Fair	Poor
—	3250	2000	1250	500

As above, in .56-62 rimfire caliber. Approximately 5,000 of this model were made.

Spencer Cartridge Model

Exc.	V.G.	Good	Fair	Poor
—	2750	1500	950	400

GAMBA, RENATO
Gardone V. T., Italy
Importer-Gamba, USA
Colorado Springs, Colorado

SIDE-X-SIDE SHOTGUNS

Hunter Super

A 12 gauge Anson & Deeley boxlock double-barrel shotgun with a variety of barrel lengths and chokes, double triggers and extractors. Engraved and silver-plated.

NIB	Exc.	V.G.	Good	Fair	Poor
1250	900	700	550	450	250

Principessa

A 12 or 20 gauge boxlock shotgun. Engraved, checkered stock.

NIB	Exc.	V.G.	Good	Fair	Poor
1850	1250	900	700	500	250

Oxford 90

A 12 or 20 gauge sidelock shotgun with various barrel lengths and chokes, the Purdey locking system, double triggers, and automatic ejectors. Walnut stock.

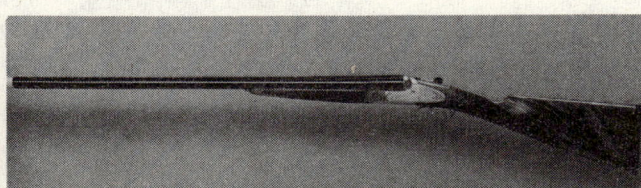

NIB	Exc.	V.G.	Good	Fair	Poor
4250	3250	1700	900	600	300

Oxford Extra

Same as above but with fine engraving.

NIB	Exc.	V.G.	Good	Fair	Poor
5200	4000	2250	1500	900	450

Gamba 624 Prince

Fitted with a Wesly Richards type frame, sel;ect walnut stock, and fine hand engraving. Offered in 12 gauge with 28" barrels.

NIB	Exc.	V.G.	Good	Fair	Poor
4800	3900	2500	1500	850	400

Gamba 624 Extra

Same as above but with deep floral engraving.

NIB	Exc.	V.G.	Good	Fair	Poor
8000	6500	4500	2500	1250	600

London

A 12 or 20 gauge Holland & Holland sidelock shotgun with various barrel lengths and chokes, double or single selective trigger, automatic ejectors. Walnut stock.

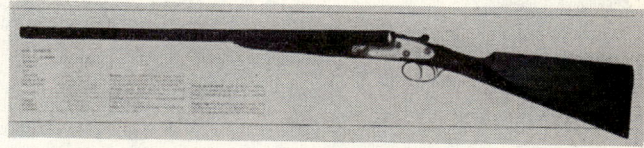

NIB	Exc.	V.G.	Good	Fair	Poor
9000	7000	4500	2500	1250	700

London Royal

As above with engraved hunting scenes.

NIB	Exc.	V.G.	Good	Fair	Poor
11000	9000	6500	3750	2000	950

Ambassador Gold and Black

A 12 and 20 gauge Holland & Holland sidelock shotgun with various barrel lengths and choke combinations, single selective trigger, automatic ejectors, and a single gold line engraved on the barrels and the frame. Walnut stocks.

NIB	Exc.	V.G.	Good	Fair	Poor
25000	19000	13500	9500	5000	2500

Ambassador Executive

Gamba's best quality shotgun produced in 12 or 20 gauge to the customer's specifications.

NIB	Exc.	V.G.	Good	Fair	Poor
34000	27000	18500	10000	5000	2500

OVER AND UNDER SHOTGUNS

Country Model

A 12 and 20 gauge Over/Under shotgun with 28" or 30" barrels with ventilated rib, double triggers, extractors, and walnut stock.

NIB	Exc.	V.G.	Good	Fair	Poor
650	550	400	300	275	200

Grifone Model

A 12 and 20 gauge Over/Under shotgun with 26", 28", or 30" ventilated rib barrels, a single selective trigger, and automatic ejectors. The boxlock action is silver-plated, with walnut stock. Available with screw-in chokes, and this would add 10% to the values.

NIB	Exc.	V.G.	Good	Fair	Poor
800	650	550	350	250	200

Europa 2000

A 12 gauge Over/Under shotgun in various barrel lengths and choke combinations, single selective trigger, and automatic ejectors. Engraved, silver-plated, boxlock action with false sideplates with walnut stock.

NIB	Exc.	V.G.	Good	Fair	Poor
1250	900	700	550	350	250

Grinta Trap and Skeet

A 12 gauge Over/Under shotgun with 26" skeet or 30" full choke barrels, a single selective trigger, automatic ejectors, and some engraving. Walnut stock.

NIB	Exc.	V.G.	Good	Fair	Poor
1350	900	700	550	350	250

Victory Trap and Skeet

As above, but more finely finished.

NIB	Exc.	V.G.	Good	Fair	Poor
1650	1150	850	600	400	250

Edinburg Match

As above, with slightly different engraving patterns.

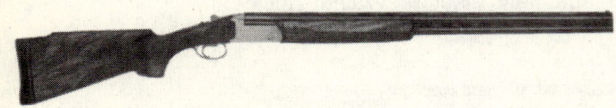

NIB	Exc.	V.G.	Good	Fair	Poor
1650	1150	850	600	400	250

Boyern 88 Combination Gun

A 12 gauge combination Over/Under rifle/shotgun with double triggers, and extractors. Engraved gamescenes and coin-finished with walnut stock.

NIB	Exc.	V.G.	Good	Fair	Poor
1250	900	700	500	400	250

Daytona Series

This is a competition shotgun, first introduced into the US in 1986 as the Type I. The Type I was available in different configurations with the base model selling for about $4,000 until 1991. In 1994 Gamba introduced the Daytona in a wide variety of configurations and grades under a new designation called the Type II. The primary difference was in the location of the stock bolt. Only about 80 Daytona Type II shotguns are allocated to the US per year. They are a high quality shotgun with an excellent reputation. Prices are listed for 12 gauge guns. 20 gauge guns are available on special request.

Daytona Trap

Offered in 12 gauge with 30" or 32" barrels. Select walnut stock with hand checkering. Removable trigger group, improved Boss lock-up, and boxlock receiver.

NIB	Exc.	V.G.	Good	Fair	Poor
5900	4750	3000	2250	1200	600

Daytona Sporting

Available in 12 gauge with 30" barrel with screw-in chokes and single selective trigger.

NIB	Exc.	V.G.	Good	Fair	Poor
6600	5250	3750	2800	1400	700

Daytona Skeet

Offered in 12 gauge with 29" barrels and single selective trigger.

NIB	Exc.	V.G.	Good	Fair	Poor
5900	4750	3000	2250	1200	600

Daytona America Trap

Offered in 12 gauge with 30" or 32" barrels, high adjustable rib, adjustable stock, and single trigger.

NIB	Exc.	V.G.	Good	Fair	Poor
7450	6000	4000	3000	1500	750

Daytona Game

Offered in 12 gauge with 28" barrels and single trigger.

NIB	Exc.	V.G.	Good	Fair	Poor
5900	4750	3000	2250	1200	600

NOTE: Add $300 for black frame with gold inlaid names and logo.

Daytona Grade 6 Engraving

Fine English scroll hand engraving edged with gold line work.

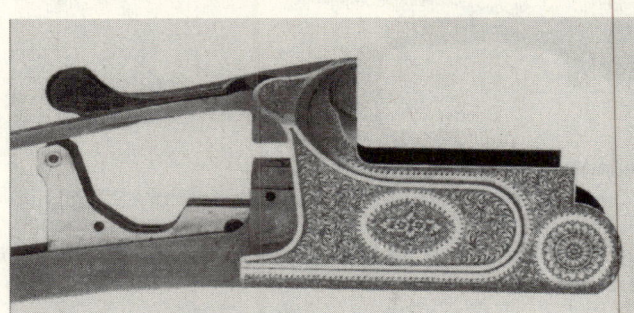

Daytona Trap and Skeet Models

NIB	Exc.	V.G.	Good	Fair	Poor
13000	10500	7500	5000	2500	1200

Daytona Sporting Model

NIB	Exc.	V.G.	Good	Fair	Poor
13500	11000	8000	5000	2500	1200

Daytona Grade 5 Engraving

Deep relief floral engraving with gold inlaid griffons.

Daytona Trap and Skeet Models

NIB	Exc.	V.G.	Good	Fair	Poor
14000	11250	8000	5000	2500	1200

Daytona Sporting Model

NIB	Exc.	V.G.	Good	Fair	Poor
14500	11500	8500	5000	2500	1200

Daytona Grade 4 Engraving

A flying eagle in a landscape and very fine English scroll by master engravers.

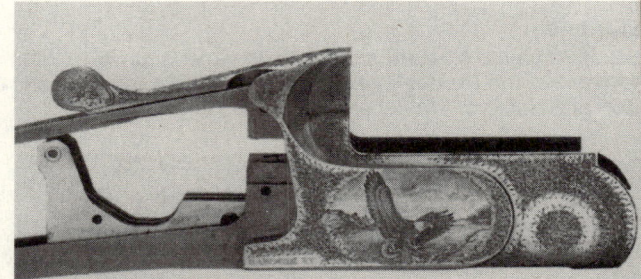

Daytona Trap and Skeet Models

NIB	Exc.	V.G.	Good	Fair	Poor
16250	13000	9000	6000	3000	1500

Daytona Sporting Model

NIB	Exc.	V.G.	Good	Fair	Poor
16750	13250	9500	6000	3000	1500

Daytona SL Grade 3 Engraving
Fitted with sideplates with engraved game scenes and fine English scroll by master engravers.

Daytona Trap and Skeet Models
NIB	Exc.	V.G.	Good	Fair	Poor
18750	15000	11000	7500	3500	1750

Daytona Sporting Model
NIB	Exc.	V.G.	Good	Fair	Poor
19250	15500	11250	7500	3500	1750

Daytona Game
NIB	Exc.	V.G.	Good	Fair	Poor
18750	15000	11000	7500	3500	1750

Daytona SLHH Grade 2 Engraving
Fitted with sideplates and Boss lock-up system, automatic ejectors, figured walnut stock, and fine game scene engraving signed by a master. Offered in 12 gauge with 28" barrels.

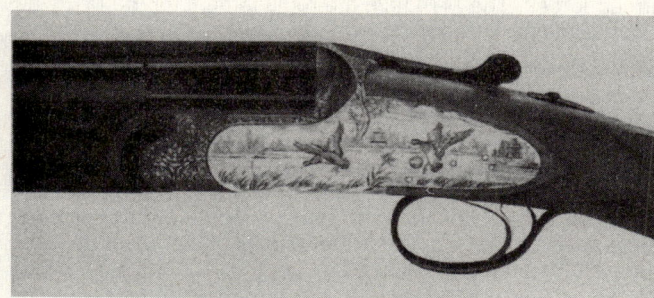

NIB	Exc.	V.G.	Good	Fair	Poor
36250	29000	20000	12500	6000	3000

Daytona SLHH Grade 1 Gold Engraving
Same as above but with gold inlaid game scenes and floral style engraving signed by master engraver. Offered in 12 gauge with 28" barrels.

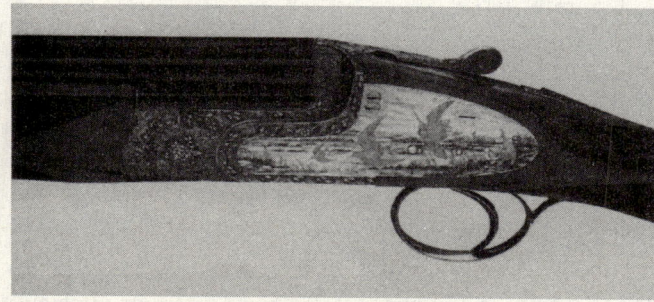

NIB	Exc.	V.G.	Good	Fair	Poor
43500	35000	25000	15000	7500	3500

Daytona SLHH "One of Thousand"
Same as above but game scene is executed at customers direction and is a totally custom ordered gun. Available in all configurations.

NIB	Exc.	V.G.	Good	Fair	Poor
106000	85000	40000	20000	10000	5000

Concorde Game Shotguns
This over and under model is offered as a slightly less expensive alternative to the Daytona Series guns. the base gun is available with a blued or chromed action. Extra barrel are interchangeable in both 12 and 20 gauges with 28" barrels and single triggers.

NIB	Exc.	V.G.	Good	Fair	Poor
5600	4500	3200	1700	950	450

Concorde Trap
Available in 12 gauge with 30" or 32" barrels with single trigger.

NIB	Exc.	V.G.	Good	Fair	Poor
5600	4500	3200	1700	950	450

Concorde Skeet
Available in 12 gauge with 29" barrels and single trigger.

NIB	Exc.	V.G.	Good	Fair	Poor
5600	4500	3200	1700	950	450

Concorde Sporting
Offered in 12 gauge with 30" barrels, screw in chokes, and single selective trigger.

NIB	Exc.	V.G.	Good	Fair	Poor
6100	5000	3500	2000	1000	500

Concorde Game Grade 7 Engraving
Game scene engraving with fine English scroll.

NIB	Exc.	V.G.	Good	Fair	Poor
8700	7000	4000	2500	1200	600

Concorde Game Grade 8 Engraving
English scroll engraving.

NIB	Exc.	V.G.	Good	Fair	Poor
6250	5000	3500	2000	1000	500

RIFLES

Safari Express
A 7x65R, 9.3x74R, or .375 H&H caliber boxlock double barrel rifle with 25" barrels, open sights double triggers, automatic ejectors, and a coin-finished scroll engraved receiver. Walnut stock.

NIB	Exc.	V.G.	Good	Fair	Poor
5500	4000	2500	1500	750	350

Mustang
A 5.6x50, 6.5x57R, 7x65R, .222 Rem., .270 Win., or.30-06 caliber sidelock single-barrel rifle with double-set triggers, engraved sidelock action and walnut stock.

NIB	Exc.	V.G.	Good	Fair	Poor
10500	8000	6000	3500	1750	800

RGZ 1000
7x64, .270 Win., 7mm Rem. Mag., and .300 Win. Mag. caliber Mauser 98 bolt action with a 20.5" barrel. Walnut pistol grip stock with a cheekpiece.

NIB	Exc.	V.G.	Good	Fair	Poor
1100	900	750	550	400	200

RGX 1000 Express
As above, with double-set triggers and a 23.75" barrel.

NIB	Exc.	V.G.	Good	Fair	Poor
1250	950	750	550	400	200

PISTOLS

SAB G90

A 7.65 Parabellum or 9 mm caliber double-action semiautomatic pistol with a 4.75" barrel, and 15-shot magazine. Blued or chrome-plated with walnut grips.

NIB	Exc.	V.G.	Good	Fair	Poor
575	450	350	300	250	175

SAB G91 Compact

As above, with a 3.5" barrel and a 12-shot magazine.

NIB	Exc.	V.G	Good	Fair	Poor
550	400	325	275	225	150

Trident Fast Action

A .32 S&W or the .38 Special caliber double-action revolver with a 2.5" or 3" barrel, 6-shot cylinder and is double-actioned. Blued, with walnut grips.

NIB	Exc.	V.G.	Good	Fair	Poor
500	400	300	250	200	150

Trident Super

As above, with a 4" ventilated rib barrel.

NIB	Exc.	V.G.	Good	Fair	Poor
550	400	325	275	225	150

Trident Match 900

As above, with 6" heavy barrel, adjustable sights and target type, walnut grips.

NIB	Exc.	V.G.	Good	Fair	Poor
850	700	550	400	350	200

GARAND
(U.S. M1 Rifle)
U.S. Rifle, CAL. M1 (Garand)

An Introduction to U.S. M1 Rifle

By Simeon Stoddard

Adopted in 1936 the M1 remained the standard issue rifle of the United States until it was replaced by the M14 in 1957. It was designed by John C. Garand, who worked for Springfield Armory from 1919 until his retirement in 1953. During this time Garand concentrated his efforts on the development of a semiautomatic shoulder weapon for general issue to the U.S. armed forces. The M14 rifle, the replacement for the M1, was a compilation of his design work as well.

With the exceptions noted, all values given are for rifles which are in original, as produced condition. Development of the M1 was an ongoing project until it was replaced, as Garand never finished perfecting his basic design. Over 5,400,000 M1 rifles were built, with the majority of them going through a rebuilding process at least once during their service life. During rebuilding, rifles were inspected and unserviceable parts replaced. Parts used for replacement were usually of the latest revision available or what was on hand.

Major assemblies and parts were marked with a government drawing size/part number. This number is often followed with the revision number (see photo above). Barrels were marked, with the exception of early Springfield Armory and all Winchester production, with the month and year of manufacture. It must be remembered that this date only refers to when the barrel was produced, and has nothing to do with when the receiver was produced or the rifle was assembled. This barrel date on "original as produced" rifles should be from 0 to 3 months, before the receiver was produced.

Restored rifles, defined as ones with parts added/replaced to more closely match what they might have been originally, are worth less money than "original as produced" rifles. This difference should be on the order of 30-40% of the values shown, and is due to the low number of rifles of this type. When in doubt, get an appraisal. To tell what parts should be correct, study chapters 5 & 6 of "The M1 Garand:WWII" and chapters 7 & 8 of "The M1 Garand:Post WWII" by Scott A. Duff.

Rebuilt Rifle, any manufacture

Value shown is for rifles with a majority of its parts mixed/replaced. Depending on the type of rebuilding that a rifle went through, rifles could be completely disassembled with no attempt to put parts together for the same rifle. Valued mainly for shooting merits. Bore condition, gaging and overall appearance are important factors.

Exc.	V.G.	Good
450	400	350

DCM Rifles

These rifles should have the correct paperwork and shipping boxes to receive the amounts listed. Prices should be considered to be base price as some DCM M1's fall into the following categories:

Exc.	V.G.	Good
550	450	400

Navy Trophy Rifles

The Navy continued to use the M1 rifle as its main rifle far into the 1960's. They were modified to shoot the 7.62x51 Nato (Winchester) round. This was accomplished at first with a chamber insert, and later with new replacement barrels in the Nato caliber. The Navy modified rifles can be found of any manufacture, and in any serial number range. As a general rule, Navy rifles with new barrels are worth more due to their better shooting capabilities. Paper work and original boxes must accompany these rifles to obtain the values listed.

AMF Rebuild

Exc.	V.G.	Good
1000	900	750

H&R Rebuild

Exc.	V.G.	Good
900	800	700

Springfield Armory Production

Gas trap sn: ca 81-50,000

Values shown for original rifles. Most all were updated to gas port configuration. Look out for reproductions being offered as original rifles! Get a professional appraisal before purchasing.

Exc.	V.G.	Good
25000	20000	12000

Gas tap/modified to gas port

These rifles should have many of there early parts.

Exc.	V.G.	Good
1200	1100	1000

pre-Dec. 7, 1941 gas port production pn sn: ca 50,000-Apx. 410,000

Exc.	V.G.	Good	Fair	Poor
1400	1000	800	600	400

WWII Production sn: ca 410,000-3,880,000

Exc.	V.G.	Good	Fair	Poor
1000	900	800	650	400

POST WWII Production sn: ca 4,200,000-6,099,361

Exc.	V.G.	Good	Fair	Poor
750	650	500	350	300

Winchester Production

Winchester produced around 513,00 M1 rifles during WWII. Their first contract was an educational order in 1939. This contract for 500 rifles and the gauges and fixtures to produce the rifles. Winchester's second contract was awarded during 1939 for up to 65,000 rifles. Winchester M1's are typified by noticeable machine marks on their parts, and did not have the higher grade finish that is found on Springfield Armory production. Watch for fake barrels, and barrels marked "Winchester" which were produced in the 1960s as replacement barrels.

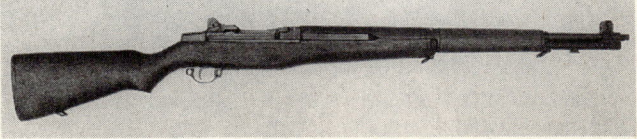

Winchester Educational Contract sn: 100,000-100,500

Exc.	V.G.	Good	Fair	Poor
3500	3300	3000	2500	2000

Winchester sn: 100,501-165,000

Rifles of this serial number range were produced from Jan 1941 until May 1942.

Exc.	V.G.	Good	Fair	Poor
1600	1400	1200	900	600

Winchester sn: 1,200,00-1,380,000

Rifles in this serial number range were produced from May 1942 until Aug 1943.

Exc.	V.G.	Good	Fair	Poor
850	700	600	500	400

Winchester sn: 2,305,850-2,536,493

Rifles in this serial number range were produced from Aug 1943 until Jan 1945.

Exc.	V.G.	Good	Fair	Poor
800	700	600	400	350

Winchester sn: 1,601,150-1,640,000

Rifles in this serial number range were produced from Jan 1945 until June 1945. These are often referred to as Win-13's because of the revision number of the right front receiver leg.

Exc.	V.G.	Good	Fair	Poor
1600	1400	1200	900	600

Harrington & Richardson Production

Between 1953 and 1956 Harrington & Richardson produced around 428,00 M1 rifles.

Exc.	V.G.	Good	Fair	Poor
750	650	500	250	200

International Harvester Corp. production

Between 1953 and 1956, International Harvester produced around 337,000 M1 rifles. International at several different times during their production purchased receivers from both Harrington & Richardson and Springfield Armory. Always check for Springfield Armory heat lots on the right front receiver leg.

International Harvester Production

Exc.	V.G.	Good	Fair	Poor
750	650	500	250	200

International Harvester/with Springfield Receiver (postage stamp)

Exc.	V.G.	Good
1200	1,000	800

International Harvester/with Springfield Receiver (arrow head)

Exc.	V.G.	Good
1250	1050	850

International Harvester/with Springfield Receiver (Gap letter)

Exc.	V.G.	Good
1000	900	750

International Harvester/with Harrington & Richardson Receiver

Exc.	V.G.	Good
1250	1050	850

M1 Experimental w/one piece upper handguard made of fiberglass-Courtesy Richard M. Kumor, Sr.

SCOPE VARIANTS (SNIPER RIFLES)

M1C

Springfield Armory production only. Serial number range is between ca 3,200,000 and 3,800,000. This variant is very rare with only around 7,900 produced. Should be mounted with M81, M82 or M84 scope with 7/8" scope rings. Ask for government relicense paperwork, and have a serial number check run before purchase is made. If provenance can not be established then rifles are worth the value of their individual parts, under $900.

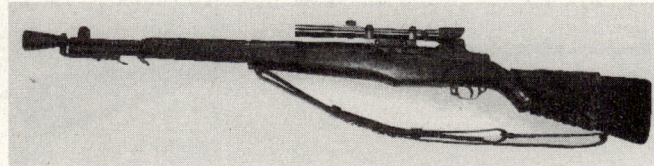

Courtesy Richard M. Kumor, Sr.

Exc.	V.G.	Good
8000	6000	3500

MC 1952 (USMC Issue)

Same production range as above. Should be equipped with 1 inch scope mount and Kollmorgen scope.

M1D

This model can be found by any manufacture and in any serial number range. This mounting system was designed by John Garand, and consists of a mounting block on the rear of the barrel. The rear hand guard is shortened and the mount attaches with a large single screw system. The modification could be made on the field repair level. It is not known how many rifles were modified, but it is very likely that they numbered into the tens of thousands. If the rifle does not come with paperwork, it is only worth the value of its parts alone, under $700.

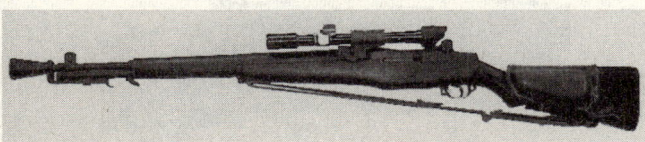

Courtesy Richard M. Kumor, Sr.

Exc.	V.G.	Good
2000	1500	1200

National Match

Type I

Produced on Springfield Armory receivers and in serial number ranges from ca 5,800,000 to around 6,090,000. All parts are available to reproduce both types of national match rifles. To obtain values listed these rifles must come with original paperwork.

Exc.	V.G.	Good
2000	1800	1500

Type II

Produced on Springfield Armory receivers, they can be found in any serial number range. These rifles should come with papers to receive values listed.

Exc.	V.G.	Good
1600	1400	1000

GARATE, ANITUA
Eibar, Spain

Charola

A 5.5mm Clement semiautomatic pistol with the magazine located in front of the trigger and having an exposed hammer. Normally encountered with a nickel-plated finish and composition grips.

Exc.	V.G.	Good	Fair	Poor
275	225	175	125	90

Cosmopolite

A .38 caliber copy of the Colt Police Positive. Manufactured from 1920 to 1930.

Exc.	V.G.	Good	Fair	Poor
200	150	125	100	75

El Lunar

Resembling the Colt Police Positive in 88mm Lebel caliber, this revolver was made for the French government in 1915 and 1916.

Exc.	V.G.	Good	Fair	Poor
225	175	150	125	100

G.A.C.

A copy of the Smith & Wesson Military & Police revolver, manufactured between 1930 and 1936, in .32-20 caliber. Marked "G.A.C. Firearms Mfg. Co."

Exc.	V.G.	Good	Fair	Poor
200	150	125	100	75

Garate, Anitua

A 7.65mm caliber "Eibar" semiautomatic pistol with 8-shot magazine.

Exc.	V.G.	Good	Fair	Poor
175	125	100	75	50

Garate, Anitua

A .455 caliber double-action break-open revolver with a 5" barrel, adopted by the Royal Army in November of 1915 and known as "Pistol OP No. 1 Mark 1".

Exc.	V.G.	Good	Fair	Poor
300	250	200	150	100

La Lira

A copy of the Mannlicher Model 1901 in .32ACP caliber with removable magazine marked "System La Lira" on the breech; "Para Cartoucho Browning 7.65mm," on the barrel; and "G.A.C.," on the grips. Produced prior to WWI.

Exc.	V.G.	Good	Fair	Poor
225	175	150	125	100

L'Eclair

A 5.5mm Velo-Dog caliber folding trigger double action revolver with 6-shot cylinder. Manufactured from 1900-1914.

Exc.	V.G.	Good	Fair	Poor
175	125	100	75	50

Sprinter

A 6.35mm caliber semiautomatic pistol marked "The Best Automatique Pistol Sprinter Patent 6.35mm Cartridge." Manufactured before WWI.

Exc.	V.G.	Good	Fair	Poor
175	125	100	75	50

Triumph

Identical to the La Lira model but marked "Triumph Automatic Pistol."

Exc.	V.G.	Good	Fair	Poor
225	175	150	125	100

GARATE, HERMANOS
Ermua, Spain

Cantabria

A 6.35mm caliber folding trigger double action revolver with a concealed hammer, cocking spur and a short barrel resembling the slide on a semiautomatic. The name "Cantabria" is stamped on the left side.

Exc.	V.G.	Good	Fair	Poor
225	175	125	100	75

Velo-Stark

A double action folding trigger revolver with concealed hammer.

Exc.	V.G.	Good	Fair	Poor
200	150	100	75	50

GARBI
Eibar, Spain
Importer-W. L. Moore and Co.
Westlake Village, California

Model 51-A

A 12 gauge boxlock shotgun with various barrel lengths and chokes, double triggers, extractors, a case-hardened receiver, and walnut stock.

NIB	Exc.	V.G.	Good	Fair	Poor
500	450	400	300	225	150

Model 51-B

As above, in 16 and 20 gauge, as well as 12 gauge, with automatic ejectors, case-hardened or coin-finished receiver.

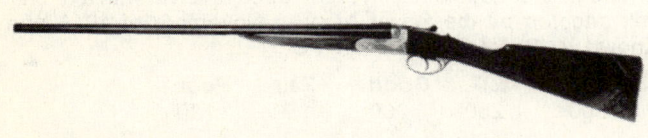

NIB	Exc.	V.G.	Good	Fair	Poor
800	725	650	500	375	200

Model 60-A

A 12 gauge sidelock shotgun with various barrel lengths and chokes, cocking indicators, engraved receiver and walnut stock.

NIB	Exc.	V.G.	Good	Fair	Poor
700	625	550	400	275	150

Model 60-B

As above, but chambered for 16 and 20 gauge as well as 12 gauge with automatic ejectors, and English-style stock.

NIB	Exc.	V.G.	Good	Fair	Poor
1250	1100	900	700	500	250

Model 62-A

A 12 gauge sidelock shotgun, with a choice of various barrel lengths and chokes, double triggers, extractors, and cocking indicators. Walnut stock.

NIB	Exc.	V.G.	Good	Fair	Poor
725	650	500	425	300	150

Model 62-B

Similar to the above, but chambered for 16 and 20 gauge as well as 12 gauge. Engraved, case-hardened or coin-finished receiver and walnut stock.

NIB	Exc.	V.G.	Good	Fair	Poor
1200	1050	850	650	450	200

Model 71

A 12, 16, or 20 gauge Holland & Holland sidelock shotgun with various barrel lengths and choke combinations, automatic ejectors and a single selective trigger. Engraved with fine English style scrollwork and walnut stock. Discontinued in 1988.

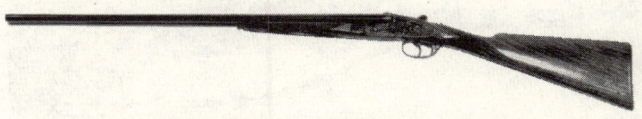

NIB	Exc.	V.G.	Good	Fair	Poor
2250	2000	1800	1500	1000	500

Model 100

A 12, 16, or 20 gauge Holland & Holland sidelock shotgun with chopper-lump barrels, automatic ejectors, and a single trigger. Engraved in the Purdy style, with walnut stock.

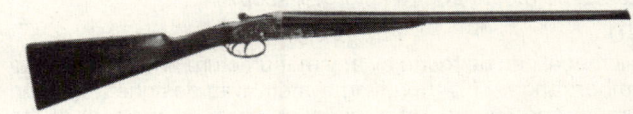

NIB	Exc.	V.G.	Good	Fair	Poor
3250	3000	2500	2000	1500	1000

Model 101

As above, with floral engraving.

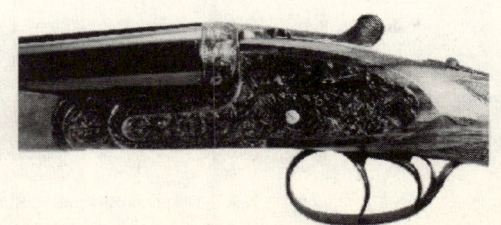

NIB	Exc.	V.G.	Good	Fair	Poor
4000	3750	3250	2500	2000	1750

Model 102

As above, with Holland & Holland style, engraving and also in 28 gauge. Discontinued in 1988.

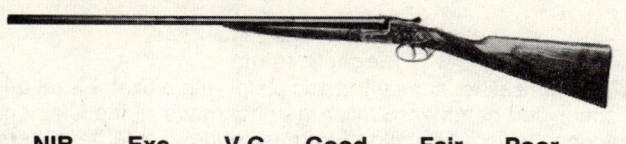

NIB	Exc.	V.G.	Good	Fair	Poor
4000	3750	3200	2500	2000	1000

Model 103A

As above with finer engraving.

NIB	Exc.	V.G.	Good	Fair	Poor
5500	5000	4500	3750	3000	1500

Model 103B

In 12, 16, 20, or 28 gauge Holland & Holland sidelock shotgun with various barrel lengths and choke combinations, chopper-lump barrels, Holland & Holland easy-opening mechanism, automatic ejectors, single selective trigger, and Purdy-type scroll engraving.

NIB	Exc.	V.G.	Good	Fair	Poor
7500	6000	4000	3000	1500	1000

Model 120

As above, with engraved hunting scenes.

NIB	Exc.	V.G.	Good	Fair	Poor
7500	6000	4000	3000	1500	1000

Model 200

As above, in Magnum gauges and with engraving.

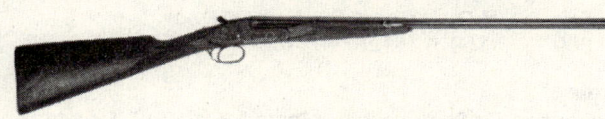

NIB	Exc.	V.G.	Good	Fair	Poor
7000	5750	3750	3000	1500	1000

Model Special AG

A 12, 16, 20, or 28 gauge Holland & Holland sidelock shotgun with various barrel lengths and choke combinations, single selective trigger, and automatic ejectors. Large scroll engraving with walnut stock.

NIB	Exc.	V.G.	Good	Fair	Poor
7500	6000	4000	3000	1500	1000

GARCIA

Garcia Bronco

A single shot .410 shotgun with swing out action. Barrel length is 18.5". Stock is a one piece metal skeltonized affair. Weight is approximately 3.5 lbs. Introduced in 1968 and discontinued in 1978. Built in Italy.

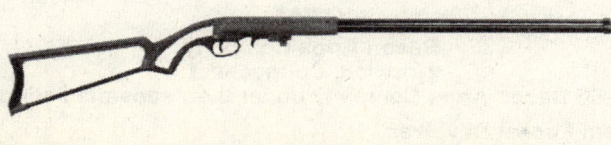

NIB	Exc.	V.G.	Good	Fair	Poor
125	100	85	75	50	30

Garcia Bronco 22/.410

This is an over and under shotgun rifle combination. The over barrel is .22 long rifle and the under barrel is chambered for .410 bore. Barrel length is 18.5". One piece metal skeltonized stock. Introduced in 1976 and discontinued in 1978. Weight is about 4 lbs.

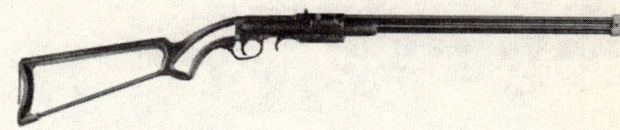

NIB	Exc.	V.G.	Good	Fair	Poor
150	125	100	80	60	40

Garcia Musketeer

This model is a bolt action rifle chambered for the .243, .264, .270, .30-06, .307 Win. Mag., .308 Norma, 7mm Rem. Mag., and .300 Win. Mag. Fitted with a checkered walnut stock, open sights, pistol grip, hinged floorplate, and adjustable trigger. Introduced in 1970 and discontinued in 1972.

NIB	Exc.	V.G.	Good	Fair	Poor
600	500	350	250	200	150

GARRET, J. & F. CO.
Greensboro, North Carolina

Garrett Single Shot Pistol

A .54 caliber single shot percussion pistol with an 8.5" round barrel, swivel ramrod, walnut stock and brass mounts. Marked on the barrel breech "G.W." or "S.R." Approximately 500 were made in 1862 and 1863.

Exc.	V.G.	Good	Fair	Poor
—	—	2500	1500	1000

GASSER, LEOPOLD
Ottakring, Austria

M1870

An 11mm caliber double-action revolver with a 14.75" or 9.3" barrel, and 6-shot cylinder. Marked "Gasser Patent, Guss Stahl." It also bears an Austrian eagle and an apple pierced by an arrow, with the words "Schutz Mark."

Exc.	V.G.	Good	Fair	Poor
375	325	250	175	125

M1870/74

As above, with a steel frame.

Exc.	V.G.	Good	Fair	Poor
375	325	250	175	125

Gasser-Kropatschek M1876

An M1870/74 weighing 1 lb., 11 oz. and 9mm caliber.

Exc.	V.G.	Good	Fair	Poor
300	225	175	125	100

Montenegrin Gasser

A 10.7mm caliber double-action revolver with 5" or 6" barrels, and 5-shot cylinder. Engraved, silver and gold inlay, and ivory or bone grips. Values given are for the plain, unadorned model. Embellished models will need individual appraisal.

Exc.	V.G.	Good	Fair	Poor
400	325	250	200	150

Rast & Gasser M1898

A 8mm caliber double-action revolver with 4.75" barrel, 8-shot cylinder, solid-frame revolver with loading gate and an integral ejector rod.

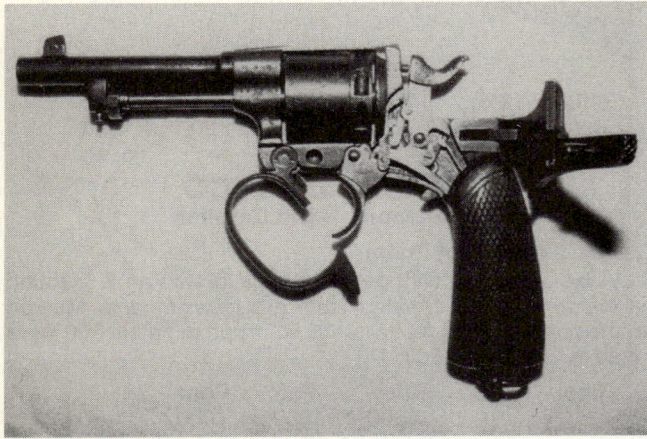

Exc.	V.G.	Good	Fair	Poor
275	225	175	125	100

GATLING ARMS CO.
Birmingham, England

Established in 1888, this company remained in operation until approximately 1890. Although primarily involved with the marketing of Gatling Guns, it did market the one revolver listed below.

Kynoch-Dimancea

A .38 or .45 caliber double-action hammerless revolver with a 6-shot cylinder. The loading system is rather unusual—a spur that resembles a hammer is pulled down, allowing the barrel and cylinder to pivot and to be pulled forward. During this motion the empty cases are ejected and new ones could be inserted. Marked "The Gatling Arms and Ammunition Co. Birmingham"; some are also marked "Dimancea Patent."

Exc.	V.G.	Good	Fair	Poor
1250	900	700	500	325

A Kynoch-Dimancea revolver was sold at auction for $3,450. It was a cut-away version used by S&W to study its function. This revolver, with a 5" barrel, was serial number 22 and chambered for 8mm cartridge. Condition was very good. Butterfield & Butterfield, July 1996.

GAULOIS
St. Etienne, France
SEE Le Francaise

GAVAGE, A.
Liege, Belgium

A 7.65mm caliber semiautomatic pistol with a fixed barrel and a concealed hammer. Similar in appearance to the Clement. Markings with "AG" molded into the grips. Some have been found bearing German Waffenamts. Manufactured from 1930s to 1940s.

Exc.	V.G.	Good	Fair	Poor
400	300	225	150	100

GAZANAGA, ISIDRO
Eibar, Spain

Destroyer M1913

A 6.35mm caliber semiautomatic pistol copied after the 1906 Browning. Produced through WWI.

Exc.	V.G.	Good	Fair	Poor
175	125	100	75	50

Destroyer M1916

A 7.65mm caliber "Eibar" design semiautomatic pistol with a 7- or 9-shot magazine. Marked "Pistolet Automatique Destroyer I Gaztanaga Eibar."

Exc.	V.G.	Good	Fair	Poor
175	125	100	75	50

Destroyer Revolver

A good quality .38 caliber copy of the Colt Police Positive.

Exc.	V.G.	Good	Fair	Poor
200	150	125	100	75

Super Destroyer

A 7.65mm caliber copy of the Walther PP. The slide is stamped "Pistola Automatica 7.65 Super Destroyer."

Exc.	V.G.	Good	Fair	Poor
200	150	125	100	75

Surete

As above in 7.65mm caliber. Marked "Cal. 7.65 Pistolet Automatique Surete" with "IG" stamped on the frame.

Exc.	V.G.	Good	Fair	Poor
200	150	125	100	75

GECO
SEE Genschow, Gustave
Hamburg, Germany

GEHA
Germany

An altered Mauser 98 rifle rebarreled for use with 12 gauge shotgun shells. Barrel length 26.5", military stock shortened to half length and the butt inlaid with a brass medallion marked "Geha". Manufactured from approximately 1919 to 1929.

Exc.	V.G.	Good	Fair	Poor
250	200	150	100	75

GEM
Bacon Arms Company
Norwich, Connecticut
SEE Bacon Arms Company under their separate listing

Gem Pocket Revolver

A .22 caliber spur trigger revolver with a 1.25" octagonal barrel. The frame is iron, engraved, nickel-plated, with walnut or ivory grips. The barrel marked "Gem." Manufactured between 1878 and 1883.

Exc.	V.G.	Good	Fair	Poor
—	1750	1000	600	300

GENEZ, A. G.
New York, New York

Located at 9 Chambers Street, Genez made a wide variety of firearms during his working life (ca. 1850 to 1875). The most commonly encountered of his arms today are single shot percussion pistols and percussion double barrel shotguns. More rarely seen are single shot percussion target rifles. A number of the arms he made were decorated by Louis D. Nimschke. Genez products signed by Nimschke command considerable premiums over the values for the standard firearms listed below and prospective purchasers of Nimschke engraved pieces are strongly advised to secure a qualified appraisal prior to acquisition.

Double Barrel Shotgun
Most often encountered in 12 gauge with varying barrel lengths; blued steel furniture, and walnut stock.

Exc.	V.G.	Good	Fair	Poor
—	—	2000	1500	500

Pocket Pistol
A .41 caliber single shot percussion pistol with a 3" barrel, German silver mountings and a walnut stock. Manufactured in the 1850s and 1860s.

Exc.	V.G.	Good	Fair	Poor
—	—	2750	1000	500

GENSCHOW, G.
Hamburg, Germany

Geco
A 6.35mm, 7.65mm, .32 long, and 8mm Lebel caliber folding trigger double action revolver.

Exc.	V.G.	Good	Fair	Poor
200	150	100	75	50

German Bulldog
A .32, .38, and .45 caliber folding trigger double action revolver with solid frames, integral ejector rods, and loading gates. The proofmarks indicate Belgian manufacture.

Exc.	V.G.	Good	Fair	Poor
200	150	100	75	50

GEORGIA ARMORY
Milledgeville, George

Established in 1862, this concern produced a rifle based upon the U.S. Model 1855 Harper's Ferry Rifle. Nearly identical in all respects to the Harpers Ferry, the Georgia Armory rifle had a lockplate patterned after the U.S. Model 1841 Rifle. Lock marked "G.A. ARMORY" over the date (1862 or 1863). Buttplate tangs marked with serial numbers. The highest known serial number is 309. These rifles were fitted with saber bayonets.

Prospective purchasers are strongly advised to secure an expert appraisal prior to acquisition.

Exc.	V.G.	Good	Fair	Poor
—	—	15000	10000	5000

GERING, H. M. & CO.
Arnstadt, Germany

Leonhardt
Identical to the "Beholla" made by Becker.

Exc.	V.G.	Good	Fair	Poor
300	250	200	150	100

GERMAN WWII MILITARY RIFLES

Model 41 Rifle(M)
First produced in 1941. Built by Mauser. Not a successful design and very few of these rifles were produced. These are extremely rare rifles today. Chambered for the 7.94mm cartridge. Gas operated.

Courtesy Richard M. Kumor, Sr.

Exc.	V.G.	Good	Fair	Poor

Correct and orginal examples will command a premium price.

Model 41(W)
Similar to the above model but produced by Walther in 1941. Correct examples will command a premium price.

Courtesy Richard M. Kumor, Sr.

Model G43
This semi-automatic rifle was built by Walther and made of stampings, castings, and forgings and machined only where necessary. Chambered for the 7.62mm cartridge. Used by the Czech army after WWII. Barrel length was 21.6" and weight is about 9.5 lbs.

NOTE: Add 150% for orginal scope.

Courtesy Richard M. Kumor, Sr.

Exc.	V.G.	Good	Fair	Poor
1000	750	500	250	100

Model VG-98
This is a poorly made single shot rifle made in the final days of WWII. It is made from parts of older often unserviceable Mausers. Chambered for 7.92 cartridge. Will command premium prices.

Exc.	V.G.	Good	Fair	Poor
—	—	—	N/A	N/A

Model VG-1
This rifle was made in the last days of WWII and is crudely made. It usd the magazine of a semi-automatic Model 43 rifle. Beware of firing this weapon. It is poorly made. Prices will bring a premium.

Courtesy Richard M. Kumor, Sr.

Exc.	V.G.	Good	Fair	Poor
—	—	—	N/A	N/A

GERMAN WWII SERVICE PISTOL THE P.38

Walther developed its German military service pistol, the P.38 or Model HP (Heerespistole), in 1937. It was adopted by the German military as its primary handgun in 1938. The background behind this adoption by the German military is an interesting one. In the 1930s, the German Army High Command wanted German arms manufacturers to develop a large caliber semiautomatic pistol to replace the Luger, which was difficult and costly to manufacture. The army wanted a pistol that was easy to manufacture as well as simple to assemble and disassemble. It also required a pistol that could be produced by several manufacturers if necessary and one whose parts would be interchangeable among manufacturers. Walther had just completed its Model HP for worldwide distribution and had the advantage over the other German companies. The German High Command approved Walther's design with only a few mechanical changes. This designation, the P.38, was not used by Walther on its commercial guns. Production began in late 1939 for both civilian and military use. Both military and commercial versions were produced throughout the war years. The civilian pistol was referred to as the MOD HP until late in the war when a few were marked MOD P.38 to take advantage of the identity of the military pistol. In late 1942, Mauser and Spreewerke began production of the P.38. Mauser was assigned the code "BYF" and in 1945 the code was changed to "SVW". Spreewerke code was "CYQ". Late in the war the die stamp broke and the code appears as "CVQ".

The P.38 is a double-action semiautomatic pistol that is short recoil operated and fires from a locked breech by means of an external hammer. It is chambered for the 9mm Parabellum and has a 5-inch barrel. The detachable magazine holds 8 cartridges and the front sight is adjustable for windage. Initially the finish was a high quality blue, but when the war effort increased less time was spent on the finish. The P.38 was equipped with two styles of plastic grips. Early pistols have a checkered grip and later grips are the military ribbed variety; the later style is much more common. The P.38 was produced by three companies and each had its own distinct markings and variations as outlined below. Despite the large number of variations that the P.38 collector will encounter, it is important for him to be aware that there are no known documented examples of P.38s that are factory engraved, nickel-plated, have barrels that are longer or shorter than standard, or built as military presentation pistols.

Collectors should be made aware of a final note. The P.38 pistol was first adopted over 50 years ago. During that period of time the pistol has seen use all over the world. After the end of WWII several governments came into possession of fairly large quantities of P.38s and used them in their own military and police agencies. Many countries have reworked these older P.38s with both original and new component parts. The former U.S.S.R. is the primary source of reworked P.38s. Many of these pistols have been completely refinished and re-proofed by a number of countries. The collector should be aware of the existence of reworked P.38s and examine closely any P.38 carefully to determine if the pistol is original German military issue. These reworked pistols bring substantially lower prices than original P.38s.

NOTE: As of 1997 the Ukraine is now the primary source of pistols. Almost all are importer marked and have been cold dipped blued. Some are reworked and others are orginal except for the finish.

WALTHER COMMERCIAL

The Commercial version of the P.38 is identified by commercial proofmarks of a crown over N or an eagle over N. Production started at around serial number 1000 and went through serial number 26659. This was the first of the commercial pistols and was a high-quality, well made gun with a complete inscription on the left slide. A few of these early pistols were equipped with checkered wooden grips. The quality decreased as the war progressed. There are many variations of these commercial models and values can vary from $1,000 to $16,000. It is suggested that these pistols be appraised and evaluated by an expert. For postwar Walther P.38 pistols see the Walther section.

A few of the Walther Commercial Model variations are listed below:

MOD HP-Early w/High Gloss Blue

Courtesy Orvel Reichert

Exc.	V.G.	Good	Fair	Poor
1800	1200	750	600	400

MOD HP-Early w/High Gloss Blue & Alloy Frame

Exc.	V.G.	Good	Fair	Poor
7500	5000	3500	2000	1000

MOD HP-Late w/Military Blue Finish

Exc.	V.G.	Good	Fair	Poor
1250	1000	750	550	350

NOTE: Add $200 for "Eagle/359" on right side.

MOD P38-Late with Military Blue (1800 produced)

Exc.	V.G.	Good	Fair	Poor
1750	1200	750	600	400

WALTHER MILITARY

Courtesy Orvel Reichert

Courtesy Orvel Reichert

ZERO SERIES

This was the first of the military P.38s and they are well made with a high polish finish. These pistols have the Walther banner and the designation P.38. The serial number began with 01 and went through about 013714. The First Zero Series has a concealed extractor and rectangular firing pin. About 1,000 First Zero Series were built. The Second Zero Series has a rectangular firing pin and standard extractor, with a production of about 2,300. The Third Zero Series has a standard firing pin and standard extractor and has the highest production with 10,000 built.

Courtesy Orvel Reichert

First Issue Zero Series

Exc.	V.G.	Good	Fair	Poor
6500	4000	3000	2500	1500

Second Issue Zero Series

Exc.	V.G.	Good	Fair	Poor
5500	3500	2750	2000	1000

Third Issue Zero Series

Exc.	V.G.	Good	Fair	Poor
2000	1300	1000	800	500

480 CODE

This code was utilized by Walther in late 1940 and represents the first true military contract pistols. There were approximately 7,250 guns produced under this code. There are two sub-variations: one with a round lanyard loop and the other with a rectangular lanyard loop.

Courtesy Orvel Reichert

Exc.	V.G.	Good	Fair	Poor
4250	3000	2250	1500	1000

"AC" CODES

This variation follows the 480 code.

"ac" (no date)

This variation has on the slide "P.38ac" then the serial number only. This is the first use of the "ac" code by Walther. There were approximately 2,700 pistols produced with this code and is the rarest of all military P.38s.

Courtesy Orvel Reichert

Courtesy Orvel Reichert

Exc.	V.G.	Good	Fair	Poor
7500	4800	3750	2800	2000

"ac40"

There are two types of "ac40s". The first variation is the ac with the 40 added, that is the 40 was hand stamped below the ac. There are about 6,000 of these produced. The second variation is the ac40 rolled on together. There are also about 14,000 of these produced as well. The "ac" 40 added is more valuable than the standard "ac40".

"ac40" (added)

Courtesy Orvel Reichert

Exc.	V.G.	Good	Fair	Poor
2250	1400	1200	900	600

"ac40" (standard)

Courtesy Orvel Reichert

Exc.	V.G.	Good	Fair	Poor
1800	1200	950	700	500

"ac41"

There are three variations of the "ac41". The first variation has "ac" on left triggerguard and features a high gloss blue. About 25,000 of this variation were made. The second variation, about 70,000 were produced, also has a high gloss blue but does not have "ac" on the triggerguard. The third variation features a military blue rather than a high gloss blue and had a production run of about 15,000 pistols.

"ac41" (1st variation)

Courtesy Orvel Reichert

Exc.	V.G.	Good	Fair	Poor
1400	900	700	500	350

"ac41" (2nd variation)

Exc.	V.G.	Good	Fair	Poor
1200	750	600	450	300

Courtesy Orvel Reichert

"ac41" (3rd variation)

Exc.	V.G.	Good	Fair	Poor
900	550	475	400	300

"ac42"

There are two variations of the "ac42" code. The first has an eagle over 359 stamped on all small parts as do all preceeding variations and a production of 21,000 pistols. The second variation does not have the eagle over 359 stamped on small parts. This second variation has a large production run of 100,000 pistols.

Courtesy Orvel Reichert

Courtesy Orvel Reichert

"ac42" (1st variation)
Exc.	V.G.	Good	Fair	Poor
850	450	400	350	275

"ac42" (2nd variation)
Exc.	V.G.	Good	Fair	Poor
700	400	350	300	250

"ac43"
This code has three variations. The first is a standard date with "ac" over 43. It has an early frame and extractor cut. The second variation has the late frame and extractor cut. Both variations are frequently encountered because approximately 130,000 were built.

"ac43" (1st variation)

Courtesy Orvel Reichert

Exc.	V.G.	Good	Fair	Poor
550	350	300	250	200

"ac43" (2nd variation)
Exc.	V.G.	Good	Fair	Poor
550	350	300	250	200

"ac43" single line slide
This variation represents the beginning of the placement of the date on the same line with the production code. There were approximately 20,000 built in this variation.

Courtesy Orvel Reichert

Exc.	V.G.	Good	Fair	Poor
650	450	400	350	250

"ac44"
This variation also has the date stamped beside "ac" and is fairly common. About 120,000 were produced.

Courtesy Orvel Reichert

Exc.	V.G.	Good	Fair	Poor
500	350	300	250	200

NOTE: Add $50 for FN frame(Eagle/140).

"ac45"
This code has three variations. The first has all matching numbers on a plum colored frame. About 32,000 of this first variation were produced. The second variation has a capital "A" in place of the lowercase "a". The third variation has all major parts with factory mismatched numbers, with a single eagle over 359 on the slide. The first variation is the most common of this code.

"ac45" (1st variation)

Exc.	V.G.	Good	Fair	Poor
500	350	325	300	250

"ac45" (2nd variation)

Courtesy Orvel Reichert

Exc.	V.G.	Good	Fair	Poor
600	350	325	300	250

"ac45" (3rd variation)

Exc.	V.G.	Good	Fair	Poor
500	350	325	300	250

NOTE: Add $50 for pistols with Czech barrels; barrel code "fnh".

"ac45" Zero Series

This is a continuation of the commercial pistols with a military marked slide. This series has "ac45" plus the 0 prefix serial number on the left side as well as the usual P-38 roll stamp. It may or may not have commercial proofmarks. A total of 1,800 of these "ac45" Zero Series guns were produced in 1945. They are often seen with a plum colored slide.

Exc.	V.G.	Good	Fair	Poor
1500	900	700	450	325

MAUSER MILITARY

The following P.38s were produced by Mauser and are identified by various Mauser codes.

Courtesy Orvel Reichert

Courtesy Orvel Reichert

"POLICE" P.38

Mauser produced the only police P.38s from 1943 to 1945. More than 8,000 were produced and there are numerous sub-variations and markings that greatly affect the value. An expert should be consulted. These Police P.38s are readily recognized by the appearance of an eagle over F or eagle over L to indicate police procurement.

"byf42"

Approximately 19,000 P.38s were manufactured in this variation. Some of these pistols will have a flat blue finish.

Courtesy Orvel Reichert

Exc.	V.G.	Good	Fair	Poor
1250	750	600	450	300

"byf43"

A common variation of the P.38 with approximately 140,000 produced.

Courtesy Orvel Reichert

Exc.	V.G.	Good	Fair	Poor
600	350	300	250	200

"byf44"

Another common variation with a total production of about 150,000 guns.

Courtesy Orvel Reichert

Exc.	V.G.	Good	Fair	Poor
600	350	300	250	200

NOTE: Add $100 for dual tone finish that is a combination of blue and gray components.

AC43/44-FN slide

Exc.	V.G.	Good	Fair	Poor
1250	850	725	600	450

"svw45"

The Mauser code is changed from "byf" to "svw". This variation was produced until the end of the war when France took over production and continued through 1946. French produced guns will have a 5-point star on the right side of the slide. A large number of these French pistols have been imported thereby depressing values.

"svw45"-German Proofed

Courtesy Orvel Reichert

Exc.	V.G.	Good	Fair	Poor
900	500	400	350	275

"svw45"-French Proofed

Courtesy Orvel Reichert

Exc.	V.G.	Good	Fair	Poor
400	300	275	250	200

"svw46"-French Proofed

Courtesy Orvel Reichert

Exc.	V.G.	Good	Fair	Poor
500	450	400	350	300

SPREEWERKE MILITARY

Production of the P.38 began at Spreewerke (Berlin) in late 1942 and Spreewerke used the code "cyq" that had been assigned to it at the beginning of the war.

"cyq" (1st variation)

The first 500 of these guns have the eagle over 359 on some small parts and command a premium. Value depends on markings and an expert should be consulted for values.

Courtesy Orvel Reichert

Exc.	V.G.	Good	Fair	Poor
1000	750	650	550	500

"cyq" (standard variation)

There were approximately 300,000 of these pistols produced in this variation which makes them the most common of all P.38 variations.

Courtesy Orvel Reichert

Exc.	V.G.	Good	Fair	Poor
450	300	275	250	200

NOTE: If "A" or "B" prefix add $250.

A "cyq" series with an "A" prefix serial number. Courtesy Orvel Reichert

"cyq" Zero Series

This variation features a Zero ahead of the serial number and only about 5,000 of these guns were produced.

Courtesy Orvel Reichert

Exc.	V.G.	Good	Fair	Poor
950	500	400	350	275

NOTE: Add $250 for AC43 or AC44 marked "FN" slide

GERSTENBERGER & EBERWEIN
Gussenstadt, Germany

Em-Ge, G.& E., Omega & Pic

A series of poor-quality revolvers sold in the U.S.A. before 1968. .22 and .32 calibers with 2.25" barrels, and 6-shot cylinder.

Exc.	V.G.	Good	Fair	Poor
125	100	70	50	25

GEVARM
St. Etienne, France

Model A-6

This .22 caliber semiautomatic rifle fires from an open bolt. It is fitted with a one piece stock. Furnished with a 10 round magazine. The E-1 20 magazine will not fit the A-6 without hand fitting.

Exc.	V.G.	Good	Fair	Poor
250	200	175	125	75

E-1 Autoloading Rifle
A .22 caliber semiautomatic rifle with a 19" barrel, 10-shot magazine, blued with walnut grips. Two piece stock. A 20-round magazine is an option.

Exc.	V.G.	Good	Fair	Poor
350	250	200	150	100

GIB
Eibar, Spain

10 Gauge Shotgun
A 10 gauge Magnum boxlock double-barrel shotgun with 32" matte-ribbed barrels. Case-hardened, blued with walnut grips.

Exc.	V.G.	Good	Fair	Poor
300	250	225	150	100

GIBBS
New York, New York

Gibbs Carbine
A .52 caliber single shot percussion carbine with a sliding 22" round barrel. Blued, case-hardened with a walnut stock. The lock marked with an American eagle and "Wm. F. Brooks/Manf New York/l863." The breech marked "L.H. Gibbs/Patd/Jany 8, 1856." There were only 1,050 produced.

Courtesy Milwaukee Public Museum, Milwaukee, Wisconsin

Courtesy Milwaukee Public Museum, Milwaukee, Wisconsin

Exc.	V.G.	Good	Fair	Poor
3250	2500	1750	1000	500

Gibbs Pistol
A caliber percussion pistol made by Hull & Thomas of Ilion, New York in 1855 or 1856.

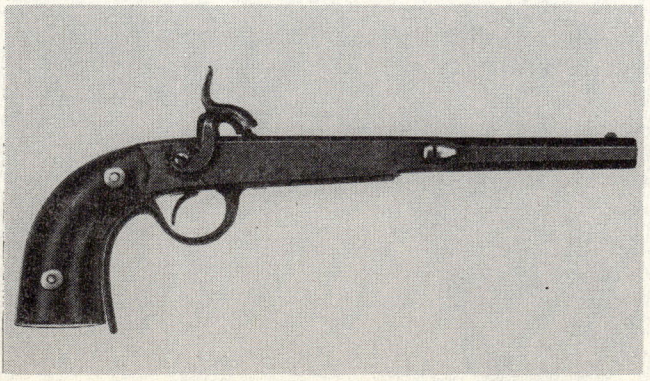

Courtesy Milwaukee Public Museum, Milwaukee, Wisconsin

Exc.	V.G.	Good	Fair	Poor
3250	2500	1500	750	400

GIBBS, J. & G.
LATER GIBBS, GEORGE
Bristol, England

Established in 1835, this concern continues in business to this day.

J. & G. Gibbs	4 Redcliffe Street	1835-1842
George Gibbs	142 Thomas Street	
	Clare Street	
	39 Corn Street	

While initially known for exceptionally accurate single shot rifles, the firm subsequently established a reputation for first quality bolt action magazine rifles in a variety of large bore calibers.

Prospective purchases are strongly advised to secure an expert appraisal prior to acquisition.

GIBBS GUNS, INC.
Greenback, Tennessee

Mark 45 Carbine
A .45 ACP caliber semiautomatic rifle with a 16.5" barrel, a 5-, 15-, 30-, or 90-shot magazine. Blued, with a walnut buttstock and forend. A nickel-plated model was available as an option and would bring approximately $25 additional. Discontinued in 1988.

NIB	Exc.	V.G.	Good	Fair	Poor
275	225	175	150	125	100

GIBBS TIFFANY & CO.
Sturbridge, Massachusetts

Under Hammer Pistol
A .28 caliber single shot percussion pistol with 3" to 8" barrels. A browned iron frame, walnut or maple pointed handle trimmed with brass. The top strap is marked "Gibbs Tiffany & Co." Active 1820 to 1838.

Exc.	V.G.	Good	Fair	Poor
—	—	600	400	250

GILLAM & MILLER
High Point, North Carolina

Established in 1862, this firm produced two types of rifles, one for the State of North Carolina and one for the Confederate Government. Six hundred and seventy six (676) were accepted by North Carolina in 1863. These arms had an overall length of 48-3/4"; barrel length 33" in .577 caliber. These rifles marked in comb of stock "GILLAM &/MILLER". Confederate contract rifles of the U.S. Model 1841 Pattern were made in .577 caliber in the same style as the state contract rifles. However, their lockplates have a pointed tail. Serial numbered inside of the lockplate. Number made in excess of 125.

Prospective purchases are strongly advised to secure an expert appraisal prior to acquisition.

GILLESPIE
New York, New York

Derringer Type Pocket Pistol
A .41 caliber single shot percussion pistol with a 2.5" barrel and a walnut stock. Manufactured from 1848 to 1870.

Exc.	V.G.	Good	Fair	Poor
—	—	2500	1200	500

GLAZE, W. & CO.
Columbia, South Carolina
SEE B. & B. M. Darling

GLISENTI
Turin, Italy

Glisenti Model 1910

A 9mm Glisenti caliber semiautomatic pistol with a 3.9" barrel, fixed sights, and 7-shot magazine. Manufactured from 1910 to 1934.

Exc.	V.G.	Good	Fair	Poor
700	550	425	300	150

GLOCK
Austria
Importer - Glock Inc.
Smyrna, Georgia

Glock Inc. is an Austrian company founded by Gaston Glock in 1963. What originally began as a commercial appliance manufacturing company developed into a line of products that involved military and police products. In 1982 Glock bid on and won the right to manufacture a new state-of-the-art semiautomatic 9mm pistol for the Austrian Army. This new pistol used polymer as a basic component material along with steel. The slide is steel, while the grip and slide base are polymer. The result is a lightweight, strong, and highly reliable military and police pistol. In 1984 the Norwegian Army chose the Glock 17 as its service pistol. With its growing success in Europe, Glock established an American subsidiary in Smyrna, Georgia in 1985 to sell its Glock 17 to American police forces and civilian shooters. By 1990 over 2,700 law enforcement agencies were using the Glock pistol as a duty weapon. One of its unusual design features is a trigger-activated safety. From its introduction as the 9mm Glock 17, the company has expanded its caliber offerings to include the 10mm, .40 S&W, and the .45 ACP.

Glock 17

This model is chambered for the 9mm Parabellum cartridge. It is a double action only semiautomatic that has a 4.49" barrel and a 17-shot detachable magazine. The empty weight of this pistol is 21.91 oz. This pistol is offered with either fixed or adjustable sights at the same retail price. The finish is black with black plastic grips. It is furnished in a plastic case with an extra magazine. This pistol was introduced in 1985 and is still currently produced.

NOTE: Add $80.00 if equipped with night sights.

NIB	Exc.	V.G.	Good	Fair	Poor
400	375	325	300	275	175

Glock 17L Competition Model

This version features a 6" compensated barrel and adjustable sights. The trigger is fine-tuned to provide between a 5 to 8 lbs. trigger pull. This model was introduced in 1988 and is still being manufactured. In 1990 this pistol won the I.P.S.C. World Stock Gun Championship.

NIB	Exc.	V.G.	Good	Fair	Poor
600	550	500	425	350	225

Glock 22

Almost identical in appearance to the Model 17, the Model 22 is chambered for the .40 S&W cartridge. It comes standard with a 15-round clip. It has a slightly larger and heavier slide. Weight is 22.36 oz.

NOTE: Add $80.00 if equipped with night sights.

NIB	Exc.	V.G.	Good	Fair	Poor
500	400	325	300	275	175

Glock 19

This is similar in appearance to the Model 17 but is a compact version with a 4" barrel and a smaller grip that will accept either a 15-round or the standard 17-round magazine that protrudes a bit. Weight for this model is 20.99 oz. empty. The grip straps on this model are serrated as they are on the other Glock models. It was introduced in 1988 and is currently in production.

NOTE: Add $80.00 if equipped with night sights.

NIB	Exc.	V.G.	Good	Fair	Poor
500	400	325	300	275	175

Model 23

Model 23 is chambered for the .40 S&W cartridge. Its slide is slightly heavier and larger than the Model 19. Weight is 21.67 oz. The Glock 23 magazine holds 13 rounds.

NOTE: Add $80.00 if equipped with night sights.

NIB	Exc.	V.G.	Good	Fair	Poor
500	400	350	325	275	175

Glock 24

Chambered for the .40 S&W cartridge it is fitted with a 6" barrel. It had a magazine capacity of 15 rounds before the Assult Weapons ban. Weight is 26.5 oz.

NIB	Exc.	V.G.	Good	Fair	Poor
550	450	400	350	300	175.

Glock 24C

Same as above but with a ported barrel.

NIB	Exc.	V.G.	Good	Fair	Poor
575	500	425	375	325	200

Glock 20 and Glock 21

Both of these models are identical in physical appearance except for the caliber: the Model 20 is chambered for the 10mm cartridge while the Model 21 is chambered for the .45 ACP. Both have a barrel length of 4.60". The Model 20 has a 15-round clip and weighs 26.35 oz. while the Model 21 has a 13-round magazine and weighs 25.22 oz.

NOTE: Add $80.00 if equipped with night sights.

NIB	Exc.	V.G.	Good	Fair	Poor
475	400	350	300	250	200

Model 26 and Model 27

Both of these models are identical except for caliber. Introduced in 1995 these are subcompact versions of the full size Glock's. The Model 26 is chambered for the 9mm cartridge, while the Model 27 is chambered for the .40 S&W cartridge. The 9mm version magazine capacity is 10 rounds and the 40 caliber version holds 9 rounds. The overall length is 6-1/4" with a barrel length of 3-1/2". The height is 4-3/16" and the width is 1-1/4". Weight for both models is about 20 oz. Standard are a dot front sight with white outline rear adjustable sight.

NIB	Exc.	V.G.	Good	Fair	Poor
550	450	300	250	200	150

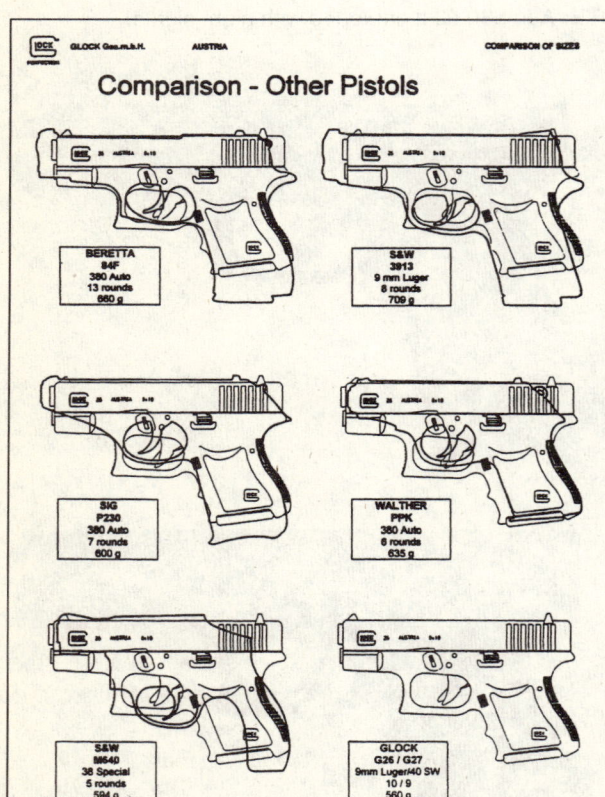

Glock 29 and Glock 30

These two pistols were introduced in 1997. The Model 29 is chambered for the 10mm cartridge while the Model 30 is chambered for the .45 ACP cartridge. Barrel length is 3.78". Weight is about 24 oz. Overall length is 6.77". The Model 29 has a magazine capacity of 10 rounds while the Model 30 has a standard capacity of 10 rounds with a optional capacity of 9 rounds. With the 10-round magazine in place the Model 30 magazine protrudes slightly below the grip. With the 9 round magazine in place the magazine fits flush with the bottom of the grip.

Model 29

Model 30 with 10 round magazine

NIB	Exc.	V.G.	Good	Fair	Poor
550	450	—	—	—	—

GODDARD
SEE B. & B. M. Darling

GOLDEN EAGLE
Tochigi, Japan
Nikko Limited

SHOTGUNS

Golden Eagle Model 5000 Grade I

A 12 or 20 gauge Over/Under shotgun with of 26", 28", and 30" barrels with ventilated ribs and various choke combinations, a single selective trigger and automatic ejectors. Blued, with a walnut stock that has an eagle's head inlaid into the pistol grip cap. Manufactured between 1976 and the early 1980s.

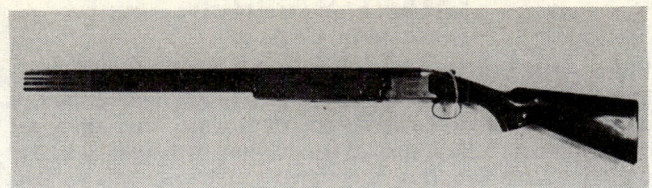

Exc.	V.G.	Good	Fair	Poor
850	750	600	475	250

Grade I Skeet

As above, with a 26" or 28" barrel having a wide competition rib.

Exc.	V.G.	Good	Fair	Poor
950	800	700	550	275

Grade I Trap

Similar to the skeet model, with a 30" or 32" barrel.

Exc.	V.G.	Good	Fair	Poor
950	800	700	550	375

Model 5000 Grade II

As above, but more finely finished with an eagle head inlaid in the receiver in gold.

Exc.	V.G.	Good	Fair	Poor
1000	850	750	600	325

Grandee Grade III

As above, but more elaborately engraved.

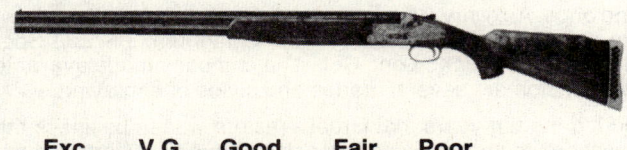

Exc.	V.G.	Good	Fair	Poor
2500	2000	1750	1400	850

RIFLES

Model 7000 Grade I

A Mauser bolt-action rifle chambered for all popular American calibers with a 24" or 26" barrel, walnut stock and a rosewood pistol-grip cap and forend tip.

NIB	Exc.	V.G.	Good	Fair	Poor
700	600	500	400	325	250

Model 7000 African

As above in .375 H&H and .458 Win. Mag. caliber with open sights.

NIB	Exc.	V.G.	Good	Fair	Poor
700	600	500	400	325	250

Model 7000 Grade II

As above, but engraved.

Exc.	V.G.	Good	Fair	Poor
625	550	475	375	300

GONCZ CO.
Hollywood, California

GC Carbine

A 7.63mm Mauser, 9mm Parabellum, .38 Super, and the .45 ACP caliber semiautomatic rifle with a 16.1" barrel. Black with a walnut stock. All current production models are now stainless steel.

NIB	Exc.	V.G.	Good	Fair	Poor
450	400	325	275	200	125

GC Stainless

As above, in stainless steel. Introduced in 1987.

NIB	Exc.	V.G.	Good	Fair	Poor
550	450	375	325	250	175

GC Collectors Edition

A limited edition with hand-polished finish.

NIB	Exc.	V.G.	Good	Fair	Poor
800	600	500	425	350	225

Halogen Carbine

The GC Carbine with a powerful light source mounted under the barrel. Chambered for 9mm and .45 ACP only.

NIB	Exc.	V.G.	Good	Fair	Poor
550	450	375	325	250	175

Laser Carbine

As above, with a laser sighting system effective to 400 yards.

NIB	Exc.	V.G.	Good	Fair	Poor
1500	1250	1000	750	650	500

GA Pistol

The GC Carbine with a 9.5" shrouded barrel and a 16- or 18-shot magazine. Black with a one-piece grip. Manufactured between 1985 and 1987.

NIB	Exc.	V.G.	Good	Fair	Poor
425	350	275	200	150	100

GAT-9 Pistol

As above, in a 9mm caliber with an adjustable trigger and hand-honed action.

NIB	Exc.	V.G.	Good	Fair	Poor
550	475	375	300	225	150

GA Collectors Edition

A hand-polished stainless steel limited production of the above.

NIB	Exc.	V.G.	Good	Fair	Poor
750	675	600	500	400	300

GS Pistol

The Model GA with a plain 5" barrel. In 1987 pistols were made in stainless steel.

NIB	Exc.	V.G.	Good	Fair	Poor
350	275	225	175	125	75

GS Collectors Edition

A hand-polished, limited-production, stainless steel version of the GS.

NIB	Exc.	V.G.	Good	Fair	Poor
725	625	550	475	350	250

GOUDRY, J.F.
Paris, France

Double action 10-shot turret pistol. Marked on barrel rib J.F. Goudry Paris and Systeme A. Norl. By raising the gate on the left side the turret can be removed and reloaded or another preloaded turret inserted.

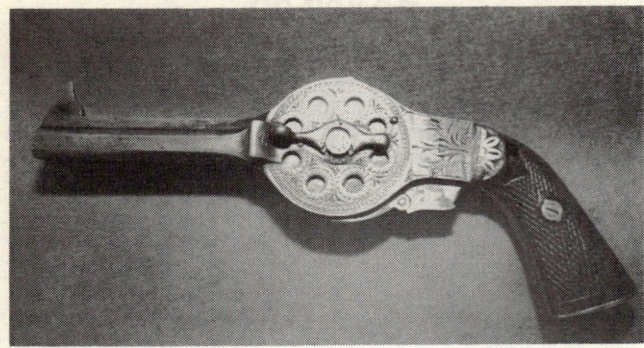

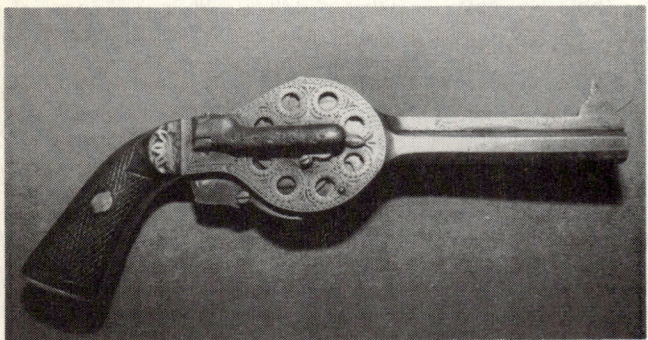

Exc.	V.G.	Good	Fair	Poor
—	5500	3500	2000	1000

GOVERNOR
Norwich, Connecticut

Governor Pocket Revolver

A .22 caliber spur trigger revolver with a 3" barrel and 7-shot cylinder. These revolvers were made from modified Bacon pepperboxes. The top strap marked "Governor". Manufactured from approximately 1868 to 1874.

Exc.	V.G.	Good	Fair	Poor
—	—	450	200	100

GRABNER, G.
Kolibri Rehberg, Austria

A 2.7mm and 3mm caliber semiautomatic pistol with a 3-grain bullet at approximately 500 feet per second and 5-shot magazine. Manufactured from 1914 to the 1920s.

Exc.	V.G.	Good	Fair	Poor
750	600	500	400	200

GRAND PRECISION
Eibar, Spain
A retailer of Spanish-made firearms

GRANGER, G.
St. Etienne, France
Importer-Wes Gilpin
Dallas, Texas

Side-x-Side Shotgun

A custom-order 12, 16, and 20 gauge boxlock double-barrel shotgun. Manufactured since 1902. This is a custom order shotgun and an independent appraisal is strongly recommended. Because the gun is imported the value of the dollar frequently determines price movement.

Exc.	V.G	Good	Fair	Poor
15000	12500	10000	7500	3500

GRANT, STEPHEN
London, England

Side-x-Side Shotgun

This old line British company produced high quality firearms on a custom order, limited-production basis. Their guns are chambered for 12, 16, and 20 gauge and are extremely scarce on today's market. The workmanship and materials were of the highest order. Manufacture has been discontinued. It is not possible to estimate the values of this rare firearm. Individual qualified appraisal should be secured.

GRAS
France

Model 1874

An 11mm caliber bolt-action rifle with a 32" barrel with a walnut stock, a barrel band and a metal tip. The bayonet is a spike blade with a wood handle and a brass butt cap.

Exc.	V.G.	Good	Fair	Poor
325	275	200	150	75

GREAT WESTERN ARMS COMPANY

A certain amount of confusion surrounds Great Western Arms Company firearms. Collectors believe that this company's Colt single action and Remington derringer look-alikes were produced in Italy or Spain and imported into the U.S. under the West Coast distributor H.Y. Hunter. In fact all major components were built of the finest alloys using investment castings and assembled in Los Angeles, California. Great Western offered an extensive variety of combinations of caliber, finish, and grips. Auxiliary cylinders were offered as well in the following chambers: .44 Special/44-40/.44 Magnum, .357/.38 Special and .45 ACP/.45 Long Colt. The company made available to its customers several grades and styles of engraving.

During the ten years that Great Western was in business the quality of its firearms was inconsistent due to uncertain management and finances. This left the company's reputation damaged and allowed Colt and Ruger to dominate the single action market. By 1961 Great Western Arms Company was no longer able to compete. Despite the company's unstable history there is a small but growing collector interest in these firearms. Approximately 22,000 single action revolvers were built and less than 3,500 derringers were manufactured from 1953 to 1961.

Standard barrel lengths were: 4-3/4, 5-1/2, and 7-1/2 inches.

Standard calibers were: .38 Special, .357 Magnum, .357 Atomic, .44 Special, 44-40, .44 Magnum, .45 Long Colt, and .22 Long Rifle.

Standard finishes were: Case-hardened frame and blued barrel and cylinder, or all blue finish.

Centerfire Single Action

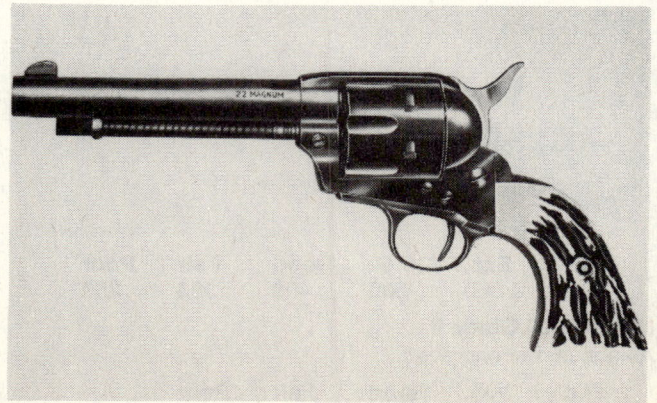

Courtesy John C. Dougan

Courtesy John C. Dougan

Exc.	V.G.	Good	Fair	Poor
500	425	350	250	200

.22 Long Rifle Single Action

Exc.	V.G.	Good	Fair	Poor
335	295	250	200	150

Target Model-Flattop with Micro Sights

Exc.	V.G.	Good	Fair	Poor
550	475	400	300	225

Fast Draw Model-Brass Back Strap and Triggerguard

Exc.	V.G.	Good	Fair	Poor
550	475	400	300	225

Deputy Model-4 inch Barrel with Full Length Sight Rib

Exc.	V.G.	Good	Fair	Poor
1000	850	750	650	550

NOTE: For calibers other than standard such as .22 Hornet, 3220, .45 ACP, .22 Magnum, .30 Carbine add 10% premium.

For factory plated pistols-Add 10%.
For factory cased pistols-Add 20%.
For Sheriff's Model or Buntline Special-Add 15%.

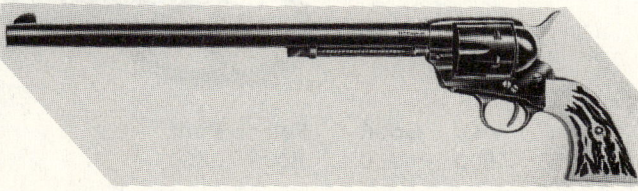

Courtesy John C. Dougan

For factory ivory grips add $175; for stag grips add $95, and for pearl grips add $150.

Factory engraved guns will add $750 to $3,500 to above prices depending on coverage.

Unassembled Kit Gun-in the White

N.I.B.	Exc.	V.G.	Good	Fair
350	300	—	—	—

NOTE: Assembled Kit Gun will bring between $100 and $200 depending on condition.

Derringer Model .38 Special & .38 S&W

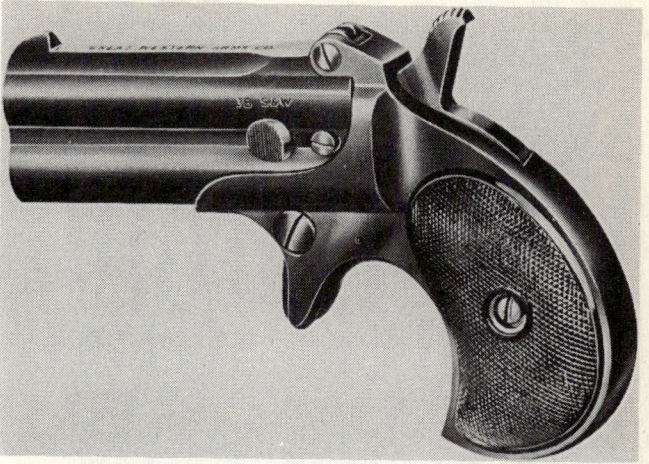

Courtesy John C. Dougan

Exc.	V.G.	Good	Fair	Poor
300	250	200	150	100

Derringer Model-.22 Magnum RF

Exc.	V.G.	Good	Fair	Poor
400	350	250	200	150

NOTE: Factory Engraved Derringers add $350 to $500.

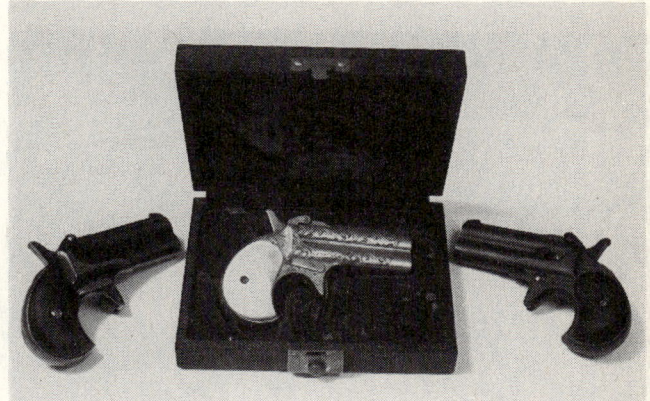

Courtesy John C. Dougan

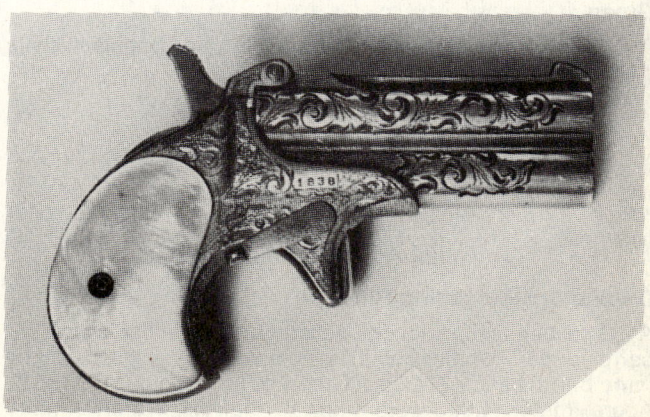

Courtesy John C. Dougan

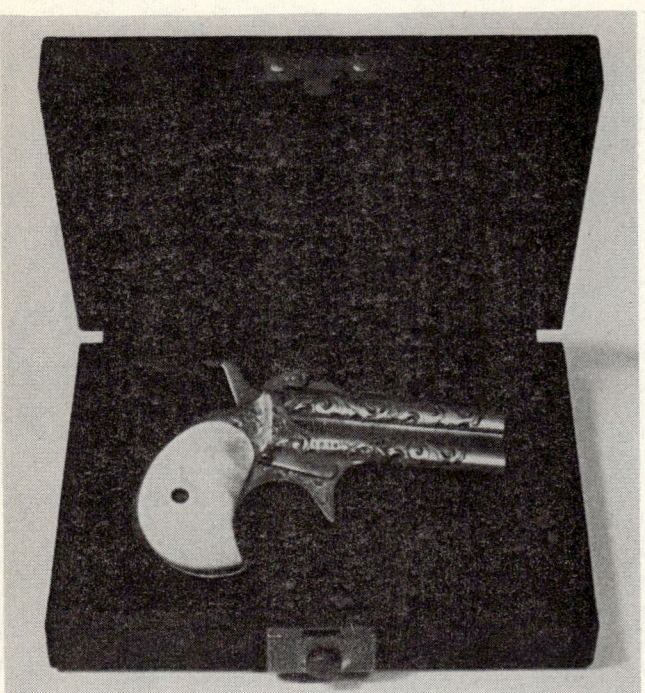

Courtesy John C. Dougan

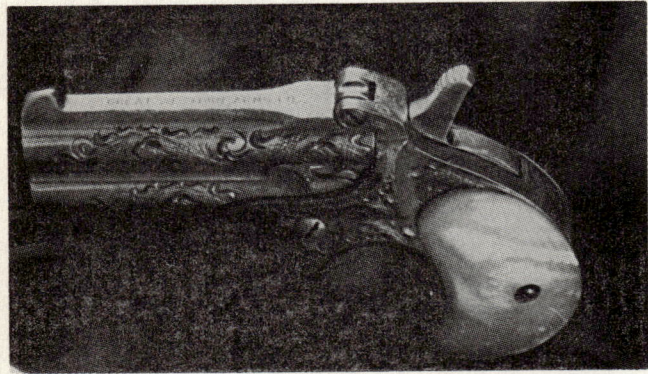

Courtesy John C. Dougan

GREEN, E.
Cheltenham, England

Green

A .450 and .455 caliber double-action revolver, popular with its military users in the late 1800s.

Exc.	V.G.	Good	Fair	Poor
450	400	350	275	150

GREENE
Milbury, Massachusetts

Greene Breechloading Rifle

A .53 caliber single shot bolt-action percussion rifle with a 35" barrel, under hammer and full length walnut stock secured by three barrel bands. Marked "Greene's Patent/Nov. 17, 1857". Approximately 4,000 were made by the A.H. Waters Armory between 1859 and 1862.

Courtesy Milwaukee Public Museum, Milwaukee, Wisconsin

Exc.	V.G.	Good	Fair	Poor
—	—	2000	950	400

GREENER, W. W. LTD.
Birmingham, England

Perhaps the best known manufacturer of double barrel shotguns in England during the nineteenth century, Greener was also a prolific author. Between the 1860s and early 1900s, W.W. Greener produced a wide variety of shotguns in grades ranging from severely plain to extremely ornate.

W.W. Greener Ltd. continued the name and has made arms such as those that follow.

General Purpose Model

A Martini action single shot 12 gauge shotgun with 26", 30", or 32" barrels. Blued, case-hardened with a walnut stock.

Exc.	V.G.	Good	Fair	Poor
400	300	250	175	100

Empire

A 12 gauge boxlock double-barrel shotgun with 2.75" or 3" chambers, 28" through 32" barrels, various choke combinations, double triggers, and automatic ejectors at an additional cost. Stock in either the straight style or pistol grip.

Automatic Ejectors-Add 20%.

Exc.	V.G.	Good	Fair	Poor
1750	1500	1250	800	550

Empire Deluxe

As above, with more finely figured wood.

Automatic Ejectors-Add 20%.

Exc.	V.G.	Good	Fair	Poor
2250	1750	1500	1000	650

F35 Grade Farkiller

A 12 gauge boxlock double-barrel shotgun with 28" to 32" barrels, various choke combinations, double triggers and optional automatic ejectors. Walnut stock, in either straight or pistol grip.

Automatic Ejectors-Add 20%.

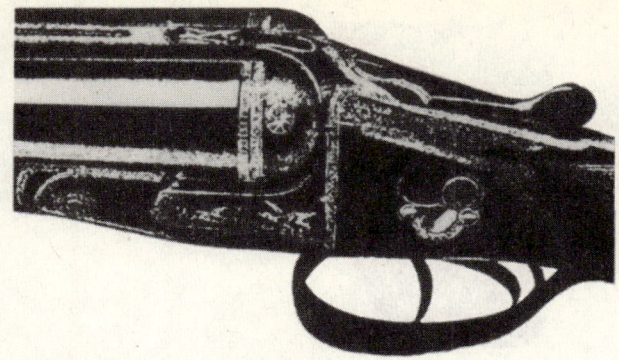

Exc.	V.G.	Good	Fair	Poor
2750	2250	2000	1500	750

F35 Farkiller Large Bore

As above in either 8 or 10 gauge.

Automatic Ejectors-Add 20%.

Exc.	V.G.	Good	Fair	Poor
2750	2250	2000	1500	750

Jubilee Grade DH35

A 12, 16, 20, 28 and .410 bore boxlock single barrel shotgun with a 26" to 30" barrel, various choke combinations, automatic ejectors, and double triggers. A single selective trigger available which adds approximately $500 to the value. Walnut stock in either a straight or pistol grip stock.

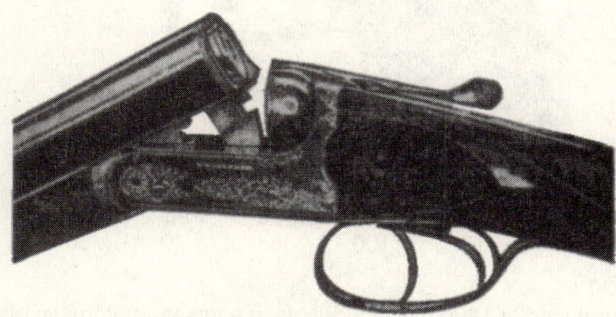

Exc.	V.G.	Good	Fair	Poor
2750	2250	2000	1500	750

Sovereign Grade DH40

As above, but more finely finished.

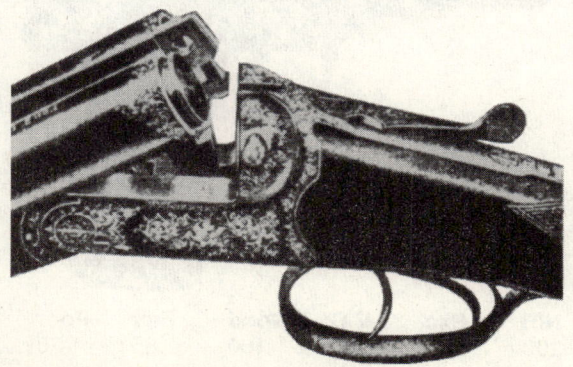

Exc.	V.G.	Good	Fair	Poor
3000	2600	2250	1750	850

Crown Grade DH55

As above, with more elaborate engraving and fancier walnut.

Exc.	V.G.	Good	Fair	Poor
3750	3200	2750	2000	1000

Royal Grade DH75

The best grade Greener similar to the Crown Grade, with more engraving and the best quality of walnut.

Exc.	V.G.	Good	Fair	Poor
4750	4200	3750	3000	1500

GREIFELT & CO.
Suhl, Germany

OVER/UNDER SHOTGUNS

Grade No. 1

A 12, 16, 20, 28 and .410 bore Anson & Deeley boxlock Over/Under shotgun with 26" to 32" ventilated rib barrels, various choke combinations, automatic ejectors, and double triggers. A single selective trigger was available and would increase the value approximately 15 percent. Walnut stock in a straight or pistol grip stock. The values are for the standard 12 gauge version.

28 Gauge and .410-Add 25%.

Exc.	V.G.	Good	Fair	Poor
3500	3000	2750	1750	1000

Grade No. 3

Similar to the No. 1, with less engraving. Manufactured prior to WWII.

28 Gauge and .410-Add 25%.

Exc.	V.G.	Good	Fair	Poor
3000	2500	1750	1250	750

Model 143E

The postwar version of the No. 1. Not made in 28 gauge or .410 bore.

Exc.	V.G.	Good	Fair	Poor
2500	2150	1500	1200	750

Combination Gun

A combination Over/Under rifle shotgun manufactured in all bores and a variety of rifle calibers with 24" or 26" barrels. Made prior to 1939.

Deduct 40% if rifle caliber is obsolete.
28 Gauge and .410-Add 25%.
Automatic Ejectors-Add 10%.

Exc.	V.G.	Good	Fair	Poor
5500	4500	3750	2500	1250

SIDE-X-SIDE SHOTGUNS

Model 22

A 12 or 20 gauge boxlock double-barrel shotgun with 28" or 30" barrels, sideplates, double triggers and extractors. Blued, case-hardened with a walnut stock. Manufactured after 1945.

Exc.	V.G.	Good	Fair	Poor
2000	1800	1500	1200	750

Model 22E

As above, with automatic ejectors.

Exc.	V.G.	Good	Fair	Poor
2250	2000	1500	1200	750

Model 103

A 12 and 16 gauge boxlock shotgun with a 28" or a 30" barrel, double triggers and extractors. Walnut stock with a pistol or straight English-style grip. Postwar model.

Exc.	V.G.	Good	Fair	Poor
2000	1800	1500	1200	750

Model 103E

As above, with automatic ejectors.

Exc.	V.G.	Good	Fair	Poor
2250	2000	1500	1200	750

Drilling

A 12, 16, or 20 gauge double-barrel shotgun fitted with a rifle barrel, chambered for a variety of cartridges. Barrel length 26", boxlock action, double triggers, extractors and folding rear sight. Manufactured prior to 1939.

Deduct 40% if rifle caliber is obsolete.
20 Gauge-Add 10%.

Exc.	V.G.	Good	Fair	Poor
3500	3000	2750	1750	1000

GRENDEL, INC.
Rockledge, Florida

P-10 Pistol

A .380 caliber semiautomatic pistol with a 3" barrel, 11-shot magazine, matte black finish with black plastic grips. The pistol has a plastic frame with plastic magazine. It is offered in electroless nickel-plate, as well as a green Teflon finish for a slightly higher price.

Green Finish-Add $5.
Electroless Nickel-Add $15.

NIB	Exc.	V.G.	Good	Fair	Poor
150	125	100	75	65	40

P-12

This semi-automatic double action pistol is chambered for the .380 ACP cartridge. Fitted with a 3" barrel, checkered polymer grips, and blued finish. Magazine capacity is 10 rounds. Weight is about 13 oz. Introduced in 1992.

NIB	Exc.	V.G.	Good	Fair	Poor
150	125	100	85	70	50

P-30

Introduced in 1990 this is a double action semi-automatic pistol chambered for the .22 WMR cartridge. Fitted with a 5" barrel or 8" barrel. Fixed sights. Magazine capacity is 30 rounds. Weight is about 21 oz. Discontinued in 1994.

NIB	Exc.	V.G.	Good	Fair	Poor
200	150	125	100	85	75

P-30L

Same as above model but in 8" barrel only. Also discontinued in 1994.

NIB	Exc.	V.G.	Good	Fair	Poor
225	175	150	100	85	75

P-30M

Similar to the P-30 but fitted with a removable muzzle brake.

NIB	Exc.	V.G.	Good	Fair	Poor
225	175	150	100	85	75

P-31

This is a semi-automatic pistol chambered for .22 WMR cartridge. Fitted with an 11" barrel, muzzle brake. Black matte finish. Weight is approximately 48 oz. Introduced in 1991 but no longer in production.

NIB	Exc.	V.G.	Good	Fair	Poor
300	250	200	150	125	100

RIFLES

SRT-20F Compact Rifle

A .308 caliber bolt-action rifle with 20" finned matchgrade barrel, 9-shot magazine, a folding synthetic stock, integral bipod and no sights.

NIB	Exc.	V.G.	Good	Fair	Poor
525	475	400	325	250	100

SRT-24

As above, with a 24" barrel. Discontinued in 1988.

NIB	Exc.	V.G.	Good	Fair	Poor
500	450	375	300	250	100

R-31 Carbine

This semi-automatic carbine was introduced in 1991 and is chambered for the .22 WMR cartridge. Fitted with a 16" barrel with muzzle brake and a telescoping tubular stock. Magazine capacity is 30 rounds. Weight is about 4 lbs. Discontinued in 1994.

NIB	Exc.	V.G.	Good	Fair	Poor
300	250	200	150	125	100

GRIFFIN & HOWE
New York, New York

Established in 1923, this firm manufactured on custom order a variety of bolt-action sporting rifles. As these arms essentially were all built to specific customer's specifications, prospective purchasers should secure a qualified appraisal prior to purchase.

GRISWOLD & GUNNISON
Griswoldville, Georgia

1851 Navy Type

A .36 caliber percussion revolver with a 7.5" barrel and 6-shot cylinder. The frame and grip straps made of brass and the barrel as well as cylinder made of iron. Approximately 3,700 were made between 1862 and 1864, for the Confederate government.

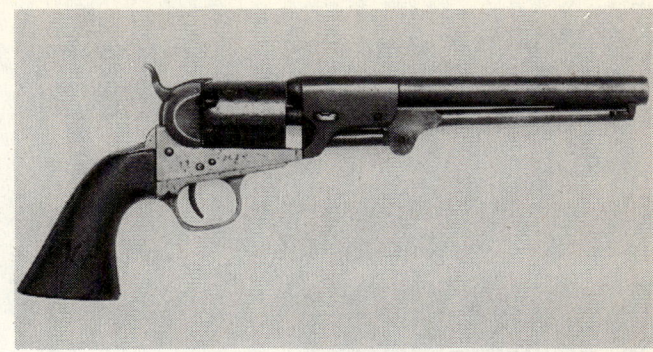

Courtesy Milwaukee Public Museum, Milwaukee, Wisconsin

Exc.	V.G.	Good	Fair	Poor
—	—	8500	4500	2500

GROSS ARMS CO.
Tiffin, Ohio

Pocket Revolver

A .25 and .30 caliber spur trigger revolver with a 6" octagonal barrel, a 7-shot cylinder and marked "Gross Arms Co., Tiffin, Ohio." Blued, with walnut grips. Only a few hundred were manufactured between 1864 and 1866.

Exc.	V.G.	Good	Fair	Poor
—	—	1000	550	300

GRUBB, J. C. & CO.
Philadelphia, Pennsylvania

Pocket Pistol

A .41 caliber single shot percussion pistol with various barrel lengths. German silver, walnut stock and engraved lock and triggerguard. The lock is marked "J.C. Grubb." Several hundred were manufactured between 1860 and 1870.

Exc.	V.G.	Good	Fair	Poor
—	—	1000	650	300

GUEDES-CASTRO
Steyr, Austria

Model 1885

An 8x60mm Guedes single shot dropping block rifle with a 28" barrel, full length walnut stock and iron mounts. Made in Austria under contract for the Portuguese army in 1885.

Exc.	V.G.	Good	Fair	Poor
650	400	350	250	125

GUIDE LAMP
Detroit, Michigan
Division General Motors

Liberator

A .45 ACP caliber single shot pistol with a 3.5" smooth bore barrel and overall length of 5.5". This pistol is made primarily of stampings and was intended to be air dropped to partisans in Europe during WWII. The hollow grip is designed to hold a packet of four extra cartridges. Originally packaged in unmarked cardboard boxes with an illustrated instruction sheet.

Courtesy Richard M. Kumor, Sr.

NIB	Exc.	V.G.	Good	Fair	Poor
1500	850	600	400	300	175

GUION, T. F.
New Orleans, Louisiana

Pocket Pistol

A .41 caliber single shot percussion pistol with a 2.5" barrel, German silver mountings, and a walnut stock. Manufactured in the 1850s.

Exc.	V.G.	Good	Fair	Poor
—	—	1750	500	275

V. GULIKERS/A LIEGE
SEE French Military Firearms

GUNWORKS LTD.
Buffalo, New York

Model 9 Derringer

An Over/Under derringer chambered in 9mm, .38 Special, .38 Super, and .357 Magnum caliber with 2.5" barrels, with a spur trigger and Millet sights. Nickel-plate, with walnut grips. Manufacturing ceased in 1986.

Exc.	V.G.	Good	Fair	Poor
125	100	90	75	50

GUSTAF, CARL
Eskilstuna, Sweden

Bolt Action Rifle

A 6.5x55, 7x64, .270, 7mm Magnum, .308, .30-06, and 9.3x62 caliber bolt-action rifle with a 24" barrel. Blued with a walnut stock in either the classic style or with a Monte Carlo cheekpiece. Manufactured between 1970 and 1977.

Exc.	V.G.	Good	Fair	Poor
500	425	350	275	150

Grade II

As above, with better walnut and a rosewood pistol grip cap and forend tip.

Exc.	V.G.	Good	Fair	Poor
600	525	450	375	175

Grade III

As above, with a high-gloss finish and a finely figured walnut stock.

Exc.	V.G.	Good	Fair	Poor
700	625	550	475	275

Deluxe Bolt Action

As above, with an engraved floorplate and triggerguard, a Damascened bolt, and a high-grade French walnut stock. Manufactured between 1970 and 1977.

Exc.	V.G.	Good	Fair	Poor
800	725	650	575	300

Varmint Model

A .222, .22-250, .243, and 6.5x55 caliber bolt-action rifle with 27" barrel and a large bolt knob made of Bakelite. Furnished without open sights and has a heavy target-type stock. Manufactured in 1970 only.

Exc.	V.G.	Good	Fair	Poor
500	425	350	275	150

Grand Prix Target

A .22 caliber single-shot, bolt-action rifle with a 27" barrel and adjustable weights. Furnished without sights and with an adjustable butt target stock. Only manufactured in 1970.

Exc.	V.G.	Good	Fair	Poor
550	475	400	325	175

Model 2000

A 6.5x55, .243, .270, .308, and .30-06 caliber bolt-action rifle with a 60 percent bolt lift and a cold swaged barrel and action. Furnished with open sights. Blued, walnut stock with a Monte Carlo cheekpiece. Manufactured until 1985.

Exc.	V.G.	Good	Fair	Poor
600	500	400	300	150

GWYN & CAMPBELL
Hamilton, Ohio

Union Carbine

A .52 caliber single shot breech loading percussion carbine with a round/octagonal 20" barrel marked "Gwyn & Campbell/ Patent/1862/ Hamilton, O." Blued, case-hardened with a walnut stock. Approximately 8,500 were made between 1862 and 1865.

Courtesy Milwaukee Public Museum, Milwaukee, Wisconsin

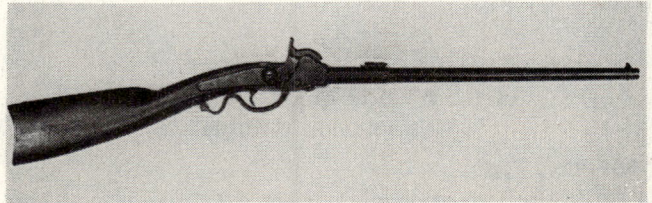

Courtesy Milwaukee Public Museum, Milwaukee, Wisconsin

Exc.	V.G.	Good	Fair	Poor
—	—	1750	750	350

H

HDH, SA.
Henrion, Dassy & Heuschen
Liege, Belgium

Cobold

A 9.4mm Dutch, 10.6mm German, .38, and .45 caliber double action five shot revolver with solid frame, octagonal barrel, and an odd safety catch that locks the cylinder.

Exc.	V.G.	Good	Fair	Poor
250	175	125	100	75

Puppy

A 5.5mm to 7.65mm caliber folding trigger, double action revolver. Most are "VeloDogs".

Exc.	V.G.	Good	Fair	Poor
175	125	100	75	50

Lincoln

A .22 caliber folding trigger, double action revolver with a solid frame, imitation pearl or ivory grips, and engraving.

Exc.	V.G.	Good	Fair	Poor
175	125	100	75	50

Lincoln-Bossu

A 5.5mm or 6.35mm caliber folding trigger double action revolver ("Velo-Dog" type) with solid-frame and hammerless.

Exc.	V.G.	Good	Fair	Poor
175	125	100	75	50

Left Wheeler

A Colt Police Positive copy in .32 or .38 caliber. The last revolver HDH manufactured.

Exc.	V.G.	Good	Fair	Poor
200	150	125	100	75

H.J.S. INDUSTRIES, INC.
Brownsville, Texas

Frontier Four Derringer

A .22 caliber four barreled pocket pistol with 2.5" sliding barrels, stainless steel frame and barrel grip and walnut grips.

Exc.	V.G.	Good	Fair	Poor
150	100	75	50	25

Lone Star Derringer

A .38 Special caliber single shot spur trigger pistol with a 2.5" barrel. Stainless steel with wood grips.

Exc.	V.G.	Good	Fair	Poor
175	125	100	75	50

HWP INDUSTRIES
Milwaukee, Wisconsin

Sledgehammer

A .500 HWP caliber double-action revolver with a shrouded 4" barrel, 5-shot, swing-out cylinder. Stainless steel with Pachmayr grips. Introduced in 1989.

Exc.	V.G.	Good	Fair	Poor
1300	1000	900	650	350

HAENEL, C. G.
Suhl, Germany

Established in 1840, this company began to manufacture semiautomatic pistols after Hugo Schmeisser joined the firm in 1921 as its chief engineer.

Model 1

A 6.35mm caliber semiautomatic pistol with a 2.48" barrel, striker fired, a 6-shot magazine and the left side of the slide is stamped "C.G. Haenel Suhl-Schmeisser Patent." Each grip panel is marked "HS" in an oval.

Exc.	V.G.	Good	Fair	Poor
375	300	225	175	100

Model 2

As above, but shorter and lighter in weight. "Schmeisser" is molded into the grips.

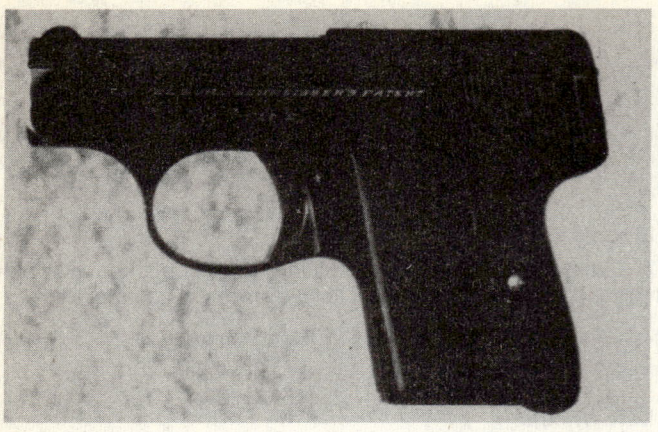

Courtesy Orvel Reichert

Exc.	V.G.	Good	Fair	Poor
400	325	250	200	125

HAFDASA
Buenos Aires, Argentina

Ballester-Molina

A copy of the Colt Model 1911 semiautomatic pistol differing only in the absence of a grip safety, smaller grip and the finger grooves on the slide. The slide stamped "Pistola Automatica Cal. .45 Fabricado por HAFDASA Patentes Internacional Ballester Molina Industria Argentina" on the slide. Introduced in 1930s.

Exc.	V.G.	Good	Fair	Poor
475	425	325	225	100

Criolla

A .22 caliber automatic pistol, similar to the Ballester-Molina. Some were sold commercially under the trademark "La Criolla."

Exc.	V.G.	Good	Fair	Poor
1000	850	650	500	250

Hafdasa

A .22 caliber semiautomatic pistol with a tubular receiver. A true hammerless, striker-fired, with an angled grip. Markings are "HA" on the butt.

Exc.	V.G.	Good	Fair	Poor
350	325	275	200	100

Zonda

As above, but marked "Zonda".

Exc.	V.G.	Good	Fair	Poor
350	325	275	200	100

HAKIM
Egypt

A 7.92x57mm caliber semiautomatic rifle copied from the Swedish Model 42 Ljungman. Manufactured by Maadi Military and Civil Industries Co.

Exc.	V.G.	Good	Fair	Poor
275	225	200	150	100

HAHN, WILLIAM
New York, New York

Pocket Pistol

A .41 caliber single shot percussion pistol with a 2.5" round barrel, German silver mountings, and a walnut stock. Manufactured in the 1860s and 1870s.

Exc.	V.G.	Good	Fair	Poor
—	—	1500	900	400

HALE, H. J.
Bristol, Connecticut

Under Hammer Pistol

A .31 caliber single shot, under hammer percussion pistol with a 5" or 6" part-round, part-octagonal barrel and an iron frame with either a pointed or a round walnut butt. Markings read "H.J.Hale/Warranted/Cast Steel." Manufactured during the 1850s.

Exc.	V.G.	Good	Fair	Poor
—	—	650	300	200

HALE & TULLER
Hartford, Connecticut

Under Hammer Pistol

A .44 caliber single shot under hammer percussion pistol with a 6" tapered round barrel and a pointed walnut grip. Manufactured at the Connecticut State Prison between 1837 and 1840.

Exc.	V.G.	Good	Fair	Poor
—	—	600	300	200

HALL, ALEXANDER
New York, New York

Revolving Rifle

A .58 caliber percussion revolving rifle with a 15-shot open centered cylinder. The frame was made of brass, the barrel and cylinder of iron and the stock of walnut. Manufactured during the 1850s in limited quantities. Prospective purchasers should secure a qualified appraisal prior to acquisition. This is a very rare firearm.

Exc.	V.G.	Good	Fair	Poor
—	—	15000	7500	3000

HALL-NORTH
Middletown, Connecticut

Model 1840 Carbine

This carbine was manufactured by Simeon North and was chambered for .52 caliber percussion. It is a single shot, breech-loading, smoothbore with a 21" round barrel. It has a full-length stock held on by two barrel bands. There is a ramrod mounted under the barrel, and the mountings are of iron. The lock is case-hardened, and the barrel is brown. The stock is walnut. The markings are "US/S. North/Midltn/ Conn." There are two distinct variations, both produced under military contract.

Type 1 Carbine

This model has a squared, right-angled breech lever mounted on the trigger plate. There were 500 of these manufactured in 1840.

Exc.	V.G.	Good	Fair	Poor
—	—	3500	2500	1200

Type 2 Carbine

This variation features a curved, breech-operating lever that is known as a fishtail. There were approximately 6,000 of these manufactured from 1840 to 1843. Some have an 8" bar and ring.

Exc.	V.G.	Good	Fair	Poor
—	—	2500	1750	750

HAMBUSH, JOSEPH
Ferlach, Austria

Boxlock Side-x-Side Shotgun

A custom-order boxlock double-barrel shotgun chambered for all gauges, single selective or double trigger and automatic ejectors. It features workmanship of a high order, and all specification could vary with the customer's wishes. Engraved with hunting scenes. This is a rare gun and is not often encountered on today's market.

NOTE: Pricing is only estimated as not enough are traded to provide accurate values.

Exc.	V.G.	Good	Fair	Poor
1500	1000	800	550	350

Sidelock Side-x-Side Shotgun

Similar to the above, but features a full sidelock action.

Exc.	V.G.	Good	Fair	Poor
2500	2000	1800	1500	1250

HAMILTON RIFLE COMPANY
Plymouth, Michigan

Manufacturer of inexpensive .22 caliber rifles established by Clarence J. Hamilton and his son Coello. The company was established in 1898 in Plymouth, Michigan. The company ceased production in 1945. Over 1 million rifles were produced between 1900 and 1911.

NOTE: Despite the fact that there were many Hamilton rifles sold, most of these little guns were used hard and many did not survive. Hamilton rifles in Exc. condition are hardly ever encountered. No prices are quoted for rifles in this condition as few exist. Further information about these rifles is gratefully accepted by the editor.

Model 7

The first rifle produced by the company, it was made entirely of castings and stampings. It was nickel plated. Chambered for the .22 Short cartridge with am 8" brass lined barrel that pivots for loading. The stock was a metal skelton. Production ceased in 1901 with a total of 44,000 rifles produced.

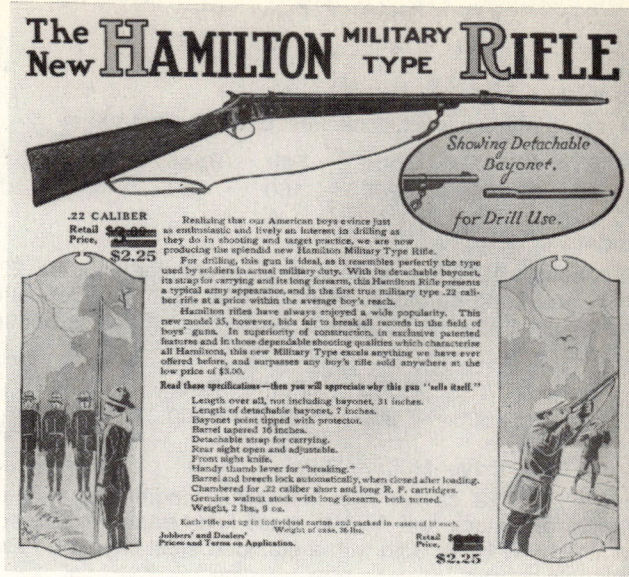

Exc.	V.G.	Good	Fair	Poor
—	350	250	200	150

Model 11

Similar to the Model 7 but fitted with a board-like walnut stock. There are markings stamped into the butt stock: HAMILTON RIFLES CO., PLYMOUTH, MICH., PAT. PENDING NO.11. The Model 11 was produced from 1900 to 1902 and approximately 22,000 were sold.

Exc.	V.G.	Good	Fair	Poor
—	400	300	200	150

Model 15

Produced from 1901 to 1910 the Model 15 was chambered for the .22 Short with an 8" brass lined barrel. Walnut stock. The design was an under lever single shot with the loading port under the barrel. The cocking knob is located at the rear of the frame. Blued finish. Approximately 234,000 of these rifles were sold.

Exc.	V.G.	Good	Fair	Poor
—	300	200	150	100

Model 19

This is similar to the Model 15 with a modified loading port and a 12" barrel. A few Model 19s have been seen with 13" barrels. these will bring a premium. Produced from 1903 to 1910 there were about 59,000 of these models sold.

Exc.	V.G.	Good	Fair	Poor
—	400	300	200	150

Model 23

This was the first bolt action rifle made by the company. The receiver is a steel tube with a loading port in the top where the barrel joins the receiver. The bolt handle is located at the extreme rear of the bolt. The cocking knob must be operated manually. Walnut stock either rounded or flat. Chamber for the .22 Short and .22 Long cartridges. 15" brass lined barrel. Blued finish. Weighs about 3 lbs. Produced from 1905 to 1909. About 25,000 guns were sold.

Exc.	V.G.	Good	Fair	Poor
—	400	300	200	150

Model 27

Single shot tip-up .22 caliber rifle with stamped steel receiver. Barrel length 16" brass lined or 14-7/8"; overall length 30". First produced in 1906.

Exc.	V.G.	Good	Fair	Poor
—	250	200	150	100

Model 27

As above with a walnut stock. First produced in 1908.

Exc.	V.G.	Good	Fair	Poor
—	250	200	150	100

Model 31

Introduced in 1910 this single shot rifle is chamberd for the .22 Short and Long cartridge. Fitted with a 15-3/4" barrel with brass liner. It is a tip-up design. Blued finish. Weighs about 2.25 lbs.

Exc.	V.G.	Good	Fair	Poor
—	500	350	250	200

Model 35 or Boys' Military Rifle

Single shot .22 caliber rifle with a full length oval walnut straight grip stock and 15-3/4" brass lined barrel. Produced from 1915 to 1918. Sold with a stamped steel bayonet. Few bayonets survive.

Exc.	V.G.	Good	Fair	Poor
—	350	250	150	100

NOTE: Add $100 for bayonet to above prices.

Model 39

This was the only repeating rifle built by the company. It is a hammerless slide action design with a tublar magazine. Magazine capacity is 15 rounds of .22 Short. Barrel length is 16" with brass liner. Walnut stock with blade front sight. Produced from 1922 to 1930. Weighs about 4 lbs.

Exc.	V.G.	Good	Fair	Poor
—	250	200	150	100

Model 43

This is a bolt action design with the loading port on the top of the barrel. There is no external cocking knob but the bolt is pulled to the rear when in the locked position. Chambered for the .22 Short and .22 Long cartridges. 15.75" brass lined barrel. Fitted with an oval walnut stock with blade front sight and open non-adjustable rear sight. Weighs about 3 lbs. Built from 1924 to 1932.

Exc.	V.G.	Good	Fair	Poor
—	250	200	150	100

Model 47

This is a bolt action single shot rifle with the loading port located on top of the barrel. It was chambered for the .22 Short and Long cartridges. The cocking knob is located at the rear of the bolt handle. Early Model 47 were built with 16" brass lined barrels. Later examples were fitted with 18.25" steel lined barrels. Early guns had an oval butt stock while later guns had a pistol grip stock. Very late guns had an all steel barrel. Produced form 1927 to 1932.

Exc.	V.G.	Good	Fair	Poor
—	400	300	200	150

Model 51

This was a conventional type bolt action rifle with the cocking knob located at the rear of the bolt. Two styles of butt stocks were used: a flat style or later an oval shape. This was the first Hamilton rifle chambered for the .22 Long Rifle cartridge. Barrel was 20" steel. Finish was blue. Weight was approximately 3.5 lbs. Produced from 1935 to 1941.

Exc.	V.G.	Good	Fair	Poor
—	350	250	200	150

Model 55

This bolt action rifle was chambered for the .22 Short, Long, and Long Rifle cartridges. Fitted with a 20" steel barrel with bead front sight and open adjustable rear sight. Walnut stock. This is the rarest Hamilton rifle. Only one example is known. Produced from late 1941 to early 1942. No price has yet been established.

HAMMERLI, SA
Lenzburg, Switzerland

RIFLES

Model 45 Smallbore Rifle

A .22 caliber bolt-action single shot, with a 27.5" heavy barrel, an aperture rear and globe target front sight and a match rifle-type thumbhole stock. Manufactured between 1945 and 1957.

Exc.	V.G.	Good	Fair	Poor
675	600	525	425	225

Model 54 Smallbore Rifle

As above, with an adjustable buttplate. Manufactured between 1954 and 1957.

Exc.	V.G.	Good	Fair	Poor
700	625	550	450	250

Model 503 Smallbore Free Rifle

Similar to the Model 54, with a free rifle style stock.

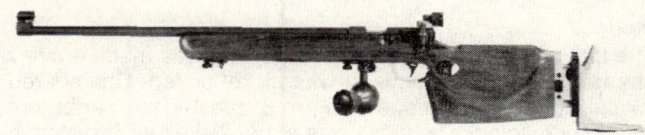

Exc.	V.G.	Good	Fair	Poor
650	575	500	400	200

Model 506 Smallbore Match Rifle.

The later version of the Smallbore target series. Manufactured between 1963 and 1966.

Exc.	V.G.	Good	Fair	Poor
700	625	650	550	350

Olympic 300 Meter

A 7x57, .30-06, or .300 H&H Magnum caliber bolt-action, single shot, rifle with a 20.5" heavy barrel, an aperture rear, globe target front sight, double-set triggers and a free rifle-type, adjustable thumbhole stock with a wide beaver tail forearm and Schutzen-style buttplate. Manufactured between 1945 and 1959.

Exc.	V.G.	Good	Fair	Poor
900	800	650	500	300

Sporting Rifle

A bolt-action, single shot rifle chambered for many popular calibers (American and European), double-set triggers and a classic-style stock.

Exc.	V.G.	Good	Fair	Poor
650	575	500	400	325

PISTOLS

Model 100 Free Pistol

A .22 caliber single shot Martini action target pistol with an 11.5" octagonal barrel, adjustable sights, single set trigger and walnut stocks. Manufactured from 1933 to 1949.

Exc.	V.G.	Good	Fair	Poor
850	725	650	500	300

Model 101

As above, with a heavy round barrel and more sophisticated target sights. A matte-blued finish and was manufactured between 1956 and 1960.

Exc.	V.G.	Good	Fair	Poor
850	725	650	500	300

Model 102

As above, with highly polished blue finish. Manufactured between 1956 and 1960.

Exc.	V.G.	Good	Fair	Poor
850	725	650	500	300

Model 103

Similar to the Model 101, with a lighter-weight octagonal barrel, high polished blued finish. Manufactured between 1956 and 1960.

Exc.	V.G.	Good	Fair	Poor
950	825	750	600	400

Model 104

As above, with a lightweight round barrel. Manufactured between 1961 and 1965.

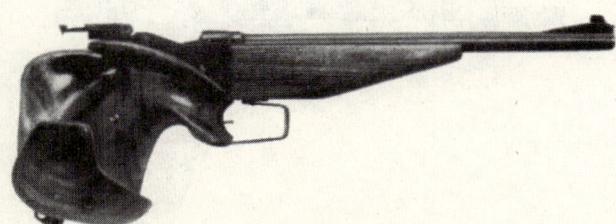

Exc.	V.G.	Good	Fair	Poor
750	625	550	450	300

Model 105

As above, with a redesigned stock and an improved action. Manufactured between 1962 and 1965.

Exc.	V.G.	Good	Fair	Poor
950	825	750	600	400

Model 106

As above, with an improved trigger.

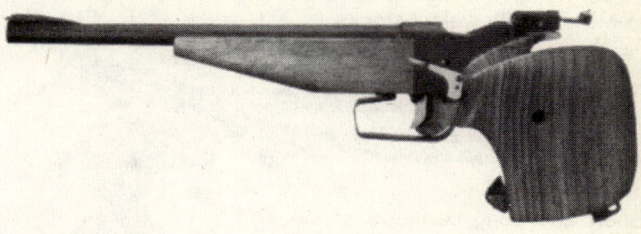

Exc.	V.G.	Good	Fair	Poor
1000	900	750	600	400

Model 107

This variation is fitted with a five-level set trigger. Introduced in 1965 and discontinued in 1971.

Exc.	V.G.	Good	Fair	Poor
750	600	500	300	—

Model 107 Deluxe

As above, but engraved and with a carved stock.

Exc.	V.G.	Good	Fair	Poor
1350	1250	900	800	500

Model 120-1 Free Pistol

A bolt-action, single shot pistol in .22 l.r. caliber with a a 9.9" barrel, adjustable target sights, activated for loading and cocking by an alloy lever on the side of the bolt. Blued, with checkered walnut grips.

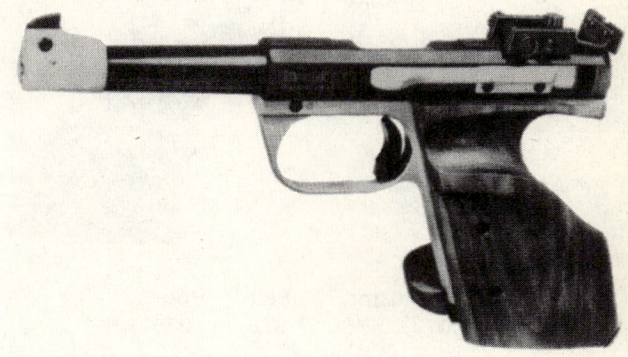

Exc.	V.G.	Good	Fair	Poor
450	375	300	225	150

Model 120-2

As above with contoured grips.

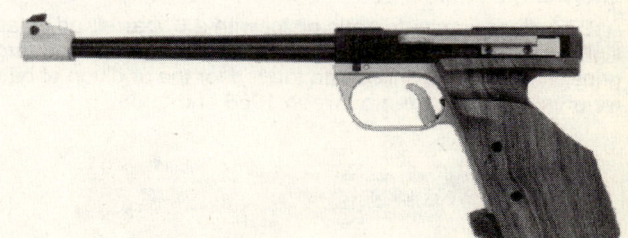

Exc.	V.G.	Good	Fair	Poor
475	400	325	250	175

Model 120 Heavy Barrel

As above, with a 5.7" heavy barrel.

Exc.	V.G.	Good	Fair	Poor
450	375	300	225	150

Model 150

A single shot, Martini action .22 caliber pistol with an 11.25" barrel, adjustable sights, contoured grips and a single-set trigger. Blued with walnut stocks.

Exc.	V.G.	Good	Fair	Poor
1950	1800	1500	1250	800

Model 152

As above, with an 11.25" barrel, and an electronic release trigger.

Exc.	V.G.	Good	Fair	Poor
2150	1950	1750	1500	900

International Model 206

A .22 caliber semiautomatic pistol with a 7.5" barrel, an integral muzzle brake, adjustable sights, and walnut grips. Manufactured between 1962 and 1969.

Exc.	V.G.	Good	Fair	Poor
700	600	475	375	275

International Model 207

As above, with adjustable grips.

Exc.	V.G.	Good	Fair	Poor
725	625	500	400	200

International Model 208

A .22 caliber semiautomatic pistol with a 6" barrel, adjustable sights and an 8-shot magazine, adjustable trigger, and target grips. The barrel is drilled and tapped for the addition of barrel weights. Manufactured between 1966 and 1988.

Exc.	V.G.	Good	Fair	Poor
1750	1550	1250	1000	750

International Model 208 Deluxe

As above, with an engraved receiver, and carved grips. Discontinued in 1988.

Exc.	V.G.	Good	Fair	Poor
3000	2750	2500	2000	1500

International Model 209

A .22 short caliber semiautomatic pistol with a 4.75" barrel, a muzzle brake, adjustable target sights, and 5-shot magazine. Blued, with walnut grips. Manufactured between 1966 and 1970.

Exc.	V.G.	Good	Fair	Poor
800	700	600	450	350

International Model 210

As above, with adjustable grips.

Exc.	V.G.	Good	Fair	Poor
800	700	600	450	350

International Model 211

As above, with non-adjustable thumb rest grips.

Exc.	V.G.	Good	Fair	Poor
1750	1550	1250	1000	750

Model 212

A .22 caliber semiautomatic pistol with a 5" barrel, and adjustable sights. Blued with walnut grips.

Exc.	V.G.	Good	Fair	Poor
1500	1275	1000	750	650

Model 230

A .22 caliber semiautomatic pistol with a 6.3" barrel, a 5-shot magazine, adjustable sights and walnut grip. Manufactured between 1970 and 1983.

Exc.	V.G.	Good	Fair	Poor
700	600	500	400	200

Model 232

A .22 short caliber semiautomatic pistol with a 5" barrel, adjustable sights, and a 6-shot magazine. Contoured walnut grips. Introduced in 1984.

Exc.	V.G.	Good	Fair	Poor
1500	1300	1150	850	550

Model 280

This is the new state-of-the-art target pistol from Hammerli. It features a modular design and has a frame of carbon fiber material. It has a 4.6" barrel with adjustable sights, trigger, and grips. It is chambered for .22 l.r. or .32 wad cutter. The magazine holds 5 rounds, and the pistol was introduced in 1988.

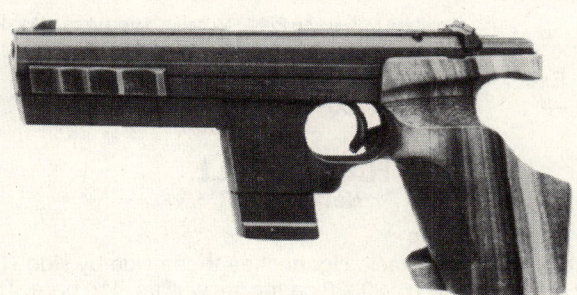

Exc.	V.G.	Good	Fair	Poor
1800	1500	1350	1000	600

Dakota

A single action revolver based on the Colt SAA design. It has a solid frame and is loaded through a gate. It is chambered for .22 l.r., .357 Magnum .44-40, and .45 Colt and was offered with barrel lengths of 5", 6", and 7.5". It has a 6-shot cylinder and is blued, with a brass triggerguard and walnut grips.

Exc.	V.G.	Good	Fair	Poor
150	125	100	75	50

Large Calibers

Exc.	V.G.	Good	Fair	Poor
225	175	150	125	100

Super Dakota

Similar to the Dakota but is chambered for .41 and .44 Magnum, with adjustable sights.

Exc.	V.G.	Good	Fair	Poor
250	225	175	150	100

Virginian

Basically a more deluxe version of the Dakota. It is chambered for the .357 and .45 Colt cartridge. The triggerguard and back strap are chrome plated, with the frame case colored and the remainder blued. This model features the "Swissafe" safety system that allows the cylinder axis pin to be locked back to prevent the hammer from falling.

Exc.	V.G.	Good	Fair	Poor
275	250	200	175	125

HAMMERLI-WALTHER
Lenzburg, Switzerland

These target pistols were produced by Hammerli under license from Walther after WWII. This project continued until approximately 1963, when production was ceased.

Olympia Model 200 Type 1952

A .22 caliber semiautomatic pistol with a 7.5" barrel, a 10-shot magazine, adjustable target sights, and a blued with walnut grips. Manufactured between 1952 and 1958.

Exc.	V.G.	Good	Fair	Poor
650	575	475	375	300

Model 200 Type 1958

As above with an integral muzzle brake. Manufactured between 1958 and 1963.

Exc.	V.G.	Good	Fair	Poor
700	625	525	425	325

Model 201

A Model 200 Type 1952 with a 9.5" barrel. Manufactured between 1955 and 1957.

Exc.	V.G.	Good	Fair	Poor
650	575	475	375	300

Model 202

Similar to the Model 201, with adjustable walnut grips. Manufactured between 1955 and 1957.

Exc.	V.G.	Good	Fair	Poor
700	625	525	425	325

Model 203

Similar to the Model 200, with the adjustable grips, available with or without a muzzle brake.

Exc.	V.G.	Good	Fair	Poor
700	625	525	425	325

Model 204

A .22 caliber semiautomatic pistol with a 7.5" barrel, a muzzle brake, and barrel weights. Manufactured between 1956 and 1963.

Exc.	V.G.	Good	Fair	Poor
750	675	575	475	375

Model 205

As above, with adjustable target grips. Manufactured between 1956 and 1963.

Exc.	V.G.	Good	Fair	Poor
850	775	675	575	450

HAMMOND BULLDOG
Connecticut Arms & Mfg. Co.
Naubuc, Connecticut

Hammond Bulldog

A .44 rimfire single shot spur trigger pistol with a 4" octagonal barrel that pivots to open. Blued with checkered walnut grips. Manufactured from 1864 to approximately 1867.

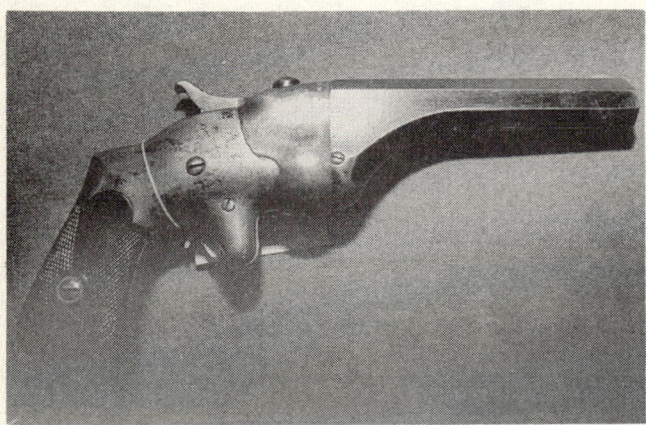

Exc.	V.G.	Good	Fair	Poor
750	600	500	375	250

HAMMOND, GRANT MFG. CO.
New Haven, Connecticut

Military Automatic Pistol

A .45 ACP caliber semiautomatic pistol with a 6.75" barrel and an 8-shot magazine. Blued, with checkered walnut grips. Marked on the right of the slide "Grant Hammond Mfg. Corp. New Haven, Conn." The left side shows the patent dates. Manufactured in 1917. As all the known specimens of this pistol exhibit differences, it is believed that they were only made as prototypes. The highest serial number known is under 20. It is strongly suggested that an expert appraisial be obtained before the sale.

Courtesy Horst Held

Exc.	V.G.	Good	Fair	Poor
8500	7850	6750	5000	4000

HANKINS, WILLIAM
Philadelphia, Pennsylvania

Pocket Revolver

A .26 caliber spur trigger percussion revolver with a 3" octagonal barrel, and a 5-shot unfluted cylinder. Blued with walnut grips. Approximately 650 were manufactured in 1860 and 1861.

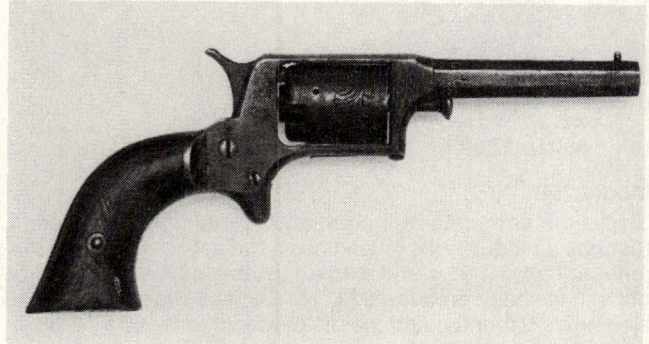

Courtesy Milwaukee Public Museum, Milwaukee, Wisconsin

Exc.	V.G.	Good	Fair	Poor
—	—	1750	1000	475

HANUS, BILL
Newport, OR

Bill Hanus Classic

Built in Spain by Ignacio Ugartechea these side by side shotgun are offered in 16, 20, 28 gauge, as well as .410 bore. They are fitted with 27" barrel with concave ribs and are choked IC/M. Stock is straight grip with splinter forearm. Double triggers are standard as are automatic ejectors.

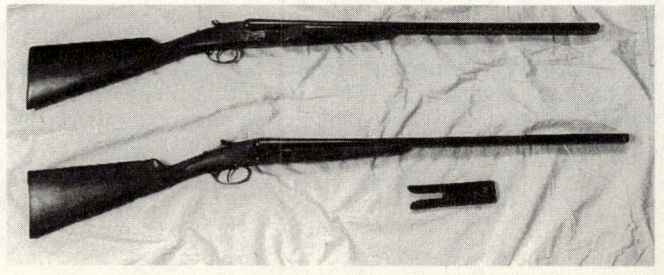

NIB	Exc.	V.G.	Good	Fair	Poor
1600	1250	—	—	—	—

HARPERS FERRY ARMORY MUSKETS AND CARBINES

Harpers Ferry, Virginia

Established at Harpers Ferry, Virginia, in 1798 as the new nation's "Southern Armory," production finally began in 1800 and continued at the "musket works" until the facilities were seized by Virginia state militia in April 1861. With the signing of a contract in 1819 between the government and J.H. Hall, the latter was permitted to construct a separate facility for the production of his patent breechloading rifles, which continued to be known as the "rifle works" after the discontinuation of Hall production until it, too, was seized by Virginia militia in 1861. The machinery of the former was sent to Richmond to be used in the manufacture of the "Richmond rifle musket" while the rifle machinery was sent to Fayetteville, North Carolina, were it was employed in making "Fayetteville rifles."

Harpers Ferry U.S. M1816 Muskets (Types I to III)

Overall length 57-3/4"; barrel length 42"; caliber .69. Markings: on lockplate eagle over "US" forward of cock, "HARPERS/FERRY/(date) on tail. Barrel tang also bears the date, and barrel should show proofmarks on upper left side near breech. The 45605 (type 1) muskets produced at Harpers Ferry from 1817 through 1821 were made with a lower sling swivel that was attached to a separate lug extending from the forward strap of the trigger guard. In 1822, this piece was eliminated and the balance of the production (216,116) officially known as the M1822 musket, incorporated the lower sling swivel directly to the triggerguard bow. Until 1832, these muskets were manufactured with a "browned" barrel to inhibit rusting. The brown barrels of these 107,684 muskets distinguish them as Type 11 production. The balance of production until 1844 (98,432) were made with bright barrel, distinguishing Type III muskets. Despite the large numbers produced, most were altered to percussion during the 1850s. Most by the "cone-in-barrel" (so called arsenal) method. Many of these were altered again during the American Civil War, usually with a "Patent Breech," and were then rifled and sighted.

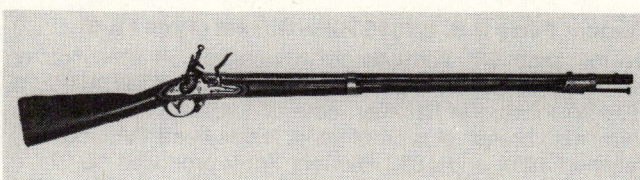

Courtesy Milwaukee Public Museum, Milwaukee, Wisconsin

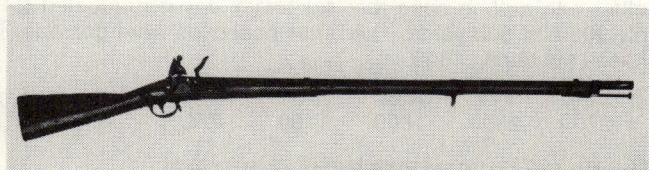

Courtesy Milwaukee Public Museum, Milwaukee, Wisconsin

(in flintlock)

Exc.	V.G.	Good	Fair	Poor
2900	2500	1650	1100	850

(altered to percussion)

Exc.	V.G.	Good	Fair	Poor
950	875	600	450	300

Harpers Ferry U.S. M1842 Musket

Overall length 57-3/4"; barrel length 42"; caliber .69. Markings: on lockplate, eagle over "US" forward of hammer, "HARP-ERS/FERRY/(date)" on tail; barrel tang also shows date; upper left quarter of barrel near breech includes proofmarks (an eagle head, a "V", and a "P") and inspector's initials. Between 1844 and 1855, Harpers Ferry manufactured 106,629 of these smoothbore muskets, many of which were subsequently rifled and sighted; the latter will bring a slight premium.

Exc.	V.G.	Good	Fair	Poor
1200	1000	850	550	400

Harpers Ferry U.S. M1819 Hall Rifle (Types I and II)

Overall length 52-3/4"; barrel (bore) length 32-5/8"; caliber .52. Markings: on top of receiver, either "J.H. HALUH. FERRY/(date)/U.S." or "J.H. HALUU.S./(date)." The 2,000 rifles manufactured between 1824 and 1826 (Type I) are distinguished by having their barrel bands retained by band springs on the right side of the stock. The balance of production (17,680), made between 1828 and 1840, have pins driven through the bands and the stock, distinguishing Type II production. Many of these rifles were altered to percussion just before and in the early months of the American Civil War. Those with evidence of having been altered in the South will command a premium.

(in flintlock)

Exc.	V.G.	Good	Fair	Poor
1800	1600	1350	1000	750

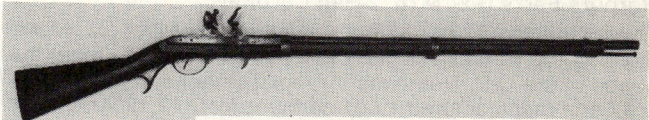

Courtesy Milwaukee Public Museum, Milwaukee, Wisconsin

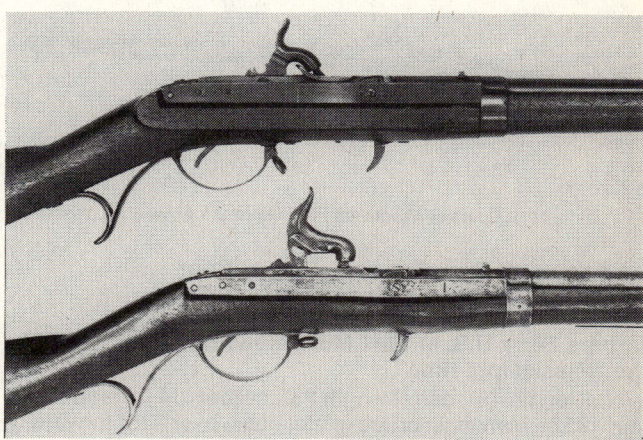

Courtesy Milwaukee Public Museum, Milwaukee, Wisconsin

(altered to percussion)

Exc.	V.G.	Good	Fair	Poor
1550	1400	1050	800	600

Harpers Ferry U.S. M1841 Hall Rifle

Overall length 52-3/4"; barrel (bore) length 32-5/8"; caliber .52. Markings: on top of receiver, either "J.H. HALUH.FERRY/US/(date)." With the general adoption of the percussion system of ignition, the manufacture of Hall's rifles was changed to conform to the new system, a cone tapped directly into the breechblock substituting for the frizzen and pan, and a hammer replacing the flint cock. The newly made percussion arms also incorporated the newly adopted "fishtail" latch for levering the breechblock. Two-thirds of the 4,213 rifles made were still in storage at the arsenal when it was burned in 1861, enhancing the rarity of the arm.

Exc.	V.G.	Good	Fair	Poor
1650	1450	1100	850	650

Harpers Ferry U.S. M1836 Hall Carbine (Types I & II)

Overall length 43"; barrel (bore) length 23"; caliber .64. Markings: on top of receiver, "J.H. HALL/U.S./(date)." To furnish the newly raised 2nd Regiment U.S. Dragoons raised in 1836, Harpers Ferry Armory was directed to construct 1,003 Hall carbines, differing in length and caliber over the M1833 model produced by the North for the 1st Regiment, but were not ready when the unit was sent to Florida. Another 1,017 were made during 1839-1840 with the addition of a tool compartment in the buttstock, distinguishing type II production.

Courtesy Milwaukee Public Museum, Milwaukee, Wisconsin

Exc.	V.G.	Good	Fair	Poor
1850	1600	1350	1050	900

Harpers Ferry U.S. M1842 Hall Carbine

Overall length 40"; barrel (bore) length 21"; caliber .52. Markings: on top of receiver, "H. FERRY/U S/1842." To meet the needs of the U.S. Dragoons for replacement carbines, Harpers Ferry manufactured 1,001 carbines in 1842, differing only from the North M1840 (Type II—"fishtail lever") carbine by being brass instead of iron mounted.

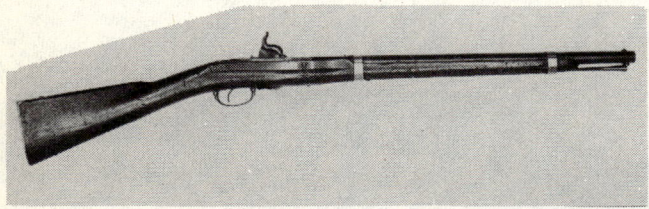

Courtesy Milwaukee Public Museum, Milwaukee, Wisconsin

Exc.	V.G.	Good	Fair	Poor
9500	9000	8000	7000	5500

Harpers Ferry U.S. M 1841 Muzzleloading Rifle- The "Mississippi Rifle"

Overall length 49"; barrel length 33"; caliber .54 (altered to .58 after 1857). Markings: on lockplate, eagle over "US" forward of hammer; "HARPERS/FERRY/(date)" on tail; date also on tang of breechplug; inspector's initials "AW/P" or "WW/P" and proofmarks (eagle head, "V" and "P" on upper left side of barrel). With the discontinuance of production of the Hall patent arms, Hall's Rifle Works was transformed into the production of the new U.S. rifle adopted in 1841. From 1846 until 1855 a total of 25,296 were manufactured at Harpers Ferry. Approximately 10,000 of these rifles were subsequently adapted for long range firing and to saber bayonets at Harpers Ferry between 1855 and 1861. The adaptations in chronological order included the adoption of the Snell bayonet and Benton long range "screw" sight, the adoption of a saber bayonet lug with guide and the Benton sight, the adoption of the saber bayonet lug with guide and the Burton "ladder" long range sights, the adoption of the U.S. M1855 (Type 1) rifle sights and bayonet lug (first in .54 and then in .58 caliber), and finally the adoption of the U.S. M1855 (Type II) rifle sights and bayonet lug (in .58

caliber). A few thousand were also adapted to the Colt revolving rifle sights and split ring bayonet adaptor in 1861-1862, but that adaptation was not restricted to Harpers Ferry-made rifles.

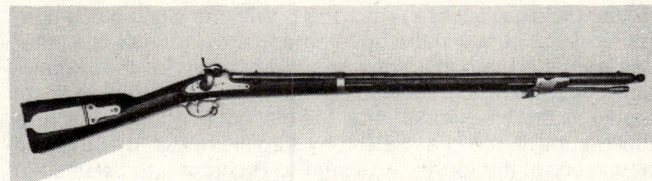

Courtesy Milwaukee Public Museum, Milwaukee, Wisconsin

Courtesy Milwaukee Public Museum, Milwaukee, Wisconsin

Exc.	V.G.	Good	Fair	Poor
2700	2550	1850	1400	850

Harpers Ferry U.S. M1842 Musket

Overall length 57-3/4"; barrel length 42"; caliber .69. Markings: on lockplate, eagle over "US" forward of hammer; "HARPERS/FERRY/(date)" on tail; date also on tang of breechplug; inspector's initials and proofmarks on barrel near breech. Harpers Ferry manufactured a total of 106,629 of these smoothbore muskets between 1844 and 1855. Many of these muskets were subsequently rifled and sighted from 1855 to 1858 or simply rifled during the early years of the American Civil War.

Exc.	V.G.	Good	Fair	Poor
2500	2200	1600	900	600

Harpers Ferry U.S. M1855 Rifle-Musket (Type I & II)

Overall length 56"; barrel length 40"; caliber .58. Markings: on lockplate, eagle on Maynard primer door; "US/HARPERS FERRY" forward of hammer; date on tail; date also on top of barrel near breech plus proofmarks (eagle head, "V", and "P"). Between 1857 and 1858 Harpers Ferry produced 15,071 of these rifles, but many were still unsighted at the end of the fiscal year. This early production (Type I) is distinguished from the later production (1859-1860) by the absence of the iron "patchbox" on the right side of the buttstock, a long range rear sight, and a brass nosecap. The "patchbox" was added in 1859 together with a short base rear sight with leaves graduated to only 300 and 500 yards. The brass nosecaps were gradually phased out during 1859.

Exc.	V.G.	Good	Fair	Poor
2600	2300	1800	1100	650

Harpers Ferry U.S. M1855 Rifles (Type I & II)

Overall length 49"; barrel length 33"; caliber .58. Markings: on lockplate, eagle on Maynard primer door; "U S/HARPERS FERRY" forward of hammer; date on tail; date also on top of barrel near breech plus proofmarks (eagle head, "V", and "P"). Designed as the replacement of the U.S. M1841 rifle, production of the U.S. M1855 rifle began at John Hall's old "Harpers Ferry Rifle Works" in 1857. The production of 1857 and 1858 (Type I), numbering only 3,645 rifles, were all brass mounted, bore a long range rear sight on the browned barrel, and bore a "patchbox" inletted for a special crosshair figure "8" detachable front sight, though many were still without their rear sights at the end of the fiscal year due to the intervention of the Secretary of War. Most of these were never issued and were subsequently destroyed when the arsenal was set afire in April 1861 to prevent the capture of its arms by Virginia forces. The 3,771 rifles produced between 1858 and April 1861 (Type II) were all iron mounted (though a transitional period continued to utilize the brass nosecaps), eliminated the special front sight (permitting the cavity to be enlarged for greased patches), and employed a short base long range rear sight similar to that of the Type II M 1855 rifle musket.

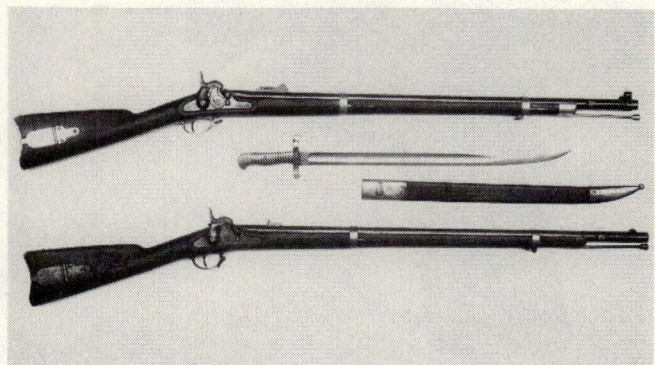

Courtesy Milwaukee Public Museum, Milwaukee, Wisconsin

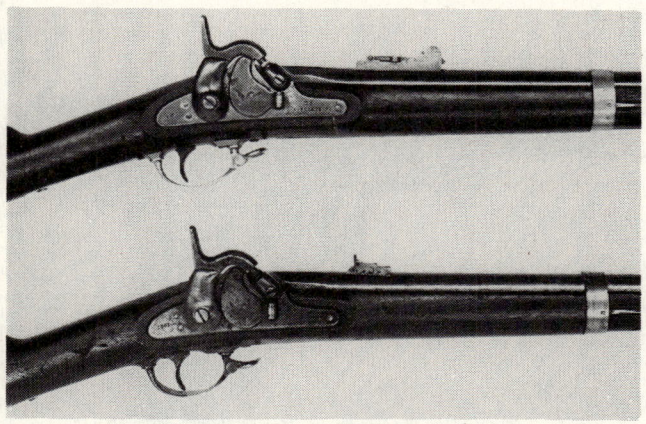

Courtesy Milwaukee Public Museum, Milwaukee, Wisconsin

(Type I)

Exc.	V.G.	Good	Fair	Poor
26,000	16,000	10,000	8000	6500

(Type II)

Exc.	V.G.	Good	Fair	Poor
2700	2500	2100	1700	950

Harrington & Richardson®

HARRINGTON & RICHARDSON, INC.
Worcester, Massachusetts

Established in 1877 by G.H. Harrington and W.A. Richardson. The arms originally produced by this company were marketed under the trade name Aetna. The firm is now located in Gardner, Massachusetts.

Model No. I

A .32 or .38 caliber spur-trigger single action revolver with a 3" octagonal barrel, solid frame, a 7-shot or a 5-shot cylinder, depending on the caliber. Nickel-plated with checkered rubber bird's-head grips. Barrel marked "Harrington & Richardson Worcester, Mass." Approximately 3,000 were manufactured in 1877 and 1878.

Exc.	V.G.	Good	Fair	Poor
300	250	200	125	75

Model 1-1/2

A .32 caliber spur-trigger, single action revolver with a 2.5" octagonal barrel and a 5-shot cylinder. Nickel-plated, round-butt rubber grips with an "H&R" emblem molded in. Approximately 10,000 were manufactured between 1878 and 1883.

Exc.	V.G.	Good	Fair	Poor
175	150	125	75	50

Model 2-1/2

As above, with a 3.25" barrel and a 7-shot cylinder. Approximately 5,000 were manufactured between 1878 and 1883.

Exc.	V.G.	Good	Fair	Poor
175	150	125	75	50

Model 3-1/2

Similar to the Model 2-1/2 except in .38 rimfire caliber with a 3.5" barrel and a 5-shot cylinder. Approximately 2,500 were manufactured.

Exc.	V.G.	Good	Fair	Poor
200	175	150	100	75

Model 4-1/2

A .41 rimfire caliber spur trigger revolver with a 2.5" barrel and 5-shot cylinder. Approximately 1,000 were manufactured.

Exc.	V.G.	Good	Fair	Poor
250	200	175	125	90

Model 1880

A .32 or .38 S&W centerfire caliber double action revolver with a 3" round barrel, a solid frame, and a 5- or 6-shot cylinder, depending on the caliber. Nickel-plated with hard rubber grips. Marked "Harrington & Richardson Worchester, Mass." Approximately 4,000 were manufactured between 1880 and 1883.

Exc.	V.G.	Good	Fair	Poor
250	200	175	125	90

The American Double Action

A .32, .28, or .44 centerfire caliber double-action revolver with a 2.5", 4.5", or 6" round or octagonal barrel, a 5- or 6-shot fluted cylinder, depending on the caliber, and solid frame, nickel-plated, with some blue models noted. The grips are of hard rubber. Marked "The American Double Action." Some noted are marked "H&R Bulldog." Approximately 850,000 were manufactured between 1883 and 1940.

Exc.	V.G.	Good	Fair	Poor
125	100	85	65	40

The Young America Double Action

A .22 rimfire or .32 S&W centerfire caliber, double-action revolver, with 2", 4.5", or 6" round or octagonal barrels, solid frame, and a 5- or 7-shot cylinder, depending on the caliber. Blued or nickel-plated, with hard rubber grips. Marked "Young America Double Action" or "Young America Bulldog." Approximately 1,500,000 were manufactured between 1884 and 1941.

Exc.	V.G.	Good	Fair	Poor
125	100	85	65	40

First Model Hand Ejector

A .32 or .38 centerfire caliber double action revolver with a 3.25" ribbed round barrel. This version does not feature the automatic ejection found on later models. Nickel-plated, with hard rubber grips. The company name is marked on the barrel. Approximately 6,000 were manufactured between 1886 and 1888.

Exc.	V.G.	Good	Fair	Poor
200	150	125	90	65

Model 1 Double Action Revolver

A .32, .32 long, and the .38 S&W caliber double action revolver with a 3.25" ribbed round barrel, and a 5- or 6-shot cylinder, depending on the caliber. Nickel-plated, with hard rubber grips. Approximately 5,000 were manufactured between 1887 and 1889.

Exc.	V.G.	Good	Fair	Poor
175	145	110	80	50

Model 2

Similar to the Model 1, with 2.5", 3.25", 4", 5", or 6" barrels. The grips feature the H&R target logo. There were approximately 1,300,000 manufactured between 1889 and 1940.

Exc.	V.G.	Good	Fair	Poor
125	100	80	65	40

Knife Model

The Model 2 with a 4" ribbed round barrel having a folding 2.25" double-edged knife mounted under the barrel. Blued or nickel-plated. Approximately 2,000 were manufactured between 1901 and 1917.

Exc.	V.G.	Good	Fair	Poor
450	400	350	250	150

Self-Loader

A 6.35mm or the 7.65mm semiautomatic pistol with a 2" or 3.5" barrel, a 6- or 8-shot magazine. The larger 7.65 model has a grip safety. Blued or nickel-plated with checkered, hard rubber grips that bear the H&R monogram. The slide is marked, "H&R Self-Loading" with 1907 or 1909 patent dates.

Approximately 16,500 were manufactured in 6.35mm between 1912 and 1916 and 34,500 in 7.65mm manufactured between 1916 and 1924.

Courtesy Orvel Reichert

Courtesy Orvel Reichert

Exc.	V.G.	Good	Fair	Poor
150	125	100	75	50

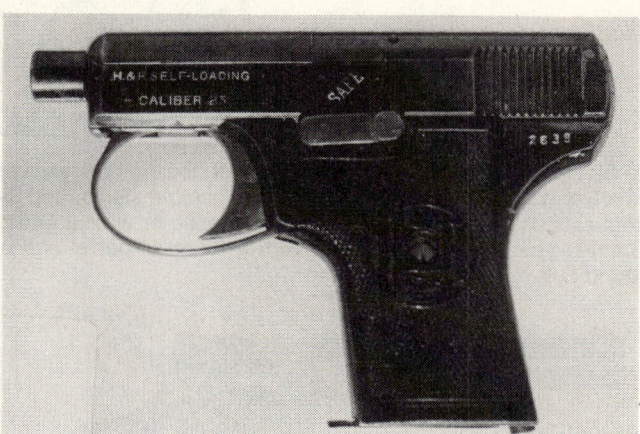

Courtesy Orvel Reichert

Exc.	V.G.	Good	Fair	Poor
300	250	200	150	100

Hunter

A .22 caliber double action revolver with a 10" octagonal barrel and a 9-shot fluted cylinder. Blued, with checkered walnut grips.

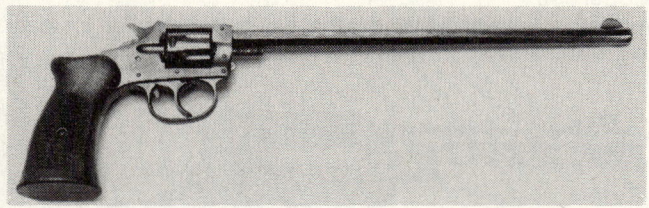

Courtesy Mike Stukslager

Exc.	V.G.	Good	Fair	Poor
200	150	125	100	75

Trapper

As above, with a 6" octagonal barrel and a 7-shot cylinder. Otherwise it is similar to the Hunter.

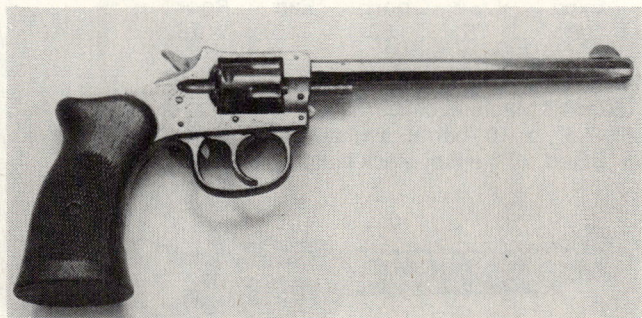

Courtesy Mike Stuckslager

Exc.	V.G.	Good	Fair	Poor
200	150	125	100	75

Model 922 First Issue

A .22 caliber double-action revolver with a 2.5", 4", or 6" barrel. Blued, with checkered walnut grips.

Target Model

A .22 l.r. or .22 rimfire Magnum caliber double-action revolver with 7-shot cylinder, a break-open frame and a 6" barrel with fixed sights. Blued, with checkered walnut grips.

Exc.	V.G.	Good	Fair	Poor
150	125	100	75	50

.22 Special

A .22 l.r. or the .22 rimfire Magnum double action, break-open revolver with a 6" barrel and a 7-shot cylinder. Blued, with checkered walnut grips.

Exc.	V.G.	Good	Fair	Poor
175	150	125	90	65

Expert

As above, with a 10" barrel.

Exc.	V.G.	Good	Fair	Poor
150	125	100	75	50

No. 199 Sportsman

A .22 caliber single action, break-open revolver with a 6" barrel, adjustable target sights and a 9-shot cylinder. Blued, with checkered walnut grips.

Exc.	V.G.	Good	Fair	Poor
200	175	150	100	75

Ultra Sportsman

As above, but more finely finished and with a special, wide target hammer and an improved action.

Exc.	V.G.	Good	Fair	Poor
225	200	175	125	90

Defender

A .38 S&W caliber double-action, break-open revolver with a 4" or 6" barrel and fixed sights. Blued, with plastic grips.

Exc.	V.G.	Good	Fair	Poor
150	125	100	75	50

New Defender

A .22 caliber double-action, break-open revolver with a 2" barrel and a 9-shot cylinder. Blued with checkered, walnut round-butt grips.

Exc.	V.G.	Good	Fair	Poor
225	200	175	125	90

.22 U.S.R.A./Model 195 Single Shot Match Target Pistol

Also called the Model 195, this pistol underwent nearly constant modifications from its inception in 1928 until production ceased in 1941. Its development was greatly influenced by the United States Revolver Association (USRA), which established certain rules for target pistol shooting. The lack of any H&R-published model chronology for the estimated 3,500 guns manufactured makes model determination by examination complicated; a further difficulty is that H&R supplied newly designed parts to owners of older variations, who would then retrofit their pistols with newer triggers, hammers, sights, and trigger guards. Extracted from the available literature, the parts represent approximately: 14 different stocks and virtually endless custom variations by Walter F. Roper; 5 different trigger guards; 3 different triggers; 2 different hammers; 2 different extractors; 3 barrel lengths (7", 8", 10"); and 3 barrel rib styles. From this array of potential characteristics, at least four distinct variations can be identified.

.22 U.S.R.A./Model 195 pistol, Variations 1 to 3

Exc.	V.G.	Good	Fair	Poor
450	350	325	275	200

.22 U.S.R.A./Model 195 pistol, Variation 4

Exc.	V.G.	Good	Fair	Poor
500	400	350	325	250

Variation 1, pre-U.S.R.A., 1928-30: Not marked **U.S.R.A.**, and known as the "H&R Single Shot Pistol." There is no finger rest between the trigger guard and front grip strap; it was advertised with "sawhandle" shape grip copied from the Model 1 or 2 smooth bore H&R Handy-Gun, manufactured with a 10" "hourglass"" barrel with a deeply undercut rib. These are the first 500 pistols.

Variation 2, U.S.R.A. Keyhole Barrel, 1930-31: This is the standard "early" model marked **U.S.R.A.**, has a finger rest, and non-sawhandle grips; however, several grip shapes were offered as options. The grip screw goes from rear of grip into threaded hold in back grip strap.

Variation 3, Modified Keyhole Barrel, 1931: Modification of Variation 2 to improve rear sight, barrel catch changed, reduced spent cartridge force by replacing cylindrical extractor with less powerful hinged type, and the hammer cocking spur and finger rest were made wider. The 8" barrel was offered as an option to standard 10" length, and the number of different grip shapes was increased. This is a transition model between "early" Variation 2 and "final" Variation 4 designs.

Variation 4, Tapered Slabside Barrel, 1931-41: New "truncated teardrop" barrel cross section shape; new standard barrel length of 7", with 10" optional; adjustable trigger; new sear; grip screw location was changed to front of grip; and front sight was adjustable for elevation. The trigger design was changed from curved to straight beveled type with relocated cocking surfaces, and the number of grip shapes increased further to 13 types. A front sight protector was supplied as standard equipment, and luggage style case offered as an option. It appears that Variation 4 was introduced around 1931; the 1932 advertisements describe the fully redesigned gun, but picture Variation 2, indicating H&R probably did not re-photograph the new design. The final variation has a special, tight bore .217" in diameter, with bullet seating .03125" (1/32") into rifling, and is among the most accurate of single-shot .22 caliber pistols. The Model 195/U.S.R.A. was relatively expensive, costing approximately $30 in 1932, and increased to slightly more than $36 by the time production ended in 1941, yet was the least expensive of all single-shot .22 target pistols of quality.

Information about specific U.S.R.A. pistols (serial number and other descriptive information) is being sought by L. Richard Littlefield, P.O. Box 9, Jaffrey, New Hampshire 03452, telephone (603) 532-8004, FAX (603) 532-4501.

Model 504

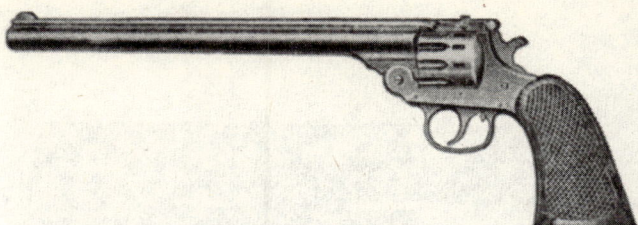

A .32 H&R Magnum caliber double-action, swing-out cylinder revolver with a 4" or 6" heavy barrel, adjustable sights, and 5-shot cylinder. Blued, with either black plastic or walnut grips. Smaller version manufactureed with a 3" or 4" barrel and a round butt.

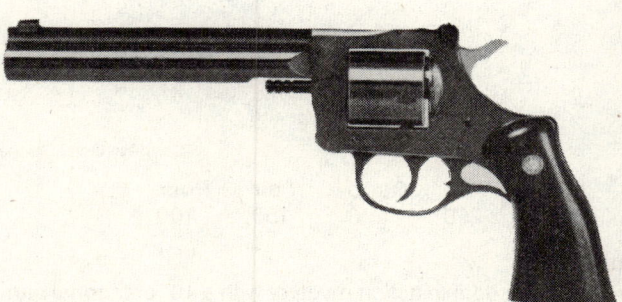

Exc.	V.G.	Good	Fair	Poor
175	150	125	90	65

Model 532
As above, but with a cylinder that has to be removed for loading. Manufactured in 1984 and 1985.

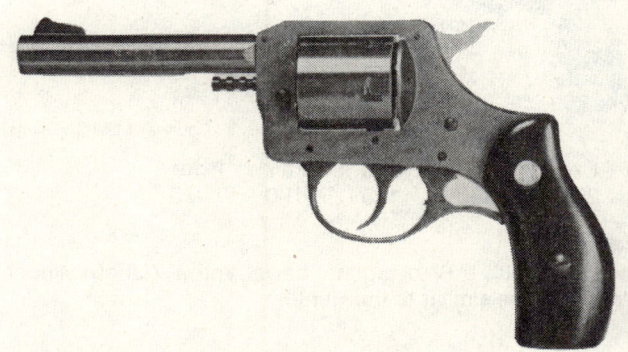

Exc.	V.G.	Good	Fair	Poor
100	75	50	40	25

Model 586
A .32 H&R Magnum caliber double action revolver with a 4.5", 5.5", 7.5", or 10" barrel, adjustable sights and a 5-shot cylinder. Blued, with either black plastic or walnut grips.

Exc.	V.G.	Good	Fair	Poor
175	150	125	100	75

Model 603

A .22 rimfire Magnum caliber double action revolver with a 6" flat-sided barrel and swing-out 6-shot cylinder. Blued, with smooth walnut grips.

Exc.	V.G.	Good	Fair	Poor
165	140	110	8 5	60

Model 604

As above, with a 6", ribbed, heavy barrel.

Exc.	V.G.	Good	Fair	Poor
175	150	125	90	65

Model 622

A .22 caliber solid-frame double action revolver with a 2.5" or 4" barrel. Blued, with round-butt plastic grips.

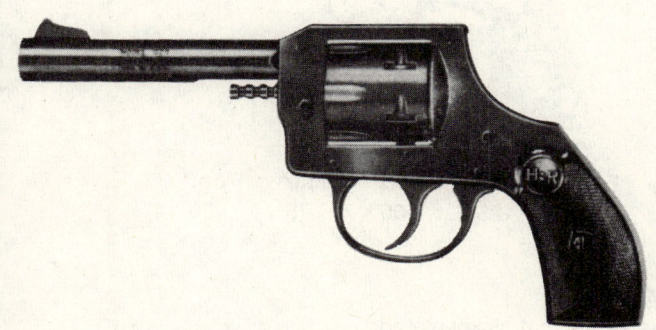

Exc.	V.G.	Good	Fair	Poor
100	80	65	50	25

Model 623

As above, but nickel-plated.

Exc.	V.G.	Good	Fair	Poor
125	100	80	60	40

Model 632

As above in .32 centerfire.

Exc.	V.G.	Good	Fair	Poor
110	90	75	60	30

Model 642

As above, in .22 rimfire Magnum.

Exc.	V.G.	Good	Fair	Poor
100	80	65	50	25

Model 649

The Model 622, with a 5.5" or 7.5" barrel.

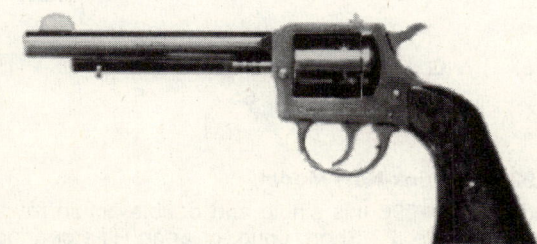

Exc.	V.G.	Good	Fair	Poor
150	125	100	75	50

Model 650

As above, but nickel-plated.

Exc.	V.G.	Good	Fair	Poor
150	125	100	75	50

Model 660

A .22 caliber solid-frame, Western-style revolver with a 5.5" barrel and is a double action. Blued, with walnut grips. It is also known as the "Gunfighter."

Exc.	V.G.	Good	Fair	Poor
100	80	65	45	25

Model 666

A .22 or . 22 rimfire Magnum caliber double action revolver with a 6" barrel and a 6-shot cylinder. Blued, with plastic grips. Manufactured between 1976 and 1982.

Exc.	V.G.	Good	Fair	Poor
100	80	65	45	25

Model 676

Similar to the Model 660. Blued, with a case colored frame. It has walnut grips. Manufactured between 1976 and 1982.

Exc.	V.G.	Good	Fair	Poor
150	125	100	75	50

Model 686

Similar to the Model 660 "Gunfighter" with a 4.5", 5.5", 7.5", 10", or 12" barrel.

Exc.	V.G.	Good	Fair	Poor
175	150	125	100	75

Model 732

A .32 caliber double action, solid-frame revolver with a swing-out cylinder, a 2.5" or 4" barrel and a 6-shot cylinder. Blued, with black plastic grips. Also known as the "Guardsman."

Exc.	V.G.	Good	Fair	Poor
125	100	80	65	45

Model 733

As above, but nickel-plated and a 2.5" barrel.

Exc.	V.G.	Good	Fair	Poor
150	125	100	75	50

Model 900

A .22 caliber solid-frame revolver with a removable cylinder, a 2.5" or 4" barrel and a 9-shot cylinder. Blued, with black plastic grips. Manufactured between 1962 and 1973.

Exc.	V.G.	Good	Fair	Poor
100	90	80	60	40

Model 901

As above, but chrome-plated with white plastic grips. Manufactured in 1962 and 1963 only.

Exc.	V.G.	Good	Fair	Poor
100	90	80	60	40

Model 903

As above, with a swing-out cylinder, a flat-sided, 6" barrel, and a 9-shot cylinder. Blued, with walnut grips.

Exc.	V.G.	Good	Fair	Poor
125	100	90	75	50

Model 904

As above, with a ribbed heavy barrel.

Exc.	V.G.	Good	Fair	Poor
150	125	100	75	50

Model 905

As above, but nickel-plated.

Exc.	V.G.	Good	Fair	Poor
165	140	110	80	65

Model 922 Second Issue

A .22 rimfire caliber solid-frame revolver with a 2.5", 4", or 6" barrel. Blued, with black plastic grips. Manufactured between 1950 and 1982.

Exc.	V.G.	Good	Fair	Poor
100	90	80	60	40

Model 923

As above, but nickel-plated.

Exc.	V.G.	Good	Fair	Poor
110	95	85	65	45

Model 925

A .38 S&W caliber double action, break-open, hand ejector revolver with a 2.5" barrel, adjustable sights and a 5-shot cylinder. Blued, with a one-piece wraparound grip. Manufactured between 1964 and 1984.

Exc.	V.G.	Good	Fair	Poor
150	125	100	75	50

Model 935

As above, but nickel-plated.

Exc.	V.G.	Good	Fair	Poor
150	125	100	75	50

Model 929

A .22 rimfire solid-frame, swing-out revolver with a 2.5", 4", or 6" barrel and a 9-shot cylinder. Blued, with plastic grips. It is also known as the "Sidekick". Manufactured between 1956 and 1985.

Exc.	V.G.	Good	Fair	Poor
125	100	85	65	45

Model 929 Sidekick-New Model

Reintroduced in 1996 this single and double action revolver chambered for the .22 Short, Long, or Long Rifle cartridges. Cylinder holds 9 rounds. Sold with a lockable storage case, nylon holster, and gun oil and gun grease samples. Weighs about 30 oz.

NIB	Exc.	V.G.	Good	Fair	Poor
150	125	—	—	—	—

Exc.	V.G	Good	Fair	Poor
100	90	80	65	45

Model 929 Sidekick Trapper Edition
Same as above but with grey laminate grips and special "NTA" Trapper Edition roll stamp on barrel.

NIB	Exc.	V.G.	Good	Fair	Poor
175	150	—	—	—	—

Model 930
As above, but nickel-plated and not available with a 6" barrel.

Exc.	V.G.	Good	Fair	Poor
125	100	85	65	45

Model 939 Ultra Sidekick
As above, with a ventilated rib, flat sided 6" barrel, adjustable sights, thumb rest grips and features a safety device whereby the pistol could not be fired unless it was unlocked by a furnished key. Manufactured between 1958 and 1982.

Exc.	V.G.	Good	Fair	Poor
125	100	85	65	45

Model 939 Premier
Similar to the above models but fitted with a 6" barrel with sighting rib, adjustable rear sight, hard wood grips, high polished blued finish. Weighs about 36 oz.

NIB	Exc.	V.G.	Good	Fair	Poor
150	125	100	85	65	45

Model 940
A round-barreled version of the above.

Model 949
A .22 caliber double action, Western-type revolver with a 5.5" barrel with an ejector rod, 9-shot, gate-loaded cylinder and adjustable sights. Blued, with walnut grips. Manufactured between 1960 and 1985.

Exc.	V.G.	Good	Fair	Poor
125	100	80	65	40

Model 949 Western
Similar to the above model this revolver is offered with a choice of 5.5" or 7.5" barrel. Drift adjustable rear sight, walnut grips, and case colored frame and backstrap with blued cylinder and barrel. Weight is about 36 oz.

NIB	Exc.	V.G.	Good	Fair	Poor
150	125	100	80	65	40

Model 950
As above, but nickel-plated.

Exc.	V.G.	Good	Fair	Poor
125	100	80	65	40

Model 976
As above, with a case-hardened frame.

Exc.	V.G.	Good	Fair	Poor
100	80	65	45	30

Model 999 Sportsman
A .22 rimfire caliber double action, break-open, self ejecting revolver with a 6"or 4" barrel ventilated rib barrel and windage adjustable sights. Blued, with walnut grips. Weighs about 30 oz. with 4" barrel and 34 oz. with 6" barrel.

Exc.	V.G.	Good	Fair	Poor
200	150	125	90	65

Engraved Model 999
As above, but engraved.

Exc.	V.G.	Good	Fair	Poor
425	350	300	200	125

Amtec 2000
This is a German designed and American built double action revolver introduced in 1996. Offered in 2" or 3" barrel and chambered for .38 Special cartridge. Pachmayr composition grips. Cylinder holds 5 rounds. Weight is approximately 25 oz.

NIB	Exc.	V.G.	Good	Fair	Poor
250	200	—	—	—	—

Hammerless Double
A 10 or 12 gauge Anson & Deeley hammerless boxlock double-barrel shotgun with a 28", 30", or 32" Damascus barrels in various choke combinations, double triggers and extractors. Engraved, case-hardened and walnut stock. Four grades were available. They differ in the amount of engraving and the

quality of materials and workmanship utilized. Approximately 3,500 were manufactured between 1882 and 1885.

D Grade

Exc.	V.G.	Good	Fair	Poor
650	550	425	300	175

C Grade

Exc.	V.G.	Good	Fair	Poor
750	650	500	400	275

B Grade

Exc.	V.G.	Good	Fair	Poor
900	750	600	500	350

A Grade

Exc.	V.G.	Good	Fair	Poor
2000	1750	1500	1000	550

Harrich No. I

A 12 gauge boxlock single-barrel shotgun with a 32" or 34", ventilated rib, full-choke barrel and automatic ejector. Engraved, blued with a checkered, walnut stock. Imported between 1971 and 1975.

Exc.	V.G.	Good	Fair	Poor
1750	1500	1150	850	650

Harrington & Richardson manufactured a series of single barrel, break-open shotguns between 1908 and 1942. They were chambered for various gauges and had various barrel lengths and chokes. The finishes were blued with walnut stocks. There is little collector interest in these guns and, if in sound condition, are desirable as shooters only. They are the Models 3, 5, 6, 7, 8, and 9, as well as a hinged-frame, folding design. Values are as follows:

Exc.	V.G.	Good	Fair	Poor
125	100	85	65	40

Turkey Mag

A single shot break-open side release gun chambered for the 12 gauge 3-1/2" shell with screw-in full choke. The hardwood stock has a Mossy Oak finish. Barrel length is 24" with a bead front sight. Weight is about 6 lbs.

NIB	Exc.	V.G.	Good	Fair	Poor
175	150	125	100	75	50

Youth Turkey Gun

Similar in appearance to the Turkey Mag but on a smaller scale. Chambered for the 20 gauge 3" shell with 22" barrel. Weighs about 5.5 lbs.

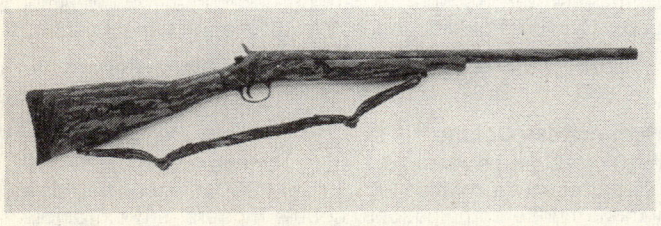

NIB	Exc.	V.G.	Good	Fair	Poor
165	140	115	90	60	40

Topper (New production)

This is a break-open side release single shot available in 12 and 20 gauge as well as .410 bore. The 12 gauge is offered with 28" barrel while the others are fitted with 26" barrels. Blued finish with hardwood stock in black finish with semi-pistol grip. Weight is approximately 6 lbs.

NIB	Exc.	V.G.	Good	Fair	Poor
125	100	80	60	45	30

Topper Deluxe

NIB	Exc.	V.G.	Good	Fair	Poor
140	115	90	70	50	40

Topper JR. in 20 Gauge and .410 Bore Only

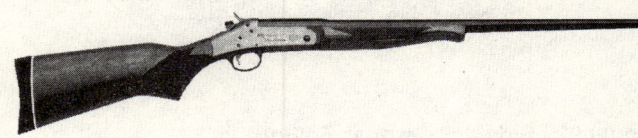

NIB	Exc.	V.G.	Good	Fair	Poor
125	100	80	60	45	30

Topper Jr. Classic

Similar to the Topper Jr. Features a black walnut stock with butt checkering. White line spacer and black recoil pad. Weighs about 7.5 lbs.

NIB	Exc.	V.G.	Good	Fair	Poor
125	100	80	60	45	30

Topper Deluxe Slug

This 12 gauge single shot has a 24" full rifles barrel with built in compensator.

NIB	Exc.	V.G.	Good	Fair	Poor
150	115	90	70	50	40

Tamer

This single shot gun is chambered for the .410 shell with 3" chamber. It is fitted with a 19-1/2" barrel and had a matte nickel finish. The stock is matte black polymer. Weighs about 6 lbs.

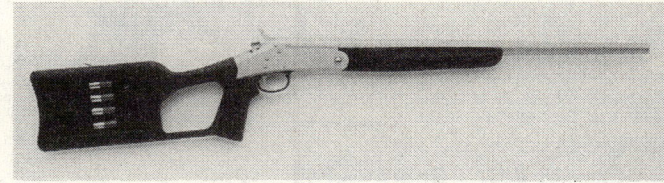

NIB	Exc.	V.G.	Good	Fair	Poor
130	100	80	60	45	30

Ultra Slug Hunter

Introduced in 1995 this model uses a heavy 10 gauge action fitted with a 24" 12 gauge barrel. Weight is about 8 lbs.

NIB	Exc.	V.G.	Good	Fair	Poor
150	115	90	70	50	40

Ultra Slug Hunter Deluxe-20 Gauge

Introduced in 1997 this model is chambered for 20 gauge shells and features a hand checkered camo laminated wood stock. Fitted with a fully rifled heavy slug barrel 24" long.

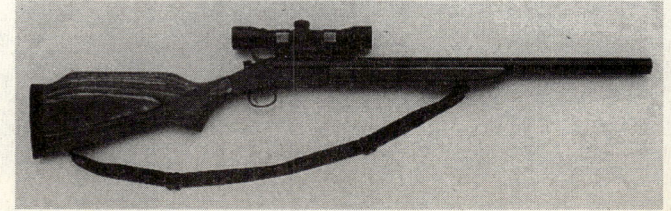

NIB	Exc.	V.G.	Good	Fair	Poor
225	175	—	—	—	—

Ultra Slug Hunter Deluxe-12 Gauge
Same as above but in 12 gauge with 3" chamber.

NIB	Exc.	V.G.	Good	Fair	Poor
225	175	—	—	—	—

Ultra Slug Youth Model
As above but chambered for 20 gauge shell. Weight is approximately 7 lbs.

NIB	Exc.	V.G.	Good	Fair	Poor
130	100	80	60	45	30

Ultra Slug Hunter-Bull Barrel
Same as above but chambered for 20 gauge.

NIB	Exc.	V.G.	Good	Fair	Poor
130	100	80	60	45	30

Ultra Slug Youth Bull Barrel
Same as above but with 22" barrel.

NIB	Exc.	V.G.	Good	Fair	Poor
130	100	80	60	45	30

H&R Handy-Gun (smooth bore)   NFA, CURIO OR RELIC
The smooth bore H&R Handy-Gun is a .410 bore or 28 gauge single-shot pistol with an 8" or 12.25" smooth bore barrel, made from 1921 to 1934 by the Harrington & Richardson Arms Co., Worcester, Massachusetts. It shares internal parts with H&R's Model 1915 (No. 5) shotgun, but the Handy-Gun's shorter receiver is designed for a pistol grip. Its barrels won't fit the No. 5, and these firearms are serial numbered separately. About 54,000 H&R Handy-Guns were manufactured, nearly all for 2.5" shells.

More than 50 H&R Handy-Gun variations exist, but their sales prices tend to be more similar. Inspection of the serial number ranges demonstrates that some variations are considerably rarer than others, and several are ultra-rare. This firearm has not achieved its full potential as a collectible mainly because ATF continues to require its registration under the National Firearms Act (NFA), although it could be administratively removed from the NFA as a collector's item. Removing the Handy-Gun from NFA requirements would probably significantly raise its value and demand among collectors; at present, they are not bought and sold frequently enough to establish reliable values. Prices below are for a typical 12.25" choked-barrel .410 (serial number on receiver and barrel lug should match), though there may be significant local variation in these prices depending upon the geographic area and collector demand.

.410 bore, Model 2, Types II and III

Exc.	V.G.	Good	Fair	Poor
500	375	300	250	175

NOTE: Rare variations command premiums: 8" barrel, 25 to 50 percent; 18" barrel (rarest), 200 to 300 percent; unchoked .410, 20 to 30 percent; 28 gauge or Model 3 (only) with factory-equipped original detachable shoulder stock, 150 percent or more; holster, $75 to $200; serial matching box, $100 to $200 or more (i.e., a box for an 8" barrel 28 gauge could be quite expensive).

Production was halted after the government ruled the H&R Handy-Gun to be a "firearm" in the "any other weapon" category under the NFA, when its retail price was about $16. An H&R Handy-Gun with an 18" smooth bore barrel is subject to the NFA, but exempt if accompanied by an original (detachable) shoulder stock.

Nine variations of the smooth bore H&R Handy-Gun have been identified. These are derived from three models which can each be further categorized according to three types, based on differences in receiver finish and markings, barrel latch levers, barrel types and markings, and trigger guards and grips. H&R termed some late-model .410 and 28 gauge Handy-Guns Models 141 and 128, respectively, but earlier variations were not assigned model numbers. During 1947-57, H&R sold the .410 Handy-Gun through its factory in Drummondville, Quebec, Canada, as the Model 625, but all these guns actually were manufactured in Worcester in or before 1934. This writer has defined the "Models" and "Types" described here arbitrarily. The number of possible combinations of characteristics noted below exceeds 50.

Model 1 has a blued receiver made of malleable (ductile) iron and a spur pistol grip, also termed the "saw-handle" grip, plain trigger guard, and a heavy cylinder bore (unchoked) barrel marked **410-12m/m** or **28 GAUGE**. Model 1, Type I has a 1.71" barrel latch lever secured by a screw, with apparently hand-cut knurling, here termed Type A. The left side of the receiver is stamped **Harrington & Richardson Arms Co/Worcester, Mass. U.S.A.** Model 1, Type II is the same as Model 1, Type I except for a smaller 1.5" barrel latch lever that is not secured by a screw, with cast knurling, here termed Type B. Model 1, Type III is the same as Model 1, Type II except that the H&R manufacturer's identification was moved to the right side of the receiver, and the left side is stamped **H&R. "HANDY-GUN."**

Model 2 has a receiver whose so-called "tiger stripe" finish was produced by hot cyanide dip, which resembles but is not true case hardening. Model 2, Type I is identical to Model 1, Type III, except for the receiver's "tiger stripe" finish. Model 2, Type II is identical to Model 2, Type I except that in .410 bore, the barrel is choked and its markings are **410-12m/mCHOKE**. In .410 bore, Model 2, Type III is identical to Model 2, Type II except for barrel markings **MADE IN U.S.A. 410 GA.CHOKE**, and a new 1.81" barrel latch lever with indented dish checkered knurling, covering the serial number, here termed Type C. In 28 gauge, the Model 2, Type I barrel marking is **28 GAUGE** (2.5" shell), with a Type B barrel latch lever. The 28 gauge Model 2, Type III is designed for 2.75" shells (the measured chamber length is 3.125"), has barrel markings **MADE IN U.S.A. 28 GA.CHOKE**, and a Type C barrel latch lever. Whether Model 2, Type II exists is currently unknown; if so, it would probably have barrel markings of **MADE IN U.S.A. 28 GA. CHOKE**, be designed for 2.75" shells, and have a Type B barrel latch lever. Some Model 2 guns have overlapping characteristics by Type; the exact number involved is unknown, but appears relatively small. Serial number 38335, classified as Model 2, Type II, has a Type B barrel latch lever but Type III barrel markings (**MADE IN U.S.A. 410 GA.CHOKE**).

Model 3 has a flat grip mounted at a 70° angle to the barrel, in contrast with the 80° bore-to-grip angle on Models 1 and 2, and the receiver was shortened about .312", probably by grinding, to accommodate it. Model 3, Type I is identical to Model 2, Type III except for the new flat grip. Model 3, Type II is identical to Model 3, Type I except that a hook was added to the trigger guard for the middle finger to assist in stabilizing recoil. Model 3, Type III is identical to Model 3, Type II except that the number **3** is stamped in the lower right-hand corner of the left side of the barrel lug, designating the barrel was H&R factory chambered for the 3" .410 shotshell of 1933. Only one 28 gauge Model 3 H&R Handy-Gun (an 8" barrel Type I with barrel markings **MADE IN U.S.A. 28 GA. CHOKE** and a 3.125" chamber) has been observed.

H&R manufactured "private-branded" or "trade-branded" H&R Handy-Guns for other distributors. One variation has **ESSEX GUN WORKS** on the left side of the receiver. Another has **HIBBARD** stamped on the left side, and **MODEL W.H.** stamped on the right; a holster with identical stampings was also available. Most have nickel-plated receivers and are serial numbered within the same ranges and have other characteristics identical to regular-production H&R Handy-Guns, by variation. None of those inspected during this research had any markings identifying H&R as the original manufacturer. Anecdotal evidence suggests H&R manufactured a Handy-Gun for an independent telephone company in Colorado; none were located during this research.

Because few factory records have been located, serial number ranges and years of manufacture for the nine variations are not well understood, although there is strong evidence that Handy-Guns were serial numbered from 1 to approximately 54,000, and that .410 and 28 gauge variations were included within this range and not numbered separately. These data are estimated, based on serial numbers of 325 H&R Handy-Guns and very limited original records, including sales records, early NFA paperwork, H&R advertisements, and other records, as shown below.

Variation	Estimated year(s) of manufacture	Observed serial number ranges .410 bore	28 gauge
Model 1			
Type I	1921-22	167 to 4981	5 to 4527
Type II	1922-23	5052 to 6588	5554 to 6274
Type III	1923-24	unknown to 6817	6973 to 7067
Model 2			
Type I	1924-25	8276 to 14660	10539 to 29731
Type II	1925-27	15159 to 38761	none observed
Type III	1927-30	39060 to 47528	44228 to 44247
Model 3			
Type I	1931	47642 to 48218	unknown to 48566
Type II	1932-33	48819 to 51655	none observed
Type III	1933-34	51920 to 53691	none observed

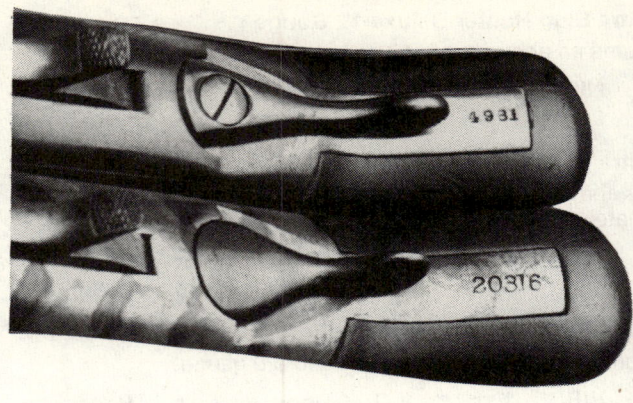

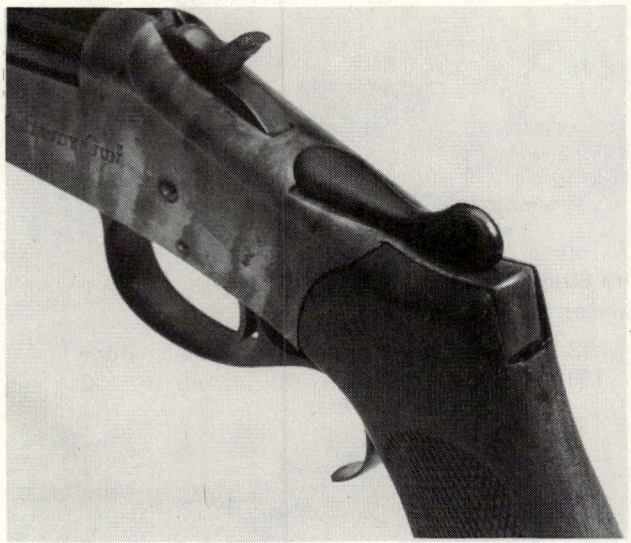

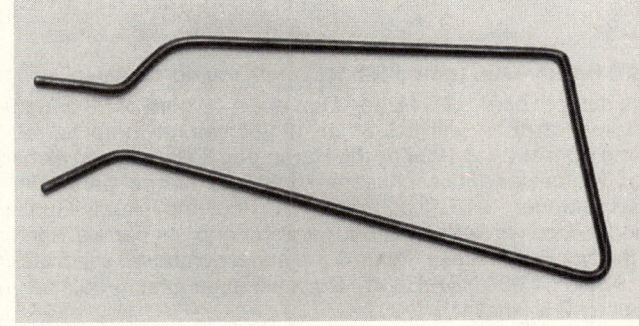

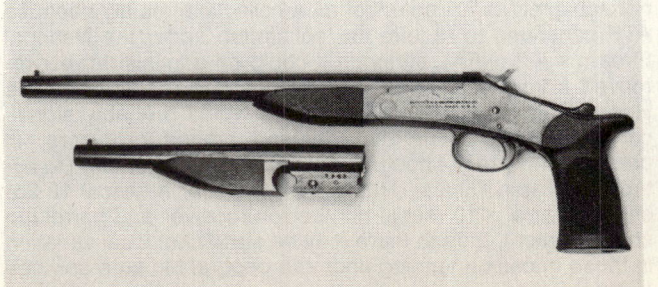

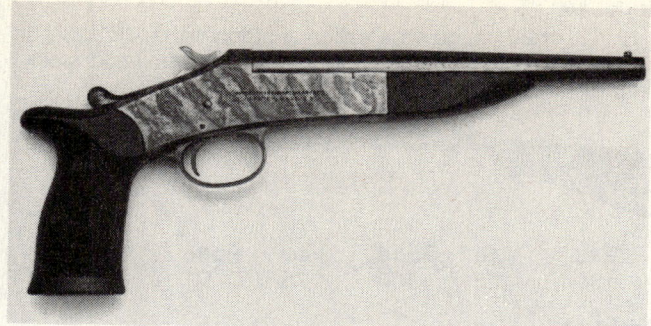

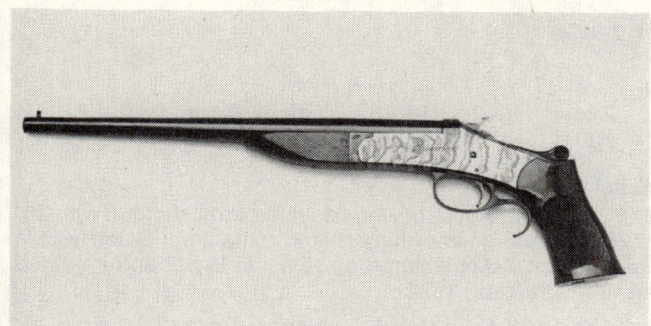

H&R Handy-Gun (rifled barrel) curio or relic

Rifled-barrel H&R Handy-Guns were manufactured about 1930-34, but details of their production are not well documented. In H&R catalogue #19 (copyright 1931) and #20, the .22 and .32-20 are listed as available with blued frame only, 12-1/4" barrel, with an optional ($1.50) detachable shoulder stock. Guns originally factory fitted for the shoulder stock have H.&R. ARMS COMPANY/WORCESTER, MASS. U.S.A./PAT. PENDIN stamped on the bottom of the grip in .125" letters. Whether the .22 W.R.F. version listed on p. 83 of the 1932 *Stoeger's Bible* was manufactured is unknown. All original shoulder-stocked Handy-Guns are extremely rare.

Known specimens of the .32-20 differ from the catalog descriptions. It is unclear whether they were serial numbered in the same run as the smooth bore H&R Handy-Gun, and its production likely predates the .22 rimfire. Observed serial number ranges for each caliber justify estimates of relatively low production totals of fewer than 250 in .22 and fewer than 100 in .32-20. Production of the rifled-barrel H&R Handy-Gun was halted in 1934 when the Bureau of Internal Revenue classified it as a "firearm" under the National Firearms Act (NFA), apparently only because it was available with a shoulder stock. As long as the shoulder stock is removed, any rifled-barrel H&R Handy-Gun is exempt from the NFA.

Because of their extreme rarity, a rifled-barrel .22 rimfire or .32-20 W.C.F. H&R Handy-Gun that was originally factory-equipped with a shoulder stock may be worth from $150 to $400 more than guns which were not, but ATF deems them illegal if they are not currently registered. While the law allows

any qualified person to "make" such a firearm (which includes "putting together" parts not controlled under the NFA) by filing ATF Form 1 (Firearms), paying a $200 tax, and obtaining ATF approval before possessing both the stock and the pistol, ATF has cautioned this writer that filing a Form 1 under these circumstances would be a prosecutable felony offense (for perjury, that is, "making a false statement to the Government.") under the reasoning that such an action would constitute reassembling a prohibited firearm, even though one part (but not the other) may be legally possessed.

The .32-20 H&R Handy-Gun has a case-hardened (hot cyanide dip) receiver and grip identical to the Model 2, Type III smooth bore H&R Handy-Gun, with a 12.25" rifled barrel marked 32-20 W.C.F. The barrel has a front target sight identical to that on the .22 rimfire variation, and a rear Partridge-type nonadjustable sight fitted into a slot milled just behind the barrel markings. Its serial number range and dates of manufacture are uncertain, but could have begun as early as 1929. Whether the .32-20s were serial numbered separately is unknown (the size of the serial numbers is the same as those on the smooth bore H&R Handy-Gun. A serial range from 43851 to 43937 can be estimated on the basis of the serial numbers of 9 guns, but total production has not yet been conclusively documented. A 10th gun, bearing serial number 46854, suggests that this range may be larger.

32-20 W.C.F. serial range mostly from 43851 (?) to 43937 (?)

Exc.	V.G.	Good	Fair	Poor
1200	900	700	600	500

Much hand fitting is evident on the .22 rimfire H&R Handy-Gun, whose rifling was made using the same high-quality machinery which produced the unusually accurate rifling perfected for H&R's .22 caliber Model 195/U.S.R.A. match target pistol. Consequently, there is significant collector and shooter demand for the .22 rimfire H&R Handy-Gun. The .15" serial numbers are smaller than the .20" serial numbers used on smooth bore H&R Handy-Guns, which probably indicates the .22 rimfire variation has its own serial number range. Based on the serial numbers of 23 guns, a serial range from approximately 1 to 223 can be established. All known commercial .22 rimfire models have blued frames with markings and grips otherwise identical to the Model 3 smooth bore H&R Handy-Gun, a 12.25" tapered barrel marked .22 RIMFIRE, and a fixed peep or flip arpeture/peep sight built into the barrel. Some nonstandard or experimental .22 caliber H&R Handy-Guns exist, but expert opinion must be sought to authenticate their originality. Some .410 bore H&R Handy-Guns have been altered to .22 rimfire, and their values approximate those for a standard 12.25" barrel .410.

.22 rimfire serial range from 1 (?) to 223 (?)

Exc.	V.G.	Good	Fair	Poor
900	700	600	500	400

Rifled-barrel H&R Handy-Guns in calibers other than .22 rimfire and .32-20 Winchester have been reported, but are controversial because (1) none have been made available for inspection, and (2) their production is not confirmed by the H&R factory. One collector has reported (but has not himself observed) that H&R Handy-Guns were manufactured in .25-20 (25 W.C.F.), 22 Hornet, and .30-30 Winchester (30 W.C.F.). The owner of a .30 caliber carbine H&R Handy-Gun, who lives in Canada, advised this writer that the gun was expertly altered by a mechanical engineer.

Topper

A single shot, break-open shotgun chambered for various gauges with various barrel lengths, chokes. Blued, with a hardwood stock. Introduced in 1946.

Exc.	V.G.	Good	Fair	Poor
110	95	75	60	40

Model 088

An external hammer single shot, break-open shotgun chambered for all gauges with various barrel lengths, chokes and an automatic ejector. Blued, with a case colored frame and hardwood stock.

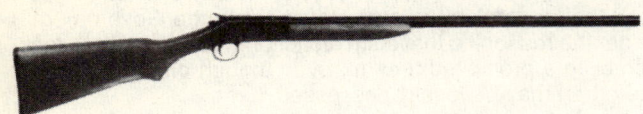

Exc.	V.G.	Good	Fair	Poor
80	65	50	40	30

Model 099

As above, but matte, electroless, nickel-plated.

Exc.	V.G.	Good	Fair	Poor
110	95	75	60	40

Model 162

A 12 or 20 gauge boxlock single shotgun with a 24" barrel with rifle sights.

Exc.	V.G.	Good	Fair	Poor
125	100	80	65	45

Model 176

A 10-gauge, 3.5" Magnum caliber boxlock single-barrel shotgun with a heavyweight 36" barrel and a full choke. Manufactured between 1977 and 1985.

Exc.	V.G.	Good	Fair	Poor
125	100	80	65	45

Model 400

A 12, 16, or 20 gauge slide action shotgun with a 28" full-choke barrel. Blued, with a hardwood stock. Manufactured between 1955 and 1967.

Exc.	V.G.	Good	Fair	Poor
150	125	100	75	50

Model 401

As above, with a variable choke device. Manufactured between 1956 and 1963.

Exc.	V.G.	Good	Fair	Poor
175	150	125	90	65

Model 402

As above, in a .410 bore. Manufactured between 1959 and 1967.

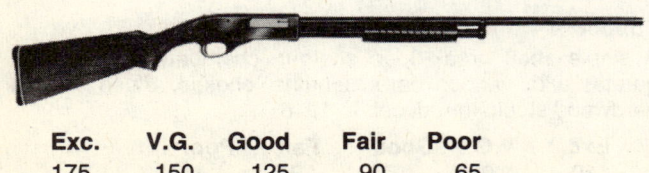

Exc.	V.G.	Good	Fair	Poor
175	150	125	90	65

Model 440

A 12, 16, or 20 gauge slide action shotgun with a 26", 28", or 30" barrel in various chokes. Blued, with a hardwood stock. Manufactured between 1968 and 1973.

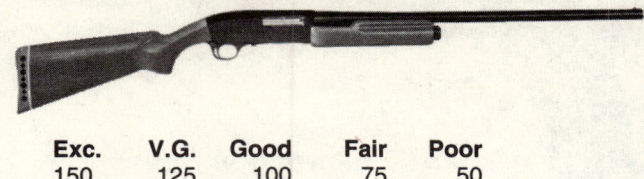

Exc.	V.G.	Good	Fair	Poor
150	125	100	75	50

Model 442

As above with a ventilated rib barrel and a checkered stock. Manufactured between 1969 and 1973.

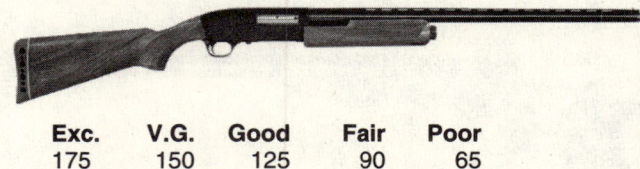

Exc.	V.G.	Good	Fair	Poor
175	150	125	90	65

Model 403

A .410 bore semiautomatic shotgun with a 26", full choke barrel. Blued, with a hardwood stock. Manufactured in 1964.

Exc.	V.G.	Good	Fair	Poor
200	175	150	100	75

Model 404

A 12, 20, or .410 bore boxlock double-barrel shotgun with 26" or 28" barrels, double triggers and extractors. Blued with a walnut stock. Manufactured by Rossi in Brazil and imported between 1969 and 1972.

Exc.	V.G.	Good	Fair	Poor
175	150	125	90	65

Model 1212

A 12 gauge Over/Under boxlock shotgun with 28" ventilated rib barrels. Blued with a walnut stock. Also available with 30" barrels having 3" chambers. Manufactured by Landbar Arms of Spain and imported after 1976.

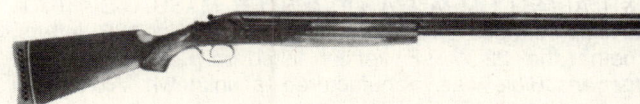

Exc.	V.G.	Good	Fair	Poor
300	250	200	150	100

Long Tom Classic

Introduced in 1996 this limited edition single barrel shotgun features a case hardened frame with 32" full choked barrel. Stock is hand checkered black walnut with crescent buttplate. Chambered for 12 gauge. Weight is about 7.5 lbs. About 1,000 of these shotguns will be built each year.

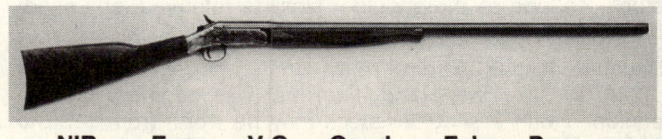

NIB	Exc.	V.G.	Good	Fair	Poor
300	250	—	—	—	—

RIFLES

Model 058

A 20 gauge, .22 Hornet, .30-30, .357 Magnum, or .44 Magnum caliber combination Over/Under rifle/shotgun. Blued, with a hardwood stock.

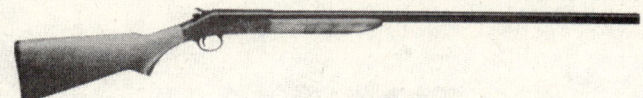

Exc.	V.G.	Good	Fair	Poor
125	100	80	65	40

Model 258

As above, but with a matte, electroless nickel-plate finish.

Exc.	V.G.	Good	Fair	Poor
175	150	125	90	65

Reising Model 60

A .45 ACP caliber semiautomatic rifle with an 18.25" barrel and a 12- or 20-round detachable magazine. Blued, with a walnut stock. It operates on a retarded blowback system and was developed to be used as a police weapon. Manufactured between 1944 and 1946.

Courtesy Richard M. Kumor, Sr.

Exc.	V.G.	Good	Fair	Poor
1200	1000	500	250	100

Model 65 Military

A .22 l.r. caliber semiautomatic rifle with a 23" barrel and Redfield peep sights. Blued, with a walnut stock. Manufactured between 1944 and 1956.

NOTE: Add 100% if USMC marked.

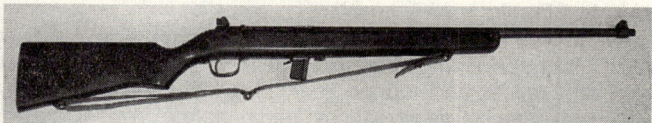

Courtesy Richard M. Kumor, Sr.

Exc.	V.G.	Good	Fair	Poor
350	300	200	125	90

Model 150

A .22 l.r. caliber semiautomatic rifle with a 20" barrel and a 5-shot magazine. Blued, with a walnut stock. Manufactured between 1949 and 1953.

Exc.	V.G.	Good	Fair	Poor
100	80	60	45	30

Model 155

This is a single shot, break-open rifle chambered for the .44 Magnum or the .45-70 cartridge. It has a 20" barrel with fixed sights. The finish is blued, with a walnut stock. It was introduced in 1972.

Exc.	V.G.	Good	Fair	Poor
125	100	80	60	40

Model 157

As above in .22 Magnum, .22 Hornet, and the .30-30 caliber.

Exc.	V.G.	Good	Fair	Poor
125	100	80	60	40

Model 158

A .357 or .44 Magnum single shot side lever rifle with a 22" barrel. Blued, case-hardened with a walnut stock. Available with an interchangeable 26" 20 gauge barrel. Manufactured prior to 1986.

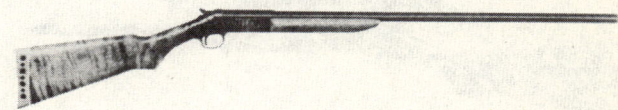

Exc.	V.G.	Good	Fair	Poor
100	80	60	45	30

Model 171

A reproduction of the Model 1873 Trapdoor Springfield Carbine with a 22" barrel. Blued, with a case colored receiver and a walnut stock.

Exc.	V.G.	Good	Fair	Poor
300	250	200	150	100

Model 171-DL

As above, but more finely finished.

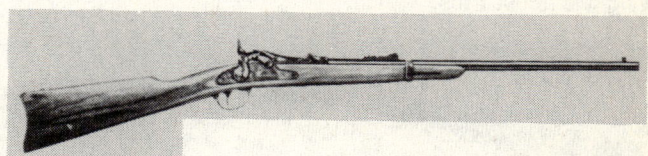

Exc.	V.G.	Good	Fair	Poor
350	300	250	200	125

Model 300 Ultra

A .22-250 up to the .300 Winchester Magnum caliber, bolt action rifle with a 22" or 24" barrel and without sights. High polished blue, and checkered walnut stock. Manufactured between 1965 and 1978.

Exc.	V.G.	Good	Fair	Poor
450	400	350	275	175

Model 301 Carbine

As above with an 18" barrel and a full-length, Mannlicher-style stock.

Exc.	V.G.	Good	Fair	Poor
450	400	350	275	175

Model 317 Ultra Wildcat

A .17 Rem., .17-223, .222 Rem., and the .223 Rem. caliber short Sako bolt action rifle with a 20" barrel furnished without sights. Blued, with a checkered walnut stock. Manufactured between 1968 and 1976.

Exc.	V.G.	Good	Fair	Poor
450	400	350	275	175

Ultra Varmint Rifle

This single shot rifle is chambered for the .223 Rem. or the .22-250 cartridge. It is fitted with a 22" heavy barrel. The stock is hand checkered curly maple with Monte Carlo cheek piece. Comes with no sights but scopes mounts are included. Weighs about 7.5 lbs.

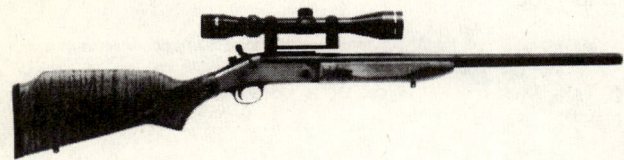

NIB	Exc.	V.G.	Good	Fair	Poor
175	150	100	80	60	40

Model 317P

As above, but more finely finished. Manufactured between 1968 and 1976.

Exc.	V.G.	Good	Fair	Poor
550	500	450	375	250

Ultra Rifle-Hunting

Single shot rifle chambered for .25-06, .308 Win., and .357 Rem. Max. The .25-06 has a 26" barrel, the other two are fitted with 22" barrels. A Cinnamon laminated stock is standard. Weight is about 7 lbs.

NIB	Exc.	V.G.	Good	Fair	Poor
225	175	125	100	75	50

Ultra Rifle-Varmint

Same as above but chambered for .223 Rem. with 22" barrel. Laminated stock with checkered pistol grip.

NIB	Exc.	V.G.	Good	Fair	Poor
225	175	125	100	75	50

Ultra Rifle-Comp

Introduced in 1997 this single shot rifle features an integral muzzle brake on the end of the barrel. Available in .270 Win. and .30-06 calibers with 24" barrels. Camo laminated stock.

V.G.	Good	Fair	Poor
275	225	—	—

Ultra Rifle Rocky Mountain Elk Foundation Commemorative

A limited edition single rifle chambered for the .35 Whelen cartridge. Selected laminated stock with Monte Carlo. Barrel length is 26".

NIB	Exc.	V.G.	Good	Fair	Poor
450	400	—	—	—	—

Ultra Rifle Whitetails Unlimited 1997 Commemorative Edition

Introduced in 1997 and chambered for the .45-70 Gov't cartridge this model features a hand chaeckered black walnut stock. Special laser engraving on the action and pewter finished medallion inletted into stock. Barrel length is 22".

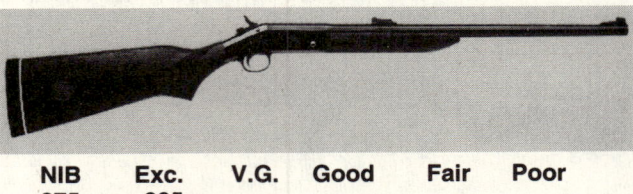

NIB	Exc.	V.G.	Good	Fair	Poor
275	225	—	—	—	—

Wesson & Harrington Brand 125th Anniversary Rifle

Introduced in 1996 this rifle commemorates the 125th anniversary of the partnership. This special rifle is chambered for the .45-70 Government cartridge. The receiver is hand engraved. The barrel length is 32". The stock is American black walnut with crescent steel butt.

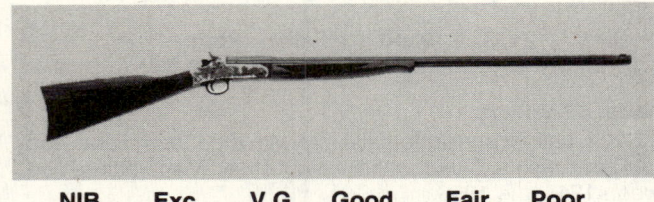

NIB	Exc.	V.G.	Good	Fair	Poor
500	400	—	—	—	—

Buffalo Classic

This rifle was first produced in 1995. It is chambered for the .45-70 cartridge. Barrel length is 32" with no sights but dovetail front and drilled and tapped rear. Hand checkered walnut stock with case colored crescent steel buttplate. Weight is approximately 8 lbs. Since its introduction in 1995 there have been about 2,000 guns produced. The factory anticipates about 1,000 of these rifles being built each year.

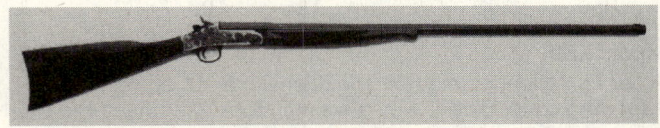

NIB	Exc.	V.G.	Good	Fair	Poor
300	250	—	—	—	—

Model 333

The Model 300 in 7mm Mag. caliber. Manufactured in 1974.

Exc.	V.G.	Good	Fair	Poor
250	200	175	125	100

Model 340

A .243 to .308 Winchester caliber bolt-action rifle with a 22" barrel and a 5-shot magazine. Blued, with a checkered walnut stock.

Exc.	V.G.	Good	Fair	Poor
400	350	300	225	150

Model 360 Ultra Automatic

A .243 Win. and the .308 Win. caliber semiautomatic rifle with a 22" barrel, adjustable sights and a 3-shot detachable magazine. Blued, with a checkered walnut stock. Manufactured between 1965 and 1978.

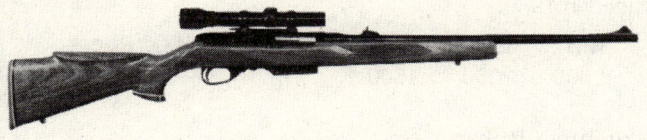

Exc.	V.G.	Good	Fair	Poor
350	300	250	175	100

Model 451 Medalist

A .22 l.r. caliber bolt-action rifle with a 26" barrel, open sights and a 5-shot detachable magazine. Blued, with a walnut stock. Manufactured between 1948 and 1961.

Exc.	V.G.	Good	Fair	Poor
175	150	125	100	75

Model 700

A .22 rimfire Magnum caliber, semiautomatic rifle with a 22" barrel, adjustable sights and a 5-round, detachable magazine. Blued, with a checkered walnut stock. Manufactured between 1977 and 1985.

Exc.	V.G.	Good	Fair	Poor
225	200	150	125	85

Model 700 DL

As above, with a checkered walnut stock and with a 4X scope. Manufactured until 1985.

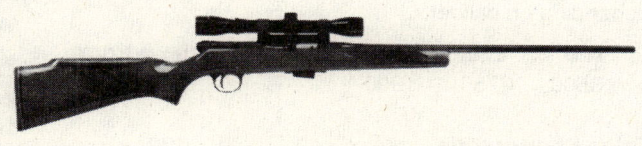

Exc.	V.G.	Good	Fair	Poor
300	250	200	150	100

Model 750

A .22 l.r. bolt-action single shot rifle with a 22" barrel with sights and a short stock. Blued, and the stock is hardwood.

Exc.	V.G.	Good	Fair	Poor
100	80	60	45	25

Model 865

A .22 l.r. caliber bolt-action rifle with a 22" barrel, open sights and a 5-shot magazine. Blued, with a hardwood stock.

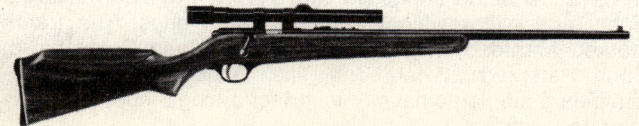

Exc.	V.G.	Good	Fair	Poor
100	80	60	45	25

Model 5200

A .22 l.r. caliber bolt-action, single shot rifle with a 28" heavy barrel without sights, and an adjustable trigger. Blued, with a target-type walnut stock.

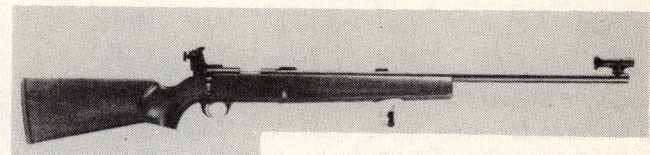

Exc.	V.G.	Good	Fair	Poor
400	350	300	225	125

Model 5200 Sporter

A .22 l.r. caliber bolt-action rifle with a 24" barrel, adjustable sights and a 5-shot magazine. Blued with a walnut stock. Not manufactured after 1983.

Exc.	V.G.	Good	Fair	Poor
400	350	300	225	125

100th Anniversary Officer's Model

A commemorative replica of the Officer's Model 1873 Trapdoor Springfield Rifle, with a 26" barrel. Engraved, and an anniversary plaque mounted on the stock. Blued, with a case-colored receiver and a pewter forend tip. There were 10,000 manufactured in 1971. As with all commemoratives, this model is desirable only when NIB with all supplied material.

NIB	Exc.	V.G.	Good	Fair	Poor
450	350	300	275	200	125

Custer Memorial Issue

A limited production issue commemorating George Armstrong Custer's Battle of the Little Bighorn. Heavily engraved and gold inlaid with a high-grade checkered walnut stock. Furnished in a mahogany display case that included two books dealing with the subject. There were two versions produced—an Officer's Model, of which 25 were issued commemorating the 25 officers that fell with Custer, and another version commemorating the 243 enlisted men who lost their lives at the Little Bighorn. As with all commemoratives, to be collectible they must be NIB with all furnished material.

Officer's Model-25 Manufactured

NIB	Exc.	V.G.	Good	Fair	Poor
2700	2000	1500	1000	600	400

Enlisted Men's Model-243 Manufactured

NIB	Exc.	V.G.	Good	Fair	Poor
1500	1000	750	500	350	250

Model 174

A plain copy of the Springfield Model 1873 Carbine in .45-70 caliber with a 22" barrel. Manufactured in 1972.

Exc.	V.G.	Good	Fair	Poor
400	350	300	250	175

Model 178

A copy of the Springfield Model 1873 rifle with a 32" barrel. Manufactured from 1973 to 1984.

Exc.	V.G.	Good	Fair	Poor
325	300	250	200	125

HARRIS GUNWORKS
Pheonix, Arizona

National Match Rifle

Introduced in 1989 this model features a bolt action rifle chambered for the 7mm-08 or .308 with 5-round magazine. It is fitted with a 24" stainless steel match grade barrel with Canjar trigger. The stock is fiberglass with adjustable butt plate. Weight is about 11 lbs.

NIB	Exc.	V.G.	Good	Fair	Poor
2600	2000	1500	750	500	250

Model 86 Sniper Rifle

Chambered for .308, .30-06, .300 Win. Mag. with 24" heavy match grade barrel. The stock is a special design McHale fiberglass with textured grip and forearm. Fitted with a recoil pad. Supplied with a bipod. Weight is about 11.25 lbs.

NIB	Exc.	V.G.	Good	Fair	Poor
2700	2100	1600	—	—	—

NOTE: Add $100 for takedown model.

Model 87 Series

These are single shot rifles chambered for 50 BMG. Fitted with a 29" barrel with muzzlebrake. Fiberglass stock. Introduced in 1987. Weight is approximately 21.5 lbs.

NIB	Exc.	V.G.	Good	Fair	Poor
3700	2900	2000	—	—	—

NOTE: For Model 87R 5 shot repeater add $400. For Model 87 5 shot repeater add $300. For Model 92 Bullpup add $300. For Model 93SN 10-shot repeater add $600

Model 89 Sniper Rifle

This bolt action rifle is chambered for .308 cartridge. Fitted with a 28" barrel. Supplied with a bipod. Stock is fiberglass with adjustable length of pull and fitted with a recoil pad. Weight is about 15.25 lbs.

NIB	Exc.	V.G.	Good	Fair	Poor
2700	2100	1600	—	—	—

Long Range Rifle

Chambered for a variety of cartridges such as the .300 Win. Mag., 7mm Rem. Mag., .300 Phoenix, .338 Lapua. This is a single shot rifle fitted with a 26" match grade stainless steel barrel. Fiberglass stock with adjustable butt plate and cheekpiece. Weight is about 14 lbs.

NIB	Exc.	V.G.	Good	Fair	Poor
2600	2000	1500	—	—	—

Antietam Sharps Rifle

This is a replica of the Sharps Model 1874 sidehammer introduced in 1994. Chambered for the .40-65 or the .45-70. Choice of 30" or 32" octagon or round barrel. Stock is fancy walnut with either straight, pistol grip, or Creedmoor with Schnabel forearm. Many optional sights offered. Weight is about 11.25 lbs.

NIB	Exc.	V.G.	Good	Fair	Poor
2000	1500	1000	—	—	—

Signature Classic Sporter

This is a left or right handed bolt action model introduced in 1987 with a choice of calibers from .22-250 to .375 H&H. Barrel lengths are 22", 24", or 26" depending on caliber. Choice of fiberglass stocks in green, beige, brown, or black. A wood stock is optional. Weight is about 7 lbs. for short action calibers.

NIB	Exc.	V.G.	Good	Fair	Poor
2600	2000	1500	—	—	—

Signature Classic Stainless Sporter

Same as above but with barrel and action made from stainless steel. A .416 Rem. Mag is available in this variation also.

NIB	Exc.	V.G.	Good	Fair	Poor
2600	2000	1500	—	—	—

Signiture Super Varminter

Similar to the Classic Sporter except fitted with a heavy contured barrel, adjustable trigger, and special hand-bedded fiberglass stock. Chambered for .223, .22-250, .220 Swift, .243, 6mm Rem., .25-06, 7mm-08, 7mm BR, .308, .350 Rem. Introduced in 1989.

NIB	Exc.	V.G.	Good	Fair	Poor
2600	2000	1500	—	—	—

Signiture Alaskan

Similar to the Classic Sporter except fitted with a match grade barrel with single leaf rear sight. Nickel finish. Walnut Monte Carlo stock with cheekpiece and palm swell grip. Chambered for .270 to .375 H&H. Introduced in 1989.

NIB	Exc.	V.G.	Good	Fair	Poor
3300	2600	1750	—	—	—

Signature Titanium Mountain Rifle

Similar to the Classic Sporter except action is made of titanium alloy and barrel of chrome molly-steel. Stock is graphite reinforced fiberglass. Chambered for .270 to .300 Win. Mag. Weight is about 5.5 lbs. Introduced in 1989.

NIB	Exc.	V.G.	Good	Fair	Poor
3200	2600	1750	—	—	—

Talon Safari Rifle

This bolt action rifle is chambered for 16 different calibers from .300 Win. Mag. to .460 Whthy. Mag. The finish is a matte black with fiberglass Safari stock. Weight is between 9 and 10 lbs. depending on caliber.

NIB	Exc.	V.G.	Good	Fair	Poor
3500	2750	1900	—	—	—

Talon Sporter Rifle

This bolt action rifle, introduced in 1991, uses a pre-64 Model 70 type action with cone breech. Barrel and action are stainless steel. Chambered for a wide variety of calibers from .22-250 to .416 Rem. Mag. Choice of walnut or fiberglass stock. Most barrel lengths are 24". Weight is about 7.5 lbs. depending on caliber.

NIB	Exc.	V.G.	Good	Fair	Poor
2600	2000	1500	—	—	—

HARTFORD ARMS & EQUIPMENT CO.
Hartford, Connecticut

Established in 1925, this firm was purchased by the High Standard Company in 1932.

Single Shot Target

A .22 caliber single shot pistol with a 6.75" round barrel, target sights and either walnut or composition grips. The frame marked "Manfd. by the Hartford Arms and Equip. Co. Hartford, Conn. Patented .22 cal. Long Rifle." Although this pistol resembles a semiautomatic, it is in fact a single shot manually operated pistol.

Exc.	V.G.	Good	Fair	Poor
750	650	500	350	275

Repeating Pistol

Identical to the above, but a manually operated repeating pistol with a 10-shot magazine.

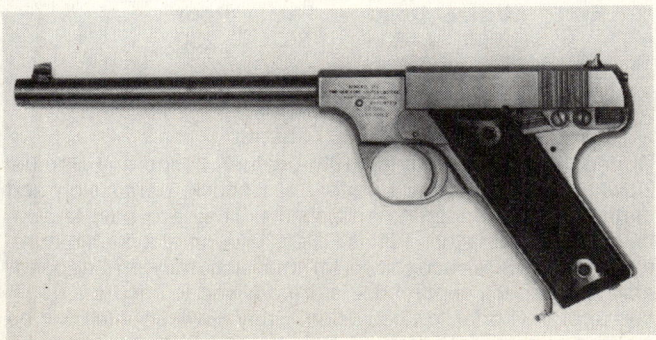

Exc.	V.G.	Good	Fair	Poor
750	650	500	350	275

Model 1925

Semiautomatic pistol chambered for .22 caliber with 6-3/4" barrel, checkered rubber grip. Approximately 5,000 were produced from 1925 to 1932.

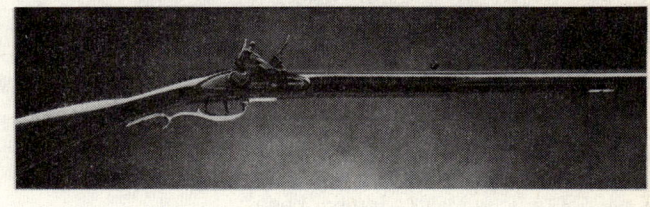

Exc.	V.G.	Good	Fair	Poor
700	600	450	375	300

HATFIELD RIFLE COMPANY
St. Joseph, Missouri

Squirrel Rifle

A flintlock or percussion rifle in .32 to .50 caliber with a 39" barrel, double set triggers, adjustable sights, brass mounts and maple stocks. Available in a wide variety of forms, which affect the values. The values listed below are for plain, standard models.

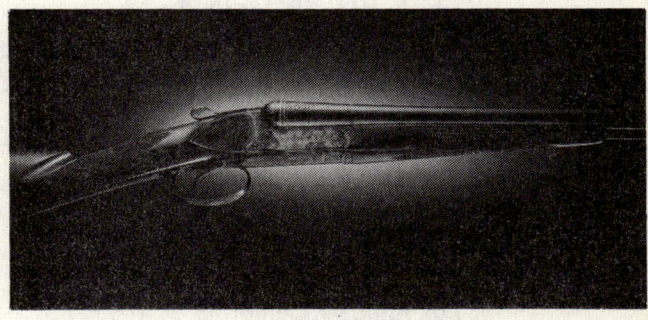

NIB	Exc.	V.G.	Good	Fair	Poor
475	400	350	300	225	150

SHOTGUNS

Uplander Grade I

A 20 gauge boxlock double-barrel shotgun with a 26" improved cylinder and modified barrel with a matte raised rib, single selective trigger and automatic ejectors. Casehardened, blued with a deluxe-grade, hand-checkered walnut stock. Introduced in 1987.

NIB	Exc.	V.G.	Good	Fair	Poor
1150	1050	750	600	475	400

Uplander Pigeon Grade II

As above, with scroll engraving with a fitted leather case.

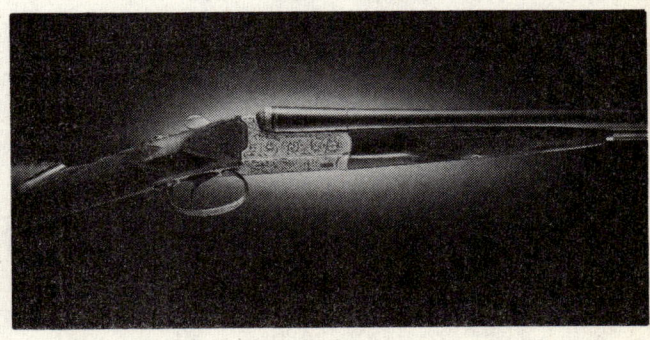

NIB	Exc.	V.G.	Good	Fair	Poor
2000	1750	1275	900	650	500

Uplander Super Pigeon Grade III

As above, with deep-relief cut engraving and a leather case.

NIB	Exc.	V.G.	Good	Fair	Poor
2500	2200	1700	1400	1000	700

Uplander Golden Quail Grade IV

A gold inlaid version of the above.

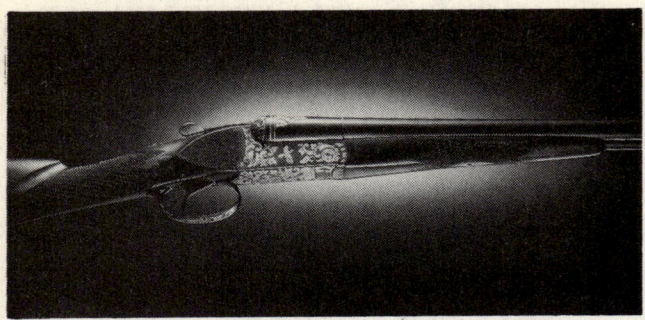

NIB	Exc.	V.G.	Good	Fair	Poor
4000	3500	2750	2000	1700	1300

Uplander Woodcock Grade V

As above, with seven 24 kt. gold inlays and best quality engraving. Furnished with a leather case.

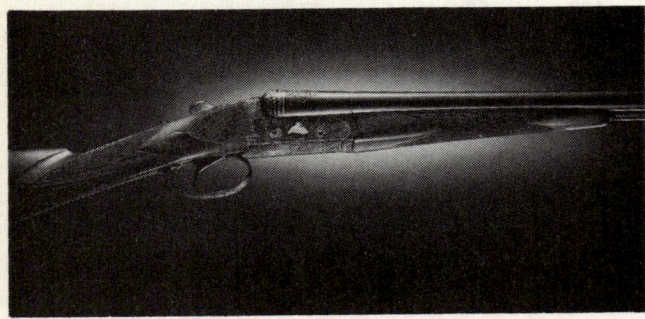

NIB	Exc.	V.G.	Good	Fair	Poor
5600	5000	4250	3500	2750	2000

HAVILAND & GUNN
Ilion, New York

Gallery Pistol

A .17 caliber rimfire single shot pistol with a 5" barrel. The barrel and frame made of one piece of iron and nickel plated. There are no markings on these pistols whatsoever. Believed to have been made during the 1870s.

Exc.	V.G.	Good	Fair	Poor
400	350	300	225	125

HAWES
Los Angeles, California
An importer of handguns primarily made in Europe

Courier

A .25 caliber, blowback, semiautomatic pocket pistol manufactured by Galesi.

Exc.	V.G.	Good	Fair	Poor
125	100	75	50	25

Diplomat

A .380 ACP pistol with an external hammer.

Exc.	V.G.	Good	Fair	Poor
150	125	100	75	50

Trophy

A J.P. Sauer & Sohn, manufactured revolver with a swing-out cylinder and a 6" barrel. Chambered for the .22 l.r. and the .38 Special. Has adjustable sights.

Exc.	V.G.	Good	Fair	Poor
250	200	175	125	90

Medalion

As above, with a 3", 4", or 6" barrel and fixed sights.

Exc.	V.G.	Good	Fair	Poor
200	175	125	100	75

J. P. Sauer also made a Western-styled series for Hawes based in appearance on the Colt Single Action Army.

Silver City Marshal

A .22 l.r. or .22 rimfire Magnum caliber single action revolver with a 5.5" barrel, 6-shot cylinder, and fixed sights.

Exc.	V.G.	Good	Fair	Poor
125	100	75	50	25

Western Marshal

A .357 Magnum, .44 Magnum, .45 Colt, .45 ACP, .44-40, 9mm, .22 l.r., and .22 rimfire Magnum single action revolver with fixed sights. Blued.

Exc.	V.G.	Good	Fair	Poor
175	150	125	100	75

Chief Marshal

A .357 Magnum, .44 Magnum, and the .45 Colt caliber revolver with a 6.5" barrel, and 6-shot cylinder and adjustable sights. Blued.

Exc.	V.G.	Good	Fair	Poor
175	150	125	100	75

Texas Marshal

As above, but nickel plated.

Exc.	V.G.	Good	Fair	Poor
185	160	135	100	75

Montana Marshal

The Western Marshal with a brass backstrap and triggerguard.

Exc.	V.G.	Good	Fair	Poor
175	150	125	100	75

Deputy Marshal

A .22 l.r. and .22 rimfire Magnum single action revolver with a 5.5" barrel, and 6-shot cylinder.

Exc.	V.G.	Good	Fair	Poor
125	100	75	50	25

Federal Marshal

A 6-shot single action revolver in .357 Magnum, .44 Magnum, and the .45 Colt caliber.

Exc.	V.G.	Good	Fair	Poor
175	150	125	100	75

HAWES & WAGGONER
Philadelphia, Pennsylvania

Pocket Pistol

A .41 caliber single shot percussion pistol with a 3" barrel, German silver mountings, and a walnut stock. Manufactured in the 1850s.

Exc.	V.G.	Good	Fair	Poor
—	1250	500	350	250

HAWKEN
St. Louis, Missouri

During the early part of the 19th century, Jacob and Samuel Hawken manufactured a variety of flintlock, percussion and cartridge rifles, shotguns and pistols. They are best known, however, for half stock Plains Rifles. Though of a plain nature, these arms were recognized for their accuracy and dependability. Prospective purchasers are advised to secure a qualified appraisal prior to acquisition. Early Hawken rifles will be worth a substantial premium over later examples. Some examples in very good condition may be worth as much as $25,000. Proceed with caution.

HECKLER & KOCH
Oberndorf/Neckar, Germany

At the end of WWII, the French dismantled the Mauser factory as part of their reparations; and the buildings remained idle until 1949, when firearms production was again allowed in Germany. Heckler & Koch was formed as a machine tool enterprise and occupied the vacant Mauser plant. In the early 1950s Edmund Heckler and Theodor Koch began to produce the G3 automatic rifle based on the Spanish CETME design and progressed to machine guns and submachine guns and eventually to the production of commercial civilian rifles and pistols. In 1990 the company got into financial difficulties because of a failed contract bid. In December of 1990 the French state consortium GIAT announced the purchase of Heckler and Koch, but a little more than a year later the contract was cancelled. Later in 1991 the company was purchased by Royal Ordnance of Britain.

Model 91

This rifle is recoil-operated, with a delayed-roller lock bolt. It is chambered for the .308 Winchester cartridge and has a 17.7" barrel with military style aperture sights. It is furnished with a 20-round detachable magazine and is finished in matte black with a black plastic stock. Some areas of the country have made its ownership illegal.

NIB	Exc.	V.G.	Good	Fair	Poor
2500	2000	1650	1100	1000	800

Model 91 A3

This model is simply the Model 91 with a retractable metal stock.

NIB	Exc.	V.G.	Good	Fair	Poor
2650	2150	1750	1100	1000	800

Model 93

This model is similar to the Model 91 except that it is chambered for the .223 cartridge and has a 16.4" barrel. The magazine holds 25 rounds, and the specification are the same as for the Model 91.

NIB	Exc.	V.G.	Good	Fair	Poor
2500	2000	1650	1100	1000	800

Model 93 A3

This is the Model 93 with the retractable metal stock.

NIB	Exc.	V.G.	Good	Fair	Poor
2650	2150	1750	1100	1000	800

Model 94

This is a carbine version chambered for the 9mm Parabellum cartridge, with a 16.5" barrel. It is a smaller-scaled weapon that has a 15-shot magazine.

NIB	Exc.	V.G.	Good	Fair	Poor
3200	2800	2500	2000	1500	1000

Model 94 A3

This model is a variation of the Model 94 with the addition of a retractable metal stock.

NIB	Exc.	V.G.	Good	Fair	Poor
3350	2950	2650	2100	1500	1000

Model 270

This model is chambered for the .22 l.r. cartridge. It is a sporting-styled rifle with a 16.5" barrel. It is furnished with either a 5- or a 20-round magazine and is blued, with a checkered walnut stock. This rifle was discontinued in 1985.

NIB	Exc.	V.G.	Good	Fair	Poor
600	500	450	350	250	150

Model 300

This model is similar to the Model 270 except that it is chambered for the .22 rimfire Magnum cartridge. It was not imported after 1988.

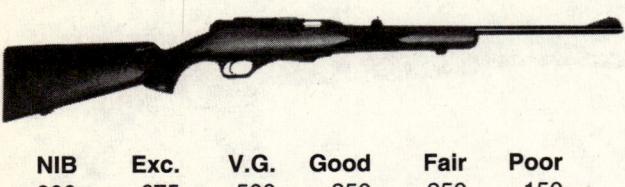

NIB	Exc.	V.G.	Good	Fair	Poor
800	675	500	350	250	150

Model 630

This model is chambered for the .223 and features the same roller-delayed semiautomatic action as found on the paramilitary-type weapons. This is a sporting style rifle that has a polished blue finish and a checkered walnut stock. The barrel is 17.7" long, and the magazines offered hold either 4 or 10 rounds. Importation was discontinued in 1986.

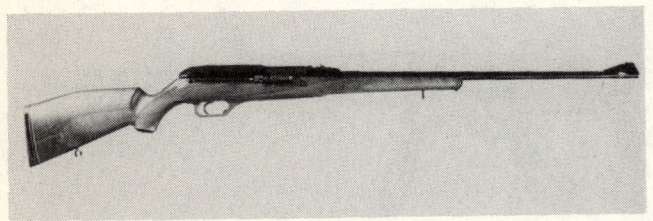

NIB	Exc.	V.G.	Good	Fair	Poor
1100	850	600	450	350	300

Model 770

This model is similar to the Model 630 except that it is chambered for the .308 Winchester cartridge and has 19.7" barrel. It was not imported after 1986.

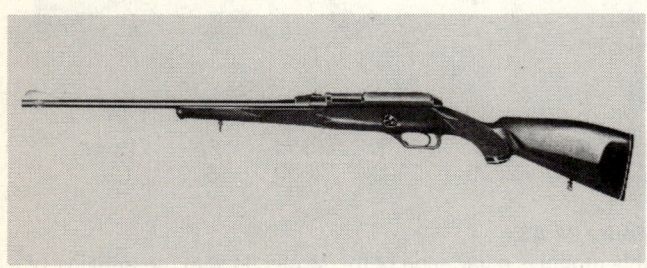

NIB	Exc.	V.G.	Good	Fair	Poor
1100	950	600	450	350	300

Model 940

This model is essentially the same as the Model 770 except that it is chambered for the .30-06 cartridge. It has a 21" barrel and was not imported after 1986.

NIB	Exc.	V.G.	Good	Fair	Poor
1450	1100	800	600	400	300

Model SL6

This is Heckler & Koch's current sporting rifle chambered for the .223 cartridge. It has a 17.7" barrel and features the same basic action as the military versions. It has a matte black finish and a walnut stock with a vented walnut hand guard. The magazine holds 4 rounds.

NIB	Exc.	V.G.	Good	Fair	Poor
1100	850	600	450	350	300

Model SL7

This model is similar to the SL6 except that it is chambered for the .308 Winchester cartridge and has a 3-round magazine.

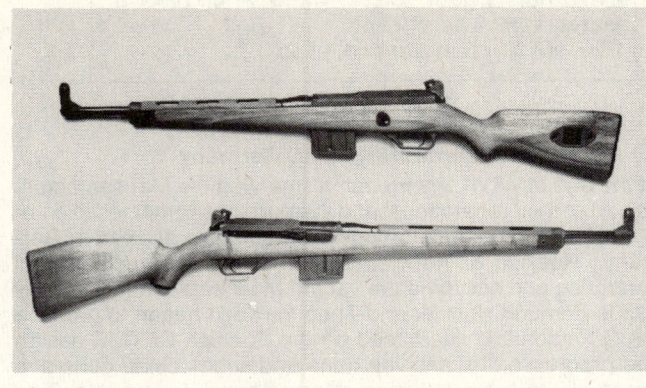

NIB	Exc.	V.G.	Good	Fair	Poor
1100	850	600	450	350	300

Model SR9

This model was introduced into the U.S. market after the federal government prohibited the importation of H&K's other semiautomatic rifles. The SR9 is similar to the HK91 but has been certified by the BATF as a sporting rifle. This model features a special thumb hole stock made of Kevlar reinforced fiberglass. The action is a delayed-roller locked bolt semi-automatic design chambered for the .308 Winchester cartridge. The barrel is 19.7" in length and features adjustable rear sight with hooded front sight. The rifle weighs 10.9 lbs.

NIB	Exc.	V.G.	Good	Fair	Poor
2000	1850	1450	1100	800	700

Model SR9 (T) Target

Similar to the standard model SR9 but with the addition of a special MSG90 adjustable butt stock, PSG 1 trigger group, and a PSG 1 contoured hand grip. Rifle weighs 10.6 lbs.

NIB	Exc.	V.G.	Good	Fair	Poor
3000	2750	2200	1500	950	800

Model SR9 (TC) Target Competition

Similar to the Model SR9 (T) but with the addition of the PSG 1 adjustable butt stock. Rifle weighs 10.9 lbs.

NIB	Exc.	V.G.	Good	Fair	Poor
3200	2800	2300	1750	1000	900

PSG-1

This rifle is a high precision sniping rifle that features the delayed-roller semiautomatic action. It is chambered for the .308

Winchester cartridge and has a 5-shot magazine. Barrel length is 25.6". It is furnished with a complete array of accessories including a 6x42-power illuminated Hensoldt scope. Rifle weighs 17.8 lbs.

NIB	Exc.	V.G.	Good	Fair	Poor
10500	8500	6500	6000	5000	3500

BASR Model

This is a bolt-action rifle chambered for various popular calibers. It has a stainless steel barrel and was essentially custom built to the customer's specifications. The stock is of Kevlar. This model is quite rare since only 100 were manufactured in 1968.

Exc.	V.G.	Good	Fair	Poor
1750	1200	900	650	400

PISTOLS

HK4

This is a blowback-operated semiautomatic pistol based on the Mauser HSc design. It is chambered for .22 l.r., .25 ACP, .32 ACP, and .380. These calibers were easily converted by switching the barrels, recoil springs and magazines. The rimfire model could be changed by rotating the breechface. The conversion kits were available for all calibers. The barrel is 3" long; and the finish is blued, with molded plastic thumb rest grips. This pistol was sold from 1968-1973 as the Harrington & Richardson HK4 and is so marked. It was completely discontinued in 1984.

.22 Caliber or .380 Caliber

Exc.	V.G.	Good	Fair	Poor
475	350	250	200	100

.25 Caliber or .32 Caliber

Exc.	V.G.	Good	Fair	Poor
350	300	250	200	100

Conversion Units

Exc.	V.G.	Good	Fair	Poor
150	125	90	60	30

P9

This is a single-action, delayed-blowback semiautomatic pistol chambered for 9mm or 7.65mm Parabellum. The action is based on the G-3 rifle mechanism. The barrel is 4" in length, and the pistol has an internal hammer and a thumb-operated hammer drop and recocking lever. There is also a manual safety and a loaded-chamber indicator. The finish is parkerized, and the grips are molded plastic and well contoured. It has fixed sights. This model was manufactured between 1977 and 1984. This model is rarer than the P9S model.

NIB	Exc.	V.G.	Good	Fair	Poor
1000	775	600	500	400	300

P9S

This model is similar to the Model P9 except that the action features a double-action capability and it is chambered for the .45 ACP and the 9mm Parabellum with a 5.5" barrel. This model was also manufactured between 1977 and 1984.

NIB	Exc.	V.G.	Good	Fair	Poor
1000	775	600	500	400	300

P9S Target Model

This version is similar to the Model P9S chambered for the 9mm or .45 ACP cartridges, with adjustable sights, and an adjustable trigger. It was discontinued in 1984.

NIB	Exc.	V.G.	Good	Fair	Poor
1350	1050	750	600	400	300

VP 70Z

This is a blowback-operated semiautomatic chambered for the 9mm Parabellum cartridge. It is striker-fired and double-action only. The barrel is 4.5" long, and the double-column magazine holds 18 rounds. The finish is blued, and the receiver and grip are molded from plastic. This model was discontinued in 1984.

NIB	Exc.	V.G.	Good	Fair	Poor
550	450	350	300	250	200

P7 PSP

This was the first of the squeeze-cocked H&K pistols. It is a single-action semiautomatic that is placed in the firing position by pressure on the front of the grip strap. This moves the striker into battery; and firing is then accomplished by a single-action pressure on the trigger, releasing the grip strap cocking device and decocking the mechanism. This particular model does not have the extended finger guard on the trigger and also does not have an ambidextrous safety. It was discontinued in 1984.

NIB	Exc.	V.G.	Good	Fair	Poor
800	700	600	500	400	200

P7 M8

This is the 8-shot newer version of the "squeeze cocker." It has the heat-shield finger guard and the ambidextrous safety. It has a 4" barrel and a 3-dot sight system. The finish is matte blue or nickel with stippled black plastic grips.

NIB	Exc.	V.G.	Good	Fair	Poor
1000	800	700	600	500	300

NOTE: For night sights, introduced in 1993, add $100.

P7 M10

A new addition to the P7 series in 1993, this variation is chambered for the .40 S&W cartridge. Magazine holds 10 rounds and the finish is available in either blue or nickel. Pistol weighs 2.69 lbs.

NIB	Exc.	V.G.	Good	Fair	Poor
1200	1000	800	650	500	300

NOTE: For night sights add $100.

P7 M13

This version is similar to the P7 M8 except that it has a double column 13-shot magazine.

NIB	Exc.	V.G.	Good	Fair	Poor
1300	1000	800	650	500	300

NOTE: For night sights add $100.

P7 K3

This is the "Squeeze Cocker" chambered for either the .380 or .22 L.R. caliber. It has a recoil buffer that is oil-filled and a 3.8" barrel. The magazine holds 8 rounds. This model was introduced in 1988.

NIB	Exc.	V.G.	Good	Fair	Poor
1000	900	750	650	500	300

.22 Caliber Conversion Kit

This unit will convert the P7 K3 to fire the .22 Long Rifle cartridge.

NIB	Exc.	V.G.	Good	Fair	Poor
575	400	350	300	150	75

.32 ACP Caliber Conversion Kit

NIB	Exc.	V.G.	Good	Fair	Poor
200	175	150	100	75	50

SP89

Introduced in the early 1990s, this is a large frame semiautomatic pistol chambered for the 9mm cartridge. It features a 15-round magazine and a square notch rear sight with a hooded front sight. The pistol has a 4.5" barrel and is 13" overall. It weighs 4.4 lbs. In August 1993 this model was no longer imported due to a ban on assault pistols. This ban will affect price, but to what degree is uncertain at this time.

NIB	Exc.	V.G.	Good	Fair	Poor
2250	1750	1250	900	500	250

USP40

Introduced in 1993 this new semiautomatic H&H pistol features a new design that incorporates a short recoil modified Browning action. Chambered for the .40 S&W cartridge this model has a 4.13" barrel and a magazine capacity of 13 rounds. Stainless steel model introduced in 1996. It weighs 1.74 lbs. Available in seven different variations from traditional double action to double action only and various safety locations and styles. These variants are numbered by H&K as follows:

1. DA/SA with safe position and control lever on left side of frame.
2. DA/SA with safe position and control lever on right side of frame.
3. DA/SA without safe position and decocking lever on left side of frame.
4. DA/SA without safe position and decocking lever on left side of frame.
5. DA only with safe position and safety lever on left side of frame.
6. DA only with safe position and safety lever on right side of frame.
7. DA only without control lever.
9. DA/SA with safe position and safety lever on left side of frame.
10. DA/SA with safety lever on the right side of frame.

NIB	Exc.	V.G.	Good	Fair	Poor
600	500	400	300	225	150

NOTE: For stainless steel model add $45.

USP9

Same as the USP40 but chambered for the 9mm cartridge. Magazine holds 16 rounds and pistol weighs 1.66 lbs. This model also has the choice of seven variations as listed above for the USP40. New for 1993.

NIB	Exc.	V.G.	Good	Fair	Poor
600	500	400	300	225	150

NOTE: For stainless steel model add $45.

USP45

Introduced in 1995 this version is slightly larger than the 9mm and .40 S&W models. Barrel length is 4.41" and overall length is 7.87". Weight is 1.9 lb. The USP45 is available in the same variants as the other USP models.

NIB	Exc.	V.G.	Good	Fair	Poor
675	575	450	350	250	200

NIB	Exc.	V.G.	Good	Fair	Poor
625	500	—	—	—	—

NOTE: For stainless steel model add $45.

H&K Stainless Steel Model

USP9 Compact

Introduced in 1997 this 9mm model is a smaller version of the full size USP9. There are some internal differences due to size. Barrel length is 3.58". Overall length is 6.81". Magazine capacity is 10 rounds. Weight is approximately 26 oz. Also available with stainless steel slide. Add $45 to NIB price.

NIB	Exc.	V.G.	Good	Fair	Poor
625	500	—	—	—	—

USP40 Compact

Same as 9mm Compact model but chambered for 40 S&W cartridge. Weight is about 27 oz. All other dimensions are the same.

From top to bottom is the USP45, the USP40, and the USP40 Compact

USP45 Match

Introduced in 1997 this model is a match grade variation of the USP. It is chambered for the .45 ACP cartridge. Fitted with a 6.02" barrel with barrel weight assembly. Adjustable rear sight and target front sight. Adjustable trigger stop. Blued finish. Weight is approximately 38 oz. Also available in a stainless steel version. Add $60.00 for stainless steel.

NIB	Exc.	V.G.	Good	Fair	Poor
1300	1000	—	—	—	—

USP Accessories

The items listed below are factory options for the USP pistol and may be encountered when a sale is contempleted. We have listed the retail price of the factory item.

Tritium Sights
MSRP-$95.00

Mark II UTL (Universal Tactical Light)
MSRP-$267.00

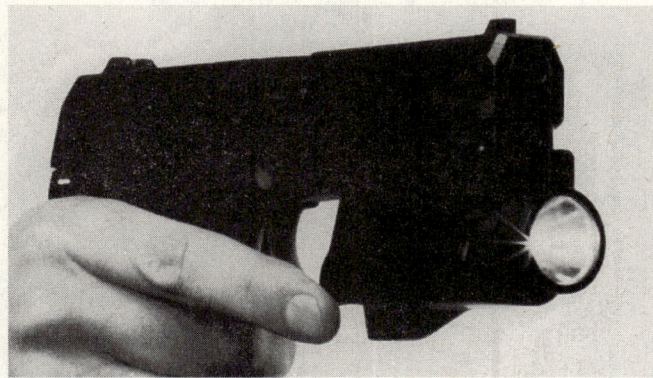

Quik-Comp
MSRP-$184.00

Optical Sight/Scope Mount

Optical sight/scope mount and Quik-Comp

MSRP-$221.00

Mark 23

Very similar to the H&K's US government contract pistol developed for special Operation Units. Chambered for the .45 ACP and fitted with a 5.87" barrel, this pistol has a polomyer frame with steel slide. Magazine capacity is 10 rounds on civilian models and 12 rounds on law enforcement models. Barrel is threaded for noise suppressor. Weight is about 42 oz. Limited availability in fall 1996 to about 2,000 pistols.

NIB	Exc.	V.G.	Good	Fair	Poor
1900	1700	—	—	—	—

HEINZELMANN, C.E.
Plochipnam Neckar, Germany

Heim

A 6.35mm semiautomatic pistol with a 2" barrel. detachable magazine holds six rounds. Manufactured during the 1930s and marked on the frame "C.E. Heinzelmann Plochingen A.N. Patent Heim-6.35."

Exc.	V.G.	Good	Fair	Poor
750	675	550	400	200

HEISER, CARL
SEE-Austrian Military Firearms

HELFRICHT
Zella-Mehlis, Germany

Model 3 Pocket Pistol

A 6.35mm semiautomatic pistol with a 2" barrel and 6-shot magazine. Blued with black plastic grips having the monogram "KH" cast in them.

Exc.	V.G.	Good	Fair	Poor
450	400	350	275	150

Model 4 Pocket Pistol

As above, without the barrel extension.

Exc.	V.G.	Good	Fair	Poor
400	350	300	225	100

HENRION & DASSY
Liege, Belgium

Semiautomatic

A 6.35mm semiautomatic pistol with a 2.5" barrel and 5-shot magazine. Blued with black plastic grips. Marked "H&D".

Exc.	V.G.	Good	Fair	Poor
600	500	450	375	275

HENRY
SEE-Winchester

HENRY, ALEXANDER
Edinburgh, Scotland

Noted for both the rifling system he developed and the falling block single shot rifles he made, Alexander Henry conducted business at the following locations:

12 South Street, Andrew Street	1853-1858
8 South Street, Andrew Street	1858-1862
12 South Street, Andrew Street	1862-1871
12 and 14 South Street, Andrew Street	1871-1875
12 South Street, Andrew Street	1875-1895
18 Frederick Street	1895-1911
22 Frederick Street	1911

Rifles made by this maker are highly sought after and prospective purchasers are strongly advised to secure a qualified appraisal prior to acquisition.

Single Shot Rifle

A high-grade single shot that features a true falling-block action that is activated by a side lever on the action. It was available in the popular European cartridges of the era, and the barrel length varies from 22" to 28" in length. This rifle exhibits fine quality materials and workmanship. The select-grade walnut stock and Schnabel forend are hand checkered. The finish of the rifle is scroll-engraved and blued. This company manufactured firearms from 1869 until 1895.

Exc.	V.G.	Good	Fair	Poor
2500	2250	1750	1250	800

Double Rifle

A side-x-side, double barreled Express Rifle chambered for the .500/450 Black Powder Express cartridge. It has Damascus barrels and double triggers. This gun is hammerless and features ornate scroll engraving as well as a high-grade hand checkered walnut stock and forend. It was furnished with a fitted leather case and accessories. This rifle was manufactured in the 1890s.

Exc.	V.G.	Good	Fair	Poor
5000	4500	3750	2900	1500

HERITAGE MANUFACTURING, INC.
Opa Locka, Florida

Stealth

This is a 9mm semiautomatic pistol. It has a black polymer frame with stainless steel slide. Barrel length is 3.9" with overall length at 6.3". Magazine capacity is 10 rounds. Weight is approximately 20 oz. A .40 S&W version is scheduled to be introduced in the summer of 1996. Offered with a black finish, two-tone black chrome with stainless steel side panels, or black chrome.

NIB	Exc.	V.G.	Good	Fair	Poor
275	225	175	150	125	100

Model H25S

A semiautomatic pistol chambered for the .25 ACP cartridge. Barrel length is 2.25" and overall length is 4.58". Weight is about 13.5 oz. Frame mounted safety. Single action only. Available in blue or nickel.

NIB	Exc.	V.G.	Good	Fair	Poor
150	125	100	85	65	50

Sentry

This is a double action revolver chambered for the .38 Special. Cylinder holds 6 rounds. Barrel length is 2". Weight is about 23 oz. Blue or nickel finish.

NIB	Exc.	V.G.	Good	Fair	Poor
130	100	85	65	50	30

Rough Rider

Single action revolver chambered for the .22 caliber cartridges. Barrel lengths are 4.75", 6.5", and 9". Cylinder holds 6 rounds. Weight is about 34 oz. Available in blue or nickel finish.

NIB	Exc.	V.G.	Good	Fair	Poor
110	85	65	50	40	30

With Combination Cylinder-.22 Mag.

NIB	Exc.	V.G.	Good	Fair	Poor
130	100	85	65	50	35

With Birds Head Grip & Combo Cylinder

NIB	Exc.	V.G.	Good	Fair	Poor
130	100	85	65	50	35

HEROLD
Franz Jaeger
Suhl, Germany

Bolt Action Rifle
A .22 Hornet bolt-action sporting rifle with a 24" ribbed barrel, adjustable sights, double set triggers and walnut stock. Imported by Charles Daly and Stoeger Arms prior to WWII.

Exc.	V.G.	Good	Fair	Poor
1150	850	700	550	375

HERTERS
Waseca, Minnesota
An importer and retailer of European made firearms. Active until approximately 1980.

REVOLVERS

Guide
A .22 caliber double action swing-out cylinder revolver with a 6" barrel and 6-shot cylinder. Blued with walnut grips.

Exc.	V.G.	Good	Fair	Poor
100	80	50	35	25

Power-Mag Revolver
A .357 Magnum, .401 Herters Power Magnum, and .44 Magnum caliber single action revolver with a 4" or 6" barrel and 6-shot cylinder. Blued, with walnut grips.

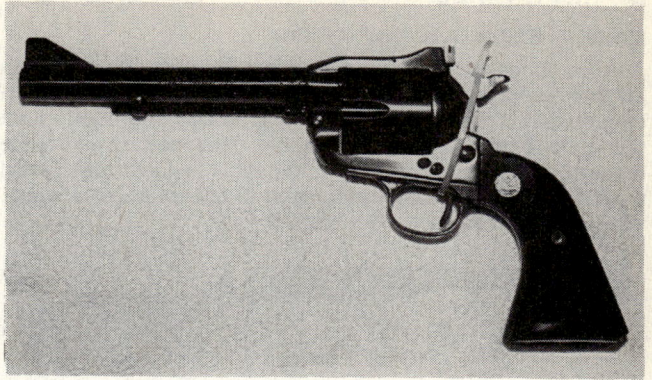

Exc.	V.G.	Good	Fair	Poor
150	125	80	60	50

Western
As above, in .22 caliber.

Exc.	V.G.	Good	Fair	Poor
85	75	60	45	25

RIFLES

J-9 or U-9 Hunter
Mauser action sporting rifles manufactured in England (J-9) and Yugoslavia (U-9), with 24" barrels and Monte Carlo-style walnut stocks.

Exc.	V.G.	Good	Fair	Poor
225	185	135	100	75

J-9 or U-9 Presentation or Supreme
As above, with checkering and sling swivels.

Exc.	V.G.	Good	Fair	Poor
250	225	200	150	100

HEYM, F. W.
Suhl, Germany
Established in 1865 in Suhl, Germany, this company was re-established after WWII in Munnerstadt. The company remained there until 1996 when it moved back to a suburb of Suhl. Postwar arms were originally imported by Paul Jaeger of Grand Junction, Tennessee. At the present time there is no American importer of Heym and the guns are not entering this country as of 1997.

SINGLE SHOT RIFLES

Model HR-30
Built on the Ruger No. 1 falling-block action and chambered for most calibers with a 24" round barrel or a 26" barrel in the magnum calibers. There is a quarter rib with express sights, and the single-set trigger is made by Canjar. The rifle is engraved with a gamescene motif, and the stock is deluxe, hand checkered French walnut with a classic European-style cheekpiece. French casehardened and blued.

Exc.	V.G.	Good	Fair	Poor
3000	2750	2250	1750	1250

Model HR-38
As above, with an octagonal barrel.

Exc.	V.G.	Good	Fair	Poor
3500	3250	2500	2000	1500

DOUBLE RIFLE

Model 77B/55B Over/Under Rifle

An Over/Under rifle manufactured in a variety of calibers with 25" barrels having open sights: and a boxlock action with Kersten double cross bolts. The action is heavily engraved with a gamescene motif and is silver plated. This model has double triggers, cocking indicators, automatic ejectors, and select walnut stock. The barrels machined to accept a Zeiss scope with claw mounts.

Exc.	V.G.	Good	Fair	Poor
5000	4500	4000	3250	2500

Model 55BSS

As above with sidelocks.

Exc.	V.G.	Good	Fair	Poor
9500	8500	7500	5000	3500

Model 55BF/77BF

Similar to the Model 55B, except one barrel is rifled and the other smooth in 12, 16, or 20 gauge.

Exc.	V.G.	Good	Fair	Poor
5000	4500	4000	3250	2500

Model 55BFSS

As above, with sidelocks.

Exc.	V.G	Good	Fair	Poor
9500	8500	7500	5000	3500

Model 88 B

A large bore double-barrel boxlock rifle with 24" barrels, automatic ejectors, double triggers, and select walnut stock.

Exc.	V.G.	Good	Fair	Poor
9500	8750	7750	5500	4000

Model 88 BSS

As above with sidelocks.

Exc.	V.G.	Good	Fair	Poor
14000	12500	9500	6500	5250

Model 88 Safari

As above, but chambered for .375 Holland & Holland, .458 Winchester Magnum, .470, or .500 Nitro Express calibers with 25" barrels.

Exc.	V.G.	Good	Fair	Poor
13500	12000	9000	6000	4750

Model 22 Safety

An Over/Under combination rifle/shotgun chambered for 16 or 20 gauge over .22 Hornet, .22 WMR, .222 Remington, .222 Remington Magnum, .223, 5.6x50Rmm, 6.5x57Rmm, and 7x57Rmm with 24" barrels. Boxlock action with a single trigger, automatic ejectors, and automatic decocking mechanism. French casehardening, blued with a walnut stock.

Exc.	V.G.	Good	Fair	Poor
2500	2000	1750	1200	900

DRILLINGS

Model 33

A boxlock drilling manufactured in a variety of American and European calibers and gauges with 25" barrels, double triggers and extractors. Casehardened, blued with a walnut stock.

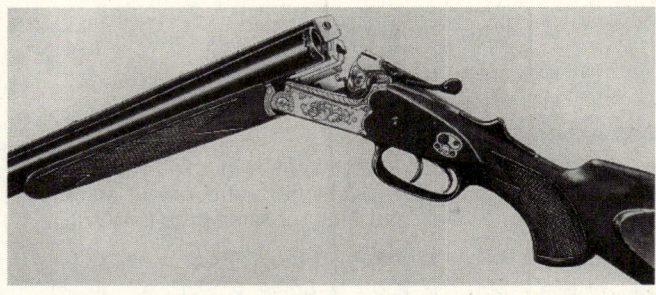

Exc.	V.G.	Good	Fair	Poor
6000	5000	4250	2750	2000

Model 33 Deluxe

Same as above but with game scene engraving.

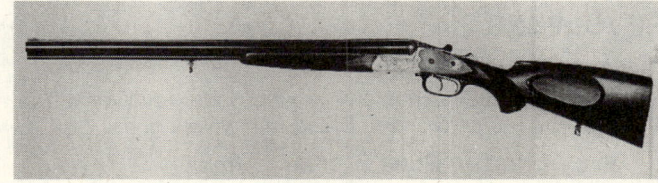

Exc.	V.G.	Good	Fair	Poor
7500	6000	4750	3500	2500

Model 37

Similar to the Model 33 Standard but with full sidelocks.

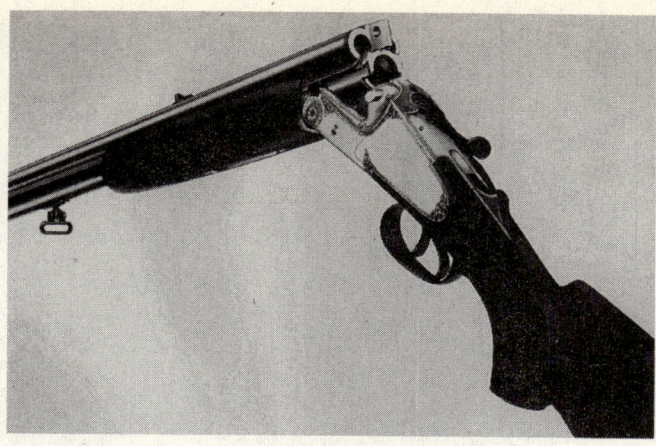

Exc.	V.G.	Good	Fair	Poor
12500	10000	7500	5000	2500

Model 37 Deluxe

Similar to the above Model 37 but with hand engraved scroll work and fancy walnut stock.

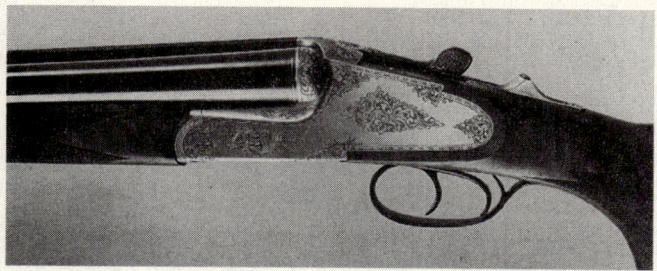

Exc.	V.G.	Good	Fair	Poor
15000	12000	8500	6000	3000

BOLT ACTION RIFLES

Model SR-20

A Mauser action sporting rifle manufactured in a variety of calibers with 21", 24", or 26" barrels, open sights, adjustable trigger or set trigger. Blued with a walnut stock.

NIB	Exc.	V.G.	Good	Fair	Poor
1450	1250	950	750	600	450

Model SR-20 Alpine

As above with a 20" barrel and Mannlicher stock. Introduced in 1989.

NIB	Exc.	V.G.	Good	Fair	Poor
2650	2250	1750	1250	850	600

SR-20 Classic Safari

As above, but chambered for .404 Jeffries, .425 Express, and the .458 Winchester Magnum with a 24" barrel having express sights. Introduced in 1989.

NIB	Exc.	V.G.	Good	Fair	Poor
3500	3000	2750	2000	1250	750

SR-20 Classic Sportsman

This model features a round barrel without sights. Chambered for many calibers from .243 to .375 H&H. Introduced in 1988. Add $100 for Magnum calibers.

NIB	Exc.	V.G.	Good	Fair	Poor
1650	1250	900	700	500	300

SR-20 Trophy

Similar to the above Classic Sportsman model but with German bead ramp sight and open quarter rib rear sight. Select walnut stock with oil finish. Octagonal barrel and rosewood grip cap.

NIB	Exc.	V.G.	Good	Fair	Poor
2500	2000	1250	800	500	300

Heym Magnum Express

This bolt action rifle is chambered for .338 lapua, .375 H&H, .416 Rigby, .500 Nitro Express.500 A-Square, and a few were built in .600 Nitro Express. Fitted with a 24" barrel. Adjustable front sight, three leaf rear express sight. Select hand checkered European walnut stock, and many other special features. Introduced in 1989.

NOTE: Add $4,000 for 600 N.E.

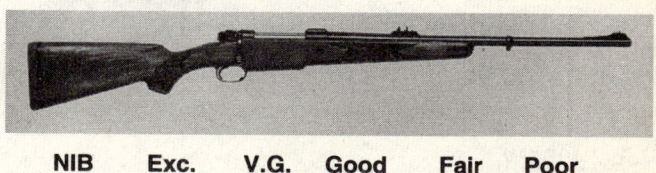

NIB	Exc.	V.G.	Good	Fair	Poor
5800	4500	3000	1500	750	500

HI-POINT FIREARMS
MKS Supply
Dayton, Ohio

Model C

This is a 9mm single action compact semi-automatic pistol with a 3.5" barrel. Magazine capacity is 8 rounds. Black or chrome finish. Weight is 32 oz.

NIB	Exc	V.G.	Good	Fair	Poor
125	100	85	75	65	50

Model C-Polymer

Same as above but with polymer frame. Weight is 28 oz.

NIB	Exc	V.G.	Good	Fair	Poor
125	100	85	75	65	50

Model JH

All steel construction chambered for .45ACP with 4.5" barrel. Magazine capacity is 7 rounds. Weight is 39 oz.

NIB	Exc	V.G.	Good	Fair	Poor
150	125	100	85	75	50

Model 40S&W

Same as above but chambered for .40S&W cartridge. 8 round magazine capacity. Weight is 39 oz.

NIB	Exc	V.G.	Good	Fair	Poor
150	125	100	85	75	50

Model CF

This pistol is chambered for the .380 ACP cartridge and is fitted with a polymer frame. Magazine capacity is 8 rounds. Barrel length is 3.5". Weight is 29 oz.

NIB	Exc	V.G.	Good	Fair	Poor
80	70	50	40	30	25

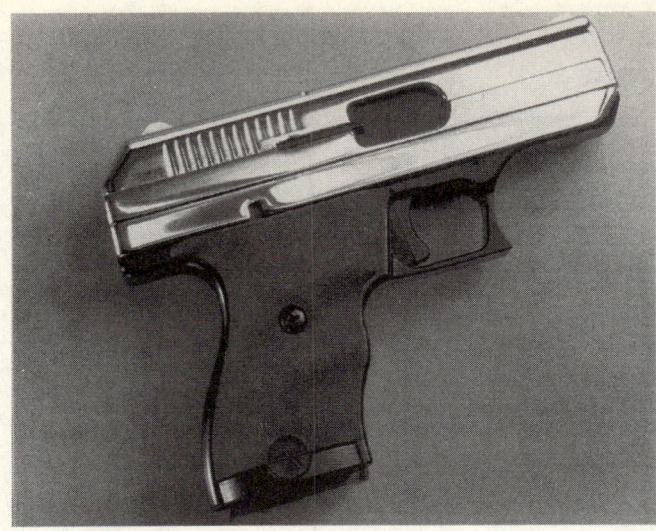

9mm Carbine

This semiautomatic carbine is chambered for the 9mm cartridge and fitted with a 16.5" barrel and a 10-round magazine. It has a polymer stock and a rear peep sight. Available in Parkerized or chrome finish.

NIB	Exc	V.G.	Good	Fair	Poor
170	150	125	100	85	65

HIGGINS, J. C.
Chicago, Illinois

The Sears, Roebuck & Company of Chicago used the trade name J.C. Higgins on the firearms and other sporting goods it sold between 1946 and 1962. Arms bearing this tradename were manufactured by a variety of American gunmakers.

HIGH STANDARD MANUFACTURING CORPORATION
New Haven and Hamden, Connecticut

The High Standard Manufacturing Company was established in 1926, by Carl Swebilius and Gustave Beck to produce drills and machine tools. In 1932, the firm purchased the Hartford Arms & Equipment Company (q.v.) and began the manufacture of the latter's Model 1925 Semiautomatic Pistol as the Hi-Standard Model "B".

Throughout the High Standard Manufacturing Corporation's business life, its products were highly regarded for both their design and quality. While the company was originally located in New Haven, in early 1950 it moved to Hamden, Connecticut. Operations ceased in 1984. **In the spring of 1993 the High Standard Manufacturing Co, Inc. of Houston, Texas acquired the company assets and trademarks as well as** the .22 Target Pistols. These orginal assets were transfered from Connecticut to Houston, Texas in July 1993. The first shipments of Houston manufactured pistols began in March of 1994. Prices listed here are separated for both the Hartford and Houston models. Collectors will pay a premium for the Hartford pistols.

Model B

A .22 caliber semiautomatic pistol with either a 4-1/4" or 6-3/4" round barrel and a 10-shot magazine. Blued with checkered hard rubber grips (later production versions have chequered grips impressed with the High Standard monogram). Introduced in 1932, with serial numbers beginning at 5000; approximately 65,000 made.

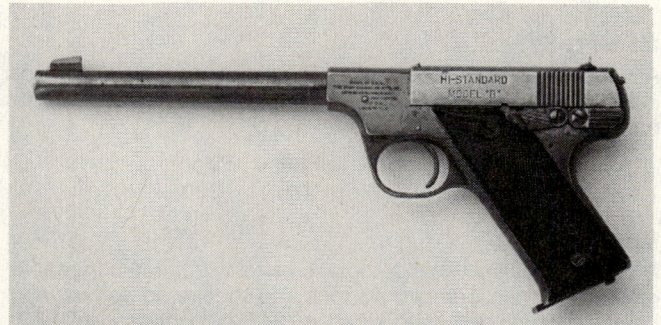

Exc.	V.G.	Good	Fair	Poor
600	450	300	200	125

Model C

As above in .22 short caliber with monogrammed and checkered hard rubber grips. Introduced in 1936; approximately 4,700 made.

Exc.	V.G.	Good	Fair	Poor
650	500	350	250	150

Model A

Similar to the Model B but with an extended grip and adjustable rear sight. Introduced in 1938; approximately 7,300 made.

Exc.	V.G.	Good	Fair	Poor
650	500	350	250	150

Model D

As above with a heavier weight barrel. Introduced in 1938; discontinued in 1942; approximately 2,500 made.

Exc.	V.G.	Good	Fair	Poor
700	550	400	300	175

Model E

As above with walnut grips having a thumb rest and a heavy target barrel. Introduced in 1938; discontinued in 1942; approximately 2,600 made.

Exc.	V.G.	Good	Fair	Poor
850	650	450	350	200

Model S

Identical to the Model A but with a smoothbore. Approximately five were made in 1939, none of which were sold commercially. A further seven were made on Model C actions at the same time. The values for both variations are equal.

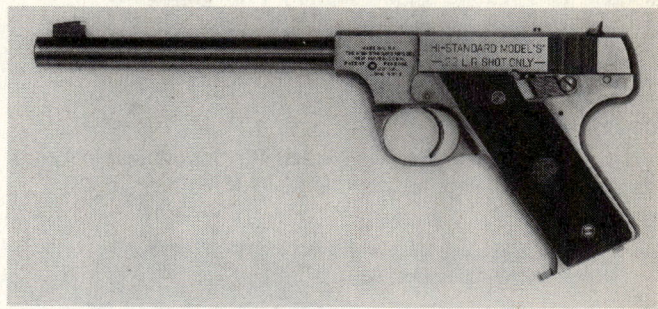

Exc.	V.G.	Good	Fair	Poor
7500	5500	4500	2500	1250

Model H-B

Identical to the Model B but with an exposed hammer. Introduced in 1940; discontinued in 1942; approximately 2,100 made of first model and 25,000 of second model.

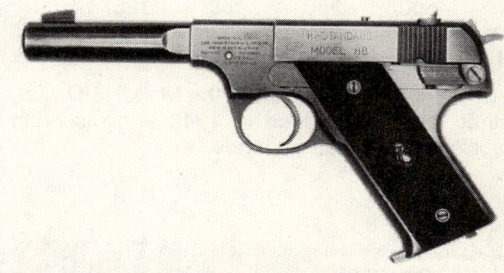

Exc.	V.G.	Good	Fair	Poor
575	425	350	250	150

Model H-A

Identical to the Model A but with an exposed hammer. Introduced in 1940; discontinued in 1942; approximately 1,040 made.

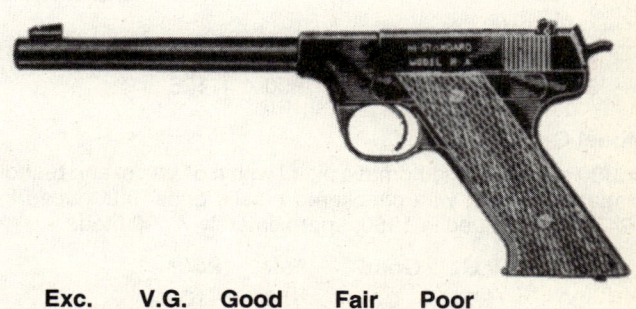

Exc.	V.G.	Good	Fair	Poor
850	700	550	400	200

Model H-D

Identical to the Model D but with an exposed hammer. Introduced in 1940; discontinued in 1942; approximately 6,900 made.

Exc.	V.G.	Good	Fair	Poor
1250	800	650	450	250

Model H-E

Identical to the Model E but with an exposed hammer. Introduced in 1940; discontinued in 1942; approximately 1,000 made.

Exc	V.G.	Good	Fair	Poor
2000	1200	950	450	250

Model B-US

A 4-1/2" barrel version of the Model B. Introduced in 1942 and discontinued in 1943. Approximately 14,000 made.

Exc.	V.G.	Good	Fair	Poor
775	550	400	300	150

Model USA-HD

A 4-1/2" barrel version of the Model H-D. Introduced in 1943; discontinued in 1946; approximately 44,000 made.

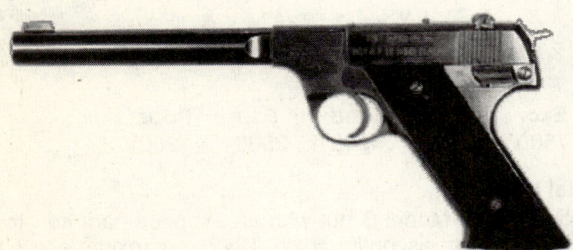

Exc.	V.G.	Good	Fair	Poor
750	500	350	250	125

Model H-D Military

A 4-1/2" or 6-3/4" barrel version of the Model H-D with checkered walnut grips. Introduced in 1946 and discontinued in 1955. Approximately 150,000 made.

Exc.	V.G.	Good	Fair	Poor
550	400	350	250	125

Model G-380

A .380 caliber semiautomatic pistol with a 5" barrel and 6-shot magazine. Blued with checkered plastic grips. Introduced in 1947; discontinued in 1950; approximately 7,400 made.

Exc.	V.G.	Good	Fair	Poor
400	350	275	150	100

Model G-B

A variation of the Model B with interchangeable 4-1/2" or 6-3/4" barrels. Introduced in 1949; discontinued in 1950; approximately 4,900 made.

Exc.	V.G.	Good	Fair	Poor
575	450	350	250	150

Model G-D

A variation of the Model D with interchangeable 4-1/2" or 6-3/4" barrels. Introduced in 1949; discontinued in 1951; approximately 3,300 made.

Exc.	V.G.	Good	Fair	Poor
750	525	400	300	175

Model G-E

A variation of the Model E with interchangeable 4-1/2" or 6-3/4" barrels. Introduced in 1949; discontinued in 1950; approximately 2,900 made.

Exc.	V.G.	Good	Fair	Poor
1250	950	700	475	250

Model G-0

A .22 short caliber semiautomatic pistol with interchangeable or 6-3/4" barrels, 5-shot magazine and checkered walnut grips having a thumb rest. Introduced in 1949; discontinued in 1950; approximately 1,200 made.

Exc.	V.G.	Good	Fair	Poor
1350	1000	750	500	275

1st Model Olympic

As above, in .22 short caliber with a lightweight alloy slide and redesigned takedown lever. Approximately 1,200 were made in 1949 and 1950.

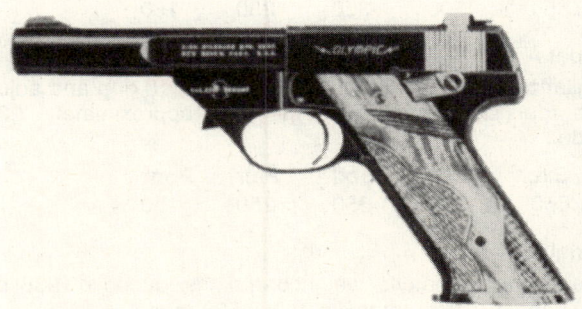

Exc.	V.G.	Good	Fair	Poor
700	600	500	375	275

1st Model Sport King

A .22 caliber semiautomatic pistol with a 4.5" or 6.75" barrel, fixed sights. Blued with plastic grips. Manufactured between 1951 and 1958.

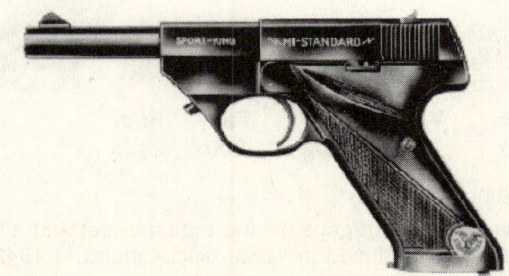

Exc.	V.G.	Good	Fair	Poor
375	325	250	175	100

1st Model Flite King

An alloy-framed version of the Sport King chambered for the .22 Short cartridge. Manufactured between 1953 and 1958. The extra barrel would add approximately 15% to the value.

Exc.	V.G.	Good	Fair	Poor
450	350	225	150	100

Field King

As above with a heavy barrel. Manufactured between 1951 and 1958. The extra barrel would add approximately 15% to the value.

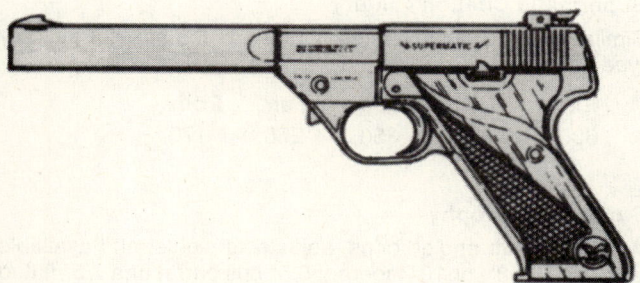

Exc.	V.G.	Good	Fair	Poor
375	325	250	175	100

Supermatic

A .22 caliber semiautomatic pistol with a 4.5" or 6.75" barrel, adjustable sights, barrel weights and 10-shot magazine. Blued with plastic grips. Manufactured between 1951 and 1958.

Exc.	V.G.	Good	Fair	Poor
600	450	350	225	125

2nd Model Olympic

As above, with an alloy slide and in .22 Short caliber.

Exc.	V.G	Good	Fair	Poor
650	550	350	250	175

Duramatic

A .22 caliber semiautomatic pistol with a 4.5" or 6.5" barrel, fixed sights, screw takedown mechanism and walnut grips. Manufactured from 1954 to 1970.

Exc.	V.G.	Good	Fair	Poor
375	325	250	175	100

2nd Model Sport King

An improved version of the Sport King that was manufactured between 1958 and 1970. The extra barrel would add approximately 15% to the value.

Exc.	V.G.	Good	Fair	Poor
350	300	225	150	100

3rd Model Sport King

Similar to the 2nd Model but available in nickel-plate. Manufactured between 1974 and 1984.

Exc.	V.G.	Good	Fair	Poor
350	300	225	150	100

Sport King-currently manufactured model

Chambered for .22 Long Rifle and fitted with a 4.5" or 6.75" barrel. Adjustable rear sight. Weight is about 44 oz.

NIB	Exc	V.G.	Good	Fair	Poor
350	300	225	150	100	80

Sport King M

As above with military-style, straight grip.

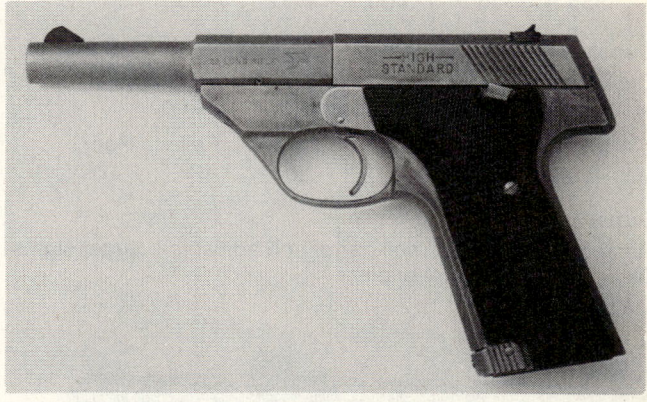

Exc.	V.G.	Good	Fair	Poor
300	250	200	125	100

2nd Model Flite King

The 2nd Model Sport King with a lightweight, alloy slide and in .22 Short caliber. Manufactured between 1958 and 1966.

Exc.	V.G.	Good	Fair	Poor
350	250	200	125	100

Sharpshooter

The 2nd Model Sport King with a 5.5" heavy barrel, adjustable sights and push-button takedown mechanism. Blued with brown, checkered plastic grips. Manufactured between 1971 and 1981.

Exc.	V.G.	Good	Fair	Poor
450	325	250	150	100

Supermatic Tournament

As above, with a a 5.5" or 6.75" heavy barrel, barrel weights, and adjustable target-type sights. Blued with checkered walnut grips. Manufactured between 1958 and 1966.

Exc.	V.G.	Good	Fair	Poor
850	550	400	300	150

Supermatic Tournament-currently manufactured model

Chambered for .22 Long Rifle and fitted with a 5.5" barrel. Matte blue finish. Weight is approximately 44 oz.

NIB	Exc	V.G.	Good	Fair	Poor
400	325	250	200	175	100

Supermatic Citation

As above, with a 5.5" bull barrel and adjustable target sights. Blued with thumb rest grips.

Exc.	V.G.	Good	Fair	Poor
600	450	350	250	175

Supermatic Citation-currently manufactured model

Chambered for the .22 Long Rifle and fitted with a 5.5" barrel. Matte blue or Parkerized finish. Weight is about 44 oz.

NIB	Exc	V.G.	Good	Fair	Poor
425	325	275	225	175	100

Supermatic Citation MS-currently manufactured model

Designed for metallic silhouette shooting and introduced in 1996. Fitted with a 10" barrel. Weight is approximately 49 oz.

NIB	Exc	V.G.	Good	Fair	Poor
675	575	425	350	250	125

Supermatic Citation Military

Similar to the Citation, except that it has the straight, military type grip frame.

Exc.	V.G.	Good	Fair	Poor
600	450	350	250	175

Supermatic Trophy

As above, with angled grips, adjustable sights, and available with a 6.75", 8", or 10" tapered, 5.5" bull barrel or a 7.5" fluted barrel. The rear sight is mounted on the frame and straddles the slide. An adjustable trigger pull and over-travel adjustment. Blued with checkered, walnut, thumb rest grips.

10" Barrel-Add 40%.
8" Barrel-Add 25%.

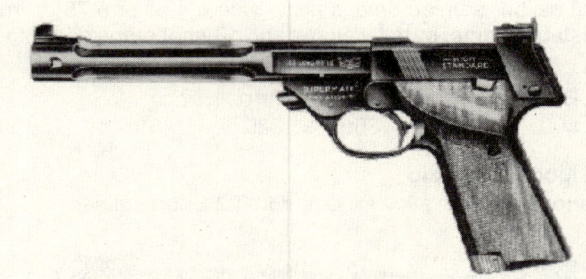

Exc.	V.G.	Good	Fair	Poor
800	600	450	300	200

Supermatic Trophy-currently manufactured model

Offered with 5.5" or 7.25" barrels and chambered for .22 Long Rifle. Adjustable trigger, barrel weights, gold plated trigger, safety, slide stop, and magazine catch. Matte blue or parkerized finish. Weight is about 45 oz.

NIB	Exc	V.G.	Good	Fair	Poor
500	425	350	250	150	100

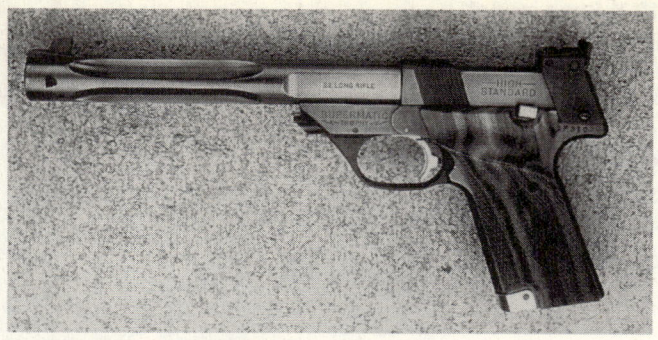

Supermatic Trophy Military

As above, with a military-type grip frame. Manufactured between 1965 and 1984.

Exc.	V.G.	Good	Fair	Poor
875	650	500	350	200

3rd Model Olympic

Similar to the Supermatic Trophy model with a lightweight, alloy slide and in .22 Short cartridge. A straight-grip, military model is also available. Manufactured between 1963 and 1966.

Exc.	V.G.	Good	Fair	Poor
950	800	550	400	250

Olympic Model-currently manufactured

Chambered for .22 Short and fitted with a 5.5" bull barrel. Blued finish. Weight is approximately 44 oz.

NIB	Exc	V.G.	Good	Fair	Poor
525	425	300	250	200	100

Olympic ISU

Similar to the Supermatic Citation, with a 6.75" or 8" barrel furnished with weights and in .22 Short caliber. A military model with the straight grip is also available. The values are the same. Manufactured between 1958 and 1984.

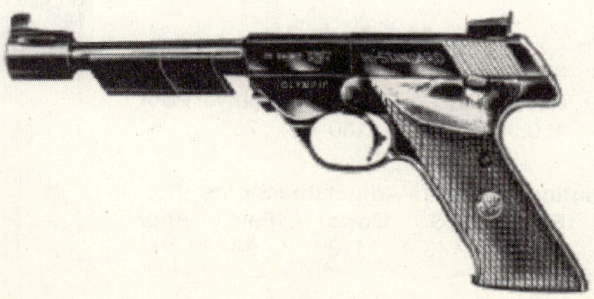

Exc.	V.G.	Good	Fair	Poor
900	700	500	400	250

Olympic ISU-currently manufactured model

Similar to the above model but fitted with a 6.75" barrel with internal stabilizer. Magazine capacity is 5 rounds. Checkered walnut grips. Weight is approximately 45 oz. This model was discontinued in 1995.

NIB	Exc	V.G.	Good	Fair	Poor
500	400	350	300	200	150

1972 Olympic Commemorative

A limited edition issued to commemorate the only American manufactured .22 pistol used to win an Olympic Gold Medal. It is heavily engraved with gold-inlaid Olympic rings and furnished in a fitted presentation case. It was manufactured in 1972 and, as with all commemoratives, must be NIB with all furnished material to be desirable from a collector's standpoint. About 200 of these pistols were produced.

NIB	Exc	V.G.	Good	Fair	Poor
2500	1000	750	600	500	300

1980 Olympic Commemorative

Similar to the above, with gold inlaid Olympic rings on the receiver. 1,000 were made in 1980 and have the serial number prefix USA.

NIB	Exc	V.G.	Good	Fair	Poor
1250	750	450	325	225	150

Olympic Rapid Fire-currently manufactured model

Introduced in 1996. Chambered for the .22 short cartridge with a 4" barrel, integral muzzle brake and forward mounted compensator. Special grips. Weight is about 46 oz.

NIB	Exc	V.G.	Good	Fair	Poor
1995	1550	—	—	—	—

Olympic Military

Chambered for the .22 Short and fitted with a 5.5" bull barrel. Adjustable rear sight. Checkered walnut grips. Detachable weights and adjustable trigger pull. Weight is about 44 oz.

NIB	Exc	V.G.	Good	Fair	Poor
525	425	300	250	200	150

Victor

A .22 caliber semiautomatic pistol with a 4.5" or 5.5" ribbed barrel, adjustable sights, push-button or screw takedown mechanism and 10-shot magazine. Blued with walnut grips.

Exc.	V.G.	Good	Fair	Poor
700	550	425	350	175

Victor-currently manufactured model

With 4.5" barrel and blue or parkerized finish.

NIB	Exc	V.G.	Good	Fair	Poor
525	425	350	300	200	125

Victor Conversion

Converts the Victor model to a .22 Short. Includes barrel with sight, slide, and 2 magazines.

NIB	Exc	V.G.	Good	Fair	Poor
400	325	275	225	175	100

10-X

A custom made semiautomatic target pistol hand assembled and signed by the employee who made the pistol. Available with either a push-button barrel release or an Allen screw release. Manufactured from 1982 to 1984.

Exc.	V.G.	Good	Fair	Poor
1850	1150	900	650	325

10-X-currently manufactured model

Fitted with 5.5" barrel. Weight is about 44 oz.

NIB	Exc	V.G.	Good	Fair	Poor
850	700	550	450	350	200

10-X-Shea model

Fitted with a 4.5" or 5.5" barrel. Limited to 150 pistol a year.

NIB	Exc	V.G.	Good	Fair	Poor
1100	850	700	500	350	200

Sharpshooter-M

Similar to the Victor, with a 5.5" heavy barrel and adjustable sights. Manufactured from 1982 to 1984.

Exc.	V.G.	Good	Fair	Poor
450	300	250	175	100

Derringer

A .22 or .22 Magnum caliber Over/Under double action pocket pistol with 3.5" barrels. Blued or nickel-plated with plastic grips.

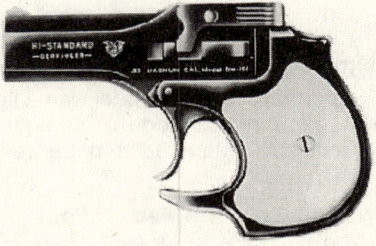

Exc.	V.G.	Good	Fair	Poor
200	165	145	100	75

Silver-Plated Derringer with Presentation Case

Exc.	V.G.	Good	Fair	Poor
250	200	150	125	100

Gold-Plated Derringer with Presentation Case

Exc.	V.G.	Good	Fair	Poor
275	225	175	150	100

SENTINEL SERIES

A .22 caliber double action swing-out cylinder revolver with a 3", 4", or 6" barrel and 9-shot cylinder. Anodized aluminum frame with blue, nickel, pink, or yellow finish.

Sentinel

Exc.	V.G.	Good	Fair	Poor
150	125	100	75	50

Sentinel Imperial - Adjustable Sights

Exc.	V.G.	Good	Fair	Poor
165	145	110	90	75

Sentinel Deluxe

Exc.	V.G.	Good	Fair	Poor
165	145	110	90	75

Sentinel Snub-2.5" Barrel, Round Butt

Exc.	V.G.	Good	Fair	Poor
150	125	100	75	50

Durango

A Western-style, double-action revolver in .22 caliber with a 4.5" or 5.5" barrel. Blued or nickel-plated with walnut grips. Manufactured between 1971 and 1973.

Exc.	V.G.	Good	Fair	Poor
150	125	100	75	50

Double Nine

As above, with a 5.5" barrel and alloy frame. Blued or nickel-plated with simulated ivory, ebony, or staghorn grips. Manufactured from 1959 to 1984.

Exc.	V.G.	Good	Fair	Poor
150	125	100	75	50

Longhorn

As above, with a 9.5" barrel.

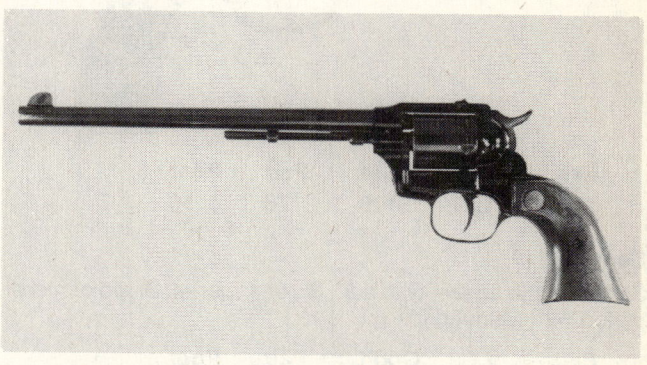

Exc.	V.G.	Good	Fair	Poor
200	175	125	100	75

Hombre

The Double Nine with a 4.5" barrel and steel frame.

Exc.	V.G.	Good	Fair	Poor
150	125	100	75	50

High Sierra

As above, with a 7" octagonal barrel and gold-plated back strap and triggerguard.

Exc.	V.G.	Good	Fair	Poor
200	175	125	100	75

Posse

As above, with a 3.5" barrel and a brass back strap and triggerguard. Walnut grips. Manufactured between 1961 and 1966.

Exc.	V.G.	Good	Fair	Poor
125	100	75	50	25

Natchez

As above, with rounded bird's-head grips.

Exc.	V.G.	Good	Fair	Poor
125	100	75	50	25

Kit Gun

A .22 caliber double action swing-out cylinder revolver with a 4" barrel, adjustable sights and 9-shot cylinder. Blued with walnut grips. Manufactured from 1970 to 1973.

Exc.	V.G.	Good	Fair	Poor
150	125	100	75	50

Sentinel I

Similar to the above, with a 2", 3", or 4" barrel. Blued or nickel-plated with walnut grips.

Exc.	V.G.	Good	Fair	Poor
225	175	125	100	75

Sentinel Mark IV

As above, in .22 Magnum.

Exc.	V.G.	Good	Fair	Poor
150	125	100	75	50

Sentinel Mark II

A .357 Magnum caliber double action revolver with 2.5", 4", or 6" barrels, fixed sights, blued finish and walnut grips. Manufactured from 1974 to 1976.

Exc.	V.G.	Good	Fair	Poor
225	175	125	100	75

Sentinel Mark III

As above, with adjustable sights.

Exc.	V.G.	Good	Fair	Poor
250	200	150	125	100

Crusader

A .357 Magnum, .44 Magnum, or the .45 Colt caliber double action, swing-out cylinder revolver with a 7.5" barrel, adjustable sights and 6-shot cylinder. Production of this model was limited.

Exc.	V.G.	Good	Fair	Poor
550	500	450	350	275

SHOTGUNS

Supermatic Field Grade

A 12 gauge semiautomatic shotgun with a 28" or 30" barrel. Blued with a walnut stock. Manufactured from 1960 to 1966.

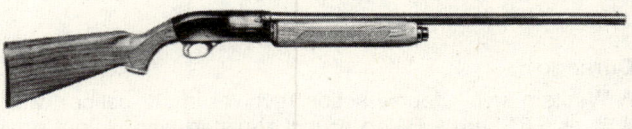

Exc.	V.G.	Good	Fair	Poor
200	175	150	100	65

Supermatic Special

As above, with a 27" barrel. Manufactured by Harrington & Richardson.

Exc.	V.G.	Good	Fair	Poor
200	175	150	100	65

Supermatic Deluxe

Similar to the Field Grade, with a ventilated rib barrel and a checkered walnut stock. Manufactured between 1961 and 1966.

Exc.	V.G.	Good	Fair	Poor
250	200	175	125	85

Supermatic Deer Gun

As above, with a 22" barrel fitted with rifle sights and the stock having a recoil pad. Manufactured in 1965 only.

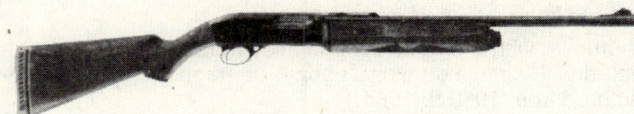

Exc.	V.G.	Good	Fair	Poor
225	175	150	100	75

Supermatic Skeet

As above, with a 26" ventilated rib barrel that is skeet bored. Manufactured between 1962 and 1966.

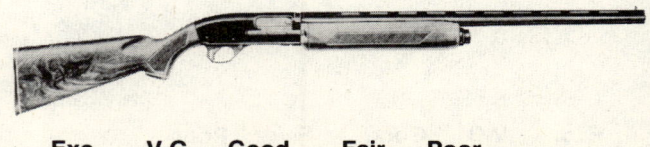

Exc.	V.G.	Good	Fair	Poor
300	250	200	150	100

Supermatic Trap

As above, with a 30" barrel and trap-style stock. Manufactured between 1962 and 1966.

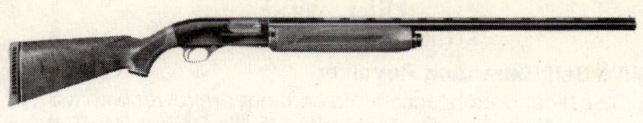

Exc.	V.G.	Good	Fair	Poor
250	200	150	100	75

Flite King Field Grade

A 12 or 20 gauge slide action shotgun with 26", 28", or 30" barrels. Blued with a walnut stock. Manufactured between 1960 and 1966.

Exc.	V.G.	Good	Fair	Poor
175	150	125	100	75

Flite King Special

As above, with a 27" barrel having adjustable choke.

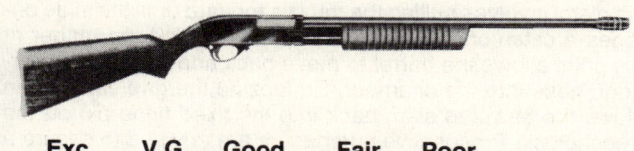

Exc.	V.G.	Good	Fair	Poor
175	150	125	100	75

Flite King Deluxe

As above, with a ventilated rib barrel and a checkered walnut stock. Manufactured between 1961 and 1966.

Exc.	V.G.	Good	Fair	Poor
200	175	150	125	100

Flite King Trophy

As above, with a 27" ventilated rib barrel with the adjustable choke. Manufactured between 1960 and 1966.

Exc.	V.G.	Good	Fair	Poor
200	175	150	125	100

Flite King Brush

As above, with an 18" or 20" cylinder-bore barrel fitted with rifle sights. Manufactured between 1962 and 1964.

Exc.	V.G.	Good	Fair	Poor
175	150	125	100	75

Flite King Brush Deluxe

As above, with an adjustable peep sight and sling swivels. Manufactured between 1964 and 1966.

Exc.	V.G.	Good	Fair	Poor
250	200	175	125	100

Flite King Skeet

As above, in 12 gauge with a 26" ventilated rib barrel that is skeet-bored. Manufactured between 1962 and 1966.

Exc.	V.G.	Good	Fair	Poor
275	225	200	150	125

Flite King Trap

As above, with a 30" ventilated rib, full-choke barrel and a trap-type stock with recoil pad. Manufactured between 1962 and 1966.

Exc.	V.G.	Good	Fair	Poor
250	200	175	125	100

Model 10B

A 12 gauge semiautomatic shotgun with an 18" barrel, pistol grip stock and bullpup design. Fitted with a folding carrying handle and a flashlight attachment on the top of the receiver. Produced in limited quantities.

Exc.	V.G.	Good	Fair	Poor
650	575	450	350	250

Supermatic Shadow Seven

A 12 gauge Over/Under boxlock shotgun with 27.5" or 29.5" ventilated rib barrels, single trigger and automatic ejectors. Blued with a walnut stock. Manufactured in Japan and imported in 1974 and 1975.

Exc.	V.G.	Good	Fair	Poor
675	600	500	425	350

Supermatic Indy

As above, with finer engraving and a better figured walnut stock. Manufactured in Japan and imported in 1974 and 1975.

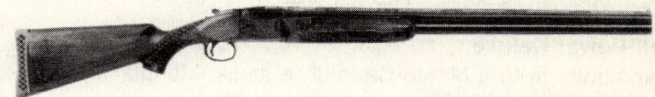

Exc.	V.G.	Good	Fair	Poor
800	700	600	500	425

Supermatic Shadow

A 12 or 20 gauge (standard or Magnum) semiautomatic shotgun with 26", 28", or 30" ventilated rib barrels. Blued with a walnut stock. Manufactured in Japan and imported in 1974 and 1975.

Exc.	V.G.	Good	Fair	Poor
350	300	275	200	125

RIFLES

Sport King Rifle

A .22 caliber semiautomatic rifle with a 22" barrel, open sights and tubular magazine. Blued with a walnut stock. Manufactured between 1960 and 1966.

Exc.	V.G.	Good	Fair	Poor
100	90	75	50	25

Sport King Special

As above, with a Monte Carlo-type stock and beavertail forearm.

Exc.	V.G.	Good	Fair	Poor
150	125	100	60	40

Sport King Deluxe

As above, with a checkered walnut stock. Manufactured between 1966 and 1975.

Exc.	V.G.	Good	Fair	Poor
175	150	125	100	75

Sport King Carbine

As above, with an 18" barrel and sling swivels. Manufactured between 1964 and 1973.

Exc.	V.G.	Good	Fair	Poor
175	150	125	100	75

Flite King

A .22 caliber slide action rifle with a 24" barrel, open sights and tubular magazine. Blued with a Monte Carlo-style stock. Manufactured between 1962 and 1975.

Exc.	V.G.	Good	Fair	Poor
125	100	80	60	40

Hi-Power Field Grade

A .270 or .30-06 caliber bolt-action rifle with a 22" barrel, open sights and 4-shot magazine. Blued with a walnut stock. Manufactured between 1962 and 1966.

Exc.	V.G.	Good	Fair	Poor
300	250	225	150	100

Hi-Power Deluxe

As above, with a Monte Carlo-style stock. Manufactured between 1962 and 1966.

Exc.	V.G.	Good	Fair	Poor
350	300	275	200	150

HILL, W.J.
Birmingham, England

Hill's Self Extracting Revolver

A .32 caliber double action folding trigger revolver with a 3.75" barrel and 6-shot cylinder. Marked "Hill's Patent Self Extractor". Blued with walnut grips.

Exc.	V.G.	Good	Fair	Poor
500	400	350	250	150

HILLIARD, D. H.
Cornish, New Hampshire

Under Hammer Pistol

A .34 caliber under hammer percussion pistol with varying barrel lengths. Blued with walnut grips. Active 1842 to 1877.

Exc.	V.G.	Good	Fair	Poor
—	—	500	350	200

HINO-KOMURA
Tokyo, Japan

A 7.65mm or 8mm Nambu semiautomatic pistol manufactured in limited quantities between 1905 and 1912. The operation of this pistol involves pulling the muzzle forward until the slide engages a catch on the trigger assembly. Pulling the trigger at this point allows the barrel to move back and engage the cartridge nose into the chamber. Squeezing the grip safety then allows the barrel to slam back into the fixed firing pin on the breechblock. Prospective purchasers are advised to secure a qualified appraisal prior to acquisition.

Exc.	V.G.	Good	Fair	Poor
3500	3250	2750	2000	1000

HODGKINS, D. C. & SONS
Macon, Georgia
SEE Bilharz, Hall & Co.

HOFER, P.
Feriach, Austria

A gunmaker specializing in double-barrel rifles made strictly to custom order. Prospective purchasers should secure a qualified appraisal prior to acquisition.

HOFFMAN, LOUIS
Vicksburg, Mississippi

Pocket Pistol

A .41 caliber percussion pocket pistol with a 3" barrel, German silver mounts and walnut stock. Active 1857 to 1886.

Exc.	V.G.	Good	Fair	Poor
—	—	750	450	200

HOLDEN, C. B.
Worcester, Massachusetts

Open Frame Rifle

A .44 r.f. single shot rifle with a 28" barrel, open sights, silver plated bronze frame and walnut stock. The barrel marked "C.B. Holden Worcester-Mass." Produced in limited quantities during the mid-1860s.

Exc.	V.G.	Good	Fair	Poor
—	—	750	475	300

HOLLAND & HOLLAND, LTD.
London, England

Established in 1835, Holland & Holland has manufactured a wide variety of shotguns and rifles during its existence. The greater part of these arms were made to custom order and, therefore, prospective purchasers are advised to secure a qualified appraisal prior to acquisition.

The following models are listed as a guide only.

A cased Holland & Holland Sesquicentennial double hammer gun was sold at auction for $23,000. It was a 12 gauge with 30" barrels and scroll engraved. Condition was new and unfired. Butterfield & Butterfield, April 1997.

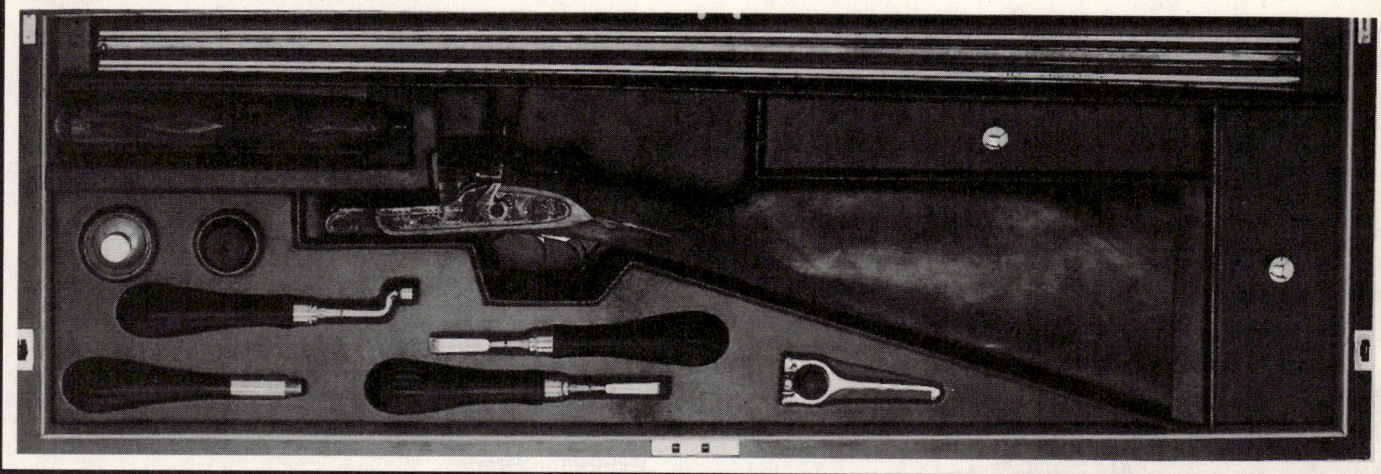

A Holland & Holland sidelock shotgun in 20 gauge with 27" barrels and 2-1/2" chambers was sold at auction for $28,750. Scroll engraved frame with double triggers. Condition was near mint. Butterfield & Butterfield, April 1997.

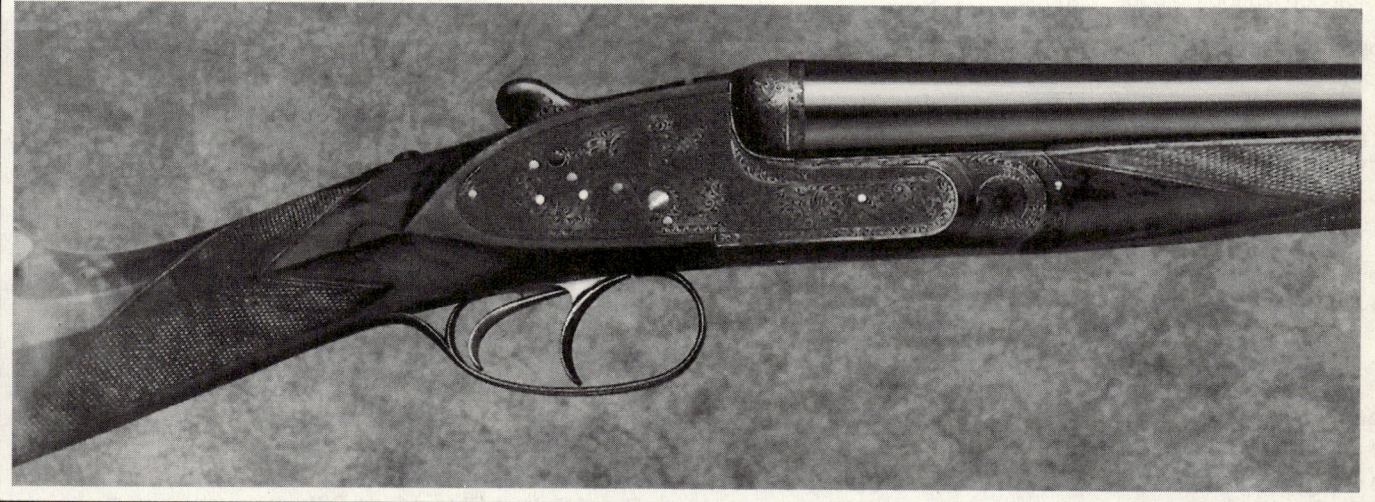

OVER/UNDER SHOTGUNS

Old Model Royal Grade

A 12 gauge sidelock double-barrel shotgun manufactured to custom order prior to 1951.

Exc.	V.G.	Good	Fair	Poor
22000	18500	15000	11000	8500

New Model Royal Grade

As above, with a slimmer action. Manufactured from 1951 to 1960.

Exc.	V.G.	Good	Fair	Poor
25000	20000	17500	12500	10000

Royal Grade Game Gun

Currently manufactured.

Exc.	V.G.	Good	Fair	Poor
45000	38000	32500	25000	20000

A cased set of two Royal Model over and under guns in 12 gauge with 28" barrels. Fine scroll engraved, sold at auction for $110,000. Built in 1955. Condition was excellent. Butterfield & Butterfield, December 1995.

SIDE-X-SIDE SHOTGUNS

Northwood Boxlock
A 12 to 28 gauge boxlock double-barrel shotgun with 28" or 30" barrels, double triggers and automatic ejectors.

20 or 28 Gauge-Add 10%.
Deluxe Version with Engraving-Add 10%.

Exc.	V.G.	Good	Fair	Poor
7500	6500	5250	4000	3000

Cavalier Boxlock
As above, but made on custom order.

20 or 28 Gauge-Add 10%.
Deluxe Model with More Engraving-Add 20%.

Exc.	V.G.	Good	Fair	Poor
12500	10000	7500	5500	4500

Dominion Sidelock
A 12, 16, or 20 gauge sidelock double-barrel shotgun with double triggers and automatic ejectors.

Exc.	V.G.	Good	Fair	Poor
5000	4250	3500	2750	2000

Dominion Game Gun
The current production model, manufactured in 12 gauge only.

Exc.	V.G.	Good	Fair	Poor
30000	25000	20000	15000	7500

Royal Ejector Grade Hammerless Sidelock
Produced strictly on custom order.

20 Gauge-Add 25%.
8 Gauge-Add 35%.
.410-Add 70%.

Exc.	V.G.	Good	Fair	Poor
12500	10000	7500	6000	3000

Deluxe Model
As above, but more finely finished with a self-opening action.

Exc.	V.G.	Good	Fair	Poor
15000	12500	10000	7500	3500

Badminton Grade
As above, without the self-opener.

20 Gauge-Add 25%.
28 Gauge-Add 35%.
.410-Add 50%.

Exc.	V.G.	Good	Fair	Poor
11000	8500	7500	5500	2500

Riviera Grade
As above, with an extra set of barrels.

20 Gauge-Add 25%.
28 Gauge-Add 35%.
.410-Add 50%.

Exc.	V.G.	Good	Fair	Poor
15000	12500	10000	7500	3500

Centenary Grade
A 12 gauge (2") sidelock double-barrel shotgun.

Royal Game Gun
Holland & Holland's best quality shotgun.

20 and 28 Gauges-Add 10%.

Exc.	V.G.	Good	Fair	Poor
42500	32500	25000	17500	8000

Single Barrel Trap Gun
A 12 gauge boxlock single barrel shotgun with 30" or 32" barrel.

Standard Grade
Exc.	V.G.	Good	Fair	Poor
5000	4500	3750	2500	2000

Deluxe Grade
Exc.	V.G.	Good	Fair	Poor
7500	6500	5500	4750	3000

Exhibition Grade
Exc.	V.G.	Good	Fair	Poor
9000	8000	7000	5500	3750

DOUBLE RIFLES

No. 2 Grade Double Rifle
A sidelock double-barrel rifle produced in a variety of calibers with 24" barrels, double triggers, automatic ejectors and express sights. Obsolete cartridges could be worth less.

Exc	V.G.	Good	Fair	Poor
15000	12500	8500	7000	4000

Royal Side-x-Side Rifle
Similar to the above, but more finely finished.

Exc.	V.G.	Good	Fair	Poor
50000	40000	30000	22500	12000

Royal Deluxe Side-x-Side Rifle
Holland & Holland's best quality double-barrel rifle.

Exc.	V.G.	Good	Fair	Poor
56000	45000	35000	25000	12500

H&H 700 Bore Side-x-Side Rifle
A .700 Holland & Holland double-barrel rifle. Currently manufactured. Due to the uniqueness of the piece, buyers should seek qualified appraisal.

> A cased engraved and enamelled gold side by side hammerless double rifle was sold at auction for $115,500. It was chambered for the .375 Express and fitted with 28" barrels. A unique engraving with enamelled gold plates and deep relief engraving with animal scenes. Condition was excellent. Butterfield & Butterfield, December 1995.

BOLT ACTION RIFLES

Best Quality Rifle

A bolt-action rifle produced in calibers up to .375 Holland & Holland with a 24" barrel, express sights and 4-shot magazine.

Exc.	V.G.	Good	Fair	Poor
7500	6500	5000	3500	2250

Deluxe Magazine Rifle

As above, but more finely finished.

Exc.	V.G.	Good	Fair	Poor
10500	8500	7000	5000	3000

HOLLIS & SONS
SEE English Military Firearms

HOLLOWAY ARMS CO.
Ft. Worth, Texas

HAC Model 7

A 7.62x54mm semiautomatic rifle with a 20" barrel, adjustable sights, integral telescope mount and 20-shot magazine. Black anodized finish with folding stock.

HAC Model 7C

As above, with a 16" barrel.

HAC Model 7S

As above, with a heavy-barrel.

HOLMES FIREARMS
Wheeler, Arkansas

MP-22

A .22 caliber semiautomatic pistol with a 6" barrel and alloy receiver. Anodized black finish with a walnut grip. Manufactured in 1985.

NIB	Exc.	V.G.	Good	Fair	Poor
375	300	275	225	200	150

MP-83

Similar to the above, but in 9mm or .45 caliber. Manufactured in 1985.

NIB	Exc.	V.G.	Good	Fair	Poor
450	350	325	275	250	200

NOTE: Several of the Holmes pistols have been declared machine guns by the BATF because of their easy conversion to full automatic. Make sure before purchase that a Class III license is not required.

HOOD F. A. CO.
Norwich, Connecticut

A manufacturer of spur trigger .22 or .32 caliber revolvers with varying length barrels and finishes. Many of these revolvers are found stamped only with trade names.

Exc.	V.G.	Good	Fair	Poor
200	175	125	100	75

HOPKINS & ALLEN
Norwich, Connecticut
ALSO SEE Bacon Arms Co.
Merwin Hulbert & Co.

Established in 1868, this company produced a variety of spur trigger revolvers in .22, .32, .38, or .41 caliber often marked with trade names such as: Acme, Blue Jacket, Captain Jack, Chichester, Defender, Dictator, Hopkins & Allen, Imperial Arms Co., Monarch, Mountain Eagle, Ranger, Tower's Police Safety, Universal, and XL.

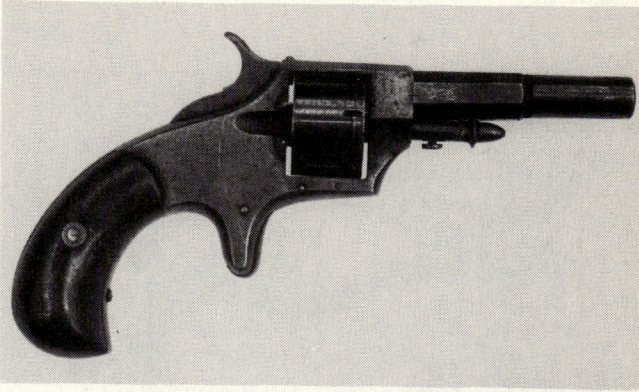

Courtesy Milwaukee Public Museum, Milwaukee, Wisconsin

Exc.	V.G.	Good	Fair	Poor
175	150	125	100	75

Some of these revolvers are hinged frame, double-action break-opens with round-ribbed barrels of various lengths. Blued or nickel-plated, with checkered plastic grips.

Exc.	V.G.	Good	Fair	Poor
150	125	100	75	50

Dictator

A .36 caliber percussion or .38 r.f. single action revolver with a 4" barrel and 5-shot cylinder. Blued with walnut grips. The barrel marked "Dictator". Approximately 6,000 percussion revolvers were made and 5,000 rimfire.

Exc.	V.G.	Good	Fair	Poor
500	400	350	250	150

Failing Block Rifle

A .22 to .38-55 caliber single shot rifle with a 24", 26", or 28" octagonal barrel. Blued with a walnut stock. Manufactured between 1888 and 1892.

Exc.	V.G.	Good	Fair	Poor
500	400	300	225	125

Schuetzen Rifle

A .22 or .25-20 caliber single shot rifle with a 26" octagonal barrel, double-set trigger and a Schuetzen-type buttplate. Blued with a walnut stock.

Exc.	V.G.	Good	Fair	Poor
850	750	650	500	300

Navy Revolver

A .38 caliber single action revolver with a 6.5" barrel marked, "Hopkins & Allen Mfg. Co., Pat. Mar. 28, 71, Apr. 27, 75" and a 6-shot cylinder. The top strap marked, "XL Navy". Blued or nickel-plated with walnut grips. Several hundred were made between 1878 and 1882.

Exc.	V.G.	Good	Fair	Poor
500	425	350	250	175

Army Revolver

As above, in .44 r.f. with a 4.5", 6", or 7.5" barrel. The top strap marked, "XL No. 8." Several hundred were manufactured between 1878 and 1882.

Exc.	V.G.	Good	Fair	Poor
650	575	475	325	225

Derringer

A .22 caliber single shot pistol with a hinged 1.75" barrel that pivots downwards for loading. Blued or nickel-plated with walnut, ivory, or pearl grips. The frame marked, "Hopkins & Allen Arms Co., Norwich, Conn. U.S.A." Several hundred were manufactured in the 1880s and 1890s.

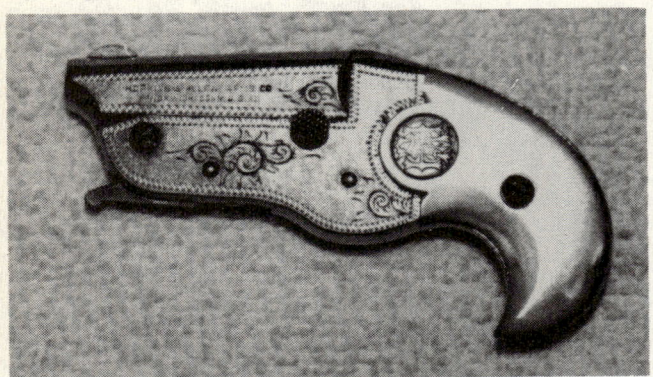

Exc.	V.G.	Good	Fair	Poor
1500	900	600	475	350

Hopkins & Allen also made single and double barrel shotguns in large numbers. Many were sold under trade names such as Siminole and King Nitro.

HOTCHKISS
Winchester Arms Co.
New Haven, Connecticut

HOWA MACHINE COMPANY
Japan

This company manufactured bolt-action rifles for Smith & Wesson until 1985 and then for Mossberg in 1986 and 1987. Presently, Howa firearms are imported by Interarms of Alexandria, Virginia.

Model 1500 Hunter

A .22-250, .223, .243, .270, 7mm Remington Magnum .308, .30-06, and .300 Winchester Magnum caliber bolt-action sporting rifle with a 22" or 24" barrel and 3- or 5-shot magazine. Blued with a checkered walnut stock. Imported by Interarms in 1988 only.

NIB	Exc.	V.G.	Good	Fair	Poor
350	300	275	225	175	100

Model 1500 Trophy

As above, but with more finely figured walnut stocks and checkering. Introduced in 1988.

NIB	Exc.	V.G.	Good	Fair	Poor
400	350	300	250	200	150

Model 1500 Varmint

As above, in .22-250 or .223 caliber with a 24" heavy barrel. Introduced in 1988.

NIB	Exc.	V.G.	Good	Fair	Poor
425	375	325	275	200	150

Model 1500 Lightning

As above, in .270, 7mm Remington Magnum, and .30-06 caliber with a composition stock. Introduced in 1988.

NIB	Exc.	V.G.	Good	Fair	Poor
500	450	400	350	250	175

Realtree Camo Rifle

Introduced in 1993 this bolt action model features a composite stock, a 22" barrel. Both the metal and stock finish are a brown leaf pattern. The receiver is a mono-block system. The floorplate is hinged and the magazine holds 5 rounds. The receiver is drilled and tapped for scope mounts. Fitted with a sling swivel and recoil pad. Offered in .30-06 and .270 calibers. Weighs 8 lbs.

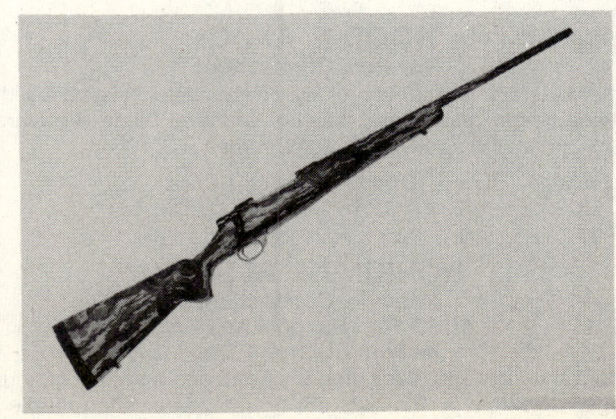

NIB	Exc.	V.G.	Good	Fair	Poor
500	450	400	350	300	200

Lighting Rifle

Introduced in 1993 this model has a black composite checkered stock with Schnabel forend. The butt stock is Monte Carlo. Offered in .223, .22-250, .243, .270, .308, .30-06, 7mm Rem. Mag., .300 and .338 Win. Mag. Weighs about 7.5 lbs.

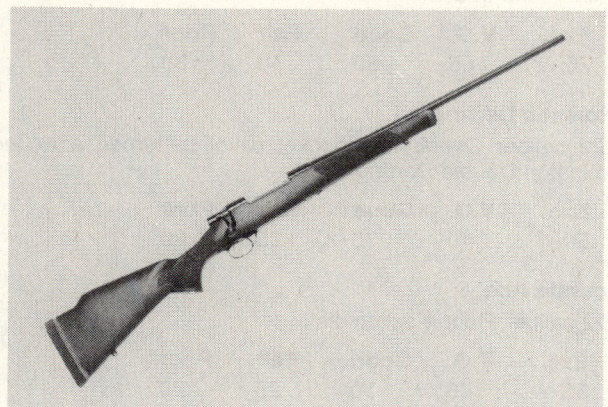

NIB	Exc.	V.G.	Good	Fair	Poor
400	350	300	250	200	125

HOWARD-WHITNEY
New Haven, Connecticut
SEE Whitney Arms Co.

HUNT
New Haven, Connecticut
SEE Winchester Repeating Arms Co.

HUNTER ARMS CO.
Fulton, New York
SEE L. C. Smith

HUSQVARNA
Husqvarna, Sweden

PISTOLS

Model 1907

This pistol is a copy of the FN Browning Model 1903 made for the Swedish Army. It is identical in every way to the FN model. Many were converted to the .380 caliber and imported into the U.S. If converted to .380 caliber reduce values by 50%.

Courtesy Orvel Reichert

Exc.	V.G.	Good	Fair	Poor
350	250	200	150	100

Lahti

A 9mm caliber semiautomatic pistol with a 5.5" barrel and 8-shot magazine. Designed by Aino Lahti and adopted as the standard Swedish sidearm in 1940.

Exc.	V.G.	Good	Fair	Poor
400	350	275	225	150

BOLT ACTION RIFLES

Hi-Power

A bolt action sporting rifle manufactured in a variety of calibers with a 24" barrel, open sights and beechwood stock. Manufactured between 1946 and 1951.

Exc.	V.G.	Good	Fair	Poor
375	300	275	200	150

Model 1100 Deluxe

As above, with a walnut stock. Manufactured between 1952 and 1956.

Exc.	V.G.	Good	Fair	Poor
450	400	325	250	200

Model 1000 Super Grade

As above, with a Monte Carlo-style stock. Manufactured between 1952 and 1956.

Exc.	V.G.	Good	Fair	Poor
450	400	325	250	200

Model 3100 Crown Grade

A bolt action sporting rifle manufactured in a variety of calibers with a 24" barrel, walnut stock with a black composition forend tip and pistol grip cap. Manufactured between 1954 and 1972.

Exc.	V.G.	Good	Fair	Poor
550	475	350	300	200

Model 4100 Lightweight

As above, with a Schnabel forend tip. Manufactured between 1954 and 1972.

Exc.	V.G.	Good	Fair	Poor
550	475	350	300	200

Model 456

As above, with a full length Mannlicher-style stock. Manufactured between 1959 and 1970.

Exc.	V.G.	Good	Fair	Poor
400	350	300	250	200

Model 6000

The Model 4100 with express folding sights and a finely figured walnut stock. Manufactured between 1968 and 1970.

Exc.	V.G.	Good	Fair	Poor
650	500	400	300	200

Model 9000 Crown Grade

A bolt action sporting rifle manufactured in a variety of calibers with a 23.5" barrel, open sights, adjustable trigger and walnut stock. Manufactured in 1971 and 1972.

Exc.	V.G.	Good	Fair	Poor
475	425	350	300	250

Model 8000 Imperial Grade

As above, with an engraved magazine floor plate, machine jeweled bolt and finely figured walnut stock. Manufactured in 1971 and 1972.

Exc.	V.G.	Good	Fair	Poor
700	550	475	400	300

HY-HUNTER, INC.
Burbank, California

Chicago Cub

A .22 caliber folding trigger double action revolver with a 2" barrel and 6-shot cylinder.

Exc.	V.G.	Good	Fair	Poor
50	40	30	25	20

Detective

A .22 or .22 WMR caliber double action revolver with a 2.5" barrel and 6-shot cylinder. Blued with plastic grips.

Exc.	V.G.	Good	Fair	Poor
65	50	40	30	25

Frontier Six Shooter

A .22 or .22 WMR caliber single action revolver with a 6-shot cylinder.

Exc.	V.G.	Good	Fair	Poor
75	65	50	40	30

Frontier Six Shooter

As above, in .357 Magnum, .44 Magnum or .45 Colt.

Exc.	V.G.	Good	Fair	Poor
125	100	85	75	50

Maxim

A .25 caliber semiautomatic pistol with a 2" barrel and 5-shot magazine.

Exc.	V.G.	Good	Fair	Poor
75	65	50	40	30

Military

A .22, .32 or .380 caliber double action semiautomatic pistol with a 4" barrel and 6-shot magazine.

Exc.	V.G.	Good	Fair	Poor
100	80	60	50	40

Stingray

A .25 caliber semiautomatic pistol with a 2.5" barrel and 5-shot magazine.

Exc.	V.G.	Good	Fair	Poor
75	65	50	40	30

Panzer

A .22 caliber semiautomatic pistol with a 4" barrel and 7-shot magazine.

Exc.	V.G.	Good	Fair	Poor
75	65	50	40	30

Stuka

Similar to the above.

Exc.	V.G.	Good	Fair	Poor
75	65	50	40	30

Automatic Derringer

A .22 caliber Over/Under pocket pistol patterned after the Remington Double Derringer.

Exc.	V.G.	Good	Fair	Poor
50	40	30	25	20

Accurate Ace

A .22 caliber Flobert action pistol.

Exc.	V.G.	Good	Fair	Poor
50	40	30	25	20

Favorite

A .22 or .22 WMR caliber copy of the Steven's single shot pistol with a 6" barrel and nickel-plated frame.

Exc.	V.G.	Good	Fair	Poor
100	80	70	50	25

Gold Rush Derringer

A .22 caliber spur trigger single shot pistol with a 2.5" barrel.

Exc.	V.G.	Good	Fair	Poor
50	40	30	25	20

Target Model

A .22 or .22 WMR bolt-action single shot pistol with a 10" barrel, adjustable sights and walnut grip.

Exc	V.G.	Good	Fair	Poor
50	40	30	25	20

HYDE & SHATTUCK
Hatfield, Massachusetts

Queen Derringer

A .22 caliber spur trigger single shot pistol with a 2.5" half octagonal barrel. Blued or nickel-plated with walnut grips. The barrel normally marked "Queen", but sometimes "Hyde & Shattuck". Manufactured between 1876 and 1879.

Exc.	V.G.	Good	Fair	Poor
—	—	450	300	150

HYPER
Jenks, Oklahoma

Single Shot Rifle

A custom made falling block action single shot rifle manufactured in a variety of calibers, barrel lengths, barrel types, and stock styles. As these rifles were made to custom order, prospective purchasers should secure a qualified appraisal prior to acquisition. Manufactured until 1984.

Exc.	V.G.	Good	Fair	Poor
2500	2000	1750	1450	800

IAB
Brescia, Italy
Industria Armi Bresciane

Imported by Puccinelli & Company of San Anselmo, California, and by Sporting Arms International of Indianola, Mississippi.

S-300

A 12 gauge boxlock single barrel trap gun with 30" or 32" barrels having a wide ventilated rib and walnut trap-style stock.

Exc.	V.G.	Good	Fair	Poor
1500	1250	1000	850	450

C-300 Combo

A 12 gauge Over/Under boxlock double-barrel shotgun with 30" or 32" barrels, single selective trigger, automatic ejectors, trap-style walnut stock, accompanied by two extra single barrels.

Exc.	V.G.	Good	Fair	Poor
2500	2250	1850	1500	800

C-300 Super Combo

As above, but more finely finished.

Exc.	V.G.	Good	Fair	Poor
3000	2750	2250	1750	900

IAR
San Juan Capistrano, California

This company is an importer of Italian made reproduction pistol and rifles. For a complete listing see *Uberti.*

IGA
Veranopolis, Brazil
Importer-Stoeger Industries
Hackensack, New Jersey

Single Barrel Shotgun

A 12 or 20 gauge or .410 bore single barrel shotgun with an exposed hammer, 28" barrel and hardwood stock.

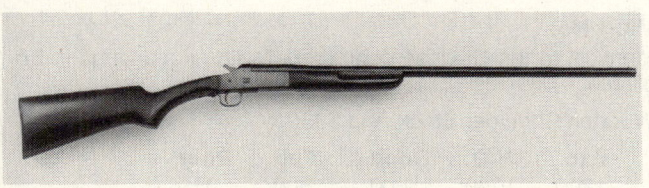

NIB	Exc.	V.G.	Good	Fair	Poor
110	90	75	50	40	30

Single Barrel Shotgun-Youth Model

Offered in 20 gauge and .410 bore this model features a 22" barrel and shorter than standard butt stock. Weighs 5 lbs.

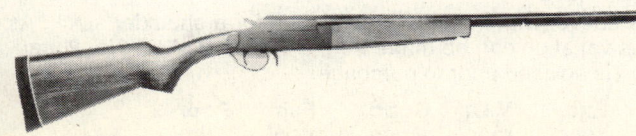

NIB	Exc.	V.G.	Good	Fair	Poor
120	100	80	60	50	35

Coach Gun

A 12 or 20 gauge boxlock double-barrel shotgun with 20" barrels, double triggers and extractors. Blued with a hardwood stock.

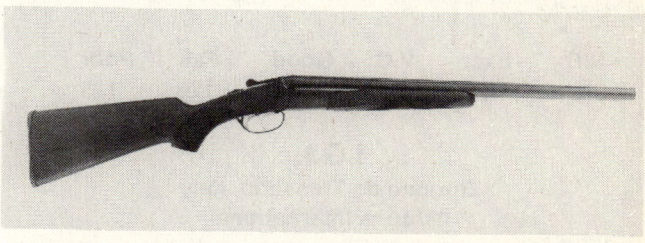

NIB	Exc.	V.G.	Good	Fair	Poor
285	225	175	150	100	75

Standard Side-x-Side-Uplander Model

Offered in 12, 20, 28 gauge, and .410 bore with 26" and 28" barrels. Checkered hardwood stock with pistol grip or straight grip in 20 gauge only. Weighs 6.75 lbs.

NIB	Exc.	V.G.	Good	Fair	Poor
250	225	200	150	100	75

Standard O/U-Condor I

This model is offered in 12 or 20 gauge with 26" or 28" barrels. Fitted with extractors and single trigger. Choke tubes are standard. Checkered hardwood stock with pistol grip and recoil pad. Weighs 8 lbs.

NIB	Exc.	V.G.	Good	Fair	Poor
275	250	225	200	150	100

Condor II

Same as above but with double triggers and plastic buttplate.

NIB	Exc.	V.G.	Good	Fair	Poor
275	225	200	150	100	75

Deluxe O/U-ERA 2000

Offered in 12 gauge only with 26" or 28" barrels. Fitted with single trigger and extractors. Choke tubes are standard. Barrels are chrome lined and stock is hand checkered.

NIB	Exc.	V.G.	Good	Fair	Poor
375	325	275	225	175	125

I.G.I.
Zingone de Tressano, Italy
Itaiguns International

Domino SP602

A .22 caliber semiautomatic target pistol with a 6" barrel and 5-shot magazine (that is inserted into the action from the top), adjustable trigger and customized grips.

Exc.	V.G.	Good	Fair	Poor
800	700	600	450	250

Domino OP601

As above, but in .22 short caliber.

Exc.	V.G.	Good	Fair	Poor
800	700	600	450	250

INDIAN ARMS CORP.
Detroit, Michigan

Indian Arms .380

A .380 caliber semiautomatic pistol with a 3.25" barrel and 6-shot magazine. Made of stainless steel and finished either in the white or blued with walnut grips. Manufactured from 1975 to 1977.

Exc.	V.G.	Good	Fair	Poor
375	325	275	175	100

INGLIS, JOHN & COMPANY
Toronto, Canada

This firm manufactured Browning Pattern .35 semiautomatic pistols for both the Canadian and Chinese governments.

Chinese Contract Pattern .35

A 9mm semiautomatic pistol with a 5" barrel and 13-shot magazine. Black anodized finish with black plastic grips, sliding tangent rear sight and the rear of the grip slotted for a shoulder stock. Manufactured in 1944 and 1945. Prices listed below are for shoulder stock as well as pistol. For pistol alone the price would be $350 less for examples in excellent condition.

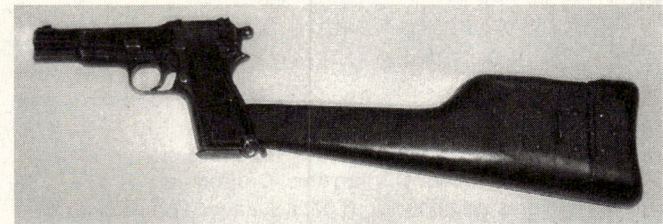

Courtesy Richard M. Kumor, Sr.

Exc.	V.G.	Good	Fair	Poor
1750	1500	1250	800	700

NOTE: Pistols of this type have been imported in large quantities and are available at low cost. The values listed above, however, are for examples not stamped with an importer's trade name or trademark.

Canadian Military

Mk. 1 No. 1

Identical to the Chinese contract but with all markings in English.

Wooden Shoulder Stock-Add $350.

Exc.	V.G.	Good	Fair	Poor
1200	1000	800	600	450

Mk. 1 No. 2

As above, with a fixed rear sight and the grip strap not slotted for a shoulder stock.

Exc.	V.G.	Good	Fair	Poor
600	500	450	350	250

Mk. I No. 2

As above, with the grip strap slotted for a shoulder stock. As this variation can be made from a standard Mk. 1 No. 2, caution is advised prior to purchase.

Exc.	V.G.	Good	Fair	Poor
1200	1000	800	600	450

INDUSTRIA ARMI GALESI
Brescia, Italy
SEE Galesi

INGRAM
Atlanta, Georgia
Military Armament Corp.

MAC10

A 9mm or .45 caliber semiautomatic pistol with a 5.75" barrel and 32-shot magazine. Anodized with plastic grips.

Accessory Kit (Barrel Extension and Extra Magazine)-Add 20%.

NIB	Exc.	V.G.	Good	Fair	Poor
1100	800	650	500	400	200

MAC 10AI

As above, but firing from a closed bolt.

Accessory Kit-Add 20%.

NIB	Exc.	V.G.	Good	Fair	Poor
450	350	250	200	150	100

MAC 11

As above in a smaller version and chambered for the .380ACP cartridge.

Accessory Kit-Add 20%.

NIB	Exc.	V.G.	Good	Fair	Poor
900	800	600	400	300	150

INTERARMS
WORLD CLASS SPORTING ARMS

INTERARMS
Alexandria, Virginia

An importer of arms made by Howa Machine, Star, Walther, and Rossi.

RIFLES

Mark X Viscount

Bolt action sporting rifle made in a variety of calibers with a 24" barrel, open sights, adjustable trigger and magazine holding either 3 or 5 cartridges. Manufactured in Yugoslavia. Blued with a walnut stock.

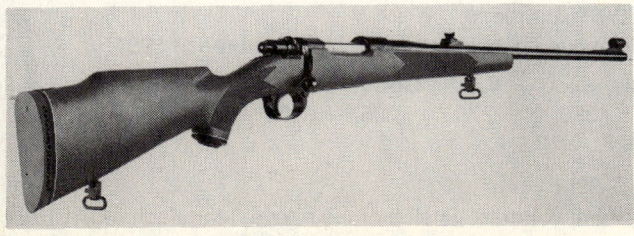

NIB	Exc.	V.G.	Good	Fair	Poor
350	300	250	200	175	125

Mark X Lightweight

As above, with a 20" barrel and composition stock. Introduced in 1988.

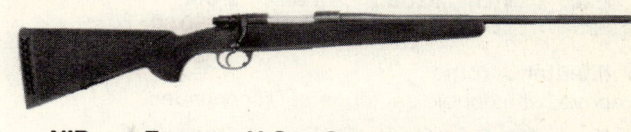

NIB	Exc.	V.G.	Good	Fair	Poor
350	300	250	200	175	125

Mini Mark X

As above, with a short action in .223 caliber only with a 20" barrel, open sights, adjustable trigger and 5-shot magazine. Introduced in 1987.

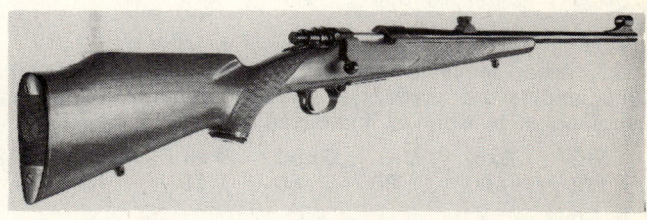

NIB	Exc.	V.G.	Good	Fair	Poor
350	300	250	200	175	125

Mark X American Field

As above, with a finely figured walnut stock, ebony forend tip, pistol grip cap, sling swivels and recoil pad. Introduced in 1984.

NIB	Exc.	V.G.	Good	Fair	Poor
450	400	350	300	250	175

Whitworth Express Rifle

A .375 Holland & Holland or .458 Winchester Magnum bolt action sporting rifle with a 24" barrel, express sights and 3-shot magazine. Blued with a walnut stock. Introduced in 1974.

NIB	Exc.	V.G.	Good	Fair	Poor
550	500	450	350	250	200

Whitworth Mannlicher Carbine

A .243, .270, 7x57mm, .308, and the .30-06 caliber bolt action rifle with a 20" barrel, open sights, sling swivels and a full length stock. Manufactured between 1984 and 1987.

Exc.	V.G.	Good	Fair	Poor
450	400	350	250	200

Cavalier

A bolt action sporting rifle made in a variety of calibers with a modern styled stock having a rollover cheekpiece. Discontinued.

Exc.	V.G.	Good	Fair	Poor
325	275	250	200	150

Mannlicher Carbine
As above, with a 20" barrel and full length stock. Discontinued.

Exc.	V.G.	Good	Fair	Poor
325	275	250	200	150

Continental Carbine
As above, with double set triggers. Discontinued.

Exc.	V.G.	Good	Fair	Poor
350	300	250	200	150

Alaskan Model
Similar to the Mark X, in .375 Holland & Holland or .458 Winchester Magnum with a 24" barrel. Discontinued in 1985.

Exc.	V.G.	Good	Fair	Poor
450	400	350	300	200

22-ATD
A .22 caliber semiautomatic rifle with a 19.4" barrel, open sights, and 11-shot magazine. Blued with a hardwood stock. Manufactured by Norinco. Introduced in 1987.

NIB	Exc.	V.G.	Good	Fair	Poor
125	100	80	60	50	40

HANDGUNS

Helwan Brigadier
A 9mm semiautomatic pistol with a 4.5" barrel, fixed sights, and 8-shot magazine. Blued with plastic grips. Introduced in 1988.

NIB	Exc.	V.G.	Good	Fair	Poor
250	225	200	175	125	100

FEG R-9
A 9mm semiautomatic pistol patterned after the Browning 35 with a 13-shot magazine. Blued with walnut grips. Manufactured in 1986 and 1987.

Exc.	V.G.	Good	Fair	Poor
275	225	185	145	100

FEG PPH
A .380 caliber double action semiautomatic pistol with a 3.5" barrel and 6-shot magazine. Blued with plastic grips.

Exc.	V.G.	Good	Fair	Poor
200	175	150	125	100

Virginian Dragoon
A .44 Magnum single action revolver with a 6", 7.5", 8.75", or 12" barrel, adjustable sights and 6-shot cylinder. Originally made in Switzerland and then in the U.S.A. Discontinued in 1984.

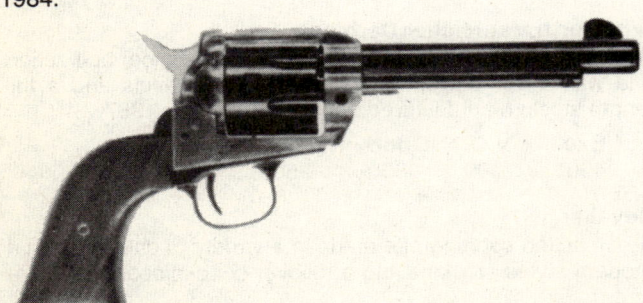

Exc.	V.G.	Good	Fair	Poor
250	150	125	100	75

Stainless Dragoon
As above, in stainless steel.

Exc.	V.G.	Good	Fair	Poor
275	175	150	125	100

Virginian .22 Convertible
As above, in .22 caliber with a 5.5" barrel.

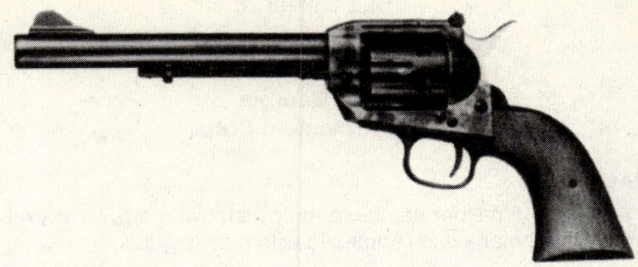

Exc.	V.G.	Good	Fair	Poor
250	150	125	100	75

Virginian Stainless .22 Convertible
As above, in stainless steel.

Exc.	V.G.	Good	Fair	Poor
275	175	150	100	80

Mauser Parabellum Karabiner
A 9mm caliber semiautomatic carbine with an 11.75" barrel and detachable shoulder stock. Fitted in a leather case.

NOTE: Only 100 were imported into the United States and this arm is subject to BATF registration.

NIB	Exc.	V.G.	Good	Fair	Poor
6500	5750	5000	4000	3000	2250

Mauser Parabellum Cartridge Counter
A reproduction of the cartridge counter Luger. Fitted in a leather case with only 100 units imported into the United States.

NIB	Exc.	V.G.	Good	Fair	Poor
3600	3000	2500	2000	1500	1000

INTERDYNAMICS OF AMERICA
Miami, Florida

KG-9
A 9mm caliber semiautomatic pistol with a 3" barrel and 36-shot magazine. Manufactured from 1981 and 1983.

Exc.	V.G.	Good	Fair	Poor
750	650	575	500	300

KG-99
As above, with a barrel shroud. Manufactured from 1981 and 1984.

Exc.	V.G.	Good	Fair	Poor
300	225	175	125	100

KG-99 Stainless
As above, in stainless steel. Manufactured in 1984.

Exc.	V.G.	Good	Fair	Poor
350	275	225	150	125

KG-99M
A more compact version of the above. Manufactured in 1984.

Exc.	V.G.	Good	Fair	Poor
250	200	150	125	100

INTRATEC USA, INC.
Miami, Florida

TEC-9

A 9mm caliber semiautomatic pistol with a 5" shrouded barrel and 36-shot magazine. Introduced in 1985.

NIB	Exc.	V.G.	Good	Fair	Poor
250	200	175	150	125	100

TEC-9C

As above, with a 16" barrel and a folding stock. Manufactured in 1987.

Exc.	V.G.	Good	Fair	Poor
275	225	200	150	100

TEC-9M

As above, with a 3" barrel and 20-shot magazine. Also made in stainless steel.

NIB	Exc.	V.G.	Good	Fair	Poor
275	200	175	150	100	75

TEC-22 "Scorpion"

Similar to the above, but in .22 caliber with a 4" barrel and 30-shot magazine.

NIB	Exc.	V.G.	Good	Fair	Poor
200	150	125	100	75	50

TEC-38

A .38 caliber Over/Under double-action derringer with 3" barrels. Manufactured between 1986 and 1988.

Exc.	V.G.	Good	Fair	Poor
125	100	80	65	45

IRVING, W.
New York, New York

Single Shot Derringer

A .22 caliber spur trigger single shot pistol with a 2.75" half octagonal barrel. Silver plated brass frame, blued barrel and rosewood grips. The barrel marked "W. Irving". Manufactured in the 1860s. The .32 caliber variation has a 3" barrel and is worth approximately 40% more than the values listed below.

Exc.	V.G.	Good	Fair	Poor
—	900	500	300	125

POCKET REVOLVER

1st Model

A .31 caliber spur trigger percussion revolver with a 3" octagonal barrel, 6-shot cylinder and brass frame. The barrel marked "W. Irving". Approximately 50 were made between 1858 and 1862.

Exc.	V.G.	Good	Fair	Poor
—	750	500	350	250

2nd Model

A .31 caliber percussion revolver with a 4.5" round barrel, loading lever and either brass or iron frame. The barrel marked "Address W. Irving. 20 Cliff St. N.Y." Approximately 600 manufactured with a brass frame and 1,500 with a frame of iron. The brass-frame version will bring a premium of about 35%.

Exc.	V.G.	Good	Fair	Poor
—	600	400	300	200

IRWINDALE ARMS, INC.
Irwindale, California
SEE AMT

ISRAELI MILITARY INDUSTRIES
Israel

Civilian firearms manufactured by this firm have been retailed by Action Arms Limited, Magnum Research, and as of 1997 by Mossberg.

ITHACA GUN CO.
Ithaca, New York

The following material was supplied by Walter C. Snyder and is Copyrighted in his name. Used with the author's permission.

The Ithaca Gun Company was founded by William Henry Baker, John VanNatta, and Dwight McIntyre. Gun production started during the latter half of 1883 at an industrial site located on Fall Creek, Ithaca, New York. Leroy Smith joined the company by 1885 and George Livermore joined the firm in 1887. By 1894 the company was under the exclusive control of Leroy Smith and George Livermore. Many of the company's assets were purchased by the Ithaca Acquisition Corporation in 1987 and moved to King Ferry, New York, where it operated until May, 1996. Ithaca Acquisition's assets were purchased in 1996 by the Ithaca Gun Company, LLC and they continue operations to this day at the King Ferry site.

HAMMER MODELS

Ithaca Baker Model

The first model produced by the company was designed by W.H. Baker and was manufactured from 1883 through 1887. It was offered in six grades; Quality A ($35.00) through Quality F ($200.00) in either 10 or 12 gauge. All Ithaca produced Baker models had exposed hammers. Grades above Quality B are seldom encountered and an expert appraisal is recommended.

Quality A

Courtesy Walter C. Snyder and C. Hadley Smith

Exc.	V.G.	Good	Fair	Poor
700	500	300	200	100

Quality B

Exc.	V.G.	Good	Fair	Poor
1000	700	350	200	100

New Ithaca Gun

The New Ithaca Gun was introduced in 1888 and discontinued during 1913. Like its predecessor, it was introduced in the same seven grades, Quality A through Quality F. Later, the Quality F was discontinued. By 1900, a steel barreled model, named Quality X, was introduced. The New Ithaca Gun was produced in gauges 10, 12, and 16. Lower grade models carried the logo, "New Ithaca Gun", usually within a banner, on each side of the frame. Expert appraisals are recommended. A Quality F grade may bring as much as $3,500 depending on condition.

Quality A

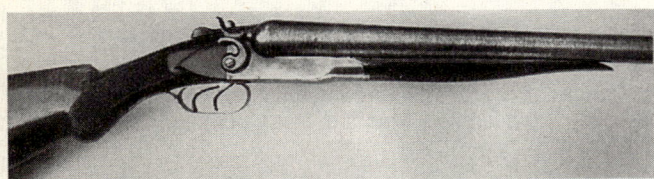

Courtesy Walter C. Snyder and C. Hadley Smith

Exc.	V.G.	Good	Fair	Poor
1000	700	300	200	100

Quality AA

Exc.	V.G.	Good	Fair	Poor
1700	1200	400	200	100

Quality B

Exc.	V.G.	Good	Fair	Poor
1700	1200	400	200	100

Quality X

Exc.	V.G.	Good	Fair	Poor
1500	1000	450	200	100

NOTE: Sixteen gauge guns command a 30% premium. the extremely rare 20 gauge model requires an expert appraisal.

The "New Double Bolted Hammer Gun"

During 1913, the Ithaca Gun Company replaced the New Ithaca Gun with a model it referred to as "our new model two bolt hammer gun". The new hammer gun had coil springs powering the external hammers. The "two bolt" lock up was accomplished by a bottom bolt and by the top lever engagement with the rear nub of the rib extension. Lower grade models were marked on both sides of the frame with a setter dog and the logo, "Ithaca Gun Co." The 1915 catalog is the last year hammer guns were advertised but the old records indicate a few were sold as late as 1919. Grades offered were X, A, AA, B, C, D, and E. The 1915 catalogue advertised a price of $29.00 for an A Quality model and $150.00 for the elaborately engraved Quality E. All grades were available in 10, 12, and 16 gauges. Like the New Ithaca Gun, grades above Quality B are seldom encountered, and an expert appraisal is recommended. Sixteen gauge guns command a 30% price premium. The extremely rare 20 gauge model requires an expert appraisal.

Quality A

Exc.	V.G.	Good	Fair	Poor
1200	800	300	200	100

Quality AA

Exc.	V.G.	Good	Fair	Poor
1700	1200	400	200	100

Quality B

Exc.	V.G.	Good	Fair	Poor
1700	1200	400	200	100

Quality X

Exc.	V.G.	Good	Fair	Poor
1500	1000	450	200	100

HAMMERLESS MODELS

The first hammerless Ithaca gun was introduced in 1888. All Ithaca double guns were discontinued in 1948.

The gauge and grade can usually be found on the left front corner of the water table of the frame, the serial number is usually found on the right side of the same water table, on the barrel flats, and on the forend iron.

Crass Model

The Crass Model, named after Ithaca's Frederick Crass who designed it, was introduced in 1888. It was offered in Quality 1 through Quality 7. The Quality 1P, a model with no engraving, was introduced in 1898. The Crass Model underwent three major frame redesigns before it was discontinued during 1901. The gun was available in 10, 12, and 16 gauge. Automatic ejectors were introduced in 1893 and were available in any quality gun at extra cost.

NOTE: Sixteen gauge guns will command a 20% price premium. Guns above Quality 4 are seldom encountered, and an expert appraisal is necessary. For automatic ejectors add $250.00. The serial number range for the Crass Model is approximately 7000 to 50000.

Quality 1

Exc.	V.G.	Good	Fair	Poor
1000	800	400	200	100

Quality 1-1/2

Exc.	V.G.	Good	Fair	Poor
1500	1000	400	200	100

Quality 1P

Exc.	V.G.	Good	Fair	Poor
80	500	350	200	100

Quality 2

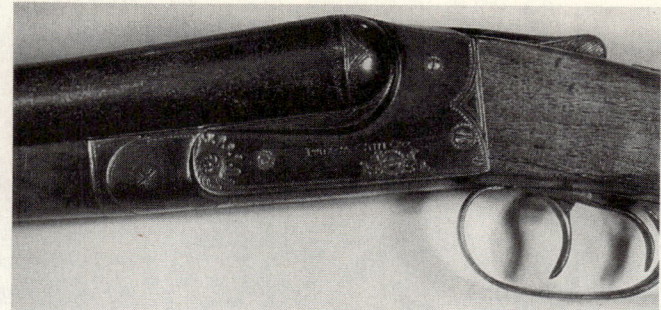

Courtesy Walter C. Snyder and C. Hadley Smith

Exc.	V.G.	Good	Fair	Poor
1200	800	550	200	100

Quality 3

Exc.	V.G.	Good	Fair	Poor
1700	1400	800	300	100

Quality 4

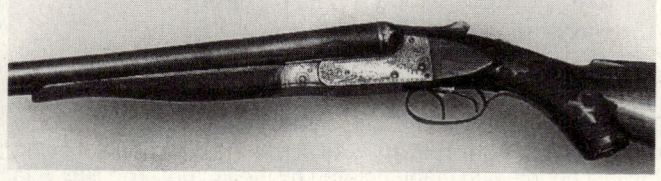

Exc.	V.G.	Good	Fair	Poor
2500	1800	1200	500	100

Lewis Model

Chester Lewis, an Ithaca Gun employee, was credited with the design of the gun that now bears his name. The gun was bolted through the rib extension in addition to the traditional under bolt. The model was available from 1901 through 1906, and was offered in Qualities 1 through 7. It was made in 10, 12, and 16 gauge, and after 1906, 20 gauge. Automatic ejectors were offered at added cost. Qualities offered: 1, 1 Special, 1-1/2, 2, 3, 4, 5, 6, 7. The 1 Special had Nitro Steel barrels.

NOTE: Automatic ejectors add about $250.00 to grades below Quality 4. The serial number range for the Lewis Model is approximately 55000 to 123,600.

Quality 1

Exc.	V.G.	Good	Fair	Poor
800	500	300	150	100

Quality 1 Special

Courtesy Walter C. Snyder and C. Hadley Smith

Exc.	V.G.	Good	Fair	Poor
800	500	300	150	100

Quality 1-1/2

Exc.	V.G.	Good	Fair	Poor
850	550	300	150	100

Quality 2

Exc.	V.G.	Good	Fair	Poor
1000	600	400	200	100

Quality 3

Exc.	V.G.	Good	Fair	Poor
1700	1400	800	400	100

Quality 4

Exc.	V.G.	Good	Fair	Poor
2500	2200	1800	400	100

Quality 5

Exc.	V.G.	Good	Fair	Poor
3500	3000	2000	700	300

Quality 6

Exc.	V.G.	Good	Fair	Poor
6000	4500	3000	1500	300

Quality 7

Exc.	V.G.	Good	Fair	Poor
6000	4500	3000	1500	300

Minier Model

The Minier Model, named after Ithaca's David Minier, was introduced in 1906 and was available through 1908. It was offered in Qualities Field through 7 and any grade could be ordered with ejectors. The Minier Model was the first Ithaca gun to use coil springs to power the internal hammers. This model was triple bolted, e.g., two fastenings at the rib extension and the under bolt. Gauges 10, 12, 16, and 20 were offered. Grades offered: Field, 1, 1 Special, 1-1/2, 2, 3, 4, 5, 6, 7.

NOTE: Automatic ejectors add $250.00 to guns below Quality 4. The serial number range for the Minier Model is approximately 130,000 to 151,000.

Field Grade

Exc.	V.G.	Good	Fair	Poor
1000	500	300	150	100

Quality 1

Exc.	V.G.	Good	Fair	Poor
800	500	300	150	100

Quality 1 Special

Exc.	V.G.	Good	Fair	Poor
800	500	300	150	100

Quality 1-1/2

Exc.	V.G.	Good	Fair	Poor
850	550	300	150	100

Quality 2

Exc.	V.G.	Good	Fair	Poor
1000	600	400	200	100

Quality 3

Exc.	V.G.	Good	Fair	Poor
1700	1400	800	400	100

Quality 4

Exc.	V.G.	Good	Fair	Poor
2500	2000	1500	400	100

Quality 5

Exc.	V.G.	Good	Fair	Poor
3500	3000	2000	700	300

Quality 6

Exc.	V.G.	Good	Fair	Poor
6000	4500	2500	1000	300

Quality 7

Exc.	V.G.	Good	Fair	Poor
6000	4500	2500	1000	300

Flues Model

The Flues Model Ithaca gun was built on a three piece lock mechanism invented and patented by Emil Flues. Introduced in 1908, it remained in production through 1926 when it was replaced by the Ithaca New Double. It was offered in gauges 10, 12, 16, 20, and 28, and enjoyed the longest production life of any Ithaca double gun. Several grades were offered beginning with the Field grade and ending with the Sousa Special. The Flues Model had the same bolting system as used on the Minier Model. Any grade could have been ordered with automatic ejectors at extra cost. A single selective trigger made by the Infallible Trigger company was offered after 1914 and was the first single trigger offered from the company. Qualities offered were: Field, 1, 1 Special, 1-1/2, 2, 3, 4, 5, 6, 7, and Sousa.

NOTE: Add $200.00 for factory ordered single trigger, add $200.00 for automatic ejectors on grades lower than Grade 4. Small gauges command a price premium. A 20 gauge field grade gun may command up to a 50% price premium; a 28 gauge filed grade perhaps as much as 100%. The serial number range for the Flues is approximately 175000 to 399000. Expert appraisals are recommended on higher grade, small gauge models as they are seldom encountered.

Field Grade

Exc.	V.G.	Good	Fair	Poor
800	600	300	150	100

Grade 1

Exc.	V.G.	Good	Fair	Poor
800	600	300	150	100

Grade 1 Special

Exc.	V.G.	Good	Fair	Poor
800	600	300	150	100

Grade 1-1/2

Exc.	V.G.	Good	Fair	Poor
850	550	300	150	100

Grade 2

Exc.	V.G.	Good	Fair	Poor
1000	600	400	200	100

Grade 3

Exc.	V.G.	Good	Fair	Poor
2000	1500	800	400	100

Grade 4

Exc.	V.G.	Good	Fair	Poor
2500	2000	1500	400	100

Grade 5

Exc.	V.G.	Good	Fair	Poor
3500	3000	2000	700	200

Grade 6

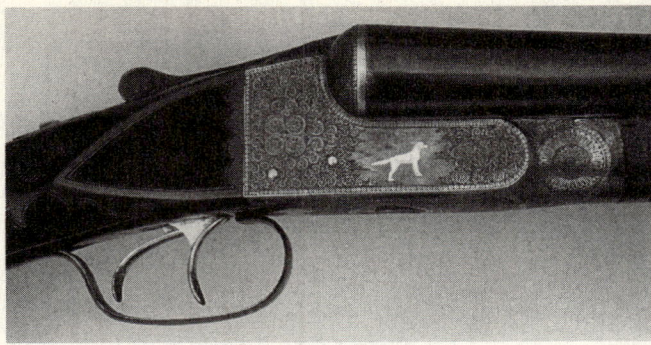

Exc.	V.G.	Good	Fair	Poor
6000	5000	3000	1000	300

Grade 7

Exc.	V.G.	Good	Fair	Poor
6000	5000	3000	1000	300

Sousa

Exc.	V.G.	Good	Fair	Poor
15000	10000	6000	3000	—

The New Ithaca Double

The New Ithaca Double, commonly referred to as the NID, was manufactured from 1926 to 1948. It has the distinction of being the last double gun manufactured by the factory. The NID was bolted by a single rotary top bolt and was considered of all Ithaca double guns manufactured up to that time. External cocking indicators were standard on all NID models until about 1934 when they were eliminated from the design. Selective and non-selective single triggers and automatic ejectors were optional at additional costs. A special variation of the NID was introduced in 1932 to accommodate 10 gauge 3-1/2" magnum ammunition and was named, appropriately, the Magnum 10. All NID were available in grades Field, 1, 2, 3, 4, 5, 6, 7, and Sousa (renamed the $1,000 grade after 1936). Gauges Magnum 10, standard 10, 12, 16, 20, 28, and .410 bore were offered.

NOTE: Like most collectable double guns, the smaller gauges command a price premium over the gauge model. A 16 gauge field grade may command a 25% price premium, a 20 gauge field grade may command up to a 50% price premium, and the 28 gauge, and .410 caliber field grade models perhaps as much as 100%. It is recommended that an expert opinion be sought for the valuation of high grade, small gauge models. Of late, the Magnum 10 gauge model also commands a price premium. Few of these guns trade, and the advise of an expert appraiser is suggested.

Non-selective Single Trigger-Add $150
Single Selective Trigger-Add $250
Ventilated Rib-Add $300
Automatic Ejectors for grade below Grade 4-Add $300.
Beavertail Forearm-Add $200

Monte Carlo butt stock-Add $300.

Field Grade

Exc.	V.G.	Good	Fair	Poor
800	600	300	150	100

Grade 1

Exc.	V.G.	Good	Fair	Poor
1000	700	400	200	100

Grade 2

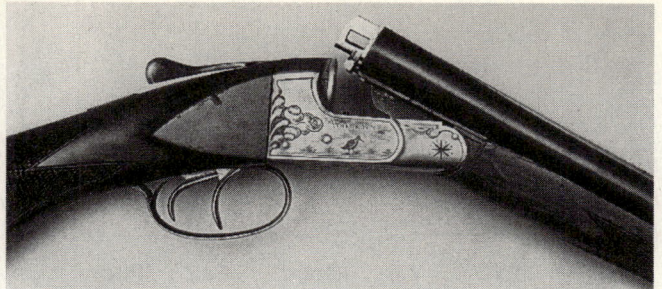

Courtesy Walter C. Snyder and C. Hadley Smith

Exc.	V.G.	Good	Fair	Poor
1200	800	650	300	100

Grade 3

Exc.	V.G.	Good	Fair	Poor
2000	1500	800	400	100

Grade 4

Exc.	V.G.	Good	Fair	Poor
2500	2000	1500	400	100

Grade 5

Exc.	V.G.	Good	Fair	Poor
3800	3200	2000	700	200

Grade 7
Exc.	V.G.	Good	Fair	Poor
7000	5000	3000	1000	—

Sousa Grade
Exc.	V.G.	Good	Fair	Poor
15000	10000	6000	3000	—

LEFEVER ARMS COMPANY, INC.

During 1921, Ithaca Gun, under the name "The Lefever Arms Company, Inc." introduced a line of lower costs, box lock guns.

See the Lefever Arms Company section of this book for prices concerning those guns.

WESTERN ARMS CORPORATION

During 1929 the Ithaca Gun Company created the Western Arms Corporation which introduced a new, low cost double gun. That new double gun was named The Long Range Double and it was produced in 12, 16, and 20 gauges, and .410 caliber. Twenty gauge guns often command a 20% premium, a .410 caliber can command up to a 50% premium. This model was last made at the start of World War II.

The Long Range Double

The Long Range Double had walnut stocks that were not checkered.

Single trigger guns will add $100 and automatic ejectors will add $300.

Exc.	V.G.	Good	Fair	Poor
450	300	200	150	—

The Long Range Double Deluxe

Usually made exclusively for the Montgomery Ward Company and sold by them under the name, Western Field Deluxe. This model had a line checkering pattern at the grip and on the splinter forend. Many of the Ithaca produced Western Field Deluxe guns had automatic ejectors and that fact was stamped into the right barrel. Add $100 for single triggers and $200 for automatic ejectors.

Exc.	V.G.	Good	Fair	Poor
450	300	250	150	—

ITHACA SINGLE BARREL TRAP GUNS

The Ithaca Gun Company introduced a single barrel trap gun in 1914. This gun was based upon the Emil Flues three piece lock design used for the double gun and has become known as the Flues Model Single Barrel Trap. The Flues Model was discontinued during 1922 and was replaced that year by a model designed by Ithaca's Frank Knickerbocker, commonly referred to as the "Knick". The Knick Model was discontinued in 1988, shortly after the Ithaca Acquisition Corp. purchased the assets of the Ithaca Gun Company. For many years, The Ithaca Single Barrel Trap Gun was the gun of choice for many champion shooters.

Flues Model Single Barrel Trap Gun (1914 to 1922)

The Flues Model trap gun was introduced in 1914 and offered in Grades 4, 5, 6, and 7. A lower cost Victory grade was introduced in 1919 and the highest cost variety, the Sousa Special was introduced in 1918. All Flues model trap guns were made within the same serial number sequence as the double guns but do have the letter "T" for Trap following the serial number. All Flues Models with the exception of the Victory Grade were produced with an automatic ejector. A rubber anti-recoil pad was an option. Guns having a pre-1916 engraving pattern will command the highest prices.

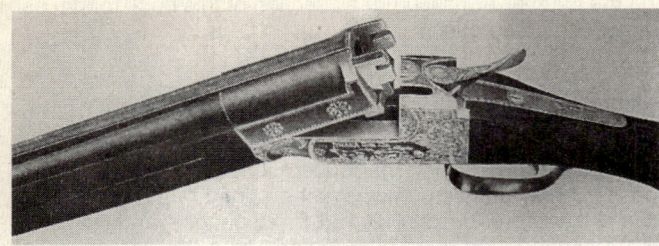

Courtesy Walter C. Snyder and C. Hadley Smith

Victory Grade

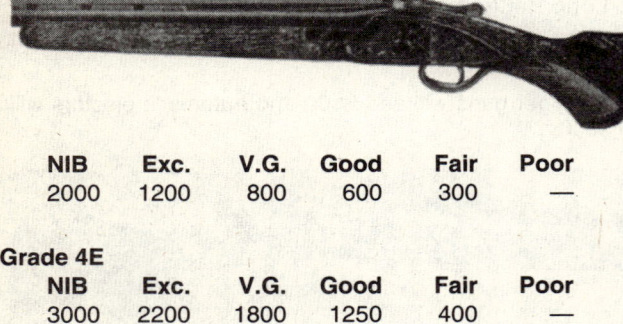

NIB	Exc.	V.G.	Good	Fair	Poor
2000	1200	800	600	300	—

Grade 4E

NIB	Exc.	V.G.	Good	Fair	Poor
3000	2200	1800	1250	400	—

Grade 5E

NIB	Exc.	V.G.	Good	Fair	Poor
6000	4000	3000	2500	600	—

Grade 6E

NIB	Exc.	V.G.	Good	Fair	Poor
10000	5000	4000	3000	800	—

Grade 7E

NIB	Exc.	V.G.	Good	Fair	Poor
12000	8000	6000	4000	1000	—

Sousa Grade

NIB	Exc.	V.G.	Good	Fair	Poor
25000	15000	10000	8000	2000	—

Knick Model Single Barrel Trap

The Knick Model trap gun was introduced during 1922 and was based on a design credited to Frank Knickerbocker. The design was simple and very serviceable, had been in continues production until 1988 when it was discontinued. The model was available in Victory, 4, 5, 7, and Sousa Special Grades. The Sousa was replaced by the $1,000 Grade in about 1936 which was replaced by the $2,000 Grade by 1952, the $2,500 Grade by 1960, the $3,000 Grade by 1965, the $5,000 Grade by 1974, and finally, the Dollar Grade in the early 1980s as the cost of production increased. All Knick models were produced with an automatic ejector and a rubber anti-recoil pad. Prospective purchasers should secure a qualified appraisal prior to acquisition.

Victory Grade

NIB	Exc.	V.G.	Good	Fair	Poor
2000	1200	800	650	300	—

Grade 4E

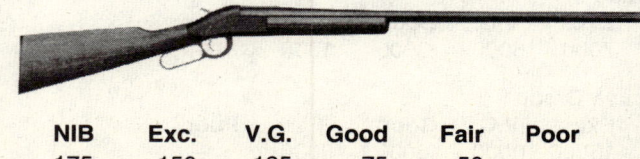

NIB	Exc.	V.G.	Good	Fair	Poor
3000	2200	1800	1000	500	—

Grade 5E

NIB	Exc.	V.G.	Good	Fair	Poor
6000	4000	3000	2500	800	—

Grade 7E

NIB	Exc.	V.G.	Good	Fair	Poor
8000	5000	4000	3000	1000	—

Sousa Grade

NIB	Exc.	V.G.	Good	Fair	Poor
25000	15000	10000	8000	2000	—

$1,000 to $2,500 Grades

NIB	Exc.	V.G.	Good	Fair	Poor
15000	12000	8000	6000	2000	—

$3,000 through the Dollar Grade

NIB	Exc.	V.G.	Good	Fair	Poor
12000	10000	6000	5000	2000	—

Century Grade Trap (SKB)

A 12 gauge boxlock single barrel shotgun with a 32" or 34" ventilated rib barrel and automatic ejector. Blued with a walnut stock. Manufactured by SKB during the 1970s.

Exc.	V.G.	Good	Fair	Poor
600	500	450	350	300

Century II (SKB)

As above, with a Monte Carlo-style stock.

Exc.	V.G.	Good	Fair	Poor
650	550	500	400	350

Model 66-1963-1978

A 12, 20 or .410 bore lever action single shot shotgun with a 24" barrel. Blued with a walnut stock. The 20 gauge and .410 bore command a 50% price premium.

NIB	Exc.	V.G.	Good	Fair	Poor
175	150	125	75	50	—

Model 66 Youth Grade

A special gun offered for the youth market in 20 gauge and .410 bore.

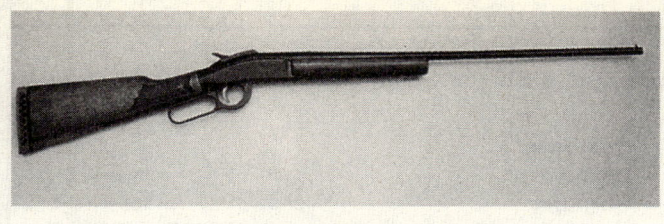

NIB	Exc.	V.G.	Good	Fair	Poor
225	150	125	100	50	—

Model 66 Buck Buster (RS Barrel)

As above, in 20 gauge with a Deerslayer 22" barrel fitted with rifle sights.

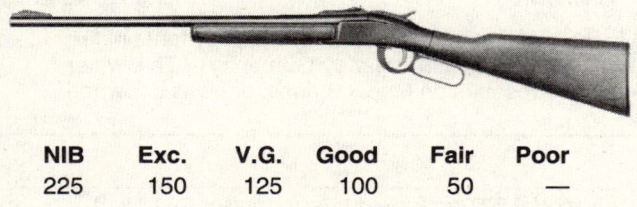

NIB	Exc.	V.G.	Good	Fair	Poor
225	150	125	100	50	—

Model 66 Vent Rib

NIB	Exc.	V.G.	Good	Fair	Poor
225	150	125	100	50	—

ITHACA AUTO & BURGLAR GUN NFA, CURIO OR RELIC

The Ithaca Auto & Burglar Gun is a double-barreled 20 gauge smooth bore pistol manufactured by Ithaca Gun Company, Ithaca, New York, from 1922 to 1934. Total production was approximately 4,500. They were made by modifying Ithaca's standard field grade double-barrel shotgun by shortening the barrels and fitting the receiver with a pistol grip. Standard factory guns had blued 10" barrels, case-hardened receivers with the legend **Auto & Burglar Gun/ Ithaca Gun Co./Ithaca, New York**, and the figure of a pointing dog stamped on each side. The barrel length on 21 guns inspected varied to 10.25" (typically in increments divisible by .125"), apparently from inexact factory quality control. Ithaca set a $37.50 retail price when the gun was in production, but some dealers sold it for $40 or more. Production was halted when the government ruled the Ithaca Auto & Burglar Gun to be a "firearm" in the "any other weapon" category under the National Firearms Act (NFA) of 1934.

There are two variations, termed Model A and Model B. Model A utilizes the so-called Flues frame (named after Emil Flues, who designed it in 1908), and its distinctive grip has a curving butt and a large spur. Model A is designed for 2.5" shells, and is not considered safe to fire using modern ammunition. Approximately 2,500 Model A Auto & Burglar Guns were manufactured from 1922 to 1925, when the Flues model was discontinued.

Model B utilizes the so-called N.I.D. frame (short for New Ithaca Double), introduced in 1926 and discontinued in 1948. The N.I.D. is designed for modern ammunition and 2.75" shells, has cocking indicators, and a different pistol grip that is perpendicular to the barrel and which lacks the distinctive spur. Some Model Bs have been observed with rosettes or "stars" engraved in each side of the receiver; their significance is unknown at this time, but they probably are decorations. Approximately 2,000 Model B Auto & Burglar Guns were manufactured from 1926 to 1934.

Model A, serial numbered from 343336 to 398365

Exc.	V.G.	Good	Fair	Poor
1,500	1,000	900	750	550

Model B, serial numbered from 425000 to 464699

Exc.	V.G.	Good	Fair	Poor
1,300	950	750	550	450

NOTE: Nonstandard or special order guns command premiums of 100 percent or more. Original holsters (marked Auto and Burglar Gun/MADE BY/ITHACA GUN CO./ITHACA, N.Y.) are extremely rare and worth $300 to $500 or more.

Ithaca Auto & Burglar Gun serial numbers are interspersed among those of sporting guns assembled during the same production runs, in lots of approximately 100. Their dates of manufacture generally correspond those by serial number reported by the Ithaca Gun Co., but some guns were assembled later than the reported years of manufacture (see *The World's Fighting Shotguns*, by Thomas F. Swearengen. Alexandria, Virginia: Ironside International Publishers, Inc., 1978, pages 80-85).

Swearengen reports approximately 20 special-order Auto & Burglar Guns were manufactured; so far 11 have been documented, and are listed below. Nonstandard (other than 10") barrel lengths were produced on special-order or were experimental or prototype guns. The 12" barrels on serial number 354442 are probably original to the gun, whose low serial number and hand engraved (rather than stamped) **Auto & Burglar Gun** legend indicates it could have been the first gun assembled. A hand-engraved legend is probably a useful diagnostic in determining the authenticity of the earliest specimens. The 18.5" barreled guns may have been exempt from the NFA when originally manufactured, but today are not because their overall lengths are less than 26" (a requirement established in 1960). Data on Model A guns, which may include experimental or prototype models, are from L. Franklin Moore, Jr. (354442); Cliff Schisler (360142); and Michael McIntosh (361452, in *Sporting Classics*, January/February 1986, page 73), respectively. Data on Model B guns, Flues and N.I.D. serial numbers, and dates of manufacture, are from Walter Claude Snyder's book *The Ithaca Gun Company From the Beginning* (Spencerport, New York: Cook and Uline Publishing Co., 1991, page 211), and reproduced here with Mr. Snyder's kind permission. Note that some N.I.D. serial numbers for 1935 and 1936 are nonsequential.

Model A (Flues frame) Factory serial number ranges			Model B (N.I.D. frame) Factory serial number ranges		
From	To	Year	From	To	Year
343336	356513	1921	425000	425299	1925
356514	361849	1922	425300	439199	1926
361900	372099	1923	439200	451099	1927
372100	390499	1924	451100	454530	1928
390500	398352	1925	454600	457299	1929
398353	398365	1926	457300	458399	1930
			458400	459139	1931
			459140	459162	1932
			459163	459195	1933
			459196	459637	1935
			459638	459649	1936
			459650	460799	1935
			460800	462899	1936
			462900	464699	1937

Nonstandard or Special Order Ithaca Auto & Burglar Guns

Serial number	Bore/Model	Barrel gauge	length	Customer	Date
354442	A	28	12"	Unknown	circa 1921
360142	A	28	10"	Unknown	circa 1921, Grade No. 1
361452	A	28	10"	Unknown	circa 1922, Grade No. 4
452245	B	.410	26"	Wray-Richards	August 17, 1928
452246	B	.410	26"	Emil F. Flues	August 17, 1928
452251	B	.410	12.5"	Leslie Hawks	March 29, 1929
452252	B	.410	10"	L. M. Armstrong	March 29, 1929
459357	B	16	18.5"	Montgomery & Crawford	September 28, 1935
460388	B	20	18.5"	Montgomery & Crawford	January 9, 1936
463375	B	20	18.5"	Lawrence D. Bell	September 2, 1937
461194	B	.410	18.5"	Unknown	June 22, 1938

These materials are copyright © 1998 by Eric M. Larson, printed in the *Catalog* by permission of the copyright holder, and will appear in a forthcoming book on pre-NFA smooth bore shot pistols (see H&R Handy-Gun entry). This writer would like to communicate with anyone who knows the significance of the rosettes on Model B guns, or owns or owned

ITHACA MODEL 37 REPEATER

The Ithaca Model 37 Repeater was introduced in 1937 in 12 gauge, 1938 in 16 gauge, and in 1939 in 20 gauge. It underwent very few design changes throughout its long life which ended 1987 when the Ithaca Acquisition Corp. acquired the assets of the Ithaca Gun Company during 1987 and renamed the gun the Model 87. The name has recently been changed again to the M37 after the assets of the Ithaca Acquisition Corp. were purchased in May of 1996 by the Ithaca Gun Company, LLC. All Model 37 guns were chambered only for 2-3/-5/4" ammunition until 1983, when the Magnum with 3" chamber was introduced to some configurations. Most Model 37 guns had blued metal and walnut stocks with the exception of the Model 37 Field Grade series which had matte finished metal and Birch stocks. Sixteen gauge guns were discontinued in 1973.

NOTE: Twenty gauge guns made before 1968 will generally command a price premium.

Model 37/Standard Grade-1937 to 1983

Guns made before 1968 will enjoy a 15% price premium; those made before World War II, a 30% price premium.

Exc.	V.G.	Good	Fair	Poor
250	200	175	125	75

Model 37S/ Skeet Grade-1937 to 1953

Guns made before World War II will enjoy a 50% price premium.

Exc.	V.G.	Good	Fair	Poor
500	400	350	250	100

Model 37T/ Trap-1937 to 1953

Guns made before World War II will enjoy a 50% price premium.

Exc.	V.G.	Good	Fair	Poor
500	400	350	250	100

A Model 37T was sold at auction for $8,050. It belonged to Admiral Chester Nimitz, U.S.N. It was a 12 gauge gun with 30" barrel choked full. A gold inscription plate was on the right side of the butt stock dated 1947. Deluxe burl walnut stock. Condition was excellent.

Model 37T/Target-1954 to 1961

Exc.	V.G.	Good	Fair	Poor
500	400	350	250	100

Model 37R/Solid Rib-1940-1967

Guns made before World War II will enjoy a 50% price premium.

Exc.	V.G.	Good	Fair	Poor
325	275	225	200	75

Model 37RD/Deluxe Solid Rib-1954 to 1962

Exc.	V.G.	Good	Fair	Poor
425	375	300	200	100

Model 37 Deerslayer-1959 to 1987

All Deerslayer models made before 1968 will enjoy a 10% to 20% price premium.

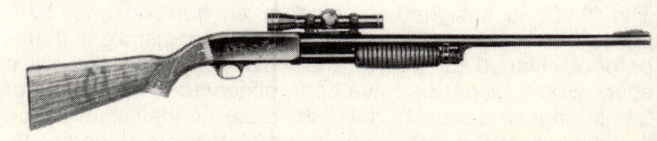

Exc.	V.G.	Good	Fair	Poor
250	225	200	125	75

Model 37 Deluxe Deerslayer-1959 to 1971

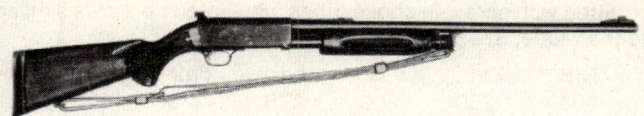

Exc.	V.G.	Good	Fair	Poor
300	250	225	125	75

Model 37 Super Deluxe Deerslayer-1959-1987

Exc.	V.G.	Good	Fair	Poor
350	325	275	200	100

Model 37 Supreme Grade-1967 to 1987

Exc.	V.G.	Good	Fair	Poor
450	400	350	200	100

Model 37 Field Grade Standard-1983 to 1985

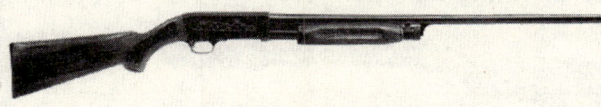

Exc.	V.G.	Good	Fair	Poor
250	200	150	125	75

Model 37 Field Grade Vent-1983 to 1986

Exc.	V.G.	Good	Fair	Poor
275	250	200	125	75

Model 37 Basic Featherlight-1979 to 1983

Manufactured in 12 gauge only.

Exc.	V.G.	Good	Fair	Poor
275	250	200	125	100

Model 37V/Vent Rib-1961-1983

Guns made before 1968 will enjoy a 10% to 20% price premium.

Exc.	V.G.	Good	Fair	Poor
250	200	175	150	100

Model 37RV/Deluxe Vent Rib-1961-1966

Exc.	V.G.	Good	Fair	Poor
425	375	300	200	100

Model 37D/Deluxe-1955 to 1977

Guns made before 1968 will enjoy a 10% to 20% price premium.

Exc.	V.G.	Good	Fair	Poor
275	225	175	125	75

Model 37DV/Deluxe Vent Rib-1961 to 1987

Guns made before 1968 will enjoy a 10% to 20% price premium.

Exc.	V.G.	Good	Fair	Poor
300	250	200	150	100

Model 37 Magnum-3" Chamber-1978 to 1987

Exc.	V.G.	Good	Fair	Poor
325	275	225	125	75

Model 37 Field Grade Magnum-1984-1987

Exc.	V.G.	Good	Fair	Poor
275	225	175	125	75

Model 37 UltraLight-1978 to 1987

The UltraLight had an aluminum alloy frame and trigger plate. The barrels are marked Ultra Featherlight and the serial number is prefaced with the mark, "ULT". Both the 12 and 20 gauges were offered.

Exc.	V.G.	Good	Fair	Poor
475	400	300	150	100

Model 37 English UltraLight-1982 to 1987

This gun is the same as the Model 37 UltraLight, but has an English style straight grip stock.

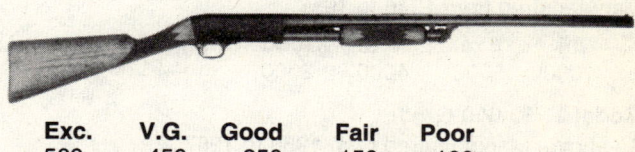

Exc.	V.G.	Good	Fair	Poor
500	450	350	150	100

Model 37 CAMO

Introduced in 1985, this model is available with either a green or brown camouflage finish and was offered only in 12 gauge.

Exc.	V.G.	Good	Fair	Poor
350	300	200	150	100

Model 37 Bicentennial

A special model produced during 1976 to commemorate the 200 year anniversary of the United States. The gun came with a full length trunk style hard case and a pewter belt buckle number to the gun. The serial number was prefaced with "U.S.A." Subtract 35% if the original case and belt buckle are missing.

NIB	Exc.	V.G.	Good	Fair	Poor
650	500	300	200	125	100

Model 37 Ducks Unlimited Commemorative, Auction Grade

Special edition made during 1977. Serial number sequence was 40-DU0001 to 40-DU1125.

NIB	Exc.	V.G.	Good	Fair	Poor
650	400	300	150	100	75

Model 37 Ducks Unlimited Commemorative, Trade Grade

Special edition made during 1977. Lower grade version of the Auction Grade. Serial number preceded with the mark, DU37040.

Model 37 2500 Series Centennial

A commemorative Model 37 12 gauge shotgun with silver-plated receiver and press checkered stocks. Manufactured in 1984.

NIB	Exc.	V.G.	Good	Fair	Poor
800	500	300	150	100	75

Model 37 Presentation Series Centennial

A commemorative Mode 37 12 gauge with a gold-plated receiver and high grade hand checkered stocks. It was manufactured during 1980, but is still available as of August, 1997.

NIB	Exc.	V.G.	Good	Fair	Poor
1500	800	500	150	100	—

Hi-Grade Ithaca Model 37 Guns

The Ithaca Gun company offered custom engraving services either from its in-house engraver, one of which was retained until about 1972, or through an outside contract engraver who was usually William Mains. Many customers requested some degree of custom work and guns with various patterns turn up from time to time. There were four standard engraving patterns offered to customers, Grade 1, Grade 2, Grade 3, and the very elaborate $1,000 Grade pattern. Increasing production costs forced the $1,000 Grade to become the $2,000

Grade, the $2,500, and finally the $3,000 Grades over the years. All factory engraved Model 37 guns are rare and require an expert appraiser to determine an accurate value.

Model 37 $1,000 Grade

The Model 37 with an engraved receiver, gold inlays, and a well-figured walnut stock. Manufactured between 1940 and 1942.

NIB	Exc.	V.G.	Good	Fair	Poor
10000	5000	4000	2000	—	—

Model 37 $2,000 Grade

Manufactured from 1946 to 1957

NIB	Exc.	V.G.	Good	Fair	Poor
10000	5000	4000	2000	—	—

Model 37 $3,000 Grade

As above. Manufactured from 1958 to 1967.

NIB	Exc.	V.G.	Good	Fair	Poor
8000	4000	3500	1500	—	—

Model 37 Law Enforcement Weapons

The Ithaca Gun Company entered the law enforcement market in 1962 when it introduced the Model 37 Military and Police (M&P) and the Model 37DS Police special (DSPS). The M&P Model was styled after the riot guns made for various military contracts. The DSPS was styled after the Ithaca Deerslayer. Both models were offered with 8-shot capacity after 1968. A chrome finish was an available option after 1976. Both models usually had ring turned slide handles. Only those models available to the general public, i.e. barrel lengths of 18" or longer, are listed.

Model 37 Military and Police (M&P)-1962-1986

Add 20% for an 8-shot model in NIB or EXC. condition, and add an additional 15% for chrome plated models in similar condition.

NIB	Exc.	V.G.	Good	Fair	Poor
350	300	250	200	125	75

Model 37 DS Police Special-1962-1986

Add 20% for an 8-shot model in NIB or EXC. condition, and add an additional 15% for chrome plated models in similar condition.

NIB	Exc.	V.G.	Good	Fair	Poor
400	350	250	200	125	75

ITHACA MODEL 87 REPEATER

During 1987 many of the assets of the bankrupt Ithaca Gun Company were purchased by the Ithaca Acquisition Corporation. Manufacture of the Model 37 was resumed that summer after the gun was renamed the Model 87. Many of the Models offered by the old company were continued. All Model 87 field guns were produced with ventilated ribs. All Deerslayer models continued the rifle sights used on the Model 37 guns.

Model 87 Basic-1989-1994

Early models had birch stocks, later production had walnut stocks. All had ring turned slide handles.

NIB	Exc.	V.G.	Good	Fair	Poor
250	200	175	150	125	75

Model 87 Magnum

A 12 or 20 gauge Magnum slide action shotgun with a 25" barrel fitted with screw-in choke tubes, ventilated rib that is similar to the Model 37. Blued with a walnut stock.

NIB	Exc.	V.G.	Good	Fair	Poor
300	250	200	175	125	100

The Model 87 was manufactured in the following styles as of 1989:

Model 87 Field Grade-1987-1990

Stocks were walnut with pressed checkering.

NIB	Exc.	V.G.	Good	Fair	Poor
300	250	200	175	125	75

Model 87 Camo-1987-1994

NIB	Exc.	V.G.	Good	Fair	Poor
300	250	200	175	125	75

Model 87 Turkey Gun-1987-1996

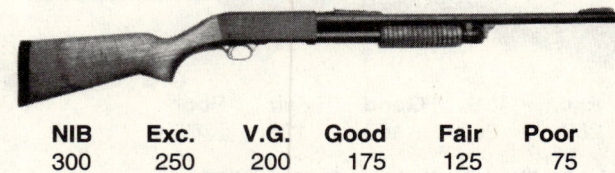

NIB	Exc.	V.G.	Good	Fair	Poor
300	250	200	175	125	75

Model 87 Deluxe -1987-1996

The butt stocks and slide handle were walnut with a machine cut checkered pattern.

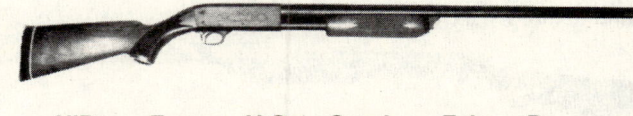

NIB	Exc.	V.G.	Good	Fair	Poor
300	275	250	200	125	75

Model 87 Ultralite-1987-1990

All IAC manufactured Ultralite guns carry the old Model 37 serial number.

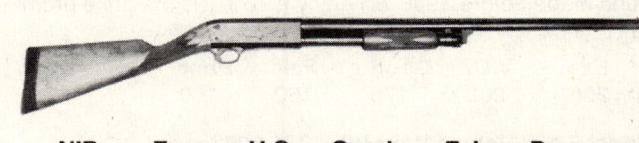

NIB	Exc.	V.G.	Good	Fair	Poor
400	350	250	175	125	75

Model 87 English-1993-1996

Hand checkered walnut stocks. The slide handle was styled after the pre-war Model 37 slide handle.

NIB	Exc.	V.G.	Good	Fair	Poor
400	350	250	175	125	75

Model 87 Ultralite Deluxe

NIB	Exc.	V.G.	Good	Fair	Poor
400	350	300	250	200	150

Model 87 Supreme Grade-1987-1996

High grade walnut stocks with hand checkering. Metal had extra fine polish and finish.

NIB	Exc.	V.G.	Good	Fair	Poor
600	500	400	300	125	75

Model 87 Deerslayer Basic-1989-1996

Walnut, oil finish butt and slide handle stocks. Slide handle was classic ring turned style.

NIB	Exc.	V.G.	Good	Fair	Poor
300	275	250	200	125	75

Model 87 Deerslayer-1989-1996

It was sometimes advertised as the Model 87 Deerslayer Field. Butt stock and slide handle were walnut and usually had a pressed checkered pattern. The slide handle was the beavertail style.

NIB	Exc.	V.G.	Good	Fair	Poor
350	300	250	200	125	75

Model 87 Deluxe Deerslayer-1989-1996

Butt stock and slide handle were walnut with a machine cut checkering pattern. The slide handle was beavertail.

NIB	Exc.	V.G.	Good	Fair	Poor
400	350	250	200	125	75

Model 87 Deerslayer II-1988-1996

This model had a fixed rifle barrel and a Monte Carlo butt stock. A small number of guns were specially made with a fast twist barrel to handle Brenneke ammunition and are marked "BRENNEKE" on the receiver. Brenneke marked guns will command a 30% price premium.

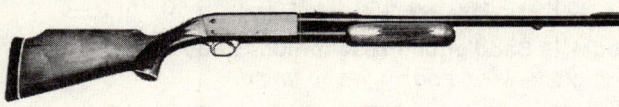

NIB	Exc.	V.G.	Good	Fair	Poor
450	400	350	200	125	75

Model 87 Home Protection and Law Enforcement models

The Ithaca Acquisition Corporation continued production of many of the law enforcement firearms produced by the Ithaca Gun Company. Only those models available to the general public are listed.

Model 87 Military & Police-1987-1996

Generally produced with a non-checkered walnut butt stock and a ring turned slide handle, both of which were oil finished. Add 20% for an 8-shot model in NIB or excellent condition. Add an additional 15% for chrome plated models in similar condition.

NIB	Exc.	V.G.	Good	Fair	Poor
350	300	250	200	125	75

Model 87 DS Police Special-1987-1996

Produced from either a pressed checkered or a non-checkered walnut butt stocks, and a ring turned slide handle, both lacquer finished. The metal was usually finished with a commercial polished blue but a chrome plated finish was also available. Add 20% for an 8-shot model in NIB or excellent condition, and add an additional 15% for a chrome plated models in similar condition.

NIB	Exc.	V.G.	Good	Fair	Poor
400	350	250	200	125	75

NEW MODEL 37

During 1996, the assets of the bankrupt Ithaca Acquisition Corporation were purchased by a new company named the Ithaca Gun Company, LLC. One of the first public actions of the new firm was to rename the Model 87 the Model 37, before resuming production later that year, the serial number of the new Model 37 is prefaced with the letter "M". A used market for the new Model 37 has not been established at this time. Suggested retail prices for each model currently produced are listed.

Model 37 Deerslayer Deluxe

Retail Price-$499.95

Model 37 Deerslayer II

Retail Price-$549.95

Model 37 Deluxe field

Retail Price-$529.95

Model 37 Turkeyslayer

Retail Price-$549.95

MODEL 51 SERIES

A 12 or 20 gauge semiautomatic shotgun with 26", 28", or 30" ventilated rib barrels. Blued with a walnut stock. Manufactured from 1970 to 1985 as follows:

Model 51A Standard-Plain Barrel

Vent Rib-Add $100.

Exc.	V.G.	Good	Fair	Poor
275	225	200	150	100

Model 51A Magnum-3" Chamber

Vent Rib-Add $100.

Exc.	V.G.	Good	Fair	Poor
300	250	225	175	125

Model 51A Waterfowler-Matte Finished

Exc.	V.G.	Good	Fair	Poor
425	375	325	250	175

Model 51A Deerslayer

Exc.	V.G.	Good	Fair	Poor
325	275	225	150	100

Model 51A Turkey Gun

Courtesy Walter C. Snyder and C. Hadley Smith

Exc.	V.G.	Good	Fair	Poor
325	275	225	150	100

Model 51A Supreme Trap

Exc.	V.G.	Good	Fair	Poor
425	375	325	250	175

Model 51A Supreme Skeet

Exc.	V.G.	Good	Fair	Poor
450	400	350	275	200

Model 51 Ducks Unlimited Commemorative

NIB	Exc.	V.G.	Good	Fair	Poor
475	400	375	325	275	200

Model 51 Presentation-Engraved Receiver

NIB	Exc.	V.G.	Good	Fair	Poor
1500	1250	1000	750	500	300

Mag-10 Series

A 10 gauge Magnum semiautomatic shotgun manufactured in a variety of barrel lengths, styles and finishes. Manufactured from 1975 to 1986 in as follows:

Standard Grade

Exc.	V.G.	Good	Fair	Poor
750	700	650	500	400

Standard Vent Rib Grade

Exc.	V.G.	Good	Fair	Poor
850	775	700	550	450

Deluxe Vent Rib Grade

Exc.	V.G.	Good	Fair	Poor
1000	850	775	600	500

Supreme Grade

Exc.	V.G.	Good	Fair	Poor
1200	1050	850	700	600

Roadblocker-Military and Police Model

Exc.	V.G.	Good	Fair	Poor
650	575	500	400	300

Presentation Grade-Engraved, Gold-inlaid, 200 Made

NIB	Exc.	V.G.	Good	Fair	Poor
1875	1500	1100	900	750	600

National Wild Turkey Federation-1985 Manufacture

NIB	Exc.	V.G.	Good	Fair	Poor
850	700	600	550	450	350

Shotguns manufactured by Perazzi and Japanese firms that were marketed by Ithaca are listed under the respective manufacturer's name.

Model X5-C

A .22 caliber semiautomatic rifle with a 7-shot magazine. A 10-shot magazine was available as an extra cost option. Blued with a walnut stock. Manufactured between 1958 and 1964.

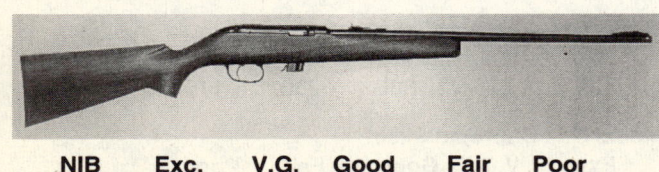

NIB	Exc.	V.G.	Good	Fair	Poor
400	175	150	100	75	—

Model X5T Lightning

A .22 caliber tubular feed auto loading rifle produced between 1959 and 1963. Some models were stocked with curly maple stocks. These guns will command a 25% price premium.

NIB	Exc.	V.G.	Good	Fair	Poor
450	175	150	100	75	—

Model X-15 Lightning

Similar to the above, but manufactured between 1964 and 1966.

NIB	Exc.	V.G.	Good	Fair	Poor
450	175	150	100	75	—

Model 49 Saddlegun-1961-1979

A .22 caliber lever action single shot rifle with an 18.5" barrel, fixed sights, alloy receiver and hardwood stock. It was offered chambered for the .22 Magnum in 1962.

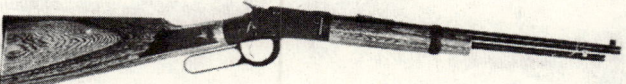

Courtesy Walter C. Snyder and C. Hadley Smith

NIB	Exc.	V.G.	Good	Fair	Poor
200	150	125	100	50	—

Model 49 Saddlegun Deluxe Grade

Fitted with gold plated trigger, hammer, and equipped with sling and sling swivels.

NIB	Exc.	V.G.	Good	Fair	Poor
300	200	150	100	50	—

Model 49 Saddlegun Presentation Grade

High grade wood and engraved frame.

NIB	Exc.	V.G.	Good	Fair	Poor
400	300	250	200	100	—

Model 49R-1968-1971

A lever action .22 caliber tubular feed rifle. Magazine capacity is 15 Long Rifle cartridges. No other chambers were offered.

NIB	Exc.	V.G.	Good	Fair	Poor
350	250	200	150	50	—

Model 72 Saddlegun-1973-1979

A .22 or .22 Magnum caliber lever action rifle with an 18.5" barrel, tubular magazine, open sights and walnut stock. Made by Erma in Germany.

NIB	Exc.	V.G.	Good	Fair	Poor
375	275	225	200	100	—

LSA-55 or 65 Series

A bolt action sporting rifle manufactured in a variety of calibers and barrel lengths by Tikka of Finland. Imported between 1969 and 1977 in the following models:

LSA-55 Standard

Exc.	V.G.	Good	Fair	Poor
400	350	300	250	175

LSA-55 Deluxe

Exc.	V.G.	Good	Fair	Poor
425	375	325	275	200

LSA-55 Varmint-Heavy Barrel

Exc.	V.G.	Good	Fair	Poor
450	400	350	300	225

LSA-65-Long Action

Exc.	V.G.	Good	Fair	Poor
400	350	300	250	175

LSA-65 Deluxe

Exc.	V.G.	Good	Fair	Poor
425	375	325	275	200

LSA-55 Turkey Gun

A 12 gauge by .22 Remington caliber Over/Under combination rifle/shotgun with 24.5" barrels, double triggers, exposed hammer and walnut stock. Manufactured in Finland by Tikka between 1970 and 1981.

Exc.	V.G.	Good	Fair	Poor
600	525	450	350	275

X-Caliber

A .22 to .44 Magnum caliber single shot pistol with 10" or 15" barrels featuring a dual firing pin system so that interchangeable barrels could be used. The Model 20 is blued, the Model 30 is Teflon coated. Introduced in 1988.

NIB	Exc.	V.G.	Good	Fair	Poor
275	225	200	175	145	100

IVER JOHNSON ARMS, INC.
Middlesex, New Jersey
ALSO SEE AMAC

Established in 1883 in Fitchburg, Massachusetts, this company has produced a wide variety of firearms during its existence.

Trade name Revolvers

A series of spur trigger revolvers were made by Iver Johnson bearing only the trade names such as those that follow: Encore, Eclipse, Favorite, Tycoon, and Eagle. In general, the value for these revolvers is as follows:

Exc.	V.G.	Good	Fair	Poor
150	125	75	50	25

Safety Automatic Double Action

A .22, .32CF, or .38CF caliber double action revolver produced in a variety of barrel lengths with or without exposed hammers. Manufactured between 1893 and 1950.

Exc.	V.G.	Good	Fair	Poor
150	125	100	75	50

Model 1900

A .22 to .38 caliber double-action revolver with a 2.5", 4.5", or 6" barrel. Blued or nickel-plated with rubber grips and no cartridge ejecting system. Manufactured between 1900 and 1947.

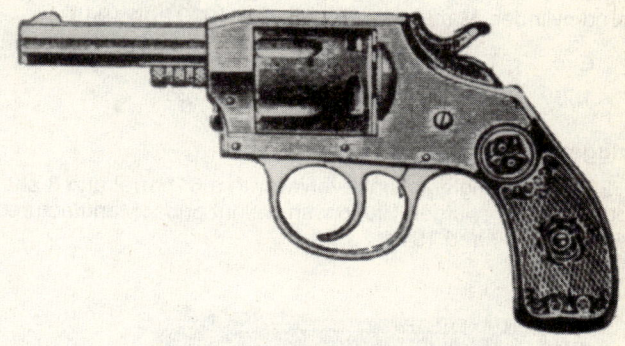

Exc.	V.G.	Good	Fair	Poor
150	125	100	75	50

Safety Cycle Automatic

Similar to the Safety Automatic with a 2" barrel.

Exc.	V.G.	Good	Fair	Poor
150	125	100	75	50

Petite

A .22 short caliber double action folding trigger revolver with a 1" barrel and 7-shot cylinder. Nickel-plated with rubber grips. Introduced in 1909.

Exc.	V.G.	Good	Fair	Poor
250	200	175	125	75

Supershot Sealed 8

A .22 caliber double action revolver with a 6" barrel and counterbored 8-shot cylinder. Blued with rubber grips. Manufactured from 1919 to 1957.

Exc.	V.G.	Good	Fair	Poor
150	125	100	50	25

Protector Sealed 8

As above, with a 2.5" barrel.

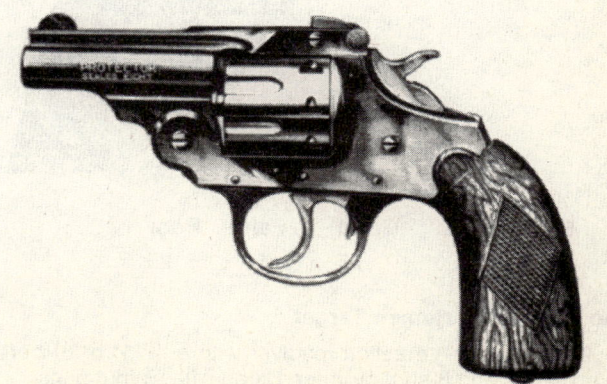

Exc.	V.G.	Good	Fair	Poor
150	125	100	50	25

Supershot 9

Similar to the Supershot Sealed 8 with a 9-shot uncounterbored cylinder. Manufactured between 1929 and 1949.

Exc.	V.G.	Good	Fair	Poor
150	125	100	50	25

Trigger Cocker Single Action

A .22 caliber single action revolver with a 6" barrel and 8-shot counterbored cylinder. Blued with walnut grips. Manufactured between 1940 and 1947.

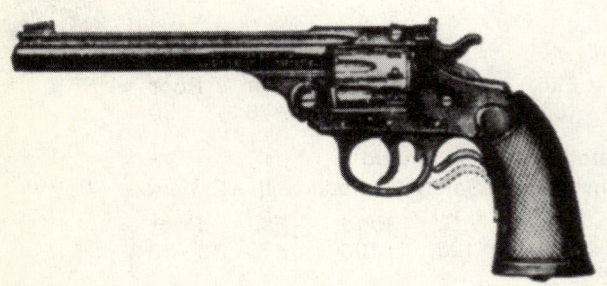

Exc.	V.G.	Good	Fair	Poor
150	125	100	50	25

.22 Target Single Action

As above, with adjustable sights and adjustable grips. Manufactured between 1938 and 1948.

Exc.	V.G.	Good	Fair	Poor
150	125	100	75	50

Model 844

A .22 caliber double action revolver with a 4.5" or 6" barrel, adjustable sights, and an 8-shot cylinder. Manufactured in the 1950s.

Exc.	V.G.	Good	Fair	Poor
125	100	75	50	25

Model 855

As above, but single action with a 6" barrel. Manufactured in the 1950s.

Exc.	V.G.	Good	Fair	Poor
125	100	75	50	25

Model 55A Sportsmen Target

A .22 caliber single action revolver with a 4.75" or 6" barrel, fixed sights and 8-shot cylinder. Blued with walnut grips.

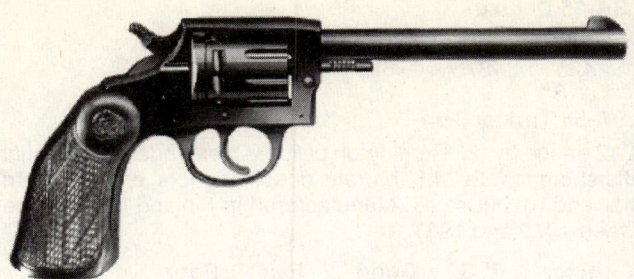

Exc.	V.G.	Good	Fair	Poor
100	75	65	50	25

Model 55S-A Cadet

A .22 to .38 caliber single action revolver with a 2.5" barrel and fixed sights. Blued with plastic grips. Introduced in 1955.

Exc.	V.G.	Good	Fair	Poor
125	100	75	60	45

Model 57A Target

As above, with a 4.5" or 6" barrel and adjustable sights. Manufactured between 1955 and 1975.

Exc.	V.G.	Good	Fair	Poor
100	75	65	50	25

Model 66 Trailsman

A .22 caliber double-action revolver with a 6" barrel, adjustable sights, and 8-shot cylinder. Blued with walnut grips. Manufactured between 1958 and 1975.

Exc.	V.G.	Good	Fair	Poor
100	75	65	50	25

Model 67 Viking
As above, with a safety hammer.

Exc.	V.G.	Good	Fair	Poor
100	75	65	50	25

Model 67S Viking Snub
Same as above but fitted with 2" barrel.

Exc.	V.G.	Good	Fair	Poor
100	75	65	50	25

Model 50
A .22 or .22 Magnum single action revolver with a 4.75" or 6" barrel, 8-shot cylinder and either fixed or adjustable sights. Also known as the Sidewinder. Manufactured between 1961 and 1975.

Exc.	V.G.	Good	Fair	Poor
100	75	65	50	25

American Bulldog
A .22 to .38 caliber double-action revolver with a 2.5" or 4" barrel and adjustable sights. Blued or nickel-plated with plastic grips. Manufactured between 1974 and 1976.

Exc.	V.G.	Good	Fair	Poor
125	100	75	50	25

Rookie
A .38 caliber revolver with a 4" barrel and 5-shot cylinder. Blued or nickel-plated with plastic grips.

Exc.	V.G.	Good	Fair	Poor
125	100	75	50	25

Cattleman Series
Manufactured by Aldo Uberti and listed under that name in this book.

Model X300 Pony
A .380 semiautomatic pistol with a 3" barrel and 6-shot magazine. Blued with plastic grips. Introduced in 1975.

Exc.	V.G.	Good	Fair	Poor
175	150	125	100	75

Trailsman
A .22 caliber semiautomatic pistol with a 4.5" or 6" barrel and 10-shot magazine. Blued with plastic or walnut grips.

Exc.	V.G.	Good	Fair	Poor
175	150	125	100	75

TP Pistol
A .22 or .25 ACP caliber double-action semiautomatic pistol with a 2.8" barrel and 7-shot magazine. Blued or nickel-plated with plastic grips.

Exc.	V.G.	Good	Fair	Poor
195	150	125	100	75

SHOTGUNS
Champion
A single barrel shotgun manufactured in a variety of gauges as well as .44 or .45 caliber with 26" to 32" barrels, external hammers, and automatic ejectors. Blued with a walnut stock. Manufactured between 1909 and 1956.

Exc.	V.G.	Good	Fair	Poor
125	100	75	50	25

Matted Rib Grade
As above, in 12, 16, or 20 gauge with a matte rib barrel. Manufactured between 1909 and 1948.

Exc.	V.G.	Good	Fair	Poor
150	125	100	75	50

Trap Grade
As above, in 12 gauge with a 32" ventilated rib barrel. Manufactured between 1909 and 1942.

Exc.	V.G.	Good	Fair	Poor
275	225	175	125	100

Hercules Grade

A boxlock double-barrel shotgun manufactured in a variety of gauges with 26" to 32" barrels, double triggers and extractors. Blued with a walnut stock.

Automatic Ejectors-Add 15%.
Single Selective Trigger-Add 15%.

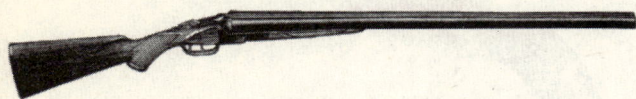

Exc.	V.G.	Good	Fair	Poor
550	450	375	300	250

Skeeter Model

As above, but more finely finished. Discontinued in 1946.

Exc.	V.G.	Good	Fair	Poor
1100	950	700	500	375

Super Trap

A 12 gauge boxlock single barrel shotgun with a 32" barrel, and extractors. Discontinued in 1942.

Exc.	V.G.	Good	Fair	Poor
1100	950	700	500	375

Silver Shadow

A 12 gauge boxlock Over/Under shotgun with a 26" or 28" ventilated rib barrels, double triggers and extractors. Blued with a walnut stock. Also available with a single trigger, which would increase the values listed below by approximately 25%. Manufactured in Italy and imported by Iver Johnson.

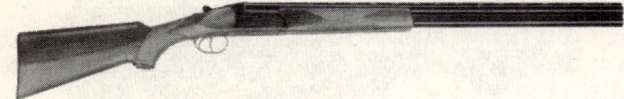

Exc.	V.G.	Good	Fair	Poor
350	300	275	200	150

IXL
New York, New York

Pocket Revolver

A .31 caliber double action percussion revolver with a 4" octagonal barrel and 6-shot cylinder. Blued with walnut grips. The barrel marked "IXL N.York." Approximately 750 were made without hammer spurs and 150 with side mounted hammers during the 1850s.

Exc.	V.G.	Good	Fair	Poor
—	—	750	500	250

Navy Revolver

As above in .36 caliber. Approximately 100 were made with both center and side mounted hammers during the 1850s.

Exc.	V.G.	Good	Fair	Poor
—	—	2750	1200	500

Courtesy Milwaukee Public Museum, Milwaukee, Wisconsin

J

JACQUEMART, JULES
Liege, Belgium

Le Monobloc

A 6.35mm semiautomatic pistol with a 2" barrel and 6-shot magazine. The slide marked "Le Monobloc/Pistolet Automatique/Brevefte." Blued with composition grips. Production ceased in 1914.

Exc.	V.G.	Good	Fair	Poor
400	300	250	200	125

JACQUITH, ELIJAH
Brattleboro, Vermont

Revolving Under Hammer Rifle

An extremely rare .40 caliber percussion revolving rifle with a 34" round-octagonal barrel and 8-shot cylinder. It is believed that approximately 25 of these rifles were made in 1838 and 1839. The barrel marked "E. Jaquith Brattleboro. Vt." Prospective purchasers should secure a qualified appraisal prior to acquisition.

Exc.	V.G.	Good	Fair	Poor
—	—	8500	4000	2000

JAGER WAFFENFABIK
Suhl, Germany

Jager Semiautomatic Pistol

A 7.65mm caliber semiautomatic pistol with a 3" barrel and 7-shot magazine. Largely made from steel stampings. Blued with plastic grips. The slide marked "Jager-Pistole DRP Angem." Approximately 5,500 were made prior to 1914.

NOTE: Add 50% for Imperial proofed examples.

Courtesy Richard M. Kumor, Sr.

Exc.	V.G.	Good	Fair	Poor
400	300	250	175	100

JAPANESE STATE MILITARY WEAPONS
Japan

NOTE: Many of the prices for Japanese military weapons are based on prices realized at an auction held by Old Town Station of the Macy Collection in March of 1996

Murata Type 18

An 11mm caliber bolt-action rifle with a 32" barrel, and full length stock secured by two barrel bands.

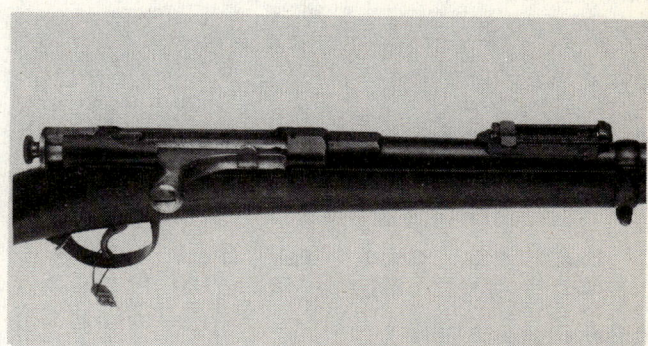

Courtesy Buffalo Bill Historical Center, Cody, Wyoming

Exc.	V.G.	Good	Fair	Poor
500	400	300	200	100

Murata Type 22

Produced circa 1889 to about 1899 in caliber 8mm Jpn. Fitted with a 29.375" barrel with 8-round tubular magazine. This was Japan's first smokeless powder military rifle.

Rifle

Exc.	V.G.	Good	Fair	Poor
800	500	400	300	200

Carbine-19.5" barrel

Exc.	V.G.	Good	Fair	Poor
900	600	450	350	200

> A Type 22 Murata rifle, serial number 15, was sold at auction for $2,750. This rifle was used at the 1890-1892 trials by the U.S. chambered for the 8mm cartridge. Condition was excellent.
> Old Town Station, Ltd., March 1996.

Murata Shotgun

A smoothbore modification of the Type 13 and 18 made during the 1920s for export.

Exc.	V.G.	Good	Fair	Poor
150	125	100	75	50

Arisaka Type 30 Rifle

A 6.5mm Arisaka caliber bolt action rifle with a 31.5" barrel, 5-shot magazine and full length stock secured by two barrel bands. Manufactured from 1897 to 1905.

Exc.	V.G.	Good	Fair	Poor
500	350	225	125	75

Arisaka Type 30 Carbine

As above, with a 19" barrel and no upper hand guard.

Courtesy Richard M. Kumor, Sr.

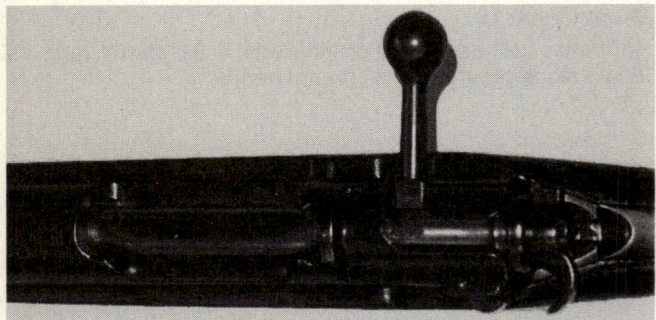

Courtesy Richard M. Kumor, Sr.

Exc.	V.G.	Good	Fair	Poor
550	400	250	150	100

Arisaka Type 38 Rifle

6.5mm Arisaka caliber bolt action rifle with a 31.5" barrel, 5-shot magazine and large bolt handle. Full length stock secured by two barrel bands. Manufactured from 1905 to 1911.

Exc.	V.G.	Good	Fair	Poor
175	150	125	90	65

> **A Type 38 Arisaka rifle was sold at auction for $1,210. Chambered for 6.5mm cartridge. Condition was excellent.**
> **Old Town Station, Ltd., March 1996.**

Arisaka Type 38 Carbine

As above, with a 19" barrel and no upper hand guard.

Exc.	V.G.	Good	Fair	Poor
250	200	175	125	85

Arisaka Type 44 Carbine

As above, with an 18.5" barrel and folding bayonet.

Courtesy Buffalo Bill Historical Center, Cody, Wyoming

Exc.	V.G.	Good	Fair	Poor
450	350	225	150	100

Japanese "Siamese Mauser" Rifle

A modified Mauser in 8x52Rmm caliber manufactured during the 1920s for the Siamese government.

Exc.	V.G.	Good	Fair	Poor
125	100	80	60	40

Arisaka Type 97 "Sniper's Rifle"

The Type 38 with a 4-power telescope and a bipod. Introduced in 1937.

Courtesy Richard M. Kumor, Sr.

Courtesy Richard M. Kumor, Sr.

Exc.	V.G.	Good	Fair	Poor
2000	1400	1000	600	300

> **A Type 97 rifle, serial number 7955, was sold at auction for $2,090. The rifle was fitted with a scope and sling. Condition was good.**
> **Old Town Station, Ltd., March 1996.**

Arisaka Type 99 Rifle

A 7.7mm caliber bolt-action rifle with a 25" barrel and full length stock secured by two barrel bands. Fitted with a monopod.

Exc.	V.G.	Good	Fair	Poor
150	125	100	80	60

NOTE: Premium paid for "last ditch" 4" long rifle variations.

Arisaka Type 99 Long Rifle

this variation is the same as the above model but fitted with a 31.4" barrel. This is a scarce variation.

Courtesy Richard M. Kumor, Sr.

Exc.	V.G.	Good	Fair	Poor
375	325	200	100	50

Test Type 1 Rifle

Bolt action rifle chambered for 6.5mm Japanese. Barrel length is 19". Cleaning rod is 17-3/16" long. The stock is a two-piece buttstock with full length handguard and a hinge attached at the wrist. Metal finish is blued. Total number produce is approximately 200-300 rifles.

Exc.	V.G.	Good	Fair	Poor
1800	1500	1000	500	125

Type 100 Paratroop Rifle

Chambered for 7.7mm Japanese cartridge. Barrel length is 25-1/4" long. Blued cleaning rod 21-5/16" long. Rear sight is adjustable from 300m to 1500m. Two piece butt stock with full handguard can be disassembled with an interrupted-thread connector. Bolt handle is detachable. Metal finish is blued. Total number produced is estimated at 500 rifles.

Exc.	V.G.	Good	Fair	Poor
4500	4000	3000	—	—

Type 2 Paratroop Rifle

Similar to the model above but with a different style of takedown. This model uses a wedge and bail wire connector. This rifle production began in late 1943.

Courtesy Richard M. Kumor, Sr.

Exc.	V.G.	Good	Fair	Poor
1000	850	650	300	100

Type 99 "Snipers Rifle"

The standard Type 99 with a 25.5" barrel and 4-power telescope.

Exc.	V.G.	Good	Fair	Poor
1800	1500	1200	500	200

Type 5 Semiautomatic Rifle

A 7.7mm semiautomatic rifle patterned after the U.S. M1. Made at the Kure Naval Arsenal in 1945. It is believed that approximately 20 were made. Prospective purchasers should secure a qualified appraisal prior to acquisition.

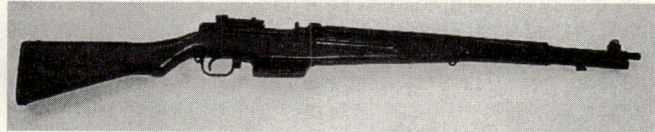

Courtesy Richard M. Kumor, Sr.

Exc.	V.G.	Good	Fair	Poor
22000	19000	14000	—	—

Type 26 Revolver

A 9mm caliber double action hinged barrel revolver with a 6-shot cylinder. As this pistol does not have a hammer spur, it only functions in double action. Manufactured from 1893 to 1924.

Exc.	V.G.	Good	Fair	Poor
400	300	200	150	100

4th Year Type Nambu Pistol

This is a quality built semiautomatic pistol chambered for the 8mm cartridge. It is fitted with a 4.7" barrel and has a magazine capacity of 8 rounds. It can be identified by the grip safety located on the front strap. The early models, serial numbers 1 to 2450, are known as "Grandpa" to collectors. Later pistols are known as "Papa" Nambu. The values shown here are only approximate. Different variations may bring different prices and an appraisal is recommended. Pistols with original wooden stocks are worth considerably more.

Exc.	V.G.	Good	Fair	Poor
750	500	400	300	150

Baby Nambu

As above, with a 3.5" barrel. 7mm cartridge is unique to the gun. A much smaller version of the Papa 8mm pistol. It is a well-made piece.

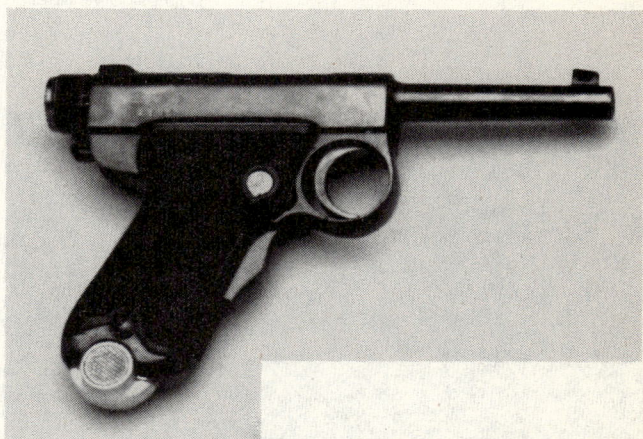

Courtesy Buffalo Bill Historical Center, Cody, Wyoming

Exc.	V.G.	Good	Fair	Poor
2250	2000	1500	1000	750

14th Year Type Nambu Pistol/T-14

Similar to the 4th Year Type but without a grip safety and with grooved grips and a larger triggerguard. Manufactured until 1945 Early guns have a small trigger guard. Later models have a much larger trigger guard. Early guns will bring a premium of 20%. The month a year of production are indicated on the right side of the receiver just below the serial numbers on both the Type 14 and Type 94 pistols. The guns are dated from the beginning of the reign of Hirohito (sho-wa period) which stared in 1925. Thus 3.12 means 1928-Dec. and 19.5 means 1944-May.

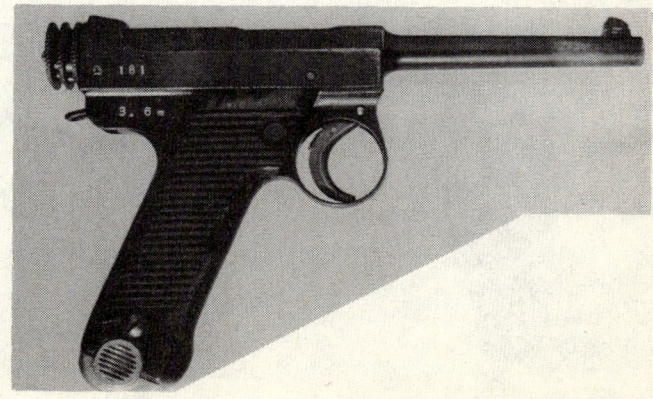

Courtesy Orvel Reichert

Courtesy Orvel Reichert

Later pistol with large trigger guard-Courtesy Orvel Reichert

Exc.	V.G.	Good	Fair	Poor
350	250	200	150	100

Type 94 Pistol/T-94

An 8mm caliber semiautomatic pistol with a 3.3" barrel and 6-shot magazine. Manufactured from 1937 to 1945.

Courtesy Orvel Reichert

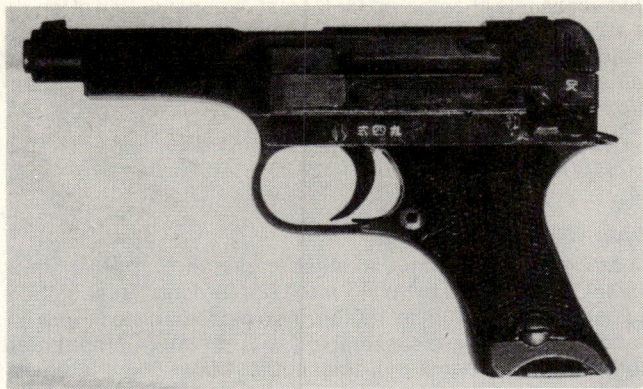

Courtesy Orvel Reichert

Exc.	V.G.	Good	Fair	Poor
350	300	250	175	125

JEFFERY, W. J. & CO. LTD.
London, England

This company produced high quality shotguns and rifles. Their products have been used by wealthy sportsmen for many years. They produced guns under their own banner and also as contractors for other distributors. They made the guns sold by the Army & Navy Department Store in London. Guns of this type were basically custom-ordered and as such are extremely hard to evaluate on a general basis. We supply an estimated value for a standard model but strongly urge that one secure an individual appraisal if a transaction is contemplated.

SHOTGUNS

Boxlock

Produced in all gauges, with barrel lengths and choke combinations to the customer's specifications. They were available with any trigger option and automatic extractors or ejectors. The materials and workmanship were of the highest order, and values would be based on options. This model was produced with exposed hammers and Damascus barrels and would be worth approximately 50 percent less in that configuration. Small gauges would add approximately 50 percent.

Exc.	V.G.	Good	Fair	Poor
4000	3500	2500	1600	900

Sidelock

The quality is similar to that of the boxlock, with the added value of the sidelock action. This was also a made-to-order gun, and values cannot be accurately estimated without an individual appraisal. Hammerguns with Damascus barrels would bring approximately 50 percent less. Small gauges would add approximately 50 percent.

Exc.	V.G.	Good	Fair	Poor
9000	7500	5000	3250	1650

RIFLES

Single Shot

Built on the Farquharson Falling Block action and was chambered for many calibers up to the .600 Nitro Express. This was also a custom-order gun, and the barrel length was optional. There are usually folding express sights; and the finish is usually blued with a select, hand-checkered walnut stock. These were high quality firearms; and the values would be determined, for the most part, by the options and embellishments on the particular specimen. Individual appraisal is definitely advised. The caliber in which a rifle is chambered will also have an effect on the value. Obsolete calibers bring less, and the larger express calibers bring more.

Exc.	V.G.	Good	Fair	Poor
4000	3250	2500	1750	900

Boxlock Double Rifle

A boxlock chambered for many different calibers. It can be found with either a top or underlever action and has folding express sights. The stock and forearm are select, hand-checkered walnut; and the finish is usually blue. This was a custom-order proposition, and values can be affected by many variables such as caliber, options, and embellishment. Damascus barreled hammerguns are worth approximately 50 percent less.

Exc.	V.G.	Good	Fair	Poor
8000	6500	4500	3500	2500

Sidelock Double Rifle

Has detachable sidelocks and otherwise is comparable to the boxlock version. Individual appraisal is recommended.

Exc.	V.G.	Good	Fair	Poor
12500	10000	7500	5000	4000

JENISON, J. & CO.
Southbridge, Connecticut

Under Hammer Pistol

A .28 caliber single shot under hammer percussion pistol with a 4" half-octagonal barrel marked "J.Jenison & Co./Southbridge, Mass." Blued with a maple or oak grip. Manufactured during the 1850s.

Exc.	V.G.	Good	Fair	Poor
—	—	650	250	150

JENKS CARBINE
Springfield, Massachusetts
N. P. Ames Manufacturer

Jenks "Mule Ear Carbine"

A .54 caliber percussion side hammer carbine with a 24.5" round barrel and full length stock secured by two barrel bands. The lock casehardened, the barrel browned and the furniture of brass. The lock marked "N.P.Ames/Springfield/Mass." The barrel stamped "Wm.Jenks/USN" followed by the inspector's initials. The buttstock carries an inspector's cartouche. Approximately 4,250 were made between 1841 and 1846. Some were marked "USR" for the "U.S. Revenue Cutter Service," and these would bring approximately an 80 percent premium over the values listed below. However, prospective purchasers should secure a qualified appraisal prior to acquisition.

Courtesy Milwaukee Public Museum, Milwaukee, Wisconsin

Exc.	V.G.	Good	Fair	Poor
—	—	2000	1000	375

Jenks Navy Rifle

As above, with a 30" round barrel and full length stock secured by three barrel bands. Approximately 1,000 were made for the U.S. Navy in 1841.

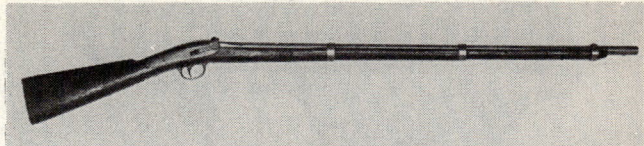

Courtesy Milwaukee Public Museum, Milwaukee, Wisconsin

Exc.	V.G.	Good	Fair	Poor
—	—	4000	2000	800

JENKS-HERKIMER
New York
Manufacturer-E. Remington & Son

Jenks Carbine

Identical to the Jenks Carbine listed in the previous entry except that the barrel length is 24.25" and the lock is fitted with a Maynard tape primer. The lock marked "Remington's/Herkimer/N.Y." The barrel is marked "W. Jenks/USN/RC/P/Cast Steel." Approximately 1,000 of these carbines manufactured circa 1846.

Exc.	V.G.	Good	Fair	Poor
—	—	2500	950	450

JENKS-MERRILL
Baltimore, Maryland

An alteration of the Jenks Carbine listed previously to a breech loading system developed by J.H. Merrill. The conventional sidelock marked "J. H. Merrill Balto./Pat. July 1858." The breech retains the mark "Wm.Jenks/USN." Approximately 300 were altered between 1858 and 1860.

Exc.	V.G.	Good	Fair	Poor
—	—	3000	1500	650

JENNINGS
Windsor, Vermont
Manufacturer - Robbins & Lawrence
SEE Winchester Repeating Arms

JENNINGS F. A., INC.
Carson City, Nevada

Distributors of arms manufactured by Calwestco in Chino, California, and Bryco Firearms in Carson City, Nevada.

J-22

A .22 caliber semiautomatic pistol with a 2.5" barrel and 6-shot magazine. Aluminum, finished in bright chrome, Teflon, or satin nickel with plastic or wood grips.

Exc.	V.G.	Good	Fair	Poor
75	65	50	35	25

Bryco Model 25

A .25 caliber semiautomatic pistol with a 2.5" barrel and 6-shot magazine. Constructed and finished as above.

Exc.	V.G.	Good	Fair	Poor
90	75	65	50	35

Bryco Model 38

A .22, .32, or .380 semiautomatic pistol with a 2.8" barrel and 6-shot magazine. Constructed and finished as above.

Exc.	V.G.	Good	Fair	Poor
90	75	65	50	35

Bryco Model 48

Similar to the above, with a redesigned triggerguard with a squared forward section. Introduced in 1988.

Exc.	V.G.	Good	Fair	Poor
90	75	65	50	35

JERICHO
Harrisburg, Pennsylvania
Israeli Military Industries Israel

Jericho

A 9mm or .41 Action Express double action semiautomatic pistol with a 4.72" barrel, polygonal rifling, ambidextrous safety and fixed sights. Blued with plastic grips.

Exc.	V.G.	Good	Fair	Poor
450	400	350	300	200

JIEFFCO
Robar et Cie
Liege, Belgium

Pocket Pistol

A .25 or .32 caliber semiautomatic pistol with a 3" barrel and 6-shot magazine. Blued with composition grips. Manufactured prior to WWI.

Exc.	V.G.	Good	Fair	Poor
300	250	200	150	100

New Model Melior

A .25 caliber semiautomatic pistol with a 2" barrel and 6-shot magazine. Blued with composition grips. Manufactured during the 1920s and imported by Davis-Warner.

Exc.	V.G.	Good	Fair	Poor
275	225	175	125	90

JOHNSON AUTOMATIC RIFLE
Cranston Arms Co.
Providence, Rhode Island

Model 1941

A 7mm or .30-06 semiautomatic rifle with a 22" barrel and 10-shot rotary magazine. Parkerized with a walnut stock. Manufactured from 1941 to 1945. Rifles of this design were purchased by the United States government, the Dutch government and various South American governments.

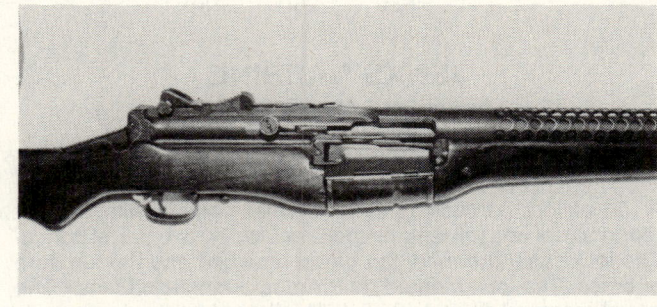

Exc.	V.G.	Good	Fair	Poor
2500	1800	1000	750	500

JOHNSON, BYE & CO.
Worcester, Massachusetts

Established in 1871 by Martin Bye and Iver Johnson. This company primarily manufactured inexpensive pistols. In 1883 Johnson assumed full control of the company and renamed it the Iver Johnson Arms Company.

Defender, Eagle, Encore, Eureka, Favorite, Lion, Smoker, and Tycoon

A .22, .32, .38, or .44 caliber spur trigger revolver manufactured with various barrel lengths and normally nickel-plated. The barrel marked with one of the above trade names.

Exc.	V.G.	Good	Fair	Poor
125	100	75	50	25

Eclipse

A .22 caliber spur trigger single shot pistol with a 1.5" barrel. Blued with walnut grips.

Exc.	V.G.	Good	Fair	Poor
125	100	75	50	25

American Bulldog

A .22, .32, or .38 caliber double action revolver with a 3" barrel. Blued or nickel-plated with walnut or composition grips.

Exc.	V.G.	Good	Fair	Poor
125	100	75	50	25

JOSEF JESCHER

SEE Austrian Military Firearms

JOSLYN

Milbury, Massachusetts

A.H. Waters-Manufacturer

Model 1855 Carbine

A .54 caliber breech loading single shot percussion carbine with a 22.5" barrel secured to the forend by one barrel band. Blued, casehardened with brass mounts. The lock marked "A.H.Waters & Co./Milbury, Mass.", and the patent dates stamped on the breech lever. Approximately 1,000 manufactured in 1855 and 1856.

Exc.	V.G.	Good	Fair	Poor
—	—	3500	1500	950

Model 1855 Rifle

Similar to the above, in .58 caliber with a 38" barrel secured by three barrel bands. Several hundred were made in 1856.

Exc.	V.G.	Good	Fair	Poor
—	—	4500	2000	1100

JOSLYN FIREARMS COMPANY

Stonington, Connecticut

Model 1862 Carbine

A .52 rimfire breech loading single shot carbine with a 22" round barrel secured by one barrel band. Blued, casehardened with brass mounts. The lock marked "Joslyn Firearms Co./Stonington/Conn.", and the patent date marked on the barrel. The trigger plate is 8" long, and the upper tang measures 4.5". Approximately 4,000 manufactured in 1862.

Courtesy Milwaukee Public Museum, Milwaukee, Wisconsin

Exc.	V.G.	Good	Fair	Poor
—	—	2500	950	400

Model 1864 Carbine

As above, with casehardened iron mounts, a 7" trigger plate and 2" upper tang. Approximately 12,000 were made in 1864 and 1865.

Courtesy Milwaukee Public Museum, Milwaukee, Wisconsin

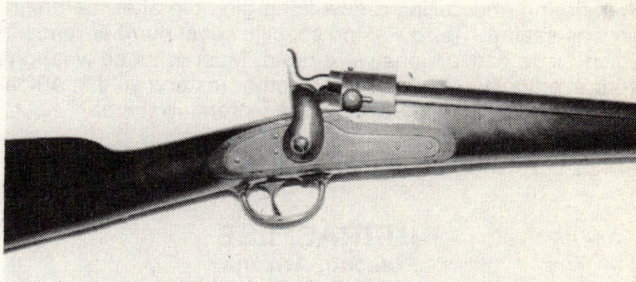

Exc.	V.G.	Good	Fair	Poor
—	—	2000	800	500

Army Model Revolver

A .44 caliber side hammer percussion revolver with an 8" octagonal barrel and 5-shot cylinder. Blued, casehardened with walnut grips. The barrel marked "B. F. Joslyn/Patd. May 4, 1858." Martially marked examples are worth a premium of approximately 25 percent over the values listed below. The two models of this revolver are as follows:

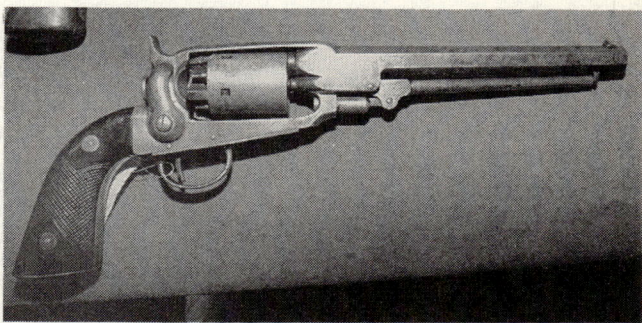

First Model

With a brass triggerguard and iron butt cap. Approximately 500 made in 1861.

Exc.	V.G.	Good	Fair	Poor
—	—	3000	1250	550

Second Model

Fitted with an iron triggerguard and without a butt cap. Approximately 2,500 were made in 1861 and 1862.

Exc.	V.G.	Good	Fair	Poor
—	—	2500	1000	400

JOSLYN

Springfield, Massachusetts

Manufacturer-Springfield Armory

Joslyn Breechloading Rifle

The first mass-produced, true breechloading cartridge firearm manufactured in a national armory. The actions were supplied by the Joslyn Firearms Company, and the rifles were chambered for the .56-50 rimfire cartridge. This rifle has a 35.5" round barrel and a full-length stock that is held on by three barrel bands. The lock is marked "U.S./Springfield" with "1864" at the back. The barrel is marked "B. F. Joslyn's Patent/ Oct. 8th, 1861 / June 24th, 1862." There were approximately 3,000 of these manufactured circa 1865. They were probably issued to Union forces, but it is unknown if they saw action before the end of the Civil War.

Exc.	V.G.	Good	Fair	Poor
—	—	1500	700	500

.50-70 Alteration

Approximately 1,600 Joslyn rifles were re-chambered to fire the .50-70 centerfire cartridge. The conversion consisted of re-chambering and drilling a new firing pin hole after the rimfire pin was sealed. There was no specific serial number range in which these conversions were done. Most of these weapons were eventually converted to smoothbores and sold in Africa. The original military specimens are extremely scarce.

Exc.	V.G.	Good	Fair	Poor
—	—	1750	1000	750

JURRAS, LEE
Prescott, Arizona
SEE Auto-Mag

While Jurras is best known for manufacturing the last model of the Auto-Mag, he also produced the following pistol sold by J. & G. Sales in Prescott, Arizona.

Howdah Pistol

A .375, .416, .460, .475, .500, and the .577. caliber single shot pistol with a 12" barrel, adjustable sights and Nitex finish, built upon a Thompson Center Contender frame.

Exc.	V.G.	Good	Fair	Poor
1200	1000	800	650	500

JUSTICE, P. S.
Philadelphia, Pennsylvania

Percussion Rifle

A .58 caliber percussion rifle with a 35" round barrel secured by two barrel bands, browned barrel, polished lock and brass furniture. The lock marked "P.S. Justice/Philada." Approximately 2,500 were manufactured in 1861.

Courtesy Milwaukee Public Museum, Milwaukee, Wisconsin

Exc.	V.G.	Good	Fair	Poor
—	—	1500	750	450

KBI, INC.
Harrisburg, Pennsylvania

PSP-25

A .25 caliber semiautomatic pistol with a 2" barrel manufactured in Charlottesville, Virginia, under license from Fabrique Nationale. Introduced in 1989.

NIB	Exc.	V.G.	Good	Fair
225	200	175	150	100

KDF, INC.
Seguin, Texas
Kleinguenther Distinctive Firearms

The former importer of Voere and Mauser rifles into the U.S.

Condor

A 12 gauge boxlock Over/Under shotgun with 28" barrels with ventilated ribs, single selective trigger and automatic ejectors. Blued with a walnut stock. Manufactured in Italy.

Exc.	V.G.	Good	Fair	Poor
650	600	525	375	275

Brescia

A 12 gauge boxlock double-barrel shotgun with 28" barrels, double triggers and extractors. Blued with a walnut stock. Manufactured in Italy.

Exc.	V.G.	Good	Fair	Poor
350	325	300	200	125

K-14 Insta Fire Rifle

A bolt action sporting rifle manufactured in a variety of calibers with 24" or 26" barrels furnished without sights. Blued with a Monte Carlo-style walnut stock.

Exc.	V.G.	Good	Fair	Poor
600	550	450	325	250

K-15

Similar to the above, with a 60-degree bolt angle and an accurized barrel guaranteed to fire a .5" group at 100 yards. Manufactured with a variety of optional features.

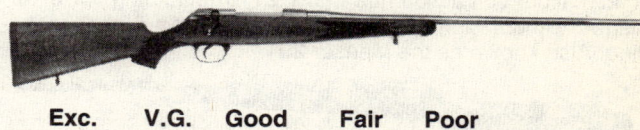

Exc.	V.G.	Good	Fair	Poor
1000	850	750	550	300

K-15 Pro-Hunter

As above, matte blued or electroless nickel-plated with a fiberglass stock.

Exc.	V.G.	Good	Fair	Poor
1400	1250	1000	700	500

K-15 Swat Rifle

A 7.62x54mm caliber bolt action rifle with a 24" or 26" barrel furnished without sights, 4-shot magazine and parkerized finish. Walnut stock.

Exc.	V.G.	Good	Fair	Poor
1500	1300	1100	800	550

K-15 Dangerous Game

As above, in .411 KDF caliber.

Exc.	V.G.	Good	Fair	Poor
2000	1600	1300	1000	700

K-16

A bolt action sporting rifle manufactured in a variety of calibers with a 24" or 26" barrel furnished without sights, single stage adjustable trigger, accurized barrel and Dupont Rynite stock. Produced with a variety of optional features.

Exc.	V.G.	Good	Fair	Poor
775	675	500	400	200

Titan Menor

A .222 or .223 caliber bolt-action rifle with a 24" or 26" barrel furnished without sights and Monte Carlo-style or standard Schnabel tipped walnut stock. Blued.

Exc.	V.G.	Good	Fair	Poor
650	600	550	400	200

Titan II Standard

As above, with a mid-sized action.

Exc.	V.G.	Good	Fair	Poor
900	800	700	500	250

Titan II Magnum

As above, with a long action. Discontinued in 1988.

Exc.	V.G.	Good	Fair	Poor
1000	850	750	550	250

Titan .411 KDF Mag.

As above, in .411 KDF with a 26" barrel having an integral muzzle brake. Blued or electroless nickel-plated with a walnut stock. Discontinued in 1988.

Exc.	V.G.	Good	Fair	Poor
1200	1050	850	650	350

K-22

A .22 caliber bolt action rifle with a 21" free floating barrel furnished without sights, adjustable trigger, and 5-shot magazine. Also known as the Mauser 201.

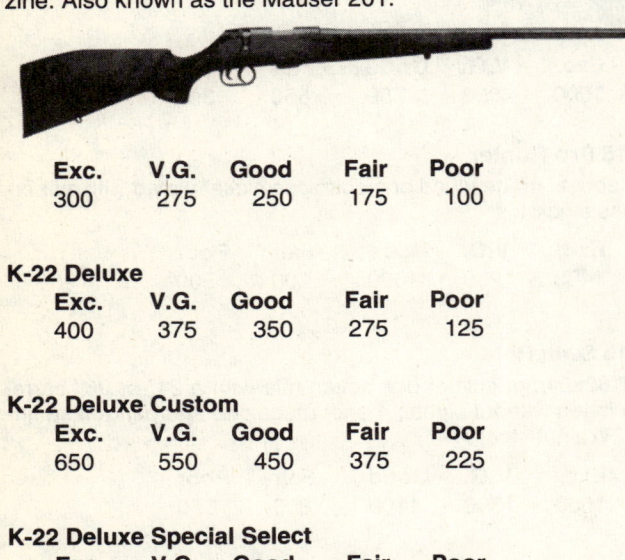

Exc.	V.G.	Good	Fair	Poor
300	275	250	175	100

K-22 Deluxe

Exc.	V.G.	Good	Fair	Poor
400	375	350	275	125

K-22 Deluxe Custom

Exc.	V.G.	Good	Fair	Poor
650	550	450	375	225

K-22 Deluxe Special Select

Exc.	V.G.	Good	Fair	Poor
1000	850	750	650	325

Model 2005

A .22 caliber semiautomatic rifle with a 19.5" barrel, open sights, and 5-shot magazine. Blued with a walnut stock. Also available in a deluxe model. Imported in 1986.

NIB	Exc.	V.G.	Good	Fair	Poor
125	100	80	60	40	30

Model 2107

A .22 or .22 Magnum caliber bolt action rifle with a 19.5" barrel, open sights, and 5-shot magazine. Blued with a walnut stock.

Exc.	V.G.	Good	Fair	Poor
175	150	125	100	75

Model 2112

The deluxe version of the Model 2107.

Exc.	V.G.	Good	Fair	Poor
250	200	175	125	90

K.F.C.
Japan
Importer-LaPaloma Marketing
Tucson, Arizona

E-I Trap or Skeet Over/Under

A 12 gauge boxlock double-barrel shotgun with 26" or 30" barrels, competition rib, single selective trigger and automatic ejectors. Engraved, blued with a walnut stock. Manufactured until 1986.

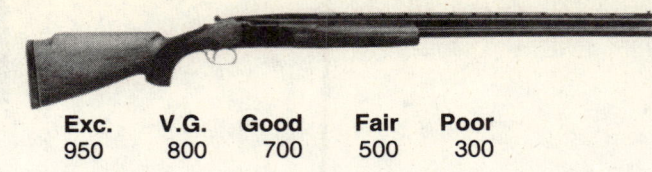

Exc.	V.G.	Good	Fair	Poor
950	800	700	500	300

E-2 Trap or Skeet Over/Under

As above, but more finely finished.

Exc.	V.G.	Good	Fair	Poor
1400	1250	1000	750	350

Field Grade Over/Under

As above, with a narrow rib and 26" or 28" barrels. Discontinuted in 1986.

Exc.	V.G.	Good	Fair	Poor
650	575	500	400	275

Model 250

A 12 gauge semiautomatic shotgun with 26", 28", or 30" barrels fitted for choke tubes. Matte blued with a walnut stock. Manufactured from 1980 to 1986.

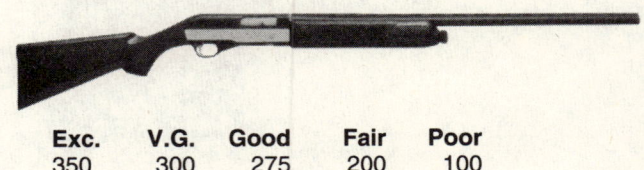

Exc.	V.G.	Good	Fair	Poor
350	300	275	200	100

KSN INDUSTRIES
Israel
Importer-J.O. Arms, Houston, Texas

Golan

A semiautomatic pistol, introduced in 1996, chambered for the 9mm or .40 S&W cartridge. Double action trigger with ambidextrous controls. Barrel length is 3.9" and magazine capacity is 10 rounds in US. In rest of the world 15 rounds for 9mm and 11 rounds for the .40 S&W. Weight is 29 oz.

NIB	Exc.	V.G.	Good	Fair	Poor
650	525	—	—	—	—

Kareen MK II

This single action semiautomatic pistol is chambered for the 9mm cartridge. The barrel length is 4.5". Ambidextrous safety and rubber grips. Steel slide and frame. Weight is about 34 oz.

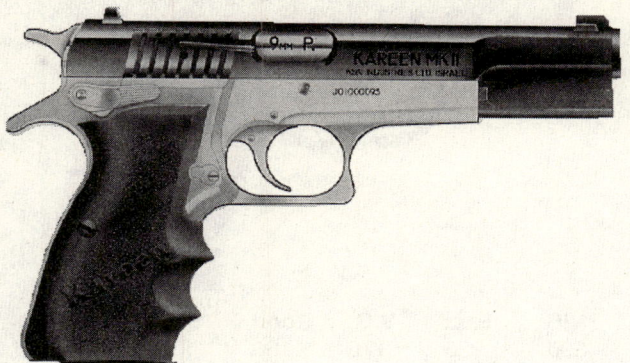

NIB	Exc.	V.G.	Good	Fair	Poor
400	325	250	200	150	100

Kareen MK II-Compact

Same as above but fitted with a 3.9" barrel. Weight is about 32 oz.

NIB	Exc.	V.G.	Good	Fair	Poor
500	400	300	250	200	150

GAL

Same as the full size Kareen but chambered for the .45 ACP cartridge.

NIB	Exc.	V.G.	Good	Fair	Poor
400	325	250	200	150	100

KAHR ARMS
Blauvelt, New York

Kahr K9

This is a semiautomatic pistol chambered for the 9mm cartridge. It is a ulta-compact size. The barrel length is 3.5" and the overall length is 6". The width at the slide is .9". The magazine capacity is 7 rounds. Available in blue or electroless nickel finish. Weight is 25 oz.

NIB	Exc.	V.G.	Good	Fair	Poor
500	425	350	300	250	150

Kahr Lady K9

Same as above but with lightened recoil spring.

NIB	Exc.	V.G.	Good	Fair	Poor
500	425	350	300	250	150

Kahr K40

This model is similar to the K9 but is chambered for the .40S&W cartridge. Weight is 26 oz.

NIB	Exc.	V.G.	Good	Fair	Poor
500	425	350	300	250	150

NOTE: For night sights add $90.00. For Nickel finish add $70.00. For Black Titanium finish add $100.00. For the K40 Stainless steel version add $50.00.

KASSNAR IMPORTS, INC.
Harrisburg, Pennsylvania
Currently the following firearms are imported by this company.

Standard Over/Under
A 12, 20, 28 or .410 bore boxlock double-barrel shotgun with 26" or 28" barrels, ventilated ribs, single trigger and extractors. Blued with a walnut stock.

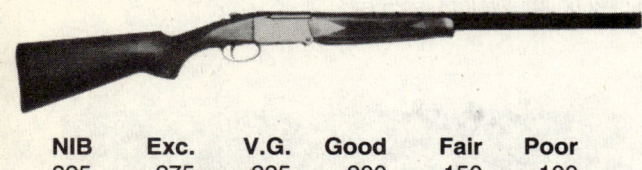

NIB	Exc.	V.G.	Good	Fair	Poor
325	275	225	200	150	100

Deluxe Over/Under
As above, with a more finely figured stock.

NIB	Exc.	V.G.	Good	Fair	Poor
375	325	250	225	175	100

Standard Side-by-Side
A 20, 28 or .410 bore boxlock folding double-barrel shotgun with 26" barrels, double triggers and extractors. Blued with a walnut stock.

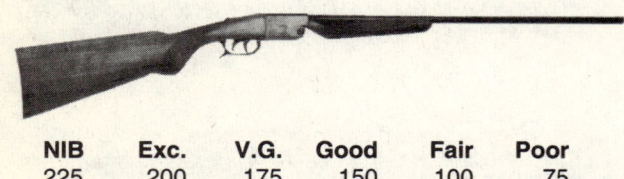

NIB	Exc.	V.G.	Good	Fair	Poor
225	200	175	150	100	75

Deluxe Side-by Side
As above, in .410 bore only and with more finely figured wood.

NIB	Exc.	V.G.	Good	Fair	Poor
250	225	200	175	125	75

KEBERST INT.
Kendall International
Paris, Kentucky

Keberst Model 1A
A .338 Lapua Magnum, .338-416 Rigby, and the .338-06 caliber bolt action rifle with a 24" barrel having an integral muzzle brake, and fitted with a 3-9 power Leupold telescope. Matte blued with a camouflaged composition stock. Manufactured in 1987 and 1988.

Exc.	V.G.	Good	Fair	Poor
3500	3000	2500	1800	900

KEL-TEC CNC INDUSTRIES
Cocoa, Florida

P-11
This is a semiautomatic pistol chambered for the 9mm cartridge. It is double action only with a barrel length of 3.1". Overall length is 5.6". Weight is 14 oz. Magazine capacity is 10 rounds. Standard model has blued slide with black grip. Stainless steel and Parkerized finish are offered as well.

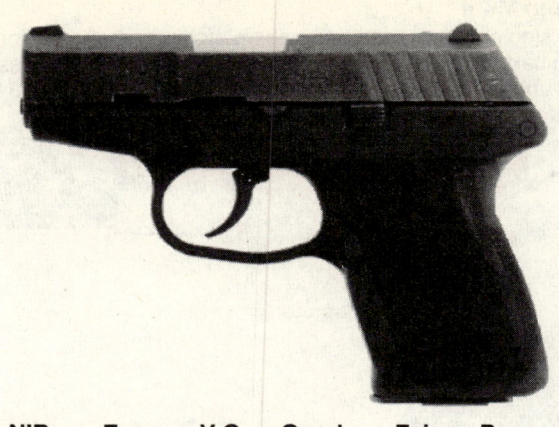

NIB	Exc.	V.G.	Good	Fair	Poor
300	225	175	150	125	100

NOTE: Add $100 for stainless steel and $50 for Parkerized finish.

SUB-9 Rifle
Introduced in 1996 this is a semiautomatic rilfe chambered for the 9mm cartridge. The barrel length is 16.1". The rifle can be folded closed with an overall length of 16". Weight is approximately 4.6 lbs. Different grip assembly can be fitted to this rifle allowing for the use of different magazines.

NIB	Exc.	V.G.	Good	Fair	Poor
650	500				

KEMPER, SHRIVER & COMPANY
Nashville, Tennessee
Delivered rifles made from sporting arm parts to the Ordnance Department at Nashville from December 1861 to March 1862. In all 150 arms were assembled. Overall length 48-1/2"; octagonal barrels shortened 33" and bored to .48 caliber; some fitted with saber bayonet lugs; stocks of military with brass furniture.

Prospective purchasers are strongly advised to secure an expert appraisal prior to acquisition.

Exc.	V.G.	Good	Fair	Poor
—	—	3500	2000	1500

KENDALL, INTERNATIONAL
Paris, Kentucky
SEE Keberst International

KENDALL, NICANOR
Windsor, Vermont

Under Hammer Pistol
A .31 to .41 caliber under hammer percussion pistol with 4" to 10" octagonal/round barrels marked "N.Kendall/Windsor,Vt." Browned or blued with brass mounts and maple grips. Manufactured in the 1850s.

Exc.	V.G.	Good	Fair	Poor
—	—	1000	400	175

KENO
Unknown

Derringer
A .22 caliber single shot spur trigger pistol with a 2.5" barrel, brass frame, and walnut grips. The barrel blued or nickel-plated and marked "Keno".

Exc.	V.G.	Good	Fair	Poor
300	250	200	150	100

KEPPLINGER, 1. HANNES
Kufstein, Austria

3-S Rifle System

A short-action rifle chambered for all popular American and European cartridges. The major parts are constructed of a high strength alloy, and it features a de-cocking lever that allows manual cocking and de-cocking of the firing-pin spring. The barrel is 23" in length, and the detachable magazine holds 3 rounds. This is essentially a custom-built gun and is rarely encountered on the market. The engraving varies with the customer's wishes; and the walnut stock, either full-length Mannlicher style or with a Schnabel forend, is made of the highest grade wood available. This company does not have an importer at this time. We are not able to evaluate, as there are too few traded. It is listed for reference only.

KERR
London, England

Kerr Revolver

A .44 caliber double-action percussion revolver with a 5.5" barrel and 6-shot cylinder. Blued with walnut grips. The frame marked "Kerr's Patent 648"; and "London Armoury Bermondsey."

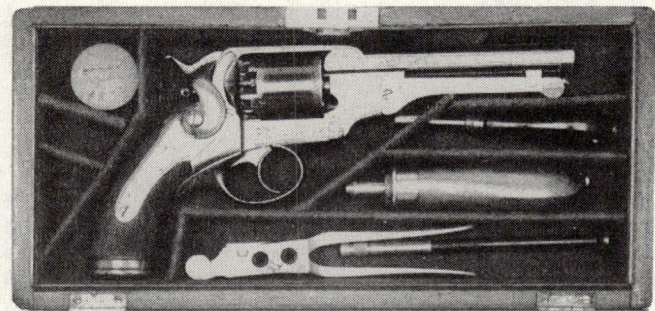

Courtesy Butterfield & Butterfield, San Francisco, California

Exc.	V.G.	Good	Fair	Poor
1850	1350	1000	750	500

KERR
SEE English Military Firearms

KESSLER ARMS CORPORATION
Silver Creek, New York

Bolt Action Shotgun

A 12, 16, or 20 gauge shotgun with 26" or 28" barrels. Blued with a walnut stock. Manufactured between 1951 and 1953.

Exc.	V.G.	Good	Fair	Poor
125	75	50	30	20

Levermatic Shotgun

A 12, 16, or 20 gauge lever action shotgun with a 26" or 28" barrel. Blued with a walnut stock. Manufactured between 1951 and 1953.

Exc.	V.G.	Good	Fair	Poor
150	100	75	50	25

KETTNER, EDWARD
Suhl, Germany

Drilling

This is a high quality three-barreled firearm chambered for 12x12 gauge or 16x16 gauge over various metric rifle cartridges. The barrels are 25" in length and feature ejectors, selective triggers, and pop-up rifle sights that appear when the rifle barrel is selected. This gun is deep-relief engraved in the German style and has a high-grade checkered walnut stock. It was manufactured between 1922 and 1939.

Exc.	V.G.	Good	Fair	Poor
2500	2000	1750	1400	850

KIMBALL ARMS COMPANY
Detroit, Michigan

Semiautomatic Pistol

A .30 carbine caliber semiautomatic pistol with a 3.5" or 5" barrel. Blued with plastic grips. Also believed to have been made in .22 Hornet and .357 Magnum, though legitimate examples have been seen. Manufactured from 1955 to 1958. Approximately 238 were made.

Exc.	V.G.	Good	Fair	Poor
850	750	650	500	275

KIMBER OF OREGON, INC.
Clackamas, Oregon

KIMBER OF AMERICA
Yonkers, New York

Kimber of Oregon was established in April 1979 by Greg and Jack Warne. The company produced high quality rimfire and centerfire rifles until going out of business in early 1991. Kimber produced approximately 60,000 rifles during its operation. In April 1993, Greg Warne opened Kimber of America in Clackamas, Oregon. This new company presently manufactures the same high quality rifles built on an improved Model 82 Sporter action and stock but in rimfire only. In 1995 the company expanded its product line to include centerfire rifles as well as a 1911 .45 ACP Semiautomatic pistol line. In 1997 the company was moved to New York state and Greg Warne no longer was involved in the operations.

CURRENT PRODUCTION MODELS

MODEL 82C SERIES

New Model 82C Classic

Bolt action rifle chambered for the .22 long rifle cartridge. Receiver drilled and tapped for sights. Fitted with a 21" barrel. Detachable magazine holds 4 rounds. Stock is plain with standard grade claro walnut. Checkering is 20 lines to the inch with 4 point side panel pattern. Red rubber butt pad and polished steel pistol grip cap are standard. Weight is approximately 6-1/2 lbs.

NIB	Exc.	V.G.	Good	Fair	Poor
775	650	500	400	300	200

New Model 82C Super America

Same as above but fitted with AAA fancy grade claro walnut with ebony tip and beaded cheekpiece. Hand checkering is 22 lines to the inch in a full coverage pattern. Steel buttplate and steel pistol grip cap are standard.

NIB	Exc.	V.G.	Good	Fair	Poor
1250	1050	700	450	300	200

Model 82C-Custom Match

This bolt action .22 caliber has a 22" barrel. The stock is AA French walnut with full coverage checkering. Finish is rust blued. Weight is about 6.75 lbs.

NIB	Exc.	V.G.	Good	Fair	Poor
2000	1600	950	700	500	250

New Model 82C Custom Shop Super America (Basic)

Same as above but furnished with a number of special order options that greatly affect the value. Seek an independent appraisal before the sale. Prices begin at $1,250.00.

Model 82C Stainless Steel Classic Limited Edition

Introduced in 1996 this limited edition Model 82C is chambered for the .22 long rifle cartridge The stainless steel barrel is 22" long. A 4-shot magazine is included. Production limited to 750 rifles whose owners may purchase a limited edition book on the history of the company for an additional $95. Book is serial numbered to the gun.

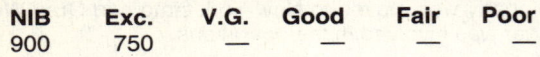

NIB	Exc.	V.G.	Good	Fair	Poor
900	750	—	—	—	—

Model 82C-Varmint Synthetic

Introduced in 1996 this .22 caliber bolt action rifle is fitted with a 20" fluted stainless steel barrel. A synthetic composite stock is black and is checkered. Weight is approximately 7.5 lbs.

NIB	Exc.	V.G.	Good	Fair	Poor
875	725	600	500	400	200

Model 82C SVT(Short/Varmint/Target)

First introduced in 1996 this .22 caliber rifle is a single shot. It is fitted with an 18" stainless steel fluted barrel. The walnut stock is a target style with no checkering. Weight is about 7.5 lbs.

NIB	Exc.	V.G.	Good	Fair	Poor
775	650	500	400	300	200

Model 82C HS (Hunting/Silhouette)

Introduced in 1997 this model features a 24" half-fluted barrel. Chambered for .22 long rifle cartridge. Stock is American walnut with high comb. Trigger is fully adjustable. Four-round magazine is standard. Weight is about 7 lbs.

NIB	Exc.	V.G.	Good	Fair	Poor
650	525	—	—	—	—

MODEL 84C SERIES

Model 84C-Classic

Reintroduced in 1996 this centerfire bolt action rifle is chamberd for the .222 Rem. and .223 Rem. cartridges. Fitted with a 22" barrel and a 5-round magazine. The stock is Claro walnut with hand checkering. Finish is blued. Weight is approximately 6.75 lbs.

NIB	Exc.	V.G.	Good	Fair	Poor
1125	875	700	500	400	200

Model 84C-SuperAmerica

This 1996 centerfire rifle is chambered for the .17 Rem., .222 Rem. and .223 Rem. cartridges. A 22" barrel is standard with AAA Claro walnut with wrap around checkering. Finish is blued.

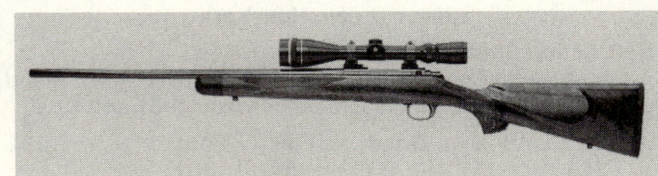

NIB	Exc.	V.G.	Good	Fair	Poor
1575	1250	850	750	550	300

Model 84C-Custom Match

Similar to the above model but stock with AA French walnut and rust blued finish. Limited availability.

NIB	Exc.	V.G.	Good	Fair	Poor
2400	1750	1200	850	600	300

Model 84C-Single Shot Varmint

Chambered for the .17 Rem. or .223 Rem. cartridge this rifle is fitted with a 25" stainless steel fluted barrel. Claro walnut stock with varmint style forearm. Weight is approximately 7.5 lbs.

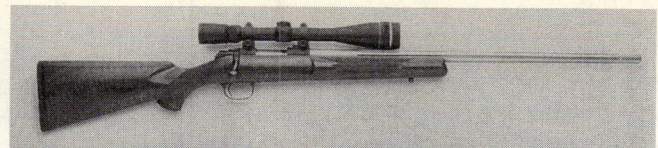

NIB	Exc.	V.G.	Good	Fair	Poor
1000	750	600	500	400	200

Model 84C Varmint Stainless

Introduced in 1997 this model features a 24" stainless steel match grade fluted barrel in medium heavy weight. Sporter style stock. Chambered for .223 Rem. Weight is approximately 7.5 lbs.

NIB	Exc.	V.G.	Good	Fair	Poor
1200	950	—	—	—	—

MODEL 770 SERIES

Model K770-Classic

This is a new 1996 Kimber design. Chambered for the .270, .300 Win. Mag., 7mm Mag., .338 Win. Mag., and .30-06 cartridges and fitted with a 24" match grade barrel. The stock is Claro walnut with hand checkering, polished steel grip cap, and hinged floorplate.

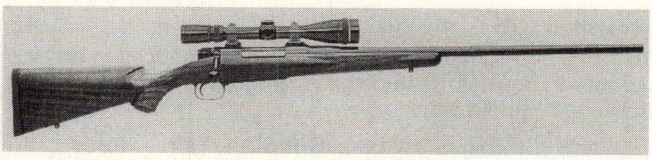

NIB	Exc.	V.G.	Good	Fair	Poor
750	575	425	350	250	125

Model K770-SuperAmerica

Same as above but fitted with AAA Claro walnut with ebony forend and beaded cheekpiece. Fine line checkering is standard on this model.

NIB	Exc.	V.G.	Good	Fair	Poor
1250	900	750	600	450	250

Kimber Sporterized Model 98 Swedish Mausers

These are reconditioned and reworked Mausers which are fitted with new match grade stainless steel fluted barrels in 24" or 26" depending on caliber. The stock is new synthetic checkered. Chambered in .257 Roberts, .270 Win., .280 Rem., .30-06, 7mm Rem. Mag, .300 Win. Mag., .338 Win. Mag., and the .220 Swift with a 25" barrel.

Suggested retail price is $535 for standard calibers and $560 for Magnums.

Kimber Sporterized Model 96 Swedish Mausers

Similar to the above in terms of reworking and reconditioning. Chambered for the following calibers:

22-250 w/stainless steel heavy barrel fluted-Retail $500
.243 Win.-$400 to $465 depending on finish.
6.5x55mm-$340 to $370 depending on finish.

7mm-08 Rem.-$415 to $465 depending on finish.
.308 Win.-$415 to 520 depending on finish and barrel configuration.

KIMBER CLASSIC .45 PISTOLS

First introduced in 1996 this is a quality built American made 1911 designed by Chip McCormick for Kimber.

Custom

Barrel length is 5" with black oxide finish fixed sights. Black synthetic grips. Magazine capacity is 8 rounds. Weight is about 38 oz.

NIB	Exc.	V.G.	Good	Fair	Poor
575	450	350	300	250	200

NOTE: For Walnut grips add $10.00.

Custom Stainless

As above but in stainless steel.

NIB	Exc.	V.G.	Good	Fair	Poor
650	500	425	350	275	225

Custom Target

The Custom Target has the same features as the Custom with the addition of an adjustable rear sight.

NIB	Exc.	V.G.	Good	Fair	Poor
745	600	525	400	300	250

Custom Royal

This has all the features of the Custom plus a high polish blue finish, hand checkered walnut grips, and long guide rod.

NIB	Exc.	V.G.	Good	Fair	Poor
700	575	475	375	300	250

Gold Match

All of the features of the Custom Royal plus Bo-Mar adjustable sights, fancy checkered diamond grips.

NIB	Exc.	V.G.	Good	Fair	Poor
900	750	600	500	400	250

DISCONTINUED MODELS

NOTE: For Model 82 Series rifles in .22 Magnum caliber add 10%. For rifles chambered for .22 Hornet add 15%.

Model 82 Classic

A .22, .22 Magnum, or .22 Hornet bolt action rifle with a 22" barrel furnished without sights and 4- or 5-shot magazine. Blued with a walnut stock. Discontinued in 1988.

Exc.	V.G.	Good	Fair	Poor
700	600	550	450	350

Cascade Model

As above, with a Monte Carlo-style stock.

Exc.	V.G.	Good	Fair	Poor
750	650	600	500	400

Custom Classic Model

As above, in .218 Bee or .25-20.

Exc.	V.G.	Good	Fair	Poor
800	725	650	400	300

Mini Classic

The Model 82 with an 18" barrel. Manufactured in 1988.

Exc.	V.G.	Good	Fair	Poor
600	550	475	400	300

Deluxe Grade

Similar to the Custom Classic. Introduced in 1989.

NIB	Exc.	V.G.	Good	Fair	Poor
1000	850	650	550	450	350

Model 82A Government

A .22 caliber bolt action rifle with a 25" heavy barrel fitted with telescope mounts. Matte blued with a walnut stock. Introduced in 1987.

NIB	Exc.	V.G.	Good	Fair	Poor
675	550	450	375	300	200

Continental

Similar to the Custom Classic with a 20" barrel, open sights, and full length Mannlicher-style stock. Introduced in 1987.

NIB	Exc.	V.G.	Good	Fair	Poor
850	750	650	500	400	300

Super Continental

As above, but more finely finished. Discontinued in 1988.

NIB	Exc.	V.G.	Good	Fair	Poor
1200	1100	1000	750	600	300

Super America

The Model 82 but more finely finished. Discontinued in 1988.

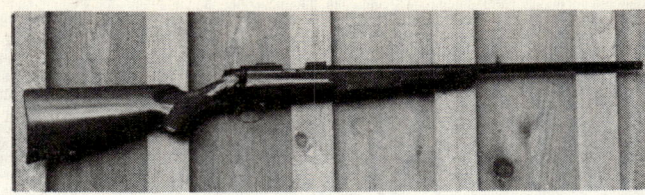

NIB	Exc.	V.G.	Good	Fair	Poor
1500	1200	950	850	650	500

Super Grade

As above, introduced in 1989.

NIB	Exc.	V.G.	Good	Fair	Poor
1200	1000	900	750	600	475

Centennial

A commemorative rifle moderately engraved including a special match barrel, skeleton buttplate, hand-selected walnut stock, and light engraving. Issued to commemorate the 100th anniversary of the 22 l.r. cartridge. One hundred were manufactured in 1987.

NIB	Exc.	V.G.	Good	Fair	Poor
2500	2250	2000	1750	1500	1150

Brownell

In 1986, 500 commemorative rifles were produced in honor of Leonard Brownell, featuring a high-grade, Mannlicher-style, full-length walnut stock.

NIB	Exc.	V.G.	Good	Fair	Poor
1500	1250	1000	800	600	500

Model 84 Series-Discontinued Models

A bolt action rifle manufactured in a variety of smallbore calibers with a 22" or 24" barrel and 5-shot magazine. Blued with a walnut stock. Variations are as follows:

Classic Model

NIB	Exc.	V.G.	Good	Fair	Poor
700	650	600	400	250	200

Custom Classic Model

NIB	Exc.	V.G.	Good	Fair	Poor
900	800	700	500	350	200

Deluxe Grade Sporter

NIB	Exc.	V.G.	Good	Fair	Poor
1200	1000	850	750	500	250

Continental

NIB	Exc.	V.G.	Good	Fair	Poor
975	900	800	700	500	250

Super Continental

NIB	Exc.	V.G.	Good	Fair	Poor
1300	1100	850	700	575	250

Super America

NIB	Exc.	V.G.	Good	Fair	Poor
1500	1000	925	825	600	300

Super Grade

NIB	Exc.	V.G.	Good	Fair	Poor
1250	1100	1000	850	650	300

Ultra Varmint

As above, with a 24" stainless steel barrel and laminated birch wood stock. Introduced in 1989.

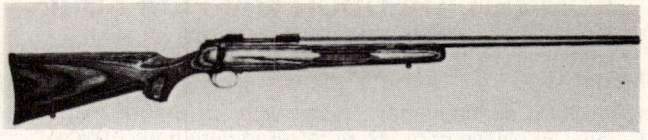

NIB	Exc.	V.G.	Good	Fair	Poor
1150	1000	900	750	550	250

Super Varmint

As above with a walnut stock. Introduced in 1989.

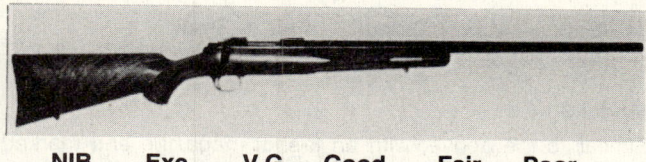

NIB	Exc.	V.G.	Good	Fair	Poor
1250	1100	1000	850	650	300

Predator

A .221 Fireball, .223 Rem., 6mm TCU, 7mm TCU, or the 6x45mm caliber single shot bolt action pistol based upon the Model 84 action with a 14.75" barrel adopted for a telescope. Blued with a walnut stock and available in two grades as follows. Manufactured in 1987 and 1988 only.

Hunter Grade

Exc.	V.G.	Good	Fair	Poor
800	650	575	400	300

Super Grade

Exc.	V.G.	Good	Fair	Poor
1000	850	675	500	400

Model 89 Series/BRG (Big Game Rifles)

A bolt action sporting rifle produced in .270 Winchester to .375 Holland & Holland caliber with a 22" or 24" barrel. Blued with a walnut stock. The variations of this model are as follows:

Classic Model

NIB	Exc.	V.G.	Good	Fair	Poor
800	650	550	400	300	200

Custom Classic Model

NIB	Exc.	V.G.	Good	Fair	Poor
1000	850	650	450	350	250

Deluxe Grade

NIB	Exc.	V.G.	Good	Fair	Poor
1400	1150	900	650	450	250

Super America

NIB	Exc.	V.G.	Good	Fair	Poor
1800	1250	900	700	500	250

Super Grade

NIB	Exc.	V.G.	Good	Fair	Poor
1800	1250	900	700	500	250

KING PIN
Unknown

Derringer

A .22 caliber spur trigger brass constructed single shot pistol with a 2.5" barrel and walnut grips. Believed to have been made during the 1880s.

Exc.	V.G.	Good	Fair	Poor
—	350	200	150	90

KIRRIKALE, ENDUSTRISI
Ankara, Turkey

Kirrikale Pistol

A 7.65 or 9mm short caliber semiautomatic pistol with a 3.5" barrel and 6-shot magazine. Blued with plastic grips. The slide marked "MKE"; and "Kirrikale Tufek Fb Cal.—-." Imported by Firearms Center in Victoria, Texas, and also by Mandall Shooting Supplies.

NIB	Exc.	V.G.	Good	Fair	Poor
400	350	275	225	150	100

KLIPZIG & COMPANY
San Francisco, California

Pocket Pistol

A .41 caliber single shot percussion pistol with a 2.5" barrel, German silver mounts and walnut stocks. Manufactured during the 1850s and early 1860s.

Exc.	V.G.	Good	Fair	Poor
—	—	1500	900	400

KNICKERBOCKER
Made by Crescent Fire Arms Co.

Knickerbocker Pistol NFA

The Knickerbocker is a 14" double-barreled 20 gauge smooth bore pistol manufactured by Crescent Fire Arms Co. of Norwich, Connecticut. On the basis of its hammerless design and the dates of production of similarly designed firearms by Crescent, the Knickerbocker was probably manufactured sometime during the early 1900s. The receiver is case-hardened, and the barrels are nickel-plated. The right side of the receiver is stamped **AMERICAN GUN CO./ NEW YORK U S A**; the left side is stamped **KNICKERBOCKER**. It probably was intended for law enforcement and/or defensive purposes, and manufactured using the same techniques used to produce the Ithaca Auto & Burglar Gun. The receiver is fitted with a checkered pistol grip resembling that of the Model 1 and Model 2 smooth bore H&R Handy-Gun. The only known specimen of the Knickerbocker bears serial number 200114. The Knickerbocker was classified as an "any other weapon" under the NFA in 1934 because it was originally designed as "a so-called shotgun with a pistol grip" and because it is concealable (see Treasury Department ruling S.T. 772, dated August 6, 1934). Its rarity precludes being able to reliably estimate its value at this time.

The Knickerbocker is a so-called "Hardware Gun" of the type produced under direct contract to distributors, mail order houses, hardware stores and other retail outlets. The Knickerbocker is apparently not listed in any Crescent or other trade catalog, and its total production is unknown at this time--but there seems little doubt it was originally manufactured in its present condition.

The design of the Knickerbocker confirms that it is an "any other weapon" rather than a short-barreled shotgun or a weapon made from a shotgun. Upon inspecting the barrels for choke using a simple plug-type gauge, both barrels were determined to be full choke, a physical impossibility had the barrels simply been cut down. The trigger guard is bent at approximately 80° and extends down the front of the grip--a design feature that is identical on the Model A 20 gauge Ithaca Auto & Burglar Gun. The pistol grip attachment is no different from that of a shoulder-fired sidelock shotgun; there is no through-bolt, but 2 screws that pass through the upper and lower tangs and the stock. Upon disassembly, no serial number is evident on the stock; the trigger guard is serialized 00114--the number 2 is missing--and the 4 is very indistinct. The complete serial number is also stamped on the left side of the barrel lug, left side of the water table, forend metal, and forend wood. The weight of the Knickerbocker is just under 5 lbs.

These materials are copyright © 1998 by Eric M. Larson, printed in the *Catalog* by permission of the copyright holder, and will appear in a forthcoming book on pre-NFA smooth bore shot pistols (see H&R Handy-Gun entry). This writer would welcome additional information concerning the Knickerbocker, and the opportunity to document additional specimens for historical research purposes.

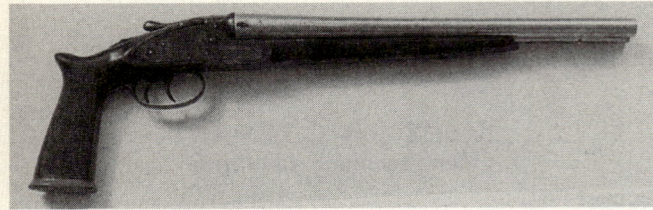

KOHOUT & SPOLECNOST
Kdyne, Czechoslovakia

Mars

A 6.35 or 7.65mm caliber semiautomatic pistol, the larger caliber having a grip safety. Blued with plastic grips impressed with the word "Mars". The slide marked "Mars 7.65 (or 6.35) Kohout & Spol. Kdyne." Manufactured between 1928 and 1945.

Exc.	V.G.	Good	Fair	Poor
300	250	200	150	100

Niva, PZK

Similar to the above in 6.35mm caliber.

Exc.	V.G.	Good	Fair	Poor
300	250	200	150	100

KOLB, HENRY M.
Philadelphia, Pennsylvania

The revolvers listed below were manufactured by Henry Kolb and Charles Foehl until 1912 when R.F. Sedgely replaced Foehl. Manufacture continued until approximately 1938.

Baby Hammerless

A .22 caliber folding trigger double action revolver with an enclosed hammer and 5-shot cylinder.

Exc.	V.G.	Good	Fair	Poor
275	225	200	150	100

New Baby Hammerless

Similar to the above, with a hinged barrel to facilitate loading.

Exc.	V.G.	Good	Fair	Poor
275	225	200	150	100

KOLIBRI
SEE Grabner

KOMMER, THEODOR WAFFENFABRIK
Zella Mehlis, Germany

Model 1

A 6.35mm semiautomatic pistol with an 8-shot magazine. Blued with plastic grips. Manufactured during the 1920s.

Exc.	V.G.	Good	Fair	Poor
275	250	200	150	100

Model 2

As above, with straight grips and a 7-shot magazine.

Exc.	V.G.	Good	Fair	Poor
275	250	200	150	100

Model 3

Similar to the above, with an 8-shot magazine and marked with the Roman numeral III after the manufacturer's name.

Exc.	V.G.	Good	Fair	Poor
250	225	175	125	90

Model 4

A 7.65mm caliber semiautomatic pistol with a 7-shot magazine and without a grip safety. The slide marked "Waffenfabrik Kommer Zella Mehlis Kal. 7.65". Manufactured between 1936 and 1940.

Exc.	V.G.	Good	Fair	Poor
275	250	200	150	100

KORRIPHILIA
West Germany
Importer-Osborne's
Sheboygan, Michigan

HSP Type I

A 7.65mm Luger, .38 Special, 9mm Police, 9mm Luger, 9mm Steyr, l 0mm ACP, and the .45 ACP caliber double action semiautomatic pistol with a 4" barrel made of stainless steel.

NIB	Exc.	V.G.	Good	Fair	Poor
2400	2000	1600	1000	850	500

HSP Type II

As above, with a 5" barrel.

NIB	Exc.	V.G.	Good	Fair	Poor
2600	2250	1750	1100	950	500

HSP Type III

As above, but single action.

NIB	Exc.	V.G.	Good	Fair	Poor
2800	2500	2000	1650	1250	500

KORTH
West Germany
Importer - Beeman Precision Arms
Santa Rosa, California

Semiautomatic Pistol

A 9mm caliber double action semiautomatic pistol with a 4.5" barrel, adjustable sights and 13-shot magazine. Matte or polished blue with walnut grips. Introduced in 1985.

NIB	Exc.	V.G.	Good	Fair	Poor
3000	2750	2000	1500	900	450

Revolver

A .22 l.r., .22 Magnum, .357 Magnum, and 9mm caliber revolver with a 3", 4", or 6" barrel and 6-shot cylinder. The barrels and cylinders are interchangeable, matte or polished blue with walnut grips.

NIB	Exc.	V.G.	Good	Fair	Poor
2450	2100	1750	1250	800	400

KRAG JORGENSEN
Springfield, Massachusetts

The first smallbore, bolt action repeating rifle that used smokeless powder that was adopted by the U.S. government as a service rifle. It was adopted as the Model 1892 and was similar to the rifle being used by Denmark as a service rifle. All of the Krag-Jorgensens were manufactured at the Springfield Armory. There are 11 basic variations of Krag Rifles, and all except one are chambered for the .30-40 Govt. cartridge. They are bolt actions that hold 5 rounds in the unique side-mounted hinged magazine. All of the Krags have walnut stocks and hand guards that are oil-finished. They all have dark gray casehardened receivers and blued barrels.

NOTE: One should be aware that there have been many alterations based on the Krag rifle by many gunsmiths through the years, and the one consistency is that all of these conversions lowered the value of the rifle and rendered it uncollectible. Proceed with caution.

Model 1892

Approximately 24,500 of these rifles produced, dated 1894, 1895, and 1896. They have 30" barrels and are serial numbered from 1-24562. Nearly all were converted to the latter Model 1896, and the original 1st Type is extremely scarce.

1st Type

Serial numbered from 1-1500 and is dated 1894 only. It features a wide upper barrel band and an iron one-piece cleaning rod mounted under the barrel. There is no compartment in the butt, and the muzzle is not crowned and appears flat. The up-per hand guard does not extend over the receiver, and the butt-plate is flat, without a compartment. One should be wary of fakes and secure expert appraisal if a transaction is contemplated. Unaltered specimens are extremely rare.

Exc.	V.G.	Good	Fair	Poor
4000	3750	3500	3000	2500

2nd Type

Similar to the 1st Type, with a front barrel band that is cut out in the center and does not appear solid. The serial range is 1500-24562, and the dates 1894 or 1895 are stamped on the receiver and the stock. Again be wary of fakes. This is a rare rifle.

Exc.	V.G.	Good	Fair	Poor
1800	1500	1000	750	600

Altered to 1896 Model

Encompassed nearly the entire production run of the Model 1892 Krag rifle. They still bear the dates 1894, 1895, and 1896 on the receiver; but they do not have the cleaning rod, and the hole in the stock has been plugged. The front barrel band was changed, and the butt has a compartment for a cleaning kit. The top hand guard covers the receiver, and the buttplate is curved at the bottom.

Exc.	V.G.	Good	Fair	Poor
300	250	200	150	100

Model 1896 Rifle

Similar to the altered Model 1892 and has a 30" barrel with the cleaning kit in the butt. The rear sight was improved, and the receiver is marked "U.S. Model 1896" and "Springfield Armory." The serial range runs from 35000-110000; and the stock is dated 1896, 1897, and 1898. There were many of these altered to the later stock configurations—in the field or at the Springfield Armory. These changes would lower the value, and one should secure expert appraisal on this model.

Exc.	V.G.	Good	Fair	Poor
450	400	350	275	175

Model 1896 Carbine

Similar to the 1896 Rifle, with a 22" barrel and half-length stock held on by one barrel band. There were approximately 19,000 manufactured between 1896 and 1898, and the serial number range is 35000-90000. There were many rifles cut to carbine dimensions—be wary of these alterations!

Exc.	V.G.	Good	Fair	Poor
650	600	500	400	250

Model 1895 Carbine (Variation)

Marked "1895" and "1896" on the receiver—without the word Model. They were produced before the Model 1896 was officially adopted, and they are serial numbered from 25000 to 35000. They are similar to the Model 1896 Carbine, with a smaller safety and no oiler bottle in the butt.

Exc.	V. G.	Good	Fair	Poor
900	700	600	500	400

Model 1896 Cadet Rifle

A rare variation produced for use by the Military Academy at West Point. The dimensions are the same as the 1896 Rifle with a one-piece cleaning rod under the barrel and the 1896-type front band. There were 400 manufactured, and most were altered to standard configuration when they were phased out in 1898.

Exc.	V.G.	Good	Fair	Poor
3000	2500	2200	1750	1250

Model 1898 Rifle

This model is similar to the Model 1896 in appearance except that the receiver is marked "U.S./Model 1898." The bolt handle was modified, and the sights and hand guards were improved. There were 330,000 manufactured between 1898 and 1903, and the serial number range is 110000-480000.

Exc.	V.G.	Good	Fair	Poor
450	400	350	250	150

Model 1898 Carbine

Similar to the rifle, with a 22" barrel and a bar and ring on the left side of the receiver. There were approximately 5,000 manufactured in 1898 and 1899. The serial range is 125000-135000. Again, be aware that many of the rifles have been converted to carbine dimensions over the years. When in doubt secure an independent appraisal.

Exc.	V.G.	Good	Fair	Poor
1500	1250	1000	700	500

Model 1898 Carbine 26" Barrel

An attempt to satisfy both the infantry and the cavalry. There were 100 manufactured for trial, and the serial range is between 387000-389000. Be wary of fakes.

Exc.	V.G.	Good	Fair	Poor
3000	2500	2200	1750	1250

Model 1898 Practice Rifle

The only Krag not chambered for the .30-40 cartridge. It is chambered for the .22 rimfire and was designed as a target-practice rifle. It has a 30" barrel and is identical in exterior appearance to the Model 1898 Rifle. The receiver is marked the same as the standard model—with "Cal .22" added. There were approximately 840 manufactured in 1906 and 1907.

Exc.	V.G.	Good	Fair	Poor
2000	1750	1500	1100	850

Model 1899 Carbine

The last of the Krags; and it is similar to the 1898, with the "Model 1899" stamped on the receiver and a 2" longer stock. There were approximately 36,000 manufactured between 1899 and 1902.

Courtesy Milwaukee Public Museum, Milwaukee, Wisconsin

Exc.	V.G.	Good	Fair	Poor
650	550	500	400	275

Model 1899 Philippine Constabulary Carbine

Approximately 8,000 altered to accept the knife bayonet at the Springfield Armory and the Rock Island Arsenal. The Springfield pieces are marked "J.F.C." on the stock. This model has a 22" barrel, with the full stock of the rifle held on with two barrel bands. One must exercise extreme care as many rifles were altered in a similar manner at later dates.

Exc.	V.G.	Good	Fair	Poor
1000	850	750	600	475

Benicia Arsenal Conversion

In the 1920s the Department of Civilian Marksmanship had a number of Krag rifles converted for their use. These are Model 1898 rifles shortened and fitted with Model 1899 Carbine stocks. These conversions are beginning to be regarded as legitimate variations by some collectors of Krag rifles.

Exc.	V.G.	Good	Fair	Poor
350	300	250	175	100

KRAUSER, ALFRED
Zella Mehlis, Germany

Helfricht or Helkra

A 6.35mm semiautomatic pistol with a 2" barrel. Produced in four models, the 4th having an enclosed barrel. Blued with composition grips. Manufactured from 1921 to 1929.

Exc.	V.G.	Good	Fair	Poor
450	400	350	250	150

KRICO
Stuttgart, West Germany
Importer-Mandall Shooting Supplies

Sporting Rifle

A .22 Hornet or .222 caliber bolt action rifle with 22", 24", or 26" barrels, single or double set trigger, adjustable sights and a 4-shot magazine. Blued with a walnut stock. Manufactured between 1956 and 1962.

Exc.	V.G.	Good	Fair	Poor
600	550	475	375	275

Sporting Carbine

As above, with a 20" barrel and full length stock.

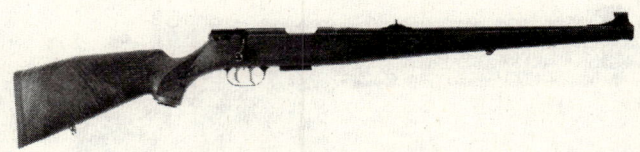

Exc.	V.G.	Good	Fair	Poor
625	575	500	400	300

Varmint Special Rifle

The Sporting Rifle with a heavier barrel.

Exc.	V.G.	Good	Fair	Poor
600	550	475	375	275

Model 300

A .22 caliber bolt action rifle with a 23.5" barrel, 5-shot magazine and grooved receiver. Blued with a walnut stock. Imported prior to 1989.

Exc.	V.G.	Good	Fair	Poor
675	600	550	400	300

Model 302 and 304

Variations of the above. Discontinued in 1986.

Exc.	V.G.	Good	Fair	Poor
675	600	550	400	300

Model 311 Smallbore

A .22 caliber bolt action rifle with a 22" barrel, double set triggers, adjustable sights and a 5- or 10-shot magazine. Blued with walnut stock. Not imported after 1988.

Exc.	V.G.	Good	Fair	Poor
325	275	225	150	100

Model 320

As above, with a 19.5" barrel and full length stock. Discontinued in 1988.

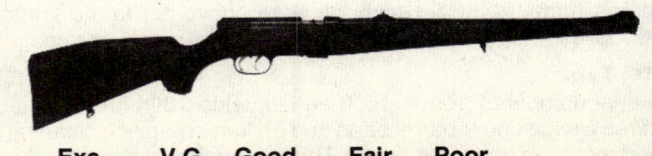

Exc.	V.G	Good	Fair	Poor
675	600	550	400	300

Model 340

A .22 caliber bolt action rifle with a 21" heavy barrel furnished without sights, adjustable trigger and 5-shot magazine. Blued with a walnut stock. Not imported after 1988.

Exc.	V.G.	Good	Fair	Poor
700	625	575	425	325

Model 340 Mini-Sniper

As above, but matte finished, the barrel fitted with a muzzle brake and the stock with a raised cheekpiece as well as ventilated hand guard.

Exc.	V.G.	Good	Fair	Poor
1000	850	750	500	400

Model 340 Kricotronic

The Model 340 fitted with an electronic trigger. Not imported after 1988.

Exc.	V.G.	Good	Fair	Poor
1250	1000	850	600	500

Model 360S Biathlon Rifle

Introduced in 1991 this model features a 22 Long rifle straight pull bolt action with 5-round magazine and fitted with a 21.25" barrel. Walnut stock with high comb and adjustable butt plate. Fully adjustable match peep sight. Fitted with 17 oz. match trigger. Weight is approximately 9.25 lbs.

NIB	Exc.	V.G.	Good	Fair	Poor
1600	1350	850	—	—	—

Model 360S2 Biathlon Rifle

Same as above but fitted with a black epoxy finished walnut stock with pistol grip. Weight is 9 lbs.

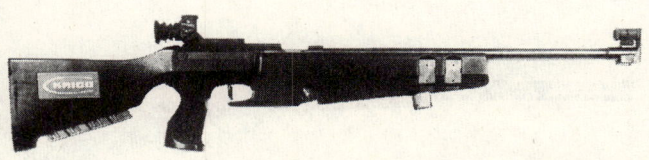

NIB	Exc.	V.G.	Good	Fair	Poor
1500	1250	800	—	—	—

Model 400 Match

Chambered for the 22 Long Rifle or the .22 Hornet this bolt action rifle is fitted with a heavy match 23" barrel and a 5-round magazine. The match style stock is of European walnut. Fitted with a double set of match trigger. Weight is about 8.8 lbs.

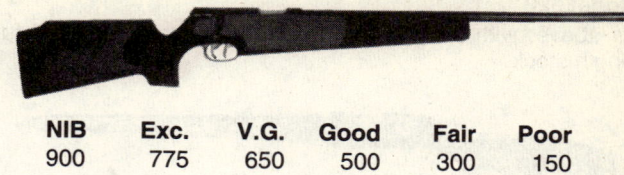

NIB	Exc.	V.G.	Good	Fair	Poor
900	775	650	500	300	150

Model 400 Sporter

A .22 Hornet caliber bolt action rifle with a 23.5" barrel, open sights and 5-shot magazine. Blued with a walnut stock. Not imported after 1988.

Exc.	V.G.	Good	Fair	Poor
700	625	550	425	325

Model 420

As above, with a 19.5" barrel, double set triggers, and a full length stock. Discontinued in 1988.

Exc.	V.G.	Good	Fair	Poor
875	750	675	500	400

Model 440

Similar to the Model 340. Not imported after 1988.

Exc.	V.G	Good	Fair	Poor
900	800	700	500	375

Model 500 Kricotronic Match Rifle

Chambered for the .22 Long Rifle this bolt action rifle is fitted with a 23.6" barrel with tappered bore. Walnut stock with match type adjustable butt plate. Electronic ignition system gives fastest lock time. Weight is approximately 9.4 lbs.

NIB	Exc.	V.G.	Good	Fair	Poor
3900	3000	—	—	—	—

Model 600 Sporter

A .17 Remington to .308 Winchester caliber bolt action rifle with a 23.5" barrel, open sights and 3-shot magazine. Blued with a walnut stock. Not imported after 1988.

Exc.	V.G.	Good	Fair	Poor
1100	950	875	700	575

Model 600 Sniper Rifle

This bolt action rifle is chambered for the .222, .223, .22-250, .243, and 308. It is fitted with a 25.6" heavy barrel with flack hider. The stock is walnut with adjustable rubber butt plate. Magazine holds 4 rounds. Weight is about 9.2 lbs.

NIB	Exc.	V.G.	Good	Fair	Poor
2600	2000	1500	—	—	—

Model 600 Match Rifle

Chambered for the same calibers as the 600 Sniper with the addition of the 5.6x50 Mag. Fitted with a 23.6" barrel. The match stock is vented in forearm for cooling. Wood is walnut with cheekpiece. Weight is approximately 8.8 lbs.

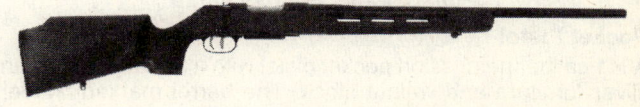

NIB	Exc.	V.G.	Good	Fair	Poor
1200	900	—	—	—	—

Model 620

As above, with a 20.5" barrel, double set triggers, and full length stock.

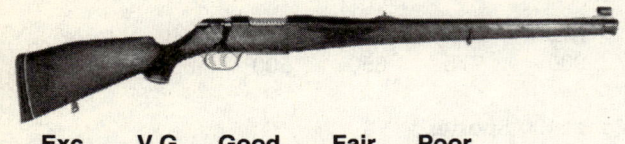

Exc.	V.G.	Good	Fair	Poor
1150	1000	900	750	600

Model 640 Varmint Rifle

Similar to the above, in .22-250, .222 or .223 caliber with a 23.5" heavy barrel. Not imported after 1988.

Exc.	V.G.	Good	Fair	Poor
1175	1025	925	775	625

Model 640 Sniper Rifle

As above, but matte finished. Discontinued in 1988.

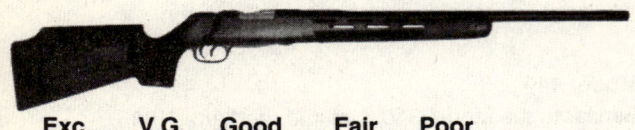

Exc.	V.G.	Good	Fair	Poor
1300	1100	950	750	600

Model 640 Deluxe Sniper Rifle

As above, in .223 or .308 caliber with a 23" barrel, stippled stock, and adjustable trigger. Not imported after 1988.

Exc.	V.G.	Good	Fair	Poor
1500	1250	1000	750	650

Model 700 Sporter

A .270 or .30-06 caliber bolt action rifle with a 23.5" barrel, open sights, single set trigger, and 3-shot magazine. Blued with a walnut stock. Discontinued in 1988.

Exc.	V.G.	Good	Fair	Poor
1000	850	750	600	500

Model 720

As above, with a 20.5" barrel, double set triggers, and full length stock. Discontinued in 1988.

Exc.	V.G.	Good	Fair	Poor
1000	850	750	600	500

Model 720 Limited Edition

As above, in .270 caliber only with gold-plated furniture and gold highlighted engraving. Not imported after 1988.

Exc.	V.G.	Good	Fair	Poor
2250	2000	1750	1400	900

KRIDER, J. H.
Philadelphia, Pennsylvania

Pocket Pistol

A .41 caliber percussion pocket pistol with a 3" barrel, German silver furniture and walnut stock. The barrel marked "Krider Phila." Manufactured during the 1850s and 1860s.

Exc.	V.G.	Good	Fair	Poor
—	—	750	400	300

Militia Rifle

A .58 caliber percussion rifle with a 39" barrel and full length stock secured by two barrel bands. The barrel browned, the lock marked "Krider". Casehardened and furniture of brass. Several hundred were manufactured in 1861.

Courtesy Milwaukee Public Museum, Milwaukee, Wisconsin

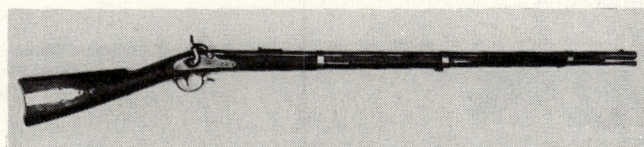

Courtesy Milwaukee Public Museum, Milwaukee, Wisconsin

Exc.	V.G.	Good	Fair	Poor
—	—	3500	1500	750

KRIEGHOFF, HEINRICH, GUN CO.
Ulm, Germany
Importer-Krieghoff International
Ottisville, Pennsylvania

NOTE: Krieghoff manufactured Lugers are listed in the Luger section.

DRILLINGS AND COMBINATION GUNS

Plus Model

A 3 barrel combination rifle/shotgun produced in a variety of gauges and calibers with 25" barrels, double triggers, and automatic ejectors. Blued with a walnut stock. Introduced in 1988.

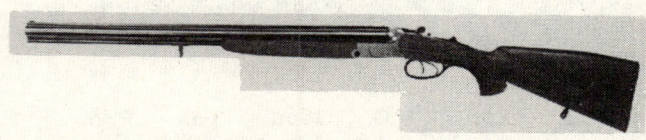

NIB	Exc.	V.G.	Good	Fair	Poor
3800	3500	2500	2000	1850	1250

Trumpf Model

A combination rifle/shotgun produced in a variety of calibers and gauges with 25" barrels and double triggers. Blued with a walnut stock.

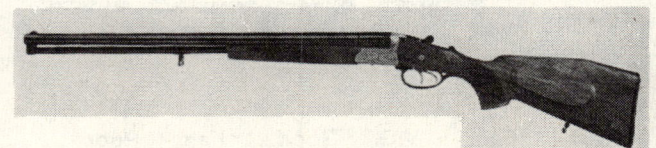

Exc.	V.G.	Good	Fair	Poor
7000	6000	4750	3200	2400

Trumpf Dural

As above, with a Duraluminum frame.

Exc.	V.G.	Good	Fair	Poor
7000	6000	4750	3200	2400

Neptun Model

A combination Over/Under rifle/shotgun with sidelocks produced in a variety of gauges and calibers. Engraved, blued with a walnut stock.

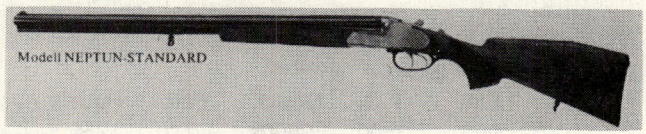

Modell NEPTUN-STANDARD

Exc.	V.G.	Good	Fair	Poor
11750	10000	7750	5000	4000

Neptun Dural

As above, with a Duraluminum frame.

Exc.	V.G.	Good	Fair	Poor
11750	10000	7750	5000	4000

Neptun Primus Model

The Neptun with relief engraving and detachable sidelocks.

Exc.	V.G.	Good	Fair	Poor
15000	12500	9500	7000	5250

Neptun Primus Dural

As above, with a Duraluminum frame.

Exc.	V.G.	Good	Fair	Poor
15000	12500	9500	7000	5250

DOUBLE RIFLES

Teck Over/Under

A boxlock Over/Under rifle manufactured in a variety of calibers with 25" barrels, double triggers, extractors, and express sights. Blued with a walnut stock.

Exc.	V.G.	Good	Fair	Poor
7500	6500	5000	3750	3000

Ulm Model

As above, with sidelocks.

Exc.	V.G.	Good	Fair	Poor
12500	10000	8000	6750	5000

Ulm Primus

As above, with detachable sidelocks.

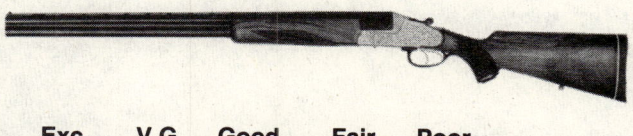

Exc.	V.G.	Good	Fair	Poor
15000	12500	10000	7500	6000

SHOTGUNS

Model 32 Standard

A 12, 20, 28 or .410 bore boxlock Over/Under shotgun with 26.5" to 32" barrels, single selective trigger and automatic ejectors. Blued with a walnut stock. Discontinued in 1980.

28 Gauge or .410 Two-Barrel Set-Add 50%.
4 barrel Skeet Set-Add 100%

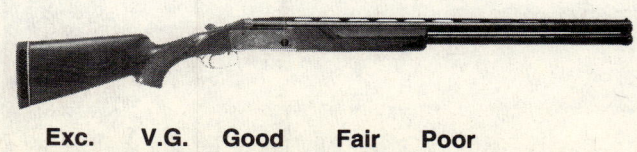

Exc.	V.G.	Good	Fair	Poor
2000	1750	1500	1000	750

Model 32 San Remo Grade

Exc.	V.G.	Good	Fair	Poor
3250	2500	1750	1250	1000

Model 32 Monte Carlo Grade

Exc.	V.G.	Good	Fair	Poor
4750	3500	2500	1500	1250

Model 32 Crown Grade

Exc.	V.G.	Good	Fair	Poor
7000	5000	3000	2000	1500

Model 32 Super Crown Grade

NIB	Exc.	V.G.	Good	Fair	Poor
10000	7000	5000	3500	2500	2000

Model 32 Single-Barrel Trap Gun

The Model 32 with a single 32" to 34" barrel.

Exc.	V.G.	Good	Fair	Poor
1750	1400	1100	750	600

KS-5 Single-Barrel Trap

This model is a boxlock 12 gauge only trap gun with 32" or 34" ventilated tapered rib barrel and casehardened frame with a satin gray finish. The barrel features an adjustable point of impact and is offered with screw-in choke tubes. Weight is approximately 8.6 lbs.

NIB	Exc.	V.G.	Good	Fair	Poor
2850	2250	1750	1500	1250	800

KS-5 Special

Same as above but furnished with adjustable rib and adjustable comb.

NIB	Exc.	V.G.	Good	Fair	Poor
3500	3000	2500	2000	1500	1000

KS-80 Trap

This is a boxlock 12 gauge shotgun built to trap dimensions. This model is offered in many variations. Available is Over/Under trap with choice of 30" or 32" vent tapered step rib barrels. Also a single barrel is offered in 32" or 34" tapered step rib lengths. These single barrels are adjustable for point of impact. A top single barrel is available as well in 34" length. Trap combos are offered also. All barrels are offered with or without choke tubes. The checkered walnut stock is offered in Monte Carlo or straight trap dimensions. Trap guns weigh approximately 8.75 lbs. Prices below are for Standard Grade.

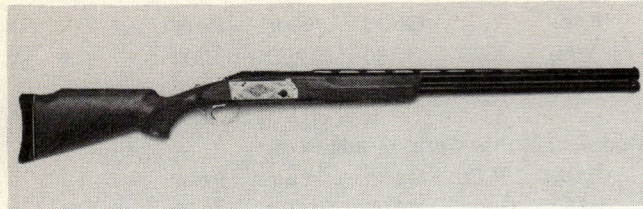

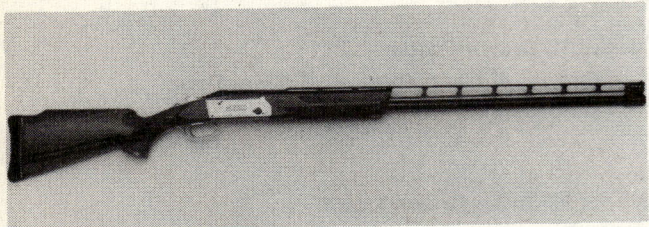

Over/Under Trap

NIB	Exc.	V.G.	Good	Fair	Poor
5400	4900	4000	3500	2000	1000

Unsingle Trap

NIB	Exc.	V.G.	Good	Fair	Poor
5800	5300	4500	4000	2250	1250

Top Single Trap

NIB	Exc.	V.G.	Good	Fair	Poor
7500	6500	5000	4000	3000	1500

Trap Combos

NIB	Exc.	V.G.	Good	Fair	Poor
8200	7000	6000	4000	3000	1500

Bavaria Grade-Add 70%.
Danube Grade-Add 100%.
Gold Target Grade-Add 200%.

K-80 Sporting Clays

The frame is the same as the trap model with the addition of a lightweight alloy model and is available in 12 gauge only. Barrel lengths for standard weight model are 28", 30", or 32" with tapered flat rib. The lightweight model is offered with 28" or 30" flat rib barrels. Select European walnut stock with hand checkering and supplied with a #3 Sporting stock with Schnabel forearm. The standard weight model weighs about 8.25 lbs. while the lightweight model weighs 7.75 lbs. Prices below are for the Standard Grade.

NIB	Exc.	V.G.	Good	Fair	Poor
5800	5250	4500	3000	2000	1000

Bavaria Grade-Add 70%.
Danube Grade-Add 100%.
Gold Target Grade-Add 200%.

K-80 Skeet

This model is offered in a number of variations. The standard weight skeet with 28" or 30" tapered or parallel ribs, lightweight skeet with 28" or 30" tapered or parallel ribs, International skeet with 28" parallel broadway rib, and the 4-barrel skeet set in 12, 20, and 28 gauge as well as .410 bore with 8mm rib. Stock is hand checkered select European walnut with a choice of several skeet dimensions. Prices below are for Standard Grade.

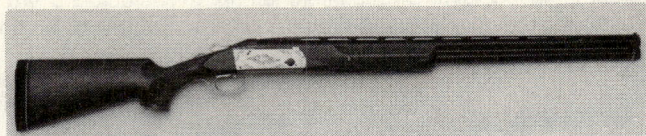

Standard Weight Skeet

NIB	Exc.	V.G.	Good	Fair	Poor
5000	4500	3500	2500	1750	1250

Lightweight Skeet

NIB	Exc.	V.G.	Good	Fair	Poor
5000	4500	3500	2500	1750	1250

International Skeet

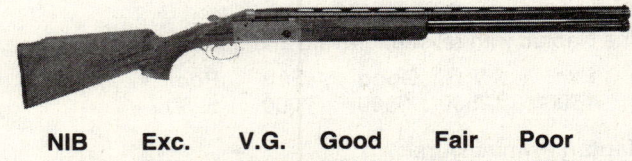

NIB	Exc.	V.G.	Good	Fair	Poor
5500	5000	3750	2750	1950	1300

4-Barrel Set

NIB	Exc.	V.G.	Good	Fair	Poor
11250	8000	6000	4000	3000	2000

Bavaria Grade-Add 70%.
Danube Grade-Add 100%.
Gold Target Grade-Add 200%.

Optional Engravings available by special order on NIB or Exc. conditions guns add:

Parcours-Add $1500.
Parcours Special-Add $2800.
Super Scroll-Add $1 100.
Gold Super Scroll-Add $2900.

Custom Bavaria $4700 over Bavaria Grade price.

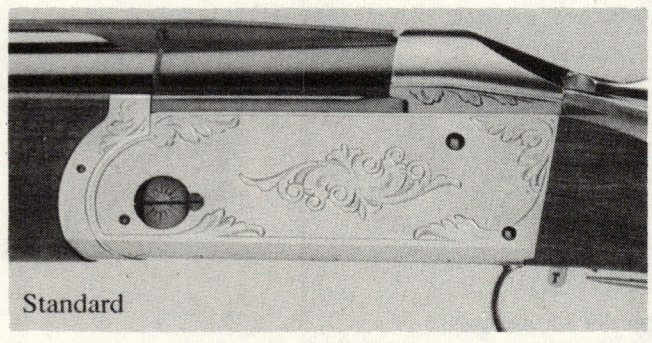

Standard

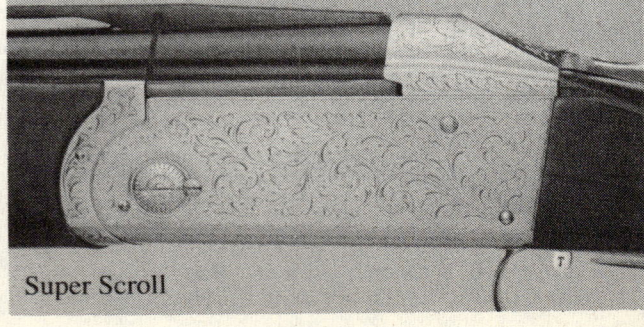

Super Scroll

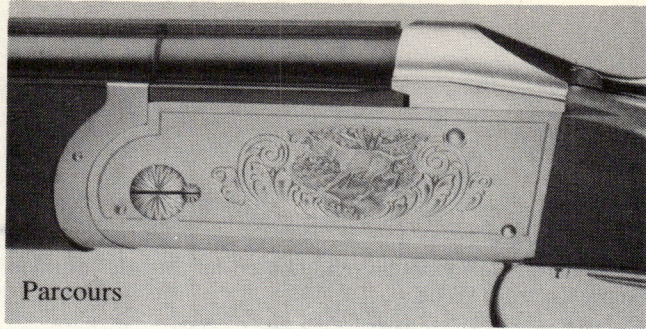

Parcours

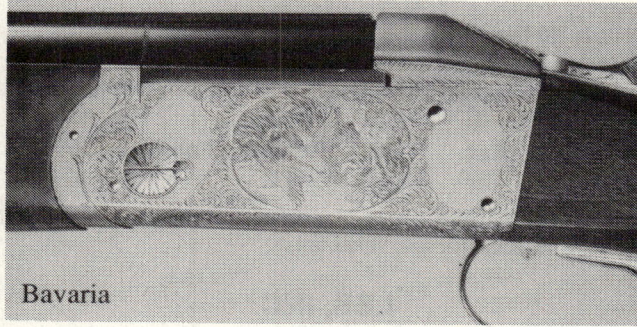

Bavaria

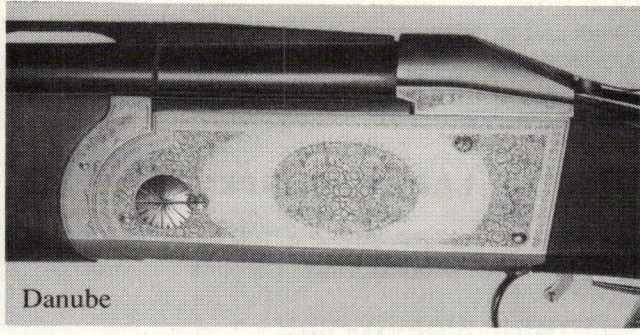

Danube

Gold Target

KRNKA, KAREL
Vienna, Austria

Karel Krnka was a talented firearms inventor born in 1858. He began his career in firearms design as a member of the Austro-Hungarian army. He made many improvements to their service rifle design. After he left the military, he took the job of head engineer with the ill-fated and short-lived "Gatling Gun Company." This company ceased operations in 1890, and then Krnka went to work for the patent office and remained there for a few years. In 1898 he became foreman of the Roth Cartridge Company and worked with Roth on firearms designs until the death of Roth in 1909. After this he became associated with the Hertenberger Cartridge Company; and finally in 1922 he moved to Czechoslovakia, where he became a firearms designer for the firm of C.Z. He remained at this post until

his death in 1926. He recorded his first firearm patent in 1888 for a mechanical repeater with a ring trigger. His best known innovations are the internal butt magazine that is loaded by means of a stripper clip and the rotating locked bolt with internal firing pin. These designs were never actually turned into a mass-marketed pistol but were major contributions in the development of a practical semiautomatic pistol design.

Model 1892

Exc.	V.G.	Good	Fair	Poor
7000	6000	5000	3000	1500

KROPATSCHEK
Steyr-Werke
Steyr, Austria

Model 1878
An 11mm caliber bolt action rifle with a 32" barrel, full length stock secured by three barrel bands, and 7-shot magazine. Finished in the white with a walnut stock.

Exc.	V.G.	Good	Fair	Poor
275	225	200	125	75

KUFAHL, G. L.
Sommerda, Germany

Kufahl Needle-Fire Revolver
Designed and patented in Britain in 1852 by G.L. Kufahl, who tried unsuccessfully to interest a British company in producing it. He then went to the firm of Rheinmettal Dreyse, where a needle-fire gun was produced in 1838. This company manufactured his design. This revolver was chambered for a unique, totally consumed .30 caliber "cartridge." A lead projectile had the ignition percussion cap affixed to its base, with the propellant powder in the rear. The firing pin had to be long enough to penetrate the powder charge and hit the percussion cap. This does not sound efficient, but realize that these were the days before cartridges. This revolver has a 3.2" barrel and an unfluted cylinder that holds six shots. It is not bored all the way through but is loaded from the front. The finish is blued, with a modicum of simple engraving and checkered wood grips that protrude all the way over the trigger. The markings are "Fv.V. Dreyse Sommerda."

Exc.	V.G.	Good	Fair	Poor
1750	1250	950	600	450

KYNOCH GUN FACTORY
Birmingham, England

Established by George Kynoch in approximately 1886, this company ceased operation in 1890.

Early Double Trigger Revolver
A .45 caliber double trigger revolver with a 6" barrel, 6-shot cylinder and enclosed hammer. Blued with walnut grips. Manufactured in 1885.

Exc.	V.G.	Good	Fair	Poor
900	750	600	450	350

Late Double Trigger Revolver
Similar to the above, but in .32, .38, or .45 caliber with the cocking trigger enclosed within the triggerguard. Approximately 600 of these revolvers were made between 1896 and 1890.

Exc.	V.G.	Good	Fair	Poor
1100	850	700	550	450

L

LAR MFG. CO.
West Jordan, Utah

Grizzly Mark I

A .357 Magnum, .45 ACP, 10mm, or .45 Winchester Magnum semiautomatic pistol with a 5.4", 6.5", 8", or 10" barrel, Millett sights, ambidextrous safety and 7-shot magazine. Parkerized, blued, or hard-chrome plated with rubber grips. Available with cartridge conversion units, telescope mounts, or a compensator. Weight is approximately 48 oz. Introduced in 1984.

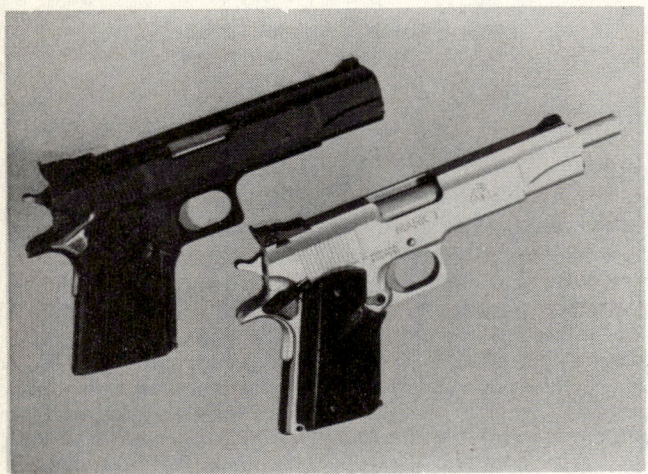

NIB	Exc.	V.G.	Good	Fair	Poor
900	775	650	500	400	200

Grizzly Mark II

As above, with fixed sights and without the ambidextrous safety. Manufactured in 1986.

Exc.	V.G.	Good	Fair	Poor
650	600	500	375	300

Grizzly Mark IV

Similar to the Mark I but chambered for the .44 Magnum cartridge. Barrel length is 5.4" or 6.5". Choice of blue or Parkerized finish.

NIB	Exc.	V.G.	Good	Fair	Poor
900	775	650	500	400	200

Grizzly Mark V

Same as above model but chambered for .50 AE cartridge. Empty weight is 56 oz.

NIB	Exc.	V.G.	Good	Fair	Poor
1100	875	700	550	425	200

Grizzly 50 Big Boar

A single shot breech loading rifle chambered for the .50 caliber BMG cartridge. The barrel is 36" in length and the rifle weighs approximately 30 lbs.

NIB	Exc.	V.G.	Good	Fair	Poor
2500	2150	1500	800	600	300

NOTE: Add $100 for parkerized finish. Add $250 for nickel frame, and $350 for full nickel finish.

LES, INC.
Skokie, Illinois

Rogak P-18

A 9mm caliber double action semiautomatic pistol with a 5.5" barrel and 18-shot magazine. Stainless steel. Discontinued.

Exc.	V.G.	Good	Fair	Poor
350	300	275	200	150

LABEAU-CORALLY
Liege, Belgium
Importer-Midwest Gun Sport
Zebulon, North Carolina

SHOTGUNS SIDE-BY-SIDE

Sologne Model

A 12, 16, or 20 gauge boxlock shotgun with 26" to 30" barrels, single trigger and automatic ejectors. Also available with false sideplates. Blued with a walnut stock.

Exc.	V.G.	Good	Fair	Poor
7500	6750	5000	4200	3750

Grand Russe Model

As above, but engraved and with a more finely figured stock.

Exc.	V.G.	Good	Fair	Poor
8500	7500	6500	4500	4000

Sidelock Ejector Grade

A 12, 16, 20, 28 gauge or .410 bore sidelock double-barrel shotgun with 26" to 30" barrels, double triggers, and automatic ejectors. Engraved, blued with a walnut stock.

28 Gauge and .410-Add 10%.

Exc.	V.G.	Good	Fair	Poor
20000	17500	12500	7500	6500

OVER/UNDERS

Sidelock Over/Under

A 12 or 20 gauge sidelock Over/Under shotgun manufactured solely to a specific customer's requirements.

Exc.	V.G.	Good	Fair	Poor
20000	17500	12500	7500	6500

Boss Model

As above, but finely engraved and with best quality walnut stock.

Exc.	V.G.	Good	Fair	Poor
30000	25000	20000	15000	11500

DOUBLE RIFLES

Boxlock Ejector Grade

A 8x57JRS, 9.3x74R, .375 H&H, and the .458 Win. Mag. caliber boxlock double-barrel rifle with a 25" barrel, double triggers, automatic ejectors and express sights. Engraved, blued with a walnut stock. Imported prior to 1989.

Exc.	V.G.	Good	Fair	Poor
9000	8000	6000	4500	3500

Sidelock Ejector Grade

As above, but with sidelocks and first quality engraving as well as a finely figured walnut stock.

Exc.	V.G.	Good	Fair	Poor
22500	18500	15000	10000	7500

LAGRESE
Paris, France

Lagrese Revolver

A large ornate revolver chambered for the .43 rimfire cartridge. It has a 6.25" barrel and a 6-shot fluted cylinder. This revolver has no top strap; and the frame, as well as the grip straps, are cast in one piece with the barrel screwed into the frame. It is loaded through a gate and has double action lockwork. The outstanding feature about this well-made revolver is its extremely ornate appearance. There are more sweeps and curves than could be imagined. It is engraved and blued, with well-figured curved walnut grips. It is marked "Lagrese Bte a Paris" and was manufactured in the late 1860s.

Exc.	V.G.	Good	Fair	Poor
—	—	2500	1150	800

LAHTI
Finland
SEE Husqvarna

Lahti

Designed by Aimo Lahti and produced by Valtion, the Finnish State Arms Factory. It was also made by Husqvarna in Sweden, and this model is found in the Husqvarna section of this book. This pistol is a locked-breech semiautomatic that features a bolt accelerator that does much to make this a reliable firearm. It is chambered for the 9mm Parabellum cartridge and has a 4.7" barrel. The detachable magazine holds 8 rounds; and the finish is blued, with checkered plastic grips. This pistol was designed to function in extreme cold and has a reputation for reliability. The Swedish version known as the M40 is a fine

pistol but is not considered on a par with the Finnish version. It was introduced in 1935.

Exc.	V.G.	Good	Fair	Poor
1250	1000	800	550	300

LAMB, H. C. & CO.
Jamestown, North Carolina

Muzzle Loading Rifle

Chambered for .58 caliber and utilizes the percussion ignition system. It has a 33" barrel and a full-length oak stock held on by two barrel bands. There is a ramrod mounted under the barrel that is made of iron. All other trim is brass, and there is a bayonet lug at the muzzle. This rifle was made for the Confederacy; and the workmanship was crude, as it was on most CSA weapons. The stock is marked "H.C.Lamb & Co., N.C." There were supposedly 10,000 rifles ordered, but actually there were approximately 250 manufactured between 1861 and 1863. The rarity of the guns of the Confederacy gives them a great deal of collector appeal. One should always be aware that there have been fraudulent examples noted, and a qualified independent appraisal is definitely advisable when dealing with weapons of this nature.

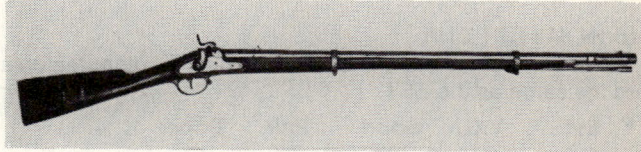

Courtesy Milwaukee Public Museum, Milwaukee, Wisconsin

Exc.	V.G.	Good	Fair	Poor
—	—	15000	7500	2000

LAMES
Chiavari, Italy

Skeet or Trap Grade

An Over/Under shotgun chambered for 12 gauge with either 26" skeet-and-skeet barrels or 30" or 32" full-choked barrels. It has a competition-style wide vent rib and automatic ejectors. The trigger is single selective, and the finish is blued. The trap gun has a Monte Carlo stock of checkered walnut. Both models feature recoil pads.

Exc.	V.G.	Good	Fair	Poor
600	525	450	350	200

California Trap Grade

This Over/Under is similar to the standard trap model, with separated barrels. All other features are the same.

Exc.	V.G.	Good	Fair	Poor
700	600	550	450	225

Field Grade

Similar in design to the standard trap model, with 3" chambers and barrel lengths of 26", 28", or 30" and a field dimensioned stock. It features various choke combinations and was also available with the separated barrels of the California Trap for an additional 20 percent in cost.

Exc.	V.G.	Good	Fair	Poor
400	350	300	225	150

LANBER ARMAS S.A.
Vizcaya, Spain
Lanber Arms of America
Adrian, Michigan

Model 844 ST

A 12-gauge Over/Under shotgun with 26" or 28" vent rib barrels. The chokes vary, and the gun features a single-selective trigger, extractors, and an engraved receiver with a blued finish and a walnut stock. This gun was manufactured until 1986, when the entire line was no longer imported.

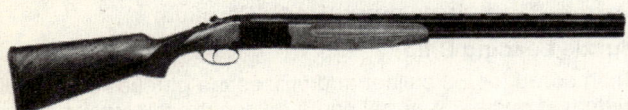

Exc.	V.G.	Good	Fair	Poor
400	350	300	250	175

Model 844 MST

Similar to the Model 844 ST except that it is chambered for 3" Magnum and has 30" full-and-modified barrels.

Exc.	V.G.	Good	Fair	Poor
400	350	300	250	175

Model 844 EST

Similar to the others, but it features automatic ejectors.

Exc.	V.G.	Good	Fair	Poor
450	400	350	300	200

Model 844 EST CHR

Has automatic ejectors and double triggers. All other features are the same as the EST.

Exc.	V.G.	Good	Fair	Poor
425	375	325	275	175

Model 2004 LCH

An Over/Under chambered for 12 gauge and features 28" vent rib barrels with screw-in choke tubes. It has a single selective trigger, automatic ejectors, and an engraved boxlock action that is matte finished, with a hand-checkered walnut stock. This model was also discontinued in 1986.

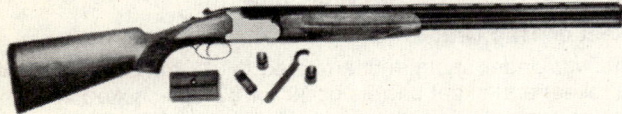

Exc.	V.G.	Good	Fair	Poor
750	650	550	475	375

Model 2008 LCH and Model 2009 LCH

The trap and skeet versions of the series. The basic differences are in the barrel lengths and the stock dimensions.

Model 2008 LCH

Model 2009 LCH

Exc.	V.G.	Good	Fair	Poor
850	750	650	575	475

LANCASTER, CHARLES
London, England

4 Barreled Pistol

A unique pistol for several reasons. It is chambered for the .476 rimfire cartridge and has four 6.25" barrels. The bore has a slightly twisted oval pattern that imparts a spin to the bullet. The barrels are hinged at the bottom and break downward for loading. It is a double action type lockwork with a long, difficult trigger pull. The pistol is well made; and the caliber, suitably heavy to insure stopping power. The primary goal was military; and it was successful, seeing action in the Sudan campaigns of 1882 and 1885. This powerful weapon was also popular with big game hunters as a backup sidearm. The finish is blued, with checkered walnut grips. It is marked "Charles Lancaster (Patent) 151 New Bond St. London." This model was introduced in 1881. There are smaller-caliber versions of this pistol with shorter barrels. They are not as well known as the large-caliber version, and the values would be similar as their rarity would be balanced by the desirability of the large bore models.

Exc.	V.G.	Good	Fair	Poor
—	—	2500	1000	750

2 Barreled Pistol

Similar to the 4-barreled version, with only two superposed barrels chambered for the .476 rimfire cartridge. The advantage to the 2-barreled pistol is that it is lighter and better balanced.

Exc.	V.G.	Good	Fair	Poor
—	—	2000	900	600

4 Barreled Shotgun

This company also produced a shotgun in the 4-barrel configuration. It is chambered for 12 or 16 gauge and has 28" barrels. The gun is, as one would imagine, quite heavy and poorly balanced; and it was not a great success.

Exc.	V.G.	Good	Fair	Poor
—	2000	1300	900	600

Bolt Action Rifle

A high-grade sporting rifle chambered for various different calibers. The barrel is 24" in length; and the finish is blued with a classic-styled, hand-checkered walnut stock. This rifle was discontinued in 1936.

Exc.	V.G.	Good	Fair	Poor
1750	1000	800	550	400

LANG, J.
London, England

Percussion Pistol

Chambered for .60 caliber percussion. It is a single-barreled, muzzle-loading pistol with a 3.25" barrel. This is essentially a defensive weapon that was well made, with Damascus barrels and an ornate engraved hammer and frame. The grips are finely checkered walnut, and there is a hinged ramrod under the barrel. There is a spring steel belt hook mounted to the left side of the frame. This pistol was manufactured circa 1836 and was marked "J. Lang."

Exc.	V.G.	Good	Fair	Poor
—	—	4000	2500	1000

Gas Seal Revolver

Chambered for the .42 caliber percussion and has a 4.75" barrel. The unfluted cylinder holds 6 shots and is spring-loaded to be forced into the barrel when cocked, in order to obtain the "Gas Seal" feature desired. This revolver was well made and finished. It is lightly engraved, with a case-colored cylinder and a blued barrel and frame. The grips are finely checkered walnut, and the markings are "J.Lang 22 Cockspur St. London." This type of firearm was the forerunner of later designs such as the Russian Nagant. This revolver was manufactured in the 1850s.

Exc.	V.G.	Good	Fair	Poor
—	2500	1250	900	550

LANGENHAN, FRIEDRICH
Zella Mehlis, Germany

Langenhan Army Model

A blowback-operated semiautomatic pistol chambered for the 7.65mm Auto Pistol cartridge. It has a 4" barrel and a detachable magazine that holds 8 rounds. The pistol was made with a separate breechblock that is held into the slide by a screw. This feature doomed this pistol to eventual failure as when this screw became worn, it could loosen when firing and allow the breechblock to pivot upwards—and the slide would then be propelled rearward and into the face of the shooter. This is not a comforting thought. This pistol was produced and used in WWI only and was never offered commercially. It is marked "F.L. Selbstlade DRGM." The finish is blued, and the grips are molded rubber, with "F.L." at the top.

Exc.	V.G.	Good	Fair	Poor
300	225	200	150	100

Model 2

A blowback-operated semiautomatic pistol chambered for the 6.35mm cartridge. It has a 3" barrel and an 8-round detachable magazine. The pistol fires by means of a concealed hammer, and the breechblock is separate from the rest of the slide and is held in place by a heavy crossbolt. The finish is blued, and the grips are molded checkered black plastic with the monogram "F.L." at the top. The slide is marked "Langenhan 6.35." This model was manufactured between 1921 and 1936.

Exc.	V.G.	Good	Fair	Poor
350	250	225	175	125

Model 3

Similar to the Model 2 except that it is somewhat smaller. The barrel is 2.25" in length, and the butt is only large enough to house a 5-round detachable magazine. The markings are the same with the addition of "Model 111" on the slide. This model was also manufactured until 1936.

Exc.	V.G.	Good	Fair	Poor
350	275	250	200	150

LASALLE
France

Slide Action Shotgun

Chambered for 12 or 20 gauge and is offered with a 26", 28", or 30" barrel with improved-cylinder, modified, or full chokes. The receiver is alloy, anodized blue; and the vent rib barrel is blued. The stock is checkered walnut.

Exc.	V.G.	Good	Fair	Poor
300	250	200	150	100

Semiautomatic Shotgun

A gas-operated semiautomatic shotgun chambered for 12 gauge only, with the same barrel length and choke combinations as are available on the Slide Action model. The receiver is also alloy, and the stock is checkered walnut.

Exc.	V.G.	Good	Fair	Poor
350	275	225	175	100

LASERAIM ARMS
Little Rock, Arkansas

Series I

Offered in 10mm or .45 ACP this single action semiautomatic pistol is fitted with a 6" barrel with compensator. Adjustable rear sight. Stainless steel frame and barrel with mate black Teflon finish. Introduced in 1993. Magazine capacity for 10mm is 8 rounds and 7 rounds for .45 ACP. Weight is about 46 oz.

NIB	Exc.	V.G.	Good	Fair	Poor
550	475	400	—	—	—

Series II

This is similar to the Series I except this model has no compensator. It is fitted with a 5" barrel and stainless steel finish. A compact version has a 3-3/8" barrel. Introduced in 1993. Weight is 43 oz. for 5" barrel and 37 oz. for compact version.

NIB	Exc.	V.G.	Good	Fair	Poor
350	300	250	—	—	—

Series III

This model is similar to the Series II except it is offered with 5" barrel only with a dual port compensator. Introduced in 1994. Weight is about 43 oz.

NIB	Exc.	V.G.	Good	Fair	Poor
500	400	300	—	—	—

LAURONA
Eibar, Spain
Importer - Galaxy Imports
Victoria, Texas

NOTE: The "G" in the model designation stands for Gemini for "twin" for the unique double selective trigger system. The "G" triggers will function either as a single or double triggers. The front trigger is non-selective firing in bottom to top sequence and the back trigger in top to bottom sequence. The "U" models are models with non-selective single triggers. The version listed first was the normal production configuration and the version listed second was the special order or optional configuration.

The list of models that appear below was compiled by Thomas E. Barker of Galaxy Imports, Ltd., Inc.

Model 67 (G&U)

The first over/under Laurona chambered for 12 gauge only with double triggers and 28" vent rib barrels with extractors. The boxlock action and barrels are blued, and the stock is checkered walnut in 20 lpi. skip line checkering.

Exc.	V.G.	Good	Fair	Poor
500	400	300	200	150

Model 71 (G&U)

Similar to the Model 67 with minor cosmetic changes and improvements to facilitate ease of manufacturing. Receiver is bright chromed with roll engraving depicting dogs on the right side and birds on the left. This model was imported and sold by Sears & Robuck in about 1973 and 1974. The earlier models had traditional solid center ribbed blued barrels, the later models having Black Chrome finished solid ribbed barrels.

Exc.	V.G.	Good	Fair	Poor
500	400	350	300	200

MODEL 82 (G&U)

Similar to the Model 71 with auto-ejectors. Chambered for 12 gauge only. All barrels seperated without center rib with Black Chrome finish and hard chrome bores with long forcing cones in chambers. Firing pins changed to traditional round type. Many internal parts improved for reliability. Checkering changed from skip diamond to standard 20 lpi. In most respects the 82 Models are representative of present day Laurona over and under shotguns and will share most internal parts.

Model 82 Game (G&U)

Barrels are 28" with 2-3/4" or 3" chambers, long forcing cones, hard chrome bores, 5mm rib, and chokes ****/**(IC/IM) or ***/*(M/F). Finish on barrels is black chrome with nickel receiver with Louis XVI style engraving. Tulip forend, field style stock with plastic butt plate. Weights approximately 7 lbs.

Exc.	V.G.	Good	Fair	Poor
550	400	350	300	200

Model 82 Super Game (G&U)

Similar to the Model 82 Game except with more elaborate and very delicate engraving

Exc.	V.G.	Good	Fair	Poor
575	450	350	300	200

Model 82 Trap Combi (U&G)

Similar to the Model 82 Game except for 28" or 29" barrels. The rib is 8mm. The Trap stock is fitted with a rubber recoil pad. Weight os about 7.4 lbs.

Exc.	V.G.	Good	Fair	Poor
550	400	350	300	200

Model 82 Trap Competition (U only)

Similar to the Model 82 Trap Combi except for the 13mm aluminum rib with long white sight. Engraving consist of motifs on sides of receiver. Beavertail fluted forend and Monte Carlo Trap stock with black rubber special Trap recoil pad. Weight is approximately 8 lbs.

Exc.	V.G.	Good	Fair	Poor
600	500	400	350	300

Model 82 Super Trap (U only)

Similar to the Model 82 Trap Competition except for special trap Pachmayr recoil pad with imitation leather face. Engraving very delicate fine scroll. Weight is 7 lbs., 12 oz.

Exc.	V.G.	Good	Fair	Poor
675	575	450	400	350

Model 82 Super Skeet

Similar to the Model 82 Super Trap except fitted with 28" barrels choked sheet with field style butt stock with plastic butt plate. Weight is approximately 7 lbs.

Exc.	V.G.	Good	Fair	Poor
600	500	400	350	300

Model 82 Pigeon Competition (U only)

Similar to the Model 82 Trap Competition except fitted with 28" barrels. Recoil pad is special competition style Pachmayr with imitation leather face. Weight is about 7 lbs., 13 oz.

Exc.	V.G.	Good	Fair	Poor
650	550	450	400	350

Model 82 Super Pigeon (U only)

Similar to the Model 82 Super Trap except fitted with 28" barrels. Weight is approximately 7 lbs., 9 oz.

Exc.	V.G.	Good	Fair	Poor
675	575	450	400	350

NOTE: The following Super Models have nickel finish receivers with delicate fine scroll engraving with black chrome relief. All barrels have a very durable rust resistance black chrome finish.

Model 84S Super Game

Similar to the Model 82 Super Game except for the new Single Selective Trigger which is designated by "S" in the model number. Chambered for the 12 gauge 3" magnum with 28" barrels with 8mm rib. Weight is approximately 7 lbs.

Exc.	V.G.	Good	Fair	Poor
800	700	650	600	500

NOTE: The following Super Game models were available with an extra set of 20 gauge multi-choke barrels in 26" or 28". Add $400 to **Exc.** value for these barrels. For models with cast-on stocks for left hand shooters add $50 to **Exc.** value.

Model 83MG Super Game

Similar to the Model 82 Super Game except this model was the advent of Laurona's new milti-choke. **CAUTION!** The Laurona multi-choke is not compatible with any other brand of screw-in chokes because the black chrome plating of the metric threads. Do not attempt to interchange with other guns. Barrel for this model in 12 gauge are 28" in length and for the 20 gauge 26" or 28". Both are chambered for the 3" shell. Rib is 8mm. Weight is about 7 lbs.

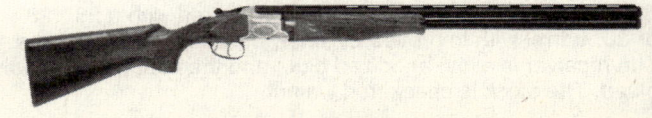

Exc.	V.G.	Good	Fair	Poor
1000	850	750	650	600

Model 85MS Super Game

Similar to the Model 83MG Super Game except for the Single Selective Trigger. Chambered for the 12 or 20 gauge 3" Magnum. Weight is about 7 lbs.

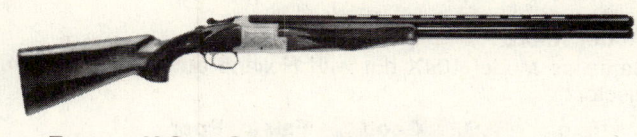

Exc.	V.G.	Good	Fair	Poor
1000	850	750	650	600

Model 84S Super Trap

Single selective trigger with 29" barrels. Chambered for 2-3/4" shells with long forcing cones. The aluminum rib is 13mm wide. Auto ejectors. Receiver is nickel plated with fine scroll engraving with black chrome relief. Beavertail forearm and choice of Monte Carlo or standard Trap stock. Weight is about 7 lbs., 12 oz.

Exc.	V.G.	Good	Fair	Poor
1250	1000	800	700	600

Model 85MS Super Trap

Similar to the Model 82S Super Trap except multi-choke in bottom barrel with fixed choke on top barrel. Weight is about 7 lbs., 12 oz.

Exc.	V.G.	Good	Fair	Poor
1250	1000	800	700	600

Model 85MS Super Pigeon

Similar to the Model 85MS Super Trap except with 28" barrels with fixed IM choke on top barrel and milti-choke on bottom barrel. Intended for live bird competition. Weight is about 7 lbs., 4 oz.

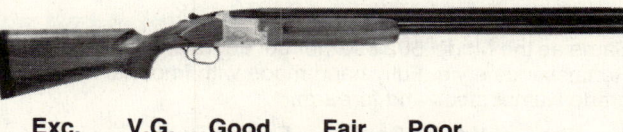

Exc.	V.G.	Good	Fair	Poor
1250	1000	800	700	600

Model 85MS Special Sporting

Similar to the Model 85MS Super Pigeon except for field style butt stock with plastic butt plate. Intended for upland game. Weight is approximately 7 lbs., 4 oz.

Exc.	V.G.	Good	Fair	Poor
1250	1000	800	700	600

Model 84S SuperSkeet

Similar to the Model 85MS Special Sporting except choked skeet and skeet. Weight is approximatley 7 lbs.

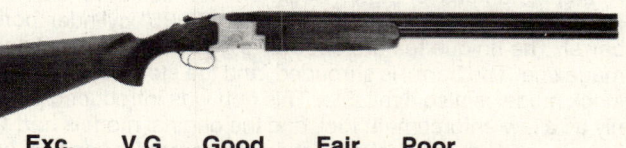

Exc.	V.G.	Good	Fair	Poor
1000	800	700	600	500

LAURONA O/U MODELS SILHOUETTE 300

These guns are basically the same as the Super series above with the exception of the following. They are readily identified by the white and black chrome stripped receiver with the model engraved on the side of the receiver. Barrels are multi-choked on both bores and have 11mm steel ribs. **NOTE:** Two types of chokes were used. Some guns came with knurl head type as in the Super models and others were made with the flush invector style. A later option for ease of changing chokes is the knurl long choke which is a flush type with a knurl head added. Both later type chokes, the flush and the knurl long type, can be used in the early multi-choke models with some extension showing.

Silhouette 300 Trap

This model has barrels 29" with 2-3/4" chambers and long forceing cones with hard chrome bores and 11mm rib. Beavertail forearm and straight comb trap stock fitted with a ventilated black rubber recoil pad are standard. Weight is approximately 8 lbs.

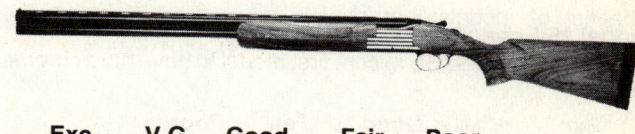

Exc.	V.G.	Good	Fair	Poor
1250	1000	800	700	600

Silhouette 300 Sporting Clays

Similar to the Model 300 Trap except with 28" barrels. Some guns came with 3" chambers. The butt stock is field style with plastic butt plate or hard rubber sporting clays pad. Weight is about 8 lbs.

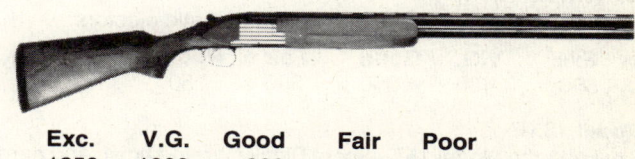

Exc.	V.G.	Good	Fair	Poor
1250	1000	800	700	600

Silhouette 300 Ultra Magnum

Similar to the Model 300 Sporting Clays except with 3-1/2" chamber in 12 gauge for waterfowl hunting. This unique gun with its ability to shoot any type and size 12 gauge ammunation along with its non-rusting Black Chrome finish makes it the most versatile O/U on the market for either hunting or competition. Weight is about 7 lbs., 8 oz.

Exc.	V.G.	Good	Fair	Poor
1265	1000	900	800	750

LAURONA SIDE BY SIDE SHOTGUNS

Models with "X" after the model number were made after 1975 and finished with non-rusting Black Chrome on barrels and action with hard chrome bores. Guns were made in 12, 16, and 20 bore. Smaller gauges were made on special order. Side by side shotguns were discontinued by Laurona after 1978 to concentrate on the O/U market.

Model 11

Box lock action with triple Greener type round crossbolt. Independent firing pins bushed into the face of the action. Barrels of "Bellota" steel. Made in 12, 16, and 20 bore.

Exc.	V.G.	Good	Fair	Poor
400	350	300	200	150

Model 13

Similar to the Mode 11 except with Purdey type bolting system. Extractor of double radius.

Exc.	V.G.	Good	Fair	Poor
400	350	300	200	150

Model 13X

Barrels and action finished in Black Chrome and hard chrome bores.

Exc.	V.G.	Good	Fair	Poor
500	400	300	250	200

Model 13E
Similar to the Model 13 except with automatic ajectors.

Exc.	V.G.	Good	Fair	Poor
500	400	300	250	200

Model 13XE
Similar to the Model 13E except Black Chrome finish and hard chrome bores.

Exc.	V.G.	Good	Fair	Poor
600	500	400	350	300

Model 15 Economic Pluma
Similar to the Model 13 except first model to have hard chrome bores.

Exc.	V.G.	Good	Fair	Poor
450	400	300	250	200

Model 15X
Similar to the Model 15 except Black Chrome finish and hard chrome bores.

Exc.	V.G.	Good	Fair	Poor
500	400	300	250	200

Model 15E Economic Pluma
Similar to the Model 15 except with automatic ejectors.

Exc.	V.G.	Good	Fair	Poor
550	450	350	300	250

Model 15XE
Similar to the Model 15E except Black Chrome finish and hard chrome bores.

Exc.	V.G.	Good	Fair	Poor
600	500	400	350	300

Model 52 Pluma
Box lock action with back of action scalloped and artistically engraved in fine English style scroll. Churchill rib and double radius extractor. Hard chrome bores. Weight is about 6 lbs.

Exc.	V.G.	Good	Fair	Poor
750	650	500	400	350

Model 52E Pluma
Similar to the Model 52 except with automatic ejectors. Weight is approximately 6 lbs., 2 oz.

Exc.	V.G.	Good	Fair	Poor
850	750	600	500	450

LAURONA SIDE BY SIDE SIDE LOCKS

Model 103
Blued side lock with some light border engraving. Triple Purdey type bolting system. Extractor of double radius. Barrels of special "Bellota" steel with hard chrome bores. Made in 12, 16, and 20 bore.

Exc.	V.G.	Good	Fair	Poor
900	800	700	500	400

Model 103E
Similar to the Model 103 except with automatic ejectors.

Exc.	V.G.	Good	Fair	Poor
1000	800	700	600	500

Model 104X
Case colored side locks with Purdey type bolting system. Extractor with double radius. Fine double safety side locks. Gas relief vents. Articulated trigger. Hard chrome bores. Demi-block barrels of special "Bellota" steel. Black Chrome barrels. Produced in 12, 16, and 20 bore with smaller bores avaiable on special order.

Exc.	V.G.	Good	Fair	Poor
1200	1000	800	700	600

Model 104XE
Same as Model 104X but with Holland automatic selective ejectors.

Exc.	V.G.	Good	Fair	Poor
1350	1100	900	800	700

Model 105X Feather
Same as the Model 104X but with concave rib. Weight in 12 gauge is approximately 6 lbs., 2 oz.

Exc.	V.G.	Good	Fair	Poor
1250	1000	800	700	600

Model 105 XE Feather
Same as Model 105X but with Holland automatic selective ejectors.

Exc.	V.G.	Good	Fair	Poor
1400	1250	1000	800	750

Model 502 Feather
Fine side lock with Purdey type bolting system. Very fine double safety side locks, hand detachable. Gas releif vents. Holland automatic selective ejectors. Articulated trigger. Inside hard chromed demi-block barrels of special "Bellota" steel. Outside Black Chrome finish. Fine English style scroll engraving. Marble gray or Laurona Imperial finish. churchill or concave type rib. Weight is 12 bore is approximately 6.25 lbs. Offered in 12, 16, and 20 bore.

Exc.	V.G.	Good	Fair	Poor
2200	1800	1600	1500	1400

Model 801 Deluxe
Same as the Model 502 Feather but engraving is a true deluxe Renaissance style. Fully hand made with Imperial finish. First grade walnut stock and forearm.

Exc.	V.G.	Good	Fair	Poor
4400	4000	3750	2750	2250

Model 802 Eagle
Same as the Model 801 Deluxe except highly artistic base relief hand engraving of hunting scenes.

Exc.	V.G.	Good	Fair	Poor
5000	4500	4000	3500	3250

LAW ENFORCEMENT ORDNANCE CORP.
Ridgeway, Pennsylvania

Striker 12
A semiautomatic shotgun designed for self-defense. It is chambered for 12 gauge and has an 18.25" cylinder bored barrel. The unique feature about this gun is its 12-round drum magazine. The barrel is shrouded, and the stock folds. A fixed-stock model is also available. This gun was introduced primarily as a law enforcement tool, and the original models had 12" barrels and were legal for law enforcement agencies and Class 3 licensed individuals only. The 18.25" version is legal for private ownership and was introduced in 1986. This shotgun is no longer imported into the U.S. This shotgun is now classified as a Class III weapon and subject to restrictions of the B.A.T.F. Be certain that the particular shotgun is transferrable before purchase. If there are any questions contact B.A.T.F. before purchase.

Striker 12 shotguns in excellent condition may sell for as much as $2,000.

LAZZERONI ARMS COMPANY
Tucson, Arizona

Model 2000 ST-F
This model, as with all Lazzeroni models, is chambered for the company's own proprietary calibers. The 6.53 (.257) Scramjet, 7.21 (.284) Firehawk, 7.82 (.308) Warbird, and the 8.59 (.338) Titan. Fitted with a 27" match grade barrel with fully adjustable trigger, and removable muzzle brake. Conventional fiberglass stock.

NIB	Exc.	V.G.	Good	Fair	Poor
3700	3000	—	—	—	—

Model 2000 ST-W
As above but fitted with a conventional black wood laminate stock.

NIB	Exc.	V.G.	Good	Fair	Poor
4800	3900	—	—	—	—

Model 2000ST-FW
As above but fitted with a conventional fiberglass stock and an additional black wood laminate stock.

NIB	Exc.	V.G.	Good	Fair	Poor
5300	4250	—	—	—	—

Model 2000SLR
This model has a 28" extra heavy fluted barrel with conventional fiberglass stock. Chambered for the 6.53 Scramjet, 7.21 Firehawk, and the 7.82 Warbird.

NIB	Exc.	V.G.	Good	Fair	Poor
3900	3100	—	—	—	—

Model 2000SP-F
This model is fitted with a 23" match grade and Lazzeroni thumbhole fiberglass stock. Chambered for all Lazzeroni calibers.

NIB	Exc.	V.G.	Good	Fair	Poor
3700	2950	—	—	—	—

Model 2000SP-W
Same as above but with black wood laminate thumbhole stock.

NIB	Exc.	V.G.	Good	Fair	Poor
4800	3850	—	—	—	—

Model 2000SP-FW
Same as above model but is supplied with two stocks: a thumbhole fiberglass stock and a black wood laminate stock.

NIB	Exc.	V.G.	Good	Fair	Poor
5300	4250	—	—	—	—

Swarovski P.H. 3-12x50 Rifle

NIB	Exc.	V.G.	Good	Fair	Poor
1400	1150	—	—	—	—

LEBEL
French State

The Lebel system was invented by Nicolas Lebel in 1886. The French replaced the single shot Gras Model 1874 rifle with this weapon. This was the first successful smallbore rifle and sent the rest of the European continent into a dash to emulate it. The Lebel system was used until it was made obsolete by the Berthier rifle in the 1890s.

Model 1886 "Lebel"
Chambered for the 8mm Lebel cartridge. It has a 31" barrel and holds 8 shots in a tubular magazine that runs beneath the barrel. This design is long and heavy and was not in use for long before being replaced by the more efficient box magazine weapons, such as those from Mauser. This rifle has a two-piece stock with no upper hand guard. It is held on by two bar-rel bands, and a cruciform bayonet could be fixed under the muzzle. Although this rifle was made obsolete rather quickly, it did have the distinction of being the first successful smokeless powder smallbore rifle; there were shortened examples in use until the end of WWII.

Courtesy Richard M. Kumor, Sr.

Exc.	V.G.	Good	Fair	Poor
400	325	200	100	50

Model 1886/M93
A shorter version of the above. Fitted with a 17.7" barrel and a 3-round tubular magazine. Issued in 1935.

Courtesy Richard M. Kumor, Sr.

Exc.	V.G.	Good	Fair	Poor
350	300	250	150	75

Model 1886/74/1917 Signal Rifle
A scarce variation of the military issue rifle.

Courtesy Richard M. Kumor, Sr.

Exc.	V.G.	Good	Fair	Poor
600	500	300	175	75

Revolver Model 1892
Chambered for an 8mm centerfire cartridge and has a 4.5" barrel with a 6-shot cylinder. It is referred to as a "Lebel," but there is no certainty that Nicolas Lebel had anything to do with its design or production. This revolver is a simple double action, with a swing-out cylinder that swings to the right side for loading. The design of this weapon is similar to the Italian Model 1889. There is one redeeming feature on this revolver, and that is a hinged sideplate on the left side of the frame that could be swung away after unlocking so that repairs or cleaning of the lockwork could be performed with relative simplicity. The cartridge for which this weapon was chambered was woefully inadequate. This revolver remained in use from its introduction in 1893 until the end of WWII in 1945, mainly because the French never got around to designing a replacement.

Exc.	V.G.	Good	Fair	Poor
200	150	125	100	75

LEE FIREARMS CO.
Milwaukee, Wisconsin

Lee Single Shot Carbine
A rare single shot break-open carbine that pivots to the right side for loading. It is chambered for the .44 rimfire cartridge and has a 21.5" barrel with a hammer mounted in the center of the frame. The carbine has a walnut buttstock but no fore-arm and is marked "Lee's Firearms Co. Milwaukee, Wisc."

There were approximately 450 manufactured between 1863 and 1865. There are few surviving examples, and one should be wary of fakes.

Courtesy Milwaukee Public Museum, Milwaukee, Wisconsin

Exc.	V.G.	Good	Fair	Poor
—	—	3500	1750	750

Lee Sporting Rifle

Similar to the military carbine except that it has a longer octagonal barrel. The barrel length was varied, and there were more of these manufactured. The survival rate appears to have been better than for the carbine model.

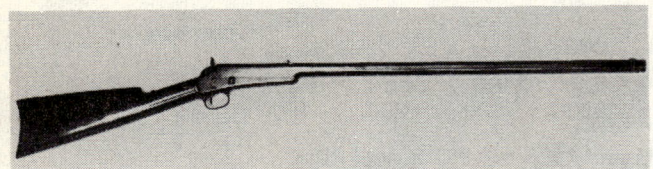

Courtesy Milwaukee Public Museum, Milwaukee, Wisconsin

Exc.	V.G.	Good	Fair	Poor
—	—	1500	900	400

LEE-ENFIELD
Middlesex, England

Royal Small Arms Factory

The British service rifle from 1895 through WWII. There are a number of minor variations, and it would behoove the potential collector to avail oneself of the material written on this weapon. We furnish descriptions and values of most of these variations.

Mark 1

Introduced on the 11th of November, 1895. Its outward appearance is similar to that of the Lee-Metford Mark 2* Rifle. The method of rifling is different, since smokeless powder had been developed. It is chambered for the .303 British cartridge and has a 30.2" barrel and a full-length stock held on by two barrel bands. There is a cleaning rod mounted under the barrel. It has military-type sights and a box magazine located in front of the triggerguard. The finish is blued, with a walnut stock with sling swivels and a stacking swivel.

Exc.	V.G.	Good	Fair	Poor
250	225	175	125	90

Mark 1*

Produced by fitting a .303 British barrel to a Mark 3 Martini Henry action. It has a 30.2" barrel and features a stripper-clip guide on the receiver. It was introduced in 1899.

Exc.	V.G.	Good	Fair	Poor
250	225	175	125	90

Mark 1**

Similar to the Mark 1 except that the cleaning rod was removed. It was introduced in 1899.

Exc.	V.G.	Good	Fair	Poor
250	225	175	125	90

Short Magazine Mark I Rifle

A carbine-length version that is chambered for the .303 British cartridge and has a 25" barrel with a 10-round, detachable box magazine. Upon its introduction it was intended to be the perfect infantryman's rifle. At first, it was not accepted because its short length was deemed to be detrimental from an accuracy standpoint. It did, however, survive; and the "SMLE" earned the reputation of one of the finest bolt action service rifles ever produced. The finish is blued, and it has a full-length walnut stock held on by two barrel bands. The stock extended nearly to the muzzle, creating a snubnose effect with the protruding barrel. It was introduced in 1903.

Exc.	V.G.	Good	Fair	Poor
225	200	150	100	75

Mark 2

Similar to the SMLE Mark I except that it has a shorter, lighter barrel, improved sights, and a stripper-clip guide on the receiver. It was also introduced in 1903.

Exc.	V.G.	Good	Fair	Poor
225	200	150	100	75

Mark 3

Similar to the Mark 1, with the addition of improved sights. It was introduced in 1907.

Exc.	V.G.	Good	Fair	Poor
225	200	150	100	75

Mark 4

A Mark 2 rifle converted by adding the features of the Mark 3. It was introduced in 1907.

Exc.	V.G.	Good	Fair	Poor
200	175	150	100	75

No. 4 Mark 1

Features the addition of a hinged aperture rear sight. The nose cap was removed from the stock. It was introduced in 1942.

Exc.	V. G.	Good	Fair	Poor
200	175	150	100	75

No. 4 Mark 2

Similar to the No. 4 Mark 1, with an improved trigger mechanism. It was introduced in 1949.

Exc.	V.G.	Good	Fair	Poor
200	175	150	100	75

No. 5 Mark 1

Known as the "Jungle Carbine." It is chambered for the .303 British cartridge and has an 18.5" barrel with a flash-hider on the muzzle. It has a shortened stock, with a rear hand guard held on by one barrel band. The stock has a rubber recoil pad. The finish is blued.

Although the weapon was light and compact for carrying, it had an excessive recoil and muzzle blast and was not popular with the soldiers who used it.

Exc.	V.G.	Good	Fair	Poor
300	250	200	150	100

LEE-METFORD
Great Britain

Mark 1

A bolt action service rifle chambered for the .303 British cartridge. It was designed by James Lee and incorporated rifling developed by William Metford. This rifling was specifically designed to alleviate the problem of black powder fouling. Ithaca 30.2" barrel and a 10-round, detachable box magazine located in front of the triggerguard. It features military-type sights and a cleaning rod mounted underneath the barrel. The finish is blued, with a full-length walnut stock held on by two barrel bands. It was introduced in 1888.

Exc.	V. G.	Good	Fair	Poor
200	175	150	100	75

Mark 1*

Similar to the Mark 1 except that the safety catch was removed from the cocking piece and a brass disc was inletted into the butt stock for regimental markings. There were a number of internal improvements, as well as the fitting of a different, blade-type front sight. It was introduced in 1892.

Exc.	V. G.	Good	Fair	Poor
175	150	125	100	75

Mark 2

Has a modified magazine that holds 10 rounds in a double column. It was introduced in 1892.

Exc.	V. G.	Good	Fair	Poor
175	150	125	100	75

Mark 2*

Has a lengthened bolt, with the addition of a safety catch. It was introduced in 1895.

Exc.	V. G.	Good	Fair	Poor
200	175	150	100	75

Mark I Carbine

Has a 20.75" barrel, and the receiver was modified to accept a stripper-clip guide. It was introduced in 1894.

Exc.	V. G.	Good	Fair	Poor
200	175	150	100	75

LEECH & RIGDON
Greensboro, Georgia

Leech & Rigdon Revolver

This Confederate revolver was patterned after the 1851 Colt Navy. It is chambered for .36 caliber percussion and has a 6-shot unfluted cylinder. The 7.5" barrel is part-octagonal and has a loading lever beneath it. The frame is open-topped; and the finish is blued, with brass grip straps and walnut one-piece grips. The barrel is marked "Leech & Rigdon CSA." There were approximately 1,500 revolvers manufactured in 1863 and 1864. These were all contracted for by the Confederacy and are considered to be a prime acquisition for collectors. Be wary of fakes, and trust in qualified independent appraisals only.

Exc.	V.G.	Good	Fair	Poor
—	—	12000	5000	2500

LEFAUCHAUX, CASIMER & EUGENE
Paris, France

Pinfire Revolver

The pinfire ignition system was invented by Casimir Lefauchaux in 1828 but was not widely used until the 1850s. It consists of a smooth rimless case that contains the powder charge and a percussion cap. A pin protrudes from the side of this case at the rear and when struck by the hammer is driven into the cap, thereby igniting the charge and firing the weapon. The pistols for this cartridge are slotted at the end of the cylinder to allow the pins to protrude and be struck by the downward blow of the hammer. This particular revolver is chambered for .43 caliber and has a 5.25" barrel. The cylinder holds 6 shots; and the finish is blued, with checkered walnut grips. This revolver was manufactured after 1865 and was selected for service by the French military.

Exc.	V. G.	Good	Fair	Poor
400	300	275	200	125

LEFEVER ARMS CO.
Syracuse, New York

Founded by Dan Lefever, who was a pioneer in the field of breech-loading firearms. This company was founded in 1884, with Lefever as the president. He was referred to as "Uncle Dan" within the firearms industry. He was responsible for many improvements in the double-barrel shotgun design. He developed the automatic hammerless system in the late 1880s. He also developed a compensating action that allowed simple adjustments to compensate for action wear. In 1901 he was forced out of the company and organized another company—the D.M. Lefever, Sons & Company—also in Syracuse. Dan Lefever died in 1906, and his new company went out of business. The original company was acquired by Ithaca in 1916. They continued to produce Lefever guns until 1948.

Sidelock Shotgun

A double-barrel, side-by-side shotgun chambered for 10, 12, 16, or 20 gauge. It was offered with 26", 28", 30", or 32" barrels with various choke combinations. The barrels are either Damascus or fluid steel. Damascus guns have become collectible and in better condition—very good to excellent—can bring nearly the same price as the fluid-steel guns. It features a full sidelock action. Double triggers are standard. The finish is blued, with a checkered walnut stock. There are a number of variations that differ in the amount of ornamentation and the quality of materials and workmanship utilized in their construction. Automatic ejectors are represented by the letter "E" after the respective grade designation. This shotgun was manufactured between 1885 and 1919. We strongly recommend that a qualified appraisal be secured if a transaction is contemplated.

20 Gauge-Add 25%.
Single Selective Trigger-Add 10%.

DS Grade

Exc.	V.G.	Good	Fair	Poor
1250	800	650	450	250

DSE Grade

Exc.	V.G.	Good	Fair	Poor
1750	1450	1100	750	400

H Grade

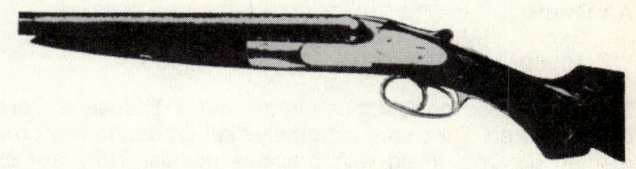

Exc.	V.G.	Good	Fair	Poor
1250	800	650	450	250

HE Grade

Exc.	V.G.	Good	Fair	Poor
2000	1650	1300	1000	500

G Grade

Exc.	V.G.	Good	Fair	Poor
1500	1300	1000	750	400

GE Grade

Exc.	V.G.	Good	Fair	Poor
3000	1800	1500	1200	650

F Grade

Exc.	V.G.	Good	Fair	Poor
1500	1000	800	650	375

FE Grade

Exc.	V.G.	Good	Fair	Poor
4500	3000	1750	1250	650

E Grade

Exc.	V.G.	Good	Fair	Poor
2000	1800	1550	1000	800

EE Grade

Exc.	V.G.	Good	Fair	Poor
5500	3500	2000	1500	1000

D Grade

Exc.	V.G.	Good	Fair	Poor
2500	2200	1650	1050	800

DE Grade

Exc.	V.G.	Good	Fair	Poor
5500	3500	2000	1500	1000

C Grade

Exc.	V.G.	Good	Fair	Poor
6000	4000	2850	2000	1250

CE Grade

Exc.	V.G.	Good	Fair	Poor
8500	6000	4000	3000	1500

B Grade

Exc.	V.G.	Good	Fair	Poor
6000	5000	4000	3000	2250

BE Grade

Exc.	V.G.	Good	Fair	Poor
10000	8000	4500	3500	2500

A Grade

Exc.	V.G.	Good	Fair	Poor
13000	9000	5000	3500	2500

AA Grade

Exc.	V.G.	Good	Fair	Poor
18500	12000	6000	4000	3000

There was also an Optimus Grade and a Thousand Dollar Grade offered. These are extremely high-grade, heavily ornamented firearms inlaid with precious metals. They are extremely rare, and evaluating them on a general basis is impossible.

LEFEVER ARMS COMPANY, INC. (ITHACA)

During 1916, the Ithaca Gun company purchased the gunmaking assets of the Syracuse, New York based, Lefever Arms Company. Between then and World War I, they continued to manufacture the same sidelock gun that had been made in Syracuse until about 1919 when they were discontinued. Prices for those guns are listed above. During 1921, Ithaca Gun Company, under the name the Lefever Arms Company, Inc., introduced a line of lower costs, boxlock guns. Eventually, six different models were produced. Ithaca's Lefever guns were produced in 12, 16, and 20 gauges, and in .410 bore. Twenty gauge guns often command a price premium of 20%, a .410 bore gun may command up to a 100% premium.

Nitro Special

A side-by-side, double-barrel shotgun chambered for 12, 16, or 20 gauge, as well as .410. The barrels were offered in lengths of 26" to 32" with various choke combinations. It features a boxlock action with double triggers and extractors standard. The finish is blued, with a case-colored receiver and a checkered walnut stock. This model was manufactured between 1921 and 1948; and incredible as it may seem, its price at introduction was $29.

Single Selective Trigger-Add $100

Automatic ejectors-Add $100.

Exc.	V.G.	Good	Fair	Poor
600	400	250	200	—

A Grade (Model 5)

Manufactured from 1936 to 1939, the A Grade was a double barreled gun. The walnut stocks had pointed checkering cut at the grip area of the butt stock and on the splinter forend. A line engraving outlined its nicely sculptured frame.

NOTE: Single trigger add $200, automatic ejectors add $200, beavertail forend add $300.

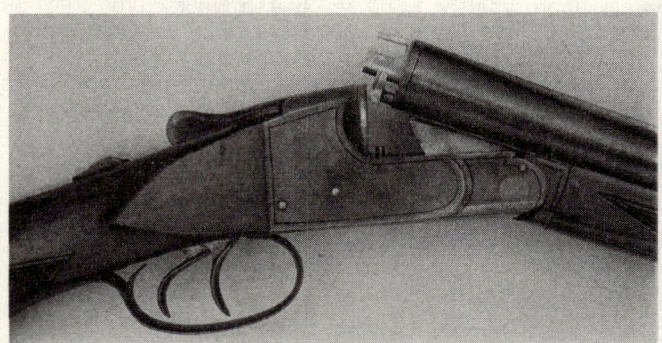

Courtesy Walter C. Snyder and C. Hadley Smith

Exc.	V.G.	Good	Fair	Poor
800	600	400	300	—

Skeet Special (Model 6)

Manufactured from 1936 to 1939, the A Grade was a double barreled gun. The walnut stocks had pointed checkering cut at the grip area of the butt stock and on the beavertail forend. A beavertail forend, single trigger, automatic ejectors, a recoil pad, and ivory center and front sight were standard. The frame was sculptured and line engraved like the Model 5.

Exc.	V.G.	Good	Fair	Poor
1500	1200	1000	400	—

Long Range Single Barrel Trap and Field (Model 2)

Manufactured from 1927 to 1947, the Model 2 was a single barrel gun with no rib. Like the Nitro Special, it had walnut stocks that were line cut checkered at the grip area of the butt stock and on the forend.

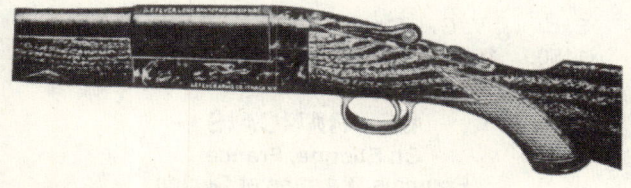

Exc.	V.G.	Good	Fair	Poor
300	250	200	100	—

Single Barrel Trap Ventilated Rib (Model 3)

Manufactured from 1927 to 1942, the Model 3 was a single barrel gun with the same ventilated rib that was used on the "Knick" trap gun. The walnut stocks had line cut checkering at the grip area of the butt stock and on the forend.

Exc.	V.G.	Good	Fair	Poor
400	300	250	100	—

Double Barrel Ventilated Rib Trap (Model 4)

Manufactured during 1929 but catalogued until 1939, the Model 4 was a double barrel gun with a ventilated rib barrel. The walnut stocks had line cut checkering at the grip area of the butt stock and on the beavertail forend. Only about 2000 units were produced.

Exc.	V.G.	Good	Fair	Poor
2000	1500	1200	700	—

LEFEVER, D. M., SONS & COMPANY
Syracuse, New York

"Uncle Dan" Lefever founded the Lefever Arms Company in 1884. In 1901 he was forced out of his company and founded the D.M. Lefever, Sons & Company. He continued to produce high-grade, side-by-side, double ceased operations. There were approximately 1,200 shotguns of all variations produced during this period, making them extremely rare and difficult to evaluate on a general basis. We list the models and average values but strongly suggest securing qualified appraisal if a transaction is contemplated.

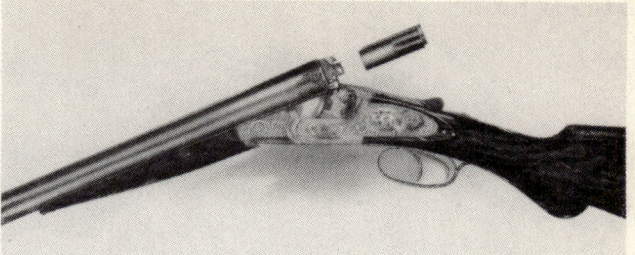

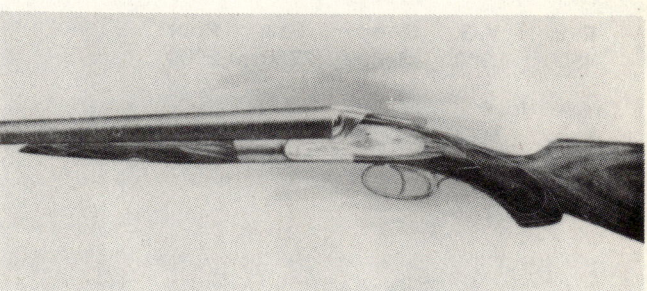

Lefever Double Barrel Shotgun

A side-by-side, double-barrel shotgun chambered for 12, 16, or 20 gauge. It was offered with various-length barrels and choke combinations that were made to order. It features double triggers and automatic ejectors. A single selective trigger was available as an option. The finish is blued, with a checkered walnut stock. The individual grades differ in the amount of ornamentation and the general quality of the materials and workmanship utilized in their construction. This model was discontinued in 1906.

Single Selective Trigger-Add 10%.
20 Gauge-Add 25%.

O Excelsior Grade-Extractors

Exc.	V.G.	Good	Fair	Poor
2500	2000	1650	950	700

Excelsior Grade-Auto Ejectors

Exc.	V.G.	Good	Fair	Poor
3000	2500	2000	1250	900

F Grade, No. 9

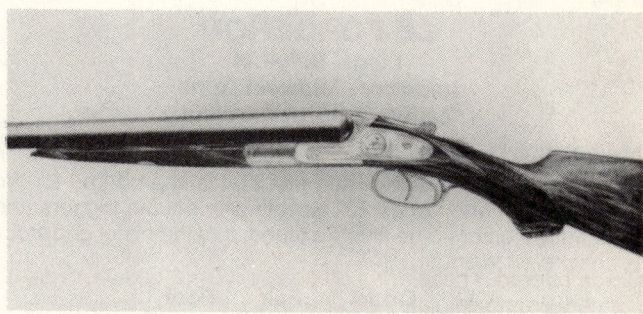

Exc.	V.G.	Good	Fair	Poor
3000	2750	2250	1500	1100

G Grade-10 Gauge, Damascus Barrels

Exc.	V.G.	Good	Fair	Poor
3500	3100	2600	2000	1350

E Grade, No. 8

Exc.	V.G.	Good	Fair	Poor
4000	3500	3000	2400	1700

D Grade, No. 7

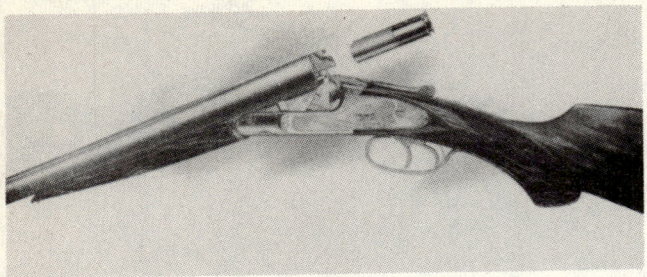

Exc.	V.G.	Good	Fair	Poor
4500	3900	3400	2750	2000

C Grade, No. 6

Exc.	V.G.	Good	Fair	Poor
5000	4500	3750	3000	2500

B Grade, No. 5

Exc.	V.G.	Good	Fair	Poor
6500	5750	4800	3500	3000

AA Grade, No. 4

Exc.	V.G.	Good	Fair	Poor
9000	7800	6500	4200	2750

There is an "Uncle Dan" grade, which is the top-of-the-line version, that features extremely high quality in materials and workmanship and a great deal of ornamentation. This firearm is extremely rare and seldom found in today's market. It is impossible to evaluate it on a general basis.

LE FORGERON
Liege, Belgium
Importer - Midwest Guns
Zebulon, North Carolina

Model 6020 Double Rifle

A boxlock-actioned side-x-side rifle that is chambered for the 9.3x74R cartridge. It has 25" barrels with double triggers and automatic ejectors. The finish is blued, and the pistol grip stock is checkered walnut.

Exc.	V.G.	Good	Fair	Poor
5000	4500	4000	3000	2500

Model 6040

Simply the Model 6020 with false sideplates. All other specifications are the same.

Exc.	V.G.	Good	Fair	Poor
5750	5200	4500	3500	3000

Model 6030

A double rifle that has a true sidelock action and is engraved. It has a deluxe French walnut stock.

Exc.	V.G.	Good	Fair	Poor
9000	8000	7250	5500	4200

Boxlock Shotgun

This is a side-x-side, double-barreled shotgun chambered for 20 or 28 gauge. The barrel lengths are optional, as are the choke combinations. This gun has a single selective trigger and automatic ejectors. It is engraved and blued, with a deluxe French walnut stock.

False Sideplates-Add 20%.

Exc.	V.G.	Good	Fair	Poor
4500	4000	3250	2250	1750

Sidelock Shotgun

Has similar specifications to the boxlock except that it has a true sidelock action and is generally more deluxe in materials and workmanship.

Exc.	V.G.	Good	Fair	Poor
11500	10500	8500	6500	5500

LE FRANCAIS
St. Etienne, France
Francais D'Armes et Cycles

Le Francais Model 28

A unique pistol chambered for the 9mm Browning cartridge. It is a large pistol, with a 5" barrel that was hinged with a tip-up breech. This is a blowback-operated semiautomatic pistol that has no extractor. The empty cases are blown out of the breech by gas pressure. The one feature about this pistol that is desirable is that it is possible to tip the barrel breech forward like a shotgun and load cartridges singly, while holding the contents of the magazine in reserve. This weapon has fixed sights and a blued finish, with checkered walnut grips. It was manufactured between 1928 and 1938.

Exc.	V.G.	Good	Fair	Poor
1250	1050	850	650	450

Police Model

A blowback-operated, double-action semiautomatic that is chambered for the .32 ACP cartridge. It has a 3.5" barrel and a 7-round magazine. It has the same hinged-barrel feature of the Model 28 and is blued, with fixed sights and molded rubber grips. This model was manufactured between 1914 and 1938.

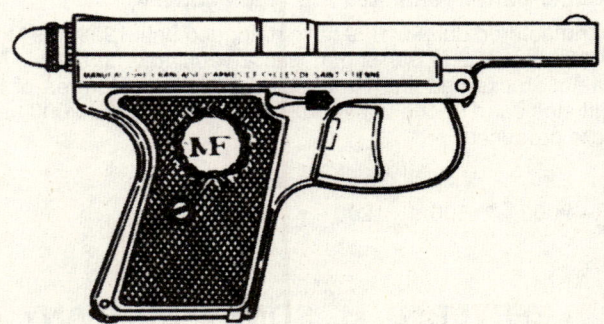

Exc.	V.G.	Good	Fair	Poor
800	700	550	375	275

Officers Model

Also a blowback-operated semiautomatic chambered for the .25 ACP cartridge. It has a 2.5" barrel and a concealed hammer. It has fixed sights and the finish is blued. The grips are molded rubber. This model was manufactured between 1914 and 1938.

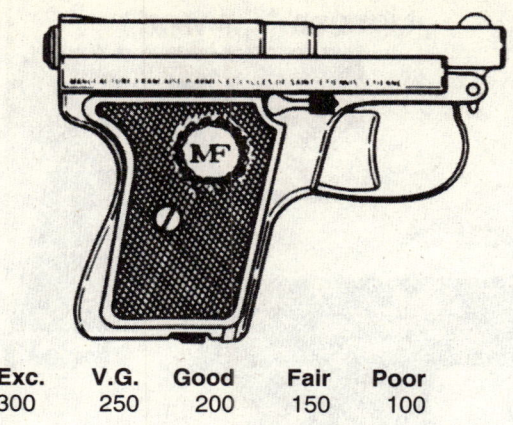

Exc.	V.G.	Good	Fair	Poor
300	250	200	150	100

LEMAN, H. E.
Lancaster, Pennsylvania

Leman Militia Rifle

A .58 caliber percussion muzzleloader that has a 33" round barrel. The stock is full-length and is held on by two barrel bands. There is a ramrod mounted under the barrel. The trim is brass; and the barrel is browned, with a case-colored lock. The lock is marked "H.E.Leman/Lancaster, Pa." There were approximately 500 manufactured between 1860 and 1864. They are believed to have been used by the Pennsylvania State Militia in the Civil War.

Courtesy Milwaukee Public Museum, Milwaukee, Wisconsin

Courtesy Milwaukee Public Museum, Milwaukee, Wisconsin

Exc.	V.G.	Good	Fair	Poor
—	—	3500	1500	650

LE MAT
Paris, France

Le Mat

Has a somewhat unique background that makes it a bit controversial among collectors. It is a foreign-made firearm manufactured in Paris, France, as well as in Birmingham, England. It was designed and patented by an American, Jean Alexander Le Mat of New Orleans, Louisiana; and it was purchased for use by the Confederate States of America and used in the Civil War. This is a curious firearm as it is a huge weapon that has two barrels. The top 6.5" barrel is chambered for .42 caliber percussion and is supplied by a 9-shot unfluted cylinder that revolves on a 5", .63 caliber, smoothbore barrel that doubles as the cylinder axis pin. These two barrels are held together by a front and a rear ring. The rear sight is a notch in the nose of the hammer, and there is an attached ramrod on the side of the top barrel. The weapon is marked "Lemat and Girards Patent, London". The finish is blued, with

checkered walnut grips. There were fewer than 3,000 manufactured, of which approximately one-half were purchased by the Confederate States of America. They were made between 1856 and 1865.

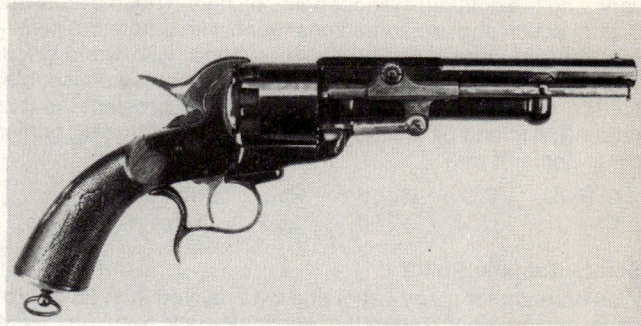

Courtesy Milwaukee Public Museum, Milwaukee, Wisconsin

Exc.	V.G.	Good	Fair	Poor
—	—	10000	5000	1750

Baby Le Mat

Similar in appearance (though a good deal smaller in size) to the standard model pistol. It is chambered for .32 caliber percussion and has a 4.25" top barrel and a .41 caliber smoothbore lower barrel. The cylinder is unfluted and holds 9 shots. The barrel is marked "Systeme Le Mat Bte s.g.d.g. Paris". It has British proofmarks and is blued, with checkered walnut grips. This is the scarcest model Le Mat, as there were only an estimated 100 manufactured and used by the Confederate States of America in the Civil War.

Exc.	V.G.	Good	Fair	Poor
—	—	20000	9500	3000

LEONARD, G.
Charlestown, Massachusetts

Pepperbox

A .31- caliber, four-barreled pepperbox with a concealed hammer. The barrels are 3.25" in length. There is a ring trigger used to cock the weapon, while a smaller trigger located outside the ring is used to fire the weapon. The barrels on this pistol do not revolve. There is a revolving striker inside the frame that turns to fire each chamber. The barrels must be removed for loading and capping purposes. The frame is iron and blued, with engraving. The rounded grips are walnut. The barrel is stamped "G. Leonard Jr. Charlestown." There were fewer than 200 manufactured in 1849 and 1850.

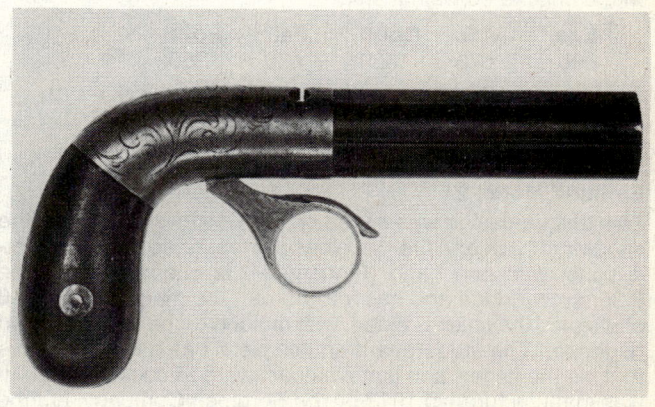

Exc.	V.G.	Good	Fair	Poor
—	—	1500	650	300

LE PAGE SA.
Liege, Belgium

Pinfire Revolver

Was in the business of revolver manufacture in the 1850s, producing a .40 caliber pinfire revolver that was similar to the Lefauchaux and other pinfires of the day. The barrel lengths vary, and the unfluted cylinder holds 6 shots. These pistols are double action and are sometimes found with ornate but somewhat crude engraving. The finish is blued, with wood grips. The quality of these weapons is fair. They were serviceable; but the ammunition created somewhat of a problem, as it is rather fragile and difficult to handle with the protruding primer pin to contend with.

Exc.	V.G.	Good	Fair	Poor
—	500	300	200	125

Semiautomatic Pistol

Was dormant for many years and was revived in 1925 to produce this blowback-operated semiautomatic with an open-topped slide and exposed barrel. It is chambered for the 7.65mm, 9mm Short, and the 9mm Browning Long cartridges. The barrel is 4" in length, and the grip is oversized, has finger grooves, and houses a 12-shot magazine. The pistol was not a commercial success, and there were not a great many manufactured.

Exc.	V.G.	Good	Fair	Poor
400	250	200	150	100

LIDDLE & KAEDING
San Francisco, California

Pocket Revolver

Manufactured by Forehand and Wadsworth and stamped with the above name. This company was a dealer in California and had nothing whatever to do with the production of this revolver. It is chambered for the .32 rimfire cartridge and has a 3.25" octagonal barrel and a 5-shot fluted cylinder. The frame is iron; and the finish is blued, with walnut grips. There were a few hundred manufactured between 1880 and 1886. The dealer's name is marked on the top strap.

Exc.	V.G.	Good	Fair	Poor
500	250	200	150	100

LIEGEOISE D ARMES
Liege, Belgium

Side-x-Side Boxlock Shotgun

This double-barreled gun is chambered for 12 and 20 gauge. The barrels are 28" or 30" in length, and the choke combinations are varied. It has a single trigger and automatic ejectors. The action is moderately engraved; and the finish is blued, with a checkered walnut stock.

Exc.	V.G.	Good	Fair	Poor
800	675	600	450	250

LIGNOSE
Suhl, Germany

Einhand Model 2A

This unique design was based on the Chelewski. It allows the shooter to cock and fire this blowback-operated semiautomatic pistol with one hand (Einhand). It is chambered for the 6.35mm cartridge and has a 2" barrel. The magazine holds 6 shots; and the finish is blued, with molded rubber grips marked "Lignose." The triggerguard on this pistol has a reverse curve that fits the finger, and it moves backward to cock the slide. It was manufactured in 1917 by the Bergman Company, but the rights were then sold to Lignose where it was produced after 1921.

Lignose "Einhand"

Model 2A

Model 3A

Exc.	V.G.	Good	Fair	Poor
300	250	200	150	100

Einhand Model 3A

Similar to the Model 2A, with a longer grip that houses a 9-shot magazine. All other specifications are the same as the Model 2A.

Courtesy Orvel Reichert

Exc.	V.G.	Good	Fair	Poor
275	225	200	150	100

Model 2

Similar to the Model 2A, with the extended grip and 9-shot capacity but no provision for one-hand cocking.

Exc.	V.G.	Good	Fair	Poor
200	175	150	100	75

LILLIPUT
SEE Menz

LINDE A.
Memphis, Tennessee

Pocket Pistol

This company manufactured a small, concealable firearm patterned after the Henry Deringer Philadelphia-type pistol. It is chambered for .41 caliber percussion and has a 2.5" barrel, German silver mountings, and a walnut stock. It was manufactured in the 1850s.

Exc.	V.G.	Good	Fair	Poor
—		1500	700	300

LINDSAY, JOHN P.
Naugatuck, Connecticut
Union Knife Company

The Union Knife Company manufactured the Lindsay 2-shot pistols for the inventor, John P. Lindsay. There are three separate and distinct models as follows.

2 Shot Belt Pistol

An oddity. It is a single-barreled, .41 caliber percussion pistol with a double chamber that contains two powder charges and projectiles that are simultaneously fired by two separate hammers. The hammers are released by a single trigger that allows them to fall in the proper sequence. The 5.5" octagonal barrel is contoured into a radical stepped-down shape, and there is a spur trigger. The frame is brass and has scroll engraving. The barrel is blued and is marked "Lindsay's Young America". There were estimated to be fewer than 100 manufactured between 1860 and 1862.

Exc.	V.G.	Good	Fair	Poor
—	2750	1500	1150	700

2 Shot Pocket Pistol

A smaller version of the Belt Pistol. It is chambered for the same caliber but has a 4" barrel. There were approximately 200 manufactured between 1860 and 1862.

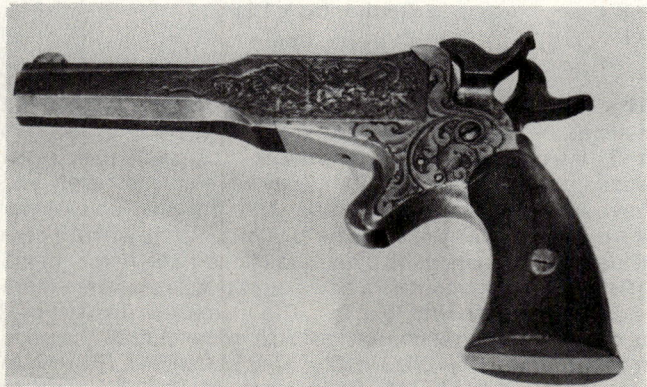

Courtesy W. P. Hallstein III and son Chip

Exc.	V.G.	Good	Fair	Poor
—	2000	1000	750	400

2 Shot Martial Pistol

A large version of the Lindsay design. It is chambered for .45 caliber smoothbore and has an 8.5" part-round, part-octagonal barrel. In other respects it is similar to the smaller models. The inventor tried to sell this pistol to the government but was unsuccessful. It was estimated that there were 100 manufactured between 1860 and 1862.

Exc.	V.G.	Good	Fair	Poor
—	2250	1500	1150	700

LINS, A. F.
Philadelphia, Pennsylvania

Pocket Pistol

Chambered for .41 caliber percussion and is a copy of the Henry Deringer pistol. It has a 3" barrel and a walnut stock and is marked "A. Fred. Lins. Philada." This pistol was manufactured between 1855 and 1860.

Exc.	V.G.	Good	Fair	Poor
—	—	1 650	750	350

Rifled Musket

A single shot, muzzleloading, percussion rifle chambered for .58 caliber. It has a 39" barrel and a full-length walnut stock held on by three barrel bands. There is an iron ramrod mounted under the barrel. The mountings are iron, and there is a bayonet lug combined with the front sight. The lock is marked "A. Fred. Lins/Philada." This is a rare weapon that was used by Union forces in the Civil War. There were approximately 200 manufactured in 1861 and 1862.

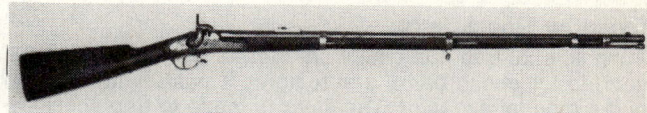

Courtesy Milwaukee Public Museum, Milwaukee, Wisconsin

Exc.	V.G.	Good	Fair	Poor
—	—	2500	1100	750

LITTLE ALL RIGHT FIREARMS CO.
Lawrence, Massachusetts

Little All Right Palm Pistol

An unusual-appearing pocket-sized palm pistol. It is chambered for the .22 Short rimfire cartridge and has a 1.75" barrel. The cylinder holds 5 shots. The trigger is mounted on the top of the barrel at the muzzle and is hinged and connected to a rod that cocks the concealed hammer, cycles the cylinder, and fires the weapon in double-action fashion. The grip was designed to be fit into the palm and not gripped as in a conventional pistol. The finish is nickel-plated, and the grips are pearl.

Exc.	V.G.	Good	Fair	Poor
—	—	1500	700	250

LJUNGMAN
Eskilstuna, Sweden
Carl Gustav

Ljungman AG-42

Designed by Eril Eklund and was placed in service with the Swedish military in 1942—less than one year after it was designed. The rifle is a direct gas-operated design with no piston or rod. It is chambered for the 6.5mm cartridge and has a 24.5" barrel with a 10-round detachable magazine. This rifle has military-type sights and a full-length stock and hand guard held on by barrel bands. There are provisions for a bayonet. There is also an Egyptian version of this rifle known as the "Hakim" and a Danish version that was manufactured by Madsen. Our AR-15 rifles use the same type of gas system.

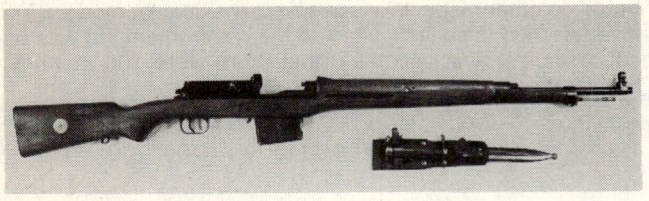

Exc.	V.G.	Good	Fair	Poor
300	250	200	150	100

Egyptian Hakim

Exc.	V.G.	Good	Fair	Poor
200	150	125	100	75

LJUTIC INDUSTRIES
Yakima, Washington

Bi-Matic Semiautomatic

A custom-built, gas-operated, semiautomatic shotgun that is known for its low level of felt recoil. It is chambered for 12 gauge and has 26" to 32" barrels choked for either skeet or trap. The stock specifications are to the customer's order. There are options available that affect the value, so we recommend an individual appraisal.

Exc.	V.G.	Good	Fair	Poor
2000	1800	1500	1200	900

Dynatrap Single Barrel

A single shot trap gun chambered for 12 gauge. It has a 33" vent rib full-choke barrel and features a push-button opener and a manual extractor. The stock is made to trap specifications. There are many options that affect the value; independent appraisal is recommended.

Exc.	V.G.	Good	Fair	Poor
2000	1800	1500	1200	900

Model X-73 Single Barrel

Similar features to the Dynatrap, with a high competition rib. Appraisal is recommended.

Exc.	V.G.	Good	Fair	Poor
2500	2250	1750	1400	1100

Mono Gun Single Barrel

Chambered for 12 gauge and has a 34" vent rib barrel. It is essentially a custom-order proposition that is available with a standard, as well as a release, trigger. There are many value-affecting options available. Appraisal is recommended.

NIB	Exc.	V.G.	Good	Fair	Poor
3800	3500	3000	2500	2000	1000

LTX Model

A deluxe version of the Mono Gun with a 33" medium-height vent rib and a high-grade walnut stock with fine hand checker-

ing. Options raise values drastically. Appraisal is recommended.

NIB	Exc.	V.G.	Good	Fair	Poor
5000	4500	4000	3500	2500	1200

Space Gun

A unique single barrel gun chambered for 12 gauge, with trap choking. It has a stock and forearm that reminds one of a crutch in appearance but which allows the shooter to have in-line control with little felt recoil. The barrel, forearm, and stock are all on one line. There is a recoil pad and a high ventilated rib.

NIB	Exc.	V.G.	Good	Fair	Poor
3750	3450	3050	2400	1750	850

Bi-Gun O/U

An Over/Under double chambered for 12 gauge. It has 30" or 32" vent ribbed barrels that are separated. The choking is to trap specifications, and the stock is deluxe hand-checkered walnut.

NIB	Exc.	V.G.	Good	Fair	Poor
10000	8500	7000	6000	5000	2500

Bi-Gun Combo

The Over/Under Bi-Gun supplied with a high-ribbed single barrel in addition to the separated Over/Under barrels. It is furnished in a fitted case, and the walnut is of exhibition grade.

NIB	Exc.	V.G.	Good	Fair	Poor
17000	15000	11000	9000	7500	4000

LLAMA
Manufactured by
Gabilondo Y Cia
Vitoria, Spain
Importers -Import Sports, Inc.

This is the same firm that was founded in 1904 and produced several inexpensive revolvers and pistols prior to 1931. In 1931 the company began to produce a semiautomatic pistol based on the Colt Model 1911. They were of high quality and have been sold around the world. After the Spanish civil war the company moved its facilities to Vitoria, Spain, where it continued to build handguns under the Llama trade name. In the 1980s the firm introduced a new line of pistols that were more modern in design and function. The Llama pistol is still produced today. For Llama pistols built prior to 1936 the slide marking reads: "GABILONDO Y CIA ELOEIBAR (ESPANA) CAL 9MM/.380IN LLAMA." For pistols built after 1936 the slide marking reads: "LLAMA GABILONDO Y CIA ELOEIBAR (ESPANA) CAL 9MM .380." Current production Llama pistols will show a slide marking with either "LLAMA CAL..." or "GABILONDO Y CIA VITORIA (ESPANA)" and the Llama logo.

LLAMA AUTOMATICS

Model I-A

This is a 7.65mm blowback design introduced in 1933. Magazine capacity is 7 rounds. The barrel was 3.62", overall length 6.3", and weight about 19 oz.

Exc.	V.G.	Good	Fair	Poor
180	150	125	100	75

Model II

Chambered for the 9mm Short introduced in the same year. Identical to the Model I. Discontinued in 1936.

Exc.	V.G.	Good	Fair	Poor
200	175	150	125	100

Model III

An improved version of the Model II. Introduced in 1936 and discontinued in 1954.

Exc.	V.G.	Good	Fair	Poor
190	170	150	125	100

Model III-A

Similar to the Model III, chambered for the .380 ACP, but with the addition of the Colt type grip safety. Introduced in 1955. Weight is about 23 oz.

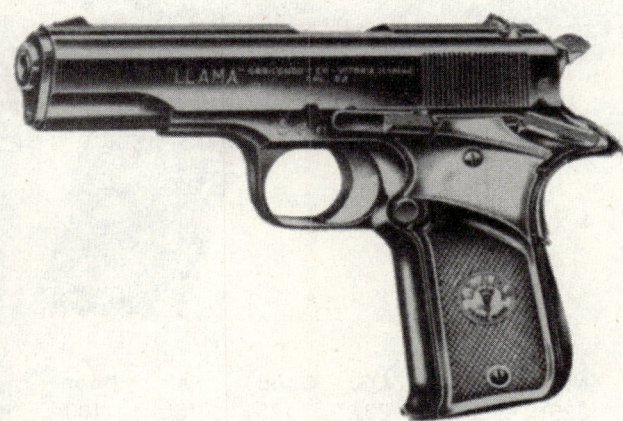

Exc.	V.G.	Good	Fair	Poor
200	175	150	125	100

Model IV

Chambered for the 9mm Largo or .380 ACP. Is not fitted with a grip safety. Introduced in 1931, it is the first of the Llama designs.

Exc.	V.G.	Good	Fair	Poor
180	150	125	100	75

Model V

The same as the Model IV but was intended for export to the United States and is stamped "made in Spain" on the slide.

Exc.	V.G.	Good	Fair	Poor
180	150	125	100	75

Model VI

Chambered for the 9mm Short and without a grip safety.

Exc.	V.G.	Good	Fair	Poor
180	150	125	100	75

Model VII

This model was introduced in 1932 and manufactured until 1954. It is chambered for the .38 Super Auto cartridge. It does not have a grip safety.

Exc.	V.G.	Good	Fair	Poor
225	200	150	125	100

Model VIII

This model was introduced in 1955 and is chambered for the .45 ACP, .38 Super, or 9mm Largo. It is fitted with a grip safety. Barrel length is 5", overall length is 8.5", and weight is about 38 oz. Magazine capacity is 7 rounds.

Exc.	V.G.	Good	Fair	Poor
250	200	150	125	100

Model IX

Chambered for the 7.65mm Para, 9mm Largo, or .45 ACP, this model has a locked breech with no grip safety. Built from 1936 to 1954.

Exc.	V.G.	Good	Fair	Poor
275	225	150	125	100

Model IX-A

This version of the Model IX is fitted with a grip safety. Current production models are chambered for the .45 ACP only. Weighs about 30 oz. with 5" barrel.

Exc.	V.G.	Good	Fair	Poor
275	225	150	125	100

Model IX-B

This version of the Model IX series is chambered in .45 ACP. It is fitted with an extended slide release, black plastic grips, and target type hammer. Offered in blue or satin chrome finish.

NIB	Exc.	V.G.	Good	Fair	Poor
325	275	225	150	125	100

Model IX-C

This is the current large frame version of the Model IX. It is chambered for the .45 ACP and is fitted with a 5.125" barrel. Blade front sight with adjustable rear sight. Magazine capacity is 10 rounds. Weight is approximately 41 oz.

NIB	Exc.	V.G.	Good	Fair	Poor
350	300	250	200	150	100

Model IX-D

This model is a compact frame version with a 4.25" barrel and chambered for the .45 ACP cartridge. Stocks are black rubber. Fixed front sight with adjustable rear. Introduced in 1995. Magazine capacity is 10 rounds. Weight is about 39 oz.

NIB	Exc.	V.G.	Good	Fair	Poor
350	300	—	—	—	—

Model X

First produced in 1935, this model is chambered for the 7.65mm cartridge. It has no grip safety.

Exc.	V.G.	Good	Fair	Poor
180	150	125	100	75

Model X-A

This version is similar to the Model X but with a grip safety. Produced from 1954 to the present.

Exc.	V.G.	Good	Fair	Poor
200	175	125	100	75

Model XI

Chambered for the 9mm Parabellum cartridge this model is different from previous models with a longer curved butt, ring hammer, and vertically grooved walnut grips. Magazine capacity is 9 rounds. Barrel length is 5". Discontinued in 1954.

Exc.	V.G.	Good	Fair	Poor
275	225	175	125	100

Model XI-B

(Currently imported by Century International Arms Co.) Similar to the Model XI but with a spur hammer and shorter barrel. Currently in production.

NIB	Exc.	V.G.	Good	Fair	Poor
200	175	150	125	100	75

Model XII-B

This model is chambered for the .40 S&W cartridge. It has a compact frame. Currently in production.

NIB	Exc.	V.G.	Good	Fair	Poor
300	275	225	175	125	100

Model XV

Chambered for the .22 long rifle this model is marked "Especial". It is fitted with a grip safety and comes in several finishes and with different grip styles. The barrel length is 3.6", the overall length is 6.5", and the weight is about 17 oz.

Exc.	V.G.	Good	Fair	Poor
225	175	150	125	100

Model XVI

This is a deluxe version of the Model XV with engraving, ventilated rib, and adjustable sights.

Exc.	V.G.	Good	Fair	Poor
300	225	175	150	100

Model XVII

This model is chambered for the .22 Short. It is small version of the Model XV with a finger-shaped grip.

Exc.	V.G.	Good	Fair	Poor
275	225	175	125	100

Model Max-I

Introduced in 1995 this 1911 design single action model features a choice of 9mm or .45 ACP chambers with a 4.25" barrel or a 5.125" barrel. Black rubber grips with blade front sight and adjustable rear sight. Weight is 34 oz. for compact model and 36 oz. for Government model.

NIB	Exc.	V.G.	Good	Fair	Poor
325	275	225	175	150	100

NOTE: For compact model add $25. For Duo-tone model add $25.

Model Minimax

This version is chambered for the 9mm, .40 S&W, or .45 ACP. Furnished with a 6-round magazine. Barrel length is 3.5". Checkered rubber grips. Introduced in 1996. Weight is about 35 oz. choice of blue, duo-tone, satin chrome, or stainless steel.

NIB	Exc.	V.G.	Good	Fair	Poor
325	275	—	—	—	—

NOTE: Add $40 for satin chrome finish. Add $60 for stainless. Add $20 for duo-tone finish.

Model Max-I with Compensator

Similar to the Max-I with the addition of a compensator. This model introduced in 1996. Weight is about 42 oz.

NIB	Exc.	V.G.	Good	Fair	Poor
450	400	—	—	—	—

Model 82

This is a large frame double action semiautomatic pistol. It features plastic grips, ambidextrous safety, 3-dot sights. The barrel length is 4.25" and overall length is 8". Weight is approximately 39 oz. Choice of blue or satin chrome finish.

NIB	Exc.	V.G.	Good	Fair	Poor
400	350	300	250	200	100

Mugica

Eibar gun dealer Jose Mugica sold Llama pistols under his private trade name. They are marked "mugica-ebir-spain" on the slide. These pistols do not seem to have any additional value over and above their respective Llama models. For the sake of clarification the Mugica models will be listed with their Llama counterparts:

Mugica Model 101	Llama Model X
Mugica Model 101-G	Llama Model X-A
Mugica Model 105	Llama Model III
Mugica Model 105-G	Llama Model III-A
Mugica Model 110	Llama Model VII
Mugica Model 110-G	Llama Model VIII
Mugica Model 120	Llama Model XI

Tauler

In an arrangement similar to Mugica a gun dealer in Madrid sold Llama pistols under his own brand name. Most of these pistols were sold in the early 1930s to police and other government officials. The most common Llama models were Models I to VIII. Slide inscriptions were in English and had the name Tauler in them. No additional value is attached to this private trademark.

REVOLVERS

Ruby Extra Models

These revolvers were produced in the 1950s and were copies of Smith & Wessons. They were marked "RUBY EXTRA" on the left side of the frame. At the top of the grips was a Ruby medallion. The barrel address is stamped: gabilondo y cia elgoeibar espana. The Ruby Extra Models represent the company's attempts to produce and sell a low cost revolver.

Model XII

This model is chambered for the .38 Long cartridge and is fitted with a 5" barrel and a squared butt.

Exc.	V.G.	Good	Fair	Poor
175	150	125	100	75

Model XIII

(Currently imported by Century International Arms Co.) Chambered for the .38 Special, this revolver has a round butt with 4" or 6" ventilated rib barrel. The 6" barreled gun was fitted with adjustable sights and target grips.

Exc.	V.G.	Good	Fair	Poor
175	150	125	100	75

Model XIV

Offered in .22 Long Rifle or .32 caliber, this model was available in a wide choice of barrel lengths and sights.

Exc.	V.G.	Good	Fair	Poor
175	150	125	100	75

Model XXII Olimpico

This model was designed as a .38 Special target revolver. It features an adjustable anatomic grip, adjustable rear sight, ventilated rib barrel, and a web that joins the barrel to the ejector shroud.

Exc.	V.G.	Good	Fair	Poor
250	200	150	125	100

Model XXVI

Chambered for the .22 Long Rifle, it features traditional grips and shrouded ejector rod.

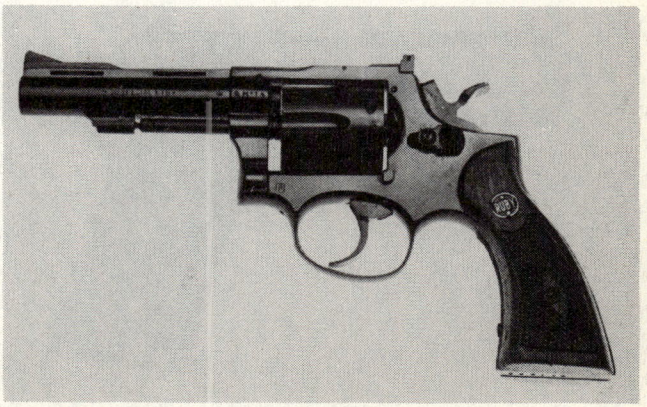

Exc.	V.G.	Good	Fair	Poor
175	150	125	100	75

Model XXVI I

Similar to the model above but fitted with a 2" barrel and chambered for the .32 Long cartridge.

Exc.	V.G.	Good	Fair	Poor
175	150	125	100	75

Model XXVIII

This model is chambered for the .22 l.r. and is fitted with a 6" barrel. It has a ramp front sight and adjustable rear sight.

Exc.	V.G.	Good	Fair	Poor
200	175	150	100	75

Model XXIX Olimpico

This is the Model XXI I chambered for the .22 Long Rifle.

Exc.	V.G.	Good	Fair	Poor
250	200	150	125	100

Model XXXII Olimpico

This model is a .32 target revolver with an unusual cylinder and frame design.

Exc.	V.G.	Good	Fair	Poor
275	225	150	125	100

Llama Omni

A .45 ACP and the 9mm caliber double action semiautomatic pistol with a 4.25" barrel and a 7-shot detachable magazine (.45 caliber) and a 13-shot magazine (9mm), a double sear bar and three distinct safeties. Steel with a blued finish. Discontinued in 1986.

Exc.	V.G.	Good	Fair	Poor
275	250	200	150	100

Llama Small Frame Semiautomatic

A .22, .32 ACP, and the .380 ACP caliber semiautomatic pistol with a 3-11/16" barrel and 7-shot detachable magazine. Either blued or satin chrome finished.

Satin Chrome Finish-Add $75.

NIB	Exc.	V.G.	Good	Fair	Poor
200	175	150	125	100	75

Llama Compact Frame Semiautomatic

A 9mm or the .45 ACP caliber semiautomatic pistol with a 4.25" barrel and either a 7- or 9-shot detachable magazine. Blued. Introduced in 1986.

NIB	Exc.	V.G.	Good	Fair	Poor
250	225	175	125	100	75

Llama Large Frame Semiautomatic

A 9mm, .38 Super or .45 ACP caliber semiautomatic pistol with a 5.25" barrel and either a 7- or 9-shot detachable magazine, depending on the caliber. Blued or satin chrome.

Satin Chrome Finish-Add $125.

NIB	Exc.	V.G.	Good	Fair	Poor
250	225	175	125	100	75

Llama Model 82

A 9mm Parabellum caliber double action semiautomatic pistol with a 4.25" barrel, a 3-dot sighting system, 15-shot detachable magazine, a loaded-chamber indicator, and an ambidextrous safety. Blued, with black plastic grips. Introduced in 1988.

NIB	Exc.	V.G.	Good	Fair	Poor
400	350	300	250	200	100

Llama Model 87 Competition

As above with a compensator special barrel bushing, a beveled magazine well, a squared and checkered triggerguard, with an adjustable trigger. Blued. Introduced in 1989.

NIB	Exc.	V.G.	Good	Fair	Poor
850	700	500	300	200	100

Llama Martial

A .22 or the .38 Special caliber double action semiautomatic pistol with a 6-round swingout cylinder, a 4" or 6" barrel and adjustable sights. Blued, with checkered hardwood grips. Manufactured between 1969 and 1976.

Exc.	V.G.	Good	Fair	Poor
225	175	150	110	85

Llama Comanche I

As above, in .22 caliber.

Exc.	V.G.	Good	Fair	Poor
250	200	175	125	100

Llama Comanche II

As above, in .38 Special caliber. Manufactured between 1977 and 1982.

Exc.	V.G.	Good	Fair	Poor
250	200	175	125	100

Llama Comanche III

As above, in .357 Magnum with a 4", 6", or 8.5" barrel and adjustable sights. Introduced in 1975.

Satin Chrome Finish-Add 20%.

NIB	Exc.	V.G.	Good	Fair	Poor
250	200	175	125	100	75

Llama Super Comanche

As above, in .44 Magnum with a 6" or 8.5" ventilated rib barrel and adjustable sights. Blued, with walnut grips.

NIB	Exc.	V.G.	Good	Fair	Poor
275	225	175	125	100	75

LOEWE, LUDWIG & CO.
Berlin, Germany
SEE Borchardt

During the 1870s and 1880s this firm manufactured a close copy of the Smith & Wesson Russian Model for the Russian government. They are marked "Ludwig Loewe Berlin" on the top of the barrel.

Loewe Smith & Wesson Russian Revolver

Exc.	V.G.	Good	Fair	Poor
250	225	200	125	75

LOHNER, C.
Philadelphia, Pennsylvania

Pocket Pistol

A .44 caliber single shot percussion pistol with a 5" barrel, German silver mounts and walnut grip. The barrel marked "C. Lohner." Manufactured during the 1850s.

Exc.	V.G.	Good	Fair	Poor
—	1200	650	450	250

LOMBARD, H. C. & CO.
Springfield, Massachusetts

Pocket Pistol

A .22 caliber single shot spur trigger pistol with a 3.5" octagonal barrel. The frame is silver plated, barrel blued and grips are of walnut. Barrel marked "H.C. Lombard & Co. Springfield, Mass."

Exc.	V.G.	Good	Fair	Poor
—	750	450	250	100

LONDON ARMOURY COMPANY
London

This firm was established in 1856, by Robert Adams. In addition to marketing revolvers based upon Adams' designs, the London Armoury Company were major retailers of other arms, particularly Enfield Pattern 53 Percussion Rifles. During the 1870's, the London Armoury distributed Colt pistols. During its business life, the London Armoury Company was located at the following addresses:

Henry Street	1857-1863
36 King William Street	1864-1868
54 King William Street	1868-1883
118 Queen Victoria Street	1884-1886
114 Queen Victoria Street	1887-1905
1 Lawrence Pounty Hill	1905-1910
31 Bury Street, St. James's	1910-1939
10 Ryder Street, St. James's	1940-1950

Although the firm continued in business after 1950, its operations were restricted to the trade of used arms.

LORCIN ENGINEERING CO., INC.
Mira Loma, California

Model L-25

A .25 caliber semiautomatic pistol with a 2.5" barrel and 7-shot magazine. Weight is 14.5 oz. Overall length is 4.8". Introduced in 1989.

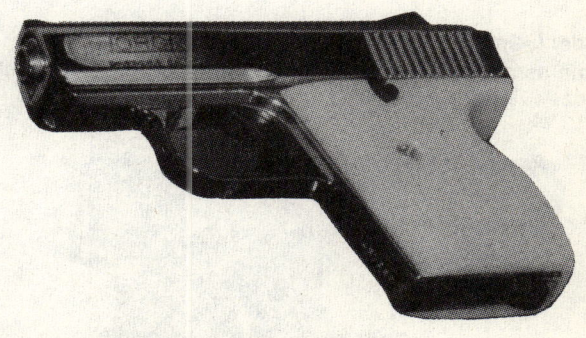

NIB	Exc.	V.G.	Good	Fair	Poor
75	60	50	40	30	20

Model LT-25

Same as above but with aluminum alloy frame. Introduced in 1989.

NIB	Exc.	V.G.	Good	Fair	Poor
100	75	60	50	40	30

Model L-22

Chambered for the .22 Long Rifle cartridge with a 2.5" barrel. Magazine capacity is 9 rounds. Introduced in 1989. Weight is 16 oz.

NIB	Exc.	V.G.	Good	Fair	Poor
90	65	55	45	35	25

Model L-380

This semiautomatic pistol is chambered for the .380ACP cartridge. Barrel length is 3.5" with a magazine capacity of 7 rounds. Introduced in 1992. Weight is about 23 oz.

NIB	Exc.	V.G.	Good	Fair	Poor
120	95	80	50	40	30

Model L-32

Same as above but chambered for the .32 ACP cartridge. Introduced in 1992

NIB	Exc.	V.G.	Good	Fair	Poor
100	80	70	50	40	30

Model LH-380

This semiautomatic pistil is chambered for the .380 ACP cartridge. The barrel length is 4.5" and the magazine capacity is 10 rounds. Offered in black, Satin or Bright Chrome finishes.

NIB	Exc.	V.G.	Good	Fair	Poor
150	125	100	75	60	50

Model L-9mm

Same as above but chambered for 9mm cartridge. Weight is 36 oz.

NIB	Exc.	V.G.	Good	Fair	Poor
150	125	100	75	60	50

Derringer

This over and under pistol is chambered for the .38 Special, .357 Magnum, and .45 ACP. Barrel length is 3.5". Overall length is 6.5".

NIB	Exc.	V.G.	Good	Fair	Poor
140	120	95	65	50	40

LOWELL ARMS CO.
SEE Rollin White Arms Co.

LOWER, J. P.
SEE Slotter & Co.

LUGERS
Various Manufacturers

Just before the turn of the twentieth century, Georg Luger redesigned the Borchardt semiautomatic pistol so that its mainspring was housed in the rear of the grip. The resulting pistol was to prove extremely successful and his name has become synonymous with the pistol despite the fact his name never appeared on it.

The following companies manufactured Luger pattern pistols at various times.

1. DWM - Deutsch Waffen und Munitions - Karlsruhe, Germany

2. The Royal Arsenal of Erfurt Germany

3. Simson & Company - Suhl, Germany

4. Mauser - Oberndorf, Germany

5. Vickers Ltd. - England

6. Waffenfabrik Bern - Bern, Switzerland

7. Heinrich Kreighoff - Suhl, Germany

Those interested in these pistols are advised to read the various books written about the marque which are listed in the bibliography at the close of this book.

DEUTSCH WAFFEN UND MUNITIONS

1899/1900 Swiss Test Model

4.75" barrel, 7.65mm caliber. The Swiss Cross in Sunburst is stamped over the chamber. The serial range runs to three digits. With less than 100 manufactured and only one known to exist, it is one of the rarest of the Lugers and the first true Luger that was produced. This model is far too rare to estimate an accurate value.

1900 Swiss Contract

4.75" barrel, 7.65mm caliber. The Swiss Cross in Sunburst is stamped over the chamber. The military serial number range is 2001-5000; the commercial range, 01-21250. There were approximately 2,000 commercial and 3,000 military models manufactured.

Wide Trigger-Add 20%.

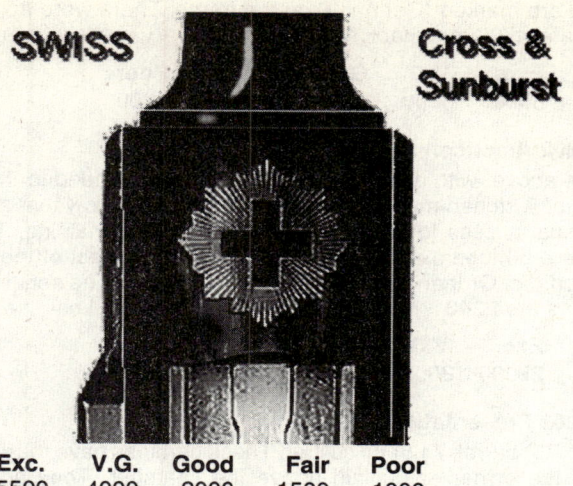

SWISS **Cross & Sunburst**

Exc.	V.G.	Good	Fair	Poor
5500	4000	2000	1500	1000

1900 Commercial

4.75" barrel, 7.65mm caliber. The area above the chamber is blank. The serial range is 01-19000, and there were approximately 5,500 manufactured for commercial sale in Germany or other countries. Some have "Germany" stamped on the frame. These pistols were imported into the U.S., and some were even stamped after blueing.

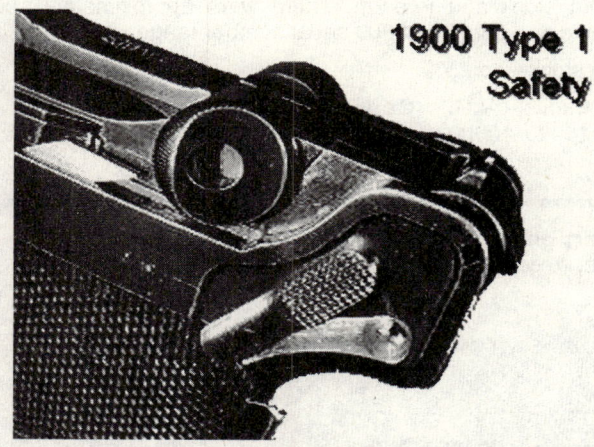

1900 Type 1 Safety

Courtesy Gale Morgan

Exc.	V.G.	Good	Fair	Poor
5000	3000	1500	1000	650

1900 American Eagle

4.75" barrel, 7.65mm caliber. The American Eagle crest is stamped over the chamber. The serial range is between 2000-200000, and there were approximately 11,000-12,000 commercial models marked "Germany" and 1,000 military test models without the commercial import stamp. The serial num-

bers of this military lot have been estimated at between 6100-7100.

Exc.	V.G.	Good	Fair	Poor
4500	3200	1500	850	600

1900 Bulgarian Contract

An old model, 1900 Type, with no stock lug. It has a 4.75" barrel and is chambered for the 7.65mm cartridge. The Bulgarian crest is stamped over the chamber, and the safety is marked in Bulgarian letters. The serial range is 20000-21000, with 1,000 manufactured. This is a military test model and is quite rare as most were rebarreled to 9mm during the time they were used. Even with the 9mm versions, approximately 10 are known to exist. It was the only variation to feature a marked safety before 1904.

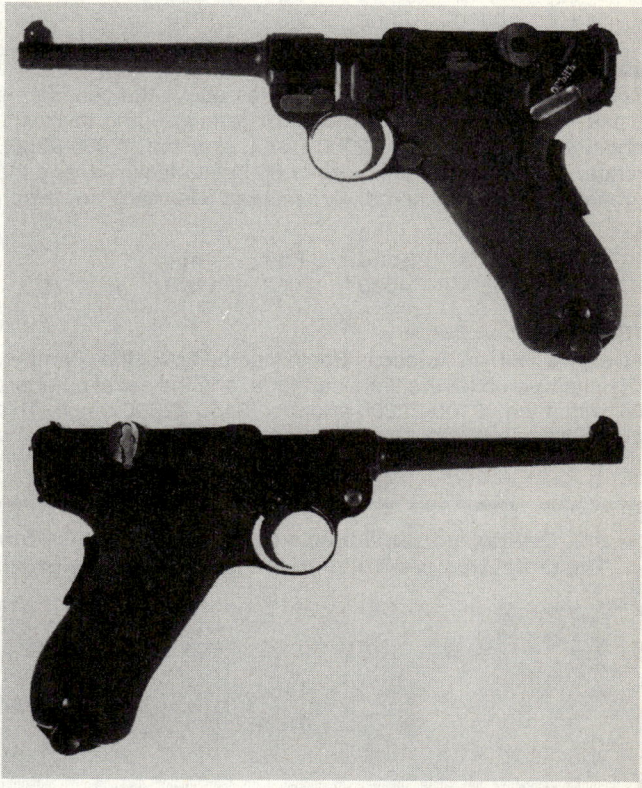

Courtesy J.C. Devine, Inc.

Exc.	V.G.	Good	Fair	Poor
12000	8000	4000	2500	1800

1900 Carbine

11.75" barrel, 7.65mm caliber. The carbines have a gracefully contoured and finely checkered walnut forearm and detachable shoulder stock. The rear sight on this extremely rare variation is a five-position sliding model located on the rear link. The area above the chamber is blank. The serial range is three digits or under, and this may have been a prototype as less than 100 were produced with only one known to exist today. This model is far too rare to estimate an accurate value.

1902 Prototype

6" barrel, 7.65mm caliber. The serial numbers are in the 10000 range with a capital B, and the chamber is blank. The 6" barrel is of a heavy contour, and there were less than 10 manufactured. The rarity of this variation precludes estimating value.

1902 Carbine

11.75" barrel, 7.65mm caliber. The sight has four positions and is silver-soldered to the barrel. A stock and forearm was sold with this weapon. The serial range was 21000-22100 and 23500-24900. There were approximately 2,500 manufactured for commercial sale in and out of Germany. Many were imported into the United States, but none here have been noted with the "Germany" import stamp.

With stock-Add 20%.

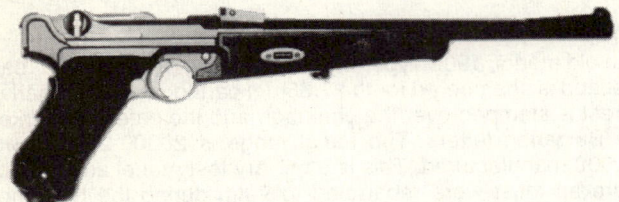

Courtesy Gale Morgan

Exc.	V.G.	Good	Fair	Poor
14000	10000	6000	3000	1500

1902 Commercial-"Fat Barrel"

Thick 4" barrel, 9mm caliber. The area above the chamber is blank. It is chambered for the 9mm cartridge, and the serial numbers fall within the 22300-22400 and the 22900-23500 range. There were approximately 600 manufactured, and the greater part of those noted were marked "Germany" for export purposes.

Exc.	V.G.	Good	Fair	Poor
8500	6500	4000	2000	1100

1902 American Eagle

As above, with an American Eagle stamped over the chamber. It is chambered for the 9mm cartridge, and the serial numbers fall within the 22100-22300 and the 22450-22900 range. This model was solely intended for export sales in the U.S.A., and all are marked "Germany" on the frame. There were approximately 700 manufactured.

Exc.	V.G.	Good	Fair	Poor
8000	6000	3500	2000	1200

1902 American Eagle Cartridge Counter

As above, with a "Powell Indicating Device" added to the left grip. A slotted magazine with a numbered window that allows visual access to the number of cartridges remaining. There were 50 lugers altered in this way at the request of the U.S. Board of Ordnance, for U.S. Army evaluation. The serial numbers are 22401-22450. Be especially wary of fakes!

Exc.	V.G.	Good	Fair	Poor
28000	18000	11000	5000	3500

1902 Presentation Carbine

11.75" barrel, 7.65mm caliber. These carbines have the initials of the owner gold-inlaid above the chamber. They are furnished with a checkered walnut stock and forearm. Only four have been noted in the 9000C serial number range. They have the initials "GL" for Georg Luger on the back of the rear toggle. They are too rare to estimate value.

1902/06 Carbine (Transitional)

11.75" barrel, 7.65mm caliber. Assembled from Model 1902 parts with a new toggle assembly. They have the four-position sliding sight, silver-soldered to the barrel, and a checkered walnut stock and forearm. There were approximately 100 manufactured in the 23600 serial number range.

With stock-Add 25%.

Exc.	V.G.	Good	Fair	Poor
15000	10000	8000	5000	3000

J.C. Devine, Inc. auctioned a cased Luger 1902 Carbine in good to very good condition for $9,775 on August 10, 1997. The pistol was presented to the governor of the province of La Plata, Argentina in 1907.

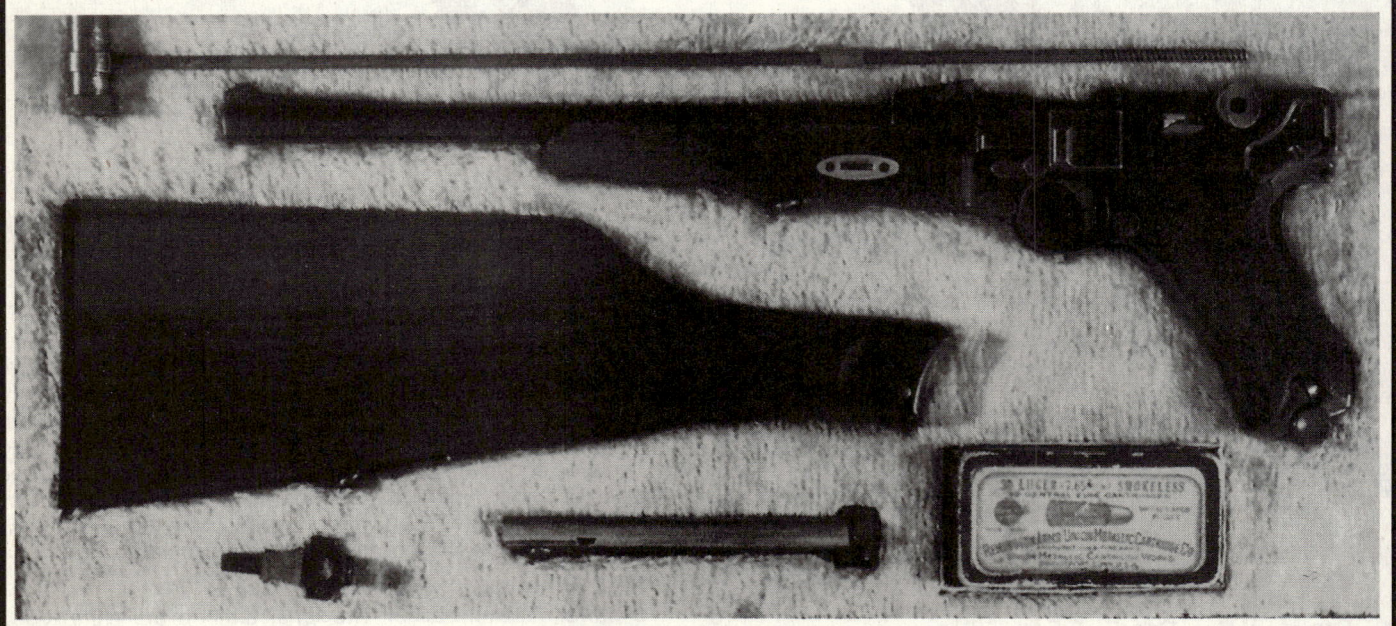

Courtesy J.C. Devine, Inc.

1903 Commercial

4" barrel, 7.65mm caliber. The chamber area is blank. There were approximately 50 manufactured for export to France, serial numbered 25000-25050. The extractor on this model is marked "CHARGE".

Exc.	V.G.	Good	Fair	Poor
12000	9000	5000	3200	2500

1904 Navy

6" thick barrel, 9mm caliber. The chamber area is blank, and the extractor is marked "Celeden". The safety is marked "Gesichert". There were approximately 1,500 manufactured in the one- to four-digit serial range, for military sales to the German Navy.

Exc.	V.G.	Good	Fair	Poor
40000	30000	16000	6000	4500

1906 Navy Commercial

This is a new model, 1906 Type, with stock lug. It has a 6" barrel and is chambered for the 9mm cartridge. The chamber is blank, and the extractor is marked "Geladin." The safety is marked "Gesichert," and some have the "Germany" export stamp. The proper magazine has a wood bottom with concentric circles on the sides. There were approximately 2,500 manufactured in the 25050-65000 serial range. They were produced for commercial sales in and outside of Germany.

Exc.	V.G.	Good	Fair	Poor
5500	4000	2700	1500	1000

1906 Commercial

4" barrel, 9mm caliber. The extractor is marked "Geleden," and the area of the frame under the safety in its lower position is polished and not blued. The chamber is blank. There were approximately 4,000 manufactured for commercial sales. Some have the "Germany" export stamp. The serial range is 26500-68000.

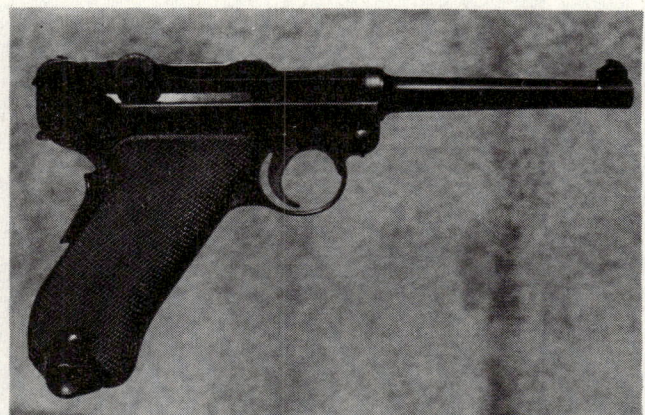

Courtesy Orvel Reichert

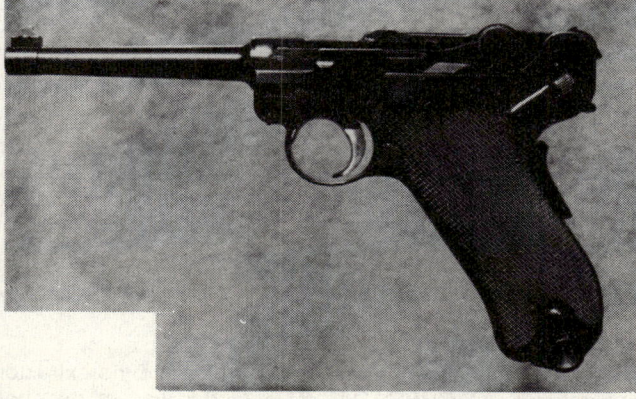

Courtesy Orvel Reichert

Exc.	V.G.	Good	Fair	Poor
3500	2500	1000	800	600

1906 Commercial (Marked Safety)

As above, with the area of the frame under the safety in its lowest position is marked "Gesichert" and the barrel is 4.75" in length and chambered for the 7.65mm cartridge. There were approximately 750 manufactured, serial numbered 25050-26800.

Exc.	V.G.	Good	Fair	Poor
4000	3000	1800	800	600

1906 American Eagle

4" barrel, 9mm caliber. The chamber area has the American Eagle stamped upon it. The extractor is marked "Loaded", and the frame under the safety at its lowest point is polished and not blued. This model has no stock lug. There were approximately 3,000 manufactured for commercial sale in the U.S.A. in the serial range 26500-69000.

Exc.	V.G.	Good	Fair	Poor
3800	2500	1200	700	500

1906 American Eagle (Marked Safety)

4.75" barrel, 7.65mm caliber. The frame under the safety at its lowest point is marked "Gesichert." There were approximately 750 manufactured in the 25100-26500 serial number range.

"Marked Safety"

Courtesy Gale Morgan

Exc.	V.G.	Good	Fair	Poor
4200	3000	1500	1200	800

1906 American Eagle 4.75" Barrel

As the Model 1906 with a marked safety. Approximately 8,000 manufactured in the 26500-69000 serial range.

Exc.	V.G.	Good	Fair	Poor
3500	2200	1100	700	450

1906 U.S. Army Test Luger .45 Caliber

5" barrel, .45 ACP caliber. Sent to the United States for testing in 1907. The chamber is blank; the extractor is marked "Loaded", and the frame is polished under the safety lever. The trigger on this model has an odd hook at the bottom. Reportedly only two of these pistols were manufactured. Serial No. 1 has never been located, and it was rumored to have been destroyed after the tests were concluded. Serial No. 2 is in a collection in the U.S.A.

In any condition, Serial No. 1 would be priceless.

1906 Swiss Commercial

4.75" barrel, 7.65mm caliber. The Swiss Cross in Sunburst appears over the chamber. The extractor is marked "Geleden," and the frame under the safety is polished. There is no stock lug, and the proofmarks are commercial. There were approximately 1,000 manufactured in the 35000-55000 serial number range.

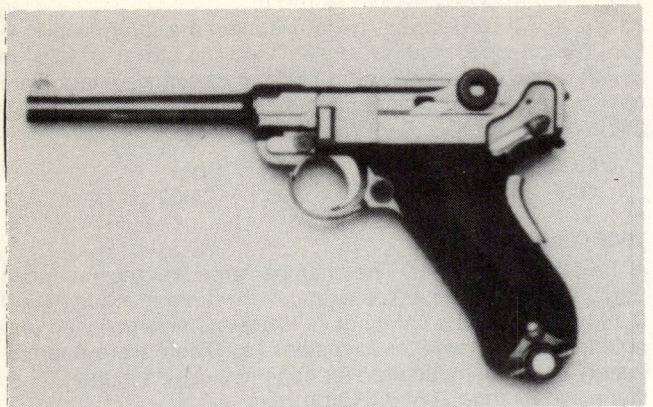

Courtesy Butterfield & Butterfield, San Francisco, California

Exc.	V.G.	Good	Fair	Poor
4000	3500	2500	1400	800

1906 Commercial

4.75" barrel, 7.65mm caliber. It has no stock lug. The chamber area is blank, and the extractor is marked "Geleden". The frame under the safety is polished and unmarked. There were approximately 5,000 manufactured for commercial sales both in and outside of Germany. They will be found in the 26500-69000 serial number range.

Exc.	V.G.	Good	Fair	Poor
3500	3000	1200	850	550

1906 Swiss Military

As the Swiss Commercial, with the Geneva Cross appearing on all major parts.

Exc.	V.G.	Good	Fair	Poor
3700	3100	2000	900	700

1906 Swiss Military Cross in Shield

As above, with a shield replacing the sunburst on the chamber marking. There were 10,215 of both models combined. They are in the 5000-15215 serial number range.

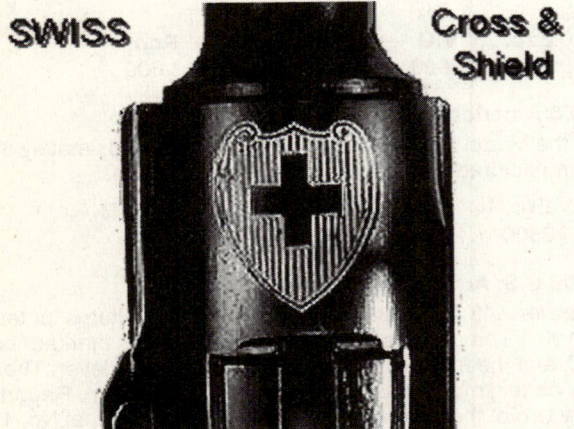

Courtesy Gale Morgan

Exc.	V.G.	Good	Fair	Poor
3800	3200	1800	1000	700

1906 Dutch Contract

4" barrel, 9mm caliber. It has no stock lug, and the chamber is blank. The extractor is marked "Geleden" on both sides, and the safety is marked "RUST" with a curved upward pointing arrow. This pistol was manufactured for military sales to the Netherlands, and a date will be found on the barrel of most examples encountered. The Dutch refinished their pistols on a

regular basis and marked the date on the barrels. There were approximately 4,000 manufactured, serial numbered between 1 and 4000.

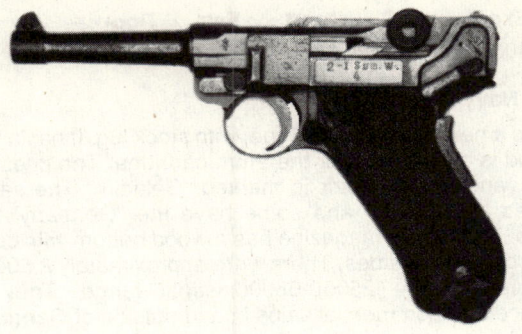

Courtesy Gale Morgan

Exc.	V.G.	Good	Fair	Poor
3500	2500	1500	800	600

1906 Royal Portuguese Navy

4" barrel, 9mm caliber, and has no stock lug. The Royal Portuguese Naval crest, an anchor under a crown, is stamped above the chamber. The extractor is marked "CARREGADA" on the left side. The frame under the safety is polished. There were approximately 1,000 manufactured with one- to four-digit serial numbers.

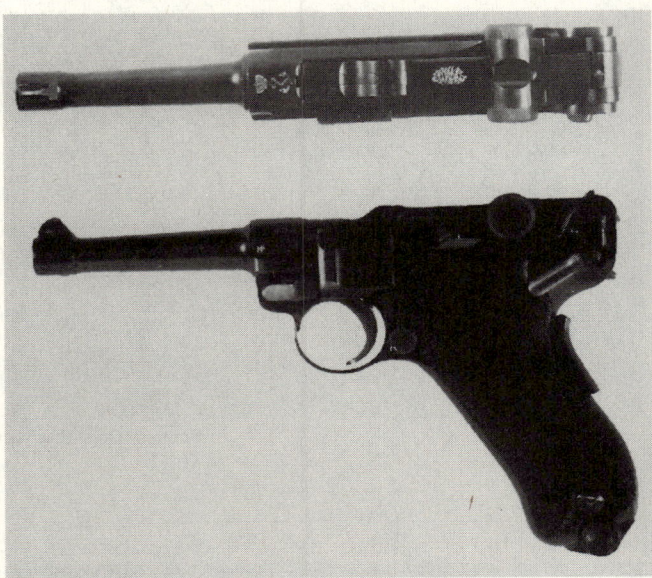

Exc.	V.G.	Good	Fair	Poor
12000	9000	6500	4000	2500

1906 Royal Portuguese Army(M2)

4.75" barrel, 7.65mm caliber. It has no stock lug. The chamber area has the Royal Portuguese crest stamped upon it. The extractor is marked "CARREGADA". There were approximately 5,000 manufactured, with one- to four-digit serial numbers.

Exc.	V.G.	Good	Fair	Poor
2500	2000	1200	600	500

1906 Republic of Portugal Navy

4" barrel, 9mm caliber. It has no stock lug, and the extractor was marked "CARREGADA". This model was made after 1910, when Portugal had become a republic. The anchor on the chamber is under the letters "R.P." There were approximately 1,000 manufactured, with one- to four-digit serial numbers.

Exc.	V.G.	Good	Fair	Poor
10000	8000	5500	3500	2500

1906 Brazilian Contract

4.75" barrel, 7.65mm caliber. It has no stock lug, and chamber area is blank. The extractor is marked "CARREGADA", and the frame under the safety is polished. There were approximately 5,000 manufactured for military sales to Brazil.

Exc.	V.G.	Good	Fair	Poor
2500	2000	1100	750	450

1906 Bulgarian Contract

4.75" barrel, 7.65mm caliber. It has no stock lug, and the extractor and safety are marked in cyrillic letters. The Bulgarian crest is stamped above the chamber. Nearly all of the examples located have the barrels replaced with 4" 9mm units. This was done after the later 1908 model was adopted. Some were refurbished during the Nazi era, and these pistols bear Waffenamts and usually mismatched parts. There were approximately 1,500 manufactured, with serial numbers of one- to four-digits.

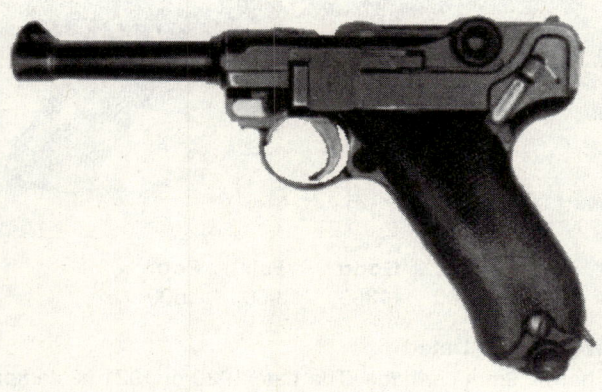

Exc.	V.G.	Good	Fair	Poor
9500	7000	5000	3500	1500

1906 Russian Contract

4" barrel, 9mm caliber. It has no stock lug, and the extractor and safety are marked with cyrillic letters. Crossed Nagant rifles are stamped over the chamber. There were approximately 1,000 manufactured, with one- to four-digit serial numbers; but few survive. This is an extremely rare variation, and caution should be exercised if purchase is contemplated.

Exc.	V.G.	Good	Fair	Poor
10000	8000	6500	4000	2500

1906 Navy 1st Issue

6" barrel, 9mm caliber. The safety and extractor are both marked in German, and the chamber area is blank. There is a stock lug, and the unique two-position sliding Navy sight is mounted on the rear toggle link. There were approximately 12,000 manufactured for the German Navy, with serial numbers of one- to five-digits. The wooden magazine bottom features concentric rings.

NOTE: Many of these pistols had their safety changed so that they were "safe" in the lower position. Known as "1st issue altered." Value at approximately 20% less.

Navy Luger 2-Position Rear Sight

Courtesy Gale Morgan

Exc.	V.G.	Good	Fair	Poor
4200	3500	2000	1300	950

1906 Navy 2nd Issue

As above, but manufactured to be safe in the lower postion. Approximately 11,000 2nd Issue Navies manufactured, with one- to five-digit serial numbers—some with an "a" suffix. They were produced for sale to the German Navy.

Crown-M Navy Proofs

Courtesy Gale Morgan

Exc.	V.G.	Good	Fair	Poor
3600	2700	1500	950	700

1908 Commercial

4" barrel, 9mm caliber. It has no stock lug, and the chamber area is blank. The extractor and the safety are both marked in German, and many examples are marked with the "Germany" export stamp. There were approximately 9,000 manufactured in the 39000-71500 serial number range.

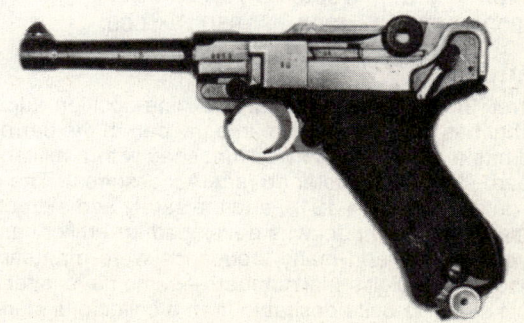

Exc.	V.G.	Good	Fair	Poor
1800	1400	750	600	450

1908 Navy Commercial

6" barrel, 9mm caliber. It has a stock lug, no grip safety, and the characteristic two-position sliding sight mounted on the rear toggle link. The chamber area is blank, and the safety and extractor are both marked. The "Germany" export stamp appears on some examples. There were approximately 1,500 manufactured, in the 44000-50000 serial number range.

Exc.	V.G.	Good	Fair	Poor
4500	3500	2500	1750	1250

1908 Navy Military

As above, with the "Crown M" military proof. They may or may not have the concentric rings on the magazine bottom. There were approximately 40,000 manufactured, with one- to five-digit serial numbers with an "a" or "b" suffix. These Lugers are quite scarce as many were destroyed during and after WWI.

Exc.	V.G.	Good	Fair	Poor
3600	2700	1500	1100	800

1914 Navy

Similar to the above, but stamped with the dates from 1914-1918 above the chamber. Most noted are dated 1916-1918. There were approximately 30,000 manufactured, with one- to five-digit serial numbers with an "a" or "b" suffix. They are scarce as many were destroyed as a result of WWI.

Exc.	V.G.	Good	Fair	Poor
3500	2500	1500	950	700

1908 Military 1st Issue

4" barrel, 9mm caliber. It has no stock lug, and the extractor and safety are both marked in German. The chamber is blank. There were approximately 20,000 manufactured, with one- to five-digit serial numbers—some with an "a" suffix.

Exc.	V.G.	Good	Fair	Poor
1300	850	600	500	350

1908 Military Dated Chamber(1910-1913)

As above, with the date of manufacture stamped on the chamber.

Exc.	V.G.	Good	Fair	Poor
1200	900	600	500	350

1914 Military

As above, with a stock lug.

Exc.	V.G.	Good	Fair	Poor
1000	800	650	500	350

1913 Commercial

As above, with a grip safety. Approximately 1,000 manufactured, with serial numbers 71000-72000; but few have been noted, and it is considered to be quite rare.

Exc.	V.G.	Good	Fair	Poor
2800	1700	1300	850	600

1914 Artillery

8" barrel, 9mm caliber. It features a nine-position adjustable sight that has a base that is an integral part of the barrel. This model has a stock lug and was furnished with a military-style flat board stock and holster rig (see Accessories). The chamber is dated from 1914-1918, and the safety and extractor are both marked. This model was developed for artillery and machine gun crews; and many thousands were manufactured, with one- to five-digit serial numbers—some have letter suffixes. This model is quite desirable from a collector's standpoint and is rarer than its production figures would indicate. After the war many were destroyed as the allies deemed them more insidious than other models, for some reason.

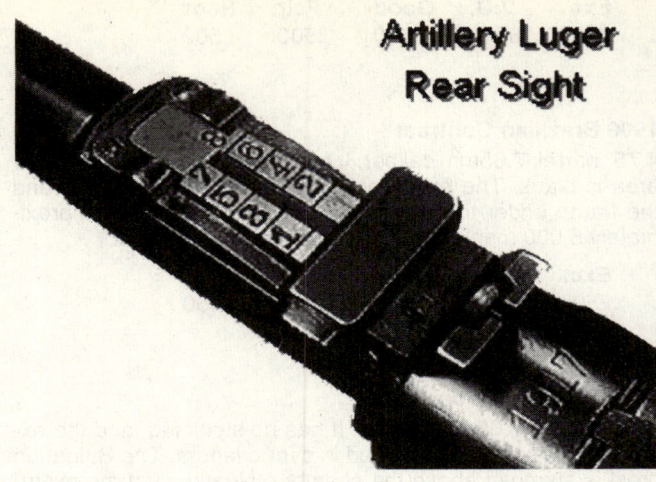

Artillery Luger Rear Sight

Courtesy Gale Morgan

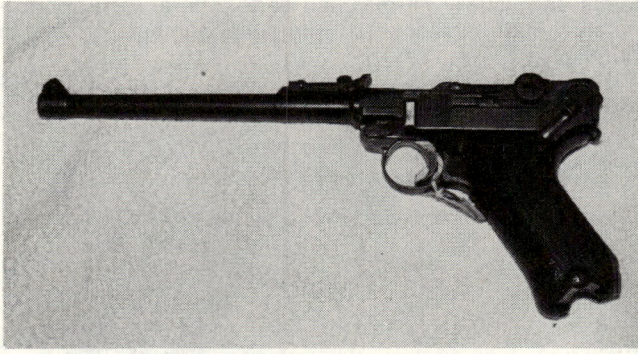

Exc.	V.G.	Good	Fair	Poor
2100	1600	1300	900	600

DWM Double Dated

4" barrel, 9mm cartridge. The date 1920 or 1921 is stamped over the original chamber date of 1910-1918, creating the double-date nomenclature. These are arsenal-reworked WWI military pistols and were then issued to the German army and/or police units within the provisions of the Treaty of Versailles. Many thousands of these lugers were produced.

Exc.	V.G.	Good	Fair	Poor
900	700	550	400	300

1920 Police Rework

As above, except that the original manufacture date was removed before the rework date was stamped. There were many thousands of these produced.

Exc.	V.G.	Good	Fair	Poor
800	650	500	350	300

1920 Commercial

Similar to the above, with 3.5" to 6" barrels in 7.65mm or 9mm and marked "Germany" or "Made in Germany" for export. Others are unmarked and were produced for commercial sale inside Germany. Some of these pistols are military reworks with the markings and the proofmarks removed; others are newly manufactured. The extractors and safety are both marked, and the chamber is blank. The serial number range is one to five digits, and letter suffixes often appear

NOTE: Add 15% for 9mm.

Exc.	V.G.	Good	Fair	Poor
850	650	500	450	350

1920 Commercial Navy

6" barrel, 9mm caliber. Some have a stock lug; others have been noted without. The chamber area is generally blank, but some have been found with 1914-1918 dates stamped upon them. These were reworked by DWM from Military Navy Lugers after WWI for commercial sales. They are marked "Germany" or "Made in Germany" and were sold by Stoeger Arms, among others. The extractor and safety are both marked, and the unique Navy sight is on the rear toggle link. No one knows exactly how many were produced, but they are quite scarce.

Exc.	V.G.	Good	Fair	Poor
3500	2750	1600	1100	850

1920 Commercial Artillery

8" barrel, 9mm caliber. Erfurt-manufactured pistols, as well as DWM-manufactured pistols, were reworked in this manner. The export markings "Germany" or "Made in Germany" are found on most examples. The number produced is not known, but examples are quite scarce.

Exc.	V.G.	Good	Fair	Poor
2500	2000	1100	700	450

1920 Long Barrel Commercial

10" to 24" barrels, 7.65mm or 9mm caliber. The extractor and safety are both marked, and an artillery model rear sight is used. This model was often built to a customer's specifications. They are rare, and the number manufactured is not known.

Exc.	V.G.	Good	Fair	Poor
2750	2000	1500	1000	800

1920 Carbine

11.75" barrel, 7.65mm caliber. The chamber is blank, and the extractor is marked either "Geleden" or "Loaded". The safety is not-marked. The carbine has a checkered walnut forearm and stock, and most have the "Germany" or "Made in Germany" export stamp. There were few of these carbines manufactured for commercial sales in and outside of Germany, and they are highly prized by collectors.

With stock-Add 25%.

Exc.	V.G.	Good	Fair	Poor
7500	6000	5000	2500	1500

1920 Navy Carbine

Assembled from surplus Navy parts with the distinctive two position, sliding navy sight on the rear toggle link. Most are marked with the export stamp and have the naval military proofmarks still in evidence. The safety and extractor are marked, and rarely one is found chambered for the 9mm cartridge. Few were manufactured.

Exc.	V.G.	Good	Fair	Poor
6250	5000	3000	1800	900

1920 Swiss Commercial

3.5"-6" barrels, 7.65mm or 9mm caliber. The Swiss Cross in Sunburst is stamped over the chamber, and the extractor is marked "Geleden." The frame under the safety is polished. There were a few thousand produced, with serial numbers in the one- to five-digit range, sometimes with a letter suffix.

Exc.	V.G.	Good	Fair	Poor
3700	3000	1600	1000	800

1923 Stoeger Commercial

3.5" to 24" barrels, 7.65mm or 9mm caliber. There is a stock lug. The chamber area is either blank or has the American Eagle stamped on it. The export stamp and "A.F.Stoeger Inc. New York" is found on the right side of the receiver. The extractor and safety are marked in German or English. This was the model that Stoeger registered with the U.S. Patent office to secure the Luger name, and some examples will be so marked. There were less than 1,000 manufactured, with one- to five-digit serial numbers without a letter suffix. Individual appraisal must be secured on barrel lengths above 6". Be wary as fakes have been noted. The values given here are for the shorter-barreled models.

Barrel lengths over 8"-Add 25%.

Exc.	V.G.	Good	Fair	Poor
4000	3000	1800	1000	700

Abercrombie & Fitch Commercial 100

Swiss Lugers were made for commercial sale in the United States by "Abercrombie & Fitch Co. New York. Made in Switzerland."—in either one or two lines—is stamped on the top of the barrel. The barrel is 4.75" in length, and there were 49 chambered for 9mm and 51 chambered for the 7.65mm cartridge. This pistol has a grip safety and no stock lug. The Swiss Cross in Sunburst is stamped over the chamber. The extractor is marked, but the safety area is polished. The serial range is four digits—some with a letter suffix. This is a rare and desirable Luger. Be careful of fakes on models of this type and rarity.

Exc.	V.G.	Good	Fair	Poor
8000	6500	4500	3000	2000

1923 Commercial

7-1/2" barrel, 7.65mm caliber. It has a stock lug, and the chamber area is blank. The extractor and safety are both marked in German. These pistols were manufactured for commercial sales in and outside of Germany. There were approximately 18,000 produced, with serial numbers in the 73500-96000 range.

Exc.	V.G.	Good	Fair	Poor
1200	1000	800	600	450

1923 Commercial Safe & Loaded

As above, except that the extractor and safety are marked in English "Safe" & "Loaded". There were approximately 7,000 manufactured in the 73500-96000 serial number range.

"Safe" Marked

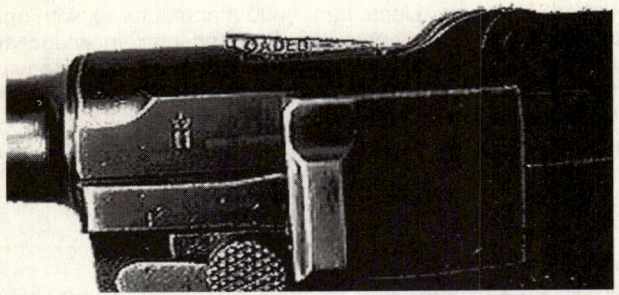

Courtesy Gale Morgan

Exc.	V.G.	Good	Fair	Poor
2000	1500	1000	800	500

1923 Dutch Commercial & Military
4" barrel, 9mm caliber. It has a stock lug, and the chamber area is blank. The extractor is marked in German, and the safety is marked "RUST" with a downward pointing arrow. This model was sold commercially and to the military in the Netherlands. There were approximately 1,000 manufactured in the one- to three-digit serial range, with no letter suffix.

Exc.	V.G.	Good	Fair	Poor
3000	2000	1000	850	550

Royal Dutch Air Force
4" barrel, 9mm caliber. Marked with the Mauser Oberndorf proofmark and serial numbered in the 10000 to 14000 range. The safety marked "RUST".

Exc.	V.G.	Good	Fair	Poor
3000	2000	1000	800	550

VICKERS LTD.
1906 Vickers Dutch
4" barrel, 9mm caliber. There is no stock lug, and it uses a grip safety. The chamber is blank, and the extractor is marked "Geleden." "Vickers Ltd." is stamped on the front toggle link. The safety is marked "RUST" with an upward pointing arrow. Examples have been found with an additional date as late as 1933 stamped on the barrel. These dates indicate arsenal refinishing and in no way detract from the value of this variation. Arsenal reworks are matte-finished, and the originals are a higher-polished rust blue. There were approximately 10,000 manufactured in the 1-10100 serial-number range.

Exc.	V.G.	Good	Fair	Poor
3500	2800	1800	1200	750

ERFURT ROYAL ARSENAL
1908 Erfurt
4" barrel, 9mm caliber. It has no stock lug; and the year of manufacture, from 1910-1913, is stamped above the chamber. The extractor and safety are both marked in German, and "ERFURT" under a crown is stamped on the front toggle link. There were many thousands produced as Germany was involved in WWI. They are found in the one- to five-digit serial range, sometimes with a letter suffix.

Exc.	V.G.	Good	Fair	Poor
1000	850	600	400	350

1914 Erfurt Military
4" barrel, 9mm caliber. It has a stock lug and the date of manufacture over the chamber, 1914-1918. The extractor and safety are both marked in German, and the front link is marked "ERFURT" under a crown. The finish on this model is rough; and as the war progressed in 1917 and 1918, the finish got worse. There were many thousands produced with one- to five-digit serial numbers, some with letter suffixes.

Exc.	V.G.	Good	Fair	Poor
1000	800	600	400	350

1914 Erfurt Artillery
8" barrel, 9mm caliber. It has a stock lug and was issued with a flat board-type stock and other accessories which will be covered in the section of this book dealing with same. The sight is a nine-position adjustable model soldered to the barrel. The chamber is dated 1914-1918, and the extractor and safety are both marked in German. "ERFURT" under a crown is stamped on the front toggle link. There were a great many manufactured with one- to five-digit serial numbers, some with a letter suffix. This model is similar to the DWM Artillery except that the finish is not as fine.

Exc.	V.G.	Good	Fair	Poor
2500	1600	1100	800	600

Double Date Erfurt
4" barrel, 9mm caliber. The area above the chamber has two dates: the original 1910-1918, and the date of rework, 1920 or 1921. The extractor and safety are both marked in German, and this model can be found with or without a stock lug. "ERFURT" under a crown is stamped on the front toggle link. Police or military unit markings are found on the front of the grip straps more often than not. There were thousands of these produced by DWM as well as Erfurt.

Exc.	V.G.	Good	Fair	Poor
750	600	500	400	350

WAFFENFABRIK BERN
See separate section on Bern.

SIMSON & CO. SUHL, GERMANY
Simson & Co. Rework
4" barrels, 7.65 or 9mm caliber. The chamber is blank, but some examples are dated 1917 or 1918. The forward toggle link is stamped "SIMSON & CO. Suhl". The extractor and safety are marked in German. Most examples have stock lugs; some have been noted without them. The only difference between military models and commercial models is the proofmarks.

Exc.	V.G.	Good	Fair	Poor
1500	1200	900	600	500

Simson Grip Safety Rework
4" barrel, 9mm caliber and a grip safety was added. There is a stock lug. The chamber area is blank; the extractor is marked but the safety is not. There were only a few of these commercial reworks manufactured, and caution should be taken to avoid fakes.

Exc.	V.G.	Good	Fair	Poor
3000	2200	1500	850	550

Simson Dated Military
4" barrel, 9mm caliber. There is a stock lug, and the year of manufacture from 1925-1928 is stamped above the chamber. The extractor and the safety are both marked in German. The checkered walnut grips of Simson-made Lugers are noticeably thicker than others. This is an extremely rare variation. Approximately 2,000 were manufactured with one- to three-digit serial numbers, and few seem to have survived.

Exc.	V.G.	Good	Fair	Poor
3200	2200	1800	900	650

Simson S Code
4" barrel, 9mm caliber. The forward toggle link is stamped with a Gothic S. It has a stock lug, and the area above the chamber

is blank. The extractor and the safety are both marked. The grips are also thicker. There were approximately 12,000 manufactured with one- to five-digit serial numbers—some with the letter "a" suffix. This pistol is quite rare on today's market.

Exc.	V.G.	Good	Fair	Poor
4000	3000	1500	1000	750

EARLY NAZI ERA REWORKS MAUSER

Produced between 1930 and 1933, and normally marked with Waffenamt markings.

Deaths Head Rework

4" barrel, 9mm caliber. It has a stock lug; and a skull and crossbones are stamped, in addition to the date of manufacture, on the chamber area. This date was from 1914-1918. The extractor and safety are both marked. The Waffenamt proof is present. It is thought that this variation was produced for the 1930-1933 era "SS" division of the Nazi Party. Mixed serial numbers are encountered on this model and do not lower the value. This is a rare luger on today's market, and caution should be exercised if purchase is contemplated.

Exc.	V.G.	Good	Fair	Poor
2500	1500	950	600	450

Kadetten Institute Rework

4" barrel, 9mm caliber. It has a stock lug, and the chamber area is stamped "K.I." above the date 1933. This stood for Cadets Institute, an early "SA" and "SS" officers' training school. The extractor and safety are both marked, and the Waffenamt is present. There were only a few hundred reworked, and the variation is quite scarce. Be wary of fakes.

Exc.	V.G.	Good	Fair	Poor
3000	2500	1100	800	600

Mauser Unmarked Rework

4" barrel, 9mm caliber. The entire weapon is void of identifying markings. There is extensive refurbishing, removal of all markings, rebarreling, etc. The stock lug is present, and the extractor and safety are marked. The Waffenamt proofmark is on the right side of the receiver. The number manufactured is not known.

Exc.	V.G.	Good	Fair	Poor
1450	1000	850	600	450

MAUSER MANUFACTURED LUGERS 1930-1942 DWM

Mauser Oberndorf

4" barrel, 9mm caliber. It has a stock lug, blank chamber area and a marked extractor and safety. This is an early example of Mauser Luger, and the front toggle link is still marked DWM as leftover parts were intermixed with new Mauser parts in the production of this pistol. This is one of the first Lugers to be finished with the "Salt" blue process. There were approximately 500 manufactured with one- to four-digit serial numbers with the letter "v" suffix. This is a rare variation.

Exc.	V.G.	Good	Fair	Poor
3800	3000	2000	1500	900

1934/06 Swiss Commercial Mauser

4.75" barrel, 7.65mm caliber. There is no stock lug, but it has a grip safety. The Swiss Cross in Sunburst is stamped above the chamber. The extractor and safety are marked in German. The front toggle link is marked with the Mauser banner. There were approximately 200 manufactured for commercial sale in Switzerland. This variation is very well finished, and the serial numbers are all four digits with a "v" suffix.

Exc.	V.G.	Good	Fair	Poor
7500	5500	4000	1800	1000

1935/06 Portuguese "GNR"

4.75" barrel, 7.65mm caliber. It has no stock lug but has a grip safety. The chamber is marked "GNR," representing the Republic National Guard. The extractor is marked "Carregada"; and the safety, "Seguranca". The Mauser banner is stamped on the front toggle link. There were exactly 564 manufactured according to the original contract records that the Portuguese government made public. They all have four-digit serial numbers with a "v" suffix.

Exc.	V.G.	Good	Fair	Poor
3200	2700	1600	900	750

1934 Mauser Commercial

4" barrel, 7.65mm or 9mm caliber. It has a stock lug, and the chamber area is blank. The extractor and the safety are marked. The Mauser banner is stamped on the front toggle link. The finish on this pistol was very good, and the grips are either checkered walnut or black plastic on the later models. There were a few thousand manufactured for commercial sales in and outside of Germany.

Exc.	V.G.	Good	Fair	Poor
3500	2800	1650	1100	700

S/42 K Date

4" barrel, 9mm caliber. It has a stock lug, and the extractor and safety are marked. This was the first Luger that utilized codes to represent maker and date of manufacture. The front toggle link is marked S/42 in either Gothic or script; this was the code for Mauser. The chamber area is stamped with the letter "K," the code for 1934, the year of manufacture. Approximately 10,500 were manufactured with one- to five-digit serial numbers—some with letter suffixes.

Exc.	V.G.	Good	Fair	Poor
4500	3500	2200	1200	1000

S/42 G Date

As above, with the chamber stamped "G", the code for the year 1935. The Gothic lettering was eliminated, and there were many thousands of this model produced.

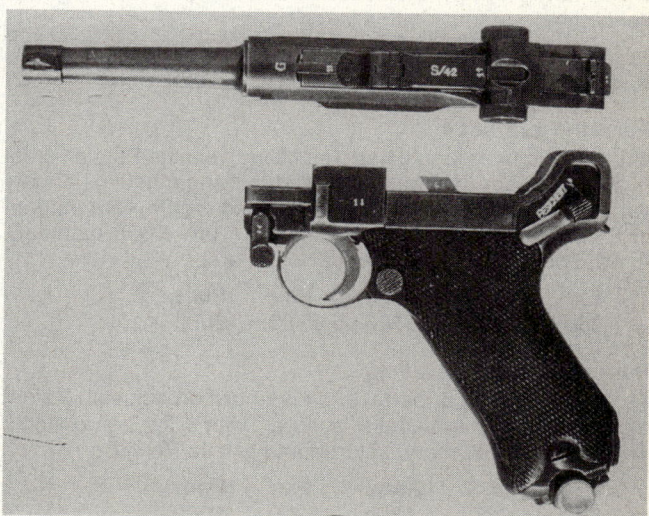

Courtesy Orvel Reichert

Exc.	V.G.	Good	Fair	Poor
1500	1250	900	650	450

Dated Chamber S/42

4" barrel, 9mm caliber. The chamber area is dated 1936-1940, and there is a stock lug. The extractor and safety are marked. In 1937 the rust blue process was eliminated entirely, and all subsequent pistols were salt blued. There were many thousands manufactured with one- to five-digit serial numbers—some with the letter suffix.

Exc.	V.G.	Good	Fair	Poor
1300	1100	750	500	400

S/42 Commercial Contract

4" barrel, 9mm caliber. It has a stock lug, and the chamber area is dated. It has a marked extractor and safety. The unusual feature is that, although this was a commercial pistol, the front toggle link is stamped S/42, which was the military code for Mauser. There were only a few hundred manufactured, so perhaps the toggles were left over from previous military production runs. The serial number range is four digits with the letter "v."

Exc.	V.G.	Good	Fair	Poor
2800	2000	1000	750	450

Code 42 Dated Chamber

4" barrel, 9mm caliber. The new German code for Mauser, the number 42, is stamped on the front toggle link. There is a stock lug. The chamber area is dated 1939 or 1940. Some are found with walnut grips; others, with black plastic. There were at least 50,000 manufactured with one- to five-digit serial numbers; some have letter suffixes.

Exc.	V.G.	Good	Fair	Poor
1100	850	650	400	350

41/42 Code

As above, except that the date of manufacture is represented by the final two digits (e.g. 41 for 1941). There were approximately 20,000 manufactured with the one- to five-digit serial number range.

Exc.	V.G.	Good	Fair	Poor
1600	1350	900	700	500

byf Code

As above, with the "byf" code stamp. The year of manufacture, either 41 or 42, is stamped on the chamber. This model was also made with black plastic, as well as walnut grips. There were many thousands produced with the one- to five-digit serial numbers— some with a letter suffix.

Exc.	V.G.	Good	Fair	Poor
1200	950	750	450	350

Persian Contract 4"

4" barrel, 9mm caliber. It has a stock lug, and the Persian crest is stamped over the chamber. All identifying markings on this variation—including extractor, safety and toggle—are marked in Farsi, the Persian alphabet. There were 1,000 manufactured. The serial numbers are also in Farsi.

Exc.	V.G.	Good	Fair	Poor
6500	5000	3500	2500	2000

Persian Contract Artillery

As above, with an 8" barrel and nine-position adjustable sight on the barrel. This model is supplied with a flat board stock. There were 1,000 manufactured and sold to Persia.

Exc.	V.G.	Good	Fair	Poor
3500	2850	1800	1300	1000

1934/06 Dated Commercial

4.75" barrel, 7.65mm caliber. It has a grip safety but no stock lug. The year of manufacture, from 1937-1942, is stamped above the chamber, and the Mauser banner is stamped on the front link. The extractor is marked, but the safety is not. There were approximately 1,000 manufactured with one- to three-digit serial numbers—some with the letter suffix.

Exc.	V.G.	Good	Fair	Poor
3000	2200	1400	900	500

1934 Mauser Dutch Contract

4" barrel, 9mm caliber. The year of manufacture, 1936-1940, is stamped above the chamber. The extractor is marked "Geleden," and the safety is marked "RUST" with a downward pointing arrow. The Mauser banner is stamped on the front toggle link. This was a military contract sale, and approximately 1,000 were manufactured with four-digit serial numbers with a letter "v" suffix.

Exc.	V.G.	Good	Fair	Poor
3500	3000	2000	1100	850

1934 Mauser Swedish Contract

4.75" barrel, 9mm or 7.65mm caliber. The chamber is dated 1938 or 1939. The extractor and safety are both marked in German, and there is a stock lug. The front toggle link is stamped with the Mauser banner. There were only 275 dated 1938 and 25 dated 1939 in 9mm. There were only 30 chambered for 7.65mm dated 1939. The serial number range is four digits with the letter "v" suffix.

Exc.	V.G.	Good	Fair	Poor
3000	1950	1600	950	700

1934 Mauser Swedish Commercial

4" barrel, 7.65mm caliber. 1940 is stamped over the chamber; "Kal. 7.65" is stamped on the left side of the barrel. The extractor and safety are both marked, and the Mauser banner is stamped on the front toggle link. There is a stock lug. This model is rare as there were only a few hundred manufactured with four digit serial numbers with the letter "w" suffix.

Exc.	V.G.	Good	Fair	Poor
2500	1800	1200	850	600

1934 Mauser German Contract

4" barrel, 9mm caliber. The chamber is dated 1939-1942, and the front toggle link is stamped with the Mauser banner. There is a stock lug, and the extractor and safety are both marked. The grips are either walnut or black plastic. There were several thousand manufactured with one- to five-digit serial numbers—some with letter suffixes. They were purchased for issue to police or paramilitary units.

Exc.	V.G.	Good	Fair	Poor
2800	2300	1500	800	550

Austrian Bundes Heer (Federal Army)

4" barrel, 9mm caliber. The chamber is blank, and there is a stock lug. The extractor and safety are marked in German, and the Austrian Federal Army Proof is stamped on the left side of the frame above the triggerguard. There were approximately 200 manufactured with four digit serial numbers and no letter suffix.

Exc.	V.G.	Good	Fair	Poor
2500	1850	1200	700	500

Mauser 2 Digit Date

4" barrel, 9mm caliber. The last two digits of the year of manufacture—41 or 42—are stamped over the chamber. There is a stock lug, and the Mauser banner is on the front toggle link. The extractor and safety are both marked, and the proofmarks were commercial. Grips are either walnut or black plastic. There were approximately 2,000 manufactured for sale to Nazi political groups. They have one- to five-digit serial numbers; some have the letter suffix.

Exc.	V.G.	Good	Fair	Poor
3000	1800	1200	900	550

KRIEGHOFF MANUFACTURED LUGERS 1923 DWM KRIEGHOFF

Commercial

4" barrel, 7.65mm or 9mm caliber. The chamber is dated 1921 or left blank. There is a stock lug. The front toggle is marked DWM, as they manufactured this luger to be sold by Kreighoff. "Kreighoff Suhl" is stamped on the back above the lanyard loop. The second "F" in Kreighoff was defective, and all specimens have this distinctive die strike. The safety and extractor are marked in German. There were only a few hundred manufactured with four-digit serial numbers with the letter "i" suffix.

Exc.	V.G.	Good	Fair	Poor
2000	1500	950	650	500

DWM/Kreighoff Commercial

As above, but marked "Heinrich Kreighoff Waffenfabrik Suhl" on the right side of the frame. Some examples have the "Germany" export stamp. There were several hundred manufactured with four-digit serial numbers with a letter suffix.

Exc.	V.G.	Good	Fair	Poor
3500	2850	2000	950	800

Kreighoff Commercial Inscribed Side Frame

4" or 6" barrel, 7.65mm or 9mm caliber. 1,000 were marked "Heinrich Kreighoff Waffenfabrik Suhl" on the right side of the frame, and 500 were devoid of this marking. All have the dagger and anchor trademark over "H.K. Kreighoff Suhl" on the front toggle link. The extractor and the safety are both marked. There is a stock lug, and the grips are of brown checkered plastic. There were approximately 1,500 manufactured with one- to four-digit serial numbers with a "P" prefix.

Exc.	V.G.	Good	Fair	Poor
6000	5000	3000	2000	1000

S Code Kreighoff

4" barrel, 9mm caliber. The Kreighoff trademark is stamped on the front toggle link, and the letter "S" is stamped over the chamber. There is a stock lug, and the extractor and safety are both marked. The grips are brown checkered plastic. There were approximately 4,500 manufactured for the Luftwaffe with one- to four-digit serial numbers.

Exc.	V.G.	Good	Fair	Poor
3750	3000	1800	950	750

Grip Safety Kreighoff

4" barrel, 9mm caliber. The chamber area is blank, and the front toggle link is stamped with the Kreighoff trademark. There is a stock lug and a grip safety. The extractor is marked "Geleden," and the safety is marked "FEUER" (fire) in the lower position. The grips are checkered brown plastic. This is a rare luger, and the number produced is not known.

Exc.	V.G.	Good	Fair	Poor
6000	4000	2800	1400	900

36 Date Kreighoff

4" barrel, 9mm caliber. It has a stock lug and the Kreighoff trademark on the front toggle link. The safety and extractor are marked, and the grips are brown plastic. The two-digit year of manufacture, 36, is stamped over the chamber. There were approximately 700 produced in the 3800-4500 serial number range.

Exc.	V.G.	Good	Fair	Poor
4500	3850	2200	1200	950

4 Digit Dated Kreighoff

As above, with the date of production, 1936-1940, stamped above the chamber. There were approximately 9,000 manufactured within the 4500-14000 serial number range.

Exc.	V.G.	Good	Fair	Poor
3750	3000	1850	950	750

2nd Series Kreighoff Commercial

4" barrel, 9mm caliber. There is a stock lug, and the Kreighoff trademark is stamped on the front link. The chamber area is blank, and the extractor and safety are marked. There were approximately 500 manufactured for commercial sales inside Germany. The date of manufacture is estimated at 1939-1940, as this variation has the dark finish that results from blueing without polishing the surface, which was done during these years. The grips are coarsely checkered black plastic. The serial number range is one to three digits with a "P" prefix.

Exc.	V.G.	Good	Fair	Poor
4000	3000	2000	1300	800

Postwar Krieghoff

4" barrel, 9mm caliber. There is a stock lug, and the chamber area is blank. The extractor and safety are marked, and the serial numbers in the one- to three-digit range are unusually larg—about 3/16ths of an inch. There were 300 of these postwar lugers produced for the occupation forces. They were assembled from leftover parts, and only 150 have the Kreighoff trademark on the front toggle link—the second 150 have blank links.

Exc.	V.G.	Good	Fair	Poor
3500	1500	1000	750	650

Krieghoff Postwar Commercial

As above, in 7.65mm caliber and the extractor not marked. Approximately 200 manufactured with standard-sized two- or three-digit serial numbers. They were supposedly sold to the occupation forces in the PX stores.

Exc.	V.G.	Good	Fair	Poor
3000	2000	1000	700	550

LUGER ACCESSORIES

Detachable Carbine Stocks

Approximately 13" in length, with a sling swivel and horn buttplate.

Exc.	V.G.	Good	Fair	Poor
3500	2500	1500	700	500

Artillery Stock with Holster

The artillery stock is of a flat board style approximately 13.75" in length. There is a holster and magazine pouches with straps attached. This is a desirable addition to the Artillery Luger. A word of caution—one must check federal laws regarding detachable stocks and short-barreled pistols; there are a number of restrictions that must be observed.

Exc.	V.G.	Good	Fair	Poor
1200	850	500	400	300

Navy Stock- without holster

As above, but 12.75" in length with a brass disc inlaid on the left side.

Exc.	V.G.	Good	Fair	Poor
1500	1000	850	500	400

Ideal Stock/Holster with Grips

A telescoping metal tube stock with an attached leather holster. It is used in conjunction with a metal-backed set of plain grips that correspond to the metal hooks on the stock and allow attachment. This Ideal Stock is U.S. patented and is so marked.

Exc.	V.G.	Good	Fair	Poor
2000	1400	1000	700	450

Drum Magazine 1st Issue

A 32-round, snail-like affair that is used with the Artillery Luger. It is also used with an adapter in the German 9mm submachine gun. The 1st Issue has a telescoping tube that is used to wind the spring. There is a dust cover that protects the interior from dirt.

Exc.	V.G.	Good	Fair	Poor
850	650	500	350	300

Drum Magazine 2nd Issue

As above, with a folding spring winding lever.

Exc.	V.G.	Good	Fair	Poor
800	600	450	350	300

Drum Magazine Loading Tool

This tool is slipped over the magazine and allows the spring to be compressed so that cartridges could be inserted.

Exc.	V.G.	Good	Fair	Poor
600	450	350	300	200

Drum Magazine Unloading Tool

The origin of this tool is unknown and caution should be exercised prior to purchase.

Drum Carrying Case

The same caveat as above applies.

Exc.	V.G.	Good	Fair	Poor
250	200	125	100	50

Holsters

Produced in a wide variety of styles.

Exc.	V.G.	Good	Fair	Poor
350	275	150	60	50

LATE PRODUCTION MAUSER LUGERS MANUFACTURED DURING THE 1970S.

P.08 Interarms

4" or 6" barrel, 7.65mm or 9mm caliber.

NIB	Exc.	V.G.	Good	Fair	Poor
850	650	500	400	350	300

Swiss Eagle Interarms

Swiss-style straight front grip strap and the American Eagle crest over the chamber. It is chambered for 7.65mm or 9mm and is offered with a 4" or 6" barrel.

NIB	Exc.	V.G.	Good	Fair	Poor
700	550	450	350	325	300

Commemorative Bulgarian

The Bulgarian crest is stamped over the chamber. There were only 100 produced.

NIB	Exc.	V.G.	Good	Fair	Poor
1900	1500	1200	950	650	450

Commemorative Russian

Crossed Nagant rifles are stamped over the chamber. There were 100 produced.

NIB	Exc.	V.G.	Good	Fair	Poor
1900	1500	1200	950	650	450

Modern Production Carbine

This splendid reproduction was produced on a limited basis. The workmanship is excellent, and the carbine and stock are furnished in a case.

NIB	Exc.	V.G.	Good	Fair	Poor
5500	4500	4000	3200	2500	2000

JOHN MARTZ CUSTOM LUGERS

Martz Luger Carbine

16" barrel. Approximately 80 were manufactured.

NIB	Exc.	V.G.
6000	5000	2500

.45 ACP

6" barrel, .45 ACP caliber. Assembled from two luger pistols that were split and welded together. 50 manufactured.

NIB	Exc.	V.G.
5500	4000	3000

Baby Luger 9mm

A compact 9mm caliber pistol. Approximately 150 were produced.

NIB	Exc.	V.G.	Good
2500	2000	1500	1000

Baby Luger .380 ACP

As above, in .380 caliber. Approximately 7 were manufactured.

NIB	Exc.	V.G.
6500	5000	4000

LUNA
Zella-Mehlis, Germany

Model 200 Free Pistol

A .22 caliber Martini action single shot pistol with an 11" barrel, adjustable sights, and walnut grips. Manufactured prior to WWII.

Exc.	V.G.	Good	Fair	Poor
1150	850	700	500	300

Model 300 Free Pistol

This model is a single shot target pistol chambered for .22 Short cartridge. Fitted with an 11" barrel, set trigger, walnut stocks and forearm with adjustable palm rest. Built from about 1929 to 1939.

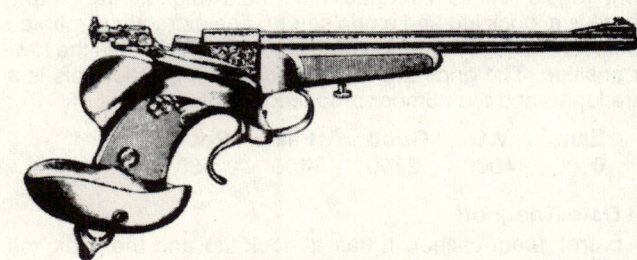

Exc.	V.G.	Good	Fair	Poor
950	750	650	400	300

Target Rifle

A .22 or .22 Hornet caliber Martini action single shot rifle with a 20" barrel, adjustable sights, and walnut stock. Manufactured prior to WWII.

Exc.	V.G.	Good	Fair	Poor
1000	850	650	500	250

M

MAB
SEE Bayonne

MAC
SEE Ingram

MAS
St. Etienne, France
Manufacture d'Armes de St. Etienne

MAS 36

A 7.5mm caliber bolt action rifle with a 22.6" barrel and 5-shot magazine. Blued with a walnut stock. The standard French service rifle from 1936 to 1949.

Exc.	V.G.	Good	Fair	Poor
250	175	150	100	75

MAS 36 CR39

As above, with an aluminum folding stock. This is a rare variation.

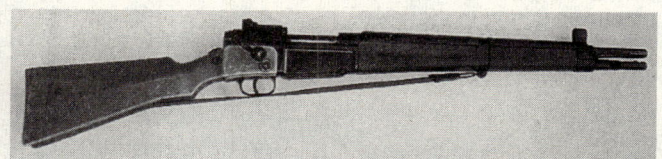

Courtesy Richard M. Kumor, Sr.

Exc.	V.G.	Good	Fair	Poor
900	800	300	125	90

Model 1917

An 8mm Lebel caliber semiautomatic rifle with a 31.4" barrel, 5-shot magazine, and full length walnut stock.

Exc.	V.G.	Good	Fair	Poor
1200	1000	800	—	—

Model 1918

As above, with a 23.1" barrel.

Exc.	V.G.	Good	Fair	Poor
1200	1000	800	—	—

MAS 44

This model was the first semi-automatic adopted by the French military. It was built in 1944. It later developed into the Model 49.

Courtesy Richard M. Kumor, Sr.

Exc.	V.G.	Good	Fair	Poor
375	300	225	150	100

MAS 49

A 7.5mm semiautomatic rifle with a 22.6" barrel and full length walnut stock.

Exc.	V.G.	Good	Fair	Poor
375	300	225	150	100

MAS 49/56

This model is a modification of the Model 49. This rifle is currently being imported.

Courtesy Richard M. Kumor, Sr.

Exc.	V.G.	Good	Fair	Poor
500	400	300	175	100

MBA GYROJET
San Ramon, California

Established in 1960, by R. Maynard and Art Biehl, MBA manufactured a pistol as well as carbine that utilized a spin stabilized rocket. Initially, these arms were of 13mm caliber and later of 12mm.

NOTE: It is reported that this ammo is selling for $20 to $25. About 20% of this ammo still functions.

Mark I Pistol

Exc.	V.G.	Good	Fair	Poor
700	600	500	400	200

Mark I Carbine

This model is similar to the pistol except that it has an 18" barrel and a buttstock with a pistol grip.

Exc.	V.G.	Good	Fair	Poor
1250	1050	850	600	300

MK ARMS, INC.
Irvine, California

K 760

A 9mm caliber semiautomatic carbine with a 16" shrouded barrel, fixed sights, and 14-, 24- or 36-shot magazine. Parkerized with a folding stock. Introduced in 1983.

NIB	Exc.	V.G.	Good	Fair	Poor
500	450	375	300	250	125

MKE
Ankara, Turkey
Importer - Mandall Shooting Supplies
Scottsdale, Arizona

Kirrikale

A 7.65 or 9mm short semiautomatic pistol with a 4" barrel and 7-shot magazine. It is an unauthorized copy of the Walther PP. Blued with plastic grips.

NIB	Exc.	V.G.	Good	Fair	Poor
400	350	275	225	150	100

M.O.A. CORP.
Maximum Dayton, Ohio

A single shot pistol manufactured in a variety of calibers with an 8.5", 10", or 14" barrel, adjustable sights, blued finish and walnut grip. Introduced in 1986.

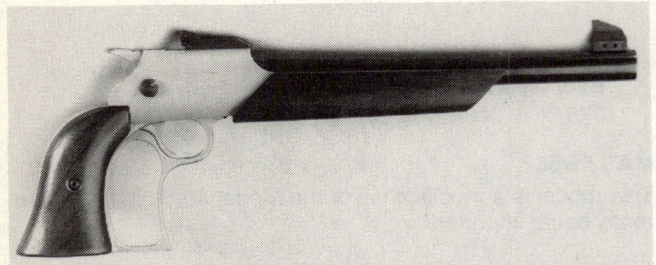

NIB	Exc.	V.G.	Good	Fair	Poor
500	425	375	300	250	125

Carbine

As above with an 18" barrel. Manufactured during 1986 and 1987.

NIB	Exc.	V.G.	Good	Fair	Poor
500	425	375	300	250	125

MAGNUM RESEARCH, INC.
SEE Desert Eagle

MAKAROV
Former Soviet Union and Warsaw Pact Nations
Importer - Centruy International Arms Co.
St. Albans, Vermont

Makarov

This semiautomatic pistol is similar in appearance to the Walther PP pistol and is chambered for the 9mm Makarov (9x18mm) cartridge. It has a double action trigger and is fitted with fixed sights. Barrel length is 3.6" and overall length is 6.4". Weight is approximately 25 oz. Magazine capacity is 8 rounds.

Exc.	V.G.	Good	Fair	Poor
125	100	80	60	50

MALIN, F. E.
London, England
Importer - Cape Horn Outfitters
Charlotte, North Carolina

Boxlock and sidelock shotguns made by Malin were imported into the United States for a number of years. As these arms were all essentially built to specific customer's requirements, standard values cannot be provided. Prospective purchasers are advised to secure a qualified appraisal prior to acquisition.

Boxlock

Features an Anson & Deeley action and high-grade walnut. All other specification were on a custom-order basis. This gun should definitely be individually appraised as values will fluctuate greatly with options.

Basic Model Estimated Value Only

NIB	Exc.	V.G.	Good	Fair	Poor
4000	3500	3000	2500	1850	1000

Sidelock

Features a Holland & Holland-type detachable sidelock action, and all other features (as on the boxlock) were on a custom-order basis. This model should also be appraised individually.

Basic Model Estimated Value Only

NIB	Exc.	V.G.	Good	Fair	Poor
5500	5000	4250	3000	2500	1250

MALTBY, HENLEY AND CO.
New York, New York

Spencer Safety Hammerless Revolver

A .32 caliber double action revolver with a 3" barrel and 5-shot cylinder. The frame and barrel made of brass and the cylinder of steel. The barrel marked "Spencer Safety Hammerless Pat. Jan. 24, 1888 & Oct. 29, 1889." Several thousand were manufactured during in the 1890s.

Courtesy Mike Stuckslager

Exc.	V.G.	Good	Fair	Poor
—	350	225	125	75

MANHATTAN FIREARMS COMPANY
Norwich, Connecticut
Newark, New Jersey

Bar Hammer Pistol

A .31, .34, or .36 caliber single shot percussion pistol with a 2" or 4" barrel. The hammer marked "Manhattan F.A. Mfg. Co. New York." Blued with walnut grips. Approximately 1,500 were made during the 1850s.

Exc.	V.G.	Good	Fair	Poor
—	—	350	250	150

Shotgun Hammer Pistol

A .36 caliber bar hammer single shot percussion pistol with a 5.5" half octagonal barrel marked as above. Blued with walnut grips. Approximately 500 were made.

Exc.	V.G.	Good	Fair	Poor
—	500	375	225	175

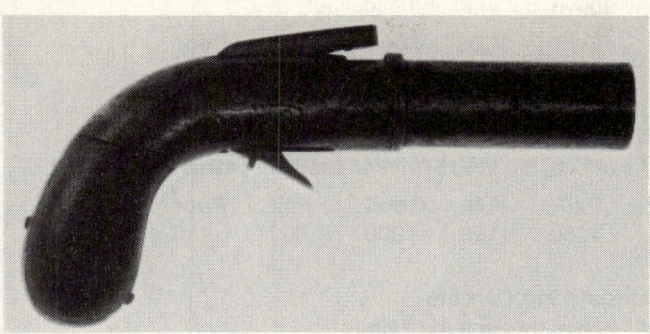

Courtesy Milwaukee Public Museum, Milwaukee, Wisconsin

Pepperbox

A .28 or .31 caliber double action percussion pepperbox with 3", 4", or 5" barrels and 5- or 6-shot barrel groups. Blued, casehardened with walnut grips. Marked as above and also "Cast Steel". The major variations of this pistol are as follows:

Three-shot with 3" Barrel
Manually rotated barrels.

Exc.	V.G.	Good	Fair	Poor
—	—	700	450	350

Five-shot with 3", 4", 5" Barrel
Automatically rotated barrels.

Exc.	V.G.	Good	Fair	Poor
—	—	600	350	250

Six-shot with 3" or 4" Barrel
Automatic rotation.

Exc.	V.G.	Good	Fair	Poor
—	—	550	350	250

Six-shot with 5" Barrel
Automatic rotation.

Exc.	V.G.	Good	Fair	Poor
—	—	750	450	350

Pocket Revolver

A .31 caliber percussion revolver with a 4", 5", or 6" barrel and either 5-shot or 6-shot cylinder. Blued, casehardened with walnut grips. The barrel marked, "Manhattan Firearms/Manufg. Co. New York" on the 5-shot model, serial numbers from 1 to approximately 1,000, and "Manhattan Firearms Mf'g. Co. New York" on the 6-shot model. The frame marked "December 27, 1859".

Courtesy Milwaukee Public Museum, Milwaukee, Wisconsin

First Model - 5-Shot

Exc.	V.G.	Good	Fair	Poor
—	—	600	250	150

Second Model - 6-Shot

Exc.	V.G.	Good	Fair	Poor
—	—	550	200	100

London Pistol Company

As above, but marked "London Pistol Company". Approximately 200 manufactured between 1859 and 1861.

Exc.	V.G.	Good	Fair	Poor
—	—	750	400	200

.36 Caliber Percussion Revolver

A .36 caliber percussion revolver with a 4", 5", or 6.5" octagonal barrel and 5- or 6-shot cylinder. Blued, casehardened with walnut grips. Approximately 78,000 were made between 1859 and 1868. There were five variations—see below.

Courtesy Milwaukee Public Museum, Milwaukee, Wisconsin

Model I

A 5-shot cylinder marked "Manhattan Firearms Mfg. Co. New York." The serial numbers from 1 through 4200. The 6" barreled version would be worth a 15% premium.

Exc.	V.G.	Good	Fair	Poor
—	—	850	400	250

Model II

As above with the 1859 patent date marked on the barrel. The serial range is 4200 to 14500.

Exc.	V.G.	Good	Fair	Poor
—	—	700	300	200

Model III

A 5-shot cylinder and marked, "Manhattan Firearms Co. Newark NJ," together with the 1859 patent date. The serial numbers are from 14500 to 45200.

Exc.	V.G.	Good	Fair	Poor
—	—	650	300	150

Model IV

As above, with a modified recoil shield and the patent date March 8, 1864, added to the barrel inscription. Serial numbers from 45200 to 69200.

Exc.	V.G.	Good	Fair	Poor
—	—	650	300	150

Model V

As above, with a 6-shot cylinder and numbered 1 to approximately 9000.

Exc.	V.G.	Good	Fair	Poor
—	—	750	350	200

.22 Caliber Pocket Revolver

A .22 caliber spur trigger revolver with a 3" barrel and 7-shot cylinder. Blued, silver plated with walnut or rosewood grips. Approximately 17,000 were made during the 1860s.

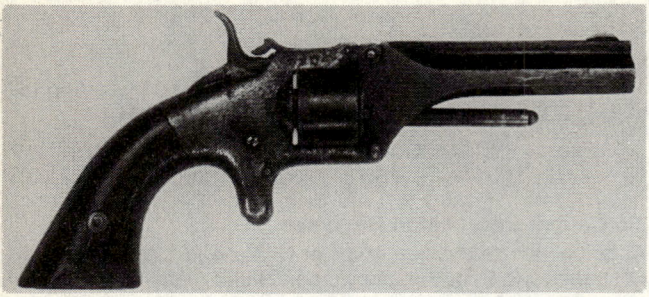

Courtesy Milwaukee Public Museum, Milwaukee, Wisconsin

Exc.	V.G.	Good	Fair	Poor
—	—	400	200	100

Manhattan-American Standard Hero

A .34 caliber single shot percussion pistol with a 2" or 3" round barrel that unscrews for loading. Blued, brass frame with walnut grips. Marked "A.S.T. Co./HERO". Made by the American Standard Tool Company, Manhattan's successor. Approximately 30,000 manufactured between 1868 and 1873.

Manhattan Manufactured

Marked, "HERO/M.F.A.Co." Approximately 5,000 were produced.

Exc.	V.G.	Good	Fair	Poor
—	—	250	150	100

American Standard Manufactured

Approximately 25,000 were produced.

Exc.	V.G.	Good	Fair	Poor
—	—	200	100	75

MANN, FRITZ
Suhl, Germany

6.35mm Pocket Pistol

A 6.35mm caliber semiautomatic pistol with a 1.65" barrel and 5-shot magazine. Blued with plastic grips having the name "Mann" cast in them. This pistol, which weighs only 9 oz., is one of the smallest semiautomatic pistols ever manufactured. Made between 1920 and 1922.

Exc.	V.G.	Good	Fair	Poor
300	250	200	150	100

7.65mm Pocket Pistol

A 7.65mm or 9mm short semiautomatic pistol with a 2.35" barrel and 5-shot magazine. Blued with plastic grips having the name "Mann" cast in them. Manufactured between 1924 and 1929.

Exc.	V.G.	Good	Fair	Poor
350	300	250	200	125

MANNLICHER PISTOL
Steyr, Austria
SEE Steyr

MANNLICHER SCHOENAUER
Steyr, Austria

Model 1903 Mountain Carbine

A 6.5x54mm caliber bolt action rifle with a 17.7" barrel, 5-shot rotary magazine, folding rear sight, double set triggers and full length walnut stock.

Exc.	V.G.	Good	Fair	Poor
1350	1100	900	700	500

Model 1905 Carbine

As above, but in 9x56mm caliber.

Exc.	V.G.	Good	Fair	Poor
1250	1100	1000	850	500

Model 1908 Carbine

As above, but in 7x57mm or 8x56mm caliber.

Exc.	V.G.	Good	Fair	Poor
1250	1100	900	600	450

Model 1910 Carbine

As above, but in 9.5x57mm.

Exc.	V.G.	Good	Fair	Poor
1100	975	850	600	450

Model 1924 Carbine

As above, but in .30-06 caliber.

Exc.	V.G.	Good	Fair	Poor
2100	1850	1600	950	650

High Velocity Rifle

As above, but in 7x64mm Brenneke, .30-06, 8x60Smm Magnum, 9.3x62mm, and the 10.75x68mm caliber with a 23.5" barrel and folding-leafsight. Half-length walnut stock.

Takedown Model-Add 75%.

Exc.	V.G.	Good	Fair	Poor
2250	2000	1750	1000	700

All of the above models were discontinued prior to WWII.

Model 1950

A .257 Roberts, .270 Winchester, and the .30-06 caliber bolt action rifle with a 24" barrel and 5-shot rotary magazine. Blued with a half length walnut stock. Manufactured between 1950 and 1952.

Exc.	V.G.	Good	Fair	Poor
1000	850	700	500	400

Model 1950 Carbine

As above, with a 20" barrel and a full-length stock.

Exc.	V.G.	Good	Fair	Poor
1250	1000	850	650	500

Model 1950 6.5 Carbine

As above, in 6.5x54mm Mannlicher Schoenauer caliber with a 18.5" barrel and full-length stock.

Exc.	V.G.	Good	Fair	Poor
1350	1100	850	650	500

Model 1952

Similar to the above, with a turned back bold handle. Manufactured between 1952 and 1956.

Exc.	V.G.	Good	Fair	Poor
1000	850	750	500	400

Model 1952 Carbine

Similar to the Model 1950 carbine, but additionally in 7x57mm caliber. Manufactured between 1952 and 1956.

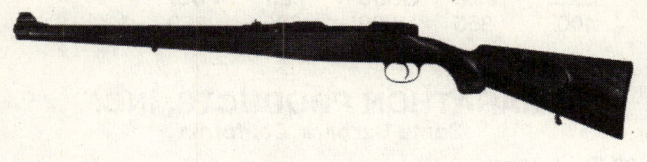

Exc.	V.G.	Good	Fair	Poor
1250	1100	950	650	550

Model 1952 6.5mm Carbine

As above, in 6.5x54mm Mannlicher Schoenauer caliber with an 18.5" barrel. Manufactured between 1952 and 1956.

Exc.	V.G.	Good	Fair	Poor
1350	1100	850	650	500

Model 1956 Rifle

A .243 or .30-06 caliber bolt action rifle with a 22" barrel and Monte Carlo-style stock. Manufactured between 1956 and 1960.

Exc.	V.G.	Good	Fair	Poor
900	800	650	500	400

Model 1956 Carbine

As above, with a 20" barrel and full-length stock. Manufactured between 1956 and 1960.

Exc.	V.G.	Good	Fair	Poor
1000	900	750	600	450

Model 1961 MCA Rifle

As above, but modified for easier use with a telescopic sight.

Exc.	V.G.	Good	Fair	Poor
900	800	650	500	400

Model 1961 MCA Carbine

As above, with a 20" barrel and half length stock.

Exc.	V.G.	Good	Fair	Poor
1100	1000	850	650	500

Model M72 LM Rifle

As above, with a 23" fluted barrel, double set or single trigger and full-length stock. Manufactured between 1972 and 1980.

Exc.	V.G.	Good	Fair	Poor
900	800	650	500	400

MANUFRANCE
St. Etienne, France
SEE Le Francais

Auto Stand

A .22 caliber semiautomatic pistol manufactured by Pyrenees and sold by Manufrance under the trade name Auto Stand.

Exc.	V.G.	Good	Fair	Poor
250	225	200	150	100

Buffalo Stand

A .22 caliber bolt action pistol with a 12" barrel and adjustable sights. Blued with a walnut stock. Manufactured prior to 1914.

Exc.	V.G.	Good	Fair	Poor
250	225	200	150	100

Le Agent

An 8mm caliber double action revolver with a 5" barrel. Blued with walnut grips.

Exc.	V.G.	Good	Fair	Poor
200	100	175	150	75

Le Colonial

As above, with an enclosed hammer.

Exc.	V.G.	Good	Fair	Poor
200	175	150	100	75

MANURHIN
Mulhouse, France

This company manufactured the Walther PP and PPK models under license and these are marked "Manufacture de Machines du Haut-Rhin" on the left front of the slide and "Lic Excl. Walther" on the left rear. These arms were imported into the U.S.A. in the early 1950s by Thalson Import Company of San Francisco, California, and later by Interarms. The latter are marked "Mark 11" and "Made in France."

New Production

Currently, the Matra Manurhin Defense Corp. is manufacturing handguns, and they are imported by Atlantic Business Organizations of New York.

Model 73 Defense Revolver

A .38 Special or .357 Magnum caliber double action swing-out cylinder revolver with a 2.5", 3", or 4" barrel having fixed sights. Blued with walnut grips.

NIB	Exc.	V.G.	Good	Fair	Poor
1150	1000	850	750	500	350

Model 73 Gendarmerie

As above, with a 5.5", 6", or 8" long barrel and adjustable sights.

NIB	Exc.	V.G.	Good	Fair	Poor
1250	1100	900	800	550	400

Model 73 Sport

Similar to the above, with a shortened lock time and target style adjustable sights.

NIB	Exc.	V.G.	Good	Fair	Poor
1250	1100	900	800	550	400

Model 73 Convertible

As above, with interchangeable .22, .32, or .38 caliber barrels and cylinders.

NIB	Exc.	V.G.	Good	Fair	Poor
2250	1850	1600	1400	950	750

Model 73 Silhouette

Similar to the Model 73 Sport, but in .22 to .357 Magnum caliber with a 10" or 10.75" shrouded barrel and formfitting walnut grips,

NIB	Exc.	V.G.	Good	Fair	Poor
1200	1050	850	750	500	350

Model PP

Similar to the Walther Model PP, with a revised safety.

Exc.	V.G.	Good	Fair	Poor
400	350	300	225	150

Model PPK/S

Similar to the Walther Model PPK/S, with a revised safety.

Exc.	V.G.	Good	Fair	Poor
400	350	300	225	150

Model PP Sports

This is a target version of the PP chambered for the .22 caliber shell. Available in various barrel lengths.

Exc.	V.G.	Good	Fair	Poor
400	350	300	225	150

MARATHON PRODUCTS, INC.
Santa Barbara, California

.22 First Shot

A .22 caliber single shot bolt action rifle with a 16.5" barrel and overall length of 31". Blued with a walnut stock. Manufactured between 1985 and 1987.

Exc.	V.G.	Good	Fair	Poor
65	55	45	30	25

.22 Super Shot

As above, with a 24" barrel. Manufactured between 1985 and 1987.

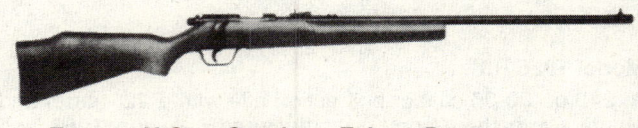

Exc.	V.G.	Good	Fair	Poor
65	55	45	30	25

.22 Hot Shot Pistol

A .22 caliber bolt action pistol with a 14.5" barrel. Blued with a walnut stock. Manufactured in 1986 and 1987.

Exc.	V.G.	Good	Fair	Poor
65	55	45	30	25

Centerfire Rifle

A bolt action sporting rifle manufactured in a variety of calibers with a 24" barrel, open sights, adjustable trigger and 5-shot magazine. Blued with a walnut stock. Manufactured in 1985 and 1986.

Exc.	V.G.	Good	Fair	Poor
300	250	200	150	125

MARBLE'S GAME GETTER
MARBLE'S ARMS & MFG. CO.
Gladstone, Michigan

Marble's Game Getter Gun NFA, CURIO OR RELIC

The Game Getter has 12", 15", or 18" separated over/under rifled/smooth bore barrels in .22/.44 or .22/.410, a manually pivoted hammer striker to select the upper or lower barrel, an attached folding steel skeleton stock, and is intended to be fired from the shoulder. The tip-up barrels are opened by pulling back the trigger guard. Two versions, Model 1908 and Model 1921, indicating their first years of production, were made. Both apparently were designed by Webster L. Marble (1854-1930), and manufactured by Marble Safety Axe Co. of Gladstone, Michigan, which became Marble's Arms & Mfg. Co. in 1911.

Marble's suspended sales of the Game Getter in the United States shortly after the government ruled it was a "firearm" under the National Firearms Act (NFA) of 1934, but continued sales abroad. Its retail price in 1934 was about $24 (12" or 15" barrels) to $26 (18" barrels). The Bureau of Internal Revenue removed the 18" barrel variation from the NFA in a Letter Ruling dated March 1, 1939. Today, the 12" and 15" barrel variations are controlled under the NFA in the "any other weapon" category. If the shoulder stock is removed from a 12", 15", or 18" barreled Game Getter, however, ATF has ruled it to be an NFA "firearm" subject to a $200 transfer tax rate.

Model 1908, serial numbered from 1(?) to 9999

Exc.	V.G.	Good	Fair	Poor
1,500	900	750	550	425

Model 1921, serial numbered from 10000 to 20000(?)

Exc.	V.G.	Good	Fair	Poor
900	750	550	450	375

NOTE: Boxed guns (wooden box, Model 1908; cardboard box, Model 1921) with accessories, or 18" barrel variations, nonstandard calibers (.25-20, .32-20, .38-40, etc.) command premiums of 50 to 200 percent or more; an original holster is $75 to $150. Two new-in-box Model 1908 with 15" and 18" barrels sold for $2,700 and $3,600, respectively, in 1994. An original wooden Model 1908 box alone may sell for $500 to $900. All 18" barrel variations are rare.

The Model 1908, whose production ended in May 1914, was available in two variations. Model 1908A has a flexible rear tang sight, and Model 1908B has a filler block. The Model 1908 is apparently serial numbered from 1 through 9999, and some confusion about its serial number range exists, in part, because of incorrect information given out informally during the 1970s by Marble's. According to some Marble's factory letters, serial numbering began with number 700 and ended with 9999; however, a number of original guns with numbers below 700 have been observed. A survey of 42 guns within the range from 731 to 9829 indicates a general absence of guns in the range between 6511 to 8023 (just one gun, a Model 1908A bearing serial number 7235, with 15" barrels, has been located within this serial number range). This apparent absence of guns could identify one or more groups that were exported. The Game Getter was listed in European catalogues, but the extent of sales there is currently unknown.

The markings on the Model 1908 are:

	Type I (serial 1 to about 4000)	Type II (about serial 4000 to 9999)
LEFT SIDE:	**?MANUFACTURED BY THE?**	**?MANUFACTURED BY THE?**
	MARBLE SAFETY AXE CO. ?GLADSTONE, MICH. U.S.A.? **MARBLE ARMS & MFG. Co.**	MARBLE SAFETY AXE CO. ?GLADSTONE, MICH. U.S.A.? SUCCESSOR
RIGHT SIDE:	*Calibers 22 & 44* *Patent Allowed*	*Calibers 22 & 44* *Patent Allowed*

Each of the markings on the right-hand side is enclosed within an elongated circle.

OTHER CHARACTERISTICS: Separate flat buttplate attached with two screws up to approximately serial number 1200; afterwards, a flattened buttplate was integrally formed from the same round steel used to form the skeleton stock. Early stocks have drop adjustment with a knurled collar 3/8" diameter by 13/16" long; at approximately serial number 2500, the collar was changed to 1/2" by 5/8" long. The hammer spur is curved down to approximately serial number 2,000, then the curve at hammer is up.

The Model 1908 was originally designed for .22 Short, Long or Long Rifle and .44 shot and ball ammunition, but the most satisfactory load was the long-cased .44-40 that held the shot in place with a disk and mouth crimp. The 1915 Marble's catalog stated the Model 1908 was available for use with the 2" .410 shotgun shell; chambering is slightly different from that of the .44-40, but is seldom encountered.

The entire Model 1908 production of this extremely popular firearm was sold out by 1917, and its manufacture was apparently discontinued mainly because of World War I. To meet continuing demand, Marble's produced a significantly redesigned gun in 1921. The serial number range for the Model 1921 was from 10000 to, apparently, about 20000, but a definitive upper range is not yet established. The grip, folding stock (made from cold-rolled sheet metal and nickeled), and other features were redesigned on the Model 1921.

The markings on the Model 1921 are:

LEFT SIDE: Marble's
Game Getter Gun
Marble Arms & Mfg.Co.
Gladstone, Mich.U.S.A.

RIGHT SIDE: *UPPER BARREL 22 S.L. LR.&N.R.A LOWER BARREL .44GG & .410 2"*

OTHER CHARACTERISTICS: Other barrel markings for the Model 1921 in .410 are *.410 2"?* and *.410 2?"*; the latter appears in the serial number range from approximately 15000 to 16600, and in the low 19000 range. Plastic grips were used in the serial range from approximately 14600 to 17000.

The Model 1921 was originally designed for the 2" .410 shotgun shell, but Marble's changed the extractor marking on some guns to **2"?** or **2?"** to indicate factory (re)chambering for the 2.5" shell, apparently on a random or special-order basis. The reason is that both 2" and 2?" marked guns have been observed in low (14000) and high (19000) serial number ranges. The lowest serial number with 2?" marking observed so far is 14601. The range from approximately 14500 to 17000 have plastic rather than walnut grips, single-bladed rear sight rather than multiple-blades, and blued rather than case hardened hammer. Outside this range, only 19288 has the 2?" marking; number 19692 is marked **2"?**. No Model 1921 Game Getters are known to have been factory chambered for the 3" .410 shotgun shell.

Marble's Game Getter Pistol and other special-order or experimental Game Getters
NFA, CURIO OR RELIC

Contemporary articles and advertisements in *Hunter-Trader-Trapper*, and some early Marble's catalogs, indicate that a few Model 1908 Game Getters were originally manufactured (with rifled barrels) for .25-20, .32-20 and .38-40 cartridges, and as pistols. Since no original factory records have apparently survived, these other materials may be the only means of independently documenting their production.

An illustrated advertisement in a 1910 issue of *Hunter-Trader-Trapper* states that 12", 15" and 18" barrel Game Getters were available for delivery in .25-20, .32-20 and .38-40, and that these firearms were designed as over/under double barreled rifles with rifled barrels. An article in the October 1913 issue of *Outdoor Life* states that Marble's was manufacturing a Game Getter pistol, with 10" barrels, and that any barrel length could be ordered. One known Model 1908 Game Getter pistol has 9" barrels, and bears serial number 3837. Inspection of this firearm (including the removal of the grips) reveals that it was never fitted with a shoulder stock, because the portion of the frame which would have held the stock was never inletted to receive one. Any Game Getter factory-manufactured as a handgun is extremely rare, and a reliable estimate of its value cannot be made.

It appears that the Game Getter pistol and other special-order or experimental Game Getters were limited to the Model 1908.

These materials are copyright © 1998 by Eric M. Larson, printed in the *Catalog* by permission of the copyright holder, and will appear in a forthcoming book on pre-NFA smooth bore shot pistols (see H&R Handy-Gun entry). This writer would like to communicate with anyone who owns several Game Getters to obtain side-by-side photographs of different variations for use in the book, and persons who own or may have owned a Model 1908 Game Getter within the serial range below 731 as well as between 6511 and 8023; Model 1921 above serial number 19692; nonstandard Game Getters in .25-20, .32-20, .38-40, and perhaps other calibers; and Model 1908 Game Getters that were originally manufactured as pistols.

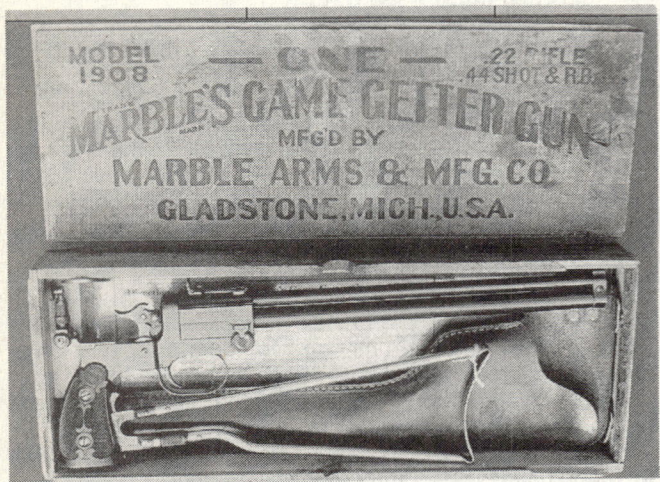

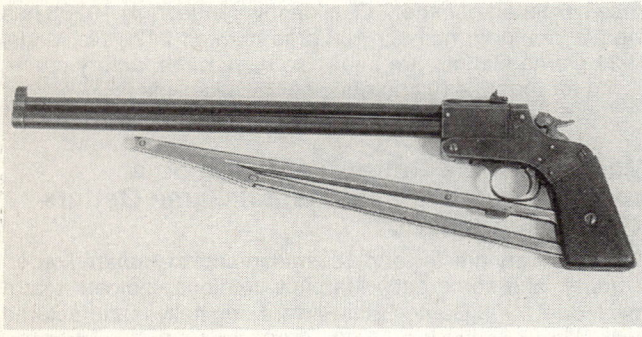

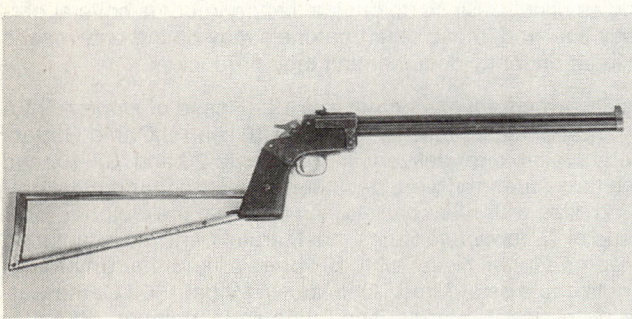

MARGOLIN
Tula, Soviet State Arsenal

Model MT Sports

This is a semiautomatic .22 caliber pistol with no barrel weights and is not threaded for a compensator. Barrel length is 7.5". Furnished with a black plastic case with spare magazine and repair parts.

Courtesy Orvel Reichert

Exc.	V.G.	Good	Fair	Poor
600	500	400	300	200

Model MTS- I

A .22 short semiautomatic pistol with a 7.5" barrel having an integral muzzle brake, adjustable walnut grips and a 6-shot magazine. Normally, accompanied by a wooden case with cleaning accessories.

Courtesy Orvel Reichert

Exc.	V.G.	Good	Fair	Poor
800	700	600	450	350

> A cased Margolin MTS-1 Target Pistol was sold at auction for $770. All accessories were included in case. Built in 1964. Condition was excellent to mint. J.C. Devine, Inc, September 1996.

Model MTS-2

As above, in .22 l.r. with a 6" barrel.

Exc.	V.G.	Good	Fair	Poor
800	700	600	450	350

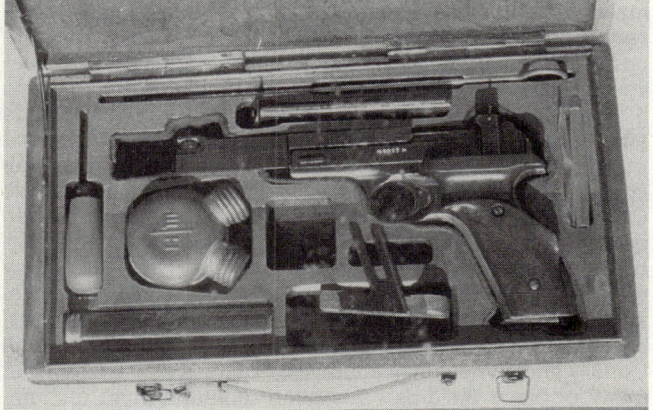

Courtesy Orvel Reichert

The above photos are of an unusual Margolin .22 caliber Olympic Model with wrap around square barrel weights and wooden case.

MARIETTE BREVETTE
Liege, Belgium

A number of European manufacturers produced percussion pepperbox pistols based upon a patent issued to Mariette during the 1840s and 1850s. These pistols have detachable barrels that are loaded at the breech, double action ring triggers, and internally mounted hammers. They are normally blued and foliate engraved.

6 Barrel Pepperbox

Exc.	V.G.	Good	Fair	Poor
2000	1700	1250	900	500

4 Barreled Pepperbox

Exc.	V.G.	Good	Fair	Poor
1750	1450	1000	750	400

MARLIN FIREARMS CO.
New Haven, Connecticut

Ballard Rifles
Established by John Mahlon Marlin in 1863. Marlin manufactured pistols until 1875 when he began production of Ballard rifles. In 1881 he made his first lever-action repeating rifle for which his company became famous.

The Marlin Firearms Company has the distinction of being the oldest family owned firearms company in the United States.

The Ballard single shot rifle was invented by C.H. Ballard of Worcester, Massachusetts. It was patented in 1861. The first of the Ballard rifles was manufactured by the Ball and Williams Co. of Worchester, Massachusetts. In 1866 Merwin and Bray purchased the firm, calling it Merrimack Arms Company, and operated until 1869, when they sold it to the Brown Manufacturing Company of New York City. This venture took a decidedly negative turn, and in 1873 mortgage foreclosure forced the sale to Schoverling and Daly of New York City. These gentlemen were arms dealers, not manufacturers, so they entered into an agreement with John M. Marlin to produce the Ballard rifle. The rifles produced during this period are regarded as some of the finest single shots ever made, and the venture finally became successful. In 1881 the business became incorporated as the Marlin Firearms Company, and the Ballard was produced under this banner until it was discontinued around the year 1891. The popularity of the repeating rifle simply eroded the demand for the fine single shot until it was no longer a profitable venture.

BALL & WILLIAMS BALLARDS
First Model
This model was the first Ballard produced. It was introduced in 1861 and was offered with a 24" or 28" octagonal barrel. The frame is case-colored, and the barrel is blued. The walnut stock is varnished. The major identifying feature of this model is the inside extractor. This was the only Ballard that had this feature before Marlin began to manufacture the rifle in 1875. The barrel is stamped "Ball & Williams/Worchester, Mass." and "Ballards Patent/Nov. 5, 1861." There were approximately 100 manufactured and serial numbered from 1-100.

Exc.	V.G.	Good	Fair	Poor
1500	1300	1000	800	550

Military Rifle
There is not enough known about these rifles and probably never will be. They were chambered most frequently for the .44 and .54 rimfire cartridges and feature the outside tangs and extractors. They were offered with a 30" round barrel and full-length forearm. There are three barrel bands and sling swivels. The government ordered only 35 of these for use in the Civil War; and if one was to be definitely authenticated as a genuine martial specimen, it would be quite valuable. Many of these rifles were marked "Kentucky" on top of the receiver because the militia of that state armed its men with the Ballard rifles and carbines. This marking was a sales aid used by the company and does not indicate militia ownership. The amount manufactured is not known. Barrel markings are as on the First Model.

Exc.	V.G.	Good	Fair	Poor
900	750	650	500	350

Civil War Military Carbine
This model has a 22" part-round, part-octagonal barrel and is chambered for the .44 rimfire cartridge. It has the outside tang and extractor. The stock and forearm are walnut with a barrel band sling swivel. The butt stock bears an oval cartouche surrounding the inspector's marks, "MM." These letters also appear stamped on major metal parts. There were 1,509 ordered by the government for use in the Civil War. The barrel was marked the same as the rifle.

Exc.	V.G.	Good	Fair	Poor
1500	1300	1000	800	550

Sporting Rifle
This model is chambered for the .32, .38, and .44 rimfire cartridges. The octagonal barrel is 24", 26", or 28" in length and is blued. The frame is case-colored. The stock and forearm

are varnished walnut, and there is a knob that protrudes in front of the frame to operate the outside manual extractor. There is a crescent buttplate standard. There were approximately 6,500 manufactured, and barrel markings are the same as on the First Model.

Exc.	V.G.	Good	Fair	Poor
800	650	550	400	300

Sporting Carbine

This model is similar in appearance to the Sporting Rifle with a 22" part-round, part-octagonal barrel. It is chambered for the .44 and .54 caliber cartridge, and the sling swivel is found on a barrel band in the front. The knob on the bottom activates the outside extractor. There have been some encountered with "Kentucky" stamped on the top, but this does not affect the value. The markings are the same as on the previous models. There are no production figures available, but some estimate approximately 2,000 were manufactured.

Exc.	V.G.	Good	Fair	Poor
900	750	650	500	350

Dual Ignition System

This system allows the use of the rimfire cartridge or percussion method by simply turning the striker on the hammer from one position to the other. This model features a percussion nipple mounted on the breechblock, and the hammer is marked "Patented Jan.5,1864." The patent was held by Merwin and Bray. This swivel system is usually found on the sporting models and would increase the value of the weapon by 20 percent.

Merrimack Arms Co. and Brown Manufacturing Co.

The values for the Ballard rifles manufactured by these two firms are the same, and the specifications are similar. The identifying difference is in the markings, "Merrimack Arms & Mfg. Co./Newburyport Mass." or "Brown Mfg. Co. Newburyport, Mass." Merrimack produced approximately 3,000 of these rifles between 1867 and 1869 serial numbered in the 18000-20000 range. Brown produced approximately 1,800 between 1869 and 1873 in the 20000-22000 serial number range.

Sporting Rifle

This model was produced in .22 (rare), .32, .38, .44, .46, and .52 caliber rimfire or percussion, as most encountered featured the dual ignition system and had the nipple in the breechblock. They have either a round or octagonal barrel in 24", 26", or 28" lengths. The appearance and finish is similar to the Ball & Williams rifles; and the major difference is the inside tang. The extractor was still outside mounted and manually activated. Exact production breakdown is unknown. There is no premium for the dual ignition system on these later guns.

Exc.	V.G.	Good	Fair	Poor
850	700	550	450	300

Sporting Carbine

This model is quite similar in appearance to the Sporting Rifle, with a 22" part-round, part-octagonal barrel.

Exc.	V.G.	Good	Fair	Poor
950	800	650	550	400

Military Rifle

The Military Rifle is similar to the sporting version except that it has a 30" round barrel and full-length forearm with three barrel bands. It is chambered for the .44 and .52 caliber rimfire or percussion with the dual ignition system.

Exc.	V.G.	Good	Fair	Poor
950	800	650	550	400

Shotgun

This model is similar to the Sporting Rifle in appearance but is chambered for 24 gauge, with a 30" round barrel. There is a groove milled in the top of the frame to use as a sight. The buttplate is shotgun-style instead of the usual crescent shape.

Exc.	V.G.	Good	Fair	Poor
650	550	450	350	250

Marlin-Ballard Rifles

Commencing in 1875 the Ballard single-shot rifle was made by John Marlin for Schoverling and Daly. In 1881 the business was incorporated and became the Marlin Firearms Co. All the Ballards made from then until 1891, when they were discontinued, were produced under this banner. The only real difference in the rifles manufactured during these periods was in the markings. The earlier rifles are stamped "J.M.Marlin New Haven. Conn. U.S.A./Ballards Patent. Nov.5, 1861"; and the post-1881 models are stamped "Marlin Firearms Co. New Haven Ct. U.S.A./Patented Feb. 9, 1875/Ballards Patent Nov. 5,1861." The major difference between Marlin-made Ballards and the earlier models is the inside tang and the internal extractor on the Marlin-made rifles. All of the Marlin-made Ballards have an octagonal frame top, and the Marlin Firearms Co. models have grooved receiver sides. The standard finish on all these later rifles is case-colored frames and blued octagonal or part-round, part-octagonal barrels. There are many variations in these rifles as to types of sights, stock, engraving, and other special order features-such as barrel lengths, weights, and contours. These rifles must be considered individually and competently appraised. There is also the fact that many of these Ballards have been rebarreled and rechambered over the years, as they were known for their shooting ability and were used quite extensively. This can seriously affect the value in a negative manner unless it can be authenticated that the work was done by the likes of Harry Pope or George Schoyen and other noted and respected gunsmiths of that era. This can add considerably to the value of the rifle. One must approach this model with caution and learn all that can be learned before purchasing.

Ballard Hunters Rifle

This model resembles the earlier Brown Manufacturing Company rifles, and it utilizes many leftover parts acquired by Marlin. It is chambered for the .32, .38, and .44 rimfire and centerfire and features John Marlin's unique reversible firing pin that allows the same gun to use both rimfire and centerfire ammunition simply by rotating the firing pin in the breechblock. This model still had the external ejector and bears the J.M. Marlin markings. There were approximately 500 manufactured in the 1 to 500 serial range. They were produced in 1875 and 1876.

Exc.	V.G.	Good	Fair	Poor
1500	1300	1000	800	550

Ballard No. I Hunters Rifle

This model bears the early J.M. Marlin marking only, as it was manufactured from 1876 until 1880 and was discontinued before the incorporation. It has a 26", 28", and 30" barrel and is chambered for the .44 rimfire or centerfire cartridge. It has the reversible firing pin and also the new internal extractor. Production figures are not available, but the serial number range is between 500 and 4000.

Exc.	V.G.	Good	Fair	Poor
900	750	650	500	375

Ballard No. 1-1/2 Hunters Rifle

This model is similar to the No. 1 except that it is chambered for the .45-70, .40-63, and the .40-65 cartridges and does not have the reversible firing pin. The barrel length is 30" and 32". It was manufactured between 1879 and 1883. This model is found with both early and later markings.

Exc.	V.G.	Good	Fair	Poor
1100	950	850	700	500

Ballard No. 1-3/4 "Far West" Hunters Rifle
This model was made by J. M. Marlin only and is similar to the 1-1/2, the difference being the addition of double-set triggers and a ring on the opening lever. It was manufactured in 1880 and 1881.

Exc.	V.G.	Good	Fair	Poor
1000	850	750	600	400

Ballard No. 2 Sporting Rifle
This model is chambered for the .32, .38 rimfire or centerfire cartridges, and the .44 centerfire. It has the reversible firing pin and was offered in 26", 28", and 30" barrel lengths. This model features "Rocky Mountain" sights and was manufactured between 1876 and 1891. It is found with both early and late markings.

Courtesy Milwaukee Public Museum, Milwaukee, Wisconsin

Exc.	V.G.	Good	Fair	Poor
850	750	600	450	300

Ballard No. 3 Gallery Rifle
This model is similar to the No. 2 rifle but is chambered for the .22 rimfire cartridge and has a manually operated external extractor. The sights are the same; and a 24" barrel was offered in addition to the 26", 28", and 30". This rifle was manufactured between 1876 and 1891.

Exc.	V.G.	Good	Fair	Poor
950	850	700	400	250

Ballard No. 3F Gallery Rifle
This is a deluxe version of the No. 3. It has a pistol grip stock, a nickel-plated Schutzen-style buttplate, and an opening lever like a repeating rifle. It features a 26" octagonal barrel and an oil-finished stock. It was manufactured in the late 1880s and is quite scarce in today's market.

Exc.	V.G.	Good	Fair	Poor
2500	1500	1000	850	650

Ballard No. 4 Perfection Rifle
This model is chambered for a number of centerfire calibers from .32-40 to .50-70. The barrel lengths are from 26" to 30", and the sights are of the "Rocky Mountain" type. This model was manufactured between 1876 and 1891.

Exc.	V.G.	Good	Fair	Poor
850	750	650	500	350

Ballard No. 3-1/2 Target Rifle
This model is similar to the No. 4 Perfection Rifle except that it has a checkered stock with a shotgun-style buttplate, a 30" barrel, and a tang peep sight with globe front sight. It was chambered for the .40-65 cartridge and was manufactured from 1880-1882.

Exc.	V.G.	Good	Fair	Poor
1200	1050	800	650	450

Ballard No. 4-1/2 Mid Range Rifle
This model is also a variation of the No. 4 Perfection model. It has a higher-grade checkered stock with a shotgun buttplate. It has a 30" part-round, part-octagonal barrel and is chambered for the .38-40, .40-65, and the .45-70 cartridges. It features a Vernier tang peep sight and a globe front sight. It was manufactured between 1878 and 1882.

Exc.	V.G.	Good	Fair	Poor
1500	1300	1150	950	675

Ballard No. 4-1/2 A-1 Mid Range Target Rifle
This is a deluxe version of the No. 4-1/2 rifle. It features scroll engraving on the frame with "Ballard A-1" on the left and "Mid-Range" on the right. It is chambered for the .38-50 and the .40-65 cartridge and has a high-grade checkered stock with a horn forend tip. The sights are the highest-grade Vernier tang sight and a spirit lever front sight. The shotgun or rifle-style butt was optional. This model was manufactured between 1878 and 1880.

Courtesy Milwaukee Public Museum, Milwaukee, Wisconsin

Exc.	V.G.	Good	Fair	Poor
2000	1800	1500	1150	850

Ballard No. 5 Pacific Rifle
This model has a 30" or 32" medium to heavyweight barrel, with a ramrod mounted underneath. It is chambered for many different calibers from .38-50 to .50-70. This model features "Rocky Mountain" sights, a crescent butt, double-set triggers, and a ring-style opening lever. It was manufactured between 1876 and 1891.

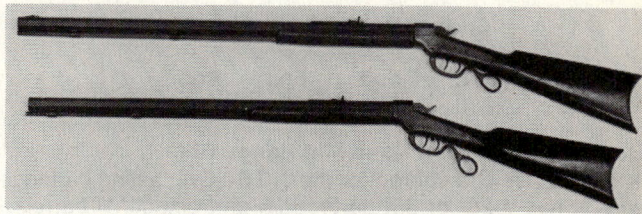

Courtesy Milwaukee Public Museum, Milwaukee, Wisconsin

Exc.	V.G.	Good	Fair	Poor
1800	1650	1300	950	650

Ballard No. 5-1/2 Montana Rifle
This model is similar to the Pacific Rifle, with an extra heavyweight barrel, and is chambered for the .45 Sharps cartridge only. It features a checkered steel shotgun-style buttplate. It was manufactured from 1882-1884 and has the late markings only.

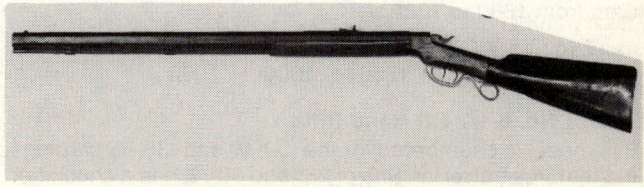

Courtesy Milwaukee Public Museum, Milwaukee, Wisconsin

Exc.	V.G.	Good	Fair	Poor
2500	2250	1750	1300	1000

Ballard No. 6 Schuetzen Off Hand Rifle

This model has a 30" or 32" octagonal barrel and is chambered for the .40-65, .44-75, and the .38-50 cartridges. The stock is of select walnut in the high-combed Schuetzen style. The buttplate is nickel-plated, and the receiver is not engraved. The sights are Vernier tang type on the rear and a spirit lever front. The triggers are double set, and the opening lever has a ring and a spur. This model is marked J.M. Marlin only and was manufactured between 1876 and 1880.

Exc.	V.G.	Good	Fair	Poor
2200	2000	1750	1300	1100

Ballard No. 6 Schuetzen Rifle

This model is similar to the Off Hand model but was produced by the later Marlin Firearms Company and was so marked. It is a more deluxe version with checkered stock, horn forend tip, and a fully engraved receiver. This model was chambered for the .32-40 and the .38-55 cartridges and was manufactured between 1881 and 1891.

Courtesy Milwaukee Public Museum, Milwaukee, Wisconsin

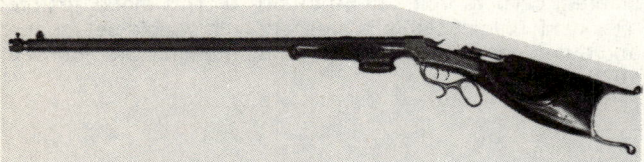

Courtesy Milwaukee Public Museum, Milwaukee, Wisconsin

Exc.	V.G.	Good	Fair	Poor
2500	2250	1750	1300	1000

Ballard No. 6-1/2 Off Hand Mid Range Rifle

This model is chambered for the .40-54 Everlasting cartridge only. It has a 28" or 30" part-round, part-octagonal barrel, a Schuetzen-style stock, and a plain non-engraved receiver. It was manufactured between 1880 and 1882.

Exc.	V.G.	Good	Fair	Poor
2000	1800	1500	1150	850

Ballard No. 6-1/2 Rigby Off Hand Mid Range Rifle

This model is chambered for the .38-50 and the .40-65 cartridges. It features the Rigby ribbed-style barrel in 26" and 28" lengths, with Vernier rear and globe front sights and a high grade, checkered walnut, Schuetzen-style stock with horn forend tip, and pistol grip cap. The buttplate is nickel-plated, and the opening lever is of the ring type with a single trigger and extensively engraved receiver. This model was manufactured from 1880 to 1882.

Exc.	V.G.	Good	Fair	Poor
2500	2250	1750	1300	1000

Ballard No. 6-1/2 Off Hand Rifle

This model is chambered for the .32-40 and .38-55 cartridges and features barrel lengths of 28" and 30". It has a checkered, high-grade walnut, Schuetzen-style stock with nickel-plated

buttplate. The forend tip and pistol grip cap are of horn, and the receiver is engraved. This model has a single trigger, full-ring opening lever, Vernier tang rear sight, and spirit lever front sight. The 6-1/2 Off Hand was made by the Marlin Firearms Company between 1883 and 1891 and is found with the later markings only.

Exc.	V.G.	Good	Fair	Poor
2250	1850	1550	1200	900

Ballard No. 7 "Creedmore A-1" Long Range Rifle

This model is commonly chambered for the .44-100 or the .45100 cartridges. It has a 34" part-round, part-octagonal barrel and a high grade checkered pistol grip stock, with a horn forend tip and shotgun-style butt. The sights are a special 1,300-yard Vernier tang rear and a spirit level front. There is another sight base on the heel of the stock for mounting the rear sight for ultra long-range shooting. The opening lever is similar to a repeating rifle, and a single trigger is featured. The receiver is engraved and marked "Ballard A-1" on the left and "Long Range" on the right. This model was manufactured between 1876 and 1886 and is found with both early and late markings.

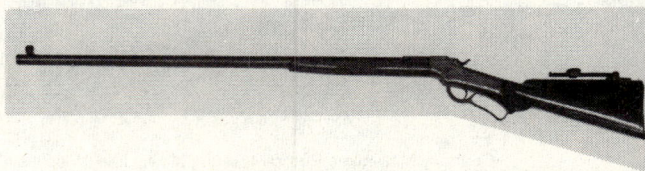

Courtesy Milwaukee Public Museum, Milwaukee, Wisconsin

Exc.	V.G.	Good	Fair	Poor
3000	2750	2250	1500	1200

Ballard No. 7 Long Range Rifle

This model is similar to the "Creedmore A-1" but is slightly less deluxe. The engraving is less elaborate, and the lettering on the receiver is absent. This model was manufactured between 1883 and 1890 and is found with the later markings only.

Exc.	V.G.	Good	Fair	Poor
2750	2500	2000	1250	1000

Ballard No. 7A-1 Long Range Rifle

This model is a higher grade version of the "Creedmore A-I," with fancier walnut and a checkered straight stock. Better sights and deluxe engraving are also featured. This model was manufactured between 1879 and 1883 and is found with both markings.

Exc.	V.G.	Good	Fair	Poor
3500	3250	2750	2000	1500

Ballard No. 7A-1 Extra Long Range Rifle

This is the highest grade version of the No. 7 rifles. It features a 34" "Rigby"-type ribbed, round barrel. This was usually a special-order rifle with most features to customer specifications. The model was manufactured in limited numbers between 1879 and 1883. It is found with both markings.

Exc.	V.G.	Good	Fair	Poor
4000	3500	3000	2250	1700

Ballard No. 8 Union Hill Rifle

This model has a 28" and 30" part-round, part-octagonal barrel and is chambered for the .32-40 and the .38-55 cartridges. It has a checkered pistol grip stock with nickel-plated buttplate; and the opening lever is fully enclosed ring, as on the repeaters. There is a double-set trigger and a tang peep with globe front sight. The receiver is not engraved. This model was manufactured between 1884 and 1890 and is found only with the late markings. This was one of the most popular rifles in the Ballard line.

Courtesy Milwaukee Public Museum, Milwaukee, Wisconsin

Exc.	V.G.	Good	Fair	Poor
1500	1250	1000	750	500

Ballard No. 9 Union Hill Rifle

This model is similar to the No. 8 except that it features a single trigger and better sights. It was manufactured between 1884 and 1891 and has the later markings only.

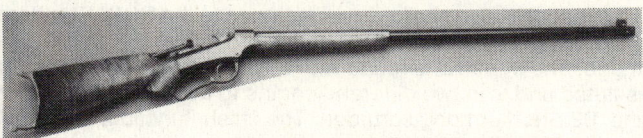

Courtesy Butterfield & Butterfield, San Francisco, California

Exc.	V.G.	Good	Fair	Poor
1800	1600	1250	1000	700

Ballard No. 10 Schuetzen Junior Rifle

This model is simply a heavier-barreled version of the No. 9. The barrel is 32" long, and the checkered pistol grip stock is of the off-hand style. The rear sight is a Vernier Mid Range model, and the front sight is a spirit-level type. This was a popular model that was manufactured between 1885 and 1891. It is found with the later markings only.

Exc.	V.G.	Good	Fair	Poor
2000	1800	1500	1150	850

Marlin Handguns

The first firearm that was manufactured by John M. Marlin was actually a derringer-type single shot that was small enough to be hidden in the palm of the hand. From this beginning evolved the company that became known for its highly accurate and dependable rifles. The Marlin Company manufactured handguns up to the turn of the century, discontinuing their last and only double action model in 1899.

1st Model Derringer

Courtesy Milwaukee Public Museum, Milwaukee, Wisconsin

This was the first handgun produced by Marlin. The barrel is 2-1/16" long and pivots to the side for loading. There is a plunger under the frame that is depressed to free the barrel. This device is a Ballard patent. This pistol is chambered for the .22 rimfire cartridge, and there is no extractor. The frame is brass and usually nickel-plated. It has two grooves milled beneath the blued barrel. The grips are of rosewood. The barrel is stamped "J.M. Marlin, New Haven, Ct." There were approximately 2,000 manufactured between 1863 and 1867. They are quite scarce on today's market.

Exc.	V.G.	Good	Fair	Poor
500	425	350	250	175

O.K. Model Derringer

The O.K. Model is chambered for .22, .30, and .32 rimfire cartridges. The barrel is 2-1/8" or 3-1/8" on the .32. There is no extractor, and it functions as the 1st Model. The frame is plated brass with flat sides, and the barrel is found either blued or nickel-plated. The grips are rosewood. The markings are the same as on the 1st Model but are located on the right side of the barrel. The top of the barrel is marked "O.K." There were approximately 5,000 manufactured between 1863 and 1870.

Exc.	V.G.	Good	Fair	Poor
450	400	325	225	150

Victor Model Derringer

This model is similar in appearance to the "O.K." Model but is larger in size and is chambered for the .38-caliber rimfire cartridge. The barrel is 2 11/16" long; and there was, for the first time, an extractor. The finish and function were unchanged. The right side of the barrel is stamped "J.M. Marlin/New Haven, Ct./Pat. April 5.1870." "Victor" is stamped on the top of the barrel. There were approximately 4,000 manufactured between 1870 and 1881.

Exc.	V.G.	Good	Fair	Poor
500	425	350	250	175

Nevermiss Model Derringer

This model was made in three different sizes chambered for the .22, .32, and .41 rimfire cartridges. The barrel is 2.5" long and swings sideways for loading. The frame is plated brass, and the barrels are either blued or nickel-plated. The grips are rosewood. The frame is grooved under the barrels as on the 1st model. There is an extractor on this model. The barrel markings are the same as on the "Victor," with the top of the barrel marked "Nevermiss." There were approximately 5,000 manufactured between 1870 and 1881.

.22 and .32 Caliber Models

Exc.	V.G.	Good	Fair	Poor
300	250	200	150	100

.41 Caliber Model

Exc.	V.G.	Good	Fair	Poor
400	350	300	250	175

Stonewall Model Derringer

This model is identical to the .41-caliber "Nevermiss," but the top of the barrel is marked "Stonewall." It is rarely encountered.

Exc.	V.G.	Good	Fair	Poor
500	450	400	350	225

O.K. Pocket Revolver

This is a solid-frame, spur-trigger, single action revolver chambered for the .22 rimfire short. The round barrel is 2.25", and the 7-shot cylinder is unfluted. The frame is nickel-plated brass with a blue or nickel-plated barrel, and the bird's-head grips are rosewood. The cylinder pin is removable and is used to knock the empty cases out of the cylinder. The top of the barrel is marked "O.K." and "J.M. Marlin. New Haven, Conn. U.S.A." There were approximately 1,500 manufactured between 1870 and 1875.

Exc.	V.G.	Good	Fair	Poor
350	300	250	200	150

Little Joker Revolver

This model is similar in appearance to the "O.K." Model except that it features engraving and ivory or pearl grips. There were approximately 500 manufactured between 1871 and 1873.

Exc.	V.G.	Good	Fair	Poor
400	350	300	250	175

J. M. Marlin Standard Pocket Revolvers

In 1872 Marlin began production of its Smith & Wesson looka-like. The Manhattan Firearms Company had developed a copy of the Model 1 S&W .22 cartridge revolver. In 1868 the company ceased business, and the revolvers were produced by the American Standard Tool Company until their dissolution in 1873. In 1872 Marlin had entered into an agreement with this company to manufacture these revolvers, which were no longer protected by the Rollin White patent after 1869. The Marlin revolvers are similar to those made by American Standard, the only real difference being that Marlin grips are of the bird's-head round configuration. A contoured grip frame and a patented pawl spring mechanism is utilized on the Marlin revolvers.

Marlin XXX Standard 1872 Pocket Revolver

This is the first in the series of four Standard model revolvers. It is chambered for the .30 caliber rimfire. The earlier model has an octagonal 3-1/8" barrel; and the later, a round 3" barrel. There are round and octagonal barrel variations (with unfluted cylinder) and round barrel variations (with short and long fluted cylinders). All of the barrels are ribbed and tip up for loading. They have plated brass frames, and the barrels are nickel-plated. The bird's-head grips are of rosewood or hard rubber, bearing the monogram "M.F.A. Co." inside a star. There is a spur trigger. The markings "J.M. Marlin-New Haven Ct." appear on the earlier octagonal-barreled models. "U.S.A. Pat. July 1. 1873" was added to the later round-barreled models. All barrels are marked "XXX Standard 1872." There were approximately 5,000 of all types manufactured between 1872 and 1887.

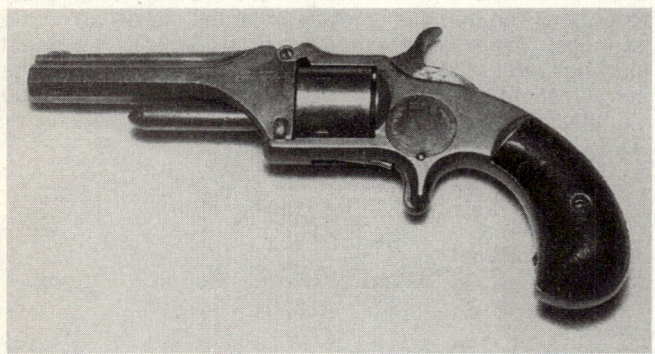

Octagon Barrel-Early Variation

Exc.	V.G.	Good	Fair	Poor
400	350	300	250	175

Round Barrel-Non-Fluted Cylinder

Exc.	V.G.	Good	Fair	Poor
375	325	275	225	150

Round Barrel-Short Fluted Cylinder

Exc.	V.G.	Good	Fair	Poor
350	300	250	200	125

Round Barrel-Long Fluted Cylinder

Exc.	V.G.	Good	Fair	Poor
300	250	200	150	100

Marlin XX Standard 1873 Pocket Revolver

This model is similar in appearance to the XXX 1872 model except that it is chambered for the .22 long rimfire and is marked "XX Standard 1873." There are three basic variations: the early octagonal barrel model with non-fluted cylinder, the round barrel model with non-fluted cylinder, and the round barrel with fluted cylinder. Function and features are the same as described for the "XXX Standard 1872" model. There were approximately 5,000 manufactured between 1873 and 1887.

Early Octagon Barrel Model

Exc.	V.G.	Good	Fair	Poor
350	300	250	200	150

Round Barrel-Non-Fluted Cylinder

Exc.	V.G.	Good	Fair	Poor
300	250	200	150	100

Round Barrel-Fluted Cylinder

Exc.	V.G.	Good	Fair	Poor
275	225	175	125	80

Marlin No. 32 Standard 1875 Pocket Revolver

This model is also similar in appearance to the "XXX Standard 1872" model except that it is chambered for the .32 rimfire cartridge. The 3" barrel is round with a rib, and the 5-shot cylinder is fluted and is in two different lengths to accommodate either the .32 Short or Long cartridge. The finish, function, and most markings are the same as on previous models with the exception of the barrel top marking "No. 32 Standard 1875." There were approximately 8,000 manufactured between 1875 and 1887.

Exc.	V.G.	Good	Fair	Poor
275	225	175	125	80

Marlin 38 Standard 1878 Pocket Revolver

This model is different than its predecessors in that it features a steel frame and flat bottom butt, with hard rubber monogram grips. There was still a spur trigger, and the 3.25" ribbed round barrel still tipped up for loading. This model is chambered for the .38 centerfire cartridge. The finish is full nickel plate, and the top of the barrel is marked "38 Standard 1878." There were approximately 9,000 manufactured between 1878 and 1887.

Exc.	V.G.	Good	Fair	Poor
300	250	200	150	100

Marlin 1887 Double Action Revolver

This is the last handgun that Marlin produced and the only double action. It is chambered for the .32 or the .38 caliber centerfire cartridges and is of the break-open auto-ejector type. The fluted cylinder holds 6 shots in .32 and 5 shots in .38 caliber. The round ribbed barrel is 3.25" in length, and the frame is made of steel. The standard finish is nickel-plated with a blued triggerguard. Many full-blued examples have been noted. The round butt grips are hard rubber, and the top of the barrel is marked "Marlin Firearms Co. New Haven Conn. U.S.A./Patented Aug. 9 1887." There were approximately 15,000 manufactured between 1887 and 1899.

Exc.	V.G.	Good	Fair	Poor
325	275	225	150	100

EARLY PRODUCTION MARLIN RIFLES

Model 1881 Lever Action Rifle

This was the first of the Marlin lever-action rifles and has always been regarded as a high quality rifle. It is capable of handling the large calibers and was well received by the shooting public. The rifle is chambered for the .32-40, .38-55, .40-60, .45-70, and the .45-85. The 24", 28", or 30" octagonal barrel is standard. Round barrels were offered and are scarce today. There is a tubular magazine beneath the barrel, and the rear sight is the buckhorn type with a blade on the front. This model ejects its empty cartridges from the top. The finish is blued, with a case-colored hammer, lever, and buttplate. The walnut stock is varnished. There were approximately 20,000 manufactured between 1881 and 1892 but this is not easy to ascertain, as the factory records on Marlin rifles are quite incomplete.

Courtesy Butterfield & Butterfield, San Francisco, California

Courtesy Butterfield & Butterfield, San Francisco, California

Exc.	V.G.	Good	Fair	Poor
2200	1300	950	650	350

Lightweight Model-Thinner Frame, Lever, and Barrel .32-40 and .38-55 Caliber Only-24" and 28" Barrel

Exc.	V.G.	Good	Fair	Poor
3000	2000	1750	1250	900

Model 1888 Lever Action Rifle

This model is chambered for the .32-20, .38-40, and the .44-40 cartridges. This is a shorter action that was designed (chiefly by Lewis Hepburn) to handle the pistol cartridges for which it was chambered. The standard barrel was octagonal, but round barrels were available as special-order items. This is a top ejecting action. It has a buckhorn rear and a blade front sight. The finish is blued with a case-colored hammer, lever, and buttplate. The walnut stock is varnished. There were approximately 4,800 manufactured in 1888 and 1889. As with most of these fine old rifles, many special-order options were available that affect today's market value. Individual appraisal would be necessary for these special models, to ascertain both value and authenticity.

Exc.	V.G.	Good	Fair	Poor
2000	1200	900	600	350

> **On December 11, 1995 a Marlin Model 1889 Exhibition Grade factory engraved rifle with 22" barrel was sold at Rock Island Auction for $30,800. The rifle was engraved by Master engraver C.F. Ulrich with gold and platinum enlays. This is a one of a kind Marlin.**

Model 1889 Lever Action Rifle

This was Marlin's first side-eject, solid-top rifle. It is chambered for .25-20, .32-20, .38-40, and the .44-40 cartridges. It features either octagonal or round barrels in lengths from 24" to 32" with buckhorn rear and blade front sights. The finish is blued with a case-colored hammer, lever, and buttplate. The plain walnut stock is varnished. The barrel is stamped "Marlin Fire-Arms Co. New Haven Ct. U.S.A./Patented Oct.11 1887 April 2.1889." This model features a lever latch, and many options were offered. Again one must urge individual appraisal on such variations. Values fluctuate greatly due to some seemingly insignificant variation. There were approximately 55,000 manufactured between 1889 and 1899.

Production Model 24" Barrel

Exc.	V.G.	Good	Fair	Poor
900	700	550	350	250

Carbine 20" Barrel and Saddle Ring on Left Side of Receiver

Exc.	V.G.	Good	Fair	Poor
1500	1300	1000	750	500

Musket 30" Barrel with Full-length Stock-68 Made in .44-40

Exc.	V.G.	Good	Fair	Poor
3500	3250	2750	2250	1500

> **Rock Island Auction sold a Deluxe Model 1889 rifle engraved by Louis Nimschke. chambered for 32-20 with a rare 28" octagon barrel. Condition is excellent. Price was $30,250.**

Model 1891 Lever Action Rifle

This was Marlin's first rifle designed to fire the .22 rimfire and the first repeating rifle to accept the .22 Short, Long, and Long Rifle cartridges interchangeably. It was also chambered for the .32 rimfire and centerfire. The 24" octagonal barrel is standard, with a buckhorn rear and blade front sight. The finish is blued with a case-colored hammer, lever, and buttplate. The stock is plain walnut. The first variation is marked "Marlin Fire-Arms Co. New Haven, Ct. U.S.A./Pat'd Nov.19.1878.April 2.1889. Aug.12 1890" on the barrel, with the solid-topped frame marked "Marlin Safety." The second variation was marked the same with "March 1,1892" added. There were approximately 18,650 manufactured between 1891 and 1897.

Ist Variation .22 Rimfire Only-Side Loading-Appr. 5,000

Exc.	V.G.	Good	Fair	Poor
2000	1250	1000	750	500

2nd Variation-.22 and .32 Rimfire, .32 Centerfire, Tube Loading, Model 1891 on Later Model Tangs

Exc.	V.G.	Good	Fair	Poor
1400	650	500	400	275

NOTE: Add 20% for .22 rifle with "1891" stamped on tang. Deduct 50% for .32 caliber.

Model 1892 Lever Action Rifle

This is basically an improved version of the Model 1891 and is similar to the second variation of the 1891. The only notable exceptions were the tang marking "Model 1892" and "Model 92" on later models. The .22 rimfire was scarce in the Model 1892. There were approximately 45,000 manufactured between 1895 and 1916. There were many options, and these special-order guns must be individually appraised to ascertain value and authenticity.

Antique (Pre-1898)-Add 20%.

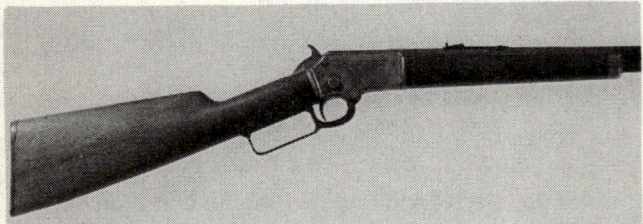

Exc.	V.G.	Good	Fair	Poor
1000	600	400	250	150

.32 Rimfire and Centerfire

Exc.	V.G.	Good	Fair	Poor
500	300	200	150	100

Model 1893 Lever Action Rifle

This model was the first rifle Marlin designed for the then new smokeless powder cartridges. It is chambered for the .25-36, .30-30, .32 Special, .32-40, and the .38-55. It was offered standard with either a round or octagonal barrel, in lengths of 24" to 32". Buckhorn rear and blade front sights were also standard. The receiver, lever, hammer, and buttplate are case-colored, and the rest is blued. The stock is varnished walnut.

As with all of these early Marlins, many options were offered and, when encountered, will drastically alter the value of the particular rifle. For this reason we supply the values for the basic model and urge securing competent appraisal on nonstandard specimens. The barrel on earlier guns is marked "Marlin FireArms Co. New Haven, Ct.U.S.A./ Patented Oct.11. 1887.April 2.1889.Aug.1.1893." In 1919 the markings were changed to "The Marlin Firearms Corporation/ New Haven, Conn.U.S.A.Patented." The rifles manufactured after 1904 are marked "Special Smokeless Steel" on the left side of the barrel. The upper tang is marked "Model 1893" on early guns; and "Model 93," on later specimens. There were approximately 900,000 manufactured between 1893 and 1935. Factory records are incomplete on the Model 1893.

> On December 11, 1995 Rock Island Auction sold a Model 1893 Marlin rifle for $57,750. It was chambered for the 38-55 cartridge and fitted with a 26" half octagon barrel. Receiver was done in the factory number 5/4 pattern with gold enlays. Condition was near mint.

Antique Production Pre-1898

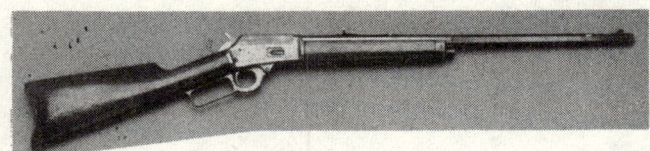

Courtesy Butterfield & Butterfield, San Francisco, California

Exc.	V.G.	Good	Fair	Poor
1400	1000	650	450	275

Modern Production 1899-1935

Exc.	V.G.	Good	Fair	Poor
1250	850	550	350	225

Model 1894 Lever Action Rifle

This model is similar to the Model 1893, with a shorter action. It is chambered for the .25-20, .32-20, .38-40, and the .44-40. 24" to 32" round or octagonal barrels with full-length magazine tubes are standard, as are buckhorn rear and blade front sights. The finish is case-colored receiver, lever, hammer, and buttplate, with the rest blued. The walnut stock is varnished. The first versions were marked "Marlin Fire-Arms Co., New Haven, Ct.U.S.A./Patented Oct.11, 1887. April 2,1889." The top of the frame is marked "Marlin Safety," and the model designation is not stamped on the tang. These early rifles were chambered for .38-40 and .44-40 only. The later rifles added the patent date "Aug. 1, 1893"; and "Model 1894" was stamped on the tang. On the latest versions this was shortened to "Model 94." There were approximately 250,000 manufactured between 1894 and 1935. This model was also produced with a great many options. Individual appraisal should be secured when confronted with these features.

> A Model 1894 Deluxe takedown rifle was sold at a December 11,1995 Rock Island Auction for $22,000. It is factory engraved and chambered for the .32-20 cartridge. Fitted with 24" half octagon barrel. Checkered pistol grip.
> Engraving pattern is No. 5 (1) style.

Antique Production (Pre-1898)

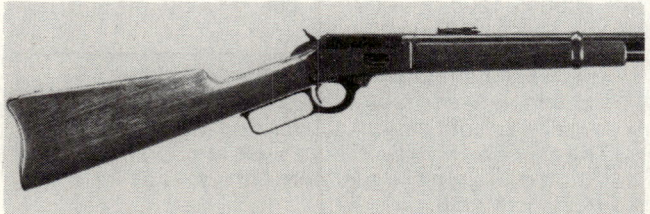

Exc.	V.G.	Good	Fair	Poor
1400	1000	650	450	275

Modern Production (1899-1935)

Exc.	V.G.	Good	Fair	Poor
1250	850	550	350	225

Model 1895 Lever Action Rifle

This is a large rifle designed to fire the larger hunting cartridges. It is chambered for the .33 W.C.F., .38-56, .40-65, .40-70, .40-83, .45-70, and the .45-90. It came standard with round or octagonal barrels from 26" to 32" in length. A bull-length magazine tube was also standard, as were buckhorn rear and blade front sights. The finish is case-colored receiver, lever, and hammer; the rest is blued with a varnished walnut stock. The barrel markings are the same as the Model 1894, and the top tang is marked "Model 1895." After 1896 "Special Smokeless Steel" was stamped on the barrel. There were also many options available for this model, and they have a big effect on the value. There were approximately 18,000 manufactured between 1895 and 1917.

> A gold inlaid factory engraved Model 1895 rifle was sold at December 11, 1995 auction for $79,750. Chambered for 45-70 with 26" half octagon barrel. This particular Marlin is considered to be the finest known to exist.
> Rock Island Auction Co.

Antique Production (Pre-1898)

Exc.	V.G.	Good	Fair	Poor
3500	2750	2000	1250	600

Modern Production (1899-1917)

Exc.	V.G.	Good	Fair	Poor
3000	2400	1600	1000	500

Model 1895 Century Limited

Introduced in 1995 to commemorate the 100th anniversary of the Marlin Model 1895, as well as the 125th anniversary of the Marlin Company. The rifle is chambered for the 45-70 Gov't cartridge. It features a 24" half round/half octagon barrel, a crescent buttplate, semi-fancy American black walnut stock, and French greyed engraved receiver. Production limited to 2,500 guns.

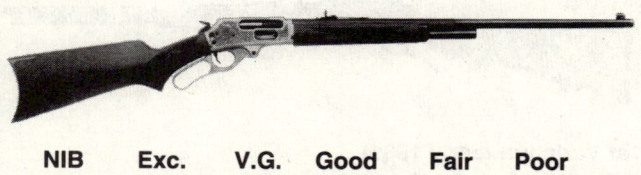

NIB	Exc.	V.G.	Good	Fair	Poor
800	650	500	350	275	200

Model 1897 Lever Action Rifle

This model is an improved version of the Model 1892. It was chambered for the .22 rimfire only and came standard with a 24", 26", or 28" round, octagonal, or part-round, part-octagonal barrel. The standard sights are buckhorn rear and blade front, and all were manufactured as takedown rifles. They have case-colored receiver, lever, and hammer. The rest is blued, and the walnut stock is varnished. There were approximately 125,000 manufactured between 1897 and 1917. In 1922 production was begun with the designation changed to Model 39 which is produced to this day. There were also options offered with this rifle that have great effect on the value; take this into consideration and seek qualified appraisal.

For First Year Production Antique-Add 40%.

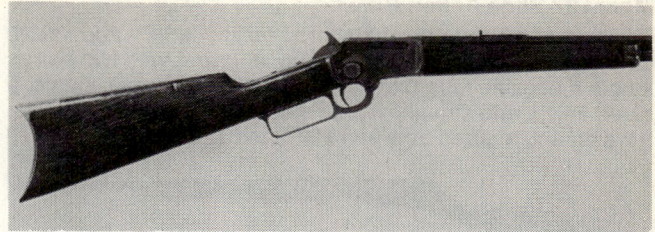

Standard Production Rifle

Exc.	V.G.	Good	Fair	Poor
1250	850	650	350	200

Deluxe Rifle with checkering and fancy pistol grip stock

> A Model 1897 Deluxe Marlin rifle was sold at Rock Island Auction on December 11, 1995, for $35,750. Executed in factory No. 10 pattern with gold enlays. This rifle is only one of two to exist in this configuration. Condition was excellent.

Exc.	V.G.	Good	Fair	Poor
2200	1500	850	500	300

MODERN PRODUCTION MARLIN RIFLES

Model 18 Slide Action Rifle

This model is chambered for the .22 rimfire cartridges. It was offered standard with a 20" round or octagonal barrel, open sights, and a straight walnut stock. It has an exposed hammer and blued finish with blued steel buttplate. There is a half-length tubular magazine, and the stock features a quick takedown screw on the top tang which was marked "Model 18." This rifle was manufactured between 1906 and 1909.

Exc.	V.G.	Good	Fair	Poor
350	300	250	150	100

Model 20 Slide Action Rifle

The Model 20 was chambered for the .22 rimfire cartridges and was offered standard with a 24" octagonal barrel and open sight, with an exposed hammer. This rifle was only made as a "Takedown" receiver model and is blued, with a straight walnut stock. It was manufactured between 1907 and 1909.

Exc.	V.G.	Good	Fair	Poor
350	300	250	150	100

Model 25 Slide Action Rifle

This model was chambered for the .22 Short only and was not a commercial success. The 23" round or octagonal barrel is standard, as are open sights. It is called a takedown model, but only the stock is removable—the receiver does not separate. It has an exposed hammer, tubular magazine, and straight walnut stock. The finish is blued. This rifle was manufactured in 1910.

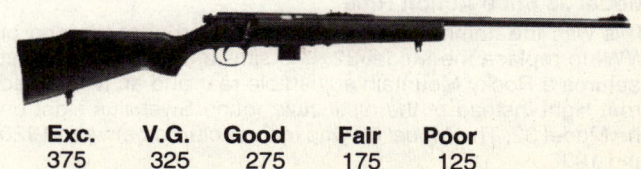

Exc.	V.G.	Good	Fair	Poor
375	325	275	175	125

Model 27 Slide Action Rifle

This is a centerfire rifle chambered for the .25-20 and .32-20 cartridges. It features a 24" octagonal barrel with two-thirds-length magazine tube that holds 7 shots. It has open sights, a blued finish, and straight walnut stock with crescent buttplate. It was manufactured between 1910 and 1932.

Exc.	V.G.	Good	Fair	Poor
350	300	250	150	100

Model 27S Slide Action Rifle

The Model 27S is similar to the Model 27 but was offered with a round or octagonal 24" barrel. The .25 rimfire cartridge was added to those already available. This model was introduced in 1913 and was manufactured until 1932.

Exc.	V.G.	Good	Fair	Poor
350	300	250	150	100

Model 29 Slide Action Rifle

This model is identical to the Model 20 with a 23" round barrel and smooth walnut forend instead of a grooved one as found on the Model 20. It was manufactured between 1913 and 1916.

Exc.	V.G.	Good	Fair	Poor
350	300	250	150	100

Model 32 Slide Action Rifle

This model was the first of the hammerless slide-action rifles. It is chambered for the .22 rimfire and has a 24" octagonal barrel and half-length magazine tube. The Model 32 is a takedown rifle with adjustable sights and features "Ballard" rifling. It is blued, with a pistol grip walnut stock. The advent of WWI and the need for Marlin to produce military arms cut short the production of this model. It was manufactured in 1914 and 1915 only.

Exc.	V.G.	Good	Fair	Poor
450	350	250	150	100

Model 37 Slide Action Rifle

This model is the same as the Model 29 with a 24" round barrel and full-length magazine tube. It was manufactured between 1913 and 1916.

Exc.	V.G.	Good	Fair	Poor
350	300	250	150	100

Model 38 Slide Action Rifle

This was the hammerless model introduced after the end of WWI to replace the Model 32. It is similar in appearance but features a Rocky Mountain adjustable rear and an ivory bead front sight instead of the distinctive round Swebilius sight on the Model 32. The Model 38 was manufactured between 1920 and 1930.

Exc.	V.G.	Good	Fair	Poor
450	350	250	150	100

Model 40 Slide Action Rifle

This model is identical to the Model 27S centerfire rifle except that the barrel is marked "Marlin-Rockwell." The top tang is stamped "Marlin/Mod. 40." This is a rare model, and not many marked in this manner have been noted.

Exc.	V.G.	Good	Fair	Poor
350	300	250	150	100

Model 47 Slide Action Rifle

This model is similar to the Model 20, with a 23" round barrel and an improved magazine tube. The Model 47 has a case-colored receiver and a checkered buttstock. This model was not offered for sale nor was it listed in Marlin's catalog but was offered free of charge to anyone purchasing four shares of Marlin stock for $100. One other fact about this model is that it was the first Marlin to be case-colored with the new cyanide method; this created a tiger-striped pattern that is peculiar to the Model 47 Rifle.

Exc.	V.G.	Good	Fair	Poor
350	300	250	150	100

Model 1936 Lever Action Carbine

This model is a direct descendant of the Model 1893. It is chambered for the .30-30 and the .32 Special cartridge. The stock is streamlined with a pistol grip added and a 20" round barrel. A barrel band and improved sights are utilized. It has a 7-shot tube magazine and a semi-beavertail forearm. The receiver, lever, and hammer are case-colored; and the rest is blued. This model was manufactured between 1936 and 1948. It was designated the Model 36 in 1937.

1st Variation (early 1936)

This variation has a slight "fish-belly" forearm, long tang, case-colored receiver, lever, and hammer, with no serial number prefix. These are rare.

Exc.	V.G.	Good	Fair	Poor
800	600	300	175	125

2nd Variation (1936-1947)

This variation has thicker forearm, short tang, and serial number prefix.

Exc.	V.G.	Good	Fair	Poor
550	400	250	150	100

Model 36 Lever Action Rifle

This model is similar to the Model 1936 Carbine, with a 24" barrel, two-thirds-length magazine tube, and steel forend tip instead of the barrel band. Is fitted with ramp sight with hood.

1st Variation (early 1936)

This variation has a slight "fish-belly" forearm, long tang, case-colored receiver, lever, and hammer, with no serial number prefix. These are rare.

Exc.	V.G.	Good	Fair	Poor
875	650	325	195	125

2nd Variation (1936-1947)

This variation has thicker forearm, short tang, and serial number prefix.

Exc.	V.G.	Good	Fair	Poor
600	450	275	175	100

Model 36 Sporting Carbine

This model is similar to the 1936 Carbine, with a 20" barrel. It features a two-thirds-length magazine tube and holds 6 shots instead of 7. The front sight is a ramp sight with hood.

Exc.	V.G.	Good	Fair	Poor
325	275	225	175	125

Model 36A-DL Lever Action Rifle

This model is similar to the Model 36A, with a deluxe checkered stock. It features sight swivels and is furnished with a leather sling.

Exc.	V.G.	Good	Fair	Poor
675	550	300	225	150

Model 336 Carbine

This model was introduced in 1948 and was an improved version of the Model 36. It features a new-type round bolt, chrome-plated with improved extractor and redesigned cartridge carrier that improved feeding. It is chambered for the .30-30 and the .32 Special cartridges and has a 20" tapered round barrel with Ballard-type rifling. The finish is blued, with the receiver top matted to reduce reflections. The pistol grip stock and semi-beavertail forend are of American walnut. It features Rocky Mountain-style rear and bead front sights, and the hammer is lowered to facilitate scope mounting.

Exc.	V.G.	Good	Fair	Poor
250	200	175	125	100

Model 336C

The same as the Model 336 Carbine. In 1951 the catalog model designation was changed. In 1953 the .35 Remington cartridge was added to the line.

Exc.	V.G.	Good	Fair	Poor
250	200	175	125	100

Model 336A

This model is similar to the 336C, with a 24" barrel and steel forend tip instead of a barrel band. The magazine tube is two-thirds-length and holds 6 shots. This model was introduced in 1948 and built until 1962. It was reintroduced in 1973 and discontinued in 1980.

Exc.	V.G.	Good	Fair	Poor
350	275	200	150	125

Model 336 ADL

This model differs from the Model 336A by having a checkered stock and forend, swivels, and a sling.

Exc.	V.G.	Good	Fair	Poor
550	375	225	150	125

Model 336 SC

This is basically a 336A with forend tip and two-thirds magazine but has a 20" barrel instead of the 24" found on the 336A.

Exc.	V.G.	Good	Fair	Poor
225	200	175	150	100

Model 336 SD

This is the 336 SC in a deluxe checkered stock version, with swivels and supplied with a sling.

Exc.	V.G.	Good	Fair	Poor
300	250	225	175	125

Model 336 Zipper

This model was advertised as a fast-handling, lever-action carbine chambered for the .219 Zipper cartridges flat trajectory, varmint-type round. It has a 20" barrel, which was the feature that doomed it to failure as this was too short to coax the maximum performance and accuracy from the cartridge. The "MicroGroove" rifling that was used did not yield long barrel life; and the model survived from 1955 through 1959, when it was discontinued. It is externally similar to the 336 SC.

Exc.	V.G.	Good	Fair	Poor
400	350	300	200	150

Model 336T (Texan)

This is a straight-stock version of the 336C, chambered for the .30-30 cartridge, with an 18.5" barrel. It was manufactured from 1954-1983.

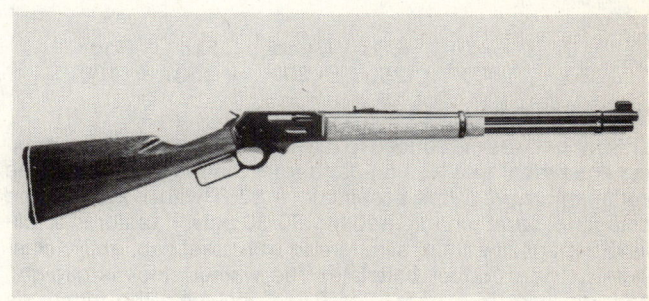

Exc.	V.G.	Good	Fair	Poor
250	200	175	125	100

Model 336 DT

A deluxe-stock version of the "Texan," with the map of Texas and a longhorn carved on the butt. It was manufactured between 1962 and 1964.

Exc.	V.G.	Good	Fair	Poor
300	250	225	175	125

Model 336 "Marauder"

This is simply a 336 T with a 16.25" barrel and a slimmer forend. It is chambered for either the .30-30 or .35 Remington cartridges, has a gold trigger, and is drilled and tapped for both scope mounts and receiver sights. It was manufactured in 1963 and 1964.

Exc.	V.G.	Good	Fair	Poor
275	250	200	150	100

Model 336 .44 Magnum

This is the 336 "Marauder" with a 20" Micro-Groove barrel chambered for the .44 Magnum cartridge. It holds 10 shots and was introduced in 1963.

Exc.	V.G.	Good	Fair	Poor
275	250	200	150	100

Model 336 T "Centennial"

In 1970 a 100th year medallion was embedded into the butt stock of every rifle manufactured.

Exc.	V.G.	Good	Fair	Poor
275	250	200	150	100

1970 100th Year Commemorative Matched Pair

This is a deluxe octagonal barreled .30-30 with an engraved receiver and deluxe wood with an inlaid medallion, accompanied by a matching Model 339 .22 rimfire rifle. They are numbered the same and are furnished in a deluxe luggage case. There were 1,000 sets manufactured in 1970. These are commemoratives, and as such it should be noted that collectors usually will only show interest if they are new and uncocked in the original packaging. All accessories and brochures should be included for them to be worth top dollar. Once a commemorative has been used, it has no more value than as a shooter.

NIB	Exc.	V.G.	Good	Fair	Poor
1000	850	650	500	400	300

Model 336 "Zane Grey Century"

This model was introduced in 1972, the 100th anniversary of the birth of Zane Grey, the famous Western author. This model has a 22" octagonal barrel chambered for the .30-30. The stock is high grade walnut and features a brass buttplate and pistol grip cap. A Zane Grey medallion is inlaid into the receiver. There were 10,000 manufactured in 1972. This is a commemorative rifle and must be new in the box to generate the top collector appeal.

NIB	Exc.	V.G.	Good	Fair	Poor
350	300	250	200	150	100

Model 336 Octagon

This model was introduced to utilize the octagonal barrel making equipment that was on hand from the manufacture of the commemoratives. It is essentially a 336T with a 22" tapered octagonal barrel chambered for .30-30 only. It features a full-length magazine tube, slim forend with steel cap, and a classic-style hard rubber buttplate. The walnut stock is straight, and the lever is square. The finish, including the trigger, is blued. This model was made in 1973 only.

NIB	Exc.	V.G.	Good	Fair	Poor
600	500	325	175	150	100

Model 336 ER (Extra Range)

This model was introduced in 1983 and was advertised as being chambered for the .307 Winchester and the .356 Winchester cartridges. The .307 was never produced. The .356 Winchester was supposed to add new capabilities to this classic rifle, but it never caught on with the shooting public and was discontinued in 1986 after only 2,441 Model ERs were manufactured. It has a 20" barrel and 5-shot tube magazine.

Exc.	V.G.	Good	Fair	Poor
400	350	300	250	150

Model 336 CS

This is the current carbine model of this line. It has a hammer-block safety and is chambered for the .30-30, .35 Remington, and until 1988 the .375 Winchester. The barrel is 20", and the magazine tube holds 6 shots. The pistol grip stock and semi-beavertail forearm are American walnut. This model has been manufactured since 1984. The 1983 model was known as the 336C and had no hammer-block safety.

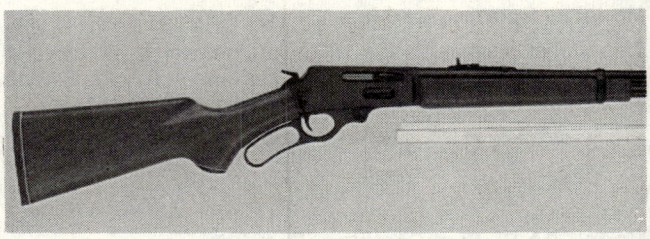

NIB	Exc.	V.G.	Good	Fair	Poor
275	225	200	175	150	100

Model 336 LTS

This is the latest version of the old "Marauder" carbine. It was dubbed the LTS or "Lightweight" model instead of the Marauder as it was feared that the latter designation would be inappropriate in today's society. The model features a 16.5" barrel with full-length tube magazine that holds 5 shots. The walnut stock has a straight grip, and there is a barrel band on the forearm. The butt has a rubber rifle pad. This model was introduced in 1988.

NIB	Exc.	V.G.	Good	Fair	Poor
350	300	250	200	150	100

Model 30 AS

This model is similar to the 336 CS, but the stock is made of walnut-finished hardwood instead of genuine American walnut. It is chambered for .30-30 only.

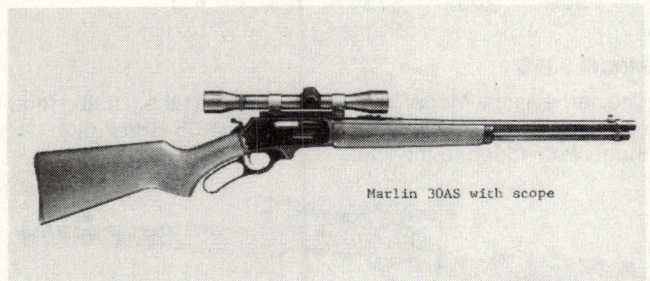

Marlin 30AS with scope

NIB	Exc.	V.G.	Good	Fair	Poor
285	250	200	175	125	100

Model 375 Lever Action

This model was introduced in 1980. It has a 20" Micro-Groove barrel and is chambered for the .375 Winchester cartridge. This should have been a popular rifle; but perhaps because of difficulty in obtaining ammunition, it was not a commercial success. Its appearance is much the same as the Model 336, with walnut pistol stock and steel forend tip. This model was discontinued in 1983 after 16,315 were manufactured.

Exc.	V.G.	Good	Fair	Poor
250	225	175	125	100

Model 444 Lever Action

This model was introduced in 1965. It is chambered for the .444 Marlin, a large and powerful cartridge that has the capability of dropping any game in North America, theoretically speaking. The rifle is essentially a Model 336 action modified to accept the larger cartridge. It has a 24" round barrel that was cut back to 22" in 1971. It holds 5 shots total and, when introduced, featured a straight-gripped Monte Carlo stock and semi-beavertail forend with barrel band. Another band holds the two-thirds-length magazine tube in place. In 1971 the stock was changed to a pistol grip without the Monte Carlo comb.

Exc.	V.G.	Good	Fair	Poor
325	250	175	125	100

Model 444 S

This model was introduced in 1972 and is essentially the later 444 with a steel forend tip instead of the barrel bands.

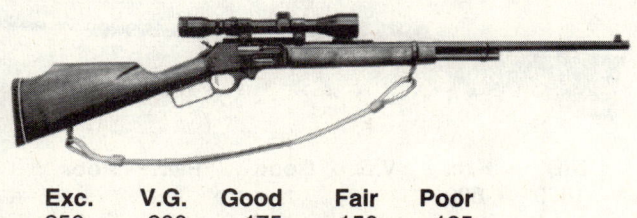

Exc.	V.G.	Good	Fair	Poor
250	200	175	150	125

Model 444 SS

In 1984 the company added a crossbolt hammer-block safety to the 444 S and redesignated it the 444 SS. This Model is currently in production.

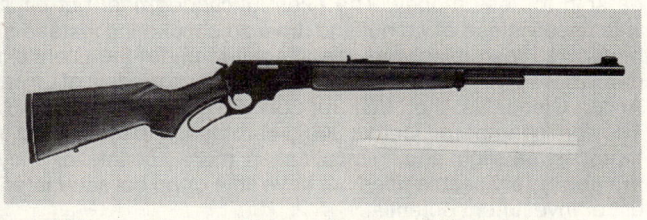

NIB	Exc.	V.G.	Good	Fair	Poor
300	250	225	175	150	125

Model 1894 Lever Action

The production of the Model 336 in .44 Magnum was a frustrating experience as the action was simply too long for a short pistol case. In 1969 Marlin reintroduced the Model 1894 chambered for the .44 Magnum cartridge. The barrel is 20", and the full-length magazine tube holds 10 rounds. It features an adjustable rear and a ramp-type front sight. The finish is blued, with a matted receiver top. The walnut stock has a straight grip; and the forend, a barrel band. From 1969 to 1971 there was a brass saddle ring.

NIB	Exc.	V.G.	Good	Fair	Poor
300	275	225	175	125	100

Model 1894 Octagon Barrel

This is basically the same as the Model 1894, with a 20" octagonal barrel and a steel forend tip instead of the barrel band. There were 2,957 manufactured in 1973 only.

Exc.	V.G.	Good	Fair	Poor
375	275	175	125	100

Model 1894 Sporter

This variation has a 20" round barrel, half-length magazine tube that holds 6 shots, and a hard rubber classic-style butt plate. Only 1,398 were manufactured in 1973.

NIB	Exc.	V.G.	Good	Fair	Poor
475	325	250	175	125	100

Model 1894 C Lever Action

This model is chambered for the .38 Special and .357 Magnum cartridges. It features an 18.5 round barrel, with full-length magazine tube and two barrel bands. It holds 9 shots and has a walnut straight-grip stock. This model was manufactured between 1969 and 1984. In 1984 a hammer-block cross-bolt safety was added, and the model number was changed to 1894 CS. All other specifications remained the same.

Exc.	V.G.	Good	Fair	Poor
275	225	175	125	100

Model 1894 M Lever Action Rifle

This model is similar to the other 1894 rifles except that it is chambered for the .22 Magnum cartridge and features an outside loading tube magazine that holds 11 shots. The barrel is 20" long, and there is a steel forend tip instead of a barrel band.

It is important to note that this model will not function properly with any cartridge except the .22 Magnum and that injury could result from attempting to chamber and fire the shorter .22 l.r. This model was manufactured between 1983 and 1988 and was only produced with the crossbolt safety.

Exc.	V.G.	Good	Fair	Poor
275	225	175	150	100

Model 1894 S Lever Action Rifle

This model was introduced in 1984. It is chambered for the .41 Magnum and the .44 Special/.44 Magnum cartridges. In 1988 the .45 Colt chambering was offered. This model has a 20" barrel and a straight-grip stock. The forend has a steel cap. This model is currently produced and features the hammer-block safety.

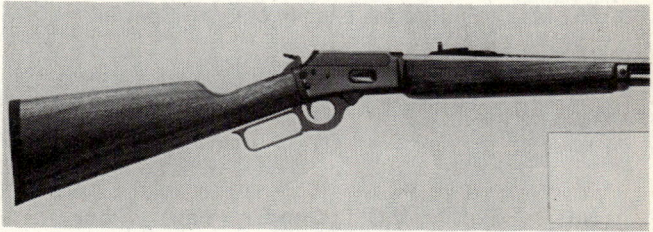

NIB	Exc.	V.G.	Good	Fair	Poor
350	325	250	200	175	125

Model 1894 CL (Classic) Lever Action Rifle

This model was introduced in 1988 and is the same basic rifle chambered for the old .25-20 and .32-20 cartridges. The rifle is also chambered for the .218 Bee cartridge. The barrel is 22", and the half-length magazine tube holds 6 shots. The walnut stock has no white spacers and has a black buttplate. Discontinued in 1993.

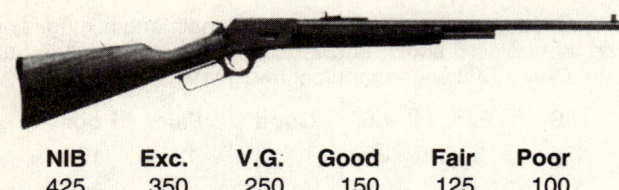

NIB	Exc.	V.G.	Good	Fair	Poor
425	350	250	150	125	100

NOTE: Collector interest has been growing in this model since it was discontinued in 1993.

Model 1894 Century Limited

An anniversary edition of the Marlin Model 1894 is limited to 2,500 rifles chambered in 44/40 caliber. Frame engraved and case colored. It is fitted with a 24" octagon barrel with 10-round magazine tube. The stock is semi-fancy walnut with straight grip and cut checkering with brass crescent buttplate.

NIB	Exc.	V.G.	Good	Fair	Poor
800	650	500	350	275	225

Model 1894 Cowboy

Introduced in 1996 this lever action rifle features a 24" tapered octagon barrel with a 10 round tubular magazine. It is chambered for the .45 Long Colt, a popular cartridge for "Cowboy Action Shooting". Straight grip checkered stock with blued steel forearm cap. Weight is approximately 7.5 lbs.

NIB	Exc.	V.G.	Good	Fair	Poor
450	375	300	—	—	—

Model 1894 Cowboy II

Introduced in 1997 and is the same as the Model 1894 Cowboy but is chambered for several cartridges. Available in .44-40, .357 Mag., .38 Special, and .44 Mag/.44 Special.

NIB	Exc.	V.G.	Good	Fair	Poor
450	375	300	—	—	—

Model 1895 Lever Action SS

The model 1895 was reintroduced on the Model 336 action that had been modified to handle the .45-70 cartridge. This was done to capitalize on the nostalgia wave that descended on the country in the early 1970s. This model features a 22" round barrel with a two-thirds-length magazine tube that holds 4 shots. The walnut stock had a straight grip until the Model 1895 S was released in 1980, when a pistol grip stock was used. In 1983 the Model 1895 SS with the crossbolt hammer-

block safety was added; and it is currently produced in this configuration.

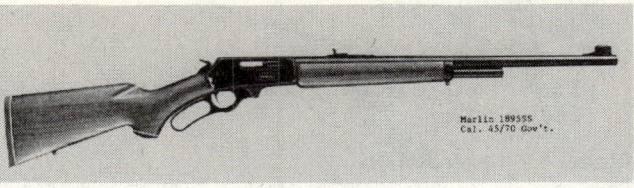

Exc.	V.G.	Good	Fair	Poor
350	275	225	150	100

NOTE: For early "B" prefix guns below serial number 12,000 add 20%.

Model 1897 Century Limited

Introduced in 1997 this model is chambered for the .22 caliber cartridge and commemorates the 100th anniversary of the Model 1897. It is fitted with a 24" half round half octagon barrel with adjustable Marble rear sight and Marble front sight with brass bead. Blued receiver is engraved and gold inlayed with semi-fancy walnut stock and hard rubber butt plate. Weight is about 6.5 lbs.

NIB	Exc.	V.G.	Good	Fair	Poor
1050	800	—	—	—	—

Marlin Glenfield Lever Action Rifles

The Glenfield line of rifles was designed to be sold in large outlet chain stores and were simply cheaper versions that were to be sold for less money. The rifles functioned fine, but birch was used instead of walnut and pressed checkering instead of handcut. These rifles were manufactured under the Glenfield name between 1964 and 1983. There are five models of Lever Action Glenfields: the 36G, 30, 30A, 30 GT, and the 30 AS. They are chambered for the .30-30 cartridge, and the basic differences are slight and, in most cases, merely cosmetic. They are good, serviceable rifles but have little or no collector interest or investment potential.

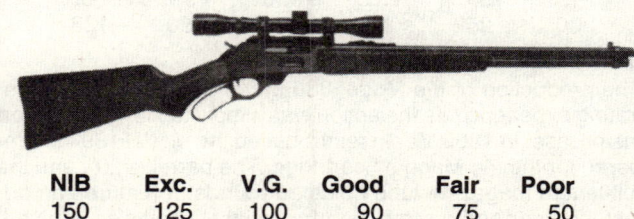

NIB	Exc.	V.G.	Good	Fair	Poor
150	125	100	90	75	50

Model 39 Lever Action Rifle

This model originally evolved from the Model 1891 invented by L.L. Hepburn. The 1891 rifle became the 1892 and eventually developed into the takedown Model 1897. The latter two were produced until 1915, when they were discontinued in favor of machine gun production for WWI. In 1922, when the company was sold to John Moran and became the Marlin Firearms Corp., the .22 rimfire lever action was reintroduced as the Model 39. It has been in production in one form or another ever since.

Model 39

As it was introduced in 1922, the Model 39 was chambered for the .22 rimfire and had a 24" octagonal barrel and a takedown receiver. It has a full-length magazine tube which holds 25 shorts, 20 longs, or 18 Long Rifle cartridges. Most Model 39s had a spring-loaded button outer magazine tube release. Very early variations had the Model '97 type knurled latch release. As the Model 39As were being phased in around 1939 many have the more modern removable inner magazine tube. It has a solid top frame and side ejection, a Rocky Mountain rear, and ivory bead front sight. The receiver, lever, and hammer are case-colored; the barrel is blued. The pistol grip stock and steel-capped forearm are varnished walnut. This model was manufactured in this form between 1922 and 1938 with a number of options that could affect value and would warrant individual appraisal. Model 39s with a "star" stamped on the tang were considered high grade guns by the factory inspector and will command a premium in better condition examples.

Standard Rifle

Exc.	V.G.	Good	Fair	Poor
1250	850	475	300	200

Deluxe Rifle-Factory checkering, fancy wood & "star" stamp on tang

Exc.	V.G.	Good	Fair	Poor
2200	1500	850	500	300

NOTE: Model 39s made prior to 1932 that have either no prefix or the prefix S to the serial number should not be used with high-speed ammunition. The prefix HS indicates the improved bolt that is safe for this ammunition.

Model 39A Lever Action Rifle

This is an improved version of the Model 39. It has a heavier, tapered round barrel and semi-beavertail forearm and a redesigned pistol grip stock. The rubber buttplate was replaced by one of a synthetic fiber; otherwise, specifications were similar to the Model 39. This model was manufactured from 1939 to 1960. Several variations are listed below:

Prewar (1939-1941)-Case-colored receiver, no serial number prefix (1939) or "B" prefix (1940-1941)

Exc.	V.G.	Good	Fair	Poor
1000	700	450	250	150

Postwar Variations (1945-1953)-Serial number prefixes up to letter "K"

Ballard Type Deep Rifling.

Exc.	V.G.	Good	Fair	Poor
500	375	275	150	100

"Golden 39A's" (1954-1963)-Gold trigger, micro groove rifling Serial number prefixes L through W

Exc.	V.G.	Good	Fair	Poor
275	225	175	125	100

Model 39A Mountie

This is basically a carbine version of the Model 39A. It features a 20" tapered round barrel, straight grip walnut stock, and slimmed-down forearm. It was manufactured between 1953 and 1960.

Exc.	V.G.	Good	Fair	Poor
275	225	175	125	100

Model 39A 1960 Presentation Model

Released in 1960, this was Marlin's 90th Anniversary model. It is similar to the 39A but has a chrome-plated barrel and receiver with a high grade, checkered walnut stock and forend. There is a squirrel carved on the right side of the butt stock. There were 500 produced in 1960. This is a commemorative and as such will be desirable to collectors only if NIB with all boxes and papers with which it was originally sold. Once used, it becomes a shooter and is not easily sold.

NIB	Exc.	V.G.	Good	Fair	Poor
600	500	400	300	175	125

Model 39M Mountie 1960 Presentation Model

This is the carbine version of the 90th Anniversary model. This is the same as the 39A with a 20" barrel and straight-grip stock. There were 500 of this model manufactured in 1960.

NIB	Exc.	V.G.	Good	Fair	Poor
600	500	400	300	175	125

Model 39ADL Lever Action Rifle

This model is the same as the 90th Anniversary issue except that it is blued instead of chrome-plated. There were 3,306 manufactured between 1960 and 1963.

Exc.	V.G.	Good	Fair	Poor
600	400	250	200	175

Golden 39A Lever Action Rifle

This model is similar to the 39A, with a gold-plated trigger and sling swivels. It was manufactured between 1960 and 1983.

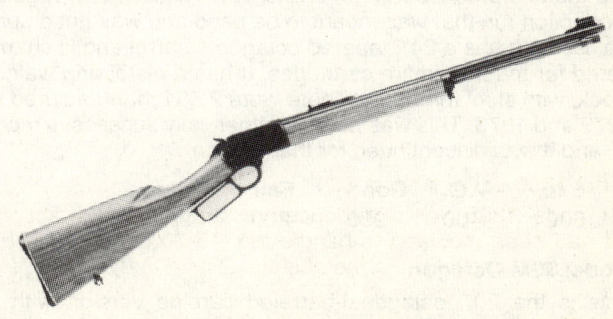

Exc.	V.G.	Good	Fair	Poor
200	175	150	100	75

Model 39 Carbine

This is a slimmer, lighter version of the Model 39A. It features a slimmer forend and thinner barrel. There were 12,140 manufactured between 1963 and 1967.

Exc.	V.G.	Good	Fair	Poor
175	150	125	90	60

Model 39 Century Limited

The introduction of this model marked the 100th Anniversary of the Marlin Company. This model features a 20" octagonal barrel with semi-buckhorn rear and brass blade front sight. The stock is fancy walnut, with a straight grip and a brass forend tip and buttplate. There is a medallion inlaid into the right side of the receiver and a brass plate on the stock. There were 34,197 manufactured in 1970. As a commemorative this model needs to be as it came from the factory to command collector interest.

NIB	Exc.	V.G.	Good	Fair	Poor
350	250	200	150	125	100

Model 39A Article II

This model commemorated the National Rifle Association's 100th Anniversary in 1971. It has a 24" octagonal barrel, high grade walnut pistol grip stock, and brass forend tip and buttplate. The right side of the receiver has the NRA's Second Amendment "Right to Keep and Bear Arms" medallion inlaid. There were 6,244 of these .22 rifles manufactured in 1971.

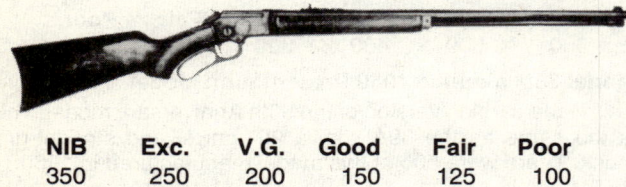

NIB	Exc.	V.G.	Good	Fair	Poor
350	250	200	150	125	100

Model 39M Article II

This model is the same as the Model 39A Article II except that it is a carbine version with a 20" octagonal barrel and a straight grip stock. There were 3,824 manufactured in 1971. As commemoratives NIB condition is essential to collector interest.

NIB	Exc.	V.G.	Good	Fair	Poor
300	250	200	150	125	100

Model 39A Octagon

This model was produced because the company had the machinery and some leftover barrels from the two commemorative models produced in 1970 and 1971. This was a regular production run that was meant to be used and was not a special issue. It has a 24", tapered octagonal barrel and is chambered for the .22 rimfire cartridges. It has a pistol grip walnut stock, with steel forend tip. There were 2,551 manufactured in 1972 and 1973. This was not a commercially successful model, and it was discontinued for that reason.

Exc.	V.G.	Good	Fair	Poor
600	400	250	200	175

Model 39M Octagon

This is the 20", octagonal-barreled carbine version with a straight-grip stock. There were 2,140 manufactured in 1973.

Exc.	V.G.	Good	Fair	Poor
600	400	250	200	175

Model 39D Lever Action Rifle

This is essentially the Model 39M carbine, 20" barrel version with a pistol grip stock. It was manufactured in 1971 and reintroduced in 1973. The 1971 version has white line spacers and pistol grip caps. The 1973 version has neither of these features.

Exc.	V.G.	Good	Fair	Poor
275	200	125	75	50

Model 39AS Lever Action Rifle

This is the current production model of this extremely popular .22 rifle. It features the hammer-block crossbolt safety and sling swivel studs. It is similar in appearance to its predecessors and still boasts a genuine walnut pistol grip stock and the same quality fit and finish we have come to expect from Marlin.

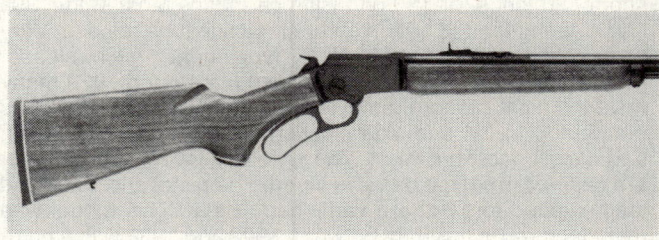

NIB	Exc.	V.G.	Good	Fair	Poor
340	275	225	200	150	100

Model 39TDS Lever Action Rifle

This is another current production model. It is similar to the Model 39AS, with a 20" carbine barrel and straight-grip stock. It replaced the Model 39M and was introduced in 1988.

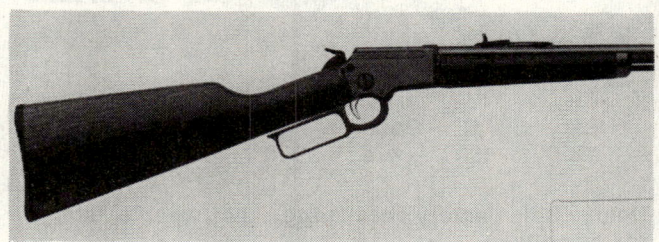

NIB	Exc.	V.G.	Good	Fair	Poor
375	325	250	225	150	100

Model 39 AWL

This is a limited edition of 2,000 rifles distributed solely through Wal-Mart. Fitted with a 24.5" octagon barrel, select checkered walnut stock, gold filled engraving, and stamped "Wildlife For Tomorrow".

NIB	Exc.	V.G.	Good	Fair	Poor
1000	—	—	—	—	—

Model 56 Levermatic Rifle

This is a streamlined version of the lever action. It features a short lever throw and a one-piece walnut stock. The 22" barrel is round and is chambered for the .22 rimfire cartridges. There is a 7-shot detachable magazine, open sights, and a gold-plated trigger. The receiver on this model was made of aluminum after 1956. There were 31,523 manufactured between 1955 and 1964.

Exc.	V.G.	Good	Fair	Poor
150	125	100	75	50

Model 56 "Clipper King" Levermatic

This is the same as the Model 56 except that it is specially packaged and comes with a 4X .22 scope. The name "Clipper King" is stamped on the barrel, and the buttplate is red hard rubber. There were only 152 of these manufactured in 1959.

Exc.	V.G.	Good	Fair	Poor
175	150	125	100	75

Model 57 Levermatic Rifle

This model is similar to the Model 56, with a tube magazine and Monte Carlo stock. In 1960 Marlin went back to a steel receiver on this model. There were 34,628 manufactured from 1959 to 1965.

Exc.	V.G.	Good	Fair	Poor
150	125	100	75	50

Model 57M Levermatic Rifle

This is the Model 57 chambered for the .22 Magnum cartridge. There were 66,889 manufactured between 1959 and 1969.

Exc.	V.G.	Good	Fair	Poor
175	150	125	100	75

Model 62 Levermatic Rifle

This model is similar in appearance to the Model 57 except that it is chambered for the centerfire .256 Magnum cartridge and has a 4-shot magazine. In 1966 the .30 carbine cartridge was added. This model has a 23" "Micro-Groove" barrel with open sights and a walnut one-piece stock. The first 4,000 Model 62s were shipped without serial numbers in violation of federal law. The company recalled the rifles for numbering; and, to this day, the owner of a centerfire Model 62 can return the rifle for numbering. There were 15,714 manufactured between 1963 and 1969.

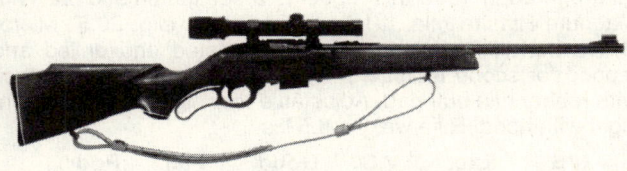

Exc.	V.G.	Good	Fair	Poor
175	150	125	100	75

It is important to note that the year of manufacture of Marlin modern production rifles made between 1946 and 1968 can be ascertained by the letter prefix on the serial number. The prefixes are as follows:

1946 - C	1951 - H	1956 - N	1961 - U	1966 - AB
1947 - D	1952 - J	1957 - P	1962 - V	1967 - AC
1948 - E	1953 - K	1958 - R	1963 - W	1968 - AD
1949 - F	1954 - L	1959 - S	1964 - Y, Z	
1950 - G	1955 - M	1960 - T	1965 - AA	

NOTE: From 1969 to 1972, the first digit of the serial number indicates the year of manufacture. In 1973, the system was changed by having the first two digits subtracted from 100 to find the year of production. For example: 2717793=100-27=1973.

The Marlin Firearms Company produced a great many bolt-action rifles, both single shot and repeaters, starting in 1930 and continuing today. These rifles were low-priced and designed primarily as utility rifles. They also manufactured many autoloaders of the same type during these years. The Glenfield name will also be found on these models, as many were produced to be marketed by the large chain outlets. These rifles have no collectible value of which I am aware, and they sell for under $100 in today's market. This list is for reference purposes.

BOLT ACTIONS	AUTOLOADERS
Model 65 - SS- 1935-37	Model 50 - 1931-34
Model 65E - SS- 1935-37	Model 50E - 1931-34
Model 100 - SS- 1935-59	Model A-1 - 1935-46
Model 80 - Rep- 1935-59	Model A-1 E - 1935-46
Model 80E - Rep- 1935-39	Model A-1C - 1940-46
Model 100S - SS- 1937-38	Model A-1 DL - 1940-46
Model 81 - Rep- 1939	Model 88-C - 1947-56
Model 81E - Rep- 1939	Model 88-DL - 1953-56
Model 80B - Rep- 1940	Model 89-C - 1950-61
Model 80BE - Rep-1940	Model 89-DL - 1950-61
Model 81B - Rep-1940	Model 98 - 1950-61
Model 81BE - Rep-1940	Model 99 - 1959-61
Model 101 - SS- 1941-77	Model 99C - 1962-78
Model 101 DL - SS- 1941-45	Model 99G - 1960-65
Model 80C - Rep-1941-71	Model DL - 1960-65
Model 80DL - Rep-1941-64	Model 60 - 1960-Pres.
Model 80 CSB - Rep-1941	Model 49 - 1968-71
Model 100 SB -SS- 1941	Model 49DL - 1971-78
Model 101 - SS- 1959	Model 990 - 1979-87
Model 122 - SS- 1962-65	Model 995 - 1979-Pres.
Model 980 - Rep- 1966-71	
Model 780 - Rep- 1971-88	
Model 781- Rep- 1971-88	
Model 782 - Rep- 1971-88	
Model 783 - Rep- 1971-88	
Model 880 - Rep- 1988—	
Model 881 - Rep- 1988—	
Model 882 - Rep- 1988—	
Model 883 - Rep- 1988—	

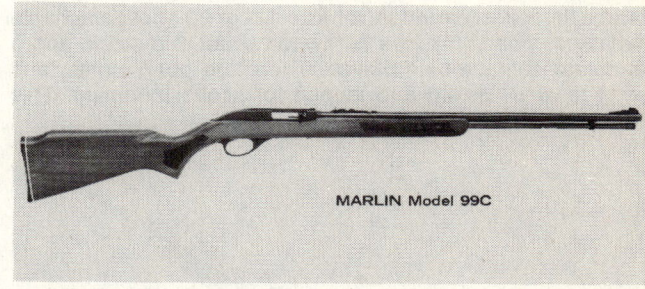

MARLIN Model 99C

Model 70P "Papoose"

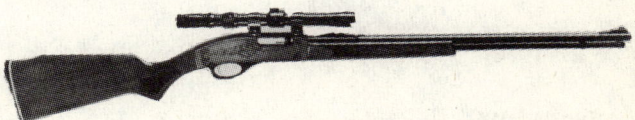

This model is quite unique in that it is a total package concept. It is a semiautomatic takedown carbine chambered for the .22 rimfire family of cartridges. It has a 16.25" barrel and a 7-shot detachable magazine. It is supplied with 4X scope and bright red case that will float if dropped overboard. The stock is walnut-finished birch, with a pistol grip and rubber buttplate. It was introduced in 1986.

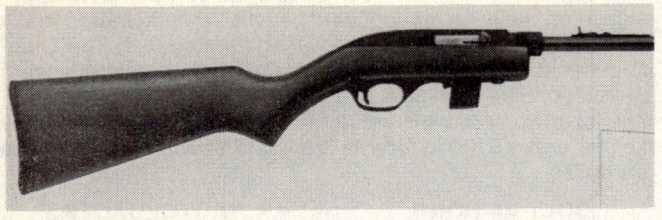

NIB	Exc.	V.G.	Good	Fair	Poor
160	140	110	85	75	50

Model 70HC

This is the Model 70 .22 rimfire that has been produced since 1983 with a high-capacity, 25-round "Banana" magazine.

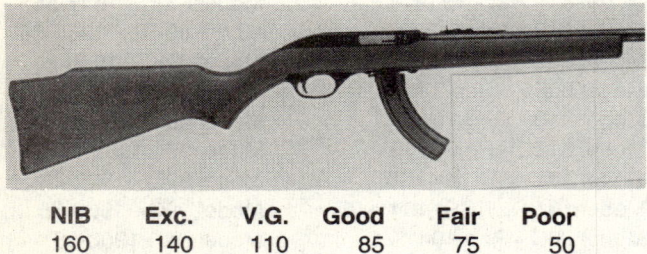

NIB	Exc.	V.G.	Good	Fair	Poor
160	140	110	85	75	50

Model 70PSS

Same as above but furnished with a 10 round magazine and finished in stainless steel.

NIB	Exc.	V.G.	Good	Fair	Poor
180	150	125	100	85	60

Model 9 Camp Carbine

This model has a 16.5" barrel and is chambered for the 9mm Parabellum pistol cartridge. It has a 12- or 20-shot detachable magazine, walnut-finished hardwood pistol grip stock, and a sandblasted matte-blued finish. There are open sights, and the receiver is drilled and tapped for scope mounting. This model was introduced in 1985.

NIB	Exc.	V.G.	Good	Fair	Poor
310	275	225	175	125	100

Model 45 Carbine

This is the same as the 9mm version but is chambered for the .45 ACP cartridge and has a 7-shot detachable magazine.

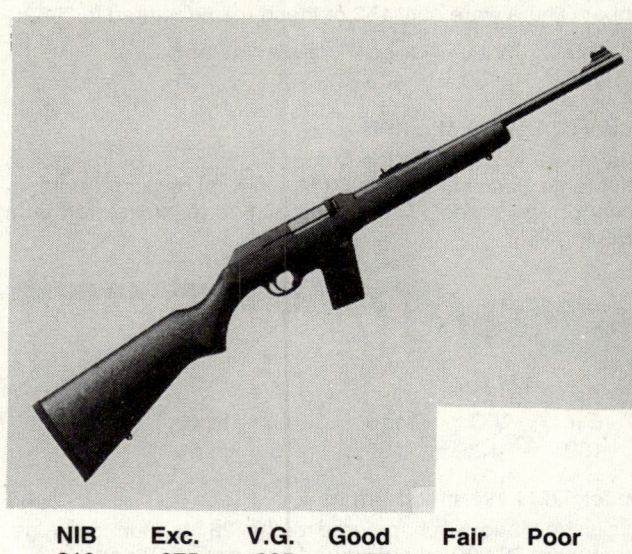

NIB	Exc.	V.G.	Good	Fair	Poor
310	275	225	175	125	100

Model 922M

First offered in 1993 this model is a semiautomatic .22 Win. Magnum Rimfire rifle. It features a 7-shot clip, 20.5" Micro-Grove barrel. The receiver is sandblasted and drilled and tapped for scope mounting. Monte Carlo black walnut stock with rubber rifle buff pad. Adjustable rear sight and ramp front sight with hood. Rifle weighs 6.5 lbs.

NIB	Exc.	V.G.	Good	Fair	Poor
275	250	200	150	125	110

Model 995

Semiautomatic .22 Long Rifle only rifle features a 7-shot clip, 18" Micro-Grove barrel. Receiver is grooved for scope mount and receiver has a serrated non-glare top. Adjustable sights. Monte Carlo American black walnut stock with checkered pistol grip and forearm. White buttplate spacer is standard. Rifle weighs 5 lbs. Introduced in 1979 and still in production.

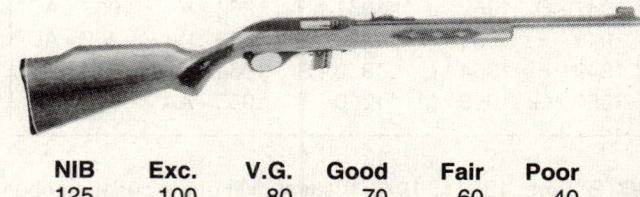

NIB	Exc.	V.G.	Good	Fair	Poor
125	100	80	70	60	40

Model 995SS

Same as above but with stainless steel finish and black fiberglass stock. Introduced in 1995.

NIB	Exc.	V.G.	Good	Fair	Poor
150	125	100	85	60	50

Model 990L

This semiautomatic .22 Long Rifle Marlin features a tubular 14-round magazine with 22" Micro-Grove barrel. The trigger is gold plated. The receiver is grooved for a scope mount while the stock is a two-tone brown birch Monte Carlo. Rubber rifle butt pad is standard. Rifle weighs 5.75 lbs.

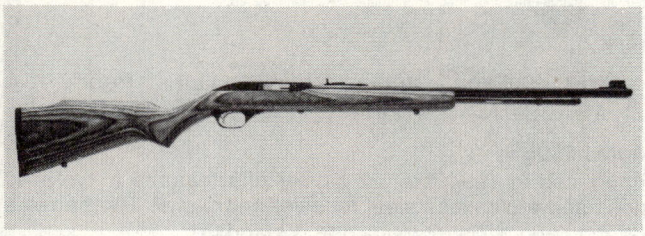

NIB	Exc.	V.G.	Good	Fair	Poor
140	120	100	80	65	50

Model 7000

This model was first offered in 1997 and is a semi-automatic .22 caliber rifle with 18" heavy barrel. Magazine holds 10 rounds. Black synthetic stock with Monte Carlo comb and molded checkering. Reciever grooved for scope mount. No sights included. Weight about 6 lbs.

NIB	Exc.	V.G.	Good	Fair	Poor
200	150	—	—	—	—

Model 795

Similar to the model above but with an 18" standard weight barrel. Weight is about 5 lbs. Also available with 4X scope. Add $5.00 for scope.

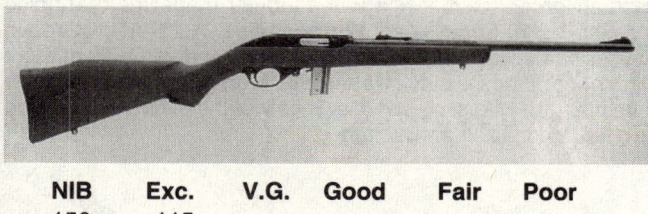

NIB	Exc.	V.G.	Good	Fair	Poor
150	115	—	—	—	—

Model 60

A Marlin promotional model. This semiautomatic 14-shot .22 caliber Long Rifle features a 22" MicroGroove barrel with adjustable rear sight. Receiver is grooved for scope mount and stock is birch with Monte Carlo comb. Rifle weighs 5.5 lbs. Introduced in 1960 and still in current production.

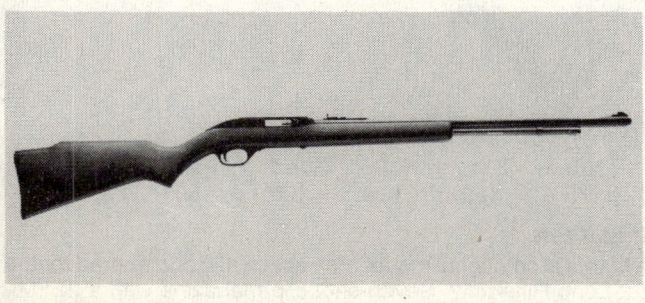

NIB	Exc.	V.G.	Good	Fair	Poor
100	85	70	60	50	40

Model 60 SS

Introduced in 1993 this model is similar to the Model 60 except that it features a stainless barrel, bolt, and magazine tube. All other metal parts are nickel plated. The stock is a two-tone black and gray laminated birch Monte Carlo.

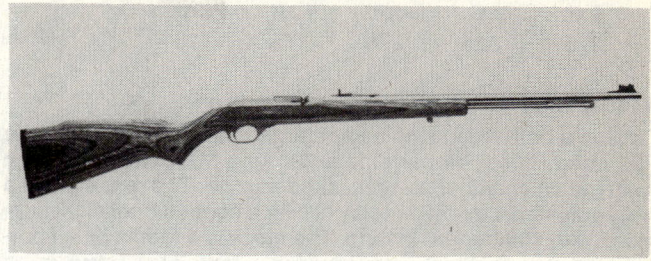

NIB	Exc.	V.G.	Good	Fair	Poor
160	135	100	80	60	50

Model 9N

Similar to the Model 9mm Carbine but furnished with nickel-plated metal parts.

NIB	Exc.	V.G.	Good	Fair	Poor
270	245	210	175	125	100

Model 322 Bolt Action Rifle

This model is chambered for the .222 cartridge and has a 24" medium-weight barrel with MicroGroove rifling. It has a checkered walnut pistol grip stock. The magazine holds 4 shots, and the adjustable trigger and sights are Sako products. The Sako receiver is fitted for Sako scope mounting bases. The Micro-Groove rifling in the barrel was not successful for this caliber, and accuracy fell off after as few as 500 shots—so this model was dropped and replaced. The serial numbers were Sako, and there were 5,859 manufactured between 1954 and 1959.

Exc.	V.G.	Good	Fair	Poor
375	325	250	175	125

Model 422 Bolt Action Rifle

This model is the successor to the Model 322. It is simply the same rifle fitted with a 24", featherweight, stainless steel barrel and named the "Varmint King." The stock features a Monte Carlo stock with a cheekpiece. There were only 354 manufactured between 1956 and 1958.

Exc.	V.G.	Good	Fair	Poor
375	325	275	175	125

Model 455 Bolt Action Rifle

This model is built on the Fabrique Nationale Belgian Mauser action. It is chambered for the .308 and the .30-06 cartridges. It has a stainless steel barrel made by Marlin and has a 5-shot magazine. It has a Bishop checkered walnut stock with detachable sling swivels and a leather sling. The rear sight is a Lyman 48, and the front is a ramp type with a detachable hood. The receiver is drilled and tapped for scope mounts. The trigger is an adjustable Sako unit. There were 1,079 manufactured in .3006 and only 59 in .308 between 1955 and 1959.

Exc.	V.G.	Good	Fair	Poor
375	325	275	175	125

Model 2000

This is a bolt action single shot target rifle chambered for the .22 Long Rifle. The barrel is a 22" long MicroGroove design with match chamber and recessed muzzle. The rear sight is a fully adjustable target peep sight with a hooded front sight supplied with 10 aperture inserts. The stock is a Marlin blue fiberglass/Kevlar material with adjustable buttplate. There is an aluminum forearm rail with forearm stop and quick detachable swivel. Rifle weighs 8 lbs.

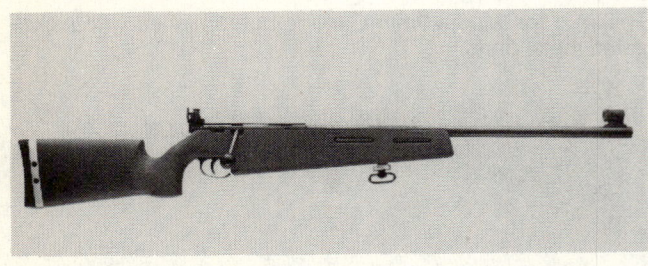

NIB	Exc.	V.G.	Good	Fair	Poor
350	300	250	200	150	125

Model 2000A

This is an ungraded 1996 version of the Model 2000 introduced in 1994 that features an adjustable comb and an ambidextrous pistol grip. A Marlin logo is molded into the side of the butt stock. Weighs approximately 8-1/2 lbs.

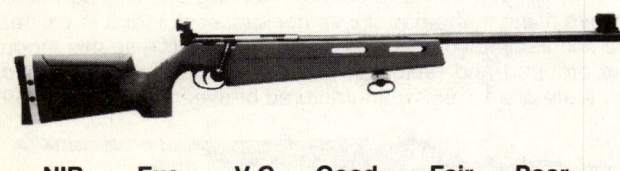

NIB	Exc.	V.G.	Good	Fair	Poor
350	300	250	200	—	—

Model 2000L

Introduced in 1996 this version of the Model 2000 features a black/grey laminated stock. It is fitted with a heavy 22" barrel with a match chamber. Fitted with a two-stage target trigger and a rubber butt plate that is adjustable for length of pull, heigth and angle. Weight is about 8 lbs.

NIB	Exc.	V.G.	Good	Fair	Poor
625	500	450	—	—	—

Model 880

This is a bolt action clip-fed rifle chambered for the .22 Long Rifle caliber. The clip is a 7-shot magazine. The MicroGroove barrel is 22" and has adjustable folding rear sight and ramp front sight with hood. Rifle weighs 5.5 lbs. and was introduced in 1988 and is still in production.

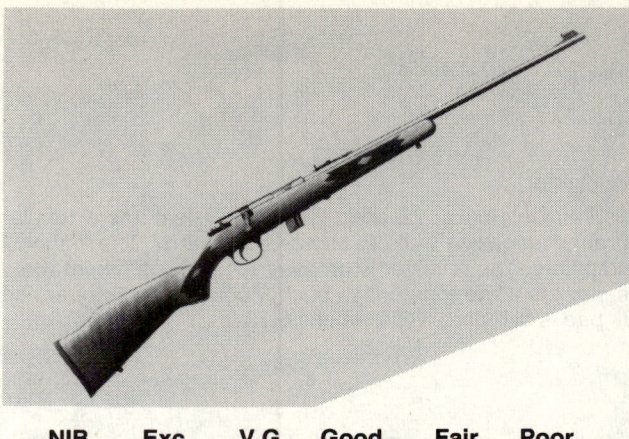

NIB	Exc.	V.G.	Good	Fair	Poor
160	135	110	90	75	50

Model 880SS

Introduced in 1994 this .22 caliber rifle features a synthetic stock and a stainless steel receiver and barrel. The barrel is 22" long and a 7-shot magazine is standard.

NIB	Exc.	V.G.	Good	Fair	Poor
225	175	150	125	75	60

Model 880SQ

Similar to the Model 880 but fitted with a 22" heavy barrel and no sights. Introduced in 1996. Weight is approximately 7 lbs.

NIB	Exc.	V.G.	Good	Fair	Poor
285	225	200	—	—	—

Model 881

Bolt action .22 caliber rifle has a tubular magazine that holds 25 Shorts, 19 Longs, and 17 Long rifles. A 22" MicroGroove barrel has adjustable folding rear sight and ramp front sight with hood. Stock is black walnut with Monte Carlo and a rubber rifle butt pad with sling swivels. Rifle weighs 6 lbs. First offered in 1988 and still in production.

NIB	Exc.	V.G.	Good	Fair	Poor
175	150	125	100	80	60

Model 25N

A Marlin promotional model. Bolt action rifle chambered for the .22 Long Rifle only. Seven-shot clip magazine with a 22" MicroGroove barrel. Receiver grooved for scope mount. Walnut finished birch stock. Gun weighs 5.5 lbs.

NIB	Exc.	V.G.	Good	Fair	Poor
100	90	80	70	50	40

Model 25MN

Same as above but chambered for the .22 Win. Magnum Rimfire cartridge. Gun weighs 6 lbs.

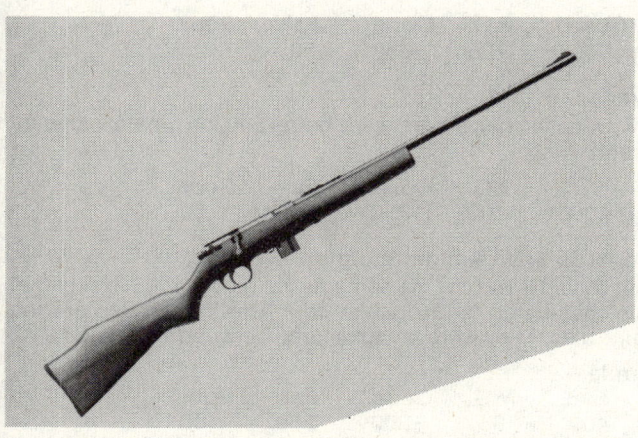

NIB	Exc.	V.G.	Good	Fair	Poor
120	100	85	75	65	50

Model 15YN

A Marlin promotional model referred to as the "Little Buckaroo". A bolt action .22 caliber single shot rifle for the beginner. Features a MicroGroove 16.25" barrel adjustable rear sight and receiver grooved for scope mount. Birch stock. Rifle weighs 4.25 lbs.

NIB	Exc.	V.G.	Good	Fair	Poor
90	80	70	60	50	40

Model 882

Bolt action rifle chambered for .22 Win. Magnum Rimfire cartridge. A 7-shot clip is standard. A MicroGroove 22" barrel with adjustable rear sight and ramp front sight with hood. Receiver grooved for scope mount. Black walnut stock with Monte Carlo and rubber rifle butt. Rifle weighs 6 lbs. Introduced in 1988 and still in production.

NIB	Exc.	V.G.	Good	Fair	Poor
150	125	100	80	65	50

Model 882L

Same as above but furnished with a two-tone brown hardwood Monte Carlo stock. Rifle weighs 6.25 lbs.

NIB	Exc.	V.G.	Good	Fair	Poor
180	155	130	100	80	60

Model 882SS

Same as above but furnished in stainless steel. With black fiberglass stock. Introduced in 1995.

NIB	Exc.	V.G.	Good	Fair	Poor
180	155	130	100	80	60

Model 882SSV

This variation of the Model 882, introduced in 1997, is all in stainless steel and chambered for the .22 WMR cartridge. It is fitted with a nickel plated 7-round magazine and 22" barrel. The stock is black synthetic with molded checkering. Receiver is grooved for scope mount. 1" brushed aluminum scope ring mounts included. Weighs about 7 lbs.

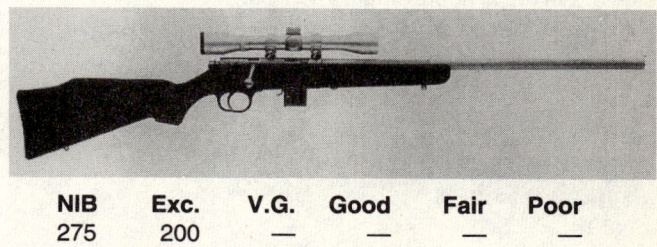

NIB	Exc.	V.G.	Good	Fair	Poor
275	200	—	—	—	—

Model 883

Bolt action rifle chambered for .22 Win. Magnum cartridge with 12-shot tubular magazine. Furnished with a 22" MicroGroove barrel and adjustable rear sight, ramp front sight with hood. Checkered American black walnut stock with Monte Carlo. Rifle weighs 6 lbs. Introduced in 1988 and still in production.

NIB	Exc.	V.G.	Good	Fair	Poor
160	125	100	80	65	50

Model 883N

Same as above but furnished with stainless steel barrel, receiver, front breech bolt, and striker. All other metal parts, except for sights, are nickel plated.

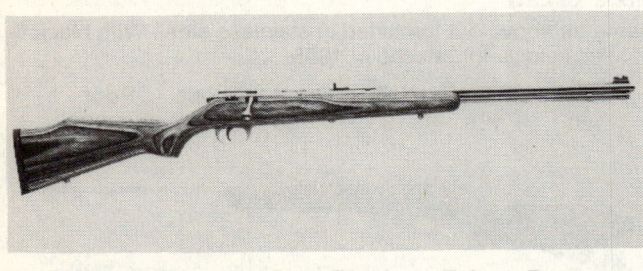

NIB	Exc.	V.G.	Good	Fair	Poor
180	155	130	100	80	60

Model 883SS

Introduced in 1993 this model is similar to the Model 883 but with all metal parts in stainless steel or nickel and the stock is a two-tone brown birch Monte Carlo that is not checkered.

NIB	Exc.	V.G.	Good	Fair	Poor
170	150	125	100	80	60

MR-7

Introduced in 1996, this is an American made bolt action centerfire rifle of a totally new design. Chambered for the .25-06 (first offered in 1997), .270 Win. or .30-06 cartridges it is fitted with a 22" barrel. It has an American black walnut stock and a 4-shot detachable box magazine. Offered with or without sights. Weight is approximately 7.5 lbs.

NIB	Exc.	V.G.	Good	Fair	Poor
400	325	—	—	—	—

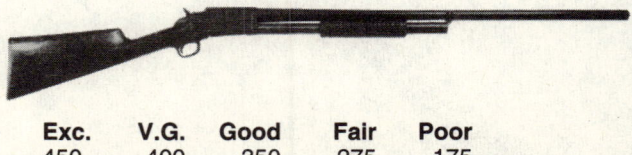

MARLIN SHOTGUNS

Model 1898 Slide Action Shotgun

This model was made in 12 gauge, with an exposed hammer. It has a takedown receiver and walnut pistol grip stock and forend.

There is a 5-shot tube magazine, and the barrel lengths are from 26" and 32". They were manufactured between 1898 and 1905.

Grade A

This variation has a 38", 30", or 32" barrel, is full choke, and is the plainest grade.

Exc.	V.G.	Good	Fair	Poor
500	450	400	300	175

Grade A Brush or Riot

This is the same shotgun with a 26" cylinder-bore barrel.

Exc.	V.G.	Good	Fair	Poor
500	450	400	300	175

Grade B

This is the same as the Grade A with a special smokeless steel barrel and a checkered stock.

Exc.	V.G.	Good	Fair	Poor
600	550	500	400	275

Model 1898 Grade C

This is a more deluxe version with engraving and fancier wood.

Exc.	V.G.	Good	Fair	Poor
800	725	650	500	400

Grade D

This variation has a Damascus barrel and the greatest amount of engraving.

Exc.	V.G.	Good	Fair	Poor
1800	1600	1250	900	700

Model 16 Slide Action Shotgun

This model is exactly the same as the Model 1898 except that it is chambered for 16 gauge only. The four grades are the same also. They were manufactured between 1903 and 1910.

Grade A

Exc.	V.G.	Good	Fair	Poor
400	350	300	250	150

Grade B

Exc.	V.G.	Good	Fair	Poor
500	450	400	350	225

Grade C

Exc.	V.G.	Good	Fair	Poor
650	575	500	425	300

Grade D

Exc.	V.G.	Good	Fair	Poor
1400	1200	1000	700	550

Model 17 Slide Action Shotgun

This model is an exposed-hammer gun with a solid frame and a straight-grip stock. It is chambered for 12 gauge, with a 30" or 32" barrel. The Model 17 was manufactured between 1906 and 1908.

Exc.	V.G.	Good	Fair	Poor
450	400	350	275	175

Model 17 Brush Gun

This variation is similar to the standard Model 17, with a 26" cylinder-bore barrel.

Exc.	V.G.	Good	Fair	Poor
475	425	375	300	200

Model 17 Riot Gun

This variation has a 20" cylinder-bore barrel.

Exc.	V.G.	Good	Fair	Poor
400	350	300	225	125

Model 19 Slide Action Shotgun

This is a takedown gun, chambered for 12 gauge. It is basically an improved and lightened version of the Model 1898. It is available in the same four grades. It was manufactured in 1906 and 1907.

Grade A

Exc.	V.G.	Good	Fair	Poor
400	350	300	250	150

Grade B

Exc.	V.G.	Good	Fair	Poor
500	450	400	350	225

Grade C

Exc.	V.G.	Good	Fair	Poor
650	575	500	425	300

Grade D

Exc.	V.G.	Good	Fair	Poor
1400	1200	1000	700	550

> A special order factory engraved Model 19 Grade 40. Engraved by C.F. Ulrich in 1906 this 12 gauge gun was fitted with a 30" barrel. Engraving is executed with gold and platinum enlays. Considered to be the finest engraved Marlin ever produced by the factory. The price for this unique Marlin was $110,000.

Model 21 "Trap" Slide Action Shotgun

This model is basically the same as the Model 19 with a straight-grip stock. The 1907 catalog listed it as a Trap model. This model was manufactured in 1907 and 1908. The four grades are similar to the previous models.

Grade A

Exc.	V.G.	Good	Fair	Poor
400	350	300	250	150

Grade B

Exc.	V.G.	Good	Fair	Poor
500	450	400	350	225

Grade C

Exc.	V.G.	Good	Fair	Poor
650	575	500	425	300

Grade D

Exc.	V.G.	Good	Fair	Poor
1400	1200	1000	700	550

Model 24 Slide Action Shotgun

This model is actually an improved version of the Model 21. It has a pistol grip stock and exposed hammer. It features an automatic recoil lock on the slide and a matte rib barrel. Otherwise, it is quite similar to its predecessor. It was manufactured between 1908 and 1917.

Grade A

Exc.	V.G.	Good	Fair	Poor
350	300	250	200	100

Grade B

Exc.	V.G.	Good	Fair	Poor
500	450	400	350	225

Grade C

Exc.	V.G.	Good	Fair	Poor
650	575	500	425	300

Grade D

Exc.	V.G.	Good	Fair	Poor
1400	1200	1000	700	550

Marlin "Trap Gun"

This model is unique in that it has no numerical designation and is simply known as the "Trap Gun." It is a takedown gun with interchangeable barrels from 16" to 32". It has a straight-grip buttstock and is quite similar in appearance to the Model 24. It was manufactured between 1909 and 1912.

Exc.	V.G.	Good	Fair	Poor
450	400	350	250	175

Model 26 Slide Action Shotgun

This model is similar to the Model 24 Grade A, with a solid frame. It has 30" or 32" barrels.

Exc.	V.G.	Good	Fair	Poor
275	225	175	125	100

Model 26 Brush Gun

This model has a 26" cylinder-bored barrel.

Exc.	V.G.	Good	Fair	Poor
300	250	200	150	125

Model 26 Riot Gun

This variation has a 20" cylinder-bored barrel.

Exc.	V.G.	Good	Fair	Poor
250	200	150	100	75

Model 28 Hammerless Slide Action Shotgun

This model was the first of the Marlin hammerless shotguns. It is a takedown 12 gauge, with barrels from 26" to 32" in length.

The stock has a pistol grip, and it comes in four grades like its predecessors. The Model 28 was manufactured between 1913 and 1922.

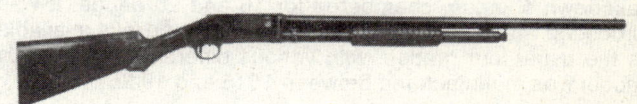

Grade A

Exc.	V.G.	Good	Fair	Poor
400	350	300	250	150

Grade B

Exc.	V.G.	Good	Fair	Poor
500	450	400	350	225

Grade C

Exc.	V.G.	Good	Fair	Poor
650	575	500	425	300

Grade D

Exc.	V.G.	Good	Fair	Poor
1400	1200	1000	700	550

Model 28 TS Trap Gun

This variation is the same as the Model 28 with a 30" full-choke barrel with matted rib and a high-comb straight grip stock. It was manufactured in 1915.

Exc.	V.G.	Good	Fair	Poor
425	375	300	225	175

Model 28T Trap Gun

This variation is the deluxe model, similar to the Model 28TS, with engraving, high-grade walnut, and hand checkering. It was manufactured in 1915.

Exc.	V.G.	Good	Fair	Poor
600	525	450	375	250

Model 30 Slide Action Shotgun

This model is an improved version of the Model 16, 16 gauge shotgun. Its features are similar, with the addition of the improved takedown system and the automatic recoil lock on the slide. This model was manufactured between 1910 and 1914.

Grade A

Exc.	V.G.	Good	Fair	Poor
400	350	300	250	150

Grade B

Exc.	V.G.	Good	Fair	Poor
500	450	400	350	225

Grade C

Exc.	V.G.	Good	Fair	Poor
650	575	500	425	300

Grade D

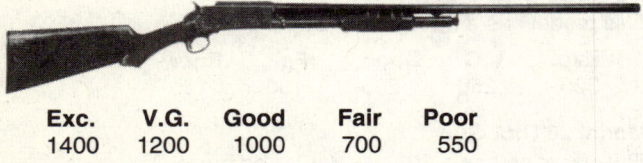

Exc.	V.G.	Good	Fair	Poor
1400	1200	1000	700	550

Model 30 Field Grade

This model is similar to the Model 30 Grade B, with a 25" modified-choke barrel and a straight-grip stock. It was manufactured in 1913 and 1914.

Exc.	V.G.	Good	Fair	Poor
400	350	300	225	150

Model 31 Slide Action Shotgun

This model is a smaller version of the Model 28 hammerless takedown shotgun, chambered for 16 and 20 gauge. It was produced with barrel lengths of 26" and 28" and was available in the usual four grades, with various different chokes. This model was manufactured between 1915 and 1922.

Grade A

Exc.	V.G.	Good	Fair	Poor
400	350	300	250	150

Grade B

Exc.	V.G.	Good	Fair	Poor
500	450	400	350	225

Grade C

Exc.	V.G.	Good	Fair	Poor
650	575	500	425	300

Grade D

Exc.	V.G.	Good	Fair	Poor
1400	1200	1000	700	550

Model 42/42A Slide Action Shotgun

This model was originally listed as the Model 42; but in the second year of production, the designation was changed to 42/A for no more apparent reason than standardization of models. This model is similar to the Model 24 except that the barrel markings are different. It is still an exposed hammer takedown gun chambered for 12 gauge. It was manufactured between 1922 and 1933.

Exc.	V.G.	Good	Fair	Poor
275	250	200	150	100

Model 43A Slide Action Shotgun

This hammerless model was quite similar to the Model 28, with different markings and less attention to finishing detail. It was manufactured between 1923 and 1930.

Exc.	V.G.	Good	Fair	Poor
350	300	250	200	150

Model 43T Slide Action Shotgun

This model is the same as the Model 43A takedown hammerless with a 30" or 32" matte-rib barrel. The straight-grip stock is of high grade walnut, with a non-gloss oil finish and fitted recoil paid. This model was manufactured between 1922 and 1930.

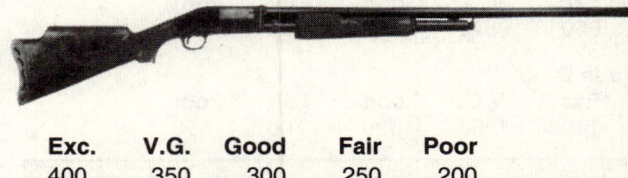

Exc.	V.G.	Good	Fair	Poor
400	350	300	250	200

Model 43TS Slide Action Shotgun

This is a custom-order version of the Model 43T, the same in all respects except that the stock could be ordered to any specifications the shooter desired. It was manufactured between 1922 and 1930.

Exc.	V.G.	Good	Fair	Poor
600	550	500	350	275

Model 44A Slide Action Shotgun

This model is similar to the Model 31 and was advertised as its successor. It is a hammerless takedown chambered for the 20 gauge. It features an improved bolt opening device located in the triggerguard area instead of at the top of the receiver and has a shorter 4-shot magazine tube. The model was manufactured from 1922 until 1933.

Exc.	V.G.	Good	Fair	Poor
375	325	275	225	175

Model 44S Slide Action Shotgun

This model is similar to the Model 44A, with a higher grade walnut stock that featured hand-cut checkering.

Exc.	V.G.	Good	Fair	Poor
450	400	350	300	225

Model 49 Slide Action Shotgun

This model is a 12-gauge, exposed-hammer takedown that combines features of the Model 42 and the Model 24. It is basically a lower-priced model that was never listed in the Marlin catalog. This model was part of Frank Kenna's money-raising program—anyone who purchased four shares of stock for $25 per share was given one, free of charge. This model was manufactured between 1925 and 1928.

Exc.	V.G.	Good	Fair	Poor
450	400	350	275	200

Model 53 Slide Action Shotgun

This model is a hammerless, takedown, 12 gauge that was not in production for long. It is theorized that the Model 53 was produced to use up old parts on hand when the Model 43 was introduced. It was manufactured in 1929 and 1980.

Exc.	V.G.	Good	Fair	Poor
350	300	250	175	125

Model 63 Slide Action Shotgun

This was the last of the slide action shotguns produced by Marlin until the Model 120 in 1971. It is a hammerless, takedown 12 gauge and replaced the Model 43A in the Marlin catalog. This model had improvements over the earlier guns, but its introduction during the Depression did little to bolster sales. This model was also offered free of charge to anyone purchasing four shares of Marlin stock at $25 per share. It was manufactured between 1931 and 1933.

Exc.	V.G.	Good	Fair	Poor
350	300	250	175	125

Model 63T Slide Action Shotgun

This is the trap-grade version of the Model 63. It has a better grade hand-checkered stock, with a fitted recoil pad and oil finish. It was manufactured between 1931 and 1933.

Exc.	V.G.	Good	Fair	Poor
375	325	275	200	150

Model 63TS Slide Action Shotgun

This variation is the same as the Model 63T except that the stock dimensions were custom-made to the customer's specifications. It was manufactured between 1931 and 1933.

Exc.	V.G.	Good	Fair	Poor
400	350	300	225	175

Model 60 Single Barrel Shotgun

This is a break-open, exposed-hammer, top lever-opening 12 gauge with either 30" or 32" full-choke barrel. It has a pistol grip stock. There were approximately 60 manufactured in 1923.

Exc.	V.G.	Good	Fair	Poor
200	175	150	125	100

Model .410 Lever Action Shotgun

This was a unique venture for the Marlin Company—a lever action shotgun based on the Model 1893 action with a longer loading port, modified tube magazine that held 5 shots, and a smoothbore barrel chambered for the .410 shot shell. The finish of this gun is blued, with a walnut pistol grip stock and grooved beavertail forend. It has a hard rubber rifle-type buttplate. The model was available with either a 22" or 26" full-choke barrel. This gun was also part of the stock purchase plan and was given free of charge to anyone purchasing four shares at $25 per share. It was also cataloged for sale and was manufactured between 1929 and 1932.

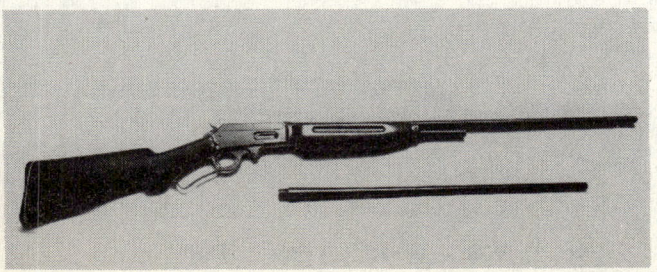

Courtesy Mike Stuckslager

Exc.	V.G.	Good	Fair	Poor
1000	500	400	300	250

Model .410 Deluxe

This variation was never cataloged and is essentially the same as the standard version with a hand-checkered stock. The forend does not have the grooves found on the standard model. Be wary of fakes!

Exc.	V.G.	Good	Fair	Poor
1500	750	650	550	400

Model 90 Over/Under Shotgun

This gun was produced in response to a request from Sears Roebuck that Marlin should manufacture an Over/Under shotgun to market in their stores. The guns produced for Sears have the prefix 103 in their serial numbers and were marked "Ranger" before WWII and "J.C. Higgins" after the war. Prior to 1945 they were not marked Marlin; after that date Sears requested that the company stamp their name on the guns. They were also produced as the Marlin Model 90 during the same period and were chambered for 12, 16, and 20 gauge, as well as .410 bore. The 16 and 20 gauge guns were first offered in 1937 with 26" or 28" barrels. In 1939 the .410 bore was first offered with 26" barrel and 3" chambers. The barrels are either 26", 28", or 30", with various chokes. The action is a boxlock with extractors. Guns made prior to 1949 had a space between the barrels; after that date they were solid. They can be found with double or single triggers and a checkered walnut stock. A ventilated rib was also offered as an option beginning in 1949. Be aware that this model was also available as a combination gun in .22 LR/.410, .22 Hornet/.410, and .218 Bee/.410. There were approximately 34,000 Model 90s manufactured between 1937 and 1963.

NOTE: Single Trigger-Add 35%. Add 25% for 20 gauge guns and 40% for .410 bores. There are other rare gauge and barrel combinations that may affect value. If in doubt seek an expert appraisal.

EDITORS NOTE: Collectors should be aware that this model has a receiver of malleable iron. It will not blue by the usual bluing methods. The barrels and ribs are soft soldered and cannot take hot bluing. Use caution.

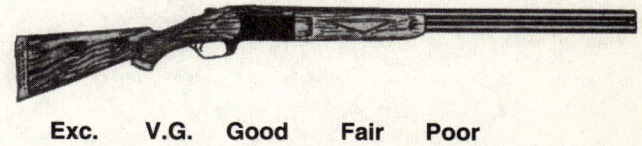

Exc.	V.G.	Good	Fair	Poor
500	425	350	275	200

Premier Mark I Slide Action Shotgun

This model was made by Manufrance and called the LaSalle. Marlin was able to purchase them without the barrels at a good enough price for them to barrel and market them under their own name. This model is 12 gauge only, with an alloy receiver and seven interchangeable barrels in 26"-30" lengths and various chokes. The plain stock is French walnut. The biggest problem with this gun is that the light weight (six pounds) produced bad recoil, and it was less than enjoyable to shoot. This model was in production from 1959 through 1963, with approximately 13,700 sold.

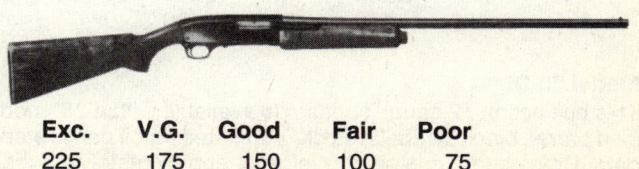

Exc.	V.G.	Good	Fair	Poor
225	175	150	100	75

Premier Mark II

This model is similar to the Mark I, with light engraving and a checkered stock.

Exc.	V.G.	Good	Fair	Poor
250	200	175	125	100

Premier Mark IV

This model is similar to the Mark II, with more engraving on the receiver.

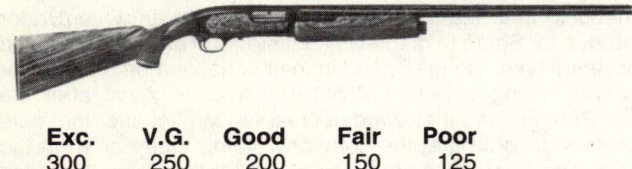

Exc.	V.G.	Good	Fair	Poor
300	250	200	150	125

Model 120 Slide Action Shotgun

This model was styled to resemble the Winchester Model 12 and was advertised as an all steel and walnut shotgun. It was offered with interchangeable barrels from 26" to 40", and various chokes were available. The checkered stock is of walnut, with a fitted recoil pad. The tube magazine holds 5 shots, 4 in 3". There was a Trap Model available (1973-1975), as well as a slug gun (1974-1984). This model was manufactured between 1971 and 1985.

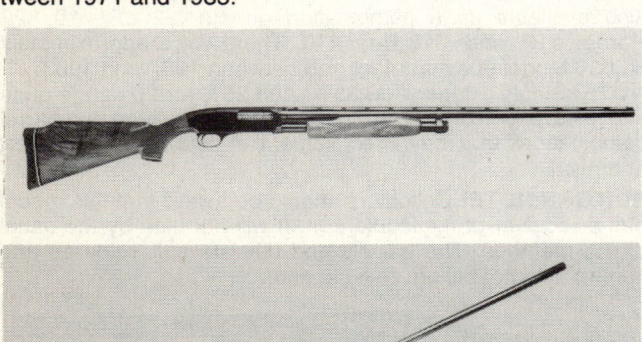

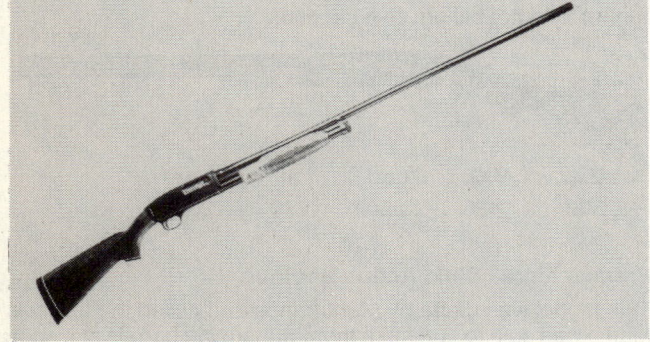

Exc.	V.G.	Good	Fair	Poor
300	250	200	150	125

Model 778 Slide Action Shotgun (Glenfield)

This model is similar to the Model 120, with a walnut finished hardwood stock instead of walnut, and the Glenfield name stamped on it. It was manufactured between 1979 and 1984.

Exc.	V.G.	Good	Fair	Poor
225	175	150	125	100

Model 50 DL

This bolt action 12 gauge shotgun is available with a 28" modified barrel, black synthetic stock. Ventilated recoil pad is standard. Brass bead front sight. Weight is approximately 7.5 lbs.

NIB	Exc.	V.G.	Good	Fair	Poor
300	275	225	150	125	100

Model 55 Bolt Action Shotgun

This model is chambered for 12, 16, and 20 gauge, with full or adjustable choke and barrels of 26" or 28". It is a bolt action with 2-shot box magazine. The pistol grip stock is plain. This model was manufactured between 1950 and 1965.

Exc.	V.G.	Good	Fair	Poor
100	75	50	35	25

Model 55 Swamp Gun

This is simply the Model 55 with a 3" Magnum, 20" barrel and an adjustable choke. It was manufactured between 1963 and 1965.

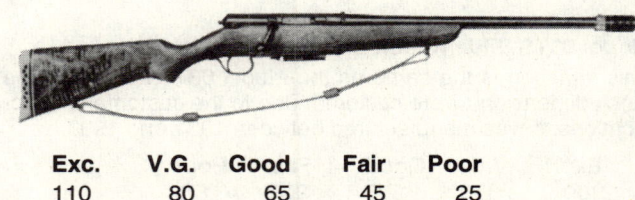

Exc.	V.G.	Good	Fair	Poor
110	80	65	45	25

Model 55 Goose Gun

This is the Model 55 with a 3" chambered, 36" full choke barrel and a recoil pad and sling. It was introduced in 1962 and is still manufactured.

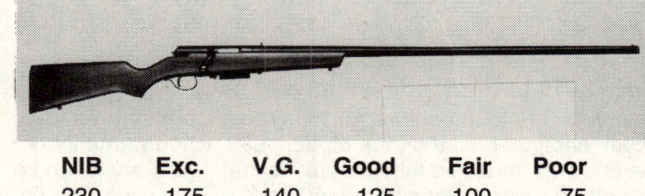

NIB	Exc.	V.G.	Good	Fair	Poor
230	175	140	125	100	75

Model 55S Slug Gun

This is the Model 55 with a 24" cylinder-bore barrel and rifle sights. It was manufactured between 1974 and 1983.

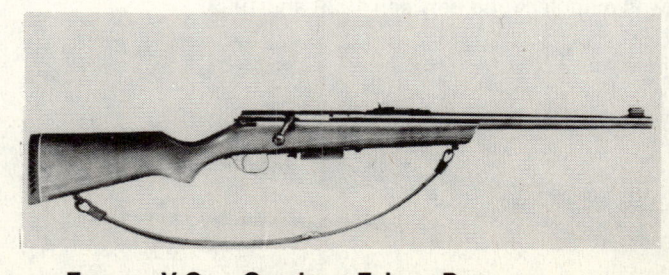

Exc.	V.G.	Good	Fair	Poor
150	125	100	75	50

Model 55 10 Bolt Action Shotgun

This model is chambered for the 3.5" 10 gauge. It has a 34" full-choke barrel and a recoil pad and sling. It was manufactured between 1976 and 1985.

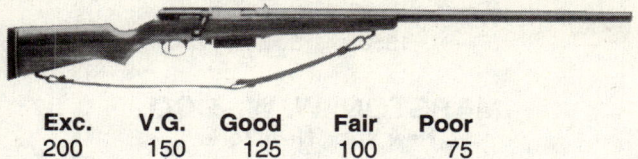

Exc.	V.G.	Good	Fair	Poor
200	150	125	100	75

Model 55 GDL

This bolt action shotgun is fitted with a 36" full choke barrel and reinforced black synthetic stock. Magazine holds two rounds. Ventilated recoil pad is standard. First introduced in 1997. Weight is about 8 lbs.

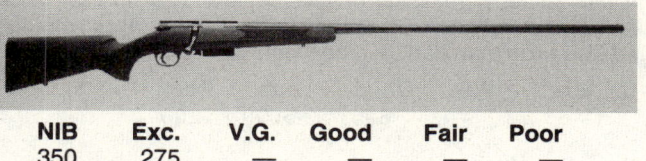

NIB	Exc.	V.G.	Good	Fair	Poor
350	275	—	—	—	—

Model 512 Slugmaster

Introduced in 1994 this bolt action shotgun features a rifled 21" barrel. It is equipped with a two-shot detachable magazine and a ventilated recoil pad. A special scope is also provided. Weight is approximately 8 lbs.

NIB	Exc.	V.G.	Good	Fair	Poor
285	250	225	200	150	100

Model 512 DL Slugmaster

Introduced in 1997 this bolt action model features a black synthetic stock with a fully rifled 21" barrel chambered for the 12 gauge shell. A two-round magazine is standard. Adjustable rear sight with ramp front sight. Receiver drilled and tapped for scope mount. Weight is about 8 lbs.

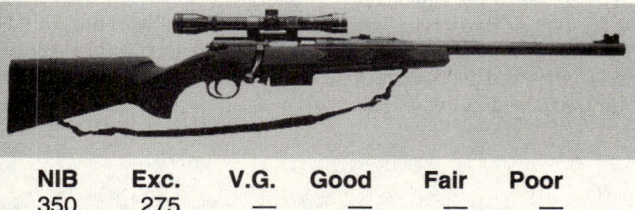

NIB	Exc.	V.G.	Good	Fair	Poor
350	275	—	—	—	—

MODERN MUZZLELOADERS

Model MLS-50/54

These Marlin in-line muzzleloaders were introduced in 1997. They are stainless steel and available in either .50 or .54 caliber. The barrel is 22" long. Adjustable Marble rear sight, ramp front sight with brass bead. Drilled and tapped for scope mount. Black synthetic stock with molded in checkering. Weight is about 7 lbs.

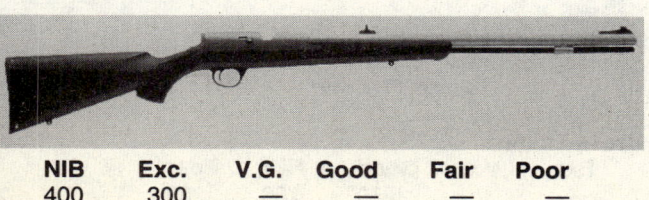

NIB	Exc.	V.G.	Good	Fair	Poor
400	300	—	—	—	—

MARROCHI, ARMI
Brescia, Italy
Importer-Precision Sales International
Westfield, Massachusetts

Model 2000

A 12 gauge Magnum single shot shotgun with a 28" barrel, exposed hammer and automatic ejector. Blued with a walnut stock.

Exc.	V.G.	Good	Fair	Poor
100	80	65	50	35

Field Master I

A 12 gauge Over/Under shotgun with 26" or 28" ventilated rib barrels fitted for choke tubes, single trigger and automatic ejectors. Blued, French casehardened with a walnut stock.

Exc.	V.G.	Good	Fair	Poor
400	350	300	200	150

Field Master 11

As above, with a single selective trigger.

Exc.	V.G.	Good	Fair	Poor
425	375	325	225	175

CONQUISTA SERIES

Offered in 3 grades:

Grade I is the standard grade with a special polished steel finish and machined engraved. The stock and forearm are select walnut and hand checkered 20 lines to the inch.

Grade II has roll engraved game scenes. The stock is select figured walnut.

Grade III is hand engraved by a master engraver featuring game scenes. Finely figured walnut stock.

Sporting Clays Model

Offered in 12 gauge with 28", 30", or 32" ventilated rib barrels. Screw in chokes are standard. Adjustable trigger. Weight is approximately 8 lbs.

Grade I

NIB	Exc.	V.G.	Good	Fair	Poor
1800	1600	1100	850	600	300

Grade II

NIB	Exc.	V.G.	Good	Fair	Poor
2200	1800	1400	950	700	350

Grade III

NIB	Exc.	V.G.	Good	Fair	Poor
3200	2750	1750	1150	800	400

Sporting Light

Same as above but slightly smaller dimensions. Available in 28" or 30" barrel length. Weight is about 7.5 lbs.

Grade I

NIB	Exc.	V.G.	Good	Fair	Poor
1900	1600	1100	850	600	300

Sporting Clays Left Model

Same as Sporting Clays Model but designed for the left-handed shooter.

Grade I

NIB	Exc.	V.G.	Good	Fair	Poor
1900	1600	1100	850	600	300

Lady Sport Model

Offered in 12 gauge only with choice of 28" or 30" vent rib barrels. Slightly smaller dimensions for women. Weight 7.75 lbs.

Grade I

NIB	Exc.	V.G.	Good	Fair	Poor
1900	1600	1100	850	600	300

Spectrum Grade-Colored frame

NIB	Exc.	V.G.	Good	Fair	Poor
1975	1650	1150	850	600	300

Lady Sport-Left Handed

Same as above but for left handed shooters.

Grade I

NIB	Exc.	V.G.	Good	Fair	Poor
1975	1650	1150	850	600	300

Spectrum-Left Handed

NIB	Exc.	V.G.	Good	Fair	Poor
2025	1700	1175	850	600	300

Trap Model

Built for the competition shooter this model features a choice of 30" or 32" vent rib barrels. Trap demension stock. Weight approximately 8.25 lbs.

Grade I

NIB	Exc.	V.G.	Good	Fair	Poor
1875	1650	1150	850	600	300

Grade II

NIB	Exc.	V.G.	Good	Fair	Poor
2275	1850	1450	1000	750	350

Grade III

NIB	Exc.	V.G.	Good	Fair	Poor
3250	2600	1850	1500	800	400

Skeet Model

This model is designed for the competition shooter. Only a 28" vent rib barrel is offered as standard. Skeet dimension stock. Skeet chokes. Weight is approximately 7.75 lbs.

Grade I

NIB	Exc.	V.G.	Good	Fair	Poor
1875	1650	1150	850	600	300

Grade II

NIB	Exc.	V.G.	Good	Fair	Poor
2275	1850	1450	1000	750	350

Grade III

NIB	Exc.	V.G.	Good	Fair	Poor
3250	2600	1850	1500	800	400

Classic Doubles Model 92

Offered in 12 gauge only with 30" vent rib barrels. Adjustable trigger. Walnut stock with 18 lines to the inch checkering. Weight is approximately 8.12 lbs.

NIB	Exc.	V.G.	Good	Fair	Poor
1500	1250	800	600	500	250

MARS
SEE-Gabbet-Fairfax or Bergmann

MARSTON, S.W.
New York, New York

Double Action Pepperbox

A .31 caliber double action percussion pepperbox with a 5" barrel group and ring trigger. Blued with walnut grips. Manufactured between 1850 and 1855.

Exc.	V.G.	Good	Fair	Poor
—	—	650	300	150

Two Barrel Pistol

A .31 or .36 revolving barrel 2-shot pistol with a ring trigger. The barrel marked "J.Cohn & S.W.Marston-New York." Blued, brass frame with walnut grips. Manufactured during the 1850s.

Exc.	V.G.	Good	Fair	Poor
—	—	1350	600	250

MARSTON, W. W. & CO.
New York, New York

W.W. Marston & Company manufactured a variety of firearms some of which are marked only with the trade names: Union Arms Company, Phoenix Armory, Western Arms Company, Washington Arms Company, Sprague and Marston, and Marston and Knox.

Pocket Revolver

A .31 caliber percussion revolver with a 3.25" to 7.5" barrel and 6-shot cylinder. Blued with walnut grips. Approximately 13,000 were manufactured between 1857 and 1862.

Exc.	V.G.	Good	Fair	Poor
—	—	500	300	200

Navy Revolver

A .36 caliber percussion revolver with a 7.5" or 8.5" octagonal barrel and 6-shot cylinder. Blued with walnut grips. Manufactured between 1857 and 1862.

Exc.	V.G.	Good	Fair	Poor
—	—	1500	650	300

Double Action Single Shot Pistol

A .31 or .36 caliber bar hammer percussion pistol with a 2.5" or 5" half octagonal barrel. Blued with walnut grips. Manufactured during the 1850s.

Exc.	V.G.	Good	Fair	Poor
—	—	325	200	100

Single Action Pistol

A .31 or .36 caliber percussion pistol with a 4" or 6" barrel. Blued with walnut grips. Manufactured during the 1860s.

Exc.	V.G.	Good	Fair	Poor
—	—	350	200	100

Breech Loading Pistol

A .35 caliber breech loading percussion pistol with a 4" to 8.5" half octagonal barrel and either a brass or iron frame. Blued, casehardened with walnut grips. Approximately 1,000 were manufactured in the 1850s.

Courtesy Milwaukee Public Museum, Milwaukee, Wisconsin

Brass Frame

Exc.	V.G.	Good	Fair	Poor
—	—	2250	750	250

Iron Frame

Exc.	V.G.	Good	Fair	Poor
—	—	1750	650	250

Double Action Pepperbox

A .31 caliber double action 6-shot percussion pepperbox with 4" or 5" barrel groups and a bar hammer. Blued, casehardened with walnut grips. Manufactured during the 1850s.

Courtesy Milwaukee Public Museum, Milwaukee, Wisconsin

Courtesy Milwaukee Public Museum, Milwaukee, Wisconsin

Exc.	V.G.	Good	Fair	Poor
—	—	600	250	100

3 Barreled Derringer

A .22 caliber 3 barreled spur trigger pocket pistol with a sliding knife blade mounted on the left side of the 3" barrel group. Blued, silver-plated with walnut grips. The barrel marked "Wm. W. Marston/New York City." Approximately 1,500 were manufactured between 1858 and 1864.

Knife Bladed Model

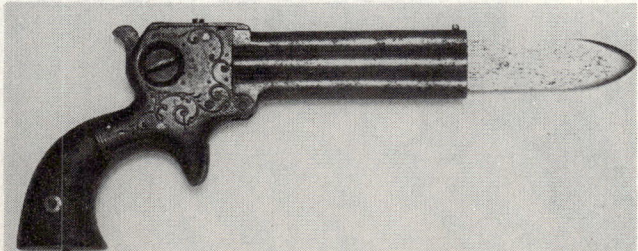

Courtesy Milwaukee Public Museum, Milwaukee, Wisconsin

Exc.	V.G.	Good	Fair	Poor
—	—	2000	950	350

Model Without Knife

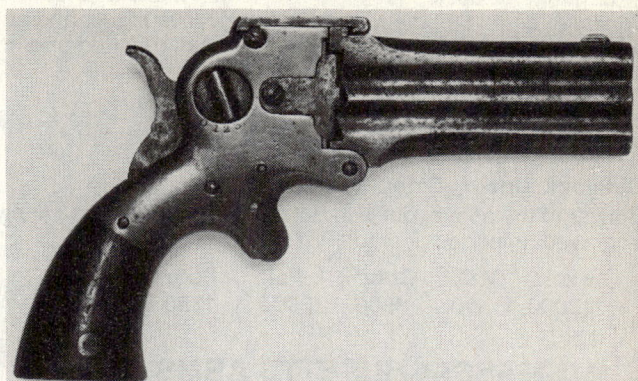

Courtesy Milwaukee Public Museum, Milwaukee, Wisconsin

Exc.	V.G.	Good	Fair	Poor
—	—	1000	550	200

.32 Caliber 3 Barrel Derringer

Similar to the above, but in .32 caliber with either 3" or 4" barrels and not fitted with a knife blade. Approximately 3,000 were manufactured between 1864 and 1872.

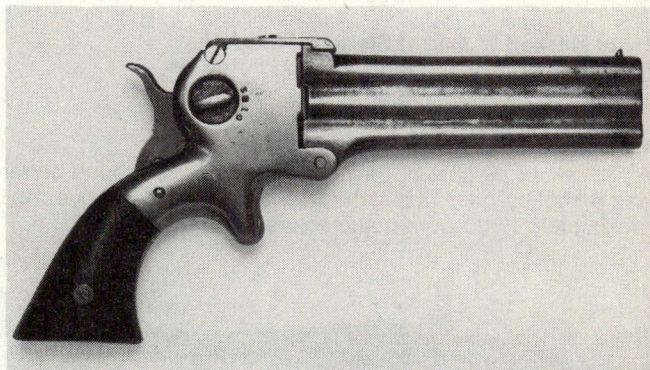

Courtesy Milwaukee Public Museum, Milwaukee, Wisconsin

Exc.	V.G.	Good	Fair	Poor
—	—	750	400	200

MASQUELIER S. A.
Liege, Belgium

Carpathe

A .243, .270, .7x57mm, 7x65Rmm, or .30-06 caliber single shot rifle with a 24" barrel, adjustable trigger and adjustable sights. Blued, with an engraved receiver and walnut stock. Imported until 1986.

Exc.	V.G.	Good	Fair	Poor
3500	3250	2750	2000	1500

Express

A .270, .30-06, 8x57JRSmm, or 9.3x74Rmm caliber Over/Under double-barrel rifle with 24" barrels, single selective trigger and automatic ejectors. Blued, engraved with a walnut stock. Not imported after 1986.

Exc.	V.G.	Good	Fair	Poor
3500	3250	2750	2000	750

Ardennes

As above, but made on custom order only. Discontinued in 1986.

Exc.	V.G.	Good	Fair	Poor
6500	5750	5000	4000	1500

Boxlock Side-by-Side Shotgun

A 12 gauge boxlock double barrel shotgun manufactured in a variety of barrel lengths with a single selective trigger and automatic ejectors. Blued with a walnut stock. Imported prior to 1987.

Exc.	V.G.	Good	Fair	Poor
4500	3750	3000	2500	950

Sidelock Side-by-Side Shotgun

Similar to the above, but with detachable sidelocks and finely engraved. Imported prior to 1987.

Exc.	V.G.	Good	Fair	Poor
13000	11500	8500	5000	1750

MASSACHUSETTS ARMS CO.
Chicopee Falls, Massachusetts

Wesson & Leavitt Dragoon

A .40 caliber percussion revolver with a 7" round barrel, 6-shot cylinder and side mounted hammer. Blued, casehardened with walnut grips. Approximately 800 were manufactured in 1850 and 1851.

Early Model with 6" Barrel-Approximately 30 Made

Exc.	V.G.	Good	Fair	Poor
—	—	4000	1750	750

Fully Marked 7" Barrel Standard Model

Exc.	V.G.	Good	Fair	Poor
—	—	3500	1250	650

Wesson & Leavitt Belt Revolver

A .31 caliber percussion revolver with a 3" to 7" round barrel and 6-shot cylinder. Similar in appearance to the above. Approximately 1,000 were manufactured in 1850 and 1851.

Courtesy Milwaukee Public Museum, Milwaukee, Wisconsin

Exc.	V.G.	Good	Fair	Poor
—	—	1000	400	150

Maynard Primed Belt Revolver

Similar to the above, with a Maynard tape primer. Approximately 1,000 were manufactured between 1851 and 1857.

Courtesy Milwaukee Public Museum, Milwaukee, Wisconsin

Exc.	V.G.	Good	Fair	Poor
—	—	1500	500	250

Maynard Primed Pocket Revolver

Similar to the above, but in .28 or .30 caliber with 2.5" to 3.5" octagonal or round barrels. Approximately 3,000 were made between 1851 and 1860.

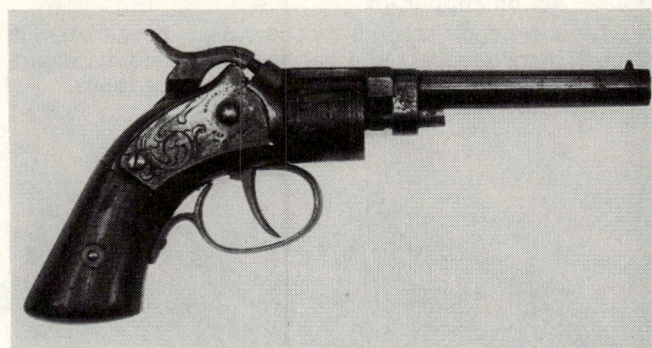

Courtesy Milwaukee Public Museum, Milwaukee, Wisconsin

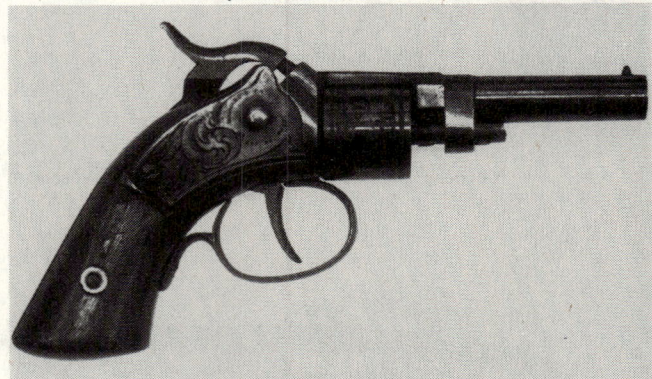

Courtesy Milwaukee Public Museum, Milwaukee, Wisconsin

Courtesy Milwaukee Public Museum, Milwaukee, Wisconsin

Courtesy Milwaukee Public Museum, Milwaukee, Wisconsin

Exc.	V.G.	Good	Fair	Poor
—	—	700	350	150

Adams Patent Navy Revolver

As above, in .36 caliber with a 6" octagonal barrel. Approximately 600 of the 1,000 made were purchased by the U.S. government. Those bearing inspection marks will bring approximately a 20% premium over the values listed below.

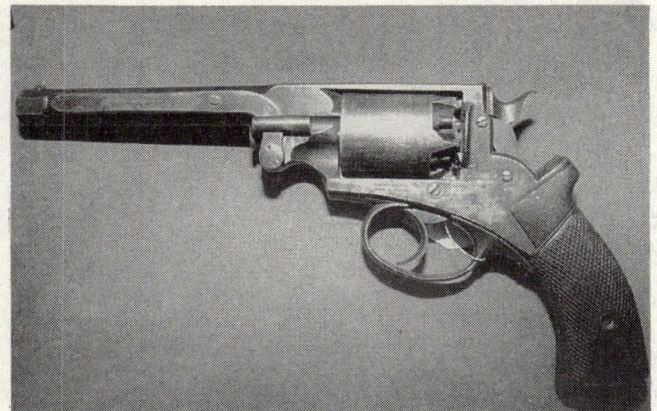

Exc.	V.G.	Good	Fair	Poor
—	—	800	400	200

Single Shot Pocket Pistol

A .31 caliber single shot percussion pistol with a 2.5" to 3.5" half octagonal barrel and a Maynard tape primer. The barrel marked "Mass. Arms Co/Chicopee Falls" and the primer door "Maynard's Patent Sept. 22, 1845." Blued, casehardened with walnut grips. Manufactured in the 1850s.

Exc.	V.G.	Good	Fair	Poor
—	—	1300	600	250

Maynard Carbine

This is a single-shot breechloader chambered for .35 or .50 caliber percussion. The barrel is round and 20" in length. The triggerguard is the lever that pivots the barrel in break-open fashion when it is lowered. The finish is blued, with a case-colored frame. The butt stock is walnut, and there is no forend. This carbine was designed by the same Maynard who invented the tape primer system. There are two models—a 1st and a 2nd. They were made for both sporting use and as a U.S. Martial carbine. The 2nd Model was used considerably during the Civil War.

1st Model

This model is marked "Maynard Patentee/May 27, 1851/June 17, 1856." It has an iron patchbox and a curved buttplate. It has a Maynard tape primer system and a tang sight. Later production was fitted with a sling swivel. There are approximately 400 of these carbines that are U.S. marked, but the total manufactured in the late 1850s is unknown.

Courtesy Milwaukee Public Museum, Milwaukee, Wisconsin

U.S. Martially Marked and AUTHENTICATED

Exc.	V.G.	Good	Fair	Poor
—	—	3000	1150	450

Commercial Model

Exc.	V.G.	Good	Fair	Poor
—	—	1500	750	350

2nd Model

This model is chambered for .50 caliber only and does not have the tape primer system or the tang sight. There is no patchbox, and the buttplate is not as curved as on the Ist Model. It is marked "Manufactured By/Mass. Arms Co./Chicopee Falls." There were approximately 20,000 manufactured between 1860 and 1865. This model was used by Union forces during the Civil War.

Courtesy Milwaukee Public Museum, Milwaukee, Wisconsin

Exc.	V.G.	Good	Fair	Poor
—	—	1000	550	350

Maynard Patent Sporting Rifles

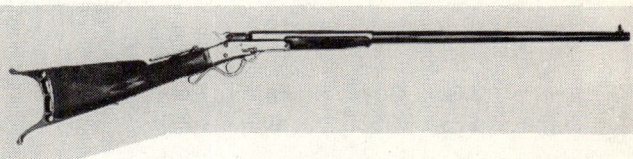

Courtesy Milwaukee Public Museum, Milwaukee, Wisconsin

Courtesy Milwaukee Public Museum, Milwaukee, Wisconsin

Sporting rifles bearing the designations Model 1865, 1873 and 1882 were manufactured in a wide variety of calibers, gauges, stock styles, finishes, and options. As these features affect the values of individual arms considerably, it is recommended that prospective purchasers are advised to secure a qualified appraisal prior to acquisition.

Exc.	V.G.	Good	Fair	Poor
—	—	800	300	125

MATRA MANURHIN DEFENSE
Mulhouse, France
SEE Manurhin

MAUSER WERKE
Oberndorf-am-Neckar, Germany

Established in 1869 by Peter and Wilhelm Mauser, this company came under the effective control of Ludwig Loewe and Company of Berlin in 1887. In 1896 the latter company was reorganized under the name Deutsches Waffen und Munition or as it is better known, DWM.

Model 1871

An 11mm caliber single shot bolt action rifle with a 33.5" barrel with bayonet lug, full length stock secured by two barrel bands and a cleaning rod. The barrel marked "Mod. 71" together with the year of production and the manufacturer's name. Blued with a walnut stock.

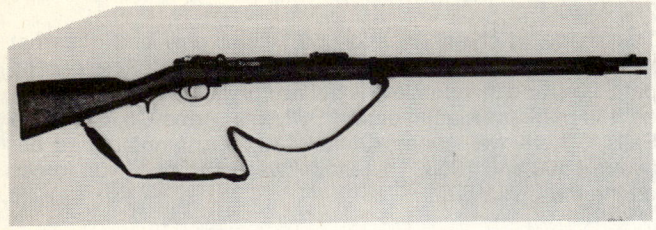

Courtesy Milwaukee Public Museum, Milwaukee, Wisconsin

Exc.	V.G.	Good	Fair	Poor
600	550	500	300	175

Model 1871 Jaeger Rifle

As above, with a 29.4" barrel.

Courtesy Bob Ball

Exc.	V.G.	Good	Fair	Poor
700	575	500	400	250

Model 1871 Carbine

As above, with a 20" barrel and no bayonet lug.

Courtesy Bob Ball

Exc.	V.G.	Good	Fair	Poor
600	500	400	300	200

Serbian Model 78/80

Identical to the Model 1871 except in 10.15mm caliber and with a 30.7" barrel. All markings in Cyrillic.

Exc.	V.G.	Good	Fair	Poor
800	500	400	325	200

Model 71/84 Rifle

The Model 71 modified by the addition of a tubular magazine. Barrel length 31.5".

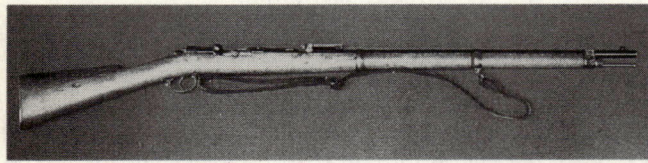

Courtesy Bob Ball

Exc.	V.G.	Good	Fair	Poor
600	500	400	250	150

Serbian Model 71/84

As above, in 10.15mm caliber with an 28.3" barrel. Marked in Cyrillic.

Courtesy Milwaukee Public Museum, Milwaukee, Wisconsin

Exc.	V.G.	Good	Fair	Poor
550	450	350	200	100

Model 1871 Jaeger Rifle

As above, with a 29.4" barrel.

Exc.	V.G.	Good	Fair	Poor
500	450	400	300	200

Model 1871 Carbine

As above, with a 20" barrel and no bayonet lug.

Exc.	V.G.	Good	Fair	Poor
500	450	400	300	200

Serbian Model 78/80

Identical to the Model 1871 except in 10.15mm caliber and with a 30.7" barrel. All markings in Cyrillic.

Exc.	V.G.	Good	Fair	Poor
350	300	250	150	100

Turkish Model 87 Rifle

Similar to the above, in 9.5mm caliber with a 30" barrel and 8-shot tubular magazine. Marked in Turkish script.

Exc.	V.G.	Good	Fair	Poor
600	500	400	250	100

Model 88 Commission Rifle

A 7.92mm caliber bolt action rifle with a 29" barrel, 5-shot magazine, full length stock, bayonet lug and cleaning rod. Marked "GEW. 88" together with the year of manufacture and the maker's name.

Exc.	V.G.	Good	Fair	Poor
225	175	150	100	75

Belgian Model 1889 Rifle

A 7.65mm bolt action rifle with a 30.6" barrel, 5-shot magazine, full length stock, cleaning rod and bayonet lug. Also made with a 21.65" barrel.

Exc.	V.G.	Good	Fair	Poor
225	175	150	100	75

Argentine Model 91 Rifle

A 7.65mm caliber bolt action rifle with a 29" barrel, 5-shot magazine, full length stock, cleaning rod and bayonet lug. Also made with a 17.6" barrel without a bayonet lug. Approximately 180,000 rifles and 30,000 carbines were made in 1891. They all are stamped with the Argentinian code of arms.

Exc.	V.G.	Good	Fair	Poor
375	300	200	125	90

Spanish Model 91

As above, but with a Spanish code of arms.

Exc.	V.G.	Good	Fair	Poor
250	200	175	125	90

Spanish Model 93

A 7x57mm caliber bolt action rifle with a 29" barrel and staggered column magazine. Adopted by the Spanish Government in 1893.

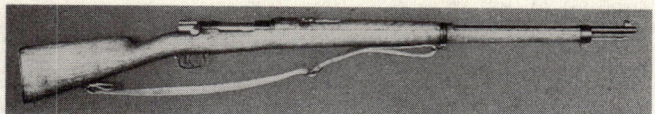

Courtesy Bob Ball

Exc.	V.G.	Good	Fair	Poor
200	150	100	70	40

Brazilian Model 94
Similar to the above, but with the Brazilian code of arms.

Exc.	V.G.	Good	Fair	Poor
200	150	100	70	40

Chilean Model 1895
As above, but marked "Mauser-Chileno Modelo 1895."

Exc.	V.G.	Good	Fair	Poor
300	200	175	100	80

Swedish Model 94 Carbine
A 6.5mm caliber bolt action carbine with a 17.7" barrel, 5-shot magazine, full length stock and bayonet lug. Marked with the Swedish Royal Crown and the date of manufacture.

Exc.	V.G.	Good	Fair	Poor
400	325	250	150	100

Swedish Model 96 Rifle
As above, with a 29" barrel.

Exc.	V.G.	Good	Fair	Poor
150	125	100	65	40

Swedish Model 38 Rifle
As above, with a 23.6" barrel and without the Swedish crown marking.

Exc.	V.G.	Good	Fair	Poor
150	125	100	70	40

Model 98 Rifle
The best known of all Mauser rifles. A 7.92mm bolt action rifle with a 29" barrel, 5-shot magazine, full length stock, hand guard, cleaning rod and bayonet lug. Marked "GEW. 98" together with the date of manufacture and maker's name.

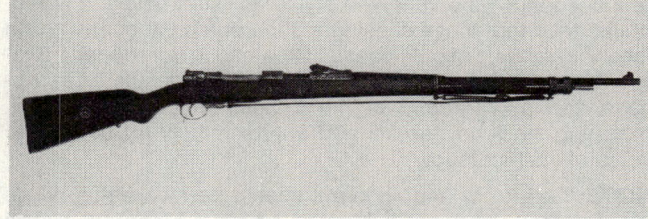

Courtesy Buffalo Bill Historical Center, Cody, Wyoming

Exc.	V.G.	Good	Fair	Poor
500	400	300	150	100

Model 98a Carbine
As above, with a 23.6" barrel and marked "KAR. 98".

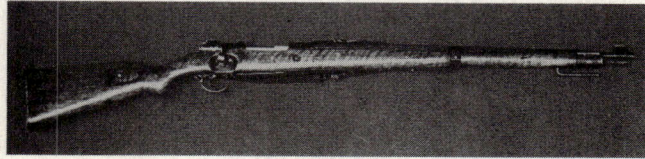

Courtesy Bob Ball

Exc.	V.G.	Good	Fair	Poor
350	250	150	110	80

Model 98k Carbine
As above, with a laminated stock and marked "Mod. 98".

Courtesy Buffalo Bill Historical Center, Cody, Wyoming

Exc.	V.G.	Good	Fair	Poor
375	250	200	125	85

> A Mauser Model 98k sniper rifle was sold at auction for $14,375. Chambered for 8mm cartridge and fitted with a Dialytan 4 power scope numbered to the rifle. Nazi proofs. All numbers match. Condition was near mint.
> Rock Island Auction Company, September 1997.

Model 33/40 Carbine
As above, with a 19.2" barrel and marked "G. 33/40" together with the year of production and the maker's code.

Exc.	V.G.	Good	Fair	Poor
850	700	600	300	200

Czech Model 98 VZ24
Assembled from Model 98k parts and identifiable by the large stamped steel triggerguard and permanent magazine floorplate. The original markings removed and replaced by Czech markings.

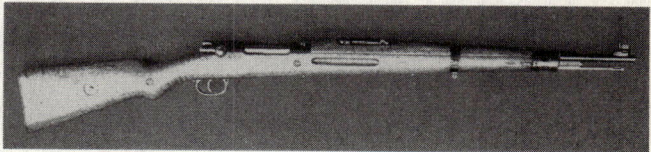

Courtesy Bob Ball

Exc.	V.G.	Good	Fair	Poor
275	200	200	175	125

French Occupation Model
Assembled from the Model 98k parts and identifiable by a hexagonal extension with a stacking rod protruding from it.

Exc.	V.G.	Good	Fair	Poor
400	350	250	150	100

Colombian Model 98
A Model 98a with a 29" barrel in .30-06 caliber.

Exc.	V.G.	Good	Fair	Poor
300	225	150	100	80

Iranian Model 98
Similar to the above, in 7.92mm caliber and also made with an 18" barrel. All markings in Farsi.

Courtesy Orvel Reichert

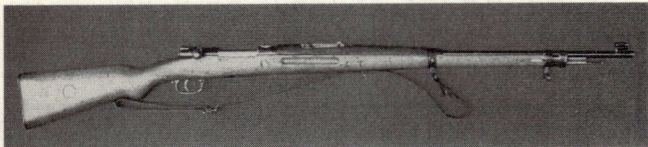

Courtesy Bob Ball

Exc.	V.G.	Good	Fair	Poor
400	250	200	150	100

Peruvian Model 1935 Rifle

Similar to the above, with a 23" barrel and in .30-06 caliber. The receiver ring stamped with a Peruvian crest.

Exc.	V.G.	Good	Fair	Poor
350	250	200	125	90

Polish Model 29

A Model 98a marked "F.B. Radom" together with the date of production. Barrel length 23.6", caliber 7.92mm.

Exc.	V.G.	Good	Fair	Poor
400	300	250	200	100

Standard Mauser Banner Rifle

A 7mm, 7.65mm, or 7.92mm caliber bolt action rifle with a 23.6" barrel and full-length stock. The receiver ring stamped with the Mauser Banner trademark.

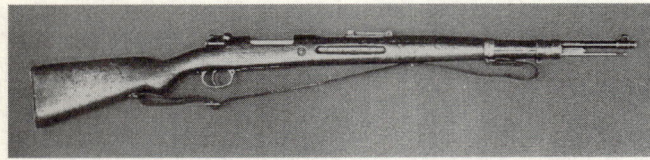

Courtesy Bob Ball

Exc.	V.G.	Good	Fair	Poor
450	400	300	225	125

Mexican Model 1910

Similar to a Model 98a, with a 23.2" barrel in 7x57mm caliber with a full-length stock and 5-shot magazine. The receiver ring stamped with the Mexican code of arms.

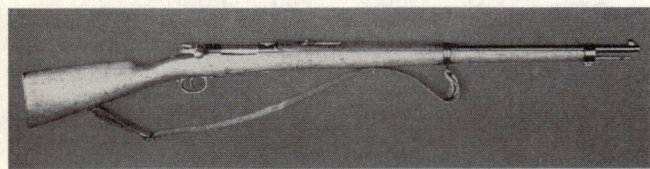

Courtesy Bob Ball

Exc.	V.G.	Good	Fair	Poor
250	150	125	85	60

Spanish Model 43

Similar to the above, with a 23.6" barrel in 7.92mm caliber. Manufactured by La Coruna Arsenal.

Exc.	V.G.	Good	Fair	Poor
225	175	150	100	75

Early Sporting Rifle

A wide variety of commercial Model 98 Sporting Rifles were made, most of which had 23.5" ribbed barrels, open sights, 5-shot magazines, single or double set triggers, and either full or semi-pistol grip stocks. While the following values are representative, it is suggested that prospective purchasers secure a qualified appraisal prior to acquisition.

Type A-Short Action

Exc.	V.G.	Good	Fair	Poor
3500	3000	2500	1500	1000

Type A-Medium Action

Exc.	V.G.	Good	Fair	Poor
2500	2000	1750	1400	1000

Type A-Long Action

Exc.	V.G.	Good	Fair	Poor
4000	3500	3000	2500	2000

Type B

Exc.	V.G.	Good	Fair	Poor
2500	2000	1500	1250	1000

Type K-21.65" Barrel

Exc.	V.G.	Good	Fair	Poor
4000	3500	3000	2250	1000

Type M-Full-length Stock, Spoon Bolt Handle

Exc.	V.G.	Good	Fair	Poor
3500	3000	2500	1500	1000

Type S-Full-length Stock, No Forend Cap

Exc.	V.G.	Good	Fair	Poor
3500	3000	2500	1500	1000

MODEL 1896 "BROOMHANDLE MAUSER PISTOL"

Manufactured from 1896 to 1939, the Model 1896 Pistol was produced in a wide variety of styles as listed below. It is recommended that those considering the purchase of any of the following models should consult Breathed & Schroeder's System Mauser (Chicago 1967) as it provides detailed descriptions and photographs of the various models. A correct, matching stock/holster will add approximately 40 percent to value of each category.

NOTE: Collectors and shooters should be aware that within the past several years a large quantity of Model 96 pistols have been imported into the United States from China.

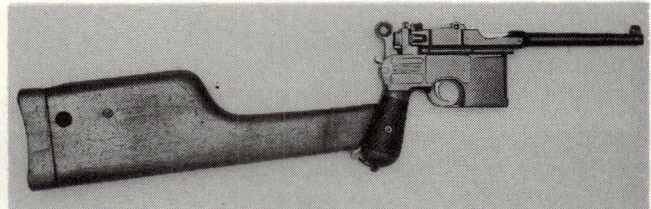

Courtesy Wallis & Wallis, Lewes, Sussex, England

Six-Shot Step-Barrel Cone Hammer

A 7.63mm semiautomatic pistol with a 5.5" barrel, fixed rear sight and checkered walnut grips. Marked "Ruecklauf Pistole System Mauser, Oberndorf am/Neckar 1896." Fewer than 200 were manufactured. Too rare to price.

Twenty-Shot Step-Barrel Cone Hammer

As above, with a 20-shot extended magazine. Too rare to price.

System Mauser Cone Hammer

As above, with the upper sides of the hammer machined with concentric rings and the grips with 22 grooves. Magazine capacity 10 rounds.

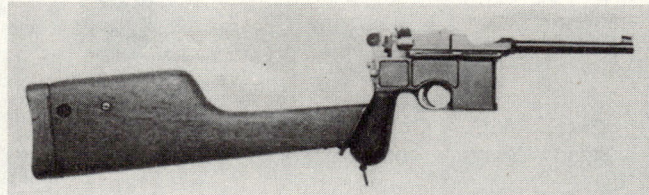

Courtesy Rock Island Auction Company

Exc.	V.G.	Good	Fair	Poor
17000	15000	10000	8000	7000

Six-Shot Cone Hammer

Similar to the above, with a 4.75" barrel, adjustable rear sight, 6-shot magazine and 21 groove grips. Marked "Waffenfabrik Mauser, Oberndorf A/N" over the chamber.

Exc.	V.G.	Good	Fair	Poor
11000	10000	6000	5000	3000

Twenty-Shot Cone Hammer

As above, with an extended magazine holding 20 cartridges.

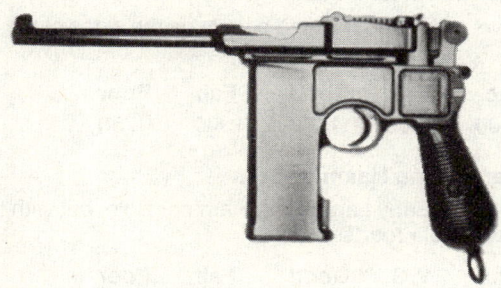

Exc.	V.G.	Good	Fair	Poor
30000	25000	15000	10000	7000

A professionally refinished 20 shot Mauser Model 1896 with stock sold at auction for $14,000. Refinished condition was mint.
Rock Island Auction Company, September 1997.

Standard Cone Hammer

As above, with a 10-shot magazine and 23 groove grips.

Exc.	V.G.	Good	Fair	Poor
3500	2750	1800	1400	800

Fixed Sight Cone Hammer

Similar to the standard Cone Hammer except that a fixed, integral sight is machined into the barrel extension.

Courtesy Gale Morgan

Exc.	V.G.	Good	Fair	Poor
4000	3000	2000	1500	1000

Turkish Contract Cone Hammer

As above, but marked in Turkish script and bearing the crest of Sultan Abdul-Hamid II on the frame. Approximately 1,000 were made.

Courtesy Gale Morgan

Exc.	V.G.	Good	Fair	Poor
11000	8000	6500	3000	2000

Early Transitional Large Ring Hammer

This variation has the same characteristics of the "Standard Cone Hammer" except the hammer has a larger, open ring.

Courtesy Gale Morgan

Exc.	V.G.	Good	Fair	Poor
3200	2400	2000	1150	800

Model 1899 Flat Side-Italian Contract

Similar to the above, with a 5.5" barrel, adjustable rear sight and the frame sides milled flat. Left flat of chamber marked with "DV" proof. Approximately 5,000 were manufactured in 1899.

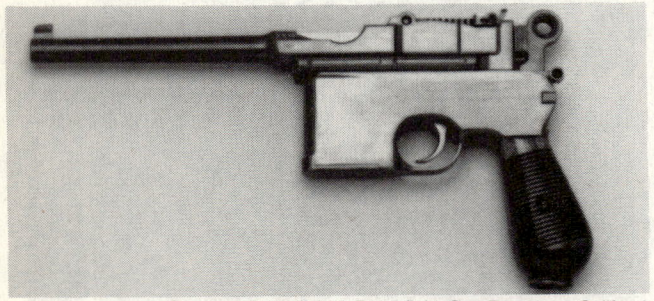

Courtesy Butterfield & Butterfield, San Francisco, California

Exc.	V.G.	Good	Fair	Poor
4000	3000	1500	1200	900

Early Flat Side

Similar to the above, except with "pinned" rear sight and without the Italian markings.

Exc.	V.G.	Good	Fair	Poor
2750	2450	1500	1000	750

Late Flat Side

Similar to the above, with an integral pin adjustable rear sight and often marked with dealer's names such as "Von Lengerke & Detmold, New York".

Exc.	V.G.	Good	Fair	Poor
2500	2000	1500	1000	750

Flat Side Bolo

Similar to the above, but with a 3.9" barrel, fixed sights, and checkered walnut grips.

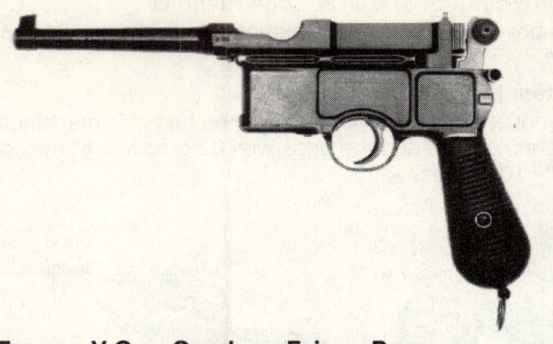

Exc.	V.G.	Good	Fair	Poor
3700	2800	2000	1500	1000

Early Large Ring Hammer Bolo

As above, with a milled frame, adjustable rear sight, and hard rubber grips cast with a floral pattern. 10-shot magazine.

Exc.	V.G.	Good	Fair	Poor
4000	3700	2000	1500	1000

Shallow-Milled Panel Model

Similar to the above, with a 5.5" barrel and either 23 groove walnut or checkered hard rubber grips.

Exc.	V.G.	Good	Fair	Poor
3000	2400	1000	750	500

Deep-Milled Panel Model

As above, with deeper milled panels on the sides of the receiver.

Exc.	V.G.	Good	Fair	Poor
2700	2000	1500	1000	750

Late Large Ring Hammer Bolo

Similar to the Early Large Ring Hammer Bolo, but with the late style adjustable rear sight.

Exc.	V.G.	Good	Fair	Poor
2500	2000	1500	1000	750

Six-Shot Large Ring Bolo

Similar to the above Large Ring Bolo but with six-shot magazine. This model is usually equipped with fixed sights.

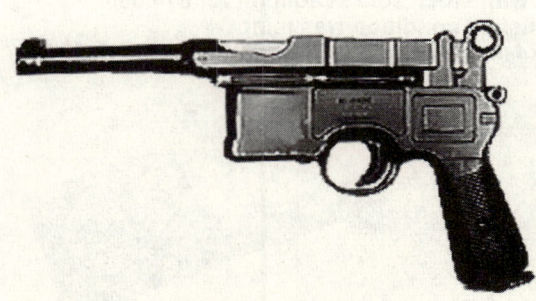

Courtesy Gale Morgan

Exc.	V.G.	Good	Fair	Poor
8000	6500	4500	3000	1800

Early Small Hammer Model, Transitional

The Model 96 with an early long extractor and a hammer having a small diameter hole and a 5.5" barrel. The grips with 34 grooves.

Small Ring Hammer

Courtesy Gale Morgan

Exc.	V.G.	Good	Fair	Poor
2500	2000	1000	750	500

Early Small Hammer Bolo Model

As above, with a 3.9" barrel and hard rubber grips cast with a floral pattern. Serial numbers in the 40,000 range.

Exc.	V.G.	Good	Fair	Poor
3000	2500	1400	950	600

Six-Shot Small Hammer Model

As above, with 27 groove walnut grips.

Exc.	V.G.	Good	Fair	Poor
7500	6500	4000	2250	1600

Standard Prewar Commercial

A Model 96 with a 5.5" barrel, late style adjustable rear sight and either 34 groove walnut grips or checkered hard rubber grips. Often found with dealers markings such as "Von Lengerke & Detmold."

Retailer Marked Panel

Courtesy Gale Morgan

Exc.	V.G.	Good	Fair	Poor
1500	1300	850	450	300

Mauser Banner Model

As above, with the Mauser Banner trademark and 32 groove walnut grips. Approximately 10,000 were manufactured.

Courtesy Gale Morgan

Exc.	V.G.	Good	Fair	Poor
3700	3200	2000	800	600

Persian Contract

As above, with Persian issuance marks. Prospective purchasers should secure a qualified appraisal prior to acquisition.

Exc.	V.G.	Good	Fair	Poor
4200	3500	2250	1400	1000

9mm Export Model

As above, in 9mm Mauser with 34 goove walnut grips.

Exc.	V.G.	Good	Fair	Poor
2500	2250	1500	1000	700

Standard Wartime Commercial

Identical to the prewar Commercial Model 96, except that it has 30 groove walnut grips and the rear of the hammer is stamped "NS" for new safety.

Courtesy Gale Morgan

Exc.	V.G.	Good	Fair	Poor
1500	1000	600	500	350

9mm Parabellum Military Contract

As above, in 9mm Parabellum caliber with 24 groove grips, stamped with a large "9" filled with red paint.

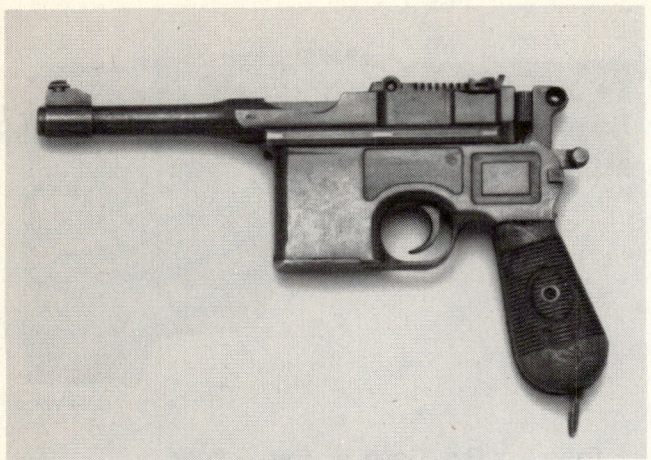

Courtesy Butterfield & Butterfield, San Francisco, California

Exc.	V.G.	Good	Fair	Poor
2000	1600	1100	600	450

1920 Rework

A Model 96 modified to a barrel length of 3.9" and in 7.63mm Mauser or 9mm Parabellum caliber. Often encountered with police markings.

Courtesy Gale Morgan

Exc.	V.G.	Good	Fair	Poor
1300	1000	500	400	350

Luger Barreled 1920 Rework

Similar to the above, but fitted with a Luger barrel of 4" in length. 23 groove walnut grips and of 9mm caliber.

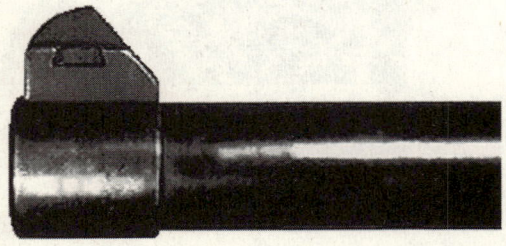

Courtesy Gale Morgan

Exc.	V.G.	Good	Fair	Poor
1800	1500	750	500	450

French Gendarme Model

A standard Model 96 fitted with a 3.9" barrel and checkered hard rubber grips. Although reputed to have been made under a French contract, no record of that has been found to date.

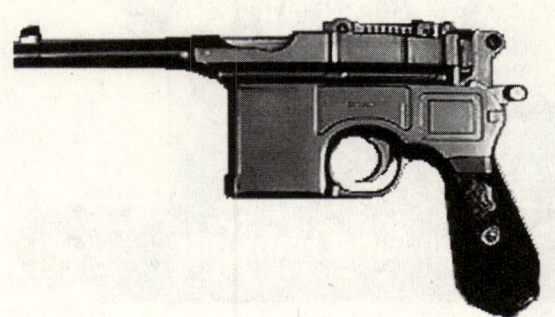

Courtesy Gale Morgan

Exc.	V.G.	Good	Fair	Poor
3700	3200	1800	1100	600

Early Postwar Bolo Model

A Model 96 in 7.63mm caliber with a 2.9" barrel, adjustable rear sight and 22-groove walnut grips.

Exc.	V.G.	Good	Fair	Poor
2000	1500	1200	650	400

Late Postwar Bolo Model

As above, with the Mauser Banner trademark stamped on the left rear panel.

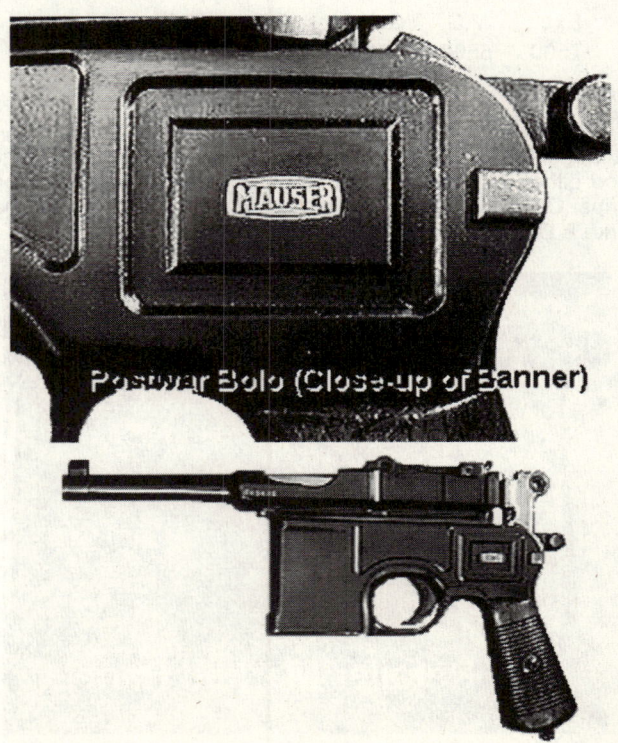

Postwar Bolo (Close-up of Banner)

Courtesy Gale Morgan

Exc.	V.G.	Good	Fair	Poor
1750	1500	1000	750	500

Early Model 1930

A 7.63mm caliber Model 96 with a 5.2" stepped barrel, 12-groove walnut grips and late style safety.

1930 Hammer

Panel Banner: Model 1930

Courtesy Gale Morgan

Exc.	V.G.	Good	Fair	Poor
2700	2000	1200	800	500

Late Model 1930

Identical to the above, except for solid receiver rails.

Exc.	V.G.	Good	Fair	Poor
2500	2000	1000	700	400

Model 1930 Removable Magazine

Similar to the above, but with a detachable magazine. Prospective purchasers should secure a qualified appraisal prior to acquisition. Too rare to price.

Cone Hammer Flat Side Carbine

A 7.63mm caliber carbine with an 11.75" barrel, early adjustable sight, flat frame and integral pistol grips/butt stock. Prospective purchasers should secure a qualified appraisal prior to acquisition. Too rare to price.

Large Ring Hammer Transitional Carbine

Similar to the above, with milled frame panels. Prospective purchasers should secure a qualified appraisal prior to acquisition.

Exc.	V.G.	Good	Fair	Poor
21000	18000	11000	5000	3000

Large Ring Hammer Carbine

Similar to the above, with a 14.5" barrel. Prospective purchasers should secure a qualified appraisal prior to acquisition.

Courtesy Gale Morgan

Exc.	V.G	Good	Fair	Poor
20000	18000	10000	4000	3000

Small Ring Hammer Carbine

Similar to the above, with the hammer having a smaller diameter hole at its tip. Prospective purchasers should secure a qualified appraisal prior to acquisition.

Exc.	V.G	Good	Fair	Poor
25000	20000	12000	5000	3000

Chinese Marked, Handmade Copies

Crude copies of the Model 96 and unsafe to fire.

Exc.	V.G.	Good	Fair	Poor
500	400	350	250	175

Taku-Naval Dockyard Model

Approximately 6,000 copies of the Model 96 were made at the Taku-Naval Dockyard. Values listed below include a correct shoulder stock/holder.

Exc.	V.G.	Good	Fair	Poor
2500	1500	1000	500	400

Shansei Arsenal Model

Approximately 8,000 Model 96 pistols were manufactured in .45 ACP caliber.

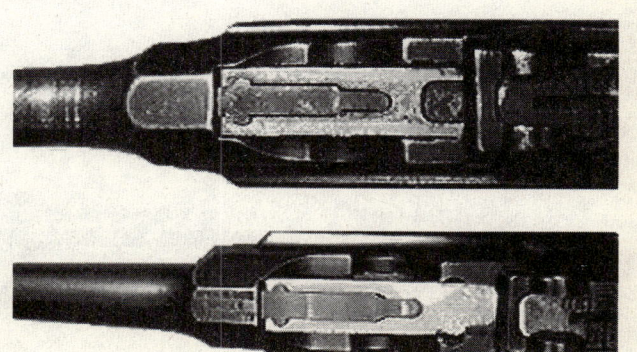

Shansei Panel Marking

Courtesy Gale Morgan

Exc.	V.G.	Good	Fair	Poor
5000	3500	2250	1500	1300

NOTE: Within the past several years, a large quantity of Model 96 pistols exported to or made in China have been imported into the United States.

Copies of the Model 96 were made by Unceta (Astra) and Zulaica y Cia (Royal) and marketed by the firm of Beistegui Hermanos. These copies are covered in their own sections of this text.

MAUSER POCKET PISTOLS

Model 1910

A 6.35mm caliber semiautomatic pistol with a 3" barrel, 9-shot magazine and either checkered walnut or hard rubber grips. The slide marked "Waffenfabrik Mauser A.-G. Oberndorf A.N. Mauser's Patent." Manufactured between 1910 and 1934.

Exc.	V.G.	Good	Fair	Poor
375	325	225	150	100

Model 1914

Courtesy Butterfield & Butterfield, San Francisco, California

A 7.65mm caliber semiautomatic pistol with a 3.5" barrel, fixed sights, and wrap-around walnut grips. The slide marked "Waffenfabrik Mauser A.G. Oberndorf A.N. Mauser's Patent" on the slide. The frame has the Mauser banner stamped on its left side. Manufactured between 1914 and 1934.

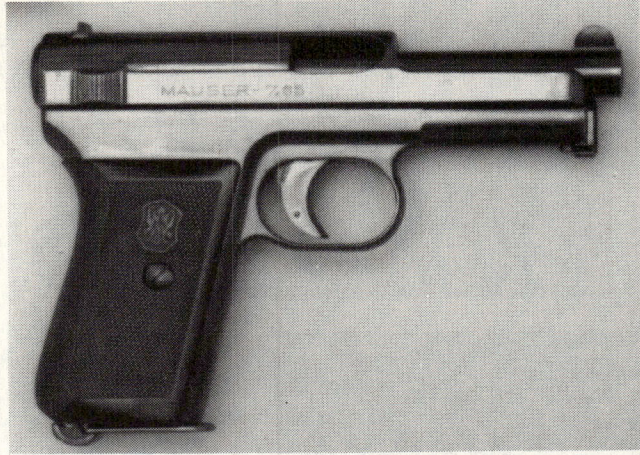

Courtesy Wallis & Wallis, Lewes, Sussex, England

Exc.	V.G.	Good	Fair	Poor
450	300	225	150	100

WTP Model I Vest Pocket Pistol

A 6.35mm semiautomatic pistol with a 2.5" barrel, 6-shot magazine and either plastic or hard rubber grips bearing the Mauser banner. The slide marked "Mauser-Werke A.G. Oberndorf A.N." Manufactured between 1922 and 1937.

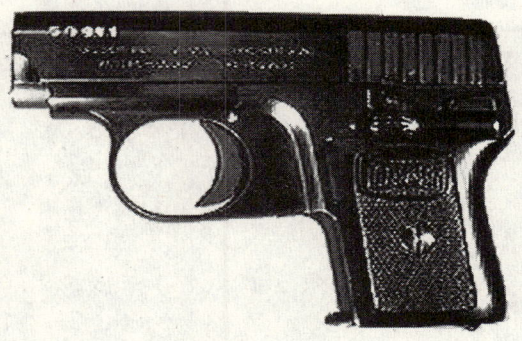

Courtesy Gale Morgan

Exc.	V.G.	Good	Fair	Poor
600	500	325	200	150

WTP Model II Vest Pocket Pistol

Similar to the above, with a 2" barrel. Manufactured between 1938 and 1940.

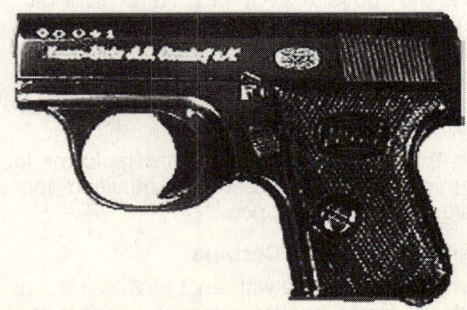

Exc.	V.G.	Good	Fair	Poor
575	500	300	225	150

Model 1934

Similar to the Model 1914, with the slide marked "Mauser-Werke A.G. Oberndorf A. N." It has the Mauser Banner stamped on the frame. The reverse side is marked with the caliber and "D.R.P. u A.P." Manufactured between 1934 and 1939. Those with Nazi Waffenamt markings are worth approximately 20 percent more than the values listed below. Those marked with an eagle over the letter "M" (Navy Marked) are worth approximately 100% more than the values listed below.

Courtesy Orvel Reichert

Courtesy Orvel Reichert

Courtesy Gale Morgan

Exc.	V.G.	Good	Fair	Poor
475	350	250	150	100

Model HSC

A 7.65mm or 9mm short caliber double action semiautomatic pistol with a 3.4" barrel, 7- or 8-shot magazine and fixed sights. Introduced in 1938 and produced in the variations listed below.

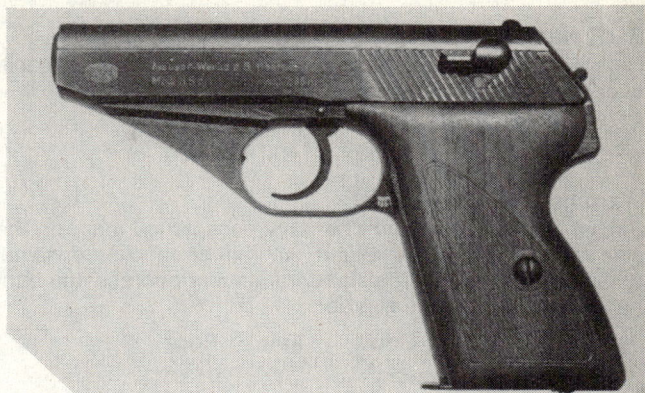

Courtesy Orvel Reichert

Low Grip Screw Model

As above, with screws that attach the grip located near the bottom of the grip. Highly-polished blue, checkered walnut grips and the early address without the lines and has the Eagle N proof. Some have been observed with Nazi Kreigsmarine markings. Approximately 2,000 were manufactured.

Exc.	V.G.	Good	Fair	Poor
3000	2500	1400	750	650

Early Commercial Model

A highly-polished blued finish, checkered walnut grips, the standard Mauser address on the slide, and the Eagle N proofmark. The floorplate of the magazine stamped with the Mauser Banner.

Exc.	V.G.	Good	Fair	Poor
450	400	350	175	125

Transition Model

As above, but not as highly finished.

Exc.	V.G.	Good	Fair	Poor
400	350	300	150	100

Early Nazi Army Model

Highly polished with Waffenamt No. 135 or 655 markings. Checkered walnut grips. Acceptance marks are located on the left side of the triggerguard.

Courtesy Orvel Reichert

Exc.	V.G.	Good	Fair	Poor
425	350	300	200	125

Late Nazi Army Model

Blued or parkerized, with walnut or plastic grips, and the 135 acceptance mark only. It also has the Eagle N proof.

Exc.	V.G.	Good	Fair	Poor
375	300	250	150	100

Early Nazi Navy Model

Highly polished with checkered walnut grips and the eagle over "M" marking on the front grip strap.

Exc.	V.G.	Good	Fair	Poor
1000	800	550	400	300

Wartime Nazi Navy Model

Similar to the above, with the navy acceptance mark on the side of the triggerguard. Blued, with either checkered walnut or plastic grips. It has the standard Mauser address and banner and also the Eagle N proof.

Exc.	V.G.	Good	Fair	Poor
700	600	500	400	200

Early Nazi Police Model

Identical to the Early Commercial Model with an eagle over "L" mark on the left side of the triggerguard.

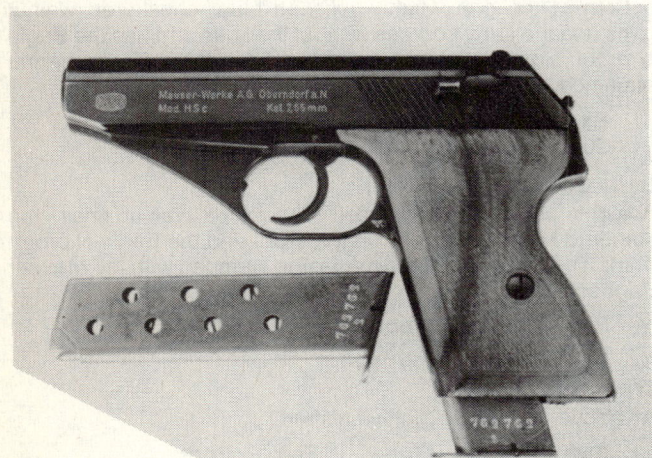

Courtesy Orvel Reichert

Exc.	V.G.	Good	Fair	Poor
475	450	350	250	175

Wartime Nazi Police Model

As above, with a three line Mauser address.

Exc.	V.G.	Good	Fair	Poor
475	400	350	250	175

Wartime Commercial Model

As above, without acceptance markings on the triggerguard.

Exc.	V.G.	Good	Fair	Poor
425	350	300	200	125

French Manufactured Model

Blued or parkerized with walnut or plastic grips and the triggerguard marked on the left side with the monogram "MR".

Exc.	V.G.	Good	Fair	Poor
325	275	225	150	100

American Eagle HSc

Only 5,000 of this pistols were produced in both .380 and .32 caliber.

NOTE: Deduct 20% for .32 caliber model.

NIB	Exc.	V.G.	Good	Fair	Poor
375	325	275	225	150	100

Late Mauser Production Model

Manufactured from 1968 to 1981, this model was almost identical to the early Commercial Model. Built in .380 and .32 caliber.

NOTE: Deduct 20% for .32 caliber model.

Exc.	V.G.	Good	Fair	Poor
325	275	225	150	100

Interarms Import Models

As above, but made by Gamba in Italy and sold by Interarms of Alexandria, Virginia, from 1983 to 1985.

Exc.	V.G.	Good	Fair	Poor
275	250	200	150	100

MAUSER RIFLES-RECENT PRODUCTION

Model 2000

A .270, .308, or the .30-06 caliber bolt action rifle with a 24" barrel, open sights and a 5-shot magazine. Blued, with a checkered walnut stock. Manufactured between 1969 and 1971.

Exc.	V.G.	Good	Fair	Poor
350	300	250	200	150

Model 3000

As above, with a 22" barrel, no sights and Monte Carlo-style stock. Manufactured from 1971 to 1974.

Exc.	V.G.	Good	Fair	Poor
450	400	350	300	250

Model 3000 Magnum

As above, in 7mm Rem. Mag., .300 Win. Mag. and the .375 H&H Mag. caliber with a 26" barrel and a 3-shot integral magazine. Blued, with a checkered walnut stock.

Exc.	V.G.	Good	Fair	Poor
500	450	400	350	300

Model 4000

Similar to the Model 3000, but in .222 or .223 caliber with folding open sights.

Exc.	V.G.	Good	Fair	Poor
400	350	300	250	200

Model 225

A .243 to. 300 Weatherby Magnum caliber bolt action rifle with a 24" or 26" barrel, no sights, adjustable trigger or 3- or 5-shot magazine. Blued with a walnut stock.

NIB	Exc.	V.G.	Good	Fair	Poor
1400	1250	1000	750	600	500

Model ES340

A .22 caliber single shot bolt action rifle with a 25.5" barrel, open sights, and walnut stock. Manufactured before WWII.

Exc.	V.G.	Good	Fair	Poor
300	250	225	175	125

Model DSM34

Similar to the above, with a 25" barrel and full-length walnut stock. Manufactured prior to WWII.

Exc.	V.G.	Good	Fair	Poor
325	275	250	200	150

Model MS420B

Similar to the above, with a 25" barrel and 5-shot magazine. Manufactured before WWII.

Exc.	V.G.	Good	Fair	Poor
375	325	300	275	200

Model ES350

A .22 caliber single shot bolt action rifle with a 27.5" barrel and checkered pistol grip walnut stock. Manufactured before WWII.

Exc.	V.G.	Good	Fair	Poor
450	400	375	350	275

Model M410

Similar to the above, with a 23.5" barrel and 5-shot magazine. Manufactured before WWII.

Exc.	V.G.	Good	Fair	Poor
375	325	300	275	200

Model M420

As above, with a 25.5" barrel.

Exc.	V.G.	Good	Fair	Poor
375	325	300	275	200

Model EN310

A .22 caliber single shot bolt action rifle with a 19.75" barrel, open sights, and plain walnut stock. Manufactured before WWII.

Exc.	V.G.	Good	Fair	Poor
250	225	200	150	100

Model EL320

As above, with a 23.5" barrel and checkered walnut stock.

Exc.	V.G.	Good	Fair	Poor
275	250	225	175	125

Model KKW

A .22 caliber single shot bolt action rifle with a 26" barrel, ladder rear sight and full-length walnut stock. Manufactured prior to WWII.

Exc.	V.G.	Good	Fair	Poor
400	350	300	225	150

Model MS350B

A .22 caliber bolt action rifle with a 26.75" barrel, adjustable rear sight and 5-shot magazine. Blued with a walnut stock.

Exc.	V.G.	Good	Fair	Poor
475	400	350	275	200

Model ES340B

Similar to the above, but in single shot form.

Exc.	V.G.	Good	Fair	Poor
375	300	250	175	100

Model MM41OBN

A .22 caliber bolt action rifle with a 23.5" barrel, adjustable sights, and 5-shot magazine. Blued with a walnut stock.

Exc.	V.G.	Good	Fair	Poor
400	350	300	200	125

Model MS420B

As above, with a 26.75" barrel and target style stock.

Exc.	V.G.	Good	Fair	Poor
400	350	300	200	125

Model 107

This is a bolt action rifle chambered for the .22 Long Rifle. Barrel length is 21.6" and box magazine has a 5-shot capacity. The beechwood checkered Monte Carlo stock is full size with pistol grip, plastic buttplate. The rear sight is adjustable. Metal finish is blue. Weighs about 5 lbs.

NIB	Exc.	V.G.	Good	Fair	Poor
265	225	180	150	125	100

Model 201 Standard

This model features a 21" medium heavy free-floating barrel. The receiver accepts all rail mounts and is also drilled and tapped for scope mount. Magazine capacity is 5-shot. Chambered for .22 Long Rifle or .22 WMR cartridge. The beechwood stock is hand checkered with plastic buttplate. The Monte Carlo stock is fitted with cheekpiece. Weighs about 6.5 lbs.

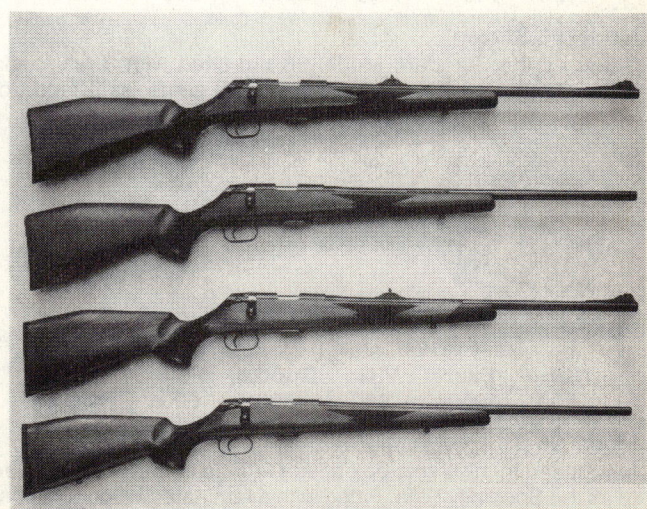

NIB	Exc.	V.G.	Good	Fair	Poor
390	370	325	275	225	175

Model 201 Luxus

Same as above but features a European walnut stock with rosewood forend, hand checkering, rubber butt pad, and 1" quick disconnect sling swivels. Available with or without sights.

NIB	Exc.	V.G.	Good	Fair	Poor
550	475	400	350	300	200

Model 66 Standard

This is a centerfire bolt action rifle fitted with a European Walnut hand-checkered oil finish stock. Stock is half stock design. Rosewood forends and pistol grip caps are standard. Fitted with rubber recoil pad and 1" quick disconnect sling swivels. Barrels are interchangeable on this model. Barrels with standard calibers is 24" and approximate weight is 7.5 lbs. Standard calibers are: .243 Win., .270, .308, .30-06, 5.6x57, 6.5x57, 7.64, and 9.3x62.

NIB	Exc.	V.G.	Good	Fair	Poor
1400	1150	850	700	550	350

Model 66 Magnum

Same as above but chambered for 7mm Rem. Mag., .300 and .338 Win. Mag., 6.5x68, 8x86S, 9.3x64. Fitted with a 26" barrel and weighs about 7.9 lbs.

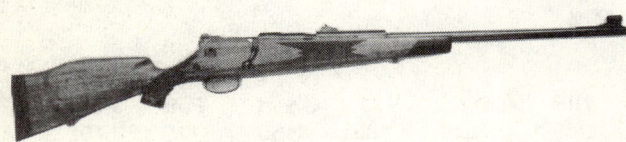

NIB	Exc.	V.G.	Good	Fair	Poor
1500	1250	950	800	600	400

Model 66 Safari

Same as above but chambered for .375 H&H and .458 Win. Mag. Fitted with a 26" barrel and weighs about 9.3 lbs.

NIB	Exc.	V.G.	Good	Fair	Poor
1650	1400	1100	850	650	400

Model 66 Stuzen

Same as the Standard Model 66 but fitted with a full stock. Barrel length is 21" and calibers are same as Standard. Weighs about 7.5 lbs.

NIB	Exc.	V.G.	Good	Fair	Poor
1500	1250	950	800	600	400

Model 86 SR

Introduced in 1993 this bolt action .308 is sometimes referred to as the Specialty Rifle. Fitted with a laminated wood and special match thumbhole stock or fiberglass stock with adjustable cheekpiece. Stock has rail in forearm and an adjustable recoil pad. Magazine capacity is 9 rounds. Finish is a non-glare blue.

The barrel length with muzzle brake is 28.8". Many special features are found on this rifle from adjustable trigger weight to silent safety. Mauser offers many options on this rifle as well that will affect the price. Weight is approximately 11 lbs.

NIB	Exc.	V.G.	Good	Fair	Poor
3300	2950	2500	1750	1250	750

Model 93 SR

Introduced in 1996 this is a tactical semiautomatic rifle chambered for the .300 Win. Mag. or the .338 Lapua cartridge. Barrel length is 25.5" with an overall length of 48.4". Barrel is fitted with a muzzle brake. Magazine capacity is 6 rounds for .300 and 5 rounds for .338 caliber. Weight is approximately 13 lbs.

NIB	Exc.	V.G.	Good	Fair	Poor
N/A	—	—	—	—	—

Model 99 Standard

This model is a bolt action centerfire sporting rifle. It is offered with two stock designs: a classic with straight oil finish stock or high luster with cheekpiece and Schnabel forend and Monte Carlo with rosewood forend tip and pistol grip cap. Chambered for standard calibers: .243, .25-06, .270, .308, .30-06, 5.6x57, 6.5x57, 7x57, 7x64. Barrel length is 24". Weight about 8 lbs.

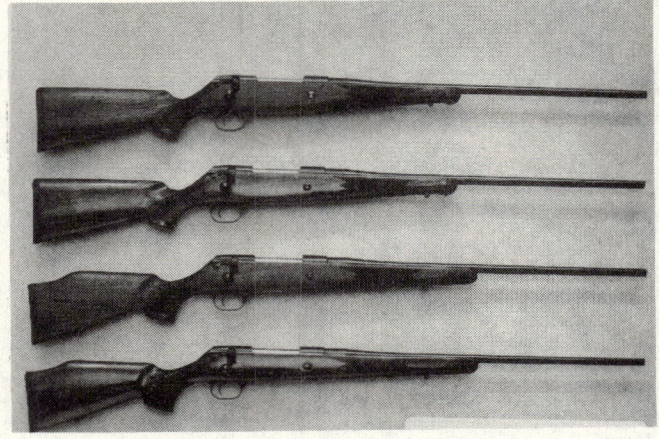

NIB	Exc.	V.G.	Good	Fair	Poor
900	700	600	500	400	300

Model 99 Magnum

Same as above but chambered for magnum calibers: 7mm Rem. Mag., .257 Wby., .270 Wby., .300 Wby., .300 and .338 Win. Mag., 8x68S, and 9.3x64. Fitted with 26" barrel. Weighs about 8 lbs.

NIB	Exc.	V.G.	Good	Fair	Poor
950	750	650	550	400	300

Model 96

This bolt action rifle is chambered for the .25-06, .270 Win., 7x64, .308, or .30-06 cartridge. It is fitted with a 22" barrel (24" Magnum calibers) and has a 5 round top loading magazine. Receiver is drilled and tapped. Checkered walnut stock. No sights. Approximately weight is 6.25 lbs.

NIB	Exc.	V.G.	Good	Fair	Poor
675	525	400	300	250	200

Model 80 SA

This single action semiautomatic pistol is based on the Browning Hi-Power design. Chambered for the 9mm Parabellum cartridge it has a barrel length of 4.66" and a magazine capacity of 14 rounds. Weighs approximately 35 oz.

NIB	Exc.	V.G.	Good	Fair	Poor
300	275	225	175	125	100

Model Compact DA
Same as above but double action trigger and shorter barrel: 4.13". Weighs approximately 33 oz.

NIB	Exc.	V.G.	Good	Fair	Poor
340	320	250	175	125	100

Model 90 DA
Similar to the Model 80 but with a double action trigger.

NIB	Exc.	V.G.	Good	Fair	Poor
310	285	235	175	125	100

MAVERICK ARMS, INC.
Eagle Pass, Texas

Model 88
A 12 gauge Magnum slide action shotgun with 28" or 30" barrels, anodized receiver and composition stock. Introduced in 1989.

NIB	Exc.	V.G.	Good	Fair	Poor
175	150	125	100	75	50

MAYNARD/PERRY
Keen, Walker & Co.
Danville, Virginia

Brass Framed Carbine
Overall length 40"; barrel length 22.5"; caliber .54. Browned, blued barrel, brass frame and walnut stock. Manufactured in 1861 and 1862. Prospective purchasers are advised to secure a qualified appraisal prior to acquisition.

Exc.	V.G.	Good	Fair	Poor
—	—	6500	2500	750

McMILLAN, G. & CO. INC.
Phoenix, Arizona

Competition Model
A custom order bolt action rifle in .308, 7mm/08, and the .300 Winchester Magnum caliber with the barrel length, stock type, and dimensions to the customer's specifications. Introduced in 1988.

NIB	Exc.	V.G.	Good	Fair	Poor
1700	1500	1150	800	600	300

Model 86 Snipers Rifle
A custom order rifle in .308 Winchester or the .300 Winchester Magnum calibers with a synthetic stock and a choice of scope systems. Introduced in 1988.

NIB	Exc.	V.G.	Good	Fair	Poor
1350	1100	900	600	400	200

Model 86 System
As above, with the Ultra scope, mounting system, bipod, and fitted case. Introduced in 1988.

NIB	Exc.	V.G.	Good	Fair	Poor
2150	1850	1500	1100	550	250

Model 87 Long Range Snipers Rifle
A large stainless steel, single shot bolt action rifle in .50 BMG caliber with a 29" barrel having an integral muzzle brake. Camouflaged synthetic stock. Weight 21 lbs. Accurate to 1,500 meters. Introduced in 1988.

NIB	Exc.	V.G.	Good	Fair	Poor
2700	2200	1800	1200	600	250

Model 87 System
As above, with a bipod and a 20X Ultra scope, mounting system, and a fitted case. Introduced in 1988.

NIB	Exc.	V.G.	Good	Fair	Poor
3350	2700	2100	1500	900	400

Signature Model
A bolt action sporting rifle manufactured in a variety of calibers up to .375 Holland & Holland with a 22" or 24" stainless barrel, composition stock and either 3- or 4-shot magazine. Introduced in 1988.

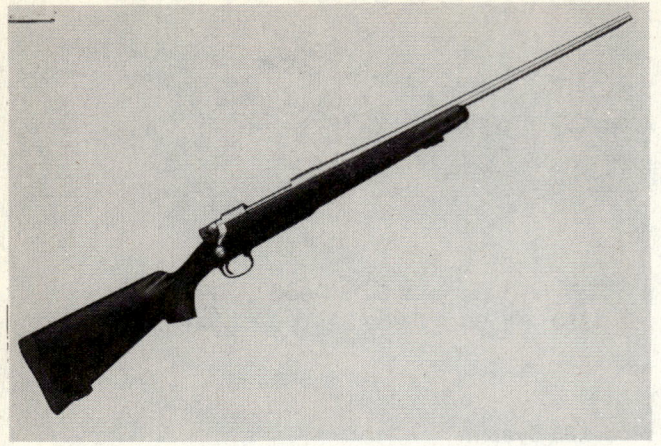

NIB	Exc.	V.G.	Good	Fair	Poor
2200	1750	1250	800	600	300

Signature Stainless

Same as model above but barrel and action made of stainless steel. Fiberglass stock. Left or right hand model. The .416 Rigby is also offered in this configuration. Introduced in 1990.

NIB	Exc.	V.G.	Good	Fair	Poor
2200	1750	1250	800	600	300

Signature Alaskan

This model, introduced in 1989, is offered in .270 .280 Rem., .30-06, 7mm Rem. Mag., .300 Win. Mag., .300 Wethby Mag., .358 Win. Mag., .340 Wethby Mag., .375 H&H. Match grade barrel from 22" to 26" in length. Single leaf rear sight and barrel band front sight.

NIB	Exc.	V.G.	Good	Fair	Poor
3000	2700	2000	1500	950	500

Signature Titanium Mountain

Offered in calibers from .270 Win. to 7mm Rem. Mag. Match grade barrel is produced from titanium. Stock is graphite. Weight is about 6.5 lbs.

NIB	Exc.	V.G.	Good	Fair	Poor
3000	2500	2000	1500	950	500

Signature Varminter

Available in calibers such as .223, .22-250, .220 Swift, .243, 6mm Rem., .25-06, 7mm-08, .308. Barrel lengths from 22" to 26". Heavy barrel configuration with hand bedded fiberglass stock. Field bipod is standard. Introduced in 1989.

NIB	Exc.	V.G.	Good	Fair	Poor
2500	2000	1500	900	600	400

Talon Safari

Bolt action rifle offered in various calibers from .300 Win. Mag. to .458 Win. Mag. Stainless steel barrel is 24". Four-round magazine. Fiberglass stock. Introduced in 1989. Weight is approximately 10 lbs.

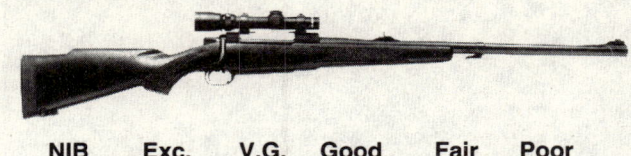

NIB	Exc.	V.G.	Good	Fair	Poor
3500	3000	2000	1500	950	500

Talon Sporter

Offered in calibers from .25-06 to .416 Rem. Mag. 24" barrel with no sights. Built on a pre-1964 Winchester Model 70 action. Choice of walnut or fiberglass stock. Weight is about 7.5 lbs.

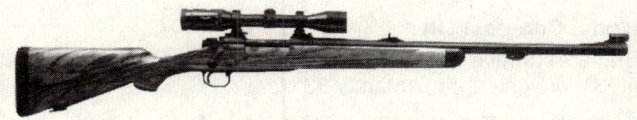

NIB	Exc.	V.G.	Good	Fair	Poor
2500	2000	1750	1250	600	250

Model 300 Phoenix Long Range Rifle

Introduced in 1992 and chambered for the .300 Phoenix cartridge. Fitted with a 28" barrel with no sights. Fiberglass stock. Weight is approximately 12.5 lbs.

NIB	Exc.	V.G.	Good	Fair	Poor
2500	2000	1750	1250	600	250

Model 40 Sniper

This bolt action rifle chambered for the .308 cartridge was introduced in1990. Fitted with a 24" match grade heavy weight barrel. No sights. Weight is about 9 lbs.

NIB	Exc.	V.G.	Good	Fair	Poor
2000	1500	1000	750	500	300

Model 92 Bullpup

This is a single shot rifle chambered for the .50 caliber BMG. Fitted with a 26" barrel and no sights. Fiberglass bullpup stock. First introduced in 1995.

NIB	Exc.	V.G.	Good	Fair	Poor
4000	3250	2500	2000	1000	500

Model 93 SN

This is a bolt action rifle chambered for the .50 BMG and fitted with a 29" barrel with muzzle brake. Magazine holds 10 rounds. No sights. Weight is approximately 21.5 lbs. Folding fiberglass stock. Introduced in 1995.

NIB	Exc.	V.G.	Good	Fair	Poor
4250	3750	3000	2250	1250	750

MEAD & ADRIANCE
St. Louis, Missouri

This company retailed a variety of single shot percussion pistols most of which were manufactured by Ethan Allen of Grafton, Massachusetts. In general, the value for pistols marked "Mead & Adriance" are as follows:

Exc.	V.G.	Good	Fair	Poor
—	—	800	400	250

MEIJA
SEE Japan State

MENDENHALL, JONES & GARDNER
Greensboro, North Carolina

Muzzle Loading Rifle
A .58 caliber percussion rifle with a 33" barrel and full-length walnut stock secured by two barrel bands. Finished in the white with the lock marked "M.J.&G.,N.C." Prospective purchasers should secure a qualified appraisal prior to acquisition.

Exc.	V.G.	Good	Fair	Poor
—	—	15000	9000	1500

MENZ, AUGUST
Suhl, Germany
Established prior to WWI to manufacture Beholla pistols, this company was purchased by Lignose in 1937.

Menta
Identical to the Beholla, which is listed separately.

Exc.	V.G.	Good	Fair	Poor
350	250	200	150	100

Liliput
A 4.25mm caliber semiautomatic pistol with a 2" barrel and 6-shot magazine. Overall length 3.5", weight 10 oz. The slide marked "Liliput Kal. 4.25". Also manufactured in 6.35mm caliber. These pistols have an overall length of 4". Blued with composition grips.

Exc.	V.G.	Good	Fair	Poor
400	300	250	200	125

Menz Model II
As above in 7.65mm caliber.

Exc.	V.G.	Good	Fair	Poor
400	300	250	200	125

Menz VP Model
Similar to the Model 2, but in 6.35mm caliber with a 2.35" barrel, 6-shot magazine and fitted with a cocking indicator.

Exc.	V.G.	Good	Fair	Poor
400	300	250	200	125

Model III
A total redesign. It has a closed-top slide, and the quality is much better than the previous Menz pistols. It has a fixed barrel and is similar to the Model 1910 Browning with an exposed hammer. This model was produced until 1937.

Exc.	V.G.	Good	Fair	Poor
450	350	300	250	150

MERCURY
Liege, Belgium

Model 622 VP
A .22 caliber semiautomatic rifle with a 20" barrel, open sights and 7-shot magazine. Blued with a walnut stock. Manufactured by Robar & Son.

Exc.	V.G.	Good	Fair	Poor
300	275	250	200	125

MERCURY
Eibar, Spain

Double Barreled Shotgun
A 10, 12, or 20 gauge Magnum boxlock double-barrel shotgun with 28" or 32" barrels, double triggers and extractors. Blued with a walnut stock.
10 Gauge-Add 25%.

Exc.	V.G.	Good	Fair	Poor
325	250	225	175	125

MERKEL, GEBRUDER
Suhl, Germany

An Introduction to Merkel Brother's Guns
by Dan Sheil
Merkel Brothers shotgun and rifle makers began production around the turn of the century in Suhl, Germany. Merkel made a number of different models but the company was most well known for its Over/Under shotgun. It also made bolt action rifles, side-by-side double express rifles, falling block single shot rifles, side by side shotguns, drillings, and just about anything in the way of firearms its customers desired.

Perhaps the company's greatest productive era fell between the end of World War I and the 1950s. During the 1930s most of the live pigeon shoots were won with Merkel shotguns. However, there seems to be a difference of opinion about when Merkel built its best quality guns. This is not an easy question to answer. Most shooters and collectors feel that pre-World War II guns are the best examples of Merkel craftsmanship. But, in my opinion, some of the finest Merkels I have seen were produced immediately after World War II. Outstanding examples of Merkel's quality continue to appear up to the construction of the Berlin Wall in 1961.

Another area of controversy is the high grade Merkel 300 series shotgun. Many have compared this gun to the Italian and British makers and believe it is a mass produced gun. This is not the case because all Merkel shotguns are handcrafted and as far as I know barrels will not interchange unless they are supplied with the gun from the factory. While the 100 and 200 series guns may be mass produced the 300 series is not, and that is easy to determine by looking at the serial number together with the date stamped on the barrel. Very few 300 series guns were produced in a given period.

In terms of durability, strength, and reliability, there is not an over and under shotgun that is built as strong as the Merkel. It has two Kersten style locking lugs on the upper barrel that fit into the face of the receiver while the bottom has two under lugs that give the gun a rugged four position locking system. I don't think I have ever heard of a Merkel being sent back to the gunmaker or a gunsmith to have the frame tightened. It just is not necessary; the guns will not shoot loose.

With respect to value, the Merkel over and under guns have been sleepers in the gun industry for a number of years. Until recently they have not brought the price that they deserve. I am specifically talking about the 300 series; the 303 Luxus and the 304. Generally speaking all of the special order Merkel over and under shotguns have done well. I think the shooting public will begin to recognize the quality and craftsmanship built into every one of these fine guns.

One last comment regarding special order Merkels and the company's reputation for building just about anything the customer wanted. It is impossible to cover all of the variations that the company produced in its long history, but the buyer should be aware that he may encounter some different and uncataloged Merkels along the way.

As of August 1993 Merkel Brothers declared bankruptcy. The assets of the company were reportedly purchased by Steyr.

Editor's Comment: The following Merkel gun prices are based on either one or two factors. First, they are no longer in production or second that the guns were built prior to the Berlin Wall, which generally bring a premium. An additional factor has been introduced as of 1994 when the factory began to use an alpha numeric serial number system. This new system dates the guns from 1994. The prices listed below for new Merkels are influenced by the value of the dollar to the German Mark.

MERKEL SIDE-X-SIDE SHOTGUNS

Model 117/117E
Offered in 12 and 16 gauge with various barrel lengths, this model featured a boxlock action with double triggers and extractors. Ejectors were available under the "E" designation. The boxlock action body was scrupled at the rear with fine line scroll engraving.

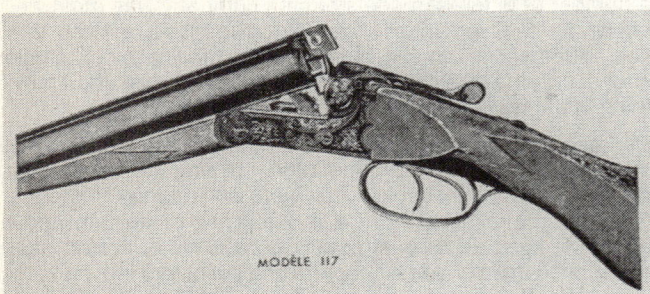

MODÈLE 117

Exc.	V.G.	Good	Fair	Poor
3000	2500	1500	1000	500

Model 118/118E
Also offered in 12 and 16 gauge this model is similar to above model with slightly more engraving and better wood. This model also has some engraving coverage on the breech end of the barrels.

Exc.	V.G.	Good	Fair	Poor
3500	2750	1700	1200	650

Model 124/125
Similar to the above models but supplied with extractors for the Model 124 and ejectors for the Model 125. Both models have more engraving coverage with game scenes. Finer checkering and fancy wood is seen on this model.

Model 124

Exc.	V.G.	Good	Fair	Poor
3900	3500	2000	1500	700

Model 125

Exc.	V.G.	Good	Fair	Poor
4500	3750	3000	2000	1000

Model 170
This model was offered in 12 gauge only with automatic ejectors. The boxlock action was engraved with fine full coverage scroll.

Exc.	V.G.	Good	Fair	Poor
5000	4000	3200	2500	1200

Model 130
This was one of Merkel's highest side-by-side shotguns. It featured a sidelock action, extra fancy wood, fine line checkering, and full coverage gamescene engraving.

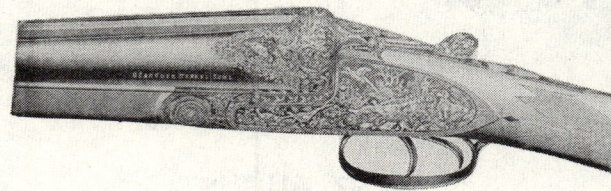

Exc.	V.G.	Good	Fair	Poor
15000	12000	7500	4500	2500

Model 126
Similar to the Model 130 but fitted with.

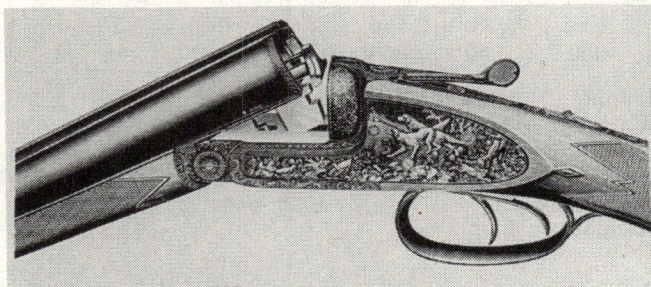

Exc.	V.G.	Good	Fair	Poor
15000	12000	7500	4500	2500

Model 127
This model was Merkel's highest and finest side-by-side shotgun. The sidelock action featured full coverage fine line scroll engraving of the best quality.

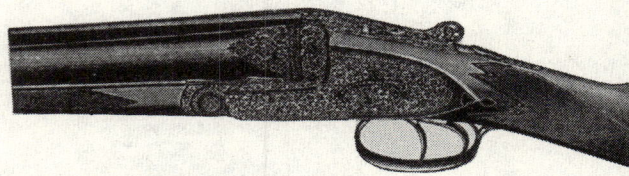

Exc.	V.G.	Good	Fair	Poor
21000	16000	12000	6000	4000

Model 8
This model has a self-cocking Deeley boxlock action side-by-side with cocking indicators. The locking mechanism is a Greener cross-bolt with double-barrel locking lug. Triggers are single selective or double. The safety is automatic and tang mounted. This model has an extractor. Offered in 12 and 16 gauge with 28" solid rib barrels or 20 gauge with 26.75" barrels. Available with straight or pistol grip oil-finished walnut stock. Receiver is case-colored with light scroll engraving. The 12 and 16 gauge guns weigh about 6.8 lbs. while the 20 gauge weighs approximately 6 lbs.

NIB	Exc.	V.G.	Good	Fair	Poor
1000	800	700	600	500	300

Model 47E

Same as above but fitted with ejectors.

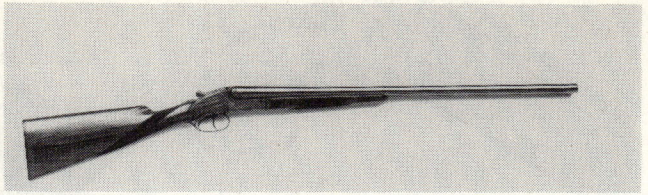

NIB	Exc.	V.G.	Good	Fair	Poor
1250	1000	800	700	500	300

Model 147

Same as Model 8 but with silver grayed receiver with fine engraved hunting scenes, engraved border, and screws.

NIB	Exc.	V.G.	Good	Fair	Poor
1500	1250	950	750	550	400

Model 147E

Same as above but fitted with ejectors.

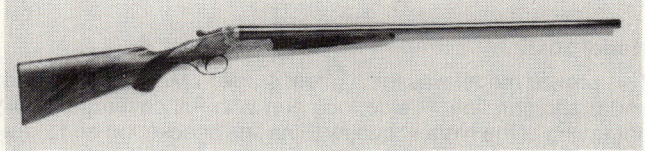

NIB	Exc.	V.G.	Good	Fair	Poor
1600	1350	1050	850	600	450

Model 122

This model features the same specifications as the above models but has false sideplates. This model is fitted with ejectors and the receiver is silver grayed with fine engraved hunting scenes on false sideplates, engraved border, and screws.

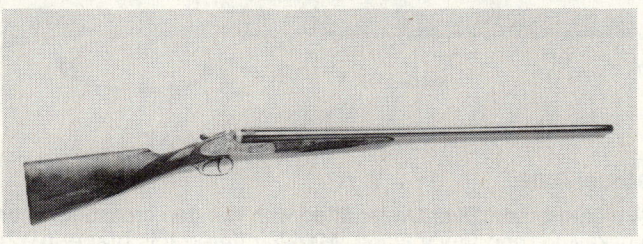

NIB	Exc.	V.G.	Good	Fair	Poor
2500	2000	1750	1200	750	600

Model 47S

Same as above but with scroll engraving in place of hunting scenes.

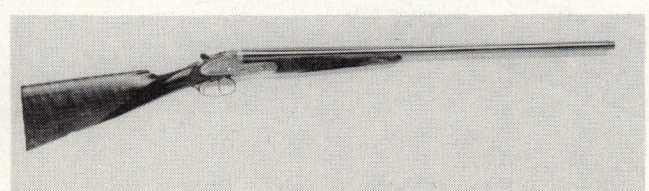

NIB	Exc.	V.G.	Good	Fair	Poor
3350	2750	2200	1750	1200	800

Model 147S

This model features true Holland and Holland style side locks with cocking indicators. Gauge and barrel lengths are as above. However, 20 gauge gun weighs 6.4 lbs.

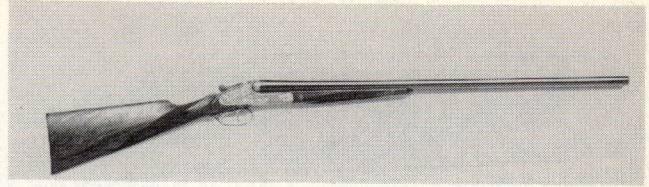

NIB	Exc.	V.G.	Good	Fair	Poor
4100	3700	3000	2000	1500	1000

Models 247S/347S/447S

These models are the same as the Model 147S with the exception of the types of engraving.

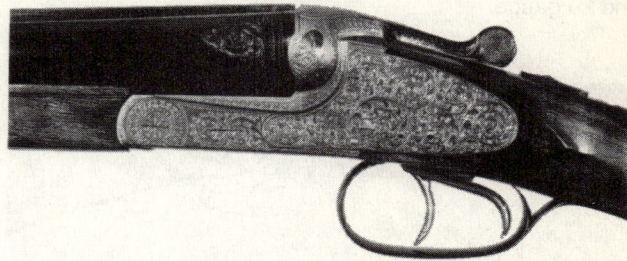

Model 247S-Large scroll engraving

NIB	Exc.	V.G.	Good	Fair	Poor
5500	4500	3500	2500	1750	1250

Model 347S-Medium scroll engraving

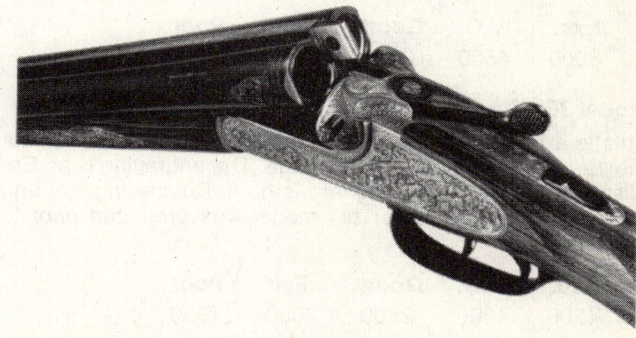

NIB	Exc.	V.G.	Good	Fair	Poor
6500	5500	4500	3500	2250	1500

Model 447S-Small scroll engraving

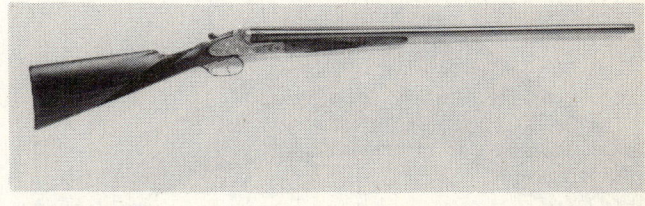

NIB	Exc.	V.G.	Good	Fair	Poor
7000	6000	5000	4000	2750	1750

MERKEL OVER AND UNDER SHOTGUNS

Model 102E

This was Merkel's standard over and under boxlock model. Offered in 12 gauge with 28" barrels or 16 gauge with 26" barrels. Both are fitted with double triggers, semi-pistol grip, and ejectors.

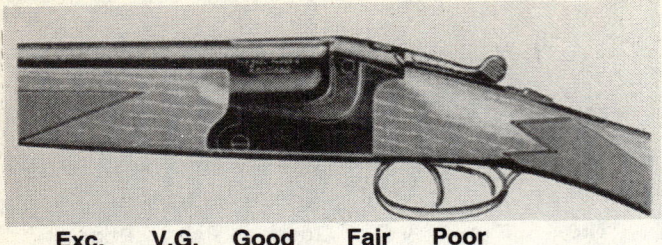

Exc.	V.G.	Good	Fair	Poor
1600	1200	1000	650	400

Model 103E

Similar to the standard but with more English scroll engraving coverage and better wood. This model was offered in 12, 16, and 20 gauge.

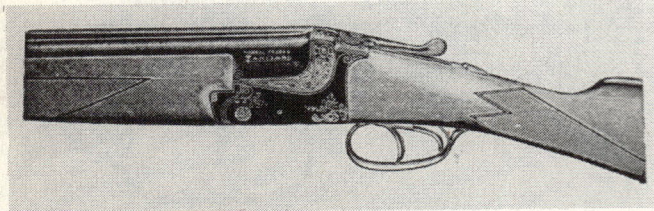

Exc.	V.G.	Good	Fair	Poor
2200	1500	1200	950	600

Model 204E

This model is essentially a Model 203E with finer engraving. This model was discontinued prior to 1939.

Exc.	V.G.	Good	Fair	Poor
6000	4500	3000	2200	1750

Model 301 E

This is a boxlock model with scrupled action chambered for the 12, 16, 20, 24, 28, and 32 gauge. The engraving is an English scroll and the triggerguard is horn. Double triggers and pistol grip are standard. This model was produced prior to 1939.

Exc.	V.G.	Good	Fair	Poor
4500	4000	2500	2000	1850

Model 302E

Similar to the Model 301E but fitted with side plates. The full coverage engraving features gamescenes. This model produced prior to WWII.

Exc.	V.G.	Good	Fair	Poor
12000	10000	7500	4000	2000

Model 303 Luxus

This over and under Merkel is custom built to the customer's specifications. Each gun is unique and should be appraised by a knowledgeable individual who is familiar with quality European shotguns.

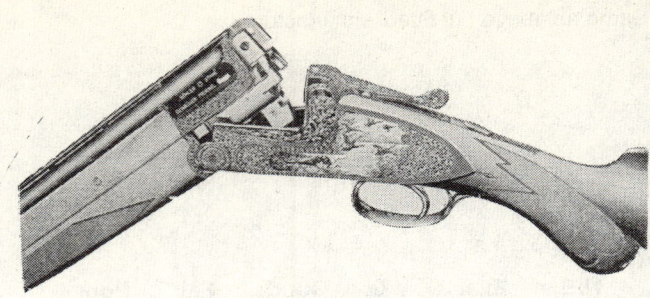

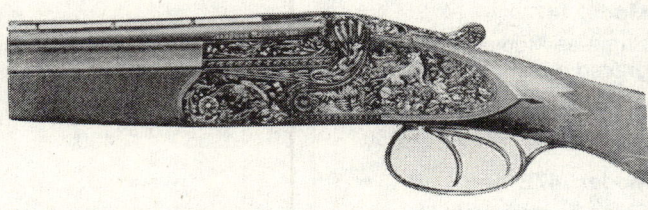

Model 304E

This prewar model was the highest grade in Merkel's over and under shotgun line. A side lock gun with full coverage scroll engraving of the highest quality. Fine line checkering and extra fancy wood make this gun difficult to appraise due to its rarity. A qualified appraisal before a sale is highly recommended.

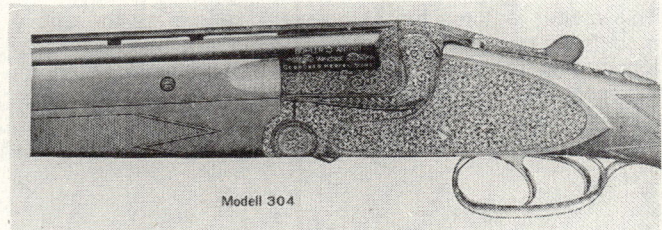

Modell 304

Model 400E

A higher grade Over/Under fitted with Kersten crossbolt, finer engraving, and fancy wood. Merkel offered this grade in 12, 16, 20, 24, 28, and 32 gauge with choice of barrel lengths. This model was produced prior to 1939.

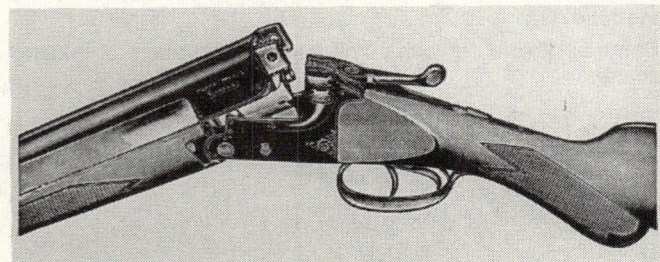

Exc.	V.G.	Good	Fair	Poor
1800	1300	1000	600	400

Model 401 E

Similar to the model above but with full coverage gamescene engraving.

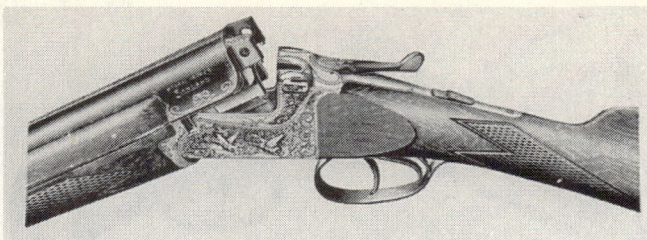

Exc.	V.G.	Good	Fair	Poor
2500	1850	1200	800	600

Model 200E

The action on this model is a self cocking Blitz where the hammers are attached to the trigger plates. The locking mechanism is a Kersten double cross bolt lock with release. Trigger may be either single selective or double. The manual safety is mounted on the tang. Fitted with coil spring ejectors. Offered in 12 and 16 gauge with 28" solid rib barrels or 20 gauge with 26.75" barrels. The oil-finished stock is offered with straight or pistol grip. The receiver is case-colored with engraved border and screws. The 12 gauge weighs 7 lbs., the 16 gauge 6.8 lbs., and the 20 gauge 6.4 lbs.

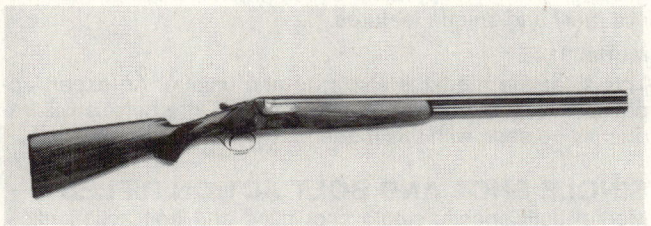

NIB	Exc.	V.G.	Good	Fair	Poor
2700	2000	1500	1000	800	500

Model 201E

Same as above but with silver grayed receiver with fine engraved hunting scenes, engraved border, and screws.

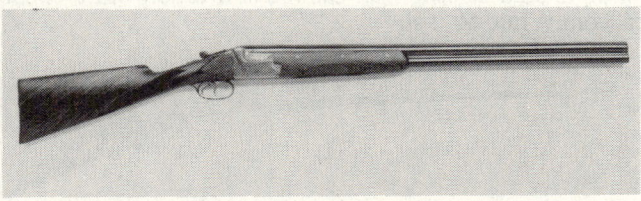

NIB	Exc.	V.G.	Good	Fair	Poor
3350	2850	2250	1500	1000	750

Model 202E

This model has the same basic specifications as the Model 201E but is fitted with false side plates with cocking indicators.

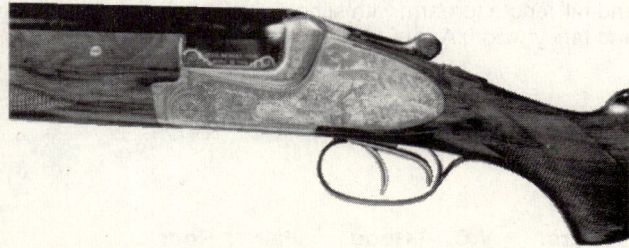

NIB	Exc.	V.G.	Good	Fair	Poor
6500	5000	3500	2500	1500	1000

Model 203E

This model has true Holland & Holland style side locks with cocking indicators. These sideplates are removable with cranked screw. The gauge selection and barrel are the same as those listed above. The silver grayed receiver as English style large scroll engraving.

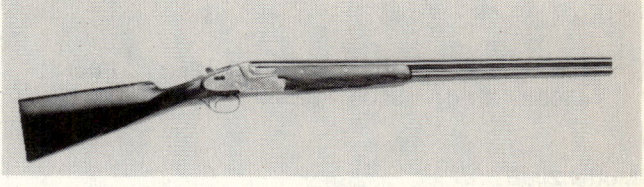

NIB	Exc.	V.G.	Good	Fair	Poor
7750	6000	4500	3000	2000	1000

Model 303E

Same as above but with detachable side lock plates with integral retracting hook. The Model 303E also has medium scroll work engraving and Holland & Holland type ejectors.

NIB	Exc.	V.G.	Good	Fair	Poor
17000	15000	12000	7500	5000	2500

Model 200ES

This model features a Blitz action with cocking indicators and Kersten double cross bolt lock with release. The trigger is single selective with tang mounted manual safety. Coil spring ejectors are standard. Offered in 12 gauge only with 26.75" or 28" ventilated rib barrel. The walnut stock has skeet dimensions with pistol grip. Receiver is silver grayed with 112 coverage scroll engraving, engraved borders, and screws. Weighs approximately 7.3 lbs.

NIB	Exc.	V.G.	Good	Fair	Poor
4000	3250	2500	2000	1500	1000

Model 200SC (Sporting Clays)

Introduced in 1995 this model is offered in 12 gauge only with 3" chambers and 30" barrels with ventilated rib. It is fitted with a single selective trigger adjustable for length of pull. It has a special walnut oil finished stock with 26 lines to the inch checkering. Pistol grip and Pachmayr Sporting Clays recoil pad is standard. Weight is approximately 7.6 lbs.

NIB	Exc.	V.G.	Good	Fair	Poor
6500	5500	3000	1500	900	450

NOTE: With Briley choke tubes add $500.

Model 201 ES

Same as model above but with full coverage scroll engraving.

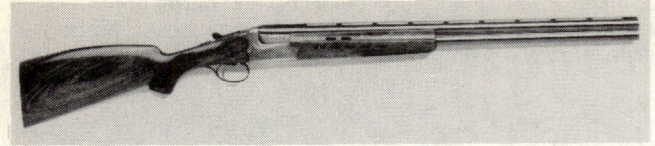

NIB	Exc.	V.G.	Good	Fair	Poor
4500	3750	3000	2500	2000	1000

Model 200ET

Same as Model 200ES, but in a trap configuration. The ventilated rib barrel length offered is 30".

NIB	Exc.	V.G.	Good	Fair	Poor
4250	3500	2750	2250	1750	1000

Model 201 ET

Same as Model 210ES but fitted with a 30" barrel and trap stock dimensions.

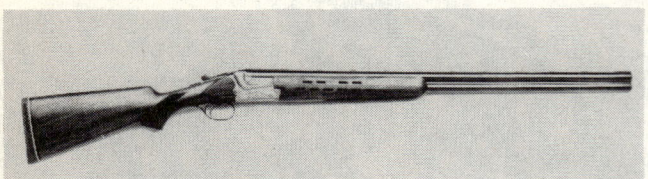

NIB	Exc.	V.G.	Good	Fair	Poor
4500	3750	3000	2500	2000	1000

MERKEL SHOTGUN CHOKE DESIGNATIONS

Choke ID	Description	Percentage
1/1	Full Choke	70 to 75
3/4	Imp. Modified	65 tp 70
1/2	Modified	60 to 65
1/4	Quarter Choke	55 to 60
VZ	Imp. Cylinder	45 to 50
S	Skeet Choke	70 to 75 (at 25 yds)

MERKEL RIFLE/SHOTGUN COMBINATIONS

Model 410E

Merkel's base boxlock model with ejectors. Produced prior to WWII.

Exc.	V.G.	Good	Fair	Poor
2250	1800	1200	750	500

Model 411 E

Similar to the above but with the addition of a small coverage of scroll engraving.

Exc.	V.G.	Good	Fair	Poor
2500	2000	1500	1000	600

Model 300

A box lock hammerless four barrel shotgun/rifle combination. The shotgun barrels were 12, 16, or 20 gauge, while the top rifle barrel was .22 rimfire with the bottom rifle barrel .30-30 or .25-35. Probably ant combination of rifle and shotgun could be used as this was a special order gun. Very rare. An independent appraisal is strongly recommended.

Model 311E

This combination gun has additional English scroll engraving.

Exc.	V.G.	Good	Fair	Poor
7900	6500	5000	2250	1700

Model 312E

This model is fitted with sideplates and gamescene engraving.

Exc.	V.G.	Good	Fair	Poor
9500	8150	6600	4000	2500

Model 313E

This model has sideplates with fine, full coverage scroll engraving. An expert appraisal is recommended due to this model's rarity and unique features.

Model 314E

This sideplate model is also rare and unique. An expert appraisal is recommended prior to a sale. Extra barrels will frequently be seen with this model.

SINGLE SHOT AND BOLT ACTION RIFLES

Merkel built special single shot rifles and bolt action rifles. These guns were produced prior to WWII and are seldom seen in the United States. The buyer should exercise caution and seek expert assistance prior to a sale.

Model 180

This is a top lever single rifle with double under lugs built on a boxlock action. The stock is 3/4 with pistol grip. Commonly referred to as a stalking rifle. Offered in a variety of European calibers. A rare Merkel.

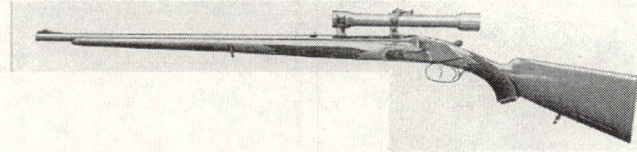

Exc.	V.G.	Good	Fair	Poor
3000	2100	1500	1000	500

Model 183

This top lever model features a Holland & Holland type sidelock action with the side lock on the left side and the removable side plate on the right side. Fitted with a straight grip stock and full length forearm with sling swivels, fine line checkering, and fancy wood. A rare rifle.

Exc.	V.G.	Good	Fair	Poor
7500	5000	3500	2000	1200

Model 190

This is Merkel's version of a Sporting rifle built on a Mauser action. Offered in a variety of European calibers. These were special order rifles and will be seen in a variety of configurations.

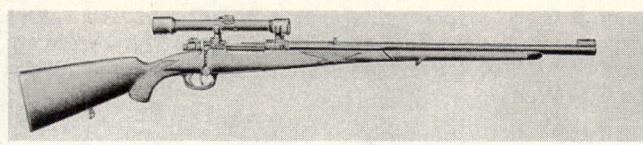

Exc.	V.G.	Good	Fair	Poor
3000	2200	1500	1000	650

DOUBLE RIFLES-COMBINATION GUNS-DRILLINGS

Merkel Side-x-Side Double Rifles Model 128E

This side-by-side rifle is a droplock design with scroll and gamescene engraving. The wood is Circassion walnut with fine line checkering. Offered in a variety of European calibers. Because of the rarity and uniqueness of each rifle a qualified appraisal should be sought prior to a sale.

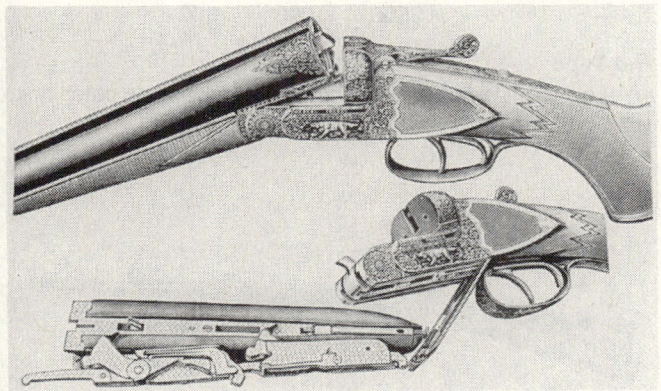

Model 132E

Similar to the Model 128E but with full coverage scroll engraving and fancy wood. This model also should have an expert appraisal done prior to a sale.

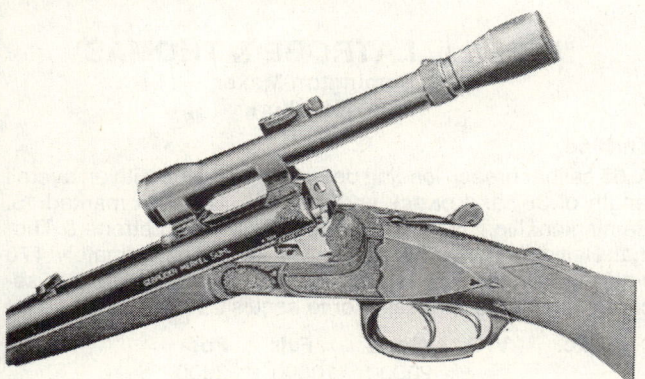

Model 220E O/U Double Rifle

This is a boxlock design with a Kersten double cross bolt, scroll engraved casehardened receiver, Blitz action, double triggers, and pistol grip stock with cheekpiece.

NIB	Exc.	V.G.	Good	Fair	Poor
8500	6000	4500	3800	2000	950

Model 221 E Over/Under Double Rifle

Similar to the model above but with gamescene engraving on a silver grayed receiver.

NIB	Exc.	V.G.	Good	Fair	Poor
9500	7000	5000	4000	2250	1200

Model 223E Over/Under Double Rifle

This model is fitted with sidelocks and features English style arabesque engraving in large scrolls on silver grayed receiver.

NIB	Exc.	V.G.	Good	Fair	Poor
14500	12500	10000	6000	3500	1500

Model 323E O/U Double Rifle

Similar to the above model but with finer engraving.

NIB	Exc.	V.G.	Good	Fair	Poor
22500	17500	12500	7500	4500	2500

Model 160S Luxus Double Rifle

This double rifle is part of the Luxus series and features on the highest quality sidelock action, wood, and fittings. It is offered in .222 Rem., 5.6x5OR Mag., .243, 6.5x57R, 7x57, 7x65, .3006, .30R Blazer, 8x57IRS, 8x57RS, .308 Win., and 9.3x74R. Weighs approximately 8 lbs. An expert appraisal should be sought prior to a sale due to the unique nature of this model.

Model 211E Rifle/Shotgun Combination

This over and under model features a gray metal boxlock action with hunting scenes. The top barrel is available in 12, 16, or 20 gauge and the bottom barrel is offered in .22 Hornet, 5.6R Mag., 5.6R, .222 Rem., .243 Win., 6.5x55, 6.5x57R, 7x57R, 7x65R, .30-06, 8x57IRS, 9.3x74R, and .375 H&H Mag. The barrel has a solid rib and the trigger is single selective. The select walnut stock is hand checkered. Weight is about 7 lbs.

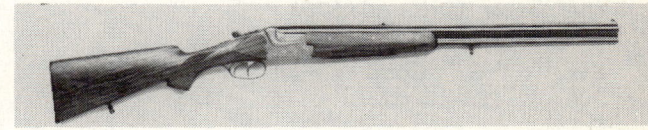

NIB	Exc.	V.G.	Good	Fair	Poor
6000	4500	3500	2250	1500	900

Model 210E Rifle/Shotgun Combination

Same as above model but features a scroll engraved case-hardened receiver.

NIB	Exc.	V.G.	Good	Fair	Poor
4750	3500	2500	1750	1200	700

Model 213E Rifle/Shotgun Combination

This combination gun features sidelocks with English style large scroll engraving on a silver grayed receiver. Also is fitted with double triggers and pistol grip with cheek piece.

NIB	Exc.	V.G.	Good	Fair	Poor
11500	9500	7500	5500	2500	1500

Model 313E Rifle/Shotgun Combination

Same as above model but with finer scroll engraving and fancy wood.

NIB	Exc.	V.G.	Good	Fair	Poor
17500	12500	7500	6500	4000	2500

Model 95K Drilling

This model is a three barrel shotgun/rifle combination. The top two barrels are chambered for 12, 16, or 20 gauge and the bottom barrel is available in rifle calibers from .22 Hornet to .375 H&H Mag. The action is a boxlock design with scroll engraving on borders and screws. The stock is select grade walnut with raised comb, pistol grip with cap, cheekpiece, and plastic buttplate. Weighs about 7.7 lbs.

NIB	Exc.	V.G.	Good	Fair	Poor
6000	4500	3500	2500	1500	1000

MERIDEN FIREARMS CO.
Meriden, Connecticut

Pocket Pistol

A .32 or .38 caliber double action revolver manufactured in a variety of barrel lengths and with either an exposed or enclosed hammer. Nickel-plated with rubber grips. The barrel marked "Meriden Firearms Co. Meriden, Conn. USA." Manufactured between 1895 and 1915.

Exc.	V.G.	Good	Fair	Poor
150	125	100	75	50

MERRILL
Fullerton, California

Sportsman

A single shot pistol manufactured in a variety of calibers with either a 9" or 12" octagonal barrel having a wide ventilated rib, adjustable sights, and integral telescope mounts. Blued with walnut grips.

Interchangeable Barrels-Add $75.
Wrist Support-Add $25.

Exc.	V.G.	Good	Fair	Poor
300	275	225	175	125

MERRILL, JAMES H.
Baltimore, Maryland

Merrill Rifle

A single-shot breechloading rifle that is chambered for .54 caliber and utilizes the percussion ignition system. The breech opens for loading by lifting and pulling back on a lever. The barrel is 33" in length, and there is a full-length walnut stock held on by two barrel bands. The mountings and patch box are brass; and the lock is case-colored, with a browned barrel. The lock is marked "J.H. Merrill Balto./Pat. July 1858." There are military acceptance marks on the stock. There were approximately 775 of these rifles manufactured and purchased by the government for use during the Civil War. They were made in 1864 and 1865.

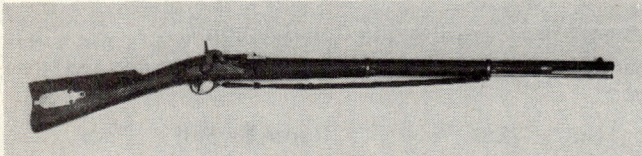

Courtesy Milwaukee Public Museum, Milwaukee, Wisconsin

Exc.	V.G.	Good	Fair	Poor
—	—	3500	1250	500

Merrill Carbine

Similar in appearance to the rifle except that the barrel length is 22" and the stock is only half-length with one barrel band. There are some variations that are quite subtle in appearance but which have a considerable effect on values. We recom-

mend that an independent appraisal be secured. The values given are for the standard 1st and 2nd Types. There were approximately 15,000 total manufactured, and most were used in the Civil War.

1st Type

No eagle stamped on the lock, and the breech lever is flat.

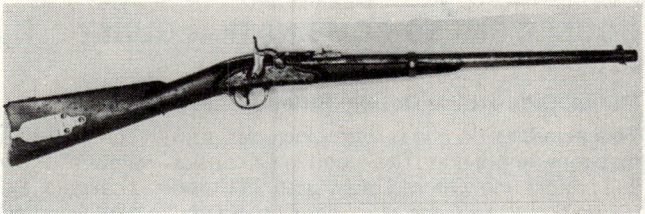

Courtesy Milwaukee Public Museum, Milwaukee, Wisconsin

Exc.	V.G.	Good	Fair	Poor
—	—	2500	1000	500

2nd Type

An eagle stamped on the lock, and the stock has no patch box. The breech lever has a round tip.

Courtesy Milwaukee Public Museum, Milwaukee, Wisconsin

Exc.	V.G.	Good	Fair	Poor
—	—	2500	1000	500

MERRILL, LATROBE & THOMAS
S. Remington-Maker
Ilion, New York

Carbine

A .58 caliber breech loading percussion carbine with an overall length of 38" and barrel length of 21". The lock marked "S. Remington/ Ilion, N.Y." and the barrel "Merrill, Latrobe & Thomas/Baltimore, Md./Patent Applied For." Approximately 170 were made in 1855. Prospective purchasers are advised to secure a qualified appraisal prior to acquisition.

Exc.	V.G.	Good	Fair	Poor
—	—	20000	10000	2000

MERRIMACK ARMS
SEE Brown Manufacturing Co.

MERWIN & BRAY
Worcester, Massachusetts

This company marketed a number of firearms produced by various manufacturers under their own name.

Merwin & Bray Pocket Pistol

A .32 caliber spur trigger single shot pistol with a 3.5" barrel. Blued, silver-plated with walnut grips. The barrel marked "Merwin & Bray New York".

Exc.	V.G.	Good	Fair	Poor
—	—	300	150	75

MERWIN & HULBERT & CO.
New York, New York

The successor to Merwin & Bray Company. Primarily known as the sales agents for Hopkins & Allen as well as the Evans Rifle Company.

NOTE: Watch out for foreign copies. They are worth 50% to 65% less than an original Merwin & Hulbert.

Army Revolver

A .44-40 or .44 M&H caliber single action revolver with a 7" barrel and 6-shot cylinder. The barrel rotates so that the cylinder and barrel unit can be pulled forward for cartridge ejection. Provided in a variety of finishes. The barrel marked with both "Merwin Hulbert & Co." and "Hopkins & Allen Manufacturing Co." A large quantity were manufactured between 1876 and 1885.

Courtesy Milwaukee Public Museum, Milwaukee, Wisconsin

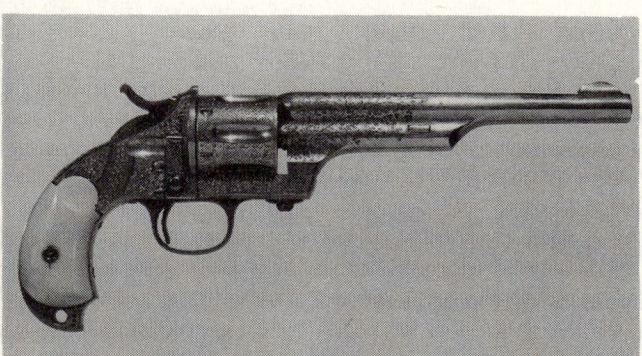

Courtesy Milwaukee Public Museum, Milwaukee, Wisconsin

Open Top Frame with the Square Butt

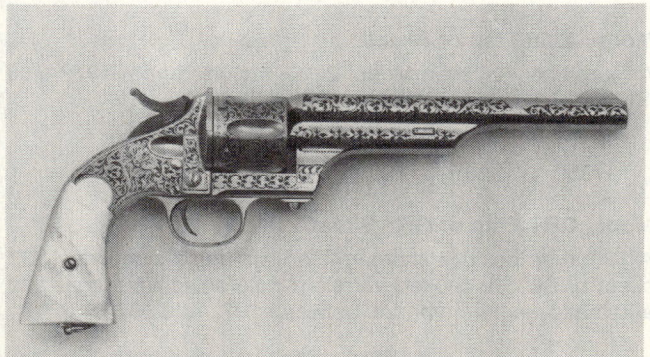

Exc.	V.G.	Good	Fair	Poor
2500	1300	800	500	250

Open Top Frame with Bird's-head Butt

Exc.	V.G.	Good	Fair	Poor
2000	1100	700	300	150

Square Butt with Top Strap

Exc.	V.G.	Good	Fair	Poor
1700	1000	700	300	150

Bird's-head Grip with Top Strap

Exc.	V.G.	Good	Fair	Poor
1600	800	650	250	100

Double Action Model

Exc.	V.G.	Good	Fair	Poor
1500	800	650	250	100

Open Top Pocket Army Revolver

As above, but additionally in .44 Russian caliber and with a 3.5" barrel and bird's-head butt. A large quantity were manufactured during the 1880s.

Courtesy Milwaukee Public Museum, Milwaukee, Wisconsin

Exc.	V.G.	Good	Fair	Poor
2000	1250	600	300	100

Top Strap Single Action Pocket Army

Exc.	V.G.	Good	Fair	Poor
1700	1000	500	350	100

Single Action Pocket Revolver

A .32 or .38 caliber spur trigger revolver with 3.5" to 5.5" barrels and either 5- or 6-shot cylinders. Nickel-plated with hard rubber grips. The barrel marked "Merwin & Hulbert & Co." with the patent dates. While the Hopkins & Allen name is marked on some examples, on others it is not present. Approximately 2,500 were made during the 1880s

Exc.	V.G.	Good	Fair	Poor
700	450	350	250	100

Single Action .22 Revolver

Tip up revolver in .22 caliber with a 3.5" barrel and 7-shot cylinder. The barrel marked "Merwin & Hulbert & Co." Nickel-plated with rubber grips. Manufactured during the 1880s.

Exc.	V.G.	Good	Fair	Poor
—	450	275	150	85

Double Action Pocket Revolver

A .32 or .38 double-action revolver with a 3.5" or 5.5" barrel and 5- or 7-shot cylinder. Nickel-plated with rubber grips. The barrel marked "Merwin & Hulbert". This model is also encountered with a folding hammer spur, which commands a slight premium. Manufactured during the 1880s.

Courtesy Milwaukee Public Museum, Milwaukee, Wisconsin

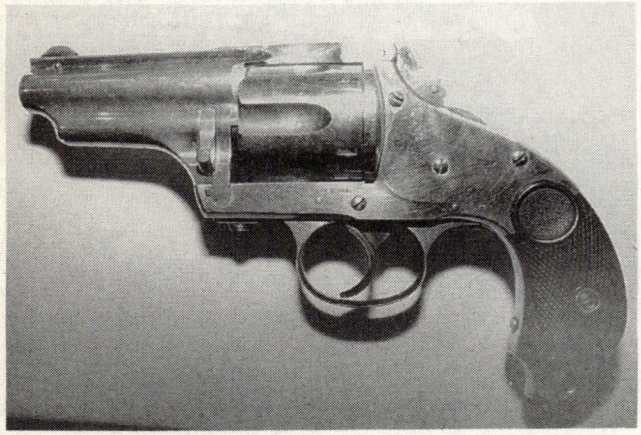

Exc.	V.G.	Good	Fair	Poor
650	400	300	200	100

METROPOLITAN ARMS CO.
New York, New York

Established in February 1864, this company manufactured copies of the Colt Model 1851 and 1861 Navy Revolvers, as well as copies of the Colt Model 1862 Police Revolver. Two of the firm's principle officers were Samuel and William Syms (formerly of Blunt & Syms) and it is believed that they were responsible for production. Curiously, although most Metropolitan pistols were produced during the 1864 to 1866 period, the company itself was not dissolved until 1920.

1851 Navy Revolver

A .36 caliber percussion revolver with a 7.5" octagonal barrel and 6-shot cylinder. Blued, casehardened with walnut grips. The barrel marked "Metropolitan Arms Co. New York." Approximately 6,000 of these revolvers were made during the 1860s. Those bearing H.E. Dimick markings are worth considerably more than the standard marked examples.

H.E. Dimick Navy Model

Exc.	V.G.	Good	Fair	Poor
—	—	4500	2000	850

Standard Navy Model

Exc.	V.G.	Good	Fair	Poor
—	—	2000	800	400

1861 Navy Revolver

A .36 caliber percussion revolver with a 7.5" round barrel and 6-shot cylinder. The loading lever of the rack and pinion type.

Blued, casehardened with walnut grips. The barrel marked "Metropolitan Arms Co. New York." Approximately 50 were made in 1864 and 1865.

Exc.	V.G.	Good	Fair	Poor
—	—	6500	3000	950

Police Revolver

A .36 caliber percussion revolver with either 4.5", 5.5" or 6.5" round barrels and a fluted 5-shot cylinder. Blued, casehardened with walnut grips. The barrel normally marked "Metropolitan Arms Co. New York," although examples have been noted without any markings. Approximately 2,750 were made between 1864 and 1866.

Exc.	V.G.	Good	Fair	Poor
—	—	900	500	200

MILDA
Japan
Marubena America Corp.

Model 612

A 12 gauge boxlock Over/Under shotgun with 26" or 28" ventilated rib barrels, single selective trigger and automatic ejectors. Blued with a walnut stock. Imported between 1972 and 1974.

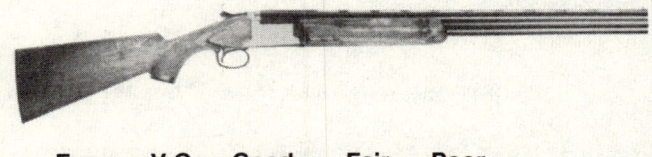

Exc.	V.G.	Good	Fair	Poor
900	800	750	600	450

Model 612 Skeet

As above, with 27" skeet choked barrels and some engraving. Imported between 1972 and 1974.

Exc.	V.G.	Good	Fair	Poor
1000	900	850	700	500

Model 2200 Trap or Skeet

As above, with either 30" trap or 27" skeet bored barrels and more finely engraved. Imported between 1972 and 1974.

Exc.	V.G.	Good	Fair	Poor
1100	1000	900	800	600

Model 2300 Trap or Skeet

A more finely finished Model 2200. Imported from 1972 until 1974.

Exc.	V.G.	Good	Fair	Poor
1350	1250	1100	1000	750

Model GRT Trap or GRS Skeet

A 12 gauge boxlock shotgun fitted with false sideplates, 27" skeet or 29" full choked barrels, single selective trigger and automatic ejector. Imported between 1972 and 1974.

Exc.	V.G.	Good	Fair	Poor
2250	1850	1650	1200	1000

MINNEAPOLIS F. A. CO.
Minneapolis, Minnesota

Palm Pistol

A .32 caliber radial cylinder pistol with a 1.75" barrel manufactured by the Ames Manufacturing Company (see the Ames entry). Nickel-plated with hard rubber grips. The sideplates marked "Minneapolis Firearms Co." and "The Protector." Several thousand were sold during the 1890s.

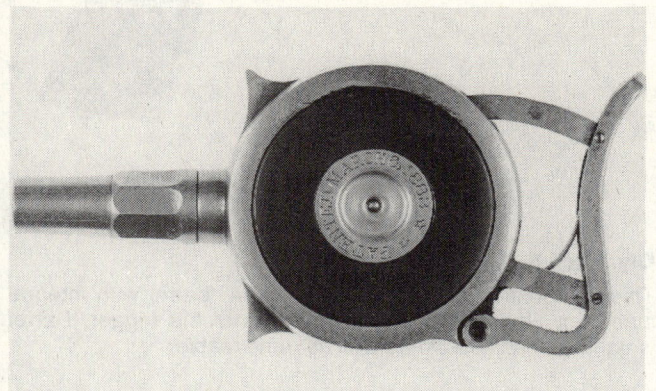

Exc.	V.G.	Good	Fair	Poor
—	1000	550	300	100

MIROKU B. C.
Miroku, Japan

Firearms produced by this manufacturer have been imported and marketed by a variety of companies such as Charles Daly, Browning, Winchester, and SKB.

MITCHELL ARMS, INC.
Santa Ana, California
An importer and distributor of foreign made firearms.

M-16

A .22 rimfire copy of the Colt AR-15. Introduced in 1987.

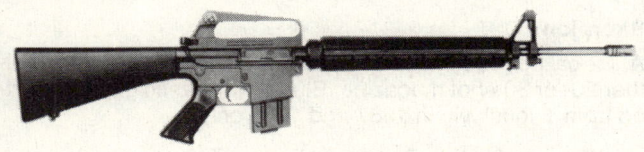

NIB	Exc.	V.G.	Good	Fair	Poor
225	200	150	125	100	75

MAS

A .22 or .22 Magnum caliber copy of the French MAS Bullpup Service Rifle. Introduced in 1987.

NIB	Exc.	V.G.	Good	Fair	Poor
275	225	200	150	125	100

Galil

A .22 or .22 Magnum caliber copy of the Galil rifle. Introduced in 1987.

NIB	Exc.	V.G.	Good	Fair	Poor
275	225	200	150	125	100

AK-22

A .22 or.22 Magnum caliber copy of the AK47 rifle. Introduced in 1985.

NIB	Exc.	V.G.	Good	Fair	Poor
225	200	150	125	100	75

PPSH-30/50

A .22 or .22 Magnum caliber copy of the PPSH Submachine gun.

NIB	Exc.	V.G.	Good	Fair	Poor
175	150	125	100	75	60

This company also imported Yugoslavian-manufactured semi-automatic AK-47 rifles in 7.62x39mm, as well as 7.62x54mm.

NOTE: The rifles listed above are banned from futher manufacture and importation under the "Assault Weapons" provisions in the 1994 Crime Law effective 9/13/94.

HANDGUNS

Trophy II

A semiautomatic pistol chambered for the .22 Long Rifle cartridge. Offered in either 7-1/4" fluted or 5-1/2" bull barrel. Barrels are interchangeable. Trigger is adjustable for weight and pull. Walnut grips with thumb rest are standard.

NIB	Exc.	V.G.	Good	Fair	Poor
400	325	275	200	150	100

Victor II

This .22 caliber pistol is built from stainless steel and has interchangeable barrels in 4-1/2" or 5-1/2" lengths. Barrels have full length ventilated ribs, checkered walnut grips with thumb rest. Gold plated trigger is adjustable.

NIB	Exc.	V.G.	Good	Fair	Poor
450	375	325	250	175	125

Victor II W/ Weaver Rib

NIB	Exc.	V.G.	Good	Fair	Poor
525	450	375	275	175	125

Citation II

Similar to the Trophy II but with a matte satin finish.

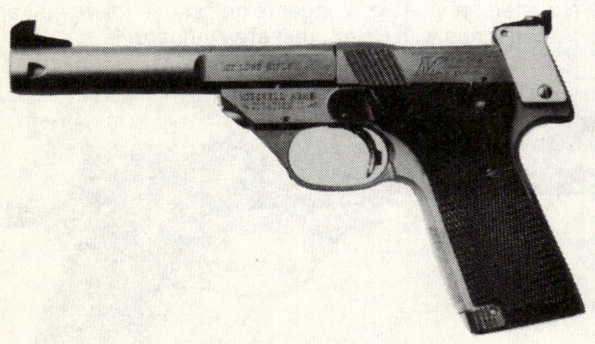

NIB	Exc.	V.G.	Good	Fair	Poor
375	300	250	200	150	100

Sharpshooter II

This is a stainless steel target pistol with 5-1/2" bull barrel to which barrel weights can be added. Fully adjustable rear sight and checkered walnut grips are standard.

NIB	Exc.	V.G.	Good	Fair	Poor
325	275	225	200	150	100

Olympic I.S.U.

This competition pistol features a 6-3/4" barrel with integral stabilizer. Rear sight is adjustable as is the trigger. Barrel weights are adjustable as well as removeable.

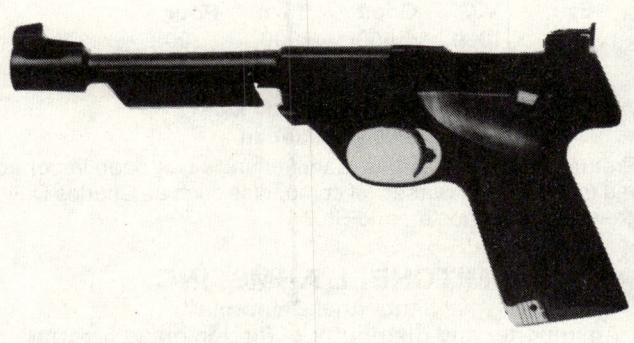

NIB	Exc.	V.G.	Good	Fair	Poor
525	475	400	300	200	100

Skorpion

A .32 caliber semiautomatic pistol with a 4.75" barrel and either 20- or 30-shot magazine. Blued with plastic grips. Imported from Yugoslavia in 1987 and 1988 only.

Exc.	V.G.	Good	Fair	Poor
600	500	425	350	175

Spectre

A 9mm caliber semiautomatic pistol with an 8" shrouded barrel and either 30- or 50-shot magazine. Blued with plastic grips. Also produced with an 18" barrel and folding butt stock. Imported from Yugoslavia in 1987 and 1988.

Exc.	V.G.	Good	Fair	Poor
600	500	425	350	175

MODESTO SANTOS CIA.

Eibar, Spain

Action, Corrientes, and M.S.

A 6.35mm or 7.65mm caliber semiautomatic pistol of low quality marked on the slide "Pistolet Automatique Model 1920." Blued with composition grips having the monogram "M.S." cast in them. Manufactured between 1920 and 1935.

Exc.	V.G.	Good	Fair	Poor
150	125	100	75	50

MONDRAGON
Mexico City, Mexico

Firearms designed by Manuel Mondragon were produced on an experimental basis first at St. Chamond Arsenal in France and later at SIG in Neuhausen, Switzerland. The latter company was responsible for the manufacture of the two known production models; the Model 1890 and 1908.

The Model 1890 Mondragon semiautomatic rifle holds the distinction of being the first self-loading rifle to be issued to any armed forces.

MONTENEGRAN-GASSER
SEE Gasser, Leopold

MOORE-ENFIELD
SEE English Military Firearms

MOORES PATENT FIREARMS CO.
Brooklyn, New York

In 1866 this company became known as the National Arms Company.

No. 1 Derringer

A .41 caliber spur trigger all metal pistol with a 2.5" barrel. Blued or silver-plated. Approximately 10,000 were manufactured between 1860 and 1865. This model was also marketed as the No. 1 Derringer by the Colt Company after they purchased the National Arms Company in 1870.

Courtesy Milwaukee Public Museum, Milwaukee, Wisconsin

1st Variation Marked "Patent Applied For"

Exc.	V.G.	Good	Fair	Poor
—	—	1700	800	350

2nd Variation Marked "D. Moore Patented Feb. 19 1861"

Exc.	V.G.	Good	Fair	Poor
—	—	900	500	250

Standard Model Marked "Moore's Pat F.A. Co."

Exc.	V.G.	Good	Fair	Poor
—	—	750	350	150

National Arms Co. Production

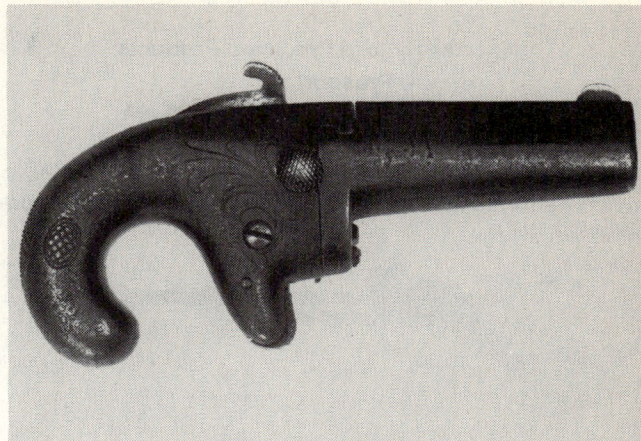

Courtesy Milwaukee Public Museum, Milwaukee, Wisconsin

Exc.	V.G.	Good	Fair	Poor
—	—	700	350	150

Iron Model

Exc.	V.G.	Good	Fair	Poor
—	—	900	450	200

Pocket Revolver

A .32 teat fire caliber spur trigger revolver with a round 3.25" barrel and 6-shot cylinder. Blued or silver plated with walnut grips. Approximately 30,000 were manufactured between 1864 and 1870.

Courtesy Milwaukee Public Museum, Milwaukee, Wisconsin

Exc.	V.G.	Good	Fair	Poor
—	—	350	200	100

Belt Revolver

A .32 rimfire caliber revolver with a 4", 5", or 6" octagonal barrel and 7-shot cylinder. The barrel and cylinder blued, the brass frame sometimes silver-plated with walnut grips. The barrel marked "D. Moore Patent Sept. 18, 1860." Several thousand were manufactured between 1861 and 1863.

Exc.	V.G.	Good	Fair	Poor
—	—	700	250	100

MORGAN & CLAPP
New Haven, Connecticut

Single Shot Pocket Pistol

A .22 or .23 caliber spur trigger single shot pistol with a 3.5" octagonal barrel. Blued, silver-plated frame with walnut grips. The barrel marked "Morgan & Clapp New Haven." Active 1864 to 1867.

Exc.	V.G.	Good	Fair	Poor
—	—	350	150	100

MORINI
Italy
Importer-Nygord Precision Products
Prescott, AZ

C-80 Standard

A .22 caliber single shot pistol with a free floating 10" barrel, match sights, adjustable frame, and adjustable grips. Discontinued in 1989.

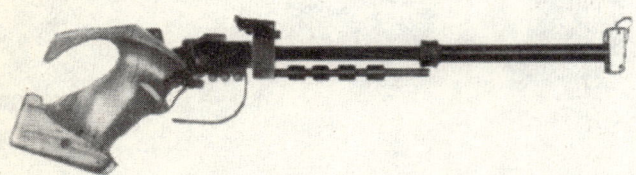

Exc.	V.G.	Good	Fair	Poor
900	800	675	550	250

CM-80 Super Competition

As above, with a trigger adjustable from 5 to 120 grams pressure, Plexiglass front sight and a polished finish. Discontinued in 1989.

Exc.	V.G.	Good	Fair	Poor
1000	900	750	650	300

Model 84E Free Pistol

Introduced in 1995 this competition pistol features an 11.4" barrel chambered for the .22 Long Rifle. It is a single shot. Adjustable sights with adjustable electronic trigger. Weight is about 44 oz.

NIB	Exc.	V.G.	Good	Fair	Poor
1450	1150	900	—	—	—

MORRONE
Hope Valley, Rhode Island
SEE Rhode Island Arms Company

MORSE
Greenville, South Carolina
State Armory

Morse Carbine

Overall length 40"; barrel length 2"; caliber.50 (other calibers are known to have been made on an experimental basis). The round barrel is blued, the frame is of brass and the stock is of either walnut or beechwood. Approximately 1,000 were manufactured during the Civil War. Prospective purchasers are advised to secure a qualified appraisal prior to acquisition.

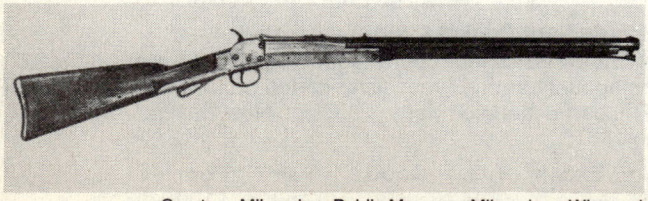

Courtesy Milwaukee Public Museum, Milwaukee, Wisconsin

Courtesy Milwaukee Public Museum, Milwaukee, Wisconsin

Exc.	V.G.	Good	Fair	Poor
—	—	8000	4000	1250

MOSIN-NAGANT
Russia

Model 1891

A .62mm caliber bolt action rifle with a 28.75" barrel, 5-shot integral magazine, ladder rear sight and a full-length stock secured by two barrel bands. Blued with a walnut stock.

Exc.	V.G.	Good	Fair	Poor
175	150	125	100	75

Model 1891/98/25 Polish Nagant

Similar to the above model but fitted with a bayonet lug and stamped with a small crowned Polish Eagle on receiver and bolt. A very rare variation. Examples will command a premium price.

Courtesy Richard M. Kumor, Sr.

Exc.	V.G.	Good	Fair	Poor
—	—	N/A	N/A	N/A

Model 1891/30 sniper rifle

This is a Model 1891/30 with a scope attached. Will command a premium price.

Courtesy Richard M. Kumor, Sr.

Exc.	V.G.	Good	Fair	Poor
—	—	N/A	N/A	N/A

Model 1910 Carbine

As above, with a 20" barrel and modified sights.

Exc.	V.G.	Good	Fair	Poor
175	150	125	100	75

Model 1930 Rifle

Similar to the Model 1891, but with a round receiver ring and improved sights.

Exc.	V.G.	Good	Fair	Poor
175	150	125	100	75

Model 1938 Carbine

As above, with a 20" barrel.

Exc.	V.G.	Good	Fair	Poor
175	150	125	100	75

Model 1944 Carbine

As above, but fitted with a folding bayonet at the barrel muzzle.

Exc.	V.G.	Good	Fair	Poor
150	125	100	75	50

Model 1895 "Gas Seal" Revolver

A 7.62mm caliber single (troopers) or double action (officers) revolver with a 4.35" barrel and 7-shot cylinder. As the hammer is cocked, the cylinder is moved forward to engage the barrel breech. Blued with either walnut or plastic grips. Manufactured from 1895 to approximately 1933.

Exc.	V.G.	Good	Fair	Poor
300	250	200	150	100

MOSSBERG, O. F. & SONS, INC.
North Haven, Connecticut

Founded by Oscar F. Mossberg in 1892 at Fitchburg, Massachusetts, this company for a time was located at Chicopee Falls, Massachusetts, and since 1919 has been in North Haven, Connecticut.

Brownie

A .22 caliber 4 barreled pocket pistol with a revolving firing pin. This pistol resembles a semiautomatic. Manufactured from 1906 to approximately 1940.

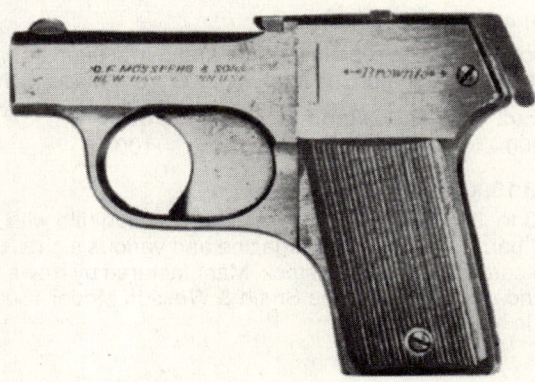

Exc.	V.G.	Good	Fair	Poor
350	325	300	225	150

RIFLES

Model K Rifle

A .22 caliber slide action rifle with a 22" barrel, tubular magazine, internal hammer and takedown system. Blued with a walnut stock. Discontinued in 1931.

Exc.	V.G.	Good	Fair	Poor
175	150	125	75	50

Model M Rifle

As above, with a 24" octagonal barrel. Manufactured from 1928 and 1931.

Exc.	V.G.	Good	Fair	Poor
175	150	125	75	50

Model L Rifle

A .22 caliber single shot takedown rifle with a 24" barrel. Manufactured from 1927 to 1932.

Exc.	V.G.	Good	Fair	Poor
300	250	200	150	100

Beginning in 1930, the Mossberg company manufactured a variety of utilitarian single shot and repeating bolt action rifles. Later they introduced a similar line of semiautomatic rifles. As these arms were intended for extensive use and were low-priced, the values for them may be categorized as follows:

Bolt Action Rifles

Model 10	Model 25	Model 340M
Model 14	Model 25A	Model 341
Model 140B	Model 26B	Model 342K
Model 140K	Model 26C	Model 346B
Model 142A	Model 30	Model 346K
Model 142K	Model 320B	Model 352K
Model 144	Model 320K	Model 450
Model 144LS	Model 321K	Model 432
Model 146B	Model 340B	Model 50
Model 20	Model 340K	Model 51
		Model 51M

Model 140 B

Exc.	V.G.	Good	Fair	Poor
100	80	65	45	20

Semiautomatic Rifles

Model 151K	Model 350K
Model 151M	Model 351C
Model 152	Model 351K
Model 152K	

Exc.	V.G.	Good	Fair	Poor
125	100	80	60	40

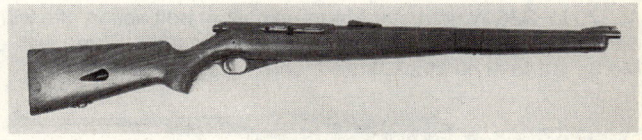

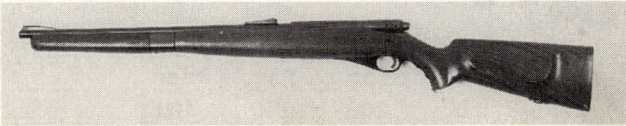

Model 400 Palomino

A .22 caliber lever action rifle with a 22" barrel, open sights and tubular magazine. Also made with an 18.5" barrel. Blued with a walnut stock. Manufactured from 1959 to 1964.

Exc.	V.G.	Good	Fair	Poor
150	125	100	75	50

Model 800

A bolt action rifle manufactured in a variety of calibers with a 22" barrel and folding leaf rear sight. Blued with a walnut stock. Introduced in 1967.

Exc.	V.G.	Good	Fair	Poor
225	200	150	100	75

Model 800D

As above, with a comb stock, rosewood forend tip and pistol grip cap. Manufactured from 1970 to 1973.

Exc.	V.G.	Good	Fair	Poor
300	250	200	150	100

Model 800V

As above, with a 24" heavy barrel not fitted with sights. Introduced in 1968.

Exc.	V.G.	Good	Fair	Poor
225	200	150	100	75

Model 800M

As above, with a Mannlicher-style stock.

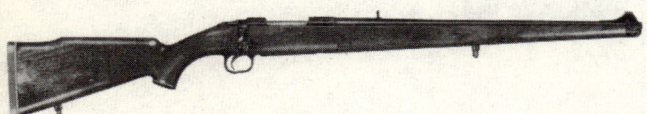

Exc.	V.G.	Good	Fair	Poor
275	250	200	150	100

Model 800SM

As above, with a 4X scope.

Exc.	V.G.	Good	Fair	Poor
300	275	225	150	100

Model 810

A .270 to .338 Winchester Magnum caliber bolt action rifle with a 22" or 24" barrel fitted with a folding rear sight. Blued with a Monte Carlo-style stock. Introduced in 1970.

Exc.	V.G.	Good	Fair	Poor
275	250	200	150	100

Model 472C

A .30-30 or. 35 Remington Caliber lever action rifle with a 20" barrel, open sights, and tubular magazine. Blued with a walnut stock. Introduced in 1972.

Exc.	V.G.	Good	Fair	Poor
200	175	150	100	75

Model 472P

As above, with a pistol grip stock and not fitted with a saddle ring.

Exc.	V.G.	Good	Fair	Poor
200	175	150	100	75

Model 472 One In Five Thousand

As above, with an etched receiver, brass buttplate, saddle ring and barrel band. A total of 5,000 were made in 1974.

Exc.	V.G.	Good	Fair	Poor
400	350	300	200	150

Model 479 PCA

Similar to the Model 472C in .30-30 caliber with a 20" barrel. Blued with a walnut stock.

Exc.	V.G.	Good	Fair	Poor
200	175	150	100	75

Model 479 RR

As above, with a gold-plated trigger and barrel band as well as "Roy Rogers" signature. A total of 5,000 were made in 1983.

Exc.	V.G.	Good	Fair	Poor
300	250	200	150	100

Model 1500 Series

A .223 to .338 Winchester Magnum bolt action rifle with a 22" or 24" barrel, 5- or 6-shot magazine and various sights. Blued with a hardwood or walnut stock. Manufactured by Howa in Japan and also known as the Smith & Wesson Model 1500. Offered in 1986 and 1987.

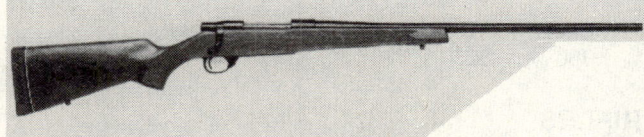

Model 1500 Mountaineer Grade I

Exc.	V.G.	Good	Fair	Poor
3050	250	225	150	125

Model 1500 Mountaineer Grade II

Exc.	V.G.	Good	Fair	Poor
325	275	250	175	125

Model 1500 Varmint-24" Heavy Barrel

Exc.	V.G.	Good	Fair	Poor
350	300	275	200	150

Model 1550

As above, but in .243, .270 or .30-06 caliber. Offered in 1986 and 1987.

Exc.	V.G.	Good	Fair	Poor
325	275	250	175	125

Model 1700 LS

Similar to the above, and in the same calibers with a 22" barrel not fitted for sights, machine jeweled bolt and knurled bolt handle. Blued with a walnut stock having a Schnabel forend. Offered in 1986 and 1987.

Exc.	V.G.	Good	Fair	Poor
400	350	275	200	150

SHOTGUNS

Mossberg manufactured a variety of shotguns that were sold at low to moderate prices. The values for these arms are approximately all the same.

Bolt Action Shotguns

Model 173	Model 190D	Model 390K
Model 173Y	Model 190K	Model 390T
Model 183D	Model 195D	Model 395K
Model 183K	Model 195K	Model 395S
Model 183T	Model 385K	Model 395T
Model 185D	Model 385T	Model 73
Model 185K		

Model 190 D

Exc.	V.G.	Good	Fair	Poor
75	65	50	40	25

Model 695

Introduced in 1969 this bolt action rifle is chambered for the 12 gauge shell. Barrel length is 22" with either a rifled bore or plain bore. Finish is matte blue or woodlands camo. In 1997 this model was offered with a 22" plain ported barrel with rifled bore.

NIB	Exc.	V.G.	Good	Fair	Poor
275	225	175	150	125	100

Model 200K

A 12 gauge slide-action shotgun with a 28" barrel and Mossberg select choke. Blued with a composition slide handle and walnut stock. Manufactured from 1955 to 1959.

Exc.	V.G.	Good	Fair	Poor
150	125	100	75	50

Model 500 Series

A 12, 20 or .410 bore slide action shotgun manufactured in a variety of barrel lengths and styles, as follows:

Model 500 Regal

Exc.	V.G.	Good	Fair	Poor
250	200	150	100	75

Model 500 Field Grade

NIB	Exc.	V.G.	Good	Fair	Poor
285	250	200	150	100	75

Model 500 Steel Shot-Chrome Bore

Exc.	V.G.	Good	Fair	Poor
300	250	200	125	100

Model 500 Slugster-Iron Sights

Exc.	V.G.	Good	Fair	Poor
275	250	200	150	100

Model 500 Camper-18.5" Barrel, Camo Case

Exc.	V.G.	Good	Fair	Poor
295	275	225	175	125

Model 500 Hi-Rib Trap

Exc.	V.G.	Good	Fair	Poor
275	250	200	150	100

Model 500 Super Grade

Exc.	V.G.	Good	Fair	Poor
200	175	150	100	75

Model 500 Pigeon Grade

Exc.	V.G.	Good	Fair	Poor
375	300	250	250	125

Model 500 Pigeon Grade Trap

Exc.	V.G.	Good	Fair	Poor
450	375	300	250	175

Model 500 Persuader-Riot Gun

NIB	Exc.	V.G.	Good	Fair	Poor
250	200	175	150	125	100

Model 500 Mariner-Marinecote Finish

NIB	Exc.	V.G.	Good	Fair	Poor
350	300	225	200	150	125

Model 500 Cruiser-Pistol Grip Only

NIB	Exc.	V.G.	Good	Fair	Poor
250	200	175	150	125	100

Model 500 Muzzleloader Combo

NIB	Exc.	V.G.	Good	Fair	Poor
350	325	275	225	200	150

Model 500 Bullpup

A 12 gauge slide action Bullpup shotgun with an 18.5" or 20" shrouded barrel. Matte black finish with a composition stock. Introduced in 1986.

NIB	Exc.	V.G.	Good	Fair	Poor
400	325	250	200	150	100

Model 500 Bantam

Introduced in 1996 this model is slightly smaller overall than the full size guns. Chambered for the 20 gauge shell it is fitted with a 22" shotgun barrel or 24" rifled vent rib barrel. Walnut stock. Weight is about 6.9 lbs.

NIB	Exc.	V.G.	Good	Fair	Poor
275	225	200	150	125	100

Model 500 Slug Gun-Viking Grade

Introduced in 1996 this model is a 12 gauge gun with 24" rifled barrel with iron sights and green synthetic stock.

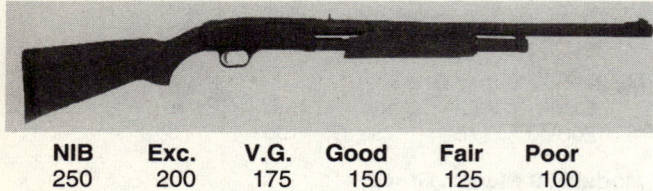

NIB	Exc.	V.G.	Good	Fair	Poor
250	200	175	150	125	100

NOTE: In 1997 Mossberg introduced ported barrels on some of its slug models. These ported barrels will be seen on rifled barrels only.

Model 500 USA

Introduced in 1997 this model is similar to the military model. It has a Parkerized finish with heavy duty sling swivels. Fitted with a plain 20" barrel choked cylinder. Stock is black synthetic. Magazine capacity is 6 rounds. Weight is about 7.2 lbs.

NIB	Exc.	V.G.	Good	Fair	Poor
250	200	175	150	125	100

Model 590

As above, with a 20" shrouded barrel, bayonet lug, parkerized or blued finish. Introduced in 1987.

NIB	Exc.	V.G.	Good	Fair	Poor
325	275	200	175	125	100

Model 590 Mariner-Marinecote Finish

NIB	Exc.	V.G.	Good	Fair	Poor
425	350	275	225	150	100

Model 590 Bullpup

The Model 500 with a 20" barrel and 9-shot magazine. Introduced in 1989.

NIB	Exc.	V.G.	Good	Fair	Poor
475	400	325	250	200	125

Model 835 Ulti-Mag

A 12 gauge Magnum slide action shotgun with a choice of 24" or 28" ventilated rib barrel fitted for choke tubes, 6-shot magazine and either composition camo or walnut stock. Introduced in 1988. Weight is 7.3 to 7.7 lbs.

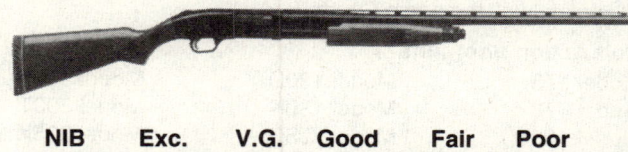

NIB	Exc.	V.G.	Good	Fair	Poor
425	350	275	25	150	100

Model 835 Ulti-Mag Crown Grade

The Crown Grade features checkered walnut stock with fluted comb. It is chambered for the 12 gauge with 3.5" chamber. Offered in 24" or 28" vent rib barrels with blued or camo finish. Weight is about 7.3 to 7.7 lbs.

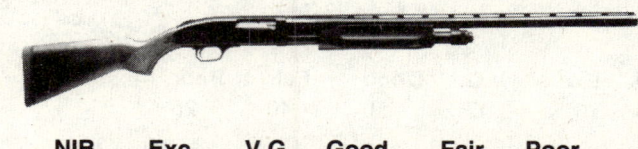

NIB	Exc.	V.G.	Good	Fair	Poor
350	275	225	200	150	100

Crown Grade Ulti-Mag Combo Model

Same as above but offered with both a 28" vent rib barrel and a 24" rifled barrel with iron sights.

NIB	Exc.	V.G.	Good	Fair	Poor
400	350	300	250	200	100

Model 835 Ulti-Mag Viking Grade

Introduced in 1996 this model features a 12 gauge 3.5" magnum chambered with green synthetic stock and modified choke tube. Furnished with 28" vent rib barrel.

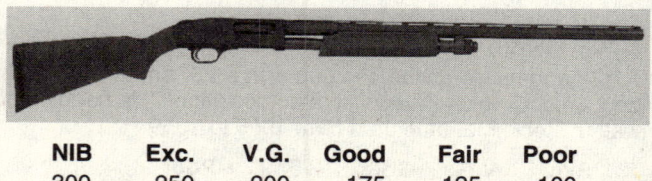

NIB	Exc.	V.G.	Good	Fair	Poor
300	250	200	175	125	100

Model 835 Wild Turkey Federation

As above, with a Wild Turkey Federation medallion inlaid in the stock. Introduced in 1989.

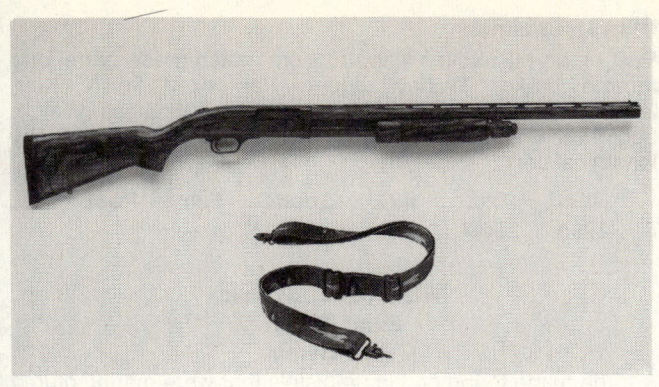

NIB	Exc.	V.G.	Good	Fair	Poor
475	400	325	250	200	125

Model 835 American Field

This 12 gauge model has a checkered walnut stock, 28" ventilated rib barrel with modified choke tube. Weight is about 7.7 lbs.

NIB	Exc.	V.G.	Good	Fair	Poor
300	275	225	200	150	100

Model 3000

A 12 or 20 gauge slide action shotgun manufactured in a variety of barrel lengths and styles. Blued with a walnut stock. Also known as the Smith & Wesson Model 3000.

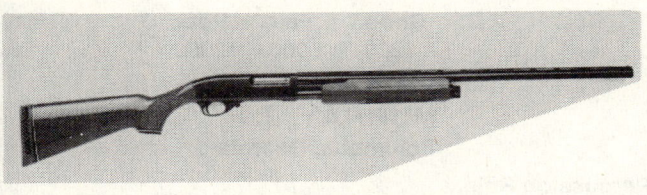

Exc.	V.G.	Good	Fair	Poor
325	250	175	125	75

Model 3000 Waterfowler

As above, but matte finished, fitted with sling swivels and accompanied by a camouflage sling. Produced in 1986.

Exc.	V.G.	Good	Fair	Poor
350	275	200	150	100

Model 3000 Law Enforcement

As above, with an 18.5" or 20" cylinder-bore barrel. Manufactured in 1986 and 1987.

Exc.	V.G.	Good	Fair	Poor
325	250	175	125	75

Model 1000

A 12 or 20 gauge semiautomatic shotgun manufactured in a variety of barrel lengths and styles, the receiver of an aluminum alloy and blued. Also known as the Smith & Wesson Model 1000. Offered in 1986 and 1987.

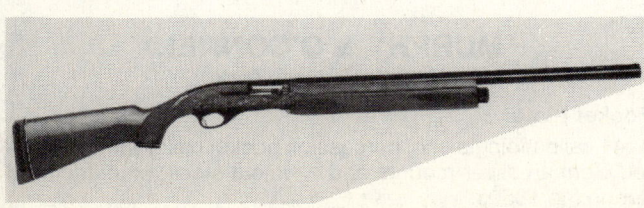

Exc.	V.G.	Good	Fair	Poor
400	325	250	200	125

Model 1000 Slug

As above, with a 22" barrel having rifle sights. Offered in 1986 and 1987.

Exc.	V.G.	Good	Fair	Poor
400	325	250	200	125

Model 1000 Super Series

As above, with a steel receiver and a self-regulating gas system that allows the use of either standard or Magnum shells.

Exc.	V.G.	Good	Fair	Poor
500	450	400	300	200

Model 1000 Super Waterfowler-Matte Finish

Exc.	V.G.	Good	Fair	Poor
500	450	400	300	200

Model 1000 Super Slug-Rifle Sights

Exc.	V.G.	Good	Fair	Poor
500	450	400	300	

Model 1000 Super Trap-30" High Rib Barrel

Exc.	V.G.	Good	Fair	Poor
475	425	350	250	175

Model 1000 Super Skeet-25" Barrel

Exc.	V.G.	Good	Fair	Poor
575	525	450	350	225

Model 5500 MKI I

A 12 gauge semiautomatic shotgun supplied with either a 26" barrel for 2.75" shells or a 28" barrel for 3" shells. Blued with a walnut stock. Introduced in 1989.

NIB	Exc.	V.G.	Good	Fair	Poor
435	375	275	225	175	125

Model 9200

This model has a variety of configurations. It is a 12 gauge semiautomatic with a choice of walnut stock or camo synthetic stock. Barrel lengths are from 22" to 28". Weights range from 7 to 7.7 lbs.

Viking Grade

NIB	Exc.	V.G.	Good	Fair	Poor
400	350	300	275	200	100

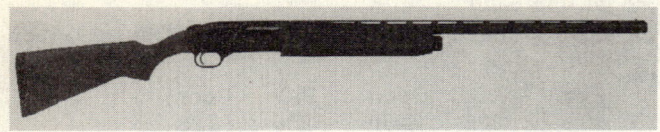

USST Crown Grade

NIB	Exc.	V.G.	Good	Fair	Poor
475	400	350	300	200	100

Combos

NIB	Exc.	V.G.	Good	Fair	Poor
550	475	425	350	300	150

Turkey Camos

NIB	Exc.	V.G.	Good	Fair	Poor
550	475	425	350	300	150

Bantam

NIB	Exc.	V.G.	Good	Fair	Poor
475	400	350	300	250	125

MOUNTAIN RIFLES, INC.
Palmer, Alaska

Mountaineer

This bolt action rifle, introduced in 1997, is built on a Remington action with Model 70 style bolt release. A factory muzzle brake is installed with open sights. A Timney trigger is standard. Stock is fiberglass. Finish is Parkerized. This model is chambered for many different calibers, from .223 Rem. to .416 Rem. Including Dakota and Weatherby cartridges. Weight starts at about 6 lbs. and is dependent on caliber. There are several options that will affect price. A left hand model is offered as an option.

NIB	Exc.	V.G.	Good	Fair	Poor
2195	1750	—	—	—	—

Super Mountaineer

Similar to the Mountaineer model but the bolt is fluted and hollow. Barrel is match grade stainless steel with muzzle brake. Kevlar/Graphite stock. Wide variety of calibers. Weight starts at about 4.25 lbs. depending on caliber.

NIB	Exc.	V.G.	Good	Fair	Poor
2895	2350	—	—	—	—

Pro Mountaineer

This model is built on a Winchester Model 70 action. Premium match grade barrel with muzzle brake. Model 70 trigger. Stainless steel matte finish. Kevlar/Graphite stock. Wide variety of calibers. Weight starts at about 6 lbs.

NIB	Exc.	V.G.	Good	Fair	Poor
2895	2350	—	—	—	—

Pro Safari

This model is built on an MRI action with controlled feed. Premium match grade barrel. Timney trigger. Matte blue finish. Exhibition grade walnut stock with custom bottom metal. Weight starts at about 7 lbs. depending on caliber. Caliber from .223 to .458 Lott.

NIB	Exc.	V.G.	Good	Fair	Poor
4495	3500	—	—	—	—

Ultra Mountaineer

Built on an MRI action with premium match grade barrel and muzzle brake. Timney trigger. Parkerized finish. Kevlar/Graphite stock. Calibers form .223 to .505 Gibbs. Weight begins at 5 lbs. depending on caliber. Add $500 for Rigby length calibers.

NIB	Exc.	V.G.	Good	Fair	Poor
2995	2500	—	—	—	—

MUGICA, JOSE
Eibar, Spain
SEE Llama

A trade name found on Llama pistols that were manufactured by Gabilondo.

MURATA
SEE Japan State

MURFEESBORO ARMORY
Murfeesboro, Tennessee

Established in 1861 by William Ledbetter. Made copies of U.S. Model 1841 Rifle complete with patchbox and double strapped nose cap. Barrel bands pinned to stock. Between 270 and 390 made from October of 1861 through March of 1862. Overall length 48-3/4"; barrel length 33"; .54 caliber. Unmarked except for serial number on various parts including the barrel.

Prospective purchasers are strongly advised to secure an expert appraisal prior to acquisition.

Exc.	V.G.	Good	Fair	Poor
—	—	1200	6000	2000

MURRAY, J. P.
Columbus, Georgia

Percussion Rifle

A .58 caliber percussion rifle with a 33" barrel, full stock and brass mounts. Also made with a 23.5" to 24" barrel as a carbine. The lock marked "J.P. Murray/Columbus Ga." Several hundred were manufactured between 1862 and 1864. Prospective purchasers are advised to secure a qualified appraisal prior to acquisition.

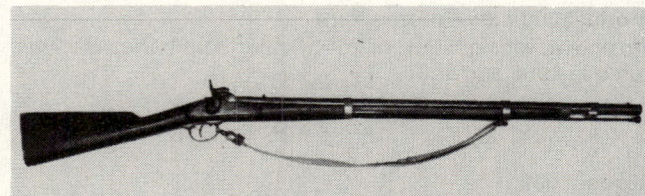

Courtesy Milwaukee Public Museum, Milwaukee, Wisconsin

Exc.	V.G.	Good	Fair	Poor
—	—	15000	7000	1500

MURPHY & O'CONNEL
New York, New York

Pocket Pistol

A .41 caliber single shot percussion pocket pistol with a 3" barrel, German silver mounts and a walnut stock. Manufactured during the 1850s.

Exc.	V.G.	Good	Fair	Poor
—	—	2000	1000	450

MUSGRAVE
Republic of South Africa

RSA NR I Single Shot Target Rifle

A .308 caliber single shot bolt action rifle with a 26" barrel, match sights, adjustable trigger and target-style stock. Made of walnut. Manufactured between 1971 and 1976.

Exc.	V.G.	Good	Fair	Poor
325	275	225	175	100

Valiant NR6

A .243, .270, .308, .30-06, and 7mm Remington Magnum caliber bolt-action sporting rifle with a 24" barrel, open sights and English style stock. Imported from 1971 to 1976.

Exc.	V.G.	Good	Fair	Poor
300	250	200	150	100

Premier NR5

As above, with a 26" barrel and pistol grip Monte Carlo-style stock. Discontinued in 1976.

Exc.	V.G.	Good	Fair	Poor
350	300	250	200	100

MUSKETEER RIFLES
Washington, D.C.
Importer-Firearms International

Sporter

A .243 to .300 Winchester Magnum caliber bolt action rifle with a 24" barrel without sights, and Monte Carlo-style stock. Imported between 1963 and 1972.

Exc.	V.G.	Good	Fair	Poor
300	250	200	175	100

Deluxe Sporter

As above, with an adjustable trigger and more finely figured walnut stock.

Exc.	V.G.	Good	Fair	Poor
350	300	250	200	100

Carbine

The Sporter with a 20" barrel.

Exc.	V.G.	Good	Fair	Poor
325	275	225	175	100

N

NAGANT, EMILE & LEON
Liege, Belgium
SEE Mosin-Nagant

Model 1878 Officers Revolver
A 9mm caliber double action revolver with a 5" octagonal barrel and 6-shot cylinder. Blued with walnut grips. Also manufactured in 7.5mm caliber for the Swedish government. Those purchased by Argentina, Brazil, and Norway bear those countries' acceptance marks.

Exc.	V.G.	Good	Fair	Poor
275	225	200	150	100

NAMBU
SEE Japan State

NATIONAL ARMS CO.
Brooklyn, New York
SEE Moore's Patent Firearms Co.
The successor to the Moore's Patent Firearms Company in 1865. Purchased by the Colt Company in 1870.

Large Frame Teat-Fire Revolver
A .45 teat fire caliber revolver with a 7.5" barrel and 6-shot cylinder. Blued or silver-plated with walnut grips. The barrel marked "National Arms Co. Brooklyn". The exact number of these revolvers made is unknown, but it is estimated to be less than 30. Prospective purchasers are advised to secure a qualified appraisal prior to acquisition.

Exc.	V.G.	Good	Fair	Poor
—	—	9000	3500	850

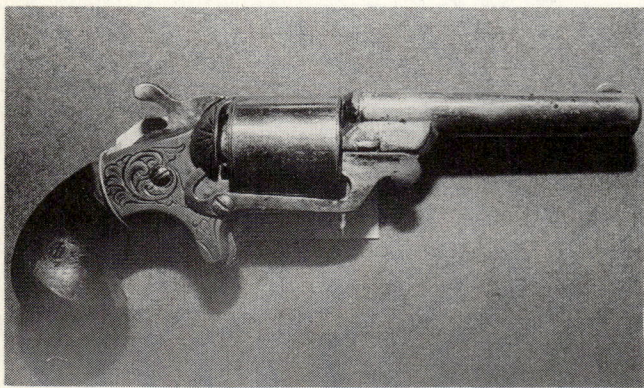

No. 2 Derringer
A .41 caliber spur trigger pocket pistol with a 2.5" barrel. Blued or silver-plated with walnut grips. Later manufactured by the Colt Company as their No. 2 Derringer.

Exc.	V.G.	Good	Fair	Poor
—	—	650	275	150

NAVY ARMS COMPANY
Ridgefield, New Jersey
Founded in 1957 by Val Forgett to enhance the shooting of black powder firearms without destroying the originals. The first replica was the Colt 1851 Navy. Thus, the name of the new company, "Navy Arms". In the early 1980s Navy Arms began importing surplus firearms from European countries. Navy Arms continues to offer both black powder replicas and foreign imports. For a short period of time the company imported double-barrel shotguns. This was discontinued in 1990.

SHOTGUNS
The shotguns listed below were no longer imported by Navy Arms in 1990.

Model 83
A 12 or 20 gauge Magnum Over/Under shotgun manufactured in a variety of barrel lengths and styles with double triggers and extractors. Blued, engraved, with a walnut stock. Introduced in 1985.

NIB	Exc.	V.G.	Good	Fair	Poor
385	25	275	200	175	125

Model 93
As above, with automatic ejectors.

NIB	Exc.	V.G.	Good	Fair	Poor
450	400	325	275	225	175

Model 95
As above, with a single trigger and screw-in choke tubes.

NIB	Exc.	V.G.	Good	Fair	Poor
475	25	350	300	250	200

Model 96 Sportsman
As above, in 12 gauge only with a gold-plated receiver.

NIB	Exc.	V.G.	Good	Fair	Poor
575	525	450	400	350	300

Model 100
A 12, 20, 28 or .410 bore Over/Under boxlock shotgun with 26" ventilated rib barrels, single trigger and extractors. Blued, chrome-plated, with a walnut stock. Introduced in 1989.

NIB	Exc.	V.G.	Good	Fair	Poor
300	250	225	200	150	100

Model 100 Side-by-Side
A 12 or 20 gauge Magnum boxlock double-barrel shotgun with 27.5" barrels, double triggers and extractors. Blued with a walnut stock. Imported between 1985 and 1987.

Exc.	V.G.	Good	Fair	Poor
375	325	275	200	125

Model 150
As above, with automatic ejectors.

Exc.	V.G.	Good	Fair	Poor
450	400	325	225	150

Model 105
A 12, 20 or .410 bore folding single barrel shotgun with a 26" or 28" barrel, chrome-plated engraved receiver, blued barrel and hardwood stock. Introduced in 1985.

NIB	Exc.	V.G.	Good	Fair	Poor
100	80	75	65	50	35

Model 105 Deluxe

As above, with vent rib barrel and a checkered walnut stock.

NIB	Exc.	V.G.	Good	Fair	Poor
120	100	85	75	60	45

REPLICA LONG GUNS

Harpers Ferry Flint Rifle

This model is a copy of the 1803 rifle in the original .54 caliber. It features a rust blued 35" barrel. Weight is 8.5 lbs.

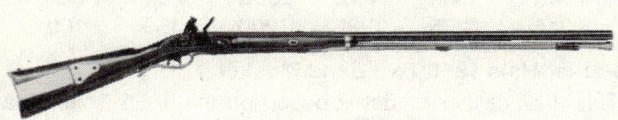

NIB	Exc.	V.G.	Good	Fair	Poor
475	400	350	300	200	100

Brown Bess Musket

This replica is a copy of the second model used between 1760 and 1776. Bright finish on metal and one piece walnut stock with polished brass locks. Barrel is 42" and weight is 9.5 lbs.

NIB	Exc.	V.G.	Good	Fair	Poor
500	450	400	300	250	100

Brown Bess Carbine

Same as above but fitted with a 30" barrel. Weighs 7.75 lbs.

NIB	Exc.	V.G.	Good	Fair	Poor
550	500	450	325	250	100

1777 Charleville Musket

Copy of French flintlock in .69 caliber. Fittings are steel with brass front sight and brass flashpan. Barrel length is 44.625" and weight is about 8.75 lbs.

NIB	Exc.	V.G.	Good	Fair	Poor
590	500	450	400	300	150

1777 Standard Charleville Musket

Same as above with polished steel barrel and select walnut stock.

NIB	Exc.	V.G.	Good	Fair	Poor
500	450	400	350	250	100

1816 M.T. Wickham Musket

Furnished in .69 caliber with steel ramrod with button head. Brass flashpan and walnut stock are standard.

NIB	Exc.	V.G.	Good	Fair	Poor
600	550	450	350	250	200

1808 Springfield Musket

This model is a U.S. copy of the 1763 Charleville musket with 1808 Springfield markings. Barrel length is 44" and weight is 8.75 lbs.

NIB	Exc.	V.G.	Good	Fair	Poor
530	475	400	300	200	100

Pennsylvania Long Rifle

This model is offered in either percussion or flintlock ignition and is offered in a choice of .32 caliber or .45 caliber. It has an

octagonal 40.5" rust blued barrel, polished lock, double set triggers, and brass furniture on a walnut stock. Weighs 7.5 lbs.

Percussion

NIB	Exc.	V.G.	Good	Fair	Poor
335	290	250	200	150	100

Flintlock

NIB	Exc.	V.G.	Good	Fair	Poor
350	300	250	200	150	100

Kentucky Rifle

Offered in either percussion or flintlock ignition it has a blue steel barrel, case-colored lockplate, and a polished brass patch box inletted into a walnut stock. The barrel length is 35" and the rifle is available in .45 oz. 50 caliber. Weight is 6 lbs., 14 oz.

Percussion

NIB	Exc.	V.G.	Good	Fair	Poor
280	250	200	150	100	75

Flintlock

NIB	Exc.	V.G.	Good	Fair	Poor
300	260	210	150	100	75

Mortimer Flintlock Rifle

Offered in .54 caliber with rust blued barrel, walnut stock with cheekpiece and checkered straight grip. It also has a external safety and sling swivels. Barrel length is 36" and weight is 9 lbs. Optional shotgun barrel.

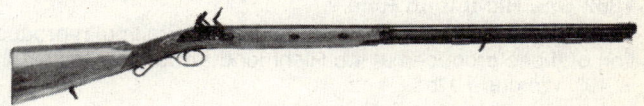

NIB	Exc.	V.G.	Good	Fair	Poor
590	550	500	450	350	200

Optional shotgun barrel-Add $240.

Tryon Creedmoor Rifle

This .45 caliber model features a heavy blued 33" octagonal barrel, hooded front sight, adjustable tang sight, double set triggers, sling swivels, and a walnut stock. Weighs about 9.5 lbs.

NIB	Exc.	V.G.	Good	Fair	Poor
580	525	450	400	300	200

Standard Tryon Rifle

Same as above but without target sights.

NIB	Exc.	V.G.	Good	Fair	Poor
400	350	300	250	200	100

Deluxe Tryon Rifle

Same as above but with polished and engraved lock and patch box.

NIB	Exc.	V.G.	Good	Fair	Poor
425	375	325	250	200	100

Parker-Hale Whitworth Rifle

This is a replica of a British sniper rifle, .451 caliber, used by the Confederates during the Civil War. Round barrel is 36" and features a globe front sight and ladder rear sight. The walnut stock is hand checkered. Weighs 9 lbs., 10 oz.

NIB	Exc.	V.G.	Good	Fair	Poor
700	650	600	450	300	150

Limited edition telescope-Add $150.

Parker-Hale Volunteer Rifle

A .451 caliber rifle with hand checkered walnut stock. Fitted with 32" barrel with globe front sight and ladder rear sight. Weighs 9.5 lbs.

NIB	Exc.	V.G.	Good	Fair	Poor
640	600	550	400	300	200

Parker-Hale 3 Band Volunteer Rifle

Same basic specifications as Whitworth rifle but furnished with Alexander Henry rifling.

NIB	Exc.	V.G.	Good	Fair	Poor
700	650	600	400	250	50

Rigby Target Rifle

The 1880s replica is chambered for the .451 caliber. It is fitted with adjustable front sight and vernier tang sight. The lock, breech plug, triggerguard, buttplate, and escutcheons are case-colored. Barrel length is 32" and weight is 7 lbs., 12 oz.

NIB	Exc.	V.G.	Good	Fair	Poor
550	500	450	300	200	100

1861 Springfield Rifle

This .58 caliber replica is fitted with an 1855-style hammer. Barrel length is 40" and weight is 10 lbs., 4 oz.

NIB	Exc.	V.G.	Good	Fair	Poor
470	425	350	300	200	100

1862 C.S. Richmond Rifle

This Confederate rifle is .58 caliber and is a faithful reproduction of those produced at the Richmond Armory. Barrel length is 40". Weighs 10 lbs., 4 oz.

NIB	Exc.	V.G.	Good	Fair	Poor
470	425	350	300	200	100

J.P. Murray Carbine

This Confederate cavalry .58 caliber carbine has a case-colored lock and brass furniture on a walnut stock. Barrel length is 23.5" and weight is 8 lbs., 5 oz.

NIB	Exc.	V.G.	Good	Fair	Poor
325	275	250	200	150	100

1863 Springfield Rifle

An exact replica of the famous Springfield Musket. Barrel is 40" with 3 barrel bands. All metal parts are finished bright. Weighs 9.5 lbs.

NIB	Exc.	V.G.	Good	Fair	Poor
470	425	350	300	200	100

1841 Mississippi Rifle

Also know as the "Yager" rifle it is offered in either .54 or .58 caliber. Barrel length is 33" and weighs 9.5 lbs.

NIB	Exc.	V.G.	Good	Fair	Poor
380	325	250	200	150	100

Zouave Rifle

This Civil War replica is a .58 caliber with polished brass hardware and blued 33" barrel. Weighs 9 lbs.

NIB	Exc.	V.G.	Good	Fair	Poor
380	325	250	200	150	100

Parker-Hale 1861 Musketoon

Made by Gibbs Rifle Company using 130-year-old gauges for reference. This .577 caliber replica features a 24" barrel with folding ladder military sight. The stock is walnut and the lock is case-colored. All furniture is polished brass. Weighs 7.5 lbs.

NIB	Exc.	V.G.	Good	Fair	Poor
380	325	250	200	50	100

Navy Arms Musketoon

Same as above but manufactured in Italy.

NIB	Exc.	V.G.	Good	Fair	Poor
315	275	225	200	150	100

Parker-Hale 1858 Two Band Musket

This .577 caliber model is based on the 1858 Enfield naval pattern. Fitted with a military sight graduated to 1,100 yards. Case-colored lock and walnut stock with brass fittings. Barrel length is 33" and weighs 8.5 lbs.

NIB	Exc.	V.G.	Good	Fair	Poor
470	425	350	300	200	100

Navy Arms 1858 Two Band Musket

Same as above but built in Italy.

NIB	Exc.	V.G.	Good	Fair	Poor
380	325	250	200	150	100

Parker-Hale Three Band Musket

This replica is based on the design produced between 1853 and 1863. The rear sight is based on an 1853 model graduated to 900 yards. Is fitted with a case-colored lock and walnut stock with brass furniture. Barrel is 39" and weighs 9 lbs.

NIB	Exc.	V.G.	Good	Fair	Poor
500	450	400	300	200	100

Navy Arms Three Band Musket

Same as above but produced in Italy.

NIB	Exc.	V.G.	Good	Fair	Poor
400	350	300	250	200	100

Navy Arms Revolving Carbine

Fitted with a 20" barrel and chambered for the .357 Magnum, .44-40, or .45 Colt cartridge. This model has a revolving 6 shot cylinder. Straight grip stock with brass butt plate and trigger guard. The action is based on the Remington Model 1874 revolver. Introduced in 1968 and discontinued in 1984.

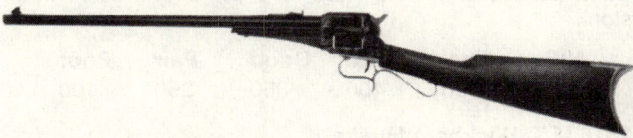

NIB	Exc.	V.G.	Good	Fair	Poor
600	500	400	300	200	100

Sharps Cavalry Carbine

A breech loading .54 caliber carbine with 22" blued barrel. Military style sights, walnut stocks, and saddle bar with ring are standard. Weighs 7 lbs., 12 oz.

NIB	Exc.	V.G.	Good	Fair	Poor
600	550	500	400	300	150

Sharps Cavalry Carbine Cartridge Model

Same as above but chambered for the .45-70 Government cartridge.

NIB	Exc.	V.G.	Good	Fair	Poor
620	570	520	400	300	50

Sharps Plains Rifle

This model features a case-colored receiver, blued barrel, and checkered walnut stock. Offered in .44-70 or .54 caliber percussion. Barrel length is 28.5". Weight is 8 lbs., 10 oz.

NIB	Exc.	V.G.	Good	Fair	Poor
600	550	500	400	300	150

1873 Winchester Rifle

This replica features a case-colored receiver, blued octagon 24" barrel, and walnut stocks. Offered in either .440-40 or .45 Long Colt. Weighs about 8 1bs., 4 oz.

NIB	Exc.	V.G.	Good	Fair	Poor
715	650	600	500	400	200

1873 Winchester Carbine

Same specifications as rifle above but fitted with a 19" round barrel, blued receiver, and saddle ring. Weighs 7 lbs., 4 oz.

NIB	Exc.	V.G.	Good	Fair	Poor
700	635	595	500	400	200

1873 Winchester Sporting Rifle

This model features a 30" octagonal barrel, case-colored receiver, and checkered pistol grip. Offered in .44-40 or .45 Long Colt. Weighs about 8 lbs., 14 oz. A 24" model is also offered.

NIB	Exc.	V.G.	Good	Fair	Poor
760	700	650	525	400	200

1866 "Yellowboy" Rifle

This model features a brass receiver, 24" octagon barrel, and walnut stocks. Weighs 8.5 lbs.

NIB	Exc.	V.G.	Good	Fair	Poor
580	525	450	400	300	150

1866 "Yellowboy" Carbine

Same as above but fitted with a 19" round barrel and saddle ring. Weighs 7 lbs., 4 oz.

NIB	Exc.	V.G.	Good	Fair	Poor
600	550	475	400	300	150

Iron Frame Henry

This is a replica of the famous and rare .44-40 Iron Frame Henry that features a case-colored frame. Barrel length is 24" and rifle weighs 9 lbs.

NIB	Exc.	V.G.	Good	Fair	Poor
750	700	650	500	400	200

Blued Iron Frame Henry

Same as above but furnished with a highly polished blued receiver.

NIB	Exc.	V.G.	Good	Fair	Poor
750	700	650	500	400	200

Military Henry

Based on the brass frame military version of the Henry rifle this model is furnished with sling swivels mounted on the left side. The buttplate is fitted with a trap door. Caliber is .44-40 and barrel length is 24". Weighs 9 lbs., 4 oz.

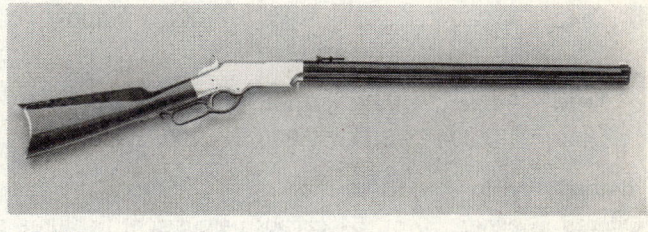

NIB	Exc.	V.G.	Good	Fair	Poor
750	700	650	500	400	200

Henry Carbine

This is the brass frame carbine version and features a 22" barrel. Chambered for the .44-40 cartridge. Weighs 8 lbs., 12 oz.

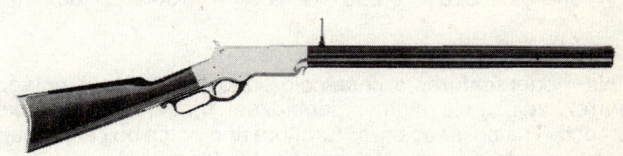

NIB	Exc.	V.G.	Good	Fair	Poor
750	700	650	500	400	200

Henry Trapper

This replica is not based on an actual Henry. Fitted with a unique 16.5" barrel, this brass frame model weighs 7 lbs., 7 oz. Chambered for the .44-40 cartridge.

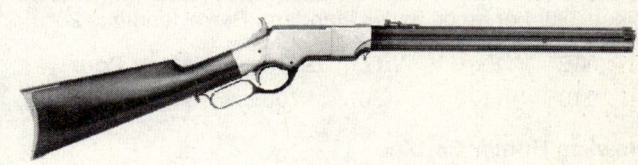

NIB	Exc.	V.G.	Good	Fair	Poor
750	700	650	500	400	200

No. 2 Creedmoor Target Rifle

This is a reproduction of the Remington No. 2 Creedmore. It features a case-colored receiver, tapered 30" octagonal barrel, hooded front sight, Creedmore tang sight, and walnut stock with checkered pistol grip. Furnished in .45-70 Government. Weighs 9 lbs.

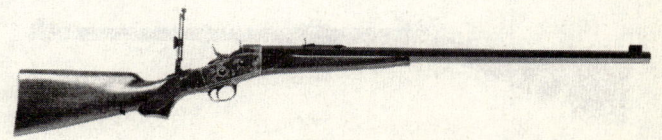

NIB	Exc.	V.G.	Good	Fair	Poor
595	550	500	400	300	150

Rolling Block Buffalo Rifle

This rifle is a replica of the Remington Buffalo rifle. It is fitted with a 26" or 30" octagonal or half octagonal barrel, casecolored receiver, blade front sight, notch rear sight, brass trigger-guard, with walnut stocks. Tang is drilled and tapped for tang sight.

NIB	Exc.	V.G.	Good	Fair	Poor
440	390	350	300	200	100

Half Octagon Barrel Model

NIB	Exc.	V.G.	Good	Fair	Poor
440	390	350	300	200	100

Ithaca/Navy Hawken Rifle

Offered in either .50 or. 54 caliber percussion. Features a 31.5" rust blued octagon barrel. The percussion lockplate is case-colored, while the rest of the hardware is blued with the exception of the nose cap and escutcheons. Weighs about 9 lbs., 13 oz.

NIB	Exc.	V.G.	Good	Fair	Poor
340	300	250	200	150	100

Hawken Rifle

This model features a case-colored lock, 28" blued octagon barrel, adjustable sights, double set triggers, and hooked breech. The polished brass furniture and patch box are mounted on a walnut stock. Weighs about 8.5 lbs.

NIB	Exc.	V.G.	Good	Fair	Poor
195	150	125	100	75	60

Hawken Hunter Rifle

Offered in .50, .54, or .58 caliber, this model features blued hardware, adjustable sights, case-colored lock, and hooked breech. The walnut stock is hand checkered with a cheek-piece. Rubber recoil pad is standard. Barrel length is 28".

NIB	Exc.	V.G.	Good	Fair	Poor
210	170	130	100	75	60

Hawken Hunter Carbine

Same as above but fitted with a 22.5" barrel. Weighs about 6 lbs., 12 oz.

NIB	Exc.	V.G.	Good	Fair	Poor
210	170	130	100	75	60

Kodiak Double Rifle

Built in Europe this model features a walnut stock with cheek-piece and hand checkering. Barrel length is 28.5" with adjustable sights. Engraved side plates are polished bright. Sling swivels standard. Weighs 11 lbs.

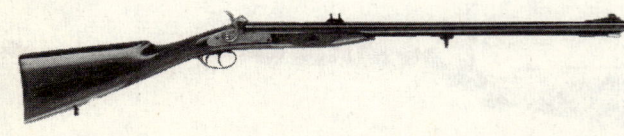

NIB	Exc.	V.G.	Good	Fair	Poor
575	500	450	300	200	100

Mortimer Flintlock Shotgun

Replica of 12 gauge English Mortimer this model features a waterproof pan, roller frizzen, external safety. All parts are case-colored. Barrel is 36" long. Weighs 7 lbs.

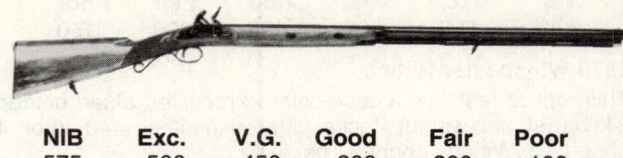

NIB	Exc.	V.G.	Good	Fair	Poor
575	500	450	300	200	100

Fowler Shotgun

This 12 gauge model is a side-by-side with straight gripstock. The gun features a hooked breech and 28" blued barrels. The side plates are engraved and case-colored. Double triggers and checkered walnut stock are standard. Weighs 7.25 lbs.

NIB	Exc.	V.G.	Good	Fair	Poor
275	225	150	125	100	75

Navy Arms Steel Shot Magnum

Same as above but chambered for 10 gauge shells. Weighs 7 lbs., 9 oz.

NIB	Exc.	V.G.	Good	Fair	Poor
440	400	350	300	200	100

T&T Shotgun

This turkey and trap model has a straight grip stock and 28" barrel choked full and full. Locks are case-colored and engraved. Walnut stock is checkered. Weighs 7.5 lbs.

NIB	Exc.	V.G.	Good	Fair	Poor
400	350	300	250	200	100

Japanese Matchlock

This model is a .50 caliber with 41" barrels. Weighs 8.5 lbs.

NIB	Exc.	V.G.	Good	Fair	Poor
420	350	300	200	100	75

HANDGUNS

Le Page Pistol

This .44 caliber percussion pistol has a 10.25" tapered octagon barrel, adjustable single set trigger. The lock, trigger-guard, and buff cap are engraved. The walnut stocks are hand checkered. Weighs 36 oz.

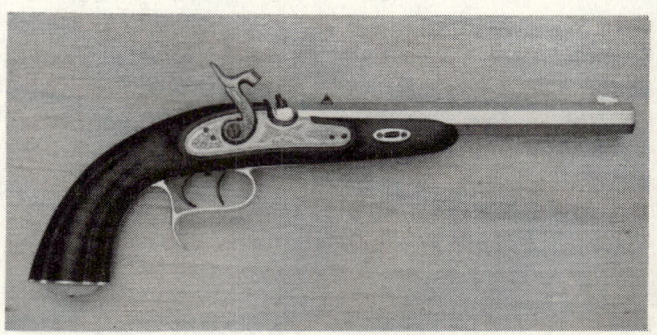

NIB	Exc.	V.G.	Good	Fair	Poor
400	350	300	250	200	100

Single Cased Set

NIB	Exc.	V.G.	Good	Fair	Poor
580	530	475	400	300	150

Double Cased Set

NIB	Exc.	V.G.	Good	Fair	Poor
995	875	750	600	400	200

Le Page Flintlock

Same as above but with flintlock ignition. Weighs 41 oz.

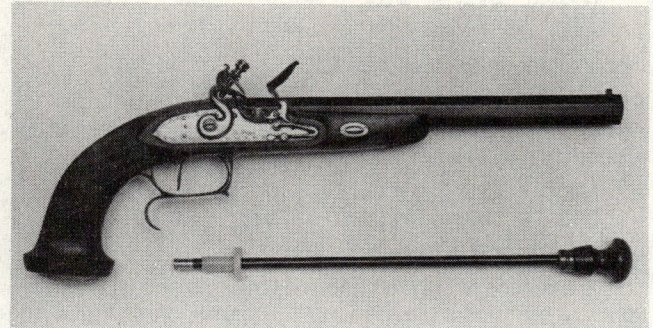

NIB	Exc.	V.G.	Good	Fair	Poor
470	425	350	250	150	100

Le Page Smoothbore Flintlock Pistol

Same as above but with a smooth bore.

NIB	Exc.	V.G.	Good	Fair	Poor
470	425	350	250	150	100

Single Cased Set

NIB	Exc.	V.G.	Good	Fair	Poor
650	600	500	400	300	150

Double Cased Set

NIB	Exc.	V.G.	Good	Fair	Poor
995	875	750	600	400	200

Kentucky Pistol

A percussion replica of a pistol developed in the 1840s. It has a 10.125" blued barrel, case-colored lock, brass furniture and triggerguard with walnut stock. Weighs 32 oz.

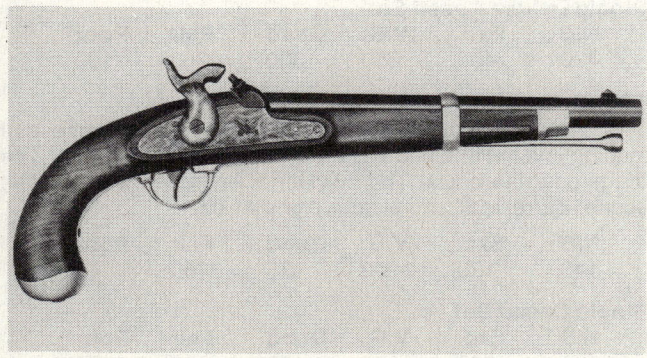

NIB	Exc.	V.G.	Good	Fair	Poor
165	150	125	100	85	60

Single Cased Set

NIB	Exc.	V.G.	Good	Fair	Poor
250	200	150	125	100	75

Double Cased Set

NIB	Exc.	V.G.	Good	Fair	Poor
420	350	300	250	150	100

Kentucky Flintlock Pistol

Same as above but with flintlock ignition.

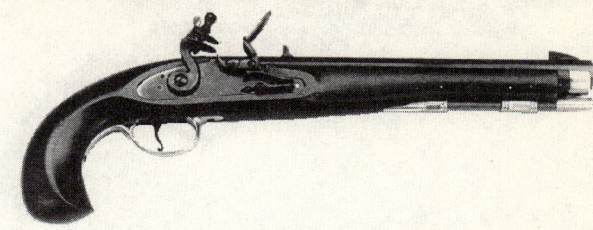

NIB	Exc.	V.G.	Good	Fair	Poor
165	150	125	100	75	60

Single Cased Set

NIB	Exc.	V.G.	Good	Fair	Poor
250	200	150	125	100	75

Double Cased Set

NIB	Exc.	V.G.	Good	Fair	Poor
440	400	350	275	175	100

18th Georgia Le Mat Pistol

This 9-shot .44 caliber percussion revolver has a 7.625" blued barrel and engraved cylinder. An engraved banner on the left side of the frame reads "DEO VINDICE". Hammer and trigger are case-colored. Stocks are checkered walnut. Comes with Le Mat mould and velvet draped French fitted case. Weighs 55 oz.

NIB	Exc.	V.G.	Good	Fair	Poor
675	600	500	400	300	50

Beauregard Le Mat Pistol

This is a replica of the Cavalry model. Comes cased.

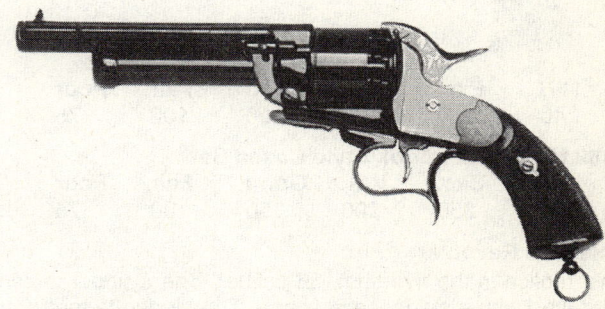

NIB	Exc.	V.G.	Good	Fair	Poor
850	800	700	550	350	200

Navy Le Mat

This model features a knurled pin barrel release and spur barrel selector.

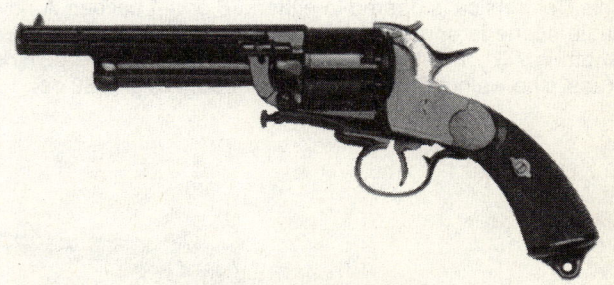

NIB	Exc.	V.G.	Good	Fair	Poor
500	450	400	350	300	150

Army Le Mat

This model features a knurled pin barrel release and cross pin barrel selector.

NIB	Exc.	V.G.	Good	Fair	Poor
500	450	400	350	300	150

Cavalry Le Mat

This model features a lanyard ring, spur trigger, lever type barrel release, and cross pin barrel selector.

NIB	Exc.	V.G.	Good	Fair	Poor
500	450	400	350	300	150

1862 New Model Police

This replica is based on the Colt .36 caliber pocket pistol of the same name. It features a half fluted and re-dated cylinder, case-colored frame and loading gate, and a polished brass triggerguard and back strap. Barrel length is 5.5" and pistol weigh 26 oz.

NIB	Exc.	V.G.	Good	Fair	Poor
240	200	175	150	100	75

1862 New Model Book Style Cased Set

NIB	Exc.	V.G.	Good	Fair	Poor
300	250	200	150	100	75

Paterson Revolver

This replica is the five-shot. 36 caliber. The cylinder is scroll engraved with a stagecoach scene. The hidden trigger drops down when the hammer is cocked. Barrel is 9" and the pistol weighs 43 oz.

NIB	Exc.	V.G.	Good	Fair	Poor
275	225	200	150	125	100

1851 Navy

This Colt replica is offered in either .36 or .44 caliber. A naval battle scene is engraved in the cylinder. The octagon barrel length is 7.5". The triggerguard, and back strap are polished brass. The walnut grips are hand rubbed. Weighs 32 oz.

NIB	Exc.	V.G.	Good	Fair	Poor
125	100	75	60	50	40

Single Cased Set

NIB	Exc.	V.G.	Good	Fair	Poor
200	150	125	100	75	60

Double Cased Set

NIB	Exc.	V.G.	Good	Fair	Poor
350	300	250	200	150	75

Optional shoulder stock-Add $100.

Augusta 1851 Navy Pistol

Available with either 5" or 7.5" barrel. Engraved with "A" coverage.

NIB	Exc.	V.G.	Good	Fair	Poor
200	150	100	75	60	50

Reb Model 1860 Pistol

This is a replica of the Confederate Griswold and Gunnison revolver. It features a blued round 7.5" barrel, brass frame, triggerguard and backstrap. Offered in .36 or .44 caliber. Weighs 44 oz.

NIB	Exc.	V.G.	Good	Fair	Poor
100	80	70	60	50	35

Reb 1860 Sheriff's Model

Same as above but fitted with a 5" barrel. Weighs 40 oz.

NIB	Exc.	V.G.	Good	Fair	Poor
100	80	70	60	50	35

Engraved Paterson Revolver

This model features hand engraving with silver inlays.

NIB	Exc.	V.G.	Good	Fair	Poor
395	350	300	250	200	50

1847 Walker Dragoon

This is a replica of the rare Colt .44 caliber revolver. The barrel and cylinder are blued while the frame and loading lever are case-colored. Barrel length is 9" and pistol weighs 75 oz.

NIB	Exc.	V.G.	Good	Fair	Poor
225	200	175	150	125	100

Single Cased Set

NIB	Exc.	V.G.	Good	Fair	Poor
325	300	275	250	200	100

Single Deluxe Cased Set

NIB	Exc.	V.G.	Good	Fair	Poor
430	400	350	300	200	100

1860 Army Pistol

This .44 caliber model features a case-colored frame and loading lever with blued barrel, cylinder, and back strap. The triggerguard is brass. The cylinder is engraved with a battle scene. Barrel is 8" and pistol weighs 41 oz.

NIB	Exc.	V.G.	Good	Fair	Poor
140	120	100	75	60	45

Single Cased Set

NIB	Exc.	V.G.	Good	Fair	Poor
225	200	175	150	100	75

Double Cased Set

NIB	Exc.	V.G.	Good	Fair	Poor
365	325	300	250	200	100

1858 New Model Remington Style Pistol

This replica has a solid frame as did the original. The frame and 8" barrel are blued while the triggerguard is brass. Walnut grips are standard. Weighs 40 oz.

NIB	Exc.	V.G.	Good	Fair	Poor
140	120	100	75	60	45

Single Cased Set

NIB	Exc.	V.G.	Good	Fair	Poor
220	180	150	125	100	75

Double Cased Set

NIB	Exc.	V.G.	Good	Fair	Poor
350	300	250	200	150	100

Stainless Steel 1858 New Model Army

Same as above but in stainless steel. Weighs 40 oz.

NIB	Exc.	V.G.	Good	Fair	Poor
220	180	150	125	100	80

Single Cased Set

NIB	Exc.	V.G.	Good	Fair	Poor
300	250	200	150	125	100

Double Cased Set

NIB	Exc.	V.G.	Good	Fair	Poor
525	475	400	300	200	150

Brass Framed 1858 New Model Army

This version features a highly polished brass frame. Barrel length is 7.75".

NIB	Exc.	V.G.	Good	Fair	Poor
100	80	70	60	50	35

Single Cased Set

NIB	Exc.	V.G.	Good	Fair	Poor
180	150	125	100	75	60

Double Cased Set

NIB	Exc.	V.G.	Good	Fair	Poor
275	250	200	150	100	75

1858 Target Model

Same as above but features a partridge front sight and an adjustable rear sight. Barrel length is 8".

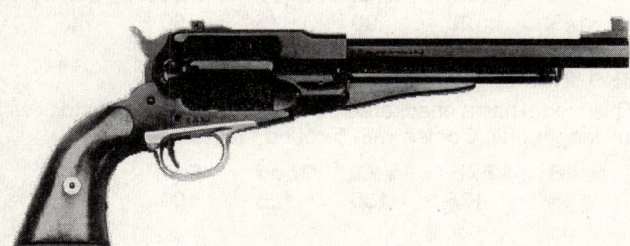

NIB	Exc.	V.G.	Good	Fair	Poor
175	150	125	100	75	50

Deluxe 1858 New Model Army

This replica is built to the exact dimensions as the original. The barrel is 8" with adjustable front sight. The triggerguard is silver plated. The action is tuned for competition. Weighs 46 oz.

NIB	Exc.	V.G.	Good	Fair	Poor
310	250	200	150	100	75

Spiller and Burr Pistol

This is a .36 caliber pistol with 7" blued octagon barrel. The frame is brass with walnut grips. Weighs 40 oz.

NIB	Exc.	V.G.	Good	Fair	Poor
115	100	80	65	50	40

Single Cased Set

NIB	Exc.	V.G.	Good	Fair	Poor
195	150	125	100	75	60

Double Cased Set

NIB	Exc.	V.G.	Good	Fair	Poor
315	250	200	150	100	50

This model features a 7.5" barrel with blued frame and barrel. Offered in .44 caliber. Walnut grips. Weighs 48 oz.

NIB	Exc.	V.G.	Good	Fair	Poor
200	150	125	100	75	50

"London Gray" Rogers and Spencer Pistol

Same as above but with a burnished satin chrome finish.

NIB	Exc.	V.G.	Good	Fair	Poor
220	180	140	125	100	80

Rogers and Spencer Target Model

Same as standard model but fitted with adjustable target sights.

NIB	Exc.	V.G.	Good	Fair	Poor
220	180	140	125	100	80

1873 Colt-Style Single Action Army

This replica features a case-colored frame and hammer with blued round barrel in 3", 4.75", 5.5", or 7.5" lengths. Triggerguard, and cylinder are blued. Offered in .44-40 or .45 Long Colt.

NIB	Exc.	V.G.	Good	Fair	Poor
315	275	200	150	125	100

Economy Model 1873 S.A.A.

Same as above but with brass trigger guard and back strap.

NIB	Exc.	V.G.	Good	Fair	Poor
275	250	200	150	125	100

Nickel 1873 S.A.A.

NIB	Exc.	V.G.	Good	Fair	Poor
370	325	275	225	150	100

1873 U.S. Cavalry Model

This .45 Long Colt model features U.S. arsenal stampings, case-colored frame, and walnut grips. Barrel length is 7.5" and pistol weighs 45 oz.

NIB	Exc.	V.G.	Good	Fair	Poor
385	350	300	250	200	100

1873 Pinched Frame Model

This is a replica of the "pinched" frame 1873 with "U" shape rear sight notch. Chambered for .45 Colt with 7.5" barrel.

NIB	Exc.	V.G.	Good	Fair	Poor
400	325	—	—	—	—

Deputy Single Action Army

Similar to the Model 1873 but with a bird's head grip. Barrel lengths are 3", 3.5", 4", and 4.75". Chambered for .44-40 and .45 Colt.

NIB	Exc.	V.G.	Good	Fair	Poor
400	325	—	—	—	—

Bisley Model

This model features the famous Bisley grip. Barrel length is 4.75", 5.5", and 7.5". Chambered for .44-40 or .45 Colt.

NIB	Exc.	V.G.	Good	Fair	Poor
425	350	—	—	—	—

1895 U.S. Artillery Model

Same as Cavalry Model but fitted with a 5.5" barrel. Weighs 42 oz.

NIB	Exc.	V.G.	Good	Fair	Poor
385	350	300	250	200	100

1875 Remington-Style Revolver

The frame is case-colored while all other parts are blued except for brass trigger guard. Available in .44-40 or .45 Long Colt. Furnished with walnut grips. Barrel length is 7.5". Weighs 41 oz.

NIB	Exc.	V.G.	Good	Fair	Poor
310	275	225	175	150	100

1890 Remington-Style Revolver

This is a modified version of the 1875 model that is also offered in .44-40 or .45 Long Colt. The web under the barrel has been eliminated. It has blued 5.5" steel barrel and frame. Lanyard loop is on bottom of walnut grips. Weighs 39 oz.

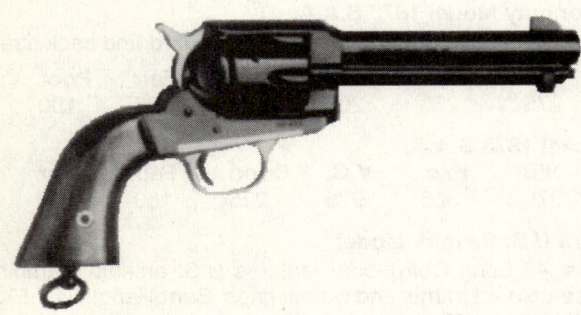

NIB	Exc.	V.G.	Good	Fair	Poor
315	280	225	175	150	100

Model 1875 Schofield-Cavalry 7" barrel

A reproduction of the S&W Model 3 top break revolver in either .44/40 or .45 Long Colt. The Cavalry model has a 7" barrel while the Wells Fargo model has a 5" barrel. Weight is about 39 oz.

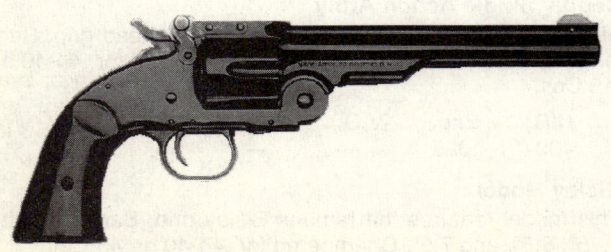

NIB	Exc.	V.G.	Good	Fair	Poor
750	600	450	350	200	100

Model 1875 Schofield-Wells Fargo 5" barrel

NIB	Exc.	V.G.	Good	Fair	Poor
750	600	450	350	200	100

MILITARY SURPLUS ARMS

SKS Type 56 W/Scope Rail

This semiautomatic gas operated rifle is chambered for the 7.62x39 cartridge. It has a 10-round clip. This model is fitted with a scope rail on the left side of the receiver. Barrel length is 20.5". Weight is 8 lbs.

NIB	Exc.	V.G.	Good	Fair	Poor
120	100	75	60	50	35

Standard SKS Type 56

Same as above without the scope rail.

NIB	Exc.	V.G.	Good	Fair	Poor
115	95	75	60	50	35

This model is fitted with a 2.75 power Type 89 scope an RPK style folding bipod.

NIB	Exc.	V.G.	Good	Fair	Poor
280	250	200	150	125	100

SKS "Cowboys Companion" Carbine

Barrel length on this version is 16.5". Weighs 7 lbs., 8 oz.

NIB	Exc.	V.G.	Good	Fair	Poor
135	110	85	70	60	40

This is the military version of the "Cowboys Companion" fitted with a short cruciform folding bayonet.

NIB	Exc.	V.G.	Good	Fair	Poor
145	120	90	75	60	40

SKS "Hunter" Carbine

This model has a checkered composite Monte Carlo stock with full length pull. Comes with 5-round magazine.

NIB	Exc.	V.G.	Good	Fair	Poor
195	175	150	125	100	75

TT-Olympia Pistol

This is a reproduction of the Walther target pistol. Chambered for .22 l.r. Barrel length is 4.625" and pistol weighs 27 oz.

NIB	Exc.	V.G.	Good	Fair	Poor
260	225	200	150	125	100

TU-90 Pistol

This model is based on the Tokagypt pistol. It features a wrap-around grip with thumb rest. Barrel length is 4.5" and pistol weighs 30 oz.

NIB	Exc.	V.G.	Good	Fair	Poor
110	90	80	70	50	40

TU-KKW Training Rifle

Based on the 98 Mauser and chambered for the .22 Long Rifle cartridge it is fitted with military sights, bayonet lug, cleaning rod and take down disc. Comes with detachable 5-round box magazine. Barrel length is 26" and weighs 8 lbs.

NIB	Exc.	V.G.	Good	Fair	Poor
180	150	125	100	80	60

TU-KKW Sniper Trainer

Same as above but fitted with a 2.75 power Type 89 scope and quick detachable mounting system.

NIB	Exc.	V.G.	Good	Fair	Poor
240	200	175	150	125	90

TU-33/40 Carbine

This model is based on the WWII Mauser G 33/40 mountain carbine. Chambered for the .22 Long Rifle or 7.62x39 cartridge. Barrel length is 20.75" and weighs 7.5 lbs.

NIB	Exc.	V.G.	Good	Fair	Poor
180	150	125	100	80	60

JW-15 Rifle

This model is a bolt action design based on the BRNO Model 5 action. Chambered for the .22 Long Rifle it features adjustable sights, sling swivels, an detachable 5-round magazine. The top of the receiver is dovetailed for easy scope mounting. Barrel is 24" long and rifle weighs 5 lbs., 12 oz.

NIB	Exc.	V.G.	Good	Fair	Poor
100	80	70	60	50	35

Martini Target Rifle

A .444 or .45-70 caliber single shot Martini-action rifle with a 26" or 30" octagonal barrel, tang sight, and walnut stock. Offered between 1972 and 1984.

Exc.	V.G.	Good	Fair	Poor
475	425	350	275	175

Parker-Hale Sniper Rifle

See Parker-Hale section of this text.

RPKS-74

A 5.56mm or 7.62x39mm caliber semiautomatic rifle with a 19" barrel patterned after the Russian AK series rifles.

Luger

A .22 caliber semiautomatic pistol with a 4", 6", or 8" barrel, fixed sights, and 10-shot magazine. Blued with walnut grips. Manufactured in the U.S.A. in 1986 and 1987.

Exc.	V.G.	Good	Fair	Poor
175	150	125	100	75

Grand Prix Silhouette Pistol

A .30-30, .44 Magnum, 7mm Special, and .45-70 caliber single shot pistol with a 13.75" barrel, adjustable sights, and an aluminum, heat-disbursing rib. Matte-blued, walnut grips and forearm. Manufactured in 1985.

Exc.	V.G.	Good	Fair	Poor
325	275	225	175	125

NEAL, W.
Bangor, Maine

Under Hammer Pistol

A .31 caliber under hammer percussion pistol with 5" to 8" barrels, iron frame and walnut grip. The barrel marked " Wm. Neal/Bangor, Me."

Exc.	V.G.	Good	Fair	Poor
—	—	750	350	150

NEPPERHAN FIREARMS CO.
Yonkers, New York

Pocket Revolver

A .31 caliber percussion revolver with 3.5" to 6" barrels and a 5-shot cylinder. Blued, casehardened with walnut grips. The barrel marked "Nepperhan/Fire Arms Co" and on some additionally "Yonkers New York". The latter are worth a slight premium over the values listed below. Approximately 5,000 were made during the 1860s.

Exc.	V.G.	Good	Fair	Poor
—	—	800	350	200

NEWBURY ARMS CO.
Catskill, New York
Albany, New York

Pocket Pistol

A .25 caliber spur trigger pocket pistol with a 4" octagonal barrel. Blued, silver-plated with walnut grips.

Exc.	V.G.	Good	Fair	Poor
—	—	950	400	200

Pocket Revolver

A .26 caliber double-action percussion revolver with a 5" barrel and C-shaped exposed trigger. Blued with an iron or brass frame and walnut grips. The barrel marked "Newbury Arms Co. Albany." Produced in limited numbers between 1855 and 1860. Prospective purchasers are advised to secure a qualified appraisal prior to acquisition.

Exc.	V.G.	Good	Fair	Poor
—	—	4000	2000	750

NEW ENGLAND FIREARMS CO.
Gardner, Massachusetts

Model R22
Magnum or .32 H&R Magnum double action revolver with a 2.5", 4", or 6" barrel and either a 6- or 9-shot cylinder. Blued or nickel-plated with walnut grips. Introduced in 1988.

NIB	Exc.	V.G.	Good	Fair	Poor
110	95	80	70	60	40

Pardner
A 12, 16, 20 or .410 bore single shot shotgun with a 24", 26", or 28" barrel. Blued with a walnut stock. Introduced in 1987.

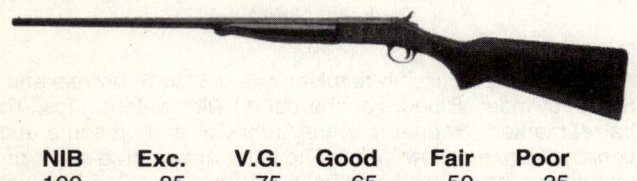

NIB	Exc.	V.G.	Good	Fair	Poor
100	85	75	65	50	35

Pardner Youth
Similar to the above model but offered only in 20 and 28 gauge as well as .410 bore. Fitted with a 26" barrel. Weight is between 5 and 6 lbs.

NIB	Exc.	V.G.	Good	Fair	Poor
100	85	75	65	50	35

Special Purpose
This is a similar model but it is offered only in 10 gauge. It is available in several different configurations. A 10 gauge model with hardwood stock with 28" barrel, a camo model with 28" barrel, a camo model with 32" barrel choked modified, and a black matte finish model with 24" barrel with screw in Turkey full choke. Weight is about 9.5 lbs.

NIB	Exc.	V.G.	Good	Fair	Poor
250	175	125	100	75	50

Special Purpose Waterfowl Model

Special Purpose Turkey Gun

Handi-Gun
.22 Hornet, .223, .243, .270, .280, .30-30, .44 Magnum, or .45-70 caliber version of the above with a 22" barrel fitted with open sights. Blued, with a walnut stock. Introduced in 1989.

NIB	Exc.	V.G.	Good	Fair	Poor
200	175	150	125	100	75

Survivor
Based on a single shot break action design this rifle or shotgun is fitted with a synthetic stock with integral storage compartments. Offered in .410/.45 Colt, 12 and 20 gauge, .223 Rem., and .357 Mag. Barrel length is 22". Weight is about 6 lbs.

NIB	Exc.	V.G.	Good	Fair	Poor
200	175	150	125	100	75

Tracker
This single shot break open shotgun is offered in both 12 and 20 gauge with rifled barrel or cylinder bore barrel. Both are 24" in length. Equipped with adjustable rifle sights. Weight is about 6 lbs.

NIB	Exc.	V.G.	Good	Fair	Poor
150	125	100	75	60	50

Super Light Rifles
This single shot rifle is chambered for the .22 Hornet or .223 Rem. It is fitted with a 20" light weight barrel. Choice of scope mount and no sights or adjustable rear sight and ramp front sight. Black polymer stock with semi-beavertail forend. Weight is about 5.5 lbs.

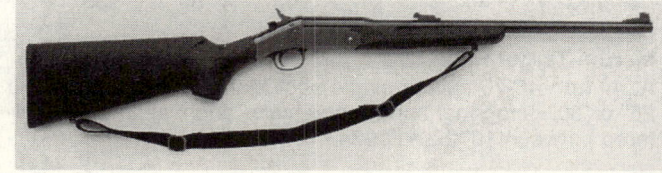

NIB	Exc.	V.G.	Good	Fair	Poor
175	125	100	75	60	50

NEWCOMB, H. G.
Natchez, Mississippi

Pocket Pistol

A .41 caliber percussion pocket pistol with a 2.5" barrel, German silver mounts and a walnut stock. Manufactured in the 1850s.

Exc.	V.G.	Good	Fair	Poor
—	—	1450	550	250

NEWTON ARMS CO.
Buffalo, New York

Also known as the Buffalo Newton Rifle Company and the Charles Newton Rifle Company. In operation from 1913 to 1932.

Newton-Mauser Rifle

A .256 Newton caliber bolt action rifle with a 24" barrel and double set triggers. Blued with a walnut stock. Manufactured circa 1914.

Exc.	V.G.	Good	Fair	Poor
750	675	550	400	275

Standard Rifle First Type

A .22, .256, .280, .30, .33, and .35 Newton as well as .30-06 caliber bolt action rifle with a 24" barrel, open or aperture sights and double set triggers. Blued with a walnut stock. Manufactured between 1916 and 1918.

Exc.	V.G.	Good	Fair	Poor
1200	1000	750	550	400

Standard Rifle Second Model

A .256, .30, or .35 Newton as well as .30-06 caliber bolt action rifle as above, but with an Enfield-style bolt handle. Manufactured after 1918.

Exc.	V.G.	Good	Fair	Poor
1000	800	650	400	350

Buffalo Newton Rifle

As above, but marked "Buffalo Newton Rifle Company".

Exc.	V.G.	Good	Fair	Poor
1000	800	650	400	350

NICHOLS & CHILDS
Conway, Massachusetts

Percussion Belt Revolver

A .34 caliber percussion revolver with a 6" round barrel and 6-shot cylinder. Blued or browned with walnut grips. It is estimated that less than 25 were made in 1838. Prospective purchasers are advised to secure a qualified appraisal prior to acquisition.

Exc.	V.G.	Good	Fair	Poor
—	—	7500	3250	1250

Revolving Percussion Rifle

A .36 or .40 caliber percussion rifle with a 22", 26", or 30" barrel and a 5-, 6-, 7- or 9-shot cylinder. Blued or browned with a walnut stock having a patch box. It is believed that approximately 150 were made between 1838 and 1840. Prospective purchasers are advised to secure a qualified appraisal prior to acquisition.

Exc.	V.G.	Good	Fair	Poor
—	—	8000	4000	1500

NOBLE
Haydenville, Massachusetts

In business between 1946 and 1971, this company manufactured a variety of plain, utilitarian firearms. In general, these arms are all worth approximately the same, that is, less than $200 in excellent condition.

RIFLES

Model 10

A .22 caliber bolt action single rifle with a 24" barrel. Pistol grip stock with no checkering. Open sights. Produced in the late 1950s.

Exc.	V.G.	Good	Fair	Poor
75	60	50	40	30

Model 20

A .22 caliber bolt action rifle fitted with a 22" barrel. Open sights. Produced from the late 1950s to the early 1960s.

Exc.	V.G.	Good	Fair	Poor
75	60	50	40	30

Model 33

This is a .22 caliber slide action rifle fitted with a 24" barrel and tubular magazine and Tenite stock. Produced from the late 1940s to the early 1950s.

Exc.	V.G.	Good	Fair	Poor
80	70	60	50	40

Model 33A

Same as above but fitted with a wood stock.

Exc.	V.G.	Good	Fair	Poor
75	60	50	40	30

Model 222

This is a single shot bolt action rifle chambered for the .22 caliber cartridge. Plain pistol grip stock.

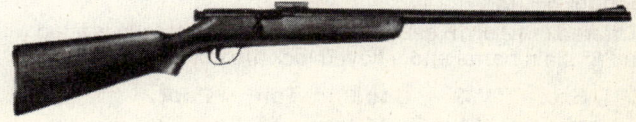

Exc.	V.G.	Good	Fair	Poor
85	75	60	50	40

Model 236

A .22 caliber slide action rifle with a 24" barrel and tubular magazine. Plain pistol grip stock and groved slide handle.

Exc.	V.G.	Good	Fair	Poor
100	85	75	60	50

Model 275

A .22 caliber lever action rifle with tubular magazine. Fitted with a 24" barrel. The plain stock has a semi-pistol grip.

Exc.	V.G.	Good	Fair	Poor
125	100	80	60	50

SHOTGUNS

Model 40

This is a hammerless slide action shotgun chambered for the 12 gauge shell. It is fitted with a tubular magazine and 28" barrel with multi choke. Plain pistol stock with grooved slide handle.

Exc.	V.G.	Good	Fair	Poor
125	100	85	70	50

Model 50

Same as above but without the multi choke.

Exc.	V.G.	Good	Fair	Poor
115	90	80	65	50

Model 60

A hammerless slide action shotgun in 12 or 16 gauge with tubular magazine and fitted with a 28" barrel with adjustable choke. Plain pistol grip stock with grooved slide handle.

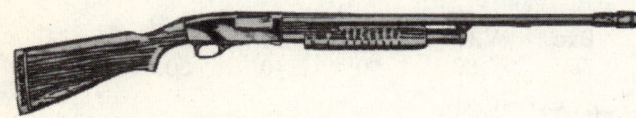

Exc.	V.G.	Good	Fair	Poor
175	150	125	100	75

Model 65

Same as above but without adjustable choke.

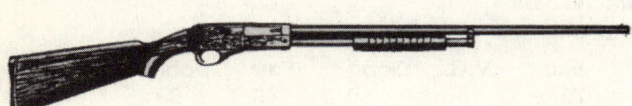

Exc.	V.G.	Good	Fair	Poor
150	125	100	75	60

Model 66CLP

Offered in 12 or 16 gauge this slide action shotgun is fitted with a 28" plain barrel and a keyed lock fire control system.

Exc.	V.G.	Good	Fair	Poor
160	140	110	85	70

Model 66RCLP

Similar to above but fitted with a 28" vent rib barrel and checkered pistol grip stock. Adjustable choke is standard.

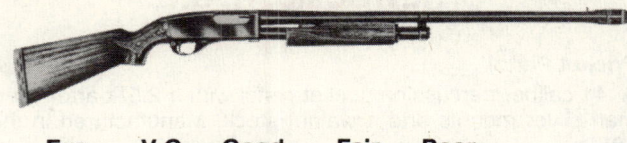

Exc.	V.G.	Good	Fair	Poor
200	175	150	125	100

Model 66 RLP

Same as above but without adjustable choke.

Exc.	V.G.	Good	Fair	Poor
175	150	125	100	75

Model 66XL

Similar to the above models but with plain barrel, and checkering only on the slide handle.

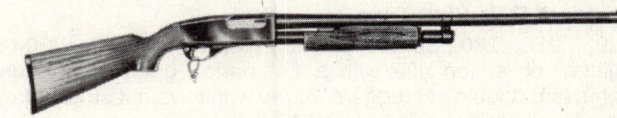

Exc.	V.G.	Good	Fair	Poor
150	125	100	75	60

Model 70CLP

Similar to the Model 66 series but offered in .410 bore with 26" barrel and adjustable choke. Both the butt stock and slide handle are checkered.

Exc.	V.G.	Good	Fair	Poor
175	150	125	100	75

Model 70RCLP

This variation is fitted with a 26" ventilated rib barrel.

Exc.	V.G.	Good	Fair	Poor
200	175	150	125	100

Model 70RLP

This model has a vent rib barrel and no adjustable choke.

Exc.	V.G.	Good	Fair	Poor
175	150	125	100	75

Model 70XL

This version has no adjustable choke but is fitted with a 26" vent rib barrel. Stock is checked.

Exc.	V.G.	Good	Fair	Poor
125	100	80	70	60

Model 602RCLP

This is a hammerless slide action shotgun chambered for the 20 gauge shell. It is fitted with a 28" vent barrel and adjustable choke. Checkered pistol grip stock with slide handle.

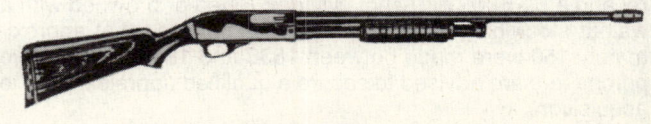

.Exc.	V.G.	Good	Fair	Poor
225	200	175	125	100

Model 602CLP

Same as above but with plain barrel.

Exc.	V.G.	Good	Fair	Poor
175	150	125	100	75

Model 602RLP

Same as Model RCLP except without the addition of an adjustable choke device.

Exc.	V.G.	Good	Fair	Poor
200	175	150	125	100

Model 602XL

Same as above but with only the slide handle checkered.

Exc.	V.G.	Good	Fair	Poor
150	125	100	75	60

Model 662

This 20 gauge slide action shotgun has a plain aluminum barrel with checkered pistol grip and slide handle. The receiver is made from aluminum. Produced in the late 1960s.

Exc.	V.G.	Good	Fair	Poor
200	175	150	125	100

Model 80

This model is a semi-automatic inertia operated shotgun chambered for the .410 shell. It is fitted with a 26" barrel, plain pistol stock with slotted forearm. Produced in the early to mid 1960s.

Exc.	V.G.	Good	Fair	Poor
250	200	150	125	100

Model 166L

This is a 12 gauge slide action shotgun with a key lock system. It is fitted with a 24" barrel bored for rifled slug. Lyman peep rear sight with post front sight. Checkered pistol and slide handle.

Exc.	V.G.	Good	Fair	Poor
250	200	150	125	100

Model 420

This shotgun is a box lock design side by side with double triggers and offered in 12, 16, 20 gauge, as well as .410 bore. Barrel lengths are 28" for all gauges except .410 where it is 26". Lightly engraved frame. Checkered walnut stock and splinter forearm.

Exc.	V.G.	Good	Fair	Poor
300	250	200	150	100

Model 450E

This model is similar to the Model 420 with the addition of automatic ejectors and not offered in .410 bore. Checkered pistol grip stock with beavertail forearm. Produced in the late 1960s.

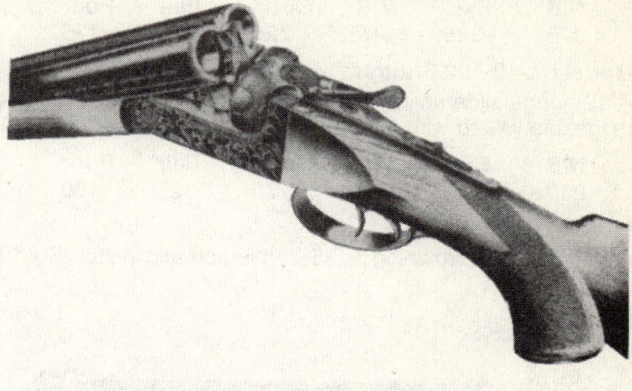

Exc.	V.G.	Good	Fair	Poor
350	275	225	175	125

NORINCO
Peoples Republic of China
China North Industries Corp.

Imported by China Sports, as well as Interarms of Alexandria, Virginia.

ATD .22

A .22 caliber semiautomatic rifle with a 19.4" barrel and 11-shot magazine located in the butt. Blued with a hardwood stock. Importation began in 1987.

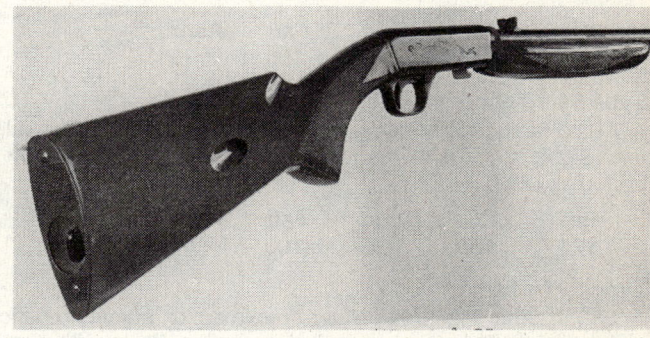

NIB	Exc.	V.G.	Good	Fair	Poor
180	150	125	100	75	50

EM-321

A .22 caliber slide action rifle with a 19.5" barrel and 10-shot tubular magazine. Blued with a hardwood stock. Introduced in 1989.

NIB	Exc.	V.G.	Good	Fair	Poor
125	100	85	75	65	50

Model HL-12-203 Shotgun

A 12 gauge boxlock Over/Under shotgun with 30" ventilated rib barrels fitted for choke tubes, single trigger and automatic ejectors. Blued with a hardwood stock. Introduced in 1989.

NIB	Exc.	V.G.	Good	Fair	Poor
375	325	275	225	175	125

Model HL-12-102 Shotgun

A 12 gauge slide action shotgun with a 28" barrel and 3-shot magazine. Blued with a hardwood stock. Introduced in 1989.

NIB	Exc.	V.G.	Good	Fair	Poor
250	225	200	75	125	100

Model 213 Pistol

A copy of the Browning P-35 semiautomatic pistol. Sold in 1988 only.

Exc.	V.G.	Good	Fair	Poor
175	150	125	100	75

Type 54-1 Tokarev

A 7.62x25mm caliber semiautomatic pistol with a 4.6" barrel, fixed sights, and 8-shot magazine. Blued with plastic grips. Imported in 1989.

Exc.	V.G.	Good	Fair	Poor
175	150	125	100	80

Type 59 Makarov

A .380 or 9mm Makarov caliber double action semiautomatic pistol with a 3.5" barrel and 8-shot magazine. Blued with plastic grips.

Exc.	V.G.	Good	Fair	Poor
275	250	225	175	125

SKS Rifle

A 7.62x39mm caliber semiautomatic rifle with a 20.5" barrel, folding bayonet and either a 10-shot fixed magazine or 30-shot detachable magazine. Blued with a hardwood stock. Importation began in 1988.

Exc.	V.G.	Good	Fair	Poor
125	100	75	65	50

Type 84S AK

Similar to the AKS service rifle, in 5.56mm caliber with a 16" barrel and 30-shot magazine.

Type 84S- 1

As above, with an underfolding metal stock.

Type 84S-3

As above, with a composition stock.

Type 84S-5

As above, with a stock that folds to the side and without a bayonet.

Type 81S

A semiautomatic copy of the AK47.

Type 81S-1

As above, with a folding stock.

NORTH AMERICAN ARMS CORP.
Toronto, Canada

Brigadier

A .45 NAACO caliber semiautomatic pistol with a 5" barrel, 8-shot magazine and alloy frame. Weight 4.5 lbs. Produced in limited quantity between 1948 and 1951. Prospective purchasers are advised to secure a qualified appraisal prior to acquisition.

Exc.	V.G.	Good	Fair	Poor
1250	1000	800	600	500

NORTH AMERICAN ARMS
Spanish Fork, Utah

Mini-Revolver

A .22 or .22 Magnum caliber spur trigger revolver with a 1" or 2.5" barrel and 5-shot cylinder. Stainless steel with plastic or laminated rosewood grips. Introduced in 1975 and made in the following styles:

Standard Rimfire Version

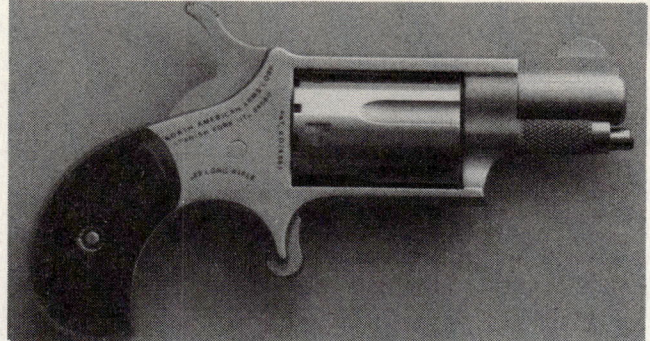

NIB	Exc.	V.G.	Fair	Poor
140	125	110	85	60

Magnum Version

NIB	Exc.	V.G.	Fair	Poor
160	145	125	100	75

2 Cylinder Magnum Convertible Version

NIB	Exc.	V.G.	Fair	Poor
185	165	150	125	100

Viper Belt Buckle Version

NIB	Exc.	V.G.	Fair	Poor
165	140	120	100	75

Standard 3 Gun Set

NIB	Exc.	V.G.	Fair	Poor
575	500	400	300	225

Deluxe 3 Gun Set

NIB	Exc.	V.G.	Fair	Poor
625	550	450	350	275

Cased .22 Magnum

NIB	Exc.	V.G.	Fair	Poor
285	250	200	150	125

Single Action Revolver

A polished stainless steel single action revolver chambered for the .45 Winchester Magnum and the .450 Magnum Express cartridge. It has a 7.5" barrel and a 5-shot cylinder. There is a transfer bar safety, and the grips are walnut. This model was discontinued in 1988.

Exc.	V.G.	Good	Fair	Poor
850	775	650	500	400

NORTH AMERICAN SAFARI EXPRESS
Liege, Belgium
SEE Francotte

A trade name used by Francotte on their double rifles imported and distributed by Armes De Chasse of Chads Ford, Pennsylvania.

NORTH & COUCH
New York, New York

Animal Trap Gun

A .28 or. 30 caliber percussion pepperbox with either a 1.75" or 2.12" barrel group and a hammer made with or without a spur. Marked "North & Couch, Middletown, Conn." or "North & Couch New York." Manufactured during the 1860s.

Disk Hammer Model

Exc.	V.G.	Good	Fair	Poor
—	—	1250	400	300

Spur Hammer Model

Exc.	V.G.	Good	Fair	Poor
—	—	1500	650	350

NORTON ARMS CO.
Mt. Clemens, Michigan
SEE Budischowsky

This firm manufactured Budischowsky Model TP-70 semiautomatic pistols prior to 1979. After that date, these arms were made by the American Arms and Amunition Company. The values for both manufacturers' products are as follows:

Exc.	V.G.	Good	Fair	Poor
350	275	200	125	100

NORWICH PISTOL CO.
Norwich, Connecticut

Established in 1875 by the New York retailer Maltby, Curtis & Company, this firm manufactured a wide variety of inexpensive spur trigger revolvers that were sold under the following trade names: America, Bulldozer, Challenge, Chieftain, Crescent, Defiance, Hartford Arms, Maltby Henley, Metropolitan Police, Nonpariel, Norwich Arms, Parole, Patriot, Pinafore, Prairie King, Protector, Spy, True Blue, U.M.C. Winfield Arms.

The company ceased operations in 1881. The value for any of its arms is approximately as follows:

Exc.	V.G.	Good	Fair	Poor
—	250	150	75	50

O

O.D.I.
Midland Park, New Jersey

Viking

A .45 caliber double action semiautomatic pistol with a 5" barrel and 7-shot magazine. Stainless steel with teak grips. Manufactured in 1981 and 1982.

NIB	Exc.	V.G.	Good	Fair	Poor
600	500	400	300	200	100

Viking Combat

As above, with a 4.24" barrel.

NIB	Exc.	V.G.	Good	Fair	Poor
600	500	400	300	200	100

O.K.
Unknown
SEE Marlin

OBREGON
Mexico City, Mexico

This is a .45 caliber semiautomatic pistol with a 5" barrel. Similar to the Colt M1911A1 but with a combination side and safety latch on the left side of the frame. The breech is locked by rotating the barrel, instead of the Browning swinging link. This unusual locking system results in a tubular front end appearance to the pistol. Originally designed for the Mexican military it was not adopted as such and only about 1,000 pistols were produced and sold commercially. The pistol is 8.5" overall and weighs about 40 ozs. The magazine holds seven cartridges. This is a rare pistol an independent appraisal is suggested proir to sale.

Exc.	V.G.	Good	Fair	Poor
4500	2000	900	750	400

O'CONNELL, DAVID
New York, New York

Pocket Pistol

A .41 caliber percussion pocket pistol with a 2.5" barrel, German silver mounts, and walnut stock. Manufactured during the 1850s.

Exc.	V.G.	Good	Fair	Poor
—	—	1500	650	250

O'DELL, STEPHEN
Natchez, Mississippi

Pocket Pistol

A .34 to .44 caliber percussion pocket pistol with a 2" to 4" barrel, German silver mounts and walnut stock. Manufactured during the 1850s. Prospective purchasers are advised to secure a qualified appraisal prior to acquisition.

Exc.	V.G.	Good	Fair	Poor
—	—	4000	2000	950

OHIO ORDNANCE INC.
Chardon, Ohio

The Model 1918A3 Self-Loading Rifle

This rifle is a semiautomatic version of the famed Browning Automatic Rifle. It is chambered for the .30-06 cartridge and has a 20-round magazine. It was introduced in this configuration in 1996.

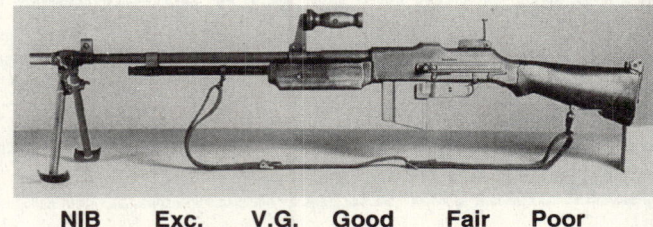

NIB	Exc.	V.G.	Good	Fair	Poor
2650	2000	—	—	—	—

OJANGUREN Y VIDOSA
Eibar, Spain

This typical Eibar company produced mediocre firearms from the early 1920s and was forced out of business during the Spanish Civil War.

Apache

A typical Eibar Browning copy that is chambered for the 6.35mm cartridge. It is of the typical low quality associated with most Spanish arms of this era. The slide is marked "Pistole Browning Automatica Cal. 6.35 Apache." The finish is blued, and the plastic grips have a head with a beret and the word "Apache" molded into them.

Exc.	V.G.	Good	Fair	Poor
175	150	125	75	50

Ojanguren

The trade name this company used to cover the line of revolvers they produced in the 1930s. They produced two in .32 caliber and two chambered for the 38 Special cartridge. They are similar in appearance and have barrel lengths of either 3" or 6". The finishes are blued, and they have plastic grips. One of the .38 caliber models—the "Legitimo Tanque"—is a reasonably well-made gun that was popular with the Spanish target shooters. These guns have little collector value and little practical value and are all valued alike.

Exc.	V.G.	Good	Fair	Poor
150	125	100	75	50

Tanque

A blowback-operated semiautomatic chambered for the 6.35mm cartridge. It has a 1.5" barrel and is actually an original design, which was rarely found on Eibar guns of this period. It has an oddly shaped slide, and the barrel is retained by means of a screw in the front of the frame. It has a 6-shot magazine, and the slide is marked "6.35 Tanque Patent." The plastic grips have a tank molded into them and the word "Tanque," as well as the letters "O&V."

Exc.	V.G.	Good	Fair	Poor
150	125	100	75	50

OLD WEST GUN CO.
Houston, Texas

An importer of reproduction firearms primarily manufactured by Aldo Uberti of Italy. In 1987 this company purchased the inventory of Allen Firearms and subsequently changed their name to Cimarron Arms.

OLYMPIC ARMS, INC.
Olympia, Washington

PISTOLS

Black Widow

A .45 caliber semiautomatic pistol with a 3.9" barrel and 6-shot magazine. Nickel-plated with ivory Micarta grips having a spider engraved on them.

Exc.	V.G.	Good	Fair	Poor
575	500	450	350	300

Enforcer

A .45 caliber semiautomatic pistol with a 3.8" barrel and 6-shot magazine. Parkerized, anodized or nickel-plated with rubber grips.

NIB	Exc.	V.G.	Good	Fair	Poor
630	575	500	425	350	300

Match Master

As above, with a 5" barrel and 7-shot magazine.

NIB	Exc.	V.G.	Good	Fair	Poor
650	600	525	450	375	300

Schuetzen Pistol Works Big Deuce

This model is made in Olympic Arms specialty shop called Schuetzen Pistol Works. Marked "Schuetzen Pistol Works" on the slide and "Safari Arms" on the frame. Introduced in 1995. This semi-automatic pistol is chambered for the .45 ACP cartridge and fitted with a 6" barrel, smooth walnut grips, and a number of other custom features. Magazine capacity is 7 rounds. Weight is approximately 40 oz. Black slide with stainless steel frame.

NIB	Exc.	V.G.	Good	Fair	Poor
950	800	700	500	—	—

Schuetzen Pistol Works Crest

Similar to the above model with the same markings. This version features a .45 ACP pistol with 4.5", 5", or 5.5" barrel Checkered walnut grips. Offered in both right and left hand configurations. Stainless steel finish. Introduced in 1993. Weight is about 39 oz. depending on barrel length.

NOTE: Left hand model will bring a small premium.

NIB	Exc.	V.G.	Good	Fair	Poor
700	600	500	—	—	—

Schuetzen Pistol Works Griffon

Similar to the above specialty models. This version is fitted with a 5" barrel and smooth walnut grips. Magazine capacity is 10 rounds. Stainless steel finish. Numerous custom features. Introduced in 1995.

NIB	Exc.	V.G.	Good	Fair	Poor
N/A	—	—	—	—	—

RIFLES

SGW Ultra Match

A match grade copy of the AR-15 with a 20" or 24" barrel and not fitted with a carrying handle. Weight is about 10 lbs.

NIB	Exc.	V.G.	Good	Fair	Poor
1000	850	750	500	400	200

Model PCR-2

Similar to the above model but fitted with a 16" match grade barrel, post front and E2 rear sight. Weight is approximately 8.2 lbs.

NIB	Exc.	V.G.	Good	Fair	Poor
950	800	600	500	400	200

Model PCR-3

Same as above model but with forged T-12 upper receiver.

NIB	Exc.	V.G.	Good	Fair	Poor
950	800	600	500	400	200

Model PCR-4

This version is fitted with a 20" steel barrel with post front sight and A-1 style rear sight. Weight is approximately 8.5 lbs.

NIB	Exc.	V.G.	Good	Fair	Poor
725	600	450	350	250	150

Model PCR-5

Similar to the above but fitted with a 16" barrel. Weight is about 7 lbs.

NIB	Exc.	V.G.	Good	Fair	Poor
700	550	400	300	200	100

Model PCR-6

This AR-15 style rifle is chambered for the 7.62x39 Russian short caliber. It is fitted with a 16" barrel with a post front sight and a A-1 style rear sight. Weight is about 7 lbs.

NIB	Exc.	V.G.	Good	Fair	Poor
700	550	400	300	200	100

Model PCR-Service Match

This .223 caliber rifle has a 20" stainless steel match barrel. It is fitted with a post front sight and a E-2 style rear sight. Weight is about 8.7 lbs.

NIB	Exc.	V.G.	Good	Fair	Poor
900	750	650	500	350	175

OMEGA
Harrisburg, Pennsylvania
Importer-Kassnar

Over/Under Shotgun

A 12, 20, 28 or .410 bore boxlock Over/Under shotgun with 26" or 28" ventilated rib barrels, single trigger and extractors. Blued with a walnut stock.

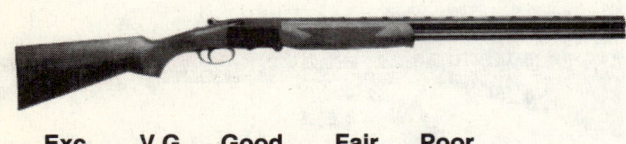

Exc.	V.G.	Good	Fair	Poor
325	275	250	200	125

Side-x-Side Double Barreled Shotgun

A 20, 28 or .410 bore boxlock double-barrel shotgun with 26" barrels, double triggers and extractors. Blued with a hardwood stock.

Exc.	V.G.	Good	Fair	Poor
250	200	150	100	75

Single Barreled Shotgun

A 12, 20 or .410 bore single barrel shotgun manufactured in a variety of barrel lengths and fitted with an extractor. Blued with a hardwood stock.

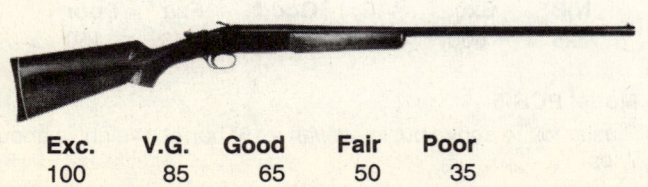

Exc.	V.G.	Good	Fair	Poor
100	85	65	50	35

OMEGA
Elbar, Spain
SEE Armero Especialistas

OMEGA
Geneseo, Illinois
Springfield Armory

Omega Pistol

A high-grade target-type pistol that is patterned after the Colt Model 1911 type pistol, with marked improvements. It is chambered for the .38 Super, 10mm, and the .45 ACP cartridges. The barrel is either 5" or 6" in length and has polygonal rifling. The barrels are furnished either ported or plain and feature a lockup system that eliminates the barrel link and bushing associated with the normal Browning design. This pistol has a dual extractor system, adjustable sights, and Pachmayr grips. It was introduced in 1987.

NIB	Exc.	V.G.	Good	Fair	Poor
850	775	675	575	400	300

OMEGA FIREARMS CO.
Flower Mound, Texas

Bolt Action Rifle

A .25-06 to .358 Norma Magnum bolt action rifle with a 22" or 24" barrel, octagonal bolt, adjustable trigger and rotary magazine. Blued with a two-piece walnut or laminated stock. Discontinued circa 1975.

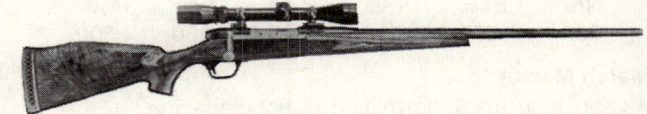

Exc.	V.G.	Good	Fair	Poor
750	650	550	400	300

OPUS SPORTING ARMS, INC.
Long Beach, California

Opus One

A .243, .270, or .30-06 caliber bolt action rifle with a 24" barrel, well figured walnut stock and an ebony pistol grip cap as well as forend tip. Built on a Model 70 Winchester action. Manufactured in 1987 and 1988.

Exc.	V.G.	Good	Fair	Poor
2000	1600	1150	700	350

Opus Two

As above, in 7mm Remington Magnum and .300 Winchester Magnum.

Exc.	V.G.	Good	Fair	Poor
2100	1700	1200	750	350

Opus Three

As above, in .375 Holland & Holland and .458 Winchester Magnum.

Exc.	V.G.	Good	Fair	Poor
2250	1800	1300	850	400

ORBEA & CIA
Eibar, Spain

Pocket Pistol

A 6.35mm semiautomatic pistol with a 2.5" barrel. Blued with plastic grips. The slide marked "Orbea y Cia Eibar Espana Pistola Automatica Cal. 6.35." Manufactured from approximately 1918 to 1936.

Exc.	V.G.	Good	Fair	Poor
175	150	125	75	50

ORTGIES, HEINRICH &CO.
Erfurt, Germany

Ortgies Pistol

A 6.35mm or 7.65mm semiautomatic pistol with a 2.75" or 3.25" barrel. Blued with walnut grips. The slide marked "Ortgies & Co. Erfurt." After 1921, these pistols were manufactured by Deutsche Werke.

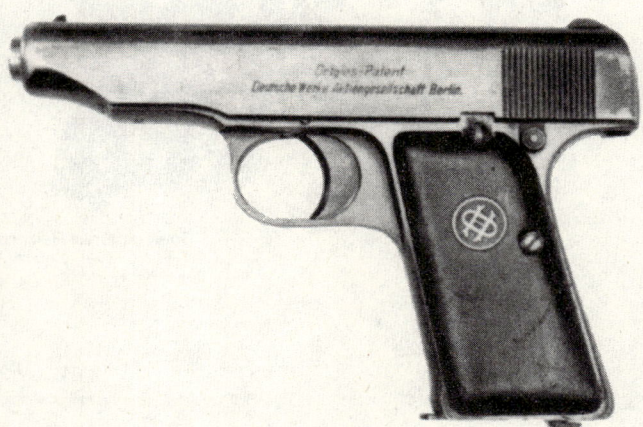

Exc.	V.G.	Good	Fair	Poor
300	225	175	125	85

ORVIS
Dallas, Texas

An importer and retailer of sporting goods including foreign manufactured firearms.

OSBORN, S.
Canton, Connecticut

Under Hammer Pistol

A .34 caliber under hammer percussion pistol with a 7" half octagonal barrel, brass mounts and a walnut grip. The barrel marked "S. Osborn/Canton, Conn."

Exc.	V.G.	Good	Fair	Poor
—	—	550	250	125

OSGOOD GUN WORKS
Norwich, Connecticut

Duplex Revolver

A .22 caliber spur trigger revolver with two super-imposed barrels, the upper most of .22 caliber and the lower a .32 caliber. The cylinder with eight .22 chambers. The hammer fitted with a moveable firing pin so that the pistol can be used either as a revolver or as a single shot with a .32 caliber barrel. Blued or nickel-plated with hard rubber grips. The barrel marked "Osgood Gun Works-Norwich Conn." and "Duplex." An unknown quantity were manufactured during the 1880s.

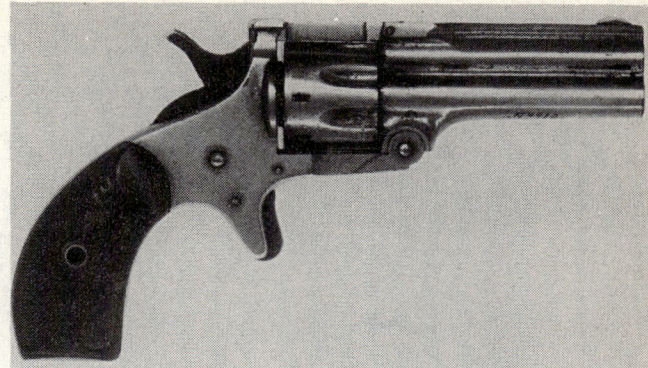

Courtesy Milwaukee Public Museum, Milwaukee, Wisconsin

Exc.	V.G.	Good	Fair	Poor
—	650	300	150	100

OVERTON, JOHN
Nashville, Tennessee

Formerly armorer at Harpers Ferry Armory. He delivered 81 rifles copying the U.S. Model 1841 but with a saber bayonet lug on the right side of the barrel. Unmarked externally but are serial numbered internally. Overall length ca. 48-3/4"; barrel length 33"; .54 caliber.

Prospective purchasers are strongly advised to secure an expert appraisal prior to acquisition.

Exc.	V.G.	Good	Fair	Poor
—	—	10000	5000	2000

OWA
Vienna, Austria
Osterreiche Werke Anstalt

OWA Pocket Pistol

A 6.35mm semiautomatic pistol with a 2" barrel. Unmarked except for "OWA" logo cast in the grips. Blued with plastic grips. Manufactured between 1920 and 1925.

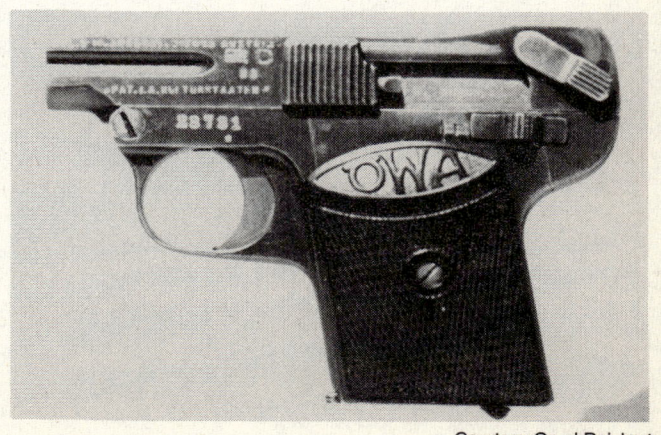

Courtesy Orvel Reichert

Courtesy Orvel Reichert

Exc.	V.G.	Good	Fair	Poor
250	200	175	100	75

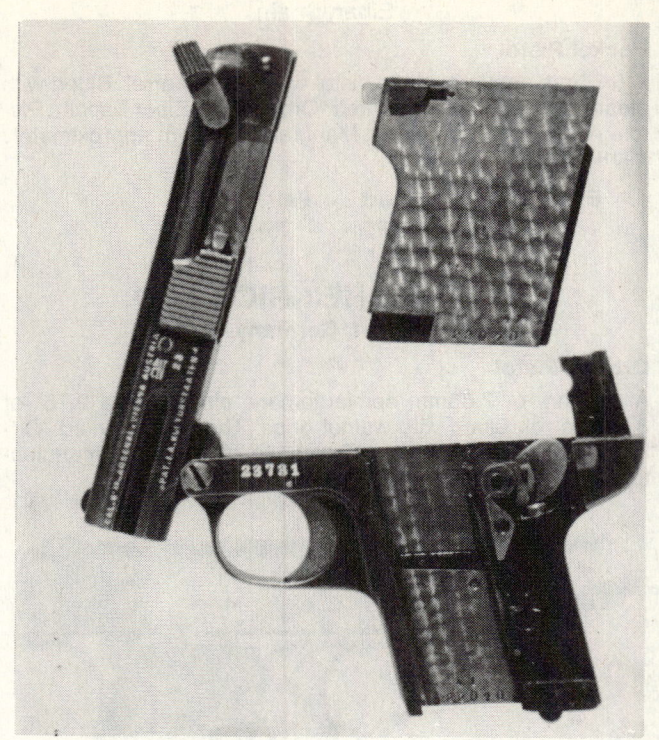

Courtesy Orvel Reichert

P

P-38
SEE German Military

P.A.F.
Pretoria, South Africa
Pretoria Small Arms Factory

P.A.F. Junior

A .22 or .25 caliber semiautomatic pistol with a 2" barrel and 6-shot magazine. Blued with plastic grips. Slide marked "Junior Verwaardig in Suid Afrika Made in South Africa". Manufactured during the 1950s.

Exc.	V.G.	Good	Fair	Poor
200	175	125	100	70

PGM PRECISION
France

Model PGM

This is a highly sophisticated semiautomatic rifle designed and built on a modular component system. Barrel change is fast and available calibers are .308 Win., .300 Savage, 7mm-08, .243, and .22-250. Match grade barrel length is 23.4". Fully adjustable trigger and butt stock with adjustable bipod. 5 round magazine is standard. Weight is approximately 13 lbs.

NIB	Exc.	V.G.	Good	Fair	Poor
8900	8000	—	—	—	—

P.S.M.G. GUN CO.
Arlington, Massachusetts

Six In One Supreme

A .22 l.r., .30 Luger, .38 Super, .38 Special, 9mm, and the .45ACP caliber semiautomatic pistol with interchangeable 3.5", 5", or 7.5" barrels, and adjustable sights. Blued or satin nickel-plated. Introduced in 1988. Conversion kits are valued at $450 per unit.

NIB	Exc.	V.G.	Good	Fair	Poor
900	800	650	500	400	250

PTK INTERNATIONAL, INC.
Atlanta, Georgia
SEE Poly-Technologies

PAGE-LEWIS ARMS CO.
Chicopee Falls, Massachusetts

Model A Target

A .22 caliber single shot lever-action rifle with a 20" barrel and open sights. Blued with a walnut stock. Manufactured from 1920 to 1926.

Exc.	V.G.	Good	Fair	Poor
275	225	175	125	100

Model B Sharpshooter

As above, with a 24" barrel and longer forend.

Exc.	V.G.	Good	Fair	Poor
275	225	175	125	100

Model C Olympic

As above, with a 24" barrel and improved sights.

Exc.	V.G.	Good	Fair	Poor
325	250	200	150	100

PALMER
Windsor, Vermont
E. G. Lamson & Co.

Palmer Bolt Action Carbine

A .50 caliber single shot bolt action carbine with a 20" round barrel, walnut half stock and full sidelock. Blued and casehardened. The receiver marked "Wm. Palmer / Patent / Dec.22, 1863" and the lock "G.Lamson & Co./ Windsor, Vt." Approximately 1,000 were made in 1865.

Exc.	V.G.	Good	Fair	Poor
—	2500	1250	650	250

PARA-ORDNANCE MFG. INC.
Scarborough, Ontario, Canada

Model P14.45

Similar in appearance to the Colt Government model this .45 ACP semiautomatic pistol features a 5" barrel, flared ejection port, combat style hammer beveled magazine well and a 13-round magazine capacity. Overall length is 8.5" and weight is 38 oz. for steel and stainless steel version and 28 oz. for alloy frame model. Finish is black except for stainless steel model.

NIB	Exc.	V.G.	Good	Fair	Poor
650	600	550	475	400	300

NOTE: Add $50 for steel frame, $45 for stainless steel, and $30 for duo-tone.

Model P16.40

This is essentially the same as the Model 14.45 except that it is chambered for the .40 S&W cartridge. The magazine capacity is 15 rounds.

NIB	Exc.	V.G.	Good	Fair	Poor
650	600	550	475	400	300

NOTE: Add $50 for steel frame, $45 for stainless steel, and $30 for duo-tone.

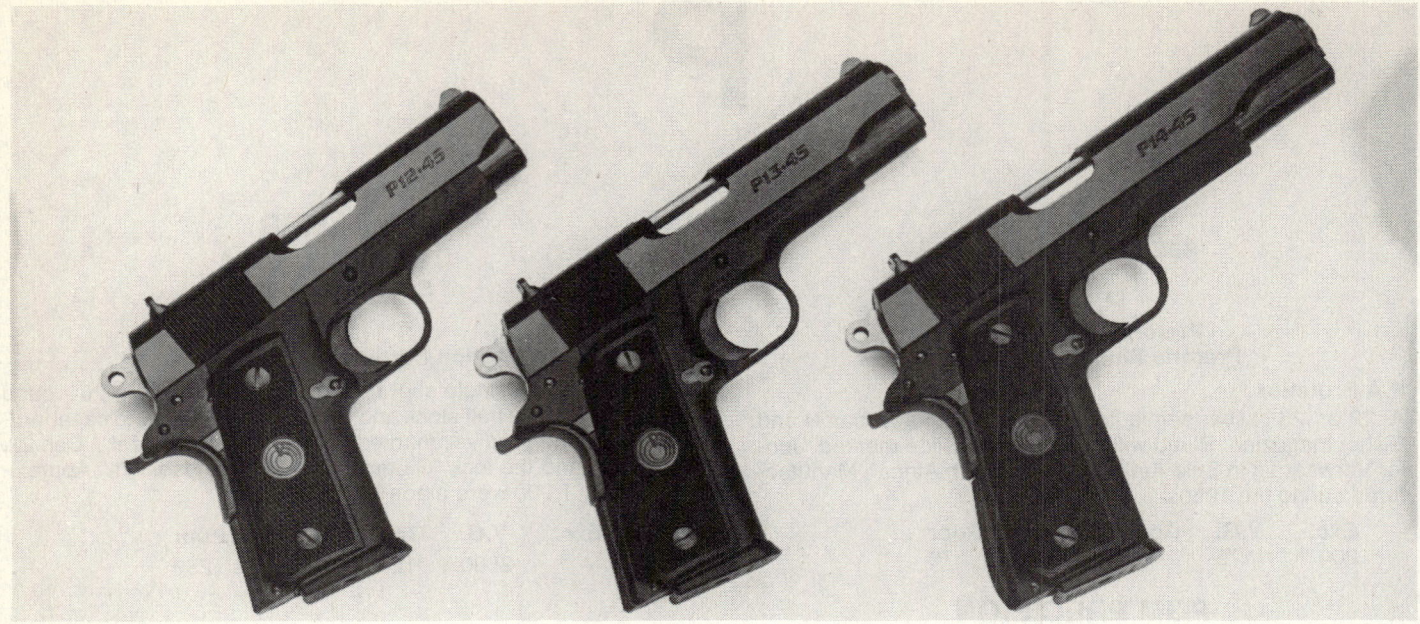

Model P13.45

Introduced in 1994 this model features a 4-1/4" barrel with a 13-round magazine. The grip is 1/4" longer than the 12.45 model. Offered in light alloy, carbon, or stainless steel. Overall length is 7-3/4" and the height is 5-1/4". Weight is about 36 oz. in steel version and 28 oz. in alloy version.

NIB	Exc.	V.G.	Good	Fair	Poor
650	600	550	475	400	300

NOTE: Add $50 for steel frame, $45 for stainless steel, and $30 for duo-tone.

Model P12.45/P12.40

Similar to the Model P14 but in a smaller package. Introduced in 1993. Has all the same features as the Model P14 but has a magazine capacity of 11 rounds. Also available in alloy, steel, or stainless steel this model weighs 24 oz. in alloy model and 33 oz. in steel models. The P12.40 is the same model but chambered for .40S&W cartridge.

NIB	Exc.	V.G.	Good	Fair	Poor
650	600	550	475	400	300

NOTE: Add $50 for steel frame, $45 for stainless steel, and $30 for duo-tone.

Model P10.45/P10.40

Introduced in 1996 this model is the smallest semi-auto .45 ACP in production. Overall length is 6.5" with height of 4.5". Magazine capacity is 10 rounds. Barrel length is 3.5". Offered in stainless steel, Duotone, or black alloy finish. Also offered chambered for .40 S&W cartridge. Weight is about 31 oz. for stainless and 24 oz. for alloy model.

NIB	Exc.	V.G.	Good	Fair	Poor
650	600	550	475	400	300

NOTE: Add $50 for steel frame, $45 for stainless steel, and $30 for duo-tone.

PARDINI
Italy
Importer-Nygord Presision Products
Prescott, Arizona

Standard Target Pistol

A .22 caliber semiautomatic pistol with a 4.7" barrel, adjustable rear sight and adjustable trigger. Blued with two sizes of walnut grips, one suitable for use by ladies. Introduced in 1986.

NIB	Exc.	V.G.	Good	Fair	Poor
950	850	700	600	500	250

Rapidfire Pistol

Similar to the above, in .22 short with an alloy bolt, 4.6" barrel and enclosed grip. Weight is about 43 oz. Introduced in 1995.

NIB	Exc.	V.G.	Good	Fair	Poor
950	850	700	600	500	250

Centerfire Pistol

Similar to the standard model, but in .32 Smith & Wesson caliber. Introduced in 1986.

NIB	Exc.	V.G.	Good	Fair	Poor
950	850	700	600	500	250

Free Pistol

A .22 caliber single shot pistol with a 9.8" barrel, adjustable sights and adjustable grip. Furnished with barrel weights. Weight is about 35 oz. Introduced in 1995.

NIB	Exc.	V.G.	Good	Fair	Poor
950	850	700	600	500	250

PARKER
Springfield, Massachusetts

4-Shot Pistol

A .33 caliber percussion pistol with a 4" half-octagonal barrel and a 4-shot sliding chamber. Marked "Albert Parker/Patent Secured/Springfield, Mass." Original finish unknown with walnut grips. Prospective purchasers are advised to secure a qualified appraisal prior to acquisition.

Exc.	V.G.	Good	Fair	Poor
—	—	12000	6000	2000

PARKER BROS.
Meriden, Connecticut

Perhaps the best known of all American shotgun manufacturers. Established by Charles Parker shortly after the Civil War, this company has produced a wide variety of shotguns in a number of different styles over the years. In the early 1930s the company was purchased by Remington Arms Company.

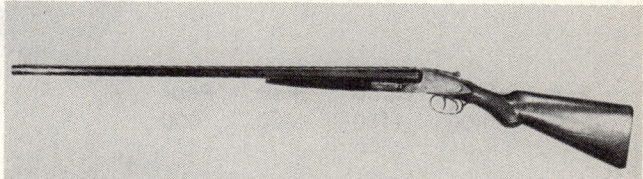

NOTE: Parker shotguns are one of the most collectible of American made shotguns. Both the beginning and the veteran collector should be aware that originality and condition are absolutely critical in establishing such high values for these shotguns. There are numerous upgraded and refinished guns that are represented as original. Beware that such misrepresentations exist because refinished and upgraded Parker guns should sell for as much as 50 to 75 percent below the price of an original gun. Extreme caution should be exercised and we would recommend that an expert be consulted. Even the most advanced collectors may benefit from such consultations. Also, the prices indicated for guns in excellent condition may fluctuate drastically, especially in high grade or small bore guns, due to their extreme rarity. In addition, uncommon extras such as single triggers, ventilated ribs, beavertail forearms, straight grip stocks, and skeleton steel buttplates may add substantial value to an individual gun.

NOTE: Letters of authenticity may be available in the near future. If so, these letters will be a must in order for any Parker gun to attain maximum value.

Trojan

A 12, 16, or 20 gauge boxlock double-barrel shotgun manufactured in a variety of barrel lengths with either single or double triggers and extractors. Blued, casehardened receiver with a walnut stock. Approximately 48,000 were made.
20 Gauge-Add 40%.

Exc.	V.G.	Good	Fair	Poor
2200	1200	900	700	500

VH

A 12, 16, 20, 28 or .410 bore boxlock double-barrel shotgun manufactured in a variety of barrel lengths with double triggers and extractors. Blued, casehardened receiver with a walnut stock. Approximately 60,000 were made.

NOTE: Also made with automatic ejectors and known as the Model VHE. The E suffix was used on all models to denote automatic ejectors.
VHE-Add 40%.
20 Gauge-Add 45%.
28 Gauge-Add 120%.
.410-Add 300%.

Exc.	V.G.	Good	Fair	Poor
2600	1400	1100	800	600

PH

Similar to the above, but not made in .410 bore. Approximately 8,500 were made.
PHE-Add 40%.
20 Gauge-Add 45%.
28 Gauge-Add 120%.

Exc.	V.G.	Good	Fair	Poor
2800	2000	1500	900	700

GH

Similar to the above, with a modest amount of engraving and the barrels marked "Parker Special Steel". Approximately 28,500 were made.
GHE-Add 35%.
16 Gauge-Add 15%.
20 Gauge-Add 40%.
28 Gauge-Add 100%.
.410-Add 300%.

Exc.	V.G.	Good	Fair	Poor
3200	2300	1800	1300	800

DH

As above, but more finely finished. Approximately 48,000 were made.
DHE-Add 35%.
16 Gauge-Add 10%.
20 Gauge-Add 40%.
28 Gauge-Add 125%.
.410-Add 400%.

Exc.	V.G.	Good	Fair	Poor
5000	4200	3000	1500	1000

CH

As above, with Acme steel barrels. Approximately 5,000 were made.
CHE-Add 35%.
16 Gauge-Add 10%.
20 Gauge-Add 40%.
28 Gauge-Add 200%.
.410-Add 700%.

Exc.	V.G.	Good	Fair	Poor
6000	4800	3500	2200	1800

BH

As above, but offered with four different styles of engraved decoration. Approximately 13,000 were made. Prospective purchasers are advised to secure a qualified appraisal prior to acquisition.
BHE-Add 35%.
16 Gauge-Add 10%.
20 Gauge-Add 40%.
28 Gauge-Add 200%.
.410-Add 800%.

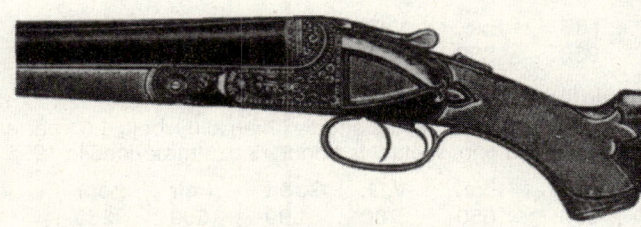

Exc.	V.G.	Good	Fair	Poor
8000	6500	4500	2800	2000

> **A BH Grade Parker with Damascus barrels was sold at auction for $18,000. The frame is #2 with 30" barrels. Cased in orginal Parker case circa 1895. Condition was excellent to mint. J.C. Devine, Inc., March 1996.**

AH

As above, but highly engraved with finely figured walnut stocks. Approximately 5,500 were made. Prospective purchasers are advised to secure a qualified appraisal prior to acquisition.
AHE-Add 30%.
16 Gauge-Add 15%.
20 Gauge-Add 50%.
28 Gauge-Add 200%.
.410-Add 500%.

Exc.	V.G.	Good	Fair	Poor
14000	10000	7000	6000	3000

AAH

As above, with either Whitworth or Peerless barrels and not made in .410 bore. The engraving is more extensive and of the first quality. Approximately 340 were made. Prospective purchasers are advised to secure a qualified appraisal prior to acquisition.

AAHE-Add 30%.
16 Gauge-Add 25%.
20 Gauge-Add 50%.
28 Gauge-Add 250%.

Exc.	V.G.	Good	Fair	Poor
25000	18000	13000	7000	5000

A cased Parker A-1 Special 20 gauge with two sets of barrels was sold at auction for $57,500. Frame size was "o". Skeleton butt. Condition was very good.
Butterfield & Butterfield, April 1997.

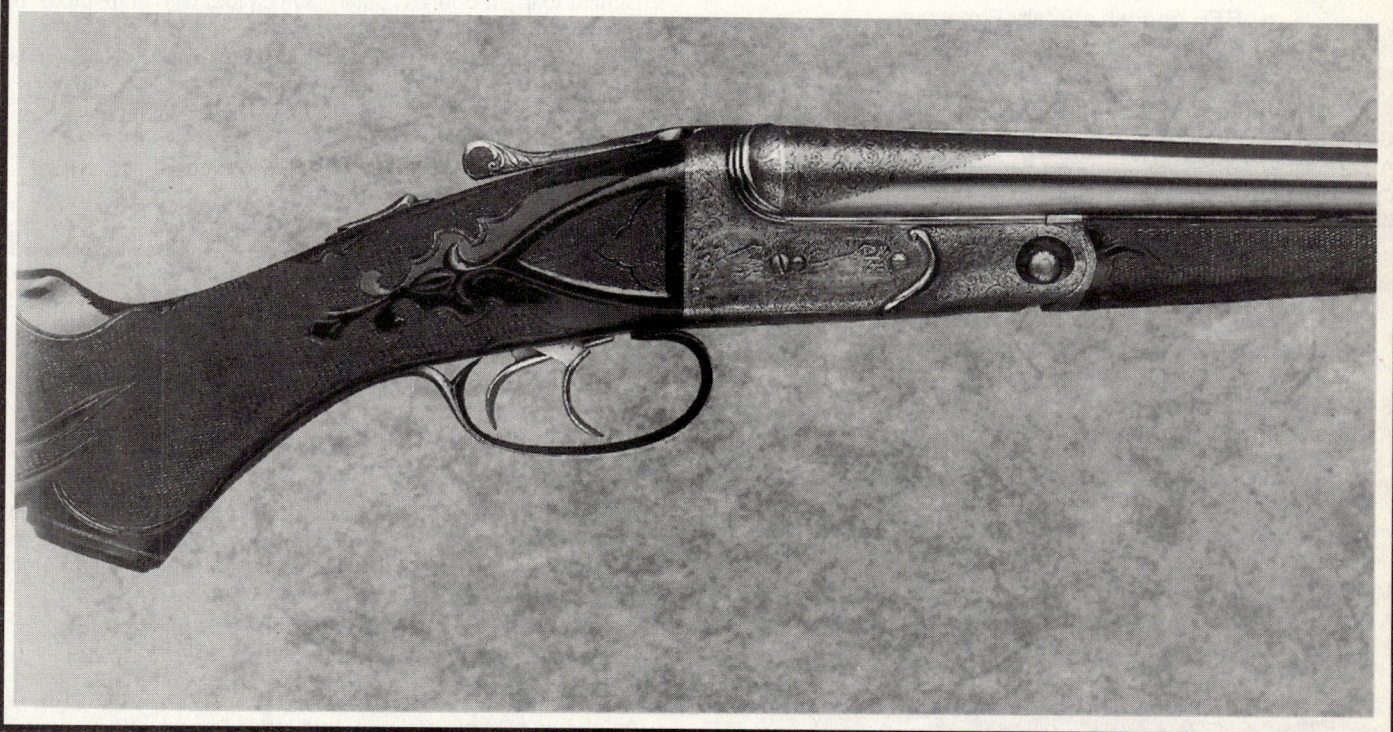

A-1 Special

As above, but made strictly on special order and not manufactured in .410 bore. Approximately 320 were made. Prospective purchasers are advised to secure a qualified appraisal prior to acquisition.
16 Gauge-Add 25%.
20 Gauge-Add 50%.
28 Gauge-Add 200%.

Exc.	V.G.	Good	Fair	Poor
50000	40000	33000	20000	13000

Single Barrel Trap

A 12 gauge single shot shotgun with a 30", 32", or 34" barrel, automatic ejector and walnut stock. Produced in a variety of grades as follows. Prospective purchasers are advised to secure a qualified appraisal prior to acquisition.

S.C. Grade

Exc.	V.G.	Good	Fair	Poor
3500	2000	1500	1000	700

S.B. Grade

Exc.	V.G.	Good	Fair	Poor
4000	3000	2500	2000	1300

S.A. Grade

Exc.	V.G.	Good	Fair	Poor
5500	4200	3000	2000	1300

S.A.A. Grade

Exc.	V.G.	Good	Fair	Poor
9000	7000	4000	2000	1300

S.A-1 Special Grade

Exc.	V.G.	Good	Fair	Poor
10000	7500	5000	3200	1800

Under Lifter Hammer Gun

A side hammer double barrel shotgun manufactured in a variety of gauges with the barrel release located in front of the triggerguards. Damascus barrels, casehardened locks, blued furniture with walnut stocks. Manufactured during the 1870s and later.

Exc.	V.G.	Good	Fair	Poor
3000	2200	1000	700	500

PARKER FIELD & SONS
SEE English Military Firearms

PARKER FIELD & SONS
London, England

Gas Seal Revolver

A .42 caliber percussion revolver with a 6" barrel and 6-shot cylinder. Blued, casehardened with walnut grips. Manufactured during the 1860s.

Exc.	V.G.	Good	Fair	Poor
—	—	1750	850	450

PARKER HALE LTD.
Birmingham, England

S&W Victory Conversion

A .22 caliber double action revolver with a 4" barrel and 6-shot cylinder. Blued with walnut grips. An alteration of the Smith & Wesson Victor model.

Exc.	V.G.	Good	Fair	Poor
250	200	150	100	75

Model 1200

A .22-250 to .300 Winchester Magnum bolt action rifle with a 24" barrel and open sights. Blued, with walnut stock.

NIB	Exc.	V.G.	Good	Fair	Poor
700	600	450	400	350	300

Model 1100 Lightweight

As above, with a 22" barrel and 4-shot magazine. Introduced in 1985.

NIB	Exc.	V.G.	Good	Fair	Poor
600	500	400	350	300	250

Model 81 Classic

A .22-250 to 7mm Remington Magnum bolt action rifle with a 24" barrel and open sights. Blued with a walnut stock. Introduced in 1985.

NIB	Exc.	V.G.	Good	Fair	Poor
875	750	600	500	400	350

Model 81 African

As above, but in .375 Holland & Holland caliber. Introduced in 1986.

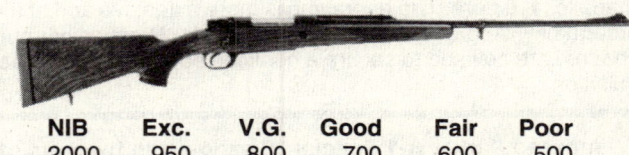

NIB	Exc.	V.G.	Good	Fair	Poor
2000	950	800	700	600	500

Model 84 Target

Similar to the Model 81, but in .308 caliber with adjustable rear sights and an adjustable cheekpiece.

NIB	Exc.	V.G.	Good	Fair	Poor
1300	1000	900	750	650	550

Model 85 Sniper

As above, with a telescope and bipod.

Exc.	V.G.	Good	Fair	Poor
2000	1550	1050	800	200

Model 640E Shotgun

A 12, 16, or 20 gauge boxlock double-barrel shotgun manufactured in a variety of barrel lengths with double triggers and extractors. Blued, French casehardened with a walnut stock. Introduced in 1986.

NIB	Exc.	V.G.	Good	Fair	Poor
575	500	450	400	300	225

Model 640A

As above, with a pistol grip, beavertail forend, and single trigger. Introduced in 1986.

NIB	Exc.	V.G.	Good	Fair	Poor
675	600	550	500	400	325

Model 645E

As above, but more finely finished and engraved.

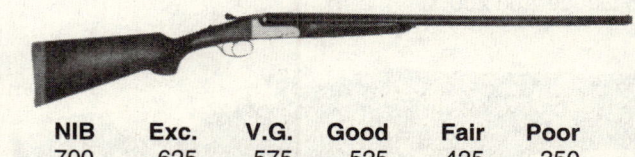

NIB	Exc.	V.G.	Good	Fair	Poor
700	625	575	525	425	350

Model 670E

A sidelock double-barrel shotgun made on special order. Introduced in 1986.

NIB	Exc.	V.G.	Good	Fair	Poor
3000	2750	2250	1750	1250	950

Model 680E-XXV

As above, with casehardened lockplates and 25" barrels.

NIB	Exc.	V.G.	Good	Fair	Poor
3000	2750	2250	1750	1250	950

PARKER REPRODUCTIONS
Japan
Importer - Regent Chemical & Research
Middlesex, New Jersey

This company had exact reproductions of Parker D, DHE, B and A-1 Special shotguns made in Japan. They are of the finest quality and workmanship. The styles of engraving and features of these shotguns correspond exactly to the original Parker Arms.

D-Grade

This side-by-side shotgun is offered in 12 gauge, 20 gauge, and 28 gauge. Barrel lengths are 26" or 28" with sold matte rib. Stocks are select walnut with choice of pistol or straight grip. Choice splinter or beavertail forearms are offered. Single or double triggers are available as well. The receiver is case-colored and scroll engraved with gamescenes to match the original Parker DHE grade. Weight of 12 gauge is 6.75 lbs., 20 gauge is 6.5 lbs., and 28 gauge weighs 5.3 lbs.

12 or 20 Gauge

NIB	Exc.	V.G.	Good	Fair	Poor
2250	1750	1250	850	600	400

16/20 Combination

Introduced in 1993 and limited to 500 sets. Offered with 28" barrels only this set features a 16 gauge barrel on a 20 gauge frame. Weighs 6.25 lbs.

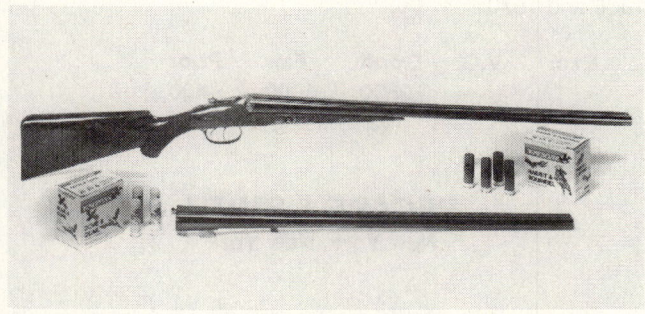

NIB	Exc.	V.G.	Good	Fair	Poor
4500	4200	3500	2500	1250	650

28 Gauge

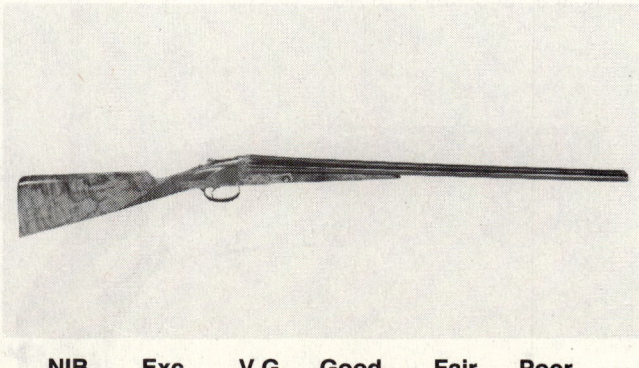

NIB	Exc.	V.G.	Good	Fair	Poor
2250	1750	1250	850	600	400

28 Gauge/.410 Bore Combination

NIB	Exc.	V.G.	Good	Fair	Poor
4750	4250	3250	1950	1000	550

NOTE: Add $990 for an additional barrel and $170 for beavertail forearm. For the D Grade three barrels sets are offered in 16/20/20 combinations for an additional $2300.

DHE Grade Steel Shot Special

Offered in 12 gauge only with 28" barrels. Fitted with 3" chambers and special chrome lined barrels. Weighs 7 lbs.

NIB	Exc.	V.G.	Good	Fair	Poor
3500	2750	2000	1200	700	400

B-Grade Limited Edition

This model features engraving similar to the original Parker BHE Grade. Fancy walnut stocks with fine line checkering was standard. It was offered in 12 gauge, 20 gauge, and 28 gauge. A 28 gauge/.410 bore combination was also offered. Only 100 shotguns in this grade were produced in 1989.

NIB	Exc.	V.G.	Good	Fair	Poor
4000	3650	2900	1750	900	450

28 Gauge/.410 Bore Combination

NIB	Exc.	V.G.	Good	Fair	Poor
5000	4500	3500	2500	1500	750

A-1 Special

Introduced in 1988 this grade fine scroll engraving and presentation French walnut with custom checkering pattern. The stock is hand carved with fleur-de-lis and features 32 lines to the inch checkering. The grip cap is rosewood and gold or gold initial plate on straight grip guns. Gold wire is used on the breech end on the barrels. Serial numbers are in gold relief as is the word "SAFE" and "L" and "R" on models with selective single trigger. Barrels flats and frame water table is jeweled. This grade is offered in 12, 20, and 28 gauge with a few early guns sold with 28 gauge/.410 bore combinations. Furnished with English style oak and leather case with canvas and leather cover, engraved snap caps, and engraved oil bottle.

12 or 20 Gauge

NIB	Exc.	V.G.	Good	Fair	Poor
9500	8000	5000	4000	2500	1000

28 Gauge

NIB	Exc.	V.G.	Good	Fair	Poor
10500	8500	6000	5000	3000	1000

A-1 Special Custom Engraved

This model is a custom hand engraved A-1 Special to each individual customer's specifications. Only a limited number of these shotguns will be built. Initial price in 1989 was $10,500. It is strongly recommended that the prospective purchaser acquire an appraisal prior to the sale due to the unique features of each gun.

PEABODY
Providence, Rhode Island
Providence Tool Company

Peabody Rifle and Carbine

A .43 Spanish, .443, .45 Peabody, .45-70, .50 or .50-70 caliber single shot rifle with a 33" or 20" (carbine) barrel and either a full length or half stock. The receiver marked "Peabody's Patent July 22, 1862 / Mann'f'd by Providence Tool Co. Prov. R.I." Blued, with a walnut stock. Produced in large quantities during the 1860s and 1870s.

Courtesy Milwaukee Public Museum, Milwaukee, Wisconsin

Exc.	V.G.	Good	Fair	Poor
—	750	350	200	100

Sporting Rifle

As above, in a sporting configuration with either 26" or 28" barrels. The frame marked, "Peabody's Patent, July 22, 1862 / Man'f'd by Providence Tool Co., Prov. R.I." Blued, casehardened with a walnut stock. Manufactured from approximately 1866 to 1875.

Exc.	V.G.	Good	Fair	Poor
—	2500	1000	500	200

PEABODY-MARTINI SPORTING RIFLES

Creedmoor

A .40-90 or .44-100 caliber Martini-action single shot rifle with a 32" round/octagonal barrel, butt-mounted vernier rear sight, combination wind gauge and spirit level front sight. The receiver marked, "Peabody & Martini Patents" and the barrel "Manufactured by the Providence Tool Co. Providence R.I. U.S.A." Blued, casehardened with a walnut stock.

Courtesy Milwaukee Public Museum, Milwaukee, Wisconsin

Exc.	V.G.	Good	Fair	Poor
—	5750	3000	1100	550

Creedmoor Mid-Range

Similar to the above, but in .40-70 or .40-90 caliber with a 28" round/octagonal barrel, vernier tang sight and wind gauge front sight. Blued, casehardened with a walnut stock.

Exc.	V.G.	Good	Fair	Poor
—	4000	2000	850	400

What Cheer

The Creedmoor without a pistol grip.

Exc.	V.G.	Good	Fair	Poor
—	4500	2500	1100	550

What Cheer Mid-Range

The Mid-Range Creedmoor without a pistol grip.

Exc.	V.G.	Good	Fair	Poor
—	3500	1750	750	300

Kill Deer

A .45-70 caliber single shot Martini-action rifle with 28" or 30" round/octagonal barrels, adjustable tang rear sight and globe front sights. Blued, casehardened with a walnut stock.

Exc.	V.G.	Good	Fair	Poor
—	5500	3500	950	500

PEAVY, A. J.
South Montville, Maine

Knife-Pistol

A .22 caliber single shot knife pistol constructed of steel and brass with a folding trigger. The side plates marked "A.J. Peavy Pat. Sept. 5, '65 & Mar. 27, '66." Produced between 1866 and 1870.

Exc.	V.G.	Good	Fair	Poor
—	—	2500	1000	400

PECARE & SMITH
New York, New York

Pepperbox

A .28 or .31 caliber 5-shot percussion pepperbox with a folding trigger and 4" barrel group. The barrel group enclosed within an iron casing. Blued, silver-plated frame with walnut grips. The barrel casing marked "Pecare & Smith." Manufactured during the 1840s early 1850s.

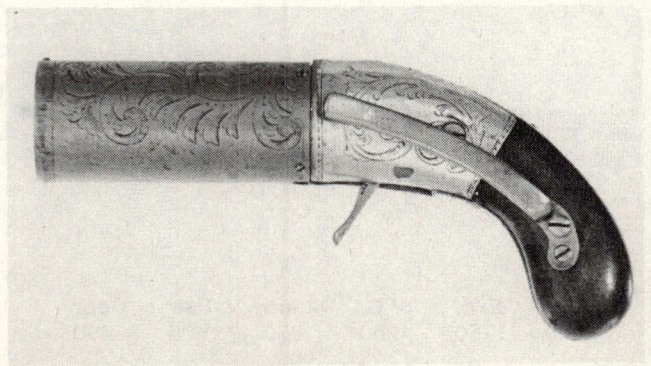

Exc.	V.G.	Good	Fair	Poor
—	—	1500	750	350

PEDERSEN CUSTOM GUNS
North Haven, Connecticut

A division of the O.F. Mossberg Company operated between 1973 and 1975.

Model 4000 Shotgun

The Mossberg Model 500 slide action shotgun in 12, 20 or .410 bore with 26", 28", or 30" ventilated rib barrels. Blued, engraved with a walnut stock. Manufactured in 1975.

Exc.	V.G.	Good	Fair	Poor
450	375	300	250	

Model 4500

As above, but with a reduced amount of engraving.

Exc.	V.G.	Good	Fair	Poor
400	350	275	225	175

Model 1500

A 12 gauge Magnum Over/Under shotgun with 26", 28", or 30" ventilated rib barrels, single selective trigger and automatic ejectors. Blued with a walnut stock. Manufactured between 1973 and 1975.

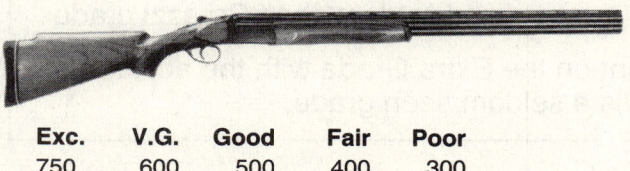

Exc.	V.G.	Good	Fair	Poor
750	600	500	400	300

Model 1000

As above, but manufactured in two grades of decoration. Manufactured between 1973 and 1975.

Grade I

Exc.	V.G.	Good	Fair	Poor
2250	2000	1750	1450	1300

Grade II

Exc.	V.G.	Good	Fair	Poor
1850	1500	1350	1150	950

Model 200A 12 or 20 gauge boxlock double-barrel shotgun with 26", 28", or 30" barrels, single selective trigger and automatic ejectors. Produced in two grades of decoration. Manufactured in 1973 and 1974.

Grade I

Exc.	V.G.	Good	Fair	Poor
2500	2000	1750	1250	1000

Grade II

Exc.	V.G.	Good	Fair	Poor
2250	1850	1500	1000	800

Model 2500

A 12 or 20 gauge boxlock double-barrel shotgun with 26" or 28" barrels, double triggers and automatic ejectors. Blued with a walnut stock.

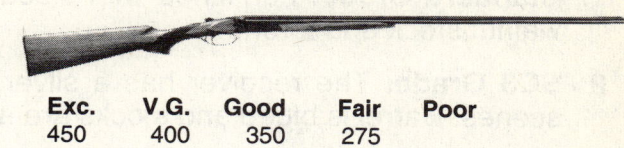

Exc.	V.G.	Good	Fair	Poor
450	400	350	275	

Model 3000

A Mossberg Model 810 bolt action rifle manufactured in .270 to .338 Winchester Magnum caliber with a 22" or 24" barrel with open sights. Produced in three grades as follows:

Grade III -Plain

Exc.	V.G.	Good	Fair	Poor
550	475	400	350	300

Grade II

Exc.	V.G.	Good	Fair	Poor
650	575	500	450	400

Grade I

Exc.	V.G.	Good	Fair	Poor
1000	800	650	550	475

Model 4700

The Mossberg Model 472 in .30-30 or .35 Remington caliber with a 24" barrel and 5-shot tubular magazine. Blued with a walnut stock.

Exc.	V.G.	Good	Fair	Poor
250	200	150	125	100

PERAZZI
Brescia, Italy
Importer - Perazzi USA, Inc.
Monrovia, California

This company was founded in 1965. During the 1970s Ithaca and Winchester imported and sold Perazzi shotguns. Perazzi has now taken over its own importation and distribution in the United States with the creation of Perazzi USA, Inc. Many shooters consider the Perazzi to be the finest currently produced shotgun in the world.

Perazzi has an extensive variety of models to choose from. In addition, each model may be available in different grades. These grades are based on the type of finish, engraving, and wood quality. The vast majority of Perazzi shotguns that are sold in this country are Standard Grade guns. According to Perazzi USA, these Standard Grade guns account for approximately 98 percent of North American sales. Therefore, it is unlikely that the shooter or collector will encounter high grade Perazzi guns. It should be pointed out that in some models no Extra Grade or Extra Gold Grade shotguns have ever been sold in the United States.

For the benefit of the reader an approximate description of each grade follows. It is a general description because the Perazzi customer may order practically any combination of finishes or engraving patterns he or she desires. Use this list as a general guide.

PERAZZI GRADES

1. **Standard Grade:** Furnished with blued receiver and barrels with hand-checkered select walnut stock and forend.

2. **SC3 Grade:** The receiver has a silver finish with scroll engraving and choice of game scenes. Barrel is blued and stocks are a higher grade of walnut.

3. **SCO Grade:** Silver receiver with choice of Continental or English scroll with choice of game scenes. Barrels are blued and fancy walnut stocks with fine line checkering are used.

4. **Gold Grade:** Customer has a choice of several different game scenes with gold inlays. Blued barrels with fancy walnut stock. Custom checkering.

5. **SCO Grade W/Sideplates:** Similar to the SCO Grade but with more coverage available due to addition of sideplates.

6. **Gold Grade W/Sideplates:** Similar to Gold Grade but with more coverage on sideplates.

7. **Extra Grade:** This is Perazzi's finest grade. The customer has a choice of almost any pattern he desires done in a fine bank note engraving style. Only the finest walnut is used on this grade with very fine line checkering. This is a rare and seldom seen Perazzi grade.

8. **Extra Gold Grade:** Similar to all of the refinement on the Extra Grade with the addition of the birds and animals are gold inlaid. Again, this is a seldom seen grade.

SC3 GRADE Engraving Patterns

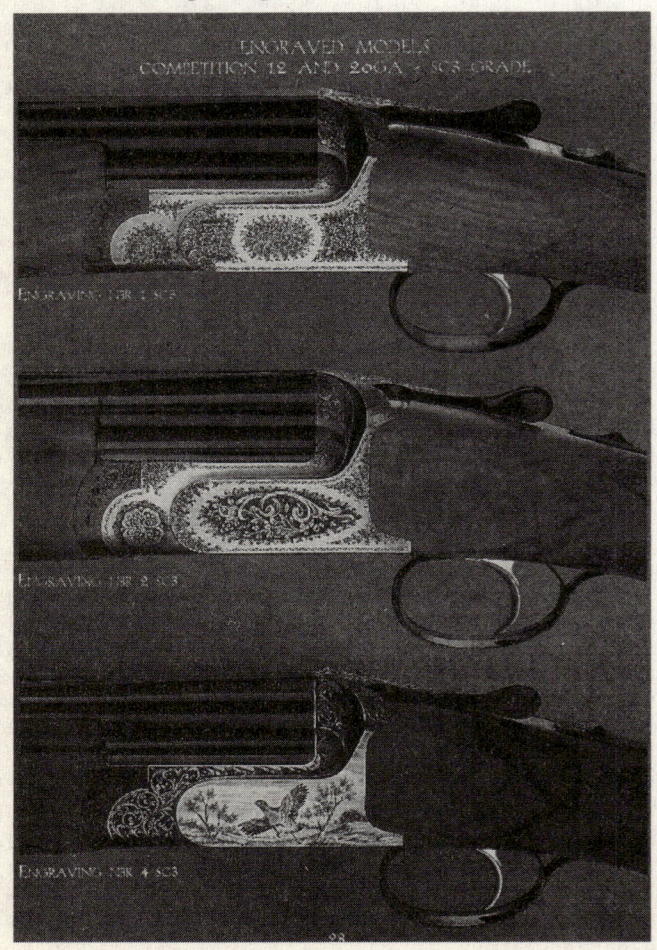

SCO GRADE Engraving Patterns

SCO GOLD GRADE Engraving Patterns

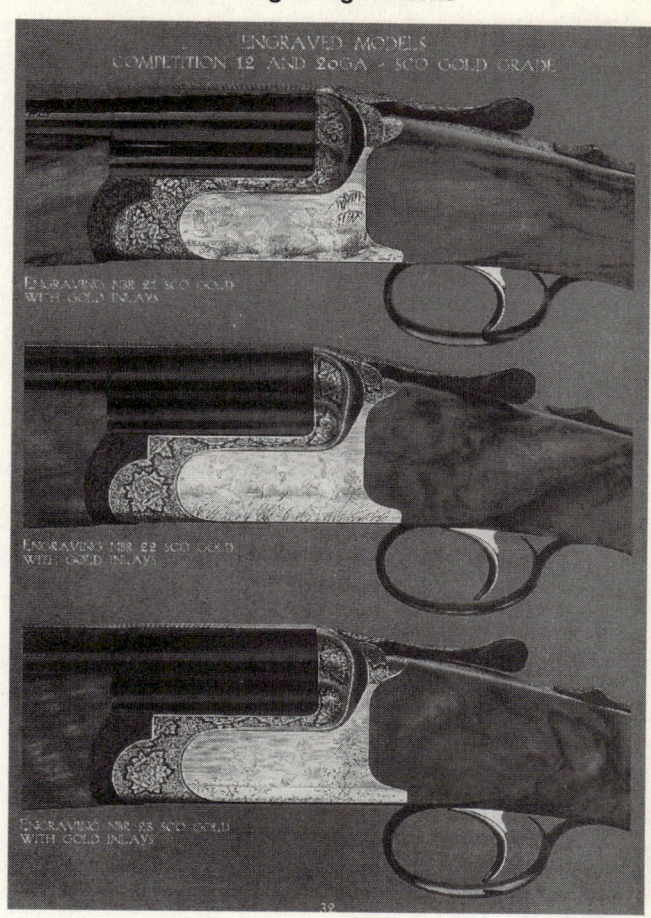

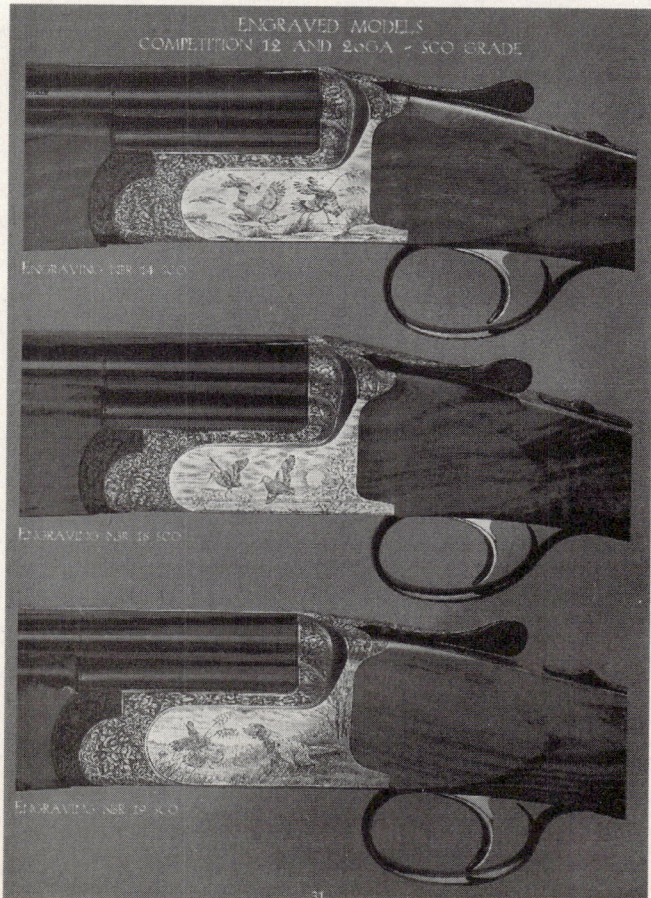

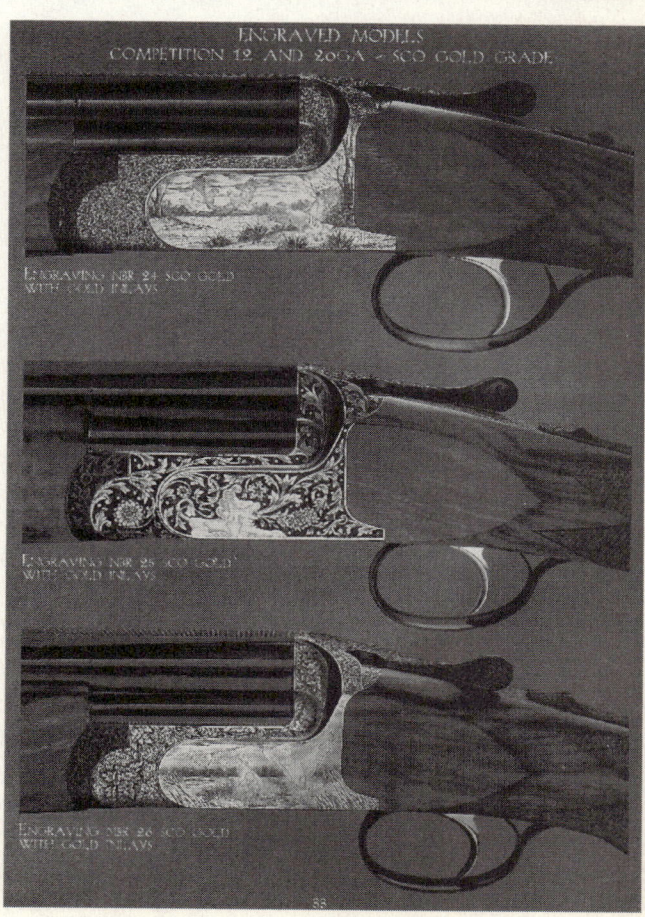

SCO GRADE With SIDEPLATES

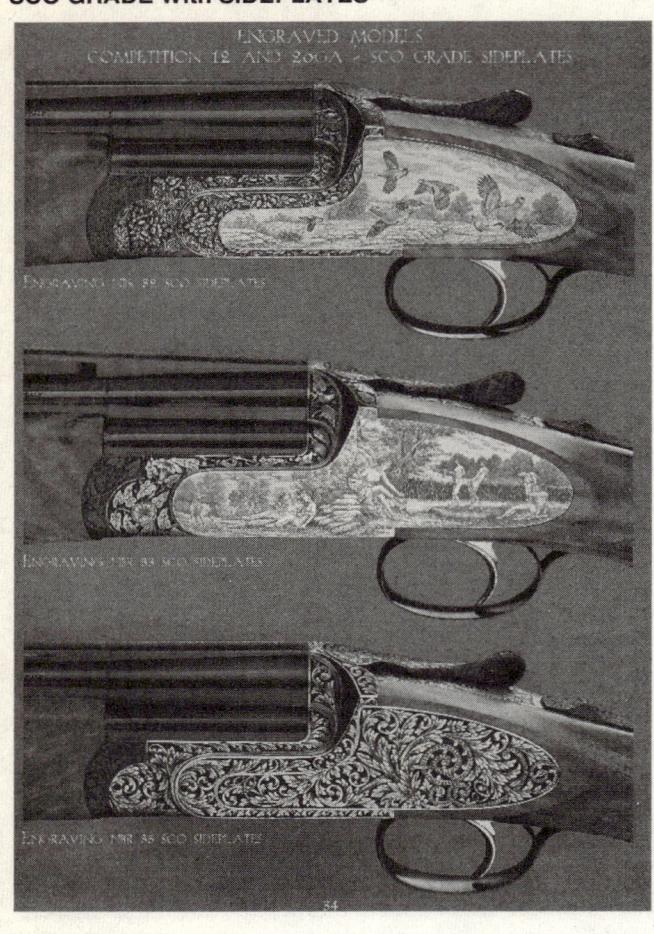

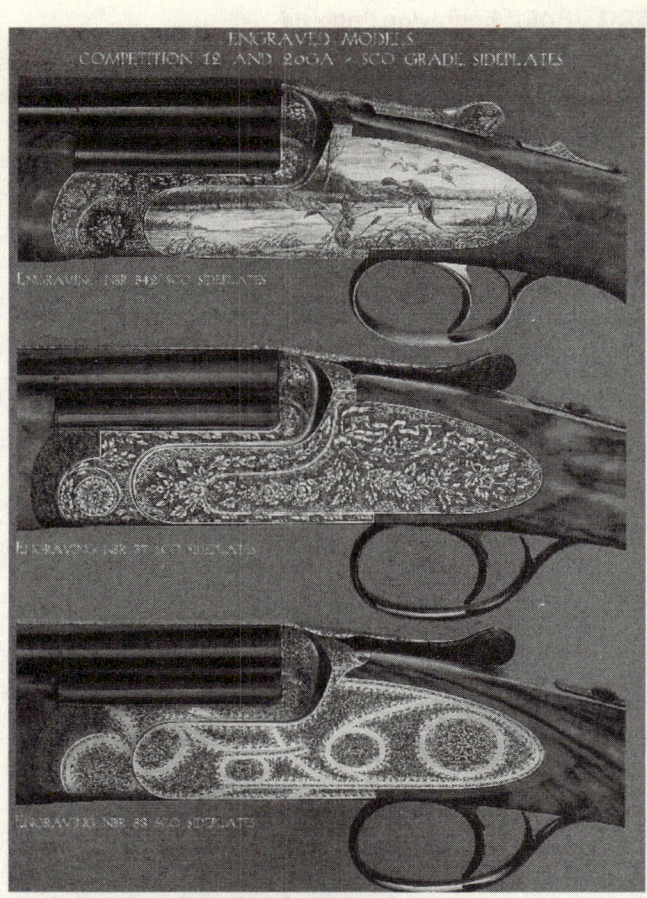

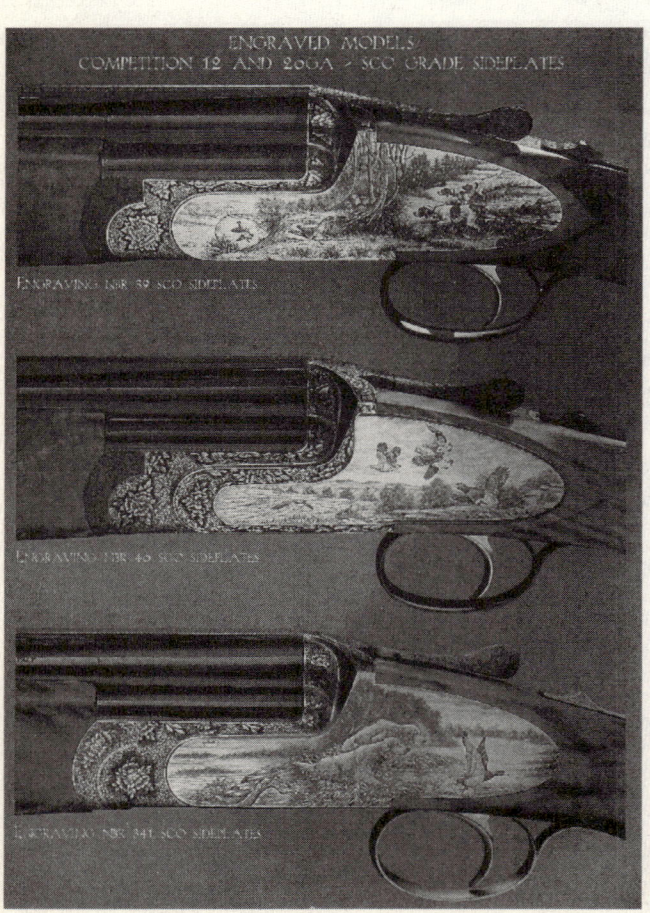

SCO GOLD GRADE With SIDEPLATES

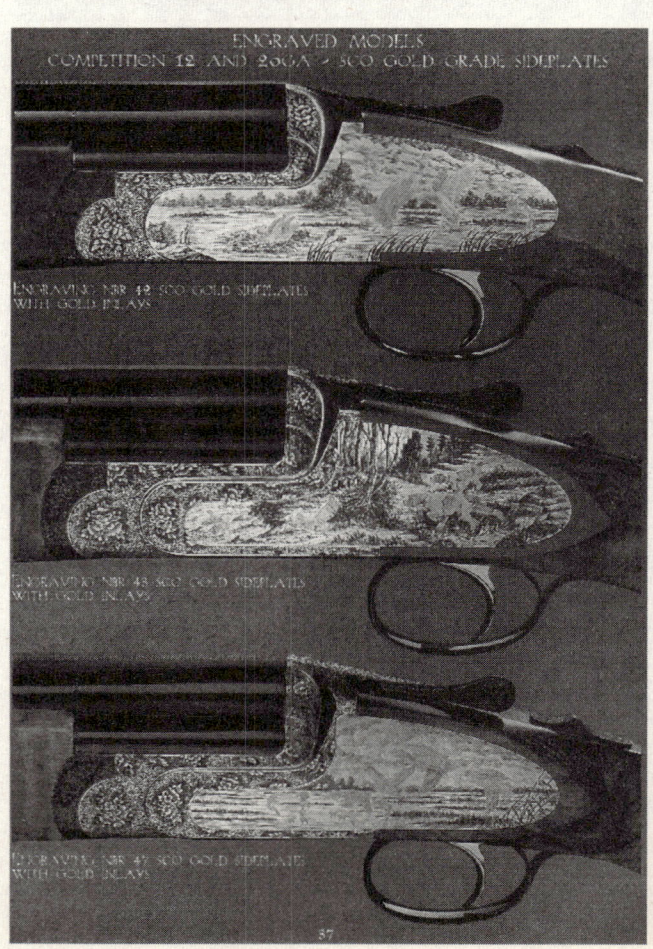

EXTRA GRADE

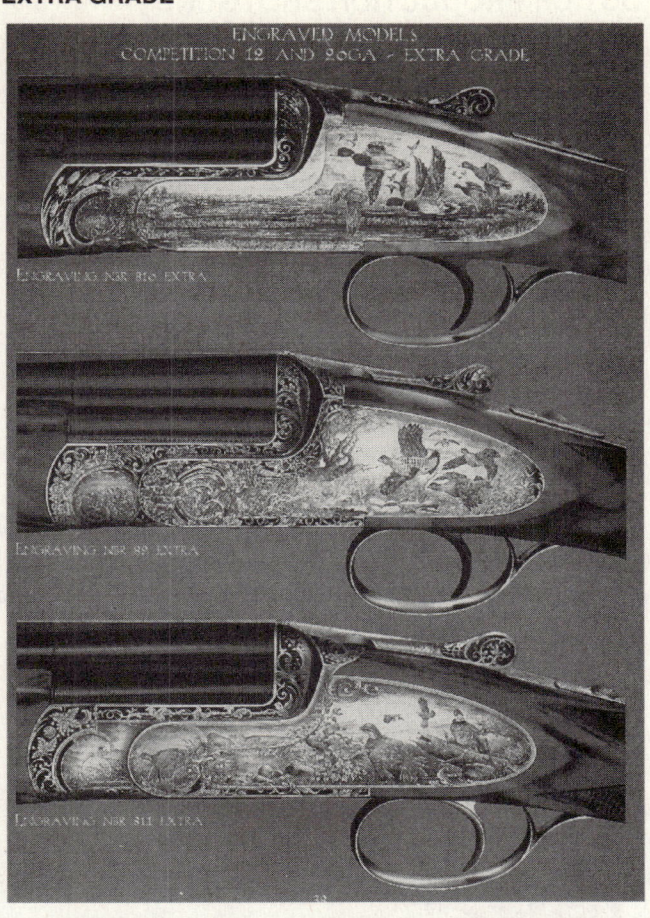

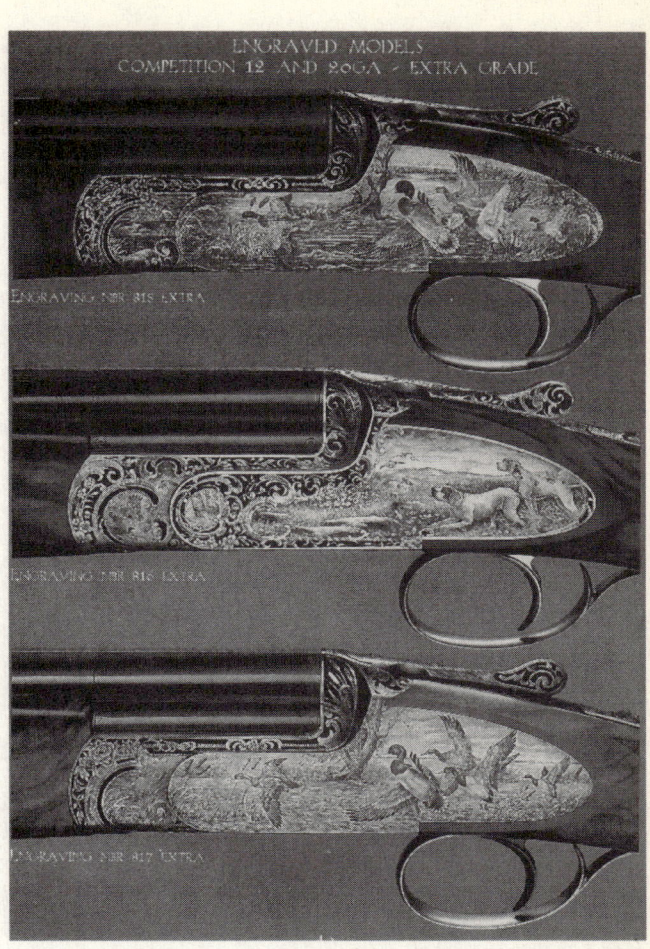

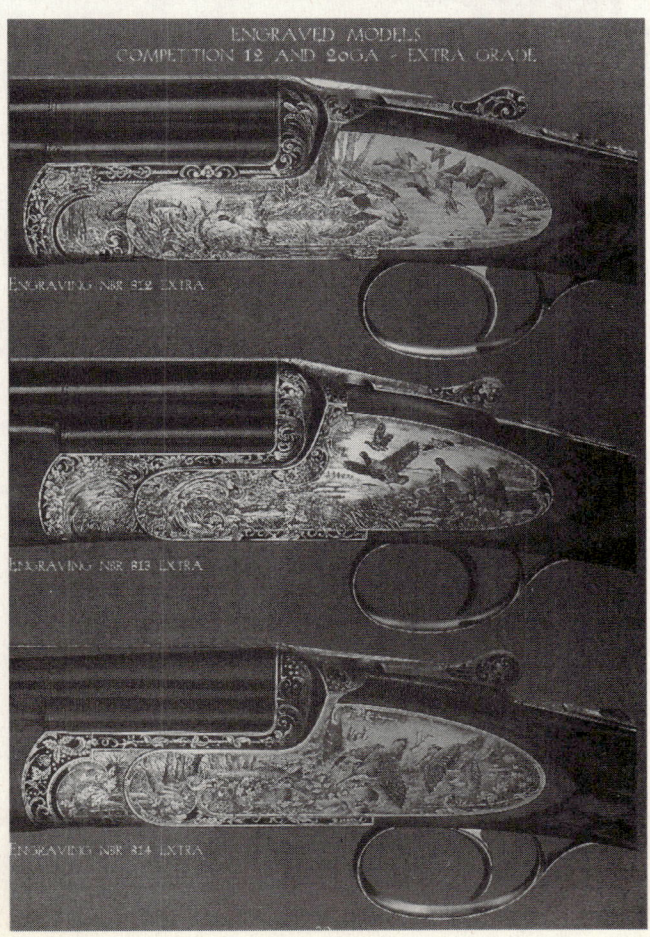

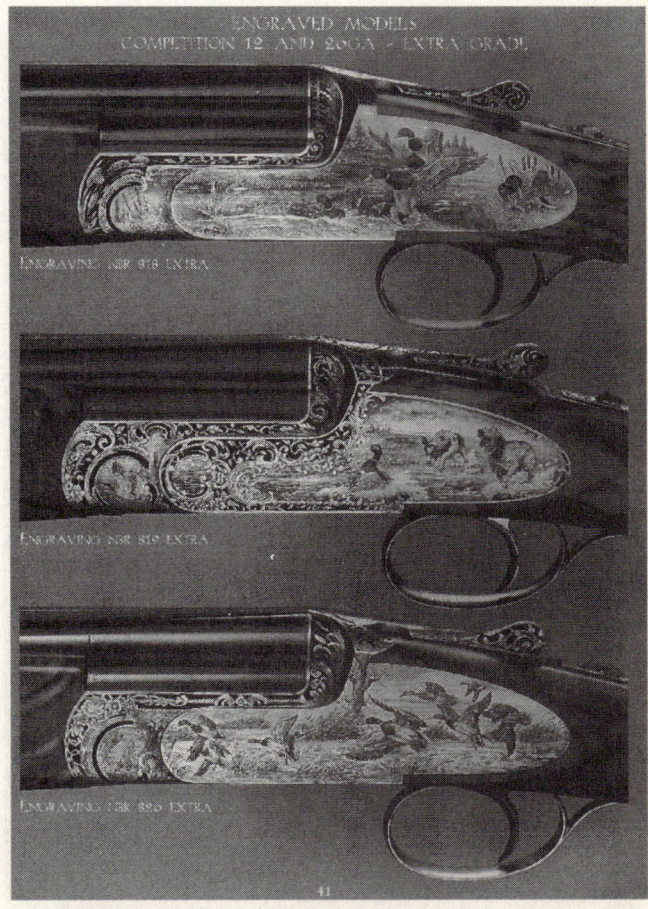

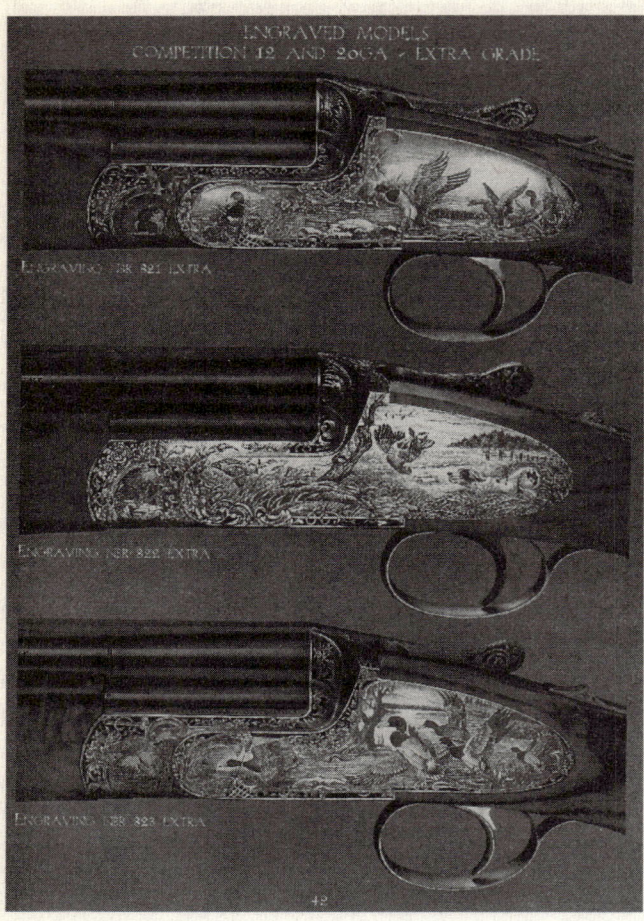

EXTRA GOLD GRADE

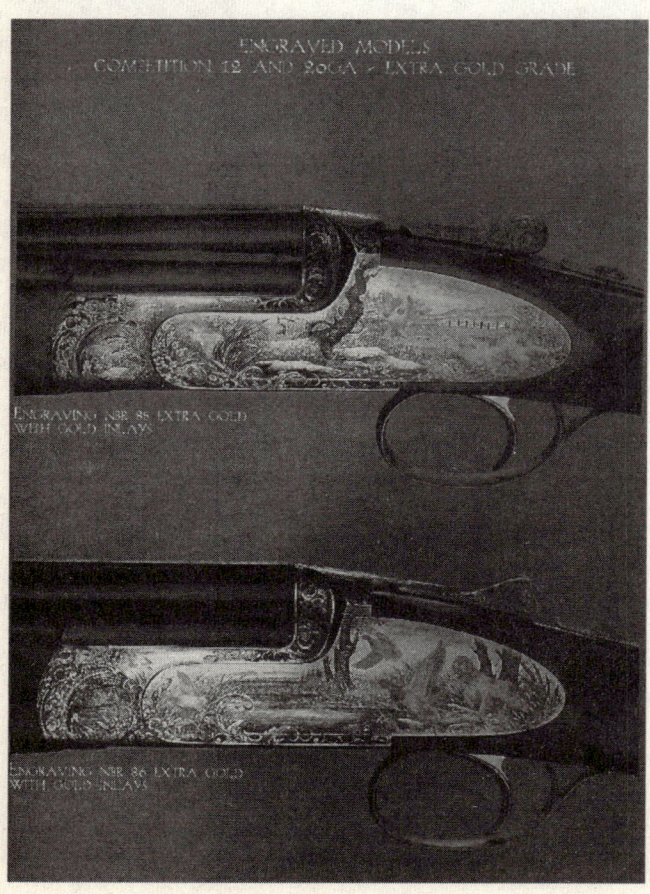

OUT OF PRODUCTION SHOTGUNS

NOTE: Very high premiums on early SCO and higher grades.

COMP1-SB TRAP

This model is a single barrel trap gun in 12 gauge only with 32" or 34" vent rib barrel.

Standard Grade

NIB	Exc.	V.G.	Good	Fair	Poor
2750	2250	1500	1000	750	500

COMP1-TRAP

This is an O/U version of the above model.

Standard Grade

NIB	Exc.	V.G.	Good	Fair	Poor
4500	3750	2750	1750	900	500

Light Game Model

Offered in 12 gauge with a 27.5" vent rib barrel. Trigger group is not detachable. Produced between 1972 and 1974.

Standard Grade

NIB	Exc.	V.G.	Good	Fair	Poor
5000	4200	3500	2500	1200	700

MT-6 Model

This model was offered in 12 gauge with a tapered vent rib. The trigger group was not removable. Discontinued in 1983.

Standard Grade

NIB	Exc.	V.G.	Good	Fair	Poor
4750	4000	3250	2300	1200	700

MX3

This model was discontinued in 1988 and was available in 12 gauge only for single barrel Trap, O/U trap, combination trap, skeet, and sporting configurations.

Standard Grade

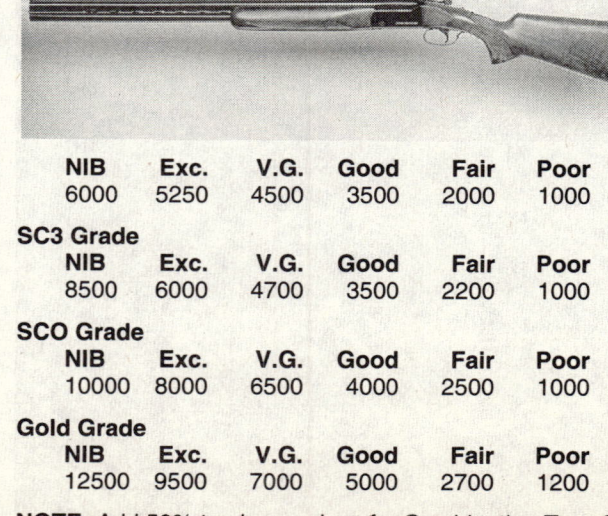

NIB	Exc.	V.G.	Good	Fair	Poor
6000	5250	4500	3500	2000	1000

SC3 Grade

NIB	Exc.	V.G.	Good	Fair	Poor
8500	6000	4700	3500	2200	1000

SCO Grade

NIB	Exc.	V.G.	Good	Fair	Poor
10000	8000	6500	4000	2500	1000

Gold Grade

NIB	Exc.	V.G.	Good	Fair	Poor
12500	9500	7000	5000	2700	1200

NOTE: Add 50% to above prices for Combination Trap Guns.

Grand American Special

This model was introduced in 1988 and features a high ramped rib similar to the MX3 model. The forend was grooved. Discontinued in 1991. It was offered in single barrel trap, combination trap, and O/U trap configurations.

Standard Grade

NIB	Exc.	V.G.	Good	Fair	Poor
5750	5000	4000	3000	1500	700

SC3 Grade

NIB	Exc.	V.G.	Good	Fair	Poor
9750	8500	5500	4000	1700	900

SCO Grade

NIB	Exc.	V.G.	Good	Fair	Poor
16500	1100	8500	5000	2000	1000

Gold Grade

NIB	Exc.	V.G.	Good	Fair	Poor
17500	13000	9000	5500	2500	1200

SCO Grade W/Sideplates

NIB	Exc.	V.G.	Good	Fair	Poor
25000	22500	11000	6000	3000	1500

Gold Grade W/Sideplates

NIB	Exc.	V.G.	Good	Fair	Poor
22500	17500	12500	6500	3200	1500

Extra Grade

NIB	Exc.	V.G.	Good	Fair	Poor
44000	35000	25000	12500	5000	2000

Extra Gold Grade

NIB	Exc.	V.G.	Good	Fair	Poor
48000	39000	26000	13000	5500	2000

SHO Model

NOTE: This O/U sidelock model is available in 12 gauge only in both Type 1 and Type 2 configurations. Type 1 does not have rebounding firing pins and is worth approximately 50% less than Type 2 models that are fitted with rebounding firing pins. There are no parts available in this country or at the factory for Type 1 guns.

The SHO model features a silver finish with fine scroll engraving with game scenes to customer's specifications. Select walnut stock built to customer's dimensions with fine line checkering. A custom built shotgun. Special order only. An expert appraisal is recommended for this model due to its unique features.

DHO Model

This is a side-by-side shotgun offered in 12 gauge only. It has full sidelocks and a silver receiver finish with scroll and game-scene engraving of the same quality as the SHO Model. Fancy walnut stock with fine line checkering. An expert appraisal is recommended for this model due to its unique features.

NOTE: There are no replacemet parts available for the model.

DHO Extra Gold

Available in any gauge and barrel length combination. Only the finest presentation walnut and checkering. A totally custom built shotgun. Special order only. An expert appraisal is recommended for this model due to its unique features.

NOTE: There are no replacement parts available for this model.

CURRENT PRODUCTION SHOTGUNS
American Trap-Single Barrel Models

MX9

Introduced in 1993 this model features removable inserts on rib to adjust point of impact and a walnut stock with adjustable comb. Offered in 12 gauge with 32" or 34" barrel with screw in chokes. The trigger group is removable. Available in several different grades of ormentation.

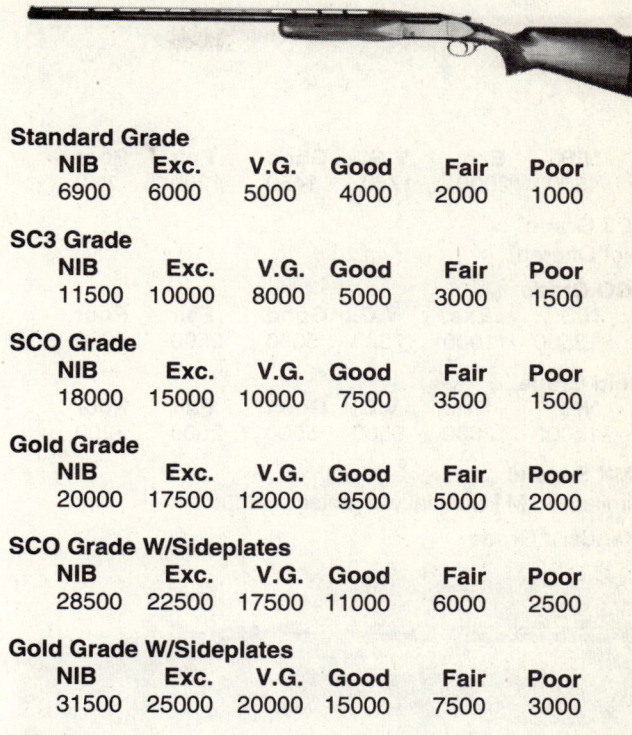

Standard Grade

NIB	Exc.	V.G.	Good	Fair	Poor
6900	6000	5000	4000	2000	1000

SC3 Grade

NIB	Exc.	V.G.	Good	Fair	Poor
11500	10000	8000	5000	3000	1500

SCO Grade

NIB	Exc.	V.G.	Good	Fair	Poor
18000	15000	10000	7500	3500	1500

Gold Grade

NIB	Exc.	V.G.	Good	Fair	Poor
20000	17500	12000	9500	5000	2000

SCO Grade W/Sideplates

NIB	Exc.	V.G.	Good	Fair	Poor
28500	22500	17500	11000	6000	2500

Gold Grade W/Sideplates

NIB	Exc.	V.G.	Good	Fair	Poor
31500	25000	20000	15000	7500	3000

MX10

This model was introduced in 1993. It features a different method of rib height and pattern adjustment. This model also has an adjustable stock. Available in 12 gauge with 32" or 34" barrels. Chokes are fixed. Trigger is removable.

Standard Grade

NIB	Exc.	V.G.	Good	Fair	Poor
6900	6000	5000	4000	3000	1200

SC3 Grade

NIB	Exc.	V.G.	Good	Fair	Poor
11700	7000	6250	5000	3000	1500

SCO Grade

NIB	Exc.	V.G.	Good	Fair	Poor
18500	10000	8000	6000	3500	1500

Gold Grade

NIB	Exc.	V.G.	Good	Fair	Poor
20300	12000	9500	6000	4000	2000

SCO Grade W/Sideplates

NIB	Exc.	V.G.	Good	Fair	Poor
28750	22750	17750	11000	6000	2500

Gold Grade W/Sideplates

NIB	Exc.	V.G.	Good	Fair	Poor
31750	25250	20000	15000	7500	3000

TM I Special

This basic single barrel Perazzi Trap model is offered in 12 gauge with 32" or 34" barrel. Trigger is adjustable.

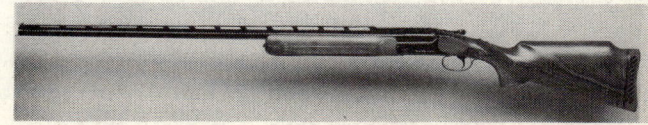

Standard Grade

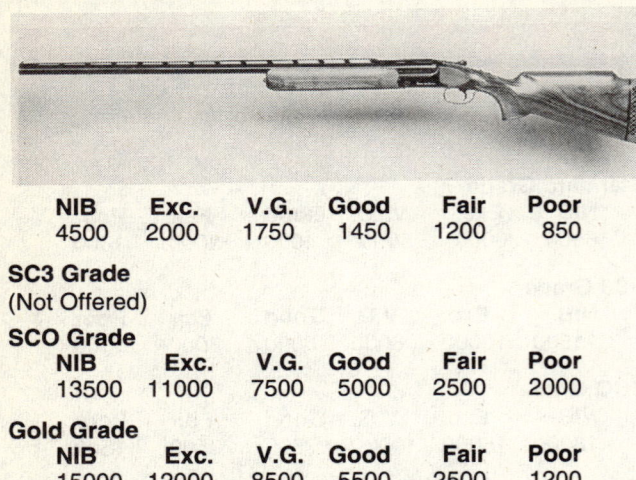

NIB	Exc.	V.G.	Good	Fair	Poor
4500	2000	1750	1450	1200	850

SC3 Grade
(Not Offered)

SCO Grade

NIB	Exc.	V.G.	Good	Fair	Poor
13500	11000	7500	5000	2500	2000

Gold Grade

NIB	Exc.	V.G.	Good	Fair	Poor
15000	12000	8500	5500	2500	1200

TMX Special
Similar to TM I Special with select walnut.

Standard Grade

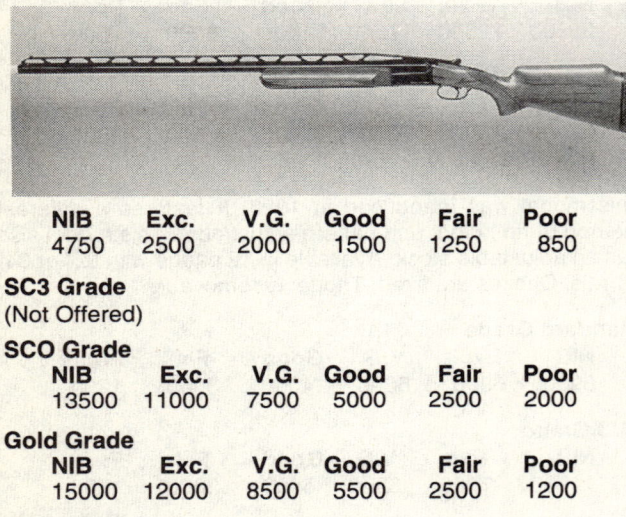

NIB	Exc.	V.G.	Good	Fair	Poor
4750	2500	2000	1500	1250	850

SC3 Grade
(Not Offered)

SCO Grade

NIB	Exc.	V.G.	Good	Fair	Poor
13500	11000	7500	5000	2500	2000

Gold Grade

NIB	Exc.	V.G.	Good	Fair	Poor
15000	12000	8500	5500	2500	1200

MX8 Special
This model features a low contour vent rib, adjustable trigger, and grooved forend.

NOTE: Some SCO engraving patterns on early models have sold in the $30,000 to $45,000 price range. Get an expert appraisial. Beware of counterfeits.

Standard Grade

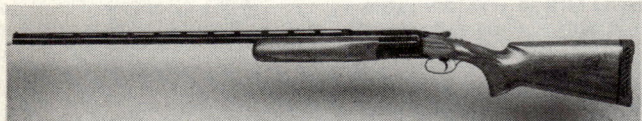

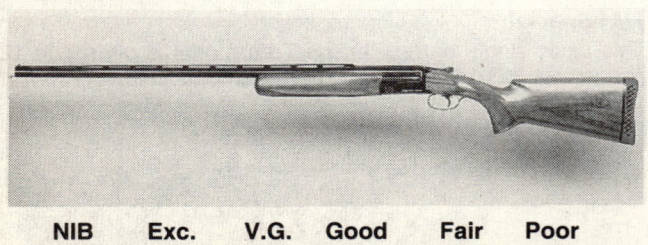

NIB	Exc.	V.G.	Good	Fair	Poor
5800	4500	3750	3000	2000	1000

SC3 Grade

NIB	Exc.	V.G.	Good	Fair	Poor
10000	8500	5000	4000	3000	1200

SCO Grade

NIB	Exc.	V.G.	Good	Fair	Poor
16500	13500	9500	6000	3000	1500

Gold Grade

NIB	Exc.	V.G.	Good	Fair	Poor
18500	14500	10000	6000	3000	1500

SCO Grade W/Sideplates

NIB	Exc.	V.G.	Good	Fair	Poor
26000	21000	15000	10000	5000	2000

Gold Grade W/Sideplates

NIB	Exc.	V.G.	Good	Fair	Poor
30000	24500	19000	12000	6000	3000

MDB81 Special
This model features a high ventilated rib.

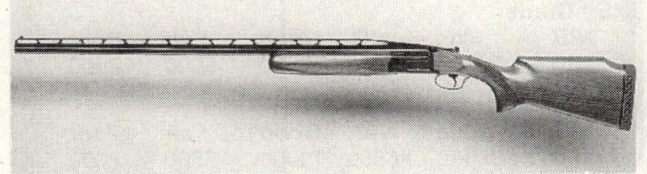

Standard Grade

NIB	Exc.	V.G.	Good	Fair	Poor
6000	5000	4000	3000	2000	2000

SC3 Grade

NIB	Exc.	V.G.	Good	Fair	Poor
10000	8500	5000	4000	3000	1200

SCO Grade

NIB	Exc.	V.G.	Good	Fair	Poor
17000	12500	8500	5000	3000	1200

Gold Grade

NIB	Exc.	V.G.	Good	Fair	Poor
18750	14750	10000	6000	3000	1500

SCO Grade W/Sideplates

NIB	Exc.	V.G.	Good	Fair	Poor
26200	21200	15200	10000	5000	2000

Gold Grade W/Sideplates

NIB	Exc.	V.G.	Good	Fair	Poor
30200	24700	19200	12000	6000	3000

AMERICAN TRAP-COMBO MODELS

MX7

Introduced in 1993. This an over and under trap model that is offered in 12 gauge with 29.5" or 31.5" O/U barrels with either 32" or 34" single barrel. This model has a nonremoveable trigger group feathering fixed coil spring trigger mechanism. The trigger is selective and works in conjunction with the safety catch. The vent rib is ramped on the Combo Trap model. The walnut is custom made to the customer's dimensions

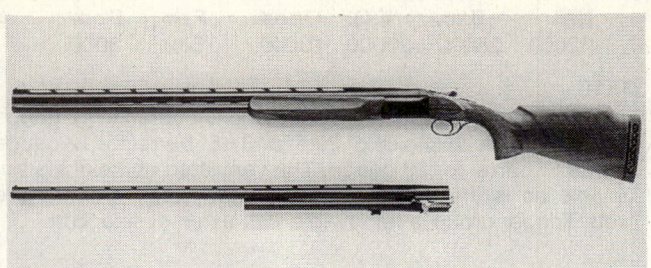

Standard Grade

NIB	Exc.	V.G.	Good	Fair	Poor
5400	3000	2500	2000	1500	1000

MX9

Offered in 12 gauge with 29.5" or 31.5" O/U barrels with 32" or 34" single barrel. All barrels are fitted with MX9 removable inserts to adjust point of impact. Walnut stock has adjustable comb. Comes with screw in chokes. Trigger group is removable.

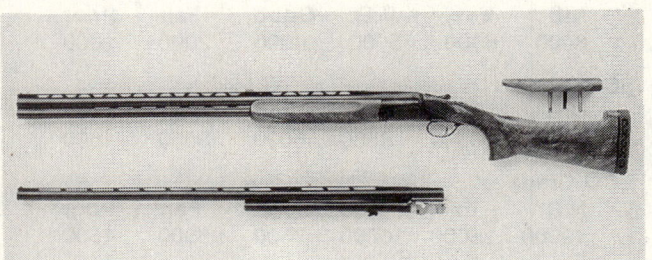

Standard Grade

NIB	Exc.	V.G.	Good	Fair	Poor
10000	7500	6000	4000	3000	1200

SC3 Grade

NIB	Exc.	V.G.	Good	Fair	Poor
15000	12500	9500	6500	3000	1500

SCO Grade

NIB	Exc.	V.G.	Good	Fair	Poor
22500	17000	14000	9000	4500	2000

Gold Grade

NIB	Exc.	V.G.	Good	Fair	Poor
25000	19000	15000	9000	4500	2000

SCO Grade W/Sideplates

NIB	Exc.	V.G.	Good	Fair	Poor
31750	25250	20000	15000	7500	3000

Gold Grade W/Sideplates

NIB	Exc.	V.G.	Good	Fair	Poor
35000	27500	22500	16000	8000	3000

MX10

Introduced in 1993 this model features a higher rib and different method of point of impact adjustment. Stock is adjustable for comb height. Offered in 12 gauge with 29.5" or 31.5" O/U barrels with 32" or 34" single barrel.

Standard Grade

NIB	Exc.	V.G.	Good	Fair	Poor
10000	7500	6000	4000	3000	1200

SC3 Grade

NIB	Exc.	V.G.	Good	Fair	Poor
15000	12500	9000	6000	3000	1500

SCO Grade

NIB	Exc.	V.G.	Good	Fair	Poor
23000	17500	14500	9000	4500	2000

Gold Grade

NIB	Exc.	V.G.	Good	Fair	Poor
25250	19250	15250	9000	4500	2000

SCO Grade W/Sideplates

NIB	Exc.	V.G.	Good	Fair	Poor
32000	25000	20000	15000	7500	3000

Gold Grade W/Sideplates

NIB	Exc.	V.G.	Good	Fair	Poor
36000	27000	2200	17000	8000	4000

MX8 Special

This model features a grooved forend, low contour ventilated rib, and adjustable trigger with internal selector. Same barrel combinations as above.

Standard Grade

NIB	Exc.	V.G.	Good	Fair	Poor
8200	7500	6000	4000	2000	1000

SC3 Grade

NIB	Exc.	V.G.	Good	Fair	Poor
13000	10000	7500	5000	2500	1500

SCO Grade

NIB	Exc.	V.G.	Good	Fair	Poor
20500	17500	2000	9500	5000	2000

Gold Grade

NIB	Exc.	V.G.	Good	Fair	Poor
23000	19000	12500	9500	5000	2000

SCO Grade W/Sideplates

NIB	Exc.	V.G.	Good	Fair	Poor
30000	25000	20000	15000	7500	3000

Gold Grade W/Sideplates

NIB	Exc	V.G	Good	Fair	Poor
33500	27500	22000	17000	8000	3000

DB81 Special

This model is similar to the above model but features a high ramped ventilated rib. Trigger is adjustable with internal selector.

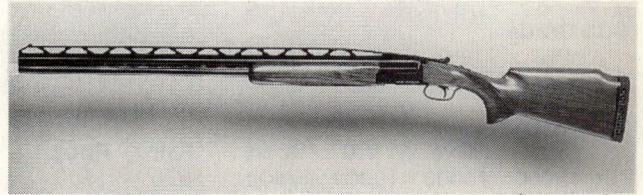

Standard Grade

NIB	Exc.	V.G.	Good	Fair	Poor
8700	7500	6000	4000	2000	1000

SC3 Grade

NIB	Exc.	V.G.	Good	Fair	Poor
13400	10500	8000	5500	2500	2000

SCO Grade

NIB	Exc.	V.G.	Good	Fair	Poor
21000	17500	12000	9500	5000	2000

Gold Grade

NIB	Exc.	V.G.	Good	Fair	Poor
23500	19000	13000	9500	5000	2000

SCO Grade W/Sideplates

NIB	Exc.	V.G.	Good	Fair	Poor
30000	24500	19000	14000	7000	3000

Gold Grade W/Sideplates

NIB	Exc.	V.G.	Good	Fair	Poor
34000	27000	20000	15000	8000	3000

COMPETITION MODELS

Competition versions are over and under shotguns in trap, skeet, pigeon, and sporting models. Stock dimensions are based on the particular model chosen. Trap models feature trap stock dimensions and forearm designed for that purpose. The other models also have their own particular specifications. However, prices are based on a common style referred to by Perazzi as Competition. Thus, all models within this group are priced the same regardless of specific type.

MX7C

Introduced in 1993 this model is offered in 12 gauge with a nonremovable trigger group. It has a coil spring mechanism, fully selective in conjunction with the safety. Offered in 27.5", 29.5", or 31.5" flat vent rib barrels. Screw in chokes are standard. Walnut stock is custom made to customer's dimensions. The forend is beavertail.

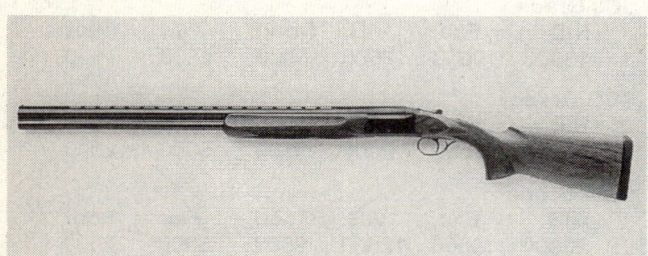

Standard Grade

NIB	Exc.	V.G.	Good	Fair	Poor
4900	3500	3000	2500	1250	750

MX9

This model was introduced in 1993 and features an adjustable comb on the stock with unique vent rib inserts to correct for point of impact. Offered in 12 gauge with 29.5" or 31.5" barrels. Trigger group is removable. Comes standard with screw in chokes.

Standard Grade

NIB	Exc.	V.G.	Good	Fair	Poor
7600	6000	5000	4000	2000	1000

SC3 Grade

NIB	Exc.	V.G.	Good	Fair	Poor
11500	10000	8000	5000	3000	1500

SCO Grade

NIB	Exc.	V.G.	Good	Fair	Poor
18000	15000	10000	7500	3500	1500

Gold Grade

NIB	Exc.	V.G.	Good	Fair	Poor
20000	17500	12000	9500	5000	2000

SCO Grade W/Sideplates

NIB	Exc.	V.G.	Good	Fair	Poor
28000	22000	17000	11000	6000	2500

Gold Grade W/Sideplates

NIB	Exc.	V.G.	Good	Fair	Poor
32000	25000	20000	15000	7500	3000

MX10

This model was introduced in 1993 and is offered in 12 gauge and 20 gauge with choice of 29.5" or 31.5" barrel for 12 gauge and 29.5" barrel for 20 gauge. The ventilated rib height is adjustable as is the comb position on the stock. Chokes are fixed. Trigger group is removable with external selection.

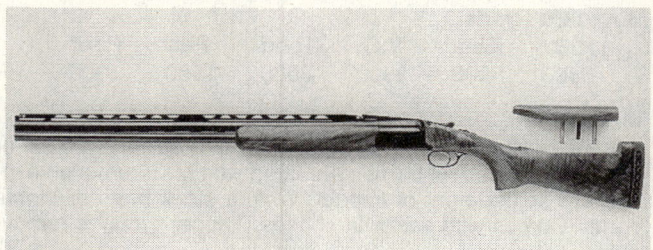

Standard Grade

NIB	Exc.	V.G.	Good	Fair	Poor
8000	6000	5000	4000	2000	1000

SC3 Grade

NIB	Exc.	V.G.	Good	Fair	Poor
12000	10500	8500	5000	3000	1500

SCO Grade

NIB	Exc.	V.G.	Good	Fair	Poor
19000	15000	10000	7500	3500	1500

Gold Grade

NIB	Exc.	V.G.	Good	Fair	Poor
21250	19500	13000	9500	5000	2000

SCO Grade W/Sideplates

NIB	Exc.	V.G.	Good	Fair	Poor
28000	22500	17500	11000	6000	2500

Gold Grade W/Sideplates

NIB	Exc.	V.G.	Good	Fair	Poor
32000	25000	20000	15000	7500	3000

MX8/20

This model was first introduced in 1993. It features a removable trigger group. Available in 20 gauge only with choice of 27.5", 28.375", 29.5" flat ventilated rib barrels. Choice of fixed or screw-in chokes on sporting model. Stock is custom made to customer's dimensions with beavertail forend.

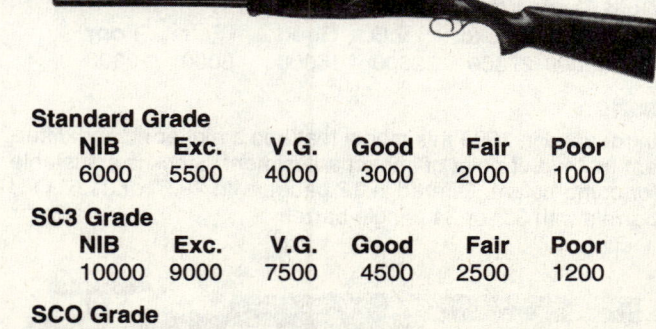

Standard Grade

NIB	Exc.	V.G.	Good	Fair	Poor
6000	5500	4000	3000	2000	1000

SC3 Grade

NIB	Exc.	V.G.	Good	Fair	Poor
10000	9000	7500	4500	2500	1200

SCO Grade

NIB	Exc.	V.G.	Good	Fair	Poor
17000	14000	9000	6500	3500	1500

Gold Grade

NIB	Exc.	V.G.	Good	Fair	Poor
19000	15000	10000	7500	3500	1500

SCO Grade W/Sideplates

NIB	Exc.	V.G.	Good	Fair	Poor
26000	19000	13000	9000	4500	2000

Gold Grade W/Sideplates

NIB	Exc.	V.G.	Good	Fair	Poor
30000	25000	20000	15000	7500	3000

Extra Grade

NIB	Exc.	V.G.	Good	Fair	Poor
48500	40000	30000	20000	10000	5000

Extra Gold Grade

NIB	Exc.	V.G.	Good	Fair	Poor
52000	42500	32500	22500	12500	6000

Extra Model

Same as MX 8/20 but available in 12 gauge only with choice of barrel lengths to 31.5".

Extra Grade

NIB	Exc.	V.G.	Good	Fair	Poor
48500	40000	30000	20000	10000	5000

Extra Gold Grade

NIB	Exc.	V.G.	Good	Fair	Poor
52000	42500	32500	22500	12500	6000

Mirage Special

This model features an adjustable trigger and is available in 12 gauge with choice of 27.5", 28.375", 29.5", or 31.5" ventilated rib barrels.

Standard Grade

NIB	Exc.	V.G.	Good	Fair	Poor
6100	5500	4500	3500	2500	1000

Mirage Special Sporting

Similar to the Mirage Special listed above, but with external trigger selection and screw-in chokes. Offered in 12 gauge only with choice of 27.5", 28.375", or 29.5" vent rib barrels.

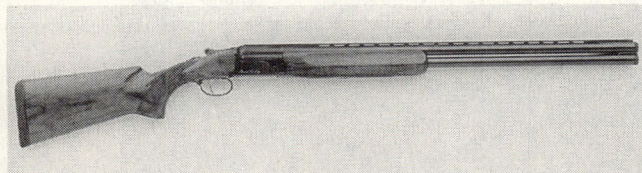

Standard Grade

NIB	Exc.	V.G.	Good	Fair	Poor
6400	5700	5000	4000	3000	1500

Mirage Special Sporting Classic

This model features the same basic specifications as the Mirage Special Sporting with the addition of a scroll border on the receiver and triggerguard. The wood is of slightly higher quality. Offered in 12 gauge only with 27.5", 28.375", or 29.5" vent rib barrels.

Standard Grade

NIB	Exc.	V.G.	Good	Fair	Poor
7500	5250	4000	3000	2000	1000

Mirage MX8

Standard Grade

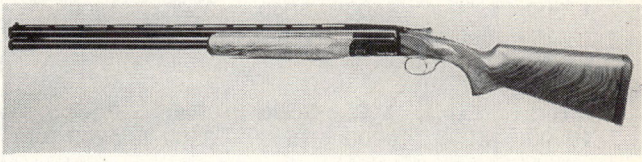

NIB	Exc.	V.G.	Good	Fair	Poor
5800	5000	4000	3000	2000	1000

MX8 Special

This model features a four position adjustable trigger. It also has a low contour rib and a grooved forearm. Offered in 12 only with choice of 29.5" or 31.5" vent rib barrels.

Standard Grade

NIB	Exc.	V.G.	Good	Fair	Poor
6100	5500	4500	3500	2500	1000

SCO Model

This model is similar to the MX8 but offered only in 12 gauge with barrel length from 27.5" to 31.5". The trigger is adjustable instead of removable.

SCO Grade

NIB	Exc.	V.G.	Good	Fair	Poor
17000	12500	8500	6000	3000	1500

Gold Grade

NIB	Exc.	V.G.	Good	Fair	Poor
19000	13500	9500	6500	3250	1500

SCO Grade W/Sideplates

NIB	Exc.	V.G.	Good	Fair	Poor
26000	21500	17000	12000	6000	3000

Gold Grade W/Sideplates

NIB	Exc.	V.G.	Good	Fair	Poor
30000	25000	19000	14000	7000	3000

DB81 Special

This model, available in 12 gauge only, features a high ramped ventilated rib. Barrel length are 29.51, or 31.5". Adjustable trigger standard.

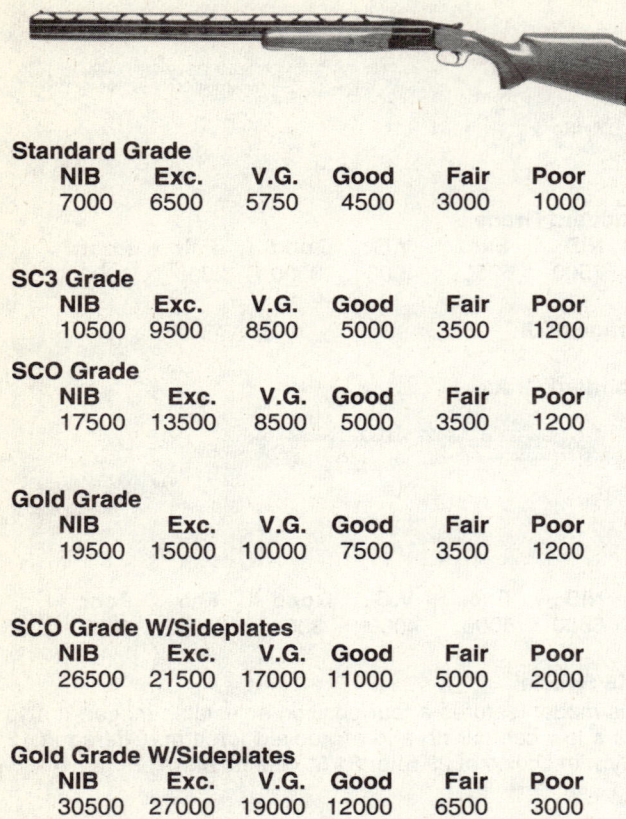

Standard Grade

NIB	Exc.	V.G.	Good	Fair	Poor
7000	6500	5750	4500	3000	1000

SC3 Grade

NIB	Exc.	V.G.	Good	Fair	Poor
10500	9500	8500	5000	3500	1200

SCO Grade

NIB	Exc.	V.G.	Good	Fair	Poor
17500	13500	8500	5000	3500	1200

Gold Grade

NIB	Exc.	V.G.	Good	Fair	Poor
19500	15000	10000	7500	3500	1200

SCO Grade W/Sideplates

NIB	Exc.	V.G.	Good	Fair	Poor
26500	21500	17000	11000	5000	2000

Gold Grade W/Sideplates

NIB	Exc.	V.G.	Good	Fair	Poor
30500	27000	19000	12000	6500	3000

Mirage Special 4-Gauge Set

Similar to the Mirage Special in appearance and specifications but fitted with four barrel sets with 27.62" barrels in 12, 20, 28 gauge, and .410 bore. For 28.37" barrels add $2,000 and for 29.5" barrels add $3,000.

Standard Grade

NIB	Exc.	V.G.	Good	Fair	Poor
14000	6500	5000	4000	3000	1500

SC3 Grade

NIB	Exc.	V.G.	Good	Fair	Poor
21000	15000	9500	4500	3500	2500

SCO Grade

NIB	Exc.	V.G.	Good	Fair	Poor
28000	22500	15000	8500	4200	2500

Gold Grade

NIB	Exc.	V.G.	Good	Fair	Poor
30000	24500	17000	9500	4500	2500

SCO Grade W/Sideplates

NIB	Exc.	V.G.	Good	Fair	Poor
40000	32500	25000	12500	6500	3000

Gold Grade W/Sideplates

NIB	Exc.	V.G.	Good	Fair	Poor
44000	35000	27000	13500	7000	3000

GAME GUN MODELS

A special set of game shotguns was especially created by Perazzi. It consists of 12, 20, 28 gauge and .410 bore guns with straight grips stocks with extra fancy walnut and special engraving. The retail price of these shotguns is $285,000.

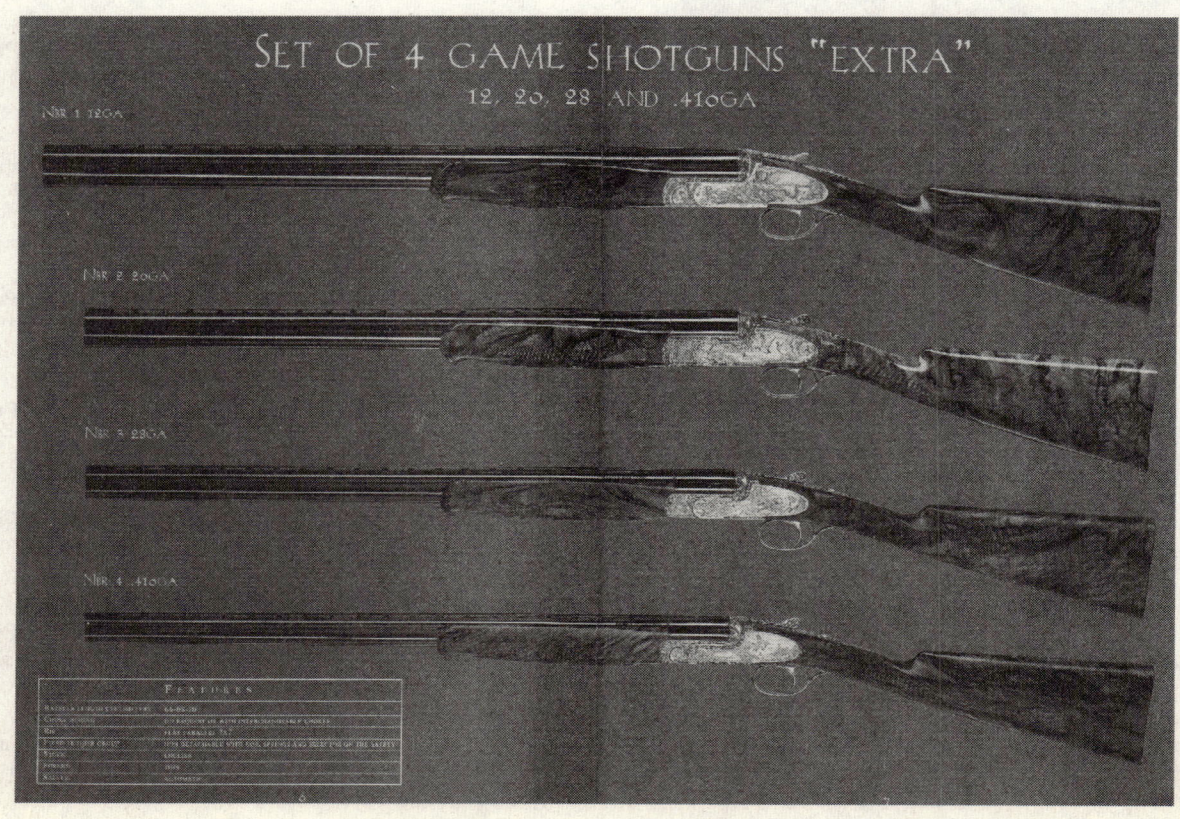

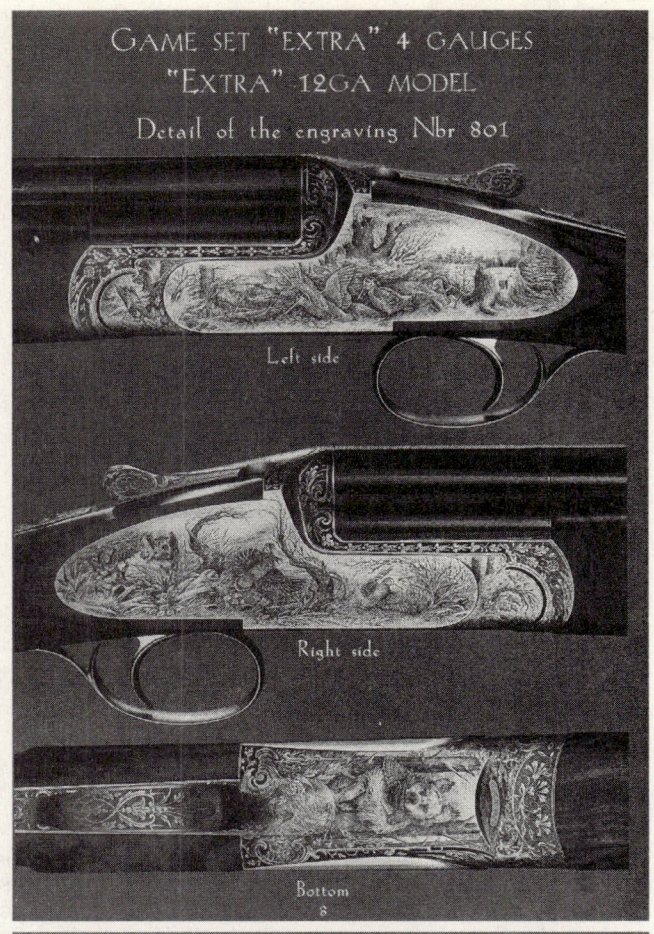

GAME SET "EXTRA" 4 GAUGES
"EXTRA" 12GA MODEL
Detail of the engraving Nbr 801

Left side

Right side

Bottom
8

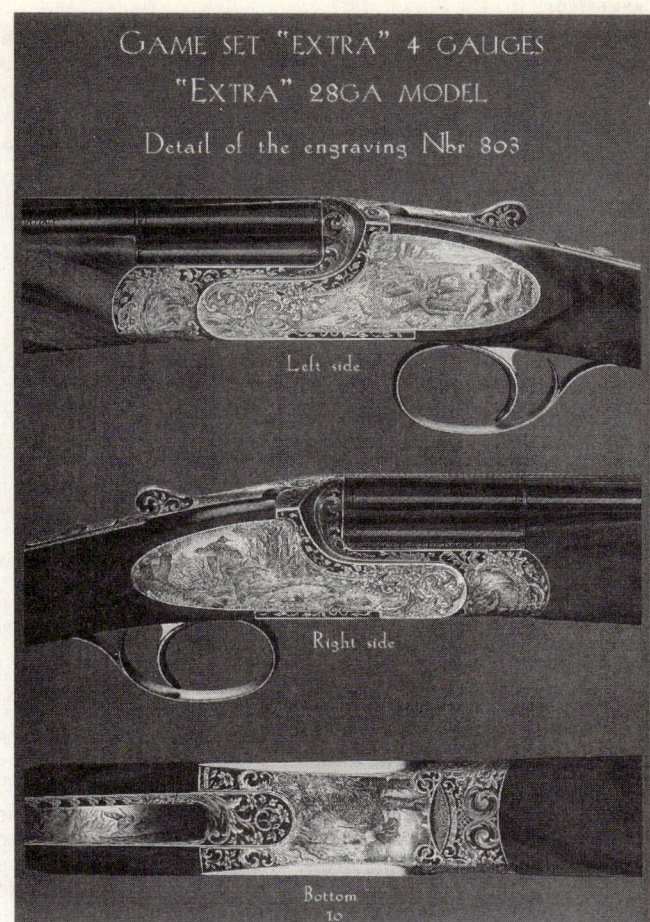

GAME SET "EXTRA" 4 GAUGES
"EXTRA" 28GA MODEL
Detail of the engraving Nbr 803

Left side

Right side

Bottom
10

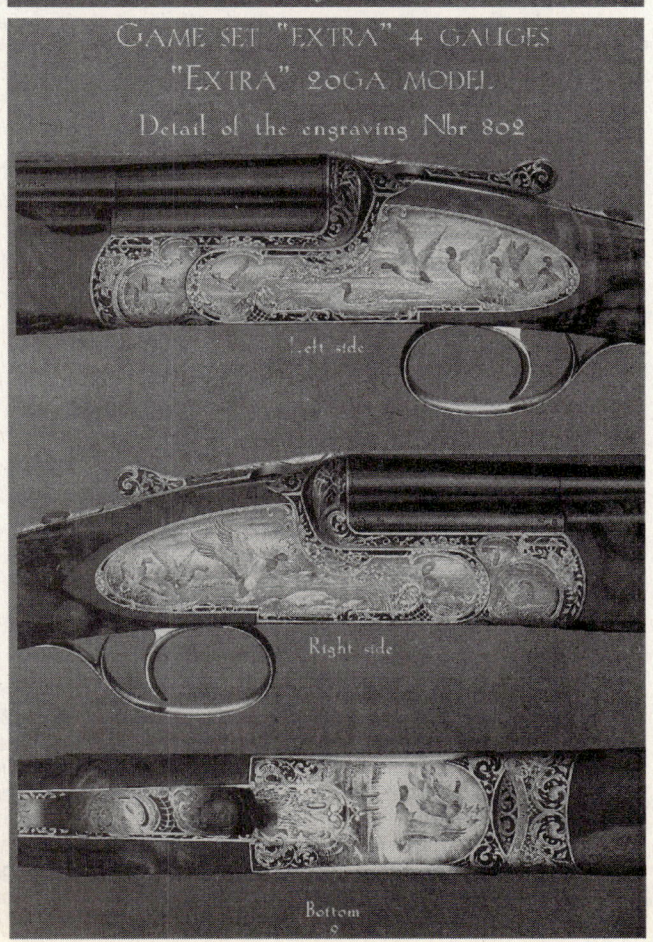

GAME SET "EXTRA" 4 GAUGES
"EXTRA" 20GA MODEL
Detail of the engraving Nbr 802

Left side

Right side

Bottom
9

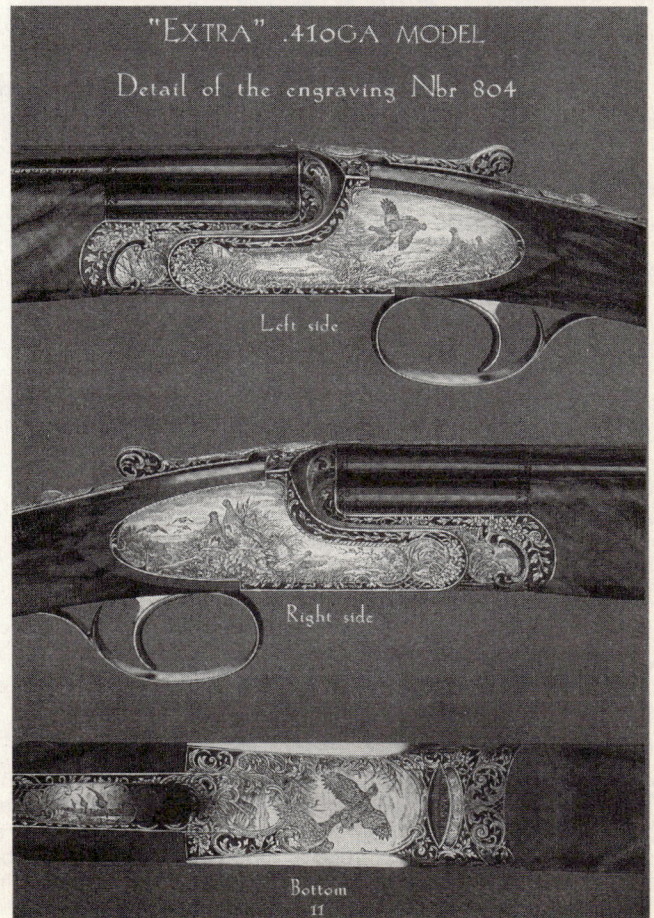

"EXTRA" .410GA MODEL
Detail of the engraving Nbr 804

Left side

Right side

Bottom
11

MXI2/12C

Offered in 12 gauge only with 26.75" or 27.5" vent rib barrels. The single selective trigger is nonremovable. The walnut stock is fitted with a Schnabel forend and the receiver gas a light scroll engraved border. The MX12 is supplied with fixed chokes while the MX12C is fitted with 5 screw-in choke tubes. Add $400 to MX12 prices to get MX12C values.

Standard Grade

NIB	Exc.	V.G.	Good	Fair	Poor
6250	5200	4500	3000	2000	1000

SC3 Grade

NIB	Exc.	V.G.	Good	Fair	Poor
9900	6500	5500	4000	3000	1200

SCO Grade

NIB	Exc.	V.G.	Good	Fair	Poor
17000	12500	9500	4500	3200	1200

Gold Grade

NIB	Exc.	V.G.	Good	Fair	Poor
19000	14500	10000	5000	3500	1200

SCO Grade W/Sideplates

NIB	Exc.	V.G.	Good	Fair	Poor
26000	22500	17000	8500	4200	2000

Gold Grade W/Sideplates

NIB	Exc	V.G.	Good	Fair	Poor
30000	22500	19000	10000	5000	2500

MX20/20C

This model is offered in 20 gauge. It features a nonremovable trigger group. The frame is smaller than 12 gauge. Offered with 26" or 27.5" vent rib barrels. The MX20 has fixed chokes while the MX20C is supplied with 5 screw-in choke tubes. Add $400 to MX20 prices to get MX20C values.

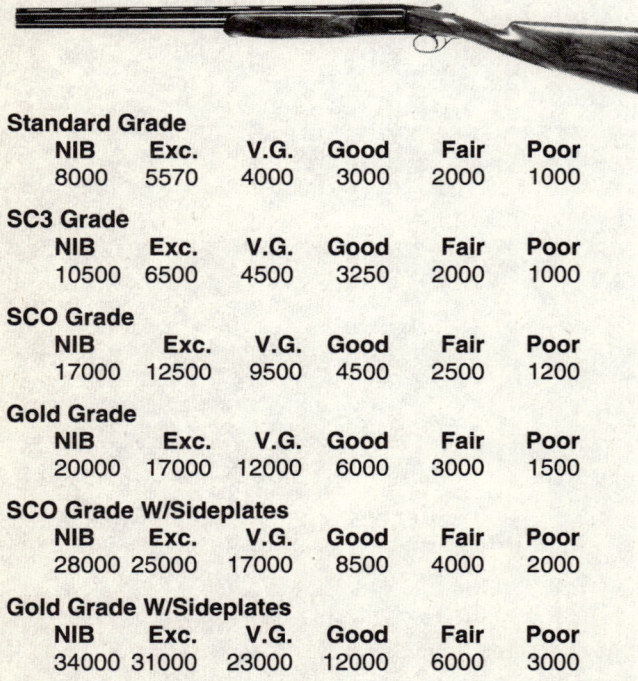

Standard Grade

NIB	Exc.	V.G.	Good	Fair	Poor
8000	5570	4000	3000	2000	1000

SC3 Grade

NIB	Exc.	V.G.	Good	Fair	Poor
10500	6500	4500	3250	2000	1000

SCO Grade

NIB	Exc.	V.G.	Good	Fair	Poor
17000	12500	9500	4500	2500	1200

Gold Grade

NIB	Exc.	V.G.	Good	Fair	Poor
20000	17000	12000	6000	3000	1500

SCO Grade W/Sideplates

NIB	Exc.	V.G.	Good	Fair	Poor
28000	25000	17000	8500	4000	2000

Gold Grade W/Sideplates

NIB	Exc.	V.G.	Good	Fair	Poor
34000	31000	23000	12000	6000	3000

MX8/20-8/20C

Introduced in 1993 and offered in 20 gauge with 26" or 27.625" vent rib barrels. The trigger group on this model is removable. The stock is a high grade walnut custom made to customer's own specifications. The forend is round. The MX8/20 is supplied with fixed chokes while the Mx8/20C has 5 screw-in choke tubes. Add $400 for MX8/20C values.

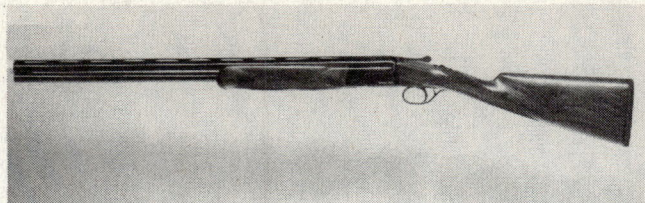

Standard Grade

NIB	Exc.	V.G.	Good	Fair	Poor
5800	5200	4500	3000	2000	1000

SC3 Grade

NIB	Exc.	V.G.	Good	Fair	Poor
9900	9000	5500	4000	3000	

SCO Grade

NIB	Exc.	V.G.	Good	Fair	Poor
17000	14000	9500	4500	3200	1200

Gold Grade

NIB	Exc.	V.G.	Good	Fair	Poor
19000	16000	10000	5000	3500	1200

SCO Grade W/Sideplates

NIB	Exc.	V.G.	Good	Fair	Poor
26000	22500	17000	8500	4200	2000

Gold Grade W/Sideplates

NIB	Exc.	V.G.	Good	Fair	Poor
30000	26500	19000	10000	5000	2500

MX28 and MX410

Introduced in 1993 these two models feature a nonremovable trigger group and a special small frame for each. The MX28, .28 gauge, weighs about 5.5 lbs. while the MX410, .410 bore, weighs slightly less. Both are supplied with fixed chokes, flat ribs, custom made stocks, and round forends. Each model is offered with a choice of 26" or 27.5" barrels. Both the MX28 and MX410 are priced the same.

Standard Grade

NIB	Exc.	V.G.	Good	Fair	Poor
11500	8000	6000	4000	3000	1500

SC3 Grade

(Not Available)

SCO Grade

NIB	Exc.	V.G.	Good	Fair	Poor
22500	19000	13000	9000	4500	2000

Gold Grade

NIB	Exc.	V.G.	Good	Fair	Poor
25000	20000	15000	10000	5000	2500

SCO Grade W/Sideplates

NIB	Exc.	V.G.	Good	Fair	Poor
31500	25250	20000	15000	7500	3000

Gold Grade W/Sideplates

NIB	Exc.	V.G.	Good	Fair	Poor
36000	30000	23000	17500	8500	3000

Extra Grade Models

There are three different configurations offered for this model. In Extra Grade they are chambered for 12 gauge and 20 gauge with nonremovable trigger group or 20 gauge with removable trigger group. In Extra Gold Grade they are offered in 12 gauge and 20 gauge with nonremovable trigger group and in 20 gauge with removable trigger group. Twelve gauge guns are offered with 26.75" or 27.5" vent rib barrels while 20 gauge guns can be had with 26" or 27.5" vent rib barrels. The 20 gauge guns with removable trigger groups were first introduced in 1993.

Extra Grade

NIB	Exc.	V.G.	Good	Fair	Poor
48500	40000	30000	20000	10000	5000

Extra Gold Grade

NIB	Exc.	V.G.	Good	Fair	Poor
52000	42000	32000	20000	10000	5000

PERRY PATENT FIREARMS CO.
Newark, New Jersey

Perry Single Shot Pistol

A .52 caliber breech loading percussion pistol with a 6" round barrel. Blued with walnut grips. The barrel marked "Perry Patent Firearms Co./Newark, N.J." Approximately 200 were made between 1854 and 1856 in two styles.

1st Type-Long, Contoured Triggerguard, Opening Lever

Exc.	V.G.	Good	Fair	Poor
—	—	3000	1500	500

2nd Type S Curved Shorter Triggerguard And An Automatic Primer Feed that Protrudes From The Butt

Exc.	V.G.	Good	Fair	Poor
—	—	2750	1250	500

Perry Carbine

A .54 caliber breech loading percussion carbine with a 20.75" barrel and half length walnut stock secured by one barrel band. Blued with a casehardened lock. Approximately 200 were made. Prospective purchasers are advised to secure a qualified appraisal prior to acquisition.

Courtesy Milwaukee Public Museum, Milwaukee, Wisconsin

Exc.	V.G.	Good	Fair	Poor
—	—	5000	2000	650

PERRY & GODDARD
RENWICK ARMS CO.
New York, New York

Derringer

A .44 caliber single shot spur trigger pistol with a 2" octagonal barrel. Blued or silver-plated with walnut or gutta-percha grips. The barrel may be swiveled so that either end can serve as the chamber and is marked "Double Header/ E.S. Renwick." Produced in limited quantities during the 1860s. Prospective purchasers are advised to secure a qualified appraisal prior to acquisition.

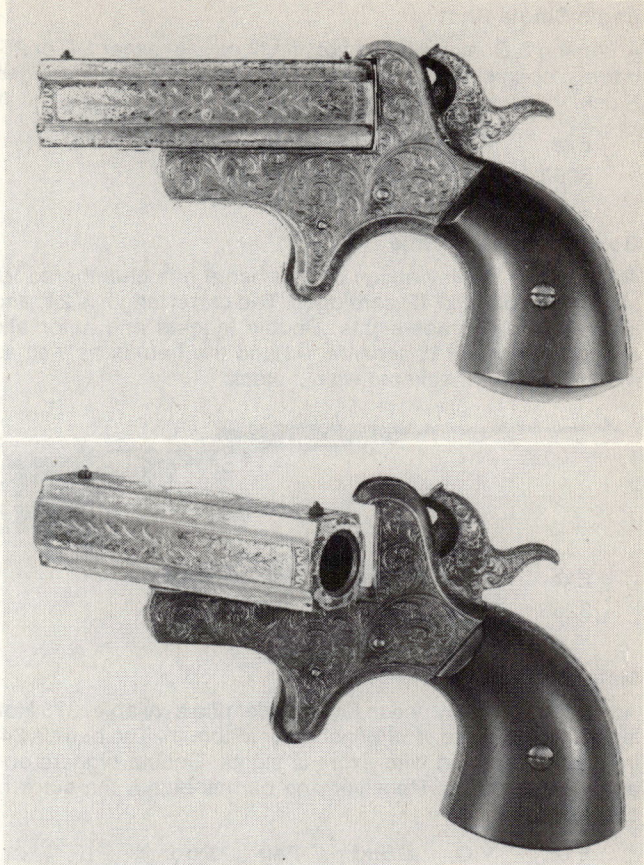

Exc.	V.G.	Good	Fair	Poor
—	—	13500	5000	1000

PERUGINI & VISINI
Brescia, Italy

Arms by this maker were imported by W.L. Moore of Westlake Village, California.

Liberty Model

A side-by-side 12, 20, 28 and .410 gauge shotgun having 28" barrels. Anson & Deeley action with a double Purdy lock. Blued overall with checkered walnut stock.

Exc.	V.G.	Good	Fair	Poor
5000	4250	3500	2750	1250

Classic Model

A 12 or 20 gauge double-barrel shotgun having a Holland & Holland style sidelock with a double Purdy lock. The barrels 28" in length. Single trigger and automatic ejectors. The sidelocks and mounts engraved and blued. Well figured and checkered walnut stock.

Exc.	V.G.	Good	Fair	Poor
11000	8500	7000	5500	2750

Bolt-Action Rifle

A Mauser type bolt-action rifle available in a variety of chamberings, with 24" or 26" barrels. Sights not furnished. Well figured checkered walnut stock.

Exc.	V.G.	Good	Fair	Poor
4000	3500	2750	2000	1000

Deluxe Bolt-Action Rifle

As above with first quality walnut stocks and a case.

Exc.	V.G.	Good	Fair	Poor
4500	3750	3000	2250	1250

Eagle Single Shot

An Anson & Deeley single shot rifle fitted with either 24" or 26" barrels, open sights, automatic ejector and adjustable trigger. Stock of checkered walnut.

Exc.	V.G.	Good	Fair	Poor
5000	4250	3500	2750	1500

Boxlock Express Rifle

An Anson & Deeley action double-barrel rifle chambered for .444 Marlin or 9.3x74R cartridges. The barrel length is 24" and is fitted with express sights. Double triggers and automatic ejectors. Receiver casehardened and the barrels as well as mounts blued. Checkered walnut stock.

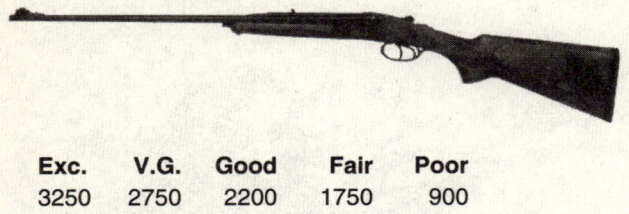

Exc.	V.G.	Good	Fair	Poor
3250	2750	2200	1750	900

Magnum O/U

An Anson & Deeley action Over/Under rifle available .375 Holland & Holland and .458 Winchester Magnum. The barrels 24" in length and fitted with express sights. Double triggers and automatic ejectors. Receiver and barrels blued, the stock of checkered walnut.

Exc.	V.G.	Good	Fair	Poor
5500	4750	3900	2750	1500

Super Express Rifle

A Holland & Holland-style sidelock double-barrel rifle. Having 24" barrels fitted with express sights. Available in a variety of chamberings. The receiver and sidelocks either casehardened or finished in the bright and fully engraved. Checkered walnut stock.

Exc.	V.G.	Good	Fair	Poor
9500	8000	6500	4000	2000

Victoria Side-x-Side Rifle

Similar to the Boxlock Express Rifle but chambered for .30-06, 7x65R, or 9.3x74R cartridges. Either 24" or 26" barrels were available. Double triggers and automatic ejectors. Blued with minimal engraving. Stock of checkered walnut.

Exc.	V.G.	Good	Fair	Poor
6500	5500	4000	3000	1500

Selous Side-x-Side Rifle

First quality double-barrel express rifle with 24" or 26" barrels. Fully detachable Holland & Holland-style sidelocks, double triggers and automatic ejectors. Fully engraved with well figured checkered walnut stocks.

Exc.	V.G.	Good	Fair	Poor
20000	15000	12500	6000	3000

PETTINGILL C. S.
New Haven, Connecticut
Rogers, Spencer & Co.
Willowvale, New York

Pocket Revolver

A hammerless, double action .31 caliber percussion revolver having a 4" octagonal barrel. The frame of brass or iron. Blued barrel, the grips of oil finished walnut. The First and Second Models are marked "Pettingill's Patent 1856" as well as "T.K. Austin." The Third Model is marked "Pettengill Patent 1856", and "Raymond and Robitaille Patented 1858." Approximately 400 were manufactured in the late 1850s and early 1860s.

1st Model with Brass Frame

Exc.	V.G.	Good	Fair	Poor
—	—	1500	800	300

2nd Model with Iron Frame

Exc.	V.G.	Good	Fair	Poor
—	—	850	400	200

3rd Model, Iron Frame and Improved Action

Exc.	V.G.	Good	Fair	Poor
—	—	850	400	200

Navy Revolver

As above but in .34 caliber with a 4.5" barrel and a 6-shot cylinder. The frame of iron, blued overall, and the grips of walnut. This model is marked "Pettengill's Patent 1856" and "Raymond & Robitaille Patented 1858." Approximately 900 were manufactured in the late 1850s and early 1860s.

Courtesy Milwaukee Public Museum, Milwaukee, Wisconsin

Exc.	V.G.	Good	Fair	Poor
—	—	1200	550	200

Army Model Revolver

As above but of .44 caliber and fitted with a 7.5" barrel. The frame of iron that is casehardened, the octagonal barrel blued, the grips of oil finished walnut. Early production models are marked as the Navy models, while later production examples are marked "Petingill's Patent 1856, pat'd July 22, 1856 and July 27, 1858." Some examples will be found with government inspector's marks and are worth approximately 25% more. It is believed that 3,400 were made in the 1860s.

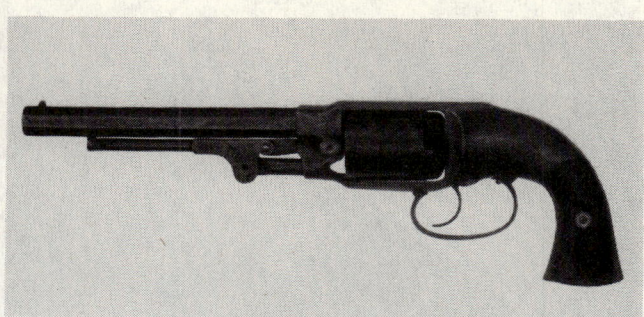

Courtesy Milwaukee Public Museum, Milwaukee, Wisconsin

Exc.	V.G.	Good	Fair	Poor
—	—	2500	750	300

PFANNL, FRANCOIS
Krems, Austria

Erika

A 4.25mm semiautomatic pistol with a hinged barrel assembly. The barrel either 1.5" or 2.25" in length. The grips are marked "Erika". Approximately 3,500 made between 1912 and 1926.

Exc.	V.G.	Good	Fair	Poor
—	400	300	200	100

PHILLIPS & RODGERS INC.
Conroe, Texas

Medusa Model 47

Introduced in 1996 this unique multi-caliber revolver is designed to chamber, fire, and extract almost any cartridge using 9mm, .357, or .38 cartridges; a total of about 25 different calibers. The barrel lengths are 2.5", 3", 4", 5", or 6". Rubber grips and interchangeable front sights. Finish is matte blue.

NIB	Exc.	V.G.	Good	Fair	Poor
900	700	—	—	—	—

Ruger 50 Conversion

This conversion, executed on a new revolver, converts a .44 Magnum Ruger into a .50 Action Express. Stainless steel or blue with 5 shot cylinder. Barrel length is 6.5".

NIB	Exc.	V.G.	Good	Fair	Poor
1000	800	—	—	—	—

Wilderness Explorer

This bolt action rifle was introduced in 1997 and features an 18" match grade barrel. The boltface and barrel are quick change so four caliber can be used in the same rifle. Synthetic stock. Chambered for .22 Hornet, .218 Bee, .44 Magnum, and .50 AE calibers. Weight is approximately 5.5 lbs.

NIB	Exc.	V.G.	Good	Fair	Poor
N/A	—	—	—	—	—

PHOENIX
Lowell, Massachusetts

Pocket Pistol

A rare .25 ACP semiautomatic pistol with a 2.25" barrel and 6-round magazine. Receiver and slide blued, the grips of hard rubber. Manufactured during the 1920s.

Exc.	V.G.	Good	Fair	Poor
500	450	400	300	150

PHOENIX ARMS
Ontario, CA

HP22

A pocket size semiautomatic pistol chambered for the .22 Long Rifle cartridge. Barrel length is 3". Magazine capacity is 11 rounds. Offered in bright chrome or polished blue finish with black checkered grips. Top of gun is fitted with vent rib. Overall length is 4.1" and weight is about 20 oz.

NIB	Exc.	V.G.	Good	Fair	Poor
80	60	50	40	30	20

HP25

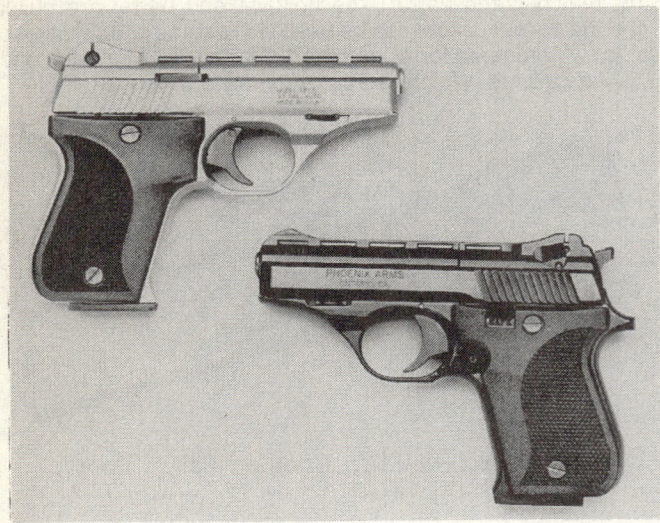

This model is the same as above but chambered for the .25 ACP cartridge. Magazine capacity is 10 rounds.

NIB	Exc.	V.G.	Good	Fair	Poor
80	60	50	40	30	20

HP22/HP25 Target

A conversion kit to convert the HP22/HP25 into a target pistol. Kit includes extended vent rib barrel and a convertible 10-round magazine. Finish is either blue or nickel.

NIB	Exc.	V.G.	Good	Fair	Poor
125	100	—	—	—	—

Raven

A small pocket size semiautomatic pistol chambered for the .25 ACP cartridge. Magazine capacity is 6 rounds. Barrel length is 2.4" with fixed sights. Offered in 3 finishes: bright chrome, satin nickel, or polished blue. Grips are either ivory, pink pearl, or black. Overall length is 4.8" and weight is approximately 15 oz.

NIB	Exc.	V.G.	Good	Fair	Poor
65	50	40	30	25	20

PHOENIX ARMS CO.
Liege, Belgium
SEE Robar et DeKerkhove

PICKERT, FRIEDRICH
Zella-Mehlis, Germany
Arminius Waffenfabrik

This firm produced revolvers bearing the trade name "Arminius". The revolvers manufactured by Pickert of the double-action type, with or without exposed hammers. Some models are fitted with ejectors, while others have removable cylinders. Calibers and barrel lengths vary. After WWII, the trade name was acquired by Hermann Wiehauch.

Exc.	V.G.	Good	Fair	Poor
175	150	125	100	75

PIEPER, HENRI & NICOLAS
Liege, Belgium

Originally founded by Henri Pieper in 1859, the company was reorganized in 1898 when his son, Nicolas, assumed control. The firm is best known for a series of semiautomatic pistols as described below.

Pieper Model 1907

A 6.35 or 7.65mm semiautomatic pistol featuring a hinged barrel assembly 2.5" in length. Receiver and barrel blued, the grips of hard rubber with the firm's trademark cast in them. The Model 1907 variation does not have a hinged barrel assembly. The Model 1908 is also known as the "Basculant", and the Model 1918 as the "Demontant".

Courtesy Orvel Reichert

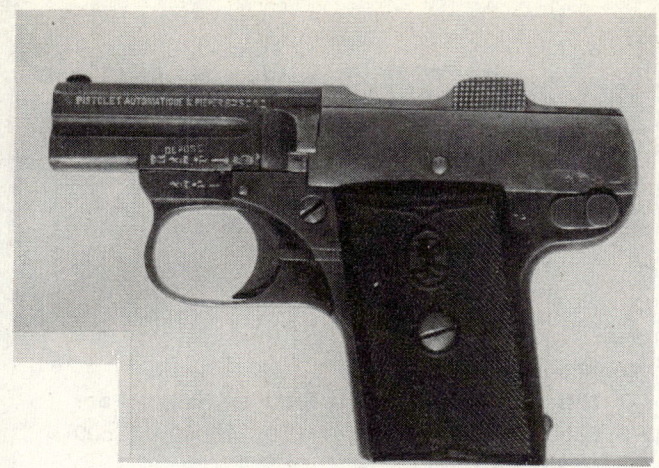

Courtesy Orvel Reichert

Exc.	V.G.	Good	Fair	Poor
175	150	125	100	75

Model 1908/Basculant

This is a tipping barrel pistol chambered for the 6.35mm Auto cartridge. Similar in appearance to the Model 1907 this model had several improvements. The front end of the barrel was retained by a pivit bolt and the recoil spring rod had a hook that engreged the lug on the slide.

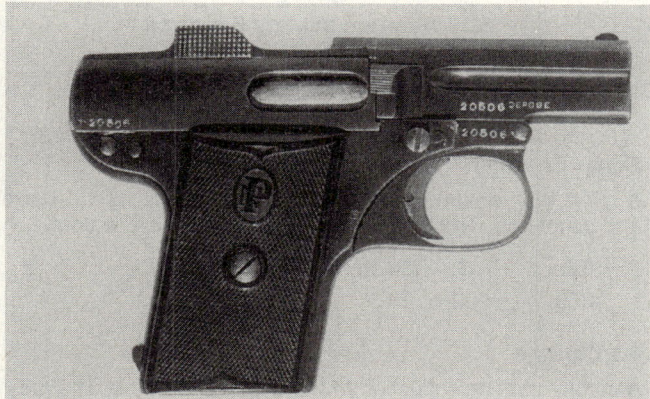

Exc.	V.G.	Good	Fair	Poor
200	175	150	125	100

Courtesy Orvel Reichert

Pieper Bayard Revolver

In competition with the Nagant gas seal revolver, Henri Pieper developed a superior design. Revolvers of this type have 5" barrels and are chambered for 8mm cartridges. The first model of this revolver had an automatic ejection system, while the second version utilized a swing-out cylinder. Standard finish is blued, with checkered hard rubber grips.

Exc.	V.G.	Good	Fair	Poor
275	250	200	150	100

Legia

This model was patterned after that of the Browning, and is chambered for the 6.35mm cartridge. The standard magazine holds 6 cartridges but a 10-round magazine was also available.

Exc.	V.G.	Good	Fair	Poor
175	150	125	100	75

Bayard

A 6.35, 7.65 or 9mm short semiautomatic pistol with a 2.5" barrel. Standard magazine capacity 6 rounds. The slide stamped "Anciens Etablissement Pieper Liege, Belgium".

Exc.	V.G.	Good	Fair	Poor
175	150	125	100	75

PILSEN, ZBROVKA

Pilsen, Czechoslovakia

Pocket Pistol

Essentially a Model 1910 Browning semiautomatic pistol without a grip safety, this pistol was of 7.65mm caliber and had a 3.5" barrel with a 6-round magazine. The slide is marked "Akciova Spolecnost drive Skodovny zavody Zbrovka Plzen." Standard finish is blued, the grips of hard rubber. Manufactured during the 1920s.

Exc.	V.G.	Good	Fair	Poor
225	200	150	125	100

PIOTTI

Brescia, Italy
Importer-W. L. Moore
Westlake Village, California

This Italian gunmaking firm is located in Gardone Val Trompia in the province of Brescia. Its shotguns are hand crafted and limited to a few each year. Each gun is made to individual specifications. Many consider them one of the best double shotguns made in the world today. Actions are either Anson & Deeley boxlock or Holland & Holland side lock. Several features are offered on these shotguns at no additional cost: type of stock and forearm, barrel length and chokes, rib, action shape and finish.

Other features are considered extra cost options and will affect the value of the gun. There are: single triggers, detachable side locks, automatic safety, recoil pads, upgraded wood, engraving, and multi-gauge sets. With the exception of a few grades Piotti guns are available in 10, 12, 16, 20, and 28 gauge, as well as .410 bore. Depending on gauge barrel lengths are from 25" to 34".

Model Piuma (BSEE)

This model is the firm's standard boxlock offering. Available in 12 gauge to .410 bore it features ejectors and a scalloped frame. Fine scroll and rosette engraving is standard.

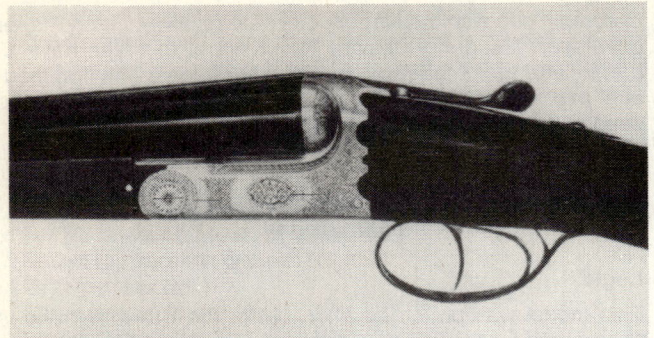

NIB	Exc.	V.G.	Good	Fair	Poor
12000	9500	6500	3000	2000	1000

Model King No. I

This model features a side lock with fine line scroll engraving with full coverage. A gold crown is inlaid on the top lever. Select walnut with hand checkering is standard. Chambered from 10 gauge to .410 bore.

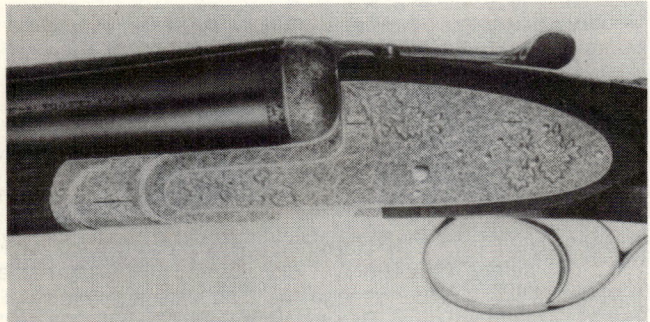

NIB	Exc.	V.G.	Good	Fair	Poor
20000	12500	8500	5000	3000	1500

Model Lunik

This model is fitted with Holland & Holland side locks. Engraving is Renaissance style relief cut scroll engraving. A gold crown is inlaid on the top lever. Offered in gauges from 10 to .410 bore.

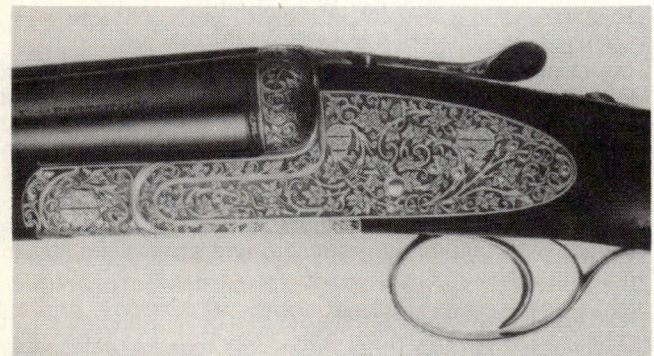

NIB	Exc.	V.G.	Good	Fair	Poor
21500	16500	11500	8500	4000	2000

Model Monaco

This side lock model features all of the best that Piotti has to offer and extra attention is paid to hand work and fitting. Only the finest European hardwoods are used. Available in 10 gauge to 410 bore. Offered with three different types of engraving designated No. 1, No. 2, and No. 4.

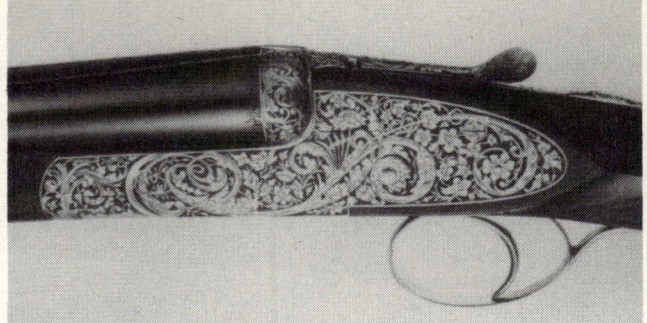

Monaco No. 1 or No. 2

NIB	Exc.	V.G.	Good	Fair	Poor
28500	22500	17000	11000	5000	2500

Monaco No. 4

NIB	Exc.	V.G.	Good	Fair	Poor
37000	31000	22000	14000	7000	3000

Model King Extra

This model is similar to the King No. 1 but with the addition of a number of engraving styles from English to gamescenes with gold inlays. Because of the wide variety of engraving patterns offered on this model it is advisable to secure a qualified appraisal before purchase.

PIRKO

SEE Austrian Military Firearms

PLAINFIELD MACHINE CO.

Dunelien, New Jersey

Super Enforcer

A cut-down version of the U.S. M1 Carbine with a 12" barrel and pistol grip. The finish is blued and stocks are walnut.

Exc.	V.G.	Good	Fair	Poor
250	200	175	125	100

M1 Carbine

A commercial reproduction of the U.S. M1 Carbine. The finish is blued. Walnut stock.

Exc.	V.G.	Good	Fair	Poor
200	175	150	100	75

MI Paratrooper Carbine.

As above with a folding wire butt stock and walnut forend.

Exc.	V.G.	Good	Fair	Poor
225	200	175	125	100

PLAINFIELD ORDNANCE CO.
Middlesex, New Jersey

Model 71
A stainless steel .22 caliber semiautomatic pistol with a 10-shot magazine and 1" barrel. Also available in .25 ACP and conversion kits were available.

Conversion Kit
Exc.	V.G.	Good	Fair	Poor
50	40	30	25	20

.22 or .25 Caliber Pistol
Exc.	V.G.	Good	Fair	Poor
150	125	100	75	50

Model 72
As above except with an alloy frame.

Exc.	V.G.	Good	Fair	Poor
150	125	100	75	50

PLANT'S MANUFACTURING CO.
New Haven, Connecticut

Army Model Revolver
A large single action revolver chambered for a .42 caliber cup primed cartridge that loads from the front of the cylinder. Barrel length 6" and of octagonal form with a rib. And the frame is made of either brass or iron. Finish is blued, with walnut or rosewood grips. Interchangeable percussion cylinders also were made for these revolvers. If present, the values would be increased approximately 30%. This revolver was marketed by Merwin & Bray, and there were approximately 1,500 of the lst and 2nd Models manufactured and 10,000 of the 3rd Model in the 1860s.

lst Model Brass Frame
Marked "Plant's Mfg. Co. New Haven, Ct." on the barrel, "M & B" on the side of the frame, and "Patented July 12, 1859" on the cylinder. Approximately 100 manufactured.

Exc.	V.G.	Good	Fair	Poor
—	—	1250	600	250

lst Model Iron Frame
As above with an iron frame. Approximately 500 made.

Exc.	V.G.	Good	Fair	Poor
—	—	1000	500	200

2nd Model Rounded Brass Frame
This model is distinguished by the markings "Merwin & Bray, New York" on the frame and the patent date "July 21, 1863". Approximately 300 made.

Exc.	V.G.	Good	Fair	Poor
—	—	900	400	150

2nd Model Iron Frame
As above with an iron frame.

Exc.	V.G.	Good	Fair	Poor
—	—	800	400	150

3rd Model
As above with a flat brass frame.

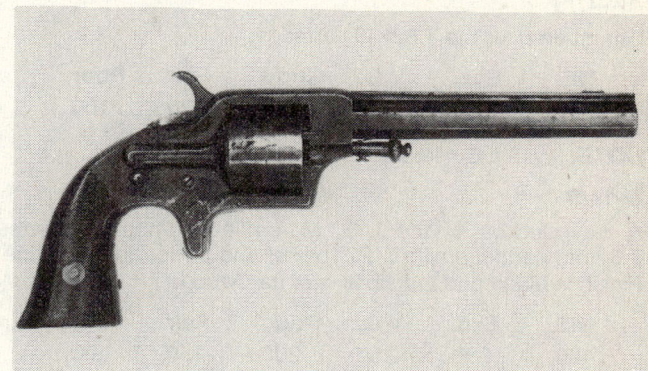

Courtesy Milwaukee Public Museum, Milwaukee, Wisconsin

Exc.	V.G.	Good	Fair	Poor
—	—	600	300	100

Pocket Revolver
Similar to the Army model described above except chambered for .30 caliber cartridges. Barrel length 3.5", five-shot cylinder. The frame normally silver plated, barrel and cylinder blued and the grips of rosewood or walnut. This model is encountered with a variety of retailer's markings: Eagle Arms Co., New York, "Reynolds, Plant & Hotchkiss, New Haven, Ct.," and Merwin & Bray Firearms Co., N.Y." Approximately 20,000 were made.

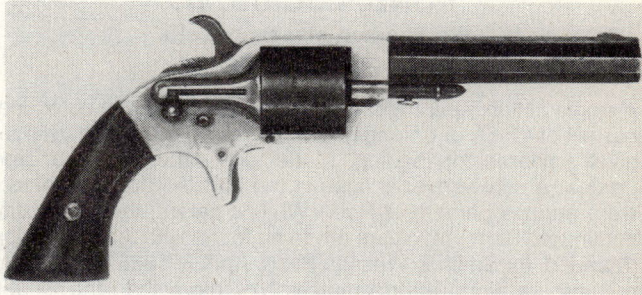

Courtesy Milwaukee Public Museum, Milwaukee, Wisconsin

Exc.	V.G.	Good	Fair	Poor
—	—	350	200	100

POLY-TECHNOLOGIES, INC.
China
Importer-Keng's
Riverdale, Georgia
Distributor-PTK Int.
Atlanta, Georgia

SKS
A semiautomatic rifle chambered for the 7.62x39mm cartridge with a 20.5" barrel and 10-shot fixed magazine, based on the Soviet Siminov carbine. Finish is blued, and the stock and hand guard are made of a Chinese hardwood.

NIB	Exc.	V.G.	Good	Fair	Poor
125	100	80	70	50	35

AKS-762

A semiautomatic version of the Chinese-type 56 Assault rifle chambered for the 7.62x39mm cartridge with a 16.5" barrel. Furnished with a 20-round magazine and a Chinese bayonet. The finish is blued, and the stock is hardwood.

NIB	Exc.	V.G.	Good	Fair	Poor
125	100	85	70	60	50

AK-47/S

Chambered for the 7.62x39 cartridge.

NIB	Exc.	V.G.	Good	Fair	Poor
475	400	325	250	200	150

NOTE: With a Soviet style bayonet-Add $15.

M-14/S

A reproduction of the U.S. M14 rifle chambered for the 7.62mm cartridge with a 22" barrel and 20-round magazine. Finish is blued and the stock is of hardwood.

NIB	Exc.	V.G.	Good	Fair	Poor
400	300	250	200	150	100

POINTER
Hopkins & Allen
Norwich, Connecticut

Single Shot Derringer

An unmarked Hopkins & Allen single shot pistol stamped "Pointer" on the barrel. Barrel length 2.75", caliber .22, frame of nickel-plated brass. The barrel swings sideways for loading. Bird's-head walnut grips. It is believed that about 2,500 were made between 1870 and 1890.

Exc.	V.G.	Good	Fair	Poor
—	—	300	150	75

POND, LUCIUS, W.
Worchester, Massachusetts

Pocket Revolver

A single action, spur trigger .32 caliber revolver with octagonal barrels of 4", 5", or 6" length. The barrel top strap and cylinder pivot upwards for loading. Made with either brass or iron frames. A screwdriver is fitted in the butt. As these revolvers were an infringement of Rollin White's patent, they were discontinued. Some revolvers are to be found with the inscription "Manuf'd. for Smith & Wesson Pat'd. April 5, 1855." These examples are worth approximately 20% more than the values listed below.

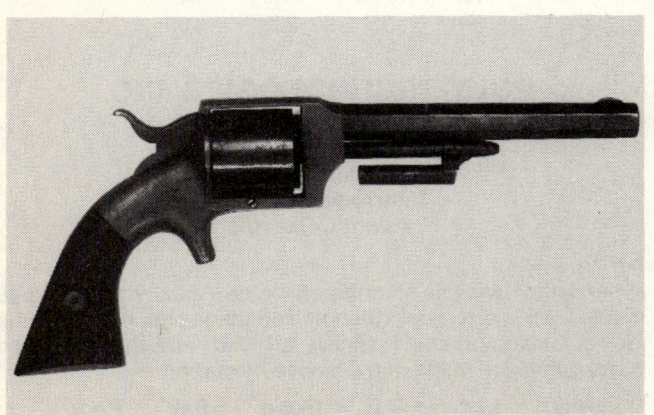

Courtesy Milwaukee Public Museum, Milwaukee, Wisconsin

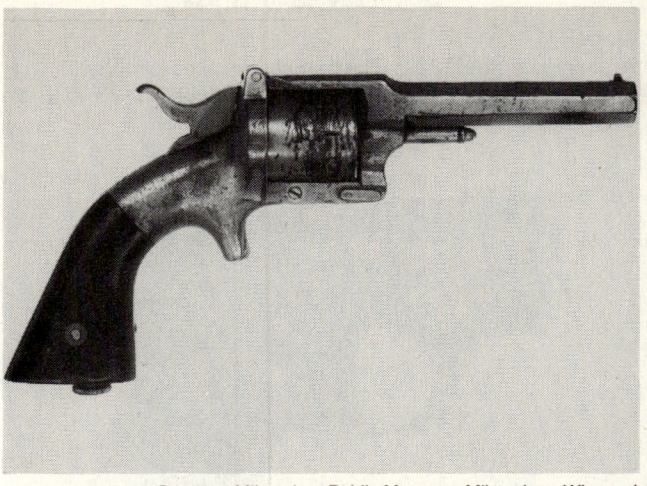

Courtesy Milwaukee Public Museum, Milwaukee, Wisconsin

Brass Framed Revolver

Exc.	V.G.	Good	Fair	Poor
—	—	500	200	100

Iron Framed Revolver

Exc.	V.G.	Good	Fair	Poor
—	—	350	150	75

Separate Chamber Revolver

To avoid the Rollin White patent, this revolver is chambered for .22 or .32 caliber rimfire cartridges that fit into separate steel chamber inserts that can be removed from the front of the cylinder for loading. The .22 caliber version has a 3.5" octagonal barrel with a 7-round unfluted cylinder; the .32 caliber version has a 4", 5", or 6" octagonal barrel and 6-shot unfluted cylinder. Frames are of silver-plated brass; and the barrels and cylinders are blued. Grips of walnut. Standard markings include "L.W. Pond, Worcester, Mass." and patent dates. Approximately 2,000 manufactured in .22 caliber and 5,000 in .32 caliber between 1863 and 1870.

.22 Caliber Version

Exc.	V.G.	Good	Fair	Poor
—	—	600	300	150

.32 Caliber Version

Exc.	V.G.	Good	Fair	Poor
—	—	600	300	150

PORTER, P. W.
New York, New York

Turret Revolver

An extremely rare 9-shot vertical cylinder .41 caliber percussion revolver with a 5.25" round barrel. The triggerguard is also a lever that turns the cylinder and cocks the hammer. An automatic primer system is also fitted to this revolver. Manufactured during the 1850s in an unknown quantity.

Exc.	V.G.	Good	Fair	Poor
—	—	12500	5000	1000

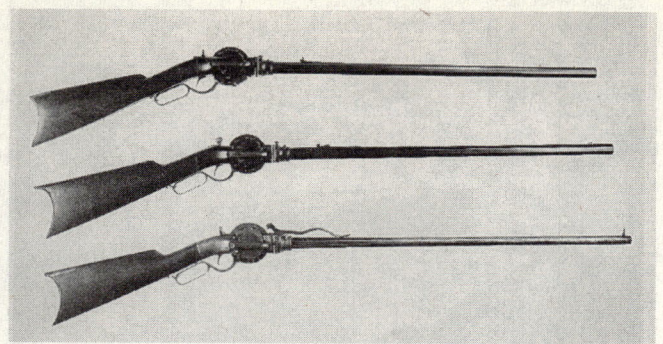

Turret Rifle

A 9-shot vertical cylinder .44 caliber rifle with either a 26" or 28" octagonal barrel. The only markings are "Address P.W. Porter/New York." Four variations of this rifle are known and the 22" barreled carbine would command a 25% premium. Approximately 1,250 were manufactured during the 1850s.

1st Model with Canister Magazine

Fitted with a 30-shot round canister magazine over the turret, this model was made in Tennessee and is extremely rare. Most often the canisters are not encountered and values reflect this. Approximately 25 were made.

Exc.	V.G.	Good	Fair	Poor
—	—	7500	3500	1000

2nd Model (New York)

Exc.	V.G.	Good	Fair	Poor
—	—	8000	3500	1000

3rd Model (New York)

This model has a screw-off cover over the magazine.

Exc.	V.G.	Good	Fair	Poor
—	—	6000	3000	750

4th Model (New York)

As above but without an automatic primer magazine and the nipples are exposed.

Exc.	V.G.	Good	Fair	Poor
—	—	6000	3000	750

POWELL, W. & SON LTD.
Birmingham, England
Importer-Jaqua's
Findlay, Ohio

Number 3 Boxlock

A custom order double-barrel shotgun available in all standard gauges, fitted with single trigger and automatic ejectors. A receiver engraved and blued. Stock of French walnut. Prospective purchasers should seek individual appraisals for these arms.

Exc.	V.G.	Good	Fair	Poor
7500	6500	5250	4000	3250

Number I Sidelock

A sidelock double-barrel shotgun of the first quality. Prospective purchasers should seek individual appraisals.

Exc.	V.G.	Good	Fair	Poor
17500	16000	12000	9000	7500

PRAGA, ZBROVKA
Prague, Czechoslovakia

Established in 1918 by A. Novotny, this company ceased operations in 1926.

Vz2I

A 7.65mm semiautomatic pistol patterned after the Model 1910 Browning, but without a grip safety. Barrel length 3.5", magazine capacity 6 rounds, grips of wood. The slide is marked "Zbrojowka Praga Praha."

Exc.	V.G.	Good	Fair	Poor
300	250	200	150	100

Praga 1921

A 6.35mm semiautomatic pistol with a slide of stamped steel cut with a finger groove at the front. Folding trigger. The barrel 2" in length. The slide is marked "Zbrojowka Praga Praha Patent Cal 6.35." The grips of molded plastic, with the name "Praga" cast in them. A dangerous feature of this pistol is that it is striker-fired with no hammer and is intended to be carried fully loaded and cocked in the pocket with absolutely no safety of any kind. The folding trigger does not spring out until the slide is drawn back slightly by using the finger groove in the front of it.

Exc.	V.G.	Good	Fair	Poor
250	225	200	150	100

PRANDELLI & GASPARINI
Brescia, Italy
Importer-Richland Arms Co.
Blissfield, Michigan

Boxlock Side-by-side Shotgun

A good quality double-barrel 12 or 20 gauge shotgun with 26" or 28" barrels. Single selective trigger, automatic ejectors and an Anson & Deeley action. Blued, stock of select walnut.

Exc.	V.G.	Good	Fair	Poor
1500	1150	900	700	450

Sidelock Side-x-side Shotgun

Similar to the above, but with full sidelocks.

Exc.	V.G.	Good	Fair	Poor
2500	2150	1500	900	500

Boxlock Over/Under Shotgun

An Over/Under double-barrel 12 or 20 gauge shotgun with 26" or 28" barrels, single triggers and automatic ejectors. Blued, with select walnut stock.

Exc.	V.G.	Good	Fair	Poor
1750	1250	950	700	350

Sidelock Over/Under Shotgun

As above with full sidelocks.

Exc.	V.G.	Good	Fair	Poor
3000	2500	1800	950	450

PRATT, GEORGE
Middletown, Connecticut

Trap Gun

A doubled-barreled, stationary burglar alarm or animal trap gun that is chambered for .38 caliber centerfire. The barrel is 4" in length, and all of the components are made of cast iron with a galvanized finish. Barrels and action are mounted on a round base, which can turn 360 degrees. The patent date "Dec. 18, 1883" is marked on the gun. There were many manufactured between 1880 and the early 1890s.

Exc.	V.G.	Good	Fair	Poor
—	—	500	250	100

PRATT, H.
Roxbury, Massachusetts

Under Hammer Pistol

A .31 caliber percussion single shot pistol with an 8.5" octagonal barrel. The frame marked "H. Pratt's/ Patent." Manufactured during the 1850s.

Exc.	V.G.	Good	Fair	Poor
—	—	800	400	200

PRECISION SMALL ARMS
Beverly Hills, California

PSA-25

This is a semi-automatic pistol chambered for the .25 ACP. The barrel length is 2.13". Magazine capacity is 6 rounds. The frame and slide is steel alloy. Weight is 9.5 oz. Overall length is 4.11". Grips are black polymer. Standard finish is black oxide.

NIB	Exc.	V.G.	Good	Fair	Poor
225	175	150	125	100	75

NOTE: For brushed chrome finish add $50 and for stainless steel add $75.

Featherweight Model

Same as above but with aluminum frame and chrome slide with gold plated trigger.

NIB	Exc.	V.G.	Good	Fair	Poor
375	300	250	200	150	100

Renaissance Model

Same as above but with hand engraved steel frame and slide. Antique stain chrome finish.

NIB	Exc.	V.G.	Good	Fair	Poor
900	700	600	450	350	200

PREMIER
Italy and Spain

A trade name used by various retailers on shotguns manufactured in Italy and Spain that were imported during the late 1950s and early 1960s.

Regent Side-x-Side Shotgun

A double-barrel shotgun with 26" to 30" barrels available in all standard gauges. Receiver blued, stock of walnut. Normally found with a pistol grip and beavertail forend.

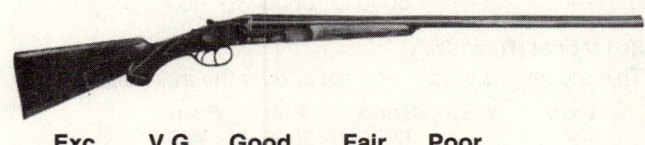

Exc.	V.G.	Good	Fair	Poor
300	275	225	175	100

Regent Magnum

As above but chambered for the 3.5" 10 gauge Magnum cartridge. Barrels 32" in length and choked full and full.

Exc.	V.G.	Good	Fair	Poor
350	300	250	200	150

Brush King

Identical to the Regent Model except that it is fitted with 22" modified and improved cylinder barrels and a straight grip English style stock.

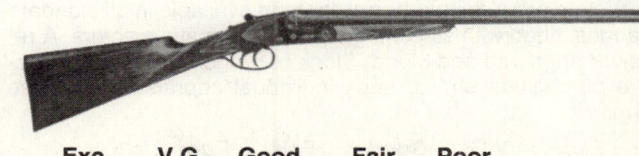

Exc.	V.G.	Good	Fair	Poor
275	250	200	150	100

Ambassador Model

A more ornate version of the Regent Model.

Exc.	V.G.	Good	Fair	Poor
400	350	300	250	175

Presentation Custom Grade

A custom-order shotgun with game scenes as well as gold and silver inlays.

Exc.	V.G.	Good	Fair	Poor
1000	750	600	500	400

PRESCOTT, E. A.
Worcester, Massachusetts

Percussion Pocket Revolver

A .31 caliber percussion spur trigger revolver with either 4" or 4.25" octagonal barrel and a 6-shot cylinder. The frame of brass, and the grips of walnut. It is believed that approximately 100 were manufactured during 1860 and 1861.

Exc.	V.G.	Good	Fair	Poor
—	—	1200	500	200

Pocket Revolver

A .22 or .32 spur trigger revolver with a barrel of either 3" or 4" length. The .22 caliber version has a 7-shot cylinder and the .32 caliber version a 6-shot cylinder. The standard markings are "E.A. Prescott Worchester Mass. Pat. Oct. 2, 1860." Approximately 1,000 were manufactured between 1862 and 1867.

Exc.	V.G.	Good	Fair	Poor
—	—	550	250	100

Belt Revolver

Although similar in appearance to early Smith & Wesson revolvers, the Prescott has a solid frame. Available in either .22 or .32 caliber, the .22 caliber model has a 3" barrel and the .32 caliber a 5.75" barrel. Markings are identical found on the Pocket Revolver. Approximately 300 were manufactured between 1861 and 1863.

Exc.	V.G.	Good	Fair	Poor
—	—	550	250	100

Navy Revolver

A single action revolver fitted with a conventional trigger, chambered for .38 rimfire cartridges with a 7.25" octagonal barrel. The unfluted cylinder holds 6 shots. The frame is of either silver-plated brass or blued iron; and the barrel and the cylinder are blued, with walnut grips. The barrel marked "E.A. Prescott, Worcester, Mass. Pat. Oct. 2, 1860." It is believed that several hundred were manufactured between 1861 and 1863.

Courtesy Milwaukee Public Museum, Milwaukee, Wisconsin

Exc.	V.G.	Good	Fair	Poor
—	—	800	350	150

PRETORIA
Pretoria, South Africa
SEE PAF

PRINZ
Germany
Importer-Helmut Hofmann
Placitas, New Mexico

Grade I Bolt Action Rifle

A high quality bolt action rifle chambered for the .243, .30-06, .308, 7mm Remington Magnum or the .300 Winchester Magnum cartridges. Barrel length 24", double-set triggers available. Finish is blued, stock of oil-finished select walnut. Introduced in 1989.

NIB	Exc.	V.G.	Good	Fair	Poor
500	450	400	350	300	225

Grade 2 Bolt Action Rifle

As above with a rosewood forend tip and pistol grip cap.

NIB	Exc.	V.G.	Good	Fair	Poor
550	500	450	400	350	250

Tip Up Rifle

A high quality single shot rifle available in a variety of American cartridges. Barrel length 24" and not furnished with sights. Finish blued, stock of select walnut.

NIB	Exc.	V.G.	Good	Fair	Poor
2200	1850	1500	1150	950	750

Model 85 "Princess"

A combination 12 gauge shotgun and rifle with 24" or 26" barrels, double triggers, and automatic ejectors. Finish blued, stock of select walnut.

NIB	Exc.	V.G.	Good	Fair	Poor
1500	1250	1000	800	750	600

PRITCHETT, POTTS & HUNT
SEE English Military Firearms

PROFESSIONAL ORDNANCE, INC.
Ontario, California

Carbon-15 Pistol

Introduced in 1996 this semi-automatic pistol is built on a carbon fiber upper and lower receiver. Chambered for the 5.56 cartridge it has a 7.25" stainless steel barrel. Ghost ring sights are standard. Magazine is AR-15 compatible. Furnished with a 10-round magazine. Weight is approximately 46 oz.

NOTE: This pistol has several options which will affect value.

NIB	Exc.	V.G.	Good	Fair	Poor
1600	1250	—	—	—	—

PROTECTION
Unknown

Protection Pocket Revolver

A .28 caliber percussion spur trigger revolver with a 3.25" octagonal barrel and 6-shot cylinder roll engraved with a police arrest scene. The frame of brass and grips of walnut. The cylinder is marked "Protection". Approximately 1,000 were manufactured during the late 1850s and early 1860s.

1st Model Roll Engraved Cylinder

Exc.	V.G.	Good	Fair	Poor
—	—	700	300	100

2nd Model Plain Cylinder Above Serial No. 650

Exc.	V.G.	Good	Fair	Poor
—	—	600	250	100

PULASKI ARMORY
Pulaski, Tennessee

Founded in 1861, this firm produced rifles for the State of Tennessee. Overall length 48-1/2" - 49-1/2"; round barrels 32-1/2" - 33-1/4"; caliber .54. Resemble U.S. Model 1841 Rifles except without patchbox; had single screw sporting locks with diamond-shaped ferrules; usually marked on barrel "PULASKI T. C.S.A. 61." Production estimated to be about 300.

Prospective purchasers are strongly advised to secure an expert appraisal prior to acquisition.

Exc.	V.G.	Good	Fair	Poor
—	—	10000	5000	1500

PURDEY, J. & SONS LTD.
London, England

Perhaps the finest manufacturer of shotguns, double-barrel and bolt action rifles in the world. Virtually all their products are made on special order and it is impossible to establish general values for their products. Prospective purchasers are advised to seek qualified guidance prior to the acquisition of any arms made by this maker.

PYRENEES
Hendaye, France

Founded in 1923 and still in operation today, this company has produced a variety of models. The most popular of which was the "Unique" series. Prior to 1939, a variety of trade names were marked on their products such as the following: Superior, Capitan, Cesar, Chantecler, Chimere Renoir, Colonial, Prima, Rapid Maxima, Reina, Demon, Demon-marine, Ebac, Elite, Gallia, Ixor, Le Majestic, St. Hubert, Selecta, Sympathique, Touriste, Le Sanspariel, Le Tout Acier, Mars, Perfect, Triomphe Francais, Unis & Vindex. Following 1939 this company's products are simply stamped "Unique".

Model 10 Unique

A 6.35mm semiautomatic pistol similar to the Model 1906 Browning. The slide is marked "Le Veritable Pistolet Francais Unique." Introduced in 1923.

Exc.	V.G.	Good	Fair	Poor
200	175	150	100	75

Model 11

As above with a grip safety and loaded chamber indicator.

Exc.	V.G.	Good	Fair	Poor
250	200	175	125	100

Model 12

As above but without the loaded chamber indicator.

Exc.	V.G.	Good	Fair	Poor
225	175	150	100	75

Model 13

As above with a 7-shot magazine.

Exc.	V.G.	Good	Fair	Poor
225	175	150	100	75

Model 14

As above with a 9-shot magazine.

Exc.	V.G.	Good	Fair	Poor
225	175	150	100	75

Model 15

As above but in 7.65mm caliber. Introduced in 1923.

Exc.	V.G.	Good	Fair	Poor
250	175	150	100	75

Model 16

As above with a 7-shot magazine.

Exc.	V.G.	Good	Fair	Poor
250	175	150	100	75

Model 17

As above with a 9-shot magazine.

Exc.	V.G.	Good	Fair	Poor
300	250	200	150	100

Model 18

A 7.65mm caliber semiautomatic pistol patterned after the Model 1920 Browning but without a grip safety.

Exc.	V.G.	Good	Fair	Poor
250	175	150	100	75

Model 19

As above with a 7-shot magazine.

Exc.	V.G.	Good	Fair	Poor
250	175	150	100	75

Model 20

As above but with a 9-shot magazine.

Exc.	V.G.	Good	Fair	Poor
275	200	175	125	100

Model 21

As above except chambered for the 9mm short cartridge.

Exc.	V.G.	Good	Fair	Poor
275	200	175	125	100

During World War 11 production at this company was taken over by the Nazis. Consequently, the various models listed above will be found with German inspection marks. These arms are worth approximately 25% more than the values listed.

POSTWAR UNIQUE

Model BCF66

A 9mm short semiautomatic pistol with a 3.5" barrel, open top slide and external hammer. The slide marked "Armes Unique Hendaye BP France." Finish blued, grips of plastic.

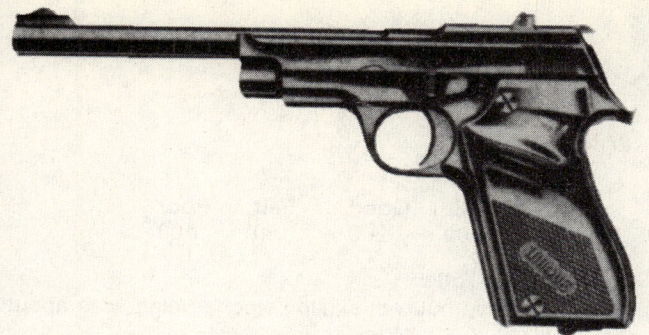

Exc.	V.G.	Good	Fair	Poor
225	175	150	125	100

Exc.	V.G.	Good	Fair	Poor
275	250	200	175	125

Model C

Virtually identical to the Model 17 listed above. The slide marked "7.65 Court 9 coups Unique." Finish blued, plastic grips with the trademark "PF" in a circle cast into them.

Exc.	V.G.	Good	Fair	Poor
200	150	125	100	75

Model D

A .22 caliber semiautomatic pistol with barrels ranging from 4" to 7.5" in length. The 7.5" barreled version fitted with a muzzle brake. Magazine capacity 10 rounds. Finish blued, plastic grips.

Exc.	V.G.	Good	Fair	Poor
225	175	150	125	100

Model Des 69

As above with better quality sights, special trigger and improved grips.

Model DES/VO

Identical to the Model D but chambered for .22 caliber short cartridges.

Exc.	V.G.	Good	Fair	Poor
225	175	150	125	100

Model F

Identical to the Model C except chambered for 9mm short cartridges. Magazine capacity 8 rounds.

Exc.	V.G.	Good	Fair	Poor
225	175	150	125	100

Model L

Similar to the Model D except chambered for .22, .32 ACP, and 9mm short cartridges. Available with either a steel or alloy frame.

Exc.	V.G.	Good	Fair	Poor
250	225	200	150	125

QUACKENBUSH
Herkimer, New York

Quackenbush Safety Cartridge Rifle

A single shot, takedown boy's rifle chambered for .22 rimfire cartridges in either .22 short or .22 long. Barrel length 18". Weight was about 4.5 lbs. All metal parts nickel-plated. The breech swings to the side for loading. Stock of walnut. Manufactured for only a few years.

Courtesy Mike Stuckslager

Exc.	V.G.	Good	Fair	Poor
500	400	200	150	100

Junior Safety Rifle

Same as above but with skelton stock. Weight was about 4 lbs.

Exc.	V.G.	Good	Fair	Poor
450	350	200	150	100

QUINABAUG MFG. CO.
Southridge, Massachusetts

Under Hammer Pistol

A .31 caliber percussion under hammer pistol with barrels from 3" to 8" in length. Frame of blued iron, the grips of walnut or maple. The top of the frame is marked "Quinabaug Rifle M'g Co. Southbridge, Mass." The barrels are normally marked "E. Hutchings & Co. Agents". Manufactured during the 1850s.

Exc.	V.G.	Good	Fair	Poor
---	---	700	350	150

R.E.
Valencia, Spain

The initials "R.E." stand for "Republica Espana". This copy of the Spanish army Model 1921, also known as the Astra 400, was produced between 1936 and 1939 during the Spanish civil war by the Republican forces. This variation can be identified by the "RE" monogram on the butt and the absence of any manufacturer's stampings.

Exc.	V.G.	Good	Fair	Poor
325	250	200	150	100

R. G. INDUSTRIES
Miami, Florida
Rohm Gmbh
Sontheim/Brenz, Germany

An importer of inexpensive handguns, which ceased operations in 1986.

RG-25

A .25 caliber semiautomatic pistol available with either a blued or chrome-plated finish.

Exc.	V.G.	Good	Fair	Poor
75	65	50	35	25

RG-16

A double-barrel .22 caliber chrome-plated derringer.

Exc.	V.G.	Good	Fair	Poor
75	65	50	35	25

RG-17

As above except chambered for. 38 special cartridge.

Exc.	V.G.	Good	Fair	Poor
90	80	70	50	25

RG-14

A .22 caliber double action revolver with a 4" barrel and 6-shot cylinder. Blued finish, plastic grips.

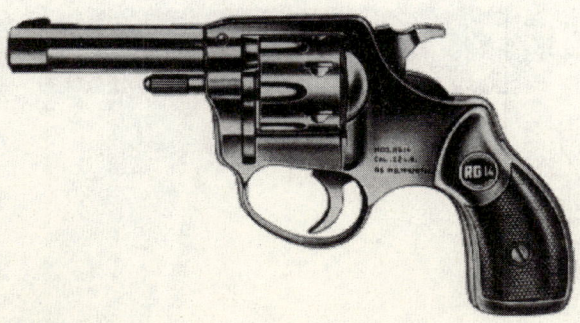

Exc.	V.G.	Good	Fair	Poor
90	80	70	50	25

RG-30

A .22 l.r. or Magnum double action revolver. Blued finish, plastic grips.

Exc.	V.G.	Good	Fair	Poor
75	65	50	35	25

RG-40

A .38 special double action revolver with swing-out cylinder. Blued finish, plastic grips.

Exc.	V.G.	Good	Fair	Poor
90	80	70	50	25

RG-57

A .357 or .44 Magnum double action revolver with 6-shot cylinder. Blued finish, checkered wood grips.

Exc.	V.G.	Good	Fair	Poor
125	100	80	65	50

RG-63

A .22 caliber double action revolver resembling a Colt Model 1873.

Exc.	V.G.	Good	Fair	Poor
60	50	40	35	25

RG-66

A .22 or .22 Magnum single action revolver patterned after the Colt Model 1873.

Exc.	V.G.	Good	Fair	Poor
60	50	40	35	25

RG-66T
As above with adjustable sights.

Exc.	V.G.	Good	Fair	Poor
65	55	45	35	25

RG-74
A .22 caliber double action revolver with swing-out cylinder.

Exc.	V.G.	Good	Fair	Poor
75	65	55	45	35

RG-88
A .357 Magnum double action revolver with swing-out cylinder.

Exc.	V.G.	Good	Fair	Poor
90	80	70	60	40

RWS
Nurenberg, Germany
Dynamit Nobel

Model 820 S
A .22 caliber target rifle with 24" heavy barrel and adjustable aperture sights. The trigger fully adjustable, three position adjustable match stock with stippled pistol grip and forend. Discontinued in 1986.

Exc.	V.G.	Good	Fair	Poor
800	700	550	450	350

Model 820 SF
As above with a heavier barrel. Discontinued in 1986.

Exc.	V.G.	Good	Fair	Poor
850	725	575	475	375

Model 820 K
Offhand "Running Boar" model of the above with a lighter barrel. Furnished without sights. Discontinued in 1986.

Exc.	V.G.	Good	Fair	Poor
775	675	525	425	325

RADOM
Radom, Poland

Fabryka Broniw Radomu
This company was established after World War I and produced military arms for Poland. During WWII the Radom factory was operated by the Nazis. Production was not recommenced after the war.

Ng 30
A copy of the Russian Nagant revolver chambered for the 7.62mm Russian cartridge. Approximately 20,000 were manufactured during 1930 and 1936.

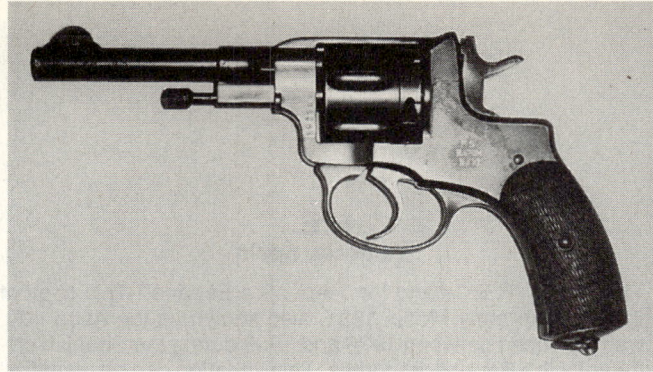

Courtesy Richard M. Kumor, SR.

Exc.	V.G.	Good	Fair	Poor
1000	750	500	200	100

VIS-35
A 9mm semiautomatic pistol with a 4.5" barrel, fixed sights and an 8-shot magazine. On this model there is no manual safety, however, a decocking lever is installed that allows the hammer to be safely lowered on a loaded chamber. Versions made prior to WWII are engraved with a Polish eagle on the slide and "FB" and "VIS" are molded into the grips. These pre-war pistols are slotted for a holster stock. German production pistols were made without the decocking lever and subsequently without the stripping catch. They also eliminated the stock slot. These pistols were stamped "P35p" and bear the Waffenamt inspector's mark "WaA77." Near the end of the war the takedown was eliminated and the grips were replaced with crude wooden grips. The slide, barrel, and frame are all numbered to each other.

Polish Eagle Model-1936 through 1939

Courtesy Richard M. Kumor, Sr.

Exc.	V.G.	Good	Fair	Poor
1500	1200	600	350	200

Nazi Captured Polish Eagle-Waffenamt Marked

Exc.	V.G.	Good	Fair	Poor
2500	1500	800	450	300

Nazi Polish Eagle (Navy Marked)

Courtesy Richard M. Kumor, Sr.

Will command a premium price.

Nazi Production Model

Exc.	V.G.	Good	Fair	Poor
450	350	250	200	175

Nazi Production Model-"bnz" code

This is a late Nazi production with no other slide markings other than "bnz". A rare variation.

Courtesy Richard M. Kumor, Sr.

Exc.	V.G.	Good	Fair	Poor
1500	1200	800	650	500

RANDALL FIREARMS CO.
Sun Valley, California
By Rick 'KK' Kennerknecht & Steve Comus
In Honor of Art Hanke

Stainless steel semiautomatic handguns are now common, but this fact of life in the 1990s would never have come to be had it not been for a small, now defunct company that dared to show the rest of the firearms industry the pathway to the future. Randall Firearms Company of Sun Valley, California, made it all happen with a line of high-quality Model 1911 derivatives.

Although Randall pistols were only manufactured from June 7, 1983, to May 15, 1985, they ushered in an entirely new era for handguns, thus carving for themselves a place in the history of firearms around the world. This historic niche, coupled with the fact that Randall pistols are exemplary specimens of their genre, has made Randall pistols collectible.

There were 24 different models with 12 variations in three different calibers. Among Randall's innovations were two significant breakthroughs in the 1911 field. One of these breakthroughs came when Randall made the first production pistol if its kind in stainless steel. The second was the introduction of a true mirror image of the 1911 in a left-hand configuration. This had never been done before on a production basis.

It began with a small company called KEN-AIR, Inc., which had been in the aircraft instrument repair business in the San Fernando Valley area of Los Angeles County in California since the mid-1950s. Then, in 1981, the company entered into a diversification program that ultimately led to the Randall pistol.

The "KEN" in KEN-AIR stands for Ken Lau, founder and chairman of the company. Lau and WWII Air Force hero, Brigadier General Russell Randall, met while working together as advisors to China Airlines.

In 1981, Lau and his KEN-AIR company received a contract from the government of South Korea to build a .45 ACP handgun. By the time production facilities at the Sun Valley manufacturing plant were established, the Korean government changed its mind and canceled the contract.

This left Lau's firm with the facilities to produce Model 1911 handguns, but no customer. By then, Lau had done more than just set up another firearms production line. He had relied on his long experience in the manufacture of parts for the aerospace industry when formulating exactly how the line would operate, and even used his knowledge of materials seen in the aerospace business as a basis for a series of decisions that helped make the Randall pistol unique.

In addition to the manufacturing hardware and engineering, Lau also assembled a team of management experts from throughout the firearms industry, people who held responsible posts at other companies such as Colt, Smith & Wesson, Remington, Winchester, Vega, Detonics, and Thomas.

Not only were Lau and Gen. Randall friends, but they were also business associates, which included Randall as a member of the board of directors of the company when it incorporated in January 1981. In addition to Randall's association with Lau in China Airlines and KEN-AIR, the general also was an advisor with Litton Industries.

Trading on the general's worldwide name identification, the new gun company was named after him: Randall Firearms Company. When the Korean government contract fell through, Lau decided to continue with the project and court the civilian markets instead. By November 1982, everything was set, and Randall announced the introduction of its first handgun—the all stainless-steel automatic.

Except for some minor changes necessitated in manufacturing, Randall pistols were much unchanged from the traditional Browning design. However, because every part except for the grips was made of aircraft quality stainless steel, this really was a new gun and quickly became known as "the only stainless steel auto fit for duty."

Although some prototype pistols were made as early as 1982, the first production Randalls came off the line on June 7, 1983. They were examples of the Service Model A111, which was a standard 1911A1. It featured the typical round-top slide with fixed sights and a five-inch, 10-groove barrel. The A111 pistols were produced throughout the life of the company and, in all, there were 3,431 produced in a serial number range of RF02000C through RF09208C. All A111 Randalls were chambered in .45 ACP. Next came the Model A121 on Sept. 14, 1983. Initially, the A121 was also called a

Service Model, but since there was some confusion with the designation, the marketing folks at Randall decided to make a change. In 1984 it became known as the Combat Model, and at that time those guns were rollmarked "Combat" just under the ejection port. The only other changes in that model at that time were cosmetic: the hammer was rounded, and Pachmayr grips were supplied as standard. Although catalogs of the era stated that it would be supplied with a flat mainspring housing, no such guns were ever actually produced.

The only other distinguishing factor between the A111 and the A121 was the A121 had a flat-top slide rather than the rounded top on the slide of the A111. Both models had fixed sights and were in .45 ACP only. Model A121 pistols were in the Randall line through June 11, 1984. In all, 1,067 of these pistols were made in a serial number range of RF02211C through RF08620C.

By Sept. 28, 1983, Randall was ready to offer a third variation in its line of .45s; this was the Service Model A131. The only difference between the A121 and A131 pistols was that the latter model sported a Millett Model 100 Gold Cup-type adjustable rear sight, which fit into a milled slot atop the rear of the slide. This model also stayed in the Randall line throughout the life of the company. In all, 2,083 of these pistols were made in a serial-number range of RF02135C through RF09201C. The last model A131 pistol was built on Oct. 22, 1984.

Collectors should note that more than 322 Service Models were made from parts outside the factory after the company closed. These pistols are not as highly collectible.

SERVICE MODEL 9MM PISTOLS

Introduced on Jan. 11, 1984, was the first Service Model A112 in 9mm Parabellum. Essentially, this was the same gun as the A111 except for caliber. In fact, the slides for the A112 pistols were made from the same 17-4 stainless steel investment casting as were the slides for the A111 in .45 ACP. This model remained in the line until July 23, 1984. In all, 301 of these 9mm pistols were produced in a serial number range of RV04666C through RF07599C.

Although there were relatively few Randall A112 pistols ever made, a change in production early on resulted in what was essentially two separate sub-models. The first Model A112 pistols employed stainless steel, six-groove standard Colt-type barrels and barrel bushings. The outside diameter of the muzzle of those barrels was 0.495 inch.

By 1984, it became apparent that the company could facilitate production by using a fatter barrel that would allow the standardization of barrel bushings. These later production Model A112 pistols featured barrels that had the same outside diameter as the standard .45 ACP. There was more of a change than simply the outside diameter of the barrel in these latter-day Model A112 handguns. Randall, at that time, went from six-groove rifling to its hallmark 10-groove configuration in these 9mm fat barrel units. The rifling was changed to enhance accuracy, and it also made the number of grooves standard throughout the Randall line as the .45s always had 10-groove barrels.

Production of the Combat Model A122 began on July 23, 1984, and ended Dec. 13, 1984. It was essentially nothing more than the Model A121 (.45 ACP) in 9mm. This meant that it differed from the Model Al12 9mm in that it had a slide with a flat top and fixed rear sight, a round hammer and Pachmayr grips. Only 18 Model A122 pistols were ever made, making it the rarest of the right-handed, full-size service pistols Randall ever produced. Of the total production of 9mm Randalls, nearly 75 percent were exported to the Euro-

pean countries of England, Germany, Austria, Switzerland, and France. Only 35% of those 9mm Randalls had the fat barrels. Of Randall's total production of full-size, right-handed service models, the 9mm pistols represented 3.2 percent.

"COMMANDER"-SIZE .45 ACP PISTOLS

By August 1983, Randall expanded its line of pistols to include the Service Model-C configuration. The "C" stood for compact. Initially, these handguns were roll-marked "Service Model-C." However, in the beginning of 1984, the company decided to give the guns a new identity, and dubbed this configuration as the "Raider," named for General Randall's unit, which had been known as Randall's Raiders.

Introduced Aug. 31, 1983, the first in the Service Model-C series was the A211, which featured a round-top slide and fixed sights. Barrel length was 4.25 inches, making the overall length .75 of an inch less than the standard A111. Magazine capacity (seven) and height remained the same. Weight of the A211 was 36 oz. compared to 38 oz. for the full-sized Model A111. After 992 of the Model A211 pistols were made, production of that model ceased on Sept. 6, 1984. The serial number range went from RF02001C through RF05808C.

Next came the Model A231, which differed from the A211 in that it had a flat-top slide and Millet Model 100 Gold Cup-type adjustable rear sight. The Model A231 was introduced on Nov. 7, 1983. Only 574 of these pistols were manufactured, with a serial number range of RF02009C through RF03814C. The last of this model was manufactured on Oct. 6, 1984.

"COMMANDER"-SIZE 9MM PISTOLS

The Model A212 was introduced on Feb. 1, 1984. Like its .45 ACP counterparts, it also went through a name change in 1984, becoming another in the "Raider" family. Primarily, the biggest difference between the A212 and the A211 (.45 ACP) was the caliber. However, the A212 also was made in two different barrel widths—the latter are rarer, being the fat barrel guns. In all, there were only 76 of the A212 pistols manufactured, of which a mere 25 had fat barrels. The serial number range was RF02359C through RF03815C. The last A212 was manufactured on Dec. 13, 1984.

Randall Model A232 came on-line on Oct. 11, 1984, and differed from the A212 in that it had a flat-top slide with the Millett Model 100 adjustable rear sight. In all, only five Model A232 pistols were ever produced, and it is believed that they all were exported to Europe since none have surfaced since in the United States. The serial number range was from RF02473C through RF03777C. The last of this model was made on Nov. 12, 1984.

This completes all of the right-handed Service Model-C and Raider pistols produced by Randall, accounting for 16.5% of total pistol production during the life of the company.

THE CURTIS E. LEMAY 4-STAR PISTOLS

In 1984, Randall expanded its line with the introduction of a true compact .45 auto that was designed by Air Force General Curtis E. LeMay. Among his many accomplishments, LeMay had been responsible for establishing the Air Force's Marksmanship Training Unit.

When LeMay created his pistol design, he intended it to be used by members of the Strategic Air Force Command. The general initially tried to have the diminutive .45 produced by Colt, but that never occurred.

As it happened, Art Hanke, who was the head of manufacturing and engineering for Randall, was a personal friend of Gen. LeMay. It was through this liaison that Randall Firearms Company came to produce the LeMay model line of pistols.

Right- and left-hand Randall LeMay and letters of authenticity. (Photo by Larry Gray)

First of the LeMay pistols was the A311. It sported a 4.25-inch, 10-groove barrel. The slide had a round top and a fixed rear sight. The handle and magazine were shortened by a half inch, limiting the magazine to six rounds. Overall weight was 35 oz. Exclusive to the LeMay models were factory-squared triggerguards.

In all, 361 of the Model A311 pistols were made in a serial number range of RF0211C through RF02011C. The first A311 was made on March 1, 1984, and production of that model ended on Oct. 25, 1984. Next came the A331, which featured a flat-top slide and Millett low-profile adjustable rear sight. The top of the slide was milled deeply so the rear sight would sit low enough to preclude its catching on clothing when drawn. There were 293 of this model produced in a serial number range of RF02010C through RF03169C. The first LeMay A311 was made on March 1, 1984, and the last one was completed on Oct. 23rd of that same year.

Among the rarest of the Randall pistols was the Model A312 that was introduced March 1, 1984, but which was never a production gun because only two sample pistols were ever made. The company intended to market this model in Europe, and had Randall Firearms Company survived, it no doubt would have made regular production runs. The company failed before any orders were taken. This pistol has a round-top slide and fixed rear sight. The only difference between the single Model A312 and the production A311 is the caliber. The A311 is a .45 ACP, and the A312 is in 9mm. Serial numbers were RF02012C and RF02031C, respectively.

Also quite rare is the 9mm Model A332. It differed from the A312 in that it had a flat-top slide with Millett low profile adjustable rear sight. Only nine were ever made, and production of this model was limited to the period between March 1, 1984, and Dec. 13, 1984.

Of all the pistols produced by Randall, 6.7% were in the right-handed LeMay family. The LeMay is also one of the most highly collectible of all Randall pistols. Randall LeMay models were shipped from the factory with a dog-leg magazine, featuring a finger extension on the bottom. For every two of the dog leg magazines, however, Randall produced one without an extension. All LeMay magazines are rare and command premiums, even moreso for the LeMay magazines without the dog leg. Also, most of the LeMay pistols were shipped in a pistol rug rather than in a factory box. Add 15% in price for LeMay pistols with a factory box.

Collectors should note that more than 225 LeMay pistols were assembled from parts outside the factory after the company closed. These pistols are not as highly collectible and do not command such high prices. A list of these guns is available from the Randall Historian.

LEFT-HANDED RANDALL PISTOLS

Randall shocked the firearms industry during the week of May 17, 1984, when it introduced the first of 10 left-handed models. These pistols were entire mirror-images of their right-hand counterparts, including the reversal of twist-in rifling from the left-to-right in the right-handed guns to right-to-left in the left-handed guns.

What the Randall company did was to make the entire breadth of its line available to southpaws in left-hand configuration. All left-handed Randalls are considered to be desirable and highly collectible, due to the fact that only 7.4% of total production was in the form of left-handed guns.

In order to make this a truly left-handed handgun, it was necessary to retool for 17 major parts changes. This meant that special left-handed magazines needed to be produced.

First among the lefties was the Service Model B111, which was a full-size government model with a five-inch, 10-groove barrel and round-top slide with fixed sights. There were 297 pistols of this model made, with a serial number range of RF02100C to RF03092C. The first Model B111 was made on May 17, 1984, and the last came off the line Sept. 7 of that same year.

Next was the B121, which sported a flat-top slide and fixed sights. Otherwise, it was the same as the B111, and differed from the right-handed A121 in that Pachmayr did not make left-handed grips, so it lacked the rubber grips of the right-handed counterpart. Randall produced 110 B121 pistols with a serial number range of RF02132C to RF03078C. The B131 was essentially the same as the B121, except that it was furnished with a Millett Model 100 adjustable rear sight. There were 225 of the B131 pistols produced in a serial number range of RF02110C through RF03092C. The first B121 was made on May 17, 1984, and the last one was completed Aug. 28, 1984. The first B131 was made on May 24, 1984, and the last one was completed Aug. 28, 1984.

Also among the most collectible of the Randall pistols were the Models B122 and B123. These left-handers were made in 9mm and .38 Super, respectively, and were otherwise counterparts to the B121. There were only two each made of these models, and those were special-order guns when they were produced. All of the full-size, left-handed pistols represented only 6.4% of Randall's entire production.

There were also three different production variations of the left-handed LeMay profile pistol. These were the B311, B312, and B331. The B311 was a LeMay with round-top slide and fixed rear sight in .45 ACP, and there were 52 manufactured in serial number range of RF02100C through RF02207C. The first B311 and B331 were made on July 13, 1984, and the last ones went off the line slightly more than a month later on Aug. 29, 1984.

The B312 was a left-handed LeMay in 9mm with a round-top and fixed rear sight. Only nine were manufactured. The B331 was the LeMay in .45 ACP, with a flat top and Millett low profile adjustable rear sight. There were 45 of these manufactured in a serial number range of RF02100C through RF02207C. All B213 pistols were made on or about Aug. 23, 1984.

The left-handed LeMay series constituted only one percent of the Randall factory's production.

FACTORY RARITIES AND VARIATIONS

Starting in 1984, Randall produced and experimented with a number of model variations. They are, by model:

1. B2/321 - Only one of these was produced, and it was made on special custom order for Texas-based collector Robert F. Mueschke, who has the largest collection of left-handed Randall pistols in the world. This variation was built on a left-hand

Raider receiver and a left-hand LeMay (B321) slide. Its serial number is RF03069C.

2. B312 with a .45 ACP Factory Conversion unit. There was only one of these produced. It was a 9mm left-handed LeMay with a .45 ACP conversion unit. Its serial number is RF02164C.

3. A 131/SO - A right-handed Service Model with a flat-top slide and adjustable sight, chambered in .451 Detonics Magnum. Only one was made with serial number RFOO451C.

4. B131/SO - A left-handed Service Model with a custom low profile Millett model 100 rear sight, custom squared triggerguard, scrimshawed ivory handles, custom metal checkering cover 40% of the gun's surface, and a special slide conversion stamped with both .38 Super and 9mm with respective barrels and ejectors.

5. A111/B111 Matched Sets - There were four such sets manufactured. These were standard government configuration pistols, and the right-hand and left-hand in each set shared a common serial number. Those serial numbers were RFOOOOOC, RFOO001C, RFOO010C and RFOO024C. Interestingly, the RFOO010 pair was originally made for the television series "Magnum P.I." However, those two guns were never delivered to the television production and have since found their way into a private collection in the state of Arizona.

6. C211 - A lightweight Raider in .45 ACP with a round top and fixed rear sights. There were five manufactured for law enforcement evaluation as off-duty carry weapons.

7. B321 Set - This set was based on the left-handed LeMay, and it was the only set to have all three slide variations fitted to a single receiver. The receiver and all three slides were identically engraved in a high relief pattern. The set was mirror-polished and was fitted with ivory grips bearing scrimshawed Randall logo on each side. The set was delivered in a custom-fitted walnut presentation case. It has the serial number of REK 1.

8. AUSTRIAN RANDALLS - Five Randall A111 pistols were sent to the Austrian government for law enforcement evaluation. Upon entering that country, the guns were processed through the Austrian proof house, where they received proofmarks on the barrels, receivers, and slides. When the Austrian government learned that Randall had gone out of business, the guns were returned to Randall's San Francisco-based exporter. Since then, all five have been acquired by a central California-based investor.

PROTOTYPES

All Randall prototype serialization begins with the letter "T" followed by a two-digit number. In all, there were 43 prototype pistols made in 15 different model designations. Prototypes included many factory variations that never saw production, such as guns with an all-black oxide finish, black oxide and silver finish, and a pink and purple LeMay.

Generally, prototypes are valued at about 150% of the same production model.

SERIALIZATION VARIATIONS

Production serial numbers on Randall pistols generally began at 02000 for right-handed models and 02100 for left-handed models. However, by special order there were 78 pistols with custom serial numbers under 02000. All but about the first 200 serial numbers started with the letters "RF" and ended with a B, C, or W. A few mismarks are in circulation. Most Randalls had serial number prefixes such as the following: RF, RFO, RFOO, 2RFO, or 2RFOOO. The breakdown of Randall serial numbers to satisfy the U.S. Bureau of Alcohol, Tobacco and Firearms is simple. The RF signified Randall Firearms, and the last letter in the serial number designated the vendor who machined the receiver. In the case of letter "B," the vendor was

Bellmore Johnson of Vermont. In the case of the letter "C," the vendor was Caspian Arms of Hardwick, Vermont. In the case of the letter "W," the vendor was Ward Machine Company of Santa Ana, California. It is believed there could have been a factory error in which the serializing machine malfunctioned, resulting in serial number suffixes of "D," "E", and "F". These would be extremely rare.

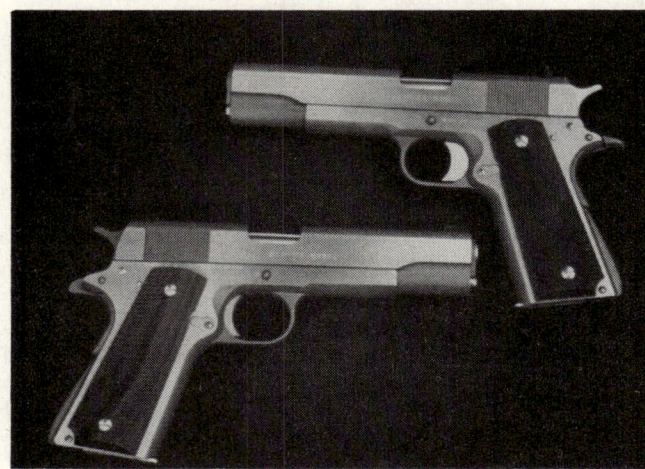

Randall matched set, serial-number RFOO010C. Made for the TV series "Magnum PI." (Photo by Steve Comus)

HOW TO IDENTIFY THE VARIOUS MODELS

Randall models are designated by a single letter prefix, followed by a three-digit number. Prefixes are A, B, or C. Prefix A designates a right-handed pistol. Prefix B denotes a left-handed configuration, and prefix C represented a right-handed, featherweight model.

In a logical sequence, the first numerical digit reflects the frame type, the second digit is for the slide configuration and the third number denotes caliber.

The first numerical digit is 1, 2 or 3. If the first number is 1, it means Service Model. A number 2 refers to Service Model-C or Raider, and a 3 denotes the LeMay Model.

The second digit is 1, 2, or 3. A 1 refers to round-top, fixed sight slide. A 2 stands for flat-top, fixed-sight slide, and 3 is for flat-top, adjustable-sight slide.

The third digit is 1, 2, or 3. A 1 refers to .45 ACP, a 2 is for 9mm Parabellum and a 3 is for .38 Super.

A marketing upgrade affected most Randall pistols made from late November 1983 through the end of production. All Randalls sold had slide stops and grip safeties upgraded to "extended" and "beavertail" types, respectively. Long triggers were installed. This was not retroactive to pistols already sold. All Randalls were shipped with extended safety locks.

Having pioneered stainless steel construction and left-handed configurations, Randall carved for itself a unique place in the history of semiautomatic handguns. In two years of production, Randall cranked out an astounding 24 models in 12 variations and three different calibers.

The Randall Firearms Company officially stopped production on Dec. 15, 1984, and closed its doors on May 15, 1985. There were many reasons why Randall did not survive. To a number of industry observers, it appeared as though the fledgling firm may have attempted to accomplish too much, too quickly. The company's agenda was packed with so many innovative approaches and ideas that the production output could not keep up with the voracious R&D appetite.

NOTE: Randall prototypes can be identified by a "T" prefix. Add 50% to the price for this variety. For serial numbers under 2000 add $100 to $150.

Randall Documentation & Collectors Club: Research letters on original Randall Letterhead are available at a cost of $25 each postpaid. Readers and collectors interested in joining the Randall Collectors Club contact the Randall Historian, Rick Kennerknecht at 228 Columbine Dr., Casper, WY 82609, 307-234-2400 or e-mail: rekenn@trib.com. A new book, *The Randall Scrapbook,* limited to 250 copies was scheduled to be available in late November 1996. Inquire for more information.

Model A111

Caliber is .45 Auto, barrel length 5", round-slide top, right-hand with fixed sights. Total production: 3,431.

NIB	Exc.	V.G.	Good	Fair	Poor
775	680	540	465	400	350

Model A121

Caliber is .45 Auto, barrel length 5", flat-slide top, right-hand with fixed sights. Total production: 1,067.

NIB	Exc.	V.G.	Good	Fair	Poor
800	690	565	485	425	375

Model A131

Caliber is .45 Auto, barrel length 5", flat-slide top, right-hand with Millett sights. Total production: 2,083.

Randall A131/SO in .451 Detonics Magnum with Randall memorabilia. (Photo by Larry Gray)

NIB	Exc.	V.G.	Good	Fair	Poor
825	725	590	515	450	400

Model A112

Caliber is 9mm, barrel length 5", round-slide top, right-hand with fixed sights. Total production: 301.

NIB	Exc.	V.G.	Good	Fair	Poor
1075	940	735	660	575	500

Model A122

Caliber is 9mm. barrel length 5", flat-slide top, right-hand with fixed sights. Total production: 18.

NIB	Exc.	V.G.	Good	Fair	Poor
1540	1400	1100	945	840	735

Model A211

Caliber .45 Auto, barrel length 4-1/4", round-slide top, right-hand with fixed sights. Total production: 922.

NIB	Exc.	V.G.	Good	Fair	Poor
875	765	615	520	450	400

Model A231

Caliber .45 Auto, barrel length 4-1/4", flat-slide top, right-hand with Millett sights. Total production: 574.

NIB	Exc.	V.G.	Good	Fair	Poor
1015	890	710	630	525	450

Model A212

Caliber 9mm, barrel length 4-1/4", round-slide top, right-hand with fixed sights. Total production: 76.

NIB	Exc.	V.G.	Good	Fair	Poor
1100	995	800	680	605	525

Model A232

Caliber 9mm. barrel length 4-1/4", flat-slide top, right-hand with Millett sights. Total production: 5.

NIB	Exc.	V.G.
1995	1750	910

Model A311

Caliber .45 Auto, barrel length 4-1/4", round-slide top, right-hand with fixed sights. Total production: 361.

A311B black oxide LeMay special order by Soldier of Fortune magazine for field testing in El Salvador. (Photo by Steve Comus)

NIB	Exc.	V.G.	Good	Fair	Poor
1325	1160	910	790	710	605

Model A331

Caliber .45 Auto, barrel length 4-1/4", flat-slide top, right-hand with Millett sights. Total production: 293.

NIB	Exc.	V.G.	Good	Fair	Poor
1460	1295	1075	920	840	735

Model A312

Caliber 9mm. barrel length 4-1/4", round-slide top, right-hand with fixed sights. Total production: 2.

NIB
3850

Model A332

Caliber 9mm. barrel length 4-1/4", flat-slide top, right-hand with Millett sights. Total production: 9.

NIB	Exc.	V.G.	Good	Fair	Poor
1930	1690	1210	890	785	735

Model B111

Caliber .45 Auto, barrel length 5", round-slide top, left-hand with fixed sights. Total production: 297.

NIB	Exc.	V.G.	Good	Fair	Poor
1475	1325	1075	945	840	735

Model B121

Caliber .45 Auto, barrel length 5", flat-slide top, left-hand with fixed sights. Total production: 110.

NIB	Exc.	V.G.	Good	Fair	Poor
1825	1600	1215	1025	920	815

Model B122

Caliber 9mm. barrel length 5", flat-slide top, left-hand with fixed sights. Total production: 2.

NIB
5775

Model B123

Caliber .38 Super, barrel length 5", flat-slide top, left-hand with fixed sights. Total production: 2

NIB
5775

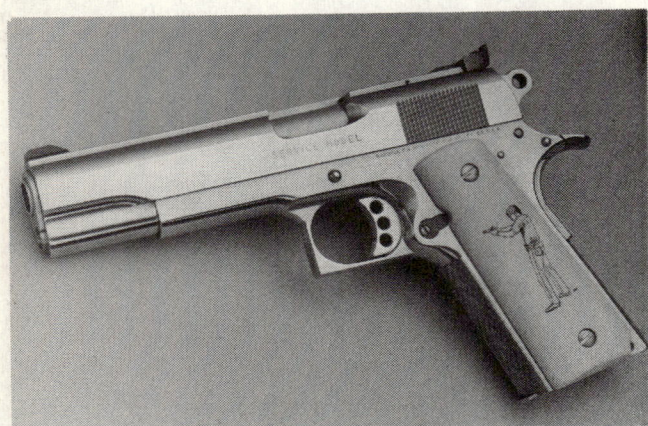

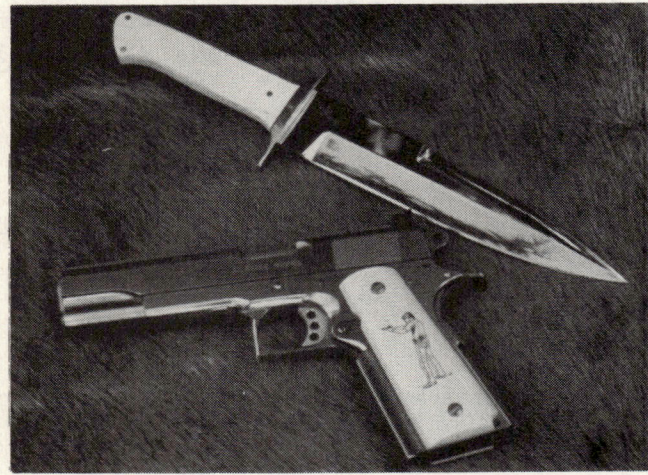

B131/SO left-hand service model with custom Chuck Stapel knife. (Photo by Steve Comus)

Model B131

Caliber .45 Auto, barrel length 5", flat-slide top, left-hand with Millet sights. Total production: 225.

NIB	Exc.	V.G.	Good	Fair	Poor
1760	1600	1270	1025	920	815

Model B311

Caliber .45 Auto, barrel length 4-1/4", round-slide top, left-hand with fixed sights. Total production: 52.

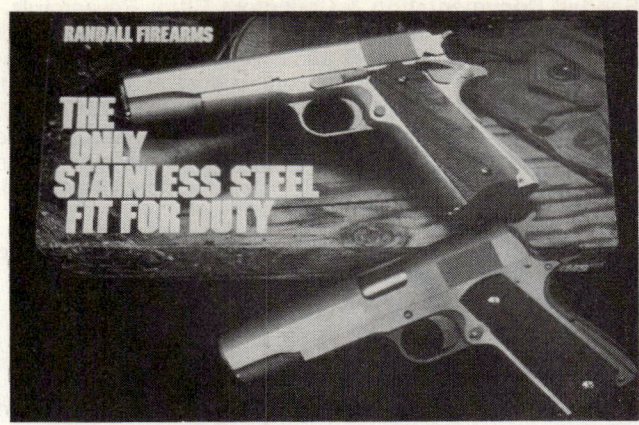

Randall left-hand B311 with original box. Few left-hand Randalls were shipped in boxes. Most were shipped in Randall pistol rugs. (Photo by Steve Comus)

NIB	Exc.	V.G.	Good	Fair	Poor
2200	1930	1375	1100	1000	850

Model B312

Caliber 9mm. barrel length 4-1/4", round-slide top, left-hand with fixed sights. Total production: 9.

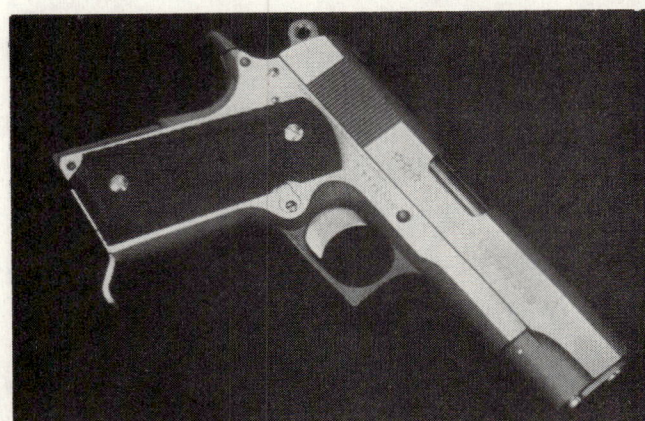

Randall B312 left-hand 9mm LeMay, one of the most sought after of the B-series guns. Only nine were manufactured. (Photo by Steve Comus)

Randall B312 with factory 45ACP conversion unit. Only one of these factory units were made. (Photo by Steve Comus)

NIB	Exc.	V.G.	Good	Fair	Poor
3350	2915	1925	1615	1340	1100

NOTE: For pistol with .45 ACP conversion in NIB 3500. Total production of this conversion is 1 pistol.

Model B331

Caliber .45 Auto, barrel length 4-1/4", flat-slide top, left-hand with Millett sights. Total production: 45.

NIB	Exc.	V.G.	Good	Fair	Poor
2150	1900	1325	1025	965	850

Model C311

Caliber .45 Auto, barrel length 4-1/4", round-slide top, right-hand with fixed sights. Total production: 1.

NIB
3350

Model C332

Caliber 9mm. barrel length 4-1/4", flat-slide top, right-hand with Millett sights. Total production: 4.

NIB	Exc.	V.G.	Good
3325	2475	1150	1000

Model B321 SET

Serial Number REK I.

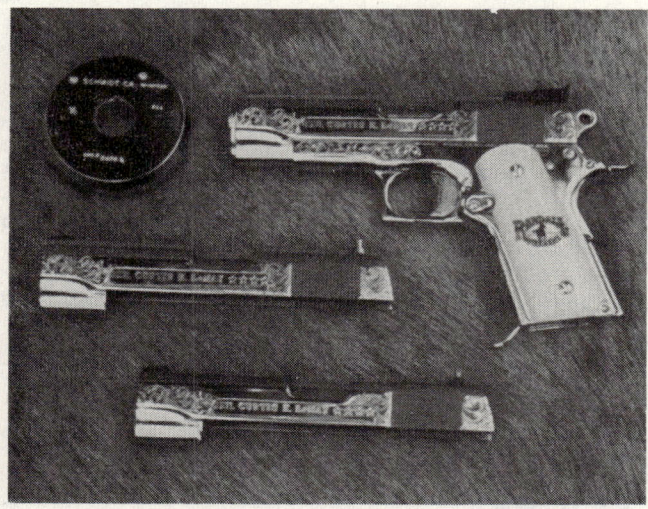

B321 set with gold-plated LeMay roll mark die. (Photo by Steve Comus)

Randall B321 of the B321 set, serial-number REK1. (Photo by Steve Comus)

NIB
23000

Model A111/111 Matched Set

Serial Numbers RFOOOOOC, RFOO001C, RFOO010-C, RFOO024C.

NIB
8600

Austrian Randall

Total production: 5.

Four of the five Austrian Randalls. Each of these A111s bear cartouches from an Austrian proof house. These Randalls were proofed for the Austrian government for law enforcement evaluation. (Photo by Christopher Todd)

NIB
3000

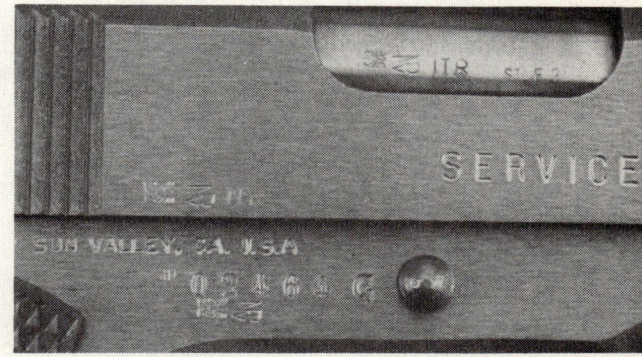

Close-up view of Austrian proof marks. (Photo by Christopher Todd)

NOTE: Prototypes with "T" serial numbers add 50%. For serial numbers under 2000 add $200 to $300. With factory box add $100 for A111, A121, and A131. Add $200 for all other right hand models and $300 for all left hand models.

RANGER ARMS, INC.
Gainesville, Texas

Statesman
A bolt action rifle produced in various calibers with a 22" barrel, no sights, and a checkered walnut stock. Standard finish blued. Manufactured in the early 1970s.

Exc.	V.G.	Good	Fair	Poor
325	250	200	150	100

Statesman Magnum
As above, but chambered for magnum calibers and with a 24" barrel.

Exc.	V.G.	Good	Fair	Poor
350	300	250	200	100

Senator
As above with a better finish.

Exc.	V.G.	Good	Fair	Poor
400	350	300	250	125

Senator Magnum

As above chambered for magnum cartridges.

Exc.	V.G.	Good	Fair	Poor
400	350	300	250	125

Governor

As above with better walnut and finer lined checkering.

Exc.	V.G.	Good	Fair	Poor
450	400	350	250	125

Governor Magnum

As above chambered for magnum cartridges.

Exc.	V.G.	Good	Fair	Poor
450	400	350	250	125

RASHID
Egypt

Rashid Carbine

A gas operated 7.62x39mm caliber semiautomatic carbine with a 20.5" barrel and 10-round integral magazine. Fitted with a folded bayonet similar to that found on the Russian SKS. Blued finish and hardwood stock. This rifle is based upon the Swedish Ljungman.

Courtesy Richard M. Kumor, Sr.

Exc.	V.G.	Good	Fair	Poor
400	375	275	150	100

RAST & GASSER
SEE Gasser

RAVELL
Barcelona, Spain

Maxim Double Rifle

A Holland & Holland-styled sidelock double-barrel rifle available in either .375 Holland & Holland or 9.3x74R with 23" barrels having express sights. Double triggers and automatic ejectors. The sidelocks and mounts engraved, stock of well figured walnut normally fitted with a recoil pad.

Exc.	V.G.	Good	Fair	Poor
4500	4000	3500	2750	1500

RAVEN ARMS
Industry, California

P-25

A .25 caliber semiautomatic pistol with a 2.75" barrel and 6-round magazine. Available with a blued, chrome or nickel-plated finish and walnut grips. Manufacture ceased in 1984.

Exc.	V.G.	Good	Fair	Poor
75	65	50	35	25

MP-25

As above with a die-cast frame and imitation ivory grips.

NIB	Exc.	V.G.	Good	Fair	Poor
75	65	55	45	35	25

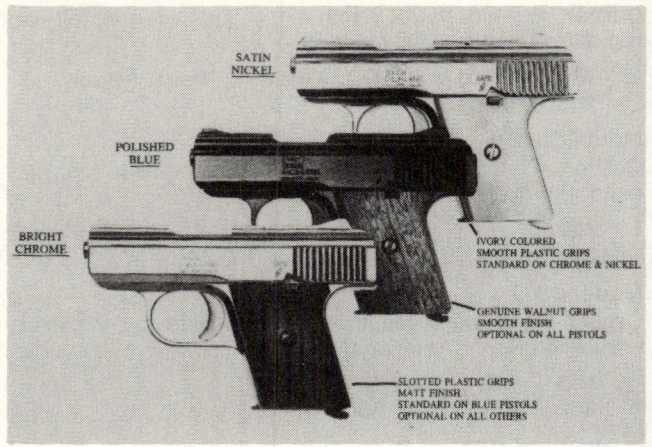

READ & WATSON
Danville, Virginia

During 1862 and 1863, Read & Watson produced approximately 900 altered Hall rifles for the State of Virginia. These arms were made from Hall rifles issued to the state prior to the Civil War. The original breech loading mechanisms were removed and a brass breech piece or receiver was secured in their place. New butt stocks were fitted and the original Hall furniture was reused. Carbines have an overall length of 42-1/8"; barrel length of 26" and are of .52 caliber. Position and style of serial numbers varies.

Prospective purchasers are strongly advised to secure a qualified appraisal prior to acquisition.

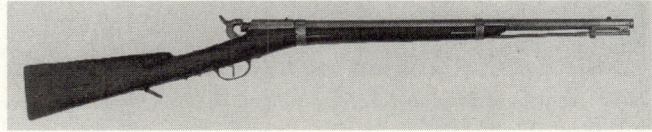

Exc.	V.G.	Good	Fair	Poor
—	—	8500	3500	1000

RECORD-MATCH ANSCHUTZ
Zelia-Mehlis, Germany

Model 210 Free Pistol

A single shot .22 caliber target pistol using a Martini falling block action. Barrel length 11", set trigger, and adjustable sights. Blued finish with checkered walnut grips and forend. Manufactured during the 1930s.

Exc.	V.G.	Good	Fair	Poor
1250	1000	850	750	400

Model 210A

As above with a lightweight alloy frame.

Exc.	V.G.	Good	Fair	Poor
1200	950	800	700	350

Model 200 Free Pistol

As above without a set trigger.

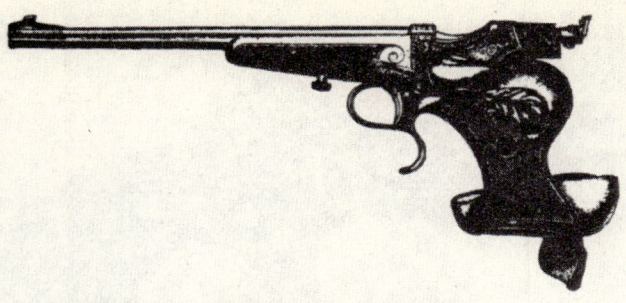

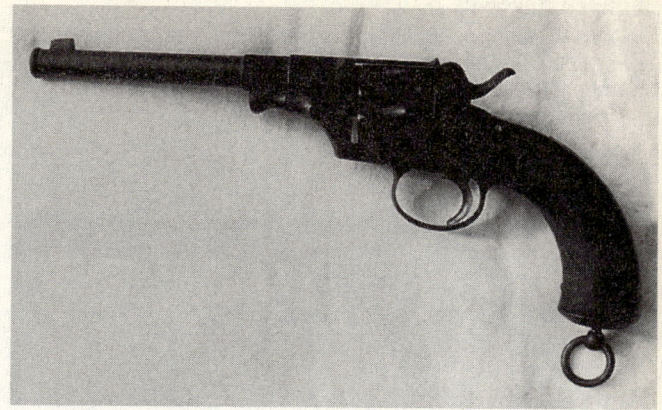

Exc.	V.G.	Good	Fair	Poor
950	850	750	550	300

REFORM
Suhl, Germany
August Schuler

Reform Pistol

A 6.35 or .25ACP fou- barreled double action pistol constructed so that the barrel unit rises upward when the trigger is pulled. It superficially resembles a semiautomatic pistol. Blued with hard rubber grips. Manufactured between 1906 and about 1913.

Exc.	V.G.	Good	Fair	Poor
600	500	375	250	175

Model 1883

As above with a 5" barrel and round bottom grips.

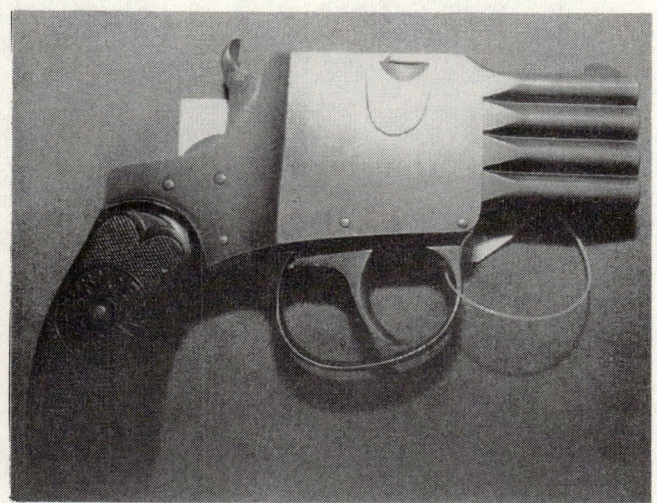

Exc.	V.G.	Good	Fair	Poor
600	500	400	300	200

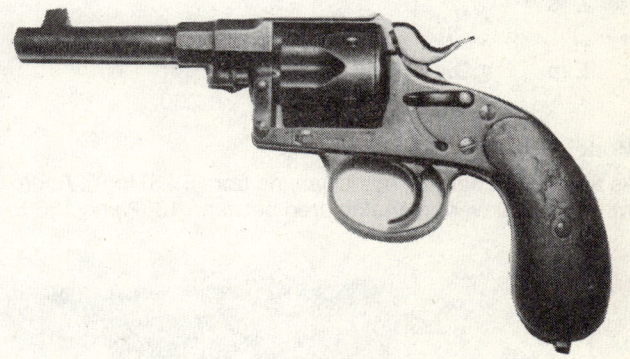

Exc.	V.G.	Good	Fair	Poor
500	400	325	225	150

REICHSREVOLVER
Germany

There are two basic versions of the German Standard Service Revolver designed by the Small Arms Commission of the Prussian Army in the 1870s. Revolvers of this type were produced by the Erfurt Royal Arsenal, F. Dreyse of Sommerda, Sauer & Sohn, Spangenberg & Sauer, and C. H. Haenel of Suhl. Normally, the maker's initials are to be found on an oval above the triggerguard.

Model 1879

A 10.55mm caliber revolver with a 7.2" barrel, 6-shot cylinder and fixed sights. Standard finish blued with walnut grips having a lanyard ring at the base. These revolvers are fitted with a safety catch.

REID, JAMES
New York, New York

Model 1 Revolver

A spur trigger .22 caliber revolver with a 3.5" octagonal barrel and 7-shot unfluted cylinder. Blued with walnut grips. The barrel marked "J. Reid, New York." Approximately 500 were manufactured between 1862 and 1865.

Exc.	V.G.	Good	Fair	Poor
—	—	500	250	100

Model 2 Revolver

As above but in .32 caliber, the barrel marked "Address W.P. Irving, 20 Cliff Street. N.Y." or "James P. Fitch. N.Y." Approximately 1,300 were manufactured between 1862 and 1865.

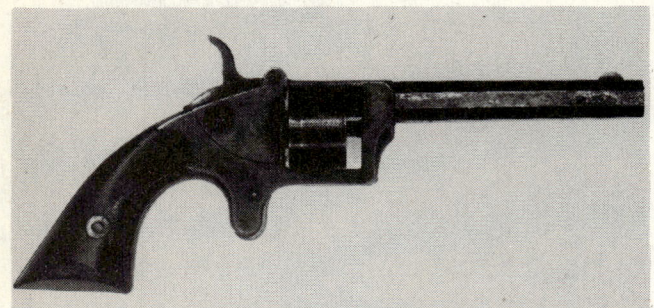

Exc.	V.G.	Good	Fair	Poor
—	—	500	200	100

Model 3 Revolver

Similar to the above, but with the grip angle sharpened. Chambered for the .32 rimfire cartridge with a 4.75" barrel. The cylinder chambers are threaded so that percussion nipples can be inserted. The barrel is marked "J. Reid N.Y. City". Approximately 300 were made between 1862 and 1865.

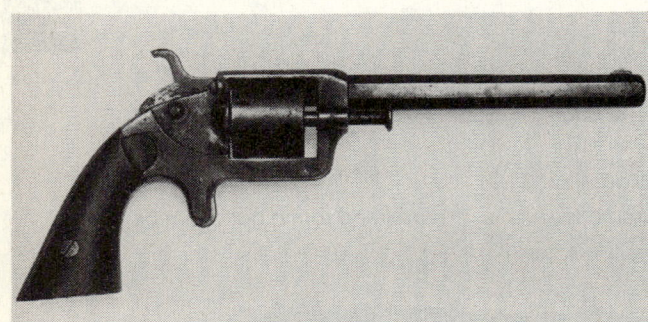

Exc.	V.G.	Good	Fair	Poor
—	—	750	400	200

Model 4 Revolver

As above with barrel lengths varying from 3.75" to 8". Approximately 1,600 were manufactured between 1862 and 1865.

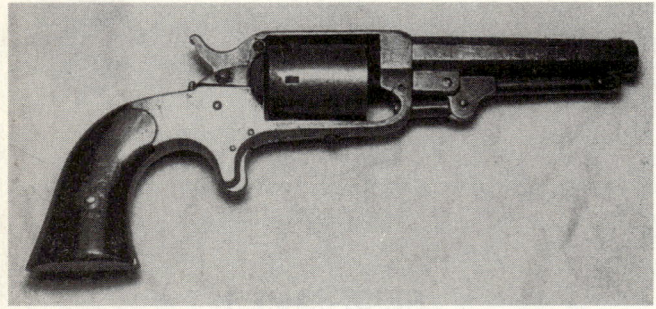

Exc.	V.G.	Good	Fair	Poor
—	—	800	400	150

"My Friend" Knuckle Duster

A 7-shot .22 caliber revolver constructed entirely of metal and without a barrel. The frame of silver-plated brass or blued iron and marked "My Friend Patd. Dec. 26, 1865." The grip is formed with a finger hole so that the pistol can be used as a set of brass knuckles.

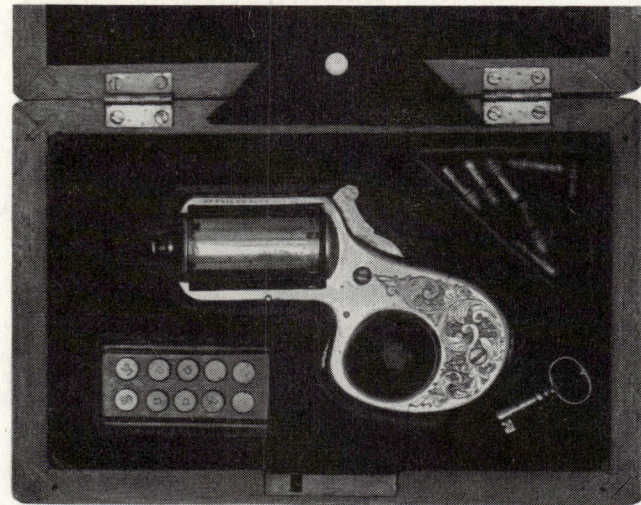

Courtesy W.P. Hallstein III and son Chip

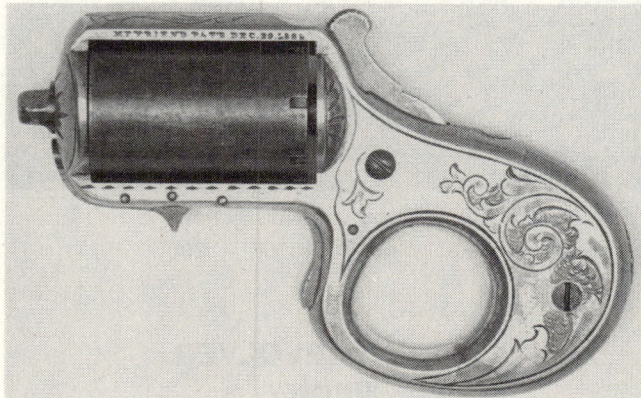

Courtesy W.P. Hallstein III and son Chip

Brass Frame

Exc.	V.G.	Good	Fair	Poor
—	—	850	400	200

Iron Frame

Exc.	V.G.	Good	Fair	Poor
—	—	1250	600	250

.32 Caliber Knuckle Duster

As above but .32 caliber. Approximately 3,400 were manufactured between 1869 and 1884.

Brass Frame

Exc.	V.G.	Good	Fair	Poor
—	—	850	400	200

Iron Frame

Exc.	V.G.	Good	Fair	Poor
—	—	1250	600	250

.41 Caliber Knuckle Duster

As above but .41 caliber and marked "J. Reid's Derringer." Approximately 300 were manufactured between 1875 and 1878.

Exc.	V.G.	Good	Fair	Poor
—	—	8000	3750	950

Model No. I Knuckle Duster

As above with a 3" barrel. Approximately 350 were made between 1875 and 1880.

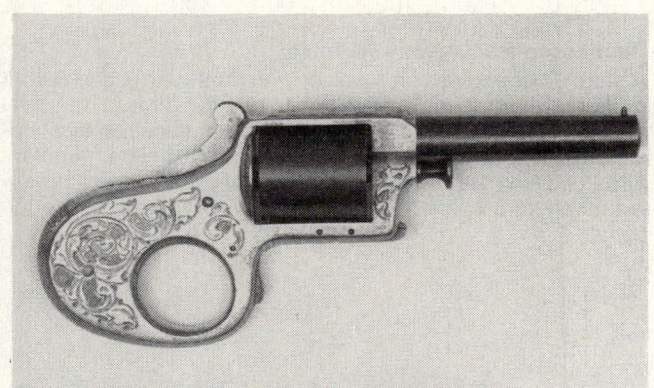

Courtesy W.P. Hallstein III and son Chip

Exc.	V.G.	Good	Fair	Poor
—	—	1500	700	250

Model No. 2 Knuckle Duster

As above with a 1.75" barrel. Approximately 150 were made between 1875 and 1880.

Exc.	V.G.	Good	Fair	Poor
—	—	1750	800	350

Model No. 3 Derringer

A .41 caliber revolver with a 3" octagonal barrel and 5-shot fluted cylinder. The frame silver-plated and the barrel as well as cylinder blued. Approximately 75 were made between 1880 and 1884.

Exc.	V.G.	Good	Fair	Poor
—	—	1500	800	350

Model No. 4 Derringer

As above but with a brass frame and walnut grips and marked "Reid's Extra." Approximately 200 were made during 1883 and 1884.

Exc.	V.G.	Good	Fair	Poor
—	—	1000	500	250

New Model Knuckle Duster

Similar to the Model 2 with a 2" barrel and 5-shot cylinder. The barrel marked "Reid's New Model .32 My Friend." Approximately 150 were made in 1884.

Exc.	V.G.	Good	Fair	Poor
—	—	1250	700	200

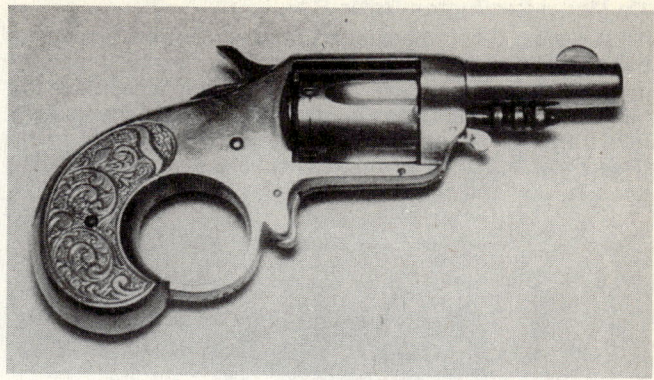

REISING ARMS CO.
Hartford, Connecticut

Standard Model

A .22 caliber semiautomatic pistol with a hinged 6.5" barrel and 10-round magazine. Standard finish is blued, however, nickel-plated versions are known. The slide marked with the company's name and patent dates. The grips of bakelite impressed with a bear's head and the motto "Reising, It's A Bear". Manufactured in both New York City and Hartford, during the 1920s. **CAUTION: High velocity ammunition should not be used in these pistols**.

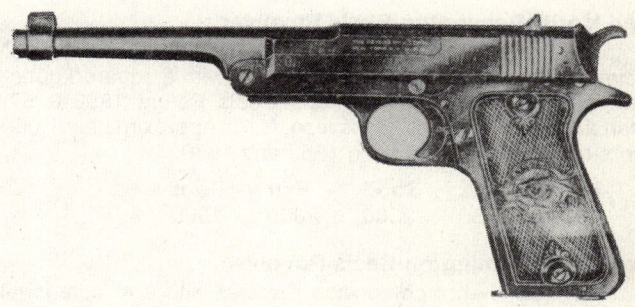

New York Manufacture

Exc.	V.G.	Good	Fair	Poor
600	400	300	200	100

Hartford Manufacture

Exc.	V.G.	Good	Fair	Poor
550	400	275	175	100

Remington.
C O U N T R Y

REMINGTON ARMS COMPANY, INC.
Wilmington, Delaware

Founded in 1816 by Eliphalet Remington, this company has the distinction of being the oldest firearms manufacturing firm in the United States. Since 1856 it has been known by four different names: between 1856 and 1888, E. Remington & Sons; 1888-1910, Remington Arms Company; 1910-1925, Remington Arms U.M.C. Company (Union Metallic Cartridge Company); and 1925 to the present, Remington Arms Company. In mid 1996 the company plans to move its headquarters to Greensboro, North Carolina.

1st Model Remington-Beals Revolver

A .31 caliber 5-shot percussion revolver with a 3" octagonal barrel. The cylinder turning mechanism is mounted on the left outside frame. Blued, case hardened, silver-plated, brass triggerguard and gutta-percha grips. The barrel marked, "F. Beal's Patent, June 24, '56 & May 26, '57" and the frame, "Remington's Ilion, N.Y." Approximately 5,000 were manufactured in 1857 and 1858.

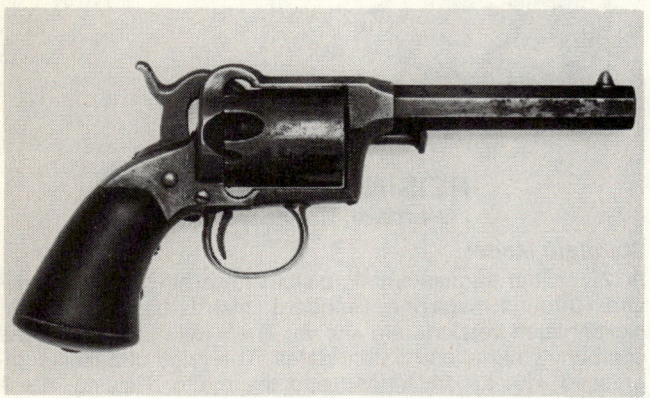

Courtesy Milwaukee Public Museum, Milwaukee, Wisconsin

Exc.	V.G.	Good	Fair	Poor
2000	1600	1000	600	300

2nd Model Remington-Beals Revolver

A spur trigger .31 caliber 5-shot percussion revolver with a 3" octagonal barrel. Blued, case hardened with a squared gutta-percha grip. The barrel marked, "Beals Patent 1856 & 57, Manufactured by Remingtons Ilion, N.Y." Approximately 1,000 were manufactured between 1858 and 1860.

Exc.	V.G.	Good	Fair	Poor
4500	3750	2500	2000	1500

3rd Model Remington-Beals Revolver

A .31 caliber 5-shot percussion revolver with a 4" octagonal barrel. A loading lever mounted beneath the barrel. Blued, case hardened with gutta-percha grips. The barrel marked, "Beals Pat. 1856, 57, 58 and also "Manufactured by Remingtons, Ilion, N.Y." Approximately 1,500 were manufactured in 1859 and 1860.

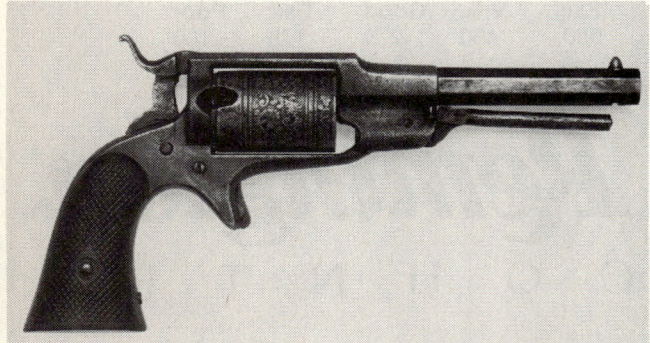

Courtesy Milwaukee Public Museum, Milwaukee, Wisconsin

Exc.	V.G.	Good	Fair	Poor
2500	2000	1200	800	500

Remington-Rider Revolver

A double-action .31 caliber percussion revolver with a 3" barrel and 5-shot cylinder. Blued, or nickel-plated, case hardened with gutta-percha grips. This model is also encountered altered to .32 rimfire. The barrel marked, "Manufactured by Remingtons, Ilion, N.Y., Riders Pt. Aug. 17, 1858 May 3,

1859." Approximately 20,000 were manufactured between 1860 and 1873. The cartridge variation is worth approximately 10% more than the percussion original version.

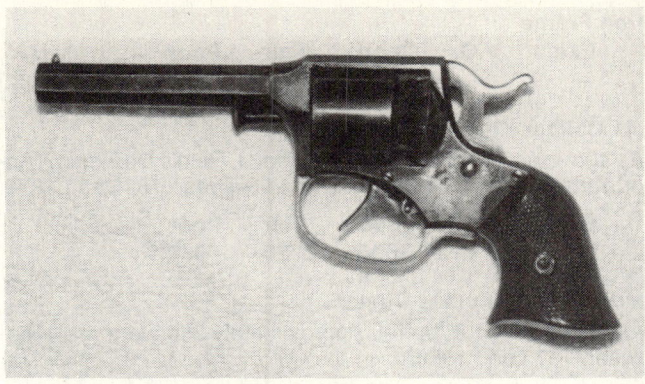

Exc.	V.G.	Good	Fair	Poor
1800	1600	1000	700	400

Remington-Beals Army Revolver

A .44 caliber percussion revolver with an 8" barrel and 6-shot cylinder. Blued, case hardened with walnut grips. The barrel marked "Beals Patent Sept. 14, 1858 Manufactured by Remington's Ilion, New York." Approximately 2,500 were manufactured between 1860 and 1862. A martially marked example is extremely rare and would be worth approximately 35% additional.

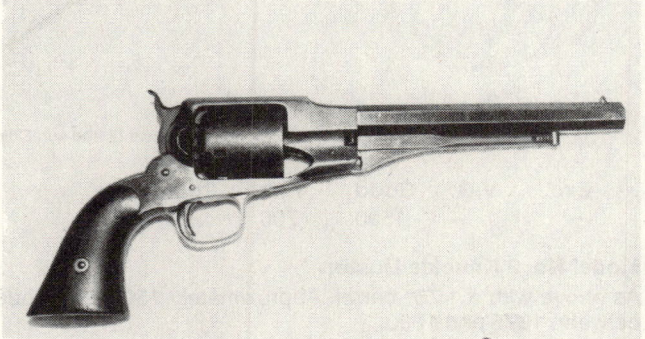

Exc.	V.G.	Good	Fair	Poor
6000	5000	3000	2000	800

Remington-Beals Navy Revolver

Similar in appearance to Remington-Beals Army Revolver, but in .36 caliber with a 7.5" octagonal barrel. The first examples of this model were fitted with a loading lever that would not allow the cylinder pin to be completely removed. These examples are worth approximately 80% more than the standard model. Approximately 1,000 of these revolvers were purchased by the United States government and marshally marked examples are worth approximately 40% more than the values listed below. Manufactured from 1860 to 1862 with a total production of approximately 15,000.

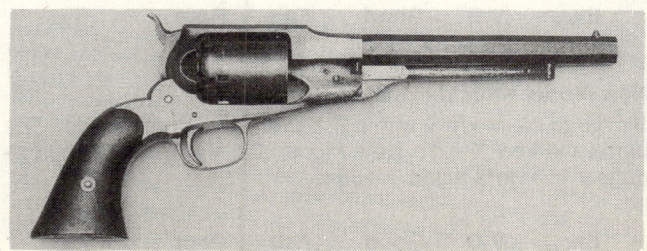

Courtesy Wallis & Wallis, Lewes, Sussex, England

Exc.	V.G.	Good	Fair	Poor
4000	3500	2500	1500	600

1861 Army Revolver

A .44 caliber percussion revolver with an 8" octagonal barrel and 6-shot cylinder. The loading lever is cut with a slot so that the cylinder pin can be drawn forward without the lever being lowered. Blued, case hardened with walnut grips. The barrel marked "Patented Dec. 17, 1861 Manufactured by Remington's, Ilion, N.Y." Some examples were converted to .46 caliber rimfire cartridge, and would be worth approximately 20% less than the original, martially marked, standard percussion model. Approximately 12,000 were manufactured in 1862. This model is also known as the "Old Army Model."

Exc.	V.G.	Good	Fair	Poor
4500	3500	1800	1200	600

1861 Navy Revolver

As above, but .36 caliber with a 7.25" octagonal barrel. Blued, case hardened with walnut grips. This model is also found altered to .38 metalic cartridge. Cartridge examples are worth approximately 35% less than the percussion versions. Approximately 8,000 were manufactured in 1862.

Exc.	V.G.	Good	Fair	Poor
4500	3500	2000	1200	500

New Model Army Revolver

A .44 caliber 6-shot percussion revolver with an 8" octagonal barrel. Blued, case hardened with walnut grips. The barrel marked "Patented Sept. 14, 1858 E. Remington & Sons, Ilion, New York, U.S.A. New Model." Approximately 132,000 were made between 1863 and 1873.

Standard Model-Military Version

Exc.	V.G.	Good	Fair	Poor
4000	3200	1400	1000	400

Civilian Model-No Government Inspector's Markings

Exc.	V.G.	Good	Fair	Poor
3500	2500	1200	800	400

.44 or .46 Cartridge Conversion

Courtesy Milwaukee Public Museum, Milwaukee, Wisconsin

Exc.	V.G.	Good	Fair	Poor
3500	3000	1500	800	400

New Model Navy Revolver

As above, but .36 caliber with a 7.23" octagonal barrel. Approximately 22,000 were made between 1863 and 1875.

Courtesy Milwaukee Public Museum, Milwaukee, Wisconsin

Military Version

Exc.	V.G.	Good	Fair	Poor
4000	3400	1800	1200	600

Civilian Version

Exc.	V.G.	Good	Fair	Poor
3500	2800	1600	1000	400

.38 Cartridge Conversion-1873 to 1888

Exc.	V.G.	Good	Fair	Poor
3000	2400	1400	800	400

New Model Single Action Belt Revolver

As above, but with a 6.5" barrel. Blued or nickel-plated, case hardened with walnut grips. This model is sometimes encountered altered to .38 cartridge. Cartridge examples are worth approximately 25% less than the values listed below. Approximately 3,000 were made between 1863 and 1873.

Exc.	V.G.	Good	Fair	Poor
3400	2800	1600	1000	400

Remington-Rider Double Action Belt Revolver

A double action .36 caliber percussion revolver with a 6.5" octagonal barrel marked, "Manufactured by Remington's, Ilion, N.Y. Rider's Pt. Aug. 17, 1858, May 3, 1859." Blued or nickel-plated, case hardened with walnut grips. This model is also found altered to cartridge and such examples would be worth approximately 20% less than the values listed below. Several hundred of this model were made with fluted cylinders and are worth a considerable premium. Approximately 5,000 were made between 1863 and 1873.

Courtesy Milwaukee Public Museum, Milwaukee, Wisconsin

Exc.	V.G.	Good	Fair	Poor
3400	2800	1600	1000	400

New Model Police Revolver

A .36 caliber percussion revolver with octagonal barrels ranging from 3.5" to 6.5" and with a 5-shot cylinder. Blued or nickel-plated, case hardened with walnut grips. This model is also found altered to cartridge and such examples would be worth approximately 20% less than the values listed below. Approximately 18,000 were manufactured between 1863 and 1873.

Exc.	V.G.	Good	Fair	Poor
2200	1800	1200	800	300

New Model Pocket Revolver

A .31 caliber spur trigger percussion revolver with octagonal barrels ranging from 3" to 4.5" in length and a 5-shot cylinder. Blued or nickel-plated, case hardened with walnut grips. The barrel marked, "Patented Sept. 14, 1858, March 17, 1863 E. Remington & Sons, Ilion, New York U.S.A. New Model." Approximately 25,000 were manufactured between 1863 and 1873.

1st Version-Brass Frame and Trigger

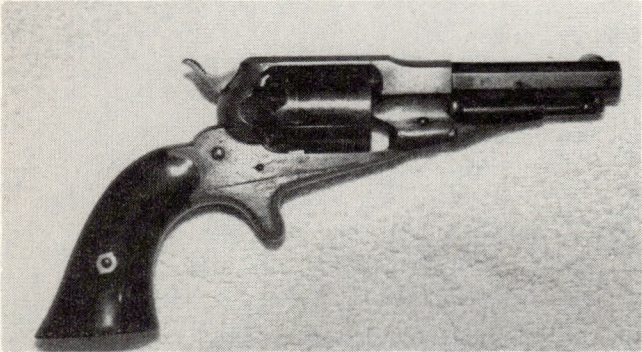

Exc.	V.G.	Good	Fair	Poor
4000	3400	1600	1200	800

2nd Version-Iron Frame, Brass Trigger

Exc.	V.G.	Good	Fair	Poor
2000	1600	1200	800	500

3rd Version-Iron Frame, Iron Trigger

Exc.	V.G.	Good	Fair	Poor
1600	1400	1000	800	400

.32 Cartridge Conversion

Exc.	V.G.	Good	Fair	Poor
1400	1200	800	500	300

Remington-Rider Derringer

A small, silver-plated brass single shot .17 caliber percussion pistol with a 3" round barrel. The barrel marked, "Rider's Pt. Sept 13, 1859." Approximately 1,000 were manufactured between 1860 and 1863. Prospective purchasers are advised to secure a qualified appraisal prior to acquisition.

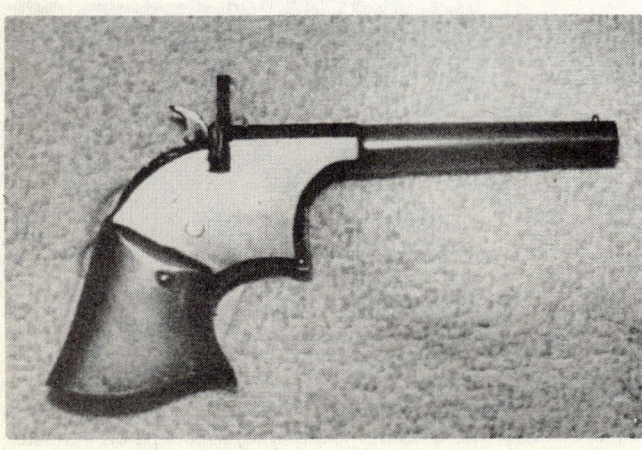

Exc.	V.G.	Good	Fair	Poor
—	—	5500	3000	900

Zig-Zag Derringer

A 6-shot .22 caliber revolving barrel pocket pistol with barrels 3.25" in length. The barrels are cut with zigzag grooves, which are part of the revolving mechanism. The trigger is formed as a ring that when moved forward and rearward turns the barrels and cocks the internal hammer. The barrel group marked "Elliot's Patent Aug. 17, 1858 May 29, 1860" as well as "Manufactured by Remington's Ilion, N.Y." Approximately 1,000 were manufactured in 1861 and 1862.

Exc.	V.G.	Good	Fair	Poor
—	—	2750	1100	450

Remington-Elliot Derringer

A 5-shot .22 or 4-shot .32 caliber pepperbox pistol with a revolving firing pin. Blued or nickel-plated with hard rubber grips. The barrel group marked " Manufactured by E. Remington & Sons, Ilion, N.Y. Elliot's Patents May 19, 1860 - Oct.1, 1861." Approximately 25,000 were manufactured between 1863 and 1888.

5-shot .22 caliber

Exc.	V.G.	Good	Fair	Poor
2000	1600	1200	600	400

4-shot .32 caliber-Courtesy W.P. Hallstein III and son Chip

4-shot .32 caliber

Exc.	V.G.	Good	Fair	Poor
1600	1400	1200	600	300

Vest Pocket Pistol

A .22 caliber single shot pistol with a 3.25" barrel. Blued or nickel-plated with walnut grips. The barrel marked "Remington's Ilion, N.Y. Patent Oct. 1, 1861." Early examples have been noted without any barrel markings. Approximately 25,000 were manufactured from 1865 to 1888.

NOTE: Add a 35% premium for blued models.

Exc.	V.G.	Good	Fair	Poor
1200	1000	600	400	200

Large-Bore Vest Pocket Pistol

As above, but in .30, .32, or .41 caliber with barrel lengths of either 3.5" or 4". Blued or nickel-plated with walnut or rosewood grips. The barrel markings as above except for the addition of the patent date, November 15, 1864. The smaller caliber versions are worth approximately 20% more than the .41 caliber. Approximately 10,000 were made from 1865 to 1888.

NOTE: Add a 35% premium for blued models.

Exc.	V.G.	Good	Fair	Poor
1600	1400	800	600	300

Remington-Elliot Derringer

A .41 caliber single shot pistol with a 2.5" round barrel. Blued or nickel-plated with walnut, ivory, or pearl grips. The barrel marked "Remingtons, Ilion, N.Y. Elliot Pat. Aug. 27, 1867." Approximately 10,000 were manufactured between 1867 and 1888.

NOTE: Add a 35% premium for blued models.

Exc.	V.G.	Good	Fair	Poor
2000	1800	1200	800	500

> An engraved Remington-Elliot derringer was sold at auction for $1,430. Fitted with pearl grips. Condition was very good.
> Butterfield & Butterfield, August 1996.

Remington Over/Under Derringer

A double barrel .41 caliber pocket pistol with 3" round barrels that pivot upward for loading. There is a lock bar to release the barrels on the right side of the frame. The firing pin raises and lowers automatically to fire each respective barrel. It has a spur trigger and bird's-head grip. The finish is either blued or nickel-plated; and it is featured with walnut, rosewood, or checkered hard rubber grips. Examples with factory pearl or ivory grips would be worth a small premium. Approximately 150,000 were manufactured between 1866 and 1935.

NOTE: Add a 25% premium for blued models.

Early Type I

Manufactured without an extractor, this type is marked "E. Remington & Sons, Ilion, N.Y." on one side and "Elliot's Patent Dec. 12, 1865" on the other side of the barrel rib. Only a few hundred were manufactured in 1866.

Exc.	V.G.	Good	Fair	Poor
4000	3500	1200	800	400

Type I Mid-Production

As above, but fitted with an extractor. Manufactured in the late 1860s.

Exc.	V.G.	Good	Fair	Poor
5000	4000	2500	1500	800

Type I Late Production

Fitted with an automatic extractor and marked on the top of the barrel rib. Manufactured from the late 1860s to 1888.

Exc.	V.G.	Good	Fair	Poor
2000	1600	800	500	300

Type II

Marked "Remington Arms Co., Ilion, N.Y." on the barrel rib. Manufactured between 1888 and 1911.

Exc.	V.G.	Good	Fair	Poor
1600	1200	600	400	200

Type III

Marked "Remington Arms - U.M.C. Co., Ilion, N.Y." on the barrel rib. Manufactured between 1912 and 1935.

Exc.	V.G.	Good	Fair	Poor
1400	1200	600	400	300

NOTE: For Type III models blue or nickel prices are the same.

Model 1865 Navy Rolling Block Pistol

A spur trigger single shot rolling block .50 caliber rimfire cartridge pistol with an 8.5" round barrel. Blued, case hardened with walnut grips and forend. The barrel marked "Remingtons, Ilion N.Y. U.S.A. Pat. May 3d Nov. 15th, 1864 April 17th, 1866." Examples bearing military inspection marks are worth approximately 25% more than the values listed below. Examples are also to be found altered to centerfire cartridge and these are worth approximately 10% less than the values listed below. Approximately 6,500 were manufactured between 1866 and 1870.

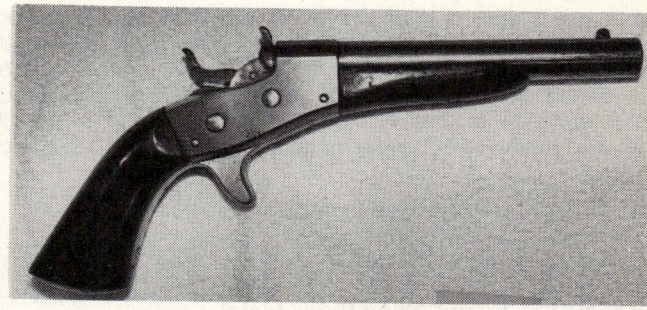

Exc.	V.G.	Good	Fair	Poor
5000	4000	3000	1500	800

Model 1867 Navy Rolling Block Pistol

A .50 caliber single shot rolling block pistol with a 7" round barrel. Blued, case hardened with walnut grips and forend. The majority of these pistols were purchased by the United States government and civilian examples without inspection marks are worth approximately 30% more than the values listed below.

Exc.	V.G.	Good	Fair	Poor
4000	3000	2000	1400	600

> In August 1995 Butterfield & Butterfield sold an engraved Remington Rolling Block pistol in .22 caliber with a 10" octagon barrel with a scroll engraved nickel plated frame. The condition was very good to excellent. The price was $3,300.

Remington Rolling Block Single Shot Smooth Bore Pistol
NFA

Also called the Remington Combination Pistol-Shotgun, this firearm is a single-shot 20 gauge smooth bore pistol with a detachable shoulder stock, and extremely rare. ATF advised this writer that the it cannot be classified as a "curio or relic," because it is an antique firearm (manufactured in or before 1898) that fires fixed shotgun ammunition that is currently available in ordinary commercial channels. ATF classifies this firearm as a short-barreled shotgun under the NFA, which requires payment of a $200 tax on each ownership transfer; it is unclear whether it qualifies as an "any other weapon" (and $5 transfer tax) if unaccompanied by a shoulder stock.

John B. McClernan's article, "The Remington Combination Pistol-Shotgun" (in *The Canadian Journal of Arms Collecting*, Vol. 5, No. 1, 1967, pages 1-12), contains the most published information about this firearm at this time. He reports the barrel length is 11.75", with "no rear sight nor any sign of milling or drilling for a rear sight [and] has [an] original brass pin front sight." The outside diameter at the joint with the receiver is .843", and .406" at the opposite end. The pistol's overall length is 18.25", and 27.5" with the shoulder stock attached. The receiver's left side bears the markings: **Remington's Ilion, N.Y.U.S.A./Pat. May 3d Nov. 15th 1864 April 17th, 1866,** which he contends "dates its production period as 1867-1875." Based on documented and exhaustive original research, McClernan states: "there is no way to escape the conclusion that this gun, if not experimental, is at least a rare, special-order Remington variation." This writer would like to communicate with persons who own or have owned one of these firearms to document them, and learn more about their current value.

These materials are copyright © 1998 by Eric M. Larson, printed in the *Catalog* by permission of the copyright holder, and will appear in a forthcoming book on pre-NFA smooth bore shot pistols (see H&R Handy-Gun entry).

Remington-Rider Magazine Pistol

A 5-shot .32 caliber magazine pistol with a spur trigger and 3" octagonal barrel. The magazine is located beneath the barrel and can be loaded from the front. Blued, nickel-plated or case hardened with walnut, pearl, or ivory grips. The barrel marked "E. Remington & Sons, Ilion, N.Y. Riders Pat. Aug. 15, 1871." Approximately 10,000 were manufactured between 1871 and 1888.

NOTE: For blued finish add a 50% premium.

Exc.	V.G.	Good	Fair	Poor
1800	1600	800	500	300

Model 1871 Army Rolling Block Pistol

A .50 caliber rolling block single shot pistol with an 8" round barrel. Blued, case hardened with walnut grips and forend. The distinguishing feature of this model is that it has a rearward extension at the top of the grip and a squared butt. Approximately 6,000 were made between 1872 and 1888. Engraved ivory-stocked versions, as pictured below, will bring considerable premiums.

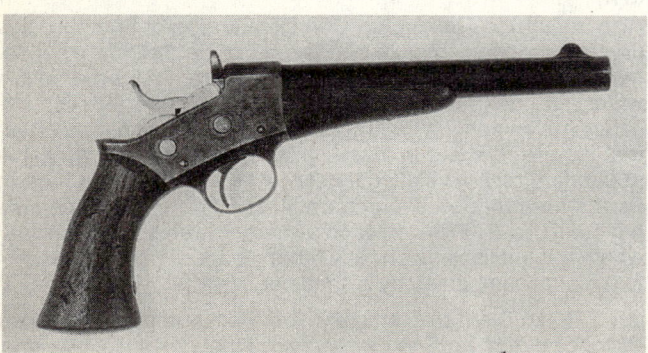

Exc.	V.G.	Good	Fair	Poor
3000	2400	1500	800	500

> A cased pair of factory engraved Model 1871s was sold at auction for $11,000. Both were fitted with 8" silver plated barrel. Grips and forend were ivory. Gilt scroll engraving. Fitted in a lined leather case. Condition was excellent.
> Butterfield & Butterfield, August 1996.

Remington-Smoot No. 1 Revolver

A .30 caliber spur trigger revolver with a 2.75" octagonal barrel and 5-shot fluted cylinder. Blued or nickel-plated with walnut or hard rubber grips. The barrel rib is marked, "E. Remington & Sons, Ilion, N.Y. Pat. W. S. Smoot Oct. 21, 1873." Examples dating from the beginning of production are found with a revolving recoil shield. Such examples would command approximately a 300% premium over the values listed below.

NOTE: For blued finish add a 50% premium.

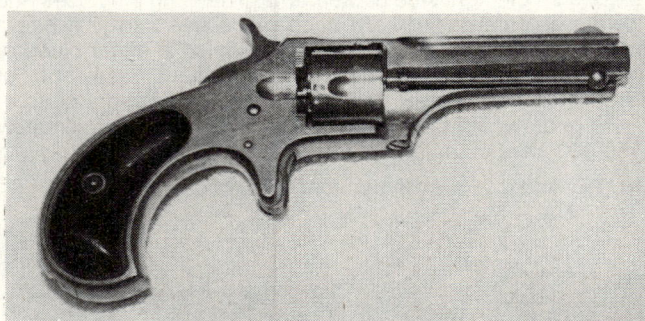

Exc.	V.G.	Good	Fair	Poor
800	600	400	200	100

Remington-Smoot No. 2 Revolver

As above, except in .32 caliber approximately 20,000 were made between 1878 and 1888.

NOTE: For blued finish add a 50% premium.

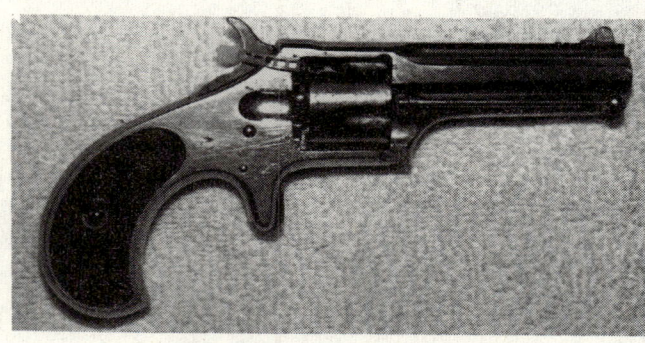

Exc.	V.G.	Good	Fair	Poor
700	600	300	200	100

Remington-Smoot No. 3 Revolver

Two variations of this spur trigger .38 caliber revolver exist. One with a rounded grip and no barrel rib, the other with a squared back, squared butt grip with a barrel rib. Centerfire versions are also known and they are worth approximately 10% more than the values listed below. Blued or nickel-plated with hard rubber grips. Approximately 25,000 were made between 1878 and 1888.

NOTE: For blued finish add a 50% premium.

Exc.	V.G.	Good	Fair	Poor
700	600	300	200	100

No. 4 Revolver

A .38 or .41 caliber spur trigger revolver with a .25" barrel and no ejector rod. Blued or nickel-plated with hard rubber grips.

The barrel marked "E. Remington & Sons, Ilion, N.Y." Approximately 10,000 were manufactured between 1877 and 1888.

NOTE: For blued finish add a 50% premium.

Exc.	V.G.	Good	Fair	Poor
600	500	300	200	100

Remington Iroquois Revolver

A .22 caliber spur trigger revolver with a 2.25" barrel and 7-shot cylinder. Blued or nickel-plated with hard rubber grips. The barrel marked "Remington, Ilion, N.Y." and "Iroquois." Some examples of this model will be found without the Remington markings. Approximately 10,000 were manufactured between 1878 and 1888.

NOTE: For blued finish add a 50% premium.

Exc.	V.G.	Good	Fair	Poor
800	600	400	300	200

Model 1875 Single Action Army

A .44 Remington or .44-40 or .45 caliber single action revolver with a 7.5" barrel. Blued or nickel-plated, case hardened with walnut grips. Some examples are to be found fitted with a lanyard ring at the butt. The barrel marked "E. Remington & Sons Ilion, N.Y. U.S.A." Approximately 25,000 were manufactured between 1875 and 1889.

NOTE: Blued Version-Add 40%.

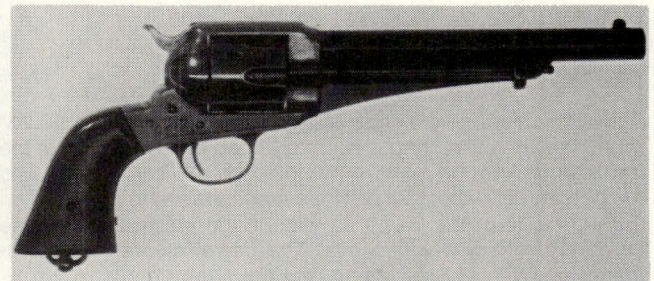

Courtesy Milwaukee Public Museum, Milwaukee, Wisconsin

Exc.	V.G.	Good	Fair	Poor
5000	4200	2000	1200	700

> A cased pair of engraved Model 1875's were sold at auction for $8,910. Engraved by Cole Agee. Engraving coverage is 100% and done in gold and silver with ivory grips. Condition is very good. Faintich Auction Service, March 1996.

Model 1890 Single Action Army

A .44-40 caliber single action revolver with a 5.5" or 7.5" barrel and 6-shot cylinder. Blued or nickel-plated with hard rubber grips bearing the monogram "RA" at the top. The barrel marked "Remington Arms Co., Ilion, N.Y." Approximately 2,000 were made between 1891 and 1894. Prospective purchasers are advised to secure a qualified appraisal prior to acquisition.

Blued Version-Add 40%.

Exc.	V.G.	Good	Fair	Poor
8000	7000	4000	2400	1500

Model 1891 Target Rolling Block Pistol

A .22, .25 Stevens, or .32 S&W caliber single shot rolling block pistol with a 10" half octagonal barrel fitted with target sights. Blued, case hardened with walnut grips and forend. The barrel marked "Remington Arms Co. Ilion, N.Y.," and the frame "Remingtons Ilion N.Y. U.S.A. Pat. May 3 Nov. 15, 1864 April 17, 1866 P S." This is an extremely rare pistol, with slightly over 100 manufactured between 1892 and 1898. Prospective

purchasers are advised to secure a qualified appraisal prior to acquisition.

Exc.	V.G.	Good	Fair	Poor
3000	2500	1500	800	600

Model 1901 Target Rolling Block

As above, with the exception that the bridge block thumb piece has been moved out of the line of sight and the rear sight is mounted on the frame instead of the barrel. Approximately 735 were made between 1901 and 1909. Prospective purchasers are advised to secure a qualified appraisal prior to acquisition.

Exc.	V.G.	Good	Fair	Poor
3000	2500	1500	1000	600

Mark III Signal Pistol

A 10 gauge spur trigger flare pistol with a 9" round barrel. The frame of brass and the barrel of iron finished matte black with walnut grips. The barrel marked "The Remington Arms - Union Metallic Cartridge Co., Inc. Mark III, Remington Bridgeport Works Bridgeport, Connecticut U.S.A." Approximately 25,000 were manufactured between 1915 and 1918.

Exc.	V.G.	Good	Fair	Poor
—	275	125	75	55

Remington 1911 and 1911A1

See the Colt section of this book for pistols of this type.

Model 51

A .32 or .380 caliber semiautomatic pistol with a 3.5" barrel and magazines capable of holding either 7 or 8 cartridges depending on the caliber. Blued with hard rubber grips having the legend "Remington UMC" in a circle at the top. The slide marked "The Remington Arms - Union Metallic Cartridge Co., Inc. Remington Ilion Wks. Ilion, N.Y. U.S.A. Pedersen's Patents Pending." Later versions carried a 1920 and a 1921 patent date. The early examples have nine grooves on the slide; later models have 15 grooves with the frame marked "Remington Trademark." Early variations are worth approximately 10% more than the values listed below and .32 caliber examples are worth approximately 25% additional. Approximately 65,000 were manufactured between 1918 and 1934.

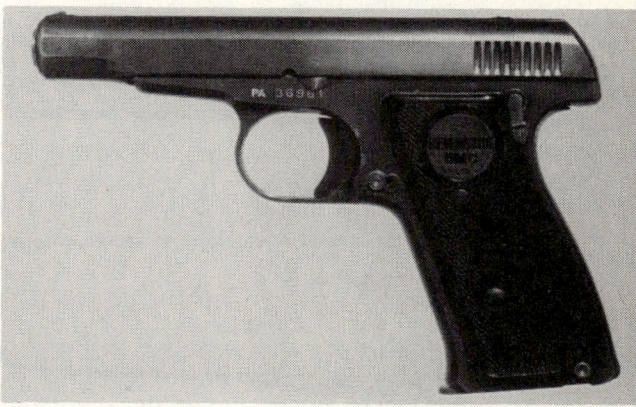

Courtesy Orvel Reichert

Exc.	V.G.	Good	Fair	Poor
—	500	275	125	75

Model 1841 "Mississippi Rifle"

A .54 caliber percussion rifle with a 33" barrel and full stock secured by two barrel bands. The lock (marked Remington's Herkimer N.Y.) case hardened, the barrel browned and the furniture of brass. The stock is fitted with a brass patch box on the right side. Approximately 20,000 were made between 1846 and 1855.

Exc.	V.G.	Good	Fair	Poor
—	—	3500	1250	450

Model 1861 U.S. Rifle Musket

A .58 caliber percussion rifle with a 40" barrel and full length stock secured by three barrel bands. The lock marked "Remington's Ilion, N.Y." Finished in the white with a walnut stock. Approximately 40,000 were made between 1864 and 1866.

Exc.	V.G.	Good	Fair	Poor
—	—	2000	850	400

Model 1863 Zouave Rifle

A .58 caliber percussion rifle with a 33" barrel and full length stock secured by two barrel bands. The lock case hardened and marked "Remington's Ilion N.Y.", the barrel blued and the furniture of brass. Approximately 12,500 were manufactured between 1862 and 1865.

Exc.	V.G.	Good	Fair	Poor
—	3000	1500	675	250

Breech-Loading Carbine

A .46 or .50 rimfire single shot rolling block carbine with a 20" barrel. Blued, case hardened with a walnut stock. The tang marked "Remington's Ilion, N.Y. Pat. Dec. 23, 1863 May 3 & Nov. 16, 1864." The .50 caliber version is worth approximately 15% more than the .46 caliber. Approximately 15,000 .50-caliber variations were made, most of which were sold to France. Approximately 5,000 carbines were made in .46 caliber. Manufactured from 1864 to 1866.

Exc.	V.G.	Good	Fair	Poor
—	—	2000	950	450

Revolving Rifle

A .36 or .44 caliber revolving rifle with either 24" or 28" octagonal barrels with a 6-shot cylinder. The triggerguard formed with a scrolled finger extension at the rear. Blued, case hardened with a walnut stock. These rifles are also encountered altered to cartridge and would be worth approximately 20% less than the percussion values listed below. The barrel marked "Patented Sept. 14, 1858 E. Remington & Sons, Ilion, New York, U.S.A. New Model." Approximately 1,000 were manufactured between 1866 and 1879.

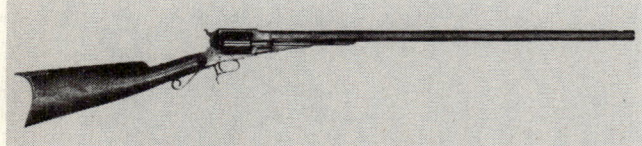

Courtesy Milwaukee Public Museum, Milwaukee, Wisconsin

Courtesy Buffalo Bill Historical Center, Cody, Wyoming

Exc.	V.G.	Good	Fair	Poor
—	—	4000	1500	650

Remington-Beals Rifle

A .32 or .38 caliber sliding barrel single shot rifle with octagonal barrels of 24", 26", or 28" length. The barrel can be moved forward by lowering the triggerguard/lever. This model is to be found with either frames made of brass or iron, the latter being worth approximately 20% more than the values listed below. Walnut stock. The barrel marked "Beals Patent June 28, 1864 Jan. 30, 1866 E. Remington & Sons, Ilion, New York." Approximately 800 were manufactured between 1866 and 1888. A few examples are known to have been factory engraved. Prospective purchasers are advised to secure a qualified appraisal prior to acquisition.

Courtesy Milwaukee Public Museum, Milwaukee, Wisconsin

Exc.	V.G.	Good	Fair	Poor
—	—	550	250	100

U.S. Navy Rolling Block Carbine

A .50-70 caliber single shot rolling block carbine with a 23.25" round barrel. A sling ring is normally fitted to the left side of the frame and sling swivels are mounted on the barrel band and the bottom of the butt. Inspector's markings are to be found on the right side of the frame as well as the stock. Blued, case hardened with a walnut stock. The barrel marked "Remington's Ilion, N.Y. U.S.A." along with the patent dates. Approximately 5,000 were manufactured in 1868 and 1869.

Exc.	V.G.	Good	Fair	Poor
—	—	1500	700	350

Model 1867 Navy Cadet Rifle

A .50-45 caliber single shot rolling block rifle with a 32.5" barrel and full length forend secured by two barrel bands. Markings identical to the above with the exception that "U.S." is stamped on the buttplate tang. Blued, case hardened with a walnut stock. Approximately 500 were made in 1868.

Exc.	V.G.	Good	Fair	Poor
1500	—	1500	700	350

Rolling Block Military Rifles

Between 1867 and 1902 over 1,000,000 rolling block military rifles and carbines were manufactured by the Remington Company. Offered in a variety of calibers and barrel lengths, the values listed below are for full length rifles. Carbines are worth approximately 40% more.

Exc.	V.G.	Good	Fair	Poor
—	2500	1000	650	300

Shotgun

As above, in 16 gauge with either a 30" or 32" Damascus or fluid steel barrels. Produced from 1870 to 1892.

Exc.	V.G.	Good	Fair	Poor
—	600	350	150	100

Baby Carbine

As above, with a 20" thin round barrel chambered for the .4440 cartridge and fitted with a saddle ring on the left side of the frame. Blued, case hardened with a walnut stock having a carbine buttplate. Manufactured from 1892 to 1902.

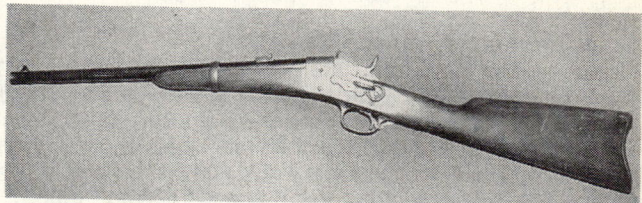

Exc.	V.G.	Good	Fair	Poor
—	2000	900	450	200

Model 1-1/2 Sporting Rifle

A lightweight variation of the above using a 1.25" wide, No. 1 rolling block action. Chambered for rimfire cartridges from .22 to the .38 extra long, as well as centerfire cartridges from .32-20 to the .44-40. Medium weight octagonal barrels from 24" to 28" in length, with open rear and a blade-type front sight. Blued, case hardened with a walnut stock. There were several thousand manufactured between 1888 and 1897.

Exc.	V.G.	Good	Fair	Poor
—	1250	500	250	100

Model 2 Sporting Rifle

As above, using a No. 2 action and chambered for various cartridges from .22 to .38 caliber with 24" or 26" octagonal barrels. Blued, case hardened with a walnut stock. This model was produced with a number of optional features that affect its value. Prospective purchasers are advised to secure a qualified appraisal prior to acquisition. Manufactured from 1873 to 1910.

Exc.	V.G.	Good	Fair	Poor
—	650	300	175	100

No. 4 Rolling Block Rifle

Built on the lightweight No. 4 action, this rifle was available in .22, .25 Stevens, or .32 caliber, with either a 22.5" or 24" octagonal barrel. Blued, case hardened with a walnut stock. A takedown version was also made and these are worth approximately 10% more than the values listed below. Approximately 50,000 were made between 1890 and 1933.

Exc.	V.G.	Good	Fair	Poor
—	400	200	100	75

Model No. 4 S Military Rifle

At the request of the United States Boy Scouts in 1913, the Remington Company designed a military style rifle having a

Courtesy Milwaukee Public Museum, Milwaukee, Wisconsin

Exc.	V.G.	Good	Fair	Poor
—	—	500	250	100

No. 1 Rolling Block Sporting Rifle
Standard No. 1 Sporting Rifle

A single shot rolling block rifle produced in a variety of calibers from .40-50 to .50-70 centerfire as well as .44 and .46 rimfire. Standard barrel lengths were either 28" or 30" and of octagonal form.

Courtesy Milwaukee Public Museum, Milwaukee, Wisconsin

Exc.	V.G.	Good	Fair	Poor
—	2000	800	375	150

Long-Range Creedmoor Rifle

A .44-90, .44-100, or .44-105 caliber rolling block rifle with a 34" half octagonal barrel, long range vernier tang sights and globe front sights. Blued, case hardened with a walnut stock having a checkered pistol grip. This rifle was available with a number of optional features and a qualified appraisal should be secured if those features are in doubt. Produced from 1873 to 1890.

Courtesy Butterfield & Butterfield, San Francisco, California

Exc.	V.G.	Good	Fair	Poor
—	4500	2500	1000	400

Mid-Range Target Rifle

As above, except chambered for .40-70, .44-77, .45-70, or .50-70 caliber with 28" or 30" half octagonal barrels. Produced from 1875 to 1890.

Exc.	V.G.	Good	Fair	Poor
—	3500	1250	650	300

Short-Range Rifle

As above, chambered for cartridges between .38 and .44 caliber with 26" or 30" round or octagonal barrels. Open rear sight with beach front sight. The walnut stock checkered. Produced from 1875 to 1890.

Exc.	V.G.	Good	Fair	Poor
—	2000	900	400	250

Black Hills Rifle

As above, in .45-60 caliber with a 28" round barrel fitted with open sights and a plain straight grip stock. Produced from 1877 to 1882.

28" barrel and full length forend secured by one barrel band. A short upper hand guard was also fitted and a bayonet stud is to be found at the muzzle. In 1915 the designation of this model was changed from "Boy Scout" to "Military Model." Approximately 15,000 were made between 1913 and 1923.

Exc.	V.G.	Good	Fair	Poor
—	1000	500	400	275

No. 5 Rolling Block Rifle

Built on the No. 5 action, this rifle was designed for smokeless cartridges and was made in a variety of barrel lengths, calibers and in a carbine version. Blued, case hardened with a walnut stock.

Exc.	V.G.	Good	Fair	Poor
—	700	350	200	100

No. 5 Sporting or Target Rifle

Chambered for the .30-30, .303 British, 7mm, .30 U.S., .32-40, .32 U.S., and the .38-55 cartridges. This rifle was offered with 28" or 30" round barrels and features a plain, straight-grip stock with a half-length forend. It has open rear sights and was available with double-set triggers that would add approximately 10% to the value. It was manufactured between 1898 and 1905.

Exc.	V.G.	Good	Fair	Poor
—	3500	1500	650	300

Model 1897

A 7x57mm and .30 U.S. caliber full stock rolling block rifle. The Model 1902 is of identical form except that it was fitted with an automatic ejector. Manufactured from 1897 to 1902.

Exc.	V.G.	Good	Fair	Poor
—	650	300	150	75

Carbine

As above, fitted with a 20" round barrel and a half-length forend secured by one barrel band.

Exc.	V.G.	Good	Fair	Poor
—	750	350	150	75

No. 6 Rolling Block Rifle

A lightweight, small rifle designed expressly to be used by young boys. It is chambered for the .22 rimfire cartridge, as well as the .32 Short or Long. It was also produced with a smoothbore barrel to be used with shot cartridges. The round barrel is 20" in length. It has a takedown action with a barrel held on by a knurled knob underneath the frame. It is a lightweight rolling block, with a thin operating knob on the breech. The finish is blued overall. Early models featured a case-colored frame, and these versions would be worth approximately 10% additional. It has a straight-grip walnut stock with a small forearm. Over 250,000 manufactured between 1902 and 1903.

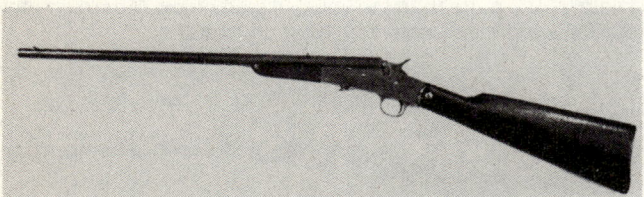

Exc.	V.G.	Good	Fair	Poor
—	300	150	100	75

No. 7 Rolling Block Rifle

Readily identifiable by its accentuated checked pistol grip, this model was available in .22 or .25-10 Stevens caliber with 24", 26", or 28" half octagonal barrels. Fitted with a tang mounted aperture rear sight. Blued, case hardened with a walnut stock. Approximately 1,000 were made between 1903 and 1911.

Exc.	V.G.	Good	Fair	Poor
—	3500	1250	600	300

Remington-Hepburn No. 3 Rifle

A lever activated falling block single shot rifle designed by Lewis Hepburn available in a variety of calibers from .22 Winchester centerfire to .50-90 Sharps with octagonal or round barrels of 26", 28", or 30" length. Blued, case hardened with a walnut stock. This model was available with a variety of optional features that affect the value considerably. Prospective purchasers are advised to secure a qualified appraisal prior to acquisition. Approximately 10,000 were made between 1883 and 1907.

Exc.	V.G.	Good	Fair	Poor
—	2250	1000	700	350

No. 3 Match Rifle

As above, but fitted with a high comb buttstock and a nickel-plated Schuetzen buttplate. Manufactured in various calibers from .25-20 Stevens to .40-65 with 30" half octagonal barrels. This model was made in two versions: "A Quality" with a plain stock, tang mounted rear sight and a Beach front sight, and; "B Quality" with a checkered walnut stock having a cheek rest, checkered forend, vernier rear sight and a combination wind gauge and spirit level front sight. Double set triggers were also available and these would add approximately 10% to the values listed below. Approximately 1,000 were made between 1883 and 1907.

A Quality

Exc.	V.G.	Good	Fair	Poor
—	2500	1250	600	350

B Quality

Exc.	V.G.	Good	Fair	Poor
—	3000	1500	700	350

No. 3 Long-Range Creedmoor Rifle

As above, in .44 caliber with a 32" or 34" half octagonal barrel, long range vernier rear sight, combination wind gauge and spirit level front sight, with a deluxe checkered walnut stock having a rubber shotgun buttplate. Produced with a number of optional features that affect the value. Prospective purchasers are advised to secure a qualified appraisal prior to acquisition. Manufactured from 1880 to 1907.

Exc.	V.G.	Good	Fair	Poor
—	5500	2500	950	400

No. 3 Mid-Range Creedmoor Rifle

As above, but chambered for the .40-65 cartridge and fitted with a 28" barrel.

Exc.	V.G.	Good	Fair	Poor
—	3000	1500	750	350

No. 3 Long-Range Military Rifle

This is a rare variation that is chambered for the .44-75520 Remington cartridge. It has a round 34" barrel and a full length forearm held on by two barrel bands. The finish is blued and case-colored, and the stock is walnut. There are two basic versions. The plain grade has an uncheckered, straight-grip stock with military-type sights. There is also a fancy grade that features a high-grade, checkered, pistol grip stock with a full-length, checkered forend, vernier tang sight, and wind gauge, spirit lever front sight. There were a few manufactured in the 1880s.

Plain Grade

Exc.	V.G.	Good	Fair	Poor
—	3500	2000	950	400

Fancy Grade

Exc.	V.G.	Good	Fair	Poor
—	6000	3500	1250	600

No. 3 Schuetzen Match Rifle

As above, with the exception that instead of the side lever, the action is raised or lowered by means of the lever on the triggerguard. Chambered for various popular cartridges and offered with a 30" or 32" part-octagonal, heavy barrel. It features a vernier tang sight with a hooded front sight. It was standard with double-set triggers and a palm rest. The finish is blued and case-colored, with a high-grade checkered walnut stock and forend. It has an ornate, Swiss-type Schuetzen buttplate and is also known as the "Walker-Hepburn Rifle." There were two versions available. One, a standard breechloader with the Remington Walker-marked barrel; and the other, a muzzle-loading variation that was fitted with a removable false muzzle. This version was supplied with a brass bullet starter and other accessories. Prospective purchasers are advised to secure a qualified appraisal prior to acquisition.

Breechloading Version

Exc.	V.G.	Good	Fair	Poor
—	20000	12500	3500	900

Muzzleloading Version

Exc.	V.G.	Good	Fair	Poor
—	35000	15000	5000	1500

No. 3 High-Power Rifle

The Model No. 3 was also made available in a variety of smokeless cartridges; .30-30, .30-40, .32 Special, .32-40 and .38-55. Standard barrel lengths were 26", 28", or 30". Produced from 1900 to 1907.

Exc.	V.G.	Good	Fair	Poor
—	2500	1000	500	200

Remington-Keene Magazine Rifle

A bolt-action rifle chambered for the .40, .43, and .45-70 centerfire cartridges with 22", 24.5", 29.25", or 32.5" barrels. It is readily identifiable by the exposed hammer at the end of the bolt. Blued, case hardened hammer and furniture, with a walnut stock. The receiver marked "E. Remington & Sons, Ilion, N.Y." together with the patent dates 1874, 1876, and 1877. The magazine on this rifle was located beneath the barrel and the receiver is fitted with a cut-off so that the rifle could be used as a single shot. Approximately 5,000 rifles were made between 1880 and 1888 in the following variations:

Sporting Rifle-24.5" Barrel

Exc.	V.G.	Good	Fair	Poor
—	1000	650	350	150

Army Rifle

Barrel length 32.5" with a full-length stock secured by two barrel bands.

Courtesy Milwaukee Public Museum, Milwaukee, Wisconsin

Exc.	V.G.	Good	Fair	Poor
—	2500	1250	600	300

Navy Rifle

As above, with a 29.25" barrel.

Exc.	V.G.	Good	Fair	Poor
—	3000	1500	750	325

Carbine

As above, with a 22" barrel and a half-length forend secured by one barrel band.

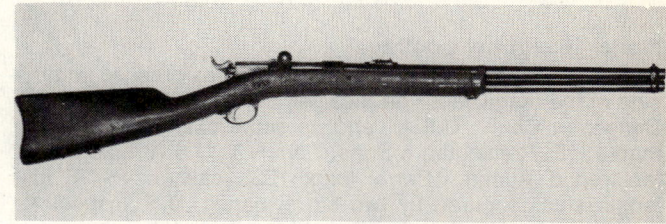

Courtesy Milwaukee Public Museum, Milwaukee, Wisconsin

Exc.	V.G.	Good	Fair	Poor
—	2500	1250	600	325

Frontier Model

As above, with a 24" barrel and half-length forend secured by one barrel band. Those purchased by the United States Department of the Interior for arming the Indian Police are marked "U.S.I.D." on the receiver.

Exc.	V.G.	Good	Fair	Poor
—	—	4000	2000	850

Remington-Lee Magazine Rifle

Designed by James Paris Lee, rifles of this type were originally manufactured by the Sharps Rifle Company in 1880. The Remington Company began production of this model in 1881 after the Sharps Company ceased operations. Approximately 100,000 Lee magazine rifles were made between 1880 and 1907. Their variations are as follows:

Courtesy Milwaukee Public Museum, Milwaukee, Wisconsin

Model 1879-Sharps Mfg.

Barrel length 28" with a full-length stock secured by two barrel bands. The barrel marked "Sharps Rifle Co. Bridgeport, Conn." and "Old Reliable" in a rectangular cartouche. Approximately 300 were made prior to 1881.

Exc.	V.G.	Good	Fair	Poor
—	—	3500	1250	600

Model 1879 U.S. Navy Model

Barrel length 28", .45-70 caliber with a full-length stock secured by two barrel bands. The barrel is marked with U.S.

Navy Inspector's Marks and an anchor at the breech. The receiver marked "Lee Arms Co. Bridgeport, Conn. U.S.A." and "Patented Nov. 4, 1879." Approximately 1300 were made.

Exc.	V.G.	Good	Fair	Poor
—	—	1500	550	250

Model 1879 Sporting Rifle

Barrel length 28" or 30", .45-70 or .45-90 caliber, checkered pistol grip stock with a sporting style forend. Markings on the receiver as above. Approximately 450 made.

Exc.	V.G.	Good	Fair	Poor
—	—	1250	650	300

Model 1879 Military Rifle

Identical to the Navy model, except chambered for the .43 Spanish cartridge. A limited number were also produced in .45-70 caliber. The Spanish versions are worth approximately 25% less than the values listed below. Approximately 1,000 were made.

Exc.	V.G.	Good	Fair	Poor
—	—	750	300	150

Model 1882 Army Contract

This model is identifiable by the two grooves pressed into the side of the magazine. The receiver is marked "Lee Arms Co. Bridgeport Conn., U.S.A." and on some examples it is also marked "E. Remington & Sons, Ilion, N.Y. U.S.A. Sole Manufactured & Agents." Barrel length 32", caliber .45-70, full-length stock secured by two barrel bands. U.S. Inspector's marks are stamped on the barrel breech and the stock. Approximately 750 were made.

Exc.	V.G.	Good	Fair	Poor
—	—	1250	600	300

Model 1885 Navy Contract

As above, with the inspection markings (including an anchor) on the receiver ring and the left side of the stock. Approximately 1,500 were made.

Exc.	V.G.	Good	Fair	Poor
—	—	1250	600	300

Model 1882 & 1885 Military Rifles

Barrel length 32", full-length stock secured by two barrel bands, chambered for .42 Russian, .43 Spanish, .45 Gardner or .45-70 cartridges. The values for those rifles not in .45-70 caliber would be approximately 25% less than those shown below. Approximately 10,000 Model 1882 rifles were made and 60,000 Model 1885 rifles. The two models can be differentiated by the fact that the cocking piece on the bolt of the Model 1885 is larger.

Exc.	V.G.	Good	Fair	Poor
—	—	700	350	150

Model 1882 & 1885 Sporting Rifle

As above, chambered for .45-70 and .45-90 caliber with 26" or 30" octagonal barrels and walnut sporting stocks. Approximately 200 were made.

Exc.	V.G.	Good	Fair	Poor
—	—	1000	500	200

Model 1882 & 1885 Carbine

As above, with a 24" barrel and a half-length forend secured by one barrel band. Prospective purchasers are advised to secure a qualified appraisal prior to acquisition.

Exc.	V.G.	Good	Fair	Poor
—	—	1150	650	300

Model 1899

Designed for use with smokeless and rimless cartridges, this model is marked on the receiver "Remington Arms Co. Ilion,

N.Y. Patented Aug. 26th 1884 Sep't 9th 1884 March 17th 1885 Jan 18th 1887." Produced from 1889 to 1907 in the following variations:

Military Rifle

Barrel length 29", 6mm USN, .30-40, .303, 7x57mm or 7.65mm caliber with a full-length stock secured by two barrel bands.

Exc.	V.G.	Good	Fair	Poor
—	750	400	200	100

Military Carbine

As above, with a 20" barrel and a 3/4 length carbine stock secured by one barrel band.

Exc.	V.G.	Good	Fair	Poor
—	1000	500	250	100

Sporting Rifle

As above, with a 24", 26", or 28" round or octagonal barrel and a half-length sporting stock with a checkered pistol grip. Approximately 7,000 were manufactured.

Exc.	V.G.	Good	Fair	Poor
—	750	400	200	100

Remington Lebel Bolt-Action Rifle

Produced for the French government, this rifle has a 31.5" barrel of 8mm Lebel caliber and a full-length stock secured by two barrel bands. The barrel marked "RAC 1907-15" and the left side of the receiver marked "Remington M'LE 1907-15." Several thousand were manufactured between 1907 and 1915.

Exc.	V.G.	Good	Fair	Poor
—	400	250	150	100

Remington Mosin-Nagant Bolt-Action Rifle

Produced for the Imperial Russian government, this rifle has a 32" barrel of 7.62mm caliber with a full-length stock secured by two barrel bands. The barrel is marked "Remington Armory" with the date of manufacture and the receiver ring is stamped with the Russian coat-of-arms. Approximately 500,000 were made between 1916 and 1918.

Exc.	V.G.	Good	Fair	Poor
—	350	200	100	75

U.S. Model 1917 Magazine Rifle

Produced for the United States government, this rifle has a 26" barrel of .30-06 caliber and a full length stock secured by two barrel bands. Those sold to the British government during WWII are often found with a 2" wide red painted stripe around their butt, which was intended to show that they were chambered for the .30-06 cartridge instead of the .303 British cartridge. Total production unknown.

Exc.	V.G.	Good	Fair	Poor
—	750	350	150	100

Remington-Whitmore Model 1874

A sidelock double-barrel shotgun, combination shotgun rifle or double-barrel rifle with 28" or 30" fluid steel barrels. Also available with Damascus barrels. The barrels released by pushing forward the top lever. Blued, case hardened with a straight or semi-pistol grip walnut stock. The barrels marked "A. E. Whitmore's Patent Aug. 8, 1871, April 16, 1872." The rib between the barrels is marked "E. Remington & Sons, Ilion, N.Y." Several thousand were manufactured between 1874 and 1882.

Shotgun

Exc.	V.G.	Good	Fair	Poor
—	1000	500	250	100

Combination Gun

Exc.	V.G.	Good	Fair	Poor
—	2000	950	450	200

Double Rifle

Prospective purchasers are advised to secure a qualified appraisal prior to acquisition. Very rare.

Exc.	V.G.	Good	Fair	Poor
—	6000	3000	1000	500

Model 1882 Shotgun

A sidelock double-barrel 10 or 12 gauge shotgun with 28" or 30" fluid steel or Damascus barrels. Blued, case hardened with a checkered pistol grip stock and hard rubber buttplate. The barrels are marked "E. Remington & Sons, Ilion, N.Y." and the lock is marked "Remington Arms Co." This model has a conventional top lever that moves to the side. Offered with optional engraving, and such models should be individually appraised. Approximately 7,500 were manufactured between 1882 and 1889.

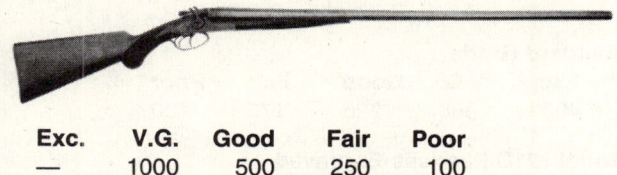

Exc.	V.G.	Good	Fair	Poor
—	1000	500	250	100

Model 1883 through 1889 Shotgun

A sidelock 10, 12, or 16 gauge double-barrel shotgun with fluid steel or Damascus barrels 28" to 32" in length. The models 1883, 1885, 1887, and 1889 are all somewhat alike, varying only in the form of their hammers and internal mechanisms. Blued, case hardened, checkered pistol grip stock with a grip cap. Available in a variety of styles including highly engraved models that should be individually appraised. Approximately 30,000 were made between 1883 and 1909.

Exc.	V.G.	Good	Fair	Poor
—	950	500	250	100

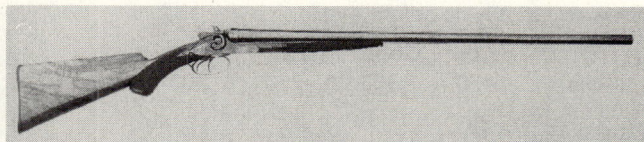

Hammerless Shotgun Model 1894

A boxlock 10, 12, or 16 gauge double shotgun with fluid steel or Damascus barrels 26" to 32" in length. Blued, case hardened with a pistol grip stock. Available in a variety of styles and it is advised that highly engraved examples should be individually appraised.

NOTE: Fluid steel barrels add 25% premium.

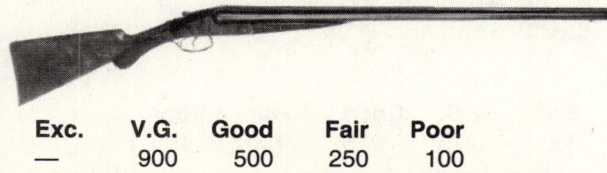

Exc.	V.G.	Good	Fair	Poor
—	900	500	250	100

> A rare engraved gold inlaid presentation Model 1894 was sold at auction for $18,700. It was chambered for 12 gauge and fitted with 30" barrels. Butt stock and forearm finely checkered with fancy walnut. Made for Marcellus O. Hartely, chairman of the Board of Remington, 1888-1902. Condition was excellent.
> Butterfield & Butterfield, December 1995.

Model 1900 Shotgun

As above, in 12 and 16 gauge only. The same cautions apply to highly engraved examples.

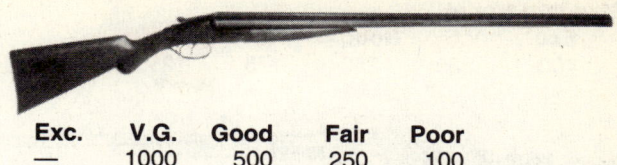

Exc.	V.G.	Good	Fair	Poor
—	1000	500	250	100

Model 8

A .25, .30, .32, or .35 Remington semiautomatic rifle with a 22" barrel having open sights. The barrel is covered by a full length tube that encloses the recoil spring. Blued with walnut stock. Approximately 60,000 were made between 1906 and 1936 in the following styles.

Standard Grade

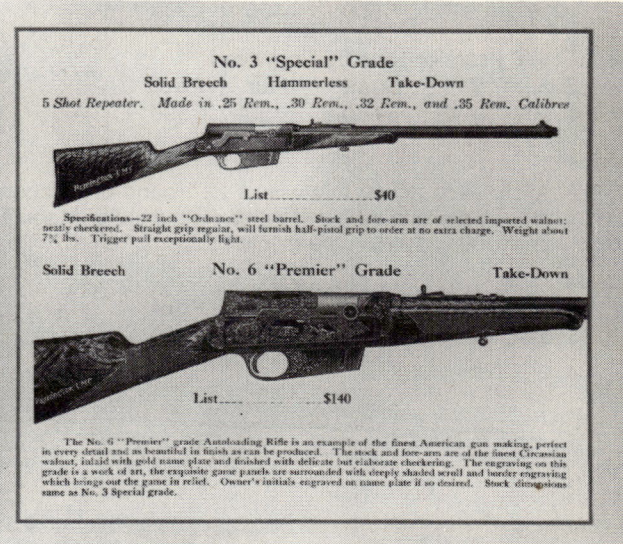

Exc.	V.G.	Good	Fair	Poor
400	325	250	175	125

Courtesy Remington Arms

Model SA-Checkered Stock

Exc.	V.G.	Good	Fair	Poor
550	450	350	225	150

Model 8C

Exc.	V.G.	Good	Fair	Poor
600	500	375	300	200

Model 8D Peerless-Light Engraving

Exc.	V.G.	Good	Fair	Poor
1200	850	500	400	300

Model 8E Expert

Exc.	V.G.	Good	Fair	Poor
1500	1200	900	600	450

Model 8F Premier-Heavily Engraved

Exc.	V.G.	Good	Fair	Poor
1800	1475	1000	750	550

Model 81 Woodsmaster

An improved variation of the Model 8, chambered for the same calibers as well as the .300 Savage cartridge. Produced from 1936 to 1950 in the following styles.

Standard Model

Exc.	V.G.	Good	Fair	Poor
400	325	250	175	125

Model 81A-Takedown

Exc.	V.G.	Good	Fair	Poor
450	375	300	225	150

Model 81D Peerless-Engraved

Exc.	V.G.	Good	Fair	Poor
1200	900	600	400	300

Model 81F Premier-Heavily Engraved

Exc.	V.G.	Good	Fair	Poor
1800	1475	900	750	550

Model 12 or 12 A

A .22 caliber slide action rifle with a 22" round or octagonal barrel having open sights. Blued with a walnut stock. Manufactured from 1909 to 1936 in the following styles.

Model 12A

Exc.	V.G.	Good	Fair	Poor
550	375	300	225	150

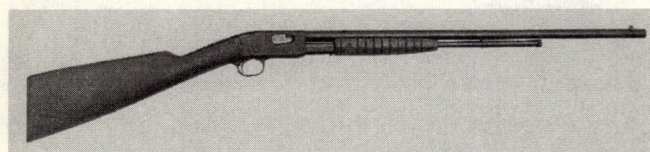

Courtesy Remington Arms

Model 12B-.22 Short, Gallery Model

Exc.	V.G.	Good	Fair	Poor
550	375	300	225	150

Model 12C-24" Octagon Barrel

Exc.	V.G.	Good	Fair	Poor
500	425	350	250	175

Model 12C N.R.A. Target-Limited Production

Exc.	V.G.	Good	Fair	Poor
750	550	450	250	200

Model 12CS-.22 Remington Special

Exc.	V.G.	Good	Fair	Poor
500	400	325	250	175

Model 12D Peerless-Light Engraving

Exc.	V.G.	Good	Fair	Poor
2250	1750	1200	1000	500

Model 12E Expert

Exc.	V.G.	Good	Fair	Poor
2500	2250	1750	1200	800

Model 12F Premier-Heavily Engraved

Exc.	V.G.	Good	Fair	Poor
3000	2250	1850	1200	800

Model 121 and/or 121A

A .22 caliber slide action rifle with a 24" round barrel. Blued with a walnut stock. Manufactured from 1936 to 1954 in the following styles.

Standard Grade

Exc.	V.G.	Good	Fair	Poor
495	350	225	175	100

Model 121D Peerless-Engraved

Exc.	V.G.	Good	Fair	Poor
2250	2000	1250	1000	750

Model 121F Premier-Heavily Engraved

Exc.	V.G.	Good	Fair	Poor
3250	2500	1750	1200	1000

Model 121S-.22 WRF

Exc.	V.G.	Good	Fair	Poor
850	700	400	350	250

Model 121SB-Smooth Bore

There are four different variations of this smooth bore rifle. Seek expert advice before a sale.

Exc.	V.G.	Good	Fair	Poor
600	450	350	250	200

Model 14 or 14A

A .25, .30, .32 or .35 Remington caliber slide action rifle with a 22" round barrel having open sights. Blued, plain walnut stock. Manufactured from 1912 to 1936.

Exc.	V.G.	Good	Fair	Poor
350	275	225	150	100

Model 14R

As above, with an 18.5" barrel.

Exc.	V.G.	Good	Fair	Poor
500	400	300	250	175

Model 14-1/2

As above, except chambered for the .38-40 or .44-40 cartridge with a 22.5" barrel. A carbine with an 18.5" barrel known as the Model 14-1/2R, would be worth approximately 10% more than the values listed below. Manufactured from 1912 to 1922.

Exc.	V.G.	Good	Fair	Poor
900	650	450	300	175

Model 141

A .30, .32, or .35 Remington caliber slide action rifle with a 24" barrel having open sights. Blued with a plain walnut stock. Later production versions of this rifle were known as the Model 141A. Manufactured from 1936 to 1950.

Courtesy Remington Arms

Exc.	V.G.	Good	Fair	Poor
500	400	300	250	175

Model 25

A .25-20 or .32-20 caliber slide action rifle with a 24" barrel having open sights. Blued with a walnut stock. Later production examples were known as the Model 25A and a carbine version with an 18" barrel as the Model 25R. Manufactured from 1923 to 1936.

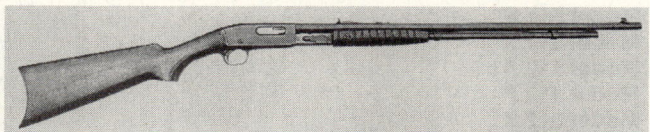

Courtesy Remington Arms-Model 25

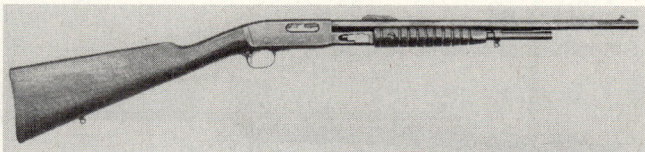

Courtesy Remington Arms-Model 25R

Exc.	V.G.	Good	Fair	Poor
550	450	350	250	200

NOTE: For rifles with 18" barrels add 100%.

Model 16

A .22 caliber semiautomatic rifle with a 22" barrel having open sights. Blued with a walnut stock. Later production examples were known as the Model 16A. Manufactured from 1914 to 1928.

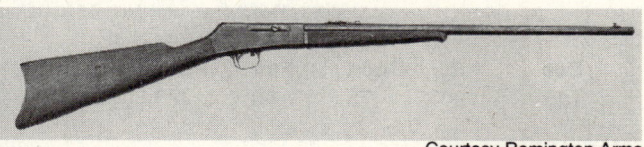

Courtesy Remington Arms

Exc.	V.G.	Good	Fair	Poor
400	350	250	125	75

Model 24

Designed by John M. Browning, this semiautomatic rifle is of .22 caliber with a 19" barrel having open sights. Blued with a walnut pistol grip stock. Later production versions were known as the Model 24A. Produced from 1922 to 1935.

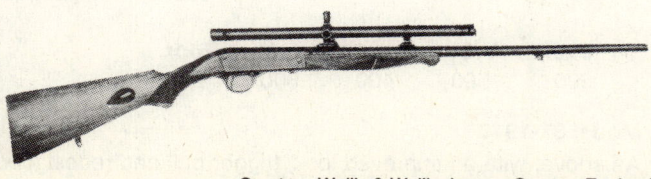

Courtesy Wallis & Wallis, Lewes, Sussex, England

Exc.	V.G.	Good	Fair	Poor
400	350	250	150	100

Model 241 Speedmaster

A .22 caliber takedown semiautomatic rifle with a 24" barrel having open sights. Blued with a walnut stock. Later production versions were known as the Model 241A. Approximately 56,000 were made between 1935 and 1949 in the following styles:

Model 241

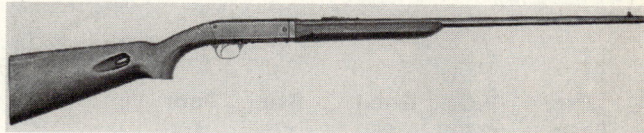

Courtesy Remington Arms

Exc.	V.G.	Good	Fair	Poor
450	350	250	200	150

Model 241 D Peerless-Engraved

Exc.	V.G.	Good	Fair	Poor
2500	2000	1500	1000	600

Model 241 E Expert

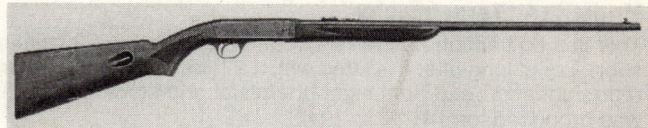

Exc.	V.G.	Good	Fair	Poor
2750	2250	1700	1000	500

Model 241 F Premier-Heavily Engraved

Exc.	V.G.	Good	Fair	Poor
3250	2500	2100	1500	1000

Model 550A

A .22 short, long, or long rifle caliber semiautomatic rifle with a 24" barrel and open sights. Blued with a walnut pistol grip stock. Approximately 220,000 were made between 1941 and 1971.

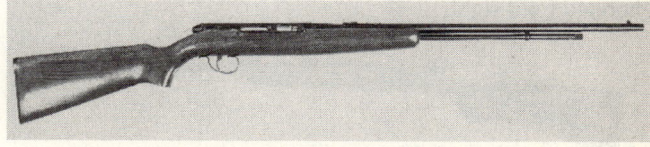

Exc.	V.G.	Good	Fair	Poor
200	175	150	100	75

Model 550P

As above, with an aperture rear sight.

Exc.	V.G.	Good	Fair	Poor
225	200	175	125	100

Model 55-2G

As above, except fitted with a shell deflector and a screw eye for securing it to a shooting gallery counter.

Exc.	V.G.	Good	Fair	Poor
200	175	150	100	75

Model 30A

A sporting rifle using the U.S. Model 1917 Enfield bolt action chambered for various Remington cartridges as well as the 7x57mm and .30-06 cartridges. Barrel length 22". Checkered walnut stock. A carbine model fitted with a 20" barrel was known as the Model 30R. Manufactured from 1921 to 1940.

Courtesy Remington Arms

Exc.	V.G.	Good	Fair	Poor
450	350	250	175	100

Model 30S

As above, chambered for the .257 Roberts, 7x57, and the .30-06 cartridges and with 24" barrel with a Lyman receiver sight. Select checkered walnut stock. Manufactured from 1930 to 1940.

Exc.	V.G.	Good	Fair	Poor
500	400	300	225	150

Model 41A "Targetmaster"

This is a bolt action rimfire rifle chambered for the .22 caliber short, Long, long rifle. It is fitted with a 27" barrel with an opean rear sight and bead front sight. the pistol grip stock is plain. It was produced form 1936 to 1940.

Exc.	V.G.	Good	Fair	Poor
150	125	85	70	50

Model 41AS

Same as above but chambered for the .22 Remington Special or .22 WRF cartridge.

Exc.	V.G.	Good	Fair	Poor
175	150	125	100	75

Model 41P

Same as Model 41A with the addition of a rear peep sight and hooded front sight.

Exc.	V.G.	Good	Fair	Poor
135	115	90	70	50

Model 41SB

Same as Model 41A except for use with .22 shot cartridge. Barrel is smoothbore.

Exc.	V.G.	Good	Fair	Poor
250	200	150	100	75

From 1930 to 1970 the Remington Company produced a variety of single shot and repeating .22 caliber rifles. The values for these are much the same so consequently we list them for reference only.

Model 33
Model 33 NRA
Model 34
Model 34 NRA
Model 341 A
Model 341 P
Model 341 SB
Model 510
Model 510 P
Model 510 SB
Model 510 X
Model 511 A
Model 511 P
Model 511 X
Model 512 A
Model 512 P
Model 512 X
Model 514
Model 514 P
Model 514 BC
Smooth-Bore Models-Add 50%.

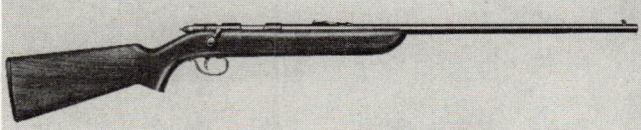

Courtesy Remington Arms-Model 510

Courtesy Remington Arms-Model 510 Carbine

Exc.	V.G.	Good	Fair	Poor
125	100	75	50	25

Model 37

A .22 caliber bolt action magazine target rifle with a heavy 28" barrel having target sights and telescope bases. Blued with a walnut target style stock. Manufactured from 1937 to 1940.

Courtesy Remington Arms

Exc.	V.G.	Good	Fair	Poor
600	500	400	300	250

Model 37-1940

As above, with an improved lock, trigger pull and redesigned stock. Manufactured from 1940 to 1954.

Courtesy Remington Arms

Exc.	V.G.	Good	Fair	Poor
650	525	400	300	200

Model 511 Scoremaster

A .22 caliber bolt action magazine sporting rifle with a 22" barrel. Blued with a walnut stock.

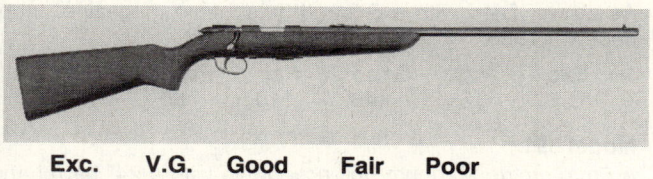

Exc.	V.G.	Good	Fair	Poor
250	200	175	125	75

Model 513 TR Matchmaster

A .22 caliber bolt action magazine target rifle with a heavy 27" barrel and Redfield aperture rear sight. Blued with a target style walnut stock. Manufactured from 1940 to 1969.

Exc.	V.G.	Good	Fair	Poor
350	300	200	150	100

Model 513 S

As above, with Marble sights and a checkered walnut sporting style stock. Manufactured from 1941 to 1956.

Exc.	V.G.	Good	Fair	Poor
600	500	400	275	225

Model 521 TL Jr.

A .22 caliber bolt action magazine target rifle with a heavy 25" barrel and Lyman sights. Blued with a target style walnut stock. Manufactured from 1947 to 1969.

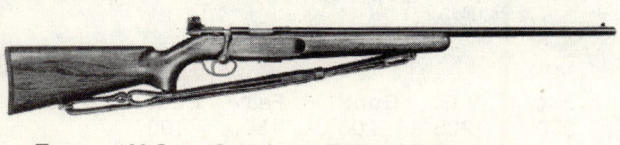

Exc.	V.G.	Good	Fair	Poor
250	200	175	125	75

Model 760

A slide-action sporting rifle chambered for various popular centerfire cartridges from the .222 up to the .35 Remington cartridge, with a 22" round barrel having open sights. It features a detachable box magazine. Blued with a checkered, walnut, pistol grip stock. Manufactured between 1952 and 1982. Examples of this rifle chambered for the .222, .223, .244, and the .257 Roberts are worth a premium over other calibers. Prospective purchasers are advised to secure a qualified appraisal prior to acquisition. This model was produced in the following styles.

Standard Model

Exc.	V.G.	Good	Fair	Poor
275	200	175	125	100

Model 760 Carbine-18.5" Barrel

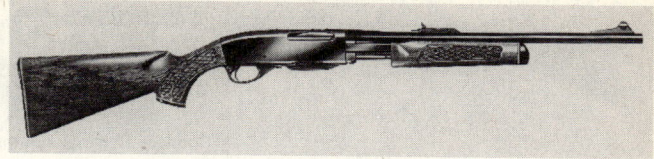

Exc.	V.G.	Good	Fair	Poor
375	300	250	175	150

Model 760D Peerless-Engraved

Exc.	V.G.	Good	Fair	Poor
1000	850	650	550	450

Model 760F Premier-Gamescene Engraved

Exc.	V.G.	Good	Fair	Poor
2500	2000	1500	1200	1000

Model 760F Gold Inlaid

Exc.	V.G.	Good	Fair	Poor
5000	4000	3000	2200	1750

Model 760 Bicentennial-1976 Only

Exc.	V.G.	Good	Fair	Poor
350	300	250	175	100

Model 760 ADL

Exc.	V.G.	Good	Fair	Poor
275	225	175	125	75

Model 760 BDL-Basketweave Checkering

Exc.	V.G.	Good	Fair	Poor
300	250	200	150	100

Model 552A Speedmaster

A .22 caliber semiautomatic rifle with a 23" barrel having open sights. Blued with a pistol grip walnut stock. Manufactured from 1959 to 1988.

Exc.	V.G.	Good	Fair	Poor
150	125	100	75	50

Model 552 BDL

As above, with a more fully figured stock and impressed checkering. Introduced in 1966.

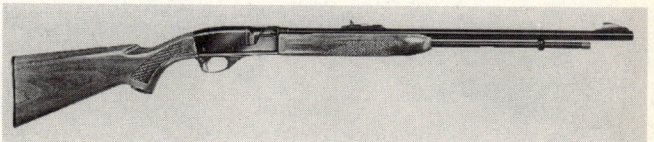

Courtesy Remington Arms

NIB	Exc.	V.G.	Good	Fair	Poor
200	175	150	125	100	75

Model 572 Fieldmaster

A .22 caliber slide-action rifle with a 21" barrel having open sights. Blued with a walnut stock. Manufactured from 1955 to 1988.

Courtesy Remington Arms

Exc.	V.G.	Good	Fair	Poor
150	125	100	75	50

Model 572 BDL

As above, but with a more fully figured walnut stock with impressed checkering. Introduced in 1966.

NIB	Exc.	V.G.	Good	Fair	Poor
210	185	165	145	110	85

Model 572SB

This is the same as the Model 572 but it has a smooth bore barrel and is chambered for the .22 Long Rifle cartridge.

NIB	Exc.	V.G.	Good	Fair	Poor
200	175	125	100	75	60

Model 580

A .22 caliber single shot bolt-action rifle with a 24" barrel having open sights and a Monte Carlo-style stock. Blued. The Model 580BR has a 1" shorter stock and would be worth approximately 10% more than the values listed below. Manufactured from 1968 to 1978.

Courtesy Remington Arms

Exc.	V.G.	Good	Fair	Poor
100	80	60	50	25

Model 580 BR

Same as above but with 1" shorter butt stock.

NIB	Exc.	V.G.	Good	Fair	Poor
130	100	75	60	50	40

Model 580SB

This is the same as the Model 580 except with a smoothbore barrel for .22 Long Rifle cartridges.

NIB	Exc.	V.G.	Good	Fair	Poor
175	125	100	75	60	50

Model 581

A .22 caliber bolt-action magazine rifle, blued with a 24" barrel and walnut stock. Manufactured from 1967 to 1983.

Exc.	V.G.	Good	Fair	Poor
150	125	100	75	50

Model 581 Left Hand

Same as above but built for a left handed shooter.

NIB	Exc.	V.G.	Good	Fair	Poor
175	150	100	75	60	50

Model 582

As above, fitted with a tubular magazine in place of the detachable box magazine. Manufactured from 1967 to 1983.

Courtesy Remington Arms

Exc.	V.G.	Good	Fair	Poor
150	125	100	75	50

Model 581-S

As above, fitted with a 5-round detachable magazine. Introduced in 1986.

Exc.	V.G.	Good	Fair	Poor
185	165	145	110	85

Model 591

A 5mm rimfire Magnum bolt-action rifle with a 24" barrel and Monte Carlo-style stock. Approximately 20,000 were made between 1970 and 1973.

Exc.	V.G.	Good	Fair	Poor
175	150	125	100	75

Model 592

As above, with a tubular magazine. Approximately 7,000 were made.

Exc.	V.G.	Good	Fair	Poor
300	250	200	150	100

Model 740

A .308 or .30-06 semiautomatic rifle with a 22" barrel and detachable box magazine. Blued with a plain walnut stock. Also available with an 18.5" barrel that would be worth approximately 10% more than the values listed below. Manufactured from 1955 to 1960.

Exc.	V.G.	Good	Fair	Poor
250	225	200	150	100

Model 740 ADL

As above, with a checkered walnut stock with a pistol grip.

Exc.	V.G.	Good	Fair	Poor
275	250	225	150	100

Model 740 BDL

As above, with a more finely figured walnut stock.

Exc.	V.G.	Good	Fair	Poor
300	275	250	150	100

Model 742

A 6mm Remington, .243, .280, .30-06, or .308 caliber semiautomatic rifle with a 22" barrel and 4-shot magazine. Also available with an 18" barrel in calibers .308 and .30-06 that are worth approximately 10% more than the values listed below. Blued with a checkered walnut stock. Manufactured from 1960 to 1980.

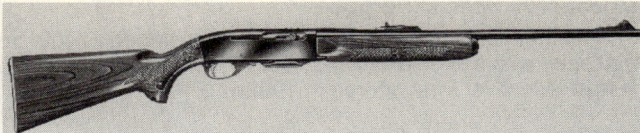

Courtesy Remington Arms

Exc.	V.G.	Good	Fair	Poor
300	275	250	150	100

Model 742 BDL

As above, with a Monte Carlo-style stock having basketweave checkering.

Standard Grade

Exc.	V.G.	Good	Fair	Poor
325	275	225	175	125

Model 742D Peerless-Engraved

Exc.	V.G.	Good	Fair	Poor
2100	1750	1500	1150	800

Model 742F Premier-Gamescene Engraved

Exc.	V.G.	Good	Fair	Poor
4000	3500	2750	1850	1300

Model 742F Premier-Gold Inlaid

Exc.	V.G.	Good	Fair	Poor
6500	5500	4000	3000	2250

Model 742 Bicentennial-Mfg. 1976 Only

Exc.	V.G.	Good	Fair	Poor
340	300	250	175	125

Model 76 Sportsman

A .30-06 slide action rifle with a 22" barrel and 4-shot magazine. Blued with walnut stock. Manufactured from 1985 to 1987.

Exc.	V.G.	Good	Fair	Poor
250	225	175	125	75

Model 7600

A variation of the above, chambered for a variety of cartridges from 6mm Remington to .35 Whelen with a 22" barrel and a detachable magazine. Also available with an 18.5" barrel. Blued with a checkered walnut stock. In 1996 fine line engraving on the receiver was offered as standard.

Courtesy Remington Arms-Model 7600 with new engraving

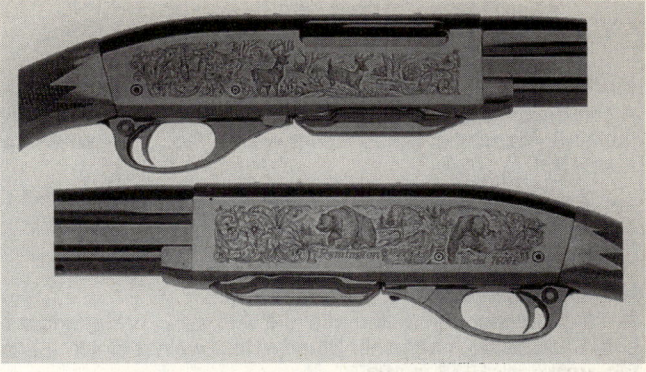

Courtesy Remington Arms-Closeup of new engraving on Model 7600

Standard Grade

NIB	Exc.	V.G.	Good	Fair	Poor
450	300	250	200	150	100

Model 7600D Peerless-Engraved

NIB	Exc.	V.G.	Good	Fair	Poor
2250	1800	1400	1200	950	750

Model 7600F Premier-Gamescene Engraved

NIB	Exc.	V.G.	Good	Fair	Poor
4750	4000	3500	2750	1850	1250

Model 7600 Premier-Gold Inlaid

NIB	Exc.	V.G.	Good	Fair	Poor
7000	6250	5000	4000	2750	1850

Model 7600 Special Purpose

The same configuration as the standard Model 7600 but equipped with a special finish on both the wood and metal that is non-reflective. First offered in 1993.

NIB	Exc.	V.G.	Good	Fair	Poor
350	300	250	200	150	100

Model 7600 Buckmasters ADF (American Deer Foundation)

Introduced in 1997 and built only for that year this model is chambered for the .30-06 cartridge and is a limited edition item. Fitted with a 22" barrel and special fine line engraved receiver.

Remington Model 7600 Buckmasters ADF

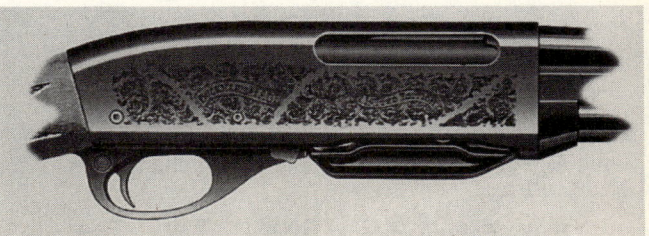

Remington Model 7600 engraving

NIB	Exc.	V.G.	Good	Fair	Poor
560	450	—	—	—	—

Model Six

A centerfire slide-action rifle with a 22" barrel and a 4-shot detachable magazine. Blued with a walnut stock. Manufactured from 1981 to 1987.

Exc.	V.G.	Good	Fair	Poor
400	350	275	200	125

Model 74 Sportsman

A .30-06 caliber semiautomatic rifle with a 22" barrel and a 4-shot detachable magazine. Blued with a walnut stock. Manufactured from 1985 to 1987.

Exc.	V.G.	Good	Fair	Poor
300	250	175	125	75

Model Four

As above, with a select Monte Carlo-style stock. Manufactured from 1982 to 1987.

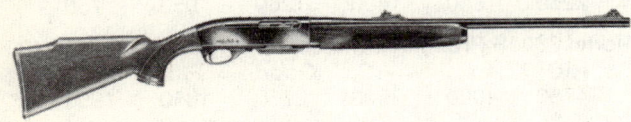

Exc.	V.G.	Good	Fair	Poor
450	400	350	275	175

Model 7400

This is a semi-automatic rifle with a 22" barrel. It is chambered for the .243, .270, .280, .30-06, .308, and the .35 Whelen. Blued with a checkered walnut stock. Average weight is about 7.5 lbs. Introduced in 1982. In 1996 this model was offered with fine line engraving on the receiver as standard.

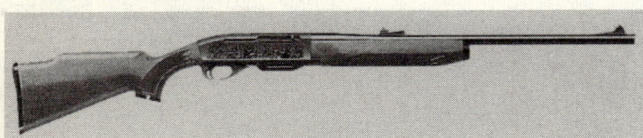

Courtesy Remington Arms-Model 7400 with new engraving

Courtesy Remington Arms-Closeup detail on engraving for Model 7400

NIB	Exc.	V.G.	Good	Fair	Poor
500	375	300	250	200	100

Model 7400 Carbine

Same as above but with 18.5" barrel and chambered for the .30-06 cartridge.

NIB	Exc.	V.G.	Good	Fair	Poor
500	375	300	250	200	100

Model 7400 Special Purpose

The same configuration as the standard Model 7400 but equipped with a special finish on both the wood and metal that is non-reflective. First offered in 1993.

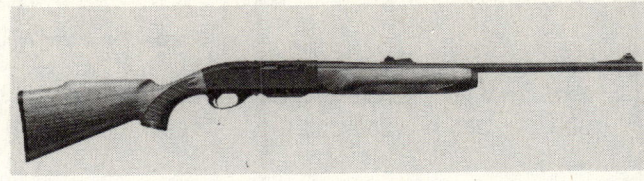

NIB	Exc.	V.G.	Good	Fair	Poor
400	350	300	250	200	100

Model 7400 Buckmasters ADF (American Deer Foundation)

Introduced in 1997 and built only in that year this model is limited. Chambered for the .30-06 cartridge and fitted with a 22" barrel. Special fine line engraving and polished blue finish. American walnut stock with Monte Carlo and cut checkering. Weight is 7.5 lbs.

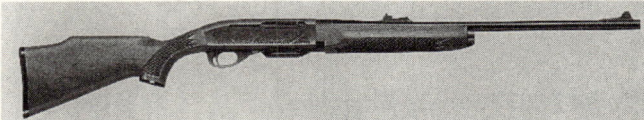

Remington 7400 Buckmasters ADF

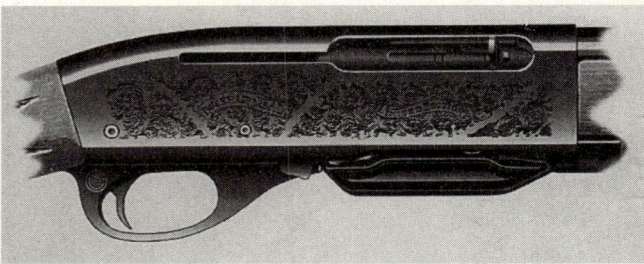

Remington Model 7400 Buckmasters ADF engraving

NIB	Exc.	V.G.	Good	Fair	Poor
600	500	—	—	—	—

Model 11

A .22 caliber bolt-action magazine rifle with a 20" barrel. Blued with a nylon stock. Manufactured from 1962 to 1964.

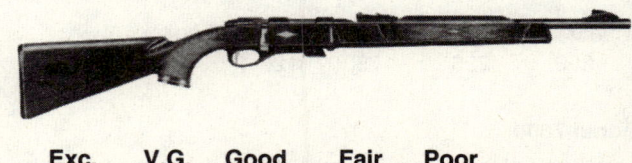

Exc.	V.G.	Good	Fair	Poor
150	125	100	75	50

Model 12

As above. Fitted with a tubular magazine. Manufactured from 1962 to 1964.

Exc.	V.G.	Good	Fair	Poor
175	150	125	100	75

Model 10

A bolt-action .22 caliber single shot rifle with a nylon stock. Manufactured from 1962 to 1964.

Courtesy Remington Arms

Exc.	V.G.	Good	Fair	Poor
125	100	75	50	25

Model 66

A .22 caliber semiautomatic rifle with a 20" barrel and tubular magazine in the butt. Black or chrome-plated finish with a black, brown or green checkered nylon stock. Manufactured from 1959 to 1988.

NOTE: Apache Black models are worth 15% more than the values listed below and the Seneca Green model is worth an additional 25%.

Exc.	V.G.	Good	Fair	Poor
150	125	100	75	50

Model 66 Bicentennial Commemorative

As above, but with a 1976 commemorative inscription on the barrel. Manufactured in 1976.

Exc.	V.G.	Good	Fair	Poor
125	100	85	70	55

Model 77

As above, with a 5-round detachable box magazine. Manufactured during 1970 and 1971.

Exc.	V.G.	Good	Fair	Poor
150	125	100	75	50

Model 76

A .22 caliber lever action magazine rifle with a nylon stock. Manufactured from 1962 to 1964.

Courtesy Remington Arms

Exc.	V.G.	Good	Fair	Poor
175	150	125	100	75

Model 522 Viper

Introduced in 1993 the Model 522 Viper is a new Remington .22 rimfire caliber semiautomatic design. The black stock is made from synthetic resin, while the receiver is made from a synthetic as well. It features a 20" barrel and a 10-shot detachable clip. The rifle weighs 4.6 lbs.

NIB	Exc.	V.G.	Good	Fair	Poor
140	120	100	80	60	40

Model 541 S Custom

A .22 caliber bolt-action magazine rifle with a 24" barrel. Blued with a scroll engraved receiver, and checkered walnut stock having a rosewood pistol grip cap and forend tip. Manufactured from 1972 to 1984.

Exc.	V.G.	Good	Fair	Poor
400	325	275	200	125

Model 541T

As above, drilled and tapped for telescopic sights. Introduced in 1986.

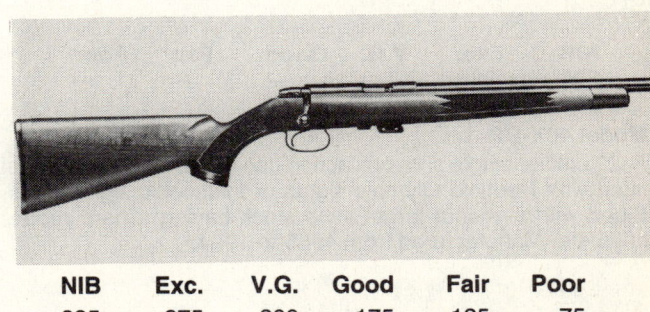

NIB	Exc.	V.G.	Good	Fair	Poor
335	275	200	175	125	75

Model 541T Heavy Barrel

This model is the same as the standard 541-T with the exception of a 24" heavy barrel. First introduced in 1993.

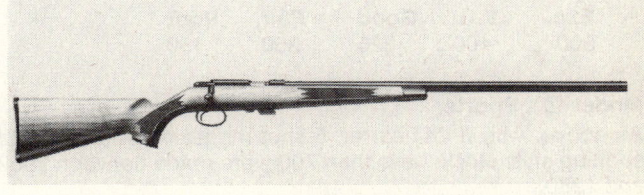

NIB	Exc.	V.G.	Good	Fair	Poor
400	350	300	250	200	125

Model 597

Introduced in 1997 this automatic .22 long rifle rimfire rifle features a carbon steel barrel with alloy receiver. All metal has a non-reflective matte black finish. Stock is dark gray synthetic. Barrel length is 20" and weight is approximately 5.5 lbs.

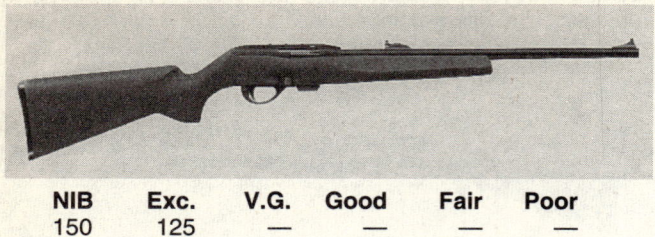

NIB	Exc.	V.G.	Good	Fair	Poor
150	125	—	—	—	—

Model 597 LSS

This version of the Model 597 is similar to the above but with the addition of a laminated stock and stainless steel finish.

NIB	Exc.	V.G.	Good	Fair	Poor
250	200	—	—	—	—

Model 597 Magnum

This model features a 20" carbon steel barrel, alloy receiver, and black synthetic stock. It is chambered for the .22 Win. Magnum cartridge. Weight is approximately 6 lbs.

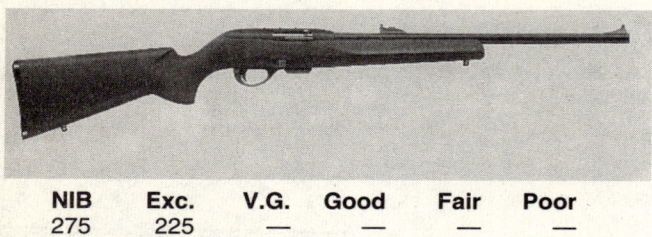

NIB	Exc.	V.G.	Good	Fair	Poor
275	225	—	—	—	—

Model 40X-BR

A .22 caliber single shot bolt action rifle with a heavy 28" barrel fitted with Redfield Olympic sights or telescopic sight bases. Blued with a walnut target style stock having a hard rubber buttplate. Manufactured from 1955 to 1964.

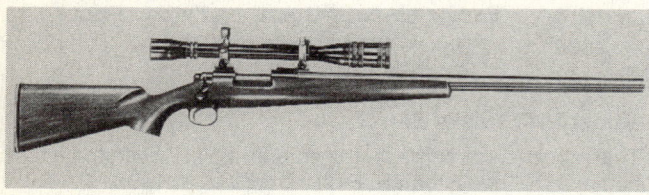

Courtesy Remington Arms

Exc.	V.G.	Good	Fair	Poor
500	400	325	250	150

Model 40X Sporter

As above, with a 24" barrel, 5-shot magazine and a walnut sporting style stock. Less than 700 were made between 1969 and 1980.

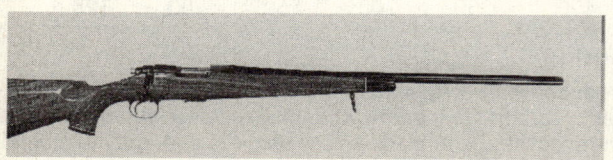

Courtesy Remington Arms

Exc.	V.G.	Good	Fair	Poor
2500	15000	1000	750	500

Model 40X Centerfire

As above, chambered for the .22, .22 Magnum, .308, or .30-06 centerfire cartridges. Manufactured from 1961 to 1964.

Exc.	V.G.	Good	Fair	Poor
550	450	350	300	200

Model 40XB Stainless

This model is built in the Custom Shop and features stainless steel barrel, receiver, and bolt. The receiver is drilled and tapped and fitted with a 27-1/4" heavy target barrel. The trigger is fully adjustable. There is a choice of walnut stock or synthetic stock. Offered in calibers from .222 to .300 Win. Mag. This rifle is built to order. Retail prices range form $1,200 to $1,500 depending on configuration and finish.

Model 40XB BR

This is a bench rest version of the above model. This rifle has a 22" stainless heavy barrel chambered for the .22 Long Rifle. Adjustable trigger. Built to order. Retail prices begin around $1,350.

Model XR KS Sporter

This version is also chambered for the .22 Long Rifle and is fitted with a 24" barrel. Fully adjustable trigger. This model is also built to special order and prices begin around $1,350.

Model 720A

A .257 Roberts, .270, or .30-06 bolt-action sporting rifle with a 22" barrel and a 5-shot integral magazine. Blued with a checkered walnut stock. Approximately 2,500 were manufactured in 1941.

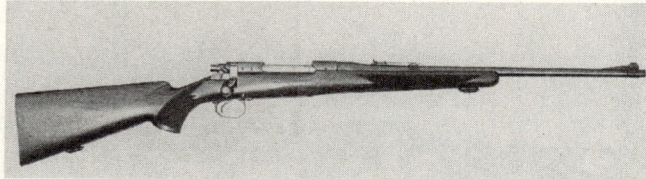

Courtesy Remington Arms

Exc.	V.G.	Good	Fair	Poor
1250	1000	800	600	475

Model 721

A .264 Magnum, .270, or .30-06 bolt action rifle with a 24" barrel and a 4-shot magazine. Blued with a plain walnut stock. Manufactured from 1948 to 1962.

Courtesy Remington Arms

Standard Version

Exc.	V.G.	Good	Fair	Poor
300	250	200	150	100

Model 721 ADL

Exc.	V.G.	Good	Fair	Poor
350	300	250	200	125

Model 721 BDL-Select Stock

Exc.	V.G.	Good	Fair	Poor
400	350	300	250	150

Model 721A Magnum-.300 H&H

Exc.	V.G.	Good	Fair	Poor
450	400	350	275	150

Model 722

As above, with a shorter action chambered for .257 Roberts, .300 Savage, or .308 cartridges. Manufactured from 1948 to 1962.

Exc.	V.G.	Good	Fair	Poor
300	250	200	150	100

Model 725 ADL

A centerfire bolt action sporting rifle with a 22" barrel, 4-shot magazine and Monte Carlo-style stock. The .222 caliber version was produced in limited quantities and should be individually appraised. Manufactured from 1958 to 1961.

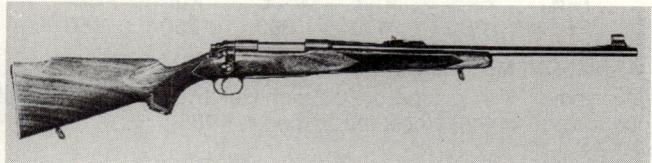

Courtesy Remington Arms

Exc.	V.G.	Good	Fair	Poor
375	325	275	225	150

Model 725 Kodiak

A .375 Holland & Holland Magnum or .458 Winchester Magnum, bolt-action sporting rifle with a 26" barrel having a muzzle brake and open sights, and 3-shot magazine. Blued with a checkered walnut stock. Manufactured in 1961.

Exc.	V.G.	Good	Fair	Poor
800	700	550	400	300

Model 600

A centerfire bolt action sporting rifle with an 18.5" ventilated rib barrel and a checkered walnut stock. Manufactured from 1964 to 1967.

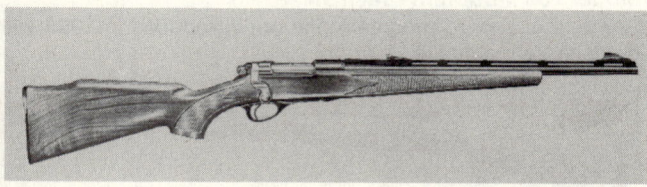

Courtesy Remington Arms

Exc.	V.G.	Good	Fair	Poor
400	325	250	175	125

Model 600 Mohawk

As above, but with a plain barrel and chambered only for the .222 Remington, .243 Winchester or .308 Winchester cartridges. Manufactured from 1971 to 1979.

Exc.	V.G.	Good	Fair	Poor
275	250	200	175	150

Model 660 Magnum

As above, chambered for the 6.5mm Remington Magnum and .350 Remington Magnum cartridges. Stock of laminated walnut and beechwood. Manufactured from 1965 to 1967.

Exc.	V.G.	Good	Fair	Poor
575	500	425	350	275

Model 660 (improved)

An improved version of the Model 600. Manufactured from 1968 to 1971.

Exc.	V.G.	Good	Fair	Poor
500	425	350	250	200

Model 660 Magnum (improved)

As above, but chambered for either the 6.5mm Remington Magnum or .350 Remington Magnum cartridges and fitted with a laminated stock.

Exc.	V.G.	Good	Fair	Poor
600	500	450	350	275

Model 78 Sportsman

A centerfire bolt action sporting rifle with a 22" barrel and 4-shot magazine. Blued with a walnut stock. Introduced in 1985.

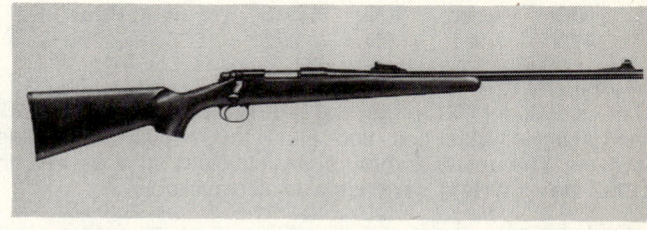

NIB	Exc.	V.G.	Good	Fair	Poor
335	275	225	200	150	100

MODEL 700 SERIES

NOTE: In 1996 Remington added fine line engraving to its Model 700 line. All Model 700 BDL rifles with have this new engraving on them at no extra charge.

Model 700 ADL

A centerfire bolt action sporting rifle with either a 22" or 24" barrel having open sights and a 4-shot magazine. Blued with a checkered Monte Carlo-style walnut stock. Introduced in 1962.

NIB	Exc.	V.G.	Good	Fair	Poor
425	325	250	200	150	100

Model 700 ADL Synthetic

This model features a black matte metal finish with 22" barrel or 24" on Magnums. The synthetic stock is black with checkering, recoil pad, and sling swivel studs. Receiver is drilled and tapped for scope. Offered in .243, 270, 30-06 and 7mm Rem. Mag.

NIB	Exc.	V.G.	Good	Fair	Poor
350	300	250	200	150	100

Courtesy Remington Arms

Model 700 BDL

Same as above, with a hinged floorplate, hand cut checkering, black forend tip and pistol grip cap.

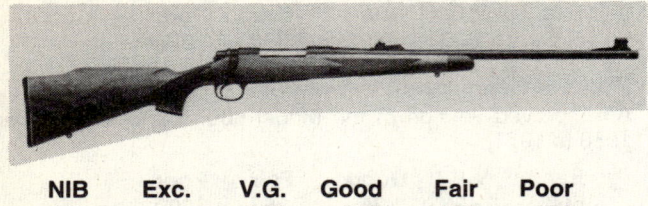

NIB	Exc.	V.G.	Good	Fair	Poor
465	400	325	275	225	150

Courtesy Remington Arms

Model 700 BDL (DM)

Same as above but introduced in 1995 with detachable magazine.

NIB	Exc.	V.G.	Good	Fair	Poor
475	425	350	275	225	150

Model 700 BDL LSS

This is a Model 700, introduced in 1996, with a synthetic stock and stainless steel bolt, floor plate, trigger guard, and sling swivels. The action and barrel are stainless steel as well. In 1997 the .260 Rem. cartridge was also available.

Courtesy Remington Arms

NIB	Exc.	V.G.	Good	Fair	Poor
600	475	400	350	300	200

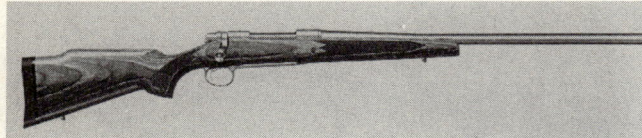

Courtesy Remington Arms

Model 700 BDL SS DM-Magnum Rifle

Introduced in 1996 this Model 700 version is fitted with a factory installed muzzle brake on its Magnum calibers; 7mm Rem. Mag., .300 Win. Mag., .300 Wthby. Mag., and the .338 Win. Mag. Weight is approximately 7.5 lbs. In 1997 the 7mm STW cartridge was added to this model.

Courtesy Remington Arms

NIB	Exc.	V.G.	Good	Fair	Poor
675	500	400	300	200	150

Model 700 Sendero

This Model 700 configuration is chambered for the .25-06, .270, 7mm Rem. Mag., .300 Win. Mag. It is fitted with a synthetic stock and a 26" heavy barrel.

NIB	Exc.	V.G.	Good	Fair	Poor
600	475	400	300	200	150

Model 700 Sendero SF

Introduced in 1996 this model features a stainless steel fluted barrel. It has a synthetic stock with full length bedding. It weighs about 8.5 lbs. Chambered for same calibers as the standard Sendero above except for the .270. In 1997 the 7mm STW cartridge was made available for this model.

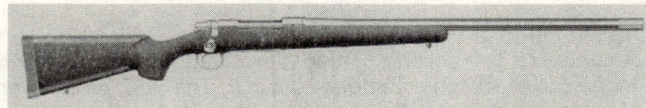

Courtesy Remington Arms

NIB	Exc.	V.G.	Good	Fair	Poor
750	600	450	350	250	150

Model 700 Mountain Rifle

As above, with a tapered 22" lightweight barrel, blued with checkered walnut stock. Introduced in 1986.

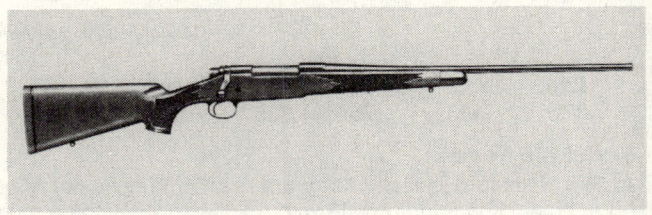

NIB	Exc.	V.G.	Good	Fair	Poor
425	325	250	200	150	100

Model 700KS Mountain Rifle

As above, with a lightweight Kevlar stock. Introduced in 1986.

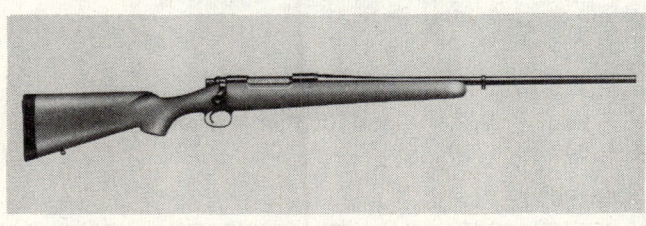

NIB	Exc.	V.G.	Good	Fair	Poor
750	700	600	500	400	300

Model 700 Mountain Rifle (DM)

Same as standard mountain rifle but introduced in 1995 with detachable magazine.

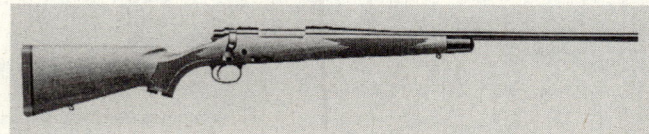

Courtesy Remington Arms

NIB	Exc.	V.G.	Good	Fair	Poor
475	425	350	300	250	175

Model 700 Safari Grade

As the Model 700BDL chambered for 8mm Remington Magnum, .375 Holland & Holland, .416 Remington Magnum or .458 Winchester Magnum cartridges, 24" barrel and 3-shot magazine. Blued with a finely figured walnut checkered stock. The Model KS Safari Grade was fitted with a Kevlar stock and would be worth approximately 20% more than the values listed below. Introduced in 1962.

NIB	Exc.	V.G.	Good	Fair	Poor
875	750	600	500	400	300

Model 700 RS

As above, chambered for the .270 Winchester, .280 Remington, or .30-06 cartridges, 22" barrel and 4-shot magazine. Blued with a DuPont Rynite stock. Manufactured during 1987 and 1988.

Exc.	V.G.	Good	Fair	Poor
500	425	350	250	150

Model 700 FS

As above, with a Kevlar stock.

Exc.	V.G.	Good	Fair	Poor
550	475	400	300	200

Model 700 BDL European

Available for the first time in 1993, this new model features an oil finish stock with Monte Carlo comb and raised cheek piece. The checkering is fine line. In addition the rifle is standard with hinged floorplate, sling swivel studs, hooded ramp front sight, and adjustable rear sight. Offered in the following calibers: .243, .207, .280, 7mm-08, 7mm Mag. .30-06, and .308.

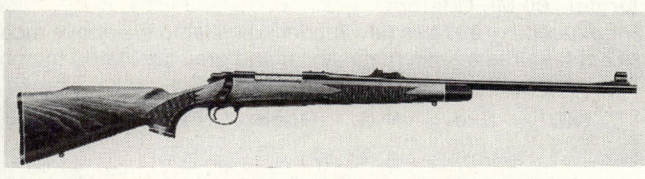

NIB	Exc.	V.G.	Good	Fair	Poor
400	350	300	250	200	125

Model 700 BDL Stainless Synthetic

Offered in 1993 this model features a stainless steel receiver, barrel, and bolt. Synthetic stock has straight comb, raised cheek piece, and hinged floor plate. Metal is finished in a black matte nonreflective finish. Available in 14 calibers from .223 to .338 Win. Mag. All barrel lengths regardless of caliber are 24".

NIB	Exc.	V.G.	Good	Fair	Poor
550	450	350	300	200	150

Model 700 BDL Stainless Synthetic (DM)

Same as above but introduced in 1995 with detachable magazine.

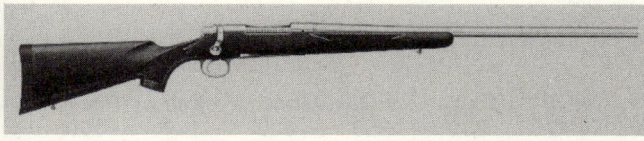

Courtesy Remington Arms

NIB	Exc.	V.G.	Good	Fair	Poor
575	475	350	300	200	150

Model 700 Mountain Rifle Stainless Synthetic

This model is the same as the Mountain rifle but with stainless steel receiver, bolt, and barrel. Offered in .25-06 Rem., .270, .280, and .30-06. All calibers are supplied with a 22" barrel.

NIB	Exc.	V.G.	Good	Fair	Poor
450	400	350	300	225	150

Model 700 Varmint Special Synthetic

The stock on this model is reinforced with DuPont Kevlar, fiberglass, and graphite. Rifle is offered with a heavy barrel and all metal has a fine matte black finish. The barrel rest on a machined aircraft-grade aluminum bedding stock. The receiver is drilled and tapped for scope mounts. Offered in .22-250, .223, and .308 calibers. In 1993 the .220 Swift was added to the line.

NIB	Exc.	V.G.	Good	Fair	Poor
500	450	400	350	300	200

Model 700 VS SF (Varmint Synthetic Stainless Fluted)

Introduced in 1994 this model features a stainless steel barrel, receiver and action. It is fitted with a 26" heavy varmint barrel that has a spherical concave crown contour. Six flutes reduce barrel weight and help cooling. A synthetic stock made from fiberglass reinforced with graphite is standard. The stock is dark gray. Offered in .223, .220 Swift, .22-250, and .308 calibers. The .243 Win. cartridge was added to this modrel in 1997. The rifle weighs about 8-3/8 lbs.

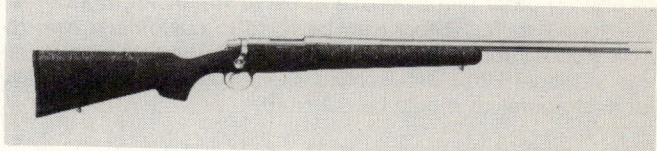

NIB	Exc.	V.G.	Good	Fair	Poor
700	575	500	400	300	200

Model 700 Varmint Special Wood

Same as above but furnished with walnut stock and offered in the following calibers: .222, .22-250, .223, 6mm, .243, 7mm-08, and .308.

NIB	Exc	V.G.	Good	Fair	Poor
450	400	350	300	250	150

Model 700 Varmint Laminated Stock (VLS)

Same as above but furnished with special laminited stock. Introduced in 1995. The 7mm-08 Rem. cartridge was added to this model in 1997.

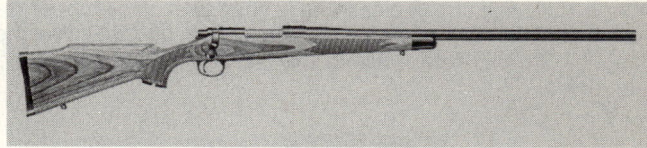

Courtesy Remington Arms

NIB	Exc.	V.G.	Good	Fair	Poor
475	400	350	300	250	150

Model 700 Classic

This limited edition model is furnished with a straight comb, satin finished walnut stock, sling swivel studs, and hinged magazine floorplate. The series began in 1981 and each year Remington has offered the Model 700 Classic in a special chambering. The following is a list of these chamberings by year.

1981-7MM	1989-.300 Wthby. Magnum
1982-.257 Roberts	1990-.25-06 Rem.
1983-.300 H&H Magnum	1991-7mm Wthby. Magnum
1984-.250-3000	1992-.220 Swift
1985-.350 Rem. Magnum	1993-.222 Rem.
1986-.264 Win. Magnum	1994-6.5X55 Swedish
1987-.338 Win. Magnum	1995-.300 Win. Magnum
1988-.35 Whelen	1996-.375 H&H Magnum
	1997-.280 Rem.

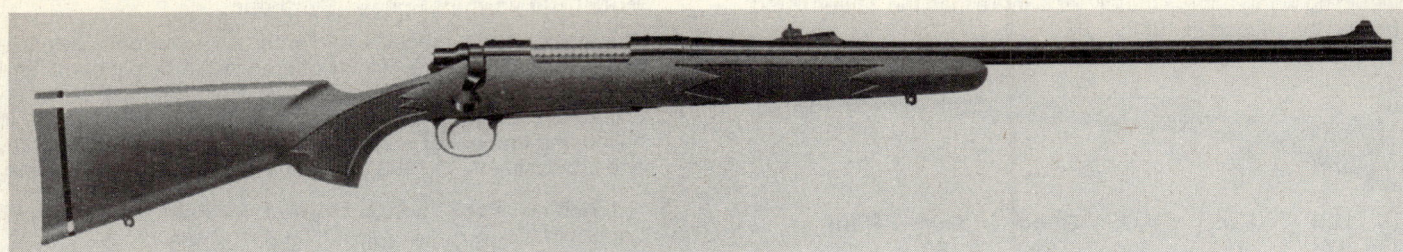

Courtesy Remington Arms

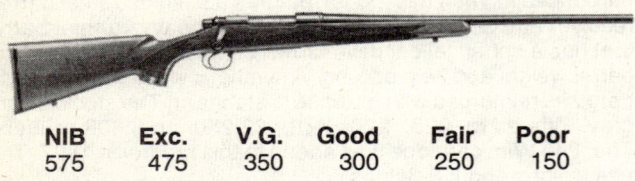

NIB	Exc.	V.G.	Good	Fair	Poor
575	475	350	300	250	150

Model 700 Custom

A special order rifle available in either American, English, or California walnut. Stock can be fitted to customer's own dimensions. Engraving is available as is a large selection of calibers. Model 700 Custom rifles should be priced individually and an appraisal should be obtained.

Model 700 AWR (Alaskan Wilderness Rifle)

This model is built in the Custom Shop and features a blind magazine and stainless steel components on a black matte synthetic stock. Fitted with a 24" barrel, all metal parts are finished in a black satin. Offered in .300 Weatherby Magnum, 7mm Rem. Mag., .300 Win. Mag., .338, and .375 calibers. Weighs about 6-3/4 lbs. Built to order with a retail price of $1,200 in 1995.

Model 700 APR (African Plains Rifle)

This Custom Shop model features a hinged floorplate, a 26" barrel, and blue metal finish. The stock is a laminated Monte Carlo style with cheek piece and is fitted with black rubber recoil pad. Offered in same calibers as Model 700 AWR. Weighs about 7-3/4 lbs. Retail price in 1995 is $1,500 on a special order basis.

Model 700 Safari KS Stainless

A new addition to the Remington line in 1993, the Safari KS Stainless has a special reinforced Kevlar stock in a nonreflective gray finish. Checkering is 18 lines to the inch. Offered in the following calibers: .375 H&H Mag., .416 Rem. Mag., and the .458 Win. Mag.

NIB	Exc.	V.G.	Good	Fair	Poor
500	450	400	350	300	150

Model 700 ML

This model was introduced in 1996. It is an in-line design and the first built on a modern action. It is chambered for the .50 or .54 caliber bullet. It is fitted with a synthetic stock and rubber recoil pad. The barrel length is 24" and the approximate weight is 7.75 lbs. A camo stock option was added to this model in 1997.

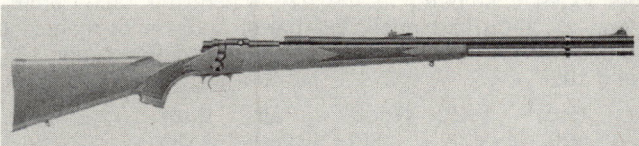

Courtesy Remington Arms

Remington Model 700 ML Camo

NIB	Exc.	V.G.	Good	Fair	Poor
350	250	200	150	100	75

Model 700 ML Custom

Introduced in 1997 this new model is similar to the above model but features a satin metal finish and gray laminated thumbhole stock with roll-over cheek piece.

NIB	Exc.	V.G.	Good	Fair	Poor
775	650	—	—	—	—

Model 700 MLS

Same as above but with stainless steel barrel and action.

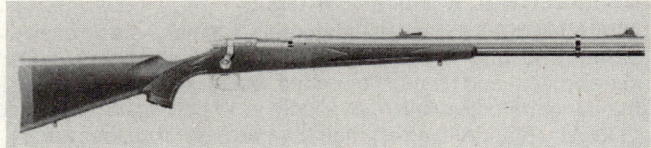

Courtest Remington Arms

Remington Model 700 MLS Camo

NIB	Exc.	V.G.	Good	Fair	Poor
400	300	250	200	150	100

Model 700 MLS Custom

Similar to the above model but with a satin stainless steel finish and a two-toned gray laminated thumbhole stock with roll-over cheekpiece. Introduced in 1997.

NIB	Exc.	V.G.	Good	Fair	Poor
875	725	—	—	—	—

Model 788

A centerfire bolt action sporting rifle with either a 22" or 24" barrel and a plain walnut stock. An 18" barrel carbine was also manufactured and is worth approximately 10% more than the values listed below. Manufactured from 1967 to 1984.

Exc.	V.G.	Good	Fair	Poor
325	275	225	150	100

Model 7

A centerfire bolt action sporting rifle with an 18.5" barrel and 4- or 5-shot magazine. Blued with a checkered walnut stock. Chambered for .223 Rem., .243 Rem., 7mm-08 Re., .308 Win., and for 1997 the .260 Rem. cartridge. Introduced in 1982.

NIB	Exc.	V.G.	Good	Fair	Poor
450	400	325	275	200	100

Model 7 FS

As above with a Kevlar stock. Introduced in 1987.

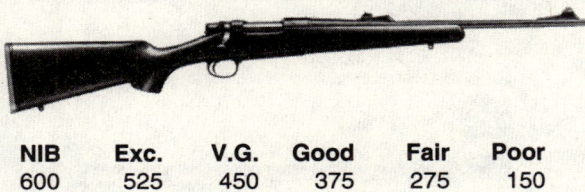

NIB	Exc.	V.G.	Good	Fair	Poor
600	525	450	375	275	150

Model 7 SS (Stainless Synthetic)

Introduced in 1994 this model features a stainless steel barrel, receiver, and bolt with a matte finish. It is fitted with a 20" barrel, and a hinged floorplate. The synthetic stock is textured black. Available in .243, 7mm-08, and .308. In 1997 the .260 Rem. cartridge was also offered. Weight approximately 6.25 lbs.

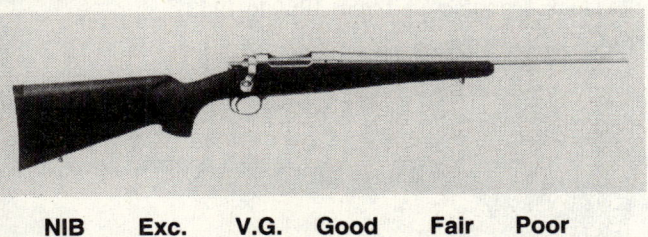

NIB	Exc.	V.G.	Good	Fair	Poor
475	400	350	300	200	150

Model 7 MS

First introduced in 1993 and available through the Remington Custom Shop. This rifle features a 20" barrel with Mannlicher stock made from select grain wood and laminated for strength. Available in calibers for .270 Rem. to .308.

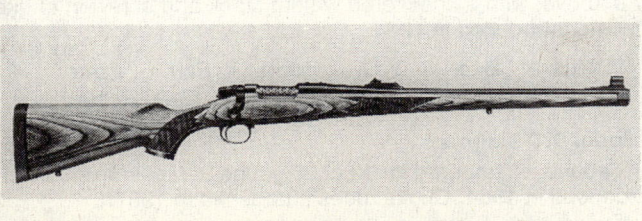

NIB	Exc.	V.G.	Good	Fair	Poor
800	700	550	350	250	150

Model 7 Youth

First offered in 1993 this variation is a youth version of the standard Model 7. The butt stock is 1" shorter than standard. Available in 6mm, .243, and 7mm-08.

NIB	Exc.	V.G.	Good	Fair	Poor
350	300	250	200	150	100

Model 1816 Commemorative Flint Lock Rifle

Introduced in 1995. It features a 39", .50 caliber octagonal barrel. Stock is hand finished extra fancy curly maple. Built for one year only. Special order only.

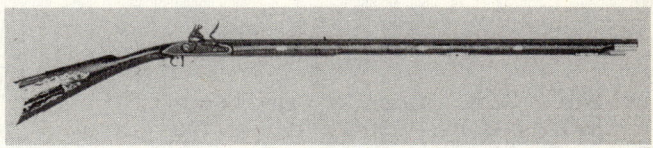

Courtesy Remington Arms

NIB	Exc.	V.G.	Good	Fair	Poor
1800	1200	850	700	500	300

Remington No. 1 Rolling Block Mid-Range

This classic rifle was reintroduced into the Remington in 1997 and features a 30" half octagon, half round barrel chambered for the .45-70 Gov't cartridge. Designed for use with black powder and lead cast bullets. The receiver is case colored. All barrel, receiver, and metalwork markings match the orginal rifle. Rear tang-mounted vernier sight and front globe sight with interchangeable inserts. A single set trigger is standard. Steel butt plate. Weight is approximately 9.75 lbs.

NIB	Exc.	V.G.	Good	Fair	Poor
2750	2250	—	—	—	—

Model 10A

A 12, 16, or 20 gauge slide action shotgun with barrels ranging from 26" to 32". Takedown, blued with a plain walnut stock. Manufactured from 1907 to 1929.

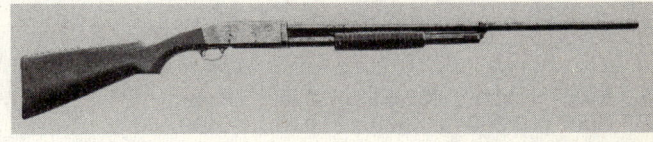

Courtesy Remington Arms

Exc.	V.G.	Good	Fair	Poor
375	300	250	200	100

Model 11

A 12, 16, or 20 gauge semiautomatic shotgun with barrels ranging in length from 26" to 32". Designed by John M. Browning and produced under license from Fabrique Nationale. Blued with a checkered walnut stock. Approximately 300,000 were made from 1911 to 1948.

Solid Rib or Vent Rib-Add 30%.

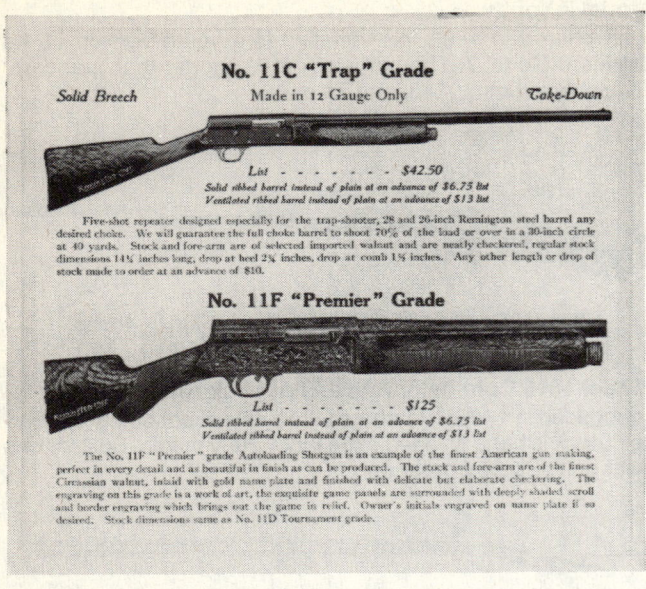

Exc.	V.G.	Good	Fair	Poor
300	250	200	150	100

Model 11B Special-Engraved

Exc.	V.G.	Good	Fair	Poor
550	475	375	275	175

Model 11D Tournament

Exc.	V.G.	Good	Fair	Poor
850	750	650	450	300

Model 11E Expert-Engraved

Exc.	V.G.	Good	Fair	Poor
1300	1150	1000	650	450

Model 11F Premier-Heavily Engraved

Exc.	V.G.	Good	Fair	Poor
2250	1900	1600	1150	600

Model 11R-20" Barrel Riot Gun

Exc.	V.G.	Good	Fair	Poor
350	300	250	175	100

Model 17

A 20 gauge slide-action shotgun with barrels ranging in length from 26" to 32". Takedown, blued with a plain walnut stock. Approximately 48,000 were made from 1917 to 1933.

Vent Rib-Add 25%.

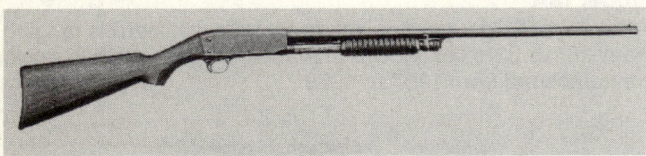

Courtesy Remington Arms

Exc.	V.G.	Good	Fair	Poor
350	300	250	175	100

Model 29

As above, chambered for 12 gauge cartridges. Approximately 24,000 manufactured from 1929 to 1933.

Vent Rib-Add 25%.

Exc.	V.G.	Good	Fair	Poor
450	350	300	200	175

NOTE: For guns with 32" barrels add 40%.

Model 31

A 12, 16, or 20 gauge slide-action shotgun with barrels ranging in length from 26" to 32" and a magazine capacity of either 2 or 4 rounds. Takedown, blued with a walnut stock. Approximately 160,000 were made from 1931 to 1949.

Solid Rib or Vent Rib-Add 25%. For early banded barrels add 25%

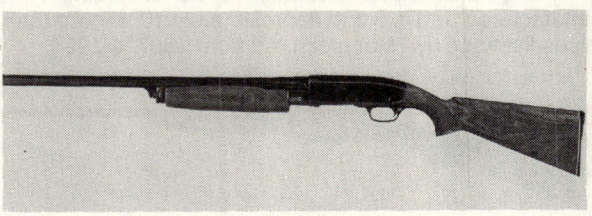

Exc.	V.G.	Good	Fair	Poor
400	325	275	200	125

NOTE: For guns with 32" barrel add 50%. For early models with checkered stocks add 40%.

MODEL 870 SERIES

In 1996 Remington offered as standard a new fine line engraving pattern on all Model 870 receivers.

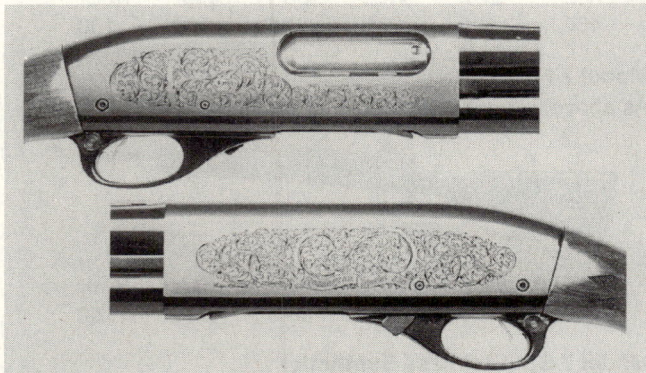

Courtesy Remington Arms-Closeup detail of new engraving on the Model 870

Model 870 Wingmaster

A 12, 16, or 20 gauge slide action shotgun with 26", 28", or 30" barrels and a 5-shot tubular magazine. Blued with a plain walnut stock. Manufactured from 1950 to 1963.

Vent Rib-Add 10%.

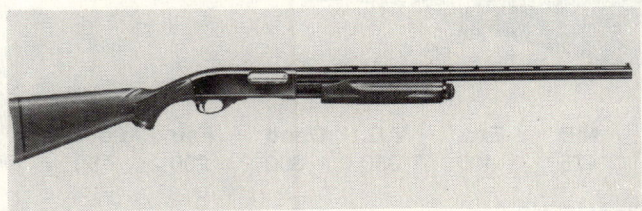

Exc.	V.G.	Good	Fair	Poor
250	225	200	150	100

Model 870 Field Wingmaster

As above, with a checkered walnut stock and screw-in choke tubes. Introduced in 1964.

NIB	Exc.	V.G.	Good	Fair	Poor
440	325	275	225	150	100

Model 870 Magnum

As above, chambered for 12 or 20 gauge 3" Magnum shells Introduced in 1964. Choke tubes introduced in 1987.

NIB	Exc.	V.G.	Good	Fair	Poor
440	325	275	225	150	100

Model 870 Express

As above, for 3", 12 gauge shells with a 28" ventilated rib and one choke tube. Parkerized with a matte finished stock. Introduced in 1987.

NIB	Exc.	V.G.	Good	Fair	Poor
235	200	175	150	100	75

Model 870TA Trap

As above, with a competition ventilated rib and checkered stock. Produced in 12 gauge only. Discontinued in 1986.

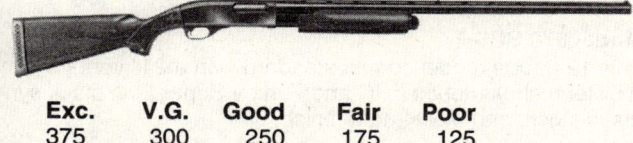

Exc.	V.G.	Good	Fair	Poor
375	300	250	175	125

Model 870TB Trap

As above, with a 28" or 30" full choke, ventilated rib barrel and a trap style walnut stock. Manufactured from 1950 to 1981.

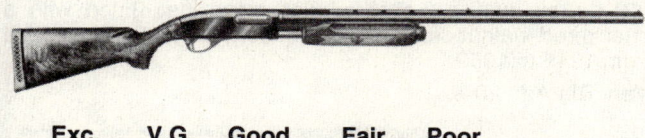

Exc.	V.G.	Good	Fair	Poor
400	325	275	200	125

Model 870TC Trap

As above, with a finely figured walnut stock and screw-in choke tubes.

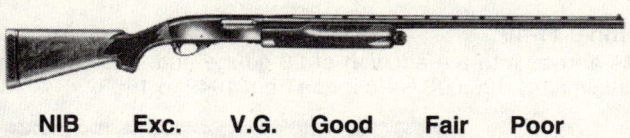

NIB	Exc.	V.G.	Good	Fair	Poor
575	475	400	350	250	150

Model 870 Special Field

This Remington pump action shotgun is available in either 12 or 20 gauge and features an English style straight grip stock, 21" vent rib barrel and slim shortened slide handle. In 12 gauge the gun weighs 7 lbs. and in 20 gauge it weighs 6.25 lbs. Comes with a set of Remington choke tubes.

NIB	Exc.	V.G.	Good	Fair	Poor
350	300	250	200	150	100

Model 870 Brushmaster Deer Gun

This 12 gauge slide action shotgun is fitted with a 20" Remington choke plain barrel and Monte Carlo stock. Available for either left-hand or right-hand shooters.

NIB	Exc.	V.G.	Good	Fair	Poor
350	300	250	200	150	100

Model 870 Express Turkey

Furnished in 12 gauge with 21" vent rib barrel with extra-full Remington choke Turkey tube.

NIB	Exc.	V.G.	Good	Fair	Poor
225	200	175	150	125	100

Model 870 Express Deer Gun

This model is fitted with a 20" fully rifled barrel, iron sights, and Monte Carlo stock. Also offered with a 20" IC rifle sighted barrel. Available in 12 gauge only.

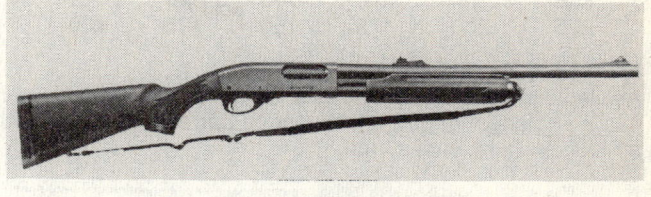

NIB	Exc.	V.G.	Good	Fair	Poor
225	200	175	150	125	100

Model 870 Express HD (Home Defense)

Introduced in 1995 this model features an 18" 12 gauge barrel with cylinder barrel with front bead sight. Weight approximately 7.25 lb.

NIB	Exc.	V.G.	Good	Fair	Poor
225	200	175	150	125	100

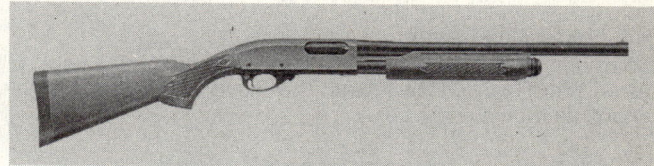

Courtesy Remington Arms

Model 870 Rifle Deer Gun

This new 20 gauge model was introduced in 1994 and features a fully rifled 20" barrel. It has a new scope rail design that is more rigid. The finish is blue and the Monte Carlo stock is walnut. Is equipped with recoil pad and checkering.

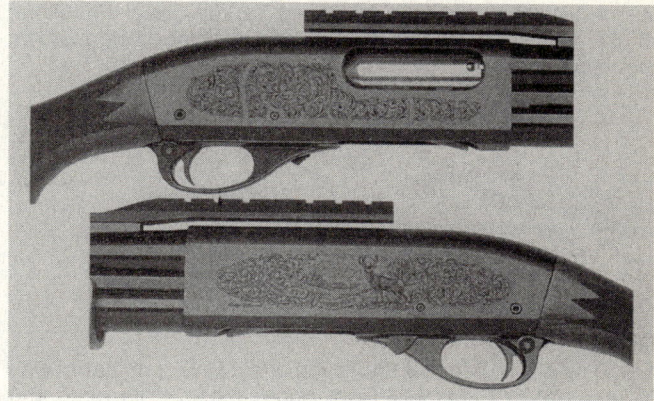

Courtesy Remington Arms-Closeup of new engraving detail on Model 870 Deer Gun

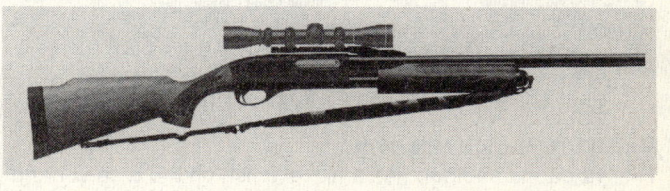

NIB	Exc.	V.G.	Good	Fair	Poor
450	400	350	300	200	100

Model 870 Express Small Game

Offered in 20 gauge or .410, this model has a nonreflective metal and wood finish. The .410 bore is furnished with a 25" vent rib full choke barrel, while the 20 gauge is available with a 26" or 28" vent rib barrel with Modified Rem. choke tube.

NIB	Exc.	V.G.	Good	Fair	Poor
225	200	175	150	125	100

Model 870 Youth Gun

Available in 20 gauge only, this shotgun is built for children. It has a 13" length of pull, a 21" vent rib barrel, and is sold with a Modified Rem. choke tube.

NIB	Exc.	V.G.	Good	Fair	Poor
225	200	175	150	125	100

Model 870 Security

Offered in 12 gauge only this personal protection shotgun has a 18.5 cylinder choked plain barrel with front bead sight.

NIB	Exc.	V.G.	Good	Fair	Poor
225	200	175	150	125	100

Model 870 SPS-Camo

Offered in 12 gauge only and a choice of 26" or 28" vent rib barrel with Rem. choke tubes. The wood and metal are finished in a brown camo color.

NIB	Exc.	V.G.	Good	Fair	Poor
325	275	225	175	125	100

Model 870 SPS-BG Camo

Available for the first time in 1993 this model features a 12 gauge 20" plain barrel with IC and Turkey Super Full Rem. choke tubes. The wood and metal are finished in a brown camo color.

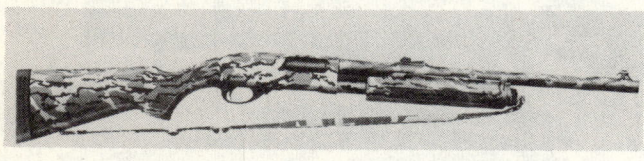

NIB	Exc.	V.G.	Good	Fair	Poor
325	275	225	175	125	100

Model 870 SPS-T Camo

Same as above with the exception of a 21" vent rib barrel with IC and Turkey Super Full Rem. choke tubes. Both wood and metal are finished in a green camo color.

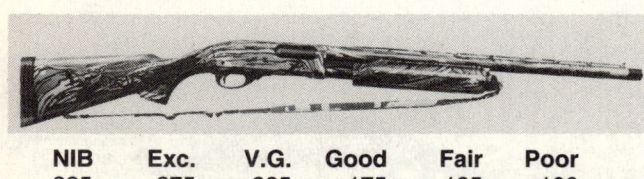

NIB	Exc.	V.G.	Good	Fair	Poor
325	275	225	175	125	100

Model 870 Marine Magnum

This 12 gauge shotgun has a nickel finish on the receiver and barrel both inside and outside. Synthetic stock is checkered. The 18" barrel is bored cylinder and is fitted with a 7-round magazine. Sling swivel studs are standard.

NIB	Exc.	V.G.	Good	Fair	Poor
325	275	225	175	125	100

Model 870 SPS

Offered in 12 gauge only with synthetic stock and black matte finish. The barrel is either 26" or 28" vent rib with Rem. choke tubes.

NIB	Exc.	V.G.	Good	Fair	Poor
325	275	225	175	125	100

Model 870 SPS-Deer

Available with a 20" rifle with plain barrel, this 12 gauge shotgun has a black synthetic stock and black matte finish. First introduced in 1993.

NIB	Exc.	V.G.	Good	Fair	Poor
300	250	225	175	125	100

Model 870 SPS-T

This 12 gauge model comes standard with a 21" vent rib barrel, Rem. choke tubes in IC and Turkey Super Full, black synthetic stock, and black matte finish.

NIB	Exc.	V.G.	Good	Fair	Poor
300	250	225	175	125	100

Model 48 Sportsman

A 12, 16, or 20 gauge semiautomatic shotgun with 26", 28", or 32" barrels and a 3-shot tubular magazine. Blued with a checkered walnut stock. Approximately 275,000 were made from 1949 to 1959.

Vent Rib-Add 20%.

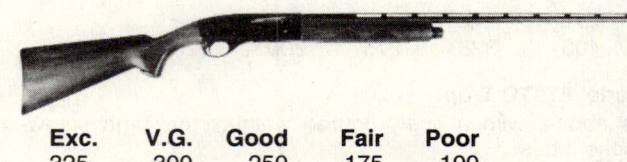

Exc.	V.G.	Good	Fair	Poor
325	300	250	175	100

Model 11-48

As above, with the addition of 28 gauge and .410 bore. Approximately 425,000 were made from 1949 to 1968.

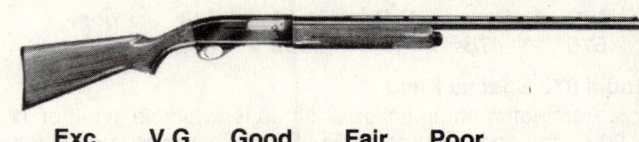

Exc.	V.G.	Good	Fair	Poor
300	250	200	150	75

Model 58 Sportsman

A 12, 16, or 20 gauge semiautomatic shotgun with 26", 28", or 30" barrels and a 3-shot tubular magazine. The receiver scroll engraved and blued, checkered walnut stock. Approximately 270,000 were made from 1956 to 1963.

Exc.	V.G.	Good	Fair	Poor
300	250	200	150	75

Model 878 Automaster

As above, in 12 gauge only. Approximately 60,000 were made from 1959 to 1962.

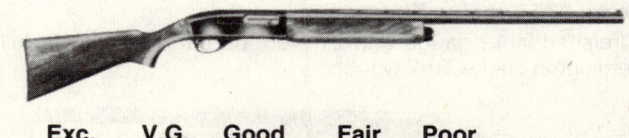

Exc.	V.G.	Good	Fair	Poor
275	225	175	125	75

MODEL 1100 SERIES

A 12, 16, 20 or 28 gauge or .410 bore semiautomatic shotgun with barrels ranging in length from 26" to 30" fitted with choke tubes after 1987. The smaller bore versions are worth approximately 20% more than the values listed below. Blued with a checkered walnut stock. Manufactured beginning in 1963.

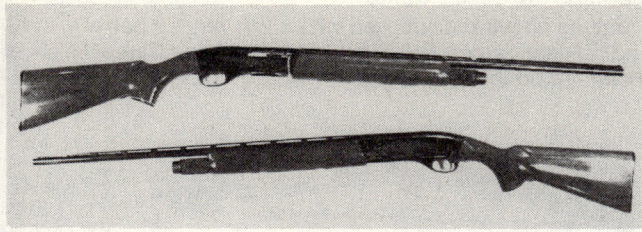

Exc.	V.G.	Good	Fair	Poor
375	300	250	200	100

Model 1100 Youth Gun
Offered in 20 gauge only with a 21" vent rib 2-3/4" barrel. The stock has a special 13" length of pull. Gun is supplied with a set of Rem. choke tubes.

NIB	Exc.	V.G.	Good	Fair	Poor
425	400	350	300	200	150

Model 1100 Small Game
Available in 20, 28 gauge or .410 bore fitted with 25" vent rib barrels. The 28 gauge and .410 have fixed chokes while the 20 gauge has Rem. choke tubes.

NIB	Exc.	V.G.	Good	Fair	Poor
500	450	400	350	250	150

Model 1100 Tournament Skeet
Offered in 20, 28 gauge, and .410 bore. The 28 gauge and .410 come with 25" Skeet choked vent rib barrels while the 20 gauge is supplied with a 26" Skeet choked vent rib barrel.

Courtesy Remington Arms

NIB	Exc.	V.G.	Good	Fair	Poor
550	475	425	350	250	150

Model 1100 Sporting 28
Introduced in 1996 this version is chambered for the 28 gauge shell. It is fitted with interchangeable chokes and a 25" vent rib barrel. The stock is walnut with Tournament grade checkering and recoil pad.

Courtesy Remington Arms

NIB	Exc.	V.G.	Good	Fair	Poor
550	475	425	350	250	150

Model 1100 LT-20
This 20 gauge model features a choice of 26" or 28" vent rib barrels with Rem choke tubes. It has a blue finish and walnut Monte Carlo stock. Recoil pad and cut checkering are standard. Weight is 6.75 to 7 lbs depending on barrel length.

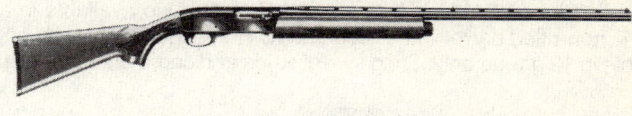

NIB	Exc.	V.G.	Good	Fair	Poor
525	450	400	300	200	150

Model 1100 LT-20 Deer Gun
Same as above but fitted with a 21" barrel with adjustable sights and an improved cylinder choke. Satin finish with American walnut stock. Weight is approximately 6.5 lbs.

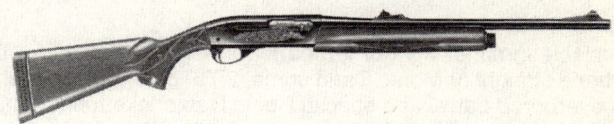

NIB	Exc.	V.G.	Good	Fair	Poor
525	450	400	300	200	150

Model 1100 LT-20 Synthetic
Same as above but fitted with a synthetic stock with recoil pad.

NIB	Exc.	V.G.	Good	Fair	Poor
425	375	325	275	200	150

Model 1100 LT-20 Magnum
This 20 gauge Model 1100 is chambered for the 3" 20 gauge shell. It is fitted with a 28" vent rib barrel with interchangeable chokes. Checkered walnut stock. Weight is about 7 lbs.

NIB	Exc.	V.G.	Good	Fair	Poor
550	475	400	300	200	150

Model 1100 Synthetic
Introduced in 1995 this model is furnished with a black synthetic stock with black matte metal finish. Available in both 12 and 20 gauge.

Courtesy Remington Arms

NIB	Exc.	V.G.	Good	Fair	Poor
400	350	300	250	200	100

Model 1100 Synthetic Deer Gun
Same as above but fitted with a 21" fully rifled barrel with can-tilever rail for scope mounting. Furnished with 2-3/4" chamber. Stock is black synthetic with checkering and Monte Carlo style cheekpiece. Recoil pad is standard.

NIB	Exc.	V.G.	Good	Fair	Poor
525	450	400	300	200	150

MODEL 11-87 SERIES

Model 11-87 Premier
A 3", 12 gauge semiautomatic shotgun with 26" to 32" ventilated rib barrels having screw-in choke tubes. Blued with a checkered walnut stock. Introduced in 1987.

NIB	Exc.	V.G.	Good	Fair	Poor
560	475	425	350	275	175

Model 11-87 Premier Cantilever Scope Mount Deer Gun

This semiautomatic model has a Monte Carlo stock and the option of a barrel mounted scope (not included). Optional with a fully rifled barrel 21" long with a 1 in 35" twist. Also available in a 21" non-rifled barrel with Rifled and IC Rem. choke tubes. Available in 12 gauge only. Sling swivel studs and camo are standard.

NIB	Exc.	V.G.	Good	Fair	Poor
500	450	400	300	200	150

Model 11-87 Premier Trap

Available in either right or left hand models. Is available with either a straight or Monte Carlo comb, 2.75" chamber, 30" vent rib overbored barrel and special Rem. Trap choke tubes. This model is set up to handle 12 gauge target loads only.

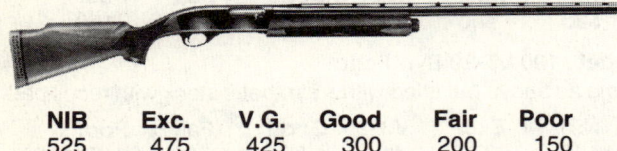

NIB	Exc.	V.G.	Good	Fair	Poor
525	475	425	300	200	150

Model 11-87 Premier Sporting Clays

This model features a special target stock with a 3.16" length of pull longer than standard and 1/4" higher at the heel. The butt pad is radiused at the heel and rounded at the toe. The receiver top, barrel, and rib have a fine matte finish on the blueing. The vent rib is a medium wide 8mm with stainless steel mid bead and a Bradley style front bead sight. Gun is supplied new with the following Rem. choke tubes: Skeet, Improved Skeet, Imp. Cyl., Model., and Full. Supplied from the factory with a two-barrel custom fitted hard case. In 1997 a nickel plated receiver and barrel porting were added to this model.

Courtesy Remington Arms-Model 11-87 Sporting Clays with new engraving

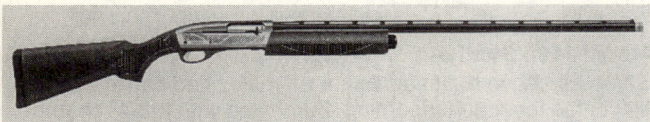

Remington Model 11-87 Sporting Clays with nickel plated receiver and ported barrel

NIB	Exc.	V.G.	Good	Fair	Poor
650	525	450	300	200	150

Model 11-87 SPS-BG Camo

This 12 gauge model is fitted with a rifle sighted 21" barrel with a brown camo finish on the stock and metal parts. Introduced in 1993.

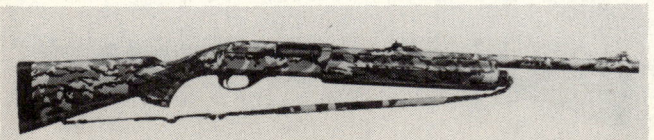

NIB	Exc.	V.G.	Good	Fair	Poor
525	475	425	300	200	150

Model 11-87 SPS-T Camo

Same as above but supplied with a 21" vent rib barrel with IC and Turkey Super Full Rem. choke tubes. Camo finish is green. Introduced in 1993.

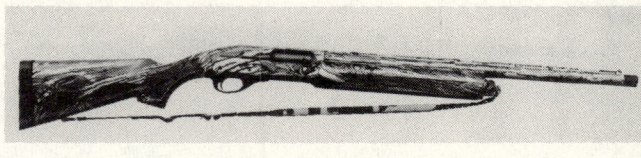

NIB	Exc.	V.G.	Good	Fair	Poor
525	475	425	300	200	150

Model 11-87 SPS

This 12 gauge model is furnished with a 26" or 28" vent rib barrel with IC, Mod., and Full Rem. choke tubes. The stock is a black synthetic material and the metal is finished in a black matte. In 1997 a camo version of this model was introduced.

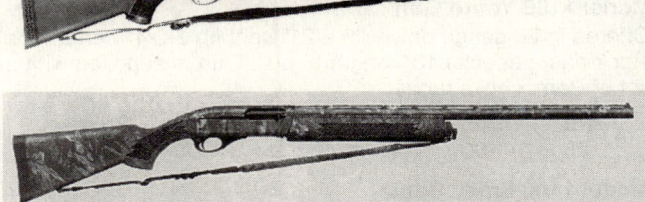

Remington Model 11-87 SPS Camo

NIB	Exc.	V.G.	Good	Fair	Poor
450	400	300	250	200	150

Model 11-87 SPS-Deer

The same as above but fitted with a 21" rifle sighted barrel. First introduced in 1993.

NIB	Exc.	V.G.	Good	Fair	Poor
525	475	425	300	200	150

Model 11-87 SPS-T

Same as above but fitted with a 21" vent rib barrel with IC and Turkey Super Full Rem. choke tubes. In 1997 a camo version of this model was introduced.

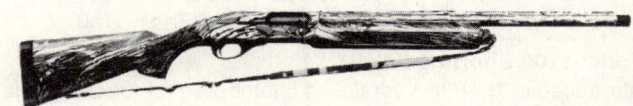

Remington Model 11-87 SPS-T Camo

NIB	Exc.	V.G.	Good	Fair	Poor
525	475	425	300	200	150

Model 11-96 Euro Lightweight

Introduced in 1996 this model is based on the Model 11-87 action. Two vent rib barrel lengths are offered: 26" and 28" supplied with 3 Rem chokes. Fine line engraving on the receiver and checkered Claro walnut stocks are standard. Blued finish. Weight is approximately 7 lbs.

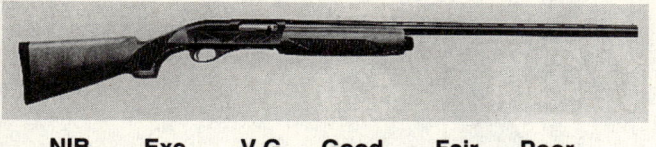

NIB	Exc.	V.G.	Good	Fair	Poor
775	700	—	—	—	—

Model SP-10

A 3.5", 10 gauge semiautomatic shotgun with 26" or 30" ventilated rib barrels having screw-in choke tubes. Matte blued with a checkered walnut stock.

NIB	Exc.	V.G.	Good	Fair	Poor
1275	1000	800	650	550	400

Model SP-10 Magnum Camo

A new model introduced in 1993, this 10 gauge semiautomatic is designed for the turkey or deer hunter. Available with either 26" or 30" vent rib barrel or a 26" vent rib barrel with a 22" deer barrel. An additional barrel option is a 23" vent rib barrel with a camo finish. All barrels are fitted with Remington choke tubes.

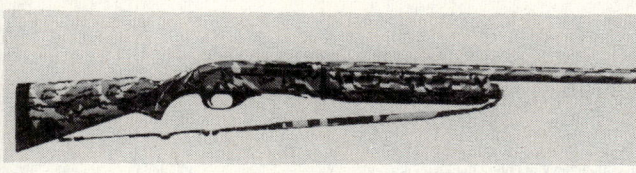

NIB	Exc.	V.G.	Good	Fair	Poor
875	800	700	500	350	200

Model 32

A 12 gauge Over/Under shotgun with 26", 28", or 30" separated barrels and a single selective trigger. Approximately 15,000 were made from 1932 to 1942.

Standard Grade

Solid or vent rib-Add 10%.

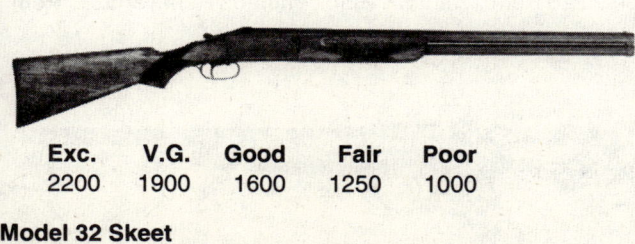

Exc.	V.G.	Good	Fair	Poor
2200	1900	1600	1250	1000

Model 32 Skeet

Exc.	V.G.	Good	Fair	Poor
2750	2250	1950	1500	1250

Model 32 TC

Exc.	V.G.	Good	Fair	Poor
2750	2500	2250	1750	1450

Model 32D

Exc.	V.G.	Good	Fair	Poor
3500	3000	2500	2000	1650

Model 32E Expert

Exc.	V.G.	Good	Fair	Poor
4500	3500	3000	2500	2000

Model 32F Premier

Exc.	V.G.	Good	Fair	Poor
7000	5500	4000	3250	2500

Model 3200

A 12 gauge Over/Under shotgun with 26", 28", or 30" separated ventilated rib barrels, single selective trigger, and automatic ejector. Blued with a checkered walnut stock. Manufactured from 1972 to 1984.

Field Grade

Exc.	V.G.	Good	Fair	Poor
800	725	600	450	300

Model 3200 Magnum-3" Chambers

Exc.	V.G.	Good	Fair	Poor
1000	850	750	550	450

Model 3200 Skeet

Exc.	V.G.	Good	Fair	Poor
800	725	600	450	300

Model 3200 4-Gauge Set

Exc.	V.G.	Good	Fair	Poor
4500	3750	3000	2250	1500

Model 3200 Trap

Exc.	V.G.	Good	Fair	Poor
850	775	650	500	350

Model 3200 Special Trap-Deluxe Wood

Exc.	V.G.	Good	Fair	Poor
1150	950	750	550	450

Model 3200 Competition Trap-Engraved

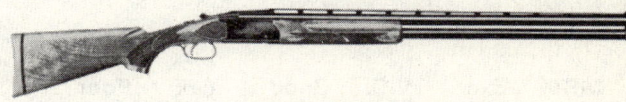

Exc.	V.G.	Good	Fair	Poor
1250	1000	850	650	550

Model 3200 Premier-Heavily Engraved

Exc.	V.G.	Good	Fair	Poor
2250	2000	1750	1500	1000

Model 3200 "One of One Thousand"-1,000 Produced

Exc.	V.G.	Good	Fair	Poor
2500	2000	1500	1100	500

Remington Peerless

Introduced in 1993 this new Remington Over/Under shotgun is offered in 12 gauge only. Available in 26", 28", and 30" vent rib barrel lengths and fitted with Remington choke tubes (IC, M,

F). The sideplates are removable and the stock is American walnut.

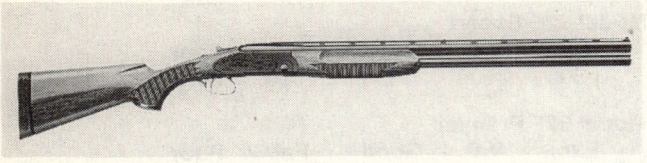

NIB	Exc.	V.G.	Good	Fair	Poor
1000	900	750	600	400	300

Model 90-T Single Barrel Trap

Offered in 12 gauge only, this single barrel Trap shotgun is fitted with either a 32" or 34" overbored full choke barrel.

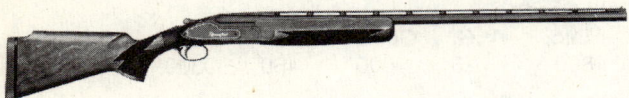

NIB	Exc.	V.G.	Good	Fair	Poor
2500	1800	1300	900	600	300

Model 90-T Single Barrel Trap (High Rib)

The same shotgun as described above with the exception of an adjustable high rib for shooters who prefer a more open target picture and higher head position.

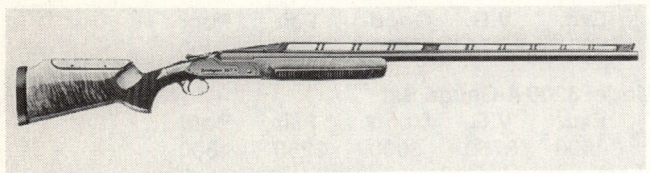

NIB	Exc.	V.G.	Good	Fair	Poor
2500	2200	1650	1200	750	400

Model 396 Sporting

Introduced in 1996 this over and under shotgun is designed for sporting clays shooting. It is offered in 12 gauge only with 30" barrels. Chokes are interchangeable Rem choke system. Fancy American stock with satin finish. Scroll engraving on the receiver and blue finish. Weight is about 8 lbs.

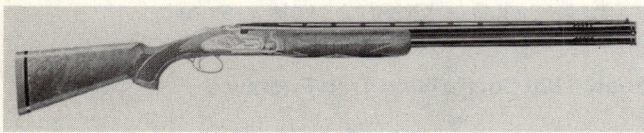

Courtesy Remington Arms

NIB	Exc.	V.G.	Good	Fair	Poor
2400	2100	1600	1200	850	500

Model 396 Skeet

Same but with a choice of 28" or 30" barrels.

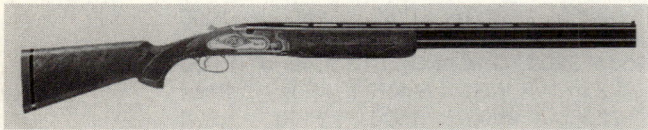

Courtesy Remington Arms

NIB	Exc.	V.G.	Good	Fair	Poor
2275	1950	1500	1150	800	500

Model XP-100

A .221 Remington Fireball or .223 Remington caliber bolt action single shot pistol with a 14.5" ventilated rib barrel and adjustable sights. Blued with a nylon stock. Introduced in 1963.

NIB	Exc.	V.G.	Good	Fair	Poor
375	325	275	225	175	100

Model XP-Silhouette

As above, chambered for either the 7mm Remington or .35 Remington cartridges and fitted with a 15" barrel drilled and tapped for a telescope.

NIB	Exc.	V.G.	Good	Fair	Poor
500	400	300	225	175	100

Model XP-100 Custom

A custom made version of the above with a 15" barrel and either a nylon or walnut stock. Available in .223 Remington, .250 Savage, 6mm Benchrest, 7mm Benchrest, 7mm-08, or .35 Remington calibers. Introduced in 1986.

NIB	Exc.	V.G.	Good	Fair	Poor
900	800	650	550	425	300

Model XP-100 Hunter

This model features a laminated wood stock, 14.5" drilled and tapped barrel, and no sights. It is offered in the following calibers: .223 Rem., 7mm BR Rem., 7mm-08 Rem., and .35 Rem.

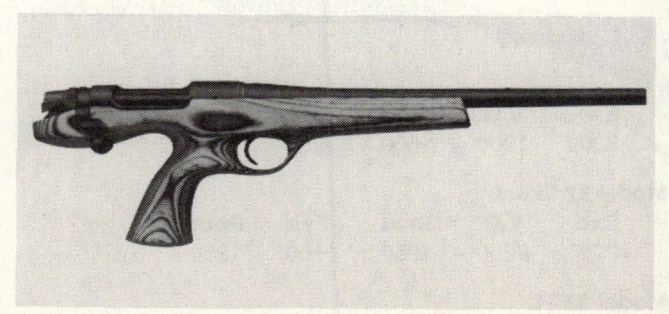

NIB	Exc.	V.G.	Good	Fair	Poor
500	400	300	225	175	100

REMINGTON 180TH ANNIVERSARY LIMITED EDITION RIFLES AND SHOTGUNS

Remington will manufacture 180 each of the following firearms to commemorate the founding of the company in 1816:

Model 700, Model 7600, Model 7400, Model 870, and the Model 11-87.

These firearms will feature fine line hand engraving with gold embellishments. The rifles will be chambered for the .30-06 cartridge with 22" barrels and the shotguns will will be chambered for the 12 gauge shell with 26" vent rib barrels with Rem chokes. All guns will feature blue finishes with high gloss semi-

fancy walnut stocks. If sold in a five gun set each will have matching serial numbers. The suggested retail price for the five gun set is $6,925. Individual guns will carry suggested retail prices as follows:

Model 700 180th Anniversary Commemorative-$1,372.00
Model 7400 180th Anniversary Commemorative-$1,372.00
Model 7600 180th Anniversary Commemorative-$1,332.00
Model 870 180th Anniversary Commemorative-$1,305.00
Model 11-87 180th Anniversary Commemorative-$1,465.00

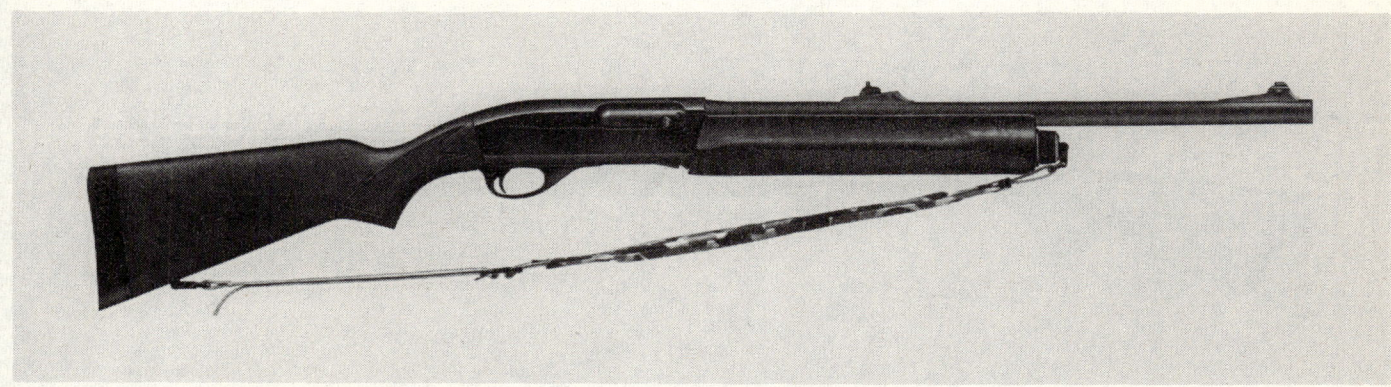

Remington Model 11-87 SP deer gun autoloading action with 3" chamber (21" barrel with rifle sights)

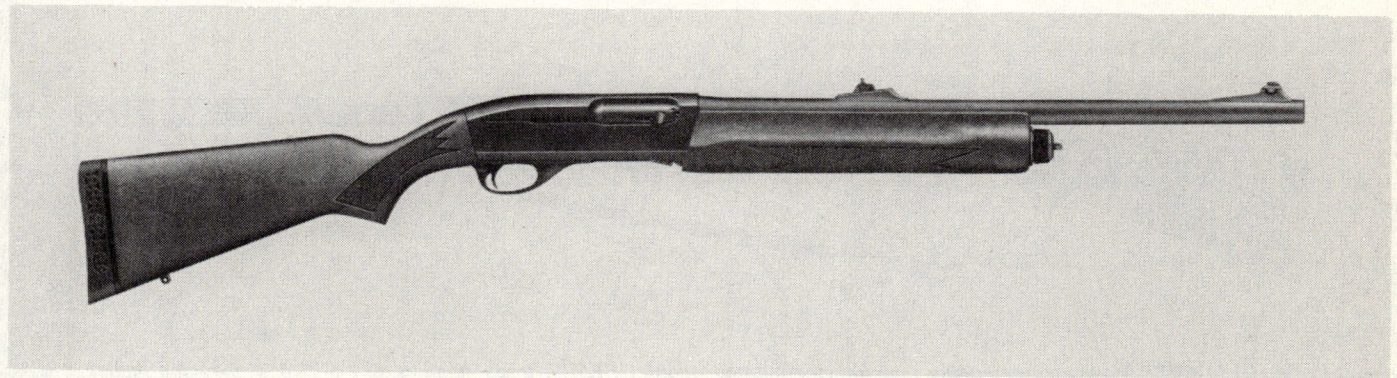

Remington Model 11-87 Police 12 gauge autoloading shotgun (21" barrel with 3" chamber and rifle sights)

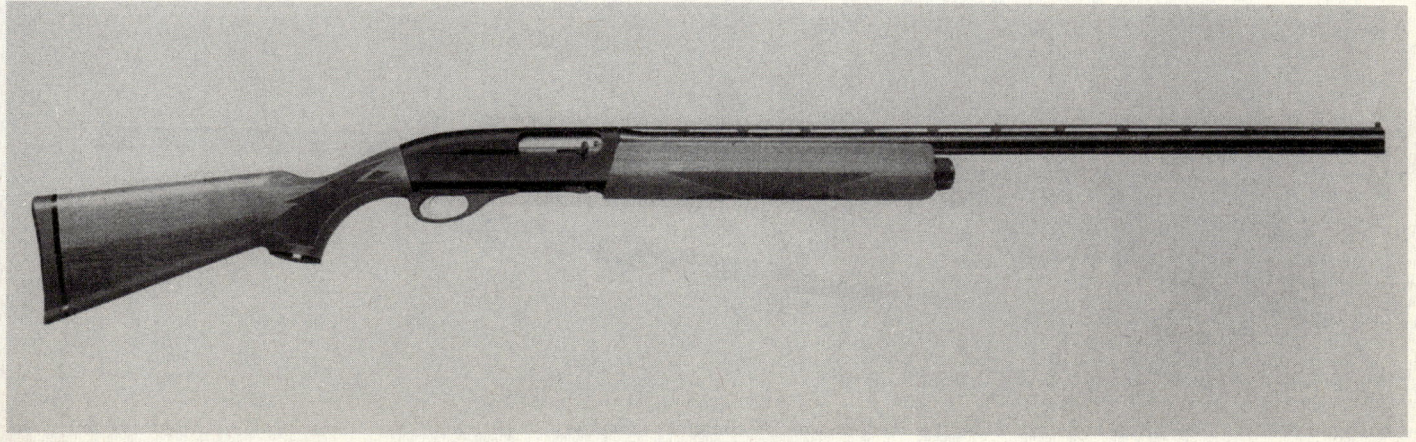

The Remington Model 11-87 Premier with new engraving. Introduced in 1996

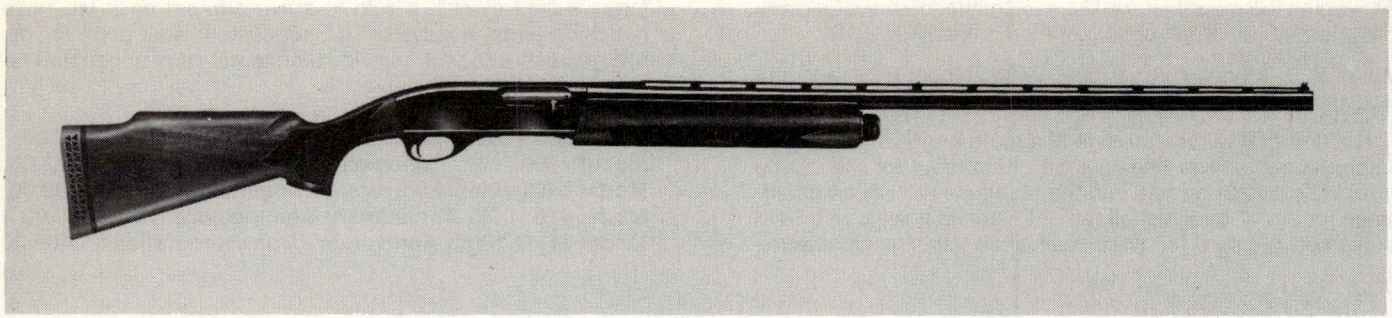

Remington Model 11-87 "Premier" autoloading trap gun with 3 interchangeable "REM" chokes (shown with Monte Carlo stock)

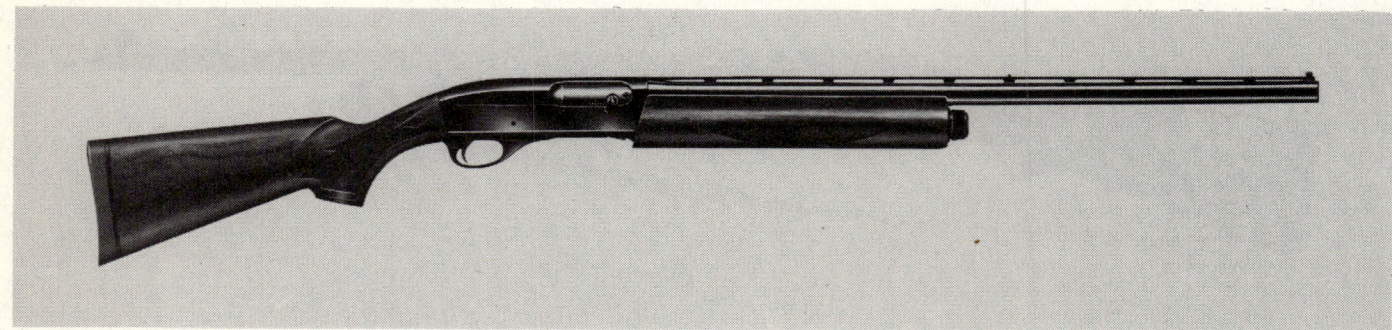

Remington Model 11-87 "Premier" 12 gauge autoloading shotgun with interchangeable "REM" chokes (handles all 2-3/4" & 3" magnum shells)

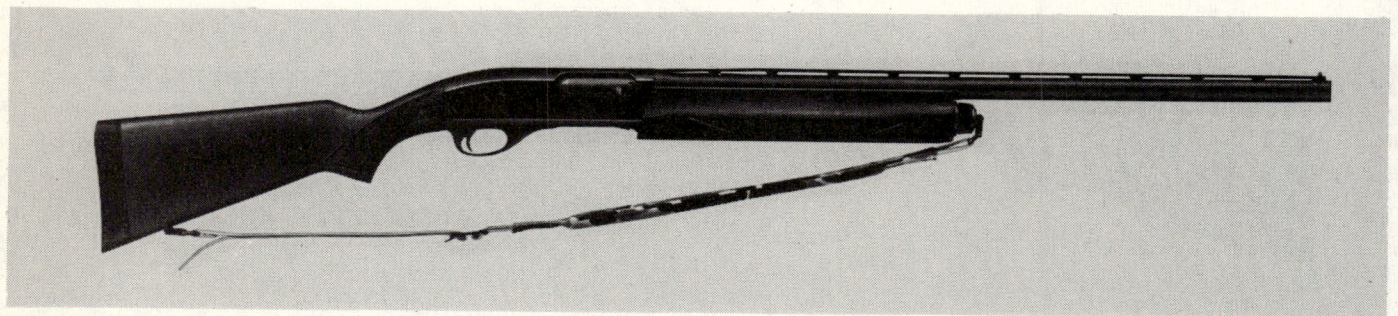

Remington Model 11-87 SP Magnum autoloading shotgun with interchangeable "REM" chokes (handles all 2-3/4" & 3" magnum shells)

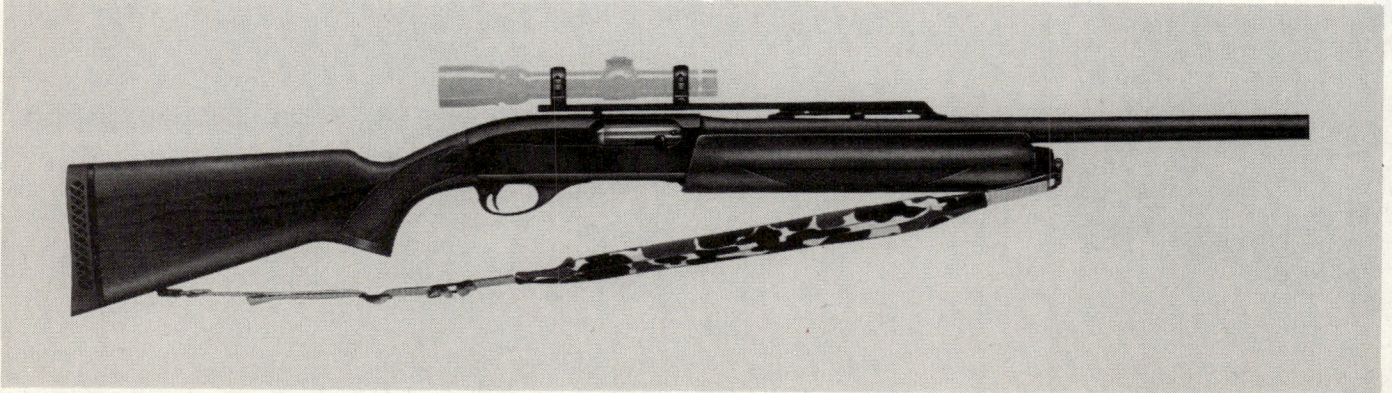

Remington Model 11-87 SP deer gun autoloading shotgun with 3" chamber, cantilever scope mount and interchangeable rifled and improved cylinder "REM" chokes

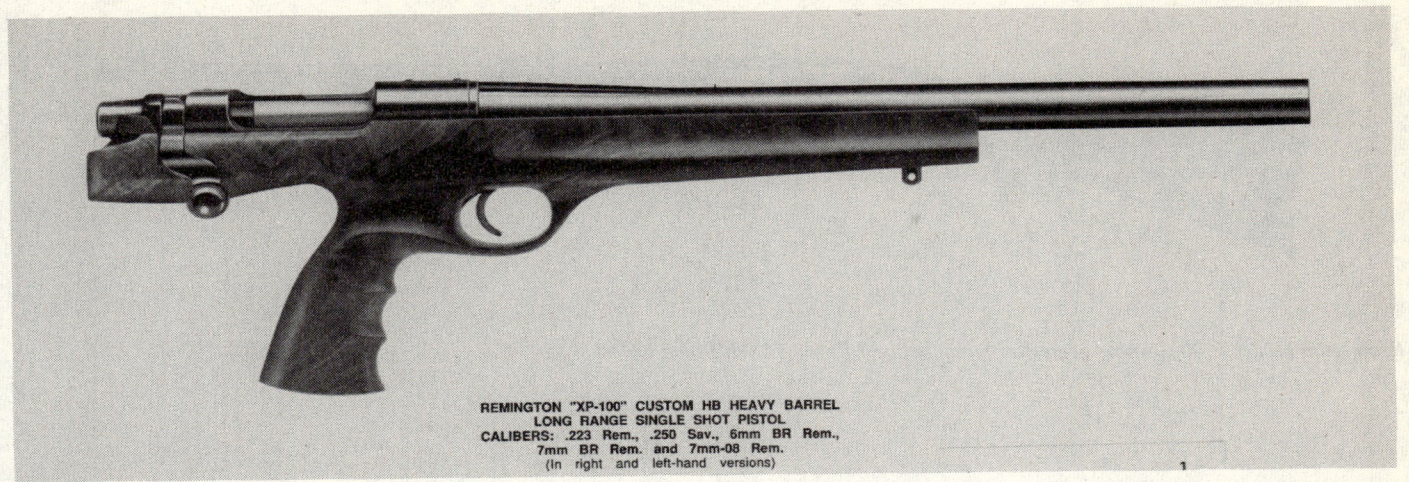

Remington "XP-100" Custom HB heavy barrel long range single shot pistol; Calibers: .223 Rem., .250 Sav., 6mm BR Rem., 7mm BR Rem. and 7mm-08 Rem. (in right and left-hand versions)

Remington XP-100R custom pistol bolt action centerfire repeater (with synthetic stock of "Kevlar" ®); Calibers: .223 Rem. (without sights), 7mm-08 Rem. & .35 Rem. (as shown)

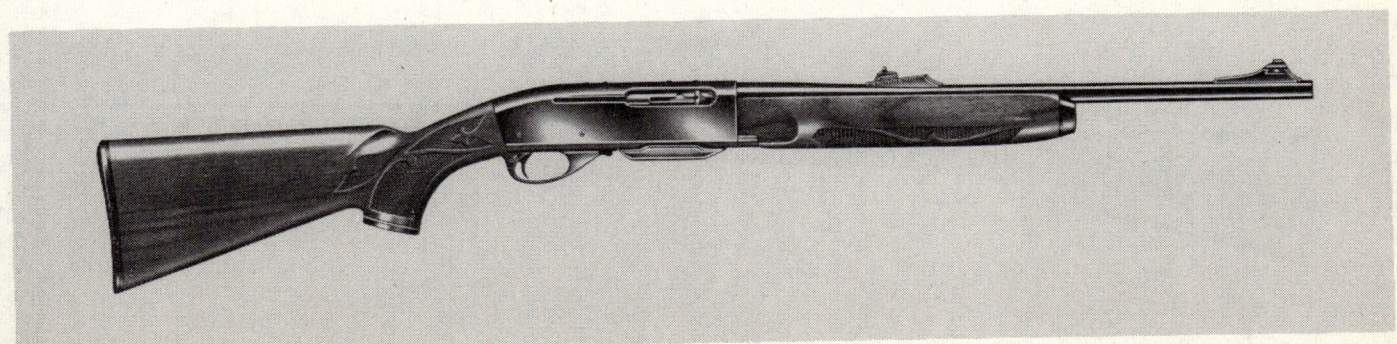

Remington Model 7400 Carbine autoloading centerfire rifle with 18-1/2-inch barrel

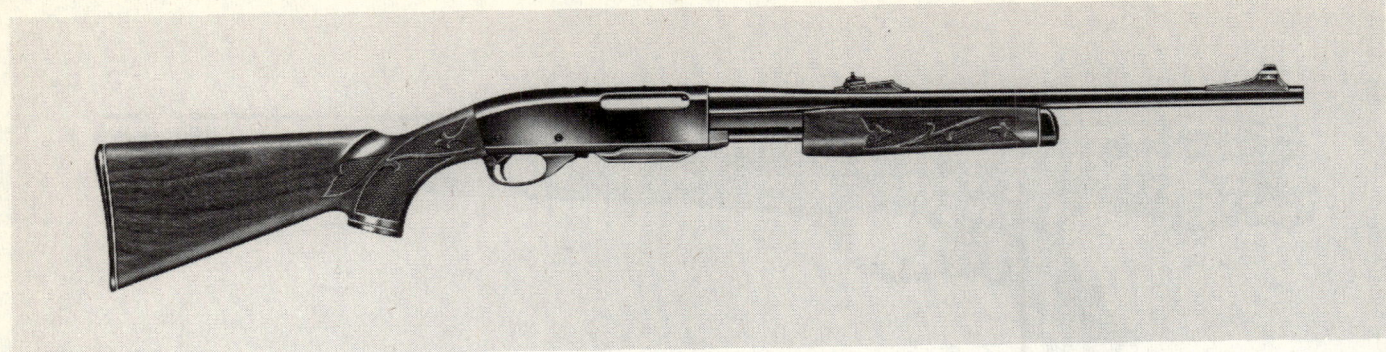

Remington Model 7600 Carbine centerfire pump action rifle with 18-1/2-inch barrel

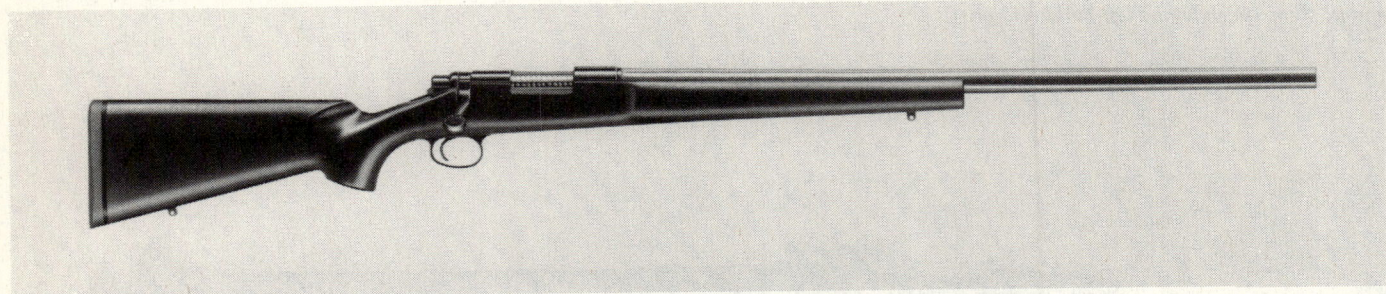

Remington Model 40-XB "Varmint Special" bolt action centerfire rifle with synthetic stock of "Kevlar"®

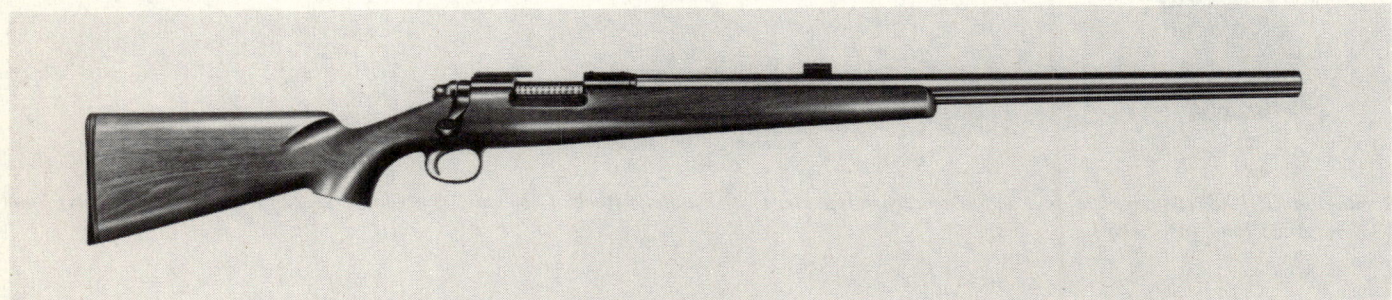

Remington Model 40-XBBR bench rest bolt action centerfire rifle

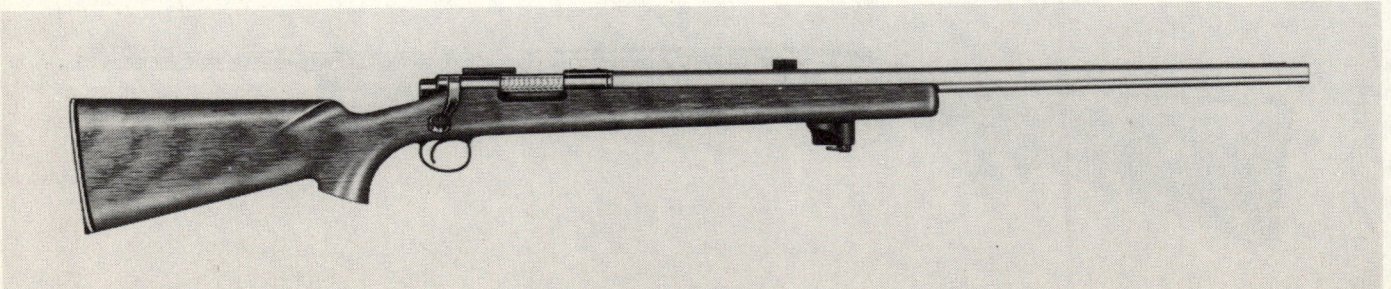

Remington Model 40-XB "Rangemaster" bolt action centerfire target rifle

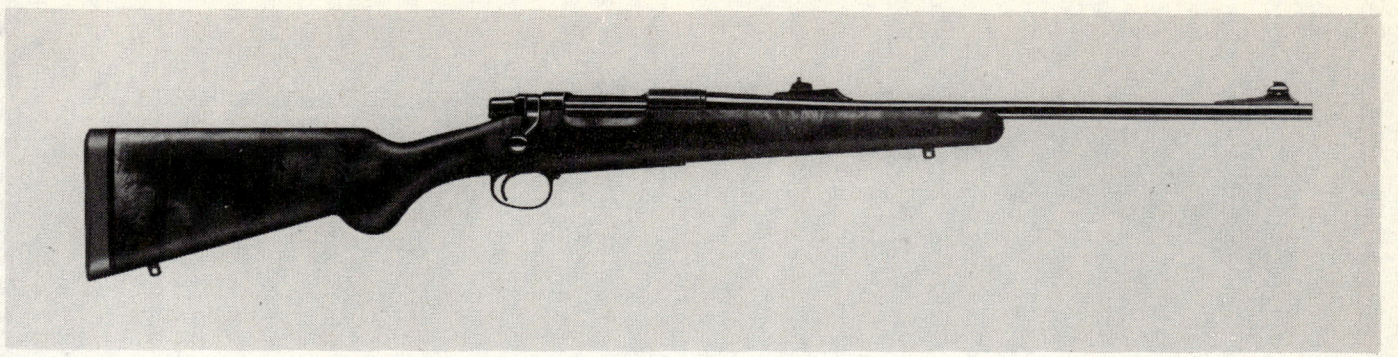

Remington Model Seven custom "KS" lightweight centerfire rifle, synthetic stock of "Kevlar" ® aramid fiber; calibers: .223 Rem., 7mm BR Rem., 7mm-08 Rem., .35 Rem. and .350 Rem. Mag.

Remington Model 700 "AS" bolt action centerfire rifle with synthetic stock

Remington Model 700 mountain rifle, short action version; Calibers: 234 Win., 7mm-08 Rem., & 308 Win.

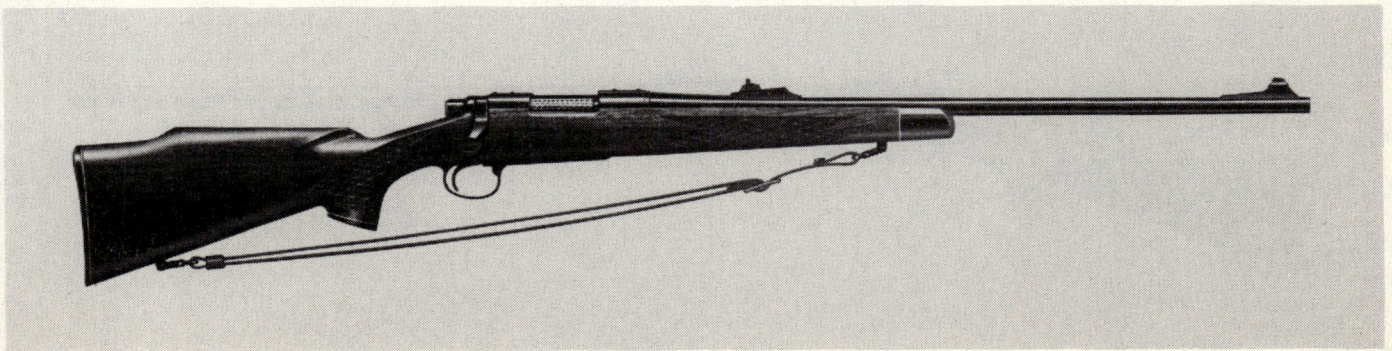

Remington Model 700 BDL, bolt action centerfire rifle (short action with 24-inch barrel)

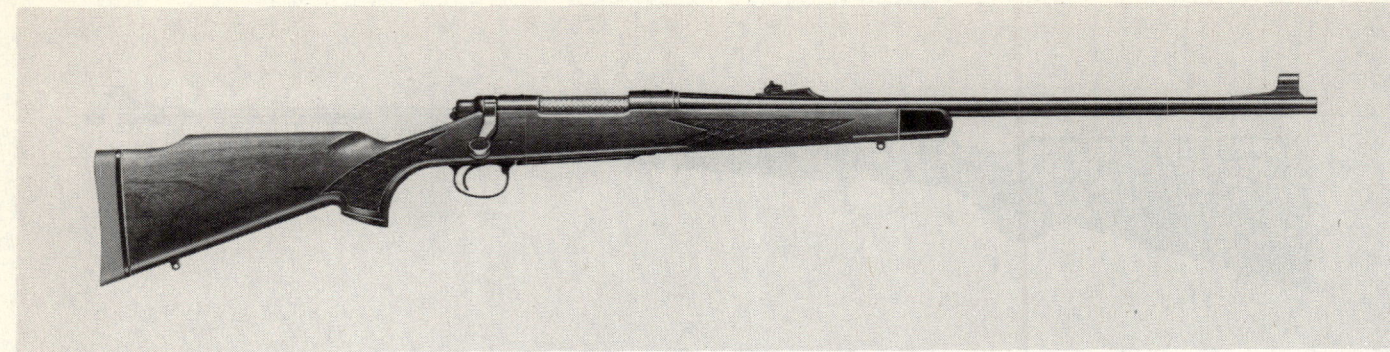

Remington Model 700 BDL Magnum; calibers: 7mm Rem. Mag., .300 Win. Mag., .338 Win. Mag. and .35 Whelen

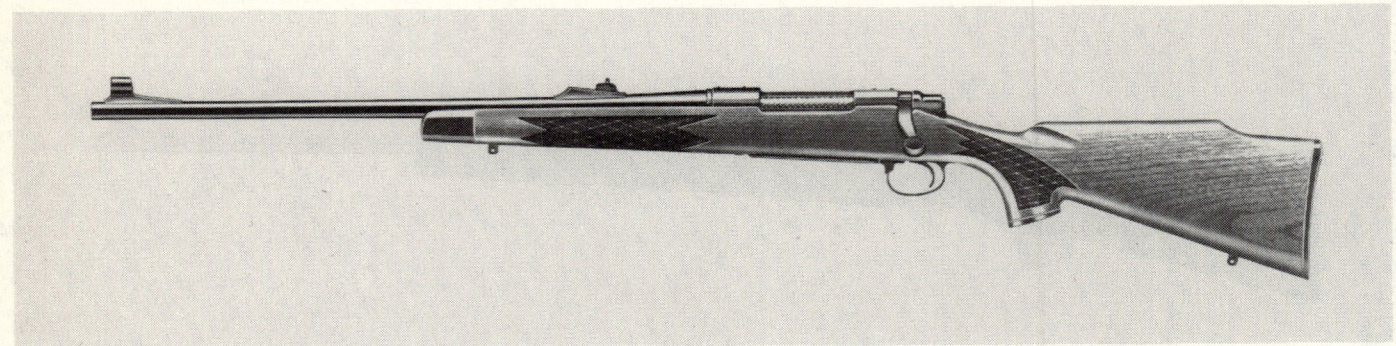

Remington Model 700 BDL left-hand bolt action centerfire rifle

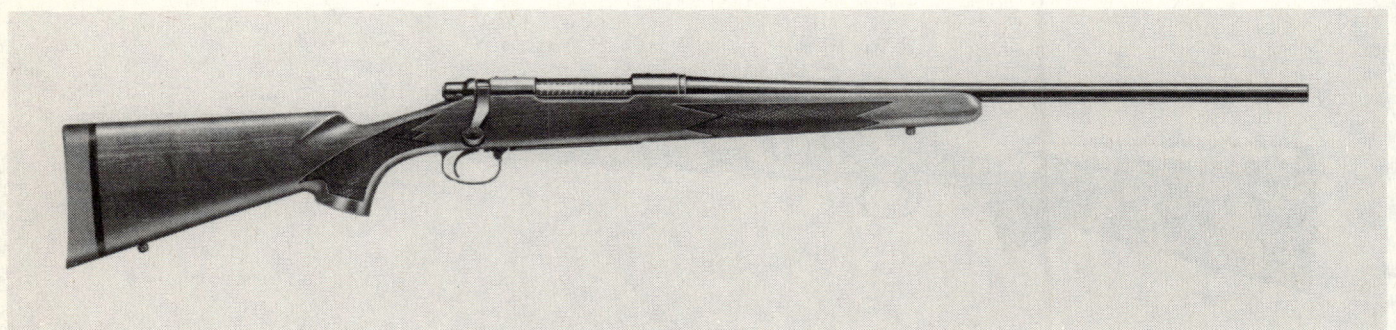

Remington Model 700 Classic bolt action centerfire rifle, Magnum caliber version

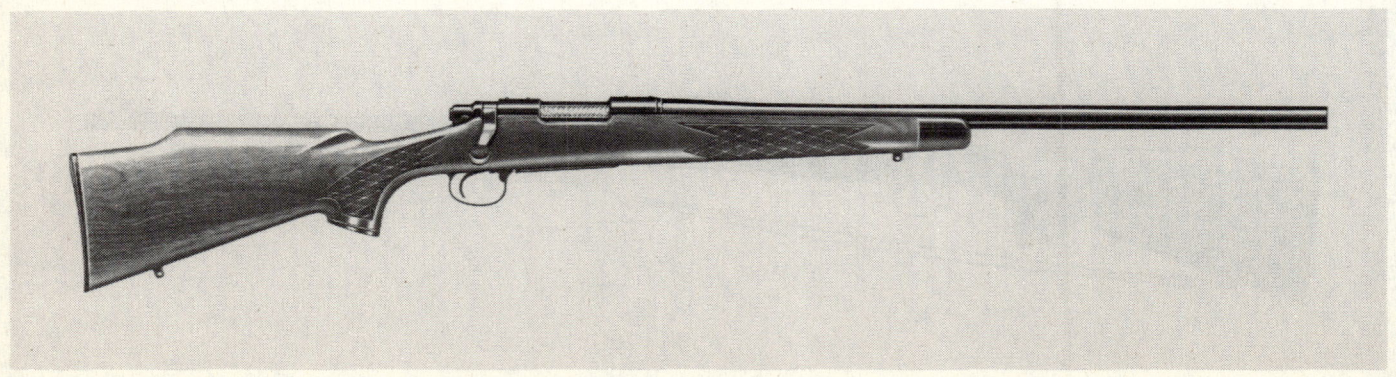

Remington Model 700 BDL "Varmint Special" bolt action centerfire rifle

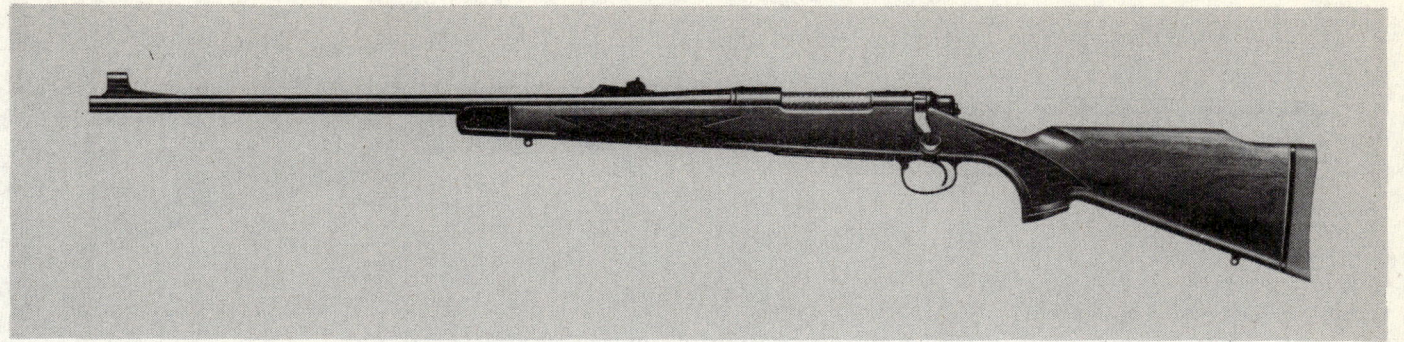

Remington Model 700 BDL Magnum, left-hand action; calibers: 7mm Rem. Mag. and .338 Win. Mag.

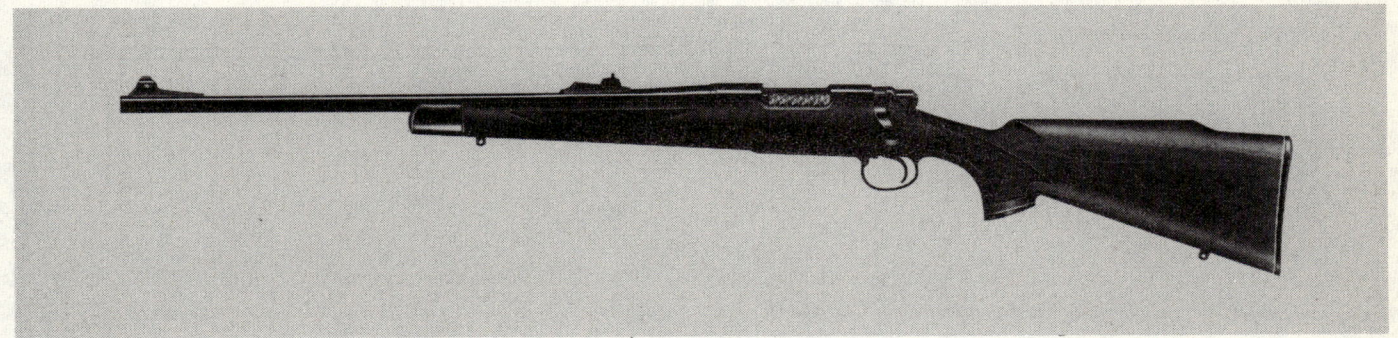

Remington Model 700 BDL left-hand bolt action (short) centerfire rifle; calibers: .22-250 Rem., .243 Win. and .308 Win.

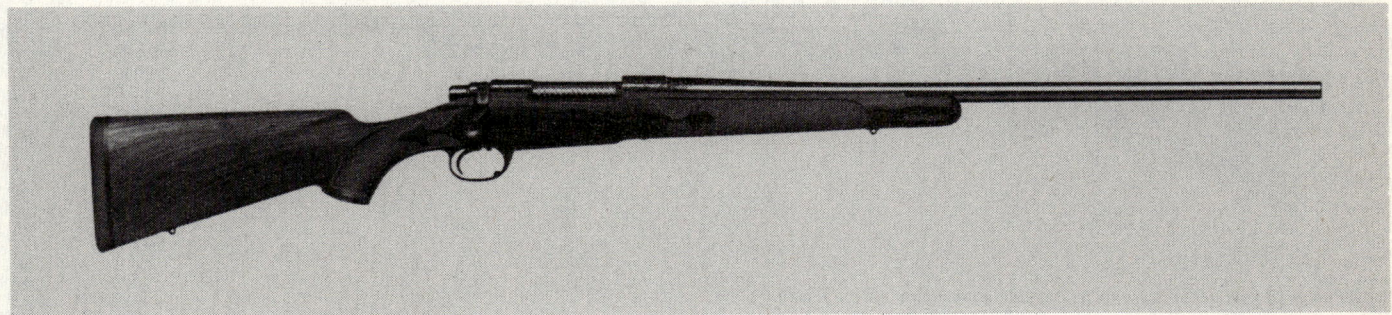

Remington Model 700 Custom bolt action centerfire rifle, Grade IV

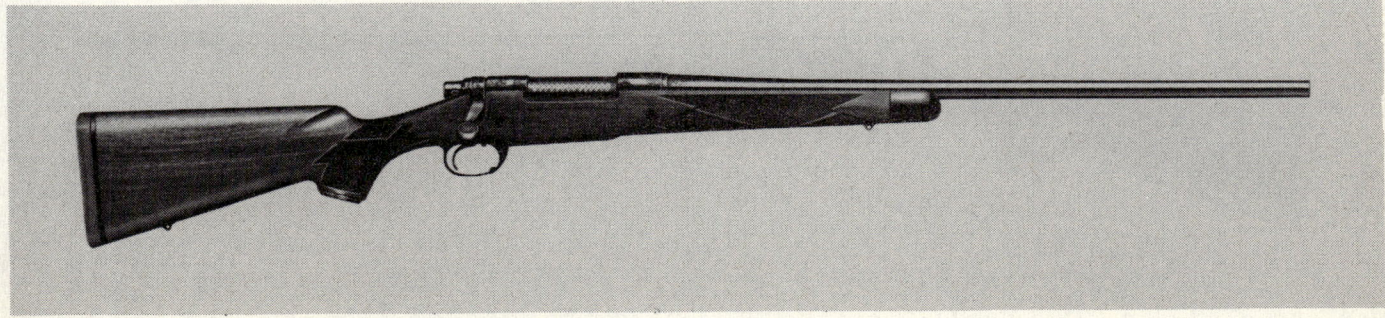

Remington Model 700 Custom bolt action centerfire rifle, Grade III

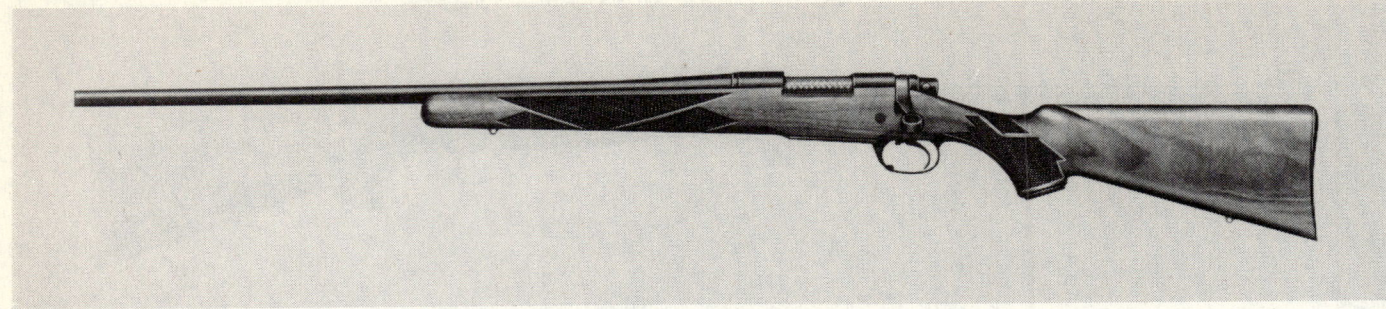

Remington Model 700 Custom Grade II, left hand short action centerfire rifle, available in grades I to IV

Remington Model 700 custom bolt action centerfire rifle, Grade II

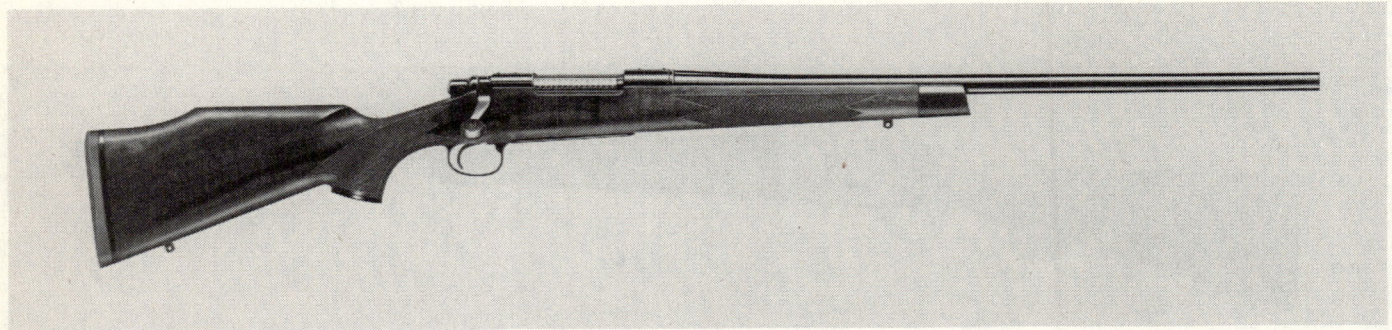

Remington Model 700 Custom bolt action centerfire rifle, Grade I

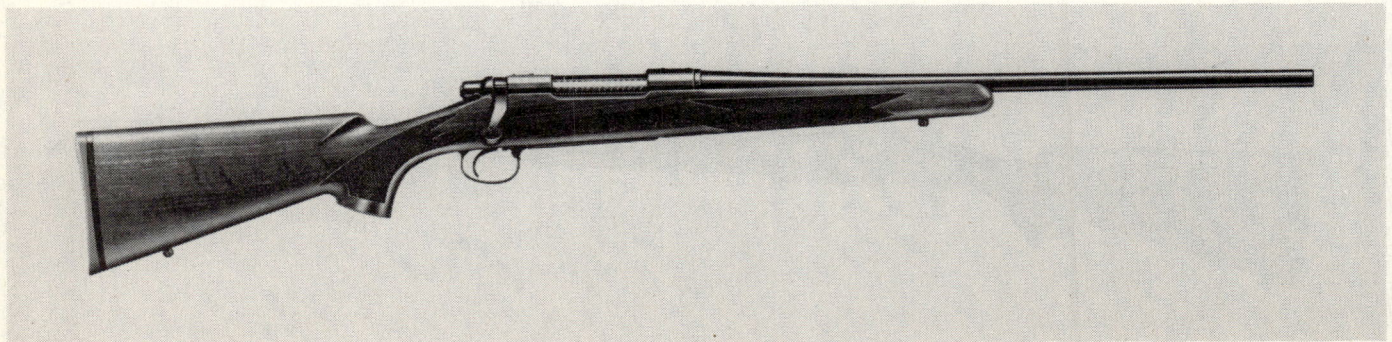

Remington Model 700 "Classic" bolt action centerfire rifle, limited edition — .25-06 Rem.

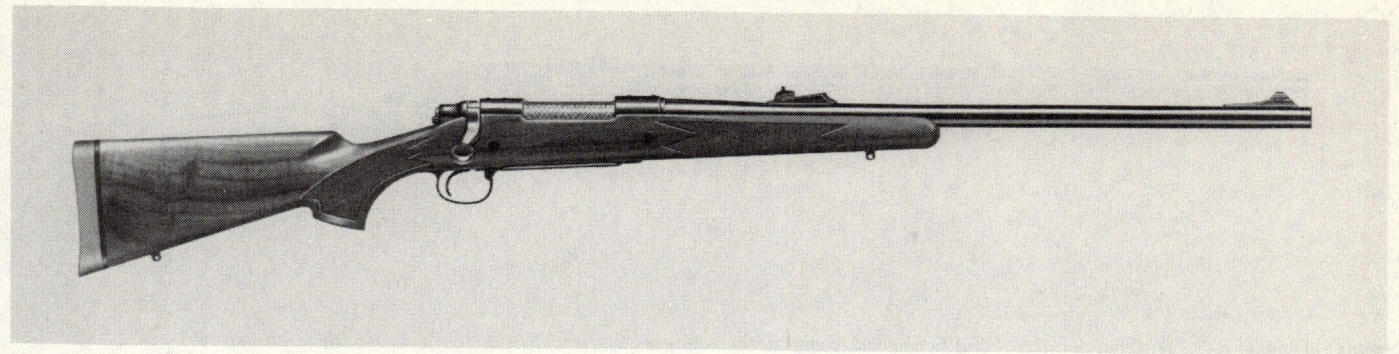

Remington Model 700 Safari Classic with sights: .416 Rem. Mag. and .458 Win. Mag.

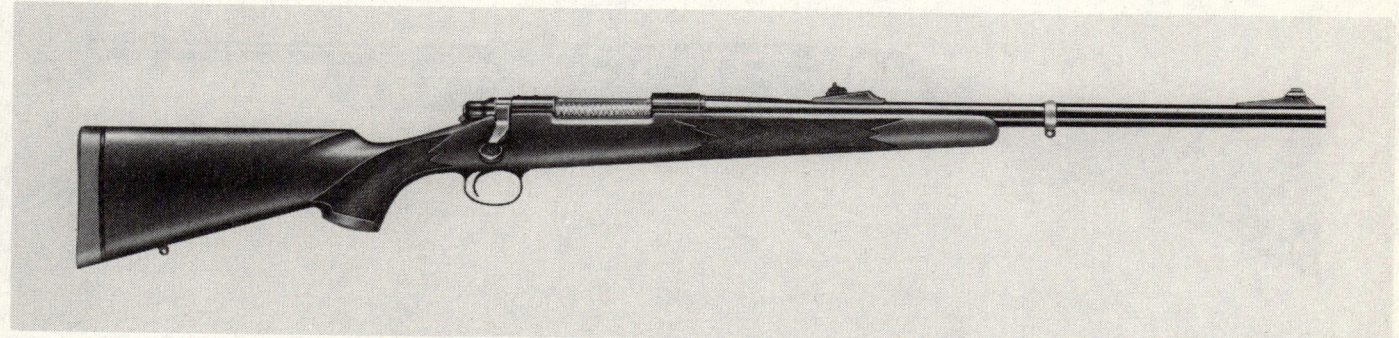

Remington Model 700 Safari KS, synthetic stock of "Kevlar" aramid fiber; Calibers: 8mm Rem. Mag., .375 H&H Mag. 416 Rem. Mag and .458 Win. Mag.

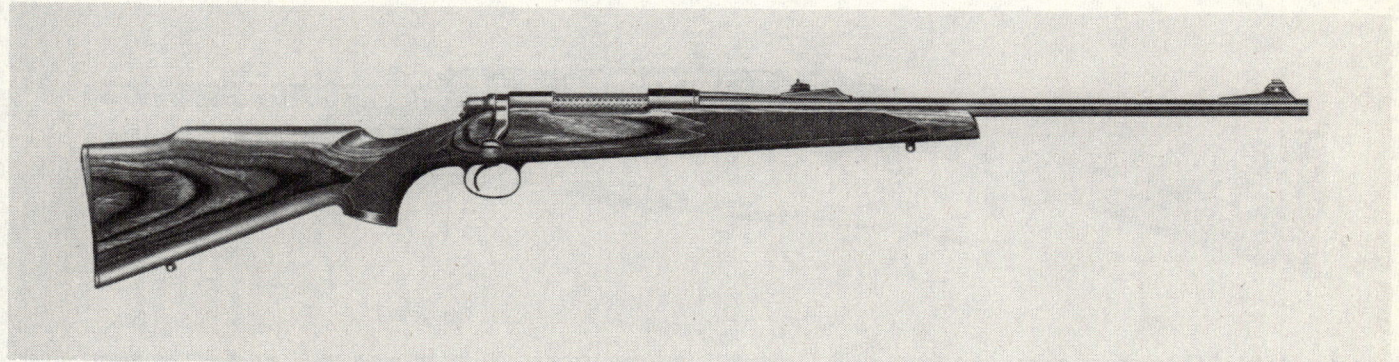

Remington Model 700 ADL "LS" bolt action centerfire rifle with laminated stock; calibers: .243 Win., .270 Win., 30-06 and 7mm Rem. Magnum

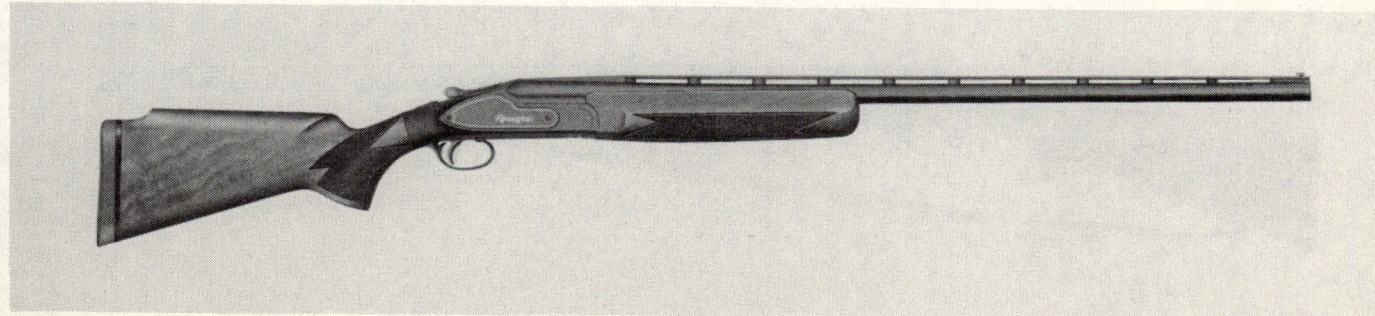

Remington Model 90-T super single trap gun, barrel lengths: 30", 32" and 34"

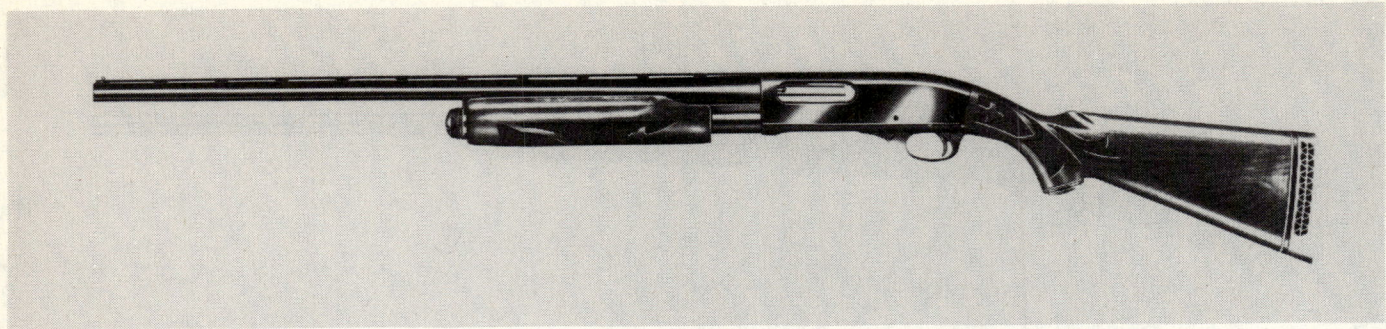

Remington Model 870 "Wingmaster" left-hand field grade pump action shotgun; 12- and 20-gauges (shown with ventilated rib)

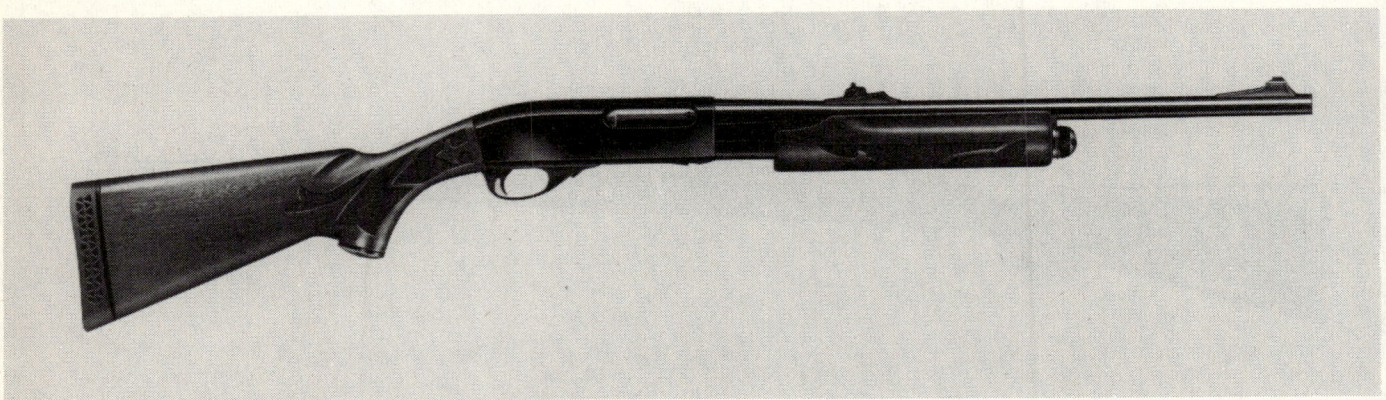

Remington Model 870 pump action 20 gauge "lightweight" deer gun

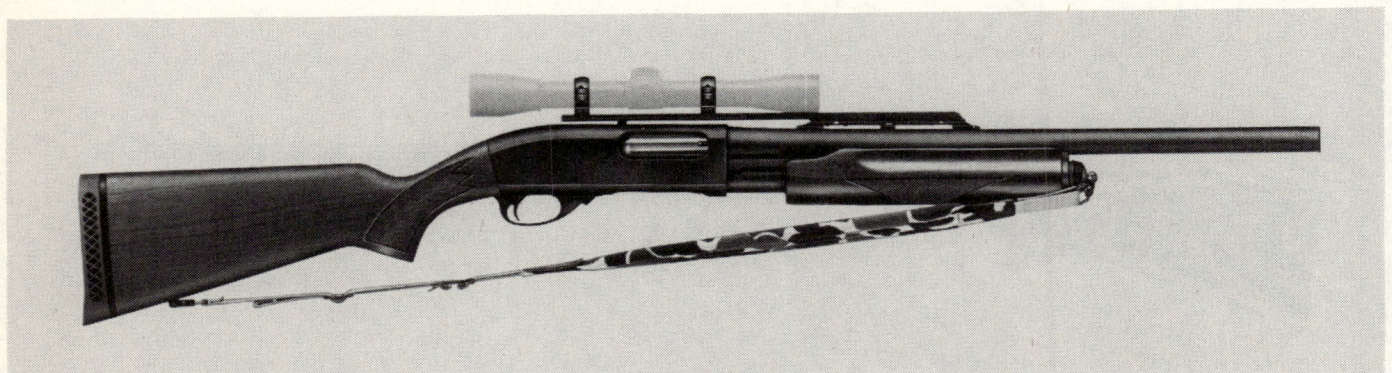

Remington Model 870 SP deer gun, pump action shotgun with 3" chamber, cantilever scope mount and interchangeable rifled and improved cylinder "REM" chokes

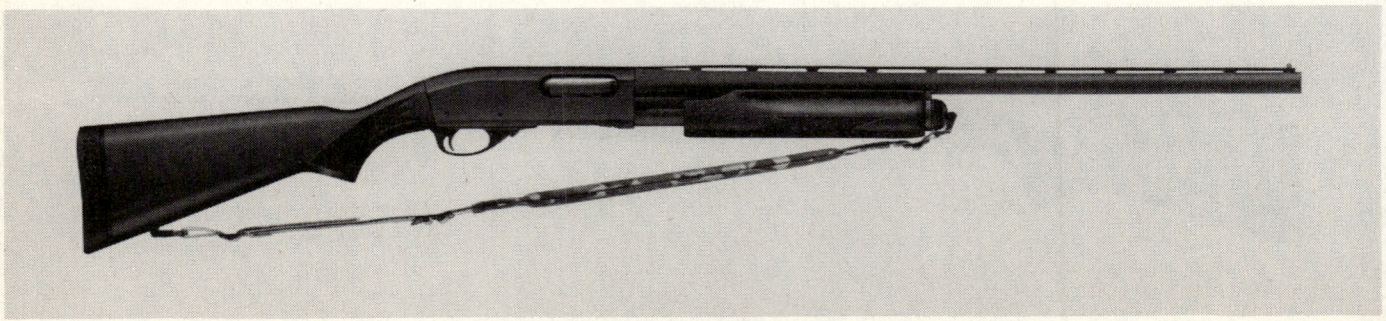

Remington Model 870 SP Magnum pump action shotgun, 3 inch chamber (shown with a 26-inch barrel)

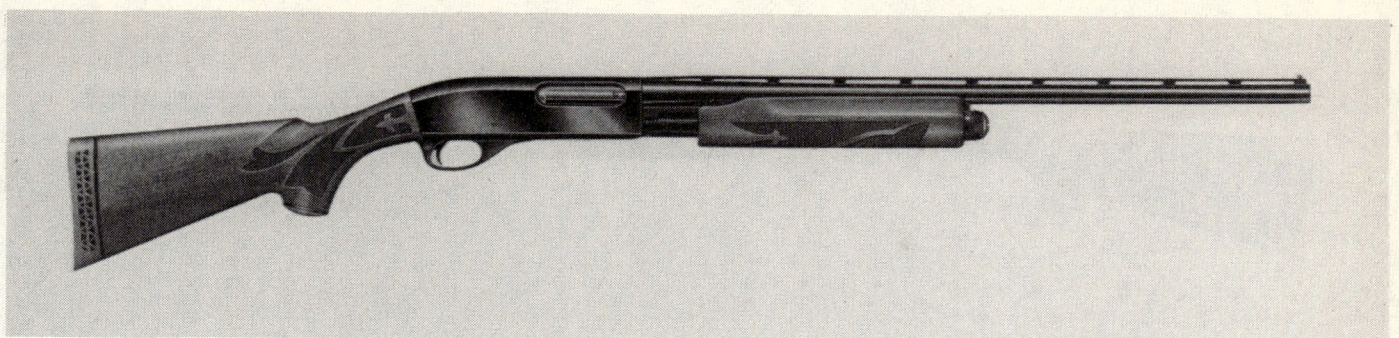

Remington Model 870 youth gun, 20 gauge lightweight pump action shotgun with interchangeable "REM" chokes. Stock: shortened 1-1/2 inches. Barrel: 21 inches

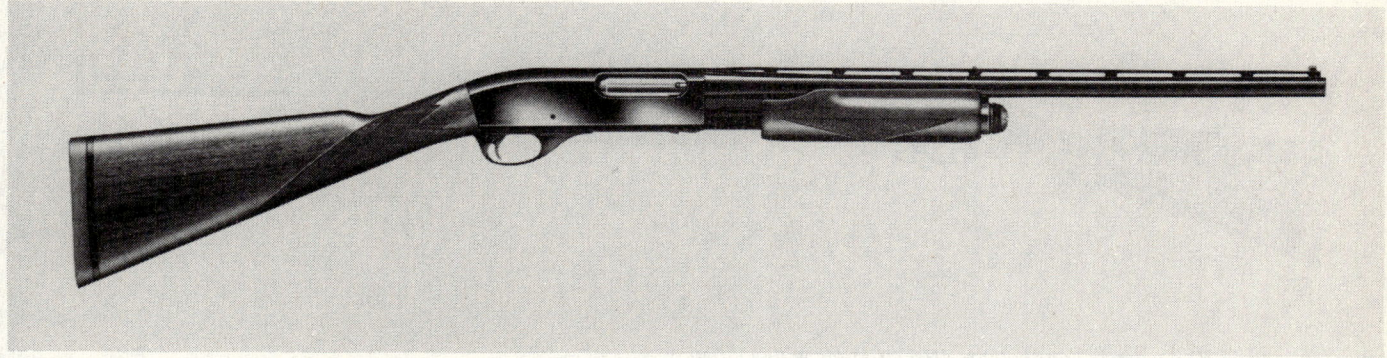

Remington Model 870 "Special Field" pump action shotgun with 21-inch vent rib barrel (20 gauge lightweight version)

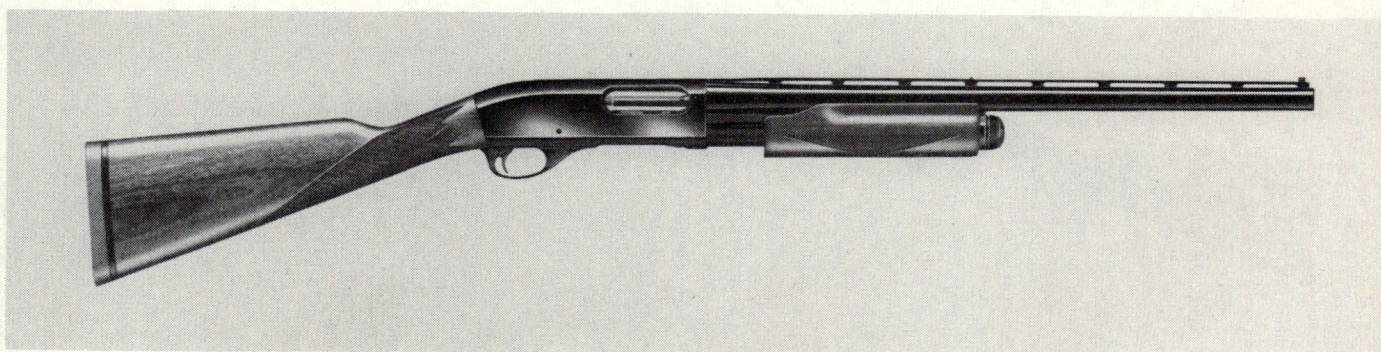

Remington Model 870 "Special Field" pump action shotgun with 21-inch vent rib barrel

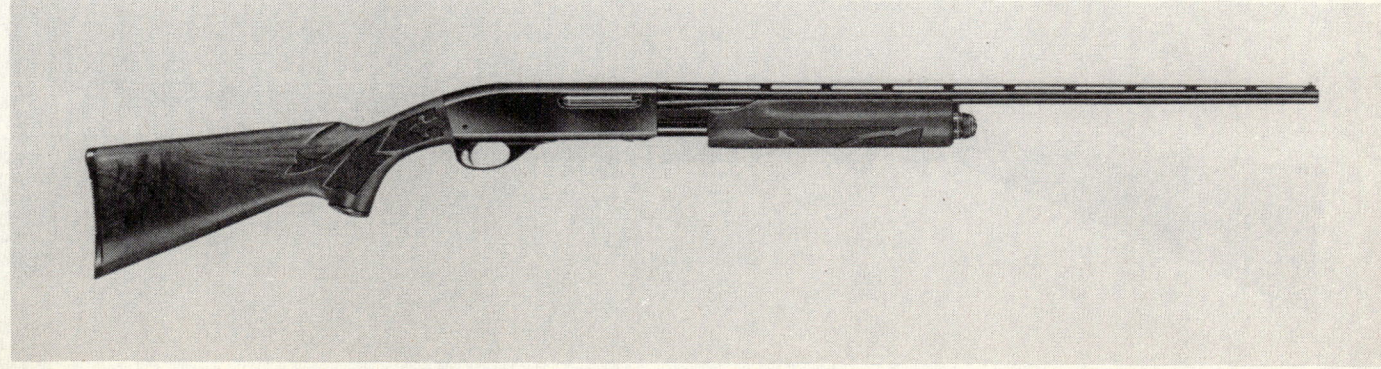

Remington Model 870 pump action shotgun, field grade small bore: 28 gauge and .410

Remington Model 870 D tournament grade pump action shotgun

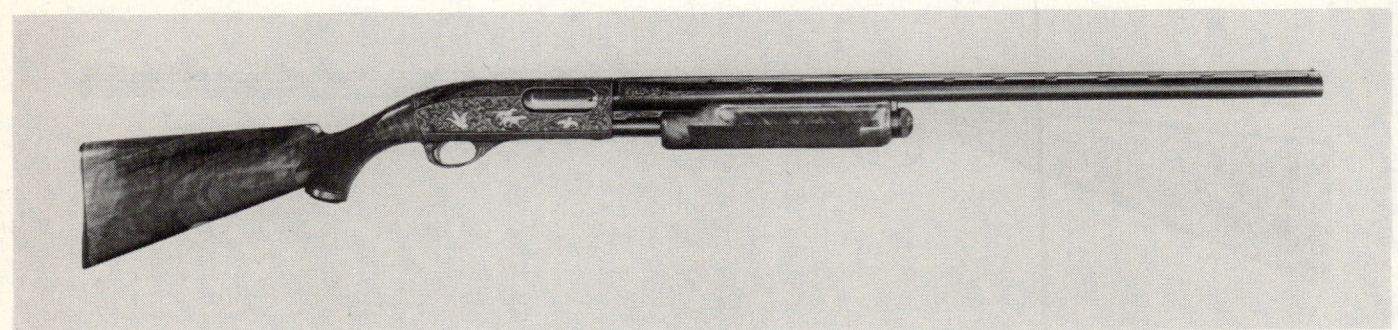

Remington Model 870 F pump action shotgun, premier grade with gold inlay

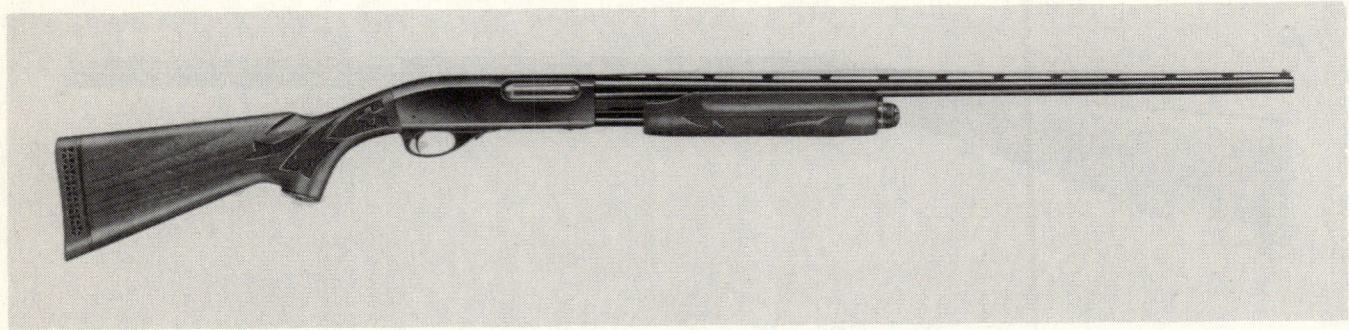

Remington Model 870 pump action shotgun, 20 gauge "lightweight" with interchangeable "REM" chokes

Remington Model 110 LT-20 "Special Field" 20 gauge autoloading shotgun with 21-inch vent rib barrel

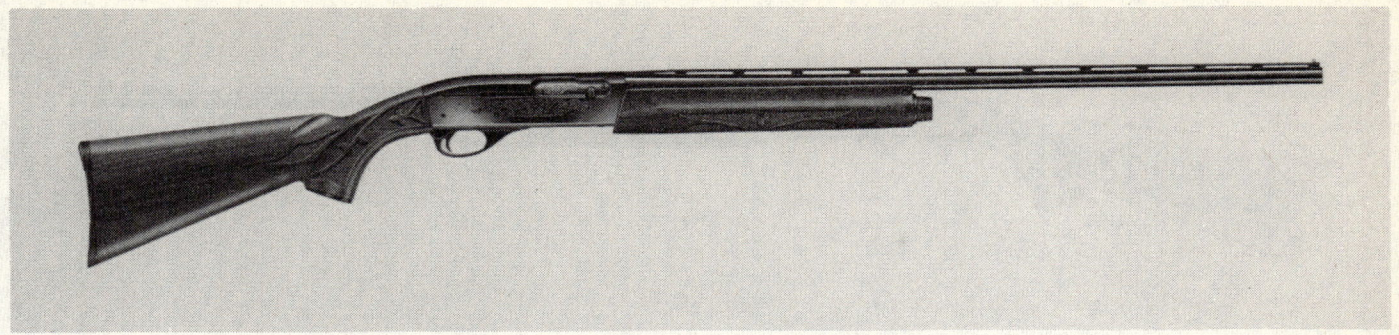

Remington Model 110 LT-20 autoloader, 20 gauge lightweight shotgun with interchangeable "REM" chokes

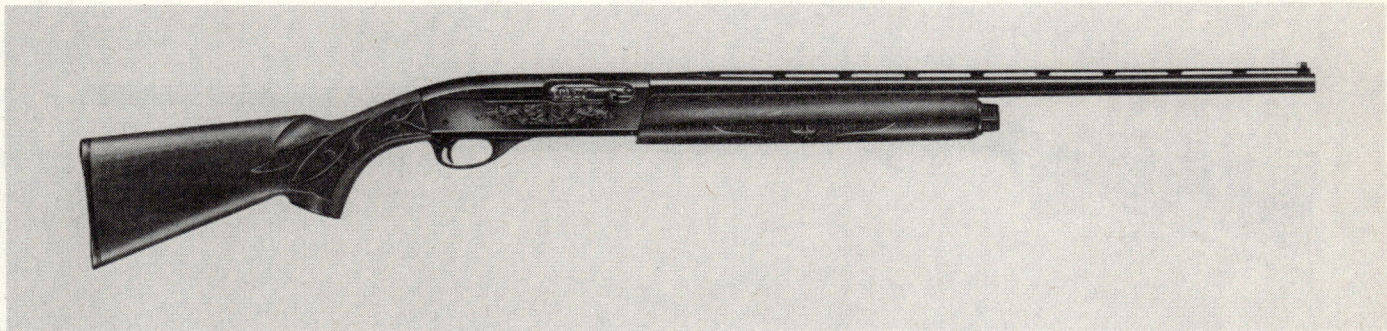

Remington Model 110 LT-20 youth gun, 20 gauge lightweight autoloading shotgun with interchangeable "REM" chokes. Stock: shortened 1-1/2 inches. Barrel: 21 inches

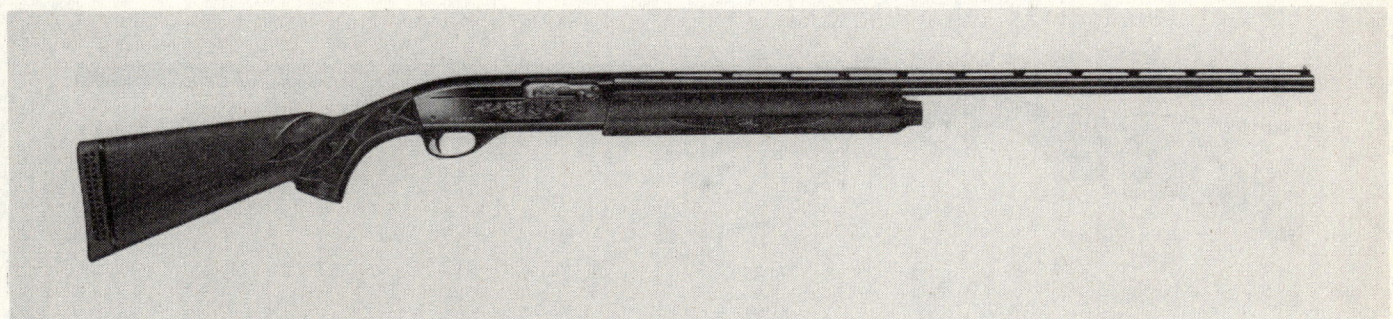

Remington Model 1100 LT-20 Magnum 20 gauge lightweight autoloader with interchangeable "REM" chokes

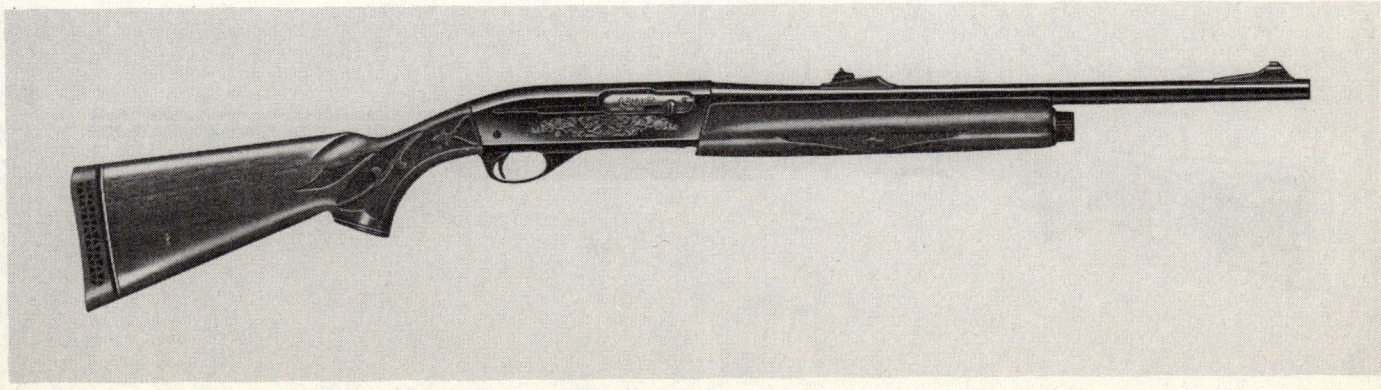

Remington Model 1100 LT-20 20 gauge lightweight autoloading deer gun

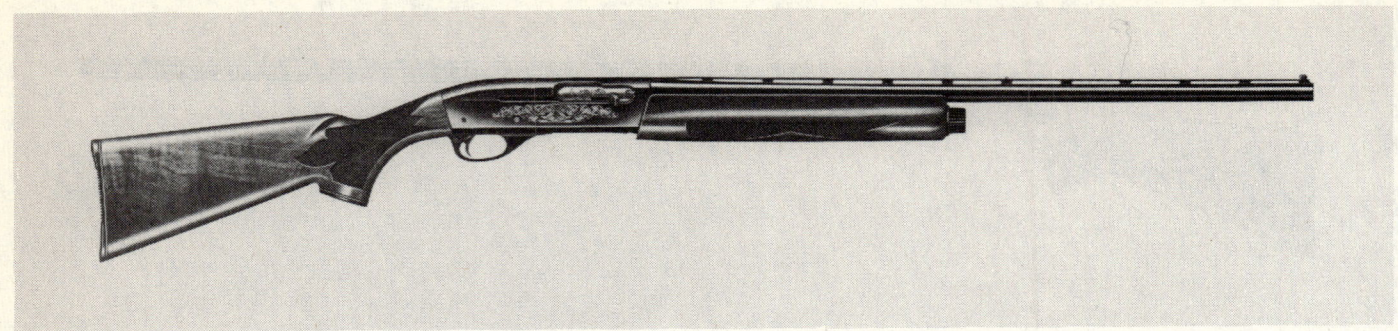

Remington Model 1100 LT-20 tournament skeet 20 gauge autoloading shotgun

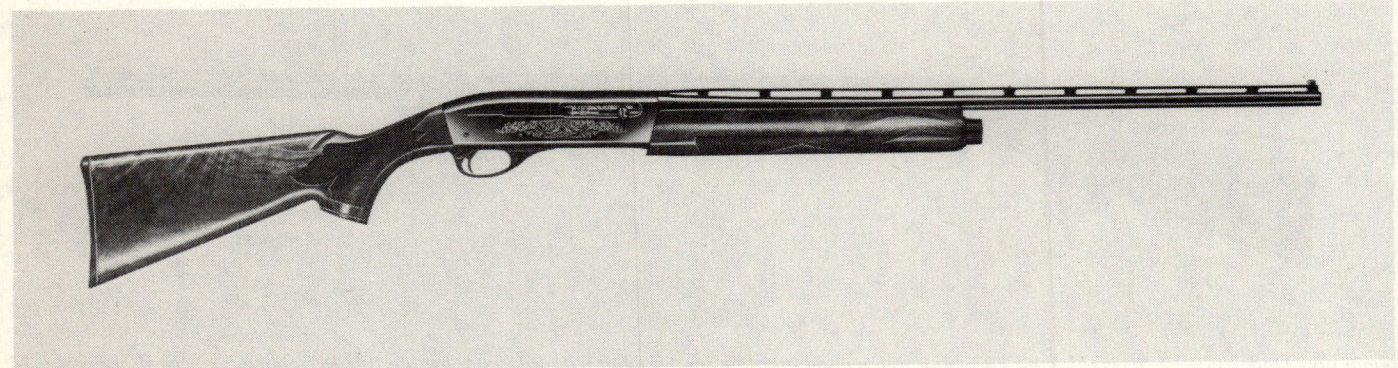

Remington Model 1100 tournament skeet autoloading shotgun, small bore version: .410 and 28 gauges

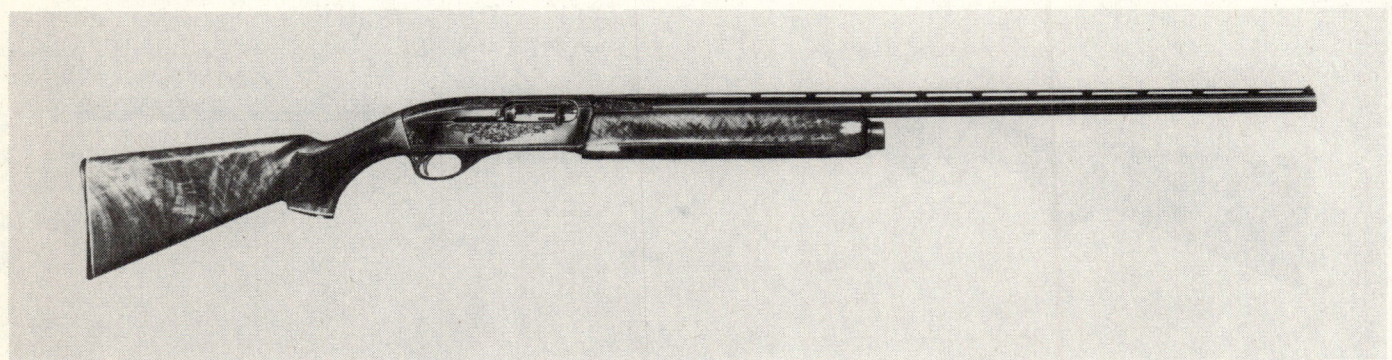

Remington Model 1100D tournament grade 12 gauge, 5 shot

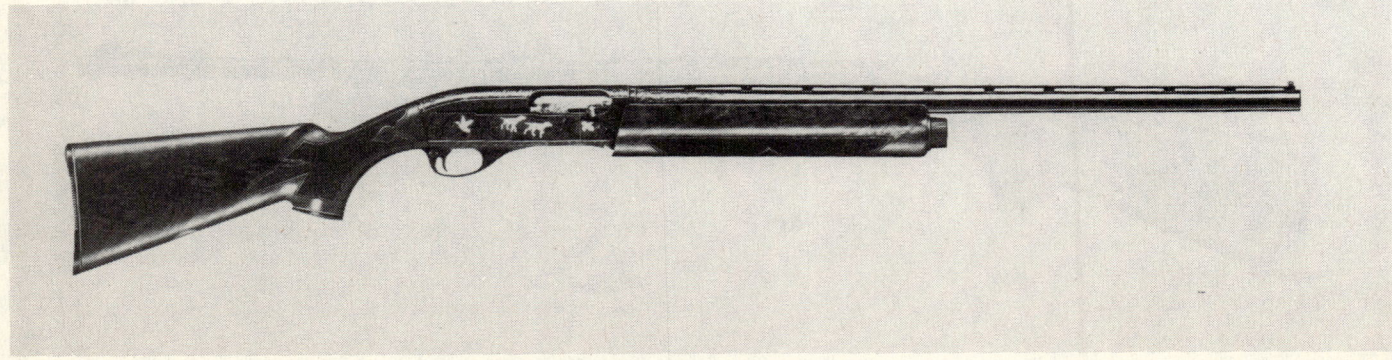

Remington Model 1100 F autoloading shotgun, premier grade with gold inlay

RENETTE, GASTINE
Paris, France

Model 105

An Anson & Deeley action 12 or 20 gauge double barrel shotgun available in a variety of barrel lengths, with double triggers and automatic ejectors. Blued, case hardened with a checkered walnut stock.

Exc.	V.G.	Good	Fair	Poor
1750	1600	1250	900	750

Model 98

As above, except more finely finished.

Exc.	V.G.	Good	Fair	Poor
2500	2250	1750	1400	1100

Model 202

A 12 or 20 gauge sidelock double barrel shotgun made only on custom order. French case hardened and blued with a checkered walnut stock.

Exc.	V.G.	Good	Fair	Poor
3500	3000	2500	1750	950

Model 353

A custom manufactured double-barrel shotgun with detachable sidelocks. Highly finished.

Exc.	V.G.	Good	Fair	Poor
9000	7500	5000	4250	2000

Type G Rifle

A .30-06, 9.3x74R, or .375 Holland & Holland double barrel rifle with 24" barrels, express sights, double triggers and automatic ejectors. Engraved, blued with a checkered walnut stock.

Exc.	V.G.	Good	Fair	Poor
2250	1850	1500	1150	650

Type R Deluxe

As above, engraved with hunting scenes and with a more finely figured walnut stock.

Exc.	V.G.	Good	Fair	Poor
2500	2250	1750	1450	750

Type PT President

As above, inlaid in gold with extremely well figured walnut stock.

Exc.	V.G.	Good	Fair	Poor
3200	2750	2000	1750	850

RENWICK ARMS CO.
SEE Perry & Goddard

RETOLAZA HERMANOS
Eibar, Spain

Brompetier

A folding trigger 6.35mm or 7.65mm caliber double action revolver with a 2.5" barrel and a safety mounted on the left side of the frame. Manufactured until 1915.

Exc.	V.G.	Good	Fair	Poor
150	100	85	70	45

Gallus or Titan

A 6.35mm semiautomatic pistol normally marked "Gallus" or "Titan". Blued with plastic grips.

Exc.	V.G.	Good	Fair	Poor
175	125	100	75	50

Liberty, Military, Retolaza, or Paramount

A 6.35mm or 7.65mm semiautomatic pistol with a 3" barrel and 8-shot magazine. The slide marked with any of the trade names listed above.

Exc.	V.G.	Good	Fair	Poor
175	125	100	75	50

Puppy

A folding trigger .22 caliber double action revolver with a 5-shot cylinder. The trade name "Puppy" stamped on the barrel.

Exc.	V.G.	Good	Fair	Poor
150	100	75	50	25

Stosel

A 6.35mm semiautomatic pistol marked on the slide "Automatic Pistol Stosel No. 1 Patent". Blued with plastic grips.

Exc.	V.G.	Good	Fair	Poor
175	125	100	75	50

Titanic

A 6.35mm semiautomatic pistol with a 2.5" barrel, the slide marked "1913 Model Automatic Pistol Titanic Eibar". Blued with plastic grips.

Exc.	V.G.	Good	Fair	Poor
175	125	100	75	50

REUNIES
Liege, Belgium

Dictator

A 6.35mm semiautomatic pistol with a 1.5" barrel, 5-shot magazine and the name "Dictator" together with the company's details stamped on the slide. This pistol features a bolt of tubular form the front end of which is hollow and encloses the barrel breech. Manufactured from 1909 to approximately 1925.

Exc.	V.G.	Good	Fair	Poor
200	150	125	100	75

Texas Ranger or Cowboy Ranger

Patterned after the Colt Model 1873 revolver. This pistol is of .38 Special caliber and has a 5.5" barrel. The barrel marked with the company's details and either the legend "Cowboy Ranger" or "Texas Ranger". Manufactured from 1922 to 1931.

Exc.	V.G.	Good	Fair	Poor
175	125	100	75	50

REUTH, F.
Hartford, Connecticut

Animal Trap Gun

A cast iron .28 to .50 caliber percussion trap gun with either single or double barrels 3.5" or 5" in length. This firearm fires a barbed arrow and is triggered by a cord attached to an animal trap or bait. The barrels marked "F. Reuth's Patent, May 12, 1857." Several hundred were made between 1858 and 1862. The double-barrel model is more common than the single barrel and is worth approximately 30% less.

Exc.	V.G.	Good	Fair	Poor
—	—	600	300	125

RHEINMETALL
Sommerda, Germany

Dreyse 6.35mm

A 6.35mm semiautomatic pistol with a 2" barrel, manual safety and 6-shot magazine. The slide marked "Dreyse". Blued with plastic grips having the trademark "RFM" cast in them. The patent for this design was issued in 1909 to Louis Scmeisser.

Exc.	V.G.	Good	Fair	Poor
300	250	200	150	100

Dreyse 7.65mm

As above, but chambered for the 7.65mm cartridge, with a 3.6" barrel and a 7-shot magazine. The slide marked "Dreyse Rheinmetall Abt. Sommerda." Blued with plastic grips.

Courtesy Orvel Reichert

Exc.	V.G.	Good	Fair	Poor
275	225	175	125	90

Dreyse 9mm

As above, but chambered for the 9mm cartridge with a 5" barrel and an 8-shot magazine. The slide marked "Rheinische Mettellwaaren Und Maschinenfabrik, Sommerda." Blued with plastic grips.

Exc.	V.G.	Good	Fair	Poor
750	650	500	400	300

Rheinmetall

A 7.65mm semiautomatic pistol with a 3.65" barrel and an 8-shot magazine. The slide marked "Rheinmetell ABT. Sommerda." Blued with walnut grips.

Exc.	V.G.	Good	Fair	Poor
275	225	175	125	90

RHODE ISLAND ARMS CO.
Hope Valley, Rhode Island

Morrone

A 12 or 20 gauge Over/Under boxlock shotgun with 26" or 28" barrels, single trigger and automatic ejectors. Blued with either a straight or pistol grip walnut checkered stock. 450 were made in 12 gauge and 50 in 20 gauge. Manufactured from 1949 to 1953.

Exc.	V.G.	Good	Fair	Poor
1250	1000	750	600	450

RICHLAND ARMS CO.
Blissfield, Michigan

This company, which ceased operation in 1986, imported a variety of Spanish-made shotguns.

Model 41 Ultra O/U

A 20, 28, or .410 bore double-barrel shotgun with 26" or 28" ventilated rib barrels, single non-selective trigger and automatic ejectors. French Case hardened receiver and checkered walnut stock.

Exc.	V.G.	Good	Fair	Poor
275	250	200	150	100

Model 747 O/U

As above, in 20 gauge only with a single selective trigger.

Exc.	V.G.	Good	Fair	Poor
425	350	300	250	175

Model 757 O/U

A Greener style boxlock 12 gauge double barrel shotgun with 26" or 28" ventilated rib barrels, double triggers and automatic ejectors. Finished as above.

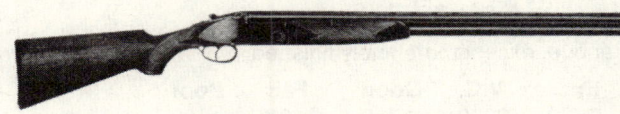

Exc.	V.G.	Good	Fair	Poor
300	250	200	175	125

Model 787 O/U

As above, fitted with screw-in choke tubes.

Exc.	V.G.	Good	Fair	Poor
450	375	325	275	200

Model 808 O/U

A 12 gauge double-barrel shotgun with 26", 28" or 30" ventilated rib barrels, single trigger and automatic ejectors. Blued with checkered walnut stock. Manufactured in Italy from 1963 to 1968.

Exc.	V.G.	Good	Fair	Poor
425	350	300	250	175

Model 80 LS

A 12, 20 or .410 bore single barrel shotgun with 26" or 28" barrels. Blued with checkered walnut stock.

Exc.	V.G.	Good	Fair	Poor
150	125	100	80	60

Model 200

An Anson & Deeley style 12, 16, 20, 28 or .410 bore double barrel shotgun with 22", 26" or 28" barrels, double triggers, and automatic ejectors. Blued with a checkered walnut stock.

Exc.	V.G.	Good	Fair	Poor
325	300	250	200	125

Model 202

As above, with an extra set of interchangeable barrels. Imported from 1963 to 1985.

Exc.	V.G.	Good	Fair	Poor
300	275	225	175	100

Model 711 Magnum

As above, chambered for 3" shells and fitted with 30" or 32" barrels.

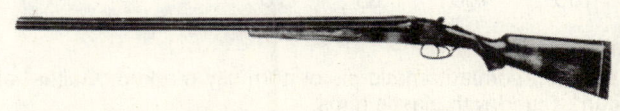

Exc.	V.G.	Good	Fair	Poor
350	300	250	200	150

Model 707 Deluxe

As above, more finely finished and fitted with well figured walnut stocks.

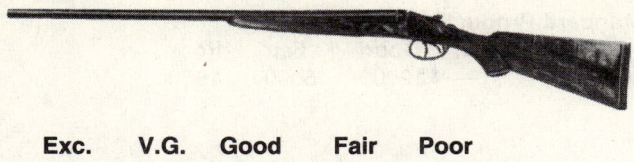

Exc.	V.G.	Good	Fair	Poor
350	300	250	200	150

RICHMOND ARMORY
Richmond, Virginia

Carbine

This weapon was manufactured for use by the Confederate States of America and is extremely collectible. We recommend qualified individual appraisal if a transaction is contemplated. This muzzle-loading carbine is chambered for .58 caliber percussion and has a 25" round barrel and a full-length stock that is held on by two barrel bands. It was manufactured from parts that were captured at the Harper's Ferry Armory in 1861. The locks are marked "Richmond, VA" and dated from 1861 to 1865. There are sling swivels in front of the triggerguard and on the front barrel band; a third swivel is on the underside of the butt stock. The quantity manufactured is not known. They were made between 1861 and 1865.

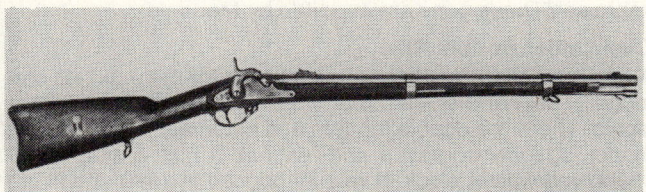

Courtesy Milwaukee Public Museum, Milwaukee, Wisconsin

Exc.	V.G.	Good	Fair	Poor
—	—	8000	4000	1000

Musketoon

This weapon is similar to the carbine except that the barrel is 30" in length and the front sight is also the bayonet lug. There is no sling swivel on the butt stock. This weapon was also manufactured between 1861 and 1865.

Exc.	V.G.	Good	Fair	Poor
—	—	8000	4000	1000

Rifled Musket

This model is also similar to the Carbine, with a 40" barrel and a full-length stock held on by three barrel bands. The front sling swivel is on the middle barrel band instead of on the front band. The Rifled Musket was also manufactured between 1861 and 1865.

Courtesy Milwaukee Public Museum, Milwaukee, Wisconsin

Exc.	V.G.	Good	Fair	Poor
—	—	9000	4000	1000

RIEDL RIFLE CO.
Westminster, California

Single Shot Rifle

This company produced custom order dropping block single shot rifles in a variety of calibers and barrel lengths. Rifles were normally fitted only with telescopic or target sight bases. Blued with a checkered walnut stock.

Exc.	V.G.	Good	Fair	Poor
500	450	400	300	225

RIGBY, JOHN & CO., LTD.
London, England

This company was established in the early 19th century and has produced a variety of shotguns and rifles over the years. Many of the arms produced by this company were custom ordered and prospective purchasers are advised to secure individual appraisals prior to the acquisition of such pieces.

Boxlock Shotgun

A boxlock shotgun manufactured in any gauge with double triggers, automatic ejectors and a hand fitted checkered walnut stock.
20 Gauge-Add 25%.
28 Gauge-Add 45%.
.410-Add 70%.

Chatsworth Grade

Exc.	V.G.	Good	Fair	Poor
4000	3000	2500	1750	1250

Sackville Grade

Exc.	V.G.	Good	Fair	Poor
5500	4500	3750	2750	2000

Boxlock Game Gun

NIB	Exc.	V.G.	Good	Fair	Poor
7500	6000	5000	4500	3000	2500

Sidelock Shotgun

A custom made double-barrel shotgun fitted with detachable sidelocks.
20 Gauge-Add 25%.
28 Gauge-Add 45%.
.410-Add 70%.

Sandringham Grade

Exc.	V.G.	Good	Fair	Poor
9000	8000	6500	4000	2750

Regal Grade

Exc.	V.G.	Good	Fair	Poor
12500	10000	7500	6500	5000

Sidelock Game Gun

NIB	Exc.	V.G.	Good	Fair	Poor
20000	17000	13500	10000	8000	6500

Magazine Rifle

Utilizing a Mauser action, this rifle is available in a number of calibers, barrel lengths and with either a 3- or 5-shot magazine. Blued checkered walnut stock.

NIB	Exc.	V.G.	Good	Fair	Poor
6500	4750	3000	2250	1500	850

Large Bore Magazine Rifle

Utilizing a Bruno square bridge Mauser action, this rifle is chambered for .375 Holland & Holland, .404 Gibbs, .416 Rigby, .458 Winchester Magnum and .505 Gibbs cartridges. Barrel lengths vary from 2" to 24" and a 4-shot magazine is standard.

NIB	Exc.	V.G.	Good	Fair	Poor
7500	5000	3750	2500	2000	1000

Single Shot Rifle

Utilizing a Farquharson dropping block action, this rifle is chambered for a variety of cartridges and has a 24" barrel. The receiver finely engraved and blued. Stock of well figured walnut.

Exc.	V.G.	Good	Fair	Poor
8000	7000	5500	4000	—

Third Quality Boxlock Double Rifle

A double barrel rifle chambered for cartridges from .275 Magnum to .577 Nitro Express with a 24" to 28" barrel fitted with express sights. Double triggers and automatic ejectors. Blued with light engraving and a checkered walnut stock.

Exc.	V.G.	Good	Fair	Poor
12500	10500	8500	7000	5000

Second Quality Boxlock Double Rifle

As above, but more finely engraved and with better quality walnut stocks.

Exc.	V.G.	Good	Fair	Poor
16000	14000	10500	8000	6000

Best Quality Sidelock Double Rifle

As above, but fitted with full sidelocks, with best bouquet engraving and finely figured walnut stocks.

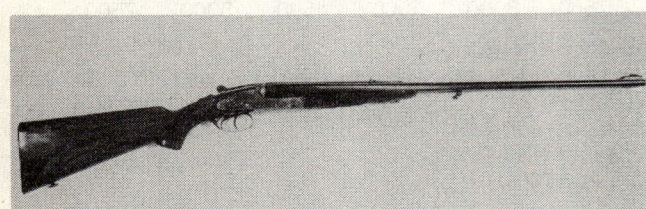

NIB	Exc.	V.G.	Good	Fair	Poor
35000	30000	25000	20000	15000	12000

RIGDON, ANSLEY & CO.
Augusta, Georgia

1851 Colt Navy Type

A .36 caliber percussion revolver with a 7.5" barrel and 6-shot cylinder. Blued with walnut grips. Initial production examples marked "Augusta, GA. C.S.A." and later models "C.S.A." Approximately 1,000 were manufactured in 1864 and 1865.

Courtesy Milwaukee Public Museum, Milwaukee, Wisconsin

Early Production Model

Exc.	V.G.	Good	Fair	Poor
—	—	13000	6000	2000

Standard Production Model

Exc.	V.G.	Good	Fair	Poor
—	—	12000	5000	1500

RIPOMANTI, GUY
St. Etienne, France
Importer - Wes Gilpin
Dallas, Texas
Morton's Ltd.
Lexington, Kentucky

Side-x-Side Shotgun

A high-grade shotgun offered on a strictly made-to-order basis. There is a boxlock model that begins at $8,500 and a side-lock that is priced from $22,500. These prices rise depending on the options and embellishments desired. These guns are rarely seen on the used-gun market; but if a transaction is contemplated, we strongly urge competent individual appraisal. The shotguns are imported by Gilpin's.

Side-x-Side Double Rifles

Extremely high-grade and basically made to order. They are rarely encountered on today's market. They have been imported since 1988. They range in price from $11,000 up. If a transaction is contemplated, we strongly urge competent individual appraisal. These guns are imported by Morton's.

Over/Under Double Rifle

A boxlock action Over/Under chambered for the 9.3x74R cartridge. The barrels are 23.5" in length and have express sights. There are double triggers and automatic ejectors. This model is highly engraved and features a high-grade, hand-checkered walnut stock. It was introduced in 1989 and is imported by Morton's.

NIB	Exc.	V.G.	Good	Fair	Poor
7000	5750	4750	4000	3000	2250

RIZZINI, FILLI
Brescia, Italy
Importer - W. L. Moore & Co.
West Lake Village, California

Early guns were manufactured with Antonio Zoli. As a result, these were off-the-shelf guns of lower prices. These early guns were imported by Abercombie and Fitch of New York. Some of these guns will be stamped with the A&F address on the barrel. These side by side guns have a box lock action.

Lusso Grade

12 gauge

NIB	Exc.	V.G.	Good	Fair	Poor
1200	850	700	600	400	200

20 gauge

NIB	Exc.	V.G.	Good	Fair	Poor
1700	1250	800	600	500	250

28 gauge and .410 bore

NIB	Exc.	V.G.	Good	Fair	Poor
2000	1600	1250	800	600	300

Extra Lusso Grade-Scalloped receiver

12 gauge

NIB	Exc.	V.G.	Good	Fair	Poor
2800	2450	1750	1200	800	400

20 gauge

NIB	Exc.	V.G.	Good	Fair	Poor
3450	3450	2000	1500	1150	600

28 gauge

NIB	Exc.	V.G.	Good	Fair	Poor
3850	3850	2250	1750	1300	700

.410 bore

NIB	Exc.	V.G.	Good	Fair	Poor
4250	4250	2400	1800	1350	750

At the present time this Italian gun company builds about 24 shotguns a year. Each gun is highly individualized for the customer. It is therefore advisable to secure a qualified appraisal before purchase. The company only produces two models. These are listed below to give the reader some idea of the value of one of these models. None of these models includes the cost of engraving and multi barrel set and multi gauge sets are extra.

Model R-1

Available in 12 to .410 bore with choice of barrels from 25" to 30". Choice of single or double trigger, pistol or straight grip, rib, barrel length and chokes are standard items on this model. This model features a Holland & Holland side lock action.

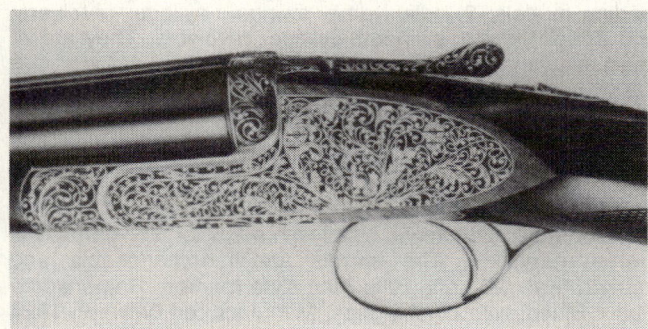

12, 16, or 20 gauge

NIB	Exc.	V.G.	Good	Fair	Poor
40000	30000	19000	10000	6000	—

.28 gauge or .410 bore

NIB	Exc.	V.G.	Good	Fair	Poor
46000	34500	22000	12000	7500	—

Model R-2

This model has a box lock action and a removable inspection plate on the bottom of the frame. The stock and forearm is fitted with Turkish Circassian walnut. Offered in 12 gauge to .410 bore.

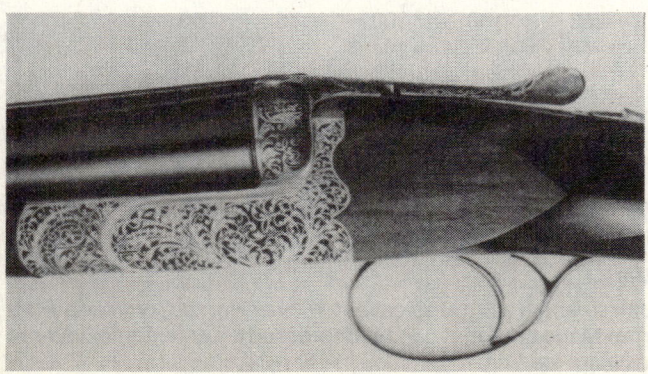

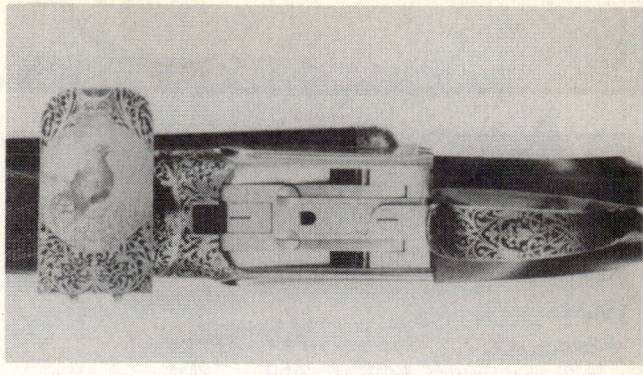

NIB	Exc.	V.G.	Good	Fair	Poor
15000	8500	8500	6000	3000	—

NOTE: Engraving extras for above models will add $8,700 for English scroll pattern and $22,000 for Fracassi style engraving. Other types of engraving are offered and it is advisable to secure a qualified appraisal of an engraved Rizzini before purchase.

Extra set of barrels in same gauge add $12,500.

ROBAR ET CIE
Liege, Belgium

Jieffeco

A 6.35mm or 7.65mm caliber semiautomatic pistol with a 3" barrel. The slide is marked "Pistolet Automatique Jieffeco Depose Brevete SGDG." Blued with plastic grips. Manufactured from 1910 to 1914.

Exc.	V.G.	Good	Fair	Poor
200	150	125	100	75

Melior

As above, with a 2.5" barrel and the slide marked "Melior Brevete SGDG." Manufactured from 1910 to 1914.

Exc.	V.G.	Good	Fair	Poor
200	150	125	100	75

New Model Melior

A .22, 6.35mm, 7.65mm, or 9mm short caliber semiautomatic pistol resembling the Browning Model 1910 with a 2" barrel. The barrel marked "Melior Brevets-Liege, Belgium." Blued, with plastic grips. Manufactured prior to 1958.

Exc.	V.G.	Good	Fair	Poor
200	150	125	100	75

Mercury

As above, in .22 caliber and imported by Tradewinds of Tacoma, Washington. The slide marked "Mercury Made in Belgium." Blue or nickel-plated. Manufactured from 1946 to 1958.

Exc.	V.G.	Good	Fair	Poor
200	150	125	100	75

ROBBINS & LAWRENCE
Windsor, Vermont

Pepperbox

A .28 or .31 caliber percussion 5 barrel pistol with the barrel groups measuring 3.5" or 4.5" in length. Ring trigger, blued iron frame with simple scroll engraving and browned barrels, which are marked "Robbins & Lawrence Co. Windsor, VT. Patent. 1849." The barrel groups for this pistol were made in two types: fluted in both calibers, and ribbed in .31 caliber only. Approximately 7,000 were made between 1851 and 1854.

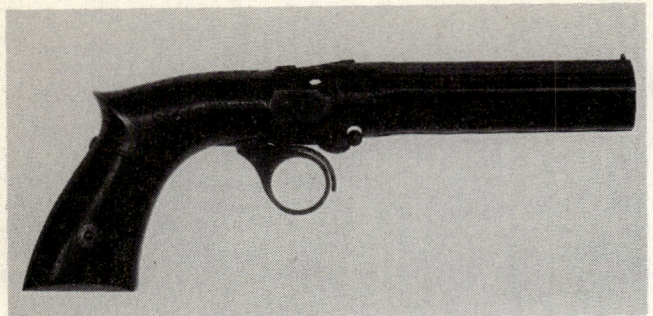

Exc.	V.G.	Good	Fair	Poor
—	—	1250	450	200

ROBERTSON
Philadelphia, Pennsylvania

Pocket Pistol

A .41 caliber single shot percussion derringer with barrels ranging in length from 3" to 4.5". The barrel marked "Robertson, Phila."

Exc.	V.G.	Good	Fair	Poor
—	—	1000	500	200

ROBINSON, ORVIL
SEE Adirondack Arms Company

ROBINSON, S.C.
Richmond, Virginia

From December of 1862 through March 1 of 1863, S.C. Robinson produced copies of the Sharps carbine. These arms had an overall length of 38-1/2", with .52 caliber barrels 21-1/2" long. The lockplates were marked "S.C. ROBINSON/ARMS MANUFACTORY/RICHMOND VA/1862" along with the serial number. The barrels were marked forward of the rear sight "S.C. ROBINSON/ARMS MANUFACTORY," as well as "RICHMOND VA/1862" to the rear of the sight. Total number made estimated to be slightly over 1900.

In March of 1863, the Robinson factory was taken over by the Confederate States Government. Carbines produced after that date are only stamped with the serial number on their lockplates and "RICHMOND VA" on their barrels. Total number made in excess of 3,400. Prospective purchasers are strongly advised to secure an expert appraisal prior to acquisition.

Robinson Sharps

Exc.	V.G.	Good	Fair	Poor
—	—	8000	4000	1500

Confederate Sharps

Exc.	V.G.	Good	Fair	Poor
—	—	8500	4500	1500

ROGERS & SPENCER
Utica, New York

Army Revolver

A .44 caliber 6-shot percussion revolver with a 7.5" octagonal barrel. The barrel marked "Rogers & Spencer/Utica, N.Y." Blued, case hardened hammer with walnut grips bearing the

inspector's mark "RPB". Approximately 5,800 were made between 1863 and 1865.

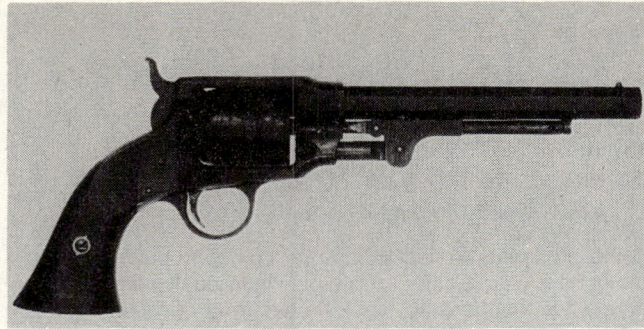

Courtesy Milwaukee Public Museum, Milwaukee, Wisconsin

Exc.	V.G.	Good	Fair	Poor
—	3000	1500	600	250

ROHM GMBH
Sonthein/Brenz, Germany

This firm produced a variety of revolvers marked with various trade names that were imported into the United States prior to 1968. Essentially, they are of three types: 1) solid-frame, gate-loading models; 2) solid-frame, swingout-cylinder revolvers; and 3) solid-frame, swingout-cylinder revolvers. They are of low quality and little collector interest.

ROMERWERKE
Suhl, Germany

Romer

.22 caliber semiautomatic pistol with a 2.5" or 6.5" barrel and 7-shot magazine. The barrels are interchangeable and marked "Kal. .22 Long Rifle," the slide marked "Romerwerke Suhl." Blued, with plastic grips. Manufactured between 1924 and 1926.

Exc.	V.G.	Good	Fair	Poor
550	450	400	300	225

RONGE, J. B.
Liege, Belgium

Bulldog

A .32, .380, or .45 caliber double-action revolver with a 3" barrel. Unmarked except for the monogram "RF" on the grips. Various trade names have been noted on these revolvers and are believed to have been applied by retailers. Manufactured from 1880 to 1910.

Exc.	V.G.	Good	Fair	Poor
200	150	100	75	50

ROSS RIFLE CO.
Quebec, Canada

Designed in 1896 by Sir Charles Ross, this straight pole rifle was manufactured in a variety of styles. Due to problems with the bolt design, it never proved popular and was discontinued in 1915.

Mark I

Barrel length 28", .303 caliber with a "Harris Controlled Platform Magazine" that can be depressed by an external lever to facilitate loading.

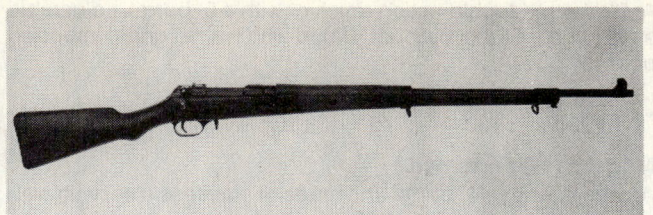

Courtesy Buffalo Bill Historical Center, Cody, Wyoming

Exc.	V.G.	Good	Fair	Poor
300	250	200	150	100

Mark I Carbine
As above, with a 22" barrel.

Exc.	V.G.	Good	Fair	Poor
350	300	250	200	150

Mark 2
As above, with a modified rear sight.

Exc.	V.G.	Good	Fair	Poor
300	250	200	150	100

Mark 3
Introduced in 1910 with improved lockwork and stripper clip guides.

Courtesy Buffalo Bill Historical Center, Cody, Wyoming

Exc.	V.G.	Good	Fair	Poor
325	275	225	175	125

Mark 3B
As above, with a magazine cut-off.

Exc.	V.G.	Good	Fair	Poor
350	300	250	200	150

Sporting Rifle
A .280 Ross or .303 caliber straight pole sporting rifle with a 24" barrel having open sights. Blued with a checkered walnut stock.

Courtesy Buffalo Bill Historical Center, Cody, Wyoming

Courtesy Buffalo Bill Historical Center, Cody, Wyoming

Exc.	V.G.	Good	Fair	Poor
275	225	200	150	125

ROSSI
F I R E A R M S

ROSSI, AMADEO
Leopoldo, Brazil
Importer - Interarms
Alexandria, Virginia

Overland Shotgun
An exposed hammer sidelock 12, 20 or .410 bore double-barrel shotgun with 26" or 28" barrels and double triggers. Manual extractors. Blued with a walnut stock. Discontinued in 1988.

NIB	Exc.	V.G.	Good	Fair	Poor
250	225	200	150	100	75

Squire Shotgun
A 12, 20 or .410 bore double-barrel shotgun with 20", 26", or 28" barrels, double triggers and manual ejectors. Blued with a walnut stock.

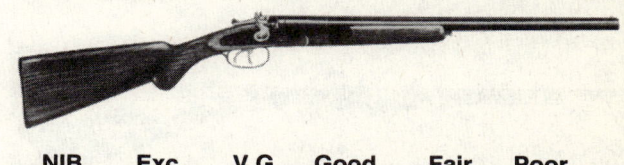

NIB	Exc.	V.G.	Good	Fair	Poor
350	300	250	200	150	100

Model 92
A copy of the Winchester Model 1892, chambered for .357 Magnum, .44 Magnum or .44-40 with either a 16" or 20" barrel. Blued with a walnut stock. The engraved version of this model is worth approximately 20% more than the values listed below. Add $50.00 for a 20" stainless steel version introduced in 1997.

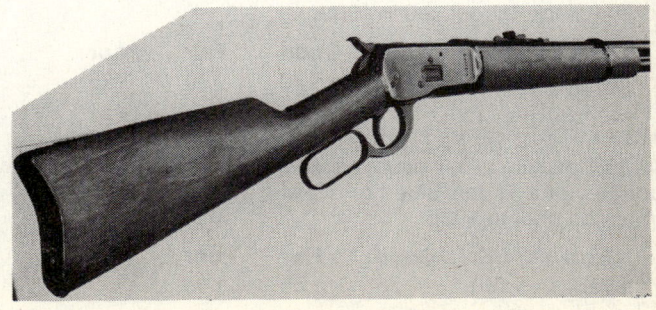

NIB	Exc.	V.G.	Good	Fair	Poor
300	225	175	150	100	75

Model 92 Rifle

Introduced in 1997 this model is fitted with a 24" half octagon barrel and brass blade front sight. Magazine capacity is 13 rounds of .45 Colt. Weight is about 6.8 lbs.

NIB	Exc.	V.G.	Good	Fair	Poor
425	350	—	—	—	—

Model 92 Large Loop

This model has a 16: barrel and is chambered for the .44 Magnum or .45 Colt cartridge. Weight is about 5.5 lbs. Finish is blue. Introduced in 1997.

NIB	Exc.	V.G.	Good	Fair	Poor
325	250	—	—	—	—

Model 62

A copy of the Winchester Model 1890 rifle with either 16.5" or 23" round or octagonal barrels. Blued or stainless steel with a walnut stock.

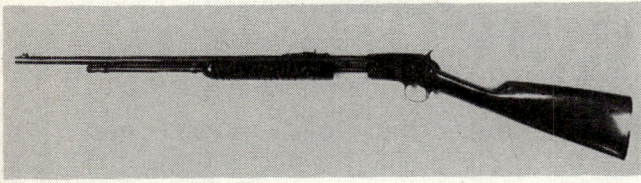

NIB	Exc.	V.G.	Good	Fair	Poor
200	175	150	125	100	75

Model 59

As above, in .22 Magnum caliber.

NIB	Exc.	V.G.	Good	Fair	Poor
210	175	150	125	100	75

Model 65

Similar to the Model 92, but chambered for either the .44 Special or .44 Magnum cartridge. Barrel length 20". Blued with a walnut stock. Introduced in 1989.

NIB	Exc.	V.G.	Good	Fair	Poor
300	250	200	175	150	125

Model 31

A .38 Special caliber double-action revolver with a 4" barrel and 5-shot cylinder. Blued or nickel-plated with walnut grips. Imported prior to 1986.

Exc.	V.G.	Good	Fair	Poor
125	100	75	50	40

Model 51

A .22 caliber double-action revolver with a 6" barrel, adjustable sights and a 6-shot cylinder. Blued with walnut grips. Imported prior to 1986.

Exc.	V.G.	Good	Fair	Poor
125	100	75	50	40

Model 511 Sportsman

As above, with a 4" barrel and made of stainless steel with walnut grips. Introduced in 1986.

NIB	Exc.	V.G.	Good	Fair	Poor
225	200	150	125	100	75

Model 677

This model was first introduced in 1997 and is chamberd for the .357 magnum cartridge. It has a matte blue finish with 2" barrel and black rubber grips. Weight is about 26 oz.

NIB	Exc.	V.G.	Good	Fair	Poor
250	200	—	—	—	—

Model 68

A .38 Special double-action revolver with a 2" or 3" barrel and 5-shot cylinder. Blued or nickel-plated with walnut grips.

NIB	Exc.	V.G.	Good	Fair	Poor
185	150	125	100	75	50

Model 68S

This new version was introduced in 1993 and features a shrouded ejector rod and fixed sights. Chambered for the .38 Special cartridge it is offered with either 2" or 3" barrel. Grips or wood or rubber. Finish is blue or nickel. Weighs about 23 oz.

	Exc.	V.G.	Good	Fair	Poor
	175	150	125	100	75

Model 851

As above, with either a 3" or 4" ventilated rib barrel and adjustable sights.

NIB	Exc.	V.G.	Good	Fair	Poor
200	175	150	125	100	75

NIB	Exc.	V.G.	Good	Fair	Poor
175	150	125	100	75	60

Model 69

As above, in .32 Smith & Wesson caliber with a 3" barrel and 6-shot cylinder. Imported prior to 1986.

Exc.	V.G.	Good	Fair	Poor
125	100	75	50	40

Model 70

As above, in .22 caliber with a 3" barrel and 6-shot cylinder. Imported prior to 1986.

Model 877

Introduced in 1996 this 6-shot revolver is chambered for the .357 magnum cartridge. It is fitted with a 2" heavy barrel. Stainless steel with black rubber grips. Weight is about 26 oz.

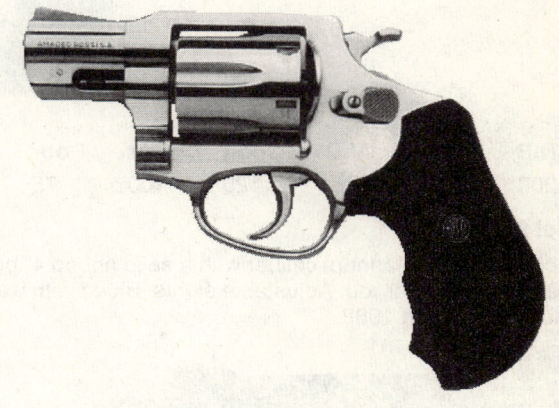

NIB	Exc.	V.G.	Good	Fair	Poor
275	200	175	150	100	80

Exc.	V.G.	Good	Fair	Poor
125	100	75	50	40

Model 84

A stainless steel, .38 Special caliber double-action revolver with ribbed 3" or 4" barrel. Blued with walnut grips. Imported in 1985 and 1986.

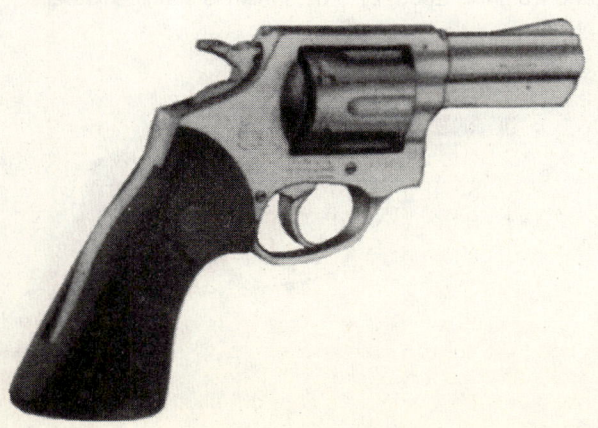

Model 88S

Introduced in 1993 this improved model has the same features of the Model 68 with the addition of a stainless finish. It is chambered for the .38 Special cartridge and is fitted with either a 2" or 3" barrel. Available with either wood or rubber grips. Cylinder holds 5 cartridges. Weighs approximately 22 oz.

NIB	Exc.	V.G.	Good	Fair	Poor
195	175	150	125	100	75

Model 89

As above, in .32 Smith & Wesson caliber with a 3" barrel.

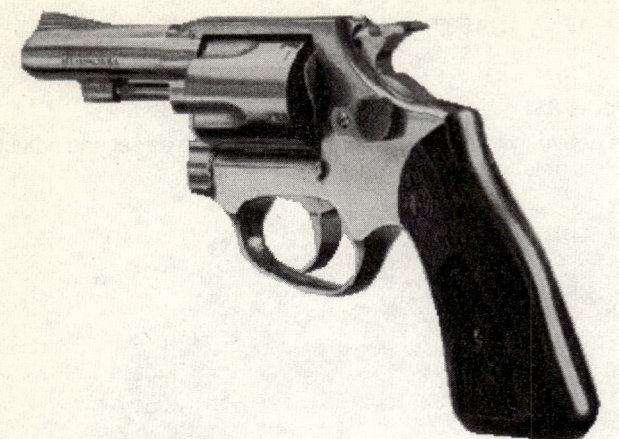

NIB	Exc.	V.G.	Good	Fair	Poor
200	175	150	125	100	75

Model 951

A .38 Special caliber double-action revolver with a 3" or 4" ventilated rib barrel and 6-shot cylinder. Blued with walnut grips. Introduced in 1985.

NIB	Exc.	V.G.	Good	Fair	Poor
200	175	150	125	100	75

Model 971

As above, in .357 Magnum caliber with a solid ribbed 4" barrel and enclosed ejector rod. Adjustable sights. Blued with walnut grips. Introduced in 1988.

NIB	Exc.	V.G.	Good	Fair	Poor
210	175	150	125	100	75

Model 971 Comp

Introduced in 1993. Similar to the Model 971 with the addition of a compensator on a 3.25" barrel. Overall length is 9" and weight is 32 oz. Chambered for .357 Magnum cartridge.

NIB	Exc.	V.G.	Good	Fair	Poor
200	175	150	125	100	75

Model 971 Stainless

As above, but constructed of stainless steel with checkered black rubber grips. Introduced in 1989.

NIB	Exc.	V.G.	Good	Fair	Poor
225	200	150	125	100	75

Model 971 VRC (vented rib compensator)

Introduced in 1996 this variation features a choice of a 6", 4", or 2.5" vent rib barrel with integral compensator. Stainless steel with black rubber grips. Weight is from 30 oz. to 39 oz. depending on barrel length.

NIB	Exc.	V.G.	Good	Fair	Poor
300	250	200	175	150	100

Model 988 Cyclops

Introduced in 1997 this model is chambered for the .357 Magnum cartridge and is fitted with four recessed compensator ports on each side of the muzzle. Offered in 8" or 6" barrel lengths this six shot double action revolver weighs about 44 ozs. for the 6" model and 51 ozs. for the 8" model. Stainless steel finish.

NIB	Exc.	V.G.	Good	Fair	Poor
425	350	—	—	—	—

Model 720

This double action revolver is chambered for the .44 Special and features a 5 round cylinder and 3" barrel. Overall length is 8" and weight is about 27.5 oz. Finish is stainless steel.

NIB	Exc.	V.G.	Good	Fair	Poor
250	200	175	150	125	100

ROTH-SAUER
SEE J. P. Sauer & Son

ROTH-STEYR
Austria-Hungary

Model 1907

An 8mm caliber semiautomatic pistol with a 5" barrel. Blued with ribbed walnut grips. This pistol is an unusual design in that the front of the bolt is hollow and encloses the barrel breech. When fired, the barrel recoils and rotates 90 degrees before the bolt is released to move rearward.

Exc.	V.G.	Good	Fair	Poor
400	350	300	200	125

TH. ROTTME
SEE Austrian Military Firearms

ROTTWIEL
Rotwiel, West Germany
Importer - Dynamit Nobel of America
Northvale, New Jersey

Model 650

A 12 gauge Over/Under shotgun with 28" ventilated rib barrels having screw-in choke tubes, single selective trigger, and automatic ejectors. The receiver engraved and in French case hardened, checkered stock of well figured walnut. Imported prior to 1987.

Exc.	V.G.	Good	Fair	Poor
700	550	400	300	150

Model 72

A 12 gauge Over/Under shotgun with 28" ventilated rib barrels having screw-in choke tubes, single selective trigger and automatic ejectors. Blued with a well figured checkered walnut stock. Imported prior to 1988.

Exc.	V.G.	Good	Fair	Poor
1750	1200	750	500	250

Model 72 American Skeet

As above, with a 26.75" ventilated rib barrel, single selective trigger, and automatic ejectors. The receiver is also engraved. Imported prior to 1988.

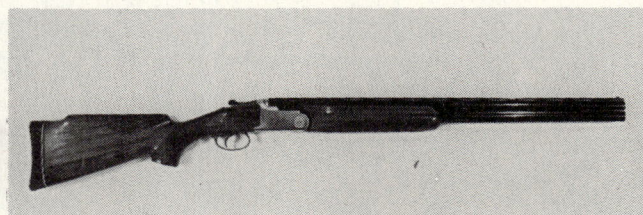

Exc.	V.G.	Good	Fair	Poor
1750	1200	750	500	250

Model 72 Adjustable American Trap

As above, with a 34" ventilated rib barrel, adjustable to point of impact. Imported prior to 1987.

Exc.	V.G.	Good	Fair	Poor
1500	1000	600	300	150

Model 72 American Trap

As above, without the barrel being adjustable to the point of impact.

Exc.	V.G.	Good	Fair	Poor
1750	1200	750	500	250

Model 72 International Skeet

As above, with 26.75" ventilated rib barrels having skeet chokes. Imported prior to 1988.

Exc.	V.G.	Good	Fair	Poor
1750	1200	750	500	250

Model 72 International Trap

As above, with 30" high ventilated rib barrels that are improved-modified and full choked. Imported prior to 1988.

Exc.	V.G.	Good	Fair	Poor
1750	1200	750	500	250

ROYAL AMERICAN SHOTGUNS
Woodland Hills, California
Importer - Royal Arms International

Model 100

A 12 or 20 gauge Over/Under shotgun with 26", 28", or 30" ventilated rib barrels, double triggers and extractors. Blued with a walnut stock. Imported from 1985 to 1987.

Exc.	V.G.	Good	Fair	Poor
350	300	250	175	150

Model 100AE

As above, with a single trigger and automatic ejectors.

Exc.	V.G.	Good	Fair	Poor
400	325	275	200	175

Model 600

A 12, 20, 28 or .410 bore double-barrel shotgun with 25", 26", 28", or 30" ventilated rib barrels, double triggers and extractors. Blued with a walnut stock. Imported from 1985 to 1987.

Exc.	V.G.	Good	Fair	Poor
375	325	275	200	175

Model 800

A 28 or .410 bore detachable sidelock double-barrel shotgun with 24", 26", or 28" barrels, double triggers and automatic ejectors. Blued, French case hardened with an English style walnut stock. Imported from 1985 to 1987.

Exc.	V.G.	Good	Fair	Poor
800	650	600	475	400

RUBY ARMS COMPANY
Guernica, Spain

Ruby

A 6.35mm or 7.35mm caliber semiautomatic pistol with a 3.5" barrel and 6-shot magazine. The slide marked "Ruby". Blued with plastic grips.

Exc.	V.G.	Good	Fair	Poor
200	150	100	75	50

RUGER
SEE Sturm, Ruger Co.

RUPERTUS, JACOB
Philadelphia, Pennsylvania

Army Revolver

This is an extremely rare revolver chambered for .44 caliber percussion. It has a 7.25" octagon barrel with an integral loading lever that pivots to the side instead of downward. The hammer is mounted on the side, and there is a pellet priming device located on the backstrap. There is only one nipple on the breach that lines up with the top of the cylinder. The cylinder is unfluted and holds 6 shots. The finish is blued, with walnut grips; and the frame is marked "Patented April 19, 1859". There were less than 12 manufactured in 1859. It would behoove one to secure a qualified independent appraisal if a transaction were contemplated.

Exc.	V.G.	Good	Fair	Poor
—	—	8000	4000	1250

Navy Revolver

This model is equally as rare as the Army model. It is chambered for .36 caliber percussion. Otherwise it is quite similar in appearance to the Army model. There were approximately 12 manufactured in 1859. Both of these revolvers were manufactured for test purposes and were not well-received by the military, so further production was not accomplished.

Exc.	V.G.	Good	Fair	Poor
—	—	8000	4000	1250

Pocket Model Revolver

This is a smaller version of the Army and Navy model, chambered for .25 caliber percussion. It has no loading lever and has a 3-1/8" octagonal barrel. There were approximately 12 manufactured in 1859.

Exc.	V.G.	Good	Fair	Poor
—	—	5000	2750	950

Single Shot Pocket Pistol

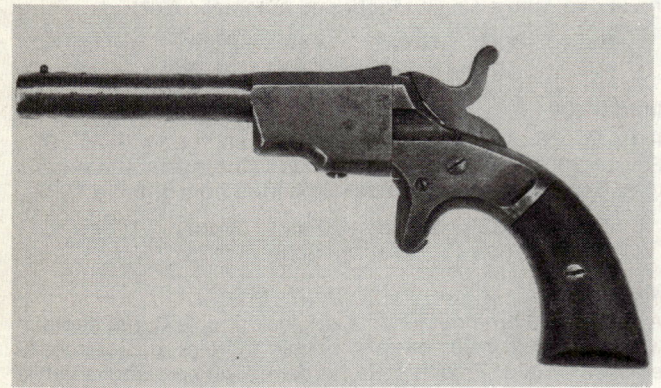

A .22, .32, .38, or .41 rimfire single shot pistol with half-octagonal barrels, ranging in length from 3" to 5". The barrel marked "Rupertus Pat'd. Pistol Mfg. Co. Philadelphia". Blued with walnut grips. Approximately 3,000 were made from 1870 to 1885. The .41 caliber variety is worth approximately 50% more than the values listed below.

Exc.	V.G.	Good	Fair	Poor
—	—	375	200	75

Double-Barrel Pocket Pistol

A .22 caliber double-barrel pistol with 3" round barrels and a spur trigger. The hammer fitted with a sliding firing pin. Blued with walnut grips.

Exc.	V.G.	Good	Fair	Poor
—	—	1250	600	200

Spur Trigger Revolver

A .22 caliber spur trigger revolver with a 2.75" round barrel and unfluted cylinder. The top strap marked "Empire Pat. Nov. 21, 71". Blued or nickel-plated with walnut grips. A .41 caliber spur trigger revolver with a 2-7/8" round barrel and a 5-shot fluted cylinder. Blued or nickel-plated with walnut grips. The top strap marked "Empire 41" and the barrel "J. Rupertus Phila. Pa." The .41 caliber variety is worth approximately 25% more than the values listed below. Manufactured during the 1870s and 1880s.

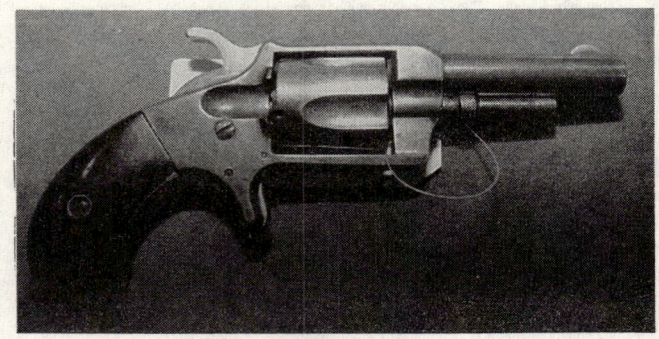

Exc.	V.G.	Good	Fair	Poor
—	—	250	125	75

S.A.C.M.
SEE French State

S.A.E.
Eibar, Spain
Importer - Spain America Enterprises,
Inc. Miami, Florida

Model 210S

A 12, 20 or .410 bore double-barrel shotgun with 26" or 28" barrels, double triggers and manual extractors. Blued, French casehardened with a checkered walnut stock. Imported in 1988.

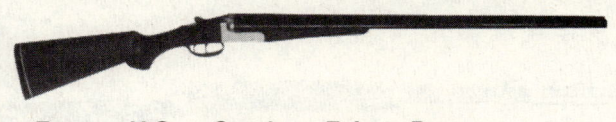

Exc.	V.G.	Good	Fair	Poor
425	375	300	225	150

Model 340X

A Holland & Holland-style sidelock 10 or 20 gauge double-barrel shotgun with 26" barrels, double triggers and automatic ejectors. Blued, casehardened with a checkered English style walnut stock. Imported in 1988.

Exc.	V.G.	Good	Fair	Poor
700	600	500	400	200

Model 209E

As above, with the exception that it was also chambered for .410 bore cartridges, and was more finely engraved. Imported in 1988.

Exc.	V.G.	Good	Fair	Poor
900	800	700	550	250

Model 70

A 12 or 20 gauge Over/Under shotgun with 26" ventilated rib barrels having screw-in choke tubes, single trigger and automatic ejectors. The modestly engraved receiver either blued or French casehardened. Stock of finely figured walnut. Imported in 1988.

Exc.	V.G.	Good	Fair	Poor
400	300	250	200	100

Model 66C

A 12 gauge Over/Under shotgun with 26" or 30" ventilated rib barrels choked for skeet or trap, single trigger and automatic ejectors. The boxlock action lifted with false sideplates, which are engraved and gold inlaid. Blued with a checkered Monte Carlo-style stock and a beavertail forearm. Imported in 1988.

Exc.	V.G.	Good	Fair	Poor
900	800	700	575	300

S.E.A.M.
Eibar, Spain

This retailer sold a number of pistols produced by the firm of Urizar prior to 1935.

Praga

A 7.65 caliber semiautomatic pistol marked "Praga Cal 7.65" on the slide. Blued with plastic grips impressed with the trademark S.E.A.M.

Exc.	V.G.	Good	Fair	Poor
175	150	125	90	65

S.E.A.M.

A 6.35mm semiautomatic pistol with a 2" barrel. The slide marked "Fabrica de Armas SEAM". Blued with black plastic grips, having the trademark "SEAM" cast into them.

Exc.	V.G.	Good	Fair	Poor
175	150	125	90	65

Silesia

As above, but of 7.65mm caliber with a 3" barrel and having the word "Silesia" stamped on the slide.

Exc.	V.G.	Good	Fair	Poor
175	150	125	90	65

SKB ARMS COMPANY
Tokyo, Japan
Importer - SKB Company USA
Manhein, Pennsylvania

Model 100

A boxlock 12 or 20 gauge double-barrel shotgun with 25" to 30" barrels, single selective trigger and automatic ejectors. Blued with a walnut stock. Imported prior to 1981.

NIB	Exc.	V.G.	Good	Fair	Poor
450	425	375	300	200	100

Model 150

As above, with some engraving, a beavertail forearm and a figured walnut stock. Imported from 1972 to 1974.

NIB	Exc.	V.G.	Good	Fair	Poor
500	450	400	300	200	100

Model 200

As above, with a French casehardened and scalloped receiver.

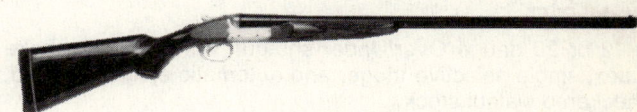

NIB	Exc.	V.G.	Good	Fair	Poor
550	500	450	375	250	150

Model 200E

As above, with an English style stock. Imported prior to 1989.

NIB	Exc.	V.G.	Good	Fair	Poor
800	675	600	475	275	150

Model 280

Same as the Model 200 but fitted with a straight grip stock.

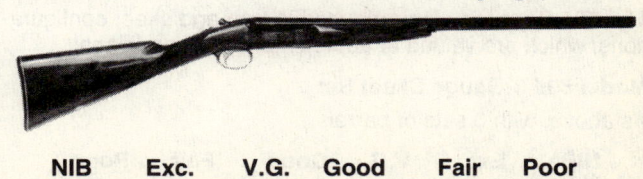

NIB	Exc.	V.G.	Good	Fair	Poor
800	675	600	475	275	150

Model 300

As above, with more engraving and a figured walnut stock.

NIB	Exc.	V.G.	Good	Fair	Poor
750	675	600	475	275	150

Model 385

Similar to the Model 300 but chambered for the 20 or 28 gauge shell. Scroll engraved frame with semi-fancy walnut. Pistol grip stock. Limited quanities imported.

NIB	Exc.	V.G.	Good	Fair	Poor
1250	900	750	600	300	150

Model 400E

As above, with engraved false sideplates and an English style stock. Imported prior to 1990.

NIB	Exc.	V.G.	Good	Fair	Poor
975	875	750	600	300	150

Model 480E

As above, with a French casehardened receiver and more finely figured walnut stocks.stocks.

NIB	Exc.	V.G.	Good	Fair	Poor
1200	1000	850	650	350	150

Model 500

A 12, 20, 28 gauge or .410 bore Over/Under shotgun with 26", 28" or 30" ventilated rib barrels. Blued with a walnut stock. Imported from 1966 to 1979. Blued with a walnut stock. Imported from 1966 to 1979.

NIB	Exc.	V.G.	Good	Fair	Poor
500	450	375	300	150	100

Model 505

A 12 or 20 gauge Over/Under shotgun with screw-in choke tubes, single selective trigger and automatic ejectors. Blued, checkered walnut stock.

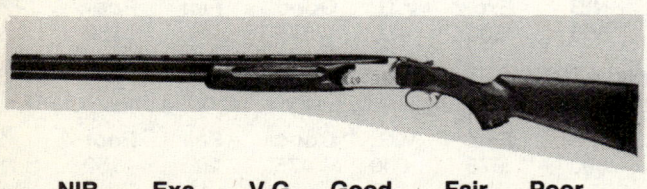

NIB	Exc.	V.G.	Good	Fair	Poor
750	675	600	500	450	375

The 505 Series is also produced in trap and skeet configurations, which are valued at approximately 5% additional.

Model 505 3-Gauge Skeet Set

As above, with 3 sets of barrels.

NIB	Exc.	V.G.	Good	Fair	Poor
1850	1650	1400	1100	900	750

Model 585

Similar to the Model 505 but offered in .410 bore as well.

NIB	Exc.	V.G.	Good	Fair	Poor
950	800	700	500	400	200

Model 585-3 barrel set

Fitted with 20, 28 gauge and .410 bore barrels. Skeet choked.

NIB	Exc.	V.G.	Good	Fair	Poor
2750	2250	1700	1200	850	400

Model 600

As above, with a silver-plated receiver and better quality wood.

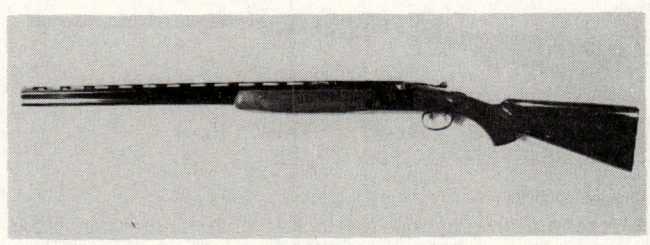

NIB	Exc.	V.G.	Good	Fair	Poor
700	625	550	450	325	150

Model 600 Magnum

As above, chambered for 3", 12 gauge cartridges. Imported from 1969 to 1972.

Exc.	V.G.	Good	Fair	Poor
725	650	575	475	350

Model 600 Trap Gun

As above, with 30" or 32" barrels trap choked, with a high comb walnut stock.

NIB	Exc.	V.G.	Good	Fair	Poor
675	600	525	425	300	150

Model 600 Skeet Gun

As above, chambered for 12, 20, 28 or .410 bore cartridges with 26" or 28" barrels that are skeet choked.

NIB	Exc.	V.G.	Good	Fair	Poor
700	625	550	450	325	150

Model 600 Skeet Combo Set

As above, with an extra set of interchangeable barrels. Furnished with a carrying case.

NIB	Exc.	V.G.	Good	Fair	Poor
700	625	550	450	325	150

Model 605

As above, with an engraved and French casehardened receiver.

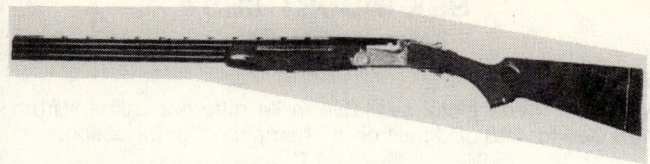

NIB	Exc.	V.G.	Good	Fair	Poor
900	750	650	550	400	350

The 605 Series is also available in trap or skeet configurations. The values are similar.

Model 605 3-Gauge Skeet Set
As above, with 3 extra sets of barrels.

NIB	Exc.	V.G.	Good	Fair	Poor
2000	1800	1550	1250	1000	850

Model 680E
Similar to the Model 600, with an engraved receiver and English style stock. Imported from 1973 to 1976.

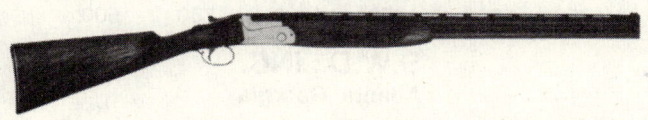

NIB	Exc.	V.G.	Good	Fair	Poor
725	650	575	475	350	200

Model 685
This over and under shotgun is offered in 12, 20, and 28 gauge as well as .410 bore. Barrel lengths are 26" or 28" with choke tubes. The engraved receiver has a silver finish with gold inlays. The walnut stock is semi-fancy.

NIB	Exc.	V.G.	Good	Fair	Poor
1400	1100	850	600	500	250

Model 700 Trap Gun
Similar to the Model 600 Trap, with a wider rib, additional engraving and a figured walnut stock. Imported from 1969 to 1975.

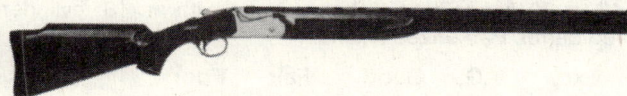

NIB	Exc.	V.G.	Good	Fair	Poor
825	750	675	575	450	250

Model 700 Skeet Gun
As above, with skeet chokes.

NIB	Exc.	V.G.	Good	Fair	Poor
850	775	700	600	475	250

Model 785
Offered in 12, 20, and 28 gauge as well as .410 bore this over and under features 26" or 28" barrels with choke tubes, single trigger, ejectors, and checkered walnut stock. the silver receiver is scroll engraved.

NIB	Exc.	V.G.	Good	Fair	Poor
1700	1450	1000	850	600	300

Model 800 Trap Gun
As above, but with trap chokes and more engraving. Imported from 1969 to 1975.

NIB	Exc.	V.G.	Good	Fair	Poor
2000	1000	850	650	550	250

Model 800 Skeet Gun
As above, in 12 or 20 gauge with 26" or 28" skeet choked barrels. Imported from 1969 to 1975.

NIB	Exc.	V.G.	Good	Fair	Poor
2000	1000	850	650	550	250

Model 880 Crown Grade
A false sidelock 12, 20, 28 or .410 bore boxlock double-barrel shotgun with a single selective trigger and automatic ejectors. The engraved sideplates and receiver French casehardened, and the figured walnut stock checkered. Imported prior to 1981.

NIB	Exc.	V.G.	Good	Fair	Poor
1700	1500	1250	1100	900	450

Model 885
A false sidelock 12, 20, 28 or .410 bore boxlock shotgun. Similar to the model 800.

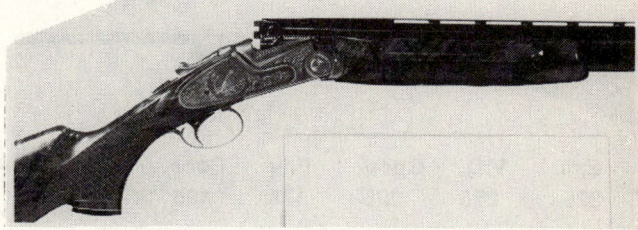

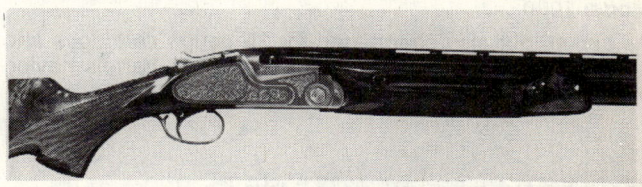

NIB	Exc.	V.G.	Good	Fair	Poor
1250	1050	900	700	600	300

Model 5600
This over and under gun is offered in 12 gauge only in either Trap or Skeet configurations.

NIB	Exc.	V.G.	Good	Fair	Poor
600	450	400	350	300	150

Model 5700
Similar to the above but with light scroll engraving on the receiver and figured walnut stock.

NIB	Exc.	V.G.	Good	Fair	Poor
750	575	500	400	300	150

Model 5800
Similar to the Model 5600 but with more engraving coverage on the receiver and fancy walnut stock.

NIB	Exc.	V.G.	Good	Fair	Poor
950	800	700	500	350	175

Model 7300
A 12 or 20 gauge slide action shotgun. Blued with a walnut stock. Imported prior to 1981.

Exc.	V.G.	Good	Fair	Poor
300	250	200	150	100

Model 7900
As above, but skeet choked.

NIB	Exc.	V.G.	Good	Fair	Poor
400	300	250	200	150	100

Model 300
A 12 or 20 gauge semiautomatic shotgun with 26", 28", or 30" barrels. Blued with a walnut stock. Imported from 1968 to 1972. Ventilated Rib Barrel-Add 20%.

Exc.	V.G.	Good	Fair	Poor
300	250	200	150	100

Model 1300

A redesigned version of the Model 300 with a ventilated rib barrel and screw-in choke tubes. Imported since 1988.

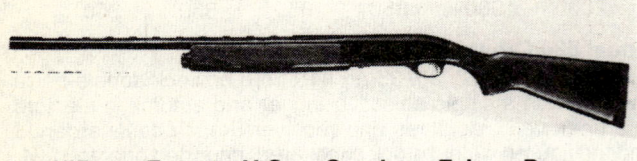

NIB	Exc.	V.G.	Good	Fair	Poor
450	400	350	300	200	150

Model XL 900 MR

A 12 gauge, semiautomatic shotgun with 26" to 30" ventilated rib barrels, and etched alloy receiver and checkered walnut stock. Imported prior to 1981.

Exc.	V.G.	Good	Fair	Poor
325	275	225	175	125

Model 1900

As above, but also chambered for 20 gauge cartridges and available with 22", 26", or 28" ventilated rib barrels having screw-in choke tubes. Blued with a walnut stock.

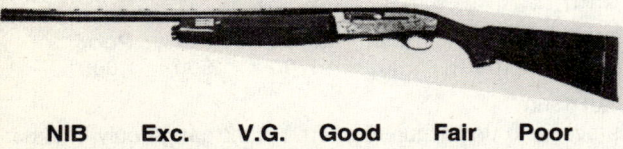

NIB	Exc.	V.G.	Good	Fair	Poor
500	425	375	300	250	175

Model 3000

Similar to the above, with a modified receiver design. Imported prior to 1990.

Exc.	V.G.	Good	Fair	Poor
475	400	350	250	150

SKS
Former Communist Bloc
Importer - Century International Arms

SKS

A 7.62x39mm semiautomatic rifle with a 20.5" barrel and 10-shot fixed magazine. Blued with oil finished stock.This rifle was a standard service arm for most Eastern Bloc countries prior to the adoption of the AK47.

NOTE: The importation of SKS rifles has resulted in an oversupply of these rifles with the result that prices are less than $100 for guns in excellent condition. However, this situation may change and if that occurs the price will adjust accordingly. Study local conditions before purchase or sale of this firearm.

SSK INDUSTRIES
Bloomingdale, Ohio

SSK-Contender

A custom made pistol available in 74 different calibers from .178 Bee to .588 JDJ built on a Thompson Center action.

NIB	Exc.	V.G.	Good	Fair	Poor
575	500	475	425	350	275

SSK-XP1OO

A custom made pistol utilizing a Remington XP1OO action. Available in a variety of calibers and sight configurations.

NIB	Exc.	V.G.	Good	Fair	Poor
650	600	550	500	400	300

.50 Caliber XP100

As above, with an integral muzzle brake and reinforced composition stock.

NIB	Exc.	V.G.	Good	Fair	Poor
1750	1500	1250	1000	750	500

S.W.D., INC.
Atlanta, Georgia

Cobray M- 11

A 9mm semiautomatic pistol with a 32-round magazine. Parkerized finish.

Exc.	V.G.	Good	Fair	Poor
225	200	175	125	100

M-11 Carbine

As above, with a 16.25" barrel enclosed in a shroud and fitted with a telescoping wire stock.

Exc.	V.G.	Good	Fair	Poor
250	225	200	150	125

Terminator

A 12 or 20 gauge single shot shotgun with an 18" cylinder bored barrel. Parkerized finish.

Exc.	V.G.	Good	Fair	Poor
100	80	70	60	50

SABATTI
SEE European American Armory

SACKET, D. D.
Westfield, Massachusetts

Under Hammer Pistol

A .34 or .36 single shot percussion pistol with a half octagonal 3" or 4" barrel marked "D. D. Sacket/Westfield/Cast Steel." Manufactured during the 1850s.

Exc.	V.G.	Good	Fair	Poor
500	400	350	250	175

SAFARI ARMS
Phoenix, Arizona

In operation from 1978 to 1987, this company was purchased by Olympic Arms of Olympia, Washington, in 1987 and the models listed below are currently produced by that company under different trade names.

Enforcer

A .45 caliber semiautomatic pistol with a 3.9" barrel and 5-shot magazine. Patterned after the Colt Model 1911. Blued, Armaloy, electroless nickel-plate or Parkerized finish with checkered walnut or neoprene grips.

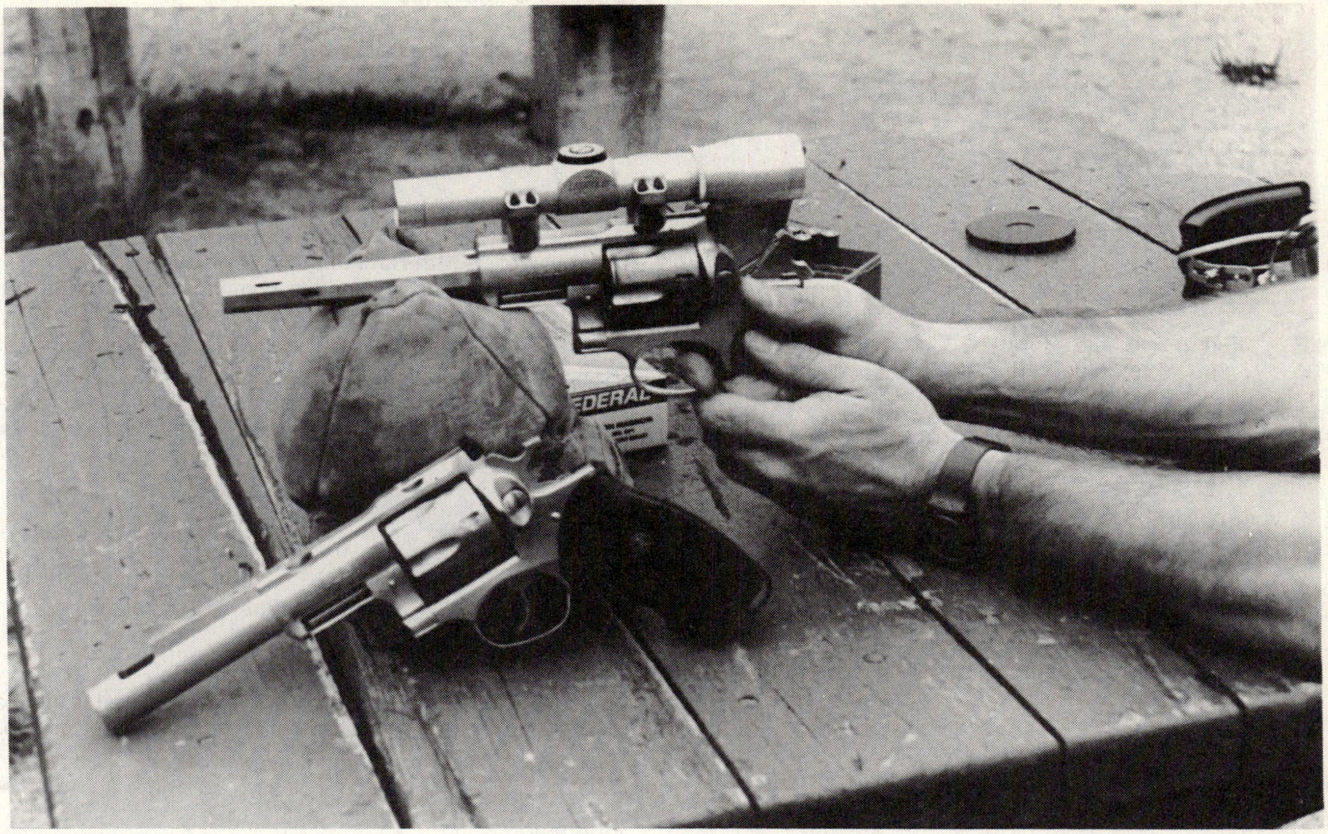

SSK Ruger Redhawk conversions.

SSK Custom Ruger Redhawk "Beast."

NIB	Exc.	V.G.	Good	Fair	Poor
700	600	500	400	350	150

Match Master

As above, with a 5" barrel.

NIB	Exc.	V.G.	Good	Fair	Poor
700	600	500	400	350	150

Black Widow

As above, with ivory Micarta grips etched with a Black Widow.

NIB	Exc.	V.G.	Good	Fair	Poor
700	600	500	400	350	150

Model 81

As above, without the grip etching and also offered in .38 caliber.

NIB	Exc.	V.G.	Good	Fair	Poor
800	700	600	500	400	200

Model 81L

As above, with a 6" barrel.

NIB	Exc.	V.G.	Good	Fair	Poor
850	750	650	550	450	200

Ultimate Unlimited

A bolt-action single shot pistol with a 15" barrel chambered for variety of cartridges. Blued with a laminated stock.

NIB	Exc.	V.G.	Good	Fair	Poor
850	750	650	550	450	200

Survivor I Conversion Unit

A conversion unit lifted to the Model 1911 frame that alters that pistol to a bolt-action carbine. Barrel length 16.25", caliber .223, folding stock.

NIB	Exc.	V.G.	Good	Fair	Poor
300	275	250	200	150	100

Counter Sniper Rifle

A .308 caliber bolt-action target rifle with a heavy 26" barrel and 20 round detachable magazine. Matte blued with a colored composite stock.

NIB	Exc.	V.G.	Good	Fair	Poor
1200	1050	850	650	450	200

SAKO
Riihimaki, Finland
Importer - Stoeger
South Hackensack, New Jersey

NOTE: Arms produced by this company prior to 1972 are worth approximately 25% more than arms of the same type produced thereafter.

Standard Sporter

A bolt-action magazine rifle produced in a wide variety of calibers with varying barrel lengths, etc. Blued with checkered walnut stocks.

Exc.	V.G.	Good	Fair	Poor
600	550	450	300	150

Deluxe Model

As above, with an engraved floorplate and checkered Monte Carlo-style stock having a rosewood pistol grip cap and forend tip.

Exc.	V.G.	Good	Fair	Poor
700	600	500	300	150

Finnbear

As above, with a long-action available in a variety of large bore calibers fitted with a 20" or 23.5" barrel. Blued with a checkered stock. .458 Winchester Magnum, 20 produced, values doubled.

Exc.	V.G.	Good	Fair	Poor
700	600	500	300	150

Forester

As above, with a shorter action suitable for use with intermediate cartridges.

Exc.	V.G.	Good	Fair	Poor
700	600	500	300	150

Vixen

As above, with a short action.

Exc.	V.G.	Good	Fair	Poor
700	600	500	300	150

FN Action

Manufactured from 1950 to 1957, this model utilized a Fabrique Nationale manufactured receiver and was chambered for .270 Winchester and .30-06 cartridges. Otherwise, as above.

Exc.	V.G.	Good	Fair	Poor
600	550	450	250	125

FN Magnum Action

As above, with a long action for .300 and .375 Holland & Holland.

Exc.	V.G.	Good	Fair	Poor
600	550	450	250	125

Finnwolf

A 4-shot lever action rifle produced in a variety of calibers. Blued, checkered walnut stock. Manufactured from 1962 to 1974.

Exc.	V.G.	Good	Fair	Poor
600	550	450	250	150

Anniversary Model

A 7mm Remington Magnum bolt-action rifle with a 24" barrel. Blued, checkered walnut stock. A total of 1,000 were manufactured. As with any commemorative firearm, this model should be NIB to realize its full resale potential.

NIB	Exc.	V.G.	Good	Fair	Poor
1200	700	550	450	250	200

Finnfire

This bolt action rifle is chambered for the .22 long rifle cartridge. It is fitted with a 22" barrel with choice of iron sights or no sights, and a European walnut stock. A 5 shot detachable magazine is standard. Weight is about 5.25 lbs.

NIB	Exc.	V.G.	Good	Fair	Poor
675	575	500	400	300	150

Courtesy Stoeger

Finnfire Heavy Barrel

Same as above but fitted with a heavy barrel.

Courtesy Stoeger

NIB	Exc.	V.G.	Good	Fair	Poor
725	650	550	450	325	150

Hunter

This model is offered in three action lengths; short, medium, and long. In the short action the calibers available are .17 Rem., .222, .223 in 21.25" barrel. In medium action the calibers are: .22-250, .243, .308, and 7mm-08 in 21.75" barrel. The long action calibers are: .25-06, .270 Win., .280 Rem., .30-06 22" barrel length. In 24" barrel the long action calibers are: 7mm Rem. Mag., .300 Win. and .300 Wby. Mag., .338 and .375 Win. Mag., and .416 Rem. Mag. In 1996 the .270 Wthby Mag., 7mm Wthby Mag., and the .340 Wthby was added to the long action calibers. Available in left-handed version for all but short action calibers. Adjustable trigger is standard. Checkered European walnut stock. Weight for short action is 6.25 lbs., for medium action 6.5 lbs., and long action calibers 7.75 to 8.25 depending on caliber.

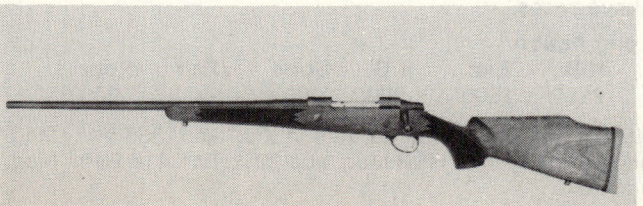

Medium Action

NIB	Exc.	V.G.	Good	Fair	Poor
795	600	500	400	300	200

Short Action

Add 10% for .222 Rem. and .223 Rem. For .17 Rem. add 20% to above prices.

Long Action

NIB	Exc.	V.G.	Good	Fair	Poor
795	600	500	400	300	200

NOTE: For long action calibers in .300 and .338 Win. Mag. add 10%. For .375 H&H Mag. add 20%. For .416 Rem. Mag. add 25%.

Carbine

As above, with an 18.5" barrel. Produced with either a medium or long-length action.

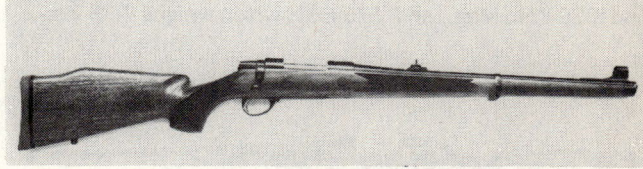

NIB	Exc.	V.G.	Good	Fair	Poor
795	600	500	400	300	200

Long Range Hunting Rifle

Similar to the long action Hunter but fitted with a 26" fluted barrel. chambered for the .25-06, .270 Win., 7mm Rem. Mag., and .300 Win. Mag. Introduced in 1996.

NIB	Exc.	V.G.	Good	Fair	Poor
1250	1000	—	—	—	—

FiberClass

This model features a black plain fiberglass stock. Offered in long action calibers only. The .25-06, .270, .280, and .30-06 are fitted with 22" barrels and weigh 7.25 lbs. The 7mm Rem. Mag., .300 Win. Mag., .338 Win. Mag., and .375 H&H are fitted with 24" barrel and weighs 7.25 lbs. The .416 Rem. Mag. has a 24" barrel and weighs 8 lbs.

NIB	Exc.	V.G.	Good	Fair	Poor
1050	800	600	500	300	200

NOTE: For long action calibers in .300 and .338 Win. Mag. add 10%. For .375 H&H Mag. add 20%. For .416 Rem. Mag. add 25%.

FiberClass Carbine

As above, with a fiberglass stock.

NIB	Exc.	V.G.	Good	Fair	Poor
1050	800	600	500	300	200

Carbine

This model features a Mannlicher-style stock with a two-piece forearm. It has a checkered walnut stock with oil finish. It is offered in both medium and short actions, all with 18.5" barrels. In medium action the .243 and .308 are available and weigh 6 lbs. The long action calibers are: .270, and .30-06 weighing 7.25 lbs.; and the .338 Win. Mag. and .375 H&H weighing 7.75 lbs.

Medium Action

NIB	Exc.	V.G.	Good	Fair	Poor
900	700	500	400	300	200

Long Action

NIB	Exc.	V.G.	Good	Fair	Poor
900	700	500	400	300	200

NOTE: For long action calibers in .338 Win. Mag. add 10%. For .375 H&H Mag. add 20%.

Laminated Model

This model features a laminated checkered hardwood stock made up of 36 layers. Solid recoil pad is standard as are quick detachable sling swivels. Available in both medium and long action calibers. Medium action calibers are: .22-250, .243, .308, and 7mm-08 with 21.75" barrel and weigh 6.5 lbs. Long action calibers are: .25-06, .270, .280, .30-06 with 22" barrel weighing 7.75 lbs. Offered with 24" barrels are: 7mm Rem. Mag., .300 and .338 Win. Mag., and .375 H&H which weighs 7.75 lbs.

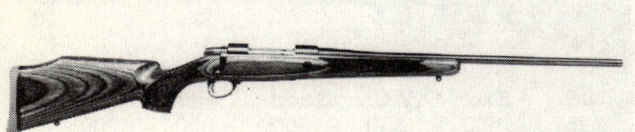

Medium Action

NIB	Exc.	V.G.	Good	Fair	Poor
950	750	600	500	300	200

Long Action

NIB	Exc.	V.G.	Good	Fair	Poor
950	750	600	500	300	200

NOTE: For long action calibers in .300 and .338 Win. Mag. add 10%. For .375 H&H Mag. add 20%. For .416 Rem. Mag. add 25%.

Varmint-Heavy Barrel

The checkered walnut stock on this model features an extra wide beavertail forearm with oil finish. Offered in both short and medium action all are fitted with a 23" heavy barrel weighing 8.5 lbs. Short action calibers are .17 Rem., .222, and .223. Medium action calibers are: .22-250, .243, 308, and 7mm-08.

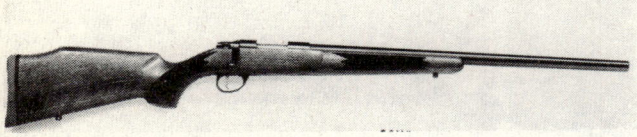

Short Action

NIB	Exc.	V.G.	Good	Fair	Poor
875	700	500	400	300	200

NOTE: Add 10% for .222 and .223 Rem. Add 20% for .15 Rem. to above prices.

Medium Action

NIB	Exc.	V.G.	Good	Fair	Poor
875	700	500	400	300	200

PPC Bench Rest/Varmint

Similar to the Varmint but single shot. Fitted with 23.75" barrel and weighs 8.75 lbs. Available in short action special calibers .22 PPC and 6mm PPC.

NIB	Exc.	V.G.	Good	Fair	Poor
1050	800	600	400	300	200

Classic-Grade

Hand checkered select grade walnut stock with matte lacquer finish are featured on this grade. Offered in medium and long ac-

tion. Long action rifles are offered in left-hand model. The medium action caliber is .243 Win. with a 21.75" barrel weighing 6 lbs. The long action calibers are: .270, .30-06, and 7mm Rem. Mag. with 24" barrels. Long action calibers weighs about 7.5 lbs.

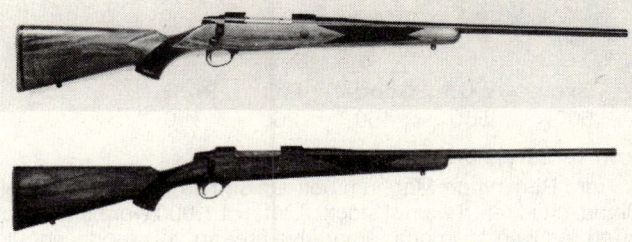

NIB	Exc.	V.G.	Good	Fair	Poor
750	600	500	400	300	200

Deluxe Grade

This grade features a high grade European walnut stock with hand cut basket weave checkering. The forend tip and grip are fitted with rosewood. English style recoil pad is standard. Long action models are offered in left-hand configuration. As with the Hunter model short, medium, and long action are available in the same calibers, barrel lengths and weights as the Hunter.

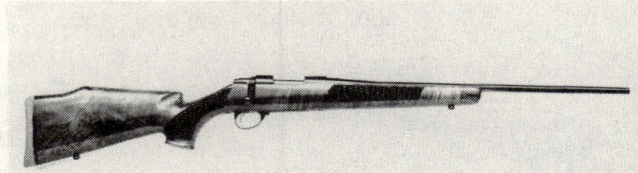

Medium Action

NIB	Exc.	V.G.	Good	Fair	Poor
1100	900	650	500	300	200

Short Action

Add 10% for .222 and .223 Rem. Add 20% for .17 Rem. to above prices.

Long Action

NIB	Exc.	V.G.	Good	Fair	Poor
1100	900	650	500	300	200

NOTE: For long action calibers in .300 and .338 Win. Mag. add 10%. For .375 H&H Mag. add 20%. For .416 Rem. Mag. add 25%. For left hand models add $100.

Super Grade/Super Deluxe

Similar to Deluxe Grade but offered with fancy walnut stock with oak-leaf carving. Floor plate and trigger guard are engraved. Pistol grip cap has inlaid silver plate. Offered in same actions and calibers as Hunter and Deluxe Grades.

Medium Action

NIB	Exc.	V.G.	Good	Fair	Poor
2250	1500	900	600	400	200

Short Action

Add 10% for .222 and .223 Rem. Add 20% for .17 Rem. to above prices.

Long Action

NIB	Exc.	V.G.	Good	Fair	Poor
2250	1500	900	600	400	200

NOTE: For long action calibers in .300 and .338 Win. Mag. add 10%. For .375 H&H Mag. add 20%. For .416 Rem. Mag. add 25%.

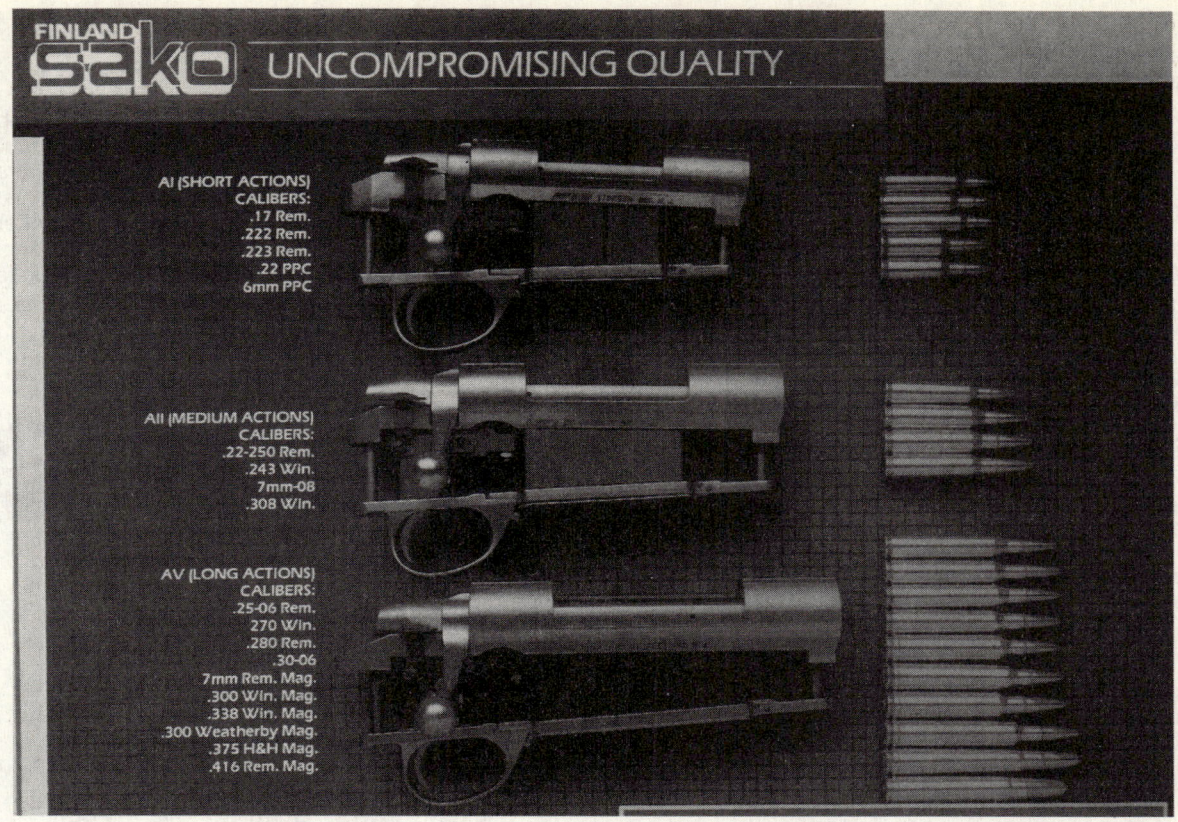

Safari Grade

As above, chambered for .300 Winchester Magnum, .338 Winchester Magnum, or .375 Holland & Holland cartridges.

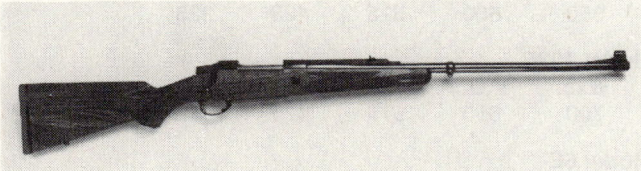

NIB	Exc.	V.G.	Good	Fair	Poor
2250	1500	900	600	400	200

Model 78

A .22 or .22 Hornet bolt-action rifle with a 22" barrel. Blued with a checkered walnut stock. Discontinued in 1986.

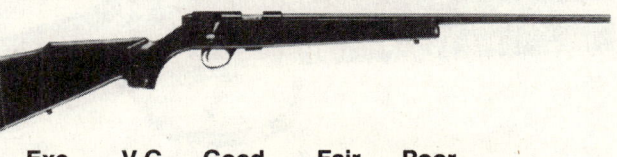

Exc.	V.G.	Good	Fair	Poor
500	450	400	300	200

Model 2700

A .270 to .300 Winchester Magnum bolt-action rifle with a 22" barrel. Blued, checkered walnut stock. Discontinued in 1985.

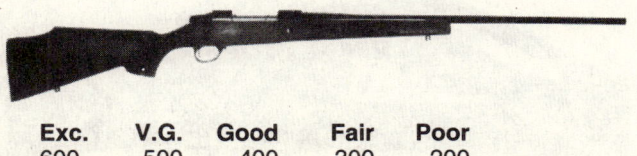

Exc.	V.G.	Good	Fair	Poor
600	500	400	300	200

TRG-S

This model features a unique cold forged receiver. The stock is a special reinforced polyurethane Monte Carlo without checkering. The recoil pad has spacer for adjustable length of pull. The trigger is adjustable and the detachable magazine holds 5 rounds. Offered in a variety of calibers from .243 to .375 H&H. Non Magnum calibers are fitted with a 22" barrel and weighs 7.75 lbs. and Magnum calibers are fitted with a 24" barrel and also weighs 7.75 lbs. In 1996 the .270 Wthby Mag., 7mm Wthby Mag., and the .340 Wthby Mag. as well as the 6.5x55S was added.

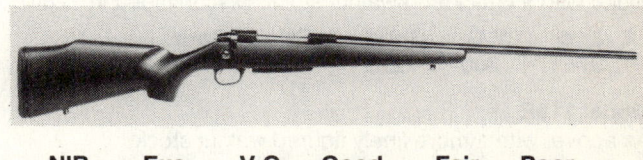

NIB	Exc.	V.G.	Good	Fair	Poor
595	500	400	300	200	100

TRG-21

The receiver is similar to the TRG-S but the polyurethane stock features a unique design. The trigger is adjustable for length and two-stage pull and also for horizontal or vertical pitch. This model also has several options that would affect the price; muzzle brake, one-piece scope mount, bipod, quick detachable sling swivels, and military nylon sling. The rifle is offered in .308 Win. only. It is fitted with a 25.75" barrel and weighs 10.5 lbs.

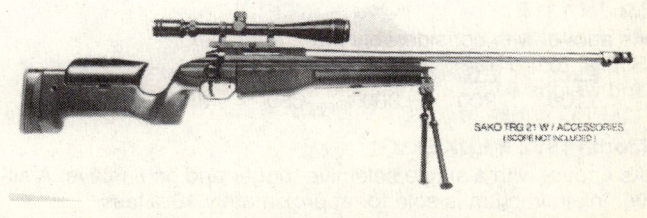

SAKO TRG 21 W / ACCESSORIES
(SCOPE NOT INCLUDED)

NIB	Exc.	V.G.	Good	Fair	Poor
3850	3200	2250	1250	700	400

TRG-41

Exactly the same as the TRG-21 except chambered for the .338 Lapua Magnum cartridge.

NIB	Exc.	V.G.	Good	Fair	Poor
4350	3750	2750	1500	950	500

SAM, INC.
Reston, Virginia
Special Service Arms Mfg., Inc.

Model 88 Crossfire

A semiautomatic combination 12 gauge .308 caliber shotgun/rifle, with a 7-shot shotgun magazine and 20-shot rifle magazine. Barrel length 20", matte black finished with a composition stock. This weapon can be fired in either mode by means of a selector switch mounted on the receiver.

SAMCO GLOBAL ARMS, INC.
Miami, Florida

This firm imports a variety of military surplus firearms that under current law are marked with the importer's name.

SARASQUETA, FELIX
Eibar, Spain
Importer - SAE, Inc.Miami, Florida

Merke

A 12 gauge Over/Under double-barrel shotgun with 22" or 27" ribbed and separated barrels, non-selective trigger and manual extractors. Blued, checkered walnut stock. Imported in 1986 only.

Exc.	V.G.	Good	Fair	Poor
275	225	200	150	100

SARASQUETA, J. J.
Eibar, Spain
Importer - American Arms, Inc.
Overland Park, Kansas

Model 107E

A 12, 16, or 20 gauge boxlock double-barrel shotgun with a variety of barrel lengths, double triggers and automatic ejectors. Blued with a checkered walnut stock. Discontinued in 1984.

Exc.	V.G.	Good	Fair	Poor
375	300	275	225	100

Model 119E

As above, with a more finely figured walnut stock.

Exc.	V.G.	Good	Fair	Poor
475	400	375	325	150

Model 130E

As above, but engraved.

Exc.	V.G.	Good	Fair	Poor
800	700	600	450	250

Model 131E

As above, with considerably more engraving.

Exc.	V.G.	Good	Fair	Poor
1100	900	800	650	350

Model 1882 E LUXE

As above, with a single selective trigger and gold inlays. A silver inlaid version is sold for approximately 10% less.

Exc.	V.G.	Good	Fair	Poor
800	700	600	450	250

SARASQUETA, VICTOR
Eibar, Spain

Model 3

A 12, 16, or 20 gauge boxlock or sidelock double-barrel shotgun available in a variety of barrel lengths, with double triggers and automatic ejectors. Blued with a checkered straight stock. The sidelock version is worth approximately 20% more than the values listed below. The basic Model 3 was offered in a variety of grades featuring different amounts of engraving and better quality wood. These shotguns are listed under the model designations of 4 to 12E below.

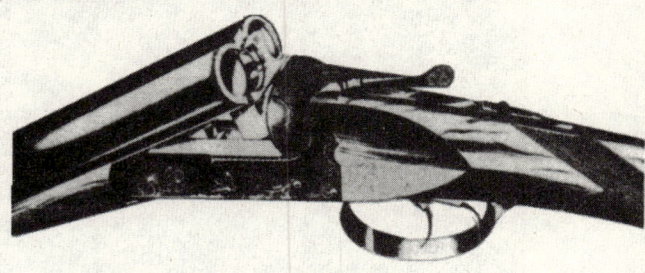

Exc.	V.G.	Good	Fair	Poor
600	500	450	350	300

Model 4

Exc.	V.G.	Good	Fair	Poor
600	550	475	400	300

Model 4E (Auto-ejectors)

Exc.	V.G.	Good	Fair	Poor
675	625	550	450	350

Model 203

Exc.	V.G.	Good	Fair	Poor
650	600	525	425	325

Model 203E

Exc.	V.G.	Good	Fair	Poor
700	650	575	475	375

Model 6E

Exc.	V.G.	Good	Fair	Poor
800	750	625	525	425

Model 7E

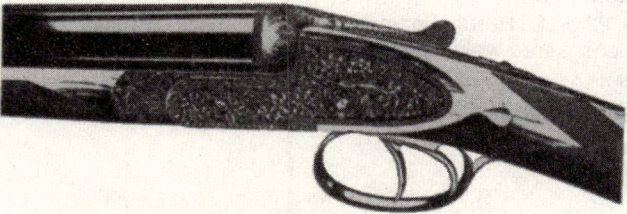

Exc.	V.G.	Good	Fair	Poor
850	800	675	575	475

Model 10E

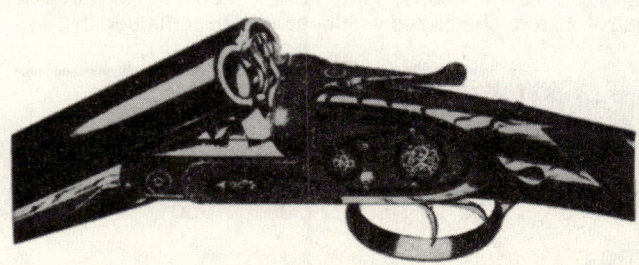

Exc.	V.G.	Good	Fair	Poor
1750	1500	1250	950	750

Model 11E

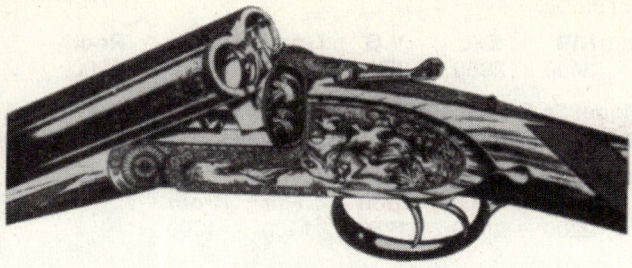

Exc.	V.G.	Good	Fair	Poor
1850	1600	1350	1150	850

Model 12E

Exc.	V.G.	Good	Fair	Poor
2200	1850	1500	1300	1000

SARDIUS
Israel
Importer - Armscorp of America, Inc.

SD-9

A 9mm double-action semiautomatic pistol with a 3" barrel and 6-shot magazine. Matte black finish with composition grips. Imported since 1988.

NIB	Exc.	V.G.	Good	Fair	Poor
350	300	250	200	150	100

SAUER, J. P. & SON
Suhl and Eckernfoerde, German

This is the oldest firearms manufacturing firm in Germany. It was founded in 1751 in Suhl. During this period the company produced high quality handguns and long guns. In 1938 it introduced a new double action semiautomatic pistol, the Sauer 38H. This pistol had the first decocking lever ever used on a mass produced pistol. In 1951 the company relocated to Eckernfoerde where it continued to produced high quality forearms.

NOTE: The Model 90 Supreme and Model 202 are currently imported by Sigarms Inc.

Bolt Action Rifle

A Mauser action sporting rifle chambered for a variety of cartridges with either a 22" or 24" barrel having a raised rib. Double set triggers, express sights, blued with a checkered walnut stock. Manufactured prior to WWII.

Exc.	V.G.	Good	Fair	Poor
700	600	500	400	300

Model 200

A bolt-action rifle chambered for a variety of cartridges with short or medium length actions, 24" barrels, set trigger, 4-round magazine. Blued, checkered walnut stock. Discontinued 1987.
Extra barrels-Add $235.

NIB	Exc.	V.G.	Good	Fair	Poor
850	650	550	500	425	350

Model 200 Lightweight

As above, with an alloy receiver. Discontinued in 1987.

Exc.	V.G.	Good	Fair	Poor
600	500	400	325	250

Model 200 Lux

As above, with a finely figured walnut stock, rosewood pistol grip cap and forend tip, gold plated trigger and a machine jewelled bolt. Imported prior to 1988.

Exc.	V.G.	Good	Fair	Poor
700	600	550	475	400

Model 200 Carbon Fiber

The Model 200 fitted with a carbon composition stock. Imported in 1987 and 1988.

Exc.	V.G.	Good	Fair	Poor
800	750	650	500	400

Model 202 Supreme

This is a bolt action rifle with a takedown feature. It is fitted with an adjustable two stage trigger, quick change barrel, black rubber recoil pad, and removable box magazine. The stock is select American claro walnut with high gloss finish and rosewood foreand and grip cap. Butt stock has a Monte Carlo comb and cheekpiece. It is offered in .243, .270, .308, and .30-06. Barrel length for these calibers is 23.6". Weight for these calibers is about 7.7 lbs. In the Supreme Magnum series it is available in 7mm magnum, .300 Win. Mag., and .375 H&H mag. Barrel for these magnum calibers is 26". Weight for these caliber is 8.4 lbs.

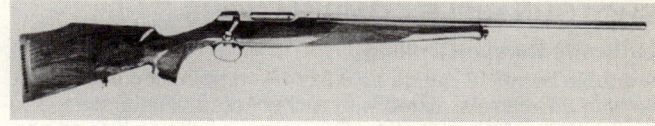

NIB	Exc.	V.G.	Good	Fair	Poor
950	800	750	—	—	—

Model 90

A bolt-action rifle produced in a number of calibers in all action lengths with 23" or 26" barrels, with a detachable magazine. Blued with a checkered walnut stock.

Exc.	V.G.	Good	Fair	Poor
800	700	600	450	400

Model 90 Stutzen

As above, with a full-length Mannlicher-style stock. Imported prior to 1990.

Exc.	V.G.	Good	Fair	Poor
825	725	625	475	425

Model 90 Safari

The Model 90 made for use with the .458 Winchester Magnum cartridge and fitted with a 24" barrel. Imported from 1986 to 1988.

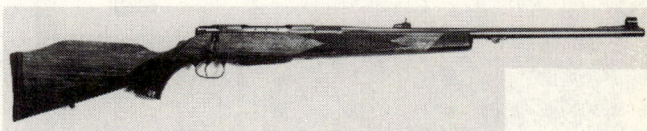

Exc.	V.G.	Good	Fair	Poor
1250	1100	950	750	600

The Model 90 Series of bolt-action rifles was available in a deluxe version that differed with the grade of workmanship and materials utilized. This deluxe series would be worth approximately 60% additional. There were optional engraved models; these should be individually appraised.

Model 90 Supreme

Similar to the above, with a gold-plated trigger, machine jewelled bolt and finely figured checkered walnut stock. Introduced in 1987.

NIB	Exc.	V.G.	Good	Fair	Poor
1500	1250	1100	950	750	650

SSG-3000

This is a semiautomatic rifle chambered for the .308 Win. cartridge. Barrel length is 24.4". It is designed for law enforcement agencies, the military, and special units. Adjustable trigger with adjustable stock. Weight is approximately 12 lbs. A Hensoldt telescope sight is standard.

NIB	Exc.	V.G.	Good	Fair	Poor
8800	8000	—	—	—	—

SG 550 Sniper

This semiautomatic rifle is chambered for the .223 cartridge. Barrel length is 24.5". Trigger and butt stock are adjustable. Comes with a 20/30 round magazine in a fitted case with accessories. Weight is approximately 15 lbs.

NIB	Exc.	V.G.	Good	Fair	Poor
14200	12500	10700	—	—	—

SHOTGUN/RIFLE COMBINATIONS

Luftwaffe Survival Drilling

A double barrel 12 gauge by 9.3x74R combination shotgun/rifle with 28" barrels. Blued with a checkered walnut stock and marked with Nazi inspection. Stampings on the stock and barrel breech. Normally, furnished with an aluminum case.

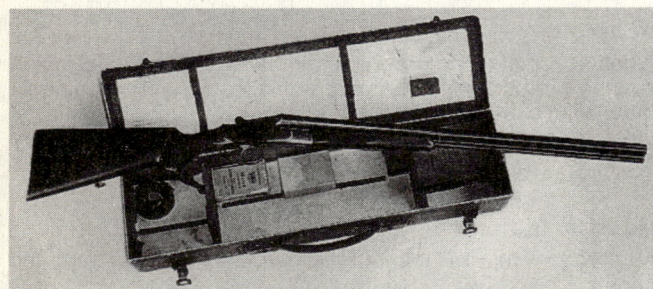

Courtesy Richard. M. Kumor, Sr.

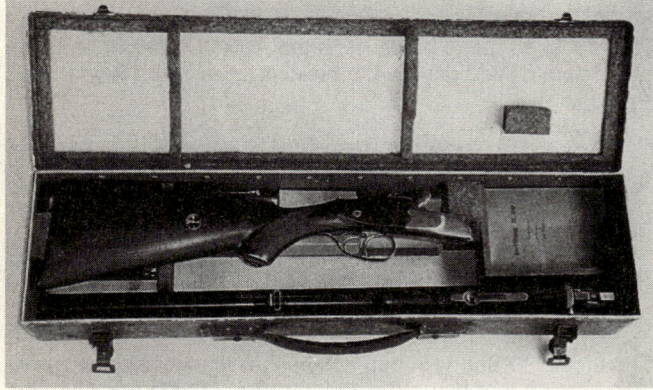

Courtesy Richard M. Kumor, Sr.

Exc.	V.G.	Good	Fair	Poor
5000	4000	3500	2500	200

Model 3000 Drilling

This model was chambered for a variety of gauges and calibers and is built upon a boxlock action having a Greener crossbolt. The action lightly engraved. Blued, checkered walnut stock.

NIB	Exc.	V.G.	Good	Fair	Poor
3400	2900	2500	2000	1500	1250

Model 54 Combo

A combination rifle/shotgun chambered for a variety of gauges and calibers with an action as above. Discontinued in 1986.

Exc.	V.G.	Good	Fair	Poor
2200	2000	1750	1400	1200

SHOTGUNS

Model 60

A 12, 16 or 20 gauge double-barrel boxlock shotgun produced in a variety of barrel lengths with double triggers and manual extractors. Blued with checkered walnut stock. Produced prior to WWII.

Exc.	V.G.	Good	Fair	Poor
700	625	550	400	300

Royal Model

A 12 or 20 gauge boxlock double-barrel shotgun with 26", 28", or 30" barrels, single selective triggers with automatic ejectors. The frame is scalloped, blued with a checkered walnut stock. Manufactured from 1955 to 1977.

Exc.	V.G.	Good	Fair	Poor
1500	1250	1000	750	500

Grade I Artemis

A 12 gauge sidelock double-barrel shotgun with 28" barrels, single selective trigger and automatic ejector. Engraved, blued with checkered walnut stock. Manufactured from 1966 to 1977.

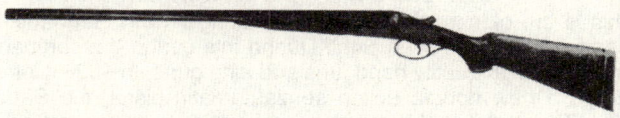

Exc.	V.G.	Good	Fair	Poor
5000	4250	3500	2500	2000

Grade II Artemis

As above, but more finely finished.

Exc.	V.G.	Good	Fair	Poor
6500	5750	4750	3500	3000

Model 66

A 12 gauge sidelock double-barrel shotgun having a 26", 28", or 30" barrel, single selective trigger and automatic ejectors. Blued, checkered walnut stock. This model was produced in three different grades that have different degrees of engraving. Produced from 1966 to 1975.

Grade I

Exc.	V.G.	Good	Fair	Poor
2000	1800	1500	1150	800

Grade II

Exc.	V.G.	Good	Fair	Poor
3000	2800	2500	2150	1800

Grade III

Exc.	V.G.	Good	Fair	Poor
3750	3500	2850	2500	2000

PISTOLS

Written and compiled by Jim Cate.

Roth-Sauer Model

The very first automatic pistol produced by J.P. Sauer & Sohn but not designed by this firm. It is available only in 7.65 Roth-Sauer caliber. It is a locked breech design, beautifully finished and extremely well made. Later this design was modified and became the Roth-Steyr military pistol which was adopted by Austria in 1907. A difficult to find pistol.

Exc.	V.G.	Good	Fair	Poor
1350	1100	700	450	300

Sauer Model 1913

First Series, which incorporates an extra safety button on the left side of the frame near the trigger and the rear sight is simply a milled recess in the cocking knob itself. The serial number range runs from 1 to approximately 4750 and this first series is found only in 7.65mm caliber. All were for commercial sales as far as can be determined. Some were tested by various militaries, no doubt.

A. European variation---all slide legends are in the German language

B. English Export variation---slide legends are marked, J.P. Sauer & Son, Suhl - Prussia, "Sauer's Patent" Pat'd May 20 1912

Both were sold in thick paper cartons or boxes with the color being a reddish purple with gold colored letters, etc. Examples of the very early European variation are found with the English language brochure or manual as well as an extra magazine, cleaning brush and grease container. These were shipped to England or the U.S. prior to Sauer producing the English Export variation.

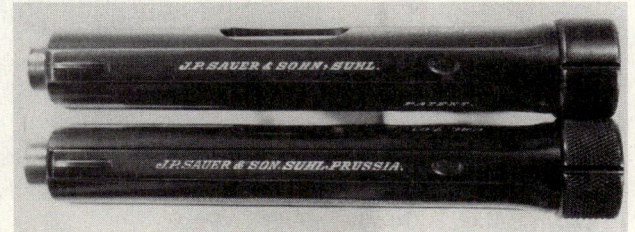

A. European variation:

Exc.	V.G.	Good	Fair	Poor
1100	900	650	400	250

B. English Export variation:

Exc.	V.G.	Good	Fair	Poor
1450	1150	800	500	300

Original box with accessories and manual: Add $500 if complete and in excellent to very good condition.

Second Series, extra safety button eliminated, rear sight acts as cocking knob retainer.

A. Commercial variation

Normal European/German slide markings. Found in 7.65mm and 6.35 (.32 and .25 acp) calibers. There are no reported examples of the English Export variation pistols in the second series. Any reference to an English Export second series Model 1913 is due to the original box and manual being printed in English rather than German. Some are noted in Spanish also.

Caliber 7.65mm variation

Exc.	V.G.	Good	Fair	Poor
450	375	300	250	100

Caliber 6.35mm variation

This particular pistol must be divided into three (3) subvariations.

This variation appears to be in a serial number range of its own. The first subvariation appears to run from 1 to 40,000. It is highly doubtful if this quantity was manufactured. The second subvariation incorporates a Zusatzsicherung or Additional Safety which can be seen between the normal safety lever and the top of the left grip. It locked the trigger bar when in use. This second range appears to run from approximately serial number 40,000 to 51,000 which probably was continuous in the number produced. Lastly, the third subvariation examples were manufactured during or after 1926. The trigger guard has a different shape; the slide has a greater area of vertical milled finger grooves; the added Additional safety (Zusatzsicherung) now acts as the hold open device as well. These are found up to approximately 57,000. Then a few examples of the first subvariation are found from 57,000 up to about 62,500. This was, no doubt, usage of remaining parts.

Caliber 6.35mm first subvariation:

Exc.	V.G.	Good	Fair	Poor
350	300	250	150	75

Caliber 6.35mm second subvariation:

Exc.	V.G.	Good	Fair	Poor
350	300	250	150	75

Caliber 6.35mm third subvariation:

Exc.	V.G.	Good	Fair	Poor
450	375	300	200	100

Please note that any commercial pistol could be special ordered with a factory nickel finish, special grip material (Pearl, wood, etc.) as well as different types of engraving. It would be in your best interest to have these pistols examined by an expert.

B. Police variations

These will be of the standard German Commercial configuration but nearly always having the Zusatzsicherung (additional safety) added to the pistol. This safety is found between the regular safety lever and the top of the left grip. Police used both calibers, 7.65mm and 6.35mm but the 7.65 was predominant. After the early part of the 1930s the 6.35 was not available to police departments. Thus the 6.35mm police marked Sauer is rather scarce in relation to the 7.65mm caliber. A few in 7.65mm are dated 1920 on the left side of the frame and were used by auxiliary policemen in Bavaria. Normal police property markings are on the front or rear gripstraps. Most were originally issued with at least two magazines and a police accepted holster. The mags were usually numbered and the holsters are found with and without pistol numbers.

Caliber 6.35mm police marked but without Zusatzsicherung

Exc.	V.G.	Good	Fair	Poor
400	350	275	200	75

Caliber 6.35mm police marked with Zusatzsicherung

Exc.	V.G.	Good	Fair	Poor
450	375	275	200	75

Caliber 7.65mm police marked without Zusatzsicherung

Exc.	V.G.	Good	Fair	Poor
375	325	275	175	125

Caliber 7.65mm police marked with Zusatzsicherung

Exc.	V.G.	Good	Fair	Poor
400	350	275	175	125

NOTE: Add 10% for one correctly numbered magazine, or 20% if found with both correctly numbered magazines. Add 30% if found with correct holster and magazines.

C. R.F.V. (Reich Finanz Verwaltung)

This Sauer variation is rarely found in any condition. The R.F.V. markings and property number could be 1 to 4 digits. This variation is found in both calibers and were used by the Reich's Customs and Finance department personnel.

Caliber 6.35mm R.F.V. marked pistols

Exc.	V.G.	Good	Fair	Poor
800	650	500	350	250

Caliber 7.65mm R.F.V. marked pistols

Exc.	V.G.	Good	Fair	Poor
750	600	400	300	200

D. Imperial Military variations

These were normal German commercial variations of the time period having either the Imperial Eagle acceptance marking applied on the front of the triggerguard and having the small Imperial Army inspector's acceptance marking (crown over a scriptic letter) on the right side of the frame close to the Nitro proof; or having just the Imperial Army inspector's marking alone. Usually these pistols are found in the 40,000 to 85,000 range. However, the quantity actually Imperial Military accepted is quite low even though thousands were privately purchased by the officer corps. There are examples in 6.35mm which are Imperial Military accepted but these are very scarce.

Caliber 7.65mm Imperial Military accepted pistols

Exc.	V.G.	Good	Fair	Poor
550	450	350	275	150

Caliber 6.35mm Imperial Military accepted pistols

Exc.	V.G.	Good	Fair	Poor
700	500	375	300	150

E. Paramilitary marked Sauer pistols, of the 1925-35 period.

A very few of the Model 1913 pistols will have been marked by paramilitary groups or organizations of this period. Usually this marking is no more than a series of numbers above another series of numbers, such as 23 over 12. These are found usually on the left side of the frame next to the left grip. Most of these numbers are indicative of property numbers assigned to a particular pistols belonging to a particular SA Group, Stahlhelm, or a rightwing organization such as the Red Front (early communist). Any pistol of this type should be examined by an expert to determine if it is an original example.

Exc.	V.G.	Good	Fair	Poor
350	300	275	200	100

F. Norwegian police usage, post World War II

After the war was over many surplus German weapons were put back into use by the government of Norway. The Germans had occupied this country and large numbers of weapons remained when the fighting ended. This included a large number of surplus Sauer pistols being utilized by the police (POLITI) forces. Most of the Sauers that were used by the Politi which have been imported into the U.S. have been the Model 1913; however there were a number of the Model 1930 pistols which reached our country as well. All examples, regardless of the model, have the word POLITI stamped on the slide as well as a rampant lion on a shield under a crown marking. Following this is the property number and this number is also stamped into the left side of the frame. Most saw much usage during the postwar period. All are in 7.65mm caliber.

Exc.	V.G.	Good	Fair	Poor
350	300	200	15	100

1926 EXPORT MODEL

This variation's name comes from actual Sauer factory records found in the Suhl Archive. It is an interim pistol produced during the 1926 to early 1929 period. It is found only in the 7.65mm caliber. This was an advancement of the normal 1913 design which included changes in (1) the safety lever's design that became a slide hold open device as well, (2) shape of the frame was altered in that the trigger guard became more streamlined and the rear of the frame was shortened, and serrations were added to the slide as well as the cocking knob. These are found in the 162,000 to 169,000 range in relatively small clusters. Two to four thousand are presumed to have been manufactured. A scarce Sauer pistol! To date, none have been seen in nickel.

Exc.	V.G.	Good	Fair	Poor
750	625	475	300	150

W.T.M.- Westentaschen Model-Vest Pocket Model

Several variations of vest pocket pistols were manufactured. The first was called a Model 1920 by the Sauer firm. We usually refer to it as the Model 1924. This pistol, as well as all other W.T.M. examples, were designed to carry in "your pocket." They are quite small in size and are found only in the 6.35mm or .25acp caliber. Later on in 1928 an updated version became available and was referred to a the Model 1928. These differed in internal parts design, slide configuration and the bottom of the grip was marked, Cal.6.35.28. The last version appeared in 1933 and still utilized the same grips but the trigger and some other small parts differed. All three were available in blue or nickel finish, as well as engraving and fancy grip material. A very few of the Model 1933 had stainless steel (NIROSTA marked) barrels.

Model 1920: Having serrations on the front and rear of the slide

Exc.	V.G.	Good	Fair	Poor
550	450	300	200	75

Model 1928: Having Cal. 6.35.28 on the black bakelite grips

Exc.	V.G.	Good	Fair	Poor
450	400	275	185	75

Model 1933: Having a different type of trigger and found in the 252,000 to 253,000 serial number range

Exc.	V.G.	Good	Fair	Poor
700	575	400	275	150

NOTE: Add $200 for factory nickel, $250 for factory engraving, $250 for exotic grip material, $500 for factory paper box with cleaning brush, extra magazine and brochure, $750 in original

factory imitation leather covered metal presentation case with accessories, $500 for NIROSTA marked stainless barrel.

Model 1930 variations

A. Dutch models: These different types of Dutch pistols will have JOH MUNTS - AMSTERDAM on the left side of the slide. The grips are usually a mottled grey color. Sauer manufactured different pistols for the Dutch police, Navy, Army, Department of Finance,

S.M.N. (Steam Ships Netherlands) and possibly other agencies.

1. Police--manufactured w/o adjustable front sight and w/o lanyard loop.

Exc.	V.G.	Good	Fair	Poor
575	450	350	250	125

2. Navy-made without adjustable sight, but with lanyard loop, and having the Anchor & Crown marked on the rear gripstrap.

Exc.	V.G.	Good	Fair	Poor
600	500	375	250	125

3. S.M.N.--found with and w/o adjustable front sights, no lanyard loop, S.M.N. marked horizontally near bottom of rear gripstrap

Exc.	V.G.	Good	Fair	Poor
600	475	375	225	100

4. Department of Finance--found with and w/o adjustable front sight, no lanyard loop, DF over date-1933-on rear gripstrap

Exc.	V.G.	Good	Fair	Poor
650	500	385	250	150

Accessories: cleaning rod, brush, aluminum oil bottle and manuals Add accordingly

B. 1930 Commercial Model

These pistols were for sale in Germany and other countries through normal commercial outlets. A very few are factory nickeled, engraved or both; some are with the NIROSTA marked barrels and a very few were made in Duralumin or Dural. The standard caliber was 7.65mm hut a very limited number were made in .22 Long Rifle (.22 lang). Standard grip material is the black bakelite material. Most of the regular pistols were purchased by military officers, some went to paramilitary group, such as the SA.

1. Standard Commercial

Exc.	V.G.	Good	Fair	Poor
600	450	300	200	125

2. Standard Commercial with NIROSTA marked barrel, 7.65mm

Exc.	V.G.	Good	Fair	Poor
700	500	350	275	150

3. Standard Commercial in .22 long rifle (.22 lang)

Exc.	V.G.	Good	Fair	Poor
1000	800	550	375	300

4. Duralumin (rural) Variation, 7.65mm

Exc.	V.G.	Good	Fair	Poor
3500	2750	2000	1200	450

For any variation above: Add: Nickel finish $100; with engraving $250; both nickel and engraving $350; with nickel, engraving, and with a fancy grip material (pearl or ebony, etc.) $500

Behorden Model

The Behorden (Authority) Model is different from the Model 1930 in that it has a trigger safety and a loaded indicator provided.

A. Behorden Commercial

These are normally found with a high polished blued finish. It was available with a nickel finish, engraving, or both, as well as fancy grip material and a NIROSTA marked barrel. The regular caliber is 7.65mm, but a very few are know in .22 L.R.

Exc.	V.G.	Good	Fair	Poor
675	550	409	350	200

NOTE: Add $100 for Nickel finish, $250 for engraving, $350 for both, $500 with nickel, engraving, and a fancy grip material; $250 for NIROSTA marked stainless barrel. Add 100% for .22 caliber

B. Late Behorden Commercial
These are actually Model 1930 pistols found in the 220,000 to 223,000 serial number range which do not have the trigger safety and/or the indicator pin.

Exc.	V.G.	Good	Fair	Poor
600	450	300	200	125

C. DURALUMIN MODEL (DURAL)
The frame and slide are made of the Duralumin material. These are rare pistols!

1. Blue anodized variation
Found with and w/o NIROSTA marked barrels. Add: $250 for the stainless barrel

Exc.	V.G.	Good	Fair	Poor
3850	3250	2500	1500	850

2. Non-anodized variation
Found with and w/o NIROSTA marked barrels. Add: $250 for the stainless barrel

Exc.	V.G.	Good	Fair	Poor
3850	3250	2500	1500	850

3. Presentation examples of a. and b. above--please consult an expert for pricing

D. Police Models
Examples will be found with police acceptance on the left side of the trigger guard and in a few cases on the front or rear grip straps. Black bakelite grips are standard.

1. Sunburst K police acceptance, with nonadjustable front sight (a round blade)

Exc.	V.G.	Good	Fair	Poor
600	500	350	275	200

2. Sunburst K police acceptance, with adjustable front sight

Exc.	V.G.	Good	Fair	Poor
750	625	450	300	225

3. Diamond in Sunburst police acceptance. All known are with the adjustable front sight.

Exc.	V.G.	Good	Fair	Poor
750	625	450	300	225

4. Grip strap marked variation.
(Having abbreviations of a city and the property number of the pistol on the grip strap.) Very few of these are known. Examples are S.Mg. 52, Sch. 78, etc.

Exc.	V.G.	Good	Fair	Poor
500	450	375	250	150

DUTCH (Netherlands) Model
Found with JOH. MUNTS AMSTERDAM on the left of the slide, as well as a lanyard ring at the bottom left grip, in regular blued steel. These pistols went to the Dutch military.

Exc.	V.G.	Good	Fair	Poor
675	550	400	325	200

MODEL 36/37
These very few pistols are all prototype Sauer pistols which preceeded the Model 38. They are in the 210,000 range. Please consult an expert to determine value! Extremely RARE

MODEL 38 AND 38-H (H MODEL) VARIATIONS

A. MODEL 38
This pistol started at 260,000. It is Crown N Nitro proofed, has a cocking/decocking lever, and a loaded indicator pin, and is double action. It has a high polish blue; is in 7.65m/m (the standard production pistol); is found without the thumbsafety on the slide; with a pinned mag release. VERY RARE

1. One Line Slide Legend variation (about 250 produced)

Exc.	V.G.	Good	Fair	Poor
1800	1600	1200	600	300

2. Two Line Slide Legend variation, C/N proofs, blued, with pinned magazine release. (about 850 produced) VERY RARE

Exc.	V.G.	Good	Fair	Poor
1500	1400	1000	500	275

3. Two Line Slide Legend variation, C/N proofs, blued, magazine release button retained by a screw. RARE

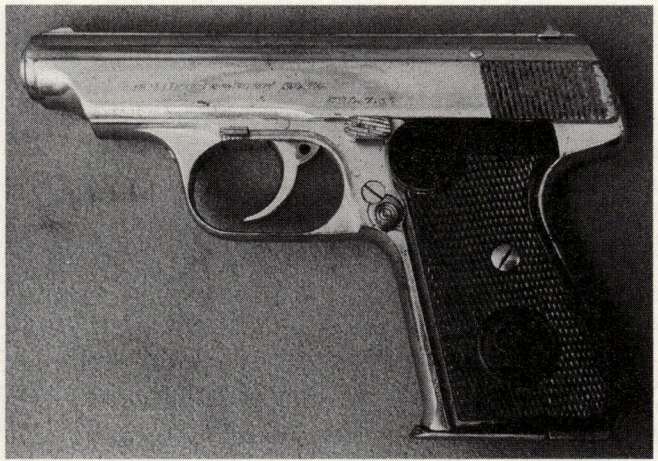

Exc.	V.G.	Good	Fair	Poor
1000	850	600	400	275

NOTE: Add $250 for factory nickel; $350 for factory chrome; $350 for engraving; $500 for NIROSTA marked barrel

4. SA der NSDAP Gruppe Thuringen marked variation blued, C/N proofs, with mag release button held by a screw. VERY RARE

Exc.	V.G.	Good	Fair	Poor
1600	1400	1000	500	275

B. MODEL 38-H or H MODEL

This model has a thumbsafety on the slide, Crown N Nitro proof-, high polish blued finish, a cocking/decocking lever, double action, and is found in 7.65m/m caliber as the standard production pistol. This model is found only with the two line slide legend or logo. Type 1, variation 2

1. Standard Commercial variation as described above:

Exc.	V.G.	Good	Fair	Poor
850	700	475	300	175

NOTE: Add $100 for factory nickel (factory chromed has not been identified); $400 for factory engraving; $250 for exotic grip material $500 for NIROSTA marked stainless barrel.

2. SA der NSDAP Gruppe Thuringia variation

Same as 1. above except having SA markings on slide, with blued finish, VERY RARE

Exc.	V.G.	Good	Fair	Poor
1100	900	650	350	200

NOTE: Add $800 for SA marked Akah holster in excellent condition

3. L.M. MODEL

(Leicht Model--lightweight model); frame and slide made of DURAL (Duralumin), in the 264800 range, with thumbsafety, and regular black bakelite grips. EXTREMELY RARE

Exc.	V.G.	Good	Fair	Poor
3850	3250	2500	1500	850

4. Police accepted variation; found with Police Eagle C acceptance on left trigger guard and having Crown N proofs. RARE

Exc.	V.G.	Good	Fair	Poor
850	700	500	300	175

TYPE TWO MODEL 38-H (H MODEL)

There are no Model 38 pistols in the Type Two description, only the H Model with thumbsafety. These begin at serial number 269,100 and have the Eagle N Nitro proofs, with a blued high polish finish and black bakelite grips. The normal caliber is 7.65m/m.

A. H Model

1. Standard Commercial

Exc.	V.G.	Good	Fair	Poor
750	550	475	300	200

NOTE: dd $1500 for boxed examples complete with factory manual, clean ring rod, all accessories, extra magazine, etc. $250 for factory nickel, $350 for factory chrome, $350 for factory engraving

2. .22 Caliber variation, found in 269,900 range.

Slide and magazines are marked CAL. .22 LANG. (Some with steel frame and slides; some with Dural frames and slides). Very Rare

Exc.	V.G.	Good	Fair	Poor
1800	1450	850	400	250

3. Jager Model

Aspecial order pistol in .22 Caliber which is similar in appearance to Walther's 1936 Jagerschafts pistol. Very Rare, and watch for fakes.

Exc.	V.G.	Good	Fair	Poor
2000	1650	1200	600	250

4. Police Eagle C and Eagle F acceptance variations.

These are the first Eagle N (post April 1940) police accepted pistols are found in the 270,000 to 276,000 ranges. (Add: 25% for E/F)

Exc.	V.G.	Good	Fair	Poor
650	500	400	325	200

5. German Military variation.

This is the first official military accepted range of 2000 pistols. It is considered a TEST range found in the 271000 to 273000 serial range. Two Eagle 37 military acceptance marks are found on the trigger guard.

Exc.	V.G.	Good	Fair	Poor
1200	900	675	475	300

6. Second Military variation.

These pistols are found with the high polish finish but have only one Eagle 37 acceptance marks. The letter H is found on all small parts.

Exc.	V.G.	Good	Fair	Poor
600	425	350	275	175

7. Police Eagle C acceptance.

This variation includes the remainder of the high polish blued police accepted pistols.

Exc.	V.G.	Good	Fair	Poor
575	425	350	275	175

NOTE: Add $50 for matching magazine, $200 for both matching mags and correct police holster; $300 for both matching mags and correct matching numbered, police accepted & dated holster.

TYPE THREE 38-H MODEL (H MODEL)

This terminology is used because of the change of the exterior finish of the Sauer pistols. Due to the urgency of the war, the order was received to not polish the exterior surfaces of the pistols as had been done previously. There was also a change in the formulation of the grip's material. Later in this range there will be found stamped parts, zinc triggers and magazine bottoms, etc. used to increase the pistol's production. Type Three has a full slide legend.

A. H Model

1. Military accepted with one Eagle 37 Waffen Amt mark

Exc.	V.G.	Good	Fair	Poor
500	450	350	275	150

2. Commercial, having only Eagle N Nitro proof marks

Exc.	V.G.	Good	Fair	Poor
450	400	350	25	150

NOTE: See Type Two Commercial info above, prices apply here also

3. Police accepted with the Police Eagle C acceptance

Exc.	V.G.	Good	Fair	Poor
500	425	350	250	150

NOTE: See Type Two Police info above, prices apply here also

TYPE FOUR 38-H MODEL (H MODEL)

This is a continuation of the pistol as described in Type Three except the J.P. Sauer & Sohn, Suhl legend is dropped from the slide and only CAL. 7,65 is found on the left side. The word PATENT may or may not appear on the right side. Many are found with a zinc trigger.

A. H Model

1. Military accepted with one Eagle 37 Waffen Amt mark

Exc.	V.G.	Good	Fair	Poor
500	450	350	275	150

2. Commercial, having only the Eagle N Nitro proofs

Exc.	V.G.	Good	Fair	Poor
450	400	350	250	150

NOTE: See Type Two Commercial info above, prices apply here also

3. Police accepted with the Police Eagle C acceptance

Exc.	V.G.	Good	Fair	Poor
500	450	350	275	150

NOTE: See Type Two Price info above, prices apply here also.

4. Eigentum NSDAP SA Gruppe Alpenland slide marked pistols.

These unique pistols are found in the 456000 and 457000 serial number ranges. They have thumbsafety levers on the slides.

Exc.	V.G.	Good	Fair	Poor
1850	1350	800	45	250

5. NSDAP SA Gruppe Alpenland slide marked pistols.

These unique pistols are found in the 465000 serial number range. They have thumbsafety levers on the slide.

Exc.	V.G.	Good	Fair	Poor
1900	1300	800	450	250

6. H. HIMMLER PRESENTATION PISTOLS

These desirable pistols have a high polish finish with DEM SCHARFSCHUTZEN - H. HIMMLER on the left side of the slide (with no other markings), and J.P. SAUER & SOHN over CAL.7,65 on the right side (opposite of normal). These pistols came in imitation leather cover metal cases with cloth interiors having a cleaning brush, extra magazine and cartridges.

Exc.	V.G.	Good	Fair	Poor
15,000	12,000	8500	3500	1000

B. MODEL 38

To speed up production even more, the thumbsafety (Handsicherung-Hammer safety) was eliminated. The side continues to be marked only with CAL. 7,65. The frame's serial number changes from the right side to the left side at 472000 with overlaps up to 489000.

1. Military accepted with one Eagle 37 Waffen Amt mark

Exc.	V.G.	Good	Fair	Poor
450	400	350	25	175

2. Commercial, having only the Eagle N Nitro proofs

Exc.	V.G.	Good	Fair	Poor
450	400	350	250	175

NOTE: See Type Two Commercial info above, prices apply here also.

3. Police accepted with the Police Eagle C acceptance

Exc.	V.G.	Good	Fair	Poor
575	450	400	300	200

4. Police accepted with the Police Eagle F acceptance

Exc.	V.G.	Good	Fair	Poor
475	400	350	250	175

NOTE: (3&4) See Type Two Police info above, prices apply here also

TYPE FIVE MODEL 38 & H MODEL PISTOLS

There are two different basic variations of the Type Five Sauer pistols. Either may or may not have a thumbsafety lever on the slide. The main criteria is whether the frame is factory numbered as per normal and follows the chronological sequence of those pistols in the preceding model. After the frames were used which were already numbered and finished upon the arrival of the US Army, the last variation came about. Neither variation has any Nitro proof marks.

A. First variation

Factory numbered sequential frames starting on or near serial number 506800. Slides and breech blocks may or may not match.

Exc.	V.G.	Good	Fair	Poor
475	350	275	225	100

B. Second variation.

Started with serial number 1; made from mostly rejected parts, generally have notched triggerguards, may or may not be blued, no Nitro proofs, slides may or may not have factory legends, etc. Approximately 300 assembled.

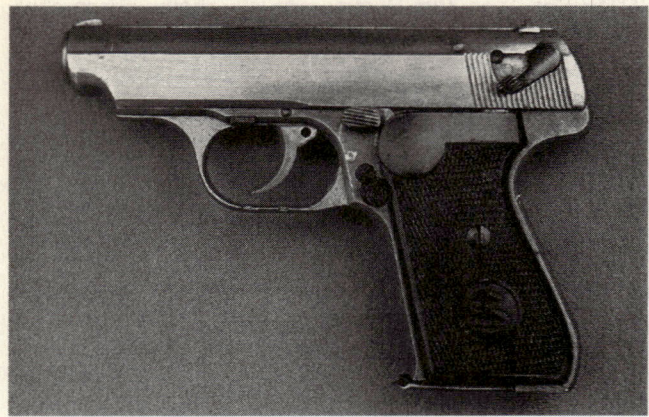

Exc.	V.G.	Good	Fair	Poor
750	500	300	200	100

NOTE: There are some pistols which have postwar Russian Crown N Nitro proofs. The Russians may have assembled a very few pistols after the US Army left this section after the war. Several have been found with newly made barrels in 7.65mm with a C/N proof.

SAVAGE ARMS CORPORATION
Utica, New York
Westfield, Massachusetts

Established in 1894 by Arthur W. Savage, this company has manufactured a wide variety of firearms of which their Model 99 is the best known. By 1915, Savage Arms was manufacturing centerfire and rimfire rifles, pistols, and ammunition. During World War I the company produced the Lewis machine guns. In 1920 Savage purchased J. Stevens Arms Company which was associated with Harry Pope, the famous barrel maker. Later in the decade the company acquired the Page Lewis Company, Davis-Warner, Crescent Firearms, and A.H. Fox. At one time Savage was the largest firearms manufacturing company in the free world. During World War II Savage/Stevens produced military small arms and machine guns. In 1947 the Sporting Arms division moved to Chicopee Falls, MA where it was incorporated into Stevens Arms Company. In 1960 the entire operation was moved to Westfield, MA.

The data on the Savage Model 1899 and 99 are provided by Doug Murry, author/publisher, and are excerpted from his book, *The Ninety-Nine: A History of the Savage Model 99 Rifle*, revised 3rd edition, and is only for the exclusive use in the *Standard Catalog of Firearms*. The pricing is provided by Murray as a reference for this publication.

Model 1895

A .303 Savage caliber lever action rifle with a 26" or 30" barrel and 5-shot magazine. Identifiable by the hole in the bolt. The barrel marked "Savage Repeating Arms Co. Utica, N.Y. U.S.A. Pat. Feb. 7, 1893, July 25, 1893. CAL. .303." Blued with a walnut stock. Approximately 8,000 were manufactured between 1895 and 1899.
22" or 30" Barrel-Add 10%.

Exc.	V.G.	Good	Fair	Poor
1500	1100	700	400	200

Model 1899-A-26" round barrel rifle

A .25-35, .30-30, .303 Savage, .32-40 or .38-55 caliber lever action rifle with 26" barrel marked "Savage Arms Company, Utica, N.Y. Pat. Feb. 7, 1893, July 25.'93, Oct.3.'99 .CAL.30." Manufactured between 1899 and 1926/27. Blued with a walnut stock. Serial number range 10000 to 300000. Block cocking indicator on bolt to s/n 90000 then changed to pin indicator on tang.

Exc.	V.G.	Good	Fair	Poor
1000	800	500	250	100

NOTE: Add 50% for .25-35, .32-40, and .38-55 calibers.

> A factory engraved Savage Model 99, caliber .303, was sold at auction for $82,500. The action was engraved with elaborate scroll and gold line work. Within the scroll are four finely executed game scenes. The stock is deluxe English walnut with five checkered panels and deep relief carving. This is one of the most elaborately engraved Model 99s known.
> Butterfield & Butterfield, December 1995.

Model 1899-A-22" barrel short rifle

Chambered for .303, .30-30, .25-35, .32-40, .38-55. Serial number range from 10000 to 220000. Produced from 1899 to 1922. Same cocking indicator as the 1899-A rifle.

Exc.	V.G.	Good	Fair	Poor
1200	900	600	300	100

NOTE: Add 50% for .25-35, .32-40, and .38-55 calibers.

Model 99-B 26" octagon barrel rifle

In calibers .303, .30-30, .25-35, .32-40, .38-55 . Manufactured between 1920 and 1915. Serial number range 10000 to 175000. Same cocking indicator as 1899-A rifle.

Exc.	V.G.	Good	Fair	Poor
1500	1100	700	350	150

NOTE: Add 50% for .25-35, .32-40, and .38-55 calibers.

Model 1899-C 26" half octagon barrel rifle

In calibers .303, .30-30, .25-35, .32-40, .38-55 . Manufactured between 1920 and 1915. Serial number range 10000 to 175000. Same cocking indicator as 1899-A rifle.

Exc.	V.G.	Good	Fair	Poor
2000	1500	1000	400	150

NOTE: Add 50% for .25-35, .32-40, and .38-55 calibers.

Model 1899-D military musket

Chambered for .303 Savage only with 28" barrel. Fitted with full military stocks. Produced from 1899 to 1915. Several hundred produced for Canadian Home Guard during WWI. These will have rack number on buttplate.

Exc.	V.G.	Good	Fair	Poor
3000	2000	1500	700	300

Model 1899-F saddle ring carbine

Fitted with 20" barrel only in calibers .303, .30-30, .25-35, .32-40, .38-55. Built from 1899 to 1919 in serial number range 19000 to 200000. Same cocking indicator as 1899-A rifle. Earliest style with barrel band is rarest variation.

Exc.	V.G.	Good	Fair	Poor
850	600	400	250	100

NOTE: Add 50% for .25-35, .32-40, and .38-55 calibers. Add 200% for barrel band carbine.

Model 1899-CD Deluxe rifle

In calibers .303, .30-30, .25-35, .32-40, .38-55. Serial number range 50000 to 175000. Built from 1905 to 1917. Same cocking indicator as the 1899-A rifle. The standard Deluxe 1899 rifle with 26" round, octagon, or half octagon barrel with pistol grip stock and checkering. Takedown barrel is 22".

Exc.	V.G.	Good	Fair	Poor
3000	2000	1500	700	300

NOTE: Add 30% for .25-35, .32-40, and .38-55 calibers.

Model 1899-H featherweight rifle
Chambered for .303, .30-30, .25-35, and .22 HP Savage in 20" barrel. Serial number range 50000 to 220000. Built from 1905 to 1919. The revolutionary .22HP cartridge was introduced in this model in 1912. Most 1899-Hs are found with takedown barrels.

Exc.	V.G.	Good	Fair	Poor
1600	1200	600	300	100

NOTE: Add 50% for .25-35.

Model 1899 .250-3000 Savage Rifle
This deluxe Model 1899 was developed to introduce the Charles Newton designed .250-3000 Savage cartridge. Fitted with a 22" featherweight takedown barrel, pistol grip, checkered perch belly stock, unique checkered trigger. Built from 1914 to 1921 in the 146500 to 237500 serial number range.

Exc.	V.G.	Good	Fair	Poor
1600	1200	700	350	100

Model 99-B 26"/24" standard weight takedown
Chambered for .303, .30-30, and .300 Savage. Serial number range 200000 to 344000. Produced from 1920 to 1934. In 1926 a new 24" barrel with ramp front sight was introduced.

Exc.	V.G.	Good	Fair	Poor
600	500	400	300	100

Model 99-C 22" standard weight short rifle
Chambered for .303, .30-30, and .300 Savage. Serial number range 238000 to 290000. built from 1922 to 1926. This model looks loke a shortened 26" rifle but with a heavily crowned muzzle.

Exc.	V.G.	Good	Fair	Poor
600	500	400	300	100

Model 99-D 22" standard weight takedown rifle
Chambered for .303, .30-30, and .300 Savage. Serial number range 238000 to 290000. Built from 1922 to 1926. Same heavily crowned muzzle as 99-C.

Exc.	V.G.	Good	Fair	Poor
600	500	400	300	100

Model 99-E lightweight rifle
Chambered for .22HP, .30-30, .303, .250-3000, and .300 Savage. Manufactured between 1922 and 1934. Serial number range 238000 to 344000. In 1926 new ramp front sight introduced.

Exc.	V.G.	Good	Fair	Poor
800	650	500	300	100

NOTE: Add 25% for .22 Hi Power and .250-3000 calibers.

Model 99-F lightweight takedown
As above, but in takedown barrels in 20", 22", and 24". these barrels were tapered lightweight barrels. Manufactured between 1920 and 1940. Serial number range 200000 to 398000. In 1926 new ramp front sight introduced. Early versions look similar to Model 1899-H featherweight. In 1938 checkered stocks offered this option is rare.

Exc.	V.G.	Good	Fair	Poor
1000	700	500	300	100

NOTE: Add 75% for 1938 checkered stocks

Model 99-G Deluxe takedown pistol grip rifle
As above, with a pistol grip checkered stock. Manufactured between 1922 and 1941. Serial number range 238000 to 407000. No takedown Model 99s made after 1941.

Exc.	V.G.	Good	Fair	Poor
1500	1000	700	300	100

NOTE: Add 50% for .22 Hi Power and 25% for .250-3000

Model 99-H standard weight barrels
Fitted with 20" or 22" barrels and chambered for .30-30, .303, .250-3000, and .300 Savage. serial number range 220000 to 400000. Built between 1923 and 1940. Distinctive plain stocks with no flat pads on side of buttstock. Curved carbine style buttplate. In 1931 barrel band added to forend. In 1935 flat pads added to buttstock sides. Also front ramp sight added.

Exc.	V.G.	Good	Fair	Poor
800	650	500	300	100

NOTE: Add 50% for 1935 barrel band carbine. Add 25% for .250-3000.

Combination Cased Set .300 Savage/.410 barrel
Fitted with 22" or 24" barrels with .410 barrels and .300 Savage in Model 99-F, 99-G, or 99-K configuration. In black fitted case. Serial number range 240000 to 350000. built from 1922 to 1934. Be aware that the barrel address on the .410 barrel matches that on the rifle barrel and that the .410 barrel takes up correctly on the receiver, and that the case fits the .410 barrel and receiver.

Exc.	V.G.	Good	Fair	Poor
2500	1800	1200	600	300

Model 99-A 24" featherweight rifle
Fitted with a 24" barrel with new 1926 ramp front sight. Chambered for .303, .30-30, or .300 Savage. Serial number range 290000 to 370000. Built from 1926 to 1937. Buttplate is older 1899 crescent style.

Exc.	V.G.	Good	Fair	Poor
600	500	400	250	75

Model 99-K Deluxe engraved rifle
The premier Savage Model 99 with an engraved receiver. Fitted with a checkered pistol grip stock of select American walnut, and a takedown frame. Hand honed and hand fitted. Chambered for .22HP, .30-30, .303, .250-3000, and .300 Savage. Fitted with 22" or 24" barrels. Serial number range 285000 to 398000. Manufactured between 1926 and 1940.

Exc.	V.G.	Good	Fair	Poor
2500	1800	1200	600	200

NOTE: Add 30% for .22 caliber Hi Power. Some of these models found with cased set with .410 barrel. Add $700 for V.G. case and barrels.

Model 99-R Heavy barrel
This model features a heavy pistol grip checkered stock with rounded forend tip. Fitted with a 24" barrel and chambered for .250-3000, .303, .300 Savage, .308, .243, and .358 calibers. Serial number range 340000 to 1060000. Manufactured between 1932 and 1960.

Exc.	V.G.	Good	Fair	Poor
875	750	600	300	100

NOTE: Add 25% for .358 and 100% for rare uncataloged .30-30. Approximately 10 made for A.F. Stoeger of N.Y.C. for N.Y. State Police in 1935 in serial number range 3486000. Most of these are found with Redfield No. 102 side peep sight and 1/4" rack number stamped in stock below pistol grip.

Model 99-RS Special Sights
As above, with a Lyman aperture rear tang sight. In 1940 this was changed to a Redfield micrometer tang sight. This was the first model fitted with Savage quick release sling swivels. No .30-30 calibers made in this model. Manufactured between 1932 and 1942.

Exc.	V.G.	Good	Fair	Poor
900	650	500	350	200

NOTE: Add 25% for .358.

Model 99-EG standard weight rifle

Produced in .243, .308, and .358 caliber with plain uncheckedered pistol grip stock until 1940. Available in .22 Hi Power, .250 Savage, .30-30, and in 1955 .300 Savage. Serial number range 350000 to 1060000. Manufactured between 1935 and 1960.

Exc.	V.G.	Good	Fair	Poor
500	400	300	200	75

NOTE: For pistol grip stocks add 20%. Add 100% for rifles chambered for .22 Hi Power and .358

Model 99-T Deluxe featherweight rifle

This is the classic short barrel deluxe Model 99 with semi-beavertail forend and distinct long checkering pattern. Fitted with 20" or 22" barrels and chambered for .250-3000, .30-30, .303, .22 HP, or .300 Savage. Serial number range 350000 to 400000. Manufactured between 1935 and 1940.

Exc.	V.G.	Good	Fair	Poor
1500	1000	700	350	100

NOTE: Add 100% for .22 Hi Power caliber.

Model 99-F featherweight rifle

The first Savage made with the model designation visible on the outside. Located at the rear on the right side of the barrel. A true featherweight with slender 22" barrel, lightweight stocks with butt end hollowed out. Chambered for .250-3000, .303, .300 Savage, .308, .243, and .358 calibers. Serial number range 755000 to present. Built from 1955 to 1973.

Exc.	V.G.	Good	Fair	Poor
700	550	400	250	75

NOTE: Add 50% for .284 and .358 calibers.

Model 99-DL Deluxe monte carlo

A deluxe version of the Model 99EG. Available in .243, .250 Savage, .300 Savage, .284, .358, and .308 calibers with a Monte Carlo-style stock. Serial number range 1000000 to present. Manufactured between 1960 and 1973.

Exc.	V.G.	Good	Fair	Poor
400	300	250	150	50

NOTE: Add 50% for .358 and .284 calibers.

Model 99-E economy

The ugly duckling of the Savage line. The Model 99-E lacked many of the standard features such as left side cartridge counter, tang sight holes, walnut stocks, and capped pistol grip. Fitted with 20", 22", or 24" barrels and chambered for .250-3000, .300 Savage, .243, and .308 calibers. Serial number range 1000000 to present. Built from 1960 to 1984.

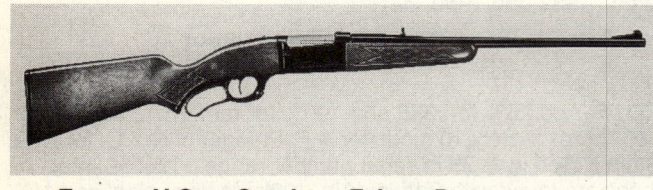

Exc.	V.G.	Good	Fair	Poor
300	250	200	150	50

NOTE: The Model 99-E was the last original rotary magazine Model 99 when production discontinued in 1984.

Model 99-C clip magazine

The current production model in .22-250, .243, .284 Winchester, 7mm-08, or .308 caliber with a 22" barrel having open sights. Blued with a walnut stock. This model features a clip magazine and is the first modification in the Model 99 in 66 years. Introduced in 1965. Dropped from production and rein-

troduced in 1995 in .243 and .308 calibers. Approximate weight is 7.75 lbs.

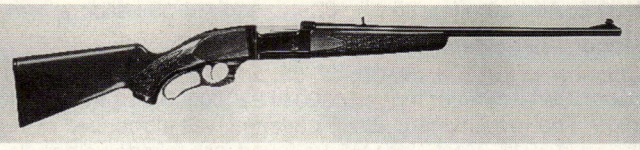

NIB	Exc.	V.G.	Good	Fair	Poor
550	350	300	250	150	50

NOTE: Add 100% for .22-250, .284, and .7mm-08.

Model 99-DE Citation grade

A premier Savage with an engraved receiver with nickel-like finish and impressed checkering on select walnut stocks. Marked 99-M. Offered in .243, .284, and .308 calibers with 22" barrel only. Serial number range 1140000 to present. Manufactured between 1965 and 1970.

Exc.	V.G.	Good	Fair	Poor
1200	800	600	—	—

NOTE: Add 30% for .284 caliber.

Model 99-PE

This model is a presentation grade Model 99 with an engraved receiver as well as a hand checkered finely figured walnut stock. Mountain lion on right side of receiver and elk on left side. Chambered for .243, .284, and .308 caliber with 22" barrel. Serial number range 1140000 to present. Manufactured between 1965 and 1970.

Exc.	V.G.	Good	Fair	Poor
1800	1200	800	—	—

NOTE: Add 30% for .284 caliber.

Model 1895 Anniversary Edition

A .308 caliber reproduction of the Model 1895 with a 24" octagonal barrel, engraved receiver and walnut stock having a Schnabel forend. Brass crescent buttplate, brass medallion inlaid in stock. There were 9,999 manufactured in 1970.

NIB	Exc.	V.G.	Good	Fair	Poor
550	300	250	200	—	—

Model 99A-Saddle Gun

A variation of the original Model 99A with a 20" or 22" barrel. Chambered for the .243, .250 Savage, .300 Savage, .308, and .375. Serial number range in new "A" series on left side. Manufactured between 1971 and 1982.

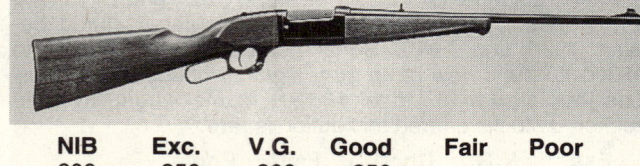

NIB	Exc.	V.G.	Good	Fair	Poor
600	350	300	250	—	—

NOTE: Add 25% for .375 caliber.

Model 99-CD Deluxe clip model

The North American classic rifle with distinct stocks of checkered walnut with long grooved forend, deep shaped pistol grip, and Monte Carlo stock with cheekpiece. Fitted with 22" barrel and chambered for .250-3000, .308, or .243. Serial number range in new "A" series on left side. Built from 1975 to 1980.

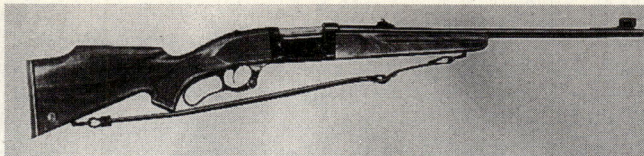

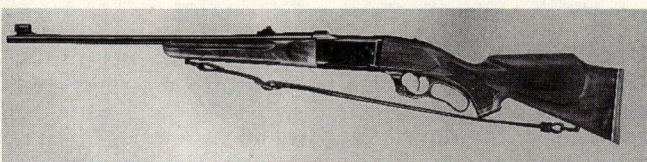

NIB	Exc.	V.G.	Good	Fair	Poor
750	550	400	300	—	

Model 99-.358 and 99-.375 Brush Guns
Similar to the Model 99-A with straight grip saddle gun, but in .358 and .375 Win. (1980) calibers. Has plain grooved forend, rubber recoil pad. Serial number range in the "A" series on left side. Built from 1977 to 1980.

NIB	Exc.	V.G.	Good	Fair	Poor
600	350	300	250	—	

NOTE: Add 25% for .358 Win. caliber.

Model 99CE (Centennial Edition)
Introduced in 1995 this limited edition rifle is chambered for the .300 Savage cartridge. Limited to 1,000 rifles with serial numbers from AS0001 to AS1000. Engraved receiver with gold inlays. Select American walnut stock with Monte Carlo comb.

NIB	Exc.	V.G.	Good	Fair	Poor
1600	1300	900	750	500	250

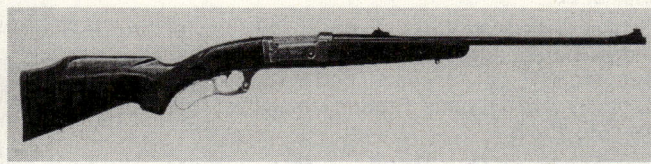

Courtesy Savage Arms

Model 1903
A .22 caliber slide action rifle with a 24" barrel having open sights. Blued with a walnut stock. Manufactured between 1903 and 1921.

Exc.	V.G.	Good	Fair	Poor
250	200	150	100	75

Model 1909
As above, with a 20" barrel. Manufactured between 1909 and 1915.

Exc.	V.G.	Good	Fair	Poor
250	200	150	100	75

Model 1914
As above, with a 24" octagonal barrel. Manufactured between 1914 and 1924.

Exc.	V.G.	Good	Fair	Poor
275	225	175	125	100

Model 25
A .22 caliber slide action rifle with a 24" octagonal barrel, open sights and tubular magazine. Blued with a plain walnut stock. Manufactured between 1925 and 1929.

Exc.	V.G.	Good	Fair	Poor
350	300	250	200	125

Model 29
Similar to above but with a 22" octagonal barrel later changed to round on post war rifles and a checkered walnut stock, later changed to plain on post war rifles. Manufactured between 1929 and 1967.

Exc.	V.G.	Good	Fair	Poor
300	250	200	150	100

Model 170
A .30-30 or .35 Remington caliber slide action rifle with a 22" barrel and 3-shot tubular magazine. Blued with a walnut stock. Manufactured between 1970 and 1981.

Exc.	V.G.	Good	Fair	Poor
200	175	125	100	75

Model 1904
A .22 caliber single shot bolt-action rifle with an 18" barrel and walnut stock. Manufactured between 1904 and 1917.

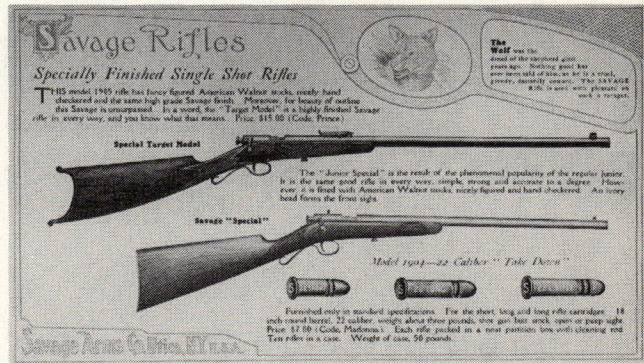

Exc.	V.G.	Good	Fair	Poor
150	125	100	75	50

Model 1905
As above, with a 24" barrel. Manufactured between 1905 and 1919.

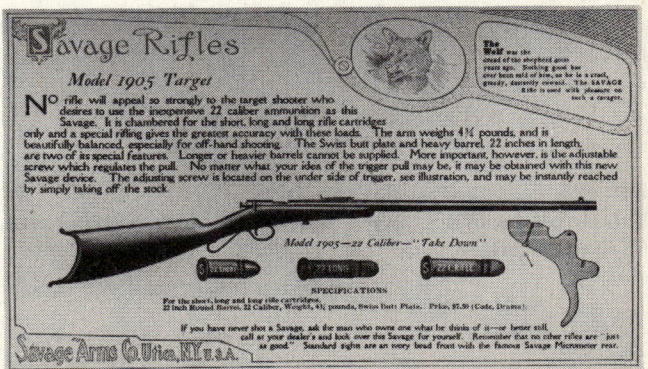

Exc.	V.G.	Good	Fair	Poor
150	125	100	75	50

Model 19 NRA

A .22 caliber bolt-action rifle with a 25" barrel, detachable magazine and full length military style stock. Approximately 50,000 were manufactured total between 1919 and 1937.

Exc.	V.G.	Good	Fair	Poor
225	175	150	100	75

Model 19L

As above, with a Lyman receiver sight. Manufactured between 1933 and 1942.

Exc.	V.G.	Good	Fair	Poor
350	300	250	200	150

Model 19M

As above, with a 28" barrel fitted with telescope sight bases. Manufactured between 1933 and 1942.

Exc.	V.G	Good	Fair	Poor
350	300	250	200	150

Model 19H

The Model 19 chambered for .22 Hornet. Manufactured between 1933 and 1942.

Exc.	V.G.	Good	Fair	Poor
500	450	350	300	200

Model 10 Target

A .22 caliber bolt-action rifle with a 25" barrel; adjustable rear sight and speed lock action. Blued with a walnut stock. Manufactured between 1933 and 1946.

Exc.	V.G.	Good	Fair	Poor
250	200	150	100	75

Model 3

A .22 caliber single shot bolt-action rifle with a 24" barrel, open sights and walnut stock. Manufactured between 1933 and 1952.

Exc.	V.G.	Good	Fair	Poor
100	80	60	50	35

Model 4

Similar to the above, with a 24" barrel and 5-shot magazine.

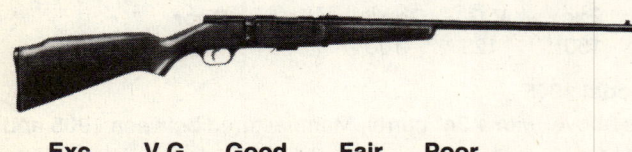

Exc.	V.G.	Good	Fair	Poor
125	100	80	60	50

Model 4M

As above, in .22 Magnum.

Exc.	V.G.	Good	Fair	Poor
125	100	80	60	50

Model 5

The Model 4 with a tubular magazine. Manufactured between 1936 and 1961.

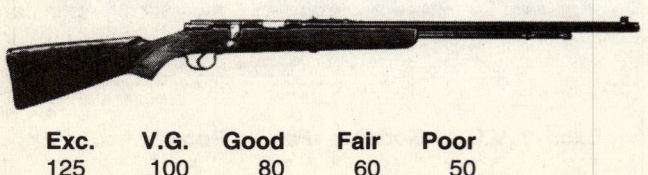

Exc.	V.G.	Good	Fair	Poor
125	100	80	60	50

Model 1920

A .250-3000 or .300 Savage caliber bolt-action rifle with a 22" or 24" barrel, open sights and 5-shot magazine. Blued, with a walnut stock having a Schnabel forend. Manufactured between 1920 and 1926.

Exc.	V.G.	Good	Fair	Poor
350	300	250	175	125

Model 23A

This bolt-action .22 l.r. rifle was introduced in 1923 and features a 5-round detachable box magazine and 23" barrel with open sights. The large loading port on the left side of the receiver permitted easy single shot loading. The stock was plain with pistol grip and a Schnabel forearm. A varnish wood finish was applied to this model. Production stopped in 1933.

Exc.	V.G.	Good	Fair	Poor
250	200	150	125	100

Model 23AA

This was an improved version of the Model 23A introduced in 1933. It features better speed lock, redesigned stock with oil finish. The receiver was tapped for No. 15 Savage extension peep sight. The rifle weighs approximately 6 lbs. Production ceased in 1942.

Exc.	V.G.	Good	Fair	Poor
290	250	200	150	125

Model 23B

Similar to the Model 23A except chambered for the .25-20 cartridge. Barrel length was 25" and forearm was a full 1.5" wide beavertail. Receiver was tapped for peep sight and magazine capacity was 4 rounds. Production on the Model 23B was from 1923 to 1942.

Exc.	V.G.	Good	Fair	Poor
250	200	150	125	100

Model 23C

The same configuration as the Model 23B with the exception of the caliber; .32-20.

Exc.	V.G.	Good	Fair	Poor
250	200	150	125	100

Model 23D

The same configuration as the Model 23B but chambered for the .22 Hornet cartridge.

Exc.	V.G.	Good	Fair	Poor
325	300	250	200	150

Model 40

Similar to the above but in .250-3000, .300 Savage, .30-30, and .30-06 caliber. Manufactured between 1928 and 1940.

Exc.	V.G.	Good	Fair	Poor
350	300	250	175	125

Model 45 Super

As above, with a Lyman receiver sight and checkered walnut stock. Manufactured between 1928 and 1940.

Exc.	V.G.	Good	Fair	Poor
400	350	300	200	150

Model 35

A .22 caliber bolt-action rifle with a 22" barrel, open sights and 5-shot magazine. Blued with a Monte Carlo-style hardwood stock.

Exc.	V.G.	Good	Fair	Poor
100	80	70	50	35

Model 46

As above with a tubular magazine. Manufactured between 1969 and 1973.

Exc.	V.G.	Good	Fair	Poor
100	80	70	50	35

Model 340

A .22 Hornet, .222 Remington, .223, or .30-30 caliber bolt action rifle with a 22" or 24" barrel, open sights and 4- or 5-shot magazine. Blued, with a plain walnut stock. Manufactured between 1950 and 1985.

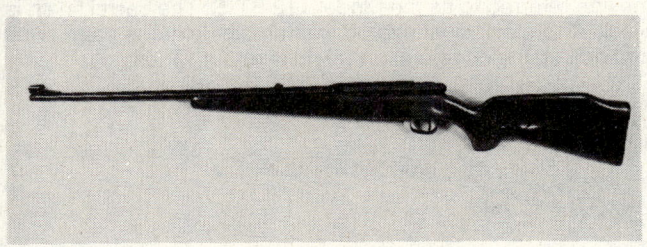

Exc.	V.G.	Good	Fair	Poor
250	200	175	125	90

Model 342

As above, but in .22 Hornet caliber. Manufactured between 1950 and 1955.

Exc.	V.G.	Good	Fair	Poor
250	200	175	125	90

Model 110 Sporter

A bolt-action rifle manufactured in a variety of calibers with a 22" barrel, open sights and 4-shot magazine. Blued with a walnut stock. Manufactured between 1958 and 1963.

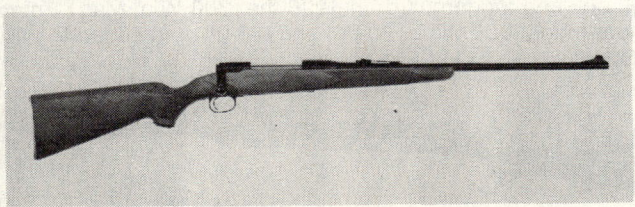

Exc.	V.G.	Good	Fair	Poor
200	150	125	100	75

Model 110-M

Similar to the above, in 7mm Magnum to .338 Winchester Magnum. Manufactured between 1963 and 1969.

Exc.	V.G.	Good	Fair	Poor
275	225	175	150	100

Model 110-D

Similar to the Model 110 in .22-250 to .338 Winchester Magnum caliber with a detachable magazine. Manufactured between 1966 and 1988.

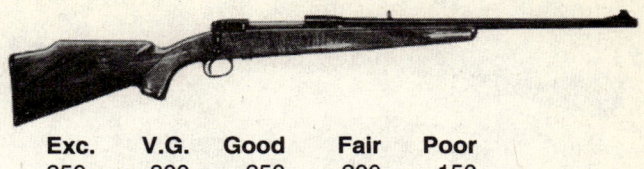

Exc.	V.G.	Good	Fair	Poor
350	300	250	200	150

Model 110-P Premier Grade

As above, with a finely figured walnut stock, rosewood forend tip and pistol grip cap. Manufactured between 1964 and 1970.

Exc.	V.G.	Good	Fair	Poor
450	375	325	250	200

Model 110-PE

As above, with an engraved receiver, magazine floorplate and triggerguard. Manufactured between 1968 and 1970.

Exc.	V.G.	Good	Fair	Poor
850	650	500	400	300

Current production Model 110-F are made in the following styles:

Model 110-F-DuPont Rynite Stock and Sights

NIB	Exc.	V.G.	Good	Fair	Poor
450	400	350	300	250	200

Model 110-FX-Without Sights

NIB	Exc.	V.G.	Good	Fair	Poor
400	350	300	250	200	150

Model 110-FP-Composite Stock and 24" heavy barrel

NIB	Exc.	V.G.	Good	Fair	Poor
400	350	300	250	200	150

Model 110-G-Checkered Hardwood Stock and Sights

NIB	Exc.	V.G.	Good	Fair	Poor
375	325	275	225	175	125

Model 110-GX-Without Sights

NIB	Exc.	V.G.	Good	Fair	Poor
350	300	250	200	150	100

Model 110-CY

A compact version of the Model 110 series. Shorter length of pull on walnut stock and 22" barrel. Overall length is 42-1/2". Weight is about 6-1/2 lbs. Chambered in .223, .243, .270, .300 Savage, and .308 calibers.

NIB	Exc.	V.G.	Good	Fair	Poor
350	300	250	200	150	100

Model 110FP-Tactical

Offered in calibers form .223 Rem. to .300 Win. Mag this bolt action rifle has a 24" heavy barrel with recessed muzzle. The synthetic stock is black as are all other surfaces. Available in both right and left hand versions. Weight is approximately 8.5 lbs.

NIB	Exc.	V.G.	Good	Fair	Poor
400	350	300	250	200	150

Model 111 Classic Hunter Series

All models under this series are fitted with a classic American designed straight comb stock with pistol grip. Chambered in 13 different calibers from .223 Rem. to the .338 Win. Mag. Weights vary with caliber and stock type but range from 6-3/8 to 7 lbs. Models are fitted with a detachable or internal magazine. All Hunter series rifles are drilled and tapped for scope mounts.

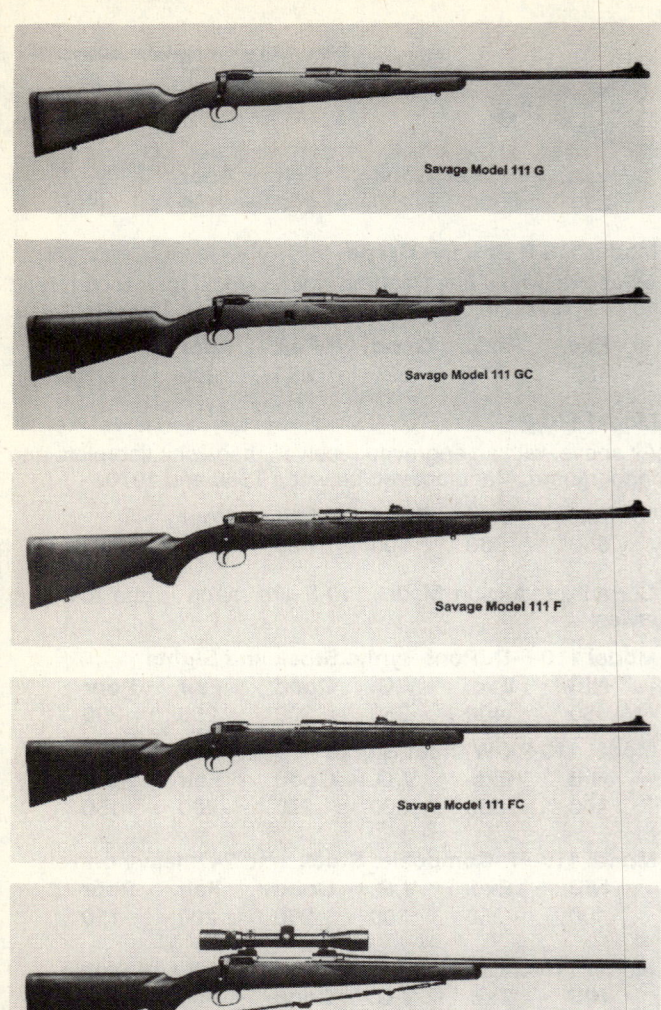

Savage Model 111 G

Savage Model 111 GC

Savage Model 111 F

Savage Model 111 FC

Savage Model 111 FXP3

Savage Model 111 FCXP3

Model 111G-Top loading with walnut stock with recoil pad.

NIB	Exc.	V.G.	Good	Fair	Poor
350	300	250	200	150	100

Model 111 GC-Detachable magazine with walnut stock and recoil pad.

NIB	Exc.	V.G.	Good	Fair	Poor
400	350	300	250	200	150

Model 111F-Top loading with graphite stock

NIB	Exc.	V.G.	Good	Fair	Poor
375	300	250	200	150	100

Model 111FC-Detachable magazine with graphite stock.

NIB	Exc.	V.G.	Good	Fair	Poor
400	350	300	250	200	150

Model 111FXP3-Top loading with graphite stock and 3x9 scope, rings, and bases, and sling.

NIB	Exc.	V.G.	Good	Fair	Poor
475	400	350	300	200	150

Model 111FCXP3-Same as above but detachable magazine.

NIB	Exc.	V.G.	Good	Fair	Poor
475	400	350	300	200	150

Model 111FAK-blued steel barrel, composite stock, muzzle brake.

NIB	Exc.	V.G.	Good	Fair	Poor
400	350	300	250	200	150

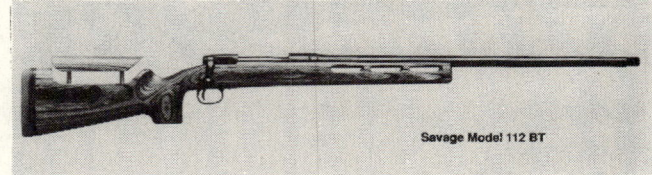

Model 112BT/112BT-S

Introduced for the first time in 1994 this model is a competition grade rifle. Chambered for the .223 Rem. and the .308 Win. it features a 26" heavy stainless steel barrel fitted to an alloy steel receiver. In 1995 the .300 Win. Magnum was added to the line referred to as the Model 112 BT-S. The barrel finish is black. The stock is laminated with ambibidextrous palm swell and adjustable cheek rest. Weight is about 11 lbs.

Savage Model 112 BT

NIB	Exc.	V.G.	Good	Fair	Poor
950	850	700	500	300	250

Model 112 Series Varmint Rifles

This series of varmint rifles features 26" barrels. Offered with either composite or laminated wood stocks all Model 112s are top loading and all are drilled and tapped for scope mounting. Available in .223, .22-250, and .220 Swift the BV configuration weighs about 10-1/2 lbs while the FV configuration weighs about 9 lbs.

Model 112 BVSS

This model has a laminated wood stock with high comb and ambidextrous palm swell. It is fitted with a stainless steel barrel, bolt and triggerguard. In 1996 the .300 Win. Mag., 7mm Rem. Mag., .308 Win., .30-06, and .25-06 was added to this model.

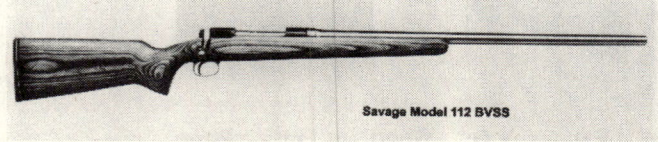

Savage Model 112 BVSS

NIB	Exc.	V.G.	Good	Fair	Poor
500	400	350	300	200	150

Model BVSS-S

Same as above but single shot.

NIB	Exc.	V.G.	Good	Fair	Poor
500	400	350	300	200	150

Model 112FVSS

This version also is fitted with a stainless steel barrel and a composite stock This version was fitted with a stainless steel "fluted" barrel in 1995. Several new calibers were added as well: 300 Win. Mag., 7mm Re. Mag., .25-06 Rem.

Savage Model 112 FVSS

NIB	Exc.	V.G.	Good	Fair	Poor
475	400	350	300	200	150

Model 112FVSS-S

This is a single shot version of the above model.

NIB	Exc.	V.G.	Good	Fair	Poor
475	400	350	300	200	150

Model 112FV

This is similar to the model above but with a blued barrel.

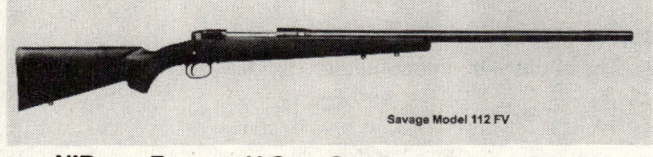

Savage Model 112 FV

NIB	Exc.	V.G.	Good	Fair	Poor
375	300	250	200	150	100

Model 112BT-Competition Grade

This model was introduced in 1996. It is a competition rifle. It features a 26" blackened stainless steel barrel and custom target style laminated stock with adjustable cheek rest. Chambered for .223 or .308 cartridges. Weight is approximately 11 lbs. The barrel is pillar bedded.

NIB	Exc.	V.G.	Good	Fair	Poor
950	850	700	500	300	250

Model 114CU

This model has a select grade walnut oil finished stock. The finish is a high polish blue and the bolt has a laser etched Savage logo. A detachable magazine is standard. The receiver is drilled and tapped for a scope mount. Offered in .270, .30-06, 7mm Rem. Mag., and .300 Win. Mag. Weights are about 7-1/8 lbs.

Savage Model 114 CU

NIB	Exc.	V.G.	Good	Fair	Poor
500	425	325	250	200	150

Model 114CE

Introduced in 1996 this rifle is chambered for the .270 Win., .30-06, 7mm Rem. Mag., and .300 Win. Mag. It has an oil finished stock with skip line checkering and cheekpiece. The forend tip is a schnable type. Rubber recoil pad and pistol grip cap are standard. High luster blue finish. Approximate weight is 7.12 lbs.

NIB	Exc.	V.G.	Good	Fair	Poor
550	475	400	350	300	150

Courtesy Savage Arms

Model 116 Series

This series of rifles feature graphite stocks and stainless steel barreled actions. An adjustable muzzle brake is also included. All rifles in the 116 series are drilled and tapped for scope mounts.

Model 116FCSAK

Features a detachable box magazine. The 22" barrel is fluted. Offered in .270, .30-06, 7mm Rem. Mag., .300 Win. Mag., and .338 Win. Mag. Weighs about 6-1/2 lbs.

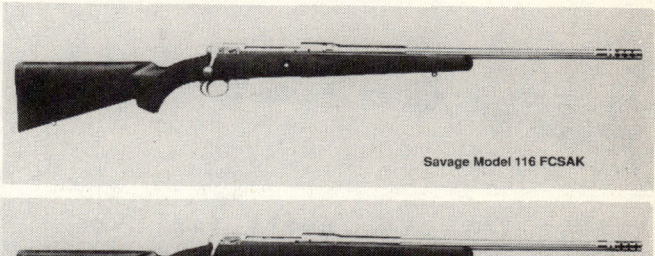

Savage Model 116 FCSAK

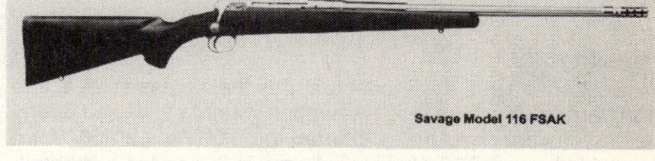

Savage Model 116 FSAK

NIB	Exc.	V.G.	Good	Fair	Poor
625	550	450	400	300	200

Model 116FSAK

Same as model above but with on-off choice given to shooter.

NIB	Exc.	V.G.	Good	Fair	Poor
575	500	400	300	200	150

Model 116FSS

This is the standard configuration for the 116 series. This model features a top loading action with 22" or 24" barrel depending on caliber. There is no muzzle brake fitted to this model. Weight is approximately 6-3/4 lbs. Offered in 7 calibers from .223 to .338 Win. Mag.

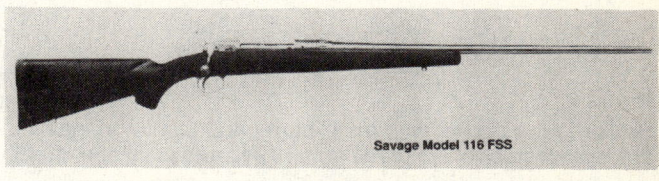

Savage Model 116 FSS

NIB	Exc.	V.G.	Good	Fair	Poor
475	400	300	200	150	100

Model 116FCS

Same as above but with stainless steel removable box magazine.

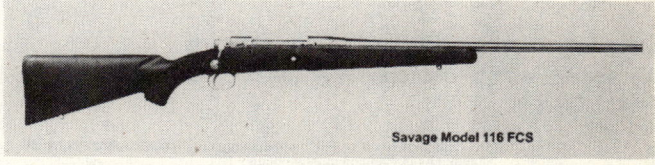

Savage Model 116 FCS

NIB	Exc.	V.G.	Good	Fair	Poor
550	475	375	300	200	150

Model 116FSK

This model features a top loading action with a 22" barrel with muzzle brake.

Savage Model 116 FSK

NIB	Exc.	V.G.	Good	Fair	Poor
550	475	375	300	200	150

Model 116SE

Introduced in 1994 this rifle features select grade walnut stock with ebony tip and deluxe checkering. Barrel and action are stainless steel with adjustable muzzle brake. Offered in .300 Win. Mag., .338 Win. Mag., and .458 calibers. In 1995 the .425 Express cartridge was added. Weight is approximately 8-1/2 lbs.

Savage Model 116 SE

NIB	Exc.	V.G.	Good	Fair	Poor
850	750	600	500	300	200

Model 116US

Introduced in 1995 this model features a stainless steel action and barrel with a high gloss American walnut stock with ebony tip and custom checkering. Offered in .270 Win., .30-06, 7mm Rem. Mag., and .300 Win. Mag. Barrel is 22" on the two smaller calibers and 24" on the magnum calibers.

NIB	Exc.	V.G.	Good	Fiar	Poor
600	500	400	300	250	200

Model 1912

A .22 caliber semiautomatic rifle with a 20" barrel, open sights and in takedown form. Blued with a walnut stock. Manufactured between 1912 and 1916.

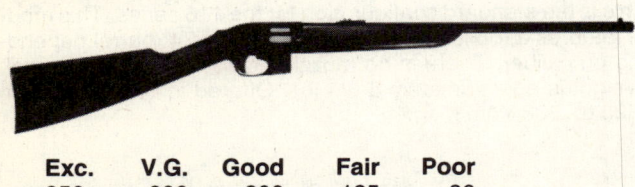

Exc.	V.G.	Good	Fair	Poor
350	300	200	125	90

Model 6

Similar to the above, with a 24" barrel and tubular magazine. The walnut stock checkered prior to 1941 and plain after 1945.

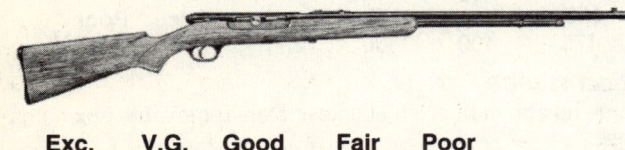

Exc.	V.G.	Good	Fair	Poor
150	125	100	75	50

Model 7

As above, with a detachable magazine. Manufactured between 1939 and 1951.

Exc.	V.G.	Good	Fair	Poor
150	125	100	75	50

Model 60

A .22 caliber semiautomatic rifle with a 20" barrel, open sights, and tubular magazine. Blued with a Monte Carlo-style walnut stock. Manufactured between 1969 and 1972.

Exc.	V.G.	Good	Fair	Poor
100	80	70	50	35

Model 64G

Introduced in 1996 this semiautomatic .22 long rifle has a 20.25" barrel and 10-shot detachable magazine. The finish is blue and the stock has a Monte Carlo with checkered pistol grip. Bead front sight with adjustable open rear sight is standard. Weight is about 5.5 lbs.

NIB	Exc.	V.G.	Good	Fair	Poor
120	95	75	60	50	40

Model 64GXP

As above but with unmounted 4x15mm scope.

NIB	Exc.	V.G.	Good	Fair	Poor
150	120	100	80	60	50

Model 64-F

Introduced in 1997 this model features a black synthetic stock with blue finish. Chambered for .22 long rifle and fitted with a 20.25" barrel. Weight is approximately 5.5 lbs.

NIB	Exc.	V.G.	Good	Fair	Poor
140	120	—	—	—	—

Model 88

As above, with a hardwood stock. Manufactured between 1969 and 1972.

Exc.	V.G.	Good	Fair	Poor
100	80	70	50	35

Model 90 Carbine

As above, with a 16.5" barrel and carbine style stock having the forend secured to the barrel by a barrel band.

Exc.	V.G.	Good	Fair	Poor
100	80	70	50	35

Model 93G

Introduced in 1996 this model is a bolt action repeating rifle chambered for the .22 WMR cartridge. It is fitted with a 20.75" barrel with 5-shot magazine. It has a walnut stained hardwood stock with cut checkering. Open sights standard. Weight is about 5.75 lbs.

NIB	Exc.	V.G.	Good	Fair	Poor
140	120	95	75	60	50

Model 93-FS

This .22 WMR model features a stainless steel finish with a 20.75" barrel and black synthetic stock. 5-round magazine. Front bead sight and sporting rear sight. Introduced in 1997. Weight is about 5.5 lbs.

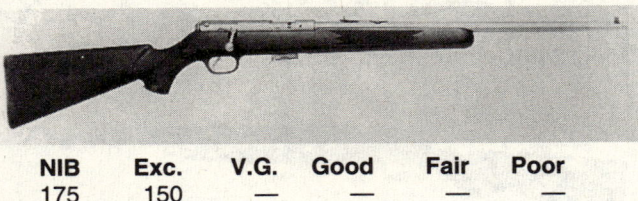

NIB	Exc.	V.G.	Good	Fair	Poor
175	150	—	—	—	—

Mark I & II Series

Introduced in 1996 this series of .22 caliber rifles feature both single shot and repeating models. They are available in both right and left hand models.

Mark I-G

This is a bolt action single shot rifle chambered for the .22 short, long, or long rifle cartridges. It is fitted with a 20.75" barrel and has a cut checkered walnut finished stock. Bead front sight and open adjustable rear sight. Offered in both right and left hand models. Weight is about 5.5 lbs.

NIB	Exc.	V.G.	Good	Fair	Poor
120	100	80	70	60	50

Mark I-GY (Youth Model)

Same as above but fitted with a 19" barrel and shorter butt stock. Weight is about 5 lbs.

NIB	Exc.	V.G.	Good	Fair	Poor
120	100	80	70	60	50

Mark I-SB

This version of the Mark I is a smooth bore model made for .22 caliber shot cartridges. Barrel length is 20.75" and weight is about 5.5 lbs.

NIB	Exc.	V.G.	Good	Fair	Poor
120	100	80	70	60	50

Mark II-G

This model is a bolt action repeater with 10 shot magazine. It is chambered for the .22 long rifle cartridge. Checkered walnut finished stock. Open sights. Barrel length is 20.75". Offered in both right and left hand versions. Weight is approximately 5.5 lbs.

NIB	Exc.	V.G.	Good	Fair	Poor
125	100	80	70	60	50

Mark II-GY (Youth Model)

Same as above but with 19" barrel and shorter stock.

NIB	Exc.	V.G.	Good	Fair	Poor
125	100	80	70	60	50

Mark II-GXP

Same as the Mark II-G model but includes an unmounted 4x15mm scope.

NIB	Exc.	V.G.	Good	Fair	Poor
130	100	80	70	60	50

Mark II-FSS

This is a stainless steel .22 caliber rifle with 20.75" barrel and 10-round magazine. Receiver is dovetailed for scope mounting. Stock is black synthetic. Weight is about 5 lbs.

NIB	Exc.	V.G.	Good	Fair	Poor
150	125	—	—	—	—

Mark II-LV

This .22 caliber is fitted with a 21" heavy barrel. It has a laminated hardwood stock with cut checkering. Blue finish and 10-round magazine. Weight is approximately 6.5 lbs. Introduced in 1997.

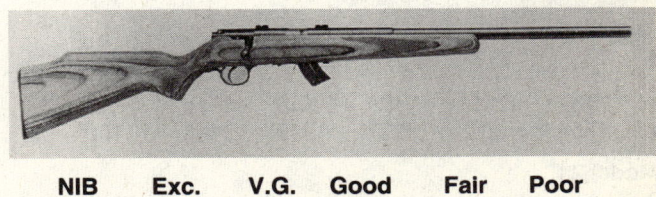

NIB	Exc.	V.G.	Good	Fair	Poor
200	150	—	—	—	—

Model 900 Series

First offered in 1996 this series consist of .22 caliber rimfire target rifles in various configurations. All are available in both right or left hand versions.

Model 900B-Biathlon

This rifle features a hardwood stock with 5 round magazine, carrying and shooting rails, butt hook, and hand stop. The barrel length is 21" and comes with a snow cover. Receiver sight are peep variety and the front sight has 7 aperture inserts as standard. Weight is about 8.25 lbs.

NIB	Exc.	V.G.	Good	Fair	Poor
475	400	350	250	200	150

Model 900 TR-Target

This model has a one piece hardwood stock with shooting rail and hand stop. Rear sight is adjustable peep and front sight has 7 aperture inserts. Barrel length is 25". Five-shot magazine is standard. Weight is about 8 lbs.

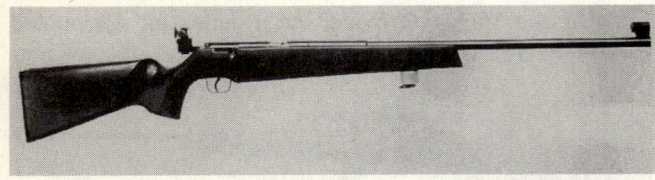

NIB	Exc.	V.G.	Good	Fair	Poor
400	325	275	225	175	125

Model 900S-Silhouette

This version features a 21" heavy barrel with recessed target style crown. Fitted with a one piece silhouette style stock with high comb and satin walnut finish. Receiver is drilled and tapped for scope mount. Weight is about 8 lbs.

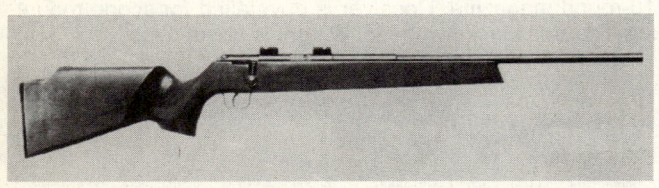

NIB	Exc.	V.G.	Good	Fair	Poor
325	250	225	175	150	100

Model 210F

Introduced in 1996 this bolt action shotgun has a 24" rifled barrel for slugs. It is chambered for the 3" 12 gauge shell. No sights. Magazine holds 2 rounds. Weight is about 7.5 lbs.

NIB	Exc.	V.G.	Good	Fair	Poor
375	300	250	200	150	100

Model 24

An external hammer combination rifle/shotgun with 24" barrels. Blued with a walnut stock. Manufactured from 1950 to 1965 in a variety of styles. The standard chambering was .22 by .410.

Exc.	V.G.	Good	Fair	Poor
150	125	100	75	50

Model 24S-20 Gauge

Exc.	V.G.	Good	Fair	Poor
160	140	125	100	75

Model 24MS-22 Rimfire Magnum

Exc.	V.G.	Good	Fair	Poor
150	125	100	75	50

Model 24DL-Satin Chrome With Checkered Stock

Exc.	V.G.	Good	Fair	Poor
150	125	100	75	50

Model 24 Field-Lightweight Version

Exc.	V.G.	Good	Fair	Poor
175	150	125	100	75

Model 24C-Nickel Finish

Exc.	V.G.	Good	Fair	Poor
200	175	150	125	100

Model 24VS-.357 Magnum/20 Gauge, Nickel Finish

Exc.	V.G.	Good	Fair	Poor
250	200	175	150	125

Model 24F-DuPont Rynite Stock

NIB	Exc.	V.G.	Good	Fair	Poor
350	300	250	200	150	100

Model 2400

A combination 12 gauge by .222 or .308 caliber Over/Under rifle/shotgun with 23.5" barrels and a Monte Carlo-style stock. Made by Valmet and imported between 1975 and 1980.

Exc.	V.G.	Good	Fair	Poor
600	525	450	350	275

SAVAGE SHOTGUNS

Model 420

A 12, 16, or 20 gauge boxlock Over/Under shotgun with 26", 28", or 30" barrels, double triggers and extractors. Manufactured between 1938 and 1942.

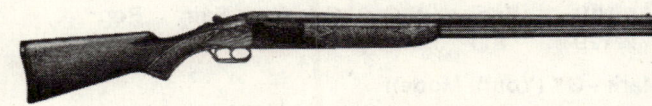

Exc.	V.G.	Good	Fair	Poor
500	400	300	200	150

Model 420 with Single Trigger

Exc.	V.G.	Good	Fair	Poor
500	400	300	200	150

Model 430

As above, with a checkered walnut stock and solid barrel rib.

Exc.	V.G.	Good	Fair	Poor
550	450	350	200	150

Model 430 with Single Trigger

Exc.	V.G.	Good	Fair	Poor
600	450	300	200	150

Model 320

This is a side by side model.

Exc.	V.G.	Good	Fair	Poor
800	650	500	400	300

Model 412

Fitted with adapter tubes.

Exc.	V.G.	Good	Fair	Poor
80	60	50	40	30

Model 412F

Fitted with adapter tubes.

Exc.	V.G.	Good	Fair	Poor
50	45	40	35	25

Model 220

A 12, 16, 20 or .410 bore boxlock single barrel shotgun with 26" to 32" barrels. Blued with a walnut stock. Manufactured between 1938 and 1965.

Exc.	V.G.	Good	Fair	Poor
100	80	70	50	35

Model 210FT

Introduced in 1997 this is a 12 gauge bolt action shotgun with a camouflage finish. Chambered for 3" shells and fitted with a 24" barrel. 2-round magazine. Approximate weight is 7.5 lbs. Drilled and tapped for scope mounting.

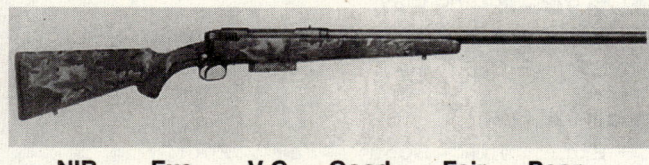

NIB	Exc.	V.G.	Good	Fair	Poor
400	325	—	—	—	—

Model 720

A 12 or 16 gauge semiautomatic shotgun with 26" to 32" barrels. Blued with a walnut stock. Manufactured between 1930 and 1949.

Exc.	V.G.	Good	Fair	Poor
300	250	200	150	100

Model 726 Upland Sporter

As above, with a 2-shot magazine. Manufactured between 1931 and 1949.

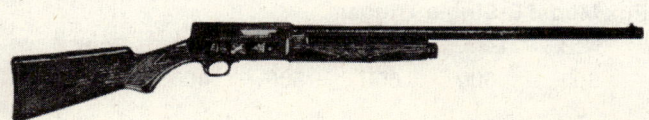

Exc.	V.G.	Good	Fair	Poor
300	250	200	150	100

Model 740C Skeet

The Model 726 with a 24.5" barrel having a Cutts compensator and skeet-style stock. Manufactured between 1936 and 1949.

Exc.	V.G.	Good	Fair	Poor
300	250	200	150	100

Model 745

The Model 720 in 12 gauge with an alloy receiver and 28" barrel. Manufactured between 1940 and 1949.

Exc.	V.G.	Good	Fair	Poor
275	225	175	125	75

Model 755

A 12 or 16 gauge semiautomatic shotgun with 26" to 30" barrels. Blued with a walnut stock. Also available with Savage Super Choke. Manufactured between 1949 and 1958.

Exc.	V.G.	Good	Fair	Poor
275	225	175	125	75

Model 775

As above, with an alloy receiver. Manufactured between 1950 and 1966.

Exc.	V.G.	Good	Fair	Poor
275	225	175	125	75

Model 750

A 12 gauge semiautomatic shotgun with a 26" or 28" barrel. The Model 750SC fitted with the Savage Super Choke and the Model 750AC with a Poly Choke. Blued with a walnut stock. Manufactured between 1960 and 1967.

Exc.	V.G.	Good	Fair	Poor
275	225	175	125	75

Model 30

A 12, 16, 20 or .410 bore slide action shotgun with 26" to 30" ventilated rib barrels. Blued with a walnut stock. Manufactured between 1958 and 1970.

Exc.	V.G.	Good	Fair	Poor
225	175	150	100	75

Model 242

A .410 bore boxlock double-barrel over and under shotgun with 26" barrels, single trigger, extractors and exposed hammers. Manufactured between 1977 and 1981.

Exc.	V.G.	Good	Fair	Poor
150	125	100	75	50

Model 550

A 12 or 20 gauge boxlock side by side double-barrel shotgun with 26", 28", or 30" barrels, single triggers and automatic ejectors. Blued with a hardwood stock. Manufactured between 1971 and 1973. Barrels were built by Valmet.

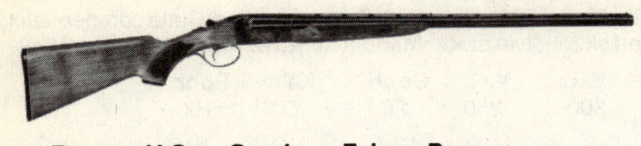

Exc.	V.G.	Good	Fair	Poor
500	400	300	200	150

Model 440

An Italian made 12 or 20 gauge boxlock Over/Under shotgun with 26", 28", or 30" ventilated rib barrels, single selective trigger and extractors. Blued with a walnut stock. Manufactured between 1968 and 1972.

Exc.	V.G.	Good	Fair	Poor
600	500	400	300	200

Model 440A

Exc.	V.G.	Good	Fair	Poor
600	500	400	300	200

Model 440B-T

Exc.	V.G.	Good	Fair	Poor
800	650	500	350	250

Model 444 Deluxe

As above, with a more finely figured stock and automatic ejectors. Imported between 1969 and 1972.

Exc.	V.G.	Good	Fair	Poor
550	475	400	300	225

Model 444

Exc.	V.G.	Good	Fair	Poor
600	500	400	300	200

Model 444B

Exc.	V.G.	Good	Fair	Poor
700	550	400	300	250

Model 440T

A 12 gauge Model 440 with 30" barrels and a trap style stock. Imported between 1969 and 1972.

Exc.	V.G.	Good	Fair	Poor
600	500	400	300	200

Model 330

A Valmet manufactured 12 or 20 gauge Over/Under shotgun with 26", 28", or 30" barrels, single selective trigger and extractors. Blued with a walnut stock. Imported between 1969 and 1980.

Exc.	V.G.	Good	Fair	Poor
800	650	500	350	250

Model 333

As above, with a ventilated rib and automatic ejectors. Imported between 1973 and 1980.

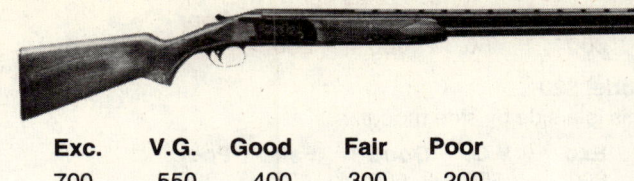

Exc.	V.G.	Good	Fair	Poor
700	550	400	300	200

Model 333T

As above, with a 30" barrel and trap style stock. Imported between 1972 and 1980.

Exc.	V.G.	Good	Fair	Poor
800	650	500	350	250

Model 312 Field O/U

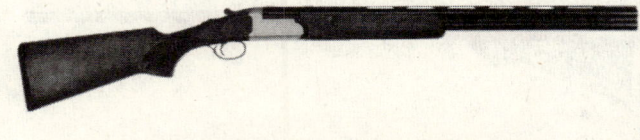

Exc.	V.G.	Good	Fair	Poor
800	600	450	300	200

Model 312 Trap

Exc.	V.G.	Good	Fair	Poor
700	600	550	350	200

Model 312 Sporting Clay

Exc.	V.G.	Good	Fair	Poor
800	600	450	300	200

Model 320 Field

Exc.	V.G.	Good	Fair	Poor
800	600	450	300	200

(SAVAGE) FOX B MODELS

The Fox Model B was introduced about 1939 by Savage for the hunter who wanted better fit and finish than offered by the Stevens brand Model 530. It was made in many variations until 1988.

Fox Model B-Utica, NY

NIB	Exc.	V.G.	Good	Fair	Poor
1000	800	600	450	400	350

Fox Model B-Chicopee Falls, Mass. (later Westfield, Mass.)

NIB	Exc.	V.G.	Good	Fair	Poor
800	750	500	400	350	300

Fox Model B-Single Trigger

NIB	Exc.	V.G.	Good	Fair	Poor
900	800	600	500	400	300

Fox Model BDL

NIB	Exc.	V.G.	Good	Fair	Poor
1000	800	700	600	400	350

Fox Model BDE

NIB	Exc.	V.G.	Good	Fair	Poor
1000	800	700	600	400	350

Fox Model BST

NIB	Exc.	V.G.	Good	Fair	Poor
800	700	600	500	400	300

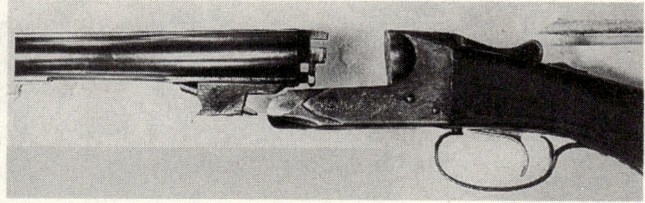

Fox Model BSE

NIB	Exc.	V.G.	Good	Fair	Poor
1000	750	650	550	450	350

Fox Model BE

NIB	Exc.	V.G.	Good	Fair	Poor
1000	800	600	450	400	350

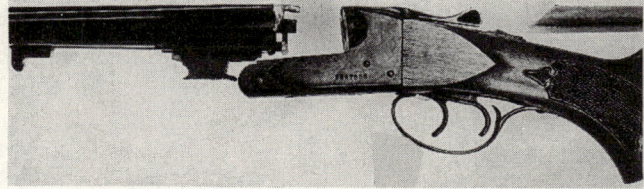

PISTOLS

Model 1907

A .32 or .380 semiautomatic pistol with a 3.75" or 4.25" barrel depending upon caliber and a 9- or 10-shot magazine. Blued with hard rubber grips. The .380 caliber model is worth approximately 20% more than the values listed below.

Courtesy Orvel Reichert

Exc.	V.G.	Good	Fair	Poor
300	250	200	125	75

Model 1915

Similar to the above, except fitted with a grip safety and having an internal hammer. Manufactured between 1915 and 1917.

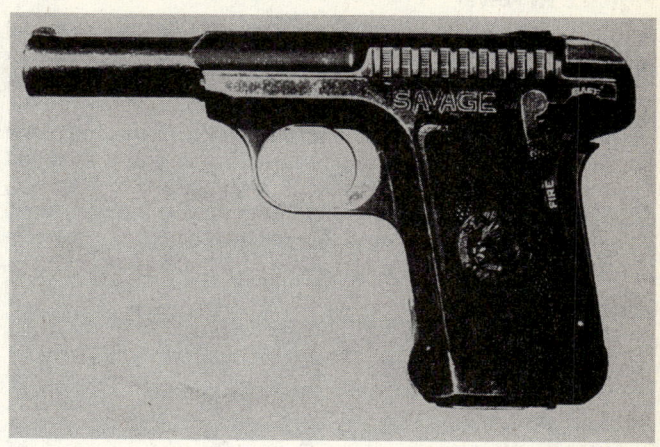

Courtesy Orvel Reichert

Exc.	V.G.	Good	Fair	Poor
375	300	250	150	100

Model 1917

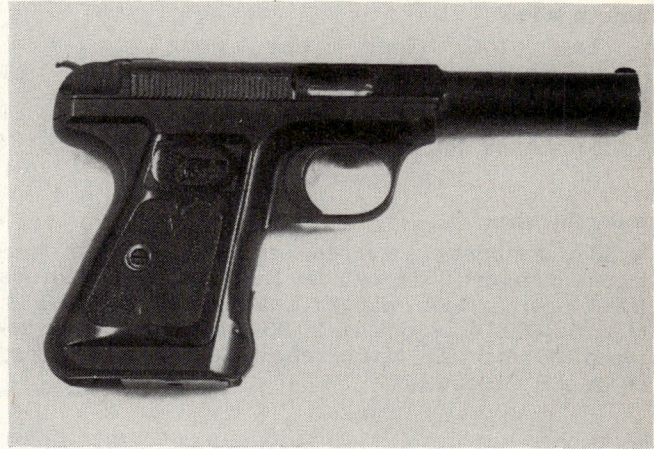

As above, with an external hammer and without the grip safety. The form of the grip frame widened. Manufactured between 1917 and 1928.

Exc.	V.G.	Good	Fair	Poor
275	225	175	100	75

U.S. Army Test Trial

A .45 caliber semiautomatic pistol resembling the above models that was made for trial by the U.S. Army Ordnance Department. Approximately 300 were manufactured. Prospective purchasers are advised to secure a qualified appraisal prior to acquisition.

Exc.	V.G.	Good	Fair	Poor
10000	4000	3000	2250	1750

Model 101

.22 caliber single shot pistol resembling a revolver with a 5.5" barrel. Blued with hardwood grips. Manufactured between 1960 and 1968.

Exc.	V.G.	Good	Fair	Poor
175	150	125	90	75

SAVAGE & NORTH
Middletown, Connecticut

Figure 8 Revolver

A .36 caliber percussion revolver with a 7" octagonal barrel and 6-shot cylinder. The barrel marked "E. Savage, Middletown. CT./H.S. North. Patented June 17, 1856." The four models of this revolver are as follows: (1) With a rounded brass frame, and the mouths of the chamber fitting into the end of the barrel breech; (2) with a rounded iron frame and a modified loading lever that is marked "H.S. North, Patented April 6, 1858"; (3) with a flat-sided brass frame having a round recoil shield; (4) with an iron frame. Approximately 400 of these revolvers were manufactured between 1856 and 1859.

First Model

Exc.	V.G.	Good	Fair	Poor
5000	4000	3500	2500	2000

Second Model

Exc.	V.G.	Good	Fair	Poor
3500	3000	2500	1800	1500

Third Model

Exc.	V.G.	Good	Fair	Poor
3750	3250	2750	2000	1750

Fourth Model

Exc.	V.G.	Good	Fair	Poor
4000	3500	3000	2250	1800

SAVAGE REVOLVING FIREARMS CO.
Middletown, Connecticut

Navy Revolver

A .36 caliber double-action percussion revolver with a 7" octagonal barrel and 6-shot cylinder. The frame marked "Savage R.F.A. Co./H.S. North Patented June 17, 1856/Jan. 18, 1859, May 15, 1860." Approximately 20,000 were manufactured between 1861 and 1865, of which about 12,000 were purchased by the U.S. Government.

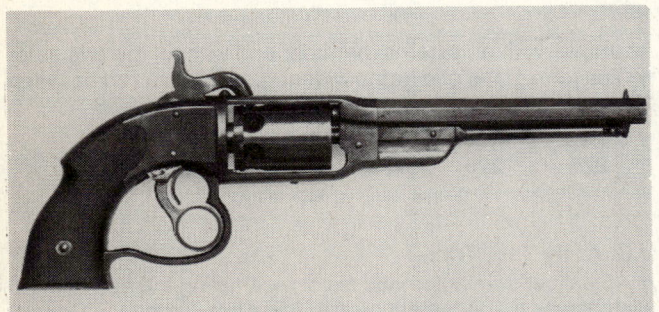

Courtesy Milwaukee Public Museum, Milwaukee, Wisconsin

Exc.	V.G.	Good	Fair	Poor
1850	1500	1250	850	500

SCHALK, G. S.
Pottsville, Pennsylvania

Rifle Musket

A .58 caliber percussion rifle with a 40" round barrel and full length stock secured by three barrel bands. The barrel marked "G. Schalk Poftsville 1861." Finished in white with a walnut stock. Approximately 100 were manufactured.

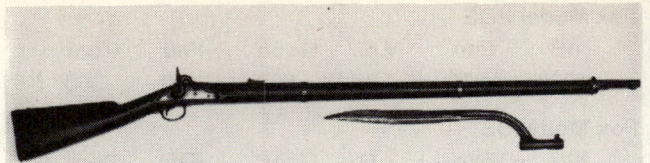

Courtesy Milwaukee Public Museum, Milwaukee, Wisconsin

Exc.	V.G.	Good	Fair	Poor
2000	1750	1500	1200	750

SCHALL
Hartford, Connecticut

Target Pistol

A .22 caliber pistol with a 5" barrel and 10-shot magazine. Blued with walnut grips.

Exc.	V.G.	Good	Fair	Poor
450	400	350	250	175

SCHMIDT, HERBERT
Ostheim, West Germany

Model 11, Liberty 11, and Eig Model E-8

A .22 caliber double-action revolver with a 2.5" barrel and 6-shot cylinder. Blued with plastic grips.

Exc.	V.G.	Good	Fair	Poor
75	65	50	40	25

Model 11 Target

As above, with a 5.5" barrel and adjustable sights.

Exc.	V.G.	Good	Fair	Poor
80	70	55	45	30

Frontier Model or Texas Scout

.22 caliber revolver with a 5" barrel and 6-shot cylinder. Blued with plastic grips.

Exc.	V.G.	Good	Fair	Poor
75	65	50	40	25

SCHMIDT, E. & COMPANY
Houston, Texas

Pocket Pistol

A .45 caliber percussion single shot pistol with a 2.5" barrel, German silver mounts and walnut stock. The barrel marked "E. Schmidt & Co. Houston." Manufactured between 1866 and 1870. Prospective purchasers are advised to secure a qualified appraisal prior to acquisition.

Exc.	V.G.	Good	Fair	Poor
2750	2250	1750	1250	1000

SCHMIDT-RUBIN
Neuhausen, Switzerland

Model 1889

A 7.5mm straight pull bolt-action rifle with a 30.75" barrel and 12-shot magazine. Blued with a full-length walnut stock secured by two barrel bands. Approximately 212,000 were manufactured.

Exc.	V.G.	Good	Fair	Poor
250	200	175	125	90

Model 1896

As above, with a shortened action. There were approximately 137,000 made.

Exc.	V.G.	Good	Fair	Poor
275	225	200	150	125

Model 1897 Cadet Rifle

Similar to the above, with a shortened stock and reduced weight. Approximately 7,000 were manufactured.

Exc.	V.G.	Good	Fair	Poor
300	250	200	150	100

Model 1900

A shortened version of the Model 1896, with a 6-shot magazine. Approximately 18,750 were manufactured between 1900 and 1904.

Exc.	V.G	Good	Fair	Poor
400	350	300	200	150

Model 1905 Carbine

Similar to the above, without a bayonet. Approximately 7,900 were manufactured.

Exc.	V.G.	Good	Fair	Poor
350	300	250	200	150

Model 1911

A redesigned Model 1896 with a 6-shot magazine and pistol grip stock. Approximately 133,000 were manufactured.

Exc.	V.G.	Good	Fair	Poor
150	125	100	80	60

Model 1911 Carbine

As above, with a 23.30" barrel. Approximately 185,000 were manufactured.

Exc.	V.G.	Good	Fair	Poor
175	150	125	100	75

Model 1931

Similar to the above, with a redesigned block work, 25.7" barrel and 6-shot magazine. Approximately 528,180 were manufactured.

Exc.	V.G.	Good	Fair	Poor
175	150	125	100	75

SCHNEIDER & CO.
Memphis, Tennessee

Pocket Pistol

A .41 caliber single shot percussion pocket pistol with a 3.5" octagonal barrel, iron or German silver mounts and a walnut stock. The lock marked "Schneider & Co./Memphis, Tenn." Manufactured 1859 and 1860.

Exc.	V.G.	Good	Fair	Poor
2500	2000	1500	800	650

SCHNEIDER & GLASSICK
Memphis, Tennessee

Pocket Pistols

A .41 caliber percussion pocket pistol with a 2.5" barrel, German silver mounts and walnut stock. The barrel marked "Schneider & Glassick, Memphis, Tenn." Manufactured 1860 to 1862.

Exc.	V.G.	Good	Fair	Poor
2500	2000	1500	1000	800

SCHOUBOE
See Dansk Rekylriffel Syndikat

SCHULER, AUGUST
Suhl, Germany

Reform

A 6.35mm caliber four-barreled pocket pistol with 2.5" barrels. The barrel unit rises as the trigger is pulled. Blued with walnut or hard rubber grips. Manufactured between 1907 and 1914.

Exc.	V.G.	Good	Fair	Poor
850	750	650	450	300

SCHULTZ & LARSEN
Ofterup, Denmark

Model 47 Match Rifle

A .22 caliber single shot bolt-action rifle with a 28" barrel, adjustable sights and adjustable trigger. Blued with an ISU style stock.

Exc.	V.G.	Good	Fair	Poor
700	650	550	400	250

Model 61 Match Rifle

As above, but fitted with a palm rest.

Exc.	V.G.	Good	Fair	Poor
900	850	750	600	300

Model 62 Match Rifle

Similar to the above, but manufactured for centerfire cartridges.

Exc.	V.G.	Good	Fair	Poor
1000	900	750	650	350

Model 54 Free Rifle

Similar to the above, with a 27" barrel and ISU stock.

Exc.	V.G.	Good	Fair	Poor
850	800	700	550	300

Model 68 DL

A .22-250 to .458 Winchester Magnum bolt-action rifle with a 24" barrel, adjustable trigger and well figured walnut stock.

Exc.	V.G.	Good	Fair	Poor
750	700	600	450	200

SCHWARZLOSE, ANDREAS
Berlin, Germany

Military Model 96

A 7.63 Mauser caliber semiautomatic pistol with a 6.5" barrel, 7-shot magazine and adjustable rear sight. Blued with walnut grips.

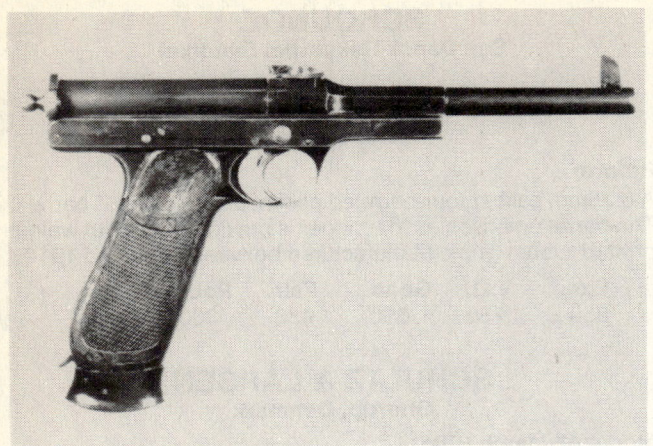

Exc.	V.G.	Good	Fair	Poor
5000	3000	2250	1500	700

Model 08

A 7.65mm semiautomatic pistol with a 4" barrel and 7-shot magazine. The right side of the frame stamped "Schwarlose" over a machine gun. Blued with plastic grips.

Exc.	V.G.	Good	Fair	Poor
475	400	350	300	200

SCOTT, W. C., LTD.
Birmingham, England
Currently offered by Holland & Holland of London.

Kinmount

A 12, 16, 20, or 28 gauge boxlock double-barrel shotgun manufactured in a variety of barrel lengths with a single non-selective trigger and automatic ejectors. Blued with a walnut stock.

NIB	Exc.	V.G.	Good	Fair	Poor
6000	5000	4000	3000	2500	1250

Bowood

As above, with a modest amount of engraving.

NIB	Exc.	V.G.	Good	Fair	Poor
6500	5500	4500	3500	2750	1350

Chatsworth

As above, but engraved in "best bouquet" style.

NIB	Exc.	V.G.	Good	Fair	Poor
8500	7000	6000	4000	3000	1500

SEARCY & MOORE
Hogans Creek, Guilford County, North Carolina

Alexander M. Searcy and Dr. J.S. Moore founded this firm in 1862. They were awarded a contract from the State of North Carolina for rifles. Out of the 500 ordered, 105 were delivered in three styles. First 15 had tumblerless locks in .50 caliber; 49 had "improved" or standard locks; and 41 had standard locks in .577 caliber. Rifles of the final style had overall lengths of 48-1/2", and barrel lengths of 33". Locks are marked "SC/1863". Serial numbered internally, as well as on the top of the barrel and top of the breech plug tang.

Prospective purchasers are strongly advised to secure an expert appraisal prior to acquisition.

Exc.	V.G.	Good	Fair	Poor
—	—	9,000	5,000	3,000

SEAVER, E.R.
New York, New York

Pocket Pistol

A .41 caliber percussion pocket pistol with a 2.5" barrel, German silver mounts and a walnut stock.

Exc.	V.G.	Good	Fair	Poor
—	—	1750	900	400

SECURITY INDUSTRIES
Little Ferry, New Jersey

Model PSS

A .38 Special double-action revolver with a 2" barrel, fixed sights and 5-shot cylinder. Stainless steel with walnut grips. Manufactured between 1973 and 1978.

Exc.	V.G.	Good	Fair	Poor
200	150	125	100	75

Model PM357

As above, with a 2.5" barrel and in .357 Magnum caliber. Manufactured between 1975 and 1978.

Exc.	V.G.	Good	Fair	Poor
250	200	175	150	100

Model PPM357

As above, with a 2" barrel and a hammer without a finger spur. Manufactured between 1975 and 1978.

Exc.	V.G.	Good	Fair	Poor
250	200	175	150	100

SEDCO INDUSTRIES, INC.
Lake Elsinore, California

Model SP22

A .22 caliber semiautomatic pistol with a 2.5" barrel. Blackened or nickel-plated with plastic grips. Introduced in 1989.

NIB	Exc.	V.G.	Good	Fair	Poor
75	65	55	50	35	25

TH. SEDERE
SEE Austrian Military Firearms

SEDGELY, R. F., INC.
Philadelphia, Pennsylvania

R.F. Sedgely produced specialized bolt-action rifles using the Model 1903 Springfield action. As these arms were for the most part custom order pieces, it is impossible to provide standardized values. It should be noted that his prime engraver was Rudolph J. Kornbrath.

SEECAMP, L. W. CO., INC.
Milford, Connecticut

LWS .25 ACP Model

A .25 caliber semiautomatic pistol with a 2" barrel, fixed sights and 7-shot magazine. Stainless steel with plastic grips. Approximately 5,000 were manufactured between 1982 and 1985.

NIB	Exc.	V.G.	Good	Fair	Poor
500	400	300	200	150	100

LWS .32 ACP Model

A .32 caliber double-action semiautomatic pistol with a 2" barrel and 6-shot magazine. Matte or polished stainless steel with plastic grips.

NIB	Exc.	V.G.	Good	Fair	Poor
900	750	650	400	200	150

Matched Pair

A matched set of the above, with identical serial numbers. A total of 200 sets were made prior to 1968.

Exc.	V.G.	Good	Fair	Poor
900	800	700	500	350

NOTE: Seecamp pistols are entirely handmade and as such production is very limited. There may be periods where demand has outstriped supply and prices will rise accordingly.

SEMMERLING
Waco, Texas
SEE American Derringer Corporation

SHARPS RIFLE MANUFACTURING COMPANY
Hartford, Connecticut

The first Sharps rifles to be manufactured were made by A.S. Nippes of Mill Creek, Pennsylvania. Later they were made by Robbins & Lawrence of Windsor, Vermont. It was not until 1855 that Sharps established his own factory in Hartford, Connecticut. After his death in 1874, the company was reorganized as the Sharps Rifle Company and remained in Hartford until 1876 when it moved to Bridgeport, Connecticut. It effectively ceased operations in 1880.

Sharps rifles and carbines were produced in an almost endless variety. Collectors should note that particular features and calibers can drastically affect the value of any given Sharps.

They are, therefore, strongly advised to read: *Frank Sellers, Sharps Firearms* (North Hollywood, California: 1978).

The following descriptions are just a brief guide and are by no means exhaustive.

Model 1849

A breechloading .44 caliber percussion rifle with a 30" barrel having a wooden cleaning rod mounted beneath it. The breech is activated by the triggerguard lever, and there is an automatic disk-type capping device on the right side of the receiver. The finish is blued and case-colored. The stock is walnut with a brass patch box, buttplate, and forend cap. It is marked "Sharps Patent 1848." There were approximately 200 manufactured in 1849 and 1850 by the A.S. Nippes Company.

Exc.	V.G.	Good	Fair	Poor
6500	4750	4000	3000	2500

Model 1850

As above, with a Maynard priming mechanism mounted on the breech. Marked "Sharps Patent 1848" on the breech and the barrel "Manufactured by A.S. Nippes Mill Creek, Pa." The priming device marked "Maynard Patent 1845." There were approximately 200 manufactured in 1850. This model is also known as the 2nd Model Sharps.

Exc.	V.G.	Good	Fair	Poor
5500	4250	3500	2500	2000

Model 1851 Carbine

A single shot breechloading percussion rifle in .36, .44, or .52 caliber with a 21.75" barrel and Maynard tape priming device. Blued and casehardened with a walnut stock and forearm held on by a single barrel band. The buttplate and barrel band are brass, and the military versions feature a brass patch box. The tang marked "C. Sharps Patent 1848," the barrel "Robbins & Lawrence," and the priming device "Edward Maynard Patentee 1845." Approximately 1,800 carbines and 180 rifles were manufactured by Robbins & Lawrence in Windsor, Vermont, in 1851. Those bearing U.S. inspection marks are worth approximately 75% more than the values listed below.

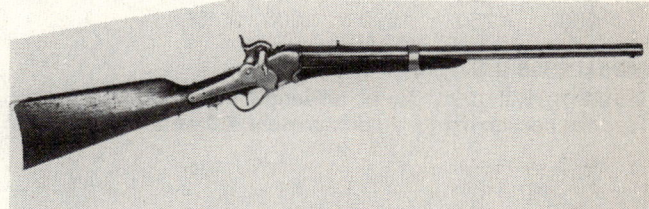

Courtesy Milwaukee Public Museum, Milwaukee, Wisconsin

Exc.	V.G.	Good	Fair	Poor
4950	3750	3000	2000	1500

Model 1852

Similar to the above, but with Sharps' Patent Pellet Primer. The barrel marked "Sharps Rifle Manufg. Co. Hartford, Conn." Blued, casehardened, brass furniture and a walnut stock. Manufactured in carbine, rifle, sporting rifle and shotgun form. Approximately 4,600 carbines and 600 rifles were made between 1853 and 1855.

Military Carbine

Exc.	V.G.	Good	Fair	Poor
1650	1350	1000	800	500

Military Rifle-27" Barrel, Bayonet Lug

Exc.	V.G.	Good	Fair	Poor
2500	2100	1750	1250	850

Sporting Rifle

Exc.	V.G.	Good	Fair	Poor
1500	1000	850	650	400

Shotgun

Exc.	V.G.	Good	Fair	Poor
1200	850	650	500	400

Model 1853

As above, but without the spring retainer for the lever hinge being mounted in the forestock. Approximately 10,500 carbines and 3,000 rifles were made between 1854 and 1858.

Military Carbine

Courtesy Milwaukee Public Museum, Milwaukee, Wisconsin

Exc.	V.G.	Good	Fair	Poor
4750	3250	1750	900	450

Military Rifle

Exc.	V.G.	Good	Fair	Poor
5500	3750	2000	1200	600

Sporting Rifle

Exc.	V.G.	Good	Fair	Poor
4750	3250	1700	900	450

Shotgun

Exc.	V.G.	Good	Fair	Poor
1000	750	550	400	250

Model 1855

As above, in .52 caliber and fitted with a Maynard tape primer that is marked "Edward Maynard Patentee 1845." Approximately 700 were made between 1855 and 1856.

Exc.	V.G.	Good	Fair	Poor
2500	1750	1500	1000	500

Model 1855 U.S. Navy Rifle

As above, with a 28" barrel, full-length stock and bearing U.S. Navy inspection marks. Approximately 260 were made in 1855.

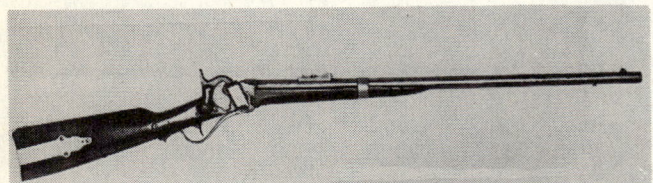

Courtesy Milwaukee Public Museum, Milwaukee, Wisconsin

Exc.	V.G.	Good	Fair	Poor
2250	2000	1750	1250	750

Model 1855 British Carbine

The Model 1855 with British inspection marks. Approximately 6,800 were made between 1855 and 1857.

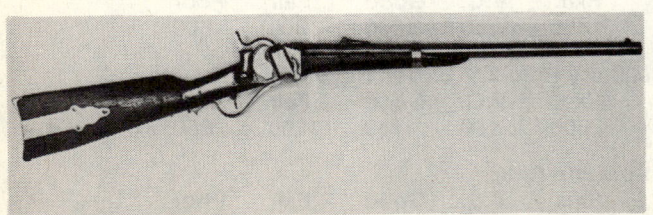

Courtesy Milwaukee Public Museum, Milwaukee, Wisconsin

Exc.	V.G.	Good	Fair	Poor
2000	1400	1000	750	500

Sharps Straight Breech Models

Similar to the above models, but with the breech opening cut on an almost vertical angle.

Model 1859 Carbine-22" Barrel, Brass Mountings

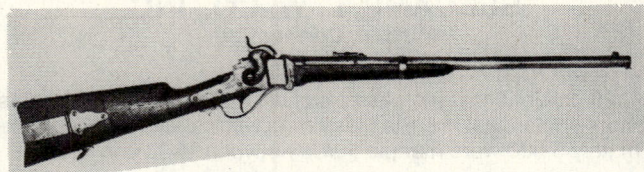

Courtesy Milwaukee Public Museum, Milwaukee, Wisconsin

Exc.	V.G.	Good	Fair	Poor
3000	1800	850	650	500

Model 1859 Carbine-Iron Mountings

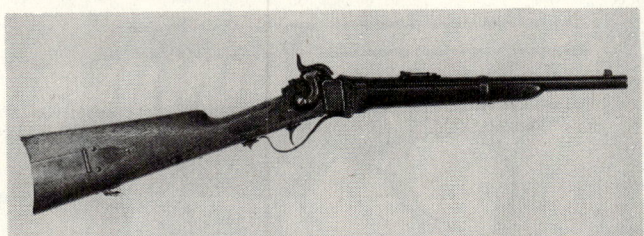

Courtesy Milwaukee Public Museum, Milwaukee, Wisconsin

Exc.	V.G.	Good	Fair	Poor
2500	1500	750	500	300

Model 1863 Carbine

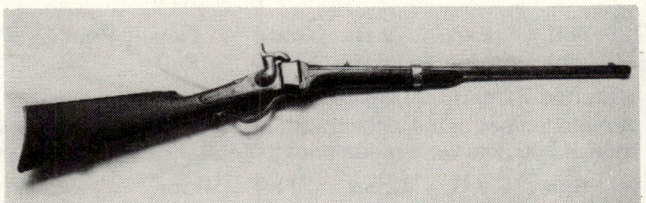

Courtesy Mike Stuckslager

Exc.	V.G.	Good	Fair	Poor
1250	800	650	500	300

Model 1865 Carbine

Exc.	V.G.	Good	Fair	Poor
1500	1000	850	650	400

Model 1859 Rifle-30" Barrel

Exc.	V.G.	Good	Fair	Poor
1500	1000	850	650	400

Model 1859 Rifle-36" Barrel

Exc.	V.G.	Good	Fair	Poor
1750	1250	1000	750	500

Model 1863 Rifle-Without Bayonet Lug

Exc.	V.G.	Good	Fair	Poor
1500	1000	850	650	400

Model 1865 Rifle-Without Bayonet Lug

Exc.	V.G.	Good	Fair	Poor
2000	1500	1250	1000	650

Sporting Rifle

As above, with octagonal barrels, set triggers and finely figured walnut stocks.

Exc	V.G.	Good	Fair	Poor
3250	2700	2000	1500	800

Coffee-Mill Model

Some Sharps'carbines were fitted with coffee-mill style grinding devices set into their butt stocks. These arms are exceptionally rare and extreme caution should be exercised prior to purchase.

Courtesy Milwaukee Public Museum, Milwaukee, Wisconsin

Exc.	V.G.	Good	Fair	Poor
11500	7500	6500	4500	3000

Metallic Cartridge Conversions

In 1867 approximately 32,000 Model 1859, 1863 and 1865 Sharps were altered to .52-70 rimfire and centerfire caliber.

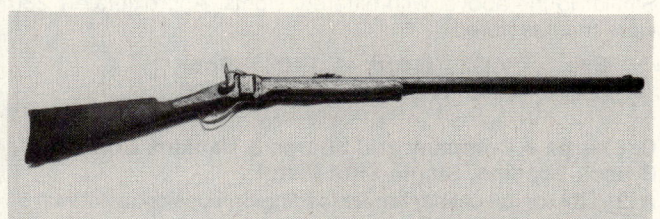

Courtesy Mike Stuckslager

Exc.	V.G.	Good	Fair	Poor
2000	1250	750	500	300

Model 1869

A .40-50 to .50-70 caliber model produced in a military form with 26", 28", or 30" barrels; as a carbine with 21" or 24" barrels and in a sporting version with various barrel lengths and a forend stock fitted with a pewter tip. Approximately 650 were made.

Carbine - .50-70, Saddle Ring on Frame

Exc.	V.G.	Good	Fair	Poor
1500	1000	800	600	400

Military Rifle - .50-70, 30" Barrel With Three Barrel Bands

Exc.	V.G.	Good	Fair	Poor
3250	2500	2000	1500	800

Sporting Rifle - 26" Barrel, .44-77 and .50-70

Exc.	V.G.	Good	Fair	Poor
2750	2000	1500	1000	700

Model 1874

This model was manufactured in a variety of calibers, barrel lengths, and stock styles. The barrel markings are of three forms: initially, "Sharps Rifle Manufg. Co. Hartford, Conn."; then, "Sharps Rifle Co. Hartford, Conn."; and finally "Sharps Rifle Co. Bridgeport, Conn." As of 1876 "Old Reliable" was stamped on the barrels. This marking is usually found on Bridgeport-marked rifles only. The major styles of this model are as follows:

Military Carbine - .50-70, 21" Barrel (460 made)

Exc.	V.G.	Good	Fair	Poor
8500	6000	3250	1250	950

Military Rifle

In .45-70 and .50-70 centerfire caliber with a 30" barrel and full-length forend secured by three barrel bands. Approximately 1,800 made.

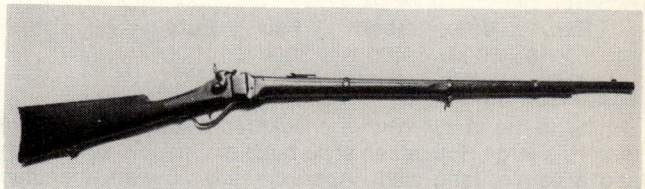

Courtesy Dennis Callender

Exc.	V.G.	Good	Fair	Poor
3750	2500	2000	1000	800

Hunter's Rifle

In .40, .44, .45-70, and .50-70 caliber with 26", 28", or 30" round barrels having open sights. Approximately 600 were manufactured.

Exc.	V.G.	Good	Fair	Poor
3750	2500	2000	1000	800

Business Rifle

In .40-70 and .45-75 Sharps caliber with a 26", 28", or 30" round barrel, adjustable sights and double-set triggers. Approximately 1,600 manufactured.

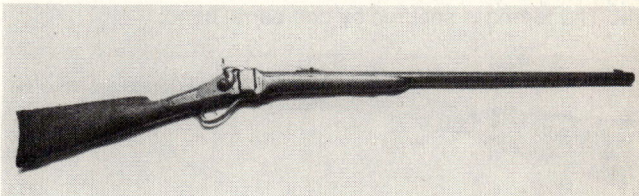

Courtesy Mike Stuckslager

Exc.	V.G.	Good	Fair	Poor
4500	3250	1500	900	750

Sporting Rifle

Offered in a variety of calibers, barrel lengths, barrel weights, barrel styles and stock styles. Approximately 6,000 were manufactured.

Courtesy Milwaukee Public Museum, Milwaukee, Wisconsin

Exc.	V.G.	Good	Fair	Poor
5500	4500	3500	2000	1000

Creedmoor Rifle

With a checkered pistol grip stock, vernier sights, combination wind gauge and spirit level front sight, set trigger and shotgun style butt. Approximately 150 were made.

Exc.	V.G.	Good	Fair	Poor
8000	6500	3000	2000	1000

Mid-Range Rifle

Similar to the above, with a crescent buttplate. Approximately 180 were made.

Exc.	V.G.	Good	Fair	Poor
6500	5500	4000	3000	1500

Long-Range Rifle

As above with a 34" octagonal barrel. Approximately 425 were manufactured.

Exc.	V.G.	Good	Fair	Poor
10000	6000	4000	3000	1500

Schuetzen Rifle

Similar to the above, with a checkered pistol grip stock and forend, a large Schuetzen style buttplate, double-set triggers and a vernier tang sight. Approximately 70 were manufactured.

Exc.	V.G.	Good	Fair	Poor
11500	7500	4000	3000	1000

Model 1877

Similar to the Model 1874, and in .45-70 caliber with a 34" or 36" barrel which is marked "Sharps Rifle Co. Bridgeport, Conn. Old Reliable." Approximately 100 were manufactured in 1877 and 1878.

Exc.	V.G.	Good	Fair	Poor
10500	7500	5000	3500	1500

Model 1878 Sharps-Borchardt

An internal hammer breechloading rifle manufactured from 1878 to approximately 1880. The frame marked "Borchardt Patent Sharps Rifle Co. Bridgeport Conn. U.S.A."

Carbine

Approximately 385 were made in .45-70 caliber with a 24" barrel. The forend is secured by one barrel band.

Courtesy Milwaukee Public Museum, Milwaukee, Wisconsin

Exc.	V.G.	Good	Fair	Poor
3750	2250	1250	1000	750

Military Rifle

Approximately 12,000 were made in .45-70 caliber with 32.25" barrels and full stocks secured by two barrel bands.

Exc.	V.G.	Good	Fair	Poor
3500	2250	1250	600	400

Sporting Rifle

Approximately 1,600 were made in .45-70 caliber with 30" round or octagonal barrels.

Exc.	V.G.	Good	Fair	Poor
3750	2250	1250	800	650

Hunter's Rifle

Approximately 60 were made in .40 caliber with 26" barrels and plain walnut stocks.

Exc.	V.G.	Good	Fair	Poor
3750	2250	900	700	550

Business Rifle

Approximately 90 were made with 28" barrels in .40 caliber.

Exc.	V.G.	Good	Fair	Poor
4000	2500	1200	700	550

Officer's Rifle

Approximately 50 were made in .45-70 caliber with 32" barrels and checkered walnut stocks.

Exc.	V.G.	Good	Fair	Poor
4250	3000	1600	1250	900

Express Rifle

Approximately 30 were made in .45-70 caliber with 26" barrels, set triggers. and checkered walnut stocks.

Exc.	V.G.	Good	Fair	Poor
4500	3000	1500	1350	1000

Short-Range Rifle

Approximately 155 were made in .40 caliber with 26" barrels, vernier rear sights, wind gauge front sight and a checkered walnut stock.

Exc.	V.G.	Good	Fair	Poor
4500	3000	1600	1350	1000

Mid-Range Rifle

Similar to the above, with a 30" barrel. Approximately 250 were manufactured.

Exc.	V.G.	Good	Fair	Poor
5500	4000	2750	1500	1000

Long-Range Rifle

Similar to the above, with different sights. Approximately 230 were manufactured.

Exc.	V.G.	Good	Fair	Poor
8000	6500	3750	1750	1000

C. Sharps & Company and Sharps & Hankins Company Breech-Loading, Single-Shot Pistol

A .31, .34, or .36 caliber breechloading percussion pistol with 5" or 6.5" round barrels. Blued, casehardened with walnut stock.

Courtesy Buffalo Bill Historical Center, Cody, Wyoming

Exc.	V.G.	Good	Fair	Poor
2750	2100	1500	1000	750

Pistol-Grip Rifle

A .31 or .38 caliber breechloading percussion rifle resembling the above. Manufactured in a variety of barrel lengths. Blued, casehardened with a walnut stock having German silver mounts.

Exc.	V.G.	Good	Fair	Poor
2750	2200	1600	1000	750

Percussion Revolver

A .25 caliber percussion revolver with a 3" octagonal barrel and 6-shot cylinder. Blued with walnut grips. The barrel marked "C. Sharps & Co., Phila. Pa." Approximately 2,000 were manufactured between 1857 and 1858.

Exc.	V.G.	Good	Fair	Poor
1650	1100	750	500	400

4-Shot Pepperbox Pistols

Between 1859 and 1874, these companies manufactured 4 barrel cartridge pocket pistols in a variety of calibers, barrel lengths and finishes. The barrels slide forward for loading. The major models are as follows:

Courtesy Buffalo Bill Historical Center, Cody, Wyoming

Model 1

Manufactured by C. Sharps & Co. and in .22 rimfire caliber.

Exc.	V.G.	Good	Fair	Poor
550	450	350	200	150

Model 2

As above, in .30 rimfire caliber.

Exc.	V.G.	Good	Fair	Poor
550	450	350	200	150

Model 3

Manufactured by Sharps & Hankins and marked "Address Sharps & Hankins Philadelphia Penn." on the frame. Caliber .32 short rimfire.

Exc.	V.G.	Good	Fair	Poor
550	450	300	175	100

Model 4

Similar to the above, in .32 long rimfire and having a rounded bird's-head grip.

Exc.	V.G.	Good	Fair	Poor
550	450	350	200	150

Model 1861 Navy Rifle

A .54 Sharps and Hankins caliber breechloading single shot rifle with a 32.75" barrel and full stock secured by three barrel bands. Blued, casehardened with a walnut stock. Approximately 700 were made in 1861 and 1862.

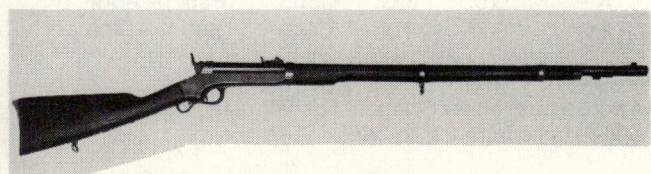

Courtesy Milwaukee Public Museum, Milwaukee, Wisconsin

Exc.	V.G.	Good	Fair	Poor
1750	1250	950	700	500

Model 1862 Navy Carbine

A .54 caliber breechloading carbine with a 24" leather covered barrel. Casehardened with a walnut stock. The frame marked "Sharps & Hankins Philada." Approximately 8,000 were manufactured between 1861 and 1862.

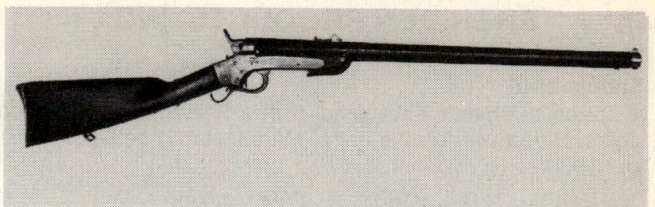

Courtesy Milwaukee Public Museum, Milwaukee, Wisconsin

Exc.	V.G.	Good	Fair	Poor
1500	1000	750	500	400

Short Cavalry Carbine

Similar to the above, with a 19" blued barrel. Approximately 500 were manufactured.

Exc.	V.G.	Good	Fair	Poor
1500	1100	900	700	500

Army Model

Similar to the above, with a 24" barrel that does not have a leather covering. Approximately 500 were purchased by the Army.

Exc.	V.G.	Good	Fair	Poor
1450	1000	800	600	450

SHATTUCK, C. S.
Hatfield, Massachusetts

Boom

A .22 caliber spur trigger revolver with a 2" octagonal barrel and 6-shot cylinder. Nickel-plated with rosewood or walnut grips. The barrel marked "Boom" and "Pat. Nov. 4. 1879". Manufactured during the 1880s.

Exc.	V.G.	Good	Fair	Poor
275	200	150	100	75

Pocket Revolver

A .32 caliber spur trigger revolver with a 3.5" octagonal barrel and 5-shot cylinder. Nickel-plated with hard rubber grips. The barrel marked "C. S. Shattuck Hatfield, Mass. Pat. Nov. 4, 1879." Manufactured during the 1880s.

Exc.	V.G.	Good	Fair	Poor
325	250	200	150	100

SHAW & LEDOYT
Stafford, Connecticut

Under Hammer Pistol

A .31 caliber under hammer percussion pistol with a 2.5" to 3.5" half-octagonal barrel. Blued with a brass mounted walnut grip. The frame marked "Shaw & LeDoyt/Stafford. Conn." Manufactured during the 1850s.

Exc.	V.G.	Good	Fair	Poor
550	400	300	200	150

SHAWK & MCLANAHAN
St. Louis, Missouri

Navy Revolver

A .36 caliber percussion revolver with an 8" round barrel and 6-shot cylinder. Blued with a brass frame and walnut grips. Marked "Shawk & McLanahan, St. Louis, Carondelet, Mo." Produced in limited quantities prior to 1860. Prospective purchasers are advised to secure a qualified appraisal prior to acquisition.

Exc.	V.G.	Good	Fair	Poor
7500	6000	5000	3000	2000

SHERIDEN PRODUCTS, INC.
Racine, Wisconsin

Knockabout

A .22 caliber single shot pistol with a 5" barrel having fixed sights. Blued with plastic grips. Manufactured between 1953 and 1960.

Exc.	V.G.	Good	Fair	Poor
125	100	90	75	50

SHILEN RIFLES, INC.
Ennis, Texas

Model DGA Sporter

A .17 Remington to .258 Winchester caliber bolt-action sporting rifle with a 24" barrel furnished without sights. Blued with a walnut stock.

Exc.	V.G.	Good	Fair	Poor
600	550	450	400	350

Model DGA Varminter

As above, in varmint calibers with a 25" barrel.

Exc.	V.G.	Good	Fair	Poor
600	550	450	400	350

Model DGA Silhouette Rifle

As above, in .308 Winchester only.

Exc.	V.G.	Good	Fair	Poor
600	550	450	400	350

Model DGA Bench Rest Rifle

A centerfire single shot bolt-action rifle with a 26" barrel and either fiberglass or walnut stock.

Exc.	V.G.	Good	Fair	Poor
700	650	550	500	450

SHILOH RIFLE MFG. CO., INC.
Big Timber, Montana

Established in Farmingdale, New York, in 1976, this company moved to Big Timber, Montana, in 1983 with the name Shiloh Products. It changed its name to ShilohRifle Manufacturing Co. in that same year. In 1985 the company began marketing its products factory direct. In 1991 Robert, Phyllis, and Kirk Bryan purchased the company. Those interested in the Sharps reproduction rifles manufactured by this company are advised to contact them in Big Timber.

NOTE: The company will build a rifle to the customers specifications. It is therefore possible that many of these rifles have special order features that are not reflected in the base model price.

Model 1863 Military Rifle

A .54 caliber percussion rifle with a 30" barrel, single or double set triggers and full-length walnut stock secured by three barrel bands.

NIB	Exc.	V.G.	Good	Fair	Poor
850	800	700	600	500	400

Model 1863 Sporting Rifle

As above, with a 30" octagonal barrel, sporting sights and a half-length stock.

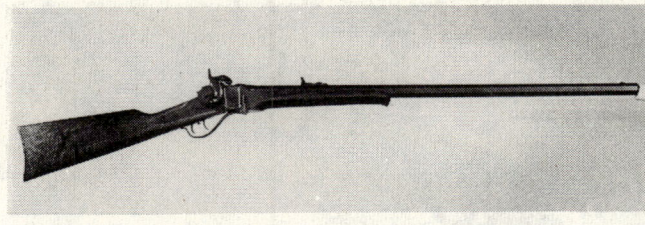

NIB	Exc.	V.G.	Good	Fair	Poor
750	700	600	500	400	350

Model 1863 Military Carbine

The Model 1863 with a 22" round barrel and carbine stock secured by one barrel band.

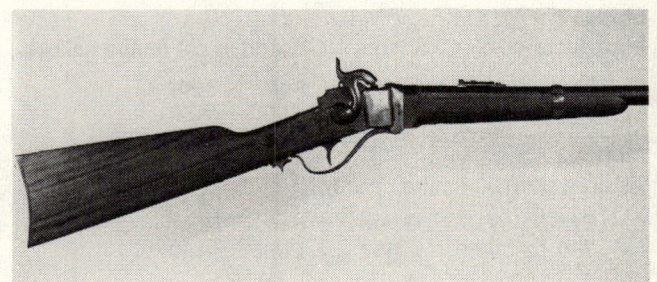

NIB	Exc.	V.G.	Good	Fair	Poor
750	700	600	500	400	350

Model 1862 Confederate Robinson

As above, with a 21.5" barrel, brass buttplate and barrel band.

NIB	Exc.	V.G.	Good	Fair	Poor
800	750	650	550	450	400

Model 1874 Express Rifle

Manufactured in a variety of calibers with a 34" octagonal barrel, double set triggers, vernier rear sight and globe front sight.

NIB	Exc.	V.G.	Good	Fair	Poor
1175	800	700	600	500	400

Montana Roughrider Rifle

As above, with either octagonal or half-octagonal barrels ranging in lengths from 24" to 34".

NIB	Exc.	V.G.	Good	Fair	Poor
1050	700	600	500	400	350

No. 1 Sporter Deluxe Rifle

Similar to the above, with a 30" octagonal barrel.

NIB	Exc.	V.G.	Good	Fair	Poor
1150	750	650	550	450	400

No. 3 Standard Sporter

As above, with a military-style stock.

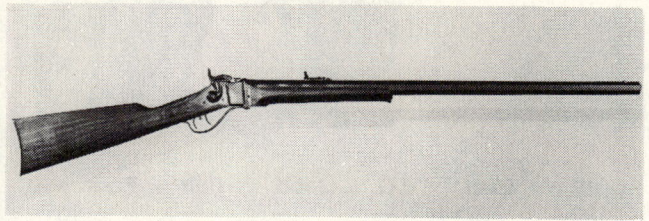

NIB	Exc.	V.G.	Good	Fair	Poor
1050	700	600	500	400	350

The Business Rifle

As above, with a heavy 28" barrel.

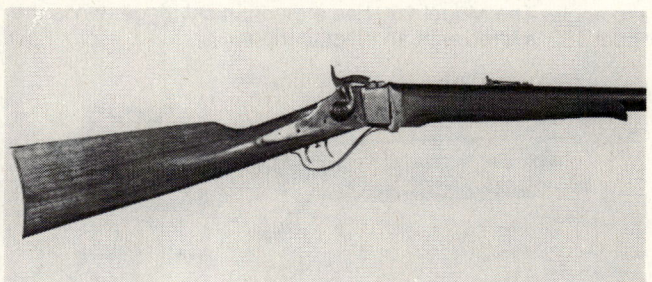

NIB	Exc.	V.G.	Good	Fair	Poor
1050	700	600	500	400	350

The Saddle Rifle

As above, with a 26" barrel and shotgun butt.

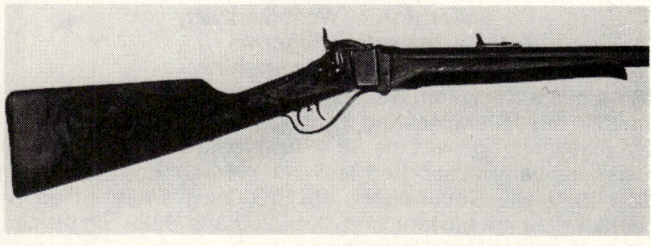

NIB	Exc.	V.G.	Good	Fair	Poor
1100	750	650	550	450	400

Model 1874 Military Rifle

The Model 1874 with a 30" round barrel, military sights and full-length stocks secured by three barrel bands.

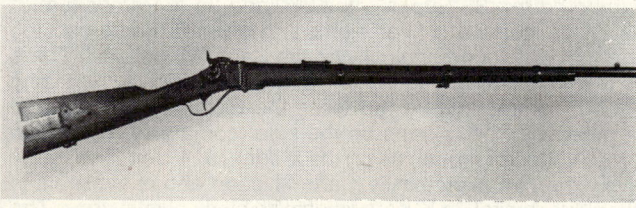

NIB	Exc.	V.G.	Good	Fair	Poor
850	800	700	600	500	400

Model 1874 Carbine

Similar to the above, with a 24" round barrel.

NIB	Exc.	V.G.	Good	Fair	Poor
750	700	600	500	400	350

The Jaeger

The Model 1874 with a 26" half-octagonal barrel, open sights and pistol grips stock having a shotgun butt.

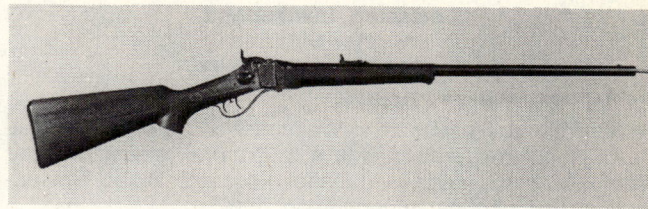

NIB	Exc.	V.G.	Good	Fair	Poor
800	750	650	550	450	400

Hartford Model

A reproduction of the Sharps Hartford Model.

NIB	Exc.	V.G.	Good	Fair	Poor
1200	900	700	550	450	350

Model 1874 Military Carbine

Similar to the Military Rifle, but with a 22" round barrel.

NIB	Exc.	V.G.	Good	Fair	Poor
750	700	600	500	400	350

SIG
Neuhausen, Switzerland
Importer - Sigarms
Exeter, New Hampshire

P210

A 7.65mm or 9mm semiautomatic pistol with a 4.75" barrel and 8-shot magazine. Blued with plastic grips. In 1996 the 9mm version was the only one imported. Weight is about 32 oz.

NIB	Exc.	V.G.	Good	Fair	Poor
2300	1500	1300	1100	800	500

NOTE: For 1996 a .22 caliber conversion unit serialized to the gun was available. Add $600 for this option.

P 210-1

As above, with an adjustable rear sight, polished finish and walnut grips. Imported prior to 1987.

Exc.	V.G.	Good	Fair	Poor
1700	1500	1150	800	400

P 210-2

NIB	Exc.	V.G.	Good	Fair	Poor
2000	1750	1350	1000	750	300

P 210-5

As above, with an extended length barrel, adjustable rear sight and walnut grips.

Exc.	V.G.	Good	Fair	Poor
1850	1650	1000	800	400

P 210-6

As above, with a 4.75" barrel.

NIB	Exc.	V.G.	Good	Fair	Poor
2750	2250	1500	1150	800	400

SIG-HAMMERLI
Lenzburg, Switzerland
Importer-Sigarms
Exeter, New Hampshire

Model P240 Target Pistol

A .32 Smith & Wesson Long Wadcutter or .38 Midrange caliber semiautomatic pistol with a 5.9" barrel, adjustable rear sight, adjustable trigger and 5-shot magazine. Blued, with adjustable walnut grips. Imported prior 1987.

Exc.	V.G.	Good	Fair	Poor
1300	1150	950	750	600

.22 Conversion Unit

A barrel, slide, and magazine used to convert the above to .22 caliber.

Exc.	V.G.	Good	Fair	Poor
500	450	400	300	200

Model 208S

This is a semiautomatic target pistol chambered for the .22 Long Rfile cartridge. The barrel length is 5.9" long with adjustable sights. Sight radius is 8.2". Trigger has adjustable pull weight, travel, slack weight, and creep. Grips are stippled walnut with adjustable palm shelf. Weight is approximately 37 oz. empty.

NIB	Exc.	V.G.	Good	Fair	Poor
1900	1600	—	—	—	—

Model 280

This model is a semiautomatic pistol chambered for the .22 Long Rifle cartridge or the .32S&W long wadcutter. Single action only. Barrel length is 4.6" with a sight radius of 8.7". Adjustable sights. Trigger is adjustable for pull weight, take-up, let-off, and creep. Stippled walnut grip with adjustable palm

shelf. Weight is 35 oz. for the .22 caliber and 42 oz. for the .32 caliber. Magazine capacity is six .22 caliber rounds and five .32 caliber rounds.

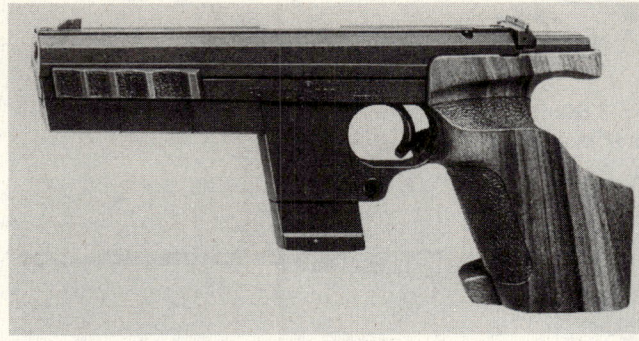

NIB	Exc.	V.G.	Good	Fair	Poor
1200	1200	—	—	—	—

Model 160/162

This .22 caliber Long Rifle single shot pistol is designed for international free pistol competition. Barrel length is 11.3" with a sight radius of 14.6". Trigger is fully adjustable as are the sights. Stippled walnut grips with adjustable palm shelp and rake angle. The Model 160 has a mechanical trigger while the Model 162 is fitted with an electric trigger.

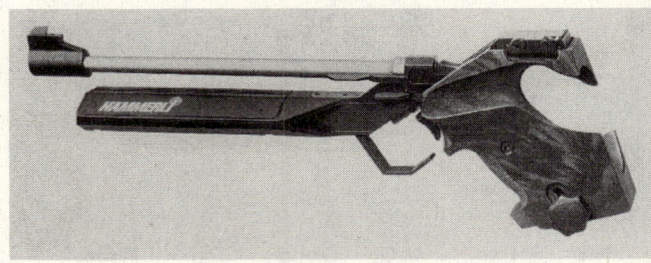

NIB	Exc.	V.G.	Good	Fair	Poor
2000	1600	—	—	—	—

SIG-ARMS
Eckernforde, West Germany
Importer - Sigarms
Exeter, New Hampshire

This old-line Swiss firm was established in 1853 and is now a broadly based engineering consortium. Its first successful commercial design was the SP 47/8 introduced in 1948. Sig, a Swiss company, associated itself with the German firm of Sauer in 1970. SIG-Sauer pistols are SIG designs assembled in Germany. At the present time the P239 and P229 Sig pistols are produced in New Hampshire.

NOTE: Maximum magazine capacity for all currently manufactured Sig pistols is 10 rounds regardless of caliber and previous capacity.

P 220

This is a high-quality, double-action semiautomatic pistol chambered for .38 Super, .45 ACP, and 9mm Parabellum. It has a 4.41" barrel and fixed sights and features the de-cocking lever that was found originally on the Sauer Model 38H. There are two versions of this pistol—one with a bottom magazine release (commonly referred to as the European model) and the other with the release on the side (commonly referred to as the American model) as on the Model 1911 Colt. The frame is a lightweight alloy that is matte-finished and is available in either blue, nickel, or K-Kote finish with black plastic grips. The .45 ACP magazine capacity is 7 rounds and the pistol weighs 25.7 oz.; the .38 Super magazine capacity is 9 rounds and the pistol weighs 26.5 oz.; the 9mm magazine holds 9 rounds and the overall weight is 26.5 oz. This model was manufactured from 1976 and is still in production. The 9mm version in this model is no longer in production. The prices listed below are for guns with a stnadard blue finish. For the K-Kote finish add $40, for nickel slide add $40.

NIB	Exc.	V.G.	Good	Fair	Poor
550	500	400	300	200	150

P225

This is similar to the Model P 220 except that it is chambered for 9mm cartridge. It is a more compact pistol, with a 3.86" barrel. It has an 8-shot detachable magazine and adjustable sights. The finish is matte blued. K-Kote, or electrolysis nickel plate with black plastic grips.The overall length is 7.1" with an overall height of 5.2". The pistol weighs 26.1 oz. For K-Kote finish add $70. For nickel slide add $70.

NIB	Exc.	V.G.	Good	Fair	Poor
625	575	500	400	200	150

P 226

This model is a full size, high-capacity pistol with a 4.41" barrel chambered for the 9mm cartridge. In 1996 this model was also available chambered for the .357 SIG cartridge. It is available with a 15- or 20-round detachable magazine and high-contrast sights. It is either blued, electrolysis nickel plated, or has a polymer finish known as K-Kote. Overall length is 7.7" and overall height is 5.5". The pistol weighs 26.5 oz. This model was introduced in 1983. Add $50 for K-Kote finish and $50 for nickel slide.

NIB	Exc.	V.G.	Good	Fair	Poor
650	600	550	450	300	200

JP 226 Jubilee Pistol

This variation is a special limited edition of the P226. Each gun carries a special serial number prefixed JP. The grips are hand carved select European walnut. The slide and frame are covered with solid gold wire inlays, while the trigger, hammer, de-

cocking lever, slide catch lever, and magazine catch are all gold plated. Each pistol comes in a custom fitted hard case of full leather. This pistol is no longer imported into the U.S. Fewer than 250 were imported between 1991 and 1992.

NIB	Exc.	V.G.	Good	Fair	Poor
1200	850	600	500	400	200

P 228

This model is a compact version of the P226 fitted with a 3.86" barrel and chambered for the 9mm cartridge. Like the P 226 it is available in blue, K-Kote, of nickel finish with black grips.Overall length is 7.1" and overall height is 5.4". Pistol weighs 26.1 oz. For K-Kote finish add $50 and for nickel slide add $50.

NIB	Exc.	V.G.	Good	Fair	Poor
650	600	550	450	350	250

P 229

This model is similar to the P 228 except that it is chambered for the .40 S&W cartridge and has a blackened stainless steel slide and lightweight aluminum alloy frame. The slide is slightly larger to accommodate the more powerful cartridge. In 1996 the 9mm chamber was also offered in this model. Its overall length is 7.1" and overall height is 5.4" Introduced in 1992. The pistol weighs 27.54 oz. and has a magazine capacity of 12 rounds. In 1994 the company introduced a new caliber for this model; the .357 SIG developed by Federal. Magazine capacity is 12 rounds. For nickel slide add $25.

NIB	Exc.	V.G.	Good	Fair	Poor
650	600	550	450	350	250

P239

Introduced in 1996 this pistol is chambered for the 9mm or .357 SIG cartridge. It is double/single action or double action only. The barrel is 3.6" long and the overall length is 6.6". Weight is 25 oz. It is fitted with a single column magazine with 7 round for the .357 SIG and 8 rounds for the 9mm.

NIB	Exc.	V.G.	Good	Fair	Poor
550	450	350	250	200	150

NOTE: All of the above SIG pistols from the P220 to the P239 are available with "SIGLITE" night sights. Add $80 for these optional sights.

P 230

This is a semiautomatic, compact, pocket-type pistol chambered for .22 l.r., .32 ACP, .380 ACP, and 9mm Ultra. It has a 3.62" barrel and either a 10, 8, or 7-round magazine, depending on the caliber chambered. The pistol weighs between 16.2 oz. and 20.8 oz. The finish is blued or stainless, with black plastic grips; and it was manufactured from 1976. In 1996 a two-tone finish was offered. The .32 ACP and the .380 ACP versions are the only ones currently available. For stainless steel finish add $85 and for stainless steel slide add $35.

NIB	Exc.	V.G.	Good	Fair	Poor
450	375	300	250	200	150

P 232

An improved model of the P 230. Incorporates numerous changes to improve function and reliability. Basic features, operation, and dimensions remain the same as the P 230.

NIB	Exc.	V.G.	Good	Fair	Poor
450	375	300	250	200	150

SSG 2000

This is a high-grade, bolt-action, sniping-type rifle chambered for .223, 7.5mm Swiss, .300 Weatherby Magnum, and .308 Winchester. It has a 24" barrel and was furnished without sights. It has a 4-round box magazine. The finish is matte blued with a thumbhole-style stippled walnut stock with an adjustable cheek piece. This model was discontinued in 1986.

NIB	Exc.	V.G.	Good	Fair	Poor
2500	2250	1750	1250	900	450

SIMPLEX
Unknown

Simplex

A German design based on the Bergmann-Mars pistol. An 8mm caliber semiautomatic pistol with a 2.6" barrel and a front mounted 5-round magazine. Blued with hard rubber grips having the trade name "Simplex" cast in them. Manufactured from approximately 1901 to around 1906. Early samples may have come from Germany and later pistols are thought to have been produced in Belgium.

Exc.	V.G.	Good	Fair	Poor
1500	950	500	400	200

SIMPSON, R. J.
New York, New York

Pocket Pistol

A .41 caliber single shot percussion pocket pistol with a 2.5" barrel, German silver mounts and walnut stock. Manufactured during the 1850s and 1860s.

Exc.	V.G.	Good	Fair	Poor
750	650	500	400	300

SIMSON & COMPANY
Suhl, Germany
SEE Luger

Model 1922

A 6.35mm semiautomatic pistol with a 2" barrel and 6-shot magazine. The slide marked "Selbstlade Pistole Simson DRP" and "Waffenfabrik Simson & Co Suhl." Blued, with black plastic grips.

Exc.	V.G.	Good	Fair	Poor
500	450	400	300	200

Model 1927

Similar to the above, with a slimmer frame stamped with the trademark of three overlapping triangles having the letter "S" enclosed.

Exc.	V.G.	Good	Fair	Poor
500	450	400	300	200

SIRKIS INDUSTRIES, LTD.
Ramat-Gan, Israel
Importer-Armscorp of America
Baltimore, Maryland

SD9

A 9mm double-action semiautomatic pistol with a 3" barrel, fixed sights and 7-shot magazine. Blued with plastic grips. Also known as the Sardius.

Exc.	V.G.	Good	Fair	Poor
325	275	225	175	125

Model 35 Match Rifle

A .22 caliber single shot bolt-action rifle with a 26" free floating barrel, adjustable rear sight and adjustable trigger. Blued with a walnut stock.

Exc.	V.G.	Good	Fair	Poor
600	550	500	400	300

Model 36 Sniper's Rifle

A 7.62x54mm caliber semiautomatic rifle with a 22" barrel. Matte blued with a composition stock.

Exc.	V.G.	Good	Fair	Poor
675	600	550	450	350

SLOTTER & CO.
Philadelphia, Pennsylvania

Pocket Pistol

A .41 caliber percussion pocket pistol with a 2.5" to 3.5" barrel, German silver mounts and walnut stock. Marked "Slotter & Co. Phila." Manufactured during 1860s.

Exc.	V.G.	Good	Fair	Poor
950	850	750	600	450

SMITH
AMERICAN ARMS COMPANY
Springfield, Massachusetts

Smith Carbine

A .50 caliber breechloading percussion carbine with a 21.75" round barrel having an octagonal breech. Blued, casehardened with a walnut stock. The barrel marked "Address/Poultney & Trimble/Baltimore, USA" and the frame "Smith's Patent/June 23, 1857" as well as "American Arms Co./Chicopee Falls." Approximately 30,000 were manufactured, most of which were purchased by the United States government. The sales agents were Poultney & Trimble of Baltimore, Maryland.

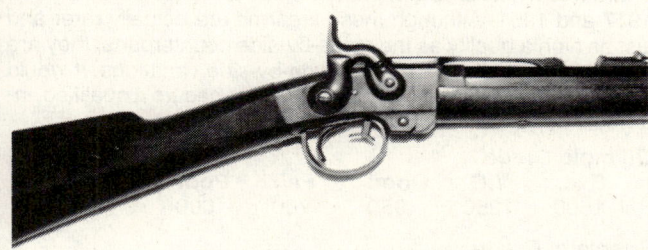

Exc.	V.G.	Good	Fair	Poor
1750	1250	1000	750	500

SMITH, L. C.
Syracuse, New York
Hunter Arms Company
Fulton, New York

One of the finest American-made double-barrel shotguns and very collectible in today's market. It was manufactured between 1880 and 1888 in Syracuse, New York; and between 1890 and 1945, in Fulton, New York, by the Hunter Arms Company. In 1945 Marlin Firearms Company acquired Hunter Arms, and the L.C. Smith was made until 1951. In 1968 the L.C. Smith was resurrected for five years, and production ceased totally in 1973. The values given are approximate for standard production models; and we strongly feel that competent, individual appraisals should be secured, especially on the rarer and higher grade models, if a transaction is contemplated.

The values given are for fluid steel, hammerless guns only. Damascus-barreled guns have become collectible if they are in very good or better condition, and values are approximately the same as for the fluid steel models. Damascus guns in less than good condition are worth considerably less.

Early Hammerless Shotguns

The following models were manufactured between 1890 and 1913. They are chambered for 10, 12, 16, and 20 gauge and were produced with various barrel lengths and choke combinations. They feature full sidelock actions. The difference in the models and their values is based on the degree of ornamentation and the quality of materials and workmanship utilized in their construction. The general values furnished are for 10, 12 or 16 gauge guns only.

20 Gauge-Add 50%.
Single-Selective Trigger-Add $250.
Automatic Ejectors-Add 30%.

00 Grade-60,000 Manufactured

Exc.	V.G.	Good	Fair	Poor
1500	1250	1000	650	400

0 Grade-30,000 Manufactured

Exc.	V.G.	Good	Fair	Poor
1600	1350	1050	700	450

No. 1 Grade-10,000 Manufactured

Exc.	V.G.	Good	Fair	Poor
2500	2000	1500	800	550

No. 2 Grade-13,000 Manufactured

Exc.	V.G.	Good	Fair	Poor
3000	2250	1750	900	700

No. 3 Grade-4,000 Manufactured

Exc.	V.G.	Good	Fair	Poor
3500	2750	1800	1000	750

Pigeon Grade-1,200 Manufactured

Exc.	V.G.	Good	Fair	Poor
3500	2750	1800	1000	750

No. 4 Grade-500 Manufactured

Exc.	V.G.	Good	Fair	Poor
10000	7500	5000	3000	2000

A-1 Grade-700 Manufactured, All Damascus, No 20-Gauge

Exc.	V.G.	Good	Fair	Poor
5000	3500	2500	1750	1000

No. 5 Grade-500 Manufactured

Exc.	V.G.	Good	Fair	Poor
8500	7000	5000	2750	2000

Monogram Grade-100 Manufactured

Exc.	V.G.	Good	Fair	Poor
11000	8500	6000	3750	2500

A-2 Grade-200 Manufactured

Exc.	V.G.	Good	Fair	Poor
15000	10000	7500	4500	3750

A-3 Grade-20 Manufactured

This is too rare to generalize a value.

Later Production Hammerless Shotguns

These were manufactured at Fulton, New York, between 1914 and 1951. They are side-by-side double-barrel shotguns chambered for 12, 16, and 20 gauge, as well as the .410. They are offered with various barrel lengths and choke combinations. They feature a full sidelock action and are available with double or single triggers, extractors, and automatic ejectors. The finishes are blued and case-colored, with checkered walnut stocks that are of either straight, semi-pistolgrip, or pistol-grip configurations. The various models differ as to the degree of ornamentation and the quality of materials and workmanship utilized in their construction. These are collectible American shotguns, and we strongly recommend securing a qualified, individual appraisal if a transaction is contemplated. The values supplied are for 12 and 16 gauge models only.

20 Gauge-Add 35%.
.410-Add 500%.
Single-Selective Trigger-Add $250.
Automatic Ejectors-Add 30%.

Courtesy Milwaukee Public Museum, Milwaukee, Wisconsin

Field Grade

Exc.	V.G.	Good	Fair	Poor
1250	1000	750	500	350

Ideal Grade

Exc.	V.G.	Good	Fair	Poor
1500	1200	900	600	450

Trap Grade

Exc.	V.G.	Good	Fair	Poor
1600	1300	1000	700	500

Specialty Grade

Exc.	V.G.	Good	Fair	Poor
3000	2500	1750	1000	600

Eagle Grade

Exc.	V.G.	Good	Fair	Poor
5000	4000	3000	1750	1250

Skeet Special Grade

Exc.	V.G.	Good	Fair	Poor
3000	2500	1750	1000	600

Premier Skeet Grade

Exc.	V.G.	Good	Fair	Poor
3000	2500	1750	1000	600

Crown Grade

With this grade, automatic ejectors became standard equipment. The .410 is extremely rare in this model and non-existent in higher grades; there were only six manufactured, and they cannot be generally evaluated.

Exc.	V.G.	Good	Fair	Poor
6000	4500	3750	2750	2000

Monogram Grade

This version is offered standard with automatic ejectors and a single selective trigger.

Exc.	V.G.	Good	Fair	Poor
12500	10000	7500	5000	3750

There were two higher grades offered—the Premier Grade and the Deluxe Grade. They are extremely rare, and there have not been enough transactions to generally evaluate them.

Fulton Model

A utility, side-by-side double-barrel shotgun chambered for 12, 16, or 20 gauge. It is offered with various barrel lengths and choke combinations. It has double triggers and extractors. Although this is technically not an L.C. Smith, it was manufactured by Hunter Arms Company.

Exc.	V.G.	Good	Fair	Poor
650	550	450	300	200

Fulton Special

A slightly higher-grade version of the utility Fulton gun.

Exc.	V.G.	Good	Fair	Poor
750	650	500	350	250

Hunter Special

A similar utility-grade gun that features the rotary locking-bolt system found on the L.C. Smith shotguns.

Exc.	V.G.	Good	Fair	Poor
600	500	400	250	175

Single Barrel Trap Guns

High-grade, break-open, single-shot trap guns chambered for 12 gauge only. They feature 32" or 34" vent rib barrels that are full-choked. They have boxlock actions and are standard with automatic ejectors. The finish is blued and case-colored, and they have a checkered walnut stock with a recoil pad. The various models differ in the amount of ornamentation and the quality of the materials and workmanship utilized in their construction. There was a total of approximately 2,650 manufactured between 1917 and 1951. Although these firearms are actually rarer and just as high a quality as their side-by-side counterparts, they are simply not as collectible as the side-by-side variations. It would still behoove the astute firearms investor to secure a qualified, individual appraisal if a transaction is contemplated.

Olympic Grade

Exc.	V.G.	Good	Fair	Poor
1500	1250	950	700	600

Specialty Grade

Exc.	V.G.	Good	Fair	Poor
2000	1750	1300	1000	800

Crown Grade

Exc.	V.G.	Good	Fair	Poor
3500	3000	2250	1500	1250

Monogram Grade

Exc.	V.G.	Good	Fair	Poor
6000	5000	3500	2500	1750

Premier Grade

Exc.	V.G.	Good	Fair	Poor
10000	8500	5500	4000	2750

Deluxe Grade

Exc.	V.G.	Good	Fair	Poor
14000	12500	9500	7500	4500

1968 Model

A side-x-side double-barrel shotgun chambered for 12 gauge with a 28" vent rib barrel, choked full-and-modified. It features a sidelock action with double triggers and extractors. The finish is blued and case-colored, with a checkered walnut stock. This shotgun was manufactured by Marlin between 1968 and 1973.

Exc.	V.G.	Good	Fair	Poor
700	600	550	450	300

1968 Deluxe Model

Similar to the 1968 model but features a Simmons floating rib and a beavertail-type forearm. It was manufactured by Marlin between 1971 and 1973.

Exc.	V.G.	Good	Fair	Poor
1000	850	750	600	400

SMITH, OTIS
Rockfall, Connecticut

This company manufactured a line of single-action, spur-trigger revolvers that are chambered for .22, .32, .38, and .41 rimfire cartridges. The pistols have varying barrel lengths. The cylinder access pin is retained by a button on the left side of the frame. The cylinder usually holds five shots. The finishes are either blued or nickel-plated, with bird's-head grips. The quality was considered to be mediocre.

Model 1883 Shell-Ejector

A single-action, break-open, self ejecting revolver with a ribbed 3.5" barrel chambered for .32 centerfire. It has a 5-shot fluted cylinder and a spur trigger. It was quite well made. The finish is nickel-plated, with black plastic grips.

Exc.	V.G.	Good	Fair	Poor
250	200	150	100	75

Model 1892

A double-action, concealed-hammer revolver chambered for the .38 centerfire cartridge. It has a 4" barrel and, for the first time, a conventional trigger and triggerguard. It is gateloaded and has a solid frame. It is nickel-plated with black plastic grips and also appeared under the Maltby, Henley & Company banner marked "Spencer Safety Hammerless" or "Parker Safety Hammerless." The Otis Smith Company ceased operations in 1898.

Exc.	V.G.	Good	Fair	Poor
250	200	150	100	75

Smith & Wesson®

SMITH & WESSON
Springfield, Massachusetts

By Roy G. Jinks
Smith & Wesson Historian

Smith & Wesson was founded by two men who shared the dream of developing a new type of firearm ... one capable of being fired repeatedly without the annoyance of having to reload it using loose powder, balls and a primer. Their idea was to direct the firearms makers out of the era of muzzleloading, which had dominated the firearms industry since the invention of hand cannons in the 14th century.

Their dream became a reality when Horace Smith and Daniel B. Wesson formed their first partnership in 1852 to manufacture a lever action pistol incorporating a tubular magazine and firing a fully self-contained cartridge. This new repeating pistol could be fired as rapidly as an individual could operate the lever that loaded the pistol and cocked the hammer, making it ready to be fired. The firing power of this lever action pistol was so impressive that, in 1854 when the gun was reviewed by *Scientific America*, it was nicknamed the Volcanic since to the reviewer the rapid fire sequence appeared to have the force of an erupting volcano.

The original site of the Smith & Wesson Arms Company was in Norwich, Connecticut, and the company operated in those facilities until it ran into financial difficulties in 1854. In the reorganization of the company during that year, a new investor, Oliver Winchester, provided the additional financial support to continue the manufacture of this particular type of pistol. The factory was moved to New Haven, Connecticut, the site of some of Winchester's holdings, and at this time the name was changed to Volcanic Repeating Arms Company and Smith &

Wesson sold the majority of their interests. It is interesting to note that this early company continued to develop using the original Smith & Wesson patents and emerged in 1866 as the Winchester Repeating Arms Company.

Horace Smith and D.B. Wesson moved from Connecticut to Springfield, Massachusetts, and in 1856 established their company for the purpose of manufacturing a revolving pistol that would fire a small .22 caliber rimfire cartridge, patented by the partners in 1854. This new rimfire cartridge was the beginning of one of the most famous cartridges developed in the world. It was originally called the "Number One Cartridge" but is today more commonly known as the .22 rimfire. The new revolver was called the Model 1 and it gained immediate popularity because of the advantages offered by the new cartridge. In 1859, finding that demand could no longer be met in the small 25-man shop, Smith & Wesson built a new factory located on Stockbridge Street, close to the United States Armory in the center of Springfield, Massachusetts. The factory continued in a progressive manner, improving on the Model 1, and introducing a larger frame gun more suitable to military and law enforcement use. This revolver was called the Model 2 and used a .32 rimfire cartridge.

The demand for the Smith & Wesson product was greatly accelerated in 1861 with the advent of the Civil War. In fact, by mid-1862, the demand for Smith & Wesson products had grown so great that it exceeded factory capacity and it was necessary to close the order books and only supply products against its heavy backlog. Wartime production helped firmly establish Smith & Wesson as one of the leading firearm manufacturers in the United States. However, in the postwar depression Smith & Wesson, like many other businesses, suffered severe business curtailments and sales dropped to only a few guns per month.

By 1867, the partners realized that a new approach was necessary. They had been experimenting with a new design but had lacked the necessary market. For this reason, in April 1867, they authorized Henry W. Hallott to negotiate contracts and establish a market in Europe, and sales agencies in England, France, and Germany. One of Hallott's first functions was to organize a display of Smith & Wesson arms at a major exposition being held in Paris. The display included the total product line as well as some of their highly engraved works of art to further illustrate the quality craftsmen employed by the firm.

The Smith & Wesson arms exhibit was extremely popular and many nations expressed interest in its products. One of the most important persons to view their product line was the Russian Grand Duke Alexis. He was so impressed with Smith & Wesson's revolvers that he purchased several small pistols for himself and his aides. This marketing approach proved highly successful and European orders helped to relieve the effects of the domestic depression. With this new marketplace and the increase in sales, Smith & Wesson introduced their first large caliber 44 revolver called the Model 3.

The Model 3 was a totally new design known as a "top break" revolver that incorporated a fully automatic ejection system allowing rapid unloading and reloading of cartridges.

One of the first customers to receive the Model 3 was the Russian military attache, General Gorloff. He promptly sent this sample to Russia for evaluation, and it was so well received that in May 1871 the Russian government signed a contract for 20,000 Model 3s, paying Smith & Wesson in advance with gold. This contract proved to be one of many signed with the Russian government but, more significantly, it influenced the total market and soon orders poured into the factory far exceeding its ability to supply handguns. The Model 3 became extremely popular throughout the world and on our own western frontier. One of the most interesting notes on the Model 3 appeared in an editorial in the *Army/Navy Journal* shortly after the Custer massacre. This article noted that if Custer and his men had been armed with Schofield's variation of the Smith & Wesson Model 3, rather than the slower loading Colt Single Action revolver, they might have possibly survived the Indian attack.

Smith & Wesson continued to grow and in 1880 expanded their line by introducing the first group of "double action" revolvers, the result of more than four years of extensive research.

In 1899, Smith & Wesson developed one of its most famous revolvers, the .38 Military & Police, which was the predecessor of the Model 10. This revolver was designed to fire another first, the .38 Smith & Wesson Special.

In the summer of 1914 at the request of the British government, Smith & Wesson began development of its first side swing revolvers in .45 caliber. As WWI was engulfing the European continent, England needed a supply of service revolvers. Smith & Wesson responded by producing more than 75,000 revolvers chambered for the .455 Mark 11 British Service cartridge in slightly more than one year, thus helping to provide the British Army with the finest revolver available in the world.

During the 1930s, Smith & Wesson introduced two more famous revolvers, the K-22 Outdoorsman for the competitive shooter and the .357 Magnum for the law enforcement officers who needed a powerful handgun to continue their fight against crime. The .357 Magnum also was significant as it was the beginning of the era of Magnum handguns; an important first in the growth of handgunning in the world.

As it had done in WWI, Smith & Wesson answered the needs of WWII's fighting forces and by 1941 its total plant production was geared to supplying arms for the United States and all her allies. By March 1945 when WWII production was ended, Smith & Wesson had supplied 568,204 .38 military and police revolvers to its close ally Great Britain. These revolvers were produced in the British Service caliber of .38/200.

At the close of WWII, Smith & Wesson continued its progressive leadership under the management of Mr. C.R. Hellstrom, who became president in 1946 and the first person outside the Wesson family to serve in this capacity. In 1949, the company moved to a totally new facility in Springfield, Massachusetts, where it has continued to expand. It introduced the first American-made 9mm double action pistol called the Model 39, followed by the introduction of a gun that has become a legend with sportsmen and gun enthusiasts throughout the world, the Model 29, .44 Magnum, the most powerful handgun.

In 1964 Smith & Wesson entered into a completely new era as the independently owned company was purchased by Bangor Panta Corporation. Bangor Panta, recognizing an even greater potential for this giant of the firearms field, encouraged the president, W.G. Gunn, to further diversify the company. William Gunn succeeded C.R. Hellstrom as president in 1963 following the death of Mr. Hellstrom at the age of 68.

Gunn soon purchased other companies to augment Smith & Wesson's line of handgun and handcuff products to further meet the needs of the law enforcement and sporting markets. By the 1970s Smith & Wesson had increased its products to law enforcement by selling riot control equipment, police Identi-Kit identification equipment, night vision, breath testing equipment and leather products. The sporting dealers were now able to purchase not only Smith & Wesson handguns but ammunition, holsters and long guns, thus allowing them to sell a complete line of Smith & Wesson products.

Even with the expansion of Smith & Wesson's product line in other areas, the management in Springfield continued to concentrate on the development of new handguns. In 1965 the firm introduced the first stainless steel revolver, thus changing again the course of firearms history. The 1970s saw the continued development of stainless models and a new 15-shot 9mm autoloading pistol called the Model 59 to meet the requirement of many law enforcement agencies. Smith & Wesson opened the market of police commemorative handguns, allowing departments to purchase specially designed handguns to commemorate department history. These commemoratives helped further establish Smith & Wessons's position with law enforcement by providing the departments with a memento of their history on a fine quality Smith & Wesson handgun.

The 1970s saw many significant improvements in Smith & Wesson; the further modernization of its manufacturing facilities in Springfield, the development of the stainless steel Model 629, .44 Magnum, the Model 547, 9mm revolver using a special patented extractor system. But most important was the development of the Smith & Wesson L frame line producing the Models 581, 586, 681, and 686, which had a significant impact on both the law enforcement and sporting markets to become the most popular new revolver introduced.

With the new L frame models and the 1980s, Smith & Wesson began to consolidate its widely diversified product line by concentrating on those lines that were most profitable and beneficial to the company. Development was begun on a 9mm autoloading pistol to meet the needs of the United States military and a new .45 autoloading pistol called the Model 645.

In January 1984, Lear Siegler Corporation of Santa Monica, California, purchased Bangor Panta, thus acquiring Smith & Wesson. Lear Siegler, in their evaluation of Smith & Wesson, recognized the fact that Smith & Wesson's total strength laid in the manufacture and sales of handguns, handcuffs, and police Identi-Kits. Under Lear's direction, Smith & Wesson divested itself of all other unrelated lines to concentrate on the product for which they were famous, thus further strengthening their position in the handgun market by concentrating Smith & Wesson's efforts in providing the highest quality, most innovative designs available to handgun users of the world.

In December 1986, Lear Siegler Corporation was purchased by Forstmann Little & Company in an agreed-upon friendly takeover. However, Forstmann Little had no interest in Smith & Wesson. Their primary interest was only in Lear Siegler holdings in the automotive and air space industry. Therefore, they offered Smith & Wesson for sale to help finance the takeover of Lear Siegler. For the first time since 1964, Smith & Wesson was going to be offered for sale on its own merits as one of the finest handgun manufacturers in the United States.

The successful bidder for Smith & Wesson was the F.H. Tomkins p.l.c. of London, England. Tomkins brings to Smith & Wesson a new strong leadership and a renewed dedication to quality and development of the finest handguns in the world.

SMITH & WESSON ANTIQUE HANDGUNS

Model 1, 1st Issue Revolver

This was the first metallic cartridge arm produced by Smith & Wesson. It is a small revolver that weighs approximately 10 oz. and is chambered for the .22 short rimfire cartridge. The octagonal barrel is 3.25" long. It holds 7 cartridges. The barrel and nonfluted cylinder pivot upward upon release of the protruding bayonet-type catch under the frame. This model has a square butt with rosewood grips. The oval brass frame is silver-plated. The barrel and cylinder are blued. The barrel is stamped with the company name and address; the patent dates also appear. The edges of the frame are rounded on the 1st Issue, and the sideplate is round. Smith & Wesson manufactured approximately 11,000 of these revolvers between 1857 and 1860. Since this was the first of its kind, it is not difficult to understand the need for the number of variations within this model designation. Many small improvements were made on the way to the next model. These variations are as follows:

1st Type

Serial range 1 to low 200s, revolving recoil shield, bayonet type catch on frame.

Exc.	V.G.	Good	Fair	Poor
12000	7500	5000	3500	2000

2nd Type

Serial range low 200s to 1130, improved recoil plate.

Exc.	V.G.	Good	Fair	Poor
6000	3000	2000	1250	750

3rd Type

Serial range 1130 to low 3000s, bayonet catch dropped for spring-loaded side catch.

Exc.	V.G.	Good	Fair	Poor
3000	1900	1400	850	450

4th Type

Serial range low 3000s to low 4200s, recoil shield made much smaller.

Exc.	V.G.	Good	Fair	Poor
2500	1750	1400	850	450

5th Type

Serial range low 4200s to low 5500s, has 5-groove rifling instead of 3.

Exc.	V.G.	Good	Fair	Poor
2500	1750	1400	850	450

6th Type

Serial range low 5500s to end of production 11670. A cylinder ratchet replaced the revolving recoil shield.

Exc.	V.G.	Good	Fair	Poor
2000	1500	1250	750	400

Model 1 2nd Issue

Similar in appearance to the 1st Issue this 2nd Issue variation has several notable differences that make identification rather simple. The sides of the frame on the 2nd Issue are flat not rounded as on the 1st Issue. The sideplate is irregular in shape—not round like on the 1st Issue. The barrel was 3-3/16" in length. The barrel is stamped "Smith & Wesson" while the cylinder is marked with the three patent dates: April 3, 1858, July 5 1859, and December 18, 1860. There have been 2nd Issue noted with full silver or nickel-plating. Smith & Wesson manufactured approximately 115,000 of these revolvers between 1860 and 1868. The serial numbers started around 1100 where the 1st Issue left off and continued to 126400. There were approximately 4,400 revolvers marked "2D Quality" on the barrels. These revolvers were slightly defective and were sold at a lesser price. They will bring an approximate 100% premium on today's market.

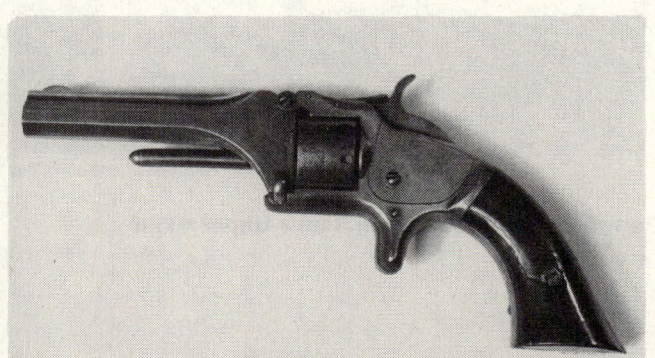

Courtesy Mike Stuckslager

Exc.	V.G.	Good	Fair	Poor
600	400	300	250	125

Model 1 3rd Issue

This is a redesigned version of its forerunners. Another .22 short rimfire, 7-shot revolver, this model has a fluted cylinder and round barrel with a raised rib. This variation was manufactured totally from wrought iron. The three patent dates are stamped on top of the ribbed barrel as is "Smith & Wesson". It features bird's-head type grips of rosewood and is either fully blued nickel-plated, or two-toned with the frame nickel and the barrel and cylinder blued. There are two barrel lengths offered—3.25" and 2 11/16". The shorter barrel was introduced

in 1872. Serial numbering began with #1 and continued to 131163. They were manufactured between 1868 and 1882. The Model 1 3rd Issue was the last of the tip-up style produced by Smith & Wesson.

Courtesy Mike Stuckslager

Shorter Barreled Version-Rare

Exc.	V.G.	Good	Fair	Poor
650	450	300	200	150

Longer Barreled Version-Common

Exc.	V.G.	Good	Fair	Poor
400	225	150	100	75

Model 1-1/2 1st Issue (1-1/2 Old Model)

This model was the first of the .32-caliber Rim Fire Short revolvers that S&W produced. It is a larger version of the Model 1 but is physically similar in appearance. The Model 1-1/2 was offered with a 3.5" octagonal barrel and has a 5-shot non-fluted cylinder and a square butt with rosewood grips. In 1866 a 4" barrel version was produced for a short time. It is estimated that about 200 were sold. The finish is blued or nickel-plated. The serial numbering on this model ran from serial number 1 to 26300; and, interestingly to note, S&W had most of the parts for this revolver manufactured on contract by King & Smith of Middletown, Connecticut. Smith & Wesson merely assembled and finished them. They were produced between 1865 and 1868.
NOTE: Add a 50% premium for the 4" barrel variation.

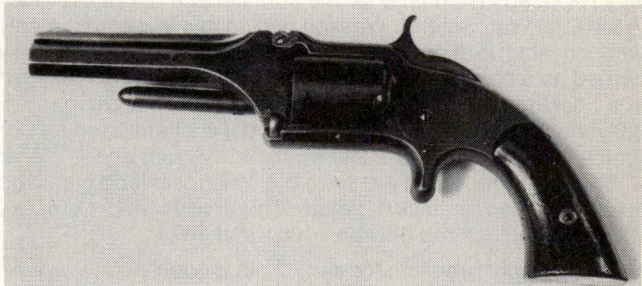

Courtesy Mike Stuckslager

Exc.	V.G.	Good	Fair	Poor
500	300	200	150	100

Model 1-1/2 2nd Issue (1-1/2 New Model)

The factory referred to this model as the New Model 1-1/2 and it is an improved version of the 1st Issue. It is somewhat similar in appearance with a few notable exceptions. The barrel is 2.5" or 3.5" in length, round with a raised rib. The grip is of the bird's-head configuration, and the 5-shot cylinder is fluted and chambered for the .32 rimfire long cartridge. The cylinder stop is located in the top frame instead of the bottom. The finish and grip material are the same as the 1st Issue. There were approximately 100,700 manufactured between 1868 and 1875.

Courtesy Mike Stuckslager

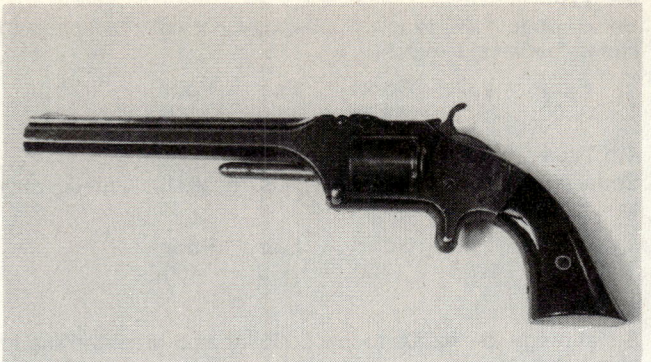

Courtesy Mike Stuckslager

3.5" Barrel

Exc.	V.G.	Good	Fair	Poor
450	300	200	150	100

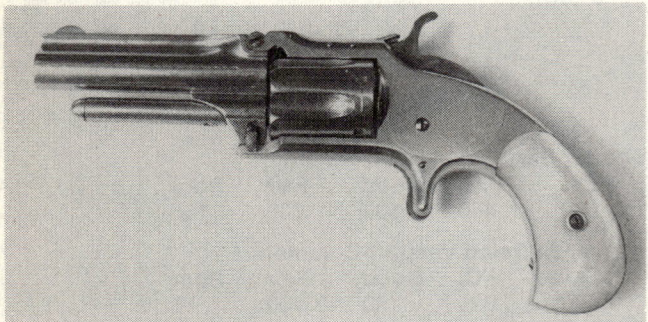

Courtesy Mike Stuckslager

2.5" Barrel

Exc.	V.G.	Good	Fair	Poor
750	500	350	300	200

Model 1-1/2 Transitional Model

Approximately 650 of these were produced by fitting 1st Issue cylinders and barrels to 2nd Issue frames. They also have 1st Model octagon barrels with 2nd Model birds head grips. These revolvers fall into the serial number range 27200-28800.

Exc.	V.G.	Good	Fair	Poor
2500	1100	800	650	400

Model 2 Army or Old Model

Similar in appearance to the Model 1 2nd Issue, this revolver was extremely successful from a commercial standpoint. It was released just in time for the commencement of hostilities in the Civil War. Smith & Wesson had, in this revolver, the only weapon able to fire self-contained cartridges and be easily carried as a backup by soldiers going off to war. This resulted in a backlog of more than three years before the company finally stopped taking orders. This model is chambered for .32 rimfire long and has a 6-shot non-fluted cylinder and 4", 5", or 6" barrel lengths. It has a square butt with rosewood grips and is either blued or nickel-plated. There were approximately 77,155 manufactured between 1861 and 1874.

NOTE: A slight premium for early 2 pin model.

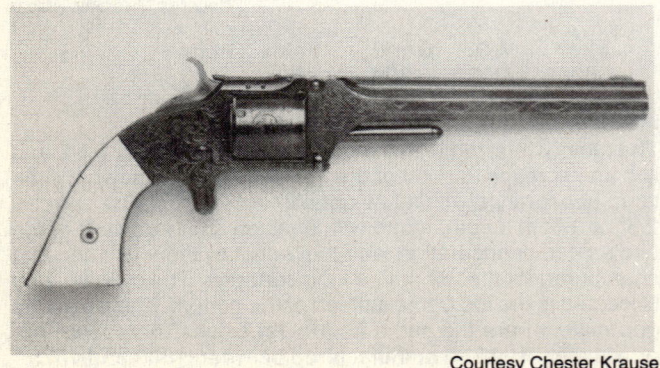

Courtesy Chester Krause

5" or 6" Barrel

Exc.	V.G.	Good	Fair	Poor
1200	650	400	300	200

4" Barrel-Rare! Use Caution

Exc.	V.G.	Good	Fair	Poor
2000	1200	800	500	300

.32 Single Action (Model 1-1/2 Centerfire)

This model represented the first .32 S&W centerfire caliber top-break revolver that automatically ejected the spent cartridges upon opening. It is similar in appearance to the Model 1-1/2 2nd Issue. This model has a 5-shot fluted cylinder and a bird's-head grip of wood or checkered hard rubber and was offered with barrel lengths of 3", 3.5", 6", 8", and 10". The 8" and 10" barrel are rare and were not offered until 1887. This model pivots downward on opening and features a rebounding hammer that made the weapon much safer to fully load. There were approximately 97,599 manufactured between 1878 and 1892.

Courtesy W.P. Hallstein III and son Chip

Early Model Without Strain Screw-Under #6500

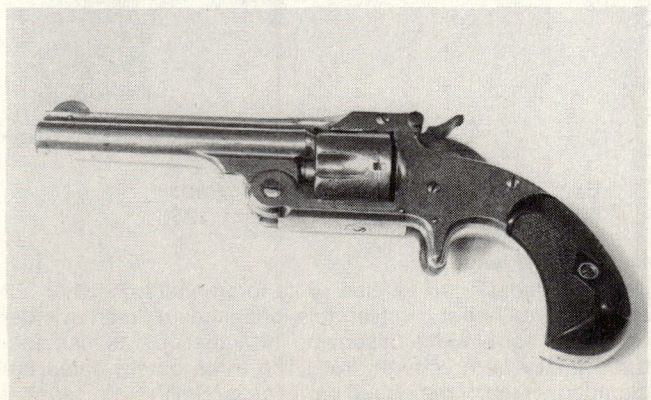

Courtesy Mike Stuckslager

Exc.	V.G.	Good	Fair	Poor
500	350	275	185	125

Later Model With Strain Screw

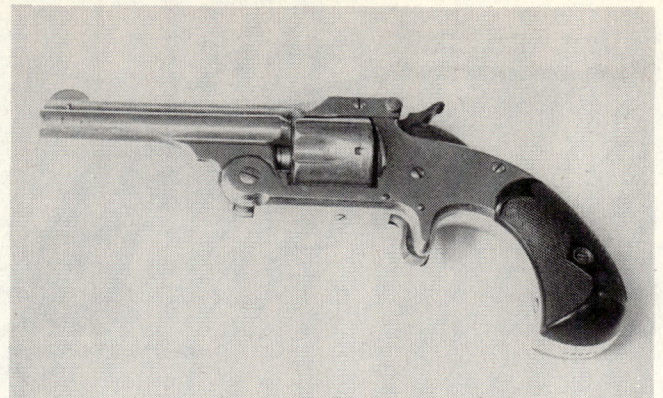

Courtesy Mike Stuckslager

Exc.	V.G.	Good	Fair	Poor
350	250	175	125	75

8" or 10" Barrel Model

Exc.	V.G.	Good	Fair	Poor
2500	1700	1000	700	400

.38 Single Action 1st Model (Baby Russian)

This model is sometimes called the "Baby Russian." It is a top break, automatic-ejecting revolver chambered for the .38 S&W centerfire cartridge. It is offered with either a 3.25" or 4" round barrel with a raised rib, has a 5-shot fluted cylinder, and is finished in blue or nickel plating. A 5" barrel was added as an option a short time later. The butt is rounded, with wood or checkered hard rubber grips inlaid with the S&W medallion. It has a spur trigger. There were approximately 25,548 manufactured in 1876 and 1877 of which 16,046 were nickel and 6,502 were blued.

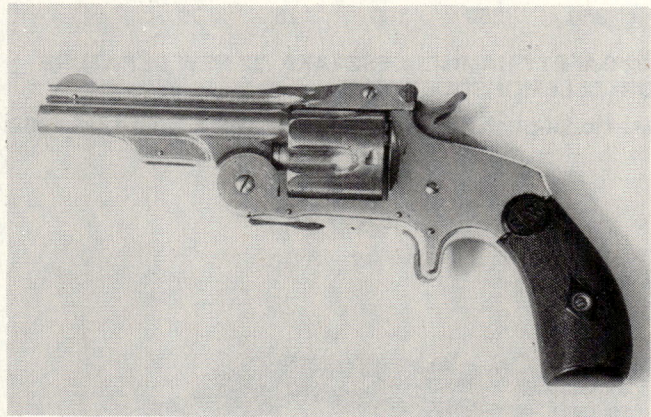

Courtesy Mike Stuckslager

Exc.	V.G.	Good	Fair	Poor
500	300	250	200	150

.38 Single Action 2nd Model

With the exception of an improved and shortened extractor assembly and the availability of additional barrel lengths of 3.25", 4", 5", 6", 8", and 10" with the 8" and 10" barrel lengths being the most rare, this model is quite similar in appearance to the 1st Model. There were approximately 108,225 manufactured between 1877 and 1891.

Courtesy Mike Stuckslager

8" and 10" Barrel

Exc.	V.G.	Good	Fair	Poor
1200	800	600	400	300

3.25", 4", 5", and 6" Barrel Lengths.

Exc.	V.G.	Good	Fair	Poor
350	225	175	125	100

.38 Single Action 3rd Model

This model differs from the first two models because it is fitted with a triggerguard. It is chambered for the .38 S&W centerfire cartridge, has a 5-shot fluted cylinder, and is a top break design with automatic ejection upon opening. The barrel lengths are 3.25", 4", and 6". The finish is blued or nickel-plated. The butt is rounded, with checkered hard rubber grips featuring S&W medallions. There were approximately 26,850 manufactured between 1891 and 1911.

Courtesy Mike Stuckslager

Exc.	V.G.	Good	Fair	Poor
1200	650	450	300	175

.38 Single Action Mexican Model

This extremely rare model is quite similar in appearance to the 3rd Model Single Action. The notable differences are the flat hammer sides with no outward flaring of the spur. The spur trigger assembly was not made integrally with the frame but is a separate part added to it. One must exercise extreme caution as S&W offered a kit that would convert the triggerguard assembly of the Third Model to the spur trigger of the Mexican Model. This, coupled with the fact that both models fall within the same serial range, can present a real identification problem. Another feature of the Mexican Model is the absence of a half cock. The exact number of Mexican Models manufactured between 1891 and 1911 is unknown but it is estimated that the number is small.

Exc.	V.G.	Good	Fair	Poor
3000	1250	900	650	450

.32 Double Action 1st Model

This is one of the rarest of all S&W revolvers. There were only 30 manufactured. It also has a straight-sided sideplate that weakened the revolver frame. Perhaps this was the reason that so few were made. This model was the first break-open, double action, automatic-ejecting .32 that S&W produced. It features a 3" round barrel with raised rib, a 5-shot fluted cylinder, and round butt with plain, unchecked, black hard rubber grips. The finish is blued or nickel-plated. All 30 of these revolvers were manufactured in 1880.

Exc.	V.G.	Good	Fair	Poor
10000	6000	4000	2000	1500

.32 Double Action 2nd Model

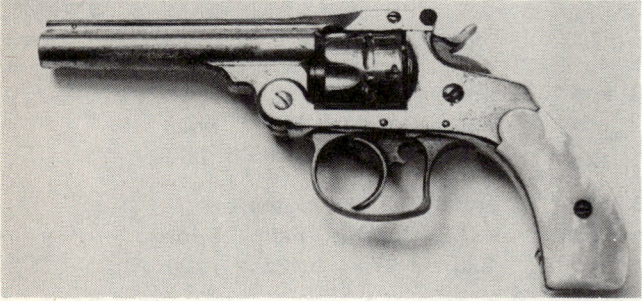

Courtesy Mike Stuckslager

This revolver is chambered for the .32 S&W cartridge and has a 3" round barrel with a raised rib. The 5-shot cylinder is fluted, and the finish is blued or nickel-plated. It is a top break design with a round butt. The grips are either checkered or floral-embossed hard rubber with the S&W monogram. This model has an oval sideplate, eliminating the weakness of the 1st Model. There were approximately 22,142 manufactured between 1880 and 1882.

Exc.	V.G.	Good	Fair	Poor
300	200	150	100	70

.32 Double Action 3rd Model

This model incorporates internal improvements that are not evident in appearance. The most notable identifiable difference between this model and its predecessors is in the surface of the cylinder. The flutes are longer; there is only one set of stops instead of two; and the free groove is no longer present. There were approximately 21,232 manufactured in 1882 and 1883.

Courtesy Mike Stuckslager

Exc.	V.G.	Good	Fair	Poor
300	200	150	100	70

.32 Double Action 4th Model

This model is quite similar in appearance to the 3rd Model except that the triggerguard is oval in shape instead of the squared back of the previous models. There were also internal improvements. There were approximately 239,600 manufactured between 1883 and 1909.

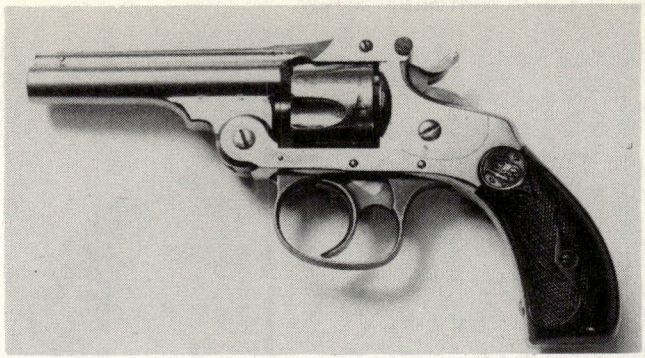

Courtesy Mike Stuckslager

Exc.	V.G.	Good	Fair	Poor
275	175	125	100	70

.32 Double Action 5th Model

The only difference between this model and its predecessors is that this model has the front sight machined as an integral part of the barrel rib. On the other models, the sight was pinned in place. There were approximately 44,641 manufactured between 1909 and 1919.

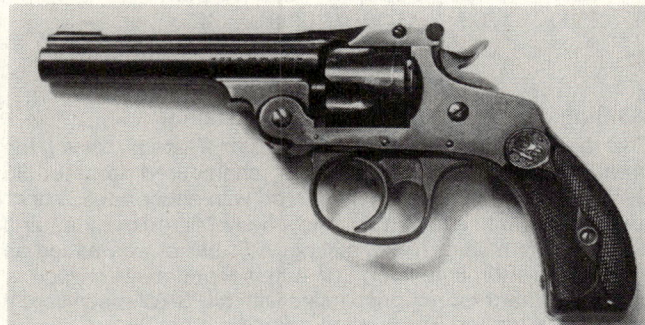

Courtesy Mike Stuckslager

Exc.	V.G.	Good	Fair	Poor
350	250	200	125	100

.32 SAFETY HAMMERLESS (AKA .32 NEW DEPATURE OR .32 LEMONSQUEEZER)

1st Model-push button latch s/n 1- 91417, built 1888-1902

Courtesy Mike Stuckslager

Exc.	V.G.	Good	Fair	Poor
325	225	175	125	75

.32 Safety Hammerless-2nd Model

T-bar latch, pinned front sight, s/n 91418-169999, built 1902 to 1909.

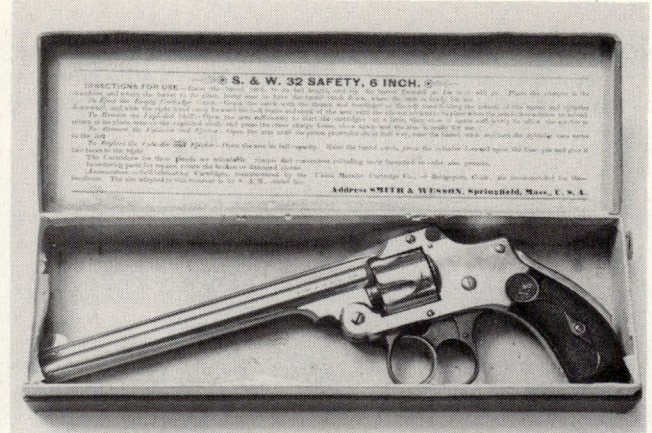

Courtesy Mike Stuckslage

.32 Safety Hammerless- 3rd Model

T-bar latch, integral forged front sight, s/n 170000-242981, built 1909 to 1937

Exc.	V.G.	Good	Fair	Poor
300	175	135	100	65

NOTE: For 2" barrel, Bicycle Model-Add 50%.

.38 Double Action 1st Model

This model is similar in appearance to the .32 1st Model, having a straight cut side-plate, but is chambered for the .38 S&W cartridge. The grips are checkered, and there were 4,000 manufactured in 1880.

Exc.	V.G.	Good	Fair	Poor
800	500	350	200	125

.38 Double Action 2nd Model

This is similar in appearance to the .32 2nd Model but is chambered for the .38 S&W cartridge. There were approximately 115,000 manufactured between 1880 and 1884.

Courtesy Mike Stuckslager

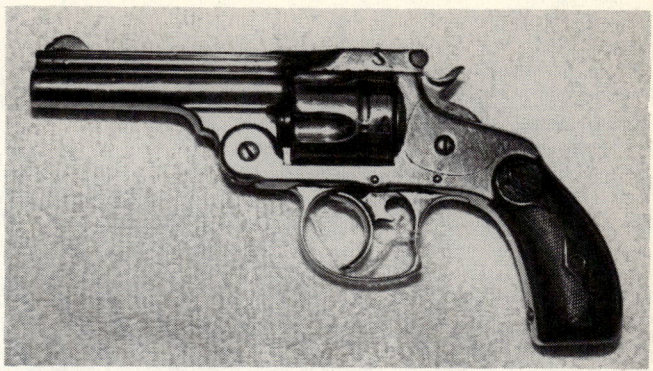

Exc.	V.G.	Good	Fair	Poor
325	225	175	125	100

.38 Double Action 3rd Model

Essentially the same in appearance as the .32 Model but chambered for the .38 S&W cartridge, it is also offered with a 3.25", 4", 5", 6", 8", and 10" barrel. There were numerous internal changes in this model similar to the .32 Double Action 3rd Model. There were approximately 203,700 manufactured between 1884 and 1895.

Courtesy Mike Stuckslager

8" and 10" Barrel

Exc.	V.G.	Good	Fair	Poor
1500	1000	700	500	350

Standard Barrel

Exc.	V.G.	Good	Fair	Poor
300	200	150	100	70

.38 Double Action 4th Model

This is the .38 S&W version of the 4th Model and is identical in outward appearance to the 3rd Model. The relocation of the sear was the main design change in this model. There were approximately 216,300 manufactured between 1895 and 1909.

Exc.	V.G.	Good	Fair	Poor
275	175	125	100	70

.38 Double Action 5th Model

This model is the same as the .32 except that it is chambered for the .38 S&W cartridge. There were approximately 15,000 manufactured between 1909 and 1911.

Courtesy Mike Stuckslager

Exc.	V.G.	Good	Fair	Poor
350	250	175	125	80

.38 Double Action Perfected

A unique top-break with both a barrel latch similar to the other top-breaks and a thumbpiece similar to the hand ejectors; also the only top-break where the trigger guard is integral to the frame rather than a seperate piece. Produced from 1909 to 1911 in their own serial number range. About 59,400 were built.

Exc.	V.G.	Good	Fair	Poor
400	275	175	130	100

Model 3 American 1st Model

This model represented a number of firsts for the Smith & Wesson Company. It was the first of the top break, automatic ejection revolvers. It was also the first Smith & Wesson in a large caliber (it is chambered for the .44 S&W American cartridge as well as the .44 Henry rimfire on rare occasions). It was also known as the 1st Model American. This large revolver is offered with an 8" round barrel with a raised rib as standard. Barrel lengths of 6" and 7" were also available. It has a 6-shot fluted cylinder and a square butt with walnut grips. It is blued or nickel-plated. It is interesting to note that this model appeared three years before Colt's Single Action Army and perhaps, more than any other model, was associated with the historic American West. There were only 8,000 manufactured between 1870 and 1872.

Standard Production Model

Exc.	V.G.	Good	Fair	Poor
5000	2250	1600	950	650

Transition Model - Serial Number Range 6466-6744

Shorter cylinder (1.423"), improved barrel catch.

Exc.	V.G.	Good	Fair	Poor
5500	2500	1600	1150	700

U.S. Army Order-Serial Number Range 125-2199

One thousand produced with "U.S." stamped on top of barrel; "OWA, on left grip.

Exc.	V.G.	Good	Fair	Poor
8000	3500	2500	1750	1000

.44 Rimfire Henry Model

Only 200 produced throughout serial range.

Exc.	V.G.	Good	Fair	Poor
10000	5000	3000	1800	1200

Model 3 American 2nd Model

An improved version of the 1st Model. The most notable difference is the larger diameter trigger pivot pin and the frame protrusions above the trigger to accommodate it. The front sight blade on this model is made of steel instead of nickel silver. Several internal improvements were also incorporated into this model. This model is commonly known as the American 2nd Model. The 8" barrel length was standard on this model. There were approximately 20,735 manufactured, including 3,014 chambered for .44 rimfire Henry, between 1872 and 1874.

NOTE: There have been 5.5", 6", 6.5", and 7" barrels noted; but they are extremely scarce and would bring a 40% premium over the standard 8" model. Use caution when purchasing these short barrel revolvers.

Courtesy Buffalo Bill Historical Center, Cody, Wyoming

.44 Rimfire Henry

Exc.	V.G.	Good	Fair	Poor
6000	3000	1500	1000	750

Standard 8" Model-.44 American centerfire

Exc.	V.G.	Good	Fair	Poor
4500	2000	1250	950	550

Model 3 Russian 1st Model

This model is quite similar in appearance to the American 1st and 2nd Model revolvers. S&W made several internal changes to this model to satisfy the Russian government. The markings on this revolver are distinct; and the caliber for which it is chambered, .44 S&W Russian, is different. There were approximately 20,000 Russian-Contract revolvers. The serial number range is 1-20000. They are marked in Russian Cyrillic letters. The Russian double-headed eagle is stamped on the rear portion of the barrel with inspector's marks underneath it. All of the contract guns have 8" barrels and lanyard swivels on the butt. These are rarely encountered, as most were shipped to Russia. The commercial run of this model numbered approximately 4,655. The barrels are stamped in English and include the words "Russian Model." Some are found with 6" and 7" barrels, as well as the standard 8". There were also 500 revolvers that were rejected from the Russian contract series and sold on the commercial market. Some of these are marked in English; some, Cyrillic. Some have the Cyrillic markings ground off and the English restamped. This model was manufactured from 1871 to 1874.

Russian Contract Model

Exc.	V.G.	Good	Fair	Poor
6000	3000	1750	1250	900

Commercial Model

Exc.	V.G.	Good	Fair	Poor
4750	2250	1400	800	600

Rejected Russian Contract Model

Exc.	V.G.	Good	Fair	Poor
4750	2250	1400	800	600

A Smith & Wesson Model 3 Russian 1st Model belonging to outlaw Cole Younger at the time of his capture following the famous Northfield bank robbery in September of 1876. The condition of the revolver was very good. Ivory grips. Auction hammer price was $190,000.
Butterfield & Butterfield, August 1997.

Model 3 Russian 2nd Model

This revolver was known as the "Old Model Russian." This is a complicated model to understand as there are many variations within the model designation. The serial numbering is quite complex as well, and values vary greatly due to relatively minor model differences. Before purchasing this model, it would be advisable to secure competent appraisal as well as to read reference materials solely devoted to this firearm. This model is chambered for the .44 S&W Russian, as well as the .44 rimfire Henry cartridge. It has a 7" barrel and a round butt featuring a projection on the frame that fits into the thumb web. The grips are walnut, and the finish is blue or nickel-plated. The triggerguard has a reverse curved spur on the bottom. There were approximately 85,200 manufactured between 1873 and 1878.

Commercial Model

6,200 made, .44 S&W Russian, English markings.

Exc.	V.G.	Good	Fair	Poor
3250	1600	950	650	400

.44 Rim Fire Henry Model

500 made.

Exc.	V.G.	Good	Fair	Poor
3750	2500	1800	1000	600

Russian Contract Model

70,000 made; rare, as most were shipped to Russia. Cyrillic markings; lanyard swivel on butt.

Exc.	V.G.	Good	Fair	Poor
3300	1750	1250	800	550

1st Model Turkish Contract

.44 rimfire Henry, special rimfire frames, serial-numbered in own serial number range 1-1000.

Exc.	V.G.	Good	Fair	Poor
5000	3000	1850	1250	900

2nd Model Turkish Contract

Made from altered centerfire frames from the regular commercial serial number range. 1,000 made. Use caution with this model.

Exc.	V.G.	Good	Fair	Poor
3750	2500	1800	1000	600

Japanese Govt. Contract

Five thousand made between the 1-9000 serial number range. The Japanese naval insignia, an anchor over two wavy lines, found on the butt. The barrel is Japanese proofed, and the words "Jan.19, 75 REISSUE July 25, 1871" are stamped on the barrel, as well.

Exc.	V.G.	Good	Fair	Poor
3300	1700	1000	700	400

Model 3 Russian 3rd Model

This revolver is also known as the "New Model Russian." The factory referred to this model as the Model of 1874 or the Cavalry Model. It is chambered for the .44 S&W Russian and the .44 Henry rimfire cartridge. The barrel is 6.5", and the round butt is the same humped-back affair as the 2nd Model. The grips are walnut; and the finish, blue or nickel-plated. The most notable differences in appearance between this model and the 2nd Model are the shorter extractor housing under the barrel and the integral front sight blade instead of the pinned-on one found on the previous models. This is another model that bears careful research before attempting to evaluate. Minor variances can greatly affect values. Secure detailed reference materials and qualified appraisal. There were approximately 60,638 manufactured between 1874 and 1878.

Commercial Model

.44 S&W Russian, marked "Russian Model" in English, 13,500 made.

Exc.	V.G.	Good	Fair	Poor
2500	1500	900	600	350

.44 Rimfire Henry Model

Exc.	V.G.	Good	Fair	Poor
3200	2000	1350	750	550

Turkish Model

Five thousand made of altered centerfire frames, made to fire .44 rimfire Henry. "W" inspector's mark on butt. Fakes have been noted; be aware.

Exc.	V.G.	Good	Fair	Poor
2600	1850	1250	700	400

Japanese Contract Model

One thousand made; has the Japanese naval insignia, an anchor over two wavy lines, stamped on the butt.

Exc.	V.G.	Good	Fair	Poor
2600	1600	1000	600	350

Russian Contract Model

Barrel markings are in Russian Cyrillic. Approximately 41,100 were produced.

Exc.	V.G.	Good	Fair	Poor
2600	1750	1250	750	375

Model 3 Russian 3rd Model (Loewe & Tula Copies)

The German firm of Ludwig Loewe produced a copy of this model that is nearly identical to the S&W. This German revolver was made under Russian contract, as well as for commercial sales. The contract model has different Cyrillic markings than the S&W and the letters "HK" as inspector's marks. The commercial model has the markings in English. The Russian arsenal at Tula also produced a copy of this revolver with a different Cyrillic dated stamping on the barrel.

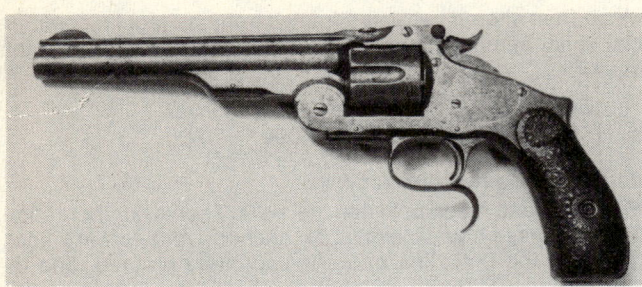

Courtesy Mike Stuckslager

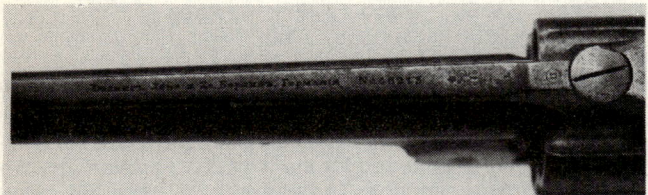

Courtesy Mike Stuckslager

Loewe

Exc.	V.G.	Good	Fair	Poor
2600	1750	1250	750	400

Tula

Exc.	V.G.	Good	Fair	Poor
3200	2250	1700	1200	800

Model 3 Schofield

In 1870 Major George W. Schofield heard about the new S&W Model 3 revolver and wrote to the company expressing a desire to be an exclusive sales representative for them. At that time S&W was earnestly attempting to interest the government in this revolver and obviously felt that the Major could be of help in this endeavor, perhaps because his brother, General John Schofield, was president of the Small Arms Board. Major Schofield was sent one Model 3 revolver and 500 rounds of ammunition free of charge. After testing the revolver, Schofield felt that it needed a few changes to make it the ideal cavalry sidearm. With the company's approval, Schofield made these changes, secured patents, and proceeded to sell them. The company eventually began production of what became known as the Model 3 Schofield 1st Model. The Major was paid a 50 cents royalty per revolver. The eventual production of this model ran to a total of 8,969, with the last one sold in 1878. What was hoped to be the adopted government-issue sidearm never materialized—for a number of reasons. First, the Colt Single Action Army being used by the cavalry had a longer chamber than the S&W and could fire the Schofield ammunition. The Schofield could not fire the longer Colt .45 cartridges. This resulted in disastrous mix-ups on more than one occasion, when Colt ammunition was issued to troops armed with the Schofields. It was eventually decided to drop the S&W as an issue weapon. At this time the company was not happy about paying the 50 cents royalty to Major Schofield. Sales of their other models were high; and they simply did not care about this model, so they eventually ceased its production. It was a popular model on the American frontier and is quite historically significant.

Model 3 Schofield 1st Model

The modifications that made this model differ from the other Model 3 revolvers were quite extensive. The Schofield is chambered for the .45 S&W Schofield cartridge. The top break latch was moved from the barrel assembly to the frame. It was modified so that the action could be opened by simply pulling back on the latch with the thumb. This made it much easier to reload on horseback, as the reins would not have to be released. A groove was milled in the top of the raised barrel rib to improve the sighting plain. The extractor was changed to a cam-operated rather than rack-and-gear system. The removal of the cylinder was simplified. There were 3,000 contract Schofields and 35 commercial models. The contract revolvers were delivered to the Springfield Armory in July of 1875. These guns are stamped "US" on the butt and have the initials "L," "P," or "W" marking various other parts. The grips have an inspector's cartouche with the initials "CW," "JRJr," or "JFEC." There were 35 1st Models made for and sold to the civilian market; these revolvers do not have the "US" markings. The Schofield has a 7" barrel, 6-shot fluted cylinder, and walnut grips. The 1st Model is blued, with a nickel-plated original finish gun being extremely rare.

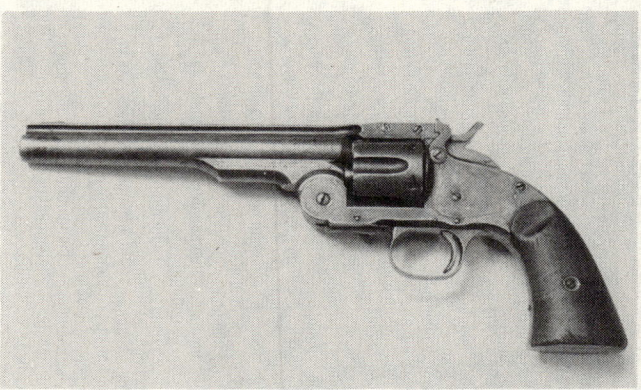

Courtesy Mike Stuckslager

"US" Contract-3,000 Issued

Exc.	V.G.	Good	Fair	Poor
7000	3000	2000	1500	900

Civilian Model, No "US" markings-35 Made-Very Rare, Caution

Exc.	V.G.	Good	Fair	Poor
15000	7000	4000	3000	2000

Model 3 Schofield 2nd Model

The difference between the 1st and 2nd Model Schofield revolvers is in the barrel latch system. The 2nd Model latch is rounded and knurled to afford an easier and more positive grip when opening the revolver. A group of 3,000 of these revolvers was delivered to the Springfield Armory in October of 1876, and another 1,000 were delivered in April of 1877. These 2nd Model contract revolvers were all blued. There were an additional 649 civilian guns sold as well. The civilian models were not "US" marked and were offered either blued or nickel-plated. A total of 8,969 Model 3 Schofield 2nd Models were manufactured. The last sale was recorded in 1878.

"US" Contract-4,000 Issued

Exc.	V.G.	Good	Fair	Poor
6500	3000	2000	1200	850

Civilian Model-646 Made

Exc.	V.G.	Good	Fair	Poor
6000	2750	1750	1100	800

Model 3 Schofield-Surplus Models

After the government dropped the Schofield as an issue cavalry sidearm, the remaining U.S. inventory of these revolvers was sold off as military surplus. Many were sold to National Guard units; and the remainder were sold either to Bannerman's or to Schuyler, Hartley & Graham, two large gun dealers who then resold the guns to supply the growing need for guns on the Western frontier. Schuyler, Hartley & Graham sold a number of guns to the Wells Fargo Express Co. These weapons were nickel-plated and had the barrels shortened to 5", as were many others sold during this period. Beware of fakes when contemplating purchase of the Wells Fargo revolvers.

Wells Fargo & Co. Model

Exc.	V.G.	Good	Fair	Poor
6500	3000	2000	1200	850

Surplus Cut Barrel-Not Wells Fargo

Exc.	V.G.	Good	Fair	Poor
2750	1500	1200	950	700

New Model No. 3 Single Action

Always interested in perfecting the Model 3 revolver D.B. Wesson redesigned and improved the old Model 3 in the hopes of attracting more sales. The Russian contracts were almost filled so the company decided to devote the effort necessary to improve on this design. In 1877 this project was undertaken. The extractor housing was shortened; the cylinder retention system was improved; and the shape of the grip was changed to a more streamlined and attractive configuration. This New Model has a 3.5", 4", 5", 6", 6.5", 7", 7.5", or 8" barrel length with a 6-shot fluted cylinder. The 6.5" barrel and .44 S&W Russian chambering is the most often encountered variation of this model, but the factory considered the 3-1/2" and 8" barrels as standard and these were kept in stock as well. The New Model No. 3 was also chambered for .32 S&W, .32-44 S&W, .320 S&W Rev. Rifle, .38 S&W, .38-40, .38-44 S&W, .41 S&W, .44 Henry rimfire, .44 S&W American, .44-40, .45 S&W Schofield, .450 Rev., .45 Webley, .455 MkI and .455 MkII. They are either blued or nickel-plated and have checkered hard rubber grips with the S&W logo molded into them, or walnut grips. There are many sub-variations within this model designation, and the potential collector should secure detailed reference material that deals with this model. There were approximately 35,796 of these revolvers manufactured between 1878 and 1912. Nearly 40 percent were exported to fill contracts with Japan, Australia, Argentina, England, Spain, and Cuba. There were some sent to Asia, as well. The proofmarks of these countries will establish their provenance but will not add appreciably to standard values.

Standard Model-6.5" barrel, .44 S&W Russian

Courtesy Mike Stuckslager

Exc.	V.G.	Good	Fair	Poor
3500	1300	950	700	400

Japanese Naval Contract

This was the largest foreign purchaser of this model. There were over 1,500 produced with the anchor insignia stamped on the frame.

Courtesy Mike Stuckslager

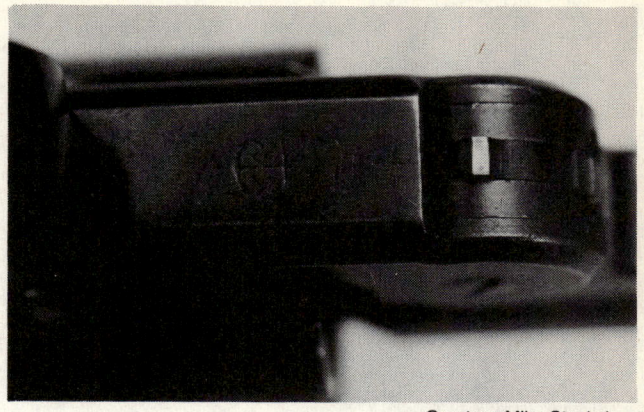

Courtesy Mike Stuckslager

Exc.	V.G.	Good	Fair	Poor
3500	1300	950	700	400

Japanese Artillery Contract

This variation is numbered in the 25,000 serial range. They are blued, with a 7" barrel and a lanyard swivel on the butt. Japanese characters are stamped on the extractor housing.

Exc.	V.G.	Good	Fair	Poor
5000	2500	1500	1200	600

Maryland Militia Model

This variation is nickel-plated, has a 6.5" barrel, and is chambered for the .44 S&W Russian cartridge. The butt is stamped "U.S.," and the inspector's marks "HN" and "DAL" under the date 1878 appear on the revolver. There were 280 manufactured between serial-numbers 7126 and 7405.

Exc.	V.G.	Good	Fair	Poor
8000	4500	3000	1750	1000

Australian Contract

This variation is nickel-plated, is chambered for the .44 S&W Russian cartridge, and is marked with the Australian Colonial Police Broad Arrow on the buff. There were 250 manufactured with 7" barrels and detachable shoulder stocks. The stock has the Broad Arrow stamped on the lower tang. There were also 30 manufactured with 6.5" barrels without the stocks. They all are numbered in the 12,000-13,000 serial range.

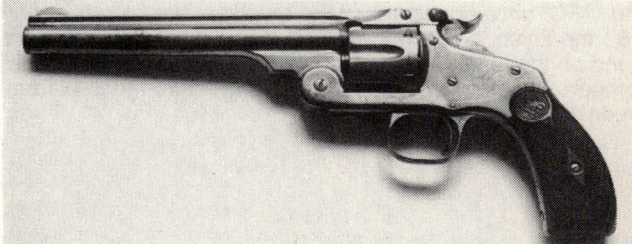

Courtesy Mike Stuckslager

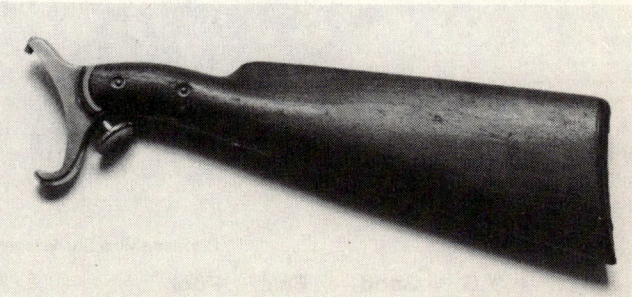

Courtesy Mike Stuckslager

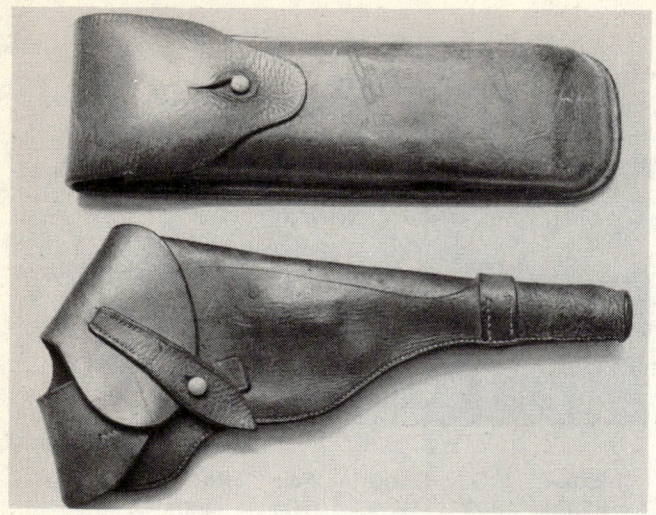

Courtesy Mike Stuckslager

Courtesy Mike Stuckslager

Revolver with stock

Exc.	V.G.	Good	Fair	Poor
6000	4000	2500	1750	1250

NOTE: Deduct 40% for no stock.

Argentine Model

This was essentially not a factory contract but a sale through Schuyler, Hartley and Graham. They are stamped "Ejer-cito/Argentino" in front of the triggerguard. The order amount-ed to some 2,000 revolvers between the serial numbers 50 and 3400.

Exc.	V.G.	Good	Fair	Poor
7000	4000	3000	1750	950

Turkish Model

This is essentially the New Model No. 3 chambered for the .44 rimfire Henry cartridge. It is stamped with the letters "P," "U" and "AFC" on various parts of the revolver. The barrels are all 6.5"; the finish, blued with walnut grips. Lanyard swivels are found on the butt. There were 5,461 manufactured and serial numbered in their own range, starting at 1 through 5,461 be-tween 1879 and 1883.

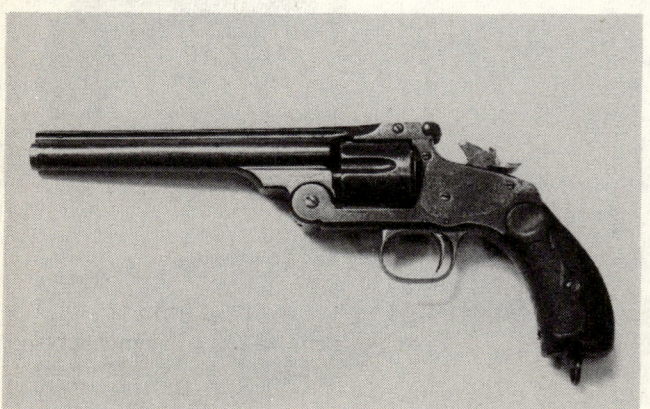

Courtesy Mike Stuckslager

Exc.	V.G.	Good	Fair	Poor
6000	3000	2000	1000	700

New Model No. 3 Target Single Action

This revolver is similar in appearance to the standard New Model No. 3, but was the company's first production target model. It has a 6.5" round barrel with a raised rib and 6-shot fluted cylinder and is finished in blue or nickel-plated. The grips are either walnut or checkered hard rubber with the S&W logo molded into them. This model is chambered in either .32 S&W or .38 S&W. The company referred to these models as either the .32-44 Target or the .38-44 Target depending on the caliber. The designation of -44 referred to the frame size, i.e. a .32 caliber built on a .44 caliber frame. This model was of-fered with a detachable shoulder stock as an option. These stocks are extremely scarce on today's market. There were approximately 4,333 manufactured between 1887 and 1910. Shoulder Stock-Add 50%.

Courtesy Mike Stuckslager

Exc.	V.G.	Good	Fair	Poor
3250	1250	850	600	300

New Model No. 3 Frontier Single Action

This is another model similar in appearance to the standard New Model No. 3. It has a 4", 5", or 6.5" barrel and is cham-bered for the .44-40 Winchester Centerfire cartridge. Because the original New Model No. 3 cylinder was 1-7/16" in length this would not accommodate the longer .44-40 cartridge. The cylinder on the No. 3 Frontier was changed to 1-9/16" in length. Later the company converted 786 revolvers to .44 S&W Russian and sold them to Japan. This model is either blued or nickel-plated and has checkered grips of walnut or hard rubber. They are serial numbered in their own range from 1 through 2072 and were manufactured from 1885 until 1908. This model was designed to compete with the Colt Single Ac-tion Army but was not successful.

Courtesy Mike Stuckslager

.44-40 Commercial Model

Exc.	V.G.	Good	Fair	Poor
4000	2500	1500	1000	750

Japanese Purchase Converted to .44 S&W Russian

Exc.	V.G.	Good	Fair	Poor
3500	1500	1200	800	500

New Model No. 3-.38 Winchester

This variation was the last of the New Model No. 3s to be introduced. It was offered in .38-40 Winchester as a separate model from 1900 until 1907. The finish is blue or nickel-plate, and the grips are checkered hard rubber or walnut. Barrel lengths of 4" or 6.5" were offered. This model was not at all popular, as only 74 were manufactured in their own serial range 1 through 74. Today's collectors are extremely interested in this extremely rare model.

Courtesy Mike Stuckslager

Exc.	V.G.	Good	Fair	Poor
7000	4500	3000	2000	1000

.44 Double Action 1st Model

This model is a top break revolver that automatically ejects the spent cartridge cases upon opening. The barrel latch is located at the top and rear of the cylinder; the pivot, in front and at the bottom. This model was also known as "The D.A. Frontier" or "The New Model Navy." The revolver is chambered for the .44 S&W Russian and was built on a modified Model 3 frame. It is also found on rare occasions chambered for the .38-40 and the .44-40 Winchester. The barrel lengths are 4", 5", 6", and 6.5", round with a raised rib. A 3-1/2" barrel was produced on this model by special request. Collectors should be aware that the barrel for this model and the New Model No. 3 were interchangeable and the factory did in fact use barrels from either model. The serial number on the rear of the barrel should match the number on the butt, cylinder and barrel latch. The cylinder holds 6 shots and is fluted. It has double sets of stop notches and long free grooves between the stops. It is serial numbered in its own range, beginning at 1. There were approximately 54,000 manufactured between 1881 and 1913.

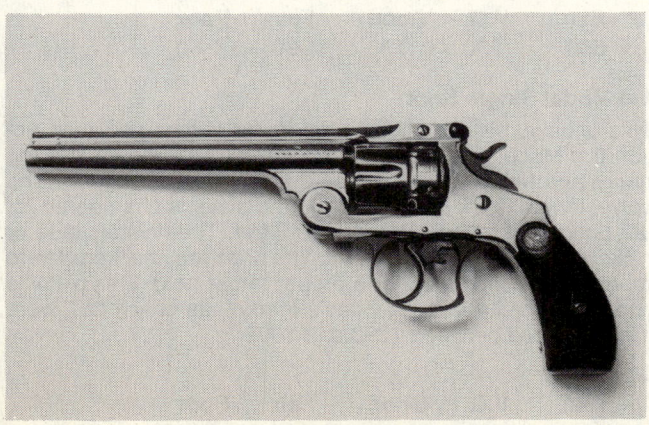

Courtesy Butterfield & Butterfield, San Francisco, California

Standard .44 S&W Russian

Exc.	V.G.	Good	Fair	Poor
1200	700	350	250	200

Model .44 Double Action Wesson Favorite

The Favorite is basically a lightened version of the 1st Model D.A. .44. The barrel is thinner and is offered in 5" length only. There are lightening cuts in the frame between the triggerguard and the cylinder; the cylinder diameter was smaller, and there is a groove milled along the barrel rib. The Favorite is chambered for the .44 S&W Russian cartridge and has a 6-shot fluted cylinder with the same double-cylinder stop notches and free grooves as the 1st Model Double Action .44. The company name and address, as well as the patent dates, are stamped into the edge of the cylinder instead of on the barrel rib. It is serial-numbered in the same range, between #9000 and 10100. The revolver was most often nickel-plated but was also offered blued. The grips are walnut or checkered hard rubber with the S&W logo molded in. There were approximately 1,000 manufactured in 1882 and 1883. Use caution when purchasing a blued model.
Blued finish-Add 25%.

Exc.	V.G.	Good	Fair	Poor
9000	6000	3500	2000	1000

Model .44 Double Action Frontier

Chambered for the .44-40 cartridge. This is a seperate model from the .44 Double Action 1st Model. It has a longer 19/16" cylinder like the later .44 Double Action 1st Model's. Produced from 1886 to 1916 with their own serial number range. Approximately 15,340 built.

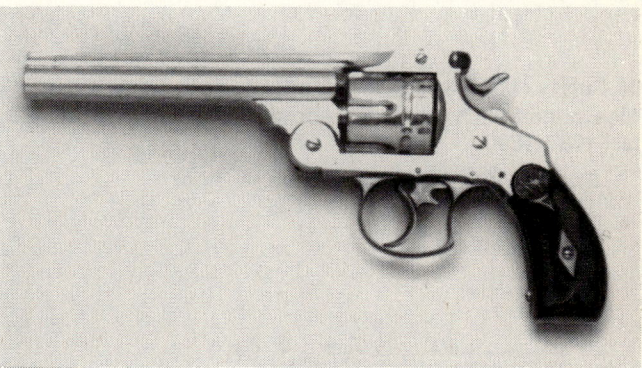

Courtesy Mike Stuckslager

Exc.	V.G.	Good	Fair	Poor
1400	750	450	300	200

Model .38 Winchester Double Action

Similar to the .44 Double Action 1st Model except for the chamber. Fitted with long cylinder. Approximately 276 produced in their own serial number range from 1900 to 1910.

Exc.	V.G.	Good	Fair	Poor
3500	2000	1500	1000	500

SAFETY HAMMERLESS

This model was a departure from what was commonly being produced at this time. Some attribute the Safety Hammerless design to D.B. Wesson's hearing that a child had been injured by cocking and firing one of the company's pistols. This story has never been proven. Nevertheless, the concealed hammer and grip safety make this an ideal pocket pistol for those needing concealability in a handgun. This is a small revolver chambered for .32 S&W and .38 S&W cartridges. It has a 5-shot fluted cylinder and is offered with a 2", 3", and 3.5" round barrel with a raised rib. The butt is rounded and has checkered hard rubber grips with the S&W logo. The finish is blue or nickelplated. The revolver is a top break, automatic-ejecting design; and the 1st Model has the latch for opening located in the rear center of the top strap instead of at the sides. The latch is checkered for a positive grip. This model is commonly referred to as the "Lemon Squeezer" because the grip safety must be squeezed as it is fired.

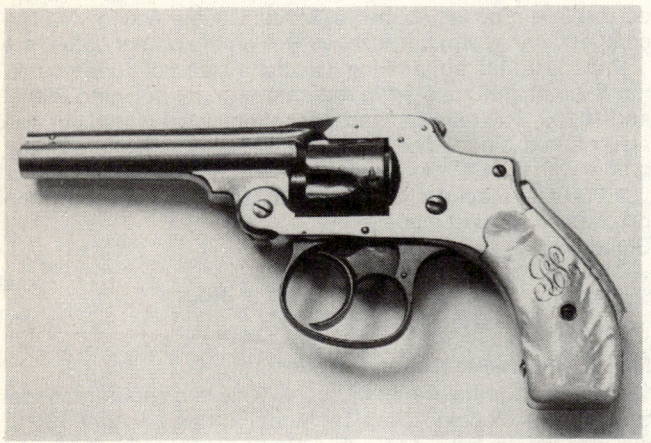

Courtesy Mike Stuckslager

.38 Safety Hammerless 1st Model

Z-bar latch, serial number range 1 to 5250, made 1887 only

NOTE: Also offered with a 6" barrel. RARE! Add 50%.

Exc.	V.G.	Good	Fair	Poor
550	450	400	250	150

.38 Safety Hammerless 2nd Model

Push button latch protrudes above frame, s/n 5251-42483, built 1887-1890.

Exc.	V.G.	Good	Fair	Poor
350	225	175	125	75

Courtesy Mike Stuckslager

.38 Safety Hammerless 3rd Model

Push button latch flush with frame, s/n 42484-116002, 1890-1898

Exc.	V.G.	Good	Fair	Poor
325	210	175	125	75

.38 Safety Hammerless 4th Model

This model was produced in .38 S&W only, and the only difference in the 4th Model and the 3rd Model is the adoption of the standard T-bar type of barrel latch as found on most of the top break revolvers. ".38 S&W Cartridge" was also added to the left side of the barrel. There were approximately 104,000 manufactured between 1898 and 1907; serial number range 116003 to 220000.

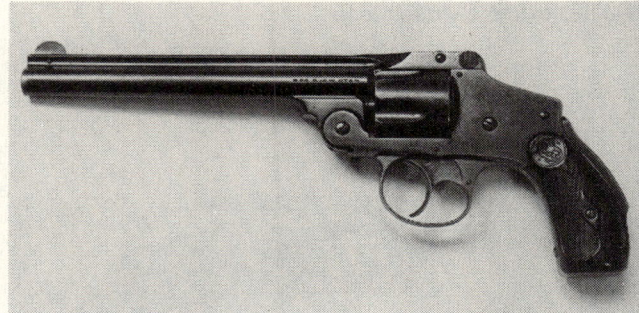

Courtesy Mike Stuckslager

Exc.	V.G.	Good	Fair	Poor
300	225	135	90	60

.38 Safety Hammerless 5th Model

This is the last of the "Lemon Squeezers," and the only appreciable difference between this model and the 4th Model is that the front sight blade on the 5th Model is an integral part of the barrel and not a separate blade pinned onto the barrel. There were approximately 41,500 manufactured between 1907 and 1940; serial number range 220001 to 261493.
2" Barrel Version-Add 50%.

Courtesy Mike Stuckslager

Exc.	V.G.	Good	Fair	Poor
350	200	135	90	60

1st Model Single Shot

This unusual pistol combines the frame of the .38 Single Action 3rd Model with a single shot barrel. This model is a top break and functions exactly as the revolver models do. The barrel length is 6", 8", or 10"; and the pistol is chambered for .22 Long Rifle, .32 S&W, and .38 S&W. The finish is blue or nickel plated, with a square butt. The grips are checkered hard rubber extension types for a proper target hold. This pistol is considered quite rare on today's market, as only 1,251 were manufactured between 1893 and 1905.

.22 L. R.

Exc.	V.G.	Good	Fair	Poor
800	650	450	250	150

.32 S&W

Exc.	V.G.	Good	Fair	Poor
950	700	500	300	200

.38 S&W

Exc.	V.G.	Good	Fair	Poor
1100	800	600	400	300

2nd Model Single Shot

The 2nd Model Single Shot has a frame with the recoil shield removed, is chambered for the .22 l.r. only, and is offered with the 10" barrel. The finish is blue or nickel plated, and the grips are checkered hard rubber extension types. There were approximately 4,617 manufactured between 1905 and 1909.

Courtesy Mike Stuckslager

Exc.	V.G.	Good	Fair	Poor
700	500	350	200	150

3rd Model Single Shot

The basic difference between this model and the 2nd Model is that this pistol could be fired double-action as well as single-action, and the frame came from the double-action perfected model. There were 6,949 manufactured between 1909 and 1923.

Courtesy Mike Stuckslager

Exc.	V.G.	Good	Fair	Poor
600	500	350	200	150

Straight Line Single Shot

This is a unique pistol that very much resembles a semiautomatic. The barrel is 10" in length and pivots to the left for loading. It is chambered for .22 Long Rifle cartridge and is finished in blue, with walnut grips inlaid with the S&W medallions. The

hammer is straight-line in function and does not pivot. There were 1,870 manufactured between 1925 and 1936.

Courtesy Butterfield & Butterfield, San Francisco, California

Exc.	V.G.	Good	Fair	Poor
2250	1600	1000	500	300

.32 Hand Ejector Model of 1896 or .32 Hand Ejector 1st Model

This model was the first time S&W made a revolver with a swing-out cylinder. Interestingly, there is no cylinder latch; but the action opens by pulling forward on the exposed portion of the cylinder pin. This frees the spring tension and allows the cylinder to swing free. Another novel feature of this model is the cylinder stop location, which is located in the top of the frame over the cylinder. This model is chambered for the .32 S&W Long cartridge, has a 6-shot fluted cylinder, and is offered with 3.25", 4.25", and 6" long barrels. It is available with either a round or square butt, has checkered hard rubber grips, and is blued or nickel-plated. Factory installed target sights were available by special order. The company name, address, and patent dates are stamped on the cylinder instead of on the barrel. There were approximately 19,712 manufactured between 1896 and 1903.

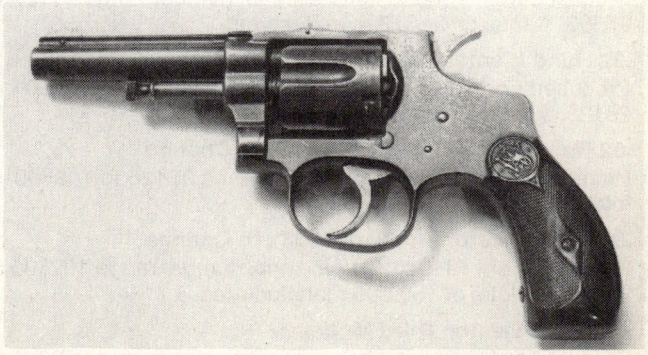

Courtesy Mike Stuckslager

Exc.	V.G.	Good	Fair	Poor
450	350	300	200	125

Hand Ejector Model of 1903

This model is quite different from its predecessor. The cylinder locks front and back; the cylinder stop is located in the bottom of the frame, and the familiar sliding cylinder latch is found on the left side of the frame. The barrel lengths are 3.25", 4.25", and 6". The 6-shot cylinder is fluted, and the revolver is chambered for .32 S&W Long. It is offered either blued or nickel-plated, and the round butt grips are checkered hard rubber. There were approximately 19,425 manufactured in 1903 and 1904; serial number range 1 to 19425.

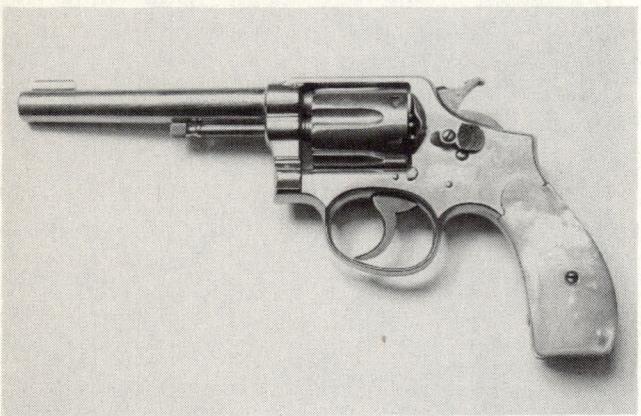

Courtesy Mike Stuckslager

Exc.	V.G.	Good	Fair	Poor
300	250	200	150	100

.32 Hand Ejector Model of 1903 1st Change

This model differs from the model of 1903 internally, and the serial number range 19426 to 51126 is really the only way to differentiate the two. There were approximately 31,700 manufactured between 1904 and 1906.

Exc.	V.G.	Good	Fair	Poor
300	200	150	125	90

.32 Hand Ejector Model of 1903 2nd Change

Produced from 1906 to 1909 in serial number range 51127 to 95500. A total of 44,373 manufactured.

.32 Hand Ejector Model of 1903 3rd Change

Produced from 1909 to 1910 in serial number range 95501 to 96125. A total of 624 manufactured.

.32 Hand Ejector Model of 1903 4th Change

Produced in 1910 in serial number range 96126 to 102500. A total of 6,374 manufactured.

.32 Hand Ejector Model of 1903 5th Change

Produced from 1910 to 1917 in serial number range 102500 to 263000. A total of 160,500 manufactured.

.32 Hand Ejector Third Model

Produced from 1911 to 1942 in serial number range 263001 to 536684. A total of 273,683 were manufactured.

Exc.	V.G.	Good	Fair	Poor
300	200	150	125	90

.22 Ladysmith 1st Model

This model was designed primarily as a defensive weapon for women. Its small size and caliber made it ideal for that purpose. The 1st Model Ladysmith is chambered for .22 Long cartridge and has a 7-shot fluted cylinder and 3" and 3.5" barrel lengths. This little revolver weighed 9-5/8 ounces. It is either blued or nickel-plated and has a round butt with checkered hard rubber grips. The 1st Model has a checkered cylinder-latch button on the left side of the frame. There were approximately 4,575 manufactured between 1902 and 1906.

Exc.	V.G.	Good	Fair	Poor
1750	1200	850	650	450

.22 Ladysmith 2nd Model

This is essentially quite similar in appearance to the 1st Model, the difference being in the pull-forward cylinder latch located under the barrel, replacing the button on the left side of the frame. The new method allowed lockup front and back for greater action strength. The 2.25" barrel length was dropped; caliber and finishes are the same. There were approximately 9,374 manufactured between 1906 and 1910; serial number range 4576 to 13950.

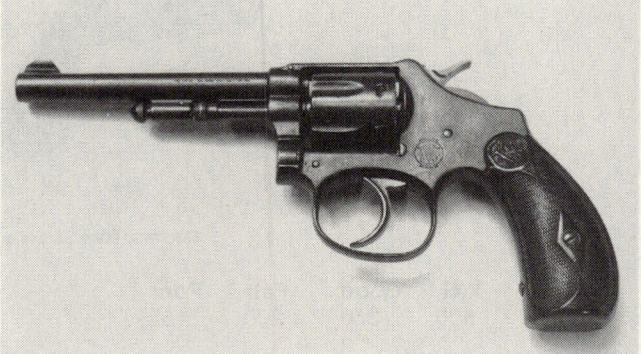

Courtesy Mike Stuckslager

Exc.	V.G.	Good	Fair	Poor
1550	900	800	600	400

.22 Ladysmith 3rd Model

This model is quite different in appearance to the 2nd Model, as it features a square butt and smooth walnut grips with inlaid S&W medallions. The barrel lengths remained the same, with the addition of a 2.25" and 6" variation. The under-barrel cylinder lockup was not changed, nor were the caliber and finishes. There were approximately 12,200 manufactured between 1910 and 1921; serial number range 13951 to 26154.

NOTE: Add a 50% premium for 2.25" and 6" barrel lengths.

Courtesy W.P. Hallstein III and son Chip

Exc.	V.G.	Good	Fair	Poor
1350	1000	800	600	400

.38 Hand Ejector Military & Police 1st Model or Model of 1899

This was an early swing-out cylinder revolver, and it has no front lockup for the action. The release is on the left side of the frame. This model is chambered for .38 S&W Special cartridge and the .32 Winchester centerfire cartridge (.32-20), has a 6-shot fluted cylinder, and was offered with a 4", 5", 6", 6.5", or 8" barrel in .38 caliber and 4", 5", and 6-1/2" in .32-20 caliber. The finish is blued or nickel-plated; the grips, checkered walnut or hard rubber. There were approximately 20,975 manufactured between 1899 and 1902 in .38 caliber; serial number range 1 to 20,975. In the .32-20 caliber 5,311 were sold between 1899 and 1902; serial number range 1 to 5311.

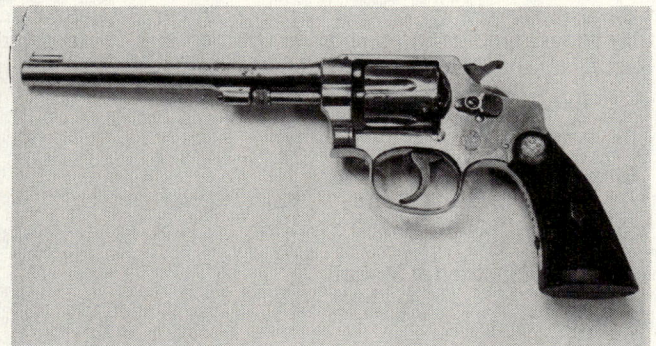

Courtesy Mike Stuckslager

Commercial Model

Exc.	V.G.	Good	Fair	Poor
750	650	600	450	350

U.S. Navy Model

One thousand produced in 1900, .38 S&W, 6" barrel, blued with checkered walnut grips, "U.S.N." stamped on butt, serial number range 5000 to 6000.

Exc.	V.G.	Good	Fair	Poor
1300	1000	700	500	300

U.S. Army Model

One thousand produced in 1901, same as Navy Model except that it is marked "U.S.Army/Model 1899" on butt, "K.S.M." and "J.T.T." on grips, serial number range 13001 to 14000.

Exc.	V.G.	Good	Fair	Poor
1300	1000	700	500	300

.38 Hand Ejector M&P 2nd Model or Model of 1902

The 2nd Model is similar in appearance to the 1st Model. The major difference is the addition of the front lockup under the barrel, and the ejector rod was increased in diameter. Barrel lengths for the .38 S&W were 4", 5", 6", or 6-1/2" while the .32-20 was available in 4", 5", or 6-1/2" barrel lengths. Both calibers were offered in round butt only configuration. There were approximately 12,827 manufactured in .38 S&W in 1902 and 1903; serial number range 20,976 to 33,803. In the .32-20 caliber 4,499 were produced; serial number range 5312 to 9811.

Exc.	V.G.	Good	Fair	Poor
500	350	300	250	100

.38 Hand Ejector M&P 2nd Model, 1st Change

Built between 1903 and 1905 this variation represents the change to the square butt, which made for better shooting control and standardized frame shape. Both the .38 S&W and the .32-20 were available in 4", 5", or 6-1/2" barrel lengths. The company manufactured 28,645 .38 calibers; serial number range 33,804 to 62,449 and produced 8,313 .32-20s; serial number 9812 to 18125.

Exc.	V.G.	Good	Fair	Poor
500	350	300	250	100

.38 Hand Ejector Model of 1905

This model was a continuation of the .38 M&P Hand Ejector series. Built from 1905 to 1906 it was available in 4", 5", 6", and 6-1/2" barrels for both the .38 and .32-20 calibers. Finished in either blue or nickel with round or square butt the .38 caliber model serial number range was from 62450 to 73250 or about 10,800 produced. The .32-20 caliber serial number range spans 18126 to 22426 or 4,300 produced.

Exc.	V.G.	Good	Fair	Poor
600	425	300	250	150

.38 Hand Ejector Model of 1905, 1st Change

Produced from 1906 to 1908 this model is similar to the original model of 1905 with regard to barrel lengths, finish and butt styles. The 1st change in .38 caliber was produced in serial number range 73251 to 120000 with 46,749 sold. In .32-20 caliber the serial-number range was 22427 to 33500 with 11,073 sold.

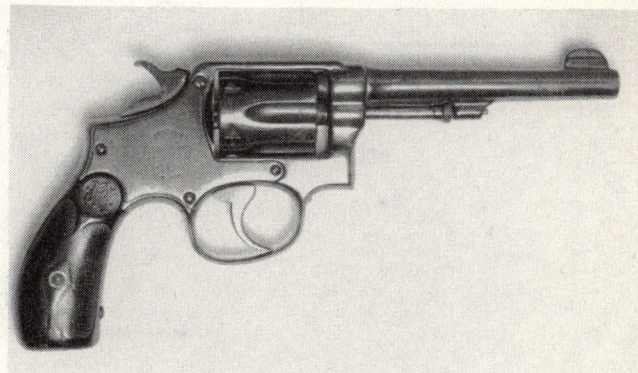

.38 Hand Ejector Model of 1905, 2nd Change

Produced from 1908 to 1909 only internal changes were made to this model. The best approach to differentiate this model is by serial number. The .38 caliber serial number range was from 120001 to 146899 with 26,898 produced. In the .32-20 caliber the serial number range is between 33501 and 45200 with 11,699 produced.

.38 Hand Ejector Model of 1905, 3rd Change

Produced from 1909 to 1915 the 3rd Change variation was available in only 4" or 6" barrel lengths for both the .38 and .32-20 models. The .38 caliber serial number range was between 146900 to 241703 with 94,803 sold.

Courtesy Mike Stuckslager

.38 Hand Ejector Model of 1905, 4th Change

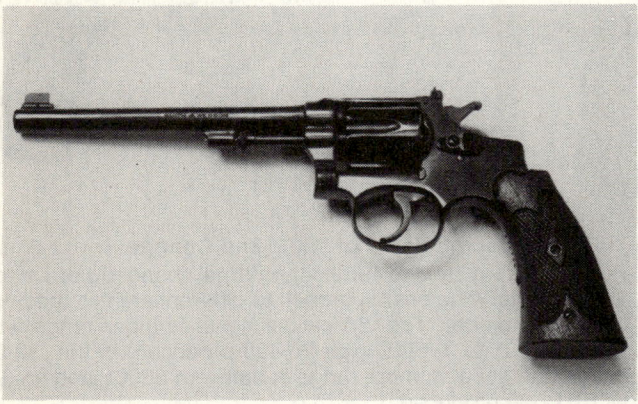

Courtesy Mike Stuckslager

This last variation was also the longest production run. Produced from 1915 to 1942 the .38 caliber model was available in 2", 4", 5", or 6", barrel lengths while the .32-20 caliber was offered in 4", 5", or 6" barrel lengths. The .38 caliber serial number range was from 241704 to 1000000. The .32-20 caliber model was produced from 1915 to 1940 in serial number range from 65701 to 144684.

.22-32 Hand Ejector

Courtesy Mike Stuckslager

This is a very interesting model from the collector's point of view. Phillip B. Bekeart, a San Francisco firearms dealer requested that S&W manufacture a .22 caliber target-grade revolver on the heavier .32 frame. He believed in his idea so passionately that he immediately ordered 1,000 of the guns for himself. This initial order is found within the serial number range 1 to 3000 and are known to collectors as the authentic Bekearts. The remainder of the extensive production run are simply .22-.32 Hand Ejectors. This model is chambered for .22 Long Rifle cartridge and has a 6-shot fluted cylinder with 6" barrel. The finish is blue, with square butt and checkered extension-type walnut grips. There were only 292 revolvers of his initial order delivered to Mr. Bekeart, but the first 1,000 pistols are considered to be True Bekearts. The production number of each respective pistol is stamped into the base of the extended wooden grips. S&W went on to manufacture several hundred thousand of these revolvers between 1911 and 1953.

"The True Bekeart"

Serial number range 138226 to 139275 in the .32 Hand Ejector series, production number stamped on butt. Professional appraisal should be secured.

Exc.	V.G.	Good	Fair	Poor
750	500	400	300	250

Standard Model

Exc.	V.G.	Good	Fair	Poor
500	300	250	200	125

.44 Hand Ejector 1st Model

This model is also known by collectors as the ".44 Triple Lock" or "The New Century." The Triple Lock nickname came from a separate locking device located on the extractor rod shroud that is used in addition to the usual two locks. This model is chambered for the .44 S&W Special cartridge or the .44 S&W Russian. On a limited basis it is also chambered in .44-40, .45 Colt, and .38-40. The fluted cylinder holds 6 shots, and the barrel was offered in standard lengths of 5" or 6.5". A limited quantity of 4" barrel was produced. The finish is blued or nickel-plated; and the grips are checkered walnut, with the gold

S&W medallion on later models. There were approximately 15,375 manufactured between 1908 and 1915.

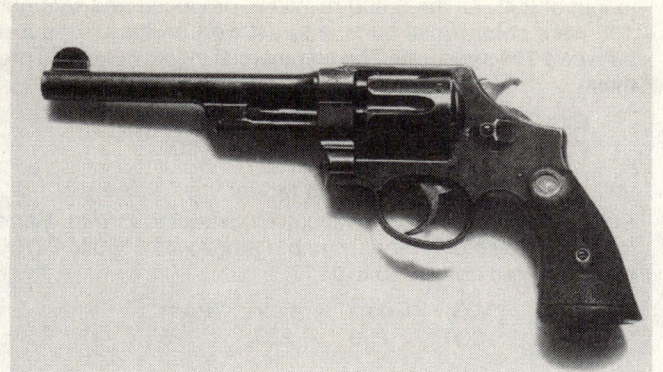

Courtesy Mike Stuckslager

.44 S & W Special and .44 S&W Russian

Exc.	V.G.	Good	Fair	Poor
900	700	500	350	200

Other Calibers (Rare)

Exc.	V.G.	Good	Fair	Poor
1100	800	600	450	300

.44 Hand Ejector 2nd Model

This model is quite similar in appearance to the 1st Model. The major difference is the elimination of the third or triple lock device and the heavy ejector rod shroud. Other changes are internal and not readily apparent. This model is also standard in .44 S&W Special chambering but was offered rarely in .38-40, .44-40, and .45 Colt. Specimens have been noted with adjustable sights in 6-1/2" barrel lengths. Standard barrel lengths were 4", 5", and 6-1/2". There were approximately 17,510 manufactured between 1915 and 1937 in serial number range 15376 to 60000.

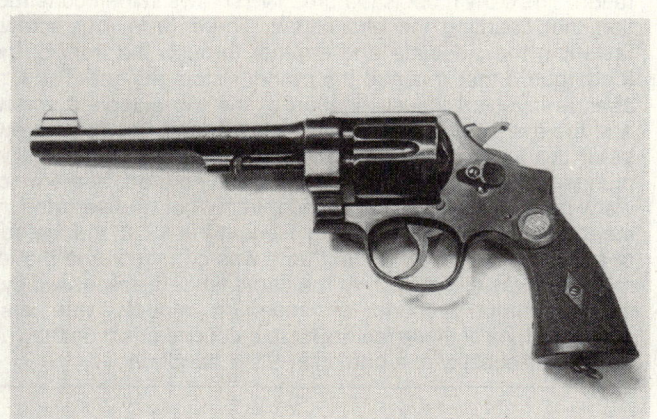

Courtesy Mike Stuckslager

.44 S & W Special

Exc.	V.G.	Good	Fair	Poor
650	600	500	350	200

.38-40, .44-40 or .45 Colt

Exc.	V.G.	Good	Fair	Poor
750	650	550	400	250

.44 Hand Ejector 3rd Model or Model of 1926

This model is similar in appearance to the 2nd Model but brought back the heavy ejector rod shroud of the 1st Model without the triple lock device. Barrel lengths were 4", 5", and 6-1/2". The .44 Hand Ejector Model was manufactured between 1926 and 1949.

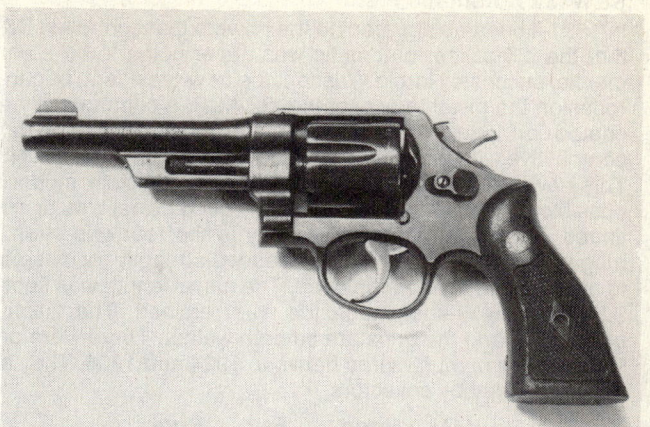

Courtesy Mike Stuckslager

.44 S & W Special

Exc.	V.G.	Good	Fair	Poor
650	450	350	275	150

.44-40 or .45 Colt

Exc.	V.G.	Good	Fair	Poor
800	550	400	300	150

.44 Hand Ejector 4th Model (Target Model)

The 4th Model featured a ribbed barrel, micrometer adjustable sight, and short throw hammer. Never a popular seller this model had only 5,050 pistol produced between 1950 and 1966.

Exc.	V.G.	Good	Fair	Poor
600	400	325	250	200

S&W .35 Automatic Pistol

Production of the .35 Automatic was S&W's first attempt at an auto-loading pistol. As was always the case, the company strived for maximum safety and dependability. This model has a 3.5" barrel and a 7-shot detachable magazine and is chambered in .35 S&W Automatic, a one-time-only cartridge that eventually proved to be the major downfall of this pistol from a commercial standpoint. There were two separate safety devices—a revolving cam on the backstrap and a grip safety on the front strap that had to be fully depressed simultaneously while squeezing the trigger. The finish is blue or nickel-plated; and the grips are walnut, with the S&W inlaid medallions. The magazine release slides from side to side and is checkered, expensive to manufacture, and destined to be modified. There were approximately 8,350 manufactured.

Exc.	V.G.	Good	Fair	Poor
500	350	250	200	150

S&W .32 Automatic Pistol

In 1921 it became apparent to the powers that controlled S&W that the .35-caliber automatic was never going to be a commercial success. Harold Wesson, the new president, began to redesign the pistol to accept the .32 ACP, a commercially accepted cartridge, and to streamline the appearance to be more competitive with the other pistols on the market, notably Colt's. This new pistol used as many parts from the older model as possible for economy's sake. The pivoting barrel was discontinued, as was the cam-type safety in the rear grip strap. A magazine disconnector and a reduced-strength recoil spring to ease cocking were employed. The barrel length was kept at 3.5", and the 7-shot magazine was retained. The finish is blued only, and the grips are smooth walnut. There were only 957 of these manufactured between 1924 and 1936. They are eagerly sought by collectors.

Exc.	V.G.	Good	Fair	Poor
2000	1500	1000	700	500

.45 Hand Ejector U.S. Service Model of 1917

WWI was on the horizon, and it seemed certain that the United States would become involved. The S&W people began to work with the Springfield Armory to develop a hand-ejector model that would fire the .45-caliber Government cartridge. This was accomplished in 1916 by the use of half-moon clips. The new revolver is quite similar to the .44 Hand Ejector in appearance. It has a 5.5" barrel, blued finish with smooth walnut grips, and a lanyard ring on the butt. The designation "U.S. Army Model 1917" is stamped on the butt. After the war broke out, the government was not satisfied with S&W's production and actually took control of the company for the duration of the war. This was the first time that the company was not controlled by a Wesson. The factory records indicate that there were 163,476 Model 1917s manufactured between 1917 and 1919, the WWI years. After the war, the sale of these revolvers continued on a commercial and contract basis until 1949, when this model was finally dropped from the S&W product line.

Military Model

Exc.	V.G.	Good	Fair	Poor
500	350	300	200	150

Brazilian Contract

25,000 produced for the Brazilian government in 1938. The Brazilian crest is stamped on the sideplate.

Exc.	V.G.	Good	Fair	Poor
300	250	200	150	100

Commercial Model

High gloss blue and checkered walnut grips.

Courtesy Mike Stuckslager

Exc.	V.G.	Good	Fair	Poor
600	450	350	275	200

.455 Mark II Hand Ejector 1st Model

This model was designed the same as the .44 Hand Ejector 1st Model with no caliber stamping on the barrel. It has a barrel length of 6.4". Of the 5,000 revolvers produced and sold only 100 were commercial guns, the rest were military. Produced betwee 1914 and 1915. The commercial model is worth a premium.

Exc.	V.G.	Good	Fair	Poor
700	575	400	300	200

.455 Mark II Hand Ejector 2nd Model

Similar to the first model without an extractor shroud. Barrel length was also 6.5". Serial number range was 5000 to 74755. Manufactured from 1915 to 1917.

Exc.	V.G.	Good	Fair	Poor
450	300	250	225	175

SMITH & WESSON MODERN HANDGUNS

With the development of the Hand Ejector Models and the swingout cylinders, Smith & Wesson opened the door to a number of new advancements in the revolver field. This new system allowed for a solid frame, making the weapon much stronger than the old top break design. The company also developed different basic frame sizes and gave them letter designations. The I frame, which later developed into the slightly larger J frame, was used for the .22-.32 and the small, concealable .38 revolvers. The medium K frame was used for the .38 duty- and target-type weapons. The N frame was the heavy-duty frame used for the larger .357 and .44 and .45 caliber revolvers. The hand ejector went through many evolutionary changes over the years. We strongly recommend that the collector secure a detailed volume that deals exclusively with Smith & Wesson (see the bibliography), and learn all that is available on this fascinating firearm. Models are catalogued the by their numerical designations, brief description are given, and current values offered. It is important to note that the S&W revolver that we see marketed by the company today has undergone many changes in reaching its present configuration. The early models featured five screws in their construction, not counting the grip screw. There were four screws fastening the sideplate and another through the front of the triggerguard that retained the cylinder stop plunger. The first change involved the elimination of the top sideplate screw, and the five-screw Smith & Wesson became the four-screw. Later the frame was changed to eliminate the cylinder stop plunger screw, and the three-screw was created. Some models were offered with a flat cylinder latch that was serrated instead of the familiar checkering. Recently in 1978, the method of attaching the barrel to the frame was changed; and the familiar pin was eliminated. At the same time, the recessed cylinder commonly found on magnum models was also eliminated. All of these factors have a definite effect on the value and collectiblity of a particular S&W handgun.

IMPORTANT PRICING INFORMATION

Values reflected below will be affected by the following factors:

Five Screw Models-Add 40 to 50%.

Four Screw Models-Add 30%. Models with flat latches-Add 20%.

Models not pinned or recessed deduct 10%.

NOTE: The pre-model number designations are listed in parenthisis after the model number.

Model 10 (.38 Military & Police)

This model has been in production in one configuration or another since 1899. It was always the mainstay of the S&W line and was originally known as the .38 Military and Police Model. The Model 10 is built on the K, or medium frame, and was always meant as a duty gun. It was offered with a 2", 3", 4", 5", or 6" barrel. Currently only the 4" and 6" are available. A round or square butt is offered. It is chambered for the .38 Special and is offered in blue or nickel-plate, with checkered walnut grips. The Model designation is stamped on the yoke on all S&W revolvers. This model, with many other modern S&W pistols, underwent several engineering changes. These changes may affect the value of the pistol and an expert should be consulted. The dates of these changes are as follows:

10-None-1957	
10-1-1959	
10-2-1961	
10-3-1961	
10-4-1962	
10-5-1962	
10-6-1962	

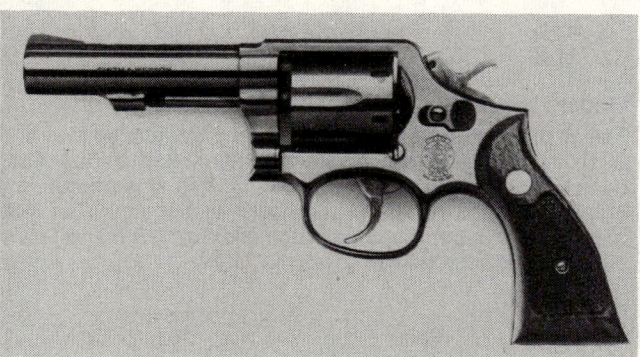

NIB	Exc.	V.G.	Good	Fair	Poor
325	250	200	150	125	90

Victory Model

Manufactured during WWII, this is a Model 10 with a sandblasted and parkerized finish, a lanyard swivel, and smooth walnut grips. The serial number has a V prefix. This model was available in only 2" and 4" barrel lengths. The Victory Model was discontinued on April 27, 1945, with serial number VS811,119.

Exc.	V.G.	Good	Fair	Poor
275	200	150	100	75

Model 11 (.38/200 British)

First produced in 1947 S&W received many contracts for this service pistol. Nicknamed the .38/200 British Service Revolver, the company sold many of these models throughout the 1950s and 1960s. There are several rare variations of this model that will greatly affect its value. Consult an expert if special markings and barrel lengths are encountered.

Exc.	V.G.	Good	Fair	Poor
250	200	150	100	75

Model 12 (.38 Military & Police Airweight)

The Model 12 was introduced in 1952, starting serial number C223,999, and is merely a Model 10 with a lightweight alloy frame and cylinder. In 1954 the alloy cylinder was replaced with one of steel that added an additional 4 ounces in weight. Discontinued in 1986.
Aluminum Cylinder Model-Add 40%.

Exc.	V.G.	Good	Fair	Poor
275	200	150	125	100

USAF M-13 (Aircrewman)

In 1953 the Air Force purchased a large quantity of Model 12s with alloy frames and cylinders. They were intended for use by flight crews as survival weapons in emergencies. This model was not officially designated "13" by S&W, but the Air Force stamped "M13" on the top strap. This model was rejected by the Air Force in 1954 because of trouble with the alloy cylinder.

Exc.	V.G.	Good	Fair	Poor
800	750	600	450	250

Model 13 (.357 Military & Police)

This is simply the Model 10 M&P chambered for the .357 Magnum and fitted with a heavy barrel. It was introduced in 1974.

Exc.	V.G.	Good	Fair	Poor
275	250	200	175	125

Model 14 (K-38 Masterpiece)

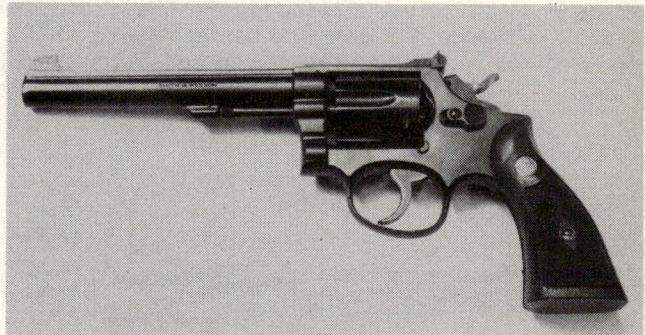

Courtesy Mike Stuckslager

This model is also known as the "K-38." In 1957 "Model 14" was stamped on the yoke. This model is offered in a 6" barrel with adjustable sights. In 1961 a single-action version with faster lock time was offered. This would be worth a small premium. This model was discontinued in 1981.
Single Action Model-Add 20%.

Exc.	V.G.	Good	Fair	Poor
275	250	200	175	125

Model 15 (K-38 Combat Masterpiece)

Also known as the "Combat Masterpiece" this model was produced at the request of law enforcement officers who wanted the "K-38" fitted with a 4" barrel. The model went into production in 1950 and was discontinued in 1987.

Exc.	V.G.	Good	Fair	Poor
300	250	200	175	125

Model 16 (K-32 Masterpiece)

Also known as the "K-32" until 1957, this model is identical in appearance to the Model 14 except that it is chambered for .32 S&W. The Model 16 did not enjoy the commercial popularity of the Model 14 and was dropped from the line in 1973. Only 3,630 K-32s/Model 16s were sold between 1947 and 1973. Reintroduced in 1990 in .32 Magnum and discontinued in 1993.

Courtesy Mike Stuckslager

Post-War

Exc.	V.G.	Good	Fair	Poor
1000	700	450	300	250

Pre-War

Exc.	V.G.	Good	Fair	Poor
2000	1400	900	600	500

Model 16 (.32 Magnum)

Reintroduced in 1990 in .32 Magnum and discontinued in 1993.

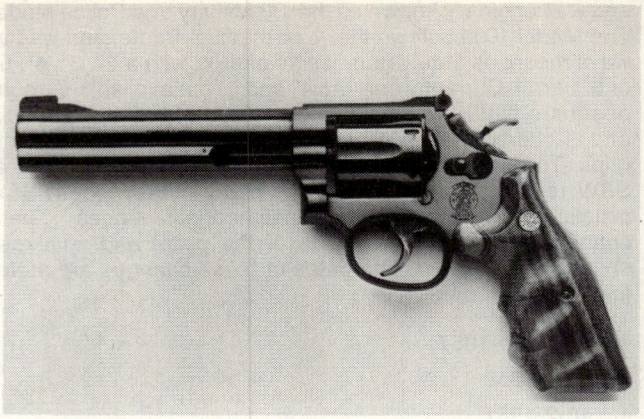

NIB	Exc.	V.G.	Good	Fair	Poor
350	300	250	200	150	100

K-32 Combat Masterpiece

S&W produced a limited number of 4" barreled K-32 revolvers. They were never given a number designation, as they were discontinued before 1957 when the numbering system began.

Exc.	V.G.	Good	Fair	Poor
1100	800	500	350	300

Model 17 (K-22)

This is the numerical designation that S&W placed on the "K-22" in 1957. This target model .22 rimfire revolver has always been popular since its introduction in 1946. It is offered in 4", 6", and 8-3/8" barrel lengths, with all target options. The 8-3/8" barrel was dropped from the product line in 1993. The finish is blued, and it has checkered walnut grips.

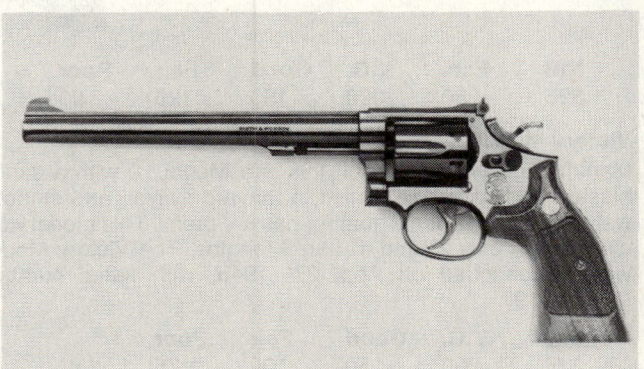

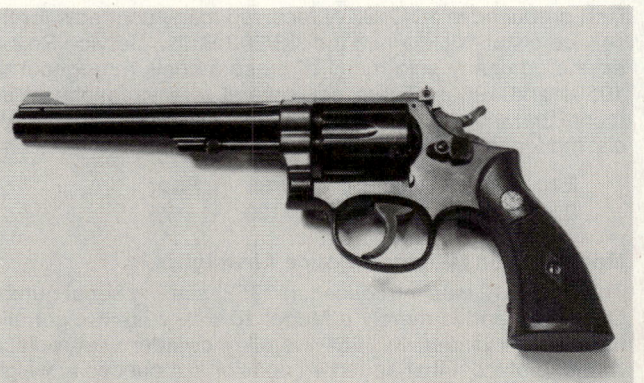

Courtesy Mike Stuckslager

NIB	Exc.	V.G.	Good	Fair	Poor
275	225	200	150	125	100

Model 17 (New Model)

Introduced in 1996 this new version of the old Model 17 has a 10 round cylinder for its .22 long rifle cartridges. It features a 6" full lug barrel with Patridge front sight and adjustable rear sight. The hammer is semi-target style and the trigger is a smooth combat style. Finish is matte black and the grips are Houge black rubber. Drills and tapped for scope mounts. Weight is about 42 oz.

NIB	Exc.	V.G.	Good	Fair	Poor
350	300	250	225	200	150

Model 617

Identical to the Model 17 but furnished with stainless steel frame and cylinder.

NIB	Exc.	V.G.	Good	Fair	Poor
300	275	250	200	150	100

Model 648

Identical to the Model 617 but chambered for the .22 Magnum rimfire cartridge.

NIB	Exc.	V.G.	Good	Fair	Poor
300	275	250	200	150	100

Model 18 (K-22 Combat Masterpiece)

This is the model designation for the 4"-barreled "Combat Masterpiece" chambered for the .22 rimfire.

Exc.	V.G.	Good	Fair	Poor
300	275	250	200	125

> **Note On "K Frame" Target Models:**
> 1. The factory eliminated the upper corner screw from the side plate in 1955. The 5-screw became a 4-screw. This change occurred around serial number K260,000.
> 2. Model number designations were stamped on the yoke in 1957.

Model 19 (.357 Combat Magnum)

Introduced in 1954 at the urging of Bill Jordan, a competition shooter with the U.S. Border Patrol, who went on to become a respected gun writer, this model is one of Smith and Wesson's most popular pistols. It was built on the "K-Frame" and was the first medium frame revolver chambered for the powerful .357 Magnum cartridge. Since its inception the Model 19 has been one of S&W's most popular revolvers. It was the first revolver to be introduced as a three-screw model. Originally it was offered with a 4" heavy barrel with extractor shroud; the 6" became available in 1963. The finish is blued or nickel-plated, and the grips are checkered walnut. The Goncalo Alves target stocks first appeared in 1959. In 1968 a 2.5" round-butt version was introduced. The Model 19 has been the basis for two commemoratives—the Texas Ranger/with Bowie Knife and the Oregon State Police/with Belt Buckle.

NIB	Exc.	V.G.	Good	Fair	Poor
275	250	225	200	150	100

Texas Ranger Cased with Knife
NIB
700

Oregon State Police Cased with Buckle
NIB
900

Model 20 (.38/.44 Heavy Duty)

Known as the "38/44 Heavy Duty" before the change to numerical designations this model was brought out in 1930 in response to requests from law enforcement personnel for a more powerful sidearm. This model, along with the .38-44 S&W Special cartridge, was an attempt to solve the problem. The revolver was manufactured with a standard 5" long barrel but has been noted rarely as short as 3-1/2" and as long as 8-3/8". It was built on the large N frame and is blued or nickel-plated, with checkered walnut grips. Eventually the popularity of the .357 Magnum made the Model 20 superfluous, and it was discontinued in 1966. Postwar production for this model was about 20,000 revolvers.

Prewar .44 Special-Add 50%.

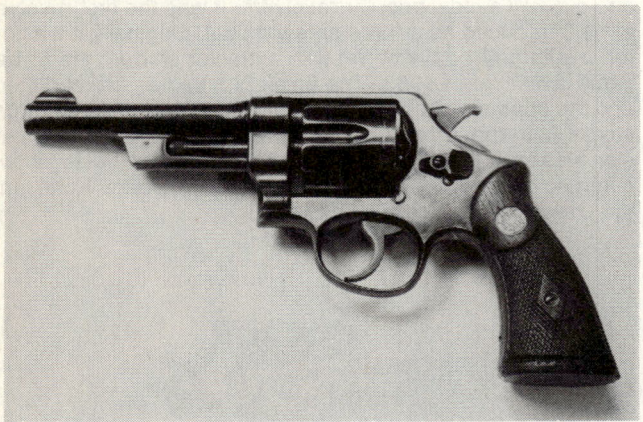

Courtesy Mike Stuckslager

Exc.	V.G.	Good	Fair	Poor
475	350	250	200	150

Model 21 (1950 Military)

This model was known as the "1950 Military" and the "4th Model .44 Hand Ejector" before the Model 21 designation was applied in 1957. The Model 21 was chambered for the .44 Special cartridge and equipped with fixed sights. The Model 21 was built on the N frame and is quite rare, as only 1,200 were manufactured in 16 years of production. It was discontinued in 1966.

Exc.	V.G.	Good	Fair	Poor
1500	1200	950	650	500

Model 696

Introduced in 1997 this model features a 3" underlug barrel. chambered for the .44 Special and fitted on an L frame, capacity is 5 rounds. Grips are Hogue black rubber. Finish is stainless steel. Weight is approximately 48 oz.

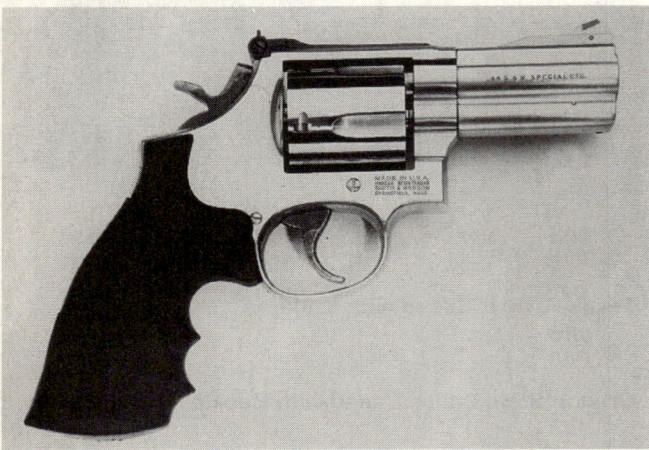

NIB	Exc	V.G.	Good	Fair	Poor
450	400	350	—	—	—

Model 22 (1950 .45 Military)

This model was known as the "1950 .45 Military" before 1957. It was actually introduced in 1951 and is similar in appearance to the Model 21 except that it is chambered for the .45 Auto Rim or .45 ACP cartridge. Half-moon clips are used with the latter. There were 3,976 manufactured between 1951 and 1966. Beginning serial number for this model was S85,000.

Exc.	V.G.	Good	Fair	Poor
750	650	550	300	200

Model 23 (.38/.44 Outdoorsman)

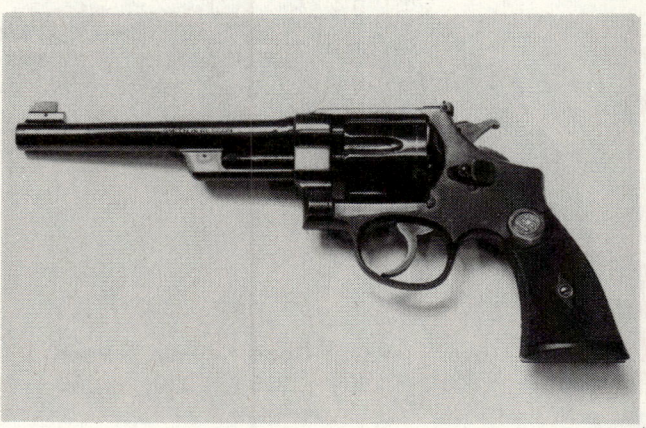

Courtesy Mike Stuckslager

The .38-44 Outdoorsman was the model name of this N-frame revolver before the 1957 designation change. This is simply the Model 20 with adjustable sights. It was introduced in 1931 as a heavy-duty sporting handgun with hunters in mind. S&W produced 4,761 of these prewar revolvers. It features a 6.5" barrel and blued finish and was the first S&W to have the new checkered walnut "Magna" grips. After 1949 this revolver was thoroughly modernized and had the later ribbed barrel. There were a total of 8,365 manufactured before the model was discontinued in 1966. 6,039 were of the modernized configuration.

Exc.	V.G.	Good	Fair	Poor
550	400	300	200	125

Model 24 (.44 Target Model of 1950)

This model was introduced as the .44 Target Model of 1950. It is simply the N-frame Model 21 with adjustable target sights. This revolver was quite popular with the long-range handgunning devotees and their leader, Elmer Keith. The introduction of the .44 Magnum in 1956 began the death knell of the Model 24, and it was finally discontinued in 1966. S&W produced a total of 5,050 Model 24s. It was reintroduced in 1983 and 1984—and then was dropped again.

Exc.	V.G.	Good	Fair	Poor
450	400	300	250	200

Model 25 (.45 Target Model of 1950)

Prior to the model designation change in 1957 this model was also known as the .45 Target Model of 1955, this was an improved version of the 1950 Target .45. The Model 25 features a heavier barrel 4", 6.5", or 8" in length with blued or nickel-plated finish. All target options were offered. The Model 25 is chambered for the .45 ACP or .45 Auto-rim cartridges. This model is still available chambered for .45 Colt as the Model 25-5.

Exc.	V.G.	Good	Fair	Poor
400	350	300	250	200

Model 25-3 125th Anniversary with Case
NIB
425

Model 25-2

This is the discontinued modern version of the Model 25 chambered in .45 ACP. The 6.5" barrel is shortened to 6" and is available in a presentation case.

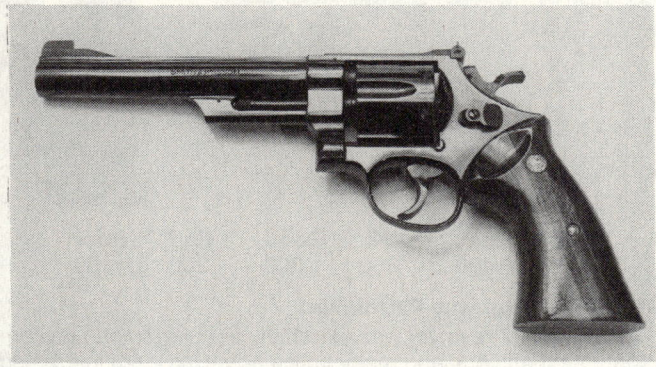

Exc.	V.G.	Good	Fair	Poor
400	350	300	250	200

Model 625-2

This is the stainless steel version of the Model 25-2. It is fitted with a 5-inch barrel and has Pachmayr SK/GR gripper stocks as standard. Designed for pin shooting.

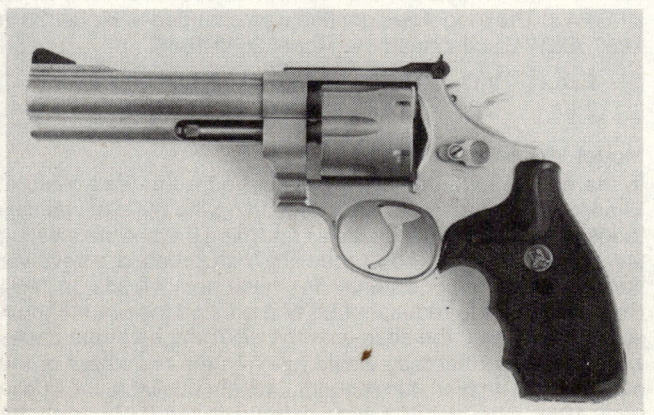

NIB	Exc.	V.G.	Good	Fair	Poor
425	350	300	250	200	150

Model 625 Mountain Gun

Offered for the first time in 1996 this model is chambered for the .45 Colt cartridge. It is fitted with a 4" tapered barrel with ramp front sight and adjustable rear sight. The frame is drilled and tapped for a scope mount.

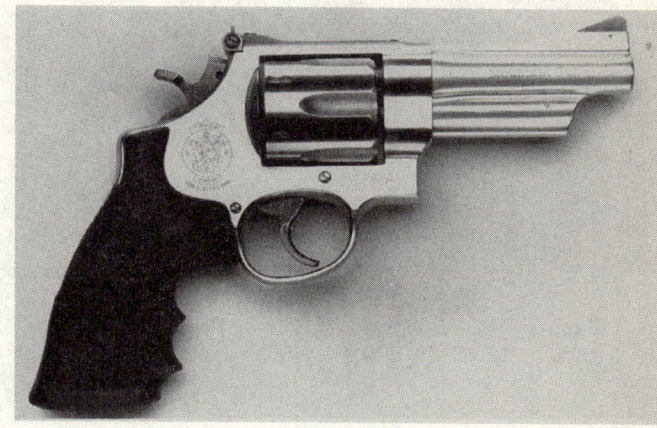

NIB	Exc.	V.G.	Good	Fair	Poor
550	500	400	350	—	—

Model 26 (1950 .45 Target)

This is the numerical designation of the 1950 .45 Target Model. This large N-frame revolver is basically the same as the Model 25 but has a lighter, thinner barrel. This caused its unpopularity among competitive shooters who wanted a heavier revolver. This brought about the Model 25 and the demise of the Model 26 in 1961 after only 2,768 were manufactured. The Model 26 also has two additional variations and are marked 26-1 and 26-2.

Exc.	V.G.	Good	Fair	Poor
750	650	500	400	250

Factory Registered .357 Magnum

In the early 1930s, a gun writer named Phillip B. Sharpe became interested in the development of high performance loads to be used in the then popular .38-44 S&W revolvers. He repeatedly urged the company to produce a revolver especially made to handle these high pressure loads. In 1934 S&W asked Winchester to produce a new cartridge that would create the ballistics that Sharpe was seeking. This new cartridge was made longer than the standard .38 Special case so that it could not inadvertently be fired in an older gun. The company never felt that this would be a commercially popular venture and from the onset visualized the ".357 Magnum" as a strictly deluxe hand-built item. They were to be individually numbered, in addition to the serial number, and registered to the new owner. The new Magnum was to be the most expensive revolver in the line. The gun went on the market in 1935, and the first one was presented to FBI Director J. Edgar Hoover. The gun was to become a tremendous success. S&W could only produce 120 per month, and this did not come close to filling orders. In 1938 the practice of numbering and registering each revolver was discontinued after 5,500 were produced. The ".357 Magnum," as it was designated, continued as one of the company's most popular items.

The Factory Registered Model was built on the N-frame. It could be custom ordered with any barrel length from 3.5" up to 8-3/8". The finish is blue, and the grips are checkered walnut. This model was virtually hand-built and test targeted. A certificate of registration was furnished with each revolver. The registration number was stamped on the yoke of the revolver with the prefix "Reg." This practice ceased in 1938 after 5,500 were produced.

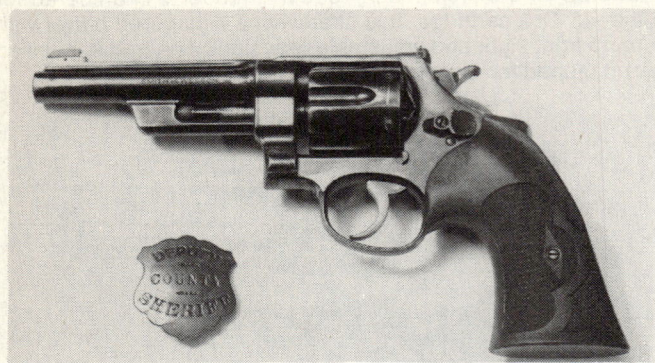

Courtesy Mike Stuckslager

Exc.	V.G.	Good	Fair	Poor
1800	1200	800	550	400

Prewar .357 Magnum

This is the same as the Factory Registered Model without the certificate and the individual numbering. Approximately 1,150 were manufactured between 1938 and 1941. Production ceased for WWII weapons production.

Exc.	V.G.	Good	Fair	Poor
750	550	450	300	250

Model 27 (.357 Magnum)

In 1948 after the end of WWII, production of this revolver commenced. The new rebound slide operated hammer block and short throw hammer were utilized, and the barrel lengths offered were 3.5", 5", 6", 6-1/2", and 8-3/8". In 1957 the model designation was changed to Model 27; and in 1975 the target trigger, hammer and Goncalo Alves target grips were made standard. This revolver is still available from S&W and has been in production longer than any other N-frame pistol. Some additional variations may be of interest to the collector. Around serial number SI 71,584 the 3 screw side plate model was first produced. In 1960 the model designation -1 was added to the model to indicate the change to a left-hand thread to the extractor rod. In 1962 the cylinder stop was changed, which disposed of the need for a plunger spring hole in front of the triggerguard. This change was indicated by a -2 behind the model number.

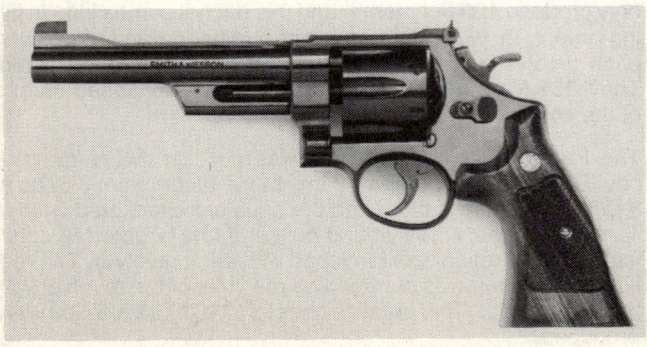

NIB	Exc.	V.G.	Good	Fair	Poor
350	325	300	250	200	150

Model 627

This is special edition stainless steel version of the Model 27 and is offered with a 5-1/2" barrel. Manufactured in 1989 only. Approximately 4,500 produced.

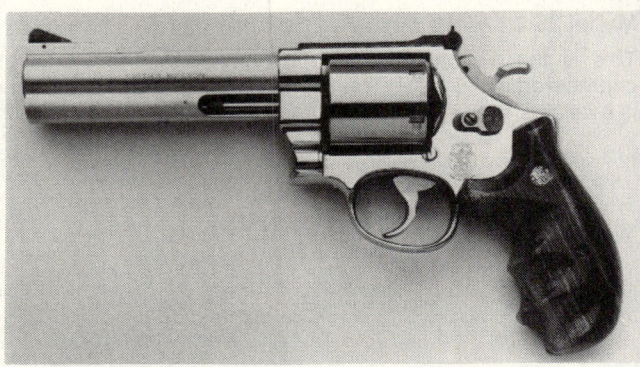

NIB	Exc.	V.G.	Good	Fair	Poor
500	400	350	300	200	150

Model 28 (Highway Patrolman)

The Model 27 revolver was extremely popular among law enforcement officers, and many police agencies were interested in purchasing such a weapon-except for the cost. In 1954 S&W produced a new model called, at the time, the "Highway Patrolman." This model had all the desirable performance features of the deluxe Model 27 but lacked the cosmetic features that drove up the price. The finish is a matte blue; the rib is sandblasted instead of checkered or serrated, and the grips are the standard checkered walnut. Barrel lengths are 4" and 6.5". On late models the 6.5" barrel was reduced to 6", as on all S&Ws. The model designation was changed to Model 28 in 1957. S&W discontinued the Model 28 in 1986.

Exc.	V.G.	Good	Fair	Poor
250	225	200	150	100

Model 29 (.44 Magnum)

In the early 1950s, handgun writers, under the leadership of Elmer Keith, were in the habit of loading the .44 Special cartridge to high performance levels and firing them in the existing .44 Hand Ejectors. They urged S&W to produce a revolver strong enough to consistently fire these heavy loads. In 1954 Remington, at the request of S&W produced the .44 Magnum cartridge. As was the case with the .357 Magnum, the cases were longer so that they would not fit in the chambers of the older guns. The first .44 Magnum became available for sale in early 1956. The first 500 were made with the 6.5" barrel; the 4" became available later that year. In 1957 the model designation was changed to 29, and the 8-3/8" barrel was introduced. The Model 29 is available in blue or nickel-plate. It came standard with all target options and was offered in a fitted wood case. The Model 29 is considered by many knowledgeable people to be the finest revolver S&W has ever produced. The older Model 29 revolvers are in a different collector category than most modern S&W revolvers. The early four-screw models can be worth a 50% premium in excellent condition. These early models were produced from 1956 to 1958 and approximately 6,500 were sold. One must regard these revolvers on a separate basis and have them individually appraised for proper valuation. In 1993 the 4" barrel was dropped from production.

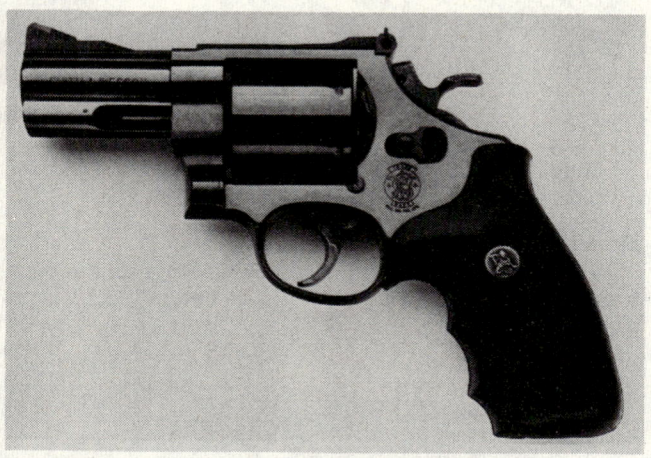

NIB	Exc.	V.G.	Good	Fair	Poor
500	400	300	250	200	150

Early 5" Barrel Model 29

This is the rarest of the Model 29s. A total of 500 were manufactured in 1958. Collectors are cautioned to exercise care before purchasing one of these rare Model 29 variations.

NIB	Exc.	V.G.	Good	Fair	Poor
2000	1500	1200	800	500	300

Notes on N Frame Revolvers:
1. N-frame models were changed from 5-screw to 4-screw between 1956 and 1958. Serial number SI75,000.
2. Triggerguard screw was eliminated in 1961.
3. The pinned barrel and recessed cylinder were discontinued in 1978.

Model 629

This revolver is simply a stainless steel version of the Model 29 chambered for the .44 Magnum.

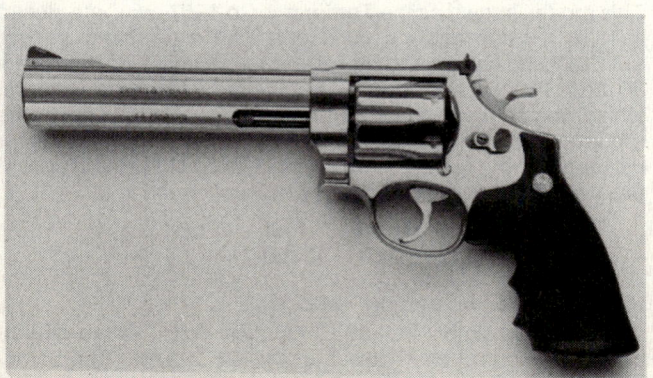

NIB	Exc.	V.G.	Good	Fair	Poor
475	400	300	250	225	200

Model 629 Backpacker

This 1994 variation of the Model 629 is built on the N-frame with round butt. Cylinders are fluted and chamfered. Barrel length is 3" with adjustable rear sight. The finish is stainless steel and Hogue rubber grips are standard. Weight is approximately 40 oz.

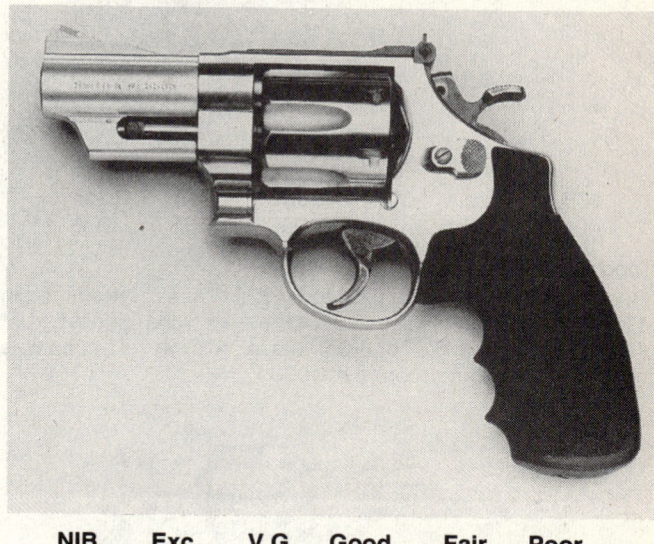

NIB	Exc.	V.G.	Good	Fair	Poor
700	600	500	400	300	200

Model 629 Mountain Gun

This limited edition 6-shot revolver, introduced in 1993, features a 4" barrel chambered for the .44 Magnum. Built on the large N-frame this pistol is made from stainless steel and is drilled and tapped for scope mounts. It is equipped with a Hogue round butt rubber monogrip. Standard sights are a pinned black ramp front sight and an adjustable black rear blade.

NIB	Exc.	V.G.	Good	Fair	Poor
500	450	400	350	300	150

Model 629 Classic

This model has additional features that the standard Model 629 does not have such as: Chamfered cylinder, full lug barrel, interchangeable front sights, Hogue combat grips, and a drilled and tapped frame to accept scope mounts.

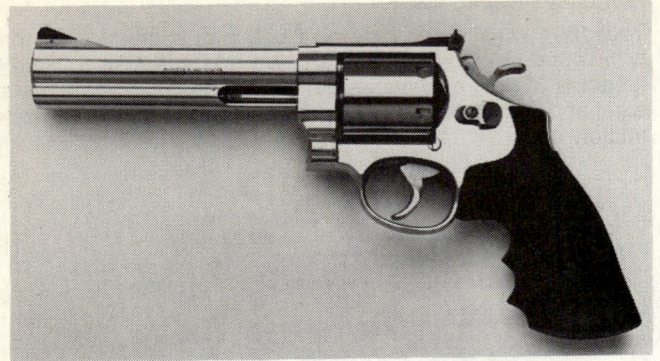

NIB	Exc.	V.G.	Good	Fair	Poor
400	375	325	250	225	200

Model 629 Classic DX

Has all of the features of the Model 629 Classic, introduced in 1991, plus two sets of grips and five interchangeable front sights. Available in 6.5" or 8-3/8" barrel. A 5" barrel option was offered in 1992 but dropped in 1993.

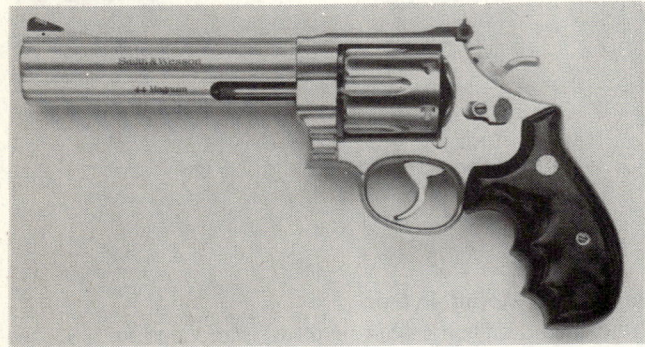

NIB	Exc.	V.G.	Good	Fair	Poor
650	500	450	350	300	150

Model 629 Classic Powerport

Introduced in 1996 this model offers a intergral compensator with a 6.5" full lug barrel. The Patridge front sight is pinned and the rear sight is fully adjustable. The frame is drilled and tapped for scope mounts. Synthetic Houge combat-style grips are standard. Weight is approximately 52 oz.

NIB	Exc.	V.G.	Good	Fair	Poor
600	550	—	—	—	—

Model 30 (The .32 Hand Ejector)

This model was built on the small I frame and based on the .32 Hand Ejector Model of 1903. This older model was dropped from production in 1942. It was re-introduced in 1949 in a more modern version but still referred to as the .32 Hand Ejector. In 1957 the model designation was changed to Model 30. In 1960 this frame size was dropped, and the J-frame, which had been in use since 1950, became standard for the Model 30. S&W stamped -1 behind the model number to designate this

important change in frame size. The Model 30 is chambered for the .32 S&W long cartridge. It has a 6-shot cylinder and 2", 3", 4", and 6" barrel lengths. It has fixed sights and is either blued or nickel-plated. The butt is round, with checkered walnut grips. It was discontinued in 1976.

Courtesy W.P. Hallstein III and son Chip

Exc.	V.G.	Good	Fair	Poor
350	250	200	150	100

Model 31 (.32 Regulation Police)

This model is the same as the Model 30 with a square butt. It was known as the .32 Regulation Police before 1957. It is now discontinued.

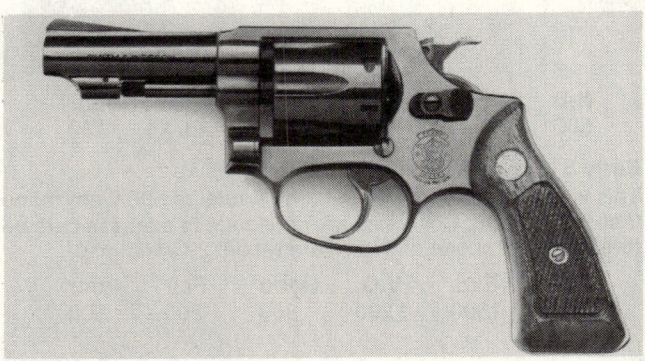

Exc.	V.G.	Good	Fair	Poor
275	250	200	150	100

Model 31 (.32 Regulation Police Target)

The Target model of the Regulation Police is rare. Only 196 of these special variations were produced in 1957. All specifications are the same as the Model 31 except for the addition of adjustable sights.

Exc.	V.G.	Good	Fair	Poor
500	400	250	200	150

Model 32 (.38/.32 Terrier)

This model, known as the Terrier prior to 1957, was introduced in 1936. It is essentially a .38 Regulation Police chambered for .38 S&W and having a 2" barrel and round butt. Like the Model 30 and 31 this revolver was originally built on the J-frame, which was changed to the I-frame in 1960. The -1 behind the model number signifies this change. It is offered in blue or nickel-plate and has a 5-shot cylinder, fixed sights, and checkered walnut grips. This model was discontinued in 1974.

Exc.	V. G.	Good	Fair	Poor
300	200	150	100	75

Model 33 (.38 Regulation Police)

This model is simply the .38 Regulation Police with a square butt and 4" barrel chambered for the .38 S & W. The factory referred to this model as the .38-.32 revolver. It, too, was built on the small I-frame and later changed to the J-frame in 1960. The Model 33 was discontinued in 1974.

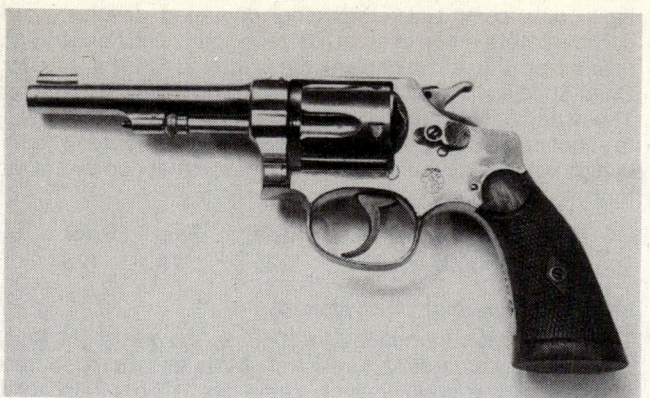

Courtesy Mike Stuckslager

Exc.	V.G.	Good	Fair	Poor
350	250	200	150	100

Model 34 (.22/.32 Kit Gun)

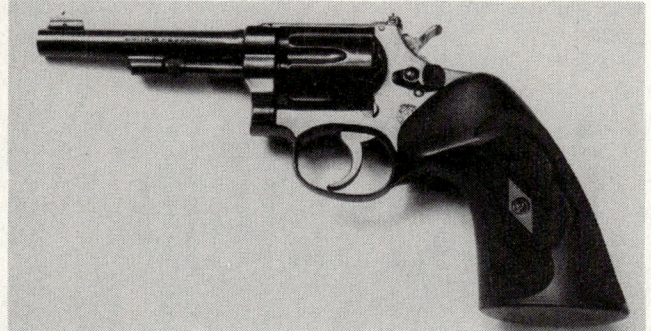

Courtesy Mike Stuckslager

Introduced in 1936 as the .22-32 Kit Gun, it has a 2" or 4" barrel, either round or square butt, and adjustable sights. This model underwent several modifications before it reached its present form. S&W modernized this revolver in 1953 with the addition of a coil mainspring and micro-click sights. The Model 34 is built on this improved version. The revolver is a .32 Hand Ejector chambered for the .22 rimfire. It is built on the I-frame until 1960 when the changeover to the improved J-frame occurred. The -1 behind the model number indicates this variation. The Model 34 is offered blued or nickel-plate and is currently in production.

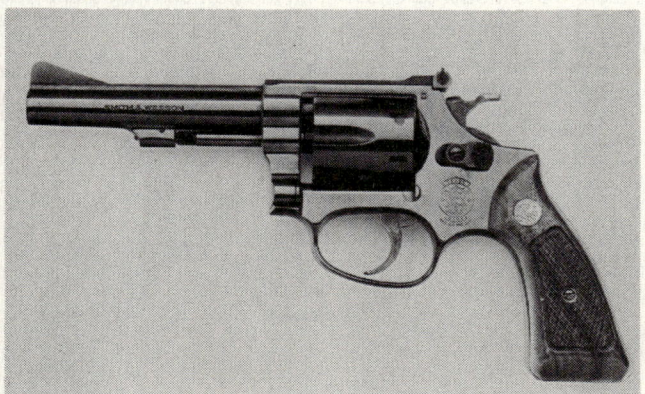

NIB	Exc.	V.G.	Good	Fair	Poor
375	300	250	225	175	100

Model 35 (.22/.32 Target)

This is a square-butt, 6"-barreled version of the .22/32 Hand Ejector. It was known prior to 1957 as the .22/32 Target. It underwent the same changes as the Model 34 but was discontinued in 1973.

Courtesy Mike Stuckslager

Exc.	V.G.	Good	Fair	Poor
350	300	250	200	100

Model 317

This 8-round revolver was introduced in 1997 and is chambered for the .22 Long Rifle cartridge. It is fitted with a 2" barrel, serrated ramp front sight, fixed rear sight, and Dymondwood boot grips. It is produced from carbon and stainless steel and also aluminum alloy on a J-frame. Its weight is about 9.9 oz.

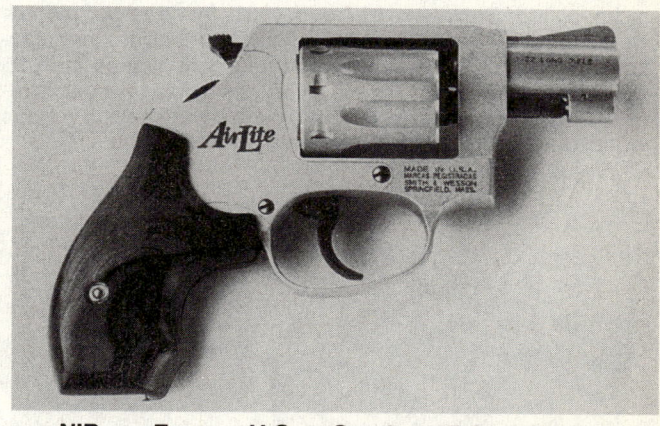

NIB	Exc.	V.G.	Good	Fair	Poor
425	375	325	—	—	—

Model 36 (.38 Chief's Special)

This model, known as the Chief's Special, was introduced in 1950. It was built on the J-frame and is chambered for the .38 Special cartridge. It holds 5 shots, has a 2" or 3" barrel, and was initially offered in a round butt. In 1952 a square-butt version was released. It is finished in blue or nickel-plate and has checkered walnut grips. A 3" heavy barrel was first produced in 1967 and became standard in 1975. The 2" barrel was dropped from production in 1993.

NIB	Exc.	V.G.	Good	Fair	Poor
300	250	200	175	125	100

Model 36LS (.38 Ladysmith)

This model is similar to the Model 36 with the exception that it is only offered with a 2" barrel, comes with rosewood grips and a soft carrying case. Weighs 20 oz.

NIB	Exc.	V.G.	Good	Fair	Poor
325	250	200	175	125	100

Model 36 (Chief's Special Target)

Since 1955 a limited number of Chief's Specials with adjustable sights have been manufactured. They have been offered with 2" or 3" barrels, round or square butts, and either blue or nickel-plated. Between 1957 and 1965, these target models were stamped Model 36 on the yoke. The revolvers manufactured between 1965 and the model discontinuance in 1975 were marked Model 50. This is a very collectible revolver. A total of 2,313 of these special target models were sold in various model designations. Some are more rare than others.

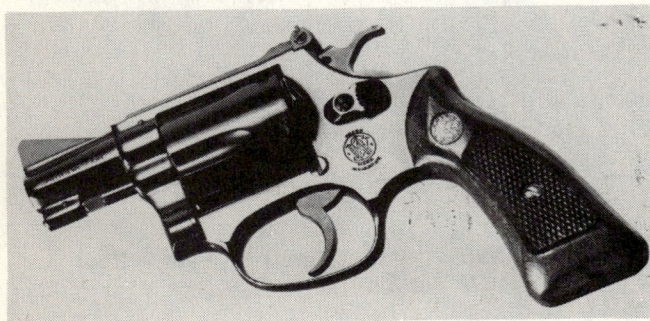

Courtesy W.P. Hallstein III and son Chip

Exc.	V.G.	Good	Fair	Poor
450	350	300	250	200

Model 37

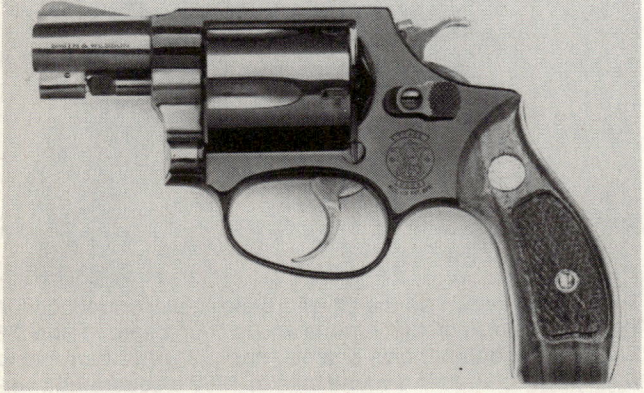

Introduced in 1952 as the Chief's Special Airweight, this revolver initially had an alloy frame and cylinder. In 1954, following many complaints regarding damaged revolvers, the cylinders were made of steel. Barrel lengths, finishes, and grip options on the Airweight are the same as on the standard Chief Special. In 1957 the Model 37 designation was adopted. These early alloy frame and cylinder revolvers were designed to shoot only standard velocity .38 Special cartridges. The use of high velocity ammunition was not recommended by the factory.

NIB	Exc.	V.G.	Good	Fair	Poor
350	300	275	225	175	125

Model 38 (Airweight Bodyguard)

This model was introduced in 1955 as the Airweight Bodyguard. This was a departure from S&W's usual procedure in that the alloy-framed version came first. The Model 38 is chambered for .38 Special and is available with a 2" barrel standard. Although a 3" barrel was offered, it is rarely encountered. The frame of the Bodyguard is extended to conceal and shroud the hammer but at the same time allow the hammer to be cocked by the thumb. This makes this model an ideal pocket revolver, as it can be drawn without catching on clothing. It is available either blue or nickel-plated, with checkered walnut grips.

NIB	Exc.	V.G.	Good	Fair	Poor
325	250	225	175	125	100

Model 49 (Bodyguard)

This model was introduced in 1959 and is identical in configuration to the Model 38 except that the frame is made of steel.

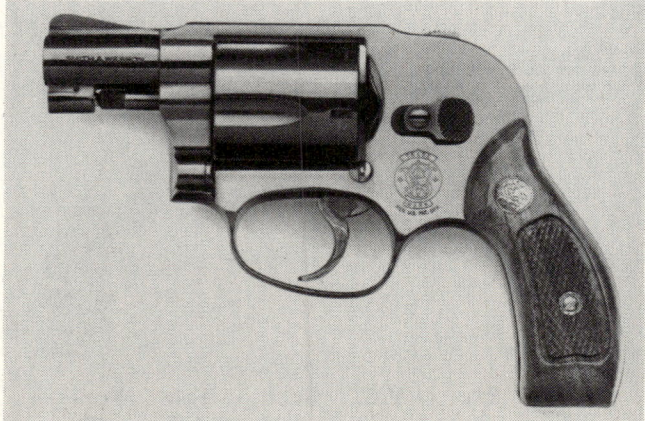

NIB	Exc.	V.G.	Good	Fair	Poor
350	250	225	200	150	100

Model 649 (Bodyguard Stainless)

This stainless steel version of the Model 49 was introduced in 1985.

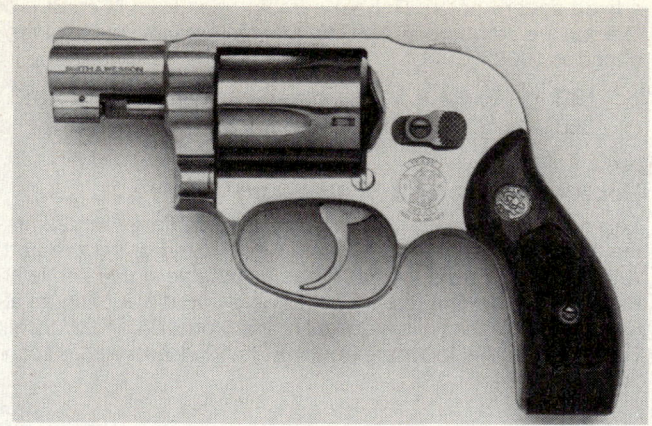

NIB	Exc.	V.G.	Good	Fair	Poor
350	300	225	200	175	125

Model 40 (Centennial)

This model was introduced in 1952 as Smith & Wesson's 100th anniversary and appropriately called the "Centennial Model". It is of the Safety Hammerless design. This model was built on the J-frame and features a fully concealed hammer and a grip safety. The Model 40 is chambered for the .38 Special cartridge. It is offered with a 2" barrel in either blue or nickel plate. The grips are checkered walnut. The Centennial was discontinued in 1974.

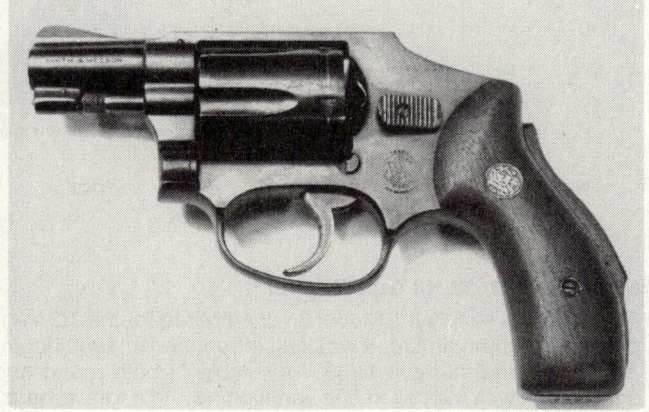

Courtesy Mike Stuckslager

Exc.	V.G.	Good	Fair	Poor
475	350	300	250	200

Model 640 Centennial

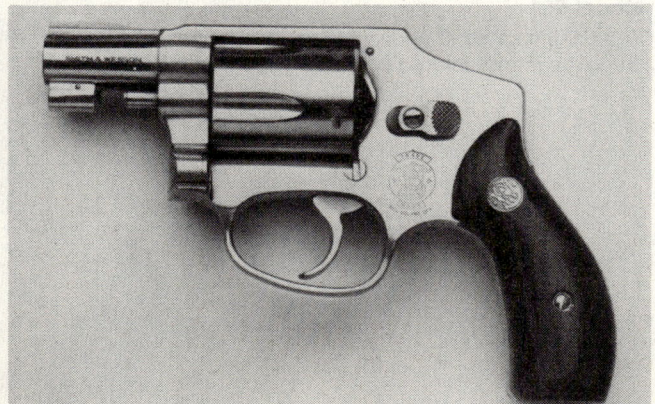

A stainless steel version of the Model 40 furnished with a 2- or 3-inch barrel. Both the frame and cylinder are stainless steel. The 3" barrel was no longer offered as of 1993.

NIB	Exc.	V.G.	Good	Fair	Poor
375	300	250	200	150	100

Model 640 Centennial .357 Magnum

Introduced in 1995 this version of the Model 640 is chambered for the .357 cartridge and fitted with a 2-1/8" barrel. The gun is stainless steel with a fixed notch rear sight and pinned black ramp front sight. It is 6-3/4" in length and weighs 25 oz.

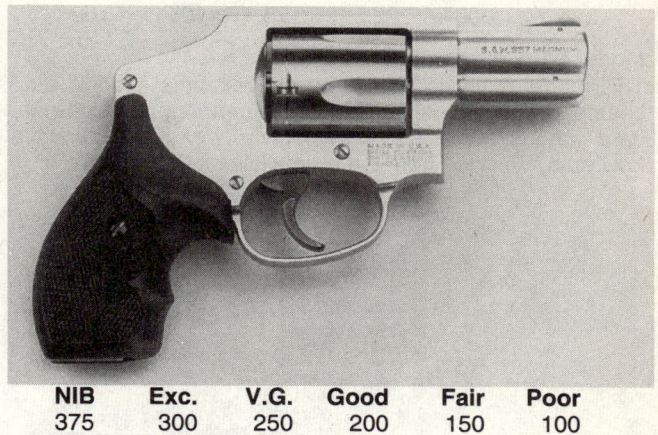

NIB	Exc.	V.G.	Good	Fair	Poor
375	300	250	200	150	100

Model 642 Centennial Airweight

Identical to the Model 640 with the exception of a stainless steel cylinder and aluminum alloy frame. Furnished with a 2-inch barrel. Discontinued in 1992. Replaced by the Model 442 which was introduced in 1993. This model was reintroduced in 1996.

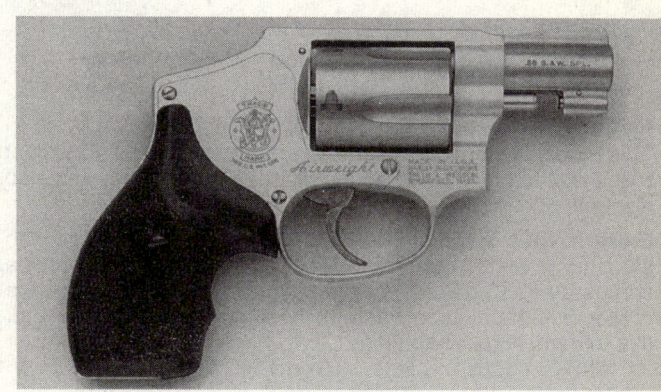

NIB	Exc.	V.G.	Good	Fair	Poor
400	300	250	200	150	100

Model 642LS

Same as above but fitted with smooth combat wood grips and a softside carry case.

NIB	Exc.	V.G.	Good	Fair	Poor
350	275	225	175	125	100

Model 940

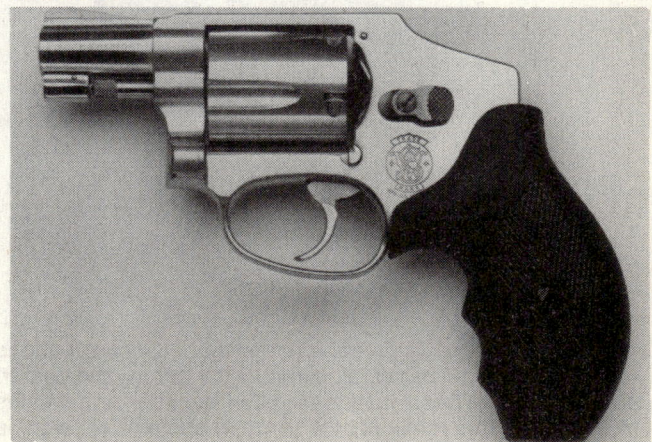

Styled like the other Centennial models, this model is chambered for the 9mm Parabellum cartridge. It has a stainless steel cylinder and frame and is furnished with a 2- or 3-inch barrel. The 3" barrel version was dropped from production in 1993.

NIB	Exc.	V.G.	Good	Fair	Poor
375	300	225	175	125	100

Model 632 Centennial

This model is similar to the other Centennial models but is chambered for the .32 H&R Magnum cartridge. It comes standard with a 2" barrel, stainless steel cylinder and aluminum alloy frame. Dropped from the product line in 1993.

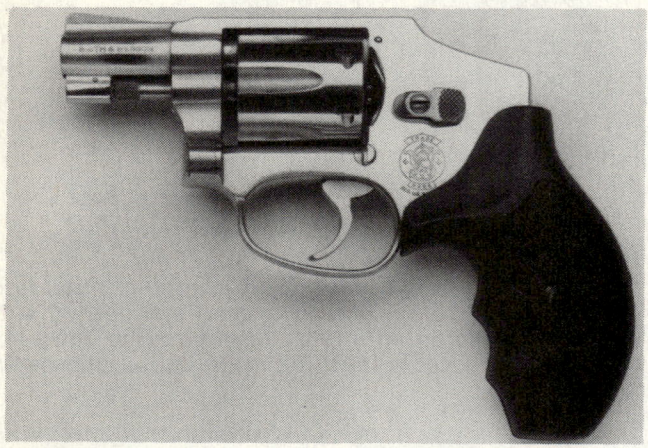

NIB	Exc.	V.G.	Good	Fair	Poor
325	275	225	175	125	100

Model 42 - Airweight Centennial

This model is identical in configuration to the Model 40 except that it was furnished with an aluminum alloy frame. It was also discontinued in 1974.

Editors Note: The first 37 Model 42s were manufactured with aluminum alloy cylinders. They weigh 11-1/4 ounces compared to 13 ounces for the standard model. The balance of Model 42 production was with steel cylinders. Add 300% for this extremely rare variation.

NIB	Exc.	V.G.	Good	Fair	Poor
450	400	325	200	150	100

Model 442 Centennial Lightweight

This 5-shot revolver is chambered for the .38 Special and is equipped with a 2" barrel, aluminum alloy frame, and carbon steel cylinder. It has a fully concealed hammer and weighs 15.8 oz. The front ramp sight is serrated and the rear sight is

a fixed square notch. Rubber combat grips from Michael's of Oregon are standard. Finish is either blue or satin nickel. Introduced in 1993.

NIB	Exc.	V.G.	Good	Fair	Poor
350	300	250	200	150	100

Model 43 (.22/.32 Kit Gun Airweight)

This model was built on the J-frame, is chambered for .22 rimfire, has a 4" barrel, and is offered in a round or square butt, with checkered walnut grips. It has adjustable sights and is either blued or nickel-plated. The frame is made of aluminum alloy. Except for this, it is identical to the Model 34 or .22/.32 Kit Gun. The Model 43 was introduced in 1954 and was discontinued in 1974.

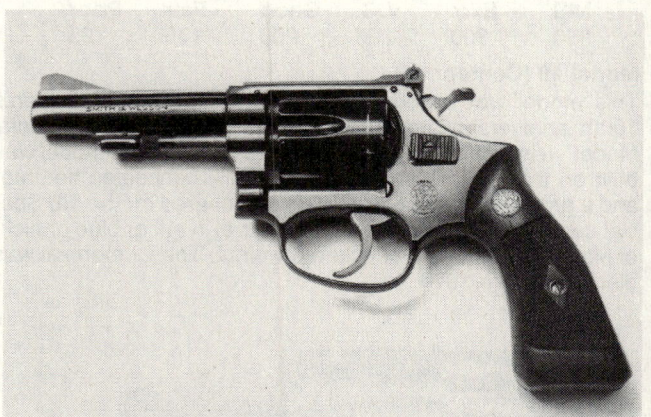

Courtesy Mike Stuckslager.

NIB	Exc.	V.G.	Good	Fair	Poor
375	300	250	200	150	100

Model 51 (.22/.32 Kit Gun Magnum)

This model is simply the Model 34 chambered for the .22 Winchester Magnum rimfire. It was first introduced in 1960 beginning with serial number 52637. Available in both round and square butt with the round butt variation having a total production of only 600. The Model 51 was discontinued in 1974.

NIB	Exc.	V.G.	Good	Fair	Poor
450	325	275	250	200	125

Model 651

This stainless steel version of the Model 51 .22 Magnum Kit Gun was manufactured between 1983 and 1987.

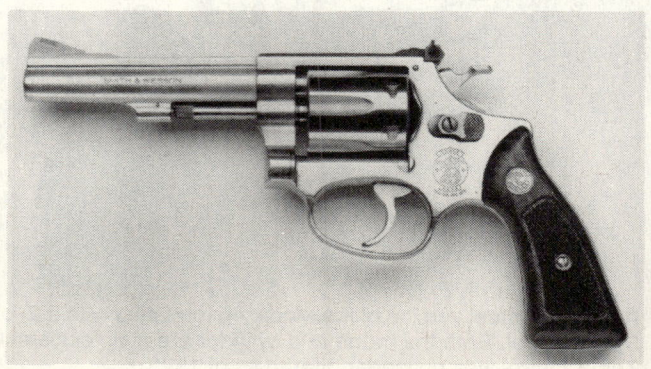

Exc.	V.G.	Good	Fair	Poor
325	275	225	175	125

<table>
<tr><td colspan="4">

Notes on J-frame Revolvers:
1. In 1953 the cylinder stop plunger screw was eliminated.
2. In 1955 the top corner sideplate screw was eliminated.
3. In 1957 the numerical model designation was stamped on the yoke.
4. In 1966 the flat latch was changed to the present contoured cylinder release.

</td></tr>
</table>

Model 45 (Post Office)

This model is a special purpose K-frame Military & Police Model chambered for the .22 rimfire. It was designed as a training revolver for police departments and the U.S. Postal Service. This model was manufactured in limited quantities between 1948 and 1957. In 1963 production abruptly began and ended again. There were 500 of these revolvers released on a commercial basis, but they are rarely encountered.

NIB	Exc.	V.G.	Good	Fair	Poor
750	600	550	350	200	100

Model 48 (K-22 Masterpiece Magnum)

Introduced in 1959 and is identical to the Model 17 or K-22 except that it is chambered for the .22 WRM cartridge. Offered in 4", 6", and 8-3/8" barrel lengths, it has a blued finish. Discontinued in 1986.

NIB	Exc.	V.G.	Good	Fair	Poor
375	300	250	200	150	100

Model 53 (Magnum Jet)

Introduced in 1961 and chambered for the .22 Jet, a Remington cartridge. The barrel lengths were 4, 6, and 8-3/8 inches and the finish is blued. Sights were adjustable and the revolver was furnished with cylinder inserts that would allow .22 rimfire cartridges to be fired. The frame had two firing pins. Approximately 15,000 were produced before it was discontinued in 1974.

NIB	Exc.	V.G.	Good	Fair	Poor
800	650	450	350	250	200

Model 56 (KXT-38 USAF)

Introduced in 1962 this is a 2" heavy barrel built on the K-frame. It is chambered for the .38 Special. There were approximately 15,000 of these revolvers built when it was discontinued in 1964. It was marked "US" on the backstrap. A total of 15,205 produced but most destroyed.

NIB	Exc.	V.G.	Good	Fair	Poor
2500	1750	1250	750	500	250

Model 57

This revolver was introduced in 1964 and is chambered for the .41 Magnum cartridge. It is built on the N-frame. Offered in 4", 6", and 8-3/8" barrel lengths, it has a blued frame and adjustable sights. Model designations are: {57-1 1982; 57-2 1988; 57-3 1990; 57-4 1993.

NIB	Exc.	V.G.	Good	Fair	Poor
450	350	275	225	200	150

Model 657

This is a stainless steel version of the Model 57 and was introduced in 1980. Still in production.

NIB	Exc.	V.G.	Good	Fair	Poor
375	325	275	225	200	150

Model 58

This model is chambered for the .41 Magnum and is fitted with fixed sights. Offered in blued or nickel finish and with 4" barrel. Checkered walnut grips are standard. Introduced in 1964.

NIB	Exc.	V.G.	Good	Fair	Poor
400	325	250	200	150	100

Model 547

Introduced in 1980 and chambered for the 9mm cartridge and offered with either 3" or 4" barrel. Finish is blued. Discontinued.

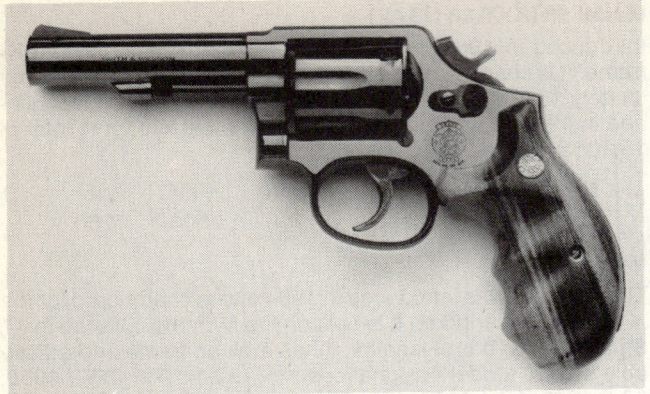

NIB	Exc.	V.G.	Good	Fair	Poor
375	300	250	200	150	100

Model 60

Introduced in 1965 this model is similar to the Model 36 but in stainless steel. Offered in 2" barrel with fixed sights, walnut grips, and smooth trigger. Some 2" Model 60s were produced with adjustable sights-Add 50%. The 3" barrel version comes with a full underlug, adjustable sights, serrated trigger, and rubber grips. The 2" version weighs about 20 oz. while the 3" version weighs approximately 25 oz. In 1996 this model was offered chambered for the .357 Magnum cartridge. This new version is fitted with a 2-1/8" barrel. The 2-1/8" barrel weighs about 23 oz.

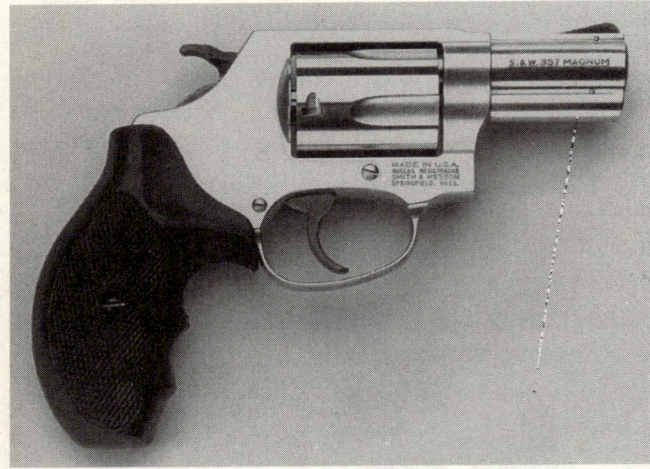

2" Barrel

NIB	Exc.	V.G.	Good	Fair	Poor
350	275	200	175	125	100

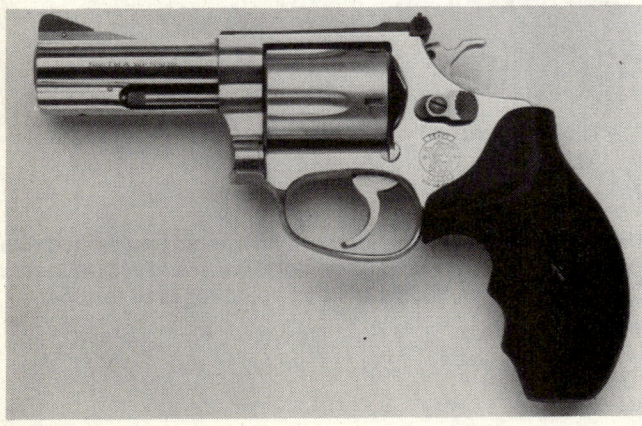

3" Barrel

NIB	Exc.	V.G.	Good	Fair	Poor
350	275	200	175	125	100

Model 60LS (LadySmith)

Chambered for the .38 Special with 2" barrel and stainless steel frame and cylinder. This slightly smaller version of the Model 60 is made for small hands. A new version offered in 1996 is chambered for the .357 Magnum cartridge.

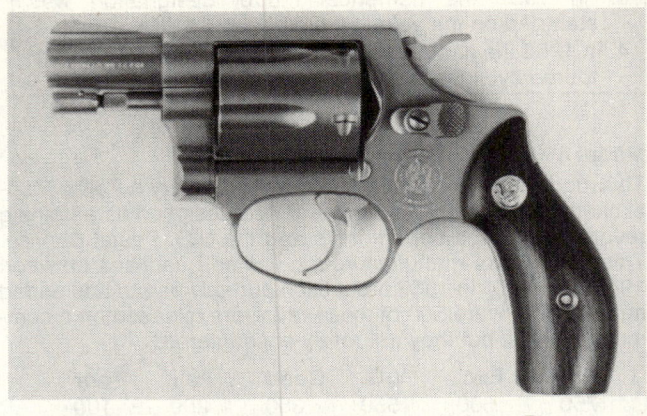

NIB	Exc.	V.G.	Good	Fair	Poor
300	275	250	200	150	100

Model 63

This model, introduced in 1977, is simply the Model 34 made of stainless steel.

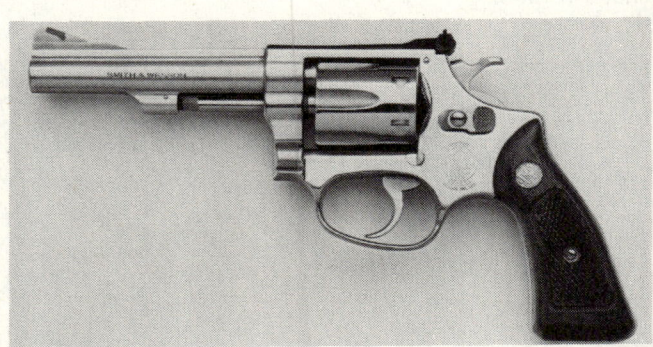

NIB	Exc.	V.G.	Good	Fair	Poor
350	275	250	225	200	150

Model 64 (Military & Police Stainless)

This model is the stainless steel version of the Model 10 M&P. It was introduced in 1970. The Model 64-1 variation was introduced in 1972 and is the heavy barrel version.

NIB	Exc.	V.G.	Good	Fair	Poor
350	300	275	225	175	125

Model 65 (.357 Military & Police Heavy Barrel Stainless)

This is the stainless steel version of the Model 13 M&P .357 Magnum. It was introduced in 1974.

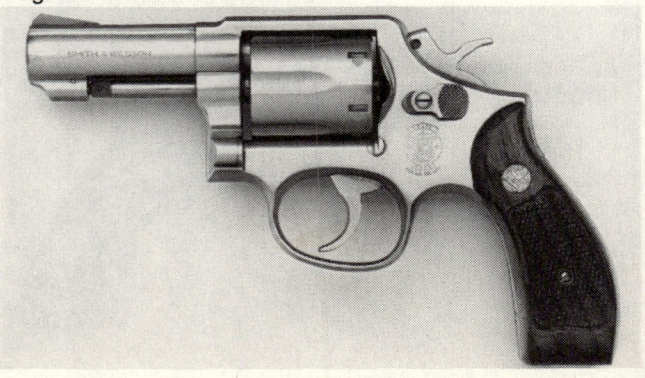

NIB	Exc.	V.G.	Good	Fair	Poor
350	300	275	225	175	125

Model 66 (.357 Combat Magnum Stainless)

Released in 1970, this is the stainless steel version of the Model 19 or Combat Magnum. It is chambered for the .357 Magnum, has adjustable sights, a square butt with checkered walnut grips, and was initially offered with a 4" barrel. In 1974 a 2.5" barrel, round-butt version was made available. It was available in a 6" barrel, as well as all target options until discontinued in 1993.

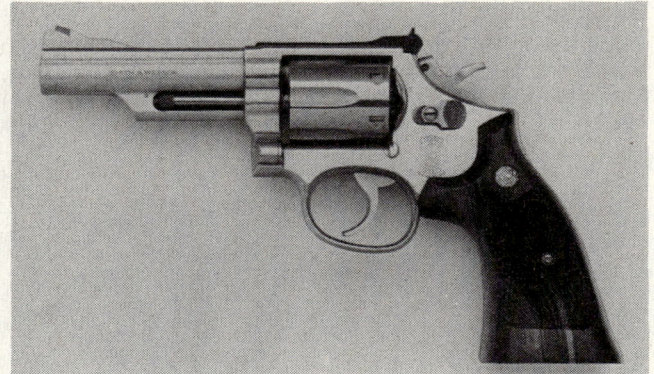

NIB	Exc.	V.G.	Good	Fair	Poor
350	300	250	200	150	125

Model 67 (.38 Combat Masterpiece Stainless)

Introduced in 1972 this is a stainless steel version of the Model 15 with a 4" barrel. It is chambered for the .38 Special cartridge. Model designation changes are as follows: {None} 1972 to 1977; {-1} 1977 to 1988; {-2} 1988 to 1993; {-3} 1993 to present.

NIB	Exc.	V.G.	Good	Fair	Poor
350	300	250	200	150	100

Model 650

Introduced in 1983 this stainless steel model is built on a J-frame with a 3" heavy barrel chambered for the .22 WRM. It has a round butt and fixed sights. Discontinued in 1988.

NIB	Exc.	V.G.	Good	Fair	Poor
425	350	250	175	125	100

Model 651

This J-frame model was introduced in 1983 and chambered for the .22 WRM and fitted with a 4" barrel. Stainless steel finish and adjustable sights. Designation changes are: {None} 1983 to 1988; {-1} 1988 to 1990; {-2} 1988 to 1990.

NIB	Exc.	V.G.	Good	Fair	Poor
400	350	250	175	125	100

Model 520

Introduced in 1980 and built on the N-frame. Chambered for the .357 Mag. cartridge with a 4" barrel. It has fixed sights, blued finish and checkered walnut grips.

NIB	Exc.	V.G.	Good	Fair	Poor
350	300	250	225	150	100

Model 581

Introduced in 1980. Built on the L-frame with a full barrel underlug. Chambered for the .357 Mag. cartridge with a 4" barrel and blued or nickel finish. Rear sight is fixed. Sometimes referred to as the Distinguished Service Magnum. Designation changes are: {None} 1980 to 1986; {-1} 1986 to 1987; {-2} 1987 to 1988; {-3} 1988 to present.

NIB	Exc.	V.G.	Good	Fair	Poor
350	300	275	225	150	100

Model 681

This model is identical as the Model 581 but with a stainless steel frame and barrel. Introduced in 1981 and discontinued in 1992.

NIB	Exc.	V.G.	Good	Fair	Poor
350	300	250	200	150	100

Model 586

Introduced in 1980 this L-frame revolver is furnished with target sights, target stocks, and target trigger. Barrels in 4", 6", or 8" lengths. Choice of blued or nickel finish. Designation changes are: {None} 1980 to 1986; {-1} 1986 to 1987; {-2} 1987 to 1988; {-3} 1988 to 1993; {-4} 1993 to present; {-5} 1993 to present (export to Brazil in .38 caliber).

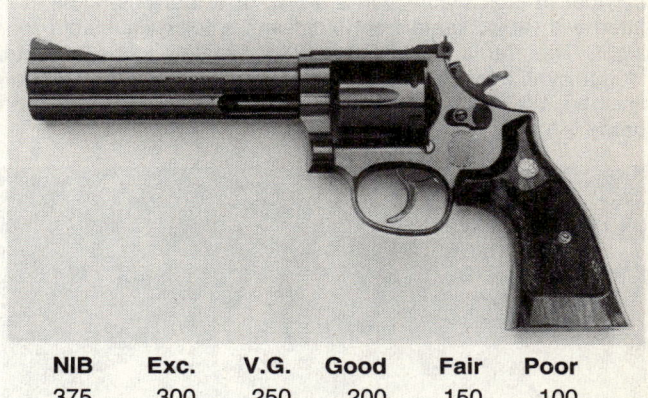

NIB	Exc.	V.G.	Good	Fair	Poor
375	300	250	200	150	100

Model 686

Introduced in 1980 this is a stainless steel version of the Model 586. There is no {-5} designation for this model.

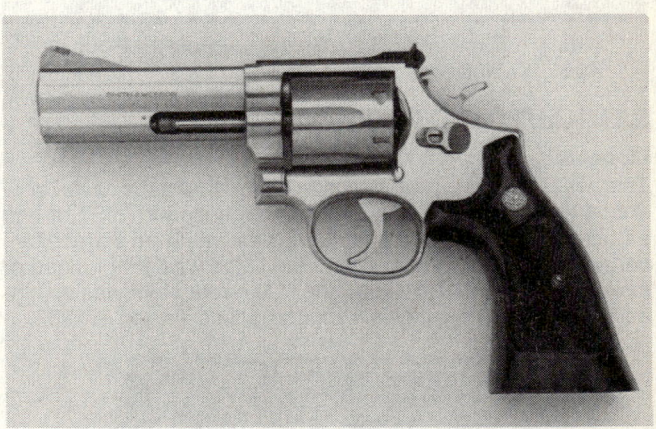

NIB	Exc.	V.G.	Good	Fair	Poor
375	300	250	200	150	100

Model 686 Powerport

Introduced in 1995 this version of the Model 686 features a 6" full lug barrel with intergral compensator. The frame is drilled and tapped for scop mounts. Hogue grips are furnished as standard.

NIB	Exc.	V.G.	Good	Fair	Poor
600	550	450	400	300	200

Model 686 Magnum Plus

Offered for the first time in 1996 this model features a 7 shot cylinder. It is available with 2.5", 4", or 6" barrel lengths. It is fitted with a red ramp front sight and a fully adjustable rear sight. The frame is drilled and tapped for scope mounts. Hogue synthetic grips are standard. The stainless steel is satin finished. Weight is between 35 oz. and 45 oz. depending on barrel length.

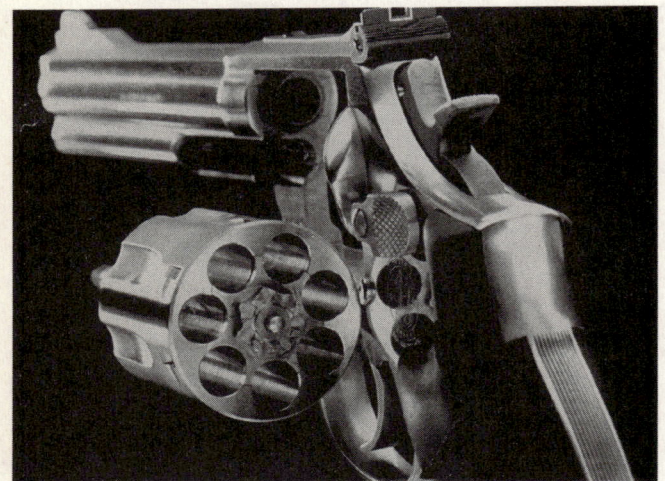

NIB	Exc.	V.G.	Good	Fair	Poor
450	400	—	—	—	—

SEMI-AUTOMATIC PISTOLS

Model 39

This was the first double action semi-automatic pistol produced in the United States. It was introduced in 1957. It had an alloy frame and was chambered for the 9mm Parabellum cartridge. The barrel was 4" and the finish was either blued or nickel with checkered walnut grips. The rear sight was adjustable. Magazine capacity is 8 rounds. Discontinued in 1982.

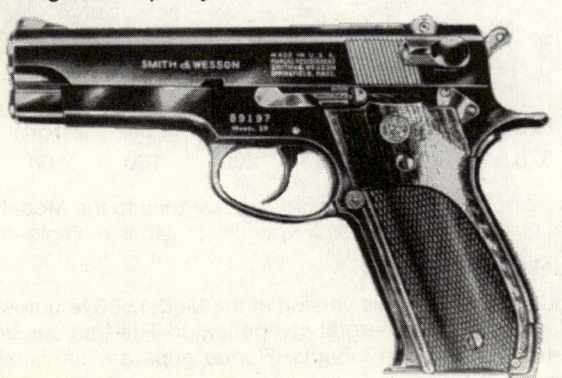

NIB	Exc.	V.G.	Good	Fair	Poor
400	350	250	200	150	100

Model 39 Steel Frame

A total of 927 steel frame Model 39s were produced. A rare pistol, use caution.

NIB	Exc.	V.G.	Good	Fair	Poor
1250	1000	700	550	400	250

Model 59

Introduced in 1971 this pistol is similar to the Model 39 but with a wide grip to hold a double column magazine of 14 rounds. Furnished with black checkered plastic grips. Discontinued in 1982.

NIB	Exc.	V.G.	Good	Fair	Poor
400	300	250	200	150	100

Model 439

Introduced in 1979 this is an improved version of the Model 39. Furnished with adjustable rear sight. Discontinued in 1988.

NIB	Exc.	V.G.	Good	Fair	Poor
450	400	350	325	250	100

Model 639

This is a stainless steel version of the Model 439. Introduced in 1984 and discontinued in 1988.

NIB	Exc.	V.G.	Good	Fair	Poor
400	325	300	250	200	100

Model 459

This improved-sight version of the 15-shot Model 59 9mm pistol was introduced in 1979 and discontinued in 1987.

NIB	Exc.	V.G.	Good	Fair	Poor
475	400	350	300	250	200

Model 659

This stainless steel version of the Model 459 9mm pistol features an ambidextrous safety and all other options of the Model 459. Introduced in 1982 and discontinued in 1988.

NIB	Exc.	V.G.	Good	Fair	Poor
475	425	350	300	250	150

Model 539

This is yet another version of the Model 439 9mm pistol. It incorporates all the features of the Model 439 with a steel frame instead of aluminum alloy. This model was introduced in 1980 and discontinued in 1983.

NIB	Exc.	V.G.	Good	Fair	Poor
450	400	350	300	250	200

Model 559

This variation of the Model 459 9mm pistol has a steel frame instead of aluminum alloy. It is identical in all other respects.

NIB	Exc.	V.G.	Good	Fair	Poor
450	400	350	300	250	200

Model 469

The Model 469 was brought out in answer to the need for a more concealable high-capacity pistol. It is essentially a "Mini" version of the Model 459. It is chambered for the 9mm Parabellum and has a 12-round detachable magazine with a finger-grip extension and a shortened frame. The barrel is 3.5" long; the hammer is bobbed and does not protrude; the safety is ambidextrous. The finish is matte blue, with black plastic grips. The Model 469 was introduced in 1983 and discontinued in 1988.

NIB	Exc.	V.G.	Good	Fair	Poor
450	375	325	275	200	150

Model 669

This is a stainless steel version of the Model 469 9mm pistol. All of the features of the 469 are incorporated. The Model 669 was manufactured from 1986 to 1988.

NIB	Exc.	V.G.	Good	Fair	Poor
475	425	350	300	250	200

Model 645

The Model 645 is a large-framed, stainless steel double-action pistol chambered for the .45 ACP cartridge. It has a 5" barrel, adjustable sights, and a detachable 8-shot magazine. It is offered with fixed or adjustable sights and an ambidextrous safety. The grips are molded black nylon. S&W manufactured this pistol between 1985 and 1988.

NIB	Exc.	V.G.	Good	Fair	Poor
500	425	375	325	250	150

Model 745 - IPSC

This model is similar in outward appearance to the Model 645 but is quite a different pistol. The Model 745 is a single-action semiautomatic chambered for the .45 ACP cartridge. The frame is made of stainless steel, and the slide of blued carbon steel. The barrel is 5", and the detachable magazine holds 8 rounds. The sights are fully adjustable target types. The grips are checkered walnut. Introduced in 1986 and discontinued in 1990.

NIB	Exc.	V.G.	Good	Fair	Poor
700	600	500	400	350	250

Model 41

The Model 41 was introduced to the shooting public in 1957. It is a high quality .22 rimfire target pistol. It has an alloy frame, steel slide, and either a 5.5" or 73/8" barrel. It has a detachable 10-shot magazine, adjustable target sights, and checkered walnut target grips. The finish is blued.

Discontinued Barrels:
5" With Extended Sight-Add $100.
5.5" Heavy With Extended Sight-Add $100.
7.5" With Muzzle Brake-Add $75.

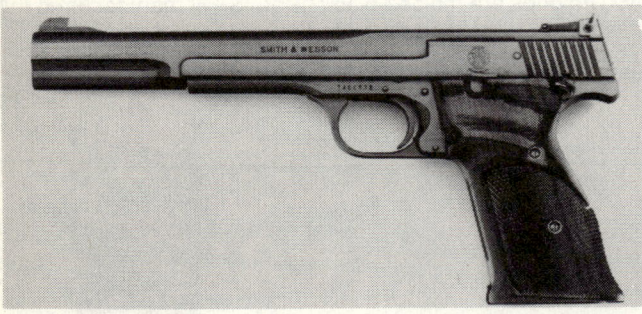

NIB	Exc.	V.G.	Good	Fair	Poor
850	600	400	300	225	150

Model 41 (New Model)

This model was restyled in 1994 featuring recontoured hardwood stocks, a Millet adjustable rear sight, and a drilled and tapped barrel for scope mounting.

NIB	Exc.	V.G.	Good	Fair	Poor
650	575	500	400	300	150

Model 41-1

This model was introduced in 1960 and is chambered for the .22 Short rimfire only. It was developed for the International Rapid Fire competition. In appearance it is quite similar to the Model 41 except that the slide is made of aluminum alloy, as well as the frame, in order to lighten it to function with the .22 short cartridge. This model was not a commercial success like the Model 41, so it was discontinued after fewer than 1,000 were manufactured.

NIB	Exc.	V.G.	Good	Fair	Poor
1200	900	725	500	375	225

Model 46

This was a lower-cost version of the Model 41. It was developed for the Air Force in 1959. Its appearance was essentially the same as the Model 41 with a 7" barrel. Later a 5" barrel was introduced, and finally in 1964 a heavy 5.5" barrel was produced. This economy target pistol never had the popularity that the more expensive Model 41 had, and it was discontinued in 1968 after approximately 4,000 pistols were manufactured.

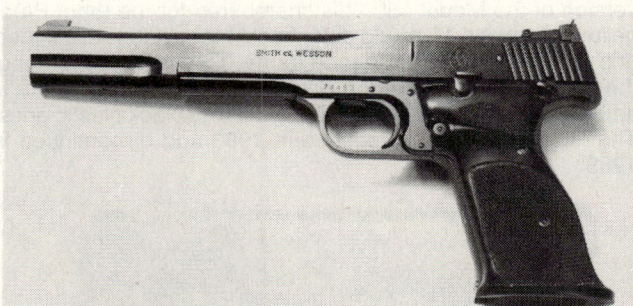

Courtesy Mike Stuckslager

NIB	Exc.	V.G.	Good	Fair	Poor
700	600	450	350	250	200

Model 61 Escort

In 1970 the Model 61 was introduced as the only true pocket automatic that S&W produced. It was chambered for the .22 l.r. cartridge with a 2-1/2" barrel and 5-round magazine. It was offered in either blued or nickel finish with black checkered plastic grips. It was dropped from the product line in 1974.

NIB	Exc.	V.G.	Good	Fair	Poor
250	175	150	125	100	75

Model 52A

Introduced in 1961 in the .38 AMU caliber for the Army marksmanship training. Army rejected the pistol and the 87 units built were released to the public. The letter "A" is stamped behind the model designation. A rare find; only 87 were produced. Use caution.

NIB	Exc.	V.G.	Good	Fair	Poor
3000	2500	2000	1500	750	500

Model 52 (.38 Master)

Introduced in 1961 as a target pistol chambered for the .38 Special mid-range wad cutter cartridge. It is similar in appearance to the Model 39 but is single action only by virture of a set screw. Fitted with a 5" barrel and a 5-round magazine. It has a blued finish with checkered walnut grips. About 3,500 of these pistols were produced in this configuration until discontinued in 1963.

NIB	Exc.	V.G.	Good	Fair	Poor
900	750	550	450	300	200

Model 52-1

In 1963 this variation featured a true single action design and were produced until 1971.

NIB	Exc.	V.G.	Good	Fair	Poor
750	650	450	350	300	200

Model 52-2

Introduced in 1971 with a coil spring style extractor. Model was discontinued in 1993.

NIB	Exc.	V.G.	Good	Fair	Poor
700	600	475	400	300	200

Model 2214 (The Sportsman)

This semiautomatic pistol is chambered for the .22 Long Rifle and designed for casual use. It is fitted with a 3" barrel and has a magazine capacity of 8 rounds. The slide is blued carbon steel and the frame is alloy. Introduced in 1990.

NIB	Exc.	V.G.	Good	Fair	Poor
200	175	150	125	100	50

Model 2206

This .22 Long Rifle pistol is offered with either a 4-1/2" or 6" barrel. Magazine capacity is 12 rounds. Adjustable rear sight. Stainless steel frame and slide.

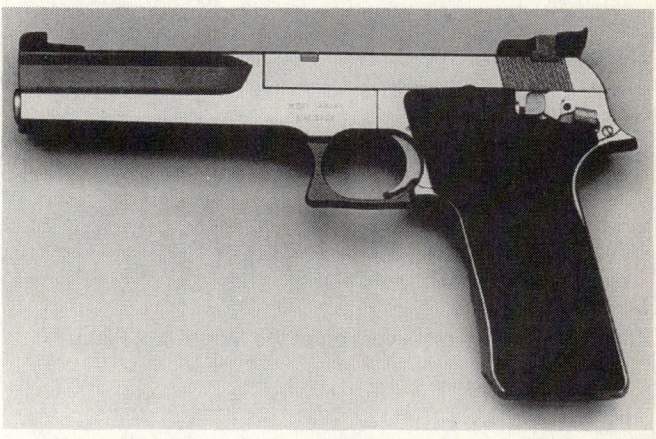

NIB	Exc.	V.G.	Good	Fair	Poor
250	200	175	125	100	50

Model 2206 TGT (Target)

Introduced in 1995 this version of the Model 2206 features a selected 6" barrel, bead blasted sighting plane and polished flat side surfaces. a Patridge front sight and Millet adjustable rear sightare standard. In addition the model has a serrated trigger with adjustable trigger stop and a 10 round magazine.

NIB	Exc.	V.G.	Good	Fair	Poor
350	300	250	200	150	100

Model 422 Field

Introduced in 1987 this .22 Long Rifle pistol has a 4-1/2" barrel or 6" barrel with an alloy frame and steel slide. The magazine capacity is 10 rounds. This model has fixed sights and black plastic grips. Finish is matte blue.

NIB	Exc.	V.G.	Good	Fair	Poor
200	175	150	125	100	50

Model 422 Target

Same as the Field model but fitted with adjustable sights and checkered walnut grips.

NIB	Exc.	V.G.	Good	Fair	Poor
250	200	175	150	100	50

Model 622 Field

This is a stainless steel version of the Model 422 Field.

NIB	Exc.	V.G.	Good	Fair	Poor
225	200	175	150	125	75

Model 622 Target

This is the stainless steel version of the Model 422 Target.

NIB	Exc.	V.G.	Good	Fair	Poor
275	225	200	175	125	75

Model 622VR

Redesigned in 1996 this .22 caliber model features a 6" ventilated rib barrel. It is fitted with a matte black trigger and a new trigger guard. The front sight is a serrated ramp style with an adjustable rear sight. Weight is approximately 23 oz. Grips are black polymer.

NIB	Exc.	V.G.	Good	Fair	Poor
300	250	200	150	100	75

Model 22A Sport

Introduced in 1997 this model features a choice of 4", 5.5", or 7" barrel. It is chambered for the .22 Long Rifle cartridge. Magazine capacity is 10 rounds. Rear sight is adjustable. Grips are either two-piece polymer or two-piece Soft Touch. Frame and slide are aluminum alloy and stainless steel. Finish is blue. Weight is approximately 28 oz for 4" model and 32 oz. for 5.5" model. Weight of 7" model is about 33 oz. Prices quoted below are for 4" model. .

NIB	Exc.	V.G.	Good	Fair	Poor
200	150	100	75	—	—

Model 22S Sport

This model, also introduced in 1997, is similar to the above model but with 5.5" and 7" barrel on stainless steel frames. Weight is about 41 oz and 42 oz. respectively.

NIB	Exc.	V.G.	Good	Fair	Poor
275	225	200	150	—	—

Model 22A Target

This .22 caliber target pistol has a 10-round magazine, adjustable rear sight, and target grips with thumb rest. The barrel is 5.5" bull barrel. Finish is blue. Weight is about 39 oz. Introduced in 1997.

NIB	Exc.	V.G.	Good	Fair	Poor
275	225	—	—	—	—

Model 22S Target

Same as above but with stainless steel frame and slide. Weight is approximately 48 oz.

NIB	Exc.	V.G.	Good	Fair	Poor
350	300	—	—	—	—

Model 3904

In 1989 S&W redesigned the entire line of 9mm semiautomatic handguns. The 3904 is chambered for the 9mm Parabellum and has an 8-shot detachable magazine and 4" barrel with a fixed bushing. The frame is alloy, and the triggerguard is squared for two-hand hold. The magazine well is beveled, and the grips are one-piece wrap-around made of delrin. The three dot sighting system is employed. This model has been discontinued.

NIB	Exc.	V.G.	Good	Fair	Poor
450	400	325	300	275	225

Model 3906

This is the stainless steel version of the Model 3904. The features are the same. It was introduced in 1989. This model has been discontinued.

NIB	Exc.	V.G.	Good	Fair	Poor
450	400	325	300	275	225

Model 3914

Offered as a slightly smaller alternative to the Model 3904, this 9mm pistol has a 3-1/2" barrel, 8-round magazine, and blued carbon steel slide and alloy frame.

NIB	Exc.	V.G.	Good	Fair	Poor
525	450	400	350	300	250

Model 3913

This version is similar to the Model 3914 but features a stainless steel slide and alloy frame.

NIB	Exc.	V.G.	Good	Fair	Poor
525	450	400	350	300	250

Model 3914LS

This is a redesigned Model 3914 that has a more modern appearance. The LS refers to LadySmith and is chambered for the 9mm cartridge. All other features are the same as the Model 3914 including the blued carbon slide and alloy frame.

NIB	Exc.	V.G.	Good	Fair	Poor
525	450	400	350	300	200

Model 3913LS

This model is identical to the Model 3914LS with the exception of the stainless steel slide.

NIB	Exc.	V.G.	Good	Fair	Poor
525	450	400	350	300	200

Model 3954

Similar to the Model 3914 but offered in double action only. Discontinued in 1993.

NIB	Exc.	V.G.	Good	Fair	Poor
525	450	400	350	300	200

Model 915

Introduced in 1993 this model is chambered for the 9mm cartridge and features a 4" barrel, matte blue finish, fixed rear sight, and wrap-around rubber grips. Overall length is 7.5" and weight is about 28 oz.

NIB	Exc.	V.G.	Good	Fair	Poor
400	350	250	200	150	100

Model 5904

This is a full high capacity, 15-shot version of the Model 3904. It was introduced in 1989 and features a slide mounted decocking lever and 4" barrel. This version has a blued carbon steel slide and alloy frame.

NIB	Exc.	V.G.	Good	Fair	Poor
525	450	375	325	275	200

Model 5906

This is a stainless steel version of the Model 5904. Both the slide and frame are stainless steel.

NIB	Exc.	V.G.	Good	Fair	Poor
525	450	375	275	200	

Model 5906 Special Edition

A double action semiautomatic pistol chambered for the 9mm with a 15-round magazine. The frame and slide have a special machine finish while the grips are one-piece wrap-around Xenoy. The front sight is a white dot post and the rear sight is a Novak L-Mount Carry with two white dots. This model has a manual safety/decocking lever and firing pin safety. Introduced in 1993.

NIB	Exc.	V.G.	Good	Fair	Poor
525	450	350	300	250	150

Model 5903

The same caliber and features as the Model 5904 and Model 5906, but furnished with a stainless steel slide and alloy frame.

NIB	Exc.	V.G.	Good	Fair	Poor
525	450	400	350	300	250

Model 5926

S&W offers a 9mm pistol similar to the 5906 but with a frame mounted decocking lever. Both the slide and frame are stainless steel. Discontinued in 1993.

NIB	Exc.	V.G.	Good	Fair	Poor
525	450	375	300	250	150

Model 5946

This 9mm pistol offers the same features as the Model 5926, but in a double action only mode. The hammer configuration on this model is semi-bobbed instead of serrated.

NIB	Exc.	V.G.	Good	Fair	Poor
525	450	400	350	300	250

Model 6904

This is the concealable, shortened version of the Model 5904. It has a 12-shot magazine, fixed sights, bobbed hammer, and a 3.5" barrel.

NIB	Exc.	V.G.	Good	Fair	Poor
525	450	400	350	300	250

Model 6906

This version has a stainless steel slide and alloy frame but otherwise is similar to the Model 6904.

NIB	Exc.	V.G.	Good	Fair	Poor
525	450	400	350	300	200

Model 6946

This is a double action version of the Model 6906.

NIB	Exc.	V.G.	Good	Fair	Poor
525	450	400	350	300	200

Model 4003

This pistol is chambered for the .40 S&W cartridge and is fitted with a 4" barrel, 11-round magazine, serrated hammer with a stainless steel slide and alloy frame.

NIB	Exc.	V.G.	Good	Fair	Poor
575	500	400	350	300	200

Model 4004
Identical to the Model 4003 except for a blue carbon steel slide and alloy frame. Discontinued in 1993.

NIB	Exc.	V.G.	Good	Fair	Poor
575	500	400	350	300	200

Model 4006
This model is identical to the Model 4003 except that both the slide and frame are made from stainless steel. This adds 8 oz. to the weight of the pistol.

NIB	Exc.	V.G.	Good	Fair	Poor
575	500	400	350	300	200

Model 4026

Similar to the Model 4006 this version has a frame mounted decocking lever.

NIB	Exc.	V.G.	Good	Fair	Poor
575	500	400	350	300	200

Model 4046
Similar to the Model 4006 but with a double action only configuration.

NIB	Exc.	V.G.	Good	Fair	Poor
575	500	400	350	300	250

Model 4013
A compact version of the 4000 series, this .40 caliber model features a 3-1/2 inch barrel, 8-round magazine, and stainless steel slide and alloy frame.

NIB	Exc.	V.G.	Good	Fair	Poor
575	500	400	350	300	200

Model 4013 TSW

Similar to the Model 4013 but traditional double action only with some improvements. Magazine capacity is 9 rounds of .40 S&W cartridges. Finish is satin stainless. Weight is approximately 26 oz. Introduced in 1997.

NIB	Exc.	V.G.	Good	Fair	Poor
700	625	—	—	—	—

Model 4014

Identical to the Model 4013 except for a blued carbon steel slide and alloy frame.

NIB	Exc.	V.G.	Good	Fair	Poor
575	500	400	350	300	200

Model 4053

Identical to the Model 4013, stainless steel slide and alloy frame, except offered in a double action only configuration.

NIB	Exc.	V.G.	Good	Fair	Poor
575	500	400	350	300	200

Model 4054

This model is the same as the Model 4053 except for a blued carbon steel slide and alloy frame. Dropped from S&W product line in 1992.

NIB	Exc.	V.G.	Good	Fair	Poor
575	500	400	300	250	200

Model 4056 TSW

This is a double action only pistol chambered for the .40 S&W cartridge. Fitted with a 3.5" barrel with white dot sights. Curved backstrap. Stainless steel and alloy frame. Stainless steel finish. Magazine capacity is 9 rounds. Introduced in 1997. Weight is approximately 36 oz.

NIB	Exc.	V.G.	Good	Fair	Poor
725	625	—	—	—	—

Model 411

This model was introduced in 1993 as a no frills model and features an alloy frame, 4" barrel, matte blue finish, fixed sights, and wrap-around rubber grips. Chambered for .40 S&W cartridge with 11-round magazine capacity. Overall length is 7.5" and weight is approximately 29 oz.

NIB	Exc.	V.G.	Good	Fair	Poor
400	350	300	250	200	150

Model 1006

This is a full size 10mm pistol with a 5" barrel, 9-round magazine, and choice of fixed or adjustable sights. Both the slide and frame are stainless steel.

NIB	Exc.	V.G.	Good	Fair	Poor
475	450	400	350	300	200

Model 1066

This is a slightly smaller version of the Model 1006 and is furnished with a 4-1/4" barrel. Discontinued in 1993.

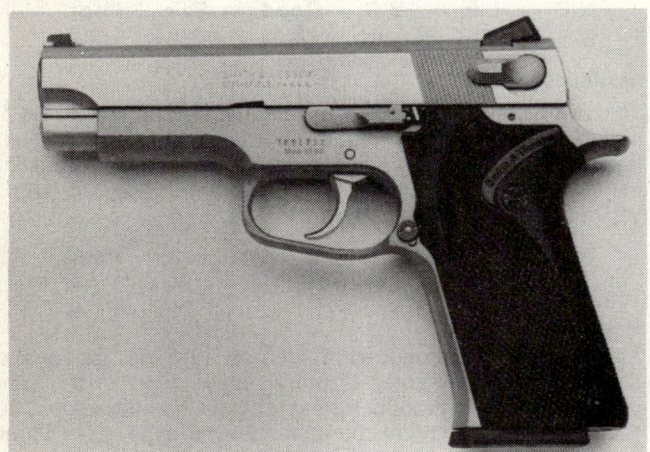

NIB	Exc.	V.G.	Good	Fair	Poor
475	450	400	350	300	200

Model 1076

Identical to the Model 1066 with the exception of the frame mounted decocking lever.

NIB	Exc.	V.G.	Good	Fair	Poor
475	450	400	350	300	200

Model 1086

Similar to the Model 1066 but offered in double action only. This model was discontinued in 1993.

NIB	Exc.	V.G.	Good	Fair	Poor
475	425	375	300	250	200

Model 1026

Similar to the Model 1006 with a 5" barrel this model has a frame mounted decocking lever.

NIB	Exc.	V.G.	Good	Fair	Poor
475	450	400	350	300	200

Model 4506

This is the newly designed double action .45 ACP pistol. It is all stainless steel and has a 5" barrel, 8-shot detachable magazine, and wrap-around black delrin grips.

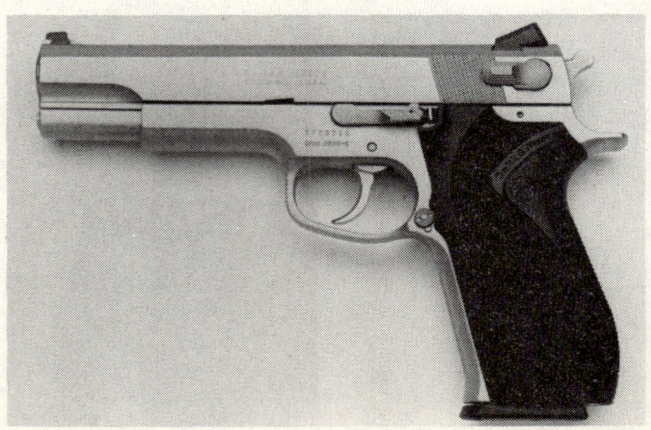

NIB	Exc.	V.G.	Good	Fair	Poor
550	475	400	350	300	250

Model 4505

This version is identical to the Model 4506 with the exception of a blued slide and frame.

NIB	Exc.	V.G.	Good	Fair	Poor
550	475	400	350	300	250

Model 4516

Offered in a .45 caliber this 4500 series is a compact version of the full size .45 caliber S&W autos. Furnished with a 3-3/4" barrel and a 7-round magazine this model has a stainless slide and frame. Discontinued in 1991. This model was reintroduced in 1994.

NIB	Exc.	V.G.	Good	Fair	Poor
550	475	400	350	300	250

Model 4546

A full size version of the Model 4506 but offered in double action only.

NIB	Exc.	V.G.	Good	Fair	Good
550	475	400	350	300	250

Sigma Series

This new pistol was introduced in 1994 and features a departure from the traditional S&W pistol. The pistol features a stainless steel barrel, carbon steel slide, and polymer frame. Offered in .40 S&W and 9mm calibers with 15 round and 17 round capacities. Magazines built after 9/13/94 will be limited to 10 rounds for all calibers per Federal law.

NIB	Exc.	V.G.	Good	Fair	Poor
550	475	425	375	300	250

Model 4536

A compact version and similar to the Model 4616 this pistol is offered with a decock lever on the frame.

NIB	Exc.	V.G.	Good	Fair	Poor
450	400	350	300	250	200

Sigma Series Compact

Same as above but with barrel and slide 1/2" shorter than full size Sigma. Offered in both .40 S&W and 9mm.

NIB	Exc.	V.G.	Good	Fair	Poor
450	400	350	300	250	200

Sigma Series SW9M

Introduced in 1996 this pistol is chambered for the 9mm cartridge. It is fitted with a 3.25" barrel and has a magazine capacity of 7 rounds. The frame is polymer and the slide carbon steel. Height is 4.5" and overall length is 6.25". Weight is 18 oz.

NIB	Exc.	V.G.	Good	Fair	Poor
450	400	—	—	—	—

Sigma SW 9V

Chambered for the 9mm cartridge this model is fitted with a 4" barrel and 10-round magazine. It has a traditional double action. White dot sights are standard. Grips are integral to the frame. Stainless steel slide. Satin stainless finish with choice of gray or black frame. Weight is about 25 oz. Introduced in 1997.

NIB	Exc.	V.G.	Good	Fair	Poor
350	300	—	—	—	—

Sigma SW40V

Same as above but chambered for .40 S&W cartridge. Weight is 25 oz. Introduced in 1997.

NIB	Exc.	V.G.	Good	Fair	Poor
350	300	—	—	—	—

Sigma SW 380

Introduced in 1995 this model is chambered for the .380 ACP cartridge. Barrel length is 3" with overall length 5.8". Empty weight is 14 oz. with a magazine capacity of 6 rounds.

NIB	Exc.	V.G.	Good	Fair	Poor
300	250	200	150	100	75

Model 410

This model was first introduced in 1996. It features an alloy frame with carbon steel slide. It is chambered for the .40 S&W cartridge. Barrel length is 4". The magazine capacity is 10 rounds and the overall length is 7.5". Weight is approximately 29 oz.

NIB	Exc.	V.G.	Good	Fair	Poor
450	400	—	—	—	—

Model 457

Introduced in 1996 this .45 ACP model features a 3.75" barrel with rounded trigger guard and double action. It is fitted with a single side decocker. Magazine capacity is 7 rounds. Overall length is 7.25" and weight is about 29 oz. The frame is alloy and the slide a carbon steel. Finish is matte black.

NIB	Exc.	V.G.	Good	Fair	Poor
450	400	—	—	—	—

Model 908

Introduced in 1996 this is an economy compact pistol. It is chambered for the 9mm cartridge and is fitted with a 3.5" barrel. The action is traditional double action. Fixed rear sight. Magazine capacity is 8 rounds. Overall length is 6-7/8" and weight is about 26 oz.

NIB	Exc.	V.G.	Good	Fair	Poor
400	350	—	—	—	—

Model 909

Introduced in 1995 this pistol is chambered for the 9mm cartridge. It has a blue carbon steel slide, aluminum alloy frame, and is double action. It has a single column magazine and curved backstrap.

NIB	Exc.	V.G.	Good	Fair	Poor
400	350	300	200	150	100

Model 910

Also introduced in 1995. Same as above model but with double column magazine and straight backstrap.

NIB	Exc.	V.G.	Good	Fair	Poor
400	350	300	200	150	100

NOTE: All detachable magazines manufactured after 9/13/94 will be limited to 10 rounds of ammunition per Federal law regardless of caliber and original capacity of the pistol.

SMITH & WESSON COMMEMORATIVES

Smith & Wesson has over the years built many special edition handguns. These guns have been to commemorate some important national or regional event or group. The company has also built a large number of special edition handguns for certain distributors such as Lew Horton which is listed below. There are well over 200 special production guns not reflected in this pricing guide. Not even Smith & Wesson has all of the information on these guns and with many the number is so small that a market price would not be possible to establish. Listed below are a number of Smith & Wesson Commemoratives that we do have information on. Due to the difficulty in determining value only the orginal retail price is listed. Remember to receive full value for these guns they must be NIB, unfired with unturned cylinders.

Model 14 Texas Ranger Comm.

Introduced in 1973. Supplied with 4" barrel and cased. Edition limited to 10,000. 8,000 of these had knives. Serial numbers TR 1 to TR 10000.

Original Retail Price: $250.00

Model 25-3 S&W 125th Anniversary Comm.
Introduced in 1977. Limited edition of 10,000. Serial numbers SW0000 to SW10000. Deluxe models marked 25-4.

Original Retail Price: $350.00

Model 26-4 Georgia State Police Comm.
Introduced in 1988/1989 and supplied with a 5" barrel. Total production of 802 guns. Known Serial numbers BBY00354 to BBY0434.

Original Retail Price: $405.00

Model 27 .357 50th Anniversary Comm.
Introduced in 1985 and supplied with a 5" barrel and cased. Limited edition to 2,500 guns. Serial numbers REG0001 to REG2500.

Original Retail Price: N/A

Model 29-3 Elmer Keith Comm.
Introduced in 1986 and supplied with a 4" barrel. Gun etched in gold. Limited edition of 2,500 guns. Serial numbers EMK0000 to EMK0100 for Deluxe models and EMK 010 to EMK2500 for standard model.

Original Retail Price: $850.00

Model 544 Texas Wagon Train 150 Anniversary Comm.
Introduced in 1986 and limited to 7801 guns. Serial numbers TWT0000 to TWT7800.

Original Issue Price: N/A

Model 586 Mass. State Police Comm.
Introduced in 1986 and fitted with a 6" barrel. Limited to 631 guns. Serial numbers with ABT-AUC prefix.

Original Issue Price: N/A

Model 629-1 Alaska 1988 Iditarod Comm.
Introduced in 1987 and limited to 545 guns. Serial numbers from AKI0001 to AKI0545.

Original Retail Price: N/A

Model 745 IPSC Comm.
Introduced in 1986 and limited to 5362 guns. Serial numbers DVC0000 to DVC5362.

Original Retail Price: N/A

Model 4516-1 U.S. Marshall Comm.
Introduced in 1990 and limited to 500 guns. Serial numbers USM0000 to USM0499.

Original Retail Price: $599.95

SMITH & WESSON PERFORMANCE CENTER HANDGUNS

The role of Smith & Wesson's Performance Center has changed since it was established in 1990. What was once a specialized tune-up and competition one-off production department has now become a separate facility in providing specialized and limited handguns to the public often with distributors participation. This change came about around 1991, when the Performance Center initiated its own limited edition designs. These editions are generally limited to between 300 and 600 pistols for each model. The Performance Center, in fact, has its own distinct product line. Performance Center pistols are made in its own shop using its own designers. One of these distributors that has played a major role in offering these special guns to the public is the Lew Horton Distribution Company. The Center still continues to offer action jobs and accurate work but no longer executes one-of-a-kind customizing. The Performance Center has built about eight to twelve different models in the last two years. Plans call for more of these unique handguns to be built in the future. Pistols that are available from a certain distributor or the Performance Center will be noted in the description of each pistol.

Limited Edition Pistols and Revolvers of 1990

One of the first limited special series of Performance Center handguns was this offering, which consisted of custom engraved S&W handguns limited to 15 units on any current (1990) production pistol or revolver. This Limited Edition featured: 24 karat gold and sterling inlays, special bright mirror finish, decorated in light scroll pattern, specially assigned serial number beginning with the prefix "PEC", tuned action, solid walnut presentation case inlaid with blue or burgundy leather insert, embossed with gold with performance center logo. Interior of case is custom fitted with a matching colored velvet. Each handgun is hand numbered and has a signed certificate of authenticity. Because of the unique nature of the Limited Edition offering it is strongly recommended to secure a professional appraisal.

.40 S&W Tactical

A limited edition semiautomatic handgun offered exclusively by Lew Horton through the Performance Center. This special pistol is fitted with a 5" match-grade barrel, hand fit spherical barrel bushing, custom tuned action, special trigger job, oversized frame and slide rails, wrap-around straight backstrap grip. Replaceable front and Novak rear sights. Special serial numbers. Offered in 1992 and limited to 200 units.

Suggested Retail Introductory Price: $1500

.40 S&W Compensated

Similar to the .40 S&W Tactical but furnished with a 4.625" barrel and single chamber compensator. This is also a Lew Horton/Performance pistol. A production of 250 units. Offered in 1992.

Suggested Retail Introductory Price: $1700

.40 S&W Performance Action Pistol

Offered in limited quantities in 1990, this Performance Center .40 S&W semiaction pistol was used by the Smith & Wesson shooting team. The frame and barrel are stainless steel with blued carbon steel slide, two port compensator, two fitted and numbered 13-round magazines, 5.25" match grade barrel extended frame beavertail, square combat triggerguard, oversize magazine release button, spherical barrel bushing, wraparound straight backstrap grip, extended magazine funnel, and Bo-Mar adjustable rear sight. The action is tuned for accuracy and precision.

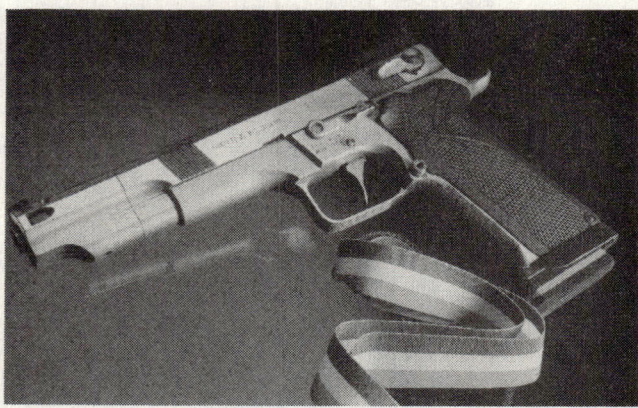

Suggested Retail Introductory Price: N/A

Model 681 Quadport

A Lew Horton revolver limited to 300 guns with special serial numbers. This 7-shot revolver has a 3" barrel underlug quadport barrel. The action is tuned cylinders are chambered and the trigger has an overtravel stop. Sights are fixed combat type.

Suggested Retail Introductory Price: $675

Model 686 Competitor

Introduced by Lew Horton and the Performance Center for 1993 this limited edition revolver features a match grade barrel and unique under-barrel weight system. The action has been custom tuned and the receiver is drilled and tapped for scope mounts. Charge holes are chambered, ejector rod housing is enclosed, and the grip is an extended competition type. Special serial numbers.

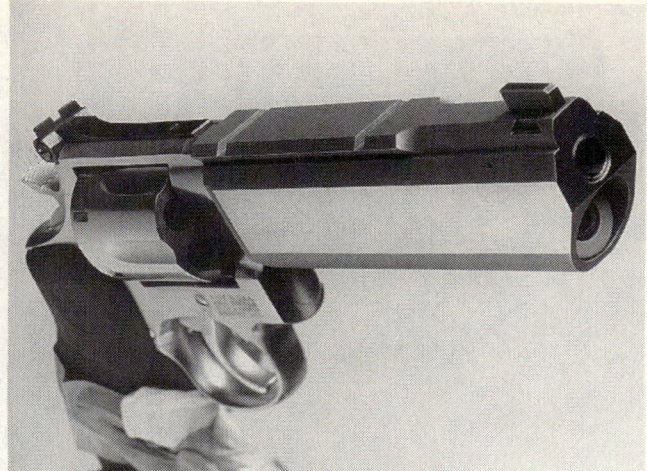

Suggested Retail Introductory Price: $1100

Model 686 Hunter

Similar to the Model 686 Competitor. This is also a limited edition Lew Horton revolver chambered for the .357 Magnum and features the under-barrel weight system, internal scope mount, and custom tuned action. Special serial numbers.

Suggest Retail Introductory Price: $1154

Model 686 Carry Comp 4"

Offered in limited quantities by Lew Horton and the Performance Center in 1992 this new design features the unique single chamber integral barrel compensator. Front is windage adjustable and the action is custom tuned. Chambered for the .357 Magnum cartridge. Special serial numbers.

Suggested Retail Introductory price: $1000

Model 686 Carry Comp 3"

The 1993 Lew Horton limited edition version of the Model 686 Carry Comp 4" model with a 3" barrel. The same features apply to both models.

Suggested Retail Introductory Price: $1000

Model 629 Hunter

Introduced in 1992 by Lew Horton and the Performance Center this limited edition revolver features a new design that utilizes a 6" under-barrel weight system, special integral barrel compensator. The action has been custom tuned and the receiver has an integral scope mount. Chambered for the .44 Magnum. Special finger groove grips are standard. Special serial numbers.

Suggested Retail Introductory Price: $1234

Model 629 Hunter II

Another Lew Horton/Performance Center limited edition revolver that features 2x Nikon scope with steel see-through rings. The barrel is Mag-na-ported and incorporates the Performance Center's under-barrel weight arrangement. The action is custom tuned and the revolver is supplied with a ballistic nylon range carry bag. Special serial numbers.

Suggested Retail Introductory Price: $1234

Model 629 Carry Comp

Introduced in 1992 by Lew Horton and the Performance Center this limited edition revolver is chambered for the .44 Magnum cartridge. It features an integral ported 3" barrel, fluted cylinder, radiused charge holes, dovetail front and fixed groove rear sight. Fitted with a rubber combat grip. The action is custom by the Performance Center. Special serial numbers.

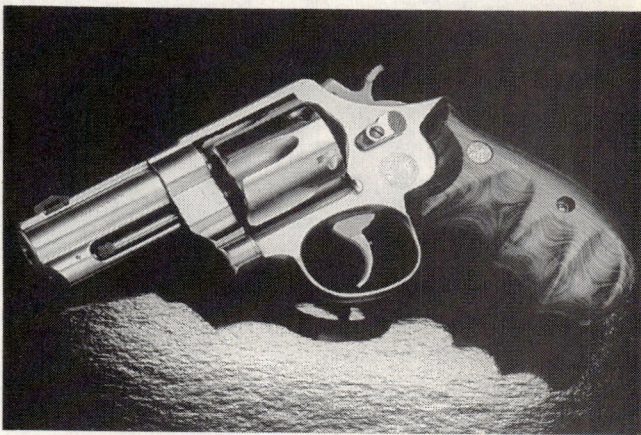

Suggested Retail Introductory Price: $1000

Model 629 Carry Comp II

A limited edition 1993 offering by Lew Horton and the Performance Center similar to the 1992 Model 629 Carry Comp with the exception that this 1993 model has a special unfluted cylider and fully adjustable rear sight. Special serial numbers.

Suggested Retail Introductory Price: $1000

Model 640 Carry Comp

Introduced in 1991 by Lew Horton and the Performance Center this revolver is chambered for the .38 S&W Special, but with a strengthened action to handle + P + loads. Fitted with a heavy 2.625" barrel with unique integral barrel compensator. The front sight is replaceable and adjustable for windage. The rear sight is a fixed groove. Custom trigger job and custom tuned action are also part of the package. Special serial numbers.

Suggested Retail Introductory Price: $750

Model 640 .357 Quad-Port

Introduced in 1996. Similar to the model above but chambered for the .357 magnum cartridge and quadported. Limited to 190 revolvers. Special serial numbers.

Suggested Retail Introductory Price: $675

Model 625 Light Hunter

This is a large frame revolver chambered for the .45 Colt. It is fitted with a 6" Mag-na-ported barrel with integral Weaver style base. It has a stainless steel finish and black Hogue rubber grips. Drift adjustable Millet front and fully adjustable rear sight. Offered in limited quantities. Introduced in 1997.

Siggested Retail Introductory Price:

Model 627-8 Shot

Chambered for the .357 Magnum cartridge this revolver has an 8-round capacity. Drilled and tapped with adjustable sights on a 5" tapered and contoured barrel. Tuned action. Hogue wood grips. Satin stainless steel finish. Weight is approximately 44 oz. A Lew Horton exclusive. Introduced in 1997.

Suggested Retail Introductory Price:

"Shorty-Forty" .40 S&W

Introduced in 1992 and available exclusively from Lew Horton, this limited edition Performance Center pistol features a light alloy frame, oversize slide rails, and spherical barrel bushing. A match grade barrel is joined to a custom tuned action. Special serial numbers.

Suggested Retail Introductory Price: $950

"Shorty Forty" Mark III

Offered in 1995 this Lew Horton exclusive features low-mount adjustable sights, hand-fitted titanium barrel bushing, checkered front strap. The action as been hand honed and the pistol is sold with two magazines; one 11 rounds and the other 9 rounds.

Suggested Retail Price: $1000

Shorty .45

Introduced by Lew Horton in 1996 this .45ACP pistol has a hand-fitted titanium barrel bushing, oversize frame and slide rails, match grade barrel, checkered front strap, hand honed double action, and special serial numbers.

Suggested Retail Price: $1095

Shorty Nine

This Lew Horton exclusive is limited to 100 units. It features a hand-fitted titanium barrel bushing, oversize slide rails, action job, low mount adjustable sights, checkered front strap, match grade barrel, and two tone finish. Furnished with two 12-round magazines.

Suggested Retail Price: $1000

Performance Center .45 Limited

This Lew Horton model is a full size single action pistol. Hand-fitted titanium barrel bushing, fitted slide lock, match grade barrel, adjustable sights, oversize magazine well, tuned action, and checkered front strap.

Suggested Retail Price: $1400

Shorty .356 TSW

This new cartridge is also available in another Lew Horton/Performance Center limited edition pistol with a 4" barrel. It features a steel frame and hand-fitted slide, with spherical barrel bushing. The double action is custom tuned by the Performance Center. Magazine holds 12 rounds. Similar in appearance to the "Shorty-Forty". Offered in 1993. Special serial numbers.

Suggested Retail Introductory Price: $1000

Model .356 TSW "Limited" Series

This is a Lew Horton gun. This model is chambered for the new .356 TSW caliber (TSW stands for Team Smith & Wesson). This is a new caliber, actually a 9mm X 21.5mm cartridge, with ballistics of around 1,235 fps. with a 147 grain bullet. Designed as a low end .357 competition pistol. Built for the competitive shooter (IPSC) it features a 15-round magazine and distinctive profile and markings. The single action trigger is adjustable for reach while the slide, frame, and barrel are custom fitted. The gun comes with a spherical barrel bushing and adjustable Bo-Mar sights. The frame grip is checked 20 line to the inch, the magazine well is extended as is the magazine release. The magazine is fitted with a pad.

Suggested Retail Introductory Price: $1350

Model 66 .357 Magnum F-Comp

A Performance Center revolver designed as a carry gun. Furnished with a 3" ported barrel and full underlug. The thumbpiece has been cut down to accommodate all speed loaders, the charge holes are countersunk, and the pistol comes standard with a stainless steel finish. The K-frame action has been custom tuned and the rear sight is a fully adjustable black blade while the front sight features a tritium dot night sight. Furnished with a round butt combat style rubber grip. This revolver has a stainless steel finish. This is a Lew Horton special limited edition, 300 units, revolver.

Suggested Retail Introductory Price: $800

Model 19 .357 Magnum K-Comp

This is the same gun as the F-Comp but furnished with a black matte finish and is sold through stocking dealers on a unlimited basis.

Suggested Retail Introductory Price: $800

Model 657 Classic

Offered in limited quantities of 350 units this Lew Horton/Performance Center revolver features an unfluted cylinder and 6.5" barrel on a drilled and tapped N-frame. Chambered for the .41 Magnum cartridge this handgun is fitted with adjustable rear sight. Special serial numbers.

Suggested Retail Introductory Price: $550

Model 657 Hunter

Introduced in 1995 this is an RSR Wholesale Guns exclusive. Fitted with an intergral waever base, Mag-Na-Ported 6" barrel with Millet red ramp front sight and adjustable rear sight this model has a stainless steel finish special serial numbers, chamfered charge holes, and adjustable trigger stop. Limited to 500 guns.

Suggested Retail Introductory Price: $600

Model 60 Carry Comp

Introduced in the summer of 1993 this J-frame revolver is fitted with a 3" full underlug barrel with integral compensator. The charge holes are radiused for quick loading and the action is tuned by the Performance Center. The pistol is rated for + P ammunition. The grips are fancy wood contoured for speed loaders. This Lew Horton revolver is limited to 300 guns and has special serial numbers.

Suggested Retail Introductory Price: $795

Paxton Quigley Model 640

This is a Performance Center offering restricted to 300 revolvers. Built around the Model 640 this limited edition handgun has a 2" compensated barrel, windage adjustable front sight, specially tuned action, and a tapestry soft gun case. Each gun has a distinct serial number range.

Suggested Retail Price: $720

Model 640 Centennial Powerport

Introduced in 1996 this model is a Lew Horton exclusive. It is fitted with a 2-1/8" barrel with integral compensator. The front sight is a black blade with Tritium insert and the rear is is a fixed notch. The cylinder holds five .357 or .38 rounds. Stainless steel with Pachmayr decelerator compact grips. Overall length is 6.75" and weight is about 25 oz. Limited to 300 units.

Suggested Retail Price: $675

Model 940 Centennial .356

Offered exclusively from Lew Horton this J-frame revolver is chambered for the new .356 cartridge and has a 2" compensated barrel. It will also fire the 9mm cartridge. This gun features a tuned action, radius hammer and trigger and special serial numbers.

Suggested Retail Price: $760

Model 13 .357

This is a Lew Horton exclusive that features a 3" barrel with 4 Magnaports, a bobbed hammer for double action only, chambered charge holes, beveled cylinder, contoured grip and thumb latch for spped loader clearance, overtravel trigger stop, and FBI grips. Limited to 300 guns.

Suggested Retail Price: $730

Model 845 Single Action

Offered by Lew Horton this pistol is chambered for the .45 ACP and is designed for the competative shooter. Adjustable reach trigger precision fitted slide, frame and barrel are some of the special features. The barrel bushing is spherical and the front sight is dovetailed. The magazine well is extended as is the magazine release and safety. Both front and rear sight are adjustable.

Suggested Retail Price: $1470

SMITH & WESSON LONG ARMS

.320 Revolving Rifle Model

This model is rare and unique—a prize to a S&W collector. The Revolving Rifle is chambered for the .320 S&W Revolving Rifle cartridge, has a 6-shot fluted cylinder and is offered with a 16", 18", and 20" barrel. Only 76 of the rifles are nickel-plated, and the remainder of the production is blued. The butt is rounded, with red hard rubber checkered grips and a forearm of the same material. There is a detachable shoulder stock with a black hard rubber buttplate featuring the S&W logo. The rifle was furnished in a leather carrying case with accessories. As fine a firearm as this was, it was a commercial failure for S&W; and they finally came to the realization that the public did not want a revolving rifle. They manufactured only 977 of them between 1879 and 1887.

NOTE: Values Are for Complete Unit. Deduct 40% Without Stock. Add 10% for 16" or 20" barrels.

Courtesy Buffalo Bill Historical Center, Cody, Wyoming

Courtesy Buffalo Bill Historical Center, Cody, Wyoming

Exc.	V.G.	Good	Fair	Poor
8000	5500	3500	2000	1500

Model A Rifle

A bolt-action with 23.75" barrel, chambered for .22-250, .243, .270, .308, .30-06, 7mm Magnum, and .300 Winchester Magnum. It has a folding rear sight and a checkered Monte Carlo stock with contrasting rosewood forend tip and pistol grip cap. It was manufactured for S&W by Husqvarna of Sweden.

NIB	Exc.	V.G.	Good	Fair	Poor
400	325	275	200	150	100

Model B

As above, with a Schnabel forend and 20.75" barrel.

NIB	Exc.	V.G.	Good	Fair	Poor
400	325	275	200	150	100

Model C

As above, with a cheekpiece.

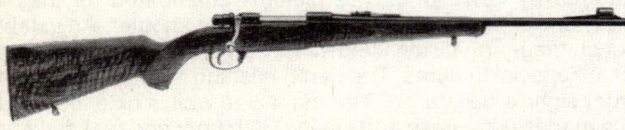

NIB	Exc.	V.G.	Good	Fair	Poor
425	350	300	225	175	125

Model D

As above, with a Mannlicher-style stock.

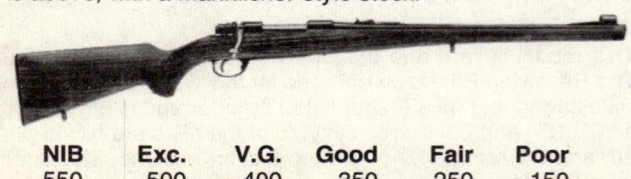

NIB	Exc.	V.G.	Good	Fair	Poor
550	500	400	350	250	150

Model E

As above, without a cheekpiece.

NIB	Exc.	V.G.	Good	Fair	Poor
500	450	400	350	250	150

Model 1500

A bolt action rifle with a 5-round magazine chambered for .222, .223, .243, .25-06, .270, .30-06, .308, .22-250. Fitted with a 22" barrel. Walnut stock. Produced from 1981 to 1985.

NIB	Exc.	V.G.	Good	Fair	Poor
375	325	250	200	175	125

Model 1500 Deluxe

Made for S&W by Howa Machine in Japan. It is chambered for .222 through .300 Winchester Magnum. It has a 22" barrel and a walnut Monte Carlo stock with skipline checkering.

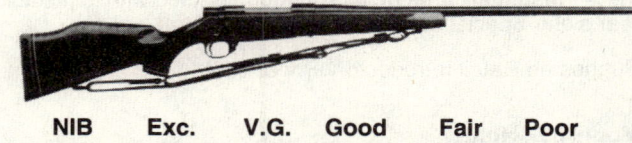

NIB	Exc.	V.G.	Good	Fair	Poor
350	300	250	200	150	100

Model 1500 Mountaineer

As above, but lighter in weight.

NIB	Exc.	V.G.	Good	Fair	Poor
400	325	275	225	175	125

NOTE: For models with factory installed recoil pads add $25.

Model 1600 Deluxe

This model is fitted with a Monte Carlo stock and cheekpiece with skip line checkering. Barrel length is 22". Caliber choices are same as those of Model 1500.

NIB	Exc.	V.G.	Good	Fair	Poor
400	350	300	250	200	150

Model 1600 Deluxe Varmint

As above with a 24" heavy barrel. Chambered for a variety of small bore calibers.

NIB	Exc.	V.G.	Good	Fair	Poor
400	350	300	250	200	150

Model 1700 Classic Hunter

This is a bolt-action rifle with 22" barrel, no sights, and a removable 5-round magazine. It has a nicely checkered walnut stock with Schnabel forend. It was imported from Howa of Japan.

NIB	Exc.	V.G.	Good	Fair	Poor
500	400	300	250	200	150

NOTE: S&W discontinued the importation of the Howa line in 1984.

Model 916 Slide Action Shotgun

This is offered in 12, 16, and 20 gauge and has barrel lengths of 20"-30" with various chokes. It has a plain stock and barrel. It was imported from Howa of Japan.

NIB	Exc.	V.G.	Good	Fair	Poor
250	175	150	125	100	75

Model 916T

As above, with interchangeable barrel capability.

NIB	Exc.	V.G.	Good	Fair	Poor
275	200	150	125	100	75

Model 3000 Slide Action

This is offered in 12 and 20 gauge. It has 3" chambers and 22"-30" barrel lengths and features a checkered walnut stock and forend.

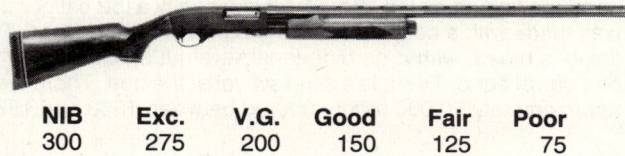

NIB	Exc.	V.G.	Good	Fair	Poor
300	275	200	150	125	75

Model 3000 Police

As above with 18" or 20" barrels, a matte blue or parkerized finish, and a combat-style finish on the stock.

NIB	Exc.	V.G.	Good	Fair	Poor
325	300	250	200	150	75

Model 1000 Autoloader

Made by Howa Machine, this gas-operated shotgun has an alloy receiver with engraving. It was offered in 12 or 20 gauge with barrel lengths from 22"-30" and various chokes. The walnut stock is checkered, and the barrel features a vent rib.

NIB	Exc.	V.G.	Good	Fair	Poor
375	325	275	225	150	100

Model 1000 Super 12

As above, with the capability of operating with different pressure cartridges.

NIB	Exc.	V.G.	Good	Fair	Poor
500	400	300	250	175	150

Courtesy Butterfield & Butterfield, San Francisco, California

This rare Smith & Wesson revolving rifle with shoulder stock is chambered for .32 caliber. It is fitted with a 16-inch barrel and has hard red rubber grips and forearm. The stock is walnut and features a factory tang sight. Serial number 902

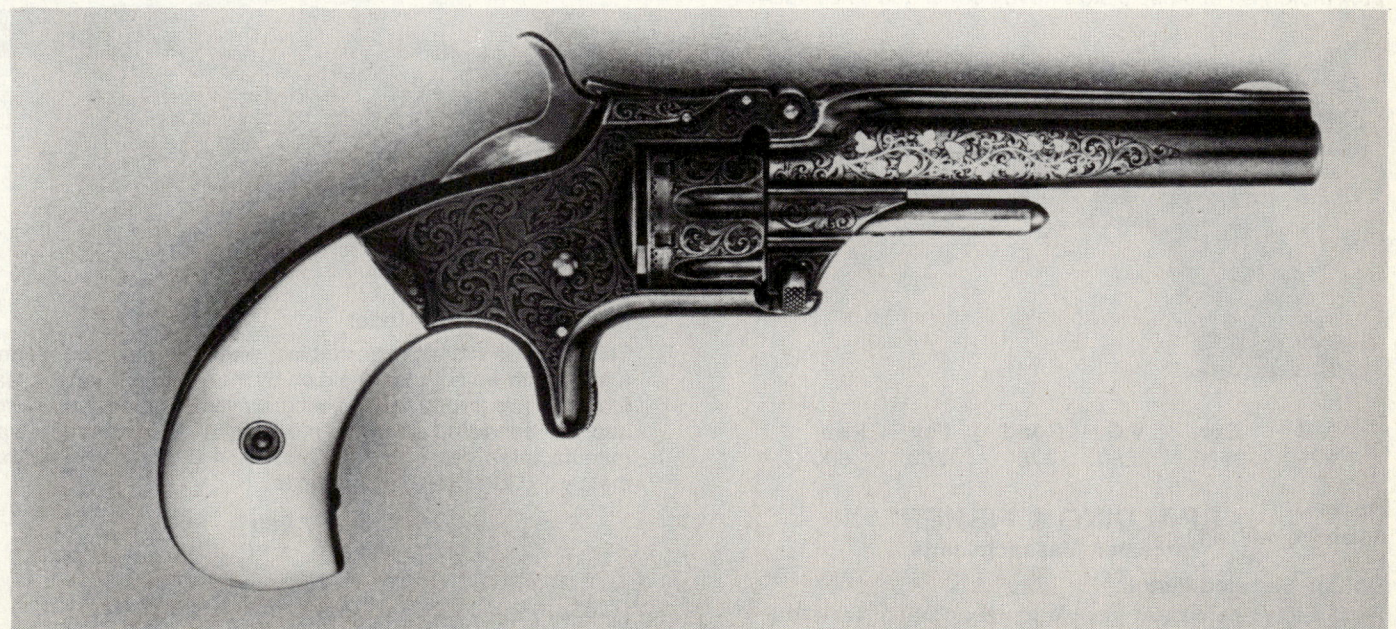

Courtesy Butterfield & Butterfield, San Francisco, California

This First Model Third Issue Smith & Wesson revolver is chambered for .22 caliber and is engraved with gold inlays by Gustave Young with mother-of-pearl grips. Its condition is excellent. Serial number 1851

SNAKE CHARMER
Little Field, Texas
Sporting Arms Manufacturing, Inc.

Snake Charmer

A .410 bore single shot shotgun with an 18.5" barrel. Stainless steel with a composition stock.

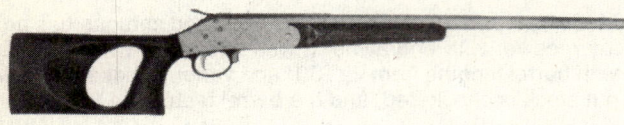

NIB	Exc.	V.G.	Good	Fair	Poor
150	125	100	75	50	25

SNEIDER, CHARLES E.
Baltimore, Maryland

2-Cylinder Revolver

A .22 caliber spur trigger revolver with a 2.75" octagonal barrel and twin 7-shot cylinders that can be pivoted. The barrel marked "E. Sneider Pat. March 1862". Produced in limited quantities during the 1860s. Prospective purchasers are advised to secure a qualified appraisal prior to acquisition.

Exc.	V.G.	Good	Fair	Poor
—	—	10000	5000	1250

SODIA, FRANZ
Ferlach, Austria

A wide variety of double-barrel shotguns, drillings, and combination shotgun/rifles are made by this maker. As these arms are essentially custom order pieces, it is advised that perspective purchasers secure individual appraisals.

SOKOLOVSKY CORP. SPORT ARMS
Sunnyvale, California

.45 Automaster

A .45 caliber stainless steel semiautomatic pistol with a 6" barrel fitted with Millet adjustable sights and 6-shot magazine. Approximately 50 of these pistols have been made since 1984.

NIB	Exc.	V.G.	Good	Fair	Poor
3250	2750	2250	1750	1250	800

SPALDING & FISHER
Worcester, Massachusetts

Double Barreled Pistol

A .36 caliber percussion double-barrel pocket pistol with 5.5" barrels, blued iron frame and walnut grips. The top of the barrels marked "Spalding & Fisher". Produced during the 1850s.

Exc.	V.G.	Good	Fair	Poor
—	—	500	250	100

SPANG & WALLACE
Philadelphia, Pennsylvania

Pocket Pistol

A .36 caliber percussion pocket pistol with a 2.5" to 6" barrel, German silver furniture and checkered walnut stock. The barrel marked "Spang & Wallace/Phila." Manufactured during late 1840s and early 1850s.

Exc.	V.G.	Good	Fair	Poor
—	—	1500	650	200

SPENCER
Boston, Massachusetts

Spencer Carbine

This was one of the most popular firearms used by Union forces during the Civil War. It is chambered for a metallic rimfire cartridge known as the "No. 56." It is actually a .52 caliber and was made with a copper case. The barrel is 22" in length. The finish is blued, with a carbine-length walnut stock held on by one barrel band. There is a sling swivel at the butt. There were approximately 50,000 manufactured between 1863 and 1865.

Courtesy Butterfield & Butterfield, San Francisco, California

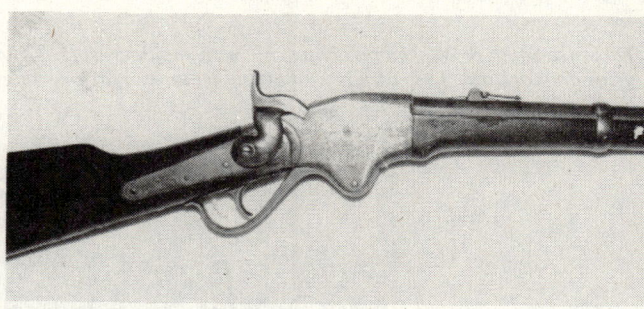

Exc.	V.G.	Good	Fair	Poor
—	—	2500	900	400

Military Rifle-Navy Model

This model is similar to the carbine, with a 30" round barrel and a full-length walnut stock held on by three barrel bands. It features an iron forend tip and sling swivels. The Civil War production consisted of two models. A Navy model was manufactured between 1862 and 1864 (there were approximately 1,000 of these so marked).

Exc.	V.G.	Good	Fair	Poor
—	—	3500	1500	600

Military Rifle-Army Model

There were approximately 11,450 produced for the Army during the Civil War. They are similar to the Navy model except that the front sight doubles as a bayonet lug. They were manufactured in 1863 and 1864.

Courtesy Milwaukee Public Museum, Milwaukee, Wisconsin

Exc.	V.G.	Good	Fair	Poor
—	—	2500	1250	600

Springfield Armory Postwar Alteration

After the conclusion of the Civil War, approximately 11,000 carbines were refurbished and rechambered for .50 caliber rimfire. The barrels were sleeved, and a device known as the "Stabler cut-off" was added to convert the arm to single shot function. Often they were refinished and restocked. The inspector's marks "ESA" will be found in an oval cartouche on the left side of the stock. These alterations took place in 1867 and 1868.

Exc.	V.G.	Good	Fair	Poor
—	—	2500	1000	400

Model 1865 Contract

This model was manufactured by the Burnside Rifle Company in 1865. They are similar to the Civil War-type carbine and are marked "By Burnside Rifle Co./Model 1865". There were approximately 34,000 manufactured. Old records show that 30,500 were purchased by the United States government, and 19,000 of these had the Stabler cut-off device.

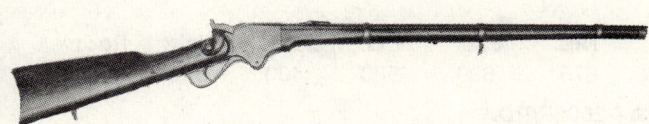

Courtesy Wallis & Wallis, Lewes, Sussex, England

Exc.	V.G.	Good	Fair	Poor
—	—	1750	850	400

NOTE: There were a number of other variations in the Spencer line. It would behoove anyone interested in collecting this fine Civil War firearm to educate oneself on these variances and to secure individual appraisal if transactions are contemplated. This is a complex model with many subtle variations.

SPENCER ARMS CO.
Windsor, Connecticut

From 1882 to 1889 they manufactured the first successful slide action repeating shotgun. Designed by Christopher M. Spencer who also designed the Civil War era Spencer military carbines. The shotgun came in both solid and takedown models in both 12 and 10 gauge. In 1890 Francis Bannerman & Sons of New York bought the patents and machinery and moved the operation to Brooklyn, New York. They produced what is known as the Spencer Bannerman models from 1890 to 1907. The takedown model is worth 20% premium and 10 gauge models are worth a 10% premium. The later Bannerman models are worth 20% less than the Spencer models.

Exc.	V.G.	Good	Fair	Poor
—	850	400	200	125

SPENCER REVOLVER
Maltby, Henley & Company
New York, New York

Safety Hammerless Revolver

A .32 caliber hammerless double action revolver with a 3" barrel. The frame and barrel made of brass, the cylinder of steel and the grips are of walnut. The barrel is marked "Spencer Safety Hammerless Pat. Jan. 24, 1888 & Oct. 29, 1889". Manufactured by the Norwich Pistol Company circa 1890.

Exc.	V.G.	Good	Fair	Poor
—	250	200	150	100

SPHINX
Sphinx Engineering SA
Porrentru, Switzerland
Imported by
Sile Distributors Inc.

This Swiss-based company was founded in 1876 and produced the first automatic turning machine. The company made small drills, tungsten carbide tools, and tool coatings. After WWII Sphinx developed more exotic machines and drills. In 1990 Sphinx Engineering SA was established for the development and production of pistols. In 1991 the AT .380 was introduced to the market. The following year the AT 2000 was placed on the market. Sphinx purchased the rights to its current line of pistols from ITM AG, a Swiss firm that experienced financial problems with the development of its pistol line, in 1989. The AT series is essentially a copy of the famous Czech CZ 75 semiautomatic pistol.

AT-380

This semiautomatic pistol is a small .380 caliber in double action only. The magazine capacity is 11 rounds. It is offered in stainless steel, blued, or two-tone finish. The barrel is 3.27" and overall length is 6.03". Sights are fixed and grips are black checkered plastic. Weight is 25 oz.

NIB	Exc.	V.G.	Good	Fair	Poor
675	600	500	400	300	200

AT-2000P/PDA

This is a slightly smaller of the AT-2000S. Magazine capacity is 13 rounds for 9mm and 11 rounds for .40 S&W. The features are the same except that the barrel length is 3.66", overall length 7.25", and weight is 31 oz.

NIB	Exc.	V.G.	Good	Fair	Poor
450	400	350	300	200	100

AT-2000

This is a series number applied to several different variations of the same basic design. Based on the CZ 75 pistol the AT-2000 is a semiautomatic pistol offered in 9mm and .40 S&W. Barrel lengths are different depending on variation, but the AT-2000 can be converted from double action to double only in just a matter of minutes.

AT-2000S/SDA

This model is chambered for the 9mm or .40 S&W cartridge. The barrel length is 4.53" and overall length is 8.12". Magazine capacity is 15 rounds for 9mm and 13 rounds for .40 S&W. Available in double action (S) or double action only (SDA). Offered with two-tone or all blued finish. Weighs 35 oz.

NIB	Exc.	V.G.	Good	Fair	Poor
650	600	500	400	300	200

AT-2000PS

This version, sometimes referred to as the Police Special, features the shorter barrel of the AT-2000P model on the larger AT-2000S frame. Barrel length is 3.66" and magazine capacity is 15 rounds for 9mm and 13 rounds for the .40 S&W.

NIB	Exc.	V.G.	Good	Fair	Poor
650	600	500	400	300	200

AT-2000H/HDA

This is the smallest version of the AT-2000 series. Magazine capacity is 10 rounds for 9mm and 8 rounds for .40 S&W. The barrel length is 3.34" and overall length is 6.78". Weight is 26 oz.

NIB	Exc.	V.G.	Good	Fair	Poor
650	600	500	400	300	200

AT-2000C

This is the competitor model. It features a competition slide, dual port compensator, match barrel, and Sphinx scope mount. Offered in double action/single action. Available in 9mm, 9x21, and .40 S&W.

NIB	Exc.	V.G.	Good	Fair	Poor
1600	1200	800	600	400	200

AT-2000CS

Same as above model but fitted with Bo-Mar adjustable sights.

NIB	Exc.	V.G.	Good	Fair	Poor
1400	1000	600	400	300	200

AT-2000GM

The Grand Master model. Features are similar to the AT-2000C but offered in single action only.

NIB	Exc.	V.G.	Good	Fair	Poor
2100	1750	1250	600	300	200

AT-2000GMS
Same as above but fitted with Bo-Mar adjustable sights.

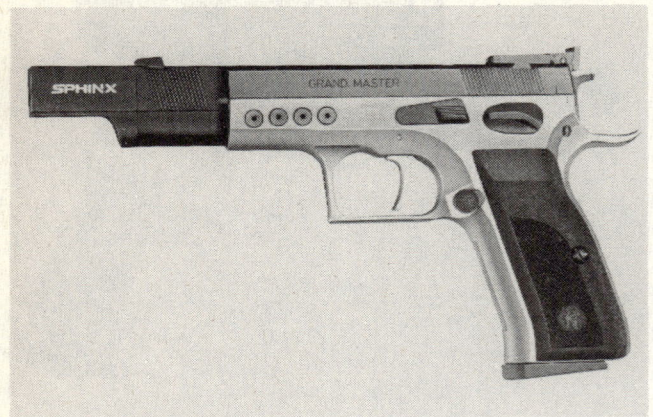

NIB	Exc.	V.G.	Good	Fair	Poor
2000	1650	1200	600	300	200

SPIES, A. W.
New York, New York

Pocket Pistol
A .41 caliber percussion pocket pistol with a 2.5" barrel, German silver furniture and a checkered walnut stock. Produced during the 1850s.

Exc.	V.G.	Good	Fair	Poor
—	—	1750	900	300

SPILLER & BURR
Atlanta, Georgia

Navy Revolver
A .36 caliber percussion revolver with a 6" or 6.5" octagonal barrel and 6-shot cylinder. The barrel and cylinder blued, the frame of brass with walnut grips. Some pistols are marked "Spiller & Burr" while others are simply marked "C.S." Approximately 1,450 were made between 1862 and 1865. Prospective purchasers are advised to secure a qualified appraisal prior to acquisition.

Courtesy Milwaukee Public Museum, Milwaukee, Wisconsin

Exc.	V.G.	Good	Fair	Poor
—	—	15000	7000	2000

SPIRLET, A.
Liege, Belgium

Spirlet was erroneously credited with inventing the top-hinged tip-up revolver. This weapon was around well before Spirlet's time. Actually, the patent that he held covers lockwork and an ejection system that was used on tip-up revolvers. Although he manufactured some of these tip-up revolvers himself, there were never enough of them to establish him as little more than a small custom gunmaker. Revolvers that he manufactured bear his name and address on the breech end of the barrel. Many other makers utilized his developments.

SPITFIRE
JSL (Hereford) Ltd.
Hereford, England
Importer - Specialty Shooters
Ft. Lauderdale, Florida

This semiautomatic pistol is a design based on the CZ 75. This is a hand-built pistol designed by John Slough and built from a solid block of steel. The stainless steel frame and slide are cut with spark erosion and diamond grinding. Barrels are built and bored in the same factory. This is primarily a competition pistol.

Spitfire Standard Model (G1)
Chambered for the 9x21, 9mm Parabellum, or .40 S&W cartridges this pistol uses the locked breech concept. The trigger system is single and double action and it is fitted with an ambidextrous safety. The barrel is 3.7" and the overall length is 7.1". Magazine capacity of the 9mm is 15 rounds. Sights are fixed. Empty weight is 35 oz. Finish is stainless steel. Comes supplied with presentation box, 2 magazines, and allen key.

NIB	Exc.	V.G.	Good	Fair	Poor
1300	900	700	500	300	200

Spitfire Sterling Model (G2)
This model is chambered for the 9x21, 9mm Parabellum, or .40 S&W cartridges. Its features are the same as the Standard Model with the exception that it has adjustable sights.

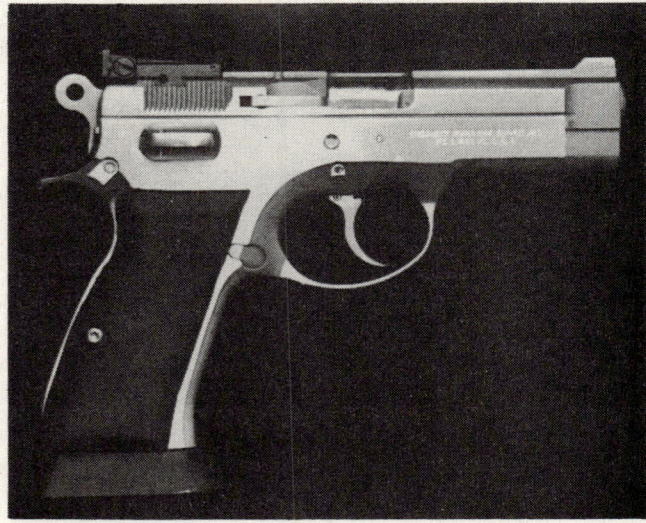

NIB	Exc.	V.G.	Good	Fair	Poor
1400	1000	800	600	300	200

Spitfire Super Sterling (G7)
Also chambered for the 9x21, 9mm Parabellum, and .40 S&W this model features a single port compensator, 4.3" barrel, and overall length of 8.25". Weight is approximately 36 oz.

NIB	Exc.	V.G.	Good	Fair	Poor
1600	1200	900	700	350	200

Spitfire Competition Model (G3)
Chambered for 9x21, 9mm Parabellum, or .40 S&W cartridge this model features a tapered slide rib, adjustable rear sight, dual pod compensator, match hammer, adjustable trigger stop with presentation box. Barrel is 5.27" with compensator and weight is 40 oz.

grips, take-down barrel design with removable weight. Limited importation.

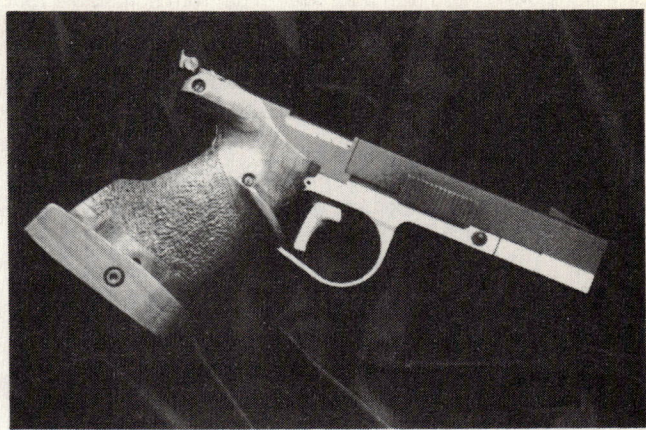

NIB	Exc.	V.G.	Good	Fair	Poor
1850	1400	1000	800	400	200

SPRINGFIELD ARMORY (MODERN)
SEE Springfield Inc.

SPRINGFIELD INC.
Colona, Illinois

RIFLES

MI Garand Rifle
A .270 (discontinued), .308 or .30-06 caliber semiautomatic rifle with a 24" barrel and 8-shot magazine. Patterned directly after the U.S. M1 Rifle.

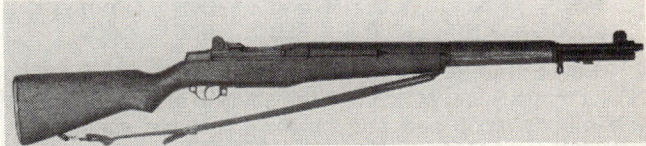

Courtesy Milwaukee Public Museum, Milwaukee, Wisconsin

Exc.	V.G.	Good	Fair	Poor
775	650	550	400	300

NOTE: As of January 1993 Springfield Inc. purchased the inventory, name, patents, trademarks, and logo of the Springfield Armory Inc. and intends to carry on the tradition of quality products and service in the future. Products, services, and distribution patterns remain unchanged. The Springfield Custom Shop, producing "Raceguns", will continue as before.

M1A Basic Rifle
Chambered for .308 Win. and fitted with a painted black fiberglass stock. Barrel length is 22" without flash suppressor. Front sights are military square post and rear military aperture (battle sights). Magazine capacity is 5, 10, or 20 box. Rifle weighs 9 lbs.

NIB	Exc.	V.G.	Good	Fair	Poor
1250	1000	850	650	400	250

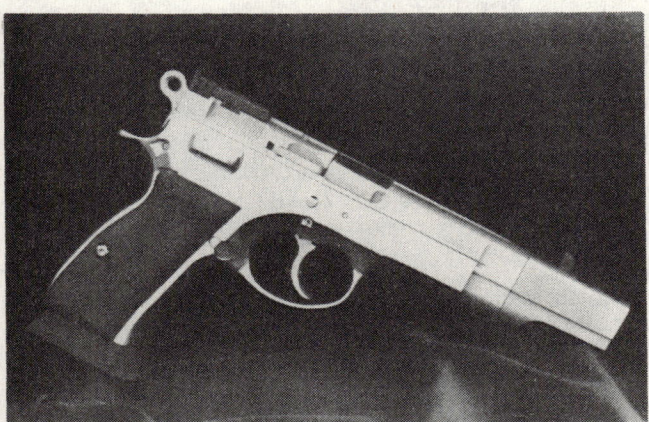

NIB	Exc.	V.G.	Good	Fair	Poor
1800	1400	1000	800	400	200

Spitfire Master Model
This is similar to the Standard Model but without sights. It is fitted with a stainless steel bridge mount to take an Aimpoint sight. Also has a dual port compensator. Supplied with presentation box and 2 magazines.

NIB	Exc.	V.G.	Good	Fair	Poor
2100	1750	1250	800	400	200

Spitfire Squadron Model
This model has a Standard Model frame, adjustable rear sight slide, adjustable rear sight slide with compensator, Master Model slide and barrel with stainless steel bridge mount and Aimpoint sight, 4 magazines, screwdriver, allen key, oil bottle, spare springs, cleaning kit, and fitted leather case.

NIB	Exc.	V.G.	Good	Fair	Poor
6000	4800	2100	900	450	200

Spitfire Battle of Britain Commemorative
This is a limited edition of 1,056 Spitfires in 9mm Parabellum. Each one represents one of the Spitfire aircraft. The stainless steel slide has the inscription "Battle of Britain-50th Anniversary", the grips are checkered walnut, log book of history of that particular aircraft, and a wooden presentation box with engraved plaque.

Retail Price: $1900.

Westlake Britarms
This is a .22 Long Rifle Match pistol. Barrel length is 5.77", sight base is 8.42", magazine capacity is 5 rounds. Weight is approximately 47 oz. Trigger is adjustable for length, front and rear trigger stops, adjustable palm rest on contoured wood

M1A Standard Rifle

This model is chambered for the .308 Win., .243, or 7mmx08 cartridges. Also fitted with a 22" barrel but with adjustable rear sight. Fitted with a walnut stock with fiberglass hand guard, it comes equipped with a 20-round box magazine. Weighs 9 lbs.

NIB	Exc.	V.G.	Good	Fair	Poor
1375	1100	850	650	400	250

M1A-A1 Bush Rifle

Chambered for .308, .243, or 7mmx08 cartridge with choice of walnut stock, black fiberglass, or folding stock(no longer produced). Fitted with 18.25" barrel. Rifle weighs 8.75 lbs.

NIB	Exc.	V.G.	Good	Fair	Poor
1400	1100	850	650	400	250

NOTE: Add $250 for folding stock.

M1A National Match

Chambered for .308 as standard with choice of .243 or 7mmx08 cartridge. Fitted with a medium weight National Match 22" glass bedded barrel and walnut stock. Special rear sight adjustable to half minute of angle clicks. Weighs 10.06 lbs.

NIB	Exc.	V.G.	Good	Fair	Poor
1700	1400	1000	700	500	250

M1A Super Match

This is Springfield's best match grade rifle. Chambered for .308 as standard and also .243 or 7mmx08 cartridge. Fitted with special oversize heavy walnut stock, heavy Douglas match glass bedded barrel, and special rear lugged receiver. Special rear adjustable sight. Weighs 10.125 lbs.

NIB	Exc.	V.G.	Good	Fair	Poor
2000	1700	1250	850	600	300

M21 Law Enforcement/Tactical Rifle

Similar to the Super Match with the addition of a special stock with rubber recoil pad and height adjustable cheekpiece. Available as a special order only. Weighs 11.875 lbs.

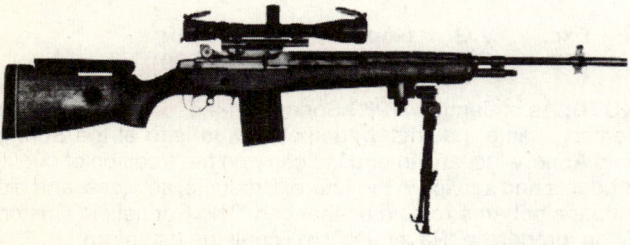

NIB	Exc.	V.G.	Good	Fair	Poor
2200	1750	1350	900	650	350

SAR-4800

This is a semi-automatic gas operated rifle, similar in appearance to the FN-FAL/LAR rifle, chambered for the .308 Win. cartridge. It is fitted with a 21" barrel and has a fully adjustable rear sight. Weight is approximately 9.5 lbs.

NIB	Exc.	V.G.	Good	Fair	Poor
1200	1000	800	600	400	250

SAR-8

This semi-automatic rifle is similar in appearance to the HK-91. It is chambered for the .308 Win. and is of the recoil operated delayed roller-lock design. Barrel length is 18" and the rear sight is fully adjustable. Weight is about 8.7 lbs.

NIB	Exc.	V.G.	Good	Fair	Poor
1200	1000	800	600	400	250

SAR-8 Tactical

Similar to the above model but fitted with a heavy barrel. Introduced in 1996.

NIB	Exc.	V.G.	Good	Fair	Poor
1600	1300	950	750	500	300

M6 Scout

A .22, .22 Magnum, or .22 Hornet and .410 bore Over/Under combination shotgun rifle with an 18" barrel. Black anodized finish with a synthetic stock.

NIB	Exc.	V.G.	Good	Fair	Poor
150	120	90	70	50	40

M6 Scout-Stainless Steel

Same as above but in stainless steel. First introduced in 1996.

NIB	Exc.	V.G.	Good	Fair	Poor
190	150	120	90	75	50

PISTOLS

Model 1911-A1

A 9mm, .38 Super or .45 caliber copy of the Colt Model 1911-A1 semiautomatic pistol. Blued or parkerized. Introduced in 1985.

NIB	Exc.	V.G.	Good	Fair	Poor
425	375	350	300	250	200

Combat Commander

A copy of the Colt Model 1911-A1 Combat Commander chambered for .45 ACP only. Introduced in 1988.

NIB	Exc.	V.G.	Good	Fair	Poor
475	425	400	350	300	250

Model Trophy Match

This model has special features such as fully adjustable target sights, match grade 5" barrel, and special wide trigger. Weight is approximately 36 oz. Available in blue, stainless steel, or bi-tone finish. In 1997 this model was offered chambered for the 9mm cartridge. Values would be the same for both .45 ACP and the 9mm models.

NIB	Exc.	V.G.	Good	Fair	Poor
850	750	650	500	400	300

NOTE: For stainless steel add $40.

Model 1911-A2 S.A.S.S.

This is a single shot pistol built on the Model 1911 frame. Available in two barrel lengths; 10.75" and 14.9". Offered in .22 Long Rifle, .223, 7mm-08, 7mmBR, .357 Magnum, .308, and .44 Magnum calibers. This conversion kit is available for those wishing to use it on their own Model 1911 pistol frames.

NIB	Exc.	V.G.	Good	Fair	Poor
225	200	175	150	100	50

Model 1911-A1 Stainless

Similar to the standard Model 1911 but chambered for the .45 ACP cartridge and offered in stainless steel. Equipped with three dot sights, beveled magazine well, and checkered walnut grips. Weighs about 39.2 oz.

NIB	Exc.	V.G.	Good	Fair	Poor
500	425	400	350	300	200

NOTE: For Bomar sights add $50.

Model 1911-A1 Factory Comp.

Chambered for the .45 ACP or the .38 Super this pistol is fitted with a three chamber compensator. The rear sight is adjustable, an extended thumb safety and Videcki speed trigger are standard features. Also checkered walnut grips, beveled magazine well and Commander hammer are standard. Weighs 40 oz.

NIB	Exc.	V.G.	Good	Fair	Poor
850	700	500	300	200	100

NOTE: Factory Comp pistols chambered for .38 Super may bring a small premium.

Model 1911-A1 Factory Comp. High Capacity

Same as above but with 13-round magazine. New pistols sold in 1996 will be supplied with 10-round magazines except to law enforcement.

NIB	Exc.	V.G.	Good	Fair	Poor
975	850	700	600	400	200

Model 1911-A1 Defender

Chambered for the .45 ACP cartridge this pistol is fitted with a tapered cone dual port compensator. It also is fitted with reversed recoil plug, full length recoil spring guide, fully adjustable rear sight, serrated front strap, rubberized grips, and Commander style hammer. Eight-round magazine capacity. The finish is bi-tone. Weighs 40.16 oz.

NIB	Exc.	V.G.	Good	Fair	Poor
850	700	500	300	200	100

Model 1911-A1 Compact

Available in blue or bi-tone this .45 ACP is fitted with a 4.5" barrel and compact compensator. It is equipped with Commander style hammer and three dot sights. Walnut grips are standard. Comes with 7-round magazine. Weighs 37.2 oz.

NIB	Exc.	V.G.	Good	Fair	Poor
500	400	300	250	200	100

NOTE: For stainless steel add $40.

Lightweight Compact Comp

Fitted with a 4-1/2" barrel and single port compensator. Magazine hold 8 rounds of .45 ACP. Frame is alloy and weight is 30 oz.

NIB	Exc.	V.G.	Good	Fair	Poor
500	400	300	250	200	100

Model 1911-A1 Compact Mil-Spec

This model is the same as the standard blued steel Compact model but with a parkerized finish.

NIB	Exc.	V.G.	Good	Fair	Poor
450	375	250	200	150	100

Model 1911-A1 Long Slide

This model features a 6" barrel, 3-dot fixed sights, checkered wooden grips, and an 8-round magazine capacity. Finish is stainless steel. Weight is about 38 oz. Introduced in 1997.

NIB	Exc.	V.G.	Good	Fair	Poor
625	550	500	—	—	—

Model 1911-A1 Champion

This .45 ACP pistol has a shortened slide, barrel, and reduced size frame. The Champion is fitted with 4" barrel, 8-round magazine, Commander hammer, checkered walnut grips, and special 3-dot sights. Weighs 33.4 oz.

NIB	Exc.	V.G.	Good	Fair	Poor
500	400	350	250	150	100

Model 1911-A1 Mil-Spec

Same as above but with a parkerized finish.

NIB	Exc.	V.G.	Good	Fair	Poor
450	375	300	200	150	100

Model 1911-A1 Stainless Champion

Same as above but offered in stainless steel. Weighs about 33.4 oz.

NIB	Exc.	V.G.	Good	Fair	Poor
525	425	375	275	200	150

Champion Compact

Includes same features as Champion but with a shortened grip frame length and a 7-round magazine. Weighs 32 oz.

NIB	Exc.	V.G.	Good	Fair	Poor
450	350	250	200	150	100

Ultra Compact 1911-A1

This model features a 3-1/2" barrel with a 7-1/8" overall length. It has a stainless steel frame, beveled mag well, speed trigger, match grade barrel, and walnut grips. Weighs 31 oz.

NIB	Exc.	V.G.	Good	Fair	Poor
550	450	350	250	200	150

Ultra Compact Lightweight MD-1

Same as above but in .380 caliber with alloy frame. Weighs 24 oz.

NIB	Exc.	V.G.	Good	Fair	Poor
375	325	275	200	150	100

Ultra Compact 1911-A1 Mil-Spec

Same as the Ultra Compact Model but with a parkerized finish.

NIB	Exc.	V.G.	Good	Fair	Poor
475	400	325	225	200	150

V10 Ultra Compact 1911 A-1

Same as the Ultra Compact 1911 A-1 but fitted with a compensator built into the barrel and slide.

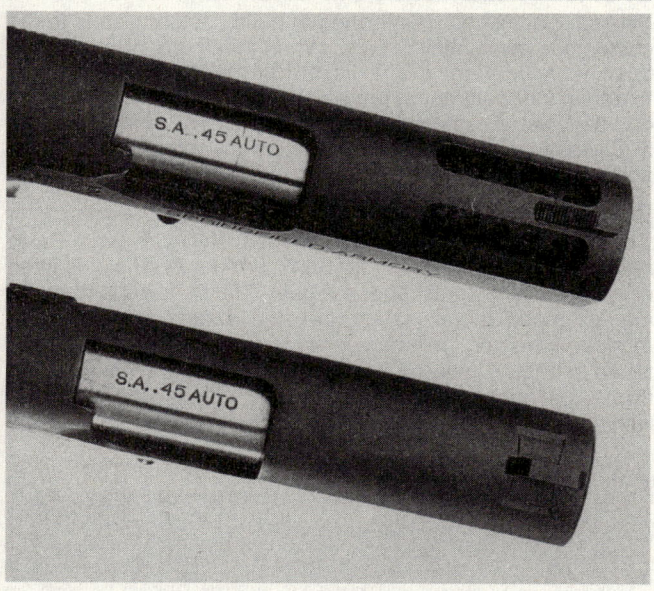

NIB	Exc.	V.G.	Good	Fair	Poor
600	525	400	300	200	150

V10 Ultra Compact 1911-A1 Mil-Spec

Same as above but with parkerized finish.

NIB	Exc.	V.G.	Good	Fair	Poor
525	425	350	300	200	150

Model 1911-A1 High Capacity

This model is chambered in .45 ACP (10-round magazine) or 9mm caliber (16-round magazine). Standard features include Commander hammer, walnut grips, and beveled magazine well. Blued finish. Weighs 42 oz. In 1997 this model was offered in stainless steel and parkerized finish.

NIB	Exc.	V.G.	Good	Fair	Poor
600	525	400	300	200	100

NOTE: For stainless steel add $40, for parkerized finish deduct $25.

Compact High Capacity

Same as above but with an 11-round magazine. New pistols sold in 1996 will have 10-round magazine except to law enforcement.

NIB	Exc.	V.G.	Good	Fair	Poor
600	525	400	300	200	150

The Springfield P9 Pistol

This is a double action 9mm, .45 ACP, or .40 S&W pistol based on the Czech CZ 75 design. It incorporates several design features including: stainless steel trigger, sear safety mechanism, extended sear safety lever, redesigned back strap, lengthened beavertail grip area, and a new high strength slide stop. This model discontinued in 1993.

NIB	Exc.	V.G.	Good	Fair	Poor
450	375	300	250	200	100

Model P9 Standard

This is the standard pistol fitted with a 4.7" barrel, low profile target sights, and a ribbed slide. The 9mm has a 16-round magazine, the .45 ACP has a 10-round magazine, and the .40 S&W holds 12 rounds. Offered in either blue or stainless finish. Weighs about 35 oz.

NIB	Exc.	V.G.	Good	Fair	Poor
425	350	300	250	200	100

Model P9 Factory Comp.

This is a competition pistol fitted with triple port compensator, extended magazine release, adjustable rear sight, slim competition wood grips, and bi-tone finish. Weighs 34 oz. Dropped from the Springfield product line in 1993.

NIB	Exc.	V.G.	Good	Fair	Poor
500	450	400	300	200	100

Model P9 Ultra (IPSC Approved)

This competition pistol features a longer slide and barrel, 5". Special target sights, rubberized competition grips. Pistol is engraved with IPSC logo. Available in bi-tone finish only. Weighs 34.5 oz. Dropped from production in 1993.

NIB	Exc.	V.G.	Good	Fair	Poor
450	400	350	300	200	100

Omega

A .38 Super, 10mm Norma, or .45 caliber semiautomatic pistol with a 5" or 6" polygon rifled barrel, ported or unported, adjustable sights and Pachmayr grips. Patterned somewhat after the Colt Model 1911. Introduced in 1987.
Caliber Conversion Units-Add $675.

NIB	Exc.	V.G.	Good	Fair	Poor
550	450	350	250	200	125

Super Tuned Champion

Introduced in 1997 this model features a 4" barrel chambered for the .45 ACP cartridge, Novak fixed low-mount sights. Tuned and polished extractor and ejector. Polished feed ramp and barrel throat. Magazine capacity is 7 rounds. Choice of blued or parkerized finish. Weight is approximately 36 oz.

NIB	Exc.	V.G.	Good	Fair	Poor
875	800	—	—	—	—

Super Tuned V10

Similar to the model above but with 3.5" barrel. Finish is bi-tone or stainless steel. Weight is about 33 oz. Introduced in 1997. Add $100 for stainless steel.

NIB	Exc.	V.G.	Good	Fair	Poor
950	825	—	—	—	—

Super Tuned Standard

This model features a 5" barrel with stainless steel finish. Weight is about 39 oz. Has all other super tune features. Introduced in 1997.

NIB	Exc.	V.G.	Good	Fair	Poor
900	775	—	—	—	—

SPRINGFIELD CUSTOM SHOP

This specialty shop was formed to build custom pistols to the customer's own specifications. When these one-of-a-kind pistols are encountered it is advisable for the shooter or collector to get an independent appraisal. The Springfield Custom also offers standard custom and Racegun packages that are readily available and in stock. These pistols are commercially available and priced below.

Custom Carry

Chambered for the following cartridges: .45 ACP, 9mm Parabellum, .38 Super, 10mm, .40 S&W, 9mm x 21. Pistol is fitted with fixed 3-dot sights, speed trigger, Match barrel and bushing, extended thumb safety, beveled magazine well, Commander hammer, polished feed ramp and throated barrel, tuned extractor, lowered and flared ejection port, fitted slide to frame, full length spring guide rod, and walnut grips. Supplied with 2 march magazines and plastic carrying case.

NIB	Exc.	V.G.	Good	Fair	Poor
1400	1200	800	600	400	200

Basic Competition Model

Chambered for the .45 ACP this model features a variety of special options for the competition shooter. Special Bo-Mar sights, match trigger, custom slide to frame fit, polished feed-ramp and throated barrel are just some of the features of this pistol.

NIB	Exc.	V.G.	Good	Fair	Poor
1500	1200	850	700	500	250

N.R.A. PPC

Designed to comply with NRA rules for PPC competition this pistol is chambered for the .45 ACP cartridge with a match grade barrel and chamber. It has a polished feedramp, throated barrel, recoil buffer system, walnut grips, and fully adjustable sights. It is sold with a custom carrying case.

NIB	Exc.	V.G.	Good	Fair	Poor
1400	1200	800	600	400	200

Bullseye Wadcutter

Chambered for .45 ACP, .38 Super, 10mm, and .40 S&W. Slide is fitted with Bo-Mar rib. Standard features include full length recoil spring guide rod, speed trigger, Commander hammer, lowered and flared ejection port, tuned extractor, fitted slide to frame, beveled magazine well, checkered front strap, checkered main spring housing, removable grip cope mount, match barrel and bushing, polished feed ramp and throated barrel, walnut grips, and two magazines with slam pads.

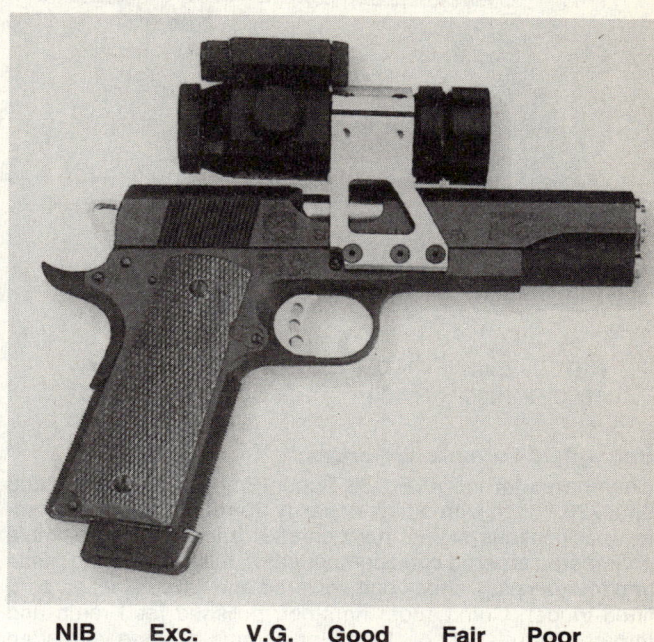

NIB	Exc.	V.G.	Good	Fair	Poor
1400	950	700	600	400	200

Trophy Master Expert Limited Class

Chambered for .45 ACP Adjustable Bo-Mar rear sight, match barrel, polished ramp and throated barrel, extended ambidextrous thumb safety, beveled and polished magazine well, full length recoil spring guide, match trigger, Commander hammer, lowered and flared ejection port, tuned extractor, fitted slide to frame, extended slide release, flat mainspring housing, Pachmayr wrap-around grips, 2 magazines with slam pads and plastic carrying case.

NIB	Exc.	V.G.	Good	Fair	Poor
1800	1500	1000	750	500	300

Expert Pistol

Similar to the above model but progressive triple port compensator.

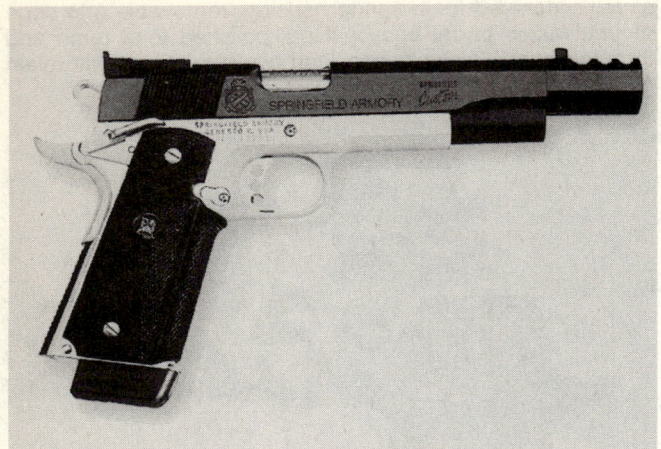

NIB	Exc.	V.G.	Good	Fair	Poor
1900	1600	1100	800	500	300

Springfield Formula "Squirtgun"

Chambered for .45 ACP, .38 Super, 9mmx19, 9mmx21, and 9mmx23. Fitted with a high capacity 20-round frame, customer specifications sights, hard chrome frame and slide, triple chambered tapered cone compensator, full recoil spring guide and reverse plug, shock butt, lowered and flared ejection port, fitted trigger, Commander hammer, polished feed ramp and throated barrel, flat checkered mainspring housing, extended ambidextrous thumb safety, tuned extractor, checkered front strap, bottom of trigger guard checkered, rear of slide serrated, cocking sensations on front of slide, built in beveled magazine well, and checkered wood grips.

NIB	Exc.	V.G.	Good	Fair	Poor
2900	2250	1250	950	400	200

Trophy Master Distinguished Pistol

This model is chambered for the following cartridges: .45 ACP, .38 Super, 10mm, .40 S&W, 9mmx21. Special Bo-Mar adjustable rear sight with hidden rear leaf, triple port compensator on match barrel, full length recoil spring guide rod and recoil spring retainer, shock butt, lowered and flared ejection port, fitted speed trigger, Commander hammer, polished feed ramp and throated barrel, flat checkered magazine well and mainspring housing matched to beveled magazine well, extended ambidextrous thumb safety, tuned extractor, checkered front strap, flattened and checkered triggerguard, serrated slide top and compensator, cocking sensations on front of slide, checkered walnut grips, 2 magazines with slam pads, and carrying case.

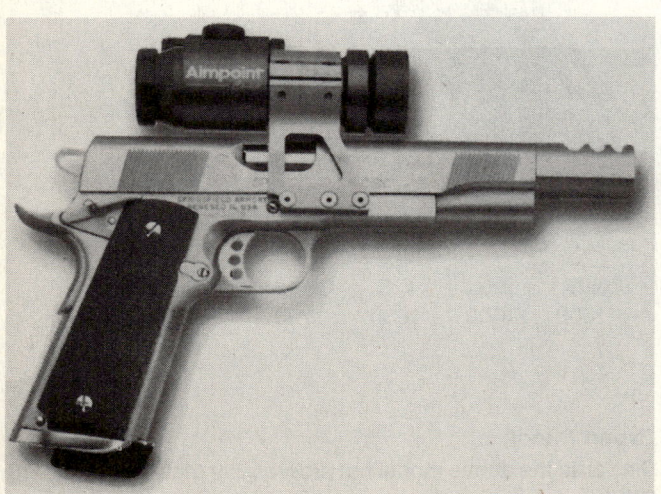

NIB	Exc.	V.G.	Good	Fair	Poor
2750	2400	1500	800	400	200

Distinguished Limited Class

Similar to the above model but built to comply with USPSA "Limited Class" competition rules. This model has no compensator.

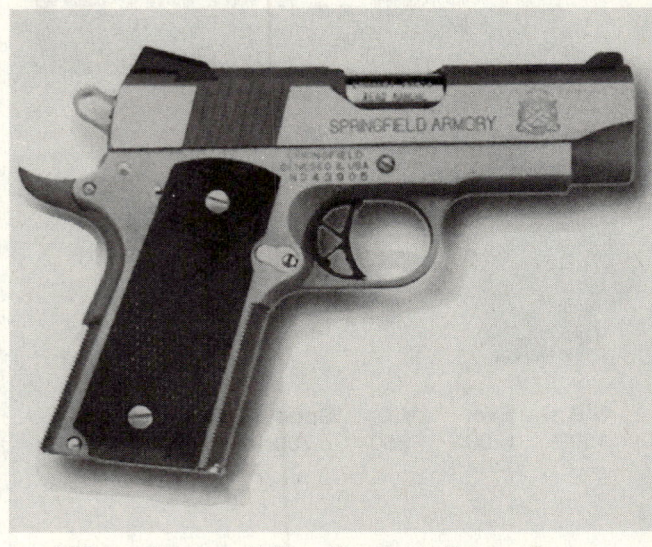

NIB	Exc.	V.G.	Good	Fair	Poor
2650	2300	1400	750	400	200

CMC Formula "Squirtgun"

Chambered for .45 ACP, .38 Super, 9mmx19, 9mmx21, 9mmx23. This pistol has a 20-round magazine and a modular frame. All other features the same as the Trophy Master.

NIB	Exc.	V.G.	Good	Fair	Poor
2750	2000	1200	800	400	200

National Match Model

As above, with a National Match barrel and bushing, adjustable sights and checkered walnut grips. Introduced in 1988.

NIB	Exc.	V.G.	Good	Fair	Poor
850	750	650	550	450	350

Competition Grade

As above, hand-tuned, Match Grade trigger, low-profile combat sights, an ambidextrous safety, and a Commander-type hammer. Furnished with Pachmayr grips. Introduced in 1988.

NIB	Exc.	V.G.	Good	Fair	Poor
1050	950	850	700	600	500

A Model Master Grade Competition Pistol

Similar to the Custom Carry Gun, with a National Match barrel and bushing. Introduced in 1988.

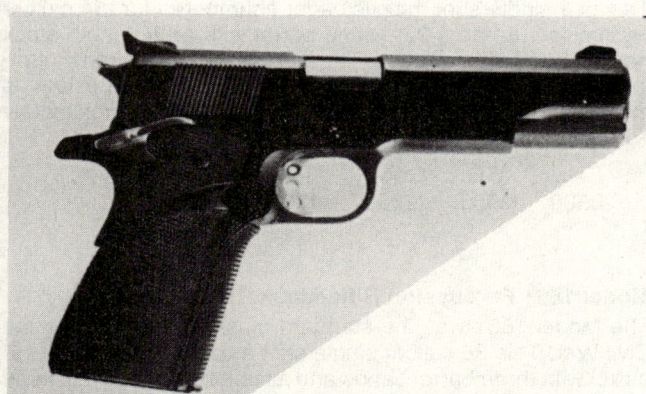

NIB	Exc.	V.G.	Good	Fair	Poor
1700	1500	1250	850	400	250

Model B-1 Master Grade Competition Pistol

Specially designed for USPSA/IPSC competition. Introduced in 1988.

NIB	Exc.	V.G.	Good	Fair	Poor
2000	1750	1250	850	400	250

High Capacity Full-House Race Gun

Built with all available race gun options. Offered in .45 ACP, 9x25 Dillon, .38 Super, and custom calibers on request.

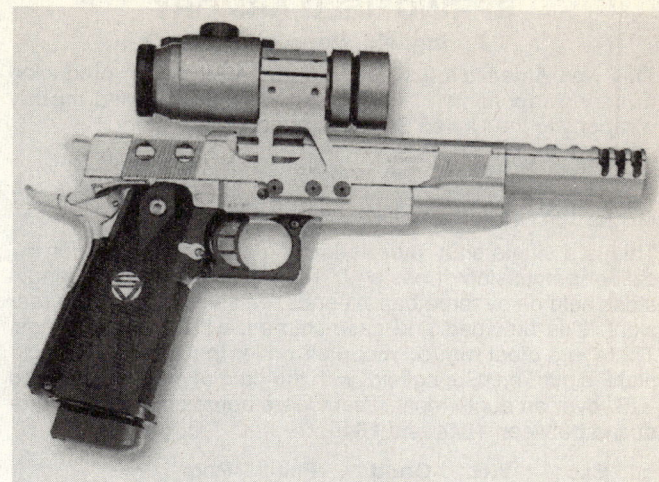

NIB	Exc.	V.G.	Good	Fair	Poor
2600	2200	1750	1250	600	300

Night Light Standard

Introduced in 1996 as a limited edition from Springfield distributor Lew Horton this full size Model 1911A1 pistol is chambered for the .45 ACP. It has a lightweight frame and slide with millett night sights with Houge rubber wrap around grips. Fitted with extented beavertail safety. Weight 29 oz.

NIB	Exc.	V.G.	Good	Fair	Poor
620	550	—	—	—	—

Night Light Compact

This model was also introduced by Lew Horton in 1996 and is similar to the above model but fitted with a 4.25" barrel and lightweight frame and slide. Weight is 27 oz.

NIB	Exc.	V.G.	Good	Fair	Poor
620	550	—	—	—	—

Night Compact

Same as above but with a steel frame and slide.

NIB	Exc.	V.G.	Good	Fair	Poor
595	525	—	—	—	—

Omega

A .38 Super, 10mm Norma, or .45 caliber semiautomatic pistol with a 5" or 6" polygon rifled barrel, ported or unported, adjustable sights and Pachmayr grips. Patterned somewhat after the Colt Model 1911. Introduced in 1987.
Caliber Conversion Units-Add $675.

NIB	Exc.	V.G.	Good	Fair	Poor
550	450	350	250	200	125

SPRINGFIELD ARMORY
Springfield, Massachusetts

This was America's first federal armory. It began producing military weapons in 1795. The armory has supplied military weapons to the United States throughout its history.

Model 1841 Cadet Musket

This is a single shot, muzzle-loading rifle chambered for .57 caliber percussion. It has a 40" round barrel with a full-length stock held on by three barrel bands. This rifle features no rear sight. It is browned and case-colored, with iron mountings. There is a steel ramrod mounted under the barrel. The lockplate is marked "Springfield" with the date of manufacture and "US" over an eagle motif. There were approximately 450 produced between 1844 and 1845.

Exc.	V.G.	Good	Fair	Poor
5000	4000	3000	2500	1850

Model 1842 Musket

This is a single shot muzzleloader chambered for .69 caliber percussion. It has a 42" round barrel and a full-length stock held on by three barrel bands. The finish is white with iron mountings and a steel ramrod mounted beneath the barrel. There were a total of approximately 275,000 manufactured between 1844 and 1855 by both the Springfield Armory and the Harper's Ferry Armory. They are so marked.

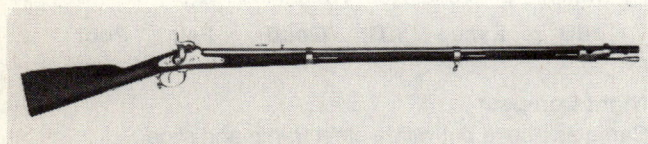

Courtesy Milwaukee Public Museum, Milwaukee, Wisconsin

Exc.	V.G.	Good	Fair	Poor
1250	1000	750	450	350

Model 1847 Musketoon

This is a single shot muzzleloader chambered for .69 caliber percussion. It has a 26" round smooth bore barrel. The finish is white, with a full-length walnut stock held on by two barrel bands. The lock is marked "Springfield". There were approximately 3,350 manufactured between 1848 and 1859.

Exc.	V.G.	Good	Fair	Poor
1750	1500	1000	850	600

Model 1851 Percussion Cadet Musket

This single shot muzzleloader in 57 caliber with 40" round barrel is almost identical with the Model 1841 Cadet Musket, the main difference and distinguishing feature is the use of the slightly smaller Model 1847 Musketoon lock. Markings are identical as shown for the Model 1841 Cadet Musket. These weapons were made at the Springfield Armory from 1851 to 1853, with total production of 4,000 guns.

Exc.	V.G.	Good	Fair	Poor
2000	1500	1000	800	300

Model 1855 Musket

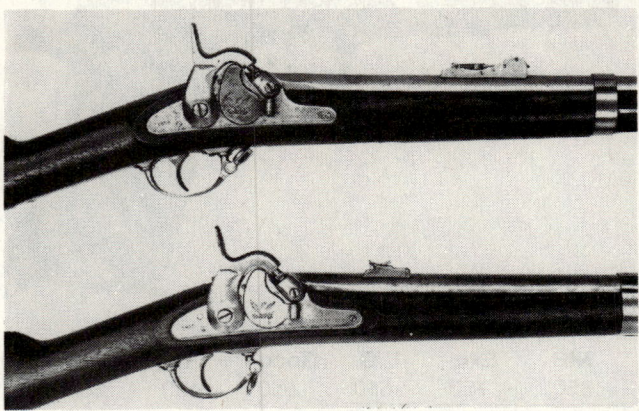

Courtesy Milwaukee Public Museum, Milwaukee, Wisconsin

This is a single shot muzzleloader chambered for .58 caliber percussion. It has a 40" round barrel with a full-length stock held on by three barrel bands. It has iron mountings and a ramrod mounted under the barrel. The front sight acts as a bayonet lug. The finish is white with a walnut stock. The lock is marked "U.S. Springfield". There was also a Harper's Ferry manufactured version that is so marked. There were approximately 59,000 manufactured between 1857 and 1861.

Exc.	V.G.	Good	Fair	Poor
1500	1250	1000	750	550

Model 1855 Rifled Carbine

This is a single shot muzzleloader chambered for .54 caliber percussion. It has a 22" round barrel with a 3/4-length stock held on by one barrel band. The finish is white with iron mountings and a ramrod mounted under the barrel. The lock is marked "Springfield" and dated. There were approximately 1,000 manufactured between 1855 and 1856.

Exc.	V.G.	Good	Fair	Poor
3500	3000	2500	1750	1250

Model 1861 Percussion Rifle-Musket

The Model 1861 was the standard musket in use during the Civil War. This 58 caliber single shot muzzleloader has a 40" barrel with three barrel bands and all iron mountings; all metal parts are finished bright (some rear sights are blued) and the stock is walnut. On the lock there is an eagle motif forward of the hammer, US/SPRINGFIELD, beneath the nipple bolster, and the date at the rear section of the lock. About 256,129 of these muskets were made at the Springfiled Armory, while almost 750,000 more were made under contract.

Exc.	V.G.	Good	Fair	Poor
2200	1500	1000	800	300

Model 1863 Rifled Musket

This is a single shot muzzleloader chambered for .58 caliber percussion. It has a 40" round barrel and a full-length stock held on by three barrel bands. The finish is white with iron mountings, and the lock is marked "U.S. Springfield" and dated 1863. There were approximately 275,000 manufactured in 1863.

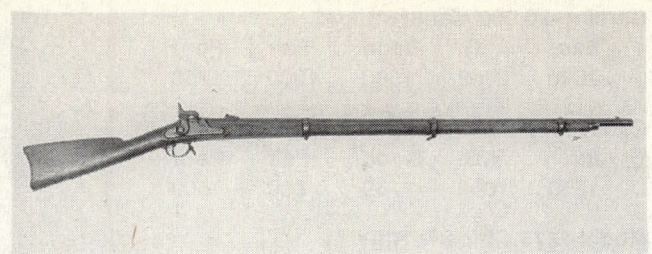

Exc.	V.G.	Good	Fair	Poor
1250	1000	750	600	400

Model 1863 Rifle Musket, Type II, a.k.a. Model 1864

This was the last U.S. marked regulation arm of muzzleloading design, and it was widely used during the latter part of the Civil War. Produced at the Springfield Armory between 1864 and 1865, with total production of 255,40 pieces. This weapon is identical to the Type I with the exception of the dating of the lock, which is either 1864 or 1865, a single leaf rear sight, and solid barrel bands secured by flat springs mounted in the stock. The ramrod was either the tulip head type, or the new knurled and slotted design.

Exc.	V.G.	Good	Fair	Poor
1800	1200	900	600	300

Joslyn Breech-Loading Rifle

Until recently, this rifle was considered a post-Civil War breechloading conversion of a muzzleloading musket, but information developed since the 1970s indicates that this was the first true breechloading cartridge rifle to be made in quantity by a national armory, circa 1864. Actions were supplied to the Springfiled Armory by the Joslyn Firearms Co. where they were assembled to newly made rifles designed for the action. In 56-60 caliber, with a 35.5" barrel with three barrel bands, the uniquely shaped lock with eagle ahead of the hammer, U.S./Springfield on the front of the lock, with 1864 at the rear. Walnut stock specially made for the barreled action and lock. Converted to 50-70 centerfire will command approximately $100 more.

Exc.	V.G.	Good	Fair	Poor
1800	1500	1000	600	300

Model 1865 U.S. Breech-Loading Rifle, Allin Conversion, a.k.a. First Model Allin

Designed in 58 caliber rimfire, with a 40" barrel with three flat barrel bands. the Breechlock is released by a thumb latch on the right side, pivoted upward, with the firing pin contained within the breechblock. 5,000 Model 1861 percussion muskets were altered using this method at the Springfield Armory circa 1865. The breechblock is unmarked, while the lock is marked with the eagle ahead of the hammer, as well as U.S./Springfield, with all specimens dated 1865 at the rear.

Exc.	V.G.	Good	Fair	Poor
3200	2500	2000	1250	750

Model 1866 U.S. Breech-Loading Rifle, Allin Conversion, a.k.a. Second Model Allin

Produced in 50 caliber centerfire, with a 40" barrel with a 50 caliber liner tube inserted and brazed, walnut stock with three barrel bands with band springs. Differences between the First and Second Model Allin include a lengthened bolt, a firing pin spring, and a stronger internal extraction system. the Breechblock is marked with 1866 over an eagle, while the lock bears standard Springfiled markings with either an 1863 or 1864 date. A total of 25,000 Model 1863 percussion muskets were thus altered at the Springfield Armory around 1866.

Exc.	V.G.	Good	Fair	Poor
1500	1100	800	500	200

Model 1867 U.S. Breech-Loading Cadet Rifle

This model is a .50 caliber centerfire, 33" barrel, two band, scaled down version of the Model 1866 Second Model Allin "trapdoor". No sling swivels; a narrow trigger guard. The breechblock has a blackened finish, with deeply arched cutouts on both sides of the underside, leaving a narrow flat ridge in the center. The breechblock is marked 1866/eaglehead. The lock plate was made especially for this rifle and is noticable thinner. The plate is marked with the usual eagle and US/Springfield, with the date 1866 behind the hammer. About 424 rifles were produced at the Springfield Armory between 1876 and 1868.

Exc.	V.G.	Good	Fair	Poor
5000	3500	2500	1000	750

Model 1868 Rifle

This is a single shot Trapdoor rifle chambered for the .50 caliber centerfire cartridge. It features a breechblock that pivots forward when a thumblatch at its rear is depressed. It has a 32.5" barrel and a full-length stock held on by two barrel bands. It has iron mountings and a cleaning rod mounted under the barrel. It features an oil-finished walnut stock. The lock is marked "US Springfield". It is dated either 1863 or 1864. The breechblock features either the date 1869 or 1870. There were approximately 51,000 manufactured between 1868 and 1872.

Exc.	V.G.	Good	Fair	Poor
800	675	500	400	250

Model 1869 Cadet Rifle

This is a single shot Trapdoor rifle chambered for .50 caliber centerfire. It is similar to the Model 1868 with a 29.5" barrel. There were approximately 3,500 manufactured between 1869 and 1876.

Exc.	V.G.	Good	Fair	Poor
1000	850	650	500	450

Model 1870

There are two versions of this Trapdoor breechloader—a rifle with a 32.5" barrel and a carbine that features a 22" barrel and a half-stock held on by one barrel band. They are both chambered for .50 caliber centerfire and feature the standard Springfield lock markings and a breechblock marked "1870" or "Model 1870". There were a total of 11,500 manufactured between 1870 and 1873. Only 340 are carbines; they are extremely rare.

Rifle

Exc.	V.G.	Good	Fair	Poor
1250	1000	750	600	500

Carbine

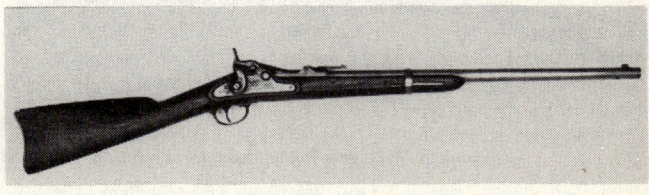

Exc.	V.G.	Good	Fair	Poor
3250	2750	2000	1500	1000

Model 1871 Rolling Block U.S. Army Rifle

This model is a .50 caliber centerfire, 36" barrel, with two barrel bands, rolling block action. Sights, sling-swivels, and most other details as for the Model 1870 Remington U.S. Navy rifle. Case-hardened frame, bright finished iron mountings. Two piece walnut stock. Known as the "locking action" as the hammer went to half cock when the breechblock was closed. No serial numbers. Left side of frame marked "Model 1871". Right side marked with eagle over U.S./Springfield/1872. On the tang, marked "REMINGTON'S PATENT. PAT.MAY 3D, NOV. 15TH, 1864, APRIL 17TH, 1868". About 10,001 rifles were produced between 1871 and 1872 under a royalty agreement with Remington Arms Co.

Exc.	V.G.	Good	Fair	Poor
1500	1200	800	600	400

Model 1871 Ward-Burton U.S. Rifle

A .50 caliber centerfire, 32.63" barrel secured by two barrel bands. This is an early bolt action, single shot rifle, with the cartridge loaded directly into the open action, with cocking on the closing of the bolt. Walnut stock, sling swivels on the forward barrel band and the front of the trigger guard. Not serially numbered. The top of the bolt marked, "WARD BURTON PATENT DEC. 20, 1859-FEB. 21, 1871". Left side of the action marked with American eagle motif and "US/SPRINGFIELD" 1,011 rifles and 316 carbines produced at the Springfield Armory basically as a trial weapon.

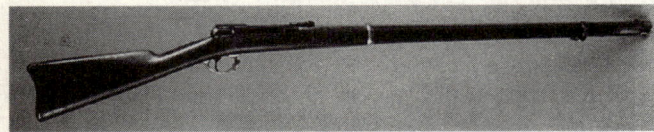

Courtesy Bob Ball

Exc.	V.G.	Good	Fair	Poor
3000	2000	1000	600	400

Model 1873

This is a Trapdoor breechloading rifle chambered for the .45-70 cartridge. The rifle version has a 32.5" barrel with a full-length stock held on by two barrel bands. The carbine features a 22" barrel with a half-stock held on by a single barrel band, and the cadet rifle features a 29.5" barrel with a full length stock and two barrel bands. The finish of all three variations is blued and case-colored, with a walnut stock. The lock is marked "US Springfield 1873". The breechblock is either marked "Model 1873" or "US Model 1873". There were approximately 73,000 total manufactured between 1873 and 1877.

Rifle-50,000 Manufactured

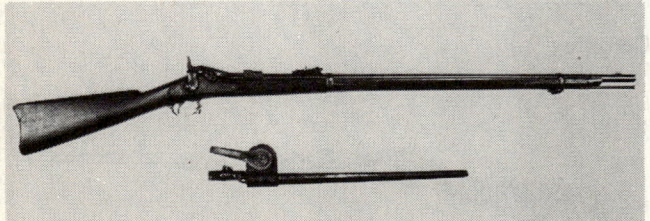

Courtesy Milwaukee Public Museum, Milwaukee, Wisconsin

Exc.	V.G.	Good	Fair	Poor
1250	1000	600	300	200

Carbine-20,000 Manufactured

Exc.	V.G.	Good	Fair	Poor
2500	2000	1500	1000	750

Cadet Rifle-3,000 Manufactured

Exc.	V.G.	Good	Fair	Poor
1250	1000	750	600	500

Model 1875 Officer's Rifle

This is a high-grade Trapdoor breechloader chambered for the .45-70 cartridge. It has a 26" barrel and a half-stock fastened by one barrel band. It is blued and case-colored, with a scroll engraved lock. It has a checkered walnut pistol grip stock with a pewter forend tip. There is a cleaning rod mounted beneath the barrel. This rifle was not issued but was sold to army officers for personal sporting purposes. There were only 477 manufactured between 1875 and 1885.

Exc.	V.G.	Good	Fair	Poor
7500	6500	5000	3500	3000

> **A U.S. Springfield Model 1875 Officers rifle was sold at auction for $30,800. An 1885 dated cartouche was stamped opposite the lock. Detachable checkered pistol grip. Condition was mint. Rock Island Auction Co., May 1996.**

Model 1875 Lee Vertical Action Rifle

A 45-70 centerfire, 32.63" barrel secured by two barrel bands. Martini-style dropping block action, with a unique, centrally mounted hammer with an exceptionally long spur. In order to open the breech, the hammer must be given a sharp blow with the heal of the hand; the insertation of a cartridge will automatically close the breech, while the hammer is cocked by hand. All blued finish. Stacking and sling swivel on upper band, with sling swivel on trigger guard. Serially numbered 1 through 143 on the internal parts only. Upper tang marked, "U.S. PAT. MAR 16, 1875", no barrel proof marks; inspector's initials "ESA" in an oval on the stock. 143 rifles produced in 1875 at the Springfield Armory basically as a trials weapon.

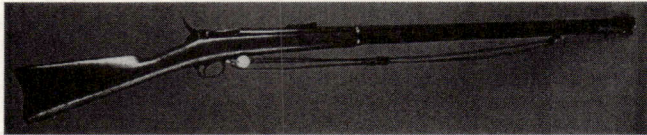

Courtesy Bob Ball

Exc.	V.G.	Good	Fair	Poor
3500	2500	1500	900	500

Model 1877

This is a Trapdoor breechloading rifle chambered for the .45-70 cartridge. It was issued as a rifle with a 32" barrel and a full-length stock held on by two barrel bands, a cadet rifle with a 29.5" barrel, and a carbine with a 22" barrel, half-stock, and single barrel band. This version is similar to the Model 1873. In fact, the breechblock retained the Model 1873 marking. The basic differences are that the stock is thicker at the wrist and the breechblock was thickened and lowered. This is basically a mechanically improved version. There were approximately 12,000 manufactured in 1877 and 1878.

Rifle-3,900 Manufactured

Exc.	V.G.	Good	Fair	Poor
1400	1200	850	700	550

Cadet Rifle-1,000 Manufactured

Exc.	V.G.	Good	Fair	Poor
1500	1300	1000	850	650

Carbine-2,950 Manufactured

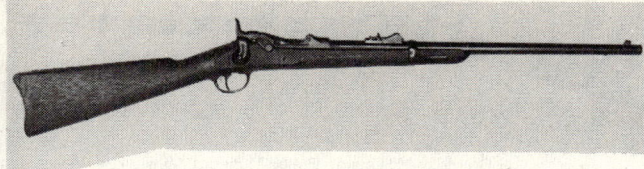

Courtesy Milwaukee Public Museum, Milwaukee, Wisconsin

Exc.	V.G.	Good	Fair	Poor
3000	2500	1800	1250	850

Model 1880

This version features a sliding combination cleaning rod/bayonet that is fitted in the forearm under the barrel. It retained the 1873 breechblock markings. There were approximately 1,000 manufactured for trial purposes in 1880.

Courtesy Milwaukee Public Museum, Milwaukee, Wisconsin

Exc.	V.G.	Good	Fair	Poor
1500	1300	1000	850	650

Model 1881 Marksman Rifle

This is an extremely high-grade Trapdoor breechloading rifle chambered for the .45-70 cartridge. It has a 28" round barrel and is similar to the Model 1875 Officer's Rifle in appearance. It features a full-length, high grade, checkered walnut stock held on by one barrel band. It has a horn Schnabel forend tip. The metal parts are engraved, blued, and case-colored. It has a vernier aperture sight as well as a buckhorn rear sight on the barrel and a globe front sight with a spirit level. There were only 11 manufactured to be awarded as prizes at shooting matches. This is perhaps the supreme rarity among the Trapdoor Springfields, and one should be extremely cognizant of fakes.

Exc.	V.G.	Good	Fair	Poor
35000	27500	22500	15000	10000

Model 1881 Shotgun

This version has a 26" round smooth bore barrel that is chambered for 20 gauge. It was used by hunters and scouts at Western forts. There were approximately 1,376 manufactured between 1881 and 1885. This version is particularly susceptible to fakery. We advise a qualified appraisal.

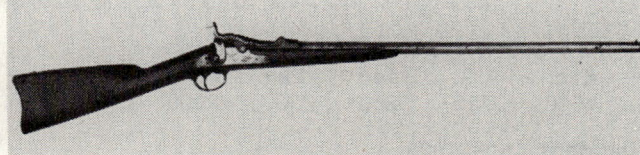

Courtesy Milwaukee Public Museum, Milwaukee, Wisconsin

Exc.	V.G.	Good	Fair	Poor
1750	1500	1200	850	700

Model 1882 U.S. Magazine Rifle, Chaffee-Reese

A 45-70 caliber centerfire, 27.78" barrel secured by two barrel bands. One of the early bolt action repeaters, with the cartridg-

es carried in a tubular feed in the butt. Iron mountings, with a blued finish, walnut stock, stacking swivel and sling swivel on the upper barrel band, and a sling swivel on the front of the trigger guard. Not serially numbered. Left side of breech marked, "US SPRINGFIELD, 1884", the barrel marked, "V.P." with eagle head proof. Unfortunately, most rifles found are lacking the feed mechanism in the butt, which lowers the value approximatley 15%. 753 rifles were produced at the Springfield Armory in 1884.

Courtesy Bob Ball

Exc.	V.G.	Good	Fair	Poor
2500	1900	1400	600	400

Model 1884

This is also a breechloading Trapdoor single shot rifle chambered for the .45-70 cartridge. It was issued as a standard rifle with a 32.75" barrel, a cadet rifle with a 29.5" barrel, and a military carbine with a 22" barrel. The finish is blued and case-colored. This model features the improved Buffington rear sight. It features the socket bayonet and a walnut stock. There were approximately 232,000 manufactured between 1885 and 1890.

Courtesy Bob Ball

Rifle-200,000

Exc.	V.G.	Good	Fair	Poor
750	650	500	350	250

Cadet Rifle-12,000

Exc.	V.G.	Good	Fair	Poor
850	750	600	400	300

Carbine-20,000

Exc.	V.G.	Good	Fair	Poor
1000	850	700	500	400

Model 1886 Experimental "Trapdoor" Carbine, aka Experimental Model 1882 third/fourth type

Apparently both of these designations are misnomers, as the weapon was officially referred to as the "24" Barrel Carbine. Collectors now call it the Model 1886 to conform to the year of manufacture. The most outstanding feature is the almost full length stock with uncapped, tapered forend. The single upper barrel band is fitted with a bent, or wraparound swivel to facilitate insertion in a saddle scabbard. Lower swivel on butt, with a sling ring and bar on the left side. Cleaning rod compartment in the butt. Buffington type Model 1884 rear sight marked XC on leaf. About 1,000 produced during 1886.

Exc.	V.G.	Good	Fair	Poor
4000	3000	2000	1000	700

Model 1888

This version is similar to its predecessors except that it features a sliding, ramrod-type bayonet that was improved so that it stays securely locked when in its extended position. The breechblock was still marked "Model 1884". This was the last Springfield Trapdoor rifle produced. There were approximately 65,000 manufactured between 1889 and 1893.

Courtesy Milwaukee Public Museum, Milwaukee, Wisconsin

Exc.	V.G.	Good	Fair	Poor
750	650	500	350	250

Trapdoor Fencing Musket

This is a non-gun that was used by the Army in teaching bayonet drills. They had no desire to damage serviceable rifles during practice, so they produced this version to fill the bill. There were basically four types produced.

Type I

This version is similar to the Model 1873 rifle without a breech or lock. The finish is rough, and it is unmarked. It was designed to accept a socket bayonet. One should secure a qualified appraisal if a transaction is contemplated. There were 170 manufactured in 1876 and 1877.

Exc.	V.G.	Good	Fair	Poor
800	650	500	400	300

Type II

This version is basically a Model 1884 with the hammer removed and the front sight blade ground off. It accepted a socket bayonet that was covered with leather and had a pad on its point.

Exc.	V.G.	Good	Fair	Poor
500	400	300	250	200

Type III

This version is similar to the Type II except that it is shortened to 43.5" in length. There were approximately 1,500 manufactured between 1905 and 1906.

Exc.	V.G.	Good	Fair	Poor
750	650	450	350	300

Type IV

This version is similar to the Type III except that the barrel was filled with lead. There were approximately 11,000 manufactured between 1907 and 1916.

Exc.	V.G.	Good	Fair	Poor
500	400	300	250	200

Model 1870 Rolling Block

This is a single shot breechloading rifle with a rolling-block action. It is chambered for .50 caliber centerfire and has a 32.75" barrel. It has a full-length forend held on by two barrel bands. The finish is blued and case-colored, with a cleaning rod mounted under the barrel. The stock and forend are walnut. The frame is marked "USN Springfield 1870". There is an anchor motif marked on the top of the barrel. It also features government inspector's marks on the frame. This rifle was manufactured by Springfield Armory under license from Remington Arms Company for the United States Navy. The first 10,000 produced were rejected by our Navy and were sent to France and used in the Franco-Prussian War. For that reason, this variation is quite scarce and would bring a 20% premium. There was also a group of approximately 100 rifles that were converted to the .22 rimfire cartridge and used for target practice aboard ships. This version is extremely rare. There were approximately 22,000 manufactured in 1870 and 1871.

Courtesy Milwaukee Public Museum, Milwaukee, Wisconsin

Standard Navy Rifle

Exc.	V.G.	Good	Fair	Poor
800	700	600	400	300

Rejected Navy Rifle

Exc.	V.G.	Good	Fair	Poor
700	600	500	350	250

.22 Caliber

Exc.	V.G.	Good	Fair	Poor
2000	1750	1250	900	750

U.S. Krag Jorgensen Rifle

NOTE: This firearm will be found listed in its own section of this text.

Model 1903

This rifle was a successor to the Krag Jorgensen and was also produced by the Rock Island Arsenal. It was initially chambered for the .30-03 cartridge and very shortly changed to the .30-06 cartridge. Its original chambering consisted of a 220-grain, round-nosed bullet. The German army introduced its spitzer bullet so our government quickly followed suit with a 150-grain, pointed bullet designated the .30-06. This model has a 24" barrel and was built on what was basically a modified Mauser action. It features a 5-round integral box magazine. The finish is blued, with a full length, straight-grip walnut stock with full handguards held on by two barrel bands. The initial version was issued with a rod-type bayonet that was quickly discontinued when President Theodore Roosevelt personally disapproved it. There were approximately 74,000 produced with this rod bayonet; and if in an unaltered condition, these would be worth a great deal more than the standard variation. It is important to note that the early models with serial numbers under 800,000 were not heat treated sufficiently to be safe to fire with modern ammunition. There were a great many produced between 1903 and 1930. The values represented reflect original specimens; WWII alterations would be worth approximately 15% less.

Courtesy Milwaukee Public Museum, Milwaukee, Wisconsin

Rod Bayonet Version (Unaltered)

Exc.	V.G.	Good	Fair	Poor
4500	3750	3250	2500	2000

Standard Model 1903

Exc.	V.G.	Good	Fair	Poor
700	575	350	275	150

Model 1903 Rifle Stripped for Air Service

Special 29" stock, 5.75 upper handguard specially made for this rifle, solid lower barrel band retained by screw underneath, rear sight leaf shortened and altered to open sight with square notch. 25-round extension magazine used. 910 rifles produced during the first half of 1918, with serial numbers ranging between 857000 and 863000; all barrel dated in first half of 1918. A very rare and desirable rifle, with the magazine almost impossible to find. Values shown include magazine.

Exc.	V.G.	Good	Fair	Poor
6000	4500	3000	2000	1500

Model 1903 Mark 1

This version is similar to the original except that it was cut to accept the Pedersen device. This device allows the use of a semiautomatic bolt insert that utilizes pistol cartridges. The rifle has a slot milled into the receiver that acts as an ejection port. The device was not successful and was scrapped. There were approximately 102,000 rifles that were produced with this millcut between 1918 and 1920. The values given are for the rifle alone—not for the device.

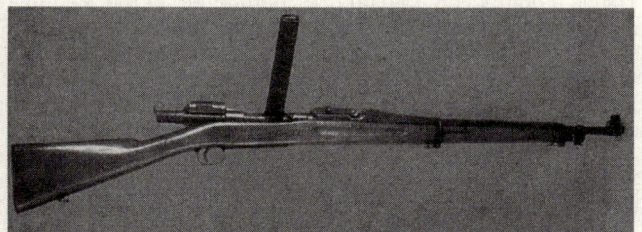

Courtesy Bob Ball

Exc.	V.G.	Good	Fair	Poor
600	450	350	275	150

Model 1903 Sniper Rifle

Selected Model 1903 rifles were fitted with telescopic sights from 1907 to 1919; apparently 25 rifles so equipped in 1906, but the type of scope has not been definitely identified. If proven original to the period, specimens would be worth more than shown in the values guide. 400 rifles were fitted with the Warner-Swasey Model 1906, 6-power telescope sight in 1911, with the sights marked Model 1908, as well as with the full Warner-Swasey markings. Scope number do not match the rifle numbers. Rifles fitted with this Model 1908 scope will bring approximatley 30% more than the values shown. Approximately 5000 rifles were fitted with the Model 1913 Warner-Swasey telescopic sight up to 1919; similar to the Model 1908, they are only 5.2 power. When originally fitted, the scopes were numberd to the rifles'; however, scopes were sold seperately from the rifles as surplus and were never numbered. These were later fitted to other weapons and the chance of finding matching numbers greatly decreases. Values shown are for original guns with original, matching telescopes.

Courtesy Bob Ball

Exc.	V.G.	Good	Fair	Poor
6500	5000	4000	2500	1500

Model 1903 A1

This version is a standard Model 1903 rifle that was fitted with a Type C, semi-pistol grip stock. All other specifications were the same.

Exc.	V.G.	Good	Fair	Poor
400	350	300	250	200

Model 1903 A3

This version was introduced in May of 1942 for use in WWII. It basically consisted of improvements to simplify mass produc-

tion. It features an aperture sight and various small parts that were fabricated from stampings; this includes the triggerguard, floorplate, and barrel band. The finish is parkerized. This model was manufactured by Remington and Smith Corona.

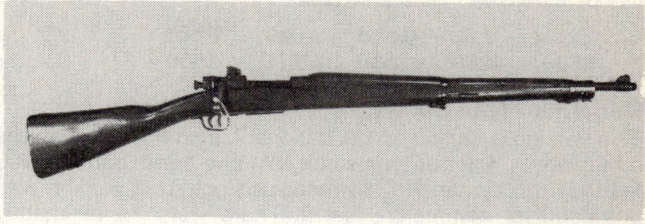

Courtesy Bob Ball

Exc.	V.G.	Good	Fair	Poor
400	350	300	200	100

Model 1903 A4

This is a sniper-rifle version of the Model 1903. It is fitted with permanently mounted scope locks and furnished with a telescopic sight known as the M73BI. This scope was manufactured by Weaver in El Paso, Texas, and was commercially known as the Model 330C. The rifle has no conventional iron sights mounted.

Courtesy Richard M. Kumor, Sr.

Exc.	V.G.	Good	Fair	Poor
1400	1200	800	550	350

Model 1903 NRA National Match

This version was based on a standard 1903 service rifle that was selected for having excellent shooting qualities. The parts were then hand-fit, and a special rifled barrel was added that was checked for tolerance with a star gauge. The muzzle of this barrel was marked with a special star with six or eight rays radiating from it. These NRA rifles were drilled and tapped to accept a Lyman No. 48 rear sight. They are marked with the letters "NRA" and have a flaming bomb proofmark on the triggerguard. There were approximately 18,000 manufactured between 1921 and 1928.

Exc.	V.G.	Good	Fair	Poor
1500	1200	1000	700	400

Model 1903 A1 National Match

Basically the same as the Model 1903 National Match rifle except for the "C" type, or pistol grip stock, without grasping grooves. Bolts and stocks numberd to the receiver. "P" in a circle proof on the underside of the pistol grip, with either a "DAL" in a rectangular cartouche, or S.A./SPG in a square cartouche. Rifles will be found with either a regular or reversed safety. Approximately 11,000 produced with a serial number range from 1285000 to 1532000.

Exc.	V.G.	Good	Fair	Poor
2300	1600	1200	700	300

Model 1903 Style National Match Special Rifle

This rifle is identical to the National Match, but with a completely different buttstock configuration identical to the Model 1922 NRA. Large shotgun type steel butt plate; full pistol grip. About 150 rifles produced during 1924.

Exc.	V.G.	Good	Fair	Poor
5500	4200	3500	2200	1500

Model 1903 Style "NB" National Match Rifle

This rifle produced with the "B" type stock with more drop than standard, suitable only for off-hand shooting; pistol grip configured with a noticably squared profile. Deep checkered butt plate. Circle "P" proof in underside of pistol grip. About 195 rifles built between 1925 and 1926.

Exc.	V.G.	Good	Fair	Poor
5500	4200	3500	2200	1500

Model 1903 NRA Sporter

This version is similar to the National Match rifle but features a half-length, Sporter-type stock with one barrel band. It also features the Lyman No. 48 receiver sight. This version was produced for commercial sales. There were approximately 6,500 manufactured between 1924 and 1933.

Exc.	V.G.	Good	Fair	Poor
1300	1150	900	700	400

Model 1903 N.B.A. Sporter Rifle

The barrel, action, and sights of this rifle are identical to the Model 1903 NRA sporter rifle above, however it is fitted with a "B" type stock. Grasping grooves and squared pistol grip profile. Circle "P" proof in the underside of the pistol grip. 589 rifles produced at the Springfield Armory during 1925 and 1926.

Exc.	V.G.	Good	Fair	Poor
5500	4200	3500	2200	1500

Model 1903 Heavy Barreled Match Rifles

These rifles were made in a bewildering number of types and variations. Commonly encountered are the style "T" with NRA type stocks. Barrels, which came in three lengths, 26", 28", and 30", measured .860" at the muzzle and 1.250" at the breech, Lyman 48 rear sight; Winchester globe front sight on a modified B.A.R. front band, telescope blocks on the receiver and barrel. Some fitted with adjustable hook type butt plates, set triggers, Garand speed locks, as well as cheekpieces (all commanding premium dollars.) INTERNATIONAL MATCH rifles (worth at least double the values shown) have many variant features which were changed annually at the request of the individual shooter: these features include palm rests, double set triggers, beaver-tail forends, checkered pistol grips, Swiss style butt plates, etc. Generally the Winchester 5A telescopic sight was used. These rifles are considered rare. Another variation is the 1922 MATCH SPRINGFILED RIFLE with NRA type stock with grasping grooves, a 24" barrel with service type front sight mount and small base integral with the barrel, as well as telescopic blocks on the barrel. 566 rifles produced at the Springfield Armory between 1922 and 1930.

Exc.	V.G.	Good	Fair	Poor
4500	3500	2500	1500	800

Model 1903 Caliber Gallery Practice Rifle "Hoffer-Thompson

This practice rifle differed from the standard issue "03 as follows: the barrel bored and rifled to .22 caliber, the breech chambered for the Hoffer-Thompson cartridge holder, the rear sight graduated to 240 yards, the mainspring shortened, the stocks generally found without cross bolts or the circle "P" on the underside of the pistol grip. Receivers produced after 1901 usually are marked with ".22" on the top of the bridge. About 15,525 rifles were produced at the Springfiled Armory between 1907 and 1918.

Exc.	V.G.	Good	Fair	Poor
3000	2000	1200	900	600

Model 1917

In 1917 when the United States entered WWI, there was a distinct rifle shortage. There were production facilities set up for the British pattern 1914 rifle. This "Enfield" rifle was redesigned to accept the .30-06 cartridge and was pressed into service as the U.S. rifle Model 1917. This rifle appears similar to the British pattern 1914 rifle. In fact, they are so similar that in WWII, when over a million were sold to Britain for use by their Home Guard, it was necessary to paint a 2" stripe around the butt so that the caliber was immediately known. The barrel length is 26", and it has a 5-round integral box magazine. The finish is matte-blue, with a walnut stock. The breech is marked "U.S. Model 1917". This was a robust and heavy-duty rifle, and many are used in the manufacture of large-bore custom rifles to this day. There were approximately 2,200,000 manufactured by Remington and Winchester between 1917 and 1918. The majority were produced at Eddystone, Pennsylvania.

Exc.	V.G.	Good	Fair	Poor
375	300	200	150	100

Model 1922

This is a bolt-action training rifle chambered for the .22 rimfire cartridge. It appears similar to the Model 1903 but has a 24.5" barrel and a half-length stock without hand guards, held on by a single barrel band. It has a 5-round detachable box magazine. The finish is blued, with a walnut stock. The receiver is marked "U.S. Springfield Armory Model of 1922 Cal. 22". It also has the flaming bomb ordnance mark. There were three basic types of the Model 1922: the standard issue type, the NRA commercial type, and the models that were altered to MI or M2. There were a total of approximately 2,000 manufactured between 1922 and 1924. The survival rate of the original-issue types is not large as most were converted.

Issue Type

Exc.	V.G.	Good	Fair	Poor
800	650	450	250	200

Altered Type

Exc.	V.G.	Good	Fair	Poor
450	350	250	200	150

NRA Type-Drilled and Tapped for Scope

Exc.	V.G.	Good	Fair	Poor
700	550	400	200	150

Model 1922 M1

This version is quite similar to the Model 1922, with a single firing pin that hits the top of the cartridge and a detachable box magazine that does not protrude from the bottom of the stock. The finish is parkerized; and the stock, of walnut. There were approximately 20,000 manufactured between 1924 and 1933.

Unaltered Type

Exc.	V.G.	Good	Fair	Poor
750	650	550	300	200

Altered to M2

Exc.	V.G.	Good	Fair	Poor
450	350	250	200	150

Unaltered NRA Type

Exc.	V.G.	Good	Fair	Poor
650	550	450	300	250

NRA Type Altered to M2

Exc.	V.G.	Good	Fair	Poor
550	500	400	300	250

Model M2

This is an improved version of the Model 1922 M1 that features an altered firing mechanism with a faster lock time. It has a knurled cocking knob added to the bolt and a flush-fitting detachable magazine with improved feeding. There were approximately 12,000 manufactured.

Exc.	V.G.	Good	Fair	Poor
600	500	400	300	200

U.S. Rifle M1 (Garand)

Springfield Armory was one of the manufacturers of this WWII service rifle. It is listed in the Garand section of this text.

SPRINGFIELD ARMS COMPANY
Springfield, Massachusetts

Dragoon

A .40 caliber percussion revolver with either a 6" or 7.5" round barrel, some fitted with loading levers, others without. The top strap marked "Springfield Arms Company". Blued with walnut grips. Approximately 110 revolvers were manufactured in 1851.

Exc.	V.G.	Good	Fair	Poor
—	—	6000	2500	950

Navy Model

A .36 caliber percussion revolver with a 6" round barrel, centrally mounted hammer, and 6-shot etched cylinder. The top strap marked "Springfield Arms Company". Blued, case hardened with walnut grips. This model was manufactured in two variations, one with a single trigger and the other with a double trigger, the forward one of which locks the cylinder. Both variations had loading levers. Approximately 250 of these pistols were made in 1851.

Exc.	V.G.	Good	Fair	Poor
—	—	2500	900	400

Belt Model

A .31 caliber percussion revolver with 4", 5", or 6" round barrels, centrally mounted hammer, and an etched 6-shot cylinder. Made with or without a loading lever. Early production versions of this revolver are marked "Jaquith's Patent 1838" on the frame and later production were marked "Springfield Arms" on the top strap. Approximately 150 were made.

Exc.	V.G.	Good	Fair	Poor
—	—	1250	500	175

Warner Model

As above, but is marked "Warner's Patent Jan. 1851." Approximately 150 of these were made.

Exc.	V.G.	Good	Fair	Poor
—	—	1000	500	150

Double Trigger Model

As above, with two triggers, one of which locks the cylinder. Approximately 100 were made in 1851.

Exc.	V.G.	Good	Fair	Poor
—	—	1000	500	150

Pocket Model Revolver

Courtesy Milwaukee Public Museum, Milwaukee, Wisconsin

A .28 caliber percussion revolver with 2.5" round barrel, centrally mounted hammer, no loading lever and etched 6-shot cylinder. Marked "Warner's Patent Jan. 1851" and "Springfield Arms Company". Blued, case hardened with walnut grips. Early production examples of this revolver do not have a groove on the cylinder and have a rounded frame. Approximately 525 were made in 1851.

Exc.	V.G.	Good	Fair	Poor
—	—	500	250	100

Ring Trigger Model

As above, but fitted with a ring trigger that revolved the cylinder. Approximately 150 were made in 1851.

Courtesy Milwaukee Public Museum, Milwaukee, Wisconsin

Exc.	V.G.	Good	Fair	Poor
—	—	750	400	200

Double Trigger Model

As above, with two triggers set within a conventional triggerguard. The forward trigger revolves the cylinder. Approximately 350 were made in 1851.

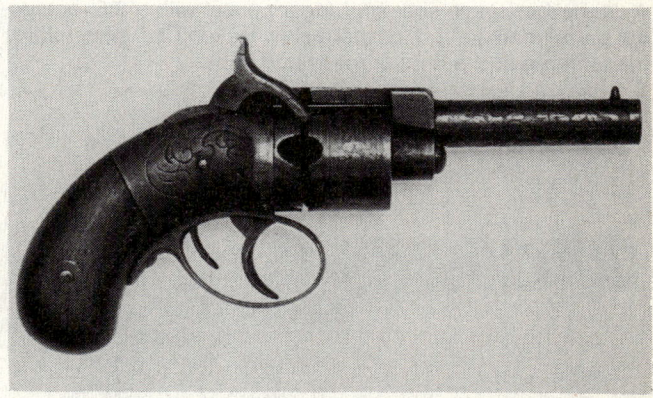

Courtesy Milwaukee Public Museum, Milwaukee, Wisconsin

Exc.	V.G.	Good	Fair	Poor
—	—	600	300	100

Late Model Revolver

As above, except that the cylinder is automatically turned when the hammer is cocked. The top strap marked "Warner's Patent/James Warner, Springfield, Mass." Approximately 500 were made in 1851.

Exc.	V.G.	Good	Fair	Poor
—	—	550	250	100

SQUIBBMAN
SEE Squires, Bingham Mfg. Co., Inc.
Rizal, Philippine Islands

SQUIRES BINGHAM MFG. CO., INC.
Rizal, Philippine Islands

Firearms produced by this company are marketed under the trademark Squibbman.

Model 100D

A .38 Special caliber double action swingout cylinder revolver with a 3", 4", or 6" ventilated rib barrel, adjustable sights, matte black finish and walnut grips.

Exc.	V.G.	Good	Fair	Poor
150	100	80	60	40

Model 100DC

As above, without the ventilated rib.

Exc.	V.G.	Good	Fair	Poor
150	100	80	60	40

Model 100

As above, with a tapered barrel and uncheckered walnut grips.

Exc.	V.G.	Good	Fair	Poor
150	100	80	60	40

Thunder Chief

As above, but in .22 or .22 Magnum caliber with a heavier ventilated rib barrel, shrouded ejector, and ebony grips.

Exc.	V.G.	Good	Fair	Poor
150	125	100	80	60

STAFFORD, T. J.
New Haven, Connecticut

Pocket Pistol

A .22 caliber single shot spur trigger pistol with a 3.5" octagonal barrel marked "T.J. Stafford New Haven Ct.," silver-plated brass frame and walnut or rosewood grips.

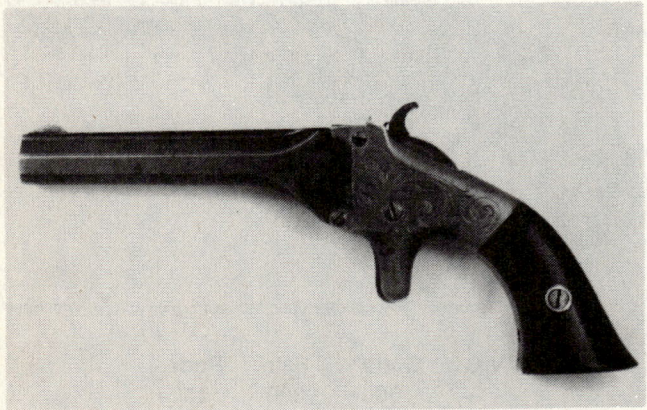

Courtesy W.P. Hallstein III and son Chip

Exc.	V.G.	Good	Fair	Poor
—	—	400	200	100

Large Frame Model

As above, but in .38 rimfire caliber with a 6" barrel.

Exc.	V.G.	Good	Fair	Poor
—	—	600	350	200

STALCAP, ALEXANDER T.F.M.
Nashville, Tennessee

First in business during the 1850's, Stalcap received a contract in 1862, to modify sporting arms for military use. Overall length 50-7/8" to 51-3/4"; octagonal barrels 35-1/4" - 36" turned round at muzzle for socket bayonets; .54 caliber. Rifles assembled with sporting locks, new stocks and brass furniture. At least 102 rifles were delivered in 1862. These arms are unmarked.

Prospective purchasers are strongly advised to secure an expert appraisal prior to acquisition.

Exc.	V.G.	Good	Fair	Poor
—	—	3500	2000	1000

STANDARD ARMS CO.
Wilmington, Delaware

Model G

Chambered for .25-35, .30-30, .25 Remington, .30 Remington, and .35 Remington, with a 22" barrel, and open sights. Integral box magazine and closeable gas port that allowed the rifle to be used as a slide action. Blued with a walnut stock. Produced in limited quantities, circa 1910.

Exc.	V.G.	Good	Fair	Poor
600	475	350	250	150

STAR, BONIFACIO ECHEVERRIA
Eibar, Spain
SEE Echeverria

STARR, EBAN T.
New York, New York

Single Shot Derringer

Courtesy Milwaukee Public Museum, Milwaukee, Wisconsin

A .41 caliber single shot pistol with a pivoted 2.75" round barrel. The hammer mounted on the right side of the frame and the trigger formed in the shape of a button located at the front of the frame. The frame marked "Starr's Pat's May 10, 1864". The brass frame silver-plated, the barrel blued or silver-plated with checkered walnut grips. Manufactured from 1864 to 1869.

Exc.	V.G.	Good	Fair	Poor
—	—	1000	500	200

Four Barreled Pepperbox

A .32 caliber 4 barreled pocket pistol with 2.75" to 3.25" barrels. The frame marked "Starr's Pat's May 10, 1864". Brass frames, silver-plated. The barrel is blued with plain walnut grips. This pistol was produced in six variations as follows:

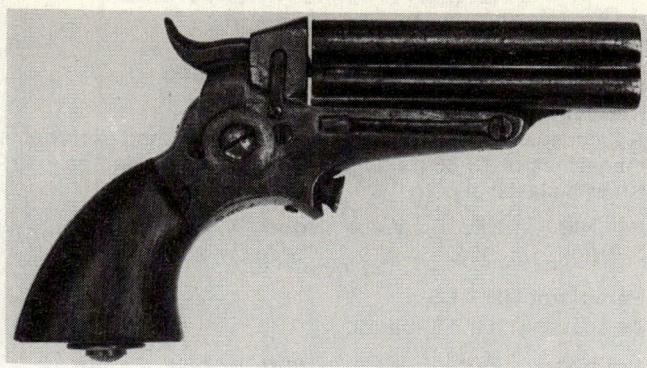

Courtesy Milwaukee Public Museum, Milwaukee, Wisconsin

First Model
Fluted breech and a barrel release mounted on the right side of the frame.

Exc.	V.G.	Good	Fair	Poor
—	—	1250	500	200

Second Model
Flat breech.

Exc.	V.G.	Good	Fair	Poor
—	—	950	400	200

Third Model
Rounded breech with a visible firing-pin retaining spring.

Exc.	V.G.	Good	Fair	Poor
—	—	800	350	150

Fourth Model
Rounded breech without visible springs.

Exc.	V.G.	Good	Fair	Poor
—	—	700	300	150

Fifth Model
A larger, more angular grip.

Exc.	V.G.	Good	Fair	Poor
—	—	650	300	150

Sixth Model
The frame length of this variation is of increased size.

Exc.	V.G.	Good	Fair	Poor
—	—	1000	500	200

STARR ARMS COMPANY
New York, New York

1858 Navy Revolver
A .36 caliber double action percussion revolver with a 6" barrel and 6-shot cylinder. Blued, case hardened with walnut grips. The frame marked "Starr Arms Co. New York." Approximately 3,000 were made between 1858 and 1860.

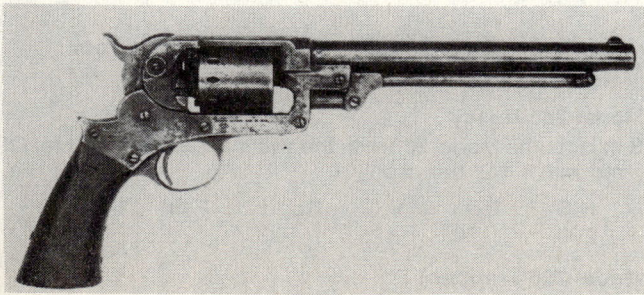

Courtesy Milwaukee Public Museum, Milwaukee, Wisconsin

Standard Model

Exc.	V.G.	Good	Fair	Poor
—	—	2000	900	300

Martially Marked (JT)

Exc.	V.G.	Good	Fair	Poor
—	—	3000	1250	500

1858 Army Revolver
A .44 caliber double action percussion revolver with a 6" barrel and 6-shot cylinder. Blued, case hardened with walnut grips. The frame marked "Starr Arms Co. New York". Approximately 23,000 were manufactured.

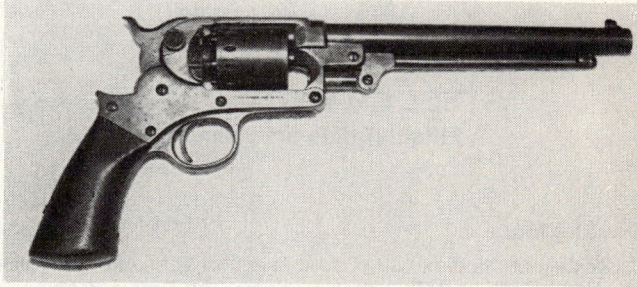

Exc.	V.G.	Good	Fair	Poor
—	—	1500	700	250

1863 Army Revolver
Similar to the above, but double action and with an 8" barrel. Approximately 32,000 were manufactured between 1863 and 1865.

Courtesy Milwaukee Public Museum, Milwaukee, Wisconsin

Exc.	V.G.	Good	Fair	Poor
—	—	2000	900	350

Percussion Carbine
A .54 caliber breechloading percussion carbine with a 21" round barrel secured by one barrel band. Blued, case hardened with a walnut stock. The lock marked "Starr Arms Co./Yonkers, N.Y."

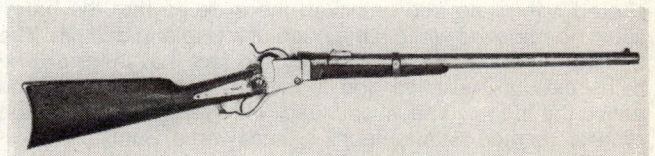

Courtesy Milwaukee Public Museum, Milwaukee, Wisconsin

Exc.	V.G.	Good	Fair	Poor
—	—	2000	950	400

Cartridge Carbine

Similar to the above, but in .52 rimfire caliber. Approximately 5,000 were manufactured.

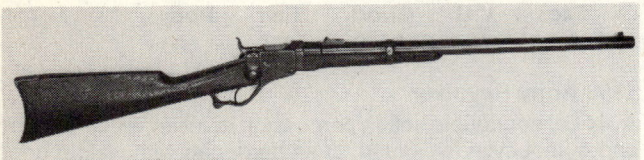

Courtesy Milwaukee Public Museum, Milwaukee, Wisconsin

Exc.	V.G.	Good	Fair	Poor
—	—	1800	700	350

STEEL CITY ARMS, INC.
Pittsburgh, Pennsylvania

Double Deuce

A .22 caliber stainless steel double action semiautomatic pistol with a 2.5" barrel, 7-shot magazine and plain rosewood grips. Introduced in 1984.

Exc.	V.G.	Good	Fair	Poor
300	250	200	150	100

STENDA WAFFENFABRIK
Suhl, Germany

Pocket Pistol

A 7.65mm semiautomatic pistol similar to the "Beholla," the "Leonhardt," and the "Menta." Stenda took over the production of the Beholla pistol design at the close of WWI. The only major difference in the Stenda design was the elimination of the Beholla's worst feature, the pin that went through the slide and retained the barrel. It was replaced by a sliding catch that anchored it in place and unlocked the slide so that the barrel could be removed without the need of a vise and drift pin. The Stenda pistol can be identified by the fact that there are no holes through the slide and there is a catch on the frame above the trigger. The finish blued, with plastic grips; and the slide is marked "Waffenfabrik Stendawerke Suhl." Approximately 25,000 manufactured before production ceased in 1926.

Exc.	V.G.	Good	Fair	Poor
300	250	200	150	100

STERLING ARMAMENT LTD.
London, England
Importer-Cassi, Inc.
Colorado Springs, Colorado

Parapistol MK 7 C4

A 9mm semiautomatic pistol with a 4" barrel, and detachable magazines of 10-68-round capacity. Black wrinkled paint finish with plastic grips.

NIB	Exc.	V.G.	Good	Fair	Poor
600	500	450	350	250	150

Parapistol MK 7 C8

As above, with a 7.8" barrel.

NIB	Exc.	V.G.	Good	Fair	Poor
625	525	450	350	250	150

Sterling MK 6

A semiautomatic copy of the Sterling submachine gun with a 16.1" barrel, folding metal stock and side mounted magazine. Finished as above.

NIB	Exc.	V.G.	Good	Fair	Poor
650	550	500	400	275	175

Sterling AR 180

A copy of the Armalite Model AR18, 5.56mm rifle. Finished with either black wrinkled paint or, more rarely, blued.

NIB	Exc.	V.G.	Good	Fair	Poor
900	800	700	500	350	200

STERLING ARMS CORPORATION
Gasport, New York

Model 283 Target 300

This pistol is similar in appearance to Hi-Standard semiautomatic pistols. Chambered for the .22 Long Rifle cartridge it was offered with 4", 4-1/2", or 8" barrels. Rear sight is adjustable and magazine holds 10 rounds. Grips are black plastic. Weight is approximately 36 oz.

NIB	Exc.	V.G.	Good	Fair	Poor
200	150	125	100	75	60

Model 284 Target 300L

Similar to the above model except for 4-1/2" or 6" tapered barrel with barrel band.

NIB	Exc.	V.G.	Good	Fair	Poor
225	175	125	100	75	60

Model 285 Husky

Similar to the Model 283 with the exception of fixed sights. Offered with 4-1/2" barrel only.

NIB	Exc.	V.G.	Good	Fair	Poor
200	150	125	100	75	60

Model 286 Trapper

Similar to the Model 284 except for fixed sights.

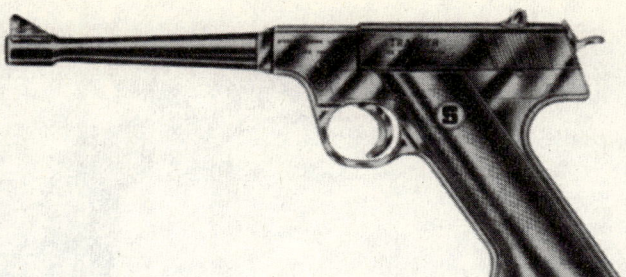

NIB	Exc.	V.G.	Good	Fair	Poor
200	150	125	100	75	60

Model 287 PPL .380

This is a pocketsize semiautomatic pistol chambered for the .380 ACP cartridge. Fitted with a 1" barrel it has a 5-1/4" length overall. Magazine holds 6 rounds. Weight is approximately 22 oz.

NIB	Exc.	V.G.	Good	Fair	Poor
125	75	60	50	40	30

Model PPL .22

This is a small pocket pistol similar to the Model 287 but chambered for the .22 l.r. cartridge. Barrel is 1" long. Pistol weighs about 24 oz.

NIB	Exc.	V.G.	Good	Fair	Poor
175	125	100	75	60	50

Model 300

Similar to the Model 287 but chambered for the .25 ACP cartridge. It has a 2-1/4" barrel with a 6-round magazine. Length is 5" overall and the weight is about 14 oz.

NIB	Exc.	V.G.	Good	Fair	Poor
150	125	100	75	50	40

Model 300S

This is the stainless steel version of the Model 300.

NIB	Exc.	V.G.	Good	Fair	Poor
165	135	115	75	50	40

Model 302

Identical to the Model 300 except that it is chambered for the .22 Long Rifle cartridge.

NIB	Exc.	V.G.	Good	Fair	Poor
150	125	100	75	50	40

Model 302S

Same as above but in stainless steel.

NIB	Exc.	V.G.	Good	Fair	Poor
165	135	115	75	60	50

Model 400

This is a double action semiautomatic pistol chambered for the .380 ACP cartridge with a 3-1/2" barrel. Magazine holds 7 rounds. Pistol is 6-1/2" overall and the weight is approximately 24 oz.

NIB	Exc.	V.G.	Good	Fair	Poor
200	175	150	125	100	75

Model 400S

This is the stainless steel version of the Model 400.

NIB	Exc.	V.G.	Good	Fair	Poor
225	200	175	125	100	75

Model 402

Similar to the Model 400 except chambered for the .22 Long Rifle cartridge.

NIB	Exc.	V.G.	Good	Fair	Poor
150	125	100	75	60	40

Model 450

This is a double action semiautomatic pistol chambered for the .45 ACP cartridge. Magazine holds 8-rounds. The barrel is 4" in length. Fitted with an adjustable rear sight. Blued finish and walnut grips are standard. Weight is about 36 oz.

NIB	Exc.	V.G.	Good	Fair	Poor
375	325	250	200	150	100

Model X-Caliber

A single shot .22 Long Rifle, .22 WMR, .357 Magnum, or .44 Magnum pistol with interchangeable barrels from 8" and 10". Adjustable rear sight. Finger groove grips.

NIB	Exc.	V.G.	Good	Fair	Poor
200	175	150	125	100	75

STEVENS, J. ARMS CO.
Chicopee Falls, Massachusetts

In 1864 this firm began doing business as J. Stevens & Company. In 1888 it was incorporated as the J. Stevens Arms & Tool Company. It operated as such until 1920, when it was taken over by the Savage Arms Company. It has operated as an independent division in this organization since. This company produced a great many firearms—most that were of an affordable nature. They are widely collected, and one interested in them should take advantage of the literature available on the subject.

Vest Pocket Pistol

This is a single shot pocket pistol chambered for the .22 and the .30 rimfire cartridges. The .22 caliber version is rarely encountered and would be worth approximately 10% more than the values illustrated. It has a 2.75" part-octagonal barrel that pivots upward for loading. It has an external hammer and a spur-type trigger. The frame is nickel-plated or blued, with a blued barrel. The odd shaped flared grips are made of rosewood. The first models were marked "Vest Pocket Pistol" only. Later models have the barrels marked "J. Stevens & Co. Chicopee Falls, Mass." There were approximately 1,000 manufactured between 1864 and 1876.

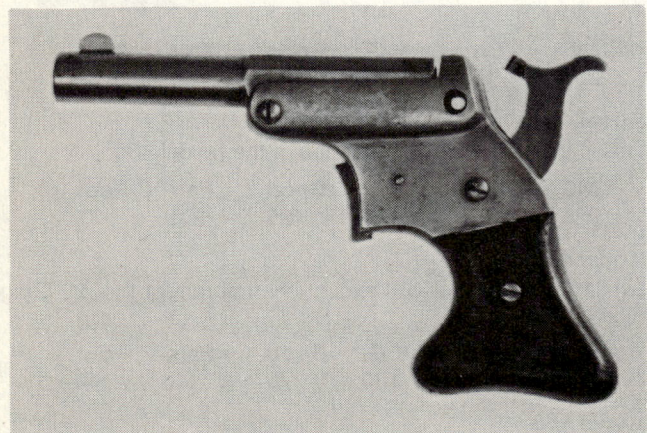

Courtesy Milwaukee Public Museum, Milwaukee, Wisconsin

Exc.	V.G.	Good	Fair	Poor
1600	1400	1200	1000	700

Pocket Pistol

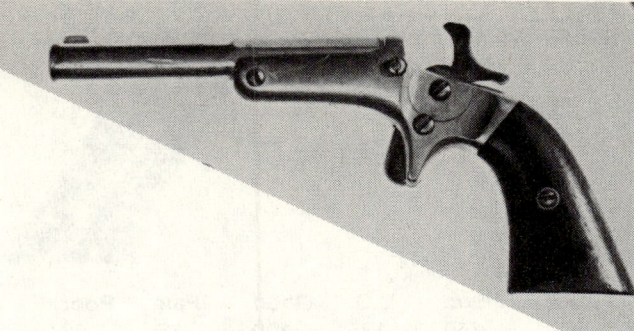

Courtesy Milwaukee Public Museum, Milwaukee, Wisconsin

This is a more conventional-appearing, single shot pocket pistol chambered for either the .22 or the .30 rimfire cartridges. It has a 3.5" part-octagonal barrel that pivots upward for loading. It features a plated brass frame with either a blued or nickel-plated barrel and rosewood, two-piece grips. The barrel is marked "J. Stevens & Co. Chicopee Falls, Mass." There were approximately 15,000 manufactured between 1864 and 1886.

Exc.	V.G.	Good	Fair	Poor
350	275	200	100	75

Gem Pocket Pistol

This is a single shot, derringer-type pocket pistol chambered for either the .22 or .30 rimfire cartridges. It has a 3" part-octagonal barrel that pivots to the side for loading. It has a nickel-plated brass frame with either a blued or plated barrel. It has bird's-head grips made of walnut or rosewood. The barrel is marked "Gem". The Stevens name or address does not appear on this firearm. There were approximately 4,000 manufactured between 1872 and 1890.

Exc.	V.G.	Good	Fair	Poor
600	500	350	300	200

.41 Caliber Derringer

This is a single shot pocket pistol chambered for the .22 or .31 Caliber rimfire cartridge. It has a 4" part-octagonal barrel that pivots upward for loading. It has a spur trigger and an external hammer. The frame is plated brass with a blued barrel. It has walnut bird's-head grips. This firearm is completely unmarked except for a serial number. There were approximately 100 manufactured in 1875.

.22 Caliber

Exc.	V.G.	Good	Fair	Poor
2600	2300	1800	1200	800

.31 Caliber

Exc.	V.G.	Good	Fair	Poor
2100	1800	1300	1000	500

Single Shot Pistol

This is a single shot pistol chambered for the .22 or .30 rimfire cartridges. It has a 3.5" part-octagonal barrel that pivots upward for loading. It is quite similar in appearance to the original pocket pistol. It has a plated brass frame and either a blued or nickel-plated barrel with walnut, square-butt grips. The barrel is marked "J. Stevens A&T Co." There were approximately 10,000 manufactured between 1886 and 1896.

Exc.	V.G.	Good	Fair	Poor
400	250	200	150	100

No. 41 Pistol

This is a single shot pocket pistol chambered for the .22 and .30 Short cartridges. It has a 3.5" part-octagonal barrel that pivots upward for loading. It features an external hammer and a spur-type trigger. It has an iron frame with the firing pin mounted in the recoil shield. It is either blued or nickel-plated, with square butt walnut grips. There were approximately 90,000 manufactured between 1896 and 1916.

Exc.	V.G.	Good	Fair	Poor
350	300	250	200	100

Stevens Tip Up Rifles

This series of rifles was produced by Stevens beginning in the 1870s through 1895. There are a number of variations, but they are all quite similar in appearance. They feature a distinctive sloped frame made of iron and nickel-plated. Most frames are similar in size, but there is a slightly lighter frame used on the "Ladies Model" rifles. These Tip Up rifles are chambered for various calibers from the .22 rimfire to the .44 centerfire cartridges. They are offered with barrel lengths of 24", 26", 28", or 30". The actions are nickel-plated, as well as the triggerguards and the buttplates. The barrels are blued, and the two-piece stocks are of walnut. They are offered with various buttplates and sights. A shotgun version is also offered. There are a number of variations that differ only slightly, and the model numbers are not marked on the rifles. We suggest securing a qualified appraisal if in doubt. The major variations and their values are as follows:

Courtesy Milwaukee Public Museum, Milwaukee, Wisconsin

Ladies Model-.22 or.25 Rimfire Only, 24" or 26" Barrel.

Exc.	V.G.	Good	Fair	Poor
2500	2000	1500	1000	500

Tip Up Rifle-Without Forend

Exc.	V.G.	Good	Fair	Poor
500	400	300	200	150

Tip Up Rifle-With Forend, Swiss-Type Buttplate

Exc.	V.G.	Good	Fair	Poor
800	600	350	250	175

Tip Up Shotgun-All Gauges, 30" or 32" Barrel

Exc.	V.G.	Good	Fair	Poor
350	300	200	150	100

Ideal Single Shot Rifle

This excellent rifle was manufactured by Stevens between 1896 and 1933. It is a single-shot, falling-block type action that is activated by a triggerguard-action lever. It was produced in many popular calibers from .22 rimfire up to .30-40. It was also manufactured in a number of special Stevens calibers. It was offered with various length barrels in many different grades, from plain Spartan starter rifles up to some extremely high-grade Schuetzen-type target rifles with all available options. In 1901 Harry Pope of Hartford, Connecticut, went to work for Stevens and brought his highly respected barrel to the Stevens Company. He remained an employee for only two years, and the firearms produced during this period have the name "Stevens-Pope" stamped on the top of the barrel in addition to the other factory markings. Rifles marked in this manner and authenticated would be worth an approximate 50% premium if they are in very good to excellent condition. Due to numerous variations and options offered, we strongly recommend securing a qualified appraisal, especially on the higher-grade Ideal series rifles, if a transaction is contemplated.

No. 44

This version is chambered for various calibers and is offered with a 24" or 26" barrel. It has an open rear sight with a Rocky Mountain-type front sight. The finish is blued and casecolored, with a walnut stock. There were approximately 100,000 manufactured between 1896 and 1933.

Exc.	V.G.	Good	Fair	Poor
900	700	400	250	150

No. 44-1/2

This rifle is similar in appearance to the No. 44 but features an improved action. It has barrel lengths up to 34" and will be found with the Stevens-Pope barrel. It was manufactured between 1903 and 1916.

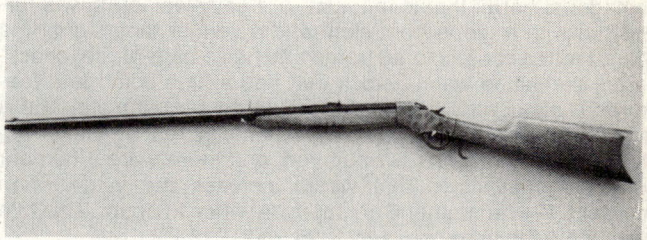

Courtesy J. B. Barnes

Exc.	V.G.	Good	Fair	Poor
1300	1100	800	600	400

No. 044-1/2

This version is also known as the English Model rifle and is similar to the No. 44-1/2 except that it has a shotgun butt and a tapered barrel. There were a number of options offered that would affect the value. It was manufactured between 1903 and 1916.

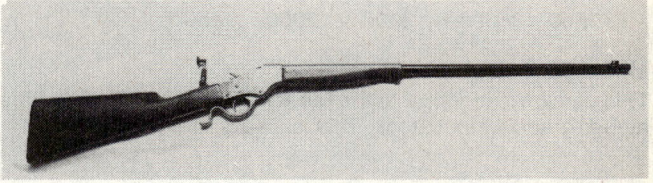

Courtesy Mike Stuckslager

Exc.	V.G.	Good	Fair	Poor
1300	1100	800	600	400

No. 45

This version is also known as the Range Rifle, It is chambered for various calibers from the .22 rimfire to .44-40. Its identifying features are the Beach sights with an additional vernier tang sight and a Swiss-type butt stock. It is offered with a 26" or 28" part-octagonal barrel. It was manufactured between 1896 and 1916. Values for a standard version are as follows:

Exc.	V.G.	Good	Fair	Poor
1400	1200	900	700	500

NOTE: Deduct 25% for .44 action.

No. 46

Same as the No. 45 but with a fancy wood stock. Manufactured from 1896 to 1902. Built in No. 44 action only.

Exc.	V.G.	Good	Fair	Poor
1800	1500	1200	1000	750

No. 47

This version is similar to the No. 45, with a pistol grip butt stock.

Exc.	V.G.	Good	Fair	Poor
2800	2500	2200	1600	1000

NOTE: Deduct 25% for .44 action.

No. 48

Same as the No. 47 but with a fancy wood checkered stock. Manufactured from 1896 to 1902. Built in a No. 44 action only. This is a very rare model.

Exc.	V.G.	Good	Fair	Poor
3000	2700	2200	1650	1100

No. 49

This model is also known as the "Walnut Hill Rifle." It is a high grade target rifle chambered for many calibers between the .22 rimfire and the .44-40. It is offered with a 28" or 30" part-octagonal barrel that is medium- or heavy-weight. It is furnished with a globe front sight and a vernier tang sight. It is blued with a case-colored frame and has a high-grade, checkered, varnished walnut stock that has a high comb and features a pistol grip, cheek piece, Swiss-type buttplate, and a loop-type triggerguard lever that resembles that of a lever-action rifle. The receiver is engraved, and there were a number of options available that would increase the value when present. We recommend an appraisal when in doubt. This rifle was manufactured between 1896 and 1916.

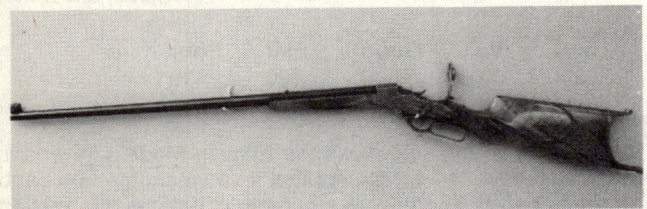

Courtesy J.B. Barnes

Exc.	V.G.	Good	Fair	Poor
5500	5000	3000	2000	1500

Model 50

This version is identical to the Model 49 but was offered with a higher-grade walnut stock. This is a very rare model.

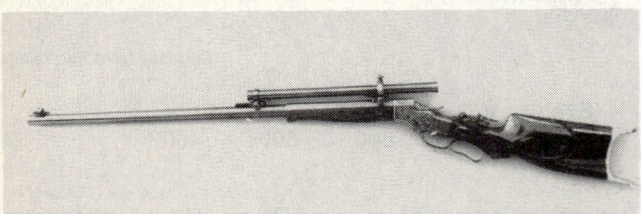

Courtesy J.B. Barnes

Exc.	V.G.	Good	Fair	Poor
6000	5500	3500	2200	1600

Model 51

This version is known as the "Schuetzen Rifle" and is quite similar to the No. 49 except that it features double-set triggers, a higher-grade walnut stock, a wooden insert in the triggerguard action lever, and a heavy, Schuetzen-type buttplate. There were many options available on this model, and we recommend securing an appraisal when in doubt. It was manufactured between 1896 and 1916.

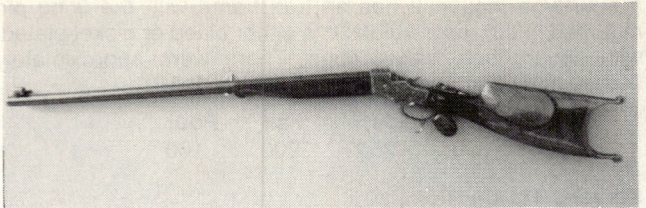

Courtesy J.B. Barnes

Exc.	V.G.	Good	Fair	Poor
9500	7500	5000	3000	2000

No. 52

This version is also known as the "Schuetzen Junior." It is similar to the No. 51 except that it features more engraving and a higher-grade walnut stock. It was manufactured between 1897 and 1916.

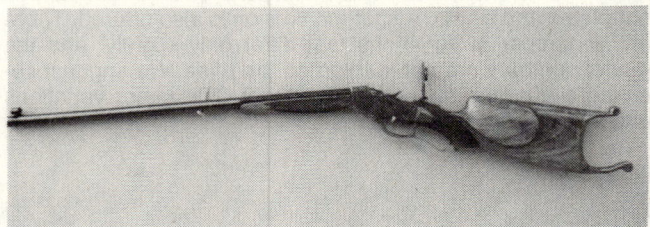

Courtesy J.B. Barnes

Exc.	V.G.	Good	Fair	Poor
9000	7000	4500	2500	1500

No. 53

This model is the same as the No. 51 except for the addition of a fancy wood stock and palm rest. Produced from 1896 to 1902 and offered only with a No. 44 action. This is a rare rifle.

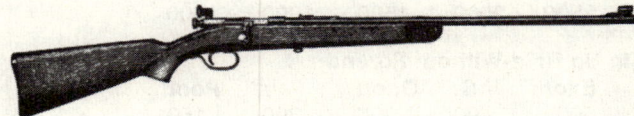

Exc.	V.G.	Good	Fair	Poor
11500	8750	6000	3750	2500

No. 54

This is similar to the No. 52 except that it has double-set triggers and a palm rest, as well as a heavy, Swiss-style buttplate. It is offered with a 30" or 32" part-octagonal heavy barrel. This was Stevens' top-of-the-line rifle. It was offered with many options, and an appraisal should be secured if in doubt. It was manufactured between 1897 and 1916.

Courtesy J.B. Barnes

Exc.	V.G.	Good	Fair	Poor
12000	10000	7000	5000	4000

NOTE: The above prices are based on a #44-1/2 action. A #44 action will bring 20% less than the prices listed above.

No. 55

This version is one of the Stevens' Ideal Ladies Models. It is chambered for the smaller rimfire calibers between .22 Short and .32 Long rimfire. It features a 24" or 26" part-octagonal barrel with a vernier tang sight. The finish is blued and case-colored, with a checkered pistol grip walnut stock that features a Swiss-type buttplate. This is a lighter weight rifle that was manufactured between 1897 and 1916.

Exc.	V.G.	Good	Fair	Poor
3000	2500	1400	800	600

No. 56

This Ladies' Model rifle is similar to the No. 55 except that it is chambered for centerfire cartridges and has a higher-grade walnut stock. It was made on the improved No. 44-1/2 action. It was manufactured between 1906 and 1916.

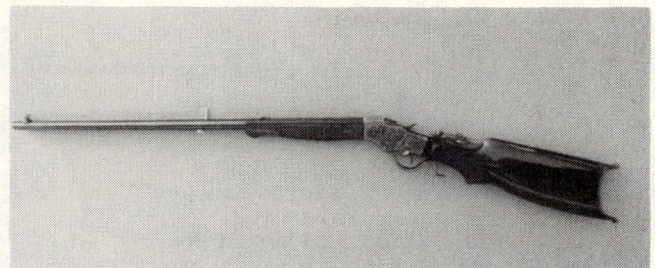

Courtesy J.B. Barnes

Exc.	V.G.	Good	Fair	Poor
3600	2900	2000	1300	700

No. 404

This version is chambered for the .22 rimfire cartridge only. It features a 28" round barrel with a globe front sight and a Lyman No. 42 receiver sight. The finish is blued and case-colored. It has a walnut straight-grip stock with a semi-beavertail forend. It features a shotgun-type buttplate. It was manufactured between 1910 and 1916.

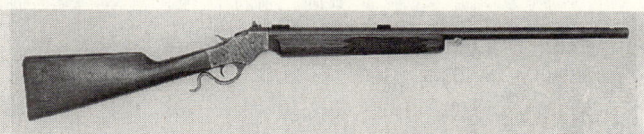

Exc.	V.G.	Good	Fair	Poor
1000	800	600	400	300

No. 414

This version is also known as the Armory Model and is chambered for the .22 l.r. cartridge only. It was built on a No. 44 action and features a 26" round barrel. It has a Rocky Mountain front sight with a Lyman receiver sight at the rear. The finish is blued and case-colored, with a straight-grip walnut stock and forend held on by a single barrel band. It was manufactured between 1912 and 1932.

Courtesy Mike Stuckslager

Exc.	V.G.	Good	Fair	Poor
650	500	400	250	250

BOYS RIFLES

The Stevens Company produced an extensive line of smaller, single shot rifles chambered for small calibers and intended primarily for use by young shooters. These firearms have become quite collectible and are considered a field of specialty by many modern collectors. There are many variations that were available with a number of options that would affect their value. We supply information and values for the major variations but would recommend securing a qualified appraisal if in doubt.

"Favorite" Rifles

This series of rifles is chambered for the .22, .25, and .32 rimfire. It has a 22" part-octagonal barrel and is blued, with a case-colored frame. It has a takedown-type action with an interchangeable barrel feature. It was available with optional sights, as well as buttplates. There were approximately 1,000,000 manufactured between 1893 and 1939. The variations are as follows:

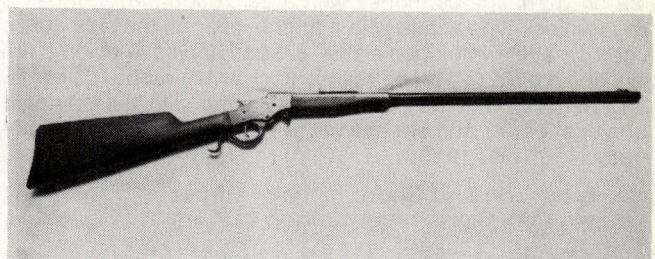

Courtesy Mike Stuckslager

Courtesy Buffalo Bill Historical Center, Cody, Wyoming

1st Model Favorite

This version is chambered for the .22 or .25 rimfire cartridge. It has a removable sideplate on the right side of the receiver not found on any other variation. There were approximately 1,000 manufactured between 1893 and 1894.

Exc.	V.G.	Good	Fair	Poor
1200	800	650	500	350

No. 17

This is the standard, plain version with open sights.

Exc.	V.G.	Good	Fair	Poor
450	300	250	175	125

No. 20

This version is chambered for the .22 or .32 rimfire shot cartridges and has a smoothbore barrel and no rear sight.

Exc.	V.G.	Good	Fair	Poor
500	350	250	175	125

No. 21

This version is known as the Bicycle rifle and features a 20" barrel with open sights standard. It was furnished with a canvas carrying case that would be worth approximately a 10% premium. It was manufactured between 1898 and 1903.

Exc.	V.G.	Good	Fair	Poor
500	300	200	150	100

No. 21 Ladies Model

This version bears the same model number as the Bicycle rifle but has a 24" barrel and a high grade, checkered walnut stock with a Swiss buttplate. It features a vernier tang sight. It was manufactured between 1910 and 1916.

Exc.	V.G.	Good	Fair	Poor
3000	2500	1400	700	400

No. 16

This version is known as the "Crack Shot." It is chambered for .22 or .32 rimfire cartridges with a 20" round barrel. It has a rolling-block-type action with a thumb lever on the side. It is a utility-type rifle with open sights, a blued and case-colored finish, and a plain two-piece walnut stock with a rubber buttplate. The barrel is marked "Crack Shot" along with the standard Stevens' barrel address markings. It was manufactured between 1900 and 1913.

Exc.	V.G.	Good	Fair	Poor
350	250	125	100	75

No. 16-1/2

This version is similar to the No. 16 except that it is chambered for the .32 rimfire shot cartridge with a smoothbore barrel. It was manufactured between 1900 and 1913.

Exc.	V.G.	Good	Fair	Poor
400	300	175	125	100

No. 23-Sure Shot

This version is chambered for the .22 rimfire cartridge. It has a 20" round barrel that pivots to the right for loading. There is a barrel release on the frame. This version is blued and case-colored, with a plain walnut buttstock and no forend. It was manufactured between 1894 and 1897.

Exc.	V.G.	Good	Fair	Poor
1500	1100	700	500	300

No. 15

This version is also known as the "Maynard Junior." It is chambered for the .22 rimfire cartridge and has an 18" part-octagonal barrel. The action is similar to the Civil War Maynard rifle with a triggerguard-activating lever. The finish is all blued, with a bored-type buttstock and no forearm. The barrel is marked "Stevens Maynard, J. R." in addition to the standard Stevens' barrel address. It was manufactured between 1902 and 1912.

Courtesy Mike Stuckslager

Exc.	V.G.	Good	Fair	Poor
450	350	200	150	100

No. 15-1/2

This is a smoothbore version of the No. 15.

Exc.	V.G.	Good	Fair	Poor
500	400	250	175	125

No. 14

This version is also known as the "Little Scout." It is a utility, takedown rifle that is blued, with a one-piece bored-type stock. It features a rolling-block-type action and was manufactured between 1906 and 1910.

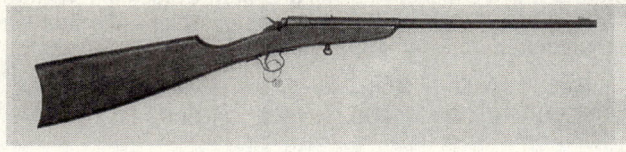

Exc.	V.G.	Good	Fair	Poor
400	350	200	150	125

No. 14-1/2

This version is similar to the No. 14 except that it has a two-piece stock. It is also marked "Little Scout." It was manufactured between 1911 and 1941.

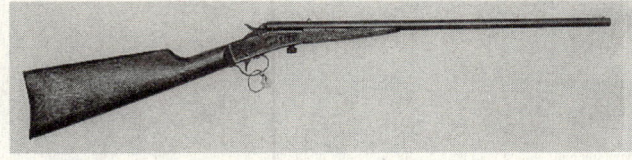

Exc.	V.G.	Good	Fair	Poor
350	250	175	100	75

No. 65

This version is known as the "Little Krag." It is a single shot bolt-action rifle chambered for the .22 rimfire cartridge. It has a one-piece stock and a 20" round barrel that was marked "Little Krag." This version is quite scarce. It was manufactured between 1903 and 1910.

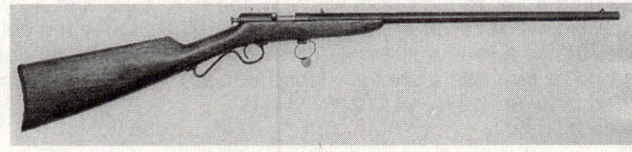

Exc.	V.G.	Good	Fair	Poor
550	450	300	200	150

No. 12

This version is also known as the "Marksman." It is chambered for the .22, .25, and the .32 rimfire cartridges. It has a 22" barrel that pivots upward for loading. It is activated by an S-shaped triggerguard lever. It was manufactured between 1911 and 1930.

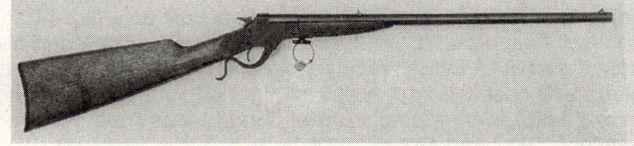

Courtesy Mike Stuckslager

Exc.	V.G.	Good	Fair	Poor
350	300	225	175	125

No. 26

This version is also known as the "Crack Shot." It has a rolling block-type action and is chambered for .22 or the .32 rimfire cartridges. It is offered with an 18" or 20" round barrel. It is blued and has a two-piece stock. It was manufactured between 1912 and 1939.

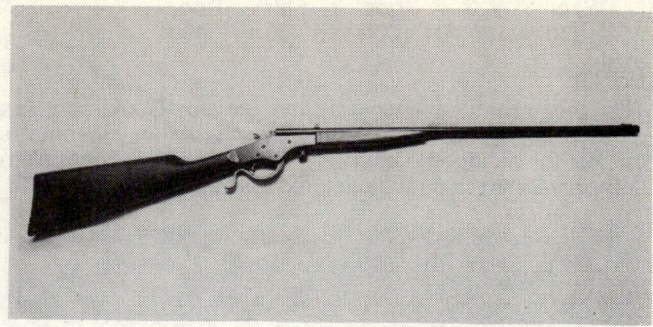

Courtesy Mike Stuckslager

Exc.	V.G.	Good	Fair	Poor
350	300	225	175	125

No. 26-1/2

This is the smoothbore version of the No. 26.

Exc.	V.G.	Good	Fair	Poor
400	350	225	175	125

No. 11-Junior

This is a single shot, rolling block rifle chambered for the .22 rimfire cartridge. It has a 20" barrel, is blued, and has a bore-type stock without a buttplate. This was the last model offered in the Boys Rifle series. It was manufactured between 1924 and 1931.

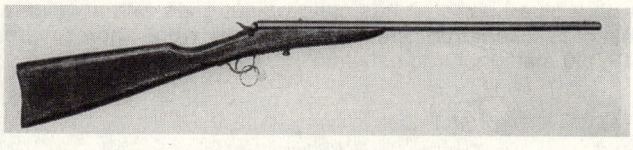

Exc.	V.G.	Good	Fair	Poor
350	300	175	100	75

Model 71

This was a reintroduced version of the "Stevens Favorite." It is chambered for the .22 l.r. cartridge and has a 22" octagonal barrel. The finish is blued and case-colored, with a plain walnut stock that has an inlaid medallion and a crescent buttplate. There were 10,000 manufactured in 1971.

Exc.	V.G.	Good	Fair	Poor
300	225	150	100	75

Model 72

This is a reintroduced version of the "Crack Shot" that features a single-shot, falling block action. It is chambered for the .22 rimfire cartridge and has a 22" octagon barrel with open sights. It is blued and case-colored, with a straight walnut stock. It was introduced in 1972.

Exc.	V.G.	Good	Fair	Poor
175	150	125	100	75

Model 70

This is a slide-action rifle chambered for the .22 rimfire cartridge. It is also known as the "Visible Loading Rifle." It features a 20" round barrel with a 3/4-length, tubular magazine. The finish is blued and case-colored, and it has a walnut stock. It features open sights but was available with other options. It was offered as the No. 70-1/2, 71, 71-112, 72, and 72-1/2. These different model numbers denote various sight combinations. Otherwise, they are identical. They were manufactured between 1907 and 1932.

Exc.	V.G.	Good	Fair	Poor
350	300	200	150	100

No. 80

This is a slide-action repeating rifle chambered for the .22 rimfire cartridge. It has a 24" round barrel with a tubular magazine. It features open sights and is blued, with a walnut stock. It was manufactured between 1906 and 1910.

Exc.	V.G.	Good	Fair	Poor
450	350	225	175	125

High Power Rifle

This is a series of lever-action hunting rifles chambered for the .25, .30-30, .32, and the .35 centerfire cartridges. It features a 22" round barrel with a tubular magazine. The finish is blued, with a walnut stock. It is available in four variations: the No. 425, No. 430, No. 435, and the No. 440. These designations denote increased ornamentation and high quality materials and workmanship used in construction. There were approximately 26,000 manufactured between 1910 and 1917.

No. 425

Exc.	V.G.	Good	Fair	Poor
600	500	400	300	200

No. 430

Exc.	V.G.	Good	Fair	Poor
750	650	550	400	300

No. 435

Exc.	V.G.	Good	Fair	Poor
1400	1100	800	600	400

No.440

Exc.	V.G.	Good	Fair	Poor
2800	2500	2100	1600	850

Model 89

This is a single shot, Martini-type, falling-block rifle chambered for the .22 l.r. cartridge. It has an 18.5" barrel and a trigger-guard loop-lever activator. The finish is blued, with a straight walnut stock. It was introduced in 1976 and is no longer manufactured.

Exc.	V.G.	Good	Fair	Poor
100	80	70	60	40

Model 987

This is a blowback-operated semiautomatic rifle chambered for the .22 l.r. cartridge. It has a 20" barrel with a 15-round tubular magazine. The finish is blued, with a hardwood stock.

Exc.	V.G.	Good	Fair	Poor
120	100	90	80	60

Beginning in 1869 the Stevens Company produced a series of single-shot, break-open target and sporting pistols that pivot upward for loading. They are chambered for the .22 and the .25 rimfire cartridges, as well as various centerfire cartridges from the .32 short Colt to the .44 Russian. These pistols were made with various barrel lengths and have either a spur trigger or conventional trigger with a guard. They are all single-actions with exposed hammers. The finishes are nickel-plated frames with blued barrels and walnut grips. These variations and their values are as follows:

Six-inch Pocket Rifle

This version is chambered for the .22 rimfire cartridge and has a 6" part-octagonal barrel with open sights. The barrel is marked "J. Stevens & Co. Chicopee Falls, Mass." There were approximately 1,000 manufactured between 1869 and 1886.

Exc.	V.G.	Good	Fair	Poor
500	400	350	200	125

No. 36

This version is known as the Stevens-Lord pistol. It is chambered for various rimfire and centerfire calibers up to .44 Russian. It is offered with a 10" or 12" part-octagonal barrel and features a firing pin in the frame with a bushing. It has a conventional trigger with a spurred triggerguard. It features the standard Stevens' barrel address. It was named after Frank Lord, a target shooter well-known at this time. There were approximately 3,500 manufactured from 1880 to 1911.

Courtesy J.B. Barnes

Exc.	V.G.	Good	Fair	Poor
1200	1000	800	500	300

First Issue Stevens-Conlin

This version is chambered for the .22 or .32 rimfire cartridges. It has a 10" or 12" part-octagonal barrel. It features a plated brass frame with a blued barrel and checkered walnut grips with a weighted buttcap. This version has a spur trigger either with or without a triggerguard. It was named after James Conlin, the owner of a shooting gallery located in New York City. There were approximately 500 manufactured between 1880 and 1884.

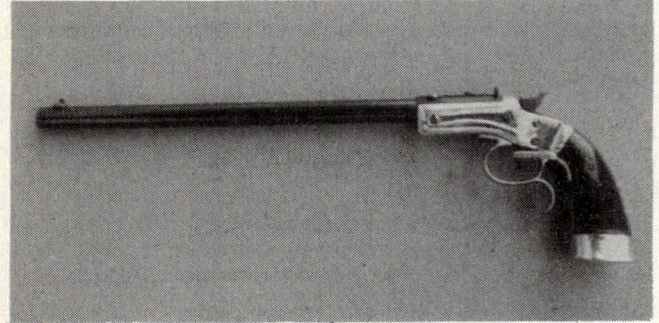

Courtesy J.B. Barnes

Exc.	V.G.	Good	Fair	Poor
2500	2100	1600	900	500

Second Issue Stevens-Conlin No. 38

This version is similar to the First Issue, with a conventional trigger and spurred triggerguard, as well as a fully adjustable rear sight. There were approximately 6,000 manufactured between 1884 and 1903.

Exc.	V.G.	Good	Fair	Poor
1400	1200	1000	700	400

No. 37

This version is also known as the Stevens-Gould and was named after a nineteenth century firearms writer. It resembles the No. 38 without the spur on the triggerguard. There were approximately 1,000 manufactured between 1889 and 1903.

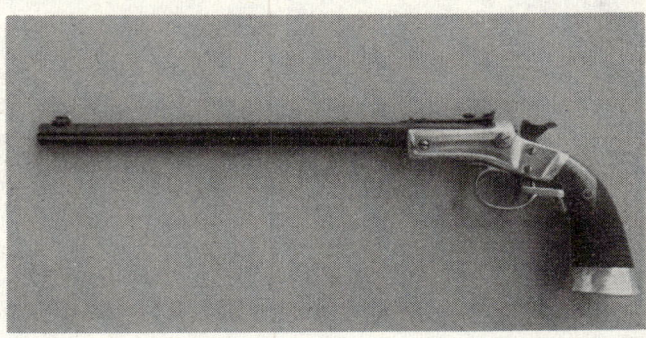

Courtesy J.B. Barnes

Exc.	V.G.	Good	Fair	Poor
1800	1600	1200	800	400

No. 35

This version is chambered for the .22 rimfire, the .22 Stevens-Pope, and the .25 Stevens cartridges. It is offered with a 6", 8", 10", or 12.25" part-octagonal barrel. The firing pin has no bushing. It features an iron frame that is either blued or plated with a blued barrel. It has plain walnut grips with a weighted buttcap. It featured open sights. There were approximately 43,000 manufactured between 1923 and 1942.

Exc.	V.G.	Good	Fair	Poor
450	325	275	175	100

NOTE: Longer barrels worth a premium.

No. 35 Target

This version is similar to the No. 35 but has a better quality triggerguard and sights. There were approximately 35,000 manufactured between 1907 and 1916.

Exc.	V.G.	Good	Fair	Poor
500	400	325	200	100

STEVENS NO. 35 OFF-HAND SHOTGUN NFA, CURIO OR RELIC

Stevens No. 35 Auto-Shot

The Stevens No. 35 is a .410 bore pistol manufactured by the J. Stevens Arms Co., Chicopee Falls, Massachusetts. It was available with an 8" or 12.25" smooth bore barrel, for 2.5" shells only, in two variations: the **Off-Hand Shot Gun** (1923 to 1929) and the **Auto-Shot** (1929 to 1934). Total production is unknown because the .410 and .22 rimfire variations of the No.

35 share the same serial number range. Researcher Ken Cope estimates total Auto-Shot production was approximately 2,000, and Off-Hand production at 20,000 to 25,000. Production was halted after the government ruled the .410 Stevens to be a "firearm" in the "any other weapon" category under the NFA in 1934, when its retail price was about $12. The Stevens does not possess the same collector appeal as other .410 smooth bore pistols, largely because (1) its relatively light weight makes it uncomfortable as a shooter, and (2) comparatively, the gun is not particularly well made.

Off-Hand Shot Gun Serial range from 1 to 43357

Exc.	V.G.	Good	Fair	Poor
300	150	100	65	50

Auto-Shot

Exc.	V.G.	Good	Fair	Poor
350	200	150	90	65

NOTE: 8" barrel commands a 25 to 50 percent premium.

These materials are copyright © 1998 by Eric M. Larson, printed in the *Catalog* by permission of the copyright holder, and will appear in a forthcoming book on pre-NFA smooth bore shot pistols (see H&R Handy-Gun entry).

No. 43

This version is also called the Diamond and was produced in two distinct variations called the First Issue and the Second Issue. The First Issue has a brass frame; and the Second Issue, an iron frame and no firing pin bushing. Otherwise they are quite similar and would be valued the same. They are chambered for the .22 rimfire cartridge and are offered with either a 6" or 10" part-octagonal barrel. The frames are either nickel-plated or blued with blued barrels and square-butt walnut grips. There were approximately 95,000 manufactured between 1886 and 1916.

Exc.	V.G.	Good	Fair	Poor
400	300	250	150	75

NOTE: Add a 25% premium for 10" barrels.

No. 10 Target Pistol

This version was a departure from its predecessors. It very much resembles a semiautomatic pistol but is, in reality, a single-shot. It is chambered for the .22 rimfire cartridge and has an 8" round barrel that pivots upward for loading. It has a steel frame and is blued, with checkered rubber grips. Instead of the usual exposed hammer, this version has a knurled cocking piece that extends through the rear of the frame. There were approximately 7,000 manufactured between 1919 and 1933.

Exc.	V.G.	Good	Fair	Poor
400	300	200	150	100

Pocket Rifles

This series of pistols is similar to the target and sporting pistols except that these were produced with detachable shoulder stocks that bear the same serial number as the pistol with which they were sold. They are sometimes referred to as Bicycle rifles. The collector interest in these weapons is quite high; but it would behoove one to be familiar with the provisions of the Gun Control Act of 1968 when dealing in or collecting this variation—as when the stock is attached, they can fall into the category of a short-barreled rifle. Some are considered to be curios and relics, and others have been totally declassified; but some models may still be restricted. We strongly recommend securing a qualified, individual appraisal on these highly collectible firearms if a transaction is contemplated. The values we supply include the matching shoulder stock. If the stock number does not match the pistol, the values would be approximately 25% less; and with no stock at all, 50% should be deducted.

Old Model Pocket Rifle

This version is chambered for the .22 rimfire cartridge and has an 8" or 10" part-octagonal barrel. It has a spur trigger and an external hammer on which the firing pin is mounted. The extractor is spring-loaded. It has a plated brass frame, blued barrel, and either walnut or rosewood grips. The shoulder stock is either nickel-plated or black. The barrel is marked "J. Stevens & Co. Chicopee Falls, Mass." There were approximately 4,000 manufactured between 1869 and 1886.

Exc.	V.G.	Good	Fair	Poor
775	575	475	300	175

Reliable Pocket Rifle

This version is chambered for the .22 rimfire cartridge and in appearance is quite similar to the Old Model. The basic difference is that the extractor operates as a part of the pivoting barrel mechanism instead of being spring-loaded. The barrel is marked "J. Stevens A&T Co." There were approximately 4,000 manufactured between 1886 and 1896.

Exc.	V.G.	Good	Fair	Poor
700	575	475	350	250

No. 42 Reliable Pocket Rifle

This version is similar to the first issue Reliable except that it has an iron frame with the firing pin mounted in it without a bushing. The shoulder stock is shaped differently. There were approximately 8,000 manufactured between 1896 and 1916.

Exc.	V.G.	Good	Fair	Poor
650	575	475	350	250

First Issue New Model Pocket Rifle

This version is the first of the medium-frame models with a frame width of 1". All of its predecessors have a 5/8" wide frame. This model is chambered for the .22 and .32 rimfire cartridges and is offered with barrel lengths of 10", 12", 15", or 18" that are part-octagonal in configuration. The external hammer has the firing pin mounted on it. It has a plated brass frame, blued barrel, and either walnut or rosewood grips. The shoulder stock is nickel-plated and fitted differently than the small-frame models in that there is a dovetail in the butt and the top leg is secured by a knurled screw. The barrel is marked "J. Stevens & Co. Chicopee Falls, Mass." There were approximately 8,000 manufactured between 1872 and 1875.

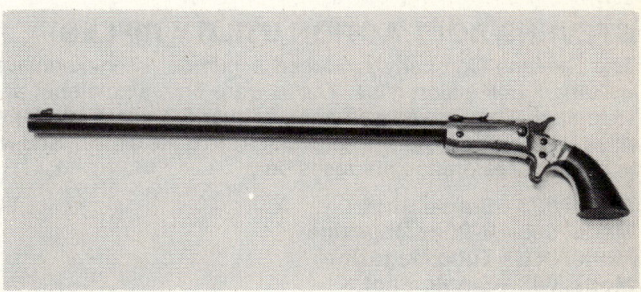

Courtesy Mike Stuckslager

Exc.	V.G.	Good	Fair	Poor
800	700	550	400	300

Second Issue New Model Pocket Rifle

This version is similar to the First Issue except that the firing pin is mounted in the frame with a bushing. There were approximately 15,000 manufactured between 1875 and 1896.

Exc.	V.G.	Good	Fair	Poor
700	600	500	400	300

Vernier Model

This version is similar to the Second Issue except that it features a vernier tang sight located on the back strap. There were approximately 1,500 manufactured between 1884 and 1896.

Exc.	V.G.	Good	Fair	Poor
850	650	550	450	200

No. 40

This version is similar to its medium-frame predecessors except that it has a longer grip frame and a conventional trigger with triggerguard. There were approximately 15,000 manufactured between 1896 and 1916.

Exc.	V.G.	Good	Fair	Poor
600	500	400	300	200

No. 40-1/2

This version is similar to the No. 40, with a vernier tang sight mounted on the back strap. There were approximately 2,500 manufactured between 1896 and 1915.

Exc.	V.G.	Good	Fair	Poor
800	700	600	500	350

No. 34

This is the first of the heavy-frame pocket rifles that featured a 1.25" wide frame. This version is also known as the "Hunter's Pet". It is chambered for many popular cartridges from the .22 rimfire to the .44-40 centerfire. It is offered with a part-octagonal 18", 20", 22", or 24" barrel. It has a nickel-plated iron frame and blued barrel. The detachable stock is nickel-plated, and the grips are walnut. There were few produced with a brass frame; and if located, these would be worth twice the value indicated. The firing pin is mounted in the frame with the bushing, and it features a spur trigger. There were approximately 4,000 manufactured between 1872 and 1900.

Exc.	V.G.	Good	Fair	Poor
950	800	500	350	250

No. 34-1/2

This version is similar to the No. 34 except that it features a vernier tang sight mounted on the back strap. There were approximately 1,200 manufactured between 1884 and 1900.

Exc.	V.G.	Good	Fair	Poor
1100	950	675	500	350

STEVENS BOLT ACTION UTILITY RIFLES

The Stevens Company produced a number of inexpensive, utilitarian, bolt-action rifles. These were both single-shot and repeaters. They have been popular over the years as starter rifles for young shooters. Their values are quite similar, and we list them for reference purposes only.

Model 053—Single Shot
Model 056—5-Shot Magazine
Model 066—Tube Magazine
Model 083—Single Shot
Model 084—5-Shot Magazine
Model 086—Tube Magazine
Model 15—Single Shot
Model 15Y—Single Shot
Model 419—Single Shot
Model 48—Single Shot
Model 49—Single Shot
Model 50—Single Shot
Model 51—Single Shot
Model 52—Single Shot
Model 53—Single Shot
Model 56—5-Shot Magazine
Model 66—Tube Magazine

Exc.	V.G.	Good	Fair	Poor
175	125	100	70	50

Model 416

This is a target rifle chambered for the .22 l.r. cartridge. It has a 24" heavy barrel with aperture sights. It features a 5-round detachable magazine and is blued, with a target-type walnut stock.

Exc.	V.G.	Good	Fair	Poor
400	350	200	150	100

Model 322

This is a bolt-action sporting rifle chambered for the .22 Hornet cartridge. It has a 20" barrel with open sights and a detachable box magazine. The finish is blued, with a plain walnut stock.

Exc.	V.G.	Good	Fair	Poor
150	125	100	75	50

Model 322-S

This version features an aperture rear sight.

Exc.	V.G.	Good	Fair	Poor
200	125	100	75	50

STEVENS SINGLE SHOT SHOTGUNS

This company manufactured a number of single barrel, break-open, single-shot shotguns. They were produced chambered for various gauges with various-length barrels and chokes. They are quite similar in appearance and were designed as inexpensive, utility-grade weapons. There is little or no collector interest in them at this time, and their values are similar. We list them for reference purposes only.

Model 100	**Model 125**	**Model 94**
Model 102	**Model 140**	**Model 944**
Model 104	**Model 160**	**Model 94A**
Model 105	**Model 165**	**Model 94C**
Model 106	**Model 170**	**Model 95**
Model 107	**Model 180**	**Model 958**
Model 108	**Model 89**	**Model 97**
Model 110	**Model 90**	**Model 970**
Model 120	**Model 93**	

Model 107

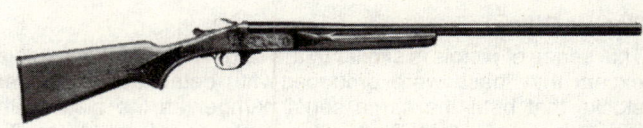

Model 94C

Exc.	V.G.	Good	Fair	Poor
130	100	75	50	25

Model 182

This is a single shot, break-open shotgun chambered for 12 gauge. It is offered with a 30" or 32" trap choked barrels and features a hammerless action with an automatic ejector and a lightly engraved receiver. The finish is blued, with a checkered trap-grade stock.

Exc.	V.G.	Good	Fair	Poor
125	100	75	50	25

Model 185

This version features a half-octagonal barrel with an automatic ejector and a checkered walnut stock.
Damascus Barrel-Deduct 25%.

Exc.	V.G.	Good	Fair	Poor
150	125	100	75	50

Model 190

This is a 12-gauge hammerless gun with an automatic ejector. It is lightly engraved with a half-octagonal barrel.
Damascus Barrel-Deduct 25%.

Exc.	V.G.	Good	Fair	Poor
150	125	100	75	50

Model 195

This is another deluxe version that features engraving, a half-octagonal barrel, and a high-grade, checkered walnut stock.
Damascus Barrel-Deduct 25%.

Exc.	V.G.	Good	Fair	Poor
275	250	200	150	100

Model 240

This over and under model features a boxlock frame with exposed hammers.

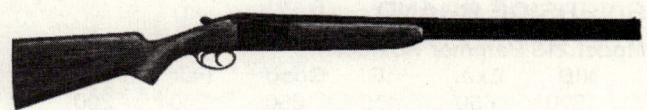

Exc.	V.G.	Good	Fair	Poor
350	300	250	200	150

STEVENS DOUBLE BARREL SHOTGUNS

The firm of J. Stevens and its successors produced a number of utility-grade, side-x-side double-barrel shotguns between 1877 and 1988. They are chambered for 10, 12, 16, or 20 gauge as well as the .410 bore. Stevens shotguns in 10 gauge and .410 bore will normally bring a premium as do guns with single triggers and ejectors. They have various length barrels and choke combinations. They feature double triggers and extractors except where noted. A complete list of Stevens brand models including the three in-house brands: Riverside, Springfield, and Super Value follow:

STEVENS BRAND

Model 1877-Hammer Boxlock

NIB	Exc.	V.G.	Good	Fair	Poor
1000	500	400	300	250	200

Model 250-Hammer Sidelock

NIB	Exc.	V.G.	Good	Fair	Poor
1000	500	400	300	250	200

Model 225-Hammer Boxlock

NIB	Exc.	V.G.	Good	Fair	Poor
1000	500	400	300	250	200

Model 260-Hammer Sidelock

NIB	Exc.	V.G.	Good	Fair	Poor
1000	500	400	300	250	200

Model 270-Hammer Sidelock

NIB	Exc.	V.G.	Good	Fair	Poor
1000	500	400	300	250	200

Model 280-Hammer Sidelock

NIB	Exc.	V.G.	Good	Fair	Poor
1000	500	400	300	250	200

Model 325-Hammerless Boxlock

NIB	Exc.	V.G.	Good	Fair	Poor
800	400	350	300	250	200

Model 350-Hammerless Boxlock

NIB	Exc.	V.G.	Good	Fair	Poor
800	400	350	300	250	200

Model 360-Hammerless Boxlock

NIB	Exc.	V.G.	Good	Fair	Poor
800	400	350	300	250	200

Model 370-Hammerless Boxlock

NIB	Exc.	V.G.	Good	Fair	Poor
800	400	350	300	250	200

Model 380-Hammerless Boxlock

NIB	Exc.	V.G.	Good	Fair	Poor
1000	500	400	350	250	200

Model 235-Hammer Boxlock

NIB	Exc.	V.G.	Good	Fair	Poor
800	400	350	300	250	200

Model 335 (Early)-Hammerless Boxlock

NIB	Exc.	V.G.	Good	Fair	Poor
800	400	350	300	250	200

Model 255-Hammer Sidelock

NIB	Exc.	V.G.	Good	Fair	Poor
800	400	350	300	250	200

Model 265-Hammer Sidelock

NIB	Exc.	V.G.	Good	Fair	Poor
800	400	350	300	250	200

Model 355-Hammerless Boxlock

NIB	Exc.	V.G.	Good	Fair	Poor
1400	700	500	400	300	250

Model 365-Hammerless Boxlock

NIB	Exc.	V.G.	Good	Fair	Poor
1600	800	550	450	350	300

Model 375 (London Proofs)-Hammerless Boxlock

NIB	Exc.	V.G.	Good	Fair	Poor
2400	1200	800	600	400	350

Model 375 (U.S.)-Hammerless Boxlock

NIB	Exc.	V.G.	Good	Fair	Poor
1800	900	600	500	350	300

Model 385 (London Proofs)-Hammerless Boxlock

NIB	Exc.	V.G.	Good	Fair	Poor
2800	1400	900	600	400	350

Model 385 (U.S.)-Hammerless Boxlock

NIB	Exc.	V.G.	Good	Fair	Poor
2000	1000	750	500	400	250

Model 345-Hammerless Boxlock

NIB	Exc.	V.G.	Good	Fair	Poor
1000	500	400	300	250	200

Model 335 (Late)-Hammerless Boxlock

NIB	Exc.	V.G.	Good	Fair	Poor
800	400	350	300	250	200

Model 330-Hammerless Boxlock

NIB	Exc.	V.G.	Good	Fair	Poor
800	400	350	300	250	200

Stevens Model 330 early Fork type cocking lever (early)

Stevens Model 330 late spade type cocking lever (late)

Model 331-Single Trigger Hammerless Boxlock

NIB	Exc.	V.G.	Good	Fair	Poor
900	450	350	300	250	200

Model 530-Hammerless Boxlock

NIB	Exc.	V.G.	Good	Fair	Poor
800	400	350	300	250	200

Model 515-Hammerless Boxlock

NIB	Exc.	V.G.	Good	Fair	Poor
1100	550	450	400	350	300

Model 515-Single Trigger Hammerless Boxlock

NIB	Exc.	V.G.	Good	Fair	Poor
1200	600	500	400	300	250

Model 500-Skeet Hammerless Boxlock

NIB	Exc.	V.G.	Good	Fair	Poor
2000	1000	800	700	600	400

Model 530M-Tenite Hammerless Boxlock

NIB	Exc.	V.G.	Good	Fair	Poor
800	400	350	300	250	200

Model 530M-Tenite Single Trigger Hammerless Boxlock

NIB	Exc.	V.G.	Good	Fair	Poor
1200	600	500	400	350	300

Model 530A-Hammerless Boxlock

NIB	Exc.	V.G.	Good	Fair	Poor
800	400	350	300	250	200

Model 530A-Single Trigger Hammerless Boxlock

NIB	Exc.	V.G.	Good	Fair	Poor
900	450	400	350	300	250

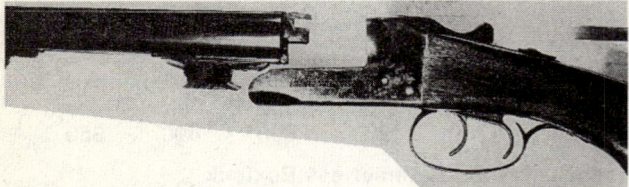

Stevens Model 311/Courtesy Nick Niles

Model 311-Tenite Hammerless Boxlock

NIB	Exc.	V.G.	Good	Fair	Poor
800	400	350	300	250	200

Model 311-Tenite Single Trigger Hammerless Boxlock

NIB	Exc.	V.G.	Good	Fair	Poor
1000	500	450	400	350	300

Model 311A-Hammerless Boxlock

NIB	Exc.	V.G.	Good	Fair	Poor
800	400	350	300	250	200

Model 311C-Hammerless Boxlock

NIB	Exc.	V.G.	Good	Fair	Poor
700	350	300	250	200	150

Model 311D-Hammerless Boxlock

NIB	Exc.	V.G.	Good	Fair	Poor
800	400	350	300	250	200

Model 311E-Hammerless Boxlock

NIB	Exc.	V.G.	Good	Fair	Poor
1000	500	400	350	300	250

Model 311 F-Hammerless Boxlock

NIB	Exc.	V.G.	Good	Fair	Poor
800	400	350	300	250	200

Model 311H-Hammerless Boxlock

NIB	Exc.	V.G.	Good	Fair	Poor
800	400	350	300	250	200

Model 311H-Vent Rib Hammerless Boxlock

NIB	Exc.	V.G.	Good	Fair	Poor
900	450	400	350	300	250

Model 311J/R-Hammerless Boxlock

NIB	Exc.	V.G.	Good	Fair	Poor
700	350	300	250	200	150

Model 311J/R-Solid Rib Hammerless Boxlock

NIB	Exc.	V.G.	Good	Fair	Poor
700	350	300	250	200	150

Model 311H-Waterfowler Hammerless Boxlock

NIB	Exc.	V.G.	Good	Fair	Poor
1200	600	500	400	300	200

RIVERSIDE BRAND

Model 215 Hammer Boxlock

NIB	Exc.	V.G.	Good	Fair	Poor
1300	650	450	350	250	200

Model 315 (Early)-Hammerless Boxlock

NIB	Exc.	V.G.	Good	Fair	Poor
1000	500	400	350	250	200

Model 315 (Late)-Hammerless Boxlock

NIB	Exc.	V.G.	Good	Fair	Poor
1000	500	400	350	250	200

SUPER VALUE BRAND

Model 511-Hammerless Boxlock

NIB	Exc.	V.G.	Good	Fair	Poor
900	450	350	300	200	150

Model 511-Sunken Rib Hammerless Boxlock

NIB	Exc.	V.G.	Good	Fair	Poor
800	400	350	300	200	150

SPRINGFIELD BRAND

Model 215-Hammer Boxlock

NIB	Exc.	V.G.	Good	Fair	Poor
1000	500	400	350	250	150

Model 311-Hammerless Boxlock

NIB	Exc.	V.G.	Good	Fair	Poor
800	400	350	300	250	150

Model 315-Hammerless Boxlock

NIB	Exc.	V.G.	Good	Fair	Poor
1000	500	400	350	250	200

Model 3150-Hammerless Boxlock

NIB	Exc.	V.G.	Good	Fair	Poor
1200	600	500	350	250	200

Model 3151-Hammerless Boxlock

NIB	Exc.	V.G.	Good	Fair	Poor
1500	750	600	400	300	200

Model 3151-Single Trigger Hammerless Boxlock

NIB	Exc.	V.G.	Good	Fair	Poor
1600	800	700	500	400	300

Model 311-Single Trigger Hammerless Boxlock

NIB	Exc.	V.G.	Good	Fair	Poor
1400	700	600	500	400	200

Model 5000-Hammerless Boxlock

NIB	Exc.	V.G.	Good	Fair	Poor
900	450	400	350	250	150

Model 5151-Hammerless Boxlock

NIB	Exc.	V.G.	Good	Fair	Poor
1000	500	400	350	250	200

Model 5151-Single Trigger Hammerless Boxlock

NIB	Exc.	V.G.	Good	Fair	Poor
1200	600	450	350	250	200

Model 311-New Style Hammerless Boxlock

NIB	Exc.	V.G.	Good	Fair	Poor
800	350	300	250	150	100

Model 311-New Style Tenite Hammerless Boxlock

NIB	Exc.	V.G.	Good	Fair	Poor
800	400	350	300	250	150

Model 5100-Hammerless Boxlock

NIB	Exc.	V.G.	Good	Fair	Poor
700	350	300	250	200	150

Model 5100-Tenite Hammerless Boxlock

NIB	Exc.	V.G.	Good	Fair	Poor
700	350	300	250	200	150

Model 511-Sunken Rib Hammerless Boxlock

NIB	Exc.	V.G.	Good	Fair	Poor
800	400	300	250	200	150

Model 511-Hammerless Boxlock

NIB	Exc.	V.G.	Good	Fair	Poor
900	450	300	250	200	150

Model 511A-Hammerless Boxlock

NIB	Exc.	V.G.	Good	Fair	Poor
900	450	300	250	200	150

STEVENS DATE CODE

Collectors will find a date code stamped on every double-barrel shotgun in the Stevens brands produced between March 1949 and December 1968. Usually, it is behind the hinge pin or ahead of the triggerguard on the bottom of the frame. It will appear as a small circle containing a number and letter. The letters correspond to the years shown in the following table. Significance of the numbers is not known.

DATE CODES	
A-1949	L-1960
B-1950	M-1961
C-1951	N-1962
D-1952	P-1963
E-1953	R-1964
F-1954	S-1965
G-1955	T-1966
H-1956	U-1967
I-1957	V-1968
J-1958	K-1959

STEVENS BOLT ACTION SHOTGUNS

The Stevens Company produced a number of bolt-action shotguns that are either single shot or repeaters. They are chambered for the 20 gauge or .410 and are blued, with walnut stocks. The values for these utility-grade shotguns are similar.

Model 237—Single Shot
Model 258—Clip Fed
Model 37—Single Shot
Model 38—Clip Fed
Model 39—Tube Magazine
Model 58—Clip Fed
Model 59—Tube Magazine

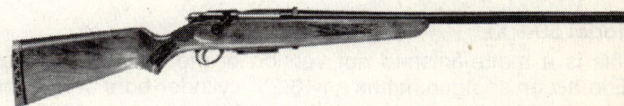

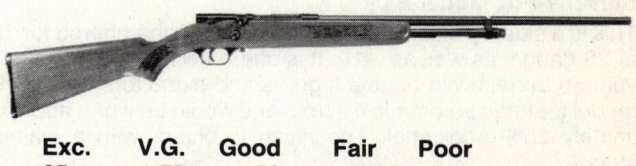

Model 58

Exc.	V.G.	Good	Fair	Poor
95	75	60	50	35

STEVENS SLIDE ACTION UTILITY GRADE SHOTGUNS

The J. Stevens Arms Company also produced a series of utility-grade slide-action shotguns. They are chambered for various gauges with various barrel lengths and chokes. The finishes are blued, with walnut stocks. The values are similar, and we list them for reference purposes as follows:

Model 520
Model 522
Model 620
Model 621
Model 67
Model 67-VR
Model 77
Model 77-SC
Model 77-AC
Model 77-M
Model 820

Model 67

Exc.	V.G.	Good	Fair	Poor
175	150	125	100	75

Model 124

This is a recoil-operated semiautomatic shotgun chambered for 12 gauge. It has a 28" barrel with various chokes, is blued, and has a brown plastic stock.

Exc.	V.G.	Good	Fair	Poor
125	100	75	65	50

Model 67

This is a slide-action shotgun chambered for 12 and 20 gauge, as well as .410. It has 3" chambers. It is offered with various length barrels and choke tubes with a 5-shot tube magazine. It features a steel receiver and is blued, with a walnut stock. It was discontinued in 1989.

Exc.	V.G.	Good	Fair	Poor
200	175	150	100	75

Model 675

This is a slide-action shotgun chambered for 12 gauge with a 24" vent rib barrel with iron sights. The finish is blued, with a hardwood stock and recoil pad. It was manufactured in 1987 and 1988.

Exc.	V.G.	Good	Fair	Poor
275	250	200	150	100

Model 69-RXL

This is a matte-finished riot version of the Model 67 series slide-action shotgun. It has an 18.25" cylinder-bore barrel and is furnished with a recoil pad. It was discontinued in 1989.

Exc.	V.G.	Good	Fair	Poor
200	175	150	100	75

Stevens-Fox Model B

This is a side-by-side double-barrel shotgun chambered for 12 or 20 gauge, as well as .410. It is offered with 26", 28", or 30" vent rib barrels with double triggers and extractors. The BDE model features automatic ejectors and would be worth approximately 25% additional. The finish is blued, with a walnut stock.

Exc.	V.G.	Good	Fair	Poor
300	275	225	175	100

Stevens-Fox Model B-SE

This is a deluxe version with single trigger and automatic ejectors. It features a select walnut stock.

NIB	Exc.	V.G.	Good	Fair	Poor
525	450	325	250	200	150

Model 311

This is a side-by-side double-barrel shotgun chambered for 12 or 20 gauge, as well as .410. It has 3" chambers. It has 28" or 30" vent rib barrels with various chokes, double triggers, and extractors. The finish is blued, with a walnut stock.

Exc.	V.G.	Good	Fair	Poor
300	275	225	175	125

Model 311-R

This is an 18.25", cylinder-bore, law enforcement version of the Model 311.

Exc.	V.G.	Good	Fair	Poor
300	275	225	175	125

STEYR
Steyr, Austria

This company began business in 1853.

Schonberger

A 8mm semiautomatic pistol with a 6" barrel and a magazine located in front of the trigger. Blued with checkered walnut grips. It is believed that approximately 36 examples of this pistol were made in 1892 and 1893.

Exc.	V.G.	Good	Fair	Poor
2750	2500	2000	1500	1250

Steyr Mannlicher Model 1894

A 7.65mm or 6.5mm Mannlicher semiautomatic pistol with a 5.5" barrel. Marked "Model 1894" or "Model 1895". Blued with checkered walnut grips.

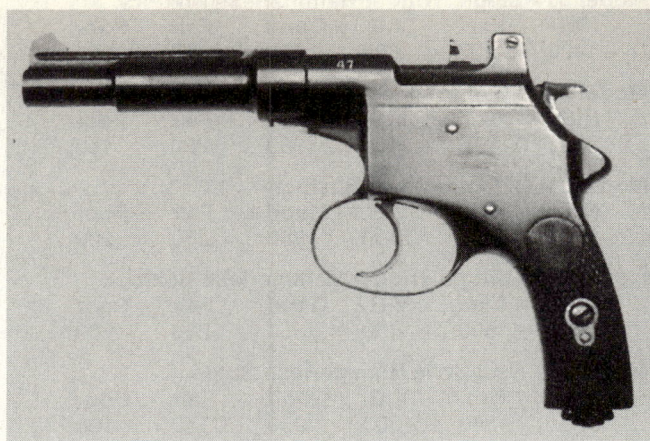

Courtesy Rock Island Auction Company

Exc.	V.G.	Good	Fair	Poor
2000	1750	1500	1000	800

Model 1900/01

A 7.63mm semiautomatic pistol with a 6" barrel and grip safety. Blued with checkered walnut grips. Adopted for use by the Argentine army in 1905.

Exc.	V.G.	Good	Fair	Poor
750	700	600	500	400

Roth-Steyr Model 1907

This is listed under its own section in this text.

Model 1911 Steyr-Hahn (Currently imported by Century International Arms Company)

A 9mm Steyr caliber, semiautomatic pistol with a 5" barrel and fixed magazine. After 1938, many of these pistols were rebarreled for use with the 9mm Parabellum cartridge and these are marked "08". Blued with checkered walnut grips, the slide marked "Osterreichische Waffenfabrik Steyr M1911 9mm." Austrian military issue examples are marked "Steyr" and the date of manufacture on the slide. Those pistols sold to Chile and Romania are marked with those country's crests.

Courtesy Orvel Reichert

Exc.	V.G.	Good	Fair	Poor
450	400	300	200	150

Model 1909 Pocket Pistol

Although marked "Oesterr Waffenfabrik Ges Steyr", this pistol was actually made by Nicolas Pieper (see first entry for Nicolas Pieper). Manufactured prior to 1914 and from 1921 to 1939.

Exc.	V.G.	Good	Fair	Poor
300	250	200	150	100

Model P18

A 9mm caliber semiautomatic pistol with a 5" barrel and 18 shot magazine. Briefly manufactured in 1974 by L.E.S. of Morton Grove, Illinois, under license. This pistol is also known as the "Rogak".

Exc.	V.G.	Good	Fair	Poor
400	350	300	250	200

Model GB

A 9mm caliber double action semiautomatic pistol with a 5-1/4" polygon rifled barrel, 18-shot magazine and black plastic grips. Blued. Imported prior to 1989.

Exc.	V.G.	Good	Fair	Poor
500	400	350	275	200

Steyr Mannlicher Model 1950

A .257 Roberts, .270 Winchester, or .30-06 caliber bolt-action sporting rifle with a 24" barrel and 5-shot rotary magazine. Blued with a checkered walnut stock having an ebony pistol grip cap and forend tip. Manufactured from 1950 to 1952.

Exc.	V.G.	Good	Fair	Poor
1000	850	700	550	300

Model 1950 Carbine

As above, with a 20" barrel and Mannlicher-style stock. Fitted with a steel forend cap. Manufactured in 1950 to 1952.

Exc.	V.G.	Good	Fair	Poor
1250	1000	850	650	300

Model 1952

Similar to the above, with a swept back bolt handle. Manufactured from 1952 to 1956.

Exc.	V.G.	Good	Fair	Poor
1000	850	750	650	300

Model 1952 Carbine

As above, with a 20" barrel and Mannlicher-style stock.

Exc.	V.G.	Good	Fair	Poor
1250	1100	950	650	350

Model 1956 Rifle

Similar to the above, in .243 and .30-06 caliber with a 22" barrel and high comb stock. Manufactured from 1956 to 1960.

Exc.	V.G.	Good	Fair	Poor
900	800	650	500	400

Model 1956 Carbine

As above, with a 20" barrel and Mannlicher-style stock. Manufactured from 1956 to 1960.

Exc.	V.G.	Good	Fair	Poor
1000	900	750	600	500

Model 1961 MCA Rifle

As above, with a Monte Carlo-style stock.

Exc.	V.G.	Good	Fair	Poor
900	800	650	500	400

Model 1961 MCA Carbine

As above, with a Mannlicher-style Monte Carlo stock.

Exc.	V.G.	Good	Fair	Poor
1100	1000	850	650	500

The Following Steyr/Mannlicher Guns are Currently Imported by GSI Inc. Trussville, Alabama

SPORTER SERIES

This series includes rifles that are lightweight and have a reduced overall length. All Sporter models have an interchangeable 5-round rotary magazine. The stock is oil-finished walnut

in either the Mannlicher full stock design or the half stock version. In both stock configurations an oval European cheek piece is standard. These rifles are offered in four different action lengths: **SL** (super light), **L** (light), **M** (medium), or **S** (magnum). They are also available with either single trigger or double set triggers.

Model M72 L/M

A .243, .270, 7x57mm, 7x64mm, .308 or .30-06 caliber bolt-action rifle with a 23" fluted barrel, and single or double set triggers. Blued, checkered walnut stock. Manufactured from 1972 to 1980.

Exc.	V.G.	Good	Fair	Poor
900	800	650	500	300

Model SL

This model features the super light action and is offered with 20" barrel in full stock version or 23-1/6" barrel in half stock version. A rubber butt pad is standard. This model does not have a forend tip on its half stock variation. Offered in the following calibers: .222 Rem., .222 Rem. Mag., .223, and 5.6x50 Mag. Weighs approximately 6.2 lbs. with full stock and 6.3 lbs. with half stock.

NIB	Exc.	V.G.	Good	Fair	Poor
1850	1650	1000	750	500	300

Model SL Carbine

As above, with a 20" fluted barrel and Mannlicher-style stock.

NIB	Exc.	V.G.	Good	Fair	Poor
1950	1750	1050	800	550	350

Varmint Model

This model features a heavy 26" barrel chambered for the .222 Rem., .223, 5.6x57, .243 Win., .308 Win., and .22-250. The forend of the stock is ventilated. The grip is enlarged and textured. Choice of single or double set triggers. Recoil pad is standard. Weighs about 8 lbs.

NIB	Exc.	V.G.	Good	Fair	Poor
1950	1750	1050	800	550	350

Model L

This rifle has the light action and is offered in the same stock configuration and barrel lengths as the Model SL. The calibers are: 5.6x57, .243 Win., .308, .22-250; and 6mm Rem. Weighs about 6.3 lbs. with full stock and 6.4 lbs. with half stock.

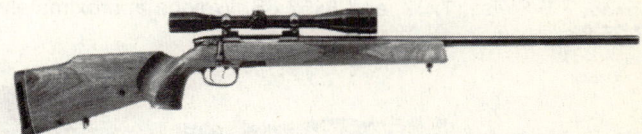

NIB	Exc.	V.G.	Good	Fair	Poor
1850	1650	1000	750	500	300

Luxus Series

This luxury model offers a choice of full or half stock variations in select walnut with fine line checkering. The pistol grip is steeply angled. The Luxus rifles are fitted with a swept back European cheek piece. A single set trigger is standard. The box magazine holds 3 rounds. Optional engraving and stock carving may be encountered on these modes that will dramatically affect price. The Luxus rifles are available with light, medium, or magnum length actions.

Luxus Model L

Same dimensions and barrel lengths as the Sporter version. The calibers are: 5.6x57, .243 Win., .308, .22-250, and 6mm Rem.

NIB	Exc.	V.G.	Good	Fair	Poor
2400	2000	1100	800	600	350

Luxus Model M

Same dimensions and barrel lengths as the Sporter Model M. Available in the following calibers: 6.5x57, .270 Win., 7x64, .30-06, 9.3x626.5x55, 7.5 Swiss, 7x57, and 8x57JS.

NIB	Exc.	V.G.	Good	Fair	Poor
2400	2000	1100	800	600	350

Luxus Model S

Same as the Sporter Model S. Offered in the following calibers: 6.5x68, 7mm Rem. Mag., .300 Win. Mag., and 8x685.

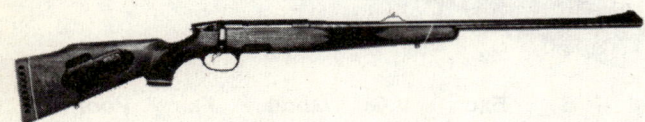

NIB	Exc.	V.G.	Good	Fair	Poor
2400	2000	1100	800	600	350

Model M

This model features the medium action and has the same barrel and stock configurations as the other two models listed above with the exception that it has no butt pad and it does have a forend tip on its half stock variation. Available in the following calibers: 6.5x57, .270 Win., 7x64, .30-06, 9.3x62, 6.5x55, 7.5 Swiss, 7x57, and 8x57JS. Weighs approximately 6.8 lbs. with full stock and 7 lbs. with half stock.

NIB	Exc.	V.G.	Good	Fair	Poor
2500	2100	1200	900	600	300

Professional Model M

This model is fitted with a medium weight action and features a black synthetic checkered stock. Comes fitted with a ventilated rubber recoil pad. Offered with 20" or 23.6" barrel it is available with single or double set trigger. Available in the following calibers: 6.5x57, .270 Win., 7x64, .30-06, 9.3x626, .5x55, 7.5 Swiss, 7x57, and 8x57 JS. Weighs approximately 7.25 lbs.

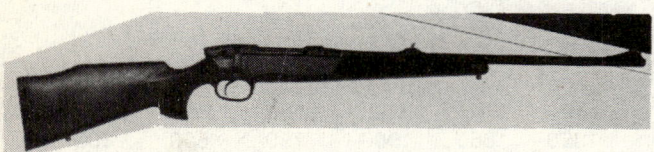

NIB	Exc.	V.G.	Good	Fair	Poor
1500	1200	950	700	600	300

Model MIII Professional

Introduced in 1995 this is an economy version of the Model M Professional. It is fitted with a 23.5" barrel, black synthetic stock, and choice of single or double set triggers. Offered in .25-06, .270 Win., .30-06, and 7x64 calibers. Weight is approximately 7 lb. 5 oz..

NIB	Exc.	V.G.	Good	Fair	Poor
900	700	500	300	200	100

NOTE: With checkered walnut stock add $100.

Model S

This rifle is offered with half stock only and is fitted with a 26" barrel. The action is magnum length and is offered in the following calibers: 6.5x68, 7mm Rem. Mag., .300 Win. Mag., and 8x685. Rifle weighs about 8.4 lbs.

NIB	Exc.	V.G.	Good	Fair	Poor
1950	1750	1150	900	700	300

Model S/T

Similar to the model above but in a heavy barreled version. Offered in the following calibers: 9.3x64, .375 H&H, and .458 Win. Mag. An optional buttstock magazine is available. Weighs about 9 lbs.

NIB	Exc.	V.G.	Good	Fair	Poor
2100	1900	1400	1100	800	500

Tropical Rifle

As above, with a 26" heavy barrel chambered for .375 Holland & Holland and .458 Winchester Magnum. Not imported after 1985.

Exc.	V.G.	Good	Fair	Poor
2000	1750	1100	650	450

Steyer SBS (Safe Bolt System)

This series was introduced in 1997 and features a newly designed bolt. It is offered in two distinct models the SBS Forester and the SBS ProHunter.

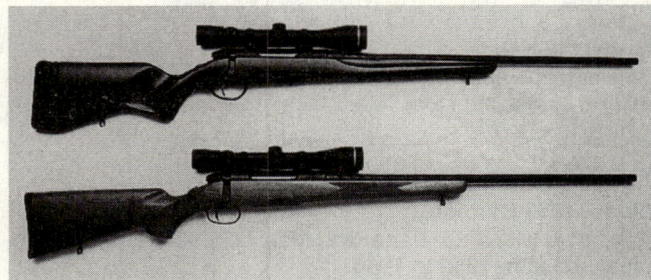

SBS ProHunter

This model has a 23.6" barrel with 4-round magazine and single adjustable trigger. Offered in .243 Win., .25-06, .270 Win., 7mm/08, .308 Win., .30-06, 7mm Rem. Mag., .300 Win. mag., and several European calibers. Weight is approximately 7.5 lbs. This model is furnished with a black synthetic stock with recoil pad and butt spacers.

NIB	Exc.	V.G.	Good	Fair	Poor
775	650	—	—	—	—

SBS Forester

Same as above model but furnished with a walnut stock with recoil pad.

NIB	Exc.	V.G.	Good	Fair	Poor
775	650	—	—	—	—

Model SSG-PI

This model features a black synthetic stock originally designed as a military sniper rifle. Fitted with a cocking indicator, single or double set trigger, 5-round rotary magazine, or 10-round magazine. Receiver is milled to NATO specifications for Steyr ring mounts. Barrel length is 26". Rifle weighs about 9 lbs. Offered in .308 Win.

NOTE: This model was originally called the SSG 69.

NIB	Exc.	V.G.	Good	Fair	Poor
2200	1650	1150	800	600	300

PII Police Rifle

This version of the SSG has a heavier 26" barrel and a larger knob style bolt handle. Weighs about 10 lbs. 11 oz.

NIB	Exc.	V.G.	Good	Fair	Poor
2250	1750	1150	800	500	300

PIIK Police Kurz

Similar to the above model but with a 20" heavy barrel. Weight is about 10 lbs.

NIB	Exc.	V.G.	Good	Fair	Poor
2250	1750	1150	800	500	300

PIV

Again similar to the above PIIK but with a 16.75" heavy barrel with a removable flash hider. Barrel is threaded. Weight is about 9 lbs 11 oz.

NIB	Exc.	V.G.	Good	Fair	Poor
2500	2200	1650	1150	800	400

Match

NIB	Exc.	V.G.	Good	Fair	Poor
3000	2500	2000	1500	800	350

Match UIT

Designed as an international target rifle this model features special shaped pistol grip, an adjustable trigger for length of pull and pressure. Enlarged bolt handle and non-glare barrel. Chambered for .308 Win. cartridge.

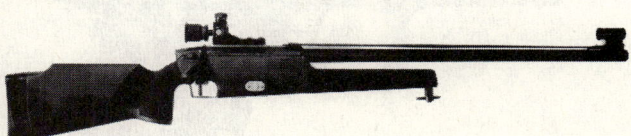

NIB	Exc.	V.G.	Good	Fair	Poor
3900	3500	3000	2000	1500	1000

JAGD Match

Introduced in 1995 this model features a choice of 23.5" or 20" barrel with sights. The stock is laminated. A full stock version is offered on 20" barrel models and a half stock is offered on the 23.5" barrel models. Available in a variety of configurations with calibers from .222 Rem. to .458 Win. Mag.

NIB	Exc.	V.G.	Good	Fair	Poor
1750	1250	900	500	350	200

Steyr AUG

A 5.56mm semiautomatic, Bullpup semiautomatic rifle with a 20" barrel incorporating a Swarovski telescopic sight. Carbon composite stock. Recommend independent, local appraisals.

NIB	Exc.	V.G.	Good	Fair	Poor
3000	2750	—	—	—	—

Steyr Zepher

This model is a .22 caliber rimfire bolt action carbine. It has a 5-round detachable magazine, dovetailed receiver for scope rings. It is fitted with a full stock. Made from 1953 to 1968.

Exc.	V.G.	Good	Fair	Poor
1250	1100	875	600	300

Model SPP

Introduced in 1993 this is a 9mm semiautomatic pistol. It is made from synthetic materials and operates on a delayed blowback, rotating barrel system. The magazine capacity is either 15 or 30 rounds. The barrel is 5.9" in length overall length is 12.75" and weight is about 42 oz. Due to its appearance and design this pistol was banned for importation into the United States shortly after its introduction. Because of this circumstance the price of this pistol may fluctuate widely.

NIB	Exc.	V.G.	Good	Fair	Poor
750	650	500	450	300	200

STEYR HAHN
SEE Steyr

STEYR MANNLICHER
SEE Steyr

STOCK, FRANZ
Berlin, Germany

Stock

A .22, 6.35mm or 7.65mm semiautomatic pistol with an open topped slide. The frame marked "Franz Stock Berlin". Blued with black composition grips impressed with the name "Stock" at the top. Manufactured from 1918 to the early 1930s.

Exc.	V.G.	Good	Fair	Poor
400	300	250	150	100

STOCKING & CO.
Worcester, Massachusetts

Pepperbox

Courtesy Wallis & Wallis, Lewes, Sussex, England

A .28 or .316 barreled percussion pepperbox revolver with barrel lengths from 4" to 6" in length. The hammer is fitted with a long cocking piece at the rear and the triggerguard may or may not be made with a spur at the rear. Blued with walnut grips. The barrel group marked "Stocking & Co., Worcester." Manufactured between 1846 and 1854.

Exc.	V.G.	Good	Fair	Poor
—	—	950	450	200

Single Shot Pistol

A .36 caliber single shot percussion pistol of the same pattern as the pepperbox with a 4" half octagonal barrel. Marked as above. Manufactured from 1849 to 1852.

Exc.	V.G.	Good	Fair	Poor
—	—	400	175	75

STOEGER, A. F.
South Hackensack, New Jersey

American Eagle Luger

This is identiical to the German design. It is chambered for the 9mm with a 7-round magazine and fitted with a 4" barrel. Checkered walnut grips. Stainless steel. Weight is about 32 oz.

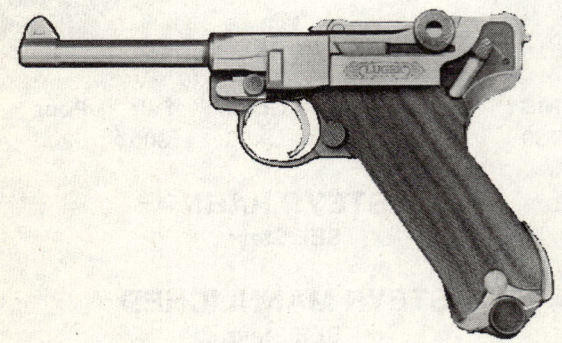

NIB	Exc.	V.G.	Good	Fair	Poor
600	450	400	250	200	100

American Eagle Navy Model

Same as above but with a 6" barrel.

NIB	Exc.	V.G.	Good	Fair	Poor
600	450	400	250	200	100

.22 Luger

A .22 caliber simplified copy of the German Model P.08 semi-automatic pistol with a 4.5" or 5.5" barrel and an aluminum

frame. The word "Luger" is roll engraved on the right side of the frame. Blued with checkered brown plastic grips.

Exc.	V.G.	Good	Fair	Poor
300	250	200	150	100

Target Luger

As above, with adjustable target sights.

Exc.	V.G.	Good	Fair	Poor
325	275	225	175	125

Luger Carbine

As above, with an 11" barrel, walnut forend and checkered walnut grips. Furnished with a red velvet lined black leatherette case. Manufactured during the 1970s.

Exc.	V.G.	Good	Fair	Poor
450	400	350	250	175

STI INTERNATIONAL
Austin, Texas

Model 4.3 Hawk

This pistol is modeled on the 1911 design and is equipped with a 4.3" barrel with steel slide. The frame of the pistol is made from polymer and features and increased magazine capacity while retaining the 1911 grip thickness. Chambered for .38 Super, .45 ACP, .40 S&W, 10mm, and 9x25 calibers. Built primarily for competition shooting.

NIB	Exc.	V.G.	Good	Fair	Poor
1500	1250	900	700	450	250

Model 3.9 Falcon

Similar to the above model but fitted with a 3.9" barrel.

NIB	Exc.	V.G.	Good	Fair	Poor
1500	1250	900	700	450	250

Model 5.1 Eagle

Similar to the Model 2011 Hawk but furnished with a 5" barrel. Comes standard with Bo-Mar adjustable sights.

NIB	Exc.	V.G.	Good	Fair	Poor
1500	1250	900	700	450	250

Model 2011 Eagle 5.5

Similar to above model but furnished with a 5-1/2" barrel with compensator.

NIB	Exc.	V.G.	Good	Fair	Poor
1650	1300	900	700	450	250

STREET SWEEPER
Atlanta, Georgia

Street Sweeper

A 12 gauge semiautomatic double action shotgun with an 18" barrel and 12-shot rotary, drum magazine. Matte black finish. Introduced in 1989.

NIB	Exc.	V.G.	Good	Fair	Poor
600	500	400	350	250	200

STURDIVANT, LEWIS G.
Talladega, Alabama

Received contract from the State of Alabama for 2,000 "Mississippi" or "Enfield" rifles. Two hundred and eighty were received on this contract. These arms resemble U.S. Model 1841 Rifles without patchboxes. Overall length 48-1/2"; barrel length 33"; .577 caliber. Unmarked.

Prospective purchasers are strongly advised to secure an expert appraisal prior to acquisition.

STURM, RUGER & CO.
Southport, Connecticut

In 1946 W.B. Ruger applied for his first patent on a blowback operated, semiautomatic, .22 caliber pistol. In 1949 Bill Ruger and Alexander Sturm released this pistol for sale, and the Ruger dynasty began. This pistol was as perfect for the American marketplace as could be. It was accurate, reliable, and inexpensive and insured the new company's success. In 1951 Alexander Sturm passed away, but Mr. Ruger continued forward. At this time the fledgling television industry was popularizing the early American West, and Colt had not reintroduced the Single Action Army after WWII. Ruger decided that a Western-style six shooter would be a successful venture, and the Single Six was born. This was not a Colt copy but a new design based on the Western look. Again Ruger scored in the marketplace, and this has been pretty much the rule ever since. With few exceptions this company has shown itself to be accurate in gauging what the gun-buying public wants. They have expanded their line to include double-action revolvers, single shots, semiauto and bolt-action rifles, percussion revolvers, and even a semiautomatic wonder nine. They have stayed ahead of the legal profession as much as possible by introducing safety devices and comprehensive instruction manuals and generally insured their future success. For such a relatively new company, collector interest in certain models is quite keen. There are a number of factors that govern Ruger collector values. All models made in 1976 were designated "200th Year of Liberty" models and if in NIB condition will bring up to a 25% premium if a market is found. The newer models that have a safety warning stamped on the barrel are generally purchased only by shooters and have no collector appeal whatsoever. The astute individual must be aware of these nuances when dealing in Rugers. There are some excellent works written on the Ruger (not as many as there are on the Colt or the Smith & Wesson), and the new collector can educate himself if he so desires. We list this company's models in chronological order.

SEMI-AUTOMATIC RIMFIRE PISTOLS

Standard Model "Red Eagle Grips"

This is a blowback semiautomatic with a fixed, exposed, 4.75" barrel. The receiver is tubular, with a round bolt. There is a 9-shot detachable magazine, and the sights are fixed. The finish is blued, and the black hard rubber grips on this first model feature a red Ruger eagle or hawk medallion on the left side. There were approximately 25,600 manufactured before Alexander Sturm's death in 1951, but this model may be seen as high as the 35000 serial number range. Because variations of this model exist an expert opinion should be sought before a final price is established.

Exc.	V.G.	Good	Fair	Poor
350	300	250	200	100

NOTE: Factory verfied plated pistols will bring between $2,500 and $5,000 depending on condition. For pistols in factory original wood "cod box" shipping carton add $750 to $1000. For pistols in original hinged cardboard box add 35%.

Standard Model

This model is identical to the Red Eagle except that after Sturm's death the grip medallions were changed from red to black and have remained so ever since. This pistol was produced from 1952-1982 in 4-3/4" and 6" barrels. There are a great many variations of this pistol, but a book dealing with this pistol alone should be consulted as the differences in variations are subtle and valuation of these variations is definitely a matter for individual appraisal.

Exc.	V.G.	Good	Fair	Poor
150	135	125	100	85

Standard Model-Marked "Hecho en Mexico"

These pistols were assembled and sold in Mexico. Approximately 200 were built with 4-3/4" barrels and about 50 were produced with 6" barrels. Only a few of these pistols have been accounted for and for this reason an expert should be consulted.

Exc.	V.G.	Good	Fair	Poor
1500	1200	850	600	400

Mark I Target Model

The success of the Ruger Standard Model led quite naturally to a demand for a more accurate target model. In 1951 a pistol that utilized the same frame and receiver with a 6-7/8", target-type barrel and adjustable sights was introduced. Early target models number 15000 to 16999 and 25000 to 25300 have Red Eagle grips. In 1952 a 5-1/4" tapered barrel model was introduced, but was soon discontinued. In 1963 the popular 5-1/2" bull barrel model was introduced. These models enjoyed well deserved success and were manufactured from 1951-1982.

For original hinged box add 35%

With Factory Supplied Muzzle Brake-Add $75-100.

Red Eagle 6-7/8" Barrel.

Exc.	V.G.	Good	Fair	Poor
450	325	250	175	125

Black or Silver Eagle 6-7/8" Barrel

Exc.	V.G.	Good	Fair	Poor
200	150	125	100	75

For other Mark I Target models under serial number 72500 in original hinged box-Add 75%.

The 5-1/4" Tapered Barrel Model

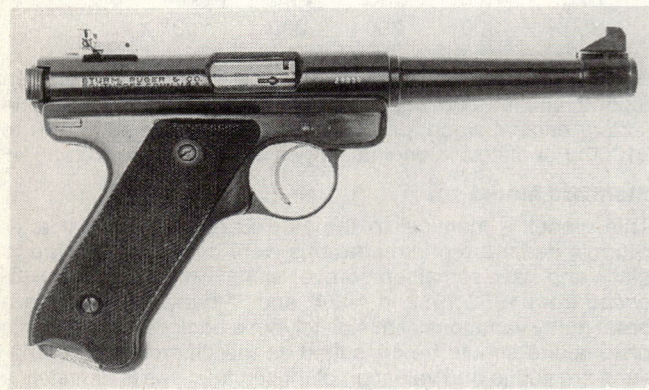

Exc.	V.G.	Good	Fair	Poor
400	325	250	175	125

Add 50% if in original 5-1/4" marked hinged box.

The 5-1/2" Bull Barrel Model.

Exc.	V.G.	Good	Fair	Poor
200	175	150	125	95

Mark I Target Model-Rollmarked With U.S. On Top Of Frame.

These pistols will have either 1/16" or 1/8" high serial numbers.

Exc.	V.G.	Good	Fair	Poor
300	250	200	175	150

Add 25% to price if pistol has 1/8" high serial numbers.

Stainless Steel-1 of 5,000

This model is a special commemorative version of the first standard with the "Red Eagle" grips. It is made of stainless steel and is rollmarked with Bill Ruger's signature on it. The pistol is encased in a wood "salt cod" case.

NIB	Exc.	V.G.	Good	Fair	Poor
425	375	300	225	175	125

MARK II .22 CALIBER PISTOL SPECIFICATIONS:

Supplied in .22 l.r. with various barrel weights and lengths. Magazine capacity is 10 rounds. Trigger is grooved with curved finger surface. High speed hammer provides fast lock time. Grips are sharply checkered and made of black gloss delrin material. Stainless steel models have a brushed satin finish. Today, each model except the MK-10 and KMK-10, come from the factory with a lockable plastic case and Ruger lock.

Mark II Standard Model

This is a generally improved version of the first Ruger pistol. There is a hold-open device, and the magazine holds 10 rounds. This model was introduced in 1982.

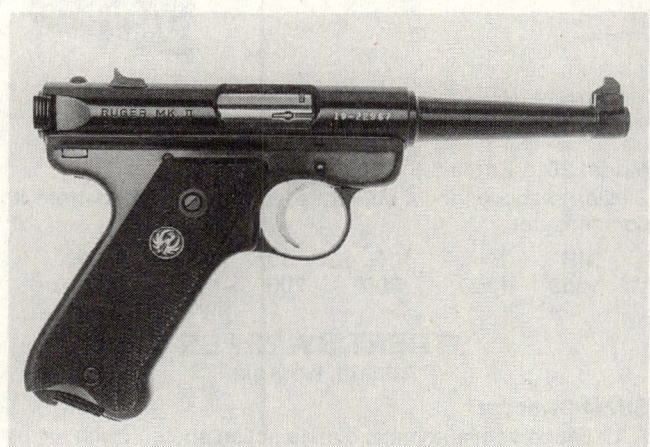

Standard Mark II Model MK-4

Blued finish with 4.75" barrel. Checkered composition grips. Weight about 35 oz.

NIB	Exc.	V.G.	Good	Fair	Poor
225	175	150	125	100	75

Standard Mark II Model MK-6

Same as above but with 6" barrel. Weight 37 oz.

NIB	Exc.	V.G.	Good	Fair	Poor
225	175	150	125	100	75

Standard Mark II Model KMK-4

This model is the same as the Mark II Standard except that it is made of stainless steel.

NIB	Exc.	V.G.	Good	Fair	Poor
300	225	200	150	125	100

Standard Mark II Model KMK-6

Same as above but with 6" barrel. Weight is about 37 oz.

NIB	Exc.	V.G.	Good	Fair	Poor
300	225	200	150	125	100

NOTE: In 1997, Ruger produced 650 of the Model MK-6 with special features for the "Friends of the NRA" auction of the same year. These guns have high polish blueing, faux ivory grips panels, a gold inlaid National Rifle Association inscription and a gold inlaid number of "1 of 650" to "650 of 650". The NIB price for these pistols is $550.00.

Mark II Target Model

This model incorporates the same improvements as the Mark II Standard but is offered with 5.5" bull, 6-7/8" tapered and 10" heavy barrel. A 5-1/4" tapered barrel was added in 1990 but discontinued in 1994. This model has adjustable target sights and was introduced in 1982.

NIB	Exc.	V.G.	Good	Fair	Poor
275	225	200	150	125	100

NOTE: In 1989, approximately 2,000 5-1/2" bull barrel Mark II pistols with blue barreled receivers and stainless steel grip frames were produced by Ruger on order from a Ruger distributor. They exist in the 215-25xxx to 215-43xxx serial number range. The NIB price for these pistols is $375.

Stainless Steel Mark II Target Model

This model is the same as the blued version but is made of stainless steel.

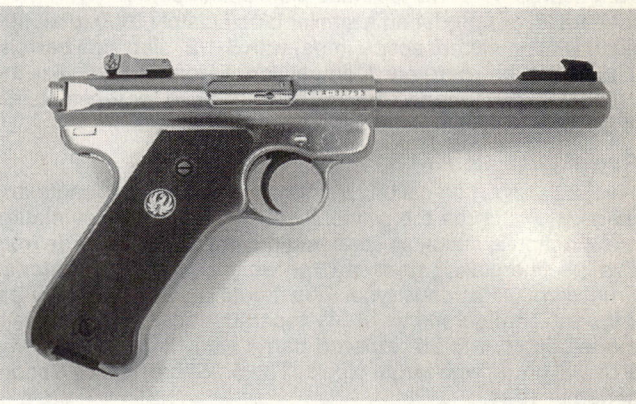

NIB	Exc.	V.G.	Good	Fair	Poor
360	300	250	200	175	125

Mark II Bull Barrel Model MK-4B

Introduced in 1996 this bull barrel variation has a blued finish with a 4" barrel. Grips are checkered composition. Weight is about 38 oz.

NIB	Exc.	V.G.	Good	Fair	Poor
325	275	225	175	150	100

Government Model

This model is similar to the blue Mark II Target, with a 6-7/8" bull barrel. It is the civilian version of a training pistol that the military is purchasing from Ruger. The only difference is that this model does not have the U.S. markings.

NIB	Exc.	V.G.	Good	Fair	Poor
330	275	225	200	150	100

Stainless Steel Government Model

Stainless steel version of the Government Model.

NIB	Exc.	V.G.	Good	Fair	Poor
400	325	250	225	175	125

NOTE: Same with U.S. markings. These are found in the serial number range of 210-00001 to 210-18600. Only a couple dozen are in civilian hands. The NIB price for these pistols is $1,000.00.

Mark II Competition Model KMK-678GC

The Competition model features a stainless steel frame with checkered laminated hardwood thumb rest grips, heavy 6-7/8" bull barrel factory drilled and tapped for scope mount, Partridge type front sight undercut to prevent glare and an adjustable rear sight. Pistol weighs 45 oz.

NIB	Exc.	V.G.	Good	Fair	Poor
420	325	250	200	125	100

NOTE: In 1997 Ruger produced 204 of these pistols in blue instead of stainless steel for one of their distributors. They are very scarce. The NIB for these pistols is $350.00.

In 1995 Ruger produced a similar blued pistol (1000 total, 500 each with or without scope rings) with 5-1/2" slab side barrels. These are not marked "Competition Target Model" like the previously described variation. The NIB price for these pistols is $350.00 and with rings $375.00.

Ruger 22/45 Model

This .22 Long Rifle caliber pistol has the same grip angle and magazine latch as the Model 1911 .45 ACP. The semiautomatic action is stainless steel and the grip frame is made from Zytel, a fiberglass reinforced lightweight composite material. Front sight is Partridge type. This model is available in several different configurations. A 4" tapered barrel and standard model sights, a 5.25" tapered barrel with target sights, or a 5.5" bull barrel with target sights. The 5.25" barrel was discontinued in 1994.

KP-4

This model features a 4.75" standard weight barrel with fixed sights. Pistol weighs 28 oz.

NIB	Exc.	V.G.	Good	Fair	Poor
250	175	150	125	100	75

KP-514

Furnished with a target tapered barrel 5.25" in length. Comes with adjustable sights. Pistol weighs 38 oz. Model now discontinued.

NIB	Exc.	V.G.	Good	Fair	Poor
300	200	175	150	100	75

KP-512

This model is equipped with a 5.5" bull barrel with adjustable sights. Weighs 42 oz.

NIB	Exc.	V.G.	Good	Fair	Poor
300	200	175	150	100	75

NOTE: In 1995 Ruger produced 500 22/45s with stainless steel 6-7/8" Government type barreled receivers for one of their distributors. They appear around the 220-59xxx serial number range. The NIB price for these pistols is $350.00.

Also in 1997 another Ruger distributor succeeded in contracting Ruger to make a similar 22/45 only in blue and with 6-7/8" slab side bull barrels. Approximatley 1,000 were produced with serial numbers extending to the 220-87xxx serial number range. The NIB price is $300.00.

P-4

A limited number, about 1,000, of this variation was produced in 1995 with a 4" bull barrel on a P frame. It was introduced into the product line as a production pistol in 1997. Weight is approximately 31 oz.

NIB	Exc.	V.G.	Good	Fair	Poor
325	250	200	150	100	75

P-512

This variation of the stainless steel version has a blued receiver with P style frame.

NIB	Exc.	V.G.	Good	Fair	Poor
210	175	125	100	75	60

SINGLE ACTION REVOLVERS

Single Six Revolver

This is a .22 rimfire, 6-shot, single-action revolver. It was first offered with a 5-1/2" barrel length and a fixed sight. In 1959 additional barrel lengths were offered for this model in 4-5/8", 6-1/2", and 9-1/2". It is based in appearance on the Colt Single Action Army, but internally it is a new design that features coil springs instead of the old-style, flat leaf springs. It also features a floating firing pin and is generally a stronger action than what was previously available. The early model had a flat loading gate and was made this way from 1953-1957, when the contoured gate became standard. Early models had checkered hard rubber grips changed to smooth varnished walnut by 1962. Black eagle grip medallions were used from the beginning of production to 1971 when a silver eagle grip medallion replaced it. No "Red Eagle" single-sixes were ever produced. This model was manufactured from 1953-1972.

Flat Gate Model

Courtesy John C. Dougan

Courtesy Know Your Ruger Single Action Revolvers 1953-63. Blacksmith Corp.

Exc.	V.G.	Good	Fair	Poor
350	250	200	165	150

NOTE: Be aware that revolvers serial numbered under 1000 will bring a premium of 25% to 125% depending on condition, low serial number, and color of cylinder frame—bright reddish purple the most desirable.

Contoured Gate Model-Introduced 1957

Exc.	V.G.	Good	Fair	Poor
265	235	185	165	130

NOTE: Be aware that 4-5/8" and 9-1/2" barrel lengths will bring a premium. There were 258 5-1/2" barrel factory engraved pistols in this model. Add $2,500 to $7,000 depending on variety and condition. For serial numbers over 360000 deduct $15.00.

Single Six Convertible

This model is similar to the Single Six but is furnished with an extra .22 rimfire Magnum cylinder.

Exc.	V.G.	Good	Fair	Poor
275	225	175	150	125

Barrel lengths in 4-5/8" and 9-1/2" will bring a premium.

Single Six .22 Magnum Model

This model is similar to the Single Six except that it is chambered for the .22 rimfire Magnum and the frame was so marked. It was offered in the 6.5" barrel length only and was manufactured for three years. An extra long rifle cylinder was added later in production. The serial numbers are in the 300000-340000 range.

Exc.	V.G.	Good	Fair	Poor
350	300	250	200	175

Lightweight Single Six

Courtesy Know Your Ruger Single Action Revolvers 1953-63. Blacksmith Corp.

This model is similar to the Single Six, with an aluminum alloy frame and 4-5/8" barrel. This variation was produced between

1956 and 1958 and was in the 200000-212000 serial number range. Approximately the first 6,500 were produced with alloy cylinders with steel chamber inserts.

Courtesy Know Your Ruger Single Action Revolvers 1953-63. Blacksmith Corp.

Silver Anodized Frame with Aluminum Cylinder Model with Martin Hardcoat Finish

Exc.	V.G.	Good	Fair	Poor
400	350	250	225	195

Black Anodized Aluminum Frame and Cylinder Model

Exc.	V.G.	Good	Fair	Poor
450	400	350	300	250

Black Anodized Frame with Blue Steel Cylinder Model

Exc.	V.G.	Good	Fair	Poor
400	350	250	225	195

Silver Anodized with Blue Steel Cylinder Model

Only a few hundred pistols in this variation were produced by the factory with an "S" suffix.

Exc.	V.G.	Good	Fair	Poor
1000	800	600	400	200

NOTE: Stamped after the serial number or on the bottom of the frame. Varieties of "S" marked lightweights exist. Individual evaluation and appraisal is recommended. These are factory seconds and are verifiable.

NOTE: For original Lightweight Single-Six boxes add 25% to 40%.

Super Single Six

Introduced in 1964, this is the Single Six with adjustable sights. Prices given below are for pistols with 5-1/2" and 6-1/2" barrels.

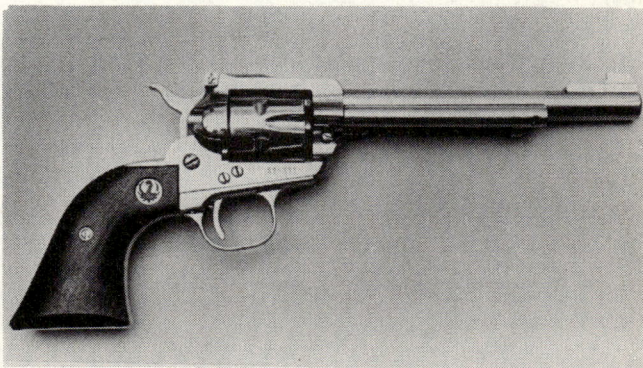

Courtesy Know Your Ruger Single Actions: The Second Decade. Blacksmith Corp.

Exc.	V.G.	Good	Fair	Poor
240	200	150	125	100

Super Single Six with 4-5/8" Barrel (200 built)

Exc.	V.G.	Good	Poor
1200	900	750	400

**Super Single Six-Nickel-Plated Model
(Approximately 100 built)**

Exc.	V.G.	Good
2,500	2,250	2,000

NOTE: The above models are factory verifiable.

Bearcat

This is a scaled-down version of the single action. It is chambered for .22 rimfire and has a 4" barrel and an unfluted, roll engraved cylinder. The frame is alloy, and it has a brass colored anodized alloy triggerguard. The finish is blue, and the grips are plastic impregnated wood until 1963, thereafter walnut with eagle medallions were used. This model was manufactured from 1958-1970.

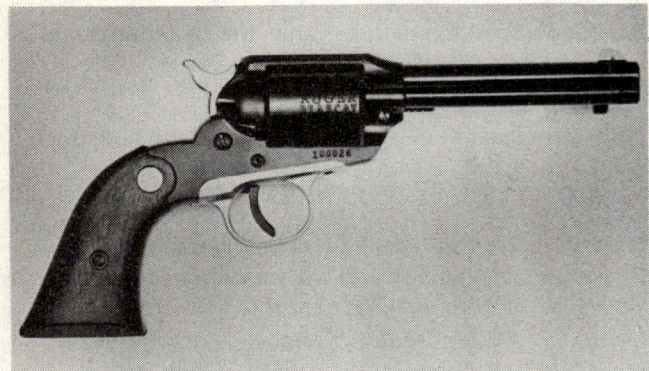

Courtesy Know Your Ruger Single Actions: The Second Decade. Blacksmith Corp.

Serial Number under 30000

Exc.	V.G.	Good	Fair	Poor
350	300	275	250	200

Alphabet Model

Exc.	V.G.	Good	Fair	Poor
375	350	295	275	225

Black Anodized Triggerguard Model (109 built)

Exc.	V.G.	Good	Fair	Poor
1000	950	900	850	750

Serial Number over 30000 or with 90-prefix

Exc.	V.G.	Good	Fair	Poor
325	300	265	225	175

Super Bearcat

This model is similar to the Bearcat, with a steel frame and, on later models, a blued steel triggerguard and grip frame. The early examples still used brass. This model was manufactured from 1971 to 1974.

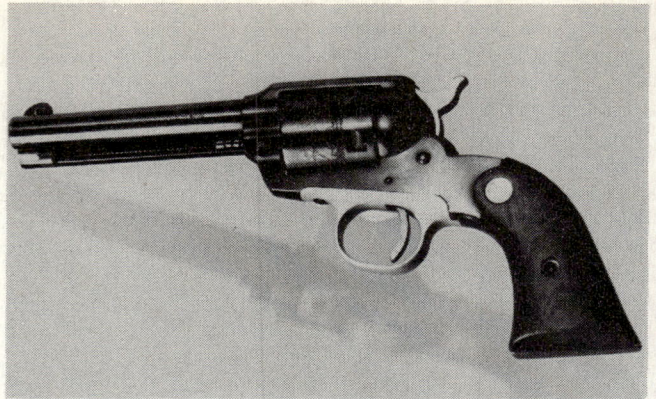

Courtesy W.P. Hallstein III and son Chip

Exc.	V.G.	Good	Fair	Poor
300	275	250	225	175

Blackhawk Flattop-.357 Magnum

The success of the Single Six led to the production of a larger version chambered for the .357 Magnum cartridge. This model is a single action, with a 6-shot fluted cylinder and a flat top strap with adjustable "Micro sight." The barrel length is 4-5/8", 6.5", and 10". The finish is blue with checkered hard rubber grips on the early examples and smooth walnut on later ones. There were approximately 42,600 manufactured between 1955 and 1962.

Courtesy Know Your Ruger Single Action Revolvers 1953-63. Blacksmith Corp.

Coutesy Know Your Ruger Single Action Revolvers 1953-63. Blacksmith Corp.

4-5/8" barrel

Exc.	V.G.	Good	Fair	Poor
475	450	275	250	225

6-1/2" barrel-6 groove rifling

Exc.	V.G.	Good	Fair	Poor
675	525	450	375	350

6-1/2" barrel-8 groove rifling

Exc.	V.G.	Good	Fair	Poor
625	500	425	350	300

10" barrel-6 groove rifling

Exc.	V.G.	Good	Fair	Poor
1100	950	850	750	650

10" barrel-8 groove rifling

Exc.	V.G.	Good	Fair	Poor
1400	1250	1100	950	750

NOTE: Add $150 for NIB

Blackhawk Flattop .44 Magnum

Courtesy Know Your Ruger Single Action Revolvers 1953-63. Blacksmith Corp.

In 1956 the .44 Magnum was introduced, and Ruger jumped on the bandwagon. This is similar in appearance to the .357 but has a slightly heavier frame and a larger cylinder. It was available in a 6.5", 7.5", and 10" barrel. It was manufactured from 1956-1963. There were approximately 28,000 manufactured.

Courtesy Know Your Ruger Single Action Revolvers 1953-63. Blacksmith Corp.

6-1/2" barrel

NIB	Exc.	V.G.	Good	Fair	Poor
725	650	575	500	375	300

7-1/2" barrel

NIB	Exc.	V.G.	Good	Fair	Poor
1025	900	800	700	575	450

10" barrel

NIB	Exc.	V.G.	Good	Fair	Poor
1150	1000	900	800	700	600

Blackhawk

This model is similar to the "Flattop," but the rear sight is protected by two raised protrusions—one on each side. It was available chambered for the .30 Carbine, .357 Magnum, .41 Magnum, or the .45 Colt cartridge. Barrel lengths are 4-5/8" or 6.5" in .357 Magnum and .41 Magnum. .45 Colt version has 4-5/8" and 7.5" barrel lengths. The .30 Carbine is furnished with a 7.4" barrel only. The finish is blue, and the grips are walnut with Ruger medallions. This model was produced from 1962 to 1972.

Courtesy Know Your Ruger Single Action Revolvers 1953-63. Blacksmith Corp.

Over serial number 60000

Exc.	V.G.	Good	Fair	Poor
250	200	175	150	125

Under serial number 60000

Exc.	V.G.	Good	Fair	Poor
300	275	200	175	150

NOTE: Original verified factory brass grip frame will add at least $150 to above prices. It was available chambered for the .357 Magnum or .41 Magnum (4-5/8" or 6-1/2" barrel), or .45 Long Colt (4-5/8" or 7-1/2" barrel).

NOTE: The .41 Magnum with factory installed brass frame will bring $800 to $1500 depending on condition.

Blackhawk Convertible

This model is the same as the Blackhawk with an extra cylinder to change or convert calibers. The .357 Magnum has a 9mm cylinder, and the .45 Colt has a .45 ACP cylinder.

.357/9mm

Exc.	V.G.	Good	Fair	Poor
275	250	225	160	135

.45 L.C./.45 ACP

Exc.	V.G.	Good	Fair	Poor
375	325	275	175	150

The 4-5/8" barrel will bring a slight premium.

NOTE: Non-prefix serial numbered .357/9mm Blackhawks will bring a premium.

Super Blackhawk

The formidable recoil of the .44 Magnum cartridge was difficult to handle in a revolver with a small grip such as found on the Blackhawk, so it was decided to produce a larger-framed revolver with increased size in the grip. The rear of the trigger-guard was squared off, and the cylinder was left unfluted to increase mass. This model was offered with a 7.5" barrel; 600 6.5" barrel Super Blackhawks were produced by factory error. This model is blued and has smooth walnut grips with medallions. The first of these revolvers were offered in a fitted wood case and are rare today. The Super Blackhawk was made from 1959-1972.

Serial number over 5000

Exc.	V.G.	Good	Fair	Poor
350	300	250	200	150

Serial number under 5000

Exc.	V.G.	Good	Fair	Poor
450	375	300	275	225

Early Model in Wood Presentation Case

Exc.	V.G.	Good	Fair	Poor
800	600	475	400	300

In Fitted White Cardboard Case

Exc.	V.G.	Good	Fair	Poor
1200	1000	950	875	675

With Long Grip Frame in Wood Case (300 guns built)

Exc.	V.G.	Good	Fair	Poor
1250	1150	1050	800	675

Factory Verified 6-1/2" barrel-about 600 guns built in the 23000 to 25000 serial number range.

Exc.	V.G.	Good	Fair	Poor
700	650	550	450	375

NOTE: For pistols with brass grip frames add $150 to above prices.

NOTE: For pistols with verefied factory installed brass grip frame add $200. Each example should be appraised.

Hawkeye Single Shot

Courtesy John C. Dougan

The shooting public wanted a small-caliber, high-velocity handgun. The Smith & Wesson Model 53, chambered for the .22 Jet, appeared in 1961; and the cartridge created extraction problems for a revolver. Ruger solved the problem with the introduction of the Hawkeye-a single shot that looked like a six shooter. In place of the cylinder was a breech block that cammed to the side for loading. This pistol was excellent from an engineering and performance standpoint but was not a commercial success. The Hawkeye is chambered for the .256 Magnum, a bottleneck cartridge, and has an 8.5" barrel and adjustable sights. The finish is blued with walnut, medallion grips. The barrel is tapped at the factory for a 1" scope base. This pistol is quite rare as only 3,300 were produced in 1963 and 1964.

NIB	Exc.	V.G.	Good	Fair	Poor
1200	1100	975	850	750	650

Editors Comment: All of the above single action Ruger pistols fitted with factory optional grips will bring a premium regardless of model. This premium applies to pistols manufactured from 1954 to 1962 only. For the following optional grips the premium is: Ivory $650, Stag $275.

NEW MODEL SERIES

The Ruger firm has always demonstrated keen perception and in 1973 completely modified their single-action lockwork to accommodate a hammer block or transfer bar. This hammer block or transfer bar prevented accidental discharge should a revolver be dropped. In doing so, the company circumvented a great deal of potential legal problems and made collectibles out of the previous models. There are many individuals who simply do not care for the "New Models," as they are called, and will not purchase them; but judging from the continued success and growth of the Ruger company, those individuals must be the exception, not the rule.

Super Single Six Convertible (New Model)

This model is similar in appearance to the old model but has the new hammer block safety system. The frame has two pins instead of three screws, and opening the loading gate frees the cylinder stop for loading. Barrel lengths are 4-5/8", 5.5", 6.5", and 9.5". The sights are adjustable; the finish is blued. The grips are walnut with a medallion, and an interchangeable .22 Magnum cylinder is supplied. This model was introduced in 1973 and is currently in production.

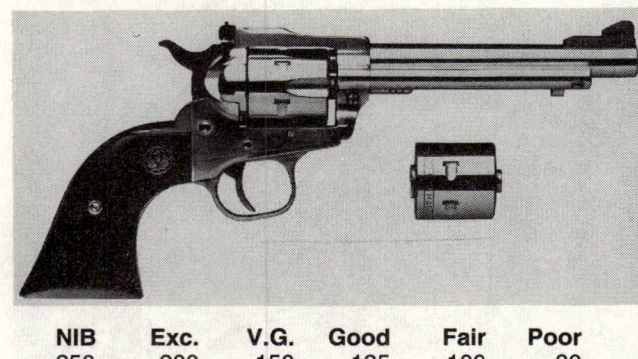

NIB	Exc.	V.G.	Good	Fair	Poor
250	200	150	125	100	80

Stainless Steel Single Six Convertible

The same as the standard blued model but made from stainless steel. Offered with a 4-5/8", 6-1/2", and 9-1/2" barrel.

NIB	Exc.	V.G.	Good	Fair	Poor
325	250	200	175	125	100

NOTE: Pistols with 4-5/8" or 9-1/2" barrel will bring an additional 40% premium. Pistols with 4-5/8" barrels with "made in the 200th year of American Liberty" rollmark on the barrel will bring at least 50% premium to the NIB prices.

New Model Single-Six (Long Rifle only) "Star" Model

This model was produced in blue and stainless for one year only in 4-5/8", 5-1/2", 6-1/2", and 9-1/2" barrel lengths.

Blue Variation

NIB	Exc.	V.G.	Good	Fair	Poor
250	200	175	150	125	100

Stainless Variation

NIB	Exc.	V.G.	Good	Fair	Poor
350	300	200	150	125	100

Pistols with 4-5/8" or 9-1/2" barrels will bring a premium of 25 to 40% to NIB prices.

Fixed Sight New Model Single Six

First made as drift adjustable rear sight (500 each in 4-5/8", 5-1/2", and 6-1/2" blue) and now a catalogued item as a pinched frmae style fixed rear sight. Barrel lengths are offered in 5-1/2" and 6-1/2" lengths. Finish is blued or glossy stainless steel. Rear sight is fixed. Weights are between 32 and 38 oz. depending on barrel length and cylinder.

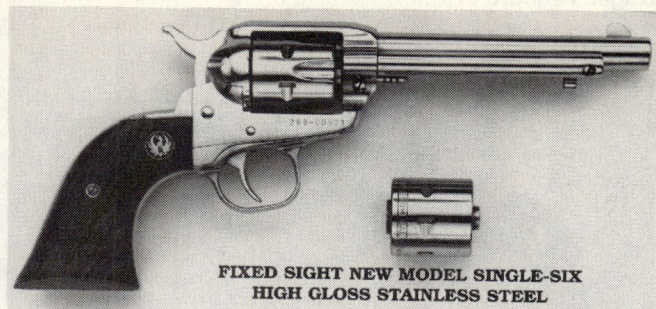

FIXED SIGHT NEW MODEL SINGLE-SIX
HIGH GLOSS STAINLESS STEEL

Blued Finish

NIB	Exc.	V.G.	Good	Fair	Poor
250	225	200	150	125	100

Stainless Steel

NIB	Exc.	V.G.	Good	Fair	Poor
325	300	250	200	150	125

Colorado Centennial Single Six

This model had a stainless steel grip frame, and the balance is blued. It has walnut grips with medallion insert. The barrel is 6-1/2", and the revolver is furnished with a walnut case with a centennial medal insert. There were 15,000 manufactured in 1975.

NIB	Exc.	V.G.	Good	Fair	Poor
300	250	200	—	—	—

NOTE: Add 50% for model with Liberty marked barrel.

Model SSM Single Six

This is the Single Six chambered for the .32 H&R Magnum cartridge. The first 800 pistols were marked with "SSM" on the cylinder frame and will bring a slight premium.

NIB	Exc.	V.G.	Good	Fair	Poor
260	205	175	150	125	100

Blackhawk (New Model)

This model is similar in appearance to the old model Blackhawk, offered in the same calibers and barrel lengths. It has the transfer bar safety device. It was introduced in 1973 and is currently in production.

NIB	Exc.	V.G.	Good	Fair	Poor
300	250	200	175	150	125

Stainless Steel Blackhawk (New Model)

NEW MODEL BLACKHAWK IN .375 MAGNUM
HIGH GLOSS STAINLESS FINISH

This is simply the New Model Blackhawk made from stainless steel. To date it has been offered in .357, .44, and .45 L.C. calibers.

NIB	Exc.	V.G.	Good	Fair	Poor
375	325	275	225	175	150

Blackhawk Convertible (New Model)

This model is the same as the Blackhawk with interchangeable conversion cylinders—.357 Magnum/9mm and .45 Colt/.45 ACP. This model was discontinued in 1985. Prices below are given for blued model.

NIB	Exc.	V.G.	Good	Fair	Poor
315	280	225	175	150	125

Stainless Model (300 guns built) .357/9mm.

Exc.	V.G.	Good	Fair	Poor
650	550	450	375	250

Model SRM Blackhawk

This is the New Model Blackhawk with a 7.5" or 10.5" barrel. It was chambered for the .357 Maximum and was intended for silhouette shooting. This model experienced problems with gas erosion in the forcing cone and under the top strap and was removed from production in 1984 after approximately 9200 were manufactured.

Exc.	V.G.	Good	Fair	Poor
450	375	350	275	250

Super Blackhawk (New Model)

This model is similar in appearance to the old model but has the transfer bar safety device. It was manufactured from 1973 to the present and commenced at serial number 81-00001.

NIB	Exc.	V.G.	Good	Fair	Poor
350	300	275	225	175	125

Super Blackhawk Stainless-Steel

This model is the same as the blued version but is made of stainless steel.

NEW MODEL SUPER BLACKHAWK .44 MAGNUM
HIGH GLOSS STAINLESS FINISH

NIB	Exc.	V.G.	Good	Fair	Poor
375	325	300	250	200	150

Bisley Model

This model has the modified features found on the famous old Colt Bisley Target model—the flat top frame, fixed or adjustable sights, and the longer grip frame that has become the Bisley trademark. The Bisley is available chambered for .22 l.r., .32 H&R Magnum, .357 Magnum, .41 Magnum, .44 Magnum, and .45 Long Colt. The barrel lengths are 6.5" and 7.5"; cylinders are either fluted or unfluted and roll engraved. The finish is a satin blue, and the grips are smooth Goncalo Alves with medallions. The Bisley was introduced in 1986.

.22 Long Rifle and .32 H&R Magnum

NIB	Exc.	V.G.	Good	Fair	Poor
300	275	225	200	150	125

.357 Magnum, .41 Magnum, .44 Magnum, and .45 Long Colt

NIB	Exc.	V.G.	Good	Fair	Poor
350	325	275	250	200	175

NOTE: Approximately 750 stainless grip frame .22 caliber Bisleys were made. These will demand a premium.

Shootists Bisley

Produced in 1994 for the Shootist organization in memory of Tom Ruger. Chambered for the .22 cartridge these revolvers were limited to 52 total produced. They were stainless steel and were fitted with 4-5/8" barrels. The barrels were marked, "IN MEMORY OF OUR FRIEND TOM RUGER THE SHOOTIST 1994". Some of these revolvers, but not all, have the name of the owner engraved on the backstrap.

Photo courtsey of Jim Taylor

NIB	Exc.	V.G.	Good	Fair	Poor
1200	—	—	—	—	—

Old Army Percussion Revolver

This model is a .45 caliber percussion revolver with a 7-1/2" barrel. It has a 6-shot cylinder, with a blued finish and walnut grips. For 1994 this model is offered with fixed sights. Weight is about 46 oz.

NIB	Exc.	V.G.	Good	Fair	Poor
300	275	250	200	150	125

NOTE: For pistols with original factory installed brass grip frame add $150 to above prices.

Old Army Stainless Steel

This model is the same as the blued version except that it is made of stainless steel.

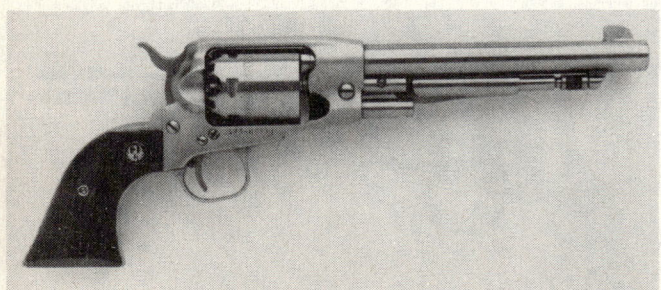

NIB	Exc.	V.G.	Good	Fair	Poor
375	300	265	210	175	150

Ruger Vaquero

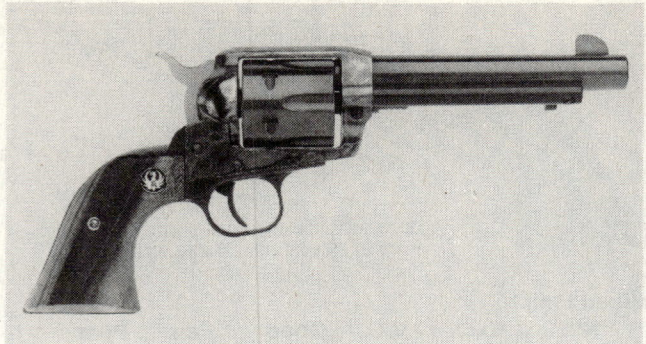

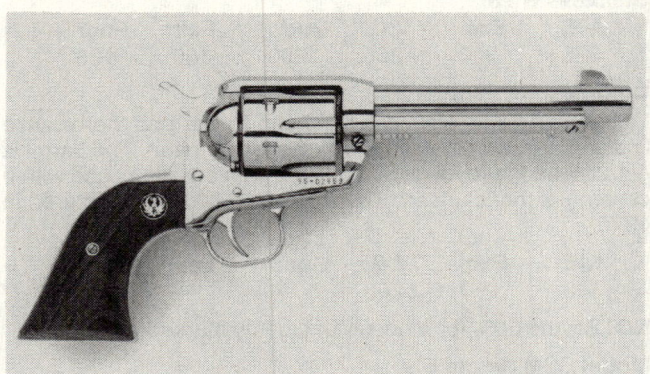

This single action pistol was introduced in 1993 and was voted handgun of the year by the shooting industry. It is a fixed sight version of the New Model Blackhawk. It is available in stainless steel or blued with case-colored frame. Offered in three different barrel lengths: 4.62", 5.5", and 7.5". Chambered for the .45 Long Colt. In 1994 the .44-40 and .44 Magnum calibers were added to the Vaquero line. Capacity is 6 rounds. Weighs between 39 and 41 oz. depending on barrel length.

NOTE: Vaqueros with 4-5/8" barrel chambered for .44 Magnum in both blue and stainless are uncatalogued and extermly rare, add 100%.

NIB	Exc.	V.G.	Good	Fair	Poor
350	300	250	200	150	100

Ruger Bisley Vaquero

Introduced in 1997 this model features a 5.5" barrel chambered for .44 Magnum or .45 Long Colt. Grips are smooth rosewood. Finish is blued with case colored frame. Blade front sight and notch rear. Weight is about 40 oz.

NIB	Exc.	V.G.	Good	Fair	Poor
425	350	—	—	—	—

New Ruger Bearcat

The return of an old favorite was made in 1993. This new version is furnished with a .22 Long Rifle cylinder and a .22 WMR cylinder. Barrel length is 4" with fixed sights. Grips are walnut. Offered in both blued finish or stainless steel.

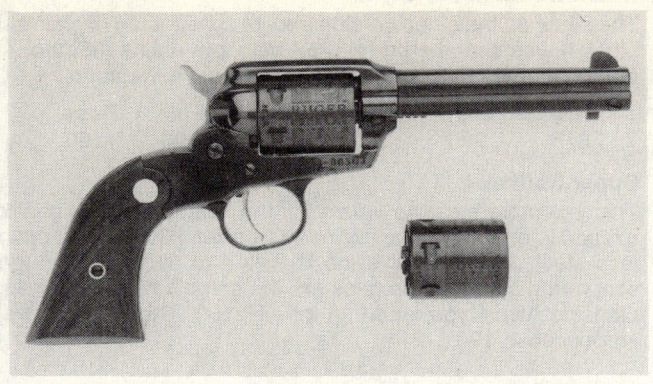

NIB	Exc.	V.G.	Good	Fair	Poor
225	200	—	—	—	—

NOTE: There was a factory recall on the magnum cylinders. Bearcats with both cylinders are very rare and will bring an additional $700-800 premium.

DOUBLE ACTION REVOLVERS

Security Six

This revolver, also known as the Model 117, is chambered for the .357 Magnum cartridge and has a 2.75", 4", or 6" barrel. It features adjustable sights and a square butt, with checkered walnut grips. It was manufactured between 1970 and 1985. Early guns with fixed sights and square butt were also marked "Security-Six". The model was later termed "Service-Six" and was so marked. The prices listed below are only for the adjustable sight and square butt "Security-Six" models. Round butt Security-Sixes with adjustable are worth a premium.

Exc.	V.G.	Good	Fair	Poor
250	225	200	150	100

NOTE: Fixed sight guns marked Security-Six and round butt Security-Sixes with adjustable sights are worth a premium.

Stainless Steel Model 717

This model is the Security-Six made from stainless steel.

Exc.	V.G.	Good	Fair	Poor
275	250	225	175	125

Speed Six

This model is known as the Model 207, chambered for .357 Magnum; Model 208, chambered for .38 Special; and Model 209, chambered for 9mm. It has a 2.75" or 4" barrel, fixed sights, and a round butt with checkered walnut grips and was blued. There are some with factory bobbed hammers. This model was introduced in 1973.

Exc.	V.G.	Good	Fair	Poor
250	225	200	150	100

Models 737, 738, 739

These are the designations for the stainless steel versions of the Speed-Six. They are the same revolver except for the material used in the manufacture.

Exc.	V.G.	Good	Fair	Poor
275	250	225	175	125

Police Service-Six

This model is also known as the Model 107, chambered for .357 Magnum; the Model 108, chambered for the .38 Special; and the 109, chambered for the 9mm. The barrel is 2.75" or 4". A few 6" barrel Service-Sixes were also produced and these are worth a premium. It has fixed sights and a square butt, with checkered walnut grips. The finish is blued. The 9mm was discontinued in 1984; the other two calibers, in 1988.

Exc.	V.G.	Good	Fair	Poor
250	225	200	150	100

Model 707 and 708

This is the designation for the stainless versions of the Police Service-Six. It was not produced in 9mm, and only the 4" barrel was offered. This model was discontinued in 1988.

Exc.	V.G.	Good	Fair	Poor
275	250	225	175	125

GP-100

This model is chambered for the .357 Magnum/.38 Special. It is available with fixed or adjustable sights in barrel lengths of 3", 4", or 6" barrel and has a frame designed for constant use of heavy magnum loads. The rear sight has a white outline, and the front sight features interchangeable colored inserts. The finish is blued, and the grips are a new design made of rubber with smooth Goncalo Alves inserts. This model was introduced in 1986.

NIB	Exc.	V.G.	Good	Fair	Poor
350	325	275	225	175	125

GP-100 Stainless

This model is the same as the GP-100 except that the material used is stainless steel.

NIB	Exc.	V.G.	Good	Fair	Poor
375	350	300	250	200	150

SP-101

This model is similar in appearance to the GP-100 but has a smaller frame and is chambered for the .22 l.r. (6-shot), 38 Special (5-shot), .357 Magnum (5-shot), and 9mm (5-shot). The grips are all black synthetic, and the sights are adjustable for windage. Barrel lengths are 2" or 3", and construction is of stainless steel. This model was introduced in 1989. 6" barrel is available for .22 caliber.

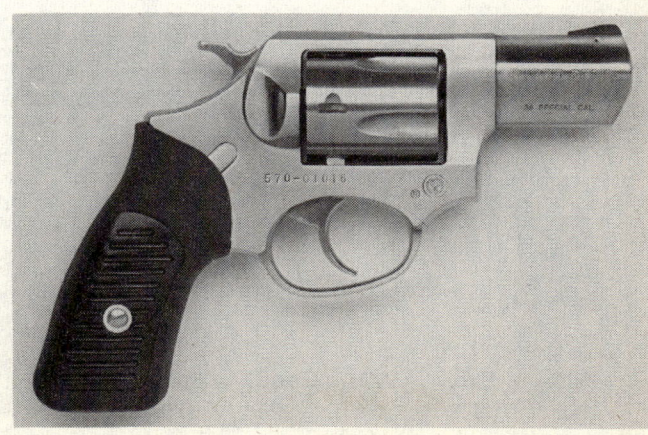

NIB	Exc.	V.G.	Good	Fair	Poor
375	350	300	250	200	150

SP-101 Spurless-Hammer

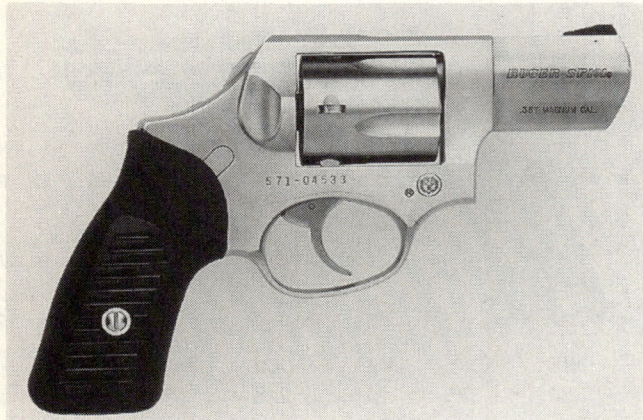

This model was introduced in 1993 and features an SP-101 without an exposed hammer spur. Available in two calibers: .38 Special and .357 Magnum with 2-1/4" barrel. This double action revolver has fixed sights, holds 5 rounds and weighs about 26 oz.

NIB	Exc.	V.G.	Good	Fair	Poor
290	250	200	150	100	80

Redhawk

This model is a large-frame, double-action revolver which was chambered for the .41 Magnum until 1992, and currently for the .44 Magnum cartridges. The barrel lengths are 5-1/2" and 7-1/2". The finish is blued, and the grips are smooth walnut. The Redhawk was introduced in 1986.

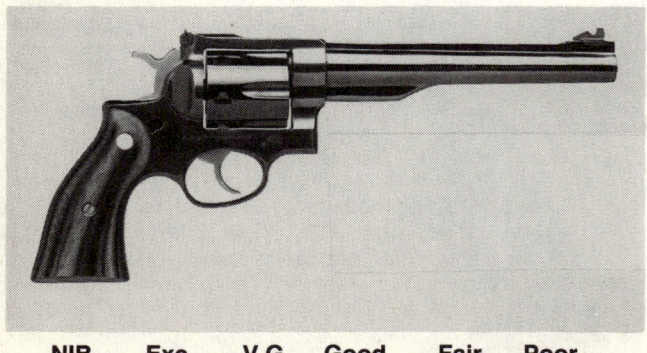

NIB	Exc.	V.G.	Good	Fair	Poor
395	325	275	225	175	125

Redhawk Stainless Steel

The same as the blued version except constructed of stainless steel. It was chambered for .357 Magnum until 1985, the .41 Magnum until 1992, and currently for the .44 Magnum.

NIB	Exc.	V.G.	Good	Fair	Poor
375	350	300	250	200	150

Super Redhawk

This is a more massive version of the Redhawk. It weighs 53 oz. and is offered with a 7.5" or 9.5" barrel. It is made of stainless steel, and the barrel rib is milled to accept the Ruger scope-ring system. The grips are the combination rubber and Goncalo Alves-type found on the GP-100. This revolver was introduced in 1987.

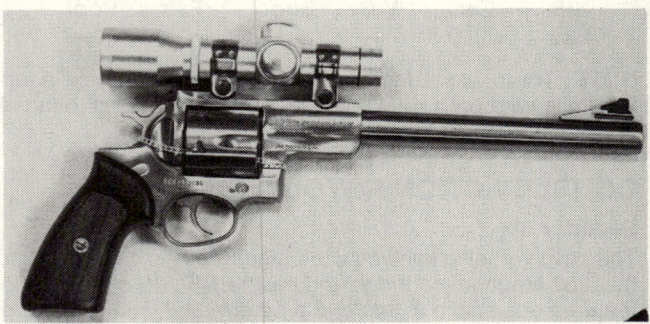

NIB	Exc.	V.G.	Good	Fair	Poor
500	450	400	350	300	225

SEMI-AUTOMATIC HANDGUNS

P-85 or P-89

This model represents Ruger's entry into the wonder nine market. The P-85 is a double-action, high-capacity (15-shot detachable magazine) semiautomatic, with an alloy frame and steel slide. It has a 4.5" barrel, ambidextrous safety, and three dot sighting system. It has a matte black finish and black synthetic grips. The latest option for this model is a decocking device to replace the standard safety. There is also an optional molded locking case and extra magazine with loading tool available. It is more reasonably priced than many of its competitors. This pistol was introduced in 1987 and was sold at large premium for some time due to limited supply and great demand. As of this writing, Ruger is producing this pistol in a new plant in Prescott, Arizona; and the premium situation no longer exists. This model is also produced in a 9x21 cartridge for non-Nato countries. In 1991 the internal mechansim was changed slightly with the result that a name change occured "P85 Mark II".

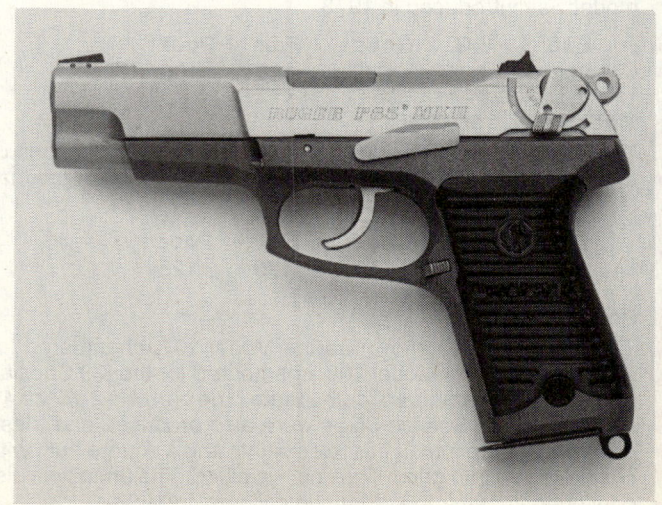

NIB	Exc.	V.G.	Good	Fair	Poor
380	300	275	250	200	150

P-85 Stainless Steel

This model is the same as the matte black version except that the receiver assembly is made of stainless steel.

NIB	Exc.	V.G.	Good	Fair	Poor
355	335	300	275	225	175

KP-89X

Introduced in 1993 this pistol features a stainless steel convertible safety model which comes with both 9mm and .30 Luger barrels. The barrels are interchangeable without the use of tools. Magazine capacity is 15 rounds. Less than 6,000 produced.

NIB	Exc.	V.G.	Good	Fair	Poor
375	325	275	200	150	100

P-89

Introduced in 1991 this semiautomatic pistol is chambered for the 9mm cartridge. It has a blued finish and a 15-round magazine. The safety is a manual ambidextrous lever type. The barrel is 4.5" and the empty weight is approximately 36 oz.

NIB	Exc.	V.G.	Good	Fair	Poor
380	250	200	150	100	80

KP-89

This model is the same configuration as the P-89 but furnished with a stainless steel finish. Introduced in 1991.

NIB	Exc.	V.G.	Good	Fair	Poor
420	300	250	200	150	100

P-89DC

This model features a blued finish and is chambered for the 9mm Parabellum cartridge but is fitted with a decock-only lever (no manual safety). After decocking the gun can be fired by a double action pull of the trigger.

NIB	Exc.	V.G.	Good	Fair	Poor
380	300	250	200	150	100

KP-89DC

This is the stainless steel version of the P-89DC with decock only.

NIB	Exc.	V.G.	Good	Fair	Poor
420	300	250	200	150	100

KP-89DAO

Chambered for the 9mm cartridge this model is the stainless steel double action only version of the above model.

NIB	Exc.	V.G.	Good	Fair	Poor
420	325	250	200	150	100

KP-90

Chambered for the .45 ACP cartridge, this model is in stainless steel and holds 7 rounds in the magazine. It is fitted with a manual safety. Introduced in 1991.

NIB	Exc.	V.G.	Good	Fair	Poor
460	350	275	200	150	100

KP-90DC

This stainless steel version of the KP-90 has a decock-only system. Chambered for the .45 ACP cartridge.

NIB	Exc.	V.G.	Good	Fair	Poor
460	350	275	200	150	100

KP-91DC

This model features a stainless steel finish and is chambered for the .40 S&W cartridge. Magazine capacity is 11 rounds. It has a decock-only system. Introduced in 1992. Discontinued.

NIB	Exc.	V.G.	Good	Fair	Poor
375	325	275	200	150	100

KP-91 DAO

Chambered for the .40 S&W with stainless steel finish it features a double action only system. Discontinued.

NIB	Exc.	V.G.	Good	Fair	Poor
375	325	275	200	150	100

KP-93DC

Introduced in 1993 this pistol is a new addition to the P series as a compact model. Stainless steel and chambered for the 9mm cartridge it has a magazine capacity of 15 rounds. Available in decock-only configuration. Barrel length is 3.9" and the weight is about 24 oz. empty.

NIB	Exc.	V.G.	Good	Fair	Poor
490	400	300	250	150	100

KP-93DAO

The double action only version of the KP-93 compact series.

NIB	Exc.	V.G.	Good	Fair	Poor
490	400	300	250	150	100

KP-94

Introduced in 1994 this model is smaller than the full size P series pistols and the compact P93 pistols. Offered in 9mm or .40 S&W calibers this pistol has an aluminum alloy frame and stainless steel slide. Barrel length is 4-1/4" and magazine capacity for the 9mm is 15-rounds and for the .40 11 rounds. Weight is approximately 33 oz. It is offered in double action only as well as traditional double action. A decock only model is available also.

RUGER'S MIDSIZED KP-94
IN 9MM AND 40 AUTO

CATALOG No. KP94 9MM (PICTURED)
CATALOG No. KP94DC 9MM
CATALOG No. KP94DAO 9MM
CATALOG No. KP944 40 AUTO
CATALOG No. KP944DC 40 AUTO
CATALOG No. KP944DAO 40 AUTO

NIB	Exc.	V.G.	Good	Fair	Poor
490	400	350	300	200	150

KP-94DC

This is similar to the model above but in decock only.

NIB	Exc.	V.G.	Good	Fair	Poor
490	400	350	300	200	150

KP-94DAO

Same as the KP-94 model but in double action only.

NIB	Exc.	V.G.	Good	Fair	Poor
490	400	350	300	200	150

KP-944

Chambered for the .40 S&W cartridge this model has a stainless steel tapered slide, an 11-round magazine , and a manual safety. Models made after September, 1994 have a 10-round magazine.

NIB	Exc.	V.G.	Good	Fair	Poor
490	400	350	300	200	150

KP-944DC

Same as a model above but fitted with a decock only system.

NIB	Exc.	V.G.	Good	Fair	Poor
490	400	350	300	200	150

KP-944DAO

Same as model above but with a double action only model of fire.

NIB	Exc.	V.G.	Good	Fair	Poor
490	400	350	300	200	150

P-95

Introduced in 1996 this 9mm pistol features a 3.9" barrel, polymer frame and stainless steel slide. Decocker only. Fixed 3-dot sights are standard. Overall length is 7.3". Empty weight is about 29 oz.

NIB	Exc.	V.G.	Good	Fair	Poor
325	275	250	200	150	100

P-95DAO

Same as above but in double action only.

NIB	Exc.	V.G.	Good	Fair	Poor
325	275	250	200	150	100

KP-95DC

This model is the same as the matte black version of the P-95, only this is in stainless steel. It has a decock only safety.

NIB	Exc.	V.G.	Good	Fair	Poor
340	300	275	225	175	125

KP-95DAO

Same as the model above but in double action only.

NIB	Exc.	V.G.	Good	Fair	Poor
340	300	275	225	175	125

SEMI-AUTOMATIC RIFLES

10/22 Standard Carbine With Walnut Stock

This model has an 18.5" barrel and is chambered for the .22 l.r. It has a 10-shot, detachable rotary magazine and a folding rear sight. The stock is smooth walnut, with a barrel band and carbine-style buttplate. This rifle enjoys a fine reputation for accuracy and dependability and is considered an excellent value. It was introduced in 1964.
Birch Stock-Deduct $20.

NIB	Exc.	V.G.	Good	Fair	Poor
185	165	125	100	75	50

10/22 Standard Carbine Stainless Steel

Same as above but with stainless steel barrel and receiver.

NIB	Exc.	V.G.	Good	Fair	Poor
225	185	150	125	100	75

10/22 Sporter

This model is similar to the Standard Carbine except that it has a Monte Carlo stock, finger-groove forend, and no barrel band. It was manufactured between 1966 and 1971.

Exc.	V.G.	Good	Fair	Poor
165	125	100	75	50

NOTE: Factory hand checkering-Add 300%.

10/22 Deluxe Sporter

The same as the Sporter with a checkered stock and better buttplate. This model was introduced in 1971.

NIB	Exc.	V.G.	Good	Fair	Poor
200	165	125	100	75	50

10/22 International Carbine

This model is similar to the Standard Carbine, with a full-length, Mannlicher-style stock. It was manufactured between 1966 and 1971 and is fairly rare on today's market.

Exc.	V.G.	Good	Fair	Poor
350	300	250	175	125

Factory hand checkering-Add 50%.

10/22 International Carbine (New Model)

This 1994 model is a reintroduction of the older version. It is offered in either a blued or stainless steel finish. Barrel length is 18-1/2". Magazine capacity is 10-rounds. The hardwood stock had no checkering when this model was first introduced. Shortly after introduced the factory began checkering these stocks. Weight is about 5.2 lbs.

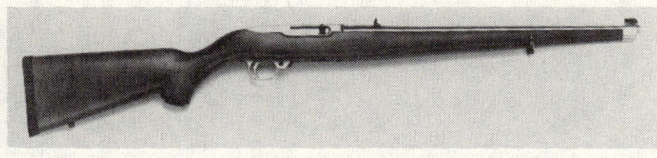

NIB	Exc.	V.G.	Good	Fair	Poor
225	200	150	125	100	75

Model 10/22T

Introduced in 1996 this model is a target version of the 10/22 line. It has a laminated American hardwood stock with blued heavy barrel with hammer-forged spiral finish. Rifle comes standard without sights. Barrel length is 20". Weight is approximately 7.25 lbs.

NIB	Exc.	V.G.	Good	Fair	Poor
375	300	250	200	150	100

Model 10/22 Canadian Centennial

In 1966 and 1967 approximately 4,500 10/22 Sporters were built for the Canadian Centennial. The first 2,000 were sold with a Remington Model 742 in .308 caliber with matching serial numbers. The Ruger Sporter may be checkered or uncheckered. The two-gun set was either boxed separately or together.

NIB For Two Gun Set
800

NIB For 10/22 Only
400

10/22 Laminated Stock Carbine

Produced in varying quantities since 1986 these models are becoming quite collectible. The stocks range in color from dark green to gray and various shades of brown. Because there are so many different variations each should be individually appraised. Prices listed are for blued carbine models.

NIB	Exc.	V.G.	Good	Fair	Poor
250	200	175	150	125	100

NOTE: In stainless steel add approximately $40 to NIB price.

10/22 Laminated Stock Sporter Model

This model has a tree bark laminated stock.

NIB	Exc.	V.G.	Good	Fair	Poor
325	275	225	175	150	100

10/22 Laminated Stock International

This stainless steel model was an exclusive Wal-Mart product. A few of these models in blue were also produced.

Blue

NIB	Exc.	V.G.	Good	Fair	Poor
400	325	250	200	150	100

Stainless Steel

NIB	Exc.	V.G.	Good	Fair	Poor
350	275	225	175	125	100

10/22 All Weather

This model is fitted with a stainless steel barrel and action and synthetic stock. Introduced in 1997.

NIB	Exc.	V.G.	Good	Fair	Poor
225	175	—	—	—	—

Model 44 Carbine

This model is a short, 18.5" barreled, gas-operated carbine chambered for the .44 Magnum cartridge. It has a 4-shot, non-detachable magazine, a folding rear sight, and a plain walnut stock. This is a handy deer hunting carbine manufactured between 1961 and 1985.

Exc.	V.G.	Good	Fair	Poor
400	350	300	200	150

Deerstalker Model

The same as the Model 44 Carbine with "Deerstalker" stamped on it. This model was manufactured in 1961 and 1962 only.

Exc.	V.G.	Good	Fair	Poor
450	400	350	300	200

Model 44RS

This is the Model 44 with sling swivels and an aperture sight.

Exc.	V.G.	Good	Fair	Poor
350	300	250	200	150

NOTE: "Liberty" marked 44RS carbines are extremely rare and will bring at least a 300% premium. An individual appraisal is recommended.

Model 44 Sporter

This version has a Monte Carlo stock, finger groove forend, and no barrel band. It was manufactured until 1971.

Exc.	V.G.	Good	Fair	Poor
400	350	300	250	200

Factory hand checkered models will bring at least a 100% premium.

Model 44 International Carbine

This version features a full-length, Mannlicher-style stock. It was discontinued in 1971 and is quite collectible.

Exc.	V.G.	Good	Fair	Poor
600	500	425	350	275

Factory hand checkered models will bring at least a 75% premium.

Model 44 25th Anniversary Model

This version is lightly engraved, has a medallion in the stock and was only made in 1985, the last year of production.

NIB	Exc.	V.G.	Good	Fair	Poor
450	400	350	300	250	200

Mini-14

This is a paramilitary style carbine chambered for the .223 Remington and on a limited basis for the .222 cartridge. It has an 18.5" barrel and is gas-operated. The detachable magazines originally offered held 5, 10, or 20 rounds. The high-capacity magazines are now discontinued, and prices of them are what the market will bear. The Mini-14 has a military-style stock and aperture sight. It was introduced in 1975.

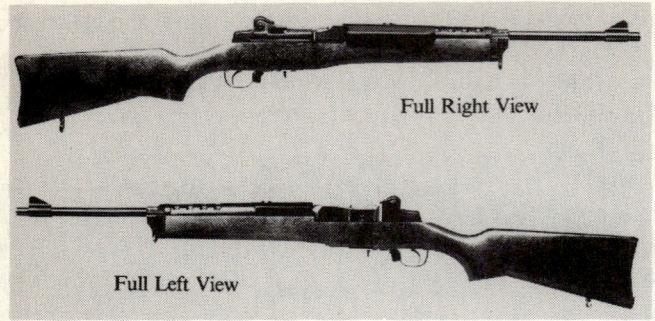

Full Right View

Full Left View

NIB	Exc.	V.G.	Good	Fair	Poor
425	375	325	275	225	150

NOTE: 10 and 20-round magazines are still offered but to law enforcement only.

Mini-14 Stainless Steel

The same as the Mini-14 except constructed of stainless steel.

NIB	Exc.	V.G.	Good	Fair	Poor
450	400	350	300	250	175

Mini-14 Ranch Rifle

This model is similar to the standard Mini-14, with a folding rear sight and the receiver milled to accept the Ruger scope-ring system. The rings are supplied with the rifle.

NOTE: Models chambered in .222 caliber will bring a premium.

NIB	Exc.	V.G.	Good	Fair	Poor
450	400	350	300	250	175

Stainless Steel Mini-14 Ranch Rifle

This model is the same as the blued version except that it is made of stainless steel.

NIB	Exc.	V.G.	Good	Fair	Poor
500	450	400	350	300	225

GB Model

This model has a factory-installed folding stock, flash suppressor, and bayonet lug. It was designed and sold by Ruger to law enforcement agencies. A number have come on the civilian market through surplus sales and police trade-ins. With the assault rifle hysteria, prices of this model have fluctuated wildly in some areas. Now that Ruger has discontinued the folding stock and the high capacity magazines, this could become even less predictable. It would behoove anyone contemplating purchase of this model to check their local ordinances and the current market in their area. Note that this is a semiautomatic and totally different than the full-auto version of this weapon available only through Class 3 dealers.

Mini-30

This model was brought out by Ruger in 1987 in answer to the influx of weapons imported from China that were chambered for this cartridge—the 7.62mm x 39 Russian. This cartridge is touted as a fine hunting cartridge for deer-sized game; and by adding this chambering, the handy Mini-14 becomes a legitimate hunting gun—and a new market opened. This model is similar in appearance to the standard Mini-14 and is supplied with Ruger scope rings.

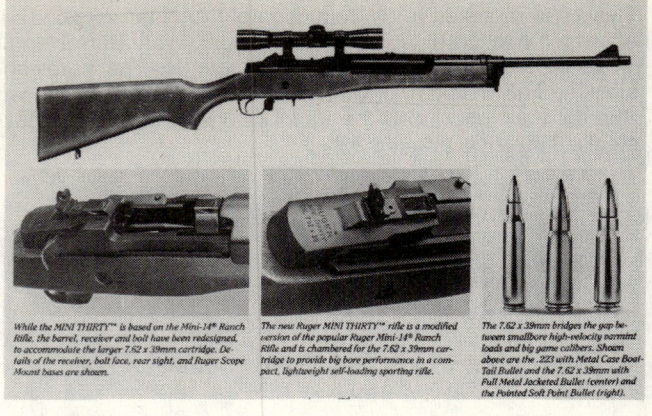

While the MINI THIRTY™ is based on the Mini-14® Ranch rifle, the barrel, receiver and bolt have been redesigned, to accommodate the larger 7.62 x 39mm cartridge. Details of the receiver, bolt face, rear sight, and Ruger Scope Mount bases are shown.

The new Ruger MINI THIRTY™ rifle is a modified version of the popular Ruger Mini-14® Ranch Rifle and is chambered for the 7.62 x 39mm cartridge to provide big bore performance in a compact, lightweight self-loading sporting rifle.

The 7.62 x 39mm bridges the gap between smallbore high-velocity varmint loads and big game calibers. Shown above are the .223 with Metal Case Boat-Tail Bullet (center) and the 7.62 x 39mm with Full Metal Jacketed Bullet (center) and the Pointed Soft Point Bullet (right).

NIB	Exc.	V.G.	Good	Fair	Poor
375	350	300	250	200	150

Mini-30 Stainless

NIB	Exc.	V.G.	Good	Fair	Poor
400	375	325	275	200	150

Ruger Carbine

This is a semi-automatic carbine chambered for the 9mm or .40 S&W cartridges. It is fitted with a 16.25" barrel and black synthetic stock. Post front sight with adjustable rear sight. Detachable magazine has 10-round capacity. Weight is approximately 6.4 lbs. Introduced in 1996.

NIB	Exc.	V.G.	Good	Fair	Poor
525	425	—	—	—	—

SINGLE SHOT RIFLES

All Ruger single shot rifles feature a sliding shotgun-type safety, that engage both the sear and the hammer, all metal parts are polished and blued, each receiver and stock is hand fitted, and the stock is American walnut with a satin finish. The pistol grip and forearm are hand checkered with 20 lines to the inch. Those No. 1 rifles offered with open sights are fitted with an adjustable folding leaf rear sight set into a quarter rib on the barrel and a dovetail-type gold bead front sight. All quarter ribs are machined to accommodate Ruger steel scope rings.

NOTE: There are many rare non-prefixed No. 1 rifles. Unique examples should be individually appraised. "Writers Club" 1 of 21 rifles that are engraved will bring $3000 to $5000 depending on the amount of engraving and gold inlay, caliber, and the person that it was presented to.

Ruger No. 1 Light Sporter (1-A)

This model features open sights, barrel band on lightweight barrel, and Alexander Henry style forearm. Offered with a 22" barrel in four calibers. Rifle weighs 7.25 lbs.

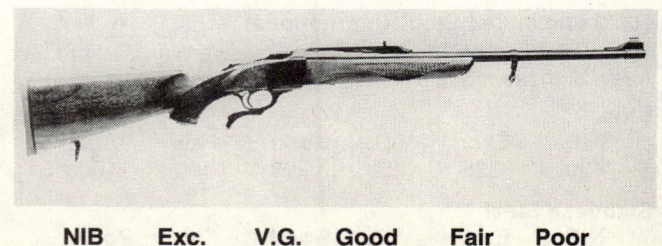

NIB	Exc.	V.G.	Good	Fair	Poor
475	425	350	300	250	200

Ruger No. 1 Standard (1-B)

This model is furnished with no sights, medium barrel, semi-beavertail forearm, and quarter rib with 1" Ruger scope rings. Weighs 8 lbs.

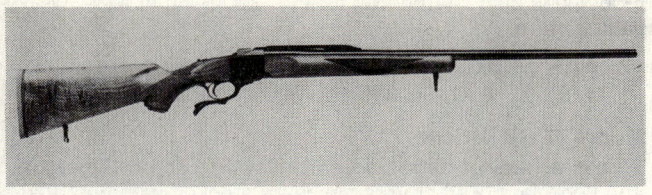

NIB	Exc.	V.G.	Good	Fair	Poor
475	425	350	300	250	200

Ruger No. 1 Tropical (1-H)

Fitted with open sights this model has a barrel band on a heavy barrel with Alexander Henry style forearm. Rifle weighs 9 lbs.

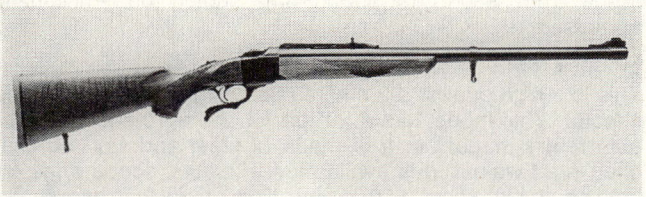

NIB	Exc.	V.G.	Good	Fair	Poor
475	425	350	300	250	200

NOTE: A few 24" heavy barrel 1-H rifles were chambered for the .45-70 Government cartridge up to 1976. These bring a substantial premium of $2000 to $4000 and should be appraised individually. The recently catalogued .404 Jeffery has been discontinued. Only a few of these rifles were produced.

Ruger No. 1 International (1-RSI)

This No. 1 rifle features a lightweight barrel with full length forearm, open sights. Rifle weighs 7.25 lbs.

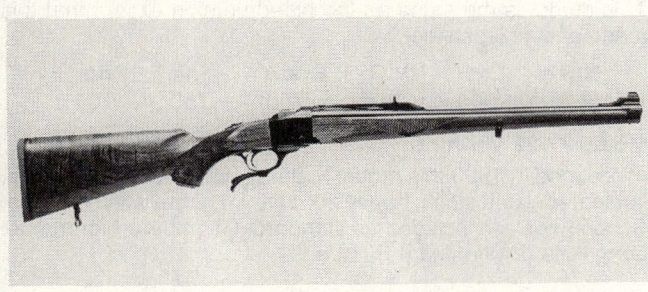

NIB	Exc.	V.G.	Good	Fair	Poor
525	475	400	300	200	150

Ruger No. 1 Medium Sporter (1-S)

The Medium Sporter is equipped with open sights, a barrel band on a medium weight barrel, and Alexander Henry style forearm. Rifle weighs 8 lbs.

NIB	Exc.	V.G.	Good	Fair	Poor
475	425	350	300	250	200

Ruger No. 1 Special Varminter (1-V)

This model is furnished with no sights, a heavy barrel, target scope blocks with 1" Ruger scope rings, and semi-beavertail forearm. Rifle weighs about 9 lbs.

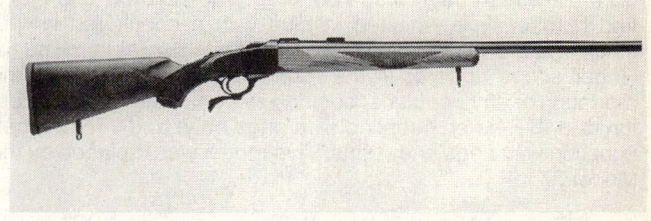

NIB	Exc.	V.G.	Good	Fair	Poor
475	425	350	300	250	200

RUGER NO. 1 SINGLE-SHOT RIFLES

Caliber, catalog number, and availability by barrel length.

Caliber	1-A	I-B	1-H	1-RSI	1-S	1-V
.218 Bee	—	26"	—	—	26"	—
.22 Hornet	—	26"	—	—	—	—
.223	—	26"	—	—	—	24"
.22 PPC	—	—	—	—	—	24"
.22-250	—	26"	—	—	—	24"
.220 Swift	—	26"	—	—	—	26"
6mm Rem.	—	26"	—	—	—	24"
6mm PPC	—	—	—	—	—	24"
.243 Win.	22"	26"	—	20"	—	—
.257 Roberts	—	26"	—	—	—	—
.25-06	—	26"	—	—	—	24"
.270 Win.	22"	26"	—	20"	—	—
.270 Wby. Mag.	—	26"	—	—	—	—
7x57mm	22"	—	—	20"	—	—
.280	—	26"	—	—	—	—
7mm Rem. Mag.	—	26"	—	—	26"	—
.30-06	22"	26"	—	20"	—	—
.300 Win. Mag.	—	26"	—	—	26"	—
.300 Wby. Mag.	—	26"	—	—	—	—
.338 Win. Mag.	—	26"	—	—	26"	—
.375 H&H Mag.	—	—	24"	—	—	—
.404 Jeffery	—	—	24"	—	—	—
.416 Rigby	—	—	24"	—	—	—
.416 Rem. Mag.	—	—	—	—	22"	—
.45-70	—	—	—	—	22"	—
.458 Win. Mag.	—	—	24"	—	—	—

Number 3 Carbine

This model is a less elaborate, inexpensive version of the Number 1. The action is the same except that the lever is less ornate in appearance and lacks the locking bar. The unchecked-ered stock is of a military carbine style with a barrel band. It is similar in appearance to the Model 44 and the 10/22. This serviceable rifle was chambered for the .45-70 when it was released in 1972. Later chamberings added the .22 Hornet, .30-40 Krag, .223, .44 Magnum, and the .375 Winchester. The barrel is 22" long, and there is a folding rear sight. This model was discontinued in 1987.

Exc.	V.G.	Good	Fair	Poor
375	325	250	200	125

BOLT ACTION RIFLES

Ruger introduced the Model 77R in 1968. It filled the need for a good quality, reasonably priced, bolt action hunting rifle. It has been a commercial success. There are certain variations of this rifle that collectors actively seek. One should avail one-self of the specialized literature on this model and secure individual appraisals on the rare variations as the differences are slight and beyond the scope of this book.

Model 77

This model was introduced in 1968. It is offered with a 22", 24", or 26" barrel. The Model 77 is chambered for most calibers from .22-250 through .458 Win. Mag. The action is of a modified Mauser type, finished in blue with a checkered walnut stock and red rubber buttplate. The rifle is available milled for Ruger scope rings or in the round-top style that allows the mounting of any popular scope ring system. This model is designated 77R when supplied with rings only; and 77RS, when supplied with rings and sights. This model was replaced by the Model 77 MK II.

NIB	Exc.	V.G.	Good	Fair	Poor
475	425	350	300	250	200

Model 77 Flat Bolt

This is an example of the slight variations that make this model collectible. This is essentially the same rifle with the knob on the bolt handle flattened. They were only produced in the configuration until 1972. Watch for fakes, and read specialized material. Calibers such as the 6.5 Rem. Mag., .284, and .350 Rem. Mag. will bring a premium especially in the RS model.

Exc.	V.G.	Good	Fair	Poor
525	450	400	350	275

NOTE: Non-prefixed rifles exists in calibers and configurations other than those advertised by Ruger. These should be individually appraised.

Model 77 RL & RLS

This variation is similar to the standard model except that it features an ultralight 20" barrel and black forearm tip. This model was also available in an 18.5" carbine version with sights designated the RLS. This model was also in an 18.5" Carbine version with sights designated the RLS. They were chambered for the .243, .270, .308, and .30-06. Weight is only 6 lbs.

NIB	Exc.	V.G.	Good	Fair	Poor
500	450	375	325	275	225

Model 77 RSI

This version of the Model 77 has a full-length, Mannlicher-style stock and was chambered for the .22-250, .250-3000, .243, .270, 7mm/08, .308 and the .30-06.

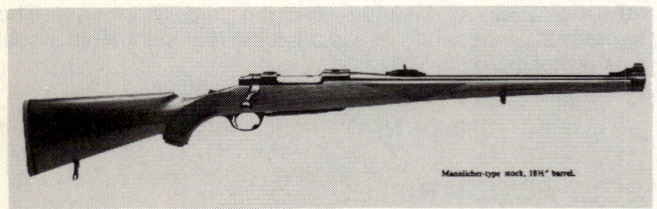

Mannlicher-type stock, 18½" barrel.

NIB	Exc.	V.G.	Good	Fair	Poor
550	475	400	350	300	250

Model 77V Varmint

This variation is similar to the standard Model 77 except that it has a 24" heavy barrel that is drilled and tapped for target scope bases and has a wider beavertail forearm. It is chambered for the .22-250, .243, 6mm, .25-06, .280, and .308. This model was also chambered for the .220 Swift in a 26" heavyweight barrel.

NIB	Exc.	V.G.	Good	Fair	Poor
475	425	350	300	250	200

Model 77 RS African

This is a heavier-barreled version, with a steel triggerguard and floorplate. Earlier versions were stocked with fine quality Circassian walnut. This rifle is chambered for the .458 Winchester Magnum.

NIB	Exc.	V.G.	Good	Fair	Poor
625	550	500	425	350	250

NOTE: Less than 50 or these rifles chambered for the .416 Taylor cartridge were produced up to 1976. Selling prices range from $3000 to $5000 and should be individually appraised.

Model 77/22

This is a high quality, .22 rimfire rifle designed for the serious shooter. This model has a 20" barrel and a 10-shot, detachable rotary magazine. It is made of steel and stocked with checkered walnut. It is available with sights, scope rings, or both as an extra cost ($20) option. This model was introduced in 1984. Early guns without the 77/22 rollmark on the receiver will bring a premium.

NIB	Exc.	V.G.	Good	Fair	Poor
365	325	275	225	175	125

Model 77/22 Synthetic Stock

This version is quite similar to the standard 77/22, with a black matte finished synthetic stock.

NIB	Exc.	V.G.	Good	Fair	Poor
300	275	225	200	150	100

Model 77/22 Stainless Steel/Synthetic Stock

This model is the same as the blued version except that it is made of stainless steel.

NIB	Exc.	V.G.	Good	Fair	Poor
350	300	250	200	150	100

Model 77/22 Varmint

Introduced in 1993 this model features a stainless steel finish, laminated wood stock, heavy 20" varmint barrel with no sights. Scope rings are included as standard. Chambered for the .22 Long Rifle or Win. Mag. Rimfire.

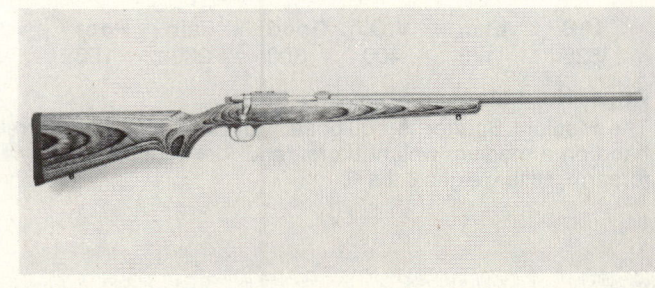

NIB	Exc.	V.G.	Good	Fair	Poor
350	300	250	200	150	100

Model 77/22M

This model is simply the 77/22 chambered for the .22 Magnum cartridge. The finish is blue, and the magazine capacity is 9 rounds.

NIB	Exc.	V.G.	Good	Fair	Poor
370	325	275	225	175	125

Model 77/22 Stainless Steel
This is the same as the blued 77/22M constructed of stainless steel.

NIB	Exc.	V.G.	Good	Fair	Poor
350	300	250	200	150	100

Model 77/22-.22 Hornet
Introduced in 1994 this version of the 77/22 series is chambered for the .22 Hornet cartridge. this model is furnished with or without sights. The barrel is 20" and it has a 6-round detachable rotary magazine. The stock is checkered walnut with sling swivels. Weight is approximately 6 lbs.

NIB	Exc.	V.G.	Good	Fair	Poor
375	325	275	225	200	150

NOTE: This model is offered with (77/22RSH) or without (77/22RH) sights.

Model K77/22VHZ
Introduced in 1995 this .22 Hornet variation features a stainless steel heavy-weight barrel and laminated American hardwood stock. Offered without sights.

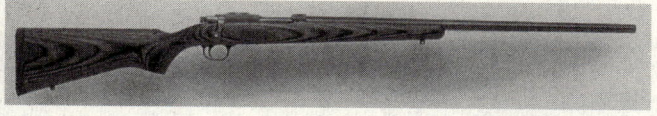

NIB	Exc.	V.G.	Good	Fair	Poor
525	475	350	250	200	150

Ruger Model 77: Mark I vs. Mark II
This Ruger bolt action was produced in the Mark I version until November 1991 when it was dropped from the product line. In December 1991 Ruger began producing a new bolt action Model 77 design referred to as the Mark II. There are several noticeable and important differences between the two versions. The Model 77 Mark I features a sliding tang safety while the Mark II has a new three-position wing safety. The Mark I designed Model 77 holds 5 rounds while the newer Mark II holds 4 rounds. The Mark I incorporates and chromemoly bolt and the Mark II has a stainless steel bolt. The Mark I has a spring loaded ejector while the Mark II has a fixed pin design. The Mark I has an adjustable trigger as opposed to the newer Mark II's nonadjustable trigger. The Mark I bolt face does not incorporate a central feed system while the Mark II does have a central feed. The Mark II design also features a slimmer action that the older Mark I design.

Model 77R MKII
Introduced in 1992 this model is the basic Model 77 rifle. Features blued metal parts and no sights. Available in 15 different calibers from .223 to .338 Win. Mag. in barrel lengths from 22" to 24" depending on caliber. Comes from factory with scope bases and rings. Rifle weighs approximately 7 lbs.

NIB	Exc.	V.G.	Good	Fair	Poor
390	350	300	250	200	150

Model 77RP MKII
This model was also introduced in 1992 and differs from the Model 77R with the addition of stainless steel barrel and receiver and synthetic stock. Available in 10 calibers.

NIB	Exc.	V.G.	Good	Fair	Poor
390	350	300	250	200	150

Model 77RS MKII
This is a blued version of the basic rifle with the addition of open sights. Available in 9 calibers from .243 Win. to .458 Win. Mag.

NIB	Exc.	V.G.	Good	Fair	Poor
450	400	350	300	250	175

Model 77RSP MKII
The stainless version of the basic rifle with the addition of a synthetic stock and open sights. Available in 6 calibers: .243, .270, 7MM Rem. Mag., .30-06, .330 Win. Mag., .338 Win. Mag. Introduced in 1993.

NIB	Exc.	V.G.	Good	Fair	Poor
450	400	350	300	250	175

Model 77RSI MKII
Also introduced in 1993 this model features a blued barrel and walnut stock. Offered in 4 calibers all with 18" barrel. The calibers are: .243, .270, .30-06, and .308.

NIB	Exc.	V.G.	Good	Fair	Poor
450	400	350	300	250	175

Model 77RL MKII
This model features a short action in six calibers from .223 to .308, all with 20" barrel. Rifle weighs about 6 lbs. Introduced in 1992.

NIB	Exc.	V.G.	Good	Fair	Poor
400	350	300	250	200	150

Model 77LR MKII
This model is a left-handed rifle furnished in long action calibers: .270, 7mm Rem. Mag., .30-06, .300 Win. Mag. Introduced in 1992.

NIB	Exc.	V.G.	Good	Fair	Poor
390	350	300	250	200	150

Model 77VT MKII
This rifle was introduced in 1993 and is a target rifle. Furnished with no sights, heavy laminated wood stock with beavertail forend, and adjustable trigger. Barrel, bolt, and action are stainless steel. Weighs approximately 9.75 lbs. Furnished in eight calibers from .223 to .308.

NIB	Exc.	V.G.	Good	Fair	Poor
475	425	350	300	250	175

Model 77RBZ MKII
This model features a stainless steel barrel and action fitted with laminated hardwood stock. No sights. Weight is approximately 7.25 lb. Offered in a wide variety of calibers from .223 to .338 Win. Mag. Introduced in 1997.

NIB	Exc.	V.G.	Good	Fair	Poor
600	500	—	—	—	—

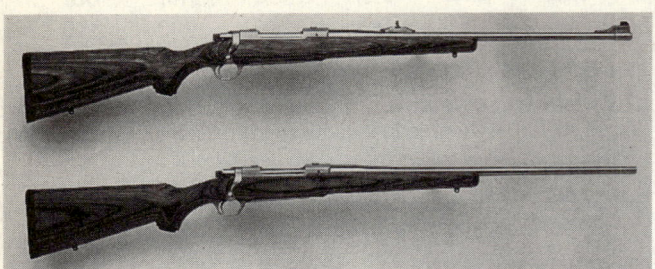

Model 77 RSBZ on top and Model RBZ at bottom.

Model 77RSBZ MKII

Same as above but fitted with open sights. Also introduced in 1997.

NIB	Exc.	V.G.	Good	Fair	Poor
650	550	—	—	—	—

Model 77 Express MKII

Introduced in 1992 the Ruger Express Mark II rifle features a select Circassian walnut straight comb checkered stock. The checkering is 22 lines to the inch and the butt stock is fitted with a rubber recoil pad. The pistol grip is fitted with a metal grip cap. The barrel length is 22" and features a blade front sight, V-notch rear express sights, and the receiver is machined for scope mounts, which are included. Available in the following calibers: .270, .30-06, 7mm Rem. Mag., .300 Win. Mag., .338 Win. Mag. Rifle weighs about 7.5 lbs.

NIB	Exc.	V.G.	Good	Fair	Poor
1100	850	650	550	400	200

Model 77 Magnum MKII

Similar in all respects to the Model 77 Express MKII except offered in the following calibers: .375 H&H and .416 Rigby The .375 and weighs about 9.25 lbs. while the .416 weighs about 10.25 lbs.

NIB	Exc.	V.G.	Good	Fair	Poor
1100	850	650	550	400	200

Model 77/44

This bolt action is chambered for the .44 Magnum cartridge. It features an 18.5" barrel with open sights. The stock is American walnut with rubber butt pad and checkering on forearm and pistol grip. Detachable rotary magazine has 4-round capacity. Weight is approximately 6 lbs. Introduced in mid-1997.

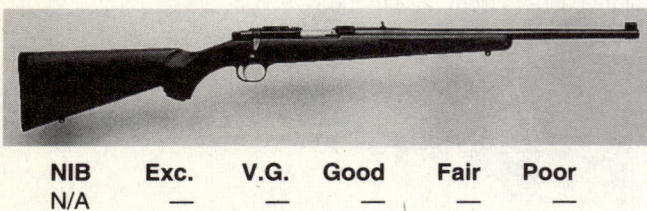

NIB	Exc.	V.G.	Good	Fair	Poor
N/A	—	—	—	—	—

Model 77/50

This model is an in-line percussion rifle chambered for .50 caliber. It is fitted with a 22" barrel with open sights. Stock is birch with rubber butt plate and no checkering. Blued finish. Weight is approximately 6.5 lbs. Introduced in mid-1997.

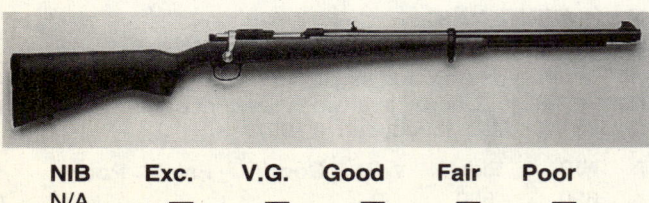

NIB	Exc.	V.G.	Good	Fair	Poor
N/A	—	—	—	—	—

LEVER ACTION RIFLES

Model 96/22

Introduced into the Ruger line in 1996 this lever action rifle is chambered for the .22 long rifle. The stock is American hardwood and the barrel length is 18.5". Magazine capacity is 10 rounds. Open sights are standard. Weight is approximately 5.25 lbs.

NIB	Exc.	V.G.	Good	Fair	Poor
300	250	200	175	150	100

Model 96/22M

Same as above but chambered for the .22 WMR cartridge. Magazine capacity is 9 rounds.

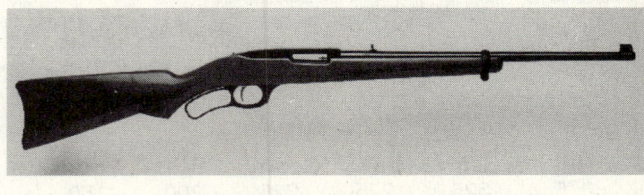

NIB	Exc.	V.G.	Good	Fair	Poor
325	275	225	175	150	100

Model 96/44

Same as the .22 caliber except chambered for the .44 Magnum cartridge. Magazine capacity is 4 rounds and the weight is about 5-7/8 lbs.

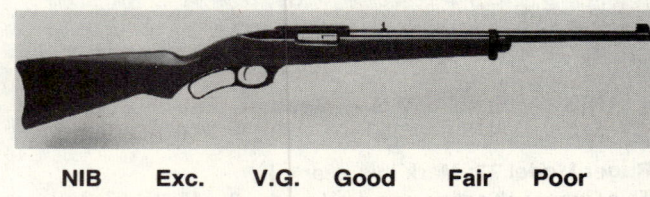

NIB	Exc.	V.G.	Good	Fair	Poor
350	300	250	200	150	100

SHOTGUNS

Red Label Over/Under Early Production

Ruger introduced the Red Label in 20 gauge in 1977; the 12 gauge followed five years later. This high quality shotgun is offered with 3" chambers in 26" or 28" barrel lengths. Various chokes are available. They are boxlocks with automatic ejectors. The stock is of checkered walnut. The finish is blue on the earlier guns.

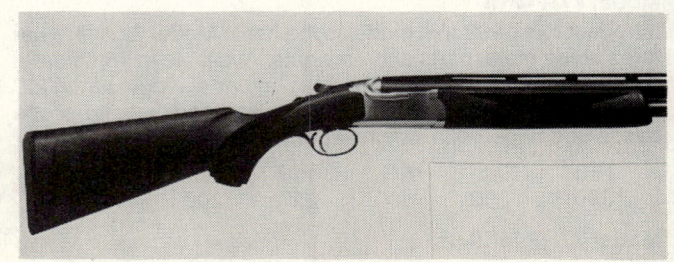

NIB	Exc.	V.G.	Good	Fair	Poor
700	575	500	400	300	250

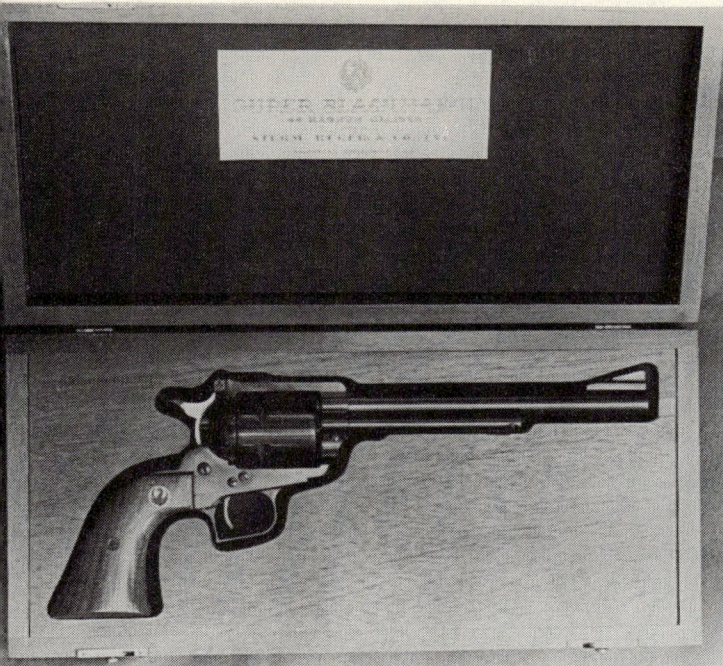

Courtesy Know Your Ruger Single Action Revolvers 1953-63. Blacksmith Corp.

Super Blackhawk in scarce mahogany case, serial numbers 1-8500.

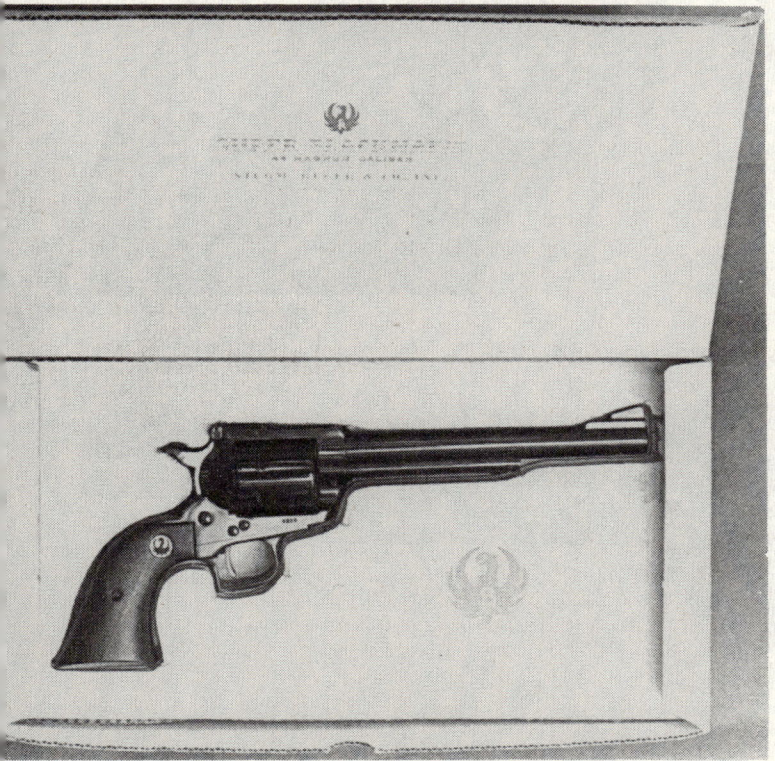

Courtesy Know Your Ruger Single Action Revolvers 1953-63. Blacksmith Corp.

Super Blackhawk in rare white cardboard case, serial numbers 3500-10500.

Red Label Over/Under Current Production

The new 12 and 20 gauge Red Label shotgun has a stainless steel receiver and blued barrels. They are offered with screw-in choke tubes. Otherwise they are similar to the earlier models. In 1994 Ruger added the 28 gauge with 26" or 28" barrels to the Red Label line.

NIB	Exc.	V.G.	Good	Fair	Poor
900	800	600	475	400	300

Red Label Over/Under Sporting Clays

Courtesy compliments of Bill Ruger, John C. Dougan

Offered in 20 gauge this model was introduced in 1994 with 3" chambers and 30" barrels. Walnut stock has checkering pistol grip. Weight is about 7 lbs.

NIB	Exc.	V.G.	Good	Fair	Poor
1050	950	750	500	400	300

NOTE: Engraved Red Label shotguns are catalogued, as of 1996, as available with three different engraving coverages.

Ruger Woodside Over/Under

Introduced in 1995 this new model features a Circassian walnut stock with either pistol grip or straight grip. Available in 12 or 20 gauge with barrel lengths of 26", 28", or 30". Screw-in chokes are standard.

NIB	Exc.	V.G.	Good	Fair	Poor
1675	1150	850	600	400	250

NOTE: The Woodside shotgun is also available in three different engraving patterns.

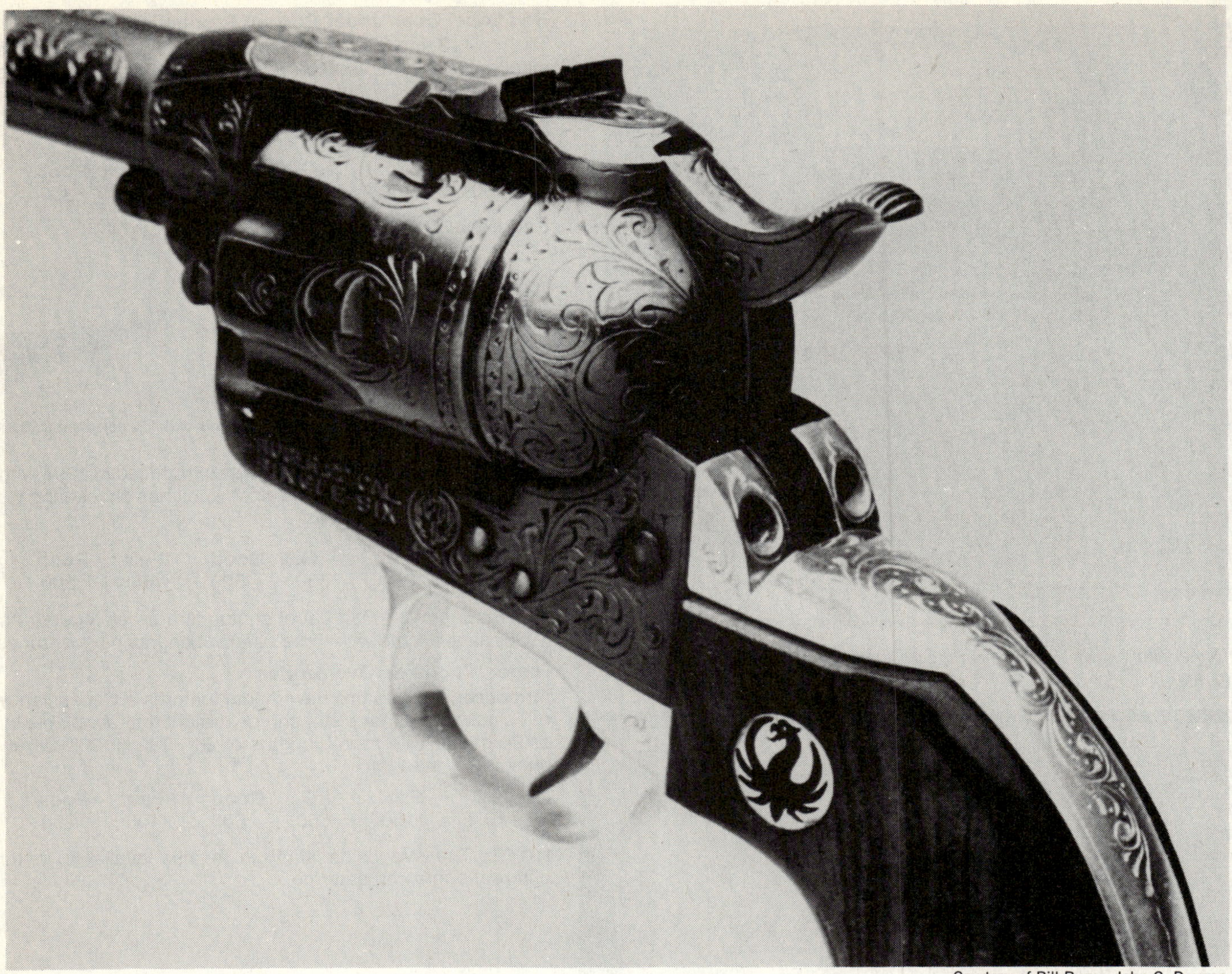

Courtesy of Bill Ruger, John C. Dougan.

.Another view of the Ruger Single Six engraved by Charles H. Jerred in 1954-1958.

Courtesy of Bill Ruger, John C. Dougan.

Factory-engraved Ruger Single Six, one of 22 such guns engraved for Ruger in Spain in 1954.

Ruger New Model Single-Six Revolver.

Ruger New Model Single-Six Revolver.

NEW MODEL BLACKHAWK®
.44 Magnum Caliber

NEW

The popular New Model Blackhawk single-action revolver is now offered in a 5½" barrel version that shoots .44 Magnum or .44 Special cartridges. This model has an all steel grip frame that accommodates walnut grip panels for comfortable and confident handling and a wide deeply serrated hammer spur that facilitates cocking. Its size, handling characteristics, and ballistic capabilities combine to make it the ideal camp and back-up gun on hunting trips.

Ruger New Model Blackhawk; .44 magnum caliber.

RUGER®
New Super Blackhawk

**.44 Magnum Stainless Steel
Single Action Revolver
Untapered Bull Barrel**

Ruger New Super Blackhawk; .44 magnum, stainless steel, single action revolver; untapered bull barrel.

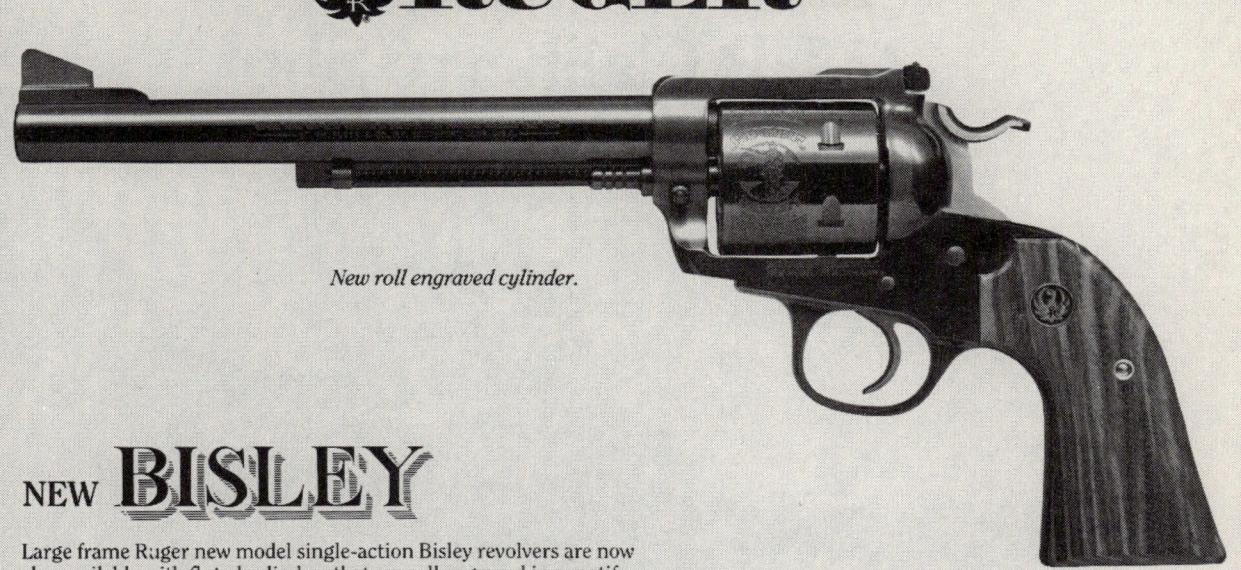

New roll engraved cylinder.

NEW BISLEY

Large frame Ruger new model single-action Bisley revolvers are now also available with fluted cylinders that are roll engraved in a motif reminiscent of the turn-of-the century Bisley era. Earlier models have fluted cylinders without roll engraving. All models are satin polished and blued. Calibers: .357 Magnum, .41 Magnum, .44 Magnum and .45 Long Colt.

New roll engraved cylinder.

NEW BISLEY

Small frame Ruger new model single-action Bisley revolvers are now also available with fluted cylinders that are roll engraved in a classic styling reminiscent of the turn-of-the century Bisley era. Earlier models have fluted cylinders without roll engraving. All models are satin polished and blued. Calibers: .22 Long Rifle and .32 H&R Magnum.

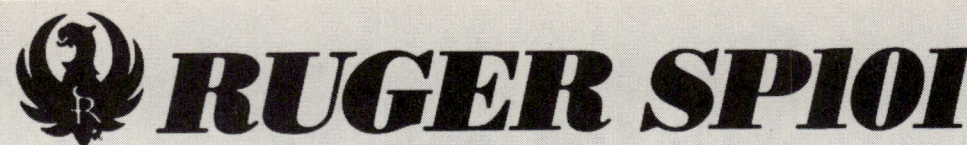

RUGER SP101

.22 LR Caliber; 6 Shot

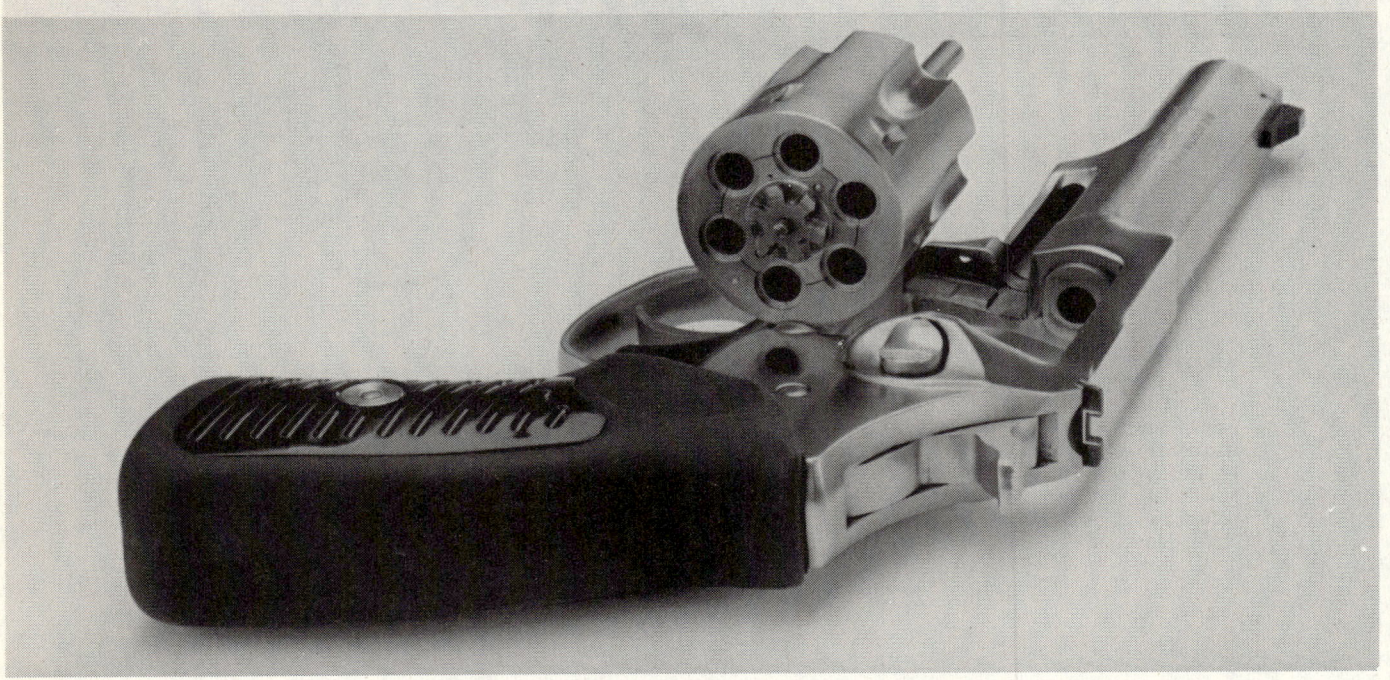

Ruger SP101 .22 LR caliber; 6 shot. The same attention to strength and secure cylinder lock-up found in the large-caliber Ruger double-action revolvers is evident in the SP101 .22 caliber.

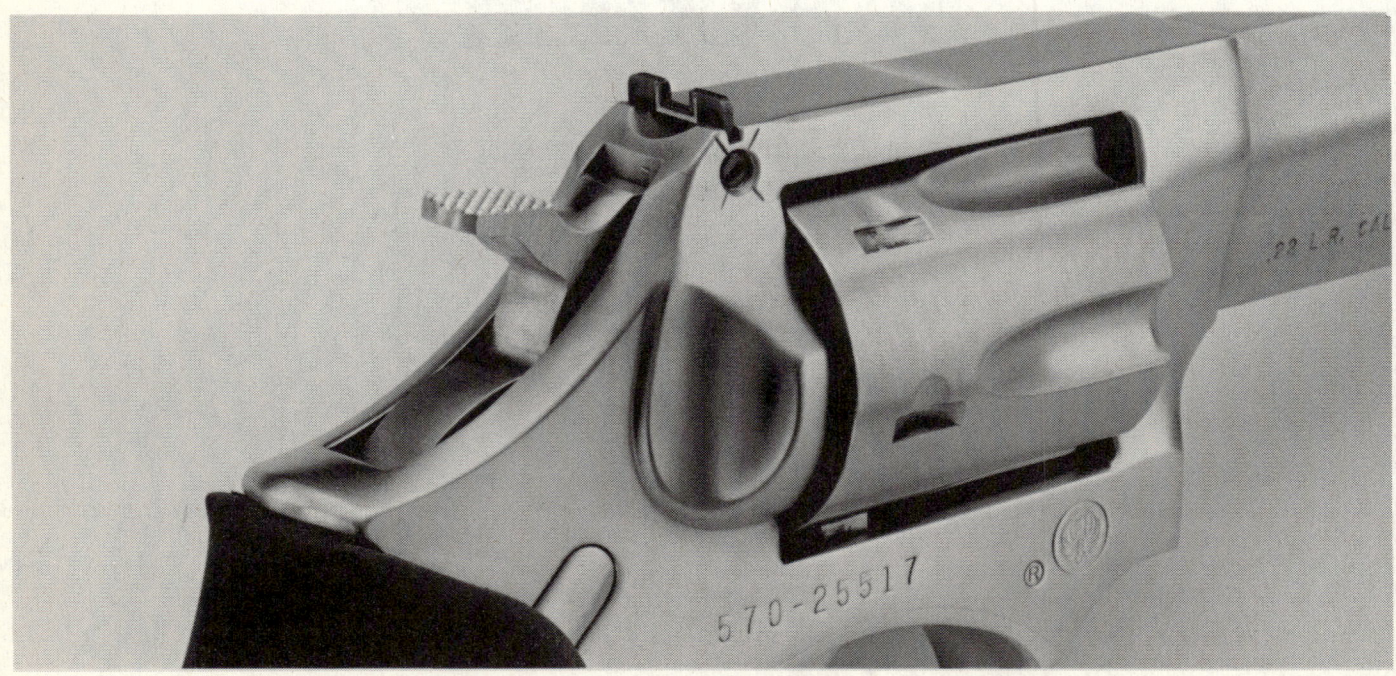

The white-outlined, square notch rear sight on the .22 caliber SP101 is adjustable for windage.

RUGER GP100®

.357 Magnum, Double Action Revolver

Ruger's GP100 Is Available in a Fixed Sight, Compact Grip Version

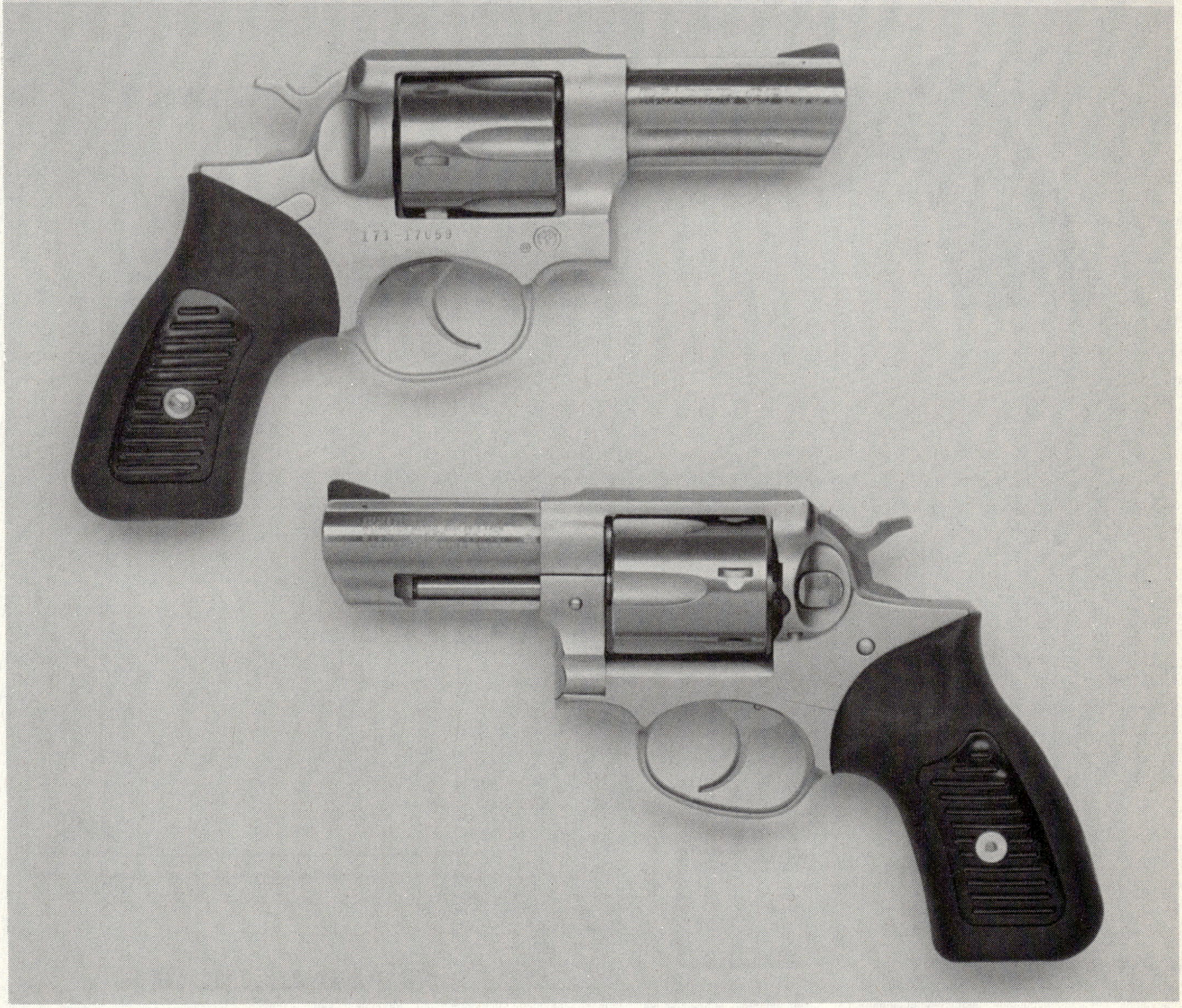

Ruger GP100 .357 magnum, double action revolver. Ruger's GP100 is available in a fixed sight, compact grip version, 3" barrel.

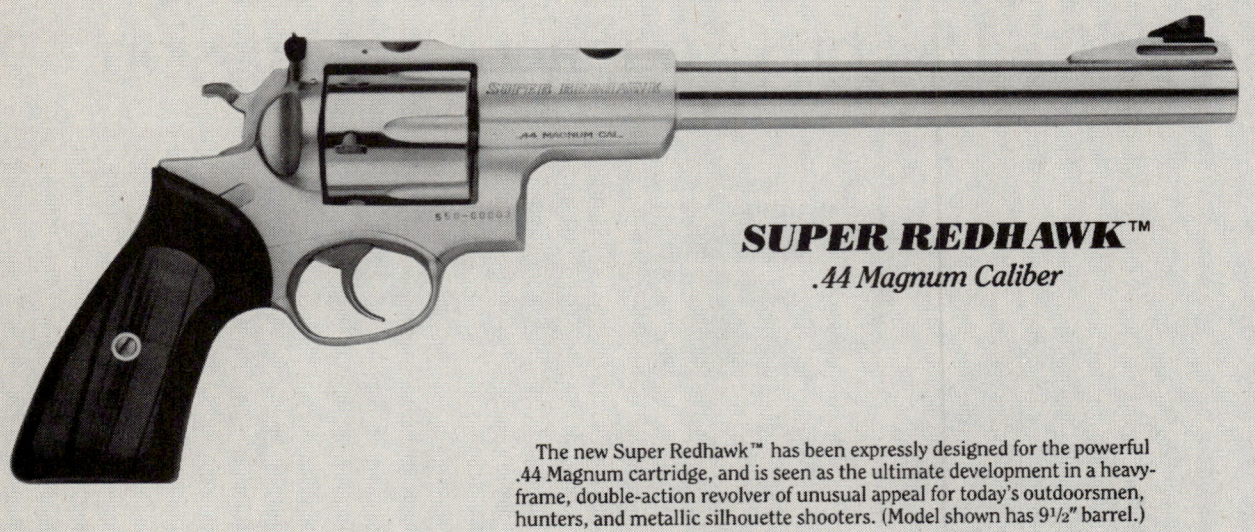

SUPER REDHAWK™
.44 Magnum Caliber

The new Super Redhawk™ has been expressly designed for the powerful .44 Magnum cartridge, and is seen as the ultimate development in a heavy-frame, double-action revolver of unusual appeal for today's outdoorsmen, hunters, and metallic silhouette shooters. (Model shown has 9½″ barrel.)

SUPER REDHAWK™
.44 Magnum Caliber

The massive new Ruger Super Redhawk™ double-action revolver incorporates the exclusive Ruger Integral Scope Mounting System. The integral scope bases on the wide top strap offer a stronger mounting with no stress on the barrel. The Ruger Cushioned Grip System (patents pending) is another important feature of the Super Redhawk revolver. (Model shown has a 9½″ barrel.)

Ruger Mark II standard model, full left view.

Ruger Mark II standard model, caliber .22 long rifle. Stainless steel.

RUGER® Redhawk®

DOUBLE-ACTION REVOLVER

Ruger Redhawk double-action revolver.

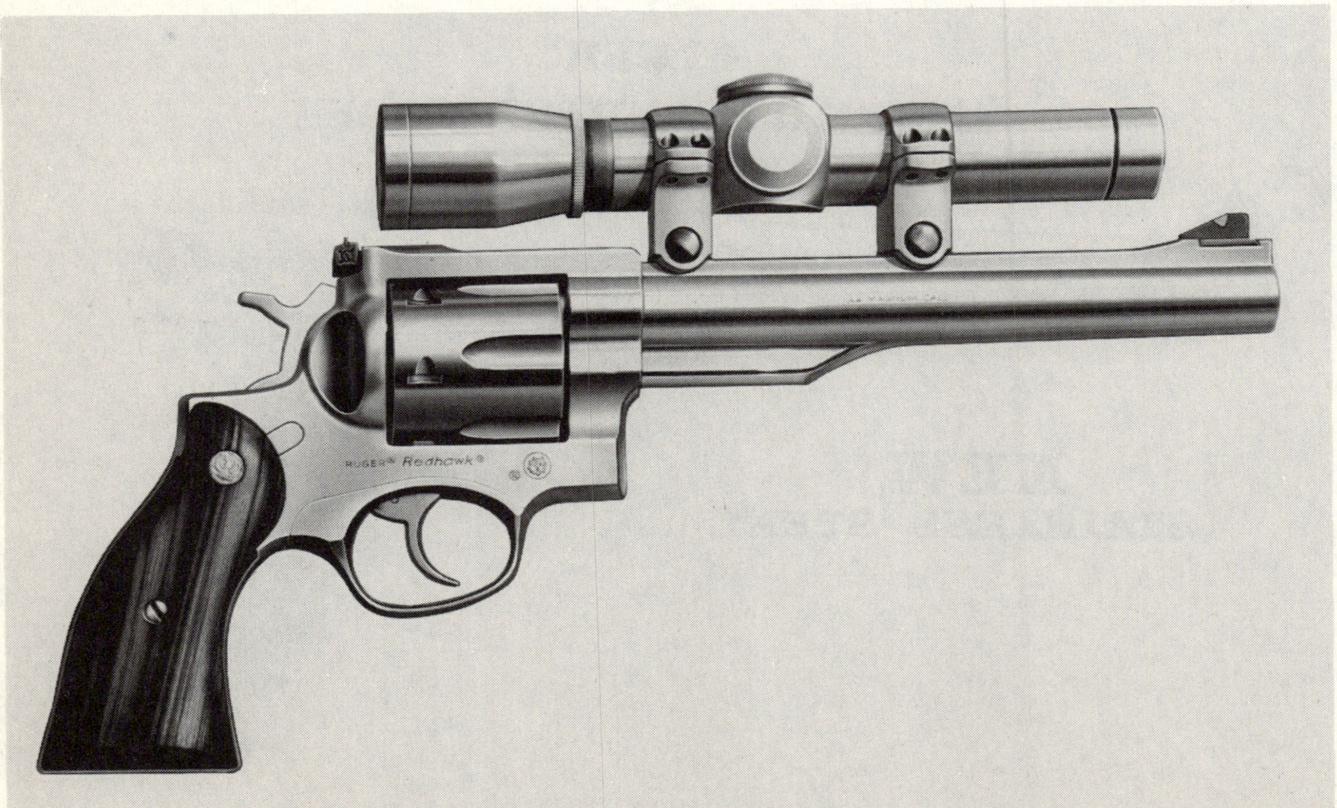

Redhawk revolver — KRH-44R with Ruger integral scope mounting system.

RUGER

MARK II BULL BARREL MODEL PISTOL
Caliber .22 Long Rifle

NEW!
STAINLESS STEEL

Ruger Mark II bull barrel model pistol, caliber .22 long rifle. Stainless steel.

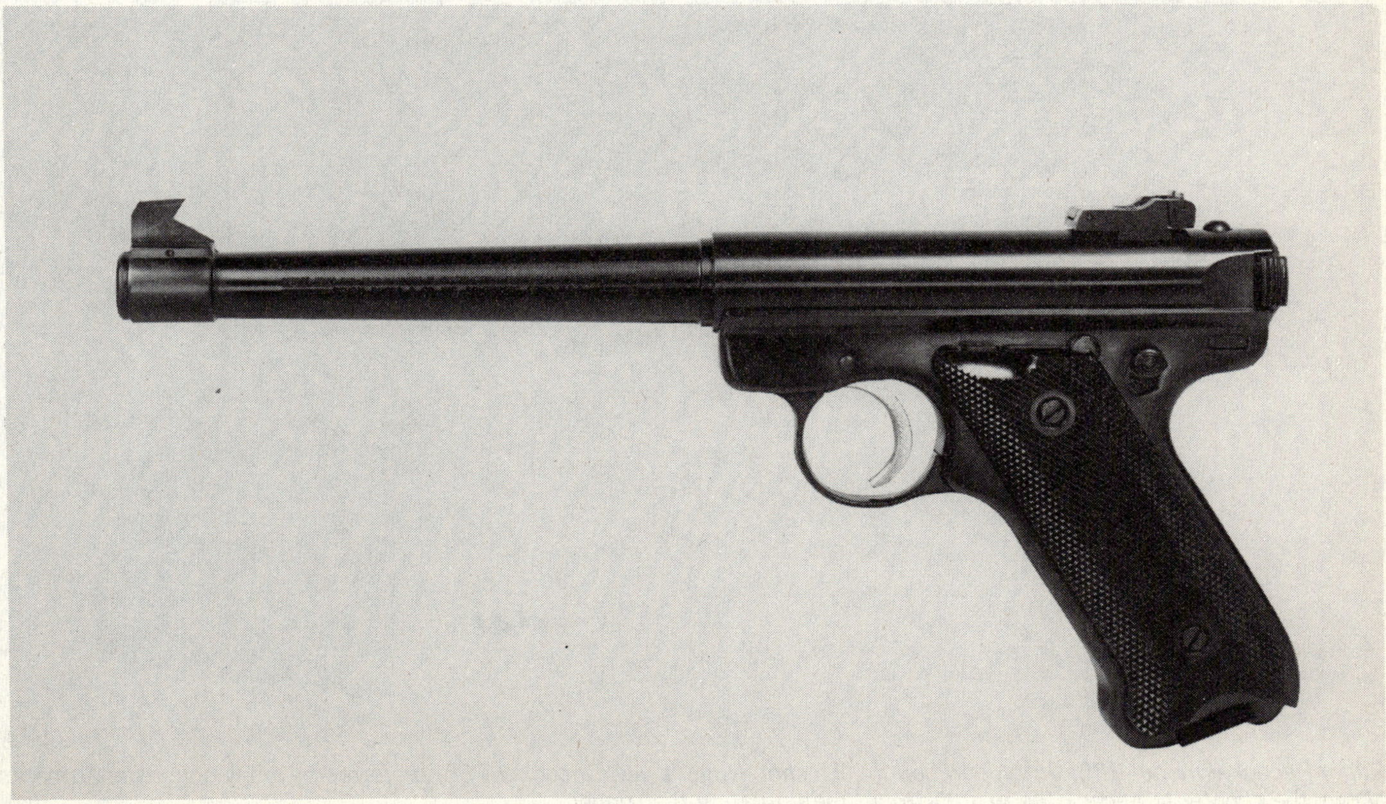

Ruger Mark II target model pistol, full left view.

Ruger Decocker model P85, 9mm, parabellum, 15 shot. Ruger's new Decocker P85, preferred by many police departments, allows the shooter to decock the pistol without manipulating the trigger.

Ruger P85 9mm automatic pistol.

RUGER P85®

9mm Automatic Pistol

Ruger P85 9mm automatic pistol.

RUGER
STAINLESS STEEL P85

9mm, 15 Shot

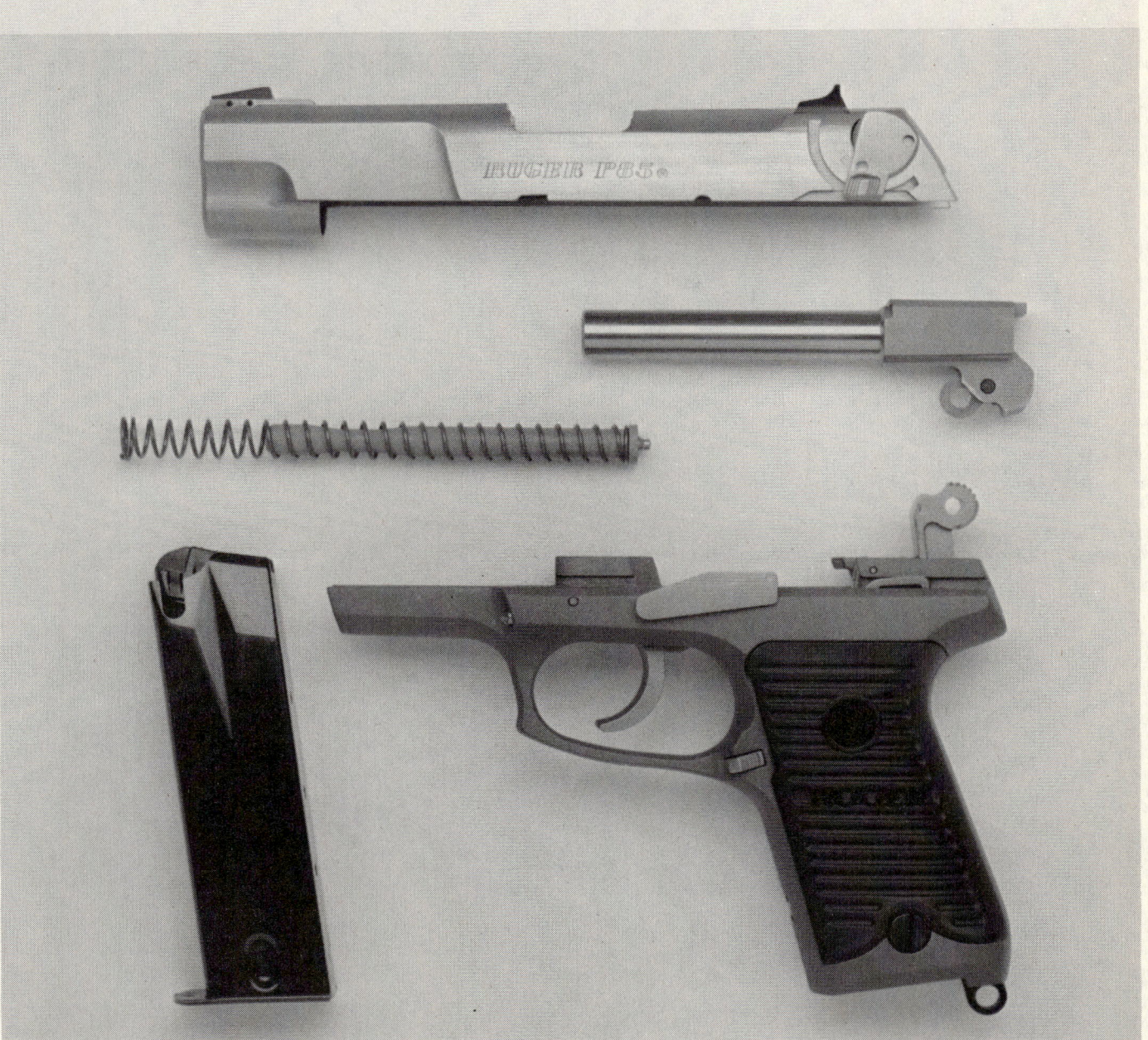

Ruger P85 9mm 15 shot. Basic fieldstripping of the stainless steel P85 is done quickly in the field without the use of tools.

Ruger .22 rimfire bolt-action rifle.

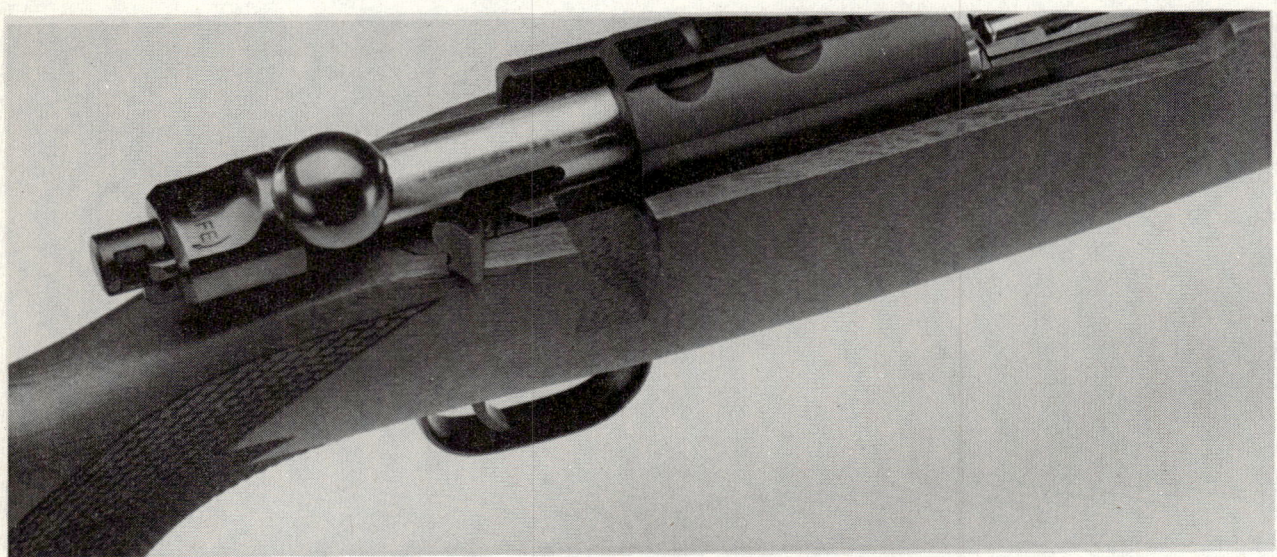

Bolt Open
Ruger 77 .22 magnum .22 rimfire bolt-action rifle; 9-shot rotary clip.

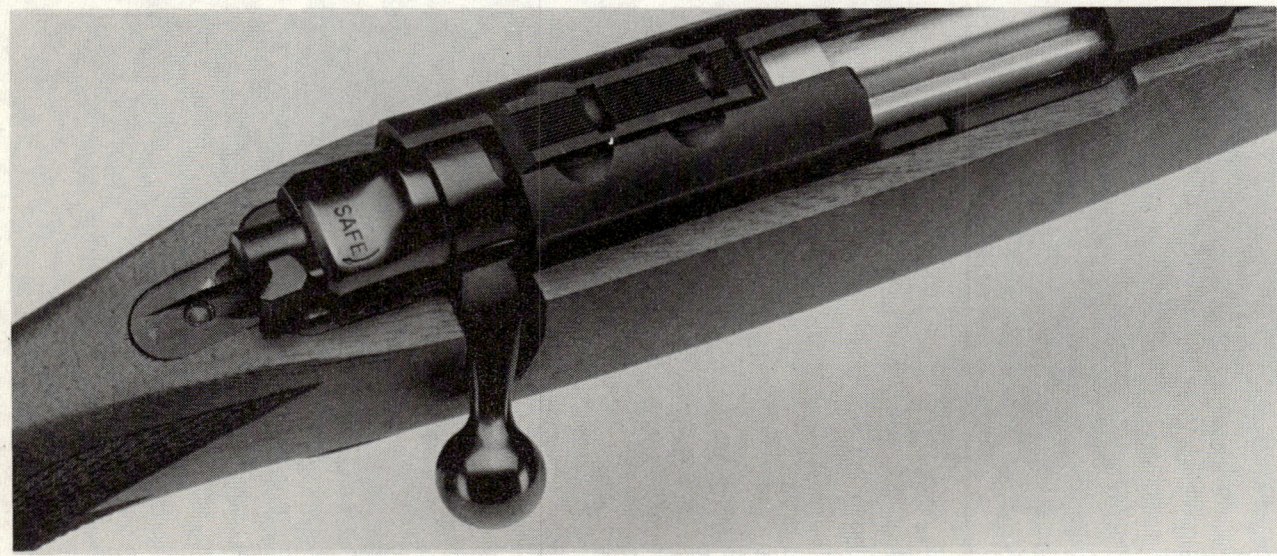

Bolt Closed
Ruger's magnum rimfire rifle is equipped with a readily accessible three-position safety that allows the shooter to unload the rifle with the safety on.

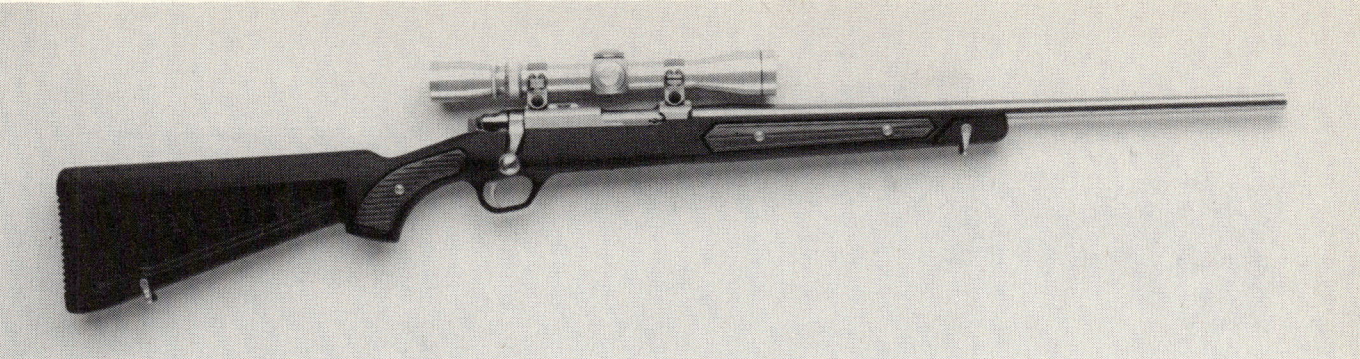

Ruger 77 / 22 .22 caliber rifle. The only all stainless steel, bolt-action rifle incorporating an impervious all-weather injection-moulded stock.

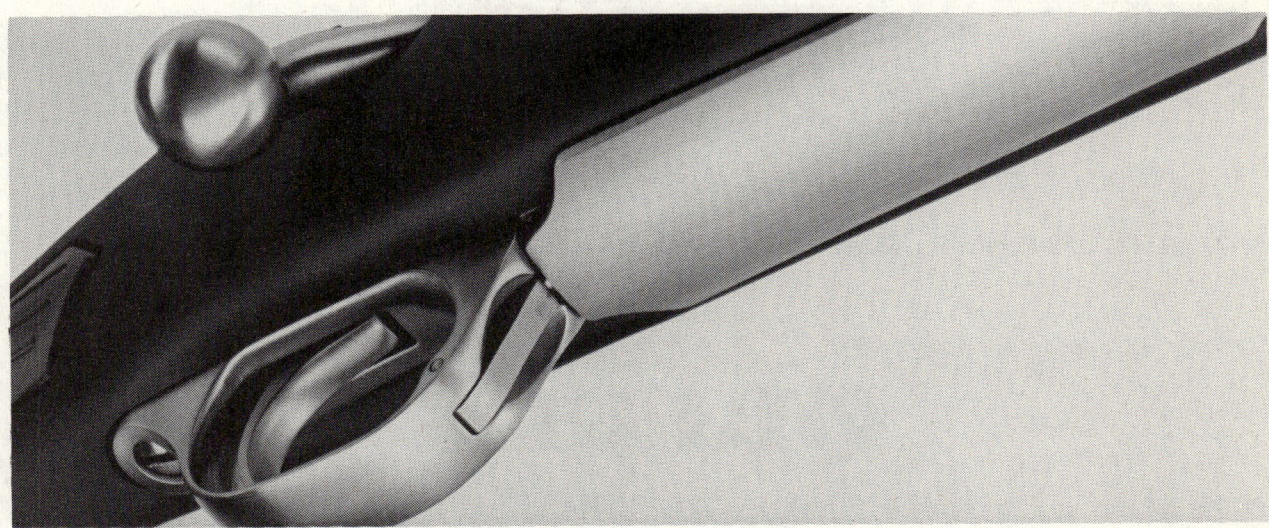

Ruger M77 Mark II stainless steel bolt-action rifle with all-weather stock. The redesigned, patented floorplate latch (flush with the contours of the trigger guard) securely holds the floorplate and prevents accidental dumping of the cartridges. The readily accessible three-position safety allows the shooter to unload the rifle with safety on for optimum convenience and security.

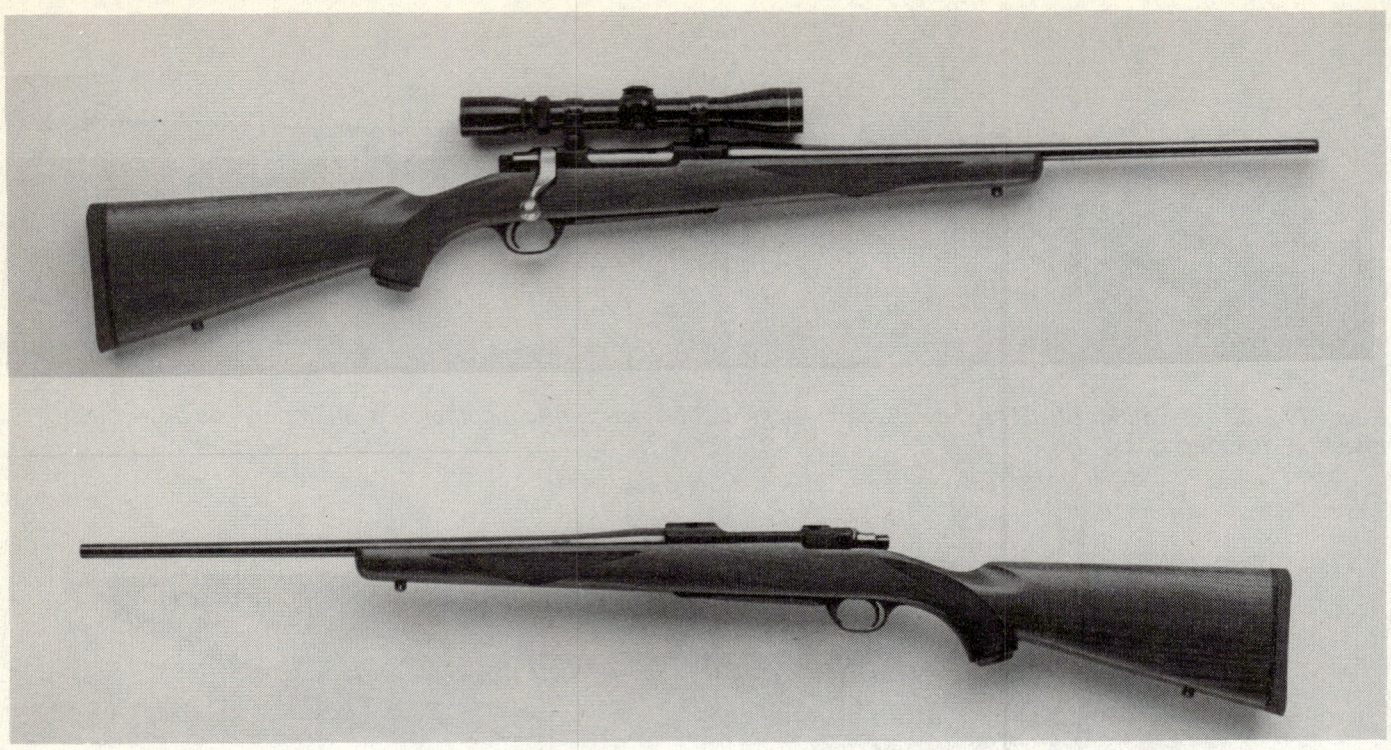

Ruger M-77 Mark II .223 Remington. Ruger's new M-77 Mark II bolt action is the slender, ideal hunter.

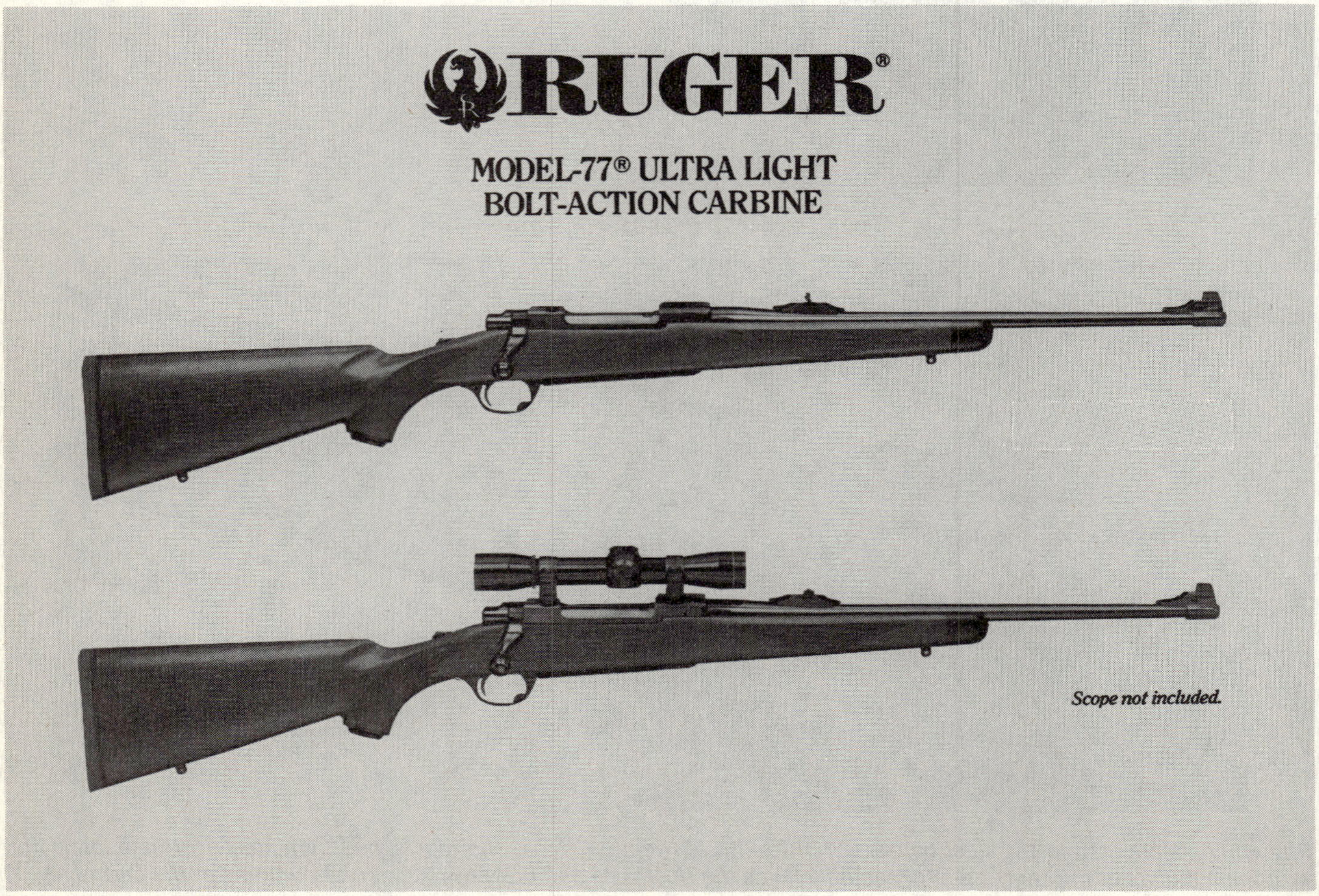

®RUGER®

MODEL-77® ULTRA LIGHT
BOLT-ACTION CARBINE

Scope not included.

Ruger Model-77 ultra light bolt-action carbine.

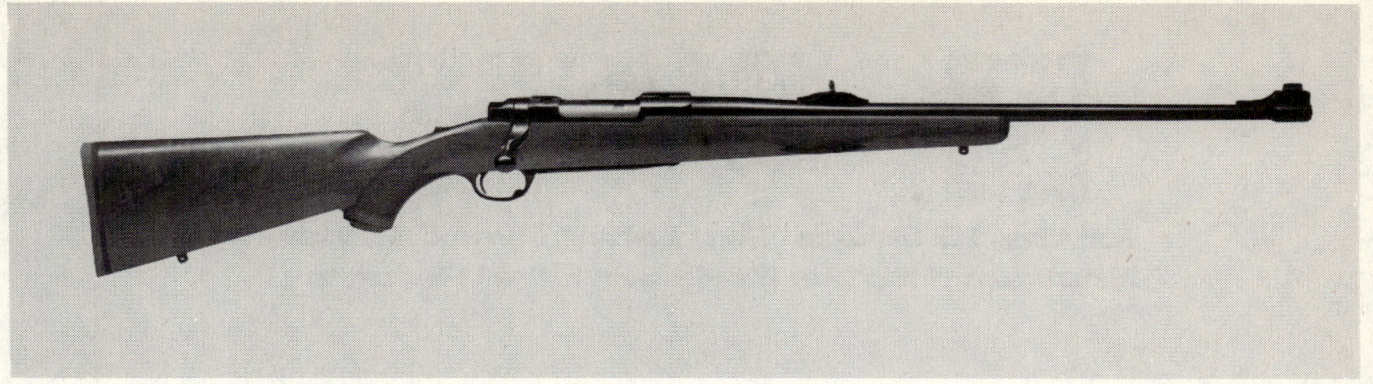

Ruger M-77RS bolt-action rifle.

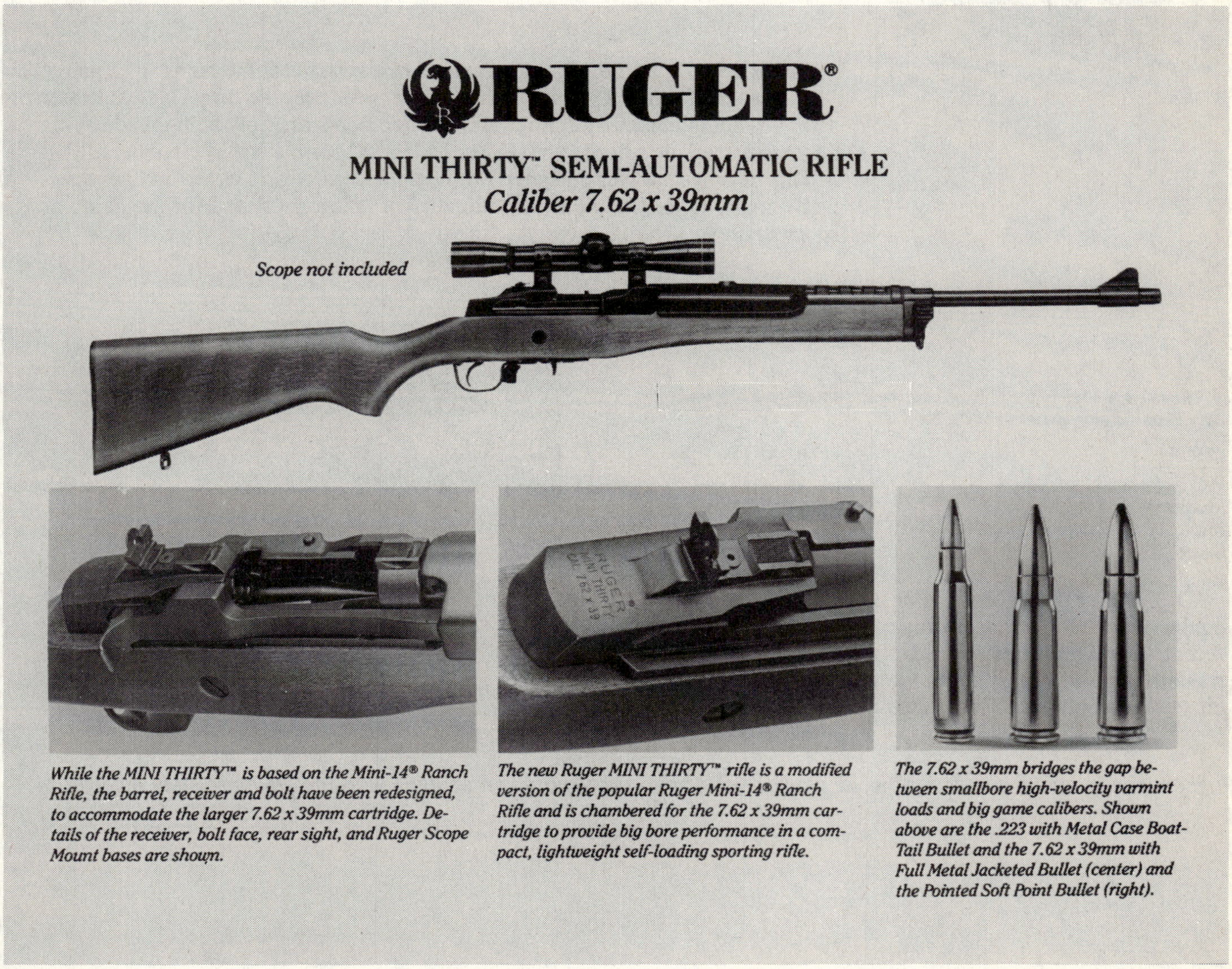

⬢RUGER®

MINI THIRTY™ SEMI-AUTOMATIC RIFLE
Caliber 7.62 x 39mm

Scope not included

While the MINI THIRTY™ is based on the Mini-14® Ranch Rifle, the barrel, receiver and bolt have been redesigned, to accommodate the larger 7.62 x 39mm cartridge. Details of the receiver, bolt face, rear sight, and Ruger Scope Mount bases are shown.

The new Ruger MINI THIRTY™ rifle is a modified version of the popular Ruger Mini-14® Ranch Rifle and is chambered for the 7.62 x 39mm cartridge to provide big bore performance in a compact, lightweight self-loading sporting rifle.

The 7.62 x 39mm bridges the gap between smallbore high-velocity varmint loads and big game calibers. Shown above are the .223 with Metal Case Boat-Tail Bullet and the 7.62 x 39mm with Full Metal Jacketed Bullet (center) and the Pointed Soft Point Bullet (right).

Ruger Mini Thirty semi-automatic rifle. Caliber 7.62 x 39mm.

RUGER®
Screw-In Choke Inserts

for the 12 Gauge "Red Label" Over & Under Shotgun with the Stainless Steel Receiver

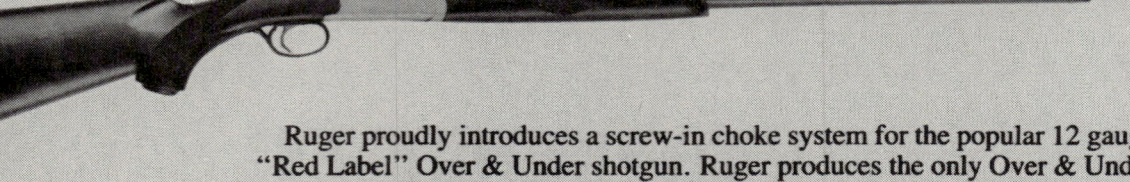

Ruger proudly introduces a screw-in choke system for the popular 12 gauge "Red Label" Over & Under shotgun. Ruger produces the only Over & Under shotgun that is made in America. Initial shipments are now being made. This new model will be offered with either 26″ or 28″ barrels and 3″ chambers.

This new system was designed for the upland game and waterfowl hunter as well as clay target shooters. Additionally, it is ideally suited for the game of sporting clays.

The muzzle edge of the chokes have been slotted for quick and easy identification in or out of the barrels.

CHOKE	NO. OF SLOTS
Full	3
Modified	2
Improved Cylinder	1
Skeet	None

The Ruger Over & Under shotguns that are equipped with the screw-in chokes have a slightly different barrel configuration from the fixed choke models. Due to dimensional variations the screw-in chokes cannot be retrofitted into existing barrels.

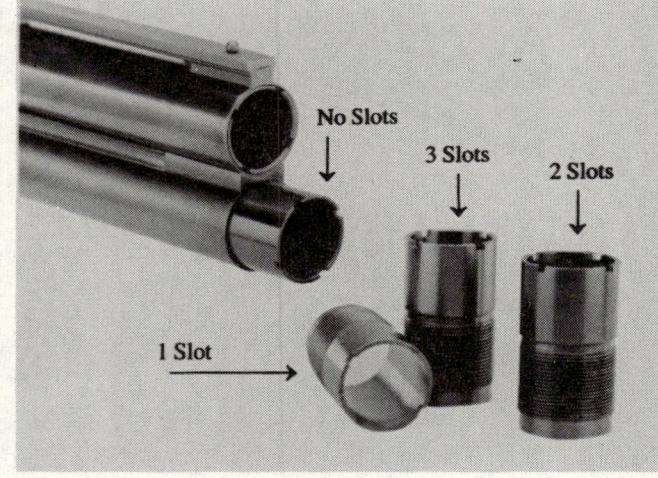

Ruger screw-in choke inserts for the 12 gauge "Red Label" over and under shotgun with the stainless steel receiver.

SUNDANCE INDUSTRIES, INC.
North Hollywood, California

Model D-22M

A .22 or .22 Magnum caliber double-barrel Over/Under pocket pistol with 2.5" barrels and an aluminum alloy frame. Blackened finish or chrome-plated with either simulated pearl or black grips. Introduced in 1989.

Exc.	V. G.	Good	Fair	Poor
225	200	150	100	80

SUTHERLAND, S.
Richmond, Virginia

Pocket Pistol

A .41 caliber percussion single shot pistol with round barrels of 2.5" to 4" in length, German silver mounts and a walnut stock. The lock normally marked "S. Sutherland" or "S. Sutherland/Richmond". Manufactured during the 1850s.

Exc.	V.G.	Good	Fair	Poor
1750	1150	800	400	300

SYMS, J. G.
New York, New York

Pocket Pistol

A .41 caliber single shot percussion pistol with 1.5" to 3.5" barrels, German silver mounts and a walnut stock. The lock normally marked "Syms/New York". Manufactured during the 1850s.

Exc.	V.G.	Good	Fair	Poor
1700	1100	750	400	300

T

TALLASSEE
Tallassee, Alabama

Carbine

A .58 caliber single shot percussion carbine with a 25" round barrel and full-length stock secured by two barrel bands. Fitted with sling swivels. Barrel and lock finished in the bright, brass furniture and walnut stock. The lock marked "C.S./Tallassee/Ala." Approximately 500 of these carbines were manufactured in 1864. Perspective purchasers are advised to secure a qualified appraisal prior to acquisition.

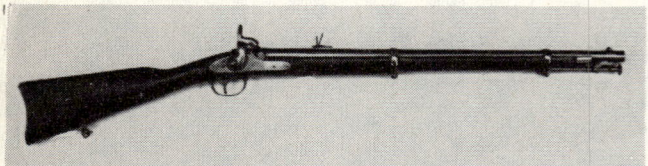

Courtesy Milwaukee Public Museum, Milwaukee, Wisconsin

Exc.	V.G.	Good	Fair	Poor
—	—	7500	3000	800

TANFOGLIO
Valtrompia, Italy

The products of this company, which was established in the late 1940s, have been imported into the United States by various companies including Eig Corporation, F.I.E. of Hialeah, Florida, and Excam.

Sata

A .22 or 6.35mm caliber semiautomatic pistol with a 3" barrel. The slide marked "Pistola SATA Made in Italy" and the grips "SATA". Blued with black plastic grips.

Exc.	V.G.	Good	Fair	Poor
175	150	125	90	75

Titan

A 6.35mm caliber semiautomatic pistol with a 2.5" barrel and external hammer. The slide marked "Titan 6.35" and on U.S. imported examples, "EIG". Blued with plastic grips.

Exc.	V.G.	Good	Fair	Poor
100	75	50	40	30

TA 90 or TZ-75

A 9mm caliber semiautomatic pistol with a 4.75" barrel and 15-shot magazine. Blued or chrome-plated with walnut or rubber grips. Those imported by Excam were known as the Model TA 90, while those imported by F.I.E. are known as the Model TZ-75.

NIB	Exc.	V.G.	Good	Fair	Poor
450	400	350	300	250	200

TA 90B

As above, with a 3.5" barrel, 12-shot magazine and Neoprene grips. Introduced in 1986.

NIB	Exc.	V.G.	Good	Fair	Poor
500	450	400	350	300	250

TA 90 SS

As above, with a ported 5" barrel, adjustable sights and two-tone finish. Introduced in 1989.

NIB	Exc.	V.G.	Good	Fair	Poor
650	600	500	450	400	300

TA 41

As above, in .41 Action Express caliber. Introduced in 1989.

NIB	Exc.	V.G.	Good	Fair	Poor
500	450	400	350	300	250

TA 41 SS

As above, with a ported 5" barrel, adjustable sights and two-tone finish. Introduced in 1989.

NIB	Exc.	V.G.	Good	Fair	Poor
650	600	500	450	400	300

TA 76

A .22 caliber single action revolver with a 4.75" barrel and 6-shot cylinder. Blued or chrome-plated with a brass back strap and triggerguard. Walnut grips.

NIB	Exc.	V.G.	Good	Fair	Poor
100	90	80	65	50	25

TA 76M Combo

As above, with a 6" or 9" barrel and an interchangeable .22 Magnum caliber cylinder.

NIB	Exc.	V.G.	Good	Fair	Poor
110	100	90	75	60	35

TA 38SB

A .38 Special caliber Over/Under double-barrel pocket pistol with 3" barrels and a hammer block safety. Blued with checkered nylon grips. Discontinued in 1985.

Exc.	V.G.	Good	Fair	Poor
100	90	80	60	40

TANNER, ANDRE
Switzerland

Model 300 Free Rifle

A 7.5mm Swiss or .308 caliber single shot rifle with varying length barrels having adjustable target sights, adjustable trigger, and a walnut stock fitted with a palm rest and adjustable cheekpiece. Blued.

NIB	Exc.	V.G.	Good	Fair	Poor
4750	3750	3250	2500	1750	900

Model 300S

As above, with a 10-shot magazine and not fitted with a palm rest. Discontinued in 1988.

NIB	Exc.	V.G.	Good	Fair	Poor
4500	3750	3250	2500	1750	900

Model 50F

As above, in .22 caliber with a thumb hole stock. Discontinued in 1988.

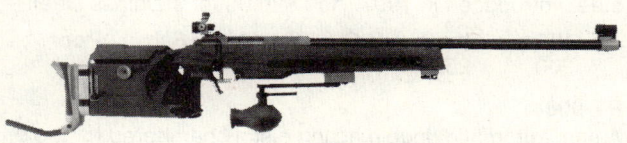

NIB	Exc.	V.G.	Good	Fair	Poor
3750	3200	2500	1750	900	500

TARPLEY J. & F. AND E. T. GARRETT & CO.
Greensboro, North Carolina

Carbine

A .52 caliber breechloading single shot percussion carbine with a 22" round barrel and a plain walnut buttstock. Blued with a case hardened frame. The tang marked "J H Tarpley's./Pat Feb 14./1863". Over 400 of these carbines were manufactured. It is advised that prospective purchasers should seek a qualified appraisal prior to acquisition.

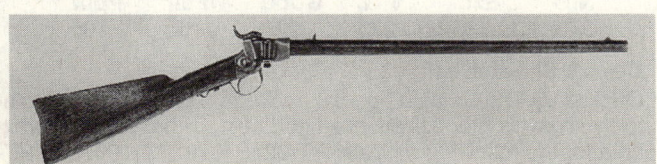

Exc.	V.G.	Good	Fair	Poor
—	—	65000	30000	—

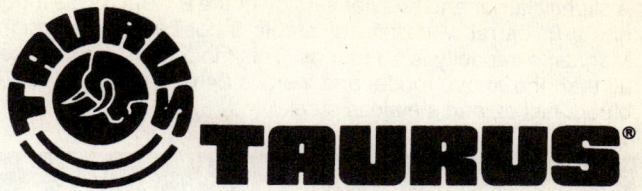

TAURUS INTERNATIONAL MFG. CO.
Porto Alegre, Brazil
Importer-Taurus, Inc.
Miami, Florida

PISTOLS

PT-92AF

A 9mm caliber double action semiautomatic pistol with a 4.92" barrel, exposed hammer, and 15-shot magazine. Blued or nickel-plated with plain walnut grips.

NIB	Exc.	V.G.	Good	Fair	Poor
400	350	300	250	200	150

PT-92C

This 9mm model is a large capacity semiautomatic pistol with a 4.25" barrel. Drift adjustable 3-dot combat rear sight. Magazine holds 13 rounds in a double column. Choice of blued, stain nickel, or stainless steel finish. Brazilian hardwood grips are standard. Weighs 31 oz.

NIB	Exc.	V.G.	Good	Fair	Poor
375	325	275	220	160	100

PT-92

A slightly larger and heavier version of the PT-92C. This model has a 5" barrel with drift adjustable 3-dot combat rear sight. Magazine capacity is 15 rounds. This model is 1" longer over-all than the above model and weighs 34 oz. Also available in blued, nickel, and stainless steel.

NIB	Exc.	V.G.	Good	Fair	Poor
375	325	275	220	160	100

PT-99

Similar in appearance and specifications to the PT-92, this version has the additional feature of fully adjustable 3-dot rear sight.

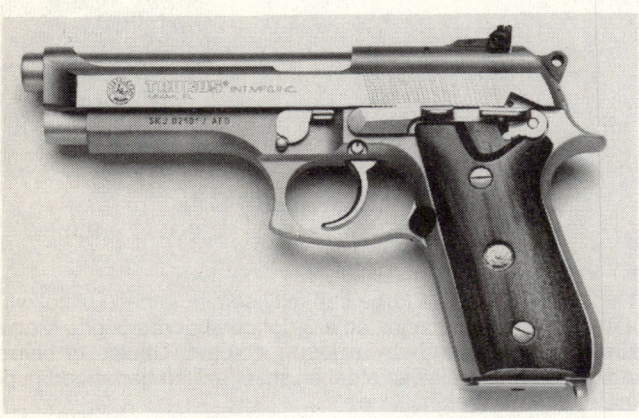

NIB	Exc.	V.G.	Good	Fair	Poor
400	350	300	250	150	100

PT-100

This model is similar to the other full size Taurus semiautomatics except that it is chambered for the .40 S&W cartridge. Sup-plied with a 5" barrel, with drift adjustable rear sight, it has a magazine capacity of 11 rounds. Also available in blued, nickel, or stainless steel. Weighs 34 oz.

NIB	Exc.	V.G.	Good	Fair	Poor
375	325	275	200	150	100

PT-101

Same as the model above but furnished with fully adjustable rear 3-dot combat sight.

NIB	Exc.	V.G.	Good	Fair	Poor
400	350	300	250	150	100

PT-111

This is a double action only pistol chambered for the 9mm car-tridge. Fitted with a 3.3" barrel. Magazine capacity is 10 rounds. Weight is about 27 oz. Choice of blue or stainless steel. Introduced in 1997. Add $20.00 for stainless steel.

NIB	Exc.	V.G.	Good	Fair	Poor
300	250	—	—	—	—.

PT-908

A semiautomatic double action pistol chambered for the 9mm Parabellum cartridge. It is fitted with a 3.8" barrel, with drift ad-justable rear 3-dot combat sight. Magazine capacity is 8 rounds in a single column. Available in blued, satin nickel, or stainless steel. Stocks are black rubber. Pistol weighs 30 oz. Introduced in 1993.

NIB	Exc.	V.G.	Good	Fair	Poor
375	325	275	225	150	100

Deluxe Shooter's Pak

Offered by Taurus as a special package it consists of the pis-tol, with extra magazine, in a fitted custom hard case. Avail-able for the following models: PT-92, PT-99, PT-100, and PT-101.

NOTE: Add approximately 10% to the above prices of these models for this special feature.

PT-911

This model was introduced in 1997 and is chambered for the 9mm cartridge. It is fitted with a 3.85" barrel and has a magazine capacity of 10 rounds. Choice of blue or stainless steel. Weight is about 28 oz. Black rubber grips are standard. Add $15.00 for stainless steel.

NIB	Exc.	V.G.	Good	Fair	Poor
375	300	—	—	—	—

PT-58

This model was introduced in 1988. Chambered for the .380 ACP cartridge it is fitted with a 4" barrel with drift adjustable rear sight. It is a conventional double action design. Available in blued, satin nickel, or stainless steel. It is fitted with Brazilian hardwood grips. Pistol weighs 30 oz.

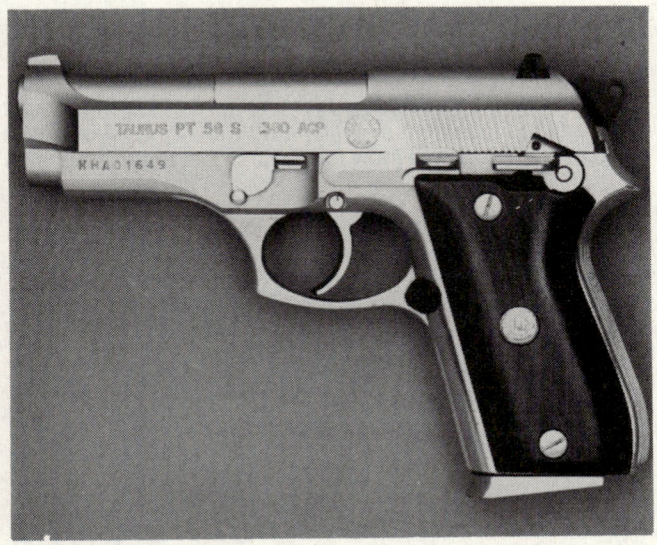

NIB	Exc.	V.G.	Good	Fair	Poor
350	300	250	200	150	100

PT-45

Introduced in 1994 this semiautomatic double action pistol is chambered for the .45 ACP cartridge. The barrel is 3-3/4" in length and the magazine capacity is 8 rounds. Offered in blued or stainless steel with grips of Brazilian hardwood. Fixed sights are standard. Overall length is 7.1" and weight is approximately 30 oz.

Blue Finish

NIB	Exc.	V.G.	Good	Fair	Poor
400	350	275	200	150	100

Stainless Steel

NIB	Exc.	V.G.	Good	Fair	Poor
475	400	325	250	200	150

PT-945

Introduced in 1995 this .45 ACP double action pistol features a 4.25" barrel with an 8-round magazine. The grips are black rubber. The sights are drift adjustable 3-dot combat style. Approximate weight is 30 oz. Offered in blue or stainless steel.

Blue

NIB	Exc.	V.G.	Good	Fair	Poor
350	300	250	200	150	100

Stainless Steel

NIB	Exc.	V.G.	Good	Fair	Poor
400	350	275	225	150	100

PT-940

Similar to the PT-945 except chambered for the .40 S&W cartridge. Fitted with a 3.85" barrel. Magazine capacity is 10 rounds. Choice of blue or stainless steel. Black rubber grips. Weight is approximately 28 oz. Introduced in 1997.

NIB	Exc.	V.G.	Good	Fair	Poor
425	325	—	—	—	—

PT-380

This model is chambered for the .380 ACP cartridge and fitted with a 3.7" barrel. Black rubber grips and choice of blue or stainless steel. Weight is about 27 oz. Introduced in 1997.

NIB	Exc.	V.G.	Good	Fair	Poor
375	325	—	—	—	—

PT-22

This is a semiautomatic double action only pistol that features a 2.75" barrel with fixed sights and a manual safety. It is chambered for the .22 Long Rifle cartridge and has a magazine capacity of 9 rounds. The stocks are Brazilian hardwood and the finish is available in either blue or nickel. Pistol weighs 12.3 oz.

NIB	Exc.	V.G.	Good	Fair	Poor
150	125	100	75	60	50

PT-25

Similar in appearance to the PT-22, this model is chambered for the .25 ACP cartridge and has a magazine capacity of 8 rounds. This model is also fitted with a 2.75" barrel. Offered in either blue finish or nickel.

NIB	Exc.	V.G.	Good	Fair	Poor
150	125	100	75	60	50

REVOLVERS

Model 73

A .32 Smith & Wesson Long double action swing-out cylinder revolver, with a 3" barrel and 6-shot cylinder. Blued or nickel plated with walnut grips.

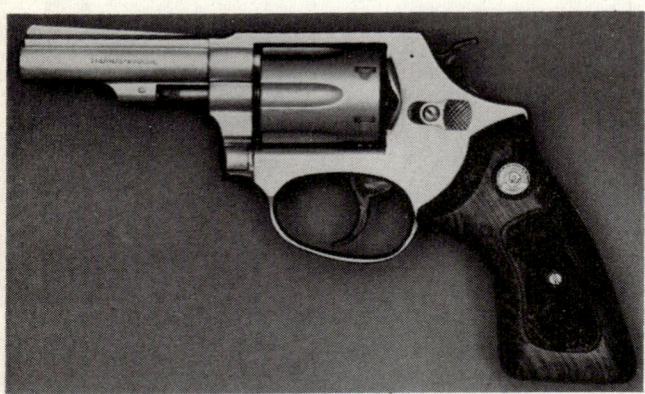

NIB	Exc.	V.G.	Good	Fair	Poor
200	175	150	125	100	75

Model 80

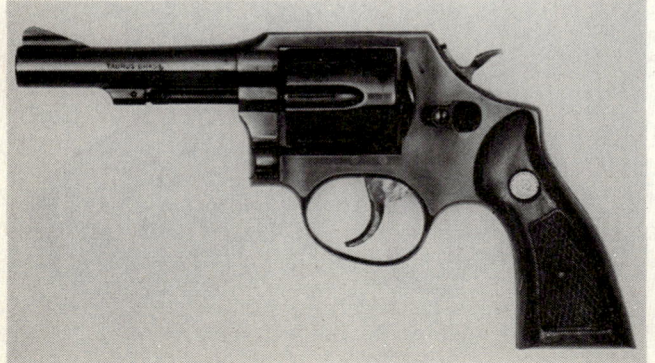

A full size 6-round .38 Special with 3" or 4" heavy tapered barrel. Supplied with fixed sights and offered with blued or stainless steel (offered new in 1993) finish. Brazilian hardwood grips are standard. Weighs 30 oz.

NOTE: Add $40 for stainless steel.

NIB	Exc.	V.G.	Good	Fair	Poor
190	175	135	110	85	70

Model 82

Nearly identical with the Model 80, the Model 82 has a 3" or 4" heavy, solid rib barrel in place of the heavy tapered barrel. Pistol weighs 34 oz.

NIB	Exc.	V.G.	Good	Fair	Poor
190	175	135	110	85	70

NOTE: Add $40 for stainless steel.

Model 83

Similar to the Model 82 except for a fully adjustable rear sight and Partridge type front sight. Offered with 4" barrel only with blued or stainless steel (new for 1993) finish. Pistol weighs 34 oz.

NIB	Exc.	V.G.	Good	Fair	Poor
200	175	150	125	100	75

Model 85

A double action revolver chambered for the .38 Special. This model is available in either a 2" or 3" heavy, solid rib barrel fitted with ejector shroud. Sights are fixed. Blued finish and stainless steel (new for 1993) are offered with Brazilian hardwood grips. Pistol weighs 21 oz. with 2" barrel.

NIB	Exc.	V.G.	Good	Fair	Poor
200	175	150	125	100	75

NOTE: Beginning in 1996 this model will be furnished with Uncle Mike's Boot Grips.

Model 85 Stainless

As above, in stainless steel.

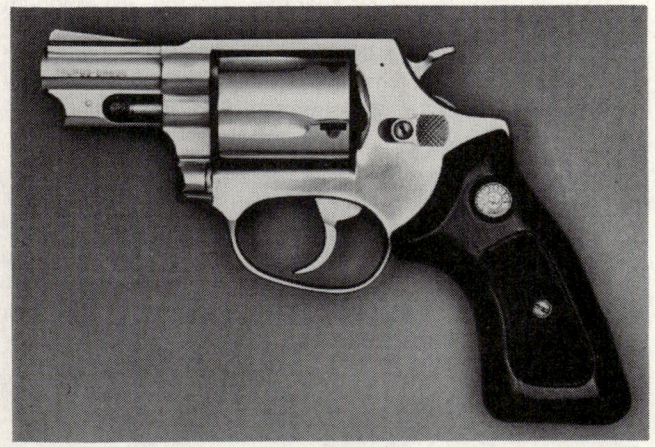

NIB	Exc.	V.G.	Good	Fair	Poor
220	190	175	150	125	100

NOTE: Beginning in 1996 this model will be furnished with Uncle Mike's Boot Grips.

Model 85CH

Same as above but offered in 2" barrel only, with shrouded hammer. Double action only.

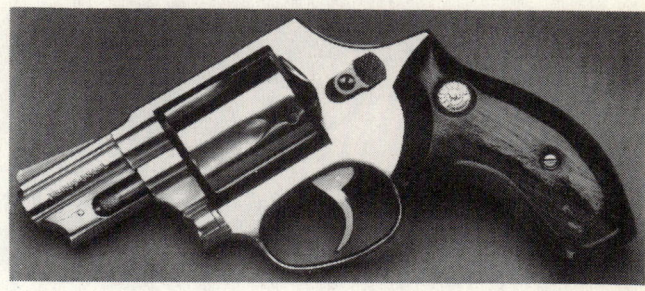

NIB	Exc.	V.G.	Good	Fair	Poor
200	175	150	125	100	75

Model 85 UL

This double action revolver is built on a small aluminum frame and is chambered for the .38 Special cartridge. It is fitted with a 2" barrel. Choice of blue or stainless steel finish. Weight is approximately 17 oz. Introduced in 1997. Add $50.000 for stainless steel.

NIB	Exc.	V.G.	Good	Fair	Poor
250	200	—	—	—	—

Model 86

Similar to the Model 83 with the exception of a 6" barrel, target hammer, adjustable trigger, and blue only finish. Weighs 34 oz.

NIB	Exc.	V.G.	Good	Fair	Poor
250	225	200	150	125	100

Model 94

This double action revolver is chambered for the .22 Long Rifle cartridge. The swing out holds 9 rounds and it is available with either a heavy, solid rib, 3" or 4" barrel. In 1996 a 5" barrel option was added to this model in both blue and stainless steel. Ramp front sight with fully adjustable rear sight. Offered in blued or stainless steel with Brazilian hardwood grips. Pistol weighs 25 oz. with 4" barrel.

Blue

NIB	Exc.	V.G.	Good	Fair	Poor
225	175	150	125	100	75

Stainless Steel

NIB	Exc.	V.G.	Good	Fair	Poor
275	225	175	150	100	75

Model 94 UL

Introduced in 1997 this model is built on a small aluminum frame with 2" barrel and chambered for the .22 Long Rifle cartridge. choice of blue or stainless steel. Weight is approximately 14 oz.

NIB	Exc.	V.G.	Good	Fair	Poor
N/A	—	—	—	—	—

Model 941

Similar in appearance to the Model 94 this version is chambered for the .22 WMR. Available with a choice of 3" or 4" heavy, solid rib barrel. In 1996 a 5" barrel option was added to this model. This model holds 8 rounds. Ramp front sight with fully adjustable rear sight. Available in blued or stainless steel with Brazilian hardwood grips. Pistol weighs 27.5 oz.

Blue

NIB	Exc.	V.G.	Good	Fair	Poor
250	200	175	125	100	75

Stainless Steel

NIB	Exc.	V.G.	Good	Fair	Poor
300	250	200	150	100	75

Model 941 UL

Same as the standard Model 941 but with an aluminum frame and 2" barrel. Weight is about 14 oz. Introduced in 1997.

NIB	Exc.	V.G.	Good	Fair	Poor
N/A	—	—	—	—	—

Model 96

A full size .22 caliber Long Rifle revolver with 6" heavy, solid rib barrel. Fully adjustable rear sight with target hammer and adjustable target trigger. Cylinder holds 6 rounds. Available in blued only with Brazilian hardwood grips. Pistol weighs 34 oz.

NIB	Exc.	V.G.	Good	Fair	Poor
250	225	175	125	100	75

Model 741

This double action revolver is chambered for the .32 H&R Mag. cartridge. It features a 3" or 4" heavy, solid rib barrel with fully adjustable rear sight. Swing out cylinder holds 6 rounds. Available in either blued or stainless steel (stainless steel model introduced in 1993) with Brazilian hardwood grips. Pistol weighs 30 oz.

NIB	Exc.	V.G.	Good	Fair	Poor
200	175	150	125	100	75

NOTE: Add $40 for stainless steel.

Model 761

Similar to the Model 741 this version has a 6" barrel, target hammer, adjustable target trigger, and is available in blued only. Weighs 34 oz.

NIB	Exc.	V.G.	Good	Fair	Poor
250	225	175	150	125	100

Model 65

This double action revolver is chambered for the .357 Magnum cartridge. It is offered with 2.5" or 4" heavy, solid rib barrel with ejector shroud. Fitted with fixed sights and Brazilian hardwood grips it is available in blued or stainless steel. The 2.5" barrel is a new addition to the Model 65 for 1993. Pistol weighs 34 oz. with 4" barrel.

NIB	Exc.	V.G.	Good	Fair	Poor
200	175	150	125	100	75

Model 605

Introduced in 1995 this revolver is chambered for the .357 Magnum cartridge. It is fitted with a 2-1/4" or 3" heavy barrel and is offered in blue or stainless steel. Weighs 25 oz.

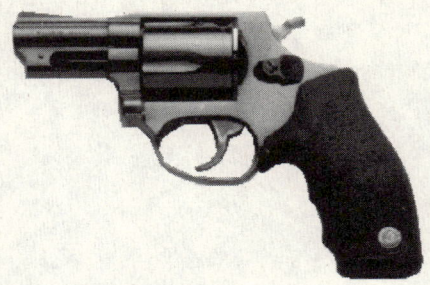

Stainless Steel

NIB	Exc.	V.G.	Good	Fair	Poor
250	200	175	150	125	100

Blue

NIB	Exc.	V.G.	Good	Fair	Poor
200	150	125	100	80	70

Model 605 Custom

Same as above but offered with a 2-1/4" compensated barrel. Prices are the same for blue or stainless steel standard Model 605.

Model 66

Similar to the Model 65 but offered with a choice of 2.5", 4", or 6" barrel with fully adjustable rear sight. Offered with either blued or stainless steel. Weighs 35 oz. with 4" barrel. The 2.5" barrel was introduced in 1993.

NIB	Exc.	V.G.	Good	Fair	Poor
225	200	175	150	125	100

Model 66CP

This model is similar to the Model 66 but features a compensated heavy, solid rib 4" or 6" ejector shroud barrel. Introduced in 1993. Pistol weighs 35 oz.

NIB	Exc.	V.G.	Good	Fair	Poor
250	225	200	150	125	100

Model 669

This model is chambered for the .357 Magnum cartridge and features a 4" or 6" heavy, solid rib barrel with full shroud. It has fully adjustable rear sight and is available with blued or stainless steel finish. Brazilian hardwood grips are standard. Pistol weighs 37 oz. with 4" barrel.

NIB	Exc.	V.G.	Good	Fair	Poor
250	225	200	150	125	100

NOTE: Add $60 for stainless steel.

Model 669CP

This variation of the Model 699 was introduced in 1993 and features a 4" or 6" compensated barrel. Fully adjustable rear sights are standard and it is offered with either blue or stainless steel finish. Weighs 37 oz.

NIB	Exc.	V.G.	Good	Fair	Poor
250	225	200	150	125	100

NOTE: Add $60 for stainless steel.

Model 689

This model is chambered for the .357 Magnum cartridge and features a heavy, vent rib barrel in either 4" or 6" lengths. Fully adjustable rear sight is standard. Offered in blued or stainless steel. Pistol weighs 37 oz.

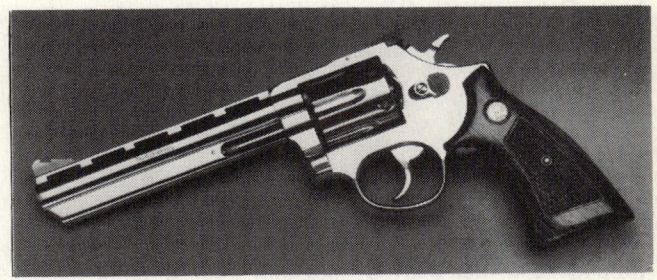

NIB	Exc.	V.G.	Good	Fair	Poor
250	225	200	150	125	100

Model 606

Introduced in 1997 this 6 round model is chambered for the .357 magnum cartridge. Fitted with a 2" solid rib barrel with ramp front sight and notched rear sight. Available in double action, single or double action only. Offered in blue or stainless

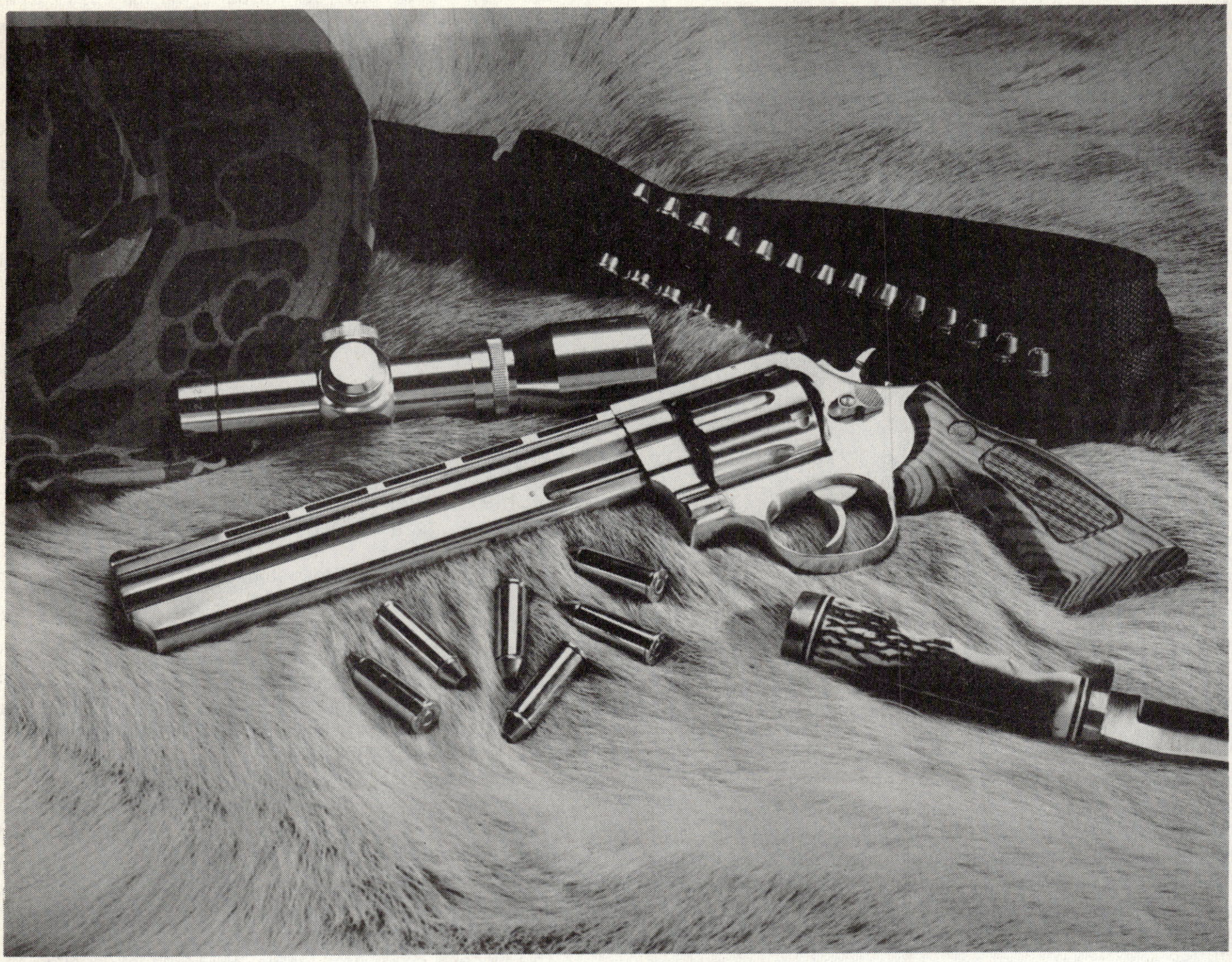

Taurus Model 44

steel. Rubber grips are standard. Weight is approximately 29 oz. A number of variations are offered on this model. For stainless steel models add $50.00.

NIB	Exc.	V.G.	Good	Fair	Poor
250	200	—	—	—	—

Model 607

Introduced in 1995 this .357 Magnum model features a choice of 4" or 6-1/2" integral compensated barrel in either blue or stainless steel. The 6-1/2" barrel is fitted with a vent rib.

Stainless Steel

NIB	Exc.	V.G.	Good	Fair	Poor
400	350	300	200	150	100

Blue

NIB	Exc.	V.G.	Good	Fair	Poor
325	275	225	200	150	100

Model 608

Introduced in 1996 this revolver is chambered for the .357 Magnum cartridge. The cylinder is bored for 8 rounds. Offered in 4" and 6.5" barrel lengths with integral compensator. The front sight is serrated ramp with red insert and the rear is ad-

front sight is serrated ramp with red insert and the rear is adjustable. Offered in both blued and stainless steel versions. Weight is approximately 51.5 oz. with 6.5" barrel.

Stainless Steel

NIB	Exc.	V.G.	Good	Fair	Poor
400	350	300	200	150	100

Blue

NIB	Exc.	V.G.	Good	Fair	Poor
325	275	225	200	150	100

Model 431

Chambered for the .44 Special cartridge this double action revolver is furnished with a 3" or 4" heavy, solid rib barrel with ejector shroud. Cylinder capacity is 5 rounds. Fixed sights are standard. Choice of blued or stainless steel finish. Pistol weighs 35 oz.

NIB	Exc.	V.G.	Good	Fair	Poor
225	200	175	150	125	100

NOTE: Add $60 for stainless steel.

Model 441

Similar to the Model 431 but furnished with an additional choice of a 6" barrel as well as a 3" or 4". Comes standard with fully adjustable rear sight. Cylinder capacity is 5 rounds. Blued or stainless steel finish. Pistol weighs 40.25 oz. with 6" barrel.

NIB	Exc.	V.G.	Good	Fair	Poor
250	225	200	175	125	100

NOTE: Add $60 for stainless steel.

Model 445

This small frame revolver is chambered for the .44 Special cartridge. It is fitted with a 2" barrel with ramp front sight and notched rear sight. Cylinder holds 5 rounds. Black rubber grips. Offered in blue or stinaless steel. Weight is about 28 oz. Add $50.00 for stainless steel. Factory barrel porting is optional. Introduced in 1997.

NIB	Exc.	V.G.	Good	Fair	Poor
250	200	—	—	—	—

Model 454

This model is chambered for the .454 Casull. It is built on a large frame with a 5-round capacity. Barrel lengths are 6.5" or 8.375" and are fitted with a ventilated rib and integral compensator. Sights are adjustable. Finish is blue or stainless steel. Black rubber or walnut grips. Weight is 53 oz with 6.5" barrel. Add $60.00 for stainless steel model. Introduced in 1997.

NIB	Exc.	V.G.	Good	Fair	Poor
650	550	—	—	—	—

Model 44

Introduced in 1994 this heavy frame revolver is chambered for the .44 Magnum cartridge. Offered with choice of three barrel lengths: 4" with sold rib barrel, 61/2" with vent rib, and 8-3/8" with vent rib. All Model 44s have a built in compensator. The

front sight is a serrated ramp with adjustable rear sight. Offered in either blued or stainless finish. Weight of 6-1/2" barrel gun is 53 oz.

Blue Finish

NIB	Exc.	V.G.	Good	Fair	Poor
300	250	200	175	150	100

Stainless Steel

NIB	Exc.	V.G.	Good	Fair	Poor
350	300	250	200	150	100

TAYLOR, L.B.
Chicopee, Massachusetts

Pocket Pistol

A .32 caliber spur trigger single shot pocket pistol with a 3.5" octagonal barrel marked "L. B. Taylor & Co. Chicopee Mass." Silver-plated brass frame, blued barrel and walnut grips. Manufactured during the late 1860s and early 1870s.

Exc.	V.G.	Good	Fair	Poor
—	—	400	150	100

TERRIER ONE
Importer-Southern Gun Distributors
Miami, Florida

Terrier One

A .32 caliber double action swing-out cylinder revolver with a 2.25" barrel and 5-shot cylinder. Nickel-plated with checkered walnut grips. Manufactured from 1984 to 1987.

Exc.	V.G.	Good	Fair	Poor
75	65	50	30	25

TERRY, J. C.
New York City

Pocket Pistol

A .22 caliber spur trigger single shot pocket pistol with a 3.75" round barrel. The back strap marked "J.C. Terry/Patent Pending." Silver-plated brass frame, blued barrel and rosewood or walnut grips. Manufactured in the late 1860s.

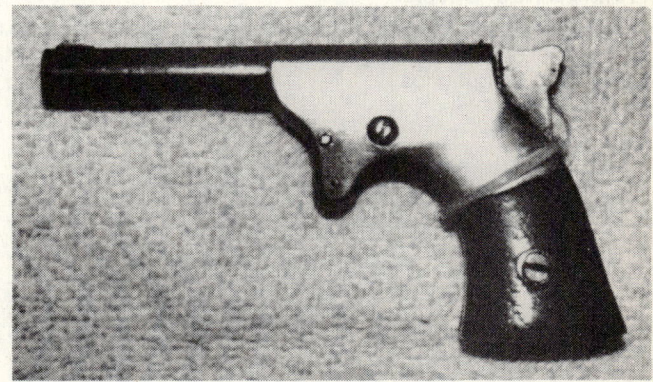

Exc.	V.G.	Good	Fair	Poor
—	—	750	350	100

TEXAS CONTRACT RIFLES

Three contractors produced rifles for the State of Texas during 1862 and 1863. One of these patterns has a sporting back-action lock, Enfield barrel bands, an overall length of 47-3/8", heavy 32" long barrel of .58 caliber. Total deliveries by all contractors amount to 1,464 rifles. Quality of these arms was decidedly inferior and often complained about.

Prospective purchasers are strongly advised to secure an expert appraisal prior to acquisition.

TEXAS GUNFIGHTERS
Ponte Zanano, Italy
Importer-Texas Gunfighters
Irving, Texas

Shootist Single Action

A .45 Long Colt caliber single action revolver with a 4.75" barrel. Nickel-plated with one-piece walnut grips. This model is made by Aldo Uberti. Introduced in 1988.

NIB	Exc.	V.G.	Good	Fair	Poor
600	550	500	400	350	200

1 of 100 Edition

As above, with one-piece mother-of-pearl grips fitted in a case with an additional set of walnut grips. 100 were made in 1988.

NIB	Exc.	V.G.	Good	Fair	Poor
1250	1000	850	700	600	300

TEXAS LONGHORN ARMS, INC.
Richmond, Texas

Jezebel

A .22 or .22 Magnum single shot pistol with a 6" barrel. Stainless steel with a walnut stock and forend. Introduced in 1987.

NIB	Exc.	V.G.	Good	Fair	Poor
225	175	150	125	100	75

Texas Border Special

A .44 Special or .45 Colt caliber single action revolver with a 3.5" barrel having Pope style rifling. Blued, casehardened with one-piece walnut grips.

NIB	Exc.	V.G.	Good	Fair	Poor
1500	1250	1000	800	600	300

South Texas Army

As above, but with a 4.75" barrel also chambered for the .357 Magnum cartridge and fitted with conventional one-piece walnut grips.

NIB	Exc.	V.G.	Good	Fair	Poor
1500	1250	1000	800	600	300

West Texas Target

As above, with a 7.5" barrel, flat top frame and in .32-20 caliber in addition to the calibers noted above.

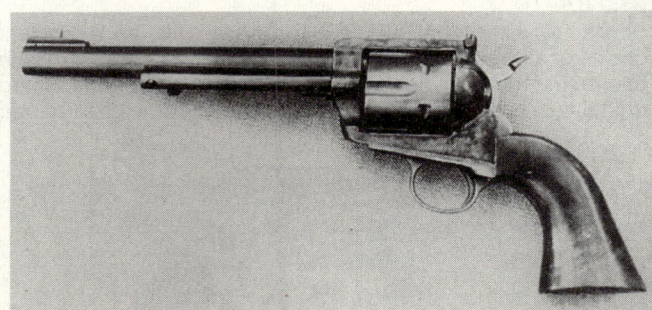

NIB	Exc.	V.G.	Good	Fair	Poor
1500	1250	1000	800	600	300

Grover's Improved Number Five

Similar to the above, in .44 Magnum with a 5.5" barrel. Serial Numbered K1 to K1200. Introduced in 1988.

NIB	Exc.	V.G.	Good	Fair	Poor
1000	800	700	600	500	250

Mason Commemorative

As above, in .45 Colt with a 4.75" barrel and having the Mason's insignia. Gold inlaid. Introduced in 1987.

NIB	Exc.	V.G.	Good	Fair	Poor
1500	1250	1000	800	600	300

Texas Sesquicentennial Commemorative

As above, engraved in the style of Louis D. Nimschke with one-piece ivory grips and a fitted case.

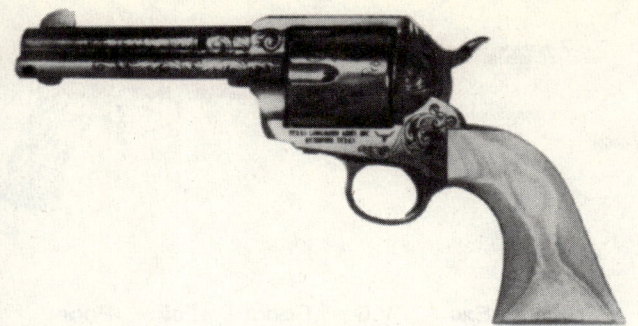

NIB	Exc.	V.G.	Good	Fair	Poor
2500	2000	1500	900	750	400

THAMES ARMS CO.
Norwich, Connecticut

A .22, .32, or .38 caliber double action top break revolver with varying length barrels normally marked 'Automatic Revolver", which refers to the cartridge ejector. Nickel-plated with walnut grips.

Exc.	V.G.	Good	Fair	Poor
175	125	100	75	50

THIEME & EDELER
Eibar, Spain

Pocket Pistol

A 7.65mm caliber semiautomatic pistol with a 3" barrel marked "T E". Blued with black plastic grips. Manufactured prior to 1936.

Exc.	V.G.	Good	Fair	Poor
175	150	100	75	50

THOMPSON
SEE Auto Ordnance

THOMPSON/CENTER ARMS
Rochester, New Hampshire

Contender

Introduced in 1967 this model is the basis for all past and present variations. The standard version is offered with a 10" octagon barrel and is available in 10" Bull barrel, 10" vent rib barrel, 14" Super models, 14" Super with vent rib, 16" Super models, and 16" Super models with vent rib. A stainless steel finish is available on all models except the 10" octagon barrel. The action on these handguns is a single shot, break open design. Unless otherwise stated the barrels are blued. The Competitor grip is walnut with rubber insert mounted on back of grip. A finger groove grip is also available made from walnut with finger notching and thumb rest. Forend is American black walnut in various length and designs depending on barrel size. Stainless steel models have rubber grips with finger grooves. Standard sights are standard Patridge rear with ramp front. An adjustable rear sight is offered as an option. Barrels with vent ribs are furnished with fixed rear sight and bead front sight. Due to the numerous variations of the Contender several breakdowns will be listed to help the reader find the closest possible handgun he may be looking for.

NOTE: Early frames with no engraving, called flatsides, and those with eagle engraving bring between $2,000 and $2,500 on the collector market.

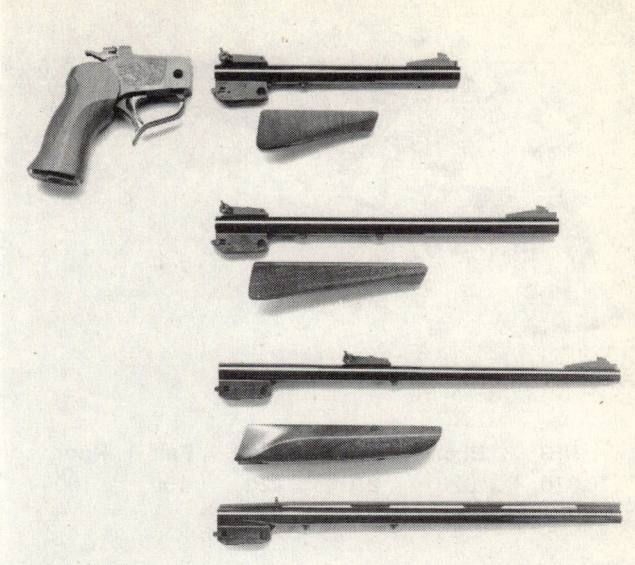

10" Octagon Barrel Model

This was the first Contender design and is offered in .22 Long Rifle only. It is supplied with adjustable rear sight and mounting holes for scope. Grips are Competitor or rubber. Weighs about 44 oz.

NIB	Exc.	V.G.	Good	Fair	Poor
360	300	250	200	150	100

10" Bull Barrel Model

Comes standard with adjustable rear sight, mounting holes for scope mounts, and Competitor grips for blued models and rubber grips on stainless models. Available in blued or stainless steel. Offered in the following calibers as complete pistols: .22 l.r., .22 l.r. Match, .22 Win. Mag. (blued only), .22 Hornet, .223, 7mm T.C.U. (blued only), .30-30, .32-20 (blued only), .357 Mag., .357 Rem. max (blued only), .44 Mag., .45 Colt, .410 bore. In 1994 Thompson/Center introduced the .300 whisper cartridge to its Contender product line. Weighs approximately 50 oz.

NIB	Exc.	V.G.	Good	Fair	Poor
350	300	250	200	150	100

10" Vent Rib Model

This features a raised vent rib and is chambered for the .45 Long Colt/.410 bore. The rear sight is fixed and the front sight is a bead. A detachable choke screws into the muzzle for use with the .410 shell. Furnished with Competitor grips or rubber grips.

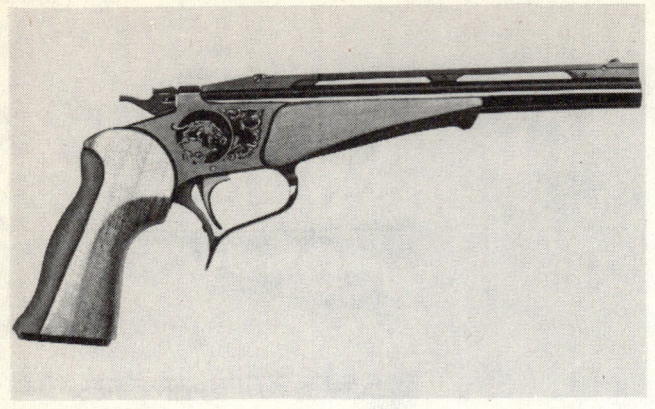

NIB	Exc.	V.G.	Good	Fair	Poor
370	320	270	220	150	100

Super 14" Model

This model features a 14" bull barrel. Furnished with adjustable rear sight and ramp front sight. Drilled and tapped for scope mounts. Competitor or rubber grips are offered. Available in blued or stainless steel finish. Furnished in the following calibers in a complete pistol only: .22 Long Rifle, .22 l.r. Match, .17 Rem. (blued only), .22 Hornet, .222 Rem. (blued only), .223 Rem., 7mm T.C.U. (blued only), 7-30 Waters, .30-30, .357 Rem. Max (blued only), .35 Rem., .375 Win. (blued only), .44 Mag. (blued only). weighs approximately 56 oz.

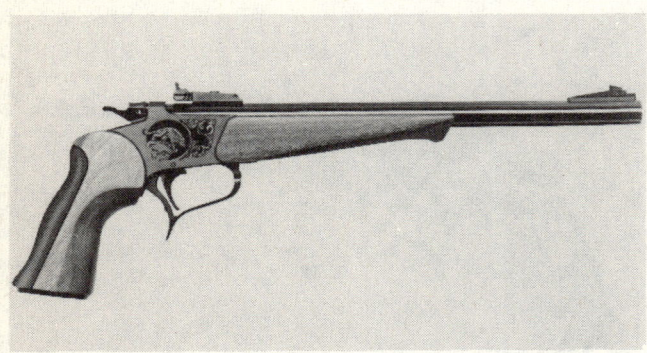

NIB	Exc.	V.G.	Good	Fair	Poor
360	300	250	200	150	100

Super 14" Vent Rib Model

Similar to the 10" vent rib model chambered for the .45 Long Colt/.410 bore but furnished with a 14" vent rib barrel.

NIB	Exc.	V.G.	Good	Fair	Poor
385	325	275	215	150	100

Super 16" Model

Fitted with a 16.25" tapered barrel, two position adjustable rear sight. Drilled and tapped for scope mount. Furnished with Competitor grips or rubber grips and choice of blued or stainless steel finish. Available in the following calibers as complete pistols only: .22 l.r., .22 Hornet, .223 Rem., 7-30 Waters, .30-30, .35 Rem., .45-70 Government. Weighs approximately 56 oz.

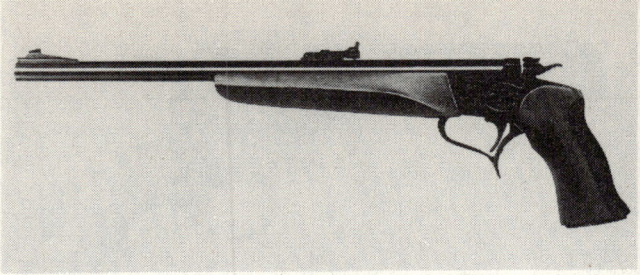

NIB	Exc.	V.G.	Good	Fair	Poor
370	320	275	215	150	100

Super 16" Vent Rib Model

Chambered for .45 Long Colt/.410 bore this model was offered for the first time in 1993. All other features are the same as the other Contender .45/.410 bore pistols.

NIB	Exc.	V.G.	Good	Fair	Poor
390	350	300	250	175	125

Contender Hunter Model

This model is designed for handgun hunting and is offered in two barrel lengths: 12" and 14". The barrels are fitted with a compensator and a 2.5 power scope. There are no iron sights fitted. A nylon carrying sling and soft leather carrying case are standard. Offered in the following calibers: 7-30 Waters, .30-30 Win., .35 Rem., .45-70 Government, .44 Mag., .223 Rem., and .375 Win. Fitted with Competitor grips and offered in blued or stainless steel finish. Weighs approximately 64 oz.

NIB	Exc.	V.G.	Good	Fair	Poor
575	500	400	300	200	100

> **NOTE:** Barrel interchangeability is acceptable for blued barrels and frames with stainless steel barrels and frames. DO NOT interchange Alloy II barrels and frames with either blued or stainless steel components.

Encore Pistol

Introduced in 1996 this single shot pistol will feature barrels chambered for the .30-06, .308 Win., 7mm-08 Rem., .223 Rem., .22-250 Rem., .44 Magnum, and 7mmBR. Offered with 10.625", 15", or 24" barrels this new handgun is designed for use with higher pressure cartridges. Barrels will not interchange with the Contender. Weight with 10.625" barrel is 56 oz., with 15" barrel about 4 lbs. and with 24" barrel about 6.75 lbs.

NIB	Exc.	V.G.	Good	Fair	Poor
500	450	—	—	—	—

Encore Rifle

Similar to the Encore pistol but with longer barrels and walnut stock and forearm. A wide variety of calibers are offered from .22-250 to .300 Win. Mag. in barrels lengths from 24" to 26". Heavy barrels are offered in 7mm Rem Mag., .300 Win. Mag., and .22-250. These are offered with no sights. Weight is about 6 lbs. 12 oz. for 7mm-08 with 24" barrel. Introduced in 1997.

NIB	Exc.	V.G.	Good	Fair	Poor
525	450	—	—	—	—

Contender Carbine Model

This model is built from the same design as the Contender Model. It features completely interchangeable barrels chambered for 12 different cartridges from .22 l.r. to .35 Rem. A .410 bore shotgun barrel is also offered. The standard model has a 21" barrel stocked with walnut. For stainless steel models a composite stock in fitted walnut is also available. All are drilled and tapped for scope mounts. Available in blued or stainless steel.

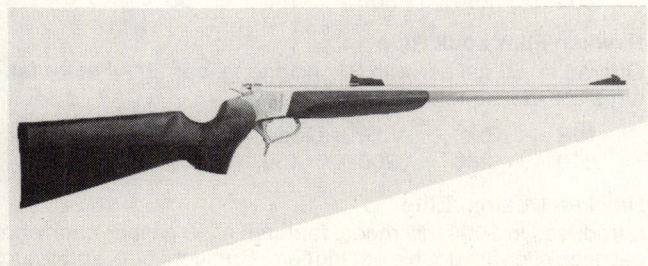

Standard 21" Carbine Model

This model is fitted with a 21" plain barrel and walnut stocks. Offered in the following calibers as a complete gun only: .22 l.r., .22 l.r. Match (blued only), .17 Rem. (blued only), .22 Hornet, .223 Rem., 7-30 Waters, .30-30, .35 Rem. (blued only), .375 Win. (blued only). Weighs 5 lbs., 3 oz.

NIB	Exc.	V.G.	Good	Fair	Poor
400	350	300	250	200	100

21" Carbine .410 Bore

Same as above but fitted with a vent rib barrel and screw in choke.

NIB	Exc.	V.G.	Good	Fair	Poor
410	360	300	250	200	100

16" Youth Model Carbine

A special walnut buttstock with 12" length of pull and 16.25" barrel. Short buttstock can be replaced with standard buttstock. Blued or stainless steel finish. Complete guns are offered in the same calibers as the 21" Carbine with the exception of the .375 Win. and the addition of the .45 Long Colt/.410 bore with vent rib barrel.

NIB	Exc.	V.G.	Good	Fair	Poor
350	300	250	200	150	100

TCR Hunter Model

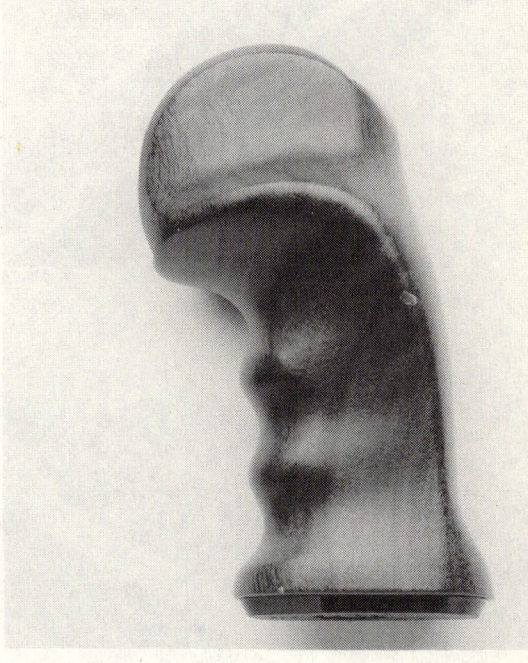

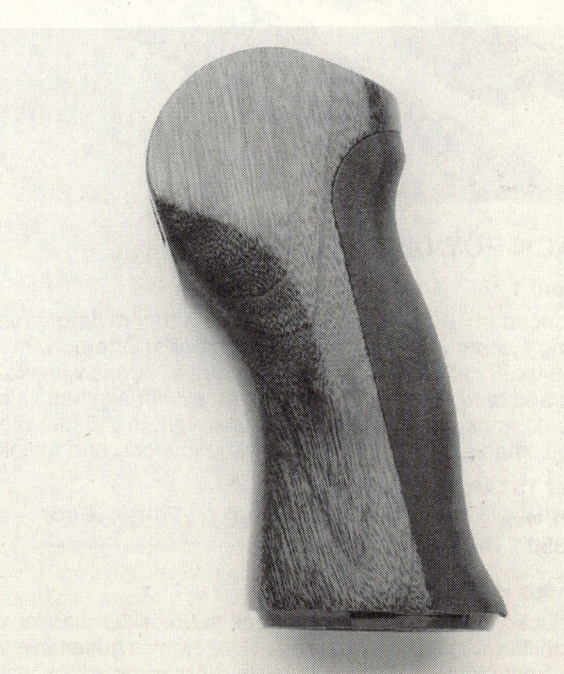

This single shot top lever rifle is chambered for cartridges from .22 Long Rifle to .308 Win. Fitted with a 23" barrel. The finish is blue with walnut stock. Discontinued as a regular production rifle in 1993 but available from the TC custom shop as a special order.

NIB	Exc.	V.G.	Good	Fair	Poor
425	375	300	250	200	100

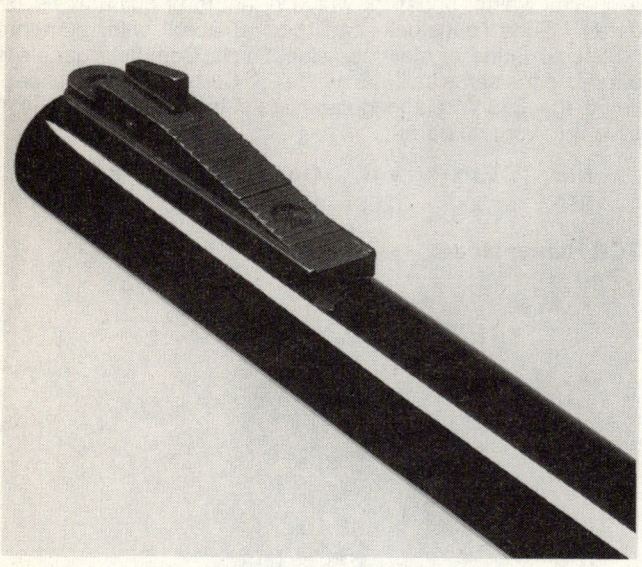

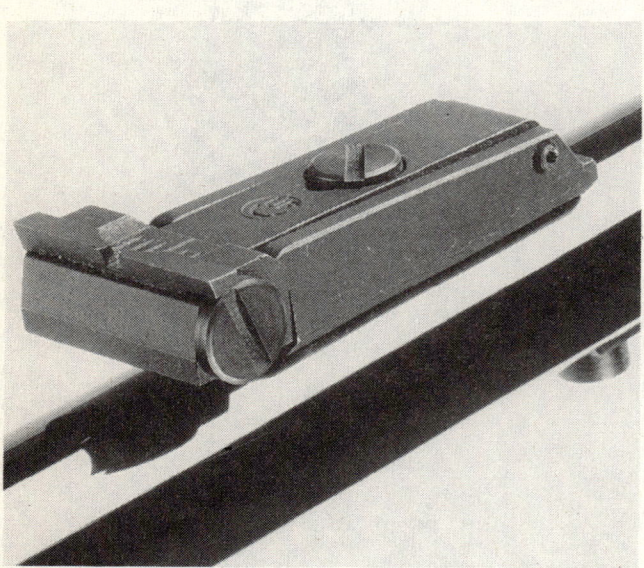

BLACK POWDER FIREARMS

System 1

Introduced in 1997 this concept features a complete muzzle-loading system with interchangeable barrels. Offered with .32, .50, .54, .58 caliber and 12 gauge shotgun barrels with walnut stock and blued finish. Or stainless steel with synthetic stock. Barrel lengths are 26". Approximate weight is 7.5 lbs. Sights are adjustable. Add $30.00 for synthetic stock and stainless steel.

NIB	Exc.	V.G.	Good	Fair	Poor
350	300	—	—	—	—

Thunder Hawk

Introduced in 1993, this rifle features a .50 caliber cap lock in-line ignition with 21" round barrel. Rear sight is adjustable with ramp front sight. The stock is a plain American black walnut

with rubber recoil pad. Trigger is adjustable. In 1994 this model was available in stainless steel. Weighs 6.75 lbs.

NIB	Exc.	V.G.	Good	Fair	Poor
225	200	175	150	100	75

Thunder Hawk Shadow

Introduced in 1996, this model features an in-line ignition in .50 or .54 caliber with a 24" round barrel. It comes standard with a black checkered composite stock. Weight is approximately 7 lbs. In 1997 this model was offered with camouflage stock and blued finish.

NIB	Exc.	V.G.	Good	Fair	Poor
300	250	200	150	100	75

Grey Hawk

This stainless steel composite stock rifle is a .50 caliber cap lock with 24" round barrel. It utilizes a hooked breech system. The lock is a heavy-duty coil spring with floral engraving pattern. Adjustable rear sight and bead front sight are standard. Weighs about 7 lbs.

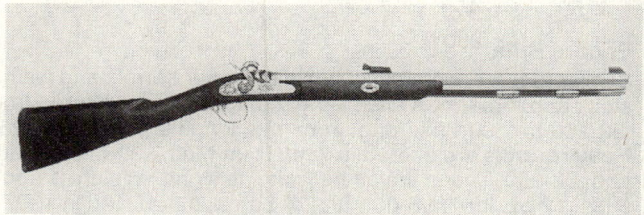

NIB	Exc.	V.G.	Good	Fair	Poor
225	200	175	150	100	75

Hawken Cap Lock Rifle

Available in .45, .50, and .54 caliber this rifle has a 28" octagonal barrel and hooked breech system. Triggers are fully adjustable and can function as double set or single stage. Adjustable sights with bead front sight are standard. Trim is solid brass and stock is select American walnut with cheek piece. Weighs about 8.5 lbs.

NIB	Exc.	V.G.	Good	Fair	Poor
300	250	200	150	100	75

Hawken Flint Lock Rifle

Offered in .50 caliber with 28" octagonal barrel. All other features are the same as above.

NIB	Exc.	V.G.	Good	Fair	Poor
310	260	200	150	100	75

Hawken Custom/Elite

Introduced in 1994 this model features a .50 caliber traditional cap lock rifle with double set triggers, Crescent butt, and select American walnut stock with no patch box. The finish is a high luster blue.

NIB	Exc.	V.G.	Good	Fair	Poor
400	350	275	175	100	75

Renegade Cap Lock Rifle

Offered in .50 or .54 caliber with 26" octagonal barrel. Adjustable triggers that can function as double set or single stage. Adjustable sights with blued trim. Walnut stock. Offered in either right hand or left hand models. Weighs about 8 lbs.

NIB	Exc.	V.G.	Good	Fair	Poor
275	225	200	150	100	75

Renegade Flint Lock

Available in .50 caliber only and right hand only. Other features are the same as Cap Lock Model.

NIB	Exc.	V.G.	Good	Fair	Poor
275	250	200	150	100	75

Big Boar Rifle

This hooked breech model features the .58 caliber with 26" octagonal barrel. Single trigger and adjustable sights are standard. Trim is blued steel. American walnut stock with rubber pad. Weighs about 7.75 lbs.

NIB	Exc.	V.G.	Good	Fair	Poor
275	250	200	150	100	75

High Plains Sporter

This is a .50 caliber cap lock with a 24" round barrel. The lock is case-colored. Choice of adjustable open sights or tang sight. Trim is blued. The stock is walnut with rubber recoil pad, pistol grip, and sling swivel studs. Weighs about 7 lbs.

NIB	Exc.	V.G.	Good	Fair	Poor
275	250	200	150	100	75

Tree Hawk

Available in either .50 caliber cap lock or 12 gauge cap lock. The .50 caliber carbine has a 21" barrel and is offered in camo colors. The 12 gauge shotgun is fitted with a 27" barrel and also comes in camo colors. Weight is about 6.75 lbs.

Rifle

NIB	Exc.	V.G.	Good	Fair	Poor
275	250	200	150	100	75

Shotgun

NIB	Exc.	V.G.	Good	Fair	Poor
275	250	200	150	100	75

White Mountain Carbine

Available in either .45, .50, or .54 caliber cap lock or .50 flint lock. Fitted with a 20-1/2" octagon barrel. The lock is case-colored and trim is blued. Stock is walnut with rubber recoil pad. Weighs about 6.5 lbs.

NIB	Exc.	V.G.	Good	Fair	Poor
250	225	200	150	100	75

Pennsylvania Hunter

Offered in .50 caliber cap or flint lock and fitted with either a 31-1/2" octagon/round barrel or a 21-1/2" octagon/round barrel. Fully adjustable sights, walnut stock, and blued trim are standard. Rifle weighs about 7.5 lbs. while the carbine weighs about 6.5 lbs.

Rifle

NIB	Exc.	V.G.	Good	Fair	Poor
250	225	200	150	100	75

Carbine

NIB	Exc.	V.G.	Good	Fair	Poor
250	225	200	150	100	75

Pennsylvania Match Rifle

Similar to the Pennsylvania Hunter Rifle except equipped with a tang peep sight and a globe front sight.

NIB	Exc.	V.G.	Good	Fair	Poor
350	275	200	150	100	75

New Englander Rifle

Offered in either .50 or .54 caliber cap lock with walnut stock and 26" round barrel. Adjustable sights. Weighs about 7 lbs., 15 oz. A 12" barrel is optional.

NIB	Exc.	V.G.	Good	Fair	Poor
200	175	150	125	90	75

NOTE: Add $150 for interchangeable shotgun barrel.

New Englander Shotgun

Same as above, but fitted with a 27" 12 gauge barrel with screw in full choke. Weighs about 6 lbs., 8 oz.

NIB	Exc.	V.G.	Good	Fair	Poor
230	200	175	150	100	75

New Englander Composite

Offered with composite stock. The .50 or .54 caliber rifle has a 24" barrel and the 12 gauge shotgun has a 27" barrel.

Rifle

NIB	Exc.	V.G.	Good	Fair	Poor
200	175	150	125	100	75

Shotgun

NIB	Exc.	V.G.	Good	Fair	Poor
225	200	175	150	100	75

Scout Carbine

This is a muzzleloading carbine of .50 or .54 caliber with an in-line ignition system. Offered with either walnut stock or composite stock (first offered in 1993) it is fitted with a 21" round barrel. Adjustable rear sight and fixed blade front sight. Brass barrel band and triggerguard on walnut stock and blued barrel band and triggerguard on composite stock model. Weighs about 7 lbs., 4 oz.

Walnut stock

NIB	Exc.	V.G.	Good	Fair	Poor
325	275	200	150	100	75

Composite stock

NIB	Exc.	V.G.	Good	Fair	Poor
250	225	175	150	100	75

Scout Rifle

Similar to the Scout Carbine but fitted with a 24" stepped half-round, half-octagonal barrel. Weight is approximately 8 lbs.

Walnut Stock

NIB	Exc.	V.G.	Good	Fair	Poor
350	300	225	175	125	100

Composite Stock

NIB	Exc.	V.G.	Good	Fair	Poor
275	250	200	150	100	75

Scout Pistol

The same design as the Scout carbine this single action pistol is available in .45, .50, or .54 caliber. Fitted with a 12" barrel, adjustable rear sight, and blued finish with brass triggerguard. Black walnut grips. Weighs 4 lbs., 6 oz.

NIB	Exc.	V.G.	Good	Fair	Poor
250	225	200	175	100	75

Fire Hawk Deluxe

Introduced in 1996 this is an in-line muzzleloader. Offered in either .50 or .54 caliber with blued or stainless steel. Semi-fancy checkered walnut stock has a cheekpiece. The round barrel is 24" long. Adjustable rear leaf sight with ramp style front bead. Weight is about 7 lbs.

NIB	Exc.	V.G.	Good	Fair	Poor
400	350	—	—	—	—

Fire Hawk

Similar to the Deluxe Fire Hawk but with standard American walnut stock or composition stock.

NIB	Exc.	V.G.	Good	Fair	Poor
300	250	200	—	—	—

Fire Hawk Thumbhole Stock

NIB	Exc.	V.G.	Good	Fair	Poor
325	275	—	—	—	—

Fire Hawk Camo Stock

NIB	Exc.	V.G.	Good	Fair	Poor
325	275	—	—	—	—

Fire Hawk Bantam

NIB	Exc.	V.G.	Good	Fair	Poor
275	225	—	—	—	—

Fire Hawk .32 & .58 caliber models

NIB	Exc.	V.G.	Good	Fair	Poor
300	250	—	—	—	—

Thompson/Center Renegade Cap Lock Rifle.

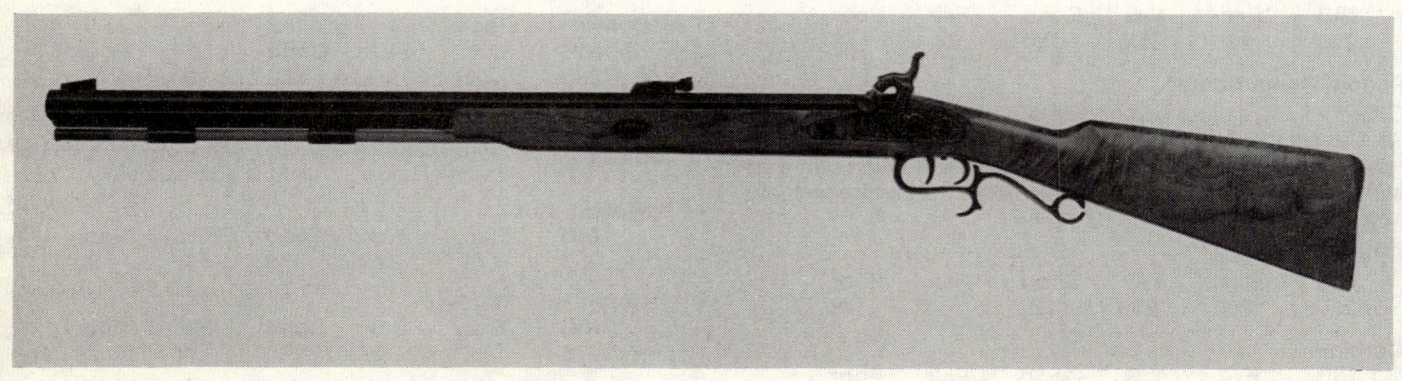

Thompson/Center Renegade Cap Lock (lefthand).

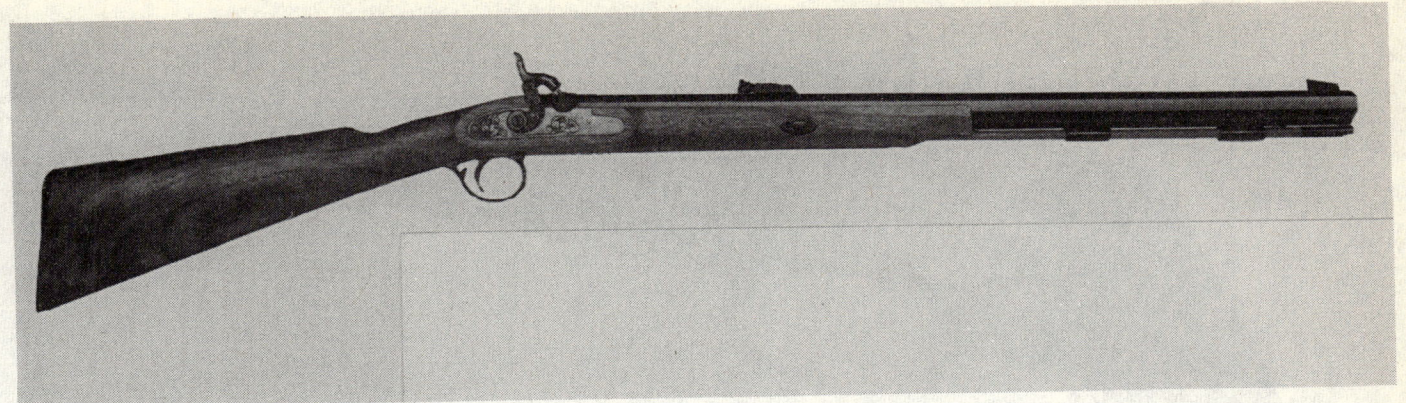

Thompson/Center Renegade Hunter Model.

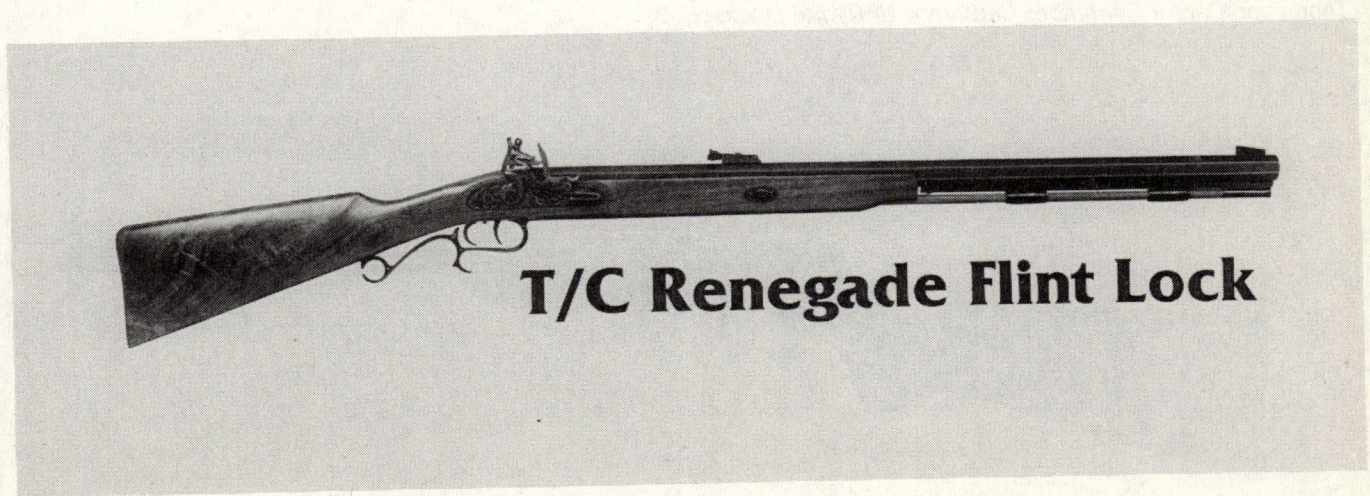

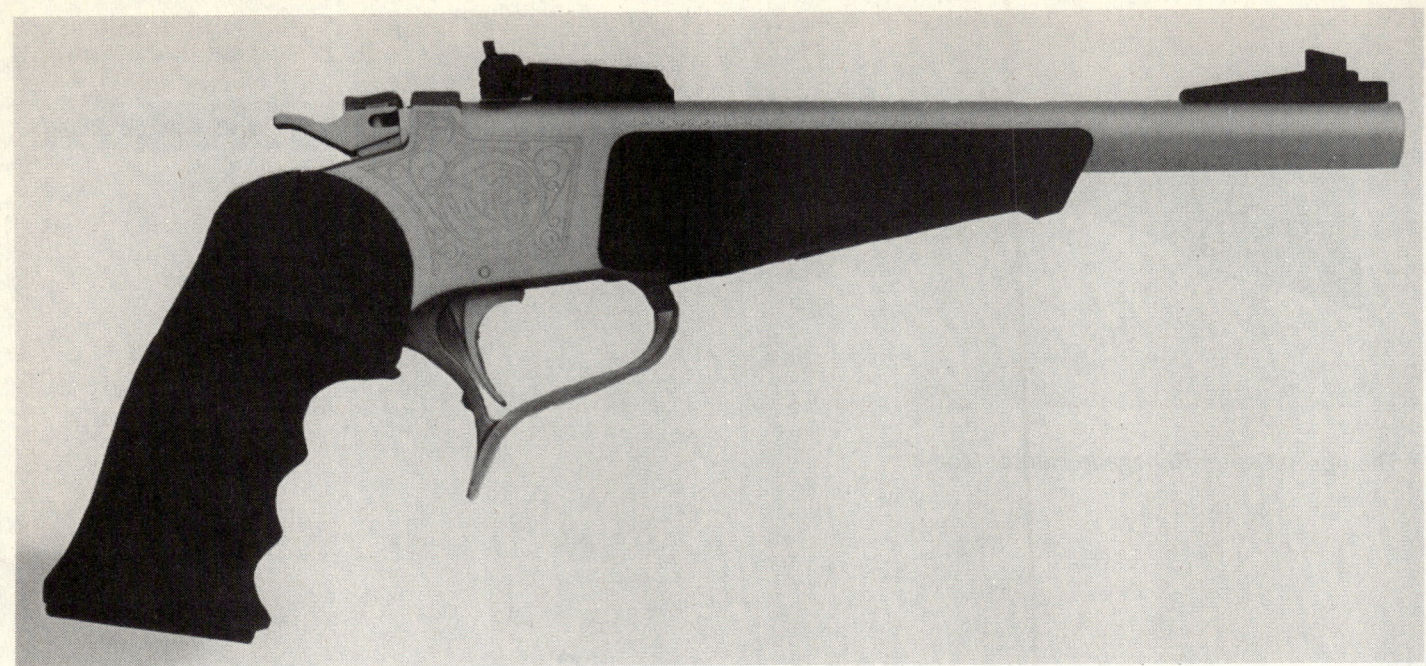

Thompson/Center Stainless Steel Contender.

Thompson/Center Contender Carbine with Rynite stock.

Thompson/Center Contender Carbine / 410 GA smoothbore with Rynite stock.

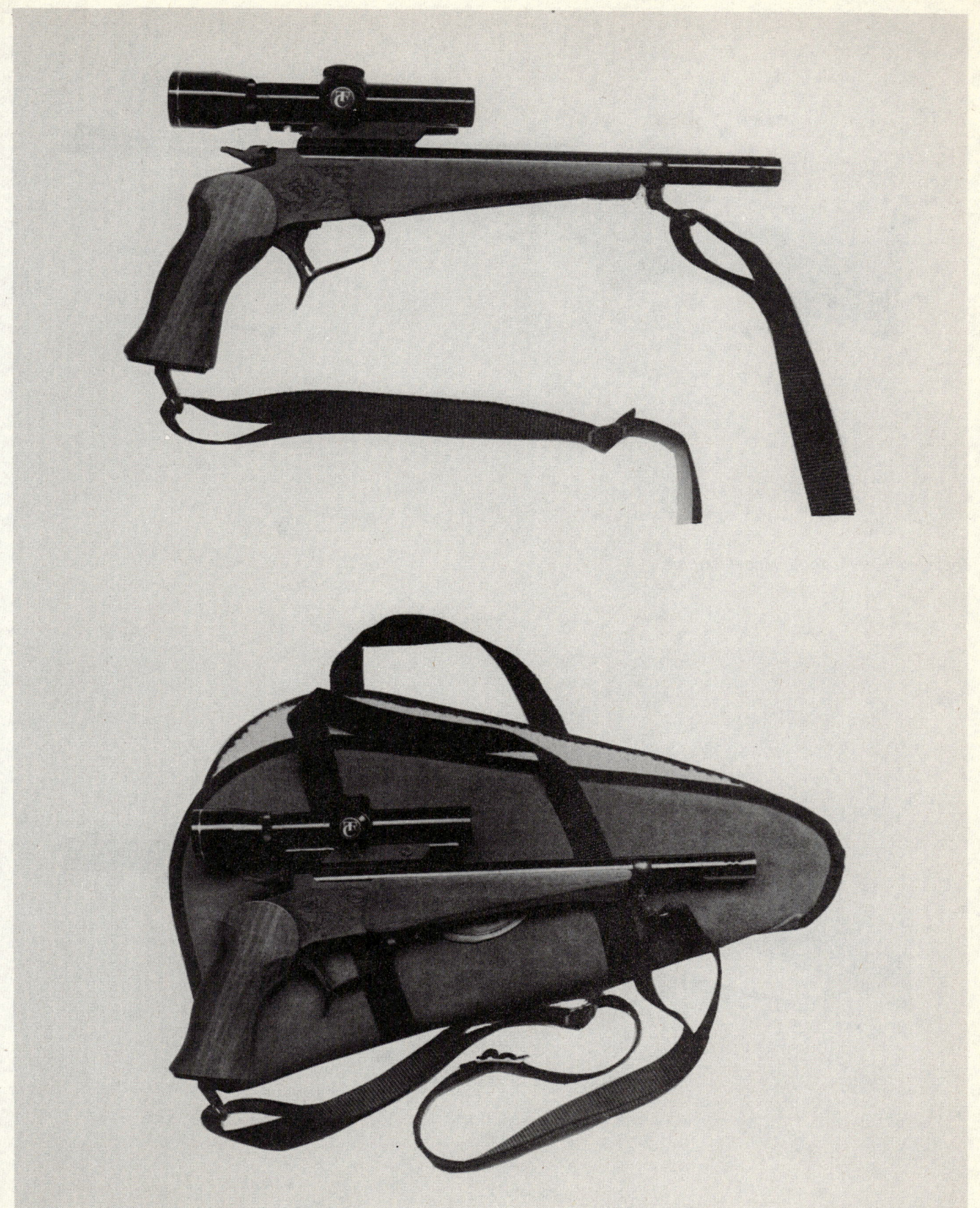

Thompson/Center Contender Hunter Package.

Thompson/Center Youth Model Carbine.

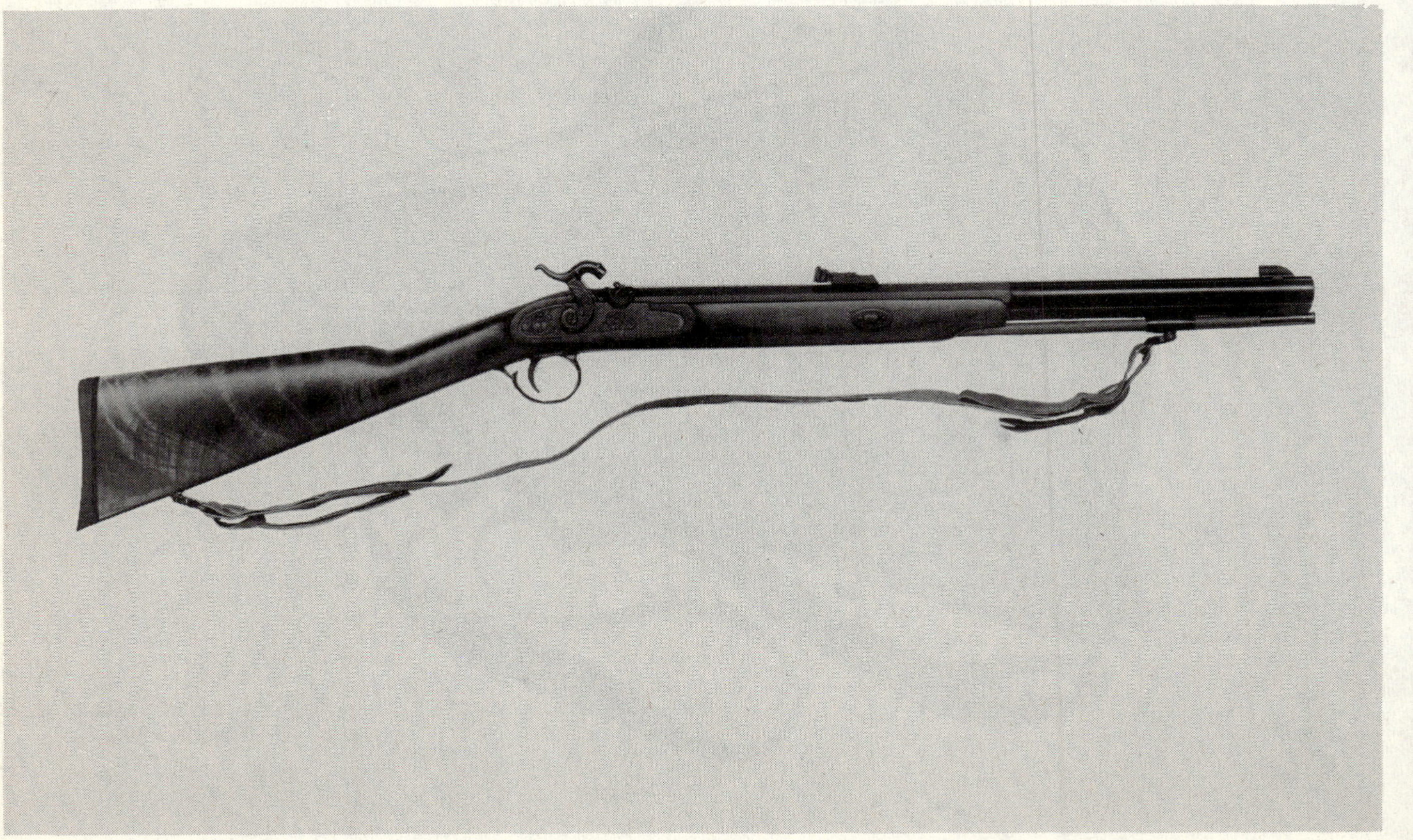

Thompson/Center White Mountain Carbine .50 caliber Cap Lock.

THUNDER FIVE
MIL Inc.
Piney Flats, Tennessee

Five shot, double action, 2" rifled barrel, matte finish, ambidextrous hammer block safety, Pachmayr grips, chambered in .45 Long Colt/.410 shotgun and .47-70 Government.

NIB	Exc.	V.G.	Good	Fair	Poor
475	400	350	300	200	100

TIKKA
Tikkakoski, Finland
Importer-Stoeger Industries
South Hackensack, New Jersey

RIFLES

New Generation Rifles

This rifle features a hand checkered walnut stock with matte lacquer finish. These rifles are furnished without sights, but receiver is grooved. Magazine is detachable box type. Two action lengths are offered: medium and long. In medium action calibers the choices are: .223, .22-250, .243, and .308 with 22.4" barrels and weigh 7 lbs. The long action calibers are: .270 and .30-06 with 22.4" barrels and weigh 7.3 lbs., 7mm Rem. Mag., .300 and .338 Win. Mag. with 24.4" barrel and weigh 7.5 lbs.

NIB	Exc.	V.G.	Good	Fair	Poor
725	600	500	400	200	150

New Generation Premium Grade

Similar to standard model above but furnished with cheekpiece, select walnut stock, rosewood pistol grip cap and forend tip. Metal surfaces are a highly polished blue. Same calibers as offered above.

NIB	Exc.	V.G.	Good	Fair	Poor
875	700	600	400	200	150

Whitetail/Battue Rifle

This rifle was originally designed for the French market. The barrel is 20.5" long and is fitted with a raised quarter rib. The walnut is checkered with rubber recoil pad standard. In the medium action the only caliber is .308. In a long action the calibers are: .270, .30-06, 7mm Rem. Mag., .300 and .338 Win. Mag. All models weigh about 7 lbs.

NIB	Exc.	V.G.	Good	Fair	Poor
750	600	500	400	200	150

Varmint/Continental Rifle

This model features a 23.5" heavy barrel without sights. The checkered walnut stock has a wide forend. Offered in .223, .22-250, .243, and .308. Weighs approximately 8.5 lbs.

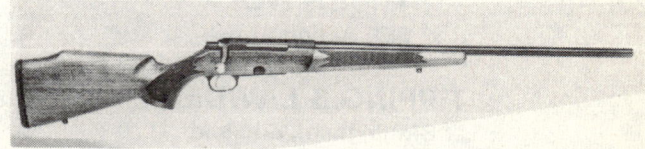

NIB	Exc.	V.G.	Good	Fair	Poor
875	700	600	400	200	150

SHOTGUNS/DOUBLE RIFLES (FORMERLY VALMET)

Tikka, Valmet and Sako have been merged into one company, SAKO Ltd. These firearms are now manufactured under the brand name Tikka and are manufactured in Italy. Parts are interchangeable between the Valmet guns, made in Finland and the Tikka guns, made in Italy.

412S Shotgun

This Over/Under shotgun is available in 12 gauge only with 26" or 28" barrels. The stock is checkered European walnut. Weighs about 7.25 lbs.

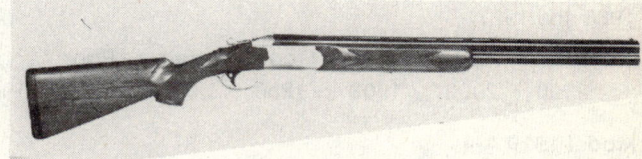

NIB	Exc.	V.G.	Good	Fair	Poor
950	800	650	500	300	200

412S Shotgun/Rifle

Same as above but with 12 gauge barrel and choice of .222 or .308 barrel. Barrel length is 24" and weighs 8 lbs.

NIB	Exc.	V.G.	Good	Fair	Poor
1000	850	700	500	300	200

412S Double Rifle

Same as above but fitted with a 24" Over/Under rifle barrel in 9.3x74R. Weighs about 8.5 lbs.

NIB	Exc.	V.G.	Good	Fair	Poor
1150	950	750	500	300	200

412S Sporting Clays

Introduced in 1993 this model is offered in 12 gauge with 28" barrels with choke tubes.

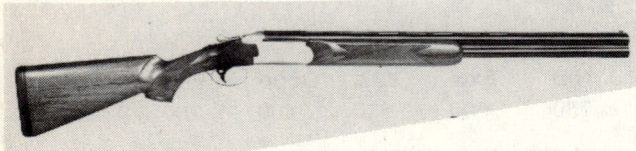

NIB	Exc.	V.G.	Good	Fair	Poor
1000	850	700	500	300	200

TIMBER WOLF
SEE Action Arms

TIPPING & LAWDEN
Birmingham, England

Thomas Revolver

A .320, .380, or .450 double action revolver with a 4.5" barrel and 5-shot cylinder, utilizing a cartridge extraction system designed by J. Thomas of Birmingham in which the barrel and cylinder may be moved forward. Manufactured from 1870 to 1877.

Exc.	V.G.	Good	Fair	Poor
—	—	600	300	175

TIPPMAN ARMS
Fort Wayne, Indiana

Model 1917

A .22 caliber semiautomatic half scale reproduction of the Browning Model 1917 water cooled machine gun. Barrel length 10". A tripod was sold with this model. Manufactured in 1986 and 1987.

NIB	Exc.	V.G.	Good	Fair	Poor
2500	2000	1500	1250	950	750

Model 1919 A-4

A .22 caliber semiautomatic half scale reproduction of the Browning Model 1919 A-4 machine gun. Barrel length 11" and furnished with a tripod. Manufactured in 1986 and 1987.

NIB	Exc.	V.G.	Good	Fair	Poor
2000	1500	1000	750	600	500

Model .50 HB

A .22 Magnum caliber semiautomatic half scale reproduction of the Browning .50 caliber machine gun. Barrel length 18.25", furnished with a tripod. Manufactured in 1986 and 1987.

NIB	Exc.	V.G.	Good	Fair	Poor
3000	2500	1750	1250	1000	750

TODD, GEORGE H.
Montgomery, Alabama

Rifled Musket

A .58 caliber single shot percussion rifle with a 40" barrel and full length stock secured by three barrel bands. Barrel and lock finished in the bright, brass furniture and walnut stock. The lock marked "George H. Todd/ Montgomery, Ala." Prospective purchasers are advised to secure a qualified appraisal prior to acquisition.

Exc.	V.G.	Good	Fair	Poor
—	—	20000	8500	1250

TOKAREV
Soviet State Arsenals

M38 Rifle

A 7.62mm caliber gas-operated semiautomatic rifle with a 24" barrel and 10-shot magazine. Blued with a two-piece hardwood stock. Manufactured from 1938 to 1940.

NOTE: Add 300% for Sniper variation.

Exc.	V.G.	Good	Fair	Poor
900	700	500	200	100

M40 Rifle

As above, with a sheet metal hand guard and muzzle brake.

NOTE: Add 50% for no importer marking.

Exc.	V.G.	Good	Fair	Poor
400	350	300	200	150

TT30 & TT33

A 7.62mm semiautomatic pistol with a 4.5" barrel and 8-shot magazine. This model was produced in a number of communist countries.

NOTE: Add 50%, for cut-aways add 200%.

TOMISKA, ALOIS
Pilsen, Czechoslovakia

Little Tom

A 6.35mm or 7.65mm caliber semiautomatic pistol with a 2.5" barrel. The slide marked "Alois Tomiska Plzen Patent Little Tom" and the grips inlaid with a medallion bearing the monogram "AT". Blued with checkered walnut grips. Manufactured from 1908 to 1918. Subsequently produced by the Wiener Waffenfabrik.

Exc.	V.G.	Good	Fair	Poor
500	425	350	250	125

TRADEWINDS
Tacoma, Washington

Model H-170

A 12 gauge semiautomatic shotgun with a 26" or 28" ventilated rib barrel and 5-shot tubular magazine. Blued, anodized alloy receiver and walnut stock.

Exc.	V.G.	Good	Fair	Poor
300	250	225	150	100

Model 260-A

A .22 caliber semiautomatic rifle with a 22.5" barrel, open sights and 5-shot magazine. Blued with a walnut stock.

Exc.	V.G.	Good	Fair	Poor
200	175	125	100	75

Model 311-A
A .22 caliber bolt-action rifle with a 22.5" barrel, open sights and a 5-shot magazine. Blued with a walnut stock.

Exc.	V.G.	Good	Fair	Poor
175	150	100	75	50

Model 5000 "Husky"
A centerfire bolt-action rifle with a 24" barrel, adjustable sights and 4-shot magazine. Blued with a walnut stock.

Exc.	V.G.	Good	Fair	Poor
350	300	275	200	100

TRANTER, WILLIAM
Birmingham, England
William Tranter produced a variety of revolvers on his own and a number of other makers produced revolvers based upon his designs. Consequently, "Tranter's Patent" is to be found on revolvers made by such firms as Deane, Adams and Deane, etc.

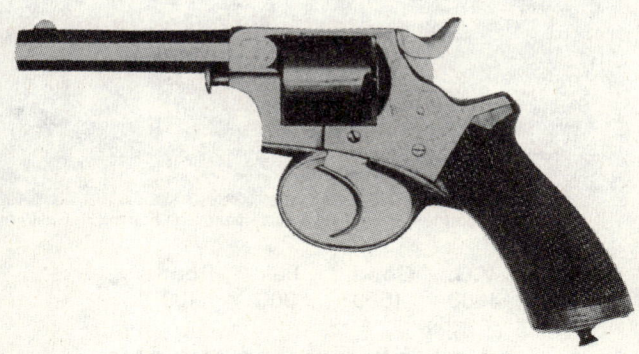

Courtesy Wallis & Wallis, Lewes, Sussex, England

Model 1872
A .38 caliber double action revolver with a 6" octagonal barrel and 6-shot cylinder. Blued with walnut grips.

Exc.	V.G.	Good	Fair	Poor
—	1000	500	300	200

Model 1878
A .450 caliber double action revolver with a 6" octagonal barrel. Blued with a walnut grip. Manufactured from 1878 to 1887.

Exc.	V.G.	Good	Fair	Poor
—	1200	500	275	175

TRIPPLET & SCOTT
MERIDAN MANUFACTURING COMPANY
Meridan, Connecticut
Repeating Carbine
A .50 caliber carbine with either a 22" or 30" round barrel and a 7-shot magazine located in the butt. This model is loaded by turning the barrel until it comes in line with the magazine. Blued, casehardened with a walnut stock. Approximately 5,000 were made in 1864 and 1865.

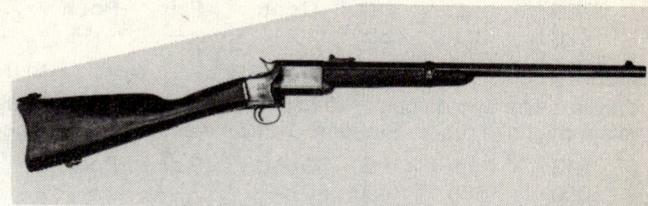

Courtesy Milwaukee Public Museum, Milwaukee, Wisconsin

Exc.	V.G.	Good	Fair	Poor
—	2000	800	500	200

TRISTAR SPORTING ARMS
N. Kansas City, MO
Model 333
This over and under gun is available in 12 or 20 gauge with 26", 28", or 30" barrels in 12 gauge. Hand engraved frame. Fitted with 3" chambers and choke tubes. Single selective triggers and auto ejectors. Fancy Turkish walnut stock. Weighs around 7.75 lbs for 12 gauge and 7.5 lbs for 20 gauge.

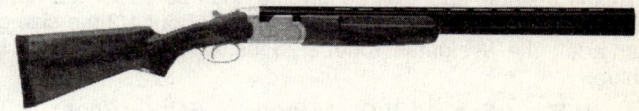

NIB	Exc.	V.G.	Good	Fair	Poor
800	650	600	—	—	—

Model 333 SC
Similar to above model but with addition of 11mm sporting rib, recoil pad, forcing cones, and ported barrels. Extended choke tubes.

NIB	Exc.	V.G.	Good	Fair	Poor
900	700	650	—	—	—

Model 333L
This shotgun has the same features as the Model 333 but with a special stock designed for women. Length of pull is shorter with special Monte Carlo comb.

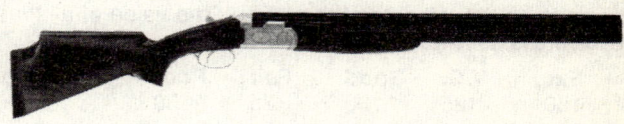

NIB	Exc.	V.G.	Good	Fair	Poor
800	650	600	—	—	—

Model 333SCL
Same features as Model 333SC but with special stock

NIB	Exc.	V.G.	Good	Fair	Poor
900	700	650	—	—	—

Model 330
This over and under model has a standard Turkish walnut stock with etched engraved frame. Offered in 12 and 20 gauge. Single trigger with extractors and fixed chokes.

NIB	Exc.	V.G.	Good	Fair	Poor
575	475	400	—	—	—

Model 330 D
This model is the same as the above but with the addition of selective auto ejectors.

NIB	Exc.	V.G.	Good	Fair	Poor
700	575	500	—	—	—

Model 300

This model features an underlug action lock with double triggers and extractors. Frame is etched. Offered in 12 gauge only with 26" or 28" barrels with fixed chokes.

NIB	Exc.	V.G.	Good	Fair	Poor
425	350	300	—	—	—

Model 311

This is a side by side gun in 12 or 20 gauge with 26" or 28" barrels with choke tubes. Standard Turkish walnut. Blued frame.

NIB	Exc.	V.G.	Good	Fair	Poor
600	500	450	—	—	—

Model 311R

Same as above but with 20" barrel choked cylinder and cylinder.

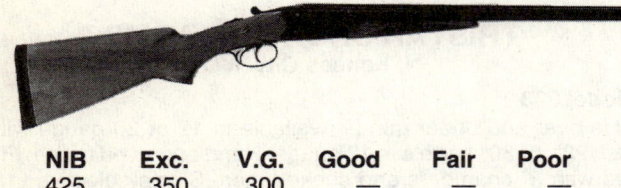

NIB	Exc.	V.G.	Good	Fair	Poor
425	350	300	—	—	—

Pee Wee

This is a single shot bolt action rifle chambered for .22 Long Rifle cartridges. Stock is walnut and it is about 1/2 the size of an adult rifle. Weight is about 2.75 lbs. Open sights. Finish is blue.

NIB	Exc.	V.G.	Good	Fair	Poor
200	150	100	—	—	—

Model 1887

This is a reproduction of the Winchester Model 1887 lever action shotgun. Offered in 12 gauge only with 30" full choked barrel. Five-round magazine. Weight is about 8 lbs.

NIB	Exc.	V.G.	Good	Fair	Poor
600	500	450	—	—	—

TROCAOLA
Eibar, Spain

This maker produced a variety of .32, .38, and .44 caliber top break revolvers between approximately 1900 and 1936. These pistols can be identified by the monogram "TAC" stamped on the left side of the frame. The value of all these revolvers is as follows:

Exc.	V.G.	Good	Fair	Poor
150	125	100	75	50

TRYON, EDWARD K. & COMPANY
Philadelphia, Pennsylvania

Pocket Pistol

A .41 caliber single shot percussion pocket pistol with a 2" or 4" barrel, German silver mounts and a walnut stock. The lock marked "Tryon/Philada." Manufactured during the 1860s and 1870s.

Exc.	V.G.	Good	Fair	Poor
—	—	1250	500	200

TUCKER SHERARD & COMPANY
Lancaster, Texas

Dragoon

A .44 caliber percussion revolver with a 7.75" round barrel fitted with a loading lever and a 6-shot cylinder. The barrel marked "Clark, Sherard & Co., Lancaster, Texas," and the cylinder etched in two panels with crossed cannons and the legend "Texas Arms." Approximately 400 revolvers of this type were made between 1862 and 1867. Prospective purchasers are advised to secure a qualified appraisal prior to acquisition.

Exc.	V.G.	Good	Fair	Poor
—	—	35000	15000	2500

TUFTS & COLLEY
New York, New York

Pocket Pistol

A .44 caliber single shot percussion pocket pistol with a 3.5" barrel, German silver mounts and walnut stock. The lock marked "Tufts & Colley" and the barrel "Deringer/Pattn". Manufactured during the 1860s.

Exc.	V.G.	Good	Fair	Poor
—	—	1250	500	200

TURBIAUX, JACQUES
Paris, France
SEE Ames

TURNER, THOMAS
Redding, England

Pepperbox

A .476 double action percussion pepperbox having 6 barrels. Blued, casehardened with walnut grips. The left side of the frame is engraved in an oval "Thomas Turner, Redding."

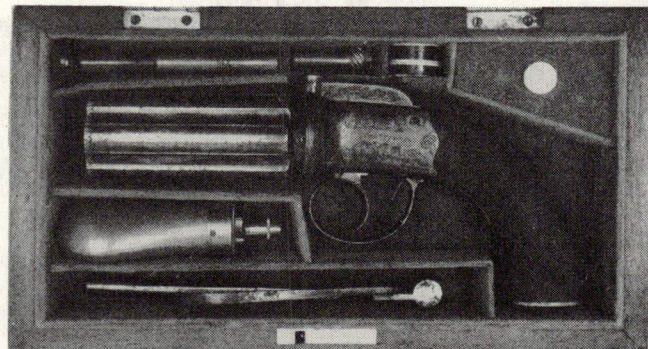

Courtesy Butterfield & Butterfield, San Francisco, California

Exc.	V.G.	Good	Fair	Poor
—	4000	1500	900	400

TYLER ORDNANCE WORKS
Tyler, Texas

This company produced 56 Austrian rifles, 508 Enfield rifles, 423 Hill rifles and 1,009 Texas rifles during the Civil War.

NOTE: Extreme caution is urged prior to purchasing any of these arms and a qualified appraisal should be sought. These rifles are very rare.

Tyler Texas Rifle

A .57 caliber single shot rifle with a 27" barrel and a full stock secured by two barrel bands. The lock marked "Texas Rifle/Tyler/Cal. .57".

Exc.	V.G.	Good	Fair	Poor
—	—	20000	10000	2500

Hill Rifle

A .54 caliber single shot percussion rifle with a 27" barrel, full stock secured by two brass barrel bands and an iron triggerguard and buttplate. The lock marked "Hill Rifle/Tyler/Tex/ Cal. .54".

Exc.	V.G.	Good	Fair	Poor
—	—	20000	10000	2500

USAS 12
DAEWOO PRECISION IND., LTD.
South Korea
Importer-Gilbert Equipment Company
Mobile, Alabama

USAS 12

A 12 gauge semiautomatic shotgun with a 18.25" cylinder bored barrel, and either a 10-shot box magazine or 20-shot drum magazine. Parkerized, with a composition stock. This model is no loner imported.

NOTE: A local appraisal of this model is strongly recommended.

U.S. ARMS CO.
Riverhead, New York

Abilene .357 Magnum

A .357 Magnum single action revolver with a 4-5/8", 5-1/2", or 6-1/2" barrel, adjustable sights and transfer-bar safety. Blued with walnut grips. Manufactured from 1976 to 1983.
Stainless Steel Version-Add 30%.

Exc.	V.G.	Good	Fair	Poor
250	225	200	150	100

Abilene .44 Magnum

As above, in .44 Magnum with a 7.5" or 8.5" barrel and a 6-shot unfluted cylinder.
Stainless Steel Version-Add 30%.

Exc.	V.G.	Good	Fair	Poor
325	300	250	200	150

U.S. REPEATING ARMS CO.
SEE Winchester

UNITED STATES REVOLVER ASSOCIATION
SEE Harrington & Richardson Arms Co.

UBERTI, ALDO
Ponte Zanano, Italy
Importers - Cimarron Firearms, E.M.F., Inc., Uberti USA, American Arms, Taylors

This company manufactures high-grade reproductions of famous Western-style American firearms. Their products have been imported over the years by a number of different companies. They produce both black powder guns and the cartridge firearms that are included in this section. This Italian manufacturer builds high quality firearms of the American West. Featured are Colt, Winchester, and Remington. Each importer stamps its name on the firearm in addition to the Uberti address.

There may be small variations in stampings on the barrel address if requested by the importer. Perhaps the most noticeable difference between importers is the exclusive use of original stampings and patent dates on Colt single actions and Winchester rifles by Cimarron Arms. This firm also has a case-hardened hammer on its Colt single action as well as a high polish charcoal blue.

The prices below represent the Uberti line as imported into the United States. Navy Arms also imports rifles and revolvers by Uberti and these are listed separately in the Navy Arms section.

Patterson Revolver

This is an exact copy of the famous and rare Colt pistol. Offered in .36 caliber with engraved 5-shot cylinder, the barrel is 7.5" long and octagonal forward of the lug. The frame is case hardened steel as is the backstrap. Grips are one piece walnut. Overall length is 11.5" and weight is about 2.5 lbs.

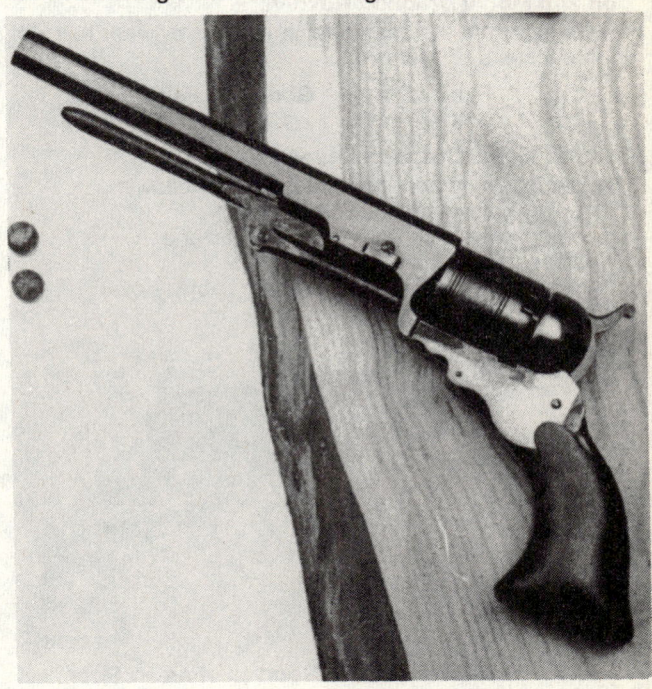

NIB	Exc.	V.G.	Good	Fair	Poor
225	200	150	125	100	75

Walker Colt Revolver

This is a faithful reproduction of the famous and highly sought after Colts. Caliber is .44 and the round barrel is 9" in length. The frame is casehardened steel and the triggerguard is brass. The 6-shot cylinder is engraved with fighting dragoons scene. Grip is one piece walnut. Overall length is 15.75" and weight is a hefty 70 oz.

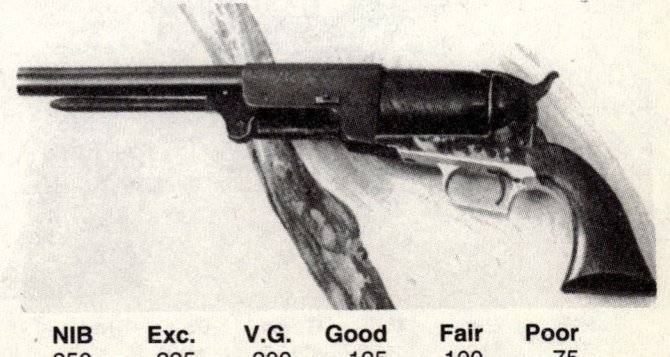

NIB	Exc.	V.G.	Good	Fair	Poor
250	225	200	125	100	75

Colt 1st Model Dragoon Revolver

This was a shorter version of the Walker and evolved directly from that original design. This model is a 6-shot .44 caliber with a 7.5" barrel. The frame is color casehardened steel while the backstrap and triggerguard are brass. Grips are one-piece walnut. Overall length is 13.5" and weight is about 63 oz.

NIB	Exc.	V.G.	Good	Fair	Poor
225	200	175	125	100	75

Colt 2nd Model Dragoon Revolver

This differs from the 1st model in that the cylinder bolt slot is square instead of oval.

NIB	Exc.	V.G.	Good	Fair	Poor
225	200	175	125	100	75

Colt 3rd Model Dragoon Revolver

This model varies from the 2nd model as follows:
a: Loading lever taper is inverted.
b: Loading lever latch hook is different shape.
c: Loading lever latch.
d: Backstrap is steel and triggerguard is brass oval.
e: Frame is cut for a shoulder stock.

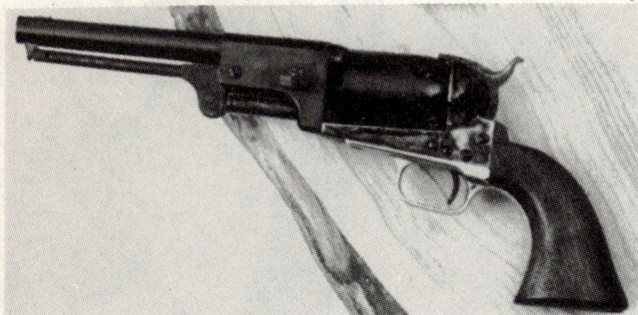

NIB	Exc.	V.G.	Good	Fair	Poor
225	200	175	125	100	75

Colt Model 1849 Wells Fargo

This model has no loading lever. Chambered for .31 caliber cartridge. The barrel is octagonal. The frame is case-colored and hardened steel while the backstrap and triggerguard are brass. Cylinder is engraved and holds 5 rounds. Grip is one piece walnut. Overall length is 9.5" and weight is 34 oz.

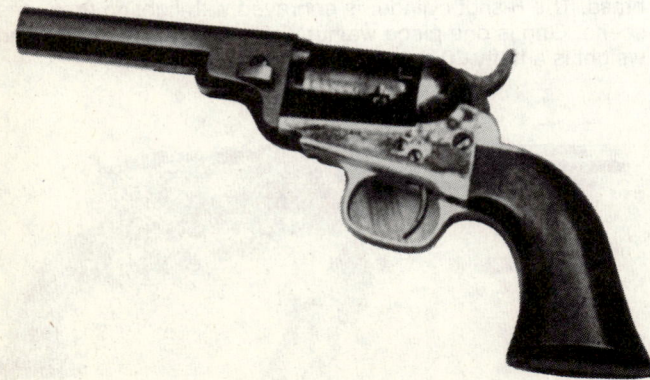

NIB	Exc.	V.G.	Good	Fair	Poor
215	180	150	125	100	75

Colt Model 1849 Pocket Revolver

Same as the Wells Fargo with the addition of a loading lever.

NIB	Exc.	V.G.	Good	Fair	Poor
215	180	150	125	100	75

Colt Model 1848 Baby Dragoon

Similar is appearance to the Model 1849 but with a 4" tapered octagonal barrel and a square back triggerguard. No loading lever. Weight is about 23 oz.

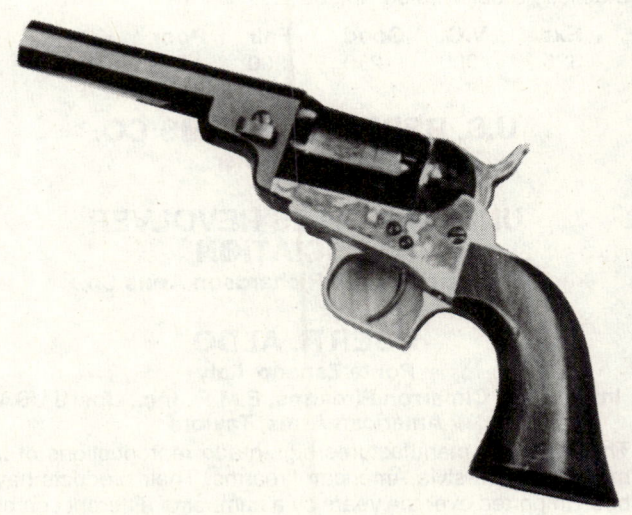

NIB	Exc.	V.G.	Good	Fair	Poor
215	180	150	125	100	75

The Model 1851 Navy Colt

Chambered for .36 caliber with an engraved 6-shot cylinder. The tapered octagonal barrel is 7.5". The frame is case-colored steel and the backstrap and oval triggerguard are brass. Grips are one-piece walnut. Overall length is 13" and weight is about 44 oz.

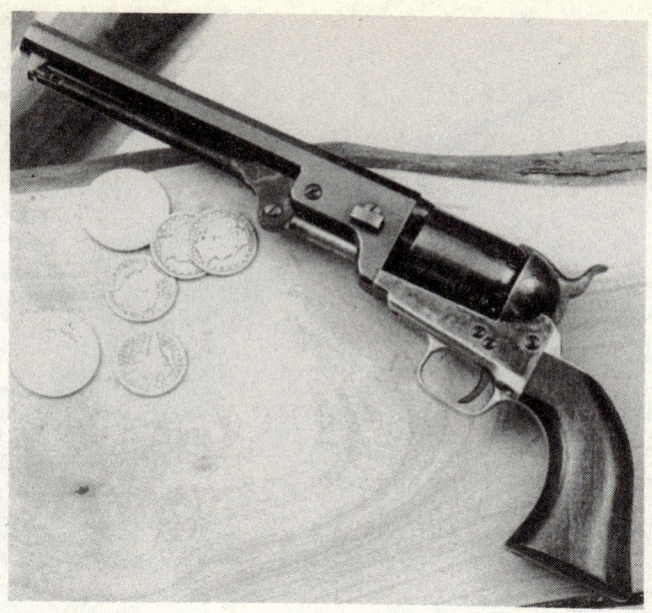

NIB	Exc.	V.G.	Good	Fair	Poor
200	175	150	125	100	75

Model 1861 Navy Colt

Sometime referred to as the "New Navy" this model is similar in appearance to the Model 1851. Offered in two variations. The military version has a steel backstrap and triggerguard and is cut for a shoulder stock. The civilian version has a brass backstrap and triggerguard and is not cut for a shoulder stock.

Military Model

NIB	Exc.	V.G.	Good	Fair	Poor
215	180	150	125	100	75

Civilian Model

NIB	Exc.	V.G.	Good	Fair	Poor
200	175	150	125	100	75

Colt Model 1860 Army

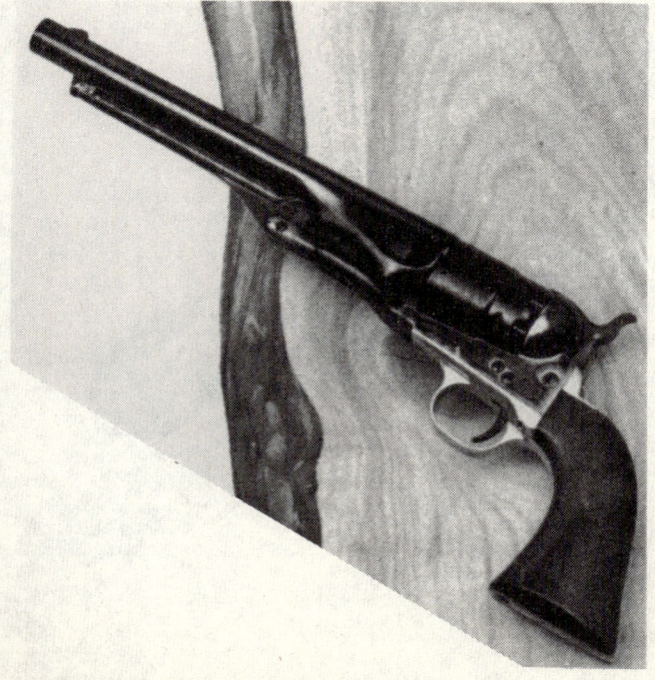

Chambered for the .44 caliber ball and fitted with a round tapered 8" barrel this revolver has a 6-shot engraved cylinder.

Grips are one-piece walnut. Overall length is 13.75" and weight is approximately 42 oz.

Military version has steel backstrap and brass triggerguard and is cut for a shoulder stock.

NIB	Exc.	V.G.	Good	Fair	Poor
200	175	150	125	100	75

Civilian version has brass backstrap and triggerguard and is not cut for a shoulder stock.

NIB	Exc.	V.G.	Good	Fair	Poor
200	175	150	125	100	75

Fluted Cylinder Version-Military

NIB	Exc.	V.G.	Good	Fair	Poor
210	185	160	125	100	75

Fluted Cylinder Version-Civilian

NIB	Exc.	V.G.	Good	Fair	Poor
185	150	125	100	80	65

Colt Model 1862 Police Revolvers

Chambered for .36 caliber and fitted with a round tapered barrel in 4.5", 5.5", or 6.5" barrel. The 5-shot cylinder is fluted, the frame color casehardened, and the backstrap and triggerguard are brass. Grips are one-piece walnut. Weight is about 25 oz.

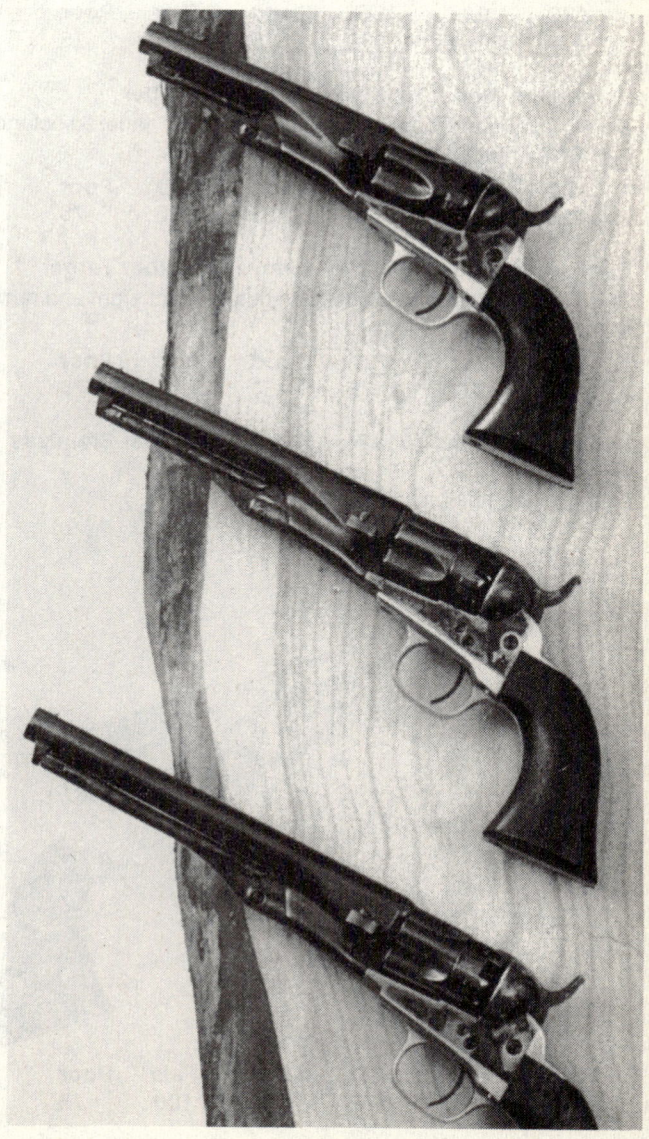

NIB	Exc.	V.G.	Good	Fair	Poor
225	200	175	150	125	100

Colt Model 1862 Pocket Navy Revolver

Similar to the Model 1862 Police model but fitted with a 5-shot engraved non-fluted cylinder. Barrel lengths are 4.5", 5.5", and 6.5". Weight is about 27 oz.

NIB	Exc.	V.G.	Good	Fair	Poor
225	200	175	150	125	100

Remington Model 1858 New Army .44 Caliber

Chambered for .44 caliber and fitted with a tapered octagonal 8" barrel. Cylinder holds 6 shots and the frame is blued steel. Triggerguard is brass. Grips are two-piece walnut. Overall length is 13.75" and weight is about 42 oz.

NIB	Exc.	V.G.	Good	Fair	Poor
200	175	150	125	100	75

Remington Model 1858 New Army .36 Caliber

Similar to above model but fitted with a 7-3/8" tapered octagonal barrel. Weight is approximately 40 oz.

NIB	Exc.	V.G.	Good	Fair	Poor
200	175	150	125	100	75

Remington Model 1858 New Army .44 Caliber Target

This version is fitted with a fully adjustable rear sight and ramp front sight.

NIB	Exc.	V.G.	Good	Fair	Poor
225	200	175	150	100	75

Remington Model 1858 New Army .44 Caliber Stainless Steel

All parts are stainless steel.

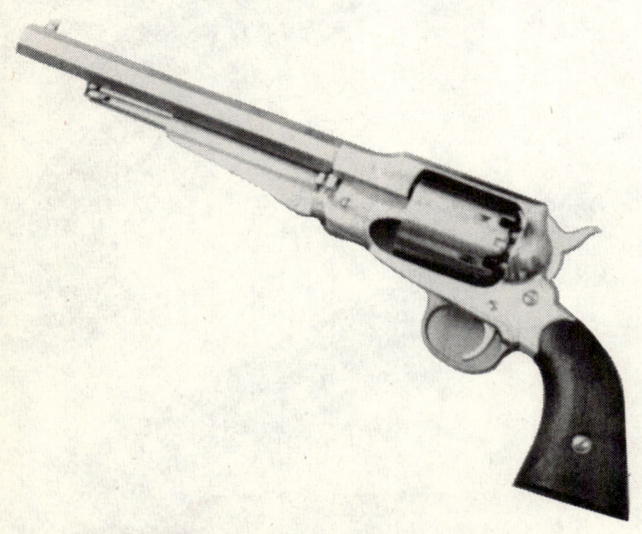

NIB	Exc.	V.G.	Good	Fair	Poor
225	200	175	150	100	75

Remington Model 1858 New Army .44 Cal. SS Target

Same as Target Model but all parts are stainless steel.

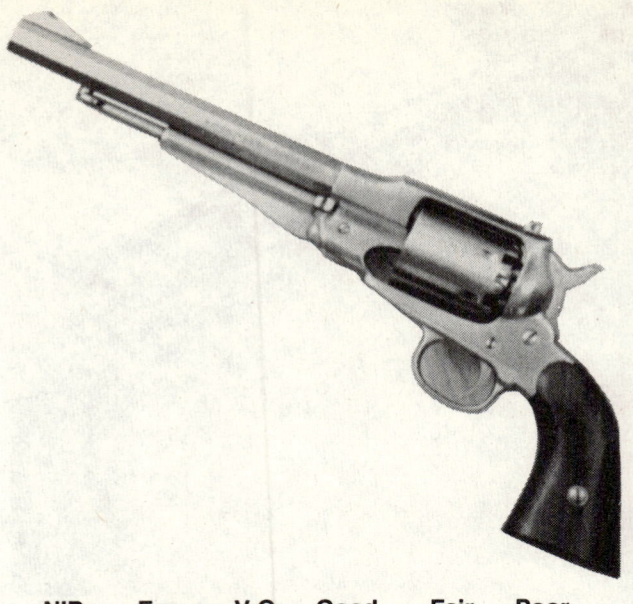

NIB	Exc.	V.G.	Good	Fair	Poor
250	225	200	175	100	75

Remington Model 1858 Target Revolving Carbine

Chambered for .44 caliber and fitted with an 18" octagon barrel. The frame is blued steel and the triggerguard is brass. Stock is select walnut. Overall length is 35" and weight is about 4.4 lbs.

NIB	Exc.	V.G.	Good	Fair	Poor
300	250	200	150	100	75

1875 Remington "Outlaw"

This is a replica of the original Remington cartridge pistol chambered for .357 Magnum, .44-40, .45 ACP, .45 ACP/.45 L.C. conversion, and .45 Colt. The frame is case-colored steel and the triggerguard is brass. It is offered with a 7.5" round barrel and is either blued or nickel-plated, with two-piece walnut grips. Overall length is 13.75" and weight is about 44 oz.

NIB	Exc.	V.G.	Good	Fair	Poor
350	300	275	225	175	125

Remington Model 1890 Police

This is a 5.5"-barreled replica of the original Remington Pistol. It is chambered for .357 Magnum, .44-40, .45 ACP, .45 ACP/.45 L.C. conversion, and .45 Colt. The frame is case-colored steel and the triggerguard is brass. It was available in either blued or nickel-plate. Grips are two-piece walnut and are fitted with a grip ring. Overall length is 11.75" and weight is about 41 oz.

NIB	Exc.	V.G.	Good	Fair	Poor
400	350	300	275	225	175

Model 1871 Rolling Block Pistol

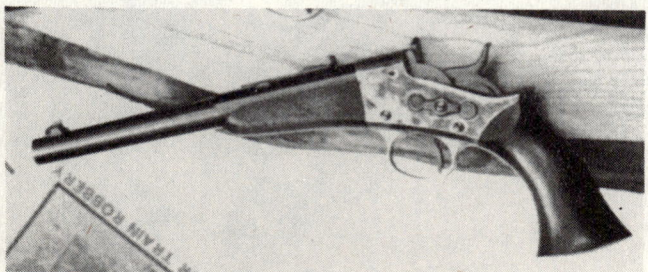

This is a single-shot target pistol chambered for .22 l.r., .22 Magnum, .22 Hornet, .222 Rem., 223 Rem., .45 Long Colt, or .357 Magnum. It has a 9.5" half-octagonal, half-round barrel and is blued, with a case-colored receiver and walnut grip and

forearm. The triggerguard is brass. Overall length is 14" and weight is about 44 oz.

NIB	Exc.	V.G.	Good	Fair	Poor
300	250	225	200	150	100

Model 1371 Rolling Block Carbine

This model is similar to the pistol, with a 22.5" half-octagonal, half-round barrel and a full-length walnut stock. Triggerguard and buttplate are brass. Overall length is 35.5" and weight is approximately 4.8 lbs.

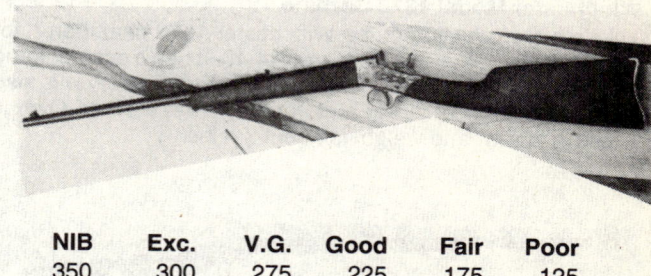

NIB	Exc.	V.G.	Good	Fair	Poor
350	300	275	225	175	125

Henry Rifle

This is a brass-framed reproduction of the famous Winchester/Henry Rifle. It is chambered for the .44-40 cartridge, and this is basically the only departure from being a true and faithful copy. The octagonal barrel is 24.25" on the rifle model and 22.25" on the carbine model. There are also two Trapper models offered; an 18.5" barrel and a 16.5" version. This is high quality rifle and amazingly close to the original in configuration. There are three grades of engraving also available. Weights are as follows: rifle 9.2 lbs., carbine 9 lbs., 18.5" trapper 7.9 lbs., 16.5" trapper 7.4 lbs. Finish can be steel, standard blued or charcoal blue.
Grade A-Add $350.
Grade B-Add $450.
Grade C-Add $600.

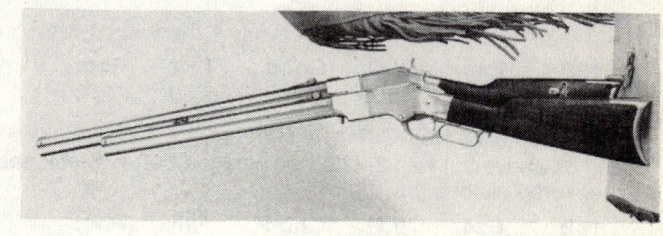

NIB	Exc.	V.G.	Good	Fair	Poor
750	650	550	450	350	200

Winchester Model 1866

This is a faithful replica of the Winchester 1866. It is chambered for .22 l.r., .22 Magnum, .38 Special, and .44-40, and .45 Long Colt. The rifle version has a brass frame and a 24.25" tapered octagon barrel. The frame finish is brass, with a walnut stock. Weight is about 8 lbs.

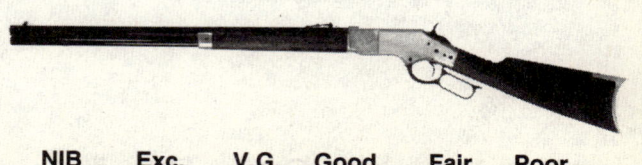

NIB	Exc.	V.G.	Good	Fair	Poor
600	550	450	400	300	200

1866 Yellowboy Carbine

This model is similar to the standard rifle, but is offered with a 19" round tapered barrel.

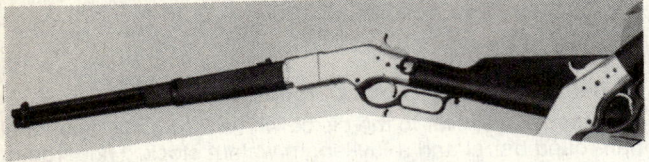

NIB	Exc.	V.G.	Good	Fair	Poor
700	600	500	450	350	200

Winchester Model 1873 Carbine

This is a reproduction of the Winchester 1873 chambered for .357 Magnum, .45 Long Colt, and .44-40. It has a case-colored steel receiver and a 19" round tapered barrel. The lever is also case-colored. The stock and forearm are walnut. Overall length is 38.25" and weight is about 7.4 lbs.

NIB	Exc.	V.G.	Good	Fair	Poor
750	600	500	450	350	200

Winchester Model 1873 Rifle

This model is similar to the Carbine, with a 24.25" octagonal barrel. Overall length is 43.25" and weight is approximately 8.2 lbs.

NOTE: Extra barrel lengths from 30" to 20" in .45 L.C. and .44-40 are also offered at extra cost.

NIB	Exc.	V.G.	Good	Fair	Poor
750	650	550	450	350	200

Winchester 1873 Half-Octagon Rifle

Same as above but with 24.25" half octagon barrel. Stock has a checkered pistol grip.

NIB	Exc.	V.G.	Good	Fair	Poor
750	650	550	450	350	200

Hawken Santa Fe

Based on the famous original rifle this reproduction is bored for .54 caliber and fitted with a 32" octagon barrel. A double set trigger and casehardened lock plate are standard. The stock ferrule and wedge plates are German silver. The stock is walnut with cheek piece. Overall length is 50" and weight is about 9.5 lbs. Also available in kit form.

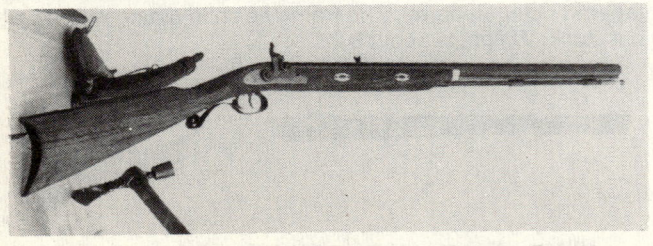

NIB	Exc.	V.G.	Good	Fair	Poor
350	300	250	200	150	100

Cattleman

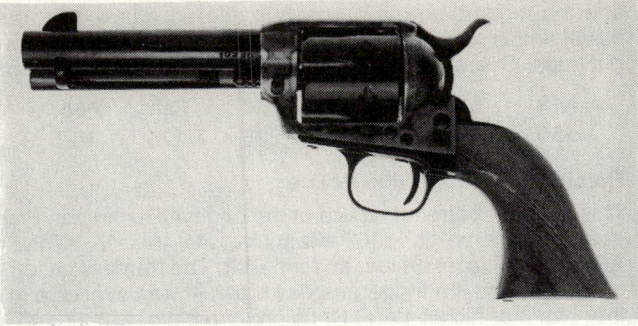

This is a single-action revolver patterned closely after the Colt Single Action Army. It is chambered in various popular calibers; .357 Magnum, .44-40, .44 Special, .45 ACP, .45 L.C./.45 ACP convertible, and .45 Colt. It is offered with barrel lengths of 4.75", 5.5", and 7.5". It is offered with either a modern or black powder-type frame and brass or steel backstraps. The finish is blued, with walnut grips. A Sheriff's Model with a 3" barrel and no ejector rod chambered for .44-40 and .45 Colt is also available and is valued the same. Weight is approximately 38 oz. for 5.5" barrel gun.

NIB	Exc.	V.G.	Good	Fair	Poor
325	275	250	200	150	100

Cattleman Target Model

This model is similar to the standard Cattleman, with an adjustable rear sight.

NIB	Exc.	V.G.	Good	Fair	Poor
350	300	275	225	175	125

New Thunderer Model

Designed and imported exclusively by Cimarron Arms for single action shooting competition. Fitted with bird's-head grip with hard rubber this model is chambered for the .357 Magnum, .44 Special, .44 WCF, and .45 Colt. Offered in barrel lengths of 3.5" and 4.75". Finish in nickel or blued with case-colored frame.

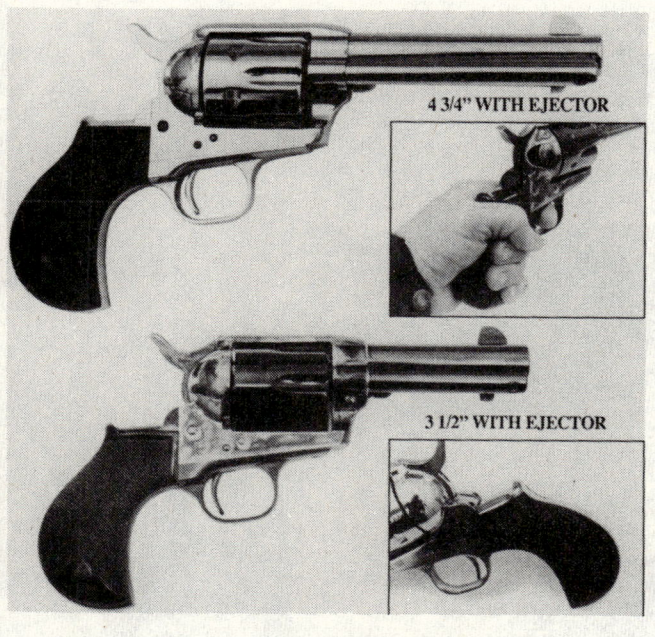

4 3/4" WITH EJECTOR

3 1/2" WITH EJECTOR

NIB	Exc.	V.G.	Good	Fair	Poor
450	350	300	250	200	100

Buckhorn Buntline

This version is chambered for the .44 Magnum. It has an 18" round barrel, and it is cut for attaching a shoulder stock. Steel backstrap and triggerguard. Overall length is 23" and weight is about 57 oz.

Detachable Shoulder Stock-Add 25%.

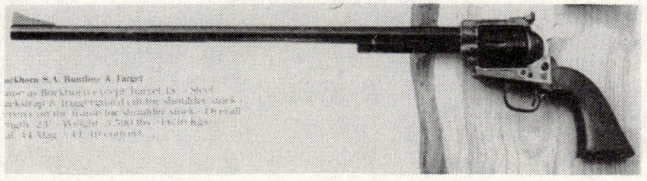

NIB	Exc.	V.G.	Good	Fair	Poor
350	325	300	250	200	100

Buckhorn Target

Same as above but fitted with an adjustable rear sight and ramp front sight. Has a flat upper frame.

NIB	Exc.	V.G.	Good	Fair	Poor
375	350	300	250	200	100

Phantom

Similar to the Buckhorn, but chambered for the .44 Magnum and the .357 Magnum. The barrel is a round 10.5" and the frame is blued with blued steel backstrap. One-piece walnut grips with anatomic profile. Adjustable sight. Weight is approximately 53 oz.

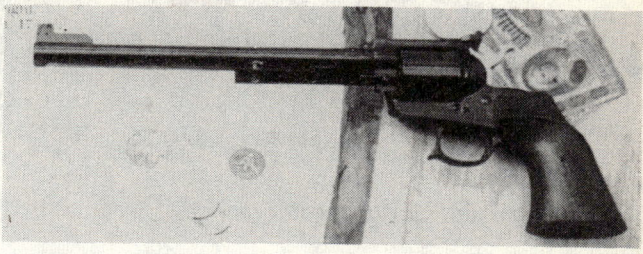

NIB	Exc.	V.G.	Good	Fair	Poor
350	325	300	250	200	100

Buntline Carbine

This version has the 18" barrel but is fitted with a permanently mounted shoulder stock with a brass buttplate and sling swivel. Chambered for .44-40, .45 Long Colt, .357 Magnum, and .44 Magnum. Offered with fixed or adjustable sights.

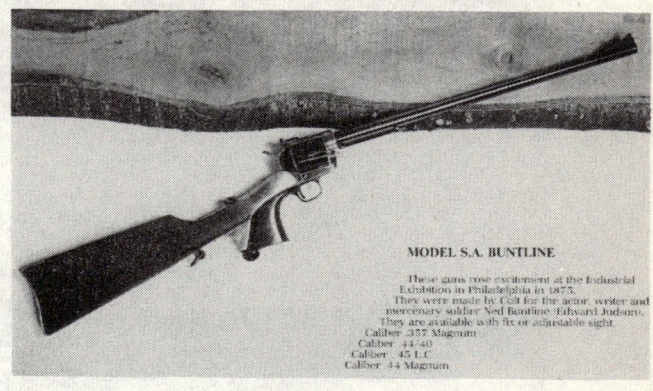

MODEL S.A. BUNTLINE

NIB	Exc.	V.G.	Good	Fair	Poor
450	400	350	300	250	200

1873 Stallion

This is a scaled-down version, chambered for .22 l.r./.22 Magnum. It is blued with a case-colored frame and features one-piece walnut grips.

NIB	Exc.	V.G.	Good	Fair	Poor
325	275	250	200	150	100

Schofield Revolver

Patterned after the original S&W revolver this model is chambered for the .44-40 or .45 Colt cartridge. It is fitted with a 7.5" barrel or a 5.5" barrel in the Wells Fargo variation. Weight with 7.5" barrel is approximately 40 oz.

NIB	Exc.	V.G.	Good	Fair	Poor
800	700	500	—	—	—

Inspector Model

This is a double action revolver built on the same general lines as the Colt Detective model. Cylinder holds 6 cartridges and is chambered for the .38 Special. Offered in the following barrel lengths with fixed sights: 2", 2.125", 2.5", 3", 4", 6" and also offered in 4" and 6" barrel lengths with adjustable sights. Grips

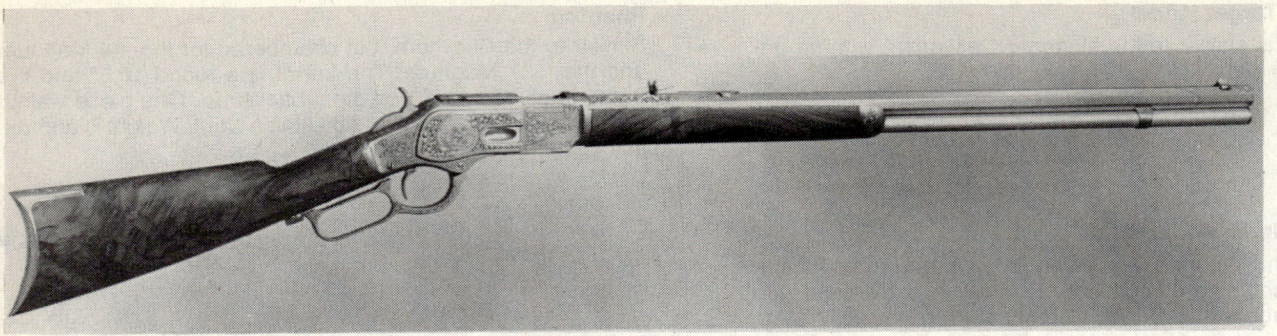

Uberti engraved 73 Winchester replica.

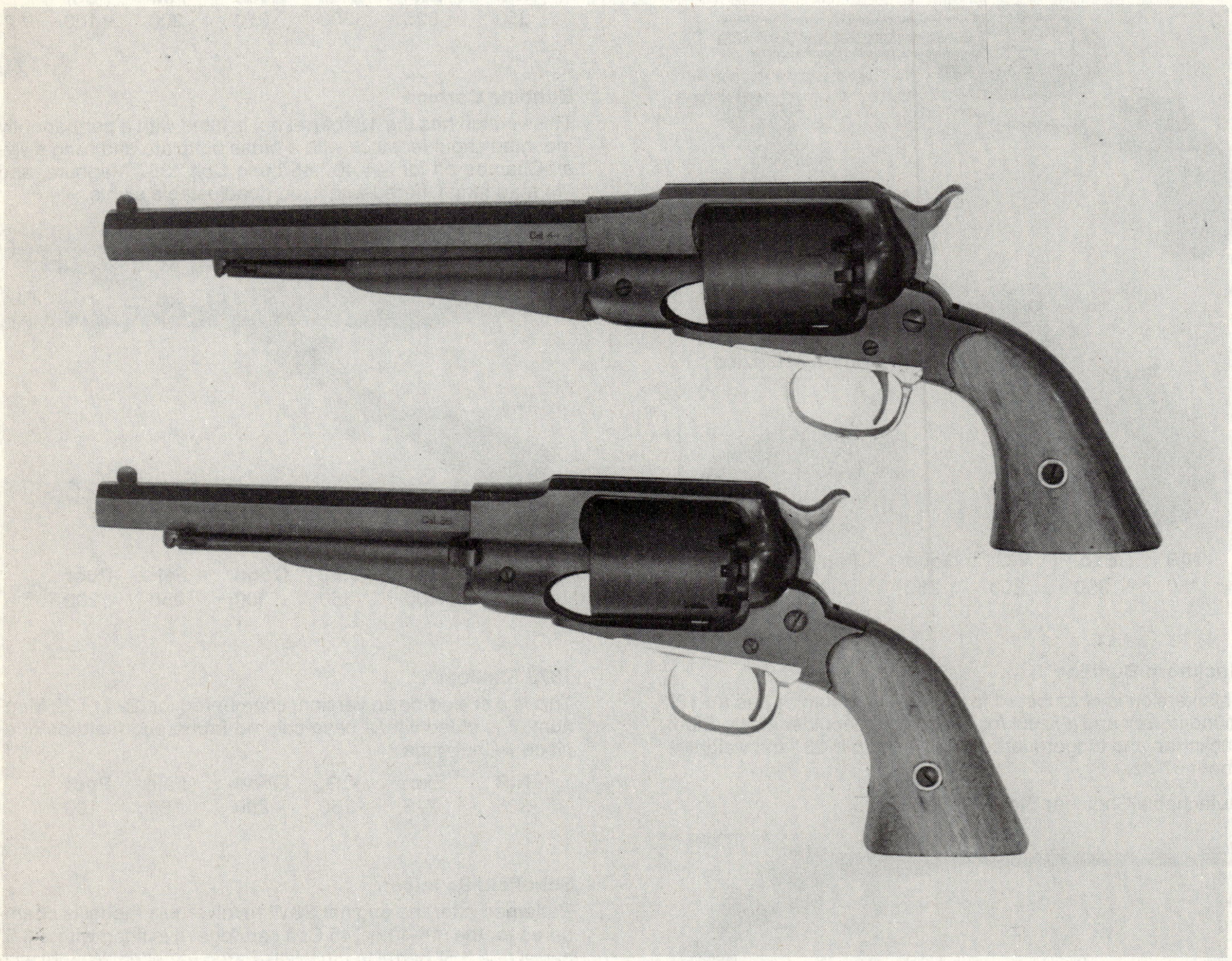

Uberti 1858 Remington replicas.

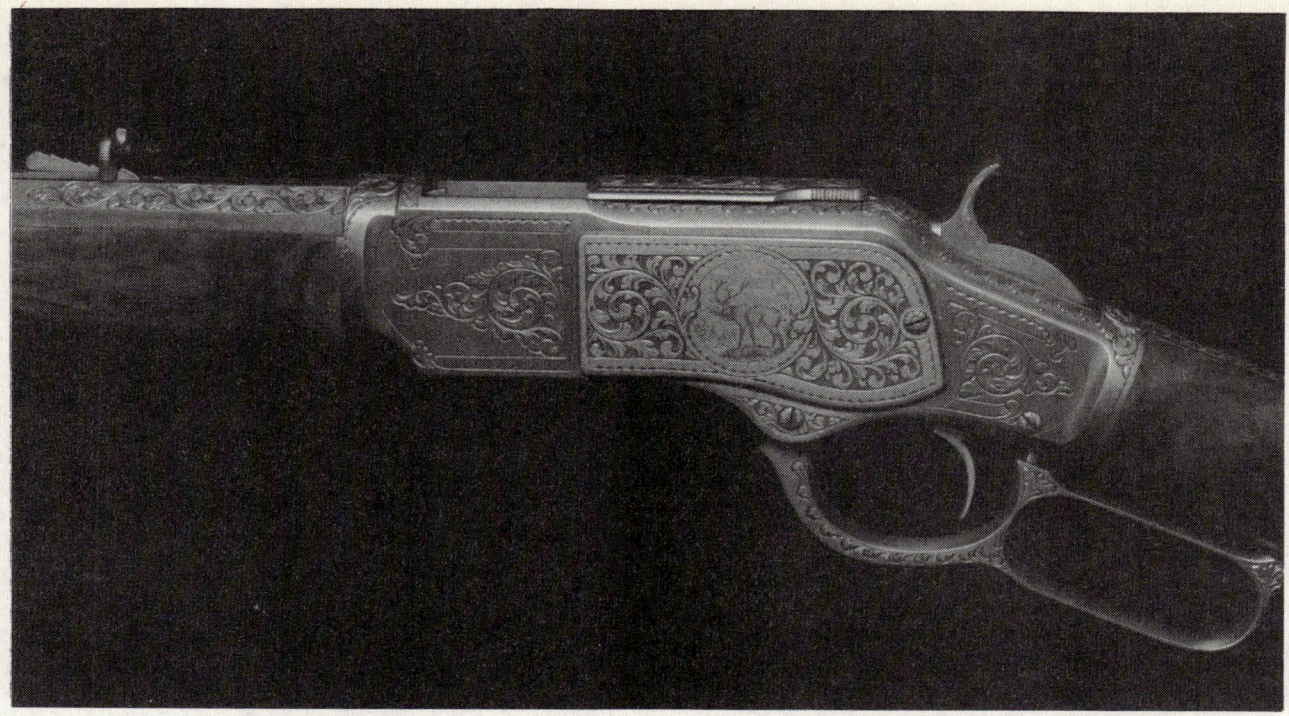

Uberti engraved 73 Winchester replica.

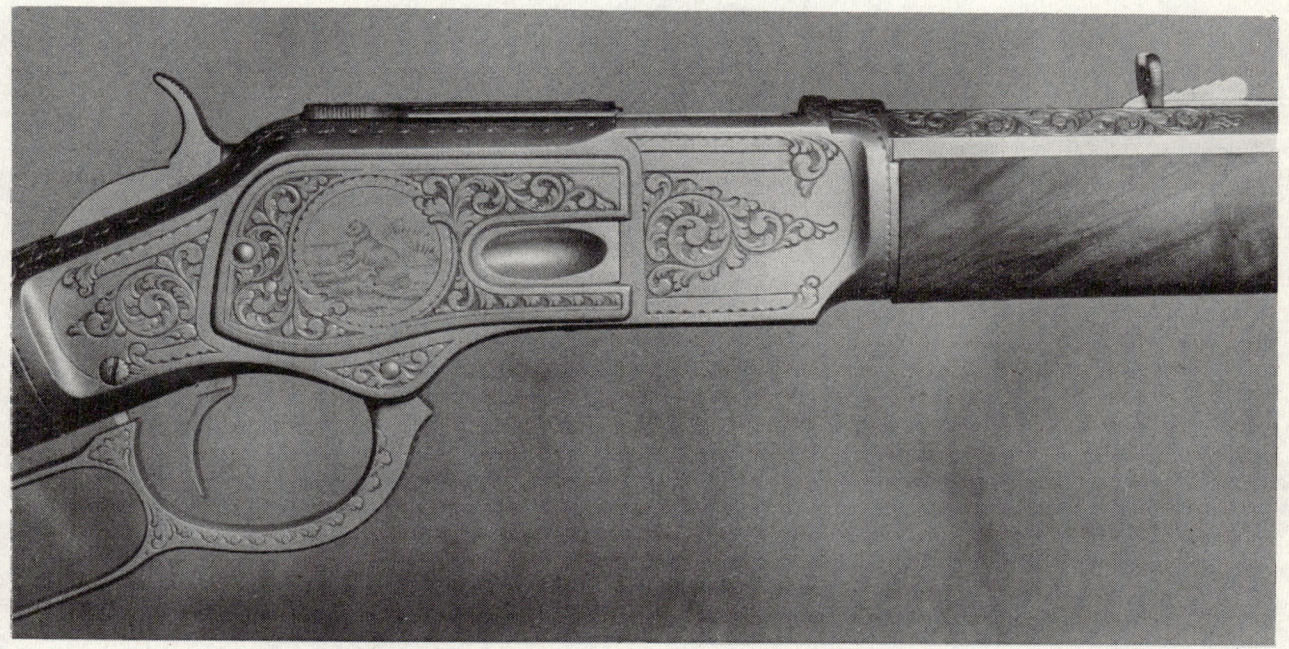

Uberti engraved 73 Winchester replica.

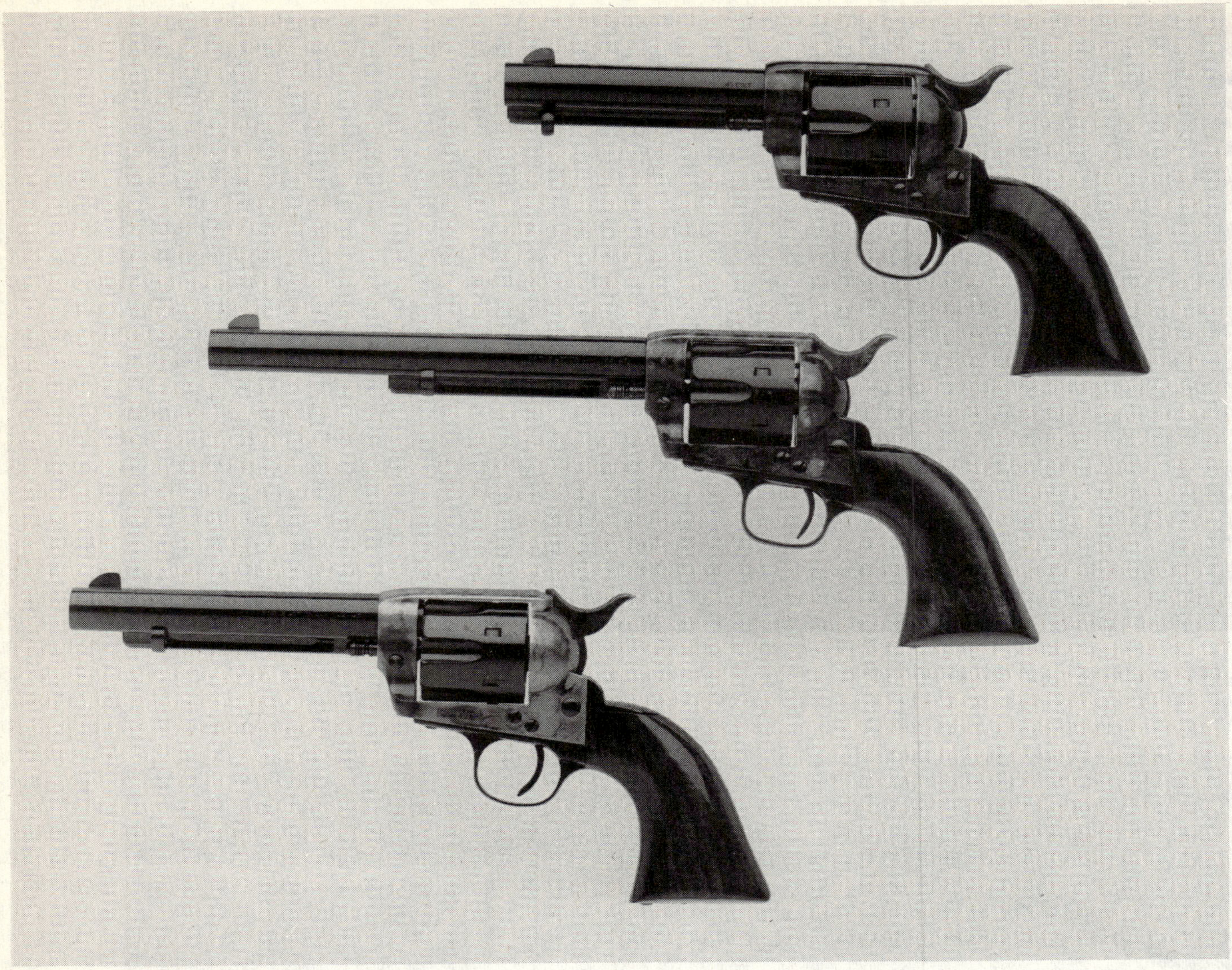

Uberti S.A.A. Colt replicas.

Uberti engraved 1860 Army Colt replica.

are walnut and finish is blued or chrome. With the 3" barrel the weight is about 24 oz.

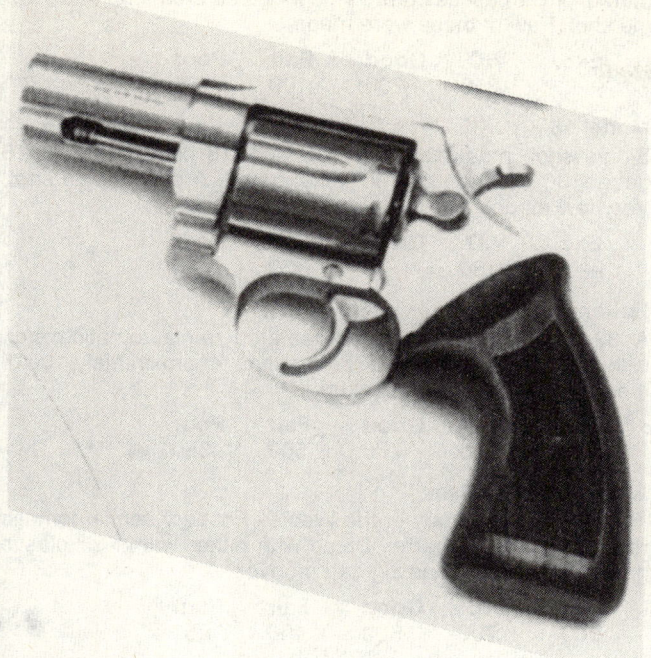

NIB	Exc.	V.G.	Good	Fair	Poor
250	200	150	125	100	75

UHLINGER, WILLIAM P.
Philadelphia, Pennsylvania

Pocket Revolver

A .32 caliber spur trigger revolver with a 2.75" or 3" octagonal barrel and an unfluted 6-shot cylinder. Blued with rosewood or walnut grips. Manufactured during the late 1860s and early 1870s.

NOTE: Uhlinger-manufactured pistols will often be found with retailer's names on them, such as: D.D. Cone, Washington, D.C.; J.P. Lower; and W.L. Grant.

Long Cylinder (1-3/16")

Exc.	V.G.	Good	Fair	Poor
—	—	400	200	100

Short Cylinder (1")

Exc.	V.G.	Good	Fair	Poor
—	—	300	150	75

.32 Rimfire Model (5", 6", or 7" Barrel)

Exc.	V.G.	Good	Fair	Poor
—	—	400	175	100

ULTIMATE
SEE Camex-Blaser

ULTRA LIGHT ARMS, INC.
Granville, West Virginia

This maker manufactures a variety of bolt action rifles fitted with Douglas barrels of varying lengths, custom triggers, and reinforced graphite stocks. The values for standard production models are as follows:

Model 20 (Short Action)
Weight is 4.75 lbs with 22" barrel.

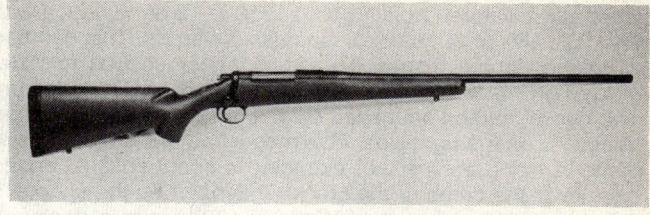

NIB	Exc.	V.G.	Good	Fair	Poor
2000	1750	1500	1250	900	700

Model 20 RF-Rimfire
Weight is about 5.25 with 22" barrel.

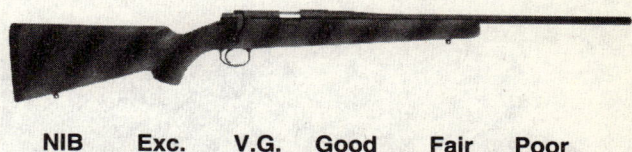

NIB	Exc.	V.G.	Good	Fair	Poor
800	650	600	500	400	300

Model 24 (Long Action)
Weight is approximately 5.25 lbs. with 22" barrel.

NIB	Exc.	V.G.	Good	Fair	Poor
2100	1850	1600	1350	900	700

Model 28 Magnum
Weight is about 5.75 lbs. with 24" barrel.

NIB	Exc.	V.G.	Good	Fair	Poor
2500	2250	1750	1500	1000	750

Model 40 Magnum
Weight is about 7.5 lbs with 26" barrel.

NIB	Exc.	V.G.	Good	Fair	Poor
2500	2250	1750	1500	1000	700

Model 20 Hunter's Pistol

A bolt action repeating pistol designed with the serious hunter in mind. It is offered in various popular calibers with a 14", high quality, Douglas heavy barrel. It has a 5-shot magazine and is matte blued, with a reinforced graphite Kevlar stock. It was introduced in 1987.

NIB	Exc.	V.G.	Good	Fair	Poor
1250	1000	850	750	600	500

UNCETA
SEE Astra-Unceta SA

UNION FIRE ARMS COMPANY
Toledo, Ohio

This company was incorporated in 1902 and used the names of Union Fire Arms, Union Arms Company, Illinois Arms Company (made for Sears) and Bee Be Arms Company. In 1917 the company was either bought up or absorbed by Ithaca Gun Company.

Model 24

Slide-action, Model 25 Peerless that was a fancy version of the Model 24 and the Model 25A, which was a trap model, were manufactured from 1902 to 1913 in 12 or 16 gauge with 24", 26", 28", or 32" steel or Damascus barrels. This gun had a unique double trigger. The front trigger cocked and decocked an internal firing pin and the back trigger fired the gun. The gun is marked on the left side of the frame and the pump release is on the right side. This model had one serious drawback, in that the slide that extracted a spent shell extended back over the comb of the stock. This often hit the shooter's thumb knuckle and caused injury. In 1907 Union redesigned their slide by reducing its length and shielding it behind a steel plate that covered the rear half of the opening. These are the Model 24, 25, and 25A improved versions. Approximately 17,000 of all models combined were made.

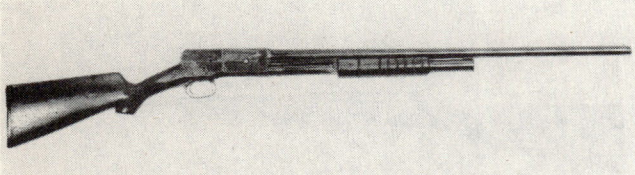

Exc.	V.G.	Good	Fair	Poor
—	600	300	200	100

Model 50

Manufactured 1911 to 1913. This was basically a redesign of the Model 24. The main distinguishing feature of the Model 50 was that the frame sloped down to meet the comb of the stock and the double trigger system was replaced by a single trigger. It came in 12 or 16 gauge with a 26", 28", 30", or 32" Krupp steel barrel. Fewer than 3,000 were made.

Exc.	V.G.	Good	Fair	Poor
—	700	400	300	200

Model 23

Hammerless double, manufactured between 1902 and 1913 with or without automatic ejectors. With some engraving, it came in both single and double trigger models; this was their top grade gun. Came in 12 and 16 gauge with 28", 30", or 32" steel, twist, or Damascus barrels.

Exc.	V.G.	Good	Fair	Poor
—	300	150	125	100

Model 22

This was essentially a no frills Model 23. It had the same barrel length and steel options, but it had a plain walnut stock and no engraving. There were fewer than 10,000 Model 22 and 23s made.

Exc.	V.G.	Good	Fair	Poor
—	200	100	75	50

Diamond Grade

Single shot, manufactured between 1905 and 1910. It had a unique octagonal breech in 12 gauge only with 30" steel, laminated, or Damascus barrel. This was their premium grade single shot. Few of these were made.

Exc.	V.G.	Good	Fair	Poor
—	350	200	100	50

Model 18

Single shot, manufactured 1906 to 1913 came in 12 or 16 gauge. 30", 32", 34", or 36" steel barrel. A plain single shot. Very few made.

Exc.	V.G.	Good	Fair	Poor
—	150	75	50	25

Reifengraber

A .32 or .38 S&W caliber gas operated semiautomatic pistol, with a 3" barrel. Blued with walnut grips, approximately 100 of these pistols were manufactured.

Exc.	V.G.	Good	Fair	Poor
1000	800	700	500	350

Automatic Revolver

.32 S&W caliber, copy of the Webley Fosbery semiautomatic revolver with a 3" barrel. Blued with either walnut or plastic grips. The cylinder has zig-zag grooves.

Exc.	V.G.	Good	Fair	Poor
900	700	500	400	250

UNION
Unknown

Pocket Pistol

.22 caliber spur trigger single shot pistol with a 2.75" barrel marked "Union". Nickel-plated with walnut grips.

Exc.	V.G.	Good	Fair	Poor
—	—	350	100	75

UNIQUE
Hendaye, France
SEE Pryrenees

UNITED SPORTING ARMS, INC.
Tucson, Arizona

Seville

A .357 Magnum, .41 Magnum, .44 Magnum or .45 caliber single action revolver with a 4-5/8", 5.5", 6.5", or 7.5" barrel having adjustable sights. Blued or stainless steel with walnut grips. Manufactured until 1986.

Exc.	V.G.	Good	Fair	Poor
400	350	300	250	200

Seville .357 Maxi

As above, in stainless steel and .357 Maximum caliber with a 5.5" or 7.5" barrel. Discontinued in 1986.

Exc.	V.G.	Good	Fair	Poor
550	500	450	350	300

Seville .375 USA

As above, in stainless steel and in .375 USA caliber. Discontinued in 1986.

Exc.	V.G.	Good	Fair	Poor
600	550	500	400	350

Seville .454 Magnum

As above, in stainless steel and .454 Magnum caliber with a 7.5" barrel and 5-shot cylinder. Discontinued in 1986.

Exc.	V.G.	Good	Fair	Poor
800	650	500	450	400

This series of revolvers was also available for silhouette shooting with 10.5" barrels and Pachmayr grips.

Sheriff's Model

Similar to the Seville Model with a 3.5" barrel. Blued or stainless steel with walnut grips. Discontinued in 1986.

Exc.	V.G.	Good	Fair	Poor
450	350	325	250	200

UNITED STATES ARMS
Otis A. Smith Company
Rockfall, Connecticut

Single Action Revolver

A .44 rimfire and centerfire single action revolver with a 7" barrel and integral ejector. The hammer nose is fitted with two firing pins so that rimfire or centerfire catridges can be used interchangeably. The barrel marked "United States Arms Company - New York", the top strap "No. 44". Blued with either hard rubber or rosewood grips. Manufactured in limited quantities. Circa 1870 to 1875.

Exc.	V.G.	Good	Fair	Poor
800	700	600	400	300

UNITED STATES HISTORICAL SOCIETY
Richmond, Virginia

The following arms are manufactured by the Williamsburg Firearms Manufactory and the Virginia Firearms Manufactory. This company ceased business under this name in 1994 and resumed business under the name of America Remembers in Mechanicsville, VA. No current prices are given for these models due to the lack of an active secondary market. Issue prices only are given.

George Washington

A reproduction of a flintlock pistol originally owned by George Washington. A total of 975 were made and were issued at a price of $3,000.

Thomas Jefferson

A reproduction of a flintlock pistol originally owned by Thomas Jefferson. A total of 1,000 were made and were issued at a price of $1,900.

Hamilton-Burr Dueling Pistols

Reproductions of the flintlock pistols used in the Hamilton-Burr duel. A total of 1,200 sets were made and sold at an issue price of $2,995.

Stonewall Jackson Pistol

A reproduction of a Colt Model 1851 Navy cased with accessories. Total of 2,500 were made in 1988. Issue Price was $2,100.

Texas Paterson Edition

A reproduction of a Colt Paterson revolver cased with accessories. Total of 1,000 were made in 1988. Issue price was $2,500.

Buffalo Bill Centennial

A reproduction of a Colt Model 1860 Army revolver with acid-etched scenes inlaid in gold, cased with accessories. Total of 2,500 were made in 1983 and issued at a price of $1,950.

U.S. Cavalry Model

A reproduction of a Colt Model 1860 Army revolver with a gold-plated cylinder and stag grips, cased with a brass belt buckle. Total of 975 were made beginning in 1988. Issue price was $1,450

Sam Houston Model

Reproduction of a Colt Model 1847 Army revolver with etched and gilt additions. Total of 2,500 were made. Issue price was $2,300.

Robert E. Lee Model

Reproduction of the Colt Model 1851 Navy revolver with gilt additions and cased with accessories. A total of 2,500 were made. Issue price was $2,100.

H. Deringer Set

Cased pair of reproduction .41 caliber Henry Deringer percussion pocket pistols available in three grades as follows:

Silver Mounted: 1,000
Issue Price $1,900

14 Kt. Gold Mounted: 100
Issue Price $2,700

18 Kt. Mounted with Gemstone: 5
Issue Price-$25,000

UNITED STATES PATENT FIREARMS MANUFACTURING COMPANY
Hartford, Connecticut

This company began business in 1995. The company imports its parts from Uberti in Italy and fits, finishes, and assembles the gun in Hartford. Produces only reproductions of Colt revolvers.

Walker Colt

A faithful reproduction of the Model 1847. Chambered for the .44 caliber ball. Half round barrel is 9". Weight is 73 oz.

NIB	Exc.	V.G.	Good	Fair	Poor
420	375	300	—	—	—

U.S. Dragoon 1st Model

Chambered for .44 caliber with a 7.5" round barrel. Weight is 66 oz.

NIB	Exc.	V.G.	Good	Fair	Poor
400	350	275	—	—	—

U.S. Dragoon 2nd & 3rd Models

Same as above but with the additional variations of the original models.

NIB	Exc.	V.G.	Good	Fair	Poor
400	350	275	—	—	—

Model 1851 Navy

Chambered for .36 caliber with a 7.5" octagonal barrel. Weight is about 42 oz.

NIB	Exc.	V.G.	Good	Fair	Poor
350	300	250	—	—	—

NOTE: For London Navy add $10. For Navy Carbine breech attachment add $250.

Model 1861 Navy

Same as above but with 7.5" round barrel. Weight is about 40 oz.

NIB	Exc.	V.G.	Good	Fair	Poor
350	300	250	—	—	—

NOTE: For Navy Carbine breech attachment add $250.

Model 1860 Army

Chambered for the .44 caliber with round 7.5" barrel. Choice of standard rebated cylinder or fluted cylinder. Weight is about 42 0z.

NIB	Exc.	V.G.	Good	Fair	Poor
370	325	275	—	—	—

NOTE: For Army Carbine breech attachment add $250.

Model 1848 Pocket Revolver

Chambered for the .31 caliber with a 4" octagonal barrel. Cylinder holds 5 shots. Offered without loading lever as was the original. Weight is about 23 oz.

NIB	Exc.	V.G.	Good	Fair	Poor
300	250	200	—	—	—

Model 1849 Pocket Revolver

Same as above but with loading lever.

NIB	Exc.	V.G.	Good	Fair	Poor
300	250	200	—	—	—

Model 1862 Navy

Chambered for the .36 caliber ball and offered with a choice of 4.5", 5.5", or 6.5" barrels.

NIB	Exc.	V.G.	Good	Fair	Poor
300	250	200	—	—	—

Model 1862 Police

Chambered for the .36 caliber bullet or ball. Choice of 4.5", 5.5", or 6.5" barrels.

NIB	Exc.	V.G.	Good	Fair	Poor
300	250	200	—	—	—

Single Action Army Revolver

Offered in a wide variety of calibers including .22 rimfire, .38 S&W, .357 magnum, .38-40, .44 Russian, .44-40, .45 Colt, and .45 ACP. Barrels lengths are 3", 4", 4.75", 5.5", and 7.5". Guns with 3" and 4" barrels are available in .44-40 or .45 Colt only. The standard gun is supplied with the original "P" frame. A modern cross pin frame is available for an additional $10. Prices below are for standard grips and finish.

NIB	Exc.	V.G.	Good	Fair	Poor
650	450	375	—	—	—

Flattop Target Model

This model is offered with the same calibers as the Single Action Army above. Barrel lengths are 4.75", 5.5", and 7.5". Grips are two piece hard rubber. Prices below are given for standard finish. Introduced in 1997.

NIB	Exc.	V.G.	Good	Fair	Poor
750	550	450	—	—	—

Henry Nettleton Revolver

This is an exact reproduction of the U.S. Government inspector model produced in the Springfield Armory. Offered in 7.5" and 5.5" models. Introduced in 1997.

NIB	Exc.	V.G.	Good	Fair	Poor
950	700	600	—	—	—

Bird Head Model

Offered with bird's head grips and available with 3.5", 4", or 4.75" barrel lengths.

NIB	Exc.	V.G.	Good	Fair	Poor
775	550	450	—	—	—

Bisley Model

Based on the famous Bisley model this reproduction features barrel lengths of 4.75", 5.5", 7.5", and 10". Add $60.00 for 10" models. Introduced in 1997.

NIB	Exc.	V.G.	Good	Fair	Poor
800	550	450	—	—	—

NOTE: This company offers a wide variety of special order options on its revolvers from special bluing to grips to engraving. These special order options will affect price to a significant degree. Seek qualified assistance prior to a sale.

UNITED STATES SMALL ARMS CO.
Chicago, Illinois

Huntsman Model Knife Pistol

Made from approximately 1918-1930.

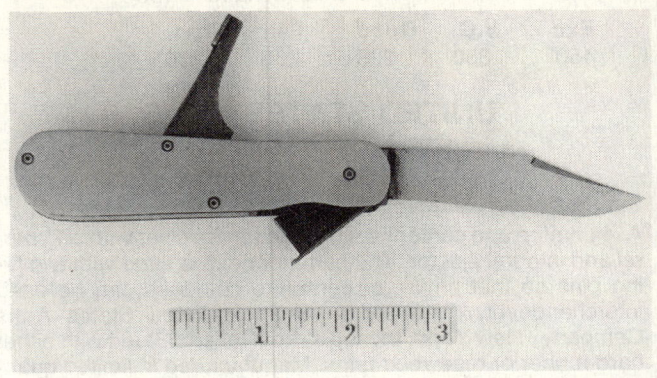

UNIVERSAL FIREARMS
Sacksonville, Arkansas

Model 7312

A 12 gauge Over/Under shotgun with separated 30" ventilated rib barrels, single selective trigger and automatic ejectors. The casehardened receiver engraved. Blued with a walnut stock. Discontinued in 1982.

Exc.	V.G.	Good	Fair	Poor
1700	1500	1250	900	450

Model 7412

As above, with extractors. Discontinued in 1982.

Exc.	V.G.	Good	Fair	Poor
1500	1250	1000	750	400

Model 7712

As above, with 26" or 28" barrels, non-selective single trigger and extractors. Discontinued in 1982.

Exc.	V.G.	Good	Fair	Poor
450	400	350	250	100

Model 7812

As above, with more detailed engraving and automatic ejectors. Discontinued in 1982.

Exc.	V.G.	Good	Fair	Poor
600	550	450	350	150

Model 7912

As above, with a gold wash frame and single selective trigger. Discontinued in 1982.

Exc.	V.G.	Good	Fair	Poor
1200	1000	750	600	300

Model 7112

A 12 gauge double barrel boxlock shotgun with 26" or 28" barrels, double triggers and extractors. Blued, casehardened with a walnut stock. Discontinued in 1982.

Exc.	V.G.	Good	Fair	Poor
350	300	250	200	100

Double Wing

A 10, 12, 20 or .410 bore boxlock double-barrel shotgun with 26", 28", or 30" barrels, double triggers and extractors. Blued with a walnut stock. Discontinued in 1982.

Exc.	V.G.	Good	Fair	Poor
350	300	250	200	100

Model 7212

A 12 gauge single barrel trap shotgun with a 30" ventilated rib ported barrel, and automatic ejector. Engraved, casehardened receiver and walnut stock. Discontinued in 1982.

Exc.	V.G.	Good	Fair	Poor
1000	850	650	450	300

Model 1000 Military Carbine

A copy of the U.S. M1 Carbine with an 18" barrel. Blued with a birch wood stock.

Exc.	V.G.	Good	Fair	Poor
350	250	200	100	75

Model 1003

As above, with a 16", 18", or 20" barrel.

Exc.	V.G.	Good	Fair	Poor
250	200	150	100	75

Model 1010

As above, but nickel-plated.

Exc.	V.G.	Good	Fair	Poor
275	225	175	125	100

Model 1015

As above, but gold-plated.

Exc.	V.G.	Good	Fair	Poor
300	250	200	150	125

Model 1005 Deluxe

As above, with a polished blue finish and Monte Carlo-style stock.

Exc.	V.G.	Good	Fair	Poor
275	225	150	100	75

Model 1006 Stainless

As the Model 1000, but in stainless steel.

Exc.	V.G.	Good	Fair	Poor
400	300	225	125	100

Model 1020 Teflon

As above, with a black or gray Dupont Teflon-S finish.

Exc.	V.G.	Good	Fair	Poor
300	225	175	125	100

Model 1256 Ferret

The Model 1000 in .256 Winchester Magnum caliber.

Exc.	V.G.	Good	Fair	Poor
275	200	175	125	100

Model 3000 Enforcer

A pistol version of the Model 1000 with an 11.25" barrel and 15- or 30-shot magazines.
Nickel Finish-Add 20%.
Gold-Plated-Add 40%.
Stainless Steel-Add 30%.
Teflon-S-Add 20%.

Blued

Exc.	V.G.	Good	Fair	Poor
300	225	200	150	100

Model 5000 Paratrooper

The Model 1000, with a 16" or 18" barrel and folding stock. This model, in stainless steel, is known as the Model 5006.

Exc.	V.G.	Good	Fair	Poor
350	250	200	125	100

1981 Commemorative Carbine

A limited production version of the Model 1000 cased with accessories. Produced in 1981.

NIB	Exc.	V.G.	Good	Fair	Poor
500	350	250	200	100	75

Model 2200 Leatherneck

A .22 caliber version of the U.S. M1 Carbine with an 18" barrel and blowback action. Blued with a birch wood stock

Exc.	V.G.	Good	Fair	Poor
200	175	150	100	75

U.S. M1 CARBINE
Various Manufacturers

This carbine was designed by William Roemer, Edwin Pugsley, and others at the Winchester Repeating Arms Company in late 1940 and early 1941. The only feature that can be credited to David Marsh "Carbine" Williams is the short stroke piston design. The U.S. M1 Carbine was produced by a number of manufacturers as listed below. The M1 A1 version was produced by Inland. The selective fire version is known as the Model M2.

Inland

Exc.	V.G.	Good	Fair	Poor
700	500	350	225	175

Underwood

Exc.	V.G.	Good	Fair	Poor
700	500	350	225	175

S.G. Saginaw

Exc.	V.G.	Good	Fair	Poor
600	450	375	250	175

IBM

Exc.	V.G.	Good	Fair	Poor
750	550	400	250	200

Quality Hardware

Exc.	V.G.	Good	Fair	Poor
600	450	375	250	175

National Postal Meter

Exc.	V.G.	Good	Fair	Poor
600	450	375	250	175

Standard Products

Exc.	V.G.	Good	Fair	Poor
600	450	375	225	150

Rockola

Exc.	V.G.	Good	Fair	Poor
800	625	500	250	175

SG Grand Rapids

Exc.	V.G.	Good	Fair	Poor
600	450	400	300	250

Winchester

Exc.	V.G.	Good	Fair	Poor
800	625	500	300	250

Irwin Pedersen

Exc.	V.G.	Good	Fair	Poor
1200	950	750	450	350

M1 A1 Paratrooper Model

The standard U.S. M1 Carbine fitted with a folding stock. Approximately 110,000 were manufactured by Inland between 1942 and 1945.

Courtesy Richard M. Kumor , Sr.

Exc.	V.G.	Good	Fair	Poor
1400	1100	750	600	400

Rock Island Auction sold a presentation Inland X Series M1 Carbine on December 11, 1995 for $2,420. The serial number had an "X" prefix. Condition is near mint.
Presented to a General Motors executive.

An example of an U.S. M1 Presentation Carbine
Courtesy Richard M. Kumor , Sr.

URIZAR, TOMAS
Eibar, Spain

Celta, J. Cesar, Premier, Puma, and Union

A 6.35mm semiautomatic pistol with a 3" barrel. The slide marked with the trade names listed above. Blued with black plastic grips, cast with a wild man carrying a club.

Exc.	V.G.	Good	Fair	Poor
175	150	125	90	75

Dek-Du

A 5.5mm folding trigger double action revolver with a 12-shot cylinder. Later versions were made in 6.35mm. Manufactured from 1905 to 1912.

Exc.	V.G.	Good	Fair	Poor
150	125	100	75	50

Express

A 6.35mm semiautomatic pistol with a 2" barrel. The slide marked "The Best Automatic Pistol Express". Blued with walnut grips. A 7.65mm variety exists with a 4" barrel.

Exc.	V.G.	Good	Fair	Poor
150	125	100	75	50

Imperial

A 6.35mm caliber semiautomatic pistol with a 2.5" barrel. This model was actually made by Aldazabal. Manufactured circa 1914.

Exc.	V.G.	Good	Fair	Poor
150	125	100	75	50

Le Secours or Phoenix

A 7.65mm semiautomatic pistol marked with either of the trade names listed above.

Exc.	V.G.	Good	Fair	Poor
150	125	100	75	50

Princeps

A 6.35mm or 7.65mm semiautomatic pistol marked on the slide "Made in Spain Princeps Patent."

Exc.	V.G.	Good	Fair	Poor
150	125	100	75	50

Venus

A 7.65mm semiautomatic pistol with the grips having the trade name "Venus" cast in them.

Exc.	V.G.	Good	Fair	Poor
150	125	100	75	50

UZI ISRAELI MILITARY INDUSTRIES
Importer-O.F. Mossberg
North Haven, CT

Uzi Carbine Model B

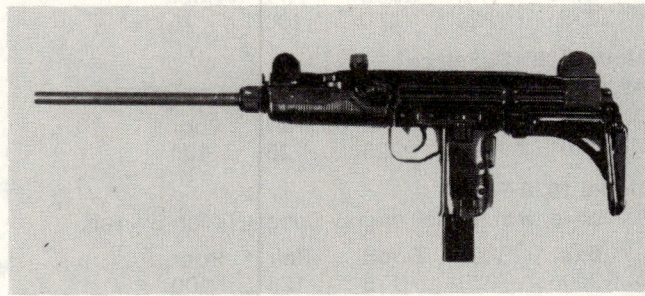

A 9mm, .41 Action Express or .45 caliber semiautomatic carbine with a 16.1" barrel and 20-, 25-, or 32-shot magazines. A 50-shot drum magazine is available in 9mm caliber. Black Parkerized finish, plastic grips and a folding stock. It is strongly suggest that a buyer or seller seek a qualified local appraisal.

NIB	Exc.	V.G.	Good	Fair	Poor
1250	900	750	600	400	300

Uzi Mini-Carbine

As above, in 9mm or .45 caliber with a 19.75" barrel.

NIB	Exc.	V.G.	Good	Fair	Poor
2000	1500	1150	800	600	400

Uzi Pistol

As above, with a 4.5" barrel, pistol grip, no rear stock and a 20-shot magazine

NIB	Exc.	V.G.	Good	Fair	Poor
850	700	550	450	350	250

V

VALKYRIE ARMS, LTD.
Olympia, Washington

Browning 1919 A4 .30 Caliber

This is a semiautomatic version of the famous Browning machine gun. It is chambered for the .30-06 or the .308 cartridge. It come equipped with a tripod, pintle, T&E, belly linker and 200 links. An A6 configuration is available. Available in late 1996.

NIB	Exc.	V.G.	Good	Fair	Poor
3850	—				—

VALMET, INC.
Jyvaskyla, Finland
Importer-Stoeger, Inc.
South Hackensack, New Jersey

M-625

A semiautomatic copy of the Finnish M-62 service rifle in 7.62 caliber that is patterned after the Russian AK47. Fitted with a walnut or tubular steel stock. Manufactured after 1962.

NIB	Exc.	V.G.	Good	Fair	Poor
2000	1750	1200	900	750	300

M-715

As above, in 5.56mm caliber and available with a composition stock.

NIB	Exc.	V.G.	Good	Fair	Poor
2000	1750	1200	900	750	300

Model 76

As above, in 5.56mm, 7.62x39mm, or 7.62x54mm with either a 16.75" or 20.5" barrel.

NIB	Exc.	V.G.	Good	Fair	Poor
1500	1250	950	750	550	200

Model 78

As above, in 7.62x54mm with a 24.5" barrel, wood stock, and integral bipod.

NIB	Exc.	V.G.	Good	Fair	Poor
1750	1500	1000	850	600	300

Lion

A 12 gauge Over/Under shotgun with 26", 28", or 30" barrels, single selective trigger and extractors. Blued with a walnut stock. Manufactured from 1947 to 1968.

Exc.	V.G.	Good	Fair	Poor
425	375	300	250	100

VALTION (LAHTI)
SEE Lahti

VARNER SPORTING ARMS, INC.
Marietta, Georgia

The rifles listed below are all patterned after the Stevens Favorite model.

Hunter

.22 caliber single shot rifle with a 21.5" half-octagonal, takedown barrel fitted with an aperture rear sight. Blued with well figured walnut stocks. Introduced in 1988.

NIB	Exc.	V.G.	Good	Fair	Poor
375	325	275	225	150	100

Hunter Deluxe

As above, with a case-hardened receiver and a more finely figured stock.

NIB	Exc.	V.G.	Good	Fair	Poor
500	400	350	275	175	150

Presentation Grade

As above, with a target hammer and trigger, and a hand checkered stock.

NIB	Exc.	V.G.	Good	Fair	Poor
575	475	425	350	250	200

Engraved Presentation Grade No. 1 Grade

NIB	Exc.	V.G.	Good	Fair	Poor
650	550	500	450	350	250

No. 2 Grade

NIB	Exc.	V.G.	Good	Fair	Poor
775	650	600	550	450	300

No. 3 Grade

NIB	Exc.	V.G.	Good	Fair	Poor
1100	950	750	650	550	400

NOTE: This company made several over and under shotguns and rifle/shotgun combination guns for the Savage Company. These are no longer being imported into this country.

VENUS WAFFENWERKE
Zella Mehlis, Germany

Venus

A 6.35mm, 7.65mm, or 9mm semiautomatic pistol with a 3.5" barrel. Slide is marked "Original Venus Patent" and the grips bear the monogram "OW". Designed by Oskar Will. Blued, plastic grips. Manufactured from 1912 to 1914.

Exc.	V.G.	Good	Fair	Poor
700	550	400	250	100

VERNEY-CARRON
St. Etienne, France
Importer-Ventura
Seal Beach, California

Concours

A 12 gauge Over/Under boxlock shotgun with 26" or 28" ventilated rib barrels, single selective triggers, automatic ejectors and profuse engraving. Blued, French case-hardened with checkered walnut stock. First imported in 1978.

Exc.	V.G.	Good	Fair	Poor
1000	850	750	600	350

Skeet Model

As above, with a 28" skeet choked barrel and a pistol grip stock.

Exc.	V.G.	Good	Fair	Poor
1100	900	800	650	450

VETTERLI
Switzerland
Various Manufacturers

Bolt Action Rifle

This rifle was invented by Friderich Vetterli at Neuhausen, Switzerland, in 1867. This was the first bolt action rifle to be used as a military service weapon. It was adopted on January 8, 1869, and predated the Fruwirth by three years. It is chambered for the 10.2 copper based Vetterli rimfire cartridge, the .41 Swiss, or the 10.4x38mm cartridges. It has a 12-round tubular magazine that is loaded through a side gate similar to a Winchester lever action. There is a swinging cover on the loading gate. The finish is blue, with a full length walnut stock secured by one barrel band and an endcap. There is a full length cleaning rod located under the barrel. The receiver has a round configuration and the triggerguard has a rear spur. The rifle was built between 1869 and 1881.
For Carbine models-Add 100%.

Exc.	V.G.	Good	Fair	Poor
500	400	300	200	100

VICKERS, LTD.
Crayford/Kent, England

Jubilee

A .22 caliber single shot Martini-action single shot rifle with a 28" barrel, adjustable sights and pistol grip walnut stock. Blued. Manufactured prior to WWII.

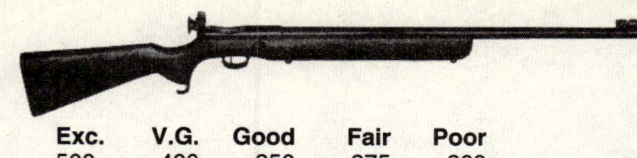

Exc.	V.G.	Good	Fair	Poor
500	400	350	275	200

Empire

As above, with a 27" or 30" barrel and a straight stock.

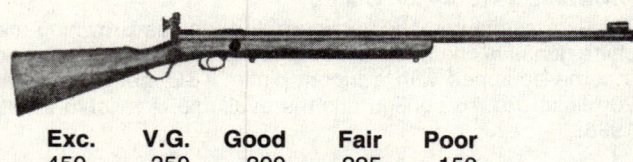

Exc.	V.G.	Good	Fair	Poor
450	350	300	225	150

VICTOR EJECTOR
See Crescent Fire Arms Co.

VICTORY ARMS COT., LTD.
North Hampton, England
Importer-Magnum Research, Inc.
Minneapolis, Minnesota

Model MC5

A 9mm, .38 Super, .41 Action Express, 10mm, or .45 caliber semiautomatic pistol with a 4.25", 5.75", or 7.5" barrel, 10-, 12-, or 17-shot magazine, decocking lever and Millett sights. Interchangeable barrels were available. Introduced in 1989.

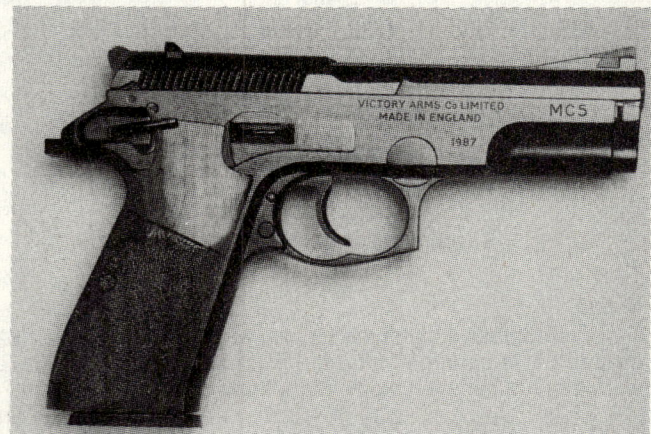

NIB	Exc.	V.G.	Good	Fair	Poor
500	450	400	300	250	100

VIRGINIAN
SEE Interarms

VOERE
Kufstein, Austria

In 1987 this company was purchased by Mauser-Werke. Voere actions are used in rifles made and sold by KDF, Inc., of Seguin, Texas. Values for older-production rifles are as follows:

Bolt-Action Rifle

A bolt-action sporting rifle made in a variety of calibers with 22" or 24" barrels, 3- or 4-shot magazines and checkered walnut stock.

Exc.	V.G.	Good	Fair	Poor
350	300	250	200	100

Semi-Auto Rifle

A .22 caliber semiautomatic rifle with a 20" barrel, adjustable sights, and a detachable magazine. Blued with a checkered walnut stock.

Exc.	V.G.	Good	Fair	Poor
250	200	150	100	75

NOTE: This rifle is a copy of the Gevarm open bolt .22 caliber rifle. It is no longer being imported into the country at the request of the BATF. Check the laws in your location before a sale.

VOLCANIC ARMS COMPANY
New Haven, Connecticut
SEE Winchester Repeating Arms Co.

VOLUNTEER ENTERPRISES
Knoxville, Tennessee
SEE Commando Arms

VOLKSPISTOLE
Various Makers
Germany

Volkspistole

Quite mysterious, as few have ever been noted. It was designed as a cheaply manufactured, last-ditch weapon that was supposed to be used to flood the German countryside and cause casualties among the invaders at the close of WWII. It is chambered for the 9mm Parabellum cartridge and features a gas-operated, delayed blowback action. It has a 5.1" barrel with an 8-round, detachable box magazine. The construction is of steel stampings. It has no safety devices and no markings whatsoever. Examples noted are in the white, and there are no sights affixed to them. It appears that this weapon never actually went into production, and it would be impossible to estimate a value. Anyone encountering such a weapon would be wise to secure a qualified appraisal.

VOUZLAUD
Paris, France
Importer-Waverly Arms Co.
Suffolk, Virginia

Model 315 E

A 12, 16, or 20 gauge boxlock shotgun with 20" barrels, double triggers, and straight gripped stock. Blued, case-hardened. Imported prior to 1988.

Exc.	V.G.	Good	Fair	Poor
7500	6500	5500	4000	2500

Model 315 EL

As above, with more engraving and also available in .28 or .410 bore, which are worth approximately $1,000 more than the values listed below.

Exc.	V.G.	Good	Fair	Poor
10000	8500	6500	5000	3000

Model 315 EGL

As above, with a French case-hardened receiver. Discontinued in 1987.

Exc.	V.G.	Good	Fair	Poor
15000	12500	10000	7500	5000

Model 315 EGL-S

As above, with engraved hunting scenes. Discontinued in 1987.

Exc.	V.G.	Good	Fair	Poor
5500	4500	3500	2500	1750

W

WALCH, JOHN
New York, New York

Navy Revolver

A .36 caliber superimposed load percussion revolver with a 6" octagonal barrel and a 6-shot cylinder fitted with 12 nipples, 2 hammers, and 2 triggers. The barrel marked "Walch Firearms Co. NY." and "Patented Feb. 8, 1859". Blued with walnut grips.

Exc.	V.G.	Good	Fair	Poor
—	—	6500	2750	950

Pocket Revolver

A spur trigger .31 caliber 10-shot percussion revolver with either a brass or iron frame and walnut grips. The iron frame version is worth approximately 50% more than the brass variety.

Exc.	V.G.	Good	Fair	Poor
—	—	1500	750	300

WALDMAN
Germany

Waldman

A 7.65mm semiautomatic pistol with a 3.5" barrel and 8-shot magazine. The slide marked "1913 Model Automatic Pistol" and some examples are marked "American Automatic Pistol". Blued with checkered walnut grips inlaid with a brass insert marked "Waldman".

Exc.	V.G.	Good	Fair	Poor
250	225	200	150	100

WALLIS & BIRCH
Philadelphia, Pennsylvania

Pocket Pistol

A .41 caliber single shot percussion pocket pistol with a 2.5" or 3" barrel, German silver furniture and walnut stock. The barrels marked "Wallis & Birch Phila." Produced during the 1850s.

Exc.	V.G.	Good	Fair	Poor
—	—	4000	2000	700

WALTHER, CARL
Zella Mehilis and Ulm/Donau, Germany

In 1886 Carl Walther set up a workshop to make sporting arms. Until 1900 his operation remained small. In 1907 he designed the 6.35mm blowback pistol. This design was offered for sale in 1908. In less than a year after the introduction of the first pistol the second model was introduced. Called the Model 2, this pistol was more advanced than the first design and became a popular handgun in Germany prior to WWI. Two years later the Model 3 was introduced and successive models were designed and produced through 1921 when the Model 9 was announced. In 1929 Walther built the now famous Model PP, Polizei Pistole, which became synonymous with quality and advanced design. The Walther legend was born and has been maintained up to this date as a fine high quality German built pistol. After WWII the Walther company relocated in Ulm/Donau, Germany.

Editors Comment: There are a large number of Walther variations, especially during the WWII era and it requires years of experience to learn the subtleties of these variations. When dealing with expensive Walther pistols it is suggested that an expert appraisal be obtained before buying or selling these highly collectable handguns.

Model 1

A 6.35mm semiautomatic pistol barrel lengths of 2-6 inches. Blued with checkered hard rubber grips with the Walther logo on each grip. Introduced in 1908.

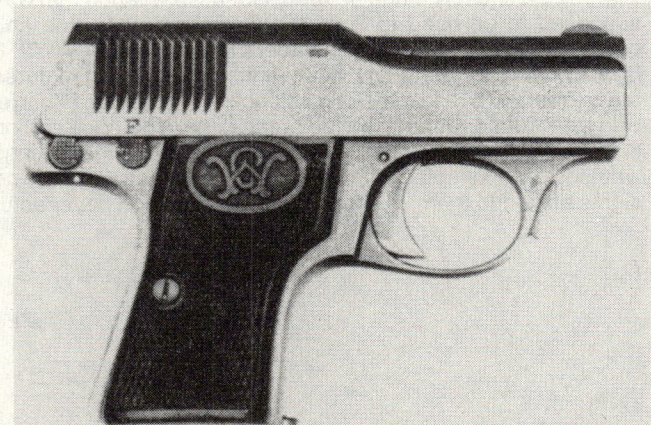

Courtesy James Rankin

Courtesy James Rankin

Exc.	V.G.	Good	Fair	Poor
650	400	350	200	200

Model 2

A 6.35mm semiautomatic pistol having a knurled bushing at the muzzle that retains the mainspring. There are two variations. One with a fixed rear sight, and one with a pop up rear sight. Blued with checkered hard rubber grips with the Walther logo on each grip. Introduced in 1909.

Courtesy James Rankin

Courtesy James Rankin

Fixed Sights

Exc.	V.G.	Good	Fair	Poor
600	375	300	200	150

Pop Up Sights

Exc.	V.G.	Good	Fair	Poor
1200	750	500	250	150

Model 3

A 7.65mm semiautomatic pistol having a smooth barrel bushing. Blued with checkered hard rubber grips with the Walther logo on each. Introduced in 1910.

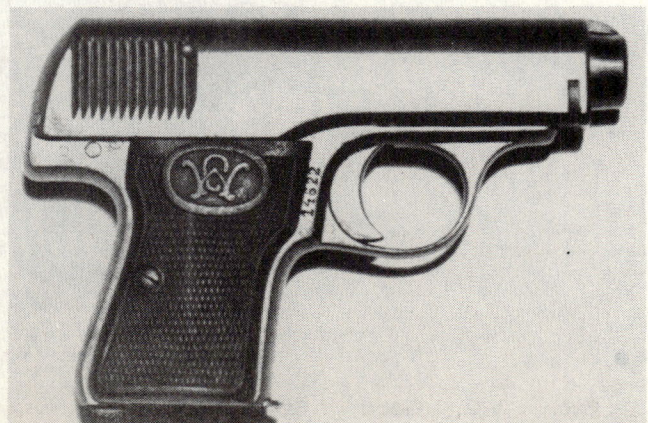

Courtesy James Rankin

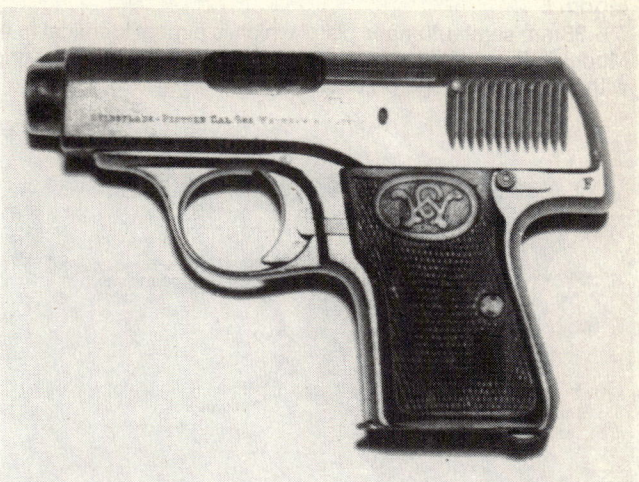

Courtesy James Rankin

Exc.	V.G.	Good	Fair	Poor
1000	700	500	350	200

Model 4

A 7.65mm semiautomatic pistol larger than the preceding models. There were many variations of this model produced. Blued with checkered hard rubber grips with the Walther logo on each grip. Introduced 1910.

Courtesy James Rankin

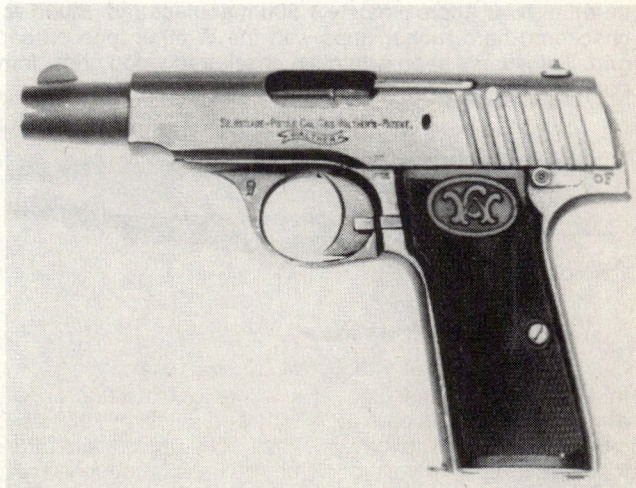

Courtesy James Rankin

Exc.	V.G.	Good	Fair	Poor
450	375	300	200	150

Model 5

A 6.35mm semiautomatic pistol which is almost identical to the Model 2. Fixed sights. Blued with checkered hard rubber grips with the Walther logo on each grip.

Courtesy James Rankin

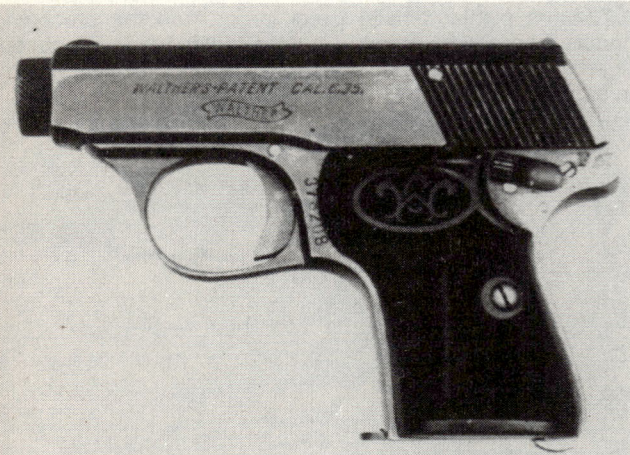

Courtesy James Rankin

Exc.	V.G.	Good	Fair	Poor
500	400	300	200	150

Model 6

A 9mm semiautomatic pistol. The largest of the Walther numbered pistols. Approximately 1,500 manufactured. Blued with checkered hard rubber grips with the Walther logo on each grip. Sometimes seen with plain checkered wood grips. Introduced 1915.

Courtesy James Rankin

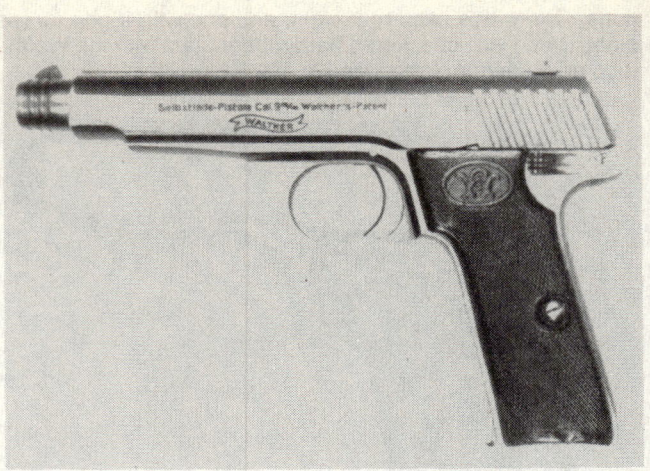

Courtesy James Rankin

Exc.	V.G.	Good	Fair	Poor
5800	3500	2200	1000	700

Model 7

A 6.35mm semiautomatic pistol in the same style as the Model 4. Blued with checkered hard rubber grips with the Walther logo on each side. Introduced in 1917.

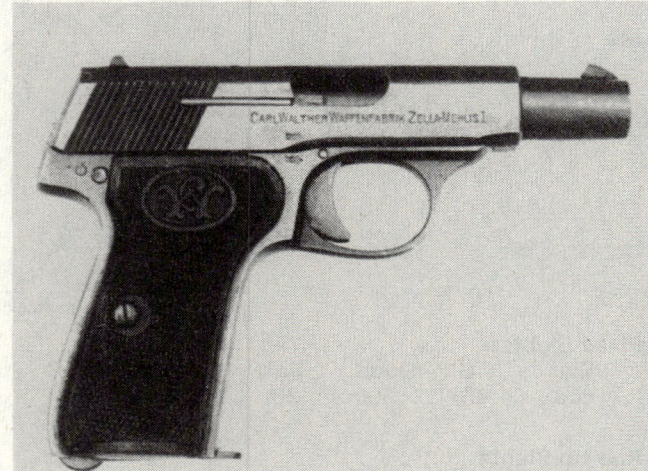

Courtesy James Rankin

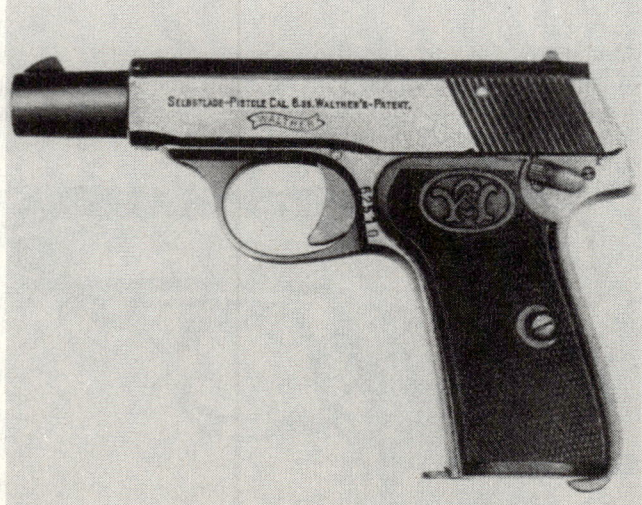

Courtesy James Rankin

Exc.	V.G.	Good	Fair	Poor
500	375	300	200	150

Model 8

A 6.35mm semiautomatic pistol. Finishes in blue, silver, and gold. Three types of engraving coverage; slide only, slide and frame and complete coverage overall. The grips are checkered hard rubber with the WC logo on one grip, and 6.35mm on the opposite side. Ivory grips are seen with many of the engraved models. Introduced in 1920 and produced until 1944.

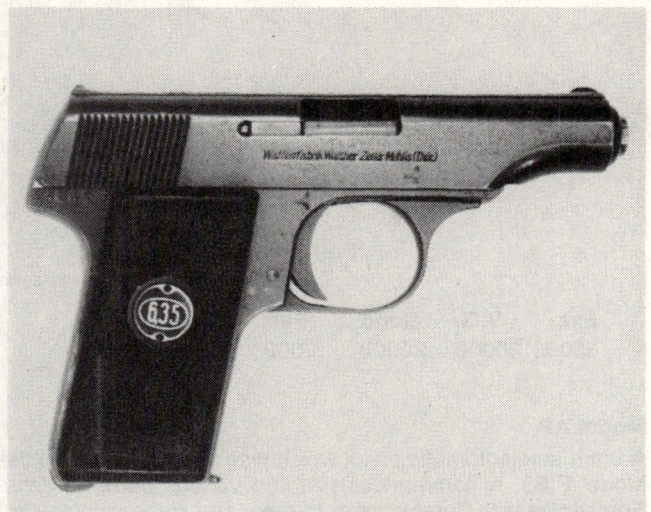

Courtesy James Rankin

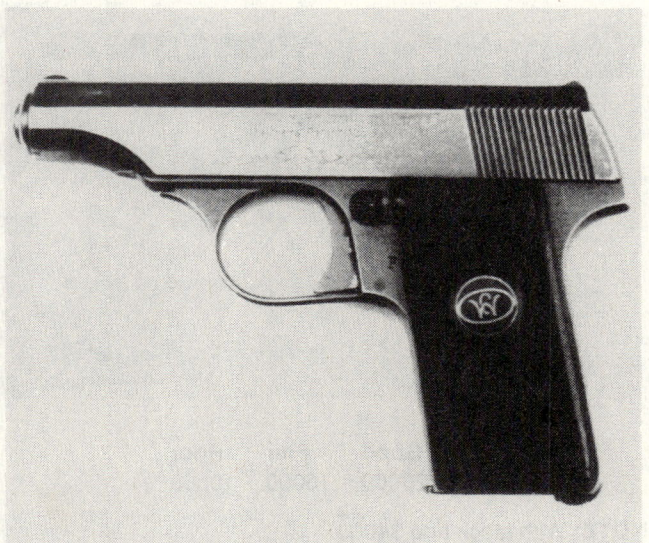

Courtesy James Rankin

Blue, Silver, and Gold Finish

Exc.	V.G.	Good	Fair	Poor
575	375	300	200	150

Engraved Slide

Exc.	V.G.	Good	Fair	Poor
1000	700	500	300	200

Engraved Slide and Frame

Exc.	V.G.	Good	Fair	Poor
2000	1400	850	450	300

Engraved, Complete Coverage

Exc.	V.G.	Good	Fair	Poor
2250	1500	900	500	300

Model 9

A 6.35mm semiautomatic pistol. Smaller than the Model 8, but built as the Model 1 with exposed barrel. Same finishes and engraving as the Model 8. Introduced 1921 and produced until 1944.

Courtesy James Rankin

Courtesy James Rankin

All values the same as the Model 8.

Sport Model 1926   Walther Hammerless Target 22
Walther Standard Sport   Walther 1932 Olympia

Sport Model Target, Special Stoeger Model

All of these 22 l.r. caliber semiautomatic pistols are the same target pistol introduced by Walther in 1926. A well-made pistol with a barrel length of between 6"-16". It has one-piece checkered wrap-around wood grips. There was also a .22 Short version of the Olympia model produced for rapid fire Olympic shooting. There was also a torpedo shape target weight available for shooters.

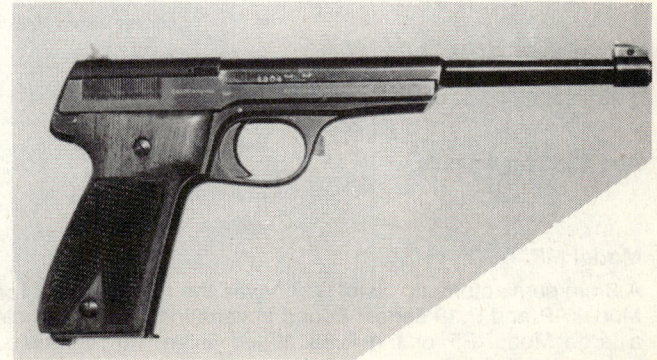

Courtesy Orvel Reichert

Courtesy James Rankin

Exc.	V.G.	Good	Fair	Poor
750	550	450	350	250

Add $200 for target weight. Add $500 for case.

Walther 1936 Olympia

This semiautomatic target pistol in .22 caliber resembled the earlier 1932 Olympia, but with many improvements. There were four standard models produced with many variations of each one. These variations included many barrel lengths, and both round and octagon barrels. There were duraluminum slides, frames and triggers. Various weight configurations to as many as four separate weights to one gun. One-piece wrap-around checkered wood grips in different configurations for the individual shooter. Produced until 1944. The four models were:

Funfklamph Pentathlon
Jagerschafts-Hunter
Sport or Standard Model
Schnellfeur-Rapid Fire

Courtesy James Rankin

Exc.	V.G.	Good	Fair	Poor
1000	750	600	475	250

Add $250 for weights.

Model MP

A 9mm semiautomatic pistol which was the forerunner of the Model AP and P.38 series. Found in variations that resemble a large Model PP or the P.38. Blued finish with one-piece wrap-around checkered wood grips.

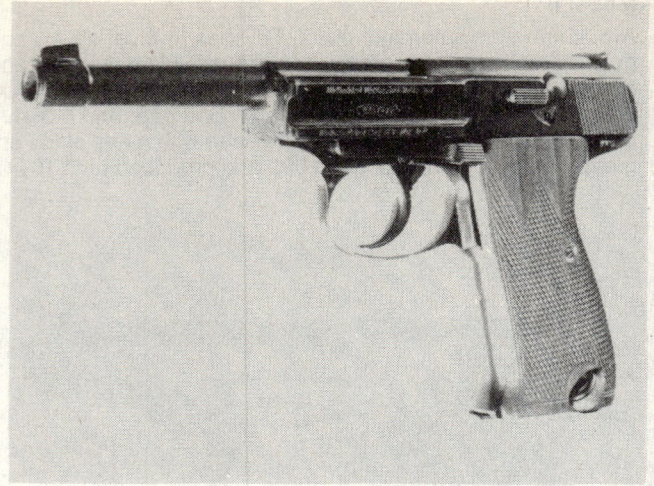

Courtesy James Rankin

Exc.	V.G.	Good	Fair	Poor
35000	30000	25000	20000	15000

Model AP

A 9mm semiautomatic pistol which was the forerunner of the Model P.38. A hammerless pistol in various barrel lengths. Sometimes with duraluminum frames, and some with stocks. Blued finish with one-piece wrap-around checkered wood grips.

Exc.	V.G.	Good	Fair	Poor
28000	25000	20000	15000	10000

NOTE: With stock add $4000.

Model PP

Courtesy James Rankin

Courtesy Orvel Reichert

Courtesy Orvel Reichert

A semiautomatic pistol in .22, .25, .32 and .380 caliber. Introduced in 1928. It was the first successful commercial double action pistol. It was manufactured in finishes of blue, silver, and gold, and with three different types of engraving. Grips were generally two-piece black or white plastic with the Walther banner on each grip. Grips in wood or ivory are seen, but usually on engraved guns. There are many variations of the Model PP and numerous NSDAP markings seen on the pre-1946 models that were produced during the Nazi regime. All reflect various prices.

Model PP .22 Caliber

Exc.	V.G.	Good	Fair	Poor
750	500	350	250	150

Model PP .25 Caliber

Exc.	V.G.	Good	Fair	Poor
5500	3500	2500	1500	600

Model PP .32 Caliber High Polished Finish

Exc.	V.G.	Good	Fair	Poor
450	325	275	225	175

Model PP .32 Caliber Milled Finish

Exc.	V.G.	Good	Fair	Poor
375	275	250	200	125

Model PP .380 Caliber

Exc.	V.G.	Good	Fair	Poor
850	650	550	475	350

Model PP .32 Caliber with Duraluminum Frame

Exc.	V.G.	Good	Fair	Poor
800	675	550	400	200

Model PP .32 Caliber with Bottom Magazine Release

Exc.	V.G.	Good	Fair	Poor
850	700	600	400	200

Model PP .32 Caliber with Verchromt Finish

Exc.	V.G.	Good	Fair	Poor
2000	1450	1000	700	400

Courtesy James Rankin

Courtesy Orvel Reichert

Model PP .32 Caliber in Blue, Silver or Gold Finish and Full Coverage Engraving

Blue

Exc.	V.G.	Good	Fair	Poor
3000	2500	2000	1200	700

Silver

Exc.	V.G.	Good	Fair	Poor
3500	3000	2500	1200	700

Gold

Exc.	V.G.	Good	Fair	Poor
4000	3500	3000	1200	700

NOTE: Add $250 for ivory grips with any of the three above.
Add $700 for leather presentation cases.
Add $500 for .22 caliber.
Add $1000 for .380 caliber.

Model PP .32 Caliber, Allemagne Marked

Exc.	V.G.	Good	Fair	Poor
850	700	550	325	250

Model PP .32 Caliber, A. F. Stoeger Contract

Exc.	V.G.	Good	Fair	Poor
2000	1450	1050	700	400

Model PP .32 Caliber with Waffenampt Proofs. High Polished Finish

Exc.	V.G.	Good	Fair	Poor
850	600	375	275	150

Model PP .32 Caliber with Waffenampt Proofs. Milled Finish

Exc.	V.G.	Good	Fair	Poor
450	375	325	250	150

Model PP .32 Caliber. Police Eagle/C Proofed. High Polished Finish

Exc.	V.G.	Good	Fair	Poor
800	475	375	250	150

Model PP .32 Caliber. Police Eagle/C and Police Eagle/F Proofed. Milled Finish

Exc.	V.G.	Good	Fair	Poor
600	400	375	275	150

Model PP .32 Caliber. NSKK Marked On The Slide

Exc.	V.G.	Good	Fair	Poor
2200	1500	850	550	300

NOTE: Add $700 with proper NSKK DRGM AKAH holster.

Model PP .32 Caliber. NSDAP Gruppe Markings

Exc.	V.G.	Good	Fair	Poor
1700	1100	750	500	300

NOTE: Add $600 with proper SA DRGM AKAH holster.

Model PP .32 Caliber. PDM Marked with Bottom Magazine Release

Exc.	V.G.	Good	Fair	Poor
850	700	550	475	300

Model PP .32 Caliber. RJ Marked

Exc.	V.G.	Good	Fair	Poor
750	600	475	400	150

Model PP .32 Caliber. RFV Marked. High Polished or Milled Finish

Exc.	V.G.	Good	Fair	Poor
700	600	475	400	150

Model PP .32 Caliber. RBD Munster Marked

Exc.	V.G.	Good	Fair	Poor
2200	1750	1200	650	400

Model PP .32 Caliber. RpLt Marked

Exc.	V.G.	Good	Fair	Poor
800	650	475	375	200

Model PP .32 Caliber. Statens Vattenfallsverk Marked

Exc.	V.G.	Good	Fair	Poor
850	700	550	375	200

Model PP .32 Caliber. AC Marked

Exc.	V.G.	Good	Fair	Poor
450	375	300	250	150

Model PP .32 Caliber. Duraluminum Frame

Exc.	V.G.	Good	Fair	Poor
700	600	500	400	150

Model PP .380 Caliber. Bottom Magazine Release and Waffenampt Proofs

Exc.	V.G.	Good	Fair	Poor
1450	1000	700	500	300

Model PPK

A semiautomatic pistol in .22, .25, .32 and .380 caliber. Introduced six months after the Model PP in 1929. A more compact version of the Model PP with one less round in the magazine and one-piece wrap-around checkered plastic grips in brown, black, and white with the Walther banner on each side of the grips. The Model PPK will be found with the same types of finishes as the Model PP as well as the same styles of engraving. Grips in wood or ivory are seen with some of the engraved models. As with the Model PP there are many variations of the Model PPK and numerous NSDAP markings seen on the pre-1946 models that were produced during the Nazi regime. All reflect various prices.

Courtesy Orvel Reichert

Courtesy James Rankin

Model PPK .22 Caliber

Exc.	V.G.	Good	Fair	Poor
1100	700	475	325	175

Model PPK .25 Caliber

Exc.	V.G.	Good	Fair	Poor
5800	3800	1850	1000	500

Model PPK .32 Caliber. High Polished Finish

Exc.	V.G.	Good	Fair	Poor
550	450	325	250	150

Model PPK .32 Caliber. Milled Finish

Exc.	V.G.	Good	Fair	Poor
500	400	325	250	150

Model PPK .380 Caliber

Courtesy Orvel Reichert

Exc.	V.G.	Good	Fair	Poor
2200	1750	1300	750	375

Model PPK .32 Caliber with Duraluminum Frame

Exc.	V.G.	Good	Fair	Poor
850	750	600	400	200

Model PPK .32 Caliber with Verchromt Finish

Exc.	V.G.	Good	Fair	Poor
2200	1750	1200	700	350

Model PPK .32 Caliber in Blue, Silver or Gold Finish and Full Coverage Engraving

Blue

Exc.	V.G.	Good	Fair	Poor
3500	3000	2500	1200	700

Silver

Exc.	V.G.	Good	Fair	Poor
3750	3250	2750	1200	700

Gold

Exc.	V.G.	Good	Fair	Poor
4500	3750	3000	1200	700

Add $750 for ivory grips with any of the three above.
Add $700 for leather presentation cases.
Add $500 for .22 caliber.
Add $1000 for .380 caliber.

Model PPK .32 Caliber Marked Mod. PP on Slide

Exc.	V.G.	Good	Fair	Poor
4000	3500	2500	1500	1000

Model PPK .32 Caliber with Panagraphed Slide

Exc.	V.G.	Good	Fair	Poor
650	550	450	300	200

Model PPK .32 Caliber. Czechoslovakian Contract

Exc.	V.G.	Good	Fair	Poor
1850	1500	1000	550	300

Model PPK .32 Caliber. Allemagne Marked

Exc.	V.G.	Good	Fair	Poor
800	700	600	400	250

Model PPK .32 Caliber with Waffenampt Proofs and a High Polished Finish

Exc.	V.G.	Good	Fair	Poor
1200	800	550	400	250

Model PPK .32 Caliber with Waffenampt Proofs and a Milled Finish

Exc.	V.G.	Good	Fair	Poor
800	600	375	300	175

Model PPK .32 Caliber. Police Eagle/C Proofed. High Polished Finish

Exc.	V.G.	Good	Fair	Poor
675	575	450	300	175

Model PPK .32 Caliber. Police Eagle/C Proofed. Milled Finish

Exc.	V.G.	Good	Fair	Poor
650	500	375	275	175

Model PPK .32 Caliber. Police Eagle/F Proofed. Duraluminum Frame. Milled Finish

Exc.	V.G.	Good	Fair	Poor
900	700	550	350	225

Model PPK .22 Caliber. Late War, Black Grips

Exc.	V.G.	Good	Fair	Poor
1200	750	600	450	300

Model PPK .32 Caliber. Party Leader Grips. Brown

Exc.	V.G.	Good	Fair	Poor
2750	2550	2350	2250	2000

Model PPK .32 Caliber. Party Leader Grips. Black

Exc.	V.G.	Good	Fair	Poor
3250	3000	2750	2550	2500

NOTE: If grips are badly cracked or damaged on the two Party Leaders above, reduce $2000 each valuation.
Add $500 with proper Party Leader DRGM AKAH holster.

Model PPK .32 Caliber. RZM Marked

Exc.	V.G.	Good	Fair	Poor
900	700	500	400	300

Model PPK .32 Caliber. NSKK Marked

Model PPK-NSKK MARKED-Courtesy Richard M. Kumor Sr.

Extremely rare WWII variation. Suggest expert appraisal before sale. Last known original example sold for $10,000.

Model PPK .32 Caliber. PDM Marked with Duraluminum Frame and Bottom Magazine Release

Exc.	V.G.	Good	Fair	Poor
2500	1800	1150	750	450

Model PPK .32 Caliber. RFV Marked

Exc.	V.G.	Good	Fair	Poor
2000	1750	1150	650	400

Model PPK .32 Caliber. DRP Marked

Exc.	V.G.	Good	Fair	Poor
800	650	550	450	275

Model PPK .32 Caliber. Statens Vattenfallsverk

Exc.	V.G.	Good	Fair	Poor
1400	1200	700	450	300

WALTHER POST WORLD WAR II

Models PP and PPK

Manufactured by the firm of Manufacture de Machines du Haut Rhin at Mulhouse, France under license by Walther.

Model PP Some with Duraluminum Frames. Model PP .22 Caliber

Exc.	V.G.	Good	Fair	Poor
650	500	350	275	175

Model PP 32 Caliber

Exc.	V.G.	Good	Fair	Poor
500	375	350	275	175

Model PP 380 Caliber

Exc.	V.G.	Good	Fair	Poor
650	500	350	275	175

Model PP. All Three Calibers Finished In Blue, Silver and Gold With Full Coverage Engraving

Blue

Exc.	V.G.	Good	Fair	Poor
1500	1100	750	450	300

Silver

Exc.	V.G.	Good	Fair	Poor
1500	1100	750	450	300

Gold

Exc.	V.G.	Good	Fair	Poor
1500	1100	750	450	300

Model PP Mark II

These Walthers were manufactured under license by Walther and produced by the Manurhin Company. They were sold exclusively by Interarms, Alexandria, Virginia. The Mark IIs were the same pistols as those above and have the same types of finish and engraving as well as the same value.

Model PP Manurhin

Manurhin Company manufactured with Manurhin logo and inscription. Usually "licensed by Walther" somewhere on the pistol. The same pistols as those above, bearing the same types of finish and engraving, and having the same values.

Model PP Sport, Manurhin

.22 caliber. This is the same gun as the Model PP with different barrel lengths running from 5-3/4" to 7-3/4". It is basically a target .22 with adjustable rear sights for elevation and windage. The front sight is also adjustable. There is a barrel bushing at the muzzle that attaches the front sight to the barrel. The grips are contoured checkered plastic and are either squared at the bottom of the grips or are in the shape of an inverted bird's head.

Exc.	V.G.	Good	Fair	Poor
800	525	450	375	275

Mode PP Sport C, Manurhin

.22 caliber. This is the same gun as the Model PP Sport but in single action with a spur hammer. It has front and rear adjustable sights and squared target grips in checkered black, brown and plastic. Blued and silver finish.

Exc.	V.G.	Good	Fair	Poor
800	600	450	375	275

Model PP Sport, Walther

A .22 caliber Sport was manufactured by Manurhin, but sold by the Walther with the Walther logo and inscription. This is the same gun as the Model PP Sport, Manurhin. Only sold for a period of two years.

Exc.	V.G.	Good	Fair	Poor
800	600	450	375	275

Model PP Fiftieth Anniversary Commemorative Model

In .22 or .380 caliber. Blued with gold inlays and hand carved grips with oak leaves and acorns. Walther banner carved into each side of the grips. Wood presentation case.

Exc.	V.G.	Good	Fair	Poor
1500	1000	750	500	300

Model PPK. Some With Duraluminum Frames

Model PPK. .22 Caliber

Exc.	V.G.	Good	Fair	Poor
700	500	350	275	175

Model PPK. .32 Caliber

Exc.	V.G.	Good	Fair	Poor
500	375	350	275	175

Model PPK. .380 Caliber

Exc.	V.G.	Good	Fair	Poor
700	500	350	275	175

Model PPK. All Three Calibers Finished In Blue, Silver and Gold With Full Coverage Engraving

Blue

Exc.	V.G.	Good	Fair	Poor
1750	1300	750	450	300

Silver

Exc.	V.G.	Good	Fair	Poor
1750	1300	750	450	300

Gold

Exc.	V.G.	Good	Fair	Poor
1850	1400	750	450	300

Model PPK Mark II

These Walthers were manufactured under license by Walther and produced by the Manurhin Company. They were sold exclusively by Interarms, Alexandria, Virginia. The Mark IIs were the same pistols as those above and have the same types of finish and engraving as well as the same value.

Model PPK Manurhin

Manurhin Company manufactured with Manurhin logo and inscription. Usually "Licensed by Walther" somewhere on the pistol. The same pistols as above, bearing the same types of finish and engraving, and having the same value.

Courtesy James Rankin

Model PPK Fiftieth Anniversary Commemorative Model

In .22 or .380 caliber. Blued with gold inlays and hand carved grips with oak leaves and acorns. Walther banner carved into each side of the grips. Wood presentation case.

Exc.	V.G.	Good	Fair	Poor
2100	1800	1250	1000	500

Model PPK/S

This Walther was manufactured in .22, .32 and .380 caliber for sale in the United States market after the introduction of the United States Gun Control Act of 1968. It is basically a Model PP with a cut-off muzzle and slide. It has two-piece black checkered plastic grips as seen on the Model PP. It was finished in blue, nickel, dull gold and verchromt.

Exc.	V.G.	Good	Fair	Poor
550	475	375	300	200

Model PPK American

In 1986 the Model PPK was licensed by the Walther Company to be manufactured in the United States. The finish is stainless steel. Caliber is .380.

Exc.	V.G.	Good	Fair	Poor
500	375	300	200	150

Model PPK/S American

Manufactured in the United States. The same as the German Model PPK/S. This pistol is finished in blue and stainless steel. **Caliber is 380.**

Exc.	V.G.	Good	Fair	Poor
500	375	300	200	150

Model TP

A Walther manufactured semiautomatic pistol in .22 and .25 calibers patterned after the earlier Model 9. Finish is blue and silver black plastic checkered grips with Walther banner medallions in each grip.

Exc.	V.G.	Good	Fair	Poor
750	600	500	375	250

Model TPH

A Walther manufactured semiautomatic pistol in .22 and .25 calibers. This is a double action pistol with a duraluminum frame. Finished in blue or silver. Two-piece black checkered plastic grips. Full coverage engraving available.

Exc.	V.G.	Good	Fair	Poor
650	500	450	350	250

Add $300 for the engraved model.

Model TPH American

This semiautomatic is produced in both .22 and .25 calibers. It is licensed by Walther and manufactured in the United States. It is produced in stainless steel and has two-piece black plastic checkered grips. It is a double action pistol.

Exc.	V. G.	Good	Fair	Poor
400	300	200	150	100

Model PP Super

This is a .380 and 9x18 caliber, double action semiautomatic manufactured by Walther. It is similar in design to the Model PP, but with a P.38 type of mechanism. Finish is blue and the grips are wrap-around black checkered plastic or a type of molded wood colored plastic.

Courtesy Orvel Reichert

Exc.	V.G.	Good	Fair	Poor
550	450	350	250	150

Model P-38

Following WWII, the P-38 was reintroduced in variety of calibers with a 5" barrel and alloy or steel frame.

.22 Caliber

NIB	Exc.	V.G.	Good	Fair	Poor
1000	800	650	500	350	200

Other Calibers

NIB	Exc.	V.G.	Good	Fair	Poor
600	500	450	400	300	200

Steel-Framed (Introduced 1987)

NIB	Exc.	V.G.	Good	Fair	Poor
1400	1250	1000	750	500	400

Factory-engraved versions of the P-38 pistol were blued, chrome, or silver or gold-plated. We suggest that a qualified appraisal be secured when contemplating purchase.

Model P-38K

As above, with a 2.8" barrel and front sight is mounted on the slide. Imported between 1974 and 1980.

Exc.	V.G.	Good	Fair	Poor
750	550	450	400	300

Model P-38 IV

A redesigned version of the above, with a 4.5" barrel and 8-shot magazine. Fitted with a decocking lever and adjustable sights. Imported prior to 1983.

Exc.	V.G.	Good	Fair	Poor
600	500	450	400	300

Model P 5

A 9mm semiautomatic pistol with a double action firing mechanism. One of the first Walthers to have a decocker lever. Finish is a combination of black matte and high polish. It has black plastic checkered grips.

Exc.	V.G.	Good	Fair	Poor
800	650	500	400	300

Model P 5, Compact

A shorter version of the standard Model P 5.

Exc.	V.G.	Good	Fair	Poor
850	700	600	375	250

Model P 5 One Hundred Year Commemorative

Blued with gold inlays and hand carved grips with oak leaves and acorns. Walther banner carved into each side of the grips.

Wood presentation case.

Exc.	V.G.	Good	Fair	Poor
2000	1500	1000	700	400

Model P88

A 9mm semiautomatic in double action with ambidextrous decocking lever. Fifteen shot magazine and two-piece black checkered plastic grips. Combination of high polish and black matte finish.

Exc.	V.G.	Good	Fair	Poor
1000	800	600	500	300

Model P88 Compact

A shorter version of the standard Model P88.

Exc.	V.G.	Good	Fair	Poor
1000	800	600	500	300

Model P99

Introduced in 1997 this is a single and double action design with a 4" barrel and polymer frame. Chambered for 9mm cartridge it has a magazine capacity of 10 rounds (16 rounds for law enforcement). Front is interchangeable and rear is windage adjustable. Total length of pistol is 7" and weight is approximately 25 oz.

NIB	Exc.	V.G.	Good	Fair	Poor
700	650	550	—	—	—

Model FP

A .22 l.r. caliber, single-shot target pistol that fires electrically. It has micro adjustable electric firing system along with micrometer sights and contoured wooden grips that are adjustable. The barrel is 11.7" and the finish is blued.

Exc.	V.G.	Good	Fair	Poor
1900	1400	900	500	400

Model GSP

A semiautomatic target pistol in .22 l.r. and .38 calibers. This target pistol has a 4-1/2" barrel, 5-shot magazine and contoured wood target grips. Blued finish and sold with attache case and accessories.

Exc.	V.G.	Good	Fair	Poor
1500	1000	750	650	300

Model GSP-C

Almost the same pistol as the Model GSP, but in .32 caliber S&W wadcutter.

Exc.	V.G.	Good	Fair	Poor
1400	900	750	650	300

Model OSP

A .22 Short semiautomatic target pistol that is similar to the Model GSP. This pistol is made for rapid fire target shooting. Blued finish with contoured wood grips.

Exc.	V.G.	Good	Fair	Poor
1400	900	750	650	300

Free Pistol

A .22 caliber single shot target pistol with an 11.7" barrel, micrometer sights, adjustable grips and an electronic trigger. Blued.

NIB	Exc.	V.G.	Good	Fair	Poor
1900	1600	1200	900	700	550

Model B

A .30-06 caliber bolt-action rifle with a 22" barrel, 4-shot magazine and single or double set triggers. Double set triggers are worth approximately 20% more than the values listed below. Blued with a walnut stock.

Exc.	V.G.	Good	Fair	Poor
450	400	350	250	175

Olympic Single Shot

A .22 caliber bolt-action rifle with a 26" barrel, adjustable target sights and a walnut stock fitted with a palm rest and adjustable buttplate. Blued.

Exc.	V.G.	Good	Fair	Poor
950	850	700	500	400

Model V

A .22 caliber single-shot bolt-action rifle with a 26" barrel and adjustable sights. Blued with a plain walnut stock. Manufactured before WWII.

Exc.	V.G.	Good	Fair	Poor
400	350	300	200	150

Model V Champion

As above, with a checkered walnut stock.

Exc.	V.G.	Good	Fair	Poor
450	400	350	250	200

Model KKM International Match

A .22 caliber single shot bolt-action rifle with a 28" barrel and adjustable sights. Blued with a walnut stock fitted for a palm rest and with an adjustable buttplate. Manufactured after WWII.

Exc.	V.G.	Good	Fair	Poor
1100	900	650	450	350

Model KKM-S

As above, with an adjustable cheekpiece.

Exc.	V.G.	Good	Fair	Poor
1100	900	700	500	400

Model KKW

As above, with a military-style stock.

Exc.	V.G.	Good	Fair	Poor
750	600	450	350	300

Model KKJ Sporter

A .22 caliber bolt-action rifle with a 22.5" barrel and 5-shot magazine. Blued with a checkered walnut stock. This model was available with double set triggers and their presence would add approximately 20% to the values listed below. Manufactured after WWII.

Exc.	V.G.	Good	Fair	Poor
600	500	450	350	300

Model KKJ-MA

As above, in .22 rimfire Magnum.

Exc.	V.G.	Good	Fair	Poor
600	500	450	350	300

Model KKJ-HO

As above, in .22 Hornet.

Exc.	V.G.	Good	Fair	Poor
750	700	600	450	350

Model SSV Varmint

A .22 caliber bolt-action single shot rifle with a 25.5" barrel not fitted with sights and Monte Carlo-style stock. Blued. Manufactured after WWII.

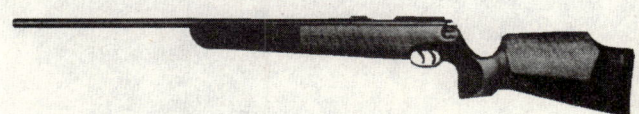

Exc.	V.G.	Good	Fair	Poor
600	550	475	375	300

Model UIT BV Universal

As above, with adjustable target sights and a walnut stock fitted with a palm rest and adjustable buttplate.

NIB	Exc.	V.G.	Good	Fair	Poor
1750	1500	1250	900	650	500

Model UIT Match

As above, with a stippled pistol grip and forend. Also available with an electronic trigger that would add approximately $50 to the values listed below.

NIB	Exc.	V.G.	Good	Fair	Poor
1250	1000	750	600	450	400

GX 1

As above, with an adjustable Free Rifle stock.

NIB	Exc.	V.G.	Good	Fair	Poor
2250	2000	1750	1250	850	700

Prone Model 400

As above, with a prone position stock.

NIB	Exc.	V.G.	Good	Fair	Poor
750	700	600	450	350	300

Model KK/MS Silhouette

A .22 caliber bolt-action rifle with a 25.5" front-weighted barrel furnished without sights and a thumb hole stock having an adjustable buttplate. Introduced in 1984.

NIB	Exc.	V.G.	Good	Fair	Poor
1300	1100	850	700	550	400

Running Boar Model 500

As above, with a 23.5" barrel.

NIB	Exc.	V.G.	Good	Fair	Poor
1550	1350	950	750	600	450

Model WA-2000

A .300 Winchester Magnum or .308 caliber bolt-action sporting rifle produced on custom order. Prospective purchasers are advised to secure an appraisal prior to acquisition. Imported prior to 1989.

Exc.	V.G.	Good	Fair	Poor
6500	4750	3500	3000	2000

Model SF

A 12 or 16 gauge boxlock double-barrel shotgun fitted with double triggers and extractors. Blued with a checkered walnut stock fitted with sling swivels.

Exc.	V.G.	Good	Fair	Poor
900	600	500	250	100

Model SFD

As above, with the stock having a cheekpiece.

Exc.	V.G.	Good	Fair	Poor
1000	750	650	425	250

WALTHER MANURHIN
Mulhouse, France

The Manurhin-manufactured Walther pistols are listed in the Walther section of this text under their respective model headings.

WANZEL
SEE Austrian Military Firearms

WARNANT, L. AND J.
Ognee, Belgium

Revolver

Modeled after pistols manufactured by Smith & Wesson, the Warnants produced a variety of revolvers in .32, .38, or .45 caliber, between 1870 and 1890.

Exc.	V.G.	Good	Fair	Poor
—	150	75	60	50

Semiautomatic Pistol

A 6.35mm semiautomatic pistol with a 2.5" barrel and 5-shot magazine. The slide marked "L&J Warnant Bte 6.35mm". Blued with black plastic grips bearing the monogram "L&JW" Manufactured after 1908.

Exc.	V.G.	Good	Fair	Poor
300	200	150	100	75

1912 Model

A 7.65mm caliber semiautomatic pistol with a 3" barrel and 7-shot magazine. The slide marked "L&J Warnant Brevetes Pist Auto 7.65mm". Manufactured prior to 1915.

Exc.	V.G.	Good	Fair	Poor
300	200	150	100	75

WARNER ARMS CORPORATION
Brooklyn, New York and Norwich, Connecticut

Established in 1912, this firm marketed revolvers, rifles, semiautomatic pistols and shotguns made for them by other companies (including N.R. Davis & Sons, Ithaca Gun Company and so forth). In 1917, the company was purchased by N.R. Davis & Company. See also Davis-Warner.

The arms marketed by Warner Prior to 1917 are as follows:

SHOTGUNS

Single Trigger Hammerless Utica Special Double Barrel
In 12 gauge with 28", 30", or 32" barrels.

Double Trigger Hammerless Double Barrel
In 12 or 16 gauge with 28", 30", or 32" barrels.

Grade X, SF, XT, SFT, XD and XDF Hammer Guns
In 12, 16 or 20 gauge with 28", 30", or 32" barrels.

Field Grade Hammer Gun
In 12 or 16 gauge with 28" or 30" barrels.

Box Lock Hammerless
In 12 or 16 gauge with 28", 30", or 32" barrels.

RIFLES

Number 522
A .22 caliber single-shot rifle with an 18" barrel.

Number 532
A .32 caliber single-shot rifle with an 18" barrel.

REVOLVERS

Double Action
.32 and .38 caliber with 4" or 5" barrels.

Double Action Hammerless
.32 and .38 caliber with 4" or 5" barrels.

SEMIAUTOMATIC PISTOLS

"Faultless": Warner-Schwarzlose Model C, .32 ACP.

WARNER, CHAS.
Windsor Locks, Connecticut

Pocket Revolver

A .31 caliber percussion revolver with a 3" round barrel and 6-shot unfluted cylinder. The cylinder marked "Charles Warner. Windsor Locks, Conn." Blued with walnut grips. Approximately 600 were made between 1857 and 1860.

Exc.	V.G.	Good	Fair	Poor
—	—	450	225	100

WARNER, JAMES
Springfield, Massachusetts

Revolving Carbines

A variety of revolving carbines were made by this maker, nearly all of which are of .40 caliber, with octagonal barrels measuring 20" to 24" in length. The most commonly encountered variations are as follows:

Manually Revolved Grooved Cylinder

This model is fitted with two triggers one of which is a release so that the cylinder can be manually turned. Not fitted with a loading lever. The top strap marked "James Warner/Springfield, Mass." Approximately 75 were made in 1849.

Courtesy Milwaukee Public Museum, Milwaukee, Wisconsin

Exc.	V.G.	Good	Fair	Poor
—	—	3000	1500	500

Retractable Cylinder Model

This version has a cylinder that fits over the breech, and it must be retracted before it can be manually rotated. The cylinder release is a button located in front of the trigger. It is marked "James Warner/Springfield Mass" and with an eagle over the letters "U.S." The cylinder is etched, and there is no loading lever. It also has a walnut stock with patch box and no forearm. There were approximately 25 manufactured in 1849.

Exc.	V.G.	Good	Fair	Poor
—	—	4000	2000	800

Automatic Revolving Cylinder

The cylinder is automatically turned when the hammer is cocked. This model is fitted with a loading lever and is marked "Warner's Patent/Jan. 1851" and "Springfield Arms Co." Approximately 200 were made during the 1850s.

Courtesy Milwaukee Public Museum, Milwaukee, Wisconsin

Exc.	V.G.	Good	Fair	Poor
—	—	3000	1500	600

Belt Revolver

A .31 caliber double action percussion revolver with a 4" or 5" round barrel and 6-shot etched cylinder. Blued with walnut grips. No markings appear on this model except for the serial number. Manufactured in 1851.

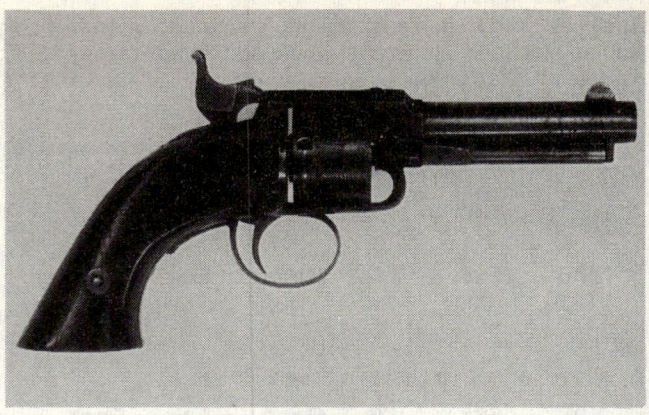

Courtesy Milwaukee Public Museum, Milwaukee, Wisconsin

Exc.	V.G.	Good	Fair	Poor
—	—	750	300	100

Pocket Revolver

A .28 caliber percussion revolver with a 3" octagonal barrel marked "James Warner, Springfield, Mass., USA" and a 6-shot cylinder. Blued with walnut grips. Approximately 500 were made.

Exc.	V.G.	Good	Fair	Poor
—	—	500	200	100

Second Model

As above, with either a 3" or 4" barrel and marked "Warner's Patent 1857."

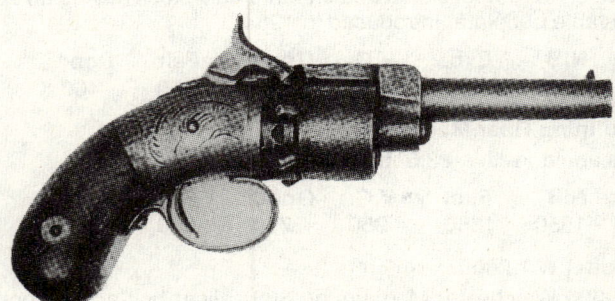

Courtesy Wallis & Wallis, Lewes, Sussex, England

Exc.	V.G.	Good	Fair	Poor
—	—	650	300	100

Third Model

As above, but in .31 caliber.

Exc.	V.G.	Good	Fair	Poor
—	—	500	250	100

Single Shot Derringer

A .41 caliber rimfire single shot pocket pistol with a 2.75" round barrel, brass frame and walnut grips. As this model is unmarked, it can only be identified by the large breechblock which lifts upward and to the left for loading.

Exc.	V.G.	Good	Fair	Poor
—	—	12000	5000	1000

Pocket Revolver

A .30 caliber rimfire revolver with a 3" barrel marked "Warner's Patent 1857" and 5-shot cylinder. Blued or nickel-plated with walnut grips. Approximately 1,000 were made during the late 1860s.

Exc.	V.G.	Good	Fair	Poor
—	—	350	150	75

WEATHERBY
Atascadero, California

This corporation was founded in 1945 by Roy Weatherby. He pioneered the high-velocity hunting rifle. His rifles were designed to fire cartridges that he also produced. They are examples of fine craftsmanship and have been used to take some of the top trophy animals from all around the world. Formerly these rifles were manufactured in West Germany. They are currently produced in Japan. Although the Japanese rifles are, in the opinion of the editors, every bit as fine a firearm as the German versions, collectors have dictated an approximate 25% premium assessed to the German-manufactured versions. The values given are for the current-production Japanese weapons. Simply add the premium for a German-manufactured rifle. There are other premiums that collectors are paying in 1994 and these are as follows:

NOTE: For German calibers .224 through .300 add 25% for 24" barrels and 35% for 26" barrels.

Mark V

This is a deluxe, bolt-action repeating rifle chambered for various popular standard calibers, as well as the full line of Weatherby cartridges from .240 Weatherby Magnum to .300 Weatherby Magnum. It is furnished with either a 24" or 26" barrel without sights. It has either a 3- or 5-round magazine, depending on the caliber. It has a deluxe, high-polish blued finish with a select, skip-line checkered walnut stock with a rosewood forearm tip and pistol grip cap. This rifle is available with a left-hand action.

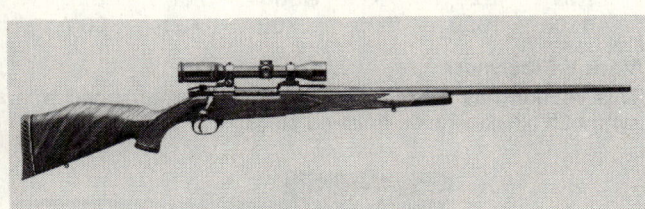

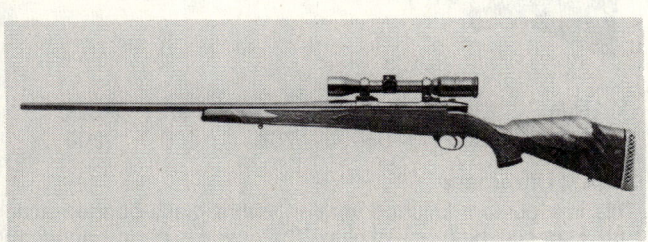

NIB	Exc.	V.G.	Good	Fair	Poor
1000	850	700	600	500	400

Mark V Sporter

Introduced in 1993 this model is identical to the Mark V Deluxe without the custom features. The metal is a low luster finish, the stock is claro walnut with high gloss finish. A Monte Carlo comb with raised cheekpiece and black 1" recoil pad are standard features on this model. Available in Weatherby calibers from .257 through .340 plus .270 Win., .30-06, 7mm Rem. Mag., .300 Win Mag., .338 Win. Mag. Weighs 8 to 8.5 lbs. depending on caliber.

NIB	Exc.	V.G.	Good	Fair	Poor
660	600	500	400	300	150

Mark V .340 Weatherby Magnum

This version is chambered for a larger magnum cartridge and is offered with the 26" barrel only.
For German guns in this caliber-Add 70%.

NIB	Exc.	V.G.	Good	Fair	Poor
1050	900	750	650	550	200

Mark V .375 Weatherby Magnum

This version was manufactured in Germany only and is chambered for the currently obsolete .375 Weatherby Magnum cartridge. This version has become very collectible.

NIB	Exc.	V.G.	Good	Fair	Poor
3000	2400	1500	900	700	500

Mark V .378 Weatherby Magnum

This version is chambered for the .378 Weatherby Magnum cartridge and is considered to be one of the most powerful rifles currently available in the world. It is furnished with a 26" barrel only.
For German guns in this caliber-Add 50%.

NIB	Exc.	V.G.	Good	Fair	Poor
1100	900	700	500	400	200

Mark V .416 Weatherby Magnum

This is an extremely powerful rifle suitable for hunting the biggest game. It is the first new caliber to be released by Weatherby since 1965. It was introduced in 1989.

NIB	Exc.	V.G.	Good	Fair	Poor
1100	900	700	500	400	200

Mark V .460 Weatherby Magnum

This is the most powerful commercial rifle available in the world. It is considered to be overkill for any game except the largest and most dangerous creatures that roam the African continent. It is available with a 24" or 26" heavy barrel with an integral, recoil-reducing muzzle brake. It has a custom reinforced stock.
For German guns in this caliber-Add 100%.

NIB	Exc.	V.G.	Good	Fair	Poor
1350	1200	1000	800	400	200

Mark V Fluted Stainless

Introduced late in 1996 this model features a fluted stainless steel barrel chambered for the .257 Weatherby Magnum to the .300 Weatherby Magnum calibers as well as the 7mm Rem. Mag. and the .300 Win. Mag. The stock is synthetic with raised comb and checkered stock. Weight varies depending on caliber.

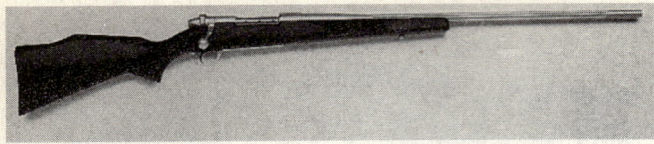

NIB	Exc.	V.G.	Good	Fair	Poor

Mark V Fluted Synthetic

This model is similar to the above model with a blued carbon steel action and barrel with synthetic stock. Introduced late in 1996.

NIB	Exc.	V.G.	Good	Fair	Poor

Mark V SLS

This model features a stainless steel barreled action with laminated wood stock fitted with a 1" black recoil pad. Rifle is chambered for .257 through .340 Weatherby Magnum calibers as well as .7mm Rem. Mag., .300 and .338 Win. Mag., and the .375 H&H mag. Weight is about 8.25 lbs depending on caliber. Introduced in late 1996.

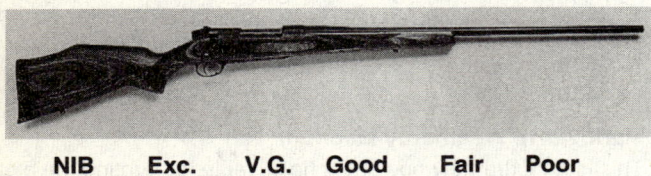

NIB	Exc.	V.G.	Good	Fair	Poor

Mark V Varmint

This version is chambered for the .22-250 and the .224 Weatherby cartridge. It is offered with a 24" or 26" heavy barrel.

NIB	Exc.	V.G.	Good	Fair	Poor
975	800	750	550	400	200

Mark V Euromark

This model features a hand-checkered, oil-finished, claro walnut stock with an ebony forend tip and pistol grip cap. It has a satin blued finish. It was introduced in 1986.

NIB	Exc.	V.G.	Good	Fair	Poor
1050	900	750	650	550	200

Mark V Lazermark

This version had a laser-carved pattern on the stock and forearm in place of the usual checkering. It was introduced in 1985.

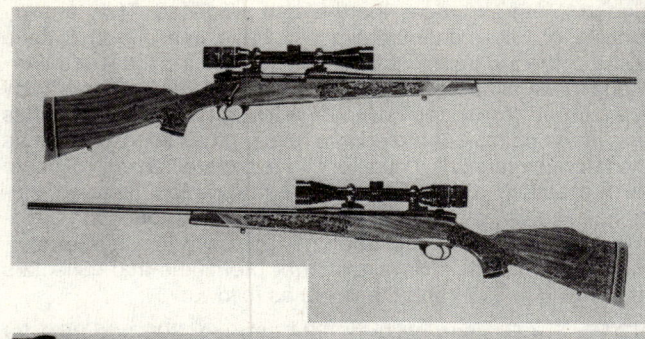

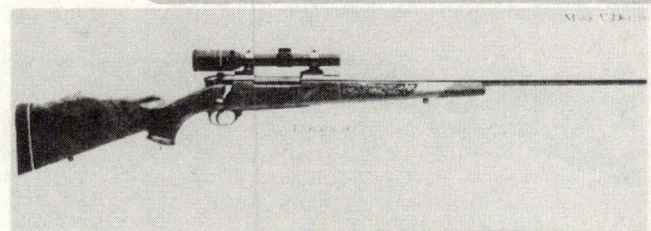

NIB	Exc.	V.G.	Good	Fair	Poor
1100	1000	800	700	400	200

Mark V Fibermark

This version has a matte blue finish and is furnished with a synthetic black, wrinkle-finished stock.

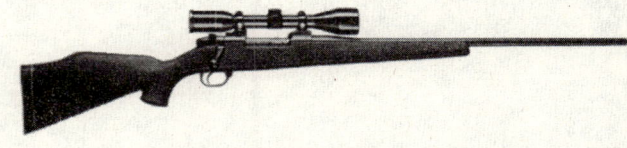

NIB	Exc.	V.G.	Good	Fair	Poor
1150	1000	850	750	400	200

Mark V Ultramark

This is a custom-finished version with a glass-bedded action and a special, high-polish blue. The action is hand-honed, and the walnut stock features basket weave checkering. It was introduced in 1989.

NIB	Exc.	V.G.	Good	Fair	Poor
1250	1150	900	750	400	200

Mark V Accumark

Introduced in 1995 this rifle features a Mark V Magnum action. The trigger is preset at the factory for 3.5 lbs of pull. It is fully adjustable for sear engagement at let-off weight. The action metal is black oxide coated with a bead blast matte finish. The stainless steel barrel is 26" in length with a low luster brushed finish. Weight is approximately 8 lbs. and is offered in caliber from .257 to .340 Weatherby Magnum, 7mm Rem. Magnum, and .300 Win. Magnum. In August the company announced that this model would also be offered in the .30-.378 Weatherby caliber. In 1997 this model was offered chambered for the 7mm STW cartridge. Available in right hand only.

Mark V Accumark

Mark V Accumark for .30-.378 Weatherby Magnum

NIB	Exc.	V.G.	Good	Fair	Poor
1100	850	—	—	—	—

35th Anniversary Commemorative Mark V

This specially embellished rifle commemorated the 35th anniversary of the company. There were 1,000 produced in 1980. As with all commemoratives, it must be NIB with all furnished materials to be worth top dollar.

NIB	Exc.	V.G.	Good	Fair	Poor
1500	1150	900	750	400	300

1984 Olympic Commemorative Mark V

This is a specially embellished Mark V rifle that has gold-plated accents and an exhibition-grade walnut stock with a star inlay. There were 1,000 manufactured in 1984. This is a commemorative rifle and must be NIB to bring premium value.

NIB	Exc.	V.G.	Good	Fair	Poor
1500	900	750	600	400	300

Safari Grade Mark V

This is a custom-order version that is available chambered from the .300 Weatherby Magnum through the .460 Weatherby Magnum. It is available with a number of custom options and can be ordered with an 8- to 10-month delivery delay.

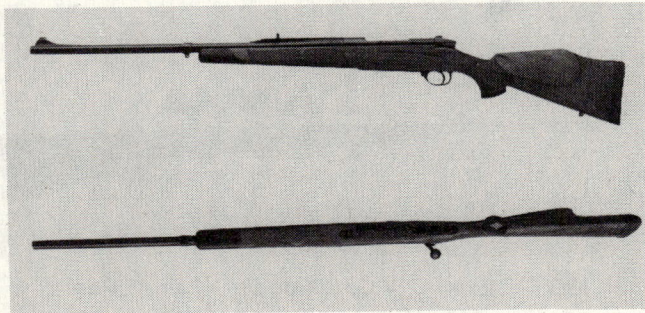

NIB	Exc.	V.G.	Good	Fair	Poor
3000	2750	2000	1200	600	300

Crown Grade Mark V

This is Weatherby's best-grade rifle and is available on a custom-order basis only. It features an engraved receiver and barrel with an exhibition-grade, hand-checkered walnut stock. It is also furnished with an engraved scope mount.

NIB	Exc.	V.G.	Good	Fair	Poor
4500	3500	2750	1500	750	300

Vanguard VGX

This was Weatherby's Japanese-manufactured economy rifle. It is chambered for various popular standard American cartridges from .22-50 to the .300 Winchester Magnum cartridge. It is a bolt-action repeater with a 24" barrel furnished without sights. It has either a 3-shot or 5-shot magazine; and the finish is polished blue, with a select, checkered walnut stock with a rosewood forend tip and pistol grip cap. This model was discontinued in 1988.

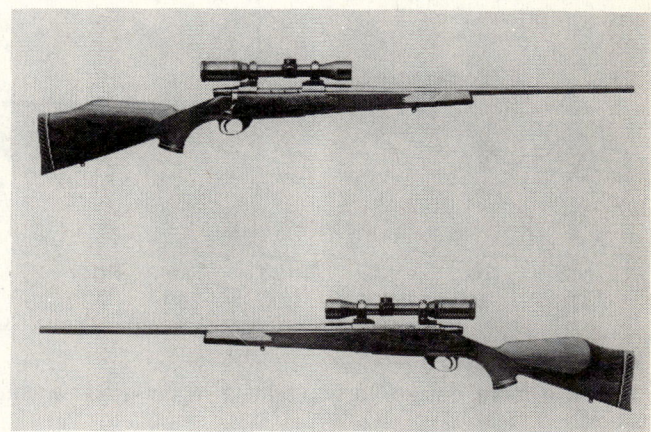

Exc.	V.G.	Good	Fair	Poor
500	400	350	300	250

Vanguard VGS

This satin-finish version was also discontinued in 1988.

Exc.	V.G.	Good	Fair	Poor
450	350	300	250	200

Vanguard VGL

This is a lightweight carbine version that has a 20" barrel. It was discontinued in 1988.

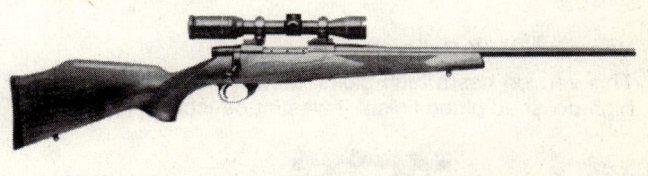

Exc.	V.G.	Good	Fair	Poor
450	350	300	250	200

Fiberguard

This version has a matte-blued finish with a green fiberglass stock. It was discontinued in 1988.

Exc.	V.G.	Good	Fair	Poor
500	400	350	300	250

Vanguard Classic I

This version is chambered for various popular standard calibers and has a 24" barrel and either a 3- or 5-shot magazine. It has a satin blue finish and a select checkered, oil-finished walnut stock. It was introduced in 1989.

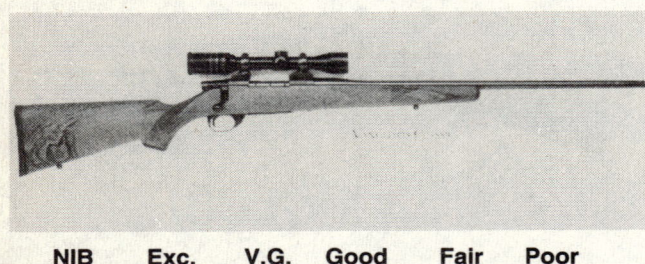

NIB	Exc.	V.G.	Good	Fair	Poor
475	400	375	300	250	200

Vanguard Classic II

This is a more deluxe version with a higher-grade walnut stock.

NIB	Exc.	V.G.	Good	Fair	Poor
600	550	475	400	300	250

Vanguard VGX Deluxe

This version has a high-gloss, Monte Carlo-type stock and a high-polished blued finish. It was introduced in 1989.

NIB	Exc.	V.G.	Good	Fair	Poor
600	550	475	400	300	250

Vanguard Weatherguard

This version has a wrinkle-finished, black synthetic stock. It was introduced in 1989.

NIB	Exc.	V.G.	Good	Fair	Poor
400	300	250	200	175	125

Weathermark

Introduced in 1993 this model features a checkered composite stock with matte blue metal finish. Available in Weatherby calibers from .257 through .340 and .270 Win., 7mm Rem. Mag., .30-06, .300 and .338 Win. Mag. Weighs 7.5 lbs.

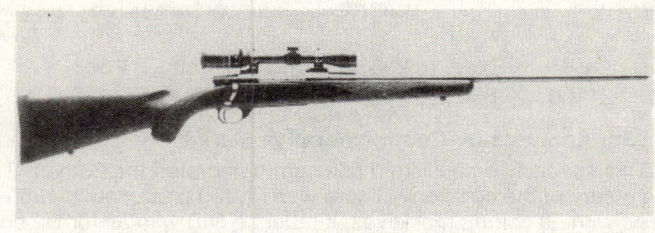

NIB	Exc.	V.G.	Good	Fair	Poor
550	450	350	300	200	150

Weathermark Alaskan

Similar to the Weathermark with checkered composite stock the barreled action is electroless nickel with non-glare finish. Muzzle brake is optional. Available in same calibers as Weathermark. Weighs 7.7 lbs.

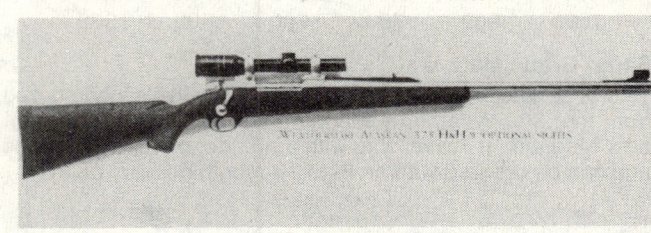

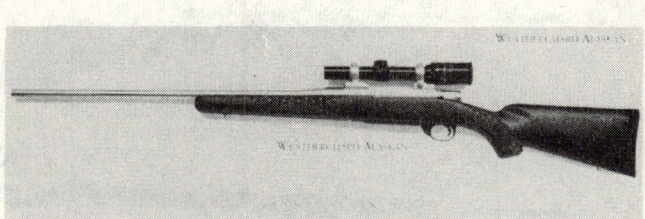

NIB	Exc.	V.G.	Good	Fair	Poor
725	600	500	400	300	150

Mark XXII

This is a semiautomatic rifle chambered for the .22 l.r. cartridge. There are two versions—one with a detachable magazine and the other with a tubular magazine. It has a 24" barrel with adjustable sights and a select checkered walnut stock with a rosewood forearm tip and pistol grip cap. This model was originally produced in Italy and was manufactured in Japan. It is now discontinued.

Mark XXII

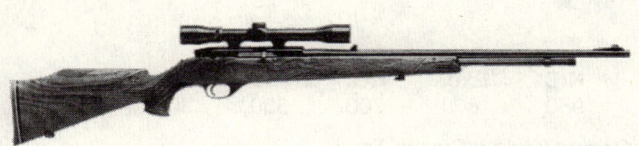

Mark XXII Tube Model

NIB	Exc.	V.G.	Good	Fair	Poor
550	350	300	250	200	150

For Italian guns-Add 35%.

SHOTGUNS

Centurion

This is a gas-operated semiautomatic shotgun chambered for 12 gauge. It is offered with various barrel lengths and chokes. It has a checkered walnut stock. It was manufactured between 1972 and 1981.

Exc.	V.G.	Good	Fair	Poor
350	300	250	200	150

Centurion Deluxe

This version is slightly engraved and features a vent ribbed barrel and higher-grade wood.

Exc.	V.G.	Good	Fair	Poor
375	325	275	225	175

Model 82

This is a gas-operated semiautomatic shotgun chambered for 12 gauge with 2.75" or 3" chambers. It has various barrel lengths with vent ribs and screw-in choke tubes. It features an alloy receiver and a deluxe, checkered walnut stock. It is also available as the Buckmaster with a 22" open-choked barrel. This model was introduced in 1983.

NIB	Exc.	V.G.	Good	Fair	Poor
500	450	400	350	300	250

Patrician

This is a slide action shotgun chambered for 12 gauge. It is offered with various barrel lengths and choke combinations. It has a vent rib barrel, a blued finish, and a checkered walnut stock. It was manufactured between 1972 and 1981.

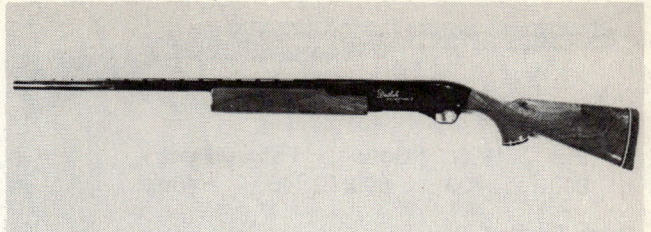

Exc.	V.G.	Good	Fair	Poor
300	250	225	175	125

Patrician Deluxe

This is a slightly engraved version with fancier-grade walnut.

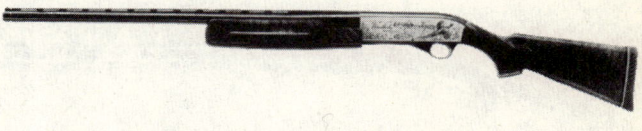

Exc.	V.G.	Good	Fair	Poor
350	300	250	200	150

Model 92

This is a slide action shotgun chambered for 12 gauge with 2.75" or 3" chambers. It is offered with 26", 28", or 30" ventilated rib barrels with screw-in choke tubes. It features a short, twin rail slide action and an engraved alloy receiver. The finish is blued, with a deluxe checkered walnut stock. A Buckmaster model with a 22" open-choke barrel and rifle sights is also available.

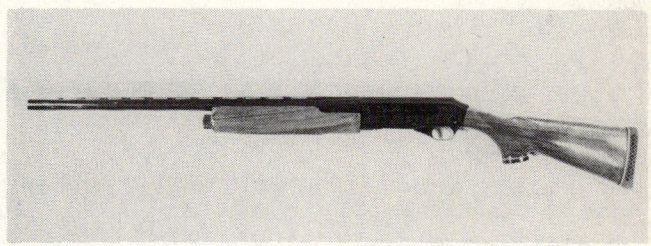

NIB	Exc.	V.G.	Good	Fair	Poor
350	300	250	200	175	125

Regency Field Grade

This is an Over/Under double-barreled shotgun chambered for 12 or 20 gauge. It has various length vent ribbed barrels and a boxlock action with engraved false sideplates. It features a single selective trigger and automatic ejectors. The finish is blued, with a checkered walnut stock. This model was imported from Italy between 1972 and 1980. It is also offered as a trap-grade with the same value.

Exc.	V.G.	Good	Fair	Poor
850	750	650	500	400

Olympian

This model is similar to the Regency, with less engraving. It was not imported after 1980. A skeet and a trap model, as well as a field-grade model, were available. The values were similar.

Exc.	V.G.	Good	Fair	Poor
800	700	600	450	400

Orion Grade I

This is an Over/Under double-barrel shotgun chambered for 12 or 20 gauge with 3" chambers. It is offered with 26" or 28" vent rib barrels with screw-in chokes. It has a single selective trigger and automatic ejectors. The boxlock action features no engraving. The finish is blued, with a checkered walnut stock. It was introduced in 1989.

NIB	Exc.	V.G.	Good	Fair	Poor
850	750	700	600	500	400

Orion Grade II Skeet

This model is supplied with a claro walnut checkered stock with full pistol grip with rosewood grip cap. The receiver is a matte blue with scroll engraving. The barrel has a matte vent rib with side vents and mid-point head with white bead front sight. Special ventilated recoil pad. Offered in 12 gauge and 20 gauge with 26" barrels. Fixed skeet chokes are standard. The 12 gauge weighs 7.5 lbs. while the 20 gauge weighs 7.25 lbs.

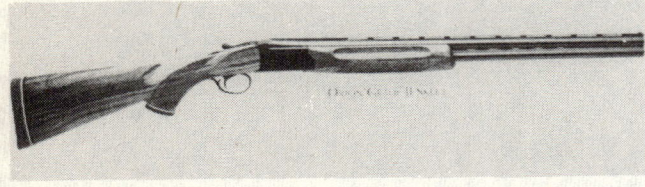

NIB	Exc.	V.G.	Good	Fair	Poor
950	800	700	550	300	150

Orion Grade II Sporting Clays

Similar to the Classic model but with a full pistol grip with rosewood grip cap. The receiver is silver gray with scroll engraving. The claro walnut stock is checkered with a high gloss finish. Offered in 12 gauge with 28" to 30" vent rib barrels. Supplied with 5 screw in choke tubes.

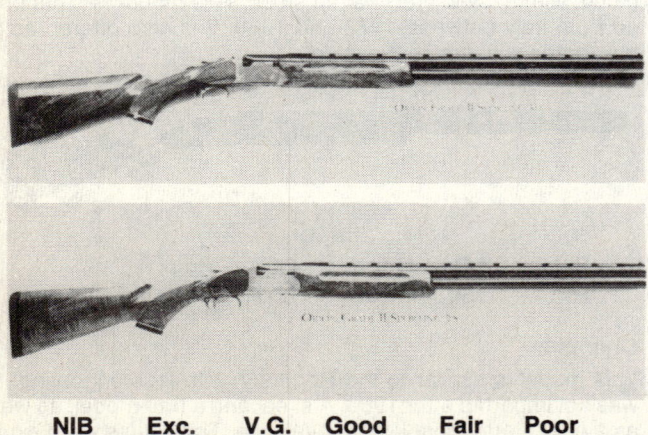

NIB	Exc.	V.G.	Good	Fair	Poor
1000	850	750	600	300	150

Orion Grade II Double Trap

This model features an integral multi-choke tube. The Monte Carlo stock has a rosewood pistol grip cap with diamond shaped inlay. The receiver is blue with scroll engraving. Available with 30" or 32" vent rib barrels. Weighs 8 lbs.

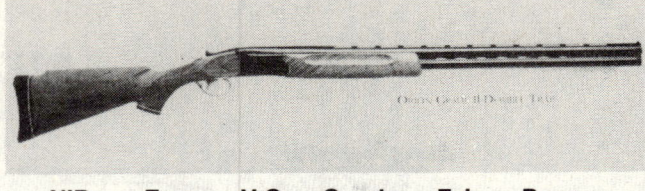

NIB	Exc.	V.G.	Good	Fair	Poor
950	800	700	550	300	150

Orion Grade II Single Trap

Similar to the Double Trap but furnished with a single 32" barrel. Weighs 8 lbs.

NIB	Exc.	V.G.	Good	Fair	Poor
950	800	700	550	300	150

Orion Grade II

This version is lightly engraved and has a high-gloss finish. Otherwise, it is similar to the Grade I.

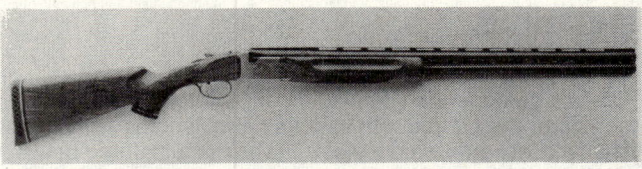

NIB	Exc.	V.G.	Good	Fair	Poor
1000	900	800	650	550	300

Orion Grade II Classic Field

Introduced in 1993 this model features a rounded pistol grip and slim forearm design. The walnut stock is oil finished. The receiver is blued with gamescene engraving. A solid recoil pad is standard. Available in 12 gauge, 20 gauge, and 28 gauge with vent rib barrel lengths from 26" to 30" depending on gauge. Screw in choke tubes standard. Weighs 6.5 lbs. to 8 lbs. depending on gauge.

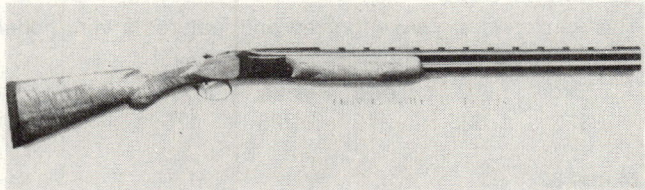

NIB	Exc.	V.G.	Good	Fair	Poor
900	800	700	550	300	150

Orion Grade II Classic Sporting Clays

Introduced in 1993 this model has a rounded pistol grip with slender forearm with an oil finished stock. The receiver is blued with scroll engraving. A stepped competition matte vent rib with additional side vents is supplied. The recoil pad has a special radius heel. Offered in 12 gauge with 28" barrel. Furnished with 5 screw in choke tubes. Weighs 7.5 lbs.

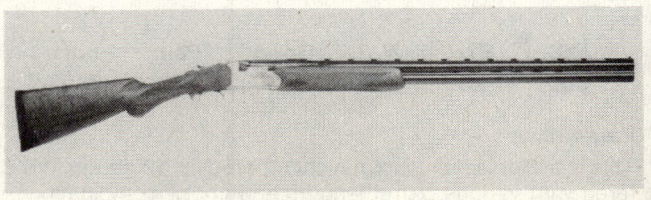

NIB	Exc.	V.G.	Good	Fair	Poor
1000	850	750	600	300	150

Orion Grade III

This version has a gamescene-engraved, coin-finished receiver and higher-grade walnut. It was introduced in 1989.

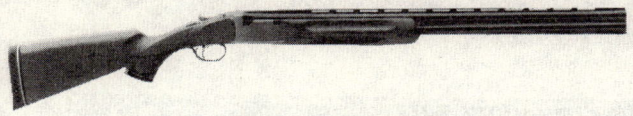

NIB	Exc.	V.G.	Good	Fair	Poor
1100	1000	900	750	650	350

Orion Grade III Classic Field

New for 1993 this model features a rounded pistol grip and slim forearm with oil finish claro walnut with fine line checkering. The receiver is silver gray with scroll engraving and gold game bird overlays. Available in 12 gauge with 28" vent rib barrels and 20 gauge with 26" vent rib barrels. Screw in choke tubes standard.

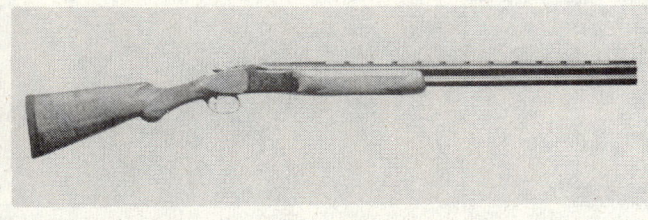

NIB	Exc.	V.G.	Good	Fair	Poor
1100	950	850	650	300	150

Orion Grade III Classic English Field

This model features an English style straight grip stock with a choice of 12 gauge with 28" barrel or 20 gauge with 26" or 28" barrels. The receiver is engraved and the oil finished is hand checkered. Weight of 12 gauge gun is about 7 lbs. and 20 gauge gun is about 6.5 lbs. Introduced in 1996.

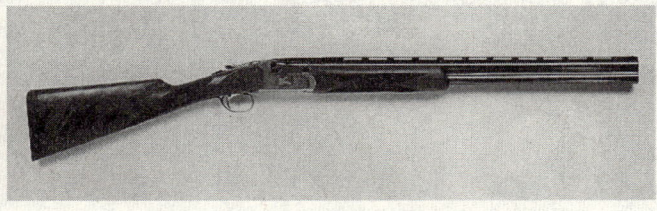

NIB	Exc.	V.G.	Good	Fair	Poor
1250	1000	800	—	—	—

Athena Grade IV

This is an Over/Under double-barrel shotgun chambered for 12, 20, and 28 gauge, as well as .410. It has 3" chambers. It is offered with various barrel lengths with vent ribs and screw-in choke tubes. It has a boxlock action with Greener crossbolt, single selective trigger, and automatic ejectors. It has engraved false sideplates and a satin nickel-plated action. The barrels are blued, with a select checkered walnut stock. This model was introduced in 1989.

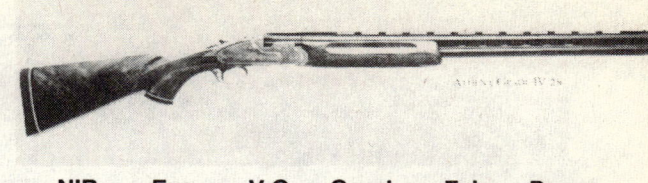

NIB	Exc.	V.G.	Good	Fair	Poor
2000	1750	1500	1200	950	750

Competition Model Athena

This is either a trap or skeet version with stock dimensions designed for either skeet or trap and competition-type ribs.

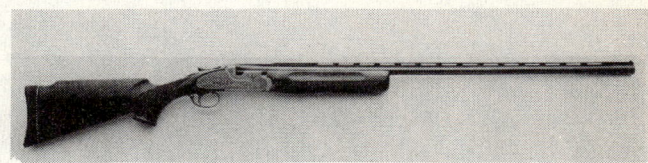

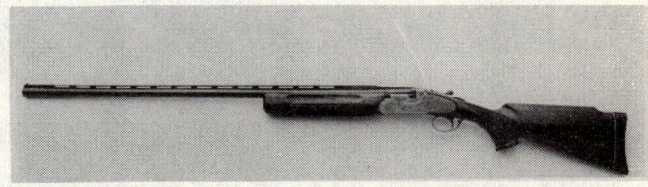

NIB	Exc.	V.G.	Good	Fair	Poor
1650	1400	1150	1000	600	300

Athena Grade V Classic Field

Introduced in 1993 this model features a rounded pistol grip with slender forearm. The high grade claro walnut stock is oil finished with fine line checkering. The receiver has a side plate that is silver gray with rose and scroll engraving. The vent rib barrels also have side vents. A solid recoil is supplied. Offered in 12 gauge with 26", 28", or 30" barrels and 20 gauge with 26" and 28" barrels. Choke tubes are standard. Weatherby Athena Master skeet tube set, 12 gauge 28" skeet shotgun, plus two each 20, 28 and .410 gauge fitted, full length Briley tubes with integral extractors. Packed in custom fitted aluminum case (not shown).

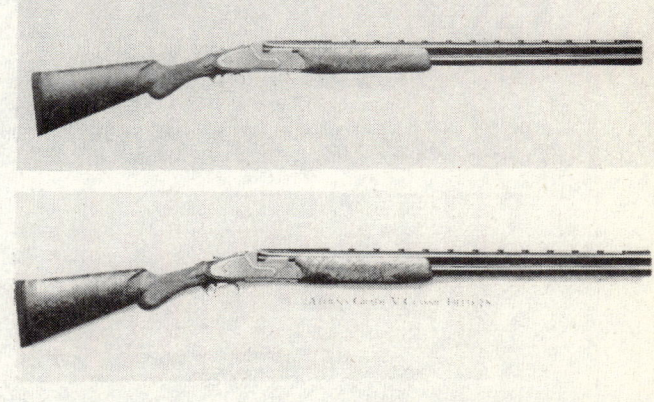

NIB	Exc.	V.G.	Good	Fair	Poor
1950	1750	1100	700	400	200

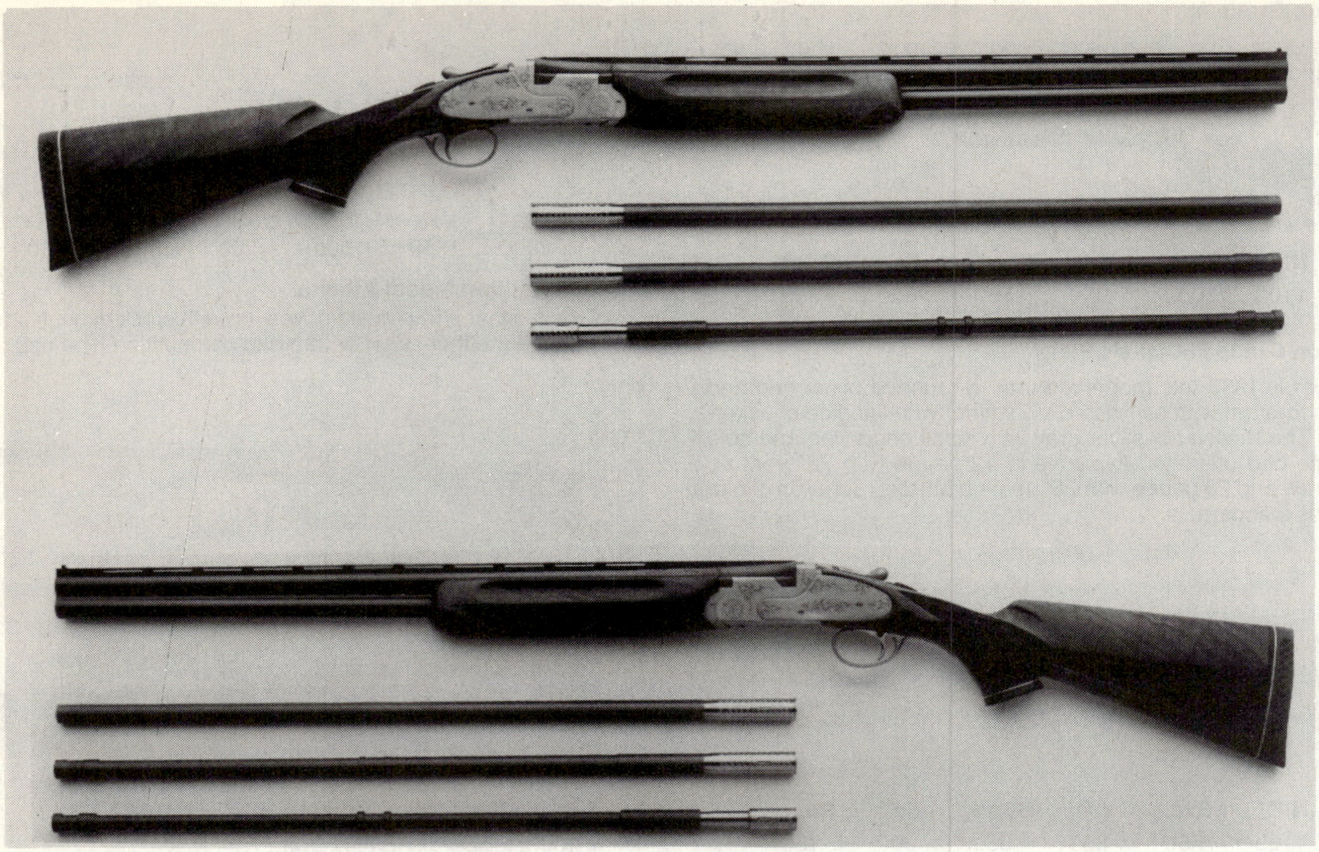

Weatherby Athena Master skeet tube set, 12 ga. 28" skeet shotgun, plus two each 20, 28 and .410 ga. fitted, full length Briley tubes with integral extractors. Packed in custom fitted aluminum case (not shown)

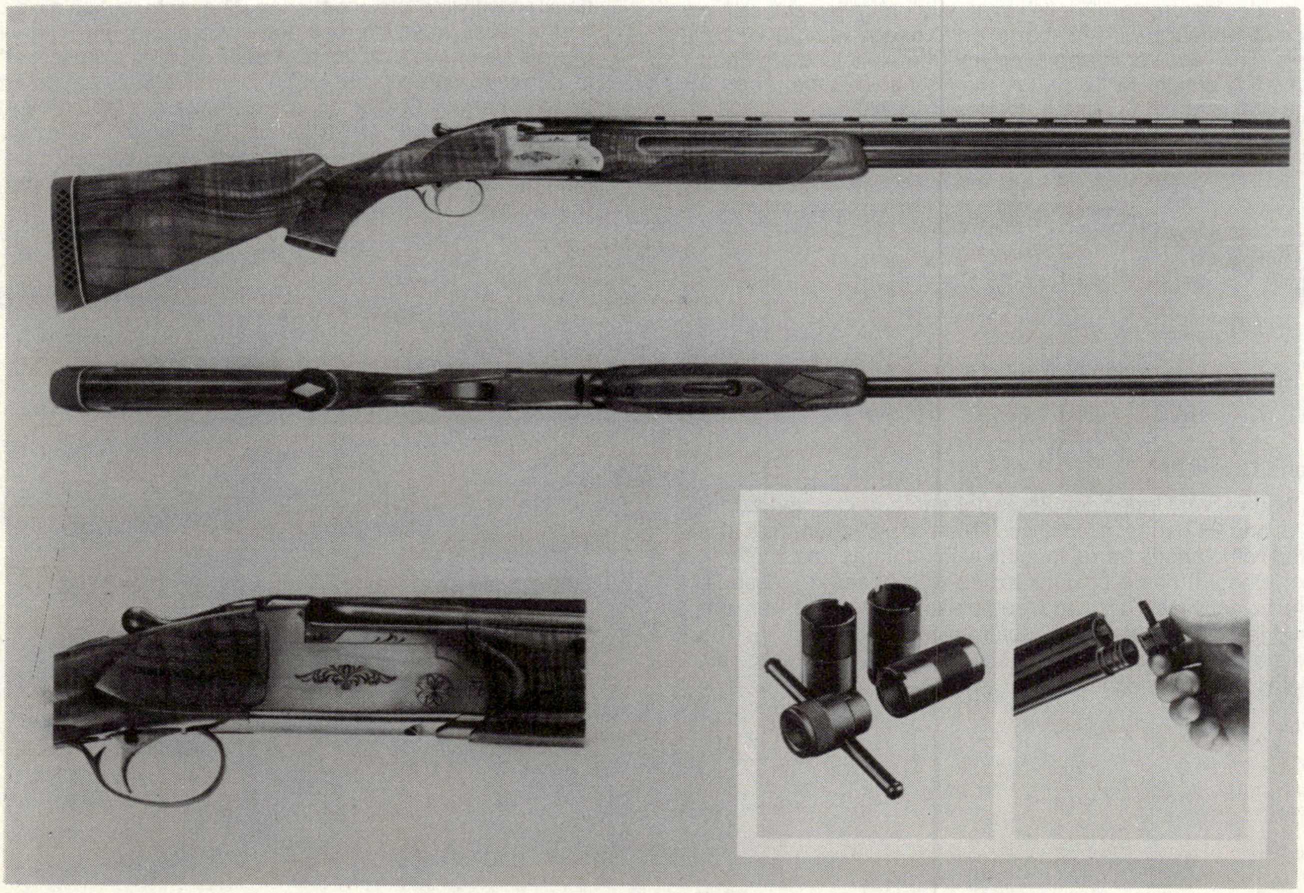

Weatherby Athena O/U Shotgun, IMC - Integral "Multi-choke" ™ flush fitting interchangeable choke tubes

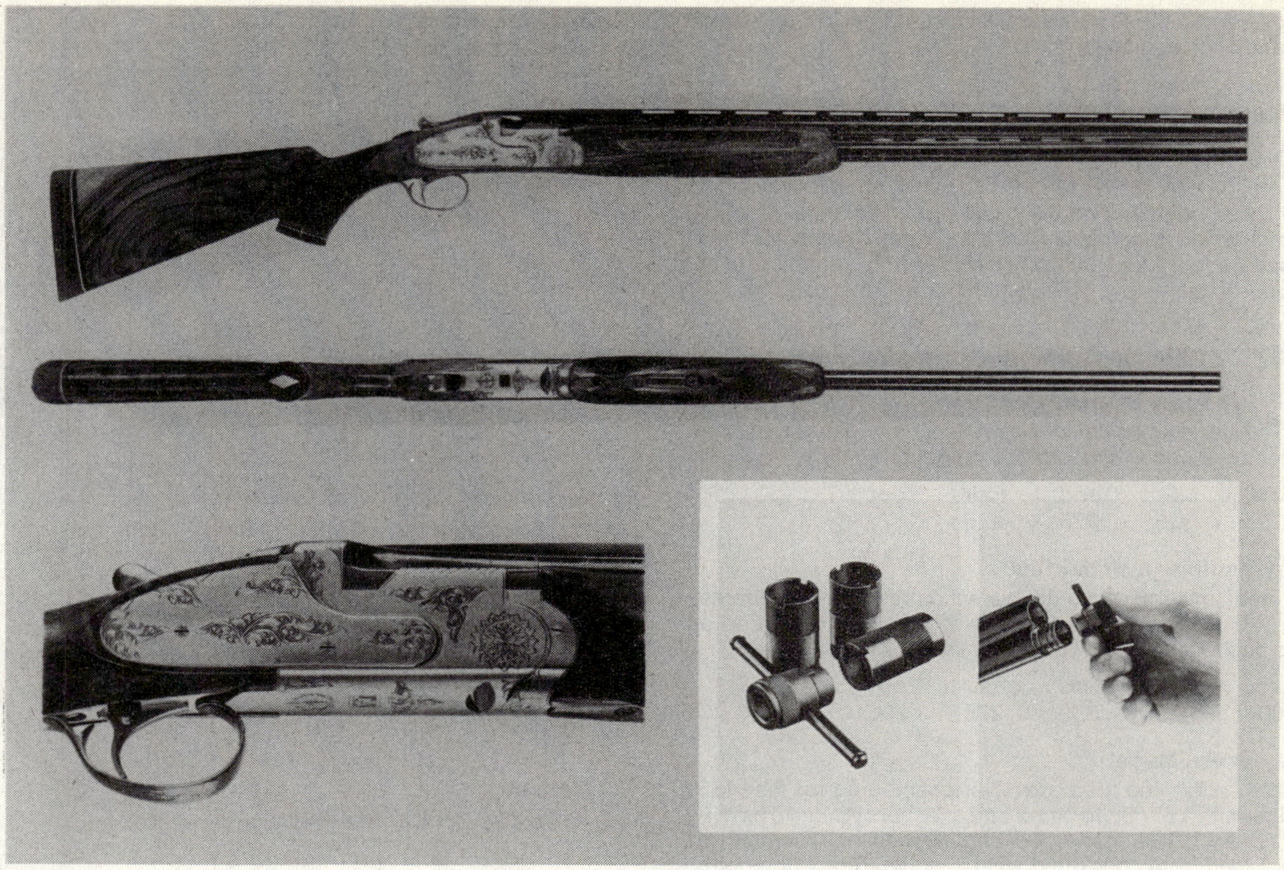

![Weatherby Orion O/U Shotgun images]

Weatherby Orion O/U Shotgun, IMC - Integral "Multi-choke"™ flush-fitting interchangeable choke tubes

WEAVER ARMS
Escondido, California

Nighthawk Assault Pistol

A 9mm semiautomatic pistol with a 10" or 12" barrel, alloy receiver and ambidextrous safety. Blackened with plastic grips. Introduced in 1987.

NIB	Exc.	V.G.	Good	Fair	Poor
500	450	400	350	300	150

Nighthawk Carbine

As above, with a 16.1" barrel, retractable shoulder stock, 25-, 32-, 40-, or 50-shot magazine. Introduced in 1984.

NIB	Exc.	V.G.	Good	Fair	Poor
550	500	450	350	300	150

WEBLEY & SCOTT, LTD.
Birmingham, England

Established in 1860, this firm has produced a wide variety of firearms over the years and has been known as Webley & Scott, Ltd. since 1906.

Model 1872 Royal Irish Constabulary

A .450 double action revolver with a 3.25" barrel, 5-shot cylinder and rotating ejector. This model was also offered with 2.5" and 3.5" barrels. Blued with checkered walnut grips.

Exc.	V.G.	Good	Fair	Poor
400	325	250	200	150

Model 1880 Metropolitan Police

As above, with a 2.5" barrel and 6-shot cylinder.

Exc.	V.G.	Good	Fair	Poor
400	325	250	200	150

Model 1880 James Hill Revolver

As above, but chambered for the .430 Eley cartridge.

Exc.	V.G.	Good	Fair	Poor
400	325	250	200	150

New Model 1883 R.I.C.

Similar to the Model 1880, but in .455 caliber with a 4.5" barrel. Also made with a 2.5" barrel.

Exc.	V.G.	Good	Fair	Poor
350	250	200	150	100

Model 1884 R.I.C. Naval

As above, with a brass frame and oxidized finish. Barrel length 2.75" and of octagonal form.

Exc.	V.G.	Good	Fair	Poor
350	250	200	150	100

British Bulldog

Similar to the new Model 1883 R.I.C. blued, checkered walnut grips. Those engraved on the back strap "W.R.A. Co." were sold through the Winchester Repeating Arms Company's New York sales agency and are worth a considerable premium over the values listed below. Manufactured from 1878 to 1914.

Exc.	V.G.	Good	Fair	Poor
350	300	250	200	150

Model 1878 Army Express Revolver

A .455 caliber double action revolver with a 6" barrel and integral ejector. Blued with one-piece walnut grips.

Exc.	V.G.	Good	Fair	Poor
375	325	275	225	175

Webley Kaufmann Model 1880

A top break, hinged-frame double action revolver chambered for the .450 centerfire cartridge, with a 5.75" barrel and a curved bird's-head butt. Blued, with walnut grips.

Exc.	V.G.	Good	Fair	Poor
500	425	350	275	200

Webley-Green Model

A double action, top break revolver chambered for the .455 cartridge, with a 6" ribbed barrel and a 6-shot cylinder. The cylinder flutes on this model are angular and not rounded in shape. Blued, with checkered walnut, squared butt grips with a lanyard ring on the butt. Introduced in 1882 and manufactured until 1896.

Exc.	V.G.	Good	Fair	Poor
500	425	350	275	200

Mark I

A .442, .455, or .476 double action top break revolver with a 4" barrel and 6-shot cylinder. Blued with checkered walnut grips. Manufactured from 1887 to 1894.

Exc.	V.G.	Good	Fair	Poor
300	200	175	125	100

Mark II

As above, with a larger hammer spur and improved barrel catch. Manufactured from 1894 to 1897.

Exc.	V.G.	Good	Fair	Poor
300	200	175	125	100

Mark III

As above, with internal improvements. Introduced in 1897.

Exc.	V.G.	Good	Fair	Poor
325	225	200	150	125

Mark IV

As above, with a .455 caliber 3", 4", 5", or 6" barrel.

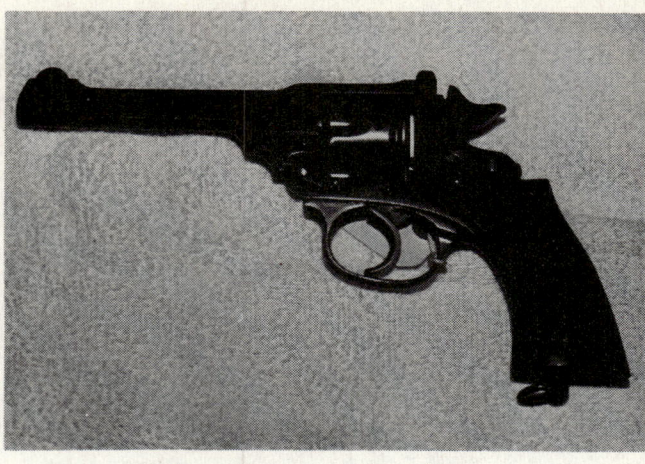

Exc.	V.G.	Good	Fair	Poor
350	300	225	175	125

Mark V

As above, with a 4" barrel. Manufactured from 1913 to 1915.

Exc.	V.G.	Good	Fair	Poor
375	325	250	200	150

Mark VI

As above, with a 4" or 6" barrel and modified grip.

Courtesy Wallis & Wallis, Lewes, Sussex, England

Exc.	V.G.	Good	Fair	Poor
350	300	250	175	125

Mark VI .22 Rimfire

A standard-size Mark V chambered for the .22 rimfire cartridge used as a training pistol. Manufactured in 1918 and quite scarce.

Exc.	V.G.	Good	Fair	Poor
450	400	300	200	150

Webley-Fosbery Automatic Revolver

A semiautomatic .38 or .455 caliber 6-shot revolver. An 8-shot variation is known and would command approximately a 100% premium over the values listed below. Blued with checkered walnut grips. Manufactured from 1901 to 1939.

.455 Caliber

Exc.	V.G.	Good	Fair	Poor
3500	2500	1500	950	450

.38 Caliber

Exc.	V.G.	Good	Fair	Poor
5000	3500	2000	1250	600

> **A Webley-Fosbery Model 1902 was sold at auction for $9,200. Chambered for .38 caliber automatic cartridge with 6" barrel. Condition was excellent. Butterfield & Butterfield, July 1996.**

Model 1904

A .455 caliber semiautomatic pistol with a 5" barrel and 7-shot magazine. Blued with walnut grips. Manufactured from 1904 to 1939.

Exc.	V.G.	Good	Fair	Poor
1500	1000	750	500	300

Model 1906

A .32 or .380 semiautomatic pistol with a 3.5" barrel and 8-shot magazine. Blued with checkered plastic grips. Manufactured from 1906 to 1939.

Exc.	V.G.	Good	Fair	Poor
250	225	200	150	100

Model 1906 .25

As above, in .25 caliber with a 2" barrel and 6-shot magazine.

Exc.	V.G.	Good	Fair	Poor
200	175	150	100	75

Model 1909

As above, with an enclosed hammer.

Exc.	V.G.	Good	Fair	Poor
250	225	200	150	100

Model 1909 9mm

As above, in 9mm Browning caliber with a 5" barrel and external hammer. Manufactured from 1909 to 1930.

Exc.	V.G.	Good	Fair	Poor
450	400	350	275	200

Model 1912 Self-Loader

Similar to the Model 1904.

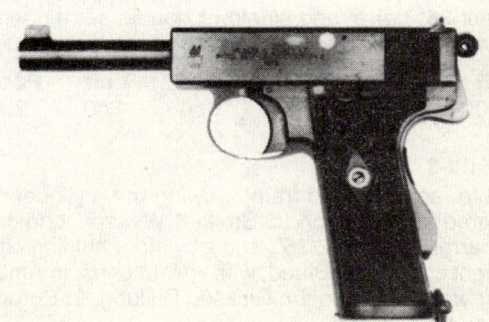

Exc.	V.G.	Good	Fair	Poor
450	400	350	275	200

Model 1915 Self-Loader

As above, with a special rear sight designed for targeting moving objects at ranges up to 200 yards. Adopted by the Royal Flying Corps in 1914. Discontinued in 1960.

Exc.	V.G.	Good	Fair	Poor
750	650	500	400	300

Model 1911 Target Pistol

A .22 caliber single shot pistol with a 4.5" or 9" barrel resembling a semiautomatic pistol.

Exc.	V.G.	Good	Fair	Poor
400	350	300	200	150

Model 700

A boxlock 12 or 20 gauge double-barrel shotgun available with either a single or double trigger. Blued, case-hardened with checkered walnut stock.

Exc.	V.G.	Good	Fair	Poor
1750	1500	1250	850	600

Model 702

As above, but more finely finished.

Exc.	V.G.	Good	Fair	Poor
2750	2500	2000	1500	1000

Model 701

As above, but heavily engraved with a finely figured, checkered walnut stock.

Exc.	V.G.	Good	Fair	Poor
3200	2750	2250	1750	1250

WEIHRAUCH, HANS HERMANN
Melrichstadt, West Germany

Model HW 60M

A .22 caliber single shot bolt action rifle with a 26.75" barrel and adjustable sights. Blued with a walnut stock.

NIB	Exc.	V.G.	Good	Fair	Poor
750	650	550	400	350	250

Model HW 66

A .22 Hornet or .222 Remington bolt action rifle with a stainless steel 26" barrel and single or double set triggers. Blued with a walnut stock.

NIB	Exc.	V.G.	Good	Fair	Poor
650	550	500	350	300	200

Model HW-3

A double action, solid-frame, swing-out cylinder revolver chambered for .22 l.r. or .32 Smith & Wesson long cartridges with a barrel length of 2.75", and a cylinder holding either seven or eight cartridges. Blued, with walnut grips. In America this revolver was known as the Dickson Bulldog. In Europe it was known as the Gecado.

Exc.	V.G.	Good	Fair	Poor
100	75	50	35	25

Model HW-5

As above, with a 4" barrel. Sold in the United States under the trade name "Omega."

Exc.	V.G.	Good	Fair	Poor
100	75	50	35	25

Model HW-7

As above, in .22 caliber with a 6" barrel and 8-shot cylinder. Sold in the United States as the "Herter's Guide Model". Also available with target sights and thumb rest grips as the Model HW-7S.

Exc.	V.G.	Good	Fair	Poor
100	75	50	35	25

Model HW-9

Similar to the HW-7, with a 6-shot cylinder and 6" ventilated rib barrel fitted with target sights and target grips.

Exc.	V.G.	Good	Fair	Poor
100	75	50	35	25

These pistols all carry the Arminius trademark, a bearded head wearing a winged helmet. The model number will be found on the cylinder crane; the caliber, on the barrel; and the words "Made in Germany" on the frame.

WEISBURGER, A.
Memphis, Tennessee

Pocket Pistol

A .41 caliber percussion single shot pocket pistol with 2.5" barrel, German silver furniture and a walnut stock. Manufactured during the 1850s.

Exc.	V.G.	Good	Fair	Poor
—	—	1000	400	150

WESSON, DAN ARMS
SEE Wesson Firearms Co., Inc.

WESSON FIREARMS CO., INC.
Palmer, Massachusetts
New Location
Greene, New York

The company was founded in 1968 by Daniel B. Wesson, the great-grandson of D.B. Wesson, co-founder of Smith & Wesson. This line of handguns is unique for its barrel/shroud interchangeability. Dan Wesson revolvers have established themselves as champion metallic silhouette competition guns. The company offers a comprehensive line of handguns for almost every use. The company will also custom build a handgun to customer specifications. Dan Wesson Arms was restructured on January 4, 1991, and is now identified as Wesson Firearms Company, Inc. Wesson handguns made after this date will be stamped with this new corporate name. In 1995 the company declared bankruptcy and is no longer in business.

NOTE: In 1996 the assets of the company were purchased by the New York International Corp. All interchangeable barrel models will be produced. There are no plans at this time to build fixed barrel models. At the present time parts and service for original Dan Wesson revolvers are available from the new company. Full production of new models is planned for 1997.

Model II

A .357 Magnum caliber double action swing-out cylinder revolver with interchangeable 2.5", 4", or 6" barrels and a 6-shot cylinder. Blued with walnut grips. Manufactured in 1970 and 1971.

Extra Barrels-Add 25% per barrel.

NIB	Exc.	V.G.	Good	Fair	Poor
200	175	150	125	100	75

Model 12

As above, with adjustable target sights.

NIB	Exc.	V.G.	Good	Fair	Poor
250	225	200	175	125	100

Model 14

As above, with a recessed barrel locking nut and furnished with a spanner wrench. Manufactured from 1971 to 1975.

NIB	Exc.	V.G.	Good	Fair	Poor
250	200	175	150	100	75

Model 15

As above, with adjustable target sights.

NIB	Exc.	V.G.	Good	Fair	Poor
275	225	200	175	125	100

Model 8

As above, in .38 Special caliber.

NIB	Exc.	V.G.	Good	Fair	Poor
225	175	150	125	100	75

Model 9

As the Model 15, with adjustable sights and in .38 Special caliber. Manufactured from 1971 to 1975.

NIB	Exc.	V.G.	Good	Fair	Poor
250	225	200	175	125	100

.22 CALIBER REVOLVERS

Model 22

This is a double action target revolver chambered for the .22 Long Rifle cartridge. It is available in 2", 4", 6", and 8" barrel length with a choice of standard rib shroud, ventilated rib shroud, or ventilated heavy rib shroud. All variations feature an adjustable rear sight, red ramp interchangeable front sight and target grips. Offered in bright blue or stainless steel finish. For revolvers with standard barrel assembly weights are: 2"-36 oz., 4"-40 oz., 6"-44 oz., and 8"-49 oz.

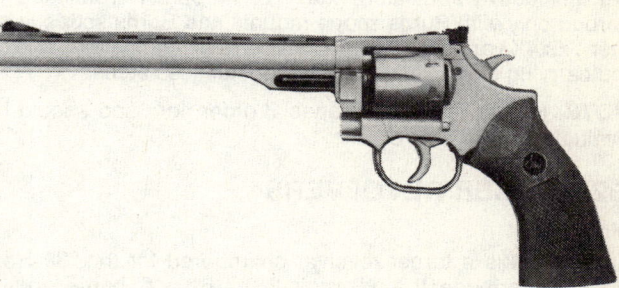

Model 722
Same as above but with stainless steel finish.

Model 22M
Same as above but chambered for .22 Magnum with blued finish.

Model 722M
Same as above but chambered for .22 Magnum with stainless steel finish.

Standard Rib Shroud

NIB	Exc.	V.G.	Good	Fair	Poor
280	250	200	150	100	75

Ventilated Rib Shroud

NIB	Exc.	V.G.	Good	Fair	Poor
300	275	225	150	100	75

Ventilated Heavy Rib Shroud

NIB	Exc.	V.G.	Good	Fair	Poor
330	280	240	200	125	100

NOTE: Add 10% to above prices for stainless steel finish.

P22 Pistol Pac

This model is also a target revolver similar to the Model 22 and its variations. Chambered for the .22 l.r. or .22 Magnum it is also offered with three types of barrel shrouds: standard, ventilated, or ventilated heavy. It is available in blued or stainless steel finish. The principal feature of the Pistol Pac is the 3 barrel assemblies in 2.5", 4", 6", and 8" with extra grips, four additional front sights, and a fitted carrying case.

Standard Rib Shroud

NIB	Exc.	V.G.	Good	Fair	Poor
500	450	400	350	300	150

Ventilated Rib Shroud

NIB	Exc.	V.G.	Good	Fair	Poor
600	550	500	450	350	150

Ventilated Heavy Rib Shroud

NIB	Exc.	V.G.	Good	Fair	Poor
650	600	550	475	350	150

NOTE: Add 10% to above prices for stainless steel finish.

HP22 Hunter Pac

This model is chambered for the .22 Magnum cartridge. The set includes a ventilated heavy 8" shroud, a ventilated 8" shroud only with Burris scope mounts and Burris scope in either 1.5x4X variable or fixed 2X, a barrel changing tool, and fitted carrying case. Finish is blued or stainless steel.

NOTE: Hunter Pacs are a special order item and should be evaluated at the time of sale.

.32 CALIBER REVOLVERS

Model 32

This model is a target revolver chambered for the .32 H&R Magnum cartridge. It is offered in 2", 4", 6", or 8" barrel lengths with choice of rib shrouds. All variations are fitted with adjustable rear sight, red ramp interchangeable front sight, and target grips. Available in blued or stainless steel finish. Weights depend on barrel length and shroud type but are between 35 oz. and 53 oz.

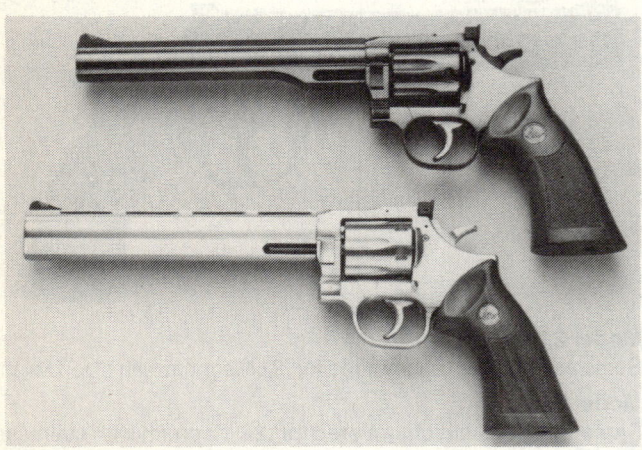

Model 732

Same as above but with stainless steel finish.

Model 322

Same as above but chambered for .32-20 cartridge with blued finish.

Model 7322

Same as above but chambered for .32-20 cartridge with stainless steel finish.

Standard Rib Shroud

NIB	Exc.	V.G.	Good	Fair	Poor
275	225	200	150	100	75

Ventilated Rib Shroud

NIB	Exc.	V.G.	Good	Fair	Poor
300	250	225	150	100	75

Ventilated Heavy Rib Shroud

NIB	Exc.	V.G.	Good	Fair	Poor
325	275	250	150	100	75

NOTE: Add 10% to above prices for stainless steel finish.

P32 Pistol Pac

This set offers the same calibers, barrel shrouds, and finishes as the above models but in a set consisting of 2", 4", 6", and 8" barrels with extra grips, four additional sights, and fitted case.

Standard Rib Shroud

NIB	Exc.	V.G.	Good	Fair	Poor
500	450	400	300	150	100

Ventilated Rib Shroud

NIB	Exc.	V.G.	Good	Fair	Poor
575	500	450	325	150	100

Ventilated Heavy Rib Shroud

NIB	Exc.	V.G.	Good	Fair	Poor
650	600	500	400	200	125

NOTE: Add 10% to above prices for stainless steel finish.

HP32 Hunter Pac

This model is chambered for the .32 H&R Magnum or .32-20 cartridge. The set includes a ventilated heavy 8" shroud, a ventilated 8" shroud only with Burris scope mounts and Burris scope in either 1.5x4X variable or fixed 2X, a barrel changing tool, and fitted carrying case. Finish is blued or stainless steel.

NOTE: Hunter Pacs are a special order item and should be evaluated at the time of sale.

.357 MAGNUM AND .38 CALIBER REVOLVERS

Model 14

This is a double action service revolver chambered for the .357 Magnum cartridge. Available with 2", 4", or 6" barrel with service shroud. It has fixed sights, service grip, and is offered in blued or stainless steel finish.

Model 714
Same as above but with stainless steel finish.

Model 8
Same as above but chambered for .38 Special cartridge with blued finish.

Model 708
Same as above but chambered for .38 Special with stainless steel finish.

NIB	Exc.	V.G.	Good	Fair	Poor
225	175	150	125	100	75

NOTE: Add 10% to above prices for stainless steel finish.

P14/8 Pistol Pac
This set consists of a 2", 4", and 6" barrel with service shroud and fixed sights. It has an extra grip and fitted carrying case. The P14 is chambered for the .357 Mag. and the P8 is chambered for the .38 Special.

NIB	Exc.	V.G.	Good	Fair	Poor
375	300	250	200	150	100

NOTE: Add 10% to above prices for stainless steel finish.

Model 15
This model is designed as a double action target revolver chambered for the .357 Magnum cartridge. It is available with 2", 4", 6", 8", and 10" barrels lengths with standard rib shroud. It features adjustable rear sight, red ramp interchangeable front sight, and target grips. Offered with blued finish. Weights according to barrel length are: 2"-32 oz., 4"-36 oz., 6"-40 oz., 8"-44 oz., 10"-50 oz.

Model 715
Same as above but with stainless steel finish.

Model 9
Same as above but chambered for .38 Special cartridge with blued finish.

Model 709
Same as above but chambered for .38 Special with stainless steel finish.

Standard Rib Shroud

NIB	Exc.	V.G.	Good	Fair	Poor
275	225	200	150	100	75

Ventilated Rib Shroud

NIB	Exc.	V.G.	Good	Fair	Poor
300	250	225	150	100	75

Ventilated Heavy Rib Shroud

NIB	Exc.	V.G.	Good	Fair	Poor
325	275	250	150	100	75

NOTE: Add 10% to above prices for stainless steel finish.

P15/9 Pistol Pac
This model is a set with 2", 4", 6", and 8" barrels with standard rib shroud. Chambered for the .357 or .38 Special with standard rib shroud, four additional sights, and extra grip, and carrying case. The P15 is chambered for the .357 Mag. while the P9 is chambered for the .38 Special.

Standard Rib Shroud

NIB	Exc.	V.G.	Good	Fair	Poor
500	450	400	350	150	100

Ventilated Rib Shroud

NIB	Exc.	V.G.	Good	Fair	Poor
575	500	450	350	150	100

Ventilated Heavy Rib Shroud

NIB	Exc.	V.G.	Good	Fair	Poor
650	575	500	400	200	100

NOTE: Add 10% to above prices for stainless steel finish.

HP 15 Hunter Pac
This model is chambered for the .357 Magnum cartridge. The set includes a ventilated heavy 8" shroud, a ventilated 8" shroud only with Burris scope mounts and Burris scope in either 1.5x4X variable or fixed 2X, a barrel changing tool, and fitted carrying case. Finish is blued or stainless steel.

NOTE: Hunter Pacs are a special order item and should be evaluated at the time of sale.

Model 40/Supermag
This model is a target revolver chambered for the .357 Maximum cartridge. It has an adjustable rear sight, red ramp interchangeable front sight, ventilated rib shroud, and target grip. Barrel lengths are 4", 6", 8", or 10". A ventilated slotted shroud is available in 8" only. For 1993 a compensated barrel assembly, "CBA", as been added to the product line as a complete gun. Finish is blued. Weighs approximately 64 oz. with ventilated rib shroud barrel.

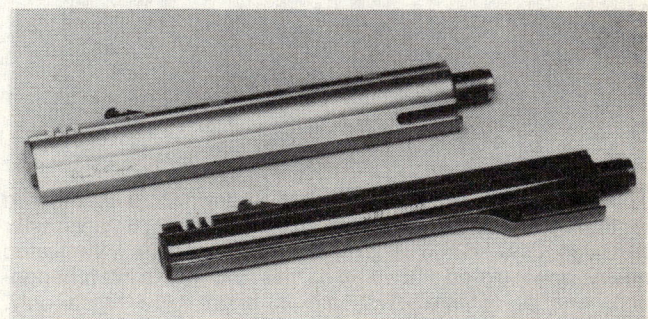

Model 740
Same as above but with stainless steel finish.

Ventilated Rib Shroud

NIB	Exc.	V.G.	Good	Fair	Poor
400	350	300	250	200	100

Ventilated Slotted Shroud-8" barrel only

NIB	Exc.	V.G.	Good	Fair	Poor
450	400	350	300	200	100

Ventilated Heavy Rib Shroud

NIB	Exc.	V.G.	Good	Fair	Poor
475	425	375	300	200	100

NOTE: Add 10% to above prices for stainless steel finish.

NOTE: For .357 Supermag with compensated barrel assembly add $30.

HP40 Hunter Pac

This model is chambered for the .357 Supermag cartridge. The set includes a ventilated heavy 8" shroud, a ventilated 8" shroud only with Burris scope mounts and Burris scope in either 1.5x4X variable or fixed 2X, a barrel changing tool, and fitted carrying case. Finish is blued or stainless steel.

NOTE: Hunter Pacs are a special order item and should be evaluated at the time of sale.

Model 375

This model, also known as the .375 Supermag, is chambered for the .357 Maximum cartridge, based on the .375 Winchester cartridge. Offered in 6", 8", 10" barrels in ventilated, ventilated heavy, or ventilated slotted rib barrels. Sights are interchangeable and adjustable. Available in bright blue finish only. Weighs approximately 64 oz. with ventilated rib shroud barrel.

Ventilated Rib Shroud

NIB	Exc.	V.G.	Good	Fair	Poor
400	350	300	250	200	100

Ventilated Heavy Rib Shroud

NIB	Exc.	V.G.	Good	Fair	Poor
450	400	350	300	200	100

Ventilated Slotted Shroud-8" barrel only

NIB	Exc.	V.G.	Good	Fair	Poor
475	425	375	300	200	100

HP375 Hunter Pac

This model is chambered for the .375 Supermag cartridge. The set includes a ventilated heavy 8" shroud, a ventilated 8" shroud only with Burris scope mounts and Burris scope in either 1.5x4X variable or fixed 2X, a barrel changing tool, and fitted carrying case. Finish is blued or stainless steel.

NOTE: Hunter Pacs are a special order item and should be evaluated at the time of sale.

.41, .44 MAGNUM, AND 45 LONG COLT REVOLVERS

Model 44

This model is a target double action revolver chambered for the .44 Magnum. It has 4", 6", 8", or 10" barrels with ventilated rib shrouds. Other features include: adjustable rear sight, red ramp interchangeable front sight, and target grips. Finish is bright blue. Weights with 4" barrel-40 oz., 6"-56 oz., 8"-64 oz., and 10"-69 oz.

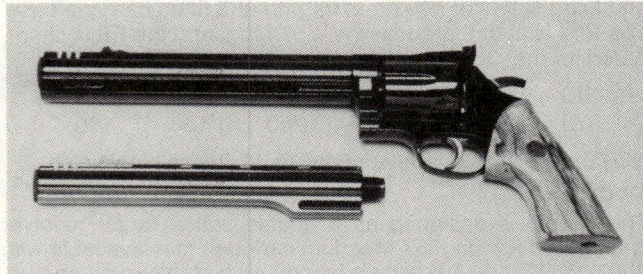

Model 744

Same as above but with stainless steel finish.

Model 41

Same as above but chambered for .41 Magnum with blued finish.

Model 741

Same as above but with stainless steel finish.

Model 45

Same as above but chambered for .45 Long Colt with bright blue finish.

Model 745

Same as above but with stainless steel finish. Ventilated rib shroud

NIB	Exc.	V.G.	Good	Fair	Poor
350	300	250	200	100	75

Ventilated Heavy Rib Shroud

NIB	Exc.	V.G.	Good	Fair	Poor
375	325	275	200	100	75

NOTE: Add 10% to above prices for stainless steel finish.

P44/P41/P45 Pistol Pac

This set features a 6" and 8" barrel assembly with ventilated rib shroud, an extra grip, two additional front sights, and a fitted carrying case. Chambered for .41 Magnum, .44 Magnum, or .45 Long Colt.

Ventilated Rib Shroud

NIB	Exc.	V.G.	Good	Fair	Poor
525	475	400	300	200	100

Ventilated Heavy Rib Shroud

NIB	Exc.	V.G.	Good	Fair	Poor
575	525	425	300	200	100

NOTE: Add 10% to above prices for stainless steel finish.

HP41/44 Hunter Pac

This model is chambered for either the .41 or .44 Magnum cartridge. The set includes a ventilated heavy 8" shroud, a ventilated 8" shroud only with Burris scope mounts and Burris scope in either 1.5x4X variable or fixed 2X, a barrel changing tool, and fitted carrying case. Finish is blued or stainless steel.

NOTE: Hunter Pacs are a special order item and should be evaluated at the time of sale.

Model 445

This double action target revolver is chambered for the .445 Supermag cartridge. Barrel lengths offered are 8" with ventilated slotted rib shroud, 8" ventilated heavy slotted rib shroud, or 10" ventilated slotted rib shroud. Barrel lengths are also available in 4", 6", 8", and 10" with choice of ventilated rib or ventilated heavy rib shrouds. Introduced in 1993 is a compensated barrel assembly available as a complete gun. This is designated the "CBA". Fitted with adjustable rear sights, red ramp interchangeable front sight, and target grips. Finish is bright blue. Typical weight with 8" ventilated rib shroud barrel is about 62 oz.

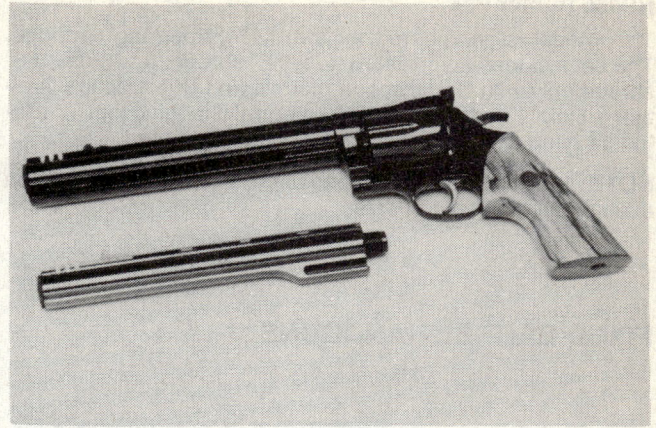

Model 7445

Same as above but with stainless steel finish.

Ventilated Rib Shroud

NIB	Exc.	V.G.	Good	Fair	Poor
400	350	300	250	200	100

Ventilated Heavy Rib Shroud

NIB	Exc.	V.G.	Good	Fair	Poor
430	380	330	250	200	100

NOTE: Add 10% to above prices for stainless steel finish.
NOTE: For .44 Magnum and .445 Supermag with compensated barrel assembly add $30.

Model 7445 Alaskan Guide Special

This limited edition model (only 500 will be produced) is chambered for the .445 Supermag cartridge. It features a 4" ventilated heavy compensated shroud barrel assembly, synthetic grips, and a matte black titanium nitride finish. Overall barrel length is 5.5" and the revolver weighs 56 oz.

NIB	Exc.	V.G.	Good	Fair	Poor
900	700	600	350	200	100

HP455 Hunter Pac

This model is chambered for the .445 Supermag cartridge. The set includes a ventilated heavy 8" shroud, a ventilated 8" shroud only with Burris scope mounts and Burris scope in either 1.5x4X variable or fixed 2X, a barrel changing tool, and fitted carrying case. Finish is blued or stainless steel.

NOTE: Hunter Pacs are a special order item and should be evaluated at the time of sale.

FIXED BARREL HANDGUNS

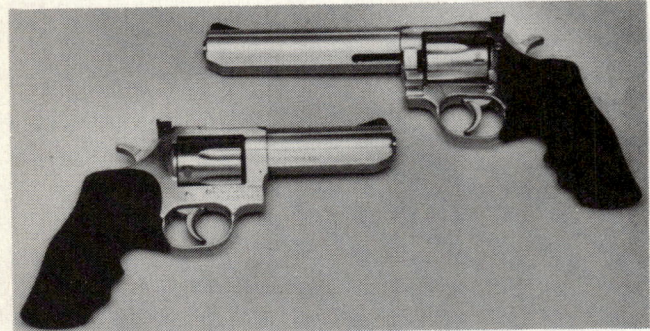

Model 38P

This model is a 5-shot double action revolver designed for the .38 Special cartridge. Barrel is 2.5" with fixed sights. Choice of wood or rubber grips. Finish is blued. Weighs 24.6 oz.

Model 738P

Same as above but with stainless steel finish.

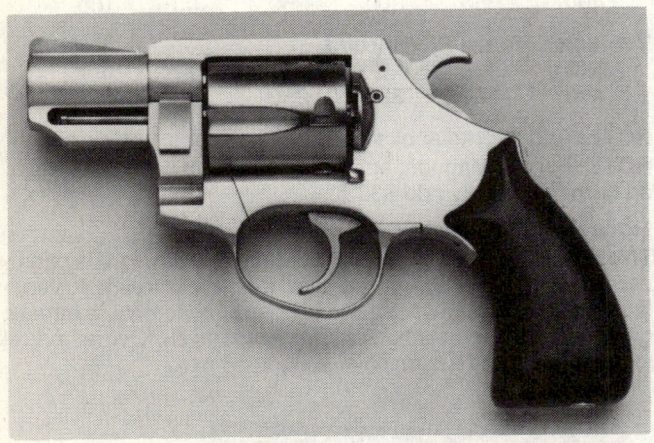

NIB	Exc.	V.G.	Good	Fair	Poor
200	175	150	125	100	75

NOTE: Add 10% to above prices for stainless steel finish.

Model 14/714 Fixed Barrel Service

Same features as the .357 Magnum Model 14 without the interchangeable barrels. Barrel length are either 2.5" or 4" with fixed sights. Offered in either blued or stainless steel. Weighs 30 oz. with 2.5" barrel and 34 oz. with 4" barrel.

NIB	Exc.	V.G.	Good	Fair	Poor
200	175	150	125	100	75

NOTE: Add 10% to above prices for stainless steel finish.

Model 15/715 Fixed Barrel Target

Same as the .357 magnum Model 15 with target sights and grips. Fixed barrel lengths are either 3" or 5". Available in blued or stainless steel. Weighs 37 oz. with 3" barrel and 42 oz. with 5" barrel.

NIB	Exc.	V.G.	Good	Fair	Poor
220	195	160	125	100	75

NOTE: Add 10% to above prices for stainless steel finish.

Model 45/745 Pin Gun

This model uses a .44 Magnum frame with 5" barrel with two-stage compensator. Choice of ventilated or ventilated heavy rib shroud configuration. Chambered for .45 ACP with or without half moon clips. Finish is blued or stainless steel. Weighs 54 oz.

Ventilated Rib Shroud

NIB	Exc.	V.G.	Good	Fair	Poor
550	500	450	400	200	100

Ventilated Heavy Rib Shroud

NIB	Exc.	V.G.	Good	Fair	Poor
600	550	500	400	200	100

NOTE: Add 10% to above prices for stainless steel finish.

Wesson Firearms Silhouette .22

This model is a 6-shot .22 l.r. single action only revolver with a 10" barrel. Fitted with compact style grips, narrow notch rear sight with choice of ventilated or ventilated heavy rib shroud. Finish is blued or stainless steel. Weighs 55 oz. with ventilated rib shroud and 62 oz. with ventilated heavy rib shroud.

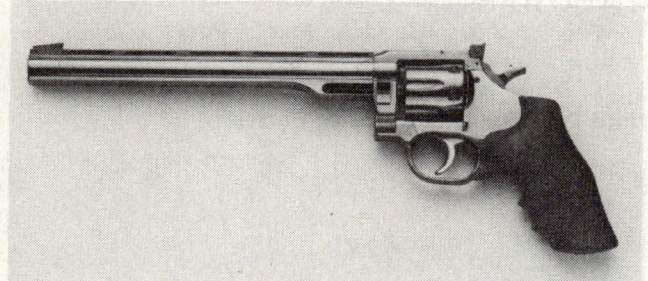

Ventilated Rib Shroud

NIB	Exc.	V.G.	Good	Fair	Poor
375	325	275	225	150	100

Ventilated Heavy Rib Shroud

NIB	Exc.	V.G.	Good	Fair	Poor
390	350	290	225	150	100

NOTE: Add 10% to above prices for stainless steel finish.

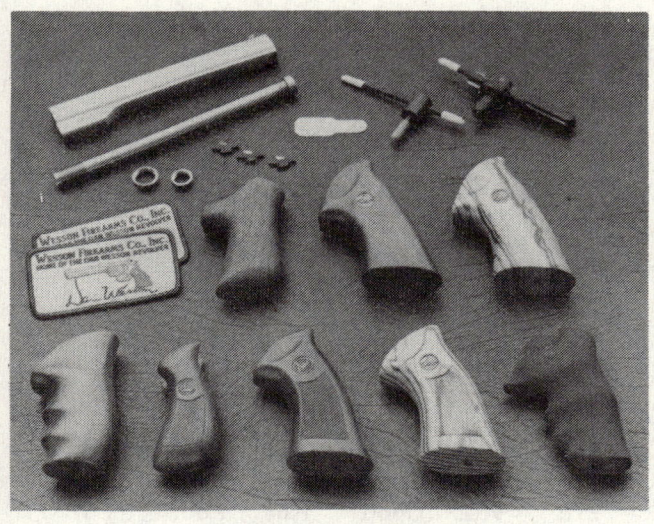

WESSON, EDWIN
Hartford, Connecticut

Dragoon

A .45 caliber percussion revolver with a 7" round barrel and 6-shot unfluted cylinder. The barrel blued, the frame case-hardened and the walnut grips fitted with a brass buttcap. Manufactured in 1848 and 1849.

Exc.	V.G.	Good	Fair	Poor
—	—	7500	4000	950

WESSON, FRANK
Worcester, Massachusetts
Springfield, Massachusetts

Manual Extractor Model

A .22 caliber spur trigger single shot pistol with a 4" octagonal barrel and thin brass frame. The barrel release is located in the front of the trigger. No markings. Approximately 200 were made in 1856 and 1857.

Exc.	V.G.	Good	Fair	Poor
—	—	600	250	100

First Model Small Frame

As above, with a 3", 3.5", or 6" half-octagonal barrel. Blued with rosewood or walnut grips. The barrel marked "Frank Wesson Worcester Mass/Pat'd Oct. 25, 1859 & Nov. 11, 1862". Serial numbered from 1 to 2500.

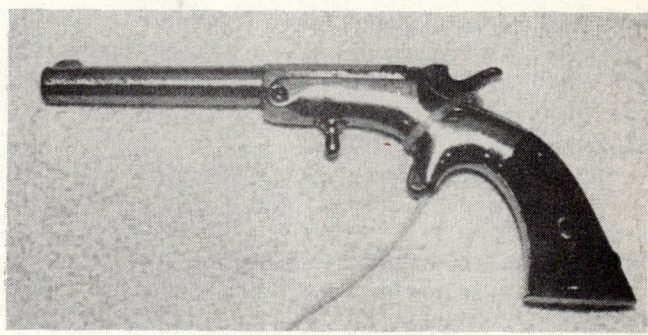

Exc.	V.G.	Good	Fair	Poor
—	—	450	200	75

Second Type

As above, with a flat sighted frame and a circular sideplate.

Exc.	V.G.	Good	Fair	Poor
—	—	350	175	75

First Model Medium Frame

As above, in .30 or .32 rimfire with a 4" half-octagonal barrel and an iron frame. Approximately 1,000 were made between 1859 and 1862.

Exc.	V.G.	Good	Fair	Poor
—	—	400	150	75

Medium Frame Second Model

As above, with a longer spur trigger and a slightly wider frame at the barrel hinge. Manufactured from 1862 to 1870.

Exc.	V.G.	Good	Fair	Poor
—	—	400	150	75

Small Frame Pocket Rifle

A .22 caliber spur trigger single-shot pistol with a 6" half octagonal barrel and narrow brass frame. This model is adopted for use with a detachable skeleton shoulder stock. The barrel marked "Frank Wesson Worcester, Mass." Manufactured from 1865 to 1875 with approximately 5,000 made.

Matching Shoulder Stock-Add 75%.

Pistol Only

Exc.	V.G.	Good	Fair	Poor
—	—	550	250	100

Medium Frame Pocket Rifle

As above, in .22, .30, or .32 rimfire with a 10" or 12" half octagonal barrel. Approximately 1,000 were made from 1862 to 1870.

Matching Shoulder Stock-Add 75%.

Pistol Only

Exc.	V.G.	Good	Fair	Poor
—	—	400	200	75

Model 1870 Small Frame Pocket Rifle

As above, in .22 caliber with a 10", 12", 15", or 18" or 20" half octagonal barrel that rotates to the side for loading. This model was made with either a brass or iron frame. It has a half cocked notch on the hammer.

Matching Shoulder Stock-Add 75%.

Pistol Only

Exc.	V.G.	Good	Fair	Poor
—	—	400	200	75

1870 Medium Frame Pocket Rifle First Type

As above, but with a slightly larger frame chambered for .32 rimfire. Approximately 5,000 were made from 1870 to 1893.

Matching Shoulder Stock-Add75%.

Pistol Only

Exc.	V.G.	Good	Fair	Poor
—	—	350	150	75

1870 Medium Frame Pocket Rifle Second Type

As above, with an iron frame and a push-button half cocked safety.

Match Shoulder Stock-Add 75%.

Pistol Only

Exc.	V.G.	Good	Fair	Poor
—	—	350	150	75

1870 Medium Frame Pocket Rifle Third Type

As above, with 3 screws on the left side of the frame.

Matching Shoulder Stock-Add75%.

Pistol Only

Exc.	V.G.	Good	Fair	Poor
—	—	350	150	75

1870 Large Frame Pocket Rifle First Type

As above, in .32, .38, .42, or .44 rimfire with an octagonal barrel from 15" to 24" in length. The barrel marked "Frank Wesson Worcester, Mass Patented May 31, 1870". Less than 250 of these rifles were made between 1870 and 1880.

Matching Shoulder Stock-Add 75%.

Pistol Only

Exc.	V.G.	Good	Fair	Poor
—	—	700	400	150

1870 Large Frame Pocket Rifle Second Type

As above, with a sliding extractor.

Matching Shoulder Stock-Add 25%.

Pistol Only

Exc.	V.G.	Good	Fair	Poor
—	—	700	400	150

Small Frame Superposed Pistol

A .22 caliber spur trigger Over/Under pocket pistol with 2" or 2.5" octagonal barrels that revolve. Approximately 3,500 were made between 1868 and 1880. On occasion this pistol is found with a sliding knife blade mounted on the side of the barrels. The presence of this feature would add approximately 25% to the values listed below.

Exc.	V.G.	Good	Fair	Poor
—	—	1250	600	250

Medium Frame Superposed Pistol

As above, in .32 rimfire with 2.5" or 3.5" barrels. As with the smaller version, this pistol is occasionally found with a sliding

knife blade mounted on the barrels that would add 25% to the values listed below. Manufactured from 1868 to 1880.

First Type Marked "Patent Applied For"

Exc.	V.G.	Good	Fair	Poor
—	—	750	300	100

Second Type Marked "Patent December 15, 1868"

Exc.	V.G.	Good	Fair	Poor
—	—	750	300	100

Third Type Full-Length Fluted Barrels

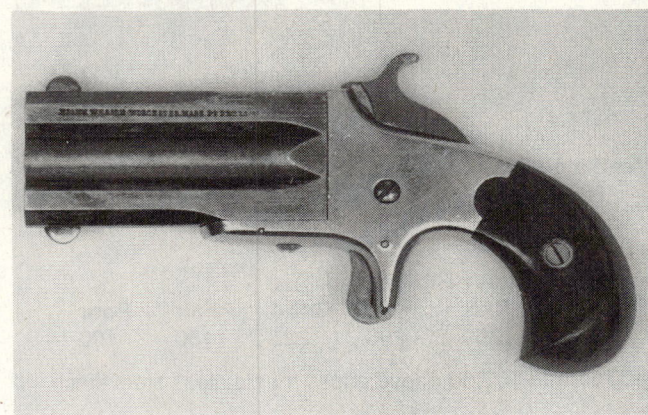

Courtesy W.P. Hallstein III and son Chip

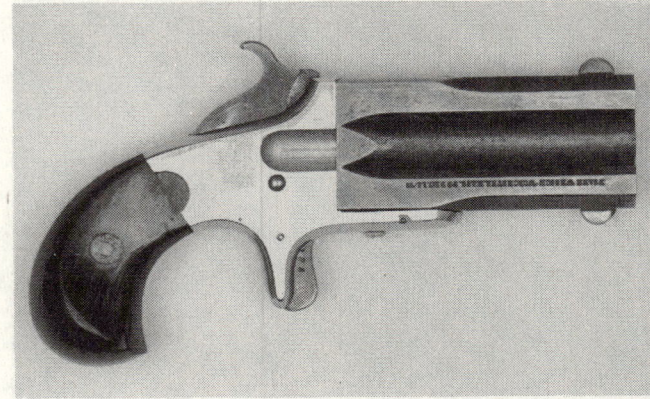

Courtesy W.P. Hallstein III and son Chip

Exc.	V.G.	Good	Fair	Poor
—	—	750	300	100

Large Frame Superposed Pistol

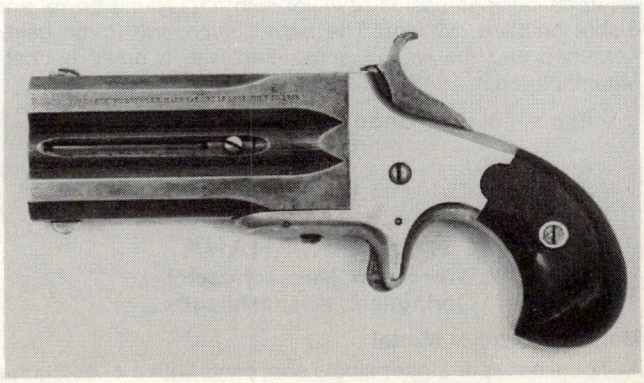

Courtesy W.P. Hallstein III and son Chip

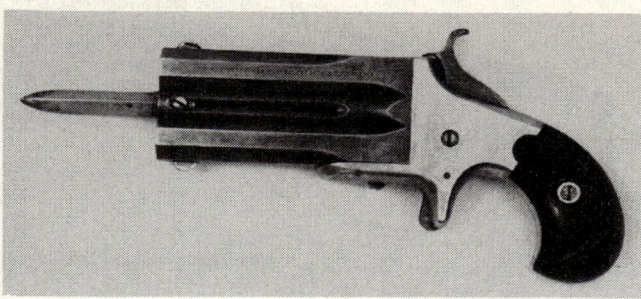

Courtesy W.P. Hallstein III and son Chip

As above, in .41 rimfire with a 3" octagonal barrel fitted with a sliding knife blade. Approximately 2,000 were made from 1868 to 1880.

Exc.	V.G.	Good	Fair	Poor
—	—	1750	750	300

No. 1 Long Range Rifle

A .44-100 or .45-100 caliber single-shot dropping block rifle with a 34" octagonal barrel. Blued with a checkered walnut stock. The barrel marked "F. Wesson Mfr. Worcester, Mass. Long Range Rifle Creedmoor". Manufactured in 1876.

Exc.	V.G.	Good	Fair	Poor
—	10000	3500	1250	500

No. 2 Mid-Range or Hunting Rifle

Similar to the above, with the firing pin located in a bolster on the right side of the receiver. The triggerguard has a rear finger loop. Standard barrel length 28", 32", and 34" and marked "F. Wesson Maker Worcester, Mass." The 32" and 34" barrels are occasionally marked "Long Range Rifle Creedmoor". Approximately 100 were made.

Courtesy Buffalo Bill Historical Center, Cody, Wyoming

Exc.	V.G.	Good	Fair	Poor
—	8000	3000	1000	500

No. 2 Sporting Rifle

A .38-100, .40-100, or .45-100 caliber single shot dropping barrel action rifle with barrels ranging from 28" to 34" in length. Approximately 25 were made.

Courtesy Buffalo Bill Historical Center, Cody, Wyoming

Exc.	V.G.	Good	Fair	Poor
—	7500	3000	1250	500

WESSON & LEAVITT
MASSACHUSETTS ARMS COMPANY
Chicopee Falls, Massachusetts

Revolving Rifle

A .40 caliber percussion revolving rifle with a 16" to 24" round barrel and 6-shot cylinder. Blued with a walnut stock. Approximately 25 were made in 1849.

Exc.	V.G.	Good	Fair	Poor
—	—	5000	3000	950

Dragoon

A .40 caliber percussion revolver with a 6.25" or 7" round barrel and 6-shot cylinder. These pistols are marked "Mass. Arms Co./Chicopee Falls". Approximately 30 were made with the 6.25" barrel and 750 with the 7" barrel. Manufactured in 1850 and 1851.

Courtesy Milwaukee Public Museum, Milwaukee, Wisconsin

Exc.	V.G.	Good	Fair	Poor
—	—	3000	1000	400

WESTERN ARMS
SEE Bacon

WESTERN ARMS CORPORATION
SEE Ithaca

WESTERN FIELD
Montgomery Ward

"Western Field" is the trade name used by Montgomery Ward & Company on arms that they retail. See Firearms Trade Names List at the end of this book.

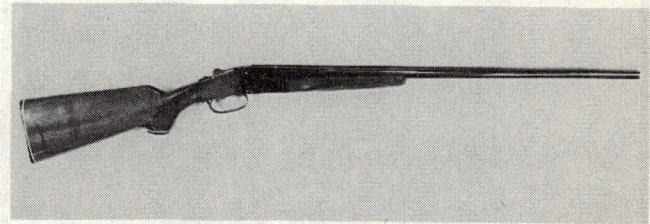

WESTLEY RICHARDS & CO., LTD.
Birmingham, England
Importer-New England Arms Co.
Kittery Point, Maine

A wide variety of firearms have been produced by this company since its founding. Presently, it produces boxlock and sidelock double-barrel shotguns of both side-by-side and Over/Under form, bolt-action rifles and double-barrel rifles. Prospective purchasers are advised to secure individual appraisals prior to acquisition.

A Westley Richards .410 bore boxlock Royal Game gun was sold at auction for $34,500. Deep relief engraving. Barrel length was 26". Butterfield & Butterfield, April 1997.

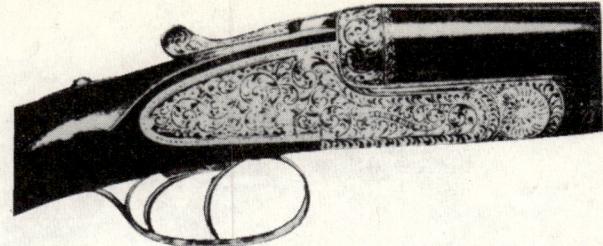

Westley Richards Deluxe Sidelock

Westley Richards Magazine Rifle

ROBERT WHEELER
SEE English Military Firearms

WHITE, ROLLIN
Lowell, Massachusetts

Pocket Pistol

A .32 or .38 rimfire spur trigger single shot pistol with a 3" or 5" octagonal barrel. Brass or iron frames with walnut grips. The .38 caliber version with the 5" barrel was not produced in large quantities and therefore is worth approximately 25% more than the values listed below. The barrels are marked "Rollin White Arms Co., Lowell, Mass."

Exc.	V.G.	Good	Fair	Poor
—	—	550	300	150

Pocket Revolver

A .22 caliber spur trigger revolver with a 3.25" octagonal barrel and 7-shot cylinder. The brass frame silver-plated, barrel blued and grips of walnut. This revolver was marked in a variety of ways including "Rollin White Arms Co., Lowell, Mass.", "Lowell Arms Co., Lowell, Mass.", or "Made for Smith & Wesson by Rollin White Arms Co., Lowell, Mass." Approximately 10,000 were made during the late 1860s.

Exc.	V.G.	Good	Fair	Poor
—	—	400	150	75

WHITNEY ARMS COMPANY
(INCLUDING)
ELI WHITNEY, SR. / P. & E.W. BLAKE / ELI WHITNEY, JR.

As the United States' first major commercial arms maker, Eli Whitney's New Haven plant, which began production in 1798 and continued under family control for the next ninety years, was one of the more important American arms manufactories of the nineteenth century. Its products, accordingly, are eminently collectible. Moreover, during its ninety years of operation, the Whitney clan produced a number of unusual arms, some exact copies of regulation U.S. martial longarms, others variations and derivatives of U.S. and foreign longarms, a variety of percussion revolvers, and finally a variety of single shot and repeating breechloading rifles in an attempt to capture a portion of the burgeoning market in these cartridge arms during the post Civil War period. Contrary to the prevailing myth, Eli Whitney, Sr., who also invented the cotton gin, did NOT perfect a system of interchangeability of parts in the arms industry. His contributions in this line were more as a propagandist for the concept that was brought to fruition by others, notably Simeon North and John Hall.

Eli Whitney, Sr. Armory Muskets, 1798-1824.1798 U.S. Contract Muskets, Types I-IV

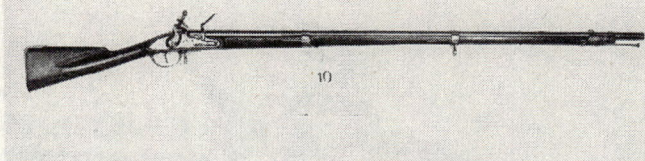

On 14 January 1798 Eli Whitney, Sr., having convinced the U.S. War Department that he could mass produce interchangeable parts muskets, was awarded a contract for 10,000 muskets following the "Charlesville" (French M1766) pattern then also being copied at the newly opened Springfield Armory and most of the U.S. musket contractors. Whitney's 1798 contract muskets measure between 58-7/8" and 57-3/4" in overall length, with the longer arms delivered earlier. The .69 caliber smoothbore barrels measure approximately 44", though most are shy of that length by anywhere from 1/16" to a maximum of 1-1/4". Lockplates are flat with a beveled edge and are marked "U.STATES" in a curve on the pointed tail and with a perched eagle with down folded wings over "NEW HAVEN" forward of the cock. Four differences in the material and manner of attachment of the pan distinguish the subtypes. The first deliver of 500 muskets in September of 1801 had an integral, faceted iron pan (Type I); the second delivery of 500 muskets in June of 1802 also had faceted iron pans, but were detachable (Type II). The 1,000 muskets delivered in September of 1802 and March of 1803 had faceted, detachable pans, but these were made of brass instead of iron (Type III). The final 8,000 muskets, delivered between 1803 and 1809, had detachable brass pans with a rounded bottom that Whitney copied from the French M1777 musket (Type IV) and a rounded cock, also copied from the French M1777 musket. Generally speaking, due to the limited production of Types I - III, they should command a higher price; prices are given for the more common Type IV 1798 contract musket. It should be noted however, that about 1804 Whitney delivered 112 Type IV muskets to Connecticut's "1st Company of Governor's Foot Guards". Although similar to the Type IV musket, these 112 arms are distinguished by the absence of the "U.STATES" on the tail of the lock and the addition of the name "CONNECTI-CUT" to the left side plate. Such an arm should demand a considerable premium over the usual Type IV musket.

Exc.	V.G.	Good	Fair	Poor
—	—	3000	1000	500

Whitney Connecticut, New York, and U.S. 1812 Contract Muskets

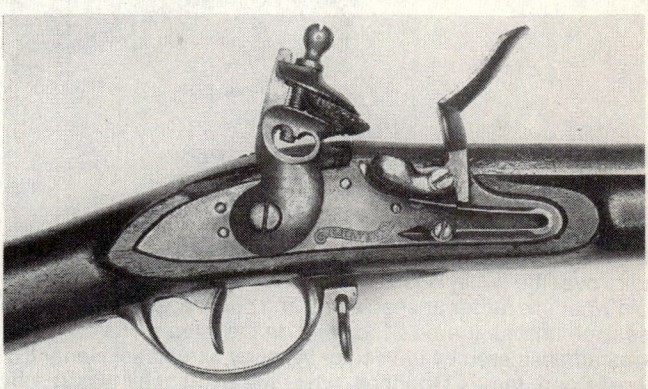

In 1808 Whitney received a contract from the state of New York for 2,000 muskets. In 1810, he received a second contract from the same source for an additional 2,000 muskets, all of which were eventually delivered by mid-1813. In the interim, in 1809, the state of Connecticut contracted with Whitney to deliver 700 muskets per year over the next three years. With the outbreak of the War of 1812, in July of 1812, a contract was let to Eli Whitney for 15,000 muskets (later extended by another 3,000 muskets), conforming to the pattern he had made for the state of New York, but with 42" long barrels. All of these contract muskets shared most of the same features. Overall length was 58". The .69 caliber smoothbore barrel was nominally 42", though the two state contracts did not rigidly enforce that dimension. The lockplate of these muskets bore the inscription "NEW HAVEN" within a curving scroll forward of the cock. Like the Type III 1798 U.S. contract muskets, the lockplates incorporated a detachable round bottomed brass pan and a round faced cock. The stock was distinguished by having a low, virtually nonextant comb similar to that of the 1816 musket pattern. The New York state contract muskets are distinguished by having the state ownership mark "SNY" on the axis of the barrel near the breech. (It should be noted that the first 1,000 muskets delivered under the U.S. 1812 contract were also delivered to New York, but these have the mark across the breech at right angles to the axis of the barrel.) The Connecticut contract muskets are distinguishable by having the state ownership mark "S.C." (for "state of Connecticut" on the barrel and the top of the comb of the stock. On Connecticut muskets in better condition, the Connecticut coat-of-arms (a shield with three clusters of grape vines) should also be visible struck into the wood on the left side of the musket opposite the lock. Verifiable Connecticut and New York contract muskets should bring a premium over the U.S. contract muskets.

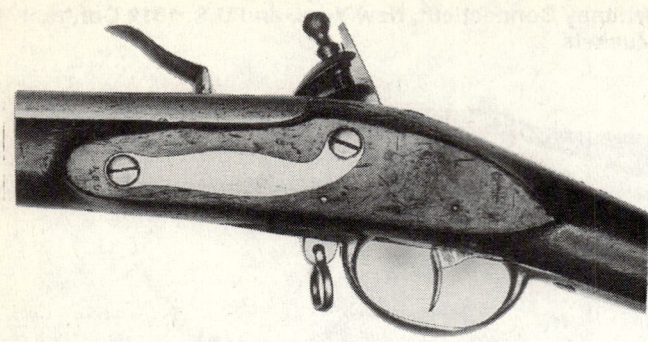

Exc.	V.G.	Good	Fair	Poor
—	—	2750	1000	500

Whitney Armory Muskets, 1825-1842

Eli Whitney died in 1825. Although he had a son destined to take over the family business, Eli Whitney, Jr. was only 5 years old when his father passed away and could assume legal possession until he turned 21 in 1842. In the interim, the company was administered by the senior Whitney's trustees, Henry Edwards and James Goodrich, while the plant itself was run by Whitney's nephews, Philo and Eli Whitney Blake. During their control of the factory, three contracts were fulfilled for the U.S. government, one awarded in August of 1822 for 15,000 muskets (delivered between 1826 and 1830), a second awarded in March of 1830 for 8,750 muskets (delivered between 1831 and 1836) and a final contract in January of 1840 for 3,000 muskets (delivered between 1840 and 1842). An additional 6,750 were delivered under annual allotments granted by the War Department between 1835 and 1839 over and above the contracts for distribution to the states under the 1808 Militia Act. Although the 1840 contract had originally called for U.S. M1840 muskets, in April of that year, the contract was altered so that Whitney's plant could continue to deliver what it had delivered consistently from 1824, the U.S. M1816/1822 flintlock musket.

Whitney (and P. & E.W. Blake) U.S. M1816/1822 Contract Muskets

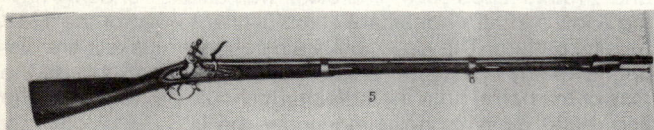

The U.S. M1816/1822 muskets manufactured at Whitney's Armory were identical to those produced at the U.S. Armories at Springfield and Harpers Ferry. The overall length was 57-3/4". The 42" long, .69 caliber smoothbore barrels were finished with a browning solution until 1831; after that date the metal was left in the polished "bright." The stock and the lock reflect Whitney's earlier attempts impart his design elements into the U.S. patterns. The stock had the low comb of his M1812 musket and the lock incorporated the rounded cock and round bottomed brass pan that he had championed from the French M1777 musket. The lock markings varied during the period that the arm was produced, though all were marked on the pointed tail with the vertical stamp: "NEW HAVEN" arced around the date (1825-1830), or in three vertical lines: "NEW / HAVEN / (date: 1831-1842)". Those made between 1825 and 1830 under the direct supervision of Whitney's nephews bore the two line mark "U.S. / P. & E.W. BLAKE" forward of the cock; those made from 1830 to 1837 bear the "U.S" over "E. WHITNEY" with a crossed arrow and olive branch between; after 1837 the crossed arrow and olive branch motif was eliminated in favor of the simple two lines. In addition to the Whitney Armory's federal contracts, Whitney executed at least one contract with the state of South Carolina in the mid-1830s for

an estimated 800 to 2,000 muskets. Basically identical in configuration to the federal contract muskets, the South Carolina muskets were distinguished by the substitution of "S.C." for "U.S." over the "E. WHITNEY" stamp of the lockplate. They also bear the state ownership mark "So. CAROLINA" on the top of the barrel. Due to their relative rarity and Confederate usage (especially if altered to percussion by means of a brazed bolster), the South Carolina contract arms should bring a considerable premium.

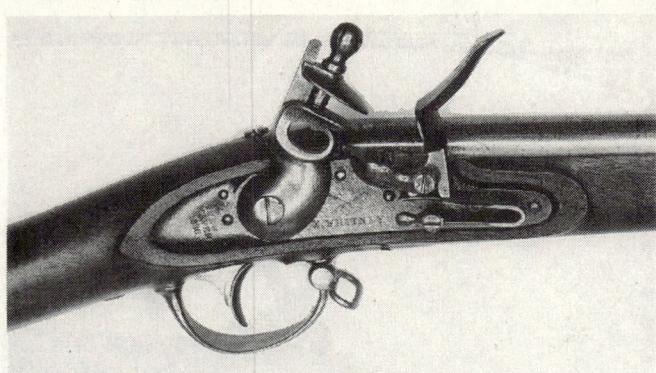

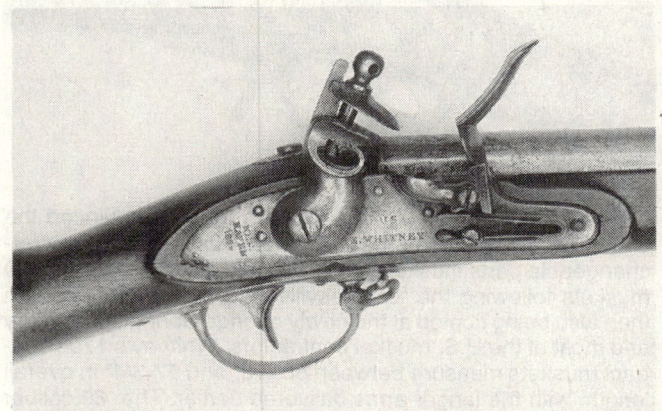

Exc.	V.G.	Good	Fair	Poor
—	—	4000	1850	600

Whitney Armory U.S. M1816/M1822 Muskets, Altered to Percussion

From 1850 through 1856, many of the contract muskets in store at the U.S. arsenals were altered from flintlock to percussion by means of the "Belgian" or "cone-in-barrel" method. The system of alteration involved the removal of the flintlock battery from the lock, filing in the screw holes from those parts, substituting a percussion hammer for the cock, plugging the vent, removing the breech plug so as to "upset" the upper, right hand side top of the barrel, drilling and threading the "upset" section for a cone, reinserting the breech plug, and screwing in a new percussion cone. The percussioned musket was effective but the barrel was considerably weakened by the process, and while some were rifled during the American Civil War, most saw service in that conflict as smoothbores. As a general rule, the muskets so altered generally command about one-third the price of the arm in original flintlock. Exceptions are those with state ownership marks (eg. "OHIO" in the stock), with regimental marks, or with the so-called "Sea Fencible" butt plate.

Whitney Armory U.S. M1816./M1822 Muskets, Flintlock or Altered to Percussion and Adapted with "Sea Fencible" Heavy Butt Plates

A number of the Whitney U.S. M1816/M1822 muskets were delivered to the Commonwealth of Massachusetts under the terms of the 1808 Militia Act. Many of these were subsequently altered to percussion at the Watertown Arsenal near Boston for the state after 1850. At some time in their career both some of the flintlock arms and those that had been altered to percussion were adapted to a heavy brass buttplate with a peculiar knob at its heel. In the process the butt stock was usually narrowed to conform to the width of the new butt plate. Because many of the muskets encountered with this butt plate bore the inspection mark of Samuel Fuller ("SF/V" within a lozenge), these arms were initially considered to have been made for the Massachusetts "Sea Fencible" organizations formed during and after the War of 1812. That appellation, however, has been dismissed, although the exact purpose of the new buttplate and the date of its application are not known. These buttplates are usually (but not necessarily) found on Whitney contract muskets and invariably marked with the Massachusetts state ownership mark "MS" on the barrel as well as rack numbers on the tang of the buttplate itself. Despite the unknown purpose of these arms, they command a considerable premium over standard flintlock or altered to percussion Whitney muskets.

Exc.	V.G.	Good	Fair	Poor
—	—	1250	650	250

Eli Whitney Jr. Armory Rifles and Rifle-Muskets, 1842-1865

Upon reaching the age of 21 in 1842, Eli Whitney, Jr. assumed command of his late father's gun making empire. Although he realized that the armory required updating to meet the improved tolerances adopted by the U.S. War Department, he also realized that a profit might be made in turning out arms of lesser standards for independent sale to the militia or the states. As a result, the younger Whitney's product line included not only several of the regulation U.S. longarms, but also a number of "good and serviceable" militia arms, including:

Whitney U.S. M1841 Contract Rifle (unaltered)

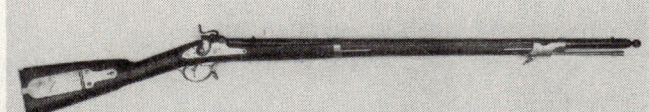

Between 1842 and 1855 Eli Whitney, Jr. received five contracts from the U.S. War Department to manufacture the newly adopted U.S. M1841 percussion rifle: 7,500 on October of 1842 (delivered between 1844 and 1847), 7,500 in March of 1848, subsequently extended to 10,000 in January of 1849 (delivered between 1849 and 1853) 5,000 (previously contracted for by Edward K. Tryon) in October of 1848 (delivered contiguous with the 1848 contract for 10,000), 5,000 in 1853 (delivered between 1853 and 1855), and 100 in 1855 (delivered that year). All except the final 1,100 delivered in 1855 conformed to the model made at Harpers Ferry, and of those 1,100, the only difference of 500 of them was the ramrod. This rifle was 49" in length, overall, having a 33" long browned barrel with .54 caliber rifled (7 groove) bore. The barrel bears the stamp of inspection at the breech, usually "U S /(inspectors' initials) / P", while the left flat (after mid-1848 for Whitney rifles) should also bear the stamping "STEEL" to indicate that the barrel had been rolled from "cast steel". Furniture is brass, the buttplate bearing the stamped letters, "U S". The lockplate is flat with a beveled edge and bears the horizontal two line inscription "E. WHITNEY" / "U S" forward of the hammer and the vertical, two line inscription "N. HAVEN" / (date) on the tail. (The date also appears on the breech plug tang). As originally made, the M1841 rifle was not adapted for a bayonet, though

several modifications were made to the rifle between 1855 and 1862 to effect that adaptation.

Exc.	V.G.	Good	Fair	Poor
—	—	3500	1250	500

Whitney U.S. M1841/1855 Contract Rifle, Adapted to Saber Bayonet & Long Range Sights

Before the final 600 rifles (of the 2,600 made in 1855) left the factory, the U.S. War Department contracted with Whitney to bring them up to the standards of the modified U.S. M1841 rifle then being produced or adapted at the Harpers Ferry Armory. The adaptation was two fold. First, a long range rear "ladder" style rear sight, having a 2-1/4" base was soldered to the top of the barrel; then a 1/2" long bayonet lug with 1" guide was brazed to the right side of the barrel, 2-1/2" from the muzzle. To permit disassembly, the old front band was removed and replaced with a shortened version. A new ramrod (also applied to 500 rifles without this adaptation), having an integral iron head cupped for the newly adopted "Minie ball" replaced the flat brass headed ramrod to complete the process; the rifle remained in .54 caliber with 7 grooves. Neither was the front sight modified. Bayonets were furnished by the Ames Manufacturing Company on a separate contract. Rifles so adapted at the Whitney Armory are among the rarer variants of the U.S. M1841 line and prices reflect that rarity.

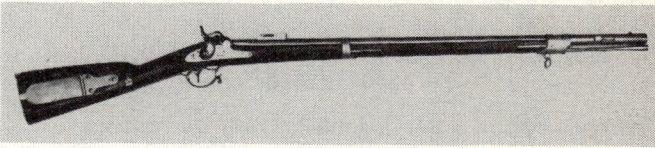

Exc.	V.G.	Good	Fair	Poor
—	—	4000	1750	650

Whitney U.S. M1841 Contract Rifles, Adapted to Saber Bayonets and Long Range rear sights (Colt 1862 Adaptation)

A large number of unaltered U.S. M1841 rifles remained on hand in U.S. Arsenals when the Civil War broke out, primarily those of Whitney's and Robbins & Lawrence's manufacture. To upgrade these rifles, revolver maker, Samuel Colt arranged to purchase 10,500 and adapt them to bayonets and long range sights. The sight that he affixed consisted of the two leaf rear sight he had been using on his revolving rifles, with one leaf flopping forward and one flopping backward from the 100 yard block. The saber bayonet lug he attached consisted of a blued clamping ring with integral 1/2" long lug attached that could fastened to the barrel so that the lug projected from the right side. These lugs were numbered both to the bayonet and the rifle's barrel, the number appearing on the lower surface of the barrel just behind the location of the clamping ring. Colt also bored the rifles up to .58 caliber, leaving some with 7 grooves but rerifling others with 3 wide grooves. An estimated half of the 10,200 rifles so modified by Colt were of Whitney's earlier production. Due to the Colt association, rifles so modified usually command slightly higher prices than other Civil War adaptations for saber or socket bayonets.

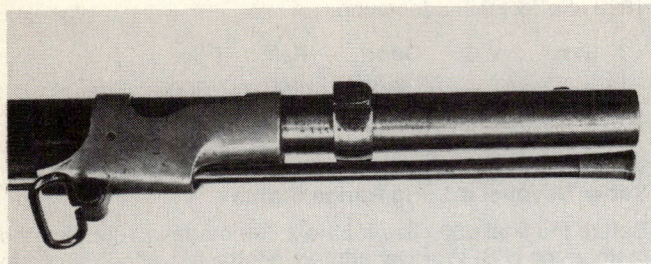

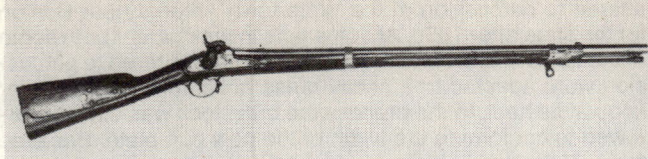

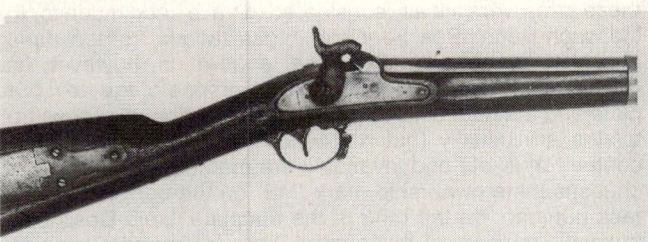

Exc.	V.G.	Good	Fair	Poor
—	—	3500	1250	600

Whitney South Carolina Contract M1841 Rifle

To meet the perceived needs of South Carolina during the anti-slavery debates following the Mexican War Annexation, Whitney produced a variant of the U.S. M1841 rifle for that state, delivering only 274 in 1849. The marking of this rifle differed only in having the letters "S C" on the plate beneath the "E. WHITNEY" stamp. Because South Carolina had previously contracted for 1,000 variant M1841 rifles from William Glaze & Co. in 1853 which accepted a socket bayonet, Whitney provided the 274 1849 dated rifles with that provision also, although the lug was located under the barrel instead of atop it. Because the socket bayonet dominated the forward 3" of the barrel, the front sight was relocated to the top of the upper strap of the front band. Rifles from this contract are exceedingly rare.

Exc.	V.G.	Good	Fair	Poor
—	—	4500	2500	950

Whitney "Good & Serviceable" M1841 Derivatives

From parts or entire rifles rejected for his federal contracts for U.S. M1841 rifles, between 1848 and 1860, Eli Whitney, Jr. assembled a number of rifles similar in overall characteristics to the federal contract rifles but differing both in quality and in a number of minor details. At least four variants were produced between 1855 and 1862 and sold to various states or independent militia companies. Distinguishing characteristics of these four are:

Type I. M1841 rifle adapted to saber bayonet but not to long range sights.

A 1/2" long saber bayonet lug (either with or without the 1" guide) brazed to the right side of the barrel; long front band replaced with short double strapped band left over from 1855 contract. Some of this type (without 1" guide) are known with "OHIO" state ownership marks and are thought to be from among the 420 purchased by the state in 1861 from Schuyler, Hartley & Graham. Examples are known with the lockplate dated 1855 and without any date or "US" stamp below "E. WHITNEY".

Type II. M1841 rifle adapted to saber bayonet and Sharps long range sight.

These rifles also bear the 1/2" brazed saber bayonet lug (with the 1" guide) and the short front band, but they also have a Sharps M1853 "ladder" rear sight added in lieu of the standard notched iron block. Moreover, rifles in this configuration lack the brass patchbox lid and its underlying cavity for implements and greased patches.

Type III. M1841 rifle adapted to socket bayonet and Sharps long range sight.

These late production (1859-1860) derivatives of the M1841 rifle are adapted to the Sharps long range sight used on the Type II. rifles but have a patch box. Unlike standard production, however, it is covered with an iron lid and hingle. The triggerguard strap is also iron. Lock plates delete both the date from the tail and the "US" under "E. WHITNEY." An iron stud is added below the barrel near the muzzle for a socket bayonet, necessitating the relocation of the brass blade front sight to the upper strap of the forward band. Probably less than 100 of this configuration were made, making it the most desirable of the derivative M1841 rifles.

Type IV. M1841 rifle unadapted using modified parts.

Rifles of this configuration use the same markings as the type III rifles but delete entirely the patch box and its lid (like the type II rifles). The triggerguard strap is iron and the lock screws seem to be the same as Whitney used for his Whitney short Enfield derivative rifles. It is suspected that these rifles were purchased from New York dealers and sold to Georgia during the secession crisis of 1860-1861, thereby enhancing their collector's value, though in general Whitney M1841 derivative rifles are equal in pricing:

Exc.	V.G.	Good	Fair	Poor
—	—	2500	1250	500

Whitney M1842 Rifled Musket Derivative

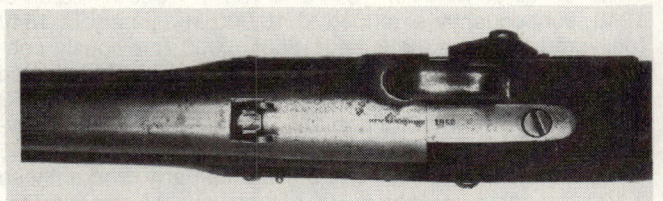

Using rejected U.S. M1842 barrels sold at auction by the Springfield Armory, Whitney assembled approximately 2,000 .69 caliber rifled muskets that he exchanged with the state of New Hampshire in 1858 for a number of old flintlock muskets owned by that state. These rifled muskets exhibit a number of anomalies from the U.S. M1842 musket, although overall length (57-3/4") and the barrel length (42") remain the same as that musket, the bores are rifles with 7 narrow grooves, and in addition to the dates and inspection marks placed at Springfield usually bear the state ownership mark "NEW HAMPSHIRE" on the top of the barrel. In finishing these rifled muskets, Whitney utilized a number of parts from other gun makers, including Sharps M1853 "ladder" style carbine rear sights, bands from the Robbins & Lawrence P1853 Enfield rifle-musket contract, and internal lock parts remaining from his M1841 rifles. Parts that are unique to these arms include the iron nosecap and the flat lockplate. The lockplates are unmarked, but the barrels usually show a letter/number code common to Whitney's production during this period. Despite a production of approximately 2,000 muskets, the survival rate for this type of arm is quite low.

Exc.	V.G.	Good	Fair	Poor
—	—	2500	950	400

Whitney P1853 "Long Enfield" Rifle-Musket Derivative

Having secured a number of bands and other furniture from the Robbins & Lawrence contract for P1853 Enfield rifle-muskets, about 1859 Whitney developed a derivative of that arm that combined those bands with a 40" barrel .58 caliber, rifled with 7 grooves that basically resembled the configuration of the U.S. M1855 rifle-musket, a copy of which Whitney was also making. The 56" long rifle-musket that resulted was sold to state militia companies and two states, Maryland purchasing 2,000 and Georgia contracting for 1,700 (of which 1,225 were delivered). Although several of the components of the furniture were from the Robbins & Lawrence contract, the nosecap was pewter (Enfield style), and the iron buttplate and brass triggerguard bow/iron strap were of a style peculiar to Whitney' Enfield series. The rear sight resembled the ladder pattern of the U.S. M1855 rifle musket. The unique flat, unbeveled lockplate simply bears the one line stamp, "E. WHITNEY" forward of the hammer.

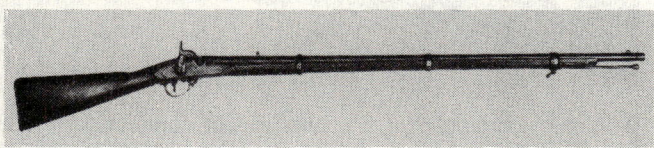

Exc.	V.G.	Good	Fair	Poor
—	—	2750	1250	600

Whitney P1853 "Short Enfield" Rifle Derivative

At the same time that Whitney developed his "Long Enfield" Derivative Rifle-Musket, he also prepared a short version of it similar to the British P1856 sergeant's rifle. Having an overall length of 49", the rifle version had a 33" long barrel in .58 caliber and rifled with 7 grooves like the rifle-musket. The furniture was basically the same as the rifle-musket as well, with a pewter nosecap, iron buttplate, and combination brass bow and iron strap triggerguard (although some variants are known with all brass P1853 triggerguards). The two iron bands were from the Robbins & Lawrence contract salvage, as were the brass lock screw washers. The flat, unbeveled lockplate is the same style as used in the Long Enfield derivative rifle-muskets and is similarly marked "E. WHITNEY" forward of the hammer. In the manufacture of the rifle, four variants evolved, as follows:

Type I. Butt stock incorporated an oval iron patch box; front and rear sights were of standard U.S. M1841 configuration and no provision was made for a saber bayonet.

Type II. Butt stock continued to incorporate an oval iron patch box; rear sight was now the long range "ladder" type on a 2-5/16" base as used on the long Enfield rifle-musket derivative. Front sight was an iron block with integral blade. A 1/2" long saber bayonet lug was added to the right side of the barrel.

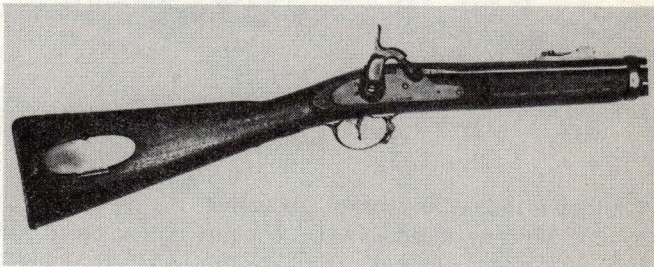

Type III. The oval iron patchbox was deleted from the butt stock. Front and rear sights remain as in Type II, as does bayonet lug.

Type IV. Identical to type III but with a new single leaf rear sight on a 1-1/4" long base.

Total production of these rifles is estimated to have been between 800 and 1,000, with approximately half of the number going to southern states. Prices should not vary between the four types; however, confirmed Confederate usage will increase the value significantly.

Exc.	V.G.	Good	Fair	Poor
—	—	3500	1250	600

Whitney M1855 Rifle Derivative

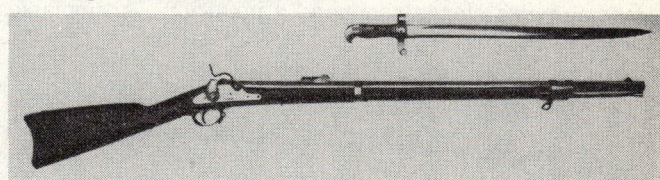

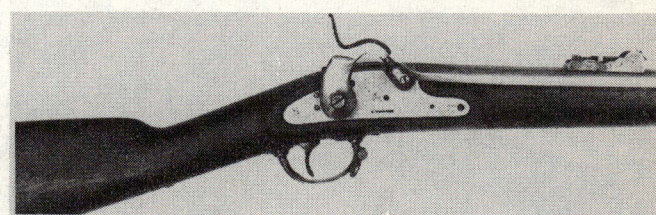

At the same time that Whitney advertised his Enfield derivative series of rifle-muskets and rifles, he also indicated the availability of a short rifle with saber bayonet. This rifle combined rejected barrels made at Harpers Ferry in 1858 for the U.S. M1855 rifles with rejected, unmilled Maynard tape primer lockplates that had been shaved of their top "hump", marked forward of the hammer with the single line stamp, "E. WHITNEY." The buttplate and the triggerguard also conform to that of the U.S. M1855 rifle, but the bands are brass, remaining from Whitney's M1841/1855 rifle contract. Early in production these rifles used round brass lock screw washers following the M1855 pattern; later production used the winged brass lock screw washers that Whitney inherited from the Robbins & Lawrence P1853 rifle-musket contract and that he used on his

Enfield series derivatives. At least two patterns of saber bayonet were used on this rifle.

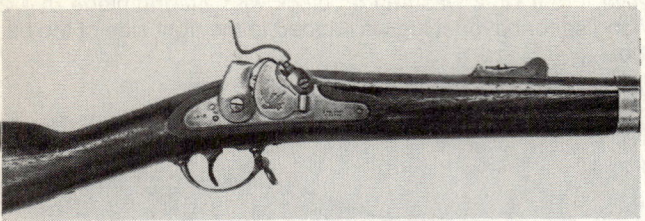

Exc.	V.G.	Good	Fair	Poor
—	—	2500	1000	500

Whitney M1855 Rifle-Musket Derivative

In 1861, Whitney accepted a U.S. contract to produce 40,000 U.S. "M1855" rifle-muskets. What Whitney had in mind under this contract and what the War Department demanded were two different arms. Whitney's product was similar to the U.S. M1855 rifle-musket but differed in a number of respects. The 40" barrel was .58 caliber but was rifled with 7 rather than 3 grooves and was adapted to the English P1853 socket bayonet he had been using on his Enfield derivative rifle-muskets. The initial rear sight, while similar to the U.S. M1855 type, was slightly shorter, having a 2-5/16" base. (On later production, Whitney substituted a shorter, 1-1/4" long base with a single, pierced leaf sight.) The nosecap, moreover was made of pewter, and followed the Enfield pattern rather than being malleable iron of the U.S. M1855 pattern. On later production, Whitney also substituted brass winged lock screw washers from his Enfield derivative series. The lockplates for these arms were drawn from complete Maynard locks made at the federal armories in 1858 and 1859 but later rejected for flaws. Upon these plates Whitney stamped "E. WHITNEY / N. HAVEN", as on his early Connecticut contract M1861 derivative rifle-muskets. Except for the letter/number code, the barrels are unmarked. Examples are known whose stocks bear indications of issue to the 8th Connecticut Infantry during the Civil War, suggesting Whitney may have sold the few made to Connecticut under his first state contract. Arms with these regimental marks should command a premium over unmarked arms.

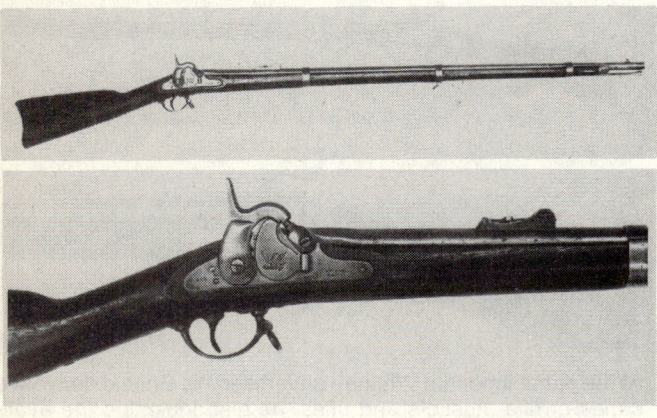

Exc.	V.G.	Good	Fair	Poor
—	—	2500	900	500

Whitney M1861 Connecticut Contract Rifle-Musket Derivative

In 1861 and 1862, Eli Whitney, Jr. entered into two contracts with his home state of Connecticut for respectively 6,000 and 8,000 rifle-muskets generally conforming to the U.S. M1861 rifle musket. A number of exceptions to U.S. model, however, were permitted. On the first contract, the 40" barrels were in .58 caliber but were made with 7 groove rifling instead of 3 groove; on the second contract the arms were made with 3 groove rifling. Nosecaps for both contracts were of the U.S. M1855/1861 pattern but were cast in pewter instead of malleable iron. An exception was also permitted in the rear sights, which initially were the same 1-1/4" long base with pierced single leaf that Whitney had used on his Type IV short Enfield derivative rifles, though later the base was changed to conform to the pattern adopted for the U.S. M1861 rifle-musket but still retaining the single leaf. Lockplates were M1861 style, marked forward of the hammer "E. WHITNEY / N. HAVEN" on early production and with an eagle surmounting a panoply of flags and trophies over "WHITNEYVILLE" on later production. The barrels bore the typical Whitney letter/number code and were adapted to the Enfield pattern socket bayonets rather than the U.S. M1855 socket bayonets. Later production occasionally bears the inspection letters "G.W.Q."

Exc.	V.G.	Good	Fair	Poor
—	—	2500	950	400

Whitney "High Humpback" Lockplate M1861 Rifle-Musket Derivative

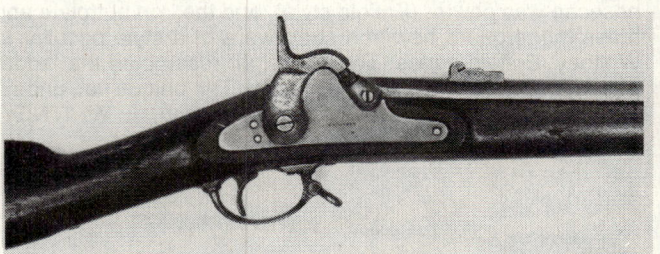

With the completion of his Connecticut contracts, Whitney combined the excess parts from its production with some of the unmilled and unshaved lockplates that he still had on hand from his M1855 Rifle Derivatives. The 56" long rifle-muskets that resulted have 40" barrels in .58 caliber with 3 groove rifling and a rear sight that conforms to the U.S. M1861 pattern that Whitney began making in 1863. The flat, beveled unmilled lockplates bear the two line stamp "E. WHITNEY / N. HAVEN" that Whitney had used on his M1855 rifle-musket derivative and on the early M1861 Connecticut contract rifle-muskets, but showing considerable wear, to the extent that the second line is often incomplete or missing entirely. Photograph evidence indicates that the 21st Connecticut Infantry received some of these rifle-muskets. They are often mistaken as a southern purchase, which artificially raises the asking prices.

Exc.	V.G.	Good	Fair	Poor
—	—	2500	950	400

Whitney "Manton" M1861 Rifle-Musket Derivative

In order to dispose of some of his inferior arms from the second Connecticut state contract, Whitney assembled at least 1,300 bearing a fictitious Old English lock stamp "Manton" forward of the hammer and the date "1862" on its tail. In most respects this arm resembled the U.S. M1861 rifle musket, complete with 3 groove rifling in its .58 caliber, 40" barrel with typical Whitney letter/number code near the muzzle (and often also marked "G.W.Q. on its left flat). Nosecaps, in typical Whitney style, were case from pewter instead of being formed from malleable iron. The rear sight closely follows the M1861 pattern but lacks the step on its side walls since it utilized a simple pierced leaf instead of the compound double leaf of the M1861 rifle-musket. These arms were disposed of in the New York City market after the 1863 Draft Riot and issued to the New York National Guard.

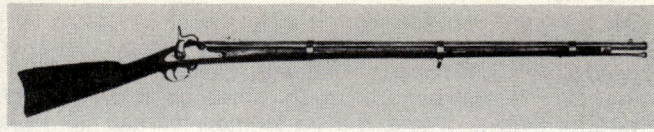

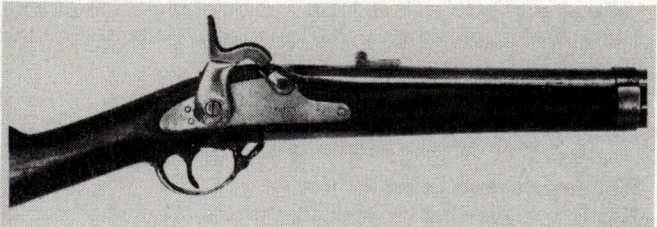

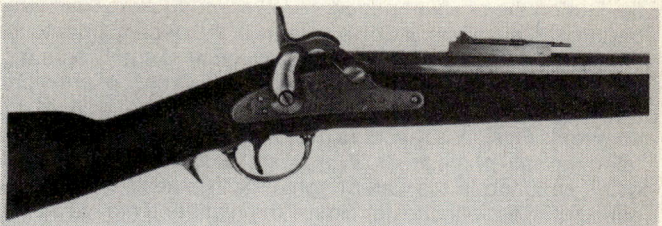

Exc.	V.G.	Good	Fair	Poor
—	—	3000	1250	600

Whitney "Direct Vent" M1861 Rifle-Musket Derivatives

In his continued efforts to dispose of surplus and rejected parts from his Connecticut and federal contracts, Whitney devised in 1863 a rifle-musket generally conforming to the M1861 rifle-musket except in two notable features. The bolster, instead of projecting considerably away from the barrel and having a clean-out screw was relatively short and flat faced. The process of making this bolster eliminated one production sequence, since it was not possible to drill the hole for the cone directly to the barrel. To accommodate the new cone position, the lockplates were made flat, without the bevel, and inletted flush with the stock. Lockplates bear the eagle surmounting the panoply of flags and trophies over "WHITNEYVILLE" stamp forward of the hammer, and are known with "1863" on the tail or without any date. The rear sight is the same as used on the "Manton" rifle-musket derivative. Arms with barrels than 40", 39", and 30" exist, all in .58 caliber with 3 groove rifling; however, the shortest of these may be postwar modifications for cadet use. Quantities made are not known, but surviving examples suggest limited production, probably to use faulty parts from the 1863 federal contract.

Exc.	V.G.	Good	Fair	Poor
—	—	2500	950	400

Whitney U.S. M1861 Contract Rifle-Musket

In October of 1863, Whitney secured a contract with the U.S. War Department to produce 15,000 U.S. M1861 rifle-muskets. The arms manufactured under this contract conform in all respects to the Springfield Model adopted in 1861. The 40" barrel is in .58 caliber and rifled with 3 grooves; its rear sight conforms to the two leaf model with stepped side walls. Nosecap is M1861 style and made of malleable iron. Socket bayonets furnished with them conform to the U.S. M1855/M1861 pattern. Marks include "US" on buttplate and standard inspection marks on barrel and stock. Lockplate marked with eagle surmounting letters "US" forward of the hammer and "WHIT-NEYVILLE" on the forward projection of the plate; date, "1863" or "1864" stamped on tail of the plate.

Exc.	V.G.	Good	Fair	Poor
—	—	2000	900	400

Whitney U.S. Navy Contract Rifle

In July of 1861, Whitney entered a contact with the U.S. Navy to produce 10,000 rifles of the "Plymouth Pattern". So called after the U.S. Navy warship whereupon the first Harpers Ferry trial rifles had been developed, the new Navy rifle borrowed many of its characteristics from the French M1846 "carbine a tige." Overall length was 50" with a 34" long barrel bearing a saber bayonet lug with guide extending nearly to the muzzle on its right side. The bore was .69 caliber, rifled with three broad lands and grooves. The rear sight copied the French M1846 and M1859 styles, i.e. it has an elevating ladder but no sidewalls. On early production the sights are serially numbered to the rifle's serial number (appearing on the breech plug tang). Barrels bear the standard U.S. inspection marks on the left quarter flat and the production date ("1863" or "1864") on the top of the barrel near the breech. Two lock markings have been encountered. The earlier production uses flat beveled plate marked with the date "1863" on its tail and an eagle surmounting a panoply of flags and trophies over the name "WHITNEYVILLE." In later (after serial no. 3,000) the lock's tail is marked "1864" and the stamping forward of the hammer matches that on the U.S. M1861 Whitney contract rifle-muskets, i.e. a small eagle over "U S" and "WHITNEYVILLE" in the forward projection of the plate. Inspector's initials (F.C.W.) appear on the barrel and in a cartouche on the stock.

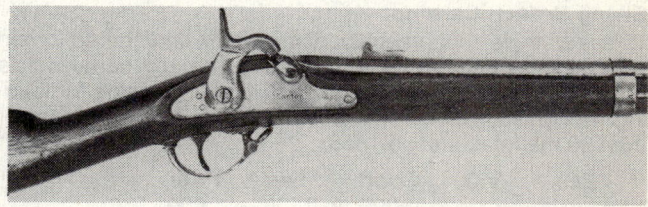

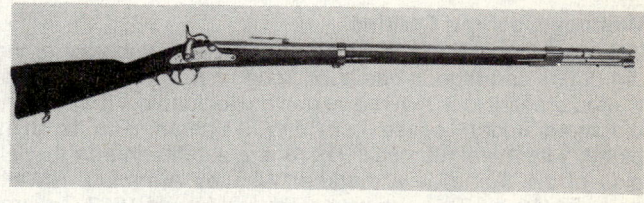

Exc.	V.G.	Good	Fair	Poor
—	—	3000	950	400

The Whitney Arms Company, 1865-1888

With the close of the American Civil War, Eli Whitney, Jr. again turned his eyes to the manufacture of inexpensive arms from parts remaining on hand from his Civil War contracts. Extra barrels were turned into inexpensive muzzleloading shotguns, and a few breechloading designs were toyed with. Following Remington's example, Whitney soon realized that a substantial profit could be made in the production of single shot martial arms for foreign governments. The result was a series of breechloading arms that copied many salient features of the Remington line, including a direct copy after the expiration of the Remington patent for the "rolling block" mechanism. Not until the late 1870's did Whitney acquire the rights to several patents that led to the production of a lever action repeating ri-

fle. During the postwar period, revolver production, which had begun with evasions of Colt's patents in the decade prior to the Civil War, mushroomed with the production of small, spur trigger rimfire cartridge revolvers. Despite the variety of arms produced, by 1883 Whitney was considering the sale of his company. Business reverses over the next five years necessitated the sale of the firm to Winchester in 1888. Primarily interested securing in the patent rights for Whitney's lever action series of rifles, Winchester closed the plant and moved its machinery to New Haven. After ninety years of production the Whitneyville Armory ceased to exist.

Single Barreled Percussion Shotgun

This firearm was manufactured by Whitney out of surplus .58 caliber rifle barrels that were opened up and converted to smoothbore .60 caliber shotgun barrels. They are offered in lengths of 28" to 36" and are marked "Whitney Arms Co., Whitneyville, Conn. Homogeneous Wrought Steel". The finish is blued, with varnished walnut stocks that are crudely checkered. There were approximately 2,000 manufactured between 1866 and 1869. These guns are rarely encountered on today's market.

Exc.	V.G.	Good	Fair	Poor
—	—	850	400	150

Double Barreled Percussion Shotgun

The specifications for this version are similar to that of the single barrel except that there are two side-by-side barrels with double locks and hammers and double triggers. They are slightly more common than the single barreled version.

Exc.	V.G.	Good	Fair	Poor
—	—	750	300	150

Swing-Breech Carbine

This is a single shot breechloading carbine chambered for the .46-caliber rimfire cartridge. It has a 22" round barrel with a button-released breechblock that swings to the side for loading. The finish is blued, with a walnut stock. There were fewer than 50 manufactured in 1866.

Exc.	V.G.	Good	Fair	Poor
—	—	3000	1500	600

Whitney-Cochran Carbine

This is a single shot breechloading carbine chambered for the .44 rimfire cartridge. It has a 28" round barrel with a lever activated breechblock that raises upward for loading. It was manufactured under license from J.W. Cochran. The finish is blued, with a walnut stock. There is a saddle ring on the left side of the frame. It is marked "Whitney Arms Co. - Whitneyville, Conn." This gun was produced for the 1867 Government Carbine Trials. There were fewer than 50 manufactured in 1866 and 1867.

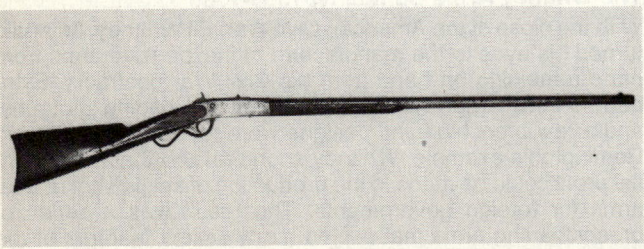

Courtesy Milwaukee Public Museum, Milwaukee, Wisconsin

Exc.	V.G.	Good	Fair	Poor
—	—	2500	1250	600

Excelsior

This is a single-shot rifle chambered for the .38, .44, or .50 rimfire cartridges. It is found with various-length octagonal or round barrels. The finish is blued, with a walnut stock and forearm held on by one barrel band. The breechblock pivots downward for loading. There is a center-mounted hammer. It is marked "Whitney Arms Co. Whitneyville Conn." The shorter barreled carbine versions have a saddle ring on the frame. There were approximately 200 manufactured between 1866 and 1870.

Exc.	V.G.	Good	Fair	Poor
—	—	1750	750	300

Whitney-Howard Lever Action

This is a single-shot breechloader that is chambered for the .44 rimfire cartridge. It has also been noted as a shotgun chambered for 20 gauge smoothbore with barrels from 30" to 40" in length. The rifle version has barrel lengths from 22" to 28". The breechblock is opened by means of a combination lever and triggerguard. There is also a carbine version with barrel lengths of 18.5" or 19". There were approximately 2,000 manufactured totally between 1866 and 1870. Values are as follows:

Shotgun

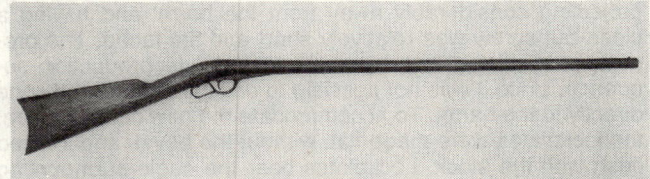

Courtesy Buffalo Bill Historical Center, Cody, Wyoming

Exc.	V.G.	Good	Fair	Poor
—	—	500	250	100

Rifle

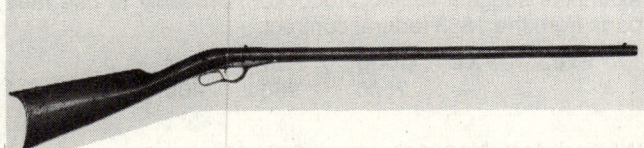

Courtesy Milwaukee Public Museum, Milwaukee, Wisconsin

Exc.	V.G.	Good	Fair	Poor
—	—	600	300	150

Carbine

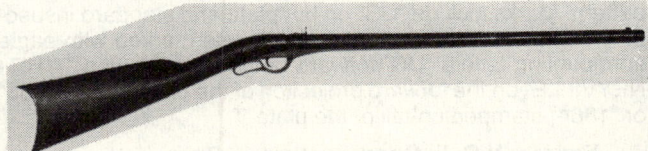

Courtesy Milwaukee Public Museum, Milwaukee, Wisconsin

Exc.	V.G.	Good	Fair	Poor
—	—	750	400	200

Whitney Phoenix

There is little known about the origin of this model. It is built on a patent issued to Whitney in 1874. There are a number of variations that are all marked "Phoenix, Patent May 24, 74." The Whitney name is not marked on any of the versions. They are all single-shot breechloaders with a breechblock that lifts to the right side and upward for loading. The barrels are all blued, with either case-colored or blued receivers and walnut stocks. There were approximately 25,000 total manufactured between 1867 and 1881. The models and values are as follows:

Courtesy Milwaukee Public Museum, Milwaukee, Wisconsin

Courtesy Milwaukee Public Museum, Milwaukee, Wisconsin

Gallery Rifle

This version is chambered for the .22 rimfire caliber and has a 24" half-octagonal barrel. Its production was quite limited.

Exc.	V.G.	Good	Fair	Poor
—	—	1000	500	200

Shotgun

This is a smoothbore version chambered for 10, 12, 14, 16, or 22 gauge. It has smoothbore barrels between 26" and 32" in length. There were approximately 5,000 manufactured.

Exc.	V.G.	Good	Fair	Poor
—	—	450	200	100

Military Rifle

This version is chambered for the .433, .45, or .50 caliber centerfire cartridges. It has a 35" round barrel with a full-length, two-piece walnut stock held on by three barrel bands. There were approximately 15,000 manufactured. Many were sent to Central or South America.

Exc.	V.G.	Good	Fair	Poor
—	—	2000	900	400

Schuetzen Rifle

This is a target-shooting version chambered for the .38, .40, or .44 centerfire cartridges. It has either a 30" or 32" octagonal barrel with a Schuetzen-type walnut stock and forearm that features hand checkering. It has a nickel-plated, Swiss-style buttplate and adjustable sights with a spirit level. This model has been noted with double-set triggers. There were few manufactured.

Exc.	V.G.	Good	Fair	Poor
—	—	2500	1000	450

Civilian Carbine

This version is chambered for the .44 caliber centerfire and has a 24" round barrel. The finish is blued, with a case-colored frame and a walnut stock and forearm held on by one barrel band. It has military-type sights, buttplate, and a saddle ring mounted on the frame. There were approximately 500 manufactured.

Courtesy Milwaukee Public Museum, Milwaukee, Wisconsin

Exc.	V.G.	Good	Fair	Poor
—	—	2000	850	400

Military Carbine

This version is chambered for the .433, .45, or .50 centerfire cartridges. It has a 20.5" round barrel and was manufactured for Central and South America. It is very rarely encountered on today's market.

Courtesy Milwaukee Public Museum, Milwaukee, Wisconsin

Courtesy Milwaukee Public Museum, Milwaukee, Wisconsin

Exc.	V.G.	Good	Fair	Poor
—	—	2000	850	400

Whitney-Laidley Model I Rolling Block

Whitney acquired manufacturing rights for this model from the inventors T. Laidley and C.A. Emery, who had received the patent in 1866. Whitney immediately started to modify the action to become competitive with the Remington Rolling Block. There were approximately 50,000 manufactured total between 1871 and 1881. There are a number of variations of this model as follows:

Military Carbine

There were approximately 5,000 manufactured chambered for the .433, .45, or .50 centerfire cartridges. It has a 20.5" round barrel with military-type sights and a saddle ring on the receiver. The finish is blued, with a case-colored frame and a walnut stock. Most of them were shipped to Central or South America.

Exc.	V.G.	Good	Fair	Poor
—	—	1000	550	250

Civilian Carbine

This version is chambered for .44 rimfire or centerfire and .46 rimfire. It has either an 18.5" or 19.5" barrel. It is blued, with a case-colored frame. The stock is walnut. A nickel-plated version is also available. There were approximately 1,000 of this version manufactured.

Exc.	V.G.	Good	Fair	Poor
—	—	850	450	200

Military Rifle

This version is chambered the same as the Military Carbine but has either a 32.5" or 35" round barrel with a full-length two-piece stock held on by three barrel bands. The finish is blued, with a case-colored receiver and a walnut stock. There were approximately 30,000 manufactured. Most were shipped to Central or South America.

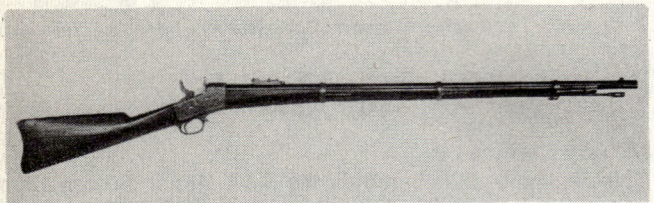

Courtesy Milwaukee Public Museum, Milwaukee, Wisconsin

Exc.	V.G.	Good	Fair	Poor
—	—	1000	550	250

Gallery Rifle

This is a .22 caliber sporting-rifle version with a 24" octagonal barrel. The finish is similar to the Military Rifle. There were approximately 500 manufactured.

Exc.	V.G.	Good	Fair	Poor
—	—	850	400	200

Sporting Rifle

This version is chambered for .38, .40, .44, .45, or .50 centerfire, as well as .32, .38, or .44 rimfire. It features barrel lengths from 24" to 30" in either round or octagonal configurations. The finish is similar to the Military Rifle, and there were approximately 5,000 manufactured.

Exc.	V.G.	Good	Fair	Poor
—	—	1250	650	300

Creedmoor No. 1 Rifle

This version is chambered for the .44 caliber cartridge and has a 32" or 34" barrel that is either round or octagonal in configuration. It has a blued finish with case-colored frame and a hand checkered, select walnut stock and forearm. It features vernier adjustable sights with a spirit level. It is marked "Whitney Creedmoor". There were fewer than 100 manufactured.

Exc.	V.G.	Good	Fair	Poor
—	—	4000	2000	850

Creedmoor No. 2 Rifle

This version is similar to the No. 1 Rifle except that it is chambered for the .40 caliber cartridge with either a 30" or 32" barrel.

Exc.	V.G.	Good	Fair	Poor
—	—	3000	1000	500

Whitney-Remington Model 2 Rolling Block

When Remington's patent for the Rolling Block action expired, Whitney was quick to reproduce the action, labeling it his "New Improved System." It is essentially quite similar to Remington's Rolling Block and is easily recognized when compared with the Model 1 because it has only two parts—the hammer and the breechblock. The frame is also rounded. The tang on this model is marked "Whitney Arms Company, New Haven Ct USA". There were approximately 50,000 total manufactured between 1881 and 1888. There are a number of variations as follows:

Shotgun

This is a smoothbore version chambered for 12, 14, 16, or 20 gauge. It is offered with barrel lengths between 26" and 30". Twenty inch barrels have also been noted.

Exc.	V.G.	Good	Fair	Poor
—	—	450	200	100

Military Carbine

This version is chambered for the .433 and .45 centerfire cartridges. It has a 20.5" barrel and is blued, with a case-colored receiver and walnut stock. There were approximately 5,000 manufactured. Most were sent to South or Central America.

Exc.	V.G.	Good	Fair	Poor
—	—	1000	550	250

Civilian Carbine

This version is chambered for the .44 rimfire or centerfire cartridge with an 18.5" round barrel. The finish is similar to the Military Carbine. There were approximately 2,000 manufactured.

Exc.	V.G.	Good	Fair	Poor
—	—	1000	550	250

Military Rifle

This version is chambered for the .433, .45, or .50 centerfire cartridge. It has a 32.5" or 35" barrel. It is finished similarly to the Military Carbine. There were approximately 39,000 manufactured.

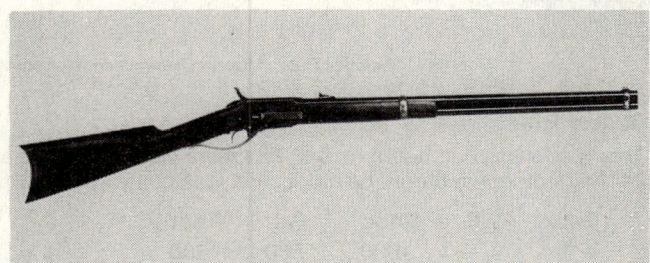

Courtesy Buffalo Bill Historical Center, Cody, Wyoming

Exc.	V.G.	Good	Fair	Poor
—	—	1000	550	250

No. 1 Sporting Rifle

This version is chambered for various popular sporting cartridges and is offered with barrel lengths from 26" to 30", either round or octagonal in configuration. The finish is blued, with a case-colored receiver and a varnished walnut stock. There were many options available that could radically affect the value, and a qualified appraisal would be advisable. There were approximately 3,000 manufactured.

Exc.	V.G.	Good	Fair	Poor
—	—	1250	650	300

No. 2 Sporting Rifle

This is a smaller version of the No. 1 Rifle, chambered for the .22 rimfire, .32, .38, and .44-40 centerfire cartridges. Again, a qualified appraisal would be helpful, as many options can affect the value.

Exc.	V.G.	Good	Fair	Poor
—	—	1000	550	200

Whitney-Burgess-Morse Rifle

This is a lever-action repeating rifle chambered for the .45-70 Government cartridge. There are three variations. All have a magazine tube mounted beneath the barrel with blued finishes and walnut stocks. The barrels are marked "G. W. Morse Patented Oct. 28th 1856". The tang is marked "A. Burgess Patented Jan. 7th, 1873, Patented Oct 19th 1873". There were approximately 3,000 total manufactured between 1878 and 1882. The variations areas follows:

Sporting Rife

This version has a 28" octagonal or round barrel. The magazine tube holds 9 rounds. There are a number of options available that can increase the value drastically; and we recommend competent, individual appraisal. Value given is for a standard model.

Exc.	V.G.	Good	Fair	Poor
—	—	1000	500	250

Military Rifle

This version has a 33" round barrel with a full-length forearm held on by two barrel bands. It features military sights and has an 11-round tubular magazine. It has a bayonet lug and sling swivels. This variation is also found chambered for the .43 Spanish and .42 Russian cartridges. There were approximately 1,000 manufactured.

Exc.	V.G.	Good	Fair	Poor
—	—	3500	1500	500

Carbine

This version has a 22" round barrel with a full-length forearm held on by one barrel band. It has a 7-round tubular magazine and a saddle ring attached to the frame. There were approximately 500 manufactured.

Exc.	V.G.	Good	Fair	Poor
—	—	3500	1500	500

Whitney-Kennedy Rifle

This is a lever-action repeating rifle that was manufactured in two sizes. It has a magazine tube mounted under the barrel and a blued finish with a case-colored lever. The stock is walnut. The barrel is marked "Whitney Arms Co New Haven, Conn. U.S.A." Occasionally, the word "Kennedy" is marked after the Whitney name. There are two major variations. One features a standard-type action lever; and the other, the same "S"-shaped lever that is found on the Burgess model. This version would be worth approximately 10% additional. As with many of the rifles of this era, there were many options available that will affect the values. We strongly recommend securing a qualified appraisal for all but the standard models if a transaction is contemplated. There were approximately 15,000 manufactured between 1879 and 1886. The variations of the Whitney-Kennedy and their values are as follows:

Courtesy Buffalo Bill Historical Center, Cody, Wyoming

Small Frame Sporting Rifle

This version is chambered for the .32-20, .38-40, and the .40-40 cartridges. It has a 24" barrel that is either round or octagonal in configuration. Examples will be noted with either a full-length or half-length tubular magazine.

Exc.	V.G.	Good	Fair	Poor
—	—	1750	750	350

Large Frame Sporting Rifle

This version is chambered for the .40-60, .45-60, .45-75, and the .50-90 cartridges. The .50-caliber version is uncommon and will bring a 20% premium. The barrel lengths offered are 26" or 28".

Exc.	V.G.	Good	Fair	Poor
—	—	2000	900	450

Military Rifle

This is a large-frame model, chambered for the .40-.60, .44-.40, and the .45-60 cartridges. It has a 32.25" round barrel At either an 11- or 16-round tubular magazine. It has a full-length walnut forend held on by two barrel bands and features a bayonet lug and sling swivels. There were approximately 1,000 manufactured. Most were shipped to Central or South America.

Exc.	V.G.	Good	Fair	Poor
—	—	3000	1100	550

Military Carbine

This is built on either the small-frame or large-frame action and is chambered for the .38-40, .44-40, .40-60, or .45-60 cartridges. It has either a 20" or 22" round barrel and a 9- or 12-round tubular magazine, depending on the caliber. It has a short forend held on by a single barrel band. There were approximately 1,000 manufactured. Most were sent to Central or South America.

Courtesy Buffalo Bill Historical Center, Cody, Wyoming

Exc.	V.G.	Good	Fair	Poor
—	—	3000	1100	550

Hooded Cylinder Pocket Revolver

This is an unusual revolver that is chambered for .28 caliber percussion. It has a manually rotated, 6-shot hooded cylinder that has etched decorations. The octagonal barrel is offered in lengths of 3" to 6". There is a button at the back of the frame that unlocks the cylinder so that it can be rotated. The finish is blued, with a brass frame and two-piece rounded walnut grips. It is marked "E. Whitney N. Haven Ct." There were approximately 200 manufactured between 1850 and 1853.

Exc.	V.G.	Good	Fair	Poor
—	—	2500	1250	600

Two Trigger Pocket Revolver

This is a conventional-appearing pocket revolver with a manually rotated cylinder. There is a second trigger located in front of the conventional triggerguard that releases the cylinder so that it can be turned. It is chambered for .32 caliber percussion and has an octagonal barrel from 3" to 6" in length. It has a 5-shot unfluted cylinder that is etched and a brass frame. The remainder is blued, with squared walnut two-piece grips. An iron-frame version is also available, but only 50 were produced. It would bring approximately 60% additional. There were approximately 650 total manufactured between 1852 and 1854.

Courtesy Milwaukee Public Museum, Milwaukee, Wisconsin

Exc.	V.G.	Good	Fair	Poor
—	—	1000	500	250

Whitney-Beals Patent Revolver

This was an unusual, ring-trigger pocket pistol that was made in three basic variations.

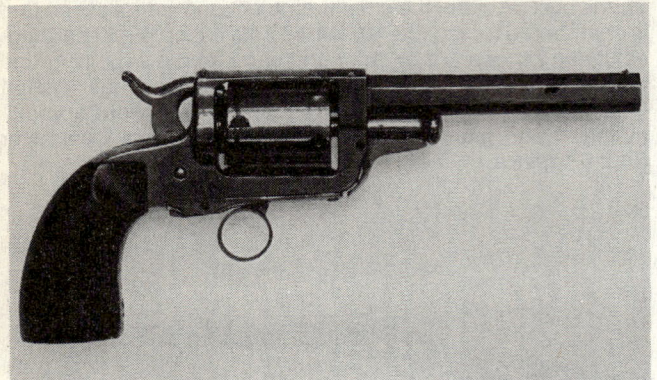

Courtesy Milwaukee Public Museum, Milwaukee, Wisconsin

First Model

This version is chambered for .31-caliber percussion and has barrels of octagonal configuration from 2" to 6" in length. It has a brass frame and a 6-shot cylinder. It is marked "F. Beals/New Haven, Ct." There were only 50 manufactured.

Exc.	V.G.	Good	Fair	Poor
—	—	2500	950	450

.31 Caliber Model

This version has an iron frame and a 7-shot cylinder. The octagonal barrels are from 2" to 6" in length. It is marked "Address E. Whitney/Whitneyville, Ct." There were approximately 2,300 manufactured.

Exc.	V.G.	Good	Fair	Poor
—	—	850	400	200

.28 Caliber Model

Except for the caliber, this model is similar to the .31 Caliber Model. There were approximately 850 manufactured.

Exc.	V.G.	Good	Fair	Poor
—	—	950	500	250

Whitney 1851 Navy

This is a faithful copy of the 1851 Colt Revolver. It is virtually identical. There is a possibility that surplus Colt parts were utilized in the construction of this revolver. There were approximately 400 manufactured in 1857 and 1858.

Exc.	V.G.	Good	Fair	Poor
—	—	3000	1500	650

Whitney Navy Revolver

This is a single action revolver chambered for .36 caliber percussion. It has a standard octagonal barrel length of 7.5". It has an iron frame and a 6-shot unfluted cylinder that is roll engraved. The finish is blued, with a case-colored loading lever and two-piece walnut grips. The barrel is marked either "E. Whitney/N. Haven" or "Eagle Co." There are a number of minor variations on this revolver, and we strongly urge competent appraisal if contemplating a transaction. There were 33,000 total manufactured between 1858 and 1862.

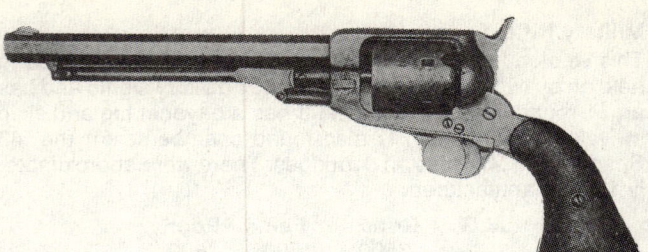

Courtesy Wallis & Wallis, Lewes, Sussex, England

FIRST MODEL

Nearly the entire production of the First Model is marked "Eagle Co." The reason for this marking is unknown. There are four distinct variations of this model. They are as follows:

First Variation

This model has no integral loading-lever assembly and has a thin top strap. There were only 100 manufactured.

Exc.	V.G.	Good	Fair	Poor
—	—	2500	1250	550

Second Variation

This version is similar to the First Variation, with an integral loading lever. There were approximately 200 manufactured.

Exc.	V.G.	Good	Fair	Poor
—	—	1750	900	400

Third Variation

This is similar to the Second, with a three-screw frame instead of four screws. The loading lever is also modified. There were approximately 500 manufactured.

Exc.	V.G.	Good	Fair	Poor
—	—	1500	600	300

Fourth Variation

This version has a rounded frame and a safety notch between the nipples on the rear of the cylinder. There have been examples noted marked "E. Whitney/N. Haven." There were approximately 700 manufactured.

Exc.	V.G.	Good	Fair	Poor
—	—	1500	600	300

SECOND MODEL

First Variation

This version features a more robust frame with a brass trigger-guard. The barrel is marked "E. Whitney/N. Haven." The cylinder pin is secured by a wing nut, and there is an integral loading lever. There were approximately 1,200 manufactured.

Exc.	V.G.	Good	Fair	Poor
—	—	1500	700	300

Second Variation

This version has six improved safety notches on the rear of the cylinder. There were approximately 10,000 manufactured.

Exc.	V.G.	Good	Fair	Poor
—	—	1000	500	250

Third Variation

This version has an improved, Colt-type loading-lever latch. There were approximately 2,000 manufactured.

Exc.	V.G.	Good	Fair	Poor
—	—	1000	500	250

Fourth Variation

This is similar to the Third except the cylinder is marked "Whitneyville". There were approximately 10,000 manufactured.

Exc.	V.G.	Good	Fair	Poor
—	—	1000	500	250

Fifth Variation

This version has a larger triggerguard. There were approximately 4,000 manufactured.

Exc.	V.G.	Good	Fair	Poor
—	—	1000	500	250

Sixth Variation

This version has the larger triggerguard and five-groove rifling instead of the usual seven-groove. There were approximately 2,500 manufactured.

Exc.	V.G.	Good	Fair	Poor
—	—	1000	500	250

Whitney Pocket Revolver

This is a single action revolver chambered for .31 caliber percussion. It has octagonal barrels between 3" and 6" in length. It has a 5-shot unfluted cylinder that is roll engraved and marked "Whitneyville". The frame is iron with a blued finish and a case-colored integral loading lever. The grips are two-piece walnut. The development of this model, as far as models and variations go, is identical to that which we described in the Navy Model designation. The values are different, and we list them for reference. Again, we recommend securing qualified appraisal if a transaction is contemplated. There were approximately 32,500 manufactured from 1858 to 1862.

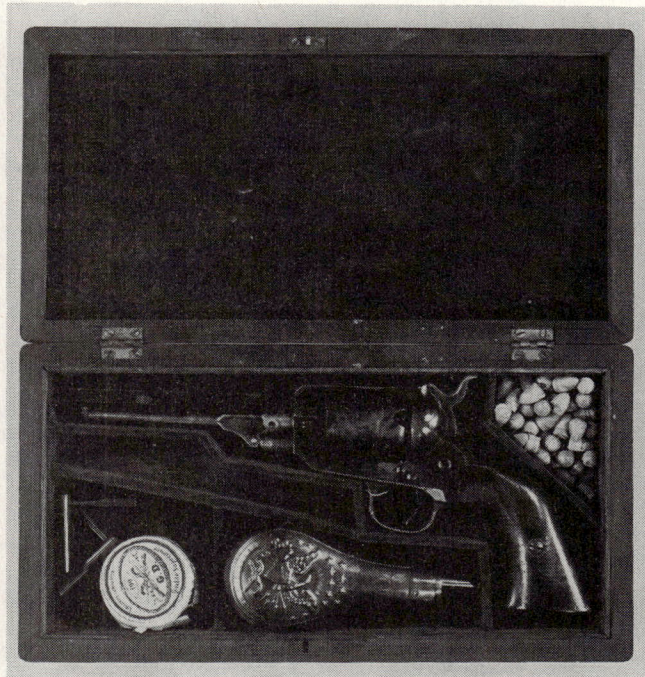

Courtesy Buffalo Bill Historical Center, Cody, Wyoming

First Model

First Variation

Exc.	V.G.	Good	Fair	Poor
—	—	1250	600	250

Second Variation

Exc.	V.G.	Good	Fair	Poor
—	—	800	400	200

Third Variation

Exc.	V.G.	Good	Fair	Poor
—	—	700	350	150

Fourth Variation

Exc.	V.G.	Good	Fair	Poor
—	—	700	350	150

Fifth Variation

Exc.	V.G.	Good	Fair	Poor
—	—	700	350	150

Second Model

First Variation

Exc.	V.G.	Good	Fair	Poor
—	—	500	250	100

Second Variation

Exc.	V.G.	Good	Fair	Poor
—	—	500	250	100

Third Variation

Exc.	V.G.	Good	Fair	Poor
—	—	500	250	100

Fourth Variation

Exc.	V.G.	Good	Fair	Poor
—	—	550	300	125

New Model Pocket Revolver

This is a single action, spur-triggered pocket revolver chambered for .28-caliber percussion. It has a 3.5" octagonal barrel and a 6-shot roll engraved cylinder. It features an iron frame with a blued finish and two-piece walnut grips. The barrel is marked "E. Whitney/N. Haven". There were approximately 2,000 manufactured between 1860 and 1867.

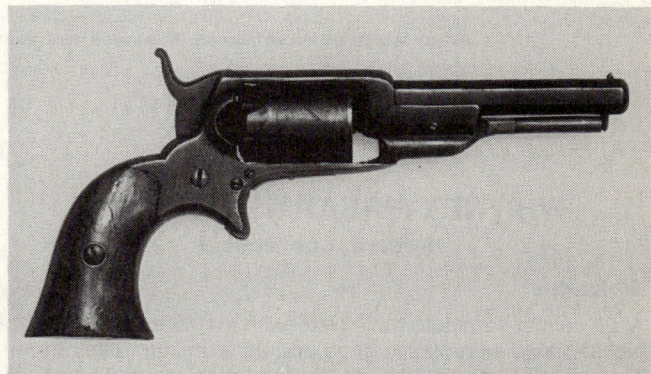

Courtesy Milwaukee Public Museum, Milwaukee, Wisconsin

Exc.	V.G.	Good	Fair	Poor
—	—	900	400	200

Rimfire Pocket Revolver

This is a spur-trigger, single action, solid-frame pocket revolver that was produced in three frame sizes, depending on the caliber. It is chambered for the .22, .32, and .38 rimfire cartridges. The frame is brass, and it is found in a variety of finishes- nickel-plated or blued, or a combination thereof. The bird's-head grips are rosewood or hard rubber; ivory or pearl grips are sometimes encountered and will bring a slight premium in value. The barrels are octagonal and from 1.5" to 5" in length. The barrels are marked "Whitneyville Armory Ct. USA". They have also been noted with the trade names "Monitor," "Defender," or "Eagle." They were commonly referred to as the Model No. 1, No. 1.5, Model 2, or Model 2.5. The values for all are quite similar. There were approximately 30,000 manufactured of all types between 1871 and 1879.

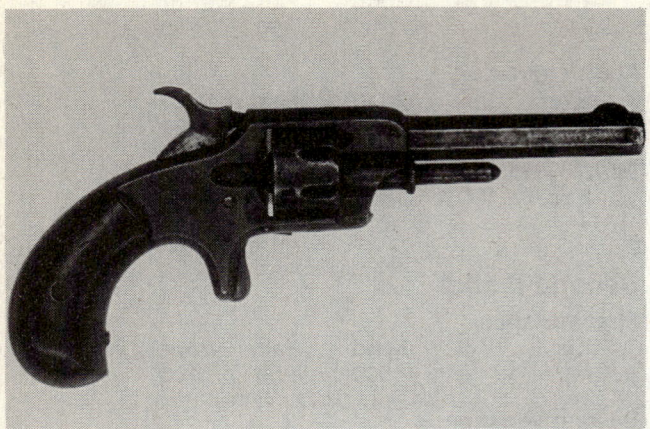

Courtesy Milwaukee Public Museum, Milwaukee, Wisconsin

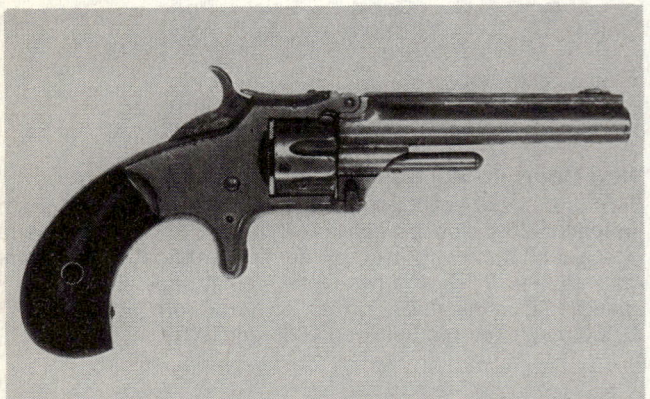

Courtesy Milwaukee Public Museum, Milwaukee, Wisconsin

Exc.	V.G.	Good	Fair	Poor
—	—	350	100	50

WHITNEY FIREARMS COMPANY
Hartford, Connecticut

Wolverine

A .22 caliber semiautomatic pistol with a 4.75" barrel. Blued or nickel-plated with plastic grips and an aluminum alloy frame. This pistol is readily distinguishable by its streamlined form. Approximately 13,000 examples were made with the blued finish and 900 with a nickel-plated finish. The slide marked "Wolverine Whitney Firearms Inc., New Haven, Conn USA". Some examples are also marked "Lightning". Manufactured from 1955 to 1962.

Blue Finish

Exc.	V.G.	Good	Fair	Poor
450	400	350	250	200

Nickel-Plated

Exc.	V.G.	Good	Fair	Poor
550	500	450	300	250

WHITWORTH
SEE Interarms

WICHITA ARMS, INC.
Wichita, Kansas

Classic Rifle

A single shot bolt-action rifle produced in a variety of calibers with a 21" octagonal barrel. Offered with Canjar adjustable triggers. Blued with a checkered walnut stock.

NIB	Exc.	V.G.	Good	Fair	Poor
3000	2500	2250	1850	1250	1000

Varmint Rifle

As above, with a round barrel.

NIB	Exc.	V.G.	Good	Fair	Poor
2000	1750	1500	1250	1000	800

Silhouette Rifle

As above, with a 24" heavy barrel, gray composition stock and 2-oz. Canjar trigger.

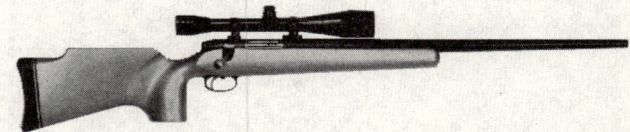

NIB	Exc.	V.G.	Good	Fair	Poor
2200	1900	1700	1000	850	650

Wichita International Pistol

A single shot pivoted barrel target pistol produced in a variety of calibers from .22 to .357 Magnum with a 10.5" or 14" barrel fitted with either adjustable sights or telescopic sight mounts. Stainless steel with walnut forestock and grips.

NIB	Exc.	V.G.	Good	Fair	Poor
500	450	400	350	300	200

Wichita Classic Pistol

A bolt-action single shot pistol chambered for a variety of calibers up to .308, with a left hand action and 11.25" barrel. Blued with a walnut stock.

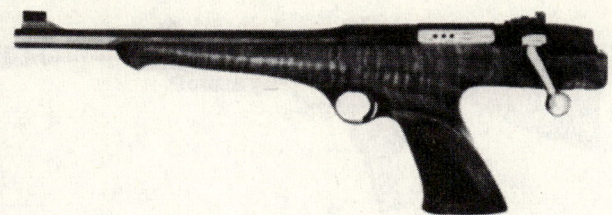

NIB	Exc.	V.G.	Good	Fair	Poor
3000	2500	2250	1850	1250	1000

Wichita Classic Engraved As Above, But Embellished

NIB	Exc.	V.G.	Good	Fair	Poor
5000	4250	3500	2500	2000	1500

Wichita Silhouette Pistol

As above, in 7mm HMSA or .308 with a 15" barrel. The walnut stock is made so that the pistol grip is located beneath the forward end of the bolt.

NIB	Exc.	V.G.	Good	Fair	Poor
1100	950	750	600	500	400

Wichita MK40

As above, with a 13" barrel having multi-range sights and either a composition or walnut stock. Standard finish is blued, however, this model was also made in stainless steel.

NIB	Exc.	V.G.	Good	Fair	Poor
1100	950	750	600	500	400

WICKLIFFE RIFLES
Triple S Development
Wickliffe, Ohio

Model 76

A single-shot falling-block rifle produced in a variety of calibers from .22 Hornet to .45-70 with a 22" lightweight or 26" heavyweight barrel. Blued with a walnut stock. Introduced in 1976.

Exc.	V.G.	Good	Fair	Poor
400	350	300	250	175

Model 76 Deluxe

As above, with a nickel-silver pistol grip cap, machine jeweled breechblock and more finely figured walnut stock. Introduced in 1976.

Exc.	V.G.	Good	Fair	Poor
450	400	350	300	200

Traditionalist

The Model 76 in .30-06 or .45-70 caliber with a 24" barrel having open sights and a checkered walnut butt stock. Introduced in 1979.

Exc.	V.G.	Good	Fair	Poor
400	350	300	250	175

Stinger

Similar to the Model 76, but chambered for .22 Hornet or .223 Remington with a 22" barrel fitted with a Burris 6X power telescope. Blued with a checkered Monte Carlo-style stock. Introduced in 1979.

Exc.	V.G.	Good	Fair	Poor
400	350	300	250	175

Stinger Deluxe

As above, with a superior grade of finish and more finely figured walnut stock.

Exc.	V.G.	Good	Fair	Poor
475	400	350	300	200

WIENER WAFFENFABRIK
Vienna, Austria

Little Tom

A 6.35mm or 7.65mm double action semiautomatic pistol with a 2.5" barrel. The slide marked "Wiener Waffenfabrik Patent Little Tom", and the caliber. Blued with either walnut or plastic grips inlaid with a medallion bearing the company's trademark. Approximately 10,000 were made from 1919 to 1925.

Exc.	V.G.	Good	Fair	Poor
500	450	400	250	175

WILDEY FIREARMS CO., INC.
Cheshire, Connecticut
New Burg, New York
Brookfield, Connecticut

Wildey Auto Pistol

A gas-operated, rotary-bolt, double action semiautomatic pistol chambered for the .357 Peterbuilt, the .45 Winchester Magnum, or the .475 Wildey Magnum cartridges. with 5", 6", 7", 8", or 10" ventilated rib barrels. The gas-operated action is adjustable and features a single shot cutoff. The rotary bolt has three heavy locking lugs. Constructed of stainless steel with adjustable sights and wood grips. The values of this rarely encountered pistol are based on not only the condition, but the caliber—as well the serial number range, with earlier-numbered guns being worth a good deal more than the later or current production models.

Cheshire CT Address

Produced in .45 Winchester Magnum only and is serial numbered from No. 1 through 2489.

Serial No. 1 through 200

NIB	Exc.	V.G.	Good	Fair	Poor
2000	1750	1500	1250	900	600

Serial numbers above 200 would we worth approximately $200 less respectively in each category of condition.

Survivor Model

This pistol is presently manufactured in Brookfield, Connecticut.

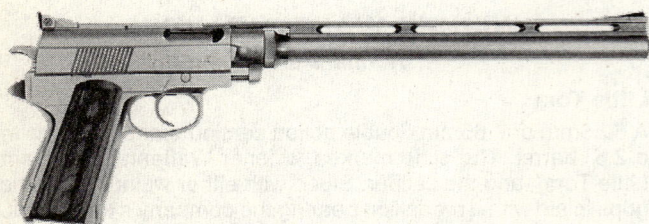

NIB	Exc.	V.G.	Good	Fair	Poor
1100	950	800	600	500	400

Presentation Model

As above, but engraved and fitted with hand checkered walnut grips.

NIB	Exc.	V.G.	Good	Fair	Poor
2500	2000	1500	1250	850	700

WILKINSON ARMS CO.
Covina, California

Diane

A .25 caliber semiautomatic pistol with a 2.25" barrel and 6-shot magazine. Blued with plastic grips.

Exc.	V.G.	Good	Fair	Poor
150	125	100	75	50

Terry Carbine

A 9mm caliber semiautomatic carbine with a 16.25" barrel, adjustable sights, and 30-shot magazine. Matte blued with either a black composition or maple stock.

Exc.	V.G.	Good	Fair	Poor
350	300	250	175	125

WILLIAMSON MOORE FIREARMS COMPANY
New York, New York

Derringer

A .41 caliber single shot pocket pistol with a 2.5" sliding barrel. Blued, with a silver-plated furniture and a checkered walnut grip. Barrel marked "Williamson's Pat. Oct. 2, 1866 New York". This pistol was fitted with an auxiliary percussion cap chamber adaptor. Manufactured from 1866 to approximately 1870.

Exc.	V.G.	Good	Fair	Poor
—	—	750	350	100

WILSON & CO.
SEE English Military Firearms

WILSON, J. P.
Ilion, New York

Percussion Alarm Gun

This unusual little device is chambered for .22 caliber percussion. It consists of approximately a 1" rectangular brass block with a chamber bored into it that accepts a black-powder charge. There is no provision for a projectile. There is a spring retained arm on top, that works as a hammer. As the device is activated by a door or a window, the hammer snaps closed, striking a percussion cap that causes the charge to fire, thereby creating an alarm notifying that the perimeter has been breached. It is marked "J. P. Wilson/Patented Feb. 8, 1859/Ilion, NY".

Exc.	V.G.	Good	Fair	Poor
—	—	500	250	100

WILSON COMBAT
Berryville, Arkansas

Wilson's began making custom 1911 style pistols using Colt slides and frames in 1977. This company produces a wide range of quality components for the 1911 pistol such as slides, triggers, safeties, barrels, etc. The models listed below are for complete factory built and assembled guns. These factory built pistols are sold with a lifetime warranty even to subsequent buyers. The pistols listed below are divided into two categories. Semi-Custom pistols are off-the-shelf guns available through participating dealers. Custom pistols are special order guns.

SEMI-CUSTOM PISTOLS

These pistols were first built in 1996 using Springfield Armory pistols as the base gun. The Protector Compact was built on the Springfield Compact pistol. In 1997 all Service Grade pistols are built on the new Wilson Combat slide and frame with the exception of the Protector compact which is built on a Colt commander slide and a Colt Officer Model frame. The semi-custom pistols are all marked with 1996A2 on the left-hand side of the slide. Service Grade pistols bear the name Protector, Protector Compact, or Classic on the rights side of the frame's dust cover.

Wilson Model 1996A2

This pistol, introduced in 1996, is offered in a number of different configurations. These configurations affect price. The base pistol is chambered for the .45 ACP cartridge, has snag free sights and blue finish. Barrel length is 5", magazine capacity is 8 rounds and weight is approximately 38 oz. There are numerous special features on the standard pistol.

NIB	Exc.	V.G.	Good	Fair	Poor
1350	1050	—	—	—	—

NOTE: Add $70 for tritium night sights, $125 for Wilson adjustable sights, $275 for nights sights, ambi safety, hard chrome frame, $325 for Wilson adjustable sights, ambi safety, hard chrome frame.

Service Grade Protector

This model is fitted to a 5" slide with match barrel adjustable sights, and numerous other special features. Weight is about 38 oz. Black polymer finish on slide and frame. Introduced in 1996.

NIB	Exc.	V.G.	Good	Fair	Poor
1695	1350	—	—	—	—

Service Grade Protector Compact

Same as above but fitted with a 4.25" match grade barrel. Weight is about 34 oz. Introduced in 1996.

NIB	Exc.	V.G.	Good	Fair	Poor
1695	1350	—	—	—	—

Service Grade Classic

This model has a 5" barrel, adjustable sights, hard chrome finish on frame, and other special features. Weight is about 38 oz. Introduced in 1996.

NIB	Exc.	V.G.	Good	Fair	Poor
1795	1400	—	—	—	—

.22 Classic Rimfire Pistol

Chambered for the .22 caliber rimfire cartridge and fitted with a 5" barrel. Hard chrome frame and black anodized slide. Weight is less than standard .45 caliber pistol. Introduced in 1996.

NIB	Exc.	V.G.	Good	Fair	Poor
1145	875	—	—	—	—

CUSTOM BUILT PISTOLS

Wilson Custom pistols bear the Wilson Combat or Wilson Custom label on the right side of the frame on the dust cover. Full custom guns are typically built on a Colt, Springfield Armory, Norinco, STI, Strayer Voight or Wilson Combat gun.

Combat Classic Super Grade

Fitted with a 5" match grade handfit stainless steel barrel. Adjustable sights, high ride beavertail safety, contoured magazine well and polymer slide with hard chrome frame. Weight is approximately 45 oz.

NIB	Exc.	V.G.	Good	Fair	Poor
3195	2475	1750	—	—	—

Stealth Defense System

Built with a 4.25" slide with match grade stainless steel barrel. This model features night sights checkered front strap and mainspring spring housing with numerous special features. Black polymer finish. Weight is approximately 34 oz.

NIB	Exc.	V.G.	Good	Fair	Poor
2695	2100	1450	—	—	—

Defensive Combat Pistol

This .45 ACP pistol is built with a 5" match grade stainless steel barrel, night sights, and numerous special features. Finish is black polymer. Weight 38 oz.

NIB	Exc.	V.G.	Good	Fair	Poor
2395	1850	1250	—	—	—

Tactical Elite

This is similar to other Wilson pistol but with the exception of the special tactical heavy tapered cone hand-NIB Exc. V.G. Good Fair Poor

2695	2100	1450	—	—	—

Defensive Combat Pistol Deluxe

This model has a 5" match grade stainless steel barrel and numerous special features. fItted with adjustable sights. Weight is about 38 oz. Finish is black polymer.

NIB	Exc.	V.G.	Good	Fair	Poor
2595	2000	1350	—	—	—

Competition Pistols

Wilson Combat offers a custom built pistol to the customer's specifications. An expert appraisal is recommended prior to sale.

WINCHESTER REPEATING ARMS COMPANY
New Haven, Connecticut

Winchester is a name that is identified with the Old West and the frontier days of America. Winchester rifles and shotguns are prized for their historical significance as well as their collectiblity. The Winchester Repeating Arms Company was formally established by Oliver F. Winchester on February 20, 1866, and the first model to bear the name of the company was the Model 1866 lever-action rifle chambered for the .44 caliber rimfire cartridge. As with any enterprise it is helpful to study the background and beginnings of the Winchester company so as to better understand the chronological sequence of various rifles and pistols that preceded the Winchester Model 1866.

The story begins with Walter Hunt of New York City who, in 1848, developed the Rocket Ball and Volition Repeater, a unique lever-action, breechloading, under-barrel magazine tube repeater. This rifle was the origin for future concepts. Hunt's business partner, George Arrowsmith, had as his machinist a man named Lewis Jennings, who improved and simplified Walter Hunt's original concept. Jennings' improvements were granted a U.S. patent in 1849. This 25-shot repeating rifle was promoted by Arrowsmith who found a willing investor in Courtland Palmer, a Connecticut merchant. Palmer bought both the Hunt and Jennings patents and had 5,000 Jennings rifles built by Robbins and Lawrence in Vermont in 1850. The foreman at Robbins and Lawrence was Benjamin Tyler Henry, a man who would play an important role in future repeating rifle developments. By 1851 two additional individuals would enter the Hunt-Jennings story: Daniel Wesson and Horace Smith. These two men improved on Lewis Jennings' design, and Smith was granted a patent in 1851, which he assigned to Palmer. Despite the initial achievements with the Jennings rifle, the action proved too complex and the cartridges too light for successful marketability.

In 1854 Horace Smith and Daniel Wesson were granted a U.S. patent for a repeating firearm similar to earlier Horace Smith design. Courtland Palmer funded the experimental work on the new pistol, which featured a 4" barrel and a full-length under-barrel magazine. Palmer, Smith, and Wesson formed a partnership incorporating the Hunt, Jennings, Smith, and new Smith & Wesson patents. The pistols were made in Norwich, Connecticut, under the name of Smith & Wesson. B. Tyler Henry was an employee of the new firm. Only about 1,000 of these pistol were produce before the company name was changed to Volcanic Repeating Arms Company, an incorporated firm, in 1855. The new company was formed by Palmer, Smith, and Wesson with the additional financial assistance of Oliver F. Winchester. Winchester was at the time a successful manufacturer of men's clothing in New Haven, Connecticut. The new company bought out Palmer and Smith, while Daniel Wesson stayed on as shop foreman to work on his metallic rimfire cartridge. Volcanic pistols and rifles were first built at the original Smith & Wesson factory in Norwich until 1856 when a new plant was located at New Haven. In 1857 the majority of stock in the Volcanic Repeating Arms Company was owned by Oliver Winchester

The New Haven Arms Company was structured in April 1857 to assume the business of Volcanic Repeating Arms Company. This new company continued the production of Volcanic pistols and rifles, but these were now marked as "NEW HAVEN CONN. PATENT FEB. 14, 1854". These Volcanics received favorable reports as to their rapidity of fire and ease of operation, but they suffered from low velocity, energy, and small calibers. These difficulties affected sales, which remained slow. Perhaps this would be the end of the story had it not been for B. Henry Tyler, who was the shop foreman at New Haven Arms Company after the departure of Daniel Wesson. Tyler had been involved with the predecessors for the past 10 years and he received a patent in 1860 for the improvement in magazine firearms. The success of Henry's new design was twofold: First, the development of a new, more powerful .44 caliber metallic rimfire cartridge was sufficiently potent enough to compete with the single shot rifles of the day, and second, the advancement in the firing pin design, the addition of an extractor, and improvements in the bolt and feeding mechanisms all helped to make the Henry rifle a success. The first production Henry rifles were delivered in 1862. In 1866 the New Haven Arms Company name was changed to Winchester Repeating Arms Company.

The subsequent models offered by Winchester are highly prized by collectors. Winchester Repeating Arms Company went on to establish itself as one of the world's leading firearms manufacturers. Winchester provided repeating rifles that played an important role in this nation's history and will forever have a place as the company that built the guns that "Won the West." By the beginning of World War I, 1914, Winchester was the leading domestic firearms producer in the United States and also exported guns around the world. After World War I ended and beginning in the early 1920s, the company began to lose its dominant position in the firearms industry. The decade of the '20s marked a difficult financial period for Winchester with the company finally being forced into receivership by the end of the decade. In 1931, Winchester was purchased by the Western Cartridge Company owned by the Olin family. Because of the changing times, the company's focus was now on sporting arms and the drive for new models and manufacturing techniques came from the vision and foresight of John M. Olin.

From 1931 until 1963, Winchester Repeating Arms regained its reputation for quality firearms, and the rifles and shotguns produced during this period are as collectible as those guns that preceded it. In 1964, the company could no longer afford to mass produce firearms that in reality were hand fitted and hand machined. Production changes were implemented that reflected the mass production psychology that was becoming so commonplace in American industry. With the exception of the Model 21 and a few other select models of Winchester rifles and shotguns, many Winchester guns produced after 1963 are not viewed by collectors necessarily as collectibles. Nevertheless, they were excellent guns for the hunting fields and duck blinds. In 1981 Winchester Repeating Arms Company sold its firearms division to U.S. Repeating Arms Company. This new company continues to the present day to build rifles and shotguns under license from Winchester. U.S. Repeating Arms Company has itself been the object of several buyouts. Nevertheless, the Winchester legend lives on; collected and respected by many.

A brief guide to the Winchester Repeating Arms Company corporate and divisional name changes will be of help to the collector to establish the proper company name on various firearms and advertising materials.

The prices given here are for the most part standard guns without optional features that were so often furnished by the factory. These optional or extra cost features are too numerous to list and can affect the price of a shotgun or rifle to an enormous degree. In some cases these options are one of a kind. Collectors and those interested in Winchester firearms have the benefit of some of the orginial factory records. These records are now stored in the Cody Firearms Museum, Buffalo Bill Historical Center, P.O. Box 1000, Cody, Wyoming (307)587-4771. For a $25 fee the museum will provide factory letters containing the original specifications of certain Winchester models using the original factory records.

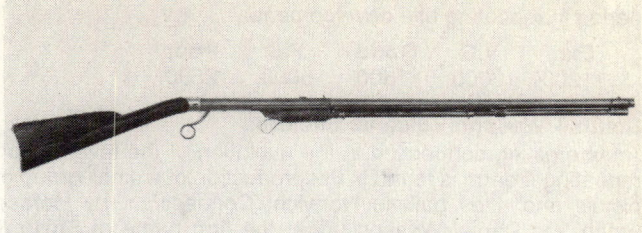

MODEL	SERIAL NUMBER
1866	124995 to l70101
1873	1 to 720496 (N/A 497-610 and 199551-199598)
1876	1 to 63871
Hotchkiss	1 to 84555
1885*	1 to 109999 (N/A 74459-75556)
1886	1 to 156599 (N/A 146000-150799)
1887 & 1901	1 to 72999
1890	1 to 329999 (N/A 20000-29999)
1906	1 to 79999
1892	1 to 379999
1893	1 to 34050
1897	1 to 377999
1894	1 to 353999
1895	1 to 59999
Lee	1 to 19999
1903	1 to 39999
1905	1 to 29078
1906	1 to 79999
1907	1 to 9999
21	1 to 35000

* Single-Shot

Hunt Repeating Rifle

Walter Hunt described his repeating rifle as the Volition Repeater. Hunt was granted U.S. patent number 6663 in August 1849 for his repeating rifle that was to pave the way for future generations of Winchester repeating rifles. Hunt's rifle design was unique and innovative as was his patent number 5701 for a conical lead bullet that was to be fired in his rifle. This ingenious bullet had a hole in its base filled with powder and closed by a disc with an opening in the middle to expel the ignition from an independent priming source that used priming pellets made of fulminate of mercury. The rifle actually worked but only the patent model was built; it is now in the Cody Firearms Museum.

Jennings

Second in the evolutionary line of Winchester rifles is the Jennings. Made by Robbins & Lawrence of Windsor, Vermont, this rifle incorporated the original concept of the Hunt design with the additional improvements utilized by Lewis Jennings. The Jennings rifle is important not only as a link in the chain of repeating rifle development but also because it introduced Benjamin Henry Tyler to the concept of the tubular magazine lever action repeating rifle. The Jennings rifle was built in three separate and distinct models. While total production of the three types was contracted for 5,000 guns, it is probable that only about 1,000 were actually produced.

First Model

The First Model Jennings was built in a .54 caliber, breech-loading, single shot configuration with a ring trigger, oval triggerguard, and 26" barrel. A ramrod was fixed to the underside of the barrel as well. This variation was made from 1850 to 1851.

Courtesy Milwaukee Public Museum, Milwaukee, Wisconsin

Exc.	V.G.	Good	Fair	Poor
7500	5000	3500	2000	1000

Second Model

The Second Model Jennings was produced adopting the improvements made by Horace Smith. This Second Model is a breech-loading repeating rifle with an under-barrel magazine tube and a 26" barrel. The frame is sculptured, unlike the First Model. The ring trigger is still present, but the triggerguard was removed as part of the design change. The caliber remained a .54, and the rifle was fitted with a 25" barrel. The Second Model was produced in 1851 and 1852.

Courtesy Milwaukee Public Museum. Milwaukee, Wisconsin

Exc.	V.G.	Good	Fair	Poor
10000	8500	6500	3000	1500

Third Model

The Third Model represents an attempt by investors to use the remaining parts and close out production. The .54 caliber Third Model was a muzzleloading rifle with a ramrod mounted under the barrel and a 26-1/2" barrel. The frame was the same as that used on the First Model, but the trigger was more of the conventional type. The triggerguard had a bow in the middle giving this model a distinctive appearance. This variation was produced in 1852 and marks the end of the early conceptual period in repeating rifle development.

Exc.	V.G.	Good	Fair	Poor
12000	10000	7500	5000	2500

Smith & Wesson Volcanic Firearms

An interesting connection in the evolution of the lever action repeating firearm is found in the production of a small group of pistols and rifles built in Norwich, Connecticut, by Horace Smith and Daniel Wesson under the firm name of Smith & Wesson. The company built two types of Volcanic pistols. One was a large frame model with an 8" barrel and chambered in .41 caliber. About 500 of these large frames were produced. The other pistol was a small frame version with a 4" barrel chambered in .31 caliber. Slightly more of these small frame pistols were built, about 700, than the large frame version. In both variations the barrel, magazine, and frame were blued. Smith & Wesson also produced a lever-action repeating rifle. These rifles are exceedingly rare with less than 10 having been built. They were chambered for the .528 caliber and were fitted with 23" barrels. Because of the small number of rifles built, no value is offered.

Courtesy Buffalo Bill Historical Center, Cody, Wyoming

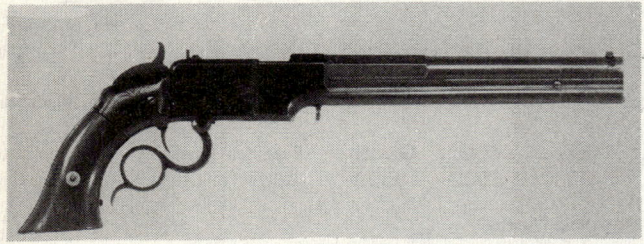

Courtesy Buffalo Bill Historical Center, Cody, Wyoming

8" Pistol

Exc.	V.G.	Good	Fair	Poor
7500	6000	4000	2000	1000

Courtesy Buffalo Bill Historical Center, Cody, Wyoming

4" Pistol

Exc.	V.G.	Good	Fair	Poor
5500	3500	2000	1500	1000

Volcanic Firearms (Volcanic Repeating Arms Company)

With the incorporation of the Volcanic Repeating Arms Company, a new and important individual was introduced who would have an impact on the American arms industry for the next 100 years: Oliver F. Winchester. This new company introduced the Volcanic pistol using the improvements made by Horace Smith and Daniel Wesson. Volcanic firearms are marked on the barrel, "THE VOLCANIC REPEATING ARMS CO. PATENT NEW HAVEN, CONN. FEB. 14, 1854". The Volcanic was offered as a .38 caliber breechloading tubular magazine repeater with blued barrel and bronze frame. These pistols were available in three barrel lengths.

6" Barrel

Exc.	V.G.	Good	Fair	Poor
9000	7100	5500	3000	1500

8" Barrel

Exc.	V.G.	Good	Fair	Poor
9500	7700	6000	3500	2000

16" Barrel

Exc.	V.G.	Good	Fair	Poor
10000	8500	7000	5000	2500

Courtesy Milwaukee Public Museum, Milwaukee, Wisconsin

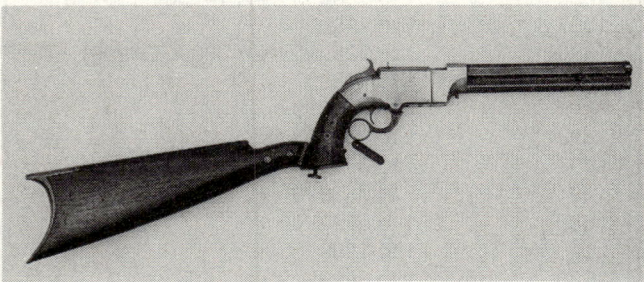

Courtesy Buffalo Bill Historical Center, Cody, Wyoming

NOTE: A few Volcanic pistols were produced with detachable shoulder stocks. These are considered quite rare. For original guns with this option, the above prices should be increased by 50%.

Volcanic Firearms (New Haven Arms Company)

In 1857 the New Haven Arms Company was formed to continue the production of the former Volcanic Repeating Arms Company. Volcanic firearms continued to be built but were now marked on the barrel, "NEW HAVEN, CONN. PATENT FEB. 14, 1854". The Volcanic pistols produced by the New Haven Arms Company were built in .30 caliber and used the same basic frame as the original Volcanic. These pistols were produced in 3-1/2" and 6" barrel lengths.

3-1/2" Barrel

Exc.	V.G.	Good	Fair	Poor
8000	6000	5200	2000	1500

Courtesy Butterfield & Butterfield, San Francisco, California

6" Barrel

Exc.	V.G.	Good	Fair	Poor
9000	7000	5500	2500	1250

Lever Action Carbine

New Haven Arms introduced, for the first time, a Volcanic rifle that featured a full length slotted magazine tube with a spring activated thumb piece follower that moved along the entire length of the magazine tube. These rifles were chambered for .38 caliber cartridge and were offered in three barrel lengths: 16", 20", and 24".

Courtesy Buffalo Bill Historical Center, Cody, Wyoming

16" Barrel

Exc.	V.G.	Good	Fair	Poor
—	15000	10000	5000	3000

20" Band

Exc.	V.G.	Good	Fair	Poor
—	17500	10000	5000	3000

24" Band

Exc.	V.G.	Good	Fair	Poor
—	20000	10000	5000	3000

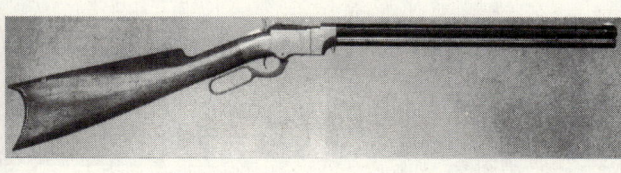

Photo by Paul Goodwin

Henry Rifle

With the development of B. Tyler Henry's improvements in the metallic rimfire cartridge and his additional improvements in the Volcanic frame, the direct predecessor to the Winchester lever-action repeater was born. The new cartridge was the .44 caliber rimfire, and the Henry rifle featured a 24" octagon barrel with a tubular magazine holding 15 shells. The rifle had no forearm, but was furnished with a walnut buttstock with two styles of buttplates: an early rounded heel crescent shape seen on guns produced from 1860 to 1862 and the later sharper heel crescent butt found on guns built from 1863 to 1866. The early models, produced from 1860 to 1861, were fitted with an iron frame, and the later models, built from 1861 to 1866, were fitted with brass frames. About 14,000 Henry rifles were made during the entire production period; only about 300 were iron frame rifles.

Iron Frame Rifle

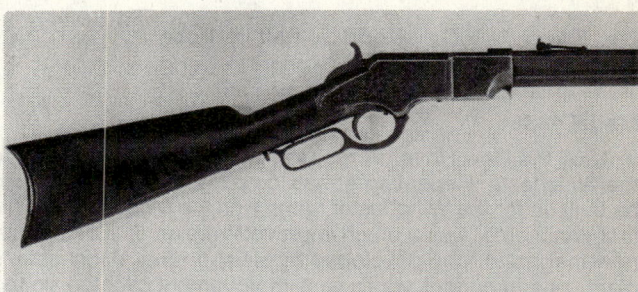

Courtesy Butterfield & Butterfield, San Francisco, California

Exc.	V.G.	Good	Fair	Poor
—	35000	25000	20000	15000

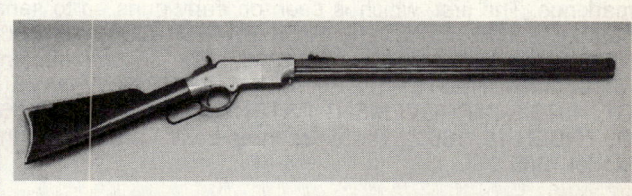

Brass Frame Rifle

Exc.	V.G.	Good	Fair	Poor
—	20000	15000	8000	4000

Martially Inspected Henry Rifles

Beginning in 1863 the Federal Government ordered 1730 Henry Rifles for use in the Civil War. These government inspected rifles fall into serial number range 3000 to 3900. They are marked "C.G.C." for Charles G. Chapman, the government inspector. These Henry rifles were used under actual combat conditions and for that reason it is doubtful that there are any rifles that would fall into the excellent condition catagory. Therefore no price is given.

NOTE: There are many counterfeit examples of these rifles. It is strongly advised that an expert in this field be consulted prior to a sale.

Exc.	V.G.	Good	Fair	Poor
—	—	25000	15000	10000

Winchester's Improvement Carbine

Overall length 43-1/2"; barrel length 24"; caliber .44 r.f. Walnut stock with a brass buttplate; the receiver and magazine cover/forend of brass; the barrel and magazine tube blued. The magazine loading port is exposed by sliding the forend forward. This design was protected by O.F. Winchester's British

Patent Number 3285 issued December 19, 1865. Unmarked except for internally located serial numbers. Approximately 700 manufactured in December of 1865 and early 1866, the majority of which were sold to Maximilian of Mexico. Prospective purchasers are strongly advised to secure an expert appraisal prior to acquisition.

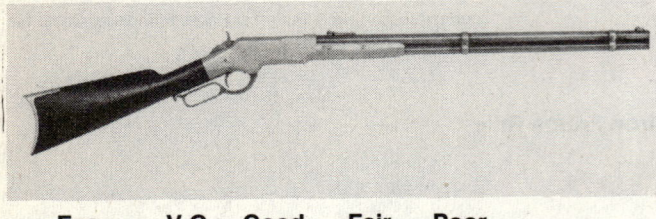

Exc.	V.G.	Good	Fair	Poor
—	—	17500	10000	7500

Model 1866

In 1866 the New Haven Arms Company changed its name to the Winchester Repeating Arms Company. The first firearm to be built under the Winchester name was the Model 1866. This first Winchester was a much improved version of the Henry. A new magazine tube developed by Nelson King, Winchester's plant superintendent, was a vast improvement over the slotted magazine tube used on the Henry and its predecessor. The old tube allowed dirt to enter through the slots and was weakened because of it. King's patent, assigned to Winchester, featured a solid tube that was much stronger and reliable. His patent also dealt with an improved loading system for the rifle. The rifle now featured a loading port on the right side of the receiver with a spring loaded cover. The frame continued to be made from brass. The Model 1866 was chambered for the .44 caliber Flat Rimfire or the .44 caliber Pointed Rimfire. Both cartridges could be used interchangeably.

The barrel on the Model 1866 was marked with two different markings. The first, which is seen on early guns up to serial number 23000, reads "HENRY'S PATENT-OCT. 16, 1860 KING'S PATENT-MARCH 29, 1866". The second marking reads, "WINCHESTER'S-REPEATING-ARMS.NEW HAVEN, CT. KING'S-IMPROVEMENT-PATENTED MARCH 29, 1866 OCTOBER 16, 1860". There are three basic variations of the Model 1866:

Courtesy Milwaukee Public Museum, Milwaukee, Wisconsin

1. Sporting Rifle round or octagon barrel. Approximately 28,000 were produced.

2. Carbine round barrel. Approximately 127,000 were produced.

3. Musket round barrel. Approximately 14,000 were produced.

The rifle and musket held 17 cartridges, and the carbine had a capacity of 13 cartridges. Unlike the Henry, Model 1866s were fitted with a walnut forearm. The Model 1866 was discontinued in 1898 with approximately 170,000 guns produced. The Model 1866 was sold in various special order configurations, such as barrels longer or shorter than standard, including engraved guns. The prices listed below represent only standard Model 1866s. For guns with special order features, an independent appraisal from an expert is highly recommended.

Courtesy Butterfield & Butterfield, San Francisco, California

First Model

This first style has both the Henry and King patent dates stamped on the barrel, a flat loading port cover, and a two-screw upper tang. Perhaps the most distinctive feature of the First Model is the rapid drop at the top rear of the receiver near the hammer. This is often referred to as the "Henry Drop," a reference to the same receiver drop found on the Henry rifle. First Models will be seen up through the 15000 serial number range.

Courtesy Butterfield & Butterfield, San Francisco, California

Rifle

Exc.	V.G.	Good	Fair	Poor
—	20000	12000	5000	2000

Carbine

Exc.	V.G.	Good	Fair	Poor
—	15000	10000	500	2000

> A First Model carbine with saddle ring and 20" barrel sold at auction for $15,820. Condition was good with traces of original finish. Caliber was .44 rimfire.
> Faintich Auction Service, June 1997.
>
> Photo by Paul Goodwin

Second Model

The second style differs from the first most noticeably in its single screw upper tang and a flare at the front of the receiver to meet the forearm. The Second Model also has a more gradual drop at the rear of the receiver than the First Model. The second style Model 1866 appears through serial number 25000.

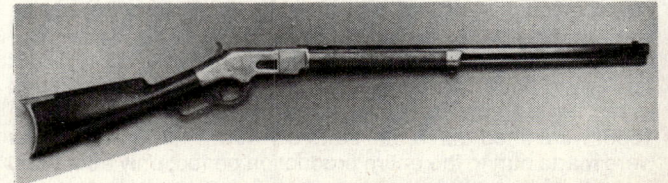

Courtesy Butterfield & Butterfield, San Francisco, California

Rifle

Exc.	V.G.	Good	Fair	Poor
—	15000	7500	4000	3000

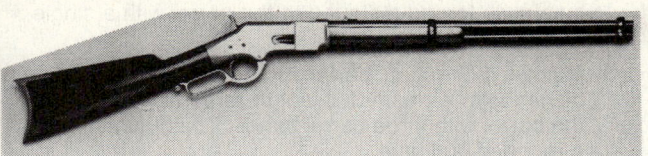

Courtesy Butterfield & Butterfield, San Francisco, California

Carbine

Exc.	V.G.	Good	Fair	Poor
—	12000	7500	5000	2000

Third Model

The third style's most noticeable characteristic is the more moderately curved receiver shape at the rear of the frame. The serial number is now stamped in block numerals behind the trigger thus allowing the numbers to be seen for the first time without removing the stock. The barrel marking is stamped with the Winchester address. The Third Model is found between serial numbers 25000 and 149000. For the first time a musket version was produced in this serial number range.

> A Nimschke engraved Model 1866 with 24" octagon barrel and full magazine was sold at auction for $110,000. Condition was excellent. Butterfield & Butterfield, December 1995.

Rifle

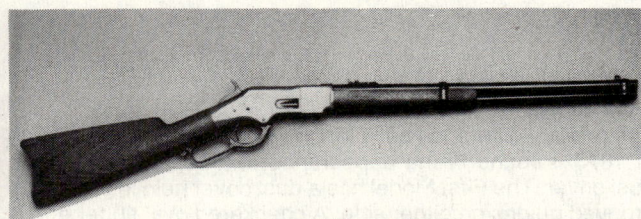

Courtesy Butterfield & Butterfield, San Francisco, California

Exc.	V.G.	Good	Fair	Poor
—	12000	7000	4000	2000

Carbine

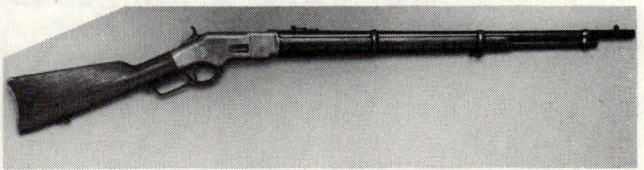

Courtesy Butterfield & Butterfield, San Francisco, California

Exc.	V.G.	Good	Fair	Poor
—	10000	7500	3500	2000

> A Model 1866 Saddle ring carbine engraved by Nimschke was sold at auction for $73,700. Fitted with a 20" round barrel with the receiver gold plated. Condition was very good and factory original. Rock Island Auction Co., May 1996.

Musket

Exc.	V.G.	Good	Fair	Poor
—	8000	5000	2000	1000

Fourth Model

The fourth style has an even less pronounced drop at the top rear of the frame, and the serial number is stamped in script on the lower tang under the lever. The Fourth Model is seen between serial number 149000 and 170100 with the late guns having an iron buttplate instead of brass.

Iron

Exc.	V.G.	Good	Fair	Poor
—	12000	7500	3500	2000

Carbine

Exc.	V.G.	Good	Fair	Poor
—	10000	5000	2000	1000

Musket

Exc.	V.G.	Good	Fair	Poor
—	9500	5000	1800	1000

Model 1866 Iron Frame Rifle Musket

Overall length 54-1/2"; barrel length 33-1/4"; caliber .45 c.f. Walnut stock with case-hardened furniture, barrel burnished bright, the receiver case-hardened. The finger lever catch mounted within a large bolster at the rear of the lever. Unmarked except for serial numbers that appear externally on the receiver and often the buttplate tang. Approximately 25 made during the early autumn of 1866. Prospective purchasers are strongly advised to secure an expert appraisal prior to acquisition. Due to the recent identification of this model pricing schedules have yet to be established.

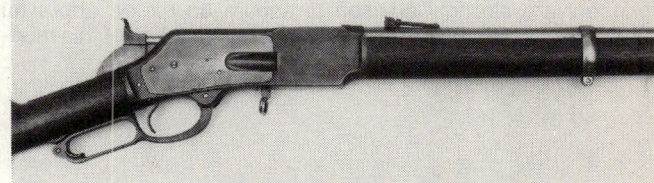

Model 1866 Iron Frame Swiss Sharpshooters Rifle

As above, but in .41 Swiss caliber and fitted with a Scheutzen style stock supplied by the firm of Weber Ruesch in Zurich. Marked Weber Ruesch, Zurich on the barrel and serial numbered externally. Approximately 400 to 450 manufactured in 1866 and 1867. Prospective purchasers are strongly advised to secure an expert appraisal prior to acquisition. Due to the recent identification of this model pricing schedules have yet to be established.

Model 1867 Iron Frame Carbine

Overall length 39-1/4"; barrel length 20"; caliber .44 r.f. Walnut stock with case-hardened furniture; the barrel and magazine tube blued; the receiver case-hardened. The finger lever catch mounted within the rear curl of the lever. Unmarked except for serial numbers that appear externally on the receiver and often the buttplate tang. Approximately 20 manufactured. Prospective purchasers are strongly advised to secure an expert appraisal prior to acquisition. Due to the recent identification of this model pricing schedules have yet to be established.

Model 1868 Iron Frame Rifle Musket

Overall length 49-1/2" (.455 cal.), 50-1/2" or 53" (.45 and .47 cal.); barrel length 29-1/2" (.455 cal.) and 30-1/4' or 33" (.45 and .47 cal.); calibers .45 c.f., .455 c.f., and .47 c.f. Walnut stock with case-hardened or burnished bright (.45 and .47 cal.) furniture; the barrel burnished bright; the receiver case-hardened or burnished bright (.45 and .47 cal.). The finger lever catch mounted on the lower receiver tang. The rear of the finger lever machined with a long flat extension on its upper surface. Unmarked except for serial number. Approximately 30 examples made in .45 and .455 caliber and 250 in .47 caliber. Prospective purchasers are strongly advised to secure an expert appraisal prior to acquisition. Due to the recent identification of this model pricing schedules have yet to be established.

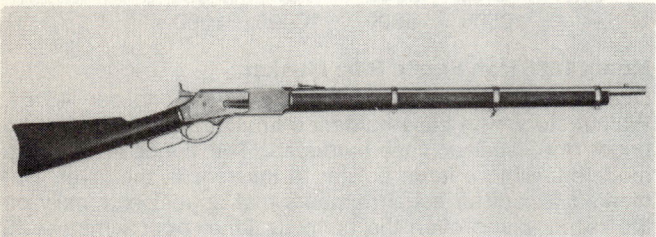

Model 1868 Iron Frame Carbine

Overall length 40"; barrel length 20"; caliber .44 c.f. Walnut stock with case-hardened furniture; barrel and magazine tube blued; the receiver case-hardened. The finger lever catch as above. Unmarked except for serial numbers (receiver and buttplate tang). Approximately 25 manufactured. Prospective purchasers are strongly advised to secure an expert appraisal prior to acquisition. Due to the recent identification of this model pricing schedules have yet to be established.

Model 1873

This Winchester rifle was one of the most popular lever actions the company ever produced. This is the "gun that won the West" and with good reason. It was chambered for the more powerful centerfire cartridge, the .44-40. Compared to the .44 Henry, this cartridge was twice as good. With the introduction of the single action Colt pistol in 1878, chambered for the same cartridge, the individual had the convenience of a pistol for protection and the accuracy of the Winchester for food and protection. The .44-40 was the standard cartridge for the Model 1873. Three additional cartridges were offered but were not as popular as the .44. The .38-40 was first offered in 1879 and the .32-20 was introduced in 1882. In 1884 the Model 1873 was offered in .22 caliber rimfire, with a few special order guns built in .22 extra long rimfire. Approximately 19,552 .22 caliber Model 1873s were produced.

Early Model 1873s were fitted with an iron receiver until 1884, when a steel receiver was introduced. The Model 1873 was offered in three styles:

1. Sporting Rifle, 24" round, octagon, or half-octagon barrel. Equipped standard with a crescent iron buttplate, straight-grip stock and capped forearm.

2. Carbine, 20" round barrel. Furnished standard with a rounded iron buttplate, straight-grip stock, and carbine style forend fastened to the barrel with a single barrel band.

3. Musket, 30" round barrel. Standard musket is furnished with a nearly full-length forearm fastened to the barrel with three barrel bands. The buttstock has a rounded buttplate.

The upper tang was marked with the model designation and the serial number was stamped on the lower tang. Caliber stampings on the Model 1873 are found on the bottom of the frame and on the breech end of the barrel. Winchester discontinued the Model 1873 in 1919 after producing about 720,000 guns.

The Winchester Model 1873 was offered with a large number of extra cost options that greatly affect the value of the gun. For example, Winchester built two sets of special Model 1873s; the 1-of-100 and the 1-of-1000. Winchester sold only 8 1-of-100 Model 1873s, and 136 of the 1-of-1000 guns that were built. In 1991 a few of these special guns were sold at auction and brought prices exceeding $75,000. The prices listed here are for standard guns only. For Model 1873 with special features, it is best to secure an expert appraisal. Model 1873s with case-colored receivers will bring a premium.

Courtesy Butterfield & Butterfield, San Francisco, California

First Model

The primary difference between the various styles of the Model 1873 is found in the appearance and construction of the dust cover. The First Model has a dust cover held in place with grooved guides on either side. A checkered oval finger grip is found on top of the dust cover. The latch that holds the lever firmly in place is anchored into the lower tang with visible threads. On later First Models, these threads are not visible. First Models appear from serial number 1 to about 31000.

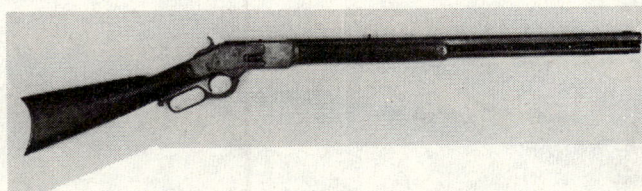

Courtesy Milwaukee Public Museum, Milwaukee, Wisconsin

Rifle

Exc.	V.G.	Good	Fair	Poor
—	7500	4000	2000	750

Carbine

Exc.	V.G.	Good	Fair	Poor
—	10000	5000	3000	1000

Musket

Exc.	V.G.	Good	Fair	Poor
—	3500	1500	1000	500

Second Model

The dust cover on the Second Model operates on one central guide secured to the receiver with two screws. The checkered oval finger grip is still used, but on later Second Models this is changed to a serrated finger grip on the rear of the dust cover. Second Models are found in the 31000 to 90000 serial number range.

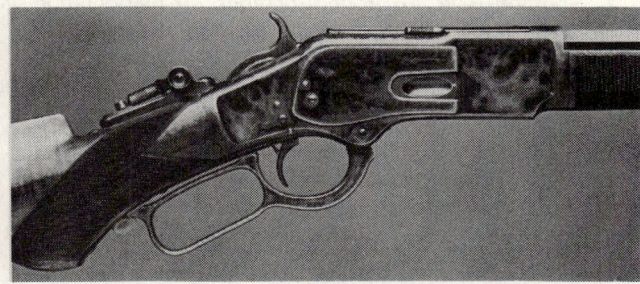

Courtesy Butterfield & Butterfield, San Francisco, California

Rifle

Exc.	V.G.	Good	Fair	Poor
9500	6000	2500	1000	500

Carbine

Exc.	V.G.	Good	Fair	Poor
12000	7500	4000	1500	800

Musket

Exc.	V.G.	Good	Fair	Poor
3500	1500	1000	750	500

Third Model

The central guide rail is still present on the Third Model, but it is now integrally machined as part of the receiver. The serrated rear edges of the dust cover are still present on the Third Model.

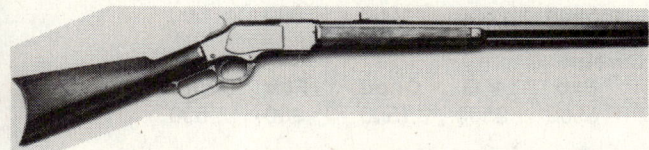

Courtesy Butterfield & Butterfield, San Francisco, California

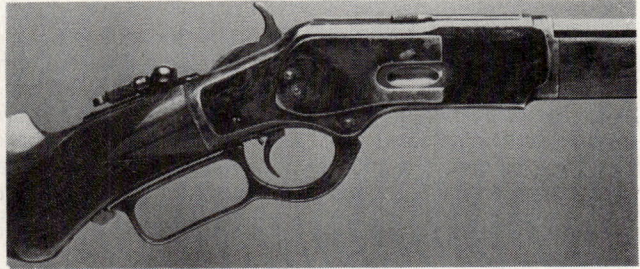

Courtesy Butterfield & Butterfield, San Francisco, California

Rifle

Exc.	V.G.	Good	Fair	Poor
9500	5000	2000	800	400

Carbine

Exc.	V.G.	Good	Fair	Poor
12000	6500	3500	1200	800

Musket

Exc.	V.G.	Good	Fair	Poor
3500	1500	1000	750	300

Model 1873 .22 Rimfire Rifle

Winchester's first .22 caliber rifle and the first .22 caliber repeating rifle made in America was introduced in 1884 and discontinued in 1904. Its drawback was the small caliber. The general preference during this period of time was for the larger caliber rifles. Winchester sold a little more than 19,000 .22 caliber Model 1873s.

Exc.	V.G.	Good	Fair	Poor
10000	5500	2500	1500	750

Model 1876

Winchester's Model 1876, sometimes referred to as the Centennial Model, was the company's response to the public's demand for a repeater rifle capable of handling larger and more potent calibers. Many single shot rifles were available at this time to shoot more powerful cartridges, and Winchester redesigned the earlier Model 1873 to answer this need. The principal changes made to the Model 1873 were a larger and stronger receiver to handle more powerful cartridges. Both the carbine and the musket had their forearms extended to cover the full length of the magazine tube. The carbine barrel was increased in length from 20" to 22", and the musket barrel length was increased from 30 to 32". The Model 1876 was the first Winchester to be offered with a pistol grip stock on its special Sporting Rifle. The Model 1876 was available in the following calibers: .45-77 W.C.F., .50-95 Express, .45-60 W.C.F., .40-60 W.C.F. The Model 1876 was offered in four different styles:

1. Sporting Rifle, 28" round, octagon, or half-octagon barrel. This rifle was fitted with a straight grip stock with crescent iron buttplate. A special sporting rifle was offered with a pistol grip stock.

2. Express Rifle, 26" round, octagon, or half-octagon barrel. The same sporting rifle stock was used.

3. Carbine, 22" round barrel with full length forearm secured by one barrel band and straight grip stock.

4. Musket, 32" round barrel with full-length forearm secured by one barrel band and straight grip stock. Stamped on the barrel is the Winchester address with King's patent date. The caliber marking is stamped on the bottom of the receiver near the magazine tube and the breech end of the barrel. Winchester also furnished the Model 1876 in 1-of-100 and 1-of-1000 special guns. Only 8 1-of-100 Model 1876s were built and 54 1-of-1000 76s were built. As with their Model 1873 counterparts, these rare guns often sell in the $75,000 range or more. Approximately 64,000 Model 1876s were built by Winchester between 1876 and 1897. As with other Winchesters, the prices given below are for standard guns.

First Model

As with the Model 1873, the primary difference in model types lies in the dust cover. The First Model has no dust cover and is seen between serial number 1 and 3000.

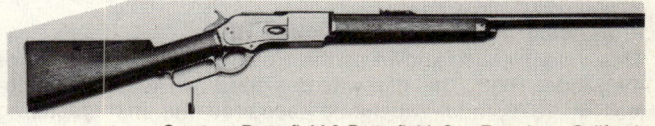

Courtesy Butterfield & Butterfield, San Francisco, California

Rifle

Exc.	V.G.	Good	Fair	Poor
—	6500	3000	1500	1000

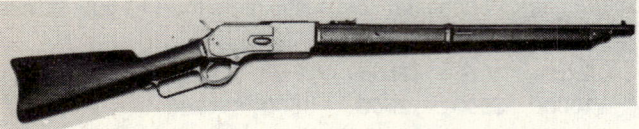

Courtesy Butterfield & Butterfield, San Francisco, California

Carbine

Exc.	V.G.	Good	Fair	Poor
—	5000	3000	1500	1000

Musket

Exc.	V.G.	Good	Fair	Poor
—	7000	4000	2000	1000

Second Model

The Second Model has a dust cover with guide rail attached to the receiver with two screws. On the early Second Model an oval finger guide is stamped on top of the dust cover while later models have a serrated finger guide along the rear edge of the dust cover. Second Models range from serial numbers 3000 to 30000.

Rifle

Exc.	V.G.	Good	Fair	Poor
—	3500	2500	1000	500

Carbine

Exc.	V.G.	Good	Fair	Poor
—	4500	2500	1500	700

Musket

Exc.	V.G.	Good	Fair	Poor
—	8000	5000	2000	1000

Third Model

The dust cover guide rail on Third Model 76s is integrally machined as part of the receiver with a serrated rear edge on the dust cover. Third Model will be seen from serial numbers 30000 to 64000.

Rifle

Exc.	V.G.	Good	Fair	Poor
6000	3500	2000	800	500

Carbine

Exc.	V.G.	Good	Fair	Poor
7000	4000	2500	1500	700

Musket

Exc.	V.G.	Good	Fair	Poor
12000	8000	4500	2000	1000

> **Three consecutive serial number Model 1876s chambered for the 45-60 cartridge with 26" octagon barrel sold at auction for $66,000. Each Deluxe rifle had a checkered pistol grip stock with fancy walnut. Each was fitted with a half magazine. Condition was excellent.**
> **J.C. Divine, Inc. April 1996.**

Winchester Hotchkiss Bolt Action Rifle

This model is also known as the Hotchkiss Magazine Gun or the Model 1883. This rifle was designed by Benjamin Hotchkiss in 1876, and Winchester acquired the manufacturing rights to the rifle in 1877. In 1879 the first guns were delivered for sale. The Hotchkiss rifle was a bolt-action firearm designed for military and sporting use. It was the first bolt-action rifle made by Winchester. The rifle was furnished in .45-70 Government, and although the 1884 Winchester catalog lists a .40-65 Hotchkiss as being available, no evidence exists that such a chamber was ever actually furnished. The Model 1883 was available in three different styles:

1. Sporting Rifle, 26" round, octagon, or half-octagon barrel fitted with a rifle-type stock that included a modified pistol grip or straight grip stock.
2. Carbine, 24" round or 22-1/2" round barrel with military style straight grip stock.
3. Musket, 32" or 28" round barrel with almost full length military-style straight grip stock. Winchester produced the Model 1883 until 1899, having built about 85,000 guns.

First Model

This model has the safety and a turn button magazine cut-off located above the triggerguard on the right side. The Sporting Rifle is furnished with a 26" round or octagon barrel while the carbine has a 24" round barrel with a saddle ring on the left side of the stock. The musket has a 32" round barrel with two barrel bands, a steel forearm tip, and bayonet attachment under the barrel. The serial number range for the First Model is between 1 and about 6419.

Sporting Rifle

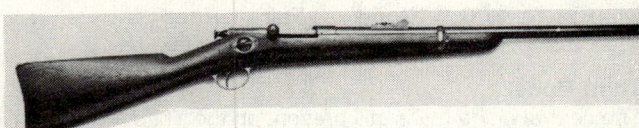

Courtesy Butterfield & Butterfield, San Francisco, California

Exc.	V.G.	Good	Fair	Poor
5500	2500	1500	900	500

Carbine

Exc.	V.G.	Good	Fair	Poor
5500	2500	1500	900	500

Musket

Exc.	V.G.	Good	Fair	Poor
5500	2500	1500	900	500

Second Model

On this model the safety is located on the top left side of the receiver, and the magazine cutoff is located on the top right side of the receiver to the rear of the bolt handle. The sporting rifle remains unchanged from the First Model with the above exceptions. The carbine has a 22-1/2" round barrel with a nickeled forearm cap. The musket now has a 28" barrel. Serial number range for the Second Model runs from 6420 to 22521.

Sporting Rifle

Courtesy Milwaukee Public Museum, Milwaukee, Wisconsin

Exc.	V.G.	Good	Fair	Poor
4500	2500	1000	750	500

Carbine

Exc.	V.G.	Good	Fair	Poor
4500	2250	1000	750	500

Musket

Exc.	V.G.	Good	Fair	Poor
4500	2250	1000	750	500

Third Model

The Third Model is easily identified by the two-piece stock separated by the receiver. The specifications for the sporting rifle remain the same as before, while the carbine is now fitted with a 20" barrel with saddle ring and bar on the left side of the frame. The musket remains unchanged from the Second Model with the exception of the two-piece stock. Serial numbers of the Third Model range from 22552 to 84555.

Sporting Rifle

Exc.	V.G.	Good	Fair	Poor
4250	2500	1000	750	500

Carbine

Exc.	V.G.	Good	Fair	Poor
4250	2500	1000	700	400

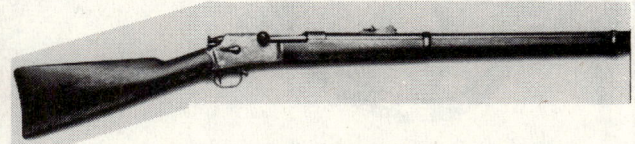

Courtesy Butterfield & Butterfield, San Francisco, California

Musket

Exc.	V.G.	Good	Fair	Poor
4250	2500	750	500	300

Model 1885 (Single Shot)

The Model 1885 marks an important development between Winchester and John M. Browning. The Single Shot rifle was the first of many Browning patents that Winchester would purchase and provided the company with the opportunity to diversify its firearms line. The Model 1885 was the first single shot rifle built by Winchester. The company offered more calibers in this model than any other. A total of 45 centerfire calibers were offered from the .22 extra long to the 50-110 Express, as well as 14 rimfire caliber from .22 B.B. cap to the .44 Flat Henry. Numerous barrel lengths, shapes, and weights were available as were stock configurations, sights, and finishes. These rifles were also available in solid frame and takedown styles. One could almost argue that each of the 139,725 Model 1885s built are unique. Many collectors of the Winchester Single Shot specialize in nothing else. For this reason it is difficult to provide pricing that will cover most of the Model 1885s that the collector will encounter. However the prices given here are for standard guns in standard configurations.

The Model 1885 was offered in two basic frame types:

A. The High Wall was the first frame type produced and is so called because the frame covers the breech and hammer except for the hammer spur.

B. The breech and hammer are visible on the Low Wall frame with its low sides. This frame type was first introduced around the 5000 serial number range.

Both the High Wall and the Low Wall were available in two type frame profiles; the Thickside and the Thinside. The Thickside frame has flat sides that do not widen out to meet the stock. The Thickside is more common on the low wall rifle and rare on the High Walls.

The Thinside frame has shallow milled sides that widen out to meet the stock. Thinside frames are common on High Wall guns and rare on Low Wall rifles.

1. The standard High Wall rifle was available with octagon or round barrel with length determined by caliber. The butt stock and forearm were plain walnut with crescent buttplate and blued frame.

2. The standard Low Wall featured a round or octagon barrel with length determined by caliber and a plain walnut stock and forearm with crescent buttplate.

3. The High Wall musket most often had a 26" round barrel chambered for the .22 caliber cartridge. Larger calibers were available as were different barrel lengths. The High Wall Musket featured an almost full length forearm fastened to the barrel with a single barrel band and rounded buttplate.

4. The Low Wall musket is most often referred to as the Winder Musket named after the distinguished marksman, Colonel C.B. Winder. This model features a Lyman receiver sight and was made in .22 caliber.

5. The High Wall Schuetzen rifle was designed for serious target shooting and was available with numerous extras including a 30" octagon barrel medium weight without rear sight seat; fancy walnut checkered pistol grip Schuetzen-style cheekpiece; Schuetzen-style buttplate; checkered forearm; double set triggers; spur finger lever, and adjustable palm rest.

6. The Low Wall carbine was available in 15", 16", 18", and 20" round barrels. The carbine featured a saddle ring on the left side of the frame and a rounded buttplate.

7. The Model 1885 was also available in a High Wall shotgun in 20 gauge with 26" round barrel and straight grip stock with shotgun style rubber buttplate. The Model 1885 was manufactured between 1885 and 1920 with a total production of about 140000 guns.

Courtesy Butterfield & Butterfield, San Francisco, California

Standard High Wall Rifle

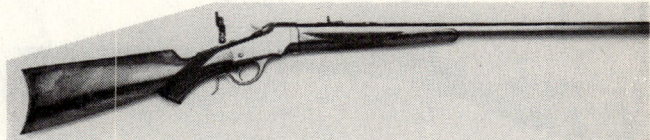

Courtesy Butterfield & Butterfield, San Francisco, California

Exc.	V.G.	Good	Fair	Poor
3750	3000	2250	1300	850

Standard Low Wall Rifle

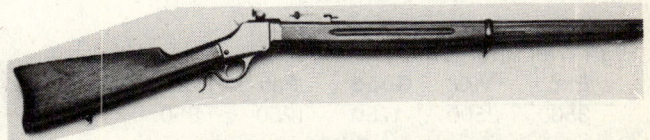

Courtesy Butterfield & Butterfield, San Francisco. California

Exc.	V.G.	Good	Fair	Poor
3500	2500	1750	1100	750

High Wall Musket

Exc.	V.G.	Good	Fair	Poor
2750	2000	1200	900	700

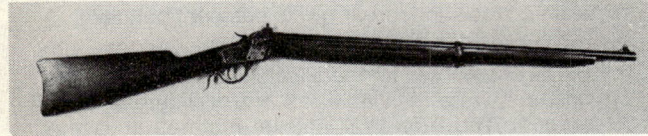

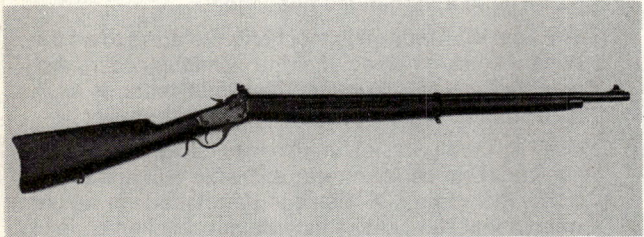

Courtesy Buffalo Bill Historical Center, Cody, Wyoming

Low Wall Musket (WinderMusket)

Exc.	V.G.	Good	Fair	Poor
2750	2000	1200	900	700

High Wall Schuetzen Rifle

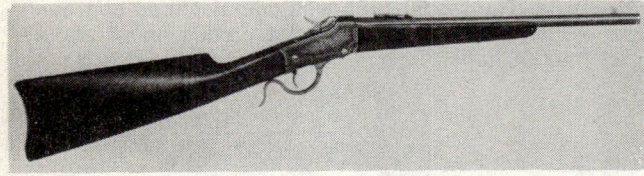

Exc.	V.G.	Good	Fair	Poor
10500	6000	4000	2000	1200

Low Wall Carbine

Courtesy Buffalo Bill Historical Center, Cody, Wyoming

Exc.	V.G.	Good	Fair	Poor
17500	10000	7000	3000	1500

High Wall Shotgun

Exc.	V.G.	Good	Fair	Poor
3500	2500	1750	1250	850

NOTE: Model 1885s with case-colored frames bring a premium of 25% over guns with blued frames.

NOTE: Model 1885s in calibers .50-110 and .50-140 will bring a premium depending on style and configuration.

In April of 1997 Rock Island Auction Company sold a custom built Model 1885 Hi Wall rifle chambered for the .22 caliber rimfire cartridge and fitted with a 28-1/2" octagon barrel. The rifle was engraved by Rudolph Kornbrath in the 1930s. Auction price was $25,300. Condition is near mint.

Model 1886

Based on a John Browning patent, the Model 1886 was one of the finest and strongest lever actions ever utilized in a Winchester rifle. Winchester introduced the Model 1886 in order to take advantage of the more powerful centerfire cartridges of the time. The rifle was available in 10 different chambers:

45-70 U.S. Gov't	50-110 Express
45-90 W.C.F.	40-70 W.C. F.
40-82 W.C.F.	38-70 W.C. F.
40-65 W.C.F.	50-100-450
38-56 W.C.F.	33 W.C. F.

The most popular caliber was the 45-70 Government. Prices of the Model 1886 are influenced by caliber, with the larger calibers bringing a premium. The 1886 was available in several different configurations.

1. Sporting Rifle, 26", round, octagon, or half-octagon barrel, full or half magazine and straight grip stock with plain forearm.

2. Fancy Sporting Rifle, 26", round or octagon barrel, full or half magazine and fancy checkered walnut pistol grip stock with checkered forearm.

3. Takedown Rifle, 24" round barrel, full or half magazine with straight grip stock fitted with shotgun rubber buttplate and plain forearm.

4. Extra Lightweight Takedown Rifle, 22" round barrel, full or half magazine with straight grip stock fitted with shotgun rubber buttplate and plain forearm.

5. Extra Lightweight Rifle, 22" round barrel, full or half magazine with straight grip stock fitted with a shotgun rubber butt-plate and plain forearm.

6. Carbine, 22" round barrel, full or half magazine, with straight grip stock and plain forearm.

7. Musket, 30" round barrel, musket style forearm with one barrel band. Military style sights. About 350 Model 1886 Muskets were produced. Model 1886 rifles and carbines were furnished with walnut stocks, case-hardened frames, and blued barrels and magazine tubes. In 1901 Winchester discontinued the use of case-hardened frames on all its rifles and used

blued frames instead. For this reason, casehardened Model 1886 rifles will bring a premium. Winchester provided a large selection of extra cost options on the Model 1886, and for rifles with these options, a separate valuation should be made by a reliable source. The Model 1886 was produced from 1886 to 1935 with about 160,000 in production.

Courtesy Milwaukee Public Museum, Milwaukee, Wisconsin

Sporting Rifle

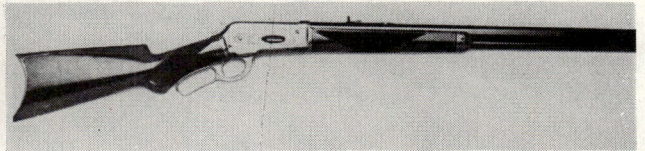

Courtesy Butterfield & Butterfield, San Francisco, California

Exc.	V.G.	Good	Fair	Poor
—	6000	3500	1500	650

Fancy Sporting Rifle

Exc.	V.G.	Good	Fair	Poor
—	9500	5000	3500	2000

This Deluxe Model 1886 rifle is chambered for the .45-90 cartridge. It is fitted with a 26" octagon barrel. Checkered stock wtih cresent butt and fancy wood. Condition is excellent. Auction price was $19,775.
Faintich Auction Service, June 1997.

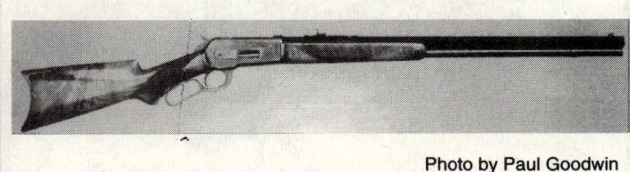

Photo by Paul Goodwin

Takedown Rifle-Standard

Exc.	V.G.	Good	Fair	Poor
—	7000	3500	1750	700

Extra Lightweight Takedown Rifle-.33 caliber

Exc.	V.G.	Good	Fair	Poor
—	2500	1250	600	400

Extra Lightweight Takedown Rifle

Exc.	V.G.	Good	Fair	Poor
—	4500	1500	1000	500

Extra Lightweight Rifle-.33 caliber

Exc.	V.G.	Good	Fair	Poor
—	2500	1100	550	400

Extra Lightweight Rifle

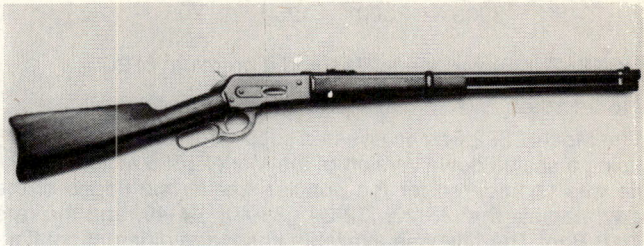

Courtesy Butterfield & Butterfield, San Francisco, California

Exc.	V.G.	Good	Fair	Poor
—	4500	1750	850	500

Carbine

Exc.	V.G.	Good	Fair	Poor
—	10000	5000	2000	1000

Musket

Exc.	V.G.	Good	Fair	Poor
—	15000	7500	3000	1500

NOTE: For .50 Express add a premium of 20%. Blued frame Model 1886 will bring 20% less than case-colored Model 1886s.

Model 71

When Winchester dropped the Model 1886 from its line in 1935 the company replaced its large bore lever-action rifle with the Model 71 chambered for the .348 caliber. The Model 71 is similar in appearance to the Model 1886 with some internal parts strengthened to handle the powerful .348 cartridge. The rifle was available in three basic configurations:

1. Standard Rifle, 24" round barrel, 3/4 magazine, plain walnut pistol grip stock and semi-beavertail forearm.
2. Standard Rifle, 20" round barrel, 3/4 magazine, plain walnut pistol grip stock and semi-beavertail forearm.
3. Deluxe Rifle, 24" round barrel, 3/4 magazine, checkered walnut pistol grip stock and checkered semi-beavertail forearm. The frames and barrels were blued on all models of this rifle.

The Model 71 was produced from 1935 to 1957 with about 47,000 built.

Standard Rifle-24" Barrel

Exc.	V.G.	Good	Fair	Poor
1000	800	600	400	300

Standard Carbine-20" Barrel

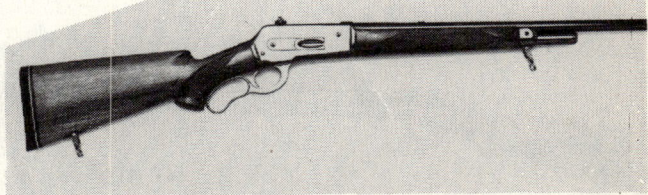

Courtesy Butterfield & Butterfield, San Francisco, California

Exc.	V.G.	Good	Fair	Poor
3250	2000	1600	1200	650

Deluxe Rifle-24" Barrel

Exc.	V.G.	Good	Fair	Poor
1600	950	700	525	425

Deluxe Carbine-20" Barrel

Exc.	V.G.	Good	Fair	Poor
3750	3000	2000	1250	700

NOTE: For prewar Model 71s add a premium of 20%.

Model 1892

The Model 1892 was an updated successor to the Model 1873 using a scaled down version of the Model 1886 action. The rifle was chambered for the popular smaller cartridges of the day, namely the .25-20, .32-20, .38-40, .44-40, and the rare .218 Bee. The rifle was available in several different configurations:

1. Sporting Rifle, solid frame or takedown (worth an extra premium of about 20%), 24" round, octagon, or half-octagon barrel with 1/2, 2/3, or full magazines. Plain straight grip walnut stock with capped forearm.

2. Fancy Sporting Rifle, solid frame or takedown (worth 20% premium), 24" round, octagon, or half-octagon barrel with 1/2, 2/3, or full magazine. Checkered walnut pistol grip stock with checkered capped forearm.

3. Carbine, 20" round barrel, full or half magazine, plain walnut straight grip stock with one barrel band forearm. Carbines were offered only with solid frames.

4. Trapper's Carbine, 18", 16", 15", or 14" round barrel with the same dimensions of standard carbine. Federal law prohibits the possession of rifles with barrel lengths shorter than 16". The Model 1892 Trapper's Carbine can be exempted from this law as a curio and relic with a federal permit.

5. Musket, 30" round barrel with full magazine. Almost full length forearm held by two barrel bands. Butt stock is plain walnut with straight grip.

The Model 1892 was built between 1892 and 1932 with slightly more than 1 million sold. The Model 1892 carbine continued to be offered for sale until 1941.

Courtesy Butterfield & Butterfield, San Francisco, California

Sporting Rifle

Exc.	V.G.	Good	Fair	Poor
3500	2500	700	450	200

Courtesy Butterfield & Butterfield, San Francisco, California

Fancy Sporting Rifle

Exc.	V.G.	Good	Fair	Poor
5500	3750	1500	700	300

A Deluxe engraved presentation Model 1892 chambered for the .38-40 was sold at auction for $11,000. Barrel length was 24.25" and octagon. half magazine. Two scroll engraved silver panels inlaid at wrist of grip. Condition was very good. Butterfield & Butterfield, August 1995.

Courtesy Butterfield & Butterfield, San Francisco, California

Carbine

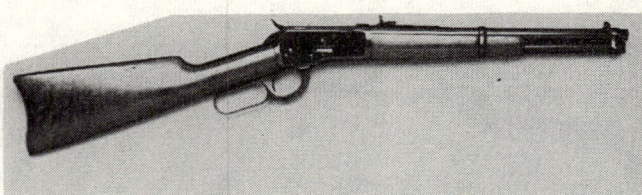

Courtesy Butterfield & Butterfield, San Francisco, California

Exc.	V.G.	Good	Fair	Poor
4000	3000	1250	700	300

A Winchester Model 1892 chambered for the .250-20 cartridge and fitted with a 20" barrel was sold at auction for $27,600. It was the property of Clyde Barrow, the outlaw. Condition was fair, refinished. Butterfield & Butterfield, April 1997.

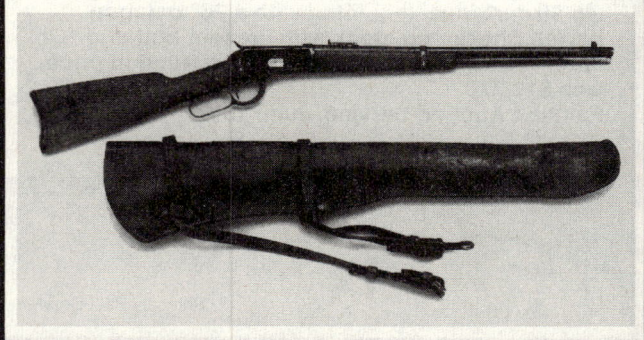

Trapper's Carbine

Exc.	V.G.	Good	Fair	Poor
7500	4800	2000	850	400

NOTE: Add 20% for 15" barrel. Add 50% for carbines chambered for 25-20 cartridge.

Musket

Exc.	V.G.	Good	Fair	Poor
—	7500	2500	1000	500

Model 53

This model was in fact a slightly more modern version of the Model 1892 offered in the following calibers: .25-20, .32-20, and the .44-40. It was available in only one style: the Sporting Rifle, 22" round barrel, half magazine, straight or pistol grip plain walnut stock with shotgun butt. It was available in solid frame or takedown with blued frame and barrel. The Model 53 was produced from 1924 to 1932 with about 25,000 built.

Sporting Rifle

Exc.	V.G.	Good	Fair	Poor
3500	2500	1000	500	300

NOTE: Add 10% for takedown model. Add 40% for rifles chambered for .44-40 cartridge. A few of these rifles were fitted with stainless steel barrel in the early 1930s. If the black paint on these barrels is in good condition they will bring a substantial premium

Model 65

This model was a continuation of the Model 53 and was offered in three calibers: .25-20, .32-20, and .218 Bee. It had several improvements over the Model 53, namely the magazine capacity was increased to 7 cartridges, forged ramp for front sight, and a lighter trigger pull. The Model 65 was available only in solid blued frame with blued barrel and pistol grip with plain walnut stock. Only about 5,700 of these rifles were built between 1933 and 1947.

Courtesy Butterfield & Butterfield, San Francisco, California

Standard Rifle

Exc.	V.G.	Good	Fair	Poor
3500	2500	1000	550	250

Model 1894

Based on a John M. Browning patent, the Model 1894 was the most successful centerfire rifle Winchester ever produced. This model is still in production, and the values given here reflect those rifles produced before 1964, or around serial number 2550000. The Model 1894 was the first Winchester developed especially for smokeless powder and was chambered for the following cartridges: .32-40, .38-55, .25-35 Winchester, .30-30 Winchester, and the .32 Winchester Special. The rifle was available in several different configurations:

1. Sporting Rifle, 26" round, octagon, or half-octagon barrel, in solid frame or takedown. Full, 2/3 or 1/2 magazines were available. Plain walnut straight or pistol grip stock with crescent buttplate and plain capped forearm.

2. Fancy Sporting Rifle, 26" round, octagon, or half-octagon barrel, in solid frame or takedown. Full, 2/3, or 1/2 magazines were available. Fancy walnut checkered straight or pistol grip stock with crescent buttplate and checkered fancy capped forearm.

3. Extra lightweight Rifle, 22" or 26" round barrel with half magazine. Plain walnut straight-grip stock with shotgun buttplate and plain capped forearm.

4. Carbine, 20" round barrel, plain walnut straight grip stock with carbine style buttplate. Forearm was plain walnut uncapped with one barrel band. Carbines were available with solid frame only. Carbines made prior to 1925 were fitted with a saddle ring on the left side of receiver and worth a premium over carbines without saddle ring.

5. Trapper's Carbine, 18", 16", 15", or 14". Buttstock, forearm, and saddle ring specifications same as standard carbine. All Model 1894s were furnished with blued frames and barrels, although case-hardened frames were available as an extra cost option. Case-colored Model 1894s are rare and worth a considerable premium, perhaps as much as 1000 per-

cent. Guns with extra cost options should be evaluated by an expert to determine proper value. Between 1894 and 1963, approximately 2,550,000 Model 1894s were sold.

Courtesy Butterfield & Butterfield, San Francisco, California

Sporting Rifle

Exc.	V.G.	Good	Fair	Poor
2500	1600	750	500	200

NOTE: Takedown versions are worth approximately 20% more.

Courtesy Butterfield & Butterfield, San Francisco, California

Fancy Sporting Rifle

Exc.	V.G.	Good	Fair	Poor
6500	2500	1400	750	400

> A Model 1894 Deluxe Sporting Rifle with 26" barrel chambered for .30 WCF. Engraved by John Ulrich in 1895. Winchester used this rifle for display at many exhibitions. Factory letters. Price $17,600. Condition very good to excellent.
> **J.C. Devine, Inc., September 1996.**

NOTE: Takedown versions are worth approximately 20% more. Fancy Sporting Rifles were also engraved at the customer's request. Check factory where possible and proceed with caution. Factory engraved Model 1894s are extremely valuable.

Extra Lightweight Rifle

Exc.	V.G.	Good	Fair	Poor
3500	2500	1100	600	300

Courtesy Butterfield & Butterfield, San Francisco, California

> A Model 1894 Deluxe rifle with 26" half round barrel and factory carved stock with gold inlaid factory engraving, Chambered for .30 WCF. Fitted with a shotgun butt, sold at auction for $66,000. Condition was very good.
> **Rock Island Auction Co., May 1996.**

Carbine

Exc.	V.G.	Good	Fair	Poor
2500	1500	600	400	200

NOTE: Above values are for guns with saddle rings. For carbines without saddle rings deduct 35%. Add 25% for carbines chambered for .25-20 cartridge.

Courtesy Butterfield & Butterfield, San Francisco, California

Trappers Carbine

Exc.	V.G.	Good	Fair	Poor
5500	3500	1500	750	400

NOTE: Add 30% for carbines chambered for 25-35 or 38-55 calibers.

Model 55

This model was a continuation of the Model 1894 except in a simplified version. Available in the same calibers as the Model 1894, this rifle could be ordered only with a 24" round barrel, plain walnut straight-grip stock with plain forend and shotgun butt. Frame and barrel were blued with solid or takedown features. This model was produced between 1924 and 1932 with about 21,000 sold. Serial numbers for the Model 55 were numbered separately until about serial number 4500; then the guns were numbered in the Model 1894 sequence.

Standard Rifle

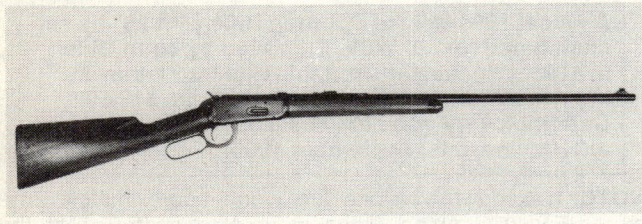

Exc.	V.G.	Good	Fair	Poor
1500	1000	650	450	200

NOTE: .25-35 caliber will bring about a 60% premium. Add 10% for models with solid frame.

Model 64

An improved version of the Model 55, this gun featured a larger magazine, pistol grip stock, and forged front sight ramp. The trigger pull was also improved. Frame and barrel were blued. chambered for the .25-35 Win., 30-30 Win., .32 Win. Special, and the .219 Zipper(added in 1938 and discontinued in the Model 64 in 1941). Serial number of the Model 64 was concurrent with the Model 1894. Built between 1933 and 1957, approximately 67,000 were sold. This model was reintroduced in 1972 and discontinued in 1973. The values listed below are for the early version only.

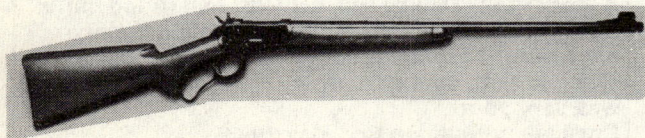

Courtesy Butterfield & Butterfield, San Francisco, California

Standard Rifle

Exc.	V.G.	Good	Fair	Poor
1200	900	500	300	200

Carbine-20" Barrel

Exc.	V.G.	Good	Fair	Poor
1550	1000	650	500	250

NOTE: For Deluxe model add 50% to above prices. For Carbine model add 50% to above prices. For rifles chambered for the .219 Zipper and .25-35 cartridges add 50%.

Model 1895

The Model 1895 was the first non-detachable box magazine rifle offered by Winchester. Built on a John M. Browning patent, this rifle was introduced by Winchester to meet the demand for a rifle that could handle the new high power, smokeless hunting cartridges of the period. The Model 1895 was available in the following calibers: .30-40 Krag, .38-72 Winchester, .40-72 Winchester, .303 British, .35 Winchester, .405 Government, 7.62 Russian, .30-03, and .30-06. The rifle gained fame as a favorite hunting rifle of Theodore Roosevelt. Because of its box magazine, the Model 1895 has a distinctive look like no other Winchester lever-action rifle. The rifle was available in several different configurations:

1. Sporting Rifle, 28" or 24" (depending on caliber) round barrel, plain walnut straight-grip stock with plain forend. The first 5,000 rifles were manufactured with flat sided receivers, and the balance of production were built with the receiver sides contoured. After serial-number 60000 a takedown version was available.

2. Fancy Sporting Rifle, 28" round barrel, fancy walnut checkered straight grip stock and fancy walnut checkered forearm. Rifles with serial numbers below 5000 had flat sided frames.

3. Carbine, 22" round barrel, plain walnut straight-grip stock with military style hand guard forend. Some carbines are furnished with saddle rings on left side of receiver.

4. Musket:

   A. Standard Musket, 28" round, plain walnut straight-grip stock with musket style forend with two barrel bands.

   B. U.S. Army N.R.A. Musket, 30-round barrel, Model 1901 Krag-Jorgensen rear sight. Stock similar to the standard musket. This musket could be used for "Any Military Arm" matches under the rules of the National Rifle Association.

   C. N.R.A. Musket, Models 1903 and 1906, 24" round barrel with special buttplate. Also eligible for all matches under "Any Military Arm" sponsored by the N.R.A. This musket was fitted with the same stock as listed above.

   D. U.S. Army Musket, 28" round barrel chambered for the .30-40 Krag. Came equipped with or without knife bayonet. These muskets were furnished to the U.S. Army for use during the Spanish-American War and are "US" marked on the receiver.

   E. Russian Musket, similar to standard musket but fitted with clip guides in the top of the receiver and with bayonet. Approximately 294,000 Model 1895 Muskets were sold to the Imperial Russian Government between 1915 and 1916. The first 15,000 Russian Muskets had 8" knife bayonets, and the rest were fitted with 16" bayonets.

The Model 1895 was produced from 1895 to 1931 with about 426,000 sold.

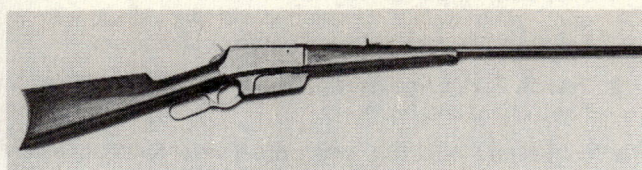

Courtesy Butterfield & Butterfield, San Francisco, California

Sporting Rifle

Courtesy Butterfield & Butterfield, San Francisco, California

Exc.	V.G.	Good	Fair	Poor
5000	3000	1200	700	300

NOTE: Flat side rifles will bring a premium of 100%. Takedown rifles will add an additional 15%.

Fancy Sporting Rifles

Exc.	V.G.	Good	Fair	Poor
6500	4500	1500	1100	500

NOTE: Flat side rifles will bring a premium of 100%. Takedown rifles will add an additional 15%.

Courtesy Butterfield & Butterfield, San Francisco, California

Carbine

Exc.	V.G.	Good	Fair	Poor
3000	1750	1050	600	300

Standard Musket

Exc.	V.G.	Good	Fair	Poor
3000	1750	1050	600	300

U.S. Army N.R.A. Musket

Exc.	V.G.	Good	Fair	Poor
4500	2000	1200	800	400

N.R.A. Musket, Model 1903 and 1906

Exc.	V.G.	Good	Fair	Poor
5500	2500	1200	800	400

U.S. Army Musket

Exc.	V.G.	Good	Fair	Poor
—	3000	1500	850	450

Russian Musket

Exc.	V.G.	Good	Fair	Poor
4000	2500	1000	500	250

Breechloading Double Barrel Shotgun

Winchester imported an English made shotgun sold under the Winchester name between 1879 and 1884. The gun was available in 10 and 12 gauge with 30" or 32" Damascus barrels. It was sold in five separate grades referred to as "classes." The lowest grade was the "D" and the best grade was called the "Match Grade." These were marked on the sidelocks. The center rib was stamped "Winchester Repeating Arms Co., New Haven, Connecticut, U.S.A." About 10,000 of these guns were imported by Winchester.

Class A,B,C, and D

Exc.	V.G.	Good	Fair	Poor
2500	2250	1250	850	500

Match Gun

Exc.	V.G.	Good	Fair	Poor
2500	2250	1250	850	500

Model 1887 Shotgun

Winchester enjoyed a great deal of success with its imported English shotgun, and the company decided to manufacture a shotgun of its own. In 1885 it purchased the patent for a lever action shotgun designed by John M. Browning. By 1887 Winchester had delivered the first model 1887 in 12 gauge and shortly after offered the gun in 10 gauge. Both gauges were offered with 30" or 32" full choked barrels, with the 30" standard on the 12 gauge and 32" standard on the 10 gauge. A Riot Gun was offered in 1898 both in 10, and 12 gauge with 20" barrels choked cylinder. Both variations of the Model 1887 were offered with plain walnut pistol grip stocks with plain forend. The frame was casehardened and the barrel blued. Between 1887 and 1901 Winchester sold approximately 65,000 Model 1887 shotguns.

Courtesy Milwaukee Public Museum, Milwaukee, Wisconsin

Courtesy Butterfield & Butterfield, San Francisco, California

Standard Shotgun

Exc.	V.G.	Good	Fair	Poor
1700	1200	850	500	300

Riot Shotgun

Exc.	V.G.	Good	Fair	Poor
2000	1500	950	600	400

Model 1901 Shotgun

This model is a redesign of the Model 1887 shotgun and was offered in 10 gauge only with a 32" barrel choked full, modified, or cylinder. The barrel was reinforced to withstand the new smokeless powder loads and the frame was blued instead of case-hardened. The stock was of plain walnut with a modified pistol and plain forearm. The Model 1901 was built between 1901 and 1920 with about 65,000 guns sold.

Standard Shotgun

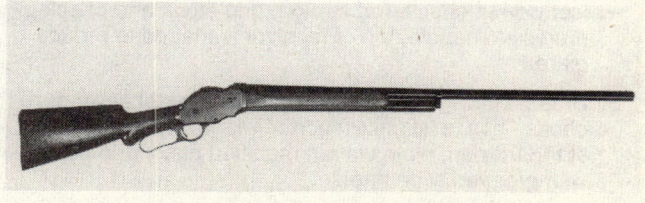

Exc.	V.G.	Good	Fair	Poor
1200	800	600	400	250

Model 1893

This was the first slide action repeating shotgun built by Winchester. It featured an exposed hammer and side ejection. Based on a John M. Browning patent this model was not altogether satisfactory. The action proved to be too weak to handle smokeless loads even though the gun was designed for black powder. The gun was offered in 12 gauge with 30" or 32" barrels choked full. Other chokes were available on special order and will command a premium. The stock was plain walnut with a modified pistol grip, grooved slide handle, and hard rubber buttplate. The receiver and barrel were blued. Winchester produced the Model 1893 between 1893 and 1897, selling about 31000 guns.

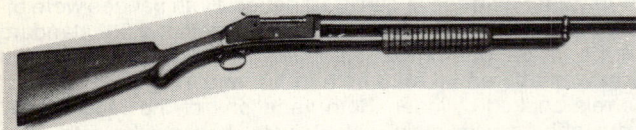

Courtesy Butterfield & Butterfield, San Francisco, California

Standard Shotgun

Exc.	V.G.	Good	Fair	Poor
1000	700	500	325	150

Model 1897

The Model 1897 replaced the Model 1893, and while similar to the Model 1893, the new model had several improvements such as a stronger frame, chamber made longer to handle 2-3/4" shells, frame top was covered to force complete side ejection, the stock was made longer and with less drop. The Model 1897 was avilable in 12 or 16 gauge with the 12 gauge offered either in solid or takedown styles and the 16 gauge available in takedown only. The Model 1897 was available with barrel lengths of 20", 28", and 30" and in practically all choke options from full to cylinder. The shotgun could be ordered in several different configurations:

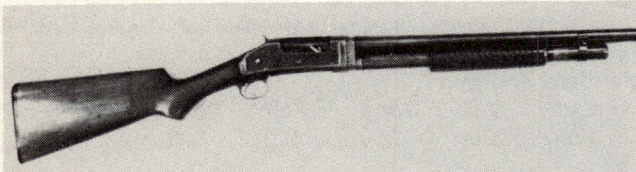

1. Standard Gun, 12 or 16 gauge, 30" barrel in 12 gauge and 28" barrel in 16 gauge, with plain walnut modified pistol grip stock and grooved slide handle. Steel buttplate standard.

2. Trap Gun 12 or 16 gauge, 30" barrel in 12 gauge and 28" barrel in 16 gauge, fancy walnut stock with oil finish checkered pistol grip or straight-grip stock with checkered slide handle. Marked "TRAP" on bottom of frame.

3. Pigeon Gun, 12 or 16 gauge, 28" barrel on both 12 and 16 gauge, straight or pistol grip stock same as Trap gun, receiver hand engraved.

4. Tournament Gun, 12 gauge only with 30" barrel, select walnut checkered straight grip stock and checkered slide handle, top of receiver is matted to reduce glare.

5. Brush Gun, 12 or 16 gauge, 26" barrel, cylinder choke, has a slightly shorter magazine tube than standard gun, plain walnut modified pistol grip stock with grooved slide handle.

6. Brush Gun, Takedown, same as above with takedown feature and standard length magazine tube.

7. Riot Gun, 12 gauge, 20" barrel bored to shoot buckshot, plain walnut modified pistol grip stock with grooved slide handle. Solid frame or takedown.

8. Trench Gun, same as Riot Gun but fitted with barrel hand guard and bayonet.

The Winchester Model 1897 was a great seller for Winchester. During its 60-year production span 1,025,000 guns were sold.

Standard Gun

Exc.	V.G.	Good	Fair	Poor
600	400	300	200	125

Trap Gun

Exc.	V.G.	Good	Fair	Poor
850	550	400	325	250

Pigeon Gun

Exc.	V.G.	Good	Fair	Poor
2700	2200	1600	1250	1000

Tournament Gun

Exc.	V.G.	Good	Fair	Poor
900	600	450	350	250

Brush Gun

Exc.	V.G	Good	Fair	Poor
850	550	400	325	250

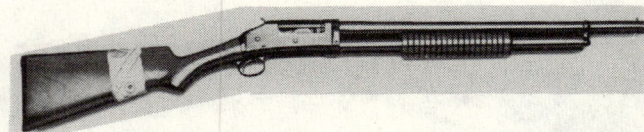

Courtesy Butterfield & Butterfield, San Francisco, California

Riot Gun

Courtesy Butterfield & Butterfield, San Francisco, California

Exc.	V.G.	Good	Fair	Poor
700	600	500	350	200

Trench Gun

Exc.	V.G.	Good	Fair	Poor
2000	1500	1000	500	300

Winchester-Lee Straight Pull Rifle

This rifle was a military firearm that Winchester built for the U.S. Navy in 1895. The Navy version was a musket type with 28" round barrel and musket style forearm and plain walnut pistol grip stock. In 1897 Winchester offered a commercial musket version for public sale as well as a Sporting Rifle. All of these guns were chambered for the 6mm Lee (236 Caliber) cartridge. The Sporting Rifle featured a 24" round barrel with plain walnut pistol grip stock and finger grooves in the forearm. Built from 1895 to 1905, Winchester sold about 20,000 Lee rifles; 15,000 were sold to the U.S. Navy, 3,000 were sold in the commercial version, and 1,700 were Sporting Rifles.

U.S. Navy Musket

Exc.	V.G.	Good	Fair	Poor
2500	2000	1500	700	500

Commercial Musket

Exc.	V.G.	Good	Fair	Poor
2500	2000	1500	700	500

Sporting Rifle

Exc.	V.G.	Good	Fair	Poor
2500	2000	1500	700	500

Model 1890

The Model 1890 was the first slide action rifle ever produced by Winchester. Designed by John and Matthew Browning, this rifle was chambered for the .22 Short, Long, and Winchester Rimfire cartridges (the WRF cartridge was developed by Winchester specifically for the Model 1890) not on an interchangeable basis. In 1919 the .22 l.r. cartridge was offered as well. The rifle was a slide action top ejecting rifle with an 18" under barrel magazine tube. All Model 1890s were furnished standard with plain walnut straight stocks with crescent buttplate and 12 groove slide handle. This rifle was one of the company's best selling small caliber firearms and was in worldwide use. The Model 1890 came in three separate and distinct variations that greatly affect its value:

1. First Model, solid frame, 24" octagon barrel, case-hardened frame, and fixed rear sight. Approximately 15,552 of these First Model guns were produced, and their distinctive feature is concealed locking lugs and solid frame. Serial numbered on the lower tang only. Built from 1890 to 1892.

2. Second Model, takedown, 24" octagon barrel, case-hardened frame, and adjustable rear sight. Serial numbered from 15,553 to 112,970 (on lower tang only) these Second Model guns feature the same concealed locking lugs but with the added takedown feature. A Deluxe version was offered with fancy walnut checkered straight or pistol grip stock and grooved slide handle.

   2A. Second Model (Blued Frame Variation), same as above but with blued frame. Serial numbered from 112,971 to 325,250 (on lower tang until 232,328, then also on bottom front end of receiver) these blued frame Second Models are much more numerous than the case-hardened variety. A Deluxe version was offered with fancy walnut checkered straight or pistol grip stock and grooved slide handle.

3. Third Model, takedown, 24" octagon barrel, blued frame, adjustable rear sight. Serial numbered from 325,251 to as high as 853,000 (numbered on both the lower tang and bottom front of receiver) the distinctive feature of the Third Model is the locking cut made on the front top of the receiver to allow the breech bolt to lock externally. A Deluxe version was offered with fancy walnut checkered stock, straight or pistol grip with grooved slide handle. Winchester offered many extra cost options for this rifle that will greatly affect the value. Secure an expert appraisal before proceeding. The Model 1890 was produced from 1890 to 1932 with approximately 775,000 guns sold.

First Model-Standard Grade

Exc.	V.G.	Good	Fair	Poor
9000	5000	2500	1250	750

Second Model-Case-hardened Frame

Standard

Exc.	V.G.	Good	Fair	Poor
5500	3500	2000	1000	500

Deluxe

Exc.	V.G.	Good	Fair	Poor
10000	7000	3500	2000	1000

Courtesy Butterfield & Butterfield, San Francisco, California

Courtesy Butterfield & Butterfield, San Francisco, California

A Deluxe with pistol grip and case colored frame was sold at auction for $22,000. This rifle featured a rare factory Swiss butt, Lyman rear tang, and Beach combination front sight. Chambered for .22 WRF. Condition was excellent.
Rock Island Auction Co., May, 1996

A Deluxe Model 1890 with pistol grip and factory engraving was sold at auction for $31,900. Condition was excellent to mint. Factory engraved Model 1890s are extremely rare. Fitted with Lyman rear tang sight and hooded front sight.
Rock Island Auction Co., May, 1996.

Second Model-Blued Frame

Standard

Exc.	V.G.	Good	Fair	Poor
4000	2250	1500	750	500

Deluxe

Exc.	V.G.	Good	Fair	Poor
7500	5500	3000	1500	1000

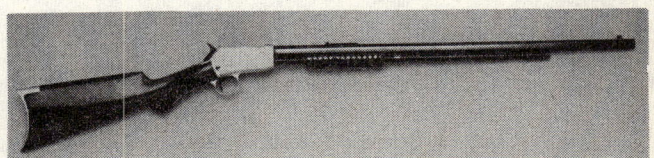

Courtesy Butterfield & Butterfield, San Francisco, California

A Model 1890 Deluxe rifle with pistol grip and checkered slide handle was sold at auction for $12,100. The 2nd model blued receiver was in excellent condition. This was one of four blued 2nd Model 90s sold with checkered slide handle and pistol grip stock by the factory.
Rock Island Auction Co., May 1996.

Third Model

Standard

Exc.	V.G.	Good	Fair	Poor
2750	1750	1200	750	500

Deluxe

Exc.	V.G.	Good	Fair	Poor
5000	3500	2000	1000	750

NOTE: For Third Models chambered for .22 Long Rifle add 25% premium.

Model 1906

In 1906 Winchester decided to offer a lower cost version of the Model 1890. The Model 1906 used the same receiver but was fitted with a 20" round barrel and plain gumwood straight grip stock. When the Model 1906 was first introduced, it sold for two-thirds of the price of the Model 1890. For the first two years the gun was chambered for the .22 Short cartridge only. In 1908 the rifle was modified to shoot .22 Short, Long, and Long Rifle cartridges interchangeably. This modification insured the Model 1906's success, and between 1906 and 1932 about 800,000 were sold. All Model 1906s were of the takedown variety. The Model 1906 is available in three important variations:

1. 22 Short Only, 20-round barrel, straight-grip gumwood stock and smooth slide handle. These were built from serial number 1 to around 113000.

2. Standard Model 1906, 20" round barrel, straight-grip gumwood stock with 12 groove slide handle. Serial numbered from 113000 to 852000.

3. Model 1906 Expert, 20" round barrel, pistol grip gumwood stock with fluted smooth slide handle. Expert was available from 1918 to 1924 and was offered in three different finishes regular blued finish, half nickel (receiver, guard, and bolt), and full nickel (receiver, guard, bolt, and barrel nickeled).

Courtesy Butterfield & Butterfield, San Francisco, California

Model 1906 .22 Short Only

Courtesy Butterfield & Butterfield, San Francisco, California

Exc.	V.G.	Good	Fair	Poor
3000	1750	750	500	200

Standard Model 1906

Courtesy Butterfield & Butterfield, San Francisco, California

NIB	Exc.	V.G.	Good	Fair	Poor
4000	2000	1000	650	400	200

Model 1906 Expert

Exc.	V.G.	Good	Fair	Poor
3250	1700	850	500	300

NOTE: Prices are for all blued Experts. Add 25% for half nickel and 100% for full nickel.

Model 62 and 62A

When the Model 1890 and Model 1906 were dropped from the Winchester product line in 1932, the company introduced the Model 62 to take their place. An updated version of the earlier slide action .22 rifles, the Model 62 was fitted with a 23" round barrel and was capable of shooting .22 Short, Long, and Long Rifle cartridges interchangeably. Winchester offered a Gallery version of the Model 62 that was chambered for .22 Short only. Some of these Gallery guns have "Winchester" stamped on the left side of the receiver. A change in the breech bolt mechanism brought about a change in the name designation from Model 62 to Model 62A. This occurred around serial number 98000. The letter "A" now appears behind the serial number. This model stayed in production until 1958, and collectors will concede a premium for guns built prior to WWII with small slide handles. The stock was of plain walnut with straight grip and grooved slide handle. Both the receiver and barrel were blued. All Model 62 and 62As were takedown. Approximately 409,000 guns were sold.

Courtesy Butterfield & Butterfield, San Francisco, California

Prewar Model 62

NIB	Exc.	V.G.	Good	Fair	Poor
2250	1500	700	400	250	150

NOTE: Barrels marked with Model 62 are worth more than barrels marked with Model 62A by approximately 15%. Gallery models will bring a premium of 400%.

Postwar Model 62

NIB	Exc.	V.G.	Good	Fair	Poor
1700	750	450	325	225	125

NOTE: Gallery models will bring a premium of 250%.

Model 61

Winchester developed the Model 61 in an attempt to keep pace with its competitors' hammerless .22 rifles. The Model 61 featured a 24" round or octagonal barrel and could be ordered by the customer in a variety of configurations. Collector interest in this rifle is high because of the fairly large number of variations. The following is a list of chamber and barrel variations found in this model:

1. 24" round barrel, .22 Short, Long, Long Rifle.
2. 24" octagonal barrel, .22 Short only.
3. 24" octagonal barrel, .22 Long Rifle only.
4. 24" octagonal barrel, .22 W.R.F. only.
5. 24" round barrel, .22 Long Rifle Shot only.
6. 24" round barrel, .22 W.R.F. only.
7. 24" round barrel, .22 Long Rifle only.
8. 24" round barrel, .22 Winchester Magnum.
9. 24" round barrel, .22 Short only.

The Model 61 was fitted with a plain walnut pistol grip stock with grooved slide handle. All Model 61s were of the take down variety. Prewar models will have a short slide handle. Manufactured between 1932 and 1963, approximately 342,000 guns were sold.

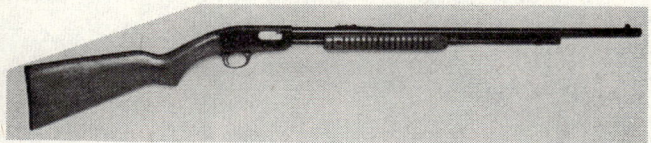

Courtesy Butterfield & Butterfield, San Francisco, California

Prewar Model 61

NIB	Exc.	V.G.	Good	Fair	Poor
2500	1500	700	400	250	150

NOTE: Single caliber models will command a premium of 50% depending on caliber. Octagon barrel models will command a premium of 75%. Shot only models will bring a premium of 250%.

Postwar Model 61

NIB	Exc.	V.G.	Good	Fair	Poor
1750	850	500	350	250	150

Model 61 Magnum

NIB	Exc.	V.G.	Good	Fair	Poor
1850	950	700	450	300	150

NOTE: This variation was produced from 1960 to 1963.

Model 1903

The first semiautomatic rifle produced by Winchester was designed by T.C. Johnson. This rifle was offered in a takedown version only and was available in a 20" round barrel chambered for the .22 Winchester Automatic Rimfire. The tubular magazine is located in the butt stock and holds 10 cartridges. The rifle was available in two different configurations:

1. Standard Rifle, 20" round barrel, plain walnut straight grip stock with plain forend. Steel shotgun butt was standard.

2. Deluxe Rifle, 20" round barrel, fancy checkered walnut pistol grip stock with checkered forearm. Manufactured from 1903 to 1932, about 126,000 were sold.

Standard Rifle

Courtesy Butterfield & Butterfield, San Francisco, California

Exc.	V.G.	Good	Fair	Poor
850	550	400	250	100

Deluxe Rifle

Exc.	V.G.	Good	Fair	Poor
2250	1000	700	500	250

NOTE: The first 5,000 guns were built without safeties, and the first 15,000 guns were furnished with bronze firing pins instead of steel. These early Model 1903s will bring a premium of 50%.

Model 63

The Model 63 took the place of the Model 1903 in 1933 in an attempt by Winchester to solve the problem of having to use a special .22 caliber cartridge in the gun to operate the blowback system. The Model 63 was chambered for the .22 Long Rifle cartridge and was available in a 20" barrel for the first four years or until about serial number 9800. Thereafter, the model was offered with a 23" round barrel for the remainder of the production period. The gun was fitted with a plain walnut pistol grip stock and forearm. The tubular magazine was located in the butt stock that came with a steel buttplate. The last 10,000 Model 63s were sold with a grooved receiver top to make the addition of a scope easier. Manufactured between 1933 and 1958, about 175,000 guns were sold.

Courtesy Butterfield & Butterfield, San Francisco, California

20" Barrel Model 63

Courtesy Butterfield & Butterfield, San Francisco, California

NIB	Exc.	V.G.	Good	Fair	Poor
2750	1400	800	500	400	250

23" Barrel Model 63

NIB	Exc.	V.G.	Good	Fair	Poor
1750	900	450	350	300	200

NOTE: Grooved top receivers command a premium of 15%.

Model 1905

The Model 1905 was a larger version of the Model 1903, developed by T.C. Johnson to handle the more powerful centerfire cartridges. It was chambered for the .32 Winchester Self-Loading and .35 Self-Loading cartridges, loading by means of a detachable box magazine. Available in takedown only, this model was offered in two different styles:

1. Sporting Rifle, 22" round barrel, plain walnut straight grip (changed to pistol grip in 1908) stock with plain forend.

2. Fancy Sporting Rifle, 22" round barrel, fancy walnut checkered pistol grip stock with checkered forend. This model was the first Winchester semiautomatic rifle to fire centerfire cartridges. Produced from 1905 to 1920 with about 30,000 rifles sold.

Sporting Rifle

Exc.	V.G.	Good	Fair	Poor
500	350	250	175	125

Fancy Sporting Rifle

Exc.	V.G.	Good	Fair	Poor
600	400	300	200	150

Model 1907

The Model 1907 was an improved version of the Model 1905 and chambered for the new .351 Winchester Self-Loading cartridge. Outward appearance was the same as Model 1905 except for 20" round barrel. This rifle was available in three different styles:

1. Sporting Rifle, 20" round barrel, plain walnut pistol grip stock with plain forend. Discontinued in 1937.

2. Fancy Sporting Rifle, 20" round barrel, fancy walnut checkered pistol grip stock and checkered forend.

3. Police Rifle, 20" round barrel, plain walnut pistol grip stock and beavertail forend. This version was fitted with a leather sling and with or without knife bayonet. First introduced in 1937. Winchester discontinued this model in 1957 after having sold about 59,000 guns.

Sporting Rifle

Exc.	V.G.	Good	Fair	Poor
400	300	250	175	125

Fancy Sporting Rifle

Exc.	V.G.	Good	Fair	Poor
550	400	300	200	150

Police Rifle

Exc.	V.G.	Good	Fair	Poor
450	350	275	200	150

Model 1910

This model was similar to the Model 1907 but the action was made stronger to handle the new Winchester .401 Self-Loading cartridge. The specifications for this model are the same as the Model 1907. Built between 1907 and 1936, only about 21,000 of these guns were sold.

Courtesy Butterfield & Butterfield, San Francisco, California

Sporting Rifle

Exc.	V.G.	Good	Fair	Poor
400	300	250	175	125

Fancy Sporting Rifle

Exc.	V.G.	Good	Fair	Poor
550	400	300	200	150

Model 55 (Rimfire Rifle)

Not to be confused with the lever-action model, this .22 caliber rifle was a semiautomatic single shot with a 22" round barrel. Fitted with a plain walnut pistol grip one-piece stock and forend. This model was not serial numbered and was produced from 1957 to 1961 with about 45,000 guns sold.

Standard Rifle

Exc.	V.G.	Good	Fair	Poor
200	150	125	90	60

Model 74

This was a semiautomatic chambered for either the .22 Short or the .22 Long Rifle. The rifle has a tubular magazine in the buttstock and a 24" round barrel. The bolt on this rifle was designed to be easily removed for cleaning or repair. The stock was plain walnut pistol grip with semi-beavertail forend. A Gallery Special was offered that was chambered for the .22 Short and fitted with a steel shell deflector. This gallery model was also available with chrome trimmings at extra cost.

Courtesy C.H. Wolfersberger

Sporting Rifle

Exc.	V.G.	Good	Fair	Poor
300	200	175	100	75

Gallery Special

Exc.	V.G.	Good	Fair	Poor
350	250	200	150	100

NOTE: For Gallery models with chrome trimmings, add a premium of 50%.

Model 77

This rifle was built on the blow-back design for semiautomatic rifles and is chambered for the .22 Long Rifle. It features a 22" round barrel and either a detachable box magazine or under barrel tubular magazine. The rifle has a triggerguard made of nylon. It has a plain walnut pistol grip stock with semi-beavertail forend and composition buttplate. Built between 1955 and 1963, Winchester sold about 217,000 of these rifles.

Standard Rifle

Exc.	V.G.	Good	Fair	Poor
175	125	100	90	75

NOTE: Models with tubular magazines will bring a slight premium of 10%.

Model 100

This rifle is gas operated, semiautomatic and chambered for the .243, .308, and .284 caliber center cartridges. It was available in a rifle version with a 22" round barrel and a carbine version with a 19" barrel. Both were furnished with a detachable box magazine. The stock was a one-piece design with pistol grip and was offered in either hand cut checkering or pressed basket weave checkering. Rifles were introduced in 1961 and the carbine in 1967. The Model 100 was last produced in 1973 with about 263,000 guns sold.

WARNING: The Model 100 has been recalled. Do not purchase this model without first determining if the problem has been repaired.

Model 100 Rifle

Exc.	V.G.	Good	Fair	Poor
475	400	300	250	200

Model 100 Carbine

Exc.	V.G.	Good	Fair	Poor
575	475	375	325	225

NOTE: Pre-1964 models 15% premium. Cut checkered add 10%. Prices given are for .308 caliber; for .243 add 15%, for .284 add 20%.

Model 88

The Model 88 was a modern short stroke lever-action chambered for the .243, .308, 284, and .358 calibers. It was available in a rifle version with 22" round barrel and a carbine version with 19" round barrel. The carbine model was not chambered for the .358 cartridge. Both were furnished with a detachable box magazine. The stock was a one-piece design with pistol grip and was offered with either hand cut checkering or pressed basket weave checkering. The rifle was introduced in 1955 and the carbine was first offered in 1968. Both versions were discontinued in 1973 with about 28,000 sold.

Model 88 Rifle

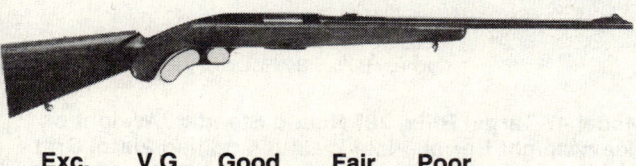

Exc.	V.G.	Good	Fair	Poor
500	400	300	250	150

NOTE: Pre-1964 models add 25% premium. Prices above are for .308 caliber; for .243 add 15%, .284 add 50%, and for 358 add 100%.

Model 88 Carbine

Exc.	V.G.	Good	Fair	Poor
950	800	650	400	300

NOTE: Add 25% for .243, add 100% for .284 calibers.

Model 1900

This single shot bolt-action .22 caliber rifle was based on a John M. Browning design. The rifle was furnished with an 18" round barrel and chambered for the .22 Short and Long interchangeably. The stock was a one-piece plain gumwood straight grip without a buttplate. The rifle was not serial numbered. It was produced from 1899 to 1902 with about 105,000 sold.

Courtesy Buffalo Bill Historical Center, Cody, Wyoming

Exc.	V.G.	Good	Fair	Poor
2500	1250	750	500	300

Model 1902

Also a single shot, this model was of the same general design as the Model 1900 with several improvements: a special shaped metal triggerguard was added, a shorter trigger pull, a steel buttplate, a rear peep sight, and the barrel was made heavier at the muzzle. The rifle was chambered for the .22 Short and Long cartridges until 1914 when the .22 Extra Long was added. In 1927 the .22 Extra Long was dropped in favor of the more popular .22 Long Rifle. All of these cartridges were interchangeable. The stock was a one-piece plain gumwood with straight grip (the metal triggerguard added a pistol grip feel) and steel buttplate, which was changed to composition in 1907. This model was not serial numbered. About 640,000 Model 1902s were sold between 1902 and 1931 when it was discontinued.

Exc.	V.G.	Good	Fair	Poor
1000	750	400	225	125

Model 99 or Thumb Trigger

This rifle was a modification of the Model 1902 without a traditional trigger. The rifle was fired by depressing the trigger with the thumb, which was part of the sear and extractor located behind the bolt. The rifle was chambered for the .22 Short and Long until 1914 when it was also chambered for the .22 Extra Long. All cartridges could be shot interchangeably. The stock was the same as the Model 1902 without the trigger or triggerguard. This model was not serial numbered. Built between 1904 and 1923. Winchester sold about 76,000 rifles.

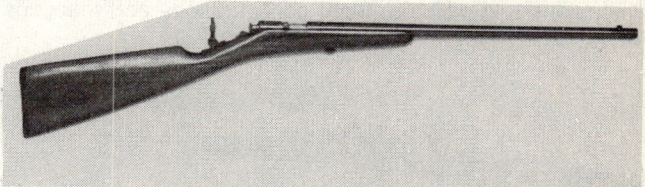

Courtesy Butterfield & Butterfield, San Francisco, California

Exc.	V.G.	Good	Fair	Poor
2250	1250	750	450	250

Model 1904

This model was a slightly more expensive version of the Model 1902. It featured a 21" round barrel, a one-piece plain gumwood straight grip stock (the metal triggerguard gave the rifle a pistol grip feel) with a small lip on the forend. Rifle was chambered for the .22 Short and Long until 1914 when the .22 Extra Long was added. The .22 Long Rifle cartridge was added in place of the Extra Long in 1927. This model was not serial numbered. Produced between 1904 and 1931, about 303,000 rifles were sold.

Exc.	V.G.	Good	Fair	Poor
850	600	350	200	100

Model D Military Rifle

Overall length 46-3/8"; barrel length 26"; caliber 7.62 mm. Walnut stock with blued barrel, receiver, magazine housing and furniture. Receiver ring over barrel breech stamped with serial number and Winchester proofmark. A total of 500 Model D Rifles were shipped to Russia for trial in March of 1917.

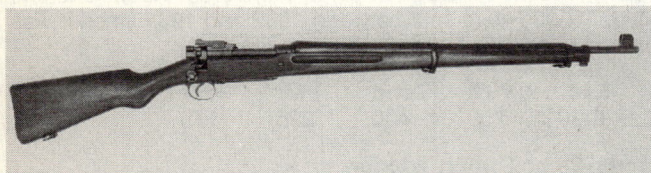

Propective purchasers are strongly advised to secure an expert appraisal prior to acquisition. Due to the recent identification of this model pricing schedules have yet to be established.

Imperial Bolt Action Magazine Rifle (Model 51)

Designed by T.C. Johnson, approximately 25 of these rifles were made during 1919 and 1920 in two different styles and three calibers. The takedown variation has an overall length of 42-1/4", barrel length 22" and was made in .27, .30-06 and .35 Newton calibers. The solid frame version is identical in form, dimensions and calibers. Sight configurations and markings vary.

Winchester Imperial Takedown

Winchester Imperial Solid Frame

Model 43

Introduced in 1949, this rifle was chambered for the .218 Bee, .22 Hornet, .25-20 Winchester, and the .32-20 Winchester. The rifle was a bolt-action with detachable box magazine, fitted with a 24" round barrel and front sight ramp forged integrally with barrel. This model was available in two styles:

1. Standard Rifle, 24" round barrel, plain walnut pistol grip stock and forend. One inch sling swivels are standard.

2. Special Rifle, 24" round barrel, select walnut checkered pistol grip stock and checkered forend. Furnished with either open sporting rear sight or Lyman 57A micrometer receiver sight.

The Model 43 was produced from 1949 to 1957 with about 63,000 sold.

Standard Rifle

Exc.	V.G.	Good	Fair	Poor
600	500	450	350	200

Special Rifle or Deluxe

Exc.	V.G.	Good	Fair	Poor
750	650	550	450	300

NOTE: For rifles chambered for .25-20 and .32-20 add a 25% premium.

Model 47

This model was a single shot bolt-action rifle chambered for the .22 Short, Long, and Long Rifle interchangeably. The rifle was furnished with a 25" round barrel, plain walnut pistol grip stock and forend. The bolt, bolt handle, and trigger are chrome plated. This model was not serial numbered. Produced between 1948 and 1954, Winchester sold about 43,000 guns.

Courtesy Buffalo Bill Historical Center, Cody, Wyoming

Model 47 Target Rifle, 28" Round Standard Weight or Heavyweight Barrel, Plain Walnut Modified Pistol Grip Stock

Exc.	V.G.	Good	Fair	Poor
275	225	200	150	100

Model 52

One of the finest small caliber bolt-action rifles ever built, the Model 52 was Winchester's answer to the increased demand for a military style target rifle following WWI. The Model 52 was a well-made quality-built bolt-action rifle. The rifle was chambered for the .22 Long Rifle cartridge. Designed by T.C. Johnson, this rifle was built in several different configurations over its production life:

1. Model 52 with finger groove in forend and one barrel band. Produced from 1920 to 1929.

2. Model 52 Target Rifle, same as above but without finger groove in forend and has first speed lock. Made from 1929 to 1932.

3. Model 52A Target Rifle, same as above with addition of reinforced receiver and locking lug. Made from 1932 to 1935.

4. Model 52B Target Rifle, same as above with addition of adjustable sling swivel and single shot adaptor. Made from 1935 to 1947.

5. Model 52C Target Rifle, same as above with addition of an easily adjustable vibration-free trigger mechanism. Made from 1947 to 1961.

6. Model 52D Target Rifle, this is a single shot rifle with free-floating barrel and new design stock with adjustable hand-stop channel.

7. Model 52 Bull Gun, same as target rifle but fitted with extra heavyweight barrel. Made from 1939 to 1960.

8. Model 52 International Match, a free style stock with thumb hole and adjustable buttstock and forend introduced in 1969 and an International Prone model with no thumb hole or adjustable buttplate and forend was introduced in 1975. Both discontinued in 1980.

9. Model 52 Sporter, 24" round barrel, select walnut checkered pistol grip stock with cheekpiece and forend with black plastic tip. Pistol grip was furnished with hard rubber grip cap. The Model 52 Sporter was introduced in 1934 and discontinued in 1958. It went through the same improvements as the Target Rifle, thus the designation Model 52A Sporter etc.

Model 52 Target

Exc.	V.G.	Good	Fair	Poor
500	400	300	275	225

Model 52 Target-Speed Lock

Exc.	V.G.	Good	Fair	Poor
550	450	350	300	250

Model 52A Target

Exc.	V.G.	Good	Fair	Poor
700	600	500	400	300

Model 52B Target

Exc.	V.G.	Good	Fair	Poor
650	550	375	325	250

Model 52C Target

Exc.	V.G.	Good	Fair	Poor
750	650	500	400	300

Model 52D Target

Exc.	V.G.	Good	Fair	Poor
750	650	550	325	275

Model 52 Bull Gun

Exc.	V.G.	Good	Fair	Poor
850	650	550	350	300

Model 52 International Match
Free Style

Exc.	V.G.	Good	Fair	Poor
1500	1250	950	600	350

Prone

Exc.	V.G.	Good	Fair	Poor
1250	1000	800	500	250

Model 52 Sporter

Exc.	V.G.	Good	Fair	Poor
2750	1750	1250	900	700

NOTE: Model 52A Sporters will being a 20% premium.

Editor's Comment: According to Winchester factory records, Model 52 barrels were, "originally drilled and tapped for Winchester telescope bases designed for use with the Winchester 3A, 5A, and Lyman telescopes. These bases had a 6.2" center to center spacing ... a change in the bases and the spacing to be used was authorized on January 11, 1933. These new bases had a specially shaped Fecker type notch added on the right hand side of both bases. They are known as Winchester Combination Telescope Sight Bases and are satisfactory for use with Winchester, Lyman, Fecker, and Unertl telescopes. Bases are spaced 7.2" center to center ... All Model 52 targets were factory drilled for scope mounting but only the "C" series Sporters were factory drilled for scopes.

Model 54

The Model 54 was to centerfire cartridges what the Model 52 was to rimfire cartridges. The Model 54 was also a quality made bolt-action rifle with a non-detachable box magazine and was chambered for a variety of calibers: .270, .30-06, .30-30, 7mm, 7.65, 9.mm, .250-3000, .22 Hornet, .220 Swift, and .257 Roberts. This was Winchester's first bolt-action rifle built for heavy, high velocity ammunition. The rifle was available in several different styles:

1. Standard Rifle, 24" or 20" round barrel (except .220 Swift which was 26"), plain walnut checkered pistol grip stock and forend.

2. Carbine, 20" round barrel, plain walnut pistol grip stock with finger groove on each side of forend.

3. Sniper's Rifle, 26" round heavyweight barrel, plain walnut pistol grip stock and forend.

4. N.R.A. Rifle, 24" round barrel, select walnut checkered pistol grip stock and forend.

5. Super Grade Rifle, 24" round barrel, select walnut checkered pistol grip stock with cheekpiece and checkered forend with black plastic tip. Pistol grip was capped with hard rubber cap. Super Grade was equipped with 1" detachable sling swivels.

6. Target Rifle, 24" round heavyweight barrel, plain walnut checkered pistol grip stock and forend.

7. National Match Rifle, 24" round barrel, plain walnut special target stock and forend.

The Model 54 was introduced in 1925 and was discontinued in 1936 with about 50,000 guns sold.

Standard Rifle

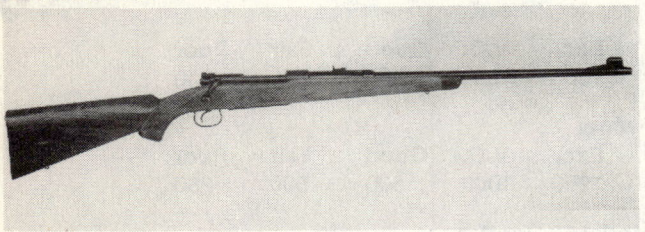

Exc.	V.G.	Good	Fair	Poor
650	550	400	300	225

Carbine

Exc.	V.G.	Good	Fair	Poor
700	600	450	350	275

Sniper's Rifle

Exc.	V.G.	Good	Fair	Poor
900	750	600	500	350

N.R.A. Rifle

Exc.	V.G.	Good	Fair	Poor
900	750	600	500	350

Super Grade Rifle

Exc.	V.G.	Good	Fair	Poor
900	750	600	450	375

Target Rifle

Exc.	V.G.	Good	Fair	Poor
900	750	600	450	375

National Match Rifle

Exc.	V.G.	Good	Fair	Poor
900	750	600	450	375

NOTE: The rare calibers are the 7.65 and the .30-30, which bring considerable premiums (in some cases as much as 250%) over standard calibers. Proceed with caution on Model 54s with rare caliber markings.

Model 56

This model was designed to be a medium priced bolt-action rimfire rifle. It featured a detachable box magazine and was chambered for the .22 Short or .22 Long Rifle cartridges. The rifle was offered in two styles;

1. Sporting Rifle, 22" round barrel, plain walnut pistol grip stock and forend.

2. Fancy Sporting Rifle, 22" round barrel, fancy walnut checkered pistol grip stock and forend.

Both styles had a forend with a distinctive lip on the forend tip. The rifle was introduced in 1926 and was discontinued in 1929 with about 8,500 rifles sold.

Sporting Rifle

Exc.	V.G.	Good	Fair	Poor
1500	1000	750	525	400

Fancy Sporting Rifle

Exc.	V.G.	Good	Fair	Poor
3000	2000	1500	900	750

NOTE: Add a 25% premium for rifles chambered for .22 Short only.

Model 57

The Model 57 was close in appearance to the Model 56 with the addition of a heavier stock, target sights, and swivel bows attached to the stock. The rifle was chambered for the .22 Short or .22 l.r. and featured a 22" round barrel with detachable box magazine. The stock was plain walnut with pistol grip and plain forend. The rifle was introduced in 1927 and dropped from the Winchester line in 1936 having sold only about 19,000 guns.

Model 57

Exc.	V.G.	Good	Fair	Poor
750	600	450	325	250

Model 58

This model was an attempt by the company to market a low priced .22 caliber rimfire rifle in place of its Models 1902 and 1904. This was a single shot bolt-action, cocked by pulling the firing pin head to the rear. It had an 18" round barrel and was chambered for the .22 Short, Long, and Long Rifle interchangeably. The stock was a one-piece plain wood with straight grip. This model was not serial-numbered. The Model 58 was introduced in 1928 and discontinued in 1931. About 39,000 were sold.

Exc.	V.G.	Good	Fair	Poor
750	600	425	250	125

Model 59

The Model 59 was essentially a Model 58 with the addition of a pistol grip stock and a 23" round barrel. Introduced in 1930, it was dropped from the product line in the same year with a total sales of about 9,000 guns.

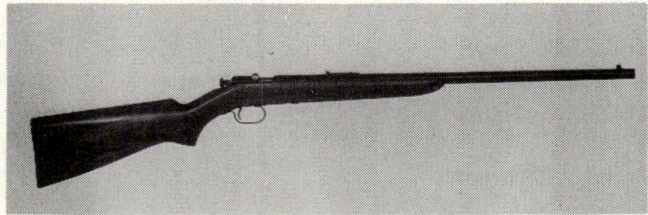

Courtesy Olin Corporation

Exc.	V.G.	Good	Fair	Poor
600	475	350	200	125

Model 60 and 60A

This rifle used the same action as that of the Model 59. When the rifle was first introduced in 1931, it was furnished with a 23" round barrel which was changed to 27" in 1933. Several other mechanical improvements were included with this model; perhaps the most noticeable were the chrome-plated bolt, bolt handle, and trigger. The stock was plain wood with pistol grip. In 1933 the Model 60A was added, which was the same rifle but in a target configuration. The front sight was a square top military blade with a Lyman 55W receiver sight. The Model 60 was discontinued in 1934 with about 166,000 rifles sold. The Model 60A was dropped in 1939 with only about 6,100 rifles sold.

Courtesy Buffalo Bill Historical Center, Cody, Wyoming

Model 60

Exc.	V.G.	Good	Fair	Poor
300	250	150	125	100

Model 60A

Exc.	V.G.	Good	Fair	Poor
400	300	225	150	100

Model 67

Winchester again upgraded and improved the Model 60 with an expansion of the styles offered to the shooting public. The standard chamber for the rifle was .22 Short, Long, and Long Rifle interchangeably with the W.R.F. only added in 1935:

1. Sporting Rifle, 27" round barrel, stock similar to the Model 60.
2. Smoothbore Rifle, 27" barrel, chambered for the .22 Long Shot or .22 Long Rifle Shot.
3. Junior Rifle, 20" round barrel and shorter stock.
4. Rifle with miniature target boring, 24" round barrel, chambered for .22 l.r. Shot.

Model 67s were not serial numbered for domestic sales but were numbered for foreign sales. Introduced in 1934 the gun was dropped from the line in 1963 having sold about 384,000. Many of these models were fitted at the factory with telescopes, and the bases were mounted on the rifle and the scope was packed separately.

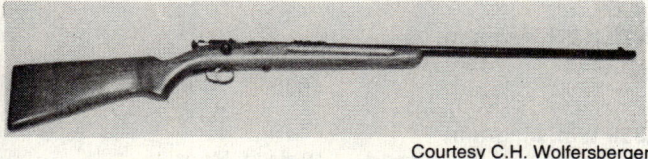

Courtesy C.H. Wolfersberger

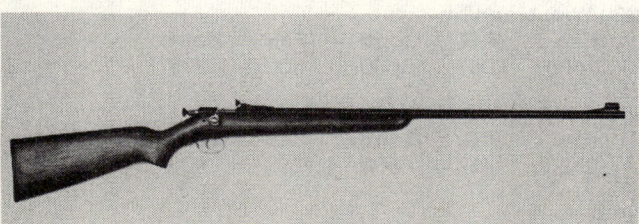

Courtesy Buffalo Bill Historical Center, Cody, Wyoming

Sporting Rifle

Exc.	V.G.	Good	Fair	Poor
200	150	125	100	75

Smoothbore Rifle

Courtesy Buffalo Bill Historical Center, Cody, Wyoming

Exc.	V.G.	Good	Fair	Poor
450	350	300	250	200

Junior Rifle

Exc.	V.G.	Good	Fair	Poor
250	200	175	150	125

Model 677

This model looked the same as the Model 67 but was manufactured without iron sights and therefore will have no sight cuts in the barrel. The rifle was furnished with either 2-3/4 power scopes or 5 power scopes. This model was not serial numbered. Introduced in 1937 and discontinued in 1939.

Exc.	V.G.	Good	Fair	Poor
1500	900	600	400	200

NOTE: Add a 50% premium for rifles chambered for .22WRF.

Model 68

Another takeoff on the Model 67, this model differed only in the sight equipment offered. Winchester fitted this rifle with its own 5 power telescopes. First sold in 1934 the Model 68 was dropped in 1946 with sales of about 101,000.

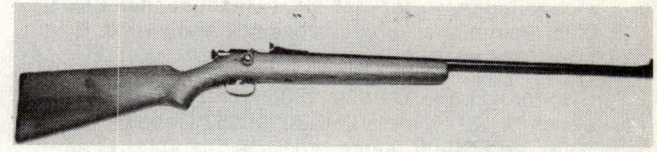

Courtesy C.H. Wolfersberger

With Scope

Exc.	V.G.	Good	Fad	Poor
500	400	250	200	150

Without Scope

Exc.	V.G.	Good	Fad	Poor
200	175	150	100	75

NOTE: Rifles with factory scopes and no sights add 40%. For rifles with factory scopes and no sights chambered for .22 WRF add 75%.

Model 69 and 69A

This model was designed by Winchester to answer the demand for a medium priced hunting and target .22 rimfire bolt-action rifle. The rifle had a detachable box magazine, and many were offered with factory-installed telescopes in 2-3/4 and 5 power. The stock was plain walnut with pistol grip and plain forend. This model was not serial numbered. The 69A version was introduced in 1937 and featured an improved cocking mechanism. Introduced in 1935 as the Model 69, this gun was dropped in 1963 with sales of about 355,000 guns.

Exc.	V.G.	Good	Fair	Poor
300	275	200	175	125

Model 697

The Model 697 was similar in appearance to the Model 69 except A was equipped exclusively for a telescope. Winchester offered either a 2-3/4 or 5 power scope with the bases attached at the factory and the scope packed separately. Built between 1937 and 1941 with small sales, this model was not serial numbered.

Exc.	V.G.	Good	Fair	Poor
1500	900	600	400	200

NOTE: For factory scopes with no sights add 50%.

Model 70

Considered by many as the finest bolt-action rifle ever built in the United States, the pre-1964 Model 70 is highly sought after by shooters and collectors alike. Its smooth, strong action has no peer. It is often referred to as "The Riflemen's Rifle." The Model 70 is an updated and improved version of the Model 54 and features a hinged floorplate, new speed locks, new safety design that does not interfere with telescope, manually releasable bolt stop, more attractive buttstock and forend, and forged steel triggerguard. Like many Winchesters, the Model 70 was available with several extra cost options that should be evaluated by an expert. The values listed below are given for pre-1964 Model 70s with serial numbers from 1 to 581471. This rifle was available in several different styles:

1. Standard Grade, 24" round barrel (except 26" round barrel for .220 Swift and .300 H&H Magnum—25-inch round barrel for .375 H&H Magnum after 1937), plain walnut checkered pistol stock and forend. Built from 1936 to 1963.

2. Standard Grade Carbine, 20" round barrel, chambered for .22 Hornet, .250-3000,.257 Roberts, .270, 7mm, and 30-06, same stock as Standard Grade. Built from 1936 to 1946.

3. Super Grade Rifle, same barrel and calibers as Standard Grade, select walnut checkered and capped pistol grip stock with cheekpiece and checkered forend with plastic tip. Built from 1936 to 1960.

4. Featherweight, 22" round barrel chambered for .243, .264, .270, .308, .30-06, and .358. Fitted with aluminum triggerguard, aluminum buttplate, and aluminum floor plate. Later versions with plastic buttplate. Built from 1952 to 1963.

5. Featherweight Super Grade, same as above except not chambered for the .358 cartridge, but fitted with Super Grade stock. Built from 1952 to 1963.

6 National Match, same as Standard Grade but fitted with target type stock and telescope bases. Chambered for .30-06 only. Discontinued in 1960.

7. Target, 24" round medium-weight barrel with same stock as National Match in .243 and 30-06 calibers. Discontinued in 1963.

8. Varmint, 26" round heavy barrel, with heavier stock, chambered for .243 and .220 Swift. Built from 1956 to 1963.

9. Westerner, 26" round barrel with Standard Grade stock, chambered for .264 Winchester Magnum. Built from 1960 to 1963.

10. Alaskan, 25" round barrel, with Standard Grade stock, chambered for .338 Winchester Magnum and .375 H&H Magnum. Built from 1960 to 1963.

11. Bull Gun, 28" round barrel, same stock as National Match, chambered for .30-06 and .300 H&H Magnum. Built from 1936 to 1963.

The standard calibers offered for the Model 70 are as follows in order of rarity: .300 Savage, .35 Rem., .458 Win Magnum, 7mm, .358 Win., .250-3000 Savage, .300 Win Magnum, .338 Win. Magnum, .375 H&H Magnum, .257 Roberts, .220 Swift, .22 Hornet, .264 Win. Magnum, .300 H&H Magnum, .308 Win., .243 Win., .270 W.C.F., .30-06.

NOTE: Prices for the Model 70 are, in many cases, based on the caliber of the rifle; the more rare the caliber, the more premium the gun will command. Many pre-1964 Model 70s are still available in new condition in the original box with all papers. Add 100% if the box is serial numberd to the gun.

Standard Rifle in .270 and .30-06 caliber

Exc.	V.G.	Good	Fair	Poor
775	675	425	350	275

NOTE: Below are prices for calibers with respect to rarity.

.243. Win.

Exc.	V.G.	Good	Fair	Poor
1150	1000	625	400	300

.300 H&H Magnum

Exc.	V.G.	Good	Fair	Poor
950	775	600	550	350

.264 Win. Magnum

Exc.	V.G.	Good	Fair	Poor
950	775	600	550	350

.22 Hornet

Exc.	V.G.	Good	Fair	Poor
1100	950	625	550	350

.220 Swift

Exc.	V.G.	Good	Fair	Poor
1100	950	625	550	350

.257 Roberts

Exc.	V.G.	Good	Fair	Poor
1250	1050	750	650	350

.375 H&H Magnum

Exc.	V.G.	Good	Fair	Poor
1700	1250	750	600	400

.338 Win. Magnum

Exc.	V.G.	Good	Fair	Poor
1400	1050	600	500	375

.300 Win. Magnum

Exc.	V.G.	Good	Fair	Poor
1400	1050	600	500	375

.250-3000 Savage

Exc.	V.G.	Good	Fair	Poor
2000	1450	800	650	400

7mm

Exc.	V.G.	Good	Fair	Poor
2850	1950	1250	950	600

.35 Rem.

Exc.	V.G.	Good	Fair	Poor
3900	2750	1850	1200	900

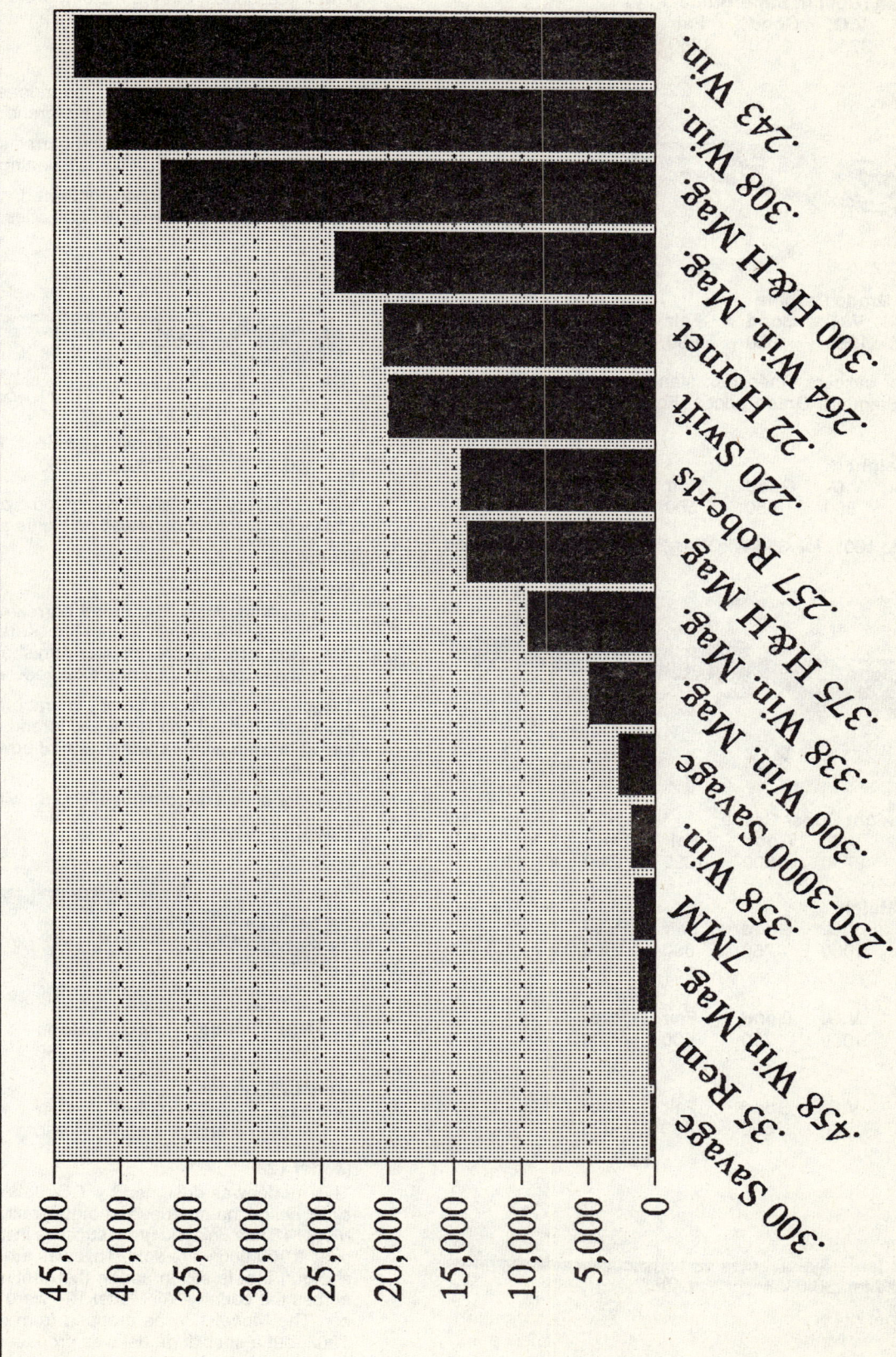

Relative Caliber Rarity*
Model 70
1936 - 1963

.243 Win.
.308 Win.
.300 H&H Mag.
.264 Win. Mag.
.22 Hornet
.220 Swift
.257 Roberts
.375 H&H Mag.
.338 Win. Mag.
.300 Win. Mag.
.250-3000 Savage
.358 Win.
7MM
.458 Win Mag.
.35 Rem
.300 Savage

45,000
40,000
35,000
30,000
25,000
20,000
15,000
10,000
5,000
0

* Excluding the .270 W.C.F.(approx. 100,000) and 30-06 (approx. 200,000) which were the most common.

.300 Savage

Exc.	V.G.	Good	Fair	Poor
3350	2750	1750	1200	900

.458 African (Built in Supergrade only)

Exc.	V.G.	Good	Fair	Poor
4750	3750	2700	1750	1000

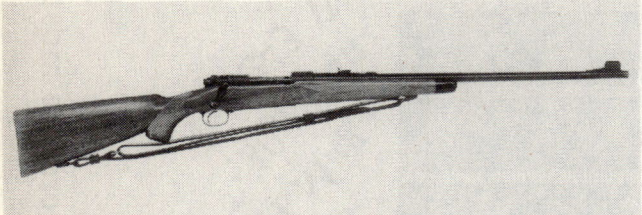

Standard Grade Carbine

Exc.	V.G.	Good	Fair	Poor
1750	1350	850	650	600

NOTE: For calibers other than standard add a premium of 100% to Standard Grade prices. For Supergrade rifles add 100%.

Featherweight

Exc.	V.G.	Good	Fair	Poor
950	800	650	500	400

NOTE: Add 100% for .358 Win. For .264 and .270 calibers add 25%.

Featherweight Super Grade

Exc.	V.G.	Good	Fair	Poor
3500	2750	1900	1250	1000

National Match

Exc.	V.G.	Good	Fair	Poor
1200	1000	750	600	500

Target

Exc.	V.G.	Good	Fair	Poor
1200	1000	750	600	500

Varmint

Exc.	V.G.	Good	Fair	Poor
800	700	550	450	325

Bull Gun

Exc.	V.G.	Good	Fair	Poor
2500	1500	1000	750	600

Model 72

This model is a bolt-action rifle with tubular magazine. It is chambered for the .22 Short, Long, and Long Rifle cartridges interchangeably. Early rifles were available with 2-3/4 or 5 power telescopes, but the majority were furnished with either open sights or peep sights. This rifle was available in two different configurations:

1. Sporting Rifle, 25" round barrel, chambered for the .22 Short, Long, and l.r. cartridges, one piece plain walnut pistol grip stock and forend.

2. Gallery Special, 25" round barrel, chambered for .22 Short only, stock same as Sporting Rifle.

This model was not serial numbered. It was built between 1938 and 1959 with about 161,000 rifles sold.

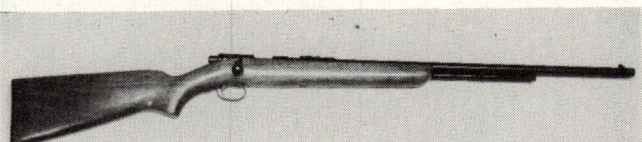

Courtesy C.H. Wolfersberger

Exc.	V.G.	Good	Fair	Poor
300	250	200	150	125

NOTE: Gallery Special will command a premium of 100%. For rifles with factory scopes and no sights add 100%.

Model 75

Styles:

1. Sporting Rifle, 24" round barrel, chambered for .22 Long Rifle, select walnut checkered pistol grip stock and forend. This rifle was furnished with either open rear sights or a Lyman 57 E receiver sight.

Target Rifle, 28" round barrel, chambered for .22 Long Rifle, plain walnut pistol grip stock and forend. The Target Rifle was furnished with either a Winchester 8 power telescope or a variety of target sights.

This model was discontinued in 1958 with about 89,000 sold.

Model 75 Sporter

NIB	Exc.	V.G.	Good	Fair	Poor
1500	750	600	450	350	200

Model 75 Target

Exc.	V.G.	Good	Fair	Poor
500	400	325	250	200

Model 12

This model was designed by T.C. Johnson and was the first slide action hammerless shotgun built by Winchester. The Model 12 has enjoyed great success in its 51-year history, and over 1,900,000 were sold. This was a high quality, well-made shotgun that is still in use in the hunting and shooting fields across the country. All Model 12s were of the takedown variety. The Model 12 was dropped from regular product line in 1963, but a special model was produced in the Custom Shop until 1979. In 1972 Winchester resurrected the Model 12 in its regular production line in 12 gauge only and ventilated rib. This reintroduced Model 12 was dropped in 1980. The prices listed below are for guns made prior to 1964 or for guns with serial numbers below 1968307. This shotgun was offered in several different styles:

1. Standard Grade, 12, 16, 20, and 28 gauge, with plain, solid rib, or vent rib round barrels of standard lengths (26", 28", 30", 32"), plain walnut pistol grip stock with grooved slide handle. Built from 1912 to 1963.

2. Featherweight, same as above with lightweight alloy triggerguard. Built between 1959 and 1962.

3. Riot Gun, in 12 gauge only with 20" round choked cylinder, stock same as Standard Grade. Built between 1918 and 1963.

4. Trench Gun, chambered for 12 gauge only with 20" round barrel with ventilated hand guard over barrel, fitted with bayonet lug. All metal surfaces are "Parkerized," and these shotguns should be U.S. marked as a military firearm. Introduced in 1918 and built for U.S. Armed Forces on special order.

5. Skeet Grade, chambered for 12, 16, 20, and 28 gauge with 26" round barrel with solid or ventilated rib, select walnut checkered pistol stock and special checkered extension slide handle (longer than standard). Built from 1933 to 1963.

6. Trap Grade, chambered for 12 gauge only with 30" round barrel with solid rib or ventilated rib, select walnut pistol or straight grip stock, checkered extension slide handle. Built from 1914 to 1963.

7. Heavy Duck Gun, chambered in 12 gauge only with 30" round barrel with plain, solid, or ventilated rib, plain walnut pistol grip stock fitted with Winchester rubber recoil pad, plain grooved slide handle. Built from 1935 to 1963.

8. Pigeon Grade, chambered for 12, 16, 20, and 28 gauges with standard barrel lengths and choice of ribs. This was a special order shotgun and will be seen in many different variations, most of these guns were factory engraved. Built 1914 to 1963.

The Model 12 shotgun will be seen in many different combinations of gauges, barrel lengths, ribs, and stocks, all of which determine value. The more rare a particular combination, the higher the price. The buyer is urged to be extremely cautious before purchasing the more rare combinations, such as a 28 gauge. The best advice is to seek assistance from an expert and get as many opinions as possible. The prices listed below are for guns in standard configurations.

Courtesy Butterfield & Butterfield, San Francisco, California

Standard Grade-12 gauge

Exc.	V.G.	Good	Fair	Poor
650	425	350	300	250

Featherweight

Exc.	V.G.	Good	Fair	Poor
500	400	325	275	250

Riot Gun

Exc.	V.G.	Good	Fair	Poor
750	650	550	400	250

Trench Gun

Exc.	V.G.	Good	Fair	Poor
1750	1200	950	550	400

Skeet Grade

Exc.	V.G.	Good	Fair	Poor
1250	750	550	400	350

Trap Grade

Exc.	V.G.	Good	Fair	Poor
800	700	600	450	400

Heavy Duck Gun

Exc.	V.G.	Good	Fair	Poor
650	500	400	325	300

Pigeon Grade

Exc.	V.G.	Good	Fair	Poor
1950	1400	1200	650	500

NOTE: For 16 Gauge add 15%. For 20 gauge add 20%. For 28 gauge add 600%. For guns with solid rib add 20%. For guns with Winchester Special Ventilated Rib add 30%. For guns with Milled Rib add 40%.

Model 25

This model is similar in appearance to the Model 12 but does not have the takedown feature. All guns were solid frame. The Model 25 was furnished in 12 gauge my with 26 or 28" plain round barrel, plain walnut pistol grip stock with grooved slide handle. This was an attempt by Winchester to introduce a less expensive version of the Model 12. Introduced in 1949 it was dropped from the product line in 1954 having sold about 88,000 guns.

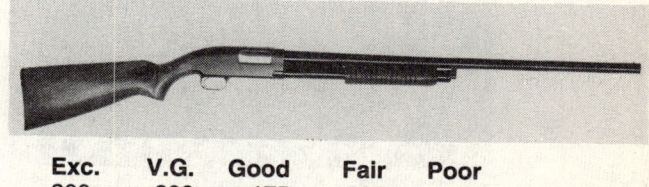

Exc.	V.G.	Good	Fair	Poor
300	200	175	125	75

Model 20

In order to utilize the expanded production facilities left over from WWI, Winchester introduced a series of three different models of single shot shotguns; the Model 20 was the first of the three. This model has a visible hammer and a top lever frame. It was the first Winchester to have this type of breakdown action. It was chambered for the .410, 2-1/2" shell. The barrel is 26" round choked full, plain walnut pistol grip stock with hard rubber buttplate. The forend has a small lip on the front end. The Model 20 was dropped from the product line in 1924 having sold about 24,000 guns.

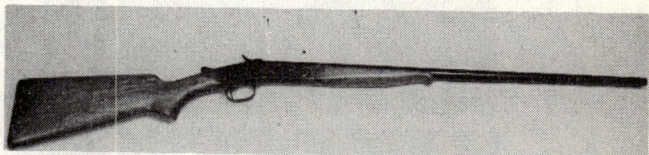

Courtesy C.H. Wolfersberger

Exc.	V.G.	Good	Fair	Poor
600	500	350	200	150

Model 36

The Model 36 was the second of the single shot shotguns to be introduced in 1920. This model features a bolt action that is cocked by pulling the firing pin head to the rear. It is fitted with an 18" round barrel, chambered for the 9mm Long Shot, 9mm Short Shot, and 9mm Ball interchangeably, plain gumwood straight-grip stock with special metal pistol grip triggerguard. Winchester referred to this model as the "Garden Gun" for use against birds and pests around the house and barn. This model was not serial numbered. It was dropped from the product line in 1927 having sold about 20,000 guns.

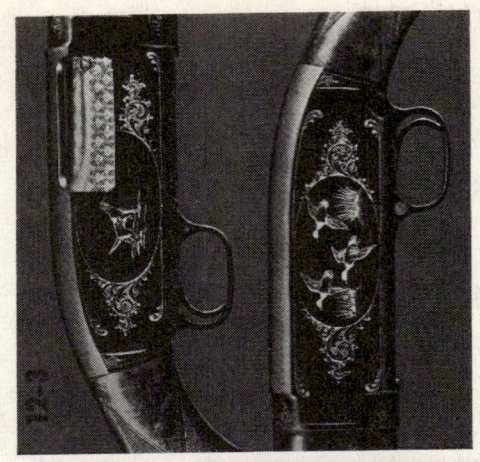

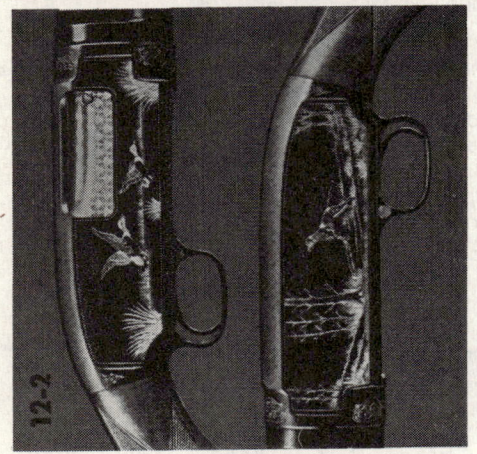

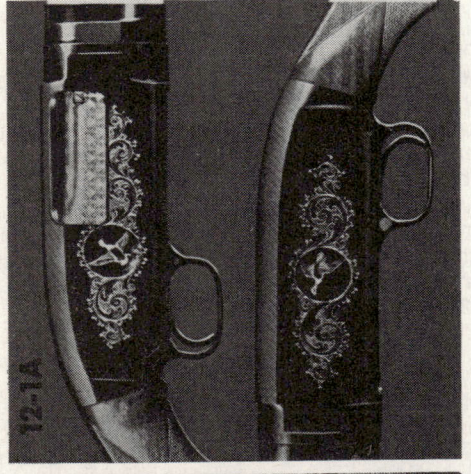

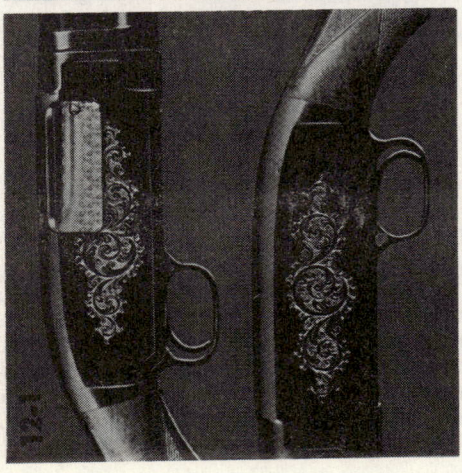

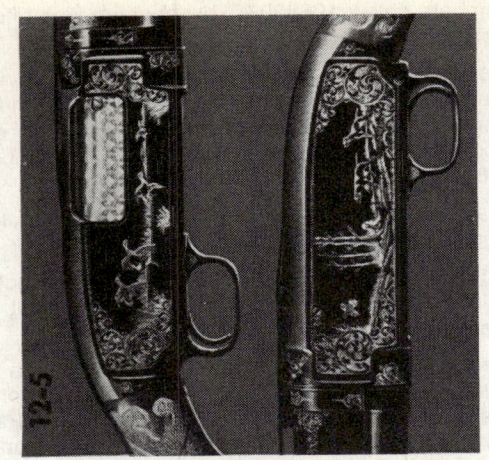

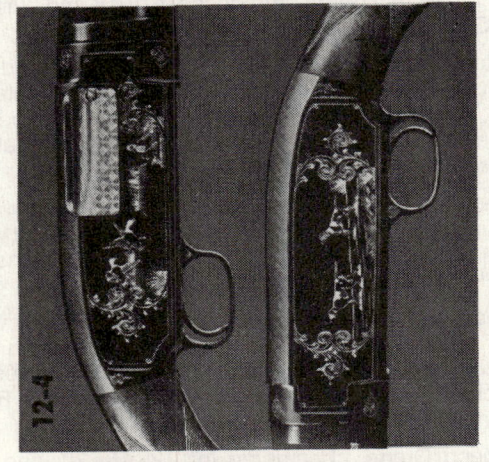

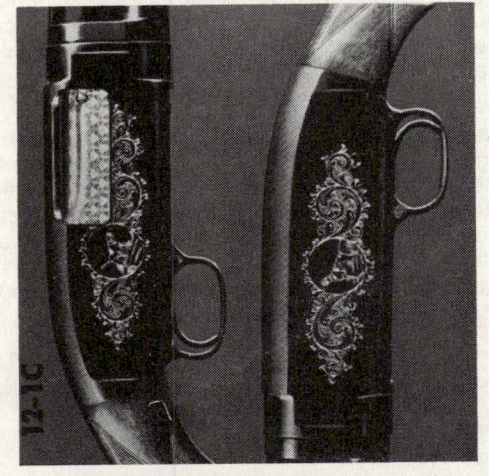

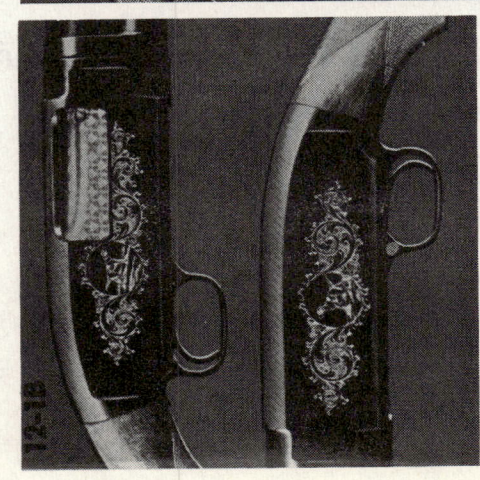

Winchester engraving patterns for the Model 12 shotgun. Winchester also used these patterns on the Model 42, but with different birds

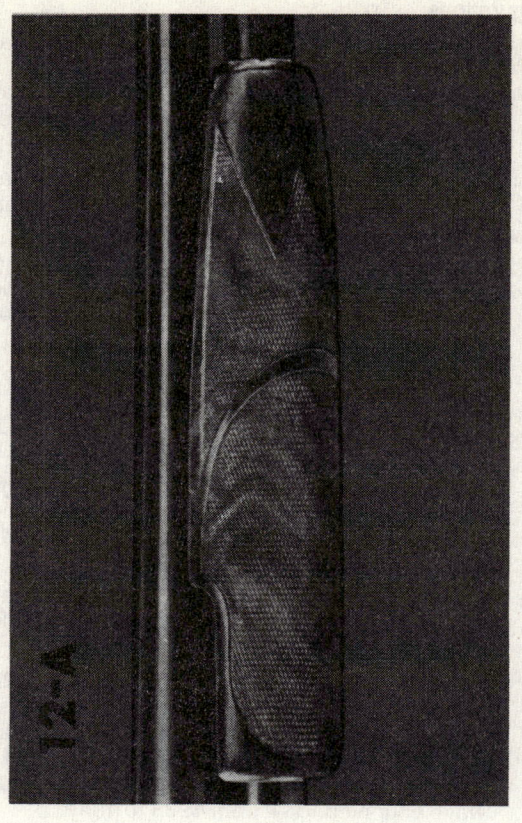

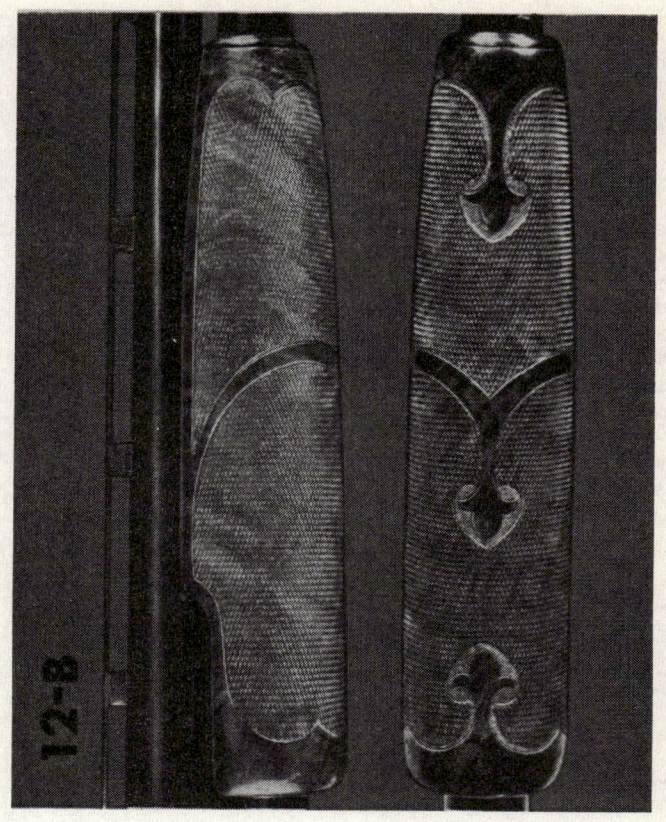

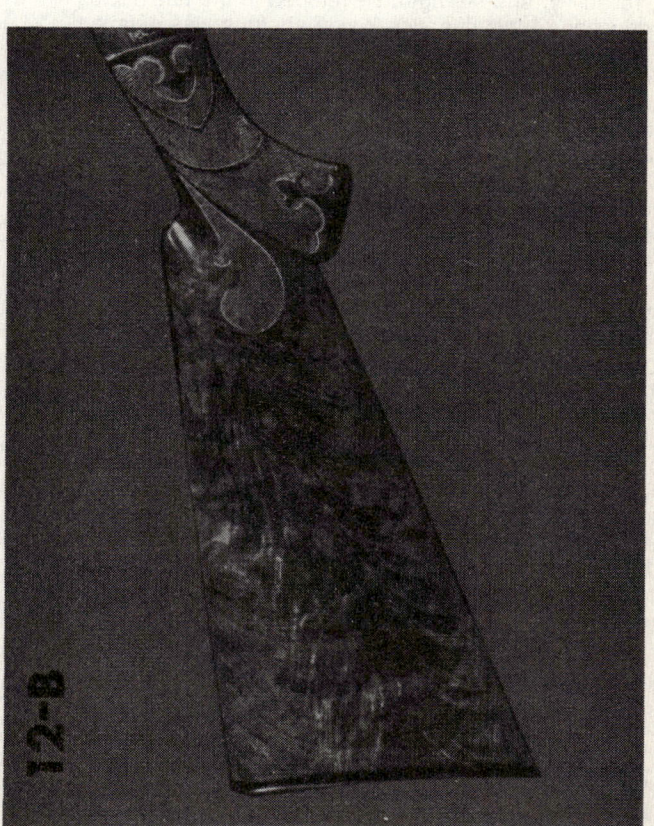

Winchester also provided optional factory stock carving for the Model 12 as well as the Model 42

Exc.	V.G.	Good	Fair	Poor
750	475	375	300	225

Model 41

This was the third of the low-priced single shot shotguns to be announced in 1920. Like the Model 36, the Model 41 was a bolt-action arrangement but of much stronger construction and design. It features a 24" round barrel, chambered for the .410 2-1/2" shell, plain walnut pistol grip stock and forend. Straight grip stock were furnished at no extra charge. This model was not serial numbered. It was discontinued in 1934 having sold about 22,000 guns.

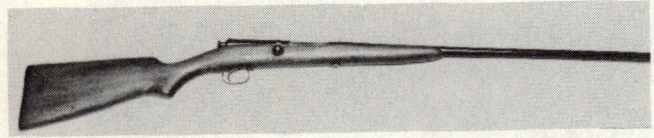

Courtesy C.H. Wolfersberger

Exc.	V.G.	Good	Fair	Poor
600	500	350	300	200

Model 21

The Model 21 was Winchester's finest effort with regard to quality, reliability, and strength. Developed in the late 1920s the introduction of this fine side-x-side shotgun was delayed by the company's financial troubles. When Winchester was purchased by the Olin family, the Model 21 was assured the attention it richly deserved due to John M. Olin's love for the gun. Despite the Model 21 being offered as a production gun it was, in fact, a hand-built custom made shotgun. Almost each Model 21 built has a personality of its own because each shotgun is slightly different with regard to chokes, barrel lengths, stock dimensions, and embellishments. The gun was introduced in 1931. From 1931 to 1959 the Model 21 was considered a production line gun and about 30,000 were sold. In 1960, when the Custom Shop was opened, the Model 21 was built there using the same procedures. Sales during the Custom Shop era were about 1,000 guns. Winchester changed the name of some of the Model 21 styles but the production methods stayed the same. In 1981 Winchester sold its firearms division to U.S. Repeating Arms Company including the right to build the Model 21. Again the production procedures stayed the same as did many of the former employees. U.S. Repeating Arms expanded and changed some of the style designations for the Model 21. Production was discontinued in about 1991. No sales figures are available for this time period. Collectors and shooters will be given the price breakdown for all three eras of production separately.

Model 21-1931 to 1959

The Model 21 was available in several different styles and configurations:

1. Standard Grade, chambered in 12, 16, and 20 gauge with barrel length from 26", 28", 30", and 32" with matted rib or ventilated rib, select walnut checkered pistol or straight-grip stock with checkered beavertail forend. Built from 1931 to 1959.
2. Tournament Grade, same as above with special dimension stock. Marked "TOURNAMENT" on bottom of trigger plate. Built from 1933 to 1934.
3. Trap Grade, same as above with slightly better grade wood and stock made to customers' dimensions. Marked "TRAP" on trigger plate. Built from 1940 to 1959.
4. Skeet Grade, same as above with the addition of the 28 gauge, stock furnished with checkered butt. Marked "SKEET" on trigger plate. Built from 1936 to 1959.
5. Duck Gun, chambered for 12 gauge 3" magnum shells, 30" or 32" barrels, Standard Grade stock except for shorter length of pull. Marked "DUCK" on trigger plate. Built from 1940 to 1952.
6. Magnum Gun, chambered for 3" 12 or 20 gauge, same stock as Duck Gun. Not marked on trigger plate. Built from 1953 to 1959.
7. Custom Built/Deluxe Grade, chambered for 12, 16, 20, 28, and .410, barrel lengths from 26" to 32", stock built to customer's specifications using fancy walnut. Marked "CUSTOM BUILT" on top of rib or "DELUXE" on trigger plate. These grades are frequently but not always engraved. Built from 1933 to 1959.

NOTE: Some early Model 21s were furnished with double triggers, extractors, and splinter forends. This combination reduces the price of the gun regardless of grade. Deduct about 25%.

Standard Grade

	Exc	V.G.	Good	Fair	Poor
12 gauge	3300	2800	2400	2200	2000
16 gauge	4000	3600	3300	3000	2500
20 gauge	5300	4900	4400	4000	3500

Tournament Grade

	Exc	V.G.	Good	Fair	Poor
12 gauge	3500	3000	2500	2300	2000
16 gauge	4500	3900	3500	3100	2500
20 gauge	5500	5100	4500	4100	3700

Trap Grade

	Exc	V.G.	Good	Fair	Poor
12 gauge	3500	3100	2700	2400	2000
16 gauge	4500	4000	3500	3100	2800
20 gauge	5700	5300	4700	4300	3900

Skeet Grade

	Exc	V.G.	Good	Fair	Poor
12 gauge	3400	2900	2500	2300	2000
16 gauge	4500	3900	3600	3100	2500
20 gauge	5500	5100	4500	4100	3700

Duck/Magnum Gun

Exc	V.G.	Good	Fair	Poor
3500	3000	2500	2300	2000

NOTE: Add 20% for 20 gauge Magnum.

NOTE: Factory ventilated ribs command a premium of about $400 on 12 gauge guns and $1,500 on 20 and 16 gauge guns. Models 21s with factory furnished extra barrels will bring an additional premium of about $1,500.

NOTE: Refinished and restored Model 21s are in a somewhat unique category of American made collectible shotguns. A gun that has been professionally refinished by a master craftsman will approximate 90% of the value of factory original guns.

Custom Built/Deluxe Grade

The prices paid for guns of this grade are determined by gauge, barrel and choke combinations, rib type, stock specifications, and engraving. Seek expert appraisal on this grade Model 21 before proceeding. It is best to secure a factory letter from the Cody Firearms Museum. With respect to such letter it is important to note that these records are incomplete and may be inaccurate in a few cases. Records for Model 21s built during the 1930s may be missing. Special order guns may have incomplete records. In such cases a written appraisal from an authoritative collector or dealer may be helpful.

Custom Built .410 Bore

Exc.	V.G.	Good	Fair	Poor
35000	30000	26000	22000	20000

NOTE: Less than 50 .410 Model 21s were built between 1931 and 1959 in all grades. The number of 28 gauge Model 21s built is unknown but the number is probably no greater than the .410 bore.

A Winchester Model 21 special order with gold inlays and chambered with a .410 bore was sold at auction for $36,800 by Rock Island Auction Company on November 18, 19 & 20 of 1996. The barrels were fitted with a factory vent rib. The stock had a straight grip. The condition was NIB with original box and papers.

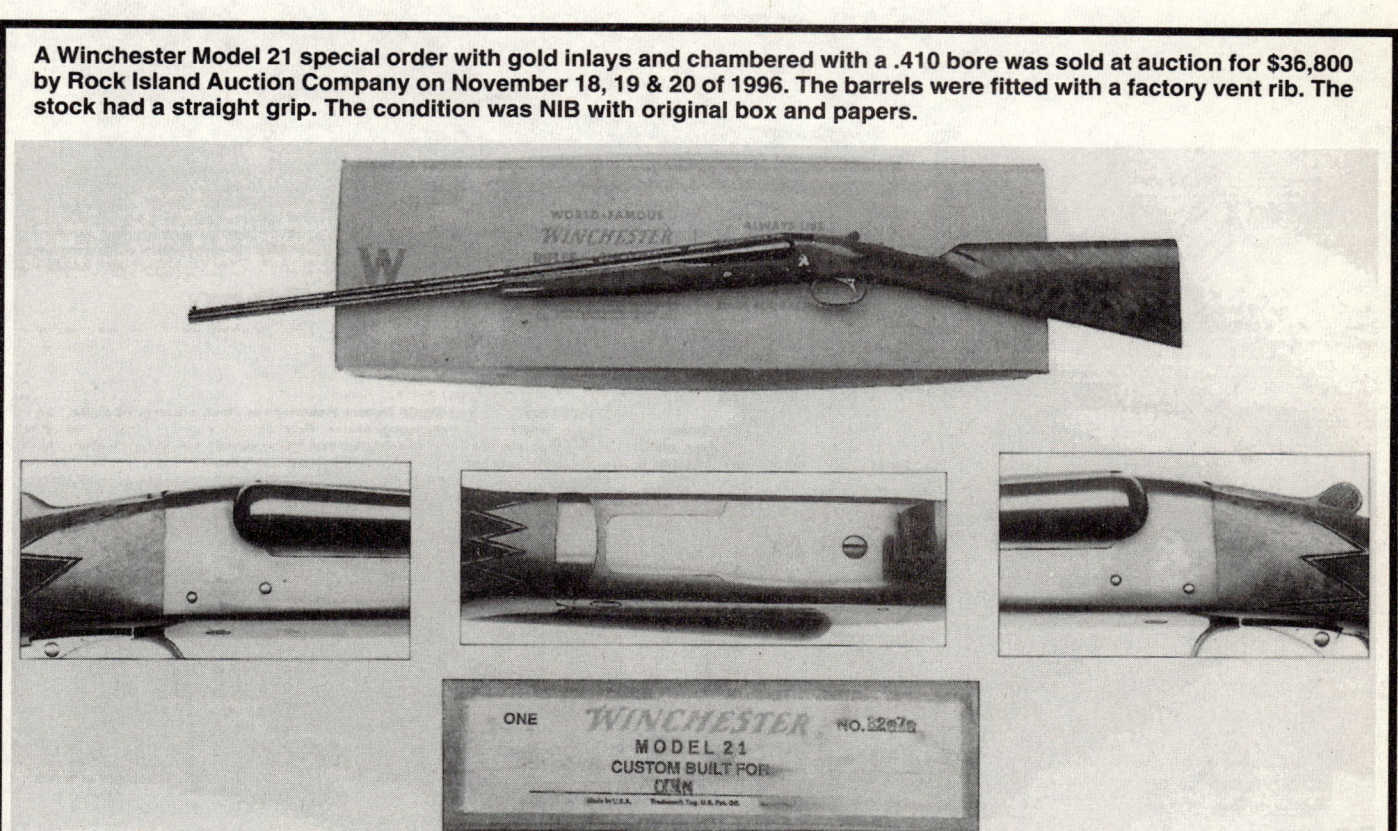

Custom Shop Model 21s - 1960 to 1981

When Winchester moved the production of the Model 21 into the Custom Shop the number of styles was greatly reduced. There were now three distinct styles:

1. Custom Grade, chambered in 12, 16, 20, 28 gauge, and .410 bore in barrel lengths from 26" to 32". Matted rib, fancy walnut checkered pistol or straight grip stock with checkered forend. Guns with pistol grips furnished with steel grip cap. A small amount of scroll engraving was provided on the frame of this grade.

2. Pigeon Grade, same chambers and barrel lengths as above with the addition of choice of matted or ventilated-rib, leather covered recoil pad, style "A" carving on stock and forend, and gold engraved pistol grip cap. The frame was engraved with the 21-6 engraving pattern.

3. Grand American Grade, same chambers and barrel lengths as Pigeon Grade with the addition of "B" carving on the stock and forend, 21-6 engraving with gold inlays, extra set of interchangeable barrels with extra forend. All of this was enclosed in a leather trunk case.

Custom Grade - 12 Gauge

Exc.	V.G.	Good	Fair	Poor
6500	5500	5000	4200	3500

NOTE: Add $4,000 for 16 gauge. Add $3,000 for 20 gauge.

Pigeon Grade - 12 Gauge

Exc.	V.G.	Good	Fair	Poor
10000	8500	6500	5000	4000

NOTE: Add $5,000 for 16 gauge. Add $4,000 for 20 gauge.

Grand American - 12 Gauge

Exc.	V.G.	Good	Fair	Poor
16000	12000	10000	9000	7000

NOTE: Add $10,000 for 16 gauge. Add $4,000 for 20 gauge.

Editor's Comment: There were eight 28 gauge Model 21s built during this period and five .410 bores built. These guns obviously command a large premium. Factory letters are available on these guns.

Custom Shop Model 21s 1982 to Present

When U.S. Repeating Arms Company took over the production of the Model 21 the Pigeon Grade was dropped from the line. The Grand American Grade was retained with all the features of its predecessor but with the addition of a small bore set featuring

Carvings for Winchester Model 21 Double Barrel Shotguns

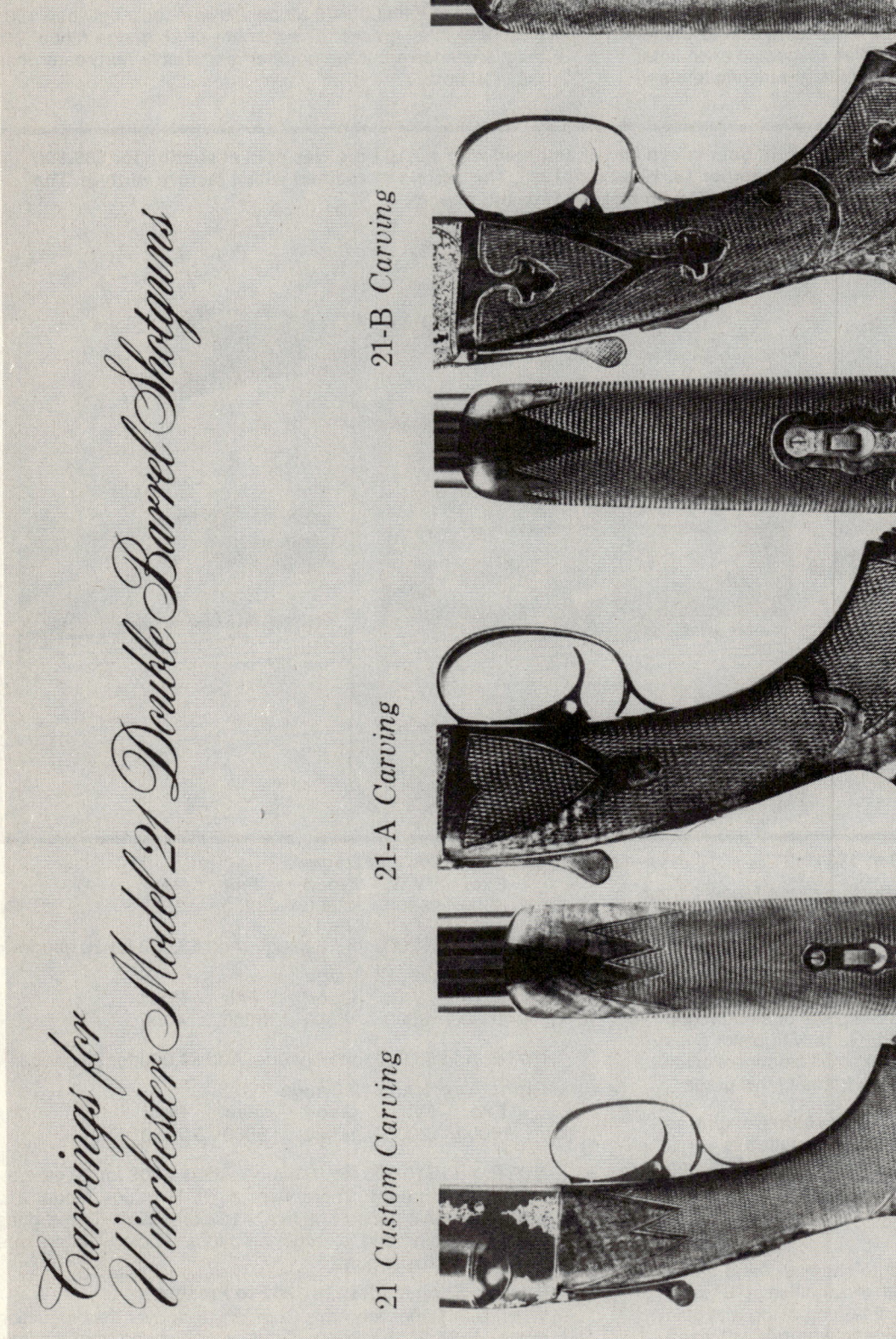

21-B Carving

21-A Carving

21 Custom Carving

Winchester factory stock carvings for the Model 21

THE lines of a double gun are particularly suited to tasteful ornamentation through genuine hand engraving. The six styles shown here and on the following pages have been executed by WINCHESTER custom engravers and designed exclusively for the Model 21. Other designs to meet a desire for something more elaborate can be submitted to our Custom Gun Department. For personalized engraving we will work from sketches or ideas offered by the purchaser.

Engravings for Model 21 Shotguns

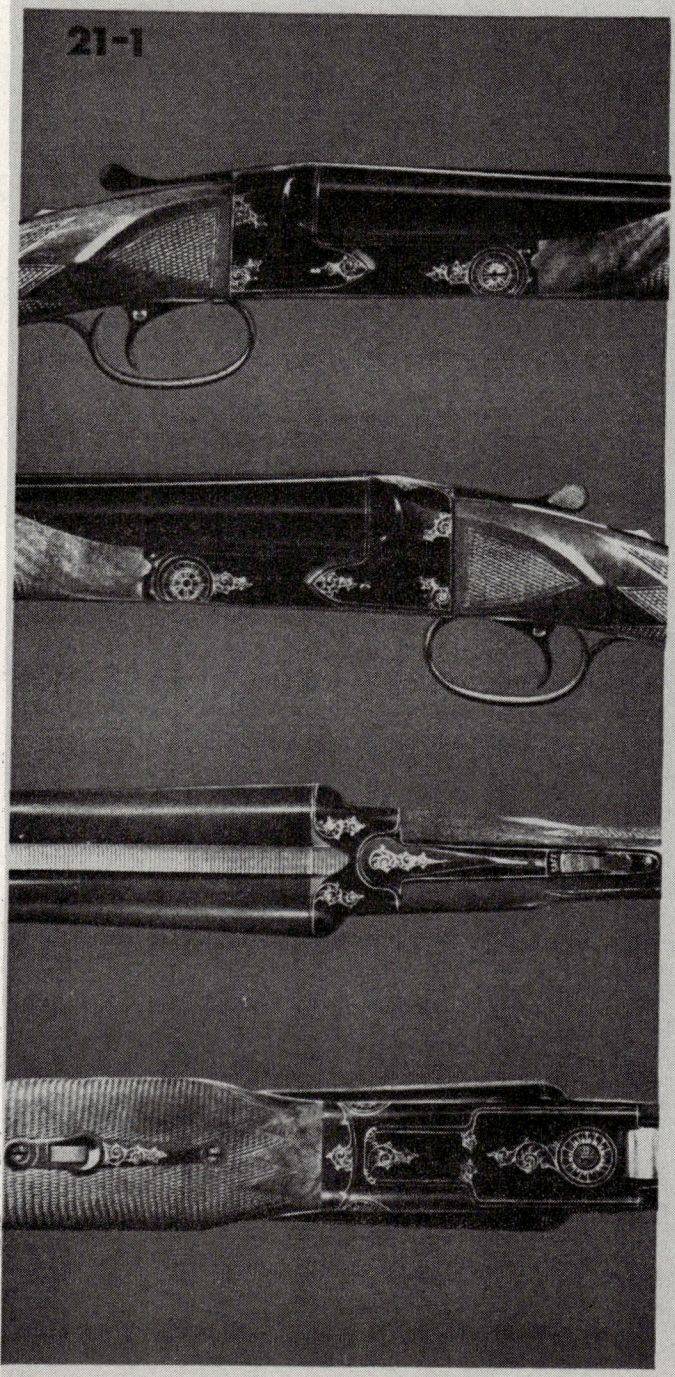

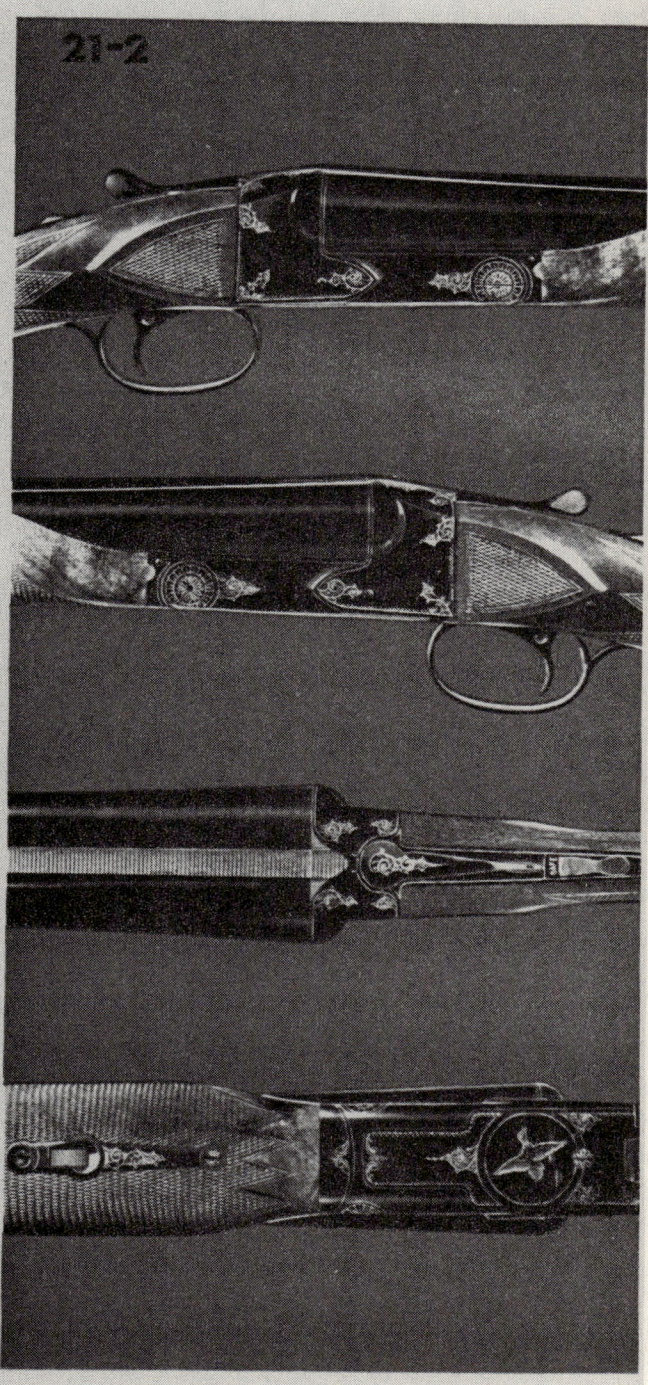

Engraving patterns used by Winchester for the Model 21 between 1932 and 1959

Engravings for Model 21 Shotguns

WINCHESTER custom engravers have specialized for many years in executing high fidelity game scenes; game animals and birds; hunting dogs; beautiful floral designs and artistic pattern or scroll work; as well as monogrammed shields or nameplates in the stock. Techniques range from very fine flat designs to heavy relief work and all types of inlay work in gold, silver or platinum.

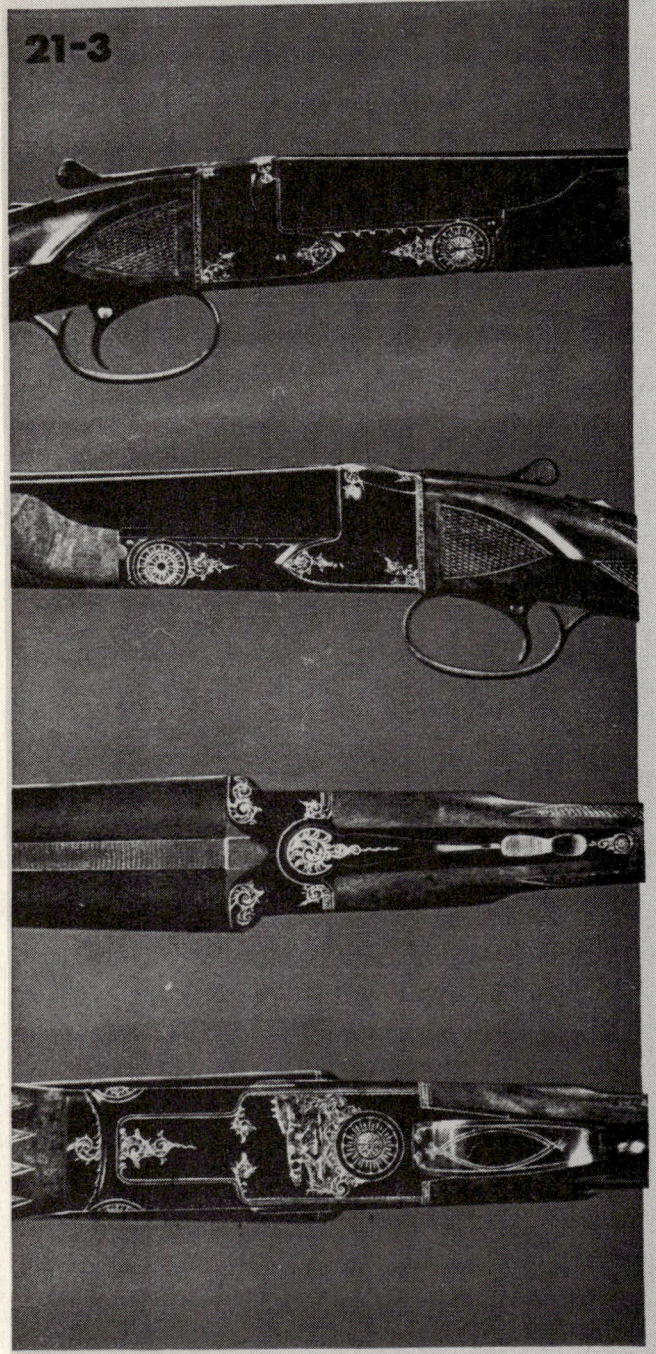

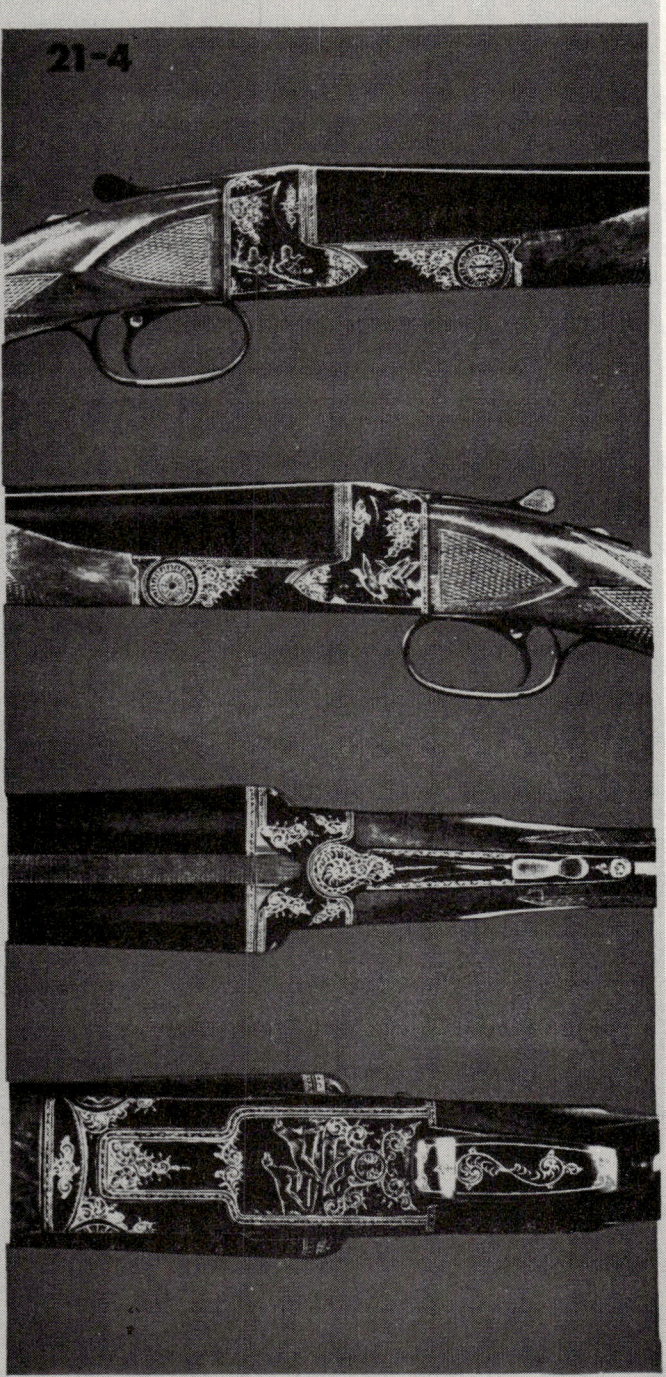

Engraving patterns used by Winchester for the Model 21 between 1932 and 1959

AMONG the parts of the Model 21 which lend themselves to a suitable distribution of ornamentation are the frame, trigger guard, fore-end shoe and catch plate, barrels at the breech and muzzle, top lever, tang and safety slide. Trigger may be checkered and either partly or fully gold-plated.

Engravings for Model 21 Shotguns

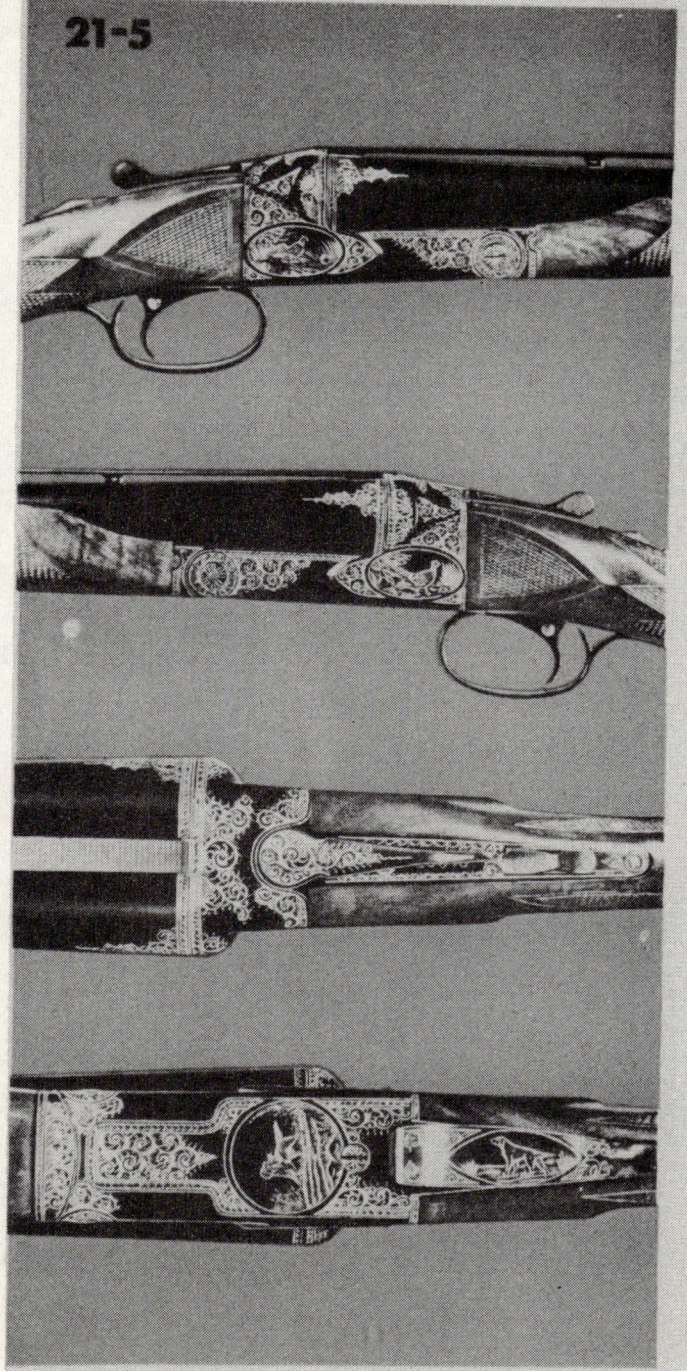

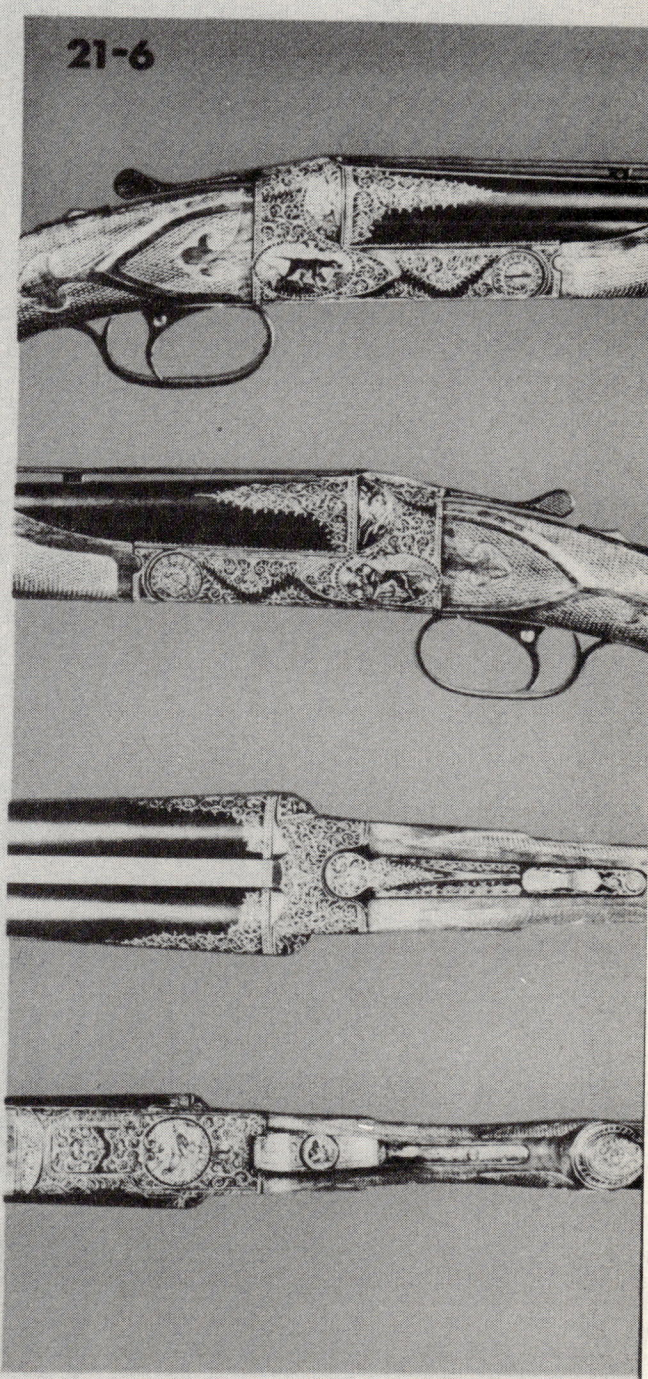

Engraving patterns used by Winchester for the Model 21 between 1932 and 1959

Engravings for
Winchester Model 21 Double Barrel Shotguns

21-3 Engraving

21 Custom Engraving

These engraving patterns were used by the factory on the Model 21 from 1960 to the present time

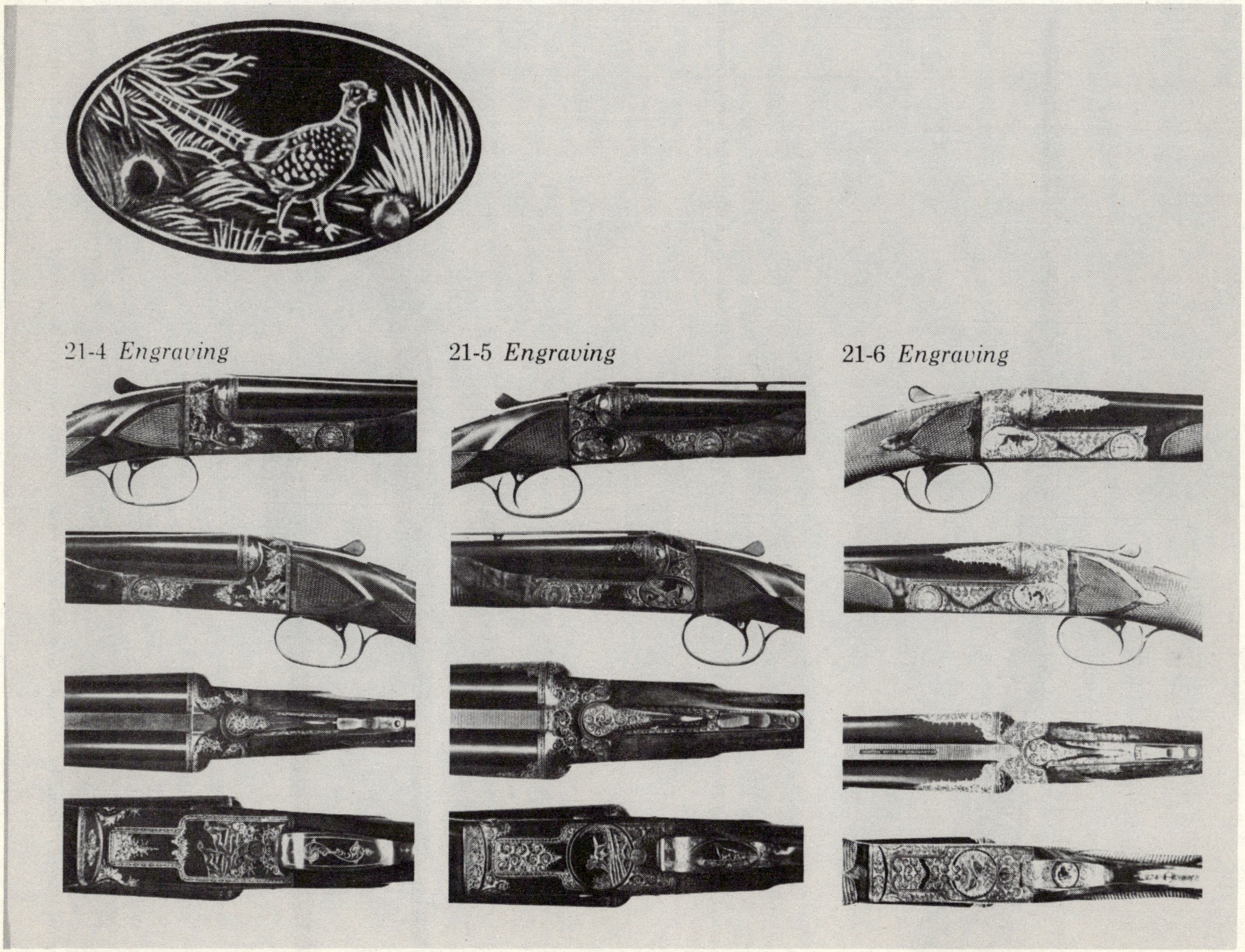

21-6 Engraving

21-5 Engraving

21-4 Engraving

These engraving patterns were used by the factory on the Model 21 from 1960 to the present time

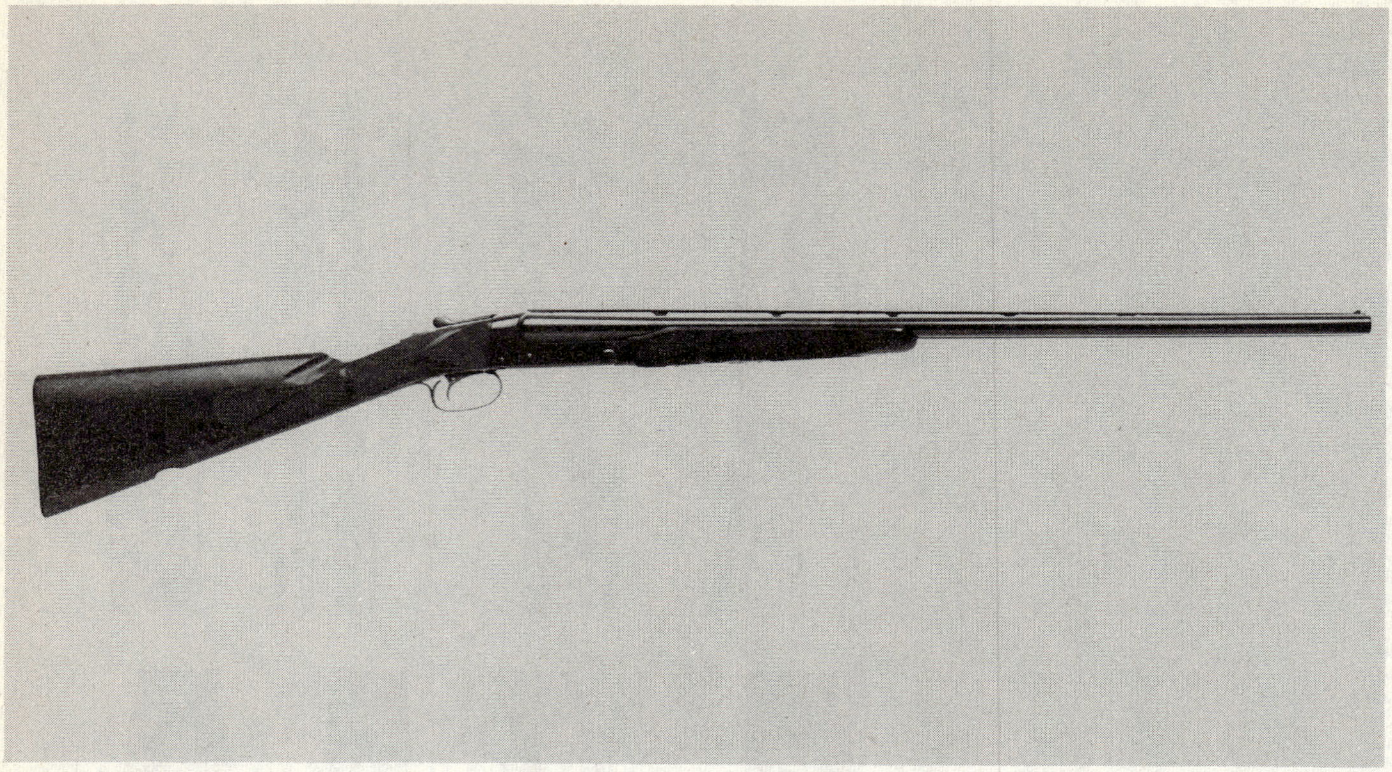

A Custom Grade Model 21 with straight trip stock and "A" carved wood. This Model 21 has no engraving which was not standard on Custom Grade guns

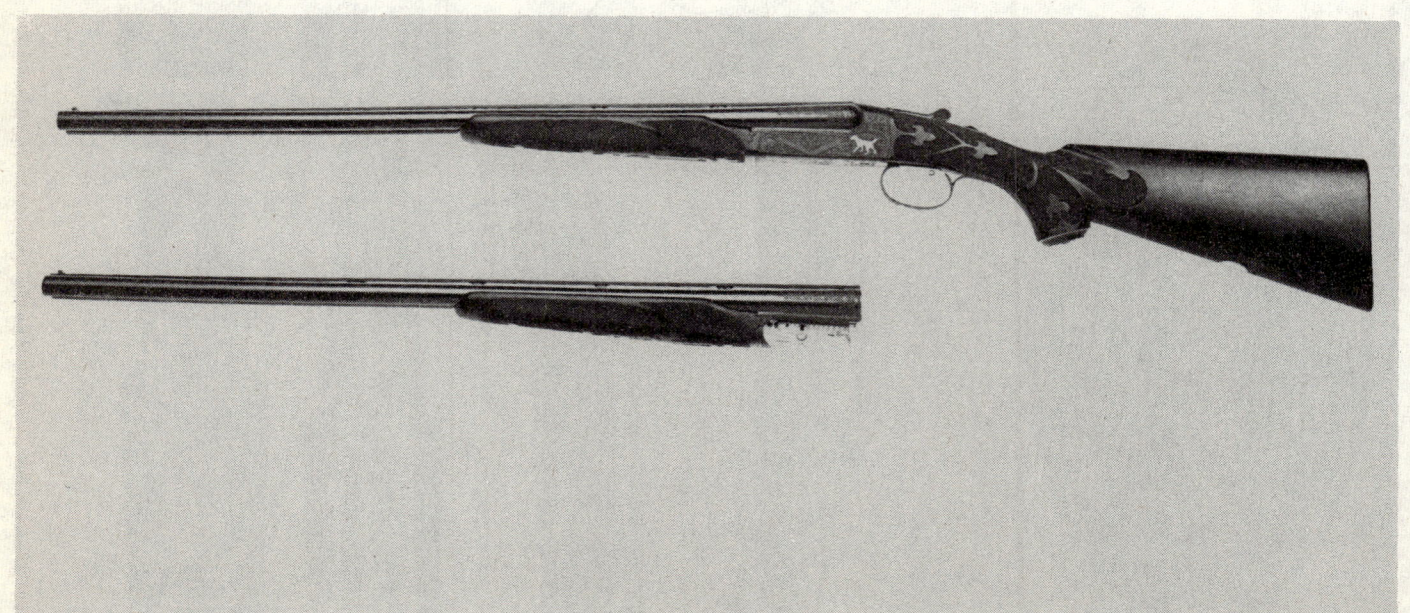

A typical Model 21 Grand American. All Grand Americans were sold with two sets of barrels and a leather trunk style case

Pigeon Grade

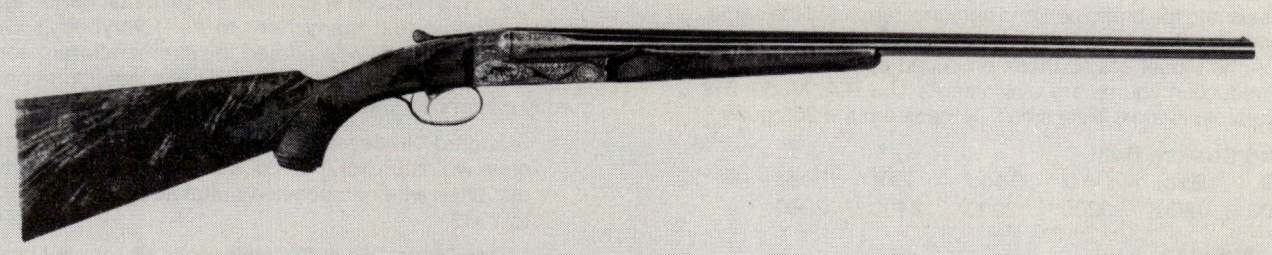

1. Choice of Gauge (12—16—20)
2. Choice of Barrel Length
   12 gauge—32", 30", 28", 26"
   16 gauge—30", 28", 26"
   20 gauge—30", 28", 26"
3. Choice of Choke Combination
4. Matted Rib or Ventilated Rib
5. 2¾ or 3" Chamber (3" Chamber not available in 16 ga.)
6. Stock and Beavertail Forearm of Grade AA Full-Fancy American Walnut
7. Style "A" carving on stock and beavertail forearm. (Style B available at extra cost— see page 8)
8. Stock built to individual specifications (within manufacturing limits). Straight or Pistol Grip —includes Cheekpiece, Monte Carlo and/or Offset
9. Choice of Forearm—Field, Skeet or Trap
10. Black insert in forearm tip
11. Gold Inlaid Pistol Grip Cap
12. Choice of composition buttplate, recoil pad, checkered butt or leather covered recoil pad
13. Panel in top rib inscribed "Custom Built by Winchester for (Customer's Name)"
14. Automatic or non-automatic safety (optional)
15. Choice of bead sights—front and middle
16. Engine turned standing breech, frame, barrel flats, barrel lug, extractors, barrel breech, forearm retainer and inside upper surfaces of forearm shoe
17. Gold plated trigger
18. Gold oval name plate or 3 initials gold inlaid on trigger guard
19. Choice of three (3) initials engraved on name plate
20. #6 engraving on frame and barrels
21. Leather trunk style gun case with canvas cover available at extra cost, (both case and cover embossed with 3 initials in gold or black)

Custom Grade

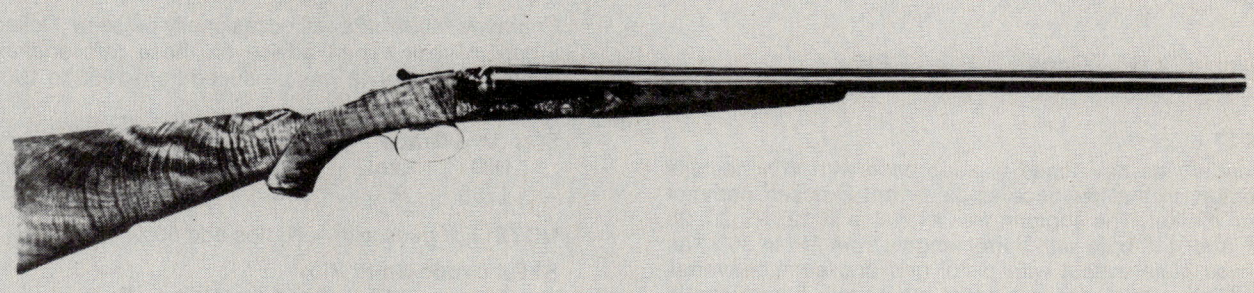

1. Choice of Gauge (12—16—20)
2. Choice of Barrel Length
   12 gauge—32", 30", 28", 26"
   16 gauge—30", 28", 26"
   20 gauge—30", 28", 26"
3. Choice of Choke Combination
4. Matted Rib
5. 2¾" Chamber
6. Stock and Beavertail Forearm of Grade AA Full-Fancy American Walnut
7. Stock built to individual specifications (within manufacturing limits). Straight or Pistol Grip — includes Cheekpiece, Monte Carlo and/or Offset
8. Choice of Forearm—Field, Skeet or Trap
9. Black insert in forearm tip
10. Custom Style Checkering on stock and forearm (Style A or B available at extra cost — see page 8)
11. Steel Pistol Grip Cap
12. Choice of composition buttplate, recoil pad or checkered butt
13. Panel in top rib inscribed "Custom Built by Winchester for (Customer's Name)"
14. Automatic or non-automatic safety (optional)
15. Choice of bead sights—front and middle
16. Engine turned standing breech, frame, barrel flats, barrel lug, extractors, barrel breech, forearm retainer and inside upper surfaces of forearm shoe
17. Custom style ornamentation
    Additional engraving available at extra cost—see patterns 3, 4 and 5 on pages 6 and 7
18. Gold plated trigger
19. Gold oval name plate (optional)
20. Choice of three (3) initials engraved on name plate
21. Leather trunk style gun case with canvas cover available at extra cost, (both case and cover embossed with 3 initials in gold or black)

a 28 gauge and .410 bore set of barrels. Two new grades were introduced in 1983; the Standard Custom Grade and the Special Custom Built. In addition to these grades the factory would undertake to build for its customers whatever was desired. Due to the unique nature of these guns it is advised that an expert appraisal be sought to establish a value. While the changeover from Winchester to U.S. Repeating Arms was a transfer of business assets and the craftsmen and personel remained the same, collectors are reluctant to assign the same values to U.S. Repeating Arms Model 21s as those produced by Winchester. No official production figures are available for U.S.R.A. Model 21s but the number is most likely small; perhaps around 200 guns.

Standard Custom Built

NIB	Exc.	V.G	Good	Fair	Poor
6000	4200	3200	2900	2400	2000

Grand American

NIB	Exc.	V.G.	Good	Fair	Poor
15000	9000	7500	6000	4500	3500

Grand American - Small Gauge Set - 28 or .410 bore

NIB	Exc.	V.G.	Good	Fair	Poor
42000	30000	25000	18000	15000	11000

Model 24

The Model 24 was Winchester's attempt to develop a medium-priced double-barrel shotgun. Like the Model 21, it was a top lever breakdown model that was available in 12, 16, and 20 gauge in various barrel lengths from 26" to 30". Offered in a Standard model only with double triggers, raised matted rib, plain walnut pistol or straight-grip stock with semi-beavertail forend, the Model 24 was introduced in 1939 and was discontinued in 1957 with about 116,000 guns sold.

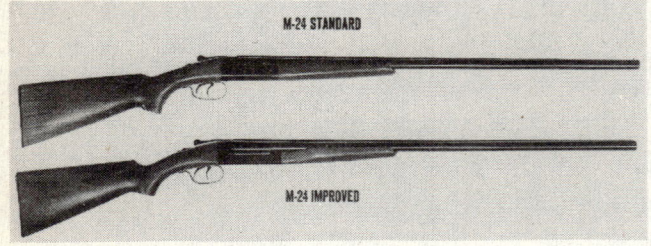

Exc.	V.G.	Good	Fair	Poor
500	400	350	250	200

Model 37

This model was developed to keep pace with Winchester's competitors in the low-price single barrel exposed hammer shotgun market. The shotgun was available in 12, 16, 20, 28 gauge, and .410 bore with barrel lengths from 26" to 30". The stock was plain walnut with pistol grip and semi-beavertail forend. This model was not serial numbered. Introduced in 1936 it stayed in the company line until 1963 having sold slightly over 1,000,000 guns.

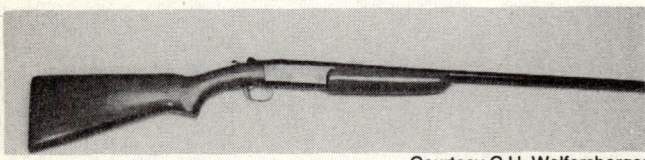

Courtesy C.H. Wolfersberger

	Exc.	V.G.	Good	Fair	Poor
12 gauge	250	200	125	100	50
16 gauge	200	175	150	125	60
20 gauge	200	200	175	150	90
28 gauge	1500	1000	800	600	450
.410 bore	300	225	200	175	100

NOTE: For 12 and 16 gauge guns add a 50% premium for 32" barrels.

Model 42

This was the first slide action shotgun ever developed exclusively for the .410 bore. Invented by William Roemer, the Model 42 was in effect, at least in outward appearance, a miniature Model 12. This shotgun was a quality built, fast handling, racy looking shotgun that many refer to as "Everybody's Sweetheart." The Model 42 was offered in several different configurations throughout its production. These configurations will greatly influence value:

1. Standard Grade, 26" or 28" plain or solid rib barrel, plain walnut pistol grip stock with grooved slide handle, fitted with composition buttplate. Built from 1933 to 1963.

2. Skeet Grade, 26" or 28" plain, solid rib, or ventilated-rib barrel, select walnut checkered pistol or straight-grip stock with checkered extension slide handle. The Skeet Grade was offered in chokes other than skeet. Skeet Grade Model 42s are seen in full, modified cylinder, improved cylinder, and skeet chokes. Built from 1933 to 1963.

3. Trap Grade, 26" or 28" plain or solid rib barrel, fancy walnut special checkered pistol or straight grip stock with special checkered extension slide handle. The Trap Grade checkering pattern has one closed diamond on each side of the pistol grip or, in the case of the straight grip, the diamond is located on the underside of the grip. The extension slide handle has two diamonds on each side. Stamped "TRAP" on the bottom of the receiver. Built from 1934 to 1939.

4. Deluxe Grade, same as above, available with ventilated rib in 1954. Some early models stamped "DELUXE" on bottom of receiver. Built from 1940 to 1963.

5. Pigeon Grade, same as above Deluxe Grade but engraved with a pigeon on the lower magazine tube. Very few of this grade were built by Winchester, and the majority were done in the late 1940s.

Engraved Model 42s will occasionally be seen. Collectors are urged to seek expert advice on these rare and expensive guns. The Model 42 was produced from 1933 to 1963. About 160,000 were sold.

Standard Grade

NIB	Exc.	V.G.	Good	Fair	Poor
1750	950	650	450	350	250

NOTE: For guns with solid ribs add 50%.

Skeet Grade-Solid Rib

Exc.	V.G.	Good	Fair	Poor
2500	1750	900	500	350

An example of a prewar Standard Grade Model 42. Notice the distinctive grip on the butt stock and the round slide handle.

A postwar Standard Grade Model 42. The pistol grip has a new shape as does the flat bottom slide handle.

A Skeet Grade Model 42 with solid rib. Notice the extension slide handle which was used on all Model 42 Skeet Grades. The pistol grip is fitted with a gripcap.

A Skeet Grade with factory ventilated rib. Winchester began to install ventilated ribs on the Model 42 in 1954 and continued until the end of production in 1963.

An example of a Deluxe Grade Model 42. Notice the single diamond in the pistol grip and the two diamonds on the extension slide handle. This particular gun has a solid rib, but Winchester built Deluxe Grades with ventilated ribs as well.
NOTE: Add 25% guns chambered for 2-1/2" shells.

An example of a prewar Standard Grade Model 42. Notice the distinctive grip on the butt stock and the round slide handle

A postwar Standard Grade Model 42. The pistol grip has a new shape as does the flat bottom slide handle

A Skeet Grade Model 42 with solid rib. Notice the extension slide handle which was used on all Model 42 Skeet Grades. The pistol grip is fitted with a grip cap

A Skeet Grade with factory ventilated rib. Winchester began to install ventilated ribs on the Model 42 in 1954 and continued until the end of production in 1963

An example of a Deluxe Grade Model 42. Notice the single diamond in the pistol grip and the two diamonds on the extension slide handle. This particular gun has a solid rib, but Winchester built Deluxe Grades with ventilated ribs as well

Skeet Grade-Ventilated Rib

NIB	Exc.	V.G.	Good	Fair	Poor
5000	3500	2500	1250	850	600

NOTE: Add 25% of guns chambered for 2-1/2" shells.

Editor's Comment: Contrary to traditional views, Winchester did install factory ventilated ribs on its Model 42. Former employees and factory drawings substantiate this fact. However, the subject of what is a factory rib and what is not has been covered in great detail in an excellent book on the Model 42. Seek expert advice before selling or purchasing any Model 42 with a ventilated rib.

Trap Grade

Exc.	V.G.	Good	Fair	Poor
8500	5500	3500	1750	700

Deluxe Grade-Solid Rib

Exc.	V.G.	Good	Fair	Poor
5500	2750	1500	750	400

Deluxe Grade-Ventilated Rib

Exc.	V.G.	Good	Fair	Poor
7500	4000	2250	900	500

NOTE: For Pigeon Grade Model 42s add 50%.

Model 1911

This was Winchester's first self-loading shotgun and was developed by T.C. Johnson in order to keep pace with the Remington Auto-Loading Shotgun Model 11, which was developed by John M. Browning with help from T.C. Johnson. Because of the delays involved in developing a brand new design, the Model 1911 was introduced on October 7, 1911. The shotgun was a recoil operated mechanism, had a tubular magazine and had the takedown feature. The shotgun was available in two styles:

1. Plain Model 1911, 26" or 28" barrel, 12 gauge, choked full, modified, or cylinder, plain birch laminated pistol grip stock and forend with hard rubber buttplate.

2. Fancy Model 1911, same as above with fancy birch laminated stock.

Because of the hurry in getting the model ready for production, the shotgun demonstrated design weakness and never proved satisfactory. It was discontinued in 1925 with about 83,000 guns sold.

Model 1911-Plain

Exc.	V.G.	Good	Fair	Poor
550	375	300	250	200

Model 1911-Fancy

Exc.	V.G.	Good	Fair	Poor
800	500	400	300	250

Model 40

This model represents Winchester's second attempt to build a self-loading long recoil-operated repeating shotgun. This shotgun was a hammerless tubular magazine gun without the hump at the rear of the receiver. Available in 12 gauge only with barrel lengths from 28" to 30". The Standard Grade had plain walnut pistol grip stock and forend. The Skeet Grade was fitted with select walnut checkered pistol grip stock and checkered forend. The Model 40 suffered from the same design problems as the Model 11, and sales were small. Introduced in 1940 and discontinued in 1941, Winchester sold about 12,000 guns.

Standard Grade

Exc.	V.G.	Good	Fair	Poor
600	500	400	275	200

Skeet Grade

Exc.	V.G.	Good	Fair	Poor
800	600	500	300	250

Model 50

The Model 50 was the company's third attempt to produce a satisfactory self-loading repeating shotgun. Winchester went to the short recoil system, utilizing a floating chamber design. This model was available in several different styles:

1. Standard Grade, 12 or 20 gauge with plain or ventilated rib in lengths from 26" to 30", plain walnut checkered pistol grip stock and forend.

2. Skeet Grade, 12 or 20 gauge with 26" ventilated rib barrel. Walnut checkered pistol grip stock and forend.

3. Trap Grade, 12 gauge with 30" ventilated rib barrel, walnut checkered Monte Carlo stock and forend.

4. Pigeon Grade, 12 or 20 gauge with barrel lengths to customers' specifications. Fancy walnut checkered stock and forend. Made on special orders only.

5. Featherweight, a lighter version of all the above except Trap Grade.

This model begins with serial number 1000. This model was successful and was built between 1954 and 1961. Winchester sold about 200,000 guns.

Standard Grade

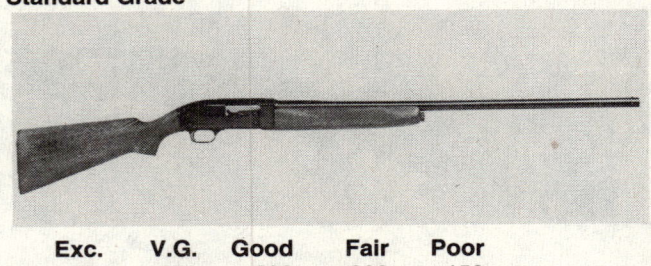

Exc.	V.G.	Good	Fair	Poor
450	350	300	200	150

Skeet Grade

Exc.	V.G.	Good	Fair	Poor
600	500	350	250	200

Trap Grade

Exc.	V.G.	Good	Fair	Poor
600	500	350	250	200

Pigeon Grade

Exc.	V.G.	Good	Fair	Poor
1250	900	750	450	250

Featherweight

Exc.	V.G.	Good	Fair	Poor
500	400	325	225	150

NOTE: Add 10% for 20 gauge.

Model 59

The fourth and final pre-1964 Winchester self-loading shotgun featured a steel and fiberglass barrel with aluminum alloy receiver. The gun was available in 12 gauge only with barrel lengths from 26" to 30" with a variety of chokes. In 1961 Winchester introduced the "Versalite" choke tube, which gave the shooter a choice of full, modified, or improved cylinder chokes in the same barrel. This model was available in two different styles:

1. Standard Grade, plain walnut checkered pistol grip stock and forend.

2. Pigeon Grade, select walnut checkered pistol grip and forend.

Winchester sold about 82,000 of these guns between 1960 and 1965.

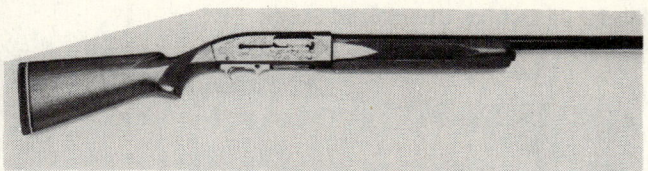

Courtesy Butterfield & Butterfield, San Francisco, California

Standard Grade

Exc.	V.G.	Good	Fair	Poor
500	375	325	225	150

Pigeon Grade

Exc.	V.G.	Good	Fair	Poor
1500	1100	850	600	300

POST-1963 RIFLES AND SHOTGUNS

RIFLES

Model 121

This is a single shot, bolt-action rifle chambered for the .22 rimfire cartridge. It has a 20.75" barrel with open sights. The finish is blued, with a plain walnut stock. It was manufactured between 1967 and 1973. A youth model with a shorter stock was designated the 121Y and is valued the same.

Courtesy Buffalo Bill Historical Center, Cody, Wyoming

Exc.	V.G.	Good	Fair	Poor
125	100	80	60	40

Model 131

This is a bolt-action repeater chambered for the .22 rimfire cartridge. It has a 20.75" barrel with open sights and a 7-round, detachable magazine. The finish is blued, with a plain walnut stock. It was manufactured between 1967 and 1973. A tubular magazine version was designated the Model 141 and is valued the same.

Exc.	V.G.	Good	Fair	Poor
140	110	90	75	50

Model 310

This is a single shot, bolt-action rifle chambered for the .22 rimfire cartridge. It features a 22" barrel with open sights. The finish is blued, with a checkered walnut stock. It was manufactured between 1972 and 1975.

Courtesy Buffalo Bill Historical Center, Cody, Wyoming

Exc.	V.G.	Good	Fair	Poor
200	150	125	100	75

Model 320

This is a bolt-action repeating rifle that is similar in configuration to the Model 310 single shot. It has a 5-round, detachable box magazine. It was manufactured between 1972 and 1974.

Exc.	V.G.	Good	Fair	Poor
350	300	250	175	125

Model 250

This is a lever-action repeating rifle with a hammerless action. It is chambered for the .22 rimfire cartridge and has a 20.5" barrel with open sights and a tubular magazine. The finish is blued, with a checkered pistol grip stock. It was manufactured between 1963 and 1973.

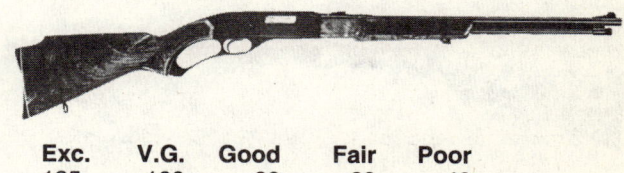

Exc.	V.G.	Good	Fair	Poor
125	100	80	60	40

Model 250 Deluxe

This version is similar to the Model 250 and is furnished with select walnut and sling swivels. It was manufactured between 1965 and 1971.

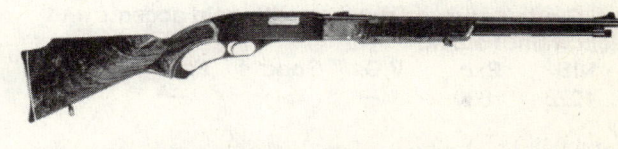

Exc.	V.G.	Good	Fair	Poor
150	125	100	75	50

Model 255

This version is simply the Model 250 chambered for the .22 WMR cartridge. It was manufactured between 1964 and 1970.

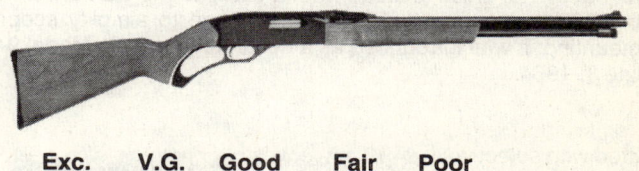

Exc.	V.G.	Good	Fair	Poor
145	120	90	70	50

Model 255 Deluxe

This version was offered with select walnut and sling swivels. It was manufactured between 1965 and 1973.

Exc.	V.G.	Good	Fair	Poor
175	150	125	100	75

Model 270

This is a slide action rifle chambered for the .22 rimfire cartridge. It has a 20.5" barrel and a tubular magazine. The finish is blued, with a checkered walnut stock. It was manufactured between 1963 and 1973.

Exc.	V.G.	Good	Fair	Poor
125	100	75	50	35

Model 490

This is a blowback-operated, semiautomatic rifle chambered for the .22 l.r. cartridge. It has a 22" barrel with open sights and a 5-round, detachable magazine. The finish is blued, with a checkered stock. It was manufactured between 1975 and 1980.

Exc.	V.G.	Good	Fair	Poor
250	200	150	100	75

Model 63

Introduced in 1997 this is a recreation of the famous Model 63 .22 caliber auto. Fitted with a 23" barrel and 10-round tubular magazine. the receiver top is grooved for scope mounting.

Grade I-engraved receiver, walnut stock

NIB	Exc.	V.G.	Good	Fair	Poor
675	525	—	—	—	—

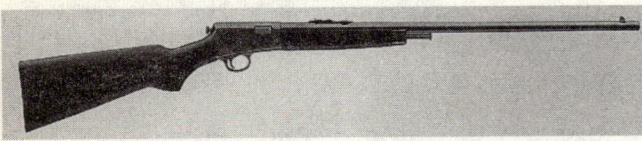

High Grade-engraved receiver with gold accents and select walnut stock.

NIB	Exc.	V.G.	Good	Fair	Poor
1075	850	—	—	—	—

Model 94

This is the post-'64 lever-action carbine chambered for the .30-30, .7-30 Waters, and the .44 Magnum cartridges. It is offered with a 20" or 24" barrel and has a 6- or 7-round, tubular magazine depending on barrel length. The round barrel is offered with open sights. The forearm is held on by a single barrel band. The finish is blued, with a straight grip walnut stock. In 1982 it was modified to angle ejection to simplify scope mounting. It was introduced as a continuation of the Model 94 line in 1964.

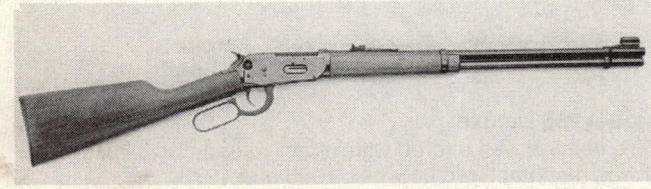

NIB	Exc.	V.G.	Good	Fair	Poor
275	225	175	125	100	75

Model 94 Ranger-Base Model

NIB	Exc.	V.G.	Good	Fair	Poor
240	200	175	150	100	75

Model 94 Deluxe-Checkered Stock

NIB	Exc.	V.G.	Good	Fair	Poor
300	250	200	150	125	100

Model 94 Win-Tuff-Laminated Stock

NIB	Exc.	V.G.	Good	Fair	Poor
300	250	200	150	125	100

Model 94 XTR-Select, Checkered Walnut Stock-Discontinued 1988

Exc.	V.G.	Good	Fair	Poor
275	225	150	100	85

Model 94 XTR Deluxe-Fancy Checkering

Exc.	V.G.	Good	Fair	Poor
350	300	200	150	110

Model 94 Trapper-16" Barrel

NIB	Exc.	V.G.	Good	Fair	Poor
300	225	175	125	100	75

Model 94 Antique Carbine-Gold-plated Saddle Ring

Exc.	V.G.	Good	Fair	Poor
250	200	175	125	90

Model 94 Wrangler-.32 Win. Special

Exc.	V.G.	Good	Fair	Poor
325	275	175	125	100

Model 94 Wrangler II-Loop Lever

NIB	Exc.	V.G.	Good	Fair	Poor
375	300	250	200	150	100

Model 94 Legacy

This Model 94 is fitted with a 20" barrel and chambered for the 30-30 Win. but it is fitted with a half pistol grip stock. Both walnut butt stock and forearm are cut checkered. Weight is 6.5 lbs.

NIB	Exc.	V.G.	Good	Fair	Poor
350	300	250	200	150	100

Model 94 XTR Big Bore

This version is chambered for the .307, .356, or the .375 Win. cartridges. It features the angle-ejection and is blued with a walnut, Monte Carlo-type stock and recoil pad. The round barrel is 20" in length. It has a 6-round, tubular magazine. It was introduced in 1978.

NIB	Exc.	V.G.	Good	Fair	Poor
300	250	200	150	125	100

Model 9422

Introduced in 1972 this model is chambered for the .22 rimfire and .22 Magnum rimfire cartridges. It was fitted with a 20.5" barrel, front ramp sight with hood, and adjustable semi-buckhorn rear sight. Tubular magazine holds 21 Shorts, 17 Longs, and 15 Long Rifle cartridges. The Magnum version holds 11 cartridges. Weight is about 6.25 lbs. Two piece American walnut stock with no checkering. Between 1972 and 1992 approximately 750,000 Model 9422s have been produced.

NIB	Exc.	V.G.	Good	Fair	Poor
275	225	200	175	150	100

Model 9422 XTR

This is a deluxe lever-action rifle chambered for the .22 rimfire cartridges. It is a takedown rifle with a 20.5", round barrel and a tubular magazine. The finish is blued with a checkered, high-gloss, straight grip walnut stock. It was introduced in 1978. A .22 Magnum version is also available and would be worth approximately $10 additional.

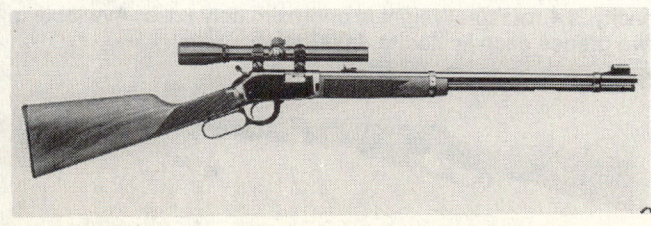

NIB	Exc.	V.G.	Good	Fair	Poor
325	275	225	175	125	100

Model 94 Centennial Limited Editions

Introduced in 1994 these models celebrate the 100-year anniversary of the Winchester Model 1894. Offered in three grades these models are of limited production. The Grade I is limited to 12,000 rifles while the High Grade is limited to 3,000 rifles. Only 94 of the Custom Limited model will be produced. Each Limited model has different grades of select walnut and engraving coverage. All are chambered for the .30-30 Winchester cartridge.

Grade I

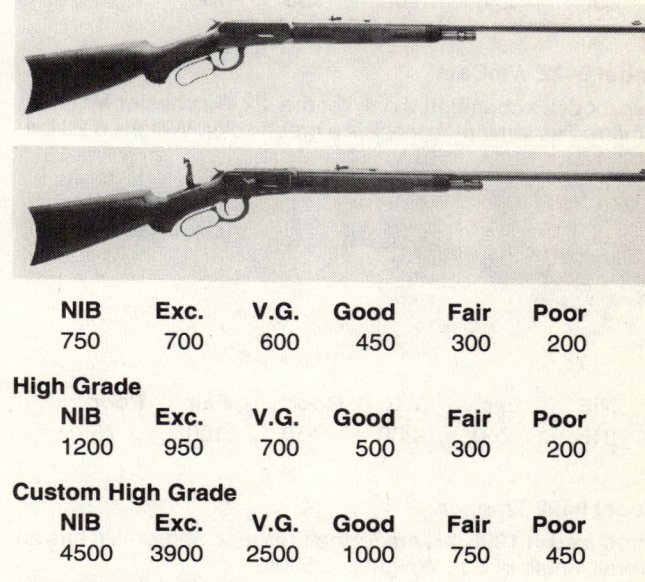

NIB	Exc.	V.G.	Good	Fair	Poor
750	700	600	450	300	200

High Grade

NIB	Exc.	V.G.	Good	Fair	Poor
1200	950	700	500	300	200

Custom High Grade

NIB	Exc.	V.G.	Good	Fair	Poor
4500	3900	2500	1000	750	450

Model 94 Trails End

This model is chambered for the .357 Mag., .44 Mag., and .45 Colt. Offered with standard size loop lever or Wrangler-style loop. Introduced in 1997.

NIB	Exc.	V.G.	Good	Fair	Poor
400	325	—	—	—	—

Model 9422 XTR Classic

This version is similar to the standard Model 9422 XTR except that it features a 22.5" barrel and a satin-finished, plain, pistol grip walnut stock. It was manufactured between 1985 and 1987.

Exc.	V.G.	Good	Fair	Poor
350	300	250	200	125

Model 9422 WinTuff

This model features an unchecked laminated wood stock that is brown in color. Chambered for both the .22 Rimfire and the .22 Winchester Magnum Rimfire. Weighs 6.25 lbs. Other features are the same as the standard Model 9422.

NIB	Exc.	V.G.	Good	Fair	Poor
300	250	200	150	100	75

Model 9422 WinCam

This model is chambered only for the .22 Winchester Magnum Rimfire. The laminated stock is a green color. Weighs 6.25 lbs.

NIB	Exc.	V.G.	Good	Fair	Poor
315	260	200	150	100	75

Model 9422 Trapper

Introduced in 1996 this model features a 16.5" barrel. It has an overall length of 33". Weight is 5.5 lbs.

NIB	Exc.	V.G.	Good	Fair	Poor
350	300	250	200	150	100

Model 9422 High Grade

This variation of the Model 9422 series features a specially engraved receiver and fancy wood stock. Barrel length is 20.5". Weight is about 6 lbs.

NIB	Exc.	V.G.	Good	Fair	Poor
450	400	300	250	175	125

Model 9422 25th Anniversary Rifle

Introduced in 1997 this model features 20.5" barrel. Limited quanities.

Grade I-engraved receiver

NIB	Exc.	V.G.	Good	Fair	Poor
600	475	—	—	—	—

High Grade-engraved receiver with silver border

NIB	Exc.	V.G.	Good	Fair	Poor
1350	1100	—	—	—	—

Model 64

This is a post-1964 version of the lever-action Model 64. It is chambered for the .30-30 cartridge and has a 24" round barrel with open sights and a 5-round, 2/3-length tubular magazine. The finish is blued with a plain walnut pistol grip stock. It was manufactured between 1972 and 1974.

Exc.	V.G.	Good	Fair	Poor
250	200	150	100	85

Model 1892

Introduced in mid-1997 this model is chambered for the .45 Colt cartridge. It features a straight grip, full magazine, and crescent butt plate.

Grade I-2,500 rifles with engraved receiver

NIB	Exc.	V.G.	Good	Fair	Poor
725	575	—	—	—	—

High Grade-1,000 rifle with gold accents.

NIB	Exc.	V.G.	Good	Fair	Poor
1275	1050	—	—	—	—

Model 1886

Introduced to the Winchester line in 1997 this was a non-catalogued item. This model features a 26" octagon barrel, semi pistol grip, and cresent butt plate.

Grade I-2,500 rifles blued receiver

NIB	Exc.	V.G.	Good	Fair	Poor
1000	800	—	—	—	—

High Grade-1,000 rifles with gold accents on receiver.

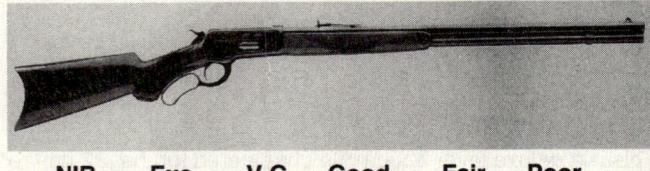

NIB	Exc.	V.G.	Good	Fair	Poor
1575	1300	—	—	—	—

Model 1895 Limited Edition

Introduced in 1995 this reproduction of the famous Model 1895 is offered in .30-06 caliber with 24" barrel. Magazine capacity is 4 rounds. Weight is approximately 8 lbs. Available in two grades each limited to 4,000 rifles.

Grade I

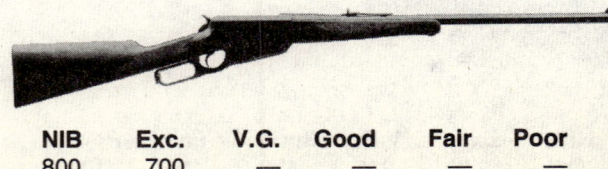

NIB	Exc.	V.G.	Good	Fair	Poor
800	700	—	—	—	—

High Grade

NIB	Exc.	V.G.	Good	Fair	Poor
1300	1000	—	—	—	—

Model 52B Sporting Rifle

A 1993 limited edition rifle (6,000 guns) that is a faithful reproduction of the famous Winchester Model 52 Sporter. Equipped with a 24" barrel, adjustable trigger, and "B" style cheekpiece. This model was reissued in 1997 and limited to 3,000 rifles.

NIB	Exc.	V.G.	Good	Fair	Poor
500	400	350	300	200	100

POST-'64 MODEL 70S

Model 70

This is a bolt-action sporting rifle chambered for various popular calibers between .22-250 and .30-06. It features a 22" barrel with open sights and a 5-round, integral box magazine. The finish is blued with a Monte Carlo-type stock furnished with sling swivels. It was manufactured between 1964 and 1980.

Exc.	V.G.	Good	Fair	Poor
350	325	250	200	125

Model 70 Mannlicher

This is a full-length, Mannlicher-type stocked version of the Model 70 bolt-action rifle that is chambered for the .243, .270, .308, and the .30-06 cartridges. It was introduced in 1969. It features a 19" barrel with open sights. The finish is blued. It was discontinued in 1972. Only 2401 were produced. Excellent quality.

Exc.	V.G.	Good	Fair	Poor
650	500	400	300	200

Model 70 Target Rifle

This version is chambered for the .308 or the .30-06 cartridges. It was offered with a 24" heavy barrel without sights. It is furnished with bases for a target scope. The finish is blued with a heavy walnut target stock with a palm rest.

Exc.	V.G.	Good	Fair	Poor
650	550	450	350	250

Model 70 International Match Army

This version is chambered for the .308 cartridge and has a 24" heavy barrel furnished without sights. It has an adjustable trigger and is blued, with a target-type heavy stock that had an accessory rail and an adjustable butt.

Exc.	V.G.	Good	Fair	Poor
750	650	500	400	300

Model 70A

This is a utility version of the bolt-action post-1964 Model 70. It was furnished without a hinged floorplate. The finish is blued, with a walnut stock. It was manufactured between 1972 and 1978.

Exc.	V.G.	Good	Fair	Poor
300	275	225	175	100

Model 70 XTR Featherweight

This gun was built after the takeover by the U.S.R.A. Company. It is a bolt-action sporting rifle chambered for various calibers from .22-250 up to the .30-06 cartridges. It has a 22" barrel that is furnished without sights and features either a short- or medium-length action. It has a 5-round, integral magazine. The finish is blued, with a checkered walnut stock. It was introduced in 1981.

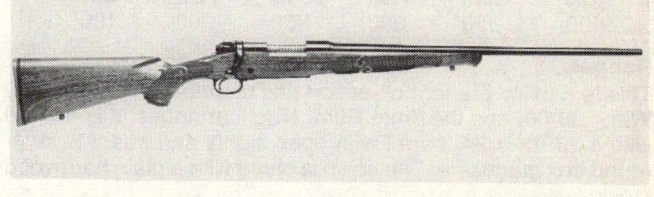

NIB	Exc.	V.G.	Good	Fair	Poor
450	400	325	300	250	200

Model 70 Fiftieth Anniversary Model

This is a commemorative version of the post-1964 Model 70 bolt-action rifle. It is chambered for the .300 Win. Mag. and is offered with a 24" barrel. It is engraved and high-gloss blued with a deluxe, checkered walnut stock. There were 500 manufactured in 1987. In order to realize collector potential, it must be NIB with all supplied materials.

NIB	Exc.	V.G.	Good	Fair	Poor
1000	800	400	300	250	200

Model 70 XTR Super Express

This is a heavy-duty version of the Post-'64 Model 70 chambered for the .375 H&H and the .458 Win. Mag. cartridges. It is offered with a 22" or 24" heavy barrel and a 3-round, integral box magazine. This version has extra recoil lugs mounted in the stock and is blued with a select, straight-grain walnut stock and a recoil pad standard.

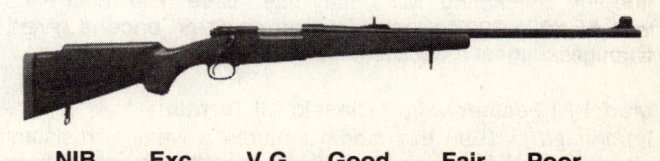

NIB	Exc.	V.G.	Good	Fair	Poor
650	500	400	300	200	100

Model 70 XTR Varmint

This version is chambered for the .22-250, .223, and the .243 cartridges. It has a 24" heavy barrel and is furnished without sights. It has a 5-round magazine and is blued with a heavy walnut stock. It was introduced in 1972.

NIB	Exc.	V.G.	Good	Fair	Poor
400	350	300	250	200	100

Model 70 Winlight

This version is offered in various calibers between .270 and the .338 Win. Mag. It features a matte-blue finish and a fiberglass stock. It is offered with a 22" or a 24" barrel and a 3- or 4-round magazine. It was introduced in 1986.

NIB	Exc.	V.G.	Good	Fair	Poor
400	350	300	250	200	100

Ranger

This is a utility-grade, bolt-action rifle chambered for the .270 Win., .30-06, and the 7mm Rem. Mag. cartridges. It is offered with a 22" or a 24" barrel with open sights and has a 3- or 4-round box magazine. The finish is blued with a plain hardwood stock.

NIB	Exc.	V.G.	Good	Fair	Poor
350	300	275	225	150	100

Model 70 Featherweight Classic

A U.S.R.A. model with 22" barrel, walnut stock, and claw controlled round feeding. The bolt is jeweled and the bolt handle knurled. Comb is straight. Available in .270, .280, and .30-06 calibers. In 1997 this model was offered in the 6.5x55mm Swedish caliber. Rifle weighs about 7.25 lbs.

NIB	Exc.	V.G.	Good	Fair	Poor
600	450	350	250	200	100

Model 70 Featherweight Ultra Grade

Limited to 1,000 rifles this model is profusely engraved with game scene and gold line inlaid. Serial number inlaid in gold. Offered in .270 caliber with very fine figured walnut stock with fine line checkering. Mahogany fitted case. The retail price was $5,000. Due to lack of active sales no price is given. Strongly suggest a qualified appraisal before sale.

Model 70 Featherweight Classic All-Terrain

Introduced in 1996 this model features a weather-resistant stainless steel barrel and action with fiberglass/graphite black synthetic stock. Offered in .270 Win., .30-06, 7mm Rem. Mag.,

.330 Win. Mag. Weight is about 7.25 lbs. Also offered with the BOSS system.

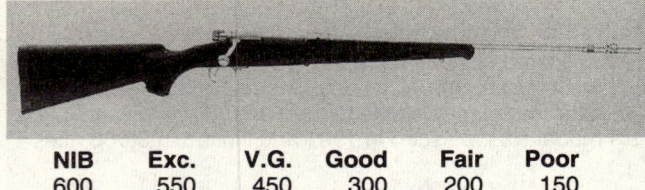

NIB	Exc.	V.G.	Good	Fair	Poor
600	550	450	300	200	150

NOTE: Add $100 for BOSS.

Model 70 Classic Laredo

First offered in 1996 this model features a heavy 26" barrel with pre-64 action on a gray synthetic stock. Chambered for the 7mm Rem. Mag and the .300 Win. Mag. The forearm is a beavertail. Finish is matte blue. In 1997 this model was offered chambered for the 7mm STW cartridge.

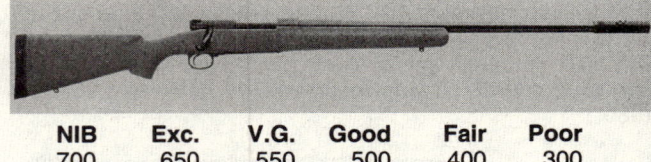

NIB	Exc.	V.G.	Good	Fair	Poor
700	650	550	500	400	300

NOTE: Add $100 for BOSS.

Model 70 Super Grade

Another U.S.R.A. rifle that features a select walnut stock, claw controlled round feed, a single reinforced cross bolt, 24" barrel shipped with bases and rings. The butt stock has a straight comb with classic cheekpiece and deep cut checkering. Available in .270, .30-06, 7mm Rem. Mag., .300 Win. Mag., .338 Win. Mag. Rifle weighs approximately 7.75 lbs. Currently in production.

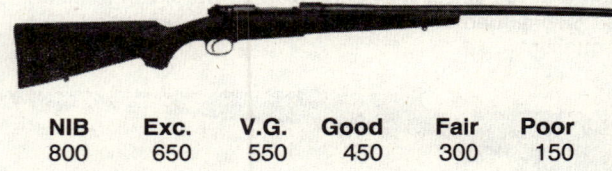

NIB	Exc.	V.G.	Good	Fair	Poor
800	650	550	450	300	150

Model 70 Super Express

A U.S.R.A. version of the post-1964 XTR Super Express. Specifications are the same as the earlier model. Rifle weighs 8.5 lbs. Introduced in 1993.

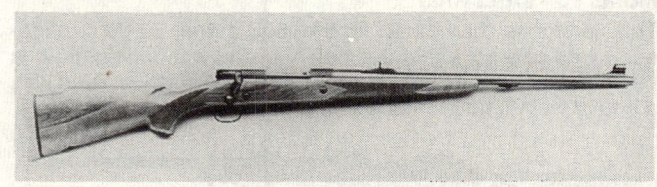

NIB	Exc.	V.G.	Good	Fair	Poor
650	500	400	300	200	100

Model 70 Custom Sharpshooter

A U.S.R.A. Custom Shop gun. This model is fitted with a stainless steel Schneider barrel with hand-honed action and hand fitted. The stock is a custom McMillan A-2 glass bedded stock. Offered in .223 Rem., .22-250 Rem., .308 Win. and .300 Win. Mag. Comes from the factory with a hard case. Currently in production.

NIB	Exc.	V.G.	Good	Fair	Poor
1300	950	750	500	300	150

Model 70 Custom Classic Sharpshooter II

Same as above but introduced in 1996 with an H-S heavy target stock, a pre-64 action stainless steel H-S barrel. Weight is about 11 lbs. Offered in .22-250, .308, .30-06, and .300 Win. Mag.

NIB	Exc.	V.G.	Good	Fair	Poor
1800	1400	—	—	—	—

Model 70 Custom Sporting Sharpshooter

Essentially a take off on the Custom Sharpshooter but configured for hunting. Fitted with a McMillan sporter style gray stock and Schneider stainless steel barrel. Offered in .270 Win., .300 Win., and 7mm STW. Introduced in 1993.

Winchester Model 70
Grey Sporting Sharpshooter

NIB	Exc.	V.G.	Good	Fair	Poor
1250	900	750	500	300	150

Model 70 Custom Classic Sporting Sharpshooter II

Introduced in 1996 this is an updated version of the model above. It features a pre-64 action with H-S special fiberglass stock and stainless steel barrel. Available in .7mm S.T.W., .300 Win. Mag. Weight is about 8.5 lbs.

NIB	Exc.	V.G.	Good	Fair	Poor
1700	1400	—	—	—	—

Model 70 Custom Grade

This custom built Model 70 is hand finished, polished, and fitted in the Custom Shop. Internal parts are hand honed while the barrel is lead lapped. The customer can order individual items to his or her own taste, including engraving, special stock dimensions and carvings, etc. Each Custom Grade Model 70 should be priced on an individual basis.

Model 70 Custom Express

Also built in the Custom Shop this model features figured walnut, hand-honed internal parts, bolt and follower are engined turned. A special 3-leaf rear sight is furnished also. Offered in .375 H&H Mag., .375 JRS, .416 Rem. Mag., .458 Win. Mag., and .470 Capstick.

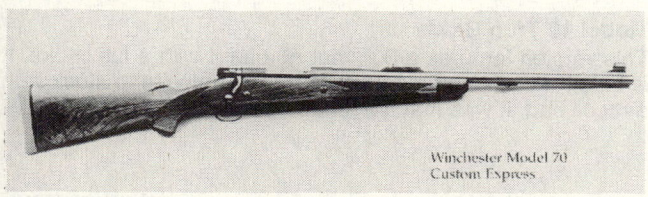

Winchester Model 70
Custom Express

NIB	Exc.	V.G.	Good	Fair	Poor
1700	1400	900	500	300	150

Model 70 Ultimate Classic

This model features a number of special options as standard. Included is a pre-64 action, choice of round, round fluted, 1/2 octagon 1/2 round barrel, full tapered octagon barrel, blued or stainless steel barrel actions, Fancy American walnut stock,

special Custom Shop serial numbers and proof stamp, inletted swivel bases, red recoil pad, fine cut checkering and a hard case. Offered in a wide variety of calibers from .25-06 to .338 Win. Mag. Weight is about 7.5 to 7.75 lbs. depending on caliber.

NIB	Exc.	V.G.	Good	Fair	Poor
2150	1900	1500	—	—	—

NOTE: In 1997 this model was introduced in a left hand version.

Model 70 Heavy Varmint

Introduced by U.S.R.A. in 1993 this rifle features a fiberglass/graphite stock with heavy 26" stainless steel barrel. Offered in .223, .22-250, .243, and .308. In 1997 this model was offered chambered for the .222 Rem. cartridge. Rifle weighs about 10.75 lbs.

NIB	Exc.	V.G.	Good	Fair	Poor
550	475	400	300	200	100

Model 70 Heavy Varmint-Fluted Barrel

Introduced in 1997 this model is similar to the above Varmint with the addition of a fluted barrel. Calibers are also the same as the above model.

NIB	Exc.	V.G.	Good	Fair	Poor
550	475	400	—	—	—

Model 70 Stainless

All metal parts are stainless steel, including the barrel, with synthetic stock. Available with 24" barrel and chambered for .270, .30-06, 7mm Rem. Mag., .300 Win. Mag., and .338 Win. Mag. Weighs about 7.5 lbs. Currently in production.

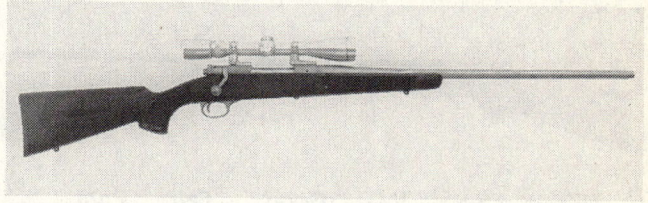

NIB	Exc.	V.G.	Good	Fair	Poor
485	425	375	300	200	100

Model 70 SM

This rifle features a synthetic stock with black matte finish. Barrel length is 24". Available in 10 calibers from .223 Rem. to .375 H&H Mag. Depending on caliber rifle weighs between 7 and 8 lbs. Currently in production.

NIB	Exc.	V.G.	Good	Fair	Poor
475	400	300	200	150	100

Model 70 DBM-S

Similar to the Model 70 SM but fitted with a detachable box magazine. The metal parts are blued and the stock is synthetic. Offered in 8 calibers from .223 Rem. to .338 Win. Mag. Furnished with scope bases and rings are open sights. Rifle weighs about 7.25 lbs. depending on caliber. Introduced in 1993

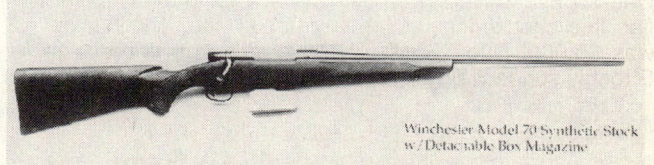

Winchester Model 70 Synthetic Stock
w/Detachable Box Magazine

NIB	Exc.	V.G.	Good	Fair	Poor
500	425	325	225	150	100

Model 70 Varmint

Similar to the Model 70 Heavy Varmint but furnished with a traditional walnut stock and 26" medium heavy barrel. Offered in .223 Rem., .22-250, .243, and .308. Weighs 9 lbs.

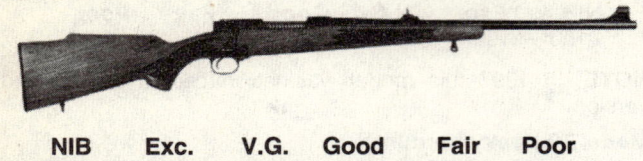

NIB	Exc.	V.G.	Good	Fair	Poor
465	400	300	200	150	100

Model 70 DBM

DBM stands for detachable box magazine. Fitted with a straight comb walnut stock. Jeweled bolt with blued receiver. Shipped with scope bases and rings or open sights. Rifle offered in 8 calibers from .223 Rem. to .300 Win. Mag. Rifle weighs about 7.35 lbs. depending on caliber. Introduced in 1993.

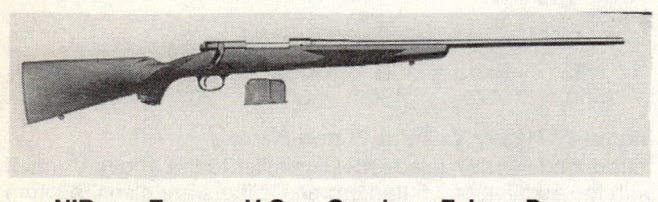

NIB	Exc.	V.G.	Good	Fair	Poor
480	425	325	225	150	100

Model 70 Sporter

U.S.R.A.'s basic Model 70 offering. Straight comb walnut stock with checkering, jeweled bolt and blued receiver and barrel are standard. Available in 12 calibers from .223 Rem. to .338 Win. Mag. including .270 Weatherby Mag. and .300 Weatherby Mag. Barrel length is 24" and is available with either scope bases and rings or open sights. Rifle weighs about 7.5 lbs.

NIB	Exc.	V.G.	Good	Fair	Poor
450	400	300	200	150	100

Model 70 WinTuff

Similar to the Sporter except fitted with a laminated hardwood straight comb stock with cheekpiece. Offered in 24" barrel lengths with a choice of 6 calibers from .270 Win. to .338 Win. Mag. Furnished with scope bases and rings. Rifle weighs about 7.65 lbs. depending on caliber.

NIB	Exc.	V.G.	Good	Fair	Poor
450	400	300	200	150	100

Model 70 Lightweight

Similar to the Model 70 Winlight. Offered with straight comb checkered walnut stock with knurled bolt and blued receiver and barrel. The barrel is 22" without sights. Offered in 5 calibers: .223, .243, .270, .308, and .30-06. Rifle weighs about 7 lbs. depending on caliber.

NIB	Exc.	V.G.	Good	Fair	Poor
400	350	300	200	150	100

Model 70 Ladies/Youth Ranger

A scaled down version of the Ranger. Length of pull is 1" shorter than standard. Rifle weighs 6.5 lbs. Chambered in .243 and .308. In 1997 this model was offered chambered for the .223 Rem. and the 7mm-08 Rem. cartridges.

NIB	Exc.	V.G.	Good	Fair	Poor
375	350	300	200	150	100

NOTE: In 1994 U.S. Repeating Arms reintroduced the pre-1963 Model 70 action on many of its Model 70 rifles. At the present time this new action does not affect values but may do so in the future depending on shooter reaction.

POST-1964 SHOTGUNS

MODEL 12 "Y" SERIES

Model 12 Field Grade

This is a later version of the slide action Model 12, chambered for 12 gauge only. It was offered with a 26", 28", or 30" vent rib barrel with various chokes. The finish is blued with a jeweled bolt and a hand-checkered, select walnut stock. This version is easily recognizable as it has the letter Y serial number prefix. It was manufactured between 1972 and 1976.

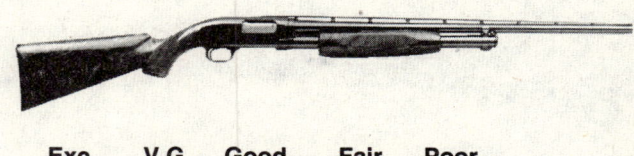

Exc.	V.G.	Good	Fair	Poor
650	550	400	350	275

Model 12 Super Pigeon Grade

This is a deluxe version that features extensive engraving and fancy checkering. It was offered with a turned action and select, fancy-grade walnut. It was a limited-production item produced between 1964 and 1972. It was briefly reintroduced in 1984 and discontinued again in 1985.

Exc.	V.G.	Good	Fair	Poor
3000	2500	1850	1400	950

Model 12 Skeet

This version is similar to the Field Grade but is offered with a 26", vent rib, skeet-bored barrel. The finish is blued, with a skeet-type stock and recoil pad. It was manufactured between 1972 and 1975.

Exc.	V.G.	Good	Fair	Poor
700	650	550	350	300

Model 12 Trap Grade

This version features a 30" vent rib barrel with a full choke. It is blued with a trap-type, standard, or Monte Carlo stock with a recoil pad. It was manufactured between 1972 and 1980.

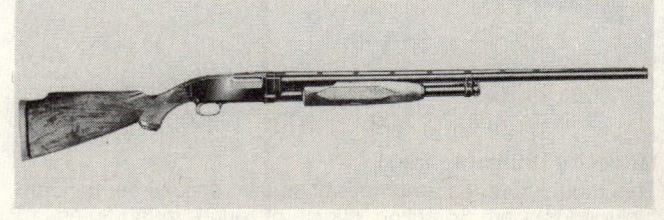

Exc.	V.G.	Good	Fair	Poor
650	600	500	300	200

Model 12 (Limited Edition)

Available in 20 gauge only. Furnished with a 26" vent rib barrel choked improved cylinder. The walnut stock is checkered with pistol grip. Introduced in 1993 and available in three different grades.

Grade 1 (4,000 guns)

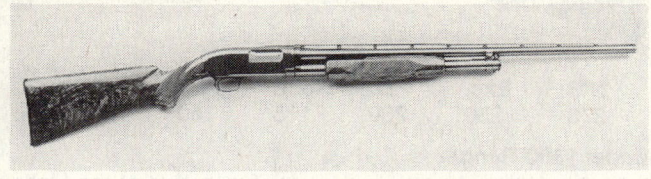

NIB	Exc.	V.G.	Good	Fair	Poor
700	600	450	350	200	100

Grade IV (1,000 guns) Gold Highlights

NIB	Exc.	V.G.	Good	Fair	Poor
1150	900	650	400	200	100

Ducks Unlimited Model

Available through Ducks Unlimited chapters. An independent appraisal is suggested.

Model 42 (Limited Edition)

A reproduction of the famous Winchester Model 42 .410 bore slide action shotgun. Furnished with a 26" ventilated rib barrel choked full. The receiver is engraved with gold border. Introduced in 1993 and limited to 850 guns.

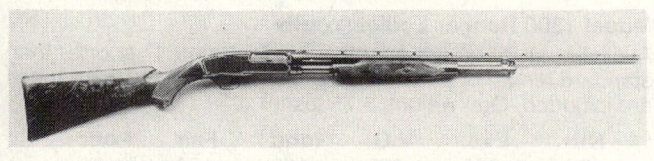

NIB	Exc.	V.G.	Good	Fair	Poor
1250	900	600	400	300	150

Model 1200

This is a slide-action shotgun chambered for 12, 16, or 20 gauge. It was offered with a 26", 28", or 30", vent rib barrel with various chokes. It has an alloy receiver and is blued, with a checkered walnut stock and recoil pad. It was manufactured between 1964 and 1981. This model was offered with the plastic Hydrocoil stock, and this would add approximately 35% to the values given.

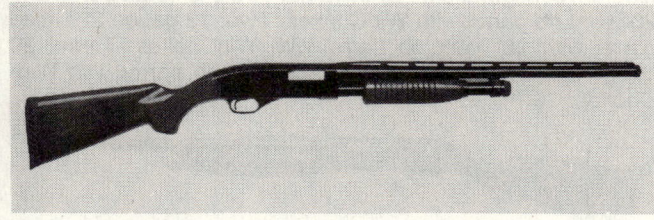

Exc.	V.G.	Good	Fair	Poor
225	175	150	100	75

MODEL 1300 SERIES

Model 1300 XTR

This is the current slide action shotgun offered by Winchester. It is chambered for 12 and 20 gauge with 3" chambers. It is a takedown gun that is offered with various-length vent rib barrels with screw-in choke tubes. It has an alloy frame and is blued with a walnut stock. It was introduced in 1978.

Exc.	V.G.	Good	Fair	Poor
300	250	200	150	100

Model 1300 Waterfowl

This version is chambered for 12 gauge, 3" only. It has a 30" vent rib barrel with screw-in choke tubes. It is matte-blued, with a satin-finished walnut stock and a recoil pad. It was introduced in 1984. A laminated WinTuff stock was made available in 1988 and would add $10 to the value.

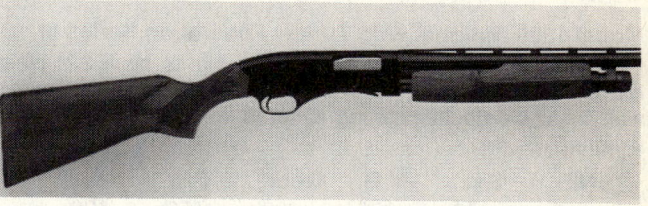

NIB	Exc.	V.G.	Good	Fair	Poor
350	300	250	200	150	100

Model 1300 WinCam Turkey Gun

This version is similar to the Model 1300 Turkey Gun, with a green, laminated hardwood stock. It was introduced in 1987. A WinTuff version is also available and would add $20 to the values given.

NIB	Exc.	V.G.	Good	Fair	Poor
375	325	250	200	150	125

Model 1300 Stainless Security

This version is chambered for 12 or 20 gauge and is constructed of stainless steel. It has an 18" cylinder-bore barrel and a 7- or 8-shot tubular magazine. It is available with a pistol grip stock, which would add approximately 50% to the values given.

NIB	Exc.	V.G.	Good	Fair	Poor
250	225	200	150	125	100

Model 1300 Turkey

This slide action model features a 22" vent rib barrel chambered for 3" 12 gauge shells. Supplied with choke tubes. Gun weighs 7.25 lbs.

NIB	Exc.	V.G.	Good	Fair	Poor
350	300	250	200	150	100

Model 1300 Realtree Turkey

Introduced in 1994 this model features a synthetic stock camouflaged with Realtree. The receiver and 22" barrel are matte finish.

NIB	Exc.	V.G.	Good	Fair	Poor
375	275	225	200	150	100

Model 1300 Black Shadow Turkey

This model was also introduced in 1994 and features a black composite stock with a non-glare finish on the barrel, receiver, bolt, and magazine. Barrel has vent rib and is 22" in length.

NIB	Exc.	V.G.	Good	Fair	Poor
250	200	175	150	125	100

Model 1300 National Wild Turkey Federation Series III

Engraved receiver, camo stock, open sights on a 22" plain barrel, and all metal and wood parts are non-glare. Comes with a quick detachable sling. Offered in 12 gauge only. Gun weighs 7.25 lbs.

NIB	Exc.	V.G.	Good	Fair	Poor
370	320	250	200	150	100

Model 1300 National Wild Turkey Federation Series IV

Introduced in 1993 this model is similar to the Series II with the addition of a 22" vent rib barrel. Stock is black laminated. Comes with quick detachable sling. Gun weight 7 lbs.

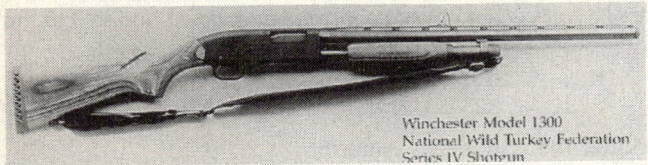

Winchester Model 1300 National Wild Turkey Federation Series IV Shotgun

NIB	Exc.	V.G.	Good	Fair	Poor
370	320	250	200	150	100

Model 1300 Whitetails Unlimited Slug Hunter

This slide action model features a full length rifle barrel chambered for 3" 12 gauge shells. Barrel is choked cylinder. Fitted with a checkered walnut stock with engraved receiver. Receiver is drilled and tapped for bases and rings, which are included. Comes equipped with camo sling. Weighs 7.25 lbs.

NIB	Exc.	V.G.	Good	Fair	Poor
350	300	250	200	150	100

Model 1300 Slug Hunter

Similar to the Whitetails Unlimited model, but without the engraved receiver.

NIB	Exc.	V.G.	Good	Fair	Poor
350	300	250	200	150	100

Model 1300 Black Shadow Deer

Introduced in 1994 this Model 1300 features a black composite stock with non-glare finish on the bolt, barrel, receiver, and magazine. Barrel is 22" with ramp front sight and adjustable rear sight.

NIB	Exc.	V.G.	Good	Fair	Poor
250	200	175	150	125	100

Model 1300 Black Shadow Field

Same as above but fitted with a 26" or 28" vent rib barrel chambered for 3" Mag. shells. Weight is about 7 lbs.

NIB	Exc.	V.G.	Good	Fair	Poor
275	225	200	150	100	80

Model 1300 Slug Hunter Sabot (Smoothbore)

Similar to the Slug Hunter but furnished with a smoothbore barrel with a special extended screw-in choke tube that is rifled.

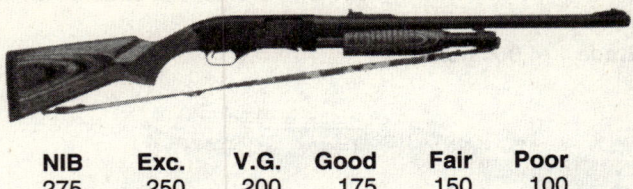

NIB	Exc.	V.G.	Good	Fair	Poor
275	250	200	175	150	100

Model 1300 Ranger

This slide action shotgun is a lower cost version of the Model 1300. Furnished With a hardwood stock and available in 12 or 20 gauge with 26" or 28" vent rib barrel. Win. chokes are included.

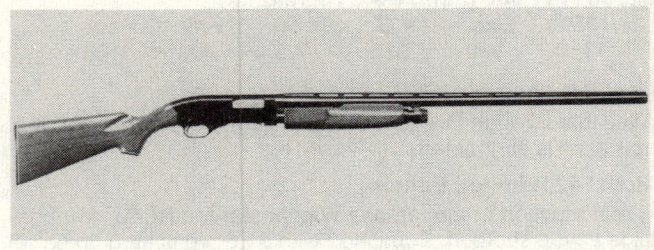

NIB	Exc.	V.G.	Good	Fair	Poor
235	200	175	150	125	100

Model 1300 Ranger Ladies/Youth

Available in 20 gauge only this model has a 1" shorter than standard length of pull and a 22" vent rib barrel. Choke tubes are included. Gun weighs 6.75 lbs.

NIB	Exc.	V.G.	Good	Fair	Poor
250	200	175	150	125	100

Model 1300 Ranger Deer Slug

Comes in two principal configurations: a 12 gauge 22" smooth barrel with cylinder choke; and a 12 gauge 22" rifled barrel. Both are chambered for 3" shells and weigh 6.75 lbs.

NIB	Exc.	V.G.	Good	Fair	Poor
250	200	175	150	125	100

Model 1300 Ranger Deer Combo

The Model 1300 Ranger Deer Combos are available in three different configurations. One: 12 gauge 22" smooth barrel and 28" vent rib barrel with WinChokes. Two: 12 gauge 22" rifled barrel with 28" vent rib barrel with WinChokes. Three: 20 gauge 22" smooth barrel with 28" vent rib barrel with WinChokes.

12 Gauge Combo

NIB	Exc.	V.G.	Good	Fair	Poor
300	250	200	175	150	100

20 Gauge Combo

NIB	Exc.	V.G.	Good	Fair	Poor
300	250	200	175	150	100

Model 1300 Defender Combo

This personal defense slide action shotgun features an 18" cylinder choked barrel and a 28" vent rib barrel with modified WinChoke and an accessory pistol grip. A hardwood stock comes fitted to the gun.

NIB	Exc.	V.G.	Good	Fair	Poor
300	250	200	175	150	100

Model 1300 Defender 5-Shot

Same as above but furnished with a hardwood stock only and 18" barrel.

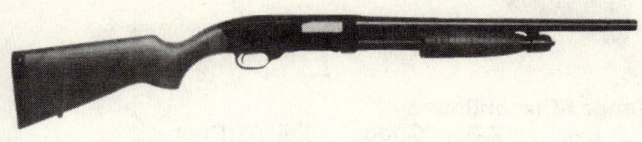

NIB	Exc.	V.G.	Good	Fair	Poor
250	200	175	150	125	100

Model 1300 Defender 8-Shot

Same as above but furnished with an 18" barrel with extended magazine tube.

NIB	Exc.	V.G.	Good	Fair	Poor
250	200	175	150	125	100

Model 1300 Defender Synthetic Stock

Same as above but fitted with a black synthetic full stock. Available in either 12 or 20 gauge.

NIB	Exc.	V.G.	Good	Fair	Poor
250	200	175	150	125	100

Model 1300 Defender Pistol Grip

Same as above but fitted with a black synthetic pistol grip and extended magazine tube.

NIB	Exc.	V.G.	Good	Fair	Poor
250	200	175	150	125	100

Model 1300 Lady Defender

Chambered for the 20 gauge shell this model features a 18" barrel with 8-round capacity. Pistol grip stock. Introduced in 1997.

NIB	Exc.	V.G.	Good	Fair	Poor
275	225	—	—	—	—

Model 1300 Stainless Marine

This 12 gauge slide action shotgun comes with a black synthetic full stock with all metal parts chrome plated. Barrel is 18" and magazine tube holds 7 rounds. Gun weighs 6.75 lbs.

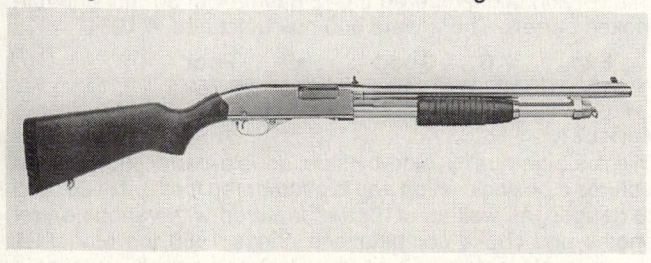

NIB	Exc.	V.G.	Good	Fair	Poor
350	300	250	200	150	100

Model 1300 Stainless Marine with Pistol Grip

Same as above with black synthetic pistol grip in place of full butt stock. Gun weighs 5.75 lbs.

NIB	Exc.	V.G.	Good	Fair	Poor
350	300	250	200	150	100

Model 1500 XTR

This is a gas-operated, semiautomatic shotgun chambered for 12 or 20 gauge, with a 28" vent rib barrel with screw-in chokes.

The finish is blued, with a walnut stock. It was manufactured between 1978 and 1982.

Exc.	V.G.	Good	Fair	Poor
300	250	225	175	125

Super X Model I

This is a self-compensating, gas-operated, semiautomatic shotgun chambered for 12 gauge. It was offered with a 26", 28", or 30" vent rib barrel with various chokes. It features all-steel construction and is blued, with a checkered walnut stock. It was manufactured between 1974 and 1981.

Exc.	V.G.	Good	Fair	Poor
400	325	250	200	150

Super X Model 1 Custom Competition

This is a custom-order trap or skeet gun that features the self compensating, gas-operated action. It is available in 12 gauge only from the Custom Shop. It is offered with a heavy degree of engraving on the receiver and a fancy, checkered walnut stock. Gold inlays are available and would add approximately 50% to the values given. This model was introduced in 1987.

NIB	Exc.	V.G.	Good	Fair	Poor
1300	1000	850	700	600	450

Model 1400

This is a gas-operated, semiautomatic shotgun chambered for 12, 16, or 20 gauge. It was offered with a 26", 28", or 30" vent rib barrel with various chokes. The finish is blued, with a checkered walnut stock. It was manufactured between 1964 and 1981. The Hydrocoil plastic stock was available on this model and would add approximately 35% to the values given.

Exc.	V.G.	Good	Fair	Poor
250	225	200	150	100

New Model 1400

This is a gas-operated, semiautomatic shotgun chambered for 12 or 20 gauge. It is offered with a 22" or 28" vent rib barrel with screw-in chokes. The finish is blued, with a checkered walnut stock. It was introduced in 1989.

NIB	Exc.	V.G.	Good	Fair	Poor
400	350	300	250	200	125

Model 1400 Ranger

This is a utility-grade, gas-operated, semiautomatic shotgun chambered for 12 or 20 gauge. It is offered with a 28" vent rib barrel with screw-in chokes, as well as a 24" slug barrel with rifle sights. The finish is blued, with a checkered stock. A combination two-barrel set that includes the deer barrel would be worth approximately 20% additional. This model was introduced in 1983 and is currently produced.

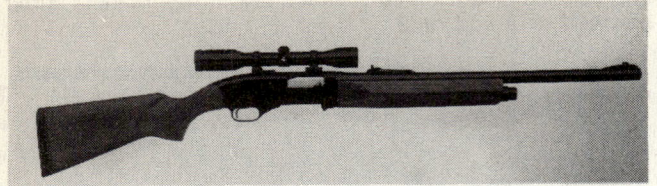

NIB	Exc.	V.G.	Good	Fair	Poor
340	300	250	200	150	100

Model 1400 Quail Unlimited

This 12 gauge semiautomatic shotgun model was introduced in 1993. It features compact engraved receiver with 26" vent rib barrel supplied with WinChoke tubes. Stock is checkered walnut. Gun weighs 7.25 lbs.

Winchester Model 1400 Quail Unlimited Shotgun

NIB	Exc.	V.G.	Good	Fair	Poor
340	300	250	200	150	100

Model 1400 Ranger Deer Combo

This model features a 12 gauge 22" smooth barrel and a 28" vent rib barrel with three WinChokes.

NIB	Exc.	V.G.	Good	Fair	Poor
340	300	250	200	150	100

Model 22

Introduced in 1975 this side by side shotgun was manufactured by Laurona in Spain to Winchester's specifications for the European market. It had an oil finished stock with checked pistol grip semi-beavertail forearm and hand engraved receiver. The finish was black chrome. The gun was fitted with double triggers, matted rib and offered in 12 gauge only with 28 unch barrels. It weighted 6-3/4 lbs.

NIB	Exc.	V.G.	Good	Fair	Poor
1250	950	700	550	400	200

Model 91

This over and under shotgun was built for Winchester by Laurona for its European markets. Offered in 12 gauge only with 28" barrels the barrels were fitted with a ventilated rib. The gun was offered with single or double triggers with hand checkered walnut stock with oil finish and hand engraved receiver. The finish was black chrome. Gun weighs 7-1/2 lbs.

NIB	Exc.	V.G.	Good	Fair	Poor
1000	800	600	500	400	200

MODEL 23 SERIES

Model 23 XTR

This is a side-by-side, double-barrel shotgun chambered for 12 or 20 gauge. It is offered with 25.5", 26", 28", or 30" vent rib barrels with 3" chambers and various choke combinations. It is a boxlock gun that features a single trigger and automatic ejectors. It is scroll-engraved with a coin-finished receiver, blued barrels, and a checkered, select walnut stock. It was introduced in 1978. This model is available in a number of configurations that differ in the amount of ornamentation and the quality of materials and workmanship utilized in their construction. These models and their values are as follows:

Grade I-Discontinued

Exc.	V.G.	Good	Fair	Poor
900	750	650	500	400

Pigeon Grade-With WinChokes

Exc.	V.G.	Good	Fair	Poor
1000	850	750	600	500

Pigeon Grade Lightweight-Straight Stock

Exc.	V.G.	Good	Fair	Poor
1300	1000	900	750	600

Golden Quail

This series was available in 28 gauge and .410, as well as 12 or 20 gauge. It features 25.5" barrels that are choked improved cylinder/modified. It features a straight grip, English-style stock with a recoil pad. The .410 version would be worth approximately 10% more than the values given. This series was discontinued in 1987.

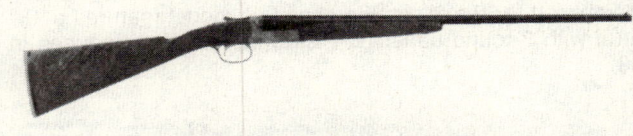

Exc.	V.G.	Good	Fair	Poor
1500	1250	1100	850	750

Model 23 Light Duck

This version is chambered for 20 gauge and was offered with a 28" full and full-choked barrel. There were 500 manufactured in 1985.

Exc.	V.G.	Good	Fair	Poor
1500	1250	1100	850	750

Model 23 Heavy Duck

This version is chambered for 12 gauge with 30" full and full-choked barrels. There were 500 manufactured in 1984.

Exc.	V.G.	Good	Fair	Poor
1500	1250	1100	850	750

Model 21

This is a high-quality, side-by-side, double-barrel shotgun that features a boxlock action and is chambered for 12, 16, 20, and 28 gauges, as well as .410. It is featured with various barrel lengths and choke combinations. Since 1960 the Model 21 has been available on a custom-order basis only. It is available in five basic configurations that differ in the options offered, the amount of ornamentation, and the quality of materials and workmanship utilized in their construction. See previous Model 21 entry.

MODEL 101 SERIES

Model 101 Field Grade

This is an Over/Under, double-barrel shotgun chambered for 12, 20, and 28 gauge, as well as .410. It was offered with 26", 28", or 30" vent rib barrels with various choke combinations. As of 1983 screw-in chokes have been standard, and models so furnished would be worth approximately $50 additional. This is a boxlock gun with a single selective trigger and automatic ejectors. The receiver is engraved; the finish, blued with a checkered walnut stock. It was manufactured between 1963 and 1987.

28 Gauge-Add 40%.

.410-Add 50%.

Exc.	V.G.	Good	Fair	Poor
750	650	500	375	300

Waterfowl Model

This version of the Model 101 is chambered for 12 gauge with 3" chambers. It has 30" or 32" vent rib barrels and a matte finish.

Exc.	V.G.	Good	Fair	Poor
1250	1000	850	650	500

Model 101 Magnum

This version is similar to the Field Grade, chambered for 12 or 20 gauge with 3" Magnum chambers. It was offered with 30" barrels with various chokes. The stock is furnished with a recoil pad. It was manufactured between 1966 and 1981.

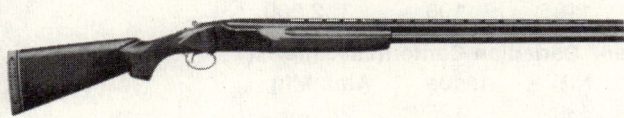

Exc.	V.G.	Good	Fair	Poor
775	675	525	400	325

Model 101 Skeet Grade

This version was offered with 26" skeet-bored barrels with a competition rib and a skeet-type walnut stock. It was manufactured between 1966 and 1984.

Exc.	V.G.	Good	Fair	Poor
950	850	750	500	400

Model 101 Three-Gauge Skeet Set

This combination set was offered with three barrels, chambered for 20 and 28 gauge, as well as .410. It was furnished with a fitted case and manufactured between 1974 and 1984.

Exc.	V.G.	Good	Fair	Poor
1850	1450	1000	750	650

Model 101 Trap Grade

This version is chambered for 12 gauge only and was offered with 30" or 32" competition ribbed barrels, choked for trap shooting. It is furnished with a competition-type stock. It was manufactured between 1966 and 1984.

Exc.	V.G.	Good	Fair	Poor
1250	1000	850	650	500

Model 101 Pigeon Grade

This is a more deluxe engraved version of the Model 101, chambered for 12, 20, or 28 gauge, as well as .410. It features a coin-finished receiver with a fancy checkered walnut stock. It was introduced in 1974.

Exc.	V.G.	Good	Fair	Poor
1500	1250	1000	800	700

Super Pigeon Grade

This is a deluxe version of the Model 101, chambered for 12 gauge. It is heavily engraved with several gold inlays. The receiver is blued, and it features a high-grade walnut stock with fleur-de-lis checkering. It was imported between 1985 and 1987.

Exc.	V.G.	Good	Fair	Poor
4000	3500	2750	2000	1650

Model 101 Diamond Grade

This is a competition model, chambered for all four gauges. It was offered in either a trap or skeet configuration with screw-in chokes, an engraved matte-finished receiver, and a select checkered walnut stock. The skeet model features recoil-reducing muzzle vents.

Exc.	V.G.	Good	Fair	Poor
1600	1250	1000	750	600

Model 501 Grand European

This is an Over/Under, double-barrel shotgun chambered for 12 or 20 gauge. It was available in trap or skeet configurations and was offered with a 27", 30", or 32" vent rib barrel. It is heavily engraved and matte-finished, with a select checkered walnut stock. It was manufactured between 1981 and 1986.

Exc.	V.G.	Good	Fair	Poor
1500	1150	950	700	550

Model 501 Presentation Grade

This is a deluxe version chambered in 12 gauge only. It is ornately engraved and gold-inlaid. The stock is made out of presentation-grade walnut. It was furnished with a fitted case. It was manufactured between 1984 and 1987.

Exc.	V.G.	Good	Fair	Poor
3000	2500	2000	1500	1250

Combination Gun

This is an Over/Under rifle/shotgun combination chambered for 12 gauge over .222, .223, .30-06, and the 9.3x74R cartridges. It features 25" barrels. The shotgun tube has a screw-in choke. It is engraved in the fashion of the Model 501 Grand European and features a select checkered walnut stock. It was manufactured between 1983 and 1985.

Exc.	V.G.	Good	Fair	Poor
2250	2000	1750	1250	1000

Express Rifle

This is an Over/Under, double-barreled rifle chambered for the .257 Roberts, .270, 7.7x65R, .30-06, and the 9.3x74R cartridges. It features 23.5" barrels with a solid rib and express sights. It is engraved with gamescenes and has a satin-finished receiver. The stock is checkered select walnut. It was manufactured in 1984 and 1985.

Exc.	V.G.	Good	Fair	Poor
1750	1500	1250	1000	750

Model 96 Xpert

This is a utility-grade, Over/Under, double-barrel shotgun that is mechanically similar to the Model 101. It is chambered for 12 or 20 gauge and was offered with various barrel lengths and choke combinations. It has a boxlock action with single selective trigger and automatic ejectors. The plain receiver is blued, with a checkered walnut stock. It was manufactured between 1976 and 1982. A competition-grade model for trap or skeet was also available and would be worth approximately the same amount.

Exc.	V.G.	Good	Fair	Poor
650	550	450	350	275

Model 1001 Field

A new addition to the U.S.R.A. product line for 1993. This Over/Under shotgun is available in 12 gauge only, with a 28" ventilated rib barrel furnished with WinPlus choke tubes. A walnut checkered pistol stock is standard. The finish is blued with scroll engraving on the receiver. The receiver top has a matte finish. The gun weighs 7 lbs.

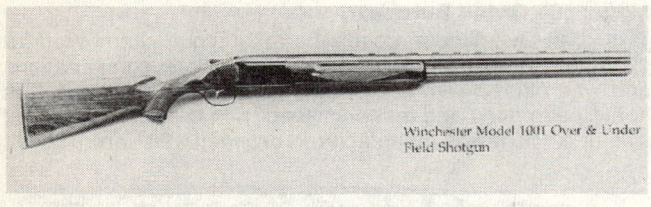

Winchester Model 1001 Over & Under Field Shotgun

NIB	Exc.	V.G.	Good	Fair	Poor
875	750	650	500	300	150

Model 1001 Sporting Clays I & II

This model features different stock dimensions, a fuller pistol grip, a radiused recoil pad, and a wider vent rib fitted on a 28" barrel (Sporting Clays I model, the Sporting Clays II features a 30" barrel). Comes complete with choke tubes. The frame has a silver nitrate finish and special engraving featuring a flying clay target. Introduced in 1993. Gun weighs 7.75 lbs.

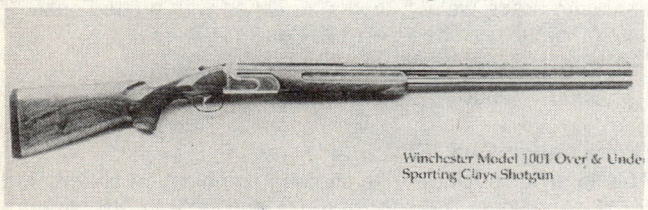

Winchester Model 1001 Over & Under Sporting Clays Shotgun

NIB	Exc.	V.G.	Good	Fair	Poor
1000	800	700	550	300	150

WINCHESTER COMMEMORATIVE RIFLES

Since the early 1960s, Winchester has produced a number of special Model 1894 rifles and carbines that commemorated certain historic events, places, or individuals. In some cases they are slightly embellished and in others are quite ornate. The general liquidity of these commemoratives has not been

as good as would be expected. In some cases they were produced in excessive amounts and could not, in all honesty, be considered limited-production items. In any case, in our opinion one should purchase weapons of this nature for their enjoyment factor as the investment potential is not sufficient reason for their purchase. As with all commemoratives, in order to realize the collector potential they must be NIB with all supplied materials including, in the case of Winchester, the colorful outer sleeve that encased the factory carton. If a Winchester commemorative rifle has been cocked leaving a line on the hammer or the lever, many collectors will show little or no interest in its acquisition. If they have been fired, they will realize little premium over a standard, Post-'64 Model 94. A number of commemoratives have been ordered by outside concerns and are technically not factory issues. Most have less collectibility than the factory-issued models. There are a number of concerns that specialize in marketing the total range of Winchester commmemorative rifles. We list the factory-issue commemoratives with their current value, their issue price, and the number manufactured.

1964 Wyoming Diamond Jubilee-Carbine

NIB	Issue	Amt. Mfg.
1295	100	1,500

1966 Centennial-Rifle

NIB	Issue	Amt. Mfg.
450	125	102,309

1966 Centennial-Carbine

NIB	Issue	Amt. Mfg.
425	125	102,309

1966 Nebraska Centennial-Rifle

NIB	Issue	Amt. Mfg.
1195	100	2,500

1967 Canadian Centennial-Rifle

NIB	Issue	Amt. Mfg.
450	125	

1967 Canadian Centennial-Carbine

NIB	Issue	Amt. Mfg.
425	125	90,301

1967 Alaskan Purchase Centennial-Carbine

NIB	Issue	Amt. Mfg.
1495	125	1,500

1968 Illinois Sesquicentennial-Carbine

NIB	Issue	Amt. Mfg.
350	110	37,648

1968 Buffalo Bill-Carbine

NIB	Issue	Amt. Mfg.
425	130	112,923

1968 Buffalo Bill-Rifle

NIB	Issue	Amt. Mfg.
450	130	

1968 Buffalo Bill "1 or 300"-Rifle

NIB	Issue	Amt. Mfg.
2500	1000	300

1969 Theodore Roosevelt-Rifle

NIB	Issue	Amt. Mfg.
450	135	—

1969 Theodore Roosevelt-Carbine

NIB	Issue	Amt. Mfg.
425	135	52,386

1969 Golden Spike Carbine

NIB	Issue	Amt. Mfg.
350	120	69,996

1970 Cowboy Commemorative Carbine

NIB	Issue	Amt. Mfg.
450	125	27,549

1970 Cowboy Carbine "1 of 300"

NIB	Issue	Amt. Mfg.
2500	1000	300

1970 Northwest Territories (Canadian)

NIB	Issue	Amt. Mfg.
850	150	2,500

1970 Northwest Territories Deluxe (Canadian)

NIB	Issue	Amt. Mfg.
1100	250	500

1970 Lone Star-Rifle

NIB	Issue	Amt. Mfg.
450	140	

1970 Lone Star-Carbine

NIB	Issue	Amt. Mfg.
425	140	38,385

1971 NRA Centennial-Rifle

NIB	Issue	Amt. Mfg.
425	150	21,000

1971 NRA Centennial-Musket

NIB	Issue	Amt. Mfg.
425	150	23,400

1971 Yellow Boy (European)

NIB	Issue	Amt. Mfg.
1150	250	500

1971 Royal Canadian Mounted Police (Canadian)

NIB	Issue	Amt. Mfg.
795	190	9,500

1971 Mounted Police (Canadian)

NIB	Issue	Amt. Mfg.
795	190	5,100

1971 Mounted Police, Presentation

NIB	Issue	Amt. Mfg.
9995	—	10

1974 Texas Ranger-Carbine

NIB	Issue	Amt. Mfg.
695	135	4,850

1974 Texas Ranger Presentation Model

NIB	Issue	Amt. Mfg.
2500	1000	150

1974 Apache (Canadian)

NIB	Issue	Amt. Mfg.
795	150	8,600

1974 Commanche (Canadian)

NIB	Issue	Amt. Mfg.
795	230	11,500

1974 Klondike Gold Rush (Canadian)

NIB	Issue	Amt. Mfg.
795	240	10,500

1975 Klondike Gold Rush-Dawson City Issue (Canadian)

NIB	Issue	Amt. Mfg.
8500	—	25

1976 Sioux (Canadian)

NIB	Issue	Amt. Mfg.
795	280	10,000

1976 Little Bighorn (Canadian)

NIB	Issue	Amt. Mfg.
795	300	11,000

1976 U.S. Bicentennial Carbine

NIB	Issue	Amt. Mfg.
595	325	19,999

1977 Wells Fargo

NIB	Issue	Amt. Mfg.
495	350	19,999

1977 Legendary Lawman

NIB	Issue	Amt. Mfg.
495	375	19,999

1977 Limited Edition I

NIB	Issue	Amt. Mfg.
1395	1500	1,500

1977 Cheyenne-.22 Cal. (Canadian)

NIB	Issue	Amt. Mfg.
695	320	5,000

1977 Cheyenne-.44-40 Cal. (Canadian)

NIB	Issue	Amt. Mfg.
795	300	11,225

1977 Cherokee-.22 Cal. (Canadian)

NIB	Issue	Amt. Mfg.
695	385	3,950

1977 Cherokee-.30-30 Cal. (Canadian)

NIB	Issue	Amt. Mfg.
795	385	9,000

1978 "One of One Thousand" (European)

NIB	Issue	Amt. Mfg.
7500	5000	250

1978 Antler Game Carbine

NIB	Issue	Amt. Mfg.
495	375	19,999

1979 Limited Edition II

NIB	Issue	Amt. Mfg.
1395	1500	1,500

1979 Legendary Frontiersman Rifle

NIB	Issue	Amt. Mfg.
495	425	19,999

1979 Matched Set of 1,000

NIB	Issue	Amt. Mfg.
2250	3000	1,000

1979 Bat Masterson (Canadian)

NIB	Issue	Amt. Mfg.
795	650	8,000

1980 Alberta Diamond Jubilee (Canadian)

NIB	Issue	Amt. Mfg.
795	650	2,700

1980 Alberta Diamond Jubilee Deluxe (Canadian)

NIB	Issue	Amt. Mfg.
1495	1900	300

1980 Saskatchewan Diamond Jubilee (Canadian)

NIB	Issue	Amt. Mfg.
795	695	2,700

1980 Saskatchewan Diamond Jubilee Deluxe (Canadian)

NIB	Issue	Amt. Mfg.
1495	1995	300

1980 Oliver Winchester

NIB	Issue	Amt. Mfg.
695	375	19,999

1981 U.S. Border Patrol

NIB	Issue	Amt. Mfg.
595	1195	1,000

1981 U.S. Border Patrol-Member's Model

NIB	Issue	Amt. Mfg.
595	695	800

1981 Calgary Stampede (Canadian)

NIB	Issue	Amt. Mfg.
1250	2200	1,000

1981 Canadian Pacific Centennial (Canadian)

NIB	Issue	Amt. Mfg.
550	800	2,000

1981 Canadian Pacific Centennial Presentation (Canadian)

NIB	Issue	Amt. Mfg.
1100	2200	300

1981 Canadian Pacific Employee's Model (Canadian)

NIB	Issue	Amt. Mfg.
550	800	2,000

1981 John Wayne (Canadian)

NIB	Issue	Amt. Mfg.
1095	995	1,000

1981 John Wayne

NIB	Issue	Amt. Mfg.
895	600	49,000

1981 Duke

NIB	Issue	Amt. Mfg.
2950	2250	1,000

1981 John Wayne "1 of 300" Set

NIB	Issue	Amt. Mfg.
6500	10000	300

1982 Great Western Artist I

NIB	Issue	Amt. Mfg.
1195	2200	999

1982 Great Western Artist II

NIB	Issue	Amt. Mfg.
1195	2200	999

1982 Annie Oakley

NIB	Issue	Amt. Mfg.
695	699	6,000

1983 Chief Crazy Horse

NIB	Issue	Amt. Mfg.
495	600	19,999

1983 American Bald Eagle

NIB	Issue	Amt. Mfg.
595	895	2,800

1983 American Bald Eagle-Deluxe

NIB	Issue	Amt. Mfg.
2500	2995	200

1983 Oklahoma Diamond Jubilee

NIB	Issue	Amt. Mfg.
1400	2250	1,001

1984 Winchester-Colt Commemorative Set

NIB	Issue	Amt. Mfg.
2250	3995	2,300

1985 Boy Scout 75th Anniversary-.22 Cal.

NIB	Issue	Amt. Mfg.
495	615	15,000

1985 Boy Scout 75th Anniversary-Eagle Scout

NIB	Issue	Amt. Mfg.
2500	2140	1,000

Texas Sesquicentennial Model-Rifle-.38-55 Cal.

NIB	Issue	Amt. Mfg.
2400	2995	1,500

Texas Sesquicentennial Model-Carbine-.38-55 Cal.

NIB	Issue	Amt. Mfg.
695	695	15,000

Texas Sesquicentennial Model Set with Bowie Knife

NIB	Issue	Amt. Mfg.
6250	7995	150

1986 Model 94 Ducks Unlimited

NIB	Issue	Amt. Mfg.
650	—	2,800

1986 Statue of Liberty

NIB	Issue	Amt. Mfg.
7000	6500	100

1986 120th Anniversary Model-Carbine-.44-40 Cal.

NIB	Issue	Amt. Mfg.
895	995	1,000

1986 European 1 of 1,000 Second Series (European)

NIB	Issue	Amt. Mfg.
7000	6000	150

1987 U.S. Constitution 200th Anniversary-44-40

NIB	Issue	Amt. Mfg.
13000	12000	17

1990 Wyoming Centennial-30-30

NIB	Issue	Amt. Mfg.
1095	895	500

1991 Winchester 125th Anniversary

NIB	Issue	Amt. Mfg.
5250	4995	61

1992 Arapaho-30-30

NIB	Issue	Amt. Mfg.
1095	895	500

1992 Ontario Conservation-30-30

NIB	Issue	Amt. Mfg.
1195	1195	400

1992 Kentucky Bicentennial-30-30

NIB	Issue	Amt. Mfg.
995	995	500

1993 Nez Perce-30-30

NIB	Issue	Amt. Mfg.
995	995	600

1995 Florida Sesquicentennial Carbine

NIB	Issue	Amt. Mfg.
1195	1195	360

1996 Wild Bill Hickok Carbine

NIB	Issue	Amt. Mfg.
1195	1195	350

Winchester 120th Commemorative Anniversary carbine

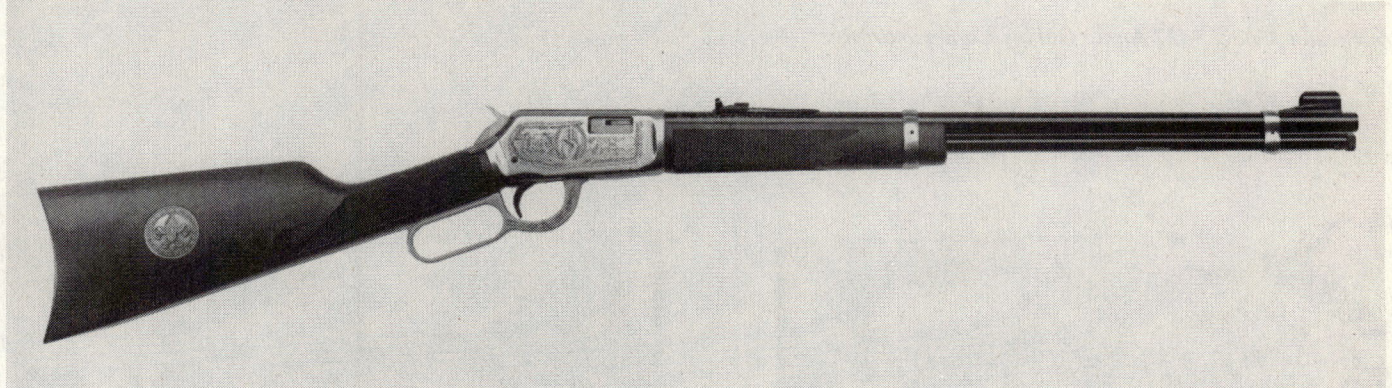

Winchester Model 9422 Boy Scouts of America Commemorative

Winchester Model 9422 Eagle Scout Limited Edition Commemorative

John Wayne Commemorative Gun

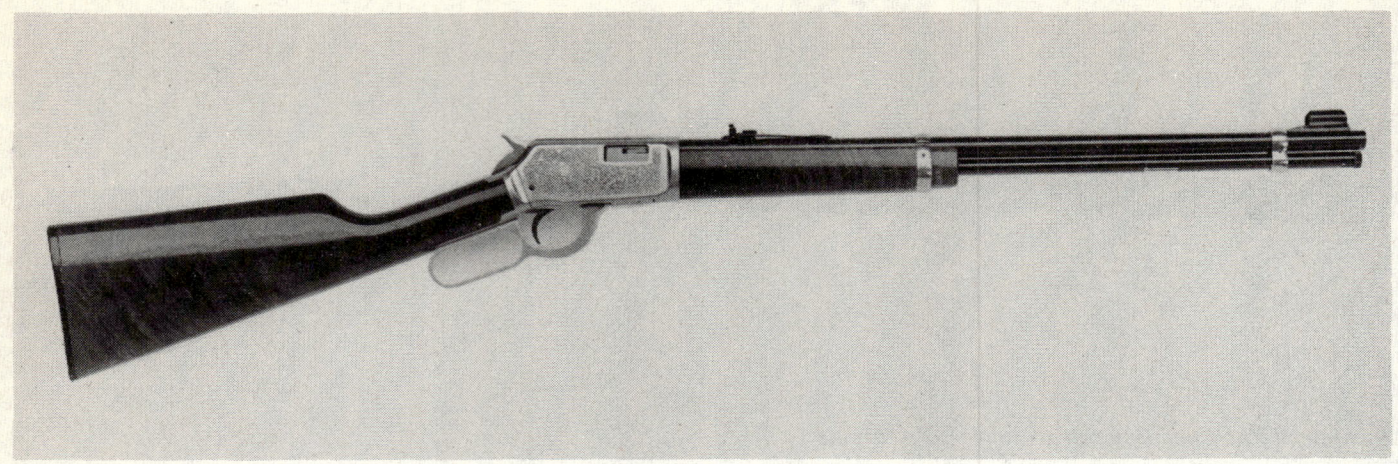

Winchester Model 9422 Annie Oakley Commemorative

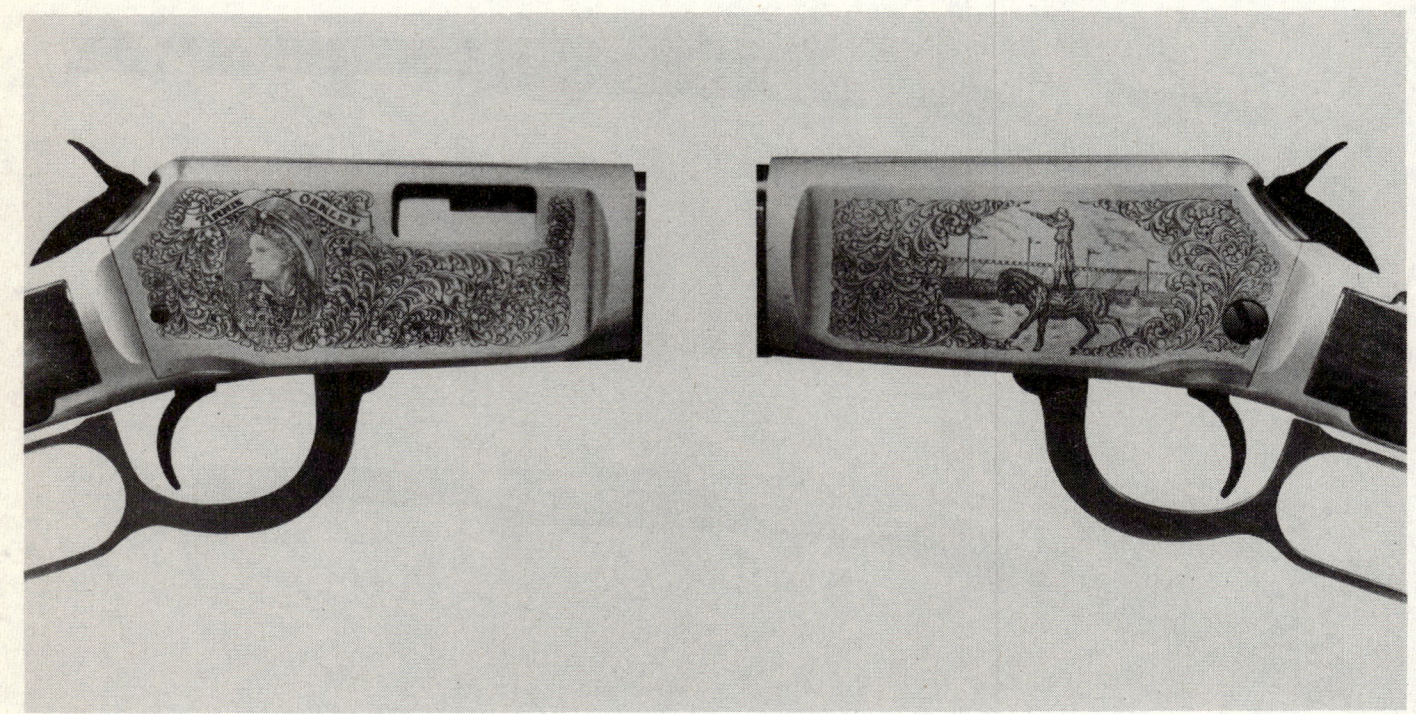

Close-up of Model 9422 Annie Oakley Commemorative engraving

Winchester Chief Crazy Horse Commemorative

Winchester Texas Ranger Commemorative

Winchester Wells Fargo & Co. Commemorative carbine

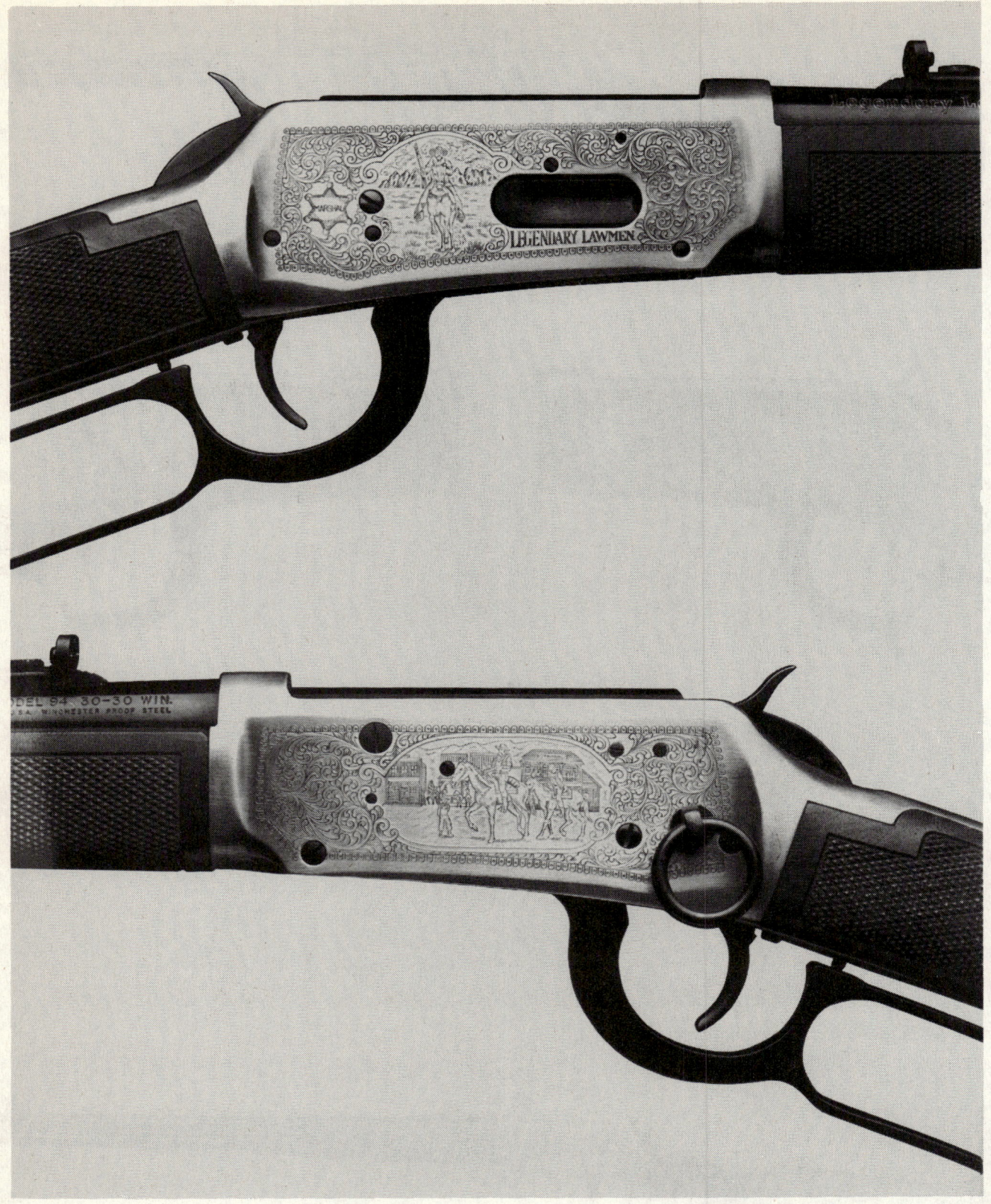

Receiver of the Winchester Legendary Lawmen Model 94 carbine. The antique silver finish is decoratively engraved on both sides

Winchester Serial Numbers

Records at the factory indicate the following serial numbers were assigned to guns at the end of the calendar year.

MODEL 100

1961 —	1 to 32189	1968 —	210053
62 —	60760	69 —	A210999
63 —	78863	70 —	229995
64 —	92016	71 —	242999
65 —	135388	72 —	A258001
66 —	145239	73 —	A262833
67 —	209498		

Records at the factory indicate the following serial numbers were assigned to guns at the end of the calendar year.

MODEL 88

1955 —	1 to 18378	1965 —	162699
56 —	36756	66 —	192595
57 —	55134	67 —	212416
58 —	73512	68 —	230199
59 —	91890	69 —	H239899
60 —	110268	70 —	H258229
61 —	128651	71 —	H266784
62 —	139838	72 —	H279014
63 —	148858	73 —	H283718
64 —	160307		

Records at the factory indicate the following serial numbers were assigned to guns at the end of the calendar year.

MODEL 74

1939 —	1 to 30890	1948 —	223788
40 —	67085	49 —	249900
41 —	114355	50 —	276012
42 —	128293	51 —	302124
43 —	None	52 —	328236
44 —	128295	53 —	354348
45 —	128878	54 —	380460
46 —	145168	55 —	406574
47 —	173524		

Records at the factory indicate the following serial numbers were assigned to guns at the end of the calendar year.

MODEL 71

1935 —	1 to 4	1947 —	25758
36 —	7821	48 —	27900
37 —	12988	49 —	29675
38 —	14690	50 —	31450
39 —	16155	51 —	33225
40 —	18267	52 —	35000
41 —	20810	53 —	37500
42 —	21959	54 —	40770
43 —	22048	55 —	43306
44 —	22051	56 —	45843
45 —	22224	57 —	47254
46 —	23534		

Records at the factory indicate the following serial numbers were assigned to guns at the end of the calendar year.

MODEL 70

1935 —	1 to 19	1950 —	173150
36 —	2238	51 —	206625
37 —	11573	52 —	238820
38 —	17844	53 —	282735
39 —	23991	54 —	323530
40 —	31675	55 —	361025
41 —	41753	56 —	393595
42 —	49206	57 —	425283
43 —	49983	58 —	440792
44 —	49997	59 —	465040
45 —	5 0921	60 —	504257
46 —	58382	61 —	545446
47 —	75675	62 —	565592
48 —	101680	63 —	581471
49 —	131580		

All post-64 Model 70s began with the serial number 700000

1964 —	740599	1973 —	G1128731
65 —	809177	74 —	G1175000
66 —	833795	75 —	G1218700
67 —	869000	76 —	G1266000
68 —	925908	77 —	G1350000
69 —	G941900	78 —	G1410000
70 —	G957995	79 —	G1447000
71 —	G1018991	80 —	G1490709
72 —	G1099257	81 —	G1537134

Records at the factory indicate the following serial numbers were assigned to guns at the end of the calendar year.

MODEL 63

1933 —	1 to 2667	1946 —	61607
34 —	5361	47 —	71714
35 —	9830	48 —	80519
36 —	16781	49 —	88889
37 —	25435	50 —	97259
38 —	30934	51 —	105629
39 —	36055	52 —	114000
40 —	41456	53 —	120500
41 —	47708	54 —	127000
42 —	51258	55 —	138000
43 —	51631	56 —	150000
44 —	51656	57 —	162345
45 —	53853	58 —	174692

Factory records indicate the following serial numbers were assigned to guns at the end of the calendar year.

MODEL 62

1932 —	1 to 7643	1946 —	183756
33 —	10695	47 —	219085
34 —	14090	48 —	252298
35 —	23924	49 —	262473
36 —	42759	50 —	272648
37 —	66059	51 —	282823
38 —	80205	52 —	293000
39 —	96534	53 —	310500
40 —	116393	54 —	328000
41 —	137379	55 —	342776
42 —	155152	56 —	357551

43 —	155422	57 —	383513
44 —	155425	58 —	409475
45 —	156073		

Records at the factory indicate the following serial numbers were assigned to guns at the end of the calendar year.

MODEL 61

1932 —	1 to 3532	1948 —	115281
33 —	6008	49 —	125461
34 —	8554	50 —	135641
35 —	12379	51 —	145821
36 —	20615	52 —	156000
37 —	30334	53 —	171000
38 —	36326	54 —	186000
39 —	42610	55 —	200962
40 —	49270	56 —	215923
41 —	57493	57 —	229457
42 —	59871	58 —	242992
43 —	59872	59 —	262793
44 —	59879	60 —	282594
45 —	60512	61 —	302395
46 —	71629	62 —	322196
47 —	92297	63 —	342001

This model was discontinued in 1963. For some unknown reason there are no actual records available from 1949 through 1963. The serial number figures for these years are arrived at by taking the total production figure of 342,001, subtracting the last known number of 115281, and dividing the difference equally by the number of remaining years available, (15).

Records at the factory indicate the following serial numbers were assigned to guns at the end of the calendar year.

MODEL 55
CENTERFIRE

1924 —	1 to 836	1929 —	12258
25 —	2783	30 —	17393
26 —	4957	31 —	18198
27 —	8021	32 —	19204
28 —	10467	33 — Clean-up	20580

Records at the factory indicate the following serial numbers were assigned to guns at the end of the calendar year.

MODEL 54

1925 —	1 to 3140	1931 —	36731
26—	8051	32 —	38543
27 —	14176	33 —	40722
28 —	19587	34 —	43466
29 —	29104	35 —	47125
30 —	32499	36 —	50145

Records at the factory indicate the following serial numbers were assigned to guns at the end of the calendar year.

MODEL 53

In the case of the Model 53 the following list pertains to the number of guns produced each year rather than a serial number list.

The Model 53 was serially numbered concurrently with the Model 92.

MODEL 53s PRODUCED

1924 —	1488	1929 —	1733
25 —	2861	30 —	920
26 —	2531	31 —	621
27 —	2297	32 —	206
28 —	1958		

This model was discontinued in 1932, however, a clean-up of production continued for nine more years with an additional 486 guns.

TOTAL PRODUCTION APPROXIMATELY - 15,100

Records at the factory indicate the following serial numbers were assigned to guns at the end of the calendar year.

MODEL 52

1920 —	None indicated	1950 —	70766
21 —	397	51 —	73385
22 —	745	52 —	76000
23 —	1394	53 —	79500
24 —	2361	54 —	80693
25 —	3513	55 —	81831
26 —	6383	56 —	96869
27 —	9436	57 —	97869
28 —	12082	58 —	98599
29 —	14594	59 —	98899
30 —	17253	60 —	102200
31 —	21954	61 —	106986
32 —	24951	62 —	108718
33 —	26725	63 —	113583
34 —	29030	64 —	118447
35 —	32448	65 —	120992
36 —	36632	66 —	123537
37 —	40419	67 —	123727
38 —	43632	68 —	123917
39 —	45460	69 —	E124107
40 —	47519	70 —	E124297
41 —	50317	71 —	E124489
42 —	52129	72 —	E124574
43 —	52553	73 —	E124659
44 —	52560	74 —	E124744
45 —	52718	75 —	E124828
46 —	56080	76 —	E125019
47 —	60158	77 —	E125211
48 —	64265	78 —	E125315
49 —	68149		

This model was discontinued in 1978. A small clean-up of production was completed in 1979 with a total of 125,419.

Records at the factory indicate the following serial numbers were assigned to guns at the end of the calendar year.

MODEL 50

1954 —	1 to 24550	1958 —	122750
55 —	49100	59 —	147300
56 —	73650	60 —	171850
57 —	98200	61 —	196400

Records at the factory indicate the following serial numbers were assigned to guns at the end of the calendar year.

MODEL 42

1933 —	1 to 9398	1949 —	81107
34 —	13963	50 —	87071

35 —	17728	51 —	93038
36 —	24849	52 —	99000
37 —	30900	53 —	108201
38 —	34659	54 —	117200
39 —	38967	55 —	121883
40 —	43348	56 —	126566
41 —	48203	57 —	131249
42 —	50818	58 —	135932
43 —	50822	59 —	140615
44 —	50828	60 —	145298
45 —	51168	61 —	149981
46 —	54256	62 —	154664
47 —	64853	63 —	159353
48 —	75142		

Records at the factory indicate the following serial numbers were assigned to guns at the end of the calendar year.

MODEL 24

1939 —	1 to 8118	1944 —	33683
40 —	21382	45 —	34965
41 —	27045	46 —	45250
42 —	33670	47 —	58940
43 —	None recorded	48 —	64417

There were no records kept on this model from 1949 until its discontinuance in 1958. The total production was approximately 116,280.

Records at the factory indicate the following serial numbers were assigned to guns at the end of the calendar year.

MODEL 12

1912 —	5308	1938 —	779455
13 —	32418	39 —	814121
14 —	79765	40 —	856499
15 —	109515	41 —	907431
16 —	136412	42 —	958303
17 —	159391	43 —	975640
18 —	183461	44 —	975727
19 —	219457	45 —	990004
20 —	247458	46 —	1029152
21 —	267253	47 —	1102371
22 —	304314	48 —	1176055
23 —	346319	49 —	1214041
24 —	385196	50 —	1252028
25 —	423056	51 —	1290015
26 —	464564	52 —	1328002
27 —	510693	53 —	1399996
28 —	557850	54 —	1471990
29 —	600834	55 —	1541929
30 —	626996	56 —	1611868
31 —	651255	57 —	1651435
32 —	660110	58 —	1690999
33 —	664544	59 —	1795500
34 —	673994	60 —	1800000
35 —	686978	61 —	1930029
36 —	720316	62 —	1956990
37 —	754250	63 —	1962001

A clean-up of production took place from 1964 through 1966 with the ending serial number 70875

New Style M/12

1972 —	Y2000100-Y2006396
73 —	Y2015662
74 —	Y2022061
75 —	Y2024478

76 —	Y2025482
77 —	Y2025874
78 —	Y2026156
79 —	Y2026399

Records at the factory indicate the following serial numbers were assigned to guns at the end of the calendar year.

MODEL 1911 S.L.

1911 —	1 to 3819	1919 —	57337
12 —	27659	20 —	60719
13 —	36677	21 —	64109
14 —	40105	22 —	69132
15 —	43284	23 —	73186
16 —	45391	24 —	76199
17 —	49893	25 —	78611
18 —	52895		

The model 1911 was discontinued in 1925. However, guns were produced for three years after that date to clean up production and excess parts. When this practice ceased there were approximately 82,774 guns produced.

Records at the factory indicate the following serial numbers were assigned to guns at the end of the calendar year.

MODEL 1910

1910 —	1 to 4766	1924 —	17030
11 —	7695	25 —	17281
12 —	9712	26 —	17696
13 —	11487	27 —	18182
14 —	12311	28 —	18469
15 —	13233	29 —	18893
16 —	13788	30 —	19065
17 —	14255	31 —	19172
18 —	14625	32 —	19232
19 —	15665	33 —	19281
20 —	Not Available	34 —	19338
21 —	15845	35 —	19388
22 —	16347	36 —	19445
23 —	16637		

A clean-up of production continued into 1937 when the total of the guns were completed at approximately 20786.

Records at the factory indicate the following serial numbers were assigned to guns at the end of the calendar year.

MODEL 1907

1907 —	1 to 8657	1933 —	44806
08 —	14486	34 —	44990
09 —	19707	35 —	45203
10 —	23230	36 —	45482
11 —	25523	37 —	45920
12 —	27724	38 —	46419
13 —	29607	39 —	46758
14 —	30872	40 —	47296
15 —	32272	41 —	47957
16 —	36215	42 —	48275
17 —	38235	43 —	None
18 —	39172	44 —	None
19 —	40448	45 —	48281
20 —	Not Available	46 —	48395
21 —	40784	47 —	48996
22 —	41289	48 —	49684
23 —	41658	**49 —	50662
24 —	42029	**50 —	51640
25 —	42360	**51 —	52618
26 —	42688	**52 —	53596
27 —	43226	**53 —	54574
28 —	43685	**54 —	55552

29 —	44046	**55 —	56530
30 —	44357	**56 —	57508
31 —	44572	**57 —	58486
32 —	44683		

Actual records on serial numbers stops in 1948. The serial numbers ending each year from 1948 to 1957 were derived at by taking the last serial number recorded (58486) and the last number from 1948, (49684) and dividing the years of production, (9), which relates to 978 guns each year for the nine year period.

Records at the factory indicate the following serial numbers were assigned to guns at the end of the calendar year.

MODEL 1906

1906 —	1 to 52278	1920 —	None
07 —	89147	21 —	598691
08 —	114138	22 —	608011
09 —	165068	23 —	622601
10 —	221189	24 —	636163
11 —	273355	25 —	649952
12 —	327955	26 —	665484
13 —	381922	27 —	679692
14 —	422734	28 —	695915
15 —	453880	29 —	711202
16 —	483805	30 —	720116
17 —	517743	31 —	725978
18 —	535540	32 —	727353
19 —	593917		

A clean-up of production took place for the next few years with a record of production reaching approximately 729,305.

Records at the factory indicate the following serial numbers were assigned to guns at the end of the calendar year.

MODEL 1905

1905 —	1 to 5659	1913 —	25559
06 —	15288	14 —	26110
07 —	19194	15 —	26561
08 —	20385	16 —	26910
09 —	21280	17 —	27297
10 —	22423	18 —	27585
11 —	23503	19 —	28287
12 —	24602	20 —	29113

Records at the factory indicate the following serial numbers were assigned to guns at the end of the calendar year.

MODEL 1903

1903 —	Not Available	1918 —	92617
04 —	6944	19 —	96565
05 —	14865	20 —	Not Available
06 —	23097	21 —	97650
07 —	31852	22 —	99011
08 —	39105	23 —	100452
09 —	46496	24 —	101688
10 —	54298	25 —	103075
11 —	61679	26 —	104230
12 —	69586	27 —	105537
13 —	76732	28 —	107157
14 —	81776	29 —	109414
15 —	84563	30 —	111276
16 —	87148	31 —	112533
17 —	89501	32 —	112992

This model was discontinued in 1932, however, a clean up of parts was used for further production of approximately 2,000

guns. Total production was stopped at serial number 114962 in 1936.

Records at the factory indicate the following serial numbers were assigned to guns at the end of the calendar year.

MODEL 1901 SHOTGUN

1904 —	64856 to 64860	1913 —	72764
05 —	66483	14 —	73202
06 —	67486	15 —	73509
07 —	68424	16 —	73770
08 —	69197	17 —	74027
09 —	70009	18 —	74311
10 —	70753	19 —	74872
11 —	71441	20 —	77000
12 —	72167		

Records at the factory indicate the following serial numbers were assigned to guns at the end of the calendar year.

MODEL 1897

1897 —	to 32335	1928 —	796806
98 —	64668	29 —	807321
99 —	96999	30 —	812729
1900 —	129332	31 —	830721
01 —	161665	32 —	833926
02 —	193998	33 —	835637
03 —	226331	34 —	837364
04 —	258664	35 —	839728
05 —	296037	36 —	848684
06 —	334059	37 —	856729
07 —	377999	38 —	860725
08 —	413618	39 —	866938
09 —	446888	40 —	875945
10 —	481062	41 —	891190
11 —	512632	42 —	910072
12 —	544313	43 —	912265
13 —	575213	44 —	912327
14 —	592732	45 —	916472
15 —	607673	46 —	926409
16 —	624537	47 —	936682
17 —	646124	48 —	944085
18 —	668383	49 —	953042
19 —	691943	50 —	961999
20 —	696183	51 —	970956
21 —	700428	52 —	979913
22 —	715902	53 —	988860
23 —	732060	54 —	997827
24 —	744942	55 —	1006784
25 —	757629	56 —	1015741
26 —	770527	57 —	1024700
27 —	783574		

Records on this model are incomplete. The above serial numbers are estimated from 1897 through 1903 and again from 1949 through 1957. The actual records are in existence from 1904 through 1949.

Records at the factory indicate the following serial numbers were assigned to guns at the end of the calendar year.

MODEL 1895

1895 —	1 to 287	1914 —	72082
96 —	5715	15 —	174233
97 —	7814	16 —	377411
98 —	19871	17 —	389106
99 —	26434	18 —	392731

1900 —	29817	19 —	397250
01 —	31584	20 —	400463
02 —	35601	21 —	404075
03 —	42514	22 —	407200
04 —	47805	23 —	410289
05 —	54783	24 —	413276
06 —	55011	25 —	417402
07 —	57351	26 —	419533
08 —	60002	27 —	421584
09 —	60951	28 —	422676
10 —	63771	29 —	423680
11 —	65017	30 —	424181
12 —	67331	31 —	425132
13 —	70823	32 —	425825

Records at the factory indicate the following serial numbers were assigned to guns at the end of the calendar year.

MODEL 94

1894 —	1 to 14579	1939 —	1101051
95 —	44359	40 —	1142423
96 —	76464	41 —	1191307
97 —	111453	42 —	1221289
98 —	147684	43 —	No Record Avail.
99 —	183371	44 —	No Record Avail.
1900 —	204427	45 —	No Record Avail.
01 —	233975	46 —	No Record Avail.
02 —	273854	47 —	No Record Avail.
03 —	291506	48 —	1500000
04 —	311363	49 —	1626100
05 —	337557	50 —	1724295
06 —	378878	51 —	1819800
07 —	430985	52 —	1910000
08 —	474241	53 —	2000000
09 —	505831	54 —	2071100
10 —	553062	55 —	2145296
11 —	599263	56 —	2225000
12 —	646114	57 —	2290296
13 —	703701	58 —	2365887
14 —	756066	59 —	2410555
15 —	784052	60 —	2469821
16 —	807741	61 —	2500000
17 —	821972	62 —	2551921
18 —	838175	63 —	2586000
19 —	870762	*1964 —	2700000
20 —	880627		2797428
21 —	908318	65 —	2894428
22 —	919583	66 —	2991927
23 —	938539	67 —	3088458
24 —	953198	68 —	3185691
25 —	978523	69 —	3284570
26 —	997603	70 —	3381299
27 —	1027571	71 —	3557385
28 —	1054465	72 —	3806499
29 —	1077097	73 —	3929364
30 —	1081755	74 —	4111426
31 —	1084156	75 —	4277926
32 —	1087836	76 —	4463553
33 —	1089270	77 —	4565925
34 —	1091190	78 —	4662210
35 —	1099605	79 —	4826596
36 —	1100065	80 —	4892951
37 —	1100679	81 —	5024957
38 —	1100915	62 —	5103248

The post-64 Model 94 began with serial number 2700000.

Serial number 1000000 was presented to President Calvin Coolidge in 1927.

Serial number 1500000 was presented to President Harry S. Truman in 1948.

Serial number 2000000 was presented to President Dwight D. Eisenhower in 1953.

Serial numbers 2500000 and 3000000 were presented to the Winchester Gun Museum, now located in Cody, Wyoming.

Serial number 3500000 was not constructed until 1979 and was sold at auction in Las Vegas, Nevada. Serial number 4000000—whereabouts unknown at this time.

Serial number 4500000—shipped to Italy by Olin in 1978. Whereabouts unknown.

Serial number 5000000—in New Haven, not constructed as of March 1983.

Records at the factory indicate the following serial numbers were assigned to guns at the end of the calendar year.

MODEL 1892

1892 —	1 to 23701	1913 —	742675
93 —	35987	14 —	771444
94 —	73508	15 —	804622
95 —	106721	16 —	830031
96 —	144935	17 —	853819
97 —	159312	18 —	870942
98 —	165431	19 —	903649
99 —	171820	20 —	906754
1900 —	183411	21 —	910476
01 —	191787	22 —	917300
02 —	208871	23 —	926329
03 —	253935	24 —	938641
04 —	278546	25 —	954997
05 —	315425	26 —	973896
06 —	376496	27 —	990883
07 —	437919	28 —	996517
08 —	476540	29 —	999238
09 —	522162	30 —	999730
10 —	586996	31 —	1000727
11 —	643483	32 —	1001324
12 —	694752		

Records on the Model 1890 are somewhat incomplete. Our records indicate the following serial numbers were assigned to guns at the end of the calendar year beginning with 1908. Actual records on the firearms that were manufactured between 1890 and 1907 will be available from the "Winchester Museum," located at The "Buffalo Bill Historical Center", P.O. Box 1020, Cody, WY 82414

MODEL 1890

1908 —	330000 to 363850	1920 —	None
09 —	393427	21 —	634783
10 —	423567	22 —	643304
11 —	451264	23 —	654837
12 —	478595	24 —	664613
13 —	506936	25 —	675774
14 —	531019	26 —	687049
15 —	551290	27 —	698987
16 —	570497	28 —	711354
17 —	589204	29 —	722125
18 —	603438	30 —	729015
19 —	630801	31 —	733178
		32 —	734454

The Model 1890 was discontinued in 1932, however, a cleanup of the production run lasted another 8+ years and included another 14,000 to 15,000 guns. Our figures indicate approximately 749,000 guns were made.

Records at the factory indicate the following serial numbers were assigned to guns at the end of the calendar year.

MODEL 1887

1887 —	1 to 7431	1993 —	54367
88 —	22408	94 —	56849
89 —	25673	95 —	58289
90 —	29105	96 —	60175
91 —	38541	97 —	63952
92 —	49763	98 —	64855

According to these records no guns were produced during the last few years of this model and it was therefore discontinued in 1901.

Records at the factory indicate the following serial numbers were assigned to guns at the end of the calendar year.

MODEL 1886

1886 —	1 to 3211	1905 —	138838
87 —	14728	06 —	142249
88 —	28577	07 —	145119
89 —	38401	08 —	147322
90 —	49723	09 —	148237
91 —	63601	10 —	150129
92 —	73816	11 —	151622
93 —	83261	12 —	152943
94 —	94543	13 —	152947
95 —	103708	14 —	153859
96 —	109670	15 —	154452
97 —	113997	16 —	154979
98 —	119192	17 —	155387
99 —	120571	18 —	156219
1900 —	122834	19 —	156930
01 —	125630	20 —	158716
02 —	128942	21 —	159108
03 —	132213	22 —	159337
04 —	135524		

No further serial numbers were recorded until the discontinuance of the model, which was in 1935 at 159994.

Records at the factory indicate the following serial numbers were assigned to guns at the end of the calendar year.

MODEL 1885
SINGLE SHOT

1885 —	1 to 375	1900 —	88501
86 —	6841	01 —	90424
87 —	18328	02 —	92031
88 —	30571	03 —	92359
89 —	45019	04 —	92785
90 —	None	05 —	93611
91 —	53700	06 —	94208
92 —	60371	07 —	95743
93 —	69534	08 —	96819
94 —	None	09 —	98097
95 —	73771	10 —	98506
96 —	78253	11 —	99012
97 —	78815	12 —	None
98 —	84700	13 —	100352
99 —	85086		

No further serial numbers were recorded until the end of 1923. The last number recorded was 139700.

Records at the factory indicate the following serial numbers were assigned to guns at the end of the calendar year.

MODEL 1876

1876 —	1 to 1429	1988 —	63539
77 —	3579	89 —	None
78 —	7967	90 —	None
79 —	8971	91 —	None
80 —	14700	92 —	63561
81 —	21759	93 —	63670
82 —	32407	94 —	63678
83 —	42410	95 —	None
84 —	54666	96 —	63702
85 —	58714	97 —	63869
86 —	60397	98 —	63871
87 —	62420		

Records at the factory indicate the following serial numbers were assigned to guns at the end of the calendar year.

MODEL 1873

1873 —	1 to 126	1897 —	513421
74 —	2726	98 —	525922
75 —	11325	99 —	541328
76 —	23151	1900 —	554128
77 —	23628	01 —	557236
78 —	27501	02 —	564557
79 —	41525	03 —	573957
80 —	63537	04 —	588953
81 —	81620	05 —	602557
82 —	109507	06 —	613780
83 —	145503	07 —	None
84 —	175126	08 —	None
85 —	196221	09 —	630385
86 —	222937	10 —	656101
87 —	225922	11 —	669324
88 —	284529	12 —	678527
89 —	323956	13 —	684419
90 —	363220	14 —	686510
91 —	405026	15 —	688431
92 —	441625	16 —	694020
93 —	466641	17 —	698617
94 —	481826	18 —	700734
95 —	499308	19 —	702042
96 —	507545		

No last number available: 1920, 21, 22, 23—720609.

Records at the factory indicate the following serial numbers were assigned to guns at the end of the calendar year.

MODEL 1866

1866 —	12476 to 14813	1883 —	162376
67 —	15578	84 —	163649
68 —	19768	85 —	163664
69 —	29516	86 —	165071
70 —	52527	87 —	165912
71 —	88184	88 —	167155
72 —	109784	89 —	167401
73 —	118401	90 —	167702
74 —	125038	91 —	169003
75 —	125965	92 —	None
76 —	131907	93 —	169007
77 —	148207	94 —	169011
78 —	150493	95 —	None
79 —	152201	96 —	None
80 —	154379	97 —	169015
81 —	156107	98 —	170100
82 —	159513	99 —	Discontinued

Winchester Ranger lever action rifle

Winchester Model 9422 walnut

Winchester Model 94 Ranger with Bushnell Sportview 4 power scope and see-through mounts

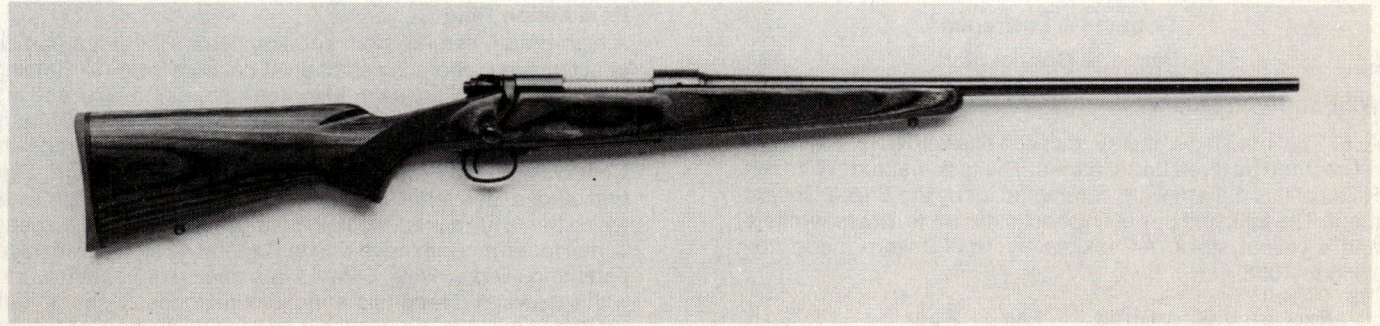

Winchester Model 70 lightweight Win-Tuff, laminated stock

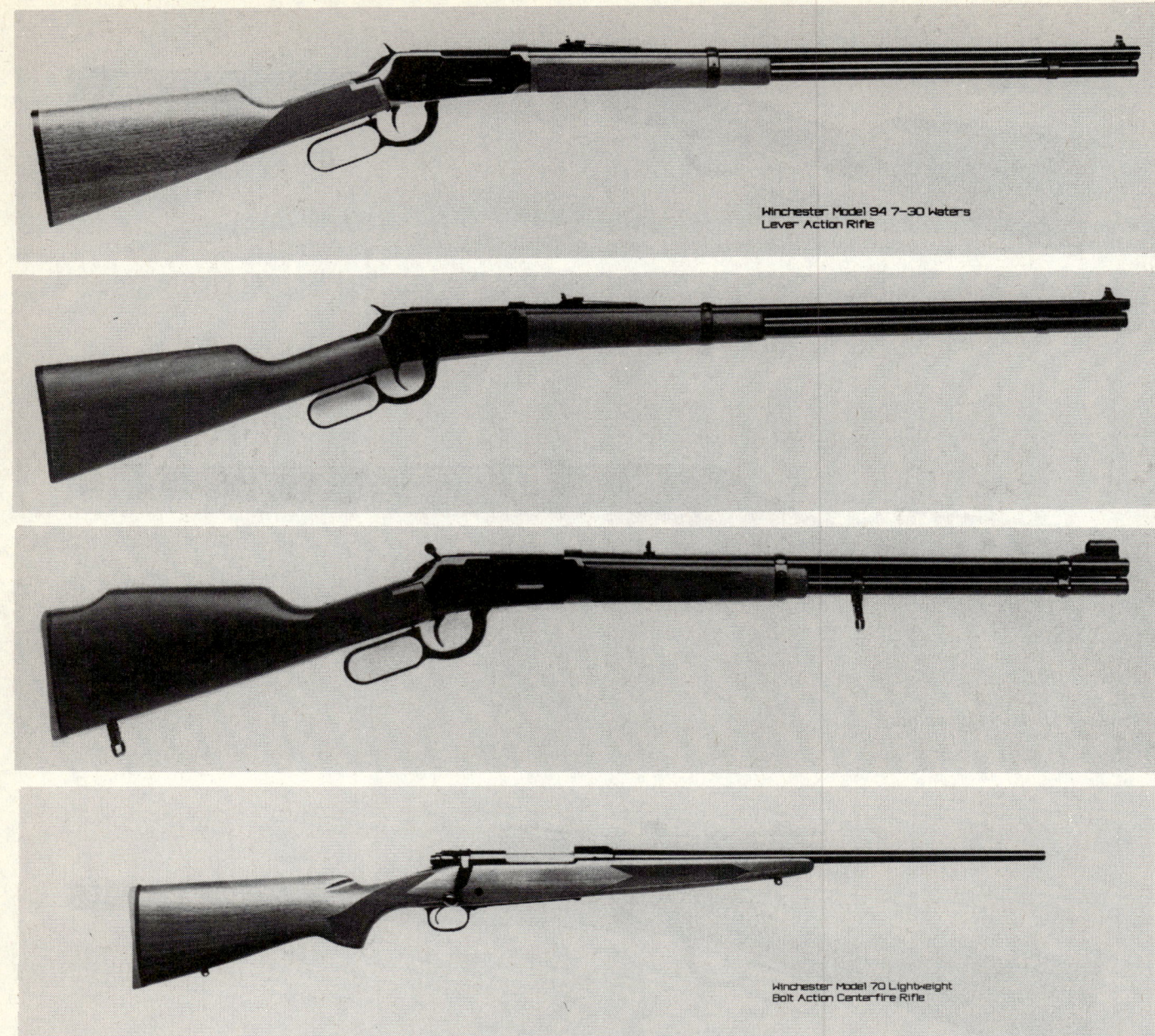

Winchester Model 94 7-30 Waters
Lever Action Rifle

Winchester Model 70 Lightweight
Bolt Action Centerfire Rifle

Winchester Model 70 lightweight bolt action centerfire rifle

WINDSOR
Windsor, Vermont
Robbins & Lawrence
Hartford, Connecticut

Windsor Rifle-Musket

A .577 caliber single shot percussion rifle with a 39" round barrel secured by three barrel bands. The lock marked "Windsor". Rifles of this pattern were contracted for by the British Government. The lock and barrel finished in the white, brass furniture, and a walnut stock. Approximately 16,000 were made from 1855 to 1858.

Exc.	V.G.	Good	Fair	Poor
—	—	2500	950	300

WINSLOW ARMS CO.
Camden, South Carolina

Bolt-Action Rifle

A high-grade, semi-custom sporting rifle built upon a number of actions and offered in all popular calibers from .17 Remington to the .458 Winchester Magnum with a 24" barrel and a 3-shot magazine. The larger Magnum models have a 26" barrel and a 2-shot magazine. Two basic stocks are offered—the Conventional Bushmaster, which features a standard pistol grip and a beavertail forearm; and also the Plainsmaster, which has a full curled, hooked pistol grip and a wide, flat beavertail forearm. Both have Monte Carlo-style stocks with recoil pads and sling swivels. Offered in a choice of popular woods with rosewood forend tips and pistol gripcaps. Eight different grades of this rifle are available and the following lists the values applicable for each.

Commander Grade

Exc.	V.G.	Good	Fair	Poor
500	450	400	350	300

Regal Grade

Exc.	V.G.	Good	Fair	Poor
600	550	450	375	325

Regent Grade

Exc.	V.G.	Good	Fair	Poor
750	700	500	450	350

Regimental Grade

Exc.	V.G.	Good	Fair	Poor
950	850	650	550	450

Crown Grade

Exc.	V.G.	Good	Fair	Poor
1400	1250	1000	750	600

Royal Grade

Exc.	V.G.	Good	Fair	Poor
1550	1400	1150	850	700

Imperial Grade

Exc.	V.G.	Good	Fair	Poor
3500	3000	2500	2000	1450

Emperor Grade

Exc.	V.G.	Good	Fair	Poor
6000	5000	4000	3000	2000

WISEMAN, BILL & CO.
Bryan, Texas

A custom order bolt-action rifle utilizing a Sako action, McMillan stainless steel barrel and laminated stock. The action components Teflon coated. It is made in four styles: the Hunter, Hunter Deluxe, Maverick, and the Varminter.

Exc.	V.G.	Good	Fair	Poor
1500	1250	1000	750	600

Silhouette Pistol

A custom made single shot pistol produced in a variety of calibers with a 14" fluted stainless steel barrel and laminated pistol grip stock. Furnished without sights. Introduced in 1989.

Exc.	V.G.	Good	Fair	Poor
1300	1000	800	600	500

WITNESS
SEE European American Armory

WOODWARD, JAMES & SONS
London, England

Prior to WWII, this company produced a variety of boxlock and sidelock shotguns that are regarded as some of the best made. Prospective purchasers should secure a qualified appraisal prior to acquisition.

WURFFLEIN, ANDREW & WILLIAM
Philadelphia, Pennsylvania

Pocket Pistol

A .41 caliber percussion single shot pocket pistol with either a 2.5" or 3" barrel, German silver furniture and checkered walnut stock. The lock marked "A. Wurfflein / Phila." Manufactured during the 1850s and 1860s.

Exc.	V.G.	Good	Fair	Poor
—	—	950	500	200

Single-Shot Target Pistol

A .22 caliber single-shot pistol with half-octagonal barrels measuring from 8" to 16" in length. The barrel pivots downward for loading and is marked "W. Wurfflein Philad'a Pa. U.S.A. Patented June 24th, 1884". Blued with walnut grips. This model is also available with a detachable shoulder stock, which if present would add approximately 35% to the values listed below. Manufactured from 1884 to 1890.

Exc.	V.G.	Good	Fair	Poor
—	—	800	400	200

Single-Shot Rifle

A single-shot rifle produced in a variety of calibers with octagonal barrels of 24" to 28" length. This rifle was available with a wide variety of optional features and a qualified appraisal should be sought if any features are in doubt.

Exc.	V.G.	Good	Fair	Poor
—	—	750	350	150

Mid-range Model

As above, with a 28" or 30" half-octagonal barrel.

Exc.	V.G.	Good	Fair	Poor
—	—	2500	950	400

Model No. 25

The highest grade rifle manufactured by Wurfflein.

Exc.	V.G.	Good	Fair	Poor
—	—	3000	1250	600

XL
HOPKINS & ALLEN
Norwich, Connecticut

Derringer

A .41 caliber spur trigger single-shot pistol with a 2.75" octagonal barrel and either iron or brass frame. Blued, nickel-plated with rosewood grips. The barrel marked "XL Derringer". Manufactured during the 1870s.

Exc.	V.G.	Good	Fair	Poor
—	—	600	300	150

Vest Pocket Derringer

As above, in .22 caliber with a 2.25" round barrel and normally full nickel-plated. The barrel marked "XL Vest Pocket". Manufactured from 1870s to 1890s.

Exc.	V.G.	Good	Fair	Poor
—	—	250	150	75

XPERT
HOPKINS & ALLEN
Norwich, Connecticut

Xpert Derringer

A .22 or .30 caliber spur trigger single-shot pistol with round barrels, 2.25" to 6" in length and a nickel-plated finish with rosewood grips. The breechblock pivots to the left side for loading. The barrel marked "Xpert-Pat. Sep. 23. 1878". Manufactured during the 1870s.

Exc.	V.G.	Good	Fair	Poor
—	—	375	150	75

Z

Z-B RIFLE CO.
Brno, Czechoslovakia

Model ZKW-465 Varmint Rifle

A Mauser bolt-action rifle chambered for the .22 Hornet cartridge. It has a 23" barrel with a three-leaf, folding rear sight. It is offered standard with double-set triggers. The finish is blued, with a select walnut checkered stock.

Exc.	V.G.	Good	Fair	Poor
1200	1000	850	700	550

ZM WEAPONS
Bernardton, MA

LR-300 sport rifle

This is a highly modified AR-15 chambered for the .223 cartridge. It is fitted with a 16.25" barrel and a true folding stock. A ghost ring rear sight and an adjustable post front sight with tritium insert is standard. Weight is approximately 7.2 pounds. Introduced in 1997.

NIB	Exc.	V.G.	Good	Fair	Poor
1995	—	—	—	—	—

ZANOTTI, FABIO
Brescia, Italy
Importer - New England Arms Co.
Kittery Point, Maine

Model 625

A 12 to .410 bore boxlock double-barrel shotgun with automatic ejectors and single selective trigger. Blued with checkered walnut stock.

NIB	Exc.	V.G.	Good	Fair	Poor
4500	3500	2500	2000	1500	750

Model 626

As above, engraved with either scroll work or hunting scenes.

NIB	Exc.	V.G.	Good	Fair	Poor
5000	4500	3000	2500	1500	750

Giacinto

An external hammer boxlock shotgun produced in a variety of gauges with double triggers.

NIB	Exc.	V.G.	Good	Fair	Poor
4750	3500	2750	2000	1200	750

Maxim

Similar to the Model 625, but fitted with detachable sidelocks.

NIB	Exc.	V.G.	Good	Fair	Poor
7500	6500	5000	3500	2250	1200

Edward

As above, but more intricately engraved.

NIB	Exc.	V.G.	Good	Fair	Poor
10000	8000	6500	4500	3000	1500

Cassiano I

As above, with exhibition grade engraving.

NIB	Exc.	V.G.	Good	Fair	Poor
11000	9000	7000	6000	4000	2000

Cassiano II

As above, with gold inlays.

NIB	Exc.	V.G.	Good	Fair	Poor
12500	10000	8500	7000	5000	2500

Cassiano Executive

A strictly custom made shotgun produced to the client's specifications. Prospective purchasers should secure a qualified appraisal prior to acquisition. Prices listed below are for base model only.

NIB	Exc.	V.G.	Good	Fair	Poor
15000	12500	—	—	—	—

ZEHNER, E. WAFFENFABRIK
Suhl, Germany

Zehna

A 6.35mm semiautomatic pistol with a 2.5" barrel and 5-shot magazine. The slide marked "Zehna DRPA," and the caliber on later production models. Blued with a black plastic grips bearing the monogram "EZ". Approximately 20,000 were made from 1921 to 1927.

Exc.	V.G.	Good	Fair	Poor
350	300	250	175	100

ZEILINGER
SEE Austrian Military Firearms

ZEPHYR
Eibar, Spain
Importer - Stoegers

Woodlander II

A 12 or 20 gauge boxlock shotgun with varying length barrels, double triggers and extractors. Blued with a walnut stock.

NIB	Exc.	V.G.	Good	Fair	Poor
500	450	400	300	200	100

Uplander

A 12, 16, 20, 28 or .410 bore sidelock double-barrel shotgun with varying length barrels, double triggers, and automatic ejectors. Blued with a walnut stock.

NIB	Exc.	V.G.	Good	Fair	Poor
800	700	500	400	300	150

Upland King

As above, in 12 or 16 gauge with ventilated rib barrels.

NIB	Exc.	V.G.	Good	Fair	Poor
1000	800	700	600	400	250

Vandalia

A 12 gauge single barrel trap gun with a 32" full choked barrel. Blued with a walnut stock.

NIB	Exc.	V.G.	Good	Fair	Poor
700	600	550	450	300	150

Sterlingworth II

Identical to the Woodlander, but with sidelocks.

NIB	Exc.	V.G.	Good	Fair	Poor
850	700	550	450	300	150

Victor Special

A 12 gauge boxlock double-barrel shotgun with 25", 28", or 30" barrels, double triggers and extractors. Blued with a walnut stock.

NIB	Exc.	V.G.	Good	Fair	Poor
450	400	300	250	175	100

Thunderbird

A 10 gauge Magnum boxlock double-barrel shotgun with 32" full choked barrels, double triggers, and automatic ejectors. Blued with a walnut stock.

NIB	Exc.	V.G.	Good	Fair	Poor
900	700	600	500	400	200

Honker

A 10 gauge Magnum single barrel shotgun with a 36" full choked and ventilated rib barrel. Blued with a walnut stock.

NIB	Exc.	V.G.	Good	Fair	Poor
500	450	400	300	200	100

ZOLI USA, ANGELO
Brescia, Italy
Importer - Same
Addison, Illinois

Slide-Action Shotgun

A 12 gauge Magnum slide action shotgun produced with a variety of barrel lengths with detachable choke tubes. Blued with a walnut stock.

NIB	Exc.	V.G.	Good	Fair	Poor
350	300	250	200	150	100

Diano I

A 12, 20 or .410 bore single-shot folding barrel shotgun. Produced in a variety of barrel lengths. Blued with a walnut stock.

NIB	Exc.	V.G.	Good	Fair	Poor
125	100	90	80	60	40

Diano II

As above, but with a bottom lever instead of a top release lever.

NIB	Exc.	V.G.	Good	Fair	Poor
125	100	90	80	60	40

Apache

A 12 gauge Magnum lever action shotgun with a 20" barrel fitted with detachable choke tubes. Blued with a walnut stock.

NIB	Exc.	V.G.	Good	Fair	Poor
450	400	350	300	250	150

Quail Special

A .410 Magnum bore double-barrel shotgun with 28" barrels and a single trigger. Blued with a walnut stock.

NIB	Exc.	V.G.	Good	Fair	Poor
225	175	150	125	100	75

Falcon II

As above with 26" or 28" barrels and double triggers.

NIB	Exc.	V.G.	Good	Fair	Poor
225	175	150	125	100	75

Pheasant

A 12 gauge Magnum double-barrel shotgun with 28" barrels, single trigger, and automatic ejectors. Blued with a walnut stock.

NIB	Exc.	V.G.	Good	Fair	Poor
400	350	300	250	200	150

Classic

As above, with 26" to 30" barrels fitted with detachable choke tubes, single selective trigger, and automatic ejectors. Blued with a walnut stock.

NIB	Exc.	V.G.	Good	Fair	Poor
850	700	600	500	300	200

Snipe

A .410 bore Over/Under shotgun with 26" or 28" barrels and a single trigger.

NIB	Exc.	V.G.	Good	Fair	Poor
275	225	200	175	150	100

Dove

Similar to the above.

NIB	Exc.	V.G.	Good	Fair	Poor
275	225	200	175	150	100

Texas

A 12, 20 or .410 bore Over/Under shotgun with 26" or 28" barrels, double triggers, and a bottom barrel release lever.

NIB	Exc.	V.G.	Good	Fair	Poor
300	250	200	150	100	75

Field Special

A 12 or 20 gauge Magnum double-barrel shotgun produced in a variety of barrel lengths with a single trigger and extractors. Blued with a walnut stock.

NIB	Exc.	V.G.	Good	Fair	Poor
500	400	300	250	200	100

Pigeon Model

As above, but more finely finished.

NIB	Exc.	V.G.	Good	Fair	Poor
500	400	300	250	200	100

Standard Model

Similar to the above but in 12 and 20 gauge only.

NIB	Exc.	V.G.	Good	Fair	Poor
450	400	300	250	200	100

Special Model

As above, with detachable choke tubes and a single selective trigger.

NIB	Exc.	V.G.	Good	Fair	Poor
500	400	300	250	200	100

Deluxe Model

As above, but engraved and with better quality walnut.

NIB	Exc.	V.G.	Good	Fair	Poor
700	600	500	400	300	150

Presentation Model

As above, with false sidelocks and finely figured walnut stock.

NIB	Exc.	V.G.	Good	Fair	Poor
800	700	600	450	350	200

St. George's Target

A 12 gauge Over/Under shotgun trap or skeet bore with various length barrels, single selective trigger, and automatic ejectors. Blued with a walnut stock.

NIB	Exc.	V.G.	Good	Fair	Poor
1000	850	700	600	550	250

St. George Competition

A 12 gauge single barrel gun with an extra set of over and under barrels.

NIB	Exc.	V.G.	Good	Fair	Poor
1750	1600	1200	950	500	300

Express Rifle

A .30-06, 7x65Rmm or 9.3x74Rmm Over/Under double-barrel rifle with single triggers and automatic ejectors. Blued with a walnut stock.

NIB	Exc.	V.G.	Good	Fair	Poor
4000	3500	2500	1750	1200	600

Express EM

As above, but more finely finished.

NIB	Exc.	V.G.	Good	Fair	Poor
5000	4000	3000	1500	1000	750

Savana E

As above, with double triggers.

NIB	Exc.	V.G.	Good	Fair	Poor
6000	5250	4500	3500	2750	1500

Savana Deluxe

As above, but engraved with hunting scenes.

NIB	Exc.	V.G.	Good	Fair	Poor
8000	7000	6000	4750	3500	2000

AZ 1900C

A .243, .270, 6.5x55mm, .308, or .30-06 bolt-action rifle with a 24" barrel having open sights. Blued with a walnut stock.

NIB	Exc.	V.G.	Good	Fair	Poor
800	700	500	400	300	150

AZ 1900M

Same as above but fitted with a Bell & Carlson composite stock.

NIB	Exc.	V.G.	Good	Fair	Poor
700	600	450	350	275	200

AZ 1900 Deluxe

As above, but more finely finished.

NIB	Exc.	V.G.	Good	Fair	Poor
950	800	650	500	400	200

AZ 1900 Super Deluxe

As above, but engraved with a finely figured walnut stock.

NIB	Exc.	V.G.	Good	Fair	Poor
1350	1000	800	600	450	250

Patricia Model

As above, in .410 Magnum bore with 28" ventilated rib barrels, various chokes, single selective trigger, and automatic ejectors. Engraved, blued with finely figured walnut stock.

NIB	Exc.	V.G.	Good	Fair	Poor
1300	1100	950	750	650	400

Condor

A .30-06 or .308 and 12 gauge Over/Under combination shotgun rifle with double triggers, extractors and sling swivels. Blued with a walnut stock.

NIB	Exc.	V.G.	Good	Fair	Poor
1250	1050	850	700	500	300

Airone

As above, with false sidelocks.

NIB	Exc.	V.G.	Good	Fair	Poor
1500	1250	1000	800	600	300

Leopard Express

A .30-06, .308, 7x65Rmm, or .375 Holland & Holland Over/Under double-barrel rifle with 24" barrels having express sights, double triggers and extractors. Blued with a walnut stock.

NIB	Exc.	V.G.	Good	Fair	Poor
1500	1250	1000	800	600	300

ZOLI, ANTONIO
Brescia, Italy
Importer - Antonio Zoli USA, Inc.
Fort Wayne, Indiana

Silver Hawk

A 12 or 20 gauge boxlock double-barrel shotgun produced in a variety of barrel lengths and chokes with a double trigger. Engraved, blued with walnut stock.

NIB	Exc.	V.G.	Good	Fair	Poor
450	400	350	300	250	100

Ariete M3

A 12 gauge boxlock double-barrel shotgun with 26" or 28" barrels, non-selective single trigger and automatic ejectors. Engraved, blued with a walnut stock.

NIB	Exc.	V.G.	Good	Fair	Poor
600	500	450	400	350	200

Empire

As above, in 12 or 20 gauge with 27" or 28" barrels. Engraved, French case-hardened, blued with a walnut stock.

NIB	Exc.	V.G.	Good	Fair	Poor
1650	1450	1200	950	750	400

Volcano Record

A 12 gauge sidelock double-barrel shotgun with 28" barrels available in a variety of chokes, single selective trigger and automatic ejectors. Engraved, French case-hardened, blued with a walnut stock.

NIB	Exc.	V.G.	Good	Fair	Poor
5500	5000	4000	3000	2000	1000

Volcano Record ELM

This model is strictly a custom ordered shotgun produced to the purchaser's specifications. A qualified appraisal is suggested prior to acquisition.

NIB	Exc.	V.G.	Good	Fair	Poor
14000	11500	8500	6500	3500	1500

Silver Snipe

A 12 or 20 gauge Over/Under shotgun produced with varying lengths, ventilated rib barrels, single trigger and extractors. Engraved, blued with a walnut stock.

NIB	Exc.	V.G.	Good	Fair	Poor
500	450	400	325	275	150

Golden Snipe

As above, but more finely finished and fitted with automatic ejectors.

NIB	Exc.	V.G.	Good	Fair	Poor
600	500	450	350	300	150

Delfino

As above, in 12 or 20 gauge Magnum with 26" or 28" ventilated rib barrels, non-selective single trigger and automatic ejectors. Engraved, blued with walnut stock.

NIB	Exc.	V.G.	Good	Fair	Poor
525	425	325	275	250	150

Ritmo Hunting Gun

As above, in 12 gauge Magnum with 26" or 28" separated ventilated rib barrels, single selective trigger and automatic ejectors. Engraved, blued with a walnut stock.

NIB	Exc.	V.G.	Good	Fair	Poor
600	500	450	400	350	200

Condor Model

As above, in 12 gauge with 28" skeet bored barrels having a wide competition rib, single selective trigger and automatic ejectors. Engraved, French case-hardened, blued with a walnut stock.

NIB	Exc.	V.G.	Good	Fair	Poor
850	800	650	500	400	200

Angel Model

As above, in a field grade version.

NIB	Exc.	V.G.	Good	Fair	Poor
900	800	600	500	400	200

Ritmo Pigeon Grade IV

As above, with 28" separated ventilated rib barrels, single selective trigger, automatic ejectors and extensively engraved. French case-hardened, blued with a finely figured walnut stock.

NIB	Exc.	V.G.	Good	Fair	Poor
1800	1600	1200	800	600	300

Model 208 Target

As above, with 28" or 30" trap or skeet bored barrels fitted with a wide ventilated rib.

NIB	Exc.	V.G.	Good	Fair	Poor
1000	850	700	600	500	250

Model 308 Target

As above, but more finely finished.

NIB	Exc.	V.G.	Good	Fair	Poor
1400	1100	850	700	500	250

Combinato

A .222 or .243 and 12 or 20 gauge Over/Under combination rifle/shotgun with an engraved boxlock action, double triggers, and a folding rear sight. French case-hardened, blued with a walnut stock.

NIB	Exc.	V.G.	Good	Fair	Poor
1700	1250	950	850	600	300

Safari Deluxe

As above, but with false sidelocks that are engraved with scrolls or hunting scenes.

NIB	Exc.	V.G.	Good	Fair	Poor
5000	4000	2850	1500	1200	650

ZULAICA, M.
Eibar, Spain

Zulaica

A solid-frame .22 caliber revolver having a 6-shot cylinder that has zigzag grooves on its exterior surface. It is fired by an external hammer and the frame is hollow with a rod inside of it that connects to the breechblock. There is a serrated cocking piece connected to this rod that is found at the top rear of the frame. When fired, the cartridge case blows from the cylinder and activates the breechblock similar to a semiautomatic pistol.

Exc.	V.G.	Good	Fair	Poor
750	600	500	350	250

Royal

The name Royal was applied to a number of pistols produced by this company, as noted below.

Royal

A 6.35mm or 7.65mm semiautomatic pistol that is normally marked on the slide "Automatic Pistol 6.35 Royal" or "Automatic Pistol 7.65 Royal".

Exc.	V.G.	Good	Fair	Poor
175	125	100	75	50

Royal

As above, in 7.65mm caliber with a 5.5" barrel and 12-shot magazine.

Exc.	V.G.	Good	Fair	Poor
200	150	125	100	75

Royal

A rather poor copy of the Mauser Model C/96 semiautomatic pistol with fixed lockwork.

Exc.	V.G.	Good	Fair	Poor
600	500	400	300	150

Vincitor

A 6.35mm or 7.65mm caliber semiautomatic pistol patterned after the Model 1906 Browning. The slide marked "SA Royal Vincitor". Blued with plastic grips.

Exc.	V.G.	Good	Fair	Poor
175	150	125	100	75

FIREARMS TRADE NAMES

A.A. Co.: Inexpensive pocket revolvers of unknown manufacture.

Acme: a) Trade name used by the W.H. Davenport Firearms Company on shotguns.

b) Trade name used by the Hopkins and Allen Company on revolvers produced for the Merwin, Hulbert and Company and the Herman Boker Company of New York.

c) Trade name used by the Maltby, Henley and Company of New York on inexpensive pocket revolvers.

Acme Arms Company: Trade name used by the J. Stevens Arms and Tool Company on pistols and shotguns produced for the Cornwall Hardware Company of New York.

N.R. Adams: Trade name used by the N.R. Davis and Company on shotguns.

Aetna: Trade name used by the firm of Harrington and Richardson on inexpensive pocket revolvers.

Alamo Ranger: The name found on inexpensive Spanish revolvers.

Alaska: Trade name used by the Hood Firearms Company on inexpensive pocket revolvers.

Alert: Trade name used by the Hood Firearms Company on inexpensive pocket revolvers.

Alexander Gun Company: Trade name believed to have been used by E.K. Tryon of Philadelphia on imported shotguns.

Alexis: Trade name used by the Hood Firearms Company on inexpensive pocket revolvers.

Allen 22: Trade name used by the Hopkins and Allen Company on inexpensive pocket revolvers.

America: Trade name used by the Crescent Firearms Company on inexpensive pocket revolvers.

American: Trade name used by the Ely and Wray on inexpensive pocket revolvers.

American Barlock Wonder: Trade name used by the H. & D. Folsom Arms Company on Shotguns made for the Sears, Roebuck Company of Chicago.

American Boy: Trade name used on firearms retailed by the Townley Metal and Hardware Company of Kansas City, Missouri.

American Bulldog: Trade name used by the Iver Johnson Arms and Cycle Works on inexpensive pocket revolvers.

American Bulldog Revolver: Trade name used by Harrington and Richardson Arms Company on an inexpensive pocket revolver.

American Eagle: Trade name used by the Hopkins and Allen Company on inexpensive pocket revolvers.

American Gun Company: Trade name used by H. & D. Folsom Arms Company on pistols and shotguns that firm retailed.

American Gun Barrel Company: Trade name used by R. Avis of West Haven, Connecticut, between 1916 and 1920.

American Nitro: Trade name used by H. & D. Folsom Arms Co. on shotguns.

Americus: Trade name used by the Hopkins and Allen Company on inexpensive pocket revolvers.

Angel: Trade name found on inexpensive pocket revolvers of unknown manufacture.

The Arab: Trade name used by the Harrington and Richardson Arms Company on shotguns.

Aristocrat: a) Trade name used by the Hopkins and Allen Company on inexpensive pocket revolvers.

b) Trade name used by the Supplee-Biddle Hardware Company of Philadelphia on firearms they retailed.

Armory Gun Company: Trade name used by H. & D. Folsom Arms Co. on shotguns.

Aubrey Shotgun: Trade name found on shotguns made for the Sears, Roebuck and Company of Chicago by Albert Aubrey of Meriden, Connecticut.

Audax: Trade name used by the Manufacture d'Armes Pyrenees on semiautomatic pistols.

Aurora: Trade name found on inexpensive Spanish semiautomatic pistols.

Autogarde: Trade name used by the Societe Francaise des Munitions on semiautomatic pistols.

Automatic: a) Trade name used by the Forehand and Wadsworth Company on inexpensive pocket revolvers.

b) Trade name used by the Harrington and Richardson Arms Company on inexpensive pocket revolvers.

c) Trade name used by the Iver Johnson Arms and Cycle Works on inexpensive pocket revolvers.

Auto Stand: Trade name used by the Manufacture Francaise d'Armes et Cycles, St. Etiene on semiautomatic pistols.

Avenger: Trade name found on inexpensive pocket revolvers of unknown manufacture.

Baby Hammerless: Trade mark used successively by Henry Kolb and R.F. Sedgley on pocket revolvers they manufactured.

Baby Russian: Trade name used by the American Arms Company on revolvers they manufactured.

Baker Gun Company: Trade name used by the H. & D. Folsom Arms Company on shotguns they retailed.

Baker Gun and Forging Company: Trade name used by the H. & D. Folsom Arms Company on shotguns they retailed.

Bang: Trade name found on inexpensive pocket revolvers of unknown manufacture.

Bang Up: Trade name used on inexpensive pocket revolvers retailed by the Graham and Haines Company of New York.

T. Barker: Trade name used by the H. & D. Folsom Arms Company of New York on shotguns they retailed.

Bartlett Field: Trade name used on shotguns retailed by Hibbard, Spencer, Bartlett and Company of Chicago.

Batavia: Trade name used on shotguns produced by the Baker Gun Company.

Batavia Leader: Trade name used on shotguns produced by the Baker Gun Company.

Bay State: Trade name used by the Harrington and Richardson Arms Company on both inexpensive pocket revolvers and shotguns.

Belknap: Trade name used by the Belknap Hardware Company of Louisville, Kentucky, on shotguns made by the Crescent Fire Arms Company, which they retailed.

Bellmore Gun Company: Trade name used by the H. & D. Folsom Arms Company on shotguns made for them by the Crescent Fire Arms Company.

Berkshire: Trade name used by the H. & D. Folsom Arms Company on shotguns made for the Shapleigh Hardware Company of St. Louis, Missouri.

Bicycle: Trade name used on firearms made by the Harrington and Richardson Arms Company.

Big All Right: Trade name used on shotguns manufactured by the Wright Arms Company.

Big Bonanza: Trade name found on inexpensive pocket revolvers of unknown manufacture.

Bismarck: Trade name found on inexpensive pocket revolvers of unknown manufacture.

Black Beauty: Trade name used by the Sears, Roebuck and Company on imported shotguns they retailed.

Black Diamond: Trade name found on Belgian made shotguns retailed by an unknown American wholesale house.

Black Diana: Trade name used by the Baker Gun Company on shotguns.

Blackfield: Trade name used by the Hibbard, Spencer, Bartlett and Company of Chicago on shotguns they retailed.

Blackhawk: Trade name found on inexpensive pocket revolvers of unknown manufacture.

Black Prince: Trade name used by the Hopkins and Allen Company on inexpensive pocket revolvers.

Bliss: Trade name believed to have been used by the Norwich Arms Company.

Blood Hound: Trade name found on inexpensive pocket revolvers of unknown manufacture.

Bluefield: Trade name used by the W.H. Davenport Firearms Company on shotguns.

Bluegrass: Trade name used by the Belknap Hardware Company of Louisville, Kentucky, on shotguns they retailed.

Bluegrass Arms Company: Trade name of shotguns made by H. & D. Folsom Arms Co. for Belknap Hardware of Louisville, Kentucky.

Blue Jacket: Trade name used by the Hopkins and Allen Company on inexpensive pocket revolvers they made for the Merwin, Hulbert and Company of New York.

Blue Leader: Trade name found on inexpensive pocket revolvers of unknown manufacture.

Blue Whistler: Trade name used by the Hopkins and Allen Company on inexpensive pocket revolvers they made for the Merwin, Hulbert and Company of New York.

Bogardus Club Gun: Trade name found on Belgian made shotguns retailed by an unknown American wholesaler (possibly B. Kittredge and Company of Cincinnati, Ohio).

Boltun: Trade name used by F. Arizmendi on semiautomatic pistols.

Bonanza: Trade name used by the Bacon Arms Company on inexpensive pocket revolvers.

Boom: Trade name used by the Shattuck Arms Company on inexpensive pocket revolvers.

Daniel Boone Gun Company: Trade name used by the Belknap Hardware Company of Louisville, Kentucky, on firearms they retailed.

Boone Gun Company: Trade name used by the Belknap Hardware Company of Louisville, Kentucky, on firearms they retailed.

Boss: a) Trade name used by E.H. and A.A. Buckland of Springfield, Massachusetts, on single-shot derringers designed by Holt & Marshall.

b) Trade name used on inexpensive pocket revolvers of unknown American manufacture.

Boys Choice: Trade name used by the Hood Firearms Company on inexpensive pocket revolvers.

Bride Black Prince: Trade name used by H. & D. Folsom Arms Co. on shotguns.

Bridge Gun Company: Registered trade name of the Shapleigh Hardware Company, St. Louis, Missouri.

Bridgeport Arms Company: Trade name used by H. & D. Folsom Arms Co. on shotguns.

Bright Arms Company: Trade name used by H. & D. Folsom Arms Company

British Bulldog: Trade name found on inexpensive pocket revolvers of unknown American and English manufacture.

Brownie: a) Trade name used by the W.H. Davenport Firearms Company on shotguns.

b) Trade name used by the O.F. Mossberg Firearms Company on a four-shot pocket pistol.

Brutus: Trade name used by the Hood Firearms Company on inexpensive pocket revolvers.

Buckeye: Trade name used by the Hopkins and Allen Company on inexpensive pocket revolvers.

Buffalo: Trade name used by Gabilongo y Urresti on semiautomatic pistols.

Buffalo: Trade name found on bolt action rifles made in France.

Buffalo: Trade name used by the Western Arms Company on an inexpensive pocket revolver.

Buffalo Bill: Trade name used by the Iver Johnson Arms and Cycle Works on an inexpensive pocket revolver.

Buffalo Stand: Trade name used by the Manufacture Francaise d'Armes et Cycles on target pistols.

Bull Dog: Trade name used by the Forehand and Wadsworth Company on inexpensive pocket revolvers.

Bull Dozer: a) Trade name used by the Norwich Pistol Company on inexpensive pocket revolvers.

b) Trade name used by the Forehand and Wadsworth Company on inexpensive pocket revolvers.

c) Trade name on Hammond Patent pistols made by the Connecticut Arms and Manufacturing Company.

Bull Frog: Trade name used by the Hopkins and Allen Company on rifles.

Bulls Eye: Trade name used by the Norwich Falls Pistol Company (O.A. Smith) on inexpensive pocket revolvers.

Burdick: Trade name used by the H. & D. Folsom Arms Company on shotguns made for the Sears, Roebuck and Company of Chicago.

General Butler: Trade name found on inexpensive pocket revolvers of unknown manufacture.

Cadet: Trade name used by the Crescent Firearms Company on rifles.

Canadian Belle: Trade name used by H. & D. Folsom Arms Co. on shotguns.

Cannon Breech: Trade name used by the Hopkins and Allen Company on shotguns.

Captain: Trade name used by Manufacture d'Armes de Pyrenees on semiautomatic pistols.

Captain Jack: Trade name used by Hopkins & Allen on inexpensive pocket revolvers.

Carolina Arms Company: Trade name used by the H. & D. Folsom Arms Company on shotguns produced for the Smith, Wadsworth Hardware Company of Charlotte, North Carolina.

Caroline Arms: Trade name used by the H. & D. Folsom Arms Co.

Caruso: Trade name used by the Crescent Firearms Company on shotguns made for the Hibbard, Spencer, Bartlett and Company of Chicago.

Centennial 1876: a) Trade name used by the Deringer Pistol Company on inexpensive pocket revolvers.

b) Trade name used by the Hood Firearms Company on inexpensive pocket revolvers.

Central Arms Company: Trade name used by the W. H. Davenport Firearms Company on shotguns made for the Shapleigh Hardware Company of St. Louis, Missouri.

Century Arms Company: Trade name used by the W. H. Davenport Firearms Company on shotguns made for the Shapleigh Hardware Company of St. Louis, Missouri.

Challenge: a) Trade name found on inexpensive pocket revolvers of unknown manufacture.

b) Trade name used by the Sears, Roebuck and Company of Chicago on shotguns made by Albert Aubrey of Meriden, Connecticut.

Challenge Ejector: Trade name used by the Sears, Roebuck and Company of Chicago on shotguns made by Albert Aubrey of Meriden, Connecticut.

Champion: a) Trade name used by H.C. Squires on shotguns.

b) Trade name used by J.P. Lovell on shotguns.

c) Trade name used by the Iver Johnson Arms and Cycle Works on shotguns and inexpensive pocket revolvers.

d) Trade name used by the Norwich Arms Company on inexpensive pocket revolvers.

Chantecler: Trade name used by Manufacture d'Armes de Pyrenees on semiautomatic pistols.

Chatham Arms Company: Trade name used by H. & D. Folsom Arms Company used on shotguns.

Cherokee Arms Company: Trade name used by the H. & D. Folsom Arms Company on shotguns made for C.M. Mclung and Company of Knoxville, Tennessee.

Chesapeake Gun Company: Trade name used by the H. & D. Folsom Arms Company of New York.

Chicago: Trade name found on shotguns retailed by the Hibbard, Spencer, Bartlett and Company of Chicago.

Chicago Ledger: Trade name used by the Chicago Firearms Company on inexpensive pocket revolvers.

Chicago Long Range Wonder: Trade name used by the H. & D. Folsom Arms Company on shotguns made for the Sears, Roebuck and Company of Chicago.

Chichester: Trade name used by Hopkins & Allen on inexpensive pocket revolvers.

Chicopee Arms Company: Trade name used by the H. & D. Folsom Arms Company of New York.

Chieftan: Trade name found on inexpensive pocket revolvers of unknown manufacture.

Christian Protector: Trade name found on inexpensive pocket revolvers of unknown manufacture.

Climax XL: Trade name used by Herman Boker and Company of New York on revolvers, rifles and shotguns.

Club Gun: Trade name used by B. Kittredge and Company of Cincinnati, Ohio, on shotguns they retailed.

Cock Robin: Trade name used by the Hood Firearms Company on inexpensive pocket revolvers.

Colonial: Trade name used by Manufacture d'Armes de Pyrenees on semiautomatic pistols.

Colonial: Trade name used by H. & D. Folsom Company on shotguns.

Columbian Automatic: Trade name used by Foehl & Weeks on inexpensive pocket revolvers.

Colton Arms Company: Trade name used by the Shapleigh Hardware Company of St. Louis, Missouri, on imported shotguns they retailed.

Colton Firearms Company: Trade name used by the Sears, Roebuck and Company of Chicago on shotguns they retailed.

Columbia: a) Trade name found on inexpensive pocket revolvers of unknown manufacture.

b) Trade name used by H.C. Squires on shotguns.

Columbia Arms Company: Registered trade name of Henry Keidel, Baltimore, Maryland.

Columbian: Trade name found on inexpensive pocket revolvers of unknown manufacture.

Columbian Firearms Company:

    a) Trade name used by the Maltby, Henly and Company on inexpensive pocket revolvers.

    b) Trade name used by the Crescent Firearms Company on shotguns.

Combat: Trade name used by Randall Firearms Co. for its service model with a flat rib top and fixed sights.

Comet: Trade name used by the Prescott Pistol Company on inexpensive pocket revolvers.

Commander: Trade name used by the Norwich Arms Company on inexpensive pocket revolvers.

Commercial: Trade name used by the Norwich Falls Pistol Company (O.A. Smith) on inexpensive pocket revolvers.

Compeer: Trade name used by the H. & D. Folsom Arms Company on firearms made for the Van Camp Hardware and Iron Company of Indianapolis, Indiana.

Competition: Trade name used by John Meunier of Milwaukee, Wisconsin, on rifles.

Conestoga Rifle Works: Trade name of Henry Leman, Philadelphia, Pennsylvania.

Connecticut Arms Company: Trade name used by H. & D. Folsom Arms Company on shotguns.

Constable: Trade name used by Astra on semiautomatic pistols.

Constabulary: Trade name used by L. Ancion-Marx of Liege on revolvers.

Continental: Trade name used by the Great Western Gun Works of Pittsburgh, Pennsylvania, on firearms they retailed.

Continental Arms Company: Trade name used by the Marshall Wells Company of Duluth, Minnesota, on firearms they retailed.

Cotton King: Trade name found on inexpensive pocket revolvers of unknown manufacture.

Cowboy: Trade name used by the Hibbard, Spencer, Bartlett and Company of Chicago on imported, inexpensive pocket revolvers they retailed.

Cowboy Ranger: Trade name used by the Rohde Spencer Company of Chicago on inexpensive pocket revolvers.

Crack Shot: Trade name used by the J. Stevens Arms and Tool Company on rifles.

Cracker Jack: Trade name used by the J. Stevens Arms and Tool Company on pistols.

Creedmoore: a) Trade name used by the Hopkins and Allen Company on inexpensive pocket revolvers.

    b) Trade name used by the Chicago Firearms Company on inexpensive pocket revolvers.

    c) Trade name used by William Wurflein on rifles.

Creedmoore Armory: Trade name used by A.D. McAusland of Omaha, Nebraska on rifles.

Creedmoore Arms Company: Trade name found on imported shotguns retailed by an unknown American wholesaler.

Crescent: Trade name used by the Crescent Arms Company on inexpensive pocket revolvers.

Crescent International 1XL: Trade name used by Herman Boker and Company of New York on shotguns.

Creve Coeur: Trade name used by the Isaac Walker Hardware Company of Peoria, Illinois, on imported shotguns they retailed.

Crown: Trade name used by the Harrington and Richardson Arms Company on inexpensive pocket revolvers.

Crown Jewel: Trade name used by the Norwich Arms Company on inexpensive pocket revolvers.

Cruso: Trade name used by the H. & D. Folsom Arms Company on shotguns made for Hibbard, Spencer, Bartlett and Company of Chicago.

Cumberland Arms Company: Trade name used by the H. & D. Folsom Arms Company on shotguns made for the Gray and Dudley Hardware Company of Nashville, Tennessee.

Czar: a) Trade name used by the Hopkins and Allen Company on inexpensive pocket revolvers.

    b) Trade name used by the Hood Firearms Company on inexpensive pocket revolvers.

Daisy: a) Trade name used by the Bacon Arms Company on inexpensive pocket revolvers.

    b) Registered proprietary trade name engraved on firearms made by the Winchester Repeating Arms Company for the F. Lassetter and Company, Limited of Sydney, Australia.

Daniel Boone Gun Company: Trade name used by H. & D. Folsom Arms Company on shotguns made for Belknap Hardware Company of Louisville, Kentucky.

Daredevil: Trade name used by Lou J. Eppinger of Detroit, Michigan, on pistols.

Dash: Trade name found on inexpensive pocket revolvers of unknown manufacture.

Davis Guns: Trade names used successively by N.R. Davis, Davis Warner, and the Crescent-Davis Arms Company on various firearms.

Dead Shot: a) Trade name found on inexpensive pocket revolvers of unknown manufacture.

    b) Trade name used by the Meriden Firearms Company on rifles.

Deer Slayer: Trade name used by J. Henry and Son of Boulton, Pennsylvania on rifles.

Defender: a) Trade name used by the Iver Johnson Arms and Cycle Works on inexpensive pocket revolvers.

    b) Trade name used by the U.S. Small Arms Company on knife pistols.

Defiance: Trade name used by the Norwich Arms Company on inexpensive pocket revolvers.

Delphian Arms Company:

a) Trade name used by the Supplee-Biddle Hardware Company of Philadelphia, Pennsylvania, on shotguns they retailed that were supplied by the H. & D. Folsom Company of New York.

b) Trade name used by the H. & D. Folsom Arms Company of New York on shotguns.

Delphian Manufacturing Company: Trade name used by the H. & D. Folsom Arms Company of New York on shotguns.

Demon: Trade name used by Manufacture d'Armes de Pyrenees on semiautomatic pistols.

Demon Marine: As above.

Dexter: Trade name found on inexpensive pocket revolvers of unknown manufacture.

Diamond Arms Company: Trade name used by the Shapleigh Hardware Company of St. Louis, Missouri, on imported shotguns they retailed.

Dictator: Trade name used by the Hopkins and Allen Company on inexpensive pocket revolvers.

Dominion Pistol: Trade name found on inexpensive pocket revolvers of unknown manufacture.

Double Header: Trade name used by E.S. Renwick on Perry and Goddard Patent derringers.

Douglas Arms Company: Trade name used by the Hopkins and Allen Company on shotguns.

Dreadnought: Trade name used by the Hopkins and Allen Company on shotguns and inexpensive pocket revolvers.

Duchess: Trade name used by the Hopkins and Allen Company on inexpensive pocket revolvers.

Duke: Trade name found on inexpensive pocket revolvers which may have been made by the Hopkins and Allen Company.

Dunlop Special: Trade name used by the Davis Warner Arms Company on shotguns made for the Dunlop Hardware Company of Macon, Georgia.

Duplex: Trade name used by the Osgood Gun Works of Norwich, Connecticut.

E.B.A.C.: Trade name used by Manufacture d'Armes de Pyrenees on semiautomatic pistols.

Eagle: Trade name used by the Iver Johnson Arms and Cycle Works on inexpensive pocket revolvers.

Eagle Arms Company: Trade name used by the Iver Johnson Arms and Cycle Works on inexpensive pocket revolvers.

Earlhood: Trade name used by E.L. Dickinson on inexpensive pocket revolvers.

Earnest Companion: Trade name found on inexpensive pocket revolvers of unknown manufacture.

Earthquake: Trade name used by E.L. Dickinson on inexpensive pocket revolvers.

Eastern Arms Company: Trade name used by the Sears, Roebuck and Company of Chicago on both shotguns and inexpensive revolvers made by the Iver Johnson Arms and Cycle Works.

Eclipse: a) Trade name found on single-shot derringers of unknown manufacture.

b) Trade name used by E.C. Meacham on imported shotguns.

Electric: Trade name found on inexpensive pocket revolvers of unknown manufacture.

Electric City Single Hammer: Trade name found on single-shot shotguns retailed by the Wyeth Hardware and Manufacturing Company of St. Joseph, Missouri.

Elector: Trade name found on inexpensive pocket revolvers of unknown manufacture.

Elgin Arms Company: Trade name used by the H. & D. Folsom Arms Company on shotguns made for the Strauss and Schram Company of Chicago.

Elita: Trade name used by the W.H. Davenport Fire Arms Company on shotguns.

Empire: a) Trade name used by the Rupertus Patented Pistol Manufacturing Company on inexpensive pocket revolvers.

b) Trade name used by the Crescent Firearms Company on shotguns.

Empire Arms Company: Trade name used by the H. & D. Folsom Arms Company on firearms made for the Sears, Roebuck and Company of Chicago.

Enders Royal Shotgun: Trade name used by the Crescent Davis Firearms Company on shotguns made for the Simmons Hardware Company of St. Louis, Missouri.

Enders Special Service: Trade name used by the Crescent Davis Firearms Company on shotguns made for the Simmons Hardware Company of St. Louis, Missouri.

Enterprise: Trade name used by the Enterprise Gun Works on inexpensive pocket revolvers.

Essex Gun Works: Trade name used by the Crescent - Davis Firearms Company on shotguns made for the Belknap Hardware Company of Louisville, Kentucky.

Eureka: Trade name used by the Iver Johnson Arms and Cycle Works on inexpensive pocket revolvers.

Excel: Trade name used by both the H. & D. Folsom Arms Company and the Iver Johnson Arms and Cycle Works on shotguns made for the Montgomery Ward and Company of Chicago.

Excelsior: a) Trade name found on inexpensive pocket revolvers of unknown manufacture.

b) Trade name used by the Iver Johnson Arms and Cycle Works on shotguns.

Expert: a) Trade name found on single-shot derringers of unknown manufacture.

b) Trade name used by the W.J. Davenport Firearms Company on shotguns made for the Witte Hardware Company of St. Louis, Missouri.

Express: Trade name used by the Bacon Arms Company on inexpensive pocket revolvers.

Express: Trade name used by Tomas de Urizar on a variety of semiautomatic pistols.

Farwell Arms Company: Trade name used by the Farwell, Ozmun, Kirk and Company of St. Paul, Minnesota, on shotguns.

Fashion: Trade name found on inexpensive pocket revolvers of unknown manufacture.

Faultless: Trade name used by the H. & D. Folsom Arms Company on shotguns made for the John M. Smythe Merchandise Company of Chicago.

Faultless Goose Gun: Trade name used by the H. & D. Folsom Arms Company on shotguns made for the John M. Smythe Merchandise Company of Chicago.

Favorite: a) Trade name used by the J. Stevens Arms and Tool Company on rifles.

b) Trade name used by the Iver Johnson Arms and Cycle Works on inexpensive pocket revolvers.

Favorite Navy: Trade name used by the Iver Johnson Arms and Cycle Works on inexpensive pocket revolvers.

Featherlight: Trade name used by the Sears, Roebuck and Company of Chicago on firearms they retailed.

Federal Arms Company: Trade name used by Meriden Firearms Company.

Folks Gun Works: Trade name of William and Samuel Folk of Bryan, Ohio on rifles and shotguns.

Freemont Arms Company: Trade name found on shotguns distributed by an unknown retailer.

Frontier: Trade name used by the Norwich Falls Pistol Company (O.A. Smith) on inexpensive pocket revolvers made for the firm of Maltby, Curtis and Company of New York.

Fulton: Trade name used by the Hunter Arms Company on shotguns.

Fulton Arms Company: Trade name used by the W.H. Davenport Firearms Company on shotguns.

Furor: Trade name used by Manufacture d'Armes de Pyrenees on semiautomatic pistols.

Gallia: Trade name used by Manufacture d'Armes de Pyrenees on semiautomatic pistols.

Game Getter: Registered trade mark of the Marble Arms and Manufacturing Company on combination rifle-shotguns.

Gaulois: Trade name used by Manufacture d'Armes et Cycles on squeezer type pistols (see also Mitrailleuse).

Gem: a) Trade name used by the J. Stevens Arms and Tool Company on single-shot pocket pistols.

b) Trade name used by the Bacon Arms Company on inexpensive pocket revolvers.

General: Trade name used by the Rupertus Patented Pistol Manufacturing Company on inexpensive pocket revolvers.

Gerrish: Trade name of G.W. Gerrish of Twin Falls, Idaho, used on shotguns.

Gibralter: Trade name of Albert Aubrey on shotguns made for the Sears, Roebuck and Company of Chicago.

Gladiator: Trade name of Albert Aubrey on shotguns made for the Sears, Roebuck and Company of Chicago.

Gold Field: Trade name found on inexpensive pocket revolvers of unknown manufacture.

Gold Hibbard: Trade name used by Hibbard, Spencer, Bartlett and Company of Chicago on firearms they retailed.

Gold Medal Wonder: Trade name used by H. & D. Folsom Arms Co. on shotguns.

Governor: Trade name used by the Bacon Arms Company on inexpensive pocket revolvers.

Guardian: Trade name used by the Bacon Arms Company on inexpensive pocket revolvers.

Gut Buster: Trade name found on inexpensive pocket revolvers of unknown manufacture.

Gypsy: Trade name found on inexpensive pocket revolvers of unknown manufacture.

Half Breed: Trade name found on inexpensive pocket revolvers of unknown manufacture.

Hamilton Arms: Registered trade name of the Wiebusch and Hilger Company, New York.

Hammerless Auto Ejecting Revolver: Trade name of the Meriden Firearms Company used on revolvers made for the Sears, Roebuck and Company of New York.

Hanover Arms Co.: If no foreign proofmarks then trade name used by H. & D. Folsom Arms Company.

Hardpan: Trade name found on inexpensive American pocket revolver.

Hard Pan: Trade name used by Hood Arms Company on inexpensive pocket revolvers.

S.H. Harrington: If no foreign proofmarks then trade name used by H. & D. Folsom Arms Company.

Frank Harrison Arms Company: Trade name used by the Sickles and Preston Company of Davenport, Iowa, on firearms they retailed.

Hart Arms Company: Trade name used by a Cleveland, Ohio, wholesaler (possibly the George Worthington Company).

Hartford Arms Company: Trade name used by the H. & D. Folsom Arms on shotguns made for the Simmons Hardware Company of St. Louis, Missouri.

Harvard: Trade name used by the H. & D. Folsom Arms Company on shotguns made for the George Worthington Company of Cleveland, Ohio.

Hercules: Trade name used by the Iver Johnson Arms and Cycle Works on shotguns made for the Montgomery Ward and Company of Chicago.

Hermitage Arms Company: Trade name used by the H. & D. Folsom Arms Company on shotguns made for the Gray and Dudley Hardware Company of Nashville, Tennessee.

Hero: a) Trade name used by the American Standard Tool Company on percussion pistols.

b) Trade name used by the Manhattan Firearms Manufacturing Company on percussion pistols.

Hexagon: Trade name used by the Sears, Roebuck and Company of Chicago on shotguns they retailed.

Hinsdale: Trade name used by the Hopkins and Allen Company on inexpensive pocket revolvers.

S. Holt Arms Company: Trade name used by the Sears, Roebuck and Company of Chicago on shotguns they retailed.

Hornet: Trade name used by the Prescott Pistol Company on inexpensive pocket revolvers.

Howard Arms Company: Trade name used by the H. & D. Folsom Arms Company on shotguns they distributed.

Hudson: Trade name used by the Hibbard, Spencer, Bartlett and Company of Chicago on shotguns they retailed.

Hunter: Trade name used by the H. & D. Folsom Arms Company on shotguns made for the Belknap Hardware Company of Louisville, Kentucky.

The Hunter: Trade name used by the Hunter Arms Company on shotguns.

Hurricane: Trade name found on inexpensive pocket revolvers of unknown manufacture.

Illinois Arms Company: Trade name used by the Rohde, Spencer Company of Chicago on firearms they retailed.

Imperial: Trade name used by the Lee Arms Company on inexpensive pocket revolvers.

Imperial Arms Company: Trade name used by the Hopkins and Allen Company on inexpensive pocket revolvers.

Infallible: Trade name used by the Lancaster Arms Company of Lancaster, Pennsylvania on shotguns they retailed.

Infallible Automatic Pistol: Trade name used by the Kirtland Brothers Company of New York on inexpensive pistols they retailed.

International: a) Trade name found on inexpensive pocket revolvers of unknown manufacture.

b) Trade name used by E.C. Meacham on shotguns.

Interstate Arms Company: Trade name used by the H. & D. Folsom Arms Company on shotguns made for the Townley Metal and Hardware Company of Kansas City, Missouri.

I.O.A.: Trade name used by the Brown, Camp Hardware Company of Des Moines, Iowa on firearms they retailed.

Invincible: Trade name used by the Iver Johnson Arms and Cycle Works on both shotguns and inexpensive pocket revolvers.

I.X.L.: a) Trade name used by B.J. Hart on percussion revolvers.

   b) Trade name used by the W.H. Davenport Firearms Company on shotguns made for the Witte Hardware Company of St. Louis, Missouri.

Ixor: Trade name used by Manufacture d'Armes de Pyrenees on semiautomatic pistols.

J.S.T. & Company: Trade name used by the Iver Johnson Arms and Cycle Works on inexpensive pocket revolvers.

Jackson Arms Company: Trade name used by the H. & D. Folsom Arms Company on shotguns made for C.M. Mclung and Company of Knoxville, Tennessee.

Jewel: Trade name used by the Hood Fire Arms Company on inexpensive pocket revolvers.

Joker: Trade name used by the Marlin Firearms Company on inexpensive pocket revolvers.

Joseph Arms Company (Norwich, Connecticut): Trade name used by H. & D. Folsom Arms Company.

Judge: Trade name found on inexpensive pocket revolvers of unknown manufacture.

Jupitor: Trade name used by Fabrique d'Armes de Grand Precision, Eibar, Spain, on semiautomatic pistols.

K.K.: Trade name used by the Hopkins and Allen Company on shotguns made for the Shapleigh Hardware Company of St. Louis, Missouri.

Keno: Trade name found on inexpensive pocket revolvers of unknown manufacture.

Kentucky: Trade name used by the Iver Johnson Arms and Cycle Works on inexpensive pocket revolvers.

Keystone Arms Company: Trade name used by the W.H. Davenport Firearms Company on shotguns made for the E.K. Tryon Company of Philadelphia, Pennsylvania.

Kill Buck: Trade name of the Enterprise Gun Works (James Bown), Pittsburgh, Pennsylvania.

Killdeer: Trade name used by the Sears, Roebuck and Company of Chicago on firearms bearing their trade name Western Arms Company.

King Nitro: Trade name used by the W.H. Davenport Firearms Company on shotguns made for the Shapleigh Hardware Company of St. Louis, Missouri.

King Pin: Trade name found on inexpensive single-shot and revolving pocket pistols.

Kingsland Gun Company: Trade name used by the H. & D. Folsom Arms Company on shotguns made for the Geller, Ward and Hasner Company of St. Louis, Missouri.

Kirk Gun Company: Trade name used by Farwell, Ozmun, and Kirk Company of St. Paul, Minnesota.

Knickerbocker: Trade name used by the Crescent-Davis Firearms Company on shotguns.

Knickerbocker Club Gun: Trade name used by Charles Godfrey of New York on imported shotguns he retailed.

Knockabout: Trade name used by the Montgomery Ward and Company of Chicago on shotguns they retailed.

Knox-All: Trade name used by the Iver Johnson Arms and Cycle Works on firearms they made for the H. & D. Folsom Arms Company of New York.

L'Agent: Trade name used by Manufacture Francaises d'Armes et Cycles on revolvers.

Lakeside: Trade name used by the H. & D. Folsom Arms Company on firearms they made for the Montgomery Ward and Company of Chicago.

Leader: a) Trade name used by the Shattuck Arms Company on inexpensive pocket revolvers.

   b) Trade name used by the Harrington and Richardson Arms Company on inexpensive pocket revolvers.

Leader Gun Company: Trade name used by the H. & D. Folsom Arms Company on shotguns they made for the Charles Williams Stores, Inc. of New York.

Le Colonial: Trade name used by Manufacture Francaises d'Armes et Cycles on revolvers.

Le Colonial: As above.

Lee's Hummer: Trade name used by the H. & D. Folsom Arms Company on firearms they made for the Lee Hardware Company of Salina, Kansas.

Lee's Special: Trade name used by the H. & D. Folsom Arms Company on firearms they made for the Lee Hardware Company of Salina, Kansas.

Le Francais: Trade name used by Manufacture Francaises d'Armes et Cycles on semiautomatic pistols.

Le Francais: As above on semiautomatic pistols.

Gen Curtis E. LeMay: Trade name used for Randall Firearms Co. for its small compact pistol made from the General's own gun.

Le Petit Forminable: Trade name used by Manufacture Francaises d'Armes et Cycles on revolvers.

Le Petit Forminable: As above on revolvers.

Le Protecteur: Trade name used by J.E. Turbiaux of Paris on squeezer pistols of the type later made by the Ames Sword Company.

Le Terrible: Trade name used by Manufacture Francaises d'Armes et Cycles on revolvers.

Liberty: Trade name used by the Norwich Falls Pistol Company (O.A. Smith) on inexpensive pocket revolvers.

Liege Gun Company: Trade name used by the Hibbard, Spencer, Bartlett and Company of Chicago on imported shotguns they retailed.

Lion: Trade name used by the Iver Johnson Arms and Cycle Works on inexpensive pocket revolvers.

Lion: Trade name used by the Iver Johnson Arms and Cycle Works on inexpensive pocket revolvers.

Little Giant: Trade name used by the Bacon Arms Company on inexpensive pocket revolvers.

Little John: Trade name used by the Hood Firearms Company on inexpensive pocket revolvers.

Little Joker: Trade name found on inexpensive pocket revolvers of unknown manufacture.

Little Pal: Registered trade name for knife pistols made by L.E. Pulhemus.

Little Pet: Trade name used by the Sears, Roebuck and Company of Chicago on inexpensive pocket revolvers they retailed.

London Revolver: Trade name found on inexpensive pocket revolvers of unknown manufacture.

Lone Star: Trade name found on inexpensive pocket revolvers of unknown manufacture.

Long Range Winner: Trade name used by the Sears, Roebuck and Company of Chicago on shotguns they retailed.

Long Range Wonder: Trade name used by the Sears, Roebuck and Company of Chicago on shotguns they retailed.

Long Tom: Trade name used by the Sears, Roebuck and Company of Chicago on shotguns they retailed.

Looking Glass: Trade name used on semiautomatic pistols of unknown Spanish manufacture.

Marquis of horne: Trade name used by Hood Arms Company on inexpensive pocket revolvers.

Mars: Trade name used by Manufacture d'Armes de Pyrenees on semiautomatic pistols.

Marshwood: Trade name used by the H. & D. Folsom Arms Company on shotguns they made for the Charles Williams Stores Inc. of New York.

Marvel: Trade name used by the J. Stevens Arms and Tool Company on various firearms.

Massachusetts Arms Company: Trade name used by both the J. Stevens Arms and Tool Company and the H. & D. Folsom Arms Company on firearms made for the Blish, Mizet and Silliman Hardware Company of Atchinson, Kansas.

Maximum: Trade name found on inexpensive pocket revolvers of unknown manufacture.

Metropolitan: Trade name used by the H. & D. Folsom Arms Company on firearms they made for the Siegal-Cooper Company of New York.

Metropolitan Police:

a) Trade name used by the Maltby, Curtiss and Company on inexpensive pocket revolvers.

b) Trade name used by the Rohde-Spencer Company of Chicago on inexpensive pocket revolvers.

Midget Hammerless: Trade name used by the Rohde-Spencer Company of Chicago on inexpensive pocket revolvers.

Mikros: Trade name used by Manufacture d'Armes de Pyrenees on semiautomatic pistols.

Minnesota Arms Company: Trade name used by the H. & D. Folsom Arms Company on shotguns they made for the Farwell, Ozmun, Kirk and Company of St. Paul, Minnesota.

Missaubi Arms Company: Trade name used by the Hunter Arms Company, possibly for the Farwell, Ozmun, Kirk and Company of St. Paul, Minnesota.

Mississippi Arms Company: Trade name used by the H. & D. Folsom Arms Company on firearms made for the Shapleigh Hardware Company of St. Louis, Missouri.

Mississippi Valley Arms Company: Trade name used by the H. & D. Folsom Arms Company on firearms made for the Shapleigh Hardware Company of St. Louis, Missouri.

Mitrailleuse: Alternate trade name of the Gauluis squeezer pistol.

Mohawk: Trade name used by the H. & D. Folsom Arms Company on firearms made for the Blish, Mizet and Silliman Hardware Company of Atchinson, Kansas.

Mohegan: Trade name used by the Hood Firearms Company on inexpensive pocket revolvers.

Monarch: a) Trade name used by the Hopkins and Allen Company on inexpensive pocket revolvers.

b) Trade name used by the Osgood Gun Works on Duplex revolvers.

Monitor: a) Trade name used by the Whitneyville Armory on inexpensive pocket revolvers.

b) Trade name used by the H. & D. Folsom Arms Company on firearms made for the Paxton and Gallagher Company of Omaha, Nebraska.

Montgomery Arms Company: Trade name used by the H. & D. Folsom Arms Company on a variety of firearms.

Mountain Eagle: Trade name used by the Hopkins and Allen Company on inexpensive pocket revolvers.

Mount Vernon Arms Company: Trade name used by the H. & D. Folsom Arms Company on firearms made for the Carlin, Hullfish Company of Alexandria, Virginia.

My Companion: Trade name found on inexpensive pocket revolvers of unknown manufacture.

My Friend: Trade name used by James Reid of New York.

Napoleon: Trade name used by the Thomas J. Ryan Pistol Manufacturing Company of Norwich, Connecticut, on inexpensive pocket revolvers.

National Arms Company: Trade name used by the H. & D. Folsom Arms Company on firearms made both for the May Hardware Company of Washington, D.C., and the Moskowitz and Herbach Company of Philadelphia, Pennsylvania.

Nevermiss: Trade name used by the Marlin Firearms Company on single-shot pocket pistols.

New Aubrey: Trade name used by Albert Aubrey of Meriden, Connecticut, on both revolvers and shotguns made for the Sears, Roebuck and Company of Chicago.

New Britain Arms Company: Trade name used by H. & D. Folsom Arms Company.

New Defender: Trade name used by Harrington & Richardson on revolvers.

New Elgin Arms Company: Trade name used by H. & D. Folsom Arms Company.

New Empire: Trade name used by H. & D. Folsom Arms Company.

New England Arms Company: Trade name believed to have been used by Charles Godfrey on shotguns made for the Rohde-Spencer Company of Chicago.

New Era Gun Works: Trade name used by the Baker Gun Company on firearms made for an unknown retailer.

New Haven Arms Company: Trade name found on Belgian shotguns imported by either E.K. Tryon of Philadelphia or the Great Western Gun Works of Pittsburgh, Pennsylvania.

New Liberty: Trade name used by the Sears, Roebuck and Company of Chicago on inexpensive pocket revolvers they retailed.

Newport: a) Trade name found on inexpensive pocket revolvers of unknown manufacture.

b) Trade name used by the H. & D. Folsom Arms Company on shotguns made for Hibbard, Spencer, Bartlett and Company of Chicago.

New Rival: Trade name used by the H. & D. Folsom Arms Company on firearms made for the Van Camp Hardware and Iron Company of Indianapolis, Indiana.

New Worcester: Trade name used by the Torkalson Manufacturing Company of Worcester, Massachusetts.

New York Arms Company: Trade name used by the H. & D. Folsom Arms Company on firearms made for the Garnet Carter Company of Chattanooga, Tennessee.

New York Gun Company: Trade name used by the H. & D. Folsom Arms Company on firearms made for the Garnet Carter Company of Chattanooga, Tennessee.

New York Club: Trade name used by the H. & D. Folsom Arms Company on rifles.

New York Machine Made: Trade name used by the H. & D. Folsom Arms Company.

New York Pistol Company: Trade name used by the Norwich Falls Pistol Company (O.A. Smith) on inexpensive pocket revolvers.

Nightingale: Trade name found on inexpensive pocket revolvers of unknown manufacture.

Nitro Bird: Trade name used by the Richards and Conover Hardware Company of Kansas City, Missouri.

Nitro Hunter: Trade name used by the H. & D. Folsom Arms Company on shotguns made for the Belknap Hardware Company of Louisville, Kentucky.

Nitro King: Trade name used by the Sears, Roebuck and Company of Chicago on shotguns of unknown manufacture.

Nitro Special: Trade name used by the J. Stevens Arms and Tool Company on shotguns.

Northfield Knife Company: Trade name used by the Rome Revolver and Novelty Works of Rome, New York, on inexpensive pocket revolvers.

Norwich Arms Company:
a) Trade name used by the Hood Firearms Company on inexpensive pocket revolvers.
b) Trade name found on shotguns retailed by the Marshall, Wells Company of Duluth, Minnesota, and Winnipeg, Manitoba, Canada.

Norwich Falls Pistol Company: Trade name used by the O.A. Smith Company on inexpensive pocket revolvers made for Maltby, Curtis and Company of New York.

Norwich Lock Manufacturing Company: Trade name used by F.W. Hood Firearms Company on inexpensive pocket revolvers.

Not-Nac Manufacturing Company: Trade name used by the H. & D. Folsom Arms Company on firearms made for the Canton Hardware Company of Canton, Ohio.

Novelty: Trade name used by D.F. Mossberg & Sons on Shattuck Unique pistols.

OK: a) Trade name used by the Marlin Firearms Company on single-shot pocket pistols.
b) Trade name used by Cowles and Son of Chicopee Falls, Massachusetts, on single-shot pocket pistols.
c) Trade name found on inexpensive pocket revolvers of unknown manufacture.

Old Hickory: a) Trade name found on inexpensive pocket revolvers of unknown manufacture.
b) Trade name used by the Hibbard, Spencer, Bartlett and Company of Chicago on shotguns they retailed.

Old Reliable: Trade name used by the Sharps Rifle Company.

Olympic: a) Trade name used by the J. Stevens Arms and Tool Company on rifles and pistols.
b) Trade name used by the Morley and Murphy Hardware Company of Green Bay, Wisconsin, on firearms they retailed (possibly made by the J. Stevens Arms and Tool Company).

Osprey: Trade name used by Lou J. Eppinger of Detroit, Michigan, on firearms he made.

Our Jake: Trade name used by E.L. and J. Dickinson of Springfield, Massachusetts, on inexpensive pocket revolvers.

Oxford Arms Company: Trade name used by the H. & D. Folsom Arms Company on firearms made for the Belknap Hardware Company of Louisville, Kentucky.

Pagoma: Trade name used by the H. & D. Folsom Arms Company on firearms made for the Paxton and Gallagher Company of Omaha, Nebraska.

Peoria Chief: Trade name found on inexpensive pocket revolvers.

Perfect: Trade name used by the Foehl and Weeks Firearms Manufacturing Company of Philadelphia, Pennsylvania, on inexpensive pocket revolvers.

Perfect: Trade name used by Manufacture d'Armes de Pyrenees on semiautomatic pistols.

Perfection: a) Trade name used by the H. & D. Folsom Arms Company on firearms made for the H.G. Lipscomb and Company of Nashville, Tennessee.
b) Trade name used by the John M. Smythe Merchandise Company of Chicago on firearms they retailed.

Pet: Trade name found on inexpensive pocket revolvers of unknown manufacture.

Petrel: Trade name found on inexpensive pocket revolvers of unknown manufacture.

Phenix: Trade name used by J. Reid of New York on revolvers.

Phoenix: a) Trade name used by J. Reid of New York on revolvers.
b) Trade name used by the Whitneyville Armory on percussion revolvers.

Piedmont: Trade name used by the H. & D. Folsom Arms Company on firearms made for the Piedmont Hardware Company of Danville, Pennsylvania.

Pinafore: Trade name used by the Norwich Falls Pistol Company (O.A. Smith) on inexpensive pocket revolvers.

Pioneer: Trade name found on inexpensive pocket revolvers of unknown manufacture.

Pioneer Arms Company: Trade name used by the H. & D. Folsom Arms Company on firearms made for the Kruse and Baklmann Hardware Company of Cincinnati, Ohio.

Pittsfield: Trade name used by the Hibbard, Spencer, Bartlett and Company of Chicago on firearms probably made by the H. & D. Folsom Arms Company.

Plug Ugly: Trade name found on inexpensive pocket revolvers of unknown manufacture.

Plymouth: Trade name used by Spear and Company of Pittsburgh, Pennsylvania, on firearms they retailed.

Pocahontas: Trade name found on inexpensive pocket revolvers of unknown manufacture.

Pointer: Trade name found on single-shot pocket pistols of unknown manufacture.

Prairie Fire: Trade name found on inexpensive pocket revolvers of unknown manufacture.

Prairie King: a) Trade name used by the Bacon Arms Company on inexpensive pocket revolvers.

b) Trade name used by the H. & D. Folsom Arms company on inexpensive pocket revolvers.

Premier: a) Trade name used by the Thomas E. Ryan Company on inexpensive pocket revolvers.

b) Trade name used by the Harrington and Richardson Arms Company on revolvers.

c) Trade name used by the Montgomery Ward and Company of Chicago on firearms they retailed.

d) Registered trade name of Edward K. Tryon and Company of Philadelphia, Pennsylvania.

Premium: Trade name used by the Iver Johnson Arms and Cycle Works on inexpensive pocket revolvers.

John W. Price: Trade name used by the Belknap Hardware Company of Louisville, Kentucky, on firearms they retailed.

Princess: Trade name found on inexpensive pocket revolvers of unknown American manufacture.

Progress: Trade name used by Charles J. Godfrey of New York on shotguns.

Protection: Trade name used by the Whitneyville Armory on revolvers.

Protector: a) Trade name found on inexpensive pocket revolvers of unknown manufacture.

b) Trade name used by the Chicago Firearms company on inexpensive pocket revolvers.

Protector Arms Company: Trade name used by the Rupertus Patented Pistol Manufacturing Company on inexpensive pocket revolvers.

Providence: Trade name found on inexpensive pocket revolvers of unknown manufacture.

Puppy: Trade name found on inexpensive pocket revolvers made by several European makers.

Quail: Trade name used by the Crescent-Davis Arms Company on shotguns.

Queen: a) Trade name used by the Hood Firearms Company on inexpensive pocket revolvers.

b) Trade name used by the Hyde and Shattuck Company on inexpensive single-shot pocket pistols.

Queen City: Trade name used by the H. & D. Folsom Arms Company on firearms made for the Elmira Arms Company of Elmira, New York.

Raider: Randall Firearms Co. Commander size pistol named after Gen Randall's flight squadron; "Randall's Raiders".

Ranger: a) Trade name found on inexpensive pocket revolvers of unknown manufacture.

b) Trade name used by the Eastern Arms Company on various firearms made for the Sears, Roebuck and Company of Chicago.

c) Trade name of the Sears, Roebuck and Company of Chicago on a wide variety of firearms marketed by that firm.

Rapid-Maxim: Trade name used by Manufacture d'Armes de Pyrenees on semiautomatic pistols.

Reassurance: Trade name found on inexpensive pocket revolvers of unknown manufacture.

Red Chieftan: Trade name used by the Supplee Biddle Hardware Company of Philadelphia, Pennsylvania, on inexpensive pocket pistols they retailed.

Red Cloud: Trade name used by the Ryan Pistol Manufacturing Company on inexpensive pocket revolvers.

Red Hot: Trade name found on inexpensive pocket revolvers of unknown manufacture.

Red Jacket. a) Trade name used by the Lee Arms Company on inexpensive pocket revolvers.

b) Trade name used by the Hopkins and Allen Company on inexpensive pocket revolvers.

Reliable: Trade name found on inexpensive pocket revolvers of unknown manufacture.

Reliance: Trade name used by John Meunier of Milwaukee, Wisconsin, on rifles.

Rev-O-Noc: Trade name used by the H. & D. Folsom Arms Company on firearms made for the Hibbard, Spencer, Bartlett and Company of Chicago.

Rich-Con: Trade name used by the H. & D. Folsom Arms Company for shotguns made for Richardson & Conover Hardware Company.

Richmond Arms Company: Trade name used by the H. & D. Folsom Arms Company on firearms made for an unknown retailer.

Charles Richter Company: Trade name used by the H. & D. Folsom Arms Company on firearms made for the New York Sporting Goods Company of New York.

Rickard Arms Company: Trade name used by the H. & D. Folsom Arms Company on firearms made for the J.A. Rickard Company of Schenectady, New York.

Rip Rap: Trade name used by the Bacon Arms Company on inexpensive pocket revolvers.

Rival: Trade name used by the H. & D. Folsom Arms Company on firearms made for the Van Camp Hardware and Iron Company of Indianapolis, Indiana.

Riverside Arms Company: Trade name used by the J. Stevens Arms and Tool Company on various types of firearms.

Robin Hood: Trade name used by the Hood Firearms Company on inexpensive pocket revolvers.

Rocky Hill: Trade name found on inexpensive cast iron percussion pocket pistols made in Rocky Hill, Connecticut.

Rodgers Arms Company: Trade name used by the Hood Firearms Company on firearms made for an unknown retailer.

Royal Gun Company: Trade name used by the Three Barrel Gun Company.

Royal Service: Trade name used by the Shapleigh Hardware Company of St. Louis, Missouri, on firearms they retailed.

Rummel Arms Company: Trade name used by the H. & D. Folsom Arms Company on firearms made for the A.J. Rummel Arms Company of Toledo, Ohio.

Russel Arms Company: Registered trade name of the Wiebusch and Hilger Company of New York.

Russian Model: Trade name used by the Forehand and Wadsworth Company on inexpensive pocket revolvers.

S.A.: Trade mark of the Societe d'Armes Francaises.

Safe Guard: Trade name found on inexpensive pocket revolvers of unknown manufacture.

Safety Police: Trade name used by the Hopkins and Allen Company on inexpensive pocket revolvers.

St. Louis Arms Company: Trade name used by the H. & D. Folsom Arms Company on firearms made for the Shapleigh Hardware Company of St. Louis, Missouri.

Scott: Trade name used by the Hopkins and Allen Company on inexpensive pocket revolvers.

Secret Service Special: Trade name used by the Rohde-Spencer Company of Chicago on inexpensive pocket revolvers.

Selecta: Trade name used by Manufacture d'Armes de Pyrenees on semiautomatic pistols.

Senator: Trade name found on inexpensive pocket revolvers of unknown manufacture.

Sentinal: Trade name found on inexpensive pocket revolvers of unknown manufacture.

Service Model C: The predecessor to the "Raider" pistol.

The Sheffield: Trade name used by the A. Baldwin and Company, Limited of New Orleans, Louisiana, on shotguns they retailed.

Sickels-Arms Company: Trade name used by the Sickels and Preston Company of Davenport, Iowa, on firearms they retailed.

Simson: Trade name used by the Iver Johnson Arms and Cycle Works on firearms made for the Iver Johnson Sporting Goods Company of Boston, Massachusetts.

Sitting Bull: Trade name found on inexpensive pocket revolvers of unknown manufacture.

Skue's Special: Trade name used by Ira M. Skue of Hanover, Pennsylvania, on shotguns.

Smoker: Trade name used by the Iver Johnson Arms and Cycle Works on inexpensive pocket revolvers.

John M. Smythe & Company: Trade name used by H. & D. Folsom Arms Company for shotguns made for John M. Smythe Hardware Company of Chicago.

Southern Arms Company: Trade name used by the H. & D. Folsom Arms Company on firearms made for an unknown retailer.

Southerner: a) Trade name used by the Brown Manufacturing Company and the Merrimac Arms Manufacturing Company on single-shot pocket pistols.

b) Registered trade name of Asa Farr of New York on pistols.

Southron: Trade name found on inexpensive pocket pistols of unknown manufacture.

Special Service: Trade name used by the Shapleigh Hardware Company of St. Louis, Missouri, on inexpensive pocket revolvers.

Spencer Gun Company: Trade name used by the H. & D. Folsom Arms Company.

Splendor: Trade name found on inexpensive pocket revolvers of unknown manufacture.

The Sportsman: Trade name used by the H. & D. Folsom Arms Company on firearms made for the W. Bingham Company of Cleveland, Ohio.

Springfield Arms Company: Trade name used by the J. Stevens Arms and Tool Company.

Spy: Trade name found on inexpensive pocket revolvers of unknown manufacture.

Square Deal: Trade name used by the H. & D. Folsom Arms Company on firearms made for the Stratton, Warren Hardware Company of Memphis, Tennessee.

Standard: Trade name used by the Marlin Firearms Company on revolvers.

Stanley Arms: Registered trade name of the Wiebusch and Hilger Company of New York on firearms they retailed.

Stanley Double Gun: Trade name used by the H. & D. Folsom Arms Company on shotguns they retailed.

Star: a) Trade name found on inexpensive single-shot pocket pistols of unknown manufacture.

b) Trade name used by the Prescott Pistol Company on inexpensive pocket revolvers.

c) Trade name used by Johnson & Bye on single-shot cartridge derringers.

State Arms Company: Trade name used by the H. & D. Folsom Arms Company on firearms made for the J.H. Lau and Company of New York.

Sterling: a) Trade name used by E.L. and J. Dickinson of Springfield, Massachusetts, on single-shot pistols.

b) Trade name used by the H. & D. Folsom Arms Company on shotguns they retailed.

Stinger: Registered proprietary trade name engraved on firearms made by the Winchester Repeating Arms Company for the Perry Brothers Limited of Brisbane, Australia.

Stonewall: a) Trade name used by the Marlin Firearms Company on single-shot derringers.

b) Trade name used by T.F. Guion of Lycoming, Pennsylvania, on single-shot percussion pistols he retailed.

Striker: Trade name found on inexpensive pocket revolvers of unknown manufacture.

Sullivan Arms Company: Trade name used by the H. & D. Folsom Arms Company on firearms made for the Sullivan Hardware Company of Anderson, South Carolina.

Superior: Trade name of the Paxton and Gallagher Company of Omaha, Nebraska, on revolvers and shotguns.

Super Range: Trade name of the Sears, Roebuck and Company of Chicago on shotguns.

Sure Fire: Trade name found on inexpensive pocket revolvers of unknown manufacture.

Swamp Angel: Trade name used by the Forehand and Wadsworth Company on inexpensive pocket revolvers.

Swift: Trade name used by the Iver Johnson Arms and Cycle Works on firearms made for the John P. Lovell & Sons, Boston, Massachusetts.

Syco: Trade name used by the Wyeth Hardware Company of St. Joseph, Missouri, on firearms they retailed.

Sympathique: Trade name used by Manufacture d'Armes de Pyrenees on semiautomatic pistols.

Ten Star: Trade name used by the H. & D. Folsom Arms Company on firearms made for the Geller, Ward and Hasner Company of St. Louis, Missouri.

Terrier: Trade name used by the Rupertus Patented Pistol Manufacturing Company on inexpensive pocket revolvers.

Terror: Trade name used by the Forehand and Wadsworth Company on inexpensive pocket revolvers.

Texas Ranger: Trade name used by the Montgomery Ward and Company of Chicago on inexpensive pocket revolvers they retailed.

Thames Arms Company: Trade name used by the Harrington and Richardson Arms Company on firearms they made for an unknown wholesaler.

Tiger: a) Trade name used by the Iver Johnson Arms and Cycle Works on inexpensive pocket revolvers.

b) Trade name used by the J.H. Hall and Company of Nashville, Tennessee, on shotguns they retailed.

Tobin Simplex: Trade name used on shotguns of unknown manufacture that were retailed by the G.B. Crandall Company, Limited of Woodstock, Ontario, Canada.

Toledo Firearms Company:

a) Trade name used by the Hopkins and Allen Company on inexpensive pocket revolvers.

b) Trade name used by E.L. and J. Dickinson on inexpensive pocket revolvers.

Toronto Belle: Trade name found on inexpensive pocket revolvers of unknown manufacture.

Touriste: Trade name used by Manufacture d'Armes de Pyrenees on semiautomatic pistols.

Tower's Police Safety: Trade name used by Hopkins & Allen on inexpensive pocket revolvers.

Townley's Pal and Townley's American Boy: Trade name used by H. & D. Folsom Arms Company for shotguns made for Townley Metal and Hardware Company of Kansas City, Missouri.

Tramps Terror: Trade name used by the Forehand and Wadsworth Company on inexpensive pocket revolvers.

Traps Best: Trade name believed to have been used by the H. & D. Folsom Arms Company on firearms made for the Watkins, Cottrell Company of Richmond, Virginia.

Triumph: Trade name used by the H. & D. Folsom Arms Company on shotguns.

Trojan: Trade name found on inexpensive pocket revolvers of unknown manufacture.

True Blue: Trade name found on inexpensive pocket revolvers of unknown manufacture.

Tryon Special: Trade name used by the Edward K. Tryon Company of Philadelphia, Pennsylvania, on shotguns they retailed.

Tycoon: Trade name used by the Iver Johnson Arms and Cycle Works on inexpensive pocket revolvers.

Uncle Sam: Trade name used by Johnson & Bye on percussion pocket pistols.

Union: a) Trade name found on inexpensive single-shot pocket pistols of unknown manufacture.

b) Trade name used by the Hood Firearms Company on inexpensive pocket revolvers.

c) Trade name used by the Prescott Pistol Company on inexpensive pocket revolvers.

Union Arms Company: Trade name used by the H. & D. Folsom Arms Company on firearms made for the Bostwick, Braun Company of Toledo, Ohio.

Union Jack: Trade name found on inexpensive pocket revolvers of unknown manufacture.

Union N.Y.: Trade name used by the Whitneyville Armory on inexpensive pocket revolvers.

Unique: Trade name used by the C.S. Shattuck Arms Company on revolvers and four barrel pocket pistols.

United States Arms Company: Trade name used by Norwich Falls Pistol Company (O.A. Smith) on inexpensive pocket revolvers.

U.S. Arms Company: Trade name used successively by the Alexander Waller and Company (1877), the Barton and Company (1878) and the H. & D. Folsom Arms Company (1879 forward) on a variety of firearms.

U.S. Revolver: Trade name used by the Iver Johnson Arms and Cycle Works on inexpensive pocket revolvers.

U.S. Single Gun: Trade name used by the Iver Johnson Arms and Cycle Works on single barrel shotguns.

Universal: Trade name used by the Hopkins and Allen Company on inexpensive pocket revolvers.

Utica Firearms Company: Trade name used by the Simmons Hardware Company of St. Louis, Missouri, on firearms they retailed.

Valient: Trade name used by the Spear and Company of Pittsburgh, Pennsylvania, on firearms they retailed.

Veiled Prophet: Trade name used by the T.E. Ryan Pistol Manufacturing Company on inexpensive pocket revolvers.

Venus: Trade name used by the American Novelty Company of Chicago on inexpensive pocket revolvers.

Veteran: Trade name found on inexpensive pocket revolvers of unknown manufacture.

Veto: Trade name found on inexpensive pocket revolvers of unknown manufacture.

Victor: a) Trade name used by the Marlin Firearms Company on single-shot pocket pistols.

b) Trade name used by the Harrington and Richardson Arms Company on inexpensive pocket revolvers.

c) Trade name used by the H. & D. Folsom Arms Company on inexpensive pocket pistols and revolvers.

Victor Arms Company: Trade name used by the H. & D. Folsom Arms Company on firearms made for the Hibbard, Spencer, Bartlett and Company of Chicago.

Victor Special: Trade name used by the H. & D. Folsom Arms Company on firearms made for the Hibbard, Spencer, Bartlett and Company of Chicago.

Victoria: Trade name used by the Hood Firearms Company on inexpensive pocket revolvers.

Vindix: Trade name used by Manufacture d'Armes de Pyrenees on semiautomatic pistols.

Viper: Trade name used on inexpensive pocket revolvers of unknown American manufacture.

Virginia Arms Company: Trade name used by the H. & D. Folsom Arms Company and later the Davis-Warner Arms Company on firearms made for the Virginia-Carolina Company of Richmond, Virginia.

Volunteer: Trade name used by the H. & D. Folsom Arms Company on inexpensive pocket revolvers made for the Belknap Hardware Company of Louisville, Kentucky.

Vulcan: Trade name used by the H. & D. Folsom Arms Company on firearms made for the Edward K. Tryon Company of Philadelphia, Pennsylvania.

Walnut Hill: Trade name used by the J. Stevens Arms and Tool Company on rifles.

Warner Arms Corporation: Trade name used by the H. & D. Folsom Arms Company on firearms made for the Kirtland Brothers, Inc. of New York.

Wasp: Trade name found on inexpensive pocket revolvers of unknown manufacture.

Wautauga: Trade name used by the Whitaker, Holtsinger Hardware Company of Morristown, Tennessee on firearms they retailed.

Western: Trade name used by the H. & D. Folsom Arms Company on firearms made for the Paxton and Gallagher Company of Omaha, Nebraska.

Western Arms Company:

a) Trade name used by the Bacon Arms on various types of firearms.

b) Trade name used by W.W. Marston on revolvers.

c) Trade name used by Henry Kolb and later R.F. Sedgly of Philadelphia, Pennsylvania, on Baby Hammerless revolvers.

d) Trade name used by the Ithaca Gun Company on shotguns believed to have been made for the Montgomery Ward and Company of Chicago.

Western Field: Trade name used by Montgomery Ward and Company of Chicago on shotguns of various makes that they retailed.

Western Field: Trade name used by Manufacture d'Armes de Pyrenees on revolvers.

J.J. Weston: Trade name used by the H. & D. Folsom Arms Company on shotguns.

Whippet: Trade name used by the H. & D. Folsom Arms Company on firearms made for the Hibbard, Spencer, Bartlett and Company of Chicago.

Whistler: Trade name used by the Hood Firearms Company on inexpensive pocket revolvers.

White Powder Wonder: Trade name used by Albert Aubrey of Meriden, Connecticut on shotguns made for the Sears, Roebuck and Company of Chicago.

Wildwood: Trade name used by the H. & D. Folsom Arms Company for shotguns made for Sears, Roebuck & Company.

Wilkinson Arms Company: Trade name used by the H. & D. Folsom Arms Company on firearms made for the Richmond Hardware Company of Richmond, Virginia.

Wiltshire Arms Company: Trade name used by the H. & D. Folsom Arms Company on firearms made for the Stauffer, Eshleman and Company of New Orleans, Louisiana.

Winfield Arms Company: Trade name used by the H. & D. Folsom Arms Company on various types of firearms.

Winner: Trade name found on inexpensive pocket revolvers of unknown manufacture.

Winoca Arms Company: Trade name used by the H. & D. Folsom Arms Company on firearms made for the N. Jacobi Hardware Company of Wilmington, North Carolina.

Witte's Expert: Trade name used by the Witte Hardware Company of St. Louis, Missouri, on shotguns they retailed.

Witte's IXL: Trade name used by the Witte Hardware Company of St. Louis, Missouri, on shotguns they retailed.

Wolverine Arms Company: Trade name used by the H. & D. Folsom Arms Company on firearms made for the Fletcher Hardware Company of Wilmington, North Carolina.

Woodmaster: Trade name found on Belgian shotguns imported by an unknown wholesaler.

Worlds Fair: Trade name used by the Hopkins and Allen Company on shotguns.

Worthington Arms Company: Trade name used by the H. & D. Folsom Arms Company on various types of firearms.

Wyco: Trade name used by the Wyeth Hardware and Manufacturing Company of St. Joseph, Missouri, on firearms they retailed.

XL: a) Trade name used by the Hopkins and Allen Company on inexpensive pocket revolvers.

b) Trade name used by the Marlin Firearms Company on single-shot pocket pistols.

XPERT: a) Trade name used by the Hopkins and Allen Company on inexpensive pocket revolvers.

b) Trade name used by the Iver Johnson Arms and Cycle Works on inexpensive single-shot pocket pistols.

XXX Standard: Trade name used by the Marlin Firearms Company on revolvers.

You Bet: Trade name used on inexpensive pocket revolvers of unknown American manufacture.

Young America: Trade name used by J.P. Lindsay of New York on superimposed - load percussion pistols.

Young American: Trade name used by the Harrington and Richardson Arms Company on revolvers.

FIREARMS MANUFACTURERS AND IMPORTERS

Action Arms, Ltd.
P.O. Box 9573
Philadelphia, PA 19124

AMAC, Inc.
2202 Redmond Road
Jacksonville, AR 72076

American Arms, Inc.
715 E. Armour Road
N. Kansas City, MO 64116

American Derringer Corp.
127 N. Lacy Drive
Waco, TX 76705

American Frontier Firearms
40725 Brook Trails Way
Aguanga, CA 92536

American Historical Foundation
1142 West Grace St.
Richmond, VA 23220

AMT
6226 Santos Diaz St.
Irwindale, CA 91702

Anschutz-Precision Sales, Inc.
P.O. Box 1776
Westfield, MA 01086

ArmaLite, Inc.
P.O. Box 299
Geneseo, IL 61254

Armes De Chasse
P.O. Box 86
Hertford, NC 27944

Arminex Ltd.
7127 E. Sahuaro Drive #107A
Scottsdale, AZ 85254

Armscorp of America
4424 John Avenue
Baltimore, MA 21227

Armsport, Inc.
3590 NW 49th St.
Miami, FL 33142

Arnold Arms Co., Inc.
P.O. Box 1011
Arlington, WA 98223

A-Square Co. Inc.
One Industrial Park
Bedford, KY 40006

Auto-Ordnance Corp.
Williams Lane
West Hurley, NY 12491

Aya-Agiurre Y Aranzabal, S.A.L.
P.O. Box 45
Eibar(Guipuzcoa), Spain

Bailons Gunmakers, Ltd.
94-95 Bath Street
Birmingham, England B4 6HG

Barrett Firearms Mfg.
8211 Manchester Highway
P.O.Box 1077
Murfreesboro, TN 37130

Beretta USA Corp.
17601 Beretta Drive
Accokeek, MD 20607

Bernardelli Vincenzo, S.p.a.
P.O. Box 74
Gardone, V.T., Brescia, Italy 25063

Charles Boswell Gunmakers
212 East Morehead Street
Charlotte, NC 28202

Brolin Arms
P.O. Box 698
LaVerne, Ca 91750

Browning
One Browning Place
Morgan, UT 84050

Browning-Parts & Service
3005 Arnold Tenbrook Rd.
Arnold, MO 63010

Calico
405 East 19th Street
Bakersfield, CA 93305

Caspian Arms, Ltd.
14 North Main Street
Hardwick, VT 05843

Century Arms
P.O. Box 714
St. Albans, VT 05478

Champlin Firearms
P.O. Box 3191/Woodring Airport
Enid, OK 73702

Charter Arms
26 Beaver Street
Ansonia, CT 06401

Charter Arms Corp.
430 Sniffens Lane
Stratford, CT 06497

Chipmunk Mfg., Inc.
114 East Jackson
Medford, OR 97501

E. J. Churchill, Ltd.
Ockley Road, Dorking
Surrey, England RH5 4PU

Cimarron Arms
P.O. Box 906
Fredericksburg, TX 78624

Colt Firearms
P.O. Box 1868
Hartford, CT 06144

Colt Blackpowder Arms Co.
110 8th Street
Brooklyn, NY 11215

Connecticut Shotgun Manufacturing Co.
A. H. Fox Shotguns
35 Woodland Street
Box 1692
New Britain, CT 06051

Connecticut Valley Arms, Inc.
5988 Peachtree Corners East
Norcross, GA 30071

Coonan Arms
1465 Selby Ave.
St. Paul, MN 55104

Cooper Arms
P.O. Box 114
Stevensville, MT 59870

Dakota Arms, Inc.
HC55, Box 326
Sturgis, SD 57785

Davis Industries
15150 Sierra Bonita Lane
Chino, CA 91710

New Detonics Mfg. Corp.
21438 N. 7th Avenue
Suite F
Phoenix, AZ 85027

Dixie Gun Works
P.O. Box 130
Union City, TN 38261

DuBiel Arms Co.
1800 West Washington Avenue
#205
Sherman, TX 75090-5359

Dumoulin Ernst-UFA
10 Rue Boclinville
Herstal, Beligium B-4041

Eagle Imports
1750 Brielle Av., Unit B1
Wanamassa, NJ 07712

Ellett Bros.
P.O. Box 128
Chapin, SC 29036

EMF Co., Inc.
1900 E. Warner Avenue 1-D
Santa Ana, CA 92705

European American Armory
P.O. Box 122
Sharpes, FL 32959

F.M.J.
P.O. Box 759
Copperhill, TN 37317

F.N. Manufacturing, Inc.
P.O. Box 104
Columbia, SC 29202

Falcon Firearms Mfg. Corporation
P.O. Box 3748
Granada Hills, CA 91344

Feather Industries
37600 Liberty Dr.
Trinidad, CO 81082

Federal Ordnance, Inc.
1443 Potrero Avenue
S. El Monte, CA 91733

Fiocchi Of American
Route 2, Box 90-8
Ozark, MO 65721

Aug. Francotte
Rue du 3 Juin, 109
Liege, Belgium B-4040

Freedom Arms
P.O. Box 1776
Freedom, WY 83120

Furr Arms
91 North 970 West
Orem, UT 84057

Galaxy Imports
P.O. Box 3361
Victoria, TX 77903

Renato Gamba
Via Michelangelo, 64
Gardone, Italy 1-25063

Gamba, USA
P.O. Box 60452
Colorado Springs, CO 80960

Glock, Inc.
6000 Highlands Parkway
Smyrna, GA 30082

Goncz Company
11526 Burbank #18
N. Hollywood, CA 91601

Griffin & Howe
36 West 44th Street #1011
New York, NY 10036

Griffin & Howe, Inc.
33 Claremont Road
Bernardsville, NJ 07924

GSI, Inc.
108 Morrow Ave.
Trussville, AL 35173

Hatfield International
224 North 4th
St. Joseph, MO 64501

Harrington & Richardson
60 Industrial Rowe
Gardner, MA 01440

Heckler & Koch, Inc.
21480 Pacific Boulevard
Sterling, VA 20166

Heritage Manufacturing, Inc.
4600 NW 135th St.
Opa Locla, FL 33054

High Standard Manufacturing Co.
4601 South Pinemont #148B
Houston, TX 77041

Hi-Power Firearms
MKS Supply
5990 Philadaphia Dr.
Dayton, OH 45415

Holmes Firearms
Route 6, Box 242
Fayetteville, AR 72703

Lew Horton Distributing Co., Inc.
15 Walkup Drive
Westboro, MA 01581

Hyper Single, Inc.
520 East Beaver
Jenks, OK 74037

Illinois Arms
2300 Central Avenue, Suite K
Boulder, CO 80301

Interarms
10 Prince Street
Alexandria, VA 22314

Intratec
12405 SW 130th Street
Miami, FL 33186

Ithaca Gun/Ithaca Acq. Corp.
891 Route 34 B
King Ferry, NY 13081

Jennings Firearms
3680 Research Way
Carson City, NV 89706

J.O. Arms Inc.
5709 Hartsdale
Houston, TX 77036

K.B.I. Inc.
P.O. Box 5440
Harrisburg, PA 17110

KDF
2485 Highway 46 North
Seguin, TX 78155

Kahr Arms
P.O. Box 220
Blauvelt, NY 10913

Kel-Tec CNC, Inc.
1485 Cox Rd.
P.O. Box 3427
Cocoa, FL 32924

Kimber
Sales & Marketing Office
2590 Highway 35
Kalispell, MT 59901
Corporate Offices
1 Lawton Street
Yonkers, NY 10705

Knight's Manufacturing Co.
7750 Ninth St., SW
Vero Beach, FL 32968

Krieghoff International
P.O. Box 549
Ottsville, PA 18942

L.A.R. Manufacturing
4133 West Farm Road
West Jordan, UT 84088

Laurona
P.O. Box 260
20600 Eibar(Guipuzcoa), Spain

Lazzeroni Arms Co.
1415 South Cherry Av.
Tucson, AZ 85726

Les Baer Custom Inc.
29601 34th Av North
Hillsdale, IL 61257

Ljutic Industries
732 North 16th Avenue
P.O. Box 2117 Suite 22
Yakima, WA 98907

Lorcin Engineering Co., Inc.
10427 San Sevaine Way
Unit A
Mira Loma, CA 91752

Magnum Research, Inc.
7110 University Avenue N.E.
Minneapolis, MN 55432

Marlin Firearms
100 Kenna Drive
North Haven, CT 06473

Maverick Arms Inc.
P.O. Box 586
Industrial Boulevard
Eagle Pass, TX 78853

G. McMillan & Co.
21421 North 7th Avenue
Phoenix, AZ 85027

Military Armament Corp.
P.O.Box 1156
Stephenville, TX 76401

Mitchell Arms Inc.
3433-B West Harvard St.
Santa Ana, CA 92704

M.O.A. Corp.
2451 Old Camden Pike
Eaton, OH 45320

William Larkin Moore & Co.
31360 Via Colinas #109
Westlake Village, CA 91301

O. F. Mossberg & Sons, Inc.
Seven Grasso Avenue
North Haven, CT 06473

Navy Arms Co.
689 Bergen Blvd.
Ridgefield, NJ 07657

New England Arms Co.
Lawrence Lane
Kittery Point, ME 03905

North American Arms
2150 South 950 East
Provo, UT 84606

Ohio Ordnance Works
P.O. Box 687
Chardon, Ohio

Olympic Arms, Inc.
624 Old Pacific Highway Southeast
Olympia, WA 98513

Para-Ordnance
980 Tapscott Rd.
Scarborough, Ontario M1X 1E7

Parker Reproductions
124 River Road
Middlesex, NJ 08846

Pedersoli Davide & Co.
Via Artigiani N. 57
Gardone Valtrompia, Brescia
Italy 25063

Perazzi USA Inc.
1207 South Shamrock Avenue
Monrovia, CA 91016

Precision Imports
5040 Space Center Dr.
San Antonio, TX 78218

Phillips & Rodgers, Inc.
100 Hilbig, Suite C
Conroe, TX 77301

Phoenix Arms
1420 South Archibald Av.
Ontario, CA 91761

P.S.M.G. Gun Co.
10 Park Avenue
Arlington, MA 02174

Raven Arms
1300 Bixby Drive
City of Industry, CA 91745

Remington Arms Co., Inc.
1011 Centre Rd.
Wilmington, DE 19805

Seecamp, L.W.C.
301 Brewster Rd.
Milford, CT 06460

Savage Arms
Springdale Road
Westfield, MA 01085

SGS Importers International
1750 Brielle Ave. Unit B-1
Wanamassa, NJ

Shiloh Rifle Mfg. Co., Inc.
P.O. Box 279
Ind. Park
Big Timber, MT 59011

SigArms, Inc.
Corporate Park
Exeter, NH 03833

Sile Distributors
7 Centre Market Place
New York, NY 10013

S.K.B.
4325 South 120th St.
P.O. Box 37669
Omaha, NE 68137

Smith & Wesson
2100 Roosevelt Road
Springfield, MA 01102

Sokolovsky Inc.
P.O. Box 70113
Sunnyvale, CA 94086

Sphinx USA, Inc.
998 North Colony Rd.
Meridan, CT 06450

Specialty Shooters
3325 Griffin Road
Suite 9M/M
Fort Lauderdale, FL 33312

Springfield Armory, Inc.
420 West Main Street
Geneseo, IL 61254

SSK Industries
721 Woodvue Lane
Wintersville, OH 43952

Steyr-Mannlicher GmbH
108 Morrow Avenue
Trussville, AL 35173

S.T.I. International, Inc.
12108-A Roxie Dr.
Austin, TX 78729

Stoeger Industries
5 Mansard Court
Wayne, NJ 07470

Sturm Ruger & Co., Inc
10 Lacey Place
Southport, CT 06490

Taurus International
16175 NW 49th Av.
Miami, FL 33014

Techno-Arms Ltd./VFI
11 Perry Dr., Unit G
Foxboro, MA 02035

Texas Longhorn Arms
P.O. Box 703
Richmond, TX 77469

Thompson/Center Arms Co.
Farmington Road
P.O. Box 5002
Rochester, NH 03867

Uberti USA, Inc.
P.O. Box 469
Lakeville, CT 06039

Ultra Light Arms, Inc.
P.O. Box 1270
Granville, WV 26534

U.S. Repeating Arms/Winchester
275 Winchester Ave.
Morgan, UT 84050

United States Patent Firearms
Manufacturing Co.
25-55 Van Dyke Av.
Hartford, CT 06106

Varner Sporting Arms Inc.
1004-F Cobb Parkway North
Marietta, GA 30062

Weatherby, Inc.
3100 El Comino Real
Atascadero, CA 93422

Westley Richards & Co. Ltd
40 Grange Road, Bournbrook
Birmingham, England B29 5A

Wichita Arms
444 Ellis
Wichita, KS 67211

Wildey, Inc.
P.O. Box 475
Brookfield, CT 06804

Wilkinson Arms
26884 Pearl Road
Parma, ID 83660

Winchester/U.S. Repeating
  Arms Co. Inc.
275 Winchester Avenue
New Haven, CT 06511

Winslow Arms
P.O. Box 783
Camden, SC 29020

ZM Weapons
203 South Street
Bernardton, MA 01337

Zoli, Antonio
Via Zanardelli,39
I-25063 Gardone V.T. (BS) Italy

GUN COLLECTORS ASSOCIATIONS

Alabama Gun Collectors
P.O. Box 59606
Birmingham, AL 35259

Alaska Gun Collectors Association
P.O. Box 101522
Anchorage, Alaska 99510

Ark-La-Tex Gun Collectors Association
919 Hamilton Road
Bossier City, LA 71111

Bay Colony Weapons Collectors, Inc.
47 Homer Road
Belmont, MA 02178

Boardman Valley Collectors Guild
County Road 600
Manton, MI 49663

Browning Collectors Association
P.O. Box 526
Aurora, NE 68818

Collectors Arms Dealers Association
P.O. Box 427
Thomson, IL 61285

California Rifle & Pistol Association, Inc.
12062 Valley View Street
Garden Grove, CA 92645

Central Illinois Gun Collectors Assn., Inc.
Box 875
Jacksonville, IL 62651-0875

Central Penn Antique Arms Association
978 Thistle Road
Elizabethtown, PA 17022

Chisholm Trail Antique Gun Association
1906 Richmond
Wichita, KS 67203

Colorado Gun Collectors
2553 South Quitman Street
Denver, CO 80219

Colt Collectors Association
25000 Highland Way
Los Gatos, CA 95030

The Corpus Christi Antique Gun Collectors Association
P.O. Box 9392
Corpus Christi, TX 78410

Dallas Arms Collectors Association, Inc.
Rt. 1, Box 282-B
DeSoto, TX 75115

Derringer Collectors Association
500 E. Old 66
Shamrock, TX 79079

Florida Gun Collectors Association
P.O. Box 43
Branford, FL 32008

Fort Lee Arms Collectors
P.O. Box 1716
South Hackensack, NJ 07606

Hawaii Historic Arms Association
Box 1733
Honolulu, HI 96806

Houston Gun Collectors Association
P.O. Box 53435
Houston, TX 77052

Indianhead Firearms Association
Route 9, Box 186
Chippewa Falls, WI 54729

Indian Territory Gun Collectors Association
Box 4491
Tulsa, OK 74159

Iroquois Arms Collectors Association
214 70th Street
Niagara Falls, NY 14304

Jefferson State Arms Collectors
521 South Grape
Medford, OR 97501

Jersey Shore Antique Arms Collectors
P.O. Box 100
Bayville, NJ 08721

Kentuckiana Arms Collectors Association
P.O. Box 1776
Louisville, KY 40201

Kentucky Gun Collectors Association
P.O. Box 64
Owensboro, KY 42376

Lehigh Valley Military Collectors Association
P.O. Box 72
Whitehall, PA 18052

Long Island Antique Gun Collectors Association
35 Beach Street
Farmingdale, L.I., NY 11735

Marlin Firearms Collectors Association
44 Main Street
Champaign, IL 61820

Maryland Arms Collectors Association
P.O. Box 20388
Baltimore, MD 21284-0388

Memphis Antique Weapons Association
4672 Barfield Road
Memphis, TN 38117

Minnesota Weapons Collectors Association
P.O. Box 662
Hopkins, MN 55343

Missouri Valley Arms Collectors Association
P.O. Box 33033
Kansas City, MO 64114

Montana Arms Collectors Association
308 Riverview Drive
East Great Falls, MT 59404

National Automatic Pistol Collectors Association
Box 15738-TOGS
St. Louis, MO 63163

National Rifle Association
1600 Rhode Island Avenue N.W.
Washington, D.C. 20036

New Hampshire Arms Collectors, Inc.
P.O. Box 6
Harrisville, NH 03450

Northeastern Arms Collectors Association, Inc.
P.O. Box 185
Amityville, NY 11701

Ohio Gun Collectors Association
P.O. Box 24F
Cincinnati, OH 45224

Oregon Arms Collectors
P.O. Box 25103
Portland, OR 97225

Pelican Arms Collectors Association
P.O. Box 747
Clinton, LA 70722

Pennsylvania Antique Gun Collectors Association
28 Fulmer Avenue
Havertown, PA 19083

Pikes Peak Gun Collectors Guild
406 E. Uintah
Colorado Springs, CO 80903

Potomac Arms Collectors Association
P.O. Box 1812
Wheaton, MD 20915

Randall Collectors Club
228 Columbine Dr.
Casper WY 82609-3948

Remington Society of America
380 South Tustin Avenue
Orange, CA 92666

Ruger Collectors Association, Inc.
P.O. Box 240
Greens Farms, CT 06436

Sako Collectors Association, Inc.
1725 Woodhill Lane
Bedford, TX 76021

Santa Barbara Antique Arms Collectors Association
P.O. Box 6291
Santa Barbara, CA 93160-6291

San Bernardino Valley Arms Collectors
1970 Mesa Street
San Bernardino, CA 92405

Santa Fe Gun Collectors Association
1085 Nugget
Los Alamos, NM 87544

San Fernando Valley Arms Collectors Association
P.O. Box 65
North Hollywood, CA 91603

Shasta Arms Collectors Association
P.O. Box 3292
Redding, CA 96049

Smith & Wesson Collectors Association
P.O. Box 321
Bellevue, WA 98009

Tampa Bay Arms Collectors Association
2461 67th Avenue South
St. Petersburg, FL 33712

Texas Gun Collectors Association
P.O. Box 9292
College Station, TX 77842

Washington Arms Collectors, Inc.
P.O. Box 7335
Tacoma, WA 98407

Weapons Collectors Society of Montana
3 1 00 Bancroft
Missoula, MT 59801

Weatherby Collectors Association, Inc.
P.O. Box 128
Moira, NY 12957

Willamette Valley Arms Collectors Association, Inc.
P.O. Box 5191
Eugene, OR 97405

Winchester Arms Collectors Association
P.O. Box 6754
Great Falls, MT 59406.

Ye Connecticut Gun Guild
U.S. Route 7
Kent Road
Cornwall Bridge, CT 06754

Zumbro Valley Arms Collectors, Inc.
Box 6621
Rochester, MN 55901

BIBLIOGRAPHY

Bady, Donald *Colt Automatic Pistols.* Alhambra, California: Borden Publishing Company, 1973.

Baer, Larry L. *The Parker Gun.* Los Angeles, California: Beinfeld Publications, 1980.

Bailey, D. and Nie, D. *English Gunmakers.* London: Arms and Armour Press, 1978.

Ball, W.D., *Remington Firearms: The Golden Age of Collecting,* Iola, WI: Krause Publications, 1995.

Ball, W.D., *Mauser Military Rifles of the World.* Iola, WI: Krause Publications, 1996.

Belford, James & Dunlap, Jack *The Mauser Self-Loading Pistol.* Alhambra, California: Borden Publishing, 1969.

Bishop, Chris and Drury, Ian *Combat Guns.* Secaucus, New Jersey: Chartwell Books, 1987.

Blackmore, H. *Gunmakers of London.* York, Pennsylvania: Geo. Shumway, 1986.

Blackmore, H. *Guns and Rifles of the World.* New York, New York: Viking Press, 1965.

Blair, C. *Pistols of the World.* London: B.T. Batsford, Ltd., 1968.

Bogdanovic & Valencak *The Great Century of Guns.* New York, New York: Gallery Books, 1986.

Bowen, T.G. *James Reid and his Catskill Knuckledusters.* Lincoln, Rhode Island: Andrew Mowbray, Inc., 1989.

Breathed, J. and Schroeder, J. *System Mauser.* Glenview, Illinois: Handgun Press, 1967.

Brophy, Lt. Col. William S., USAR, Ret. *The Krag Rifle.* Los Angeles, California: Beinfeld Publications, 1980.

Brophy, Lt. Col. William S., USAR, Ret. *L.C. Smith Shotguns.* Los Angeles, California: Beinfeld Publications, 1977.

Brophy, W. *Marlin Firearms.* Harrisburg, Pennsylvania: Stackpole Books, 1989.

Browning, J. and Gentry, C. *John M. Browning; American Gunmaker.* Ogden, Utah: Browning, 1989.

Butler, David F. *The American Shotgun.* New York, New York: Winchester Press, 1973.

Buxton, Warren *The P 38 Pistol.* Dallas, Texas: Taylor Publishing Company, 1978.

Carr, J. *Savage Automatic Pistols.*

Chant, Christopher *The New Encyclopedia of Handguns.* New York, New York: Gallery Books.

Conley, F.F. *The American Single Barrel Trap Gun.* Carmel Valley, California: F.F. Conley, 1989.

Cope, K.L. *Stevens Pistols and Pocket Rifles.* Ottawa, Ontario: Museum Restoration Service.

Cormack, A.J.R. *Small Arms, a Concise History of Their Development.* Profile Publications, Ltd.

Cormack, A.J.R. *Small Arms in Profile, Volume I.* Garden City, New York: Doubleday & Company, Inc.,1973.

deHass, Frank *Bolt Action Rifles.* Northfield, Illinois: Digest Books, Inc., 1971.

deHass, Frank *Single-shot Rifles and Actions.* Northfield, Illinois: Digest Books, Inc., 1969.

Eastman, Matt, *Browning Sporting Arms of Distinction; 1903-1992.* Fitzgerald, Georgia, 1994.

Eberhart, L. D. & Wilson, R. L. *The Deringer in America: Volume Two - The Cartridge Era.* Lincoln, RI: Andrew Mowbray Inc., 1993.

Goddard, W. H. D. *The Government Models.* The Development of the Colt Model of 1911. Lincoln, RI: Andrew Mowbray Inc., 1988.

Graham, R., Kopec, J., Moore, C. *A Study of the Colt Single Action Army Revolver.* Dallas, Texas: Taylor Publishing Co., 1978.

Greener, W. *The Gun and Its Development.* Secaucus, New Jersey: Chartwell Books, 1988.

Gun Digest 1967 through 1989 Editions. Northfield, Illinois: DBI Books.

Guns of the World Los Angeles, California: Petersen Publishing Company, 1972.

Dance, T. *High Standard: A Collector's Guide to the Hamden & Hartford Target Pistols.* Lincoln, RI: Andrew Mowbray Inc., 1991.

Dunlap, J. *Pepperbox Firearms.* Palo Alto, California: Pacific Books, 1964.

Ezell, Edward C. *Small Arms Today.* Harrisburg, Pennsylvania: Stackpole Books.

Frasca & Hill *The 45-70 Springfield.* Northridge, California: Springfield Publishing Company, 1980.

Fuller, C. *The Whitney Firearms.* Huntington, West Virginia: Standard Pub., Inc., 1946.

Gaier & Francotte, *FN 100 Years; The Story of a Great Liege Company, 1889-1989.* Brussels, Belgium, 1989.

Hayward, J.F. *Art of the Gunmaker, Vol.* 1. London: Barrie & Rockliff, 1962; Vol. 2. London: Barrie & Rockliff, 1963.

Henshaw, Thomas, et. al., *The History of Winchester Firearms 1866-1992, 6th Ed.* Winchester Press, 1993.

Hiddleson, C. *Encyclopedia of Ruger Semi-Automatic Pistols: 1949-1992.* Iola, WI: Krause Publications, 1993.

Hinman, Bob *The Golden Age of Shotgunning,* New York, N.Y., Winchester Press, 1975.

Hoff, A. *Airguns and Other Pneumatic Arms.* London: Barrie & Jenkins, 1972.

Hoffschmidt, E.J. *Know Your. 45 Auto Pistols Models 1911 & Al.* Southport, Connecticut: Blacksmith Corporation, 1974.

Hoffschmidt, E.J. *Know Your Walther PP & PPK Pistols.* Southport, Connecticut: Blacksmith Corporation, 1975.

Hogg, Ian V. *German Pistols and Revolvers 1871-1945.* Harrisburg, Pennsylvania: Stackpole Books, 1971.

Hogg, Ian V. and Weeks, John *Military Small Arms of the 20th Century.* Fifth Edition. Northfield, Illinois: DBI Books, 1985.

Hogg, Ian V. and Weeks, John *Pistols of the World. Revised Edition.* Northfield, Illinois: DBI Books, 1982.

Honeycutt, Fred L., Jr. *Military Pistols of Japan.* Lake Park, Florida: Julin Books, 1982.

Houze, H. *The Winchester Model 52: Perfection in Design,* Iola, WI: Krause Publications, 1997.

Houze, H. *To The Dreams Of Youth: Winchester .22 Caliber Single-shot Rifle.* Iola, WI: Krause Publications, 1993.

Houze, H. *Winchester Repeating Arms Company Its History and Development 1865 to 1981.* Iola, WI: Krause Publications, 1994.

Houze, H. *Colt Rifles & Muskets: 1847-1870.* Iola, WI: Krause Publications, 1996.

Jamieson, G. Scott *Bullard Arms.* Erin, Ontario: Boston Mills Press, 1988.

Jinks, R.G. *History of Smith A. Wesson.* Beinfeld Pub., Inc., 1977.

Karr, C.L. and C.R. *Remington Handguns.* Harrisburg, Pennsylvania: Stackpole Co., 1956.

Kenyon, C. *Lugers at Random.* Glenview, Illinois: Handgun Press, 1990.

Kindig, J., Jr. *Thoughts on the Kentucky Rifle in its Golden Age.* New York, New York: Bonanza Books, 1964.

Laidacker, John S. *Collected Notes Concerning Developmental Cartridge Handguns In .22 Calibre As Produced in the United States and Abroad From 1855 to 1875.* Bloomsburg, PA: J.S. Laidacker, 1994.

Larson, Eric *Variations of the Smooth Bore H&R Handy-Gun.* Takoma Park, Maryland: 1993.

Leithe, Frederick E. *Japanese Handguns.* Alhambra, California: Borden Publishing Company, 1968.

Lenk, T. *The Flintlock, Its Origins and Development.* New York, New York: Bramhall House, 1965.

Lugs, J. *Firearms Past and Present.* London: Grenville, 1975.

Madis, George *The Winchester Model 12.* Brownsboro, Texas: Art & Reference House, 1982.

Madis, George *The Winchester Book.* Brownsboro, Texas: Art & Reference House, 1977.

Marcot, R. *Spencer Repeating Firearms.* Irvine, California: Northwood Heritage Press, 1990.

Markham, George *Japanese Infantry Weapons of World War Two.* New York, New York: Hippocrene Books, Inc., 1976.

McDowell, R. *Evolution of the Winchester.* Tacoma, Washington: Armory Pub., 1985.

McDowell, R. *A Study of Colt Conversions and Other Percussion Revolvers,* Iola, WI; Krause Publications, 1997.

McIntosh, Michael *A.H. Fox; The Finest Gun in the World.* Countrysport Press, 1992.

Moller, G. D. *American Military Shoulder Arms, Volume 1, Colonial and Revolutionary War Arms.* Niwot, CO: University Press of Colorado, 1993.

Murphy, J. M.D. *Confederate Carbines & Musketoons.* J. Murphy, M.D., n.p.: 1986.

Murray, Douglas P. *The 99: A History of the Savage Model 99 Rifle.* Murray, 1976.

Myatt, Major Frederick, M.D. *Pistols and Revolvers.* New York, New York: Crescent Books, 1980.

Nutter, W.E. *Manhattan Firearms.* Harrisburg, Pennsylvania: Stackpole Co., 1958.

Olson, Ludwig *Mauser Bolt Rifles.* Third Edition. Montezuma, Iowa: Brownell & Sons, 1976.

Parsons, J. E. *Henry Deringer's Pocket Pistol.* New York, New York: Wm. Morrow & Co., 1952.

Pender, Roy G. *III Mauser Pocket Pistols 1910-1946.* Houston, Texas: Collectors Press, 1971.

Peterson, H.L. *Arms and Armor in Colonial America.* New York, New York: Brandhall House, 1956.

Petty, Charles E. *High Standard Automatic Pistols 1932-1950.* Highland Park, NJ: The Gun Room Press, 1989.

Rankin, J. *Walther Models PP and PPK.* Coral Gables, Florida: Rankin, 1989.

Rankin, J. *Walther Volume III,* 1908-1980. Coral Gables, Florida: Rankin, 1981.

Reese, Michael *11 Luger Tips.* Union City, Tennessee: Pioneer Press, 1976.

Reilly, R. *United States Martial Flintlocks.* Lincoln, Rhode Island: Andrew Mowbray, Inc., 1986.

Reilly, R. *United States Military Small Arms 1816-1865.* Baton Rouge, Louisiana: Eagle Press, Inc., 1970.

Renneberg, R.C. *The Winchester Model 94: The First 100 Years.* Iola, WI: Krause Publications, 1992.

Riling, R. *The Powder Flask Book.* New York, New York: Bonanza Books, 1953.

Rosenberger, R.F.& Kaufmann, C. *The Long Rifles of Western Pennsylvania-Allegheny and Westmoreland Counties.* Pittsburgh, PA: University of Pittsburgh Press, 1993.

Rule, R. *The Rifleman's Rifle: Winchester's Model 70, 1936-1963.* Northridge, California: Alliance Books, 1982.

Ruth, L. *War Baby! Comes Home-The U.S. Caliber .30 Caliber Carbine Volume II.* Toronto, Ontario: Collector Grade Publications, Inc., 1993.

Ruth, L. *War Baby! The U.S. Caliber .30 Carbine.* Toronto, Ontario: Collector Grade Publications, Inc., 1992.

Schroeder, Joseph J. *Gun Collector's Digest, Volume II* Northfield, Illinois: Digest Books, Inc., 1977.

Schwing, N. *Winchester's Finest, The Model 21.* Iola, WI: Krause Pub., 1990.

Schwing, N. *The Winchester Model 42.* Iola, WI: Krause Pub., 1990.

Schwing, N. *Winchester Slide Action Rifles, Vol. Model 1890 and Model 1906.* Iola, WI: Krause Publications, 1992.

Schwing, N. *Winchester Slide Action Rifles, Vol. Model 61 and Model 62.* Iola, WI: Krause Publications, 1993.

Schwing, N. *The Browning Superposed: John Browning's Last Legacy.* Iola, WI: Krause Publications, 1996.

Sellers, F. *Sharps Firearms.* North Hollywood, California: Beinfeld Pub., Inc., 1978.

Sellers, F. *American Gunsmiths.* Highland Park, New Jersey: Gun Room Press, 1983.

Sellers, F. and Smith, S. *American Percussion Revolvers.* Ottawa, Ontario: Museum Restoration Service, 1971.

Serven, James E. *200 Years of American Firearms.* Chicago, Illinois: Follett Publishing Company, 1975.

Serven, J. *Collecting of Guns.*

Sharpe, P. *The Rifle in America.* Funk and Wagnalls Co., 1953.

Sheldon, Douglas G. *A Collector's Guide to Colt's. 38 Automatic Pistols.* Sheldon, 1987.

Smith, W. *The Book of Pistols and Revolvers.* Harrisburg, Pennsylvania: Stackpole Co., 1962.

Stadt, R.W. *Winchester Shotguns and Shotshells.* Tacoma, Washington: Armory Publications, 1984.

Stevens, R. *The Browning High Power Automatic Pistol.* Toronto, Canada: Collector Grade Publications, 1990.

Stoeger's Catalog & Handbook. 1939 Issue. Hackensack, New Jersey: Stoeger Arms Corporation.

Supica J. & Nahas R., *Standard Catalog of Smith & Wesson.* Iola, WI: Krause Publications, 1996.

Sutherland, R.Q. & Wilson, R. L. *The Book of Colt Firearms.* Kansas City, Missouri: R.Q. Sutherland, 1971.

Tivey, T. *The Colt Rifle, 1884-1902.* N.S.W. Australia: Couston & Hall, 1984.

Vorisek, Joleph T *Shotgun Markings:* 1865 to 1940, Canton, CT: Armsco Press 1990.

Wahl, Paul *Wahl's Big Gun Catalog II.* Cut And Shoot, Texas: Paul Wahl Corporation, 1988.

Walter, John *The German Rifle.* Ontario, Canada: Fortress Publishing, Inc., 1979.

Whitaker, Dean H. *The Winchester Model 70 1937-1964.* Dallas, Texas: Taylor Publishing Company, 1978.

Wilkerson, Don *The Post War Colt Single Action Army Revolver.* Dallas, Texas: Taylor Publishing Company, 1978.

Wilson, R.L. *Colt An American Legend.* New York, New York: Abbeville Press, 1985.

Wilson, R.L. *Colt Engraving.* Beinfeld Publishing, Inc., n.p., 1982.

Wilson, R.L. *Winchester Engraving.* Palm Springs, California: Beinfeld Books, 1989.

Wilson, R.L. *The Colt Heritage.* New York, New York: Simon & Schuster, 1979.

Wilson, R.L. *Winchester An American Legend.* New York, New York: 1991.

Winant, L. *Early Percussion Firearms.* New York, New York: Wm. Morrow & Co., 1959.

Winant, L. *Firearms Curiosa.* New York, New York: Greenburg Pub., 1955.

Workman, W.E. *The Ruger 10/22,* Iola, WI: Krause Publications, 1994.

Zhuk, A.B. *The Illustrated Encyclopedia of Handguns.* London, England, Greenhill Books, 1995.

ABOUT THE EDITOR

Ned Schwing has spent most of his life around sporting guns and hunting. As a college history instructor his interest was devoted to English and American eighteenth century military. He has studied and written on eighteenth century British naval history. His knowledge of military history, particulary armor and adminstration, led to a blending of history with his fondness for sporting arms, namely shotguns.

His first commercial book on Winchester shotguns was the popular and best selling *The Winchester Model 42*, now in its fourth printing. This effort was followed shortly by the highly regarded *Winchester's Finest: The Model 21*, designated the official history of the Winchester Model 21 by the Olin Corporation. His history of the Model 21 is considered the definitive work on this distinguished and prestigous American shotgun. Turning his attention to Winchester slide action rifles, his first love, Mr. Schwing wrote an extensive and comprehensive two volumne work on these rifles. The result of his research was the *Winchester Slide Action Rifles, Volume I: The Model 1890 and Model 1906* followed by the second companion volume, *Winchester Slide Action Rifles, Volume II: The Model 61 and Model 62*. His latest work, published in 1996, is the sweeping history of the Browning Arms Company and its flagship shotgun the Superposed entitled, *The Browning Superposed: John M. Browning's Last Legacy*.

During this period he has also expanded his efforts into broader efforts with his appointment as co-editor of the *Standard Catalog of Firearms*. He has served in that capacity from the 2nd through the 6th editions, and he now serves as the editor of the 7th and 8th editions. Mr. Schwing's articles have appeared in the *American Rifleman*, *Shooting Sportsman*, *Waffen Digest*, and other firearms publications.

MANUFACTURER & MODEL INDEX

KEEP UP-TO-DATE WITH THE LATEST GUN REFERENCE